THE TROUSER PRESS RECORD GUIDE

Fourth Edition

THE TROUSER PRESS RECORD GUIDE

Fourth Edition

IRA A. ROBBINS, Editor

COLLIER BOOKS
Macmillan Publishing Company • New York

Maxwell Macmillan Canada • Toronto

Maxwell Macmillan International
New York • Oxford • Singapore • Sydney

Collier Books
Macmillan Publishing Company
866 Third Avenue
New York, NY 10022

Maxwell Macmillan Canada, Inc.
1200 Eglinton Avenue East
Suite 200
Don Mills, Ontario M3C 3N1

Macmillan Publishing Company is part of the Maxwell Communication
Group of Companies.

Library of Congress Cataloging-in-Publication Data
The Trouser Press record guide/Ira A. Robbins, editor.—4th ed.,
  1st Collier Books ed.
      p.   cm.
    Rev. ed. of: The New Trouser Press record guide. 3rd ed., Rev. ed.
  c1989.
    Includes bibliographical references.
    ISBN 0-02-036361-3
    1. Popular music—Discography.   2. Sound recordings—Reviews.
  I. Robbins, Ira A.   II. New Trouser Press record guide.
  ML156.4.P6T76   1991   91-18564   CIP
  016.78164'026'6—dc20   MN

Revised edition of *The Trouser Press Guide to New Wave Records* and *The New
Trouser Press Record Guide*

Macmillan books are available at special discounts for bulk
purchases for sales promotions, premiums, fund-raising, or
educational use. For details, contact:

                   Special Sales Director
                   Macmillan Publishing Company
                   866 Third Avenue
                   New York, NY 10022

First Collier Books Edition 1991

10 9 8 7 6 5 4 3 2 1

Printed in the United States of America

CONTENTS

PREFACE

This book began as an almost-successful attempt to review all of the significant albums with a direct connection to new wave music—records that either directly led to or resulted from the 1976–'77 upheaval spearheaded by the Sex Pistols, Clash, Ramones, Television, Blondie, etc. (Although it came to be—and remains—a derisive designation for watered-down bands who affected hip style but were bland enough for American pop radio, "new wave" was originally a general and non-judgmental description of bands upsetting the norm in the late '70s.)

The first edition, published by Scribners in 1983 as *The Trouser Press Guide to New Wave Records*, was a logical outgrowth of *Trouser Press* magazine. Armed with a well-established anti-mainstream editorial stance, it was easy to map out the book's contents by simply including anything that was adventurous, rebellious, esoteric or simply uncommercial, in any idiom that could be considered rock-based. As a result, the original book was fairly parochial in scope, essentially reviewing every American or imported rock album we could get ahold of that had some connection—even plainly superficial or fraudulent—to a genre that was then fairly well circumscribed and not that densely populated.

The first book was fine for what it was, but the ceaseless development and cross-fertilization of styles (not to mention the proliferation of independent label releases) quickly rendered the focus unduly narrow and the central theme rather outdated. By the time of the second edition, times had changed. For one thing, *Trouser Press* had ceased publishing. For another, the music that had once been considered anti-commercial in this country was being given enormous exposure by MTV, where a colorful image and a good spiel was all it took to reach a new and growing "new music" audience.

The second edition (Scribners, 1985) broadened the essential concept and abandoned the by-then-outmoded notion of new wave for a more general slice of the musical hemisphere, one that extrapolated stylistically (and genealogically) from the groups covered in the original book. This book was bigger and more far-reaching, but it lacked an easily definable aesthetic basis. (It also lacked, for reasons of space, the compilation section that had appeared in the first edition. An effort to include it in the third edition was fruitless as well; by this point it's almost a book in and of itself.) As no better title emerged, the book was published as *The New Trouser Press Record Guide*.

A revised version of the book was published in the United Kingdom in late 1987 as *The New Music Record & Tape Guide* (Omnibus). It updated and expanded on the 1985 edition, but deleted a lot of internationally obscure bands on American independent labels. In exchange, substantial coverage of reggae, rap, hardcore and African artists was added. That edition has never been distributed in the US and isn't counted in the American numbering.

Building on all of the previous versions, the book's third edition (Collier, February 1989) caught up with new releases through the spring of 1988 while increasing and extending the scope of bands and records covered. Most of what was excised for the British book was restored, and a smattering of indie metal records and new folk music was added, resulting in an eclectic 654-page volume. For the first time, information on compact discs was included.

By both plan and circumstances, this fourth edition (for statisticians, the final count is

1,600 entries covering 2,500 artists and about 9,500 records) wound up being very different from the others. There were several goals at the outset: to add entries on a number of really major artists of quality and influence, to improve or replace existing entries where needed, to deepen the coverage of obscure but significant bands and to cope with rap's format shift from 12-inch singles (which are outside the book's scope) to full-length albums. A major effort was made to rectify past shortcomings by covering relevant bands that had been overlooked, adding EPs to both discographies and text, reviewing records that had previously been listed but not covered and correcting errors both tiny and glaring. Although it meant accepting a varied set of critical sensibilities, a passel of new writers with expertise in specific areas were invited to provide more informed and artistically sympathetic coverage of genres—metal, industrial, goth, dance, hardcore—that had previously been given short aesthetic shrift. (While it would have been great to include substantial world music coverage, that idea proved to be logistically out of the question.) Writers were encouraged to be as detailed as possible, to suggest and cover bands they felt were essential and to follow family trees through solo projects and offshoots. Compounding such journalist profligacy with the unexpectedly huge number of records released over the past three years that had to be reviewed as updates, the net result was a text that initially came in around 800,000 words, roughly double the size of the last edition and about a hundred pages beyond what was publishable.

That meant a lot had to come out. This edition cuts a number of old entries that would have simply been repeated unchanged from the 1989 book. On the principle that new material is better than old, I took the opportunity to prune entries that now seem trivial or hopelessly irrelevant, and to excise those in which I felt the writing, coverage and/or discographies were substandard. It was a difficult decision-making process, but I don't think many of the deleted entries will be much missed, and then only by those who can refer to the previous edition.

The new entries on George Clinton, Faust, Bob Marley, Sky Saxon, Tom Waits, and Neil Young were overdue; for reasons beyond our control, planned coverage of Frank Zappa and John Zorn didn't happen. (As a pre-emptive reply to those who can't understand omissions of clearly deserving artists, the following would have been included had circumstances (meaning records, writers, knowledge and time) allowed: African Head Charge And Also the Trees, Band of Holy Joy, Cassandra Complex, Chrysanthemums, Death in June, Deep Freeze Mice, Drowning Pool, Etron Fou, Fourwaycross, Front Line Assembly, Lemon Kittens, Magma, Youssou N'Dour, Rhythm Pigs, Rose of Avalanche, Salt'n'Pepa, 7 Seconds, Peter Stampfel and the Bottlecaps, Subhumans, Tail Gators, Theatre of Hate, 3 Mustaphas 3. Oh well.)

Although opinion will undoubtedly be split on the subject, I think rap music fully fits the book's context and criteria. In this edition, I've attempted to cover as many noteworthy rap (but not other African-American pop styles, like new jack swing or house) artists as possible, omitting the blandest and least distinguished figures but including a couple of commercial titans whose work demands critical examination. Following the classic rebel template of an autonomous and self-willed form created by and for a young, alienated segment of society, the hip-hop explosion is one of pop music's most profound upheavals and very much a conceptual echo of the late '70s punk/new wave era. Despite a difference of social and cultural values, there are a lot of points at which the only essential difference between hip-hop and rock records is the beat.

While dance music has, in the past, fallen outside the stylistic framework of this book, there's no getting around its current dominance—so much more so now than during the disco era—of the pop life. In light of the Manchester rave scene, the rise of DJ/performers, industrial music and, of course, hip-hop, the '80s proved that rock'n'roll and dance music can't escape each other. Following the disco-sucks era when bitter rock fans felt disenfranchised by the commercial dominance of unpalatable records that denied the primacy of song and artist, musical innovators set about crafting hybrids that would make disco—in all its crass, simplistic, dance-oriented glory—enticing to a wider musical audience by appealing to familiar sensibilities. "New romantics" recycled glam-rock sensibilities and art-rock trappings; industrial noise purveyors harnessed punk's brutality to danceable rhythms; techno-pop got heavier and funkier and moved from rock clubs to dance clubs. Ultimately, it became obvious that too much criss-crossing of stylistic boundaries is going on to count bands in or out solely on the basis of a rhythm.

Partially as a result of that development, the book's longstanding (I can't bring myself to claim tradition at this early juncture) criteria—bands and artists who favor experimentation, radicalism, innovation and self-expression, those who embrace music as something beyond its potential financial or ego-massaging rewards—don't really apply to some of the bands here. Finding myself out on this stylistic limb, I tried to concoct some editorial guidelines as I went along, but wound up just winging it.

Looking over this edition, I think the heart of what the book now covers is eccentricity: from mild intellectual dabblings to bizarre religious statements to full-blown screeching insanity. If that means pop with a twist, rock with a different kind of roll, ear-splitting noise, amateurish home-brew dabblings or bizarre tape manipulations, it's all part of a shared belief that music need not be ordinary, and that—despite what the charts say—defiance of the established order is still a highly prized element to many music lovers. As long as *The Trouser Press Record Guide* can help support and encourage risk-taking and rule-breaking in a wide variety of styles, it will uphold the spirit that originally inspired its creation.

INTRODUCTION

The format is straightforward: entries are arranged purely alphabetically by the last name of individuals and the first word of group names, with no precedence given to acronyms, abbreviations, numerals, etc. Groups who have taken their collective name from an actual member (even a pseudonymous one) are alphabetized as if an individual; fabricated group names that don't refer to a person within the group are treated as band names. (For instance: Brinsley Schwarz is in "S" and Ed Hall is in "E.")

Articles are ignored and omitted from headings unless considered an actual and essential part of a name. Bands that get to keep their articles are alphabetized by them (A Flock of Seagulls, Thee Hypnotics, The Scene Is Now). English-language groups with non-English names (Das Damen, Die Kreuzen) are alphabetized by their articles; groups who use their own language (Die Haut, Les Thugs) aren't. One-letter surnames are ignored in favor of first names (Simon F is under S), and rappers are filed by first letter (including titular designations like MC, DJ or Queen) unless there's a clearly understood surname (Big Daddy Kane is under K) that suggests a more appropriate location.

Groups that have gone under more than one name (including solo efforts and side projects) are listed under all the recording names (and cross-referenced as such), but alphabetized under the most recent and/or significant. This edition does more ganging up of related families, with location being a compromise between chronological comprehension and best-known name. Every attempt has been made to make it easy and logical to find things quickly, but if an artist isn't listed where you where you expect, keep looking.

Each heading includes as-complete-as-possible album listings (US, UK or whatever else applies without being redundant; general geographical precedence is domestic, British and then everywhere else) through March 1991, with a smattering of listings of scheduled releases as late as June. Reviews run up through early-'91 releases (the end of '90 for imports), with the absolute cut-off being the end of April. Some records that were received too late—or not located at all—are merely listed in the headings without being discussed in the text. Discographies do not reflect current availability of records (i.e., deletions are not deleted) and indicate cassette releases only when other formats are not available.

In the interests of reference completeness, discographies occasionally include second-hand information gleaned from catalogue listings, reviews or advertising. Those records are, of course, not reviewed in this work, merely listed and mentioned in the text if there's reliable info regarding content (compilations, concerts, outtakes, etc.). However, release dates and exact titles of such records are sometimes impossible to determine or confirm. In cases of severe dubiousness, listings are omitted to avoid sending fans on wild-goose chases; in the absence of a firm release date, a "c." indication precedes the year to acknowledge the possibility of error. Every effort was made to resolve such questions, but in some cases we were unable to do so. Any corrections brought to our attention will be incorporated into the next edition.

Albums that have been released on compact disc are noted with a bullet (●) at the end of the heading line. However, the ● indication does not mean that a domestic (US) CD exists or that the CD was issued by the record's original album label, merely that the title has been issued *somewhere* by someone in the format. (Admittedly, coverage of Japanese CD releases is very sketchy, and there are undoubtedly records that have been issued on CD there and not acknowledged here.) Differences between US, UK, European and Pacific CD releases are covered when such information is available, but don't assume that the lack of such discussion means they're all the same. Every effort has been made to note differences between album, CD and cassette releases, although there are undoubtedly plenty that were overlooked.

CD-only releases are indicated as [CD] between title and label; for consistent scannability, a ● follows such listings as well. In cases where one CD incorporates another listed piece of vinyl, both are marked ● regardless of whether a compact disc was issued under that title: if it's on CD, it's on CD. (The exception to that rule is when a CD issued under a unique title includes several records; it would be too confusing if the individual records were also marked ●.)

The increasing unavailability of vinyl has complicated format matters considerably. While the new φ designation indicates that a record was released *only* on tape and CD, that doesn't quite nail down this hellishly confusing situation. As of 1991, most British and European record companies continue to issue vinyl on a lot of releases, and some American labels who don't still do limited vinyl runs for college radio. With the legal roadblocks to imports preventing a British band's vinyl from being distributed in America even if the group's American label has decided against a three-format release, it's fairly pointless to acknowledge foreign vinyl issue. As a result, records marked φ may indeed be available somewhere—but not, most likely, in your local record store—on vinyl. And with retail distribution making it nearly impossible to find vinyl releases even when they exist, such knowledge may be virtually useless to traditionalists.

Records that have been issued in the US will note only the US label. UK releases are given as (nr/Label). However, records issued in different countries under alternate titles or with substantially different contents may be listed twice. Records that have not been released in the US or the UK include a country of origin before the label name: (Fr. New Rose), (Aus. Au-go-go). One exception: Canadian releases sometimes take precedence over British, so a Canadian label may be indicated on a record that indeed has had a British release. Label names are given as accurately as possible, although several space-saving adaptations must be noted: IRS is listed without periods, Les Disques du Crépuscule is reduced to Crépuscule, and the words International and Communications are abbreviated.

In previous editions, the year given in headings was the earliest release date the album was originally issued, anywhere. An effort was made to note both American release dates and foreign releases in a prior year for records added to this edition, but it was generally impossible to go back and correct this for earlier releases. (This occasionally results in confusing anomalies. A record released in the UK in 1985 and in the US a year later will have the US company but the UK date. An effort has been made to treat lengthy gaps as reissues, but consistency in this regard is not guaranteed.)

Succeeding issues and reissues are noted by a second date (and new label information, for those records not reissued by the original label). CD releases of old records are not considered reissues and the ● CD notation does not indicate a year of such release. Reissues that don't improve on geographical precedence are excluded unless the reissue is far more likely to be found or there are notable differences from the original.

The ''[tape]'' notation signifies a cassette-only release. (Tapes listed without label information are home-brew self-releases that are/were commercially available to some degree but don't carry a company name.) The ''EP'' designation covers everything from a three-song 7-inch to a six-song mini-album, regardless of how a record is billed. There are a few exceptions. Albums with six or fewer long tracks that are clearly full-length LPs are considered as such; 7-inches with eight or ten tracks are, by the same logic, not albums.

Otherwise, anything with six or fewer tracks is an EP here; a 12-inch record or a CD with seven or more is an album. CD singles are ignored unless they contain four different songs (remixes excluded), but the converse is not necessarily true. A major effort was made to expand the book's EP coverage this time, and a lot more items were reviewed and/or listed, including many from the mid-'80s.

With one or two exceptions, promo-only releases, bootlegs and interview records are omitted. Although every effort has been made to precisely list record titles as they appear—with all weird spellings, made-up words and odd punctuation preserved—quotation marks around complete titles are generally removed in order to minimize confusion with the handful of singles that are listed. The final right to resolve inconsistencies (when the front cover, spine and label don't agree) rests with the judges.

Confusion of another sort may be unavoidable: In the spring of 1990, a Warner Bros.-related record company named Giant was launched and the company that had been called Giant up till then switched its name to Rockville; the discographies have not been retroactively corrected. Furthermore, England and America each has unaffiliated labels called Jungle and Link.

Because many entries have been updated or revised by people other than the original reviewers, there are multiple bylines. (Bylines appear as lower-case initials in brackets at the end of each entry. Refer to the list of contributors to decode names.) Cross-references at the bottom of entries (greatly expanded this time) provide direction to other related entries of interest that may not be obvious; the text of an entry may suggest other artists worth investigating.

Political note: Music critics often refer to "black music" and "white music" as if skin color determined the sound of music one is obliged to make. In the hopes of avoiding the patent racism inherent in such simpleminded generalizing, when those phrases are used here, they're in quotes to stress that a musical style, not a performer's race, is being addressed.

Comments, criticisms, corrections, quibbles, quarrels and kudos are gladly accepted. Please address all correspondence to:

The Trouser Press Record Guide
c/o Collier Books—21st floor
866 Third Avenue
New York NY 10022

ACKNOWLEDGMENTS

This book could not have been created without the enthusiasm and efforts of many people. First and foremost, my thanks go to all the contributors (past and present), who did great work for lousy money, some coming through with fine work despite major life-type obstacles. Special mention goes to those who shouldered more than their part of the undertaking and those who did much more than just what was asked of them: Jem Aswad, Art Black, Doug Brod, Harold DeMuir, Greg Fasolino, Glenn Kenny, Jack Rabid, Andrea 'Enthal, Dave Sprague and Wif Stenger. The official *Trouser Press* cabal—Jim Green, Dave Schulps and Scott Isler—and honorary member David Sheridan not only contributed reviews, but provided significant input to the direction of this edition.

Many people provided records and information, but Alan Fielding set new standards for being really fantastic and assisted in hundreds of ways for which he will never be adequately compensated. Ron Decker was amazingly helpful on a number of fronts, as were many other publicists and friends: Bill Ashton, Cary Baker, Ron Bally, Rich Bauer, Danny Beard, Beth Bellis, Debbie Bennet, Janet Billig, Mark Brennan, Joanne Brown, Sophia Chang, Irwin Chusid, Jason Cohen, Ron Coleman, Neil Cooper, Tom Cording, Crypt, Nick Cucci, Steve Daly, Joshua Davis, Nick DeBenedetto, Monica Dee, Fran DeFeo, Fred Dellar, Sue Drew, Bruce Duff, Alan Duffy, Andy Dunkley, Alvin Eng, Lisa Fancher, Delores Fernandez, Jill Fonaas, Pete Frame, Jack Frank, Kathy Gillis, Scott Givens, Kenn Goodman, Milhan Gorkey, Lisa Gotthiel, Huw Gower, Michelle Gutenstein, Robert Haber, Daniel Haesen, Michael Hafitz, Chryste Hall, Dave Hall, Lisa Hayes, Jerry Jaffe, Chris Kamatani, Steve Karas, Kenyatta, Peter Koepke, Kramer, Michael Krumper, Maggie Krupka, Arthur Levy, Miriam Linna, Marilyn Lipsius, Sharon Liveten, Jocelynn Loebl, Marty Maidenberg, Mary Marcus, Sue Marcus, Lisa Markowitz, J.D. Martignon, Steve Martin, Patrick Mathé, Jill McLean, Mary Melia, Joe Metcalfe, Brett Milano, Billy Miller, Tracey Miller, Luigia Minichiello, Andrea Mulrain, Pat Naylor, Bo Orloff, Deborah Orr, Dino Ostacinni, Dino Paredes, Sue Patel, Anne Patteson, Robert Perlman, Lisa Pollan, Jonathan Poneman, Albert Ragusa, Cindy Redmond, Bettina Richards, Raymond Rodriguez, Melani Rogers, Scott Schinder, Andy Schwartz, Camille Sciara, Kevin Sharp, Greg Shaw, John Silva, Gary Stewart, Carrie Ann Svingen, Tom Timony, Eileen Treacy, Leyla Turkkan, Michel Vidal, Robert Vodicka, Ken Weinstein, Meryl Wheeler, Vicky Wheeler, Peter Wright, Howard Wuelfing, Lauren Zelisko.

I'd also like to acknowledge the publications that yielded the largest amounts of essential discographical and background information: *Option, CMJ New Music Report, Bucketfull of Brains, Q, New Musical Express, Melody Maker, Billboard, Spin, Forced Exposure, Catalogue, Entertainment Weekly, The Music Master Record Catalogue, Schwann Spectrum, The Random House Dictionary, The Essential Guide to Rock Records, Christgau's Record Guide, Rolling Stone Record Guide, Pete Frame's Rock Family Trees, International Discography of the New Wave, New Rock Record, The Rolling Stone Encyclopedia of Rock & Roll, The New Rock'n'Roll, The Illustrated Encyclopedia of Black Music, Harmony Illustrated Encyclopedia of Rock, Hachette Guide to Great Britain, Rock Movers & Shakers* and *The Guinness Book of British Hit Albums.* And kudos to Maxum computers and Xywrite word processing, both of which smoothed the technical path this time.

Thanks to everyone—especially Robert Christgau and Greg Sandow—whose generous and encouraging comments originally helped me undertake another edition and who stayed in my thoughts throughout the project, providing a jolt of resolve when my own wavered. I'd also like to acknowledge the unique contributions of Wendy Harte on behalf of the last edition as well as this one.

Most of all, I'd like to express my deepest gratitude to my wife, Regina Joskow, for her role in this enterprise. I have no doubt that I could not (and most assuredly would not) have done it without her.

I dedicate this book to my extraordinary parents, Louis and Estelle Robbins, who provided me with all the tools anyone ever needed for a successful life, are always there when the going gets rough and have never asked me when I'm going to get a real job.

Ira A. Robbins
New York City
1 May 1991

THE
TROUSER PRESS
RECORD GUIDE

Fourth Edition

THE CONTRIBUTORS

ab	Art Black
ag	Altricia Gethers
aw	Amy Wachtel
bc	Byron Coley
bk	Bud Kliment
cpl	Charles P. Lamey
db	Doug Brod
df	David Fricke
dgs	David Sheridan
ds	Dave Schulps
dss	David Sprague
'e	Andrea 'Enthal
ep	Elizabeth Phillip
gef	Greg Fasolino
gf	Graham Flashner
gk	Glenn Kenny
hd	Harold DeMuir
i	Ira Robbins
icm	Ian McCaleb
ja	Jem Aswad
jg	Jim Green
jl	John Leland
jr	Jack Rabid
jw	John Walker
jy	Jon Young
kh	Kathy Haight
kl	Kate Lewis
ks	Karen Schlosberg
kss	Karen Schoemer
mf	Mark Fleischmann
mg	Marlene Goldman
mp	Michael Pietsch
pn	Paul Nash
rg	Richard Gehr
rj	Regina Joskow
rnp	Robert Payes
rs	Rich Shupe
sg	Steven Grant
si	Scott Isler
sk	Steve Korté
sl	Scott Lewis
sm	Scott McCaughey
tf	Tony Fletcher
tr	Terry Rompers
wk	Wayne King
ws	Wif Stenger

ABBREVIATIONS

●: available on compact disc
φ: available only on CD and cassette
[CD]: CD-only release
[tape]: cassette-only release
EP: maxi-single, extended-play single, mini-album (up to six songs)
nr: not released
c.: circa
DIY: do-it-yourself
aka: also known as
b/w: backed with
Comm.: Communications
Int'l: International
Aus.: Australian
Bel.: Belgian
Braz.: Brazilian
Can.: Canadian
Dan.: Danish
Fin.: Finnish
Fr.: French
Ger.: German
Gr.: Greek
Hol.: Dutch
Ice.: Icelandic
It.: Italian
Jam.: Jamaican
Jap.: Japanese
Nor.: Norwegian
NZ: New Zealand
Port.: Portuguese
Sp.: Spanish
Sw.: Swiss
Swed.: Swedish
UK: British
US: American

ABC

The Lexicon of Love (Mercury) 1982 ●
Beauty Stab (Mercury) 1983 ●
How to Be a ... Zillionaire! (Mercury) 1985 ●
Alphabet City (Mercury) 1987 ●
King Without a Crown EP (nr/Neutron) 1988 ●
The Real Thing EP (nr/Neutron) 1989 ●
Up (Mercury) 1989 ●
Absolutely (Mercury) 1990 φ

ABC revolves around the talented but often misguided Martin Fry, a onetime fanzine editor whose detailed notions of style include, on the Sheffield band's first album, setting his own Ferry/Bowiesque vocals in lustrous pop production (by Trevor Horn) laden with keyboards and strings, mostly to a supple techno-soul disco pulse. He succeeds admirably with "Poison Arrow" and "The Look of Love," but an entire album on the same subject—Fry is stuck in the lexicon's lack-of/loss-of love section—can be a strain. Taken in toto, the melodies seem like retreads, and his attempts at urbane metaphoric wit seem forced.

Fry unexpectedly converted ABC into a rock band for **Beauty Stab**, making guitar the main instrument on most tracks. Fielding the same core lineup as latter-day Roxy Music (vocals, guitar, sax) and, coincidentally (?), joined by the session bassist and drummer (Alan Spenner and Andy Newmark) used on **Flesh + Blood**, ABC offers a remarkable impression (discounting Fry's usual howler lyrics) of that band on "That Was Then but This Is Now." ABC makes additional overtures towards Roxyish guitar rock but with little aptitude in direction, identity or grace. Quotes from Bo Diddley, the Move and other rock icons abound, but ABC has no idea how to use them.

By then reduced to a duo of Fry and guitarist/keyboardist Mark White, ABC took a long hiatus as Fry overcame a serious illness. In '85, the group re-emerged with **Zillionaire!**, a mixed bag of sarcasm ("So Hip It Hurts," "Vanity Kills," "How to Be a Millionaire") and sweetness ("Be Near Me") on which the prime new influence is American hip-hop. (Sugar Hill techno-rhythm vet Keith LeBlanc figures prominently on the record.)

ABC returned to its (adopted) roots on **Alphabet City**, a confident modern soul record which draws from various contemporary genres but basks from start to finish in a soothing wash of strings, horns and heavenly background vocals. Fry and White have clearly matured, dropping the arch lyrical humor and selfconscious stylistic adventures to concentrate on painstaking pop craft. The clear highlight is "When Smokey Sings," a touching and slyly tributary ode to William Robinson, but the remainder of the record is as easily enjoyable.

If **Alphabet City** put the band back on track, **Up** sent ABC down the home stretch, completing the stylistic oval interrupted by the second album. Returning to

glibly clever techno-soul with a prominent and persistent beat, Fry and White use the peppy dance rhythms and irritating lyrics of their youth, lending the economical-sounding LP a similarity to Bowie's Philadelphia period. Fry's singing is deeper and more sincerely emotional than ever before; if the idealistically romantic songwriting wasn't so overdone, the likable **Up** would have been a dandy.

Absolutely samples the band's five albums for such ABC essentials as "Poison Arrow," "The Look of Love," "That Was Then but This Is Now," "Be Near Me" and "When Smokey Sings." The CD and tape contain bonus tracks. [jg/i]

A-BONES

See *Zantees*.

ABOVE THE LAW

Livin' Like Hustlers (Ruthless-Epic) 1990 ●

Over handsome tracks constructed from '70s soul classics as well as live guitar, bass and keyboards, these belligerent (in content, not delivery) self-styled LA hustlers—Cold 187um (Gregory Hutchinson), KM.G the Illustrator (Kevin Dulley), Go Mack (Arthur Goodman) and Total K-oss (Anthony Stewart)—rhyme about cold-blooded violence on the Mega Side and cold-hearted sex (and other topics) on the Ranching Side. Capable but not especially clever and certainly not entertaining, these would-be gangsters (joined, on "The Last Song," by label boss Eazy-E) are less intimidating than unpleasant. [i]

ABSOLUTE GREY

Green House (Earring) 1984 (Midnight) 1986
What Remains (Midnight) 1986
Painted Post EP (Midnight) 1987
A Journey Thru the Past (Greek Di-Di Music) 1988
Sand Down the Moon (Greek Di-Di Music) 1989

PAT THOMAS

Pat Thomas (Heyday) 1988

Long before self-reflective female singers became the hip trend on the alternative music scene, Beth Brown of Rochester, NY's Absolute Grey was writing and singing about loneliness and the challenge of independence. What Brown lacked in vocal range, she more than made up for in guts and naked emotion. **Green House** (six studio tracks and a pair of live numbers, including the Velvet Underground's "Beginning to See the Light") defines the quartet's garage-pop approach, with the bass carrying most of the melodies and the guitar adding color with Peter Buck-ish arpeggios.

The denser, darker **What Remains**, produced by Tim Lee of the Windbreakers, is a humble masterpiece in which Brown alternately deplores her weakness and

1

musters up strength in the face of a failing relationship. The performances are crude, and drummer Pat Thomas sometimes sounds as though he's being piped in from a different state, but neither can suffocate the album's intrinsic dignity.

Absolute Grey pared down to a two-piece for most of the **Painted Post** EP; the four songs on which Brown is accompanied only by Mitch Rasor on bass and acoustic guitar are frighteningly beautiful. Without the competition of a full rhythm section, her voice can be softer and more expressive, and her lyrics articulate pain without ever stooping to self-pity. "Closer Apart," "Sylvia" and "Abandon Waltz" are touching little adventures into her soul.

A **Journey Thru the Past** is a live album (recorded in Rochester in 1984) containing all previously unreleased material. In the summer of '87, all four original members reformed briefly and cut another studio record, **Sand Down the Moon**. Thomas' solo album finds the drummer instead singing and playing acoustic guitar.

[kss]

ACCELERATORS

Leave My Heart (Dolphin) 1983
The Accelerators (Profile) 1987 ●
Dream Train (Profile) 1991 φ

One of numerous Southeastern bands nurtured in the Mitch Easter/Don Dixon pop bosom (both play on the quartet's first album; Dixon produced the first and two cuts on the second), North Carolina's Accelerators blend crisp, energetic, well-mannered rock with a little 'billy and some mild R&B to give **Leave My Heart** just enough grit and soul to make it both memorable and charming. Guitarist/songwriter Gerald Duncan sings pleasantly enough (although more spunk would be an asset); simplicity and restraint make Doug Welchel's drumming noticeably good.

There's even better-sounding guitar rock on **The Accelerators**' dozen uneven cuts, including a remake of the tuneful "Two Girls in Love" from **Leave My Heart**. Duncan and Welchel are the lineup's only holdovers; new lead guitarist Brad Rice adds excitement and extra vocals to strong, melodic numbers like "Radio," "(Why You) Hang Up on Me" and "Tears." Unfortunately, the band's lyrics are often simpleminded, and a fiery guitar solo can't salvage the ill-conceived funeral-speed cover of "Black Slacks." (A version of the Box Tops' "The Letter" flies at a brisk clip, but gets them nowhere.) **The Accelerators** has its fine qualities, but still leaves plenty of room for improvement. [i]

A CERTAIN RATIO

The Graveyard and the Ballroom [tape] (nr/Factory)
 1979 + 1985
Do the Du EP (Factory) 1980
Blown Away EP (nr/Factory) 1980
To Each ... (nr/Factory) 1981
Sextet (nr/Factory) 1981
I'd Like to See You Again (nr/Factory) 1982
The Old and the New (nr/Factory) 1985
Force (nr/Factory) 1986 ●
A Certain Ratio—Live in America (nr/Dojo) 1986 ●
Good Together (nr/A&M) 1989 ●
MCR (nr/A&M) 1990 ●

Manchester's A Certain Ratio (ACR) were one of the first new wave-era outfits to use horns and other instruments to play a soulful brand of contemporary music that defied prevalent trends but proved significantly influential. The **Graveyard** cassette compiles '79 material—half studio work produced by Martin Hannett, the rest live from their hometown's famed Electric Ballroom. With the subsequent **Do the Du**, an exciting and original post-punk dance record that does ACR proud (check out "Shack Up" for the decay of modern social values), it seemed certain that ACR would quickly join Public Image in the vanguard of the new rock left.

The studied tedium of **To Each . . .** , however, snuffed the early promise, as the band buried itself in dreary rhythms and astonishing self-indulgence. Leader Simon Topping—he of the free-form trumpet that stamped songs like "The Fox" (here on a subdued remake from **Do the Du**)—evidently believed that ACR would fill the gap left by Joy Division. Unfortunately, while Joy Division was at least lyrical in its despair, A Certain Ratio is merely monotonous. **Blown Away** is a three-song 12-inch of non-LP blasts of horns and rhythms.

ACR relocated their energy on **Sextet**, but didn't apply it in the right places. There's no real focus to the discoid beats and wailing female vocals (Martha Tilson); ACR don't seem especially motivated by the music they're making. **I'd Like to See You Again** suffers from Tilson's absence, and stumbles about, evincing self-consciousness and conservatism in place of the previously aggressive experimental attitude.

The Old and the New is a compilation, originally released with a bonus 45 of "Shack Up."

ACR maintained a low profile after the early '80s, but continued releasing new records. **Force** follows in the footsteps of **I'd Like to See You Again**, abandoning the raw, stark and chilling sound of the band's seminal work. Professionally executed but completely boring and devoid of spontaneity, there's little here that Chuck Mangione fans might not enjoy. Occasional sonic experimentation isn't enough; the backwards bass on "Bootsy" and the odd drones of "Take Me Down" can't mask the fact that the songs go nowhere.

Live in America is a basic greatest-hits run-through. The sound quality is amazingly good, but it has all the soul of a conservatory jazz ensemble playing from sheet music. The inclusion of cuts that sounded so great just half a decade earlier ("Shack Up," "Knife Slits Water") now only serves to degrade ACR's reputation even further. Yawn. [gf/dgs]

A CONFEDERACY OF DUNCES

Tsk Tsk Tsk [CD] (Old School) 1989 ●

Although its name comes from a novel about New Orleans, this charming Queens, New York pop quartet takes its basic stylistic cues from **Village Green**-era Kinks. Singing in a plain but pleasant voice, John Dunbar (also the band's songwriter, guitarist and pianist) displays a keen traditional melodic sense (hindered a bit by imperfectly pitched background vocals) and a pointed ear for social observation that makes him something of an American Glenn Tilbrook. From a rueful critique of modern music ("The Filler Years") to well-drawn portraits of common people ("Live for Lotto," "She Hates Good Looking Guys," "Ophelia"), Dunbar and the Dunces bring a realistic modern outlook to old-fashioned musical virtues.   [i]

ACOUSTINAUTS
Inhale Einstein (PopLlama Products) 1987

It's easy to imagine this offbeat quartet, guitars in hand, striding through the streets of Seattle, regaling the local folks—even those backing away in confused fear—with their intelligently loopy songs. Keeping things light and folky, the vocal foursome comes on like Devo's hick cousins on the semi-amusing **Inhale Einstein**, playing unaffected country ("Don't You Dare Walk Out of My Life (Without Me)," "Strangers When We Met") and singing about weird science ("Inhale Einstein"), weird religion ("Children of Macedonia") and weird romance ("Big Sexin'").   [i]

ACT
Too Late at 20 (Hannibal) 1981

Impeccable production gives singer/songwriter Nick Laird-Clowes' controlled passion and the band's tight, tasteful playing a clearly deserved chance to be heard. Elvis Costello and Tom Petty appear to be the Act's major influences (there are also nods to the Byrds and Springsteen) but the quartet rises above derivation, giving such songs as "Touch and Go" and "The Long Island Sound" indelible emotional authenticity.   [mf]

See also *Dream Academy*.

ADAM AND THE ANTS
Dirk Wears White Socks (nr/Do It) 1979 (Epic) 1983
Kings of the Wild Frontier (Epic) 1980 ●
Prince Charming (Epic) 1981 ●
Antmusic EP (nr/Do It) 1982
Peel Sessions (Strange Fruit-Dutch East India) 1991 ɸ

ADAM ANT
Friend or Foe (Epic) 1982 ●
Strip (Epic) 1983 ●
Vive le Rock (Epic) 1985 ●
Hits (nr/CBS) 1986 ●
Manners & Physique (MCA) 1989 ●
Antics in the Forbidden Zone (Epic) 1990 ɸ

VARIOUS ARTISTS
Jubilee (nr/Polydor) 1978

When London art-school escapee Adam (Stuart Goddard) turned up with the Ants on the awful **Jubilee** movie soundtrack in 1978, you'd never have guessed he'd amount to anything. Like much of the record, his two cuts were just ordinary meatgrinder punk. Nor was the ambitious **Dirk Wears White Socks** all that encouraging, despite the considerable effort Adam obviously expended on it. The self-produced LP's word-heavy tunes examine sexual excess ("Cleopatra"), bizarre visions ("Day I Met God"), alienation ("Digital Tenderness") and the like. Adam's dour, uncomfortable vocals find compatible backing from his band, which sounds nearly dead and far too slow. It's as if the nastiest portion of **Ziggy Stardust** had come to life full-blown. After he'd made it big, Adam obtained the rights to the record, remixed and resequenced the tracks—replacing

"Catholic Day" and "Day I Met God" (is there a theme to this revisionism?) with "Zerox" and "Kick" (from 45s) and exchanging the album's "Cartrouble (Parts 1 & 2)" for the far better second version—and had it reissued with a new cover.

Adam's old Ants subsequently left for the employ of Malcolm McLaren, transmuting (more or less) into Bow Wow Wow. In their place, Adam teamed up with guitarist Marco Pirroni (who proved to be a significant collaborator) and recruited drummer/producer Chris Hughes (aka Merrick). A re-recorded single of **Dirk**'s "Cartrouble" b/w "Kick" got Adam's new era off the ground in the mid-'80. (The exploitatively titled **Antmusic** EP, issued by Do It to cash in on Adam's success elsewhere, contains remixes of the original two-part "Cartrouble," an outtake of "Kick" and two other early rarities.)

Adam found his groove with **Kings of the Wild Frontier**. Goodbye heaviness and failure, hello hit parade. Dressed in flamboyant pirate gear, Adam and his merry crew bounce through a delightful program of modern bubblegum with shrewd underpinnings. "Dog Eat Dog" uses the rampaging pseudo-tribal drums Adam picked up from McLaren. "Antmusic" shamelessly self-promotes (as do many of Adam's early lyrics) to the accompaniment of an irresistible stop-start melody. The sourness of **Dirk** survives on **Kings**, but there's so much exuberant fun on the surface that it's hard not to have a good time.

Prince Charming is a letdown. "Stand and Deliver" offers more percussive entertainment à la "Dog Eat Dog," and the title track is florid melodrama, but much of the LP seems forced, ill-tempered and silly. Adam hits bottom on "Ant Rap," an embarrassing stab at rap filled with braggadocio.

After dumping all the Ants except for Marco, Adam went solo and came up with the neat **Friend or Foe**, an LP with energy and plenty of variety. Adam and Marco try a little of everything—soul, rockabilly, his usual weightless pop—with convincingly joyful results. Highlights include "Goody Two Shoes" (a spirited, cheeky self-defense) and the Doors' "Hello, I Love You." This may be junk, but it's classy junk.

After that triumph, time for another bad album? No problem! **Strip** is pathetic. Adam's attempt to grow up was recorded at Abba's state-of-the-art studio in Stockholm and features two cuts produced by Phil Collins. (Richard Burgess, Adam and Marco co-produced the remainder.) By taking a less sensational approach, Adam exposes the weakness of his melodies and the inherent silliness of his sleazoid attitudes. Best suited for emotionally stunted *Playboy* readers.

Adam pulled in his horns and, with the production suss of Tony Visconti, made a big-league pop album even a mother could endure. **Vive le Rock**'s spirited title track is a perfect send-up of ELO's Dave Edmunds phase; "Rip Down" likewise recalls Marc Bolan. Other songs ("Razor Keen," "Miss Thing") proffer Bolanesque lyrics but suffer from characterless backing. "Apollo 9," a wonderfully gimmicky single (also included in an a cappella version), proves that the old boy's still got it, whatever *it* may be. "Yabba yabba ding ding," indeed!

Monsieur Ant spent a few years concentrating his

energies on an acting career. His best role was in 1987's stylish *Slamdance*, but he also appeared in *Trust Me* (1989) and *Nomads* (1986) as well as on television and in the theater. In the meantime, his British label issued **Hits**, a compilation of his biggest singles, from "Kings of the Wild Frontier" through "Vive le Rock."

In 1990, Adam resurfaced in Los Angeles with the confident and entertaining **Manners & Physique**, diving into electronic dance music without drowning in synthesized rubbish. Marco contributed to the songwriting (as did ex-Dexys leader Kevin Rowland, surprisingly enough) and plays guitar; producer/co-writer André Cymone did everything else but sing. Walloping techno beats and monotonous funk-rock grooves occasionally dislocate the album's pop spine, but Adam's melodic vocals and ridiculous lyrics remain a reassuring constant.

Drawing five tracks from **Kings of the Wild Frontier** and selecting notable tracks from each of Adam's group and solo albums prior to **Manners & Physique** (plus "Beat My Guest," from the B-side of "Stand and Deliver"), **Antics in the Forbidden Zone** compiles 21 tunes with few serious lapses in taste. (Four songs from the American **Dirk** is, however, at least two too many.)

Historically interesting if not exactly entertaining, the ten-song **Peel Sessions** documents the **Dirk**-era band (which included future Monochrome Set bassist Andy Warren) in January and July of 1978 and March 1979, doing "Animals and Men" and "Never Trust a Man (With Egg on His Face)" from the LP, along with "Zerox," "You're So Physical" (later a B-side) and otherwise unwaxed material.   [jy/i/kl]

See also *Bow Wow Wow, Monochrome Set, Wide Boy Awake, Wolfgang Press.*

ADAMSKI

Liveandirect (MCA) 1989 ●
Doctor Adamski's Musical Pharmacy (MCA) 1990 φ

At a time when it seemed Britain's "rave" culture of vast warehouse and outdoor acid house parties might cultivate a generation oblivious to the concept of live performance, the then-teenage Adamski hauled his synthesizers up onstage alongside the star DJs and reintroduced the notion. This novel approach made him an overnight star, the catchy debut single "N-R-G" immediately became an anthem and his debut album, recorded live at various raves and full of short, sharp snippets of interchangeable acid melodies and techno beats, serves as a valuable souvenir of an important flashpoint in British musical history. While it may not improve with age, **Liveandirect** will hold up better than the efforts of such Adamski imitators as Guru Josh.

Adamski's good fortunes continued when a young vocalist called Seal added a melancholic plea for racial harmony to an otherwise unspectacular instrumental, and the resulting "Killer" took up residence at the top of the UK singles charts. Adamski ran off to Los Angeles to record the rest of **Doctor Adamski's Musical Pharmacy**, and it's been downhill from there. "Killer" and the occasional serviceable instrumental fail to redeem his efforts as a vocalist, particularly on the disastrous cover versions of "All Shook Up" (reworked as "Space Jungle") and "Soul Kitchen."   [tf]

OLETA ADAMS

See *Tears for Fears*.

BARRY ADAMSON

The Man with the Golden Arm EP (nr/Mute) 1988 ●
Moss Side Story (Mute-Restless) 1989 ●
The Taming of the Shrewd EP (nr/Mute) 1989 ●
Delusion (Mute) 1991 φ

Best known for his tenures in Magazine and the Bad Seeds, bassist Adamson proves himself an adept composer and arranger on his own records, which are more orchestral works than conventional solo discs. Beatniky jazz, surf-rock and industrial *sturm und drang* are just a few of the manifold genres he enters to produce rich aural tableaus.

"Directed and produced by Barry Adamson," the 54-minute **Moss Side Story** is an exquisite soundtrack to a nonexistent film noir. Sampled newscasts, period sound effects and a great, throbbing version of Elmer Bernstein's "The Man with the Golden Arm" (previewed on a four-song 1988 EP) imbue the album with a strong aura of '60s mod London. A stellar cast of performers (including the Fall's Marcia Schofield, possessed diva Diamanda Galas and assorted Bad Seeds) contribute to this odd and inventive project, which surely has no correlative in most "alternative" record collections. (Perhaps as a result, Adamson got the nod to score a real film, the thriller *Delusion*, in 1991.)

Limited to EP length, the four fascinating new pieces on **Taming of the Shrewd** are nowhere near as cohesive or satisfying as the LP. With twangy guitar and thick polyrhythms dominating one side and full-bodied bebop on the other, Adamson teases with stylistic complexity that deserves to be fleshed out in a full-length effort.

[db]

KING SUNNY ADÉ AND HIS AFRICAN BEATS

Juju Music (Mango) 1982 ●
Synchro System (Mango) 1983 ●
Aura (Island) 1984 ●
The Return of the Juju King (Mercury) 1988 ●
Live Live Juju (Rykodisc) 1988 ●

Following a decade spent establishing himself as one of Africa's most prolific and successful pop artists, Nigeria's King Sunny Adé (Sunday Adeniyi) came to prominence in Europe and the US in 1982. Almost unanimously embraced by critics (if not consumers), he plays juju, a flowing, sonorous musical style which has its origins in the Yoruba people of Nigeria. Adé has made around 50 albums; only a handful have been released in the US.

The music is almost as formulaic as it is intoxicating; Adé's long songs (often filling an entire side on African releases) contain some of the most irresistible grooves anywhere. As many as a half-dozen guitarists and an equal number of percussionists playing simple figures collectively weave an intricate web that serves as background for call-and-response vocals. Within this framework, Adé—borrowing from many other cultures—adds his own touches. **Juju Music**, culled from several prior LPs, relies heavily on synthesizers,

Hawaiian steel guitars and reggae dub techniques. It is the densest of the first three domestic releases: ghostlike guitars float through one another with near-vocal textures for perhaps as organic a sound as can be produced with electric instruments.

Synchro System is more melodically stripped-down. Percussion dominates, especially the bubbling sound of the talking drum, an African instrument of variable pitch. On **Aura**, Adé sets his pan-cultural sights even further, and the rhythm tracks are almost pure beatbox in style. The vocal harmonies in his work have a distinctive Latin feel.

After it became clear that Adé was not to inherit the late Bob Marley's role as preeminent Third World musical/cultural ambassador, he returned to being just a Nigerian national treasure. **The Return of the Juju King** compiles tracks from three mid-'80s albums released on his own Atom Park label. Shaking off his failure to win Western hearts, Adé sounds like a happy man again; the joyous juju reaffirms his status as one of the most captivating and important musical talents anywhere in the world today.

As it turns out, Adé's major contribution in the West has been to open doors for others. Not having appeared on records by platinum-selling yuppie faves (as Youssou N'Dour and Ladysmith Black Mambazo have), Adé has had to watch as "world beat" became a hip way for white people to assuage their guilt and/or impress their friends. Regardless, he has continued to produce quality work; one noteworthy release is **Live Live Juju**, recorded in Seattle in 1987.

As much as Adé's music flows in the studio, it is really meant to be heard live. Songs are allowed to go on longer, and the interaction between his many band members (and the audience) is far more playful and intricate. In concert, the emphasis is shifted away from the synthesizers and steel guitars and towards the real roots of juju: drums, rhythm guitars and massed voices. **Live Live Juju** reprises material from previous US albums, but most of the songs are new (or at least previously unissued in the US). The recording quality is excellent, and the liner notes, concerning Adé as well as the social and cultural history of Nigerian pop music, are very informative. [dgs]

HASIL ADKINS
Out to Hunch (Norton) 1986
The Wild Man (Norton) 1987
Peanut Butter Rock and Roll (Norton) 1990
Moon Over Madison (Norton) 1990

Granted that rockabilly is a musical form with few rules, Hasil Adkins still comes on like a crazed lunatic; by comparison, Gene Vincent resembles Herbert von Karajan. Then again, West Virginian Adkins has rarely played by the rules. His recordings—the bulk of them dating from the late '50s/early '60s—are homemade one-man-band affairs, originally released, if at all, as singles on tiny and/or private labels. With literally no one to answer to, he has created one of the most idiosyncratic soundscapes to be shoehorned into the category of "popular music": a Bizarro-world of uncertain meters, irregular phrases, grungy guitar and wacked-out, over-modulated vocals on even more wacked-out songs.

Out to Hunch collects Adkins' best-known (if that's the right term) songs: "She Said" (later recorded by the Cramps), two not-quite-dance-crazes ("The Hunch" and "Chicken Walk"), the grisly "No More Hot Dogs" and its Guignolish spinoffs "We Got a Date" and "I Need Your Head." But with genius of this sort, inspiration can strike anywhere. "Come on Along" (on **Peanut Butter Rock and Roll**) features a chirping female voice mindlessly repeating the title phrase in the background. **Moon Over Madison**, a concept album spotlighting Adkins' quieter side, displays his authentic vocal twang on some affecting, moody originals.

But for the title track on **Moon Over Madison**, those three albums were all assembled from vintage recordings. **The Wild Man**, recorded in 1986, finds the 49-year-old as vital as ever. Whether exhorting hordes to "Do the Scalp" or turning wistful on "Still Missing You," Adkins—and a truly inimitable electric guitar—confirms that he's an American original. You'll never wrench these sounds from a synthesizer. [si]

ADOLESCENTS
Adolescents (Frontier) 1981 •
Brats in Battalions (S.O.S.) 1987 •
Balboa Fun*Zone (Triple X) 1988 •
Live 1981 and 1986 (Triple X) 1989 •
RIKK AGNEW
All by Myself (Frontier) 1982
RIKK AGNEW'S YARD SALE
Emotional Vomit (Triple X) 1990 •

Adolescents is one of the better longplayers to come out of the early Southern California hardcore punk scene. With the legendary Rikk Agnew on guitar, the first album by this high-energy Orange County quintet (drawing some of its teenaged membership from Agent Orange and Social Distortion) has a crisp, metallic guitar sound and clear, comprehensible vocals.

The group fell apart soon after the first album, but Rikk, singer Tony Montana (né Cadena) and bassist Steve Soto put it back together in 1986, leading the first of several revolving lineups. The self-released **Brats in Battalions**, a hard-hitting but sloppy rush of punk, rock, demi-metal and speedskating near-core, credits six members (including guitarist Alfie Agnew standing in for his older brother, Frank) and contains covers of "House of the Rising Sun" and "I Got a Right." (The fragmentary "Do the Freddy," however, is an original.)

With Montana and two Agnew siblings gone, Rikk and Soto co-wrote the songs and share the vocals on **Balboa Fun*Zone**, a lyrically provocative rock record of substantial merit. Agnew sings "Alone Against the World," a strongly cautionary tale about heroin addiction; Soto takes charge on "It's Tattoo Time," a paean to the epidermal art. Even an uncalled-for version of "Instant Karma" receives reverent, intelligent treatment. Topped off with crisp production of the quartet's thick guitar sound, the green-vinyl **Balboa** is an impressively mature record. (The cassette appends "Surf Yogi"; the CD adds that song plus two more.)

The crappy-sounding but nonetheless exciting **Live 1981 and 1986** (apparently a side of each, although the notes don't specify who-where-when) features three different Agnews singing and playing guitar in classic garage thrash. The sixteen cuts (eighteen on cassette; 21 on CD) cover most of the first album's material, giving such high-school concerns as "L.A. Girl," "No Friends" and "Word Attack" full-throttle stagings complete with bratty joke introductions. ("Hi, we're the Bangles . . . ")

Between the Adolescents' two lives (and a stint in Christian Death), Rikk Agnew made a nifty one-man solo album of enjoyable loud pop and demi-punk songs played with spunk and variety. Despite clumsy lyrics and rudimentary production, **All by Myself** proves that Agnew's budding abilities were not likely to be restrained by any simple genre formula.

Following the Adolescents' final (?) farewell in '89, Agnew began the new decade with another solo outing. Except that yesterday's punk now favors mildly metalized hard rock and has access to better production, **Emotional Vomit** has many of the same qualities as **All by Myself**. Brothers Alfie and Frank are among the few guests on this uneven collection of originals (plus a steely cover of Depeche Mode's "Never Let Me Down Again"). [cpl/i]

See also *Christian Death*.

ADRENALIN O.D.

Let's Barbeque with Adrenalin O.D. EP (Buy Our) 1983
The Wacky Hi-Jinks of . . . Adrenalin O.D. (Buy Our) 1984 ●
Humungousfungusamongus (Buy Our) 1986 ●
Cruisin' with Elvis in Bigfoot's U.F.O. (Buy Our) 1988
Ishtar (Restless) 1990 φ

VARIOUS ARTISTS

4 Bands That Could Change the World! (Gasatanka) 1987

It's always nice to encounter punks with a sense of humor. Although A.O.D. got off to a slow start on **Let's Barbeque**—six songs on seven inches recorded in fifteen minutes—these New Jerseyites have grown into a far better band. The first record's sound is barrel-bottom, but the playing has a nice industrial buzz; creative use of spoken and shouted vocals punctuates the drone.

"Middle-aged Whore" on **Wacky Hi-Jinks** was, as noted on the back cover, "recorded in our underwear." Musically, however, A.O.D. is no joke, a fact immediately apparent from "A.O.D. vs Godzilla," the killer stun-guitar instrumental that opens the album. Unfortunately, muddy production buries mediocre vocals spewing funny, satiric lyrics in fuzzy speedrock, leaving incisive numbers like "White Hassle" (alienation at the Castle) and the sketchy "Rock & Roll Gas Station" half of what they might have been.

The improved studio sound of **Humungousfungusamongus**, which opens with another monster movie instrumental ("A.O.D. vs. Son of Godzilla"), allows the warp-speed quartet to vent their wits and expanding musical imagination with greater clarity than ever before. "Fishin' Musician," "Pope on a Rope," "Bugs" and "The Nice Song (In the Key of D)" all put a full-frontal guitar assault to semi-clever lyrics. But A.O.D. has other ideas: "Masterpiece" gives punks their own version of the theme music from PBS's *Masterpiece The-*

atre (composed in 1729 by J.J. Mouret!), while "Pizza-n-Beer" changes gears entirely for all-percussion instrumentation. Above-average hardcore for suburban smartasses. (The CD also contains **Wacky Hi-Jinks**.)

On **4 Bands That Could Change the World**, a goofy concept platter shared with 7 Seconds, White Flag and F, A.O.D. whips off three rockingly entertaining covers (Bay City Rollers, Sex Pistols and Kiss) and "Rock & Roll Gas Station."

Teaming up with guitarist/producer Daniel Rey (Shrapnel, Ramones), A.O.D. then made an enormous musical leap into the punk-pop mainstream. A neat pre-LP 12-inch ("Theme from an Imaginary Midget Western" b/w "Coffin Cruiser" and Kiss' "Detroit Rock City") revealed the band's new direction—towards clear, medium-speed rock'n'roll—with conviction. Well-played and almost tuneful, the post-hardcore **Cruisin' with Elvis** contains "Theme" and other deadly potshots ("Something About . . . Amy Carter," "Bulemic Food Fight," "Flipside Unclassified") that thunder along with concise energy and the group's typical whimsy.

Despite a change of label and producer (Andy Shernoff, the ex-Dictator now in Manitoba's Wild Kingdom), A.O.D. are still their jocular rocking selves on **Ishtar**. Unfortunately, they're running low on inspiration: the mildly sarcastic lyrics aren't very clever and the music is utterly routine. After an auspicious beginning with the brief "My Achin' Back" and "Twenty Dollar Bill" (a melodic tune about finding money on the street), **Ishtar** downshifts into a terrible rendition of Queen's "Sheer Heart Attack" and slides sideways from there. Better luck next time. [i]

ADULT NET

Take Me EP (nr/Fontana) 1989 ●
The Honey Tangle (Fontana-PolyGram) 1989 ●

American guitarist/singer Brix Smith originally formed the Adult Net in 1985 as a flower-powery side project to the Fall, recording singles with a flexible lineup drawn from past/present members of the Fall and Smiths. **Take Me** has a great rendition of the Strawberry Alarm Clock's "Incense and Peppermints" and three originals, two of which take a pointless country turn.

Having ended her marriage to Mark E. in early '89, Brix left the Fall shortly after the release of **The Honey Tangle** that summer. Ex-Blondie drummer Clem Burke, erstwhile Smiths guitarist Craig Gannon and bassist James Eller back her on this catchy power-folk-pop collection that sounds like a flashback to 1981 Los Angeles. Polished by Craig Leon's mild paisley production, Smith's songs (plus a joyous cover of P.F. Sloan's "Where Were You (When I Needed You)") and wispy vocals recycle classic styles to no special effect, but the familiar setting helps sell the tuneful material. The American CD and cassette include four bonus tracks, including "Incense and Peppermints." [i]

See also *Fall*.

ADVENTURES

Theodore and Friends (nr/Chrysalis) 1985 ●
The Adventures (Chrysalis) 1985

The Sea of Love (Elektra) 1988 ●
Trading Secrets with the Moon (nr/Elektra) 1989 (Elektra)
   1990 ●

Vocalist Terry Sharpe and guitarist Pat Gribben began the sophisticated harmony-pop Adventures in London after their former group, Belfast's spunky Starjets, split up in 1980. On its classy if overproduced debut, the quintet—boasting three singers (including Gribben's wife, Eileen) and no on-board drummer—crafts crisp, commercial guitar/keyboards music distinguished by attractive melodies and striking harmonies. Slickly mainstream without being hollow or obnoxious (despite a stack of guest synthesists), **Theodore and Friends** (issued in the US as **The Adventures**) has a couple of great songs—the sweeping "Send My Heart" (which sounds like it was written for a synth-pop band) and the falsetto-sung African-accented "Another Silent Day"—plus pleasantly diverting also-rans.

Adding a drummer and adopting a warmer, semi-acoustic adult-rock sound, the Adventures essayed **The Sea of Love** with less artistic success. The songs aren't as good (Gribben's lyrical pretensions are such that he can base a song here on *The Trip to Bountiful*), and the performances lack the first LP's instrumental sparkle.

Stemming a drift towards becoming a bookish Abba, the again-drummerless Adventures engaged producers Clive Langer and Alan Winstanley, who gave **Trading Secrets with the Moon** an intimate sound colored with bits of fiddle, organ, horns, pedal steel and traditional Irish instruments. Unfortunately, the tasteful arrangements also minimize the band's backing vocals, leaving Gribben alone in the spotlight to sing his bland poetry. Lloyd Cole co-wrote one song, the countryish "Desert Rose." [i]

ADVERTISING
Jingles (nr/EMI) 1978

Britain's Advertising was a clever young pop quartet with a penchant for quirky but catchy tunes, punny teenager lyrics and the color pink. They had a near brush with UK chart success via a 45 called "Lipstick" (included on **Jingles**); failure to win a large following caused an early breakup. This album (produced separately by Andy Arthurs and Kenny Laguna) is chock-a-block with engaging numbers, cheery vocals and snappy, clean playing; the songs (written by guitarists Tot Taylor and Simon Boswell) are literate and charming. Since leaving Advertising, Tot Taylor has recorded under his own name, while Boswell became a producer and formed Live Wire. [i]

See also *Live Wire, Tot Taylor*.

ADVERTS
Crossing the Red Sea with the Adverts (nr/Bright) 1978
   (nr/Butt) 1982 (nr/Link Classics) 1990 ●
Cast of Thousands (nr/RCA) 1979
The Peel Sessions EP (nr/Strange Fruit) 1987
Live at the Roxy Club (nr/Receiver) 1990 ●

When the four Adverts (including female bassist Gaye Advert) debuted on a 1977 Stiff 45 with "One Chord Wonders," the young Londoners could barely play their instruments, but that didn't keep vocalist Tim (T.V.) Smith's song from offering a witty commentary on earnest incompetence. By the time they re-recorded the tune for their first LP, the Adverts had acquired just enough proficiency to make a positive difference.

In its own way, **Red Sea** is the equal of the first Sex Pistols or Clash LP, a hasty statement that captures an exciting time. Smith's tunes almost all offer a new wrinkle on issues of the day; when they fall into a rut, as in "Bored Teenagers," his breathy, urgent vocals compensate. It's too bad the original album didn't include the ghoulishly funny "Gary Gilmore's Eyes," a wicked single about a blind person who receives a transplant from you-know-(but-may-not-remember)-who. (That omission was rectified on the 1982 reissue but then repeated when a pressing boo-boo left it off the vinyl version of the '90 reissue. The CD, however, does contain that tricky little item.)

Oddly, **Cast of Thousands** is as feeble as **Red Sea** is vital. Fatigue and depression permeate the LP, suggesting that Smith's muse had made a hasty exit. One need only read the back-cover quote from 1 John 2:15 to get the picture: "Love not the world, neither the things that are in the world." Pretty punky, huh?

The Adverts' John Peel broadcast session EP was recorded in early 1977 and contains live-in-the-studio run-throughs of all the aforementioned songs plus two others. For a full-length live Adverts album, try the **Roxy** record, a '77 show that reviews the group's repertoire with appropriately raunchy sound. [jy/i]

See also *T.V. Smith's Explorers*.

AFGHAN WHIGS
Big Top Halloween (Ultrasuede) 1988
Up in It (Sub Pop) 1990

There's a surprising amount of subtlety—sophistication, even—rustling beneath the boozy, gutter-rat surface of this Cincinnati quartet's debut. While Greg Dulli's desperate, breathless rasp recalls **Hootenanny**-era Paul Westerberg (as does his uncommon wordsmithery: check out the bittersweet "Here Comes Jesus"), the rest of the band stirs '70s rock—from punk to pomp—into an aural hurricane with one hypnotic eye. An altogether terrific debut.

Typically gauzy Jack Endino production instantly brands **Up in It** as a Sub Pop issue. And while the increased volume (and hair length) are requisite, the Whigs still wax more lyrical than their thrash'n'burn labelmates. There's more implied in the affecting "I Know Your Little Secret" and the disjointed country swing of "Son of the South" than mere sonic overkill, an effect somewhat reflected in the sleeve art's understated creepiness. Repeated listens reveal a creeping Heartbreakers (as in J. Thunders) fixation, which might not be a bad thing to cultivate. [dss]

A FLOCK OF SEAGULLS
Modern Love Is Automatic/Telecommunication EP
   (Jive-Arista) 1981
A Flock of Seagulls (Jive-Arista) 1982 (Jive-RCA) 1986 ●
Listen (Jive-Arista) 1983 (Jive-RCA) 1986
The Story of a Young Heart (Jive-Arista) 1984 ●
Dream Come True (Jive-Arista) 1986 (Jive-RCA) 1986
Best of A Flock of Seagulls (Jive-RCA) 1987 ●

Amid all the talented and adventurous bands of the second Liverpool explosion, A Flock of Seagulls was ironically the first to snag a gold record in the US. Led by singer/keyboardist/guitarist Mike Score (he of the ludicrous hairdo) and including his brother Ali on drums, the quartet's first break came when Bill Nelson produced a single for them and released it on his Cocteau label.

The five-song **Telecommunication** EP has a catchy tune or two, but it wasn't until AFOS entered the studio to make **A Flock of Seagulls** with producer Mike Howlett that they developed a style of their own. Relying on guitarist Paul Reynolds' U2-influenced textural wash, distended strains of synthesizer and some fancy studio maneuvers, the band's inadequacies (mainly dumb lyrics and limited conceptual range) fade into the background on their debut LP, overtaken by listenable, danceable techno-rock that proved to have broad commercial appeal.

Attempting to follow that hugely successful album, the Seagulls recorded **Listen** with Howlett (except for one cut) and hit some real highs. Retreating from gimmicky sci-fi themes (notwithstanding the circuit-board cover), they found an affecting path in the lushly pretty, languid "Wishing (If I Had a Photograph of You)" and the understated "Nightmares," but fouled out on several boring tracks and "What Am I Supposed to Do," which starts well but winds up repeating the title endlessly. Score does the same thing on "(It's Not Me) Talking," but a propulsive synth-dance-beat and some neat sonic maneuvers keep it exciting.

Made without Howlett, **The Story of a Young Heart** is decidedly inferior. The bland romantic ballads on the first side lack character, have tedious vocals and point up the group's finite songwriting skill. "The More You Live, The More You Love" comes closest to creative merit but is plodding and forgettable. The rockier songs on the flipside are marginally better, but can't carry the record alone. A vain attempt at artistic maturity and sophistication, the real story here is one of ambition at odds with ability.

Reynolds left and AFOS made their next record as a trio (augmented by half a dozen different guitarists), with Mike Score in charge of production. Although somewhat short on personality, the almost modestly appointed **Dream Come True** is reasonably listenable, a collection of simpleminded romantic numbers led by "Heartbeat Like a Drum."

The ten-song compilation leans heavily on the first ("Telecommunication," "Space Age Love Song," the Top 10 "I Ran") and second ("Wishing," "Nightmares," "(It's Not Me) Talking") albums, with nothing later than 1985's "Who's That Girl (She's Got It)." The CD adds a nine-minute remix of "Wishing" and the third LP's title track.

In 1989, a new version of AFOS—with only Mike Score remaining from the original band—launched a vain comeback try, touring the US in support of a hopeless new single, "Magic." [i]

AFRIKA KORPS
Music to Kill By (Iron Cross) 1977
God It's Them Again! (Fr. New Rose) 1987

Fielding a five-man wedge of rhythm guitarists, the Afrika Korps was a casually constituted underground supergroup whose fifteen-person lineup included fanzine writers, Slickee Boys and other assorted Washington DC-area garagepunks. **Music to Kill By** boasts 22 songs (including the Slickee Boys' "Jailbait Janet," covers of the Kinks and Yardbirds, and such culturally profound outpourings as "Iggy," "Death to Disko!" and "N.Y. Punk."). Although badly recorded and mastered—the guitar army often sounds more like one kid playing through a Pignose amp—the band's unflinching musical integrity and enthusiasm make this a significant memento of punk's early independent label surge.

Reuniting on a smaller scale five years later, the Korps roared back into action with a punchy second album. Solomon Gruberger (who does a pretty good Joey Ramone imitation on "Tonight") shares lead vocal duties on the half-dozen songs with ex-Slickee Boys singer Martha Hull and SB guitarist Kim Kane. The clear production is certainly welcome, but the energetic performances are squandered on weak original material. See also *Slickee Boys*. [i]

AFROS
See *Run–DMC*.

AGENT ORANGE
Living in Darkness (Posh Boy) 1981 ●
Bitchin' Summer EP (Posh Boy) 1982 ●
When You Least Expect It ... EP (Enigma) 1984
  (Aoki-Restless) 1987 ●
This Is the Voice (Enigma) 1986 ●

Picture a band that combines the best elements of the Sex Pistols, the Ventures and early Blue Öyster Cult. Got that? Then you've got Agent Orange, a Fullerton, California trio who hybridized surf-twang sounds, smart-metal chops and punky drive. **Living in Darkness** is a short, concise collection of seven originals (like "Bloodstains") plus an appropriate memory-tweaker: the instrumental classic "Miserlou." **Bitchin' Summer** contains three previously released guitar instrumentals and a new song. (Both records are contained on one CD.)

The four songs on the 1984 EP display relative restraint, subordinating Mike Palm's guitar in favor of his echoed vocals on the pop "It's Up to Me and You." The two instrumentals are likewise less inflamed, although that doesn't stop "Out of Limits" from being great. A tepid cover of the Jefferson Airplane's "Somebody to Love," however, is a total mistake.

Established high enough in the skate-rock pantheon to offer an official band board for sale, Agent Orange issued **This Is the Voice**, a dynamic collection of high-energy vocal numbers that benefit greatly from (ex-Berlin) Daniel Van Patten's crisp electric production. The echo on Palm's strong voice, the lush guitar roar and the stiff-backed power drumming collectively suggest a slight '60s/'80s mod influence, but this impressive outing has a sound all its own. The record steers clear of punk overdrive to stand as Agent Orange's finest and most popular-sounding release. [rnp/i]

AGE OF CHANCE

Crush Collision EP (Virgin) 1987
One Thousand Years of Trouble (Virgin) 1987 •
Mecca (Charisma) 1990 ф

Age of Chance dresses up harsh British beatbox-metal-pop with colorful, vaguely apocalyptic sloganeering. Despite all the shouting, the Leeds quartet's biggest problem is the lack of a cohesive identity to match their records' careening sonic stew. The six-track **Crush Collision** is generally shrill and undistinguished, but it does include a pretty decent cover of Prince's "Kiss" (as well as a really awful one of the Trammps' "Disco Inferno").

One Thousand Years of Trouble benefits from being more gimmicky and over-the-top, with *lots* more sampling; even so, an album's worth of this stuff is pretty grating. You'd be better off going no further than Side Two, song one: the insistent "Who's Afraid of the Big Bad Noise?," which was a small UK hit.

With a fairly soulful new singer (Charles Hutchinson) and more polished songwriting, **Mecca** is a better focused, more listenable album which, in its own modest way, comes closer than its predecessors to realizing Age of Chance's idealized sonic melting pot. A more conventional effort, but a more enjoyable one.   [hd]

AGITPOP

Feast of the Sunfish (Community 3) 1985 •
Back at the Plain of Jars (Community 3-Rough Trade) 1986 •
Open Seasons (Twin/Tone) 1988
Stick It! (Twin/Tone) 1989 •
Po-Town Tea Party EP (Twin/Tone) 1989
The Comm3 Sessions [CD] (Community 3) 1990 •

For the past seven years, this Poughkeepsie, NY-spawned trio has been hacking up exceedingly dense hairballs of frat-boy-*cum*-trade-unionist fusion-punk. Heavily indebted to, if slightly to the right of (aesthetically) the Minutemen and Gang of Four, Agitpop operates on the age-old principle of "free your ass and your mind will follow." The thing is, unlike the bulk of their boho brethren, Agitpop navigate those hip joints as though they were doctors of chiropractic.

Feast of the Sunfish makes the most of the band's strengths; a love of open space, an aggressively jazzy rhythm section and a frontman, John DeVries, who's not altogether crazy about being in the spotlight. DeVries is choosy about where to spray his terse, atonal guitar leads (rhythm is almost totally absent) and he buries his pointed lyrics with the glee of someone sending pals off on a killer scavenger hunt. Make particular effort to exhume the contents of "Loaded with Blanks" and the chilling (no pun intended) "Icicles."

Back at the Plain of Jars is palpably riper. The sympathetically austere production (by Comm3 honcho Albert Garzon) adds a sinister edge to the odd instruments (wind chimes, squeeze toys, kiddie xylophones) all three members wield with exponentially increased dexterity. Not as twee as Pianosaurus, songs like "Snowdrift Over 4 Feet Tall" and the clever anti-Reagan jab "His Worst Movie Ever" verge on the sweet bad-seed menace of *The Little Girl Who Lives Down the Lane*.

For some reason, inking to Minneapolis' Twin/Tone label invested Agitpop with a yen for janglepop—after a fashion. **Open Seasons** grafts more florid playing onto their stolid Minutemen roots and ends up making you pine for what fIREHOSE could have been had the right third hand stirred the soup. **Stick It**, unfortunately, could be fROMOHIO outtakes; a monotonous landscape (most obviously the flat remake of **Sunfish**'s "On the Hudson") with precious few surprises, although "Crack in Her Heart" is a spry mod nugget.

The four-song **Po-Town Tea Party** contains a bracing cover of Gang of Four's "Not Great Men" and a rather hazy take on Cream's "Badge." **The Comm3 Sessions** combines the first two LPs on a single CD, adding a pair of extra tracks. Agitpop broke up in late '90.   [dss]

RIKK AGNEW

See *Adolescents*.

AGNOSTIC FRONT

Victim in Pain (RatCage) 1984 (Combat Core) 1986 •
Cause for Alarm (Combat Core) 1986 •
Liberty & Justice For ... (Combat) 1987 •
Live at CBGB (In Effect-Relativity) 1989 •

MADBALL

Ball of Destruction EP (In Effect-Relativity) 1989

This pioneering skinhead outfit which has been on the New York hardcore scene since the early '80s debuted (following a 1982 EP entitled **United Blood**) with an album of standard-issue punk—fast and blurry, but not absurdly so—and well-intentioned, if simpleminded, lyrics about unity, authority and justice. Roger Miret is an adequate run-of-the-mill shouter; like him, little about **Victim in Pain**, beyond its embossed all-black cover, is especially distinguished. (Remastering the LP for its 1986 reissue doesn't clear things up much; one CD contains both **Victim in Pain** and **Cause for Alarm**.)

Agnostic Front's demi-metal second album has a relentless kick-drum sound and a pernicious right-wing outlook. Songs about Bernhard Goetz ("Shoot His Load") and racist resentment of welfare recipients ("Public Assistance") join typical bonehead musings about killing, war, youth and the failings of the public education system. The one random moment of lucidity is "Toxic Shock," a protest against dioxin pollution.

A lineup change that retained only Miret and guitarist Vinnie Stigma then enlarged the quartet into a five-piece. With drums and guitars filling up every nanosecond, **Liberty & Justice** is a dull, onrushing storm of flailing limbs and incinerating transistors. Bottom-heavy and routine to the max, the music is utterly disposable; Miret's vocals dissolve in an incomprehensible hysterical gurgle. Even worse are the vague religious references.

The live record, cut with a new bassist in August 1988, strikes a balance between the energy and discipline of punk to deliver a taut, clear rock barrage that gallops and moshes along in close formation. The nineteen-song selection pretty much covers AF's high (and low) career points; the strangest moment is when

9

Miret leads the audience in reciting the Pledge of Allegiance.

Madball is a side project in which members of Agnostic Front back Roger's kid brother, Freddie. On the 7-inch **Ball of Destruction**, the younger Miret barks out eight indistinguishable shardcore tunes in under a minute each. You'd never know it from listening to this overcompressed buzz, but the program includes a couple of AF songs and the Animals' "It's My Life." [i]

A HOUSE
On Our Big Fat Merry-Go-Round (Sire-Reprise) 1988 ●
I Want Too Much (Sire-Reprise) 1990 ●

Ireland's A House will probably never attain the stadium status of U2, nor influence as many bands as the Undertones. But that's not to say the Dublin quartet's contribution to the history of shamrock'n'roll will be insubstantial. The first LP is a sprightly collection of literate guitar rock, made all the more endearing by Dave Couse's melodramatic (and often hilariously off-key) vocals. The joyous, charging "Call Me Blue" and the torchy "My Little Lighthouse" introduce an idea-filled band that isn't afraid to wear its heart (among other organs) on its sleeve.

I Want Too Much inadvertently answers the burning musical question, "What if the Violent Femmes aspired to be an honest-to-goodness electric rock group and *not* a jumped-up jug band?" An oversimplification, perhaps, but this is one amazing record. From the gentle folky strum of the opening "13 Wonderful Love Songs" to the thesaurus-busting "Small Talk," **I Want Too Much** reveals a band with an uncanny knack for writing witty pop tunes that actually mean something. Songs like "The Patron Saint of Mediocrity" and "I Think I'm Going Mad" provide a fair idea of the mindset at work here. [db]

JANE AIRE AND THE BELVEDERES
Jane Aire and the Belvederes (nr/Virgin) 1979
EDGE
Square One (nr/Hurricane) 1980
Complete Works of the Edge (nr/Preset) 1987

Another talented singer from Akron, Ohio whose career really got started outside her homeland. Accompanied here by a sharp four-piece English band otherwise known as the Edge, Aire works confidently through a solid set of tunes that includes the oft-recorded "Breaking Down the Walls of Heartache," Pearl Harbor's "Driving," Holland-Dozier-Holland's "Come See About Me," plus some of producer Liam Sternberg's better original compositions.

The Edge (the group) came about when guitarist Lu Edmonds and drummer Jon Moss (formerly of punk slouches London) left a brief and unrecorded incarnation of the Damned in 1978. With the addition of keyboardist Gavin Povey (who had played with Lew Lewis) and bassist Glyn Havard (whose long career has included stints with the Yachts and, er, Jade Warrior), the Edge fell together. They played behind Jane Aire as the Belvederes on her LP and appeared, nearly intact, on Kirsty MacColl's first album. Subsequent to the Edge, Lu has

worked in a number of bands, including Shriekback, the Spizzles and Public Image Ltd., while Jon Moss went on to temporary fame and fortune in Culture Club. Povey has done some additional recording with MacColl.

Oh yeah—about the music on **Square One**. Never quite blending into any particular style, the Edge's eclectic, melodic rock has flashes of the Jam, Boomtown Rats, Deep Purple, Police and Stranglers—all united by the satirical outlook of amusing lyrics. [i]

AJAX
Mind the Gap EP (Wax Trax!) 1989
One World EP (Wax Trax!) 1990
Ajax (Wax Trax!) 1990 ●

Among the bands who purvey industrial house music, this New York trio goes about it with a lighter, more accessible sensibility than most. Rather than concentrating on noisy ways to overpower a synthesized beat, Ajax uses natural-sounding percussion, open-air production (by Ajax and bigtime DJ Mark Kamins), busy bass lines and intriguing stylistic ingredients to dress up its starkly functional dance accompaniment. Unfortunately, numbingly monotonous repetition, routine found-sound samples and the songs' skimpy content render Ajax's records pretty useless outside the club environment.

The title tracks of the two 12-inch EPs (which otherwise contain remixes and filler) both appear on the band's full-length album, alongside several similar rhythmic workouts and a couple of genuine song-type things. While Mitchel (who's generally prone to shouts) does a bit of wispy singing in "Fast Cars," she really goes to town on "Haze" and "B Box," which actually boast lyrics (!) and melodies (!!). More promising than genuinely entertaining, **Ajax** suggests the group won't stay in the limited move'n'groove world forever. (Quality control footnotes: **One World** is marked as 33 but plays at 45 rpm, and **Ajax**'s track listing is completely out of order on the cover and inner sleeve.) [i]

ALARM
The Alarm EP (IRS) 1983 ●
Declaration (IRS) 1984 ●
Strength (IRS) 1985 ●
Eye of the Hurricane (IRS) 1987 ●
Presence of Love EP (nr/IRS) 1988
Compact Hits EP [CD] (A&M) 1988 ●
Electric Folklore Live EP (IRS) 1988 ●
Change. (IRS) 1989 ●
Newid. (nr/IRS) 1989 ●
A New South Wales EP (nr/IRS) 1989 ●
Standards (IRS) 1990 φ
Raw (IRS) 1991 φ

If these four young Welshmen weren't so studiedly intense, the Alarm might be able to drop the Clash/U2 pretensions and use their evident talent to make enjoyable records. Singer Mike Peters and bassist Eddie MacDonald write catchy, anthemic songs, but the tireless exhortations are tiring and, worse, can become ludicrous.

The Alarm compiles pre-LP UK singles: "The Stand," the first (but not last) pop song based on a

Stephen King novel, "Marching On" and three more slices of roughed-up folk-rock. **Declaration** further exploits the pose (and the big haircuts) with a batch of memorable tunes ("Sixty Eight Guns," "Blaze of Glory," "Where Were You Hiding When the Storm Broke?"), all smeared with Peters' melodramatic bawling. The Alarm's got an excess of passion; what they lack is the subtlety that keeps U2 from becoming histrionic.

Mike Howlett produced **Strength** and managed to rein in some of the Alarm's brassiness, slowing them down, focusing Peters' vocals and opening up the sound with dynamics and silence. Keyboards and stronger songs also contribute to the overall improvement, but it's still an Alarm LP. Highlights: the title track, which rips off Billy Idol to amusing effect, and "Spirit of '76," a Springsteenish crypto-ballad about the group's punk roots. Other tracks sound like old Gen X and Mott the Hoople. Weird but encouraging.

U2's ascendancy to global domination did not pass unnoticed in the Alarm camp, and the dull and disappointing **Eye of the Hurricane** has its share of echoed guitars and sweeping vocal theatrics. (Although, to be fair, most of the songs have too little personality—of any sort—to warrant comparison.) "Rain in the Summertime," an energetic dance-rocker with a catchy melody, is the album's standout; the oddest piece of inanity here is "Shelter," which mixes Pete Townshend's riff from "The Good's Gone" with lyrics lifted (in part) from various Stones songs.

The six-song, 42-minute **Electric Folklore Live** (in Boston, April '88) captures the most sanctimonious excesses of the Alarm's live show, not to mention those of the band's unaccountably fawning devotees. The overall effect is a bit ghoulish.

The Tony Visconti-produced **Change.** was supposedly intended as a poignant lament on the dying Welsh language, but the Alarm lacks the lyrical subtlety or musical finesse to pull off such an ambitious conceit. Instead, the band sounds more desperately derivative than ever, taking half-cocked stabs at techno-glam ("Sold Me Down the River"), blue-collar wisdom ("Devolution Workin' Man Blues") and power-balladry ("Love Don't Come Easy") amidst the usual barrage of mock-messianic boot-stomping. Oddly, **Change.**'s only affecting track is also its most over-the-top: the heartfelt choir-and-orchestra-accompanied "A New South Wales." (In a commendably unusual move, the Alarm also released **Newid.**, a complete Welsh-language version of the album.)

The pompously titled **Standards** collects thirteen (fifteen on the CD) of the band's near-hits plus three new recordings: the self-aggrandizing and self-explanatory "The Road," a slick remake of an early single ("Unsafe Building") and a pointless run-through of John Lennon's "Happy Christmas (War Is Over)." The CD bonus tracks are "Marching On" and "Blaze of Glory."   [i/hd]

WILLIE ALEXANDER AND THE BOOM BOOM BAND
Willie Alexander and the Boom Boom Band (MCA) 1978
Meanwhile ... Back in the States (MCA) 1979

WILLIE ALEXANDER
Solo Loco (Bomp!) 1981
Tap Dancing on My Piano (Fr. New Rose) 1986

WILLIE LOCO ALEXANDER & THE CONFESSIONS
Autre Chose (Fr. New Rose) 1982
A Girl Like You (Fr. New Rose) 1982

WILLIE "LOCO" ALEXANDER
Taxi-Stand Diane EP (Fr. New Rose) 1984
Greatest Hits (nr/New Rose) 1985
The Dragons Are Still Out (Fr. New Rose) 1988

Long-time Boston scene patriarch Alexander is an intriguing figure whose redoubtable three-decade résumé includes such groups as the Lost, Bagatelle, Grass Menagerie—even a stint in the post-Lou Reed Velvet Underground. With countless club gigs under his belt, Alexander's credentials are impressive; unfortunately, his inconsistent records aren't. (The appellation is a tribute to Latin pianist Joe Loco.)

Willie Alexander and the Boom Boom Band is dedicated to Jack Kerouac, and includes Alexander's tributary "Kerouac," a cult hit when it first appeared on a 1975 independent single. The song's a heartfelt standout; the rest of the record is routine bar-band rubbish, wanting for both songs and style. **Meanwhile** follows the same path, but is notably better, thanks to Alexander's looser singing. For him, sloppiness is definitely an asset.

Willie left the Boom Boom Band behind for **Solo Loco**, relying instead on his own keyboards and percussion, with some outside guitar assistance. The record is a real departure, using occasional synthesizers to support extended, moody numbers that refer back to his earliest recorded work, and a voice that seems at once weary and sanguine. The material is uneven; when it's good, the record shines brightly. (**Solo Loco** was originally released on French New Rose; the American version is slightly different.)

Autre Chose—two disques of live Willie—was recorded in France during a March/April 1982 tour with a new backing trio. The choice of material is eclectic, beginning with "Tennesse [sic] Waltz" performed a cappella and including all of his best(-known) songs, plus some new things.

The Confessions on **A Girl Like You** (recorded in an American studio but unreleased outside France) include a saxophonist, the same bassist and guitarist from the live LP, but no drummer; Willie (a qualified percussion practitioner) picks up the sticks for this effort. Like a low-key version of a '70s Rolling Stones album, there's a little rock'n'roll, a blues number, lots of sex, a few choice covers and some good times. A career high-water mark, **A Girl Like You** (dedicated to Thelonious Monk) shows various sides of this mature—if limited—performer.

Continuing along his odd Boston-and-Paris path, Alexander recorded a spare album that excludes guitar and rock in favor of keyboards for a bluesy, late-night sound: **Tap Dancing on My Piano** has the loose, funky feel of old friends tinkering in the studio. Basically, Willie accompanies himself on piano with varying amounts of harmonica, sax and drums thrown in for accent. There's nothing here you would call arranged: even the busiest tracks sound like a first rehearsal. The boozy, seemingly extemporaneous "I'm So Lonesome I Could Cry" is a heartwarming highlight; the rest varies from Randy Newmanesque ("The Ballad of Boby Bear," named after a drummer of Willie's acquaintance who does spell it that way) to the bizarre ("Me & Stravinsky Now"). A modest and appealing slice of sincerity.

The Dragons Are Still Out finds Alexander back to rocking with a full-strength rock trio, horns, co-producer/co-writer Erik Lindgren on keyboards and even a cellist. Fearlessly covering a wide range of styles—from a unique interpretation of "Slippin' and Slidin'" to the improvised weird-piano autobiography of "Me and Dick V." and the inadvisable (but not *completely* embarrassing) "WA Rap"—as well as more typical (and more exotic) fare, **The Dragons** proves that this old-timer is neither out of touch nor out of tricks.   [i]

ALGEBRA SUICIDE
Algebra Suicide EP (Buzzerama) 1982
An Explanation for That Flock of Crows EP (Buzzerama) 1984
Big Skin [tape] (Cause & Effect) 1986 (Buzzerama) 1988
The Secret Like Crazy (RRR-DOM) 1988
Real Numbers [CD] (Ger. Pursuit of Market Share) 1989 ●
Alpha Cue (Bel. Body) 1990

Of the many vocalist/instrumentalist duos to emerge in and around the new wave, this Chicago team is quite unique, a fascinating marriage of Don Hedeker's music and Lydia Tomkiw's poetry. Over the course of its career, Algebra Suicide has flirted with pop forms and occasionally shared stylistic ground with both Laurie Anderson and the Velvet Underground but never wavered from its own individual path.

The eponymous debut—a four-song 7-inch—puts a sketchy but atmospheric mix of guitar and rhythm box behind Tomkiw's coolly intoned short texts, which include the haunting "True Romance at the World's Fair." **That Flock of Crows**, also a 7-inch EP, adds bass, better sound and new vocal inflections (Tomkiw nearly sings "Tonight") to the recitation of four more pieces made accessible—even catchy—through tangible, occasionally narrative ideas and strong internal tempos. Algebra Suicide isn't rock'n'roll, but even those with an aversion to poetry should try the pair's concise records.

Issued on cassette with a lyric booklet, **Big Skin** introduces piano and simple synthesizers to Hedeker's increasingly complex and dynamic musical contributions. The duo stumbles in several efforts to synchronize the verbal/instrumental rhythms, but both the song-form music and the lyrical content (like a fascinating, wry discussion of death entitled "Little Dead Body Poem," also released on a contemporaneous single with two other **Big Skin** selections) are typically engrossing.

The Secret Like Crazy is a generous compilation, containing three tracks from each EP, half of **Big Skin** and four items from various sources and three new cuts. The German CD-only **Real Numbers** is a convivial live album, recorded (with tapes supplementing Hedeker's onstage guitar work) in Chicago in April 1988. Premiering new material and revisiting more than a dozen oldies

(all with the benefit of new backings/presentations and Tomkiw's brief introductions), **Real Numbers** is a significant addition to the Algebra Suicide catalogue.

The couple's first full-fledged studio album, **Alpha Cue**, is their most ambitious production to date. (And the first to employ a guest musician, who plays bass and piano on two numbers.) Except for the robotic electronic drumming, Hedeker's carefully formed tracks have a credible band sound and enough chordal structure to easily support melodies; additionally, some of Tomkiw's multi-tracked vocals resemble tune-shy singing a lot more than recitation. Is Algebra Suicide on the verge of finding a way to infiltrate the pop mainstream?   [i]

ALICE DONUT
Donut Comes Alive (Alternative Tentacles) 1988
Bucketfulls of Sickness and Horror in an Otherwise Meaningless Life (Alternative Tentacles) 1989
Mule (Alternative Tentacles) 1990 ●
Revenge Fantasies of the Impotent (Alternative Tentacles) 1991 ●

Although this New York quintet writes and plays punky junk-culture pop with considerable skill, singer Tomas Antona has one of those hate-it-or-leave-it voices, an obnoxious high-register wheedle that could earn him the understudy role in Jane's Addiction. (The writer who described his singing as Jello Biafra on helium pretty much nailed it.) A belated East Coast response to the Dickies and Redd Kross, the crude but funny **Donut Comes Alive** boasts mean-spirited songs about Tipper Gore, three different child stars (Linda Blair, Mason Reese and Joan of Arc) and a noisy rewrite of Donovan's "Sunshine Superman."

When the inconsistent production of **Bucketfulls of Sickness and Horror** falters, the sloppy guitar smear obscures everything but Antona's voice. (As on the first LP, bassist Ted Houghton sings a couple of numbers, but his inoffensive strivings in that department aren't much of an improvement.) Rather than target specific icons (with the exception of the intelligently critical "Sinead O'Connor on MTV"), the lyrics take broader aim at groups like celebrities, jocks, shoppers, etc.

With **Mule**, Alice Donut sheds its juvenile skin to reveal tight, bracing musical intricacy and intelligently incisive social commentary. Tomas' discovery of more listenable ways to express himself, coupled with the band's vastly improved playing, makes the record challenging and invigorating. The dark vision running through provocative songs about death, religion, menial labor, urban anomie and man-induced genetic plague is powerful stuff, and the sturdy music backs it up with authority.   [i]

ALICE IN CHAINS
Facelift (Columbia) 1990 φ

Alice in Chains might as well be Seattle's 999, a second-wave also-ran in the mighty Northwest's late-'80s surge of grungy, woolly bands. While the scene was pretty well along by the time of **Facelift**, Alice in Chains' clever combination of balls and hooks adds a distinct twist to the genre. Although the songs do tend to sound similar, Dave Jerden's excellent production and the quartet's ability to loft lasting melodies above the craggy power-crunch riffs make **Facelift** (and especially the single "We Die Young") one of the better in its breed.　　　　　　　　　　　　　　　　　　　　[ja]

ALIEN SEX FIEND

Who's Been Sleeping in My Brain? (Relativity) 1983 ●
Acid Bath (Epitaph) 1984 (Chameleon) 1988 ●
Liquid Head in Tokyo (nr/Anagram) 1985
Maximum Security (nr/Anagram) 1985
I Walk the Line EP (nr/Flicknife) 1986
"It" the Album (nr/Plague-Anagram) 1986
"It" the Album/Maximum Security [tape]
(nr/Plague-Anagram) 1986
The Impossible Mission Mini L.P. (PVC) 1987
Here Cum Germs (PVC) 1987 ●
The First A.S.F. CD [CD] (nr/Plague-Anagram) 1987 ●
All Our Yesterdays (nr/Plague-Anagram) 1988 ●
Another Planet (Caroline) 1988 ●
Too Much Acid? (nr/Plague-Anagram) 1989 ●
A.S.F. Box (nr/Plague-Anagram-Windsong) 1990
Curse (Sinclair) 1990 ●

Although they came out of England's early-'80s Batcave movement, Alien Sex Fiend were (and are) a far cry from the era's typical gothicism. "Ignore the Machine," the band's debut single, established their unique sound, as ghoulish frontman Nik Fiend's creepy Cockney-accented ravings meld to the pulsing cosmic keyboards of his consort, Mrs. Fiend; Johnny Ha-Ha's drums are integrated with a burbling rhythm box, while Yaxi High-rizer spins off primitive Link Wray-via-the-Cramps guitar riffs. Neither did they fit into the decadent glam image propagated by Specimen: theatrical enough to be their own horror movie, Nik's Herman Munster/Alice Cooper synthesis is an original and enjoyable musical persona.

Undisturbed by mainstream trends, the Fiends have made a lunatic career out of a comic-book aesthetic and their own hallucinogenic strain of humor; through a long string of releases, the only thing they ever seem to take seriously is having a freaky old time.

The first LP is a charming collection of punky psycho-tunes like "Wish I Woz a Dog" and "Wild Women." The most concise ASF record, it's like a '50s monster-movie soundtrack returned from the dead. The US edition subtracts one tune in favor of the catchy and audacious B-side "Drive My Rocket (Up Uranus)"; a live track and "Crazee" were added to the later CD.

The less guitar-driven production emphasizes Mrs. Fiend's gloriously spooky synth blips on **Acid Bath**, an inspired dose of mesmerizing, brain-frying insanity. The spacey "E.S.T. (Trip to the Moon)" and "Attack!" (a surging rocker) lead the pack of cool cuts. (The CD adds a psychobilly B-side, "Boneshaker Baby," a live cut and a dub mix.)

The lack of a substantial repertoire at that point makes **Liquid Head**, recorded live in Tokyo, pretty unnecessary, although completists will want it for the otherwise unrecorded "Back to the Egg."

Maximum Security is a big departure from the first two albums, and the least of all Fiend works. Bleak and predominantly slow, the material is based heavily around drum machine beats (replacing Ha-Ha's human touch) and suffers from a somewhat monotonous same-

ness. The title track (also released as a 45) is a notable exception.

The Fiends came right back, though, with **I Walk the Line**, a robust four-song 12-inch which struck a new singles mold for the band: danceable rhythms overlaid by aerodynamic guitar riffs. (The EP also contains a smoking Fiendization of the Coop's "School's Out.") This set the stage for **"It" the Album**, unquestionably the group's most creative, mind-expanding undertaking. The sound is far looser and more organic ("Get into It" is a particularly loopy example), and many of the songs—like the entrancing "Manic Depression"—are stretched to psychedelic lengths. The cassette version pairs it with **Maximum Security**.

The Impossible Mission Mini L.P. combines "The Impossible Mission" 45 (a groovy instrumental) and its fuzzbuster Cramps-like B-side, "My Brain Is in the Cupboard Above the Kitchen Sink," with two previous singles—the driving "Smells Like . . . " (also on **"It"**) and a cover of Red Crayola's "Hurricane Fighter Plane"—and their B-sides, seven tracks in all. The subsequent **Here Cum Germs** (which also contains both sides of the "Impossible Mission" single) is a good album, but increasing friction with guitarist Yaxi led to a somewhat thrown-together, incomplete feel. Nonetheless, the title cut, the acoustic-flavored "Isolation" (the closest they've come to a ballad) and the epic "Boots On!" are high spots.

Yaxi departed after **Germs**, leading to **All Our Yesterdays**, a consistently high-quality end-of-an-era singles compilation that should definitely be the first choice for those new to Fiendom. **The First A.S.F. CD** is just **Maximum Security** with a lot of extra stuff tacked on: "E.S.T.," "Attack!," a different version of "Boneshaker Baby" and a remix of "Ignore the Machine."

Another Planet is an Alien Sex Fiend watershed; the revitalized duo (and some capable new cohorts) come up with their most entertaining album to date. The wacky, sample-based "Bun-Ho!" sits among such gripping, streamlined rockers as "Sample My Sausage," "Nightmare Zone" and "Everybody's Dream." Meanwhile, studio pranks like "Wild Green Fiendy Liquid" and "Instant Karma Sutra" add to the overall psychotronic aura. (The CD version adds a searing cover of Hawkwind's "Silver Machine" and the Stones' "Satisfaction.")

Too Much Acid? is a splendid double-live album from a spring '89 European jaunt. The reconstituted band (the Fiends are joined officially by Rat Fink Jr. and Doctor Milton, who both play various permutations of guitar, drums and keyboards) is a boon, and it's great to hear the material—mainly singles, including the then-current 45 "Haunted House" (a Fiends-on-45 medley set to house beats)—flow with such free-form elasticity. The **A.S.F. Box** contains a fun mixture of previously issued material: three 12-inches, the **R.I.P.** 10-inch EP and an *11-inch* historical curio (the **E.S.T.** EP). There's also a booklet, a poster, a T-shirt and, last (but certainly not least), a plastic turd.

Returning to the more experimental **"It"** mold, **Curse** emphasizes longer tracks like the monstrous three-part masterpiece "Katch 22," whose creeping, neo-orchestral bounce suggests Laibach on acid. Such hypnotics as "Ain't Got Time to Bleed" and the bug-eyed-boogie single "Now I'm Feeling Zombiefied" alternate with faster, maniacal blasts like "Eat! Eat! Eat!" and "Burger Bar Baby." The CD and cassette add five, including a Cramps semi-cover, "Mad Daddy Drives a U.F.O.," and an insane gig announcement, "Radio Jimi." [gef]

ALL

Allroy Sez .... (Cruz) 1988 ●
Allroy for Prez EP (Cruz) 1988 ●
Allroy's Revenge (Cruz) 1989 ●
Trailblazer (Cruz) 1990 ●
Allroy Saves (Cruz) 1990 ●

In 1987, the Descendents parted ways with singer Milo Aukerman, bringing ex-Dag Nasty singer Dave Smalley in to take over, and transmuted into All, drummer Bill Stevenson's long-brewing caffeine concept quartet. Whether or not anyone actually knows what the concept is, All puts a melodic spin and a goofy lyrical twist on punky, clear guitar rock. At the first LP's silliest, All sings a Dickiesish ode to "Alfredo's," a crummy Mexican fast food joint, in the hopes of getting free food. But All's no joke: "Just Perfect," "#10 (Wet)" and "Hooidge" have killer hooks and a beach-blanket sound energized by unexpected hardcore-derived moves. At once summarizing and surpassing the Descendents, All offers a spunky, electric post-punk alternative for those who miss Generation X and despise Billy Idol. Totally excellent.

Allroy for Prez dispenses with the humor for a half-dozen rocking love songs written individually by all the Alls. The playing and production are killer, but the material doesn't consistently connect with equal potency. From Smalley's bitter "Wrong Again" through bassist/cover artist Karl Alvarez's cynical "I Hate to Love," the record gains melodic momentum, peaking on "Postage," an overdriven Shoes-like power pop hummer penned by Stevenson. The CD and cassette add a new version of "Just Perfect" and "Wishing Well," both from a prior 12-inch single.

Scott Reynolds replaced Smalley in time for **Allroy's Revenge**, a speedy, punkier-sounding album of broadening artistic ambition that lacks the production clarity, melodic strength and carefree demeanor of All's best work. Existential anxieties and problems with women (even "Copping Z," an intriguingly syncopated number about sleeping late, asks "What can I expect from the years ahead?") set a serious tone that is hardly leavened by the hard-edged music. (The delightful "She's My Ex," which puts romantic regrets to a tuneful bop, is the exception that best demonstrates the problem.) A snappy rendition of "Hot Rod Lincoln" (one of two CD/tape bonus tracks) proves that All hasn't lost its taste for fun, but this powerful, occasionally enlightening record should have been made by another band.

In a nice bit of continuity, the live **Trailblazer**, recorded at New York's CBGB on a Tuesday night in July 1989, opens with the same song that closes the **Revenge** CD. Named after a portable toilet that (according to the stomach-turning liner notes) vastly improved All's quality of life on the road, **Trailblazer** draws more than half of its fourteen songs from **Revenge**. An adequate but unessential document, the sound is mushy and flat, and the performances are nothing special.

The pursuit of the mythic All has most recently brought the group to **Allroy Saves**, a complex and sophisticated album that trades in difficult rhythms and intricate guitar figures, as well as pop melodies and thoughtful lyrics. With Reynolds taking the lead writing role, conversational narratives about losers, fools, cops and frogs make **Saves** fascinating and provocative; the rough music alternates All-some catchiness (as on Milo Aukerman's Gen X-y "Just Like Them") with a challenging attack that approaches an unpretentious punk Police. [i]

See also *Dag Nasty, Descendents, DYS, Last.*

ALL ABOUT EVE

All About Eve (Mercury) 1988 ●
Scarlet and Other Stories (Mercury) 1989 ●

This London quartet features the rather lovely (and often multi-tracked) voice of Coventry-born Julianne Regan (an early bassist in Gene Loves Jezebel!) and utilizes, of all people, former Yardbird bassist Paul Samwell-Smith in the producer's chair. With dreamy-looking cover art and songs about children, angels and clouds, one might expect lots of wispy, ethereal music, but 1988's **All About Eve** mostly offers up mainstream, big-guitar rockers. Even the quieter moments, such as "Like Emily" and "Shelter from the Rain" (with Wayne Hussey of the Mission adding vocals), sound like arena fare by some U2 support act. (The CD adds three.)

Samwell-Smith gives **Scarlet and Other Stories** a much lighter, more acoustic sound. This setting is better suited to Regan's voice, but the LP drags along laboriously; the softer spots come dangerously close to resembling Renaissance. In comparison to this, the debut's variety is a real asset.

Guitarist Tim Bricheno left in '90 and resurfaced later that year in the Sisters of Mercy. [dgs]

See also *Sisters of Mercy.*

ALLEY CATS

Nightmare City (Time Coast) 1981
Escape from the Planet Earth (MCA) 1982

ZARKONS

Riders in the Long Black Parade (Time Coast-Enigma) 1985
Between the Idea and the Reality ... Falls the Shadow (Atlantic) 1988 ●

The Alley Cats—Dianne Chai (bass/vocals), Randy Stodola (guitar/vocals) and John McCarthy (drums)—were an early fixture on the Los Angeles punk scene, churning out loudhardsemifast rock with awful, predictable lyrics. Proceeding from independent label land to the majors, the group's two LPs show some progress—i.e., **Nightmare City** is more samey and less imaginatively produced than **Escape from Planet Earth**.

Parting company with both MCA and their original name, the trio reappeared in 1985 as the Zarkons. The diabolical production on the eight-song **Riders in the Long Black Parade** sinks the heavily echoed vocals deep into the wall behind your speakers; although nearly inaudible, Chai's reasonably dramatic rendition of Grace Slick's "White Rabbit" (in march-time, no less) is the album's only sign of life.

Joined by two new sidepersons (a female vocalist and a different drummer), Stodola and Chai then raised their pretensions tenfold. **Between the Idea and the Reality** (title courtesy of T.S. Eliot)—a slick and vapid radio wannabe—begins by ruining the Yardbirds' "Heart Full of Soul" with synth drums and a noxious sax solo and then proceeds to desecrate the memory of Dylan Thomas, setting one of his poems ("The Hunchback in the Park") to atrocious fake folk music. Beyond contempt. [i]

GG ALLIN AND THE JABBERS
Always Was, Is, and Always Shall Be (Orange) 1980
    (Black & Blue) 1988
Public Animal #1 EP (Orange) 1982
No Rules EP (Orange) 1983
Banned in Boston (Black & Blue) 1989 φ

GG ALLIN AND THE SCUMFUCS
Eat My Fuc (Blood) 1984 (Black & Blue) 1988
Hard Candy Cock EP (Blood) 1984
I Wanna Fuck Your Brains Out EP (Blood) 1985

GG ALLIN AND THE SCUMFUCS/ARTLESS
GG Allin and the Scumfucs/Artless (Ger. Starving
    Missle-Holy War) 1985

GG ALLIN
Live Fast, Die Fast EP (Black & Blue) 1984 + 1987
Hated in the Nation [tape] (ROIR) 1987
Freaks, Faggots, Drunks & Junkies (Homestead) 1988
Doctrine of Mayhem (Black & Blue) 1990

GG ALLIN AND THE HOLY MEN
You Give Love a Bad Name (Homestead) 1987

For better or worse, GG Allin is a legend. This self-immolating jockstrap-clad mace-spraying dung-heaving aberration has somehow survived his own berserk reputation (not to mention his recklessly self-destructive instincts) to become the worst nightmare the Dead Boys and Iggy never had, a relentlessly obnoxious, coarse and lewd extremist who can send even the most generous-minded liberal over the edge. His catalogue is a juggernaut of puerile mania, demented concupiscence and *Hustler*-level humor.

All moral and artistic judgment aside, Allin is due some credit for managing to do what he's done with so much conviction for so long. GG's long and storied career began in 1978, deep within New Hampshire's rolling hills, when somebody foolishly fronted this Hookset, NH kook some green to press an LP. A decent though badly produced record, **Always Was, Is, and Always Shall Be** (which sold like hotcakes in Sweden) mixes a variety of influences—most notably the Stooges and the Dolls, but also 1980-vintage punk and new wave pop—into a fairly appealing rock sound. But Allin has a fatal weakness for extremely vulgar lyrics. How can a relatively straight song like "Unpredictable" be taken seriously in the vicinity of "Beat, Beat, Beat" and the fatuous "Pussy Summit Meeting"? Allin clinched his commercial fate with unwavering offense, and whatever promise flashed on the first LP faded on subsequent releases.

David Peel's Orange Records saw fit to add to the GG Allin and the Jabbers library in 1982 and '83, issuing two 7-inch EPs, **Public Animal #1** and **No Rules**. The former merely consists of three album tracks plus "You Hate Me and I Hate You," a new cut which sounds like a small-town guesstimate of big-city hardcore. **No Rules**, however, isn't all that bad. Gone for a fleeting three-song moment are the sodomic and anatomical references, replaced by the apt punk strains of "No Rules," "New York City Tonight" and "Up Against the Wall." (GG regains his vile composure on "A Fuckup," but it's a good-humored rant.) The Jabbers disbanded soon after, but GG reunited with two of them in '84 for the **Live Fast, Die Fast** EP.

After a brief run as frontman of Manchester, NH's Cedar Street Sluts, Allin organized the Scumfucs, a trashy trio indeed. The pairing's three releases on Blood are among the most intensely unlistenable offerings ever spewed into the rock underground. As **Eat My Fuc** (co-produced by—get this—Dick Urine) captures the totally skill-less Scumfucs in flat and murky sound, it becomes apparent that GG's lyrics have taken a considerable turn towards true derangement—where they have since remained.

Although the music is a little more interesting, **Hard Candy Cock** tenders five more songs of similar caliber and mentality. Only "Convulsions"—an interesting rhythmic departure from GG's usual invective pattern—strays from the profane path. **I Wanna Fuck Your Brains Out** continues the scatological tirade, and merits no descriptive amplification.

Allin laid low for a while, but 1987 brought a sudden surge in his hip credibility, and a few independent labels saw fit to encourage him into further ignobility and profligacy. ROIR issued **Hated in the Nation**, a tape which collects some prior EPs and singles, including "Hard Candy," "Drink, Fuck and Fight" and "Gimme Some Head" (a 1981 45 on which GG is accompanied by two ex-members of the MC5). The cassette includes some live stuff, sessions with "the New York Superscum" (which includes J Mascis of Dinosaur Jr.) as well as a few of the more articulate messages left on GG's answering machine.

Homestead endured GG for two offerings, and label head Gerard Cosloy even played guitar on the Holy Men LP, **You Give Love a Bad Name**. Whatever vestiges of a singing voice Allin once had are lost to the ravages of self-abuse; his raspy whinings are blanketed over the usual backdrop of punk-*cum*-grunge metal. "Tough Fuckin' Shit" is a sure-fire original winner, as are covers of Bad Tuna Experience's "Beer Picnic" and Charles Manson's "Garbage Dump." (Be sure to check out the liner notes detailing GG's sexual exploits.) Although he is joined by different sidemen on **Freaks, Faggots, Drunks & Junkies**, the album is virtually a carbon copy of **Love**.

With Allin languishing in a Michigan jail after one of his excesses got way too excessive, his recording career has been on ice of late. But a number of reissues, retrospectives and compilations have appeared recently. **Banned in Boston**, for one, consists of early studio cuts, '82 live matter and radio interviews. [icm]

STEVE ALMAAS
See *Beat Rodeo*.

MARC ALMOND AND THE WILLING SINNERS

Vermin in Ermine (nr/Some Bizzare) 1984 ●
Tenderness Is a Weakness EP (nr/Some Bizzare) 1984
Stories of Johnny (nr/Some Bizzare) 1985 ●
Stories of Johnny EP (nr/Some Bizzare) 1985 ●
The House Is Haunted EP (nr/Some Bizzare-Virgin) 1986

MARC ALMOND

Melancholy Rose EP (nr/Some Bizzare-Virgin) 1987
Mother Fist ... and Her Five Daughters (nr/Some
    Bizzare-Virgin) 1987 ●
Singles 1984–1987 (nr/Some Bizzare-Virgin) 1987 ●
The Stars We Are (Some Bizzare-Capitol) 1988 ●
Jacques (nr/Some Bizzare) 1989 ●
Enchanted (Some Bizzare-Capitol) 1990 ●

MARC AND THE MAMBAS

'Untitled' (nr/Some Bizzare) 1983
Torment and Toreros (nr/Some Bizzare) 1983

Leaving the evident confines of Soft Cell behind—during, and subsequent to the dissolution of, his partnership with Dave Ball—singer Marc Almond assembled various associates to be the Mambas on his first two solo albums. **'Untitled'** (an LP plus a three-song 12-inch) is a swell hodgepodge of originals, covers, collaborations and excesses, all sung in Almond's appealing but pitch-poor voice. With Annie Hogan and Matt (the The) Johnson as his main collaborators, Almond ventures into summery soul ("Angels"), ambient balladry ("Big Louise") and obvious source material (Lou Reed's "Caroline Says," Syd Barrett's "Terrapin," Jacques Brel's "If You Go Away"), covering phenomenally varied terrain. More an audio sketchbook than a coordinated album, **'Untitled'** is nonetheless a fine excursion outside the techno-pop corridors of Soft Cell.

Torment and Toreros, on the other hand, is a vile and pathetic attempt to ape '30s German cabaret decadence with mostly piano/orchestral backing and calculated-to-shock vulgar lyrics. A sleazy two-record drag.

That digression over and done with, Almond moved on to the Willing Sinners, and began a far more entertaining segment of his career. Playing his campy gutter queen persona to the hilt, he is pictured on the cover of **Vermin in Ermine** perched on a garbage can, wearing devil's horns and a spangled jacket he could only have borrowed from Liza Minnelli. While the songs typically reflect Almond's seamy, negativist taste ("Ugly Head," "Tenderness Is a Weakness," "Crime Sublime," "Shining Sinners," etc.), the Sinners and sidemen provide theatrical, often sarcastically caricatured music to accompany his stylized singing. **Vermin** isn't all that involving—the jolly presentation works against the grungy intent, leaving a sense of aimlessness rather than artistic tension. (The cassette and CD have three extra cuts.)

Stories of Johnny is more on track, matching moody, sometimes pretty atmospherics with Almond's disconsolate (but brightening) outlook. The backing sporadically includes slick synthesizer maneuvers, bringing him full circle, demonstrating once again just how important Soft Cell was to earning its place in pop music. The title track (a deserving British hit) is a full-scale Spectorized production number with excellent singing.

Presaged by a double 7-inch of the album's "Melancholy Rose," **Mother Fist** (dedicated to Truman Capote, whose work provided the LP's title) finds Almond reflecting on pleasure and pain in characteristically graphic fashion. The generally sparse and often pleasant arrangements co-exist uneasily with Almond's decadent balladry but, given his outlook, that's as it should be. The one total downer is the somber "Saint Judy" (as in Garland), which ends with a chilling minor-key refrain of "Get Happy" (a song she originally sang in 1950's *Summer Stock*) interlaced with Almond's own doleful refrain. Amid the record's lighter-weight fare, it's a powerful centerpiece. Not for the fainthearted, **Mother Fist** is both rewarding and disturbing.

The singles compilation offers a solid non-Cell A-side retrospective: ten songs, including "Stories of Johnny," "Mother Fist," "Tenderness Is a Weakness" and "The House Is Haunted."

Paring the Willing Sinners down from a sextet to a trio (and renaming the group La Magia), Almond recorded **The Stars We Are**, a sensual, romantic antidote to **Mother Fist**'s bleak earthiness, lush with synthesized strings and horns. This is an essential album for those looking for insights into the Almond persona: "These My Dreams Are Yours" and "Bittersweet" both serve as apologias of sorts. A duet with Nico on "Your Kisses Burn" and an emotional rendition of Gene Pitney's "Something's Gotten Hold of My Heart" are also highlights.

Jacques is a tribute to Jacques Brel, the Belgian singer/poet whose influence pervades Almond's work. Mostly recorded with an augmented Willing Sinners lineup back in '86 (some tracks are as recent as '89), it's a real showcase for his abilities as an interpretive singer, especially as the vocals are mixed way up front over spare backgrounds. Regardless of how you feel about Almond or Brel—although it does help to appreciate both here—**Jacques** is an ambitious undertaking by an increasingly confident and always adventurous artist.

Almond made **Enchanted** without longtime keyboardist Annie Hogan or a live drummer; the use of both Fairlight synthesizer and an orchestra (not to mention guest brass players) creates a not entirely attractive tension between sterility and warmth. Lacking a strong stylistic hand, the arrangements (by Almond and stalwart keyboardist/bassist Billy McGee) are hit-and-miss, too often overzealous when a little bit of restraint would have done the trick. Almond's singing and writing, however, are unpretentiously entertaining, uniting past notions with subtle cohesion and as little overt camp as the listener cares to enjoy. Best track: the faux-Balkan bounce of the satanic "Deaths Diary." [i/ds]

ALPHAVILLE

Forever Young (Atlantic) 1984 ●
Afternoons in Utopia (Atlantic) 1986 ●
The Singles Collection (Atlantic) 1988 ●
The Breathtaking Blue (Atlantic) 1989 ●

Berlin's Alphaville plays simpleminded, obnoxious synthesizer rock. On **Forever Young**, the trio's slickly polished songs and vapid English lyrics ("Big in Japan," "The Jet Set") are at best inconsequential but often overbearingly dumb. The self-importance of singer Marian Gold's overdramatic delivery only contributes to the band's absurdity. While the title track comes within hailing range of a bewitchingly textured Ultravox sound, the album is otherwise insipid.

Whether it's a language barrier or a lack of talent, the idealistic science-fiction concept of **Afternoons in Utopia** (which credits 31 musicians and vocalists in addition to the group itself—wasn't technology supposed to make humans more self-reliant and efficient?) falls apart in a jumble of vague, frequently comical non sequiturs. While their imagination may be sailing off to Mars, Alphaville's music (notably improved over the first LP, possibly the result of lineup changes and a new producer) remains firmly planted in a simple, tuneful generic dance idiom.

The Singles Collection assembles two mixes each of two tracks each from the trio's two albums. (That means eight all together.) If you need to hear ten minutes (each) of "Forever Young," "Red Rose," "Big in Japan" or "Dance with Me," help yourself.

The Breathtaking Blue, co-produced by the venerable Klaus Schulze (Tangerine Dream), introduces a new, suavely continental aspect to Alphaville's music. Gold's attempts to ape and mix Bryan Ferry, Freddie Mercury and David Bowie are appalling; the band's concomitant efforts to swing on a jazzy acoustic tree prove equally futile. Typical of Alphaville's haplessness, the album's best track ("Ariana") is an utter anachronism, a giddy echo of Abba-styled new wave pop. (For those equipped with the proper equipment, the CD is graphics-encoded with hundreds of still photographs and illustrations.)   [i]

ALTER BOYS
Soul Desire (Big Time) 1987 ●

Former Dictator Andy Shernoff may have produced the only LP by New York's Alter Boys, but the group's roots seem closer to two other great erstwhile Gotham bands—Television and the Velvet Underground. The two guitarists seem promising enough, but they often seem held back by the relatively stiff rhythm section; the band sounds most comfortable on its best (and most Television-like) number, "One Eye Only," and "Sweet Blossom Mary," which borrows its chorus from "Anarchy in the UK." Depressives may enjoy the more VU-oriented gloom-and-doom of numbers like "Mid-Winter Deathtrip" and "Dry-Out Center."   [ds]

ALTERED IMAGES
Happy Birthday (Portrait) 1981 (Epic) 1990 ●
Pinky Blue (Portrait) 1982
Bite (Portrait) 1983
Collected Images (nr/Epic) 1984

Led by baby-voiced singer Claire Grogan, this twinky Scottish nuevo pop quintet hit high in the British singles charts with catchy, uncomplicated tunes like "Happy Birthday" and "Dead Pop Stars." Grogan's cutesy-poo vocals, however, were not universally appreciated; many found the group more precious than charming. Four different producers are credited on the three original albums; they clearly wielded powerful influence on these impressionable youngsters.

Except for the Martin Rushent-produced title track, the first LP (otherwise produced mainly by Banshees

bassist Steve Severin) shows no signs of life. The songs drag along, refusing to make any instrumental impression, relying on the singing, which just isn't enough.

Rushent produced all of **Pinky Blue**, revealing Altered Images to be a clever dance-pop force. With gleaming, bouncy sound, the songs jump out in classic hit single fashion—"See Those Eyes" and "I Could Be Happy" especially provide the joyous setting that Grogan's voice needs to succeed. (The cover of Neil Diamond's cloying "Song Sung Blue," however, should have been nixed.)

Bite is something of a departure. From the mature-young-sophisticate photo of Grogan on the front cover to the lush disco sound—strings, chorus, sax, wah-wah guitar, the works—of "Bring Me Closer," the album foolishly attempts to haul Altered Images out of their adolescent innocence and make them a Scottish Blondie. Worse, the equal division of production responsibilities between Tony Visconti and Mike Chapman leaves the record with a wicked case of schizophrenia. Visconti's tracks are basically heartless dance numbers—Abba gone funky. While Chapman's also trespass in the same terrain, "Change of Heart," "Another Lost Look" and the memorable "Don't Talk to Me About Love" are attractive pop tunes that retain some of the band's winsome charm. (The English cassette has extra tracks and bonus remixes.) **Collected Images** is a reasonable posthumous compilation.

After the band's end, members formed Hipsway and Texas. Grogan released a single (the only public results of a shelved solo album) and acted on film, stage and TV. Her new band is called Universal Love School. See also *Texas*.   [i]

ALTER NATIVES
Hold Your Tongue (SST) 1986
Group Therapy (SST) 1988 ●
Buzz (SST) 1989 ●

The Alter Natives are a frantic, improv-minded combo from Richmond, Virginia's hop-crazed art community. During SST's expansionist days of '86, their all-instrumental, sax-lead spazz-attack was among the most promising noise the label released. The band's first two LPs, recorded as a quartet, feature sax and flute-playing (Eric Ungar) of a remarkably non-fusionoid stripe; by the time of the third LP, however, the configuration was rock-basic (guitar/bass/drums), and **Buzz** is an excellent album of aggressive space Hunch. [bc]

ALTERNATIVE TV
The Image Has Cracked (nr/Deptford Fun City) 1978
Vibing Up the Senile Man (Part One) (nr/Deptford Fun City) 1979
Live at the Rat Club '77 (nr/Crystal-Red) 1979
Action Time Vision (nr/Deptford Fun City) 1980
Strange Kicks (IRS) 1981
Peep Show (nr/Anagram) 1987
Splitting in 2 (nr/Anagram) 1989
Sol EP (nr/Chapter 22) 1990
Dragon Love (nr/Chapter 22) 1990

HERE & NOW/ALTERNATIVE TV
What You See ... Is What You Are (nr/Deptford Fun City) 1978

GOOD MISSIONARIES
Fire from Heaven (nr/Deptford Fun City) 1979

MARK PERRY
Snappy Turns (nr/Deptford Fun City) 1981

The hipness and success of London punk-explosion photocopy fanzine *Sniffin' Glue* was almost entirely due to the irreverent, pugnacious sincerity of its founder/sparkplug Mark P(erry). That Perry should form a band seemed a natural progression; that it was any good at all a surprise; that it maintained a stance utterly disdainful of compromise a small miracle. Unfortunately, this musical Diogenes had neither adequate vision nor foresight to avoid the pitfalls of Striving for Artistic Expression.

Live at the Rat Club '77 (an authorized bootleg) consists of messy-sounding live material taped before co-founder/guitarist Alex Fergusson split. (Temporarily replaced by the Police's then-road manager Kim Turner, Fergusson rejoined in time for **Strange Kicks**.) By **The Image Has Cracked**, Perry's urge to experiment was taking intriguing turns (e.g., a half-studio, half-live attempt at meaningful audience participation). Although the abstract stuff doesn't hold up so well, it's still an amazing document of a time and place. The straighter efforts are better: an early Buzzcocks/Clash sock is well-exercised on the band's rousing manifesto, "Action Time Vision." It's also why the compilation of the same name, including non-LP singles sides (through '79) on which Perry's righteously vented spleen is effectively displayed, works better than **Image** as entertainment if not artifact.

What You See . . . Is What You Are is also live (from the summer of '78), but shared half-and-half with tour partners Here & Now, a horrid hippie offshoot of Gong. Worse (even discounting the tinny sound) still, such disillusion had set in that Perry remade his song as "Action Time Lemon" in sheer disgust. While a move towards edge music could be seen coming—further spurred by Mick Linehan (later in the Lines) replacing Kim Turner—ATV here sounds aimless and desperate. **Vibing Up the Senile Man** was made by Perry and stalwart bassist Dennis Burns; while some of the lyrics are eloquently impassioned, Perry's tuneless vocals ride atop music that's up the pseudo-avant creek without a paddle.

Come 1981, Perry, Burns and the more pop-minded Fergusson reunited (adding a drummer and a keyboard player) for **Strange Kicks**, an album that's a different proposition altogether. The one-time quasi-nihilist says, "What the hey!" and rattles off smart, vernacular humor, easygoing if still reasonably cynical, thereby unifying ATV's snappy romp through an assortment of styles (ska, pop-punk, even electro-dance), produced by Richard Mazda. Still, "There must be more to life than a heading in a record store."

Perry launched the Good Missionaries—who were, unfortunately, nothing special—during one period of ATV's dissolution. This band recalls Frank Zappa at his most pointless; the music meanders without form or reason. Creating this chaos may have been enjoyable for the people involved (including Henry Badowski), but that doesn't justify its release. Perry's subsequent solo outing belies its title by dishing up more of his semi-tortured recitation of what-a-bloody-world-it-is to the tune of . . . well, no recognizable tune at all.

What a surprise that, come 1987, a new lineup of ATV should rise up again with **Peep Show**. From the back cover: "It's happening again/The angels and demons have dragged me out." Yes, folks, it's back to the bile and the same old semi-anarchic self-indulgence that characterized much of ATV's non-Fergusson work. Yet if you can bear with him, Perry still strikes a few chords and touches a few nerves; his increased knowledge of musical forms and formats enables him to vary the tempo and style, adding horns and keyboards to good effect. Fans of the first ATV LP will probably enjoy this one, too.

By **Sol**, ATV had changed again (just Perry and one James Kyllo), so forget musical progress or even continuity. Plus, the sound stinks. "Every Day" is a decent enough number rendered nearly unlistenable by strange guitar distortion (like an uncorrectable technical glitch); a similar problem mars "The Word." The most succinct and catchy track, "Pain Barrier," is undercut by cymbal echo. The sound of "Affecting People" is merely mediocre but, as with the other three, the all-important words just aren't clear. For fans only.

Offering five tracks from the first LP plus eight sides from non-LP singles, **Splitting in 2** is an excellent collection. (But it should have included "Life After Life.") [cpl/jg]

See also *Psychic TV*.

DAVE ALVIN
Every Night About This Time (nr/Demon) 1987
Romeo's Escape (Epic) 1987 ●

VARIOUS ARTISTS
Border Radio (Enigma) 1987

Following his long tenure as the Blasters' guitar-slinging songwriter and a brief stay with X, Dave Alvin struck out on his own with the very fine **Romeo's Escape** LP (originally released in the UK, titled after another one of its songs). His first try as a lead singer won't win Dave any awards, but his hoarse delivery is more expressive than many technically superior vocalists. The contents are familiar roots rock and country, ranging from scorching boogie ("New Tattoo") to the weary testimony of a union man ("Brother on the Line"). Other highlights include gritty versions of tunes first recorded by the Blasters ("Long White Cadillac") and X ("Fourth of July"). They're less polished here, and plenty persuasive.

The **Border Radio** soundtrack is a decent bunch of odds'n'ends featuring Alvin, Chris D., Green on Red and members of X and Los Lobos. Tony Kinman of Rank and File delivers a nice, lazy version of Dave's title track (originally on Alvin's own LP); Alvin and Steve Berlin contribute ambient instrumentals. Mainly for completists. [jy]

See also *Blasters, X*.

PHIL ALVIN
Un"Sung" Stories (Slash) 1986

Without brother Dave's stirring songs, what on earth will Blasters frontman Phil Alvin sing? Not to worry, 'cause this traditional music buff assembles an enticing lineup of blues, jazz and gospel goodies on his solo debut. Good ol' Phil wraps his homey vocals around such venerable delights as Cab Calloway's "Minnie the Moocher" and "Brother, Can You Spare a Dime?" in this engaging tour of classic styles, making Un"Sung" Stories a delightful history lesson. Sun Ra and the Arkestra even guest on three, nicely complementing Phil with their own loopy charm. [jy]

See also *Blasters*.

ERIC AMBEL
See *Del-Lords*.

AMBITIOUS LOVERS
See *Arto Lindsay*.

AMERICAN MUSIC CLUB
The Restless Stranger (Grifter) 1986
Engine (Grifter-Frontier) 1987 ●
California (Grifter-Frontier) 1988 ●
United Kingdom (nr/Demon) 1990 ●

Rock'n'roll, especially the fringier areas thereof, has always been awash with beautiful losers. Maybe that's why AMC mastermind Mark Eitzel is so refreshing. His desperate confessional songs reveal a man with little doubt that he's a loser, but can't for the life of him see any beauty in said condition. With a no-frills Bay Area aggregation providing bare-bones backing, Eitzel's pointedly non-metaphorical writing sails past self-revelation on its way to self-evisceration.

The singer's unipolar, Ian Curtis-like vocal drone dominates **The Restless Stranger**'s tales of solitude and delirium tremens to perhaps too great a degree. That affectation, and occasionally ponderous arrangements (he's cited, without irony, early Yes as an influence), blunt some of the songs' impact, though "Room Above the Bar" and "$1,000,000 Song" bull through.

A lineup juggle that preceded **Engine** (producer Tom Mallon stepped in to handle bass—and, more importantly, arranging—chores) nudges the band towards stark but gently applied folk-rock structure. On "Outside This Bar," a Bukowski-like attempt to maintain the hermetic seal around the singer's world, Eitzel wails almost unaccompanied; in this context, when the backing grows more strident (as on the harrowing "Art of Love"), the edge becomes even sharper.

Like a particularly cruel maze, **California** is exceedingly difficult to enter and all but impossible to extricate oneself from. Though it incongruously contains the spitting brawler "Bad Liquor," **California** is even more austere than previous AMC efforts. The cumulative emotional overload (particularly on "Laughingstock") is positively anesthetizing.

Dispensing with its predecessors' vague adherence to folk-rock structure, **United Kingdom** lacks obvious songs and melodies as such and, in its starkness, recalls nothing so much as Big Star's **Sister Lovers**. Perhaps the most interesting thing (besides the fact that the three live tracks lack any standard concert-album evidence of an audience's presence) is "The Hula Maiden," the first recording of Eitzel's occasional stage retreat into the safe harbor of broad Vegas schmaltz. With its wild mood swings—from morose to mocking—**United Kingdom** is the best microcosmic document yet of an erratic, invigorating and frightening band. [dss]

DANNY AMIS
See *Raybeats*.

ANARCHY 6
See *Red Cross*.

BRUCE ANDERSON
See *MX-80 Sound*.

LAURIE ANDERSON ET AL.
You're the Guy I Want to Share My Money With (Giorno Poetry Systems) 1981

LAURIE ANDERSON
Big Science (Warner Bros.) 1982 ●
Mister Heartbreak (Warner Bros.) 1984 ●
The United States Live (Warner Bros.) 1984 ●
Home of the Brave (Warner Bros.) 1986 ●
Strange Angels (Warner Bros.) 1989 ●

Balanced above a high-wire above performance art and art pop, Laurie Anderson's **Big Science** is perhaps the most brilliant chunk of psychedelia since **Sgt. Pepper**. She combines singsong narrative (often electronically treated) with a strong musical base that evokes, yet postdates, traditional musical forms. **Big Science**, featuring the surprise answering-machine hit single, "O Superman," is a most enjoyable work of genius. (Anderson had previously appeared on several compilation albums, the most prominent being **You're the Guy I Want to Share My Money With**, a two-record set also featuring John Giorno and William S. Burroughs.)

With the help of co-producers Bill Laswell, Roma Baran and Peter Gabriel (who sings on "his" cut), Anderson continues merging not-readily-identifiable morsels of '60s psychedelia and '70s progressivism into a blinding studio-perfect maelstrom of oddity on **Mister Heartbreak**, an excellent LP that was overshadowed in the year of its release by the five-record (!) **United States Live**, a summation of the state of Anderson's bewildering but popular performance art. Anderson and crew performed **United States** whole in London, Zurich and New York, where the Brooklyn Academy of Music, which commissioned the last of its four parts, provided the site (in February 1983) for recording the whole kit and kaboodle. Perhaps better suited for videotape, the album mixes spoken-word monologues, music and noise (in that order) with snippets of film, slides, lighting and other visual effects that are inevitably lost here. Anderson's impressionistic multimedia portrait of the USA makes a good case for her talents as standup comedian ("There are ten million stories in the naked city, but nobody can remember which is theirs"), yet reveals its miscellany of truths slowly and coolly. Although it's a little like having an artsy friend over who always talks *at*, rather than *to*, you, **United States Live** remains a definitive statement of what a clever artist can get away with—and that's a compliment. (Years later, the set was reissued as a four-CD box.)

Home of the Brave is the digitally recorded soundtrack to Anderson's performance film. Joined by an all-star collection of players (Adrian Belew, David Van Tieghem, Nile Rodgers, Bill Laswell), she proffers technically exquisite versions of familiar items as well as new compositions, all imbued with her usual blend of dadaist humor and bemused social criticism.

Besides demonstrating Anderson's future as an urban Judy Collins (check the title track), **Strange Angels** goes to a lot of trouble—and uses such sidepersons as the Roches, Bobby McFerrin, Anton Fier and Van Tieghem—to uncover its few gems: "Baby Doll," in which a bossy brain orders the protagonist around via scribbled notes, the wittily feminist "Beautiful Red Dress" and "The Day the Devil." It would be nice to say that Anderson doesn't need theatrical vocal inflections or intellectual songwriting gimmicks to make memorable, significant music, but she does. Despite the unfailingly high level of craft and taste, songs without meaty hooks glide right by without leaving a trace.

[jw/mf/i]

AN EMOTIONAL FISH

An Emotional Fish (Atlantic) 1990 φ

If there are any young rock bands in Dublin that don't want to be U2, you'd never know it from some of the ones who have debuted recently. The only glimmers of personality on this quartet's first album are patently derivative; except for the lead-off track, a building drone (with hooks) entitled "Celebrate," An Emotional Fish proves incapable of weaving anything remotely engaging from its borrowings. The CD adds a bonus track.   [pn]

ANGELIC UPSTARTS

Teenage Warning (nr/Warner Bros.) 1979
We Gotta Get Out of This Place (nr/WEA) 1980
2,000,000 Voices (nr/EMI) 1981
Live (nr/EMI) 1981
Still from the Heart (nr/EMI) 1982
Reason Why? (nr/Anagram) 1983
Angel Dust (The Collected Highs 1978-1983) (nr/Anagram) 1983 ●
Last Tango in Moscow (nr/Picasso) 1984 (nr/Razor) 1988
Power of the Press (nr/Gas) 1986 (nr/Link Classics) 1990
Bootlegs and Rarities (nr/Dojo) 1986
Blood on the Terraces (nr/Link) 1987
Brighton Bomb (Chameleon) 1987
Live and Loud!! (nr/Link) 1988
England's Alive EP (nr/Skunx) 1988

With the commanding Mensi (Tommy Mensforth) as singer and spokesperson, the Angelic Upstarts came down from Newcastle in 1978—after self-releasing a powerful and controversial protest single, "The Murder of Liddle Towers"—and found a patron in Sham 69's Jimmy Pursey, who produced their first album. As one of the groups responsible for the continued strength of '70s punk in England, it is to the Upstarts' credit that they have avoided the demagogic stupidity of other skinhead bands by maintaining a progressive attitude and speaking out against racism and fascism.

Through shifting lineups (several of which included ex-Roxy Music drummer Paul Thompson), the band's early albums—effectively culled on the excellent **Angel Dust** compilation—are classic/standard working-class thrash, a predictable and hardly timeless jolt of accented electric rabble-rousing, but no less effective for it.

Reason Why? is the Upstarts' great leap forward, a blend of angry socio-political lyrics with a controlled and melodic rock attack (broken on the title track with a reggae digression and on the a cappella folk ballad, "Geordies Wife") that is punky only in Mensi's unpolished bellow and the band's gang-shouted backing vocals. Otherwise, the guitars build an attractive base—like the Clash on **Give 'Em Enough Rope**—that is embellished by guest sax and keyboards. The songs are competent enough and the production, by guitarist Mond, captures it all with clarity and energy. A surprisingly good record for all rock tastes.

The (old) Clash comparison carries through on the equally listenable **Brighton Bomb** (the American equivalent of **Power of the Press**), which actually contains a song addressed specifically to Strummer: "Joe Where Are You Now?" quotes assorted Clash tunes to make its point about punk traditionalism. As modern electric folksingers, the Upstarts' unprepossessing but palatable musical approach may be excused in consideration of the lyrics' good intentions: simplicity is in direct proportion to the sincerity. Two appropriate non-originals ("Soldier" and Eric Bogle's "Greenfields of France") show a healthy broadening of scope and a fearless respect for folk music in all its many variants.

The picture of Mensi on the back cover of **Blood on the Terraces** (the title track is about football hooliganism) shows him smiling and short-haired (not crew-cut) in a Nike T-shirt, looking for all the world like a cheerful suburban brother-in-law. Typical of the increasingly diverse and intelligent quartet (which here includes Splodgenessabounds' Max Splodge on drums), the album includes a reggae tune ("It's Your Life"), a punked-out Mel Tillis cover ("Ruby"), a rejection of cold war mythology ("I Don't Wanna Fight the Soviet") and a touching prison drama ("Four Grey Walls").   [i]

ANGRY SAMOANS

Inside My Brain EP (Bad Trip) 1980 (PVC) 1987 (Triple X) 1990 ●
Back from Samoa (Bad Trip) 1982 (PVC) 1987 (Triple X) 1990 ●
Yesterday Started Tomorrow EP (PVC) 1987 (Triple X) 1990 ●
Gimme Samoa: 31 Garbage-Pit Hits [CD] (PVC) 1987 ●
STP Not LSD (PVC) 1988 (Triple X) 1990 ●
Live at Rhino Records (Triple X) 1990 ●
Return to Samoa (nr/Shakin' Street) 1990

METAL MIKE

Plays the Hits of the 90's EP (Triple X) 1991 ●

Hypothetically following in the Richard Meltzer/early Dictators tradition at first, this Los Angeles quintet led by erstwhile rock critics Metal Mike Saunders and Gregg Turner (both vocals/guitar) mucks around in the self-conscious gutter of conceptual punk satire. Unfortunately, besides being off-brand musicians, the Samoans aren't very funny. The six-song **Inside My Brain** manages to spit out some snickering lyrics on "Get off the Air," a vituperative attack on DJ Rodney Bingenheimer, but otherwise offers nothing to get excited about. The brief, well-played songs on **Back from Samoa** have cool titles ("My Old Man's a Fatso," "Tuna Taco," "They Saved Hitler's Cock," etc.), but the lyrics are rarely as clever.

Yesterday Started Tomorrow adds another half-dozen terse items to the catalogue; neither the words nor the plain-issue rock tracks evince effort or imagination beyond the bare essentials. Hardly amateurish, this impersonal recording is adequate only in a technical sense.

The **Gimme Samoa** CD consolidates the entire 31-track contents of the band's first three records on one disc.

Proceeding from there, **STP Not LSD** has great snarly guitar tone and utterly competent playing, but Saunders and bassist Todd Homer still sing the dumbass lyrics like they're reading them upside down in a mirror. Although these guys are obviously intelligent junk culture junkies, their inability to follow the prime directive—garbage in, garbage out—remains an insurmountable obstacle.

Those who just can't get enough of the Samoans' magic will probably be anxious to own the band's live album, an atrociously bad sounding document of a short 1979 (!) show before an audience of—judging by the uncontrollable applause—five or six. Playing standard-issue mid-tempo punk, the quintet thrashes its way through "My Old Man's a Fatso," "I'm in Love with Your Mom" (co-written by Meltzer), the Ramones' "Commando" and six more.

The archival **Return to Samoa** consists of eight previously unissued studio tracks originally recorded for **Back from Samoa**, with Jeff Dahl doing the vocals. (He joined after Saunders had left the band. The group cut the LP, Saunders returned and redid the vocals, leaving only Dahl's bass playing on one **Back from Samoa** song.) **Return** also contains eight live tracks recorded in New York City in 1981.

In early '91, Metal Mike Saunders issued a six-song solo debut. [i]

See also *Jeff Dahl Group*.

ANGST

Angst EP (Happy Squid) 1983 (SST) 1986
Lite Life (SST) 1985
Mending Wall (SST) 1986
Mystery Spot (SST) 1987
Cry for Happy (SST) 1988 ●

This Denver-to-San Francisco artpunk trio of brothers Joe Pope (bass/vocals) and Jon E. Risk (guitar/vocals) plus drummer Michael Hursey serves up uncompromising, driving music in a number of directions on their debut EP. They get funky on "Pig," a heartwarmingly old-fashioned song about the law, drone on the junked-out "Another Day" and drive straight ahead on a would-be political anthem, "Die Fighting." Throughout, Angst manage to stay just one step ahead of their pretensions. Credit a sense of humor, exercised at the expense of some great Americans: "Neil Armstrong" is a goofy look at a space cadet; "Nancy" asks, chanting over a drum beat, "Does Nancy perform acts of oral copulation?"

The articulate lyrics on **Lite Life** again prove Angst's prowess for turning politically informed ideas into mature and witty tunes. Plain sound and no-frills arrangements underscore the preeminence of function over form. "Glad I'm Not in Russia," delivered as dustbowl country-rock, is a fairly incisive comment on the cultural divisions between the superpowers; the skit-

tish and busy dance-funk of "This Gun's for You" mixes up several topics but stays sharp; personal emotional issues ("Friends," "Turn Away," "Never Going to Apologize") receive the same coldly objective analysis.

Stylistic variety also underpins **Mending Wall**, another dose of Angst's tense and rough-edged musical simplicity, enhanced this time with noticeably stronger vocal harmonies by Risk and Pope. The lyrics are less specific and more thoughtful; individual alienation, confusion and anomie are transformed into powerful, uniquely directed songs. A cover of Paul Simon's "Richard Cory," however, goes wrong, pruning the melody and bare-bonesing it into an ugly ghost of the original.

Angst took a calculated risk on **Mystery Spot**, engaging producer Vitus Mataré to help flesh out and upgrade the sound. It almost worked. Multi-tracked guitars and dynamic arrangements bring the songs into near-pop focus, with unprecedented melody, sensitivity, structure and vocal appeal, but atrocious recording quality (and/or a heinously bungled mix) buries them in a flat, muddy swamp. Pope and Risk continue to reveal themselves in emotionally resonant songs—too bad their ambitious effort was spoiled by a technicality.

With Andy Kaps replacing Hursey, Angst and Mataré continued working in the same vein on **Cry for Happy**, a fine-sounding (except for the drums) record that encompasses semi-acoustic countryish pop, nervous rock funk, boogie, desolate electric blues ("Motherless Child") and straight Angst-rock with pretty harmonies. With lyrics of loneliness and joy that are as emotionally ambivalent as the album title, **Cry for Happy** brings Angst out into the open as never before. [jl/i]

ANIMAL LOGIC

See *Stewart Copeland*.

ANNABELLA

See *Bow Wow Wow*.

ADAM ANT

See *Adam and the Ants*.

ANTHRAX

Fistful of Metal (Megaforce) 1984 ●
Armed and Dangerous EP (Megaforce) 1985 ●
Spreading the Disease (Megaforce Worldwide-Island) 1985 ●
Among the Living (Megaforce Worldwide-Island) 1987 ●
I'm the Man EP (Megaforce Worldwide-Island) 1987 ●
State of Euphoria (Megaforce Worldwide-Island) 1988 ●
Persistence of Time (Megaforce Worldwide-Island) 1990 ●

Disproving the fantasy that New York bands were too cool to play heavy metal, Anthrax abandoned the hardcore scene early enough to get in on the ground floor of the underground movement that eventually spawned such estimable headbanging ensembles as Megadeth and Metallica. The quintet's debut, **Fistful of Metal** is fast and furious, but not overbearingly so, holding to a near-rock sound punctuated by dizzying guitar solos. Singer Neil Turbin has a good strong voice but lets fly with stereotypical falsetto howls far too often for adult audio comfort.

Turbin and bassist Dan Lilker were subsequently replaced in what became Anthrax's permanent lineup. (Lilker went on to form Nuclear Assault.) The **Armed and Dangerous** mini-LP unveiled the new lineup on five unassuming cuts: a pair of studio previews for **Spreading the Disease**, two live renditions of songs from the previous LP and a reverent, hard-hitting version of "God Save the Queen." The album that followed is, all things considered, much better, a scalding assault that reasserts the band's punk bearings with chunky chords, varying tempos and searing vocals.

The back cover of **Among the Living**, co-produced by Eddie Kramer, shows Anthrax looking relaxed in a New York subway station, wearing sneakers, jeans and leather jackets. The album focuses the band's sound and attitude to arena-scale, replacing old-fashioned metal clichés with a demi-hardcore approach—shifting tempos, gang vocals—that translated well to larger venues. Besides "Caught in a Mosh," two songs based on Stephen King prose and one inspired by a British comic character, Anthrax trots out a bit of common Bronx street slang to humorous effect in "Efilnikufesin (N.F.L.)," while using the word "dissin'" in "Indians." An entirely different sort of post-metal record that is uniquely New York.

Anthrax's merry cross-cultural adventure stretches even further afield on **I'm the Man**, a six-cut EP with three versions—"Censored," "Def Uncensored" and "Extremely Def Ill Uncensored"—of the hysterical Beasties-styled rap-rocking title track. The EP also contains live takes of "Caught in a Mosh" and "I Am the Law," plus a convincing rendition of "Sabbath Bloody Sabbath."

By 1988, however, the *Mad* magazine-style band portrait on **State of Euphoria**'s back cover wasn't Anthrax's only cartoonish element. Although the album went gold faster than any of its predecessors and showed a reasonable amount of progression (especially in the lyrics: "Who Cares Wins" is a hard-hitting depiction of Manhattan's homeless), the riffs bounce around on pogo sticks, and the band sounds aware that, stylistically, they were moshing themselves into a corner.

Anthrax took some time off before returning with the bruising **Persistence of Time**; a leaner, tougher band attacks the revitalized songs with more energy than any effort since **Spreading the Disease**. The self-parodic element remains, but Anthrax fights it with a roaring second wind, confronting the real world (family abuse, racism) with music as tough as the subject matter. And if you really want to know what time it is as far as the post-punk world goes, they cover Joe Jackson's "Got the Time" (from his first album) as if it were a hard-rock classic.

Like all movements, the trash-metal thing was done within three years, leaving five (or so) first-class bands and hundreds of mediocre ones. Anthrax is unquestionably one of the best, adding a sense of fun and humor to a genre that far too often tried to be scary and succeeded only in being ridiculous. [i/ja]

ANTIETAM

Antietam (Homestead) 1985
Music from Elba (Homestead) 1986
Burgoo (Triple X) 1990 ●
Everywhere Outside (Triple X) 1991 ●

Although the genealogical successor to Louisville, Kentucky's Babylon Dance Band, Antietam—named after an 1862 Civil War battle—actually came together in New York. The first album rushes madly through artlessly raucous neo-pop; guitarist Tara Key's strident voice clashes with her three male bandmates' (everybody sings), obliterating intelligent lyrics and potentially nice melodies in the fray. Michael Weinert's clumsy time-keeping never locks into the beat; flashes of mellifluous invention teasingly suggest what Antietam might accomplish if they practiced.

The improvements on **Music from Elba** can be traced to a new drummer, more coordinated playing and wisely moderated tempos. Still, the discordant dual vocals by Key and husband/bassist Tim Harris (shades of X) and their dull songwriting limits the LP's appeal to those immune to bad singing. Danna Pentes of Fetchin Bones guests on violin.

With production by Yo La Tengo's Ira Kaplan and Georgia Hubley, Key and Harris made the gently grating **Burgoo** (pressed on clear blue vinyl for those old-fashioned enough to notice), removing any lingering doubt about their inclination or ability to progress. The songs hold more water than before but, after all this time, Key is no closer to singing in tune, their playing is still one-take amateurish and Charles Schultz's unsteady drumming is as helpful to the songs as a rusty threshing machine. If 10,000 Maniacs had younger siblings, they might sound like Antietam. [i]

ANTI-NOWHERE LEAGUE

Anti-Nowhere League EP (WXYZ) 1982
We Are ... the League (WXYZ) 1982 (nr/ID) 1984
Live in Yugoslavia (nr/ID) 1983
Long Live the League (nr/ABC) 1985 ●
The Perfect Crime (GWR-Profile) 1987
Live & Loud!! (nr/Link) 1990
Fuck Around the Clock EP (nr/Link) 1990

At first, it was awfully hard to take this cartoonish punk quartet from Tunbridge Wells seriously. The songwriting team of Animal (Nick Karmer) and Magoo penned irate diatribes aimed at what they called the "nowheres" of the world: straights, nine-to-fives, etc. Although one can't doubt them when they spit "I Hate . . . People," they do manage to inject a sense of humor on the first album, which can soften even the most potentially offensive song, such as the ragingly misogynist "Woman." And anyone who doubts their ingenuity should listen to the blazing (but surprisingly appropriate) treatment of Ralph McTell's folkie chestnut, "Streets of London." (That number also appears on the prior American EP, joined by two other tunes from the album and a bonus cut.)

The live album was indeed recorded in Tito-land (April 1983) and features a full airing of the band's repertoire, including "I Hate People," "Woman," "We Are the League," "Streets of London" and "Let's Break the Law." The Zagreb audience is surprisingly enthusiastic as the quartet puts on a no-holds-barred rock show, captured in trebly but adequately clear sound. **Long Live the League** is a compilation, containing outtakes and remixes.

Four years on, the League evidently decided to try a new approach—or ten. Like an '80s rock jukebox gone out of control, tracks on **The Perfect Crime** imitate Big Country, the Stranglers, Alarm, Buzzcocks and others, with surprisingly good results. "(I Don't Believe) This Is My England," which actually doesn't sound like anybody, is a touchingly anthemic folk ballad that couldn't be further from dumb punk. Overall, the album boasts reasonably sturdy melodies, plus intelligent and positive-minded political lyrics—a likable new chapter in this unlikely saga.

The public, used to a far less respectable League, didn't take to the LP, and the group split up in 1988. The following year, however, a one-off reunion gig in the band's hometown was recorded and released as **Live & Loud!!** The three **Perfect Crime** songs get first-album treatment (no synthesizers), and the album rocks in the band's old style from start to finish. Kicking off with the classic "For You," the League's characteristic humor, insouciance and gusto are in full effect, particularly on a version of Eddie Cochran's "Something Else" copied from the Sex Pistols' version, "We Are the League" and "Streets of London." A worthy finale, bidding adieu with a loud belch rather than a whimper.
[ks/i/jr]

ANY THREE INITIALS
See *Flipper*.

ANY TROUBLE
Where Are All the Nice Girls? (Stiff) 1980
Live at the Venue (nr/Stiff) 1980 ●
Wheels in Motion (Stiff) 1981
Any Trouble (EMI America) 1983
Wrong End of the Race (EMI America) 1984

Stiff Records had great commercial hopes for this Manchester quartet, led by balding, bespectacled singer/guitarist/pianist Clive Gregson, whose songs—mostly about the unhappy side of love—have always shown real talent. It unfortunately took the group a long time to escape their basic facelessness and locate a sound, a slow start that may be why Any Trouble ended without ever receiving the acclaim they deserved.

The first LP suffers from (reasonable) comparisons to early Elvis Costello, and shows Any Trouble to be a pub band five years after the end of that era, playing competent, melodic rock with no special character. Only "The Hurt" and the stunningly derivative "Second Choice" (a retread of "Less than Zero") leave any lasting impression beyond overall nice-guy swellness.

Live at the Venue, recorded onstage in London in May '80, includes performances of both aforementioned songs (and five more from the first album), plus a rendition of Springsteen's "Growing Up" (shades of Greg Kihn). The band shows a helpful increase in spunk and velocity, but still falls short of being exciting. (Although **Live at the Venue** never came out in America as such, six selections were issued as the promo-only **Live and Alive** 12-inch.)

Wheels in Motion, produced by Mike Howlett (later a hitmaker for A Flock of Seagulls), evinces further improvement, adding impressive intricacy and dynamics to the arrangements. Gregson's growing confidence as a singer helps put across his pessimistic (but not cynical) lyrics on songs like "Trouble with Love," "Another Heartache" and the outstanding "Walking in Chains." **Wheels in Motion** still isn't a record to make you stop in your tracks, but an extremely likable collection of intelligently written rock songs performed ably and without pretense.

Any Trouble, by a half-new lineup, is the band's first great album, a wonderful new blend of soul and pop strengthened by Gregson's sharpening melodic sense and lightening lyrical outlook. "Please Don't Stop," "Man of the Moment," "Northern Soul" and other tracks resemble a non-obnoxious Hall and Oates crossed with Costello and recorded in Motown; production by David Kershenbaum provides the sonic variety and sophistication previously lacking. Gregson's development into a powerful, sensitive singer is merely the icing on the cake.

The group inexplicably re-recorded three early (and not timeless) songs for **Wrong End of the Race**, adding a rousing cover of the Foundations' "Baby Now That I've Found You," and a bunch of new Gregson compositions. (The US edition deletes "Lucky Day" and "Yesterday's Love," a reprise of the group's first single, to make way for three tracks not on the UK version.) Featuring an illustrious cast of guests (Richard Thompson, Billy Bremner, Geoff Muldaur), the LP is less stylized than its remarkable predecessor, but bristles with renewed vigor and rich horn-and-vocal-filled arrangements. Without fanfare, that was the end of Any Trouble. Gregson carried on, making a solo album, working closely with Richard Thompson and forming a remarkably fruitful partnership with Christine Collister. [i]
See also *Clive Gregson*.

APACHE DANCERS
War Stories (Happy Hermit-IRS) 1990 ●

Bernadette Colomine has one of those ooh-la-la French accents that can make grown men blush; guitarist Tom Durbin sings in the lonesome voice of someone who wishes he were raised on a strict diet of Hank Williams. That wild cultural contrast is what makes this LA-based cowboy-rock quartet (which includes Rank and File's old drummer) so uncommon and, in one spot, uncommonly good: "You're the Reason," the non-original duet which opens **War Stories**, is a left-field country-rock grabber. Unfortunately, most of the album (haphazardly co-produced by Earle Mankey) is an either/or proposition, offering Colomine's unsteady pitch (in English and French) without Durbin's rugged resonance (his melodic skills are only a little better) or vice versa. Additionally impaired by Durbin's terrible guitar playing and dumb-ass lyrics, Apache Dancers can be as incomprehensible and off-putting as their namesakes. [i]

APB
Something to Believe In (Link) 1985 ●
Cure for the Blues (Link) 1986
Missing You Already EP (Link) 1986

23

A popular member of Scotland's neo-funk movement, this Aberdeen group found a friend in American college radio, where the quintet's pressurized dance-rock was very well-received. The ten 1981-'85 singles compiled on **Something to Believe In** are either effectively claustrophobic and offbeat ("Shoot You Down") or trite and obnoxious ("Rainy Day"). The CD has bonus tracks.

Cure for the Blues is a fine album of new tunes, not all of which follow the band's basic pattern—"Part of the Deal" is light pop that resembles Aztec Camera. Iain Slater's intense bass playing and mildly adenoidal (if pleasantly accented) vocals drive the songs, leaving the rest of the band in a subsidiary role.

Slater switched instruments with guitarist Glenn Roberts in time for the four-track **Missing You Already** 12-inch, nicely evening out the sound and providing more variety in the stylistic mix. While half the tunes are pretty routine, "Best of Our Love" uses piano and strong rhythm guitar to propel the beat into a soulful shake. [i]

A POPULAR HISTORY OF SIGNS
A Popular History of Signs EP (Wax Trax!) 1984
Comrades (nr/Jungle) 1985
Taste (nr/Jungle) 1987
England in the Rain EP (nr/Jungle) 1988

Led by singer/bassist/keyboardist Andrew Jarman (vocally something of a David Byrne student), this London quartet drifts between arty synth-dance and lightly played mood music. Using dinky electronic percussion rather than a drummer in the early days, the enigmatic group's records alternately wax chilly, funky, humorless and clever.

Save for a few exceptions on Side Two, the poorly structured songs on **Comrades** typically work one groove for several minutes and then fade out with the vocals still going. Despite the nicely spare arrangements, provocative subject matter ("Lenin," for instance), crystalline production and flawless playing, this is a mighty boring way to spend an afternoon.

Ministry's Al Jourgensen remixed "Ladder Jack" and "House" for the eponymous American 12-inch, a four-song sampling of the band's pre-**Comrades** 45s. Both of those remixes also appear on **Taste**, a 1980-'87 singles compilation that presents an absurdly bloodless trashing of Lou Reed's "Rock & Roll" and adds two previously unreleased items, including an awfully strange cover of John Fogerty's "Run Through the Jungle."

Fielding a solid five-man lineup, APHOS comes out of the woods on the obviously commercial **England in the Rain**. Unlike its previous unpredictable self-indulgences, the band now reveals a clear-cut focus: the half-dozen peppy songs are all standard stylish modern dance rock that compares favorably to Wang Chung and that whole post-Ultravox ilk. If Jarman weren't such a duff singer, these attractively produced tracks might be really appealing. [i]

AQUANETTAS
Love with the Perfect Stranger (Nettwerk-IRS) 1990 ●

A cross between Josie and the Pussycats and the Replacements, this all-female New York outfit's debut album (named after a Natalie Wood movie) offers a better peek into girlworld than a hundred issues of *Vogue*. "Faults" teaches a lesson in how to blow off a bad date; "15 Men" iterates a hilarious catalogue of conquests. With guitarist Jill Richmond tossing off some mean leads, the music is a slightly glossed-up version of garage rock, with hints of surf. Although the album turns predictable by the middle of Side Two, laconic putdowns like "Larry and Pete are just typical guys/ Blasting their music and watching the thighs" make **Love** a rewarding affair. [kss]

ARABIAN PRINCE
See *N.W.A.*

ARCADIA
See *Duran Duran*.

A R KANE
Sixty Nine (Rough Trade) 1988 ●
"i" (nr/Rough Trade) 1989 ●
rem'i'xes EP (nr/Rough Trade) 1990 ●

Rising to prominence in 1987 as Colourbox's collaborators on M/A/R/R/S's surprise club hit "Pump Up the Volume," Britain's A R Kane—Alex and Rudi—have lived up to their apt name, which is not just a cute pun but an accurate summation of everything about the enigmatic duo. The only musical influence they cop to is Miles Davis, but you can be sure they're not referring to any of his famous quintets: A R Kane harks back to the deep atmospherics and funk noise of Davis' mid-to-late-'70s work. Co-produced with Ray Shulman, **Sixty Nine** is, as one might surmise, mostly concerned with sensuality, but an enervated sensuality—the grooves here are submerged, the singing like some strange male siren calling from a cave. The sense of desperate menace hidden amid calm recalls another singular work, Robert Wyatt's **Rock Bottom**.

Mixing sixteen proper songs with ten sound snippets, **"i"** runs a wider gamut of song genres than the debut. While "Love from Outer Space" seems like a conventional techno-dance number, "Crack Up" offers some amusing off-kilter piano and "Snow Joke" serves up Philly soul strings. Deeper into the record, though, the music turns harsher, then downright hostile, although the vocals remain implacable and drained of personality.

Five **"i"** songs appear in new versions ("Crack Up" gets two makeovers) on **rem'i'xes**, an EP which further demonstrates the band's enjoyable willfulness: remixes are generally intended to pep up the originals for better dance-floor consumption, but most of the songs are more restive here than they were on **"i"**. (Robin Guthrie of the Cocteau Twins did half the honors; the band did the rest themselves.) Unfortunately, a few numbers sound more weak-kneed than stripped-down, and their removal from the album's context doesn't help. [gk]

JOAN ARMATRADING
Whatever's for Us (nr/Cube) 1972 (A&M) 1973 ●
Back to the Night (A&M) 1975 ●
Joan Armatrading (A&M) 1976 ●

Show Some Emotion (A&M) 1977 ●
To the Limit (A&M) 1978 ●
Steppin' Out (A&M) 1979
How Cruel EP (A&M) 1979
Me Myself I (A&M) 1980 ●
Walk Under Ladders (A&M) 1981 ●
The Key (A&M) 1983 ●
Track Record (A&M) 1983 ●
Secret Secrets (A&M) 1985 ●
Sleight of Hand (A&M) 1986 ●
The Shouting Stage (A&M) 1988 ●
Compact Hits EP [CD] (nr/A&M) 1988 ●
Hearts and Flowers (A&M) 1990 ●
The Very Best of Joan Armatrading (nr/A&M) 1991 ●

For two decades, singer/guitarist/songwriter Joan Armatrading—born in the West Indies and raised in Birmingham, England—has been making records of warm, emotionally resonant music that has earned her a devoted following on at least two continents. Despite brushes with chart stardom, Armatrading remains an independent-minded cult star whose remarkable and individual voice, regardless of her albums' assorted settings, never wavers. In recent years, newcomers like Suzanne Vega (the two share a label) and Tracy Chapman (the two seemingly share one voice) have found success holding to much the same folk-based traditions as Armatrading, underlining her achievements by following in their path.

Whatever's for Us, produced between Elton John albums by Gus Dudgeon, was a collaborative effort with lyricist Pam Nestor; on her own, with Dada/Vinegar Joe member Pete Gage at the helm, **Back to the Night** proved equally uncommercial. She then teamed up with Glyn Johns, who brought in ex-members of Fairport Convention as backing musicians for **Joan Armatrading**, an extraordinarily thoughtful and moving album that contains "Down to Zero" and "Love and Affection," two of her most enduring and powerful compositions.

The intimate, upbeat **Show Some Emotion** is warm and lovely, an unaffected, casual-sounding album of songs that, if not among her best, are more than presentable and occasionally captivating. Continuing with Johns, Armatrading made the harder-rocking **To the Limit**, a slightly dated-sounding collection of strong songs (which includes the notable "Bottom to the Top," set to a gentle reggae beat) played by a small electric band that, at its most exuberant, resembles a modest Mad Dogs and Englishmen. Johns also produced **Steppin' Out**, a live document drawn from American performances: backed by a five-piece band, Armatrading delivers nine songs, including "Love and Affection" and "Cool Blue Stole My Heart." **How Cruel** is a four-song 12-inch containing some non-LP material.

Me Myself I was produced by Richard Gottehrer and performed by a stellar cast of Anglo-American rock musicians (including Chris Spedding, Clarence Clemons, Danny Federici and three members of David Letterman's band). Even in this all-electric setting, Armatrading and her songs hold up nicely. "Me Myself I" is brilliant, a chillingly beautiful declaration of independence with a memorable pop melody; the rest of the record explores the vagaries of love and percolates with energy, grace and sensitivity.

Steve Lillywhite took the production reins for **Walk Under Ladders**, engaging a fascinating selection of players—XTC's Andy Partridge, King Crimsonites Tony Levin and Mel Collins, Sly and Robbie and Thomas Dolby. Although the stylized results short-change Joan's personality a bit, successful numbers like "I Wanna Hold You" and "At the Hop" affirm her courageous desire to explore uncharted areas.

The Key is a slick package that employs many of the same players as **Walk Under Ladders** to recapture the potent melodic pop elements of **Me Myself I**. "(I Love It When You) Call Me Names" is a should-have-been-a-hit single with spectacular multi-tracked harmonies and a hair-raising Adrian Belew guitar solo. "The Game of Love" has an Edge-like echoed guitar sound and a memorable chorus. Motels starmaker Val Garay produced the bristling "Drop the Pilot" (Lillywhite did all but one other track) with loud power chords and a stomping backbeat; although spoiled by ill-advised synths, "I Love My Baby" ends the record with a tender lullaby.

Track Record basically compiles Armatrading's most popular songs from six of her prior albums, but also includes a pair of otherwise non-LP items ("Frustration" and "Heaven") and a track from **How Cruel**.

Secret Secrets is Armatrading's admission of pain and suffering. In "Persona Grata" she announces, "I'm your whipping boy," adding "I'm in love with you" in a resigned, grim tone. "Love by You" and "Friends Not Lovers" mourn the end of a relationship with tragic depth. In "Strange," she realizes "I am not missing you"; other songs ("Moves," "One Night") allow more hope to shine through the tears. Pino Palladino's inimitable fretless bass provides the most notable instrumental character; other than on "Moves," the sophisticated modern backing is rather faceless.

Armatrading produced **Sleight of Hand**, using just a drummer, bassist and keyboardist (with a few minor guest contributions). She acquits herself well, both on guitar and behind the board, with songs that suggest more personal happiness and stability than **Secret Secrets**. Without falling into any easily identifiable musical department, **Sleight of Hand** has only fascinating sounds, able songwriting and the peerless performing talents of Ms. Armatrading to recommend it. Not bad.

Served up on a sensuous plate dominated by horns, Palladino's bass and flashy guitar work by Phil Palmer and Mark Knopfler, **The Shouting Stage**—another self-production, this time in a smooth and jazzy adult contemporary vein—explores romance from both ends of the emotional spectrum. The rapture of "Did I Make You Up" and "Watch Your Step" quickly gives way to "Words" and culminates in "The Shouting Stage." Although decent and tasteful, this anxious-sounding effort is not among Armatrading's most musically compelling.

The **Compact Hits** EP features a non-representative quartet of tracks ("Love and Affection," "Willow," etc.), none of which were actually big hits.

Armatrading selected another one of England's most expressive bassists, Mick Karn, to play on **Hearts and Flowers**, a handsomely slick and modern realization of her traditional artistic values. After announcing that there's "More Than One Kind of Love" and overtly expressing her spiritual awakening in "Promise Land," Armatrading uses intentionally ambiguous lyrics to convey deep adoration that could just as easily be for a person as for a deity.   [i]

ARMOURY SHOW

See *Richard Jobson*.

ARSENAL

See *Big Black*.

ART & LANGUAGE

See *Red Crayola*.

ART BEARS

See *Henry Cow*.

ARTICLES OF FAITH

Give Thanks (Reflex) 1984
In This Life (Can. Lone Wolf) 1987

VIC BONDI

The Ghost Dance (Wishing Well) 1988

JONES VERY

Words and Days (Hawker) 1989 •

Articles of Faith gave singer/guitarist Vic Bondi—a Chicago punk luminary and an articulate thinker more than willing to speak his mind—a podium from which to spout his vision, and spout he does on the Bob Mould-produced (and released) **Give Thanks**. The quintet wastes no time in cutting to the core of its anger; each song is masterfully crafted, from the pounding and ironic "Give Thanks," the finger-pointing "In Your Suit," and the embittered "American Dreams" to the tragically tender "Everyman for Himself." Though AOF played hardcore, the songs are fully developed, and occasionally run well over the genre's usual time limits. AOF consistently demonstrates superior talent, exploring various branches from the punk mainstream without stepping across the line to either pop or heavy metal.

Mould produced AOF's second LP in 1985, but it wasn't released until early '87; parts of it sound a lot like contemporaneous Soul Asylum. Some songs scale back the percussion; an acoustic guitar is added to strengthen songs like "Nowhere"; the vocals are imaginatively layered on all thirteen tracks. Highbrow hardcore?

After AOF's demise, Bondi—by then a University of Massachusetts history instructor—returned with a surprising, dry-as-dust solo album. Strumming an acoustic guitar (with overdubbed electric accents on a few songs) and singing in a hoarse, unmusical voice, he fills **The Ghost Dance** with plaintive, obliquely poetic songs about relationships, in settings like "Montana," "Cambridge" and "Abilene Sunset." Proceeding from the album title (a carefully explained reference to a Native American religious movement of the late 1800s), "Mister Noon" is a striking piece of evocative prose that doesn't work as a song.

Joining up with a powerful rhythm section, Bondi formed Jones Very (named after a 19th-century Unitarian minister) and cut the impressive but uneven **Words and Days**, a loudly textured rock album with intelligently sophisticated lyrics. Bondi occasionally unleashes a frightening guttural shriek, making several songs unlistenably harsh. But when he and bassist Jeff Goddard jam (as on "Cut") or harmonize on tuneful material (like the excellent title track), Jones Very turns into an exciting, invigorating proposition, a taut bundle of hyped-up melodic rock that packs a serious headkick.

[icm/i]

ART OF NOISE

Into Battle with the Art of Noise EP (ZTT-Island) 1983
(Who's Afraid Of?) The Art of Noise! (ZTT-Island) 1984 •
In Visible Silence (China-Chrysalis) 1986
  (China-PolyGram) 1989 •
Re-works of Art of Noise (China-Chrysalis) 1986 •
In No Sense? Nonsense! (China-Chrysalis) 1987
  (China-PolyGram) 1989 •
The Best of the Art of Noise (China-Polydor) 1988 •
Below the Waste (China-Polydor) 1989 •
The Ambient Collection (China-Polydor) 1990 φ

Originally a pop producer's idea of nouveau hip-hop instrumentals, the Art of Noise—a brilliant post-rock meld of studio/tape wizardry, floor-shaking dance percussion and adventurous audio experimentation—has turned into a hardy, self-sufficient organization with a distinctive creative outlook. The group began as a semi-anonymous studio band directed by Trevor Horn, who issued the records as an art statement on his Zang Tuum Tumb label. **Into Battle** has the aptly named "Beat Box," with choral vocals and crazy effects (including, repeatedly, a car starting) punctuating typically booming electronic drums. But it also has far lighter essays: "The Army Now," with cut-up Andrews Sisters-style vocals, and "Moments in Love," an obsequious, lush backing track (for Barry White, perhaps?) that goes nowhere for an unconscionably long time. Produced to some incomprehensible blueprint, bits from one track often turn up in the midst of another.

The full-length **Who's Afraid Of?** album contains some of the same cuts, but most notably adds the brilliant "Close (to the Edit)," a furious and unforgettable march of highly organized rhythm, effects and jagged musical/vocal ejaculations. Elsewhere, spoken-word collages mingle with the disjointed assemblages to create newsreel-inflected dance music of enormous vitality and originality. Remarkable and significant, with an electronic language all its own.

Proving their autonomy, the heart of Art of Noise— Anne Dudley, J.J. Jeczalik and producer Gary Langan—split from Horn and ZTT in 1985. Forming the China label, the group issued the "Legs" single, revealing a desire to invade the pop market by locating a functional compromise with it. A full new album, **In Visible Silence**, followed several months later. Although no individual track is as gripping as "Close (to the Edit)," a semi-straight version of "Peter Gunn," with twang legend Duane Eddy playing the unforgettable guitar line, became a substantial international hit; the rest is typically intriguing, aggravating and entertaining.

A long 12-inch mix of "Peter Gunn," joined by two other previously issued 45s—"Legacy" (a drastic variation on "Legs") and "Paranoimia," recorded with the voice of Max Headroom breaking the usual vocal silence—comprise one side of **Re-works**. The rest of the long mini-album documents Art of Noise onstage in London, playing "Legs," "Paranoimia" and the ten-minute "Hammersmith to Tokyo and Back." The concert format has its obvious hazards for a painstaking group which is so reliant on the studio, but the results are more unsatisfying than disappointing. In any case, the ability to put this stuff over in front of an audience is noteworthy.

Shelving their pop ambitions, Art of Noise outfoxed themselves on **In No Sense? Nonsense!**, an overreaching undertaking that incorporates an orchestra, choir, horn section and guest rock musicians. The flaccid tracks are short on rhythmic power and wander all over the stylistic map with little logic or focus. Taken as a whole, this indeed makes no sense. The handful of numbers which indifferently plunder past adventures manage to be dull even when they resemble things that were exciting. Sonic quality is shortchanged by the technical considerations of recording so many musicians: abandoning modern high-tech claustrophobia for the inappropriately warm, open ambience of a cathedral ranks as a gross creative mistake.

The Best of the Art of Noise is a fine compilation, covering all of the band's high points—alone ("Beat Box," "Close (to the Edit)," "Legacy," "Dragnet '88") and in collaboration with Max Headroom, Duane Eddy (a different mix than appears on **Re-works**) and Tom Jones (an endless rendition of Prince's "Kiss" of more conceptual than musical merit). Although some of the tracks run on way too long, this colorful résumé offers a fine summary of the band's unique experimentation. (The vinyl edition contains 7-inch mixes; the CD and cassette contain 12-inch versions.)

Below the Waste dabbles with world music (using South African vocal group Mahlathini and the Mahotella Queens on several songs) and a Western orchestra, but the material simply doesn't meet the challenge and succumbs to frequent film-score dullness. Beyond one energetically rhythmic hybrid ("Chain Gang"), this weak album shortchanges Art of Noise's audio personality and fails to supplant it with anything equally potent.

Already covered by a half-remixes album and a greatest hits collection, Art of Noise undertook a more radical recycling program on **The Ambient Collection**, opening their tape library to producer Youth (ex-Killing Joke/Brilliant) who, to paraphrase the liner notes, "compiled, defiled and remixed" a selection of the band's gentlest efforts (mostly from **In No Sense? Nonsense!** and **In Visible Silence**) into an album of new age wallpaper. The process involves editing tracks, either to brief snippets or lengthy loops, and adding real-world sounds (the word atmospheric has literal significance here) and other ephemera.   [i]

A'S

The A's (Arista) 1979
A Woman's Got the Power (Arista) 1981
Four Dances EP (Straight A's) 1982

One of the first bands on Philadelphia's new wave club scene to sign with a major label, the A's made their reputation through an energetic stage show which featured singer Richard Bush's Jerry Lewis-like antics. On the group's first album, Bush shows an equal aptitude for playing the comedian ("Teenage Jerk Off," an affectionately tongue-in-cheek nod to punk) and the straight man (the outstanding "After Last Night"). If anything, **The A's** resembles the Boomtown Rats'

Tonic for the Troops in the way it combines wit, street savvy and relatively intricate hard-pop arrangements.

On **A Woman's Got the Power**, the group's sound and material changed drastically, and not for the better: The album is an exercise in misplaced bombast. Bush's occasional excesses are charming on the first outing, but here he consistently over-emotes, imbuing the songs with angst they don't really merit. While the big sound works well enough for the first couple of tracks (the soulful title tune and the pretty "Electricity"), the bluster then begins to grate; there isn't another listenable cut on the album.

Back on their own, the A's pulled in their horns with a 12-inch of four modestly presented rock songs. On the plus side, the likable "Do the Dance" sounds like a techno-pop club tune without the electronics, while "Girl That I Love" is crisp skinny tie Beatle-pop. But when "Ain't No Secret" devolves into a blithering jam of arena guitars and synthesizer riffing, it's time for the B's.   [ds/i]

DANIEL ASH

See *Love and Rockets*.

A SPLIT-SECOND

Ballistic Statues (Bel. Antler) 1987 ●
A Split-Second EP (Wax Trax!) 1988 ●
... From the Inside (Wax Trax!) 1988 ●
Another Violent Breed EP (Bel. Antler) 1989 ●
Firewalker EP (Caroline) 1990 ●
Kiss of Fury (Antler-Subway-Caroline) 1990 ●

The Belgian duo of Mark Ickx (ex-Extraballe) and Chrismar Chayell first emerged in 1986 with an imaginatively upbeat instrumental dance track, "Flesh." Despite the promise of a bright future in that vein, A Split-Second wanted desperately to be perceived as a band, and on their next record ("Rigor Mortis") introduced deep, morbid vocals to prove the point. By the time Wax Trax! in America compiled these initial efforts into a six-track EP, A Split-Second had already issued an album (**Ballistic Statues**) that indicated a determination to match body music with song structure.

Ickx and Chayell have gradually honed a studio sound built upon electronic drums, fleshed out with prominent synthesizer melodies, caustic guitars and vocals alternating unevenly between the bass-heavy growls favored by many Euro rockers and conventional pop choruses. Still capable of enticing grooves when the mood is right, the best moments on **From the Inside** are its dance singles—"Scandinavian Bellydance" (also included on **A Split-Second**) and "The Colosseum Crash"—although the torchy "Last Wave" and the gentle title track indicate some songwriting ability.

Following a live EP (**Another Violent Breed**), **Kiss of Fury** shows AS-S pushing towards conventionality; the opening "Backlash" is its most commercial offering to date. A fascination with the darker side is maintained, however, in the moody vocals, visual imagery and a continuing obsession with erotica ("Crash Course in Seduction"). Awkwardly juggling gothic rock, industrial and pop-dance, A Split-Second doesn't quite excel in any of those arenas.   [tf]

See also *Extraballe*.

27

ASSOCIATES

The Affectionate Punch (nr/Fiction) 1980 + 1982
Fourth Drawer Down (nr/Situation Two) 1981
  (nr/Beggars Banquet) 1982
Sulk (Sire) 1982 ●
Perhaps (nr/Associates-WEA) 1985
Take Me to the Girl EP (nr/Associates-WEA) 1985
Heart of Glass EP (nr/WEA) 1989 ●
The Peel Sessions EP (nr/Strange Fruit) 1989 ●
Wild and Lonely (Circa-Charisma) 1990 φ
Popera: The Singles Collection (Sire-Warner Bros.)
  1990 φ

ALAN RANKINE

The Day the World Became Her Age (Bel. Crépuscule)
  1986 ●
She Loves Me Not (nr/Virgin) 1987 ●
The Big Picture Sucks (Bel. Crépuscule) 1989 ●

The Associates—Billy Mackenzie (most words and all vocals, eventually everything) and Alan Rankine (most music and all instruments except drums)—once attempted brilliance, but later settled for playing at being clever. **The Affectionate Punch** boldly tried to stake a claim for some of the no-man's land between Bowie's theatrical, tuneful rock and Talking Heads' semi-abstract, intellectual dance approach, with a slight flavoring of the pair's native Scottish traditional music. Not fully mature, and sometimes almost burying its own best points, the band seemed a promise of riches to come.

Unfortunately, the Edinburgh-based duo veered off in a more art-conscious—at times willfully obscure—direction, with harsh musical textures often dominating the melodies. **Fourth Drawer Down**, a compilation of singles, gives the somewhat redeeming impression of determined experimentation that is, however, lessened by the exclusion of certain B-sides in favor of later tracks which reveal Mackenzie's growing preference for pose over accomplishment.

By **Sulk**, such talent as comes through seems strained under the weight of Mackenzie's selfconsciousness. Rankine's emphasis on keyboards over guitar is symptomatic of the defection away from rock and towards a sort of neo-pop, but the melodies are hindered by tinny sound, arrangements that muddle rather than clarify and vocal excesses that make Bowie's worst sound tame. The US edition subtracts three cuts, inserting instead a pair from **Fourth Drawer Down** and two subsequent singles. Net result: Associates (no article) are a shrill, non-synth Human League for emotional infants. The title's all too accurate—Mackenzie comes across as a callow, shallow poseur. On the eve of its first major British tour, the band splintered.

Putting the article back in the name, Mackenzie completed an album with Martin Rushent that WEA rejected in 1983; some of it emerged two years later on **Perhaps**. To write it off with a snide "perhaps not" would be a cheap shot, but more than generous. Mackenzie has many associates here, including guitarist Steve Reid—who co-wrote half the songs—but whether any given track was produced by Heaven 17's Martyn Ware, Martin Rushent or the team of Mackenzie and Dave Allen, it all sounds like Heaven 17 or the Human League—*with* synths, now—making undanceable dance

music with a few ho-hum twists. The lyrics include strange, gratuitous, incomprehensible non sequiturs; the music is at best uninvolving, even if you listen for sheer sound and ignore the pose. At seven minutes, the one all-around good track ("Waiting for the Loveboat") overstays its welcome by half; the cassette edition needlessly adds instrumental versions of four album cuts.

A surprisingly strong new single, "Take Me to the Girl," emerged later in the year, and—shortly after it flopped—was re-released on a five-track 10-inch, combined with a remix of "Perhaps" and three live cuts recorded in London that find Mackenzie crooning heartfelt if histrionic versions of songs like "God Bless the Child" and (ulp) "The Little Boy That Santa Claus Forgot."

Four years and another rejected LP (**The Glamour Chase**) later, Mackenzie re-emerged with a non-LP EP and, the following year, a garish Eurodisco album, **Wild and Lonely**. While the songs reprise the moods and melodies (not to mention the keyboardist) of **Perhaps**, producer Julian Mendelsohn straps on a similarly dated saccharine straitjacket. (Have these guys been living on Mars?) Still, Mackenzie's voice occasionally shines through the marzipan, particularly on the atmospheric title cut.

The five-track **Peel Sessions** EP (from April '81) contains rougher, rock-oriented versions of '81-'82 material and would be highly recommended if it actually included "Me, Myself and the Tragic Story" (which is listed) instead of the far inferior "Arrogance Gave Him Up" (which isn't).

Popera compiles nearly all of the essential material (including a track from **The Glamour Chase** and a song recorded with Yello) from the Associates' seemingly deliberate anti-career, resulting in the group's most satisfying and wildly schizoid release ever. (That nothing from **Wild and Lonely** appears is no loss.)

Since leaving the band in 1982, Alan Rankine has been living in Brussels, working extensively with Paul Haig and releasing solo albums. **She Loves Me Not**, the only one of his efforts to be issued outside of Belgium, offers clever dance-pop and impressively sung balladry, a smooth and appealing concoction akin to mid-period Thompson Twins but dolled up with a bit of continental suaveness. [jg/ja]

See also *Paul Haig, Holger Hiller, Yello.*

VIRGINIA ASTLEY

Love's a Lonely Place to Be EP (nr/Why Fi) 1982
From Gardens Where We Feel Secure (nr/Happy
  Valley-Rough Trade) 1983
Promise Nothing (Bel. Crépuscule) 1983
Hope in a Darkened Heart (Geffen) 1986 ●

A classically trained pianist and flautist less known for her own work than for the illustrious company she keeps, Astley has played sessions for Siouxsie and the Banshees, Richard Jobson and Troy Tate, among others. Her father, Ted Astley, is an accomplished composer best known for television themes; her brother is artist/producer Jon Astley; her brother-in-law is Pete Townshend. (She played piano on his "Slit Skirts.") Her late-'70s band, the three-woman Ravishing Beauties, included Nicky Holland, later known for her work with Tears for Fears and Ryuichi Sakamoto. However, Astley's own pastoral and tranquil records are markedly different from those of family and friends.

Evoking images of summer afternoons in the countryside, **From Gardens Where We Feel Secure** is, superficially at least, soothing sonic wallpaper. Except for a few syllables, it's entirely instrumental, consisting basically of piano, flute, clarinet and tape loops. Upon closer scrutiny, the tapes (animal sounds, church bells, etc.) build subliminal tension; there's more to Ms. Astley than initially meets the ear.

Promise Nothing is a compilation, including cuts from **Gardens** and various singles. The orchestration on the earlier work is thicker—synthesizers, sax and percussion place the material more in the rock realm—but her choir-boy soprano keeps things from getting too raucous. Standouts: the irresistible "Love's a Lonely Place to Be" and "Arctic Death," as haunting as any John Cale effort. An impressive record from an intriguing artist.

In 1985, Astley signed to Elektra in the United Kingdom and released a pair of singles, neither of which broke any new musical ground for her. **Hope in a Darkened Heart**, her US debut, was mostly produced by Sakamoto, who adds more synths and drum machines. David Sylvian sings on the opening "Some Small Hope." While it's still very pretty, there's more substance as well. The angry lyrics by this single mother (the baby's father left Astley during her pregnancy) are made even more effective by the charm of her voice and the delicacy of the music. I wouldn't want to be the guy to whom "A Father" or "So Like Dorian" are directed. Remixes of earlier tracks, including "Love's a Lonely Place to Be," round out Side Two.

She may never be prolific or commercially popular, but Virginia Astley is one of the most unique talents around these days.   [dgs]

ASWAD

Aswad (Mango) 1976 ●
Hulet (nr/Grove) 1978 (nr/Grove-Island) 1979 (Mango) 1990 ●
Showcase (nr/Grove-Island) 1981 (Mango) 1990 ●
New Chapter (nr/CBS) 1981
Not Satisfied (nr/CBS) 1982 ●
A New Chapter of Dub (Mango) 1982 ●
Live and Direct (Mango) 1983 ●
Rebel Souls (Mango) 1984 ●
To the Top (nr/Simba) 1986 (Mango) 1990 ●
Distant Thunder (Mango) 1988 ●
Renaissance (nr/Stylus) 1988 ●
Crucial Tracks (Best of Aswad) (Mango) 1989 ●
Too Wicked (Mango) 1990 ●

Though they've never really caught on in the States, Aswad is one of Britain's best and most popular reggae bands. The trio's work is characterized by consistently excellent musicianship (Aswad's adjunct horn section is superlative) and a sound that is modern yet authentic. (Although it's become less so as the group has become increasingly oriented to the pop mainstream.) Their easygoing groove may resemble UB40's, but Aswad is thoroughly unique; after fifteen years, their continued growth and versatility are remarkable. Along with Linton Kwesi Johnson and Dennis Bovell, Aswad represents the flowering of British reggae. Their recording history, however, is disjointed and reflects shifts in personnel, musical direction and labels.

The debut album (with "Back to Africa") is of mixed quality, but showcases the band's stylistic variety, featuring lovers rock, dub and Marley-inspired roots. **Hulet**, released two years later, is much better—assured and capable—but indecision about direction is clearly audible. Shortly after this release, bassist George Oban left; Tony Gad (Robinson), who had played keyboards in the group, took over on bass. A stint with British CBS yielded two albums, **New Chapter** and **Not Satisfied**, both (particularly the latter) rich with fine songs and performances. **A New Chapter of Dub**, while decent enough, is for fans only.

Rebel Souls has a genial consistency and includes significant covers of Toots Hibbert's "54-46 (Was My Number)" and Marvin Gaye's "Mercy Mercy Me." Wisely, Aswad were linking themselves to tradition as they geared up for the future.

The group's full yet rootsy sound continued on **To the Top**; strong and full of punch, the album is one of their best, with top-notch writing, singing and playing throughout. With the band operating at peak power, the record is probably their most representative studio effort.

Distant Thunder marks a distinct change in direction. Feeling perhaps that they had pushed their old sound to its limit, the band experiments here with funk and soul, as well as keyboards. The lightweight, crossover-geared approach was bound to alienate some fans but, while several of the new songs sound tentative, others (like the pop-soul single "Don't Turn Around") are engaging and credible, featuring the same musical craftsmanship that has always characterized Aswad's work.

To some extent, Aswad's strongest releases have been their singles. No proper greatest hits package existed prior to 1989, but two albums had partially filled that gap. **Showcase**—remixes of their most popular non-LP numbers, including "Rainbow Culture," "Warrior Charge" and "Babylon" (the title theme of a film which starred Aswad's Brinsley Forde)—is excellent, and a fine place for novices to start. In addition, **Live and Direct** (London, 1983) contains some of Aswad's best-loved songs and gives a hint of the band's live power. "Rockers Medley" stands out, but the whole LP is great.

The **Renaissance** compilation, issued by a UK label marketed through TV advertising, attempts to cram in 20 selections from the group's long history, but unceremoniously edits the numbers down, making this a must to avoid.

Crucial Tracks (Best of Aswad) has six fewer cuts than **Renaissance** but preserves the songs' full running times. The compilation includes some single sides, including "Gimme the Dub," the B-side of 1988's "Give a Little Love."

Too Wicked finds the group in an even more serious crossover bid, pushing towards funk, pop, soul and even dancehall, with beatbox drumming, hi-tech samples and house grooves all reeking of commercial aspirations. The best track is "Fire," on which Aswad is joined by

Shabba Ranks, 1990's ruler of the dancehall DJs. While "Just Can't Take It" maintains Aswad's socio-political awareness, the record could have done nicely without an Eagles cover ("Best of My Love"). [bk/aw]

ATHLETICO SPIZZ 80
Do a Runner (A&M) 1980
SPIZZLES
Spikey Dream Flowers (A&M) 1981
SPIZZ
Spizz History (nr/Rough Trade) 1982
SPIZZOIL
The Peel Sessions EP (nr/Strange Fruit) 1987

Whatever band British vocalist Kenneth Spiers led—Spizzoil, Spizzenergi, Spizzles, Athletico Spizz 80—he'll always be best remembered for one novelty hit, 1979's "Where's Captain Kirk?" The charm and wit of that single was nowhere to be found on the subsequent **Do a Runner**, which was mired in the band's predilection for science fiction imagery. If it seems tough to conceive an album of time warps, time machines and almost nine minutes of "Airships," imagine how tough it would be to repeat that formula; **Spikey Dream Flowers** offers robots, deadly war games and incessant runaway guitar (by recent arrival Lu Edmonds) with no place to go.

Spizz History compiles tracks from various Spizz eras, reaching all the way back to a 1978 single; "Where's Captain Kirk?," "Soldier Soldier," a version of Roxy Music's "Virginia Plain" and a 1982 single, "Megacity," are all worth hearing, but that's about it. The **Peel Sessions** EP was recorded in the summer of '78. [gf]

ATLANTICS
Big City Rock (ABC) 1979
BALL AND PIVOT
Ball and Pivot EP (Z Club) 1983

The only album by this talented Boston rock band with strong, melodic material and a slightly overdramatic vocalist was unfortunately issued on a label that was breathing its corporate last. Two standout songs—"When You're Young" and "One Last Night"—suggest abundant power-pop promise, but weak production and a crucial lack of promotion kept the quintet a local phenom.

The Atlantics' songwriters—guitarist Tom Hauck and bassist Bruce Wilkinson—returned a few years later fronting a synth-pop trio called Ball and Pivot. The EP, which echoes Duran Duran, Spandau Ballet and Red Noise, is pleasant enough. The most interesting track, however, is "Two O'Clock Jump," which mixes the pair's new sound with the Atlantics' Yardbirds stylings. [i/ds]

A TRIBE CALLED QUEST
People's Instinctive Travels and the Paths of Rhythm (Jive-RCA) 1990 ●

Junior members of the Native Tongues—the pacific Afrocentric New York area rap family that includes the Jungle Brothers and De La Soul—A Tribe Called Quest build their wonderful, easygoing debut on a solid platform of warm humor and classic soul (and other) music. Over smoothly percolating tracks more suited to swaying than any more athletic motion, the witty and personable young quartet—Q-Tip, Shaheed, Phife and Jarobi—tells shaggy dog stories ("I Left My Wallet in El Segundo"), romances fantasy figures ("Bonita Applebum"), warns about lice ("Pubic Enemy") and cholesterol ("Ham'n'Eggs"), and criticizes a variety of anti-social archetypes ("Description of a Fool"). Except for several instances in which good ideas give way to tiresome repetition, **People's Instinctive Travels** is a thoroughly enjoyable trip. [i]

ATTRACTIONS
See *Elvis Costello*.

BILLY ATWELL
See *Th'Inbred*.

AUDIO TWO
What More Can I Say? (First Priority Music-Atlantic) 1988 ●
I Don't Care (First Priority Music-Atlantic) 1990 ●

One controversial flashpoint in 1990's censorship free-for-all was this Brooklyn rap duo's second album; more specifically, the homophobic "Whatcha' Lookin' At?," which announces that "I hate faggots . . . gay mothers get punched in the face." Lacking real rhyming talent or good voices, these sons of First Priority president Nat Robinson (and the brothers of MC Lyte, who guests on two **I Don't Care** tracks) outgrew (?) the innocuous B-boy boasts of the dull **What More Can I Say?** by becoming outrageously obnoxious, delivering witless ultra-attitude ("I Get the Papers") and crude sexuality ("Undercover Hooker," "Build Up Back Up," "The Nasty"). Not for nothing does **I Don't Care** stoop to bathroom sounds. [pn]

AU PAIRS
Playing with a Different Sex (nr/Human) 1981
Sense and Sensuality (nr/Kamera) 1982
Live in Berlin (nr/a.k.a.) 1983

Although the quartet was evenly divided between the sexes, the trademarks of Birmingham's Au Pairs were singer/guitarist Lesley Woods' husky vocals and her feminist themes. They favored stripped-down, generally tuneless dance-rock, perhaps the better to drive home ironic messages like "We're So Cool," "Set-Up" (both on the first album), "Sex Without Stress" and "Intact" (on **Sense and Sensuality**). A female viewpoint is, unfortunately, still novel for pop music; Woods is humorless and sometimes oozingly graphic, but usually thought-provoking in her romantic analyses. Au Pairs' few overtly political songs ("Armagh," "America") are less successful.

The live album, recorded at the Berlin Women's Festival, finds the group in good form, running through their best songs with careful intensity. The rhythm section is especially good, but Woods predictably dominates the proceedings. [si/i]

AVENGERS
Avengers EP (White Noise) 1978 + 1981
Avengers (CD Presents) 1983 ●
PENELOPE HOUSTON
Birdboys (Subterranean) 1988

What allegedly began as an excuse for punk fashions became, briefly, the most powerful band in the San Francisco area; the Avengers' original EP was a minor classic of its time, indicating that they might have become America's best straight-ahead punk (not hardcore) band had they lasted. The four-song **Avengers** boasts tight, memorable cuts instrumentally akin to Johnny Thunders and the Sex Pistols, though it's Penelope Houston's intoning words of some depth that makes the difference. Like X without any pretensions; too bad Steve Jones couldn't finish the production (the mix needed him).

The posthumous album reprises the entire contents of that EP, adding a stack of ace punk tunes recorded (with one subsequent exception) in 1977 and 1978. Houston clearly prefigures Chrissie Hynde as the archetypal indomitable rock'n'roll woman—her strength and aggression are what elevates these tracks from energetic but typical punk to remarkable personal statements. Whether anyone outside of San Francisco realized it at the time, the Avengers were a major national musical asset. (The CD and cassette contain two bonus cuts.)

After the Avengers folded in 1979, the Los Angeles-born and Seattle-bred Houston worked with Alex Gibson and Howard Devoto. In 1986, her cleverly named group, Dash Thirty Dash (journalists will get the reference), issued a smart and melodic single, "Full of Wonder." That song and its B-side also appear on her subsequent album, a folky acoustic collection produced by (and dedicated to) the late Snakefinger and played with a four-person band. While the lyrics are astute, and Houston's skillful voice—an airy, mature soprano—fills **Birdboys** with lovely character, much of the simple music (self-composed with various collaborators, none of them as worthy as her Dash Thirty Dash partner) just isn't that good. [jg/i]

JOHN AVERY
See *Hula*.

AZTEC CAMERA
High Land, Hard Rain (Sire) 1983 ●
Oblivious EP (Sire) 1984
Knife (Sire) 1984 ●
Still on Fire EP (nr/WEA) 1984
Backwards and Forwards EP (Sire) 1985
Love (Sire) 1987 ●
Somewhere in My Heart EP (nr/WEA) 1988 ●
Stray (Sire-Reprise) 1990 ●

The Glaswegian guitarist-singer-songwriter Roddy Frame leads/is Aztec Camera, whose delicate pop conveys his poetic sensibility and rampant originality. **High Land, Hard Rain** is a magnificent debut, airy yet somehow lush, filled with lovely melodies and thoughtful, impressionistic lyrics. "Oblivious," "Walk Out to Winter" and "We Could Send Letters" are all memorable, distinguished by layered acoustic guitars, beautiful vocal arrangements and jazzy rhythms; "Down the Dip" displays Frame's playful side.

There are two **Oblivious** EPs. Both include the same remix of the title tune, but the US version has three British B-sides, while the earlier UK edition contains one B-side, an LP track and a live take.

Knife, produced by Dire Straits' Mark Knopfler, is a lot less ethereal, employing a stronger backbeat, sterner vocals and horns. Frame's lyrics continue to walk the line between profound and ludicrous but, for the most part, manage to stay within the realm of lucidity. His writing shows the influence of Elvis Costello and also incorporates a mild R&B feel. Typical of the record's approach, the lead-off "Still on Fire" faintly recalls the Jackson 5's "I Want You Back." (That song's 12-inch release adds four live cuts.)

It's rare to encounter a marketing gimmick worthy of special mention, but the commercially available **Backwards and Forwards** EP is brilliant. The folder covering the 10-inch record contains the band's complete discography and history, plus profiles and photos. The swell record offers four live tracks (only two encores from the **Still on Fire** EP) plus the band's ingeniously languid acoustic cover of Van Halen's "Jump."

Reduced to a name for Frame's solo career, Aztec Camera returned to action three years later with **Love**, a heartfelt but colorless Philly soul record made with studio musicians and half a dozen producers. (Think of Boy George or Paul Young, with music supplied by Steve Winwood.) Although Frame's singing and songwriting don't quite suit this musical style, his low-key charm and basic talent keep him from embarrassing himself.

In some ways, **Stray** is Frame's return to form, a mature retake on some of **High Land**'s themes. "The Crying Scene" is a verdant burst of electric guitar pop; the title track, with its dizzying wordplay and tender sentiments, ponders the pain of lost innocence. But Frame has yet to settle into a particular genre, and the album swings between jazzy cabaret ballads, ballsy rock'n'roll and more blue-eyed soul ("Notting Hill Blues" could be an outtake from **Love**). The profound lyrics and emotive vocals hold things together, though, and **Stray** contains some of Frame's finest work to date. [i/kss]

BABES IN TOYLAND

Spanking Machine (Twin/Tone) 1990 ●

Gut-grinding music from three Minneapolis women, as powerful as it is agitating. In line with the jackhammer rhythm section, Kat Bjelland beats the shit out of her guitar (which seems to be fighting back), and matches that aggression with cathartic screeching: these babes didn't just fall off the toy-truck. With monstrous production by Jack Endino, **Spanking Machine** is a forceful, uncompromising opening statement. [sm]

BABY FLIES

Rain (Hol. Resonance) 1988
A Colorful View (Resonance) 1989 ●

If nothing else, bands with an established producer in their lineup can be assured of good-sounding records. That's certainly the case with New York-scene studio-star-*cum*-bassist Jim Waters (Das Damen, Missing Foundation, etc.), whose Hoboken-sound pop trio makes a handsomely presented but nearly generic debut on **Rain**. For most of the album, Pat Waters' thin, plain singing leaves the overly restrained (and laboriously paced) material at the starting gate. But then she cranks up a neat multi-voiced part on the chorus of "Iza Dream" and pumps handsome life into the song.

Although stronger, Pat's folky delivery is still inadequate on **A Colorful View**, an occasionally lively record of simply attractive tunes arranged—with impressive new maturity and sophistication—for chiming guitars and subtle keyboards. A nice try, but the Baby Flies still need better singing and songwriting. (The CD adds six **Rain** songs.) [i]

BABY OPAQUE

See *Bomb*.

BACKBONES

See *Senders*.

BAD BRAINS

Bad Brains [tape] (ROIR) 1982 (Dutch East Wax) 1991
Bad Brains EP (nr/Alternative Tentacles) 1982
I and I Survive/Destroy Babylon EP (Important) 1982
Rock for Light (PVC) 1983 (Caroline) 1991 ●
I Against I (SST) 1986 ●
Live (SST) 1988 ●
Attitude: The ROIR Session [CD] (ROIR-Important) 1989 ●
Quickness (Caroline) 1989 ●
The Youth Are Getting Restless (Caroline) 1990 ●

H.R.

Its About Luv (Olive Tree) 1985 (SST) 1988
Human Rights (SST) 1987 ●

HR Tapes '84-'86 (SST) 1988 φ
Singin' in the Heart (SST) 1989 ●
Charge (SST) 1990 ●

RAS MICHAEL

Zion Train (SST) 1988 ●

In their quest to become a crossover band, these black jazz-rock fusionists from Washington DC (later based in New York) turned to orthodox speedpunk and released the memorable 1980 super-fast single "Pay to Cum" (1:33 of free-fire guitar rage, produced by Jimmi Quidd of the Dots) that established their mastery of that genre. Bad Brains' hardcore is a more distinctively modulated roar than most, but what really sets them apart are radically contrasting excursions into dub and reggae. Hardcore's dogmatic streak makes it harder on chameleons than most rock subgenres; these guys get away with it.

On the **Bad Brains** cassette album (and the four-song **Bad Brains** EP excerpted from it), the quartet excels in both fields: loping, Rastafarian reggae ("I Luv I Jah," "Leaving Babylon," "Jah Calling") and powerhouse political slam-rock (a re-recorded "Pay to Cum," "Banned in D.C.," "Big Takeover"). The album was later reissued on CD under the title **Attitude** and later on vinyl as **Bad Brains**.

The Ric Ocasek-produced **Rock for Light**, which includes new versions of five **Bad Brains** songs, offers the same dualism, with subject matter covering everything from angry politics ("Riot Squad") to minor pop culturisms ("At the Movies"), stretching from Rasta topics to "How Low Can a Punk Get" sociology. Throughout, Joseph I's (aka H.R.) reedy vocals set off the hardcore roar led by guitarist Dr. Know (Gary Miller) and sweetly color the reggae rumble. A fascinating and truly unique blend. (Ocasek and bassist Darryl Jenifer remixed the album for its 1991 reissue, which also adds three outtakes from the original sessions.)

I Against I is a bracing all-rock explosion, a mature collection of well-written originals played, at varying speeds, with authority and enthusiasm. Dr. Know trots out a number of different effects, sounds and approaches; H.R. has likewise never been better. Shrugging off punk conventions, Bad Brains explore sophisticated and subtle terrain all their own. At its most explosive, the record crosses Van Halen with Black Flag; more restrained passages resemble an energized, younger Police. The quartet holds reggae rhythms to a bare minimum, although lyrics continue to reflect their religious and political convictions.

Playing punk, thrashy rock and reggae with equal command and conviction (Earl Hudson's deft drumming is crucial to the band's gear-shifting ability), the Bad Brains fill the impressive **Live** with familiar repertoire items documented at a handful of dates on an '87 tour. The CD bonus track is a reggae version of "Day Tripper."

Like many hardcore stars, Bad Brains took a turn towards metal (on the mighty **Quickness**, a mid-speed rock record with just one reggae number), accepting the genre's brutish intensity but rejecting its clichés. Dr. Know's spiraling near-jazz leads and Hudson's thundering percussion (fortified by a second drummer) give H.R. a mighty platform from which to deliver the band's obscure socio-religious analyses—of AIDS ("Don't Blow Bubbles" contains the memorable exhortation, "Don't blow no fudge buns"), genetics, musical trends and Rastafari faith.

The Youth Are Getting Restless is another '87-vintage concert album, this one a punky explosion recorded at an Amsterdam show. Although there's lots of material overlap with **Live**, this eighteen-song selection offers a more extensive review of the first three albums, downplaying dub for such charged classics as "Rock for Light," "Pay to Cum" and "Big Takeover."

H.R. (Paul Hudson) has left and rejoined the group several times, releasing solo albums along the way. The fascinating if indifferently recorded **Its About Luv** (on his own Olive Tree label) offers chaotic punk—class of '77 UK division, with anthemic melodies ("Let's Have a Revolution")—on one side and upbeat Caribbean funk ("Who Loves You Girl?"), jazzy reggae ("Happy Birthday My Son") and a live rocker ("Free Our Mind") on the back. (Expanded by the three-song **Keep Out of Reach** 12-inch, **Its About Luv** was issued on cassette—and CD—as **HR Tapes**.)

The high-tech **Human Rights**—featuring, among others, Oscar Brown Jr. and H.R.'s brother, drummer Earl—is a bizarre but captivating pastiche of funk, reggae-based rock-pop, carefully arranged and delicately textured rock, studio experimentation and other offbeat manifestations of H.R.'s beliefs.

Most of **Singin' in the Heart** is straight Rasta reggae and dub—easygoing grooves nicely played and warmly sung, with some neat guitar work thrown on top—but then there's "Singin' in the Heart" and "Don't Trust No (Shadows After Dark)," on which a different group of musicians (Oscar Brown Jr. performs the entire title track on keyboards and a drum machine) support H.R. in a suavely soulful pop mode.

With Earl on drums, four guitarists, backing vocalists and a two-man horn section, H.R. sings nothing but old-style reggae originals with little stylistic variation on **Charge**, a handsome but dull album that praises the lord so often it might as well be a church service.

H.R. produced, co-wrote and sings (Earl plays drums) on the deeply atmospheric **Zion Train**, one of many albums by Ras Michael, a legendary Jamaican figure whose career dates back to the '60s.   [mf/i]

See also *Token Entry*.

BAD MANNERS

Ska'n'B (nr/Magnet) 1980
Loonee Tunes! (nr/Magnet) 1980
Bad Manners (MCA) 1981
Gosh It's . . . (nr/Magnet) 1981
Forging Ahead (Portrait) 1982
The Height of Bad Manners (nr/Telstar) 1983
Klass (MCA) 1983
Can Can (nr/Hallmark) 1984
Mental Notes (Portrait) 1985
Live and Loud!! (nr/Link) 1987 ●
Return of the Ugly (Blue Beat-Relativity) 1989 φ
Anthology–Bad Manners (nr/Blue Beat) 1989 ●

This rollicking nine-piece London neo-ska nonsense ensemble is fronted by a cartoon-character vocalist dubbed Buster Bloodvessel (well, it's a more colorful name than Doug Trendle), an immense bald hulk. The rest of the lineup—three horns, guitar, bass, drums, keyboards and harmonica (played, but of course, by Winston Bazoomies)—churns out smooth, tight bluebeat like early Madness or Specials, while embracing all manner of musical silliness for humorous effect. Bad Manners is strictly entertainment; their records, juvenile though they may sometimes be, consistently provide smile-inducing, good-natured, toe-tapping value in every groove.

Ska'n'B (the band's original musical self-description) has fewer originals than subsequent LPs; versions of "Monster Mash," "Scruffy Was a Huffy Chuffy Tug Boat," the "Magnificent Seven" theme and "Ne-Ne Na-Na Na-Na Nu-Nu" are ludicrous but engaging. Their first American escape, **Bad Manners**, draws tracks from **Ska'n'B** as well as **Loonee Tunes!**, released in the meantime. **Gosh It's . . .** squeezes in a frisky instrumental rearrangement of "Can Can" amid pleasing originals like "Gherkin" (giddily described on the back cover as a "deeply moving tribute to Charles Aznavour") and "Ben E. Wriggle," plus some almost serious numbers that suggest insidious maturation.

Forging Ahead, the group's finest record, has a (thankfully) instrumental version of "Exodus," a cover of "My Boy (Girl) Lollipop" and an original called "Samson and Delilah (Biblical Version)." When released in the US two years later, a great subsequent single, "That'll Do Nicely," had been added.

Two compilations were issued in 1983. The American one has a truly disgusting pig-out cover and most of the band's best early tracks; the British release offers a different selection, with only six songs in common. While the following year's **Can Can** collection overlaps both, it's not that similar to either. Of the three, **Height** offers the strongest program.

With **Mental Notes**, B.M. pulls away from their original concept, managing to cover Todd Rundgren's "Bang the Drum All Day" without serious damage. Like Madness' transitional period (which came a lot earlier, careerwise), the bluebeat tempos remain, but they're under a slick coat of restraint, sophistication and—dare it be said?—maturity. Bring back giddy stupidity!

During the band's lengthy studio lay-off, a 1987 "official bootleg" album appeared: poorly recorded but dynamic live performances of the band's best originals and favorite covers. The CD adds two extra cuts.

Amid further compilations, Bad Manners managed to record the all-new **Return of the Ugly**, a serious fun album with traditional ska values and no stylistic mucking about. Covering two Laurel Aitken songs (now that's bluebeat cred!), giving the *Bonanza* theme a rock steady twist and contributing a bunch of generic originals, Bad Manners put their digressions aside and party like it's 1979. Skank on!   [i]

BAD RELIGION

How Could Hell Be Any Worse? (Epitaph) 1982
Into the Unknown (Epitaph) 1983
Back to the Known EP (Epitaph) 1984
Suffer (Epitaph) 1988 ●
No Control (Epitaph) 1989 ●
Against the Grain (Epitaph) 1990 ●

On their first album, this Southern California hardcore quartet adds such unexpected attributes as piano, dynamics and university-level lyrics to an otherwise traditional sore-throat-vocals/maximum-overload-guitar sound. The well-recorded LP meets the minimum daily requirement of loud and fast rock without sacrificing basic human intelligence in the process. **Into the Unknown**, a mini-album, is even better, a swirling blizzard of noisy, catchy psychedelia and paisley rock, with real songs and a sound that resembles Nazz tunes played by early Deep Purple. A masterpiece.

After that great leap forward, half the original lineup, joined by guitarist Greg Hetson (on loan from the Circle Jerks) and a guest bassist, made a conscious reversal on the one-sided 12-inch EP, **Back to the Known**, which banishes the stylish keyboard sound in favor of an unreconstructed punk attack. Still, Greg Graffin's articulate vocals are way above average, and the stun-volume chords don't swamp out the melodies or lyrics. Not bad at all.

The first-LP quintet reunited in 1988. Considering the years elapsed since **Back to the Known**, **Suffer**'s new-found fury is a revelation. The album is faster, meaner and leaner than any in the band's past, the attack ablaze with unusual hooks, pointed riffs and pseudo-erudite lyrics ("The masses are obsequious contented in their sleep/The vortex of their minds contented in the murky deep"). Unfortunately, with two slower exceptions ("Best for You" and "What Can You Do"), the relentless velocity makes it hard to tell the songs apart.

Suffer was just a warmup, however, for **No Control**, an awesome achievement in an otherwise moribund genre. Arguably one of the best hardcore albums ever, **No Control** recaptures all of the form's exhilarating attributes, with inspired songwriting, vocal harmonies, transfixing highbrow lyrics ("The automatic man is the quintessential mindless modern epicene"), explosive playing and Graffin's soaring, pleading, tearing voice. The lack of rhythmic and stylistic variety can't sabotage this firecracker, as the sheer power of might meeting melody is too satisfying.

Against the Grain maintains **No Control**'s pace, another deranged rollercoaster ride without a seat belt. Smoking hot production makes Graffin's sensational voice seem even more sinister on such tracks as "Get Off," "Anesthesia" and a scathing indictment of the anti-abortion movement, "Operation Rescue." The few slow songs (like "Faith Alone") test his range, but he delivers dramatic performances. In offering a heavy dose of the danger modern rock so rarely possesses, Bad Religion has become not only the best (by far) contemporary hardcore band, but one of the best current rock-'n'roll bands, period. [i/jr]

BAGS

Rock Starve (Restless) 1987 ●
The Bags (Stanton Park) 1990

SWAMP OAF

Swamp Oaf (Stanton Park) 1989

The product of a city with a tremendous underground musical heritage, this Boston trio plays a hybrid of common punk and '70s heavy-guitar rock, but writes surprisingly sensitive songs with memorable hooks and singalong choruses. On **Rock Starve**, the Bags demonstrate a singular ability to analyze and describe relationships and emotions with searing but subtle simplicity. (How often do you hear a hardcore number sincerely, even lovingly, describe a woman's beauty?) The album doesn't contain a bad tune.

Guitarist Crispin Wood and bassist Jon Hardy's dual vocals show substantial maturity on the follow-up, and the material (like "Evil," an examination of a recently severed relationship) is just as solid. The peculiarly danceable "Atomic Coconuts," the hardcore "Superpower," the moving "Closer Than" and the clever "Beauty of the Bud" are all terrific.

The Swamp Oaf album finds the Bags posing as a mythical lost monster band (à la Spinal Tap). **Swamp Oaf** was recorded in eighteen hours, uniting a variety of sounds (including a sort of goofy jazz improv) to create a very un-Bagsy platter. [icm]

CHRIS BAILEY
See *Saints*.

BAILTER SPACE
See *Gordons*.

JOE BAIZA & THE UNIVERSAL CONGRESS OF
Universal Congress Of (SST) 1987
UNIVERSAL CONGRESS OF
Prosperous and Qualified (SST) 1988 ●
This Is Mecolodics EP (SST) 1988
The Sad and Tragic Demise of Big Fine Salty Black Wind
  (Ger. Enemy) 1990

Saccharine Trust guitarist Baiza's first solo record contains two endless studio jams, sans vocals. "Certain Way" covers the entire first side and part of the second; whether you'll actually turn the record over to hear how it finishes depends entirely on your ability to remain awake during nineteen enervating minutes of four guys dicking around formlessly in the studio. But his band's next outing, **Prosperous and Qualified**, is much better—a jazzy, spacious rock record that contains actual songs, credible sax riffing (by Steve Moss) and other good stuff.

The luxuriantly post-bop vocabulary of the five-song **This Is Mecolodics'** lengthy, tongue-in-cheek liner essay doesn't, ultimately, go very far towards explaining just what the term (the use of which Baiza is nominally serious about) means. One pigeonhole to eliminate immediately—parodistic packaging aside—is the fake jazz once espoused by semi-kindred spirit John Lurie. This is as real (spiritually, at least) as jazz gets. Baiza's as hell-bent on improv as ever: garroting his axe Sonny Sharrock-style on the virulent "Joey," softening the tone and lending a mariachi feel to Ornette Coleman's "Law Years," even sitting out a round as Steve Moss and Jacob Kuhn tussle in the steel cage sax matchup "Niños de la Tierra."

Sad and Tragic Demise returns to tighter structures, emphasizing the band's formidable new rhythm section. Versions of Ronald Shannon Jackson and Henry Threadgill numbers reveal more precision *and* swing than anything in UCO's past. Baiza, however, downplays his guitar work (probably a bad idea) and sings on a number of tracks—definitely a bad idea, aside from "Uh-Huh," an oddball Donald Fagen soundalike.

See also *Saccharine Trust.* [i/dss]

ARTHUR BAKER AND THE BACKBEAT DISCIPLES
Merge (A&M) 1989 ●

Hip-hop's first star producer in the early '80s and a major figure in the introduction of record remixing to mainstream rock artists, Arthur Baker was just a face in the studio crowd by decade's end. So he made an album of his own. Collaborating with everyone from ABC and OMD to the Force M.D.'s, Baker (whose limited role here involves songwriting, percussion and occasional instrumental contributions) doesn't so much merge styles as stack them up. Essentially a sampler album, **Merge** offers slick techno soul, new jack swing, mushy adult rock, hip-house, suave pop and more, none of it particularly noteworthy. [i]

BALAAM AND THE ANGEL
Love Me EP (nr/Chapter 22) 1985
Day and Night EP (nr/Chapter 22) 1985
She Knows EP (nr/Virgin) 1986
The Greatest Story Ever Told (Virgin) 1987 ●
Live Free or Die (Virgin) 1988 ●
I Took a Little EP [CD] (nr/Virgin) 1989 ●
Days of Madness (Virgin) 1989 ●

Despite their goth garb, Scotland's Morris brothers—singer/bassist Mark, guitarist Jim and drummer Des—are popsters at heart, a fact which they take pains to disguise on these unremarkable albums. **The Greatest Story Ever Told** does have some charm, but the trio's melodies are too often buried in feeble attempts to whip up a vague air of menace. (Balaam started as protégés of the Cult's Ian Astbury.) **Live Free or Die**, produced by former Cult boardman Steve Brown, is closer to Van Halen-styled AOR metal. (The CD adds two tracks.)

Day and Night is a four-song 12-inch of pre-LP material, the title track of which wound up as one of two bonus cuts on the British **Greatest Story** CD. Built around a song from the first LP, **She Knows** is a double 7-inch with two radio session tracks of songs that appeared on the second album. The 1989 CD-3 EP (offering a one-song preview of **Days of Madness**) joins the titular LP track with three live cuts.

With the band now a quartet, **Days of Madness** continues Balaam's descent into metal mediocrity, unironically recycling every commercial hard-rock cliché in the book, without even the mild diversion of its predecessor's pop hooks. [hd]

BALANCING ACT
New Campfire Songs EP (Type A) 1986 (Primitive Man) 1987 ●
Three Squares and a Roof (Primitive Man) 1988 ●
Curtains (IRS) 1988 ●

This semi-electric LA rock quartet is earnest enough on its Peter Case-produced debut EP but, with the exception of "Wonderful World Tonight," a likable and evocative update of the "Goin' Up the Country" ethos, none of these half dozen **New Campfire Songs** is likely to show up alongside "Blowin' in the Wind" at the next weenie roast. Give the Balancing Act credit for a unique blend of acoustic and electric elements, though. Also, they've got a melodica, and they know how to use it!

Three Squares and a Roof is a lot less precious and more interesting than the EP. The playing and production are better, the material vastly improved, revealing songs that cover substantial lyrical territory, nearly all of it previously uncharted. The **Three Squares** CD also contains **New Campfire Songs**.

Deftly produced by ex-Gang of Four guitarist Andy Gill, **Curtains** could be a sampler of classic '60s and '70s harmony vocal styles. Echoes of the Beatles, Hollies and especially Crosby, Stills and Nash abound, as well as the Bee Gees (on a cover of Funkadelic's "Can You Get to That," no less!), the Monkees and jazzers Lambert, Hendricks and Ross. Gill's adventurous hightech production not only keeps the album from sounding too retro, but helps put some punch into material which occasionally leans towards wimpiness. [ds]

BALCONY DOGS
See *Echo & the Bunnymen.*

B.A.L.L.
Period (Another American Lie) (Shimmy-Disc) 1987 ●
Bird (Shimmy-Disc) 1988 ●
Trouble Doll (Shimmy-Disc) 1989 ●
Four (Hardball) (Shimmy-Disc) 1990 ●

GUMBALL
Special Kiss (Primo Scree) 1991 ●

Everything you really need to know about B.A.L.L. is that **Bird** contains a smirking cover of George Harrison's "Bangla Desh." This dual swipe at rock star pomposity and sacred cow causes pretty much defines the B.A.L.L. worldview. How funny you find the joke depends on how resonant the whole post-Beatles era of rock self-importance was to you, and how tolerant you are of grown men who think that lampooning it is a meaningful activity.

Formed by Velvet Monkeys singer/guitarist Don Fleming and drummer Jay Spiegel, along with producer/bassist Kramer and percussionist Dave Licht, B.A.L.L. fills **Period** with amusing, grungy, guitar-driven crude-pop tunes like "The French" and "My TV Is Broke" (so what else is new?). The joke behind the band comes to full flower on **Bird**, the cover art of which is a re-creation of the Beatles' infamous butcher sleeve. Besides "Bangla Desh," the tunes here include Ringo Starr's "It Don't Come Easy," Harrison's "Wah-Wah" and Marc Bolan's "Buick Mackane"; all of them are kind of funny but none shed any light on the original songs. The band's own material is mildly entertaining but generally faceless.

The back cover of **Trouble Doll** calls it "the disappointing third LP," but that's not the half of it. The cover drawing is blatantly racist and without discernible context; the faux-protest song "African Sunset" (on CD only) doesn't promote intercultural understanding, either. While some songs are moderately diverting, other stuff is barely of demo quality. (One side was recorded live at CBGB, and includes material from **Bird** as well as covers.) The very deliberate attempt to make sloppiness a virtue backfires as often as it clicks here.

Strangely enough, in the midst of a reportedly acrimonious breakup, the band (which later reassembled as Gumball) completed its best album, **Four (Hardball)**. Side One offers fully fleshed-out, fast, funny and energetic songs, while the flip comprises a trash suite of sorts, with five grunge-guitar-heaven instrumentals. (It's likely these were meant to be complete vocal numbers and that Fleming quit before finishing them, but that's not how it sounds.) All in all, a worthy precursor to **Rake**, the LP Fleming next made with a reformed Velvet Monkeys. [gk]

See also *Velvet Monkeys*.

DAVE BALL
In Strict Tempo (nr/Some Bizzare) 1983
GRID
Electric Head (nr/East West) 1990 ●

Without erstwhile Soft Cell partner Marc Almond supplying the sleaze, shy keyboard man Dave Ball is a cold-hearted bore on his solo album. **In Strict Tempo**'s drab mood pieces strain with little success for wry wit to leaven the pretentiousness, but wind up just a jumble of undeveloped ideas. Genesis P-Orridge of Psychic TV warbles on two tracks.

Making up for lost time, Ball's first album with Grid partner Richard Norris (a former P-Orridge collaborator who does a bit of vocalizing besides poking at an assortment of machines and guitar) runs through a wide variety of related electronic dance musics: techno-pop (dinky and lush), environmental ambience, go-get'em house, prog-rock and found-sound fooling around. The few songs and the most focused instrumental pieces are fine for what they are, but a seemingly random track sequence badly blunts **Electric Head**'s impact. [jy/i]

OTIS BALL
I'm Gonna Love You 'Til I Don't (Bar/None-Restless) 1990 ●

A transplanted Midwesterner who joined the Hoboken scene, singer/guitarist Ball has a whiny voice perfectly suited to songs that poke fun at celebs from Buddha to Charles Manson, as well as several women who are no doubt nearer to his heart. The two exceptional songs that make this light, warm self-produced pop record worth many a return visit are the rollicking "Walk on Water" (They Might Be Giants provide the insidious chorus vocal hook) and the anthemic title track, a wondrous let's-live-for-today credo that's somehow both sad and strongly optimistic. [sm]

BALLAD SHAMBLES
See *LeRoi Brothers*.

BALL AND PIVOT
See *Atlantics*.

AFRIKA BAMBAATAA & THE JAZZY 5
"Jazzy Sensation" (Tommy Boy) 1981
AFRIKA BAMBAATAA & SOULSONIC FORCE
"Planet Rock" (Tommy Boy) 1982
"Looking for the Perfect Beat" (Tommy Boy) 1982
"Renegades of Funk" (Tommy Boy) 1983
Planet Rock—The Album (Tommy Boy) 1986
"Return to Planet Rock" (York's) 1990
TIME ZONE
"The Wildstyle" (Celluloid) 1983
"World Destruction" (Celluloid) 1984 ●
SHANGO
Shango Funk Theology (Celluloid) 1984 ●
AFRIKA BAMBAATAA & JAMES BROWN
"Unity" (Tommy Boy) 1984
AFRIKA BAMBAATAA AND FAMILY
"Funk You!" (Tommy Boy) 1985
Beware (The Funk Is Everywhere) (Tommy Boy) 1986
Death Mix Throwdown (nr/Blatant) 1987
The Light (Capitol) 1988 ●

Bronx DJ-turned-hip-hop-godfather Bambaataa not only created the record that thrust beatbox electro-funk into the '80s and brought Kraftwerk onto the dancefloor, he has made pioneering sides with numerous performers and established himself as a major figure in contemporary music. Working mainly in the 12-inch format, Bam's ascent began with a routine boast rap, "Jazzy Sensation," but got into gear with "Planet Rock," the Arthur Baker-produced (and co-written, with the band and John Robie) explosion of scratch cuts, electronic gimmickry, processed vocals and solid-state rhythms. (Both tracks were later compiled on the Tommy Boy label retrospective, **Greatest Beats**.) "Looking for the Perfect Beat" is even better, with Baker mostly soft-pedaling the monolithic pounding in favor of a skittish electronic metronome and tacking on fancier effects, vocals and mix tricks to create an ultra-busy urban symphony. The mega-rhythmic "Renegades of Funk" adds social/historical/political lyrics to the dance-floor dynamism and delivers a really bizarre blend of rap, synthesizers and oppressive electronic percussion.

As a precursor to a long-promised album (which ultimately included it), Bambaataa released "Funk You!," a corny rap idea stretched out over a 12-inch in four very different mixes, with borrowings from James Brown and Queen. When it finally appeared, **Beware** proved that the LP format presents no obstacle to the imposing Overseer: variety and invention make it an exciting electro-beat vision of a freewheeling stylistic future. "Funk Jam Party" is exactly that; "Tension" sounds like Bowie comes to Harlem; "Rock America" incorporates howling electric guitars, a munchkin chorus and chintzy organ without ever losing the funk. Easily the highlight, and another amazing cross-cultural accomplishment by Bambaataa, is Bill Laswell's earthy, energized production of the MC5's "Kick Out the Jams." Awesome.

In a fascinating cross-generational culture mix, Bambaataa teamed with the Godfather of Soul to record "Unity," a positive political message released in six alternate versions (connected by studio patter) on one disc. Hitting a funky compromise between classic soul and modern hip-hop, the record works on a number of levels and is certainly a significant milestone in rap. Taking another startling detour, Bambaataa wrote and recorded "World Destruction" with Bill Laswell, sharing the vocals with John Lydon, jump-cutting the Englishman's no-wave keen into an intense, ominous funk-rock maelstrom for one of the most remarkable dance singles in recent memory.

Bambaataa also records as a member of Shango, a vocal trio that is supported by Material (for this purpose, Laswell and Michael Beinhorn). The album-length **Funk Theology** offers five sophisticated party creations that also feature guitarist Nicky Skopelitis. The originals get no heavier, lyrically, than "Let's Party Down"; a version of Sly Stone's "Thank You" is utterly appropriate. Good for dancing but a bit dull for listening.

Extending the Family way out there, **The Light** features UB40, Nona Hendryx, Boy George, George Clinton, Bootsy Collins, Yellowman and others. At times, the appealing and diverse pan-ethnic album involves Bam only tangentially, like a brief rap on UB40's "Reckless" track, or a few interjections on the Hendryx/George rendition of Curtis Mayfield's "Something He Can Feel." The only credit he takes on "Shout It Out" is as co-publisher of the composition. The individual tracks are fine, but the lack of focus leaves this plainly commercial effort more a various artists sampler than a cohesive Bambaataa creation.

Planet Rock–The Album is a compilation of the three classic 12-inch records with Soulsonic Force plus previously unreleased tracks featuring Melle Mel and Trouble Funk.   [i]

BAMBI SLAM

Is ... EP (Product Inc.-Rough Trade) 1987
The Bambi Slam (Blanco y Negro-Warner Bros.) 1988 ●

Admittedly inspired by the Jesus and Mary Chain, this Canadian-British quartet (guitar/bass/drums/cello!) takes a less claustrophobic and more rhythmic approach to noise-laden echo-pop than the Reids but still winds up sounding a lot like **Psychocandy** on **Is**, a six-track American compilation of British singles. Although not prominent in the mix, the big fiddle adds a nice touch to songs like "La, La, La (It's Out of Hand)" and "Hit Me with Your Hairbrush." Redundant but amusing.

Singer/guitarist Roy Feldon is all that remains of the Bambi Slam on the album, although his former bandmates add some cello, backing vocals and one drum track. Running the one-man show, Feldon gets an irritatingly raw sound from a rhythm machine and lots of equally coarse guitar; his singing is no mellifluous prize,

either. Where the EP had a certain spirit and excitement, the album is draggy, ineffectual and repetitive, a parade of sounds rather than songs.   [i]

BANANARAMA

Deep Sea Skiving (London) 1983 ●
Bananarama (London) 1984 ●
True Confessions (London) 1986 ●
Wow! (London) 1987 ●
The Greatest Hits Collection (London) 1988 ●
Pop Life (London) 1991 ●

SHAKESPEAR'S SISTER

Sacred Heart (ffrr-PolyGram) 1989 ●

Keren Woodward, Sarah Dallin and Siobhan Fahey became a trio in London in 1979. They first gained notoriety singing with the Fun Boy Three, who later returned the favor by producing and backing them on their earliest singles. **Deep Sea Skiving** essentially compiles their first string of infectious 45s, encompassing a panoply of styles: percussive Afro-beat ("He Was Really Sayin' Somethin'"), girl-group soul ("Shy Boy"), '60s chart silliness ("Na Na Hey Hey Kiss Him Goodbye") and lush pop ("Cheers Then"). Additionally, **Deep Sea Skiving** offers Paul Weller's "Doctor Love," the charming and light "Hey Young London" and the morose "What a Shambles." An assortment of producers yields little uniformity of sound, but the ensemble vocals provide the crucial character regardless of setting.

For their first real album, Bananarama gave the ball to hitmakers Swain and Jolley (Spandau, Alison Moyet, Imagination) who, as is their custom, co-wrote the material. Over the lush, highly arranged backing, the ladies croon two wonderful singles—the evocatively tropical "Cruel Summer" (a hit, one year apart, in the UK and US) and "Robert De Niro's Waiting." Otherwise, the album deflects much of the trio's engaging individuality and substitutes a vacuous sheen that's too functional and defeats their ingenuous image. **Bananarama** isn't bad—the vocals are charming in any case—but it is forgettable.

Although Swain and Jolley still held the reins for **True Confessions**, they lost their franchise to the up-and-coming Stock-Aitken-Waterman team, who placed two sides on the LP, including an irresistibly catchy disco remake of Shocking Blue's "Venus" that topped the American charts. Overall, **True Confessions** is a limp outing that sculpts a refined adult sound, evaporating the group's youthful vitality and charm in the process.

Capitalizing on their Moroder-based sequencer formula, Stock, Aitken and Waterman wrote, produced and programmed **Wow!**, a peppy synth-driven dance record that disguises Bananarama's vocal limitations in an overwhelming wash of electronic music simulation. The crass gimmickry and mock-Supremes arrangements of "I Heard a Rumour" and "I Can't Help It" are as predictable as the tunes are unshakable; the rest of the album's tracks resemble those two so closely they might as well be remixes. (The UK CD and cassette actually include bonus remixes.) Sure it's total trash, but what else does a car need to keep it running in the hot summer sun?

In late '87, following **Wow!**'s success, Fahey (by

then married to Dave Stewart of Eurythmics) left the band and was replaced by Jacquie O'Sullivan, formerly of the Shillelagh Sisters. It would have been nice if the resulting compilation album had carefully sealed the original group's best and biggest tunes in a time capsule, but **The Greatest Hits Collection** mixes in a couple of items by the new lineup and includes before-and-after photos as well. Considered as an overall oeuvre (well . . .), there's a lot more crap than quality here; the handful of charming pop gems are swamped by craven trash.

If Dave Stewart had, as claimed, no hand in crafting the synthesized dance-rock of **Sacred Heart**, then precisely mimicking Eurythmics' sound must be easier than one would imagine. Joined in Shakespear's Sister by Marcella Detroit (who, in her '70s life as Marcy Levy, toured and recorded with Eric Clapton), the post-Bananarama Fahey (sporting a deeper, more serious voice) kisses off her ex-bandmates with the nasty "You're History," but isn't above recreating their harmony signature on several tunes. Although she does a fair Chrissie Hynde impression on "Heaven Is in Your Arms" and echoes other contemporary vocalists elsewhere, frequent, detailed nods to Annie Lennox give the record an overwhelming sense of déjà entendu. Even "Primitive Love," a goofy six-line shoutalong with raging fuzz bass, sounds like Eurythmicized Gary Glitter.

[i]

BAND OF BLACKY RANCHETTE
See *Giant Sandworms*.

BAND OF OUTSIDERS
See *Certain General*.

BAND OF SUSANS
Blessing and Curse EP (Trace Elements) 1987
Hope Against Hope (Furthur-Blast First) 1988 ●
Love Agenda (Blast First-Restless) 1989 ●
The World and the Flesh (Restless) 1991 ●

ROBERT POSS
Sometimes [tape] (Trace Elements) 1986

ROBERT POSS/NICOLAS COLLINS
Inverse Guitar [tape] (Trace Elements) 1988

HELMET
Strap It On (Amphetamine Reptile) 1990

Indeed there were, for a time, three Susans (Stenger, Tallman and Lyall) in this New York sextet that has its roots in Glenn Branca's and Rhys Chatham's experimental downtown ensembles. The four songs on **Blessing and Curse**, produced by (ex-Western Eyes) guitarist/songwriter/vocalist Robert Poss, locate an exciting niche between anti-music chaos and accessible rock by setting simple, repetitive chord/bass patterns in motion and then slathering on layers of vocals and noisy guitar. Dense without being forbidding, "You Were an Optimist" and the speeding "Where Have All the Flowers Gone" (an original) clearly indicate the Susans' intriguing direction and skill.

Hope Against Hope (titled after an EP track that was remixed and included; a second appears in a new version here) is an improvement on all fronts, revealing a bracingly loud—but never actually strident—band that seemingly can't put enough guitar electricity on vinyl to satisfy itself. Besides Poss' febrile production, his songs are better formed here, with chord progressions that actually resolve. (In a touching show of pop cognizance, "I the Jury" quotes the Stones' "Last Time.") Anchored by a solidly plain rhythm section, the storm of strings continues to rage unabated, making **Hope Against Hope** something of a rockier American response to **Psychocandy**. (Just ignore the band's English-major lyrics.) The CD adds the two remaining songs—"Where Have All the Flowers Gone" and "Sometimes"—from **Blessing and Curse**.

With the departure of two Susans (following **Hope Against Hope**'s mid-'87 sessions), a five-piece/three-guitar lineup made **Love Agenda** with no diminution in power. Although it sounds unlikely the songs would amount to much musically in a different context—these aren't twinky little pop ditties given a radioactive-waste bath—the band's ability to harness distortion, wall-shaking volume and feedback (keeping things just below the chaos line) into reasonably melodic forms remains a marvelous achievement. The barreling "Because of You" and the droney "It's Locked Away" are the album's most impressive tracks. The CD adds a loud but unconvincing cover of the Stones' "Child of the Moon."

Made while Poss was still a member of Chatham's band, **Sometimes** predates the Susans' first record but features two of its members—Alva Rogers on backing vocals and drummer Ron Spitzer on piano. A tentative and transitional bridge between career stages, the eight songs—which include early versions of "Sometimes" and **Hope Against Hope**'s "Throne of Blood," as well as an otherwise unrecorded song entitled "Blessing and Curse"—cover both regular rock and surging noise.

Poss fills one side of **Inverse Guitar** with formless, ear-splitting 1987 guitar-damage improvisations; the other documents his (and Susan Tallman's) collaboration with electronic music composer Nicolas Collins on three failed experiments that employ familiar life sounds and backwards manipulation of guitar and bass.

Guitarist/shouter Page Hamilton—a **Love Agenda** Susan—leads the far less melodic Helmet, a brutal noise quartet that clearly isn't in it for the songs. Like an uptempo Black Sabbath record with a bad skip, Helmet repeats lockstep guitar/bass riffs endlessly on **Strap It On**, erecting a crudely effective brick wall of sound.
See also *Rhys Chatham*. [i]

BANGLES
Bangles EP (Faulty Products) 1982 (IRS) 1982
All Over the Place (Columbia) 1984 ●
Different Light (Columbia) 1986 ●
Everything (Columbia) 1988 ●
Greatest Hits (Columbia) 1990 φ

SUSANNA HOFFS
When You're a Boy (Columbia) 1991 φ

These four young women from Los Angeles—originally known as the Bangs—display an odd collection of influences on their five-track debut EP, neatly produced by Craig Leon. The swell harmonies on several cuts come straight from the Mamas and the Papas, while the music alternates between evoking **Rubber Soul** and energetic, bantamweight Yardbirds-styled garage rock. The playing's fine and the vocals are great—the songs just aren't up to snuff.

The Bangles' young career was temporarily derailed when Faulty Products went out of business and bassist Annette Zilinskas left to join Blood on the Saddle. Come 1984, the group swung back into action, fortified with a new bassist, a more reliable record contract, the best American power-pop producer money can buy (David Kahne) and a passel of brilliant new songs (mostly by guitarist Vicki Peterson, but also Kimberley Rew's "Going Down to Liverpool," a cover which indirectly led to *his* group, Katrina and the Waves, finally securing an American deal). **All Over the Place** has everything a pop album needs: exceptional harmony vocals, catchy, memorable and intelligent tunes and a full dose of rock-'n'roll guitar energy. Unlike the Go-Go's, who never fully clarified their lyrical stance, the Bangles offer an adult play-fair-or-take-a-hike independence that is a lot more contemporary than their joyously evocative sound. The best cuts other than "Liverpool"—"Hero Takes a Fall," "Tell Me" and "James"—feature guitarist Susanna Hoffs' alluring vocals and are unassailable gems; the worst tracks only fall short of that by a smidge. Simply wonderful.

Prince became a fan, and gave the rising band a song, "Manic Monday" (written pseudonymously by "Christopher"), for **Different Light**. Despite trivial lyrics, it became a gigantic hit single, establishing the quartet's stardom but causing many to overlook the LP's finer points: Jules Shear's "If She Knew What She Wants," Alex Chilton's classic "September Gurls" and bassist Michael Steele's harrowing "Following." If not as consistently top-notch as **All Over the Place**, it's nonetheless enjoyable and often memorable.

Taking a dive from the precipice of quality pop, the Bangles sacrificed **Everything** to the gods of radio programming. Studiously produced by Davitt Sigerson into a weak imitation of artistic pretension, the mellifluous album contains one great song (the sexy "In Your Room"), lots of bad ideas ("Bell Jar," a Sylvia Plath tribute so idiotic that the grim lyrics and peppy arrangement almost hit together; "Glitter Years," a sheepish glam-rock recollection that ends with a Bowie quote; the merry death wish of "Crash and Burn") and the group's creative nadir: the blatant pandering song-factory schmaltz of Hoffs' showcase "Eternal Flame," a test-run for her impending solo career.

Besides a short list of obvious LP tracks (that manages to overlook "September Gurls," "James," and other personal faves), the compilation appends the Bangles' ripping version of Paul Simon's "Hazy Shade of Winter" (from the **Less Than Zero** soundtrack), a bland folky romp through the Grass Roots' "Where Were You When I Needed You" (rescued from an early B-side) and an insignificant **Everything** outtake.

Hoffs' solo album (named for a lyric from the Bowie song that closes the record) is a no-holds-barred commercial bore, with painstaking adult-pop overproduction by Kahne and a strange hodgepodge of demographically designed material. Besides the hollow products of hit hacks, the scattered program includes Cyndi Lauper's "Unconditional Love" (with "new lyrics written expressly for Susanna Hoffs"!), E∗I∗E∗I∗O's fine "This Time," Pearl Harbor and the Explosions' "So Much for Love" and "That's Why Girls Cry," a presentable collaboration between singer, producer and Juliana Hatfield of Blake Babies. Donovan Leitch is one of the numerous backing singers; John Entwistle guests on the appalling misreading of "Boys Keep Swinging." [i]

See also *Blood on the Saddle*.

LESTER BANGS AND THE DELINQUENTS
Jook Savages on the Brazos (Live Wire) 1981
DELINQUENTS
The Delinquents (Live Wire) 1981
LESTER BANGS AND BIRDLAND
Birdland (Add On) 1986

Elevated (strung up?) as the newest breed of rock-'n'roll hero—martyred chronicler—Lester Bangs was a timely victim for the perennial personality cult, which seized upon his accidental death in April 1982 to resurrect his seminal rock writing for a new fanzine audience. By turns introspective and scathing, his dissection of music was frequently intense and insightful, occasionally misguided and paltry, but it was *always* soul-searching and achingly personal, crypto-musical characteristics that have endeared him to subsequent generations and which, not surprisingly, infuse his own recorded work.

Following the nakedly bleary emotion of his "Let It Blurt" 45 (with backing by members of the Patti Smith Group, Voidoids and Raybeats), Bangs somehow hooked up with the Delinquents (Texas version), locally infamous for relinquishing their sociopathic vocalist Layna Pogue to a quiet room with rubber walls. That brief intersection yielded an LP not unlike Richard Hell's first—if recorded impromptu during second rehearsal, with Hank Williams and Pere Ubu puppeteering overhead. Classic or erratic, depending on your skew of vision.

The Delinquents also released a self-titled LP sans frontperson, with the guitarists sharing vocals atop vaguely B-52'sish new wave surf. After they disbanded, bassist/Live Wire boss Brian Curley went on to work with yet another certifiably abnormal intellect, Roky Erickson, in Evil Hook Wildlife ET., before forming 27 Devils Joking.

In 1986, **Birdland** denigrated the Bangs legend with its posthumous reflection on Lester's band of the same name, generally despised during its existence as a worthless live unit with ties to Lower East Side little brothers the Rattlers. Basically pop with dulled hooks, even Lester's jagged vocals and lyrics seem to have lost all edge and point, not least in the remakes (from **Jook Savages**) of the previously nervy "I'm in Love with My Walls" and "Accidents of God." [ab]

See also *Rattlers*.

PATO BANTON
Never Give In (nr/Greensleeves) 1987 (Primitive Man) 1988
Pato & Roger Come Again EP (Primitive Man) 1988
Visions of the World (IRS) 1989
Wize Up! (No Compromize) (IRS) 1990 ●

A dozen years after making his album debut (on the Beat's **Special Beat Service**) duetting with Ranking Roger on "Pato and Roger a Go Talk," Pato Banton (born Patrick Murray) returned to these shores with **Never Give In**. Mainly backed by Birmingham's Studio Two house band, which provides strong reggae riddims punctuated by colorful horns and rock-oriented lead guitar, Banton sings, toasts and speed-raps against war, poverty and drugs (except one, of course). Fortunately, his advice on how to behave in Babylon is laced with humor—his impersonations of his mother (on three songs), wife and a scared riot victim are hilarious. Also fun are duets with Paul Shaffer, another go-round with Ranking Roger and a wonderful high speed toast titled "Gwarn!"

The **Pato & Roger Come Again** EP contains two versions of the title track, one longer and one shorter than the one on **Never Give In**; "Don't Sniff Coke" (also from the LP), which features a rap about Pato's encounter with a dope dealer on a train; and the gritty non-LP "King Step."

While **Visions of the World** and **Wize Up!** remain fairly similar to **Never Give In** in terms of subject matter, the music is slicker, leaning more towards smooth dance rock, bland soul and synthesized pop reggae. Pato's added a bit more boast to his toast, but both albums lack the humor and flair of the first. Switching styles (and accents) in most unnerving manner, Banton makes a number of faint political statements on **Visions of the World**, adding only one amusing toast, "Ready Me Ready," about a romantic misadventure in London.

Steel Pulse's David Hinds duets on the title track of **Wize Up!**, which also features Banton's rendition of "Spirits in the Material World." (In a fitting stylistic payback, the Police song became an alternative radio hit for him.) Judging from this album, Banton could be the first toaster to become a pop star in America.   [ds/i]

BARNES & BARNES

Voobaha (Rhino) 1980
Fish Heads: Barnes and Barnes Greatest Hits EP (Rhino)
  1981
Spazchow (Rhino) 1981
Soak It Up EP (Boulevard-CBS) 1983
Amazing Adult Fantasy (Rhino) 1984
Sicks (Rhino) 1987
Zabagabee: The Best of Barnes & Barnes (Rhino) 1988 ●

Art and Artie Barnes (one of whom had a highly public former life as Billy Mumy, child actor) are a sick pair of perverts you would not want to know personally. At your party, they would stage disgusting practical jokes; they would tell obscene lies to your parents just to get a laugh. Both **Voobaha** and **Spazchow** offer heavy doses of dark-hued novelty music that chews up modern culture and spits it back, producing an equal number of chuckles and shudders. The first features the underground hit "Fish Heads" plus "Boogie Woogie Amputee" and "Party in My Pants." On **Spazchow** you get "Spooky Lady on Death Avenue," "Swallow My Love" and a merciless dissection of (the group) America's "I Need You."

In what clearly was the only possible response, two members of America provided backing vocals on the pair's next effort, **Soak It Up**, a relatively restrained

five-song EP. (The earlier retrospective EP is a fish head-shaped picture disc.)

Amazing Adult Fantasy offers further proof that age is softening the Barnes boys. Not only does Steve Perry of Journey sing on the utterly presentable "Don't You Wanna Go to the Moon," but the pair makes a vain stab at commercial accessibility with "I Don't Remember Tomorrow" and other wimpolinos. **Sicks**, however, returns them to the disgustatorium, with such garbage pail tunes as "Pizza Face," "Pussy Whipped" and "Sit on My Lap and Call Me Daddy."

Reprising only two of the five songs comprising the appropriately shaped **Fish Heads** picture disc, **Zabagabee** contains many of the pair's finest and most essential moments, including "Fish Heads," "Party in My Pants," "Boogie Woogie Amputee," "Pizza Face" and a fine reading of "What's New Pussycat?" produced by kindred weirdo Bob Casale. (The CD throws in five more.) Lovers of absurdist, sleazy humor should consider Barnes & Barnes highly recommended. All others should proceed with extreme caution.   [jy/i]

See also *Crispin Hellion Glover*.

RICHARD BARONE
See *Bongos*.

BARRACUDAS
Drop Out with the Barracudas (Voxx) 1981 ●
Mean Time (Fr. Closer) 1983
House of Kicks EP (nr/Flicknife) 1983
Live 1983 (Fr. Coyote) 1983
Endeavour to Persevere (Fr. Closer) 1984
The Big Gap (Fr. Coyote) 1984
Live in Madrid (Sp. Impossible) 1986
I Wish It Could Be 1965 Again (Fr. GMG) 1987
The World's a Burn EP (nr/Flicknife) 1988
The Garbage Dump Tapes! (nr/Shakin' Street) 1989 ●

FORTUNATE SONS
Rising (nr/Bam Caruso) 1986
Karezza (nr/Bam Caruso) 1987

JEREMY GLUCK WITH NIKKI SUDDEN & ROWLAND S. HOWARD
I Knew Buffalo Bill (nr/Flicknife) 1987
Burning Skulls Rise EP (nr/Flicknife) 1988

Despite a cheerfully self-deprecating stance, London's Barracudas offer quite an enjoyable sentimental journey through assorted American traditions on **Drop Out**. Some tunes plunge headlong into dense, ringing folk-rock—see "Violent Times" or "I Saw My Death in a Dream Last Night" for an update of the Byrds on a gloomy day. Surf tunes like "Summer Fun" and "His Last Summer" strive a little too hard for laughs to overcome fundamental flimsiness, but are fun and can't be faulted on attitude. (The UK and US versions of the LP differ by a track.)

After abandoning a second album (four tracks from which were salvaged and released as **House of Kicks**) and losing drummer Nick Turner to the nascent Lords of the New Church, singer Jeremy Gluck and guitarist Robin Wills assembled a new Barracudas and recorded the wonderful **Mean Time**, produced by Pete Gage (ex-Vinegar Joe), who also adds evocative keyboards to the LP. Reclaiming more than half of the unreleased album's songs, the Barracudas here sound like a younger Flamin Groovies. (In fact, this five-piece lineup—easily the Barracudas' best—features ex-Groovie guitarist Chris Wilson.) An effortless and catchy '60sish blend of punky pop, vintage rock'n'roll, mock Mersey-beat, snarly mild psychedelia and Byrdsy 12-string folk-rock.

The 1983 live LP, packaged and recorded so ama-teurishly as to resemble a bootleg, has a few original songs from the two preceding albums but mostly consists of covers like "Seven and Seven Is," "You're Gonna Miss Me" and "Fortunate Son." The performances rock out enthusiastically, but the miserable sound quality is an insurmountable obstacle to enjoyment.

After making a third album, **Endeavour to Persevere**, the Barracudas disbanded at the end of '84. While assorted European labels issued compilations (**I Wish It Could Be 1965 Again**), outtake collections (**The Big Gap**) and archival concert albums (**Live in Madrid**, a terrible 1984 show with better sound than the French live LP), Gluck made a musically unrelated solo LP in collaboration with Nikki Sudden and Epic Soundtracks (both ex-Swell Maps), Rowland S. Howard (Birthday Party, etc.) and Gun Club leader Jeffrey Lee Pierce (on guitar). Various permutations of that gang play Gluck/Sudden compositions in simple recordings that have a nice, casual feel. Stylistic variety—from acoustic guitars ("Gone Free," the nicest tune here) to near-noise (the last portion of the epic "All My Secrets")—keeps **Buffalo Bill** interesting, but Gluck's artless voice doesn't really suit the material. Intriguing but unsatisfying. (The same crew later reassembled to cut an EP, **Burning Skulls Rise**.)

For his part, Wills made a pair of albums with a group called the Fortunate Sons (originally a trio, but later a quartet with Chris Wilson), whose bassist wound up in the Barracudas when Wills and Gluck decided to restart the band in early '89. The first order of business was to polish up the tapes of the lost second album from 1982. **House of Kicks**' belated release as **Garbage Dump** isn't exactly the Rosetta Stone of '80s music, but it is a potent dose of solid garage rock, albeit without the same tuneful charm as **Mean Time** (with which it shares eight songs); in hindsight, that underscores the roles Chris Wilson and Pete Gage played on that album. Overall, the biggest failings are the vocals, which are hoarsely unattractive and rather weak in the harmony department, and the unimaginative, overly nostalgic production style. **The World's a Burn** is a six-track compilation of singles.

By the end of 1990, the Barracudas had recorded an album's worth of new material produced by Andy Sher-noff and were looking for a label.   [jy/i]

SYD BARRETT

The Madcap Laughs (nr/Harvest) 1970 (Capitol) 1990 ●
Barrett (nr/Harvest) 1970 (Capitol) 1990 ●
The Madcap Laughs/Barrett (Harvest) 1974
The Peel Sessions EP (nr/Strange Fruit) 1987 (Strange
   Fruit-Dutch East India) 1991 ●
Opel (nr/Harvest) 1988 (Capitol) 1989 ●

VARIOUS ARTISTS
Beyond the Wildwood (nr/Imaginary) 1987 ●

One of rock's legendary living dead casualties, guitarist/songwriter Syd [Roger] Barrett formed Pink Floyd in 1965 and made it one of the first art-school bands to abandon blues for druggified psychedelia. Syd fell out of Pink Floyd after a debut album that put the band on the verge of major international success; having grown erratic, withdrawn and unpredictable, he pretty much retired in 1968, and has since lived a private, reclusive existence—except for making two solo records in 1970. Barrett has influenced many bands and remains an enduring rock icon for the chronically dislocated. Twenty years later, his unselfconscious looniness continues to set a framework in which artists can explore updated acid-rock with little more than an acoustic guitar. The Television Personalities have sung about him, Robyn Hitchcock, Anthony More, Edward Ka-Spel (of the Legendary Pink Dots) and others have been compared to him, and numerous art, psychedelic and neo-mod bands have invoked his name, recorded his songs or acknowledged his impact. Tormented but unquestionably brilliant, Barrett left a musical legacy which is wholly contained on Floyd's first LP and these four discs. (The two original records were issued separately but subsequently repackaged as a double album. When it came to CDs, however, they were split up again.)

The Madcap Laughs sounds as though it was a difficult record to make. Ex-bandmates David Gilmour and Roger Waters obviously had to expend some effort to get Barrett organized enough to produce releasable tracks, and they only did half the record. (The remainder was produced by the label manager of Harvest Records.) The inclusion of false starts and between-take discussions make it clear this was no easy task. Still, the songs (e.g., "Terrapin," "Octopus") are wonderful, and Syd's delicate but clumsy singing lends charm to the effort, which alternates between one-man performances and subtly played group efforts (several of which were actually solo takes overdubbed by Hugh Hopper, Mike Ratledge and Robert Wyatt of the Soft Machine).

Gilmour and Floyd keyboardist Richard Wright produced **Barrett**, using Humble Pie drummer Jerry Shirley as the album's fourth musician. This more consistent-sounding record—relatively confident and upbeat—offers Barrett's idiosyncratic view of life in songs like "Waving My Arms in the Air" and "Effervescing Elephant." Confusion and anger lurk just below the surface of misleadingly chipper bits of Carnaby Street flower-power music.

The outtakes and leftovers from those two projects, combined with 1968 demo sessions, were culled for **Opel**, an excellent appendix to Barrett's oeuvre. Considering the uncommon qualities of **The Madcap Laughs** and **Barrett**, this collection of early/alternate/unaccompanied versions and otherwise unreleased material—including "Golden Hair," "Octopus" (then titled "Clowns & Jugglers"), "Dark Globe" (aka "Wouldn't You Miss Me")—make just as cohesive an album. None of these tracks shed any new light on Barrett as a person or an artist, but this is a major addition to his slim solo catalogue.

The excellent Peel EP dates from February 1970 and contains cogent renditions of "Terrapin," "Gigolo

41

Aunt," "Baby Lemonade," "Effervescing Elephant" and the otherwise unissued "Two of a Kind," performed energetically and reasonably cogently with simple accompaniment by Gilmour and Shirley. The EP's US release (on CD and tape only) has a different cover and a singular title.

One of the very first entrants in the recent rash of tribute albums, **Beyond the Wildwood** contains interpretations of Barrett songs by an assortment of neo-psychedelic bands, including the Soup Dragons ("Two of a Kind"), Shamen ("Long Gone") and the TV Personalities ("Apples and Oranges"). Highlights: the Mock Turtles' unnervingly Syd-like version of "No Good Trying," Plasticland's straightforward "Octopus" and SS-20's wispily sung/enthusiastically played "Arnold Layne." [i]

WILD WILLY BARRETT
See *John Otway*.

ROB BASE & D.J. E-Z ROCK
It Takes Two (Profile) 1988 ●
ROB BASE
The Incredible Base (Profile) 1989 ●

New York MC Rob Base (Ginyard) shook more than dancefloors with his first LP: rapping against contrasting refrains of non-sampled soul singing (most notably on the title cut—blithely named the best single of all time by *Spin* magazine—and "Joy and Pain"), he made an exciting style-busting innovation that helped spread serious hip-hop sounds into the "black music" mainstream. Other than those extraordinary achievements (and "Crush," a croony romantic ballad Base more or less sings), **It Takes Two** matches powerfully simple rhythm tracks to masterful PG-rated rhymes. Where some rappers revel in the violence of contemporary urban life, Base—a positive self-promoter devoted only to pumping up a good time—has the sense to acknowledge that "Times Are Gettin' Ill" and reject the temptation of drugs and guns.

With his partner temporarily out of the picture, Base followed his gold-selling debut with **The Incredible Base**, an entertaining stream of high-velocity/high-ideals egocentric rhymes and cushy soul singing. Taking two distinct stylistic directions, the album pushes straight rap—the killer "Turn It Out (Go Base)" and "If You Really Want to Party" hype up the mix with chanted backing vocals, while "The Incredible Base" throws in the kitchen sink to move the jam along—and loosely swinging grooves that borrow music from 20-year-old classics (like "War," "Come and Get Your Love" and "Ain't Nothing Like the Real Thing"). As Base himself immodestly notes, **The Incredible Base** is "Outstanding." [i]

BASEMENT 5
1965–1980 (Antilles) 1981
In Dub (nr/Island) 1981

Basement 5 came out of Island Records' London art department playing a blend of reggae and synth-pop under the production auspices of Martin Hannett. **1965–1980** waffles between both forms, never quite achieving the hoped-for marriage, but does sport a number of light ditties with heavy political overtones. The contrast between roots and futurism gives Basement 5 a fascinating, if ephemeral, flavor. Even more interesting is **In Dub**, a paean to Hannett's control-booth genius, which naturally features dub versions of some material from the first LP. Bassist Leo Williams later surfaced in Big Audio Dynamite. [sg]

See also *Big Audio Dynamite*.

BASSOMATIC
See *William Orbit*.

BASTRO
Rode Hard and Put Up Wet EP (Homestead) 1988
Bastro Diablo Guapo (Homestead) 1989 ●
Sing the Troubled Beast (Homestead) 1990 ●

Guitarist/singer David Grubbs (who also plays in Bitch Magnet) formed Bastro after the end of Squirrel Bait; he recorded the six-song debut with only a former bandmate, bassist Clark Johnson, and a rhythm machine. Bringing drummer John McEntire into the lineup, the trio made **Bastro Diablo Guapo**, an above-average LP that embraces—but isn't consumed by—Chicago-styled thrash noise. Rather than career around like a rhinoceros plugged into an electric socket, Bastro stays tight, well-structured and musical, even when engaging in meltdown firepower.

Sing the Troubled Beast tempers Grubbs' extremist instincts to reveal a rough but stately melodic side, and an affecting poetic sensibility. The guitar has the rich textures of a Hammond organ (an instrument which, like piano, makes an occasional appearance); the rhythm section demonstrates the facility to dig trenches or drop back to small-scale time-keeping. While "The Sifter" is either a disastrous mastering mistake or just a pointless bit of transistorized foolishness, the haunting, somber "Tobacco in the Sink" crystallizes Bastro's achievements to date, and sets the stage for a promising future.

See also *Bitch Magnet*. [i]

MARTYN BATES
See *Eyeless in Gaza*.

BATFISH BOYS
The Gods Hate Kansas (nr/Batfish) 1985
Crocodile Tears EP (nr/Batfish) 1985
Head (Twilight) 1986
Lurve: Some Kinda Flashback (Twilight) 1987
BATFISH
Batfish Brew (GWR-Restless) 1989

When singer Simon Denbigh was booted from March Violets, he wasted little time in assembling a more conducive outfit. On **The Gods Hate Kansas**, the Batfish Boys take the Violets' dark post-punk and give it a traditional rock setting. Several of the best moments ("The Tumbleweed Thing," "Mrs. Triffid" and the terrific single, "Swamp Liquor") are reminiscent of the Cramps or Gun Club, utilizing creepy, twanging riffs and Denbigh's weird, roughly grumbled lyrics to create a bluesy, desolate atmosphere. While the tunes are passable, **Crocodile Tears** suffers from a lack of this intrigue.

By **Head**, the group had devolved into muddy, guitar-driven rock with psychedelic blues overtones. They display plenty of panache, but the material is all too familiar. **Lurve** illustrates the problem. Chronologically assembling their British EPs from '85 (including most of the tracks from **Crocodile Tears**) to '87 ("The Bomb Song"), it reveals a downward spiral from imaginative swamp rock to mediocre pseudo-metal.

Apparently not boys anymore (and presumably aware how dumb the Batfish Men would sound), the group simply became Batfish with the release of the 1989 album. The generic, mid-tempo arena-metal on **Batfish Brew** is completely indistinguishable from scores of other practitioners. The only track that stands out does so for its utter inanity: a cover of Queen's "Another One Bites the Dust" with a feeble attempt to insert bits of Hendrix's "Purple Haze," an exercise even more pointless than it sounds.   [dgs/gef]

See also *March Violets*.

STIV BATORS

Disconnected (Bomp!) 1980 •
The Church and the New Creatures (Fr. Lolita) 1983

So what does a typecast Dead Boy do when his band breaks up? He moves to Los Angeles, hires local musicians and cuts a tremendous album of melodic rock tunes. Playing down his outrageous side, Bators' first solo record maintains an Iggy-like persona while replacing chaotic garage-punk with thoughtful music that owes power pop a sizable debt. Originals like "Evil Boy" and "The Last Year" mask their dark messages with pretty tunes; a great cover of the Electric Prunes' classic "I Had Too Much to Dream (Last Night)" clarifies Bators' roots and caps the album off nicely. The French LP contains all of **Disconnected**, adding three sides from a pair of Bomp! singles and one other cut.

In 1987, Bators released a 12-inch ("Have Love Will Travel" b/w a sharp swipe at the Moody Blues' "Story in Your Eyes") on Bomp!, with musical assistance from various co-conspirators. He later sang with Jeff Conolly on a Lyres song, issued as a 12-inch and included on that band's 1988 LP. In June 1990, Bators was struck by a car in Paris, returned home and died of his injuries the next day.   [i]

See also *Dead Boys, Lords of the New Church, Wanderers*.

BATS

By Night EP (NZ Flying Nun) 1984
"And Here Is 'Music for the Fireside'I" (NZ Flying Nun) 1985
Made Up in Blue EP (nr/Flying Nun) 1986
Compiletely Bats [tape] (NZ Flying Nun) 1987 (Communion) 1991
Daddy's Highway (NZ Flying Nun) 1988 (Communion) 1988 •
Four Songs EP (NZ Flying Nun) 1988
The Law of Things (NZ Flying Nun) 1990 (Communion) 1990 •

When the former bass players for New Zealand legends Toy Love and the Clean—Paul Kean and Robert

Scott, respectively—decided in 1983 to form a band together, Scott (also perpetrator of the *Every Secret Thing* fanzine and cassette label) switched to guitar and led the group into the studio to record six of his melodic melancholic odes. **By Night** is paradoxically morose and exhilarating; each song a moody pop gem, with hints of the hard-strummed countryisms of Gram Parsons. The seven-song **Fireside** 12-inch is even better, spanning a wider stylistic spectrum, from lackadaisical laments to sweeping, enticing rushes of pure pop satisfaction, each made all the more appealing by Scott's nasal, high register vocals.

Recorded in a 24-track London studio during a 1986 European trip, **Blue** (the first Flying Nun UK release) lacks some of the alluring immediacy of its predecessors. All three tracks were reprised on the following year's **Compiletely**, along with all of **Fireside** and five-sixths of **By Night**.

The Bats' first proper album, begun in Scotland and finished in NZ, is a bit of a disappointment. Generally softer and less heady, as well as less identifiably Bat-like, **Daddy's Highway** finally brought the group an American release (and prompted a US tour). **Four Songs** excerpts the standout track, spreading it flatteringly across twelve full inches with a B-side trio harking back to the sound of the **Blue** EP.

Following time devoted to other pursuits—like the Clean reformation and singer/multi-instrumentalist Kaye Woodward's motherhood—the Bats returned to action, releasing several singles and the monumental **Law of Things** LP. Capturing all the hooky appeal and personal charm of their first records, it updates the recipe with seven years of instrumental mastery and superior sonics, becoming, along with **Compiletely**, one of the two essential Bats releases, as well as a high-water mark of New Zealand musicmaking.   [ab]

See also *Clean, Tall Dwarfs*.

LES BATTERIES

See *Fish & Roses*.

BAUHAUS

Bela Lugosi's Dead EP (nr/Small Wonder) 1979 •
In the Flat Field (nr/4AD) 1980 •
Mask (nr/Beggars Banquet) 1981 •
Searching for Satori EP (nr/Beggars Banquet) 1982
The Sky's Gone Out (A&M) 1982 •
Press the Eject and Give Me the Tape (nr/Beggars Banquet) 1982 •
Ziggy Stardust EP (nr/Beggars Banquet) 1982
Lagartija Nick EP (nr/Beggars Banquet) 1982
Burning from the Inside (Beggars Banquet-A&M) 1983 •
The Singles 1981–1983 EP (nr/Beggars Banquet) 1983 •
4.A.D. EP (nr/4AD) 1983
1979–1983 (nr/Beggars Banquet) 1985 •
Swing the Heartache: The BBC Sessions (Beggars Banquet-RCA) 1989 •

Though their career was over in a mere four years, Bauhaus are the acknowledged godfathers of gothic rock, following the art movement for which they were named in seeking to use minimalism as a powerful mood-setting tool. Combining guitars and electronics into a bleak backdrop for Peter Murphy's angst-driven vocals, Bauhaus ignited what was already a volatile mix by throwing dark, energetic theatrics into the pot.

"Bela Lugosi's Dead" (gloom's own "Stairway to Heaven") is an unlikely debut single which melds brisk dub reggae rhythms, Daniel Ash's creepy, atmospheric guitar technique and Murphy's Nosferatu vocal performance. If the record created any stylistic expectations, however, Bauhaus was quick to defy them, as the group's subsequent records were all significantly different from each other.

The self-produced **In the Flat Field** is a dense, disjointed patchwork of sounds and uncertain feelings, supported by a pressured, incessant beat. Delving deep into the dark side of the human psyche, Bauhaus conjures up unsettling images of a world given over to death and decay. **Mask**, their finest achievement, explores a variety of styles, incorporating airs of heavy metal, funk brass and Tangerine Dreamy electronics into an organic whole. Though still weighty, the lyrics make occasional stabs at humor and reveal an increasingly romantic side.

Searching for Satori offers a wholly different version of 1981's funky "Kick in the Eye" 45, a dub mix of a **Mask** track and a pair of reggae-influenced new cuts, "Harry" and "Earwax."

The Sky's Gone Out opens with a lively, bright version of Brian Eno's "Third Uncle," signaling a more upbeat period for Bauhaus, offsetting the ongoing themes of death and destruction. Good production opens up the sound considerably and, in a flash of ambition, the album includes a three-part mini-opera, "The Three Shadows." (The CD adds four bonus tracks.) **Press the Eject and Give Me the Tape**, a live LP recorded in London and Liverpool, was first included as a second disc in UK copies of **The Sky's Gone Out**, then reissued as a separate album.

The late-'82 release of a copycat live-in-the-studio version of "Ziggy Stardust" (joined on the 12-inch by a bizarre, funny original consisting of Faustian film dialogue over cool instrumental backing, "Third Uncle" and a live recording of "Waiting for the Man," with guest vocals by Nico) supported Bauhaus' self-image as latter-day glam-rockers (the group had released a single of T. Rex's "Telegram Sam" in 1980), taking an intentional poke at critics who had accused the group of imitating Bowie. Besides the tart, enigmatic title cut, **Lagartija Nick** (another non-LP 12-inch) has a horn-dominated dance track, a live take of "In the Flat Field" and the weird in-joke of "Paranoia, Paranoia."

A bout with pneumonia forced Murphy to miss several recording sessions, leaving Ash and bassist David J(ay) to sing almost half the songs on the final Bauhaus album, **Burning from the Inside** (no doubt a pivotal development towards their work as Love and Rockets). There are plenty of swell numbers, some in a more acoustic vein (Ash's haunting "Slice of Life," the optimistic "Hope" and the delicately chanted "King Volcano"); still, the individualized songwriting weakened the band's sense of unity.

Bauhaus split up in mid-1983. Ash continued a side project he'd begun in 1981, Tones on Tail, soon joined by Bauhaus drummer Kevin Haskins. Jay did a hefty amount of solo recording, briefly joined the Jazz Butcher, then got together with Ash and Haskins (when a planned Bauhaus reunion fell through) to form Love

and Rockets. Peter Murphy teamed with ex-Japan bassist Mick Karn to form Dalis Car, then went solo.

In death, Bauhaus has become more popular (and influential) than ever, a phenomenon exploited by numerous posthumous collections. **The Singles** EP consolidates six A-sides, including "Ziggy Stardust," "Kick in the Eye" and "Lagartija Nick." **4.A.D.** compiles several 1980 singles, including "Telegram Sam," "Dark Entries" and a rare version of John Cale's "Rosegarden Funeral of Sores." The double disc set **1979–1983** functions as both a comprehensive overview of Bauhaus' work—spotlighting both the popular singles and more obscure album tracks and flipsides—and as a one-stop sampler, though it does include the memorable "Sanity Assassin" (which was to be their last single), previously available only on a fan club 45. The more intriguing **Swing the Heartache** joins all four of the group's UK radio sessions, which (roughly) chronologically correspond to the four original studio albums (all of which have since been issued on CD with non-LP singles tacked on). Of particular note are two previously unknown songs ("Poison Pen," a sinister piece of anti-drug funk that had been recorded for **Mask**, and a sizzling off-the-cuff version of the Strangeloves' '66 garage rocker "Night Time") and a version of "Third Uncle" at a tempo much closer to the original.   [sg/i/gef]

See also *Jazz Butcher, Love and Rockets, Peter Murphy, Tones on Tail*.

BEARS
See *Adrian Belew*.

BEASTIE BOYS
Polly Wog Stew EP (Rat Cage) 1982 + 1988
Rock Hard EP (Def Jam) 1984
Licensed to Ill (Def Jam-Columbia) 1986 ●
Paul's Boutique (Capitol) 1989 ●

The Beastie Boys began in 1979 as a jokey New York University hardcore band starring Adam Yauch, Michael Diamond and drummer Kate Schellenbach. Although the group quickly fell apart, the Beasties reformed in 1981 to cut and release the eight-song **Polly Wog Stew**, a 7-inch of average but occasionally rambling punk salvos ("Egg Raid on Mojo," "Transit Cop," "Jimi," "Beastie Boys"), later reissued as an import 12-inch of dubious legal standing.

Abandoning the sound of punk while delving further into its snotty attitude, the Beastie Boys stripped down to a trio—Yauch (aka MCA), Diamond (aka Mike D) and Adam Horovitz (aka King Ad-Rock)—and set a course for the big time. Pointing the way to the group's hip-hop future, the 1983 "Cooky Puss" single laid down a tremendous beat pulsing with rock energy, adding sharp mix tricks and puerile spoken-word jive centered on a crank telephone call. Ridiculous but undeniably funny and danceable, the 12-inch includes a bogus reggae song ("Beastie Revolution") that mugs Musical Youth and Rasta culture.

In 1984, the Beasties moved into rap with the release of **Rock Hard**, a 12-inch produced by NYU chum Rick Rubin. Unmistakably white and middle class, the group acknowledged its '70s rock heritage in hunks of guitar—AC/DC riffs pop up in "Rock Hard" and "Party's Gettin' Rough," shards of Led Zeppelin fill "Beastie Groove." The Beasties then appeared in the film *Krush Groove*, for which they cut "She's on It," a fun, dumb stomper with a great guitar hook and obnoxious couplets like "She'd get down on her knees/If we'd only say *please*." The Beasties had reached the heights of offensiveness and were squinting upwards.

The release of **Licensed to Ill** caught the guardians of popular culture napping. Within months, the album and its attendant 45s were skyrocketing towards astronomical sales levels as kids of all colors in countless countries rapped and danced to such intentionally moronic celebrations of self-indulgent stupidity and trash culture as "Fight for Your Right (To Party)," "No Sleep till Brooklyn," "Brass Monkey," "Time to Get Ill" and the absurdly catchy "Girls." Rubin's brilliant stew of dodgy bits lifted from records by the Stones, Led Zep, Clash (and dozens more still unidentified), combined with the whining nasal roar of the three stooges' inventive sexist drivel, somehow hit that perfect beat, and made the Beasties mondo stars, dragging controversy, anger and damage reports in their wake.

By the time the Beasties came off the road, engineered a disputed label switch and got around to making a record (with time out for Horovitz to star in 1989's *Lost Angels*), the rap world was a very different—and far more competitive—place. Recognizing the fragile oddness of their stylistic position, the trio abandoned **Licensed to Ill**'s rock'n'rap formula and reached for street credibility on **Paul's Boutique**. What they wound up with was a dull collection of simple rhythm tracks over which the terrible three's verbose raps (and the record's innumerable samples) drop endless cultural references to no memorable effect. Lacking Rubin's furious imagination, the Dust Brothers (California producers responsible for monster records by Tone-Lōc and Young MC) leave the Beasties yakking among themselves on an album that is neither effective hip-hop nor amusing parody. The deluxe fold-out sleeve—two panoramic four-panel photographs of the Lower East Side—is easily the best thing about this disappointing dud.   [dgs/i]

BEASTS OF BOURBON
The Axeman's Jazz (Aus. Green) 1984 (Big Time) 1985 ●
Sour Mash (Aus. Red Eye) 1988 ●
Black Milk (Aus. Red Eye) 1990
SALAMANDER JIM
Lorne Green Shares His Precious Fluids (Aus. Red Eye) 1985
VARIOUS ARTISTS
Waste Sausage (Aus. Black Eye) 1987
Leather Donut (Aus. Black Eye) 1988
THUG
Mechanical Ape/Proud Idiot's Parade (Aus. Black Eye) 1987
Electric Wooly Mammoth (Aus. Black Eye) 1988
BUTCHER SHOP
Hard for You EP (Aus. Black Eye) 1988
Pump Action (Aus. Black Eye) 1990

The connecting factor here is Tex Perkins, but really we're talking about a hefty chunk of Australia's ugliest, least velvet underground. On **Axeman's Jazz**, the Beasts of Bourbon—Tex (vocals), Spencer Jones (guitar) and three past or present Scientists—play lazy, garagey nihilistic C&W with moderately straight faces. Highly Crampsian in feel, the material and restraint (not to mention prominent slide and scree guitar) invent a new category for the band, one that garnered a considerable worldwide indie following back in '84, particularly amongst chronic thrashaholics. (The live B-side added to the US edition features an alternate selection of Scientists.)

Salamander Jim posits Tex in front of a new band with similarly anti-social proclivities, making C&W just one facet of a mash rampant with James White/Brownisms, jagged Beefheartian R&B and even a Stooge cop or three, adding up to a (short) LP that may not be original, but lurches and sputters to a peculiarly intriguing internal heartbeat.

At this point, things really begin to fragment and fester. Australia's Red Eye label caught a whiff of what the ex-Salamanders were doing and promptly formed Black Eye to isolate them from the rest of the species. Salamander Jim's Lachlan McLeod assembled **Waste Sausage** (and later **Leather Donut**), two dangerously inbred collections of real and spurious "bands" populated by former Jims and diseased cohorts playing brutal and scato-sexual music spanning the lizard lounge to the hardcore pit. Naturally uneven, the overall tone of disgust and DIY invests even the weaker tracks with a sense of place and purpose; the same sort of contextual value that makes **Live at the Roxy** a genuinely endearing historical document instead of just a shittily recorded live compilation.

Meanwhile, as Stuart Grey from Salamander Jim was turning up the volume to become Stu Spasm of Lubricated Goat, Tex joined with Peter Read to complete the original Black Eye roster in Thug, who may not have planned to crack the local alternative charts with their deliciously malicious debut 45 "Fuck Your Dad," but unexpectedly found themselves with a genuine hit partway through 1987. **Mechanical Ape/Proud Idiot's Parade**, even less cohesive and coherent than **Waste Sausage**, is the aural equivalent of a dying man's life flashing before his eyes—assuming said life to be foul and filthy, filled with discord and turmoil—conveniently condensed for the incumbent psycho into 40 or so minutes of snippets combined and maligned for maximum discomfort. **Electric Wooly Mammoth** varies the recipe only in titling the snippets rather than merely the side, adding McLeod as the third Thug, and being belligerently more juvenile. And clownish. And obvious. And inferior.

The Butcher Shop reunited Tex with Spencer Jones, adding Kid Congo Powers (Cramps, Bad Seeds, Gun Club), first for a much heavied-up Beastlike-*cum*-Jimian EP, the extended tribal drone of the B-side being its sole mesmerizing factor, while the 1990 LP (with no personnel overlap save Tex and bassist Phil Clifford, supplemented by assorted Sausages and Salamanders) is almost confusing in context for its rote simplicity. Tough in pose but weak in delivery, it sounds like an LP of B-sides and filler.

45

Which perhaps it is, as Tex reformed the original Beasts concurrent with the Butcher Shop; the only difference between the new group and the old one is that it's angrier, meaner, more spiteful, more vicious and more capable of flaying with sound. Including the title track from the Butcher Shop's debut—here splayed out expansively and nine times ballsier—the songwriting on **Sour Mash** echoes the band's earlier C&W misanthropy but finally interpolates it into a singular black-eyed drive that invests the hateful narratives with the sort of power, immediacy and personal threat inherent in the best country blues.

Black Milk, with an extended cast that includes pianist Louis Tillet from Wet Taxis, is closer to a Chicago sort of blues LP, the anger and attack subdued, the band subservient to familiar style. Which is not to deny the individual elements—sometimes striking for their respective instants—but taken as a whole the third LP is only modestly rewarding.   [ab]

See also *Lubricated Goat*.

BEAT
The Beat (Columbia) 1979
To Beat or Not to Beat EP (Passport) 1983

PAUL COLLINS' BEAT
The Kids Are the Same (CBS) 1982

Paul Collins, once a third of SF-to-LA's fabled Nerves (the other two were Peter Case, later of the Plimsouls, and tunesmith-to-the-stars Jack Lee), writes songs calling to mind the early Hollies (except grittier and American) and a more down-to-earth, less poetic Byrds. Though never scaling the heights of either band, **The Beat** (issued prior to the name conflict with the English Beat) is simple, satisfying power pop, all meat and no filler. If anything, though, it's a little too no-frills, with unimaginative production; the lack of idiosyncrasy and variation gives it a monotonous feel.

This problem was remedied somewhat on the Beat's second album, which is quite a bit heavier. Although they seem to run out of steam—and songs—halfway through **The Kids Are the Same**, the band shows a high degree of musical volatility up to that point.

Collins refurbished the Beat's lineup for the 1983 EP. The new combo includes ex-Patti Smith Group drummer Jay Dee Daugherty and guitarist Jimmy Ripp, both of whom have played on Tom Verlaine LPs. The band smokes and the songs are stylistically varied, but this glorified demo surprisingly failed to get Collins a new major-label deal.   [jg]

(ENGLISH) BEAT
I Just Can't Stop It (Sire) 1980 (IRS) 1983 ●
Wha'ppen? (Sire) 1981 (IRS) 1983 ●
Special Beat Service (IRS) 1982 ●
What Is Beat? (IRS) 1983 ●

Although lumped in with the 2-Tone crowd upon emerging in 1979, the wonderful Beat (known in America as the English Beat) proved far more versatile and broadly talented than most of their skanking contemporaries. True, **I Just Can't Stop It** has its share of ska-influenced upbeats—a delightful reworking of "Tears of a Clown" (on the US release only) and patois-tinged toasting ("Rough Rider") by Ranking Roger—but the

Birmingham band's furious drive and pumping bass ("Two Swords," "Click Click," "Twist & Crawl") relate more to the rock tradition. A recording of Andy Williams' warm-bath "Can't Get Used to Losing You" is a nice gesture, regardless of the outcome. (The US release also includes another track not on the original British album.)

By **Wha'ppen?**, the Beat had mellowed out, preferring midtempo grooves drawn from various Third World cultures. Loping music, playful combinations of voices (Roger and lead singer/guitarist Dave Wakeling) and Saxa's effervescent sax almost obscure the songs' depressing views of personal and social troubles ("Drowning," "All Out to Get You," "Cheated").

Special Beat Service is the band's slickest offering. The polished music generates more light than heat, but lyrics—dwelling more on romantic than political problems—depict believably complex scenarios. Ranking Roger's lighthearted showcases are now isolated from the group's main concerns, but the Beat here remains a fine band committed to pan-cultural understanding.

The **What Is Beat?** farewell compilation is actually three different records. The fourteen-track English album is a straight greatest-hits collection of their most memorable work; early copies (and the cassette) added a bonus disc's worth of eight extended remixes. Although there's a lot of overlap in material, the American release is altogether different—single sides, two live renditions, a couple of remixes, etc. Collect 'em all!

Following the Beat's lamentable dissolution, Ranking Roger and Dave Wakeling stuck together to form General Public; David Steele and Andy Cox assembled Fine Young Cannibals.   [si/i]

See also *Pato Banton, Fine Young Cannibals, General Public*.

BEAT FARMERS
Tales of the New West (Rhino) 1985 ●
Glad'n'Greasy EP (nr/Demon) 1986 (Rhino) 1991 ●
Van Go (Curb-MCA) 1986
The Pursuit of Happiness (Curb-MCA) 1987 ●
Poor & Famous (Curb-MCA) 1989 ● ˙
Loud and Plowed and ... LIVE!! (Curb) 1990 ●

JOEY HARRIS AND THE SPEEDSTERS
Joey Harris and the Speedsters (RDM-MCA) 1983

JACKS
Jacks Are Wild (Rounder) 1988

BUDDY BLUE
Guttersnipes 'n' Zealots (Rhino New Artists) 1991 φ

You can tell a lot about musicians by the company they keep. On **Tales of the New West**, produced by Steve Berlin, this San Diego quartet gets vocal assistance from Peter Case (ex-Plimsouls), Chip and Tony Kinman (Rank and File) and Sid Griffin (Long Ryders). The Farmers do the '50s-come-'80s neo-country-rock stomp with enthusiasm, economy and not a hint of phoniness or selfconsciousness. The mock-cowboy nonsense of "California Kid" (disregarding its uncharacteristic resemblance to the Bonzo Dog Band) proves they're not sensitive about the genre; post-punk roots even show on a cover of Lou Reed's

"There She Goes Again." An honest album from an honest band.

Glad'n'Greasy, a six-song studio recording made during the Farmers' first UK tour ('85), comes even closer than the debut album in capturing the band's down-and-dirty essence. With no intrusive tinkering from producers Bob Andrews (ex-Rumour) and Colin Fairley, they rip into Neil Young's "Powderfinger" and attack Rod McKuen's "Beat Generation" with a rocking combination of humor and humanity that would be in shorter supply on subsequent studio efforts.

A re-recorded "Powderfinger" is one of the few highlights of **Van Go**, a halfbaked, halfhearted outing that doesn't step in anything odious but falls flat on its bum anyway—even as guitarist Buddy Blue's energetic slide work threatens to save the day. A wry Blue tune called "Gun Sale at the Church" offers faint breath in the mirror, but otherwise this one's ready for burial.

Guitarist/singer Joey Harris replaced Blue on **The Pursuit of Happiness**, a commercially minded record that meanders further from the simple glories of **The New West**. Echoes of Springsteen, Jeff Lynne and John Cougar Mellencamp don't exactly improve the originality quotient, but Harris' witty songwriting—gossiping about cow-pokers in "Texas" and expressing religious skepticism in "God Is Here Tonight"—does; Covers of Tom Waits and Johnny Cash are beneficial; guest pianist Nicky Hopkins does his bit with typical aplomb.

The band's continuing misguided efforts to tone down their eccentricities on record resulted in **Poor & Famous**, the most schizophrenic item in the Beat Farmers' catalogue. Though there are some memorable songs—including Harris' "Wheels" and "Girl I Almost Married" and singer/guitarist Jerry Raney's "Socialite"—the album's barren personality deprives them of intensity. Meanwhile, bear-voiced singer/drummer (and ex-Crawdaddy) Country Dick Montana's showcases—always a highlight of live shows—seem completely out of place in this context. **Poor & Famous** is a disorientingly lopsided listen.

The double **Loud and Plowed and . . . LIVE!!** temporarily solves the Farmers' record-making dilemma by capturing them in front of a hometown crowd on New Year's weekend '89/'90. The band is in fine form on a selection of highlights from the studio albums, plus well-chosen covers of George Jones, the Kinks and Kenny Rogers. Montana's beer-soaked clowning, never properly integrated on the three previous LPs, fits in perfectly here.

Harris' lone album with the Speedsters is well-crafted but overly conventional commercial rock-pop, distinguished by his soulful vocals and some strong songwriting.

Blue re-emerged as leader of the Jacks, whose one LP features likable bar-band country-rock in a style not unlike the first Beat Farmers disc. The rest of the Jacks (plus Dave Alvin, Mojo Nixon and Richard "Louie Louie" Berry) contributed to Blue's solo debut, **Guttersnipes 'n' Zealots**, which casts the singer/guitarist as a mature, thoughtful songwriter without sacrificing his rock'n'roll grit. "Blind Monkeys," "Somethin' Inhuman" and a superior remake of "Gun Sale at the Church" demonstrate a rare combination of social conscience and ironic satire. [i/hd]

BEAT HAPPENING

Beat Happening EP [tape] (K) 1984
Three Tea Breakfast EP [tape] (K) 1984
Beat Happening (K) 1985
Crashing Through EP (nr/53rd & 3rd) 1988
Jamboree (K-Rough Trade) 1988
Black Candy (K) 1989 ●
1983–85 (K-Feel Good All Over) 1990 φ
Dreamy (Sub Pop) 1991 ●

BEAT HAPPENING/SCREAMING TREES

Beat Happening/Screaming Trees EP (K-Homestead) 1988

Overweening ambition is such a common component of contemporary music that it's nice to find a young band that truly doesn't have any. Beat Happening, a talented trio of minimalists from Olympia, Washington, write and sing swell songs, accompanied only by shards of guitar and rudimentary drum(s). To their credit, Bret, Heather and Calvin Johnson (all three switch off playing; Heather and Calvin alternate vocals) consistently sail past the Scylla and Charybdis of rock'n'roll primitivism and never sound pathetic or precious.

After releasing two five-song tapes (**Beat Happening** contains the band's debut single, "Our Secret"; the rudimentary and easily skipped **Three Tea Breakfast** was recorded in Tokyo) via Calvin's K label, Beat Happening made a great debut album, produced (well . . .) by Greg Sage of the Wipers. This fresh breeze of one-take pop ingenuity is remorselessly amateurish but loaded with charm and invention. Some songs ("I Spy," "Down at the Sea" and the Crampsy "Bad Seeds," presented in both studio and noisy live renditions) are fully developed and could easily bear complete arrangements, while others ("In Love with You Thing") are a little too eccentric for their own good.

Just prior to the release of their second album, Beat Happening issued a four-song UK 12-inch. Along with **Jamboree**'s "Crashing Through" and an alternate version of the same LP's "The This Many Boyfriends Club," **Crashing Through** contains both sides of a non-LP single.

Repeating the first LP's gambit of ending with a live cut, **Jamboree**—co-produced by Mark Lanegan and Gary Lee Conner of Screaming Trees—is a bit more intricate and electric than **Beat Happening**, but not enough to hurt. What makes the group so special is its innate ability to turn raw, crude ingredients into friendly, nice music without getting all mushy about it. So, while "Hangman" gets a ferocious Cramps roar going, the vocals are totally mild. Similarly, the alluring "Indian Summer" paints an idyllic lyrical picture over a Velvet Underground drone relieved of all sinister implications. On the other end of the spectrum, the Jonathan Richman-like pathos of "Cat Walk" has enough of a spine not to whimper.

The four songs on the joint Beat Happening/Screaming Trees 12-inch (the record melds the two groups without specific credits) suggest that someone in Olympia's been listening to **Disraeli Gears** a lot. (The wah-wah and mock-Ginger Baker drumming is a dead giveaway.) "Polly Pereguin" and the pointedly titled "Tales of Brave Aphrodite," a loopy confessional, are rough-cut electric pop with definite '60s ambience.

Beat Happening lost its poise on **Black Candy**, a disappointing album that's more careless than casual, with vocals (almost all by Calvin) that wander nervously around melodies over guitars and drums that are too often intrusively aggressive (and, in "Knick Knack," gravely out of tune). While the Crampsian grind of "Pajama Party in a Haunted Hive" and the driving intensity of "Ponytail" are impressive, there isn't enough winsome pop ("Cast a Shadow" and the folky "Other Side" are pretty much it) to balance out the mood. Sung over snapped fingers and brushes on a snare, the somber "Grave Digger Blues" has the record's lightest sound, but not a shred of innocence or vulnerability. Has maturity overtaken our young heroes?

Produced by Steve Fisk, the darkly painted **Dreamy** continues the stylistic direction introduced on **Black Candy** but is a much better, more consistent LP with none of its predecessor's sloppy shortcomings. Calvin's resonantly deep voice is the concise (30 minutes) disc's dominant feature (Heather sings three: the lightly tuneful "Left Behind," the wistful "Fortune Cookie Prize" and a feedbacky droner, "Collide"); the simple electric music supports him with easy grace, making the most of inspired—and only occasionally Crampsy (check "Nancy Sin")—minimalism.

The 26-song **1983–85** combines the band's first single, first album, **Three Tea Breakfast**, several compilation contributions and some previously unreleased tracks. [i]

BEATNIGS
The Beatnigs (Insight-Alternative Tentacles) 1988 ●
Television EP (Alternative Tentacles) 1988

On their debut album, this striking San Francisco quintet explodes in a tight and danceable riot of industrial percussion, vocals and tape manipulations. According to an enclosed booklet ("Aural Instruction Manual"), the word "nig" is defined as "a positive acronym . . . [it] has taken on a universal meaning in describing all oppressed people who have actively taken a stand against those who perpetuate ethnic notions and discriminate on the basis of them." Assailing "Television" (the medium, not the band), poverty and hunger ("Burritos"), the "CIA" and South Africa ("Control"), the Beatnigs cross Devo, Test Dept. and the Dead Kennedys in a brilliant, original coincidence of extremist musical ideas and radical politics. "Television" was subsequently given a pair of head-spinning remixes by Adrian Sherwood, Gary Clail and Mark Stewart and issued on a four-version 12-inch. [i]

BEATNIK BEATCH
See *Jellyfish*.

BEATNIKS
See *Yukihiro Takahashi*.

BEAT RODEO
Staying Out Late with Beat Rodeo (IRS) 1985
Home in the Heart of the Beat (IRS) 1986 ●

CRACKERS
Sir Crackers! EP (Twin/Tone) 1980

STEVE ALMAAS
Beat Rodeo EP (Coyote) 1982

Following the breakup of the Suicide Commandos (in which he played bass), Minneapolis' Steve Almaas turned to guitar and formed the Crackers (not the New Mexico band with the same name). Unfortunately, the trio's EP is of little consequence except to vaguely indicate the rough-hewn melodic rock direction he'd pursue: **Sir Crackers!** threatens to take off, but just fizzles.

After working with the Bongos, Almaas and boss Bongo Richard Barone headed down to North Carolina to visit Mitch Easter at his Drive-In Studio. The three of them whipped up the **Beat Rodeo** EP, finally showing Almaas off to great advantage. If Marshall Crenshaw's early treatment of the Buddy Holly legacy irks you for being wrapped in candy floss, this charming, rocking disc should be right up your alley—swell tunes, Almaas' straight-as-an-arrow vocals and Easter's clear production that lets the natural sweetness shine through.

Almaas almost immediately formed a quartet named for the EP but not including any of its other participants. **Staying Out Late** (originally issued in Germany in 1984) shows a country bent implicit in its name (but absent from the EP) and integrates it (countryish guitar sound, even a dash of fiddle) rather well into the already established pop-rock context. But there's little memorable content and insufficient élan: "Without You" almost rocks out, but shortcircuits the power with an overloaded arrangement. Also, lyrical tension is never conveyed by Almaas' vocals, which run the emotional gamut from A(miable) to B(oringly benign).

Staying Out Late was produced by Don Dixon (with two tracks by Richard Gottehrer). Whether resulting from the switch to Scott Litt or simply the educational benefit of past mistakes, **Home in the Heart of the Beat** is a definite improvement. The band tends to play more to its strengths and avoid (or compensate for) its weaknesses. The countryness is now a feel rather than a form, and as such suits them far better; the songs are more mature and less awkward. The record's title may be a tad pretentious, but in several ways Beat Rodeo really *is* more at home—with themselves, at any rate. Solid, enjoyable fare. [jg]

See also *Bongos*.

BEATS INTERNATIONAL
Let Them Eat Bingo (Go Beat-Elektra) 1990 ●

After the Housemartins disbanded, bassist Norman Cook returned to his original career as a DJ and became one of England's most successful remixers; that led him to form Beats International, less a group than a conglomeration of singers, musicians and, most important, samples. The music tracks on **Let Them Eat Bingo** are constructed almost entirely out of other people's songs and recordings. The dub-inspired bass line of the Clash's "Guns of Brixton" is used as the bottom for a cover of the SOS Band's classic "Just Be Good to Me"; a Billy Bragg up/down electric guitar stroke from "Levi Stubbs' Tears" is vamped into the basis for "Won't Talk About It"; and so on. At its best, this is clever stuff that, beyond being enjoyable strictly on its own, provocatively recontextualizes its sources and creates an endlessly fascinating cross-cultural weave—dig how well the African drums fit in with the imitation-Billie

Holiday moaning on "Burundi Blues." At its worst—the tiresome "Babies Making Babies"—it's just boring and silly. (The CD contains a bonus 12-inch mix of the album's "For Spacious Lies.") [gk]

BEAUTIFUL SOUTH
Welcome to the Beautiful South (Go! Discs-Elektra) 1990 ●
Choke (Go! Discs-Elektra) 1990 φ

The two groups that arose from the Housemartins' ashes are as dissimilar to each other as they are from the original group. Unlike Beats International, the Beautiful South is mildly identifiable with the Housemartins, as it also features the acerbic lyrics and sweet vocals of Paul Heaton. But while the old pop jangle has been replaced by a jazzier, keyboard-driven sound that could easily suck in any lite-music-loving yuppie who happened by it, the songs' unrepentant nastiness puts a sharp hook inside such alluring bait.

On Welcome to the Beautiful South, the catchy "You Keep It All In" deftly skewers pop-psych truisms, while "Woman in the Wall" is a grisly, perhaps Poe-inspired tale of wife abuse. The South's special target, though, is the pop machine itself, and "Song for Whoever" unflinchingly dissects the cynicism that goes into the making of so many silly love songs. Welcome can be too clever for its own good, and becomes particularly annoying when it draws a bead on sitting ducks—the potshot at Simon Le Bon is not just predictable, but dated as well.

Expanding from a quintet to a sextet, the Beautiful South returned the same year with the even more bilious Choke, a collection of eleven acerbic, pointed songs that is over and done in 37 minutes. The group's disgust with just about everything but its seductive music—tinged with horn parts straight from the Bacharach/David songbook and distinguished by a loping, easy groove—is palpable from the very first cut, "Tonight I Fancy Myself," where the singer recoils from the sight of icky-cooey lovers and bluntly states, "I choose/self-abuse." On another cut, Brian Corrigan describes a horrible scene of domestic violence and then sings, with perfect insouciance: "I should have kept my eyes shut/My mouth should've closed/But the mixture of vomit and blood/Just crept up through my nose." In "I've Come for My Award," a disgusting, thieving captain of free enterprise allows that "Jesus was my greatest accomplice." Choke makes it clear that the Beautiful South has ample pop sense and pure venom to keep its unique act going for quite a while. [gk]

JEAN BEAUVOIR
Drums Along the Mohawk (Columbia) 1986 ●
Jacknifed (Columbia) 1988 ●

This onetime Plasmatic (more recently a producer and Little Steven sideman) did almost everything on his first solo album—writing, playing, producing, arranging, etc. Side One of Drums Along the Mohawk (the reference is tonsorial) owes a huge debt to Prince (see the "Little Red Corvette" chapter), but the mainstream rock LP makes chameleonic room for other soundalikes: "Rockin' in the Street" favors Eddy Grant, while most of "This Is Our House" could be Foreigner with better

vocals. And darned if that ain't Tom Petty singing "Drive You Home." Welcome to the wax museum . . .

Recorded in New York, Paris, Stockholm and elsewhere, Jacknifed lets a few musicians share in the fun. Beauvoir thankfully downplays the stylistic clone action (although the Prince influence is far from gone), but forgets to replace it with anything sufficiently original or substantial. His lyrics—clever and provocative—are the best aspect of this highly accomplished and salable album which is neither diverting nor memorable. [i]

BEFOUR THREE O'CLOCK
See *Three O'Clock.*

BEL CANTO
White-Out Conditions (Bel. Crammed Discs) 1987 (Can. Nettwerk) 1988 ●
Birds of Passage (Can. Nettwerk) 1989 (Nettwerk-IRS) 1990 ●

The name is Italian ("beautiful song"), but this trio hails from Norway, sings mostly in English and was originally signed by an artsy Belgian label. Bel Canto's songs are delicate soundscapes that effectively blend orchestral and folk instruments with electronic keyboards and computer-driven synths. On the first LP, Anneli Marian Drecker sings in a fairly limited but not unpleasant alto, a new age Siouxsie Sioux with a slight accent and voice lessons. White-Out Conditions offers a decent variety of material, from Enoesque pop ("Blank Sheets") to somewhat clichéd electro-noodling ("Upland"), but the surprise is "Agassiz," an Arabic-flavored dancefloor oddity.

Drecker stretches out her falsetto more on Birds of Passage, but she has all she can do to keep from being buried in the thick orchestration crafted by bandmates Nils Johansen and Geir Jenssen (plus guests playing everything from flugelhorn to bouzouki). Fans of the Cocteau Twins, Minimal Compact, Virginia Astley and other chamber-rock artists should feel at home with Bel Canto, although the trio adds more bite where necessary. Intriguing stuff. [dgs]

ADRIAN BELEW
Lone Rhino (Island) 1982
Twang Bar King (Island) 1983
Desire Caught by the Tail (Island) 1986 ●
Mr. Music Head (Atlantic) 1989 ●
Young Lions (Atlantic) 1990 ●
Pretty Pink Rose EP [CD] (Atlantic) 1990 ●

BEARS
The Bears (Primitive Man) 1987 ●
Rise and Shine (Primitive Man) 1988 ●

Having served with David Bowie, Talking Heads, the Tom Tom Club and King Crimson, guitarist Belew echoes famous associates on his first solo LP without staking out any turf to call his own. The Kentucky native employs pre-stardom friends from Midwestern bands rather than big names, serving up a varied program of calculated weirdness, straight rock and semi-funk. Mildly charming and rather unfocused, the tenuous unifying thread on Lone Rhino is his David Byrne-influenced voice.

On his second outing, Belew shows much more self-assurance in putting over the same ingredients—an assurance that spills over into self-indulgence long before the album is over. But this record does underscore his contributions to King Crimson: the distinctive vocabulary of extra-musical noises, the personality and especially the humor, which is in abundant evidence here. When it all works, it works incredibly well.

Before taking a solo hiatus in the Bears, Belew issued a one-man instrumental record, **Desire Caught by the Tail**. The simply overdubbed guitars and percussion have a casual home-studio air but no discernible direction. Unlike his ex-bandmate's obsessively controlled Frippertronics, these excursions, while occasionally evocative, hold scant listener appeal.

Seemingly designed to discover how his catalogue of eccentric guitar noises would sound in the context of a traditional pop-rock band—like, say, the Beatles, Hollies, Squeeze or XTC—Belew hooked up with pre-Crimson bar buddies the Raisins to form the Bears. And what a revelation the group's two wonderful records are! Challenging, muscular, tuneful, idiosyncratic and accessible, **The Bears** (complete with group cover portrait by *Mad* magazine's inimitable Mort Drucker) is a superlative record. Everyone contributes and it all works—songs, playing, vocals and production. The only catch: it's too pop for weirdo purists, too weird for pop purists. You figure out why it didn't sell lots of copies.

Rise and Shine is nearly as good. While a bit more adventurous in song structure and playing, it also contains the occasional heavy-handed lyric (especially when bassist Rob Nyswonger writes alone) and one or two fewer memorable songs than **The Bears**. You'd be foolish to pass up either of these, though—get 'em while you can. As a bonus, the CD adds remixed versions of two songs ("Man Behind the Curtain" and "Figure It Out") that were on **The Bears**.

Belew returned to the one-man-band approach of **Desire Caught by the Tail** for his Atlantic albums, making allowances for a few guest performers on each. The main difference between them and his work for Island is that the newer material is far more accessible. **Mr. Music Head**, Belew's most pop-oriented album to date, shows the Bears' influence. Written mostly on piano, it's definitely more song-oriented than any of his earlier solo records, though containing enough of his signature guitar demonstrations to please the faithful. Still, a pure pop ditty like "Oh Daddy" (with guest vocals by daughter Audie) would have been hard to imagine on any of his prior records.

Belew finished **Young Lions** just before going out on David Bowie's globe-trotting *Sound + Vision* tour, in which he served as guitarist and musical director. Bowie's presence is strongly felt here, not just because he wrote and sings two songs (including the catchy "Pretty Pink Rose," also issued on a CD with two non-LP cuts and the previous album's "Oh Daddy"), but in the album's generally heavier—but somehow more ethereal—tone. If **Mr. Music Head** was an earthbound journey with a nostalgic edge (typified by "Motor Bungalow" and "1967"), **Young Lions** constantly looks skyward in the present, whether for salvation on "Looking for a U.F.O." or at "Men in Helicopters" shooting rhinos from the sky. Only the album's two covers seem out of touch with Belew's strong vision here: a reworking of "Heartbeat," which he originally sang on King Crimson's **Beat**, and a faithful-but-faster rendition of the Traveling Wilburys' "Not Alone Anymore." [jy/mf/ds]

See also *David Bowie, King Crimson, Talking Heads*.

BELLE STARS
The Belle Stars (Stiff-Warner Bros.) 1983

Offering a self-contained, funkier alternative to early Bananarama, London's seven-woman Belle Stars played and sang neo-soul and dance-rock. At their most glamorous (the excellent "Sign of the Times") they resemble that era's ABC, but with added spunk and less chrome. Much of the material on the album is, however, much plainer. Far more enjoyable than the band's originals are covers of "Mockingbird," "Needle in a Haystack," "The Clapping Song" and "Iko Iko" (a huge hit when recycled on the soundtrack of 1988's *Rain Man*) which provoke a good time largely through the band's own evident enjoyment. [i]

BELOVED
Where It Is (nr/Flim Flam) 1988
Happiness (Atlantic) 1990 ●
Blissed Out (nr/East West) 1990 φ

As a dark and moody British independent rock act, Camberwell, London's Beloved floundered in obscurity for much of the late '80s, releasing a series of unsuccessful singles (eventually compiled as **Where It Is**). Comparisons to early New Order are inevitable, not just because of the similarity between Jon Marsh's plain-but-comforting vocals and those of Bernard Sumner, but by dint of the band's jolting instrumentation (as on "This Means War") and furtive experiments with drum boxes and synthesizers. The beautiful ballad "Surprise Me" aside, the most remarkable thing about the original Beloved was that they persisted for so long with such mediocre results.

The group then split in half, leaving Marsh and keyboardist Steve Waddington to pursue a growing fascination with dance music. After several further unspectacular singles, they re-emerged on a major label, still casting reflections to New Order, but suddenly—and spectacularly—as peers rather than from a distance. Building on layers of luscious synthesizer and relaxed dance beats, still utilizing guitars (but without aggression), the duo came up with a mellow anthem for the rave generation ("The Sun Rising"), quickly followed it up with a list of their own reference points ("Hello") and then unleashed a debut album that lived up to its title in all respects. Every song on **Happiness** sounds like a single; with its inviting melodies, relaxed grooves and a feel for commercial appeal that never sacrifices subtlety, it is the perfect pop souvenir of Britain's turn-of-the-decade dance movement.

A fondness for remixes and the procession of singles drawn from **Happiness** led to the equally joyful listen of **Blissed Out**, which reprises most of the album's tracks in extended form(s). (The cassette has five bonus mixes.) [tf]

BERLIN

Pleasure Victim (M.A.O.-Enigma) 1982 (Geffen) 1983 ●
Love Life (Geffen) 1984 ●
Count Three & Pray (Geffen) 1986 ●
Best of Berlin 1979–1988 (Geffen) 1989 ●

BIG F

The Big F (fff-Elektra) 1989 ●

Los Angeles' Berlin had been active for several years—an almost totally different lineup issued a 1980 single—before bursting onto the national scene with the impressively slick **Pleasure Victim**, a seven-song mini-album which commercializes routine synth-rock with singer Terri Nunn's audio pornography. The record's most blatant (and hence, popular) track, "Sex (I'm a . . .)," is tasteless and offensive, with crude lyrics and ridiculous moaning. There are two likably atmospheric tunes ("Masquerade" and "The Metro"); otherwise this ranges from bland to inept. (The CD adds a track.)

Berlin serves up more singles-bar smarm on **Love Life**, which makes a bid for respectability as a techno-dance band. Unfortunately, bassist/singer John Crawford is too shallow a songwriter; at best, Berlin can only manage a polished Mike Howlett-produced noise (Giorgio Moroder co-produced a pair of tracks as well) to glamorize a vapid and depressing view of sex. Pathetic.

Between them, Nunn, Crawford and drummer Rob Brill brought only vocals and a rhythm section to **Count Three & Pray**. With unannotated guitar work by Ted Nugent, Dave Gilmour and Elliot Easton, plus a heap of other session players, Berlin made what thankfully proved to be their last record. (The band ended its miserable existence in 1987, perhaps to make way for Pretty Poison.) While Brill's "Like Flames" is an adequate song with a catchy singalong chorus, Crawford's "Sex Me, Talk Me" is straight from the stunted rut of his attitudes about copulation. Originally co-written and produced by Moroder for the soundtrack of *Top Gun*, "Take My Breath Away" is a terrible, characterless ballad that somehow became a forgettable hit single.

Besides the obvious hits and album tracks, the non-chronological compilation also contains the group's otherwise non-LP debut single, "A Matter of Time."

Although the hard-rocking power trio is carefully swathed in mystery, no one has ever seen Big F bassist/singer John Shreve and ex-Berlin bassist/singer John Crawford in the same room. (Coincidentally, the Big F drummer's first name is Rob.) Despite its studied goth pretensions, **The Big F** is merely another noisy soldier in the sub-Cult army of '70s metal wannabes, and not an especially skilled one at that. Shreve's unpleasant growl and Mark Christian's derivative guitar demonstrations give the din-o-meter a good push, but one would have to be a pretty indiscriminate and gullible Led Zep fan to think anything of this shuck.   [i]

CINDY LEE BERRYHILL

Who's Gonna Save the World? (Rhino) 1987 ●
Naked Movie Star (Rhino) 1989 ●

On her debut, Cindy Lee comes off as an endearing flake who at times may remind you of a folky Patti Smith or a female Jonathan Richman in his Modern Lovers days. Like them, she's no great singer or musician, but her songs, mostly about middle-class adolescent and post-adolescent life crises (alienation, drug addiction, suicide) not only ring true, but do so without lapsing into cliché or self-pity. There's also an ironic sense of humor at work, best seen in "Damn, Wish I Was a Man," a catalogue of reasons for penis envy that contains such gems as "Wish I was a man, I'd be sexy with a belly like Jack Nicholson."

For **Naked Movie Star**, producer Lenny Kaye beefs up Berryhill's musical surroundings, expanding and amplifying the lineup (an acoustic trio on the debut) on a number of songs. In fact, after a couple, you may think Cindy Lee's working on becoming Southern California's female Springsteen. Fortunately, the first album's spirited quirkiness eventually re-emerges, complete with a new set of purposeful musical reference points that include **Blonde on Blonde**-era Dylan, Peggy Lee, the Beach Boys and Patti Smith. With **Naked Movie Star**, Berryhill moves into new areas while remaining true to what made her interesting in the first place.   [ds]

ADELE BERTEI

Little Lives (Chrysalis) 1988 ●

Sporting a résumé that includes stints with the Contortions, Thomas Dolby and Jellybean Benitez, New York singer Bertei made a surprisingly accessible and enjoyable solo debut with **Little Lives**. Collaborating on both the fine songs and imaginatively diverse production with keyboardist Ian Prince (and others), Bertei dishes out a warm platter of engagingly substantial dance music, adult rock and jazzy soul-pop. Several numbers gain rich, theatrical character from a backing chorus providing answers to her strong lead vocals. Following Laura Nyro into the '80s, **Little Lives** establishes Bertei as an intelligent and independent voice.

See also *Thomas Dolby, Jellybean.*   [i]

BEVIS FROND

Miasma (Reckless) 1987 ●
Inner Marshland (Reckless) 1987 ●
Triptych (Reckless) 1988 ●
Bevis Through the Looking Glass (Reckless) 1988
Acid Jam (nr/Woronzow) 1988
The Auntie Winnie Album (Reckless) 1989 ●
Any Gas Faster (Reckless) 1990 ●
Ear Song EP (Reckless) 1990

BEVIS AND TWINK

Magic Eye (nr/Woronzow) 1990

Trading under the one-man banner of the Bevis Frond, London's prolific Nick Saloman traffics in unreconstructed, unrepentant psychedelia. His procession of remarkable (and mostly homemade) albums could get by, if necessary, on their sheer monomaniacal obsession to the form. Fortunately, the guitarist (and other instruments) is a master craftsman, adept at fashioning quirkily expressive cottage-industry epics out of psychedelia's most overworked conventions.

Miasma, Inner Marshland, Triptych and **The Auntie Winnie Album** are more or less interchangeable, mixing gently twisted melodic pop, aggressive Hendrixian jamming, moments of reflective introspection and flashes of absurdist humor. (The authentically anachronistic sound is apparently due in part to the fact that much of the material was written and/or recorded years before its release.) The CD versions of these four albums offer excellent value for money, each running beyond 70 minutes, with bonus tracks drawn from two vinyl-only releases: **Bevis Through the Looking Glass** and **Acid Jam**, both of which concentrate on Saloman's guitar-freakout expertise.

The upgraded production values of **Any Gas Faster** (recorded in a real studio for a change) make it a fine forum for Saloman's iconoclastic artistry. A subsequent EP of two **Any Gas Faster** tracks ("Ear Song" and "Olde Worlde") also contains four live songs from a 1990 Copenhagen show, at which Saloman ably leads a four-man group.

Looking very much like father and son in the cover snap, Saloman and ex-Pink Fairy drummer Twink unite two generations of British psychedelia on **Magic Eye**, alternating vocals for an inconsistent but frequently fab batch of unstylized (nonetheless retro-sounding) songs, like Bevis' Hüsker Düish "Flying Igloos," the two-chord "Fractured Sky," Twink's deliciously sludgy "The Fairy" and the no-it's-not-the-Stooges "Bag Drip." Despite an overabundance of wanky noodling (all that's lacking at the most aimless points is a voice going "check . . . check . . . "), there's plenty here to enjoy.   [hd/i]

See also *Social Deviants*.

BEWITCHED
See *Sonic Youth*.

B-52'S
The B-52's (Warner Bros.) 1979 ●
Wild Planet (Warner Bros.) 1980 ●
Party Mix! EP (Warner Bros.) 1981
Mesopotamia EP (Warner Bros.) 1982
Whammy! (Warner Bros.) 1983 ●
Bouncing off the Satellites (Warner Bros.) 1986 ●
Cosmic Thing (Reprise) 1989 ●
Dance This Mess Around: The Best of the B-52's
    (nr/Island) 1990 ●
Party Mix/Mesopotamia (Reprise) 1991 φ

FRED SCHNEIDER & THE SHAKE SOCIETY
Fred Schneider & the Shake Society (Warner Bros.) 1984
    (Reprise) 1991 ●

Just when new wave seemed to be bottoming out, along came Athens, Georgia's B-52's to rev it back up again, with distinctive junk-store '60s visuals (Kate Pierson and Cindy Wilson sport bouffant wigs—"B-52's" in Southern regional slang) and stark, highly danceable songs with appropriately surreal kitsch lyrics. The B-52's' wacky sense of humor made their self-titled first album a sleeper that was finally certified gold in 1986. Now a cult classic, it contains such cornerstones of the repertoire as "52 Girls," "Dance This Mess Around," "6060-842" and the ever-popular "Rock Lobster."

The B-52's have been wondering what to do for an encore ever since. The eagerly awaited **Wild Planet** has its inspired moments: "Private Idaho" and "Devil in My Car" mesh a firm beat with dark and/or silly senti-

ments. "Give Me Back My Man" takes a new direction—a serious (!) showcase for Cindy Wilson's Patsy Cline-influenced singing. (Vocalist Fred Schneider is usually up front for comic relief.) But too much of the album, with its short length and recycled ideas, comes across as a pale imitation of its predecessor.

Apparently the band felt the same way, and stayed away from the recording studio for the next year and a half. **Party Mix!**, issued in the interim, takes three songs each from the two LPs and—through the miracle of tape loops, overdubs and other studio tomfoolery—inflates them to nearly 30 minutes of playing time. The result is functional for discos but antithetical to the B-52's' minimalist precepts.

The band was next "officially" heard from with another mini-LP, **Mesopotamia**, salvaged from sessions produced by Talking Head David Byrne. Whether under Byrne's humorless influence or not—he plays on the record and engages a couple of Heads-family percussionists to help out—the B-52's get serious, with dire results. "Loveland" and "Deep Sleep" sacrifice élan for slickness—not a fair trade. "Cake" and the title cut (one of only two Schneider vocals) come off as self-conscious parodies of the old, carefree B-52's. Only "Throw That Beat in the Garbage Can" taps the zany reservoir that made the group popular in the first place.

After the curious abortion of **Mesopotamia**, **Whammy!** came as a reassuring return to form, or perhaps formula. On some cuts ("Whammy Kiss," "Trism," "Butterbean"), the band goes through the by-now-well-worn motions. Elsewhere ("Big Bird," "Queen of Las Vegas"), horns—introduced on **Mesopotamia**—and intriguing narratives show the B-52's are only on semi-automatic pilot. Drummer Keith Strickland and guitarist Ricky Wilson (Cindy's brother) play all the instruments save horns; the sound is more electronic than funky-human.

Schneider's solo project hardly discouraged fears about the state of the B-52's. (Kate Pierson helps Fred out with vocals.) The *pro tem* Shake Society is a fine stopgap for the parent band's looniness. Schneider's lyrics continue to dwell on campy sci-fi ("This Planet's a Mess," "Orbit") and campy fantasy ("Summer in Hell," "Boonga"), with campy sex ("Monster," "It's Time to Kiss") thrown in for good measure. The remixed reissue is billed and titled without mention of the Shake Society.

Ricky Wilson died of AIDS in October 1985, shortly after the recording sessions for **Bouncing off the Satellites**. Produced by British popmeister Tony Mansfield (who also plays Fairlight on every track) and with Schneider hardly in evidence, the bittersweet record was eventually completed and released in late 1986. The first side is entirely delightful, filled with such classic B-52 silliness as "Wig," "Detour Thru Your Mind" and "Girl from Ipanema Goes to Greenland," but the flip is overly smooth, limp and uninspired. Typifying the record's structural oddness, Schneider is the only band member on the lengthy "Juicy Jungle," co-written and largely played by one John Coté.

Although the B-52's seemed likely to toss in the towel after **Satellites**, they pulled together (Strickland having switched to guitar), worked out their problems and managed an amazing come-from-behind victory. Don Was and Nile Rodgers (two seemingly odd studio choices that panned out beautifully) each produced half of **Cosmic Thing**, which relocates the group's old fun-filled groove and gives it a commercially snug berth. Preserving the band's kitschy spirit but eliminating its rhythmic eccentricity, the platinum **Cosmic Thing** puts the quartet's signature vocals and whimsical lyrics center stage in a slickly mainstream recreation of '60s party music. While the sound is as consistent as TV dinners, the material runs from fabulous ("Roam," "Love Shack," "Deadbeat Club") to fair ("Bushfire") to flat ("Channel Z," "Dry County").

The B-52's and **Wild Planet** have been repackaged as a double-length cassette (but individual CDs). In 1991, a remixed version of **Mesopotamia** was issued on a joint CD with **Party Mix!** The skimpy eleven-song **Dance This Mess Around** compilation offers a far-from-definitive sampling of the band's albums through **Satellites**.   [si/i]

JELLO BIAFRA
No More Cocoons (Alternative Tentacles) 1987
High Priest of Harmful Matter—Tales from the Trial
   (Alternative Tentacles) 1989
VARIOUS ARTISTS
Terminal City Ricochet (Alternative Tentacles) 1989
JELLO BIAFRA WITH D.O.A.
Last Scream of the Missing Neighbors EP (Alternative
   Tentacles) 1990 ●
JELLO BIAFRA WITH NOMEANSNO
The Sky Is Falling and I Want My Mommy (Alternative
   Tentacles) 1991 ●

Since the end of the Dead Kennedys, Jello Biafra has continued to ply his missionary trade with spoken word records. **No More Cocoons** contains four sides of political satire recorded at college appearances, radio interviews, readings and in-stores. Biafra has found his ideal medium here, and this is as sharp, funny and informative as any DK record. Biafra applies his acerbic wit, endless outrage, abundant intelligence and dramatic skills to a variety of concerns, making the record highly worthwhile and grimly amusing. Those old enough to remember Lenny Bruce or even Mort Sahl in his prime may consider this a topical comedy record in the grand tradition; younger listeners are likely to hear it as a chilling reintroduction to what the DKs' songs were saying all along.

As someone whose outspoken opinions and free-thinking actions are enough to bring down the legal wrath of the land's moral guardians, it's convenient that Biafra has an independent record label on which to rebut his accusors. Following his 1987 acquittal for "distribution of harmful matter to minors" in the **Frankenchrist** trial, Biafra released a post-mortem on that absurd brush with the justice system. Besides a typically intelligent and amusing 1988 lecture on the general topic of contemporary censorship, the two-disc **High Priest** offers his detailed account of the events that began on April 15, 1986, when police raided his San Francisco apartment.

Biafra stars in and performs on the soundtrack of 1989's *Terminal City Ricochet*; the soundtrack album of this Canadian film contains tracks by assorted AT bands as well as Biafra's musical collaborations with D.O.A., Nomeansno and Keith LeBlanc. While working on that project, he took a step towards resuming his musical career with **Last Scream of the Missing Neighbors**, a roaring rock record that puts Biafra's trademark vocals and songs to D.O.A.'s meat-and-potatoes guitar power. With a half-dozen numbers like "Wish I Was in El Salvador," "Attack of the Peacekeepers" and the epic "Full Metal Jackoff," **Last Scream** proudly rehoists the DK flag in all but name.   [i]

See also *Dead Kennedys, Ice-T, Lard*.

BIBLE
Walking the Ghost Back Home (nr/Backs) 1986 ●
Eureka (Chrysalis-Ensign) 1988 ●
The Bible (nr/Ensign-Chrysalis) 1989 ●
BOO HEWERDINE AND DARDEN SMITH
Evidence (Chrysalis) 1989 ●

This Cambridge, England-based band includes a jazz drummer on keyboards and Kirsty MacColl's brother Neill on guitar. On **Walking the Ghost Back Home**, the Bible covers a lot of musical territory, from airy Bruce Hornsby-esque rock ("Graceland") to Traffic-like jazz-rock (the title track) to a U2-ish tribute to Mahalia Jackson ("Mahalia"). One song recalls early Bowie; another almost goes back to the days of dole queue punk. While the whole enterprise is earnest and competent, only "Graceland" and "Mahalia" are truly compelling.

The Steve Earle-produced **Eureka** is a more focused record. Clean and crisply played, it has pretty moments, but also suffers from a real lack of rhythmic dynamism; the songs tend to plod on too long. **The Bible** is a compilation that contains all but three of **Eureka**'s tracks and adds five more, including "Graceland" (again) and a version of "Abraham, Martin and John" that—believe it or not—is even more sentimental than Dion's original. Initial quantities of the UK release contained a bonus 12-inch of four acoustic cuts.

Bible vocalist Boo Hewerdine teamed up with Texas singer-songwriter Darden Smith on **Evidence**, a far more interesting and affecting album than anything the Bible's done to date. The unpretentious Smith (who has also done albums on his own) is a perfect foil for Hewerdine; the vocal excesses Hewerdine indulges in the Bible are checked here, and his voice is instead channeled into arresting harmonies in the bare-bones tunes. A winner.   [ds]

BIFF BANG POW!
Pass the Paintbrush, Honey.. (nr/Creation) 1985 ●
Love's Going Out of Fashion EP (nr/Creation) 1986 ●
The Girl Who Runs the Beat Hotel (nr/Creation) 1987 ●
Oblivion (Creation-Relativity) 1987 ●
Love Is Forever (Creation-Relativity) 1988 ●
The Acid House Album (nr/Creation) 1989 ●
Songs for the Sad Eyed Girl (nr/Creation) 1990 ●

Besides doing his part to influence the sound of British music by founding and running the influential Creation label, Glasgow native Alan McGee leads this hip neo-pop quartet, which he formed in London. Although Biff Bang Pow! has much to recommend it, fans of the band for which it and the record company are named, however, will find little evidence of the Creation's peerless '60s art-rock here.

Psychedelia and nostalgia inform Biff Bang Pow!'s records but, as often as not, the wiry guitar pop sounds like a compromise between Josef K, Orange Juice and Haircut One Hundred. Although they would seem spiritually in synch with the Television Personalities or Times (indeed, the latter's Edward Ball is an occasional member), Biff Bang Pow! doesn't share those groups' winsome charm or demonstrative cultural resonance.

The cover photo of **Pass the Paintbrush** shows a set of Vox gear that would do any revivalist band proud. The first side offers little such personality; noisy interludes of non-chromatic harmonica provide the most noticeable component of the short ditties. Side B has the real goods, containing the rushing Kinksy "Colin Dobbins" and the outstanding "A Day Out with Jeremy Chester," a lengthy acid-rock trip loaded with wild feedback and exciting guitar crashes. The **Paintbrush** CD also contains the band's next album.

Poorly produced with thin, shrill sound, **The Girl Who Runs the Beat Hotel** reveals much stronger, more attractive songwriting. "Someone Stole My Wheels" and "The Happiest Girl in the World" are convincing period pieces colored in with, respectively, prominent organ and female vocals; "Five Minutes in the Life of Greenwood Goulding" uses crazy backwards guitars. Strangely, McGee's vocals suggest Robert Smith on "Love's Going Out of Fashion" and Lloyd Cole on "He Don't Need That Girl." The melodies and varied arrangements are stylishly appropriate, but the botched mix prevents them from being fully appreciated. The 12-inch of "Love's Going Out of Fashion" avoids that sonic pothole and includes three atmospheric non-LP tracks.

Almost all of the band's remaining sharp edges have been polished off of **Oblivion**, a handsome effort with brilliant vocals and sparkling guitar uplifting the finely constructed songs. Still, it's heartwarming to hear "A Girl Called Destruction" devolve into a noisy old-fashioned raveup; "I See the Sun" contrasts acoustic strumming with massive distortion on the solo. If Paul Weller had grown up listening to the Hollies as much as the Who, the Jam might have made an album like **Oblivion**; fortunately, Biff Bang Pow! did.

Side One of **Love Is Forever** mixes electric and acoustic guitars (played by McGee and stalwart bandmate Richard Green) with pretty harmonica to yield music akin to the Bluebells' sprightly folk-rock (but not songs of that group's caliber). The other side—all-electric and at times *loud*—is bracing but largely unfathomable, despite the inclusion of such delicacies as "She Went Away to Love." While remnants of **Oblivion**'s appeal and clarity are evident, **Love Is Forever** is comparatively dull and uninspired.

The Acid House Album is nothing of the sort, but rather an exceedingly enjoyable compilation containing one side of alternate versions (demos, outtakes, etc.). Surprisingly consistent production sound and wise programming makes this a fine place for neophytes to begin and fans to revisit. (A demo of "The Girl from Well Lane" provides a teaser for the group's next release.)

The seven romantic **Songs for the Sad Eyed Girl** may be heartfelt, but casual folky underproduction leaves the record a bit listless. (Some of the tracks are effectively McGee solo acoustic turns.) Only the marvelous massed harmonies of "She Kills Me," "Baby, You Just Don't Care" and "Hug Me Honey" offer reasons to be cheerful. [i]

BIG AUDIO DYNAMITE
This Is Big Audio Dynamite (Columbia) 1985 ●
No. 10, Upping St. (Columbia) 1986 ●
Tighten Up Vol. 88 (Columbia) 1988 ●
Megatop Phoenix (Columbia) 1989 ●

BIG AUDIO DYNAMITE II
Kool-Aid (nr/CBS) 1990 ●
The Globe (Columbia) 1991 ●

The rote replay of the unClash's **Cut the Crap** only underscores the accomplishment of Mick Jones' subsequent band, originally formed with filmmaker-*cum*-musician Don Letts. Joe Strummer attempted to purify the Clash by purging Jones, but wound up liberating the guitarist's muse and (for a while) misplacing his own. The original B.A.D.—which included ex-Basement 5 bassist Leo Williams in its uncommon lineup—takes off from various things the Clash had tried on **Sandinista!** and **Combat Rock**, but goes much further with audio vérité, sonic effects and beatbox funk. The adventurous band's recordings are creatively ambitious crazy quilts of half-baked songs with fascinating lyrics, slathered over with shards of film dialogue and news reports. Although flimsy and gimmicky on first exposure, the meandering dance grooves on **This Is Big Audio Dynamite** (especially "E=MC2" and "The Bottom Line") prove far more alluring and resilient with repeated exposure. Jones' monochromatic vocals can be a negative factor in spots, but they're generally adequate to the task, and occasionally perfectly suited.

In a truly startling development, Strummer wound up co-producing (and co-writing half of) B.A.D.'s second album with Jones. Appraising the nature of his contribution or understanding the pair's ongoing synergy is impossible, but finding this uniquely conceived pancultural record fascinating is easy. Similar to the first album, but improved by greater studio mastery and better writing, **No. 10, Upping St.** deconstructs modern culture and politics in a wild soup of sounds and lyrics. The shuffling "Beyond the Pale" and the attractively melodic "V. Thirteen" (reprised in an instrumental version as "The Big V.") are the closest things to Clash songs since **Combat Rock**, while "C'mon Every Beatbox" quotes Jeff Beck and Eddie Cochran over a powerful groove with ricocheting drumbeats. ("Badrock City," the B-side dub of the "Beatbox" single, became a surprise dance hit, and was tacked onto later pressings of the album.) A unique, danceable hybrid of art and life.

The disappointing **Tighten Up Vol. 88** reaches no such peaks and now sounds like a fairly brazen attempt to get hip commercial airplay. The fault is seldom with Jones' songwriting but more with the slick sheen laid over the leaner, less aggressive beats. The LP yielded "Just Play Music" and "Other 99," but a pall was thrown on the release as Jones fell deathly ill shortly after its appearance; having contracted pneumonia, he was hospitalized for months.

Less than a year after **Tighten Up**, however, Jones

miraculously returned with **Megatop Phoenix**. Arguably B.A.D.'s best, this dense, quick-cut audio collage weaves its songs through enough studio wankery to summon flashbacks of **Sandinista!**; the claustrophobic sequencing makes the invention of CD remotes especially welcome. Not unlike his early '80s funk fetish, Jones mixes acid house in to both surprisingly good ("Contact," "House Arrest") and embarrassingly bad ("James Brown") effect. However, his flair for melody is as strong as ever and, although the fun samples ("Honky Tonk Women" and "I Can't Explain," among dozens) are often cluttered, the cinematic mixes collude to create evocative soundscapes for the London-centric cyberpunk/Colin MacInnes lyrics.

Megatop was, in many ways, the culmination of B.A.D.'s original concept, and the band split in early '90. Letts, Williams and drummer Greg Roberts formed Screaming Target, releasing a single called "Who Killed King Tubby?" late that year; keyboardist Dan Donovan joined Tony James—Jones' pre-Clash bandmate in the London SS—in Sisters of Mercy. Jones recruited three street-looking lads (one of whom alarmingly resembles Sid Vicious), adopted the name Big Audio Dynamite II and issued **Kool-Aid**, a stopgap prior to **The Globe**. With a relatively loose feel and concept, **Kool-Aid** is his most diverse outing ever, offering two acoustic ballads, acid-dance, techno-rock, Kraftwerk samples and even Laurie Anderson-styled poltergeist vocals, as well as a remixed (and retitled) version of "Free," the band's contribution to the *Flashback* soundtrack.   [i/ja]

See also *Basement 5, Clash, Jah Wobble*.

BIG BAM BOO
Fun, Faith, & Fairplay (Uni) 1987

Catchy pop tunes, nicely harmonized joint vocals, heartily strummed acoustic/electric guitars and reverb-heavy drums make this personable (if overly commercial) Anglo-Canadian duo something of an '80s Everlys descendant. Although Richard Manwaring's production frequently drowns the pair in sappy modern arrangements (not that it's an unwelcomed imposition: Big Bam Boo is not at all rootsy or nostalgic in concept), the album's few modestly presented songs (like "Fell off a Mountain" and "Wicked Love") are delightful.   [i]

BIG BLACK
Lungs EP (Ruthless) 1983
Bulldozer EP (Ruthless-Fever) 1984
Racer-X EP (Homestead) 1984
Atomizer (Homestead) 1986 ●
The Hammer Party (Homestead) 1986 ●
Headache EP (Touch and Go) 1987
Sound of Impact (nr/Walls Have Ears) 1987
The Rich Man's Eight-Track Tape [CD] (Homestead) 1987 ●
Songs About Fucking (Touch and Go) 1987 ●
ARSENAL
Manipulator EP (Touch and Go) 1989 ●
Factory Smog Is a Sign of Progress EP (Touch and Go) 1990 ●

"The only good policeman is a dead one/The only good laws aren't enforced/I've never hung a darkie but

I've fed one/I've never seen an Indian on a horse." With these gentle words, acerbic Chicago fanzine writer Steve Albini began his extremely serious adventures in the rock'n'roll skin trade. For a while, Albini assembled makeshift lineups from other bands (Big Black subsequently stabilized a lineup of its own); regardless of who, they make music that's grating, angular, humorless and very intelligent—sort of a cross between Gang of Four, PiL and the Great Crusades (not a band). Albini's self-righteousness sometimes causes him to be as much unaccommodating as uncompromising, but his bile is generally well-directed, and he's immune to corruption, except from within. All these records are challenging and rewarding.

Lungs is at once the most homegrown and overwrought Big Black release. Over a skeletal art-funk background, Albini creates bleak, tough images of recessioned industrial America. While "I Can Be Killed" is almost laughable for its delusionary self-importance, "Steelworker" is intensely muscular. **Bulldozer** goes for a chunkier sound and more violent imagery. The recording quality and playing are more sophisticated, making it less alluring than the spartan **Lungs**. "Cables" is about voyeurs at a slaughterhouse; "The Pigeon Kill" is about poisoning birds; "Seth" is about a dog trained to attack black people. Overambitious, but sincere and scary. (A limited number of copies of **Bulldozer** were packaged in a sheet metal sleeve, with the band's name etched in acid.) The CD of **The Hammer Party**, which on vinyl is simply a combined reissue of the first two EPs, adds the third, **Racer-X**.

Racer-X is less obsessively cranky than the first two records (a positive development). The basic elements remain: one-riff industrial funk grooves, coarse vocals, jagged guitar. But this EP fills out the sound without sacrificing any of its amateur appeal. The musicians, while skilled technicians all, keep the sound raw. And if Albini is still something of a cartoon curmudgeon in his boasts about being "The Ugly American," he at least includes a James Brown cover and a tribute to Speed Racer's cooler brother. Not as idiosyncratically brilliant as **Lungs**, but fine stuff nonetheless.

Atomizer comes thundering out of the starting gate like a wounded rhino, charging around madly with awesome, claustrophobic rock power. Albini leads his troupe through such angry slices of niho-philosophy, depravity and arson as "Big Money," "Stinking Drunk," "Fists of Love," "Jordan, Minnesota," "Kerosene" and "Bazooka Joe" (for which the liner notes note "part of the drum track is an M1 carbine being fired in a field exercise by a guy named Joe"). A magnificently rugged record and a major sourcebook for countless bands to come.

As a sticker prudently warns, **Headache** is nowhere near as good as **Atomizer**. With the exception of the slow-to-fast chugger "Ready Men," nothing approaches the same level of excellence. Although **Headache** is the weakest Big Black LP or EP, it will forever be remembered for its original (fortunately?) limited edition sleeve: the most gruesome, disgusting photo imaginable, an accident victim's head so grotesque the record had to be sold with a covering black jacket.

Sound of Impact is a rather mysterious, extraordinarily limited edition live LP. Big Black's name appears nowhere on the sleeve or spine; many are unaware of the record's existence. Recorded live in Muncie, Indiana and Minneapolis, it includes early versions with different lyrics of later material, and is as jarring and unrelenting as their concerts were.

The CD-only **Rich Man's Eight-Track Tape** (ha-ha) is a sixteen-track compilation containing all of **Atomizer** and **Headache** plus both sides of the "Heartbeat"/"Things to Do Today" single.

As Big Black was splitting up, they released their finest work: a second actual LP, **Songs About Fucking.** As if to go out kicking, screaming, howling and biting, it's their most raging, abrasive, pulverizing record, with only an excellent and ironic guitar take of Kraftwerk's "The Model" providing any relief. Albini's screeched vocals are so low in the mix they're just another instrument. Obsessing as usual on the excessive and bizarre side of human life, his stories remain mini horror movies set to the punishing, scathing guitar attack. Lyrically and aurally like **Atomizer**, it's liable to alter your perceptions. (The CD and cassette add Big Black's cover of Cheap Trick's "He's a Whore," originally released as a 45, complete with parodic sleeve photo.)

Following Big Black's windup, Albini got busy producing records (usually without taking sleeve credit) for the Pixies and zillions of other bands. He also formed Rapeman and discovered entire new vistas of aural and conceptual antagonism that have proven astonishingly influential.

Although the main reason Big Black split was because guitarist Santiago Durango enrolled in law school, he's since found the time to record two EPs as Arsenal, assisted on the second by Naked Raygun's Pierre Kezdy. (Durango was in Raygun's original lineup, prior to Kezdy's arrival.)

Manipulator is too experimental, as if Durango hadn't decided what sort of music he wanted to make. "Little Hitlers" could be a Big Black outtake, but the rest sounds like an afternoon of self-indulgent knob twisting. The vocals, delivered in a barely discernible Darth Vader growl and deliberately hidden behind the instruments, make Albini's anti-singer mixes sound like a U2 album.

Factory Smog is much better. Including songs originally done by the legendary Strike Under and Trial by Fire (Kezdy's two old bands), this EP carries on Big Black's harsh wallop, with big-fuzzed instrumental passages that also bring to mind Breaking Circus. While the vocals are still nowhere near the front of the mix, the harrowing riffs make for real drama. (One CD contains both EPs.)   [jl/i/jr]

See also *Rapeman*.

BIG BOYS/DICKS
Recorded Live at Raul's Club (Rat Race) 1980

BIG BOYS
Where's My Towel (Wasted Talent) 1981
Fun, Fun, Fun ... EP (Moment) 1982
Lullabies Help the Brain Grow (Moment-Enigma) 1983
No Matter How Long the Line Is at the Cafeteria, There's Always a Seat! (Enigma) 1984
Wreck Collection (Unseen Hand) 1988 + 1989

Initially another bunch of misfit goodfernaughts in thrall of shock, volume and outrage, Austin, Texas' Big Boys were well matched with cross-dressing nascent blues revisionists the Dicks on the LP they shared, recorded loud and dirty at their hometown's premier end-of-the-'70s punk showplace.

The self-released **Where's My Towel** better indicates the band's ultimate strengths: Randy "Biscuits" Turner's melodic rasp and shriek, the surprising musical prowess and singularity of the instrumentalists (particularly guitarist Tim Kerr) and, most significantly, the proto-funk leanings that would later dominate the group. They continued to hone/splinter their approach on the two Moment releases, paralleling the anti-metal punk bent of Mission of Burma and, more specifically, those fractured funk political missionaries, the Minutemen.

By the time of the schizo **No Matter How Long the Line Is at the Cafeteria** LP, the Big Boys encompassed everything from pure 'core to Hüsker Dü-inspired overdrive pop to horn-flatulent dance dreck. Unsurprisingly, this was their last LP; members scattered to units as diverse as Doctor's Mob, Bad Mutha Goose and the Brothers Grimm, Scratch Acid, Poison 13, Rapeman and, most ignominiously, Junkyard. In 1988, longtime producer/collaborator Spot released (first on tape and second on vinyl) the **Wreck Collection** of odds and ends, beginning with the impossibly rare (until recently bootlegged) debut 7-inch and running through outtakes and alternate mixes.   [ab]

See also *Dag Nasty*.

BIG COUNTRY
The Crossing (Mercury) 1983 ●
Wonderland EP (Mercury) 1984
Steeltown (Mercury) 1984 ●
The Seer (Mercury) 1986 ●
Peace in Our Time (Reprise) 1988 ●
Broken Heart EP (nr/Mercury) 1988 ●
Through a Big Country (nr/Mercury) 1990 ●

Guitarist Stuart Adamson—the unsung hero and sound shaper of the Skids—survived that once-wonderful band's miserable end to form a down-to-earth rock quartet unhampered (at the outset, anyway) by grandiose artistic pretensions. Rounded out by guitarist Bruce Watson and the ace rhythm section of Tony Butler and Mark Brzezicki (who have also played, individually and collectively, on records by Pete Townshend, the Pretenders, Roger Daltrey and others), Big Country quickly jumped into the vanguard of resurgent guitar-hero bands.

Retaining some of the Skids' pseudo-Scottish six-string-bagpipe effects, **The Crossing**, brilliantly produced by Steve Lillywhite, offers rousing anthems ("In a Big Country," "Inwards" and "Fields of Fire," its riff cleverly lifted from "The Guns of Navarone") and moving romantic ballads ("The Storm," "Chance") that neatly intertwine Celtic folk traditions with blazing guitar riffs. (The UK tape edition has extra tracks.) The **Wonderland** EP consists of four songs, including an early B-side and the uplifting, catchy title track, one of the band's best efforts.

Steeltown breaks no new ground and is basically a formulaic reprise, but the band is so unique, passionate and skilled at what they do that you don't really mind. Best selections: "East of Eden," "Where the Rose Is Sown" (a virtual rewrite of "In a Big Country," itself not all that different from "Fields of Fire") and "Just a Shadow."

Well-crafted, with melancholy lyrics and a guest vocal appearance by Kate Bush on the title track, **The Seer** holds close to the band's by-now-standard sound, with no loss in appeal. Even if they don't vary much in content or style, Big Country's records offer an original and invigorating brand of modern rock'n'roll with deep cultural resonance.

After carefully establishing their rockist guitar-army aesthetic, Big Country took a surprising detour on the deliriously overproduced **Peace in Our Time**, which submerges the band's trademark sound in sanitized, synthesized musical settings that bear scant evidence of what made their previous efforts so appealing. While a few decent songs—"Thousand Yard Stare," "From Here to Eternity," the title track—shine through, **Peace in Our Time**'s drastic recasting of the band feels like commercial desperation rather than artistic restlessness. More to the point, it just isn't much fun.

Through a Big Country is a fine fourteen-track career summary, with material from all four albums, plus "Wonderland" and the non-LP "Save Me." The CD and tape contain three more bonus cuts, all previously released. [i/hd]

See also *Skids*.

BIG DIPPER

Boo-Boo EP (Homestead) 1987 ●
Heavens (Homestead) 1987 ●
Craps (Homestead) 1988 ●
Slam (Epic) 1990 ●

Boston's Big Dipper came together in 1986 when bassist Steve Michener and guitarist Gary Waleik (both from the original lineup of the Volcano Suns) joined up with former (and future) Embarrassment vocalist Bill Goffrier and local drummer Jeff Oliphant. The six-song **Boo-Boo** is an extremely jovial combination of retro-punk guitar and loopy rhythms and vocals. It bounces like a goddamn superball.

The **Heavens** LP, which shows the group beginning to rely more heavily on layered vocals than string-croak, features such college-rock classics as "Younger Bums" and "All Going Out Together." (The cassette appends one song; **Boo-Boo** is contained on the CD.)

Subsequent recordings have seen Big Dipper move even further into the college-rock hard-pop mainstream (**Slam** contains an ambiguous cover of Mott the Hoople's "All the Way from Memphis"), and their initial, odd bite seems to have softened. [bc]

See also *Embarrassment*.

BIG DISH

Swimmer (Virgin-Warner Bros.) 1986 ●
Creeping Up on Jesus (Virgin-Warner Bros.) 1988 ●
Satellites (East West) 1991 φ

Singer/songwriter Steven Lindsay leads the Big Dish, a tasteful and basically unstylized Scottish pop trio. With subtle soul inflections in the roomy guitar-plus-horns arrangements, the handsome, intelligent songs on **Swimmer** consistently tumble into the dead zone between youthful freshness and mature restraint.

Using an impressive list of session players—including Blair Cunningham (drums) and Gary Barnacle (horns)—producer Bruce Lampcov fleshed out Big Dish's sound on the second album, but to no avail. Despite twinkling layers of guitar, keyboards and vocals, Lindsay's songs are steadfastly underwhelming, and the album is merely an attractive but characterless noise.

The Big Dish finally got off the ground with **Satellites**, an effectively commercial adult-pop record that makes good use of stylistic borrowings (soul, rock, country) and guest players (bassist Pino Palladino, drummer Manu Katché) to flavor the bright (if not illuminating) material. Lindsay's faint vocal resemblance to Sting, and Warne Livesey's sterile Steely Dan-style production keep the record a small-scale entertainment, but at least the tunes don't all evaporate as soon as they reach the air. [i]

BIG DRILL CAR

Small Block EP (Varient) 1988 (Cruz) 1990 ●
Album Type Thing (Cruz) 1989
Tape Type Thing [tape] (Cruz) 1989
CD Type Thing [CD] (Cruz) 1989 ●

Like labelmates All and Chemical People, Huntington Beach, California's Big Drill Car specializes in bouncy punk-pop full of hooks, harmonies and exuberant playing. To its credit, BDC wisely eschews the former's atonal excesses and the latter's porno fetish.

Frank Daly's earnest and clear vocals and Mark Arnold's sharp, efficient guitar work (both are ex-M.I.A.) brighten the six-song **Small Block**, a near-perfect introduction to a very likable quartet. The inexplicably French-titled "Les Cochons sans Poils," which suggests the group has listened to as much Cheap Trick as Black Flag, stands out on a record whose only disappointment is its brevity.

The band's first full-length opus (the title of which is format-specific) mines similar terrain, though only a couple of the tracks are as immediately catchy as those on the EP. Still, as the jaunty "16 Lines," "No Need" and "About Us" prove, you'd be hard-pressed to find a band straddling the hardcore, power-pop and hard-rock fences with more finesse and enthusiasm. (Compulsives may want to consult "I Scream" from the Brigade's 1986 **The Dividing Line** to trace the ancestry of the great hook on "About Us.") [db]

See also *M.I.A.*

BIG F

See *Berlin*.

BIG IN JAPAN

From Y to Z and Never Again EP (nr/Zoo) 1978

As the band Budgie drummed in before the Slits (or Siouxsie and the Banshees), as Ian Broudie's group long before he was a hotshot producer or a Lightning Seed, as the first recorded sighting of wild Bill Drummond (future mastermind of the JAMS/KLF) and as an early proving ground for bassist (!) Holly Johnson (later the vocalist in Frankie Goes to Hollywood), Liverpool's Big in Japan deserves a lasting place in rock history merely for existing.

Between the group's formation in the summer of '77 and its dissolution fifteen months later, the entirety of its vinyl output was one half of a single (backed by a pseudonymous Yachts track credited to the Chuddy Nuddies). The rest of its oeuvre was issued posthumously: two compilation cuts and a four-track 7-inch, **From Y to Z and Never Again**. Singer Jayne Casey (who later led the dub-tinged pop band Pink Military and the ethereal Pink Industry) takes inspiration here from Japanese girl pop singers, adopting a choppy and chirpy boopsie-doll voice in "Suicide a Go Go," a sing-song foray into an underworld of prostitution. While "Taxi" hints at the kind of full-echo drumming that Budgie would later exploit as a Banshee, "Cindy and the Barbi Dolls" is a Martian surf samba with Drummond mumbling Rod McKuen-esque poetic love junk over '50s guitar while a kitschy choir of double-speed munchkins oh-oh-ohs and yeah-yeahs its way behind the chords.   ['e]

See also *Frankie Goes to Hollywood, Justified Ancients of Mu Mu, Lightning Seeds, Original Mirrors, Pink Military.*

BIG PIG

Bonk (A&M) 1988 •

From the cruel metaphor of the opening "Iron Lung" to the weary conclusion of "Devil's Song," **Bonk** is one angry record. Although technically an Australian group, Big Pig began in London around 1985, and hatred of Margaret Thatcher's England seems to fuel the bittersweet material. Lead singer Sherine has a dark alto that complements the songs' often depressing tone. But vocals aren't the half of Big Pig. The instrumentation is keyboards, harmonica and drums—lots of drums, played by three out of seven members. The trundling, tribal rhythms give the songs the effect of steamrollers extinguishing their protagonists' burned-out lives. Sparse musical textures, including group chants and that anomalous bluesy harmonica, help make **Bonk** compelling listening. Big Pig's obviously got attitude to burn, and who couldn't use a healthy blast of protest?   [si]

BIG STAR

See *Alex Chilton.*

BIG TROUBLE HOUSE

See *Breaking Circus.*

BIG WHEEL

East End (Giant) 1989

With two of his ex-bandmates off to weird noiseville in Slint and another joining the Lemonheads, onetime Squirrel Bait singer Peter Searcy formed this Louisville quartet to play impassioned and intelligent heartland rock with no more than a hint of its punk roots. Sharing the skillful songwriting with guitarist Glenn Taylor, Searcy belts out intriguingly bemused lyrics about friends and loners over rough but unchallenging music with a few light interludes (the album includes one acoustic number). Despite Searcy's dramatic voice, **East End** is strong but never striking.   [i]

BIG YOUTH

Screaming Target (nr/Trojan) 1973 •
Dreadlocks Dread (nr/Klik) 1975 (nr/Front Line) 1978 (Front Line) 1989 •
Natty Cultural Dread (nr/Trojan) 1976
Hit the Road Jack (nr/Trojan) 1976
Isaiah, First Prophet of Old (nr/Front Line) 1978
Everyday Skank—The Best of Big Youth (nr/Trojan) 1980
Some Great Big Youth (Heartbeat) 1981
The Chanting Dread inna Fine Style (Heartbeat) 1983
Live at Reggae Sunsplash (Sunsplash) 1984
A Luta Continua (Heartbeat) 1985 •
Manifestation (Heartbeat) 1988 •
Jamming in the House of Dread [tape] (ROIR) 1991

His front teeth inlaid with red, green and gold gems, Big Youth (Manley Buchanan) is probably the best-known and most popular of all reggae DJs, with a career that's been going strong since the early '70s. He began toasting in the early '70s, after working as a cab driver and a mechanic. His success was quick: records like "The Killer" and "S.90 Skank" (named after a motorcycle) scaled the Jamaican charts with ease, demonstrating his power and versatility. Many years and albums later he remains a major reggae presence, an influence on an entire generation of toasters. (He's credited with coining the term "natty dread.") If U-Roy laid the foundation, Big Youth made it happen—he gave toasting style as well as something to say.

Eccentric and startling, all of Big Youth's early records sounded radical when they first appeared, and have held up marvelously well. Featuring instrumental tracks from songs by Dennis Brown, Gregory Isaacs and others, **Screaming Target** boasts two versions of the wild title cut, along with "The Killer" and "Solomon a Gunday." **Natty Cultural Dread** features the amazing "Every Nigger Is a Star" and "Jim Squashy," which invokes John Coltrane. **Hit the Road Jack** has several loopy covers of American soul hits, including Marvin Gaye's "What's Going On," the titular Ray Charles song and Teddy Pendergrass' "Wake Up Everybody." You've never heard these songs this way—offbeat and wonderful. Although all of the Trojan releases are worth owning, **Everyday Skank** is an invaluable compilation of LP tracks and early singles.

Dreadlocks Dread (reissued by Virgin in the **Crucial Cuts** series) features "Marcus Garvey Dread" (a toast of the Burning Spear classic), "Train to Rhodesia" and "House of Dread Locks." The LP marks Big Youth's development as a composer, and his increased reliance on Rasta subject matter. Side Two has a couple of filler instrumentals, but the record is widely considered his best.

Isaiah continues the evolution heard on **Dreadlocks Dread**. Youth does more singing (or sing-jaying, as it's called) than toasting; originals outnumber covers. The groove is steady and appealing. Big Youth's recent releases are also marked by their consistency. All four Heartbeat titles boast a variety of styles, tough and relevant protest lyrics and rootsy playing. Not as wild as his early sides, these records are nonetheless some of the best contemporary reggae—authentic and uncorrupted, personal and moving. He's mellowed a bit with age—parts of **Manifestation** are downright sluggish—but Big Youth remains as formidable an artist as ever.

Rounding out the canon, **Live at Reggae Sunsplash**

(from a 1982 festival) proves he hasn't lost his ability to work a crowd, and provides a decent document of one of his better shows.   [bk]

BIRDHOUSE
Burnin' Up (nr/Vinyl Solution) 1987 (Link) 1988
Raw & Alive! (Ger. Glitterhouse) 1988
Meglamania (Link) 1989

Prominent among US-worshipping foreigners, London's Birdhouse managed to amass a sizable following for their slavishly imitative Motor City drone with a 1986 single, "My Birdman." **Burnin' Up** was released as a six-song EP in the UK and a ten-song album in America; except for Vic Maile's crunching production and an obnoxious slap at metal/rap, the quintet's second studio album, **Meglamania**, is indistinguishable.

Arguably superior to your average Athens-by-numbers or Belgium-by-numbers, the Birdhouse's Detroit-by-numbers shtick suffers only for lack of power, chops and originality; every cold, stolen nuance, every feigned emotion, every fake climax merely confirms that they've spent too much time studying French bootlegs. **Raw & Alive!** is a red vinyl live 10-inch (eight songs, mostly from the two albums) that illustrates why one should, in seeking Detroit's *real* progeny, turn to Halo of Flies or early Motörhead.   [ab]

BIRDSONGS OF THE MESOZOIC
Birdsongs of the Mesozoic EP (Ace of Hearts) 1983
Magnetic Flip (Ace of Hearts) 1984
Beat of the Mesozoic EP (Ace of Hearts) 1986
Sonic Geology [CD] (Rykodisc) 1987 •
Faultline (Cuneiform) 1989 ϕ

BIRDSONGS OF THE MESOZOIC
—ERIK LINDGREN—PINK INC.
Soundtracks (Arf Arf) 1987

ERIK LINDGREN
Polar Yet Tropical (Arf Arf) 1987

Launched in 1980 as a one-off experimental keyboard collaboration between two former Boston bandmates—Mission of Burma guitarist Roger Miller and producer/synthesist Erik Lindgren—the all-instrumental Birdsongs of the Mesozoic expanded to a real band with the addition of keyboardist Rick Scott and another Burmite, tape manipulator-turned-guitarist Martin Swope. The group (which described itself as "the world's hardest rocking chamber music quartet") remained a part-time sideline until Miller developed tinnitus and decided to continue his musical career at a lower volume, thus forcing an end to Burma. Often compared to new minimalist composers like Philip Glass and Terry Riley—who do a lot with a little—Birdsongs seem to be doing a lot with more. And probably going right over the heads of many old Burma fans in the process.

The debut EP finds Birdsongs taking quite a different tack from Burma's impassioned, chaotic noise-on-the-brink, with six instrumentals ranging from the achingly pretty romance of "The Orange Ocean" to juxtaposed chords played as much against as with each other. **Magnetic Flip** improves substantially on the first record's flat production, allowing the band's whole idea and execution to become bolder and more aggressive.

The opening of "Shiny Golden Snakes" is pure rock power chording, while the variations on Stravinsky's "The Rite of Spring" pile one thundering dissonance over another and the austere keyboard repetition starting off "Ptoccata" does recall Glass. (The loopy rendition of "Theme from Rocky and Bullwinkle" proves that the band's highbrow inclinations are only one facet of its personality.)

The five songs on **Beat of the Mesozoic** take a generally less radical approach, allowing beauty to be a prime directive. Still, "Scenes from a . . . " layers taped voices and bells over the soothing piano cant; the title piece employs numerous types of sonic effects. The tense "Lost in the B-Zone" is the most unsettling track, a complex conflation of synthesizer lines going off in a half-dozen directions, with syncopated electronic percussion tripping over itself in the background. The CD-only **Sonic Geology** retrospective draws large portions from those three records, adding two new items to complete a rewarding 72-minute package.

Side One of **Soundtracks** consists of the Birdsongs' improvised 1986 score for Michael Burlingame's independent film, *To a Random*. With Lindgren on synth, Miller on piano, Scott on Farfisa and Swope on guitar, the quietly anxious piece lacks some of the group's off-beat studio invention but maintains the usual standards of taste and musicianship. The rest of the album contains a witty Lindgren suite entitled "The Last 68 Million Years Summed Up in Less Than 13 Minutes" and "Flames in Trains," his varied 1984 collaboration with two female vocalists.

With Miller off to a fulltime solo career, Birdsongs made its 1989 album without him, adding two hornmen (Ken Field and occasional past collaborator Steve Adams) to the Swope-Lindgren-Scott core. The hour-long **Faultline** (composed individually by four of the musicians) runs the complete continuum from jazz to noise, delicate subtlety to unendurable wall-shaking chaos. Building up from the Birdsongs' past, **Faultline** shows the group to be not only alive but well on its way to forging a new stylistic synthesis.

Recorded sporadically between 1975 and 1987, Lindgren's **Polar Yet Tropical** contains an entire side of '60s (loosely defined) covers. Showing moderate wit and maximum reverent enthusiasm—these are mid-tech garage renditions rather than smugly modern reinterpretations—he confronts such classics as "I Wanna Be Your Dog," "Iron Man" and "In-a-Gadda-Da-Vida," armed with sophisticated keyboard instruments and occasional assistance by his bandmates. ("Out of Limits" is, in fact, played by Birdsongs.) The original keyboard instrumentals—colored by guest horns, reeds, strings, etc.—on the other side show Lindgren's diverse compositional skills.   [ep/i]

See also *Roger Miller, Mission of Burma*.

BIRTHDAY PARTY
The Birthday Party (Aus. Missing Link) 1980
Prayers on Fire (Thermidor) 1981 (nr/4AD) 1988 •
Drunk on the Pope's Blood EP (nr/4AD) 1982
Junkyard (nr/4AD) 1982 •
The Bad Seed EP (nr/4AD) 1983 •
The Birthday Party EP (nr/4AD) 1983 •
Mutiny! EP (nr/Mute) 1983 (nr/4AD) 1989 •

59

It's Still Living (Aus. Missing Link) 1985
A Collection ... (Aus. Missing Link) 1985 (Suite Beat)
  1986 ●
The Peel Sessions EP (nr/Strange Fruit) 1987 ●
The Peel Sessions EP (nr/Strange Fruit) 1988
Hee Haw [CD] (nr/4AD) 1989 ●
Peel Session Album (Strange Fruit-Dutch East India)
  1991 φ

BOYS NEXT DOOR
Door Door (Aus. Mushroom) 1979
Hee Haw EP (Aus. Missing Link) 1979 + 1983

LYDIA LUNCH
Honeymoon in Red (Widowspeak) 1987 ●

This intensely challenging and influential Australian band put everything it had into making inhospitable and unyielding records and wound up as the yardstick by which countless bands have since been judged. With partial comparisons possible to such noisy free-formists as the Fall, Pere Ubu and Public Image Ltd., the Birthday Party's unique sensibility sprang from singer Nick Cave (who wrote most of the lyrics) and guitarist Rowland S. Howard, who took care of a good chunk of the songwriting.

Before relocating to London from Melbourne, the Birthday Party released several Australian-only records, the first two under their original name, the Boys Next Door. **Door Door** and the five-song **Hee Haw** are surprisingly normal-sounding aggressive rock with traditional song structures and musical values. Cave's vocals invest the album with an ominous undercurrent, but the overall ambience hardly suggests the insanity that lay ahead.

That began to take form on their next release, **The Birthday Party** (the label credits the band under both monikers). Whatever their name, though, serious derangement was setting in fast. Cave's vocals and Howard's newly developed wall of feedback make **Door Door** sound positively inhibited; each track here is deeply unsettling. The LP's opening kick, "Mr Clarinet," presents an ultra-distorted organ sitting atop a stiff goose-step beat. The second side is even more crazed: "The Friend Catcher" (relentless and hypnotic) and "Happy Birthday" both contain some of the most frenzied guitar work ever captured on vinyl.

After moving to the UK, the Birthday Party recorded and released their first international LP, **Prayers on Fire**, a raging beast filled with agonized howling, braying Cave vocals flung against a backdrop of violently attacked guitars and no-wave horn noise. Drums and bass alone toe the line of established patterns; everything else ignores the song at hand and goes flat out in competition with Cave's literate invective.

The live **Drunk on the Pope's Blood** followed, half of a disc that also contains a side of live Lydia Lunch (who later formed the Immaculate Consumptives with Cave, and worked with Howard and others in the axis). Recorded in London at the end of 1981, the disc is honestly described on the jacket as "16 minutes of sheer hell!" Drawing two of its four songs from **Prayers on Fire**, Cave and Co. growl and shriek through the slow pieces with stunning gruesomeness—incomprehensibility aside, no one else has ever suffered with a more effective sonic display than what's in these grooves. **Junkyard** has less energy to the sound, but still man-ages to lift blood pressure with such assaults as "Dead Joe," "Big-Jesus-Trash-Can" and "6" Gold Blade."

Three BP EPs (plus a reissue of the Boys Next Door's **Hee Haw**) were released in 1983, the same year the band broke up. The first was **The Bad Seed**, four concise cuts of incredible visceral impact. From the slow psycho-blues of "Deep in the Woods" to the frenzied blur of "Sonny's Burning," it leaves the listener helpless and enthralled. **The Birthday Party** EP compiles five tracks from singles: the A-side ("The Friend Catcher") of the band's 1980 UK debut plus 1981's "Release the Bats" b/w "Blast Off" and "Mr Clarinet" b/w "Happy Birthday." Finally, the posthumous **Mutiny!** was released at the correct time: it wouldn't have been easy to follow. Like **The Bad Seed**, it mixes two furious numbers with a pair of funereal dirges. "Jennifers Veil," a harrowing lament, is perhaps the band's finest song ever—neither John Cale nor Alfred Hitchcock was ever this scary.

Released in Australia two years later, **It's Still Living** (recorded in Melbourne in 1982) offers spirited performances of material from **Prayers on Fire** and **Junkyard** and, although decried by the band, is recommended for fans. The first **Peel Sessions** EP dates from April 1981; the second from December of the same year; the LP joins 'em up. Tracks include "Release the Bats," "Pleasure Heads Must Burn" and "Rowland Around in That Stuff."

A Collection . . . (also known as **The Best and the Rarest**) takes its tracks from **Junkyard**, **Hee Haw**, **Prayers on Fire** and some singles, adding a few alternate versions and other rarities. The American CD is somewhat different.

Having already issued CDs of **Prayers on Fire** (with two bonus tracks from an Australian 45) and **Junkyard**, 4AD brought the rest of the band's post-**Door Door** studio catalogue into the laser age with two 1989 reissues. One disc contains **Mutiny!** and **The Bad Seed**, adding two vintage outtakes previously issued on an Australian 45. **Hee Haw** pairs that EP's five songs with **The Birthday Party** EP, adding "The Friend Catcher"'s two B-sides and three more songs to create an expanded version of the **Birthday Party** album.

Prior to packing it in for other projects, bits and pieces were recorded for what was supposed to have been a Birthday Party/Lydia Lunch album. Shelved and subsequently tinkered with by Lunch and Clint Ruin, **Honeymoon in Red** finally saw the light of day in 1987 on Lunch's label. (Slow tempos and sparse arrangements suggest that Lunch dominated the proceedings and/or had plenty of input come mixing time.) Howard and bassist Tracy Pew (an epileptic who died in 1986) are credited, but Cave and guitarist/keyboardist/drummer Harvey appear under pseudonyms (Cave is Lunch's "dead twin" on "Done Dun" and "a drunk cowboy junkie" on "Dead in the Head"). The tracks all employ different personnel permutations, with guests—including Thurston Moore, Ruin and Genevieve McGuckin (These Immortal Souls)—adding to the morbid racket. The lyrics are real storybook/fairytale fodder (it rains blood, people cry blood, etc.), but the music is eminently suitable for such visions. The best cut is McGuckin's "Three Kings," on which Howard and Moore combine for some of the most haunting guitar noise ever recorded five years apart. [i/dgs]

See also *Barracudas, Blue Ruin, Nick Cave and the Bad Seeds, Crime and the City Solution, (Die) Haut, Lydia Lunch, Nikki Sudden, These Immortal Souls.*

BISHOPS
See *Count Bishops.*

BITCH MAGNET
Star Booty (Roman Candle-Communion) 1988 ●
Umber (Communion) 1989 ●
Ben Hur (Communion) 1990 ●

On **Star Booty**, this North Carolina-based trio (originally formed at Oberlin College in Ohio) lays out eight sheets of feedback-heavy fuzz-punk, well-played and raucous but lacking in any real personality that would make it stand out among others offering similar wares.

Things get a bit more streamlined on **Umber**, where songs with real melodies emerge from the loud miasma. With ex-Squirrel Bait guitarist David Grubbs (who splits his time between Bitch Magnet and his own band, Bastro) contributing mightily to the din, the anthemic "Motor" sets the pace for a collection of ten noisefests, some of which are painted in a deep shade of Big Black. Though the record's slow tracks sound quite a bit like contemporaries Nice Strong Arm, Bitch Magnet finally manages to overcome this excessive familiarity by serving up a thick guitar-rich soup that splashes by quite powerfully on its own. (The **Umber** CD and cassette append **Star Booty**.)

Ben Hur includes a lyric sheet, but with lines like "What beats the taste of lye on a swollen tongue raw with sores" it probably shouldn't have. Thankfully, the lyrics are unintelligible and decidedly secondary to the seismic rumblings of the industrial-strength rhythm section and slices of noise-funk guitar. "Dragon," the excellent nine-minutes-plus opener, lives up to the album's epic title, but Bitch Magnet's derivativeness (right down to the bullhorned vocals) will do nothing to shake its well-earned Little Black tag. [db]

See also *Bastro.*

BIZ MARKIE
Goin' Off (Cold Chillin'-Warner Bros.) 1988 ●
DIABOLICAL BIZ MARKIE
The Biz Never Sleeps (Cold Chillin'-Warner Bros.) 1989 ●

Rap's reigning clown prince, Long Island's Biz Markie (Marcel Hall), has a juvenile sense of humor and a pronounced speech impediment, but his relaxed rhyming style and uninhibited silliness make him a winning entertainer. Produced by long-time associate Marley Marl and co-written by the Biz, Marl and Big Daddy Kane, **Goin' Off** is a dubious debut, opening with a supremely obnoxious ode to something too tasteless to go into before settling down to a mildly entertaining program of inoffensive nonsense.

Although it also begins on a worthless note ("Dedication") and includes a number about body odors, **The Biz Never Sleeps** is a much better record that solidly establishes Biz Markie's unique character. Producing (with disconcertingly abrupt fades) and writing it all himself, the Biz re-emerges as an ingenious nut, punctuating his winsome romantic stories with odd musical bits and wholesome wit. A dinky piano line and a hopelessly off-key refrain keep popping up in the sad/funny tale of a faithless lover ("Just a Friend"), while an equally inane bit of crooning (in a goony Barry White voice) breezes through "Spring Again," an infectious hymn to warm weather. But the Biz isn't only geared for laughs: with a neat horn sample adding to the evocative groove, he dips into nostalgic recollection for the tender tribute of "My Man Rich." [i]

BLACK & WHITE
Don't Know Yet (Atlantic) 1989 ●

This LA rap duo mixes more than races: the rhythm tracks on **Don't Know Yet** are uncut heavy metal with a booming drum sound. Unfortunately, the MCs, both ostensibly gang-connected, are not especially convincing (although only one of them has a lame Val-boy accent); the pair doesn't so much rap as shout inane and atonal lyrics in crude rhythmic synch with the music. Despite the credible notion of two relevant covers—Sly Stone's "Don't Call Me Nigger. . .Whitey" and Jimi Hendrix's "I Don't Live Today"—this attempt at a novel hybrid is a gimmicky failure. [i]

BLACKBEARD
See *Dennis Bovell.*

BLACKBIRD
Blackbird (Iloki) 1988 ●
Blackbird (Iloki) 1989

After the proto-cowpunk Rank and File failed to make its way through the music-industry maze and reach a mainstream audience, brothers Chip and Tony Kinman (originally of the punk Dils) more or less told the business to take a flying leap by reinventing themselves once again as a ridiculously uncommercial post-industrial drone-pop duo. Ironically, by the time Blackbird had released a couple of records, there was actually a sizable audience for industrial music, and the Kinmans' concept no longer seemed so weird.

Mixing guitar and bass with bargain-basement drum machines and other low-tech noisemakers, Blackbird makes dark, clattery music that's not as far removed from the brothers' punk and country roots as it might appear. Their strong songwriting and the humanity of their off-kilter vocal blend consistently bubbles beneath the noise.

Blackbird's two eponymous Iloki albums are completely separate entities. The first (red cover) is the noisier and riffier of the two, and contains Blackbird's most memorable song, "Howl." The second (black cover with pink lizard) leans more towards melody, with the uncharacteristic love song "Hold Me" and an interesting version of Lou Reed's "What Goes On." [au]

See also *Dils, Rank and File.*

BLACK FLAG
Nervous Breakdown EP (SST) 1978 ●
Jealous Again EP (SST) 1980 ●
Damaged (SST) 1981 ●
Everything Went Black (SST) 1983 + 1984 ●
The First Four Years (SST) 1984 ●

My War (SST) 1984 ●
Family Man (SST) 1984 ●
Slip It In (SST) 1984 ●
Live '84 [tape] (SST) 1984 φ
Loose Nut (SST) 1985 ●
The Process of Weeding Out EP (SST) 1985 ●
In My Head (SST) 1985 ●
Who's Got the 10 1/2? (SST) 1986 ●
Wasted ... Again (SST) 1987 ●
I Can See You EP (SST) 1989 ●

Black Flag was, for all intents and purposes, America's first hardcore band. They emerged from Southern California to gain international prominence, touring enough to become a major attraction in virtually every city where a scene existed and undoubtedly inspiring others to get in the game. Via the band's still-thriving SST label, Black Flag played an essential role in the development and popularization of American punk. Through countless revolving-door personnel changes—which spawned numerous spinoff bands along the way—Black Flag persevered until 1986, finally dissolving after locating and exploring the zone where punk and heavy metal intersect and overlap.

The four-song 7-inch **Nervous Breakdown** (SST 001) and the five-song 12-inch **Jealous Again** offer brief but convincing blasts of primal punk roar by two early lineups; the ghost of the Sex Pistols comes floating through the brazen blare of guitars and vocals. **Damaged** features a superior cast (most significantly, Washington DC singer Henry Rollins, ex-S.O.A., had joined) and includes the culture classic "TV Party," as well as other goofy paeans to dissipated suburban life ("Six Pack," "Thirsty and Miserable") and the classic American punk anthem, "Rise Above." Rollins' hoarse shout grates, but the barely contained rock energy and tongue-in-cheek lyrics make **Damaged** a great rock'n'roll LP that isn't beholden to any clichéd genre. (The **Damaged** CD also contains the contents of **Jealous Again**.)

In the midst of a horrible legal dispute with Unicorn Records, the group found itself enjoined from using the Black Flag name and logo on any new records, and resorted to releasing the double-album outtakes-and-more career retrospective, **Everything Went Black**, with only a listing of band members on the cover for identification. (It was later reissued with all the proper nomenclature and unexpurgated liner notes.) The tracks, which date from 1978 to 1981 (the album's European edition is substantially different), feature various configurations of the Black Flag gene pool attacking a motley collection of songs. ("Police Story," "Gimmie Gimmie Gimmie," "Damaged" and "Depression" all get done twice.) As a developmental Black Flag sampler, **Everything Went Black** is both illuminating and entertaining, but the real treat is Side Four, "Crass Commercialism," a hysterically funny collection of crazed radio spots for Flag gigs, most with music, that say a lot about the cultural milieu in which the band existed. **The First Four Years** is an extensive compilation of early releases, including the 1981 **Six Pack** maxi-single, **Jealous Again** and two tracks from a New Alliance compilation.

Following the resolution of their litigation (Unicorn helpfully went bankrupt), a new and prolific Black Flag—Rollins, guitarist Greg Ginn (who doubled in the studio on bass, using the pseudonym Dale Nixon) and

Descendents drummer Bill Stevenson—drifted vaguely towards metal on **My War**, a mediocre album with some interminably long songs. (One plodding side has a grand total of three!) There *are* some good punk tunes ("I Love You") but elsewhere, a labored heavy-bottomed sound and appallingly bad guitar solos cross the line from sarcasm into sheer awfulness. Rollins' vocals are the same as ever, which makes the bad tracks even stranger.

Kira Roessler (sister of 45 Grave keyboardist Paul Roessler) took over on bass for **Slip It In**. With far clearer sound on the eight tracks, the LP further blurs the line between moronic punk and moronic metal. Songs are mostly built on trite riffs repeated endlessly; the rude lyrics of the title song are performed complete with enthusiastic sex noises for anyone who fails to grasp the point and/or be offended by it. Other songs are less tasteless but little more interesting. **Family Man** deconstructs Black Flag into a side of Rollins reading his poetry and a side of group instrumentals.

Live '84 puts the band's recent creative output and selected oldies onstage for an hour of wanton loud fun. Black Flag concerts were typically an utter mess, which suits the songs perfectly, making this chaotic explosion naturally one of their best releases.

Black Flag continued their torrid pace in 1985, releasing three new records: **Loose Nut**, **The Process of Weeding Out** and **In My Head**. **Weeding Out** is a Henryless instrumental EP: four lengthy improvs displaying unexpected technical prowess (especially Kira, on "Your Last Affront") and a new side to the band. There's a certain nostalgia factor for those who remember Canned Heat or Ten Years After in the old days, but on its own merits, little here would entice you into multiple listenings. The other two records feature the complete Rollins-Ginn-Kira-Stevenson lineup and are fairly similar: nine songs each of varied but mostly medium-tempo guitar rock that keeps a safe distance from metal, hardcore *and* sleaze. **Loose Nut** has clean sound, Rollins' brutally self-hating "This Is Good" and lyrics on the inner sleeve—the best Black Flag LP of 1985. (The **In My Head** cassette contains three bonus tracks.)

With new drummer Anthony Martinez, Black Flag recorded the live **Who's Got the 10 1/2?** in Portland, Oregon on 23 August 1985. Besides a great cover photo of the band's actual tour calendar that says more about the rock'n'roll life than any half-dozen magazine articles, the album features hot versions of '84-'85 material, plus a genuine oldie, "Gimmie, Gimmie, Gimmie." (The cassette and CD add 24 more minutes of fun.)

The posthumous **Wasted . . . Again** neatly recapitulates Black Flag's high career points with a dozen essential tracks, from "Wasted" to "Drinking and Driving." Everything you'd want in a single disc is included, and brief annotation adds the veneer of history.

In 1989, SST quietly issued **I Can See You**, an EP of four previously unreleased studio tracks by the '84-'85 quartet, probably recorded around the time of **In My Head**. The music isn't extraordinary for that era of Black Flag, but Rollins' colorful vocal performances —on the complacent "Kickin' & Stickin' " and the aggrieved "You Let Me Down" especially—make this a surprisingly rich nugget.   [i]

See also *Circle Jerks, D.C.3, Dos, Gone, Minutemen, Henry Rollins, S.O.A., SWA*.

BLACKGIRLS

Speechless EP (Tom Tom-Black Park) 1987
Procedure (Mammoth) 1989 ●
Happy (Mammoth) 1991 ●

No, they're not and, yes, they are. The three white North Carolina women of Blackgirls perform intricate chamber music on acoustic guitar, violin and piano, creating an uncommon art-folk/classical hybrid with occasional Celtic inflections. But singer/songwriters Eugenia Lee and Dana Kletter both have dry, unsteady voices and a taste for cuteness and/or neurotic hypersensitivity in their lyrics. Combined with the dizzying polyrhythmic tides of the instrumental/vocal arrangements on **Procedure**, the accomplished music is charmless and uninviting.

With Joe Boyd (of Fairport Convention fame) again providing a crystalline production job, Blackgirls refine and smooth out their art (if not their diary-entry lyrics) on **Happy**, a sophisticated and accomplished-sounding record that seems, for the first time, to acknowledge the possible presence of an audience. While a lot of the album sticks to its predecessor's choppy complexity, the arrangement of "Charleston" is simplified to the point of easy appeal.   [i]

BLACK UHURU

Love Crisis (nr/Third World) 1977
Showcase (Heartbeat) 1979
Sinsemilla (Mango) 1980 ●
Black Sounds of Freedom (Greensleeves) 1981 ●
Red (Mango) 1981 ●
Black Uhuru (nr/Virgin) 1981 ●
Guess Who's Coming to Dinner (Heartbeat) 1981 ●
Tear It Up–Live (Mango) 1982
Chill Out (Mango) 1982
The Dub Factor (Mango) 1983
Anthem (Mango) 1983 ●
Reggae Greats (Mango) 1985 ●
Brutal (RAS) 1986 ●
Brutal Dub (RAS) 1986
Positive (RAS) 1987 ●
The Positive Dub (RAS) [tape] (ROIR) 1988
Live in New York City (Rohit) 1988 ●
Now (Mesa) 1990 ●
Now Dub (Mesa) 1990 ●
Iron Storm (Mesa) 1991 ●

JUNIOR REID

One Blood (Big Life-Mercury) 1990 φ

MICHAEL ROSE

Proud (nr/RCA) 1990 ●

The leading second generation reggae vocal group, Black Uhuru was formed in Jamaica in 1974 by Derrick "Duckie" Simpson; after a couple of false starts, he enlisted Michael Rose, whose quivery voice makes him sound like a Rasta cantor, and recorded **Love Crisis**—competent but hardly distinctive (although the best track, "I Love King Selassie," survived to become a live staple). (**Black Sounds of Freedom** is a remix of the same album.) After American expatriate Puma (Sandra) Jones joined to add haunting high harmony, Black Uhuru joined forces with Sly and Robbie; their riddims pushed the singing along with the force of a tank.

Showcase, a compilation of their early singles

("Abortion," "General Penitentiary," "Guess Who's Coming to Dinner," etc.), is an unqualified classic. In 1981, the album was reissued by Heartbeat as **Guess Who's Coming to Dinner** and by Virgin as **Black Uhuru**.

Sinsemilla firmly established Uhuru as an album act. The record delivers a level of consistency only Bob Marley himself had achieved. Their breakthrough, however, came with **Red**. From the first track, "Youth of Eglington," listeners—even those not particularly interested in reggae—had a compelling reason to discover Black Uhuru.

The band spent considerable time on the road. A live album (**Tear It Up**) recycles a lot of the material from **Showcase** and is only a so-so approximation of their in-concert excitement. But **Chill Out**, the next studio effort, is great. Rose had moved to New York and takes on the city in the title cut; "Darkness," "Emotional Slaughter" and others reveal a departure from Rasta subject matter. **The Dub Factor** is a ferocious dub disc, more of which can be found on Sly and Robbie's **Raiders of the Lost Dub**.

The release of **Anthem** was troubled. The original issue was remixed and revised for America; that version was subsequently re-released in Europe. In any case, it's a spotty record, despite a couple of killer tracks ("Party Next Door" and Steve Van Zandt's "Solidarity"). Sly and Robbie's synthetics are more pronounced, perhaps to compensate for the weak material and convictionless performances. (Ironically, it won a Grammy award in the US.) A decent hits collection in the **Reggae Greats** series followed. Then Michael Rose left to go solo. After five years of scattered singles (and a short-lived change of name spelling to Mykal Roze), he finally released an album at the end of 1990.

On **Brutal**, Black Uhuru unveiled their new lead singer, Junior Reid, who displays an awkward tendency to mimic Rose. Sly and Robbie still provide backup; Arthur Baker is among the producers. While the Reid/Simpson songs attempt a number of different styles, not all are successful. (A companion dub LP, featuring mixes by Baker, Scientist and Steven Stanley is also available.)

Live in New York City, recorded at the old Ritz in the fall of 1987, is the last Black Uhuru album to feature the Reid-Simpson-Jones lineup. With backing provided by some of Jamaica's top players (including guitarist Earl "Chinna" Smith, who now plays with Ziggy Marley, and drummer Santa Davis, who played with Peter Tosh), Reid's spicy lead vocals and between-song improvs make this a perfect souvenir of the band's '86-'87 era. The set includes a lot of material from **Brutal**, as well as some of Reid's solo numbers ("Shock-a-Lock," "Foreign Mind") and items dating back to Michael Rose's days ("Emotional Slaughter," "Solidarity").

Puma Jones left the lineup and was replaced by Olafunke, a Jamaican-born soundalike; **Positive** shows the reconstituted group moving forward. The LP finds Reid coming into his own as a vocalist, and features a few songs that are strikingly original (Simpson's apocalyptic "Fire City," for example). Sly and Robbie continue to be the featured musicians, but producer Steven Stanley offers flourishes and variations on their familiar martial drums and bass lines. While there are echoes of the old Black Uhuru on **Positive**, a new band identity and sound are slowly emerging. An okay dub version of the LP has also been released, first as a limited-pressing LP, then on cassette with an added cut. (The **Positive** CD contains four dub mixes.)

On 28 January 1990, Puma Jones, 36, died of cancer and was buried in South Carolina, her birthplace. She was one of the great women of reggae, Rasta, black pride and women's rights, and one of the only females to be part of a predominantly male group that reached such international acclaim.

Ironically, around the time of Jones' death, Black Uhuru released **Now**, featuring what is considered to be the band's original lineup: founder Duckie Simpson, Don Carlos (a solo artist for many years) and Garth Dennis (ex-Wailing Souls). Revisiting the group's early vocal-trio sound, this reunion album is highlighted by more richly produced remakes of three songs from **Love Crisis**: "Army Band," "Peace and Love" (originally titled "Willow Tree") and "Heathen" (aka "Eden"). Despite the different sound (compelling, but less biting than usual), the message—militancy, prophecy, truth and rights—remains, as does the lyrical punch, in songs like the anti-crack "Reggae Rock," the romantic "Thinking of You" and "Take Heed." A cover of "Hey Joe" rounds out the album, with roots reggae, pop harmony and rock guitar.

Now Dub is a dub version of the LP that stretches the limits of the form. A Guy Called Gerald's genre-bending remix of "Reggae Rock" is a crazyhouse version that fixes Uhuru's floating vocals to pounding bass and a wall-pulverizing drum beat. The dub of "Hey Joe" is even more astonishing.

Resuming his solo career, Junior Reid had a massive Jamaican hit in 1989 with "One Blood," which became the title track of his slick, electro-reggae album the following year. (Puma Jones sings backup on a bizarre cover of "Eleanor Rigby.") Covering a few other bases, Reid appears on Coldcut's 1988 "Stop This Crazy Thing" and did a guest turn on the Soup Dragons' "I'm Free." [bk/aw]

See also *Sly and Robbie*.

RUBÉN BLADES
Maestra Vida: Primera Parte (Fania) 1980
Maestra Vida: Segunda Parte (Fania) 1980
Nothing but the Truth (Elektra) 1988 ●
RUBÉN BLADES Y SEIS DEL SOLAR
Greatest Hits (Musica Latina Int'l) 1983
Buscando America (Elektra) 1984 ●
Escenas (Elektra) 1985 ●
Agua de Luna (Elektra) 1986 ●
RUBÉN BLADES Y SON DEL SOLAR
Antecedente (Elektra) 1988 ●
Live! (Elektra) 1990 φ
VARIOUS ARTISTS
Crossover Dreams (Elektra) 1986 ●

Rubén Blades is the first major salsa performer to integrate rock aesthetics into his music. After a successful stint with Willie Colón, the Panamanian-born New Yorker went solo, rocketing to the top of salsa charts with songs that avoided the music's clichés in favor of topical narratives and carefully crafted imagery. The best of these, including the classic gangster tale "Pedro Navaja," are found on **Greatest Hits**.

In 1984, Blades signed two contracts with Elektra, one for Spanish-language recordings, the other for English-language ones. **Buscando America** stands as the finest of his major-label recordings to date. His group, Seis del Solar, includes four percussionists and two electric keyboardists. Instead of salsa's traditional horn section, Blades sings frank songs about abortion, Latin America's political disappeared and the banality of evil.

Blades is also a screen actor. His first starring role was in *Crossover Dreams*, which charted the rise and fall of a *salsero* who denies his roots in search of American chart success. The soundtrack LP includes two pop tunes by Blades, plus a healthy selection of salsa standards performed by some of the field's finest players.

Escenas finds Blades making first steps towards the sort of crossover (he calls it "convergence") acceptability he so obviously desires. Joe Jackson and Linda Ronstadt make guest appearances, but except for "Muévete," things don't sizzle quite so much as before. In an audacious experiment with tepid results, some of Blades' songs on **Agua de Luna** were inspired by Gabriel García Márquez short stories.

Setting his band aside, Blades collaborated with Elvis Costello, Lou Reed and Sting on **Nothing but the Truth**, his first all-English album. Recorded with studio journeymen, the music ranges from hard-core salsa to mainstream rock to political doo-wop. The tunes co-written by Costello hold up the best, but that's to be expected. Following that record, as if to atone for an apparent sell-out (sorry, "crossover"), Blades quickly rejoined the newly aligned five-man Son del Solar and made the rewardingly rootsy **Antecedente**.

The following year, with eleven musicians suavely mixing trombones, timbales, piano *and* synthesizer, Blades recorded a vibrant live album at New York's Lone Star Roadhouse. Ignoring recent albums, the material (with the exception of "Pedro Navaja" and one other) is drawn entirely from **Escenas** and **Buscando America**. [rg/i]

See also *Sting*.

BLAKE BABIES
Nicely, Nicely (Chew-bud) 1987
Slow Learners (nr/Utility) 1989 ●
Earwig (Mammoth) 1989 ●
Sunburn (Mammoth) 1990 ●
Rosy Jack World EP (Mammoth) 1991 ●

With singer/bassist (and former Berklee music student) Juliana Hatfield's voice as the pivotal love-'em/leave-'em factor, Boston's Blake Babies play peppy post-mod pop that has a few teeth. On the first album, drummer Freda Boner and guitarist John Strohm (both natives of Indiana), Hatfield and a bassist run through collegiate numbers like "Let Them Eat Chewy Granola Bars," "Swill and the Cocaine Sluts" and "Better 'n You" (a handsomely harmonized duet with Evan Dando of the Lemonheads, a band for whom Strohm moonlighted on drums), demonstrating a facility for tunefully presentable songs and the unsettling range of Hatfield's all-over-the-place singing. The habit of suddenly abandoning a nice mid-range melody to search out a high note that may elude her makes Hatfield an unpredictable and inconsistent quantity.

Dando played bass on **Slow Learners** (Hatfield didn't take over that responsibility until sessions for the next LP), a more accomplished and refined seven-song collection—incorporating a country accent—that is entirely duplicated on **Earwig**. That album, which contains two other 1988 recordings (with a different guest bassist) and a half-dozen 1989 products of the now-autonomous trio (including a fair sexual inversion of the Stooges' "Loose"), sets its sternly judgmental attacks ("You Don't Give Up," "Take Your Head off My Shoulder," "Outta My Head," "Your Way or the Highway," etc.) into consistently attractive textured guitar pop.

The burst of feedback that begins both **Sunburn** and Hatfield's "I'm Not Your Mother" isn't nearly as abrasive as the song's venomously petulant lyrics. In general, though, Juliana's off the offensive on the Blakes' best album: her casually blunt lyrics range from resigned victimization ("A Million Years") to haunting desolation ("Gimme Some Mirth") to frightening fantasies of self-destruction ("Watch Me Now, I'm Calling"). Meanwhile, Strohm's songs ("Girl in a Box," a rare vocal turn, and "Train," a duet) and his collaborations (the exceptional "Out There") provide a much needed lyrical alternative. With some of the band's catchiest tunes ("Look Away" for one) and fewer vocal misadventures (effective harmonies mask some of those remaining), **Sunburn** is an ironic and frequently moving mixture of beauty and sadness. [i]

See also *Lemonheads*.

BLANCMANGE

Happy Families (Island) 1982
Mange Tout (London-Sire) 1984 ●
Believe You Me (London-Sire) 1985 ●
Second Helpings: The Best of Blancmange (nr/London) 1990 ●

WEST INDIA COMPANY

Ave Maria EP (nr/London) 1984
Music from New Demons (Editions EG) 1989 ●

One of the synth-pop era's more individual and original duos, Stephen Luscombe and Neil Arthur mixed dominant percussion with bizarre, often exotic seasonings to create tracks with abundant personality and enormous dance potential. The one major drawback is Arthur's voice: a rough, unpleasant instrument which becomes riddled with melodrama when he gets excited.

On **Happy Families**, Blancmange offer typically eccentric concepts—"God's Kitchen," "Living on the Ceiling"—in varied settings that fall into two general styles: (1) Loud, rhythmic and derivative of Talking Heads. These tunes, especially "Feel Me," suffer from extreme monochromatic tediousness. (2) Delicate and reserved. "I've Seen the Word" and others are quite lovely, resembling the spare grace of mid-period Orchestral Manoeuvres in the Dark.

Mange Tout (a brilliant bilingual pun) is simultaneously a bit sillier and grander overall, using more horns, woodwinds and strings than before. Largely neglecting option 2 but not sounding much like the Heads

either, Blancmange opt to let the beat send the message, while thankfully maintaining better song quality and, thus, less boredom. The four major tracks—"Don't Tell Me," "My Baby," "Blind Vision" and "That's Love That It Is"—all offer different levels of melodiousness (most pretty high) with Arthur's vocals, though improved, still an occasional stumbling block.

Believe You Me is an ambitious undertaking, recorded in seven different studios with four producers and zillions of guest musicians. The results are hardly as inconsistent as they might have been; in fact, the restrained album is quite agreeable, reasonably free of the overzealousness, busyness and absurdity that diminished some of the duo's prior work. The songs aren't consistently wonderful, but simplicity and understatement make inquisitive tracks like "Don't You Love It All" (with flugelhorn played by Hugh Masekela), "What's Your Problem?" and "Why Don't They Leave Things Alone?" pleasant, if not immediately memorable.

Second Helpings is a straightforward (albeit incomplete) compilation of UK chart singles—from 1982's "God's Kitchen" through 1985's "What's Your Problem?"—that pretty much covers the high points of Blancmange's recording career. But considering that all ten tracks (including two B-sides) come from the band's three albums, fans can skip this serving with impunity.

Following Blancmange's 1986 split, Luscombe devoted himself to the poly-cultural West India Company, an experimental trio whose 1984 vinyl debut employed the voice of famed Bombay film singer Asha Bhosle. Created as the performance soundtrack for a show by Montreal avant-dance company La La La Human Steps (known for their work on Bowie's '90 tour), **New Demons** alternates vocal selections and instrumentals, putting traditional Indian music (and other sources) through a sympathetic British art wringer. Despite the similarity of their basic components, the decidedly non-pop WIC bears no resemblance to Monsoon; the trio's rich and cerebral blend—both in terms of instrumentation and presentation—is quite original. [i]

BL'AST!

The Power of Expression (Wishing Well) 1984 (SST) 1987 ●
It's in My Blood (SST) 1987 ●
Take the Manic Ride (SST) 1989 ●

Formed in 1982 as M.A.D., this Santa Cruz quartet was obviously touched by the message of Black Flag's mid-period work. The rumble on the bottom, the elliptical scrambling of Mike Neider's guitar and the bellicose roar of Clifford Dinsmore's vocals all bring post-**Damaged** Flag to mind. Considering the lame thrash that many of their skate-punk peers were purveying at the time, Bl'ast! should be saluted for taking a far less generic stance. (The CD of **It's in My Blood** includes both sides of the "School's Out" single.) [bc]

BLASTERS

American Music (Rollin' Rock) 1980
The Blasters (Slash-Warner Bros.) 1981
Over There: Live at the Venue, London EP (Slash-Warner Bros.) 1982
Non Fiction (Slash-Warner Bros.) 1983

Hard Line (Slash-Warner Bros.) 1985
The Blasters Collection (Slash-Warner Bros.) 1991 φ

They say everything old becomes new again, and California's Blasters proved it in 1981 by jumping into the national spotlight with an utterly familiar brew of blues, rockabilly and rock'n'roll. Detractors might call them little more than an updated Canned Heat—as if anything were wrong with that—but such criticism ignores their strengths: tight ensemble work, swingin' original tunes in the classic mold and Phil Alvin's ageless, confident vocals.

American Music appeared on an independent rockabilly revival label, which is probably one reason it didn't reach a larger audience. The band already had total control of R&B and rock conventions, fusing them into a supple, flowing style. Although there's not quite as much sting here as later on, Dave Alvin's guitar work displays plenty of spirit. Oldies like "Buzz Buzz Buzz" and "I Wish You Would" (Billy Boy Arnold via the Yardbirds) mingle with catchy new tunes like "Marie, Marie," later a big UK hit for Shakin' Stevens.

The Blasters established the quintet nationwide. Originally released on LA independent Slash, it did so well that the label was able to strike a licensing/distribution deal with Warner Bros. No wonder: it smokes. The band is tighter than a drum, and Dave Alvin's songs—including "No Other Girl," a re-recorded "Marie, Marie" and "Border Radio"—have a joyous, irresistible momentum. R&B legend Lee Allen guests on sax.

Highlighted by a crackling hot sound, the six-cut live in London EP serves as a good introduction to the Blasters, but offers no new wrinkles. Definitely suitable for parties, though.

Any lingering suspicions that the Blasters were just an oldies band at heart were surely dispelled by the fine **Non Fiction**. Dave Alvin's essay on real life, the LP presents a series of well-crafted vignettes reminiscent of Robbie Robertson's work with the Band. Songs like "One More Dance" and "Fool's Paradise" depict the trials and tribulations of the little people, while "Long White Cadillac" laments Hank Williams. The playing on the self-produced record is smoother and not as quaint as before.

A shade less stirring than **Non Fiction**, **Hard Line** reprises that LP's formula, but also includes a blatant stab at commercialism. Although "Colored Lights," penned for the Blasters by John Cougar Mellencamp, isn't bad, other songs are more heartfelt. Highlights include "Trouble Bound" and "Help You Dream," both featuring the Jordanaires (of Elvis Presley fame for you young'uns).

In 1986, Dave Alvin left to join X, briefly replacing Billy Zoom; he soon moved on to launch his own solo career. But he also worked on other people's projects; for instance, backing Syd Straw on her '89 tour. Alvin's replacement in the Blasters was a guitarist known as Hollywood Fats (Michael Mann), who tragically died a few months later, bringing Alvin briefly back into the fold. Ironically, Billy Zoom later joined the Blasters, who have been less active since Phil Alvin began attending graduate school.

The Blasters Collection assembles 20 tracks, including three previously unreleased numbers.   [jy]

See also *Dave Alvin, Phil Alvin, X*.

PETER BLEGVAD

The Naked Shakespeare (nr/Virgin) 1983
Knights Like This (nr/Virgin) 1985
Downtime (nr/Recommended) 1988
King Strut and Other Stories (nr/Silvertone) 1990 ●

SLAPP HAPPY

Sort Of (Ger. Polydor) 1972
Acnalbasac Noom (Ger. Polydor) 1973
  (nr/Recommended) 1982 (Cuneiform) 1988 ●
Slapp Happy (nr/Virgin) 1974

SLAPP HAPPY/HENRY COW

Desperate Straights (nr/Virgin) 1975 (nr/Recommended) 1982
In Praise of Learning (nr/Virgin) 1975 (Red) 1979 [CD] (East Side Digital) 1991 ●

JOHN GREAVES & PETER BLEGVAD

Kew. Rhone. (nr/Virgin) 1977

If Peter Blegvad is one of America's most underrated songwriters, it's partly due to the fact that the New Yorker—who is also an accomplished illustrator—has lived in England for most of the past two decades, and few of his records have been issued in the US. An affecting singer and a fine guitarist, Blegvad has an uncanny knack for creating literate lyrics—a golden triangle of emotion, intellect and humor—and combining them with enduring melodies. A restless spirit that displays no patience for cliché runs through all of his work. And while Blegvad has hiked with many stellar companions, he has always blazed an utterly personal trail.

In Germany in the early '70s, the Connecticut-born Blegvad, British keyboardist/composer Anthony Moore and his wife, German singer Dagmar Krause, began working their own little corner of the obscure-pop tapestry as Slapp Happy. On the liner notes to the trio's first album, **Sort Of**, Blegvad wittily tags the band as "champions of Naïve Rock, the Douannier-Rousseau sound," which pegged them perfectly—sort of. With its slightly discordant guitars, deliberately simple lyrics and Dagmar's naturally doomy voice trying to come off winsome or chipper as the song may demand, **Sort Of** is willfully naïve and, at its worst, a bit affected.

At its best, though, the band was refreshing, diverting and sometimes moving. The second Slapp Happy LP, **Acnalbasac Noom**, is a gem from start to finish. Blegvad crafts some wonderful, offhandedly literary lyrics while Moore provides sophisticated tunes to match. (As the group didn't contain a rhythm section, both albums feature the rhythm section from Faust, not that you'd ever guess.) **Slapp Happy**, using anonymous studio musicians as needed, includes a handful of previously recorded songs in drastically rearranged versions, some including ambitious but unsuccessful string backing.

Following those three records, Slapp Happy and labelmates Henry Cow—a symbiotic blend of art and politics united by equally offbeat sensibilities about musicmaking—joined forces to produced a pair of highly rated albums. Several years later, Blegvad and Henry Cow bassist John Greaves made a record together. In the early '80s, Blegvad began a solo career.

Andy Partridge's production of **The Naked Shakespeare** is entirely too slick and busy. Only the songs given relatively simple arrangements are delightful, particularly "You Can't Miss It," "Vermont" and the pensive title track. Also noteworthy is the chilling rape-nightmare of "Irma," a mostly spoken piece set to Eno-ish ambient synth.

Engaged by Virgin in an unabashed effort to sell Blegvad to UK pop radio, David Lord (Peter Gabriel, etc.) did a spectacular misproduction job on **Knights Like This**. (Shades of Phil Spector's off-base pairing with Leonard Cohen.) Like Cohen, Blegvad is an idiosyncratic writer whose songs work best in uncomplicated settings. Here, most of his luminous lyrics are lost amid the overwrought pop arrangements, full of strings, backup choruses and synthesized percussion.

Back in New York during the early '80s, Blegvad fell in with the burgeoning downtown improv scene. He recorded with John Zorn and, through his friendship with Anton Fier, became part of the Golden Palominos family. Blegvad served as "vocal coach" on the group's first album, and co-wrote half the songs of the third (**Blast of Silence**), on which he also performed. In 1989, Blegvad played on sometime-Palomino Syd Straw's solo album, the highlight of which is one of the two songs they wrote together. (Anthony Moore also contributed to Straw's LP.)

In comparison to Blegvad's first solo efforts, the folky and countryish rock settings (there's even a Louvin Brothers cover) of **Downtime** are much more successful at capturing the intimacy of his music. Chris Cutler (ex-Henry Cow/Pere Ubu), Tony Maimone (Pere Ubu) and members of Greaves' current band, the Lodge (which includes Blegvad's brother Kristoffer and, lately, Peter himself), provide warm backing to a set of powerful songs, including the hilarious "Card to Bernard" and improved readings of two songs from the Palominos' **Blast of Silence**. This splendid album closes with the whimsical bossa nova of "Crumb de la Crumb," a self-deprecating poke at Blegvad's own obscurity.

King Strut puts it all together for Blegvad, combining the warmth of **Downtime** with the pop smarts of his first two LPs. Partridge produced three tracks (not two, as indicated on the label), including the unfortunate closer, an irritating reprise of the title track. (The rest of the album receives sympathetic treatment from Chris Stamey, who brought in ex-partner Peter Holsapple, rekindling a collaboration that led to *their* 1991 album.) The treasures of **King Strut** are five mostly acoustic pearls on Side Two, particularly the deeply romantic "Northern Lights" and "Shirt & Comb."

[ws/gk]

See also *Golden Palominos, John Greaves, Anthony More, Syd Straw, Victoria Williams.*

BLIND IDIOT GOD

Blind Idiot God (SST) 1987
Undertow (Enemy) 1989 ●
Purged Specimen EP (Enemy) 1989

Refusing to compromise their chops with some cut-rate rock vocalist, this young instrumental trio (originally from St. Louis but now living in Brooklyn) constructs a huge, brash sound influenced (consciously or not) by Blue Cheer, Jimi Hendrix, the Velvet Underground, the Meters (Blind Idiot God covers the Cres-

cent City funk geniuses' "More Time"), the Sex Pistols, Glenn Branca and Jamaican dub (their first LP concludes with a trio of dubwise treats). Simultaneously leaning towards heavy metal (with less ego) and reggae (with more voltage), these demonic decibel gluttons are having the time of their lives in hammer-of-the-gods territory. [rg]

BLONDIE

Blondie (Private Stock) 1976 (Chrysalis) 1977 ●
Plastic Letters (Chrysalis) 1977 ●
Parallel Lines (Chrysalis) 1978 ●
Eat to the Beat (Chrysalis) 1979 ●
Autoamerican (Chrysalis) 1980 ●
The Best of Blondie (Chrysalis) 1981 ●
The Hunter (Chrysalis) 1982 ●

DEBBIE HARRY/BLONDIE

Once More into the Bleach (Chrysalis) 1988 ●

JIMMY DESTRI

Heart on a Wall (Chrysalis) 1982

That Blondie may be remembered as perhaps the best singles band to emerge from the new wave—in fact, a world-class hitmaking powerhouse—is extraordinary for those who recall the group's humble genesis and occasionally appalling early efforts. Even after the New Yorkers had secured a recording contract, few expected they could ever surpass the commercial level of, say, Lou Reed—i.e., a moderate fluke hit single, perhaps a charting album, but mainly cult status. How could the torpid, immovable, generally disgusting commercial music establishment of the day somehow reverse itself and open up to *Blondie*? Like the rest of the us they were part of, it seemed they'd always be on the outside looking in.

Yet the core members (singer Debbie Harry, guitarist Chris Stein, keyboard player Jimmy Destri and drummer Clem Burke) always had a vision that anything was possible. So what if they weren't slick studio musicians? They'd still be able to put the sounds in their heads on plastic, sounds that weren't just "Pure Pop for Now People" but pure pop for hit radio—in the most sincere, uncynical and popularly resonating tradition. So they engaged in inspired, positively subversive, musical "pilferage" and synthesis in ways few others have consistently sustained. And through all of that (until the last album, anyway), Blondie maintained a distinctive group identity.

Some of their dabblings weren't successful, but if Blondie could be called a bunch of dilettantes, it's only fair to note that many others wet their musical toes in the same exotic waters only after Blondie set the precedent. Moreover, Blondie largely pursued their commercial and artistic goals in nonconformist fashion, often to the dismay of their record company and even some of their fans.

Blondie effervesces with exuberance which, at points, extends the band's reach beyond its grasp. Still, it's a guileless classic, and arguably the group's best album. They create a series of charming musical Frankenstein monsters—stitched together from salsa, funk, Broadway pop and thrill-flick soundtracks—in addition to their more typical girl-group/surf/Anglopop hybrids, as on "X Offender," the debut single included here. Any lapses in expertise are counterbalanced by the sense of ebullient abandon, as captured by producer Richard Gottehrer.

Plastic Letters reflects not only professional seasoning and a better rapport with Gottehrer, but also the turmoil of changes in personnel, management and record label. The resulting LP—fuller, tighter and more authoritatively rocking than the debut—includes the band's first two UK hits, "(I'm Always Touched by Your) Presence, Dear" (written by, and recorded as a sort of tribute to, departed bassist Gary Valentine) and "Denis" (a revamp of the 1963 Randy & the Rainbows oldie). There's also a brooding feel to many of the tracks—the hard, riffy stuff and the thoughtful experimentation ("Cautious Lip") alike. More conservative than **Blondie**, and less exciting.

By **Parallel Lines**, the new lineup had already jelled, and producer Mike Chapman (looking to repeat the massive success he enjoyed during the early-'70s English glitter-pop days) took over the console, imposing his exacting, disciplined approach. The band seems totally in control of every musical form it takes on, from zombie metal to pop-a-billy, from quasi-avant spaciness to the hitbound electro-disco flirtation, "Heart of Glass." Compared to Gottehrer's first-take spontaneity, some of the LP seems a tad clinical, but it's easily good enough to be considered America's answer to Nick Lowe's first solo LP.

Eat to the Beat, surprisingly, proved less artistically and commercially successful than an album that recapitulates a soaring band's strong points should have been, but it does have some of the best sheer rock'n'roll the group ever produced. **Autoamerican** goes in precisely the opposite direction; breaking out of a stylistic cul-de-sac, Blondie jumped out in a number of new directions again: cocktail jazz, Eurodrama, country (sort of) and rap. An "A" for effort, but Blondie's most uneven album, ranging from obvious boo-boos to the hits "Rapture" and "The Tide Is High."

Within two years after that ambitious LP, the "successful rock band collapses under its own weight" syndrome had apparently set in. **The Hunter** sounds as though their excitement about musical recombination had simply degenerated into a polished but sterile capability of manipulating a wide variety of stylistic devices. Bereft of things to say, or ways to say nothing with style and grace, the LP is aimless, elephantine—its largely impenetrable pretentiousness not that far removed from dinosaurs like Jefferson Starship or Yes.

The Best of Blondie should really be called **The Singles Album**, since that's exclusively what's on it and what limits the view it gives of the group. It doesn't include the spiffy version they did of Johnny Cash's "Ring of Fire" on the soundtrack of the movie *Roadie*, but it does have three special remixes and the otherwise non-LP hit, "Call Me" (from *American Gigolo*). The US and UK editions differ according to Blondie's chart successes in those markets.

Although it shares five songs in common with **The Best of Blondie**, **Once More into the Bleach**—a mixture of group songs and Harry's solo work—offers most of them (and eight others) in drastically remixed and elongated form. Considering this music from a decidedly dance-oriented perspective overlooks its historical context, eliminating the friendly openness of Blondie's new wave pop records for the distant sound of anonymous star product—an effect the original albums, regardless of their hits, always avoided. Clubbing up already rhythmic jams like "Heart of Glass," "Call Me" and "Rapture" involves no great stylistic leap, but cutting the joy out of "Denis" is unforgivable, and the Coldcut dub mix (complete with seagulls) of "The Tide Is High" (inexplicably credited here to Harry solo) is idiotic. Oddly, the set ends with the group's delightful (and previously rare) French rendition of the third album's "Sunday Girl," mercifully unsullied by studio second-guessers.

Keyboardist Destri's solo outing, produced by Lou Reed/Pink Floyd cohort Michael Kamen and featuring Clem Burke, takes traditional pop values and updates them with decidedly Bowiesque leanings. Destri had already proved himself a creative and occasionally inspired musician and songwriter in the group context (and beyond—in 1980 he produced an album by Joey Wilson); here, he proves solid, if not exemplary, in those capacities. But his lack of vocal ability or even identity is a definite drag on the proceedings.   [jg/i]

See also *Chequered Past, Debbie Harry*.

ALPHA BLONDY

Jah Glory (Fr. Celluloid) 1985
Apartheid Is Nazism (Shanachie) 1987 ●
Cocody Rock!!! (Shanachie) 1988 ●
Revolution (Shanachie) 1989 ●
The Prophets (Capitol) 1989 ●
The Best of Alpha Blondy (Shanachie) 1990 ●

ALPHA BLONDY AND THE WAILERS

Jerusalem (Shanachie) 1987 ●

Since the death of Bob Marley, numerous Third World performers have been proposed to succeed him as the world's leading reggae exponent. Ziggy Marley is one obvious choice; Alpha Blondy (born Kone Seydou) is another, more unusual, candidate. For starters, Blondy is from the Ivory Coast; he performs reggae in French, English, Hebrew, Arabic and other African languages. Rather than Rasta and Jah, he sings about the Middle East and South Africa, on records which he writes, produces and arranges himself. He's enormously popular in Europe and Africa, where he tours frequently. Because of his global success, Blondy has come to signify the internationalization of reggae as a music and phenomenon—the true world beat.

Blondy's LPs—beginning with 1982's **Jah Glory**, later issued in France—are genuinely exciting, and should definitely be heard. Among his first few American releases, **Jerusalem** has the slight edge, if only because the Wailers play behind him (strengthening the comparisons to Marley) and they always sound so good. On **Apartheid Is Nazism**, he's backed by members of his touring group, the Solar System Band, who are less distinctive but just as tight. **The Best of Alpha Blondy** contains both arrangements, offering such exemplary tracks as "Cocody Rock," "Apartheid Is Nazism," "I Love Paris" and "Jerusalem." Combining roots rhythms and exotic foreign lyrics, the music is at once familiar and strange, but its depth of feeling never falters, and needs no translation. Delightfully haunting—this is reggae and then some.

Moving to a major American label, Blondy made the weird-sounding **The Prophets**, dedicating it to the planet Earth. Mixing synthesizers, horns, a female chorus and way too much reverb, he deftly shifts in and out of reggae rhythms with political and religious songs in English, French and Dioula. Adventurous but a bit too odd, **The Prophets** is not the ideal ticket to broaden Blondy's audience.   [bk/i]

BLOOD ON THE SADDLE

Blood on the Saddle (New Alliance) 1984
Poison Love (Chameleon) 1986
Fresh Blood (SST) 1987

These California cow-punks are less concerned with revering C&W icons than trashing them at a furious pace: Blood on the Saddle's idea of country is Hank Williams OD-ing in the back of his car; their western, that of spaghetti flicks. On the quartet's first album, ragged harmonies, yodelled vocals and the slap of stand-up bass lend authenticity, making the record a rodeo where even the horses are doing speed. One of the band's three lead singers, ex-Bangle Annette Zilinskas, vocalizes on the best songs, including "Do You Want to Dance?" and "(I Wish I Was a) Single Girl (Again)," where she sounds like a real down-home country singer trying to stay straight while her band, out of control, beats her to the finish.

Poison Love refines the group's stylistic balance, clarifying the energetic country-rock side while reducing the first album's more wanton rock impulses. The resulting cross-breed is easygoing and colorful, a post-adolescent barn dance with enough electricity to make a deep impression and enough credible cultural resonance to survive the style-mongering. Zilinskas and guitarist/banjo-picker Greg Davis both bring more enthusiasm than skill to the microphone, but their delivery (better solo than their X-like harmonies) is perfectly adequate for kick-up-your-heels songs like "Police Siren," "Steal You Away" and "Promise Your Heart to Me." Slow numbers like "Johnny's at the Fair" and speeders like "Colt 45," however, elude the band's grasp.

With one acoustic rest period, the band's blood runs hotter on the third album, an uneven race with the devil that uses flat-out tempos on hard-rocking originals related to country music more by structural inspiration than content. (Indicative of the shifting personality, covers of "Rawhide" and "Folsom Prison Blues" are crazed but bland, hand-me-downs that no longer fit.) As a singer, Davis thrives in this exciting environment, but Zilinskas' efforts to keep pace with the charging rhythms and skillet-licking solos strip the twangy character from her voice.   [ep/i]

See also *Bangles, ¡Screamin' Sirens!*

BLOOD ORANGES

Corn River (East Side Digital) 1990 φ

Defying geographical prejudices, this Boston quartet plays twangy country rock, setting Mark Spencer's fancy electric guitar pickin' against singer Jim Ryan's skillful mandolin work, driving it all with a crisp rhythm section. Displaying a polite cowpunk sensibility as well as an appreciation for traditional Appalachian music (e.g., "Shady Grove"), the Blood Oranges are more folky-reverent than most of the West Coast groups known for similar hybrids, but **Corn River** doesn't shy away from electricity at all: "Incinerator" has guest slide guitar by Dumptruck's Seth Tiven, "Western Man" is a loud Creedence-style blues-rock choogle and "Time Takes Away" distributes a roar of measured guitar power that nearly crushes tinkly bits of mandolin and guest piano.   [i]

BLOODSPORT

I Am the Game (Homestead) 1985

Part of the mid-'80s Chicago scene (alongside Big Black, Effigies et al.), Bloodsport features guitarist Chris Björkland, a veteran of Strike Under, the early Chi-town punk band (its 1981 EP was the first-ever Wax Trax! record) that also included his brother Steve (later of Breaking Circus) and Naked Raygun bassist Pierre Kezdy.

Björkland, singer Dave Bergeron, bassist Tom Woods and drummer Joe Haggerty (brother of Raygun's John) cut Bloodsport's only record, the seven-song **I Am the Game**, in 1985. Inspired by the same Ruts/Killing Joke/Stranglers sources as Bloodsport's counterparts, the slabs of innovative, guitar-dominated walls of post-punk power-rock ("Better and Best," "Sixes and Sevens," the instrumental "Killing Floor" and the chilling "Rhymes of Reason") are just what one would expect: solid and invigorating.

The group has been a study in inertia ever since. Bloodsport continued as an unrecorded trio after Bergeron left; all three members currently back singer John Kezdy in the Effigies. Although Bloodsport still exists, Björkland moonlights in the re-formed Defoliants and Haggerty is in Pegboy, a new band with his ex-Raygun brother John.   [jr]

See also *Effigies, Naked Raygun.*

LUKA BLOOM

Riverside (Reprise) 1990 ●

Barry Moore, brother of famed Irish singer Christy Moore, moved to New York after releasing three folk albums in Ireland. With joking nods to James Joyce's Leopold Bloom and Suzanne Vega's bestselling kid, he changed his name to Luka Bloom and earned a fast following as a riveting live performer. **Riverside** is admirably underproduced for a major-label product, relying mostly on an amplified acoustic guitar, subtly assisted by such guests as Liam O'Maonlai (Hothouse Flowers) on *bodhrán*, Ed Tomney (Rage to Live) on electric guitar, Jane Scarpantoni (Tiny Lights) on cello and Ali Fatemi on Iranian finger drum. A few songs, like "The Man Is Alive" (an elegy for his father), are set in Ireland, but most of them take place in New York—or in Bloom's hopelessly romantic heart. A tendency towards obviousness occasionally leads him astray, as in the heavyhanded "Hudson Lady" (apparently about the Statue of Liberty) and in the silly wet-dream fantasy of "An Irishman in Chinatown." While those songs become annoying after repeated listens, other tracks—like "Gone to Pablo," "This Is for Life" and "You Couldn't Have Come at a Better Time"—prove Bloom to be an extraordinarily sensitive lyricist and singer.   [ws]

69

BLOTTO

Hello! My Name Is Blotto. What's Yours? EP (Blotto) 1980
Across and Down EP (Blotto) 1980
Combo Akimbo (Blotto) 1982
I Wanna Be a Lifeguard (Performance) 1987

Albany, New York's whimsical comic-pop sextet made a big splash with the silly summer song, "I Wanna Be a Lifeguard," included on the first EP. All three original records have witty observations and skillfully played parodic music, but Blotto reached its peak on the pre-Spinal Tap brain-banger, "(I'm Turning into a Heavy) Metal Head," from **Combo Akimbo**.

I Wanna Be a Lifeguard is a fair career summary, putting the best items from both EPs and **Combo Akimbo** on one easy-to-use record, with a bonus flexi-disc of "I Wanna Be a Lifeguard" (live) and a studio cut. [i]

KURTIS BLOW

Kurtis Blow (Mercury) 1980
Deuce (Mercury) 1981
Tough (Mercury) 1982
Party Time? EP (Mercury) 1983
Ego Trip (Mercury) 1984 ●
America (Mercury) 1985
Kingdom Blow (Mercury) 1986 ●
Back by Popular Demand (Mercury) 1988 ●

One of rap's earliest and most enduring stars, New York's Kurtis Blow consistently makes solid records with workable grooves and lyrics that alternately address topics of social and socializing interest. In doing so, Blow has become something of a modern African-American culture maven, singing the praises of Harlem ("One-Two-Five (Main Street, Harlem, USA)" on **Party Time?**), waxing eloquent about hoops ("Basketball" on **Ego Trip**) and competing Grandmaster Flash's "The Message" in discussing the urban challenge ("Tough" on the LP of the same name, "Street Rock" on **Kingdom Blow**). All of the records are state-of-the-art in an almost mainstream vein; **Ego Trip** makes a concerted effort to get hipper by having Run–DMC do a guest rap on "8 Million Stories." (**Kingdom** tops that in the cameo stakes: the first voice you hear belongs to Bob Dylan.)

Taking a turn towards patriotism in the title cut of **America**, Blow (who also produced) shows off his dichotomous musical goals. In the same song he uses aggressive electronic percussion and mixing techniques to mimic the Bambaataa/Lydon Time Zone sound (with Art of Noise effects) *and* sings like Kool and the Gang. The rest of the album is passable but only the catchy and soulful strut of "If I Ruled the World" is worth remembering. (And "Super Sperm" is well worth forgetting.)

Kingdom Blow not only has Dylan and a homely but sincere paean to "The Bronx," but George Clinton and "Zip-a-Dee-Doo-Dah" to boot. Kurtis is nothing if not open-minded and adventurous. The eight long cuts, some more compelling than others, throw in just about everything (TV bites, Donald Duck, party sounds, Emulator gimmickry, etc.) except the London Philharmonic.

Dispensing with most of **Kingdom Blow**'s ambitious frivolity, **Back by Popular Demand** finds the venerable but passé rapper in an understandably insecure mood, circling his wagons in a vain attempt to get with the new hip-hop generation. Boasting is traditional, but Blow spends far too much of this mild old-school record (that contains a few melodic soul excursions, including an appealingly sung version of Charles Wright's old "Express Yourself"—is this Blow's future?) claiming his preeminence in the field and too little proving it. [i]

BLOW MONKEYS

Limping for a Generation (nr/RCA) 1984 ●
Forbidden Fruit EP (RCA) 1985
Animal Magic (RCA) 1986 ●
She Was Only a Grocer's Daughter (RCA) 1987 ●
Whoops! There Goes the Neighbourhood (nr/RCA) 1989 ●
Choices: The Singles Collection (nr/RCA) 1989 ●
Springtime for the World (nr/RCA) 1990 ●

Moving in to fill the vapid-soul vacancy left by Culture Club during that band's terminal creative drought, England's Blow Monkeys whipped up a disturbingly familiar-sounding bit of fluff, "Digging Your Scene," for their second album. While the absurdly named bowler-wearing Dr. Robert (Howard) manages a passable imitation of George's vocals and songwriting, his subordinates are no match for the Clubbers, and the rest of **Animal Magic** is equally redundant and stupid. The title track is an appalling T. Rex knock-off; "Sweet Murder" attempts to rewrite Talking Heads' "I Zimbra." The LP's most consistent feature is its pathetic lack of originality.

As an introduction to America, **Forbidden Fruit** mixes "Atomic Lullaby" and the Smithsy "Wild Flower" from **Limping for a Generation** with four foretastes of **Animal Magic**. The only items of note are a pair of crazed Eek-a-Mouse dub mixes that largely obscure the songs.

The uncontrollably egotistical Dr. R. sorted out his stylistic desires in time for **She Was Only a Grocer's Daughter**, which consistently focuses on a danceable pop-soul format that crosses Culture Club's basic ideas with lush ABC-like production, including enough strings and backing vocals—the credits list a dozen session singers—to pack a stadium. If the band can't hack it instrumentally on their own, a studio full of players are on hand to help. The trivial songs at least *sound* fine; the peerless Curtis Mayfield provides a huge (if underserved) credibility boost by duetting on the appropriately derivative "The Day After You." The album title is an effete slap at Margaret Thatcher; the CD adds two extra tracks.

Most of **There Goes the Neighbourhood** sounds frighteningly like ABC, but a variety of producers (Stephen Hague, Leon Sylvers III, Julian Mendelsohn and the godlike talents of a certain Blow Monkey) prevents any consistent sound from jelling. Continuing his strange habit of setting strongly motivated left-wing criticisms of the state of contemporary England into ultra-commercial arrangements, Dr. Robert doesn't so much share his political thoughts as allude to them coyly while his three bandmates and guests effortlessly and energetically pump out forgettably glib mush.

The Blow Monkeys followed **Neighbourhood** with a compilation of their UK hits. The **Choices** CD and tape add extended remixes and other bonus tracks.

Extending the misbegotten limits of pretentious conceptual insanity, **Springtime for the World** begins with blandly commercial pop-soul (the title track is a nifty Style Council imitation) but then turns absurdly global. "Reflections '89" is an instrumental with soundbites from assorted world leaders; other songs appropriate Afrobeat accents, absurdly cramming them into a schmaltzy orchestral arrangement on "If You Love Somebody." These confused fellas really need to straighten themselves out.   [i]

BUDDY BLUE
See *Beat Farmers*.

BLUE AEROPLANES
Bop Art (nr/Abstract) 1984
Action Painting and Other Original Works EP (nr/Fire) 1985
Lover and Confidante and Other Stories of Travel, Religion and Heartbreak (nr/Fire) 1986
Tolerance (nr/Fire) 1986 ●
Spitting Out Miracles (Restless) 1987 ●
Friendloverplane (nr/Fire) 1988 (Fire-Restless) 1989 ●
Swagger (Ensign-Chrysalis) 1990 ●
Loved EP (nr/Ensign) 1990 ●
World View Blue (Ensign-Chrysalis) 1990 φ

GERARD LANGLEY + IAN KEAREY
Siamese Boyfriends (nr/Fire) 1986

Aided by numerous friends, this eccentric Bristol quintet often has as many as a dozen people playing on its records; the diversity of ideas shows in the rich sound. Referents such as the Velvets, Fall, Pere Ubu, Feelies and others ricochet from all sides, topped off by Gerard Langley's poetic lyrics.

From the hard funk of "Pinkies Hit the Union" to the sonic landscape of "Owls," **Bop Art** has something for everyone. Along with a barrage of guitars, bass and percussion, the instrumentation includes saxes, bagpipes and several 16th-century guitar ancestors. The band is such an effective ensemble that, even with all the masterful variety, the LP manages a logical progression.

The **Action Painting** EP builds some nice Velvets-*cum*-early Cabaret Voltaire drones; **Lover and Confidante**, another four cuts, is a trailer for **Tolerance**. Not quite as kaleidoscopic as **Bop Art**, **Tolerance** trades much of the oddness and idiosyncrasy of previous work for some psychedelic touches, adding just enough characteristic embellishment to prevent deep identification with the paisley bandwagon.

By the time of their first American release, **Spitting Out Miracles**, the Blue Aeroplanes were up to an eight-piece (if you count the dancer and the guy who contributes tapes and records), with an equal number of guests (including Michelle Shocked on mandolin). Amazingly, with all those ingredients, it often manages to sound like a singer/songwriter album; the musicianship is so controlled and artistic that the focus stays on Langley's beat-influenced wordplay and Dylanesque delivery. On "Bury Your Love Like Treasure," the artistes rock out fine and everybody gets home happy. All of the aforementioned records are highly recommended.

Friendloverplane is a compilation of non-LP tracks, half of them previously unreleased. As is typical of such efforts, it's a hit or miss assemblage, with song and sound quality varying quite a bit. (Ironically, most of the better-produced numbers are inferior songs, such as "Etiquette!" and the single "Veils of Colour.") While the first side is mostly slower quasi-blues, Side Two opens up more. Highlights are "Tolerance" and "Old Men Sleeping on the Bowery," but neither ranks among the band's best. For devotees only.

Swagger contains the Blue Aeroplanes' first new material in three years. Gil Norton's clear production allows the multi-layered guitars to create an uncluttered backdrop for tales of interpersonal relationships. (Langley provides lyrics for ten of the twelve tracks; guitarist Rodney Allen contributes "Careful Boy" and Sylvia Plath's "The Applicant" is effectively tuned up.) Guests include Michael Stipe and ex-Belle Stars saxophonist Clair Hirst. The Blue Aeroplanes remain one of rock's hidden treasures, intelligent and mature without being pretentious or stodgy.

Named for the **Swagger** track presented here in an acoustic version, **World View Blue** is an eight-song collection of live tracks, leftovers and covers (a concert run-through of Dylan's "I Wanna Be Your Lover" rocks as much as anything the group has ever done). "You (Are Loved)" sounds like a potential breakthrough single; the sole low point is a completely unnecessary "Sweet Jane."

Langley and in-again-out-again Aeroplanes guitarist Ian Kearey recorded the six-song **Siamese Boyfriends** in 1986. Kearey is quite the multi-instrumentalist here, finding a part for everything from toy pianos and melodica to bowed psaltery and banjimer (!). "Joe Taylor's/La Morisque" is a nicely played but not very interesting instrumental; "Dear, Though the Night Is Gone" is a W.H. Auden poem mumbled almost inaudibly over Kearey's accompaniment. **Siamese Boyfriends** isn't so much produced as just recorded; that results in the participants jockeying for position and stepping on each other's contributions. Not a major work.   [dgs]

BLUE ANGEL
Blue Angel (Polydor) 1980 + 1984

As crass trash goes, you could certainly do worse than New York City's Blue Angel. Their painfully obvious mixture of '50s hokum, '60s girl-group theatrics and '70s detachment might have been more noteworthy if Blondie hadn't issued their own, more original version a few years earlier. The singer warbles and trills skillfully, but without much charm. The album was reissued in 1984, after said warbler, Cyndi Lauper, topped the charts with "Girls Just Want to Have Fun."   [jy]
See also *Cyndi Lauper*.

BLUEBELLS
The Bluebells EP (Sire) 1983
Sisters (Sire) 1984

MCCLUSKEY BROTHERS
Aware of All (nr/Thrush) 1987

In a brief career, Glasgow's rustic pure-pop Bluebells—whose small output was concentrated on singles made with a procession of producers—never had anywhere near the impact their marvelous music plainly deserved. Guitarist and ex-fanzine publisher Robert Hodgens (aka Bobby Bluebell) wrote instantly memorable classics (some in collaboration with the two brothers who completed the Bluebells' essential troika) and Kenneth McCluskey sang 'em in a likably unaffected voice, making every track count. The five-song EP and the album have three songs in common (Brendan Behan's moving folk classic, "The Patriot's Game," the beautiful and romantic "Cath" and different versions of "Everybody's Somebody's Fool"), all of them winners. **Sisters** also boasts "I'm Falling (Down Again)" and six others, all subtly shaded with country fiddles and mandolins, ringing guitars, a light bouncy beat and choruses that you'll be humming all the way home. Utterly wonderful.

After the Bluebells ended, brothers Kenneth (vocals) and David (drums) McCluskey picked up different instruments, formed a duo and continued to record airy originals with more of a folky feel and none of Hodgens' power pop leanings. Bluebells bassist Laurence Donegan, meanwhile, surfaced in Lloyd Cole's Commotions.   [i]

BLUE HIPPOS

Blue Hippos (Twin/Tone) 1987
Forty Forty (Twin/Tone) 1988

OTTO'S CHEMICAL LOUNGE

Spillover (Homestead) 1985

On the seven-song **Blue Hippos**, this Twin Cities trio, led by singer/guitarist Paul Osby (late of Otto's Chemical Lounge), wavers between garage thrash and tentative funk, with competent but unexceptional results. **Forty Forty** sounds more confident, and shows a somewhat greater mastery of funk dynamics, but the band still lacks the musical and/or lyrical bite that would give its R&B appropriations more authority.

Like the Blue Hippos' discs, the sole release by Otto's Chemical Lounge (with Osby as guitarist and songwriter but not lead vocalist) fails to capture on vinyl what was reputedly a powerful live act. The eight-song, 22-minute disc is basically competent but pedestrian indie guitar rock with avant-gardsy pretensions. The jams don't go anywhere in particular, and the covers of Johnny Kidd and the Flamin Groovies are flat and obvious. Grant Hart sings backup on three songs. [hd]

BLUE IN HEAVEN

All the Gods' Men (Island) 1985
Explicit Material (Island) 1986
Rock'n'Roll R.I.P EP (nr/Solid) 1988

Although this young Irish quartet debuted on 45 with a fiery guitar anthem ("Julie Cries"), an inappropriate choice of producer (Martin Hannett) for their first album turned them into bass-heavy doom mongers. A remix of the single on **All the Gods' Men** tells the whole sordid tale. A little light does shine through in "Sometimes," "The Big Beat" and "In Your Eyes," but Hannett's lush atmospherics detract from, rather than complement, the effort.

The second record was co-produced by Island Records chief Chris Blackwell, Eric Thorngren and the band, to far more appealing effect. Guitars power the mostly melodic songs along without overly coloring them; Shane O'Neill's vocals provide the strongest character. Amidst the attractive pop, Shane's avowed Iggy fixation comes through on the grungy "Be Your Man" (which also mentions a familiar canine variation).

The multi-personality EP chronologically straddles the band's major-label career, with a derivative 1983 track ("On and On") produced by the Edge and three '87 studio efforts (light pop, ponderous plodding *and* Iggy-styled rock). Rounding off this strange package is a dull live '87 take on the Stooges' "Loose." [ag/i]

BLUE NILE

A Walk Across the Rooftops (Linn-Virgin-A&M) 1984 ●
Hats (Linn-Virgin-A&M) 1989 ●

This unique Glaswegian trio has considerable creative depth, building atmosphere with lots of empty space and well-controlled conflicting musical maneuvers. The first album's title track mixes strings, horns, drum and bass with a meandering, disjunct vocal for something like a blend of Robert Wyatt, Joni Mitchell and John Cale. Although **A Walk Across the Rooftops** isn't easy to love, at its most accessible point ("Stay," which actually has a chorus and more of a verse melody than the others), it's quite appealing.

Hats was five years in the making, but the band's relentless perfectionism paid off: the album's seven songs are as dense and moving as a midnight sky. With sweeping synths and the pristine click of electronic percussion, "The Downtown Lights" and "Over the Hillside" are as moody as film music, while "From a Late Night Train" and "Saturday Night" are impressionistic vignettes that creep along in slow motion. There's hardly a guitar or live drum to be heard, but seldom has studio technology been used to such warm and personal results. [i/kss]

BLUE ORCHIDS

The Greatest Hit (Money Mountain) (nr/Rough Trade) 1982
Agents of Change EP (nr/Rough Trade) 1982

This Manchester quartet, which included two early members of the Fall—guitarist/singer Martin Bramah and keyboardist Una Baines—used organ as its main instrument, but at times on **The Greatest Hit** it sounds as if Baines is playing a different song from the rest of the band. There are many overlapping layers in the deceptively simple sound; the long organ washes are interrupted by guitars lurching to the fore. Bass and drums keep the steady beat, but the others don't necessarily fall in line behind them. Vocals are half-sung, half-spoken and full of poetic pretense, but it's the mesmerizing music that captures the listener in bright swirling folds. While **The Greatest Hit** can be simply tagged as neo-psychedelia, that doesn't cover the full scope of this fascinating band's music.

The EP, packaged in a printed plastic shopping bag, offers four very nice subsequent tracks that are at once subtler and more conservatively structured, sounding like nothing so much as the pretty side of early Velvet Underground.

The Blue Orchids didn't last long, and the members dropped out of the spotlight. In 1989, however, occasioned by Brix Smith's departure, Bramah rejoined the Fall in time to play on **Extricate**.   [i]

See also *Fall*.

BLUE PEARL
See *Youth & Ben Watkins*.

BLUE RODEO
Outskirts (Can. Risqué Disque) 1987 (Risqué
   Disque-Atlantic) 1988 ●
Diamond Mine (Risqué Disque-Atlantic) 1989 ●
Casino (East West America) 1991 φ

BOB WISEMAN
Bob Wiseman Sings Wrench Tuttle: In Her Dream (Risqué
   Disque-Atlantic) 1990 ●

There's an undeniable '60s flavor to Toronto's Blue Rodeo. On **Outskirts**, that means Beatlesque harmonies, Dylan-influenced songwriting, down-home Band-like musicianship and a touch of Doorsy organ. Fortunately, the quintet's two singer/songwriter/guitarists—Jim Cuddy and Greg Keelor—possess excellent and distinctive voices and a knack for writing songs that transcend the obvious comparisons.

Diamond Mine continues the stroll down the "boulevard of broken dreams" (as the first album's liner notes put it), but also expands to include some political songs, including "God and Country," a thinly veiled swipe at Ollie North and his ilk. Recorded pretty much live in an empty theater in Toronto, it lacks both the punch and especially the neat harmonizing of **Outskirts**. In attempting rawness, the band may have sacrificed some of its best assets.

Producer Pete Anderson must have thought so. On **Casino**, he brings back the harmonies with a vengeance, pushes the group's pop side to the fore, and turns up the guitars. This one may remind you a lot of **Rubber Soul** at times, or at least that period in which the ideas of the Beatles and Dylan seemed to converge. Blue Rodeo, however, brings that sound clearly into the '90s.

Keyboard/accordion player Bob Wiseman's solo album probably won't appeal to everybody, and that's a pity. On **In Her Dreams**, he puts to music lyrics purportedly sent to him in the mail by a fellow named Wrench Tuttle. (Actually, Wiseman writes them himself, but it's a good story.) In fact, Wiseman doesn't have much of a voice, but what he lacks in tunefulness he more than makes up in personality and charm. The songs are topical, quirky, bluesy, heartfelt, clever and more; obviously a real labor of love. Wiseman plays guitar as well as keyboards here, and is helped out by a coterie of Canadian musicians, including k.d. lang sideman Ben Mink and the wonderful Mary Margaret O'Hara.   [ds]

See also *Crash Vegas*.

BLUE RUIN
Such Sweet Thunder (Aus. Major) 1985
Flame (Aus. Rampant) 1987
Strange Things in the Corner (Aus. rooArt-PolyGram)
   1988 ●

Although the lone Birthday Party alumnus in this dark and bluesy Australian quartet is drummer Phill Calvert, it's singer Ian "Quinsy" McLean and his obvious Nick Cave fixation that establishes the stylistic bond between **Such Sweet Thunder** and **From Her to Eternity**. With Blue Ruin providing the basic guitar-bass-drums framework and dramatic vocals, guests add the sax, harmonica and keyboards coloration that make hard-edged numbers like "She's Murder," "Waterhole" and "Love Me When I'm Low" engrossingly atmospheric.

Other than guitarist Mulaim Vela's organ work, **Flame** again relies on session players (trombone, strings, sax) for its musical flavoring. Overall, Blue Ruin's second album takes a better-adjusted path, relegating a chunk of the group's jagged intensity and bleakness to the downcast—not quite dissolute—and violent lyrics. (Strangely, **Flame** includes a new rendition of the first album's vindictive "What a Hell'uva Woman.")

The powerfully live **Strange Things in the Corner** was recorded over a pair of May 1988 nights in Melbourne. Other than Willie Dixon's "I Just Wanna Make Love to You" (given an alternately slow/fast but consistently tuneless reading) and one band original, all of the tunes come from the two studio albums. (Yep, "Hell'uva Woman" makes its third appearance.)   [i]

BLURT
In Berlin (Ruby) 1981
Blurt (nr/Red Flame) 1982
Bullets for You (Fr. Divine) 1984
Six Views in Black (Sixty Minutes of Blurt in Blighty) [tape]
   1985
Friday the 12th (nr/Another Side) 1985 (PVC) 1985
Poppycock (nr/Toeblock) 1986
Smoke Time (Moving Target) 1987 ●
Kenny Rogers' Greatest Hit (Take 2) (nr/Toeblock)
   1989 ●
The Body Live! (Ger. Heute) 1989 ●

VARIOUS ARTISTS
A Factory Quartet (nr/Factory) 1981

TED MILTON
Confessions of an Aeroplane Farter EP (nr/echtl) 1982
Love Is Like a Violence (nr/Embryo) 1984
"Ode: O to Be Seen Through Your Eyes!" EP
   (nr/Toeblock) 1985

JEAN-FRANCOIS PAUVROS
Le Grande Amour (Fr. Nato) 1986

Ted Milton is a direct and honest guy. "I will lead the world over the end of the Santa Monica Pier," he declares in "No Go Dada" (originally on **Bullets for You**, but also on several of the live records: two Blurt credos are recycling and documenting each new lineup in performance), "but not until you've raised the temperature of the Pacific Ocean to blood temperature and provide warm towels in the dressing room." (He's practical, too.) Making a saxophone honk, screech and generally giving the impression of Mother Goose meeting armageddon, Milton, his drummer brother Jake and guitarist Pete Creese debuted in the summer of 1980 with the "My Mother Was a Friend of the Enemy of the People" single, followed it with a live debut album the following year and have been squawking their way through a noisy avant-garde netherworld between jazz and rock ever since. Ted's voice is just what his band's name would suggest, a grumbling, gurgling, bleating (if not bleeding) blurt of a sound, silenced only when his mouth is wrapped around a saxophone reed. That saxophone would just as soon imitate fingernails down a chalkboard or elephants in heat as conform to the jazzy warmth the instrument might yield in other hands.

A lover of wordplay, the iconoclastic Milton is capable of *serious* irreverence. In the title track of **Bullets for You**, a song about JFK's assassination, he grunts, "I am a donut. There's a hole in my head. Ich bin ein Berliner. That's what Jack said . . . and now Jack is dead." Blurt lyrics (as well as those on Milton's solo works) are dada ga-ga woven around some kind of derailed spark. Behind that spark is a literate and educated sense of nonsense. You either love Blurt or hate them; there's plenty of validity to both views.

Blurt is one of the trio's artiest and most orderly works. Creese's minimalist guitar spews out repeating patterns of stark chords that function almost like a backing samba in "The Ruminant Plinth" (against Ted's incoherently belching screams and squirming sax) and double as a rhythm track, as well as the melody, at other times.

Bullets for You is Blurt at its most accessible, and the final release by the original lineup. Featuring lyrics that are actually decipherable, song structures from Earth instead of Mars, and even hooks such as the mutilated two-syllable "you-ooo" in the title track, Ted twists his voice (between saxophone tweetings) into a yodel-edged squeal that is as catchy and memorable as any pop refrain. Jake counters with some equally infectious drumming.

After Creese left, the brothers hired keyboardist Herman Martin for a short time. The cassette-only **Six Views in Black**, compiled from four live performances in March of 1985, contains the band's only known recordings with synthesizer. (Blurt's live documentation also includes a four-song side of **A Factory Quartet**.)

Martin alone accompanies Milton on the solo 12-inch rendition of "Ode: O to Be Seen Through Your Eyes!" (a band version of which appears on **Kenny Rogers' Greatest Hit (Take 2)**), a recitation set to a harsh synthesized drumbeat. Like Foetus, whose twisted intonations his vocals resemble, Milton is a master of mood when allowed out on his own. Martin's synth work is anything but traditional, veering from the silicon chip gone amok of "Skies Are Blue" to percussive layers and textures.

Guitarist Steve Eagles replaced Martin for **Friday the 12th**, another live album that contains almost the same selections as the twelve-track **Six Views**, but returns the arrangements to guitar.

By the time of **Poppycock**, Paul Wigens had taken over the drum seat. Though the only dance-step possible to a Blurt record is the quadriplegic head-bob, **Smoke Time** almost reaches a dance-club orientation. With Wigens contributing violin as well as percussion, the album features a big, clear beat on the title cut and more upfront drumming in the unbelievably intense "Nights Before." A smorgasbord of Blurt's various sounds, it revives the band's early-period sound in "Bullet-Proof

Vest," while "Aboule Ton Fric" returns the band to the simpler textures of "The Ruminant Plinth."

With new drummer Nic Murcott, **Kenny Rogers' Greatest Hit (Take 2)** is a sparser recording; Milton grumbles intelligibly (in a mixture of English and French) while a smoother, clarinetish tone sneaks out of his sax bell. Murcott also appears on **The Body**, a live retrospective that includes "Enemy Ears" (dating back to the first Blurt lineup) but concentrates on post-Creese material. The majestically spacious live recording finds Milton back to his honk-and-babble vocals, Murcott drumming with crashing precision and everything else harsh and grungy.

In another extra-Blurt-ial project, Ted collaborated with Arto Lindsay, Terry Day and Jean-Francois Pauvros on the avant-experimental **Le Grande Amour** LP.

['e]

BOBS
The Bobs EP (Safety Net) 1983
White Gazebo (Safety Net) 1984

This Ft. Lauderdale trio (not to be confused with the San Francisco a cappella group of the same name) led by future Silos co-founder Bob Rupe plays quirky, satiric music with an edge, steeping their hard pop in reggae and funk, occasionally interrupting it with a distorto-guitar solo. If the Bobs weren't as engagingly clever as some of their TV-culture-commentary peers, at least they were occasionally louder.

The crucial tracks on the sprightly six-song 12-inch debut (recorded in 1981 by Rupe and two other guys named Bob) are "Sneaking T.V." and "Sounds of People" (eating). Working with a different drummer and guitarist (neither of whom is named Bob), bassist/singer Rupe finds fewer original avenues for the band's satire on **White Gazebo**, a more accomplished seven-songer that has better tunes and such accents as pedal steel (on "The Beer Tune," an ingenuous country lament from the lighter side of the roots movement). [jl/i]

See also *Silos*.

BODEANS
Love & Hope & Sex & Dreams (Slash-Warner Bros.) 1986 ●
Outside Looking In (Slash-Reprise) 1987 ●
Home (Slash-Reprise) 1989 ●
Black and White (Slash-Reprise) 1991 φ

Despite the unappetizing roots-rock-saviors hype, Waukesha, Wisconsin's BoDeans (not to be confused with Britain's Bodines) are "new music" by default, simply because the rock mainstream at which they aim their earnest, plain-spoken tunes no longer exists. (If it ever did.) And while a lack of pretension is the BoDeans' principal charm, it's also their biggest liability, as the band rarely strives for much more than competent tunefulness.

Love & Hope & Sex & Dreams—on which all four members adopt the BoDean surname—is an agreeably modest debut, thanks to T-Bone Burnett's homey production and the downright bizarre interplay of singers Sammy Llanas and Kurt Neumann (the band's only concession to eccentricity). But even at this early stage, the material is alarmingly thin, with memorable singles like "Fadeaway," "She's a Runaway" and "Angels" contrasting obvious filler.

Depending upon your reference points, **Outside Looking In**—on which the BoDeans lose a drummer but regain their real names—either suffers or benefits from Talking Head (and fellow Wisconsinite) Jerry Harrison's radio-ready production, which smooths out most of the rough edges and leaves the band sounding suspiciously like everybody else. Still, the combo's natural grit shines through the gloss on "Only Love," "What It Feels Like" and a few others. It's significant that **Outside Looking In**'s most appealing and memorable numbers are a trio of self-produced four-track demos included on the CD and cassette.

Surprisingly, the even glossier **Home** uses space-age studio technique to the band's advantage, showing off mature songwriting and strong vocals (not to mention guest drummer Kenny Aronoff's usual fine work). "When the Love Is Good" and "Beautiful Rain" are unpretentiously soulful, while "Good Work" and "Worlds Away" rock righteously. The album's only major misstep: the echoey U2-ish guitar effects on the anthemic "You Don't Get Much," which only serve to subvert an otherwise worthy song.

Black and White continues in more or less the same vein as **Home**, balancing gritty performances and slick production by David Z. The material shows continued growth, with some fine adult love songs ("Good Things," "Naked") and a few successful stabs at social comment ("Paradise," "Black, White and Blood Red"). [hd]

BOLLOCK BROTHERS

The Last Supper (nr/Charly) 1983 ●
Never Mind the Bollocks 1983 (nr/Charly) 1983 ●
Live Performances: Official Bootleg (nr/Charly) 1983
'77 '78 '79 (nr/Konexion) 1985
The 4 Horsemen of the Apocalypse (nr/Charly) 1985 ●
Rock'n'Roll Suicide (nr/Konexion) 1986
Live in Public in Private (nr/Charly) 1987 ●
The Prophecies of Nostradamus (Blue Turtle) 1987 ●

Under the enthusiastic (mis)guidance of singer Jock McDonald, the semi-serious Bollock Brothers will try anything once, and make an art out of artless prole absurdity. Over the years, this unpredictable and virtually undefinable band has wavered between conceptual brilliance and total creative failure. **The Last Supper**, a double studio album, rambles easily from "Horror Movies" (a corny Munsterized dance theme) to attempted political criticism ("The Act Becomes Real," with regard to Reagan), plus lots more, all characterized by inept singing and ept playing.

The bizarre **Never Mind the Bollocks 1983** parodically reprises the entire contents (and cover design) of the Sex Pistols' 1977 album. Rather than attempt to mimic the Pistols, however, the Bollock Bros. simply borrow the material in toto, adding a few lyrics of their own, and employ synthesizers to convert most of the tunes into a sub-New Order update with McDonald's blandly artless vocals serving in lieu of Rotten's sneering bile. Not exactly a piece of timeless musical history, but an amusing novelty record made just a bit weirder

by the guest vocal appearance of Michael Fagin (a headcase once arrested for sneaking into Buckingham Palace) on "God Save the Queen" and "Pretty Vacant." Fagin also appears on one side of the "official bootleg" **Live Performances**, a two-record collection of various concert appearances which revisits the band's catalogue, including a set of Pistols tunes. Ridiculous.

The 4 Horsemen employs three of the least likely songwriters you'd ever expect to find sharing one album—McDonald, the late Alex Harvey and Vangelis—yet this well-produced studio job isn't as wacky as that might indicate. Jock still can't sing worth a damn, although his dumb B-movie lyrics remain as crazed and offbeat as ever; combined with the conservative rock backing, it makes for a regrettably tepid and laborious album.

Each side of **The Prophecies of Nostradamus** leads off with a typically devolved and irreverent cover version (Steppenwolf's "Magic Carpet Ride" and Led Zeppelin's "Heartbreaker"). Although mysteriously retitled "God Created Woman," Berlin's "Sex (I'm a . . .)" is also featured, complete with a brief interpolation of "Satisfaction." There are a few good originals, but McDonald's cloying metaphysics on the title track and proselytic religious numbers like "Ceremony" and "The Beast Is Calling" degrade the music, appealingly played by a proficient five-person European band. (But what are we to make of Genevieve French's credit for "backing vocals & special entertainment"?) [i]

BOLSHOI

Giants EP (nr/Situation Two) 1985 (IRS) 1986 ●
Friends (IRS) 1986 ●
Lindy's Party (Beggars Banquet-RCA) 1987 ●
Bigger Giants (nr/Situation Two) 1990 ●

Sounding like a modest cross between U2 and early Cult, this Leeds trio isn't exactly good (vocalist Trevor Tanner ain't got what it takes), but they're not dead in the water, either. The six-track **Giants** has some promising ideas and intriguing production qualities, but nothing else going for it.

Keyboardist Paul Clark joined the Bolshoi in time for **Friends**, which takes more of a glossy guitar-and-synth dance path, colored by sporadic echoes of Big Country, a crisp drum sound and Tanner's alternately Antlike/Bonoesque overtones. While the American **Friends** CD incorporates the contents of **Giants**, the UK tape and CD merely add one bonus track ("A Funny Thing . . . ").

After such slow beginnings, the quartet finally located a workably thick equilibrium between guitar and keyboards on the self-produced **Lindy's Party**, ten new slices of threadbare lyrical pretension delivered in Tanner's usual semi-tolerable voice. Less specifically derivative than the group's previous records, **Lindy's Party** should have been the Bolshoi's debut.

Released in 1990, **Bigger Giants** consists of **Giants** plus two 12-inch singles of the same vintage. With a weird cover of Hendrix's "Crosstown Traffic," a wretchedly Bowiesque rendition of Jacques Brel's "Amsterdam" and two different versions of "Happy Boy," this record proves conclusively that—in the Bolshoi's case at least—bigger isn't necessarily better. [i]

BOMB

To Elvis ... in Hell (Bogadigga) 1987
Hits of Acid (Boner) 1988
Happy All the Time EP (Boner) 1989
Lucy in the Sky with Desi [CD] (Boner) 1989 ●

BABY OPAQUE

Fugue in Cow Minor (Catch Trout) 1986

Back in Charlottesville, Virginia, singer/bassist Michael Dean was in Baby Opaque, a trio whose lone album applies tight punk unity and a bit of jazzy aggression to imaginative rock songs with slightly deranged vocals. Although guitarist Todd Wilson keeps threatening to run off into noiseland, Baby Opaque never loses control, and winds up in some surprisingly subtle territory. Ian MacKaye (Minor Threat/Fugazi) guests on the trio's version of "Long Black Veil."

Moving to San Francisco, Dean became one-third of Bomb, a similar but more incendiary and self-amused outfit whose open-space rock thrashings (like "Healthfood and Heroin" and "I Loved You and Then I Died") fill the first two albums with an odd semi-psychedelic mixture of Buttholian frantics and rough flower-powery atmosphere.

The well-produced and stronger-sounding **Happy All the Time** has two songs (including "Lucy in the Sky with Desi," which became the title of a CD compiling the band's two Boner releases) on the 45 rpm side and four (including a remake of "Healthfood and Heroin") on the 33 rpm reverse. [kl]

BOMB THE BASS

Into the Dragon (nr/Rhythm King) 1988 ●

Tim Simenon was only 19 years old when he recorded a relentless dance collage of stolen sounds and break beats entitled "Beat Dis" in early 1988. Released under the name Bomb the Bass, the single was not just a major hit in Britain and a club smash in America, but the birth of the DJ record and the UK dance explosion. Bomb the Bass led the charge of anonymous hi-tech groove producers; unmoved by the lure of pop stardom, Simenon hid behind other vocalists and rappers on subsequent hits, which ranged from the urgent hip-hop of "Megablast" to the updated cover of Aretha Franklin's "I Say a Little Prayer." On album, this mishmash sounds a little confused, a sense perhaps shared by Simenon, who attempted to cement **Into the Dragon** together with radio segues. [tf]

VIC BONDI

See *Articles of Faith*.

BONEDADDYS

Ä-Koo-De-Ä! (Chameleon) 1988 ●
Worldbeatniks (Chameleon) 1989 ●

Uplifting Afrobeat, uptight contemporary funk and sizzling rock'n'roll collide with delightful results on the merry gumbo of the Bonedaddys' first LP. The large interracial LA outfit—essentially a citywide sideband—takes a knowledgeable approach to exotica (confidently covering two Manu Dibango songs) and a witty pen to localism. "Zouk Attack," co-written by Bonedaddy guitarist Paul Lacques (whose main band is the polka-crazy Rotondi, but he also has a group called the Underthings) and ex-Motels/Burning Sensations leader Tim McGovern, critiques the trendy club scene; "Dumpster Girl," penned by singer Kevin Williams, is a twisted love song. Other bands—like the Red Hot Chili Peppers and Oingo Boingo—have confronted the challenge of rampant cross-culturalization and large-ensemble organization, but the Bonedaddys have a musical nationality all their own.

The party continues on **Worldbeatniks**, as the group (here an octet with guests; McGovern is no longer involved) offers up three more Afrobeat numbers (including Fela Kuti's "Zombie" and Afro National's "Jokenge"), some New Orleans-style R&B (Allen Toussaint's "Shoo-rah, Shoo-rah") and an eclectic array of originals, among them the (first?) neo-hippie anthem "Hippie Children," also recorded by Rotondi. Fun'n'funky. [i/ds]

BONE ORCHARD

Stuffed to the Gills EP (nr/Jungle) 1983
Swallowing Havoc! EP (nr/Jungle) 1984
Jack (nr/Jungle) 1984
Penthouse Poultry EP (nr/Vax) 1985

The artwork on this Brighton quintet's debut LP employs the same scratchy/violent style as Batcave bands like Specimen and Alien Sex Fiend; the music on **Jack** is similarly gloomy and intense, but generally less clichéd and more engaging. Credit singer Chrissy McGee (an original, intelligent lyricist—check the story-like "Five Days in the Neighborhood" for details), whose deep, deadpan voice sounds a little like Siouxsie's, and the use of four guest musicians augmenting the guitar-based lineup with piano, strings and sax. Bone Orchard's other strength is a sense of dynamics—they can thunder oppressively or drop back for contrast. **Jack** may not be an overly pleasant disc, but it is a well-crafted one with several nice touches.

The two earlier EPs are of the same caliber, if less artful, with lots of aggressive songs with exclamation points in the titles. The band definitely has a major Birthday Party jones but, unlike many other Party pretenders, they bring a fresh perspective to the psychobilly sound (McGee wasn't called the female Nick Cave for nothing). **Stuffed to the Gills'** best track is "Shall I Carry the Budgie Woman?," a meld of surf guitar, tribal drums and a strange outro with bird sounds. **Swallowing Havoc!**'s highlights are the Crampsian "I'm Boned! (Boneabilly Party)" and the slow, sexy "Love Has Sin."

Bone Orchard followed **Jack** up with the "Princess Epilepsy" 12-inch—consisting of two more psychobilly cuts (McGee's assertive "You Don't Press My Pants" is pretty funny) and a long, burning blues on the B-side—which fails to raise as many hackles as the earlier EPs. Ironically, the band's final release, **Penthouse Poultry**, is a breakthrough, diverging off into all sorts of weirdness: "Scenic Cruiser" is cocktail jazz with tingling sax, "Eyesore" nicks its riff from the Stooges' "TV Eye" and the eerie ballad, "Dumb Poet," could be a sibling of the Birthday Party's "She's Hit." [i/gef]

BONE SYMPHONY

See *Scott Wilk + the Walls.*

BONGOS

Time and the River (nr/Fetish) 1982
Drums Along the Hudson (PVC) 1982
Numbers with Wings EP (RCA) 1983
Beat Hotel (RCA) 1985

RICHARD BARONE/JAMES MASTRO

Nuts and Bolts (Passport) 1983

RICHARD BARONE

Cool Blue Halo (Passport) 1987 •
Primal Dream (Paradox-MCA) 1990 •

Led by enthusiastic guitarist/singer Richard Barone, this Hoboken, New Jersey pop band makes no effort to conceal its roots. On **Drums Along the Hudson** (an expanded version of the **Time and the River** mini-album, itself a compilation of singles), mixed among original songs is a breathy cover of T. Rex's "Mambo Sun"; elsewhere, Barone spins out streamlined Byrds guitar licks and maintains a brisk pace throughout. Tuneful originals like "In the Congo" and "Video Eyes" may trade a certain amount of substance for easy appeal, but there's no better musical equivalent of whipped cream anywhere.

The Bongos subsequently expanded from a trio with the fulltime addition of guitarist James Mastro. In an offbeat variation on the solo record concept, Barone and Mastro dropped down to North Carolina to record **Nuts and Bolts** in collaboration with Mitch Easter. Each Bongo takes a side to showcase his own writing and singing, while helping the other out as well. Barone's results are bland and resemble unfinished band demos or outtakes, with dull sound matching uninspired material; Mastro takes a more idiosyncratic approach, using the opportunity to express some individuality and clearly delineate his contribution to the Bongos.

Recording for the first time as a quartet, the Bongos cut five new songs for **Numbers with Wings**, produced by Richard Gottehrer. "Barbarella" and the title track are prime, filled with swell harmonies, driving acoustic guitars and subtle structural tricks; the rest is adequate but dispensable.

Produced by John Jansen (Lou Reed, Television), **Beat Hotel** is the Bongos' most rocking record, a sparkling explosion of guitar pop. "Space Jungle" has a nagging hook and a full-blown arrangement; "Apache Dancing" is similarly ambitious in a different vein; "Come Back to Me" and "A Story (Written in the Sky)" hark back to the band's simpler days; "Totem Pole" sounds a bit like the dB's except for the overblown big-band finale. Given the best audio treatment of their career, the Bongos prove their mettle, simultaneously exposing their main inadequacy: inconsistent songwriting.

Barone recorded his first solo album onstage at New York's Bottom Line, trading the Bongos' big pop for airy chamber music, leading a scaled-down attack flanked by a cellist, acoustic guitarist and a percussionist-pianist-vibraphonist. **Cool Blue Halo**'s gentler approach shows off his romanticism to good effect, especially on well-chosen covers as the Beatles' "Cry Baby Cry" and Bowie's "The Man Who Sold the World" and Bongos classics ("The Bulrushes" and "Numbers with Wings"). A perfect three a.m. record, though it sounds a tad precious in broad daylight.

In contrast, **Primal Dream** is a full-blown studio job that applies overly smooth production (half by Richard Gottehrer, half by Don Dixon) to Barone's subtle song craft. Though it's consistently tasteful and tuneful, **Primal Dream** lacks the rocking playfulness of the Bongos' best work, veering dangerously close to MOR blandness. Still, taken in small enough doses, the pleasures of such tunes as "River to River" and "Where the Truth Lies" (not to mention a gracefully unslick cover of Lou Reed's "I'll Be Your Mirror") are undeniable. See also *Beat Rodeo.* [jy/i/hd]

BONGOS, BASS, AND BOB

Never Mind the Sex Pistols, Here's Bongos, Bass, and Bob! (What on Earth Were They Thinking?) (50 Skidillion Watts) 1988

Sixteen terribly amusing songs about oral hygiene, used duds ("Clothes of the Dead"), rent-control romance, Thorazine and girls with guns, all done to a golden-brown turn by magician-comedian-label-proprietor Penn Jillette (Bass), Dean J. Seal (Bongos) and Rob "Running" Elk (guitar), with Kramer kind of at the kontrols. Loose'n'lively in a hip, know-it-all, post-frat singalong sort of way. [rg]

BONGWATER

Breaking No New Ground! EP (Shimmy-Disc) 1987
Double Bummer (Shimmy-Disc) 1988 •
Too Much Sleep (Shimmy-Disc) 1989 •
The Power of Pussy (Shimmy-Disc) 1991 •

What's in a brilliant name? Some of the funniest, smartest and messed-up ultra-psychedelia ever invented. Almost all of Bongwater's music comes courtesy of Mark "Maul of Sound" Kramer, the former Shockabilly linchpin, king of the Shimmy-Disc label and in-house workaholic producer/owner of Noise New York studios. Performance artist-*cum*-actress Ann Magnuson contributes onstage attitude and her dreams, transcriptions of which provide many of the group's lyrics. Frequent associates include guitarist Dave Rick (Phantom Tollbooth, etc.) and former Shockabilly percussionist David Licht (who sat out **Too Much Sleep**, replaced by a drum machine). Bongwater is not so much a rock band as a particularly disturbing dream of one.

With its chorus of songs by the Moody Blues, Led Zep and the Beatles, the six-track **Breaking No New Ground!** was but a suggestive whiff of the surreal, parodistic skullfuck of **Double Bummer**, a monumental two-LP set. (The **Double Bummer +** CD adds the EP and an inspirational cover of Roky Erickson's "You Don't Love Me Yet.") **Double Bummer** breaks down into songs constructed around Magnuson's rock dreams, translucently sludgy Kramer originals that take post-pot Beatles as zero-base inspiration and an assortment of adroit covers.

Slapp Happy's "The Drum" is transmogrified into a poignant group anthem on **Too Much Sleep** (the cassette of which *also* contains **No New Ground**). Even better, Magnuson and Kramer—by this point the thinking person's Eurythmics—have integrated their songwriting abilities to even more troubling and hilarious ends, with sampled voices and head-spinning effects a specialty. Thick, rich and satisfying.

As is **The Power of Pussy**, which turns cock-rock on its head in nearly every song and breaks virgin ground with Magnuson's nine-minute opus of apocalyptic acquiescence, "Folk Song." [rg]

See also *Carney-Hild-Kramer, Shockabilly*.

BONZO GOES TO WASHINGTON
See *Jerry Harrison*.

BOOGIE DOWN PRODUCTIONS
Criminal Minded (B-Boy) 1987 ●
By All Means Necessary (Jive-RCA) 1988 ●
Ghetto Music: The Blueprint of Hip Hop (Jive-RCA) 1989 ●
Edutainment (Jive-RCA) 1990 ●
Ya Know The Rules EP (Jive-RCA) 1991
Live Hardcore Worldwide (Jive-RCA) 1991 φ

MS. MELODIE
Diva (Jive-RCA) 1989 ●

HARMONY
Let There Be Harmony (Virgin) 1990 φ

D-NICE
Call Me D-Nice (Jive-RCA) 1990 ●

STOP THE VIOLENCE MOVEMENT
Self Destruction EP (Jive-RCA) 1989

Chris Parker was homeless on the streets of New York for six years before he met Scott Sterling, a counselor at a Bronx men's shelter. As Blastmaster KRS-One (a loose acronym for Knowledge Reigns Supreme Over Almost Every One) and DJ Scott LaRock, the duo formed Boogie Down (slang for the Bronx) Productions as an umbrella organization for various musical endeavors and cut the self-financed single "Crack Attack." They followed it with **Criminal Minded**, one of the most stunning hip-hop debuts ever. The record clearly revealed Parker as an eloquent and serious social commentator, one who would go well beyond rap's standard concerns, tempering his didactic preachiness with humor and humility. Indeed, he has grown into one of the most influential and respected artists of his generation, largely responsible for the rise of positive-message rap and the blending of reggae and hip-hop.

The title track of **Criminal Minded** is as good as rap gets. Witty, compassionate lyrics bust out gracefully over hard beats as ghostly (opera?) samples float in the background. The waking-nightmare "9mm Goes Bang," set to a chattering reggae beat, takes us deep inside the mind of a drug dealer—and begins a BDP tradition of painting psychological profiles of street life.

That life struck home all too vividly when LaRock was shot to death on 25 August 1987, just as the album was growing into a major underground hit. (It went on to sell nearly a million copies.) Undeterred, KRS-One

returned with **By All Means Necessary**, noticeably more confident and politically conscious than on the debut. His brother Kenny Parker (and posse member D-Nice) ably shouldered the DJ responsibilities, laying down killer reggae rhythms and sampling everything from Deep Purple to a street person mumbling "What can we get for 63 cents?" (As every future BDP release would, the sleeve declared that **By All Means Necessary** was "Overseen by D.J. Scott LaRock.") While Chris Parker posed with an Uzi on the cover in emulation of Malcolm X, his lyrics made it clear that he advocates violence only in self-defense. The song "Stop the Violence" led to **Self Destruction**, an all-star benefit 12-inch produced by KRS-One and D-Nice and featuring an impressive cast: Kool Moe Dee, Just-Ice, MC Lyte, members of Stetsasonic and Public Enemy, plus Parker's wife, Ramona "Ms. Melodie" Parker.

The best of the post-LaRock albums so far, **Ghetto Music** presents a startling blend of provocative politics and hard-edged reggae-rap, mostly played by live musicians. Highlights include the stark, explosive police story, "Who Protects Us from You?," the rapid-fire Dylanesque images of "Jack of Spades" and the dubwise "Jah Rulez," which showcases impassioned singing by Ms. Melodie's younger sister, Pamela "Harmony" Scott.

Edutainment is indeed educational, but hardly as entertaining as previous BDP albums. The thirteen barebones tracks are interspersed with six excerpts from lectures by KRS-One and Kwame Touré (formerly Stokely Carmichael). Allowing some bitterness and sarcasm to mingle with his thoughtful commentary, KRS lashes out at meat-eaters, the music industry and "house niggas." But few of the tracks have musical hooks as strong as their stories. The two most musically successful are "100 Guns," a relentless account of driving across the country with a trunk full of weapons, and "The Homeless," a bitter state-of-the-black-nation address ("Not fully American/We're getting there slowly") set to an African-styled rhythm. (The CD and cassette contain three bonus tracks, including "7 Dee Jays," a nineminute reggae number that features various posse members.)

Ya Know The Rules includes three mixes of the **Edutainment** track for which it's named plus live versions (all from **Live Hardcore Worldwide**) of "Criminal Minded" and "The Bridge Is Over" (from the debut) and the second album's "Jimmy."

Although losing out to the 2 Live Crew as the first group to release a live rap album, BDP proves even more explosive on stage than in the studio. Including six raps from the debut album and several impassioned speeches by KRS-One, **Live Hardcore Worldwide**—recorded at clubs in New York, London and Paris—offers a solid introduction to the band's career.

Besides working the lecture circuit, KRS-One has become an in-demand producer, working with both hiphop and reggae artists, including Sly and Robbie, Ziggy Marley and Mikey Dread. He's also taken an active role in BDP's expanding roster, producing albums for both Ms. Melodie and Harmony. While the former's **Diva** is simply mediocre, **Let There Be Harmony** is an intriguing, if erratic, effort. Harmony alternately applies her rich gospelly voice to mushy love songs and raps about tough revolutionary politics—and Christian piety.

Displaying more production skills than lyrical depth, D-Nice (Derrick Jones) steps out on **Call Me D-Nice**, a great-sounding mix of hip-hop, soul and reggae that—with the positive edutainment exceptions of "A Few Dollars More" and "Glory"—stays pretty close to kiss/dis clichés. KRS-One makes an avuncular guest appearance on "The TR 808 Is Coming."

In yet another facet of BDP's business, toaster/rapper Jamal-ski is featured on one side of a 1990 12-inch, speeding his way through "Let's Do It." [ws]

BOOK OF LOVE
Book of Love (I Square-Sire) 1986 ●
Lullaby (I Square-Sire) 1988 ●
Candy Carol (I Square-Sire-Warner Bros.) 1991 φ

Produced by Ivan Ivan for his own label, this New York art-school quartet's first album is a clever synthesis of catchy electro-pop minimalism and dance-driven rhythmatics. Susan Ottaviano's breathy, almost spoken vocals on atmospheric tunes like "Boy" and "Happy Day" neatly offset the simple, spacious arrangements; others aren't quite as memorable. A bit like Trio without the irony or Dominatrix cleaned up for mass appeal, **Book of Love** is an alluring if insignificant way to while away time in clubland. (Special note to aficionados of esoteric cover versions: Book of Love tackles Liliput's "Diematrosen.")

From such fringey beginnings, Book of Love made the mistake of abandoning the first record's stylish economy and reaching for mainstream success on **Lullaby**. The group's knowing junk-culture side surfaces on the driving club interpretation of "Tubular Bells" that opens the album, but Susan O's sex-kitten singing, Ted Ottaviano's dumb lyrics and the routine sound of hyperactive sequencers nearly adds up to Berlin reborn.

The all-keyboards-and-vocals quartet (with a few guest guitarists) found its place again on the toned-down **Candy Carol**, a fairly enticing application of flowerpower style and lush pop harmonies. The synth arrangements run from trite ("Butterfly") to subtle ("Candy Carol," which makes cute use of a melody that comes pre-programmed on every $30 Casio) as do the lyrics: "Quiver" is simple and dumb, while "Flower Parade" consists of an a cappella list of floral species, and "Orange Flip" is a kicky little ode to lipstick colors. [i]

SONIC BOOM
See *Spacemen 3*.

BOOM CRASH OPERA
Boom Crash Opera (Warner Bros.) 1987 ●
These Here Are Crazy Times (Giant) 1990 ●

On Boom Crash Opera's debut album, the Melbourne, Australia quintet plays heavy drum-driven dance-oriented rock much in the manner of INXS, but with just enough angst and bombast to live up to their name.

Wide-screen sound characterizes the crisply produced (in part by Jimmy Iovine) **Crazy Times**, even though many of the numbers are pushed by acoustic guitars. There's a dash of U2's spiritualism here and the Alarm's romanticism there (especially on the anthemic

"Dancing in the Storm"), a couple of bright big-beat dance-rock numbers, even a Zeppelin-style riff or two thrown in for good measure. Not a bad record, but the band has yet to establish a vision of its own. [ds]

BOOMTOWN RATS
The Boomtown Rats (Mercury) 1977
A Tonic for the Troops (Columbia) 1978 ●
The Fine Art of Surfacing (Columbia) 1979 ●
Mondo Bongo (Columbia) 1980 ●
Rat Tracks EP (Can. Vertigo) 1981
V Deep (Columbia) 1982 ●
The Boomtown Rats EP (Columbia) 1982
Ratrospective EP (Columbia) 1983
In the Long Grass (Columbia) 1984
Greatest Hits (Columbia) 1987 ●

Like Madness and the Jam, the Boomtown Rats generally matched considerable Anglo-European success with near-total American commercial obscurity. Despite a string of intelligent, irresistible pop singles and intricate, skillful, unpredictable albums filled with assorted musical styles and sounds, the only US hit the Rats ever had was the morbid ballad "I Don't Like Mondays." While their albums are not uniformly excellent, the band's commitment to quality and growth, plus singer/songwriter Bob Geldof's magnetic personality, help elevate even lesser efforts to listenability, and much of their work is downright brilliant.

The six future Rats left the unemployment lines in Dublin to enter the rock sweepstakes and had become a going concern on the Irish concert circuit by the time new wave came along. While the resulting upsurge in record-industry openness towards young, energetic bands undoubtedly helped them get a contract, it was clear from the start that the Rats were a different musical breed. Produced in Germany by pre-metal Mutt Lange, the first album is more tradition-minded than punky, but there's no mistaking the verve and independence which tied the Rats solidly to less accomplished, more enraged outfits. From the Springsteenish "Joey's on the Street Again" to the Dr. Feelgoody "Never Bite the Hand that Feeds" to a Mott the Hoople-styled ballad, "I Can Make It If You Can," and the album's sarcastic standout, "Lookin' After No. 1," the ambience is hip, but the rock is fairly routine. Geldof's incisive lyrics and the entire band's credible musicianship invest the stylistically diverse selections with character, making this a top-notch, timeless record.

Assumptions about the Rats' musical intent were dispelled with **A Tonic for the Troops**. Taking giant steps forward in invention and sophistication, Geldof turned from a junior rock singer into a skilled vocalist with a recognizable style; the band likewise exhibited new-found intricacy and multifaceted versatility, thanks in large part to Johnnie Fingers' keyboard cleverness and Lange's layered production. **Troops** is not a total departure—"Rat Trap" picks up precisely where "Joey" left off, and "She's So Modern" merely improves on "Mary of the 4th Form"—but "Me and Howard Hughes," "Like Clockwork" and "Living in an Island" display development on all fronts: writing, singing, performing, arranging. (The American version deletes "Can't Stop" and "(Watch Out for) The Normal People" in favor of two tracks retrieved from the first

LP, which had sunk without a trace upon its release by the Rats' previous US label.)

The Rats took another big leap on **The Fine Art of Surfacing**, but with less rewarding results. Substandard songs get unenthusiastic treatment, and an overwhelming sense of self-importance highlights the ennui, despite impressive technical aptitude and obviously strengthened confidence and stylistic reach. The record does contain the powerful "I Don't Like Mondays" and a few other standouts—"Someone's Looking at You," which is clumsy but melodic and charming, and "When the Night Comes," a showstopper with ace Geldof lyrics and a swell arrangement that uses Latin-flavored acoustic guitar for color—but otherwise **Surfacing** is a slick drag.

On first listen, **Mondo Bongo** is even more outlandish, but a little application reveals a number of great tracks in a percussion-laden Afro-Carib style, delivered up in gonzo fashion by co-producer Tony Visconti. "Up All Night," "The Elephants Graveyard" and "Don't Talk to Me" are rollicking good fun, but "Mood Mambo" takes the genre detour too literally, and a totally unnecessary rewrite of an old Rolling Stones tune ("Under Their Thumb . . . Is Under My Thumb") adds to the record's shortcomings. Neither a triumph nor a disaster, **Mondo Bongo** is a halfbaked but entertaining digression. The Canadian-only **Rat Tracks** has a live cut, a remix of "Up All Night" and several otherwise UK-only obscurities: five tracks in all.

Total confusion as to the band's direction and frustration at the disinterest shown by the American audience may have been the reasons why Columbia tried to avoid releasing **V Deep**, opting instead for a 12-inch condensation of it. (The company eventually came around and issued the entire LP, including the EP's contents.) Although heavily stylized and partially overproduced, **V Deep** (the band's fifth LP and its first as a quintet, following the departure of guitarist Gerry Cott, who then released a couple of solo singles) contains some of the Rats' strangest songs, but also some of their most evocative and moving efforts. Geldof is at his driven best, and the band keeps pace in a number of styles (including an encore of **Mondo Bongo**'s sound and a Dennis Bovell dub mix of one track) that don't neatly hang together, but paint the group in a most fascinating light. A fine album to be savored repeatedly.

After **V Deep**, the Rats dropped out for several years, prompting the US issue of **Ratrospective**, a minialbum containing "I Don't Like Mondays," "Up All Night," "Rat Trap" and three other familiar cuts. In late 1984, Geldof surfaced as the co-instigator of Band Aid, an all-star 45 fundraiser for Africa that inspired a wave of similar ventures throughout the music world. The band returned to action in early 1985 with a new single, followed several months later by an entire new album, **In the Long Grass**, which had actually been recorded in 1983 but initially rejected by their label. (The inner sleeve thanks people "For making an unbearable year tolerable . . .") The Rats look miserable and spent on the cover; the lyrics are unremittingly bitter, defiant and angry. Matching the verbal onslaught, the music is as dense and rugged as any they have ever made, yet uplifting in the band's stalwart refusal to buckle. An extraordinarily powerful record. (In an ironic final bit of tampering, Columbia forced the Rats to rewrite the lyrics of "Dave," a song on the UK LP, resulting in an entirely different vocal and title: "Rain.")

Later that year, Geldof organized the massive Live Aid charity concert/telecast and was mooted for Nobel Prize consideration, but it hardly aided the Rats, who met 1986 without an American label and decided to call it quits. Acknowledging the group's demise and taking fair (and dignified) advantage of the attention Geldof had earned, Columbia expanded **Ratrospective** by four tracks and called it **Greatest Hits**, a fair compilation improved by Arthur Levy's enthusiastic liner notes. [i]

See also *Bob Geldof*.

DUKE BOOTEE
Bust Me Out (Mercury) 1984

Duke Bootee (Edward Fletcher, in his other life a Newark, NJ schoolteacher) is one of the unsung heroes of rap. As a member of the Sugar Hill label's extraordinary house band, he wrote the tune, "chorus" and half the raps for "The Message." Although that groundbreaking single came out under the name of Grandmaster Flash and the Furious Five, the raps belong to Bootee and Melle Mel. The two paired up less successfully (and more formulaically) on "Message II" and "New York, New York," before Bootee rediscovered the urban claustrophobia groove on the title track of his solo LP. The album boasts aggressive playing and production from his old Sugar Hill friends, and the rap side (as opposed to the song side) smokes. [jl]

BOOTHILL FOOT-TAPPERS
Get Your Feet Out of My Shoes EP (nr/Go! Discs) 1984
Ain't That Far from Boothill (nr/Mercury) 1985

In yet another installment of "Musical Styles Traverse the Ocean," these seven rustic English lads and lassies play a charming and catchy version of oldtimey folk (banjo, fiddle, guitar, washboard, accordion) on the wonderful title track of their five-song 12-inch. But it doesn't stop there: they also essay a soulful choral arrangement of Curtis Mayfield's "People Get Ready" and a rousing assault on Margaret Thatcher called "True Blues." The only duff item is the rushed, tuneless "Milk Train."

Unfortunately, the album makes a crime of eclecticism: the band dabbles in everything from ska to country-western, connecting emotionally with none of it. Flat, insipid production (mostly by Dick Cuthell) matches the performances' lack of spunk; the net result is a record without depth or charm. Even a new version of "Get Your Feet Out of My Shoes" sounds tedious and contrived. The Boothill Foot-Tappers disbanded at the end of 1985. [i]

BOOTSTRAPPERS
See *fIREHOSE*.

BOO-YAA T.R.I.B.E
New Funky Nation (4th & B'way) 1990 ●

The "Six Bad Brothas" of Los Angeles' Boo-Yaa crew are, in fact, an imposing family of mean-looking Samoan-Americans named Devoux who sing and deliver tough gangster raps over a full band of live musicians. As a result of that innovation and the band's considerable abilities, **New Funky Nation** is an extraordinarily powerful and uncommon hip-hop LP, a rhythmic soul assault of horns, Boo-Yaa bass and violence-prone street rhymes that have an unsettling ring of truth.

[i]

BOREDOMS
Soul Discharge (Shimmy-Disc) 1990

This totally inexplicable noise band from Japan boasts six members: P-We YY, God Mama, Human Rich Vox Y, Hila Y, Eye Y and No. 1 Y. **Soul Discharge**, which contains such songs as "JB Dick + Tin Turner Pussy Badsmell" and "Bubblebop Shot," amounts to lumbering stop-start drums, distorted thrusts of bass and guitar, and people shrieking, chattering, yelling and groaning goodnaturedly. For a vague reference point, the Boredoms' essential notions fall somewhere between the Butthole Surfers, the B-52's and a band of bag ladies. You have been warned. [i]

BORGHESIA
Love Is Colder Than Death (It. Materiali Sonori) 1985
Their Laws, Our Lives (It. Materiali Sonori) 1986
No Hope, No Fear EP (Play It Again Sam) 1987 •
Escorts And Models (Play It Again Sam) 1988 •
Resistance (Play It Again Sam) 1989 •

CLICK CLICK/BORGHESIA
Doublebill (Play It Again Sam) 1988

Understandably for a trio of sociology and philosophy students who began as a theater group, Borghesia's music is arty, grandiose and pretentious; however, as a band emerging from a repressed society (Yugoslavia) to create its own movement (the New Slovenian Art scene, along with Laibach), Borghesia is also intriguing and provocative.

Lacking Laibach's fascistic bent, Borghesia also uses symphonic keyboard arrangements and morbid beats to create a similar Teutonic and military feel. The group's early output is quite rare: cassette-only releases (including one, apparently, of purely classical music) and two European albums, **Love Is Colder Than Death** and **Their Laws, Our Lives**.

Borghesia's trans-Atlantic calling card, the **No Hope, No Fear** mini-album, presents a group whose classical background merges comfortably with a digital sensibility. Though certainly not easy listening, the six tracks are far more mainstream than might be expected of a group so far removed from the familiar environs of rock and pop.

Escorts and Models is far better. This collection of songs about the darker side of sex combines melodic vocals with spoken phrases (only partly in English), utilizes samples to excellent effect and embraces both funereal tempos ("Beat and Scream") and industrial disco ("A.P.R."). A tantalizing musical venture by any standards, it proves that, in their genre, Borghesia have the skills and creative tools to compete with the world's best.

Exposure to Western audiences through touring and (self-produced) videos resulted in the mutated 12-inch cover of Sonic Youth's "She Is Not Alone." Borghesia then returned to their own culture for **Resistance**, loosely an album of protest songs. Dropping the playful aspects of **Escorts and Models**, this venture is sinister through and through, an often unsettling voyage into the heart of totalitarianism. The beats pound ominously, the lyrics are direct and the choruses have a martial feel. While Borghesia is clearly capable of doing the commercial tango, **Resistance** is a battle with evil.

Doublebill is a joint 12-inch shared with England's Click Click: Borghesia's side consists of two mixes of "Naked Uniform Dead" (from **Escorts**) and two non-LP cuts. [tf]

ADRIAN BORLAND AND THE CITIZENS
See *Sound*.

BOSS HOG
See *Pussy Galore*.

ANNE RICHMOND BOSTON
See *Swimming Pool Q's*.

BOUNTY HUNTERS
See *Nikki Sudden*.

DENNIS BOVELL
Brain Damage (nr/Fontana-Phonogram) 1981
BLACKBEARD
Strictly Dub Wize (nr/Tempus) 1978 (nr/Ballistic-UA) 1978
I Wah Dub (nr/More Cut-EMI) 1980
DENNIS BOVELL AND THE DUB BAND
Audio Active (Moving Target) 1986 •

Guitarist Dennis "Blackbeard" Bovell has long been a reggae musician and producer of high standing. (He co-founded Matumbi, defunct for several years now but still remembered as one of England's first and best self-contained reggae bands; try their **Point of View** LP on EMI America.) Bovell also happened to have been a school chum of white jazz-pop keyboardist Nick Straker and musician/producer Tony Mansfield (New Musik, Captain Sensible, etc.), with whom he maintained contact; such eclectic musical connections have enabled him to bring a fresh perspective to the production of early new wave bands like the Slits and the Pop Group.

This same eclecticism informs his dub LPs in conceptual outlook and willingness to take chances beyond the usual electronic overkill. Bovell creates strong instrumentals that are mainly written and arranged for dub; the catchy melody lines are dissected but not disintegrated. **Strictly Dub Wize** (mostly performed by Bovell, with some help from Matumbi and others) exhibits cleverness and humor by the bagful (one track even bases itself on "Surrey with the Fringe on Top"!). **I Wah Dub** carries Bovell's creation of aurally pungent tracks infused with musical witticisms from merely excellent to brilliant. Aside from some drumming, the odd

81

piano part here or melodica toot there, Bovell plays everything.

Brain Damage and **Audio Active** are also both consistently enjoyable, though less spectacular: neither uses much dub at all. The former adds a mixed bag of boogie-woogie, rock'n'roll and R&B to the reggae, and Bovell's homely but good-humored vocals adorn several tracks. (A bonus dub LP—all new tracks, similar to **I Wah Dub**, though not as engrossing—is included.) Good lightweight groove music, ideal for summer.

The later record—a band effort, including Straker and Matumbi's horn duo—is mostly vocal and almost all reggae. Surprisingly, the instrumental and dub tracks are less interesting than the vocal tunes; Bovell's songwriting has grown and his singing's matured. If Eddy Grant stuck to reggae for most of an LP it might sound like this. Durably likable, it goes by too darn fast—all ten tracks are between three and four minutes long.

[jg]

DAVID BOWIE

Man of Words/Man of Music (Mercury) 1969
The Man Who Sold the World (Mercury) 1970 (RCA)
   1972 (Rykodisc) 1990 ●
Hunky Dory (RCA) 1971 (Rykodisc) 1990 ●
The Rise and Fall of Ziggy Stardust and the Spiders from
   Mars (RCA) 1972 (Rykodisc) 1990 ●
Space Oddity (RCA) 1972 (Rykodisc) 1990 ●
Images 1966–1967 (London) 1973
Aladdin Sane (RCA) 1973 (Rykodisc) 1990 ●
Pin-Ups (RCA) 1973 (Rykodisc) 1990 ●
Diamond Dogs (RCA) 1974 (Rykodisc) 1990 ●
David Live (RCA) 1974 (Rykodisc) 1990 ●
Young Americans (RCA) 1975 (Rykodisc) 1991 ●
Station to Station (RCA) 1976 (Rykodisc) 1991 ●
Changesonebowie (RCA) 1976 ●
Low (RCA) 1977 ●
Starting Point (London) 1977
Heroes (RCA) 1977 ●
Stage (RCA) 1978
Lodger (RCA) 1979 ●
Scary Monsters (RCA) 1980 ●
Changestwobowie (RCA) 1981 ●
Let's Dance (EMI America) 1983 ●
Golden Years (RCA) 1983 ●
Tonight (EMI America) 1984 ●
Fame and Fashion (RCA) 1984 ●
Never Let Me Down (EMI America) 1987 ●
Sound+Vision (Rykodisc) 1989 ●
Changesbowie (Rykodisc) 1990 ●

TIN MACHINE

Tin Machine (EMI) 1989 ●

Throughout his lengthy career, David Bowie has worked in many widely disparate musical areas, and virtually all of them have proven enormously influential, even if sometimes it's taken years for the rest of the rock world to catch up with him. Nonetheless, the mercurial star continues to shift gears, styles and fashions almost as often as shirts and, by example, helps keep pop and rock developing and changing. (Unfortunately, long after he's abandoned some excessive dalliance or another, his camp followers trundle on, missing the ephemeral and transitory essence of Bowie's work.) Even if only as the source of unreproachably hip songs

to cover, Bowie has played an essential role in glam-rock, new wave, post-punk, neo-soul, dance music, etc.

Although he actually began recording in the late '60s, we join the Bowie show in progress at the dawn of the '70s, when he dropped some of his more theatrical Anthony Newley affectations and got down to rock'n'roll cases. (The discography omits some of the less significant compilations and repackages, as well as film soundtracks, collaborations, EPs and spoken-word records.)

The Man Who Sold the World begins Bowie's affair with guitar-heavy rock'n'roll, courtesy Mick Ronson. Tony Visconti's compressed production gives the album an utterly synthetic audio quality; few records this simply played sound as studio-created. In retrospect, the grim futurist imagery of "Saviour Machine," "The Supermen" and "Running Gun Blues" seems far more prescient than the thrilling but unadventurous band's music. Still, a shockingly strong debut for the electrified Bowie. (Besides illustrating the album's various covers, the Ryko reissue adds a previously unreleased track and the "Holy Holy" single from 1970, as well as both sides of the 1971 Arnold Corns single: early versions of "Moonage Daydream" and "Hang on to Yourself," both of which would get full play on **Ziggy Stardust**.)

Hunky Dory was a detour of sorts, briefly returning a seemingly innocent Bowie to his hippie-folkie-cabaret days for the catchy "Changes" and the obnoxiously precious "Kooks," plus such atypically direct tributes as "Song for Bob Dylan" and "Andy Warhol." But the album also contains the redemptive "Life on Mars," "Queen Bitch" and "Oh! You Pretty Things," all essential cornerstones in the burgeoning glam-sci-fi-decadence world Bowie was assembling. (The reissue adds an alternate mix of the album's "Bewlay Brothers" and a demo of its "Quicksand," as well as a second version of the previous LP's "Supermen" and an unreleased '71 song, "Bombers.")

Bowie began his fey alien role-playing in earnest on **Ziggy Stardust**, a classic rock'n'roll album. He introduces this new persona via the pseudo-biographical title track; otherwise, songs paint a weird portrait of an androgynous (but sexy) world ahead. Armed with supercharged guitar rock and truly artistic production (Bowie and Ken Scott), and mixing rock'n'roll stardom imagery with a more general *Clockwork Orange* outlook, the peerless set (including "Suffragette City," "Hang on to Yourself," "Rock'n'Roll Suicide" and "Moonage Daydream") outlines some of the concerns that underpinned a lot of rock songwriting in the '70s and '80s. (The reissue—also available in a deluxe edition with a slipcase and book of liner notes—adds demos of the title track and "Lady Stardust," the otherwise unreleased "Sweet Head," a '71 B-side, "Velvet Goldmine," and a remix of the 1972 single "John, I'm Only Dancing.")

Bowie's label then dredged up an oldie, reissuing 1969's lightweight **Man of Words/Man of Music** as **Space Oddity** (after the memorable lead-off track, but clearly in the hopes of cashing in on **Ziggy**'s sci-fi content). The Ryko edition adds a 1970 B-side ("Conversation Piece" and a two-part single version, with Mick Ronson's first appearance, of the album's hippydippy "Memory of a Free Festival"). In another dose of déjà vu, an American corporate relative of Bowie's old UK label put together a two-disc set of even earlier recordings (primarily from the 1967 **David Bowie** LP), titling it **Images 1966-1967**. Years later, London condensed **Images** into the single-record **Starting Point**.

Having peaked so gloriously with a character that could not last indefinitely, Bowie adjusted Ziggy a bit on **Aladdin Sane** and came up with a weird set of tunes—some tremendous, some minor—and a distant, unpleasant left-field studio sound. "Panic in Detroit," "Watch That Man," "The Jean Genie" and "Drive-In Saturday" are some of his greatest songs, painting bleak pictures of detached existences, with cinematic strokes and killer riffs. Rather than singing about apocalypse, Bowie captures the barren feel of a dead world, and feeds it into the music. **Aladdin Sane** is also notable for allowing a serious crooner side to re-emerge—as on "Time," a foreshadow of future developments. That said, it must be noted that Bowie's revisionist cover of "Let's Spend the Night Together" is utterly misguided.

In a surprisingly guileless gesture, Bowie next made an all-covers album of songs by great mid-'60s English bands. Although not easily related creatively to Bowie's creative flow, **Pin-Ups** is a wonderful, loving tribute that contains generally ace renditions of classic but, in America at least, largely unknown songs by the Pretty Things, Pink Floyd, Them, Mojos, Merseys, Kinks, Yardbirds, Easybeats and Who. If nothing else, Bowie's reverent consideration helped gave the songs and artists much-deserved cachet in the new rock world. (The Rykodisc edition adds two worthless items: a previously unissued rendition of Bruce Springsteen's "Growing Up" and a drippy version of a Jacques Brel/Mort Shuman composition—"Port of Amsterdam"—that had been used as a B-side.)

Bowie then jettisoned his band and drafted a new bunch of sidemen to further explore his trendily somber vision of a doomed future on **Diamond Dogs**. Although the LP contains one of Bowie's most incredible and concise songs—"Rebel Rebel," perfectly describing his followers and their role in the new society—and such significant items as "1984" and "Rock 'n Roll with Me," it also has a pompously overblown and underdeveloped concept. In retrospect, **Diamond Dogs** isn't so bad, but it does suffer significantly from eccentric, seemingly unfinished, production and strident sound. The 1990 reissue addresses the latter concern with much-improved remastering, unexpurgates the cover painting to its intended form and adds two tracks: an intricate demo of the album's "Candidate" and 1973's previously unreleased soul stomp "Dodo."

Bowie's first concert record, the two-record **David Live**, was recorded in Philadelphia at two 1974 shows with a ten-piece band featuring guitarist Earl Slick. Featuring a fine song selection broadly drawn from the preceding albums, the program also includes renditions of the Stax classic "Knock on Wood" and "All the Young Dudes," a song Bowie had graciously given Mott the Hoople. The reissue adds "Time" and "Here Today, Gone Tomorrow."

Dropping his gimmicky costumes, Bowie donned a fine suit and made **Young Americans**, an album mainly composed of phony (but pleasant) Philadelphia soul/rock mixed with other oddities, like a truly awful collaboration with John Lennon, "Fame." It took five years for the British new wave, finally bereft of their own new ideas, to ape Bowie and start reflecting African-American idioms into their work.

Following that brief infatuation, Bowie launched an experimental phase that directly influenced far more bands, especially the "new romantics" and arty minimalists. **Station to Station** is a strangely impersonal mixture of chilly show ballads, techno-pop and whatever was passing for disco that year. The album features the hit "Golden Years," but also the experimental and challenging "TVC15." It also marked the beginning of Bowie's artistic distance from his former rock-idol role.

That trend was formally instigated with **Low**, on which Bowie arranged to co-opt the modernistic sensibility of Brian Eno (his collaborator on three consecutive studio LPs) and present a selection of tracks that are not so much songs as word-paintings or, in many cases, simply mood pieces. Moving from the grandiosity of **Young Americans** to the art-noise sketches here, Bowie took heart from intellectual, bare-bones rock bands like Wire and, in turn, helped legitimize and promote such spartan stylings.

As the follow-up to **Low**, **Heroes** has slightly fleshier production, though nearly one full side is comprised of whizzing synthesizers and amorphous textural noodling. Robert Fripp contributes lead guitar, and his presence adds a bit of sinew to the overall sound, something lacking in the less-forceful **Low**. The album leans heavily on chilly, European affectations (with a large debt owed to Kraftwerk), but also has room for a genuine and spectacular pop single, the atmospheric, concertedly European title track (also released in French and German).

Bowie's second double-live LP, **Stage**, features a Carlos Alomar/Adrian Belew guitar lineup and includes hits ("Ziggy Stardust," "Fame") as well as Eno-era album tracks ("Warszawa," "Beauty and the Beast").

Lodger, the third installment of the Bowie-Eno trilogy, finds Bowie drifting back into a solid song-oriented context. Though much of the material seems to be stream-of-consciousness, there are a couple of pure poppers, such as "D.J." and "Boys Keep Swinging," that recall a more commercial time. Also of interest is Bowie's version of "Sister Moonlight," rewritten as "Red Money."

Scary Monsters is Bowie's most consistent LP since the pre-**Low** period, a culmination of the styles that had been showcased individually on previous discs. The tone is up-front, a confrontation with the real world of alienation Bowie always ascribed to his fictional settings. **Scary Monsters** contains two soon-to-be standards: "Ashes to Ashes" and "Fashion."

Having tired of years of acclaim matched with only sporadic, middling glimmers of the kind of success that superstars are supposed to enjoy, Bowie changed labels and made **Let's Dance**, a calculated effort (with the production assistance of Nile Rodgers) to get in step with the sound of today, rather than tomorrow or yesterday, his usual habitats. Not surprisingly, Bowie succeeds at whatever he sets his mind to, and the record was a worldwide smash. "Let's Dance," "Modern Love" and "China Girl" may not be the Thin White Duke's finest creations, but they do hit a solid compromise between art and commerce, and don't harm his reputation nearly as much as expand his audience (and bank balance).

Several years later, Bowie regained the rights to his back catalogue and attempted to arrange for his entire oeuvre to be reissued by his new label. The plan backfired, and all of the RCA albums—on vinyl, tape and CD—went out of print. Fortunately, Bowie was able to strike a deal that led to a full-scale, top-notch reissue program, beginning in 1989 with the extraordinary **Sound + Vision** boxed set, a beautifully appointed collection of classics, obscurities, previously unissued outtakes, 1972 concert recordings, etc. Except for the inclusion of too many tracks from the live albums, this is a monumental and fascinating way to rediscover Bowie.

After a mega-tour to consolidate the album's huge success, Bowie banged out **Tonight**, a casual, smug cookie-cutter job geared for easy chart ascent. (What other recording challenges are left for Bowie? He's tried self-indulgent art and go-for-the-jugular commercialism, scoring just what he wanted on both fronts.) In its losing defense, the album does include a duet with Tina Turner and a remarkably swell pop hit, "Jazzin' for Blue Jean," that recalls far earlier times in his career.

The styleless **Never Let Me Down** was released to general indifference and critical derision. Although this casual loud-rock outing—Peter Frampton and Carlos Alomar share guitar responsibilities with Bowie—seems on first blush to be slapdash and slight, the first side is actually quite good, offering provocative pop-culture lyrics delivered with first-take enthusiasm and carefree backing. "Day-In Day-Out" is silly but charming in its way; the verses' catchy ticktock pop on "Beat of Your Drum" makes it resemble a Cars song; the Lennonish title track is equally weird and likable. Bowie has rarely sounded so unconcerned and relaxed. The inferior second side starts off with the subsequent tour's fantasyland nonsense theme song ("Glass Spider") and ends with Iggy's "Bang Bang," a cute digression in keeping with the record's flip attitude.

After that fiasco, Bowie went off and formed a collaborative modern-rock quartet with guitarist Reeves Gabrels and the fraternal rhythm section of Hunt and Tony Sales. Taking pages from Bowie's loose-sounding work with Iggy as well as **Diamond Dogs**, Tin Machine's first album (a follow-up was reportedly recorded in late '89 but still not released by early '91) is loud and blunt—occasionally a bit brutish—with provocative songs that are credible but (with the exception of "Baby Can Dance" and "Crack City") not especially memorable. While the results of the experiment are equivocal and it's hardly a significant item in Bowie's catalogue, as a noisy and exciting rock album, **Tin Machine** is better than most.

The **Changesonebowie** compilation covers a lot of stylistic ground in eleven tracks: from "Space Oddity" and "Changes" to "Rebel Rebel" and "Golden Years." **Changestwobowie** is weaker, but still has such amazing tracks as "Sound and Vision," "Starman," "D.J." and "1984." The eighteen-track **Changesbowie**, issued to coincide with the 1990 greatest-hits tour, includes all of the first **Changes** LP (replacing the original "Fame" with a remix), adds "Fashion" and "Ashes to Ashes" from the second, and then tops it off with such tunes as "Heroes," "Let's Dance," "China Girl," "Modern Love" and "Blue Jean." **Fame and Fashion**—drawing only from RCA albums—straddles all three, with a half-dozen or so in common with each and only one song ("TVC15") that doesn't appear on any of the others. The pointless and unnecessary **Golden Years** repeats **Fame and Fashion**'s "Fashion," "Golden Years" and "Ashes to Ashes," but also contains things like "Joe the Lion," "Wild Is the Wind" and "Scary Monsters." [jw/i]

See also *Adrian Belew, Iggy Pop, Lou Reed.*

BOW WOW WOW

Your Cassette Pet [tape] (nr/EMI) 1980
See Jungle! See Jungle! Go Join Your Gang Yeah! City All Over, Go Ape Crazy (RCA) 1981
The Last of the Mohicans EP (RCA) 1982
I Want Candy (RCA) 1982
Twelve Original Recordings (Harvest) 1982
When the Going Gets Tough the Tough Get Going (RCA) 1983
The Best of Bow Wow Wow (nr/Receiver) 1989 ●

ANNABELLA

Fever (RCA) 1986 ●

Bow Wow Wow may have been easily dismissed by some as rock entrepreneur Malcolm McLaren's creation, but the band deserved better. Combining musicians lured away from Adam and the Ants (with whom McLaren had briefly worked) and fifteen-year-old singer Annabella Lwin, the ever-provocative McLaren formed the band, launching their career via a 45, "C-30, C-60, C-90 Go," which espoused the virtues of home taping at a time when the band's record company (and virtually all others) were beginning to bitterly oppose it. True to McLaren's precepts (although it should be noted that tapes at that time were not as commonly copied as discs), **Your Cassette Pet** is a tape-only collection of eight songs. Except for "I Want My Baby on Mars" and a painful rendition of "Fools Rush In," the material is marked by Annabella's breathless ranting and incessant drumming style "borrowed" from the African Burundi tribe. The results are cheerful if smarmy.

The first full-length album, **See Jungle! See Jungle!**, isn't as wound up as **Cassette Pet**, but does show artistic growth. By downplaying the leering football chants, Bow Wow Wow was able to investigate subtler lyrics and rhythms. And fueled by drummer Dave Barbarossa, they pack quite a wallop.

Last of the Mohicans is a four-song EP whose producer (Kenny Laguna, of Joan Jett fame) and lead-off track (the Strangeloves' "I Want Candy") were chosen presumably for their American commercial potential. If nothing else, the sound is cleaner than before.

The discographical plot thickens with **I Want Candy**, released in two distinctly different versions. The American LP is comprised of the **Mohicans** EP, four tracks from **See Jungle!** (three of them remixed) and two new cuts. The UK album of the same title makes **Your Cassette Pet** available on vinyl, except for "Louis Quatorze." It also includes a few British single sides and the US-only EP, with its re-recorded "Louis Quatorze." Got that?

Not to be outdone, EMI's American affiliate issued **Twelve Original Recordings**. This is essentially the British **I Want Candy** LP minus several tracks. Pay your money and take your choice.

McLaren and Bow Wow Wow parted company in

1982 and the all-new **When the Going Gets Tough** was recorded free of his machinations. On their final album, Bow Wow Wow delivered much the same musical barrage as before, but without any of the propagandistic pretense. The band subsequently ejected Annabella and regrouped as the Chiefs of Relief. **The Best of Bow Wow Wow** neatly compresses Bow Wow Wow's entire career—with hits and album selections from **Your Cassette Pet** through **When the Going Gets Tough**—onto a single sixteen-track album.

Having outgrown her traumatic youth, Annabella's solo album is basically high-gloss rubbish, despite the efforts of six very different producers (including Slade's Jim Lea, hip-hop heavy John Robie and Zeus B. Held). It's not that Annabella can't sing, it's just that she's foundering here without purpose or personality. Even a cover of Alice Cooper's "School's Out" goes appallingly wrong.   [si/i]

See also *Adam and the Ants, Chiefs of Relief.*

BOX

The Box EP (nr/Go! Discs) 1983
Secrets Out (nr/Go! Discs) 1983
Great Moments in Big Slam (nr/Go! Discs) 1984
Muscle In EP (nr/Doublevision) 1985
Muscle Out (nr/Rough Trade) 1985

One of the few bands capable of effectively combining the spontaneity and musicianship of jazz with the urgency and rough-edged sound of rock, the Box were a five-piece spin-off from Sheffield industrial funksters Clock DVA. Comparisons to Captain Beefheart, Gang of Four, the Minutemen and Ornette Coleman are all appropriate; execution is first-rate (especially by ex-Clocks Paul Widger on guitar and saxophonist Charlie Collins), the material frantic.

The Box EP contains five manic cuts, setting instruments on wild collision courses behind Peter Hope's vocals. **Secrets Out** improves on that formula by injecting unexpected subtleties and an underlying murkiness that give even more impact to the hyperactive guitar/sax counterpoint. A solid, frenzied album guaranteed to keep listeners on their toes.

Great Moments in Big Slam, however, is quite a letdown. The pace is slower and the band really doesn't get a chance to cut loose, but that's not the problem so much as the heavy-handed percussion and grossly exaggerated vocals which dominate the production. After releasing the **Muscle In** EP, the Box announced a trial separation to pursue other projects. The posthumous **Muscle Out** was recorded live at the Leadmill in Sheffield.   [dgs]

See also *Cabaret Voltaire.*

BOY GEORGE

Sold (Virgin) 1987 ●
Tense Nervous Headache (nr/Virgin) 1988 ●
Boyfriend (Ger. Virgin) 1989 ●
High Hat (Virgin) 1989 ●
The Martyr Mantras (Virgin) 1991 φ

Following Culture Club's dissolution—not to mention a public bout with drug addiction and a series of lurid and tragic tabloid scandals—formerly flamboyant frontman Boy George (O'Dowd) attempted to resume his career but could only come up with the wretched **Sold**. Away from his former bandmates, George and Club producer Stewart Levine whipped up a forgettable, overblown concoction possessing none of the flair of the band's better work. Indicative of the Boy's total creative bewilderment, the album's dubious high point is an absurd reggaefied version of Bread's "Everything I Own" (styled after a Ken Boothe rendition which topped the British charts in 1974).

The singer's next American album, stitched together from two overseas releases (one of which didn't even come out in England), finally appeared as **High Hat**. Under any title, it's slick, assembly-line R&B with nary a shred of personality. How odd that a performer who built a huge career on stylized outrage should end up making music this anonymous. Four tracks produced by former Prince drummer Bobby Z (including the almost-successful tortured-diva move "Whisper") show a bit more musical and lyrical character but, in this context, that's not saying much.

The Martyr Mantras, a dance-oriented compilation of non-LP singles and newer tracks recorded with a variety of producers (including one collaboration with ex-Culture Club confrère Jon Moss), is a significant improvement. Though most of the material is more functional than inspired, the uncluttered extended dance-mix settings allow George to deliver some genuinely soulful vocal performances, particularly on the disco number "Generations of Love" (included in two versions) and the ballad "One on One." Of equal note is the return of his sociopolitical conscience on "No Clause 28," an effective and good-humored anti-oppression rant.

See also *Culture Club.*   [i/hd]

BOYS

The Boys (nr/NEMS) 1977 (nr/Link Classics) 1990 ●
Alternative Chartbusters (nr/NEMS) 1978 (nr/Link
    Classics) 1990 ●
To Hell with the Boys (nr/Safari) 1979
Boys Only (nr/Safari) 1980

YOBS

The Yobs Christmas Album (nr/Safari) 1980 (nr/Great
    Expectations) 1989 ●

Too unseriously pop-minded for the punks and too punky for the power-poppers, well received nearly everywhere in Europe except at home in England, beset with label woes in the UK and name confusion in the US, the star-crossed Boys were perennially in the wrong place at the wrong time.

Norwegian expatriate Casino Steel (the band's keyboard player and co-writer of much of their first three albums) was already a veteran of this sort of thing, having been a member of the Hollywood Brats, a London glitter band styled after the New York Dolls.

The Boys' first album is an inconsistent (if promising) mélange of Steel's Bratisms, standard punkarama and the stirrings of a Beatle (and other pop) influence. **Alternative Chartbusters**, though, presents infectiously rocking tunes played with irreverent élan, featuring Duncan "Kid" Reid's engagingly adolescent readings of the mostly humorous lyrics (often, as on **To Hell with the Boys**, playing the punk schlemiel), culminating in a pair of classic pop-punk singles, "Brickfield Nights" and "First Time." The third album (recorded in the tiny Norwegian town of the punny title) delivers more of the same, but with slicker and fuller sound—organ in addition to piano, more dual guitars—and more variety. Sadly, reverses (among them, Steel's deportation) took their toll, and the Boys, as a quartet, made a fourth album that's flatter than stale soda.

Under a not-very-obscure pseudonym, the Boys recorded an LP of Yuletide favorites (plus their own seasonal compositions) in various variations on pop-punk, sometimes just cute, but mostly skipping irreverence and heading straight for sheer tastelessness, e.g., "Silent Night" by Nazi-punks and "Twelve Days of Christmas" translated by "Oi" brigands into locker-room scatology. Subsequently, Boys guitarist Honest John Plain cut an LP, **New Guitars in Town**, with Lurker Pete Stride, supported by other members of both bands, who had formed an alliance of sorts.   [jg]

See also *Lurkers*.

BOYS NEXT DOOR
See *Birthday Party*.

BPEOPLE
See *Alex Gibson*.

BRADFORD
Shouting Quietly (Sire) 1990 ●

Bradford's Ian H. is a talented chap. He writes better-than-average melodic pop-rock songs (mostly about life and love in northern England), his lyrics display a wit and verbal ability worthy of Elvis Costello and he sings them in a way that'll remind you a lot of Morrissey (Bradford comes from a Manchester suburb, not the nearby town for which the group is named, and were discovered by producer Stephen Street—who did the honors here—opening a show for Morrissey). So why isn't **Shouting Quietly** a better album? Consider the title. The record is just too low-key for its own good; the band never delivers the punch to make the songs involving. These days, shouting quietly just may not be enough.   [ds]

BILLY BRAGG
Life's a Riot with Spy vs. Spy (nr/Utility) 1983
  (nr/Utility-Go! Discs) 1983
Brewing Up with Billy Bragg (CD Presents) 1984
Between the Wars EP (nr/Go! Discs) 1985
Life's a Riot Etc (CD Presents) 1985
"Days Like These" EP (nr/Go! Discs) 1985
Talking with the Taxman About Poetry (Go! Discs-Elektra) 1986 ●
Back to Basics (Go! Discs-Elektra) 1987 ●
The Peel Sessions EP (nr/Strange Fruit) 1987 ●
Help Save the Youth of America EP (Go! Discs-Elektra) 1988 ●
Workers Playtime (Go! Discs-Elektra) 1988 ●
The Internationale (Utility-Elektra) 1990 φ

Playing a solitary electric guitar and singing his pithy compositions in a gruff voice, Billy Bragg reintroduced the essence of folksinging—not the superficial trappings, but the deep-down Woody Guthrie activist/adventurer archetype—to the modern rock world.

Although his tools are utterly simple, Bragg is capable of enormous strength and depth in his writing and performing, spinning off touching, warm love songs as well as trenchant social satire and socialist political commentary.

On the seven tracks of **Life's a Riot** (recorded originally as songwriting demos), Bragg waxes tender ("The Milkman of Human Kindness"), bitter ("A New England") and sarcastic ("The Busy Girl Buys Beauty"), keeping things blunt and one-take spartan, making it an ultimate no-frills pop record. Combining the wordplay wit and strong emotions of Elvis Costello with the grumpy melodic charm of Paul Weller, it's a small, articulate masterpiece.

Brewing Up, a relatively ambitious full-length undertaking with a tiny bit of organ and trumpet (not to mention—gasp!—overdubbed guitars and vocals), finds Bragg retaining all of his rugged pop appeal while sharpening his pen. The songs focus on romance, offering nervous but perceptive angles on love and lust ("Love Gets Dangerous," "The Saturday Boy," "A Lover Sings"). He also shreds Fleet Street journalism with "It Says Here."

Bragg then turned his attentions to another traditional subject for angry young men with guitars: politics. He's done countless benefit concerts, played in Communist countries and, via Red Wedge, the musicians' organization he helped found, campaigned for the Labour Party. **Between the Wars**, an extraordinarily powerful 7-inch EP, is Bragg at his finest, singing of England's peacetime recessions ("Between the Wars"), chronicling a 17th century rebellion ("The World Turned Upside Down") and reviving the 1940s union classic, "Which Side Are You On."

"Days Like These," a subsequent three-song single, shows Bragg's deepening commitment to socialist political activities. This latter-day Woody Guthrie belts out sincere (if occasionally awkward) constructs like "I see no shame in putting my name to socialism's cause/ Nor to seek some more relevance than spotlight and applause."

Talking with the Taxman About Poetry ("the difficult third album") is a great leap forward, the deft application of understated instrumental accompaniment on some of Bragg's best-ever songs. "Greetings to the New Brunette" (widely known as "Shirley") is an airy love song with serious underpinnings; "Levi Stubbs' Tears" tells chillingly of a tragic couple, colored with a touch of flugelhorn, trumpet and percussion; "Ideology" consciously paraphrases Dylan's "Chimes of Freedom" for a scathing look at the old-boy buddy club of British government; rinky-tink piano provides the setting for "Honey, I'm a Big Boy Now," a sharp-eyed appraisal of marital failure; "Help Save the Youth of America" is a powerful—and not ill-considered—indictment from abroad. The only false step is a cover of the Count Bishops' tuneless "Train Train," which interrupts the flow of Side One.

Subtitled "live and dubious," the 1988 EP, issued to coincide with an American tour, contains four live recordings (including the title track, captured in Moscow, complete with translated intro), "There Is Power in a Union," done bluegrass style with accompaniment by the Pattersons, an alternate studio version of "Days Like These" and a leaflet promoting voter registration

86

and electoral responsibility. **Life's a Riot Etc** is a handy American-only release that combines all of the first mini-album with **Between the Wars** for a Bragg then-and-now extravaganza, complete with lyric sheet. **Back to Basics** goes that effort one better by putting **Life's a Riot, Between the Wars** and **Brewing Up** on two discs, billed as "the first 21 songs from the roots of urbane folk music." **The Peel Sessions** EP was recorded live in 1983 for radio broadcast and contains renditions of "A New England," "Love Gets Dangerous," John Cale's "Fear" and a hilarious Britain-specific exploration of "Route 66."

On the Costello-esque **Workers Playtime**, veteran folk-rock producer Joe Boyd stretches Bragg's sonic palette, setting that undisguisable voice and irrepressible wit into utterly appealing frames without undermining his homespun integrity. (Frequent sidewoman pianist Cara Tivey again plays a major role.) Although Bragg's political consciousness is such that the proletarian Chinese art cover absurdly carries the slogan, "Capitalism is killing music," most of these excellent new creations ("She's Got a New Spell," "The Price I Pay," "Life with the Lions") are about the ups and downs of personal affairs. When he mentions Marx in "The Short Answer," a truly beautiful love song, it's only to locate Mary in the dictionary. Indicative of Bragg's unpretentious maturity, the cynical "Waiting for the Great Leap Forwards" (which invokes Camelot and Castro, and quotes Mott the Hoople to boot) offers this sardonic couplet: "Mixing pop and politics he asks me what the use is/I offer him embarrassment and my usual excuses."

No such self-effacement troubles Bragg on **The Internationale**, a well-meaning but misbegotten seven-song collection of left-wing anthems and Bragg's own dubious contributions to the genre. An a cappella tribute to Phil Ochs that rewrites "I Dreamed I Saw Joe Hill Last Night" is a sanctimonious embarrassment, and Bragg's ambitiously orchestrated rendition of "The Internationale" is neither impressive nor amusing. Likewise, the tra-la-la merriment with which Bragg sings "The Marching Song of the Covert Battalions," his ode against imperialism, fails to achieve the desired ironic effect. [i]

BRIAN BRAIN

Unexpected Noises (nr/Secret) 1980
Fun with Music! EP (Plaid) 1985
Time Flies When You're Having Toast (Moving Target) 1987 ●

Although Brain—or, more accurately, Martin Atkins—was the drummer in Public Image for a time (more recently he's toured with Ministry), his solo career has taken a much less dour direction. So while **Unexpected Noises**—mostly his own work—is of little consequence, at least it attempts to be anarchic and funny rather than anarchic and glum. Biggest problem here is the poor production, which leaves the sound muddled and flat.

Five years later, Atkins emerged from a period of inactivity and returned to the concert circuit and vinyl world in Brian Brain (the Group), an outfit including original Go-Go's bassist Margot Olavarria. **Fun with Music!** is a four-song 12-inch recorded in New York.

Brain's body may be in America (the cut-up tribal chant of "U.S.A." is a jaundiced cultural appraisal) but his brain is on clean living: two numbers pitch anti-drug-use messages. Interestingly, the ex-PiLer does a song called "Happy?" two years before the album of that name.

The subsequent **Time Flies** album (which sounds a bit like a modernized cross between Captain Sensible and John Otway) reprises a pair of songs from the EP and adds eight more, all recorded with Olavarria, guitarist Geoff Smyth and others. The rhythm-heavy hip-hop/massed-drums tracks—with jungle ambience, found sounds and other sonic ephemera keeping things appropriately offbeat—are a bit short on melody, but not concept or wit. Atkins isn't a great singer, but he has a lively mind and an absurdist outlook to keep things stimulating even when the music drags. [i]

See also *Ministry, Public Image Ltd.*

BRAINS

The Brains (Mercury) 1980
Electronic Eden (Mercury) 1981
Dancing Under Streetlights EP (Landslide) 1982

The Brains' story is typical of many independent bands who signed to not-so-swift big labels. Led by lanky Tom Gray, this Atlanta-based quartet first garnered widespread attention with a striking homemade single, "Money Changes Everything." The Brains subsequently recorded two LPs for Mercury, but neither sold a speck. Following a divorce by mutual consent, the group returned, poorer and wiser, to the independent label scene.

On both albums, producer Steve Lillywhite concocts a thick, heavy sound that subjugates Gray's synthesizers and Rick Price's aggressive guitars to the tunes themselves. And for good reason: Gray's songs are tart accounts of love and confusion perfectly suited to his dry, sardonic voice. The Brains offer a rougher and less glib variant of the Cars' ironic sensibility, which is probably why they never achieved widespread popularity. Gray and crew unsettle rather than divert.

The Brains includes a re-recording of the cynical "Money Changes Everything" and "Gold Dust Kids," a pithy, unsentimental portrait of decadence. **Electronic Eden** features the bitter romanticism of "Heart in the Street," covered (badly) by Manfred Mann and "Collision," a humorously tasteless look at a brain-damaged car-crash survivor.

The four-song EP is more of the same intense longing and hidden passion. If the Brains sound a bit weary, chalk it up to the record biz blues. **Dancing Under Streetlights** isn't the best starting point, but it's a worthy continuation. The Brains have since disbanded. (As an undoubtedly lucrative footnote, Cyndi Lauper covered "Money Changes Everything" on her first LP.) [jy]

GLENN BRANCA

Lesson No. 1 (99) 1980
The Ascension (99) 1981
Symphony No. 1 (Tonal Plexus) [tape] (ROIR) 1983
Symphony No. 3/Gloria (Neutral) 1983
Symphony No. 6 (Devil Choirs at the Gates of Heaven) (Blast First) 1989 ●

GLENN BRANCA/JOHN GIORNO

Who You Staring At? (Giorno Poetry Systems) 1982

Many artists have had their music described as a wall of sound, but few have deserved it as much as New York composer/guitarist Glenn Branca. One of the first to realize that a classical-rock fusion need not involve technique-crazed keyboardists soloing away to the accompaniment of rehashed Brahms or Stravinsky, Branca writes music of orchestral richness that retains—intact—all of rock's danger, urgency and impact.

With his roots in the downtown no-wave movement of the late '70s, Branca's **Lesson No. 1** was the first release on the influential 99 label. Slow, repetitive harmonic changes and hidden sub-motifs invite comparisons to minimalists like Philip Glass, but Branca's music is more dissonant, primitive and—above all—loud.

The Ascension is the closest he's ever come to an out-and-out rock album. Atop pulverizing bass/drum combinations, Branca and three other guitarists build a thick, layered mass of shifting textures, sometimes all on one chord, sometimes in a dense cacophony of six-string clusters. Suffice to say, it packs quite a wallop.

Branca's side of the joint disc with poet John Giorno is music commissioned for a dance piece (*Bad Smells*) by Twyla Tharp. Except for very brief sections of quiet, most of it resembles **The Ascension**.

Only three of Branca's seven symphonies have been recorded and released commercially so far, but that's the format in which he is most effective. Played by large ensembles, the pieces incorporate a plethora of amplified instruments of his own design (primarily dulcimer-like things strung with steel wire and hammered with mallets) in addition to guitars, horns and a battery of percussion. He builds intense drones and ear-shattering crescendos while exploring the sonic possibilities of large tonal clusters and the resultant overtones. **Symphony No. 1** alternates between one relentless, thundering chord and primal rhythmic pounding. As instrumental layers build, overtones clash to produce melodies of their own, and can even trick the listener into hearing instruments that aren't there. **Symphony No. 3** adds homemade keyboards, giving an orchestral and almost Oriental sound to the piece—delicacy amidst the thunder. Both recordings are hindered in that it is impossible to capture the full effect of his live performances, where the volume generally runs around wake-the-dead level.

After a long recording hiatus, Branca's **Symphony No. 6** (subtitled **Devil Choirs at the Gates of Heaven**) was released in 1989. Maybe an ear specialist suggested he turn things down a notch; several of the old ideas are in effect, but volume levels, compositional techniques and textures are much more varied than on previous works. No fewer than ten guitarists, ranging from Swans/Of Cabbages and Kings bassist Algis Kizys to conservatory-trained classicists, plug away at a million and one riffs, leaving space for fairly prominent keyboard parts. Branca doesn't renounce volume, but he arrives at it by way of crescendos rather than instant deafness. [dgs

BRAND NUBIAN

One for All (Elektra) 1990 ●

MASTERS OF CEREMONY

Dynamite (4th & B'way) 1988 ●

Mixing delightful daisy-age soul, funk and go-go grooves with engaging rapid-fire rapping, this exceptionally talented New Rochelle, New York trio provides a nearly irresistible setting for its promotion of the Five-Percent Nation's bizarre Islamic racism. Some of the articulate tracks on the self-produced **One for All** push a positive message of education, self-preservation and peace, but others are loaded with the usual cryptic references to obscure religious beliefs that can ruin the party for nonbelievers.

Before forming Brand Nubian, rapper/producer Grand Puba Maxwell (Dixon) led the non-religious Masters of Ceremony. **Dynamite** displays some promising signs of life in some of the grooves (like the title track and the deconstructed PE style of "Rock Steady"), but most of the lyrics are pretty pedestrian. [i]

BRAVE COMBO

Music for Squares (Four Dots) 1981
World Dance Music (Four Dots) 1984
No Sad Faces (Four Dots) 1985
People Are Strange EP (Rogue) 1986
Musical Varieties (Rounder) 1987 ●
Polkatharsis (Rounder) 1987 ●
Humansville (Rounder) 1988 ●
A Night on Earth (Rounder) 1990 ●

Formed by Denton, Texas homeboy Carl Finch in 1979, Brave Combo are witty and wise purveyors (and perverters) of polkas and musics of many nations. A highly successful tour of local mental institutions honed their chops, and each record reveals an ever-more-adventurous and itinerant package of sounds. By exploring and exploiting the least hip music on god's green earth—the polka—Finch and Co. demonstrate that everything most people know about pop music is wrong.

The aptly titled debut album, **Music for Squares**, finds them grinding out polka, cha-cha, twist, waltz and tango standards and originals with rockish energy. On **World Dance Music** they began to take rock standards, such as the Doors' "People Are Strange," and twist them into weird ethnic shapes (such as the Romanian hora). You'll hear an African-ska version of a Perez Prado hit, as well as the usual assortment of *cumbias*, *norteñas*, *schottisches* and, of course, polkas. "If we missed your part of the world," suggests the cover, "please check future releases."

The live **No Sad Faces** contains an unforgettable "In-a-Gadda-Da-Vida," a cha-cha version of "O Holy Night," a ska take on "Little Bit of Soul" and much more. The **Musical Varieties** compilation is an excellently produced and generous introduction to the band which sets the stage for **Polkatharsis**, the Combo's brave return to its roots. They play hardball with eleven polkas—from "Happy Wanderer" to "Who Stole the Kishka"—on this all-trad collection, adding a couple of sweet waltzes and a *schottische*.

Like their European (conceptual) cousins 3 Mustaphas 3, the Combo has evolved from being merely a good joke into a fine band. On **Humansville**, the playing is tighter, the originals are serious (space is important, money isn't everything) and the conceits seem less forced. That's maturity for you.

Guaranteeing plenty of smiles, **A Night on Earth** follows the Brave Combo on another delightfully capricious stylistic smorgasbord (in English, Spanish and instrumental Italian) of witty originals (like the anti-complacency "Do Something Different") and a smooth cover of "Hey There" (Rosemary Clooney et al.). Imagine what might happen if these guys made a record with Kid Creole . . .   [rg/i]

BREAKING CIRCUS
The Very Long Fuse (Homestead) 1985
The Ice Machine (Homestead) 1987
Smokers' Paradise EP (Homestead) 1987

BIG TROUBLE HOUSE
Afghanistan (Horse Latitudes) 1989
Mouthful of Violence (Horse Latitudes-Community 3) 1990 φ

Breaking Circus began as a vehicle for Steve Björklund, veteran of the '80-'83 Chicago punk explosion (as a member of the seminal Strike Under and, later, Terminal Beach). The eight-song 45 rpm **Very Long Fuse** is terse, post-punk vitriol set to a banging dance-beat drum machine. "The Imperial Clawmasters' Theme" and "Precision" are sharp, jagged and guitar-powered, unique for such dancefloor bop. (The closest stylistic reference is the Three Johns, whose songs Breaking Circus have played live.)

Björklund then relocated to Minneapolis and put together a more stable band-type environment, borrowing the rhythm section of Rifle Sport when that group isn't working. **The Ice Machine** contains sinister and methodical blows like "Song of the South," "Ancient Axes" and "Took a Hammering." Trading fire for poisoned darts, **Ice Machine** gets under the skin with repeated listenings.

Smokers' Paradise offers similar fare (complete with another imposing hammer adorning the cover), only better. The instrumental title track adds smoky, ghostly acoustic and tiptoeing piano, a walk through a haunted graveyard; the trademark saber-toothed guitars on "Eat Lead" and "Three Cool Cats" (not the 1959 Coasters hit) are equally hair-raising. An eerie and innovative pleasure.

Although the group split around '88, Björklund has since used the Breaking Circus name to release a solo single of Naked Raygun and U.K. Subs covers done as electro-pop. While the rhythm section continues on in Rifle Sport, second guitarist Phil Harder formed Big Trouble House, a trio in which his vocals lean more towards Steve Albini than Björklund; with constant tempo changes, **Afghanistan**'s overall feel is less spooky and more meandering than Breaking Circus. A somewhat formative effort, this interesting and generally good album was largely overshadowed by the excellent "Watered Down" single (produced by Albini) that followed in '90.

Though as haphazard and as woefully inconsistent as its predecessor, **Mouthful of Violence** is indeed an improvement. With meatier production by Albert Garzon, the more succinct songs (like "Union Feed Grain Mill") show Big Trouble House capable of a rocking edge and intensity that compares favorably to the Did-

jits. The CD also includes "Watered Down," an unreleased track and, for some reason, four tracks from **Afghanistan**.   [jr]

BREEDERS
Pod (4AD) 1990 ●

In this appealing side-project supergroup, Kim Deal (the Pixies bassist, here playing guitar) and guitarist Tanya Donelly of Throwing Muses are joined by bassist Josephine Wiggs (who left the Perfect Disaster soon after) and drummer Britt Walford (using the pseudonym Shannon Doughton) of Slint. Everybody sings. Deal, responsible for such Pixies highlights as "Gigantic" and "Silver," wrote most of **Pod**, the sound of which (as "engineered" by Steve Albini) favors the Pixies far more than the gentler Muses. Side One's a bit shaky, saved by a wry remake of "Happiness Is a Warm Gun" and Deal's blazing "Hellbound" (describing an aborted fetus that survives). But the second half of the album is damn near perfect, kicking off with the scrumptious lilting pop of "Fortunately Gone," churning through "Iris" (a wrenching account, with majestic guitars, of menstruation) and on to the intoxicating magical-realism of "Opened," the frankly sexual "Only in 3's" and Wiggs' Wire-y mutterings on "Metal Man."   [ws]

BILLY BREMNER
Bash! (nr/Arista) 1984

Erstwhile Rockpile guitarist Bremner is far more talented than his low profile would indicate; insecurities have hampered him considerably. In many ways, **Bash!** is the Dave Edmunds album Edmunds never made (and more consistent than anything Dave's done since **Repeat When Necessary**, which included three Bremner songs). Billy's a bit poppier and a better, more prolific songwriter than his former bandmate.

Ex-Records drummer Will Birch produced and supplied the lyrics on **Bash!**, which also benefits from previously unrecorded donations (one each) from Elvis Costello (brilliant!) and Difford/Tilbrook (they should have finished writing it first). The album doesn't contain Bremner's Stiff 45, "When Laughter Turns to Tears," but still delivers the goods track after track.   [jg]

See also *Pretenders, Rockpile*.

JACK BREWER BAND
See *Saccharine Trust*.

BRILLIANT
See *Youth & Ben Watkins*.

BRILLIANT CORNERS
Growing Up Absurd (nr/SS20) 1985
Fruit Machine EP (nr/SS20) 1986
What's in a Word (nr/SS20) 1986 (nr/McQueen) 1988
Somebody Up There Likes Me (nr/McQueen) 1988 ●
Everything I Ever Wanted (nr/McQueen) 1988
Joyride (nr/McQueen) 1989 ●

Bristol's Brilliant Corners are capable of the most joyous of pop sounds—bright, ringing guitars skipping through a mix of peppy drums, tight bass, trumpet and piano. By the same token, the group is also capable of the most depressing lyrics. Like Morrissey, singer/songwriter Davey Woodward has curious preoccupations—with death and dying and lost and unrequited loves. The Brilliant Corners' music is beyond reproach, but Woodward is one miserable boy.

Growing Up Absurd, while not as striking as it might have been, sets the course for the quintet's releases—bouncy pop with the unusual novelty of a full-time trumpeter. The **Fruit Machine** EP sparkles with invention: piercing guitar lines, nimble trumpeting and keyboards make "Meet Me on Tuesdays" and "Jim's Room" the best of these four tracks.

Brilliant Corners continued their creative expansion on **What's in a Word**, adding strings and female backing vocals. The band's greatest songs are here: "Laugh I Could've Cried," "A Very Easy Death" and "Egotistical Me." The delightful "Boy and a Cloud" suggests that Davey may not be as miserable as we think he is.

Somebody Up There Likes Me shows the Brilliant Corners at their most accomplished; musically *and* lyrically, they are unnervingly precise. A dozen ardent testimonials on life and love in the '80s—"She's Dead," "Never a Young Girl" and "With a Kiss" are a far cry from the trite pop ditties we've come to expect from this kind of musical backing. It's rare to find such soul-baring honesty in pop music.

Everything I Ever Wanted is a compilation of **Growing Up Absurd** and **Fruit Machine**.　　[ag]

BRITISH ELECTRIC FOUNDATION
Music for Stowaways [tape] (nr/Virgin) 1981
Music for Listening To: (nr/Virgin) 1981
Music of Quality and Distinction Volume One (nr/Virgin) 1982

HOT GOSSIP
Geisha Boys and Temple Girls (nr/DinDisc-Virgin) 1981

In search of more meaningful dance music, Martyn Ware and Ian Craig Marsh abandoned the about-to-be-enormous Human League in 1980 to form the more experimental (musically and structurally) British Electric Foundation. The core members—Marsh, Ware and singer Glenn Gregory—also work as Heaven 17, a "division" of B.E.F. Confused? While Heaven 17 is geared for dance funk'n'soul, B.E.F. (for a while, at least) pursued one-off concept projects with a variety of other people, like the suddenly vocal TV dance troupe Hot Gossip.

Music for Stowaways—released only on cassette—consists of moody instrumentals, ranging from funk-rock to icy Germanic synth-garde to electro-bop and sound experiments. Much of it was reissued on the seven-track **Music for Listening To:**, which also includes an extra track, "A Baby Called Billy."

Music of Quality and Distinction, B.E.F.'s first venture into pop experimentation, brings in a number of interesting people (including Tina Turner, Gary Glitter, Sandie Shaw and Paul Jones) to perform cover versions of well-known and not-so-well-known oldies, from "These Boots Are Made for Walking" and "Wichita Lineman" to David Bowie's "The Secret Life of Arabia" and Lou Reed's "Perfect Day." Older songs hold up better under this treatment than new ones but, over-

all, choices of singers and musicians are on the mark. Despite any social implications (or lack thereof), a good time.　　[sg]

See also *Heaven 17, Human League*.

DAVE BROCK
See *Hawkwind*.

BROKEN BONES
Dem Bones (nr/Fall Out) 1984 ●
Seeing Thru My Eyes EP (nr/Fall Out) 1985
Live at the 100 Club (nr/Subversive Sounds) 1985
Bonecrusher (Combat Core) 1986
F.O.A.D. (Combat Core) 1987
Decapitated (nr/Fall Out) 1987 ●
Losing Control (nr/Heavy Metal) 1989 ●

This quartet (originally comprising ex-Discharge guitarist Bones, Baz, Oddy and Nobby) may not be good spellers, but they certainly have a clear idea which end of a guitar to bash. Playing at maximum stun volume, Broken Bones' lack of literacy presents no obstacle to the blunt protest songs with clear and indomitable rock power on **Dem Bones**. An early and distinctly British center ground between parochial punk (BB generally play too slow) and modern metal (but more topical and fiery), Broken Bones could be the modern answer to the MC5. Or just another would-be Black Sabbath.

By the time of the half-studio/half-live **F.O.A.D.** (suffice to say three of the initials stand for **Off And Die**), Tezz had taken over bass chores from Oddy and the band had grown older and louder, finding a niche in the pre-dinosaur echelon of indie metal. The seven studio tracks sound pretty routine—all muddy bottom and squalling guitars—while the boiling nine-song speed-metal/Oi! live side (London, 1986) is treblier but equally indistinct.

Decapitated, which shares a single CD with **Dem Bones**, compiles the contents of four singles (a dozen tracks in all), including 1983's "Decapitated" and the 1985 10-inch, **Seeing Thru My Eyes**.　　[i]

BRONSKI BEAT
The Age of Consent (London-MCA) 1984 ●
Hundreds & Thousands EP (London-MCA) 1985 ●
Truthdare Doubledare (London-MCA) 1986 ●

Playing only electronic instruments and singing unequivocal gay lyrics in a window-rattling falsetto, this London trio burst full-blown onto a complacent music scene in 1984. Jimmy Somerville (who left the following year to form the Communards) has a piercing voice which he can modulate for greater appeal (as on "Junk"); the band plays a powerful and unique breed of techno-dance, with room for such digressions as George and Ira Gershwin's "It Ain't Necessarily So" and Giorgio Moroder-for-Donna Summer's "I Feel Love." Far more blunt and sexy (the cover image and sleeve notes are similarly plain-spoken) than Tom Robinson's old records (to which the group surely owes a cultural debt of gratitude), **The Age of Consent** is an invigorating, courageous and memorable album.

Underscoring the Bronskis' club and dance orientation, **Hundreds & Thousands** offers lengthy remixes of four album cuts ("Why," "Smalltown Boy," "Junk," "Heatwave") plus the non-LP "Run from Love" and "Hard Rain." Horns have been added, and all the tunes extended to the six-minute-plus range; the cassette and CD contain two more.

Replacing Somerville with John Jon, a competent but far less distinctive singer, Bronski Beat managed to make **Truthdare Doubledare**, a halfbaked progression from the first album. "Hit That Perfect Beat" is exactly the same kind of hi-NRG dance excitement favored by post-Bronskis Somerville, but the rest of the record attempts to diversify in upscale dance directions that don't quite pan out. While the songs continue to address gay issues ("Dr John" is about AIDS; "We Know How It Feels" and "Punishment for Love" both concern societal pressures), the lyrics are vague and subtle enough to be overlooked by casual listeners.   [i/tr]

See also *Communards*.

JACQUI BROOKES

See *Fingerprintz*.

BROTHERHOOD OF LIZARDS

See *Cleaners from Venus*.

DENNIS BROWN

See *Gregory Isaacs*.

BRYGADA KRYZYS

Brygada Kryzys (Polish Tonpress) 1982
Brygada Kryzys (nr/Fresh) 1982

This semi-underground (and I don't mean that figuratively) Polish band is not exactly in the mainstream of world punk rock, but does play a slightly toned-down version of high-octane guitar (and sax) raunch that compares favorably to bands from Bauhaus to the Sex Pistols. While not breaking any new creative ground, Brygada Kryzys is a fascinating and credible example of stylistic transliteration from one culture to a rather different one.   [i]

BUCK PETS

The Buck Pets (Island) 1989 •
Mercurotones (Island) 1990 •

Blasting out of a suburban Dallas garage with guitars blazing, the Buck Pets made their debut in a fury of loudly textured hard rock. A bit punky in approach (guitarist Chris Savage knows his way around feedback; the bratty lyrics are sung with youthful verve) but scaled for stadiums, the quartet shares some traits with other young bands rooted in the likes of Led Zeppelin. While the songs on **The Buck Pets** are rarely memorable ("A Little Murder" is a neat exception), Ron St. Germain's dynamic production captures the exciting guitar sound in all its overmodulated glory. (The CD adds a bonus track.)

While most ex-punks head straight for metal's commercial slipstream, the Buck Pets actually pulled back on the arena tendencies and made a punky street-level

second album. With Michael Beinhorn producing (and playing keyboards), **Mercurotones** reflects a strong Replacements influence, throws off the same sort of rambunctious riff-rock favored by Soul Asylum and employs acoustic guitars and a few acid-house shuffle rhythms. Indicative of how open to new ideas the Buck Pets have grown, "Libertine" (a track produced by the Dust Brothers) features horns and a syncopated dance beat.   [i]

HAROLD BUDD

See *Cocteau Twins, Brian Eno*.

BUDDY LOVE

See *Alan Milman Sect*.

BUFFALO TOM

Buffalo Tom (Hol. Megadisc) 1989 (SST) 1989 •
Crawl EP (Hol. Megadisc) 1990
Birdbrain (Beggars Banquet-RCA) 1990 •

Sometimes jokingly called Dinosaur Jr. Jr., this trio from western Massachusetts features a brand of scree-hyped guitar rock based in the post-Burma/Dü tradition, and has spent a lot of its studio time with Dinosaur Jr.'s guitar-honey, "Jake" Mascis. Buffalo Tom's first LP actually came out in Europe before it was picked up by SST, but the second was released by a major label as a possible wedge into the college market. Buffalo Tom's oink has a kinda student/hippie charm, and the band's sound is moving away from its derivative beginnings into more original (if still distinctly college-rock) terrain. It's hard to imagine them ever spreading out too far, but the first album might provide a nice soundtrack for your next late-night pot party. (The **Birdbrain** CD includes two bonus cuts, including acoustic versions of the Psychedelic Furs' "Heaven" and **Buffalo Tom**'s "Reason Why.")   [bc]

BUGGLES

The Age of Plastic (Island) 1980 •
Adventures in Modern Recording (Carrere) 1982

After "Video Killed the Radio Star" changed the course of electro-pop forever, it was straight downhill for the Buggles as a group. The two members, however, proved a lot more durable on their own: Geoffrey Downes went on to grand success with Yes and Asia; Trevor Horn became a hit record producer (for ABC and Malcolm McLaren) before founding ZTT Records and foisting Frankie Goes to Hollywood on an unsuspecting world.

While **The Age of Plastic** was a disappointment to fans of the Buggles' cogent 45s, **Adventures** amounts to little more than a self-explanatory post-mortem. Both albums are technically stunning, reasonably catchy and crashingly hollow.   [i]

See also *Art of Noise, Frankie Goes to Hollywood*.

BULLET LAVOLTA

Bullet LaVolta EP (Taang!) 1988 •
The Gift (Taang!) 1989 (RCA) 1989 •
Gimme Danger EP (Metal Blade-RCA-Restless) 1990 φ

On its initial outing, this Boston five-piece spews up a metallic-hardcore rainbow comprised of equal parts AC/DC and Circle Jerks. Small in stature yet possessing a wail bigger than Moby Dick, Indiana banshee Yukki Gipe makes up for his lack of singing ability with sheer scream pyrotechnics. By no means groundbreaking, the raucous six-song debut is an excellent intro to a band gleefully making the kind of racket your parents always told you to turn off. (The cassette contains a bonus track.)

Bullet LaVolta's assault continues on **The Gift**, a swell, chandelier-shattering collection of powerfully noisy rock songs punctuated by blasts from the lethal twin guitars of Clay Tarver and Ken Chambers (on loan from his other band, Moving Targets). The best cuts—the vaguely psychedelic yowlathon "Blind to You" and the near-pop title song (which cops part of its melody from "You Shook Me All Night Long")—fairly define the notion of punk-metal crossover, a fact that helped BLV to a major label deal shortly after **The Gift**'s release. (The RCA reissue adds two songs from the EP; the Taang! CD appends the whole thing.)

Apparently intended as a stopgap until the second LP, **Gimme Danger** is actually a worthwhile purchase that delivers two new explosive studio tracks ("Every Hungry Rabbit" and "Transparent Man") along with three live numbers, including Kiss' "Detroit Rock City." [db]

See also *Moving Targets*.

BUREAU

See *Dexy's Midnight Runners*.

J.J. BURNEL

See *Stranglers*.

T-BONE BURNETT

Truth Decay (Takoma) 1980 (nr/Demon) 1986 ●
Trap Door EP (Warner Bros.) 1982
Proof Through the Night (Warner Bros.) 1983
Behind the Trap Door EP (nr/Demon) 1984
T Bone Burnett (Dot-MCA) 1986 ●
The Talking Animals (Columbia) 1988 ●

Singer, songwriter, ace producer (Los Lobos, Marshall Crenshaw, etc.), Christian moralist and pal of Elvis Costello, T(-)Bone Burnett has wielded a steady and growing influence on the music scene since the late '70s. Whether his inconsistent records leave any lasting mark or not, he's likely to make his presence felt in some role for a long time to come.

Burnett debuted on disc as a member of the Alpha Band, part of the extended family surrounding Bob Dylan during his mid-'70s Rolling Thunder period. Following three Alpha Band LPs, he went solo on what remains his best full-length album, **Truth Decay**. The loose rockabilly and blues grooves offer a sympathetic backdrop for Burnett's sweet (countryish)'n'sour (Dylanish) vocals, as he delivers romantic laments and scathing commentaries on the sorry state of contemporary life. His moral essays generally don't grate ("Madison Avenue" being an exception), thanks to the sheer musicality of the sounds.

The **Trap Door** EP is even better, with the gleaming folk-rock of "Hold on Tight" and "I Wish You Could Have Seen Her Dance" making an exhilarating tonic for troubled souls. And the sly, sarcastic "Diamonds Are a Girl's Best Friend" gets his point across perfectly.

Guess the boy's head got turned by too many good reviews and famous fans, 'cause things then got tainted with smug self-righteousness. **Proof Through the Night** boasts a stellar supporting cast that includes Ry Cooder, Richard Thompson and Pete Townshend. However, the big arrangements and epic pretensions grow tiresome, especially his attempts to encapsulate an era in "The Sixties," "Hefner and Disney," et al. Burnett's got some valid points, but who made him judge and jury?

While **Behind the Trap Door** may be a sequel to his successful EP, it plays more like outtakes. A waste. Far better is **T Bone Burnett**, a sparse, largely acoustic country LP that marks his first outing without a hyphen. Songs tend to be more personal than preachy, with the standard "Poison Love" and "Oh No Darling" among the highlights. (The CD adds three bonus Burnetts.)

The Talking Animals is a return to the mainstream attempts of the Warner discs, and features creative input by such folks as Bono and Tonio K. Some of the songs rock tougher than anything he's done before (see "Monkey Dance" and "You Could Look It Up"); others succeed only in scaling new heights of pretension. Sung in four languages, "Image" could be a Brecht castoff, while "The Strange Case of Frank Cash and the Morning Paper" is a tedious five-minute spoken-word tale. Skip instead to "The Killer Moon," a mid-period Beatles soundalike, and the aptly titled "Relentless." All in all, worth hearing, though one wishes this talented jerk weren't so impressed with himself. [jy]

BURNING SENSATIONS

Burning Sensations (Capitol) 1983

After a one-album stint in the Motels, ex-Pop guitarist Tim McGovern formed an intriguing but unrealized rock band with pan-cultural aspirations. A few of the songs (most notably the wonderful "Belly of the Whale" and "Afrobilly (Live It Up)," which conflates a vague adaptation of high-life and noise-guitar) make real use of the group's assets and ambitious ideas; the rest of the record (like covers of Creedence's "Down on the Corner" and Hendrix's "I Don't Live Today") just sink into an unfocused fog. Several of Burning Sensations' six members went on to play in the more world-oriented Bonedaddys, for whose first album McGovern co-wrote one song. [i]

See also *Bonedaddys, Pop*.

BURNING SPEAR

Marcus Garvey (Mango) 1975 ●
Man in the Hills (Mango) 1976 ●
Garvey's Ghost (Mango) 1976 ●
Dry & Heavy (Mango) 1977
Live (Island) 1978
Social Living (nr/Island) 1978
Hail H.I.M. (nr/Burning Music-EMI) 1980
Farover (Heartbeat) 1982 ●
Fittest of the Fittest (Heartbeat) 1983 ●

Resistance (Heartbeat) 1984 ●
Reggae Greats (Mango) 1984 ●
People of the World (Slash) 1986 ●
Mistress Music (Slash) 1988
Live in Paris: Zenith '88 (Slash) 1989 ●
Mek We Dweet (Mango) 1990 ●
100th Anniversary [CD] (Mango) 1990 ●

For more than 20 years, Winston Rodney—better known as Burning Spear—has been one of reggae music's most consistent and enduring forces, if not its most essential embodiment. Singing in a unique, soulful growl, the beloved Spear is known for his commitment to the African chant style, as well as his potently heavy, penetrating sound. He has largely devoted his life and art to the teaching of black history, in particular the work of Marcus Garvey. (Like Garvey and Bob Marley, Rodney was born in St. Ann's, Jamaica.)

Spear's recording career began in 1969, but he became a local legend in the mid-'70s with the release of "Marcus Garvey" and the classic album of the same name. Soon after, a London appearance that found him backed by members of Aswad made him the toast of England, and he has remained a major international figure ever since.

All three of Spear's early-'80s albums on Heartbeat are excellent. **Farover** contains two of his best songs: "O'Jah" and "Jah Is My Driver," with his haunting vocals and trance-inducing music. **Fittest of the Fittest** is another typical Spear effort, highlighted by the title track. Keyboard stabs, creative percussion and intriguing arrangements provide a solid background to his cries and moans of passion. The soulful and sensuous **Resistance** (which got a Grammy nomination) matches his voice to a stellar horn section, with Burning Band drummer Nelson Miller providing a strong backbone. The record contains some of his most memorable songs, including the title track, "Queen of the Mountain," "We Been There" and "The Force." Turning in a surprising new direction, "Love to You" finds Spear scatting and singing almost like a bluesman.

Signing to Slash, Spear made one of 1986's most far-reaching reggae records, **People of the World**. Taking its title from the Starship hit, "Built This City" relocates the idea to Kingston and shifts the music to reggae, and combines Spear's lyrical gifts with the incredible instrumental sounds of the Burning Band. Featuring an all-female horn section, they manage to integrate a multitude of musical styles—borrowing from calypso, rock, jazz and African—while staying within the dub context. The trumpet solo on "Winner," the sax on "Little Love Song" and the blues jammin' on other tracks combine to make this quite an LP.

Mistress Music finds the production (by Spear and Miller) and orchestration reaching a new level. In a lyrical departure, the album predominantly contains love songs (not that it doesn't include the tributary "Love Garvey"). A Spear attempt at commerciality is almost a contradiction in terms, but the record does serve to expand his parameters.

Spear's concerts are legendary; he frequently reaches unknown heights in a hypnotic trance. The extraordinarily clean-sounding two-LP **Live in Paris**—his first concert album since 1978's **Live** (which was done in London, with Aswad behind him)—captures Spear in the throes of his 1988 tour, performing songs from **Mistress Music** and **People of the World**, as well as some early classics. The Burning Band lays out the groove and blazes the path for Spear's lift-off.

Spear returned to Mango (the label which issued his most classic works) for **Mek We Dweet** ("make we do it"). Impeccably recorded at Bob Marley's Tuff Gong Studios in Kingston, Spear delivers a message that's both state-of-the-union and state-of-art. With a vision that encompasses both families and the greatest crises of social injustice, Spear focuses on a panorama of topics, repeatedly underscoring the album's roots theme, preaching respect and awareness for heritage and origins.

100th Anniversary is a CD pairing of **Marcus Garvey** and its dub counterpart, **Garvey's Ghost**. Although never issued in the US, **Hail H.I.M.** is worth seeking out, as it contains two Spear classics—"Columbus" and "African Postman." [aw]

CHARLIE BURTON & THE CUTOUTS
Is That Charlie Burton ... or What?!?! (Wild) 1982

CHARLIE BURTON
Don't Fight the Band that Needs You!!!! (Wild) 1983

CHARLIE BURTON AND THE HICCUPS
I Heard That (Wild) 1985
Green Cheese (Wild) 1990 φ

This crazed rock'n'roller from Lincoln, Nebraska does it the old-fashioned way: he and three bandmates (bassists come and go but guitarist/pianist Phil Shoemaker and drummer Dave Robel are on all of these self-released albums) play wonderfully unpretentious hopped-up/stripped-down rockabilly/R&B originals, with offbeat, often funny, lyrics. Burton's a colorful vocalizer from the unstoppable howler school; the music barrels along with loose-limbed energy yet never runs off the road. Nothing fancy or remotely contemporary—just gutsy and great! (And don't forget those exclamation points!!!)

The first album has touching odes to cigarettes ("The Pack Song") and Elvis ("Breathe for Me, Presley!"), as well as a disconcerting song about dog bites ("Rabies Shots"). The sound is thick and muddy—just the way it oughta be. **Don't Fight the Band That Needs You!!!!** is marginally fancier (maybe it's just the addition of piano and a guest violin on one song that makes it sound more accomplished) but just as great. Charlie's in a distinctly Presleyesque mood here, crooning the romantic "It's Not Polite" and hiccuping through the cynical "I, 4 1, Don't Care." Strangest creation: "Succubus." Most winsome thought: "(Can't Find My) Niche."

Talk about slick: **I Heard That**'s lyric sheet is typed! Produced to a nice clear turn by Missouri's estimable Lou Whitney, the album—solid but restrained fun with above-average lyrics—takes Charlie and 'Cups up the country and into unstylized traditional pop. "All Time Low" takes a page from the Johnny Cash songbook; the catchy "Is That Wishful Thinking (On My Part)" has a blistering lap-steel solo, while "Road Kill" ("god's will/my thrill") is tight trucker-country rock.

We'll overlook the high-falutin' weirdness of Charlie Burton on compact disc to note that **Green Cheese** (produced by Shoemaker) sets to pumping out rock and country with redoubled vim and a new taste for puns. Alongside such sure-to-be-classics as "Brand New Mom" and "Girl with the Artificial Heart," Charlie cracks cheap jokes like "Party Trained" and "(You're Not Playing Fair) Elise!!," complete with the relevant Beethoven citation. Highbrow, lowbrow or nobrow, Charlie Burton comes from a cultural state all his own.

[i]

KATE BUSH

The Kick Inside (Harvest) 1978 ●
Lionheart (EMI America) 1978 ●
Live on Stage EP (nr/EMI) 1979
Never for Ever (EMI America) 1980 ●
The Dreaming (EMI America) 1982 ●
Kate Bush EP (EMI America) 1983
Hounds of Love (EMI America) 1985 ●
The Whole Story (EMI America) 1986 ●
The Sensual World (Columbia) 1989 ●
Aspects of the Sensual World EP (Columbia) 1989 ●
This Woman's Work (nr/EMI) 1990 ●

Kate Bush's literate, masterful, enchanting records have won her enormous popularity, even if she can be overbearingly coy and preciously self-indulgent. Over the years, she has become increasingly ambitious, turning what might have been a career dominated by others into a singleminded and fascinating pursuit of her own muse. The young piano-playing singer on **The Kick Inside** bloomed into a fully autonomous artist.

The Kick Inside is dominated by Bush's startling falsetto and such imaginative songs as "Them Heavy People," "Wuthering Heights" and "Kite." Top-notch sessionmen and Andrew Powell's sparkling production provide a rich setting for the songs. The record's huge popularity didn't seem to faze Bush, who returned before the end of the same year with another well-crafted album, **Lionheart**. Subtler, more jazz-inflected arrangements keep it less immediate, but the cinema-minded "Hammer Horror" and theater-minded "Wow," as well as the fondly nationalistic "Oh England My Lionheart," make it memorable.

Bush's next release was a live 7-inch EP of four songs from her first two albums. Demonstrating newfound studio expertise, she arranged and co-produced **Never for Ever**, which yielded three British hits ("Breathing," "Babooshka" and "Army Dreamers") and further proved her compositional depth. Songs about dead rock stars ("Blow Away"), a murder ("The Wedding List") and a tribute to the "Violin" are among her strange lyrical concerns. A credit line thanking Richard Burgess and John Walters for "bringing in the Fairlight" gains significance in hindsight, given how integral the sampling instrument subsequently became to her music-making.

Self-produced, **The Dreaming** offers Bush's first truly rock-oriented work, tinted with strong rhythms and clever Fairlight sounds. Almost free of her little-girl voice, Bush is revealed her as a highly skilled, controlled singer capable of abundant drama and personality. While the artistic resemblance to Peter Gabriel—in terms of what can be done artfully within the song

form—is obvious, it's all Kate Bush and perhaps her first really extraordinary album.

Hounds of Love divides into separately titled halves. The "Hounds of Love" side contains one of Bush's most impressive songs, "Running Up That Hill (A Deal with God)," plus other similarly complex and enticing creations; "The Ninth Wave" side offers an overextended contemplation on drowning—impressive, but not really enjoyable.

Kate Bush is an American mini-album: one track from the live EP plus a pair of cuts from **The Dreaming** and one each from the two preceding LPs. **The Whole Story** is a fine career compilation (not in chronological order) of a dozen singles, from "Wuthering Heights" (with new vocals) to 1986's energetic "Experiment IV."

After four years of LP silence, Bush reemerged on a new label with **The Sensual World**, a major effort that was (incorrectly) expected to become her American commercial breakthrough. Early mentor David Gilmour is back on guitar; other such luminaries as Alan Stivell (Celtic harp), Davey Spillane (uillean pipes), Eberhard Weber (bass) and the otherworldly Bulgarian Trio Bulgarka (backing vocals) also contribute. The title track ushers the listener into a lush, erotic space where Celtic and Middle Eastern sounds mingle with lyrics inspired by *Ulysses*' Molly Bloom. It's an enchanting welcome, but the album never fulfills its promise. The rest varies from cool delicacy to overwrought byzantine indulgence. Ultimately, **The Sensual World** is a noble disappointment, never achieving the intended directness, too restrained and enigmatic to reward the listener's emotional investment.

Aspects of the Sensual World includes an instrumental version of the album's title track plus three unreleased songs, all of which appear on **This Woman's Work**, a luxurious, extensively annotated boxed set: eight CDs or cassettes (nine LPs) that contain the six original albums plus 29 B-sides, 12-inch mixes, video versions and live tracks. [tr/ws]

BUSH TETRAS

Rituals EP (Stiff) 1981
Wild Things [tape] (ROIR) 1983
Better Late Than Never [tape] (ROIR) 1989

FLOOR KISS

Goodnight Moon EP (Fr. Sourmash-L'Invitation au Suicide) 1985

LOVELIES

Mad Orphan (109) 1988

Arising from the New York post-rock scene (Pat Place had been one of James White's Blacks), the Bush Tetras attempted a synthesis of African sensibilities (as perceived by white Americans) with the modern dance to form a global tribal music. The 12-inch **Rituals** (produced by then-Clash drummer Topper Headon) sets songs against a funk/reggae beat with horns and punchy guitar work tossed in liberally. "Can't Be Funky" and its doppelgänger, "Funky Version," are the most explicitly Third World tunes; "Cowboys in Africa" rushes along with punk intensity and "Rituals" employs a threnody pace.

The **Wild Things** cassette is a concert compilation of late '82 performances in and around New York. The band is in fine ferocious form, and Cynthia Sley spits and scowls her vocals as if the songs really meant something. The material reprises most of the Tetras' slim recorded repertoire, plus a couple of appropriately savage covers.

Better Late Than Never gathers together all of the Bush Tetras' studio work—**Rituals**, two prior singles and two otherwise unreleased demos (the earlier of which finds the group pushing a funky and reasonably accomplished dance groove)—on one digitally remastered cassette. On the band's last session (from '83), Place and Sley are backed by a new rhythm section.

After leaving the Tetras, drummer Dee Pop and his singing wife, onetime John Cale sidewoman deerfrance, launched Floor Kiss with former 8 Eyed Spy guitarist Michael Paumgardhen and a bassist. Hampered by crude self-production, the band's six-song 12-inch pairs simple rock-*cum*-power pop backing and breathy vocals in service of reasonably diverting material. A minor pleasure that might have developed into something.

The Lovelies are Sley's quintet with guitarist Ivan Julian (ex-Voidoids/Outsets), an unpleasant pairing of his common rock and her uncommon voice. On the "Thrash" side of **Mad Orphan** (the Mad Orphans were a Lovelies precursor), the flat, muddy production manages to hide Julian's guitar sparks but not Sley's artlessly abrasive singing. On the "Gash" side (what a charming title), keyboards, lower volume and more musical vocals (especially when multi-tracked) make several of the songs far more palatable. [sg/i]

See also *Outsets*.

BUTCHER SHOP
See *Beasts of Bourbon*.

BUTTHOLE SURFERS
Butthole Surfers (Alternative Tentacles) 1983
Live PCPPEP (Alternative Tentacles) 1984
Psychic . . . Powerless . . . Another Man's Sac (Touch and Go) 1985 ●
Cream Corn from the Socket of Davis EP (Touch and Go) 1985 ●
Rembrandt Pussyhorse (Touch and Go) 1986 ●
Locust Abortion Technician (Touch and Go) 1987 ●
Hairway to Steven (Touch and Go) 1988 ●
Double Live (Latino Bugger Veil) 1989 ●
Widowermaker! EP (Touch and Go) 1989 ●
"The Hurdy Gurdy Man" EP (Rough Trade) 1990 ●
Piouhgd (Rough Trade) 1991 ●

JACKOFFICERS
Digital Dump (Rough Trade) 1990 ●

PAUL LEARY
The History of Dogs (Rough Trade) 1991 ●

There are few experiences in this life that leave one feeling as sullied as a spin through the grooves of a Butthole Surfers record. Unlike so many nouveau scuzzbos, Austin's Buttholes don't descend into the depths of squalor to make a point about the human condition—they just like it down there. Splotches of Paul Leary's guitar noise and Gibby Haynes' tortured

screams are these enigmatic Texans' bread and butter. When the noise revs up really fast, it sounds almost like hardcore, but this band relies more on filth than speed or power. The Butties inflict and exorcise pain like other people eat potato chips, and whatever debts they owe to Flipper and PiL would probably be forgotten if they'd just go away. There's clearly no one like 'em.

The debut mini-LP (also issued on colored vinyl under the title **Brown Reason to Live**) poses its threat to the social order through a varied thrash-to-Beefheart-blues attack and an inspired/inspiring set of lyrics. "The Shah Sleeps in Lee Harvey's Grave" is the obvious anthem while, on "Suicide," Gibby sets political matters aside for an intensely personal statement: "I'm not fucking kidding man, it hurts!" On the other hand, "Hey" is almost subdued, Feelies-style material—extremism sometimes takes the oddest forms, don't it?

The seven-song **Live PCPPEP** offers denser and dirtier treatments of some of the first record's non-hits. The biggest improvement is the new brother and sister standup drumming team. **Another Man's Sac** (originally pressed on clear vinyl) shows an addled creative sensibility—you were expecting them to develop into Hall and Oates? The faint-at-heart may not survive this assault, but then they probably don't deserve to.

The 12-inch **Cream Corn** EP hauls more sediment and sludge up from the gutter and onto the turntable, hitting its high point with "Moving to Florida," a cloying ear nuzzle imparted over Crampsian dirtabilly. (The CD of **Another Man's Sac** and the cassette of **Rembrandt Pussyhorse** both tack on the EP's four songs.) Mixing deranged blues, metal-punk and an overriding sense of anarchy, these loonies don't make guitars scream, they make 'em vomit and choke on it.

Rembrandt Pussyhorse takes a gonzo psychedelic approach that is (dare it be said) downright arty in its bizarre sonic experimentation. With some of the bowel-grinding dregs toned down, piano, organ, violin and a plethora of guitar techniques make the album a real diversion. Of special note is a cover of the Guess Who's "American Woman," which, in the Butties' bloody hands, sports a huge drum sound and metallic guitar, with tinny, atonal voices—imagine Nile Rodgers producing the Residents.

Locust Abortion Technician—which typically offers absolutely no information about the parties responsible—ebbs and flows like organic waste, an unpredictable flux of noise, movie score politeness, grating grunge-rock, fake folk, chirping birds, voices, tape manipulations and words, done at various recording speeds. "Sweat Loaf" launches the record with silence, speaking and then manic rock gusto; "22 Going on 23" ends it with grinding radio vérité.

With an incredible cover and numerous nods to the '60s, **Hairway to Steven** is as varied as it is entertaining: the program includes acoustic guitars competing with bowling alley sounds, half-speed vocals mixed (shades of "Third Stone from the Sun") with Hendrixy guitar psychedelia, live (maybe) cowbunk storytelling, straightforward (well . . .) melodic songsmithery and flat-out audio hysteria. Reactionary times demand inspirational rebels like the Buttholes.

The double-live **Double Live** is a self-released authorized bootleg, a monumental nineteen-song (29 on

CD) sampling of the Surfers' oeuvre (plus an R.E.M. cover!), recorded—for the most part—as clearly as such distorted music ought to be. Largely removed from the manipulative possibilities of the studio (although things do manage to turn very weird on "The One I Love"), the Butties aren't the ultimate sonic bizarros, but Gibby's madman vocals plus the chaotic onslaught of two drummers and Leary's endless guitar noise still make this a reasonable facsimile of party night at the nuthouse.

Three of the four new songs chucked up on **Widowermaker!** cover the usual terrain, with processed vocals, gross-out lyrics, vehement guitar noise and buzzing sound effects. But then there's the restrained melody and delivery of "The Colored F.B.I. Guy," on which a quiet bit of feedback is as strident as things get.

The Butties' only 1990 product was an adequate if witless remake of Donovan's "Hurdy Gurdy Man," issued with an inane stripped-down house mix—thereby proving that, even in the iconoclast's world, there are rights and wrongs. Instead, Gibby and bassist Jeff Pinkus spent their time on a side project, releasing an album as the Jackofficers. Uniting samples, beats, noise and occasional lyrics, **Digital Dump** applies the Surfer sensibility to dance music but comes up on the imaginative end of ordinary. Steady electronic rhythms and electronic keyboards pin the duo down to the same sound and structures as everybody else, reducing whatever is thrown into the mix—whether it's Oliver North's voice, *Mission Impossible* music, chipmunk vocals, noise guitar or sex sounds—to a colorful variation on very common themes. Only the crazed "Swingers Club" and "Don't Touch That," both of which more or less transmute Butthole Surfers music whole onto synthesizer, really demonstrate the concept's potential.

Considering how long it's been since the band's last studio LP, the uneven **Piouhgd** (pronounced "p-o'd") is a well-produced disappointment that wastes too much time on halfbaked ideas like "Hurdy Gurdy Man" and "Revolution," one part of which consists of an unobtrusive stew of synthetic strings, noise-guitar, a ringing phone and police sirens over which Gibby keeps calling out Garry Shandling's name. Besides that nonsense, and "Lonesome Bulldog," a comedic cowboy ballad in three parts, **Piouhgd** stoops to a spot-on parody of the Jesus and Mary Chain (funny, but so what?). The reassuring appearance of several slabs of typical Buttholian psychoacoustics (one of which sounds like a Move song in hell) prove that our mad anti-heroes aren't getting soft; still, **Piouhgd** lacks a certain psumbthaenng. (The CD bonus, "Barking Dogs," is an extended sound collage with brief canine contributions.) [jl/i]

See also *Fearless Iranians from Hell.*

BUZZCOCKS

Spiral Scratch EP (nr/New Hormones) 1977 + 1981
Another Music in a Different Kitchen (nr/UA) 1978 ●
Love Bites (nr/UA) 1978 ●
A Different Kind of Tension (nr/UA) 1979 (IRS) 1989 ●
Singles Going Steady (IRS) 1979 ●
Parts One, Two, Three EP (IRS) 1984 ●
Total Pop 1977–1980 (Ger. Weird Systems) 1987 ●
The Peel Sessions EP (nr/Strange Fruit) 1988
Lest We Forget [tape] (ROIR) 1988

Live at the Roxy Club April '77 (nr/Absolutely Free) 1989 (nr/Receiver) 1990 ●
The Fab Four EP (nr/EMI) 1989 ●
Product (Restless Retro) 1989 ●
The Peel Sessions Album (nr/Strange Fruit) 1989 (Strange Fruit-Dutch East India) 1991 ●

Inspired by the Sex Pistols, Manchester's Howard Devoto and Pete Shelley formed the Buzzcocks in 1976, specializing in high-energy, staccato delivery of stripped-down pop songs. With John Maher (drums) and Steve Diggle (bass), the Buzzcocks cut **Spiral Scratch**, the UK's first self-released punk record. Though ragged and rudimentary, the 7-inch features the frantic, minimalistic pop stylings that would characterize the group's work and, with songs like "Breakdown" and "Boredom," remains a seminal artifact of '70s DIY.

Devoto departed shortly thereafter to form Magazine. Garth Smith joined, taking over bass while Shelley switched to vocals (in addition to guitar) and Diggle to lead guitar. The band signed to United Artists and, after one frenetic and controversial single ("Orgasm Addict"), sacked Smith; the arrival of Steve Garvey fixed the lineup that would remain unchanged throughout the band's original existence.

Another Music in a Different Kitchen expands on the stark three-minute pop song and themes of confusion, alienation and betrayal, adding a new emphasis on harmony and humor and a growing coordination of the players in contrast to the earlier inspired chaos. "Fast Cars," the jagged waltz "Sixteen" and the tom-tom pounder "Moving Away from the Pulsebeat" are all mini mindblowers.

Love Bites demonstrates both the Buzzcocks' perfection of their particular brand of pop and their disillusionment with its restrictions. Producer Martin Rushent clarifies the elements of the sound even further, and Shelley's songwriting continues to improve, including the band's highest-charting UK single, "Ever Fallen in Love" (later covered badly by Fine Young Cannibals). Other cuts, like "Sixteen Again" and "Real World," would have made great pop singles as well, but much of the album (which includes two instrumentals) finds the Buzzcocks mired in repetitive structures.

A Different Kind of Tension makes tentative maneuvers into the new, as the Buzzcocks attempt to throw off the yoke of pop music. This schizophrenic album features some of Shelley's finest songs, notably "You Say You Don't Love Me" and "I Believe." With Diggle providing some of the material, the band reaches a zenith of effortless craft, especially on Side Two (subtitled "The thorn beneath the rose"), where Shelley dives into the challenging waters of paranoia, selfconscious despair and harrowing uncertainty, climaxing in the title track. That's followed by "I Believe," a seven-minute summation of reasons to be cheerful continually undercut by a chorus of "There is no love in this world any more." Powerful stuff.

After three more singles in '80 and '81 (later compiled as the **Parts One, Two, Three** EP), Shelley decided to go solo and the Buzzcocks came to an end. Maher and Diggle went off to form Flag of Convenience; following a brief stint on Shelley's '81 solo tour, Garvey moved to New York and eventually quit the music business.

Singles Going Steady is a stunning compilation of the band's eight classic UA 45s, proving conclusively that the Buzzcocks *were* an amazing singles band, perhaps one of the best ever. From the teen angst of the Devoto/Shelley "Orgasm Addict" to the 20th-century malaise of "Something's Gone Wrong Again," the songs are across-the-board great, and the album is a non-stop hit parade.

Containing all six tracks (written half-and-half by Shelley and Diggle) from the group's last efforts, **Parts One, Two, Three** is a postscript to **Singles Going Steady**, a transition away from big-pop structures into a more elusive, subversive form that still possesses plenty of octane and odd hooks. "What Do You Know?" introduces horns; the relaxed pace of "Running Free" and the odd "Are Everything" (later covered by Heaven 17) are equally novel. (IRS later issued a CD combining **Parts One, Two, Three** and **A Different Kind of Tension**.)

Total Pop, an offbeat German collection, draws from **Singles Going Steady, One, Two, Three, Love Bites** and **Tension**, adding the band's two live tracks ("Breakdown" and "Love Battery") from **The Roxy London WC2**, a classic 1977 scene document. (The CD and cassette have three bonus cuts.)

The **Peel Sessions** EP, which dates from September '77, contains only three songs: "Fast Cars," "(Moving Away from the) Pulsebeat" and "What Do I Get." The long-delayed **Lest We Forget** is a fine-sounding live compilation tape recorded at—with one Mancunian exception—various US gigs in 1979 and 1980.

Live at the Roxy Club April '77, the first in an archival series of releases of recordings made at the legendary London venue, is eminently skippable. Unlike **Lest We Forget**'s maturity, this documents the Buzzcocks at a weak point, playing one of the first gigs without Devoto. The band is an engaging shambles—sloppy, out of tune, sometimes downright awful.

Released as a teaser for the **Product** boxed set, **The Fab Four** EP consists of four consecutive A-sides (all included on **Singles Going Steady**), from "Ever Fallen in Love" to Diggle's "Harmony in My Head."

Product is brilliant. Except for the **Spiral Scratch** EP, this three-CD (or three-cassette or four-LP) extravaganza, complete with a detailed historical booklet, contains the Buzzcocks' complete studio works: every track of the band's three albums and twelve singles. The boxed set also includes "I Look Alone," a fantastic basher that was an outtake from the **Parts One, Two, Three** series, and eight songs from a 1978 gig at London's Lyceum. All better than **Lest We Forget**, these tracks offer the best released evidence of the band's wall-of-guitar concert power.

The release of **Product** was one of the factors that contributed to the Buzzcocks' 1989 reunion. Shelley, Diggle, Maher and Garvey undertook brilliant tours of the US and England. (Drummer Maher then returned to his Volkswagen repair business, replaced for subsequent dates in Australia and Japan by ex-Smith Mike Joyce.) It appears nearly certain that the Buzzcocks will resume recording in the '90s.

The **Peel Sessions Album** (which subsumes the previously issued **Peel** EP) offers four different looks at the band between 1977 and 1979. While the regular studio recordings are generally better than these radio broadcasts, there is a searing "E.S.P." that is more gripping than the version on **Love Bites**, while two instrumentals from the same LP and **Tension**'s "Mad Mad Judy" are all notably—and nicely—dissimilar to their subsequent renderings. [sg/i/jr]

See also *Howard Devoto, Flag of Convenience, Magazine, Pete Shelley, Teardrops.*

BUZZ OF DELIGHT
See *Oh-OK.*

DAVID BYRNE AND BRIAN ENO
My Life in the Bush of Ghosts (Sire) 1980 + 1980 ●
DAVID BYRNE
Songs from the Broadway Production of "The Catherine Wheel" (Sire) 1981 ●
Music for *The Knee Plays* (ECM) 1985
Rei Momo (Luaka Bop-Sire) 1989 ●
The Forest (Luaka Bop-Sire-Warner Bros.) 1991 φ
DAVID BYRNE ET AL.
Sounds from True Stories (Sire) 1986
RYUICHI SAKAMOTO, DAVID BYRNE AND CONG SU
The Last Emperor (Virgin Movie Music) 1988 ●
VARIOUS ARTISTS
Brazil Classics Vol. 1: Beleza Tropical (Fly-Sire) 1989 ●
Brazil Classics Vol. 2: O Samba (Luaka Bop-Sire) 1989 ●
Brazil Classics Vol. 4: Tom Zé (Luaka Bop-Sire) 1990 φ
Brazil Classics Vol. 3: Forró Etc./Music of the Brazilian Northeast (Luaka Bop-Sire) 1991 φ

As a Talking Head, David Byrne—guitarist, songwriter, singer—has long shown an inquisitive, intelligent interest in unusual applications of, and exploratory cultural variations on, pop music. His solo musical work revolves around transfiguring pop through the infusion of alien elements or by injecting it into foreign situations. **My Life in the Bush of Ghosts**, a continuation of his (and the band's) collaboration with Eno, blends found vocal tapes with electronic music centering on Third World (notably African) rhythms to interesting effect and uneven results. (After strenuous Islamic objections were raised, the record was reissued with "Very Very Hungry" in place of "Qu'ran.")

Byrne created the music on **The Catherine Wheel** for a dance production by the renowned Twyla Tharp. Listeners can get either a selection of tracks on the album, or the complete score on the cassette version. The pace and instrumentation on the poppier material bears a strong resemblance to Talking Heads' work of the **Remain in Light** period, with volatile rhythms and jazz inflections; other songs are more experimental, drawing heavily on Eno's ambient and tape-editing techniques.

Byrne next forayed into theatrical music by writing and producing the Dixieland-inflected horn score for **The Knee Plays**, a section of director/avant-garde opera conceptualist Robert Wilson's stage work **The Civil Wars**. Inspired by the Dirty Dozen Brass Band, Byrne created angular pieces that remove the swing from ragtime, turning New Orleans jazz into engaging machine music over which he occasionally recites lyrics.

Although Talking Heads released an album of songs to coincide with Byrne's *True Stories*, a soundtrack record of incidental music for the film was also issued. Byrne produced and wrote the majority of **Sounds from True Stories** (subtitled ''Music for Activities Freaks''), earning his star billing while performing on just two tracks. The rest of the musical cast—the Kronos Quartet, Carl Finch (of Brave Combo), Steve Jordan, Terry Allen, the Heads, Prairie Prince and others—plays his (and their) instrumentals in a panoply of styles, from country to polka to electronics to jazz.

Working individually on separate segments of it, Sakamoto, Byrne and Cong Su shared a Golden Globe award and an Oscar for the score of Bernardo Bertolucci's *The Last Emperor*. Byrne's segment—fifteen instrumental minutes on Side Two—avoids trite Oriental clichés while managing to adequately evoke the cultural locale with gongs, strings and woodwinds. Lovely.

Having made his artistic peace with North America, Africa and Asia, Byrne next turned his continental attentions southward, compiling and annotating two albums of contemporary Brazilian pop (singers like Milton Nascimento, Gilberto Gil and Caetano Veloso) and dance music. (The third, a one-artist anthology, was numbered out of order; **Brazil Classics Vol. 3** didn't appear until early '91.)

Almost free of his usual intellectual aloofness, the summery **Rei Momo** (produced by Steve Lillywhite and performed by a large group of top Latin players) is lively and enjoyable, with an infectious light feel, lyrics that have nothing to do with the record's style and appealing songs (including three co-written with Johnny Pacheco or Willie Colon) that make little effort to sound Latin. Instead, Byrne uses percussion, rhythms and appropriate instrumentation (not to mention occasional backing vocals in Spanish) to give exemplary tunes like ''Dirty Old Town,'' ''Marching Through the Wilderness'' and ''Make Believe Mambo'' a delightful dash of salsa.   [sg/i]

See also *Talking Heads*.

CABARET VOLTAIRE

Extended Play EP (nr/Rough Trade) 1978
"Mix-Up" (nr/Rough Trade) 1979 (Mute-Restless) 1990 ●
Live at the YMCA 27-10-79 (nr/Rough Trade) 1980
   (Mute-Restless) 1990 ●
Three Mantras (nr/Rough Trade) 1980 (Mute-Restless)
   1990 ●
The Voice of America (Rough Trade) 1980
   (Mute-Restless) 1990 ●
1974–1976 [tape] (nr/Industrial) 1980
3 Crépuscule Tracks (Rough Trade) 1981
Live at the Lyceum [tape] (nr/Rough Trade) 1981
   (Mute-Restless) 1990 φ
Red Mecca (Rough Trade) 1981 (Mute-Restless) 1990 ●
2 X 45 (nr/Rough Trade) 1982 (Mute-Restless) 1990 ●
Hai! Live in Japan (Rough Trade) 1982 (Mute-Restless)
   1990 ●
The Crackdown (nr/Some Bizzare-Virgin) 1983 ●
Johnny YesNo (nr/Doublevision) 1983 (Mute-Restless)
   1990 ●
Micro-Phonies (nr/Some Bizzare-Virgin) 1984 ●
Drinking Gasoline (Caroline) 1985
The Arm of the Lord (Caroline) 1985 ●
The Drain Train EP (Caroline) 1986 (Mute-Restless)
   1990 ●
The Golden Moments of Cabaret Voltaire [CD] (nr/Rough
   Trade) 1987 ●
Code (EMI Manhattan) 1987 ●
Eight Crépuscule Tracks (Giant) 1988 ●
Listen Up with Cabaret Voltaire (Mute-Restless) 1990 ●
The Living Legends (Mute-Restless) 1990 φ
Groovy, Laidback and Nasty (nr/Parlophone) 1990 ●

PRESSURE COMPANY

Live in Sheffield 19 Jan 82 (nr/Solidarity-Paradox) 1982

RICHARD H. KIRK

Disposable Half-Truths [tape] (nr/Industrial) 1980
Time High Fiction (nr/Doublevision) 1983
Black Jesus Voice (nr/Rough Trade) 1986
Ugly Spirit (nr/Rough Trade) 1986

PETER HOPE & RICHARD KIRK

Hoodoo Talk (Native-Wax Trax!) 1987 ●

STEPHEN MALLINDER

Pow-Wow (nr/Fetish) 1982
Pow-Wow Plus (nr/Doublevision) 1985

The prolific Cabaret Voltaire is one of the most energetic, progressive and dissonant forces in modern music. Working primarily in the electronic form, specializing in found sounds and tape manipulations, Cabaret Voltaire has relentlessly pushed at the outer edges of style, shedding an early primitivism for a subsequent accessibility that plays on the (almost) familiar. Coming from the industrial city of Sheffield, they have spent years attempting to make a music that reflects their experience and perceptions.

Extended Play launched Cabaret Voltaire—Richard H. Kirk (guitar, synth, horns, clarinet), Stephen Mallinder (bass, vocals) and Christopher Watkins (organ, tapes)—and gave an early boost to Rough Trade (it was the label's third single). It highlights the Cabs' main features—unpredictable sounds and eerie, disembodied vocals manipulated over a very physical beat—and is particularly notable for a distorted cover version of Lou Reed's "Here She Comes Now."

The more professionally produced **"Mix-Up"** has better coordinated use of electronics, increasing the bizarre intensity of the sound. Bass, guitar and flute are evident (but deformed) in the mix, and Cabaret Voltaire makes visible use of other people's material, as with the Seeds' "No Escape."

Live at the YMCA (as well as the later **Live at the Lyceum** tape) dispels any notions of Cab Volt as a sterile studio group. Wisely, they don't seek to precisely duplicate their recorded sound, but convert it into outré-populist dance music that is almost improvisational in nature. Though the live recordings are more fragmented than their studio counterparts, they compensate for it in added energy.

Three Mantras is the group's first explicit venture into non-Western musical forms. The Arabic material used is successfully developed into a chant, and then its structure is applied to a new work. The record also marks a shift in technique, as musical demands take precedence over production to strange and beautiful effect.

The Voice of America is an uneven release, combining older material with much more assured newer work, such as the political "The Voice of America/Damage Is Done," which uses found tape and sparse electronics to juxtapose the repressive and libertarian aspects of American life. The new material shows much greater focus and cleaner production than the older, with the mantra technique rising in place of the former chaotic electro-noise.

For serious fans, **1974–1976** is a series of curious and intriguing false starts and experiments from the band's earliest days.

3 Crépuscule Tracks captures the band in transition between their found-vocals/art-noise period and a commitment to dance-floor electronics. "Sluggin' fer Jesus (Part One)" is a masterful combination of the two, as a right-wing TV preacher demands large cash contributions over a powerful, trance-inducing synth beat.

On **Red Mecca**, the trio tightens its focus to produce an album more coherent than its predecessors, underscored by a reworking of Henry Mancini's score for Orson Welles' *Touch of Evil*. As their music reaches a new level of maturity and polish in both production and performance, Cabaret Voltaire focus and extend their film noir theme through all the material, making this an odd, deceptively accessible record.

Two 12-inch EPs packaged as an album, **2 X 45** picks up the trends begun on **Red Mecca** and compresses them into a new form. Also interesting is the move away from obvious electronics and manipulations to a more naturalistic sound, with emphasis on acoustic instruments, like saxophone and clarinet. This is the closest the group has come to making a rock'n'roll album.

Like earlier live albums, **Hai! Live in Japan** marks time, playing with recent developments, funky in nature and far more coherent than **Live in Sheffield**. The latter was a one-off show to raise funds for the Polish Solidarity union, and was released under the Pressure Company name for contractual reasons. Disordered and trenchant, it is a reminder that the band is still capable of electrifying cacophony.

In 1983, Cabaret Voltaire signed with that noted asylum for eccentrics, Some Bizzare, a move criticized by some as a sell-out. The resulting LP, **The Crackdown**, is perhaps the most left-field record ever accused of commercial compromise. Sticking mostly to a funk format, the songs are more structured than those on **2 X 45**, and the band displays a plethora of high-tech but dark electronic textures. Probably the strongest of their many albums.

Johnny YesNo is a soundtrack to Peter Care's film about a junkie. Released on the band's own Doublevision label, it was recorded in 1981, prior to Chris Watkin's departure. Like most soundtracks, it's not designed for careful listening, and consists primarily of eerie electronic noodling. **Micro-Phonies** is similar to **The Crackdown**, except that the sound is a bit sparser and decidedly more rhythm-conscious. Much of the material would be very much at home coming from a beat-box, particularly "Sensoria" and "James Brown," the 12-inch remixes of which are both highly recommended.

Drinking Gasoline is a double 12-inch (running over 30 minutes) recorded primarily as a video soundtrack. The four numbers are entirely interchangeable, the sort of hard electro-funk found on previous LPs. Fans will enjoy it, but the Cabs seem stuck in a rut, an unsurprising problem after so many releases. **The Arm of the Lord** (reissued on CD as **The Covenant, The Sword and the Arm of the Lord**) proves that no band could be so productive without a few tricks up its sleeve. Titled after an American neo-Nazi religious organization, the record crossbreeds trademark electro-rhythm attack with odd breaks, varied tempos, the return of eerie found voices, unpolished production and harsh dissonance. "I Want You" and "Motion Rotation" actually have catchy melodies—a band first!

The Drain Train, a two-disc 12-inch, consists mostly of three not vastly different versions of a track quite similar to other recent material. The other two tracks don't do much groundbreaking, either. **Code**'s admission of outside assistance (Bill Nelson on guitar and Adrian Sherwood as co-producer) makes for some interesting but rather subtle touches, as the band reaches for crystal-clear, state-of-the-art sound. But the material is a stylistic reprise of **The Arm of the Lord**: tempos are varied quite a bit, but each track has the same feel. Artsy British industrialists or computerized hip-hoppers?

Obviously sensing the need for a rest and a rethink, the duo took their first extended vacation following

Code. The late '80s saw the release of several compilations. Those nostalgic for the Cabs' white noise and distortion period will appreciate **The Golden Moments of Cabaret Voltaire** (and agree with the title) and **Eight Crépuscule Tracks**. The first is a CD-only release of material from the band's Rough (Trade) days; there's nothing more recent than **2 X 45**, and most of it predates that. The juxtaposition inherent in digital reproduction of primitive music makes it a very interesting collection. **Eight Crépuscule Tracks** draws from the same approximate time frame, taking the original **3 Crépuscule Tracks** and adding some singles and a previously unreleased cover of "The Theme from *Shaft*," which sounds as if it was recorded around the time of **Voice of America**.

The two-LP/two-CD **Listen Up with Cabaret Voltaire** is an essential item, containing rarities and unreleased selections spanning the length of the Cabs' recorded history. Even the previously released material is obscure, rescued from *NME* compilation cassettes, early Factory samplers and videos; the "new" cuts would have stood proudly in contemporaneous works—"This Is Our Religion," for instance, would have fit in perfectly on **Voice of America**, while "Enough's Enough" or "Why" could be from any recent LP.

The Living Legends consists of A- and B-sides from the band's days as a trio on Rough Trade, fourteen tracks that underscore the enormous influence Cabaret Voltaire's music has had on virtually every industrial and/or experimental band of the past decade. (Three items overlap **Golden Moments**, which is mostly culled from albums.) Real treats include the disassembled cover of the Velvets' "Here She Comes Now" and the prehistoric "Is That Me (Finding Someone at the Door Again)," recorded live in 1975.

Three years after **Code**—by which point many had presumed the group no longer existed—Kirk and Mallinder returned with **Groovy, Laidback and Nasty**. Recorded partly in Chicago, the LP employs a number of co-producers and backup singers, all sorts of house-style arrangements and Mallinder's warmest and most tuneful vocals ever; the result is an entirely updated Cabaret Voltaire, a group whose dance music has never sounded better. An EP of four remixes plus one extra cut is also included. Welcome back.

Both members have done solo work, which is especially interesting as it allows identification of who brings what to the band. Mallinder's **Pow-Wow** mini-album is dominated by muscular bass and drum combinations, tapes and his husky voice. On his own, he seems to prefer electronically treated acoustic instruments rather than synthesizers. **Pow-Wow Plus** repackages that record with the addition of 1981's "Temperature Drop" single. Kirk's **Time High Fiction** is a one-man double album recorded over a three-year period; it's richer in texture (mostly electronic) and less rhythmic than his partner's work. The two-side-long "Dead Relatives" is even more dissonant than anything the two have done together.

Kirk released a pair of solo LPs in 1986: **Black Jesus Voice** and **Ugly Spirit**. (Both were combined on a single cassette under the title of the former.) **Black Jesus Voice** is not a drastic departure from Cabaret Voltaire; rhythmically similar but with slightly harsher sounds. Most of the vocals are from tapes rather than sung by Kirk himself. **Ugly Spirit** changes gears completely, however, and takes a sound-sculpture approach with often very effective results.

In 1986, Kirk joined forces with former Box singer Peter Hope for **Hoodoo Talk**, which wasn't released until two years later. Playing all the instruments, Kirk provides varied but familiar synth/guitar/drum machine patterns, from busy, booming rhythms with swelling layers of noise to minimalist sound bites. Hope adds disjointed, vaguely nightmarish lyrics sung in the same ingratiating, exaggerated way that made later Box material such rough going. The desire to spend studio time with someone new after so many years is understandable, but this probably would have worked better with Mallinder as a Cab Volt LP. [sg/dgs]

CHRIS CACAVAS AND JUNKYARD LOVE

See *Green on Red.*

JOHN CALE

Vintage Violence (Columbia) 1969 ●
Church of Anthrax (Columbia) 1971
The Academy in Peril (Reprise) 1972 (nr/Edsel) 1986 ●
Paris 1919 (Reprise) 1973
Fear (Island) 1974 ●
Slow Dazzle (Island) 1975 ●
Helen of Troy (nr/Island) 1975
Guts (Island) 1977
Animal Justice EP (nr/Illegal) 1977
Sabotage/Live (Spy) 1979
Honi Soit ... (A&M) 1981
Music for a New Society (ZE-Passport) 1982
Caribbean Sunset (ZE-Island) 1984
John Cale Comes Alive (ZE-Island) 1984
Artificial Intelligence (Beggars Banquet-PVC) 1985 ●
Words for the Dying (Opal-Warner Bros.) 1989 ●
Even Cowgirls Get the Blues [tape] (ROIR) 1991

KEVIN AYERS–JOHN CALE–ENO–NICO

June 1, 1974 (Island) 1974 ●

LOU REED/JOHN CALE

Songs for Drella (Sire-Warner Bros.) 1990 ●

ENO/CALE

Wrong Way Up (Opal-Warner Bros.) 1990 ●

John Cale's musical career since leaving the Velvet Underground—after two albums on which his viola-scraping and genuine musical training played a pivotal role—has been diverse and unpredictable, exploring both classical/avant-garde "serious" music as well as more shoot-from-the-hip rough rock. Throughout, the inscrutable Welshman has surrounded himself with able and distinguished cohorts, and has produced music of real challenge and quality.

His first solo efforts after the Velvets were effectively collaborations: **Vintage Violence**, with Garland Jeffreys and New York rock group Grinder's Switch; **Church of Anthrax**, with avant-garde titan Terry Riley; **Academy in Peril**, with the Royal Philharmonic Orchestra. Also in much the same vein, Cale made **Paris 1919** with backing by members of Little Feat. It wasn't until he signed to Island that his music became weird

and abrasive, signifying a partial return to the chaos of his Velvet days.

His first such release was as a member of the **June 1, 1974** project, a one-off concert documented on an LP and featuring Kevin Ayers, Brian Eno and Nico as well as Cale, Robert Wyatt and others. It's a wonderful album, with Cale taking a vocal on "Heartbreak Hotel" and elsewhere contributing viola and piano.

Cale emerged into pre-new wave weirdness with **Fear**, an aggressively wild record made with assistance from the likes of Eno and Roxy Musician Phil Manzanera. Clean production only heightens the anxiety inherent in Cale's voice and created by the skittering, modified guitar sounds. "Fear Is a Man's Best Friend" and "Gun" build a claustrophobically intense aura; quieter efforts like "Ship of Fools" only slightly diminish the queasiness level. A brilliant record full of neat surprises and great, unsettling songs.

Slow Dazzle adds Chris Spedding to the lineup and pursues some curious pathways: "Heartbreak Hotel," recast as a haunted-house dirge; "Mr. Wilson," an homage to the Beach Boys' Brian; "The Jeweller," a recitation reminiscent of the Velvets' "The Gift." More restrained, but no less entrancing than **Fear**.

Helen of Troy, featuring Phil Collins as well as Spedding and Eno (but not Manzanera), is a gripping, morbid collection of songs, including Jonathan Richman's "Pablo Picasso," powered by Cale's commanding vocals and whining slide guitars, and "Leaving It All Up to You," which has a reference to Sharon Tate that caused it to be removed from the album when first issued; it was subsequently replaced. A dark and pained album.

Animal Justice—three cuts on a 45 rpm 12-inch—features what remained of a touring band after half had quit in protest of a legendary onstage chicken-chopping incident. The EP's leadoff track ("Chicken Shit") concerns that brouhaha; the other songs are a pointless version of Chuck Berry's "Memphis" and a stunning Cale original, "Hedda Gabbler." **Guts** is an excellent collection of tracks from the three preceding LPs.

Sabotage/Live, recorded onstage at New York's CBGB in June 1979, presents almost all new material. The sound's just passable, and the album never jells. **Honi Soit** used an outside producer (Mike Thorne) for a change and a totally new band as well; some tracks are good, but it's not on a par with Cale's best. With **Music for a New Society**, Cale retreated from nakedly aggressive music and turned to a more orchestrated style that owes something to his early pre-punk efforts, like **Paris 1919**. Cale's lyrics, however, have rarely been as grim or violent as they are here. The arrangements prominently feature keyboards and the music effectively matches the darkly moody subject matter.

Caribbean Sunset is Cale's least interesting album to date. Even if the puzzlingly muddy self-production hadn't stifled everything but his jagged-edged vocals, the songs themselves are too flimsy to support his words or passion.

Perhaps sensing this, Cale released **Caribbean Sunset** back-to-back with another LP showcasing his in-concert strengths with the same band. Though he self-defeatingly begins *and* ends **Comes Alive** with half-assed studio efforts, that's the extent of the disappointment. The live core of the album consists of

101

gripping versions of vintage material like "Fear" and "Leaving It All Up to You," a death-rattling "Heartbreak Hotel" performed solo at the electric piano, a bouncily tongue-in-cheek "Waiting for the Man" as a tip of the hat to Lou Reed, and a couple of **Sabotage Live** songs minus the overly metallic sound that made them almost unlistenable on that LP. Cale should record *all* his material this way: live and with a solid band.

Artificial Intelligence has the solid band: a trio of James Young, Graham Dowdall and David Young. It also has Cale co-writing lyrics with journalist Ratso Sloman, whose Dylan fixation comes through clearly on the articulately verbose "Everytime the Dogs Bark" and other songs. Elsewhere, a mild island lilt suggests a well-read Jimmy Buffett. Moody and contained, but energetic and occasionally stimulating, **A.I.** is a reasonable if unspectacular addition to Cale's extensive catalogue.

After an extended recording hiatus, Cale reappeared in non-rock mode with the classically oriented Brian Eno-produced **Words for the Dying**. The album is divided into three sections: the 31-minute "Falklands Suite" (Cale singing four Dylan Thomas poems with a Russian orchestra and a Welsh choir), a two-part piano solo ("Songs Without Words") and "The Soul of Carmen Miranda" (a ghostly semi-pop collaboration with Eno). Though **Words for the Dying** doesn't equal Cale's most intense work, it's not meant to, and marks a welcome return to action for this perennially underrated artist.   [i/mf/hd]

See also *Brian Eno, Lou Reed*.

ROBERT CALVERT
See *Hawkwind*.

CAMOUFLAGE
Voices & Images (Atlantic) 1988 ●
Methods of Silence (Atlantic) 1989 ●
Meanwhile (Atlantic) 1991 φ

Considering that British synth-pop has its roots in German prog-rock, there's something faintly just about this Hamburg trio's real-or-Memorex Depeche Mode imitation on **Voices & Images**. Although several songs do digress from the overtly familiar, there's little chance that anyone favorably disposed towards **Speak & Spell** (and unperturbed by the notion of hand-me-downs) won't like this.

The DM sound reappears frequently on **Methods of Silence**, but Camouflage adds other elements that are less specifically derivative. Every track incorporates guest guitar; electronic piano, oboe, sax and cello also make beneficial appearances. While the maturing trio's functional but mediocre songwriting (the lyrics, in English, rarely hit the mark) limits its ability to develop, the intriguing inter-generational leap of covering New Musik's "On Islands" at least suggests an alternate path to explore.   [kl]

LUTHER CAMPBELL FEATURING THE 2 LIVE CREW
See *2 Live Crew*.

STAN CAMPBELL
See *Specials*.

CAMPER VAN BEETHOVEN
Telephone Free Landslide Victory (Independent
    Project-Rough Trade) 1985 ●
Take The Skinheads Bowling EP (Pitch-A-Tent-Rough
    Trade) 1986 ●
Camper Van Beethoven II & III (Pitch-A-Tent-Rough
    Trade) 1986 ●
Camper Van Beethoven (Pitch-A-Tent-Rough Trade)
    1986 ●
Vampire Can Mating Oven EP (Pitch-A-Tent-Rough Trade)
    1987 ●
Our Beloved Revolutionary Sweetheart (Virgin) 1988 ●
Key Lime Pie (Virgin) 1989 ●

MONKS OF DOOM
Soundtrack to the Film: "Breakfast on the Beach of
    Deception" (Pitch-A-Tent-Rough Trade) 1988
The Cosmodemonic Telegraph Company
    (Pitch-A-Tent-Rough Trade) 1989 ●

JONATHAN SEGEL
Storytelling (Pitch-A-Tent-Rough Trade) 1988 ●

Because they understand why middle-Eastern ethnic music isn't really all *that* different from rock'n'roll, and because they realize that the indie-rock underground is every bit as stupid and petty as the mainstream, the mere existence of playfully eclectic post-hippie California surrealists Camper Van Beethoven validates the very concept of pop music. Unselfconsciously absorbing inspiration from any musical style that strikes them, and adding leader David Lowery's dizzy absurdist lyrics, Santa Cruz's Campers make records that suggest what the Grateful Dead might sound like if they had a sense of humor and knew how to write pop songs.

The band has gradually downplayed the giddy shifts in style that distinguished their early LPs, integrating their disparate influences into a more cohesive individual voice. Still, the Camper catalogue is a remarkably consistent one, showcasing a unique aesthetic that seemed to emerge fully developed on **Telephone Free Landslide Victory**.

In addition to the underground in-jokes "Take the Skinheads Bowling" (the EP of which pairs that college-radio hit with five non-LP tracks of varying length) and "Where the Hell is Bill?," **Telephone** includes a woozy cover of Black Flag's "Wasted" and self-explanatory instrumentals like "Border Ska," "Yanqui Go Home," "Balalaika Gap" and "Mao Reminisces About His Days in Southern China." The 20-track **II & III** features lots of country references and a hoedown version of Sonic Youth's "I Love Her All the Time," plus the raga-pop "Circles," the phony anti-rock protest anthem "No More Bullshit" and the delightful "ZZ Top Goes to Egypt."

Camper Van Beethoven displays a more integrated band style and an emerging political consciousness on "Good Guys & Bad Guys" and "Joe Stalin's Cadillac"; there's also a respectful cover of Pink Floyd's "Interstellar Overdrive" and "Une Fois," the most impressive Indian-cajun fusion in recent memory. (A 1987 CD combines **Camper Van Beethoven** and **Vampire Can Mating Oven**.)

Closing out the band's indie-label career, the six-song **Vampire Can Mating Oven** collects up some enjoyable odds and ends, including a jolly remake of Ringo Starr's "Photograph."

Judging by **Our Beloved Revolutionary Sweetheart**, Camper Van's move to the majors didn't dampen the combo's iconoclasm, and the addition of a sympathetic producer (Dennis Herring) has made for a more ambitious sonic palette. Highlights include the catchy, self-deflating "Never Go Back" (previewed on the **Vampire Can Mating Oven** EP), the picturesque "Eye of Fatima," the Zep-like "Waka" and an oldie, "O Death," borrowed from '60s kindred spirits Kaleidoscope.

Key Lime Pie—the group's final album prior to an acrimonious breakup—is a decidedly bittersweet swansong, trading the exuberance of prior outings for a crushing sense of disillusionment. Still, the record's gloomy vibe makes for sporadically interesting listening on "When I Win the Lottery," the appropriately titled closer ("Come on Darkness") and particularly the stunning "Sweethearts," a resigned assessment of the Reagan era. A cute remake of Status Quo's 1968 "Pictures of Matchstick Men" seems to have wandered in from another album.

The mostly instrumental first Monks of Doom LP is a side project featuring three Campers—guitarist Greg Lisher, bassist Victor Krummenacher and drummer Chris Pedersen—and Ophelias guitarist David Immergluck (who became an end-time Camper) playing mildly psychedelic improvisational guitar rock, with occasional forays into jazzy ethnicity. The more song-oriented **Cosmodemonic Telegraph Company** is a big improvement over its predecessor, with the Monks having developed a distinct identity apart from their parent bands. Drawing on a seemingly bottomless well of mainstream-rock and avant-garde clichés, they produce personalized art-rock that's both artful and rocking, with covers of Eugene Chadbourne and the Residents that are conceptually consistent with the quartet's surprisingly concise originals.

Longtime Camper violinist Jonathan Segel—who left the band during the early stages of **Key Lime Pie**—released the 28-track **Storytelling** double-LP while still a member of the group. The leisurely song cycle moves easily between quiet folk tunes, gentle psychedelia and flat-out prog-rock, with the multi-instrumentalist getting musical help from all four Monks of Doom and various other San Francisco scenesters. Though Segel is only a passable vocalist, his matter-of-factly gee-whiz lyrics are functional, and the music makes for fine late-night/pre-dawn listening. [hd]

See also *Eugene Chadbourne, Harm Farm, Ophelias.*

CAN

Monster Movie (nr/UA) 1969 (Spoon-Mute-Restless Retro) 1990 ●
Soundtracks (nr/UA) 1970 (Spoon-Mute-Restless Retro) 1990 ●
Tago Mago (nr/UA) 1971 (Spoon-Mute-Restless Retro) 1990 ●
Ege Bamyasi (UA) 1972 (Spoon-Mute-Restless Retro) 1990 ●

Future Days (UA) 1973 (Spoon-Mute-Restless Retro) 1990 ●
Limited Edition (nr/UA) 1974
Soon Over Babaluma (UA) 1974 (Spoon-Mute-Restless Retro) 1990 ●
Landed (nr/Virgin) 1975 (Spoon-Mute-Restless Retro) 1990 ●
Unlimited Edition (nr/Caroline) 1976 (Spoon-Mute-Restless Retro) 1990 ●
Opener 1971–1974 (nr/Sunset) 1976
Flow Motion (nr/Virgin) 1976 (Spoon-Mute-Restless Retro) 1990 ●
Saw Delight (nr/Virgin) 1977 (Spoon-Mute-Restless Retro) 1990 ●
Out of Reach (Peters Int'l) 1978 ●
Cannibalism (nr/UA) 1978
Can (nr/Laser) 1979 (Spoon-Mute-Restless Retro) 1990 ●
Cannibalism 1 (Ger. Spoon) 1980 (Spoon-Mute-Restless Retro) 1990 ●
Incandescence 1969–1977 (nr/Virgin) 1981
Delay 1968 (Ger. Spoon) 1981 (Spoon-Mute-Restless Retro) 1990 ●
Onlyou [tape] (Ger. Pure Freude) 1982
Prehistoric Future–June, 1968 [tape] (Fr. Tago Mago) 1984
Rite Time (nr/Mercury) 1989 ●
Cannibalism 2 (Spoon-Mute-Restless Retro) 1990 φ
Cannibalism 3 (Spoon-Mute-Restless Retro) 1990 φ

HOLGER CZUKAY
Movies (nr/EMI) 1980
On the Way to the Peak of Normal (nr/EMI) 1982
Der Osten Ist Rot (nr/Virgin) 1984
Rome Remains Rome (nr/Virgin) 1987 ●
Radio Wave Surfer (nr/Virgin) 1991 ●

HOLGER CZUKAY/ROLF DAMMERS
Canaxis (Ger. Spoon) 1982

A German group that arose during the psychedelic movement of 1968 from jazz, avant-garde and rock sources, Can (essentially Holger Czukay, Irmin Schmidt, Jaki Liebezeit, Michael Karoli) developed (and perfected) electronic collage in rock music and actively absorbed a number of musical traditions into their eclectic work. In addition to providing an example of individualistic behavior remote from commercial music, Can's output influenced a number of more modern figures, including Pete Shelley and John Lydon, while Can's Holger Czukay has worked with musicians as disparate as Eurythmics and Jah Wobble.

Monster Movie is a decent 1969 psychedelic album that reflects the influence of early Pink Floyd, and displays the sparse, repeating percussion patterns that became a trademark. Synth and fuzzbox guitar wail over Liebezeit's drums and Czukay's bass. As with most of Can's later releases, vocals are present but secondary.

By **Soundtracks**, Can had refined its sound, bringing the rhythms further to the foreground and working guitar and synthesizer around them. Several tracks feature impressive psychedelic guitar textures; others tone the guitar down and concentrate on rhythm. The addition of Japanese singer Kenji "Damo" Suzuki (replacing the highly inappropriate American vocalist Malcolm Mooney) leads to several rather beautiful songs here.

Can burst free of its formalism on the double-album

Tago Mago, kicking out the jams on the nearly structureless "Aumgn," seventeen minutes of texture and eerie mood. Other tracks feature long improvisations built around hypnotic rhythm patterns, backwards vocals, tape effects and other innovations. (Ironically, the LP's shortest track, the four-minute "Mushroom," has become something of a post-punk staple.) At this point, Can began making the albums that would wield enormous influence on '80s groups as diverse as the Fall, Einstürzende Neubauten and Zoviet France.

Ege Bamyasi is a tighter, more sophisticated version of **Tago Mago**, though it lacks some of the earlier album's sense of excitement. The group integrates textures, rhythms and experiments into an almost jazz-like form on the two longer pieces, while also producing more concise songs of lyrical beauty like "Sing Swan Song" and "I'm So Green." One of Can's best.

Future Days is so laid back and sparsely beautiful that it could have been recorded in California rather than Germany. (Indeed, one of the four lengthy tracks is entitled "Bel Air.") Liebezeit's patterns are quicker and even more in the foreground, but played with great restraint. As Schmidt's synthesizer washes like ocean air, Karoli either twangs and picks guitar in the foreground or drones off in the distance. Mellow yet hardly boring, there's plenty going on here if you listen for it. Suzuki left following **Future Days**, and Karoli and Schmidt took on vocal responsibilities.

The quartet regained its abrasive edge on **Soon Over Babaluma**, which introduces reggae-like rhythms and Karoli's sawing violin. "Splash" uses insistent drums and distorted lead guitar, while "Chain Reaction" and "Quantum Physics," which jointly fill the second side, improvise guitar around quirky drums and all kinds of synthesizer noises.

Following the darkly perverse **Landed**, Can exposed a fascination with non-Western musics on **Limited Edition**, which unveils several pieces in the Ethnological Forgery Series, more of which appear on **Unlimited Edition**, **Flow Motion** and **Can**. The inclusion of Rosko Gee and Reebop Kwaku Baah in the group gave a Jamaican voodoo flair to **Saw Delight** that prefigured the reggae absorption of the Clash, the Police and other groups.

A relative degree of popular success with "I Want More" from **Flow Motion** strained the group to the point where they opted to break up. They have, however, reunited occasionally. Recorded in 1986 as a premature 20th anniversary commemoration, **Rite Time** finds Can again working with Mooney, fitting him into their sophisticated atmospherics as well as can be expected (i.e., hideously).

Opener and the two-disc **Cannibalism** both anthologize work from 1968 to 1973 (containing performances by both Mooney and Suzuki); the latter features five tracks in re-edited versions and liner notes by Pete Shelley, in which he credits Karoli as a pivotal influence. **Cannibalism 1** is the same record minus two tracks. **Delay 1968** features heretofore-unreleased work by the original group (meaning Mooney) from 1968/69, a weird mixture of accessible (but spacey) guitar psychedelia, fairly straight rock and funky soul vamps (!). **Incandescence** (enough with the corny puns already!) is also a compilation.

While Irmin Schmidt has issued a stack of would-be soundtrack albums on his own, of all the Canmen, Holger Czukay's solo career (including recent joint projects with David Sylvian) has proven the most internationally prominent as well as the most artistically inspiring. He first continued his tape collage experiments on the excellent **Movies** and then **On the Way to the Peak of Normal**, the latter with Jah Wobble guesting. (**Canaxis**, which actually dates from 1969, consists of two long pieces of environmental mood music incorporating various ethnic components.)

Der Osten Ist Rot (**The East Is Red**), with Liebezeit and Conny Plank helping out, takes a lighthearted and often amusing tack, splicing found tapes to fairly straightforward songs that run the gamut from cabaret crooning to demented instrumentals. A wonderfully foolish excursion with serious undercurrents of political satire.

The guest sidemen on Czukay's winningly loopy **Rome Remains Rome** include Liebezeit and Karoli, making it virtually a Can reunion record, as well as Wobble and his associate, Olli Morland. Playing everything from guitar to french horn to radio, Czukay takes his usual jaundiced view, deflating musical convention ("Hey Baba Reebop" puts a hysterical electro twist on big-band swing) as he experiments with sounds, including a lot of vocals (some in English, many sung by a chameleon-like female chorus) this time. (The CD includes tracks from **Der Osten Ist Rot**.) [sg/i/sl]

See also *Eurythmics, David Sylvian, Jah Wobble.*

CAPTAIN BEEFHEART AND THE MAGIC BAND

Safe as Milk (Kama Sutra) 1967 (Buddah) 1970 ●
Dropout Boogie (nr/Buddah) 1967
Strictly Personal (Blue Thumb) 1968
Trout Mask Replica (Straight) 1969 (Reprise) 1970 ●
Lick My Decals Off, Baby (Straight) 1970 (Reprise) 1970 (Enigma Retro) 1989 ●
Mirror Man (Buddah) 1970 + 1974 (nr/Demon) 1986 ●
Clear Spot (Reprise) 1972
Unconditionally Guaranteed (Mercury) 1974 (Blue Plate) 1990 ●
Bluejeans & Moonbeams (Mercury) 1974 (Blue Plate) 1990 ●
Shiny Beast (Bat Chain Puller) (Warner Bros.) 1978 (Enigma Retro) 1990 ●
Doc at the Radar Station (Virgin) 1980 ●
Ice Cream for Crow (Virgin-Epic) 1982 (Blue Plate) 1990 ●
The Legendary A&M Sessions EP (A&M) 1984
Safe as Milk/Mirror Man (nr/Castle Comm.) 1988 ●

CAPTAIN BEEFHEART
The Spotlight Kid (Reprise) 1972
The Captain Beefheart File (nr/Pye) 1977

CAPTAIN BEEFHEART WITH FRANK ZAPPA AND THE MOTHERS
Bongo Fury (Discreet) 1975 (Rykodisc) 1989 ●

VARIOUS ARTISTS
Fast'n'Bulbous (nr/Imaginary) 1988 ●

Possessor of a five-octave vocal range, fluent on saxophone and harmonica, intuitively musical enough to compose for, play (after a fashion) and even teach other instruments so as to enable sidemen to function in his rarefied musical world, Captain Beefheart (alias Don Van Vliet) is one of rock's genuine geniuses. He's also an accomplished poet, sculptor and painter. Starting with a mixture of blues and rock, Beefheart has dismembered and reassembled rhythms, song structure, harmony and tonality, adding in quantities of free jazz—all without getting academic, flashy or selfconsciously pompous about it.

Beefheart's awesome yet idiosyncratic (as well as groundbreaking) talent has deeply influenced bands like Devo, Pere Ubu, the Residents, Public Image and others, each in a different way. Bridging the worlds of free-form jazz and modern rock, Beefheart has demolished conventions and paved the way for much of rock's recent adventurousness.

Awarded a two-single A&M contract as the grand prize in a Vox battle of the bands, Beefheart—from Southern California's Mojave Desert—made the first a regional hit with a footstomping version of Bo Diddley's "Diddy Wah Diddy," but A&M judged his album demos too unsettling to keep him on the roster. (Nearly 20 years later, the two original 45s plus one hitherto unissued track were packaged as **The Legendary A&M Sessions**; the producer, who also wrote one song, was David Gates, founder-to-be of pap-rockers Bread.)

Another label gave him a shot and, with 19-year-old guitar wiz Ry Cooder, Beefheart spewed out **Safe as Milk**, which cannily redefined what white boys could do with the blues, not to mention rock'n'roll. Although Buddah released it, the label—then best known as the purveyors of the bubblegum sounds of the 1910 Fruitgum Co. et al.—evidently wasn't thrilled about it. Cooder departed just in time to force the cancellation of an appearance at the fabled Monterey Pop Festival.

Beefheart got another record deal with a hip, maverick independent label and recorded **Strictly Personal**, an even punchier and more irreverent version of what he'd essayed on **Safe as Milk**. But the LP was remixed while he was away on a European tour; Beefheart was understandably disgusted by the results. At this remove, however, the silly effects added without his consent merely date the record a bit; looking past that, it's virtually the equal of its more celebrated predecessor.

Beefheart may have felt like his third strike had been thrown while he wasn't looking, but along came childhood friend and former (albeit briefly) bandmate Frank Zappa, who'd wangled a custom label deal that allowed him to offer Beefheart complete creative control. What popped out was **Trout Mask Replica**, generally regarded as his first masterpiece. The minimalist rock blossomed, mated at times with free jazz. (Between cuts, he can faintly be heard telling visitors that he calls it "bush music.") The lyrics (and straight-up poetry) received, and warranted, increasing prominence. **Decals** was a consolidation of artistic gains that suffers only in comparison to **Trout Mask**. Both attracted enough attention that Buddah brought out **Mirror Man**, an LP consisting of four extended live tracks (from '65) that was derided as a sub-par exploitation move. Regardless, it's damn good stuff, and didn't do much exploiting, either: all three albums were commercial stiffs. (Two songs from **Mirror Man** were later re-recorded for **Strictly Personal**.)

The Spotlight Kid reverted to a simpler, bluesier sound (à la the first two LPs), though sonically enriched by the Captain's subsequent explorations. Further changes and commercial pressures resulted in **Clear Spot**, which sported a more stylized, heavy-rock style (varied by an excellent, if uncharacteristic, Memphis-style soul number).

On the other hand, **Unconditionally Guaranteed** and **Bluejeans & Moonbeams** are even more simplified, sometimes to the point of inanity, and the musicians on the records don't seem to have a clue about Beefheart or his music. (The second—allegedly outtakes from the first—is actually better.) He made some money for a change and won new European fans, but some of the faithful felt he'd sold out.

Beefheart cut an album called **Bat Chain Puller** for Virgin, but legal problems prevented its release. With a new band that included ex-Mothers of Invention trombonist Bruce Fowler, he signed to Warners and released **Shiny Beast**, which incorporated much of the material first cut for **Bat Chain Puller** (and therefore used that name as a subtitle). It's a progression from **Decals**, as if the intervening albums had never happened, and stands as one of his best. The words are more direct than on **Decals**; the music smoother and more orchestral.

He then proceeded to top himself with **Doc at the Radar Station**. A minor shift in the band had toughened the sound, and the LP combined his continuing refinement with a touch of **Clear Spot**'s hard-nosed attack.

Beefheart went still further with **Ice Cream for Crow**, the height of his career's most sustained upward creative swing, despite (because of?) a near-total lineup turnover right after the recording of **Doc**. **Crow** is Beefheart at his most distinctively and beautifully melodic, his most frightening and his most danceable. And it's apparently his musical swan song. The painter/sculptor has made the sad but understandable decision that visual, not audio, art is his best means of support—a depressing comment on the record business and our culture.

Fast'n'Bulbous offers twelve (fourteen on CD) versions of the Captain's songs, by the Scientists, Sonic Youth, XTC, That Petrol Emotion, the Membranes and eight lesser lights. As with all such tributes, the danger is that contributors often haven't a clue how to do justice to the subject, and wind up trivializing the artist being canonized; in this case, it's true in spades. Some reduce Beefheart to snappy garage rock, some (like XTC) just simulate the originals with the benefit of better sound. A good idea on paper, it lacks vision and effort in execution. [jg]

CAPTAIN SENSIBLE
Women and Captains First (nr/A&M) 1982
The Power of Love (nr/A&M) 1983
A Day in the Life of ... Captain Sensible (A&M) 1984
One Christmas Catalogue EP (nr/A&M) 1984
Sensible Singles (nr/A&M) 1984
Revolution Now (nr/Deltic) 1989 ●
CAPTAIN SENSIBLE/
BROTHERHOOD OF LIZARDS
Smash It Up Part 4 EP (nr/Deltic) 1990

When not playing guitar and keyboards in the Damned, the good Captain (Ray Burns to his parents) spent the early '80s making lighthearted hit records with producer Tony Mansfield. His two best weird'n' wonderful chart-toppers—the joke-rapping "Wot" and "Happy Talk" (from the musical *South Pacific*)—are included on **Women and Captains First**, alongside other equally ridiculous concepts ranging from country-western to cabaret. Aided and abetted by such divergent talents as Robyn Hitchcock and female vocal trio Dolly Mixture, Sensible's homely singing is ingratiating, if not always on key.

The Power of Love is less varied and novelty-filled, but nonetheless contains a few subtler gems: "It's Hard to Believe I'm Not" and "Secrets," both co-written with Hitchcock, "Stop the World" and "The Power of Love," all distinguished by Sensible's engaging vocals and silly/serious lyrics.

In a vain attempt to introduce Sensible to America, **A Day in the Life** compiles tracks from both English albums (plus a previously non-LP single) and has most of what you would want to hear by the lad. But you should also be aware of the seasonal EP, **One Christmas Catalogue**, which came complete with a plastic Santa beard and, amidst three great originals, Sensible's puzzling *nearly* straight version of Frankie Goes to Hollywood's "Relax." For completists, there's also **Sensible Singles**, a thirteen-cut collection that largely overlaps the albums.

Resuming his solo career in the late '80s, Sensible reached some sort of artistic peak on the excellent **Revolution Now**, an all-new album of originals (some co-written by Cleaner from Venus/Brotherhood of Lizards' Martin Newell) recorded with such comrades as Rat Scabies, Henry Badowski and Paul Gray. Although hampered a bit by Sensible's minimalist singing and the obvious use of synthesizers where real instruments would have sounded better, the record is still full of catchy melodies and nearly serious left-field lyrics. (Not to mention spoken-word TV bites that help express Sensible's chagrin at modern consumerism.) There isn't a bad song here, and the best ones—"Missing the Boat," "The Toys Take Over," "Revolution Now," "Phone-In"—cover amazing stylistic ground with ease and flair.

[i]

CAPTAINS OF INDUSTRY

See *Wreckless Eric*.

CARBON

See *Elliott Sharp*.

CARCASS

Reek of Putrefaction (nr/Earache) 1988 ●
The Peel Sessions EP (nr/Strange Fruit) 1989 ●
Symphonies of Sickness (nr/Earache) 1989
  (Earache-Relativity) 1990 ●

Although thought to be a Napalm Death side-project, Liverpool's Carcass was actually formed by guitarist Bill Steer, drummer Ken Owen and an Indian vocalist named Sanjiv in 1985, well before Steer joined Napalm. Participating in both bands more or less simul-taneously, he and Owen were joined in '87 by bassist/biology student Jeff Walker, whose anatomy studies play a large role in his job: claiming to be "particularly interested in the digestive system," his lyrics and album artwork are among the most revoltingly graphic imaginable. (For what it's worth, the three are devout vegetarians.)

Reek of Putrefaction contains sixteen tracks of the trio's distinctive "medi-core": skull-pulverizing riffs, cardiac-arrest time-changes, guttural vocals and charming titles like "Vomited Anal Tract," "Feast on Dismembered Carnage" and the fitting "Psycho-pathologist." Steer left Napalm Death in mid-'89 to concentrate on Carcass, and the ensuing **Symphonies of Sickness** contains ten tracks ("Excoriating Abdominal Emanation," "Cadaveric Incubator of Endoparasites," "Crepitating Bowel Erosion") of even more brutal grind. The two albums are combined onto one CD.

See also *Napalm Death*. [ja]

BELINDA CARLISLE ●

Belinda (IRS) 1986 ●
Heaven on Earth (MCA) 1987 ●
Runaway Horses (MCA) 1989 ●

Following the breakup of the Go-Go's, Belinda Carlisle stuck with guitarist Charlotte Caffey and recorded a mixed-up solo album whose cover shows the newly glamorized singer striking a stylish Cyd Charisse pose. Inside **Belinda,** however, the mock-girl groupisms, misbegotten Motown take-offs and lush quasi-Ronstadt rock are easy on the ears but utterly lacking in conviction or charm. Carlisle's voice was never the Go-Go's' strongest feature; with training, her skills have improved over the years, but she still isn't very appealing. Dull material and unimaginative production adds little to her first bid for acceptance as an adult artist.

Carlisle's second album—an absurd but stylistically focused big-budget studio concoction on which hit-bound rock-pop production numbers like "I Get Weak" and "Heaven Is a Place on Earth" mingle with such bizarrities as a lame cover of Cream's "I Feel Free"—turned her into a huge, meaningless star. The limits of Carlisle's voice are obvious on some songs; producer-mastermind Rick Nowels' slim repertoire of ideas (mainly loud electric guitars thrown against synthesized strings and heavenly backing chorus) is also a problem. The album's only hint of wit is Carlisle's credit for air guitar.

Again directed by Nowels, **Runaway Horses** is another hollow melodrama of contrivance and cliché. The record's calculated hooks are hard to resist, but Carlisle's studied delivery—check the exuberant title track, the pseudo-Latin "La Luna" and the idiotic "Leave a Light On" (to which George Harrison adds inappropriate slide guitar)—has all the come-on conviction of phone sex. Next stop: the Go-Go's reunion! [i]

See also *Go-Go's*.

CARMEL

Carmel EP (nr/Red Flame) 1982
The Drum Is Everything (Warner Bros.) 1984 ●
The Falling (nr/London) 1986 ●
Everybody's Got a Little ... Soul (nr/London) 1987 ●

Set Me Free (nr/London) 1989 •
Collected (nr/London) 1990 •

Brassy belter Carmel McCourt and her two-man band (drummer Gerry Darby and stand-up bassist Jim Paris), plus various organists, singers, drummers and hornmen, make the Mike Thorne-produced **The Drum Is Everything** a joyous and raucous outing that has a bit in common with nouveau jazz-pop crooners like Sade, but is far more adventurous and ambitious in scope. "More, More, More" and "Willow Weep for Me" are inspiring, near-gospel outbursts of enthusiasm; "Tracks of My Tears" (no, not that one) and "Stormy Weather" (yes, that one) show a bluesier, more reserved side that isn't as appealing in this setting. Carmel doesn't modulate all that well—for her, singing is a full-blooded pastime with no room for pussyfooting—and tends to overpower the more subtly played songs.

Using four different producers (including Brian Eno and Chris Porter), **The Falling** runs a similar gamut, from the sinuous blues of "I'm Not Afraid of You" to the boisterous chorus-and-horns ebullience of "Let Me Know" to "Mercy," a nothing song electrified by a bravura vocal performance. While Carmel's improved control is a plus, even the sparing use of electronic percussion seems like a serious breach of stylistic integrity. And the syncopated deconstruction of Randy Newman's "Mama Told Me Not to Come" is just too weird.

Carmel reunited with Thorne for the trio's glossed-up third album, which gives synthesizers a firm toehold in the arrangements. Taking a disappointing (and tense-sounding) detour towards urbane pop, McCourt allows guest keyboardist Ugo Delmirani to share in the songwriting, resulting in blander material with obvious commercial aspirations. If not quite a fatal artistic concession (the schmaltzy "Nothing Good," which she can't even sing, comes darn close to it), the misbegotten **Everybody's Got a Little . . . Soul** lacks most of what made its robust predecessors so rewarding.

Further removed from the early records' unaffected simplicity, the uneven **Set Me Free** lifts any remaining barriers to modern technology and slathers on the drum programs, MIDI processors and synthetic strings. With Delmirani thankfully out of the picture, McCourt and a variety of collaborators deliver a reasonably good set of songs, individually produced by Eno, Thorne, Pete Wingfield and Jim Parris (new spelling). Singing over a busy rush of danceable jazz-pop-rock, a seemingly reinvigorated McCourt comfortably throws her voice into high gear, cutting through the arrangements with ease. But putting on the melodramatic chanteuse act for songs like the grim "God Put Your Hand on Me" still doesn't suit her at all. The new Carmel may not be as wonderful as the old Carmel, but **Set Me Free** provides reason enough to keep listening.

The **Collected** compilation—a fair album summary that leans a bit too heavily towards **Set Me Free** material—has the added attraction of one alternate version and a duet Carmel sang with Johnny Hallyday on his 1987 LP.   [i]

CARNEY-HILD-KRAMER

Happiness Finally Came to Them (Shimmy-Disc) 1987

What happens when uninhibited musicians get together for a creative brainstorm? Ralph Carney (sax, guitar) is a veteran of Tin Huey and the Swollen Monkeys. Daved Hild (vocals, drums) has percussionized with David Thomas. Kramer is the ex-Shockabilly bassist/keyboardist who runs Shimmy-Disc and plays in Bongwater and other groups. With such guests as Michael Cudahy (guitar; Christmas), the trio has a blast on **Happiness**, writing and playing up a raucous storm of flighty fun, arty seriousness and utter rubbish. That it's nearly impossible to tell which is which may be this one-off album's greatest achievement.   [i]

See also *Bongwater, Shockabilly, Swollen Monkeys, Tin Huey.*

PAUL CARRACK

Nightbird (nr/Vertigo) 1980
Suburban Voodoo (Epic) 1982 •
One Good Reason (Chrysalis) 1987 •
Ace Mechanic (nr/Demon) 1987
The Carrack Collection (Chrysalis) 1988 •
Groove Approved (Chrysalis) 1989 •

One of rock's more circuitous success stories: Carrack was the lead-singing keyboardist in Ace, a pub-rock outfit before "pub-rock" became a rock press subgenre—strictly background music for soaking up suds. Ace hadn't the faintest idea what to do when Carrack's catchy (if banal) "How Long" became an international hit in 1975, and proved it with three LPs of boring laid-backism. Carrack hung on through Ace's dissolution and his all-too-pat first solo LP, **Nightbird**. He got a real boost, though, when Squeeze hired him to replace Jools Holland. It was only for the **East Side Story** album—just one Carrack lead vocal, but that's on "Tempted," one of Squeeze's most popular numbers. The song became a Carrack calling card, too.

That LP also brought him into contact with the Elvis Costello/Nick Lowe axis (EC produced the Squeeze LP, Lowe had produced Elvis, both were managed by Jake Riviera). Carrack and Lowe then formed Noise to Go, a Rockpilish arrangement in which the two alternated top billing. No surprise, then, that **Suburban Voodoo** sounds like the souled-up flipside of **Nick the Knife**—if anything, it's better. Yet it succeeds because of Lowe's production and composing presence, which complements Carrack's excellent voice with the kind of pop smarts that bring out his best.

Carrack next found employment with Mike & the Mechanics (Mike Rutherford's extra-Genesis sideline), and wound up singing strangely anonymous-sounding lead on that group's big hit, "Silent Running." This exposure got Carrack a 1987 touring-band job with Roger Waters after Pink Floyd's split.

Half of **One Good Reason** is decent-to-good, and the rest is mediocre-to-poor. Produced by former Hall and Oates overseer Christopher Neil, it's got more radio-music slickness than Carrack's had in years, but at the cost of some identity. (Although Carrack is clearly to blame for the demolition of "When You Walk in the Room.") It did yield a genuine not-bad pop hit ("Don't Shed a Tear").

Groove Approved is a pretty fair title: lots of good old-fashioned R&B grooves, often garnished with Carrack's tasty Hammond organ licks. Unfortunately, the synthetic drums sometimes slicken or stiffen the rhythm too much (they just don't get greasy, y'know?). Despite such co-writers as Lowe, Chris Difford, John Wesley Harding and ex-Doobie Michael McDonald, the songs aren't unforgettable, but they're mostly painless. Bassist T-Bone Wolk, with whom Carrack co-authored three tracks, produced.

The fourteen-track Demon compilation samples everything (Ace, Squeeze, M + the Ms, solo) Carrack recorded before signing with Chrysalis; *that* label's compilation covers the same stuff, but less of it. [jg]
See also *Squeeze*.

JOE "KING" CARRASCO AND EL MOLINO
Joe "King" Carrasco and El Molino (Lisa) 1978
Tex-Mex Rock-Roll [tape] (ROIR) 1989

JOE "KING" CARRASCO AND THE CROWNS
Joe "King" Carrasco and the Crowns (Hannibal) 1980
Party Safari EP (Hannibal) 1981
Synapse Gap (Mundo Total) (MCA) 1982
Party Weekend (MCA) 1983
Tales from the Crypt [tape] (ROIR) 1984
Bordertown (nr/Big Beat) 1984 ●
Viva San Antone EP (nr/Big Beat) 1985
Royal, Loyal & Live (Rio's Royal Texacali) 1990 ●

JOE KING CARRASCO Y LAS CORONAS
Bandido Rock (Rounder) 1987 ●

Austin's Joe "King" Carrasco (né Teutsch) grew up in the Lone Star state under the spell of Tex-Mex border music. El Molino, his first band, straddled this tradition (with horns and marimba) and rock (with Doug Sahm's keyboard player, Augie Meyers, and songs like "Rock Esta Noche"). El Molino's only album (reissued a decade later on cassette as **Tex-Mex Rock-Roll**) is pleasant enough, but sounds pale compared to what followed.

Whether influenced by new wave or reverting to more adolescent taste, Carrasco traded in El Molino for the Crowns. This no-nonsense backing trio, dominated by Kris Cummings' cheesy organ, is built for speed. The Crowns' debut album touches on rockabilly ("One More Time"), polka ("Federales") and border influences ("Buena," "Caca de Vaca"). Their forte, though, is performing "96 Tears" under a variety of thin guises, all of them delightful ("Let's Get Pretty," "Betty's World," you name it). The tempos are revved-up punk, the feeling, Southwestern *mestizo*. (The Stiff LP has two numbers not on the American album, but Hannibal's release has three songs not on the English version, and a funnier cover as well.)

Party Safari is a four-song EP further displaying Carrasco's cultural dementia; the Crowns' next album, **Synapse Gap**, finds them only slightly more subdued. Besides re-recording two of **Party Safari**'s songs, Carrasco dabbles in reggae rhythms and somehow got Michael Jackson (!) to sing along on "Don't Let a Woman (Make a Fool Out of You)."

In a last-ditch effort to sell out (well, to sell a few records at least), Carrasco made **Party Weekend**, a non-stop heap o' fun. Richard Gottehrer produced it, and tunes like "Let's Go" and "Burnin' It Down" (not to mention a spiffy remake of "Buena") perfectly crystallize all of the group's strengths. Murderously infectious and upbeat—attitudinally the Southwest's answer to the Ramones—**Party Weekend** seemed perfectly designed to introduce the world to Carrasco's abundant talent and charm. But it didn't take off, and so Carrasco unceremoniously returned from his safari in the majors.

Joe's next release was the tape-only **Tales from the Crypt**, a marvelous set of demos from 1979 with embryonic (read: raw and exciting) versions of many of Carrasco's best tunes, from "Let's Get Pretty" to "Caca de Vaca" to "Federales." Although not intended as such, it's an ideal introduction to a world of boundless spirit and infectious fun.

By **Bordertown**, Carrasco's act is getting kind of, er, familiar: too many of the songs employ not only the same chords and melody, but a lot of 'em stick to the same Spanglicized rhyming patterns. Adding to the fatigue is a new-found political sensibility, yielding well-intentioned bores like "Who Buys the Guns" and "Current Events (Are Making Sense)." If you haven't been following the Carrasco saga for long, **Bordertown** is as good as any of his prior records; however, those with a large collection can survive without it.

Bandido Rock finds the increasingly politicized Carrasco (note retitled band) mouthing sentiments like "Juarez and Zapata/Stood for love of the people." Just a glance at the album's song list—including "Fuera Yanqui" and "Hey Gringo 'No Pasaran' "—confirms suspicions of monomania. Too bad, because the band, now mostly accordion-led, still sounds fine. But with only three out of ten songs in a *yanqui* 4/4, **Bandido Rock** is strictly for the musically converted and/or anyone ready to follow Joe into Nicaragua.

Enjoyment of **Royal, Loyal & Live**—recorded with a loud, tight quartet in early '89—has no such prerequisites. The seriously sweaty rock'n'roll show begins weakly with "Hey Joe" and that unofficial Texas anthem, "96 Tears," but then shifts into high gear as Carrasco—surging with contagious enthusiasm—delivers an impressive program of mostly new material. (The handful of JKC oldies are, thankfully, items like "Mañana" and "Parti [*sic*] Weekend" rather than more obvious and overplayed numbers.) Amid greater stylistic and rhythmic diversity than Carrasco's records usually muster, **Bandido Rock** alumnus Marcelo Gauna (accordion/keyboards) and Tom Cruz, a piercingly good lead guitarist, provide ample instrumental flavor. Joe King does the rest. [si/i]

CARS
The Cars (Elektra) 1978 ●
Candy-O (Elektra) 1979 ●
Panorama (Elektra) 1980 ●
Shake It Up (Elektra) 1981 ●
Heartbeat City (Elektra) 1984 ●
Greatest Hits (Elektra) 1985 ●
Door to Door (Elektra) 1987 ●

RIC OCASEK
Beatitude (Geffen) 1982
This Side of Paradise (Geffen) 1986 ●

GREG HAWKES
Niagara Falls (Passport) 1983

ELLIOT EASTON

Change No Change (Elektra) 1985

BEN ORR

The Lace (Elektra) 1986 ●

For an example of shifting perceptions, consider the Cars. When their debut LP appeared in 1978, the Boston-based quintet was tagged as a prime commercial *and* critical prospect of the emerging post-punk phenomenon called new wave. In other words, they were cool and potentially popular. Then, presto! Upon release of an album, the Cars became an immediate smash and entered the ranks of platinum-sellers, where they remained. Quickly, they lost all artistic credibility among critics, despite their remarkable consistency on disc.

The Cars changed little after that first record established the ground rules. On their debut, singer/songwriter Ric Ocasek pursues the trail of ironic, sometimes wistful romanticism blazed by David Bowie and especially Bryan Ferry. "Good Times Roll," "My Best Friend's Girl" and other tunes contradict blithe surfaces with nervous undercurrents. As sparely produced by Roy Thomas Baker, virtually interchangeable lead singers Ocasek and bassist Ben Orr ride a slick, pulsing current generated by Elliot Easton's skittish guitar, Greg Hawkes' poised synths and ex-Modern Lover David Robinson's booming drums. Here, and on subsequent albums, the alluring glibness serves as a gateway to underlying emotional anguish.

Candy-O's main flaw is that it offers the same accomplished style. Emotions are more directly expressed on the title track and the frankly sentimental "It's All I Can Do," but the polish remains. "Let's Go" and "Dangerous Type" express a muted ambivalence that allows the Cars to continue pleasing superficial listeners. **Panorama** tampers with the formula slightly, though not enough to jeopardize the band's enormous popularity. Many tunes are murkier and less immediate, giving greater play to the creeping desperation that permeates Ocasek's writing. More unsettling, though still highly listenable.

Shake It Up is the lightest album in the Cars' collection. The title track comes as close as they ever got to a conventional good-time tune, and others are less haunting than you might like Ocasek's songs to be. Highlight: the feverish, blatantly Roxyesque "This Could Be Love." Then the Cars took a group vacation.

For his first solo album, Ocasek enlisted Hawkes, handpicked musicians from various semi-underground bands (Bad Brains, New Models, Ministry, etc.) and created a moody collection of stimulating but only semi-commercial new songs. **Beatitude** bears an unavoidable resemblance to the Cars' sound, but the prevalence of synthesizer over guitar and an avoidance of choppy, driving rhythms make it different enough. While several Cars tracks have worked similar languid terrain ("Since You're Gone" on **Shake It Up** and "You Wear Those Eyes" on **Panorama** are two), Ocasek's solo approach is subtler and texturally richer; his lyrics here are also exemplary. Best track: "Jimmy Jimmy," a sympathetic portrait of a troubled teen.

Niagara Falls confirms keyboardist Hawkes' role in shaping the Cars' instrumental sound, but it's mighty dull fare all the same. Take away the band's lyrics, vocals and tension and you get this sort of muzak.

After that dalliance, the Cars reconvened for **Heartbeat City**, a more substantial LP than **Shake It Up** and the band's most commercially potent record to date. The disc yielded no less than three major hits: the dreamy "Drive," the ebullient "You Might Think" and "Magic," which might best be described as the Cars meet the Electric Light Orchestra. The lyrics are Ocasek's usual neurotic doodlings, though he shows more compassion for his "lost generation" characters than before.

Buoyed by that album's stellar performance, the Cars took another solo break. Easton's **Change No Change** is a minor work to be sure, but a surprisingly good record nonetheless. A more immediate and electric record than the band would ever dare make, it contains some pithy harmonies, some snarling boogie and even a Costello soundalike. Irrepressible Jules Shear co-wrote all the tunes.

Joined by co-producer/drummer Chris Hughes (ex-Ants), Ocasek drafted another set of famous friends (including most of his bandmates, guitarists Steve Stevens, Tom Verlaine and G.E. Smith) to help him imitate the Cars some more on **This Side of Paradise**. The man's stylistic consistency is indeed amazing. Orr's tepid record is also Cars-like, but with a lighter, more vocal-oriented feel and a warmly non-mechanical pop approach. That's not to say the songs—co-written by Orr and Diane Grey Page—are any good, but **The Lace** is nice and harmless.

The final Cars album, **Door to Door**, which Ocasek wrote and produced, is likable but irrelevant. (The group's audience evidently agreed: it was the only Cars LP to fall short of a million sales.) Ocasek has never before allowed this much noisy guitar rock to corrupt the chilly tension of the Cars' formula; the overenthusiastic intrusion on the group's familiar sound is noticeable but not unpleasant. [jy/i]

See also *Jonathan Richman and the Modern Lovers, Suicide*.

CHRIS CARTER

See *Chris and Cosey*.

PETER CASE

Peter Case (Geffen) 1986
The Man with the Blue Postmodern Fragmented
    Neo-Traditionalist Guitar (Geffen) 1989 ●

Setting aside the rock approach of Case's former bands (the Nerves and the Plimsouls), the talented singer/songwriter/guitarist's eponymous solo debut is a portrait of the artist as a literate young troubadour, baggy suit, fedora and all. Downplaying the Plimsouls' frantic guitar jangle in favor of lean, diverse arrangements, Case and co-producers T-Bone Burnett and Mitchell Froom focus squarely on the material (some of it co-written by Burnett) and Case's soul-on-fire vocals. The barbed Americana of Case's best songs—"I Shook His Hand," "Steel Strings" (later recorded by Marshall Crenshaw), "Old Blue Car"—points to greatness around the corner. However, other tunes (the contrived "Small Town Spree," arranged by Van Dyke Parks, the sub-Mellencamp "Horse & Crow") demonstrate the need for a good editor. **Peter Case** closes with a good cover of the Pogues' "Pair of Brown Eyes," with Roger McGuinn on guitar.

Case's second solo effort fulfills much of the promise hinted at on its predecessor. The songwriting is more fluent and self-assured, as is his singing; with contributions from David Lindley, Jim Keltner and Los Lobos' David Hidalgo, the musical settings are more varied and distinctive. Case delivers some startlingly precise character studies ("Poor Old Tom," "Travellin' Light"), stark emotional dramas ("Put Down the Gun," "Two Angels") and sharply observed sense-of-place vignettes ("This Town's a Riot," "Entella Hotel"). Perhaps most notable, though, is the born-again artist's new-found deftness at bridging spiritual and secular concerns, which he does effectively on "Hidden Love."

See also *Nerves, Plimsouls*.   [i/hd]

CATERWAUL
The Nature of Things (Lost Arts) 1987
Beholden EP (IRS) 1988
Pin & Web (IRS) 1989 ●
Portent Hue (IRS) 1990 ●

Formed in Phoenix, this talented, hard-to-pin-down band—a versatile rock/folk trio plus singer Betsy Martin (also the band's lyricist and occasional mandolin player)—made its debut on an indie album before relocating to Los Angeles and hooking up a bigger deal. Following a three-song trial run with Camper Van producer Dennis Herring on **Beholden**, Caterwaul (especially Martin, who can deliver a country croon, a cowgirl yodel and a chilling rock howl, but never does anything quite like the band's name) exorcised some extremist tendencies and continued on to **Pin & Web**. As self-centeredly enigmatic as early R.E.M. but with in-your-ear vocals and a different regional orientation, **Pin & Web** lacks top-notch songs, instead relying on clear, carefully crafted music (Mark Schafer is evidently an open-minded student at the Edge school of electric guitar textures) and Martin's exciting excursions. (The CD adds the two **Beholden** tracks not already included on the LP.)

The dramatic, full-blooded rock (balanced by acoustic mandolin interludes) of **Portent Hue** matches Martin's inventive vocals strength for strength, cutting an uneven path but scoring points along the way. Kevin Pinnt wallops the skins convincingly as Schafer weaves busy guitar patterns in which Martin can throw her many voices at various odd angles. When the band's songwriting is in full effect (as on "Alex' Aphrodisiac" or "Bulldosage") Martin's theatrics are a neat bonus; elsewhere (as on "Manna and Quail," where she performs amazing Siouxsiesque octave jumps) she's the whole show.   [i]

CAT HEADS
Hubba (Restless) 1987 ●
Submarine (Restless) 1988

(EX) CAT HEADS
Our Frisco (Twitch City) 1989

If anything, this San Francisco quartet suffers from an excess of talent: three members write, all four sing. **Hubba** is all over the place style-wise, from the agreeably noisy post-folk/rock of "Hangin' Around" to the stately romanticism of "Final Letter" to the mock-country of "Saved by the Bottle" to the playful hippie-punk of "Golden Gate Park." Most of it's quite good, but the jarring lack of focus makes the album an unnecessarily distracting listen.

The winsome **Submarine**, on the other hand, wisely concentrates on the band's strengths, sticking to more melodic material and allowing drummer Melanie Clarin (concurrently a member of Donner Party) to sing more. As a result, **Submarine** (co-produced by Dave Lowery of Camper Van Beethoven) consistently captures the haunting melody of **Hubba**'s best moments (as on "Postcard" and "Sister Tabitha") without ditching the goofy humor ("Jiggy Sawdust/Gumshoe") or the melodic rock edge ("Upside Down," "Apologize").

Though the band split up after **Submarine**, charter members Sam Babbitt and Alan Korn recruited a third singer/guitarist/bassist and Flying Color's ex-drummer to record **Our Frisco** as the (Ex) Cat Heads. The inscrutably packaged and annotated album—an enjoyably casual-sounding set—is not all that different from the original band's quirky electric-acoustic mix. Former bandmate Clarin returns to sing harmony on the most memorable track, the cheerfully self-mocking "Anti-Song."   [hd]

See also *Donner Party, Harm Farm*.

CATHEDRAL OF TEARS
See *True Sounds of Liberty*.

NICK CAVE AND THE BAD SEEDS
From Her to Eternity (nr/Mute) 1984 ●
The Firstborn Is Dead (Mute-Homestead) 1985 ●
Tupelo EP (Homestead) 1985
Kicking Against the Pricks (Homestead) 1986 ●
Your Funeral ... My Trial (Mute-Homestead) 1986 ●
Tender Prey (Mute-Enigma) 1988 ●
The Good Son (Mute-Enigma) 1990 (Mute-Elektra) 1990 ●
The Weeping Song EP [CD] (Mute-Enigma) 1990 ●

ANITA LANE
Dirty Sings EP (nr/Mute) 1988 (Mute-Restless) 1989 ●

NICK CAVE/MICK HARVEY/ BLIXA BARGELD
Ghosts ... of the Civil Dead (Mute) 1989 ●

Following the Birthday Party's self-destruction, singer/lyricist Nick Cave formed the Bad Seeds as a new vehicle for his foreboding visions of love and death. While his passionate bellowing certainly fit in well with his former mates' wall of noise, **From Her to Eternity** sounds like the record he always wanted to make. The Bad Seeds—an all-star unit including ex-Magazine bassist Barry Adamson, ex-Birthday Party guitarist/keyboardist-turned-drummer Mick Harvey and guitarist Blixa Bargeld on loan from Einstürzende Neubauten—provide a sparse twisted-blues setting that gives Cave plenty of room for his vocal pyrotechnics. The guitars are bizarre but subdued, bass and drums slow and deliberate; rudimentary piano fills the gaps. While the album relies less on shock effects than any the Birthday Party ever made, the explosive parts are that much more effective. The title track, "A Box for Black Paul" and a chilling rendition of Leonard Cohen's "Avalanche" stand up to anything Cave did with the Birthday Party. (A contemporaneous single of "In the Ghetto" is also highly recommended.)

The Firstborn Is Dead takes Cave's fixations on the blues and Elvis Presley one step further, this time with somewhat mixed results. A resident of London and Berlin, the Melbourne native leaves himself open to accusations of romanticizing a culture he's never known, but this doesn't sound like a man singing out of ignorance. Slow-moving and perhaps as self-indulgent as it is heartfelt, **The Firstborn** is a mature work which may at first disappoint those awaiting another "Big-Jesus-Trash-Can," but the patient listener will find Cave's emotional range intact, albeit in a subtler setting. The American **Tupelo** EP takes the album's opening track as its title and adds "In the Ghetto," "The Moon Is in the Gutter" and a drastically different version of the old Birthday Party live staple, "The Six Strings That Drew Blood."

Kicking Against the Pricks is an all-covers LP on which Cave really makes his mark as a song stylist. He performs passionate takes of blues standards ("Muddy Water," "I'm Gonna Kill That Woman"), gospel ("Jesus Met the Woman at the Well"), rock classics ("Hey Joe," "All Tomorrow's Parties") and, surprisingly enough, "By the Time I Get to Phoenix." His voice has never sounded stronger, and no musical style among those selected is beyond his grasp. Some interpretations are faithful to originals, others (especially "All Tomorrow's Parties") are completely unique, and the album's success owes as much to the work of the Bad Seeds as it does to Cave's talents. (Thomas Wydler is now the band's drummer, with Harvey returning to his jack-of-all-trades role; the late Tracy Pew, Birthday Party's bassist, makes his final recorded appearance on "Hey Joe.") An almost flawless album.

Your Funeral . . . My Trial is an eight-song album issued as a pair of 12-inches. The expanded format enhances the production, which is the clearest and most up-front of any Cave release. That in turn augments the melodicism and increased energy level of the music. With the notable exception of the blunt "Hard on for Love," **Your Funeral** also stands as Cave's best lyrical effort. He takes the persona of old Nick the storyteller, and the images are haunting.

After a two-year hiatus, Cave and his troupe (a five-man ensemble, including Harvey, Bargeld and guitarist Kid Congo Powers) returned in 1988 with **Tender Prey**. One need not get any further than the opening track, "The Mercy Seat" (perhaps Cave's strongest song ever), to recognize that the LP is a scorcher. Cave's voice is mixed high and out front in the incredibly thick, bottom-heavy production (quite unlike the spartan sound of most of his previous discs). Even more surprising are his melodic vocals; without any forfeit of passion, it really sounds as if he's taken singing lessons. But nothing else has changed: "Deanna" is a **Nuggets**-style rocker, but the lyrics plot a murder spree in a Cadillac. (You were expecting moon-June-spoon?) Although the songs weaken a bit towards the end, this is a challenging work of extraordinary quality.

In the two years prior to **The Good Son**, Cave kicked a junk habit and finished his first novel, *And the Ass Saw the Angel* (a morbid tale originally conceived as a screenplay). Perhaps he mellowed by saving his own life or released his crazed energy via the book, but this is more akin to the Cave who covered "By the Time I Get to Phoenix." **The Good Son** is sedate and lachrymose, filled with religious references and orchestrated with strings, piano and background vocals. Recorded in Brazil, the opening "Foi Na Cruz" is sung partly in Portuguese; the most uptempo cut is the gospel-flavored "The Witness Song." Easy listening compared to other things he's done, but an emotional album not many other artists could have pulled off. (Initial quantities of the British album came with either a 7-inch single or a 5-inch CD containing acoustic versions of "The Mercy Seat," "City of Refugee" and "Deanna.")

Anita Lane's claim to fame is that she's Nick Cave's girlfriend and has supplied him with occasional lyrics for solo and Birthday Party records. (Her picture is on the back cover of **From Her to Eternity**, making it appear she was then a Bad Seed.) For those who need to know more than that, **Dirty Sings** is a four-song EP with spoken, groaned and badly sung Lydia Lunch-like vocals above slow-moving but interestingly arranged backing (anonymous musicians, but Cave's Bad Seeds are readily identifiable and receive songwriting credits). She covers Chic's "Lost in Music," but the "I'm a Believer" here isn't the Monkees tune. Dark without being too gloomy or morbid, Lane does have an intriguing presence on vinyl. Not a bad little record.

Besides the band's appearance in Wim Wenders' *Wings of Desire* (performing "The Carny"), Cave, Bargeld and Harvey composed and performed the soundtrack to *Ghosts . . . of the Civil Dead*, an Australian film (in which Cave had a dramatic role) about a maximum security prison in Marion, Illinois. The jail is brutal enough to be known as the new Alcatraz, and while the slow-moving accompaniment is eerie, it's not at all violent. Much of the LP is dominated by spoken accounts from guards and inmates and Bargeld's subdued industrial guitar; the oft-repeated main theme also includes cello, Lane's mostly lyric-less vocals and a shrill tin whistle. Probably effective within the context of the film, but two "songs" and little compelling content doesn't make for much listening allure.   [dgs]

See also *Barry Adamson, Birthday Party, Einstürzende Neubauten, (Die) Haut, Lydia Lunch*.

CAVEDOGS

Tayter Country EP (Restless) 1990 Φ
Joyrides for Shut-Ins (Enigma) 1990 (Capitol) 1991 Φ

The Cavedogs know their psyche-power-pop and, on **Joyrides for Shut-Ins**, they turn up with multi-tracked Rickenbackers blazing. Producer Ed Stasium (and others who worked on the previously released singles included here) gives the trio a BIG sound; while quotes from summer-of-love sources (Move, Floyd, Beatles and Monkees to name but a few) abound you'll also hear enough echoes of the Jam, dB's, R.E.M. and the Smithereens to know the Boston-based trio has progressed past pure paisley. What it all adds up to is glorious power-pop with the emphasis squarely on power, though the three-part harmonies will please picky popsters no end. If the sheer energy and tunefulness aren't enough, you can have fun deciphering the lyrics behind the guitars. Occasionally, you'll rewarded with gems like "We're just three white rich kids bitchin' 'bout the world/We think we got problems, but we ain't got problems" (from "La La La") that prove the Cavedogs know where it's at in the here and now.

The **Tayter Country** EP features the blistering title track (a single that also appears on the LP) and three more, including a version of "What's New Pussycat?" rife with power chords and feedback.   [ds]

CELEBRITY SKIN

See *45 Grave*.

CELIBATE RIFLES

But Jacques, the Fish? EP (Aus. no label) 1982
Sideroxylon (Aus. Hot) 1983 ●
The Celibate Rifles (Aus. Hot) 1984 ●
Quintessentially Yours (What Goes On) 1985
The Turgid Miasma of Existence (Hot-Rough Trade) 1986
Mina Mina Mina (What Goes On) 1986
Kiss Kiss Bang Bang (What Goes On) 1987
Roman Beach Party (What Goes On) 1987
Dancing Barefoot EP (What Goes On) 1988
Blind Ear (Aus. True Tone-EMI) 1989 ●
Platters du Jour (Ger. Hot-Rattlesnake-Normal) 1990

EASTERN DARK

Long Live the New Flesh! EP (What Goes On) 1986
Girls on the Beach (With Cars) (Aus. Waterfront) 1990

DAMIEN LOVELOCK

It's A Wig, Wig, Wig, Wig World (Aus. Hot-Survival) 1988

CRENT

Crent (Aus. Waterfront) 1990

The antithesis of a sex pistol is a celibate rifle, but Australia's Celibate Rifles are anything but the opposite of loud, snotty and fast. A fusion between Detroit-style straight-ahead hard rock and Ramones pop, steeped in Stooges and Radio Birdman milk, the Rifles began as a party-time Sydney band, racing through deliberately silly and simple Ramonesque lyrics ("What about the kids? Get a baby sitter . . . and some kitty litter") with three fast/loud chords. But unlike the Ramones, the Rifles insert loud, sinewy guitar solos between the slash-'n'burn verses and, on tracks like the 7-inch **Jacques'** "24 Hours," warped and warbly guitar effects.

By **Sideroxylon**, the Rifles had dropped most of early punk's stripped-down economy for the heavy guitar sound—more Hendrix than Kiss—that would follow them through the rest of their career. (An obvious Hendrix reference pops up in the middle of **Sideroxylon's** "God Squad.")

Three of the four tracks from **Jacques** and five of **Sideroxylon's** eleven were later issued as **Quintessentially Yours**. **Mina Mina Mina** is also a compilation, featuring four more **Sideroxylon** selections and all but "Electric Snake River" from **The Celibate Rifles** (aka **Les Fusiles Célibataires**). If that's not confusing enough, **Sideroxylon** and **The Celibate Rifles** are on a single CD.

Turgid Miasma sums up the band's past without reissuing any material and takes them in new directions (some of which they've never again tried). Split almost evenly between early-style fast, poppy rockers, metallic guitar excursions and a new style which encompasses everything from piano through zither and glockenspiel, **Miasma** is anything but turgid. Lead singer Damien Lovelock adds a sinisterly effective soft deadpan to his vocal repertoire—a deep, dark grumble which meshes into the guitar texture in "No Sign" and stands out in contrast with the bright chugga chords at the opening of "Conflict of Instinct." **Miasma** is one of the Rifles' most interesting LPs.

Lest their new-found studio prowess convince fans they had a secret craving to become sons of Steely Dan, their next release, **Kiss Kiss Bang Bang**, is a straight-ahead live album recorded at New York's CBGB. Most of the material comes from **Celibate Rifles** and **Miasma**, with covers of the Only Ones' "City of Fun" and Radio Birdman's "Burn My Eye." No keyboards. No soft thinky-feely moments. Just hearty rock'n'roll.

Roman Beach Party and **Dancing Barefoot** take the band in an even harder direction, back to the metallic '70s music they first admired. On "The More Things Change" and "Junk" (from the **Barefoot** EP), loud twists of feedback meet fuzzy scuzzy chords that are deep and dark—heavy as molasses and powered by 200 proof adrenaline. "Dancing Barefoot" itself couples twisted solos with Patti Smith's lyrics about heroin for an acid-hard '60s revivalist version of the song.

Despite the noisy washes of swirling wah-wah/fuzz/feedback guitar, the rough'n'ripping **Blind Ear** transcends any particular stylistic era for a bracing adult punk rush. Alternately wry, angry and compassionate, the intelligent lyrics concern politics, global responsibility, losers (like drug-dealing "Johnny") and progress (check the ultra-catchy "Wonderful Life" and the new-age spoof "Dial Om for Murder"), giving the exciting music a good run for album honors.

The double-album **Platters du Jour** career retrospective begins with "Kent's Theme" (which incorporates the Marlboro jingle) and the rest of **Jacques** and runs through the **Dancing Barefoot** EP. With numerous band classics (mostly singles), rarities, outtakes and informative annotation by guitarist Dave Morris, this is the ideal starting point for discovering (or rediscovering) the Rifles.

When bassist James Darroch left the Rifles in 1984, he formed the Eastern Dark, a trio in which he played guitar and sang. The five-song EP, released shortly after Darroch was killed in a 1986 automobile accident, has plenty of noisy electric excitement, but his songwriting isn't quite strong enough to make the band special. Mixing acoustics and electrics in a Woodentopsy rush, "I Don't Need the Reasons" comes the closest. **Girls on the Beach** is a two-record set of live performances, plus a pair of unreleased studio tracks from '85.

Lovelock is backed on his first solo album by colleagues from the Rifles and friends from the Church. The record by Crent, a slightly adventurous side duo formed by Rifles guitarist Kent Steedman, is promising but dull, fitting a few clever bits in amid such trippy but pointless '70s rock exercises as the side-long "9K?" jam.   ['e/i]

See also *New Christs*.

CERTAIN GENERAL

Holiday of Love EP (Labor) 1982
November's Heat (Fr. L'Invitation au Suicide) 1984

112

These Are the Days (Fr. New Rose) 1986
Cabin Fever (Fr. Barclay) 1988
Jacklighter (Fr. Barclay) 1990

CERTAIN GENERAL/BAND OF OUTSIDERS

Far Away in America (Sourmash) 1984
Far Away in America (The Live Side) EP (Fr. L'Invitation au Suicide) 1985

BAND OF OUTSIDERS

Up the River EP (nr/Flicknife) 1985
Everything Takes Forever (Fr. L'Invitation au Suicide) 1985
I Wish I Was Your Kid EP (nr/Flicknife) 1985
Longer Than Always EP (Fr. L'Invitation au Suicide) 1985
Act of Faith (Fr. Barclay) 1986
Acts of Faith (Sourmash) 1987
Armistice Day (Nocturnal) 1989

CORVAIRS

Temple Fire EP (Sourmash) 1984
Sad Hotel EP (Sourmash) 1985
Rio Blanco (Cryptovision) 1988
Hitchhiker (Fr. New Rose) 1989 ●

PHIL GAMMAGE

Night Train (Fr. New Rose) 1990 ●
Kneel to the Rising Sun (Fr. New Rose) 1991 ●

MARC JEFFREY/PLAYTIME

Marc Jeffrey/Playtime (nr/Conviction) 1990 (Behemoth) 1991

While every one of these bands has indisputably defined its own singular identity, the restless, incestuous pool of members and intents forming the core of each renders them analogous to a single beast with multiple heads pointing in different directions. Evolving from late-'70s CBGB teenage power-poppers the Limit, Band of Outsiders began by self-releasing a no-big-deal '81 single of spiky two-guitar indie rock. A year later, hot downtowners Certain General came out with their five-song debut, **Holiday of Love**, a fresher and more immediate mix of spartan semi-funk, drifting/scattershot guitar and male/female vocals akin to a reserved Peter Murphy (admittedly a contradiction in terms) duetting with Exene. Despite a borderline tendency to then-typical new wave conventions, the songs still sound fresh—even refreshing—today, as befits what must be the only record in history to be co-produced by Peter Holsapple and Michael Gira.

Come 1984, with both bands established as NYC club regulars, they joined forces to form Sourmash Records and release **Far Away in America**, an album to which each contributed two live and two studio songs. By this point, the groups had grown closer in sound; Band of Outsiders in particular evincing an atmosphere and range barely hinted at on the previous 45.

Minus drummer/co-vocalist Marcy Saddy, Certain General eschews much of their jagged arhythm for a more straightforward pop moodiness on **November's Heat**, which includes new versions of several **Far Away** songs. The album emphasizes the band's morose poetic imagery (especially vocalist Parker DuLany) in a manner paralleling R.E.M. (with whom they'd shared tiny stages) while continuing to chart a characteristically oblique course.

That same year, Band of Outsiders released the six-song **Up the River**, further developing a sound that

compared favorably to both Television and the then-nascent Cali-zona bands (True West, Green on Red, Thin White Rope): heartland songsmithery with guitars in uneasy collaboration and/or comfortable rivalry. Dropping the raucous but poorly recorded live cover of "Child of the Moon," the remaining **Up the River** songs reappeared on **Everything Takes Forever**, along with the two **Far Away** studio tracks and three outtakes from those sessions.

The all-new **I Wish I Was Your Kid** offered their best material to date, particularly the somnolent yet barbed title cut. Bringing all of the group's preceding efforts to a head, **Longer Than Always** is a soft, sizzling set of songs to sing through clenched teeth while handcuffed in the back seat of a patrol car.

Certain General, meanwhile, had more or less crumbled, prompting guitarist Phil Gammage to nab a new rhythm section and take center stage in the Corvairs. **Temple Fire** is quite similar to latter-day Certain General, albeit less arty and tortured (thanks to his Gene Pitneyesqe vocals). The latent/blatant Morricone/Scotty Moore rhythms retreated a bit for **Sad Hotel**, an undistinguished and ill-conceived extended dance track backed by a competent surf instrumental and little else of consequence.

Reflecting the bands' growing European following, New Rose released **These Are the Days**, a half-finished compendium of material recorded by Parker DuLany and a new backing group (notably Sprague Hollander), under the Certain General name. By 1988's **Cabin Fever**, the band had effectively condensed to just the duo plus incidental musicians; Hollander produced this slick and seamless set of lyrically haughty, musically specious tunes. **Jacklighter** offers superior material and comfortable production by (alternately) Fred Maher and Lloyd Cole, positing the band as neo-soft-rockers, comparable to Giant Sand if that group were drained of all grit and attack.

Back to Band of Outsiders: **Act of Faith** recycles all three tracks from **I Wish I Was Your Kid** in different versions, along with a new "Conviction" from the live half-album. **Acts of Faith** (the pluralized US edition) drops two tracks and adds the **Longer Than Always** EP in its entirety. Like the subtler concurrent New Zealand bands couching their pop in muted tones and colors, Band of Outsiders relied not so much on hooks or abandon as an ensnaring ambience.

Armistice Day catches Band of Outsiders in a November 1988 one-shot reunion—eighteen months after their split—airing the archives, but also doing a few newies and covers. Recorded in almostereo, the miserable US pressing undermines the relaxed versions of—inexplicably—the band's *non*-hits, focusing mostly on less-memorable material. A visiting Nikki Sudden plucks a few guitar chords and warbles undiscernibly on the last two tracks; Jeremy Gluck did the liner notes. (Members of the BOO/CG axis had previously played on both Sudden and Gluck records and tours, and continue to do so.)

The Corvairs released their first full LP, **Rio Blanco**, in 1988, a distillation/reduction of Gammage's career to date, as produced by Fleshtone Keith Streng. With all the initial spikiness gone, the Corvairs here play familiar rock'n'roll, from worn heels to fuzzy chins. **Hitchhiker** spreads out a bit sonically, allowing for a better sounding version of the same old thing. In its finer moments, **Hitchhiker** presents a likable band playing forgettable material.

The opposite is true of Gammage's solo debut, **Night Train**, wherein a more fluid and versatile group (comprised largely of familiar gene-pool faces) puts some personality into oddly underwrought darkside Americana echoing Nick Cave's fascinations minus the melodrama. Which might well make Gammage this generation's Hank Williams.

Meantime, Band of Outsiders singer/guitarist Marc Jeffrey—on his way to becoming this generation's Nick Drake—delivered his best LP yet. On **Playtime**, he delves deeply into melancholy, utilizing axis backing for non-rock instrumentation and approaches, neatly avoiding any maudlin and/or baroque temptations. **Playtime** unfolds like a series of stark confessionals, morose romanticism curiously reminiscent of Peter Perrett's England's Glory; low-key, unfinished yet attractive blueprints just waiting for that dose of electroshock to kick them into the annals of greatness. [ab]

EXENE CERVENKA

See *X*.

EUGENE CHADBOURNE

There'll Be No Tears Tonight (Parachute) 1980 ●
Chicken on the Way [tape] (Parachute) 1983
The President: He Is Insane (Iridescence) 1985
Country Music of Southeastern Australia (RRRecords)
1986 ●
Country Protest (Fundamental Music) 1986 ●
198666 EP (Ralph) 1986
Calgary Exile [tape] (Parachute) 1986
Megadeath [tape] (Parachute) 1987
Third World Summit Meeting [tape] (Parachute) 1987
Corpses of Foreign Wars (Fundamental Music) 1987 ●
Tucson, Arizona [tape] (Parachute) 1987
LSD C&W (Fundamental Music) 1987 ●
Kill Eugene (Placebo) 1987
Fuck Chuck [tape] (Parachute) 1988
I've Been Everywhere (Fundamental Music) 1988 ●
The Eddie Chatterbox Double Trio Love Album
(Fundamental Music) 1988 ●
Wichita, Kansas [tape] (Parachute) 1988
Country Music in the World of Islam (Fundamental Music)
1990

EUGENE CHADBOURNE WITH EVAN JOHNS AND THE H-BOMBS

Vermin of the Blues (Fundamental Music) 1987 ●

EUGENE CHADBOURNE WITH CAMPER VAN BEETHOVEN

Camper Van Chadbourne (Fundamental Music) 1987 ●

On his compulsive own, the guitarist/leader of the late, lamented Shockabilly has spewed forth a ceaseless stream of records and cassettes (the latter on his own Parachute label) that easily represent the oddest version of country and folk music ever. While the notable left-winger's guitar playing is looser than clams, it harbors wildly unique energy. The North Carolinian is also the master of several different voices, some of them deceptively sincere. Harsh, funny, irritating and packed with ideas, Chadbourne often suggests a politically correct Frank Zappa.

There'll Be No Tears Tonight lovingly takes on thirteen country-western standards. Eugene acts out his "free improvised country & western bebop" with several game free-music experts on everything from Carl Perkins' "Honey Don't" to Merle Haggard's "Swingin' Doors." The results are hilarious and touching.

The President contains Chadbourne's own politically charged ditties, many in a Phil Ochs-ish bag. His targets include Jerry Falwell, Women Against Pornography and his arch-nemesis, Senator Jesse Helms.

Country Music of Southeastern Australia mixes ten country standards and ten originals, played freeform style with such noted noisemongers as Rik Rue, John Rose and David Moss. **Country Protest** features the quintessential Chadbourne cover-version collage, "Medley in C." He's joined by Lenny Kaye on steel guitar and the Red Clay Ramblers for 11:25 of everything from "Imagine" to "TV Party" to "Dang Me" to "The Shah Sleeps in Lee Harvey's Grave."

The 7-inch **198666** EP, released on the Residents' label, is a rustic little artifact containing country-folk renditions of "You Can't Roller Skate in a Buffalo Herd" and four other songs.

Corpses of Foreign Wars is an all-protest vehicle featuring Violent Femmes Victor DeLorenzo and Brian Ritchie; highlights include a wonderful Phil Ochs medley and originals that range from verbal assaults on despicable neighbors to the "KKKremlin." Somehow, it all fits together.

Chadbourne then cleaned out his closet, using the two-record **LSD C&W** as the merry receptacle. Much of the material here—including a Beatles medley, "In a Sentimental Mood," a Roger Miller medley and other free-jazz, blues and rock faves—derives from mid-'80s sessions featuring former Shockabilly members Kramer and David Licht, plus John Zorn, Tom Cora, Toshinori Condo and many others. It also includes some of EC's finest originals sung solo. **LSD C&W** is the most of EC on vinyl, and possibly the best.

Chadbourne goes it alone on **Kill Eugene** (the complete title of which is **Dear Eugene What You Did Was Not Very Nice So I Am Going to Kill . . .**), although a nutty old lady on the radio and a few appreciative audiences (for the tracks recorded live) do make guest appearances. Covers on this mostly acoustic outing include "8 Miles High," "Purple Haze," "Oh Yoko," "Lucifer Sam," "Ramblin' Man" and the *Pee-wee's Playhouse* theme, which gets a topical rewrite as "Ollie's Playhouse."

Top-notch Austin stompers Evan Johns and the H-Bombs provide authentic rock'n'roll accompaniment on **Vermin of the Blues**, which covers ground from Count Basie to the Count Five, along with Chadbourne's usual amusing rants.

Eugene almost comes off as a father-figure on the joint **Camper Van Chadbourne**, although he easily out-eccentrics the Santa Cruz eclecticians. Check out their Zappa medley, the long-inevitable cover of Pink Floyd's "Careful with That Axe, Eugene," Tim Hardin's "Reason to Believe," Joe South's "Games People Play" and Chadbourne's own witty'n'wise originals.

Though not credited as such, the **Double Trio Love Album**—one side of Chadbourne originals and a side of Tim Buckley songs—is more or less a second volume of Camper Van Chadbourne whimsy. Unfortunately for Chadbourne fanatics, he relinquishes the driver's seat for the bulk of this road trip. There's a bit more politicking (and a few inside jokes), but the real flaw (as Eugene's lectures so often warn) lies in the democratic process.

I've Been Everywhere (credited to the Doctor Eugene Chadbourne) is as near to pure autobiography as the avant-rock form will allow; Eugene trots out both his (many) noise-making apparati and some of his most tender licks in a collection of songs that cut deep. In another way, so does **Country Music in the World of Islam**. This salvo, aimed pretty squarely at the evils of United States foreign policy, finds both Chadbourne's medium *and* message growing shrill—but it's hard to discount his arguments.

Chadbourne's voluminous tape cache is truly astounding, in terms of scope and overall quality. Sure, there are some duds among the dozens of selections the man himself proffers by post, but even a blind stab is likely to yield something of interest. A few samples:

Chicken on the Way ranks with the best of his fully structured cassette releases. Recorded around the time of Shockabilly's birth, there's really no reason this couldn't be a bona fide vinyl album (although that would preclude the finger-lickin' fast-food packaging). **Calgary Exile**'s mélange of obscure and/or unreleased tracks from '75-'76 is a little tougher sledding (so to speak). Recorded when Mr. C. was indeed exiled (by Selective Service persecution) to friendlier tundra, it's nonetheless a useful document of his "outside" material.

Megadeath is one of the least song-oriented collections here. Bits of a surreal AM-radio talk show pitting Eugene against some bewildered North Carolinian homemakers provide breathers between the (mostly) rake-and-plunger—he's played pickup-equipped versions of both for years—material. **Third World Summit Meeting** is a virtual obscure-rail pass through a plethora of little-explored ethnic styles. The individual numbers tend to drag but, in small doses, this is fascinating.

Both **Tucson** and **Wichita** document live sets from those cities (the Arizona tape actually combines a pair of shows) in all their rollercoaster glory. **Tucson** is a bit milder and more pensive (in part due to its solo circumstances), while **Wichita** osterizes anarcho-syndicalist rhetoric, bitter, almost Lenny Bruce-like barbs and plenty of feedback to fine effect. And though it's not clear who "Chuck" is, he abets Chadbourne on a crazy-quilt of material, including works by Charlie Parker and Duane Eddy. [rg/dss]

See also *Camper Van Beethoven, Evan Johns and His H-Bombs.*

CHAINSAW KITTENS
See *Defenestration.*

CHAMELEONS (UK)
Script of the Bridge (MCA) 1983 ●
What Does Anything Mean? Basically? (nr/Statik) 1985 ●
Strange Times (Geffen) 1986 ●

The Fan and the Bellows (Caroline) 1989 ●
Tripping Dogs (nr/Glass Pyramid) 1990
Tony Fletcher Walked on Water (nr/Glass Pyramid) 1990
The Peel Sessions (nr/Strange Fruit) 1990 (Strange
    Fruit-Dutch East India) 1991 ●

SUN AND THE MOON
The Sun and the Moon (Geffen) 1988 ●
Alive; Not Dead EP (nr/Midnight Music) 1988

This stylish Manchester pop quartet somehow managed to bring something of its own to much-traveled terrain, making songs like the melodic "Up the Down Escalator" and the far denser "Don't Fall" moody and memorable. Bassist Mark Burgess recalls Psychedelic Fur Richard Butler's world-weariness in his singing; the band's playing is, however, generally lighter in tone and simpler in design than that band's. **Script of the Bridge** isn't a great album, but it has very appealing moments. (US and UK editions differ.)

What Does Anything Mean? Basically? is even better, with much stronger production underscoring both the band's direct power and the ghostly atmospherics of its icy church keyboards and delay-ridden guitars. More than just songs, the Chameleons build meticulous puzzles, forests of sound with heartfelt melodies. "Intrigue in Tangiers" and "On the Beach" show the muscle beneath the beauty, while "Perfume Garden" and "One Flesh" spring with such fresh life they're instantly enveloping.

Strange Times was produced by Dave Allen, who instills a dark edge in the normally bright sound. The dreamy undercurrents add a luster to the three epic tracks, "Caution," with its odd 6/8 time swing, "Soul in Isolation," an emotional piece of knowing loneliness, and "Swamp Thing," a delicious, building mini-masterpiece. "Time" and "In Answer" are aggressive, no-holds barred post-punk rockers that such sound architects as these are supposed to be neither capable of or inclined towards, and they add a breathless whoosh to the proceedings. (Early US copies came with a not-to-be-missed six-song bonus 12-inch containing such covers as the Beatles' "Tomorrow Never Knows" and Bowie's "John, I'm Only Dancing.")

After the Chameleons split up in the summer of '87, Burgess and drummer John Lever joined with a pair of guitarists to form a new quartet, the Sun and the Moon, which debuted in mid-'88 with an eponymous album that sounds a lot like the Chameleons. Burgess evinces even more imploring emotionality than in the past, and it's a very solid LP, if no challenge to the Chameleons' general brilliance (inventive guitarists Dave Fielding and Reg Smithies are greatly missed).

The Sun and the Moon followed that record with the much-improved **Alive; Not Dead** EP, which sounds like a new group rather than a second-rate Chameleons. More acoustic and dreamy, three of the four songs are gently soothing, and almost submerge Burgess' sophisticated melodies. A raucous, madcap bluster through Alice Cooper's "Elected" (peppered with speeches from *The Prisoner* and updated anti-Tory lyrics) closes out the record.

Despite this promising relaunch, the Sun and the Moon fell apart in April '89. The group has since reassembled (without Burgess) as Weaveworld; Burgess has staked out a solo career. Fielding and Smithies have formed the Reegs (with a drum machine) and have released two singles, including a stunning rendition of the Kinks' "See My Friends."

Meanwhile, archival Chameleons material continues to leak out. **The Fan and the Bellows** is a set of '82 demos, mostly produced by Steve Lillywhite. Statik had attempted to release the album as early as '86, but the Chameleons went to court and blocked it. With no band left to maintain the legal challenge, the LP finally appeared in 1989. Though the primitive post-punk doesn't sit comfortably with the three real Chameleons LPs, **The Fan and the Bellows** nevertheless documents a stage in the group's creative development.

Burgess then formed Glass Pyramid Records and began (against Fielding's objections) releasing old Chameleons material in '90. **Tripping Dogs** is a live rehearsal from '85; not terribly earthshaking in light of better-known studio versions, but interesting for its early versions of two songs that later appeared on **Strange Times**.

Far more exciting is **Tony Fletcher Walked on Water** (named in tribute of the band's late manager), which collects the original group's last tracks: four long songs that are among the Chameleons' best. The epic sweep of "The Healer" and the chaotic "Free for All" pick up from **Strange Times**, and capture the band peaking as it shattered.

No controversy surrounds **The Peel Sessions** LP, a collection of three appearances ('81, '83 and '84) in a special sleeve by Smithies, artist for all of the band's covers. This mix of primal **Fan and the Bellows**-era material and full-bloom incandescence is well worth hearing.   [i/jr]

JAMES CHANCE
Theme from Grutzi Elvis EP (ZE) 1979
JAMES CHANCE AND THE
CONTORTIONS
Live aux Bains Douches (Fr. Invisible) 1980
Live in New York [tape] (ROIR) 1981
Soul Exorcism [tape] (ROIR) 1991
CONTORTIONS
Buy (ZE-Arista) 1979
JAMES WHITE AND THE BLACKS
Off White (ZE-Buddah) 1979
Sax Maniac (Animal) 1982
JAMES WHITE AND THE
CONTORTIONS
Second Chance (ZE-PVC) 1980
JAMES WHITE
Flaming Demonics (nr/ZE-Island) 1983
VARIOUS ARTISTS
No New York (Antilles) 1978

Arriving from Milwaukee with a saxophone on his knee, James (Siegfried) Chance/White/Black quickly became the linchpin of the budding New York no wave movement, appearing in Teenage Jesus and the Jerks with Lydia Lunch. More than any of his contemporaries, Chance turned harsh, abrasive music into an art form; at one time or another, almost everyone of any importance on the New York art-rock scene was in his band.

No New York, produced by Brian Eno and shared by three other bands, features four tracks by Chance and the Contortions (drummer Don Christensen, guitarist and future Bush Tetra Pat Place, guitarist Jody Harris, bassist George Scott III and keyboardist Adele Bertei) at their most cacophonous, shattering the limits of taste and anti-commerciality with a mixture of punk and jazz. Recommended in all its jangle. **Buy** lacks the jagged edge of the **No New York** material, but expands the Contortions into a first-class, no-holds-barred act, with every note and vocal oozing out Chance's deranged contempt for man and society in passionately cold renditions of normally pleasant dance music, epitomized by his anthemic "Contort Yourself."

Theme from Grutzi Elvis separates Chance's haranguing, bitter vocals from what turns out to be unusual, colorful music. Notably, Chance sings a subdued, oddly touching version of "That's When Your Heartaches Begin." **Live aux Bains Douches** features Chance and the Contortions live in Paris; **Live in New York** demonstrates that there is real emotion energizing Chance's savage, solipsistic music. (A decade later, ROIR brought out a second live tape, this one from Holland, 1980.)

Off White is a set of funky, demented disco tunes performed with Scott, Harris, Christensen and Place. Though milder and more accessible than his Chancework, **Off White** plays freely with his attempts at sexual ennui ("Stained Sheets") and racial ambiguity ("Almost Black"), and features a wonderfully weird and erotic version of Irving Berlin's "(Tropical) Heat Wave." Recommended. After White/Chance left the label, ZE compiled material from **Off White** and **Buy** to make **Second Chance**.

Sax Maniac, which he produced, proved that several years' absence hadn't harmed White at all, and that he is a wonderful, inventive sax player. Similar in all respects except personnel to **Off White**, **Sax Maniac** (complete with a cover of "That Old Black Magic") is a fevered masterpiece of white funk.   [sg]

See also *Bush Tetras, Defunkt, False Prophets, Jody Harris, Teenage Jesus and the Jerks.*

SHEILA CHANDRA
See *Monsoon.*

CHANNEL THREE
CH3 EP (Posh Boy) 1981
Fear of Life (Posh Boy) 1982
I've Got a Gun (nr/No Future) 1982
After the Lights Go Out (Posh Boy) 1983
Airborne EP (Enigma) 1984
Last Time I Drank … (Enigma) 1985

Cerritos' Channel Three (aka CH3) was one of the Southern California suburban hardcore bands signed to the pioneering Posh Boy label. An aggressive, speedy mixture of West (Black Flag) and East (early Ramones), the **CH3** EP and **Fear of Life** album are fairly typical genre fare, and not very inspired at that. The young quartet's lyrics predictably concern school, girls and the angst of growing up middle-class. The one-take-live-in-the-studio feel of **After the Lights Go Out** benefits from crisp, balanced sound and charged-up performances. Singer/guitarist Mike Magrann's wordy originals are routine enough that a burning version of the Stones' "Stupid Girl" is easily the record's highlight.

The trio on **Airborne** is far more proficient and creatively developed than any prior CH3 lineup; the songs—three of the four written by Magrann with ex-Stepmother Jay Lansford (who likely has a lot to do with the band's improvement)—are strong aggro-folk of some note.

The even-better **Last Time I Drank** finds the Magrann/Lansford writing/singing partnership firing on all rockets. Putting a mature post-punk sensibility to melodic hard-rock with an occasional Southwestern twist, CH3 comes through with an exciting record that packs a punch yet keeps both feet on the ground. Making memorable music this energetic without collapsing into raucousness or resorting to metallic precision isn't easy, but every song on the album finds a way to do it. Perhaps the Aerosmith cover ("Lord of the Thighs") is a clue. Of all the early punk bands, CH3 is one of the few that outgrew the genre without sacrificing its credibility.   [i]

CHANT
Three Sheets to the Wind (Safety Net) 1985 ●
Two Car Mirage (Safety Net) 1990 ●

On their first album, Florida's four-man Chant plays energetic and sparkling Southern folk-pop with a strong R.E.M. influence. The peppy tempo and flat-picked guitars of "All Behind Me" make that band's overwhelming impact evident from the very start; Walter Czachowski's husky (but articulate) singing furthers the comparison. But the loose-limbed guitar jam of " . . . For You," the striking country feel of "Heaven Assumes" and a spectacular cover of "Little Black Egg," the classic late-'60s obscurity by Florida's Nightcrawlers, help give **Three Sheets to the Wind** a legitimacy all its own.

Recorded in '87 (good) and '88 (very good) by two different lineups, **Two Car Mirage** contains more fine examples of the Chant's unpretentious Byrdsy rock: sturdy and appealing originals energetically played and sung with plenty of guitar sparkle. The CD includes all but one song from the first album.   [i]

TRACY CHAPMAN
Tracy Chapman (Elektra) 1988 ●
Crossroads (Elektra) 1989 ●

Singer/songwriter Chapman's powerful lyrics and extraordinarily powerful voice give her first album—unquestionably the most impressive solo debut of 1988—the impact of a rock wrapped in cotton. Tasteful electric backing and simple, clear production allows the uncomplicated songs to be the record's focus, and what a sharp image they draw! "Fast Car" considers the obstacles to escaping urban poverty; "Behind the Wall" paints a chilling picture of domestic violence; "Talkin' Bout a Revolution" has the uplifting symmetry of a classic folk anthem. Meanwhile, songs about romance ("Baby Can I Hold You," "For My Lover," "For You") leave the anger with undiminished intensity and conviction.

Acknowledging the intrusive challenge of sudden and massive success, Chapman resiliently channeled the threat to her own privacy and independence (most bluntly addressed in the title song) into broadly relevant songs of personal freedom (romantic, social and political) on the highly satisfying second album. Beyond that, **Crossroads**—which features more varied and expansive arrangements—maintains her tasteful artistic commitment to social protest, supporting Nelson Mandela ("Freedom Now") and idealism ("All That You Have Is Your Soul"), while drawing a critical bead on governmental neglect ("Subcity") and upward mobility ("Material World"). But Chapman saves the most affecting lyrics on **Crossroads** for relationships, where her wounds and anxieties fill the resonant songs with love and loneliness.   [i]

CHARGED G.B.H
Leather, Bristles, Studs and Acne EP (nr/Clay) 1981 + 1990 ●
City Baby Attacked by Rats (nr/Clay) 1982 (Clay-Combat) 1987 ●
Leather, Bristles, No Survivors and Sick Boys ... (Clay-Combat) 1982 ●
City Baby's Revenge (Relativity) 1984 ●
The Clay Years 1981 to 84 (Clay-Combat) 1986 ●
Diplomatic Immunity (nr/Clay) 1990 ●

G.B.H
Oh No It's G.B.H. Again! EP (Combat Core) 1986
Midnight Madness and Beyond ... (Combat Core) 1986 ●
No Need to Panic! (Combat) 1987 ●
Wot a Bargin' EP (Combat) 1988 φ
No Survivors (nr/Clay) 1989 ●
A Fridge Too Far (nr/Rough Justice) 1989
From Here to Reality (Restless) 1990 ●

First appearing in 1980, Birmingham's G.B.H (Grievous Bodily Harm)—Charged was appended to prevent confusion with a British metal band of the same name—quickly joined the top ranks of England's second-generation buzzsaw punk firmament. Enraged if not especially enlightened, the quartet tears through **City Baby Attacked by Rats** with chops and venom, throwing off sparks on dubious numbers like "Slut" and "The Prayer of a Realist." **Leather, Bristles, No Survivors and Sick Boys** compiles the similarly titled 1981 EP and two subsequent releases in a bracing storm of morbid speedcore. Ignore the dismal lyrics and enjoy the sweeping, trebly adrenaline rush.

The photos on **City Baby's Revenge** show singer Colin Abrahall and guitarist Jock Blyth sporting extraordinary hair-like extremities; the record is, conversely, marginally more restrained and less garishly violent than before. "Vietnamese Blues," "Christianised Cannibals," "Diplomatic Immunity" and other songs display a refined and more intelligent political punk sensibility, along with a slightly slower and easier-to-grasp sound. A blazing Stooges cover ("I Feel Alright") adds to the fun; on the downside, "Womb with a View" is an inexcusable anti-feminist diatribe.

With G.B.H. off to another label for a few years, Clay issued a compilation: tracks from EPs, singles and the albums, plus a strong pair of previously unreleased items, "Children of Dust" and "Do What You Do"—

which fairly condenses the band's primal punk catalogue. Four years later, the label also issued **Diplomatic Immunity**, a poorly mastered and undocumented 21-song compilation that repeats all but the two rarities from **The Clay Years** and adds seven other selections from the band's first three albums.

The speaker-busting **Oh No** EP is one of the most explosive rock records ever, a blistering quartet of tunes that are easily among G.B.H's best. The unexpectedly melodic "Malice in Wonderland" is a revelation that pairs the old sound of Generation X and the Pistols with Megadeth production. Wow!

Taking a sidestep on **Midnight Madness**, G.B.H. replaced the shrill top with a thundering bottom and mixed speedmetal rhythms in with the breakneck hardcore tempos. It's still essentially a punk record, and a pretty good one at that, although the notion of these hard hooligans writing songs about New York's Iroquois Hotel, horror movies and international touring is a bit disconcerting. The inclusion of "Limpwristed" shows the still-undeveloped state of the band's egalitarian humanist sensibilities.

G.B.H got themselves a new drummer with twin bass pedals and went all metal on **No Need to Panic!** Echo on the vocals and blurry guitar on top of an over-eager rhythm section typify the sonic approach; sporadic spoken bits, sound effects and TV bites don't add as much as the band might imagine. Another reason not to be cheerful: the dull and unfocused lyrics.

Avoiding **Panic**'s ill-advised fripperies, the four new songs on **Wot a Bargin'** are simply more thundering thrash metal; winding up to deliver a killer blow, G.B.H. can't get themselves tight or focused enough to make any real impact. Much the same problem plagues the self-produced **From Here to Reality**, an album on which glimmers of melody and an accessible rock sensibility are buried in an endless roar of undifferentiated noise. Get these guys a real metal producer and stand back! [i]

CHARLATANS (UK)
The Only One I Know EP (Dead Dead Good-Beggars
    Banquet-RCA) 1990
Some Friendly (Dead Dead Good-Situation Two-Beggars
    Banquet-RCA) 1990 φ

Friendly neighbors of the Stone Roses/Happy Mondays rave-pop scene, this young quintet from Northwich (equidistant from Manchester and Liverpool) uses Hammond organ, an evocative echo chamber and the neo-psychedelic fad's maddening drum beat to effectively flavor tuneful '60s-styled numbers. Not as lame as Inspiral Carpets or as danceably ambitious as Happy Mondays, the Charlatans keep things simple, assuring maximum chart potential with a light, unchallenging approach. Equipped with Tim Burgess' appealing voice and Rob Collins' varied organ work, the Charlatans have the tools for major flavor-of-the-month stardom.

The four-song EP's catchy title track—which sounds an awful lot like Deep Purple's version of "Hush"—was a huge British hit, and helped move the Charlatans well ahead of the critically favored Stone Roses in the commercial stakes. Although not originally included on **Some Friendly**, the song was added to the album's American issue, joining the moody "You're Not Very

Well," the dense "Then" (another UK hit), the jumping "Sonic" and several other likably disposable diversions with prickly lyrics. [i]

CHARLES DE GOAL
Algorhythmes (Fr. New Rose) 1981
Ici l'Ombre (Fr. New Rose) 1982
3 (Fr. New Rose) 1984
Double Face (Fr. New Rose) 1986

Stylish but awkward, this French artist is at his best on weird, moody synthesizer workouts—those songs that rely on choppy guitar and weak singing aren't as effective. A version of Bowie's "Hang on to Yourself" (on **Algorhythmes**) is skittish and tense, but not especially different from the original; its inclusion seems purposeless.

Ici l'Ombre has very little in the way of electronics; most of the tracks use only electric guitar, bass and drums. Among the haphazard collection of styles played poorly here: garden-variety punk ("Atout Mineur"), glum solemnity ("Rouge sur Blanc"), acoustic piano ("Face/Coma"), gothy noise ("Self Control") and squiggly synth-pop ("Kling Klang"). Hopeless.

Charles gets his cabinet properly organized on **3**, but the well-produced and reasonably focused mixture of guitars, synthesizers and Linndrum still isn't very entertaining. Dramatic singing doesn't improve the weak material; while the cute melodic rock ("Hop Hop Hop Hop," "Technicolor") and a clumsy English cover of Wire's "A Question of Degree" are amusing enough, the barren dance experiments that otherwise fill the album are fairly dismal. [i]

RHYS CHATHAM
Factor X (Ger. Moer Music) 1984
Die Donnergötter (Ger. Dossier) 1987 (Homestead)
    1989 ●
Do It Twice (Ger. Dossier) 1988 ●

For years, folks even marginally acquainted with NYC's downtown music scene have been treated to an ongoing dialogue about which came first, the chicken or the egg. What's unique about this particular debate is that the chicken and egg themselves—Rhys Chatham and Glenn Branca—have been doing all the shouting about just which composer/performer caught the no wave first. One thing's for certain: Chatham's tightrope walk across the rock/classical gorge began firmly on the "legitimate" side, so his work has often courted rockists with an assumed thumbs-up from "serious" music fans—the reverse of Branca's approach.

Factor X is an aberration. The volume's certainly there, but the free jazzers who are called upon to deliver the goods simply don't have that swing (with the notable exception of drummer Anton Fier, at his most authoritarian here).

Die Donnergötter comprises three wildly different pieces (written and recorded several years apart). The earliest, "Guitar Trio" (on which Chatham and future Ordinaire Joe Dizney are axepeople) is the most visceral, with a slack, extended-time structure that pulls taut at the most unexpected moments. "Waterloo, No. 2" dispenses with guitars entirely, using an art-damaged drum and trombone corps (Chatham again) to create a rather rote bit of militaria. The side-long title track, however, is a real jewel. Using six guitars playing interlocking melodies, Chatham weaves an intricate tapestry that's alternately ear-splitting and nearly Eastern in its delicacy (not to mention a recurring theme that sounds exactly like the coda of "Marquee Moon"). Participants in the piece include future members of the Band of Susans.

Recently, Chatham has upped the pain-threshold ante by performing a piece ("An Angel Moves too Fast to See") with one hundred electric guitars. Get the fuses and the earplugs ready! [dss]

See also *Band of Susans*.

CHEAP TRICK

Cheap Trick (Epic) 1977 ●
In Color (Epic) 1977 ●
Heaven Tonight (Epic) 1978 ●
At Budokan (Epic) 1979 ●
Dream Police (Epic) 1979 ●
Found All the Parts EP (Epic) 1980
All Shook Up (Epic) 1980 ●
One on One (Epic) 1982 ●
Next Position Please (Epic) 1983 ●
Standing on the Edge (Epic) 1985 ●
The Doctor (Epic) 1986 ●
Lap of Luxury (Epic) 1988 ●
Busted (Epic) 1990 ●

At a time when heavy metal had lost its menace and was fading into side-show stupidity, Rockford, Illinois' Cheap Trick blew out of the Midwest, where they had long been dominating clubs and bars, and set about proving that commercial rock writ large enough for football fields could also be relaxed, witty and sarcastic. Rick Nielsen stepped right through the guitar hero stereotype, wringing out glorious garbage while upholding the punk ethos by refusing to take the pose seriously. Although the quartet went wrong by buying into the expectations raised by large-scale success, Trick's early records and live performances positively influenced a generation of future bands growing up American in the late '70s. Many of today's post-punks (Replacements, Soul Asylum, Das Damen, Redd Kross, etc.—even Big Black went to the trouble of covering "He's a Whore" on a 1987 single) took something from them. While the self-important, phony and coldly efficient Kiss also influenced the same generation, Cheap Trick managed to make rock stardom look like fun, providing an alternative American archetype at a time when big-league success was almost a guarantee of total timidity and tedium.

After proving that a certain dose of commercial savvy was cool, Cheap Trick discovered that too much could be deadly. Failing to keep pace with what they had launched, the quartet wound up as dinosaurish and irrelevant as the arena reptiles they had originally displaced.

Drawing primary inspiration from the Move and Beatles, Cheap Trick synthesized a loud and brilliant rock powerdrive and backed it up with shows that, while formulaic and gimmicky in the extreme, had all the punch and spirited good humor that older, tired arena bands lacked. **Cheap Trick** is an absolute stunner, an immediately recognizable onslaught of Tom Petersson's

8- and 12-string basses, Nielsen's guitar overachiever theatrics, Robin Zander's nuclear assault voice and Bun E. Carlos' Watts-like steady drumming. Well-honed songs explode under Jack Douglas' all-electric production. "Taxman" turns the Beatles upside down with a twist; "He's a Whore" rocks with a ragingly melodic chorus; "The Ballad of TV Violence (I'm Not the Only Boy)" displays a healthy nasty streak by concerning Chicago mass murderer Richard Speck (albeit in the vaguest terms); "Oh Candy" laments a depressed male friend's suicide. One of the world's all-time greatest albums. (But don't put too much faith in the fabricated biography of the liner notes by future superstar novelist Eric Van Lustbader.)

In Color (And in Black and White), produced by Tom Werman (who went on to score metal with Ted Nugent, Mötley Crüe and Poison), is another spectacular record which reduces the buzzy guitar raunch in favor of a cleaner, more clearly pop-oriented sound. Trick maintained its anti-establishment coolness by including "Downed," an undisguised paean to barbiturates, and offering the bitchy "You're All Talk." Meanwhile, the LP contained the band's first hit single: the twinky "I Want You to Want Me."

Heaven Tonight hit a new pinnacle with the brilliant "Surrender" and a new low with the gimmicky "On the Radio." In between, the LP covers the Move ("California Man"), conveys the ambience of depressant use in song ("Heaven Tonight") and paraphrases arena rock in the leering "Stiff Competition."

As a result of burgeoning Asian popularity, the band's Japanese label recorded a pair of April 1978 Tokyo shows and released a live album, **At Budokan**. The concert version of "I Want You to Want Me" caught American radio programmers' attention and they jumped on the record—especially a dynamic rendition of Fats Domino's "Ain't That a Shame"—forcing its domestic release the following year and providing the group's first hit album.

Dream Police (also available on picture disc) continues the dedication to diversity. The wimpy ballad "Voices" and the paranoid mega-produced title track are pure pop; "Gonna Raise Hell," meanwhile, builds a rock disco groove with a powerful bass riff and overlays melodramatic vocals about the massacre at Jonestown, fading out with Zander's anguished shrieks. "I Know What I Want" is quintessential three-chord rock with a delightfully goofy Petersson vocal; the magnificent "Need Your Love" starts out slow and restrained, but builds to an intense boogie-based climax that closes the LP—and the essential segment of Cheap Trick's career.

As if to celebrate that juncture, a four-song 10-inch EP (later repackaged as a 12-inch) was released with a previously unissued track from each year, 1976–1979. "Take Me I'm Yours" is a worthwhile studio number; "Daytripper," ostensibly recorded live, lets the group display its affection (if not exactly reverence) for the Beatles.

The George Martin-produced **All Shook Up** is a bewildering array of production tricks, inferior material, halfbaked experiments and self-conscious mimicry of the Faces and the Rolling Stones. A few songs ("Baby Loves to Rock," "Can't Stop It but I'm Gonna Try") do withstand the overall botch, but the LP—Petersson's last—remains best unheard. **One on One**, produced by Roy Thomas Baker, is more realistic in its aspirations but suffers from second-rate material. Only the lascivious "She's Tight" and the obligatory ballad ("If You Want My Love") make strong impressions in this lackluster outing. New bassist Jon Brant adds nothing to the group's sound.

Nielsen had played with post-Rundgren remnants of Nazz around 1970, so the choice of Todd as the producer of the refreshing **Next Position Please** was a circle closer of sorts. (Given Cheap Trick's evident studio uncertainty the LP could have been titled **Next Producer Please**.) Returning somewhat to the straight rock-pop of **In Color**, but with Rundgren's unique imprint, songs like "Borderline," "I Can't Take It," "Won't Take No for an Answer" and Rundgren's contribution, the stunning "Heaven's Falling," make it a welcome return (almost) to form. On the downside, the LP also contains an atrocious self-produced version of the Motors' "Dancing the Night Away" inserted at the label's unfortunate insistence. The cassette adds "You Talk Too Much" and the slide-guitar blues festival, "Don't Make Our Love a Crime."

The next two LPs find Cheap Trick flailing about with skimpy ideas, no self-confidence and little enthusiasm. Reuniting with Jack Douglas for **Standing on the Edge** yielded a likable rote ballad ("Tonight It's You"), a charged riff-rocker ("She's Got Motion") and one good pop tune ("This Time Around"), all co-written with professional song doctor Mark Radice, who also plays the LP's keyboards. **The Doctor**, produced by metal-man Tony Platt (who mixed **Standing on the Edge**), is loud and abrasive, with the barest of worthy tunes ("Rearview Mirror Romance," "The Doctor," "Good Girls Go to Heaven") and almost no trace of lyrical personality.

Petersson rejoined the group in time for **Lap of Luxury**, Cheap Trick's creative nadir and (natch) commercial renaissance. Produced by the bombastic Richie Zito, with songs from all sorts of hacks (Nielsen only *co-wrote* four; Petersson and Zander collaborated on two others), the album gets off to a great start with "Let Go" but runs straight downhill from there. The hit-bound version of "Don't Be Cruel" is a nice touch, but no great achievement; "Wrong Side of Love" indicates they can still rev up the engines. Despite the promise of the original lineup and the sales figures, this album runs on empty.

Reclaiming some of the songwriting responsibility on the similarly structured but less obnoxious **Busted**, Cheap Trick demonstrates a facility for connecting the dots on the contemporary compositional template: the band's own "Can't Stop Fallin' into Love" is interchangeable with **Lap of Luxury**'s treacly store-bought hit ("The Flame"). Still, several of the original rockers ("I Can't Understand It," "Busted") are encouraging to the point of enjoyability, despite worthless lyrics and deep-seated insincerity. But the appearance of two miserable demographic song-factory ballads, a guest role for Foreigner's Mick Jones, an uninspired Roy Wood cover (now that's a low) and a self-conscious *Hard Day's Night*-era Beatles knock-off are continued evidence of the bottomless well of insecurity that keeps anything risky or inventive from appearing on a Cheap Trick record.   [i]

CHEEPSKATES

Run Better Run (Midnight) 1984
Second and Last (Midnight) 1986
Remember (Ger. Music Maniac) 1987 ●
It Wings Above (Ger. Music Maniac) 1988 ●
Waiting for Unta (Ger. Music Maniac) 1989 ●
Perry Como: Songs Vol. 1 EP (Ger. Music Maniac) 1989
Confessional (Ger. Music Maniac) 1990 ●

HERRERA & THE HANDOUTS

A Handout from a Cheepskate (Midnight) 1989

SHANE FAUBERT

Kalkara (Ger. Music Maniac) 1989 ●

The mercurial Cheepskates began life as an anomaly on New York's garage-rock scene: when most of their peers were scouring exurbia for vintage paisleys and vinyl (the more primitive the better, on both counts), this low-key quartet was creating some of the most carefully crafted pure pop to escape from those Seed-y halls. **Run Better Run**, dominated by Shane Faubert's bouncy (but not overly retro) Farfisa organ and clear, expressive voice, attests to the group's originality. Usually smart, occasionally precious songs like "Gone for Good" and "That's When I Say Goodbye" are reminiscent of the Zombies' art-school pop. Refreshingly cover-free (all four members write; three swap lead vocals), the disc is a timeless pleasure.

The original lineup split while recording the follow-up (hence the title), and the attendant tension is audible. The songs are looser in structure (though not overlong) and rely a bit too heavily on David Herrera's whammy-bar fills. The diffusion does yield some positive by-products, notably Herrera's "Good Life" (essentially a rewrite of Neil Young's "Barstool Blues") and bassist Tony Low's "Every Man's a King," the album's best song. Still, novices should stick to the debut.

After a year's hiatus, Faubert and Low revamped the band as a trio and recorded **Remember**, a spare, atmospheric collection of dark pop that would forever put the revivalist tag behind them. Although the songs are still shaded with Farfisa, Faubert proves himself a very good guitarist in the Roger McGuinn vein on songs like "Backwards Boy" and the moody "Better off Alone." **It Wings Above** is more intricate (there are swatches of saxophone and glockenspiel) and a bit brighter. Songs like the stunning "Goodbye Princess" and "From Light to Pouring Rain" occasionally swirl in a heady Game Theory (or even "Ride My See-Saw"-era Moody Blues) direction.

Recorded live in Berlin, **Waiting for Unta** indicates that the Cheepskates might have more aces in their deck. Besides their well-documented pop intuition, the trio—here augmented by ex-Wind guitarist Lane Holland (né Steinberg)—reveals a harder, Quicksilver-like side with plenty of guitar interplay. And just to keep everyone off balance, the set closes with a spot-on rendition of the Everly Brothers' "Bye Bye Love." To further complicate critical matters, the band's next release consisted of six songs popularized by Perry Como. "Catch a Falling Star," "Round and Round" and the rest are handled with a blend of subtle irony and heartfelt appreciation worthy of NRBQ. Perfect for parties.

The aptly titled **Confessional** is the edgiest Cheepskates disc yet, with stark shifts between the sugary

("Bear Down," "Come Close to Me") and the cyanide-laced ("Sorry," "It's Up to You") being made between almost every pair of tracks. Newly added second guitarist Rich Punzi makes his presence felt with some heartily feedback-drenched riffs.

Original guitarist Herrera indulges his dual fascinations—spacey, Santana-styled jamming and British blues—on his solo LP. If you can bypass the fact that he has nothing even resembling a singing voice, you'll find his fluid playing more attuned to the former (as evidenced by "Frog Booth"). **Handout**'s meanderings, however, merit little more than a cursory listen.

Faubert, on the other hand, stakes out a patch of territory midway between early solo John Cale and the more mannered work of R. Stevie Moore. Strings, stately keyboards and minimal, orchestral percussion dominate the drony, hypnotic **Kalkara**, which serves as a rejoinder to—rather than an alternately arranged rehash of—his poppier work within the band.   [dss]

CHELSEA

Chelsea (nr/Step Forward) 1979
Alternative Hits (nr/Step Forward) 1980
No Escape (IRS) 1980
Evacuate (IRS) 1982
Just for the Record (nr/Step Forward) 1985
Original Sinners (nr/Communique) 1985
Rocks Off (nr/Jungle) 1986
Backtrax (nr/Illegal) 1988
Underwraps (nr/IRS) 1989 ●
Unreleased Stuff (nr/Clay) 1989

Dismissed by more than a few as a bad joke, the never-say-die Chelsea was one of the few original punk groups to forge a unique sound *and* survive. Their distinctiveness stems from the grunt'n'groan vocals of Gene October, the guiding force and only constant member through enough lineup changes to rival John Mayall's role in a different musical realm.

Even in the early days, Chelsea didn't pursue the buzzsaw punk stereotype, instead favoring a less-fevered, sometimes lumbering intensity, redolent of an ignorant, lower-class background. **Chelsea** does offer plenty of thrills, however. James Stevenson's guitar enlivens slashing rockers like "I'm on Fire," and October constantly seems about to burst from the pressure. On a cover of Jimmy Cliff's exquisite "Many Rivers to Cross," he renders a vivid portrayal of someone suffering extreme pain who can't articulate it properly. It's poignant.

Alternative Hits (aka **No Escape**), produced by onetime Who manager/producer Kit Lambert, consists largely of tracks originally (and better) heard on singles. Collected on an album, these songs betray the band's lack of versatility. But at least it includes Chelsea's electrifying debut 45, "Right to Work."

Evacuate brings Gene October about as far into the modern age as he can go. In a bid for relative respectability, the bull-in-a-china-shop approach is toned down a bit. Somehow, it just doesn't seem right.

Like a beaten punch-drunk fighter who doesn't know enough to lay down, Chelsea slips further with its 1986 studio LP, **Rocks Off**. The record opens with an eyebrow-raising candied Hare Krishna chant, followed by its only enjoyable song, "Fools' Paradise," an engaging, harpsichord-laced ballad that might have been a radio hit in a more hospitable dimension. October's voice fits the flavor of the song, his clumsiness conveying an appropriate sense of confusion. From there, Chelsea retreats into "Revolution #9": a Beatles title, a Stones riff and 999's sound. The remainder is utterly pedestrian and dismal. Some legends are best left in the past.

Underwraps begins and ends on weird notes: "Somebody Got Murdered," a surprisingly accurate replica of the Clash song (from **Sandinista!**), and a coherent rendition of "Let the Good Times Roll," on which some of Chelsea is joined by ex-Clash drummer Topper Headon and original Police guitarist Henry Padovani (who sounds like he hasn't been practicing much lately). In between, October and his three current cohorts run warm (the Professionals soundalike of "Nice Girls," the mid-speed '77 punk of "Life of Crime") and cold (most everything else, all of it simple rewrites of familiar melodies) in a generic exercise that couldn't mean anything to anyone other than relatives and girlfriends.   [jy/icm/i]

CHEMICAL PEOPLE

So Sexist! (Cruz) 1988 ●
Ten-Fold Hate (Cruz) 1989 ●
The Right Thing (Cruz) 1990 ●
Overdosed On ... (nr/Vinyl Solution) 1990

Hooky punk to the last decimal place: pure pop for impure people. While reveling in pornography (see the first few LP covers), LA's Chemical People nonetheless uphold a simpler, purer comic-book music and style. Energetic and insistent yet clean and uncluttered (without being didactically straight-edge), Chemical music is hardly unfamiliar or unexpected, but a hi-test sugar rush (not unlike the Descendents' caffeine crank) that will make latent pogoers snap their rods.

So Sexist! (with intro and outro by notorious horn-dog Tesco Vee) is split into sides "Blair" and "Dave," the former documenting the group's relatively unremarkable beginnings as a four-piece led by the titular guitarist/vocalist, while the flip marks the uneven launch of the *real* Chemical People, with drummer Dave Naz(worthy; also of the Last) taking charge of the songwriting and Mike Ness-like vocalizing.

Ten-Fold Hate (cover star: Taija Rae) leaps ahead with immeasurably better production and tunes, more power and personality. **The Right Thing** only continues the trend (excepting the porn-queen idolatry, abandoned when it began to overshadow the music), while **Overdosed** consists of the second through fifth of the band's 7-inch EPs, augmented by one new studio track and three cuts recorded in '89 at CBGB.

With Jeff Dahl as frontman, the Chemical People transformed into the Chemical Dolls on "Sympathy for GG," a recent one-off 7-inch of GG Allin covers to benefit the imprisoned raver.   [ab]

See also *Last*.

CHEQUERED PAST

Chequered Past (EMI America) 1984

Although listening to this run-of-the-mill Bad Company arena rock may not, a glance at the credits indicates why Chequered Past was one of the most depressing groups/albums of recent years. Clem Burke and Nigel Harrison (both ex-Blondie) and Steve Jones (ex-Pistols) formed three-fifths of the band, proving conclusively that even talented new wavers, no matter how idealistic and rebellious, were merely a few years away from becoming just as bogus as the musicians they originally set out to dethrone.   [i]

See also *Blondie, Sex Pistols*.

NENEH CHERRY

Raw Like Sushi (Virgin) 1989 ●

After stints singing with Rip Rig + Panic and Float Up CP, Cherry (born of a Swedish artist and an African percussionist, she uses the surname of her stepfather, renowned trumpeter Don Cherry) teamed up with UK hip-hop producer Bomb the Bass for the single "Buffalo Stance." An infectious, sassy and savvy pop/rap hybrid, "Buffalo Stance" benefited as much from Cherry's persona—sexy and autonomous sensualist with a social conscience and crossover appeal—as it did from the jingly/scratchy backing track, singalong chorus and what-does-*that*-mean? title.

Raw Like Sushi, the album that followed, never matches the single's initial rush, but when it hits (about a third of the time) it's funky, refreshing fun. Cherry's more convincing when she sticks to the sex and sass—among the LP's memorable moments are "Outré Risqué Locomotive" (a churning paean to coitus and commitment) and the breathless protests of "I came already" at the end of "So Here I Come." But "The Next Generation" amply demonstrates Cherry's ability to make a statement without sacrificing a sense of fun. You wind up admiring her so much you wish the album were a little better.   [gk]

See also *Rip Rig + Panic*.

CHESTERFIELD KINGS

Here Are the Chesterfield Kings (Mirror) 1983
stop! (Mirror) 1985 + 1987
Don't Open Til Doomsday (Mirror) 1987
Night of the Living Eyes 1979-1983 (Mirror) 1989 ●
The Berlin Wall of Sound (Mirror) 1990 ●
Drunk on Muddy Water [CD] (Mirror) 1990 ●

Unless you check the copyright date, you'll swear that this upstate New York band with pudding bowl haircuts and Beatle boots existed two decades back. The Kings' faithful re-creation of '60s guitar rock and garage punk (the first album's material is strictly covers, most of it so esoteric that only a fanatic record collector would recognize more than one or two tunes) is so spot-on that it's impossible to discern from the real thing. In their chosen idiom, the group's records are as consistent and reliable as early Ramones.

The Kings' staggeringly true alternation of merseybeat and sneery trash remains uncompromised on **stop!**; surprisingly, the high proportion of originals scarcely diminishes the lifelike effect. (Two extra songs were added when Mirror remastered **stop!** for its 1987 reissue.)

The shag haircuts on the cover of **Don't Open Til Doomsday** offer fair warning that the quintet (having undergone a lineup adjustment) has loosened the stylistic strings. Leavening the slavish fundamentalism with a little modern sonic character, they hit on something comparable to late-'70s Flamin Groovies. As a concession to the less obscure-minded, the waning proportion of non-originals draws on T-Bone Burnett and Ray Davies and Dee Dee Ramone. The album is enthusiastically played and cleanly recorded but, once a band has painted itself up such a stylistic tree, musical development may mean a straight path down. (Esoterica note: "They were never born/they were thrown out of hell" is inscribed in the run-off groove.)

Night of the Living Eyes temporarily avoids the issue of musical direction by reaching into the vaults, compiling material (all covers, natch) recorded in the four years before the Kings started making LPs: both sides of their first three singles, a rehearsal outtake featuring manager/label chief/cult-figure-in-his-own-right Armand Schaubroeck and an early-'83 NYC live set. A fine document of the band's savage youth.

The Berlin Wall of Sound finds frontman Greg Prevost and bassist Andy Babiuk, joined by two new members, making further moves towards a more contemporary approach. Save for a version of Bo Diddley's "Pills" and another Dee Dee tune, the songs are all originals. Sporting a raw, Stonesy sound that suits swaggering tunes like "Love, Hate, Revenge" and "(I'm So) Sick and Tired of You" (not to mention the rather questionable "Richard Speck"), **Berlin Wall** presents the Chesterfield Kings as a fine, non-anachronistic hardrock band. For weirdness' sake, there's also "Coke Bottle Blues," a distinctly bizarre stab at delta-blues fetishism.

The band apparently liked that track enough to attempt an entire album's worth of twelve-bar standards: **Drunk on Muddy Water**, released in a numbered limited edition of one thousand. Though Greg (billed here as Yardbird) Prevost is no Leadbelly, the loose, lo-fi renditions of classics by Muddy, John Lee Hooker, etc. are entertainingly demented.   [i/hd]

CHICKASAW MUDD PUPPIES

White Dirt (Wing-Texas Hotel-PolyGram) 1990 φ
8 Track Stomp (Wing-Mercury) 1991 ●

Thirsty for a little Southern musical comfort, amateur swamp-grunge variety? This conscientiously rustic Athens, Georgia duo of Ben Reynolds (electric guitar, vocals, percussion) and Brant Slay (vocals, harmonica, percussion) may not be authentic anything, but their brief debut LP's carefully cruddy sound (produced by Michael Stipe and John Keane) and rudimentary performances do convey the backporch feel of a couple of boys singing, stomping and banging out rough tunes with raw spirit (and an echo chamber). If **White Dirt** could kick up anything besides a little atmosphere, there might be a reason to recommend it.

The full-length **8 Track Stomp**, produced separately by Stipe and Chicago blues legend Willie Dixon, fits more songwriting effort into the duo's minimalist clatter-and-strum fantasies and comes out substantially more invigorating. Slay's yip'n'holler vocals find a real home in "Night Time (Ain't Got No Eyes)," the

Stonesy "Superior" and Dixon's "Moving So Fast"; the restrained pop of "Cold Blue" shows the Puppies in a captivatingly pretty light. Now there's something to stomp about. [i]

CHIEFS OF RELIEF
Chiefs of Relief (Sire) 1988 ●

Bow Wow Wow guitarist Matthew Ashman (now also a vocalist) formed the Chiefs of Relief as the post-Annabella version of that band, but it took a few years before anything came of it. By that time, he had teamed with ex-Pistols/Professionals drummer Paul Cook and, joined by a bassist and keyboard player, begun playing a pop-safe hybrid of rap, beatbox funk and loud rock. At times resembling a tamer Big Audio Dynamite (a bit too closely), the Chiefs are nonetheless an agreeable dance-powered outfit that draws on the varied experiences of its creative team to kick the songs into fun gear. Richard Gottehrer's production accommodates the assorted directions handily, making Chiefs of Relief an easy pill to swallow. [i]

See also Bow Wow Wow, Professionals, Sex Pistols.

BILLY CHILDISH
See Pop Rivits, Thee Mighty Caesars.

D.J. CHUCK CHILLOUT & KOOL CHIP
Masters of the Rhythm (Mercury) 1989 ●

Venerable old-school DJ Chuck Chillout and his rapping partner Kool Chip run a graduate class in hip-hop tradition on Masters of the Rhythm, a solidly entertaining party record that skirts rugged language and any ideas more serious than "Rhythm Is the Master." Over modest beats that sample Kool and the Gang, Cameo, Herbie Hancock and Talking Heads' "Once in a Lifetime," the duo drops energetic rhymes on familiar topics (with relevant soundbites from Public Enemy, the Fat Boys and Run–DMC), reliving rap's recent past with engaging enthusiasm. [i]

CHILLS
The Lost EP (NZ Flying Nun) 1985 (Homestead) 1988 ●
Kaleidoscope World (nr/Creation) 1986 (Homestead) 1990 ●
Brave Words (NZ Flying Nun) 1987 (Homestead) 1988 ●
Submarine Bells (Slash-Warner Bros.) 1990 ●

New Zealand's Chills make lightweight, non-controversial pop with such fresh-scrubbed integrity that it's hard not to like them. Guitars may twinkle like harps and jangle over angelically whispery vocals but somehow the love songs are never gooey. Gooey bands do not write lines like "Oh god this white ward stinks, sterilized stench of sticky death, sniveling relatives at the feet of another moist corpse, but that corpse is Jayne and Jayne can't die" (from Brave Words' "16 Heart-throbs"). Soppy sentimentalists aren't honest enough to admit "I'd like to say how I love you but it's all been said in other songs" as singer/guitarist Martin Phillipps (after a decade, the only original Chill) does on the same album's "Night of Chill Blue."

The Chills write mostly love songs. They love women, rain, the Otago Peninsula at the southern tip of New Zealand's southern island and their leather jackets. They even love to be hurt because out of hurt comes growth. They love cool, clean production with sparkling high notes, keeping just enough homestyle dustiness to avoid slickness. At times, their music seems like a low-budget answer to the Moody Blues. Other times they sound like they just stepped out of a renaissance market square with folky acoustic guitars and delicate drums.

Kaleidoscope World is the record for Chills and Kiwi-pop purists, as it compiles most of the band's early singles and compilation tracks on one disc; the CD version of the belated American release adds the Lost EP, both sides of a subsequent 12-inch and two songs from a compilation. If nothing else, the record—in any format—is worth owning for 1982's "Pink Frost," one of the most haunting songs about death ever recorded by a pop group, and the band's masterpiece.

Sympathetically produced by Gary Smith, Submarine Bells (a far better album than the flawed Brave Words) graduates the Chills from being just a first-rate singles band. Andrew Todd's ghostly keyboards abound on such graceful yet eerie gems like "Effloresce and Deliquesce"; a tinge of knowing, slow heartbreak slings its way through "Part Past Part Fiction" and "Don't Be–Memory." Others, like the should-have-been-a-smash "Heavenly Pop Hit" (quite) and the splendorous title track, show a decided late-'60s Brian Wilson influence. And for all of the Chills' charm, pristine textures and cool atmosphere, Phillipps' roots in late-'70s punk still show in such uncharacteristic blasters as "The Oncoming Day" and "Familiarity Breeds Contempt." ['e/jr]

ALEX CHILTON
Singer Not the Song EP (Ork) 1977
Like Flies on Sherbert (Peabody) 1979 (nr/Aura) 1980 (Ger. Line) 1981 ●
Bach's Bottom (Ger. Line) 1981 + 1985 ●
Live in London (nr/Aura) 1982 ●
Feudalist Tarts EP (Big Time) 1985 ●
Document (nr/Aura) 1985
No Sex EP (Big Time) 1986
Stuff [CD] (Fr. New Rose) 1987 ●
High Priest (Big Time) 1987 ●
Black List (Fr. New Rose) 1990 ●
19 Years: A Collection of Alex Chilton (Rhino) 1991 φ

BIG STAR
#1 Record (Ardent) 1972
Radio City (Ardent) 1974
#1 Record/Radio City (nr/Stax-EMI) 1977 (nr/Big Beat) 1987 (Ger. Line) 1987 ●
3rd (PVC) 1978 (nr/Aura) 1978
Sister Lovers (PVC) 1985 (Ger. Line) 1987 ●
Big Star's Biggest [CD] (Ger. Line) 1987 ●

VARIOUS ARTISTS
Alex Chilton's Lost Decade (Fr. Fan Club) 1985

A seemingly unlikely figure for a new wave progenitor, Memphis-born ex-Box Tops singer Chilton nonetheless exerted tremendous influence on many groups via his unconventional early '70s recordings with Big Star. If not the best of Big Star's three LPs, #1 Record is at least the most cohesive. Recorded in 1972, when its Beatlesque four-part harmonies, early Byrds/Kinks guitar sound and crisp, tight, live-sounding production were decidedly out of vogue, the album was an early rejection of then-dominant bloated "progressive" rock, which had already fallen victim to the giant ego-tripping of not-so-giant talents.

Where **#1 Record** is a collaborative effort in every sense of the word (Chilton co-wrote and shares lead vocals with the talented Chris Bell; all four members sing), **Radio City** is more a showcase for Chilton's increasingly quirky talents. Bell had left the group (he died in a December 1978 car crash), and Chilton, whose gruff tenor epitomized the Box Tops' Top 40 sound, sings at the very top of his range, straining at times to reach high notes in his own songs. The well-organized production values of **#1 Record** give way to a more emotional and spontaneous sound, a middle ground between Lennon's **Plastic Ono Band** and early Sun records. If the material on **Radio City** is spotty, it's never uninteresting, and the best songs—"September Gurls" and "Back of a Car"—are as good as any rock-'n'roll produced in the first half of the '70s. (While Big Beat's joint CD of **#1 Record/Radio City** deletes two tracks from the first album, the German Line edition contains both complete LPs.)

Recorded in 1974 but unreleased until 1978—by which time Big Star had broken up—**3rd**, reissued much later under its original title of **Sister Lovers**, is almost a Chilton solo album. Alex, Big Star drummer Jody Stephens and a host of Memphis friends and sessioneers (Jim Dickinson and Steve Cropper among them) comprise the band. Capturing Chilton at a point when his creative powers were still strong enough to effectively chronicle the spiritual pain which would eventually sideline him for an extended stretch, it's an eclectic mix, alternately depressing and uplifting, ugly and beautiful. Though the various released versions were assembled without input by Chilton or producer Dickinson, **3rd/Sister Lovers** is—in its own fragile, ragged way—Chilton's most compelling (not to mention influential) album. Unlike the halfbaked material he'd produce during the ensuing decade, **3rd/Sister Lovers** does a brilliant job of balancing madness and genius, with classic tracks like "Holocaust," "Dream Lover" and "Stroke It Noel" standing as some of the most chillingly beautiful music ever produced in the pop medium. (The Aura and PVC versions originally featured different track selections; the PVC and Line CDs each include the same seventeen songs, but in a different sequence and with different cover art.)

Between the release of **Radio City** and **3rd**, Chilton had recorded an album's worth of material in a series of stormy sessions in Memphis with rock critic/musician Jon Tiven producing. Chilton was reportedly so out of it during the recording that Tiven ended up playing all the guitar. Some of the results of those sessions were released in 1977 on an Ork Records EP: **Singer Not the Song** includes versions of the titular Stones song and a 59-second "Summertime Blues," plus a couple of decent Chilton co-compositions that might have sounded better under other circumstances. In 1981, the EP's contents plus more material from the same wild sessions (including five more minutes of "Summertime Blues")

were released in Germany as **Bach's Bottom**. Only the really faithful will want to know.

Despite leading bands in New York (with Chris Stamey) and Memphis between 1975 and 1979—the years when he was rediscovered and lionized by critics and musicians—Chilton released only one single (1978's "Bangkok"/"Can't Seem to Make You Mine") during that period. Live shows did serve to increase his reputation as an erratic and eccentric performer, and the 1979 release of **Like Flies on Sherbert** painfully confirmed the degradation of a once-major talent. Produced in Memphis by Dickinson, the LP sounds (not surprisingly) like a bunch of drunken louts running amok in a studio. Some potentially good Chilton material is trampled to death in the process, as well as some covers. In short, it stinks. (The 1980 British edition on Aura apparently utilized the wrong master tapes; the original mix from the tiny Peabody release, most widely available on a German Line issue, is far superior.)

Live in London captures a 1981 performance at Dingwalls on what is, for Chilton, a fairly good night. Backed by the Soft Boys rhythm section (Matthew Seligman and Morris Windsor) and Vibrator Knox on guitar, Chilton runs through material from all three Big Star LPs and **Like Flies on Sherbert**. Although characteristically sloppy and erratic, the album has moments that indicate there may be life in the old boy yet.

After spending several years drying out and laying low in New Orleans and Memphis, Chilton returned to active duty in late 1984, touring with a new pair of sidemen and recording his first new studio release in many years. **Feudalist Tarts** is a delight, six sides marked by control, easy confidence and entertaining variety. Chilton even sounds like he's enjoying the work for a change. Among the originals are a humorously raunchy blues, "Lost My Job," and the absurdist jivey "Stuff" (with horns); covers include a slow, lazy take on Carla Thomas' "B-A-B-Y" and a funky slide number from the Slim Harpo songbook. The EP is a bit insubstantial, but most encouraging.

Big Star's Biggest is a good eighteen-track sampler drawn from all three of the band's albums; **Document** is a thirteen-cut 1985 compilation covering both Big Star and solo tracks. **Lost Decade** is an interestingly conceived collection of '70s work: one disc of rare and semi-rare Chilton solo recordings (some predating Big Star) plus an album's worth of material Chilton produced for singer Scott Adams and three other obscure artists. **Stuff** is an amazing French CD-only collection that contains all of **Feudalist Tarts**, the three songs on the 1986 "No Sex" 12-inch and seven more solo items, including "Bangkok" and its B-side, a version of the Seeds' "Can't Seem to Make You Mine."

Having influenced scores of garage rockers from the Replacements (only one of several bands to write a song about him) on down, Chilton can be forgiven for calling his next album **High Priest**. The record—which contains only four Chilton compositions—finds him tackling virtually every type of song you can imagine him playing (and some you wouldn't, like "Volaré"), from the Memphis soul of his Box Tops days to Brill Building pop to Jimmy Reed-style blues to gospel to Big Star to a twisted version of the Bill Justis instrumental "Raunchy," all lovingly delivered in a casual live-or-near-live garage style. What it lacks in polish, it more than makes up in charm, verve and just plain ol' soul. This could be what rock'n'roll is all about. (Big Time's American CD adds all of **Feudalist Tarts**, "No Sex" and one of its two B-sides. In France, where those EPs had already been collected on the **Stuff** CD, New Rose affixed four previously unreleased bonus tracks, including a knowingly creepy remake of Porter Wagoner's "Rubber Room.")

The six-song **Black List** continues in **High Priest**'s archivist/craftsman/lounge-lizard mode, with a slinky blues cover ("I Will Turn Your Money Green"), a cheerfully nonsensical take on Ronnie and the Daytonas' "Little GTO" and the laconic social commentary of Chilton's own "Guantanamerika."

With the benefit of clear annotation and the inclusion of a Troggs cover recorded for a New Rose compilation, **19 Years**, Chilton's first proper American retrospective, is basically culled from **3rd**, **High Priest**, **Feudalist Tarts** and **Like Flies on Sherbert**, with some of the same esoterica collected on **Stuff**. The cassette contains fourteen tracks; the CD goes five better.

See also *Panther Burns*. [ds/i/hd]

CHINA CRISIS

Difficult Shapes & Passive Rhythms, Some People Think It's
  Fun to Entertain (nr/Virgin) 1982 (Virgin) 1987 •
Working with Fire and Steel EP (Warner Bros.) 1983
Working with Fire and Steel Possible Pop Songs Volume
  Two (Warner Bros.) 1983 •
Flaunt the Imperfection (Virgin-Warner Bros.) 1985 •
What Price Paradise (Virgin-A&M) 1986 •
Best Kept Secret EP (nr/Virgin) 1988 •
Diary of a Hollow Horse (Virgin-A&M) 1989 •
The China Crisis Collection (nr/Virgin) 1990 •

The weird title of the first album by this Liverpool group—essentially a duo of Gary Daly (words, keyboards, vocals) and Eddie Lundon (guitar and music), plus Dave the percussionist—does convey a sense of what China Crisis is about. The rhythms—R&B, funk, reggae, Afro-gypsy, bossa nova—are so gently, modestly, melodiously proffered that it goes down *too* smoothly. Then you notice that the dreamily enunciated sentiments interface the political and the personal, with hopeful dreams and admissions of self-doubt and inner struggle. The cohesive feel is maintained despite four different producers; China Crisis' sturdy intellectual backbone emerges often enough to avoid wimpiness.

Working with Fire and Steel has just as much going for it. Sax and/or oboe (!) appears on all but two tracks, with more horns on occasion and even strings (real and synth). Mike Howlett's production, plus a new drummer and a permanent bassist, help the group attain a bit more sonic snap; the lyrics are less tortured, if just as thoughtfully and melancholically personal. (The EP of the same name unites two versions of the title track with a pair of pretty, wistful instrumentals originally released as British 45 B-sides.)

Flaunt the Imperfection was produced by Steely Dan's Walter Becker but, while displaying a bit of Dan influence (see "The Highest High" and "Black Man

Ray," both memorable pieces of modern art-pop), it's far more obviously a refinement of the band's own style. The lyrical art seems so artless, the musical airiness so effortless; like the first album, it's almost too subtle for its own good. (Almost.)

By **What Price Paradise**, Daly had handed the keyboards over to a fifth band member, but that had no audible, directly traceable influence compared to the switch to the production team of Clive Langer and Alan Winstanley. The sound has more edge to it, yet is somehow less delicate, less distinctive than on previous albums. In fact, the vocals (lead and backing) on one track are so different that the group is nearly unrecognizable. Still, it pretty much is China Crisis; if the songs occasionally seem more conventionally written, they're still attractive, even almost (gulp) commercial. What'll they think of next?

On **Diary of a Hollow Horse**, aside from three tracks overseen by Mike Thorne, a return to Becker is what. While Thorne uses a sparer sound, Becker often opts to add sax, flute, extra guitar and female backing vocalists. But the album is more familiarly typical of China Crisis (again with a taste of musical Danishness), and grows with repeated plays. In an uncharacteristic break with the usual conscious self-control, the group releases some tension in the nearly anthemic (by these standards) "All My Prayers." **Diary** is no match for their finest work, but a gratifying effort all the same.

The China Crisis Collection is a balanced overview, but contains only one track from the '89 LP.

[jg]

CHOIR INVISIBLE

Choir Invisible (Frontier) 1981
Sea to Shining Sea EP (PVC) 1984

FLYBOYS

The Flyboys EP (Frontier) 1980

Drummer Danny Benair, onetime mainstay of LA's Quick and later in the Three O'Clock, was—between those two outfits—one-fourth of Choir Invisible, known as the Flyboys when they released the trebly EP which was Frontier's first record. The band bears some resemblance to early U2 on **Choir Invisible**—credit the guitar work by Thames Sinclair (later half of a duo called Wonderwall)—but singer John Curry's melodramatic voice doesn't put the songs across convincingly. There's variety and depth, but also some problems that need to be resolved.

Adding a keyboard player and switching drummers, Choir Invisible made the much-improved **Sea to Shining Sea**, adopting a lush dance-synth style that sounds very British. Feigning the same mid-Atlantic accent (but pruned of its excesses), Curry's voice better suits this material, although he's still not a great singer. Sinclair's textures keep the midtempo tunes from dragging too much; he *is* a great guitar player. "I Walked Away," with its surprising Association-like harmonies, is the best of the disc's six offerings. There's nothing essential here, but it's more amusing than records by many likeminded outfits, and there are certainly enough of them. [i]

See also *Flesh Eaters*.

CHORDS

So Far Away (nr/Polydor) 1980
No One's Listening Anymore (nr/Unicorn) 1988

The Jam parented a 1979-'81 UK mod revival, as Secret Affair, the Purple Hearts, Merton Parkas, Gas, Lambrettas, Mods and Jolt all scrambled to join the hit parade. Though each left behind credible singles, only the Chords (no relation to the '50s doo-wop band) had the punk balls that made the Jam more than '67 wannabes. The Chords have been better remembered than most of their contemporaries, cited by no less than the Stone Roses as an early influence.

So Far Away's crashing power-pop singles ("Maybe Tomorrow" and "Something's Missing") approach the same tuneful heights as such contemporaneous Jam tunes as "Going Underground" and "Funeral Pyre." The album otherwise joins inspired originals ("It's No Use," "I'm Not Sure," "Happy Families") with two properly reverent oldies ("She Said She Said" and "Hold on, I'm Coming") updated in a twin guitar attack led by Chris Pope.

Recorded live at London's Rainbow in June 1980, No One's Listening Anymore captures the Chords at the height of their popularity. The concert versions don't improve on the walloping originals, but the album does showcase a punchy stage quartet, and the packaging includes concert posters and a band chronology.

After unwisely sacking popular vocalist/guitarist Billy Hassett (cousin of bassist Martin Mason) and replacing him with an ex-Vibrator, the Chords released a pair of excellent 45s and then folded in November 1981, leaving an album's worth of second-LP demos that occasionally turns up in bootleg racks.   [jr]

CHRIS AND COSEY

Heartbeat (nr/Rough Trade) 1981 (Wax Trax!) 1990 ●
Trance (nr/Rough Trade) 1982 (Wax Trax!) 1990 ●
Songs of Love + Lust (nr/Rough Trade) 1984 (Wax Trax!) 1990 ●
European Rendezvous (nr/Doublevision) 1984
Techno Primitiv (nr/Rough Trade) 1985 (Wax Trax!) 1990 ●
Take Five EP (Can. Nettwerk) 1986 ●
Exotika (Can. Nettwerk) 1987 (Nettwerk) 1990 ●
Action (nr/Licensed) 1987
Trust (Bel. Play It Again Sam) 1989 (Nettwerk) 1990 ●
Chris and Cosey (Bel. Play It Again Sam) 1989 ●
Allotropy (Staaltape) 1989 φ
Reflection (Wax Trax!) 1990 ●
Pagan Tango (Wax Trax!) 1991 ●

CREATIVE TECHNOLOGY INSTITUTE

Elemental 7—The Original Soundtrack (nr/Doublevision) 1984

CHRIS CARTER

Mondo Beat (nr/Conspiracy Int'l) 1986

COSEY FANNI TUTTI

Time to Tell (nr/Cathexis) 1988

CORE

Core (Can. Nettwerk) 1988 ●

CONSPIRACY INTERNATIONAL

Collectiv One [CD] (Austrian CTI) 1988 ●

Rising in the very early '80s from the corpse of Throbbing Gristle, Chris Carter and Cosey Fanni Tutti (aka CTI, the Creative Technology Institute) infuse their electronic mantras with the beat of the factory to create a desolate industrial vision. Much of the work on Heartbeat follows solidly in Throbbing Gristle's footsteps, with found voices playing over pulsating synthesizer sounds, while the remainder strives towards lightweight Kraftwerkian metal pop. (The cassette has extra tracks.)

Trance's songs unfold more slowly and deliberately, only reaching their final rock forms after passing through stages that frequently bear an uncanny resemblance to Gregorian chant warped into the future. As the title suggests, the mood is dark and contemplative; within the inventive and apparently emotionless electronics lie deep wells of terror and claustrophobia. Worth looking into.

Songs of Love and Lust has a distinctively icy sound, with precise, percussive synths not very far to the left of Depeche Mode. Cosey's cold, distant voice, paying only passing attention to intonation at times, fits in perfectly amidst the machines. The problem is the songs—they're highly repetitive and go nowhere. (Five of the LP's nine tracks exceed five minutes.) Considering the pair's background, this record takes few chances.

CTI's Elemental 7, the soundtrack to a long-form video, consists primarily of tempo-less washes of synthesizers, bordering on '70s-style space rock. Not very listenable as an album. European Rendezvous is a live set recorded throughout the continent in 1983.

Techno Primitiv is interchangeable with Songs of Love and Lust, dominated by unchallenging, mechanical electro-pop. Tempos and textures vary, but each track has an air of familiarity. One could possibly find some interest if the production were at least good, but the album has a really dead sound.

Still without a US record deal, Chris and Cosey signed with Canada's Nettwerk and released Take Five in 1986. It begins with "October Love Song," a song worthy of the Human League; the four other tracks fall between that approach and the pair's previous work. The production is much improved (two numbers are remixes of early material).

The liner notes on Exotika explain, "Today we have tremendously diverse kinds of music," but the grooves contain very little to demonstrate that these two are actually aware of that fact; each (lengthy) cut is an electro-Eurodisco variation on the same theme, introduced long ago. Again, the sound is nice, but other bands have done (and overdone) this same stuff much better. Chris and Cosey are just about up to the point of being permanently dismissible. (The Exotika CD adds Take Five.)

Trust earns them a temporary reprieve. The tracks are more diverse than those on Exotika, and Cosey's voice doesn't, for once, sound like a recorded message, which makes a world of difference. "Watching You" might go on forever, but at least she gives the impression of feeling the lyrics' paranoia. The title cut is a haunting, predominantly spoken tone poem more reminiscent of the less abrasive moments of Throbbing Gristle; other tracks concentrate on sexuality and get fairly funky—in a sense. (The CD adds a remix of the song "Hypnotika.")

The long, repetitive grooves on Pagan Tango are—

structurally at least—not that dissimilar to industrial music. (In other words, Chris and Cosey are catching up to their own influence.) But as the techno dance beats and synthesized washes are trancey/pretty rather than bludgeoning/cruel, Cosey's insignificant vocal contributions seem more instrumental than intellectual.

The **Reflection** compilation contains two selections each from the duo's four Rough Trade LPs. The earlier work is refreshing to hear, as it serves to remind that Chris and Cosey have produced a variety of quality material over the years. **Collectiv One** compiles twelve tracks from 1983-'85.

Core is a project in which the duo collaborates with a half-dozen other artists, among them Robert Wyatt, Boyd Rice and Coil (thereby reuniting with former Gristle-mate Peter Christopherson). The variety of colleagues is reflected in the material; Chris and Cosey (as CTI) allow others plenty of input. "Feeder," recorded with Coil, sounds cinematic; "Unmasked" is a chilling ballad with Wyatt; a cut with Rice marks a return to their industrial roots. Very little of **Core** revisits previous C&C releases; even a cut without guests steers clear of familiar territory, and features a (real? Fairlighted?) orchestra. An unexplained minute or so of quiet electronics separates each track. Very impressive.

[sg/i/dgs]

CHRIS D.

See *Divine Horsemen, Flesh Eaters*.

CHRISTIAN DEATH

Only Theatre of Pain (Frontier) 1982 ●
Deathwish EP (Fr. L'Invitation au Suicide) 1984 ●
Catastrophe Ballet (Fr. L'Invitation au Suicide) 1984 (It. Contempo) 1987 (Nostradamus) 1990 ●
Ashes (Nostradamus) 1985 (Ger. Normal) 1988 ●
The Wind Kissed Pictures EP (It. Supporti Fonografici) 1985 (Nostradamus-Chameleon) 1986 ●
The Decomposition of Violets [tape] (ROIR) 1985 (It. Contempo) 1990 ●
An Official Anthology of "Live" Bootlegs (nr/Nostradamus) 1986
Atrocities (Ger. Normal) 1986 ●
Jesus Christ Proudly Presents Christian Death (Ger. Normal) 1987
The Scriptures (nr/Jungle) 1987 ●
The Wind Kissed Pictures (past & present) [CD] (It. Supporti Fonografici) 1988 ●
Sex and Drugs and Jesus Christ (nr/Jungle) 1988 (Nostradamus-Dutch East India) 1989 ●
The Heretics Alive (nr/Jungle) 1989 (Nostradamus-Dutch East India) 1990 ●
All the Love All the Hate Part One: All the Love (nr/Jungle) 1989 ●
All the Love All the Hate Part Two: All the Hate (nr/Jungle) 1989 ●
The Wind Kissed Pictures (past present & future) (It. Supporti Fonografici) 1990 ●
Insanus, Ultio, Proditio, Misericordia Que (It. Supporti Fonografici) 1990 ●

POMPEII 99

Look at Yourself (Nostradamus) 1981
Ignorance is the Control EP (Nostradamus) 1982

Formed originally in Los Angeles as a theatrical shock-horror outgrowth of the punk scene (guitarist Rikk Agnew was a recent refugee from the Adolescents), Christian Death has survived to flourish into a multinational organization with a vast catalogue of pretentious gothic records.

Only Theatre of Pain is hampered by singer Rozz Williams' ghastly voice, but the loud/not-too-fast music is appropriately doomy'n'gloomy, with inventive arrangements and clear sound to capture the mood in full B-movie fidelity. The lyrics irreverently address horror topics and religion: they're overwrought and dumb (the backwards masking of "Mysterium Iniquitatis" being one clever exception) but easy to overlook in the wash of inspired rock noise. (The CD appends the menacing synth-rocker "Dogs," rescued from the first **Hell Comes to Your House** compilation, as well as **Deathwish**—a grainy-sounding five-song EP of pre-LP demos that includes early versions of three songs that made it onto the original album as well as two punky tracks that didn't.)

Fronting an entirely different lineup on the stylish-looking **Ashes**, Williams evidently learned to temper his harsh voice by burying it low in the mix. Unfortunately, keyboardist Gitane DeMone also sings, creating a bit of internal controversy over which key any given song should employ. The ponderous Bauhausian music, which sets its solid foundation on David Glass' drumming, is more mature and sophisticated; lyrics (some in German) drop religion for vague evocations of medieval debauchery and evil. **The Decomposition of Violets**, a contemporaneous live tape of that same lineup onstage in Hollywood, is loud and enthusiastic but suffers greatly from the blatant overuse of synthesizers and terribly recorded vocals.

With guitarist Valor taking over the vocals and songwriting, Christian Death became a trio on **The Wind Kissed Pictures**. Occasionally colored by gusty vampire movie ambient effects, the clear, open music makes the would-be decadence of "Believers of the Unpure" and the title track easier to endure, if not actually enjoy. Valor's singing, alone and combined with DeMone's, is also something of an improvement, although his lyrics are actually worse than Williams'. The American edition adds an English-language "Lacrima Cristi," while the first Italian CD, lengthened to **The Wind Kissed Pictures (past & present)**, adds three cinematic instrumentals. The third Italian version, **The Wind Kissed Pictures (past present & future)**, adds the Italian and English renditions of "Lacrima."

Taking the band's name as its literal mission, Valor set out to destroy organized religion. Thus motivated, he began to really distinguish himself as a pompous prat on **Atrocities**, Christian Death's darkhearted return to the somber cesspool of slow-paced grimness. "Herein contained are the emotional remains of millions," his liner notes to the impenetrable concept album exclaim, but that's hard to believe. **Jesus Christ Proudly Presents** (another dubious assertion, to be sure—*proudly?*) is a lavish box set, spreading a concert's worth of live cuts and an interview over six 7-inch EPs.

Raging ego and unchecked ambition allow Valor to attempt a laughable comparative history of religion on **The Scriptures**, subtitled "A Translation of World Beliefs by Valor." (Thanks, Val!) After beginning the LP with a fundamentalist preacher, V. goes on to crib lyrics from the Bible and sing—with an audibly straight face—of Huns, horsemen and Ma'gog, pontificating in a most truly offensive manner. The trio also manages to cover a Jimi Hendrix song (''1983'') and play the relatively incidental (but agreeable) rock music with a bit of outside assistance. The original pressing included a bonus 7-inch single of ''Jezebel's Tribulation'' and ''Wraeththu,'' both also added to the CD.

Christian Death claims to have assembled **An Official Anthology** by collecting and culling illicit concert recordings made of them between 1981 and 1986. Shows from London, Amsterdam and Los Angeles are included, as are three previously unrecorded tracks.

Like its British edition's intentionally offensive cover photograph (of the messiah jacking up), the contents of **Sex and Drugs and Jesus Christ** are awful, a rudimentary and barely musical mix of (what sound like synthetic) drums, bass and loud guitar that could have been knocked off in an afternoon by just about anybody with hands. Lyrically, Valor and DeMone continue to prattle crypto-religious imprecations and apocalyptic mumbo jumbo. To get an idea just how bad this is, try singing ''Your church makes me vomit into the vertiginous abyss'' or ''In the chambers of unguiculate sacciform/From the Almighty avenging words of pernicious thoughts'' and see where it gets you.

Recorded as a five-piece at the Marquee London in mid-1989 (hence the prominence given to material from **Sex and Drugs**), **The Heretics Alive** contains on-site interviews with fans explaining their fondness for—and understanding of—Christian Death. Given the devilishly grungy sound and sloppy, impotent performances, the irrational comments make a better case for the band than anything else on the record.

After DeMone departed to pursue her jazz club singing in Holland, Valor made some changes. Aided by a drummer and new multi-instrumental cohort Nick the Bastard, he came up with an ambitiously simpleminded concept project, released as two separately packaged LPs. **All the Love**, which begins with a Martin Luther King quote—now *that's* artistic presumption—takes an ambivalent stance on the subject of l'amour, from respectful (''We Fall Like Love'') to hostile (''Love Is Like a Bitchin' in My Heart,'' revising the Holland/Dozier/Holland classic without credit) to bent (''Deviate Love''). The casually played, occasionally atmospheric music likewise shifts gears (none of them especially accomplished or attractive) without ever finding one worthy of attention.

All the Hate, a third-rate heavy metal record whose cover shows a swastika in a black heart ringed by Jewish stars, uses shock value symbols, inflammatory lyrics and sound bites of Hitler and the KKK in a supposed commentary about the evil that men do. Hardly. While ''Climate of Violence'' does indeed mention numerous historical forms of prejudice, from Jim Crow laws to Salman Rushdie, Valor merely lists them without comment; the sound of Nazi salutes is equally meaningless in this lame context. Strip away the pretense, and **All the Hate** is just a standard lurid metal maniac fantasy, with only one redeeming item. In ''I Hate You,'' Sevan Kand (Valor and Gitane's five-year-old son) unleashes a bratty British-accented spew of four-letter words and cranky opinions (''I hate going to bed/And I hate sting-ing nettles/And I hate . . .'' ad nauseum) in a fine pre-pubescent echo of punk-rock solipsism.

Insanus, Ultio, Proditio, Misericordia Que is a compilation.

Before joining Christian Death, the Valor/DeMone/Glass crew had been a band known as Pompeii 99. Also part of the LA death-rock scene, the group released an album and EP that are—unsurprisingly—very similar to Christian Death. Pompeii 99 was scheduled to do a European tour opening for Christian Death; when Rozz Williams lost his group, the two bands merged under the better-known name. [i/gef]

See also *Adolescents*.

CHRISTIANS
The Christians (nr/Island) 1987 (Island) 1988 ●
Colour (Island) 1990 ●
ROGER CHRISTIAN
Checkmate (nr/Island) 1989 ●

Brothers Garry and Russell Christian (formerly an a cappella soul trio with Roger, another sibling) and ex-Yachts helmsman Henry Priestman (who left It's Immaterial to join them) comprise the core of this Liverpool group. (Roger Christian appeared on the group's earliest singles, but quit prior to the first Christians album and eventually surfaced as a solo act.)

Sonically, **The Christians** is a treat, with airy harmonies floating angelically above and around Priestman's crisp keyboards and percolating percussion, while Garry C. sings with restrained soul about life in a (depressed) Northern town. Unfortunately, the messages of songs like ''Forgotten Town,'' ''When the Fingers Point,'' ''Hooverville'' and ''Ideal World'' are almost undermined by the prettiness and pop sparkle of it all, as if they've muted the passion the songs require in an effort not to overstate the case. With a few more memorable melodies and a bit more punch, this record might have been something special. (As it was, the LP spent well over a year in the UK charts.)

Colour continues in the same vein as **The Christians**, and the same criticism applies. If anything, the sound is even prettier here, but the generally overlong songs lack the dynamics needed to keep them interesting. As well-intentioned as the Christians are—and to their credit, the group's sound is definitely distinctive—they seem locked into an MOR sheen that, despite moments of real beauty, inevitably turns tedious. [ds]

CHRISTMAS
In Excelsior Dayglo (Big Time) 1986
Ultraprophets of Thee Psykick Revolution (IRS) 1989 ●

On their first album, an enjoyable folk-rock escape into wry absurdity that owes an emotional debt to Redd Kross (repaid in 1990 when guitarist Michael Cudahy co-wrote a song for that band's **Third Eye** LP), Boston's kooky Christmas eulogizes Pee-wee Herman, ''Tommy the Truck'' and ''Pumpkinhead.'' Drummer Liz Cox and guitarist Michael Cudahy alternate appealing lead vocals over simple, well-played music that is far from skeletal. If the trio comes up a bit short on identifiable personality here, considerable wit and ability almost make up for it.

Following a relocation to Las Vegas, Christmas released **Ultraprophets**, an across-the-board improvement with better songs, fuller production and a stronger Xmas spirit than the first record. The excellent "Stupid Kids," "This Is Not a Test" and "My Operator" are all catchy, melodic rock with Cheap Trick undertones and bizarre lyrics; the incongruity of Cox's Banglesque vocals (supported nicely by Cudahy's singing) adds both direct and ironic merits to "Richard Nixon," "Warhog" and "Great Wall of China." But as alluring as the record can be, Christmas never seems as off-the-wall weird as it ought to be, and half of the songs don't amount to anything. [i]

CHROME
The Visitation (Siren) 1977
Alien Soundtracks (Siren) 1978 (Touch and Go) 1990 ●
Half Machine Lip Moves (Siren) 1979 (Touch and Go) 1990 ●
Read Only Memory EP (Siren) 1979
Red Exposure (Siren) 1980
Inworlds (Siren) 1981
Blood on the Moon (Siren) 1981 ●
3rd from the Sun (Siren) 1982 ●
No Humans Allowed (Siren) 1982
Chrome Box (Subterranean) 1982
Raining Milk (Fr. Mosquito) 1983
Chronicles (Ger. Dossier) 1984 ●
Into the Eyes of the Zombie King (Fr. Mosquito) 1984 ●
The Lyon Concert (Ger. Dossier) 1985 ●
Another World (Ger. Dossier) 1986 ●
Dreaming in Sequence (Ger. Dossier) 1987
Live in Germany (Ger. Dossier) 1989
Alien Soundtracks II (Ger. Dossier) 1989

HELIOS CREED
X-Rated Fairy Tales (Subterranean) 1985
Superior Catholic Finger (Subterranean) 1989
The Last Laugh (Amphetamine Reptile) 1989 ●
Boxing the Clown (Amphetamine Reptile) 1990 ●

DAMON EDGE
Alliance (Fr. New Rose) 1985 ●
The Wind Is Talking (Fr. New Rose) 1985
Grand Visions (Fr. New Rose) 1986
The Surreal Rock (Ger. Dossier) 1987 ●

DAMON EDGE AND CHROME
Eternity (Ger. Dossier) 1986 ●

Under the innocuous name of Chrome, two San Franciscans—Damon Edge (vocals, synths, etc.) and Helios Creed (vocals, guitar, etc.), with part-time rhythm-section assistance by the Stench brothers of Pearl Harbor's band—created an often awesome series of pre-industrial LPs that explore a dark state of mind only hinted at by '60s psychedelia. Taking cues from Suicide, Can, Pink Floyd, Jimi Hendrix, the Residents and anyone who ever made home tapes in their bedroom, the pair's dense, chaotic science-fiction epics are vivid vinyl nightmares—a thick blend of mechanical noises, filtered, twisted voices and fantastic, bizarre lyrics—that flesh out a frightening world both absorbing and repellent. Though conventional song structures are preserved to the point where tracks can be distinguished (indeed, the duo's early efforts

aren't all that far from semi-normal guitar rock), Chrome's strength is its ability to create sounds of horrible beauty that transcend discrete musical units. If Chrome isn't as conceptually out there or as ear-splitting as the noisemongers and goth-rockers that followed, the duo's sonic intensity is still something to behold.

After the tentativeness of the first two albums, apart from early refinements, Edge and Creed pretty much stuck to the same uniquely nerve-shattering style—metal-drone-punk—throughout their time together. The utterly fearless are recommended to begin with the **Chrome Box**, a limited-edition set of six albums, including **Alien Soundtracks**, **Half Machine Lip Moves**, **Blood on the Sun**, **No Humans Allowed** and the previously unreleased two-disc **Chronicles**.

Following Chrome's dissolution in 1983, Creed and Edge each launched solo careers. Creed's first album finds him leading a noisy quartet that drops the science-fiction content but retains Chrome's sonic density and mild dissonance. Kind of low-rent and faintly cheesy, **X-Rated Fairy Tales** has to contend with Creed's ponderous singing and the superficial synthesized chaos; occasionally the LP wins. **Superior Catholic Finger** is much better, an inspired collage of found sounds, noise, tape manipulation and overdriven punky assault, played by a trio lineup that leans towards guitar, keyboards and drums. (The diminution of vocals is duly noted and appreciated.) Gonzo and gripping.

Produced by Jack Endino, **The Last Laugh** is a heaping helping of frenzied but terse psychedelia. Creed's gothic, incantory lyrics ebb and flow much like computer-era Gregorian chants—invoking spirits of Gehenna and sundry other fearsome creatures. While some stretches (like the skulking three-part opener) are heavily processed, selections like "Nirbasion Annasion" and "Road Out of Hell" would be palatable to fans of Voivod. **Boxing the Clown** adds the machine shop drumming of ex-Scratch Acid pounder Rey Washam which, if anything, clarifies the focus of obsessive tracks like "Hyperventilation" and "Go Blind." As *Reefer Madness* warned, one puff of Creed's powerful stuff will give you the fear!

Disinterring the Chrome moniker for a series of new albums released by Dossier in the second half of the '80s was not a wise move on Edge's part; the only possible benefit is that dozens of disaffected cyberpunks might be inspired to learn the phone number of their local Better Business Bureau. In point of fact, the post-Creed Chrome LPs aren't terrible, they're simply not Chrome. Returning to the unabashed UFO (not the band)-isms of the pre-Creed **Visitation**, Edge couches his obsessions in ambient (albeit decibel-heavy) sonic cocoons. **Live in Germany** is the low point—and somewhat ironic, since the original band dissolved over Edge's refusal to tour.

Dossier has issued a number of CDs that pair up Chrome albums. **Into the Eyes of the Zombie King** is joined with Edge's first solo undertaking, **Alliance**; **Blood on the Moon** is on a disc with **Eternity**; **Half Machine Lip Moves** goes with Edge's **The Surreal Rock**; **The Lyon Concert** and **Another World** round off the selection. Meanwhile, back in the States, Touch and Go paired **Half Machine** with **Alien Soundtracks**.

[jy/i/dss]

CHURCH

Of Skin and Heart (Aus. Parlophone) 1981 (Arista)
1988 ●
The Church (Capitol) 1982 (nr/Carrere) 1985 ●
Temperature Drop in Downtown Winterland EP
(nr/Carrere) 1982
The Blurred Crusade (nr/Carrere) 1982 (Arista) 1988 ●
Sing-Songs EP (Aus. Parlophone) 1982
The Unguarded Moment EP (nr/Carrere) 1982
Seance (nr/Carrere) 1983 (Arista) 1988 ●
Persia EP (Aus. Parlophone) 1983
Remote Luxury EP (Aus. Parlophone) 1984
Remote Luxury (Warner Bros.) 1984 (Arista) 1988 ●
Heyday (Warner Bros.) 1986 (Arista) 1988 ●
Starfish (Arista) 1988 ●
Conception (nr/Carrere) 1988 ●
Hindsight (Aus. EMI) 1988 ●
Gold Afternoon Fix (Arista) 1990 ●

STEVE KILBEY

Unearthed (Enigma) 1987 ●
Earthed (Rykodisc) 1988 ●
The Slow Crack (Aus. Red Eye) 1988 (Rough Trade)
1989 ●
Transaction EP (Aus. Red Eye-Polydor) 1989
Remindlessness (Aus. Red Eye-Polydor) 1990

PETER KOPPES

Manchild & Myth (Rykodisc) 1988 ●
From the Well (TVT) 1989 ●

MARTY WILLSON-PIPER

In Reflection (Aus. Chase) 1987
Art Attack (Rykodisc) 1988 ●
Rhyme (Rykodisc) 1989 ●

At first, the Church seemed like a promising blend of the Beatles (musically) and early Bowie (vocally and lyrically). Peter Koppes and Marty Willson-Piper explored the guitar territory first mapped out by Harrison and Lennon, but in greater detail and with perhaps a more practiced—if less inspired—hand. Bassist Steve Kilbey chanted/sang articulate lyrics with a world-weary melancholy similar to early Bowie, but colder and less melodramatic.

The band's American debut, **The Church**, consists of most of **Of Skin and Heart** plus the best three songs from a subsequent double-45 release. (Arista's belated CD of **Of Skin and Heart** includes those three tracks as well.) The gorgeous guitar soundscapes and occasionally evocative verbal imagery seemed to promise bright things to come. The blatant Beatleness of "The Unguarded Moment" is so offset by its other virtues that it's easily the album's high point. Still, Kilbey's worst lyrical instincts flowered on **The Blurred Crusade**. You can add some Byrds and perhaps a touch of post-Floyd Barrett into the mix, but you can also toss in some pointless obscurity, non sequiturs and confessional windiness.

Lyrically, **Seance** is both more superficial and more straightforward, which is partly why it succeeds. At its best, the band achieves something akin to mid-'60s British pop psychedelia: nothing timeless, but a neat trip. The Church isn't as poppy here, and **Seance**'s most obviously retroid psychedelic number ("Travel by Thought") is more atmosphere than song, but stuff like "Fly" and "Dropping Names" is still a groove (man).

(But the pistol-shot snare-drum sound on much of the LP is a real bummer.)

Remote Luxury, which combines the two preceding Australian EPs, has less range than **Seance**; its shimmering folk-rock textures are hampered once again by Kilbey's overly oblique lyrics. A step sideways at best.

Well-produced by Peter Walsh, **Heyday** (which was actually recorded as an album) is another step forward: straight-ahead guitar pop housed in an ironically paisleyfied cover. Although titles like "Tristesse" and "Myrrh" suggest otherwise, Kilbey's lyrics are engagingly vague and easier to comprehend. Likewise, the melodies are stronger and catchier than any since the first album.

The production of **Starfish**, by LA session guitarists Waddy Wachtel and Danny Kortchmar, may have something to do with its shortcomings. Superficially, the LP seems pleasant but thin; look past the ziplessness, however, and you'll discover the band's most consistently engrossing and memorable tunes yet. Even Kilbey's off-the-wall lyrics seem to be better integrated and more to the point (or some point, anyway). Willson-Piper's unexpected but delightful '60s Anglo-pop-rock concoction, "Spark," is a bonus.

The double best-of **Hindsight** offers a fairly balanced selection from the various albums, but more than half of the album consists of non-LP tracks. Many of those are pretty good, though, although some lyrics still arouse the usual reservations ("ornamental or warm and gentle/on the way to paradise," indeed). Following **Starfish**'s enormous Stateside success, Arista issued the group's Australian albums and made them available on CD. (**Conception** is a ten-song compilation.)

Co-produced by the group and Wachtel, **Gold Afternoon Fix** is the most sonically pleasing Church album yet, varied but cohesive. For once, melodrama is effective, as on the opening "Pharoah." Also, Kilbey's lyrics are coherent and focused for almost the entire album, notably on the back-to-back "You're Still Beautiful" (a "walking picture of Dorian Gray" set to a strident beat) and "Disappointment" (a dreamy evocation of feeling out of phase with the rest of the world). The CD and cassette add two bonus tracks.

The Church's outside projects, at least the earlier ones, are more genuinely solo than most, with only small contributions from wives, girlfriends, brothers, etc.

Kilbey's **Unearthed** (originally an '86 Australian issue) is a mixed bag of songs (some solid, if short on polish) interlarded with brief, generally forgettable instrumentals. **Earthed** goes one better than all the other Churchmen's solo LPs: the band's prime lyricist concentrates on purely instrumental ideas, many of which would fall beyond the Church's purview, even *with* lyrics. While the worst of it sounds like intros in search of actual songs, the good stuff ranges from a sonic montage to a queer but fetching little waltz. (A 76-page booklet of poetry meant to complement the music accompanies some copies.)

The US version of **The Slow Crack** includes three tracks not included on the original Australian release, and it's a good thing too: "Transaction," the lead-off cut, is one of the most tightly focused rockers that Kilbey had done in or out of the band prior to **Gold**

Afternoon Fix. "Fireman" is enjoyable folk-rock-*cum*-wall-of-sound (guitars, synth, strings, sax). The rest of Side One is at least pleasant, but Side Two ranges from dull to dreary, even when he turns to Shakespeare for inspiration ("Ariel Sings") or the Bible for lyrics ("Song of Solomon").

The double-album **Remindlessness** (the single CD deducts two cuts) is Kilbey's best solo work to date. There's too much of it, and some tracks go on too long, but even his relative failures are more interesting than before. Lyrically, his "stories" are more to the point, but even better are his portrayals of people and situations, often enlivened by incisive lists of items ("Life's Little Luxuries," "The Amphibian"). What also makes it work are widely varied instrumental textures, which efficiently create atmospheres and moods (echoing the advances made by the group). In fact, sometimes the sound is so seductive that it doesn't matter what he's saying! And sometimes he doesn't say anything at all: several tracks are instrumentals, like the title track (a wordless progression on the big sound of "Fireman"). Well done. The **Transaction** EP contains the US **Slow Crack**'s "Transaction," a track from **Remindlessness** and two unexceptional but otherwise unreleased items.

The songs on all three Willson-Piper albums are mostly softish folk-pop—virtually no real rock—with sparse instrumentation, sometimes (on the first two) without bass or drums. In **Reflection** seems like (justifiably) unused demos, while the other two are more clearly finished. Despite a cottony airheadedness that runs through all of his albums, **Art Attack**, which is extremely self-indulgent but frequently intriguing, is easily the most varied and stimulating of the three. "You Whisper" is like Peter Frampton imitating Elvis Costello gone psychedelic ("Your marzipan skin in a crystal stare/Your chocolate box of fears"); "Word" is eight-and-a-half minutes of one-syllable words spoken over a melody vaguely reminiscent of Pachelbel's "Canon." Cleverly created mood, willful obscurity or just plain twaddle? "Evil Queen of England" offers nifty lyrical bile accompanied only by an acoustic bass. (The US cassette and CD include six tracks from **In Reflection**.)

Rhyme dispenses with experimentation to return to folk-pop as a steady ration. It's much more polished than **In Reflection** and, after a while, a bit tedious, especially since Willson-Piper's lyrics are sometimes as obscure as Kilbey's, and sometimes just inane. But four tracks do mix it up a bit musically, including bouncy, exceptionally infectious pop-rockers for fans of **Starfish**'s "Spark." Ignore the verses of "Melancholy Girl" and "Cascade," just revel in the sound.

Guitarist Peter Koppes' solo work has a strike against it straightaway: he can barely carry a tune (although he's trying). On **Manchild & Myth**, he's surrounded by other voices and buried in the mix (his monotone mumble can't cut through anyway), but that does nothing for the vocal melodies and lyrics. Worse, the LP's arrangements and production lack dynamism. The only good tracks on the album are two stylistically routine ones that are simply a cut above the rest and one atypically moody Eurosynth instrumental. (The US CD and cassette include his so-so 1987 three-track **When Reason Forbids** EP.)

From the Well, Koppes' next album, actually follows that Eurosynth direction more thoroughly, and profitably so. In fact, the whole LP is a step forward. No more burying his voice—although he's not averse to singing duets with his sweeter-voiced lady, Melodie (!)—and he no longer makes Leonard Cohen sound like Pavarotti (only just). The synth (drums and keyboard textures) plus bass and guitars often assume a dark tone, but the tunes aren't bad, and overall it's quite listenable, if a bit on the dark, moody side.   [jg]

See also *Hex*.

CICCONE YOUTH
See *Sonic Youth*.

CINECYDE
Black Vinyl Threat EP (Tremor) 1978
Positive Action EP (Tremor) 1979
I Left My Heart in Detroit City (Tremor) 1982
Who Goes There? (Tremor) 1989

Detroit has been the site of several musical generations of punk; Cinecyde emerged on the local scene there in the late '70s, gigging and releasing records (by several bands as well as compilations) on their own label. Following a sneery pair of rudimentary 7-inch EPs and some singles, **I Left My Heart** unleashes enough raw power to stun, but a superior sense of song structure, the group's skilled musicianship and non-topical lyrics prevent it from falling into the stylistic clutches of simple hardcore or heavy metal.

Keeping the rock'n'roll faith (not to mention the first album's lineup!), Cinecyde issued a long-come second album in early 1989. Now more inclined to play loud power-pop than tuneful punk, Cinecyde has tempered the pace, but not the spirit or electricity of its music. **Who Goes There?** is a welcome return from these talented and sturdy Midwest musicians. (The LP doesn't include a subsequent sign-of-the-times 45, "Burn the Crack House Down.")   [i]

CIRCLE JERKS
Group Sex (Frontier) 1980 ●
Wild in the Streets (Faulty Products) 1982 (Frontier) 1988 ●
Golden Shower of Hits (LAX) 1983 ●
Wönderful (Combat Core) 1985 ●
VI (Relativity) 1987 ●

Singer Keith Morris left Black Flag after appearing on that group's debut single ("Nervous Breakdown") and formed this popular and durable LA slam band with ex-Redd Kross guitarist Greg Hetson. First immortalized on celluloid in *The Decline of Western Civilization* punk documentary, the Circle Jerks' vinyl success (via the film soundtrack and their own releases) came later. Typically crude and undisciplined, despite occasional offbeat choices of material (**Wild in the Streets** contains a hyper remake of Jackie DeShannon's "Put a Little Love in Your Heart"), these Jerks managed to become a live success; their shows generate some of the most intense slam-dancing and stage-diving anywhere. (In 1988, Frontier remixed and reissued **Wild in the Streets**, appending **Group Sex** to the CD.)

With a joyously tasteless urinal cover photo, **Golden Shower of Hits** offers a new batch of tuneless kinetic guitar rock, built around the funnier-in-concept-than-execution "Jerks on 45" medley, which dismembers a number of well-known wimp classics, including "Along Comes Mary," "Afternoon Delight," "Having My Baby" and "Love Will Keep Us Together."

Joined by a new rhythm section, Morris and Hetson cut **Wönderful**, a tepid self-produced imitation of a punk record by a band that, while bearing a passing resemblance to the Dictators, sounds old, tired and bored. Amazingly, the identical lineup is also responsible for **VI**, a far better high-burn collection (this one *really* sounds like the Dictators) that gets off to a great start with "Beat Me Senseless" and continues from there, going so far as to strip down and speed up Creedence's "Fortunate Son" for a fun cover. After eight years, the self-aware Circle Jerks have a sharp focus; the charged-up enthusiasm is tempered by a sense of musical responsibility. Some of the songs suck but, in general, **VI** is cogent, powerful and thoughtful—punk the old-fashioned way. [rnp/i]

See also *Bad Religion, Black Flag, Red Cross.*

CIRCUS MORT
Circus Mort EP (Labor) 1981

These New Yorkers—led by future Swans founder/guitarist Michael Gira—sound like they want to back you into a corner and harangue you into a screaming fit. They're not some punks on a rampage, though—this is amphetaminized dance music with a faint European tinge and cool, discreet keyboards. As a hectoring vocalist, Gira is, under the circumstances, quite articulate. I'll be good—honest! [jg]

See also *Swans.*

CITIZEN FISH
See *Subhumans.*

GARY CLAIL
See *Tackhead.*

CLAN OF XYMOX
The Clan of Xymox (4AD-Relativity) 1985 ●
Medusa (nr/4AD) 1987 ●

XYMOX
Twist of Shadows (Wing-PolyGram) 1989 ●
Phoenix (Wing-Mercury) 1991 ●

Despite competent musicianship and complexity, this Dutch quartet's gothic dance gloom is more imitative than distinctive. On **The Clan of Xymox**, the right components are present but the record is disappointingly short on personality. Despite three alternating vocalists (deeply anguished to breathlessly fragile), jutting electric and acoustic guitars, sinewy bass and a wealth of synths, Clan of Xymox can't seem to make anything extraordinary happen, and only three songs approach memorability. What would have made a commendable EP flounders as an album.

Medusa wallows even deeper in bland Eurodisco gloom; "Michelle," a bouncy psychedelic pop tune, offers the only relief. Obviously out of place on this depressing LP, that song would serve as an excellent starting point for Xymox's future endeavors.

"Evelyn," which opens **Twist of Shadows**, lifts the murk and clattering percussion from "Michelle" to reveal an attractive mixture of piano, electronics and stilted vocals. Elsewhere, the group works to locate a functional commercial form, keeping rhythms, melodies and arrangements accessibly simple and allowing Tony Visconti to score strings for two songs. As easily endurable as this album is, Xymox—here revealed as just another lightweight electronic dance band of the post-romantic era—still lacks any compelling personality. [ag/i]

JOHN COOPER CLARKE
Où Est la Maison de Fromage? (nr/Rabid) 1978
    (nr/Receiver) 1989
Disguise in Love (nr/CBS) 1978
Walking Back to Happiness EP (nr/Epic) 1979
Snap, Crackle [&] Bop. (nr/Epic) 1980
Me and My Big Mouth (nr/Epic) 1981
Zip Style Method (nr/Epic) 1982

The first acknowledged new wave poet, Manchester's John Cooper Clarke created a genre all on his own, reciting trenchant, often hilarious poetry in a thickly accented, adenoidal voice; a deviant British precursor of rap. Looking like **Blonde on Blonde**-era Dylan (but skinnier) and suggesting a mindset lifted from Jack Kerouac or Lenny Bruce, Clarke exists with one foot in literature and the other in rock music, using both but succumbing wholly to neither. On most of his recordings, musical backing is provided by a nebulous organization known as the Invisible Girls, which—besides a nucleus of keyboardist Steve Hopkins and producer Martin Hannett—has included such name-brand players as Pete Shelley and Bill Nelson. When combined on vinyl, the two forces—Clarke as satiric commentator and the Invisible Girls as musical adventurers—make for a unique listening experience.

Où Est la Maison de Fromage?, originally released by an early Manchester independent, is a sloppy, ragged, (almost) unaccompanied, poorly recorded but enthralling hodgepodge—demos, rehearsals and recitations—of pieces that wound up on later albums. Clarke's major-league debut, **Disguise in Love**, contains such classic inventions as "(I Married a) Monster from Outer Space," "Psycle Sluts 1 & 2" and "I Don't Want to Be Nice." The collaboration between words and music works splendidly, although it should be noted that Clarke's approach doesn't vary on two tracks performed a cappella. The music leans heavily to electronics, but varies the sound with guitar and weird noises.

Walking Back to Happiness is a live recording released as a 10-inch EP on clear vinyl. For over twenty minutes, Clarke goes one-on-all against a generally appreciative but partially hostile audience, reciting, jousting, cracking deadly one-liners, dealing with hecklers and being captivating with scathing, funny numbers like "Majorca" (an attack on tourists) and "Twat." As a bonus, the EP closes with a studio track called "Gimmix."

Snap, Crackle [&] Bop. matches impressive packaging (the front cover, of the original edition at least, is a photo of a sports coat with working pocket containing a lyric book) with awesomely powerful songs like "Beasley Street," recalling nothing so much as Dylan's "Desolation Row." And while "Conditional Discharge" is a cheap pun about venereal disease, the notable "Thirty Six Hours" is Clarke's most songlike effort to date. On it, the Invisible Girls' backing matches the bard's intensity dram for dram, creating dense waves of electronics and electrics that fit the words perfectly.

Me and My Big Mouth collects Clarke's greatest non-hits, drawing equally from the three previous records, and suffices as an ideal introduction and overview.

Zip Style Method, still JCC's most recent release, finds him in a more upbeat humor, and includes a pair of love songs amidst the remorseless satire. The Invisible Girls are at their best, working in a number of idioms. More than any of the other albums, this seems to be a cooperative venture—more organically entwined than autonomous—between poet and players. That's a major development, because it makes Clarke's words stand out less, but convey more. There aren't any bad tracks; although the intensity level isn't up there with "Beasley Street," songs like "Midnight Shift," "The Day the World Stood Still" and "Night People" present different, entertaining sides to Clarke's musical persona. Clarke has continued to perform as a poet, but regrettably has not recorded anything of late.   [i]

CLASH

The Clash (nr/CBS) 1977 (Epic) 1979 ●
Give 'Em Enough Rope (Epic) 1978 ●
The Cost of Living EP (nr/CBS) 1979
London Calling (Epic) 1979 ●
Black Market Clash (Epic) 1980
Sandinista! (Epic) 1980 ●
Combat Rock (Epic) 1982 ●
Cut the Crap (Epic) 1985 ●
12" Tape EP [tape] (nr/CBS) 1986
I Fought the Law EP (nr/CBS) 1988 ●
The Story of the Clash Volume 1 (Epic) 1988 ●
Crucial Music: The Clash Collection (CBS Special
    Products-Relativity) 1989 φ
Crucial Music: 1977 Revisited (CBS Special
    Products-Relativity) 1990 φ
Return to Brixton EP [CD] (Epic) 1990 ●

TOPPER HEADON

Waking Up (nr/Mercury) 1986

HAVANA 3 A.M.

Havana 3 A.M. (IRS) 1991 φ

That the Clash survived as long as they did and, in fact, proved commercially viable in both the UK and US is a clear testament to rugged integrity and a stubborn refusal to buckle despite enormous adversity, much of it self-induced. The Clash were formed to fall apart, but it took better than seven years for the inevitable Joe Strummer-Mick Jones bust-up to finally occur.

If any rock band ever insisted on doing it their way, the Clash takes first-place honors, despite the price their nonconformity exacted. Nonetheless (or as a result), they became enormously popular, even in America, where their Top 20 chart success stands as redemptive proof of an indomitable spirit. The Clash received no small amount of criticism over the years: damned for

their integrity (or lack thereof); assailed for absorbing black musical styles; attacked for injecting politics into their songs; blamed for changing; blamed for not changing; ridiculed for having ideals; branded sell-outs, hypocrites, rockists, opportunists and worse. Through it all, the Clash consistently proved equal to the task of confounding everyone that ever followed or dealt with them, offering contradictory and inconsistent statements in classic Bob Dylan obfuscatory oratory and generally failing to act in their own self-interest.

With continuous chaos and controversy swirling around them, the Clash still managed to make some of the most brilliant, absorbing, potent and staggering rock'n'roll of all time. Alone save for Elvis Costello and the Sex Pistols, Joe Strummer, Mick Jones and Paul Simonon (plus two different drummers) stand as new wave's original and most significant trendsetters; the original Clash never made an album that isn't worth owning.

The Clash, 1977's finest LP bar none, was not issued in the US until 1979, and then in radically altered form, adding subsequent single sides (the apocalyptic, autobiographical "Complete Control," the groundbreaking reggaefied "White Man in Hammersmith Palais" and others) and deleting four original tracks, making it paradoxically fragmentary but stronger. In the album's original form, the fourteen songs explode in a scathing frenzy of venom and sardonic humor, ranging in subject from unemployment ("Career Opportunities") to the underground music scene ("Garageland") to cultural imperialism ("I'm So Bored with the U.S.A.") to rebellion ("White Riot," "London's Burning," "Hate & War"). Strummer's incomprehensible bellow exudes focused rage, while Jones' flaming guitar work both sets and supersedes the style for countless derivators who followed. Since the original album lacks a lyric sheet (the US label couldn't resist adding one), the exact words were appropriately undiscernible, but there's no missing the power of the music. A full disc of classics, including the Clash's first stab at reggae: a brilliant rendition of Junior Murvin's "Police and Thieves." (Initially, the American LP also included a bonus 45 with two numbers recorded for **The Cost of Living** EP: Jones' rocking "Gates of the West" and Strummer's Dylanesque semi-acoustic "Groovy Times." The EP's "I Fought the Law" was included on the album itself.)

The pairing of the fiercely English and (then) anti-commercial Clash with American big-shot producer Sandy Pearlman (Blue Öyster Cult, but also the Dictators) proved controversial but fruitful on **Give 'Em Enough Rope**. By exchanging the band's garageland raunch for heavily overlaid, crystal clear guitars and drums, Pearlman delivered a supercharged rock sound and Strummer and Jones came up with some of their best songs—"Safe European Home," "Tommy Gun," "English Civil War," "Stay Free" and "All the Young Punks." The band's new-found studio sophistication did nothing to blunt their power—quite the opposite, especially in terms of Topper Headon's stunningly authoritative drumming—and their defiant confidence to mix in more liberal amounts of sensitivity and cleverness only adds to the album's appeal. Jones' vocal on "Stay Free" casts him as the tenderhearted member of the band but, as a guitarist, his work throughout goes against punk's early egalitarian precepts, proudly standing up as a genuine guitar hero for the new age.

The Cost of Living EP is a small but mighty 7-inch that contains the Clash's blistering remake of "I Fought the Law," a second (and otherwise unavailable) version of "Capital Radio" and the aforementioned "Gates of the West" and "Groovy Times."

London Calling established the Clash's major-league stature, regardless of commercial considerations. The two records, produced by the legendary (and now late) Guy Stevens (Mott the Hoople), stretch over an enormously expanded musical landscape with few weak tracks. Unlike most double albums, **London Calling** needs all four sides to say its piece; while not especially coherent or conceptual, the tracks share a maturity of vision and a consistency of character. Whichever way the band turns, the record bears their unique stamp—from the anti-nuclear throb of the title track to the updated blues oldie, "Brand New Cadillac," to the bebop of "Jimmy Jazz" and the anthemic "Rudie Can't Fail." And that's just the first side! Some of the other stunners are "Death or Glory," "Koka Kola," "Lost in the Supermarket" (Jones' spotlight), "The Guns of Brixton" (a powerful reggae rumble featuring Simonon), "Spanish Bombs," "The Right Profile" (about actor Montgomery Clift—how's that for a change of pace?) and "Clampdown," collectively proof positive that the Clash would not be limited by anyone's expectations. A masterwork.

The Clash's many singles contained as much exciting music as their albums, and a lot of non-LP tracks were issued along the way. Since very few of their early 45s were even released in the US, Epic assembled an odds-and-ends collection, **Black Market Clash**—nine tracks on a 10-inch platter, subsequently reissued as a 12-inch. Tracks appended to the US release of the first album were left off here; the two records collectively fill in the non-LP gaps through 1980. Essential items like "Capital Radio One" (the original), "Armagideon Time," "The Prisoner" and "City of Dead" join interesting but less crucial tracks like covers of "Time Is Tight" and "Pressure Drop." **Black Market Clash** is a worthwhile and entertaining record, not a collection of inferior scraps.

Whatever self-restraint the Clash might once have had evaporated on **Sandinista!**, six sprawling sides (two CDs without any of the original record's inner artwork) of wildly varied styles and maddeningly uneven quality. Besides the proper songs—some of which are absolutely first-rate—there are silly (but entertaining) kiddie renditions of "Guns of Brixton" and "Career Opportunities," assorted self-indulgent toss-offs, audio experiments (the backwards "Mensforth Hill"), bizarre stylistic digressions ("Look Here" is swing jazz, "Let's Go Crazy" is mock-calypso and "The Sound of the Sinners" is ambiguous Strummer gospel), dub mixes and guest artists (toaster Mikey Dread, violinist/singer Tymon Dogg) taking center stage. You name it, it's here, with only the faintest structural outline holding the whole shebang together. Basically, **Sandinista!** unnecessarily saddles one-and-a-half great albums with an equal amount of material that ranges from disposable nonsense to endurance-defying crap.

Side One ("The Magnificent Seven," "Hitsville U.K.," "Ivan Meets G.I. Joe," "Something About En-

gland") and Side Four (Eddy Grant's "Police on My Back" given a devastating high-pressure rip, "The Call Up," "Washington Bullets") are the two strongest chunks, but there's good stuff ("Somebody Got Murdered," "Charlie Don't Surf," "Up in Heaven (Not Only Here)," "Corner Soul," Simonon's hideously sung "The Crooked Beat") strewn throughout. Overall, the wide stylistic swath is more provocative than rewarding; a better-focused album would have been much more powerful, both musically and politically.

Returning to a manageable one-disc format, **Combat Rock** found the Clash taking a new musical detour, absorbing and regurgitating American rap and funk with more conviction than ever before (**Sandinista!** contained a few test runs) and also becoming arty enough to invite poet Allen Ginsberg to appear on the record. A bizarre collection of material that seems to be diverging at a blinding rate, the dozen tracks proved extremely popular, yielding two bona fide US chart hits (the simple "Should I Stay or Should I Go?" and the danceable "Rock the Casbah"). Despite slick production possibilities (ace studio hand Glyn Johns "mixed"), the Clash sound more ragged than ever, getting dolled up only for the dance numbers like "Overpowered by Funk," which features a guest rap by Futura 2000. A perplexing but partially entertaining set of sounds from the world's most unpredictable rock band.

Although it wasn't well known at the time, the Clash had split into two musical camps. With commercial success tugging on one side, abiding fascination for "black music" on the other, and problematic idealism presenting a genuine challenge up the middle, the Clash finally rended, with Strummer and Simonon unexpectedly booting Jones out of the band. Joined by three young players, the remaining pair later toured and recorded **Cut the Crap**, ostensibly a Clash album. With one notable exception (a movingly mournful anthem, "This Is England"), **Crap** is just that, a painfully tired and hopelessly inept attempt to catch up with an elusive, fading legend. Strummer and manager Bernard Rhodes co-wrote the songs (a dead giveaway of major creative problems right there), but they needn't have bothered: Sham 69 outtakes would've been preferable to these prosaic, forgettable shouters. "We Are the Clash," indeed. Shortly after the album appeared, the lineup dissolved. Jones played with General Public in the studio during that band's formative months, and unveiled his new group, Big Audio Dynamite, to great critical acclaim, in late 1985. (The story doesn't quite end there: Strummer wound up taking a significant role in B.A.D.'s second album.)

Since then, it's been reissue time all the way. The first releases were a couple of British EPs: the cassette-only **12″ Tape** (extended mixes of "London Calling," "This Is Radio Clash," "Rock the Casbah" and three others) and the four-song **I Fought the Law** (with "City of the Dead," "Police on My Back" and "48 Hours"). The two-record **Story of the Clash** compilation followed, thankfully overlooking **Crap**'s existence. The running order is far from chronological; still, the 28-song selection, despite some notable omissions, conveys the band's diversity and depth. The only rarity is the 1977 London tube interview portion of "Capital Radio One," originally released on an early giveaway flexidisc. Overall, the remastered sound quality is fairly clear and hot, even on the old stuff; liner notes by one Albert Transom (undoubtedly Strummer) may shed little light for neophytes, but are amusing enough. Suggestions for **Volume 2**: "Hate and War," "I'm So Bored with the U.S.A.," "The Prisoner," "Jail Guitar Doors," "All the Young Punks" and "Hitsville U.K."

More recent reissues: the **Clash Collection**'s ten tracks (only one of them not on **Story**) favor songs that got American airplay ("Tommy Gun," "Train in Vain," "Clampdown," "Police and Thieves"). With no **Story** overlap, **1977 Revisited** (aka **A Collection of Rare Tracks & B-Sides**) collates the four songs deleted from the first album's belated American edition, two non-LP tracks from **The Cost of Living**, "1977" and the live "London's Burning" from the backs of early singles and two less noteworthy B-sides.

The British chart-topping success of Beats International's "Dub Be Good to Me," a dance number built around Simonon's mighty bass riff from "The Guns of Brixton," prompted the release of **Return to Brixton**: the original track plus three useless house remixes by Jeremy Healy (ex-Haysi Fantayzee).

The following year, Simonon returned to action as the leader of Havana 3 A.M., a rootsy/modern Los Angeles quartet with local new wave perennial Gary Myrick and singer Nigel Dixon, formerly of English rockabilly band Whirlwind. The band's eponymous debut album—an exceedingly clever commercial sublimation of unassailable source material (rockabilly, reggae, punk, power-pop) stripped of any edge or conviction—is clearly the work of experienced pros making something presentably adult out of what they can recall of their long-gone youth. "The Hardest Game" sounds like Squeeze on an uninspired day; "Surf in the City" is a fairly obnoxious rewrite of Elvis Costello's "This Year's Girl" as if done by a Del-Lords cover band; the Stray Catsy "Blue Gene Vincent" is one tribute the late rocker could have done without.

Topper Headon, who vanished from the Clash and the music business soon after the release of **Combat Rock**, reportedly because of drug problems (Terry Chimes—"Tory Crimes" of the first LP—replaced him for live work), launched a solo career in 1986 with **Waking Up**. Ambitious and plucky but surprisingly underwhelming, this horn-soul album is so humble his drums aren't even mixed high enough. Despite an impressive talent roster (including ex-Blockhead and frequent Clash collaborator Mickey Gallagher and ex-Beck guitarist Bobby Tench), Headon's songs are amateurish, and the arrangements routine and uninvolving; even another version of Booker T's can't-miss "Time Is Tight" doesn't hit a nerve. (Chimes went on to form the Cherry Bombz with former members of Hanoi Rocks and Toto Coelo.)

In March 1991, spurred by its use as a commercial jingle for Levi's jeans, "Should I Stay or Should I Go?" was re-released (with a Big Audio Dynamite II B-side!) and promptly topped the British singles charts, making it the long-defunct band's biggest UK hit ever. "Rock the Casbah" was also successfully reissued. [i]

See also *Big Audio Dynamite, Mikey Dread, Ellen Foley, Ian Hunter, 101ers, Joe Strummer*.

CLAWHAMMER
Poor Robert EP (Aus. Grown Up Wrong) 1989
Clawhammer (Sympathy for the Record Industry) 1990
Double Pack Whack Attack EP (Sympathy for the Record Industry) 1990

With a moniker cribbed from Captain Beefheart, you wouldn't suspect ex-Pontiac Brother guitarist Jon Wahl's new baby to mewl forth much in the way of pub-rock revivalism. And you'd be mostly right. Locked into a stupefyingly precise dada-blues/hard-rock fusion on **Poor Robert**, the quartet zooms along like a dragster doing 110 mph with cruise control (particularly on a hard-as-nails version of the Fab Four's less-than-robust "Everybody's Got Something to Hide . . .").

Unfettered by standard song structure on much of the first longplayer, Wahl's mercurial yelp skitters across measures like Richard Hell at his most dislocated. At times ("Papa's Got Us All Tied in Knots"), Clawhammer sounds like fellow Beefheart-throbs Half Japanese gone classic rock. Then again, at the end of the LP's closer, the group indulges in a spate of angular jamming that's like nothing so much as a newly unearthed Allman Brothers session. That they never actually parrot the good Captain is to their credit; that they can evoke his spirit as convincingly as on "Warm Spring Night" is nothing short of eerie.

On **Double Pack Whack Attack**, Clawhammer inflicts varied degrees of damage to Patti Smith's "Pumping," Pere Ubu's "Final Solution," Eno's "Blank Frank" and Devo's "Uncontrollable Urge." (There's talk of a cassette-only cover of the first Devo LP—in its entirety.) Definitely a band for these post-post-modern times. [dss]

CLEAN
Boodle Boodle Boodle EP (NZ Flying Nun) 1981
Great Sounds EP (NZ Flying Nun) 1982
Oddities [tape] (NZ Flying Nun) 1983
Live Dead Clean EP (NZ Flying Nun) 1986
Compilation (NZ Flying Nun) 1986 (Homestead) 1988 ●
In-a-Live EP (NZ Flying Nun) 1989
Vehicle (Flying Nun-Rough Trade) 1990 ●

GREAT UNWASHED
Clean Out of Our Minds (NZ Flying Nun) 1983
Singles (NZ Flying Nun) 1984

If all Flying Nun bands sound alike to you, don't feel bad: they're supposed to. Peter Gutteridge, for instance, began with the Clean, helped form the Chills, returned to join the Great Unwashed, then spent some time in the Alpaca Brothers and the Puddle. Clean drummer Hamish Kilgour continued on to the Great Unwashed and then formed Bailter Space (where he was joined by the formerly Unwashed Ross Humphries). Hamish also has a guitar-playing brother named David who was with him in the Clean and also involved in the Chills. The Clean's five-song **Boodle Boodle Boodle** EP was produced by Tall Dwarf Chris Knox, adding legitimacy to the sonic similarity between the two bands. The list goes on. Figuring it all out is like dissecting a family tree where every other bandmember is a Siamese twin. But if you could put all the information together to make some semblance of sense, you'd find the Clean somehow at the center of the whole story.

"Tally Ho!," a 1981 single, was Flying Nun's first

release. A fuzz-encrusted do-it-yourself slice of rough pop with deliberately unmelodic, sing-songy male vocals and scratchy lead guitar, it jangles through dramatic pace changes before ending in sparse applause. Sales funded a follow-up EP, the equally poppy **Boodle Boodle Boodle**, which was meticulously recorded on Knox's home tape recorder. Those and other early tracks are assembled on **Compilation**, where the percussively hard-strummed acoustic guitar of "Billy Two" meets the hesitantly squirmy soft psychedelia of "Point That Thing Somewhere Else" (slow-paced single-stroke drum beat and sitaresque '60s guitar lines). A thoroughly enjoyable and lighthearted festival of pop fuzz, it ranges from the silliness of a Donald Duck guest appearance through artful backward-tracking.

What it doesn't do is show how great the trio was live. **Live Dead Clean** does. From the melodically scratchy guitar dips of "Happy Birthday John" (which Hamish Kilgour describes as being "about time passing, people dying and nuclear bombs going off") through the powerfully Western-tinged "Attack of the Teddy Bears," it's a high-energy (though sometimes lo-fi) excursion into pleasantly scraped pop guitar.

The first incarnation (actually, the one that made records) of the Clean didn't last long. Their whole vinyl career was over within eighteen months. But the split with bassist Robert Scott (who wound up forming the Bats) was amicable and, since the two founding Kilgours were still brothers, they became the Great Unwashed, the name a jokey response to numerous puns that had plagued the old band in reviews. The Unwashed had (pun unintentional) a cleaner sound than the original band but still made vigorously vibrant rock with poppy chords, avant twists, fragile vocals and infectious warmth. **Clean Out of Our Minds** has a loose and friendly feel, as the Kilgours strum autoharps and guitars, bang on household items and generally croon and ramble through charming little songs of no fixed structure with a lot more genial enthusiasm than concern for details.

On 13 July 1988, Scott and the Kilgours reunited for a concert at the Fulham Greyhound in London; five tracks from it were released as the **In-a-Live** EP. A seductively slinking spin through the band's early material ("Fish," "Anything Could Happen," "Flowers," "Point That Thing Somewhere Else," "Whatever I Do Is Right"), the performances are every bit as good as the '81-'82 tracks on **Live Dead Clean**. The guitars are as warmly fuzzy as ever; the darker bass sets off the shimmering leads. But where **Live Dead** was culled from technically crude sources, **In-a-Live** has the advantage of 16-track sound.

Vehicle, a new studio album of happy harmony, both vocal and instrumental, followed a year later. Texture is what it's about. Bass contrasts against the guitar's peal-through chime; although influenced by a decade's worth of dance club bands, the crisp, hard beat never turns robotic or rhythm-boxy. The album flirts with acoustic plinking, continues the band's use of warm electric organ and emphasizes casual harmonies in the boy-next-door vocals. They ain't the Beach Boys, but in the Clean's own strange way, **Vehicle** is an excursion of cool guitar sunshine, an audio dose of endless summer. ['e]

See also *Bats, Gordons*.

CLEANERS FROM VENUS

Blow Away Your Troubles [tape] 1981
On Any Normal Monday [tape] 1982
Midnight Cleaners [tape] 1982
In the Golden Autumn [tape] 1983
Under Wartime Conditions [tape] (nr/Acid Tapes) 1984 (Ger. Modell) 1986 ●
Songs for a Fallow Land [tape] 1985
Living with Victoria Grey [tape] 1986
Going to England (nr/Ammunition Comm.) 1987
The Brotherhood of Lizards [tape] 1988
Town and Country (Ger. RCA) 1988

BROTHERHOOD OF LIZARDS

Lizardland (nr/Deltic) 1989 ●

Go ahead, call me prejudiced, but it seems that "English" and "eccentric" have more in common than just the letter e. It's easy to envision a nation of oddball limeys—encouraged by technology that lets loopy ideas flow straight onto portastudios—sequestered in their scattered rural cottages, brewing up cassette albums for the delectation of a select and similarly offbeat audience. While no match for America's national treasure, R. Stevie Moore, Martin Newell's work throughout the '80s offers a delightful diary of one man's pop obsessions.

The Cleaners from Venus—Newell (vocals, guitars, keyboards) and Lol Elliot (drums)—began issuing tapes in 1981, the fifth of which (**Under Wartime Conditions**) wound up becoming the band's first vinyl—in Germany. Rudimentary and casual, but musically substantial and indicative of anything-goes pop talent, the LP has elements of XTC, Mike Oldfield ("The Winter Palace" instrumental, which sounds like it's being played on water glasses, bears a resemblance to "Tubular Bells"), odd bits of talking and sonic ephemera and, significantly, a "Song for Syd Barrett."

Newell recorded the accomplished **Living with Victoria Grey** aided by a new collaborator (keyboardist Giles Smith); some of the songs from the tape were reworked onto the Cleaners' engaging first UK LP, **Going to England**. With wonderful Carnaby Street pop ("Living with Victoria Grey"), catchy TV kitsch ("Illya Kurayakin [sic] Looked at Me," on which Captain Sensible plays guest guitar) and delightful '60s Farfisa-beat soul ("What's Going on in Your Heart?"), the album is gently nostalgic and entirely likable.

By the time of the relaxed and rustic pure-pop **Town and Country**, the Cleaners had added a bassist (Peter Nelson) and drummer and were pursuing an explicitly XTC-oriented sound (in Beatlesque settings) with some of Newell's smartest, loveliest English-culture songs: "Let's Get Married," "The Beat Generation and Me," "Tenpenny Hill" and "I Was a Teenage Idiot Dancer." Great!

Retiring the Cleaners moniker, Newell resurfaced the following year in the Brotherhood of Lizards, a duo in which Nelson (soon to join New Model Army) plays both bass and drums. Melodic and clever without fuss, **Lizardland** (the contents of which are unrelated to the cassette entitled **The Brotherhood of Lizards**) offers another dozen unprepossessingly poetic vignettes ("Market Day," "The World Strikes One," "Love the Anglian Way," "Dear Anya") of life in these British Isles. The bubbly '60s psychedelipop of "She Dreamed

She Could Fly," the catchy chorus of "It Could Have Been Cheryl" and the Turtlesque "ba-ba-ba" refrain of "The Happening Guy" are positively brilliant; the rest of the album is merely splendid.   [i]

See also *Captain Sensible*.

JOHNNY CLEGG & SAVUKA
Third World Child (Capitol) 1987 ●
Shadow Man (EMI-Capitol) 1988 ●
Cruel, Crazy, Beautiful World (EMI-Capitol) 1989 ●

JULUKA
Scatterlings (Warner Bros.) 1982 ●
Stand Your Ground (Warner Bros.) 1985
The Best of Juluka (Rhythm Safari) 1991 φ

In a well-intentioned gesture of political unity, singer/guitarist Johnny Clegg (an English academic raised in Zimbabwe and South Africa) joined forces with Sipho Mchunu, a black South African street musician, to form Juluka, a failed experiment in combining rock with Zulu chants and the *mbaqanga* sound of the South African township. The results, heard on both of the interracial group's Warner Bros. records, are a mush of sweet, laid-back California style harmonies over a loping backbeat, with mild anti-apartheid sentiments. (The Best of Juluka, which compiles the group's American albums with a sampling from its four African-only releases, dating back to 1979, paints an incrementally more compelling image of the group.)

Clegg's subsequent band Savuka (which retains two members—not Mchunu—from Juluka) is even more Western-oriented. The slick production of Third World Child relieves it of the simple, unassuming emotionality of township music, and the selfconscious, breast-beating lyrics of the title track and "Berlin Wall" suggest that Clegg's gunning for the Nobel peace prize while attempting to forge a calculated commercial sound. Too bad Paul Simon beat him to the bank.

By Shadow Man, Clegg is starting to sound a bit like Sting, a catchy pop hybrid of synthesizers and African percussion. Attempting to join the Anglo-American mainstream without abandoning his homeland (for which his love seems genuine enough), Clegg drops Zulu phrases and instrumentation like a social climber mentioning famous names at a party. Unfortunately, he can't have it both ways, and this fusion sounds more like an American effort to sound African than vice versa.

Like many other artists, Clegg was electrified by the tumultuous political events of the late '80s. Cruel, Crazy, Beautiful World has songs of both anger and optimism, presented with a more comfortable blend of musical idioms than ever before. (Although the Sting comparison still applies.) There's nothing traditional about Savuka's sound, but the stylistic weave serves both ingredients nicely for a change, and the album finds a satisfying midpoint between disparate cultures.   [rg/i]

CLICK CLICK
Wet Skin and Curious Eye (Play It Again Sam) 1987 ●
Rorschach Testing (Play It Again Sam) 1988 ●
Bent Massive (Play It Again Sam) 1989 ●

CLICK CLICK/BORGHESIA
Doublebill (Play It Again Sam) 1987

Snarling dyspeptic lyrics over beats that can only be described as dance-oriented (though I dread to think who would actually find this stuff conducive to booty-shaking), Bedfordshire, England's Click Click falls well short of Foetusian intensity *and* lacks the subtlety to get by on cleverness. Wet Skin and Curious Eye, a boring compilation of remixed singles ("Sweet Stuff," "Skripglow," etc.), finds brothers Adrian (synths, vocals) and Derek (drums) Smith, with help from a second synthesist, drummer/engineer Alan Fisch and a guitarist, working familiar tricks of the industrial trade with modest efficiency.

Doublebill pairs a long three-song Click Click 12-inch (the transitional "I Rage I Melt," plus two more non-LP items) with a Borghesia EP (Naked Uniform Dead) on the flipside.

Dropping the heavy rhythms and exaggerated vocals, Rorschach Testing brings the trio (Smith, Smith and guitarist Graham Stronach) into the realm of accessible techno-rock, suggesting a couple of Depeche Mode/Soft Cell fans on lithium. Neither appealing nor awful, tracks like "Perfect Stranger" and "Whirlpool" display skill but no imagination at all.

One LP was evidently enough light relief for Click Click. Adrian is partially back on the growl prowl with Bent Massive, an otherwise more open-minded musical adventure. Dynamic synthesizer/guitar arrangements (with samples and surprising variety) generally leave rhythms in a subsidiary role (although not on "Moist," a mighty, ominous dance number); the tracks are less songs than sonic experiments with words. Not bad.   [i]

GEORGE CLINTON
Computer Games (Capitol) 1982
You Shouldn't-Nuf Bit Fish (Capitol) 1983
Some of My Best Jokes Are Friends (Capitol) 1985
R&B Skeletons in the Closet (Capitol) 1986
The Best of George Clinton (Capitol) 1986 ●
The Cinderella Theory (Paisley Park-Warner Bros.)
    1989 ●

GEORGE CLINTON/ PARLIAMENT-FUNKADELIC
The Mothership Connection (Live from Houston) (Capitol)
    1986

P-FUNK ALL-STARS
Urban Dancefloor Guerrillas (Uncle Jam-CBS Associated)
    1983 ●

INCORPORATED THANG BAND
Lifestyles of the Roach and Famous (Warner Bros.)
    1988 ●

This national treasure's musical concepts are so wide-ranging and generous that he's needed an entire roster of groups—creating dozens of albums—to work them out. During Clinton's '70s heyday, one of the two main exponents for his genius was Parliament (an outgrowth of the Parliaments, a doo-wop group dating back to the mid-'50s that had a 1967 hit with "(I Wanna) Testify"), which played idiosyncratic R&B with an initial emphasis on harmony vocals. Meanwhile, Funkadelic played exactly what its name implied—psychedelic funk. Clinton invented the form, and subsequent practitioners of it—from Prince to the Red Hot

Chili Peppers (whose second album Clinton produced) and beyond—are deeply in his debt.

Numerous members of the huge Parliament/Funkadelic crew have also wielded enormous influence. Having reinvented funk bass playing for James Brown in the late '60s, Bootsy Collins did it again for Clinton, and without keyboardist Bernie Worrell the lexicon of synth bass licks would be substantially thinner.

While Clinton really didn't distinguish himself as a great player or singer, his ideas (both verbal and musical) have always been audacious, uninhibited and ahead of their time. As the '70s went on, Funkadelic got deeper and deeper. The classic **One Nation Under a Groove** (1978) remains a touchstone for many musical cultures. In the meantime, Parliament got sillier and sillier, putting out albums replete with high voices and squiggly sounds. Still, P-Funk (as the whole shebang came to be known) hits—monsters like "Tear the Roof off the Sucker" (now an essential hip-hop sample) and "Flash Light"—are simply unstoppable.

Clinton closed the P-Funk umbrella in the early '80s, but continued to give up the funk under his own name. **Computer Games**' title gave the nod to the burgeoning wave of techno-funk that was beginning to overtake almost every other form of dance music; rather than reject the new technology, he adapted it here in his own unique way, resulting in the ace hit single, "Atomic Dog." **You Shouldn't-Nuf Bit Fish**'s title cut refers to the splitting of the atom—a scientific fish that shouldn't have bit, leading mankind into the terrifying age of nukes. The rest of the record is more lighthearted and dance-oriented and, like all of Clinton's records, boasts an all-star cast of funkateers, here including former Parliament vocalist Phillippe Wynne.

Clinton briefly convened the P-Funk All Stars in '83; **Urban Dancefloor Guerrillas** is a monstrous dance record pretty much defined by its single, "Generator Pump."

Some of My Best Jokes Are Friends is a likable but fairly undistinguished effort featuring guest Thomas Dolby. What results from the pairing isn't quite tension, but one does get the sense that while Clinton wanted the (then) hot Dolby for added commercial viability, Dolby would like nothing better than to be Clinton.

R&B Skeletons in the Closet has vocals by ex-Miss America (and soon-to-be-a-star-solo-singer) Vanessa Williams; here immortal phrasemaker Clinton asked the musical question "Do Fries Go with That Shake?" Otherwise, it was business as usual, with very little of the roots alluded to in the title overtly evident in the grooves.

In 1986, Capitol issued an ersatz best-of that reproduced one whole side (but not the title track) of **Fish**. Unnecessary to be sure, but if it was the only Clinton record available, you'd find it entertaining enough. **The Mothership Connection (Live in Houston)** pairs a side of vintage live P-Funk with three selections (including "Atomic Dog," which is also on **The Best Of**) from the Capitol studio LPs.

After laying low for a while (but doing theme music for *The Tracey Ullman Show*), Clinton resurfaced to co-produce the Incorporated Thang Band's **Lifestyles of the Roach and Famous** with Bootsy Collins. The following year, signed to Prince's Paisley Park label, he made the excellent (and slightly purple-tinted) **The Cin-**derella Theory**, with guest shots by such young admirers as Chuck D. and Flavor Flav of Public Enemy. (The album includes another canine-based hit, "Why Should I Dog U Out?") Various co-productions and an appearance on Prince's **Graffiti Bridge** soundtrack followed.
[gk]

CLINTS
No Place Like Home (Skyclad) 1989

This Southern California-based foursome's long-playing debut has certain commendable points, specifically Dan Matovina's dense, offbeat production and guitarist Clint Wade's strange, meandering songs ("The Grey Receiver," "Mysterious Clints"). On the downside, fellow tunesmith/guitarist Clint Ambuter's earnest, soul-searching efforts are lyrically less interesting, and some of the arrangements have a dated new-wavy quality. While the Clints, to their credit, sound like no other band, this album is less than awe-inspiring. [sm]

CLOCK DVA
White Souls in Black Suits [tape] (nr/Industrial) 1980 (It.
　Records from Around the World) 1982 + 1990
Thirst (nr/Fetish) 1981 (nr/Doublevision) 1985
Advantage (nr/Polydor) 1983 (Wax Trax!) 1990 ●
Breakdown EP (Relativity) 1983
The Hacker/The Act [CD] (Wax Trax!) 1988 ●
Buried Dreams (Wax Trax!) 1990 ●

Appearing in 1980 and allied with industrial bands like Throbbing Gristle and Cabaret Voltaire, Sheffield's Clock DVA aped the sound of British white soul groups of the day on the wholly improvised **White Souls in Black Suits**—although the mock-soul energy is strangely vitiated by urban metal noise that distorts the songs around the edges. Eerie but captivating, with a punchy beat. (Although initially available only on cassette, **White Souls** was subsequently released on Italian vinyl.)

On **Thirst**, the band maintained an interest in dance music, but abandoned soul pretensions for electro-noise, and the album is a playground of startling, unearthly machine chants. Clock DVA's initial lineup then collapsed, losing most of its members to the Box. But leader Adi Newtown pressed on with new sidemen.

Advantage is their strongest, most powerful LP, a funky concoction of intense dance-powered bass/drums drive with splatters of feedback, angst-ridden vocals by Newton, tape interruptions and dollops of white-noise sax and trumpet. The band also digresses into devolved bebop. Released as a British single from **Advantage**, "Breakdown" also formed the basis for an American EP, which added an extended remix, another great LP cut and a mesmerizing take on the Velvet Underground's "Black Angel's Death Song."

After the group dissolved again, Newton formed the Anti-Group, an industrial jazz project whose 1985 debut single was produced by Cabaret Voltaire. In 1989, he revived Clock DVA as a sample-oriented electronic tool for dramatic techno-cultural commentary. Taking cues from contemporary industrial groups but aiming much higher, both the music and the non-music on **The Hacker/The Act** are colorful and engrossing, an imaginative, dynamic and rhythmic blend of art and reality.

As opposed to the more oblique and challenging pieces ("The Hacker," "The Connection Machine") on the record, "The Act," "Re/Act" and "Re/Act 2" (three slight lyrical variations on the same track) are sung in relatively traditional fashion.

If you can survive the stifling intellectual pretensions of the package, **Buried Dreams**—an audio essay on death, fetishism and decadence—is another entertaining nightmare on wax. Both "The Act" and "The Hacker" make repeat appearances, preceded by creations ostensibly inspired by a genocidal 16th-century countess, Albert Camus and a case history from *Psychopathia Sexualis*. Regardless, the slow, moody synthesizer noises and unpleasantly treated vocals give the album a potent theatrical power.   [sg/i]

See also *Box*.

CLOSE LOBSTERS
Foxheads Stalk This Land (Fire-Enigma) 1987 ●
What Is There to Smile About EP (Fire-Enigma) 1988 ●
Headache Rhetoric (Fire-Enigma) 1989 ●

In a world overrun by samey janglepop, this Scottish quintet has managed to establish a distinctive sound by melding the aggro bounce of Britpunk's first wave with the mellower melodic strains of such groups as the Church. The band's four instrumentalists construct a dense wall of guitars and drums on which Andrew Burnett hangs his plaintive, dreamy crooning.

Foxheads is a fine introduction, an album full of sunny pogoable songs ("Sewer Pipe Dream" and the title track) and epic axe assaults (the eight-minute "Mother of God"). The succeeding EP offers a half-dozen additional tracks, showcasing an even more mature sense of melody (especially on the haunting "Let's Make Some Plans") and all-around songwriting excellence.

No news is good news on **Headache Rhetoric**, another fine record which highlights Graeme Wilmington and Tom Donnelly's full-bodied guitars and the sturdy rhythm section (Andrew's brother Bob and Stewart McFayden). The vocals still obscure the lyrics, but no matter. However you slice them, songs like "Lovely Little Swan" and "Nature Thing" stay with you long after the album has ended.   [db]

CLUB FOOT ORCHESTRA
Wild Beasts (Ralph) 1986
Kidnapped (Ralph) 1987
The Cabinet of Doctor Caligari [tape] (Ralph) 1989
Nosferatu [tape] (Ralph) 1989

In the years since the Lounge Lizards and Pigbag first made jazz a fashionable post-rock commodity, things have settled down enough that this eight-to-ten-person San Francisco horn-based ensemble can take some of its basic style from '40s swing bands without making a heavy ironic statement. (That Club Foot Orchestra records for Ralph is more emblematic of the label's changes than any fringeworthiness on the band's part.) Trombonist Richard Marriott writes jazzy modern numbers that have nothing to do with Benny Goodman or Harry James, and the group arranges them for horns, violin, drums, etc. That's about it. The results fall somewhere between Frank Zappa and the Ordinaires; a bit bland at times, but generally good, imaginative fun.

Wild Beasts is strictly instrumental and features contributions from the late Snakefinger; **Kidnapped** is dedicated to him, and has fine vocals by clarinetist Beth Custer on some tracks. The latest two tape-only releases are Marriott's original scores composed for Ralph's videocassette issues of the 1919 and 1921 German cinema classics.   [i]

CLUSTER
See *Brian Eno*.

COCKNEY REJECTS
Greatest Hits Vol. 1 (nr/EMI) 1980
Greatest Hits Vol. II (nr/EMI) 1980
Greatest Hits Vol. 3 (nr/EMI) 1981
The Power & the Glory (nr/EMI) 1981
The Wild Ones (nr/a.k.a.) 1982
Unheard Rejects (nr/Wonderful World) 1985
We Are the Firm (nr/Dojo) 1986
Live and Loud!! Bridgehouse Tapes (nr/Link) 1987

This obstreperous lot of working class kids from London's East End were discovered in the early days of post-Pistols punk by Sham 69 leader Jimmy Pursey, who co-produced their first album with Peter Wilson. The Rejects gained immortality of a sort on **Vol. II** by coining a name for UK skinhead rock with the chanted refrain of the song "Oi Oi Oi." **Vol. 3** (reasonably subtitled **Live & Loud!**) was recorded in a studio with a unnaturally vociferous audience of fans adding background vocals to the quartet's fast rock'n'roll noise. Besides songs drawn from the first two LPs ("Join the Rejects," "Bad Man," "The Greatest Cockney Rip-off," "Hate of the City"), the album includes a sloppy rendition of "Motorhead."

While retaining the aggressiveness and spunk, **The Power & the Glory** took a big chance by trying such experimental ventures as acoustic guitar, melodies, musicianship and semi-tasteful artwork. The album contains impressive moments, especially noteworthy given the Rejects' prior blitzkrieg approach. Not stunning, but their best effort, and an LP of interest not solely to punk aficionados.

Having gotten "art" out of their systems (and switching labels), the Rejects' next move (subsequently not such an uncommon gambit for punk bands) was into heavy metal. Produced by UFO bassist Pete Way, **The Wild Ones** is unfortunately terrible; although the distance from teen punk sludge to adult metal sludge is not very far, this lot was much better suited for numbers like "Greatest Cockney Ripoff."

If the sound quality were even remotely adequate, the blistering 1981 London gig retrieved from the vaults for **Live and Loud!!** would be a real humdinger. What was originally planned as the group's **Vol. 3** live album is an intense explosion of classic prole punk, flat-out renditions of the Rejects' early repertoire that are even more rousing than those cut live in the studio.   [i]

COCONUTS
See *Kid Creole and the Coconuts*.

139

COCTEAU TWINS

Garlands (nr/4AD) 1982 ●
Lullabies EP (nr/4AD) 1982
Peppermint Pig EP (nr/4AD) 1983 ●
Head Over Heels (nr/4AD) 1983 ●
Sunburst and Snowblind EP (nr/4AD) 1983 ●
Pearly-Dewdrops' Drop EP (nr/4AD) 1984
Treasure (nr/4AD) 1984 ●
Aikea-Guinea EP (nr/4AD) 1985
Treasure/Aikea-Guinea (Can. Vertigo) 1985
Tiny Dynamine EP (nr/4AD) 1985 ●
Echoes in a Shallow Bay EP (nr/4AD) 1985
Tiny Dynamine/Echoes in a Shallow Bay (nr/4AD) 1986 ●
The Pink Opaque (4AD-Relativity) 1986 ●
Victorialand (nr/4AD) 1986 ●
Love's Easy Tears EP (4AD-Relativity) 1986 ●
Blue Bell Knoll (4AD-Capitol) 1988 ●
Heaven or Las Vegas (4AD-Capitol) 1990 ●
Iceblink Luck EP (4AD-Capitol) 1990 ●
Heaven or Las Vegas EP (4AD-Capitol) 1990 ●

HAROLD BUDD/ELIZABETH FRASER/ROBIN GUTHRIE/ SIMON RAYMONDE

The Moon and the Melodies (4AD-Relativity) 1986 ●

The Cocteau Twins are actually a Scottish trio who, on their first album, add a borrowed drum synthesizer to vocals, bass and heavily treated guitar, producing atmospheric dirges with rich textures and little structure. Elizabeth Fraser's vocals are essentially tuneless, and the backing goes nowhere, but it's all artily agreeable enough for those with the patience to wade through the murk and mire. (The UK **Garlands** CD adds a 1983 John Peel radio broadcast and two previously unreleased studio tracks.)

Bassist Will Heggie then left (resurfacing in Lowlife), and Simon Raymonde joined Fraser and guitarist Robin Guthrie. **Head Over Heels** shows marked improvement, both in terms of songwriting technique and vocal performances. "Sugar Hiccup" (a different version of which appears on **Sunburst and Snowblind**) exhibits a stronger melodic sense, and Fraser's voice soars on songs like "In the Gold Dust Rush" and "Musette and Drums." The record also offers more varied tempos: the rather Bansheelike "In Our Angelhood" rocks more than anything the Cocteaus had previously done.

Sunburst and Snowblind is a strong four-song EP, well-honed for those who'd rather meet the Cocteau Twins in smaller doses. Delicate, precious yet accessible, the instrumental backing is a little thinner and the vocals more confident. **Head Over Heels** and **Sunburst and Snowblind** were issued together on CD and cassette.

Pearly-Dewdrops' Drop strips down the sound a little further; "The Spangle Maker" and the title track even forgo much of the reverb that permeates their records. By this point, the Cocteau Twins had become ubiquitous figures in the alternative record charts and a major live attraction as well. **Treasure** stands as their finest hour. It contains no black and white sounds—just intriguing shades of gray—immersing the listener in a full range of emotions, with Fraser's now-powerful voice alternately full of sorrow, joy, calm and fury. The production is meticulously detailed; increased use of keyboards and drums provides a wider range of tone colors. All ten diverse tracks work well; "Persephone" and "Ivo" are particularly noteworthy.

After **Treasure**, the Cocteaus ran a little short on new ideas. In 1985, they released three four-song EPs. **Aikea-Guinea** could pass as outtakes from previous albums, while **Tiny Dynamine** and **Echoes in a Shallow Bay** are virtually identical, in cover art as well as sound. On the following year's **Victorialand**, almost all the instrumental backing is psychedelic-tinged treated acoustic guitar. While that opens things up and gives Fraser's voice more room, the material again recalls earlier records. All of these works, if heard individually, are pleasant, effective mood music; taken as a whole, however, they're all cut from the same cloth.

The Moon and the Melodies enlists pianist/minimalist composer/Eno collaborator Harold Budd and gives him equal billing. Let's just say that the results don't exactly kick butt; the band's remaining redeeming feature, Fraser's voice, sounds noticeably uninspired on the (only) three tracks where she appears. Those familiar with the band's recent work, firmly entrenched in the dangerous realm of new age mush, will know what this one sounds like before the laser beam hits the CD.

Love's Easy Tears is four tracks of déjà vu. **The Pink Opaque**, a career-spanning compilation, was originally issued as a British CD; the vinyl version became the band's first American release. For **Blue Bell Knoll**, a 35-minute major-label debut, the band seemed content to stick with its well-defined formula of pleasant, florid aural wallpaper; the album is smoothly produced and utterly forgettable.

Whether it was Guthrie and Fraser's parenthood, Guthrie's outside production work with such groups as the Veldt and Lush or a visitation from aliens, something lit a fire under this somnolent band. Delivered at a point when the Cocteaus were veering dangerously close to self-parody, **Heaven or Las Vegas** reasserts their artistic respectability and then some. The most obvious shock is that Fraser's lyrics are in understandable English (well, at least part of the time); there are more actual *songs* here than on their past half-dozen releases combined. While the pacing isn't drastically different, energetic playing, Fraser's deeper range and new-found expressiveness, and imaginative, less florid songwriting make **Heaven or Las Vegas** the first Cocteau Twins album to climb out of the trendy-muzak bin.

Iceblink Luck showcases a catchy song (with the clearest words of any Twins single yet) from the LP and two non-album tracks, including the nearly funky "Watchlar." The **Heaven or Las Vegas** EP includes one non-album track, the ambient "Dials." [dgs/ws]

See also *Lowlife, This Mortal Coil*.

COIL

How to Destroy Angels EP (Bel. Laylah) 1984 ●
Scatology (nr/K.422-Some Bizzare) 1984 ●
The Anal Staircase EP (Some Bizzare-Relativity) 1987
Horse Rotorvator (Some Bizzare-Relativity) 1987 ●
Unreleased Themes from *Hellraiser* (nr/Solar Lodge) 1988 ●
Gold Is the Metal with the Broadest Shoulders (nr/Threshold House) 1988 ●
Unnatural History (nr/Threshold House) 1990
Love's Secret Domain (Wax Trax!) 1991 ●

140

CURRENT 93/COIL

Nightmare Culture (Bel. Laylah) 1985

Although its output has been sporadic, Coil is the most consistently excellent of the three groups formed from the dissolution of Throbbing Gristle. After TG disbanded in 1981, Peter Christopherson (keyboards, programming) worked with Genesis P-Orridge in Psychic TV, but split in 1982 to join John Balance (vocals, percussion), who was already recording under the name Coil. With frequent help from Clint (Foetus) Ruin and others, the pair exercises an obvious fascination with sonic textures and sound manipulation, and program some mean rhythms.

Scatology, the subject of which is a strange mix of fetish, fantasy and religion, finds Christopherson and Balance working with Ruin, Stephen Thrower and ex-Alternative TV guitarist Alex Fergusson. Most of the tracks are built around simple but forceful electronic percussion, with sampler and synthesizer overdubs adding a mood of spiritual despair and decaying grandeur. "The Sewage Worker's Birthday Party" uses sampled guitar feedback to create a melancholy mood piece of shocking beauty, showcasing the group's skill at audio sculpture.

With far richer production and almost none of **Scatology**'s heavy rhythms, **Horse Rotorvator** (which contains two of **The Anal Staircase**'s three cuts) is a mélange of electronic tone poems of varying textures and styles, from haunting drones to film noir jazz (complete with a Clint Ruin horn section) to quasi-Middle Eastern/African modalities. Rather than falling into the trap of making an academic exercise of the whole thing, though, Coil breathes life into the proceedings with upfront spoken/sung vocals and the use of acoustic instruments.

Composed for—but not used in—Clive Barker's 1987 horror film, **Unreleased Themes from** *Hellraiser* contains some of the best mood music recorded during the 1980s, slowly building layers of awesome creepiness. One side contains eleven short bits of incidental music, some of which are quite good, but most are too brief to leave a lasting impression.

Gold Is the Metal with the Broadest Shoulders collects outtakes and alternate versions of material from **Hellraiser**, **Horse Rotorvator**, **Scatology**, plus tracks from some of the many compilations on which Coil has appeared. While it doesn't hang together as well as the other albums, most of the eighteen tracks are well worth hearing. The versions here are often quite different—and sometimes notably better—than the originals. If nothing else, **Gold** offers an overview of Coil's history, from simplicity to sophistication.

Unnatural History assembles more ephemera from the Coil archives. The first three tracks, recorded with Boyd Rice, were originally released as one side of the **Nightmare Culture** album (shared with Current 93), and present a strange combination of noise experiments, Casio ditties and atmospherics. The collection also includes seventeen minutes of ambient gong music, designed "for the accumulation of male sexual energy," that initially appeared as a one-sided 1984 EP, **How to Destroy Angels**.

Love's Secret Domain makes some acknowledgment of related trends in modern music, with hip-hop scratching, acid house beats and other contemporary sounds thrown into the band's more characteristic ambient experiments. (The sore-thumb referent here is vintage Kraftwerk, which one track strongly resembles.) While the LP is occasionally ear-catching, Coil seems to be rather short on striking ideas and creative energy this time out, and a lot of the LP drifts by too blandly to notice. [sl/dgs/i]

See also *Psychic TV, Throbbing Gristle*.

SCOTT COLBY

See *Zoogz Rift*.

COLDCUT

What's That Noise? (nr/Ahead of Our Time-Big Life) 1989 (Tommy Boy-Reprise) 1989 ●

London DJs Matt Black and Jonathan More were at the vanguard of the British warehouse party scene, and their dissection of popular dance music into "bootleg" records full of samples made them a name on trendsetters' lips from the start. Yet had these collagists never done anything after pairing the wailing of Ofra Haza to the slinky bass riff of Eric B. & Rakim's "Paid in Full" (on a commissioned remix of that number, some of which later ended up on M/A/R/R/S' "Pump Up the Volume" and is heard in a non-vocal form on **What's That Noise?**), they'd still have an enduring place in music history.

When the duo pulled in then-unknown singer Yazz to add celebratory vocals to their dancefloor cut "Doctorin' the House," Coldcut hit on a winning formula and became major instigators of the acid house scene. A Top 10 British hit in early 1988 and a classic of its time, the song didn't make it onto the US version of the duo's debut album (it had previously been issued Stateside on a different label); the improvement in the US release is the addition of Queen Latifah's vocals to "Smoke Dis One." If Coldcut should be noted for anything, it's their impeccable taste in singers: Junior Reid ("Stop This Crazy Thing"), Lisa Stansfield ("People Hold On") and Mark E. Smith ("(I'm) In Deep") of the Fall, who then proceeded to cover the album's "My Telephone" as "Telephone Thing." In between the vocal tracks are various "Beats & Pieces," as one title has it: samples, melodies and grooves that help flesh out **What's That Noise?**, a patchy but generally rewarding debut. [tf/gk]

JUDE COLE

See *Records*.

LLOYD COLE AND THE COMMOTIONS

Rattlesnakes (Geffen) 1984 (Capitol) 1988 ●
Easy Pieces (Geffen) 1985 (Capitol) 1988 ●
Mainstream (nr/Polydor) 1987 (Capitol) 1987 ●
1984–1989 (Capitol) 1989 ●

LLOYD COLE

Lloyd Cole (Capitol) 1990 ●

Bursting with promise as both singer and writer on his first LP, Scotland's Lloyd Cole puts the post-beatnik lyrical outlook of a young Bob Dylan to textured backing. **Rattlesnakes'** strength lies in Cole's well-constructed folk-rock tunes and casually emotive vocals; the four Commotions make a tight, talented unit capable of subtlety and power in many voices. Cole's prose occasionally overreaches (but never by much); lyrics that hit their mark do so sharply. Those hypersensitive to creeping Dylanitis will find **Rattlesnakes** a bit hard to accept; openminded adventurers will be immediately engrossed.

Easy Pieces, smoothly produced by Langer/Winstanley, succumbs to hazards threatened on the first LP. While the solid band remains unprepossessing, Cole's vocals are overly stylized; quoting Bolan and the Beatles, his lyrics veer towards meaningless self-importance. Given that it's not strikingly different from **Rattlesnakes**, **Easy Pieces** makes you wonder why you liked the band in the first place. (The CD has three extra tracks.)

Cole regained his footing and momentum on **Mainstream**: factoring in maturity and experience (his and the band's), it actually winds up a better album than the first. Subtly cast and deftly played arrangements that range from Aztec Camera airiness to fleshed-out light rock keep songs like "Sean Penn Blues" and "Mister Malcontent" from drifting into ponderousness; Cole's affecting singing is likewise finely wrought. The shimmering "From the Hip" and "Hey Rusty," an ace song that builds tension slowly, are highlights of this welcome return.

Moving to New York without the Commotions, Cole put the band concept in his past with **1984–1989**. The compilation contains four cuts from each of the three albums plus a couple of non-LP B-sides—a decent retrospective, but it would have been better to pick the best songs overall rather than give each record equal representation.

For his solo debut, Cole reunited with Commotion keyboardist Blair Cowan (who'd left after **Mainstream**, and thus didn't miss any of Cole's recordings) and hooked up with Bob Quine and Fred Maher, early '80s cohorts of another major Cole influence, Lou Reed. (The album's bassist is Matthew Sweet.) Though there's no great stylistic difference between **Lloyd Cole** and his Commotions work, Maher's way with a groove helps Cole to swing just a bit freer than before, making this his warmest, most personal and confident outing to date.

Bloomsday, a band formed by two ex-Commotions—guitarist Neil Clark and drummer Stephen Irvine—surfaced in 1990.   [i/ds]

EDWYN COLLINS
See *Orange Juice*.

HENRIETTA COLLINS AND THE WIFEBEATING CHILDHATERS
See *Henry Rollins*.

NICOLAS COLLINS
See *Band of Susans*.

PAUL COLLINS' BEAT
See *Beat*.

CHRISTINE COLLISTER
See *Clive Gregson*.

COLORBLIND JAMES EXPERIENCE
The Colorblind James Experience (Earring) 1987 (Fundamental) 1987 •
Why Should I Stand Up? (nr/Death Valley-Cooking Vinyl) 1989 (Death Valley-Cooking Vinyl-Gold Castle) 1990 •
The Peel Sessions EP (nr/Strange Fruit) 1989 •

COLORBLIND JAMES AND THE DEATH VALLEY BOYS
Strange Sounds from the Basement (nr/Death Valley-Cooking Vinyl) 1990

The Colorblind James Experience sounds like a polka band on an acid trip, which is to say that this wild bunch from Rochester, New York isn't like too many other bands in your record collection. But how to describe them . . . The Jazz Butcher meets Guy Clark? Robyn Hitchcock falls Asleep at the Wheel? Or maybe as the group that picked up where the Bonzo Dog Band's "Rhinocratic Oaths" left off? How about just saying they're unique, silly, surreal and wonderful.

On the self-titled debut, the Experience is a quartet led by the estimable Mr. James, who sings, talks and plays a mean vibraphone (and some guitar to boot). The album pretty much lays the groundwork for everything to come, as Colorblind delivers his story-songs over repetitious-but-very-sprightly figures, containing hints of country, blues, lounge jazz, polka and Tex-Mex in assorted permutations and combinations. The whole enterprise reaches its pinnacle on "Considering a Move to Memphis," wherein James ponders the consequences of relocation ("I'm considering a move to Memphis/That's Memphis, Tennessee/It worked for Elvis Presley/Why can't it work for me?"). "Dance Critters" and "Gravel Roads" explore the group's country side, while other numbers concern a visit by some German girls, camel walking, an inept circus attendant and more.

With the addition of two horn players, the Experience expanded to six pieces on **Why Should I Stand Up?**, but the general formula remains the same. If anything, the album is a little more country flavored than its predecessor, but there's also plenty of polka and even some rock'n'roll. (Though not on a song called "Rockin' as Fast as I Can," about James' confrontation with angry fans shouting "Let's Rock!" at him.) Once again, it's the twisted songs that'll get ya.

The Peel session, recorded in '88, features two songs from **Why Should I Stand Up?** and a couple of non-album tracks. Easy to skip.

Strange Sounds from the Basement finds Colorblind and crew (now dubbed the Death Valley Boys, even though the only personnel change from the last Experience album is one trombonist) delving further into the country side of things, and relying more on traditional verse-chorus song structures than on ad infinitum repetition. Fortunately, the wit and bizarre subject matter remain unchanged.   [ds]

COLOR ME GONE

See *Marti Jones*.

COLOURBOX

Colourbox EP (nr/4AD) 1983 ●
Colourbox (nr/4AD) 1985 ●

Although this London trio's music is not particularly avant-garde, the group does fit in with the uncompromising 4AD family due to their steadfast determination to totally redefine a musical style. Instrumentalists Martyn and brother Steven Young, along with vocalist Lorita Grahame, take soul places it's never been—and is unlikely to go again.

The eponymous EP—three hours of sessions edited down to a half-hour of hip-hop/scratch and reggae/dub experiments, with a graphic depiction of horses mating on the cover—largely earned its negative reception. The **Colourbox** LP, however, is a vast improvement, an eclectic display that embraces the entire realm of dance music: reggae, vibrant industrial, hard'n'heavy funk, '50s R&B. Screeching guitar on the near-metal "Maniac" segues into the highlight, a sparkling remake of the Supremes' "You Keep Me Hanging On." (The cassette of **Colourbox** is double-length, adding an LP's worth of remixes; initial quantities of the LP contained the same on a bonus disc.)

Other than the occasional one-off single, Colourbox remained unexpectedly dormant following the release of its LP. However, Steven and Martyn did achieve notoriety in 1987 due to their role in M/A/R/R/S (the "S" for Steven and the "M" for Martyn; the A and R come from the two members of A R Kane), the studio concoction responsible for the massively influential club smash "Pump Up the Volume." [ag]

COLOUR FIELD

Virgins and Philistines (Chrysalis) 1985 ●
The Colour Field EP (Chrysalis) 1986
Deception (Chrysalis) 1987 ●

TERRY, BLAIR AND ANOUCHKA

Ultra Modern Nursery Rhymes (nr/Chrysalis) 1989 ●

Vocalist Terry Hall's post-Fun Boy Three band started out slowly, with just an eponymous single in 1984. But the trio's first album a year later was well worth the wait. **Virgins and Philistines** kicks off brilliantly with the mock-"96 Tears" organ intro to "Can't Get Enough of You Baby," itself a fine imitation of Georgie Fame-era beat music. The music mixes its metaphors, from stripped-down Fun Boys rock to samba, folk and jazzy '60s R&B; Hall's sharp tongue and the band's intelligent creativity make each track different. Of special note: a shimmering acoustic version of the Roches' "Hammond Song" and "Pushing Up Daisies," a vicious condemnation of celebrity. Drama, beauty, ideas and energy make **Virgins and Philistines** provocative, stylish and memorable.

The EP—unveiling an expanded four-piece lineup—contains a pair of live cuts ("Pushing Up Daisies" and "Yours Sincerely") plus four excellent new tracks, including the memorable "Faint Hearts," an almost psychedelic folk tune, and "Things Could Be Beautiful," a soulful rocker.

Hall is the only person pictured on the disappointing **Deception**, a subdued and mechanical-sounding LP that employs a guest drum programmer, a keyboard player and Tears for Fears guitarist Roland Orzabal. Producer Richard Gottehrer misplaces the resonant stylistic variety and energy that previously typified the group, leaving pale jazzy support—occasionally resembling a less constipated Dream Academy—for Hall's characteristically wispy singing. The material ("Badlands," "Confession," Boyce/Hart's "She") isn't bad, but the facile arrangements leave Hall moaning up the wrong tree.

Ultra Modern Nursery Rhymes—the first album by Hall's new trio with Blair Booth (vocals/keyboards) and Anouchka Groce (guitar/vocals)—drapes his usual lyrical dyspepsia in superficially simple light pop music that's too subtle for its own good. While several songs recall the Fun Boys' old partnership with Bananarama (minus the rhythmic intensity), there are fewer echoes of Hall's subsequent adventures: the faint accents here are Dixieland, swing and Latin. Booth, who shares songwriting and lead vocals, is a versatile, sympathetic collaborator, but the album is a bit down-the-middle dull, lacking any strong stylistic personality. After years of making music neck-deep in atmosphere, Hall isn't served well by such understatement; as pleasant as these tunes are, none of them has the memorable mettle of his best. [i]

See also *Fun Boy Three, Specials*.

SHAWN COLVIN

Live Tape [tape] 1988
Steady On (Columbia) 1989 ●

The career of this South Dakota-born New Yorker offers an object lesson in the danger of major labels. Colvin's eight-song **Live Tape**, recorded in Massachusetts in 1988, is as enchanting a collection of acoustic songs as one could imagine. Accompanying her extraordinary pipes with just a guitar, Colvin hurls herself into folky material with an utterly distinctive, jazzy voice that flutters and swoops in a most affecting way. And aside from occasional forays into the Joni Mitchell/Suzanne Vega school of precious, self-indulgent lyrics, each of these eight songs is hauntingly, simply beautiful.

So what happened? Featuring new versions of six **Live Tape** songs, **Steady On** is bland, overproduced, radio-ready drivel. Vega producer Steve Addabbo and John Leventhal (Colvin's songwriting partner and guitarist) layer on schlocky session playing and synthesizers to the point where the individuality of Colvin's voice and songs is all but lost.

Colvin sang backup on "Luka," and Vega returns the favor here. It's ironic that while Colvin has more vocal range and expressiveness, not to mention melodic imagination, than Vega, **Steady On** attempts to emulate her. It's also worth noting that "Another Long One," the one track Colvin produced by herself, is the album's sparest and most moving moment. [ws]

COMATEENS

Comateens (Cachalot) 1981
Pictures on a String (Virgin-Mercury) 1983
Deal with It (Virgin-Mercury) 1984

This New York trio played a bouncy brand of dance rock rooted in chintzy '60s Farfisa organ pop and spooky horror-movie soundtrack music. The group first gained recognition in 1979 with a homemade single that featured a stripped-down version of Bowie's "TVC 15," which they re-recorded for their first LP. After a number of personnel changes, the lineup solidified at Lyn Byrd (keyboards), Oliver North (guitar, not international subterfuge), Nic North (bass) and synthetic drums. **Comateens** is a delightful distillation of the aforementioned influences, with neat contrasts between the thin-sounding synth fills and the chunky, rhythmic guitar. There's also a three-track 12-inch—on the same label—of the hypnotic "Ghosts," the pure pop "Late Night City" and the theme for TV's *The Munsters*, which pretty much sums up the Comateens' music.

Signed to a major label, the Comateens made **Pictures on a String**, which diverges into rock quirkiness and danceable commercialism, pushing a powerful disco beat on "Get off My Case," "Cinnamon" and other numbers. The rock-oriented material, especially the Beatlesque "Comateens," with its awesome fuzz-blizzard guitar solo, and a weird overdrive cover of the oldie "Uptown," are more intriguing; the dance tracks don't really go anywhere.

With a guest drummer and veteran hitmaker Pete Solley producing, **Deal with It** sublimates the big beat into various styles, much the way Blondie often did. Rather than base tunes on rhythms, these songs explore widely differing pop modes, welded to strong, emphasized drum tracks, resulting in a fascinating mix full of unexpected, delightful juxtapositions. This is the album that finally and fully realizes the Comateens' hybridizing potential.

After Oliver North's death in 1987, Nic North and Lyn Byrd continued to work together, recording for French Virgin under the name of West & Byrd. [ds/i]

COMMUNARDS
Communards (London-MCA) 1986 ●
Red (London-MCA) 1987 ●
JIMMY SOMERVILLE
Read My Lips (nr/London) 1989 (London) 1990 ●
The Singles Collection 1984/1990 (nr/London) 1990 (London) 1991 ●

When Scottish-born falsetto vocalist Jimmy Somerville split from Bronski Beat in 1985 and formed the Communards with classically trained pianist Richard Coles, many assumed the new group would take an even more determined political stance than the Bronskis' gay activism. Indeed, the pair participates in the Socialist Red Wedge movement but, graphics aside, you'd never know it from their records.

The first track on **Communards** is an over-the-top hi-NRG remake of "Don't Leave Me This Way," Thelma Houston's 1977 hit; the remainder mixes boring dance music with overly precious arrangements (strings, horns and the orchestral kitchen sink in spots) of songs that occasionally lean towards light opera. Except for those whose homophobia intrudes, the lyrics about sex and romance are merely tired and trivial. Worse, the group's best asset is squandered: Somerville's inimitable voice is totally unsuited for this halfbaked material. (The CD adds a song and a remix.)

Endorsing disco's ongoing commercial viability, the duo did a breathless version of "Never Can Say Goodbye" (following Gloria Gaynor's interpretation, not the Jacksons) on **Red**, a thoughtful, melodic album that is as likable as the first is cloying. Stephen Hague's keyboard-oriented Eurodance production (half of the record; Somerville and Coles did the rest) is more conducive to the much improved material, trimming the rococo excess for a slicker, more appealing sound.

By the end of 1987, the format-happy duo had issued 34 discrete singles and EPs. The deluge persevered until Somerville quit to go solo.

While reasserting his outspoken social and political stance, Somerville's first solo album maintains the non-stop modern dance momentum with catchy percolating hi-NRG grooves (played and produced by a variety of collaborators, including Hague and Steve Parr) over which he engagingly delivers romantic lyrics of love and loss. (The album also includes a version of Sylvester's "You Make Me Feel (Mighty Real)" and a French number which Somerville does twice.) The anthemic and catchy "Read My Lips (Enough Is Enough)" specifically addresses the fight against AIDS; "And You Never Thought That This Could Happen to You" artfully makes a gay-rights statement. Using the combined power of dance and pop to argue for rational behavior could be nightmarish, but Somerville pulls it off with amazing skill.

Covering all three phases (and four albums) of Somerville's career to date, **The Singles Collection** begins with "Smalltown Boy" and ends with "Read My Lips," sandwiching fifteen tracks by the Bronskis, Communards and JS solo in between. The only non-LP tune is a lovely soul-reggae cover of the Bee Gees' "To Love Somebody." [i]

COMPTON'S MOST WANTED
It's a Compton Thang! (Orpheus) 1990 ●

This interracial quartet (two rappers, two writer/producers) from NWA's 'hood runs its low-key cold gangster raps (available in both explicit and expurgated editions) in a relentless stream of B-boy slang over swaying funky soul grooves. Beyond the high quality of the beats, **It's a Compton Thang!** seems like the over-anxious work of kid brothers trying to catch up with the big boys. CMW are a talented crew (check the kitchen sink production of the intense "I Give Up Nuthin"), but if they weren't trying so hard to prove how cool they feel, they might find out just how cool they are. [i]

COMSAT ANGELS
Red Planet EP (nr/Junta) 1979
Waiting for a Miracle (nr/Polydor) 1980
Eye of the Lens EP (nr/Polydor) 1981
Sleep No More (nr/Polydor) 1981
Fiction (nr/Polydor) 1982
Land (Jive) 1983
Independence Day EP (nr/Jive) 1984
Enz (nr/Polydor) 1984
7 Day Weekend (Jive) 1985
Chasing Shadows (Island) 1987 ●
DREAM COMMAND
Fire on the Moon (Island) 1990

Like Joy Division and the Cure, Sheffield's Comsat Angels mastered the art of atmospherics; only nominally involved in rock'n'roll at the outset, they were actually interested in creating haunting mood music. Firm beats play against melancholy melodies and hushed vocals to create the impression of eavesdropping on someone's inner turmoil, an approach which is morosely fascinating on **Waiting for a Miracle** (hailed in one UK paper as the greatest debut LP of all time, it remains a stunning masterwork) and tunes like "Total War" and "Independence Day" (both included live on the 1984 EP).

The **Eye of the Lens** 12-inch consists of four non-LP cuts (one later re-recorded for **Sleep No More**; the other three compiled on the **Enz** collection) highlighted by the surprisingly straight driving title track, one of the heaviest recordings of the group's career. The rest are dark, smoky and blood-curdling, a prelude to the second album. The Comsats at their best.

Sleep No More is a tightly wound hotbed of tension, frayed edges, shattered nerves and spilled coffee. Although criticized for its bleakness, its dark and disturbing tone, this is a fascinating, underrated and often misunderstood work, ambitious rather than accommodating or immediately accessible.

On the quartet's next album, **Fiction**, an unsettling sense of tension underlies Stephen Fellows' dejected vocals and guitar on "Ju-Ju Money" and "Zinger." However, even this artistic success raises questions about how much longer the band could prosper working in such a seemingly uncommercial style.

They did attempt to expand, trying their hand in the synth-pop market, a radical departure. Switching labels and getting their first American release, the Comsat Angels were forced to use the name C.S. Angels for the US. **Land**, produced by Mike Howlett, fails in an effort to cast them as a variant on A Flock of Seagulls, but it does contain a number of upbeat, memorable tunes that resemble a poppier, less serious Simple Minds. The subsequent EP takes two good songs off the LP and adds three early tracks; **Enz** is a compilation of pre-Jive releases.

The liner notes on the back cover of **7 Day Weekend** are downright sad ("We had a stretch of good luck, which rapidly turned into bad . . ."); the music fortunately is more self-assured and dignified. Produced variously by the totally dissimilar James Mtume, Chris Tsangarides and Mike Howlett, there is scant sonic continuity, but that causes overall little damage.

Dissatisfied with their musical progress, the Comsats retrenched, switched labels (Island signed them on the advice of singer Robert Palmer) and totally abandoned their four-year synth-pop experiment. **Chasing Shadows** picks up where **Fiction** left off (in fact, the group has called it their fourth LP), with the return of thudding drums, booming bass and echo guitar, while mixing in some of the poppier melodies of the better tracks on **Land** and **7 Day Weekend**. If not nearly as impressive as the early LPs, it's still a strong record with a few choice cuts, the best being "Under the Influence."

Finally tiring of the name game, Comsat Angels became Dream Command in '89. Unfortunately, the first album released under this new moniker is something of a dud. While the band's songwriting touch is still evident on "Venus Hunter," "Reach for Me," "Whirlwind" and "Phantom Power," the record is drowned in glossy production, a soul-sapping sound unheard even during the group's mid-'80s work. [jy/jr]

CONCRETE BLONDE
Concrete Blonde (IRS) 1987 ●
Free (IRS) 1989 ●
Bloodletting (IRS) 1990 φ

DREAM 6
Dream 6 EP (Happy Hermit) 1983

Earle and Jim Mankey were, respectively, the original guitarist and bassist in Halfnelson/Sparks. When the band's other pair of brothers left for England without them, Earle wasted no time in becoming a well-known record producer. It took Jim a lot longer to re-enter the spotlight, but Concrete Blonde proved, at least commercially, to be worth the wait.

Jim's collaboration with singer/bassist Johnette Napolitano began in Dream 6, whose six-song 12-inch EP (co-produced by Earle) is an intriguing, unassuming item. Using the same organizational chart as the Police, Dream 6 draws on various styles, offering little personality besides the vocals, which are plain but pleasant.

Replacing drummer Micheal Murphy with Harry Rushakoff, Dream 6 became Concrete Blonde and released a terrible album that sounds like half-finished demos no one with ears would give a second listen. Napolitano's untrained voice is remarkably unattractive (especially when she tries too hard to ape Chrissie Hynde); the guitar work (Mankey and Napolitano) imitates everyone from Mark Knopfler to Andy Summers on duff songs that thrust along with neither focus nor flair. Even George Harrison's "Beware of Darkness" is left for dead in a pointless cover version.

Expanding to a quartet, Concrete Blonde—well on its way to becoming Napolitano's showcase—made the better-sounding **Free**, a loud, textured rock record with clunky drumming and occasionally overzealous singing. The weak material seems to spring from a late-'60s ex-hippie sensibility, an impression that isn't discouraged by the Phil Lynott cover ("It's Only Money"), the 1970 Leon Russell quote reproduced on the inner sleeve or the run-off grooves' yippie exhortations. The two songs that stand out are the sweet and catchy "Happy Birthday" and the grave stylistic miscalculation of "Roses Grow," a bizarre, inept stab at rap.

The third incarnation of Concrete Blonde finds Napolitano (now taking sole songwriting credit) and Mankey joined only by ex-Roxy Music drummer Paul Thompson. Erstwhile metal producer Chris Tsangarides makes a tentative attempt to move the group towards mainstream rock on **Bloodletting**, roughing up and punching up the sound a bit, adding instrumental and vocal layers without appreciably raising the band's volume. But the songs—almost all of which are about a recently failed relationship—haven't got the melodic content to hold the charge. The closest this record comes to Top 40 power is "Joey," a Heart-like ballad that rewrites "Love Hurts" with some really heinous lyrics. [i]

See also *Sparks*.

CONCRETE BULLETPROOF INVISIBLE

See *Doll by Doll*.

CONFLICT

Live at the Centro Iberico EP (nr/Xntrix) 1982
(nr/Mortarhate) 1984
It's Time to See Who's Who (nr/Corpus Christi) 1983
To a Nation of Animal Lovers EP (nr/Corpus Christi) 1983
The Serenade Is Dead EP (nr/Mortarhate) 1984
Increase the Pressure (nr/Mortarhate) 1984
The Ungovernable Force (nr/Mortarhate) 1986
Only Stupid Bastards Help EMI (nr/New Army) 1986
Turning Rebellion into Money (Mortarhate-Rough Trade) 1987
The Final Conflict (nr/Mortarhate) 1989
Standard Issue 82-87 (nr/Mortarhate) 1989
Against All Odds (nr/Mortarhate) 1989

I'm not sure what to think about the music of a band that informs me that "three members are vegetarians" and then tattles on the one—Paco—who isn't. The sleeve of the second album by these Crass-family Anglo-anarchists (Steve Ignorant, who became, along with mainman Colin Jerwood, one of Conflict's three simultaneous lead vocalists, was a founding member of Crass) also notes that the band "still wear articles of leather" but they've gotten down to "just boots," which "they will continue to wear until they are useless" but "will not buy more." I certainly respect people with a highly developed and self-disciplined political consciousness, but I can't shake the feeling that a record album should do more than announce how deep the musicians' commitment runs. In the real/rock world, only the young and the gullible expect their favorite bands to abide by lofty personal standards.

That aside, Conflict (not to be confused with an Arizona band of the same name which recorded for Placebo) is a pretty good political punk band, powered by fire and intelligence. **It's Time to See Who's Who** has incredibly ornate artwork and songs about media, Vietnam, vegetarianism (Smiths fans should note Conflict's "Meat Means Murder" here) and related issues. **Increase the Pressure** is a more proletarian production with black and white artwork; the LP itself is half-studio (dynamic) and half-live (raucous). This time out, the prominent issue illustrated on the graphics is Save the Seals; songs attack cruise missiles, the music press, the police, etc. with undiminished zeal and venom.

The Ungovernable Force, a self-descriptive slogan Conflict has repeated on subsequent releases, uses news reports, riot noises and spoken-word ingredients (as well as a musical quote from "Anarchy in the UK") in its relentless attack on Thatcher's England and its equally stubborn support of the Animal Liberation Front. Blistering.

The double-live **Turning Rebellion into Money** was recorded in April 1987 at a London show known as the "Gathering of the 5,000"; the back cover enumerates the progressive organizations sharing—as per the title's promise—the proceeds. The 32 artless punk tunes, a veritable best-of-Conflict collection, bark out with righteous guitar-and-sax rage at every topic imaginable, from specific events to assorted socio-economic-political issues. **Only Stupid Bastards Help EMI** is another live record.

Muddy sound and a horn player are the two distinguishing characteristics of **The Final Conflict**, a well-played but poorly recorded ten-track collection that looks inward, offering lyrics about the band: "I Heard a Rumour" repeats absurd gossip about Conflict's integrity, replying "Drop it/forget it/you've got it fucking wrong." (**The Final Conflict** cassette is backed with **The Ungovernable Force**.)

In mid-'89, Conflict issued two simultaneous albums. **Standard Issue** is an annotated compilation of album tracks and rare singles, including "Conflict," from the group's 1982 debut, and three powerful mid-tempo tracks from **The Serenade Is Dead**, a 1984 EP that actually reached the British pop charts. (The **Standard Issue** cassette is backed with **Increase the Pressure**.) One side of the other record, **Against All Odds**, is given over to the extended titular piece, which begins with a chilling machine-guns-and-choir introduction and then continues into familiar speed-guitar raunch, only to turn quiet and slow halfway through. The remainder of the album is equally unpredictable, with somewhat more accessible songs that have actual melodies, electronic keyboards and sound effects. [i]

CONNELLS

Darker Days (Black Park) 1986 (Black Park-TVT) 1987 ●
Boylan Heights (TVT) 1987 ●
Fun & Games (TVT) 1989 ●
One Simple Word (TVT) 1990 ●

This North Carolina combo, led by guitarist/songwriter Mike Connell and his bassist brother David, possesses a fragile, vaguely Celtic melodic sense that nicely complements the introspective lyrics, making for music that combines the best impulses of Southern guitar jangle and the sensitive singer-songwriter tradition.

Darker Days broods a bit too intently, and suffers from Doug MacMillan's awkward, affected vocals. The band sounds too inexperienced to properly execute their sophisticated songwriting and arranging ideas, but enough obvious talent shines through to make the album a standout in the new-Southern-pop sweepstakes.

The Mitch Easter-produced **Boylan Heights** is altogether more graceful, as the band has matured into a distinctive enough unit to do justice to Michael's yearning collegiate considerations of love, war and alienation. MacMillan's vocals are likewise substantially more effective, lending emotional authority to swirling folk-rockers like "Scotty's Lament" and "Try," as well as fragile specters like "Pawns" and "Choose a Side."

On **Fun & Games**, producer Gary Smith gives the band a slightly harder-edged sound, to the benefit of such Mike Connell compositions as "Something to Say," "Upside Down" and "Hey Wow," whose intermittent lyrical preciousness is mitigated by their melodic invention. Five tunes written and sung by guitarist George Huntley, while stylistically compatible with the rest of the group's material, are much less satisfying.

England's Hugh Jones, who took over the production reins on **One Simple Word**, is apparently the arbiter the Connells have always needed, as this is the band's tightest, catchiest and least wimpy effort to date. The guitars ring out more distinctively than ever, Mac-Millan's singing is more confident, and the best songs—"Stone Cold Yesterday," "Get a Gun," the title track—are the strongest that the group has recorded. Even Huntley's contributions ("The Joke" and "What Do You Want?") are superior. [hd]

CHRIS CONNELLY
See *Revolting Cocks*.

CONTORTIONS
See *James Chance*.

CONTROLLED BLEEDING
Wall of China Love Letter EP (Souptime) 1979
Knees and Bones (Swed. Psychout) 1983
Body Samples (Ger. Dossier) 1984
Between Tides (Swed. Multimood) 1985
Head Crack (nr/Sterile) 1986
Curd (Ger. Dossier) 1986
Core (Subterranean) 1987
Songs from the Drain (Ger. Dossier) 1988
Music from the Scourging Ground (Bel. Play It Again Sam) 1988
Songs from the Grinding Wall EP (Wax Trax!) 1989 ●
Songs from the Ashes (C'est la Mort) 1989 ɸ
Les Nouvelles Mistiques de Chambre (Bel. Sub Rosa) 1989
Trudge (Wax Trax!) 1990 ●
Controlled Bleeding [CD] (nr/Kunst=Kapital) 1989 ●
Hog Floor (Subterranean) 1991 ●

JOINED AT THE HEAD
Joined at the Head EP (Wax Trax!) 1990
One of the earliest and most prolific industrial noise bands, Controlled Bleeding—generally a trio led by multi-instrumentalist/singer Paul Lemos, who also teaches high school English—first existed in Boston in the mid-'70s but was reconvened in the New York City suburb of Massapequa, Long Island and began releasing cassettes of remarkable audio brutality around the turn of the decade. (The debut 7-inch, by an otherwise un-recorded incarnation of Controlled Bleeding, is in an entirely different vein; there's also a 1979 live-at-CBGB album by Body Sink, which was another early version of the band.) Since **Knees and Bones** (generally de-scribed as abrasive, aggressive and amateurish), Lemos has never looked back.

He has, however, looked sideways a few times. Af-ter several LPs of unmitigated aggression, the group began (around **Between Tides**) to explore quieter forms of atmosphere; by the point of their first domestic LP, the nearly vocal-less **Core**, the trio (Lemos, drummer Joe Papa and keyboardist Chris Moriarty) had devel-oped into a sophisticated and intriguingly accessible out-fit, capable of mixing semi-classical and semi-jazzy instrumentals with sepulchral pseudo-operatics and driv-ing rock dynamism.

Despite this positive new direction, Controlled Bleeding didn't lose its taste for industrial noise, as demonstrated by "Crack the Body," the first of four **Songs from the Grinding Wall**. But that's only one facet of the EP, a mixed platter of considerable stylistic depth.

Leaving behind **Core**'s ambient expeditions, **Trudge** is nonetheless diverse and extraordinarily en-tertaining, with substantial melodies and arrangements that are strong but rarely hyper-intense. The album cov-ers a lot of ground: except for the typical profanity-laced lyrics about killing women and crushing lives (high school English, huh?), "Crimes of the Body" is per-fectly delightful dancefloor techno-rock with a dramatic bridge. "The Fodder Song," previously issued as a 12-inch single, is a piledriver with growly vocals; "Healing Time" could be the soundtrack of a medieval war movie.

Hog Floor is a five-year retrospective of rarities and unreleased material; the cassette and CD contain three bonus tracks.

Attempting to separate the band's multiple person-alities into clear-cut stylistic entities, Lemos and Mori-arty launched Joined at the Head, a side project that is strictly for electronic club kids; the four-song EP offers orthodox Wax Trax! horrorshow noise, with distorted lyrics hissed/roared over simple, repetitive rhythm tracks.

Lemos has also assembled several compilations of other bands under the **Dry Lungs** title and released col-laborative albums under other names. [i]

COO COO ROCKIN TIME
See *Half Japanese*.

COOLIES
dig..? (DB) 1986
Doug (DB) 1988 ●
These Atlanta jokesters made an underground splash with **dig..?**, a collection of goofy Simon & Garfunkel covers (plus a version of Paul Anka's "Having My Baby"). Great concept for a frat-party set; the psychedelic-funk "Scarborough Fair" and surf-instru-mental "Mrs. Robinson" would have made chuckle-worthy B-sides, but the idea of devoting an entire LP to such tomfoolery is a product of the same sort of thinking that produced **Having Fun with Elvis on Stage.**

Amazingly, the Coolies followed the one-joke **dig..?** with the brilliant **Doug**, a trenchant "rock opera" about a skinhead who murders a transvestite short-order cook, gets rich by publishing his victim's recipes, falls into paranoia and substance abuse and ends up in the gutter. The sad tale is related through ingenious knock-offs of the Who ("Cook Book"), John Lennon ("Pov-erty"), the Replacements ("Coke Light Ice"), rap ("Pussy Cook") and metal ("The Last Supper"), and in a comic book—not included with the cassette or CD, alas—designed by Jack Logan, of *Pete Buck Comics* fame. A quantum leap from its predecessor's one-dimensional silliness, **Doug** is a work of demented genius. [hd]

JULIAN COPE
World Shut Your Mouth (nr/Mercury) 1984 ●
Fried (nr/Mercury) 1984 ●

Julian Cope EP (Island) 1986
Saint Julian (Island) 1987 ●
Eve's Volcano EP (nr/Island) 1987 ●
My Nation Underground (Island) 1988 ●
Skellington (nr/CopeCo-Zippo) 1989 ●
Droolian (nr/MoFoCo-Zippo) 1990 ●
Peggy Suicide (Island) 1991 φ

Welsh-born Liverpool legend (now resettled in the ancient English town of Tamworth) Julian Cope called a halt to The Teardrop Explodes during 1983 sessions for the band's third album and decided it was time to set off on a solo career instead. Aided by the Teardrops' drummer and a guitarist, Cope took the songs he'd written and finished them as **World Shut Your Mouth** (which does not contain the song of that title), a highly inventive take on '60s psychedelia. Mainly blending weird sounds with charming pop, his acceptably inelegant voice and period organ playing add substantial personality to the non-nostalgic venture. The humorous and sensitive lyrics may be a touch *too* sensitive in spots, but Cope's openness and fanciful streak undercut any semblance of pretentiousness.

The title and sleeve photos (he's pictured on all fours, nude, under a huge tortoise shell) of **Fried** suggest Cope's Syd Barrett-like mental state at the time. This flaky collection is energetic and less stylized than the first; rocking forthrightness, intuitive musicianship and a strong backing quartet keep it from drifting away on disoriented meanderings like "Bill Drummond Said," "Laughing Boy" and "O King of Chaos." A fine, disturbing and bewildering document of a man on the edge.

The confident stomp of "World Shut Your Mouth," a brilliant 1986 British hit first issued in the US on the waters-testing **Julian Cope** EP and the following year included as the centerpiece of the triumphant **Saint Julian** album, proudly announced Cope's recovery and return to action. The rip-roaring eponymous EP adds two originals and brilliant covers of Pere Ubu ("Non Alignment Pact") and the 13th Floor Elevators ("I've Got Levitation"). **Saint Julian**, produced by Ed Stasium, proceeds from there, a loud and melodic collection of uniformly delectable tunes that reflect Cope's idiosyncratic personality and imagination.

My Nation Underground follows in the same vein as **Saint Julian**, with Cope sounding more confident and dynamic than ever, striking a brilliant balance between his dual personae as serious artiste and preening pop star. The album opens with an ingeniously apocalyptic reading of the Vogues' 1966 "5 O'Clock World" (intercut with the old Petula Clark hit "I Know a Place"). The originals are equally effective, examining various pet themes, most notably Cope's ongoing artist-as-con-man obsession.

Finally released as an authorized bootleg years after its recording (right after **Fried**), the mostly acoustic **Skellington** is a primal-scream folk record: twelve short, primitive and sporadically fascinating demo-quality ditties. Basically a footnote for devoted fans, but an enjoyable and revealing one.

An equally far cry from Cope's usual well-crafted studio output is the mysterious **Droolian**, on which Cope's name does not actually appear. Walking the thin line between demystification and pretension that's inspired much of his work, the artist—with spare instrumental backing this time—messes around on thirteen songs with varying degrees of seriousness. In its own casual way, **Droolian** is nearly as compelling as Cope's official releases, with the addition of a mischievous sense of experimentalism.

The epic double-length **Peggy Suicide** brings all of Cope's charmingly artful eccentricities to bear on an over-the-top cavalcade that, while deeply uncommercial, amounts to a twisted artistic triumph, a passionate meditation on sanity and ecology. [i/hd]

See also *The Teardrop Explodes*.

STEWART COPELAND
Rumble Fish (A&M) 1983
The Rhythmatist (A&M) 1985 ●
The Equalizer & Other Cliff Hangers (IRS No Speak) 1988 ●
KLARK KENT
Music Madness from the Kinetic Kid (Kryptone-IRS) 1980
ANIMAL LOGIC
Animal Logic (IRS) 1989 ●
II (IRS) 1991 φ
RAY LEMA
Nangadeef (Mango) 1989 ●
Gaia (Mango) 1991 ●

Though possessing competence on all the necessary instruments, not to mention a homely yet winning boy-next-doorish voice, Police drummer Stewart Copeland—in his first solo turn, a one-off in the guise of Welsh looney Klark Kent—turns in less a DIY showcase than a mildly amusing show of self-indulgence, pressed on ten inches of green vinyl in a K-shaped jacket, no less! There are plums to be found in the tongue-in-cheek pop-punk of "Don't Care" and a clever Zappaesque instrumental, "Theme for Kinetic Ritual," but the other six tracks are merely variations on those two styles.

Three years later, with the Police nearing an end, Copeland launched a career in film and TV soundtracks by writing, producing and playing (except horns and strings) the music for Francis Coppola's *Rumble Fish*. The atmospheric instrumentals downplay drums; some are strongly enough structured that they could support lyrics. "Don't Box Me In," an actual song co-written and vocalized by ex-Wall of Voodooer Stan Ridgway, is easily the album's highlight.

Copeland's second solo record is the soundtrack to an African safari video. Described on the sleeve as "a curious blend of musical snatches from Tanzania, Kenya, Burundi, Zaire, the Congo and Buckinghamshire," **The Rhythmatist** is variously a rock album with Africanisms layered on and a rock interpretation (or imitation) thereof. The blurry line between what is genuine and what Copeland has made of whole Anglo-American cloth is disturbing, to say the least, and there's obviously real African music where this dubious rock star contraption came from. Still, the invigorating record sounds lovely, especially thanks to his collaborator, Zairean vocalist Ray Lema. (**Nangadeef**, the veteran's subsequent American solo debut, offers an uneasy, occasionally attractive commercial blend of *soukous*, jazz, pop and computerized dance-funk.)

The Equalizer, another one-man-orchestra instrumental outing, collects Copeland music done for the titular TV show, along with unrelated but harmonious new compositions. Favoring keyboards (seemingly piano and organ; the sketchy credits indicate reliance on a Fairlight synthesizer) and strong rhythms, Copeland's technically impressive work here occasionally recalls some of Keith Emerson's lighter crypto-classical moments.

Copeland's next long-term project was Animal Logic, an ill-conceived sophisto-rock trio with singer/songwriter Deborah Holland and master bassist Stanley Clarke. On **Animal Logic**, the superstar rhythm section (which actually doesn't blend very well: Copeland is far more suited to work with a hacker like his old bandmate Sting than an overachiever like Clarke) takes an accomplished back seat to Holland, guest guitarist Michael Thompson and jazzy guests. A strange and uneasy blend of instrumental excellence and creative mediocrity.

See also *Police*. [jg/i]

COP SHOOT COP

Headkick Facsimile EP (Jap. Supernatural Organization) 1988
Consumer Revolt (Circuit) 1990

Calculatingly deconstructing rock'n'roll in a manner spiritually akin to Pussy Galore (whose Jon Spencer briefly played metal percussion in the band Shithaus with Cop's Tod A.), if sonically opposite (CSC uses two basses and no guitar), Cop Shoot Cop shares the same taste for indulging in pain, filth, disillusion and discontent. Unfortunately, that stance reduces their otherwise potent strain of subversive diversion to a cliché of sorts. Rarely do they achieve the serrated poetry of decadence skirted most prominently these days by Nick Cave and Henry Rollins (after Burroughs and Bukowski), more often settling for a showoff revelry of *attitude* easily pegged as Little Black.

Consisting partly of ex-members of NYC sublegends the Undead, Black Snakes and Dig Dat Hole, Cop Shoot Cop's wall-of-noise sampling, odd stuttered timings and belligerent anti-structures illustrate a conceptual ambition underscored by such psychotic psychedelic sound collages as "Disconnected 666," somewhat less structurally/sonically intricate than Pere Ubu's "Sentimental Journey" but drawn from the same dark core of industrial paranoia. Harking back in some ways to the days of New York no wave, Cop Shoot Cop are currently three toes idiot, seven toes savant—an improvement over their debut EP's ratio of five to five. [ab]

TOM CORA

See *Skeleton Crew*.

CORE

See *Chris and Cosey*.

HUGH CORNWELL

See *Stranglers*.

CORPSE GRINDERS

The Legend of the Corpse Grinders (Fr. Fan Club) 1983
Valley of Fear (Fr. New Rose) 1984

A trivial footnote to New York's new wave underground, the Corpse Grinders were a useless hard rock group formed in 1977 by ex-Brats guitarist Rick Rivets and ex-Dolls bassist Artie Kane (who didn't stay for much of the Grinders' year-long existence). The original quartet's few recordings—which amount to badly dated sub-Dolls R&B-punk with impressively stupid lyrics—were posthumously compiled on **The Legend**, joining 1983 tracks by the reincarnated group.

The all-new **Valley of Fear** finds Rivets joining his Johnny Thunders-style guitar work and Bob Casper's ivory-tinkling in a diverse assortment of originals and a pair of credibly played Stones covers. Although much of the album is given over to boppy vintage rock'n'roll and acoustic ballads, the title track breaks away for lightweight goth with a hooky chorus. [i]

CORVAIRS

See *Certain General*.

COSEY FANNI TUTTI

See *Chris and Cosey*.

ELVIS COSTELLO

My Aim Is True (Columbia) 1977 • —
New Amsterdam EP (nr/F-Beat) 1980
Taking Liberties (Columbia) 1980 •
Spike (Warner Bros.) 1989 •
Veronica EP (nr/Warner Bros.) 1989 •
Baby Plays Around EP (nr/Warner Bros.) 1989 •
Mighty Like a Rose (Warner Bros.) 1991 ◌

ELVIS COSTELLO AND THE ATTRACTIONS

This Year's Model (Columbia) 1978 •
Armed Forces (Columbia) 1979 •
Get Happy!! (Columbia) 1980 • —
Ten Bloody Marys & Ten How's Your Fathers (nr/F-Beat) 1980 (nr/Demon) 1984 •
Trust (Columbia) 1981 •
Almost Blue (Columbia) 1981 •
Imperial Bedroom (Columbia) 1982 •
Punch the Clock (Columbia) 1983 •
Goodbye Cruel World (Columbia) 1984 •
The Best of Elvis Costello and the Attractions (Columbia) 1985 •
The Man: The Best of Elvis Costello (nr/Telstar) 1985 (nr/Demon) 1987 •
Elvis Costello EP (nr/Stiff) 1985
Blood & Chocolate (Columbia) 1986 •
Girls + £ ÷ Girls = $ & Girls (nr/Demon) 1989 (Columbia) 1990 •

THE COSTELLO SHOW

King of America (Columbia) 1986 •

VARIOUS ARTISTS

Out of Our Idiot (nr/Demon) 1987 •
The Courier (Virgin Movie Music) 1988 •

ATTRACTIONS

Mad About the Wrong Boy (nr/F-Beat) 1980 (nr/Demon) 1984

Elvis Costello has become the King Kong of contemporary music, looming so large over everything that admirers and detractors alike feel compelled to take note of his most trivial actions. A remarkable performer with a cutting voice, he's charted a consistently fascinating course in an intensely productive career and shows no sign of fatigue. He's arguably the most significant individual creative voice to emerge in rock'n'roll since Bob Dylan, and definitely one of pop music's most unforgettable characters.

My Aim Is True quickly established Elvis as an angry young man armed with cleverly worded insults and taut melodies. Although the backing (by American band Clover, sans future star Huey Lewis, the group's harmonica player) lacks his intensity, the bespectacled one's passion comes through full force. Many of the songs are already standards: "Watching the Detectives," a sizzling, disorienting excursion into reggae (not included on the original UK version of the LP); "Alison," a searing ballad, and "Less Than Zero," Elvis' first single and a wry attack on one of his preferred targets, fascism. The overall effect is that of an updated Buddy Holly, neurotic and tormented by sexual insecurity. For more information, consult "Miracle Man" and "No Dancing."

This Year's Model improves significantly on Costello's stunning debut by winding the music uncomfortably tight. Elvis gained confidence from the addition of an outstanding permanent backing band: Bruce Thomas on bass, Pete Thomas (no relation) on drums and Steve Nieve, whose piano and organ, rather than Elvis' guitar, generally fill in melodies. The album finds Costello's anger and insecurity grown harsh and nasty. The surging "No Action," "Pump It Up" (something of a re-write on Dylan's "Subterranean Homesick Blues") and "Lipstick Vogue" bristle with ingeniously stated, hard-rocking vitriol. "Radio Radio" (not on the UK edition) became Costello's unofficial theme song, a daring and snotty attack on the powers that rule the airwaves.

Costello avoids sneering himself into a dead end on **Armed Forces**, with the help of producer Nick Lowe. The prettier, less demanding and more varied sound still allows him freedom of expression. The lyrically potent "Oliver's Army" borrows from Abba's pop lushness; "Accidents Will Happen" mixes a beautiful melody with a driving arrangement; Lowe's "(What's So Funny 'Bout) Peace, Love and Understanding" offers an unironic, unexpected and agitated plea for tolerance. **Armed Forces** was the "nicest" of Costello's first three LPs.

Get Happy!! marks the beginning of Elvis' concerted stylistic fiddling and his first serious attempt to shift the emphasis to the music and away from the overpowering persona. The watchword here is simplicity, with 20 short songs and borrowings from such soul greats as Booker T & the M.G.'s and Sam & Dave, whose "I Can't Stand Up for Falling Down" gets disheveled but earnest treatment. Other highlights include "Motel Matches," an early flirtation with Nashville country; the moving "King Horse"; and a rip-snorting version of the Merseybeats' "I Stand Accused." By

lessening the intensity somewhat, Elvis comes up with a most personable LP. (The three non-LP tracks on the **New Amsterdam** 7-inch, billed to Costello alone and also available as a picture disc, later appeared on **Ten Bloody Marys**.)

Reflecting Costello's prolific nature, **Taking Liberties** collects an amazing twenty previously non-LP odds and ends in wildly divergent styles. (The UK counterpart, **Ten Bloody Marys & Ten How's Your Fathers**, is altogether different, part of a consistent plan to enforce alternate international releases. Originally issued only on cassette, it appeared on vinyl four years later and subsequently on CD.) Despite a few dull entries, there's plenty of remarkable stuff. The classic "My Funny Valentine" is a harbinger of **Imperial Bedroom**; "Talking in the Dark" gaily recalls "Penny Lane"; "Stranger in the House," dating from the period of **This Year's Model**, masterfully reflects his growing obsession with country music. Chaotic and marvelous.

Trust exhibits new self-confidence, blending some of the polish of **Armed Forces** with the straightforward delivery of **This Year's Model**. Though few tracks stand out individually, the LP packs a powerful, coherent punch. "Clubland" is an impassioned lament while "Lovers Walk" overlays a Bo Diddleyish motif with Latin piano and heaps of anxiety. On the fierce "From a Whisper to a Scream," Costello engages in a spirited dialogue with Squeeze's Glenn Tilbrook, reaffirming his presence in the real world.

Elvis was bound to goof eventually, and **Almost Blue** is a dud. This album of country cover versions, recorded in Nashville with veteran producer Billy Sherrill (Tammy Wynette, George Jones, just about everyone else), is surprisingly clumsy in light of Costello's previously demonstrated ability to come up with fine originals in the same genre. Curiously, he succumbs to the urge to oversing instead of finesse the vocals, a mistake his obvious model, the late Gram Parsons, never made.

Imperial Bedroom is a resounding return to form, and indicates Costello's interest in becoming a classic tunesmith in the Tin Pan Alley tradition instead of just a venerated rocker. This is certainly his most subdued LP, with songs such as "Beyond Belief," "Kid About It" and "Town Cryer" more suitable to a cocktail lounge torch singer than a garage band. How time flies.

Punch the Clock is yet another tour de force. Produced by Madness architects Clive Langer and Alan Winstanley, the disc continues in the pop vein of **Imperial Bedroom**, but with considerably more attention paid to mixing up styles and textures. Hence you get politically motivated ballads like the brooding "Pills and Soap" and the ethereal, desperately angry "Shipbuilding" (co-written with Clive Langer), as well as swaggering raveups ("The World and His Wife"), classic Costello angst ("Charm School") and much more. Best of all is the lilting "Everyday I Write the Book," a winning tune worthy of being sung by Aretha Franklin (and the closest Costello's come to a US hit single).

By contrast, **Goodbye Cruel World** seems awkward and forced. The playing's overly baroque, the melodies mild and too much of Costello's edge is sublimated by the Langer/Winstanley cushion of sound. (On "The Only Flame in Town," for instance, they bathe a fine song in swanky saxophones and duet vocals by Daryl Hall, watering down Costello's individual power.) However, "Sour Milk-Cow Blues" has a cranky charm, "The Deportees Club" has old-fashioned Attractions' bite and "Peace in Our Time" brilliantly captures the chilling madness of nuclear politics. Otherwise, Costello sounds like he needs a vacation.

Perhaps the nineteen-song **Best Of** (the similarly extensive UK counterpart of which—initially offered via TV advertising on a discount label but later reissued by Costello's real record company—has only a dozen tracks in common) did the trick. Or maybe it was the decision to shelve the Attractions temporarily. Then again, maybe his burgeoning romance with (soon-to-be-ex-)Pogue bassist Cait O'Riordan was the reason.

In any case, the extraordinary **King of America**—billed as the Costello Show and recorded with co-producer T-Bone Burnett and a clutch of top American sessioneers, including sidemen from another Elvis—returned him to masterful top form. MacManus (as he then wished to be known) banged together fifteen intelligent, mature creations in a variety of idioms, many recalling styles he had already tried and abandoned (C&W, R&B, nightclub sophistication) and some (folk, blues) not so familiar. The sound often recalls the Band in its unique blending of country and urban traditions; elsewhere, it's latter-day Elvis Presley, played by his own musicians. As articulate and clear-headed as he's ever been, MacManus dissects several major themes—the British perception of America, alcoholism, his own stardom—each from more than one vantage point. Not only do all these forays work individually, the songs fit together with surprising ease. In addition, he's never sung better, with such subtlety and control. A career highlight.

Released before the same calendar year's end, **Blood & Chocolate** brought the Attractions back into the picture, joined on a few tunes by guest vocalist O'Riordan. (More nomenclatural absurdity: while the name Elvis Costello appears on the front cover, the composer of all but one track is MacManus and the vocalist/guitarist is named Napoleon Dynamite.) Although the LP has no characteristic sound, overall theme or discernible organizational logic, the individual songs are quietly excellent—simply played gems performed with restrained enthusiasm, if little color. Eschewing any new stylistic statement, Elvis the unnameable ambles back into personal commentary with subdued eloquence. A bit underwhelming at first, but substantial nonetheless.

The 1987 **Out of Our Idiot** crypto-compilation serves up a brace of singles, B-sides, outtakes and side projects employing enough different monikers to justify the record's "various artists" billing. Besides assorted undertakings as Costello variations, the hodgepodge of good-to-incredible tracks credit such ensembles as Napoleon Dynamite & the Royal Guard, the Emotional Toothpaste and the Coward Brothers. Besides alternate versions of "Blue Chair" and "American Without Tears," and familiar-to-fans collaborations with Jimmy Cliff, T-Bone Burnett and Nick Lowe, the record's highlight is "So Young," an infectious bluebeat bouncer borrowed from Jo Jo Zep and evidently omitted from **Armed Forces**. The 21-track CD adds another E.C. & the Attractions outtake (1982's "Little Goody Two Shoes") as well as cuts by the MacManus Gang (from the *Straight to Hell* soundtrack) and the Imposter. (In another piece of film work, Costello—as Declan

MacManus—scored, produced and played music for *The Courier*, in which O'Riordan has a starring role. His dramatic instrumental efforts occupy nearly a side of the soundtrack album.)

Costello bills himself as The Beloved Entertainer—stuffed and mounted—on the front cover of **Spike**, his first new album since **Blood & Chocolate**. Following **King of America**'s blueprint, each of the fifteen tracks employs a different assortment of players, from the Dirty Dozen Brass Band (on "Deep Dark Truthful Mirror" and "Stalin Malone") to Paul McCartney (on the tender and touching "Veronica," one of two songs he and Costello co-wrote). Regardless of which sort of tasteful arrangement (Irish folk, acoustic pop, jazz, rock, jagged noise) or star collaborator (Chrissie Hynde, Christy Moore, Benmont Tench) he chooses for any individual song, however, the record is a testament to Costello's complete mastery. For most of the record, Costello is in rare form, conversing with the deity ("God's Comic"), ripping the lynch-mob mentality in a fact-based tale ("Let Him Dangle"), sending a withering blast at Margaret Thatcher ("Tramp the Dirt Down") and wallowing in romantic regrets ("Baby Plays Around," whose joint marital authorship lends a reassuring fictional sense to its troubled lyrics). For concerned Attractions fans, Pete Thomas puts in an appearance on one solitary song.

The two EPs taken from **Spike** contain four songs each. On 12-inch and CD-3, **Veronica** adds the album's CD bonus track ("Coal-Train Robberies"), a B-side (a cover of Clint Ballard's "You're No Good," on which E.C. plays kalimba and drum machine) and "The Room Nobody Lives In." Likewise, **Baby Plays Around** has "Almost Blue" (from **Imperial Bedroom**), "My Funny Valentine" (originally on the flip of "Oliver's Army") and "Point of No Return."

Taking discographical perversity to new extremes, the **Girls + £ ÷ Girls = $ & Girls** compilation (covering 1976-'86) was originally issued in the UK in four formats: as a 31-track double album, two individual cassettes with a combined 51 songs, a double-CD with 47 songs and a digital audio tape containing 31 songs. To compound the confusion, the different configurations aren't simply related: not all of the CD tracks, for example, appear on the cassettes. The American release skipped DAT and vinyl and stuck the cassettes together in a cardboard longbox, but preserved the alternate tape and CD programs. Building on a common—albeit not entirely logical—core of 36 familiar songs (selected by the artist, who also provided amusing liner notes), the tape and CDs offer two different views of the Costello catalogue, neither of them entirely fair or complete.

Despite his evident stylistic and intellectual ambition, Costello reveals some creative fatigue on the mildly disappointing **Mighty Like a Rose**, a collection of colorful stylistic threads woven into a frequently familiar fabric. One reason the catchy "Other Side of Summer" is so immediately likable is that it's strikingly self-derivative, recalling the Attractions' era right down to the vintage Steve Nieve piano and organ quotes. Except for a few subtle instrumental elements, the memorable "How to Be Dumb"—a ripping attack apparently aimed at Bruce Thomas for his tacky play-and-tell "novel," *The Big Wheel*—could very easily have been on **This Year's Model**. The raucous massed-drum "Hurry

Down Doomsday (The Bugs Are Taking Over)" owes a more oblique debt to that same album. (And check the bass thrusts at the end of "Harpies Bizarre.") A remarkable simulation of the Band ("Playboy to a Man") is oddly effective; other highlights include the boppy "Georgie and Her Rival" and the solemn piano-with-horns ballad, "Sweet Pear."

On their own in 1980, the Attractions sound more like Nick Lowe than their then-boss. The sixteen snappily executed ditties on **Mad About the Wrong Boy** feature bright, breezy surfaces and very little depth, which isn't so bad in light of the cheerful atmosphere. The title cut, "La-La-La-La-La Loved You" and others offer agreeably washed-out harmonies reminiscent of UK flower-power pop of the late-'60s. Decent.   [jy/i]

See also *Steve Nieve*.

COUCH FLAMBEAU

Curiosity Rocks [tape] (no label) 1982
Mammal Insect Marriage (Ludwig Van Ear) 1983
The Day the Music Died (It's Only a Record) 1985
Rock with Your Sock On [tape] (It's Only a Record) 1987
Models EP (It's Only a Record) 1987
Ghostride (It's Only a Record) 1989

Education is a dangerous thing, and these Wisconsin smartboys have been in school far too long for public safety. Armed with Jay Tiller's rapier wit, dadaist visions, squawky voice and ear-busting guitar work, the group's records are hysterically funny exercises in eminently enjoyable noise-to-go.

The lyrics of **Mammal Insect Marriage**'s opening track, "ADM 12," immediately make it clear you've checked into a real hellhouse of collegiate weasel weirdness: "I saw a car accident near the zoo. There were mangled bodies all over. I felt sick, but I found a finger. I still have it in my freezer." Recorded in seven fun-filled hours, **Mammal Insect Marriage** has thirteen additional warped and funny B-movie haikus. Brilliant and extraordinary.

The tape-only **Rock with Your Sock On** combines the entire contents of **Curiosity Rocks** (recorded and mixed in a single eight-hour session just months after the band's formation) and **Mammal Insect Marriage**. The former contains sketchy versions of "ADM 12" and "I Don't Want to Be an Eddie," as well as "Mobile Home," "Satan's School for Girls" and "Curtains for You," all of which resurfaced on Couch's third album.

The Day the Music Died gets off to a slow start with the instrumental title track, but revs into high gear with "We'll Go Through the Windshield Together," a romantic tale of vehicular homicide (complete with sound effects) told from the victim's perspective. Other highlights include the pessimistic "Life's Rough," a feedback-filled mantra that recasts an old 7-Up slogan ("You Hate It, It Hates You") and bassist Neil Socol's "Curtains for You," in which the protagonist makes a major educational discovery: "I hate Shakespeare/He's too hard to read/I wish he were dead/Oh, he is?"

Continuing as a duo (Socol and Tiller, who doubles on drums), Couch made the five-song **Models** EP, going easy on the radical sounds. Instead, the pointed cultural sarcasm of "Models," "White Boy Blues" and "Vipers" are laid over relatively easygoing music that paradoxically undercuts the lyrics by failing to match their absurdity. The one exception is "Song with a Message," a wimpy dance groove underlying a random series of messages left on Socol's answering machine.

Beneath the unpredictable lyrics and Tiller's brain-spasm vocals, **Ghostride**—a full sixteen-song dose—cranks up equally unpredictable (although tight and well-played) rock noise that flirts with metal. In Couch's world, nothing is ever perfect: "We're Not So Smart" describes the joy and heartbreak of being an underground rock group (the related "Scene Report" dismembers punk-rock poseurs), while "Think Twice" is equally realistic about the hazards of dating and "Summer Vacation" is, predictably, a complete disaster. Great!   [i]

COUNT BISHOPS

Speedball EP (nr/Chiswick) 1975
Good Gear (Fr. Dynamite) 1977 (Fr. Lolita) 1984
The Count Bishops (nr/Chiswick) 1977 ●

BISHOPS

Bishops Live (nr/Chiswick) 1978
Cross Cuts (nr/Chiswick) 1979

Although they never attained major popularity, hits or even a US release, the Count Bishops played a small but important role in the development of British punk. First, they provided a stylistic and chronological link between the raw R&B revivalism of Dr. Feelgood and early demi-punk flailings by Eddie and the Hot Rods. Second, the four-song 7-inch **Speedball** was the debut release by the first independent new wave label in England, Chiswick (which preceded Stiff by a matter of months).

The group's only recording with American (Brooklyn, no less) singer Mike Spencer (replaced by the gravel-throated Dave Tice soon after, for reasons that are audibly obvious), **Speedball** clearly defines the group's style. Combining rock-a-boogie raveups of mid-'60s-style material with mid-'70s chops and energy, the Bishops re-cover the same R&B and rock'n'roll songs favored by the first wave of British beat groups (Stones, Yardbirds, Kinks) and American punks (Standells, Strangeloves). The idea was obviously to recapture the rawness and spontaneity of that period and, although the concept is both limited and doomed almost by definition, **Good Gear** (probably drawn from live-in-the-studio demos) is so raunchy and spirited that it succeeds, even if it is essentially a copy of a copy.

Trouble set in with the first *real* album, **The Count Bishops**. How do you convey a style that works best after a few beers and really offers nothing new to vinyl? Even with two solid guitarists and a fine rhythm section, the Bishops were never quite able to resolve the problem. Though it sounds nasty as hell on **Bishops Live** (issued on both 12-inch and 10-inch vinyl), Tice's growl is hard to take over two sides of a recording made in the rarefied atmosphere of the studio. And where most bands use cover versions to fill space, the filler here is the Bishops' self-penned stuff. With rare exception, their originals are sub-Status Quo boogie, which just about destroys most of **Cross Cuts**. Following the death of guitarist Zenon de Fleur in an auto accident just prior to the release of **Cross Cuts**, the Bishops called it a day.   [ds]

WAYNE COUNTY AND THE ELECTRIC CHAIRS

The Electric Chairs (nr/Safari) 1978
Storm the Gates of Heaven (nr/Safari) 1979
Things Your Mother Never Told You (nr/Safari) 1979
The Best of Jayne/Wayne County and the Electric Chairs
  (nr/Safari) 1982

JAYNE COUNTY

Rock 'n' Roll Resurrection (nr/Safari) 1981
Private Oyster (nr/Revolver) 1986
Amerikan Cleopatra (nr/Konnexion) 1987
Betty Grable's Legs! EP (nr/Jungle) 1989

Georgia-born transsexual County was a (male) fixture on the budding New York club scene in the early '70s, stretching the limits of vulgarity and outrage on stages alongside the New York Dolls. After writing and recording the theme song for the legendary venue Max's Kansas City, County migrated to England, just as the London punk scene was getting underway. Having been commercially unappreciated at home, County found a sympathetic British label and recorded a series of albums, none of which were ever released Stateside.

High camp posturing and foul-mouthed (but not unfunny) lyrics form the basis of County's work. Along with a skillful trio playing routine rock, **The Electric Chairs** finds County singing (with more enthusiasm than talent) touching ballads ("Eddie & Sheena," a minor hit single recounting a love story between a teddy boy and a punk), catty putdowns ("Bad in Bed") and trotting out the old narcissistic scene celebration of "Max's Kansas City."

Storm the Gates of Heaven has a great cover, was pressed on sickly colored lavender vinyl and showcases two new guitarists hired to replace one left behind. The songs are less contrived and more interesting; the beginnings of a band sound can be discerned. All in all, a vast improvement that even includes a smoking version of "I Had Too Much to Dream Last Night." Flying Lizard David Cunningham produced the subsequent **Things Your Mother Never Told You** with the same lineup, but came up with a flat-sounding, dull LP.

A New Year's Eve gig in Toronto yielded the live **Rock'n'Roll Resurrection**. Fronting a largely new band, Jayne (following the surgery) belts out a shambling selection of non-hits, including such gutter faves as "Cream in My Jeans" and "F . . . Off." Pretty dire. A nicely packaged best-of collection (pressed on white vinyl) finally brought together everything you'd ever want to hear by Wayne or Jayne.

In the mid-'80s, County made the self-produced **Private Oyster** (reissued as **Amerikan Cleopatra**). Proof that some things really never change, Jayne sounds exactly the same as ever on **Betty Grable's Legs!**: five songs recorded with an old-style rock trio. County still has the identical voice (and singing ability), songs like "Paranoia Paradise" are the same trashy junk she/he's always written and the hapless band sounds totally unaware that the '80s have come and gone. [i]

COWBOY JUNKIES

Whites off Earth Now!! (Can. Latent) 1986 (RCA) 1991 ●
The Trinity Session (RCA) 1988 ●
The Caution Horses (RCA) 1990 ●

How slow can you go? No doubt that's what the unsuspecting listener will ask after a close encounter with Canada's Cowboy Junkies. Like folk-rockers on Quaaludes, this elegant Toronto quartet specializes in hushed, atmospheric tunes delivered at a dirge-like tempo. Whether you consider this an annoying gimmick or an ingenious creative strategy, there's no denying it's original.

Whites off Earth Now!! finds the quartet in the process of forging an identity. While Margo Timmins already practices floating vocals (see Sandy Denny for roots), the overall result is more boring than evocative. The LP is dominated by covers, including Springsteen's "State Trooper" and Robert Johnson's "Me and the Devil."

The ultimate three a.m. listening experience, **The Trinity Session** constitutes a quantum leap forward. Recorded on a single day in a Toronto church, this shimmering triumph has the impact of a deep, haunting dream. Timmins imitates a heavenly spirit on potent originals like "Misguided Angel" and (on the CD) "Blue Moon Revisited (Song for Elvis)," while more than doing justice to Lou Reed's "Sweet Jane" and Patsy Cline's "Walking After Midnight." A goosebump special.

Following the commercial as well as artistic success of **The Trinity Session**, the Junkies wisely concluded they'd already carried the catatonic approach to a logical conclusion. They became somewhat more aggressive emotionally and musically on **The Caution Horses**—with partial success. On one of the best tracks, "Sun Comes Up, It's Tuesday Morning," Timmins bitterly dismisses a lover to a snappy country tempo; the acid monologues "'Cause Cheap Is How I Feel" and "Where Are You Tonight?" sustain the bad, riveting vibes. Elsewhere, the band is less impressive, spoiling the mood with erratic material and a leaden cover of Neil Young's "Powderfinger." [jy]

COWS

Taint Pluribus Taint Unum (Treehouse) 1987
Daddy Has a Tail! (Amphetamine Reptile) 1989
Effete and Impudent Snobs (Amphetamine Reptile)
  1990 ●
Peacetika (Amphetamine Reptile) 1991

Minneapolis' Cows don't fool around when it comes to raising a holy ruckus. Besides throwing off a frenzied psycho-guitar roar, the quartet takes a viciously crude view of the world (enunciated in a tuneless shout by Shannon Selberg, who also provides the Cows with the surprising sound of trombone and bugle), all mitigated by a wry undercurrent of humor. The badly recorded **Taint Pluribus Taint Unum** is an elementary introduction, a noisy storm of electrified steel wool that rushes through roughly cut songs like "Mother (I Love That Bitch)" and the instrumental "Summertime Bone" (Eddie Cochran sent to trombone hell) with more enthusiasm than effect.

A second ancient rock classic turns up on **Daddy Has a Tail!**, only the Cows' version of Johnny Kidd's "Shakin' All Over" has different lyrics: "Yo girl, I love it when you make my asshole bleed . . . I'm shakin' in my colon." Ha ha ha. Overall, this horrible exercise in juvenile dementia makes the Cows' first

153

record sound like **Dark Side of the Moon**. With production that couldn't be worse if the studio had been underwater, the murky rumble of Thor Eisenstrager's overdriven guitar is an all-consuming swamp that muffles the entire effort.

Except for a mix that makes the distorted vocals nearly subliminal at times, **Effete and Impudent Snobs** shreds speakers with far more clarity and focus. Using trebly shards of layered guitar and thrusting fuzz bass, the Cows rock out snorting chunks of unhinged grunge with lyrics; some of the tracks ("Big Mickey," "Nancy Boy Cocaine Whore Blues," "Cartoon Corral") even coalesce into vague song shape. If you've ever been tempted to find out what it would be like to stick your head in a blender, don't bother—the Cows have already done it for you.   [i]

CRACKERS
See *Beat Rodeo*.

CRAMPS
Gravest Hits EP (Illegal) 1979 ●
Songs the Lord Taught Us (Illegal-IRS) 1980 ●
Psychedelic Jungle (IRS) 1981 ●
... Off the Bone (nr/Illegal) 1983 ●
Smell of Female EP (Enigma) 1983 + 1990 (Dutch East
    Wax) 1991 ●
Bad Music for Bad People (IRS) 1984 ●
A Date with Elvis (nr/Big Beat) 1986 (Enigma) 1990
    (Dutch East Wax) 1991 ●
Stay Sick! (Enigma) 1990 (Dutch East Wax) 1991 ●
All Women Are Bad EP (nr/Enigma) 1990 ●

Predating and never quite participating in the early '80s rockabilly revival, the Cramps used that genre's primal sound as a jumping-off point for a uniquely weird pastiche of rock'n'roll, psychedelia and a monster movie/junk food/swamp-creature aesthetic. Led by uninhibited vocalist Lux Interior (Erick Purkhiser) and guitarist Poison Ivy Rorschach (Kirsty Wallace), the band had its roots in Cleveland but was actually formed in New York. After two self-released 45s in '77, the Cramps crashed the 12-inch barrier with **Gravest Hits**, reissuing all four songs from those records plus a fifth track from the same time, all produced by Alex Chilton.

Like a seance or voodoo session, the Cramps' music needs time to work its spell, and so the albums make a better introduction. **Songs the Lord Taught Us** is a delirious invocation to the demons behind rock'n'roll. Besides horror-comic originals like "TV Set," "The Mad Daddy" and "Zombie Dance," the band overhauls classics like "Tear It Up" and "Strychnine" to emphasize their Dionysian inheritance. A minimal approach—no bass, rudimentary drumming, Lux's monotonous vocals—underlines the music's incantatory power. (The 1989 CD adds four alternate versions of tracks from the LP and an otherwise unavailable original entitled "Twist and Shout.")

As a result of slower tempos, **Psychedelic Jungle** is not quite as intense; still, it contains prime Cramps psychobilly ("Goo Goo Muck," "Voodoo Idol," "Can't Find My Mind") as well as related phenomena ("The Crusher," "Rockin Bones"). The CD adds **Gravest Hits**.

On **Smell of Female**, a six-song live EP recorded at New York's Peppermint Lounge, the group's maniacal sense of humor comes through loud and clear on well-recorded mung like "Thee Most Exalted Potentate of Love" and "I Ain't Nuthin' but a Gorehound." The reissues (red vinyl on one label; CD and cassette on another) add three non-LP tracks, including alternate versions of "Beautiful Gardens" (originally on **Psychedelic Jungle**) and "She Said."

Amid rotating guitarists and disputes with their record label, the Cramps then temporarily submerged. IRS issued **Bad Music for Bad People**, a kiss-off collection of singles sides (both LP and non-LP) and other obscure gems, like the hilariously offensive "She Said." Meanwhile, the Cramps' foreign cult following was temporarily sated by **Off the Bone**, a fifteen-track compilation including all of **Gravest Hits** and the contents of **Bad Music for Bad People**, with two earlier album cuts replacing the latter's "TV Set" and "Uranium Rock."

The Cramps returned to the living dead in late '85 with a wonderfully smarmy single ("Can Your Pussy Do the Dog?"), followed by an all-new sex-crazed studio album, **A Date with Elvis**, dedicated to Ricky Nelson. A bit more professional (Ivy breaks tradition and plays bass as well as guitar!) and less stylized than usual, but as happily crazed as ever, **Elvis** contemplates such Interior/Ivy designs as "What's Inside a Girl?," "(Hot Pool of) Womanneed" and "The Hot Pearl Snatch." (Although initially unreleased in the Cramps' homeland, **A Date with Elvis** was subsequently issued, with four bonus tracks collected from European B-sides, on CD/cassette by Enigma and colored vinyl by Dutch East.)

With fulltime bassist Candy Del Mar joining the lineup and Ivy in the producer's chair, **Stay Sick!** maintains the Cramps' high low-culture standards with colorful enthusiasm. While "Bikini Girls with Machine Guns," "All Women Are Bad" and "Journey to the Center of a Girl" all demonstrate Lux's ongoing bewildered bedevilment by the opposite sex, "Mama Oo Pow Pow" takes a good swig from the cultural trashcan that originally fueled the Cramps' wild-eyed vision. (The artistic reasons for covering "Shortnin' Bread" and "Muleskinner Blues" are, however, completely open to debate.) The CD adds a nifty version of Carl Perkins' "Her Love Rubbed Off." The 12-inch of "All Women Are Bad" contains three additional B-music tracks: "King of the Drapes," "Teenage Rage" and "High School Hellcats."   [si/i]

See also *Beasts of Bourbon, Nick Cave and the Bad Seeds, Electric Eels, Gun Club, Pagans, Veil, Zantees*.

CRASH VEGAS
Red Earth (Risqué Disque-Atlantic) 1989 φ

This Toronto quartet (including Daniel Lanois' bass-playing sister, Jocelyn, once of Martha and the Muffins) plays a lovely brand of spartan atmospheric folk-rock that falls somewhere between the Cowboy Junkies and 10,000 Maniacs. On **Red Earth**, what's not played seems nearly as important as what is; the ample sonic space makes the sound feel big without a lot being played. It's a perfect setting for Michelle McAdorey's supple voice to shine, and it does. A cover of Buffalo

Springfield's "Down to the Wire" provides another good point of reference. Blue Rodeo's Greg Keelor (a former member of Crash Vegas) co-wrote nearly half the cuts. [ds]

See also *Blue Rodeo*.

CRASS

The Feeding of the Five Thousand, The Second Sitting
  (nr/Crass) 1978 •
Stations of the Crass (nr/Crass) 1979 •
Penis Envy (Crass) 1981 •
Christ–The Album (nr/Crass) 1982 •
Yes Sir, I Will. (nr/Crass) 1983 •
10 Notes on a Summer's Day (nr/Crass) 1986 •
Best Before (nr/Crass) 1986 •

PENNY RIMBAUD & EVE LIBERTINE

Acts of Love (nr/Crass) 1985

Lords of English punk's extreme left, the Essex-based Crass didn't just sing about anarchy in the UK—they *did* something about it. Formed in 1977 as a band much in the Sex Pistols/Sham 69 image, they saw themselves as a more righteous alternative to those bands, and soon evolved into an anarchist commune, a broadsheet publisher, several record labels and an information service. Crass espouse all the proper causes—anti-war, anti-nuclear, feminism, flushing out hypocrisy in organized religion—with blood-curdling vehemence on their own records and on the numerous singles and albums by likeminded bands they've released (or inspired). The group was frequently embroiled in legal battles with various government agencies but, in an era largely typified by apathy, Crass stands as a remarkably successful model of dead-serious political commitment in rock.

The Feeding of the Five Thousand is a reissue of the group's debut EP on Small Wonder. Fitting eighteen songs on a 12-inch 45, it is typical of Crass' shock tactics: the first cut is a sneering recitation of "Asylum," an irreverent dismissal of Christ as anybody's lord over droning guitar feedback. The rest is mostly raw faster-louder punk spiked with protest demagoguery, four-letter words and harsh Cockney ranting.

Stations of the Cross is even harder going—three studio sides and a live side containing a full seventeen numbers. Almost in spite of the oppressive, relentless punk bluster, Crass often wrote anthemic songs (like the ironic "Banned from the Roxy" and "Do They Owe Us a Living?" from **Five Thousand**), but over the course of this album (all of the studio material was cut in one day!), they blur into white noise. "White Punks on Hope" forcefully summarizes their scorn of punk as fashion; the Sham 69 parody, "Hurry Up Garry," is a wicked snipe at the music press.

Better production and more expansive arrangements distinguish **Penis Envy**. Drawing an ugly parallel between rampant sexism and man's rape of nature and society, the album bounces vibrantly from the strident bash of the ironic rape fantasy "Bata Motel" to the LP's unsettling church-organ coda.

Christ–The Album is quintessential Crass. This boxed two-record studio/live set comes with a 28-page booklet packed with emotionally charged fine print about the revolution and one man who died for it. Mu-sically, it builds on the daring of **Penis Envy**, going so far as to include a mock string arrangement in "Reality Whitewash" without tempering the band's brute punk rage. The severity of their sound and the belligerent politics can be predictable, even petulant, but **Christ–The Album** proves the band's courage and conviction.

Yes Sir, I Will. is a bitter response to the Falklands War, a series of musical speeches covering the conflict and indicting Prime Minister Thatcher for the deaths. Although most of the backing is typically abrasive, a couple of passages are quite beautiful.

Drummer Penny Rimbaud and singer Eve Libertine put together **Acts of Love**, an album of romantic poetry, "in an attempt to demonstrate that the source of our anger was love rather than hate." After making a final album, **10 Notes on a Summer's Day**, Crass retired from performing and recording (keeping the Crass label in business, and reissuing the band's catalogue on CD) to continue the struggle in more personal ways. The 20-song **Best Before** compilation begins with 1977's "Do They Owe Us a Living?" and runs through the band's singles before ending with that same song performed in 1984 at Crass' final gig. [df/i]

CRAWDADDYS

Crawdaddy Express (Voxx) 1979
Still Steamin' (Ger. Line) 1980
Here 'Tis! (Voxx) 1987
Mystic Crawdads (Ger. Wired-Line) 1989 •

This San Diego band delivers a 1979 record straight from 1964. Taking their name from the London R&B club where the Stones and Yardbirds began, the Crawdaddys copy those and other appropriate groups of the period (like the Pretty Things). Unfortunately, the group's sincerity and enthusiasm don't excuse lame renditions of various R&B and rock'n'roll classics, blues obscurities and two originals from the same mold; **Crawdaddy Express** may be a well-intentioned tribute, but it amounts to little more than nostalgia-mongering.

Over the course of the next five years, the Crawdaddys recorded one unreleased album and went through a batch of lineups (leaving drummer Dan McLain free to become Country Dick Montana and co-found the Beat Farmers). Three years after the band called it quits, the lost second LP (vintage 1984) was finally released, expanded with five previous outtakes. Offering a fair reflection of the group's early '60s eclecticism, **Here 'Tis!**—a sharper and more convincing LP than **Express**—relies heavily on singer Ron Silva's originals, but also covers Chuck Berry, Leiber/Stoller, soul legends and British Invasion stars. **Mystic Crawdads** is a compilation of early material. [wk/i]

See also *Beat Farmers*.

CRAWLSPACE

Silent Invisible Conversation EP (Aus. Grown Up Wrong)
  1989
In the Gospel Zone (Bona Fide) 1989
Solitude Crawlspace Head EP (Sympathy for the Record
  Industry) 1990

Mid-'70s fanzine guru (and former Gizmo) Eddie Flowers leads this loosely constructed Los Angeles aggregation through a variety of blaring, but somehow pacific improv-rock styles, all of which reinforce the band's implicit motto: "The chemicals go in before the name goes on." **Silent Invisible Conversation** takes its name from a line in the Can song ("Little Star of Bethlehem") that fills Side Two and hints that the three adrenal, Germs-ish tracks on the flip were but a stepping stone to the harder-to-shake stuff.

In the Gospel Zone peddles a much slower-working, but ultimately more lethal, brew. Ricocheting in white-water-rapids-of-consciousness fashion, between beatnik nihilism, full-leather-jacket biker hate-mongering and White Panther positivism, Flowers' rants reproduce the spirit of utter drug-rock derangement like no one since the (NYC) Godz. A public-service announcement for some, a call to arms for others. **Solitude** narrows the focus a bit, with the rambling "Solitude Smokestack Head" overtly advocating the use of cannabis (simultaneously discouraging it via the unmistakable evidence of brainpan burnout). The almost zen-like "Ocean = You," however, is actually quite beautiful. [dss]

See also *Gizmos*.

CRAZY BACKWARDS ALPHABET

See *Henry Kaiser*.

CRAZYHEAD

Desert Orchid (Food-EMI) 1988 •

Taking its cues from grebo mongrels Zodiac Mindwarp and the Love Reaction, this cheeky Leicester quintet—whose personnel employ such sobriquets as Porkbeast and Reverb—gleefully gooses heavy metal with a poppy irreverence that is absolutely infectious. Bolstered by two superb singles ("Time Has Taken Its Toll on You" and "What Gives You the Idea That You're So Amazing Baby?"), **Desert Orchid** is a fine debut that somehow manages to sound both fresh *and* classic. Producer Mark Freegard (who's worked with New Model Army) lends the requisite punch to songs like "In the Sun," "Down on You (Dragon City)" and a rambunctious cover of the Sonics' "Have Love Will Travel." [db]

CRAZY PINK REVOLVERS

See *Spear of Destiny*.

CREATIVE TECHNOLOGY INSTITUTE

See *Chris and Cosey*.

CREATURES

Wild Things EP (nr/Polydor) 1981
Feast (nr/Wonderland-Polydor) 1983
Boomerang (Geffen) 1989 •

Soon after the Banshees released **Juju**, Siouxsie Sioux and drummer Budgie, calling themselves the Creatures, collaborated on a five-song double-45 of voice-and-percussion pieces, including a nasty reworking of the Troggs classic "Wild Thing." The full-length **Feast**, however, is a dilettantish excursion into the only previously untested flavor-of-the-month: Hawaiian. The instrumentation incorporates marimba, while an ethnic choir adds bogus authenticity to the messy proceedings. Even worse, the lyrics are bad acid visions written by people evidently unfamiliar with their subject matter. The Creatures did make one great 1983 single, "Right Now" (covering an old Mel Tormé tune), which is not on the LP.

Six years passed before the duo issued another album. Recorded in Spain, **Boomerang** (thankfully) makes no attempt at contributing to the musical heritage of any world culture. Augmented by horns, harmonicas, synths, etc., the Creatures produce (along with Mike Hedges) a varied collection of fine, if not earth-shaking work. Each of the fourteen tracks has something different to offer, from the Euro-electronics of "Pluto Drive" to the bluesy "Killing Time." Budgie also gets to practice his marimba, steel drums and the like on several cuts. A much better idea the second time around.

See also *Siouxsie and the Banshees*. [rnp/dgs]

HELIOS CREED

See *Chrome*.

CREEPERS

See *Marc Riley with the Creepers*.

CREEPS

Enjoy the Creeps (Swed. Tracks on Wax) 1986 (Can. Star) 1987
Now Dig This! (Ger. WEA) 1988 •
Blue Tomato (Atlantic) 1990 •

When organist Hans Ingemansson relinquished songwriting and lead vocals to guitarist Robert Jelinek in the mid-'80s, picking up a new rhythm section in the bargain, Sweden's premier modern beat-psych combo offhandedly changed names from the Backdoor Men to the Creeps and made a big splash in the small pond of garage punk devotees with the wickedly soulful and melodic **Enjoy**. The album includes several covers and numerous copped riffs, all interpolated into a powerful attack blatantly imitative of the Lyres while concurrently possessed of more range and greater attention to mood mechanics.

Several years later, the follow-up jettisoned virtually all the dirt and raunch in favor of an early funk bias to match the heavy soul pump and attitude now permeating the music. Still a terrific songwriter and strong vocalist, Jelinek rallied his backdoor troops in a high energy romp through the underside of the pop and "black" charts circa mid-to-late-'60s, albeit with '80s urgency and production values. An interesting development, but **Now Dig This!** isn't as good as the first LP, substituting style for rage, budget for exuberance.

Blue Tomato, the quartet's first LP with an outside producer, only exacerbates the problem, offering up '80s dancefloor style to further modify the gutsy, gusty organ-pumped brew for mall-goers in designer tags. Quite possibly the best Stax-oriented club band operating today, the Creeps are still a great loss in terms of compromised potential. [ab]

MARSHALL CRENSHAW

Marshall Crenshaw (Warner Bros.) 1982 ●
Field Day (Warner Bros.) 1983
Our Town EP (nr/Warner Bros.) 1984
Downtown (Warner Bros.) 1985
The Distance Between EP (nr/Warner Bros.) 1986
Mary Jean & 9 Others (Warner Bros.) 1987 ●
Good Evening (Warner Bros.) 1989 ●
Life's Too Short (Paradox-MCA) 1991 φ

Detroit native Crenshaw spent some time in a road company of *Beatlemania* before moving (with drummer brother Robert) to New York, where his own songs became local new wave faves. Following an independent 12-inch with a major-label recording contract, Crenshaw made a debut album of sparkling, tuneful gems that are instantly memorable and remain every bit as enjoyable after a decade. Clean and crisp, free of frills and pretense, **Marshall Crenshaw**'s scrubbed pop style makes the record sound like a test of studio audio quality. Notwithstanding the reasonable Buddy Holly comparisons (renewed when Crenshaw portrayed Buddy in 1987's *La Bamba*), songs like "Someday, Someway," "She Can't Dance," "Cynical Girl" and "Brand New Lover" make it clear that Crenshaw is an enormously talented original.

Field Day, rather overproduced by Steve Lillywhite, has a walloping drum sound, lots of sonic holes and a few of Crenshaw's best songs. Although not an artistic success in toto, joyous numbers like "Whenever You're on My Mind," "All I Know Right Now" and "Our Town" mine Crenshaw's shuffle-pop resources effectively. Mindful of the criticism **Field Day** engendered, "Our Town" and two other tracks from it were given a simplifying remix by John Luongo, attached to a live oldie ("Little Sister") and issued as an impressive second-chance 12-inch in the UK.

With production assistance by T-Bone Burnett and a large bunch of savvy sidemen in place of his usual band, Crenshaw filled **Downtown** with extraordinarily memorable and intelligent pop songs in a number of musical veins. Easily the finest, most mature of his first three albums, **Downtown** swings with easy confidence through heartbreakers ("The Distance Between," "Like a Vague Memory"), lovemakers ("Yvonne," "Terrifying Love"), country laments and blues struts. It also features an incisive reading of Ben Vaughn's hauntingly wistful "I'm Sorry (But So Is Brenda Lee)." (The **Distance Between** 12-inch pairs two **Downtown** tracks with two songs from the first LP.)

Continuing on his onward and upward path, Crenshaw returned to the small-combo format, cutting the brilliant, often beautiful **Mary Jean** with two sidemen—brother/drummer Robert Crenshaw and longtime Joe Jackson bassist Graham Maby. Don Dixon's simple but full production sparkles, with just the right echo on the snare and spring in the strings. Even when shockingly manic guitar solos erupt in "'Til That Moment" and "This Street," they work for the songs, not against them. Guest crooners (including Tom Teeley and Marti Jones) pitch in to enrich winsome, well-crafted tunes— "Wild Abandon"; "Mary Jean"; a thoughtfully reflective Crenshaw/Dixon composition, "Calling Out for Love (At Crying Time)"; Peter Case's atmospheric

(and metaphoric) ode to the guitar, "Steel Strings"— with exquisite harmonies that wordlessly convey both the ecstasy and misery of romance.

The frustration and anxiety caused by long-term commercial neglect haunts the lightweight **Good Evening**, a disappointing creative sidestep that smacks of compromise and a lack of inspiration (not to mention over-use of whiny slide guitar). Other than well-chosen and delightfully performed songs by Richard Thompson ("Valerie"), Bobby Fuller ("Let Her Dance"), John Hiatt ("Someplace Where Love Can't Find Me") and the Isley Brothers ("Live It Up"), the pickings are slim: two so-so Crenshaw songs, three fair collaborations and an unwelcome contribution by the dreaded Diane Warren.

Nicely produced by Ed Stasium, **Life's Too Short**—almost all originals—is a lightweight but consistent pleasure. No instant classics (although the dopey-enough-to-be-real romanticism of "Fantastic Planet of Love" comes close), but even the lesser tracks are just too much fun to pick on. Marshall (mostly with bassist Fernando Saunders and drummer Kenny Aronoff) stretches nearly every cut a bit longer than necessary (no track's less than four minutes, which used to be his upper limit), but the songs—including one by Chris Knox of the Tall Dwarfs—are strong enough not to sound attenuated.

Extracurricular activities: Crenshaw compiled and annotated **Hillbilly Music . . . Thank God!** and produced a 1989 album for Nashville's rocking Thieves.

[i/jg]

CRENT

See *Celibate Rifles*.

CRIME AND THE CITY SOLUTION

The Dangling Man EP (nr/Mute) 1985
Just South of Heaven EP (nr/Mute) 1985
Room of Lights (nr/Mute) 1986 ●
Shine (Mute-Restless) 1988 ●
The Bride Ship (Mute-Restless) 1989 ●
Paradise Discotheque (Mute-Elektra) 1990 φ

Although singer Simon Bonney had led a series of groups under this odd name, it was only in the wake of the Birthday Party—when guitarist Rowland S. Howard, drummer Mick Harvey and Howard's bass-playing brother Harry joined—that the Australian band gained international access and recognition.

The Dangling Man, a four-track disc, picks up where the Party ended—a slow, stripped-down, blues-flavored horror show. (Considering that Cave did much the same on his first solo recordings, one wonders if the band didn't break up out of boredom rather than any serious musical differences.) None of the songs really take off, but it does show promise.

With ex-Swell Map drummer Epic Soundtracks in the lineup, Harvey returned to his old BP role as multi-instrumentalist. **Just South of Heaven** is cleaner and more powerful: all six tracks work well. Howard's guitar is as strong as ever, but piano and organ figure just as prominently. A hauntingly beautiful record by a well-integrated band.

Room of Lights, Crime's first full-length LP, features a noticeably heavier and thicker sound. With the predominance of slow tempos, Bonney's somewhat unattractive voice and the overly serious lyrics, supplied mostly by violinist Bronwyn Adams, the disc is laboriously endurance-defying. The band seems to be somewhat stunted developmentally: these eight songs are merely variations on previously introduced themes.

Following **Room of Lights** and an appearance in Wim Wenders' *Wings of Desire*, Soundtracks and the Howards split to form These Immortal Souls; Bonney, Harvey and Adams resettled in Berlin where they recruited three local musicians (including Einstürzende Neubauten guitarist Alexander Hacke) and recorded **Shine**. With Adams' violin prominent throughout, the overall tone is surprisingly much lighter and livelier; "Fray So Slow" could almost be old Simple Minds. Several other tracks move along nicely and melodically. Listeners who mistakenly thought Howard had been the band's major creative force will be caught off-guard by this impressive disc.

After **Shine**, Crime and the City Solution took a decidedly artsy turn, but in an odd throwback direction. Although not as outrageously dramatic as, say, Doctors of Madness nor as elegant as post-Eno Roxy Music, those comparisons are not completely off base. The enhanced melodic sense is supplemented by Bonney's much improved vocals (or is it vice versa?) on the baroque **Bride Ship**. While the embellished, fussy production utilizes an intriguing sonic palette, tempos plod along incessantly and the end result is just a distant, detached-sounding band.

Paradise Discotheque is an improvement, with much more warmth and blood in the sound. Several cuts, especially the folksy "I Have the Gun," are produced simply enough to stand on their own merits. On the down side, the band reveals a penchant for multipart suite-songs—"The Last Dictator" needs four segments and an entire side to get its point across.   [dgs]

See also *Birthday Party, These Immortal Souls*.

CRIMONY
See *D.C.3*.

CRIPPLED PILGRIMS
Head Down–Hand Out EP (Fountain of Youth) 1984
Under Water (Fountain of Youth) 1985

Most of the music on this Maryland quartet's EP and album is fairly undistinguished folk- and garage-rock—sketchy songs roughly produced on two guitars, bass and drums. Lead singer Jay Moglia seems to be trying to convey something about how people underestimate themselves and settle for less than they're worth, and about the difficulty of honest self-expression. But either he gets too angry and the songs turn into shapeless inchoate rants, or he turns dreamy and blathers on without really saying much. Then, for a few beautiful and perfect moments on **Under Water**, he gets it right. In "Down Here," "Undone" and "Pretend Not to Care," the guitar chords slip softly by like leaves in a pool, and Moglia's tentative, unsure voice finds its balance of desperation and desire. Rough, sullen and unyielding, with

a kick drum pounding like an accelerated heartbeat, "Oblivious and Numb" is his most beautiful and perfect moment of all.   [kss]

CRISPY AMBULANCE
Live on a Hot August Night EP (Bel. Factory Benelux) 1981
The Plateau Phase (Bel. Factory Benelux) 1982
Open Gates of Fire [tape] (nr/CSBT) 1983
The Blue & Yellow of the Yacht Club [tape] (nr/CSBT) 1983
Sexus EP (Bel. Factory Benelux) 1984 ●
Fin (Bel. Les Temps Modernes) 1984 + 1990 ●
Crispy Ambulance [CD] (Bel. Factory Benelux) 1990 ●

Manchester's Crispy Ambulance was one of the indie-label explosion bands that formed in the late '70s after such ensembles as Throbbing Gristle and the abrasively punky Mekons helped dig a niche for music that wasn't oriented to the rock'n'roll lifestyle or chart success. Despite a reputation as part of the city's gloom movement—thanks to an early association with Factory, a Joy Division gig at which Crispy Ambulance singer/synthesist Alan Hempsall subbed for Ian Curtis, and one studio foray with producer Martin Hannett—on the misleadingly titled **Live on a Hot August Night** 12-inch: two JD wannabe studio tracks that run a combined total of 22 minutes, including droning ambient passages—the quartet could actually be quite perky, even danceable, as on the posthumously issued "Sexus" single.

More soundsters than popsters, Crispy Ambulance at first produced landscapes of timbre and texture featuring canted vocals and sharp-edged guitar; the group later moved on to drawn-out moanings and synthesizer-produced textures mixed with shimmering guitar. At its best, Crispy Ambulance could create deceptively unobtrusive sci-fi scores; at worst, the music is little more than a pretentious sea of echoed din.

Recorded live (with occasionally dodgy sound) at various European shows in 1981 and '82, **Fin** shows just how active and abrasive the group's experiments with synthesizer and guitar textures could be, and acknowledges its stylistic foundations in a cover of Throbbing Gristle's "United."

Despite absurdly over-echoed percussion, **Plateau Phase** is pretty and introspective, with engrossing shifts in texture, tempo and tone and enough guts to ballast the gloomy elegance.

When the post-punk/gloom genre ended, so did Crispy Ambulance, closing up shop in late '82. (Although a subsequent incarnation named Ram Ram Kino put out a single on UK Temple.) In 1990, two CDs reissued virtually everything the group ever released (save for the two 1983 cassettes of live material and demos). **Crispy Ambulance** contains **The Plateau Phase** and both EPs; the new edition of **Fin** adds both sides of the band's 1980 debut single and a B-side.   ['e/i]

CRO-MAGS
The Age of Quarrel (Rock Hotel-Profile) 1986 ●
Best Wishes (Profile) 1989 ●

Although led by a Hare Krishna devotee, these New York hardcore kings neither jangle finger cymbals nor chant religious mantras on **The Age of Quarrel**, a blaze of state-of-the-art punk aggro. Vocalist John Joseph (co-lyricist with bassist Harley Flanagan) roars through humanist lyrics about peace, trust, independence and justice as the band keeps up the mid-speed speaker-shredding with two guitarists doing their best to update Ritchie Blackmore's throaty Deep Purple sound. Drummer Mackie regulates the tempo enough to ensure an adequate proportion of mosh parts (generally at the beginning of songs rather than the middle), but often unnervingly sounds like he's playing an entirely different song from his bandmates.

With varied tempos, extended song lengths, more guitar solos and effectively threatening atmosphere, an overhauled lineup—now featuring Flanagan on vocals (in place of the departed Joseph) and ex-Kraut guitarist Doug Holland sharing the axe duties with Parris Mitchel Mayhew—made an effective stylistic transition from metallic punk to punky metal on **Best Wishes**. While most of the tightly structured tracks thunder along with little subtlety (except in the lyrics), Flanagan does deliver his devotional sentiments in "The Only One" with dramatic flair. [i]

See also *Kraut*.

CROSSFIRE CHOIR

Crossfire Choir (Passport) 1986 •
Back to the Wall (Track) 1988

A major American label signed this up-from-Florida New Jersey quartet but never released their album; after the band was dropped, tracks recorded in England with producer Steve Lillywhite were retrieved and issued (along with three subsequent items) as a belated debut. Although the group had built a club reputation for punky outrageousness, this is far more familiar fare: urgent pop/rock with keyboards and a hint of potential pomposity. The music isn't bad, but guitarist J Pounders' grating dramatic warble is more memorable than his songs.

Nicely produced by Ed Stasium, **Back to the Wall** reduces the group's weaknesses (mainly by cranking up the rhythm guitars and mixing down Pounders' voice), but still doesn't find anything particularly worthwhile in the music. A petulant chorus of "Why can't we be on MTV?" reveals the Choir's problem: more ambition than talent. [i]

CROWDED HOUSE

Crowded House (Capitol) 1986 •
World Where You Live EP (nr/Capitol) 1987 •
Temple of Low Men (Capitol) 1988 •
I Feel Possessed EP (Capitol) 1989 •
Woodface (Capitol) 1991 •

Songwriter/singer/guitarist Neil Finn's post-Split Enz group follows the trend of that band's later albums towards simplification. Despite occasional keyboards (added on disc by Finn and producer Mitchell Froom and onstage by ex-Enzman Eddie Rayner, who co-wrote one of the first LP's songs), the trio's sound is a bit thin. Yet the melodic mix of tunes about dreams and nightmares, aching for love and the aching love causes, does prove enjoyable and affecting, given time; for its modest first impressions, **Crowded House** gradually developed into a substantial commercial success. (The **World**

Where You Live EP is four LP tracks plus a non-LP bonus.)

On **Temple of Low Men**, Froom's growing rapport with the group (and greater ability to integrate his keyboards) yields fuller, more varied musical textures. Ironically, some melodies seem unfinished, or maybe deliberately oblique. So while the album *sounds* much better, the quality of the best material here still doesn't match the debut's standouts. Finn's painful or ugly stream-of-consciousness fragments contribute to the overall loss-of-innocence feel: "I Feel Possessed" leads off, followed by "Kill Eye" (late-period Beatles from hell) and "Into Temptation"—you get the idea. A pretty dark album from such a seemingly light band. One gem, "Never Stay the Same," however, scintillates with possibilities both good and ill. Richard Thompson provides a guest guitar solo on "Sister Madly."

Rather than just release "I Feel Possessed" as a CD single, Capitol added three Byrds classics faithfully reproduced onstage by Byrdhouse (the band backing Roger McGuinn, get it?). Nice, but for fans only.

Bassist Nick Seymour, who also painted both Crowded House album covers, happens to be the brother of Hunters and Collectors leader Mark Seymour. In late '90, Tim Finn joined his brother's band, and the quartet began working on its third album. [jg]

See also *Split Enz*.

CRUCIFUCKS

The Crucifucks (Alternative Tentacles) 1985
Wisconsin (Alternative Tentacles) 1987

DOC CORBIN DART

Patricia (Alternative Tentacles) 1990

In pursuit of the ultimately offensive band name, these confrontational Michiganders were so successful that their first album incorporates actual spoken-word comments and run-ins with the law over it. Unfortunately, little else about the record is amusing: rudimentary slow-to-mid-speed punk with a truly obnoxious vocals by Doc Corbin Dart and obvious topical songs like "Hinckley Had a Vision," "Cops for Fertilizer" and "Go Bankrupt and Die."

Eulogizing the cheese state (where it was recorded) on their second LP, the Crucifucks unveil a surprising bit of wit and musical development. Dart still sounds like Pete Shelley's tuneless nerd cousin, but intelligent, politically correct lyrics ("Laws Against Laughing," "The Savior") and well-recorded electric and acoustic guitar raunch ("Concession Stand," "Pig in a Blanket") make **Wisconsin** commendable to, say, fans of the Dead Kennedys.

Whatever the band might have achieved, Dart's solo album is an altogether darker and more disturbing affair. The simple rock and folk (by Dart and two other multi-instrumentalists) may sound lighter and more appealing, but the lyrics' self-analytic torrent of fear, bitterness and withdrawal turn the album into a harrowing real-life nightmare. Imagine a wobbly ex-Buzzcock singing his emotional problems on a psychiatrist's couch and you'll get a sense of this unsettling exploration into a damaged psyche. That **Patricia** is both articulate and—dare it be said—oddly entertaining is a testament to Dart's talent and honesty. [i]

JULEE CRUISE
Floating into the Night (Warner Bros.) 1989 ●

In 1985, Iowa native Julee Cruise was a talent scout for soundtrack composer Angelo Badalamenti when he began working with David Lynch on *Blue Velvet*. She fit the spacey-baby-doll sound the director wanted, and wound up recording "Mysteries of Love"—lyrics by Lynch and music by Badalamenti—for the movie. The song set a format which the three have repeatedly explored: on Cruise's album, her appearances on *Twin Peaks*, an inane "avant-garde" stage production and home video (*Industrial Symphony No. 1*) and the *Twin Peaks* soundtrack LP, which contains three tracks lifted directly from **Floating into the Night**. (Besides numerous film scores, Badalamenti—who had a minor hit in the '60s as Andy Badale and the Nashville Beer Garden Band—has written songs for George Benson, Patti Austin and others.) Admittedly, it's a supremely seductive sound, marrying walking bass lines to dark, enveloping film noir jazz and swelling strings, with Cruise's ethereal come-hither vocals cooing coolly through it all. As produced by the Lynch/Badalamenti songwriting duo, some of the tracks veer dangerously close to elevator music but others, like "Rockin' Back Inside My Heart," are truly idiosyncratic and contain moments of real drama.   [ws]

CRUMBSUCKERS
Life of Dreams (Combat Core) 1986
Beast on My Back (Combat) 1988 ●

Life of Dreams is second-rate New York (Long Island) hardcore with a metal crossover edge: the Crumbsuckers have the essential audio elements (speed, volume, chops, croaked vocals) but nothing much on their minds. The LP has one oddity—a discussion of the 1984 Presidential campaign in "Super Tuesday"—but otherwise offers such routine middle-class contemplations as "Live to Work" and "Bullshit Society."

Beast on My Back (aka **B.O.M.B.**) turns the Crumbsuckers on their heads, stylistically speaking. This time out, armed with a new flight-of-the-bumblebee lead guitarist and high-def production (Randy Burns, remixed by Genya Ravan), they're a speedmetal band with some recalcitrant 'core tendencies. The nine long songs (none under three minutes, two over five) have mosh parts and shouted vocals, but don't all rely on breakneck down-strumming or double-bass foot-pedaling. More impressive than listenable, **B.O.M.B.** is an exhausting ride to nowhere.   [i]

CRUZADOS
Cruzados (Arista) 1985 ●
After Dark (Arista) 1987 ●

Despite the quartet's impressive non-mainstream pedigree—Tito Larriva and Chalo Quintana were in the Plugz, Steven Hufsteter was involved with various Kim Fowley-related ventures, including the Quick—Cruzados is a rather familiar-sounding melodic rock album with few distinguishing characteristics and no evident Southwest influences. Perhaps it's the fault of producer Rodney Mills, veteran of countless .38 Special albums. Or maybe the work these guys did on film scores or backing Bob Dylan on TV made them too slick. In any case, **Cruzados** is nothing to get excited about.

Envisioning chart possibilities in the post-Mellencamp world of simple heartland rock, the Cruzados replaced Hufsteter and augmented Mills with four more producers (including Waddy Wachtel) for their second LP. With guest appearances by everyone from the late Paul Butterfield to Pat Benatar to Don Henley, **After Dark** is a plain but solid effort. (Except for Larriva's "Time for Waiting," which sounds nauseatingly like the Eagles.)   [i]

See also *Havalinas, Plugz, Quick*.

CUCUMBERS
Fresh Cucumbers EP (Fake Doom) 1983
Who Betrays Me ... and Other Happier Songs (Fake Doom) 1985
The Cucumbers (Profile) 1987 ●

Charming, original pop from Hoboken, New Jersey. Guitarist Deena Shoshkes' lead vocal on "My Boyfriend" is Brenda Lee magic set to a dB's-like tune; elsewhere, the blend includes more edgy guitar work (by Jon Fried) and less fizzy charm. The other three songs on **Fresh** sacrifice some catchiness for added complexity, but all are likable.

The half-new quartet's **Who Betrays Me** is a full album of peppy melodies, thoughtful lyrics, semi-intricate guitar-based arrangements and appealing harmonies by Shoshkes and Fried. The spare "Everything Goes" blends a sultry melody and a fine dual vocal; "Desperation" sounds like an update on the Everly Brothers; "Walking and Talking" mixes and matches rhythms for a kicky B-52's effect; "Want to Talk" grafts on a mild Latin feel for a danceable slice of summer.

Recorded in London with a new bassist in the lineup, **The Cucumbers** leads off with a new version of "My Boyfriend" and then fails to deliver anything else equal to it. Overall, fancier production reduces the group's amateurish appeal and obscures its quirky personality; smoothed out and spruced up, the entirely presentable songs blur together. There are some acute lyrics, however: "My Town" is a clever ode to 'Boken, while "Shower" makes a cogent observation about men, women and water temperatures.   [i]

CUD
When in Rome, Kill Me (nr/Imaginary) 1989 ●
Elvis Belt (nr/Imaginary) 1990 ●
Leggy Mambo (nr/Imaginary) 1990 ●

Dadaistically detached from reality and selfconsciously eclectic, Cud matches obscure lyrical wit and simple parodic music on the jukebox-blender longplaying debut. The 21-minute title track of **When in Rome, Kill Me** is a series of seven dry jokes (the Morrissey tweak of "Only (A Prawn in Whitby)," the quirky-pop "Bibi Couldn't See," the vintage Britbeat of "Push and Shove," the garage psychedelia of "When in Rome, Kill Me Again," etc.) all linked by spoken drama. Elsewhere, the Leeds-area quartet trundles merrily through blistering fuzz-rock ("Van Van Van"), Pink Floyd pop ("Alison Springs") and a careful Dexys imitation ("Wobbly Jelly").

The second LP mostly collects up Cud's unfocused and dull early singles (going all the way back to 1987— wow!) and covers. (Imaginary is the label behind the tribute album fad, and Cud has appeared on its share.) While a previously unissued high-speed interpretation of the Bonzo Dog Band's "Urban Spaceman" is annoying but worth hearing, **Elvis Belt** (which contains one new number and an early version of **When in Rome**'s "I've Had It with Blondes") is unlikely to attract any new Cud-ettes.

Produced by XTC's Dave Gregory, **Leggy Mambo** brings Cud's surreality closer to serious accessibility with good playing, clear sound (finally) and less specific musical satire. Unfortunately, left to its own semi-nostalgic stylistic devices, Cud hasn't got enough personality or imagination to sustain an album. Despite a few cool pop tracks (the Buddy Hollyesque "Not Exactly D.L.E.R.C.," the inevitable Madchester spoofs of "Magic" and "Syrup and Sour Grapes"), **Leggy Mambo** is pointless and dull.   [i]

CUDDLY TOYS
See *Raped*.

CULT
Dreamtime (nr/Beggars Banquet) 1984 ●
Love (Sire) 1985 ●
Revolution EP (nr/Beggars Banquet) 1985
Electric (Beggars Banquet-Sire) 1987 ●
Lil' Devil EP (nr/Beggars Banquet) 1987 ●
The Manor Sessions EP [CD] (nr/Beggars Banquet)
   1988 ●
The Love Mixes EP [CD] (nr/Beggars Banquet) 1989 ●
The Electric Mixes EP [CD] (nr/Beggars Banquet) 1989 ●
Sonic Temple (Beggars Banquet-Sire-Reprise) 1989 ●

SOUTHERN DEATH CULT
The Southern Death Cult (nr/Beggars Banquet) 1983 ●

DEATH CULT
Death Cult EP (nr/Situation Two) 1983 ●

RITUAL
Kangaroo Court EP (nr/Red Flame) 1982

Less is more . . . or the saga of a British band whose fame grew as its name shrunk. The story begins in early '83, as the Southern Death Cult (from Bradford, a northern city near Leeds) has just broken up without releasing an album; various sessions and live takes were, however, compiled for a posthumous LP. As such, **The Southern Death Cult** paints an inconsistent picture of ominous and dense doom-punks with a serious power supply and few original ideas. The songs aren't much to brag about—drum-dominated drones at various tempos—and the performances, given their mongrel origins, are too muddy to really judge the band.

Singer Ian Astbury then formed Death Cult, which released two 1983 12-inches, one of them a four-songer containing "Brothers Grimm" and "Ghost Dance." (The EP's subsequent CD reissue contains the Death Cult's entire six-song oeuvre.) The following year, with its name finally reduced to just the Cult, the quartet got around to releasing a proper album. **Dreamtime**, an extremely intense and well-produced (by John Brand) outing, reveals Astbury's true intentions: hip heavy

metal. Domineering drums blend with Billy Duffy's layered lead guitar figures and Astbury's drama-drenched vocals on pseudo-poetic songs that oddly connect with the Doors and other bands of the first psychedelic era. Impressive in its clear-headed strength and attractive for its electric sound, **Dreamtime** is, like a lot of metal, exciting but empty and not a little stupid. (Initial quantities came with a bonus live LP.)

Love also chugs along enthusiastically, awash in Duffy's guitars and Astbury's sweeping vocals. The material—except for the atmospherically powerful and catchy "She Sells Sanctuary"—is pretty naff, with simple chord riffs providing a loud bed for draggy melodies and too much pointless riffing. (A lot of the drive and precision is due to drummer Mark Brzezicki, on loan from Big Country.) The invocation of '60s hard-rock and grunge-punk bands is subtle enough not to be obnoxious, but the Cult's relevance to modern times remains marginal at best. A subsequent EP adds non-LP tracks to **Love**'s "Revolution" (not the Beatles tune); **The Love Mixes** offers two variations on "She Sells Sanctuary" (including a dub dissection with—get this— baying wolves) and remixes of "Revolution," "Rain" and a track from the previous LP.

In these high concept times, it made perfect sense for the Cult to hook up with that great gazoo of '70s revisionism Rick Rubin, the production svengali behind numerous rap and metal acts, including the Beastie Boys and Slayer. On **Electric**, Rubin kitted out the Cult with a gargantuan drum sound and a frenetic guitar maelstrom, partially succeeding in having the band mimic AC/DC, although Astbury's vocals occasionally favor Leslie West on steroids, and the opening guitar of "Love Removal Machine" replicates the Stones' "Start Me Up." As sensually gratifying as it is cornball retromoronic, **Electric** can lay claim to one of history's worst versions of "Born to Be Wild." Not too surprisingly, the first track, "Wild Flower," is virtually a rewrite of "She Sells Sanctuary." The **Lil' Devil** EP contains the LP track, two live cuts (including "She Sells Sanctuary") and the previously unreleased "Zap City."

The Cult didn't plan on making **Electric** with Rubin. After recording a dozen tracks with Steve Brown (the producer of **Love**), the band decided they didn't like the results and asked Rubin for a remix, which turned into a redo. Left holding an entire alternate version of the record, the Cult used four tunes from it for B-sides and then put five remaining tracks out as **The Manor Sessions**. For what it's worth, Brown's work is less clearly articulated and focused than Rubin's, but in truth the Cult is the Cult is the Cult. **The Electric Mixes** completes the collection with extended edits of "Love Removal Machine" and "Wild Flower," another LP track and lumbering radio session takes on "King Contrary Man" and the non-LP "Conquistador."

Fully anointed as major stars in the post-Zeppelin hard-rock universe, the Cult parted ways with Rubin and drummer Les Warner, making the platinum **Sonic Temple** with a guest skin-beater and ex-Payola Bob Rock as producer. Beginning with a remark borrowed from Pete Townshend (as documented in *Monterey Pop*), the album is standard-issue Cult: Astbury bellows, Duffy squalls and bassist Jamie Stewart makes like John Paul Jones by doubling on keyboards. The closest the album comes to a stylistic groundbreaker—

"Edie (Ciao Baby)," a pseudo-poetic tribute to Edie Sedgwick complete with strings and an acoustic guitar intro—is one of the stupidest songs in the Cult's low-brow compositional closet. Meanwhile, "Soul Asylum," another idiotically clichéd lyrical display whose labored tempo makes it ideal for accompanying calisthenics, has nothing in common with the group of the same name.

Jamie Stewart, who was in on the formation of Death Cult and stuck with the Cult through 1989, began his musical career as the guitarist in a young Harrow post-punk band called Ritual. Following the 1982 "Mind Disease" 45, **Kangaroo Court** bears a strong resemblance to Theatre of Hate (a band which, coincidentally and simultaneously, included Billy Duffy for a year), with prominent sax riding over a simple doom drone. Ritual did record a full-length LP (**Songs for a Dead King**) which, like ToH and U.K. Decay, melded Brit-punk aggro and political/goth aesthetics; the record was never commercially released. While Stewart and drummer Raymondo jumped on board the Death Cult train, two other Ritualists hooked up with ex-U.K. Decay guitarist Spon in 1983 to form In Excelsis.   [i/gef]

See also *U.K. Decay*.

CULTURE

Two Sevens Clash (Lightning) 1978 (Shanachie) 1987 ●
Baldhead Bridge (nr/Magnum Force) 1978 ●
Africa Stand Alone (nr/April) 1978
Harder Than the Rest (nr/Front Line) 1978
Cumbolo (nr/Front Line) 1979 (Shanachie) 1988 ●
International Herb (nr/Front Line) 1979
Vital Selection (Virgin Int'l) 1981
Lion Rock (Heartbeat) 1982 ●
Culture in Culture (Jam. Blue Track) 1986 (Heartbeat) 1991 ●
Culture at Work (Shanachie) 1986 ●
The Peel Sessions EP (nr/Strange Fruit) 1987
Nuff Crisis! (Jam. Blue Mountain) 1988 (Shanachie) 1989 ●
Good Things (RAS) 1989 ●
Too Long in Slavery (Front Line) 1989 φ

Formed in Jamaica in 1976 and comprised of Joseph Hill, Kenneth Dayes and Albert Walker, Culture is one of reggae's greatest roots harmony trios. Lead singer Hill invokes the passion of a Burning Spear, while the others are reminiscent of the earthen and soulful rootical wails of the Itals. Despite a string of fine albums, Culture is most closely identified with their debut LP, **Two Sevens Clash**, and its apocalyptic title track. And rightly so: the song, first released in 1977, is a reggae classic, a perfect marriage of Rasta ideology and musicianship that struck a chord in punk England and became an influential scene staple. The music on the LP is smoky and mysterious—the keyboards are mixed way up front—but also rhythmically dynamic, with drummer Sly Dunbar turning in some of his best work. But the center is Hill's high, wavering voice. In song after song, he conveys his own distinctive blend of conviction and dread. Reissued a decade later, the album is every bit as consistent and compelling.

Besides his Rastafarian faith and African heritage, Hill's lyrics typically address the oppressed and the suffering. "Crack In New York" (**Nuff Crisis!**) will make

you want to dance because the music is so lively, but if you check the lyrics you really ought to cry. Similarly, the title track of **Good Things** is a warning to "make good use of good things" because the time will come when we or they won't be around.

The beauty of Culture is the group's ability to be contemporary and traditional at the same time. But while adhering to old-time standards and traditions, Culture is very much in the flow of things: **Culture in Culture**'s "Capture Rasta" acknowledges the popular "Sleng Teng" riddim of the mid-'80s.

Cumbolo is another Culture classic, loaded with the trio's trademark social commentary and prophetic, inspirational cantations. Among the highlights: "Natty Dread Naw Run," a handsome adaption of the folk-music standard "This Train," "Mind Who You Beg for Help" and the extraordinary title track.

The Peel BBC broadcast material dates from 1982 and includes "Two Sevens Clash" alongside three other tracks. **Too Long in Slavery** is a compilation of tracks from **Harder Than the Rest**, **International Herb** and **Cumbolo**.   [bk/aw]

CULTURE CLUB

Kissing to Be Clever (Virgin-Epic) 1982 (Virgin) 1990 ●
Colour by Numbers (Virgin-Epic) 1983 (Virgin) 1990 ●
Waking Up with the House on Fire (Virgin-Epic) 1984 (Virgin) 1990 ●
From Luxury to Heartache (Virgin-Epic) 1986 ●
This Time—The First Four Years (Virgin-Epic) 1987 ●

For a time England's biggest pop sensation, ludicrously heralded in America as leaders of a second British Invasion, Culture Club capitalized on Boy George's outrageous nightlife cross-dressing and aimed-to-shock intelligence to slip their mushy mainstream soul-pop into respectable homes the world over. Phenomenology aside, the foursome never sounded anywhere near as bizarre as they originally appeared; regarding their albums in coldly critical terms reveals them to be nice but meaningless: sophisticated dance pop that is insidiously memorable but utterly disposable.

Kissing to Be Clever has such Club standards as "Do You Really Want to Hurt Me," a warm reggae pulse supporting the catchy melody, and "I'll Tumble 4 Ya," a boppy, upbeat dance number. Spurred by the American success of the former as a single, the US label switched the LP's track order to highlight it, and later reissued it with a subsequent 45, "Time (Clock of the Heart)," appended.

Dropping the silly "white boy" crypto-sociology that threads through the first album, **Colour by Numbers** gets right to the business at hand, which is the creation of irresistible pop hits in a variety of molds. And in that regard, the album is a real success, containing as it does the mildly folk-rock-psychedelicized "Karma Chameleon" and "Church of the Poison Mind," as well as the more soul-oriented "Miss Me Blind" and "Black Money." Easily the best of the four albums, **Colour by Numbers** prominently features singer Helen Terry, who provides a powerful foil to George's smooth crooning.

Riding high on stardom, Culture Club blew their rock credibility and career momentum totally with the ultra-dull **Waking Up with the House on Fire**.

George's voice is fine and the band—drummer Jon Moss (ex-London), guitarist/keyboardist Roy Hay and bassist Mikey Craig—plays with maximum slickness and sophistication. But the songs are irredeemably awful. From the torpid velveeta of "Mistake No. 3" (apt title, that) to the juvenile stupidity of "The War Song" ("War is stupid . . . ") and the inane stop-start mess of "Hello Goodbye," there's no material equal to the early singles. With misguided intentions of achieving political relevance *and* added MOR acceptance, the album is an unmitigated disaster.

At that point, it seemed likely that the Club was on the verge of splitting up, and the lengthy delay in producing a new album only fueled speculation about the group's future. Nevertheless, the quartet managed to deliver **From Luxury to Heartache**, which isn't awful at all. Culture Club's new problem is their irrelevance: lacking controversy, a style to call their own or truly catchy songs, the LP offers nothing to hold onto, just a bunch of well-produced (Arif Mardin and Lew Hahn) mild soul/funk disposables. Given that Culture Club had never really changed musically, **From Luxury to Heartache** underscores the inexplicability of their original reception: it was ever thus.

Billed as "Twelve Worldwide Hits," **This Time—The First Four Years** consolidates all the essential 45s, plus "Love Is Love" from the *Electric Dreams* soundtrack. Despite occasionally brittle sound and the obligatory inclusion of dimwitted later material, "Karma Chameleon," "I'll Tumble 4 Ya," "Church of the Poison Mind," "Do You Really Want to Hurt Me" and "Time (Clock of the Heart)" just about covers Culture Club's basics for all but the most devoted aficionados. (The CD adds two cuts.)

George went solo in the wake of the band's long-anticipated 1987 collapse. Jon Moss attempted to launch a new band, Heartbeat UK, and released a debut single called "Jump to It." [i]

See also *Boy George*.

CULTURE SHOCK

See *Subhumans*.

DAVID CUNNINGHAM

See *Flying Lizards*.

C∗NTS

It Came from Out of the Garage (Disturbing) 1984
A Decade of Fun: 1978–1988 (Pravda) 1988

The Cunts (or C∗nts) latched severely onto '60s punk long before (or after) it was fashionable, steadfastly refusing to budge any way but laterally ever since, even as nominally parallel bands nationwide (and wider) have "discovered" the '70s, glitter, funk, metal, you-name-it. **It Came from Out of the Garage** is awash in grungy guitars, pumping keys and sneering attitudes, but sorely lacks the spark of inspiration that distinguished the band's obvious antecedents, like the Standells, Count Five, ? and the Mysterians, etc.

A Decade of Fun, by dint of its scattered sources, paints a slightly more varied portrait of the Chicago quintet—quirkier and less tunnel-visioned, consequently higher in its peaks and more turgid in its depths.

At best, the early singles (some of which make up Side One), the band echoes the sort of jagged '60s revisionism that characterized Cleveland in the mid-to-late-'70s. The later (previously unreleased) tracks on Side Two subtract most of the edginess from the equation, adding a poppier slant in direct proportion to the year of recording. [ab]

CURE

Three Imaginary Boys (nr/Fiction) 1979 •
Boys Don't Cry (Fiction-PVC) 1980 (Elektra) 1988 •
Seventeen Seconds (nr/Fiction) 1980 (Elektra) 1988 •
Faith (nr/Fiction) 1981 (Elektra) 1988 •
Carnage Visors [tape] (nr/Fiction) 1981
. . . Happily Ever After (Fiction-A&M) 1981
Pornography (Fiction-A&M) 1982 (Elektra) 1988 •
The Walk EP (Fiction-Sire) 1983
Japanese Whispers (Fiction-Sire) 1983 •
The Top (Fiction-Sire) 1984 •
Concert: The Cure Live (nr/Fiction) 1984
Concert and Curiosity (nr/Fiction) 1984 φ
The Head on the Door (Elektra) 1985 •
Quadpus EP (Elektra) 1986
Standing on a Beach: The Singles (Elektra) 1986
Staring at the Sea: The Singles [CD] (Elektra) 1986 •
Kiss Me Kiss Me Kiss Me (Elektra) 1987 •
The Peel Sessions EP (nr/Strange Fruit) 1988 (Strange Fruit-Dutch East India) 1991 •
Disintegration (Elektra) 1989 •
Pictures of You EP [CD] (Elektra) 1990 •
Integration [CD] (Elektra) 1990 •
Mixed Up (Fiction-Elektra) 1990 •
Entreat (nr/Fiction) 1991 •

FOOLS DANCE

Fools Dance EP (nr/Lambs to the Slaughter) 1985

Though catapulted to some early success with the pop hit "Boys Don't Cry," the Cure—led by obsessive singer/guitarist Robert Smith, originally with Michael Dempsey on bass (replaced after one LP by Simon Gallup) and Laurence (Lol) Tolhurst on drums—originally specialized in the presentation of a gloomy, nihilistic world view.

Three Imaginary Boys (released in America—and later England—as **Boys Don't Cry**, with several LP tracks replaced by singles) shows the Cure to be masters of the three-minute form, and includes some amazingly terse and effective musical dissertations on loneliness ("10:15 Saturday Night"), war and hatred ("Killing an Arab," "Fire in Cairo"), the precariousness of urban life ("Subway Song") and trendiness ("Jumping Someone Else's Train"). An intelligent, unique halfway point between Gang of Four and the Jam.

Seventeen Seconds moved the Cure—temporarily a quartet with Matthieu Hartley on keyboards—further into terra incognita, away from the pop song and into the angst epic. Some songs ("Play for Today," "In Your House") still offer a fading element of hope, but the title track, "The Final Sound" and "A Forest" all take a turn towards disconsolateness.

Despair arrives in **Faith** as an element of style. Sacrificing any pretense of fun, the music is strengthened by an impassioned but sedated mood, its themes as powerful and defiant as any in recent music. (**Carnage Visors**, which appears only as a bonus on the UK cassette version of **Faith**, is the hastily assembled instrumental soundtrack of a short film made for use on tour by Simon Gallup's brother, and provides even stronger reasons for locking up the razorblades while listening.)

The sarcastically titled **Happily Ever After** combines **Seventeen Seconds** and **Faith** into a double album for American release.

Pornography seems to be the climax of Smith's obsessions, by now coalesced into resigned paranoia; the music firmly establishes the group as superior if idiosyncratic. As usual, the true star here is the phobic, morbid atmosphere. Recommended, but not for the suicide-prone.

With Smith temporarily splitting his time between Siouxsie and the Banshees and his own band (which by this point revolved entirely around him and Tolhurst), a far different Cure emerged. The playful "Let's Go to Bed" heralded a new era of stylistic innovation and sporadic whimsy, played out on a series of singles beginning in late 1982. **The Walk** EP—four songs of New Orderish synth-based music that's more solemn than miserable—was also issued in the US with the earlier "Let's Go to Bed" and its flipside added. **Japanese Whispers**, a compilation of recent 45s, then appeared in both countries, reprising the entire American EP plus a subsequent bit of jazzy froth, "The Lovecats," and its similar B-side, "Speak My Language."

Having almost fully exercised their dalliance with light relief, Smith and Tolhurst, joined by a drummer and sax player, recorded **The Top**, which basically returns them to more familiar corners of gloomy self-indulgence. Except for "The Caterpillar," which is upbeat and likable pop, the record is not among the Cure's best, and disjointed excursions into psychedelia, heavy rock and dance rhythms only punctuate its shortcomings.

Over the course of the following two years, the Cure issued a lot of music, although only one new studio album arrived in the onslaught. The UK-only live record—drawn from a week of shows in May 1984—contains some of the group's most significant tracks to that point but is most notable in its cassette and CD versions, which add a bonus album's worth of demos (including a positively winsome May '78 rendition of "Boys Don't Cry," a full year prior to the song's release), live audience tapes and other curios ("from Robert's cassette collection") entitled **Cure Anomalies 1977–1984**.

The fine career-long singles compilation, **Standing on a Beach**, is also worth finding in its non-vinyl format. The tape adds a dozen B-sides; the CD edition, falling in line with the video-clip compilation, is titled **Staring at the Sea** and adds four tracks. (In a bizarre development, the LP's inclusion of "Killing an Arab" created an enormous tumult when an American pro-Arab organization, ignoring that the song had been in circulation since 1979, took its title from a famous Albert Camus novel and in no way advocates violence to Arabs, launched a political campaign against the band.)

With "In Between Days," **The Head on the Door** opens sounding exactly like New Order. By the second song, of course, Smith's fickle idiom dabbling returns the band—here a revamped quintet, with Simon Gallup back in the fold—to an entirely different world, via the mildly oriental "Kyoto Song," and follows in flamenco style with "The Blood." Toeing a line between pop and sullenness keeps the Cure from achieving maximal creative impact, but it's an altogether listenable album that is sporadically ("Push" and "Close to Me," for example) as eclectically brilliant as can be. The **Quadpus** EP joins two B-sides—including the bizarre "A Man Inside My Mouth"—to "Close to Me" and "A Night Like This" from the album.

Doubtless encouraged by growing international stardom, the Cure released an ambitious and challenging double-album, **Kiss Me Kiss Me Kiss Me**. Sporting a dense and dynamic arena-scaled rock sound and adding such touches as wah-wah guitar, sitar, strings and horns, the organically coherent album surges with gloomy power but also percolates with occasional bits of charming low-key pop. Smith's resolutely miserable, ironic lyrical visions ("The Kiss," "Shiver and Shake," "How Beautiful You Are . . .") fill even some of the musically lighter songs, although a few (including "Catch," "The Perfect Girl," "Hey You!!!" and "Why Can't I Be You?") do offer giddy love sentiments.

The Cure repeats the expansive, gauzy sonic approach of **Kiss Me** on **Disintegration**, but slows down and stretches out the material even more, perhaps enjoying the lazy rhythms and rich textures a bit too much. Despite the enervatingly trancey ambience that suffuses the record, Smith does come through with a few great songs—"Pictures of You," "Lovesong," the driving "Fascination Street"—that still take forever to get where they're going. (The CD and cassette add "Homesick" and "Last Dance.")

Remixing the seven-minutes-plus "Pictures of You" down to under five, the Cure attached four intricate, atmospheric live renditions (from a 1989 London show) of **Disintegration** songs and released it all as a CD EP. (In the UK, a collection of eight live **Disintegration** tracks from the same source were issued as **Entreat**, initially as a limited retail giveaway and later as a commercial item.)

Integration boxes up the four CD EPs (as originally issued) from **Disintegration**, throwing in a small group poster as an added incentive to indecisive consumers. Besides **Pictures of You**, there's **Lullaby** (adding a remix and two live tracks), **Fascination Street** (two remixes and a pair of non-LP studio creations) and **Lovesong** (also two mixes and two non-LP songs).

After years of keeping a very firm grip on the Cure's creative output, Robert Smith took the unprecedented step of inviting a variety of studio hounds to have a go at remixing the band's 12-inch catalogue and issuing an album of the ones that worked out to his satisfaction. The extremely uneven **Mixed Up** is a strange package, with one brand new song (the hard-rocking "Never Enough"), newly recorded and mixed re-creations of "The Walk" and "A Forest," a few previously issued versions of familiar singles and, most provocative, disfiguring reworkings of several Cure classics. "Close to Me" gets a shuffling house beat and horns; "Pictures of You" undergoes a complete dub/house remodeling; the dancefloor "Inbetween Days" is nearly unrecognizable. (In an amusing bit of format perversity, the bonus track of "Why Can't I Be You?" is *only* on vinyl.)

The Peel session from December 1978 records the original trio giving four early classics—including "Killing an Arab" and "Boys Don't Cry" (on which over-dubbed guitars ruin the illusion of it being a completely live effort)—skeletal readings that lack the familiar studio renditions' urgent excitement.

Bassist Simon Gallup, who left the Cure in 1982 (between **Pornography** and **The Walk**), is the leader of Fools Dance, a quintet whose lamely selfconscious five-song 12-inch EP was released shortly after Gallup rejoined the Cure.   [sg/i]

See also *Glove, Siouxsie and the Banshees.*

CURRENT 93

Lashtal (Bel. Laylah) 1983
Nature Unveiled (Bel. Laylah) 1984 ●
Dog's Blood Rising (Bel. Laylah) 1984 ●
In Menstrual Night (nr/United Dairies) 1986
Live at Bar Maldoror (nr/Mi-Mort Records) 1986 ●
Dawn (nr/Maldoror) 1987 ●
Imperium (nr/Maldoror) 1987
Swastikas for Noddy (Bel. Laylah) 1987 ●
Earth Covers Earth (nr/United Dairies) 1988
Looney Runes (nr/Durtro) 1991

CURRENT 93/COIL

Nightmare Culture (Bel. Laylah) 1985

Named after some theory or other of English mage Aleister Crowley, Current 93's early work used Crowley and Lautréament's *Maldoror* as the starting points for an occult trip tinged with tragic grandeur. David Michael Bunting (aka David Tibet) is the group's core, with significant assistance from Steve Stapleton of Nurse with Wound. The motto on early albums is "How can there be pleasure, how can there be joy, when the whole world is burning?" On later albums, Tibet finds some joy, though the listener may not, as the music is far less compelling.

Lashtal, a three-track EP recorded with Fritz Haaman of 23 Skidoo and John Balance of Coil, is ritualistic music using Tibetan thighbone, slow, trance-like drumming, droning electronics and tapes of chanting (perhaps old recordings of Crowley). **Nature Unveiled** is more fully developed and points the way of the next several albums. Stapleton's production is evident on both side-long pieces, which use layers of Gregorian chants and modified requiems, menacing electronic drones and Tibet's own chantings and moanings, cut up and reassembled. The perfect soundtrack for a documentary (shot in murky black and white) about the inner lives of Notre Dame gargoyles.

Dog's Blood Rising takes the concept a stage further, with more sophisticated production and less reliance on the plundering of pre-existing music. At once angrier *and* more restrained, **Dog's Blood** is the best Current 93 album to date. "Jesus Wept" and "Falling Back in Fields of Rape" (each of which runs about fourteen minutes) rise with agonizing screams and fall back to near silence, intermingling the 12th century and science fiction to lament the cruelty and abnegation of responsibility in the contemporary world. "From Broken Cross Locusts" takes its form from Tibetan liturgical music, but uses electronically modified vocals and electronic drums. The album closes with a humorous but chilling a cappella medley of Simon & Garfunkel hits.

Current 93 shares **Nightmare Culture** with Coil,

employing Eastern chanting, growling electronics and tapes to create a mood similar to **Dog's Blood**. **Live at Bar Maldoror** recycles many of the same tapes used on **Nature Unveiled** and **Dog's Blood** but plays them in a different order, often mixing tapes from both albums together, and layering new electronics over them. Not as essential as either of the albums from which it draws, but quite good and different enough. (The CD adds two excellent tracks from a compilation album.)

In Menstrual Night, originally a limited-edition picture disc but later reissued as a regular LP (Current 93 habitually puts out limited editions which are subsequently re-released), has a gentler sound, with a steady drumbeat all the way through one side and pleasant electronics and tape loops with religious themes. The other half consists of tape loops and processed old English folk melodies. This record, which sounds similar to later Nurse with Wound records, is on that band's label.

Compared to prior Current 93 releases, **Imperium** is almost a folk album, though a strange and decidedly moody one. Tibet pretentiously intones ecclesiastical lyrics over muted, faux-Elizabethan flute, electronic growling, lute plucking, a simple drumbeat (on one track) and some bass (on another), all cloaked in a fog of production. Not the band's best.

Dawn temporarily reversed the gentleness trend. The title track is an abrasive, highly structured tour de force, a recurring loop of a man saying "destruction destruction" followed by slabs of guitar feedback, then various electronics. The other side is a live version of "Maldoror is Dead," the best rendition yet of a song that can also be found on **Nature Unveiled** and an early cassette-only release.

With **Swastikas for Noddy**, Simon & Garfunkel get the last laugh. Tibet had written some folkish songs for Death in June, but always kept to a more occult mood for his Current 93 work. On **Swastikas**, he delivers traditional numbers like "Oh Coal Black Smith" and originals in the same vein. Most of the folk songs retain a melancholy feel, though strummed guitar replaces the Gregorian chants. While the electronics and eeriness remain on tracks like "Panzer Rune," the upbeat "Beausoleil" could be played by any but the most cowardly college radio station. (A couple of 12-inch singles released around the same time attempted to weld the new folk orientation with the older kind of lyrics and an almost danceable beat, yielding decidedly awkward results.)

For **Earth Covers Earth**, Tibet slipped further into the land of the Incredible String Band, going so far as to pay homage to that duo's 1968 LP, **The Hangman's Beautiful Daughter**, in the cover photo. Unfortunately, Tibet's talents don't nearly equal those of his icons. Nice but vacuous.   [sl]

See also *Nurse with Wound.*

BILLY CURRIE

See *Ultravox.*

CURTISS A

Courtesy (Twin/Tone) 1980
Damage Is Done (Twin/Tone) 1984
A Scarlet Letter (Twin/Tone) 1988

SPOOKS

1980–1990 EP (Twin/Tone) 1978

Curt Almsted is a talented songwriter with a great sense of humor, an adequate if colorless voice and connections with every other local Minneapolis musician (except maybe Prince), many of whom played on his first album. The tracks are energetic rockers in a niche between Marshall Crenshaw, Bruce Springsteen and George Thorogood, but much rawer and less predictable.

Damage Is Done is a more mature record that draws further on sources like primal soul to stretch Almsted's expanding skills (most notably as a singer, now showing signs of Van Morrison and Willy DeVille as well) and to better display eleven well-drawn, heartfelt songs. The production is generally quite sympathetic, but the drums sound like distant cardboard boxes, and that significantly cuts down on the album's impact. There's still something missing—maybe a grander setting—that keeps Almsted a minor-leaguer, but he certainly has the wherewithal to move on up.

Almsted then went through a bad patch, losing longtime sideman Bob Dunlap to the Replacements, suffering a death in the family and ultimately winding up in jail on a battery charge involving an ex-girlfriend. Piling up years of bitterness over a number of women, Almsted spews out his pain on **A Scarlet Letter**, with NRBQ guitarist Al Anderson producing and heading up the backing band. Nakedly emotional missives like "I Wanna Make You Happy," "Starting to Cry," "I Can't Call Mary Anymore" and the brilliantly titled "(I Feel Just Like George Jones When He Was a) Heel to Tammy" get soulful treatment from Almsted's impassioned voice, which has really come to resemble DeVille's. Easily his best record, **A Scarlet Letter**—unironically dedicated to Ike Turner—avoids hysteria for deep feelings that translate into resonant roots rock.

Almsted's early band, Spooks, debuted in '78 with a 7-inch EP of weird, punkish rock'n'roll (including "Scum of the Earth," a tribute to Travis Bickle) that bears little (but not no) resemblance to his subsequent work.   [i]

CHRIS CUTLER

See *Henry Cow, Pere Ubu, David Thomas.*

ANDRE CYMONE

Livin' in the New Wave (Columbia) 1982
Survivin' in the 80's (Columbia) 1983
AC (Columbia) 1985 ●

An early member of Prince's touring ensemble, Cymone did his own "look ma, no band" musical crossover LP in 1982. Less horny and inspired than his former employer's contemporaneous approach, Cymone is nonetheless a strong contender in his own right and seems exhilarated (note the title of his first album) by the possibilities inherent in the same area of musical commingling.

Although **Survivin' in the 80's** still shows a lot of Prince's influence (especially imagewise—check the costumed male/female black/white band photo on the cover), Cymone is working more typical dancefloor terrain than the Purple One, with processed vocals and mild scratch production adjusting the slow funk grooves of numbers like "Make Me Wanna Dance" and "Body Thang." Slick and functional, but no creative landmark.

Back on his own in the studio, Cymone created **AC** with only skimpy outside assistance. Prince wrote and co-produced one easily recognizable track ("The Dance Electric") that also features backing vocals by Wendy and Lisa; Cymone allowed others to add a few jots of percussion and vocals as well. Otherwise, Cymone remains perfectly capable—like his ex-boss—of working easily and independently in a number of styles, from languid reflection ("Pretty Wild Girl") to pretty balladry ("Sweet Sensuality") to kinetic dance music ("Book of Love," "Satisfaction").

Although Cymone hasn't made a record under his own name in a while, his full-service production/writing work with Jody Watley and Adam Ant has kept him busy and successful through the late '80s.   [jg/i]

See also *Adam and the Ants, Prince.*

CYNICS

Blue Train Station (Get Hip-Skyclad) 1986
Twelve Flights Üp (Get Hip-Skyclad) 1988
Blue Train Sessions [CD] (Get Hip-Skyclad) 1989 ●
Rock'n'Roll (Get Hip-Skyclad) 1989 ●
Sixteen Flights Up [CD] (Get Hip-Skyclad) 1990 ●

Neo-garage-psychedelia from a Pittsburgh quintet weaned on "the punk explosions of '66 and '77." Standouts in an overworked genre, the Cynics achieve a quintessential evocation of their ancestors' glorious sound on **Blue Train Station** and **Twelve Flights Üp**. Gregg Kostelich's guitars buzz with primal distortion as Michael Kastelic blurts out the lyrics in a sneery whine from somewhere deep within the sonic blur. Grungier than a seedy bar and more energetic than a class of sugared-up toddlers, the Cynics pack both albums (an evenhanded mix of strong originals and vintage obscurities) with surefooted atmosphere and excitement.

Blue Train Sessions and **Sixteen Flights Up** are remixed, expanded CD versions of the Cynics' first two albums, with improved sound quality and added tracks. The latter disc also features some entertaining snatches of pissed-off studio chat.

Rock'n'Roll presents an altered band lineup (with a change in drummers and no replacement for departed organist Beki Smith), an increased emphasis on original material and a slightly updated recording approach. More than ever, the songs are catchy and to-the-point, and the band performs them with an intensity that renders questions of revivalism irrelevant.   [i/hd]

HOLGER CZUKAY

See *Can, David Sylvian, Jah Wobble.*

D D D D D D D

DAG NASTY
Can I Say (Dischord) 1986
Wig Out at Denkos (Dischord) 1987
Field Day (Giant) 1988 ●

JUNKYARD
Junkyard (Geffen) 1989 ●
Sixes, Sevens & Nines (Geffen) 1991 ●

With Dave Smalley of Boston's DYS on vocals and Brian Baker (ex-Minor Threat/Meatmen) on guitar, this DC quartet began as something of a supergroup; with co-production by Ian MacKaye, the debut sounds a lot like Minor Threat. Hardcore pop with heart and harmonies, it's still much rougher than Smalley's next stop, All. Pithy and articulate, with a share of straight-edge sentiments, this is music for moshers and homebodies alike.

With a new singer and bassist, **Wig Out at Denkos** is a more streamlined affair that replaces most of the first LP's frantic tempos with rockier dynamics. Peter Cortner's vocals are much more musical than Smalley's, which only enhances the noticeably sharper material, especially the neat title track.

With another lineup change (this time it's the drummer), **Field Day** is an excellent punky pop record that is by turns soulful ("The Ambulance Song") and aggressive ("Dear Mrs. Touma"). The Ruts' influence on DC punk bands shows up in an exciting cover of "Staring at the Rude Boys" and Dag Nasty's own foray into dub lite, "Never Green Lane." A re-recorded "Under Your Influence" (from **Can I Say**) and (as one of the four CD bonus tracks) Wire's "12 XU," a staple from Baker's Minor Threat days, are well-integrated into this diverse and tunefully accessible collection that has penetrating personal lyrics.

The following year, Baker resurfaced in LA metallurgists Junkyard, teamed with, of all people, former Big Boy Chris Gates. Despite the pedigree, the band's first LP is a horrible major-label bomb. [db]

See also *All, DYS, Meatmen, Minor Threat.*

JEFF DAHL GROUP
Vomit Wet Kiss (Sympathy for the Record Industry) 1987
Scratch Up Some Action (Aus. Dog Meat) 1989
(nr/Shakin' Street) 1990

JEFF DAHL
I Kill Me (Triple X) 1990 ●
Ultra Under (Triple X) 1991 ●

VOX POP
The Band, the Myth, the Volume EP (Goldar) 1982

POWERTRIP
When We Cut We Bleed (Public) 1983 (PVC) 1987

JESTERS OF DESTINY
Fun at the Funeral (Dimension-Restless) 1986
In a Nostalgic Mood EP (Dimension-Metal Blade-Restless) 1987 ●

A decade after releasing an inept debut single on Washington DC's Doodley Squat label, guitarist/singer Dahl—by then a Los Angeles-based veteran of several local bands, including Vox Pop (with Paul B. Cutler), the Angry Samoans, the Mentors (briefly) and his own Powertrip (pioneering speedmetal)—made his first solo album, **Vomit Wet Kiss**. Fronting an adjustable lineup that, on some tracks, includes ex-Dead Boy guitarist Cheetah Chrome, Dahl revisits the Stooges in competent but undistinguished loud rock with metal/punk fringes. (Just skip the clenched-teeth version of "Paint It, Black" and the acoustic "Lustful Glances.")

Leading a quartet of Amy Wichmann (guitar), Bruce Duff (bass) and Del Hopkins (drums)—with assists from Cheetah and Rikk Agnew—Dahl returned with the better-produced, excellently played **Scratch Up Some Action**. This **Raw Power**-styled roar of razor-edge rock makes rocket fuel out of obvious covers ("White Light/White Heat," "1970," "Two-Headed Dog") but runs into trouble with some of Dahl's originals.

Named for a song on the second album, **I Kill Me** was actually recorded prior to the first and includes (on the LP, and as cassette/CD bonuses) some of the same tracks as **Vomit Wet Kiss**. Dahl airs his Iggy aspirations with obvious vocal inflections on "Goin' Underground" (a song he co-wrote with Chrome) and a spot-on cover of "Search and Destroy"; otherwise the potent but uneven album focuses on self-preservation, with songs like "This Stuff Is Killin' Me," "Haven't Had a Drink in a Long Time" and "The Boy Who Self-destroyed" (with most of the Angry Samoans guesting).

Bassist Duff, another longtime LA scene vet and rock critic, and guitarist Ray Violet led the Jesters of Destiny, unseriously metalesque cultural scavengers who, on **Fun at the Funeral** (a title which pretty well conveys the band's innocuous attitude), cleverly crib song plots from exploitation movies ("God Told Me To") and other horror stories ("Incubus"), with enough wit to quote "Eleanor Rigby" while they're at it.

In a Nostalgic Mood is a pointless all-covers EP: humorless hard-rock renditions of classics by Hendrix, Creedence, Sabbath and two others. [i]

See also *Angry Samoans, Chemical People.*

DALE
See *Missing Persons.*

167

DALIS CAR

See *Peter Murphy*.

ROLF DAMMERS

See *Can*.

DAMNED

Damned Damned Damned (nr/Stiff) 1977 (nr/Demon) 1986 (Frontier) 1989 ●
Music for Pleasure (nr/Stiff) 1977 (nr/Demon) 1986 ●
Machine Gun Etiquette (nr/Chiswick) 1979 (nr/Big Beat) 1982 (Emergo) 1991 ●
The Black Album (IRS) 1980 ●
Friday the 13th EP (nr/NEMS) 1981
The Best of the Damned (nr/Big Beat) 1981 (Emergo) 1991 ●
Strawberries (nr/Bronze) 1982 (nr/Dojo) 1986 ●
Live at Shepperton 1980 (nr/Big Beat) 1982 ●
Live in Newcastle (nr/Damned) 1983
Damned EP (nr/Stiff) 1985
Damned but Not Forgotten (nr/Dojo) 1985 ●
Phantasmagoria (MCA) 1985 ●
Is It a Dream? EP (nr/MCA) 1985
Damned Damned Damned/Music for Pleasure (nr/Stiff) 1986
The Captain's Birthday Party (nr/Stiff) 1986
The Peel Sessions EP (nr/Strange Fruit) 1986 ●
Not the Captains Birthday Party? (nr/Demon) 1986
Anything (MCA) 1986 ●
The Peel Sessions EP (nr/Strange Fruit) 1987 ●
Mindless, Directionless, Energy. Live at the Lyceum 1981 (ID-Revolver) 1987 ●
The Light at the End of the Tunnel (MCA) 1987 ●
The Long Lost Weekend: Best of Volume 1 1/2 (nr/Big Beat) 1988
Final Damnation (Restless) 1989 ●
The Peel Sessions Album (nr/Strange Fruit) 1990 (Strange Fruit-Dutch East India) 1991 ●
EP (nr/Deltic) 1990

NAZ NOMAD & THE NIGHTMARES

Give Daddy the Knife Cindy (nr/Big Beat) 1984 ●

Noted for being the very first British punk band to issue an album (Stiff's first LP) as well as the first to tour America, the Damned hold a special position in history, if not always in music. Over an exceedingly checkered multi-label career—breakups, reformations, side projects, farewell gigs, a spell as the Doomed, vast popularity, near obscurity—the Damned have consistently managed to shatter expectations and defy the odds, wreaking havoc and nonchalantly tweaking convention. But getting a cogent critical perspective on their large recorded oeuvre is as elusive as attempting to read the label on a spinning 45.

Damned Damned Damned was a major groundbreaker, a stripped-down punk album of high-speed songs filled with raunchy guitar rock and equally aggressive sentiments. With Nick Lowe producing, the Damned trounced such then-hard-to-challenge traditional recording values as musical precision and studio-quality sound. Unfailingly energetic and vital, it's the only Damned studio album to feature the original lineup of Dave Vanian (vocals), Brian James (guitar), the ex-

ceptionally skillful Rat Scabies (drums) and Captain Sensible (bass). Just to heighten the bratty iconoclasm, early copies of the sleeve "goofed"; the back cover pictured rivals Eddie and the Hot Rods in lieu of the Damned.

Surprisingly enough, the second Damned opus was produced by Nick Mason of Pink Floyd. With added guitarist Lu Edmonds and no stylistic plan, the attack sounds blunted, and there aren't as many great songs as on the first LP. Despite a great cover, **Music for Pleasure** doesn't live up to the title. (Stiff reissued both LPs as a mail-order-only double in 1986.)

The Damned broke up and reformed several times before cutting **Machine Gun Etiquette** with a new lineup. Sensible had traded bass for guitar, Lu had departed (to join a number of bands, including Public Image) and ex-Saints bassist Algy Ward had joined. (Ward left after the one album, going on to form a grebo metal band, Tank, which has released at least five LPs.) Despite the tumult, the band is totally revitalized and on top of things—more mature, but no less crazy—tearing through great numbers like "Love Song," "I Just Can't Be Happy Today" (both UK hits), "Smash It Up" and the anthemic "Noise Noise Noise." A great record by a band many had already counted out. The 1991 CD/cassette reissue has a new cover, cool liner notes by Jack Rabid and bonus tracks: a six-minute edit of 1983's "White Rabbit" plus three erstwhile B-sides: "Ballroom Blitz," "Suicide" and "Rabid (Over You)."

With ex-Hot Rod bassist Paul Gray joining the lineup, the **Black Album**—a two-record set in the UK, one disc in America—takes off in a totally different direction, displaying unexpected character traits. The first two sides (the entire US release) are packed with melodic rock verging on power pop, using acoustic guitar, vocal harmonies, mellotron and synthesizers, as well as other seemingly inconceivable components. "Wait for the Blackout" and "Dr. Jekyll and Mr. Hyde" indicate how far the debonair Damned had traveled; other tracks prove that they had not abandoned the roar'n'roll with which they began. But the last two sides are dead weird: one is a single composition, strung together by church organ, that doesn't work; the other a live best-of that's impressive but halfbaked. (**Live at Shepperton 1980** comes from the same gig, but runs for two sides, not one, offering such additional tunes as "Neat Neat Neat" and "Help.")

Friday the 13th, a four-song 7-inch of new non-LP material released during the band's brief (and unproductive) liaison with the NEMS label, features "Disco Man," "Billy Bad Breaks" and a cover of the Stones' "Citadel." Meanwhile, the band's former label put together **The Best of the Damned**—not exactly that, but rather a reasonable collection of '76-'80 singles (A-sides and some B-sides) from "New Rose" to "Wait for the Blackout," including Sensible's worthless 1982 solo cover of Elton Motello's "Jet Boy, Jet Girl." (As **Damned Damned Damned** had finally been released in the States, the worthless '91 reissue of **The Best of the Damned** deletes "Neat Neat Neat," replacing it with the "White Rabbit" single, and swaps the classic "New Rose" for a live version.)

Mindless, Directionless, Energy was recorded live in London (1981) with the Scabies-Sensible-Vanian-Gray lineup and boasts crummy sound and an indifferent set of songs. "Smash It Up," "Love Song" and "I Feel Alright" are fair inclusions that receive exciting performances, but a terrible rendition of Sweet's "Ballroom Blitz" (dedicated to Lady Di and sung with a chorus of "great big tits") and other duff items make this dodgy record worth burying, not buying. (The CD adds a blistering "New Rose.") Yet another live album, **Not the Captains Birthday Party?** documents an earlier era, capturing the original band running through some of the first album onstage at London's Roundhouse in late 1977. A show from Newcastle was released as an authorized bootleg in '83.

The two EPs (later joined on a single disc and issued in the US) of live-in-the-studio material were recorded for John Peel's BBC radio show in November 1976 and May 1977 and provide solid evidence of the young band's playing abilities away from Nick Lowe's compressed/accelerated production. The earlier date (released second) offers punchy renditions of "Neat Neat Neat," "Stab Your Back," "New Rose" and two more. Besides shoddy performances and flat sound, the choice of material for the '77 session is weak, capped by "Fan Club" and "Sick of Being Sick."

Despite a humorous porcine cover shot, **Strawberries** is a gormless, old-sounding affair that drags itself along with neither bite nor character. Short of truly terrible, it's merely forgettable. (Outtakes from this album were later packaged as a 1990 EP on Sensible's Deltic label.)

Another compilation, **Damned but Not Forgotten** covers roughly '81 to '84, with tracks from assorted singles (including B-sides), **Friday the 13th** and elsewhere.

Phantasmagoria is mainly Vanian's show. His imposing singing on graveyard items like "Grimly Fiendish" and "Sanctum Sanctorum" provides the character the songs themselves lack. Jon Kelly's production (complete with horror-film effects and phantom-of-the-opera organ) is adequate, but the Damned no longer has a unique sound beyond Vanian, so it's fairly academic. (The LP was also issued in the UK with a bonus blue vinyl 12-inch of the subsequent "Eloise," a drippy Paul Ryan song which became a hit for them.) An EP of the album's "Is It a Dream" adds four live tracks.

Released pseudonymously by Naz Nomad & the Nightmares, **Give Daddy the Knife Cindy** is the Damned's imaginary '60s psychedelic film soundtrack, filled with covers of such classics as "I Had Too Much to Dream (Last Night)," "Kicks," "Nobody but Me," Kim Fowley's "The Trip," plus a pair of originals. The material is great, but the unembellished studio performances are merely functional. A nice thought anyway.

Stability—the Damned's lineup of Vanian, Rat, guitarist/keyboardist Roman Jugg (who joined in 1981) and bassist Bryn Merrick lasted from 1984 until 1987—evidently had a negative effect on the band's creativity. **Anything** boasts a neat version of Love's "Alone Again Or," but otherwise falls well short of achieving anything memorable. Despite the Damned's proven ability to alternately rock gothic and play nice, there's no audible point to the music; it's hard to imagine who would find this LP pleasurable.

The Light at the End of the Tunnel is a haphazardly sequenced two-record decade-spanning compilation with a dandy family tree by that British national treasure, Pete Frame. The unassailable 27-cut selection includes hits, album cuts, non-LP mixes, B-sides (like "Help" from '77) and other rarities, but what possible illogic guided the track order? ("New Rose," "Neat Neat Neat," "I Feel Alright" and "I Feel the Pain" are all on different sides!)

The Long Lost Weekend is a fairly useless compilation of odds and ends from '79-'84: singles, three tracks from **Friday the 13th**, four cuts from **Strawberries**, even a joint recording ("Over the Top") with Motörhead.

In the late '80s, with Sensible's solo career off the charts, the Damned—Vanian, Scabies, Sensible, James, Merrick and Jugg—began doing reunion shows, culminating in a triumphant ten-date US tour in 1989. The live **Final Damnation**, taped the previous year in London, has seventeen of the songs you want to hear performed at reasonable tempos in a powerful mix of musical skill and self-amused abandon. With nothing left to prove, the Damned merrily live the legend without making a fuss about it. Easily their best live record and the only one truly worth owning.

The album title was evidently serious. (No, really. We mean it this time . . .) The Damned have apparently called it quits, as latest reports have Vanian, Jugg and Merrick working together in a new band called the Phantom Chords. [i]

See also *Captain Sensible, Lords of the New Church*.

DANGTRIPPERS
Days Between Stations (Dog Gone) 1989 ●

Byrdsy Midwest power-pop bands are a dime a dozen, but when the occasional one with that special something (could it be . . . talent?) comes along, it makes up for all the uninspired strivers. This unassuming rock-pop quartet from Iowa City, Iowa, doesn't do anything out of the ordinary on **Days Between Stations**, but the consistently fine songs and the able-bodied performances make it an eminent delight. Tunes? Strong and memorable. Harmonies? Alluring and modestly employed. Lyrics? Simple but not simpleminded. Playing? Guitars weave in and around each other over a sturdy rhythm section. (Kenn Goodman of the Service provides guest keyboards.) Just wonderful. [i]

DANNY & DUSTY
The Lost Weekend (A&M) 1985

This one-off studio bender assembles the cream of LA's cowpunk society for a batch of rowdy tunes about drinkin', lovin', gamblin' and losin'. The cast: Dan Stuart and Chris Cacavas of Green on Red, Steve Wynn and Dennis Duck of Dream Syndicate and most of the Long Ryders. Produced by Paul Cutler, **The Lost Weekend** offers a saucy good time, short on significance, but long on ambience and spirit. For reference, a version of Dylan's "Knockin' on Heaven's Door" typifies the tenor of Wynn/Stuart's collaborative songwriting. [i]

DANNY AND THE DOORKNOBS
See *Trotsy Icepick*.

DANSE SOCIETY

Seduction EP (nr/Society) 1982
Heaven Is Waiting (Arista) 1984
Looking Through (nr/Society) 1986

Selfconsciously arty and needlessly dramatic, this quintet from England's southwest occasionally mixes almost straightforward rock into its dense techno-dance rhythms, yielding a reasonably good song now and again. **Seduction** is a longwinded six-track 12-inch with busy Bauhaus-strength mud supporting sporadic vocals and gimmicky sound effects. Tuneless and tedious.

Danse Society reached America with the full-length **Heaven Is Waiting**: further plodding nonsense that can claim the abrasive but catchy dance-rock of the title track and a weirdly modernized reading of the Stones' already spacey "2000 Light Years from Home."

Billed as the band's final album (but claiming ominously that "the end is only the beginning"), **Looking Through** is more tedious and repetitive new wave disco for the doomy haircut-and-mascara brigade. Lacking any striking material, this is functional genre fare for yesterday's club kids. [i]

DANZIG

Danzig (Def American-Geffen) 1988 ●
Danzig II—Lucifuge (Def American-Geffen) 1990 ●

At the very crest of Misfits cult mania, producer Rick Rubin decided to help ex-'Fits vocalist Glenn Danzig realize his dream of making his current group, Samhain, more professional and focused. As Danzig, the band has achieved significant commercial success while remaining true to fans' sanguinary tastes.

Cleaving Glenn's signature groaning and pagan-demono-sexuality lyrics to a more basic hard-rock foundation, **Danzig** ends up as a crunchy cross between the Doors, Misfits and Black Sabbath. With the benefit of a real band—tasteful, metallic guitarist John Christ, Samhain holdover Eerie Von (bass) and dexterous vet Chuck Biscuits (ex-D.O.A., Black Flag and Circle Jerks, perhaps the greatest punk rock drummer ever)—behind him, Danzig's amazing voice has never sounded as clear or as dominant. While roughly half of the album is ominous and mighty ("Twist of Cain," "She Rides," "Soul on Fire" and "Mother"), the rest proves shallow on repeated listenings, displaying the weak side of Rubin's thinly homogeneous production.

Lucifuge corrects the flaws: Rubin's production is far fleshier, the theatrically demonic muscle-stud angle is entertainingly exercised, the songs (especially the cool, dank beauty of "Her Black Wings," with its subtly menacing riff, and a '50s-style melodic tearjerker, "Blood and Tears") are consistently stronger, and a heavy dose of voodoo blues (check out the stripped-down "I'm the One") is wisely incorporated into the thematic and musical brew. [gef]

See also *Misfits*.

TERENCE TRENT D'ARBY

Introducing the Hardline According to Terence Trent D'Arby (Columbia) 1987 ●
Terence Trent D'Arby's Neither Fish nor Flesh (Columbia) 1989 ●

THE TOUCH WITH TERENCE TRENT D'ARBY

Early Works (Ger. IMP-Polydor) 1989 ●

Once he topped the US charts with "Wishing Well," the press was full of talk about hype but, hit or not, expatriate American Terence Trent D'Arby is an outstanding soul singer. Versatile, too, with the ability to produce a compelling gospel wail ("If You All Get to Heaven"), a funky shout ("Dance Little Sister") or a sultry romantic come-on ("Sign Your Name"). Confident down to his toenails, D'Arby inspires favorable comparisons to such luminaries as Al Green, Sam Cooke and Smokey Robinson, and he rocks out, to boot. (Fans of early-'70s British rock may recognize the Roger Chapman influence on "If You Let Me Stay.")

Of course, true artistes don't pander to the marketplace. With that in mind, TTD threw a major-league curve on his second LP, rejecting the commercial strengths of his debut for moody experiments. As he announces in the opening track, "I will not be defined." No kidding! **Neither Fish nor Flesh** (modestly subtitled **A soundtrack of love, faith, hope & destruction**) showcases creepy falsetto vocals and downbeat tunes à la later Marvin Gaye mixed with screwy, skeletal rockers, psychedelic funk and, to add a touch of normalcy, a few shots of (more or less) southern-fried soul. Individually, most of the tracks have virtues; collectively, they add up to the most unfocused record in the history of western civilization.

The Touch's album is routine pop-soul recorded in Germany in '83, when TTD was still developing his moves. Such are the skeletons that plague the famous. [jy]

DARK DAY

See *DNA*.

DARKSIDE

All That Noise (nr/Situation Two) 1990 (Beggars Banquet-RCA) 1991 ●

The ex-Spacemen 3 rhythm section of this Rugby, England, trio (which became a quartet after making **All That Noise**) has the Doors' old rainy-night bass/drums sound down cold; the remaining elements on this atmospheric but routine debut are lazy artless-pop vocals (by bassist Pete Bassman), bits of wheedly organ and guitar work that ranges from a translucent drizzle to a flood of distortion. This sort of bland and derivative mock-'60s tedium may go down like soda in the UK nowadays, but that doesn't make it right. [i]

DARLING BUDS

Pop Said ... (Columbia) 1988 ●
Tiny Machine EP (nr/Epic) 1990 ●
Crawdaddy (Columbia) 1990 ◊
Erotica Plays EP [CD] (nr/Epic) 1991 ●

This Welsh quartet emerged in the late '80s as part of Britain's resurgent girl-group update. Along with Voice of the Beehive, Transvision Vamp and the very similar Primitives, the Buds looked to the past (not that far: they settled on Blondie) and forged a derivative yet likable sound that, taken in small bites, should satisfy the cravings of any neo-bubblegum fan.

On the relentlessly chirpy debut produced by Pat Collier, singer/lyricist Andrea Lewis and guitarist/songwriter Harley Farr offer a dozen upbeat songs about love (of the puppy, crummy and lost varieties), all solidly played and well sung. The gorgeous "Let's Go Round There" and the Bo Diddley bop of "Things We Do for Love" (not the 10cc song) highlight an album full of highlights. But proceed cautiously, as repeated listenings may cause a sugar rush.

Opening with distorto-feedback reminiscent of the Jesus and Mary Chain, **Crawdaddy** reveals a more mature Buds, a group that has learned the value of a little variety. With longtime Smiths producer Stephen Street twiddling the knobs, there's a lushness on such tracks as "You Won't Make Me Die" and "So Close" that was absent from **Pop Said . . .** In addition, the band hops aboard the Madchester bandwagon, coming up with "Tiny Machine" and "Crystal Clear," the LP's most memorable tracks. Some now-tired Blondie-isms remain, but this fine sophomore effort is mostly a forward-looking, groove-heavy delight. (The subsequent EP features "It Makes No Difference" plus three self-produced non-LP tracks.)   [db]

DOC CORBIN DART

See *Crucifucks*.

DAS DAMEN

Das Damen EP (Ecstatic Peace) 1986 (SST) 1986
Jupiter Eye (SST) 1987
Triskaidekaphobe (SST) 1988 ●
Marshmellow Conspiracy EP (SST) 1988 + 1988 ●
Mousetrap (Twin/Tone) 1989 ●
Entertaining Friends (Ger. City Slang) 1990 ●

Like many other young bands of the '80s, New York's Das Damen cavalierly crosses decades of musical influences to inbreed contemporary whateverism with '60s acid rock, '70s arena metal and '80s postpunk. The quartet relies on loud guitars, unrestrained energy and their college educations to produce music that has volume and intelligence, if not always impact.

The group's debut EP, originally released on a label run by Sonic Youth's Thurston Moore but quickly reissued by SST, offers six badly mixed long songs that are noisy but fun. Roaring guitar chords, above-average vocals, solid drumming and an invaluable sense of dynamics balance off the unfocused sonic wash and formless songwriting.

The dodgy sound quality on **Jupiter Eye** is similarly haphazard, but the album reveals enlarged stylistic ambition and sophistication. With the shambling electrified chaos of live improvisation, hard-driving instrumental sections are enthralling; the poorly recorded vocals are effective additions only some of the time. "Girl with the Hair" and "Name Your Poison" find a functional equilibrium; the mild-mannered "Do" offers a most appealing low-key antidote. **Jupiter Eye** contains all the ingredients for excellence, but Damen is still fitting the pieces together. (A good producer wouldn't hurt.)

The well-rehearsed organization and clear, balanced audio fidelity of **Triskaidekaphobe** removes some of the rampant wildness in favor of syncopated hard-rocking power and disarmingly melodic tunes. "Bug"

and "Candy Korn" are pop songs with feedback; "Spider Birds" crosses Lynyrd Skynyrd with Cheap Trick; "Reverse into Tomorrow" updates sprightly power-pop with augmented chords and a knee-twisting time shift; "Pendant" takes a driving and textured Hüsker Dü approach and cuts it up with an unexpectedly delicate bridge. Though this impressive LP diverges out of focus, it seems likely that Damen's growing bag of tricks will eventually yield a completely satisfying record.

When certain parties and their legal representatives discovered that "Song for Michael Jackson to \$ell"—one of the four tracks on the **Marshmellow Conspiracy** pink-vinyl 12-inch—was, in fact, "Magical Mystery Tour," the record was withdrawn from the market. Too bad. Although the song doesn't get much respect from the absurdly accented vocal performance, the elongated psychedelic finish is an amusing display of one generation's interpretation of another's trippy noise. (After the dust settled, SST reissued the three remaining songs—including two from the previous LP, one in a new version featuring ex-MC5 guitarist Wayne Kramer—as a 12-inch and a CD-3.)

Mousetrap puts Damen one step closer to demi-monde greatness. The songs (especially on the West Coast side) are by far their best ("Sad Mile" has a killer chorus; the Blue Cheerish "Demagnetized" and the gently tuneful "Hey, Angel" are also highlights); the band's instrumental work and arrangements are both better developed and more varied than ever. A better **Mousetrap** to be sure, the album solidifies Damen's stylistic development, setting a terrific musical plateau from which the band can continue to progress.

Recorded live at CBGB in early 1990, **Entertaining Friends** has good sound and a fine retrospective selection of album tracks, but the warts'n'all performances are totally uneven, fluctuating between potent waves of confident wah-wah power to wobbly vocals and arrangements on the brink of collapse. Damen's live performances aren't exactly peanut butter consistent, and this live document is all too accurate. The CD adds a nifty cover of Television's "Friction."   [i]

DASH RIP ROCK

Dash Rip Rock (688) 1986 (Mammoth) 1989 ●
Ace of Clubs (Mammoth) 1989 ●
Not of This World (Mammoth) 1990 ●

Taking their name from a character on *The Beverly Hillbillies* (Elly May's movie-star paramour), this trio from Baton Rouge, Louisiana puts a bloodboiling flame under a peppery pot of rhythm & blues, old-time rock-'n'roll and tradition-minded country. Given mighty support by bassist Ned "Hoaky" Hickel and drummer Fred LeBlanc, guitarist/singer Bill Davis is a talented and powerful frontman; all three write. Dash is the kind of rough-and-ready band you imagine tearing up a roadhouse somewhere in your romantic dreams of highway adventures; **Dash Rip Rock** has a few flaws but bears the unmistakable imprint of a significant find.

The white-hot center of **Ace of Clubs**—"Money Love Time," the vintage-sounding "Leave Me Alone (With My Bottle)" and "Johnny Ace" (great biographical lyrics set to sizzling high-speed guitar energy)—is surrounded by equally entertaining tracks in a variety of less incendiary styles: chunky power pop ("Go Home

Little Girl''), acoustic country-folk (''Blue Moon at Midnight''), herky-jerky rock-pop (''Legacy,'' ''Lisa''). The album would have benefited from a more clearly cut personality, but the well-written and sharply played songs make it a fine second showing.

With producer Jim Dickinson and a new drummer taking over from LeBlanc, Dash grew up and got loud (and a bit raunchy) on **Not of This World**, a smooth high-octane blend of the band's rootsy rock-R&B-country ingredients. Whether Davis is using guitar metaphors in a lusty love song (''String You Up''), issuing crude putdowns (''Rich Little Bitch,'' ''Rattle Trap'') or pledging to follow a woman to the ends of the earth (in a song delicately mistitled ''Bum for Egypt''), the band—augmented on some songs by a guest keyboard player—plays hot enough to light a small studio conflagration. Get that fire extinguisher out before you drop the needle.   [i]

DATE BAIT
See *Slickee Boys*.

DATURA SEEDS
See *Zero Boys*.

DAVID J
See *Bauhaus, Love and Rockets*.

DANIELLE DAX
Pop-Eyes (nr/Initial) 1983 (nr/Awesome) 1985
Jesus Egg That Wept (nr/Awesome) 1984 + 1985
Inky Bloaters (nr/Awesome) 1987 ●
The Janice Long Session EP (nr/Nighttracks-Strange Fruit) 1988
Dark Adapted Eye (Sire) 1988 ●
Blast the Human Flower (Sire) 1990 ◊

Emerging from the ashes of the Lemon Kittens (formed at Surrey University; 1979-'82), England's Danielle Dax, Our Lady of the Arabic dance slink, has a voice like vanilla yogurt: cool, high and honey-sweet with a tartly mysterious flavor that keeps her work from sounding the slightest bit mainstream. From the old Hebrew inscription of her Awesome Records logo (apparently gibberish) through the lyrics on **Inky Bloaters** (where ''Big Hollow Man'' reaps the wages of his materialistic hypocrisy), there's an underlying current of Biblical mysticism embedded in her work and an infectiously droney middle-Easternness to many of her melodies.

An eclectic collision between arty and rootsy, Dax's work ranges from the almost scientifically crisp and clinical ('' . . . In Wooden Brackets,'' which she recorded while still a Lemon Kitten, introduces backward instrumental tracks to warbling pseudo-Chinese vocal chirps) to mutant blues/gospel. In ''Evil-Honky Stomp,'' from **Jesus Egg That Wept**, a moaning, off-kilter saxophone evokes images of Mississippi riverboats as she sings of branding slaves with all the sweetness of a Scarlett O'Hara wafting down a staircase.

The bright bop and twinkle of ''Here Come the Harvest Buns'' (included on both **Jesus Egg** and **Pop-Eyes**) bounces with perky electronic keyboard percussion, triangle and bottle plinks, disguising its dark message to cheating spouses: ''Spin we go with a hi-de-ho, with a knee in the place where the hero roamed.'' The sweeter she sounds, the more sinister her ideas. (The reissued version of **Jesus Egg** contains an additional track.)

Dax has a million sounds and at least as many visions to cram onto vinyl. After the utterly unaccompanied **Pop-Eyes** (amazingly recorded, using more than a dozen different instruments, on a four-track tape machine!), her visions were explored with the help of collaborator Karl Blake, who shared vocals, writing, performing and production duties in the fecund Lemon Kittens. (He appears as a guest musician on **Jesus Egg**'s ''Ostrich''). Around 1984, she began to work with guitarist/keyboardist David Knight; he appears on some of **Jesus Egg**'s tracks. Dax later added guitarist Ian Sturgess, who plays numerous other instruments, including jaw harp and harmonica, to her band.

The absolutely brilliant **Inky Bloaters** finds the Dax troika merrily plundering the sounds of the '60s (as well as ancient slinky Middle-Easternisms) with mock-sitars, giddy fuzz guitars and a by-the-numbers songbook that helps recall everyone from Mungo Jerry (''Inky Bloaters'') to T. Rex (''Big Hollow Man'') to the Jefferson Airplane (''Brimstone in a Barren Land''). ''Flashback'' and ''Sleep Has No Property'' are among the enticing potions Dax delivers in this remarkably inventive stylistic encapsulation of the Woodstock generation.

The Janice Long Session, an impressive December 1985 radio showing by Dax plus four sidemen, features four selections from her extensive catalogue. Dax's wavery singing lacks some of its usual studio flair and polish, but the version of ''Fizzing Human Bomb'' (from **Inky Bloaters**) is quite extraordinary.

Dark Adapted Eye, Dax's excellent introduction to America, mixes more than half of **Inky Bloaters** (all the songs mentioned above except ''Sleep'') with five new tunes, most notably the T. Rexy drama of ''Cat-House'' and the droney percussive pop of ''Whistling for His Love.'' Although the credits omit mention of Sturgess (seemingly a prominent figure on **Inky Bloaters**) in favor of newcomer Pete Farrugia, his contributions don't appear to have been wiped off the tracks.

After such a string of wonderful records, Dax took a dive. A deeply disappointing commercial sell-out, the dreadful **Blast the Human Flower** (produced by Stephen Street) foolishly suppresses Dax's eccentricity in anonymous modern guitar-rock performed by such trusted associates as Knight, Farrugia and Blake. Although relieved of its sinuous character, her voice is the album's only familiar element—the nearly witless lyrics are no help. Having erased Dax's boundless panculturalism, a routine sitar-house cover of the Beatles' ''Tomorrow Never Knows'' lamely pays lip service to it.   ['e/i]

MORRIS DAY
Color of Success (Warner Bros.) 1985 ●
Daydreaming (Warner Bros.) 1987 ●

Longtime friend Prince raised Morris Day to stardom by helping his band, the Time, and later by casting

Morris in a starring role as his musical arch-enemy in *Purple Rain*. Soon after that, when the Time collapsed, Day went solo. Ironically, **Color of Success** has less of his personality than the group's last LP, and points him in a rather familiar pop-soul direction. Things turn ridiculous when Morris introduces a dance called "The Oak Tree" in a seemingly endless display of self-amusement; on stronger footing, he rocks steady with "Love Sign" and waxes smoothly romantic on "Don't Wait for Me."

Day got his ultra-successful ex-Timemates Jimmy Jam and Terry Lewis to co-write and produce a pair of songs on **Daydreaming**, turning the tracks into a dry run for the Time reunion as Jerome Benton, drummer Jellybean Johnson and Jesse Johnson all put in guest appearances. Overall, the album's material is dire, a mix of dull ballads (including the macho bullshit of "A Man's Pride") and unexciting dance movers—even the Jam/Lewis efforts fail to connect. Despite an evident lack of conviction, Day's smooth singing is appealing; insubstantial material is **Daydreaming**'s undoing.   [i]

See also *Time*.

DB'S
Stands for Decibels (nr/Albion) 1981 (IRS) 1989 ●
Repercussion (nr/Albion) 1982 (IRS) 1989 ●
Like This (Bearsville) 1984 (Rhino) 1988 ●
Amplifier (nr/Dojo) 1986
The Sound of Music (IRS) 1987 ●

WILL RIGBY
Sidekick Phenomenon (Egon) 1985

PETER HOLSAPPLE & CHRIS STAMEY
Mavericks (Rhino New Artists) 1991 φ

It's difficult to understand why the dB's' first two albums—both well-conceived and entirely accessible—had such a hard time getting released in the band's own country. On the New York-based band's debut, the four North Carolina emigrants draw inspiration from '60s pop psychedelia (and '70s pop disciples like Big Star) and quote freely from such sources as the Beatles, Move, Nazz and even the Beau Brummels. However, Peter Holsapple and Chris Stamey, the group's two guitar-playing singer/songwriters, each have too individual a style to merely parrot, and nearly every song has some new twist, whether through production effects (few pop records are as consistently aurally interesting as this without resorting to gimmickry), or an unusual instrumental or lyrical approach. Produced in London by Scott Litt, **Stands for Decibels** is not a happy record—often as not the songs are about deteriorating relationships—but the playing is so exuberant that it's uplifting.

Repercussion adds a number of flourishes to the group's style. Litt achieves a fuller, more modern overall sound; instrumentation on many of the tracks is denser than anything on its predecessor. The Rumour Brass makes an appearance on "Living a Lie." In addition, drummer Will Rigby—one of a mere handful of current rock drummers with a sound of his own beyond mere beat-keeping—is brought more to the fore on numbers like "Ask for Jill" and "In Spain." Depending on

one's preferences in production style, **Repercussion** can be seen either as a great advance over **Decibels** or as a glossing-up of the group's sound. (The poorly packaged, carelessly programmed **Amplifier** is a pointless fourteen-track regurgitation of the Albion era.)

Just as the dB's *finally* signed to an American label, Chris Stamey left for a solo career. With a little instrumental realignment, they recorded **Like This** as a trio, adding a new bassist afterwards. Although the reliance on Holsapple's songwriting cuts down on the band's eccentricities, unpretentious intelligence, wit and ineffable pop smarts make it a wonderful album with no weak spots or inadequate songs. Dropping much of the British influence in favor of an Americanized, country-fied air, tunes like "Love Is for Lovers," "Lonely Is (As Lonely Does)" and "White Train" carry the banner of romance disappointed into memorable settings. An instantly lovable gem.

Bearsville dissolved shortly after the release of **Like This**, leaving the group again label-less. (**Like This** was subsequently licensed by Rhino, gaining a CD release with two bonus tracks, including an extended remix of the excellent "A Spy in the House of Love.") By the time IRS finally signed the band, the lineup had returned to a quartet, with the addition of New Orleans bassist Jeff Beninato.

The Sound of Music finds the dB's continuing in the style of **Like This**, with similarly fine results. The previously introduced country elements appear on tracks like "Bonneville" (complete with fiddles and mandolins), "Never Before and Never Again" (a brilliant Holsapple duet with Syd Straw) and "Looked at the Sun Too Long," which could easily be mistaken for a Gram Parsons tune. There's still plenty of great pop, too, and the group gets heavy on "Any Old Thing." Guitarist Gene Holder left to join the Wygals shortly after **The Sound of Music**'s release; following one tour without him, the dB's quietly split up. Holsapple subsequently performed and recorded with R.E.M. as auxiliary guitarist and keyboardist.

Following a long unscheduled delay while errant master tapes were being located, IRS reissued the band's first two albums in late 1989, finally making the entire catalogue available domestically. Consumers should note that the IRS CDs are far superior to the now-deleted import versions, with improved sound quality and non-LP bonus tracks ("Judy" on the first LP and "pH Factor" on the second).

Drummer Rigby's solo record is a loopy laugh, a ramshackle one-man-band collection of country covers and likewise originals on which his kit is often the most prominent item in the mix. The singing is informal but engaging (as are his skills on piano, guitar, harmonica and other instruments); Holsapple's occasional contributions don't interrupt the casualness of this delightfully unselfconscious romp.

After occasional gigs with Stamey, Holsapple helped out on a Peter Blegvad session that Stamey was producing, and the two old friends wound up collaborating on a new album. The acoustic-flavored **Mavericks** is a major career highlight for both, a heartfelt and deeply moving collection that neatly sums up everything they've done singly and together. The songs (especially "Angels," "I Want to Break Your Heart" and "She

Was the One'') are no less than memorable; the masterful performances are loaded with handsome harmonies and painterly production touches. Magnificent. [ds/i/hd]

See also *Katrina and the Waves, Sneakers, Chris Stamey, Wygals.*

D.C.3
This Is the Dream (SST) 1985
The Good Hex (SST) 1986
You're Only as Blind as Your Mind Can Be (SST) 1986
Vida (SST) 1989 ●

TWISTED ROOTS
Twisted Roots (CD Presents) 1987

PAUL ROESSLER
Abominable (SST) 1988

CRIMONY
The Crimony E.P. EP (New Alliance) 1988

Erstwhile Black Flag guitarist Dez Cadena's current band (a trio for one LP, a quartet still named D.C.3 ever since) makes albums, to quote him, "in the style of the records that used to excite us when we were young." Unfortunately, what he and his friends (including ex-45 Grave keyboardist Paul Roessler) remember fondly is Deep Purple and Humble Pie, and the first two releases resemble various '60s and '70s nightmares, from Blue Öyster Cult to Black Sabbath. There's actually some fine music and an amusing undercurrent to both, although the subtle satirical value may be missed by those too young (or too old).

With the dated influences toned down, leaving a state of pleasantly mild nostalgia, the third LP turns up the lyrical power. As Cadena's liner notes note, "I ended up hurting someone who is very close to me. This album is about life without that person." With single-minded dedication, selections like "Baby, You Know Where I Live," "Party for One," "I Ain't Got You," "Lost Someone" and "Talkin' to the Mirror" verbalize his anguished cry with an intensity the upbeat music lacks.

Compiling LA performances from '87 and '88, **Vida** mixes D.C.3 originals with covers of John Lee Hooker, Hawkwind and Black Flag for an electrifying slab of smart and gutsy guitar rock that owes no debt to any era but the present. While Cadena's vocals and playing hit just the right noisy mix of casual concentration, Roessler contributes to the din without making a fuss.

Roessler enlisted Cadena and Jeff Dahl's rhythm section to make the enjoyable **Twisted Roots**, a solo album in all but name. Playing and singing melodic originals (plus the Stones' "She's a Rainbow") with a slightly theatrical bent, Roessler keeps things upbeat and pleasant with chipper keyboards and enthusiastic vocals, even as Cadena sets to rocking out feverishly in the background. Is this man punk's answer to Elton John?

Recorded with a drummer and three people rotating on bass and guitar, **Abominable** is a jolly instrumental romp through somber film-less scores, skating rink music, phantom-of-the-punk-club eccentricities and pompless ELP-styled classics ("Prokofiev Boogie" takes *Peter and the Wolf* out of the woods), all solidly composed and proficiently played. I wouldn't want to hear too many more records like this, but **Abominable** is quite entertaining on its own terms.

Except for brother-in-law Mike Watt playing bass and co-producing the five simple tracks, **The Crimony E.P.** is more solo work from Roessler, who tickles the ivories and sings jaunty numbers like "Life Is Too Short" and "Vampire Party" and solemn ballads like "Prison Blues." There isn't much interaction between the two men, but the songs and performances are enjoyable enough. [i]

See also *Black Flag, Jeff Dahl Group, 45 Grave.*

DEAD BOYS
Young Loud and Snotty (Sire) 1977 ●
We Have Come for Your Children (Sire) 1978
Night of the Living Dead Boys (Bomp!) 1981 ●
Younger, Louder and Snottier (nr/Necrophilia) 1989 ●

Although originally from Cleveland, the Dead Boys earned their lasting international reputation in New York starting in early '77 by outpunking everyone else on the Bowery circuit. Having absorbed what had already happened in England (the Sex Pistols, Damned) and America (the Stooges), the Dead Boys took it a dozen steps further, uncovering new levels of violence, nihilism, masochism and vulgarity. Their two studio albums have aged well and have served as guideposts to an entire new generation of fans and bands.

Young Loud and Snotty, one of the earliest punk albums released on a US label, benefits from the production skill of Genya Ravan, who made it loud and raw—an onslaught of sizzling guitars and Stiv Bators' sneering whine. Classic tracks include tasteless originals like "Sonic Reducer," "All This and More" and "Caught with the Meat in Your Mouth," as well as a dynamic rendition of the Syndicate of Sound's archetypal "Hey Little Girl." (Twelve years after the fact, someone came across a cassette of rough mixes for the LP and, adding a live Stooges cover, issued it as the legally dubious **Younger, Louder and Snottier.**)

We Have Come for Your Children, produced by the late Felix Pappalardi, has inferior sound, but equally strong playing. The material suffers from second-LP drought and an onset of self-parodic punk typecasting, leading to such dumb tunes as "Flame Thrower Love," the topical "Son of Sam" and "(I Don't Wanna Be No) Catholic Boy." The record's best track is the reflective "Ain't It Fun," co-written by guitarist Cheetah Chrome and Cleveland legend Peter Laughner.

Night of the Living Dead Boys was recorded live at CBGB in New York in 1979, and captures the end-time band flailing through classic numbers in ragged-but-right fashion. Although the mix is trebly and muddled (a rare combination), this is still a punk documentary of some merit.

The Dead Boys—Bators, Chrome, Johnny Blitz and Jeff Magnum—reformed in 1987 and issued a single, "All the Way Down (Poison Lady)." Following his years in Lords of the New Church, Stiv recorded a 1988 single with the Lyres. The Dead Boys' saga came to an end in June 1990, when Stiv died of automobile injuries in Paris. [tr]

See also *Stiv Bators, Peter Laughner, Lords of the New Church, Lyres, Wanderers.*

DEAD CAN DANCE

Dead Can Dance (nr/4AD) 1984 •
Garden of the Arcane Delights EP (nr/4AD) 1984 •
Spleen and Ideal (nr/4AD) 1985 •
Within the Realm of a Dying Sun (nr/4AD) 1987 •
The Serpent's Egg (nr/4AD) 1988 •
Aion (nr/4AD) 1990 •

Mesmerizing (if a bit laborious), Dead Can Dance's eponymous debut finds the Australian-born/London-based quintet spinning slow webs of drum-driven but mostly shapeless guitar music with chanting, singing and howling by the two (male and female) singers; the LP is of possible interest only to undiscriminating fans of moody psychedelia and/or the Cocteau Twins. The more intriguing four-song **Garden of the Arcane Delights** EP (included on the **Dead Can Dance** CD) has crisper production than the album, although similar musical stylings.

By the time **Spleen and Ideal** was released, DCD were down to a duo of vocalists Brendan Perry and Lisa Gerrard. Some of the guitars have given way to ethereal keyboards, with tympani, cellos and trombones blended in; much of the LP sounds as though it belongs in a cathedral rather than a concert hall. The songs are more structured than before, but things do get a bit precious, and the three hymnalesque cuts that open the album are pretty tough to sit through. The music gets meatier as it progresses, though, and the end result is a record of haunting and solemn beauty.

With song titles such as "Xavier" and "Dawn of the Iconoclast," and credits for such instruments as bass trombone, oboe and military snare, there's no way that **Within the Realm of a Dying Sun** (and how about that title?) could be quite as boring as its sounds. (Comes close at times, mind you.) Major mistake: segregating the Perry-sung material on one side of the LP and the (somewhat superior) songs Gerrard sings on the other forces the listener to compare the two quite different solo vocal styles, rather than uniting the often spectacular compositions into one overall mood.

Building on its predecessor's shift towards an awareness of ancient musics—European, Celtic and Middle Eastern predominate—**The Serpent's Egg** has some scintillating moments. Still, it's a lesser, transitional work, without much sense of flow, serving mainly to pave the way for the fully developed medievalisms of **Aion**. Minstrels Perry and Gerrard now bear scant resemblance to the more trad 4AD-style neo-goths of the first album. Jettisoning any ties to the present, this masterfully organized recording whirls headlong into the Renaissance, to a sonic realm where somber Gregorian chants (and there's a lot of them here) and jaunty maypole dances like "Saltarello" have never left the hit parade. Utilizing authentic folk instruments (hurdy gurdy, lutes, bagpipes, etc.) and letting Gerrard's lovely voice soar unimpeded, Dead Can Dance has finally found a distinct sound of its own.   [dgs/gef]

See also *This Mortal Coil*.

DEAD KENNEDYS

Fresh Fruit for Rotting Vegetables (IRS) 1980 •
In God We Trust, Inc. (Alternative Tentacles-Faulty
    Products) 1981 •
Plastic Surgery Disasters (Alternative Tentacles) 1982 •
Frankenchrist (Alternative Tentacles) 1985 •
Bedtime for Democracy (Alternative Tentacles) 1986 •
Give Me Convenience or Give Me Death (Alternative
    Tentacles) 1987 •

WITCH TRIALS

The Witch Trials EP (Subterranean-Alternative Tentacles)
    1981

KLAUS FLOURIDE

Cha Cha Cha with Mr. Flouride (Alternative Tentacles)
    1985
Because I Say So (Alternative Tentacles) 1988 •
The Light Is Flickering (Alternative Tentacles) 1991

It took a while, but in the Dead Kennedys, America finally produced a powerful, self-righteously moral band to match the fury of the Sex Pistols. Led by audacious and inimitable singer Jello Biafra (who once ran—and received a substantial number of votes—for mayor of San Francisco, the band's base), the DKs combine blunt and sardonic discussions of touchy issues with crushing, high-speed guitar and drums. Generally acknowledged as prime pioneers of American hardcore, the Kennedys have been influential, not only by setting a style, sensibility and commendable standards, but with their productive Alternative Tentacles label and active support for grassroots rock activity. Biafra's legal confrontation over the poster included in **Frankenchrist** effectively ended the band, but left a powerful anti-censorship legacy for others to uphold.

Despite a few weak songs, **Fresh Fruit** is explosive and gripping (also controversial—a borrowed photo used on the back cover led to some funny but unpleasant legal trouble). Jello's political sarcasm erupts on "Kill the Poor" and "California über Alles," offering a funny but chilling condemnation of then-governor Jerry Brown and "zen fascists" in the latter. The bracing and tightly focused "Holiday in Cambodia" echoes the Pistols' "Holidays in the Sun" and became a DKs standard. In typically unsubtle broadside fashion, Jello nails another popular target with "Let's Lynch the Landlord."

In eight very brief songs, **In God We Trust, Inc.** offers additional valid statements about the religious right. But the music is stripped of dynamics and reduced to routine hyperactive punk; scrap the record and keep the lyric sheet.

Plastic Surgery Disasters, with a gruesome mock-E.T. cover, enlarges the musical blend to include more three-dimensionality while retaining the Kennedys' typical rock energy. Songs like "Terminal Preppie," "Winnebago Warrior," "Trust Your Mechanic" and "Well Paid Scientist" mix humor and activism for pointed and intelligent observations on social absurdity. (The CD also contains **In God We Trust**.)

The DKs stopped recording for several years while the members worked on outside projects. Bassist Klaus Flouride was the busiest boy, producing other bands for release on Alternative Tentacles and recording his own one-man seven-song mini-album, **Cha Cha Cha with Mr. Flouride.** Displaying not the slightest trace of political consciousness, Klaus lets down his hair on a straight rock'n'billy (with a guest drummer and pianist) love ode, "My Linda." Elsewhere, he laments a serious social problem, "Dead Prairie Dogs," and takes an amusing cowboy jaunt with "Ghost Riders." The simple music—mostly guitars and cheap-sounding electronics—is lighthearted and goofy, showing more spirit than originality, but cute nonetheless. And the cover is great.

In early 1985, the band hit the road again with **Frankenchrist**, which generally repeats the psycho-punk of **Plastic Surgery Disasters**. There are some bad tracks with forced, awkward lyrics, but the LP does contain two of the DKs' finest moments: "MTV Get off the Air" and "Stars and Stripes of Corruption," one of the most powerful political statements ever committed to vinyl. Instead of just bellyaching about problems (a common habit of politico-punks), Biafra offers possibilities for constructive change, demonstrating real American patriotism as opposed to jingoist commie-bashing.

Bedtime for Democracy—21 strong cuts and an eight-page clip-art newspaper—ended the Kennedys' recording career on a high note. A full-tilt platform of targets, including working poverty, Reagan, toxic waste, macho attitudes, conformity and more, are decimated with energetic, well-played music and Biafra's uniquely quivery voice. The Kennedys' knowing cover of "Take This Job and Shove It" is also good for a chuckle.

In mid-'86, Biafra and others were charged by California authorities with "distribution of harmful matter to minors"—i.e., a reproduction of H.R. Giger's *Landscape #20*, which was included in **Frankenchrist**. More than a year later, the case—which might have led to a jail term—ended in a mistrial. The charges were dismissed but the Dead Kennedys had it.

The final chapter in the saga was **Give Me Convenience or Give Me Death**, a posthumous career recap, which contains fifteen examples of the DKs' best work (hits, live performances and obscurities), a two-song flexi-disc ("Buzzbomb from Pasadena" and "Night of the Living Rednecks"—both added to the cassette and CD editions) and a newsprint art/lyric book. Essential.

The bulk of Flouride's second album, **Because I Say So**, is devoted to atmospheric instrumental soundtrack music corrupted by assorted streams of noise that wander in and out of the mix. The diverse vocal songs are likewise a mixed blessing: while "Keep on Walking" is a politely Beatlesque piano ballad, Norman Greenbaum's "Charlies Friends" gets a twisted acoustic country interpretation and "Dominating Baby" copies (and acknowledges) Leon Redbone. "Bus Thru the Barrier," meanwhile, is a sloppy mash that repeats the same meaningless couplet ad nauseum, pausing only for two blitzed out fuzz guitar solos. (The CD adds three bonus tracks.)

The Witch Trials was an early Biafra studio one-off, recorded in England and shrouded in mystery. With DK guitarist East Bay Ray, Sound vocalist Adrian Borland and California's Christian Lunch providing the uncredited backing—an atmospheric drone on one side, jarring unpleasantness on the other—Biafra recites two dramatic tales of mayhem and chants two more pieces of madness that exhibit his characteristic venom and wit.

See also *Jello Biafra, Lard*. [jy/dgs/i]

DEADLY HUME

Basement Tapes EP (Aus. Bulb) 1985
Me, Grandma, Iliko and Hilarian (Aus. Phantom) 1987
Lonely Mr. Happy EP (Aus. Phantom) 1988

The Deadly Hume takes its name from the Hume Highway, a dangerous and desolate stretch of roadway between Melbourne and the band's hometown, Sydney. The band's sound derives from the clash and grind of urban Australia and the swampy darkness of American blues, although the records encompass everything from a cappella spiritual choruses to acoustic guitar. On tracks like "Fine Line" (from **Me, Grandma, Iliko and Hilarian**), the rhythm-sticks-from-hell percussion clatter and sawing bass lines could almost let the music pass for a lost outtake from **Fireman's Curse**-era Hunters and Collectors (Hume lead vocalist Greg Perano was in H&C at the time) while the swampy fuzz guitar and squealing chords of "My Head Feels Like It's Been Hit by a Train" drag the band through an intense and slithery Amer-Aussie version of '80s blues-rock.

The Nick Cave-esque "48 Coffees in 24 Hours" intersperses shouts of "I'm nervous nervous nervous" with brash striptease horns and mumbled stream-of-caffeine vocals, capturing the wiped-out frazzle anyone who's overdosed on java will recognize. "The Trains Kept Shunting" (from **Grandma**) pounds with a soft, insistent drum pulse as what sounds like a box filled with sand shuffles and guitars peal out sheets of feedback and hard, clear chimes. Like impressionist painters working in sound instead of oils, the Deadly Hume have the marvelous ability to turn pop songs into art without leaving a stuffy aftertaste.

Besides a reprise of "48 Coffees," the six-song **Lonely Mr. Happy** 12-inch contains such equally colorful Hume-isms as "Miss Haversham," "Bed, Bread and Humour" and the absurdly political "The Queen and the President." ['e]

DEAD MILKMEN

Big Lizard in My Back Yard (Fever-Enigma) 1985 ●
Eat Your Paisley! (Fever-Restless) 1986 ●
Bucky Fellini (Fever-Enigma) 1987 ●
Instant Club Hit (You'll Dance to Anything) EP
   (Fever-Enigma) 1987 ●
Beelzebubba (Fever-Enigma) 1988 ●
Metaphysical Graffiti (Enigma) 1990 φ

Philadelphia has been the subject of many jokes, but the mildly punky Milkmen, a homegrown insult machine with a snotty attitude and a grasp of modern society's cultural monstrosities, bring their own whoopie cushion to the party. On a lightweight foundation of plain, unfancy rock music, the Milkmen don't focus on individual victims so much as unleash their bratty irreverence in scattershot volleys.

The reckless insults and putdowns on **Big Lizard in My Back Yard** connect most memorably on "Bitchin Camaro," a catchy cocktail-jazz/hardcore hybrid that tastelessly makes light of AIDS while satirizing teenagers, the Doors and sports car owners. Overall, the record's sense of humor is stupid and only spottily amusing.

Eat Your Paisley! makes no great effort to be funny or offensive, yet manages to convey a sense of satire by painting bizarre B-movie tales like "Moron," "Beach Party Vietnam" and "The Thing That Only Eats Hippies." The group's wacky observations of stereotypes and artifacts are vague but astute; the music is expendable but never less than presentable.

Bucky Fellini is a relatively expansive effort with guest musicians, improved songwriting and such dementedly parodic cultural concepts as "Nitro Burning Funny Cars," "Going to Graceland," "(Theme from) Blood Orgy of the Atomic Fern" and "Instant Club Hit (You'll Dance to Anything)." Rodney Anonymous is a self-assured if unmusical vocalist; Joe Jack Talcum leads the guitar-based band through the artless tunes with easygoing aplomb.

The **Instant Club Hit** EP offers three mixes of that vindictively funny number (including the all-percussion "Boner Beats"), plus the previously unreleased "Ask Me to Dance" and tracks that were CD bonuses on the first two albums.

The Milkmen's skimpy charms run very thin on **Beelzebubba**, an album with precisely three assets: a great title, amusing artwork and the catchy but stupid "Punk Rock Girl." (Who told these guys that the Beach Boys did "California Dreaming"?) Otherwise, the lyrics are totally unfunny, and the music is too dull to matter. Although **Metaphysical Graffiti** can likewise manage some clever song titles ("If You Love Somebody, Set Them on Fire," "In Praise of Sha Na Na," "I Tripped Over the Ottoman"—a song about Rob Petrie), the songs (some merely other-joke fragments) they refer to are disappointingly lame. Gibby Haynes makes a guest appearance on "Anderson, Walkman, Buttholes and How!"   [i]

DEAD OR ALIVE

Dead or Alive EP (nr/Black Eyes-Rough Trade) 1982
Sophisticated Boom Boom (Epic) 1984 ●
Youthquake (Epic) 1985 ●
Mad, Bad, and Dangerous to Know (Epic) 1987 ●
Rip It Up (Epic) 1988 ●
Nude (Epic) 1989 ●

Pete Burns, Dead or Alive's cross-dressing poseur/leader/singer, can claim historical credit in the second Liverpool explosion—he was in a brief but seminal band with Julian Cope and Pete (Wah!) Wylie before founding Nightmares in Wax, the developmental predecessor to Dead or Alive. The early EP finds him searching for meaning and truth while attempting to appropriate Jim Morrison's vocal style; it's murky, to say the least.

Sophisticated Boom Boom includes a totally horrible and gratuitous remake of KC and the Sunshine Band's "That's the Way (I Like It)"—and that's as good as the album gets. Burns sings as if his atavistic urges ("What I Want," "You Make Me Wanna," "I'd Do Anything") were the stuff of Shakespearian drama; the backing is slickly competent dance-rock bereft of personality. (Of possible interest to fact fans: Mission founder Wayne Hussey was a onetime Dead or Alive member and co-wrote much of the album's material.)

Burns' bunch subsequently issued a couple of better 45s, including "You Spin Me Round (Like a Record)," that cut a lot of the crap and substituted a kinetic, catchy pop sensibility. Produced by the frighteningly shallow but super-successful Stock, Aitken and Waterman team, **Youthquake** contains "You Spin Me Round," as well as the equally appealing "Lover Come Back to Me" and a few others that show how much fun Dead or Alive can be. On the other hand, the record has its bad patches,

proving the impossibility of pinning Burns down to any steady style or quality level.

Mad, Bad, and Dangerous to Know employs the same hitmaking mechanics to conjure up a consistent—*extremely* consistent—synthesized pop-dance groove which is easy to grasp and hard to hold. That the pulsing sequencer patterns on the nine lengthy soundalikes vary little may be seen as either a functional advantage or a mark of limited creative effort. "Brand New Lover" is giddily hummable for the first three or four minutes but then gets dead boring; the rest of this shoddy effort isn't as catchy.

For **Rip It Up**, Dead or Alive selected eight songs (which means all of the good ones—and then some) from the two preceding albums and gave them a new coat of studio paint, adding and subtracting bits to make the originals more dancer-friendly. Leaving that apt monument to the S-A-W hit factory, Burns took control and produced **Nude** with drummer Steve Coy. In step with the disco times, the album's percolating hi-NRG songs acknowledge both house music and glib techno-soul, downplaying Burns' more melodic pop instincts for a peppy, unchallenging dance record.   [jg/i]

See also *Mission (UK), Sisters of Mercy*.

DEAF SCHOOL

2nd Honeymoon (nr/Warner Bros.) 1976
Don't Stop the World (nr/Warner Bros.) 1977
2nd Honeymoon/Don't Stop the World (Warner Bros.) 1977
English Boys/Working Girls (Warner Bros.) 1978
2nd Coming: Liverpool '88 (nr/Demon) 1988

Liverpool's sprawling nine-strong (later eight) Deaf School seemed like an ideal candidate for success in the quiet pre-punk doldrums of 1976. Visually, the group had more than enough going for it to guarantee a high profile in the British press. The cast included pasty-faced guitarist Clive Langer, who sported wire-rims and wrote most of the melodies; the Rev. Max Ripple, a keyboardist done up like a parson; and no less than *three* lead vocalists: mustachioed Enrico Cadillac, a Bryan Ferry disciple; Bette Bright, who suggested a somewhat frumpy torch singer; and the suave, acid-voiced Eric Shark, who sang as Humphrey Bogart might have.

Despite its slick, full sound, **2nd Honeymoon** has the clear markings of a first effort. The band cleverly mixes the melodrama of Roxy Music with the music hall vivacity of middle-period Kinks, but many of the songs are bloated and their intent unclear. As on later LPs, crooner Cadillac takes the lion's share of the vocals, making tales of modern desperation ("What a Way to End It All") and lost love ("Room Service") into intriguing, if incomplete, exercises in style.

Deaf School came into its own on **Don't Stop the World**, trimming the excesses of **2nd Honeymoon** and adding impressive new elements. While Cadillac continues to warble romantically, Shark belts out a vicious rocker ("Capaldi's Cafe") and Bright shines in a rare solo spot, the after-hours ballad, "Operator." (The two LPs were issued in the US as a double-pack in 1977.)

Although **English Boys/Working Girls** offers more of the same, it's the product of a band running out of steam. In a return to the clutter of their debut, Deaf School favors theatrics over substance; accounts of modern violence like "Ronny Zamora (My Friend Ron)" and "English Boys (With Guns)" are more exploitation than insight.

The Deaf School alumni remained busy after the band folded, making it—in retrospect—a startling fount of promise. Enrico Cadillac formed the Original Mirrors under his civilian name, Steve Allen, and recorded two albums. Bassist Steve "Average" Lindsey founded the Planets and did the same. Bette Bright cut a delightful solo record, produced by Clive Langer who, with his partner Alan Winstanley, earned additional production credits (not to mention scads of money, no doubt) with Madness, Elvis Costello and Dexys Midnight Runners. Langer also formed a band and released records.

Most of the original cast—including Langer and all three singers—reunited for **2nd Coming**, a surprisingly solid live set of the band's "hits" ("Taxi!," "What a Way to End It All," etc.), as well as a robust cover of the Flamin Groovies' "Shake Some Action" and an elegantly corny "Blue Velvet." A great souvenir for fans who felt Deaf School never got enough attention in its prime, this might even gain 'em some new admirers, though probably not too many: the curious blend of Roxy Music-style drama and vaudeville hokum seems as reassuringly offbeat as ever.   [jy]

See also *Clive Langer and the Boxes, Original Mirrors*.

DEATH COMET CREW

See *Dominatrix*.

DEATH CULT

See *Cult*.

DEATH FOLK

See *Pat RuthenSmear*.

DEATH OF SAMANTHA

Strungout on Jargon (Homestead) 1986
Laughing in the Face of a Dead Man EP (Homestead) 1986
Where the Women Wear the Glory and the Men Wear the Pants (Homestead) 1988 ●
Come All Ye Faithless (Homestead) 1989 ●

This Cleveland quartet won't get anywhere on its clothes sense. The goofy garb displayed on record covers (drummer Steve-O's wardrobe is particularly egregious) constantly undercuts the seriousness of purpose in their music, but maybe that's the idea. Regardless, they're one of the strongest rock bands around, with an ace double-guitar attack that can satisfy the most fundamental riff-lust but never descends to sodden cliché. Singer/guitarist John Petkovic has always been a sharp and acerbic songwriter, and lately his lyrics have taken on a literary cast that suits them very well.

After a couple of singles on the band's own label, **Strungout on Jargon** displays the pronounced influence of Cleveland gods Pere Ubu, particularly on "Coca Cola & Licorice," where Petkovic's clarinet squeals recall the soprano sax and recorder yelps on various Ubu LPs. Too much of the record falls into a generic alter-

native slot but, as debuts go, **Strungout** is definitely promising.

Although the group sounds as if it's in a holding pattern, **Laughing in the Face of a Dead Man** is quite an entertaining circle. The cover of "Werewolves of London" is hysterical in several senses of the word, and the tape-and-instrumental "American Horoscope and the Bad Prescription" shows more **Dub Housing**-era Ubu influence.

The group laid off for two years before recording **Where the Women Wear the Glory** and delivered a real stunner. Aside from Petkovic's choked-sounding-because-he-can't-do-it-any-other-way vocals (DOS's only potentially off-putting feature), the band divests itself of any outré tendencies and just rocks out with fire, anger and intelligence. The opening "Harlequin Tragedy" is Petkovic's best song, wrapping a perfect hook around a dour, on-target metaphor for modern life and summing it up with "We're living for nothing/and dying for less." Every cut is outstanding; in one last bow to tradition, the album includes a fairly lavish (strings and everything!) cover of Peter Laughner's "Sylvia Plath."

Come All Ye Faithless is considerably denser—even darker and more difficult than **Women**—but equally rewarding. Not as rollicking as the previous record, it presents a terrific set of songs with which to crawl into a dark corner.   [gk]

DEEE-LITE

World Clique (Elektra) 1990 ●

The celebutante scene of New York nightlife—a narcissistic world of put-on glamour that elevates club-goers, record-spinners and obsessive poseurs of all outrageous stripes into creative entities whose only talent is for self-promotion—is bound to feed on itself from time to time. Jumping off the dancefloor to become momentary pop stars, this colorful trio—a female singer and two exotic male DJs—is really good at vogueing in ginchy psychedelic clothes and (with help from folks like Bootsy Collins and sax legend Maceo Parker) arranging for a solid, bass-driven technotronic club beat with various accents. But that's all there is to Deee-Lite, and **World Clique**, a smug and artless in-joke, boils down to "Groove Is in the Heart," an irritating tagline that managed to become a huge hit single.   [i]

DEFENESTRATION

Defenestration EP (Slow Iguana) 1986
Dali Does Windows (Relativity) 1987

TODD WALKER

Thrown Away EP (Owl House) 1989

CHAINSAW KITTENS

Violent Religion (Mammoth) 1990 ●

Born in Norman, Oklahoma, a college town whose other '80s musical export is the astoundingly strange Flaming Lips, Defenestration had an approach to complement their odd name (it means "the throwing out of a person or thing through a window"). Lead singer Tyson Meade was weaned on B-movies, Janis Joplin and the Birthday Party; the rest of the band combined influences from T. Rex and Cheap Trick to the Byrds. Recorded for almost no money and released on a loan from Meade's mom, **Defenestration** is quirky and brilliant, a result of being far more ambitious than its means. "Cut Your Soul in Half" has grand ideas and sprawling gothic piano; "Slaughterville" is a showcase for Meade's Joplinesque shriek; "Heartthrob" is a subtly written and beautifully melodic discourse on the politics of being an outcast.

Mismatched with heavy-metal producer Randy Burns, Defenestration sacrificed some of its originality on **Dali Does Windows** in favor of enjoyable but less imaginative rock-pop. Traces of the title's surrealist bent crop up in "Tripping Drag Queens" and "Cars in Trees"; "Bedlam Revisited" is as sad and truthful a love song as anyone could want. "D.Y. Wanna (Bubblegum)" is a friendly mutation of "Bang a Gong (Get It On)."

Guitarist Todd Walker split in 1987 and resurfaced two years later, trailing some other Defenestration defectors, with **Thrown Away**, a modest collection of country-rock numbers. Upon the original band's official demise, Meade formed a new quartet, the Chainsaw Kittens. The self-produced **Violent Religion** is a glam-rock sewer of cross-dressing, trash culture, Freudian psychology ("Mother (of the Ancient Birth)") and horror film scenarios. Although Meade remains an inventive songwriter, the most interesting thing about the Kittens is their lipstick and gimmicky hangups. [kss]

DEF JEF
Just a Poet with Soul (Delicious Vinyl) 1989 ●

Articulate and clear-spoken, with varied, warm soul-funk tracks that layer percussion and samples over bouncing bass and drums, fast-talking California rapper Def Jef (Fortson) makes a fine first showing on the largely self-produced **Just a Poet with Soul**. But egotism is its own reward, and Jef's endless boasts about his rhyming skill make the first side and most of the flip a lyrical snore. Only the Afrocentric "Black to the Future" (biting the Steve Miller Band's "Fly Like an Eagle") and the urban tableau of "Downtown" break the mold, demonstrating the kind of material that should be the rule—not the exception—next time. [i]

CARMAIG DE FOREST
I Shall Be Released (Good Foot) 1987
CARMAIG DE FOREST + BAND
6 Live Cuts EP (Fr. New Rose) 1988

Undoubtedly the rockingest singer/songwriter ever to exercise his muse on ukulele, San Francisco' (more recently Los Angeles') Carmaig de Forest emerges on his debut album (produced with creative electric ferocity by Alex Chilton) as a strong, independent voice with plenty on his mind. Following in the tradition of John Hiatt and Billy Bragg, de Forest is a brilliant folk-based tunesmith who synthesizes rock and other influences into a characteristically wry style that owes something to both Jonathan Richman and the Violent Femmes. (Not coincidentally, de Forest has toured with two of the three Femmes.) Chilton surrounds his (Lou) Reedy singing and polite ukework with a simple, effective band that deftly realizes such sharp-tongued originals as "Big Business," "Hey Judas" and "Crack's No Worse Than the Fascist Threat" at assorted energy levels. **I Shall Be**

Released exudes confidence, righteous political anger and enormous originality.

The French live EP was recorded at a pair of October 1987 San Francisco gigs with a bassist, drummer and guitarist. The material includes two tracks from the album, a thrilling cover of "You Can't Always Get What You Want" and three previously unwaxed tunes, one of them quite good. [i]

DEFUNKT
Defunkt (Hannibal) 1980 ●
Thermonuclear Sweat (Hannibal) 1982
In America (Antilles New Directions) 1988 ●
Avoid the Funk ... A Defunkt Anthology
(Hannibal-Carthage) 1988 ●

Led by singing trombonist Joe Bowie (younger brother of famed jazz trumpeter Lester Bowie), the seven-man Defunkt peddled black funk with dry bounce. Originally formed as James Chance's horn section, Defunkt also had ties with the world of avant-garde jazz, putting it in a unique and culturally resonant position. **Defunkt** isn't a revolutionary breakout, but does include the super-catchy (if obtusely titled) "Blues," a number which was extremely popular around New York at the time. **Thermonuclear Sweat**, named for a track from the first LP, is sweeter-sounding and jazzier, smoothed out by Joe Boyd's sage production.

Following a two-year stint spent living in the Caribbean, Bowie returned to New York and formed a new six-piece Defunkt, which debuted on vinyl in mid-'88. Except for a drum sound that suggests tin cans in a carpet showroom, **In America** is brilliant, a dynamic rock-funk-jazz concoction of popping bass, neck-melting guitar (by Bill Bickford, Ronnie Drayton and Tomas Doncker) and Bowie's inventive trombone figures and up-close-and-personable vocals. Stretching further afield, "In America" uses found-sound comments from Richard Nixon, John Kennedy and others to make its political point. While Defunkt has nothing at all to do with heavy metal, fans of Living Colour would do well to check out this alternate mixture of overlapping ingredients.

Avoid the Funk revisits Defunkt's early-'80s work with one track from **Defunkt** ("Make Them Dance"), three from **Thermonuclear Sweat** (including "Avoid the Funk" and a version of the O'Jays' "For the Love of Money," both of which feature Vernon Reid as one of two guitarists), a 1981 single ("The Razor's Edge"/ "Strangling Me with Your Love (Revisited)") and smoking 1983 live performances of two songs from the first LP. [jw/i]

DEL AMITRI
Del Amitri (Chrysalis) 1985 ●
Waking Hours (nr/A&M) 1989 (A&M) 1990 ●

This Glasgow quartet fell victim to excessive hype before the release of its debut album. Many who went overboard praising the group on the strength of two singles and a few live performances unjustly criticized the LP—ten quirky, country-flavored tracks, drenched in crystalline Rickenbacker guitar and Hugh Jones' spare production—for being too traditionalist. Although admittedly a conventional construct, few play this style with as much heart as Del Amitri. These lads love what they do, and you can hear (and feel) it in such rollicking songs as "Crows in the Wheatfield" and "Sticks and Stones Girl."

Apparently chastened by public indifference to the first album, Del Amitri returned with a more "adult" set of tight, commercial tunes the second time around. **Waking Hours**' clean vocal harmonies and smooth craftsmanship suggest careful attention to middlebrow faves like the Police and Dire Straits, though the LP is nowhere near as stuffy. The acoustic lament "This Side of the Morning" has the rough, heartrending beauty of early Rod Stewart and could provide somebody with a big mainstream hit. [ag/jy]

DE LA SOUL

3 Feet High and Rising (Tommy Boy) 1989 ●
Me Myself and I EP (Tommy Boy) 1989 ●
De La Soul Is Dead (Tommy Boy) 1991 ●

If you could put a jigsaw puzzle together in such a way that a completely different picture appeared, you'd have an idea about De La Soul's originality, about how the trailblazing trio blends standard rap elements into something totally unique. Humorous without being too goofy, libidinous without being sexist and sociopolitically aware while steering clear of any doctrinaire posturing, these three young Long Islanders—Posdnous (Kelvyn Mercer), Trugoy the Dove (David Jolicoeur) and P.A. Pasemaster Mase (Vincent Mason) cross a number of musical boundaries on their debut album, ingeniously produced by the studio architect of the daisy age, Prince Paul of Stetsasonic. Laid-back tempos and dayglo graphics paint the group as hip-hop hippies. (But a borrowing from the Turtles' "You Showed Me" earned De La the legal ire of Flo and Eddie: ain't the '80s a bitch?)

Where other bands use samples as rhythmic backdrops or musical exclamation points, De La Soul employs what it can find on records by everyone from Steely Dan to Otis Redding to the Coasters to shape melodies: this is one rap album you can hum. With over twenty tracks, it's easy to find highlights on **3 Feet High and Rising**. For giggles, try "Jenifa Taught Me" or "Do as De La Does"; the former takes the surprising position of a man being sexually victimized by a smarter, more experienced woman, while the latter lambastes everything about hip-hop's language and performance styles in just under two minutes. If you just want to dance to a soulful groove, check out "Tread Water," "Say No Go" or "Me Myself and I." More than anything, **3 Feet High and Rising**—uncovering a previously unknown oasis between gang wars, party people and Saturday morning cartoons—is further proof of rap's diversity and creative vitality. A must.

The **Me Myself and I** 12-inch contains four versions of the the title cut: two instrumentals, the original LP track and a drastically different beat-heavy mix with enough samples replaced to give it a completely new feel and melody. The three other tracks are all great, with messages dissing clichéd hip-hop lingo, violence, drugs and status symbols. [dgs]

DEL-BYZANTEENS

Del-Byzanteens EP (nr/Don't Fall off the Mountain) 1981
Lies to Live By (nr/Don't Fall off the Mountain) 1982

Up from the murky pit of New York's art-punk scene came the Del-Byzanteens, a quartet with stylistic threads running back through Television and the Velvet Underground and the ability to give their dark, urgent arrangements a cinematic pan. (Not a surprising attribute, considering the future career of keyboardist Jim Jarmusch.) An unsettling cover of the Supremes' "My World Is Empty" on the three-track EP is a slice of jungle paranoia with voodoo percussion, ominous group vocals that sound like a satanic mass and a guitar quotation from *Perry Mason*.

The group's inventive resources are spread a little thin, though, on **Lies to Live By**. The quirky B-52's guitarisms and hyper-disco thump of "Draft Riot" and dour facelessness (Joy Division variety) of the title track dull the impact of both "War," a clever union of funk-punk drive with protest lyrics from Caribbean calypso records, and the gray soul of the old Jaynettes' shuffle, "Sally Go Round the Roses." Both "Lies to Live By" and a new version of the EP's "Girl's Imagination" were used by Wim Wenders in his movie *The State of Things*. [df]

DEL FUEGOS

The Longest Day (Slash) 1984
Boston, Mass. (Slash-Warner Bros.) 1985 ●
Stand Up (Slash-Warner Bros.) 1987 ●
Smoking in the Fields (RCA) 1989 ●

The Longest Day is a solid album bursting with high-energy beat'n'billy-inflected guitar rock. The songs are memorable without pandering; the playing is simple but never simpleminded. From the quivering "Nervous and Shakey" (which opens the LP) to the ominous hipshake "Call My Name" (which ends it), this is a full, therapeutic dose of mature, unaffected rock'n'roll recalled from the '50s and '60s built strictly in and for the '80s.

Besides atrocious art direction, the Boston band's second LP is a hair more selfconscious than its first. In view of the momentary popularity of "working class" rock, **Boston, Mass.** sounds like it was designed to please a wide audience, although it actually recalls the old Animals more than anything else. On the other hand, the Del Fuegos can't be accused of making any radical readjustment.

The stupid fold-out back cover gimmick of **Stand Up** should serve as a warning: this messy indulgence (with guest appearances by Tom Petty, James Burton and others) hasn't got any worthwhile songs or intrinsic personality. Dan Zanes' voice is largely shot; the spunky band of music-crazy street kids has turned into a grizzled bunch of oldtimers who run through this tired assortment of horned-out grit-rockers like a rejected beer commercial. Following the album, drummer Woody Giessmann (ex-Embarrassment) became an ex-Del Fuego.

It isn't the illusion of reclaimed youth that makes **Smoking in the Fields** such a welcome improvement over **Stand Up**, it's the discovery that maturity isn't such a bad thing. Secret weapon harp demon Magic

Dick (ex-J. Geils Band) sends out waves of soulful moaning on some of the songs as horns and tasteful strings gussy up others; the lively variety show of smoking R&B, Stonesy guitar rock, rugged pop and whiskey-scarred soul (shades of Mink DeVille) scores on all four fronts. The record gets on such a roll that even a tender love song Zanes croons (with guest harmony by Rick Danko) over acoustic guitar, cello and mandolin backup turns up in the middle of Side B without any loss in momentum. Producer Dave Thoerner deserves plenty of credit for fitting the Fuegos' music into appropriate arrangements (that couldn't simply be worked out onstage) and still coming up with a full-bodied album that sounds completely natural.   [i]

See also *Embarrassment*.

GABI DELGADO

See *Deutsche Amerikanische Freundschaft*.

DELINQUENTS

See *Lester Bangs*.

DEL-LORDS

Frontier Days (Enigma-EMI America) 1984
Johnny Comes Marching Home (Enigma-EMI America) 1986
Based on a True Story (Enigma) 1988 ●
Howlin' at the Halloween Moon (Restless) 1989 φ
Lovers Who Wander (Enigma) 1990 φ

ERIC AMBEL

Roscoe's Gang (Enigma) 1988 ●

Musical pioneers at the East Coast's westernmost boundaries, New York City's Del-Lords stand in the forefront of back-to-the-roots countryfied urban rock-'n'roll, skipping any particular stylistic imitation to enthusiastically bang out perceptive tunes of hard times and true love. With guitarist Scott Kempner (once Top Ten of the Dictators) penning the material but occasionally relinquishing lead vocals to guitarist Eric "Roscoe" Ambel, the Del-Lords embrace rock's basic components with such skill and verve that they outshine most everyone else on the scene. The best tracks on **Frontier Days**—"Burning in the Flame of Love," "Feel Like Going Home" and a cover of Alfred Reed's "How Can a Poor Man Stand Such Times and Live"—are true-blue and brilliant.

The songs on **Johnny Comes Marching Home**—produced with no ill effects by Pat Benatar's husband, Neil Geraldo—are better and the playing is even more confident and enthusiastic. Lyrical topics stretch from the sunny optimism of "Heaven" to the misery of "Love Lies Dying," with stops along the way for a kidnapped victim of terrorism ("Against My Will"), a love letter to a real-life '60s radio DJ ("Saint Jake") and a veteran's wistful view of militarism ("Soldier's Home"). The music runs from a greasy Link Wray instrumental to a wittily disguised rewrite of "If I Had a Hammer." Not trendy, twangy, corny or selfconscious, the Del-Lords simply play the old-fashioned way, with a sharp ear for melody and choruses that don't evaporate after a few listens. Considering that the quartet's roots are essentially a quarter-century old, they sure make it sound fresh and young.

Geraldo's commercially conscious production work loses sight of the Del-Lords' essence—making them sound in spots like a bland bar band straining to cop a chart hit—but **Based on a True Story** is generally another proud blast from the Bronx heartland. "We don't follow fashion," writes Kempner (in "The Cool and the Crazy"), "Who needs it when you got style?" Oddly, the band's intrinsic savoir faire is less apparent than ever before, perhaps a casualty of too many guest stars. Mojo Nixon's participation in "River of Justice" adds helpful absurdity to the proceedings, but when a multi-tracked Syd Straw and others sing the chorus, it's easy to forget exactly whose record this is. "Judas Kiss" (a Kempner composition sung by Ambel) is a tremendous song despite the wrongheaded treatment, and others—"Whole Lotta Nothin' Goin' On," "Cheyenne" and the twelve-bar "A Lover's Prayer"—find the Lords firmly in charge.

Despite a good head of electric steam, the seven live cuts captured on **Howlin' at the Halloween Moon** don't raise much dust. Somewhere between the weak choice of material (so-so originals like "I Play the Drums" and "The Cool and the Crazy," plus the Flamin' Groovies' "Jumpin' in the Night" and "Tallahassee Lassie") and the energetic but ineffectual performances, the record winds up flat and plain. Even the magnificent "Judas Kiss" comes off routine. And who stole the Del Lords' hyphen?

With Kempner delivering the most passionate and mature songs of his career, **Lovers Who Wander**, co-produced by Thom Panunzio and bassist Manny Caiati, eliminates the commercial anxiety to focus all of the band's strengths onto one great record. Besides the haunting "Learn to Let Go" (lyrics by David Roter), the melancholy "Wild Boys" and the sensuous, organ-cheesed "About You," the album features a remarkable choogling translation of the Dictators' classic "Stay with Me," slowing the song down to reveal new emotional depths that make it wholly appropriate to this resonant, downcast album.

Soon after the release of **Lovers Who Wander**, Ambel left the Del Lords to devote himself to a fulltime solo career. He had already tested the waters in 1988 with **Roscoe's Gang**, a casual good-time rock'n'roll session with the Skeletons, Peter Holsapple and like-minded friends. Co-produced by Ambel and Lou Whitney, cover versions of Swamp Dogg, Bob Dylan and Neil Young songs meld with Whitney, Kempner and Ambel originals in the joyful party atmosphere.   [i]

See also *Dictators, David Roter Method*.

DELMONAS

Comin' Home Baby EP (nr/Big Beat) 1984
Hello, We Love You EP (nr/Big Beat) 1984
Dangerous Charms (nr/Big Beat) 1985
Delmonas 5! (nr/Empire) 1986 (nr/Hangman) 1988
The Delmonas (nr/Hangman) 1989
Do the Uncle Willy (Skyclad) 1989

Originally known as the Milkboilers, Sarah, Hilary and Louise first clustered around a microphone to sing girl-group backup on records by the Milkshakes, for whom they doubled as groupies and squeezes. After taking lead chores on "Boys," they cut their own two-volume set of four-song 7-inches "with musical accompaniment by Thee Milkshakes" for Big Beat (then the 'Shakes label), collecting these songs plus three outtakes and five new tracks cut for a radio program into a debut album, **Dangerous Charms**. The predominance of '60s classics only emphasizes their flat vocals, but on the Hampshire/Childish tunes, written with such limitations well in mind, they ignite, sparkle (and sputter) with undeniable enthusiasm and, well, charm.

Following a short period of inactivity resulting from a clash of headstrong personalities regarding leadership and direction, the band resurfaced as Delmonas 5!, now down to two members (renamed Miss Ida Red and Ludella Black) with the original Caesars lineup as backing. Recorded louder, harsher and with considerably more confidence, the mood on **Delmonas 5!** is darker, with a greatly bolstered Nancy Sinatra tuff-girl quotient.

The Delmonas has the same raw immediacy, perhaps even accentuating it, and includes the first album's lost title track plus a pair of songs redone with French lyrics, again relying two parts on real oldies and one part on *new* oldies from assorted Childish bands—the most darkly melodic tunes thereof. **Do the Uncle Willy** collects slightly less crisp sounding tracks from the two previous LPs plus a pair of alternate versions and a previously un-Monaed Billytune for their most "flattering" LP, a spirited soundtrack for dreary afternoons and bleary aftermidnights.   [ab]

See also *Pop Rivits, Thee Mighty Caesars*.

VICTOR DE LORENZO

See *Violent Femmes*.

DEL RUBIO TRIPLETS

Three Gals, Three Guitars (Cabazon-Blue Yonder Sounds) 1988

Too talented and successful an act for Broadway Danny Rose (but almost as kitschily inspired as piano-pecking birds), these three middle-aged sisters create a delicious platter of unintended camp by blithely bringing their '40s vocal stylings to bear on a bizarre program of material. After covering easy-listening classics like "Hey Jude" and "Light My Fire" for starters, the guitar-strumming Del Rubios move right into sublime weirdness with selections from the Bangles ("Walk Like an Egyptian"), Pointer Sisters ("Neutron Dance") and Pet Shop Boys ("What Have I Done to Deserve This?").   [i]

DEPECHE MODE

Speak & Spell (Mute-Sire) 1981 ●
A Broken Frame (Mute-Sire) 1982 ●
Construction Time Again (Mute-Sire) 1983 ●
People Are People (Mute-Sire) 1984 ●
Some Great Reward (Mute-Sire) 1984 ●
The Singles '81–'85 (nr/Mute) 1985 ●
Catching Up with Depeche Mode (Mute-Sire) 1985 ●
Black Celebration (Mute-Sire) 1986 ●
Music for the Masses (Mute-Sire) 1987 ●
101 (Mute-Sire) 1989 ●
Violator (Mute-Sire-Reprise) 1990 ●

MARTIN L. GORE

Counterfeit EP (Mute-Sire) 1989 ●

RECOIL

Hydrology and 1 + 2 (Mute-Enigma) 1989 φ

Born in England's new romantic movement, Basildon's Depeche Mode (a French magazine translation of "fashion dispatch") immediately proved capable of making flawlessly captivating electro-pop tunes with simple formulae. What set them apart at the outset (how times change) was their complete reliance on synthesizers, offering post-modernistic gloss to comfortably familiar (but new) material. Over the years, the increasingly successful—and not deeply talented—group has grown pompous and gloomy, embracing heavier and denser sounds, but they've never abandoned the singles format or lost their appeal to teenage girls.

Not coincidentally, the best songs on **Speak and Spell** were the UK hits: "New Life," "Dreaming of Me" and the smash "Just Can't Get Enough." Oblivious to innovation or deep thinking, the album is simply a good, catchy collection of modern dance tunes.

Despite the dire predictions that followed songwriter Vince Clarke's departure to form Yazoo (and later Erasure), Depeche Mode pressed on, essentially unhampered, as a trio to make **A Broken Frame**, which has similar virtues, tempered with some deviation from course. David Gahan's vocals are stronger, and while funk forms the rhythmic base of "My Secret Garden," a Japanese tinge is given to "Monument" and "Satellite" centers around a ska beat. The rest of the album varies to a small degree from the dancemania of earlier work without abandoning it—a characteristic midpoint between experimentation and repetition.

Expanding back to a quartet, with Martin Gore continuing as the main songwriter, **Construction Time Again** exposes a mature outlook, dropping the simplistic pop tunes for a more intellectual, challenging approach. The transition is not altogether smooth. "Everything Counts" offers a bitter denunciation of the (presumably music) business world and "Shame" is a heartfelt confrontation with responsibility. Other tunes ("Pipeline," "More Than a Party") are less probing, although the former has interestingly industrialized music and chanted vocals. (The **Construction Time Again** CD adds a bonus cut.)

Although the reasons for its assembly are unclear, **People Are People** (not released in the UK) is a compilation of post-Clarke tunes, drawing five of its tracks from the two preceding LPs and the rest from singles. Not a cohesive album, it does contain prime material blending synth-rock with real-life and industrial noises to make truly modern pop music.

Some Great Reward is Depeche Mode's best record, containing everything from the bitter religious doubt of "Blasphemous Rumours" to the socio-sexual role playing of "Master and Servant" and the egalitarian "People Are People." Seamlessly blending unsettling concrète sounds—like synthesized factory din and clanking chains—into the music, the group achieves a masterful music/life mix few of the same mind have approached.

As Depeche Mode's international stature grew to awesome proportions, two compilation albums—**The Singles** and **Catching Up**—were released. The former, issued in the UK, is a fine collection of thirteen familiar items; the cassette and CD add two more. The American release has most of the same tracks (excluding those already compiled on **People Are People**), but includes "Fly on the Windscreen" (also on **Black Celebration**) and "Flexible." Complicated enough? (Actually, the quartet's discography is far more involved, thanks to numerous EPs. "Blasphemous Rumours," "Everything Counts," "Get the Balance Right," "Love, in Itself," "A Question of Time," "Never Let Me Down Again" and others have all been issued on 12-inch and CD with non-LP bonus tracks, many of them live.)

Depeche Mode has tackled many different lyrical concerns in the past, but never have they done such a consistently downcast record as **Black Celebration**. Except for intermittent bouts of romanticism and a bluntly political protest ("New Dress"), the songs are filled with doubt, disgust and depression, an attitude reinforced by their dirgelike, minor-chord constructions. Unfortunately, many of the tunes resemble each other; shards of the same melody turn up repeatedly. There's a certain grim power to this work, but it's not one of their more appealing or accomplished albums.

Music for the Masses is marginally brighter in temperament, but shows the band running low on creative juice. Unambitious, bland and forgettable, the album displays little beyond Gore's emotional anxieties and Gahan's vocal limitations. The tense "Behind the Wheel" and "Never Let Me Down Again" are the only powerful songs here, and both have dumb lyrics and skimpy, underdeveloped melodies. "Pimpf," a turgid piece of operatic nonsense, ends the album on a most unpromising note. The CD has four bonus tracks.

Given the band's underwhelming concert presence —a woeful mixture of pre-programmed synthesizers and Gahan's unsteady vocals—the advisability of a live album (and a theatrical documentary filmed by D.A. Pennebaker) can only be weighed against the potential for profit. Young Depechites undoubtedly could care less about the inadequacies of **101**—four sides of hits, etc., recorded at a 1988 stadium show in Pasadena, California—but this is hardly a significant item in the canon. (The CD adds three.)

Possibly the result of extensive touring, the dismal **Violator** matches **Music for the Masses** for shallow blandness. Gore's obvious dearth of meaningful ideas dominates this handsomely performed, tuneless waste; the lack of external input locks the insular group in a closed creative circle that shows no signs of opening or expanding. Worse than routine music (the LP's best song, "Enjoy the Silence," is totally self-derivative; the idiotic "Clean" uses a monotonous sequencer line borrowed from Kraftwerk), the vague egocentric lyrics ("Blue Dress," "World in My Eyes," "Clean") no longer make any effort to be about anything. In the record's sole flash of wit, "Personal Jesus" (also released on a five-mix CD) uses a jaunty rock'n'roll swing, but "reach out and touch faith" isn't a very profound message.

Gore gave songwriting a rest for his solo EP, an insubstantial 12-inch of obscure cover versions. (The traditional "Motherless Child" and Sparks' "Never Turn Your Back on Mother Earth" are the most familiar songs in his repertoire; other selections come from Durutti Column and Tuxedomoon.) Skillful but occasion-

ally running too contrary to the material, **Counterfeit** demonstrates two things: that Gore can carry a tune and that he has no artistic ambitions beyond Depeche Mode's usual style.

Alan Wilder debuted his solo project, Recoil, in 1986 with **1 + 2**, a British 12-inch later expanded by further efforts and reissued on the longwinded **Hyrdrology and 1 + 2**. Accented with ephemeral electronic and vocal noises, Recoil's monotonous instrumentals drone aimlessly in several idioms: loud synthesizers, soft synthesizers, pinging synthesizers, chanted vocals and piano. The first track recalls **Tubular Bells**, and that's the most provocative feature of this hissy-sounding record. [sg/i]

See also *Erasure, Yazoo*.

DESCENDENTS

Fat EP (New Alliance) 1981 (SST) 1988 ●
Milo Goes to College (New Alliance) 1982 (SST) 1988
Bonus Fat (New Alliance) 1985 (SST) 1988
I Don't Want to Grow Up (New Alliance) 1985 (SST) 1988 ●
Enjoy! (New Alliance-Restless) 1986
All (SST) 1987 ●
Liveage! (SST) 1987 ●
Two Things at Once (SST) 1988 φ
Hallraker (SST) 1989 ●

In search of the metaphysical All, LA's Descendents did their growing up in public. The group debuted as a young power-pop trio on a likable 1979 single ("Ride the Wild") but then didn't return to vinyl until 1981, when a four-piece lineup issued the smart, fast and punky 7-inch **Fat EP**: six fleeting (total time 5:52) Black Flag-like culture statements like "Wienerschnitzel," "I Like Food" and "My Dad Sucks." (Besides **Fat**'s re-release on 12-inch, cassette and CD-3, the EP and preceding single were combined as **Bonus Fat**.)

When singer Milo Aukerman left the band to study biochemistry in San Diego, the Descendents pressed on and issued **Milo Goes to College**, a promising hardcore album with a few dumb bummers amidst the fun. Then drummer Bill Stevenson—the primary Descendent, as it were—went off to join Black Flag, and the group evaporated for a while.

When they reassembled in mid-1985, Milo, Stevenson, bassist Tony Lombardo and ex-SWA guitarist Ray Cooper (who had switched to vocals after Milo's departure) recorded **I Don't Want to Grow Up**. This excellent, surefooted punk album knowingly uses the hyperkinetic musical idiom as a disguise for intelligent, sarcastic songwriting. Melodies (a few border on power pop) and substantial lyrics drift around the edge of obnoxiousness without entirely giving in to it.

Enjoy! features a new bassist and proves that even talented bands with positive attitudes are not immune to gratuitous vulgarity and base stupidity. The title song is a childish paean to farting, complete with audio vérité effects; two others reveal a deeply juvenile attitude towards women. On the other hand, a peppy version of Brian Wilson's "Wendy" is spectacular; most of the originals—including the satirical "Hürtin' Crüe," the Anglo-popping "Get the Time" and the surly noise of the seven-minutes-plus "Days Are Blood"—are at least near-excellent, reflecting the band's loping musical strides. (Curious art note: the titles listed on the back cover have virtually nothing in common with the record's contents.)

The disappointing **All** starts with one of the shortest songs on record: the 1-second title track. Leading new bandmates, Milo and Stevenson take a raunchy guitar-rock excursion (excepting the almost acoustic "Impressions") that downplays the band's melodic side. "Clean Sheets" and "Pep Talk" have solid tunes and invigorating performances, but "Van," "Coolidge," "Iceman," the high-concept "All-o-gistics" and lengthy "Schizophrenia" are basically loud and witless, substituting routine guitar work for character. (After the Descendents arrived on SST, the label reissued their prior work. **Two Things at Once** is a CD/cassette pairing of **Milo Goes to College** and **Bonus Fat**.)

Before vanishing into All (get the drift?), the Descendents released a live album, recorded in 1987 at First Avenue in Minneapolis. **Liveage!**'s eighteen rushed songs (more on the cassette and CD) review the band's entire repertoire in a noisy, frenzied attack that's both fun and exciting.

As Stevenson explains in the informative liner notes, **Hallraker** ("the other live Descendents LP") was released to redress fan complaints about material that wasn't on **Liveage!** Partially recorded at the same Minneapolis show (the remainder is from a California date a few months earlier), **Hallraker** serves up sixteen different songs with exactly the same sloppy punk panache.

See also *All, Black Flag, Last*.   [i]

DESPERATE BICYCLES
New Cross New Cross EP (nr/Refill) 1978
Remorse Code (nr/Refill) 1979

Along with the far more heralded Soft Boys, this legendary post-punk Chocolate Watch band predated the neo-psychedelic movement by several years with a series of self-released singles and an LP of ten pop gems. The interplay of agile bass and near-perfect guitar on **Remorse Code** helps kick things along, and songs like "Sarcasm" and "It's Somebody's Birthday Today" are utter classics. Sly humor is exhibited with silly tape and sound effects, not to mention the guitarist's savvy pseudonym: Dan Electro.   [dgs]

JIMMY DESTRI
See *Blondie*.

DESTROY ALL MONSTERS
See *New Order*.

DEUTSCHE AMERIKANISCHE FREUNDSCHAFT
Ein Produkt der D.A.F. (Ger. Warning-Atatak) 1979
Die Kleinen und die Bosen (nr/Mute) 1980
Alles Ist Gut (nr/Virgin) 1981 ●
Gold und Liebe (nr/Virgin) 1981 ●
Für Immer (nr/Virgin) 1982 ●
Deutsche Amerikanische Freundschaft (nr/Virgin) 1988 ●

GABI DELGADO
Mistress (nr/Virgin) 1983
ROBERT GÖRL
Night Full of Tension (Elektra) 1984

Originating as Düsseldorf art-punk cacophony cultists in the holdout hippie culture of late 1970's Germany, D.A.F.—originally a group, but generally known internationally as the duo of instrumentalist Robert Görl and singer Gabi Delgado-Lopez—broke away to find success in Europe as a synthesizer-and-dance band.

Ein Produkt der D.A.F. is an apocalyptic eruption of sound announcing the end of the German Republic, with shrieking, colliding overdubbed synths and guitars. The electro-metal is simultaneously repellent and compelling. **Die Kleinen und die Bosen**, D.A.F.'s first international release (following the group's relocation to London), modifies the electronic chaos with an eye towards the modern dance. Material is more polished, with anarchic synthesizer work slowly integrating a solid, defined beat.

Alles Ist Gut abandons the band's Faustian tendencies for cerebral dance music, polished to a metallic shine by producer Conny Plank. Typical funk rhythms are replaced by industrial pulses (trains, etc.); some vocal experimentation casts the band onto shrewd pop turf, despite decidedly libidinous lyrics. **Gold und Liebe** perfects the advances of **Alles Ist Gut**, emphasizing the punchy use of drum-box and de-emphasizing other instruments, creating a robot void that eerily strands the guttural vocals.

D.A.F.'s final album, **Für Immer**, breaks the pattern, with a variety of styles from funk to rock'n'roll to distorted metal drone before returning to a dance blowout for the final track. While it's all interesting, none of these excursions are displayed long enough to be truly impressive. The inner spaces of earlier work are filled by a range of instruments, including very gentle bells. Like all of D.A.F.'s LPs, it is sung in German. The 1988 release is a fourteen-song compilation from the band's three Virgin albums; the CD adds two alternate versions as bonus tracks.

Delgado and Görl dissolved their partnership to pursue solo careers (reuniting temporarily in 1985). For his album, Gabi enlisted some top names in modern German music—Conny Plank and Can's Jaki Liebezeit among them—to make slick but expendable disco, topped off with obsequious lyrics, mostly about sex.

Görl's flat singing (mostly in English) on **Night Full of Tension** leaves a lot to be desired. The fact that he wrote all of D.A.F.'s music doesn't appreciably aid these dull lumps of spare, rhythmic, go-nowhere electronics. The LP's only notable success is "Darling Don't Leave Me," an angst-ridden duet with Annie Lennox (returning a favor—Görl was the drummer on one track of Eurythmics' first LP) that bears an unpleasant air of sado-masochism. Lennox appears on several other songs as well.   [sg/i]

DEVIANTS
See *Mick Farren, Social Deviants*.

WILLY DEVILLE
See *Mink DeVille*.

DEVINE & STATTON

The Prince of Wales (Bel. Crépuscule) 1989 (Rockville)
1990 ●

Cardiffians (Bel. Crépuscule) 1990 ●

This bewitching team-up of two soft-spoken conjurers—Ian Devine from the obscure-but-rated-by-Morrissey early-'80s Manchester group Ludus, and Allison Statton, the unforgettably nondescript voice of Wales' Young Marble Giants and Weekend—has produced the apotheosis of well-bred, thoughtful, slightly neurotic folk-pop. Devine writes sharply observed songs about his polite, slightly pampered, rather befuddled peers and the ordinary heartbreaks and tragedies that attend their daily lives. As voiced by Statton, the songs' ironies register tenderly, while her intelligence whisks away any wistful treacle a lesser interpreter might bring to them. **The Prince of Wales** has very spare, guitar-based arrangements which give the simple melodies a nice lilt; the duo manages to keep things sounding light but not wispy.

Cardiffians adds NYC downtowners Curtis Fowlkes, Roy Nathanson and Marc Ribot on, respectively, trombone, sax and guitar, and New Order's Peter Hook joins on bass (presumably he approved of the duo's much-softened cover of "Bizarre Love Triangle" on **The Prince of Wales**). Despite the expanded lineup, the sound is still remarkably spare, and all of the songs have a lingering quality that goes beyond the incisive lyrics and deceptively simple music. In light of Devine's first-rate material here, the cover of Crystal Gayle's "Don't It Make My Brown Eyes Blue" is cute but rather pointless, although it does allow the duo to demonstrate that sensitive, insightful treatment can't salvage a fundamentally bad song. That misstep aside, **Cardiffians** is wonderful. [gk]

See also *Young Marble Giants*.

DEVO

Q: Are We Not Men? A: We Are Devo (Warner Bros.)
1978 ●

Be Stiff EP (nr/Stiff) 1978

Duty Now for the Future (Warner Bros.) 1979

Freedom of Choice (Warner Bros.) 1980 ●

Dev–o Live EP (Warner Bros.) 1981

New Traditionalists (Warner Bros.) 1981

Oh, No! It's Devo (Warner Bros.) 1982

Shout (Warner Bros.) 1984

E-Z Listening Disc [CD] (Rykodisc) 1987 ●

Total Devo (Enigma) 1988 ●

Now It Can Be Told (Enigma) 1989 ●

Smooth Noodle Maps (Enigma) 1990 (Dutch East Wax)
1991 ●

Hardcore Vol. 1 74–77 (Rykodisc) 1990 φ

Devo Greatest Hits (Warner Bros.) 1990 φ

Devo Greatest Misses (Warner Bros.) 1990 φ

MARK MOTHERSBAUGH

Muzik for Insomniaks Volume 1 (Enigma) 1988 φ
Muzik for Insomniaks Volume 2 (Enigma) 1988 φ

VARIOUS ARTISTS

KROQ-FM Devotees Album (Rhino) 1979

When the new wave floodgates opened in the mid-'70s, all sorts of strange things flowed out. From Ak-ron, Ohio, came five neurotic overachievers (the Mothersbaugh and Casale brothers on guitars and bass, plus a drummer) armed with an ambitious and effective robotic sound, and a carefully contrived (but intentionally inarticulate) theory about the de-evolutionary state of things to come. Beginning with a pair of groundbreaking 1977 singles on the group's own Booji Boy label, the efficiently organized quintet delivered itself encased in a self-willed pseudo-culture, with industrial uniforms, loopy graphics, promotional films, lingo, merchandise, etc. Whether sharp social commentators on the breakdown of modern life or just canny media marketers selling a total pop package (a distinction that was soon revealed to be essentially meaningless), the spudboys quickly won a revered place in rock's brave new world, serving as a major influence for many.

Produced with energetic precision by Brian Eno, Devo's first album is the most concentrated presentation of the band's nebulous theories. "Jocko Homo," "Mongoloid" and "Shrivel Up" employ a cold, assembly-line jerkiness to drive home their defeatist attitudes and post-modern morality. The same nervous energy fuels more emotional messages like "Uncontrollable Urge," "Gut Feeling," "Sloppy (I Saw My Baby Gettin')," the science-fiction paranoia of "Space Junk" and a hilariously high-strung (and de-sexed) version of the Rolling Stones' "Satisfaction," with a mechanical-sounding drum beat that would frizz Charlie Watts' hair.

Be Stiff collects Devo's two indie 45s—four tunes that had been re-recorded for **Are We Not Men?**—and the third single, done for Stiff.

The second full-length album, **Duty Now for the Future** (produced by Ken Scott), doesn't score as many bull's-eyes as the first, but includes two Devo anthems of malaise, "Blockhead" and "S.I.B. (Swelling Itching Brain)." Amid disturbing signs of portentousness, Devo turns their bemused eyes to the mating ritual on "Strange Pursuit," "Triumph of the Will" and "Pink Pussycat."

The self-produced **Freedom of Choice** is the band's most evocative pairing of words and music. Setting aside metaphysical foofaraw, the flowerpot-wearing fivesome contrast choppy keyboard licks ("Girl U Want," "It's Not Right," "Snowball") and ironic but unalienated perceptions ("Gates of Steel," "Planet Earth," "Freedom of Choice"). Their tolerance was rewarded with a subversive hit single from the LP, "Whip It."

Issued to milk the success of "Whip It," **Dev–o Live** is thoroughly redundant. Five of the six songs, including you-know-what and an instrumental version of "Freedom of Choice," are from the preceding LP; only "Be Stiff" is new to album buyers. Hardly a jamming band, Devo live sounds just like Devo in the studio, except maybe a bit sloppier.

Devo's been soft-pedaling their philosophy (on record, at least) since **Freedom of Choice**'s breakthrough. Musically they're still held back by a stunted sense of melody, although the dance-rock movement created a favorable climate for a rhythmic orientation and probably led to Devo's increasing emphasis on a whomping beat. Unfortunately, the conducive atmosphere coincided with reduced artistic ambition; Devo has never made another album half as good as any of the first three.

New Traditionalists has a couple of attention-getting songs ("Love Without Anger," "Going Under," the extraordinarily attractive "Beautiful World") and, for early birds, a bonus 45 of Lee Dorsey's "Working in the Coal Mine." Most of it, though, is clinical-sounding laissez-faire techno-dance stuff, less-than-compelling lyrics set to a metronomic 4/4 beat.

After wobbling through that uneven effort, Devo went straight to the dogs. **Oh, No! It's Devo**, pointlessly produced by Roy Thomas Baker, failed to slow the creative slide; the mocking optimism of "That's Good" and the nonsense lyrics of "Peek-a-Boo!" are the sole songs worth recalling from it.

Shout's only memorable contribution is a version of the Jimi Hendrix oldie, "Are You Experienced?" Songwriters Mark Mothersbaugh (guitar/keyboards) and Gerald Casale (bass/keyboards) are evidently going through a dry spell of drought proportions, substituting clichés for the razor-sharp observations that used to keep Devo intriguing as well as danceable. Did Devo succumb to its own devolution?

Little was heard from the group proper for years after **Shout**, although Casale and the Mothersbaughs remained active, writing and performing music for films and television (including *Pee-wee's Playhouse*; in '90, Mark M. reached prime time with the theme to *Davis Rules*) and producing outside projects. Their Los Angeles (where the group relocated in the early '80s) recording studio has also been busy. Under the Devo banner, however, the only music to surface during this era was the woefully mistitled **E-Z Listening Disc**—an hour-plus CD containing the group's smugly straight-faced (and barely recognizable) schlocky instrumental remakes of nineteen Devo songs—originally available on the mail-order-only **E-Z Listening** cassettes.

Returning to active duty in the late '80s, the group made the self-produced **Total Devo**, the most notable aspect of which (besides the replacement of drummer Alan Myers by ex-Gleaming Spire/Spark David Kendrick) is its simultaneous four-format release: LP, cassette, CD and digital audio tape (DAT). Otherwise, it's little more than a timid and bland imitation of the countless bands Devo inspired. Lost and confused, Devo attempts to sound like Human League, sings of being a "Disco Dancer" with far too little irony and essays a witless cover of "Don't Be Cruel" that reveals a rather profound absence of humor. (The release of a "Disco Dancer" 12-inch with "3 Ivan Ivan remixes unavailable elsewhere" underscores just how far the once-visionary group has fallen.)

Dead in the water and sinking fast, Devo cast out **Now It Can Be Told**, a three-sided live album recorded in Los Angeles at the end of 1988. Lackluster, impotent performances turn what should have been a holding action into a total waste of time. Kendrick's unimaginatively routine drumming derails "Gut Feeling" and "Satisfaction," while a drastically revised arrangement of "Jocko Homo" turns it into an annoyingly slow, acoustic sway.

The appearance of a song called "Devo Has Feelings Too" on **Smooth Noodle Maps** might have promised some sort of cathartic statement about the group's mental state, but the lyrics add nothing to the title. Still, the keyboard-heavy album gets back to muscular techno-dance music with less ambition and more success. Although the hi-NRG bounce of "When We Do It" is as numbingly bad as anything in Devo's past, **Smooth Noodle Maps** is not without its moments. Maybe it's the result of reduced expectations, but "Post Post-Modern Man" and "Spin the Wheel" have some of the melodic freshness and enthusiasm (if not the ironic intelligence) long absent from Devo's records. But why cover "Morning Dew" in sequencers and rhythm machines?

The home-brew 4-track recordings (many of songs that have never surfaced in any other authorized form) from the band's formative years that comprise **Hardcore** demonstrate how strong a stylistic foundation Devo had constructed before revealing itself to the world. Besides the Booji Boy versions of "Satisfaction," "Mongoloid," "Jocko Homo" and "Social Fools" and a few half-baked duds, this frequently fascinating document reveals such intriguing castoffs as the lyrically twisted "Uglatto" (Gene Vincent meets Marc Bolan in the next century), "Stop Look and Listen," the boogie-happy "I'm a Potato" and "Buttered Beauties."

Serving as both a reminder of Devo's past greatness and the evident futility of its continued existence, a matching pair of compilations was issued at the end of 1990. Rather than assemble one full-fledged retrospective, the band created two halves that don't add up to much, for real fans *or* casual spuds. Cherrypicking the early albums, finding the few good bits in the later ones and then adding on some token representatives of albums that contain nothing of merit, **Greatest Hits** (the titular reference obviously isn't strictly commercial) gathers up sixteen tunes, from "Jocko Homo" and "Satisfaction" through a remixed version of **Shout**'s "Here to Go." Except for the overly generous inclusion of three tracks from **Oh, No!**, the selection isn't bad, but anyone owning the first four albums can skip this package without missing anything significant.

For slightly more serious Devophiles, **Greatest Misses** puts together early LP tracks (some of which—"Blockhead," "S.I.B.," "Devo Corporate Anthem" —could rationally have replaced later stinkers on the **Hits** volume), such artifacts as the Booji Boy singles of "Be Stiff" and "Mechanical Man" (a minute shorter than the version on **Hardcore**) and a rude 1979 UK B-side, "Penetration in the Centerfold." The standard stuff is nice but redundant, and most of the rarities aren't rare enough (a couple of them are on **Hardcore**) to make this record a necessity.

Far removed from his work in Devo, Mothersbaugh's two **Muzik for Insomniaks** releases consist of simple synthesizer instrumentals selected from what is evidently a massive cache of similar works. (One presumes the titles' sleeplessness refers more to the artist than the listener.) That many of these peppy exercises basically sound alike—some on **Volume 1** pointedly suggest Asian musical styles and others take a jazzy turn, but none would sound awfully out of place accompanying the *Pee-wee's Playhouse* credits—isn't really a hindrance, although two volumes is really one too many. Most of Mothersbaugh's non-verbal haikus are pleasant and relaxing, with enough compositional backbone to warrant attention. Each volume ends with an audio index: a brief snippet of each track.

The **Devotees Album** is a compilation of goofball cover versions, parodies of and tributes to Devo submitted to an LA radio station by a motley assortment of local amateur musicmakers.   [si/i]

HOWARD DEVOTO
Jerky Versions of the Dream (IRS) 1983
LUXURIA
Unanswerable Lust (Beggars Banquet-RCA) 1988 ●
Beast Box (Beggars Banquet-RCA) 1990 ●

Following influential and estimable careers with the Buzzcocks and Magazine, singer/writer Devoto continued his quest for independence as a solo artist. Using Dave Formula and Barry Adamson from Magazine, as well as other players, Devoto offers his idiosyncratic worldview and original musical outlook on ten tunes that range from funky ("Topless," "Way Out of Shape") to ethereal ("Rainy Season") to playful ("I Admire You") and beyond. Full appreciation of **Jerky Versions of the Dream** requires a bit of forbearance and effort, but few artists make music this careful and intelligent.

Five years on, Devoto's next project—Luxuria, a duo with a Liverpudlian musician known as Noko—leads him deep into the waters of overbearing pretension. On **Unanswerable Lust**, his lyrics quote Proust, spout *français*, mention Rimbaud and announce such silliness as "I am the street where you live." Even when the music—an unfocused mix of acoustic delicacy and walloping techno-dance crud—takes hold, it's swamped by Devoto's melodramatic quaver.

Beast Box has a higher proportion of quality tracks (credit better songwriting) but the music occasionally slips into a dull void, despite some excellent guitar work by Noko. Worse, Luxuria's dalliance with dance beats (as on "The Beast Box Is Dreaming" and the old "Jezebel") falls flat. But Devoto's specialty—spare, turgid tundras—still pervades tracks like "Stupid Blood," "Ticket" and "We Keep on Getting There," and numerous quietly dramatic touches lurk in the album's shadows.   [i/jr]

See also *Buzzcocks, Magazine.*

DEXY'S MIDNIGHT RUNNERS
Searching for the Young Soul Rebels (EMI America) 1980 ●
Don't Stand Me Down (Mercury) 1985 ●
KEVIN ROWLAND AND DEXYS MIDNIGHT RUNNERS
Too-Rye-Ay (Mercury) 1982 ●
Geno (nr/EMI) 1983 + 1986 ●
KEVIN ROWLAND
The Wanderer (nr/Mercury) 1988 ●
Young Man EP (nr/Mercury) 1988 ●
BUREAU
The Bureau (Atlantic) 1981

Although changing Dexy's from a nouveau American-soul band to an ethnic Irish folk group may make singer/mastermind Kevin Rowland seem a tad fickle, his singleminded devotion to whatever direction he selects gives the Birmingham group's first two albums a powerful sense of care and dedication that many infinitely more consistent musicians never achieve.

Searching for the Young Soul Rebels, recorded by the original eight-man lineup, boldly challenged the direction new wave had taken in 1979 and '80, long before soul music and horns became trendy. Taking inspiration from soul men like Sam & Dave and Geno Washington, onetime punk singer Rowland anted up a batch of emotionally powerful songs that work equally well as heartfelt tributes and modern creations. Despite the enormous amount of image-building that surrounded it, **Searching** is a fine, expressive album with no bad tracks.

Following a rancorous disagreement with Rowland, five bandmembers (including ex-Merton Parka keyboardist Mick Talbot) split with him at the end of 1980 and formed the Bureau, augmenting their instrumental resources with singer/songwriter Archie Brown, a guitarist and a trombone player. While Rowland began rebuilding Dexys, the Bureau cut an eponymous LP (produced by Pete Wingfield) that has some of the old band's signature horn sound and rhythmic punch but not much else of note.

Too-Rye-Ay, overalls and country instruments notwithstanding, is not as radically different at its core from **Searching** as it might first appear. Fronting a totally new band (including ex-Secret Affair drummer Seb Shelton) augmented with a two-piece fiddle section and a vocal trio, Rowland retains some of the earlier throaty horn work to make a few tracks (one a spot-on cover of Van Morrison's "Jackie Wilson Said") sound a lot like the first LP. Elsewhere, fiddles, banjos, accordion and tin whistle take over to make jolly, rollicking jug band fare—the enormous worldwide hit "Come on Eileen" and "The Celtic Soulbrothers," for instance. Other songs mix metaphors and become something more indescribable. Although a truly weird smorgasbord, the clever melodies and arrangements keep it consistently entertaining.

Dexys' only album release in either 1983 or 1984 was **Geno**, a worthwhile compilation of early singles (A- and B-sides) assembled by the band's former label.

To everyone's lasting discredit, the band didn't evaporate then and there: **Don't Stand Me Down** (forever to be recalled, if at all, as the "accountants" album due to yet another image change, this time into conservative pinstripes) is a torpid snore that denies entertainment on every level. With titles like "Knowledge of Beauty" and "Reminisce Part Two," the seven lengthy songs with absurd lyrics aim for a literate Van Morrison-like looseness, but end up just falling asleep or apart.

As if **Don't Stand Me Down** hadn't made the hairline between pop prodigy and pretentious twit abundantly clear, **The Wanderer** (credited to "Kevin Rowland of Dexys Midnight Runners," with a cover depicting the artist as a mustachioed dandy) treads that border as selfconsciously as ever. Recorded in New York with MOR fusion-jazz specialist Deodato producing, it's a fairly restrained collection of relatively unpretentious lounge-pop, a bit samey but not entirely without charm. Ironically, these songs cry out for the Big Pop treatment that Rowland might have felt more comfortable giving them prior to the critical debacle of **Don't Stand Me Down**.   [i/hd]

DHARMA BUMS

Haywire (PopLlama Products) 1989 (PopLlama
Products-Frontier) 1989
Bliss (Frontier) 1990 ●

Nothing fancy or stylish about this unassuming Portland, Oregon, quartet—just tight little melodic rock (plus country and punk) tunes played with youthful enthusiasm and sung with endearingly gangly harmonies. On the band's promising but not quite convincing debut, the mixture of Jeremy Wilson's mislocated drawl and guitarist Eric Lovre's kinetic inventiveness sets the Dharma Bums on a college-radio road between non-Byrdsy R.E.M. and a soft-center Replacements.

Bliss finds the band sporting a trebly guitar attack (with occasional feedback), erasing the first album's twinkier tendencies in an uncut aggressive rock attack. Several songs are tersely effective ("Pumpkinhead," "Far From Gone," "B-Sting," the countryfied "A Place to Be"), but too many others are tunelessly below the good-to-go level for this samey-sounding record to be anything like its title. [i]

DHARMA BUMS

Everything Is Always Alright (Telegraph Hill) 1987

This trio from the Boston area might have had the name first, but it's unlikely that their LP ever got distributed much beyond Rhode Island. Owing little to contempo trends, **Everything Is Always Alright** is solid, post-pub folk-rock that would surely bring a smile to the lips of diehard Brinsley Schwarz fans. (All six of 'em.) [bc]

D.I.

Team Goon (Reject) 1981 (Triple X) 1986 ●
Ancient Artifacts (Reject) 1984 (Triple X) 1986 ●
Horse Bites Dog Cries (Reject) 1985 (Triple X) 1986 ●
What Good Is Grief to a God (Triple X) 1988 ●
Tragedy Again (Triple X) 1989 ●

Like other bored suburban youths in Southern California, Orange County's D.I. voices disgust with a stagnant society through sarcastic humor, cynicism and punk's tension-relieving pace. Despite a revolving-door lineup that, for a time, featured Adolescents guitarist Rikk Agnew, D.I.'s general sound—propulsive melodies, careening guitars and snide upfront vocals by Casey Royer—has remained fairly constant.

Team Goon finds Royer, Agnew and future guitarist John Bosco (here on bass) delivering an open-palmed critique of the '80s degeneration. "Nuclear Funeral" inserts Biafran spoken satire, while "Venus De Milo" and the ironically understated "Richard Hung Himself" (a song D.I. contributed to Penelope Spheeris' wasted-youth movie, *Suburbia*, in 1984) both discuss suicide. The 1986 reissue adds three songs; the CD includes a rendition of Devo's "Uncontrollable Urge."

Ancient Artifacts has thin production and uneven material, but manages to come through powerfully in spots. While "(I Hate) Surfin' in H.B." is merely a teenage whine, "Spiritual Law" unplugs the TV generation's vacuous culture, and "Hang Ten in East Berlin" brings subtle harmonies into play. (The cassette and CD tack on a batch of live tracks, including a cover of the Adolescents' "Kids of the Black Hole.")

The much-improved **Horse Bites Dog Cries** (which includes remakes of "Hang Ten" and "Spiritual Law") best showcases D.I.'s gripping intensity. "Living in the U.S.A." jabs at the nation's bleakest qualities, while "Johnny's Got a Problem" portrays a troubled youth about to explode. The lightning tempo on "Youth in Asia" offsets the vocals' robotic repetition, a contrast to the sweeping "oh-oh" chorus in "Pervert Nurse." The CD and cassette add "Bedrock."

With Royer and guitarist Bosco as D.I.'s core, **What Good Is Grief to a God** intermittently maintains **Horse**'s song quality but is elsewhere lackluster. "No Mistakes" shakes a clenched fist at the world; "Girl Scout Camp" again rings with Jello-like satire. Overall, it's a good record impaired by predictable songwriting and guitarist Mark Cerneka's unimaginative solos. The cassette and CD add "She's Obscene"; the CD also boasts a remake of "Johnny's Got a Problem."

If nothing else, **Tragedy Again** (which throws "On Our Way," an odd '60s hippie send-up, into the usual hydrospeed attack) vouches for the band's stamina. Bonus track: "Cocktail Flu." [mg]

DIAGRAM BROTHERS

Some Marvels of Modern Science (nr/New Hormones)
1981
Discordo 45 EP (nr/New Hormones) 1982

Something like XTC (but lacking their musical smarts or stellar wit), the Diagram Brothers—of the Manchester art-noise family encircling the Buzzcocks' New Hormones label—play dissonant weirdness with lyrics about current events. Song titles pretty much say it all: "Isn't It Interesting How Neutron Bombs Work," "I'm a Policeman," "I Didn't Get Where I Am Today by Being a Right Git." While the poorly produced music only hints at talent hidden behind the quartet's anti-music self-indulgence, it's actually the four-sheet insert, containing detailed fold-cut-paste directions for assembly into a portfolio about the record, that evinces real cleverness.

The 10-inch EP adds four more episodes of whimsical wordplay ("I would like to make/A special toast/To my new toaster") and more appealing instrumental oddity (do I hear a tuba?) to the Diagram Brothers' legend. [i]

DICKIES

The Incredible Shrinking Dickies (A&M) 1979 ●
Dawn of the Dickies (A&M) 1979 ●
Stukas Over Disneyland (PVC) 1983 (Restless) 1988 ●
We Aren't the World! [tape] (ROIR) 1986
    [CD] (ROIR-Relativity) 1990 φ
Killer Klowns EP (Enigma) 1988 ●
Great Dictations (A&M) 1989 ●
Second Coming (Enigma) 1989 ●

For some reason, the lovable Dickies—a *Mad* magazine-flavored punk self-parody—never endeared themselves to as large an international cult as the Ramones have. Perhaps this mob of San Fernando Valley zanies has always been too unserious and knowing of their own idiocy, while their New York counterparts may well be playing it straight. (That's cooler, apparently.)

The Incredible Shrinking Dickies is a burst of late-'70s hyperactive California punk. But while most such bands display surly conviction, giddy good humor dominates here. Seven of the thirteen tracks clock in at under two minutes each, and everything sounds the same, from covers of "Eve of Destruction," the Monkees' "She" and Black Sabbath's "Paranoid" to originals like "Mental Ward" and "Rondo (The Midget's Revenge)."

On **Dawn of the Dickies**, the title of which, like that of its predecessor, alludes to a junk-movie classic, something wonderful happens: the Dickies get genuinely good. By slowing down the tempo a half step and coming up with strong melodies, guitarist Stan Lee and crew manage to reel off one maniacally catchy gem after another. The pop-culture slant is the same as before (check the delirious "Manny, Moe and Jack" and "Attack of the Mole Men"), and the mood is equally flippant, but this is a record with staying power.

After a prolonged absence, the boys next popped back into view with a frisky eight-song mini-album. Half of **Stukas Over Disneyland** dates from 1980, and includes a delightfully garbled version of Led Zeppelin's "Communication Breakdown." The high point of the remaining tracks (cut around 1983) is "Pretty Please Me," a power-pop pearl. Not a work of demented genius like **Dawn**, but damn good fun.

More oddities and endities can be found on **We Aren't the World!**, 21 doses of live Dickiedom recorded between 1978 and 1985, plus the raw four-song demo from '77 that, according to Lisa Fancher's belligerent liner notes, got them signed to A&M. Although the recording quality is as varied as the locales, this is a potent dose for fans of chaotic smartassitude.

In 1988, amid endless touring, an apparently recharged (and realigned) Dickies returned with a five-song EP built around the theme song for the cheesy sci-fi comedy *Killer Klowns from Outer Space*. Included on this fun (if less than inspired) release is a gimmicky remake of Jet Screamer's *Jetsons* rockabilly classic "Eep Opp Ork (Uh, Uh)," one more item in the Dickies' ever-expanding catalogue of daffy covers. That same year, Restless reissued **Stukas** with three additional songs, including the long-unavailable "Gigantor."

Concurrent with the release of the first new Dickies album in years, the group's old label unleashed **Great Dictations**, a haphazard collection of hard-to-find singles and tracks from the first two LPs.

Although hindered by overly fussy production and a worthless, atypically straight rendition of Gene Pitney's "Town Without Pity," **Second Coming** (only the band's third full-length studio effort in ten years) contains a solid dose of typical nuttiness. A shaggy cover of "Hair" opens the record on an up note which continues through such comic-pop gems as "Cross-Eyed Tammy" and "Dummy Up." Even "Goin' Homo," the normally lighthearted band's sole detour into wrongheaded crudity, is a lowbrow hoot. Oddly, the album repeats two **Killer Klowns** tracks (one improved by the addition of guest dialogue from singer Leonard Phillips' mom). While hardly the promised resurrection, **Second Coming** is still a perfectly (dis)respectable showing from one of our national treasures. [jy/i/db]

JAMES LUTHER DICKINSON
See *Panther Burns*.

DICKS/BIG BOYS
Recorded Live at Raul's Club (Rat Race) 1980
DICKS
Kill from the Heart (SST) 1983
These People (Alternative Tentacles) 1985
SISTER DOUBLE HAPPINESS
Sister Double Happiness (SST) 1988 ●

Much of the Dicks' early output can most flatteringly be described as forgettable political punk, yet Gary Floyd's mongrel Texas blues howl and some genuinely hooky snippets certainly snag attention (see **Live at Raul's** "Hate Police," also recorded as the Dicks' first single and later covered by Mudhoney). **These People**—recorded following a lineup shift occasioned by the Austin band moving to San Francisco and then everyone but Floyd moving back—displays a massive power shift into amphetamine blues territory, still riddled with hardcore violence but also embracing mood, pacing and proficiency. Including a much-improved tune from the live album the quartet shared with the Big Boys, it qualifies in retrospect as one of the hinge pins in punk's metallic boomerang at the end of the '80s.

Changing name and personnel to further escape the limitations of their past, **Sister Double Happiness** elaborates on all of the band's previous trends, but bluesier, more melodic, more metallic and more enduring. Heavily steeped in booze and depression and including a serious and sensitive examination of AIDS and its distancing mystique, the debut was also a farewell, as the band broke up soon after; in spiritual disarray, Gary Floyd exited music altogether. After a successful reunion gig in 1990, however, the band (with yet another bassist) released a mediocre Sub Pop 45 pairing a nondescript hard rocker with a tastier, simplified bottleneck blues; an LP on SST was announced for the following year. [ab]

See also *Frightwig*.

DICTATORS
The Dictators Go Girl Crazy! (Epic) 1975 ●
Manifest Destiny (Asylum) 1977
Bloodbrothers (Asylum) 1978
Fuck 'Em If They Can't Take a Joke [tape] (ROIR) 1981
   (Fr. Danceteria) 1991 ●

Considering that the first Dictators album came out in 1975, scads of credit is due these hearty pre-punk New Yorkers for blazing a trail, melding junk culture—wrestling, fast food, TV, beer, cars, scandal sheets—with loud/hard/fast rock'n'roll and thus creating an archetype that has been adopted and adapted by countless other bands. Although originally formed as a response to the MC5, Flamin Groovies and the Stooges, the Dictators wound up playing a similarly crucial and inspirational role to the generations that followed *them*.

Although wavering wildly in terms of style and track-to-track consistency, all four of the band's albums (including the posthumous live tape) are great. As protégés of genius music journalist Richard Meltzer, the Dictators helped translate a lot of intellectual fandom's

189

crazed hypothetical theorizing about rock'n'roll's possibilities into wretchedly wonderful reality.

The Dictators began as a quartet: *Teenage Wasteland Gazette* publisher Adny Shernoff (vocals/bass), monster guitarist Ross the Boss, Scott "Top Ten" Kempner (rhythm guitar) and Stu Boy King (drums). Crazy-roadie-turned-crazy-singer Handsome Dick Manitoba was photographed in wrestling regalia for the cover of their first LP, guested on some of the tracks and was listed in the credits as "secret weapon." Produced by the Sandy Pearlman/Murray Krugman team responsible for the Blue Öyster Cult, **The Dictators Go Girl Crazy!** is a wickedly funny, brilliantly played and hopelessly naïve masterpiece of self-indulgent smartass rock'n'roll, proof that regular kids could make the major-label record (as if there were an alternative at the time) always imagined. The album has covers ("I Got You Babe," "California Sun") that unravel history, Shernoff slices of "Teengenerate" life, the Manitoba signature song ("Two Tub Man") and even an original surf-rock gem, "(I Live for) Cars and Girls." An absolute classic doomed to utter commercial oblivion.

Immediately after the album's release, King took a hike and various troubles beset the band, resulting in a two-year delay before a follow-up was issued. By then, Manitoba had become the fulltime vocalist, drummer/singer Ritchie Teeter had come on board and bassist Mark "The Animal" Mendoza had joined, allowing Shernoff to switch from bass to keyboards. Although the sonic quality was mortally damaged in the original mastering (and a CD reissue has yet to appear), **Manifest Destiny** comes across with another helping of brilliant Shernoff songs like "Steppin' Out," "Science Gone Too Far!" and "Sleepin' with the TV On," plus a stunning rip through the Stooges' "Search and Destroy." The musical approach is less tongue-in-cheek and sounds nearly adult, but any band fronted by Manitoba could hardly fall prey to rock-star pretension.

Falling in with novelist Richard Price, the Dics made some concessions on **Bloodbrothers** in a last-ditch attempt to turn the band into a commercially viable proposition. Mendoza had already left for greener metal pastures (specifically Twisted Sister); the five-man lineup sent Shernoff back to bass. Despite the band's halfhearted attempt to sell out, the record has its share of great tracks—a heartfelt love song ("Stay with Me"), a tribute to Meltzer ("Borneo Jimmy"), a seamy tale of teenage prostitution ("Minnesota Strip") and an electric statement of purpose ("Faster and Louder," an expansion on the previous album's "Young, Fast, Scientific"). A blinding cover of the Flamin' Groovies' "Slow Death" closes the album, putting a lid on the Dictators studio days and, shortly thereafter, the band as well.

A few reunion gigs played around the New York area in late 1980 and early '81 resulted in the album-length live cassette, which finds the group in fine form, with Manitoba doing a riotous star turn as singer, ringleader and MC. The Dictators played a tenth anniversary reunion concert in New York in January 1986 and another show the following year. By that point, Top Ten had formed the Del-Lords; Manitoba and Shernoff have continued working together in Manitoba's Wild Kingdom.   [i]

See also *Del-Lords, Manitoba's Wild Kingdom.*

DIDJITS

Fizzjob (Bam Bam-Touch and Go) 1986
Hey Judester (Touch and Go) 1988 ●
Hornet Piñata (Touch and Go) 1990 ●
Full Nelson Reilly (Touch and Go) 1991 ●

Give a sarcastic kid a guitar and a mic, and watch out. This Champaign, Illinois, trio blurts intelligent dumbness over thrashy midtempo rock with an above-average chordal backbone. Showing more enthusiasm than concern for musical precision, singer/guitarist Rick Sims praises "Wingtips" while poking fun at Jerry Lee Lewis and "California Surf Queen" on Fizzjob, co-produced by Iain Burgess. The album's one-take roughness suits the off-the-cuff lyrics; while Sims' rhythm guitar playing has room to develop, he does show plenty of hyperactive promise.

The Didjits ramped up the velocity, focus and ferocity for **Hey Judester**. Amid a sharply defined rock powerdrive (drummer/brother Brad Sims gets the most-improved star), Rick sings (the surly "Dad"), shouts ("Max Wedge") and shrieks (a frantic freakout cover of Little Richard's "Lucille," to which he adds key-busting piano) increasingly demento lyrics. A powerful dose of Midwest madness (the fishing songs are priceless) that packs a serious punch. The CD contains **Fizzjob** as a bonus.

Hornet Piñata is a slamming melody-rock LP that—except for the vocals—belies the Didjits' jokey beginnings. Sims' decisive guitar work shoots spears with stunning velocity and intensity as the pounding rhythm section deftly keeps pace. While most of the blitzed-out songs concern automotive topics (from "Evel Knievel" to "Gold Eldorado"), the 'Jits stop to cover the MC5 ("Call Me Animal") with considerable skill and Jimi Hendrix ("Foxey Lady") with, er, enthusiasm (and car sounds).   [i]

DIED PRETTY

Died Pretty EP (nr/What Goes On) 1984
Next to Nothing EP (What Goes On) 1985
Free Dirt (What Goes On) 1986
Pre-Deity (Aus. Citadel) 1988
Lost (Beggars Banquet-RCA) 1989 ●
Every Brilliant Eye (Beggars Banquet-RCA) 1990 ●

There aren't many bands whose names convey their sound as accurately as Australia's Died Pretty. The coupling of dark and hard-hewn guitar chords with light and lilting jangles make the Sydney quintet's records both delicately pretty and devastatingly loud (not at the same time). That contrast and the interplay between scream and shiver is what gives Died Pretty its appeal. One moment Ronald S. Peno is screeching like he's tried on Robert Plant's too-tight pants, the next he's got the voice of Jim Morrison calling from the grave. The band likewise essays both the cat-mating squeals of post-Hendrix guitar with sinister horns and crashing cymbals *and* a delicate church organ picking out a melody as their voices meld into a vanilla smooth background chorus.

The **Died Pretty** 12-inch is a compilation of their first two 45s, "Out of the Unknown" and "Mirror Blues." The four-song **Next to Nothing**, Died Pretty's debut US release, does not contain the song of that name—it's on **Free Dirt**. The highly recommended album—which contains glimmers of the '60s, Dylan,

Gram Parsons, folk-rock and neo-psychedelic—uses guest contributions of mandolin, violin, pedal steel and sax to magnify the band's own essential variety.

Lost opens with two glorious pop tunes that give way to the usual slate of heart-wrenching acoustic numbers ("As Must Have") and pummeling rockers ("Winterland," complete with introductory gob). Sparkling production by ex-Radio Birdman Rob Younger helps put across the alternately delicate and roaring songs. This is the work of a band that, in a perfect world, would rule the album-rock airwaves.

Died Pretty went LA (sort of) on **Every Brilliant Eye**, replacing its longtime bassist and keyboardist and hooking up with producer Jeff Eyrich (Legal Weapon, Rank and File). But as the nine tracks attest, a change of scenery didn't dilute the band's power. In particular, "The Underbelly" (all sprawling six-plus minutes of it) seems a perfect summarization of this fine record's sound: imagine Ian Curtis fronting Crazy Horse. That the cuts on the two most recent albums are practically interchangeable is the mark of either an astonishingly consistent band or one caught in a creative rut. One would like to imagine the former. ['e/db]

DIE HAUT
See *(Die) Haut*.

DIE KREUZEN
Cows and Beer EP (Version Sound) 1982
Die Kreuzen (Touch and Go) 1984 •
October File (Touch and Go) 1986 •
Century Days (Touch and Go) 1988 •
Gone Away (Touch and Go) 1989

Milwaukee's Die Kreuzen is simultaneously one of the most thrilling and conservative exponents of American hardcore. While many quality thrash bands have escaped the genre's brutally circumscribed conventions by delving into metal, psychedelia, funk or bohemianism, this quartet plays punk strictly by the book. **Cows and Beer**, a six-song 7-inch debut (all of which is reprised on **Die Kreuzen**), contains such numbers as "Hate Me," "Pain" and "In School." Although well-played, the music of these brief songs is as familiar as the titles.

On the first LP, armed with an antagonistic attitude and a predilection for velocity, the band burns through 21 explosive songs (riffs, really) that are interchangeable but not redundant. The primary ingredient, hyperkinetic energy, remains constant throughout **Die Kreuzen**, but the riffs are all different and uncommonly well-articulated. As loud and fast as these guys are, their playing remains crisp. (Dan Kubinski's vocals, however, are utterly unintelligible. What works for Couch Flambeau doesn't fit so well here.)

October File pushes the envelope a bit, diverting the thrash energy into slower, more conceptual outpourings. (It's still loud, raunchy rock, but few of the fourteen songs could be characterized as hardcore.) While Kubinski's impassioned shrieking binds the quartet to a limited realm, the other members—especially guitarist Brian Egeness and bassist Keith Brammer—seem to have other musical directions in mind. (Indeed, the latter joined the more intentionally abrasive Wreck in

1989.) **October File** and **Die Kreuzen** were released on a single CD.

With Kubinski's desperate off-key screech still a frequent hazard, Die Kreuzen takes several intriguing detours on **Century Days**, an album of impressive dynamic range and sonic control. As the band's playing has grown into an atmospheric and powerful noise, the ability to do other things—like drop back for the nearly acoustic plaint of "These Days" and the handsome pop textures of "Slow" (on which Kubinski's singing is perfectly fine), or deliver a serious melodic kick, as in "Elizabeth"—has emerged. Several tracks even part the curtain to reveal horns and piano.

The **Gone Away** 12-inch has two strong new songs (on a 45 rpm side) of measured rock and (on the 33 rpm reverse) five live'n'loud tracks—including three **Century Days** numbers—also recorded in January 1989.

See also *Wreck*. [jl/i]

DIE WARZAU
Disco Rigido (Fiction-PolyGram) 1989 •

The Chicago duo of Van Christie and Jay Marcus possesses a wide range of stylistic interests (the former has a guitar-rock background; both have experience in house and techno music and a fondness for samples, industrial percussion and a pounding dance beat), all of which come together on the promising **Disco Rigido**. Though the opening song "Welcome to America" immediately announces "This is a racist nation," the group's political agenda never gets in the way of the fun. Melody is minimal; vocal tracks like "Jackhammer" and "Strike to the Body" tend to involve the shouted repetition of simple phrases (à la Nitzer Ebb). Die Warzau's forte is pure rhythm and samples, and the album offers up many inspired examples, including "Free Radio Africa" and "Y Tagata en Situ." (The CD and cassette contain six bonus tracks.) [tf]

DIFFORD & TILBROOK
See *Squeeze*.

DIF JUZ
Huremics EP (nr/4AD) 1981 •
Vibrating Air EP (nr/4AD) 1981 •
Who Says So EP (nr/Red Flame) 1983
Extractions (nr/4AD) 1985 •
Out of the Trees (nr/4AD) 1986

The cover of **Huremics** offers no information whatsoever about this British quartet; the disc consists of four obliquely titled mood-setting improvisational guitar/drums/bass instrumentals. **Vibrating Air** continues the enigmatic graphic pose and style, featuring four new diminutive atmospherics. While not exactly captivating fare, these slight records are actually quite nice and seem custom-made for scratch mixes, or for use as backing tracks of unwritten songs. **Who Says So** contains a third quartet of pieces.

The Cocteau Twins help out on the full-length **Extractions** LP: Robin Guthrie produced, and Liz Fraser became the first vocalist on a Dif Juz record. With the addition of prominent keyboards and sax, it's not as ambient as prior work, shooting instead for a big, echoey sound, not unlike Simple Minds. As an instrumental band, Dif Juz must be vigilant not to fall into the nice-sound-few-ideas trap. They get by on **Extractions**, but just barely.

Out of the Trees combines **Huremics** in its original form with a partially re-recorded (and entirely remixed) version of **Vibrating Air**.   [i/dgs]

DIGITAL SEX
Essence (Post-Ambient Motion) 1985
Essence & Charm [CD] (Fr. Sordide Sentimental) 1986 ●

STEPHEN SHEEHAN
Eyes of the Wilderness (Fr. New Rose) 1990 (Emigre) 1990 ●

Working at a safe distance from the music world's stylistic hotspots, this Omaha, Nebraska, trio recasts the delicate art-rock of recent English progressives (the Durutti Column and Eyeless in Gaza come to mind) and the gentler side of Ultravox-y techno-pop with unpretentious Midwest sincerity and small-scale forthrightness. **Essence** offers nine diverse songs tastefully crafted in shifting instrumental permutations of Dereck Higgins (bass, keyboards, drums, guitar), John Tingle (guitar) and Steve Sheehan (vocals, keyboards). Although colorless at times, the excellently played material is soothing and substantial, and occasionally quite pretty.

The nineteen-track **Essence & Charm** CD includes the LP, both sides of a mediocre 1983 single, one slightly Devoesque Sheehan solo effort and another album's worth of previously unreleased material that lacks the earlier work's appealing tastefulness. While some of the songs merely overheat the guitar-rock (drummer Kevin Kennedy is no smoothie), things really nosedive on the Cure-accented "Without Hesitation," which inexplicably contains the sound of someone belching.   [i]

DIGITAL UNDERGROUND
Sex Packets (Tommy Boy) 1990 ●
This Is an E.P. Release EP (Tommy Boy) 1990 φ

While Digital Underground's debut album—much of it a sustained conceptual fantasy about safe sex-substitute drugs—isn't as consistently entertaining as the wonderful singles ("Doowutchyalike" and "The Humpty Dance") it contains, this lighthearted Bay Area crew led by the charismatic Shock-G does offer more brain-tickling wit than any other rap band around. Over insinuating party tracks assembled from melodic rock and soul samples (as well as original piano-borne music), the group creates its own land and lingo with true left-field originality. While the Underground has the ingenuity and charm to make even plain creations worth hearing, numbers that feature Shock-G's alter-ego Humpty Hump (a joke-voiced Groucho Marx-mask character with a winning line in self-promotion) delivering his grin-inducing stream of intricate wordplay are simply amazing.

This Is an E.P. Release remixes "The Way We Swing" and "Packet Man" from the LP, adding two excellent new tracks (the safe-sex/universal harmony "Same Song" and the fear-of-matrimony "Tie the Knot") from the soundtrack of *Nothing but Trouble* (the EP cites the disastrous 1991 film in which the Under-

ground appears by its working title, *Valkenvania*), an amusing boast ("Nuttin' Nis Funky") and a silly historical debate between Shock-G and Humpty Hump entitled "Arguin' on the Funk."   [i]

DILS
Live! (Iloki-Triple X) 1987
The Dils (Lost) 1990

That the Dils' first LP or EP (and first 12-inch) would come out seven years after the group called it quits should serve as a reminder how comparatively small and ineffectual the independent record scene was in the late '70s. Although the now-legendary Dils were one of the best and largest-drawing West Coast punk groups of the original '77-'80 punk explosion, they released only three 7-inch singles during four years of existence.

The trio played 90-second primal-scream maximum punk ditties with fiery politics (a real rarity in '77 Los Angeles); Army brat brothers Chip and Tony Kinman topped them off with Everlyesque harmonies. Culled from two cassette recordings, the sound on the posthumous **Live!** is hotter than most bootlegs, and the album offers a parade of neo-classics: "I Hate the Rich," "Class War" and an incredibly improved (slowed down) "You're Not Blank." (Fans will also recognize "The Sound of the Rain," a Dils single the Kinmans re-recorded for the second Rank and File LP.) As John Silvers, the longest-running of four drummers who served with the pair, makes his vinyl debut here, even the material that's familiar from the singles (about half) sounds tighter and more powerful. Rarely has a historical document seemed so timely or so current.

Side One of the second posthumous Dils LP compiles the seven tracks from the band's three original singles plus "Blow Up" (previously included on the first **Rat Music for Rat People** compilation). Where **Live!** unearthed seven never-before-heard songs, the live Side Two of **The Dils** adds an additional eight new numbers from a different show (again with Silvers). Although the sound quality isn't as good, the murk can't hide Chip Kinman's lashing guitar on the brutal "Citizen," or the overall vintage punk aggression on "National Guard" and the catchy "You Don't Matter Anymore." Long before Billy Bragg, the Dils mixed crackling socialist politics and personal lyrics, but it's the trio's tight fire that rides it home. **The Dils** is thus a more complete retrospective, encompassing primitive '77 slam-punk, the band's later, more accomplished attack and the final "Les Dils" single, a stylistic prelude to the Kinmans' subsequent bands, Rank and File and Blackbird.   [jr]

See also *Blackbird, Rank and File.*

DIMENTIA 13
Dimentia 13 (Midnight) 1985
Mirror Mind (Midnight) 1987
Disturb the Air (Midnight) 1989
T.V. Screen Head (Midnight) 1990

The Ohioan behind these simple demi-psychedelic garage romps is Bradley S. Warner, a resourceful Syd Barrett fan who frequently displays ingenuity yet never quite ascends to the magical heights (depths?) of retro-pop resonance. With minor assists from keyboardist/ singer/bassist Louanne Varholick (and, on the third LP, a drummer), the singer/guitarist indulges his nostalgic passions and intellectual interests on songs that have grown from obvious selfconsciousness (e.g., "Can You Hear the Walls Melting?" and "Psychedelic Mushroom Cloud Explosion," both from the underwhelming **Mirror Mind**) to broader, more idiosyncratic concerns.

Produced by Glenn Rehse of Plasticland and featuring a guest appearance by John Fallon of the Steppes, **Disturb the Air** is Dimentia's most impressive effort yet, a record that drops the derivative pretensions for what seems to be a heartfelt expression of Warner's sensitive personality and choppy guitar work.

Revealing an intriguing singer/songwriter side, **T.V. Screen Head** compiles a dozen previously unreleased four-track solo demos into something less like a Dimentia 13 LP than a musical letter from a friend. Accompanying himself simply on acoustic and electric guitar and acoustic and electronic drums, Warner (whose annotation is crucial to enjoyment of the record) muses about old age ("Cannot Compare to This"), quotes at random from a zany magazine article ("The Little Things That Kill You"), takes inspiration from Karl Marx ("All That Is Solid Melts into Air") and makes an oblique art stab at hip-hop ("Ah! Lightning Bolt!").

[i]

DINOSAUR
Dinosaur (Homestead) 1985
DINOSAUR JR.
You're Living All Over Me (SST) 1987 ●
Bug (SST) 1988 ●
Just Like Heaven EP (SST) 1989 ●
The Wagon EP (nr/Blanco y Negro) 1991 ●
Green Mind (Blanco y Negro-Sire-Warner Bros.) 1991 φ

Modern masters of high-decibel manipulation, this Amherst, Massachusetts, power trio once had difficulty playing more than a single gig in any one club because of their ear-damaging attack. Prior to forming Dinosaur, J Mascis and bassist Lou Barlow played together in Deep Wound (featured on the 1984 Conflict compilation **Bands That Could Be God**); Mascis switched from drums to guitar and recruited Murph, formerly of All White Jury.

Dinosaur finds the group sounding like ten different bands on as many songs. Mascis, also the primary singer and songwriter, employs an array of electronic devices to squeeze a myriad of variations from harmonic structures, utilizing a variety of tones from loud to louder to loudest. Meat Puppets, Neil Young and Sonic Youth comparisons are inevitable, but Dinosaur's raucous individuality is beyond dispute. After legal threats from the West Coast summer-of-love vets calling themselves the Dinosaurs, Dinosaur politely became Dinosaur Jr.

The band further reduced their already minimal pop factor on the deafening **You're Living All Over Me**, a brilliant, brutal hailstorm of hyper-distorted riffs and pulverizing basslines that is harder, louder and meaner than nine out of ten heavy metal albums. The multi-sectioned songs change direction so frequently that it's hard to tell them apart, as the power-trio assault is modulated by graceful, looming melodies that rise like mist out of the pedal-mess. The monolithic album is marred

only by Barlow's self-indulgent "Poledo." (The CD tacks on the band's tongue-in-cheek B-side rendition of Peter Frampton's "Show Me the Way," a bizarre incongruity, to say the least.)

Bug was preceded by "Freak Scene," J's greatest pop song to date and one of the most enduring indie singles of the decade—the band's bruising delivery of such an accessible melody is half of its enormous appeal. Largely a continuation and expansion upon **Living**, **Bug** wanders into folkier pastures with the lilting "Pond Song" and experiments with primal scream on the electric axe-murder of "Don't," a lease-breaker if ever there was one. The album was followed by yet another ironic single, this time a cover of the Cure's "Just Like Heaven" (which fits Dinosaur's style perfectly) and two rough B-sides.

Barlow left to concentrate on his band Sebadoh, and Dinosaur increasingly became the J Mascis Experience. An attempt at an indie-rock supergroup pairing J and Murph with Don Fleming and Jay Spiegel fell apart almost as soon as it was announced (although the ex-B.A.L.L.istics did play on "The Wagon"), and Mascis distracted himself for months with the Velvet Monkeys and Gobblehoof (on whose debut EP he played drums). Emerging nearly three years after its predecessor, **Green Mind** resolves the personnel problems: Mascis did almost everything (including drums on all but three tracks) himself. The old snarl and brawn are there, but distilled from an older/wiser viewpoint. "The Wagon" is the excellent and inevitable follow-up to "Freak Scene," but the stirring "Thumb" parts previously uncharted waters in the realm of hypnoriff (live dates in early '91 deputised Screaming Trees bassist Van Conner to stunning effect), "Muck" is "our disco song" and "Flying Cloud" sounds like an outtake from **Led Zeppelin III**. A mature effort from a rare talent who hasn't lost his primal urgency.   [rg/ja]

See also *Gobblehoof, Sonic Youth, Velvet Monkeys.*

DIRTY ROSEANNE
See *Sex Gang Children.*

DISCO 2000
See *Justified Ancients of Mu Mu.*

DISTRACTIONS
You're Not Going Out Dressed Like That EP (nr/TJM) 1979
Nobody's Perfect (nr/Island) 1980

Decades from now, rock historians will scratch their heads in bewilderment that the Distractions' fine body of work didn't ensure the Manchester quintet a longer lifespan. The 1979 EP (which contains rougher versions of two songs that would later turn up on **Nobody's Perfect**, plus a live pair—"Too Young" and "Maybe It's Love"—unavailable elsewhere) hints that the group was working from an abnormally broad palette, a sense confirmed by its one fine album.

A lot of records belong to a specific time, but **Nobody's Perfect** continues to measure up as an ace slab of educated pop rock, right in tune with the ground rules laid down by Blondie, Squeeze and others of that ilk. Part of the problem may be that **Nobody's Perfect** is too weighty to be passed off as a simple diversion. The band's eclecticism draws on everything from Chuck Berry to Phil Spector to psychedelia—often within the same song—and the vocals tend to be more somber than carefree. "Boys Cry" comes on like a Ronettes tune but delivers none of the upbeat emotional release seasoned pop listeners are trained to expect. Regardless, **Nobody's Perfect** very nearly is.   [dss/jy]

DIVINE HORSEMEN
Time Stands Still (Enigma) 1984
Devil's River (SST) 1986
Middle of the Night (SST) 1986
Snake Handler (SST) 1987 ●
Handful of Sand EP (SST) 1988

STONE BY STONE W/ CHRIS D
I Pass for Human (SST) 1989 ●

Following his work with the Flesh Eaters, California's Chris D(esjardins) formed the Divine Horsemen, who debuted on the mostly acoustic **Time Stands Still**. Without an electric band churning away steadily behind him, he's more appallingly effective than ever. The attractive, understated music belies such sentiments as "Past All Dishonor" and "Hell's Belle"; the all-star supporting cast includes Blasters, Gun Clubbers, an X and Texacala Jones of the Horseheads.

A no-star electric lineup made the similarly low-key and driven **Devil's River**, a record which, like its predecessor, leaves the major responsibility for conveying fear and loathing to the lyrics, here geared to Western/cowboy topics. Chris shares the vocals with Julie C(hristensen), who adds an X-like harmony to the proceedings. A dusty road, but a fascinating one.

Predominately recorded in and around the same sessions as **Devil's River**, the oddly compiled and countryfied **Middle of the Night** features the same crew, with John Doe and D.J. Bonebrake of X guesting on two of the eight cuts. Chris and Julie perform most of the vocals as a relatively mellifluous duo, making this the Horsemen's most attractive album. The title tune is a sweet lullaby; there are also alternate recordings of two previously issued Chris D. efforts, an acoustic version of David Allen Coe's country classic "Field of Stone" and two other covers: a slow but accurate "Gimmie Shelter" and the Cramps' "Voodoo Idol."

Guitarist Peter Andrus replaced two departing members on **Snake Handler**, bringing the Horsemen into the light with a trimmed-down, tightened-up rock sound. Comparisons to X at this point are more than fair, although these joint vocals are far more divine than that band's. The lyrics don't bear a lot of scrutiny—they may be poetic, but aren't about much of anything. (The harrowing escape-from-heroin saga, "Fire Kiss," is a significant exception.) Chris' grip on the gritty fear-film idiom is intact, but lines like "Fire is my home/and if you let me die alone/the fire will eat my bones" or "I been waiting for someone like you since I was just thirteen years old" don't pack any punch.

The Divine Horsemen and Chris D.'s longterm relationship with Christensen dissolved at about the same time, which (as borne out by **I Pass for Human**'s more chilling moments) certainly gave the guy plenty to write about. Not surprisingly, there's little in the way of standard jilted-lover self-pity in Mr. D.'s psyche. Borrow-

ing "Time Stands Still" from an earlier work, he effectively closes the book on that era by retooling it with bitter clinical precision. Indeed, the overall tone of the one-shot Stone by Stone is darn close to the violently lurching blood-Catholic beat-poesy of primo Flesh Eaters (especially the ghost-town atmosphere of the epic "Pale Fire"). No surprise then, that a resurrected version of that very combo came together months after this disc's release.   [jy/i/dss]

See also *Flesh Eaters*.

DIVINE STYLER FEATURING THE SCHEME TEAM
Word Power (Rhyme Syndicate-Epic) 1989 φ

Rapping like a hyped Islamic math teacher prone to free association, Divine Styler drops a brief lecture on the speed of light into "Koxistin U4ria" on his ambitious but dull debut, released via Ice-T's label. The verbose expositions on Afrocentricity, faith in Allah and racism (white and black) are loaded with intriguing, frequently obscure content, but Styler can't make them musical, and the sketchy tracks (co-produced by Bilal Bashir) don't help.   [i]

DIVINYLS
Monkey Grip EP (Aus. WEA) 1982
Desperate (Chrysalis) 1983 ●
What a Life! (Chrysalis) 1985 ●
Temperamental (Chrysalis) 1988 ●
Divinyls (Virgin) 1991 φ

Sydney, Australia's Divinyls couple Christina Amphlett's unusual vocal mannerisms with the band's rowdy pop sound—kind of like AC/DC meets the Pretenders, with a soupçon of Lene Lovich and a few subtle, unexpected chord-progression shifts. The thick guitar and keyboard textures pack a marvelous rock-'n'roll punch; the downside is the band's occasional flirtation with arena clichés.

Amphlett appeared in the movie *Monkey Grip*, for which the group recorded the six songs contained on the EP; some were redone for **Desperate**. The LP's standouts include "Only You" (all the above comparisons applicable in one song, and it works!) and the goofily lovable "Science Fiction." Even the weakest songs get by on sheer gusto. The Easybeats' "I'll Make You Happy" is given a hard-rock update, as Amphlett blithely assumes the song's assertive role which had, after all, been written for a man.

Intentionally or not, all three producers (Mark Opitz, Mike Chapman, Gary Langan) of **What a Life!** appear to have been determined to sell the group to US radio by polishing away their idiosyncrasies (dousing the spark in the songs too, if there was any). The result comes awfully close to Anybandism. The worst offender is "Pleasure & Pain," the only track produced and co-written by Mike Chapman, which veers towards the territory of his onetime charge, Pat Benatar.

That's why it's all the more surprising that Chapman not only produced **Temperamental**, he also allowed the quirky, rough-edged charm shown on **Desperate** to come through. There are some nifty little touches, like clever usage of backing choruses as aural coloring. Divinyls is now reduced to the songwriting team of Amphlett and lead guitarist Mark McEntee, but the hired hands on bass and drums provide a superbly compatible loose-limbed wallop. The title track is the killer; the others are also generally strong right off the bat. The Syndicate of Sound's "Hey Little Girl" gets an impressive reading: the original is definitive, but Amphlett's rare ability to make the tune hers (as "Hey Little Boy") is an entertaining angle.

What a disappointment, then, that the duo's self-titled fourth LP falls so flat. The co-production by erstwhile Chapman protégé Dave Tickle (who also worked with Split Enz) is okay but, on the whole, the music is pedestrian and the performances lackluster. Even the vocals: you really have to pay attention to what Amphlett's singing to notice anything offbeat going on, e.g., the not-so-coy naughtiness of "I Touch Myself"—which was co-written by Hollywood hitmeisters Billy Steinberg and Tom Kelly ("Like a Virgin," etc.). The most interesting tracks are "If Love Was a Gun" and (coincidence?) "Bullet"—but they're just near misses.

[jg]

DON DIXON
Most of the Girls Like to Dance but Only Some of the
    Boys Like To (Enigma) 1985 ●
Praying Mantis EP (nr/Demon) 1986
Romeo at Juilliard (Enigma) 1987 ●
Chi-Town Budget Show (Restless) 1989 φ
EEE (Enigma) 1989 φ

Before his name started showing up as a producer on albums by R.E.M., the Smithereens, Let's Active and many others, Don Dixon spent fourteen years as bassist/singer/songwriter in a hot North Carolina band called Arrogance. On the solo debut from this jack-of-all-musical-trades, Dixon offers an uneven but engaging five-year patchwork of singles and demos from his personal archives—some from the Arrogance days, others done at home on his 4-track and one recorded at Mitch's Drive-In Studio—that display his affection for '60s pop and R&B. Sometimes cynical, sometimes whimsical, his views of love and lust are delivered with a soulman's vocal passion. The wonderfully oddball images of kissing insects and claw action in "Praying Mantis" make it an instant gem; Mitch Easter contributes lead guitar to a cover of Nick Lowe's "Skin Deep." (The original British edition has a few different tracks, song annotation and alternate artwork than the subsequent American release.) The four-song EP packages the title song with another album track and two more from the Arrogance library, including a sweat-drenched live version of Percy Sledge's "When a Man Loves a Woman," which also appears on the US album.

The all-new Romeo at Juilliard fulfills the first album's promise in spades. Aided by a few guests (mainly drummers, but also Easter, Dixon's wife and frequent musical partner Marti Jones and Spongetones guitarist Jamie Hoover), Dixon rocks confidently in a country/pure pop/Atlantic soul/R&B style that equally suggests the gritty side of John Hiatt and the gloss of Nick Lowe. Expressing deep bitterness at a former loved one, his songs are well-written and brilliantly executed; each arrangement varies the approach without straying far from the LP's overall sound. Dixon's voice is wonderfully rich and emotional; that he's distinguished himself as a producer and not a singer/songwriter (yet) hardly seems believable from the evidence here. "Borrowed Time," "Your Sister Told Me" and "Swallowing Pride" are pained outpourings that channel the man's soul right through your speakers.

Chi-Town Budget Show is a fine, unadorned document of a March '88 live radio broadcast, with Dixon backed by Marti Jones and North Carolina's Woods. It's smart, ingratiating fun; the two Dixon/Jones acoustic tracks which open the disc provide a keepsake of the duo's endearing live presence.

EEE adds the Uptown Horns to the mix with predictably appealing results. Dixon's originals—"Oh Cheap Chatter," "Roots of Truth," "Silent Screen"—mine quirky rock-soul territory more persuasively than ever, and he also wraps his pipes around some well-chosen covers, including an adorable duet (with Jones) on Brenton Wood's 1967 hit, "Gimme Little Sign." There's even a bit of avant-garde audio collage ("EEE/T.O.T.T.V.") that actually works. [kh/i/hd]

See also *Marti Jones, Sneakers*.

DMZ
DMZ EP (Bomp!) 1977
DMZ (Sire) 1978
Relics (Voxx) 1981
DMZ!! Live at Barnabys!! 1978!! (Crypt) 1986
Live! 1978! EP (Pryct) 1986

One of Boston's primary punk bands, DMZ was led by the maniacal Mono Mann (aka Jeff Conolly, later of the Lyres), an organist/singer whose '60s roots (garage punk and psychedelia) and Iggy Pop fixation formed the basis for the group's influential stylings. Their first album, produced by Flo and Eddie, has bad sound, sloppy playing and little character, despite the raveup playing and general enthusiasm.

On the other hand, Relics—released four years after being recorded on a 4-track by Craig Leon—has the intensity and cutting sonic attack to effectively re-create the weird sounds of Mann's idols. Anyone that can do justice to a Roky Erickson number (as in the 13th Floor Elevators' "You're Gonna Miss Me") is alright by me. Four of Relics' cuts first appeared on the cool 1977 7-inch; the other five had not previously been released.

The two 1986 releases—recorded at a single June 1978 club date—document the DMZ concert experience. One is a full-length LP; the other is a supplementary (no overlap) four-track 7-inch that covers both the Chocolate Watch Band and the Beatles. [i]

See also *Lyres, Barrence Whitfield and the Savages*.

DNA
A Taste of DNA EP (American Clavé) 1981
VARIOUS ARTISTS
No New York (Antilles) 1978
The Fruit of the Original Sin (Bel. Crépuscule) 1981
DARK DAY
Exterminating Angel (Lust/Unlust) 1980
Dark Day EP (Lust/Unlust) 1981
Window (Plexus) 1983
Beyond the Pale [tape] (Nigh Eve) 1985

This controversial noise trio was a fixture on the New York scene for several years, initially tagged as part of the avant-garde no wave wing of the city's punk movement. Despite a minuscule recorded output, DNA was a major presence of startling originality.

DNA's genius and power were immediately evident when the group entered four cuts on the **No New York** compilation album. Arto Lindsay—once described as James Brown trapped in Don Knotts' body—pits scratch-slash-kill guitar against Robin Crutchfield's sinister Suicidal electric piano and contributes two vocals showing his unique (if unintelligible) singing style in embryonic form. On "Not Moving," Lindsay's playing approximates Syd Barrett with an amphetamine edge.

The band matured on **A Taste of DNA**. Six pithy, polished statements show Kabuki-painted drummer Ikue Mori coming into her own as a tight, tireless master of shifting asymmetrical rhythm; Lindsay drawls, yells, yelps, gulps, burbles and gurgles his way to left-field legend. Replacing Crutchfield's monolithic riffing is the sensitive, painterly bass of Tim Wright. This is no formless anarchic blare—each piece is a painstakingly crafted kernel of ideas organized with fearless unorthodoxy.

The three live performances ("Taking Kid to School," "Cop Buys a Donut," "Delivering the Goods") on **The Fruit of the Original Sin** compilation are a poor epitaph. They suffer from crummy sound quality—one shifts from stereo to mono right in mid-song!—and bizarre editing, though Wright's bass solo on "Delivering the Goods" is typically exquisite.

For the last encore of its final performance, DNA did Led Zeppelin's "Whole Lotta Love," fittingly capping an iconoclastic career with the utterly unexpected.

Keyboardist Robin Crutchfield formed Dark Day as a trio after his departure from DNA; **Exterminating Angel** uses machine-like riffs as the foundation for moody, Teutonic music. By the release of **Dark Day**, he had jettisoned his backing band, shifting the music into the twilight of ambient Eno or Dome. Never a complete original, Crutchfield manages to get extra mileage out of the styles he borrows.   [mf/rnp]

See also *Golden Palominos, Arto Lindsay/Ambitious Lovers, Lounge Lizards, UT.*

D-NICE

See *Boogie Down Productions.*

D.O.A.

Triumph of the Ignoroids EP (Can. Friend's) 1979
Something Better Change (Can. Friend's) 1980
Hardcore 81 (Can. Friend's) 1981
War on 45 EP (Alternative Tentacles) 1982
Bloodied but Unbowed (CD Presents) 1984
Don't Turn Yer Back (on Desperate Times) EP (Alternative Tentacles) 1985
Let's Wreck the Party (Alternative Tentacles) 1985
True (North) Strong & Free (Rock Hotel-Profile) 1987 ●
Murder. (Restless) 1990 ●

RANDY RAMPAGE

Randy Rampage EP (Can. Friend's) 1982

Vancouver's premier punk outfit has never abandoned its righteous yet hedonistic spirit, as embodied by founding guitarist/vocalist/songwriter Joey Shithead (Keighley). (Indeed, D.O.A. is one of the few original punk bands that has never wandered off into metaldom.) After early personnel shifts, the lineup stabilized and the other members eventually began complementing Keighley's singing and songwriting with their own.

Triumph of the Ignoroids is raw and live, like stripped-down Dead Boys; **Something Better Change** is tighter, with more anthemic material fleshed out by two guitarists; **Hardcore 81** is faster and looser.

War on 45 sounds like a keyboardless Stranglers and includes a humorous (and highly charged) reworking of Edwin Starr's "War" ("good god y'all!!") that makes Springsteen's attempt sound pathetic. Although D.O.A. isn't above confusing vulgarity with rebellion (e.g., the "Let's Fuck" rewrite of Chris Montez's 1962 hit), this is mainly above-average punk. (The UK version of **War on 45** substitutes two tracks from **Something Better Change**.)

Subtitled "The Damage to Date: 1978–1983," **Bloodied but Unbowed** is a nineteen-track career recap (remixed and remastered) which convincingly confirms D.O.A.'s hard-won status as Canada's top punks, a raging behemoth of tightly organized high-compression rock aggression. Incredible, intense and essential.

Don't Turn Yer Back is a ten-minute, four-song 12-inch cut in 1984 for a John Peel radio session but released by the band well before the launch of that series. Dedicated to striking miners, it's more angry and political than ever. **Let's Wreck the Party** includes two of those tracks, but is overall more lighthearted. The clear, professional sound and occasional slowed tempos may turn off hardcore fanatics, but it's a cutting and witty record nonetheless.

True (North) boasts similar sonic variations and maturity—these guys are almost growing up! Topics include Canada's inferiority complex ("51st State"), an equation of Ramboid jingoism with nascent fascism ("Nazi Training Camp"), their gonzo work/play ethic (note the version of Bachman-Turner Overdrive's "Takin' Care of Business" with the lead riff played on guitar plus trumpet!) and a longstanding commitment to political activism and freedom. (The band's mechanical royalties from the song "Ready to Explode" go to South Africa's then-outlawed African National Congress.) Weird angle: "Bullet Catcher," the grim tale of a woman cop who died in a hail of bullets; D.O.A.'s song is critical but sympathetic.

The three biggest changes on **Murder.** are a new (mis-?) spelling for Joe K.'s surname (Keithley), the arrival of new guitarist Chris Prohom in place of stalwart Dave Gregg and the acknowledgment of Nelson Mandela's release (in a sore-throat rewrite of "The Midnight Special"). Otherwise, the LP is strictly high-octane/mid-tempo business as usual, but without the fiery inspiration to make it sizzle. (The CD and cassette add one track.)

On his solo record, early D.O.A. bassist Randy Rampage—with assists from ex-D.O.A. drummer Chuck Biscuits and former members of California's Dils and Avengers—shows he can almost approximate solid, even (gasp) "musical" punk rock, if he'd just tighten up his wig (and get a producer).   [jg/dgs/i]

See also *Jello Biafra, Dead Kennedys.*

D.O.C.

See *N.W.A.*

DOCTOR & THE MEDICS

Doctor & the Medics (nr/Illegal) 1985
Spirit in the Sky EP (nr/Illegal) 1985
Laughing at the Pieces (IRS) 1986 ●
I Keep Thinking It's Tuesday (IRS) 1987 ●

If you're going to be a one-joke band, you'd better pick a doozy. England's absurd glam-psychedelic Doctor & the Medics chose to record a carefully unreconstructed version of the greatest god-rock bubblegum hit of all time, Norman Greenbaum's "Spirit in the Sky," and let the wave of '60s nostalgia do the rest. Defying all logic, it proved to be a brilliant commercial gambit, catapulting this ridiculously dressed trifle of a band into the charts on two continents. The quintet's otherwise self-penned first album has little else to recommend it, although Craig Leon's production (XTC's Andy Partridge takes easily audible credit for one song) and attractively musical vocal interplay between the Doctor (Clive Jackson) and Medics Wendi and Colette keep it listenable.

The American edition of the second LP contains the group's spot-on re-creation of Abba's "Waterloo," with saxual contributions by living legend Roy Wood, as well as the Doc's awful gussied-up version of "Burning Love." Other than one William Orbit remix that employs soon-to-be-trendy acid house rhythms, **I Keep Thinking It's Tuesday** lacks any discernible personality or reason for existing.   [i]

DR. FEELGOOD

Down by the Jetty (nr/UA) 1975 (nr/Fame) 1982
   (nr/Edsel) 1984 ●
Malpractice (Columbia) 1975 ●
Stupidity (nr/UA) 1976 (nr/Liberty) 1985
Sneakin' Suspicion (Columbia) 1977 (nr/Fame) 1987
Be Seeing You (nr/UA) 1977 (nr/Edsel) 1987
Private Practice (nr/UA) 1978 ●
As It Happens (nr/UA) 1979
Let It Roll (nr/UA) 1979
A Case of the Shakes (Stiff America) 1980 (nr/Edsel)
   1986
On the Job (nr/Liberty) 1981
Casebook (nr/Liberty) 1981
Fast Women and Slow Horses (nr/Chiswick) 1982 ●
Doctors Orders (nr/Demon) 1984 ●
Mad Man Blues EP (nr/ID) 1985 ●
Mad Man Blues (Can. Star) 1986
Brilleaux (nr/Grand) 1986 ●
Case History–The Best of Dr. Feelgood (nr/EMI) 1987 ●
Singles (The UA Years+) (nr/Liberty) 1989 ●
Live in London (nr/Grand) 1990 ●

To suggest that all of Dr. Feelgood's records sound alike would be less than generous; there are, however, groups that have explored varying modes of musical expression with greater diligence. The band has been utterly true to its original aims; few contemporary groups can challenge this veteran outfit when it comes to playing basic, energetic R&B. Over the course of fifteen years, through numerous studio LPs, live sets and compilations, the Feelgoods'—or, more precisely, singer/harmonicat Lee Brilleaux, for it is he who has kept the group going through various lineups—dedication to preserving the gritty spirit of groups like the early Rolling Stones has scarcely wavered.

Regardless of inventiveness (or lack thereof), Dr. Feelgood deserves a place of respect in modern music annals by being the commercially successful leader of English pub-rock at its zenith, drawing huge crowds into small clubs all over Europe in the mid-'70s. By playing grassroots music that pleased not only critics but fans in large numbers, the Canvey Island quartet helped set the stage for the transitional—younger, more rock-oriented—Eddie and the Hot Rods, as well as the more radical punk outburst that followed *them*. Without Dr. Feelgood, there would have been fewer venues for these populist groups to play, less likelihood of a successful indie label scene (Stiff's founding was financed, in part, by Brilleaux) and a much smaller audience receptive to groups without dry ice and laser beams.

The original Dr. Feelgood lineup—Brilleaux, singer and shock-guitarist extraordinaire Wilko Johnson (John Wilkinson), drummer "The Big Figure" and bassman John Sparks—made four albums together. Johnson left the band in 1977; Sparks and the Figure in 1982. Mixing Johnson's original tunes with a hefty selection of classics from the catalogues of Chuck Berry, Willie Dixon, Rufus Thomas, Leiber/Stoller, Sonny Boy Williamson and Muddy Waters, the first three studio records had the same R&B/primal rock/blues character as the original Stones. (The band's fanatic devotion to the past led them to mix the first album in mono!) While **Down by the Jetty** has a certain amateurish charm, **Malpractice** has a stronger, more confident sound, and includes better material, like "Back in the Night," "Riot in Cell Block #9" and "You Shouldn't Call the Doctor (If You Can't Pay the Bills)." Johnson's playing—a frantic, choppy, rhythm/lead style adapted from Mick Green and John Lee Hooker, mixed with a riveting spasmodic stage presence—and Brilleaux's hoarse singing may sound a bit out-of-date, but there's no mistaking the energy and honesty they brought to their work.

The live **Stupidity**, although an effective representation, suffers from its similarity to their studio efforts and lack of the exciting visual factor that made their early gigs so great.

Sneakin' Suspicion is the last LP to feature Johnson; although he appears on the whole thing, a disagreement over musical purity led to a split during the recording. (He formed the Solid Senders and then continued on as a solo artist.) In fact, it's equally good as **Malpractice**, with strong originals ("Walking on the Edge," in particular) and nifty covers ("Nothin' Shakin' (But the Leaves on the Trees)," "Lights Out"). The next Dr. Feelgood album, **Be Seeing You** (title and graphics borrowed from *The Prisoner* TV series), features new six-stringer John Mayo—a strong player with his own sound, but not an even swap for the inimitable Johnson—and Nick Lowe as producer. The change in guitarists is obvious; the band's overall style, however, survives nearly intact, and some of the tracks are good enough to carry the day.

Private Practice, a studio LP produced by Richard Gottehrer, has nothing on the ball, and is played too slow to avoid tedium. **As It Happens**, another live outing, is a *real* stiff, drawing its material almost totally from **Private Practice** and **Be Seeing You**. Completing this naff trilogy is **Let It Roll**, an inconsistent (not worthless) collection produced by blues veteran Mike Vernon.

Proving that they could still cut it, Dr. F. reunited with Lowe for **A Case of the Shakes**, a revitalized treat that brings the group up-to-date (relatively speaking) and in line with the likes of Rockpile, giving their traditionalist approach a more modern setting. Mayo's playing is great and the songs are surprisingly impressive and enjoyable.

On the Job is a needless concert rehash with all but one number drawn from the two preceding albums. **Casebook** is a compilation containing enough of the Feelgoods' best to make it worthwhile. **Fast Women and Slow Horses**, produced by Vic Maile, is the last LP to feature the original Figure/Sparks rhythm section. The follow-up, **Doctors Orders**, puts the Feelgoods—Brilleaux, guitarist Gordon Russell, bassist Phil Mitchell and drummer Kevin Morris—back in league with producer Mike Vernon for a program that includes Eddie Cochran's "My Way" and Muddy Waters' "I Can't Be Satisfied."

Sticking it out for another release, that lineup tears through six blues covers on the down-and-dirty **Mad Man Blues**. Brilleaux and the others sound just great, and the readings of Elmore James' "Dust My Broom," Willie Dixon's "My Babe" and John Lee Hooker's title growl are unfussy and packed with power. Not since the glory days of Canned Heat and Paul Butterfield has white blues sounded this wonderful and unselfconscious. (The Canadian reissue, with entirely different artwork, adds four previously non-LP tracks—including a new original, "I've Got News for You"—produced by Mike Vernon, probably at the '84 sessions for **Doctors Orders**.)

Case History and **Singles (The UA Years +)** are, respectively, single and double-album career compilations with a lot of overlap. The latter (which deducts a pair of tracks, including a 1989 remake of "Milk and Alcohol," from the CD version) has liner notes by Will Birch and is highly recommended as a concise summary of the band's best work. [i]

DOCTOR ICE

See *UTFO*.

DOCTORS CHILDREN

Rose Cottage EP (nr/Upright) 1986
King Buffalo EP (nr/Upright) 1987
Girl with Green Eyes EP (nr/Buffalo) 1987
King Buffalo (Down There-Restless) 1987 ●

Combining two UK-only mini-albums—**Rose Cottage** and **King Buffalo** (**Girl with Green Eyes** is a song from the latter joined by an early demo and two radio session tracks)—into a full American longplayer, this British quartet shows off leader Paul Smith's clever songwriting and artless singing on **King Buffalo**, as John Leckie's production does justice (but little more) to arrangements which lean towards the hard-pop guitar sound of Robyn Hitchcock and the Egyptians. Matthew

Woodman's Hammond organ adds the only notable sonic element to these competent but rarely ear-catching tracks. For what it's worth, the earlier, less-polished material from **Rose Cottage** has more bite and backbone in the playing, and leaves a stronger impression. [i]

DOCTORS' MOB

Headache Machine (Wrestler) 1985
Sophomore Slump (Relativity) 1987

Headache Machine, the debut album by this gutsy power pop quartet from Austin, Texas, shows abundant promise with melodies, roughly ringing guitars, electricity and a certain nascent stylistic flair. But **Sophomore Slump**, produced to order by Tommy Erdelyi, is definitely the record to get by these guys. Singer/guitarist Steve Collier's writing shows marked improvement; the band rushes at his songs with youthful eagerness and the self-confidence of seasoned roadhogs. Crossing an attractive Athens influence, a hint of folk and a dusty Southwestern truth those California cowboys would dearly love to borrow, Doctors' Mob get onto something good. [i]

DOCTORS OF MADNESS

Late Night Movies, All Night Brainstorms (UA) 1976
Figments of Emancipation (UA) 1976
Sons of Survival (nr/Polydor) 1978
Revisionism 1975–1978 (nr/Polydor) 1981

This odd excuse for a rock group was essentially the warped musical vision of Kid (Richard) Strange, as realized in posh, over-the-top pretentious style by a manager who spent scads of money in an unsuccessful attempt to make them the Next Big (Ultra-Outrageous) Thing. Although the blue hair, silly theatrical gear and transparent glam pose were awfully out-of-step with the younger and faster safety-pinned hordes who stole their thunder, the Doctors did possess a unique style, thanks in large part to Urban Blitz's (no kidding) eerie violin work, an unlikely instrument in a band hoping to be perceived as Bowie's post-Ziggy disciples.

Late Night Movies (released in the US only as a double-record set with **Figments of Emancipation**) is the wildest and freshest of the group's three albums, going all out to be—or at least seem—weird and exciting. It's hard to take seriously, but there is something worth hearing in terms of the creepy ambience, substantial songs and subtle musical shadings. **Sons of Survival** and **Figments** refine the approach but lack the gonzo originality of the first record. **Revisionism** is an adequate career summary.

After a stint that saw Dave Vanian (on furlough during one of the Damned's collapses) a member, public response—a mixture of apathy and ridicule—proved terminal, and Strange embarked on a solo career. Whatever the verdict on the Doctors of Madness while they were in business, the fact that the new romantics later shouldered the same foolish mantle of narcissism, ludicrous costumes and stage names—an aberration also adopted by American nouveau-glam-metal bands like Mötley Crüe—proves that this band was indeed ahead of its time. [i]

See also *Richard Strange*.

JOHN DOE

See *X*.

DOGBOWL

See *King Missile (Dog Fly Religion)*.

THOMAS DOLBY

The Golden Age of Wireless (Capitol) 1982
(Capitol-Mobile Fidelity) ●
Blinded by Science EP (Capitol) 1983
The Flat Earth (Capitol) 1984 ●
Music from the Film Gothic (Virgin) 1987 ●

THOMAS DOLBY AND THE LOST TOY PEOPLE

Aliens Ate My Buick (EMI Manhattan) 1988 ●

VARIOUS ARTISTS

Howard the Duck (MCA) 1986

After years of session work and part-time employment with Lene Lovich, Bruce Woolley & the Camera Club, Thompson Twins, Foreigner and Joan Armatrading, Thomas Dolby helped revitalize a largely moribund and redundant synth-pop scene with his own recordings. **The Golden Age of Wireless** avoids the usual tactical error and gives the songs prominence over the instruments. Besides demonstrating an unfailing flair for sharp, snappy compositions, Dolby shows himself unusually capable of getting warm, touching feeling out of his synthesizers and his voice, creating an evocative sound that magnificently straddles nostalgia and futurism.

Although his first album contains some really lovely tunes (e.g., "Radio Silence," "Europa and the Pirate Twins"), Dolby followed it with an execrable moron-funk single, "She Blinded Me with Science" (evidently written about his archaeologist father), which became a Top 5 hit. After the album was reissued with that song added on, a five-cut mini-album appeared, combining it with three LP tracks and another lovely new song, "One of Our Submarines." *That* was subsequently appended to the album for its third American variation.

Dolby has never concentrated solely on his own recordings. After the debut's success, he worked on various projects, producing tracks for Whodini and others before getting around to making a new LP of his own. **The Flat Earth** contains nothing really memorable, but does feature nicely restrained pieces of inviting atmospheric charm (including "The Flat Earth" and "Screen Kiss"). Unfortunately, it also contains the strident "Hyperactive!"

Dolby then put his own pop career on hold. He did film soundtracks, collaborated with Ryuichi Sakamoto on an EP, played on Belinda Carlisle's **Heaven on Earth** and co-produced and played on albums by George Clinton (**Some of My Best Jokes Are Friends**), Joni Mitchell (**Dog Eat Dog**) and Prefab Sprout. In cinema land, Dolby wrote, performed and produced five unexceptional new rock songs for George Lucas' misbegotten mega-flop *Howard the Duck*, filling one side of the soundtrack album. (The rest is a John Barry score.) For Ken Russell's equally atrocious *Gothic*, Dolby composed and performed (on Fairlight) appropriately menacing and dramatic accompaniment, actually using a real orchestra on five of the brief selections.

Aliens Ate My Buick, the long-awaited follow-up to **The Flat Earth**, suggests that the now-LA-based musical artist (married to an American TV actress) may be a little out of touch with the real world. The obnoxiously overcrowded '40s swing of "The Key to Her Ferrari" is only the most obvious self-important gaffe here; other lengthy tracks like "Airhead" and "Hot Sauce" are production-driven dance-rock creations with smarmy lyrics. "My Brain Is Like a Sieve" touches on reggae to no avail; "The Ability to Swing" announces Dolby's shortcomings in the music noir area; "Budapest by Blimp" is every bit as annoying as the title would suggest. [sg/i]

See also *Lene Lovich, Prefab Sprout, Ryuichi Sakamoto*.

DOLL BY DOLL

Remember (nr/Automatic) 1979
Gypsy Blood (nr/Automatic) 1979
Doll by Doll (MCA) 1981
Grand Passion (nr/Magnet) 1982

CONCRETE BULLETPROOF INVISIBLE

Big Tears EP (Dimension-Restless) 1988

The only constant on Doll by Doll's four albums is singer/guitarist Jackie Leven, who began as the leader of a quartet and wound up its only member. On the first three LPs, his presence is so commanding—thanks to a deep, rich, expressive voice that leaps into falsetto or descends to an ominous whisper as the moment dictates—that everyone around him takes a back seat. An impressive but flawed debut, **Remember** needlessly limits Doll by Doll's obvious electric strength. Although some tracks rock out, the group's folk roots place song before the performance, occasionally blunting the excitement. A sophisticated work that serves mainly to introduce Leven's startling voice.

After some personnel changes, a reconstituted Doll by Doll made the fine **Gypsy Blood**. With all restraint lifted and the emotional intensity cranked up high, tunes like "The Human Face" and "Teenage Lightning" are simply magnificent—crystal clear, intricately arranged and full of rock fire. Leven's voice and poetic lyrics invest the record with dramatic grandeur. A bit overblown, but a real stunner.

Long delayed by contractual problems, **Doll by Doll** suffers from creeping relaxation. The flame burns less brightly; although songs are strong and affecting, the reach isn't as expansive, and the results not as attention-grabbing.

In partnership with vocalist Helen Turner, Leven made **Grand Passion** using studio sidemen, attempting something in a different vein. Unfortunately, the experiment—whatever it may have been—failed. Turner's singing is like bad Nico, and the songs are filled with pretentious and obnoxious lyrics. Musically adequate but totally unappealing. Doll by Doll played its last gig in late '84.

Years later, Leven rejoined former bandmates Jo Shaw (guitar, vocals) and Dave McIntosh (drums) in Concrete Bulletproof Invisible, a promising but short-lived rock quartet with ex-Pistol bassist Glen Matlock. The nifty title track of CBI's 12-inch **Big Tears** EP lifts the chorus from "White Light/White Heat" but has its own ideas as well; the other tracks (two in the UK, three in the US) sound a bit forced and clunky.   [i]

DOLPHIN BROTHERS

See *Japan*.

DOME

Dome (nr/Dome-Rough Trade) 1980
3R4 (nr/4AD) 1980
Dome 2 (nr/Dome-Rough Trade) 1981
Dome 3 (nr/Dome-Rough Trade) 1981
MZUI/Waterloo Gallery (nr/Cherry Red) 1982
Will You Speak This Word (Nor. Uniton) 1983
8 Time [CD] (nr/4AD) 1988 ●

DUET EMMO

Or So It Seems (nr/Mute) 1983

BRUCE GILBERT

This Way (nr/Mute) 1984
The Shivering Man (nr/Mute) 1986 ●
This Way to the Shivering Man (Mute-Restless) 1990 φ
Insiding (Mute-Elektra) 1991 φ

HE SAID

Hail (nr/Mute) 1985 (Mute-Restless) 1989 ●
Take Care (nr/Mute) 1988 (Mute-Enigma) 1989 ●

During Wire's lengthy hiatus (1980 to 1986), bassist Graham Lewis and guitarist B.C. (Bruce) Gilbert continued their partnership—often under the name Dome—to explore the outer reaches of studio technique and synthetic sound, sidestepping Wire's arcane hitmaking tendencies and Colin Newman's more classical aspirations.

Dome abandons conventional song form for a hodgepodge of treated instruments and voices, with lurching mechanical noises infrequently keeping a vague beat; melodies fragment under studio manipulation. Eerie. **3R4** moves into the ambient drone music pioneered by Brian Eno, and its four tracks achieve an almost symphonic effect. **Dome 2** continues the ambient/minimalist experimentation of the first two albums, painting audio expressions of modern ennui, but **Dome 3** breaks stride, lifting the beats of other cultures and mixing them with abstracted bits of psychedelia and disembodied noises. The 71-minute **8 Time** CD combines the contents of **3R4** with two singles released around the time under the name Cupol.

MZUI/Waterloo Gallery, done in conjunction with Russell Mills, makes extensive use of found noises and self-made instruments. Microphones placed around a London art gallery collected intentional and unintentional sounds from inside and out. The arhythmic result isn't music per se, but a curious examination of the relationship between environment and sound.

Will You Speak This Word combines some of **Dome 3**'s ethnic borrowings with the repetitive minimalism of earlier works. The suite-like "To Speak" takes up all of one side; it begins with quasi-Arabic violin and random, atonal sax, moving into an acoustic guitar/sax/pseudo-African drum drone with slowly shifting textures before ending with extraterrestrial electron-

ics. An interesting and well-composed piece. The other side's six tracks mix primal drum rhythms with light touches of art-noise generated on a variety of instruments, building intriguing trances. A progressive album in the truest sense of the term.

Duet Emmo was a one-off project by Gilbert, Lewis and Mute Records chief Daniel Miller (the name is an anagram of Dome and Mute). **Or So It Seems** fluctuates between atonal, electronic sound collages and stiff, monotonous synth-funk reminiscent of D.A.F., with no track ever getting off the ground. Fun studio noodling no doubt, but not of lasting import.

Gilbert's **This Way** features a three-part suite ("Do You Me? I Did") commissioned by Michael Clark, leader of England's hippest dance troupe (the company has worked with the Fall and performed in New Order's "True Faith" video). Part of the Clark's uniqueness lies in his selection of music: much of "Do You Me?" is about as arhythmic as **Music for Airports**, but more dissonant. The remaining two tracks are mostly percolating electronics that move in and out of synch.

Much more in line with Dome's experimental approach, **The Shivering Man** is a meandering instrumental collection of spare sonic doodles. (Some of the tracks were commissioned by artist Angela Conway, a vocalist on He Said's **Hail**, and the Paris Opera Ballet.) Employing the kind of electronic production devices that often enliven adventurous modern music, the only component missing from **The Shivering Man** is the music itself. (**This Way to the Shivering Man** is a compilation containing about half the tracks from Gilbert's first two albums.) **Insiding** consists of two side-long pieces created for dance pieces by choreographer Ashley Page.

Released the same year as Wire's reformation, the first album by He Said, Lewis' flexible studio project, includes contributions by Gilbert, co-producer/programmer John Fryer, Eno and others. The well-organized music—essentially effects-laden electro-beats with ethereal vocals—never quite finds its stylistic voice, although individual passages are impressive.

The follow-up, **Take Care**, is basically another collaboration with Fryer (only two cuts feature anyone else). While the general approach is similar to the thinking person's atmospheric electro-pop (at times not unlike Wire) on **Hail**, the album contains a surprising detour into rap ("A.B.C. Dicks Love"); otherwise, the long (five or six minutes each) songs sound—or at least feel—kind of samey. The final two tracks were composed as music for an avant-garde ballet.   [sg/dgs]

See also *A.C. Marias, Wire*.

DOMINATRIX

The Dominatrix Sleeps Tonight EP (UpRoar-Streetwise) 1984

DEATH COMET CREW

At the Marble Bar EP (nr/Beggars Banquet) 1984

DEATH COMET

"Mystic Eyes"/"Death Comet Drive" (J-Mark-Elektra) 1986

Charming and catchy, Dominatrix's one New York club hit consists of passionless dada femme recitation over light atmospheric music by Stuart Arbright (ex-Ike Yard) and Ken Lockie (ex-Cowboys International), with scratch mix effects by Ivan Ivan and Lockie. The 12-inch offers two full-scale versions plus two additional remixes ("Chants" and "Beat Me").

Collaborating again with Lockie as co-producer and joined by a few other musicians, Arbright became the Death Comet Crew for a 12-inch electro-funk exercise that's not as exceptional as Dominatrix, but still amusing and offbeat. "At the Marble Bar" offers a varied collection of percussion sounds; "Exterior St." has rap vocals by Rammellzee; "Funky Dream" is an amusingly reductionist cut-up edit of the word "funky."

Taking a rocking Billy Idolish approach without much dance-club potential, Arbright and the same crew from DCC—guitarist Michael Diekmann and bassist Shinichi Shimokawa—did a nice cover of Van Morrison's "Mystic Eyes" on the Death Comet 12-inch, sticking a similar-sounding but inferior original on the flip.   [i]

ANNA DOMINO

East and West EP (Bel. Crépuscule) 1984
Anna Domino (Bel. Crépuscule) 1986
This Time (Bel. Crépuscule) 1987 (Giant) 1988 ●
Colouring in the Edge and the Outline EP (Bel.
    Crépuscule) 1988 (Giant) 1989 ●
Mysteries of America (Bel. Crépuscule) 1990 ●

Transcontinental chanteuse Domino was born in Tokyo, but lived in Italy and Canada before moving to New York, where she played in an early version of Polyrock. She later fell in with the Brussels art-quiet crowd and began a career writing and recording dignified pop songs. Following the **East and West** mini-LP, Domino made her full-length debut, produced half-and-half by Alan Rankine of the Associates and Marc Moulin of Telex.

The first Domino record to see American release, **This Time**, was co-written with Belgian multi-instrumentalist Michel Delory (her creative partner ever since) and produced by UK technologist Flood (Erasure, etc.). A weak collection of diversely dull music, nice but unambitious singing and sensitive lyrics that fall just short of imaginative, **This Time** is not that far from a synthesized Motels album.

Colouring in the Edge unearths a much more productive approach. Domino's vocals reach an understated eloquence (doubling herself on "Luck" adds to the handsome effect) over music that alternates light naturalism ("Clouds of Joy," "Perfect Day–No, He Says") and jittery but intimate sequencers ("88"). This time, Domino comes off like a suave Suzanne Vega minus the urban poetry. (On the 12-inch record's original Belgian release, all five songs are mastered on one side, leaving the other to an artistic engraving.)

For most of **Mysteries of America**, acoustic guitar, incidental string accents and the merest bits of percussion (bongos are the loudest rhythm element) set off Domino's wispiest singing and most involving lyrics. The continental folk of "Paris," the jazzy "Tamper with Time," the courtly lullaby "Dust" and "Isn't That So" (a Jesse Winchester cover) are all quite lovely, drawing the listener further into Domino's world. But she hasn't completely broken off her affair with synthesizers, and allows the mildly overactive chatter of several numbers ("Bonds of Love," for one) to interrupt the album's otherwise beguiling mood.   [i]

DONNER PARTY

Donner Party (Cryptovision) 1987
Donner Party (Pitch-A-Tent-Rough Trade) 1988

This trio's amiable mix of thrashily melodic folk-rock and loopy acoustic pop was not unlike that of another San Francisco group, the Cat Heads. (The two shared drummer/singer Melanie Clarin.) What distinguishes Donner Party is the agreeably twisted sensibility of main writer/vocalist Samuel Coomes, whose absurdist meditations are endearing without being cloying.

Though both Donner Party albums are eponymously titled, they're distinctly different. The first (the one with the cartoon-montage cover art) is a rough gem, with scrappy rockers like "Oh Esmerelda" and "Godlike Porpoise Head of Blue-Eyed Mary" combining propulsive tunes with whimsical lyrics. The self-explanatory "When You Die Your Eyes Pop Out" reveals a bent for rustic fatalism.

The second release (with the 19th-century Edward Hicks cover painting) boasts better sound quality, more stylistic variety and shows the band moving comfortably from DIY inspiration to versatile craftsmanship with no loss of energy or personality. The songwriting is likewise more accomplished, alternating wonder ("Up & Down," "Try to Imagine a Terrible World") and dread ("Boxfull of Bones," "Sickness"), often finding a place where the two overlap.   [hd]

See also *Cat Heads, Harm Farm*.

DOS

Dos (New Alliance) 1986
Numero Dos EP (New Alliance) 1989

Dos—meaning, of course, two—consists of husband-and-wife bassists Mike Watt (Minutemen, fIRE-HOSE) and Kira Roessler (ex-Black Flag). Since Kira has also composed for fIREHOSE, several of the short compositions comprising the pair's charming album hint at that fine trio's signature sound. A dose of **Dos** entails little more (and nothing less) than two basses sniffing around one another like curious animals, making it an atmospheric, playful, even loving pleasure to hear.

The two get groovier on their 1989 EP by covering Billie Holiday ("Don't Explain") and Sonic Youth ("Pacific Coast Highway"). But more singing apparently means less bassing: except for two awesomely intelligent instrumentals, the deep-down sound tends to get lost in breathy melancholy.   [rg]

See also *Black Flag, D.C.3, fIREHOSE, Minutemen*.

DOTS

Return of the Dots . . . (Ger. Rebel) 1985
I Can See You (Ger. Rebel) 1986
Live in West-Germany: 15 Songs, 15 Stories (Ger. Rebel)
    1986

This longstanding on-off secret of the NYC scene has been able to pack clubs in certain Eastern US cities and in Germany (not to mention Holland and Yugoslavia), but can barely get a booking in their hometown. Such topsy-turvyness is part and parcel of Dotsongs, underlined by an unclassifiable grab-bag approach.

After a very brief stint in a precursor to the Ramones, guitarist and chief songwriter Rick Garcia founded the Dots in 1978 with singer Jimmi Quidd; early guitarists (Garcia began on bass) included the late Alison East, but the lineup finally jelled when Garcia became sole guitarist. Most of **Return of the Dots** had been cut as demos, more than six years before a German label put it out. This phase of the band was punk energy, a heavy dose of Anglo-pop (especially early Who and Move), *The Honeymooners* and *Huckleberry Hound*. The musical styles are sort of jumbled, as are song topics (intra-office romance, marrying a monkey, a "Legend" in his own mind, etc.), yet it all somehow hangs together, partly through Quidd's high, reedy vocals. Plain and simple, it's a lot of fun.

The early Dots' high-speed battiness helped inspire some fans at a Washington DC gig; next thing, Quidd found himself producing "Pay to Cum!," the Bad Brains' landmark debut. He also produced an EP for the Undead (led by an ex-Misfit). Then came **Return**, followed quickly by the other two LPs. Unfortunately, what makes the live album so fine is what makes the second studio LP unnecessary. The live LP has three fab reworkings (of the Beatles, the Count Five and Maxine Nightingale!), five new songs and seven numbers from previous Dots discs. Six of those are from **I Can See You**.

On the live LP, the nucleus of Quidd, Garcia and bassist Leigh Sioris was joined by Nat Seeley on drums (replacing Jeff Formosa, who was on **I Can See You**) and guitarist Al Maddy (ex-Nitecaps). The two guitars work together well, and the album's sound is full and punchy—in fact, better than the studio LP. Anyway, it's as much fun as **Return**; where else can you find out why some people go to hell ("Hard Times"), what to do with a drunken sailor ("I Won't Cry 'Cause You Want Me To") or where "exceptionality" went ("Crime of Passion"). Dottiness may be an acquired taste, but it's quite savory in its own odd way. Quidd died of an aneurysm in 1990.   [tr]

DOW JONES & THE INDUSTRIALS

See *Gizmos*.

DOWNY MILDEW

Downy Mildew EP (Texas Hotel) 1986
Broomtree (Texas Hotel) 1987
Mincing Steps (Texas Hotel) 1988 ●

Those who like R.E.M. and 10,000 Maniacs, and rush out to get everything new on 4AD will find the shimmering acoustic/electric guitars and gauzy ambience of Southern California's Downy Mildew as refreshing as a cool sprinkle on a hot summer night. The first EP contains four songs written by the quartet's two singing guitarists, Charlie Baldonado and Jenny Homer, and introduces the band's two early sides: peppy folkpop (he) and moodier rock balladry (she).

Broomtree is more accomplished, adding keyboards, autoharp, violin and dissonantly bowed cello to the acoustic guitars and buffered drums. Unfortunately, the slower tempos and improved production reveal a faint resemblance to **Dark Side of the Moon**; a mild and dry jazzy side comes through as well. The alterna-

tion of lead vocals creates a certain tension, but the band's unassailable delicacy and taste provide enough stylistic unification to hold the album together.

Downy Mildew's increasingly refined escape from Planet Rock continues on **Mincing Steps**, a shimmering collection that reflects the group's transition into a distinguished chamber quartet. Touching on some of the ways '60s rock bands introduced baroque classical elements into their sound, Downy Mildew hit the right blend of energy and eclecticism about half the time. When it clicks, the record is a rare treat.   ['e/i]

DRAGONS

Parfums de la Révolution (Fr. Blitzkrieg) 1982

A piece of punk exotica: three underground musicians from mainland China recorded in secret by a visiting Frenchman. (Done, thankfully, before the brief 1985 tour there by Wham!) Using only vocals, electric guitar, rudimentary drums and Chinese violin, the trio attempts "Anarchy in the UK" and "Get off My Cloud" with truly bizarre results; the remaining seven tracks are originals in a more traditional Oriental vein. A fascinating transliteration of rock from a country not generally considered in terms of modern music.   [i]

DRAGSTERS

See *Ronald Koal and the Trillionaires*.

DRAMATIS

See *Gary Numan*.

MIKEY DREAD

Dread at the Controls (nr/Trojan) 1979
African Anthem (Jam. Dread at the Controls) 1979 (RAS) 1989
World War III (Jam. Dread at the Controls) 1980 ●
Beyond World War III (Heartbeat) 1981 ●
S.W.A.L.K. (Heartbeat) 1982
Pave the Way (Heartbeat) 1983 ●
Pave the Way (Parts 1 & 2) (nr/DEP Int'l) 1985
Happy Family (RAS) 1989 ●
Evolutionary Rockers (Jam. Dread at the Controls) 1989
Best Sellers (Rykodisc) 1991 ф

Jamaican disc jockey Michael Campbell changed his name, moved to England and made it as a recording artist. **Dread at the Controls** (the name of his radio show and, later, record label) is a modest debut, but **World War III** is an out-and-out sonic adventure. Mixed up (and down) by Scientist, the LP features Dread's dancehall-style toasting, beefed up with ultraheavy production and sonic effects. The album tied into punk rockers' enthusiastic acceptance of both reggae's outlook and its techniques; Dread was thus considered a new wave reggae artist, a link he affirmed when he recorded (on **Sandinista!** and singles) and toured with the Clash. (**Beyond World War III** is a slightly revised American edition.)

Unfortunately, none of his later releases are as impressive as **WWIII**. **S.W.A.L.K.** is a halfhearted imitation filled with unconvincing lovers rock made worse by Dread's nasal singing. **Pave the Way (Parts 1 & 2)** is just as inconsistent. Although it offers stylistic variety, Dread's capable production and Paul Simonon on background vocals, the LP's best tracks are chant-down cuts like "Roots and Culture," the theme of a UK children's show. The two-LP British version is impressive at least for its ambition; the prior American single record seems spare in comparison.

African Anthem is Mikey Dread at his best, tripping out with sound and dub, visiting hemispheres no one else has ever been. Digging into his library of tapes from his years as a JBC DJ, he includes his zany station IDs, drop-ins and samplings amid the already wild-style dubtronics. **Evolutionary Rockers** (a reissue of Dread's first LP) also features superstar remix engineers King Tubby and Prince Jammy; while it has a surreal feel, it isn't as dubby. More than anything else, these two albums define Dread at the Controls, an originator of sheer genius.

On the other hand, **Happy Family** suggests that his strength may lie behind the scenes, not behind the mic. While his message and lyrics are still strong, Dread's singing is ofttimes mediocre.   [bk/aw]

DREAD ZEPPELIN
Un-led-Ed (IRS) 1990 φ
5,000,000* (IRS) 1991 φ

Proving that a joke doesn't have to be funny to be successful as long as it exploits popular prejudices, this California novelty act—which had previously self-released a cassette album—hit the charts by covering Led Zeppelin songs in an Elvis Presley impersonator voice over reggae rhythms with dub production accents. The sextet gets some smileage out of mixing icons (sticking "Heartbreaker" and "Heartbreak Hotel" together, and running "Black Dog" into "Hound Dog"), but the concept—an idea *SCTV* could have squeezed dry in a five-minute skit—is hardly adequate for an entire debut album, much less an ongoing career.   [i]

DREAM ACADEMY
The Dream Academy (Warner Bros.) 1985 ●
Remembrance Days (Reprise) 1987 ●
A Different Kind of Weather (nr/Blanco y Negro) 1990
   (Reprise) 1991 φ

In a shocking success story, Dream Academy's easy listening, generally dull pop found its way to the top of America's record charts in 1985. "Life in a Northern Town," the atmospheric Association-like '60s novelty tune (acoustic guitars, chanted vocals, cellos, tympani), is pleasant, pretentious and shallow, but nothing else on the first LP comes close to being as catchy or characteristic. Nick Laird-Clowes (ex-Act) is at best a bland vocalist; his partners (Gilbert Gabriel, keyboards; Kate St. John, woodwinds, horns) are equally inadequate to his Thompson Twins fantasies. The LP employs many guest musicians; David Gilmour co-produced most of the tracks.

The riot of credits on **Remembrance Days** acknowledges production work by Hugh Padgham, Lindsey Buckingham and others. It's another airy record—stunningly clean, precise, sophisticated and of absolutely no significance. Dream Academy has thankfully abandoned the nostalgia gimmick, but Laird-Clowes' songs are still trifles, with clumsy lyrics that smack more of education than imagination. If Prefab Sprout didn't exist, Dream Academy would still be second-rate, an ornate frame for a missing picture.

Other than a disrespectful acid house rendition of John Lennon's "Love" (with guest chanting by Poly Styrene!) and the reasonably catchy "Mercy Killing," **A Different Kind of Weather** offers little vitality or stylistic variation on the trio's lush pop formulae. St. John's oboe and soprano sax is an effective antidote to blandness, but the languid material is almost characterless, relegating the album to handsomely accomplished ambience for the old at heart.   [i]

See also *Act*.

DREAM COMMAND
See *Comsat Angels*.

DREAM 6
See *Concrete Blonde*.

DREAMS SO REAL
Father's House (Coyote) 1986
Rough Night in Jericho (Arista) 1988 ●
Gloryline (Arista) 1990 ●

This tuneful Athens threesome, produced on its first album by Peter Buck, uses a bit of piano and close vocal harmonies—the Kingston Trio and Buffalo Springfield come to mind—to differentiate itself from That Other Local Band. Although guitarist/singer Barry Marler does favor Buck, Dreams So Real's light, airy pop doesn't really reflect an R.E.M. influence at all. (Cover your ears when "Capitol Mall" comes on.) In any case, **Father's House** is too mild to truly matter: while the summery ambience is pleasant enough, the songs are insubstantial and many of the performances rush along in an overeager blur.

Moving to a major label, the trio toughened its sound and commercialized its approach for **Rough Night in Jericho**, putting stronger rhythms behind the ringing guitar strums and arena-ready drama into the vocals. The melodies are okay, but the dynamic delivery exaggerates the weakness in Marler's lyrics.

Gloryline wisely backtracks a little, simplifying the drums to a snappy backbeat and tempering the electric intensity with a folkier sensibility, acoustic guitar strums and more effective use of guest keyboards. Dreams So Real are still caught between two conflicting impulses—big-league rock power and carefully detailed grassroots richness—but this album puts them on the way to finding a singable solution. Cindy Wilson of the B-52's guests on one track.   [i]

DREAM SYNDICATE
The Dream Syndicate EP (Down There) 1982 (Enigma)
   1984
The Days of Wine and Roses (Ruby) 1982
Tell Me When It's Over EP (nr/Rough Trade) 1983
Medicine Show (A&M) 1984 ●

This Is Not the New Dream Syndicate Album ... Live! EP
(A&M) 1984 ●
Out of the Grey (Big Time) 1986 ●
50 in a 25 Zone EP (Big Time) 1987 ●
Ghost Stories (Enigma) 1988 φ
Live at Raji's (Restless) 1989 φ

STEVE WYNN
Kerosene Man (Rhino) 1990 ●
Kerosene Man EP [CD] (RNA) 1991 ●

Dream Syndicate was one of the first bands from the Los Angeles psychedelic revival (misleadingly dubbed the paisley underground) to reach a national audience. While many of the movement's bands plumbed the Byrds/Buffalo Springfield or Pink Floyd archives for inspiration, Dream Syndicate's weird, obsessive lyrics, relentless noise maelstroms—mixed with eerie/pretty otherworldly dirges and ballads—and singer Steve Wynn's nasal rasping and ranting recalled the Velvet Underground, though (of course) they steadfastly denied that to be their intent. Following the release of a four-song demo on Wynn's Down There label, the quartet made its proper debut on **The Days of Wine and Roses**, rawly produced by Chris D. (Flesh Eaters/Divine Horsemen). With driving, feedback-drenched guitars and stream-of-consciousness lyrical spume, the record appealed to sensitive English-major college radio programmers too young to shoot up to the Velvets the first time around. (The UK-only **Tell Me When It's Over** EP adds three live cuts to the title track, drawn from the album.)

Original bassist Kendra Smith left; the band signed to A&M and recorded a second album, produced by Sandy Pearlman. Wynn's songs remain driven and obsessive, but he seems more inclined to ape Mick Jagger than Lou Reed this time. Also, guitarist Karl Precoda cuts back on the feedback and the entire album has more of a traditional rock'n'roll feel. Early fans cried sell-out, but with eight-minute jam/raps like "John Coltrane Stereo Blues" included, that accusation doesn't hold much water.

Nine-and-a-half minutes of that song also appear on **This Is Not the New Dream Syndicate Album ... Live!**, a dismal document recorded live in Chicago during the 1984 tour that followed **Medicine Show**. (The two records were later paired on a domestic CD.)

After guitarist/producer Paul B. Cutler (ex-45 Grave) replaced Precoda, a revitalized Dream Syndicate released **Out of the Grey**, nine rugged rock-cowboy songs characterized by Wynn's worn but hopeful vocals and Cutler's obsessive distorto-guitar madness. Proceeding from Neil Young's Crazy Horse period, songs like "Forest for the Trees," "Now I Ride Alone," "Slide Away" and "50 in a 25 Zone" (also released on a 12-inch with a bare-bones remix and three added tracks, including a maudlin version of "The Lonely Bull") hum with enough coarse energy and stylistic insouciance to cover their compositional deficiencies. (The **Out of the Grey** CD contains the EP's extra tracks.)

For **Ghost Stories**, the band actually enlisted Neil Young's old producer (Elliot Mazer) and, whether through his guidance or their own maturity, transcended previous inconsistencies to make a great album. While still mainly offering the usual dirges and ballads (Blind

Lemon Jefferson's "See that My Grave Is Kept Clean" is a perfectly apt cover), Wynn's songs here are lean and concise, his singing controlled and effective. The instrumental excesses have been stripped away, and solid music replaces noise excursions. If soul-in-torment songs and "traditional" rock song structures don't appeal to you, skip this. Otherwise, it's well worth checking out.

Unfortunately, after the **Ghost Stories** tour, the band itself checked out, leaving **Live at Raji's**, recorded in January '89 at the noted Hollywood nightspot, as a rough'n'ready document of this band in its best—and final—stage. (The group's fan club actually got in the last word, releasing a 1989 collection of outtakes and live tracks entitled **It's Too Late to Stop Now**.)

With a gang of session players and LA luminaries in tow, Wynn began work on **Kerosene Man** immediately after the split, but many of the songs seem to chronicle a breakup of a more personal nature. Covering a number of musical settings—ranging from Dylanesque folk-rock ("Tears Won't Help" and "Carolyn" are the best) to **Transformer**-era Lou Reed soundalikes (check out his phrasing on "The Blue Drifter" and "Conspiracy of the Heart") to more abrasive pieces reminiscent of early Dream Syndicate ("Younger" and "Anthem")—**Kerosene Man** showcases both the best and worst of what Wynn has to offer. The EP contains the album's title track and four items—including a version of Sonic Youth's "Kool Thing" recorded in Holland—from various 1990 radio broadcasts.   [ep/i/ds]

See also *Danny & Dusty, Human Hands, Opal*.

D.R.I.
Dirty Rotten LP (Rotten) 1984 ●
Dealing with It! (Death-Metal Blade-Enigma) 1985 ●
Crossover (Metal Blade-Enigma) 1987 ●
Four of a Kind (Metal Blade-Enigma) 1988 ●
Thrash Zone (Metal Blade-Enigma) 1989 ●

Arguably the first punk-to-metal crossover band, D.R.I. was formed in Texas as Dirty Rotten Imbeciles, playing basic raw hardcore (as evidenced on the self-issued debut). Shortly after, the group relocated to the San Francisco area, and **Dealing with It!** blurs their sound into more of a speed metal category. By **Crossover**, a major blow to the few remaining boundaries between the by then very similar genres, D.R.I. had practically become a full-on heavy metal band. The next two albums expand on D.R.I.'s sound, bringing the group—which has undergone numerous personnel changes—into a genre otherwise populated by the likes of Suicidal Tendencies and Bad Brains.   [ja]

DRIVIN' N' CRYIN'
Scarred but Smarter (688) 1986 (Island) 1988 ●
Whisper Tames the Lion (Island) 1987 ●
Mystery Road (Island) 1989 ●

DRIVIN-N-CRYIN
Fly Me Courageous (Island) 1991 φ

KEVN KINNEY
MacDougal Blues (Island) 1990 ●

FRANK FRENCH AND KEVN KINNEY

Everything Looks Better in the Dark (Twilight) 1987

Though often misidentified as part of the R.E.M.-led new-Southern-rock posse, Atlanta's drivin' n' cryin' actually embraces an eclectic mix of styles, from hard rock to bluegrass, with singer/guitarist Kevn Kinney's thoughtful (if occasionally melodramatic) lyrics contributing a romantic working-class Everyman sensibility that rarely seems forced.

Scarred but Smarter is a promising, if somewhat murky, debut whose principal charm lies in the way the trio mines contrasting genres as if they can't tell the difference. The enjoyably mixed bag features country-rockers ("Another Scarlet Butterfly"), pastoral ballads ("You Mean Everything"), anthemic blue-collar rock ("Stand Up and Fight for It") and Sabbathy metal ("Saddle on the Side of the Road"), all united by Kinney's salt-of-the-earth lyrics.

Produced by Anton Fier (who also did most of the drumming), **Whisper Tames the Lion** focuses the trio's musical attack while maintaining the polystylistic approach. The resulting disc is surprisingly balanced and dynamic; highlights include the tense title track, the garagey "Powerhouse" and the delicately acoustic "On a Clear Daze."

Mystery Road shows the band (now a four-piece with the addition of former R.E.M. roadie Buren Fowler as second guitarist) growing more fluent in their varied idioms. Full-throttle fast'n'loud tunes like "Toy Never Played With" and "You Don't Know Me" suggest that drivin' n' cryin' could probably make a nice living as a metal band if so inclined, but such folkier numbers as "Peacemaker" and "Straight to Hell" make you glad they're not.

Accompanied by a streamlined spelling of the band's handle, **Fly Me Courageous** (with hard-rock producer Geoff Workman behind the board) finally whips the band's divergent elements into a cohesive style. Kinney and Fowler emerge as a distinctive guitar team, lending riffy authority to such Kinney compositions as the title track, "Around the Block Again" and "Chain Reaction."

Kinney's solo **MacDougal Blues** actually features his entire band (as well as R.E.M.'s Peter Buck, who also produced) in supporting roles. Though the album has its moments, this attempt to recast Kinney as an acoustic New York folkie is misguided; he's a lot more convincing in the group context.

Everything Looks Better in the Dark is a collection of fifteen tracks recorded by Kinney (who wrote and sings all but one) and former partner Frank French between 1984 and 1986. The tunes sound like what they apparently were: a blueprint for drivin' n' cryin' (the album contains one song bearing the band's name, and another that was re-recorded for **Whisper Tames the Lion**). [hd]

DROOGS

Heads Examined EP (Plug-n-Socket) 1983
Stone Cold World (Plug-n-Socket) 1984 (PVC) 1987
Kingdom Day (PVC) 1987 ●
Anthology (Ger. Music Maniac) 1987
Mad Dog Dreams (Ger. Music Maniac) 1989 ●

Want Something (Skyclad) 1990 ●
Live in Europe EP (Ger. Music Maniac) 1990

On their first EP, LA's Droogs—who started playing together as pre-teens in 1966 and began issuing singles in the mid-'70s—pound out bluesy garage rock which variously resembles the early Stones (thanks mostly to the harmonica wailing in "99 Steps"), the Yardbirds and the Seeds; a faithful cover of "Born to Be Wild" is both obligatory and superfluous. The first album, well-produced by Earle Mankey, sets a more ambitious course, relying on period-evocative psychedelic originals and mixing in different instrumental flavors and textures, while never straying far from recognizable clichés. The quartet deftly avoids genre slavishness but, a few notable exceptions (the solid title track, for instance) aside, still falls a bit short of being exciting on their own recorded merits.

With Mankey again manning the board, **Kingdom Day** drops the nostalgia shtick and mixes electric (kudos to Roger Clay) and acoustic guitars to good effect while keeping the focus on Ric Albin's growly vocals. Dynamic arrangements and enthusiastic, inspired playing make up for material that isn't all inherently memorable. The band's shorter songs work best, roughing up R&B and boogie stylings into modern rock, but the one non-original—"Call off Your Dogs," written by Jeffrey Lee Pierce and Peter Case—is the record's high point. This hot date proves the Droogs need no longer long to sound like anyone else.

The German **Anthology** is a well-annotated diary of the first decade in the history of America's first proto-punk combo: a full five years before such genre "forefathers" as the Chesterfield Kings and the Unclaimed, the Droogs were spreading the gospel according to Question Mark with a series of spottily distributed 7-inch manna wafers. All of that early issue appears here, for the most part in lo-fi that attests to the band's purity *and* poverty. Proof that a modern lifeline—however thin—has always been connected to the body of '60s raunch.

Initially set for release a couple of years earlier on the ill-fated PVC label, surfacing first in Europe as **Mad Dog Dreams** and then expanded by two tracks, **Want Something** essentially crystallizes what the Droogs have been moving towards for the past few years. The album layers sinewy, decidedly Western slabs of open-highway hard rock ("Long Dark Night," John Hiatt's "Zero House") with moodier, folk-tinged atmospherics ("Mad Dog Dreams" and "Devil Left to Pay," the latter written by LA rock scribe/rocker Robert Lloyd). That the multitude of guests—including ex-Code Blue honcho Dean Chamberlain, Dream Syndicaters Steve Wynn (who sings lead on his own composition, "Maria"), guitarist Karl Precoda and Paul Cutler (who also produced the LP)—never obscures the Droogs' character is a tribute to the group's forceful personality. (The CD adds three.) [i/dss]

BILL DRUMMOND

See *Big in Japan, Justified Ancients of Mu Mu.*

DUB SYNDICATE

See *New Age Steppers.*

DUCK AND THE PONDS

See *Alan Milman Sect.*

DUCKS DELUXE

Ducks Deluxe (RCA) 1974
Taxi to the Terminal Zone (nr/RCA) 1975
Don't Mind Rockin' Tonite (RCA) 1978
Last Night of a Pub Rock Band (nr/Blue Moon) 1981

Heard in the cold light of the present, England's pub-rockin' Ducks Deluxe sound rather inconsequential (if amiable). Back in the dark ages of 1974, however, they were manna from heaven. Along with Brinsley Schwarz and Dr. Feelgood, the Ducks championed a much-needed return to basics by playing in traditional American styles diametrically opposed to the glitter and art trends then in vogue. And that paved the way for punk.

The Ducks' first (and best) LP captures the ultimate pub-rock band in all its glory—great for dancing and drinking, not critical analysis. Bursting with boisterous pride and spirit, the quartet careens through covers of songs by Eddie Cochran and the Stones, plus "originals" that borrow heavily from Chuck Berry, Lou Reed's "Sweet Jane," Otis Redding and so on. Three of the four sing: Nick Garvey is the rough-hewn romantic and Martin Belmont the awkward crooner, but it's Sean Tyla's growling boogie that sets the tempo.

Taking its title from a line in Chuck Berry's "Promised Land," **Taxi to the Terminal Zone** beats the sophomore jinx but also exposes the band's limitations. Many of the tracks are simply rewrites of songs from the first LP, which themselves were hardly groundbreakers. A cover of the Flamin Groovies' "Teenage Head" is inspired, however. The album benefits from Dave Edmunds' production and the addition of keyboardist Andy McMaster(s), author of the surprisingly poppy "Love's Melody," a foretaste of the work he and Garvey would pursue in one of the Ducks' many outgrowths, the Motors.

In 1978, RCA sensed that the Ducks could be tied to the growth of new wave, and released **Don't Mind Rockin' Tonight**, a collection titled after one of the standout boogie tracks on the first album. A must for the band's fans, as it contains some previously non-LP B-sides; expendable for everyone else.

Last Night of a Pub Rock Band—that is, July 1, 1975—is so abysmally recorded that even aficionados should skip it.   [jy]

See also *Motors, Graham Parker, Rumour, Sean Tyla Gang.*

DUET EMMO

See *Dome.*

STEPHEN "TIN TIN" DUFFY

The Ups and Downs (nr/10-Virgin) 1985 ●

STEPHEN DUFFY

Because We Love You (nr/10-Virgin) 1986 ●

If awards were handed out for foresight, Birmingham's Stephen Duffy would not likely be considered for one. At the turn of the decade, he parted company with a trendy young new romantic band, saying they were just too reliant on synthesizers for his taste. Never mind that his own subsequent work has included plenty of electronics; the band he left was Duran Duran.

It took a little while, but Duffy did eventually get his own career off the ground. Using the ludicrous nom de rock Tin Tin, he had big international dance hits with "Kiss Me" and "Hold Me," both annoying, stereotypical synth-pop ditties. The former was re-released several times and (two years later) included on **The Ups and Downs**, his long-delayed solo debut.

Because We Love You drops the Tin Tin tag and much of the electronic orchestration, replacing the latter with generic pop/rock/soul from the Wham!/Spandau school. With such ingenious titles as "I Love You," "Love Station" and "Unkiss That Kiss," almost every track is a predictable mélange of horns and standard bass/drums patterns, topped with Duffy's wimpy, emotionless voice. He can write good hooks, but neither of these albums offers anything you haven't already heard.

See also *Lilac Time.*   [dgs]

DUKES OF STRATOSPHEAR

See *XTC.*

DUMPTRUCK

D Is for Dumptruck (Incas) 1983 (Big Time) 1985
Positively Dumptruck (Big Time) 1986 ●
For the Country (Big Time) 1987 ●

An interesting partnership from Massachusetts: Kirk Swan and Seth Tiven each sing, write and play guitar and bass on **D Is for Dumptruck**, with only a drummer for company. The dozen songs fall somewhere between Joy Division and the dB's—too bleak and intense to be happily engaging, yet rooted in a jagged pop melodicism. Insecure, downcast lyrics support the pair's darker side; occasionally chipper guitar bits elevate the mood. Although some tracks are disorientingly dense and chilly, Dumptruck can be a most entertaining and stimulating proposition. (The reissue is identical save for the back cover.)

With a full two-man rhythm section and producer Don Dixon on keyboards, Dumptruck firmly pushed **Positively** towards the Chris Stamey facet of its personality, playing rugged guitar pop with the same intelligence but more melodicism. Although Swan and Tiven write separately, their musical styles meld together without seams. The strained, mildly anguished vocals definitely suggest the ex-dB, but the busy drumming, swirling guitars and raggedly Byrdsish harmonies give Dumptruck a sound of its own.

Swan is gone from the third album, replaced by another singing guitarist; the lineup sports a new bassist as well. In a vain bid for commercial acceptance (Big Time having pacted with RCA for distribution and marketing), **For the Country** was produced in Wales by Hugh Jones. Dumptruck sounds stronger than ever: Tiven, now the sole writer, sings his dejected lyrics with a surprisingly determined edge, as a wall of strummed guitars and a loudly echoing backbeat surge behind him. He's certainly not a happy fellow: the irony of "Carefree," disgust of "Friends," anxiety and resignation of the delicately haunting "Dead Weight" are merely the tip of his melancholy iceberg. Involving and unsettling.   [i]

SLY DUNBAR
See *Sly & Robbie*.

DUNCAN DHU
Canciones (Sire) 1989 ●
Autobiografía (Sire) 1990 ●

Far from being the Basque revolutionaries of their press notices, this mild-mannered Spanish duo plays simple, hearty guitar pop (frequently with nothing more than a single acoustic) in a willy-nilly variety of idioms: bare-bones rockabilly, early Elvis Presley and the Everly Brothers, as well as more modern designs. (The only musical traditions that seem to have been overlooked are any that would reflect the group's national origin.) A compilation of the band's first three Spanish albums, **Canciones** wobbles all over the place with charming enthusiasm and great vocals, frequently suggesting a destylized translation of the Stray Cats or House of Freaks.

Under the tutelage of British producer Colin Fairley, Mikel Erentxun (guitar, vocals) and Diego Vasallo (vocals, bass) made **Autobiografía** with such sympathetic rockers as Nick Lowe, Brinsley Schwarz, Pete Thomas, Bruce Thomas and the Rumour Brass. Regardless of good crossover intentions, however, the tasteful assistance all but buries the band's personality, eliminating its eccentricities and erasing the look-ma-we-made-a-record! giddiness that surges through every groove of **Canciones**. As a further inducement to Anglo-American pop consumers, the LP includes a bonus EP (added to the CD and cassette as well) containing accented English renditions of three album tracks and one **Canciones** number.   [i]

DURAN DURAN
Duran Duran (Harvest) 1981 (Capitol) 1983 ●
Rio (Harvest) 1982 (Harvest-Mobile Fidelity) ●
Carnival EP (Harvest) 1982 ●
Seven and the Ragged Tiger (Capitol) 1983 ●
Arena (Capitol) 1984 ●
Notorious (Capitol) 1986 ●
Big Thing (Capitol) 1988 ●
Decade (Capitol) 1989 ●
Liberty (Capitol) 1990 ●

ARCADIA
So Red the Rose (Capitol) 1985 ●

ANDY TAYLOR
Thunder (MCA) 1987 ●
Dangerous (nr/A&M) 1990 ●

Although conceived as a mix of the Sex Pistols and Chic, Birmingham's Duran Duran was in fact launched as another pretty-boy-new-romantic-haircut-clothes-synth-pop-dance ensemble and became an unimaginably popular teen sensation, drawing young fans into the world of techno-dance music. Taking cues (sound and image) from early Roxy Music and using simple electronics to flavor the lush but powerful rock sound, Du-

ran Duran crossbred pop craft with a strong visual consciousness (using videos as a major strategic tool) to create records that are at once high-sheen disco and semi-inventive rock, even if that's not how the band and their followers view it.

Duran Duran introduced the dance attack in a remarkable sonic setting produced by Colin Thurston. Tracks like "Planet Earth," "Girls on Film" and "Is There Anyone Out There" meld the basic attributes of '70s disco—preeminent beat, repetition and studio gimmickry—to a variant on post-Ultravox rock to create something that was, at the time, fairly original. The elongated strains of synthesizer and syncopated tempos cover a multitude of creative shortcomings, but it's still an extraordinary album filled with now-classic songs.

Rio fulfills the band's potential, displaying stronger songwriting and far more intricate arrangements. The music's clearly danceable, but brilliantly listenable as well. Singer Simon Le Bon handles tantalizing melodies and obtuse lyrics with confidence (if not profound ability), while honestly proficient musicianship by the other four defines each song's character differently. There isn't anything less than good, and "Rio," "Last Chance on the Stairway" and "New Religion" are downright astonishing in their melodic excellence. Thanks to a remix that features prominent female moaning (and an exotic video), "Hungry Like the Wolf" caught American radio programmers' attention, and lofted the band high into the charts, where they long remained a well-appointed fixture.

Quick to recognize Duran's essential role as a dance band with rising commercial appeal, the group's US label released a package of four remixes ("Hungry Like the Wolf," "Girls on Film," "Hold Back the Rain" and "My Own Way") as **Carnival**.

Parting ways with Thurston, Duran attempted to expand their musical horizons beyond the lush ambience of **Rio** and developed a herky-jerky rhythmic style aimed at creating catchy singles in a variety of modes. Unfortunately, this led them to make the utterly detestable **Seven and the Ragged Tiger**, a sorry collection of half-baked melodies, meaningless lyrics (their earlier work, while not poetry, at least *sounded* clever) and over-active studio foolishness. Basically, the songs ain't no damn good. And even a passable item like "The Reflex" gets twisted with exaggerated, comical vocals; "Union of the Snake" sounds only half-written. The only truly noteworthy song, "New Moon on Monday," actually sounds like an outtake from **Rio**. Still, the album proved extremely successful among the audience who cheered the video monitors, not the band, during the tour that followed it.

Arena, the audio documentary of a mammoth coast-to-coast American trek, features surprisingly good playing (but extremely bad singing) on nine hits; additionally, the package (and I do mean package) includes a studio cut, "The Wild Boys," produced by Nile Rodgers, which resembles a possible theme song for *Lord of the Flies*. This album is irrelevant to anyone over the age of fifteen.

Duran Duran spent the next two years split into two camps. Taylor and Taylor (Andy and John) formed Power Station, while Simon, Nick and Roger stuck together, dubbing their sub-group Arcadia. Not surpris-

207

ingly, with the artistic troublemakers out of the picture, Arcadia's **So Red the Rose** (produced by the late Alex Sadkin and featuring guest spots by Sting, Herbie Hancock, David Van Tieghem, David Gilmour, Andy Mackay and others) is virtually an old-fashioned Duran Duran album. Not an especially good one, mind you, but it does sound a lot more like **Rio** than **Seven and the Ragged Tiger** does.

Although they had a number one single in mid-'85 with the theme song for a James Bond film ("A View to a Kill"), the group was in a transitional state. Roger left in 1986; Andy stayed long enough to play on four tracks on the next album before splitting for a solo career. That left Simon, Nick and John Taylor to carry the tattered but marketable banner, supported on **Notorious** by producer/guitarist Nile Rodgers (talk about realizing career ambitions), Missing Person guitarist Warren Cuccurullo and session drummer Steve Ferrone. A lack of material, a surplus of horns and the overall sterile pop/ funk precision leave Duran resembling a dull, toned-down Power Station with no songs. The title track isn't entirely horrible, but that's not much to hang an album on. (That same year, John Taylor wrote and recorded a big-selling solo single, "I Do What I Do," for the film *9 1/2 Weeks*.)

Critics might have written the group off by that point, but somebody bought a million copies of **Notorious**, granting the group license to make the even worse **Big Thing**. Again towing Cuccurullo and Ferrone, the trio sleepwalks through an utterly unmemorable collection of rote retreads, complete with premature middle-age-crisis sexual stupidity (from the same school as the Who's similarly titled **It's Hard**) and brief instrumental interludes. A total waste of time.

The appearance of **Decade**, a selective but solid singles compilation with cover by fashion designer Stephen Sprouse, underscored the group's flagging creative momentum and raised the possibility that the not-so-wild boys might have called it quits.

No such luck. The best that can be said about **Liberty** (unveiling Cuccurullo and drummer Sterling Campbell as permanent members) is that it doesn't sound much like **Notorious** or **Big Thing**. Chris Kimsey's lively, down-to-business production avoids those albums' obvious sonic vapidity. A senseless collision of standard Duran/Power Station funk, tuneless guitar raunch (!), Motown-inflected soul pop ("Violence of Summer (Love's Taking Over)" sounds like the B-52's interpreting Joe Jackson), numbing dance grooves, **Rio**-style lushness and even (now here's a great idea) found-sound audio collage, **Liberty** is accessibly idiotic, with lyrics that set new standards for pretensions gone out of bounds. Typical of Le Bon's crimes against intelligence, taste and dignity: "Divine blasphemer tempting/holy beads of jism/with the scarlet catechism . . . " Yeuch!

Andy Taylor's solo career got off to a quick and weird start in mid-'86 when he scored a minor hit single with "Take It Easy," a song for the *American Anthem* soundtrack. Unlike anything else in his past work, the song unnervingly resembles the Bellamy Brothers' 1976 easy-listening smash, "Let Your Love Flow."

Although Taylor's name alone graces the cover of **Thunder**, ex-Pistol Steve Jones co-wrote, co-produced and played half the guitar on it. Impressionable Durannies must have plotzed upon hearing their beloved fash-

ion plate roaring through demi-metal rock songs. Pathetic stabs at incorporating echoes of Duran and Power Station aside, the pair's power chords (and even some of the solos) ring loud and true, giving the louder songs conviction, if not artistic merit.   [i]

See also *Power Station*.

DURANGO 95
Lose Control (Can. Star) 1983
Dreams and Trains EP (Stonegarden) 1986
Mothers Day (Can. Star) 1990

PURPLE TOADS
Purple Toads (Can. Star) 1986
Love Songs for the Hard of Hearing (Can. Star) 1988

These five garage-punk wiseacres from Oshawa, Ontario, must have been raised on a strict diet of the Shadows of Knight. Greg Weir has a semi-whiny teen voice that blends efficiently with the band's restrained roar on **Lose Control**. Not spectacular, but good fun.

Before splitting (the two guitarists and bassist went on to form the Purple Toads) in 1984, the Durangos cut a fun-filled second album that wasn't issued until six years later. **Mothers Day** pushes less-stylized/less-funny/more-confident/more-mature rock'n'roll (Weir's voice is a lot easier to take this time around) on such charging originals as "Cats Aren't Like People," "Hangin' from a Tree" and "Waking Up Stoned."

The Purple Toads play '60s punk classics ("You're Gonna Miss Me," "Sometimes Good Guys Don't Wear White," "Nobody but Me," etc.) and garagey originals ("You Got Money") with unfettered enthusiasm and solid skill on the excellent **Purple Toads**; guitarists Paul MacNeil and Rob Sweeney can get a good Yardbirds-style R&B fire going. With the exception of "Tobacco Road" and three others, the raunchier-sounding **Love Songs** is entirely (and effectively) self-penned.   [i]

DURUTTI COLUMN
The Return of the Durutti Column (nr/Factory) 1979 ●
LC (nr/Factory) 1981 ●
Another Setting (nr/Factory) 1982 ●
Live at the Venue, London (nr/VU) 1983
Amigos in Portugal (Portuguese Fundacio Atlantica) 1984
Without Mercy (nr/Factory) 1984 ●
Say What You Mean, Mean What You Say EP
    (nr/Factory) 1985 ●
Domo Arigato [CD] (nr/Factory) 1985 ●
Circuses and Bread (nr/Factory) 1985 ●
Valuable Passages (Factory-Relativity) 1986 ●
Live at the Bottom Line New York [tape] (ROIR) 1987
The Guitar and Other Machines (Venture-Virgin) 1988 ●
The First Four Albums [CD] (nr/Factory) 1988 ●
Vini Reilly (nr/Factory) 1989 ●
Obey the Time (nr/Factory) 1990 ●

VINI REILLY
The Sporadic Recordings [CD] (nr/Sporadic) 1989 ●

Durutti Column—the historical name comes from the Spanish Civil War—is essentially guitarist Manchester Vini Reilly (who began his career as a punk, in the late-'70s Ed Banger & the Nosebleeds), although he has used other musicians in the studio and tours with other players. In the late '80s, Reilly branched out, backing

Morrissey (another Nosebleeds alumnus, as it happens) on his first solo record and working on an assortment of projects.

Producer Martin Hannett deserves equal credit on **The Return of the Durutti Column**, a perversely titled debut of evocative guitar instrumentals, many multi-tracked and accented with environmental, synthetic and studio-created percussive effects. Occasionally reminiscent of Mike Oldfield's **Tubular Bells** and some of the Frippertronics recordings, Reilly pretty much creates his own style—a gentle, uncluttered amalgam of acoustic and electric guitar textures.

Hannett is absent from the self-produced **LC**, Bruce Mitchell plays drums in spots and Reilly, regrettably, "sings" on a couple of the tracks, all of which makes it the lesser of Reilly's first two works, although the instrumentals still provide pleasant listening.

Continuing to experiment with various approaches, Reilly incorporated a cor anglais (English horn) player on **Another Setting**. The first of the two side-long pieces that comprise **Without Mercy** is like modern chamber music, an ambitious and shifting mixture of piano, horns, strings and electronic percussion. The second, which favors guitar, employs an entire studio group, including Blaine Reininger of Tuxedomoon.

While hardly raucous, Reilly moved further away from his ambient roots on **Say What You Mean**: deep, heavy electronic (or treated) percussion is annoyingly high in the mix on most of the six tracks. The record's highlight, "Silence," starts out sparsely, with electronic piano and marimba, and builds nicely with the addition of drums, trumpet, slide guitar and Reilly's much-improved voice. Although his vinyl output is perhaps more prolific than his creativity, Reilly is capable of producing rewarding music.

The airy and alluring 70-minute-long **Domo Arigato** CD, recorded live at a 1985 Tokyo concert appearance by Reilly (singing and playing a bit of piano), drummer Mitchell (doubling on xylophone), John Metcalfe (viola) and Tim Kellett (trumpet), draws its material from all of DC's prior releases and has beautifully clear sound. Offering an equally comprehensive review of the studio albums, the smartly compiled **Valuable Passages** adds a previously unreleased item and assorted rarities (from singles, etc.), making it the perfect introduction to Reilly's soothing atmospherics. For the complete review of the Durutti Column's early work, **The First Four Albums** is a four-CD repackage (in one jewelbox) of **The Return**, **LC**, **Another Setting**, **Without Mercy** and **Say What You Mean**.

Circuses and Bread finds Reilly again constructing layers of repetitive guitar figures with varying mixtures of other ingredients—drums, viola, piano, vocals, horns, sound effects—to help differentiate the tracks. In two groundbreaking tracks, "Hilary" is the loudest, most aggressive thing he has ever recorded, while "Royal Infirmary," a somber mood piece played on piano and punctuated by the sound of automatic rifle fire, has no guitar at all.

The live-in-New York cassette finds Reilly, backed by Mitchell and Metcalfe, playing piano and treated guitar on a career-spanning program (with little overlap of **Domo Arigato**'s song selection) of tasteful instrumentals that suffers from an inordinate amount of tape hiss.

Some of the new material presented at that late-'86 show wound up being recorded for **The Guitar and Other Machines**, which also relies on Mitchell and Metcalfe (plus others to a lesser degree) for studio support. The eleven pieces (three with guest vocals) are as sonically adventurous as anything Reilly has ever attempted. While remaining inside the group's traditional parameters, this ambitious record increases his emotional reach.

Using three guest vocalists, **Vini Reilly** (also available on DAT) is Reilly's most accomplished effort yet, but it also reveals his creative dilemma (or options, depending on one's point of view). While the strong infrastructure of "Love No More" shows real compositional development, "Pol in G" is just another meandering doodle with no backbone. But then there's the suave theatricality of "Opera I," the bass-driven funk of "People's Pleasure Park" and the Stonesy chord work of "Red Square." Each approach (echoed on other tracks) is valid and intriguing in its way, but such haphazard variety leaves the album—and, by extension, the artist—without any clear direction or focus. [ds/dgs/i]

See also *Morrissey*.

IAN DURY

New Boots and Panties!! (Stiff) 1977 (nr/Demon) 1986 ●
Lord Upminster (Polydor) 1981 (nr/Great Expectations) 1990 ●
Apples (nr/WEA) 1989 ●

IAN DURY & THE BLOCKHEADS

Do It Yourself (Stiff-Epic) 1979 (nr/Demon) 1990 ●
Laughter (Stiff-Epic) 1980
Jukebox Dury (Stiff America) 1981
Greatest Hits (nr/Fame) 1982
Sex & Drugs & Rock & Roll (nr/Demon) 1986 ●
Warts'n'Audience (nr/Demon) 1991 ●

IAN DURY AND THE MUSIC STUDENTS

4000 Weeks' Holiday (nr/Polydor) 1984 (nr/Great Expectations) 1990 ●

Stunted in growth, crippled by polio and unrepentantly Cockney, Ian Dury is one of rock's most memorable (and certainly lovable) figures. Hardly a newcomer in 1977—the 35-year old had already been around with Kilburn and the High Roads—Dury came into his own with **New Boots and Panties!!**, an album whose energy almost defies it to stay on the turntable. With the motley but talented Blockheads, Dury trounces merrily through outrageous odes like "Plaistow Patricia," "Billericay Dickie," "Blockheads" and the anthemic "Sex & Drugs & Rock & Roll" (not on the original UK LP, but added to the American edition and later to the British as well). A more sensitive side emerges lyrically on "Sweet Gene Vincent," "My Old Man" and "If I Was with a Woman" and musically on "Wake Up and Make Love with Me."

Dury and the Blockheads' disco leanings came to the fore on the dazzling **Do It Yourself**. The band's rich interweaving behind Dury's playfully obscure vocals may have meant sensory overload for some, and the more sophisticated music (compared to **New Boots**' often raucous blare) must have turned away the punk cadres. With hindsight, though, **Do It Yourself** can be heard as a trailblazing fusion of dance musics, in both upbeat ("Sink My Boats," "Dance of the Screamers") and relaxed ("Inbetweenies," "Lullaby for Francies") modes.

Blockhead musical director Chaz Jankel left after **Do It Yourself**, but the band carried on with thinner textures and ex-Feelgood guitarist Wilko Johnson. (Jankel subsequently pursued a dull solo career as a pianist/singer.) **Laughter** is an uneasy and uneven mix of whimsical concepts like "Yes & No (Paula)," "Dance of the Crackpots" and "Over the Points," as well as less-inspired funk-rock like "(Take Your Elbow Out of the Soup You're Sitting on the Chicken)" and "Sueperman's Big Sister."

Dury abandoned Stiff and scuttled the Blockheads, but reunited with Jankel for **Lord Upminster**, recorded in the Bahamas with reggae rhythm kingpins Robbie Shakespeare and Sly Dunbar. After the Blockheads' joyful noise, **Lord Upminster**'s funk sounds ascetic. (Keyboard player Tyrone Downie is the only other musician.) Disappointingly, Dury scales down his writing for the occasion, approaching minimalist levels on "Wait (For Me)" and "Trust (Is a Must)." Aside from the exceedingly frank "Spasticus (Autisticus)," the record amounts to a creative holding pattern.

It took Dury three years to bang out another, this time with a mostly unfamiliar set of sidemen working under the ironic Music Students moniker. The homemade-look cover of **4000 Weeks' Holiday** belies the slickly produced soul tracks inside; only Dury's homey speak-singing connects the songs to a non-mainstream aesthetic. Lyrically conservative as well, Dury waxes romantic ("You're My Inspiration"), treacly ("Friends"), political ("Ban the Bomb") and noirish ("The Man with No Face") and whimsical ("Take Me to the Cleaners").

Reuniting with Mickey Gallagher, Davey Payne and a host of other old mates (Steve Nieve and Wreckless Eric both guest), Dury broke a five-year recording silence with the charming and gentle **Apples**. While the lightly flavored arrangements leave the songs (mostly Dury/Gallagher compositions) on the pleasant side of mild, Dury's personable vocals provide all the character needed. (Frances Ruffelle duets on several tracks and sings one solo.) In any case, Dury's lyrics—with the exception of "Love Is All" ("My fevered brow is bursting till I choke"???)—are wonderful. Besides satiric slaps at tabloid reporters ("Byline Browne") and novice policemen ("Pc Honey"), he considers the labor problems faced by criminals ("The Right People"), offers a laundry list of British celebrities ("England's Glory") and rewrites the Lord's Prayer with homonymic place names ("Bus Driver's Prayer").

In his prime, Dury worked best outside the album format. "Hit Me with Your Rhythm Stick" was hastily added to **Do It Yourself** as a bonus 45; "Reasons to Be Cheerful (Part 3)" fell between **Do It Yourself** and **Laughter**. Although it could be ungenerously interpreted merely as Stiff's last chance to cash in, **Jukebox Dury** (reissued as **Greatest Hits**) is also the best and most consistent Dury LP. Besides the two hits just mentioned, it has other fine 45 sides ("What a Waste," "Razzle in My Pocket," "Common as Muck") and a few choice album cuts. Dury's humanism comes through loud and clear, and the record is programmed swell.

Created as a complement to **New Boots and Panties!!**, the **Sex & Drugs** compilation is almost identical to **Jukebox Dury** except that it omits "Sweet Gene Vincent" and "Wake Up and Make Love to Me" in favor of "Sueperman's Big Sister" and "You're More Than Fair." The CD has four bonus tracks. **Warts'n' Audience** is a live LP from December 1990.   [si/i]

DWARVES
Horror Stories (Voxx) 1986
Toolin' for a Warm Teabag (Nasty Gash) 1988
Astro Boy EP (Sub Pop) 1990
Blood Guts & Pussy (Sub Pop) 1990 ●
Lucifer's Crank EP (No. 6) 1991

SUBURBAN NIGHTMARE
A Hard Day's Nightmare (Midnight) 1985

Proponents of an extremist wing of the less-is-more school of thought, the Dwarves have wreaked much underground havoc with highly confrontational (often blood-soaked) live sets that are over in ten minutes, and "longplayers" of acute political incorrectness which don't last even twice that. If there weren't so much action here—imagine watching *The Evil Dead* on fastforward—these San Francisco-via-Chicago neo-punks might be just another bunch of exhibitionists.

The Dwarves downplay the existence of **Horror Stories** which, all things considered, is solid reasoning. Captured in transition from teen Zappaphiles to circusfreak speedballers, the quartet strains against the flowerpower leash, but never manages to break free. What followed, however, is a metamorphosis as ungodly as any in the annals of rock'n'roll. **Toolin' for a Warm Teabag** lasts but nine minutes, but that's enough time for the Dwarves to slash through seven post-hardcore incantations ("Free Cocaine," "Let's Get Pregnant," etc.) that effectively exorcise any prior embarrassments.

You might think that **Blood Guts & Pussy**'s title (along with the calculated offense of a cover that depicts two women and a *real* dwarf, all nude and drenched in type-O claret) tells you all you need to know about the disc. Think again. Unexpectedly tight and musicianly (especially guitarist He Who Cannot Be Named), the Dwarves reveal themselves as informed pop students. Pushed along by the yammering vocals of Blag Jesus (aka Julius Seizure), these eleven tracks (fifteen minutes this time) are constantly on the verge of falling apart. But somehow, that translates into immensely powerful forward propulsion. The CD includes two non-LP tracks from the 7-inch **Astro Boy**.

A Hard Day's Nightmare is the real wild card here. Recorded before the renamed band's move to California, it's more or less a drug-sodden update of **Cruisin' with Ruben and the Jets**, sound-collage splatter oozing between relatively straightforward bits of Farfisa-tinged psychobilly. The disc is more clever than outrageous; a song called "6" brags "I ain't gonna be no average dick." And while a cover of "Brand New Cadillac" may have appealed to revivalists, there's nothing old-fashioned about an album whose sides are titled "Sex" and "Sex & Drugs."

The **Lucifer's Crank** 7-inch compiles seven alternate takes of songs from the past three records, plus a devolved obliteration of Red Crayola's "Hurricane Fighter Plane."   [dss]

DYS

Wolfpack (Taang!) 1983
DYS (Taang!) 1984

Although probably better known for his stints in Washington DC's Dag Nasty and California's All, Dave Smalley began his career in Boston, with a hardcore band ironically named for the city's Department of Youth Services. On **Wolfpack**, as DYS expounds the judgmentally self-righteous straight-edge ethos (i.e., no drugs, no drink) that became popular in both Boston and DC, Smalley comes off as an admirable idealist and a terrible singer. Though the debut could simply be tagged and shelved as a chunk of tolerable hardcore, it does contain some bright spots, most notably "Escape," a metalized dirge with heavily delayed vocals. The album also displays a sense of humor—not a common straight-edge commodity—in an ad-libbed cover of "Ironman" and a pair of parodies ("Dirty Dog" and "Rub a Dub").

Satire seemed to suit the band, and **DYS** is pure metal mockery. (Or is it?) Either a good joke badly executed or a bad idea through and through, the record has a real scary cover and appropriately styled vocals. Funny or not, it just isn't any good. [icm]

See also *All, Dag Nasty.*

211

EASTERHOUSE

In Our Own Hands EP (nr/London) 1985
Inspiration EP (nr/Rough Trade) 1986
Contenders (Rough Trade-Columbia) 1986 ●
Waiting for the Redbird (Rough Trade-Columbia)
1989 ●

Easterhouse's original incarnation—a Manchester quintet led by argumentative brothers Andy (vocals/lyrics) and Ivor (guitar) Perry—turned strident leftist rhetoric into bracing, cathartic music before predictably imploding over ideological conflicts. The band's demise was a shame, since Easterhouse seemed well on its way towards perfecting a brand of explicitly political rock that compromised neither music nor message.

The four-track **In Our Own Hands** is a commanding debut, bursting with musical energy and topical fervor. **Inspiration** examines the troubles in Northern Ireland with convincing passion, while giving Ivor a convincing framework for his spidery guitar lines. Two **Inspiration** numbers—the title song and "Nineteen Sixty Nine"—later showed up on Easterhouse's longplay debut.

Contenders, Easterhouse's abortive shot at US success, almost makes good on the band's lofty goals. Their lyrical concerns are compelling and clear without falling prey to sloganeering or anthem-mongering. The music is both melodic and muscular, lending authority to Andy's regret-tinged broadsides. Songs like "Out on Your Own," "To Live Like This" and "Cargo of Souls" vilify various institutions (including England's Labour Party) without losing sight of the human cost of governmental oppression. (The English CD adds two songs not on the American LP or CD.)

Ruminations on the contradictions inherent in a revolutionary communist band's affiliation with a multinational entertainment megalith were put on hold when Easterhouse's initial lineup fell apart not long after **Contender**'s US release. Ivor Perry and drummer Gary Rostock briefly (one single on UK Rough Trade) reemerged in a new band called the Cradle, with ex-Aztec Camera/Smiths guitarist Craig Gannon.

Andy Perry, meanwhile, held onto the Easterhouse name and released **Waiting for the Redbird**, a virtual solo album whose slick, processed studio sound couldn't be further from the five piece's bare-wires approach. Perry's lyrics remain singleminded and lucid enough for his extremism to be intermittently compelling. Ultimately, though, without a commanding musical identity to match his exhortations, the one-dimensional dogma rings hollow. Wicked Irony Department: **Redbird**'s anthemic "Come Out Fighting" was briefly adopted as an all-purpose go-for-it anthem by unsuspecting American TV sports programs. [hd]

EASTERN BLOC

Wall to Wall EP (Chetnick) 1986
Eastern Bloc (Paradox-Passport) 1987 ●

These three New York scene veterans—bassist Ivan Kral, guitarist Mark Sidgwick and drummer Frankie LaRocka—have individually backed the likes of Patti Smith, Iggy Pop, David Johansen, Holly Vincent, Tim Scott and John Waite. Their own band's album, while not exactly a groundbreaker, is a thoroughly respectable melodic rock collection that reflects the years they've spent in the trenches. Sidgwick has a pleasant if limited voice and his guitar playing is both fiery and flexible; the rhythm section is dexterous and inventive. A Pink Floyd-speed version of Kral's estimable 1979 Smith collaboration, "Dancing Barefoot," is odd enough to work; the Sidgwick/Kral originals could use smarter lyrics, but don't want for hooks or commercial craft. [i]

See also *Holly and the Italians, David Johansen, Patti Smith.*

EASTERN DARK

See *Celibate Rifles.*

EAST OF EDEN

East of Eden (Echo Chamber-Capitol) 1989 ●

Slick and soul-free, this Boston quintet (with a recycled name: no relation to the '70s British rock-with-violin band) fronted by singer/songwriter Cinde Lager displays an efficiently modern keyboard/guitar sound—equally beholden (indirectly) to the Pretenders and Simple Minds—and weak material on its dull debut, produced by Roy Thomas Baker. [i]

ELLIOT EASTON

See *Cars.*

EAT

Sell Me a God (Fiction-PolyGram) 1989 ●

Lauded in Britain but virtually unknown in the States, this Bath-born/London-formed quintet's first LP is one of the most impressive debuts of recent years. Merging elements from bands as diverse as the Doors, Gang of Four and Big Audio Dynamite, Eat created an instantly familiar record that ultimately sounds like no one else. From the spaghetti western blues crunch of "Tombstone" and "Walking Man" to the swampy rap of "Stories" and "Things I Need," Eat marries hip-hop technology to an ersatz bayou-bred instinct. Lyrically, **Sell Me a God** conjures up seamy abstract imagery in the tradition of scuzz-poet Jim Morrison; what may read as pretentious drivel on paper *sounds* just right. (The

CD adds two sweaty funk tracks and a strong, hard take on the Lovin' Spoonful's "Summer in the City.")

Eat recorded a second album, but split up in November 1990, leaving its release in limbo. [db]

EATER
The Album (nr/The Label) 1977
Get Your Yo Yos Out EP (nr/The Label) 1978
The History of Eater Vol. I (nr/DeLorean) 1985

British punk became a true youth movement in 1976 upon the arrival of Eater, a London group with 13-year-old drummer Dee Generate. (The other members were 15 at the time.) Although not taken seriously at first, the unwitting stars of Don Letts' *Punk Movie* (responsible for the ridiculous pig-head scene) released two credible and likable 45s: "Outside View" (after which Generate was replaced by the more talented, and slightly older Phil Rowland, who joined Slaughter and the Dogs when Eater split in '78) and the punk classic "Thinking of the U.S.A."

The album that followed is uneven but spirited. "Lock It Up" (another choice 45), "Public Toys," "No More" and an improved version of "Outside View"'s B-side ("You") join hilariously trashy sped-up covers of the Velvets' "Waiting for the Man" and "Sweet Jane," Bowie's "Queen Bitch" and Alice Cooper's "18" rejuvenated as "15." Andy Blade's vocals are Lou Reed deadpan, Brian Chevette's guitar is raspy and simple, and Ian Woodcock's bass runs along with stunning velocity.

Get Your Yo Yos Out is an unremarkable four-song live outing, though it does contain two numbers never released in studio form. While **The History of Eater** is mostly a reprise of **The Album** with a few added 45 tracks, it includes a bonus 7-inch, credited to Eater, of a Blade solo single, recorded in the mid-'80s with ex-Damned guitarist Brian James. A second volume of rare and live Eater material was announced but never appeared. [jr]

EAZY-E
See *N.W.A.*

ECHO & THE BUNNYMEN
Crocodiles (Sire) 1980 ●
Shine So Hard EP (nr/Korova) 1981
Heaven Up Here (Korova-Sire) 1981 ●
Porcupine (Korova-Sire) 1983 ●
Echo and the Bunnymen EP (Korova-Sire) 1983
The Cutter [tape] EP (nr/Korova) 1983
Seven Seas EP (nr/Korova) 1984
Ocean Rain (Korova-Sire) 1984 ●
Songs to Learn & Sing (Korova-Sire) 1985 ●
Echo & the Bunnymen (Sire) 1987 ●
Bedbugs & Ballyhoo EP (Sire) 1988
The Peel Sessions EP (nr/Strange Fruit) 1988 ●

WILL SERGEANT
Themes for Grind (nr/92 Happy Customers) 1982

BALCONY DOGS
Trip (nr/Bloodline-Island) 1988 ●

IAN MCCULLOCH
Candleland (Sire-Reprise) 1989 ●
Faith & Healing (Remix) EP (nr/WEA) 1989 ●
Candleland (The Second Coming) EP (nr/East West) 1990 ●

This vanguard foursome—at its late-'78 start a trio plus Echo the drum machine—emerged from Liverpool's new wave renaissance with a debut album stunning in its starkness and power. Unlike also-rans with the same idea, Ian McCulloch's specter-of-Jim Morrison vocals are no mere pilferage; where Morrison would have ordered you on your knees, Mac does it himself, alternately writhing in resistance or slumped in resignation to the agonies of an entirely different decade. On **Crocodiles**, Will Sergeant's scratchy, yet ringing, guitar and Pete De Freitas' unhurriedly relentless pounding drums set the sonic scene for McCulloch's ambivalently delivered existential crises. (The US album adds "Do It Clean" and "Read It in Books," both originally UK B-sides.)

The four songs on **Shine So Hard** come from the soundtrack to a half-hour film of a specially staged concert (admittedly a logistic and musical disappointment), and mostly serves to preview the upcoming LP in lackluster fashion. But in its own right, the gloom engulfing **Heaven Up Here** seems to have smothered the band's cogency, with McCulloch less a fist-shaker than a whiner. The old potency is still audible at times (mainly on Side One) but, like McCulloch, the guitars sound fragile, even brittle; overall, it's a dreamy, depressed and depressing effort.

Echo's third LP is far more enthralling, an invigorating collection of bizarre, challenging songs given surprising but fitting color by the addition of violinist Shankar's offbeat wailings. Sweeping creations like "The Cutter" and "The Back of Love" are tremendously exciting; the rest of **Porcupine**, if not as consistently memorable, captures the band's unique essence with grace and style. New-found efficiency dispatches past self-indulgent inaccessibility.

The even-better **Ocean Rain** exchanges Shankar's unique contribution for more routine string accompaniment, but offers an amazing skein of great songwriting. "Silver," "Crystal Days," "Seven Seas" and "The Killing Moon" all achieve the ideal marriage of pop with drama, using McCulloch's strong vocal presence and Sergeant's varied and textural guitar work to imbue the songs with majesty and subtlety.

Concisely recapitulating the band's first five years, **Songs to Learn & Sing** is a welcome retrospective: nine essential items, a fine new tune ("Bring on the Dancing Horses") and "The Puppet," Echo's third single (from 1980), which had not been on any previous US release. The CD and cassette have four bonus tracks.

The all-great eponymous 1983 EP contains "The Cutter" and "Back of Love" (from **Porcupine**), "Rescue" (from **Crocodiles**), "Never Stop" (a 1983 single) plus a live version of "Do It Clean" from the Royal Albert Hall. **The Cutter** cassette, which contains the title tune plus four live Peel session tracks, was also packaged in with initial UK quantities of **Porcupine**. The **Seven Seas** EP is available as a five-song 12-inch (with LP tracks from **Ocean Rain** and **Crocodiles**) and as a seven-song doublepack 45. The Peel session EP predates the first LP, and contains live-in-the-studio renditions of "Read It in Books," "Villiers Terrace" and two other songs.

De Freitas briefly left Echo (ex-Haircut One Hundred drummer Blair Cunningham took his place) in 1986 but was back in the lineup in time for **Echo & the Bunnymen**, a solid and mature album which gains momentum as it plays. Produced by Laurie Latham, engaging, reflective songs—"Lips Like Sugar," "Lost and Found," "New Direction" and "All in Your Mind"—show the Bunnymen's ongoing refinement and consistent quality; the band acknowledges its debt to the Doors by prominently featuring Ray Manzarek, one of several guest keyboardists the record employs, on the distinctly reminiscent "Bedbugs and Ballyhoo." That track (in its LP version and an elongated remix) was subsequently issued as one side of an EP, the flipside of which offers three spiffy live covers: "Paint It Black," the Velvet Underground's "Run, Run, Run" and Television's "Friction." (In a similar vein, Echo contributed a version of the Doors' "People Are Strange" to *The Lost Boys'* soundtrack.)

In 1982, Sergeant self-released **Themes for Grind**, a noodly instrumental solo album originally created to accompany a film project that was never completed. In 1988, the Balcony Dogs (successor to the abortive Sex Gods, the band De Freitas formed with two members of the Bunnymen road crew during his sabbatical) released **Trip**, a surprisingly good record on which the drummer plays only a minor role. Putting an intermittent psychedelic '60s spin on casual guitar pop (with strong nods to Echo, the Doors and other relevant referents), the Balcony Dogs—with genealogical connections to many Liverpool luminaries—sound a bit like Bunnymen fans trying to impress themselves, but the playing and singing displays such ingenuous enthusiasm that the LP is hard to resist.

McCulloch quit in mid-'88, picked up a guitar and began writing songs for his first solo album. Released late the following year, The alluring **Candleland**, atmospherically produced by Ray Shulman, distills the dreamy rock sound of **Echo & the Bunnymen** while preserving the band's sweeping melodies and guitar hooks. His expressive vocals, surprisingly good guitar playing and resonantly emotional lyrics (the haunting "Start Again" bids farewell to his late father, De Freitas, who died in a 1989 accident, and another friend who passed away) make such excellent new songs as "Flickering Wall," "White Hotel" and "Proud to Fall" immediately familiar; varied arrangements turn others (like "Faith and Healing," "The Cape" and the waltz-time "I Know You Well") into everything from orchestrated balladry to New Orderized dance-pop. With only one serious flaw—the songs' elementary chord patterns—**Candleland** is a magnificent record.

Besides an incidental remix of the title song, the **Faith & Healing** EP offers a trio of non-LP tracks produced by McCulloch and performed with his hard-rocking touring band, the Prodigal Sons. Two of the tunes are lame, but "Rocket Ship" is brilliant. The **Candleland** EP contains a sturdier version of the album's evanescent title track (again featuring vocals by Cocteau Twin Elizabeth Fraser) as well as three fine new songs. [jg/i]

ECHO & THE BUNNYMEN
Reverberation (Korova-Sire) 1990 ●
ST. VITUS DANCE
Love Me Love My Dogma (nr/Probe Plus) 1987

When Ian McCulloch left Echo and the Bunnymen, he fully expected that the group's decade-long saga had ended and that his bandmates would go their separate ways. He was wrong: the other three opted to keep the name and get themselves a new vocalist. Although De Freitas was killed in a June 1989 motorcycle accident (on the way to a rehearsal), Sergeant and bassist Les Pattinson pressed on with Irish singer/lyricist Noel Burke, longtime Echo adjunct Jake Brockman on keyboards and drummer Damon Reece. Unveiled in late '90, the new-look/new-sound Echo and the Bunnymen—unable to preserve the past *or* create anything substantially original—weakly attempt to catch up with history on the Geoff Emerick-produced **Reverberation**. Suspended between the familiar and the unreachable, and seemingly motivated mostly by bitterness towards McCulloch, the album offers imaginative performances of dull melodies and obvious second-person lyrics, all sprinkled with familiar musical moves. (Burke comes closest to aping Mac on "Thick Skinned World.") The sparkling "Enlighten Me" effectively kicks Madchester acid pop further into folky flower-power (with tabla and sitar for authenticity!); the rest of **Reverberation** is, as its title suggests, merely the decaying echo of an original sound.

Burke's prior band, St. Vitus Dance (not to be confused with the similarly named American group), was a charming Belfast sextet with good, simple songs and an abundance of shaggy personality. **Love Me Love My Dogma** is no technical masterpiece, but the clever common-sense lyrics ("I was a stable boy who grew to be a most unstable man") about Irish life, the jolly rock (credit Haydn Boyle's colorful piano/organ playing) music and Burke's lively vocals make this nifty item well worth finding. [i]

EDDIE AND THE HOT RODS
Live at the Marquee EP (nr/Island) 1976
Teenage Depression (Island) 1976
Life on the Line (Island) 1977
Thriller (nr/Island) 1979
Fish'n'Chips (EMI America) 1980
One Story Town EP (nr/Waterfront) 1985
The Curse of the Hot Rods (nr/Hound Dog) 1990

It may be difficult to hear now, but London's Eddie and the Hot Rods played a crucial role in the birth of new wave. If the Rods hadn't been out there playing wild and fast rock'n'roll in the clubs at a time when superstar pomposity was the currency of pop music, bands like the Sex Pistols would never have had the opportunity to join, intensify and broaden that rebellious spirit into a national—and international—musical upheaval.

Today, **Teenage Depression** sounds like a fairly tame set of R&B-influenced rock tunes, like early Flamin Groovies or Dave Edmunds, but in 1976 it had a major impact on the British music scene. The title track (a hit single there) is the record's finest moment. (The American album replaced two soul covers with four tracks that had appeared on the prior live 7-inch.)

For **Life on the Line**, the Rods expanded to a five-piece with the addition of ex-Kursaal Flyer Graeme Douglas. It was a wise move, as Douglas gave the band a smart kick in the pop direction, best exemplified on the wonderful "Do Anything You Wanna Do," which he co-wrote. Overall, a strong album (thanks to good songs and enthusiastic playing) that stands up much better than its predecessor.

By the time of **Thriller**, the Hot Rods weren't much more than an artifact. Rendered redundant by the bands they had inspired, they hadn't been able to keep pace with the changes. The album reeks with bitterness; although competent, it has neither the freshness of **Life on the Line** nor anything substantial to replace it. As a sign of the band's "maturity," Linda McCartney sang some backup parts.

With Al Kooper producing, a revised quartet (without Douglas or bassist Paul Gray) turned out an unnecessary fourth album that is best forgotten. Five years later, following a stint in the Inmates, two original Hot Rods—singer Barrie Masters and drummer Steve Nicol—put a new band together long enough to perform such classics as "Teenage Depression," "Quit This Town" and "Do Anything You Wanna Do" on the surprisingly good six-song **One Story Town**, recorded live and peppy in France.

Rounding things off, **The Curse of the Hot Rods** is an entertaining (if not especially illuminating) collection of 1979 studio outtakes and demos: the original group's last productive breath. A version of the Small Faces' "I Got Mine" is neat, as are some of the originals, especially those penned by Douglas (pop) and Gray (rock'n'roll). [i]

See also *Damned, Inmates*.

EDGE

See *Jane Aire and the Belvederes*.

DAMON EDGE

See *Chrome*.

ED GEIN'S CAR

Making Dick Dance (Ed Gein's Car) 1985
You Light Up My Liver/Live at CBGB! (CBGB-Celluloid) 1987

The lovable Ed Gein's Car epitomizes the spirit of New York punk. Not hardcore or speed-thrash, just good ol' greasy, gritty punk rock with a working class aesthetic. Despite a pronounced Misfits influence and the use of a gruesome serial killer's name, the band's lyrics shun the horror angle. Instead, the songs on **Making Dick Dance** focus on things like topical social problems ("Boo Fuckin' Hoo," about the Bernhard Goetz case), Ramonesian goofball humor (the nifty "Go Down on My Dog") and crude songs about women ("A Girl Just Like You"). Good Clash-like harmonies and Scott Weiss' rough, melodic lead vocals help put the tunes over.

Fittingly enough, the second album was recorded live at CBGB. While reprising most of **Making Dick Dance**, the program also includes a cool version of the Misfits' "Last Caress," two songs from the group's 1985 7-inch debut and a healthy batch of newies, led by the anti-Live Aid anthem "We're Not Your World." [gef]

ED HALL

Albert (Boner) 1988
Love Poke Here (Boner) 1990 ●

More noisy bizarros from Texas. On **Albert**, this obliquely named Austin trio—a tamer party-band alternative to the Butthole Surfers—throws out a goodnaturedly disorganized roar: Gary Chester's riffy distorto-guitar collapsing over Larry Strub's wobbly bass and Kevin Whitley's semi-sturdy drumming. The humorous lyrics on such topics as literature and dates are a lot more intellectually diverting than the inflamed (but not explosive) music.

Love Poke Here (actually, the cover leaves the title wide open to interpretation) continues the band's giddy blare, with louder, more conscientious arrangements and equally mischievous songs—about rich people's houses, "Buddha" and "Hearty Tom Foolery." [pn]

DAVE EDMUNDS

Rockpile (MAM) 1972
Subtle as a Flying Mallet (RCA) 1975
Dave Edmunds, Rocker: Early Works 1968/1972 (Fr. Parlophone-EMI) 1977
Get It (Swan Song) 1977 ●
Tracks on Wax 4 (Swan Song) 1978 ●
Repeat When Necessary (Swan Song) 1979 ●
Twangin . . . (Swan Song) 1981 ●
The Best of Dave Edmunds (Swan Song) 1981 ●
D.E. 7th (Columbia) 1982 ●
Information (Columbia) 1983
Riff Raff (Columbia) 1984
The Dave Edmunds Band Live: I Hear You Rockin' (Columbia) 1987 ●
Closer to the Flame (Capitol) 1990 ●

VARIOUS ARTISTS

Stardust (Arista) 1974
Porky's Revenge (Columbia) 1985 ●

Can traditional rock'n'roll survive in the modern world? As long as Dave Edmunds is around, the answer will be yes. A rousing singer, superlative guitarist and wizard producer, the Welsh native has preserved the simplicity and directness of '50s rock without ever sounding like a slavish revivalist. Along the way, he's also performed tricks with country music and even Phil Spector's elaborate constructions. Edmunds has had his ups and downs on record, but the one thing he's never been is pretentious.

Dave prefaced his solo career with two LPs as the leader of manic blues-psychedelic trio Love Sculpture. Those days are well documented on numerous compilations, the best being a two-disc French set, **Dave Edmunds, Rocker**.

Rockpile was recorded because Edmunds needed to make an LP to capitalize on his worldwide smash single, a one-man remake of "I Hear You Knockin'," a Dave Bartholomew number from the mid-'50s. This LP established the boundaries of the first phase of his solo career: a Chuck Berry tune, a Willie Dixon blues, a country stomp (by Neil Young, no less) and so on. **Rockpile** is a mishmash in terms of recording dates—one track was cut in 1966—and creation, with Edmunds playing almost all the instruments himself. No matter—it rocks like crazy.

Of the 40 cuts on the two-LP soundtrack/compilation for the David Essex film *Stardust*, seven are fine covers of oldies by Edmunds. A point to note here: six of those tracks are credited to the Stray Cats—years in advance of Brian Setzer's group.

By 1975, the unprolific Edmunds had a few more UK hits and enough other odds and ends to assemble another LP; unfortunately **Subtle as a Flying Mallet** doesn't hold together. The Everly Brothers' "Leave My Woman Alone" and a few other individual tracks work, but this is otherwise a largely lifeless record. The intricate one-man Spector homages ("Maybe," "Baby I Love You," etc.) are pretty but strained. Two tracks recorded live with Brinsley Schwarz point to the end of Edmunds' hibernation in the studio.

Get It lets air into the musty, old room of Edmunds' musical mind. Dave still laid down a lot of the tracks unaided, but also utilized the services of members of the Rumour and the now-defunct Brinsleys, forming a significant partnership with the latter's Nick Lowe. Highlights of this bright-sounding LP include Lowe's Chuck Berry rewrite, "I Knew the Bride," and the Lowe/Edmunds sprightly salute to the Everly Brothers, "Here Comes the Weekend."

Tracks on Wax 4 hardens and intensifies the attack, fully freeing Edmunds from the negative aspects of his nostalgic leanings. Give credit for that to the formation of Rockpile, a hard-working band composed of Edmunds, Lowe on bass, guitarist Billy Bremner and drummer Terry Williams; over the following few years, Rockpile recorded both Lowe and Edmunds solo albums, then cut one under the group name before splintering. On **Tracks on Wax 4**, they drive Dave to new heights of rock'n'roll glory.

Perhaps his best effort, **Repeat When Necessary** follows the course set by **Tracks on Wax**, with a bit of country sweetening. Standouts: Elvis Costello's "Girls Talk," "Queen of Hearts" (later a hit for Juice Newton) and the sultry "Black Lagoon."

Following the acrimonious breakup of Rockpile, Edmunds rushed out **Twangin . . .** , a resounding disappointment. Despite the presence of a few pearls, this is clearly an inferior patchwork. Outtakes deserve to remain outtakes. The return to the claustrophobic one-man-band sound of his early days is particularly disheartening.

The Best of Dave Edmunds, thirteen tracks from the four Swan Song LPs, makes no chronological sense, but offers an impressive musical overview.

D.E. 7th marks a return to form. With a hot new supporting cast, Edmunds boogies like a happy man again. Springsteen's "From Small Things (Big Things One Day Come)" and a rip-roaring version of NRBQ's "Me and the Boys" lead the parade.

Information and **Riff Raff** comprise Edmunds' Jeff Lynne period: a horrendously ill-advised attempt to concoct slick, saleable "contemporary" product, with ELO leader Lynne acting as unlikely production/songwriting svengali. Though both albums have some good moments (the undeniably catchy "Slippin' Away" and an-

other fine NRBQ cover on the former; good Paul Brady and Four Tops tunes, plus the demented roller-rink extravaganza "Rules of the Game" on the latter), they're largely characterized by a glib, crass sensibility that's fundamentally at odds with the unselfconscious enthusiasm that's always driven Edmunds' best work.

In contrast to those discs, the **Porky's Revenge** soundtrack is—believe it or not—a fine collection of rootsy, unpretentious rock'n'roll. In addition to some sharp cuts of his own, Edmunds produced worthy tracks for Jeff Beck, George Harrison (a new Dylan tune), Clarence Clemons and a studio supergroup featuring Edmunds' former Swan Song mentor, Robert Plant.

Edmunds' artistic productivity may have dipped in the mid-'80s, but his career as a producer stayed hot all decade. He guided the latter-day Stray Cats to the top of the charts and fulfilled a longstanding ambition of working with the Everly Brothers by producing their 1984 comeback album. He produced k.d. lang's debut and a new Dion album, and even reunited with old cohort Nick Lowe to produce Basher's **Party of One**.

The unprepossessing but delectable **I Hear You Rockin'** was recorded live in London, New York and New Jersey with Edmunds' post-Rockpile band: veteran pub-rock pianist Geraint Watkins, guitarist Mickey Gee, bassist John David and drummer/engineer Dave Charles. Edmunds touches all the obvious bases with little fanfare (save some intrusive synthesizer), reprising the better half of his Swan Song compilation while adding "I Hear You Knocking," "Information," "Paralyzed," "Slipping Away" and a fine reading of Dion's "The Wanderer."

Closer to the Flame, Edmunds' first solo studio effort in six years, isn't quite the resounding comeback that one would hope for, but it's a big improvement over the Lynne-influenced discs, with convincing stops at rockabilly ("King of Love," "Sincerely") and R&B (the title song, "Test of Love"), plus a pair of songs each by pub-rock legend Micky Jupp and NRBQ's Al Anderson. [jy/i/hd]

See also *Rockpile*.

EEK-A-MOUSE

Wa-Do-Dem (Greensleeves) 1982 ●
Skidip! (Greensleeves) 1982 ●
The Mouse and the Man (Greensleeves) 1983
Mouseketeer (Greensleeves) 1984
Assasinator (RAS) 1984 ●
The King and I (RAS) 1985 ●
The Very Best of Eek-A-Mouse (nr/Greensleeves) 1987 ●
Mouse-a-Mania [CD] (RAS) 1988 ●
Eek-a-Nomics (RAS) 1988 ●

One of the biggest new solo reggae stars in the '80s, Eek-a-Mouse (Ripton Joseph Hylton) has no trouble maintaining a high profile. Not only is he six-foot-six, his distinctive voice is hard to miss: he sings with a nasal twang (like a higher-pitched version of Michael Rose), but punctuates his vocals with all sorts of syllabic thrusts, like reggae's answer to scat. The effect is both melodic and percussive—it keeps the groove moving forward. Eek's success is also attributable to the high quality of his records. He works primarily with Roots Radics, a popular Jamaican session band that's played behind Gregory Isaacs and countless others.

With Eek, however, the chemistry is unique—they seem to play better with him—and the power of their collaboration helps keep his albums consistent and special.

Above all, Eek is funny, a comic as well as social critic. **Wa-Do-Dem**, a smart debut, features the hit single of the same name. ("Wa do dem stare? Because she's too short and he's too tall.") **Skidip!** also has its share of hits ("Modelling Queen" and "You Na Love Reggae Music"), though the second side is a little thin. **Assassinator** is steady and strong, but boasts no outstanding tracks.

The Mouse and the Man and **Mouseketeer** are his best albums—assured and versatile. The first includes the epic tale of Eek's meeting with Mickey Mouse, "Modelling King" (a follow-up to his earlier hit) and a curious ditty called "Hitler." **Mouseketeer** features the journalistic "Star, Daily News or Gleaner," a song about anorexia and, for all who wondered, "How I Got Me Name." Not to be missed.

Eek's reign continues on **The King and I**, but he's stretching out a bit. Working with a number of musicians besides Roots Radics, the instrumentation is fuller (and includes some synthesizer), but hardly a drastic departure from his successful formula. **Mouse-a-Mania** is a CD-only compilation of tracks from **The King and I** and **Assassinator**.

The front cover of **Eek-a-Nomics** shows Mouse decked out in a tux, top hat and champagne; the back finds him on the skids, with ripped hand-me-down clothes. Besides the "The Freak," a hilarious, out-there dance single with *Addams Family* overtones, the album contains more of Eek-a-Mouse's usual stories and ravings.   [bk/aw]

EFFIGIES

Haunted Town EP (Autumn) 1981
We're Da Machine EP (Ruthless-Enigma) 1983
The Effigies EP (Ruthless-Enigma) 1984
For Ever Grounded (Ruthless-Enigma) 1984
Fly on a Wire (Fever-Enigma) 1985
Ink (Fever-Restless) 1986
Remains Nonviewable (Roadkill) 1989

The Effigies were the first band from Chicago's bald-'n'booted brigade to gain any out-of-town recognition, and rightfully so. The quartet's five-song debut EP (later reissued with an extra track as **The Effigies** EP) showcased their bold, taut, spare punk attack on real songs about adult concerns, with prophetic (for punk) metal guitar lacing through their best material, including the anthemic "Mob Clash."

Although flat production obscured the disc's strong points, the Effigies fuzzed up the guitar (simultaneously experimenting with acoustic) and moved it to the fore on **We're Da Machine**. The best songs on **For Ever Grounded**—a lyrically and rhythmically more diverse LP that even adds dance beats—wail with the urgency of a siren at night. Earl Letiecq's guitar screeches like whitewalls on sodden pavement—the raw nerve that keeps the Effigies' sound permanently on edge. Though sometimes seen as humorless and uncharismatic, the Effigies are solid and reliable.

Robert O'Connor stepped in to replace Letiecq, and the Effigies made a satisfying second album. One misguided disco-y track and a couple of wanky guitar solos

aside, **Fly on a Wire** (which includes a cover of Joy Division's "No Love Lost") is an arresting LP, characterized by singer John Kezdy's venomous delivery and the band's punky melodicism on such tracks as "Forever, I Know" and "The Eights."

More than any of the previous outings, **Ink** spotlights the Effigies' canny command of tuneful (if not exactly hooky) postpunk songwriting. "The Sound That Moves" and "Yes!" rock like nobody's business, and O'Connor's edgy playing and Kezdy's nervy shout keep everything just this side of speaker-shredding. The Effigies' most assured and accessible work, **Ink** cements the group's rep as one of Chi-town's finest.

Remains Nonviewable, which compiles the 1981 "Body Bag" single and selected cuts from the early records, is a must for folks unable to score those rarities. **Haunted Town**'s "Below the Drop," heard in this historical context, seems as potent a punk epiphany as has emerged from the movement.

Letiecq eventually rejoined the band, but 1990 saw Kezdy (whose law-school sabbatical led to the Effigies' low profile in the late '80s) joined in the Effigies by all three members of Bloodsport.   [ep/i/db]

See also *Bloodsport*.

EGGPLANT

Monkeybars (Dr. Dream) 1989 ●
Sad Astrology (Dr. Dream) 1990 ●

In an eternal quest for true human tenderness in song, this unassuming Southern California quartet explores avenues paved by Jonathan Richman and Daniel Johnston. Guitarists Jon Melkerson and Jeff Beals have the uncanny ability to spin tales of cheerful wistfulness.

On **Monkeybars**, Eggplant proves the Richman axiom that excessive volume and force are not required for soul-stirring rock'n'roll; an almost celebratory cover of Lou Reed's "Vicious" grooves comfortably nearby the not-too-vicious slagging of "Rolling Stones" and the mundane fantasy travelogue of "Goin to Maine." **Sad Astrology** sports bigger-budget, brighter production (by Russ Tolman) and more happy/sad beauties like "Unexpected" and "If You See the Real World Coming." The title cut deserves an award for Best Apocalyptic Love Song of 1990.   [sm]

MAX EIDER

See *Jazz Butcher*.

E∗I∗E∗I∗O

Land of Opportunity (Frontier) 1986
That Love Thang (Frontier) 1988 ●

Wisconsin's E∗I∗E∗I∗O is an "American Music" band in the tradition of Creedence Clearwater Revival and the Blasters. Like those two bands, their sound is an amalgam of rock'n'roll, rockabilly, country, blues and folk. They've also got a strong singer with an unmistakably individual voice in Steve Summers, two good songwriters (Summers and bassist Richard Szeluga) and a pair of shit-hot guitarists (one of whom had been in Off Broadway) and harmony vocalists who can sing like Byrds.

The uniformly excellent material on **Land of Opportunity** (co-produced by Steve Berlin) ranges from flat-out ravers ("Tear It Down," "Go West Young Man," "The Middle of November") to songs about the ups and downs of the road ("Me and Jesus Christ," "White Lines, Blue Skies, Black Top"), country life ("Blue Mountaintop") and, of course, love ("This Time," "Hello Heartache," "Get Back to Arkansas," "Every Word True"). The music's emotional intensity and physical excitement make this an essential record. (The cassette adds "Stars Are Out and the Moon Is High" and "No Father in the Family.")

With guitarist Mike Hoffman gone off to form Semi-Twang, the group uses **That Love Thang** to expand its sound further, adding a propulsive R&B-type horn section (on the wonderful "Hey, Cecelie" and the title track) and strings (for the LP's ambitious closer "Brother Michael"). While some of the songs here are a bit less involving than on **Land of Opportunity**, this is another fine record. (The cassette and CD append "You Can't Stay Here.") [ds]

8 EYED SPY
Live [tape] (ROIR) 1981
8 Eyed Spy (nr/Fetish) 1981
LYDIA LUNCH
Hysterie (nr/Widowspeak) 1986 (CD Presents) 1986

Perhaps the acme of New York no wave groups, 8 Eyed Spy briefly collected the talents of Lydia Lunch, bassist-turned-drummer Jim Sclavunos, ace bassist George Scott, sax and guitar player Pat Irwin and guitarist Michael Paumgarden. Considerably less shrill than other similarly conceived groups, 8 Eyed Spy was nonetheless dominated by Lunch's confrontational vocals and lyrics and Irwin's insistent quasi-jazz sax. On **Live**, it becomes apparent that Lunch's style is mutilated blues (especially on the Beefheart-inspired opener, "Diddy Wah Diddy") and that Sclavunos and Scott's flawless collaboration is the band's axis. The blend of influences (jazz/blues/rock) creates exciting music that is beyond description.

8 Eyed Spy contains much of the same material as the cassette and is split into a live side and a studio side. While the former (which includes a hilarious version of "White Rabbit") shows the same gifted chaos apparent on **Live**, the latter proves 8 Eyed Spy capable of considerable restraint and polish. While the tone of the studio work implies an increasing reliance on jazz, the drumming rivets it to danceable rock. There is the hint of an impending breakthrough in these recordings, but the band dissolved in the wake of George Scott's 1980 death.

Lydia's **Hysterie** compilation contains an entire side of previously released 8 Eyed Spy, including live and studio tracks, all from 1980. [sg]

See also *Lydia Lunch, Raybeats*.

808 STATE
Newbuild EP (nr/Creed) 1988
Quadrastate EP (nr/Creed) 1989
808:90 (nr/ZTT) 1989 ●
The EP of Dance EP (nr/ZTT) 1989 ●
Utd. State 90 (ZTT-Tommy Boy) 1990 ●
ex:el (ZTT-Tommy Boy) 1991 ●

MC TUNES
The North at Its Heights (nr/ZTT) 1990 ●

This four-man troupe of Manchester synthesists and sampler wizzes (who take their name from the Roland drum machine that can be heard in countless contemporary records) made its rep with "Pacific," a soprano-sax-led instrumental dance groove that led to an unfortunate coinage, new age house. The mixture of Enoesque ambience and a solid beat proved to be a significant development in the progress of British dance music, but there's a lot more to 808 State conceptually than one groundbreaking sound.

While the **Newbuild** EP (featuring acid house's own future Rick Wakeman, A Guy Called Gerald) heralded nothing more impressive than an imaginative New Order/Kraftwerk synthesis, the release of "Pacific" (contained on the **Quadrastate** EP) promised much more, and the album **808:90** delivered. Expanded substantially for its American release (as **Utd. State 90**) by Tommy Boy, this is a brilliantly kaleidoscopic dance record that recycles a couple of basic melodic themes into trancelike variations, spicing them up with peculiar noises while maintaining a steady beat. The combination of musical minimalism with sonic maximalism is heady and witty, constantly exhilarating and fresh.

In 1990, the band produced and wrote the music for **The North at Its Heights**, an album by Manchester rapper MC Tunes. While most of the numbers display 808's characteristic drollery, many of Tunes' raps are serious indeed, depicting Mancunian street violence, junkiedom and other social ills with surprising conviction and credibility. The contrast yields a provocative sense of alienation; on lighter numbers like "Tunes Splits the Atom," the effect is more familiarly amusing.

Genealogical footnote: Graham Massey of 808 State was the guitarist in Biting Tongues, an early-'80s Joy Division wannabe. [gk]

801
See *Phil Manzanera*.

EINSTÜRZENDE NEUBAUTEN
Schwarz EP (Ger. Zick Zack) 1981
Kollaps (Ger. Zick Zack) 1981 ●
Drawings of Patient O.T. (nr/Some Bizzare) 1983 (ZE-PVC) 1985 ●
80–83 Strategies Against Architecture (nr/Mute) 1984 (Homestead) 1986 ●
2 X 4 [tape] (ROIR) 1984
1/2 Mensch (Some Bizzare-Rough Trade) 1985 ●
Fuenf auf der Nach Oben Offenen Richterskala (Some Bizzare-Relativity) 1987 ●
Haus der Luege (Some Bizzare-Rough Trade) 1989 ●
Strategies Against Architecture II [CD] (Mute) 1991 ●
EINSTÜRZENDE NEUBAUTEN/ LYDIA LUNCH/ ROWLAND S. HOWARD
Thirsty Animal EP (Ger. GEMA) 1982

Words such as "noisy," "raw," "primitive" and "radical" have been used to describe many a band, but few have earned these labels more than Berlin conceptual anti-artists Einstürzende Neubauten (Collapsing

New Buildings). Their instrumentation includes power tools and large metal objects beaten with hammers, pipes, wrenches and axes. What traditional musical implements they use receive similar treatment; Blixa Bargeld's pained vocals and guitar are often blurred to the point of white noise. Their live shows are even more daring, and many a club owner has stopped performances and/or barred them from returning after watching a stage practically demolished under the band's creative supervision.

While Einstürzende Neubauten built a reputation in the German avant-garde underground via the 1980 "Fuer den Untergang" single and **Schwarz** (the following year's double-pack 7-inch), these records are products of the group's creative infancy. Thus, several of the EP's five tracks have a haphazard, aimless quality far removed from the exquisitely controlled noise that was to follow. The precocious "Kalte Sterne," however, is a wholly realized song (comparable to the Gang of Four's "Anthrax"), one of the best they've ever recorded.

Kollaps combines guitar and bass drones with a barrage of metallic pounding, both rhythmic and random. Topped off with tortured howls (and titles like "Hear with Pain"), it is one of the most shocking visions ever committed to vinyl. Not recommended for dancing or romantic interludes.

Neubauten soon became the darlings of the UK press. In 1983, they signed to Some Bizzare and released **Drawings of Patient O.T.** While no more melodic than **Kollaps**, the production is less primeval and the band shows a wider degree of textural variety. At times the sound is rather stripped down, and a few of the cuts are actually songs. (The title track *even has a chord progression!*) Two years later, the record was released in the US, adding four non-LP items on a bonus EP.

Strategies Against Architecture is a compilation of five tracks from **Kollaps**, two from **Schwarz**, the B-side of "Fuer den Untergang" and some brilliant previously unreleased works, three of them live. The itemization of instrumentation is amusing, including as it does an air conditioning duct, smashing glass, an amplified spring and a bridge. For more live material, the cassette-only **2 X 4** is an admirable attempt to capture the mood of Neubauten on stage, recorded throughout Europe between 1980 and 1983. Like **Drawings**, it leaves more space in the sound, which makes the shock effects that much more shocking. "Armenisch Bitter" is, by their standards, a ballad, with plaintive sax warbling along with Bargeld's voice in a quasi-Middle Eastern style.

1/2 Mensch (aka **Halber Mensch** and **Half Man**) is the band's strongest record yet, displaying a wide range of creative compositional technique. Putting some of the junkyard orchestration aside, the title track is a cappella, sounding like some avant-garde opera; "Letztes Biest (am Himmel)" uses quiet bass harmonics as its only pitched instrument. Add such things as grand piano, inside-out dance beats and Neubauten's characteristic thunder, and **Halber Mensch** is truly remarkable.

The band temporarily broke up in 1986, then reformed to record **Fuenf auf der Nach Oben Offenen Richterskala** (**Five on the Open-Ended Richter Scale**), the most low-key LP they've ever done. Vocals, often almost at a whisper, frequently predominate. A whole plethora of instruments (or whatever) are plunked, strummed and smashed way down in the mix, almost as though Neubauten was trying not to wake up the old lady next door. Quite a contrast to much of their previous work, **Fuenf**'s quiet intensity leaves one waiting for noise which never comes.

After another lengthy sabbatical during which Bargeld concentrated on his work with Nick Cave & the Bad Seeds (while other members played in Crime and the City Solution and Sprung aus den Wolken), Neubauten re-emerged with **Haus der Luege** (**House of Lies**), a much stronger album than **Fuenf**. Though the volume is still restrained, the higher intensity level makes all the difference; the semi-ballad "Der Kuss" is quietly explosive, while the opening "Prolog" demands an acceptance of the band's sometimes schizophrenic approach (it's hard to avoid jumping out of your skin whenever the naked recitative is punctuated by colossal bursts of crashing noise). Their experimentation with heartbeat dance pulses continues to good effect on "Feurio!" [dgs/gef]

See also *Nick Cave and the Bad Seeds, Crime and the City Solution.*

ELECTRIC BLUE PEGGY SUE AND THE REVOLUTIONIONS FROM MARS

You Say You Want a Revolutionion (Fin. Gaga Goodies) 1987
You Tell Me That It's Evolutionion (Fin. Gaga Goodies) 1987
But When You Talk About Destruction (Fin. Gaga Goodies) 1988
All Family (Fin. Gaga Goodies) 1989
Music for McDonalds (Fin. Sonet) 1990

Finland's Electric Blue Peggy Sue and the Revolutionions from Mars may not be big on evolution(ion) but, if you got it, why change it? What Peggy Sue's got is a big, hard, all-dark-meat sound with lots of grit and grimy gristle. Lead vocalist Ray Katz has a voice that sounds like he drinks Drano for breakfast and washes it down with lighter fluid, tossing in the lighter for good measure. His voice grumbles and growls out the band's English-language lyrics with cackled and shrieked high-pitched edges. (Chris D of the Flesh Eaters is a fair comparison, but so is the Wicked Witch of the West.)

The 10-inch **Revolutionion** (named for the Beatles song, but that's the extent of that band's role here) contains short, hard tracks of post-Stoogescore (plus a similarly treated cover of Alan Vega's "Speedway") delivered grunge first, with Farfisa and a Seedsy '60s sensibility filtered through '70s punk experience.

The band's formula (as well as the specific source of its LP titles) remains the same through **Evolutionion** and **Destruction**, both of which rock as hard as a cement wall.

By **Music for McDonald's** though, change is afoot. Adding horns and other new instruments to the previous sonic package, the album has a Fast Side which preserves the group's old perspective and a Food Side, where anything goes. "The Amazing Chronicle of Josef's Family" slinks cat-like at its opening, tough and measured, with tantalizingly tangoesque hesitation. It whispers and pauses and hides, then reveals a swelling, almost traditional pop song in its midst, only to degenerate in a glorious sea of barking half-speed vocals, backward trackings and studio babble before the hard, smooth nugget of the song makes its return. Having stopped referencing the Beatles in titles, Electric Blue Peggy Sue has begun to reflect their influence in the grooves.   ['e]

ELECTRIC EELS

Having a Philosophical Investigation with the Electric Eels (Tinnitus) 1989 •

Recorded in 1975, this is one lost recording by a legendary band that actually lives up to its hype. Cleveland's Electric Eels bridge the gap between **Trout Mask Replica**-era Beefheart/**Love It to Death**-era Alice Cooper and punk rock proper. It would certainly be safe to say that there would be no Pere Ubu without this band which, at various points (none chronicled on this record), contained future Ubu members; the album does, however, have future Cramp Nick Knox as its drummer. But that's not even the half of it. **Having a Philosophical Investigation** is a wonderful, careening and genuinely surreal record, a terrific example of just how far a band can go with lots of squealy amplification and a rotten attitude. Once heard, tunes like "Cyclotron," "Agitated" and "Refrigerator" will not easily go away. And that's *still* not the half of it. In his liner notes, psychotronic chronicler (and one-time Eels crony) Michael Weldon half-facetiously ranks the Eels' music with that of other local legends, citing LaWanda Page, Jim Backus and Albert Ayler. Play this LP back to back with an Ayler platter and see how apt the juxtaposition is—it's that good.   [gk]

ELECTRIC LOVE MUFFIN

Playdoh Meathook (Buy Our) 1987
Rassafranna (Fever-Restless) 1989 •
Second Third Time Around (Buy Our) 1990

Given the name and jokey trappings, it's no small surprise that this Philadelphia quartet can really play. If the songs on **Playdoh Meathook**—a clear self-produced rip of punk-pop guitars, strong melodies and easily understood vocals—were a couple of notches cleverer, this would be an impressive debut. (A goofy version of "Norwegian Wood" also falls just short.)

Produced with Joe "The Butcher" Nicolo (known for his work with Schoolly-D), **Rassafranna** all but eliminates ELM's punk element in favor of a loud, tight rock sound that meanders between the Replacements and charged jangle-pop, with excursions into not-exactly-soul, loopy cow-punk and Meat Puppets territory, instrumentally ("Club Car") and songwise ("Down Easy"). Overall, the material is strong: "Diamonds & Glass" is the kind of song that would sound great on acoustic guitar, while "Drunk & Horny" is funny for all the right reasons.

Rejoining its original label, the Muffin (again with Nicolo) made **Second Third Time Around**, a fine, if slightly dispirited, seven-song return visit to the Midwest, Southwest and Motown styles explored on **Rassafranna**. In what is becoming the band's formula, the record includes singer/guitarist Rich Kaufmann originals, an instrumental ("Mr. Softy's Wild Ride") and a cover (the Temptations' "Get Ready").   [i]

ELECTRONIC

See *New Order*.

ELEVENTH DREAM DAY

Eleventh Dream Day EP (Amoeba) 1987 •
Prairie School Freakout (Amoeba) 1988 •
Beet (Atlantic) 1989 •
Lived to Tell (Atlantic) 1991 ф

FREAKWATER

Freakwater (Amoeba) 1989 •
Dancing Underwater (Amoeba) 1991 •

With their jagged guitars, unruly playing, rough-hewn songs and Rick Rizzo's tense, terse vocals, Chicago's Eleventh Dream Day make art in the raw. The band is about anti-craft—the idea that four people bashing away in a garage (or a barn, or a field) can pull some essential beauty out of the unbridled heat of the moment. At their best, EDD capture a glorious immediacy, a feeling of movement, the rush of watching something unexpected unfold.

"Walking Through the Barrel of a Gun," the first track on the debut EP (which is, surprisingly, the quartet's most temperate effort) defines the Dream Day style. Mixing trashy '60s psychedelia with a drop of country-western blood, the song places an anonymous character into a surreal crisis; imagine a Jim Thompson novel sung by Gene Pitney with Neil Young on guitar.

Prairie School Freakout puts the band's rock'n'roll primitivist thesis into execution. The entire album was recorded in six hours one night, "half of the time spent trying to fix the wild buzz coming out of Rick's amp," according to the liner notes. "We finally gave up and decided to make amp buzz the theme of the record." The album is slightly more elegant than roadkill. Guitarists Rizzo and Baird Figi trade leads that could saw down a petrified forest; the lyrics, when decipherable through Rizzo's strangulations, depict lonesome roads, empty rooms and horror-film traumas filled with the same eerie dread as the original *Texas Chainsaw Massacre*.

Beet is less extreme, though still vital; producer Gary Waleik (Big Dipper) coaxes the songs out of hiding without losing the intrinsic noisiness of the Eleventh Dream Day experience. Both Rizzo and his wife, drummer/singer Janet Beveridge Bean, are splendid lyricists, writing cagey little narratives that trace characters through the gloomy and mysterious recesses of their own minds and the weird America around them. Bean's "Bagdad's Last Ride" follows a lonelyheart named Hank from the bus to the racetrack, where he risks it all; Rizzo's "Love to Hate to Love" takes a two-second moment when a girl curses at her boyfriend and dissects the layers of thought and emotion. As with **Prairie School Freakout**, the lack of textural variation becomes a bit daunting after a while; listen to these albums while driving, and let the clogged, chaotic sounds fly loose through an open window. (The CD adds Figi's "Seiche" as a bonus.)

Lived to Tell offers more good stuff to wallow in, but a bit less to grab onto. The violently echoing slide guitar in "Dream of a Sleeping Sheep" is as sick and mean as anything on **Prairie School Freakout**, and the power-rocking "Rose of Jericho" builds to its moment of release with scientific precision. But other songs waver instead of stampede; for the first time, the band seems to know where they're going, and that takes some joy out of the ride.

Freakwater, a rootsy side project by the Kentucky-born Bean and another bluegrass state homegirl, guitarist (and Dream Day cover artist) Catherine Ann Irwin, is EDD's rural folkie flipside. With the spare accompaniment of upright bass, violin, cello, dobro and minimal percussion, the pair twang and warble through six originals plus a few covers (like the Louvin Brothers' "Childish Love") on **Freakwater**. The rich spontaneity and crumminess of the recording define the spirit of uncontrived good fun. Bean and Irwin are welcome around my campfire any day.   [kss]

DANNY ELFMAN
See *Oingo Boingo*.

ELLEN JAMES SOCIETY
Reluctantly We (Daemon) 1990

It should be a safe assumption that a band named for *The World According to Garp*'s imaginary organization of self-mutilated mutes would be all-instrumental, but that's not the case with this Atlanta quartet. (At least not by the point of this debut album.) For better or worse, guitarists Chris McGuire and Cooper Seay dramatically sing their grim romantic lyrics in, respectively, harsh and amelodic voices on **Reluctantly We**, co-produced by Indigo Girl Amy Ray and released by her indie label. (Both Indigo Girls make guest appearances here.) The EJ Society's tasteful folk-rock playing isn't bad at all, but the two frontwomen have all the grating habits of Ray's band (selfconsciously hypersensitive romantic lyrics, occasionally unpleasant singing) and none of its finer vocal qualities.   [i]

ELVIS BROTHERS
Movin' Up (Portrait) 1983
Adventure Time (Portrait) 1985

This trio from Champaign, Illinois, has roots in many local bands of that area (some credible, others cringeable); together, they play a marvelous (and deceptively simple) concoction of slicked-up rockabilly, stripped-down Cheap Trick-tinged melodic rock'n'roll and pristine pure pop that boasts superbly articulated energy, occasionally goofy lyrics and enough hooks to catch a school of minnows. **Movin' Up** traverses a panoply of mildly bent styles, from mock-Stray Cats ("Fire in the City") to Dave Edmunds-ish rock'n'roll ("Hey Tina") to Anglo-pop ("Hidden in a Heartbeat") to countryfied rock ("Santa Fe") and much more. Sure they futz around a lot (especially onstage), but their silliness never interferes with the serious task—playing catchy pop with maximum gusto. It may not mean a lot, but the album is truly mega-fun.

Adrian Belew produced **Adventure Time**, but didn't do too much damage to the E-Bros.' essentially lighthearted spirit. There are a couple of socially responsible messages about gun control and insanity in the

modern world but, by and large, the Elvises go about their business with typical happy-go-lucky aplomb. From the high-powered rock of "Burnin' Desire" and "Somebody Call the Police" to the beauty of "Crosswinds" and "Akiko Shinoda," they effortlessly toss off tune after tune of infectious should-be-hits.   [i]

See also *Darren Robbins*.

EMBARRASSMENT
The Embarrassment EP (Cynykyl) 1981
Death Travels West (Fresh Sounds) 1983
Retrospective [tape] (Fresh Sounds) 1984
The Embarrassment LP (Time to Develop) 1987
God Help Us (Bar/None) 1990 ●

Before they broke up in 1983, this quartet from Wichita, Kansas, could rock furiously, with less brittle/more melodic guitar than the Scottish nouveau pop bands (like Orange Juice and Josef K) to whom the Embos were sometimes compared. While John Nichols' vocals weren't incredible (Bill Goffrier's guitar work nearly was), the Embarrassment did convey a promising array of nuances—from wistfulness to sarcasm—and an inquisitive, adventurous way with arrangements. The lyrics vary in quality, but "Don't Choose the Wrong Song" and "Elizabeth Montgomery's Face" show budding verbal pithiness, "Wellsville" a laconic melodic strength. Best of all, most of the debut EP's five songs grow on you with each listen.

The ambitious **Death Travels West** is essentially a historical concept album—on several levels—about a voyage. The melodic songs benefit from hot performances; while getting the thematic point requires some effort and attention, the charged, raw-edged pop is immediately likable, showing the Embarrassment's facility for creating memorable tunes.

The posthumous **Retrospective** tape is even more impressive, a collection of otherwise unissued studio recordings from 1979 to 1983, plus a side of live '82-'83 performances. It's a treasure trove that shows the Embarrassment in command of a wide stylistic range—from catchy pop to gutsy punk—and in possession of broad-based songwriting talent. The best of many fine songs is "Woods of Love," a mesmerizing slice of anti-imperialism played with Feeliesque folksy pop-psychedelia, recorded onstage.

One side of **The Embarrassment LP** reissues the debut EP; the other, salvaged from a 1983 live-in-the-studio session, consists of previously unreleased recordings, except for the insidious version of "Age of Five" that was included on **Retrospective**. Full-bodied, confident one-take performances of "Woods of Love," "Picture Women" and the pulsing "Rhythm Line" make the Embos' demise all the more regrettable. After the split, drummer Brent Giessmann joined the Del Fuegos; Goffrier formed Big Dipper.

In late '88, Goffrier began splitting his time between Big Dipper and the reactivated Embarrassment, who recorded a brilliant album and toured the following year. With great new material and wonderful edgy-pop performances, **God Help Us** effortlessly picks up where the quartet left off: older, wiser, but even better than before. Shuffling and sorting out the '80s (there are flashes of the Suburbs, Devo, Talking Heads, R.E.M. and others), the group arrives at a stylistic focus that puts starch into the sensitively muscular tunes. While Nichols' voice exhibits new-found confidence and control, he still possesses a boyish zeal that makes the witty songs even more dynamic. [jg/i]

See also *Big Dipper, Del Fuegos*.

EMBRACE
See *Minor Threat*.

JACK ENDINO
See *Skin Yard*.

ENGLAND'S GLORY
See *Only Ones*.

ENGLISH BEAT
See *(English) Beat*.

BRIAN ENO
Here Come the Warm Jets (Island) 1973 (EG) 1982 ●
Taking Tiger Mountain (By Strategy) (Island) 1974 (EG) 1982 ●
Another Green World (Island) 1975 (EG) 1982 ●
Discreet Music (Antilles) 1975 (EG) 1982 ●
Before and After Science (Island) 1977 (EG) 1982 ●
Music for Films (Antilles) 1978 (EG) 1982 ●
Music for Airports (Ambient) 1979 (EG) 1982 ●
On Land (EG) 1982 ●
Music for Films Volume 2 (EG) 1983
Working Backwards 1983–1973 (EG) 1984
Thursday Afternoon [CD] (EG) 1985 ●
More Blank Than Frank (EG) 1986
Desert Island Selection [CD] (EG) 1989 ●
Boxed Set (nr/EG) 1989 φ

KEVIN AYERS—JOHN CALE—ENO—NICO
June 1, 1974 (Island) 1974 ●

CLUSTER & BRIAN ENO
Cluster and Eno (Ger. Sky) 1977
Old Land (Relativity) 1985 ●

ENO WITH MOEBIUS AND ROEDELIUS
After the Heat (Ger. Sky) 1978

JON HASSELL/BRIAN ENO
Fourth World Vol. 1: Possible Musics (Editions EG) 1980 ●
Power Spot (Ger. ECM) 1986 ●

HAROLD BUDD/BRIAN ENO
The Plateaux of Mirror (EG) 1980 ●
The Pearl (EG) 1984 ●

BRIAN ENO WITH DANIEL LANOIS & ROGER ENO
Apollo Atmospheres & Soundtracks (EG) 1983 ●

ROGER ENO & BRIAN ENO
Voices (EG) 1985 ●

ROGER ENO
Between Tides (Opal) 1988 ●

VARIOUS ARTISTS
Music for Films III (Opal) 1988 ●

ENO/CALE
Wrong Way Up (Opal-Warner Bros.) 1990 ●

From his original role as electronics dabbler and art-rocker with Roxy Music in the early 1970s, Brian Eno has become the epitome of the independent artist—articulate, intelligent, serious and intent on following his own impulses. He has progressed from a tight, wry pop music into more difficult forms, incorporating aspects of many different disciplines. As well as a solo artist, Eno has collaborated with many people; he became a major force in the emerging music of the '80s as producer of such adventurers as Ultravox, Talking Heads, New York no-wave bands, Devo, U2 and others.

Here Come the Warm Jets, Eno's first foray as a solo artist, features sharply crafted, cerebral pop songs that put equal emphasis on quirky music and chatty, surrealistic lyrics—an endearing novelty record with bizarre but affecting songs that no one else could have made.

Taking Tiger Mountain (By Strategy) finds Eno flirting with Chinese communism and dream psychology as grist for his lyric mill. The tone of the music is darker overall than on the first album; though Eno was already beginning to show a mistrust of pop forms, the songs here are filled with humor and joy and his continuing taste for experimentation.

By **Another Green World**, Eno was enhancing his work with crystal-clear production. Much of the album features beautiful, fragile instrumentals, leaving the manic rock tone of the first two albums behind. Electronics play a greater role, and Eno all but abandons standard pop forms for a less-formulaic sound that presages his future ambient work.

Discreet Music (as well as his two collaborations with Robert Fripp) was first devised while Eno was recovering from an auto accident, and it marks his experimental break from pop forms, using classical structures as the basis for tape loops and manipulations. The result is striking and haunting, filled with beauty and apprehension, paralleling the minimalist music being made by Steve Reich and Philip Glass.

Before and After Science was the apex of Eno's pop work, a collection of ten lyrical songs—ranging from bouncy, eccentric pop ("King's Lead Hat") to wistfully pastoral songs ("Spider and I," "Through Hollow Lands")—that smack of vast distances. The pivotal work of Eno's career, it sees him spanning whole musical worlds, but from this point on, his involvement with pop music was, for a long time, relegated to production work.

Music for Films, which introduced Eno's subsequent focus, consists of fragments done over the years as possible soundtracks for imaginary movies. (Eno's work has since appeared on several actual soundtracks.) Totally instrumental, the album features a return, with greater sophistication, to the work of **Discreet Music**—a conscious attempt to imply subtle moods and settings through electronically manipulated sound.

Ambient music, which goes directly against Western tradition by not demanding explicit attention from the listener, was introduced on **Music for Airports**, a stark but hypnotic collection of sounds especially composed for airport sound systems to inure passengers to flying and death. Whether successful (or even ever used) in that setting or not, the album's spare and delicate sounds open up the meditative possibilities of music.

Beginning in the mid-'70s, Eno began forging numerous collaborations (with 801, Ayers–Cale–Nico, Bowie, Cluster, Jon Hassell, Talking Heads, etc.) that allow him to dabble in (as well as influence) various strains of popular music, from fusion rock to electropop. In 1977, he teamed up with the atmospheric German duo Cluster (aka Moebius and Roedelius)—who first joined him on a modest track on **Before and After Science**—on an eponymous LP which made tentative steps in the direction of mood-evoking electronics. More successful is the 1978 collaboration, **After the Heat**, an alluring—occasionally compelling—collection of instrumentals that deftly avoid the pitfalls of ambient music, plus three tracks with vocals of varying value (one declaimed, one sung, a third sung but played backwards). (**Old Land** is a selection of tracks from both LPs.)

The Plateaux of Mirror, with Harold Budd, finds Eno expanding his ambient work to multi-dimensional proportions, while **My Life in the Bush of Ghosts**, with David Byrne, allows him to indulge his fascination with African and other Third World rhythms, with the latter made more intriguing through the mixture of these rhythms and found speech and music tapes. **Possible Musics** is an exploration of different areas of ethnomusicology with experimental Canadian trumpéter Jon Hassell.

By **On Land**, Eno had polished his ambient music into a dense, evocative representation of terra incognita. Though sometimes obscure and always devoid of lyrics, the work shows Eno at his most expressive, with sound paintings that exist somewhere between ancient mantra and avant-garde.

Invited to do the music for a film about the Apollo space missions, Eno used all of his inspiration about the grandeur and mystery of man's walking on the moon to create **Apollo Atmospheres & Soundtracks**, recorded in conjunction with his brother Roger and longtime collaborator, Daniel Lanois (also known for his solo production work with Martha and the Muffins and others; he issued a solo album in the late '80s). Avoiding any sensationalistic (or even typical space/rocketry) sounds, it's another hauntingly poetic collection of ambient pieces, written and played variously by all three musicians.

Thursday Afternoon is a 61-minute instrumental piece (logically enough issued only on CD) created to accompany a VHS cassette of "video paintings" by Christine Alicino. The soothing spaciousness of the soundtrack ambience belies its compositional sophistication, as explained in the liner notes.

Roger Eno's **Between Tides** sounds even more like movie soundtrack music than much of the **Music for Films** LPs—if you play it at 45 rpm. The undynamic arrangements of the soft sounds of a clarinet, a string quartet and a dash of flute frame piano melodies that capture a plaintive, oddly American feel (at least some of that intentional). Roger chipped in on the **Music for Films III** LP, the first of that series featuring some tracks not primarily by Brian. Standout cuts are those by Harold Budd, John Paul Jones and Brian himself (though not the ones teaming him with his U2 co-producer Daniel Lanois). Also of note is the track licensed from Soviet artistes Misha Mahlin and Lydia Theremin.

Working Backwards 1983–1973 is the ultimate Eno collection—an eleven-disc boxed set containing all of his solo albums through **Music for Films Volume 2**, plus an otherwise unavailable LP of **Rarities**, featuring such items as "Seven Deadly Finns" and "The Lion Sleeps Tonight." Issued to coincide with the publication of the *More Dark Than Shark* book, the one-LP **More Blank Than Frank** is a modest and idiosyncratic compilation—ten of the artist's own faves from his first four solo records (excluding **Discreet Music**) with careful annotation. (The cassette adds two tracks.) **Desert Island Selection** is the CD issue of **More Blank Than Frank**. The pointless **Boxed Set** contains **Another Green World**, **Before and After Science** and **Apollo**.

Working together for the first time in years, Eno produced John Cale's **Words for the Dying** in 1989; the following year, Eno found himself unexpectedly inclined to resume singing, and the two collaborated on an album. For all the things a joint effort by the two could have been, it's a small miracle that **Wrong Way Up** turned out to be an absolutely wonderful pop record, a subversion of Top 40 formulae to the pair's own idiosyncratic (but utterly accessible) ends. Blending Eno's ambience and Cale's classical lyricism, as well as the pair's contrasting voices (and capturing the whole thing in a masterfully subtle studio effort), **Wrong Way Up** is a marvel, a tuneful and catchy collection whose instant likability belies its highbrow origins (not to mention the partners' reported disharmony, reflected in the cover art's dagger graphics). It's hard to remember when either Cale or Eno has sounded happier or warmer, and their co-writing has an easy, relaxed feel. With the American Southwest surfacing as a repeated theme in such songs as the rollicking "Crime in the Desert" and "The River," variations in the partnership's balance keep the album in constant stylistic motion. "In the Backroom," the irresistible "Been There, Done That" and "Spinning Away" take their cues from three different decades of R&B, while "Lay My Love" and "One Word" follow that same dance-pop arc into the technologized present. Magic.   [sg/i/jg]

See also *David Bowie, David Byrne, Fripp & Eno, Phil Manzanera, Talking Heads.*

EPMD

Strictly Business (Fresh) 1988 ●
Unfinished Business (Fresh) 1989 ●
Business as Usual (Def Jam-Columbia) 1991 ●

K-SOLO

Tell the World My Name (Atlantic) 1990 ●

While Long Island rappers Erick Sermon and Parrish Smith—aka EPMD—have modestly adequate writing/production skills, a generally positive outlook and realistic values, a bad habit of repeating themselves and Sermon's cotton-mouthed delivery are significant impediments to enjoying their records. Why they've been so successful is something of a mystery.

Strictly Business uses routine samples (Steve Miller, Bob Marley, etc.) without much imagination; except for the title track's anti-drug message and the idea of a dance called "The Steve Martin," this unambitious debut is no thing.

The casually amateurish self-production of **Unfinished Business** is its most engaging asset: Sermon and Smith sound like a couple of kids fooling around in their basement, rapping about nothing in particular, attempting to sing a line or two, using some favorite records for cut-in jokes and generally amusing themselves while the tape deck runs. But other than a jokey and commendable condemnation of drunk driving ("You Had Too Much to Drink"), the winsomely autobiographical "Please Listen to My Demo" and a second installment of the first LP's "Jane" sex saga, **Unfinished Business** is pretty lame.

Despite the title, **Business as Usual** is anything but: EPMD turns up the heat with a newly aggressive stance and smoothly charged-up backing tracks. While Sermon's rapping has improved a bit, he's no match for his partner, who comes on like an angry linebacker in rugged no-slang-barred cuts like "I'm Mad," "Hardcore" and "Brothers on My Jock." The pair seems a little unsteady with their new power, however: a cautionary track about sexually transmitted disease is mostly an excuse for a dumb-ass bragging session between a man and his bozack (penis).

K-Solo (Kevin Madison), another Long Island native, had been in a pre-EPMD group with Smith, who arranged for him to appear on **Unfinished Business** ("Knick Knack Patty Wack") and produced and played keyboards on **Tell the World My Name**. The rough-edged rapper's a-n-n-o-y-i-n-g gimmick of spelling rhymes on "Spellbound" is a terrible opener, and "The Messenger" praises (and includes a speech by) Minister Farrakhan, but the stark strength of the autobiographical "Fugitive" and the anti-drug "Tales from the Crack Side" are memorably effective, and "Your Mom's in My Business" offers a witty perspective on parental meddling. [i]

ERASURE

Wonderland (Mute-Sire) 1986 ●
It Doesn't Have to Be EP (nr/Mute) 1987 ●
The Circus (Mute-Sire) 1987 ●
The Two Ring Circus (Mute-Sire) 1987 ●
The Innocents (Mute-Sire-Reprise) 1988 ●
Crackers International EP (Mute-Sire-Reprise) 1988 ●
Wild! (Mute-Sire-Reprise) 1989 ●

Vince Clarke's post-Yazoo band is a duo with Andy Bell, a tremulously melodramatic singer who initially bore a creepy vocal resemblance to Clarke's former partner, Alison Moyet. The music on **Wonderland** likewise sounds like Yazoo (bizarre, considering that Bell co-wrote most of them). On one hand, it's disconcerting; on the other, Yazoo was a fine band, and Clarke's more than welcome to keep up the good work, regardless of who with. The best tracks ("Heavenly Action" and "Oh l'Amour") are memorable pop confections. (The CD adds two tracks.)

Erasure's second album was released twice: the one-disc **The Circus** and, later, as a double 12-inch set of remixes and re-recordings. (The second version's CD has seven extra tracks.) Although the original LP's material is mostly cut from the same synth-dance cloth as the first record, the arrangements here are richer, more intricate and inventive. Unfortunately, Bell's flat delivery of the pessimistic and strife-ridden romance lyrics

leaves them unaffecting and whiny; he even renders the plainly lascivious "Sexuality" and "Sometimes" with a sickening lack of enthusiasm. This is the sort of misery that deserves to be left alone. ("It Doesn't Have to Be," which leads off the album, was first released on a pre-LP 12-inch.)

The Two Ring Circus—an abridged set of songs with a revamped running order and a side of orchestral versions—is a significantly better record, as the elongated remixes open up the instrumentation while downplaying the vocals. The powerful "Hideaway," a sweepingly melodic number about a young person coming out of the closet, gets the most-improved award. Three songs (one reprised from Erasure's first LP) that eschew synthesizers for strings, pianos, horns and timpani not only indicate healthy stylistic catholicism, they coax Bell into far more emotive performances.

Stephen Hague produced **The Innocents**, an OMD-like textured dance-pop collection that hasn't got many good songs beyond "A Little Respect" and "Heart of Stone." But clever arrangements that don't all sound exactly the same render the nebulous romantic lyrics superfluous; toning down Bell's maddening delivery helps immeasurably. (The CD adds "When I Needed You" and the probably inevitable "River Deep, Mountain High.")

The self-produced **Crackers International** mini-album contains four new (and otherwise non-LP) songs, highlighting Bell's flamboyant vocals on the hi-NRG "Stop!" and "Knocking on Your Door" (presented in two mixes each).

Emboldened by global stardom, Erasure stretched themselves a bit in the vastly superior **Wild!**, which adds a welcome dynamic assortment of styles to the duo's usual disco chugalug. Revealing new-found restraint, variety and artistry, **Wild!** has delicate ballads, a piano instrumental and gentle techno-pop to recommend it. Standouts: the giddy "Star" and the Latinesque "La Gloria." [i]

See also *Depeche Mode, Yazoo.*

ERIC B. & RAKIM

Paid in Full (4th & B'way) 1987 ●
Follow the Leader (Uni) 1988 ●
Let the Rhythm Hit 'Em (MCA) 1990 ●

Queens homeslice Eric B. (Barrier) is the DJ and Strong (Long) Islander Rakim (William Griffin) is the rapper; as the latter sings in "I Ain't No Joke," "I hold the microphone like a grudge/Eric B. hold the record so the needle don't budge." Beginning with a brilliant summer of '86 single, "Eric B. Is President," on an obscure Harlem label, Eric B. and Rakim proved themselves if not the hardest, certainly the most technically intricate—both musically and lyrically—rap duo around. Their follow-up, "Paid in Full," inspired more than 30 (!) different mixes; the standout was Coldcut's "Seven Minutes of Madness," which introduced Yemenite singer Ofra Haza to the international pop audience through the miracle of sampling. (Eric B. and Rakim themselves pioneered the musical appropriation of James Brown in their mixes, initiating hip-hop's almost obligatory homage to the Godfather of Soul.)

Paid in Full is a spectacular debut LP that includes new mixes of "Eric B. Is President" and its flipside,

"My Melody." Rakim's lyrics focus on the duo's prodigious talents and celebrate the joy of money, with the accumulation of wealth's material accoutrements seemingly serving as an artistic end in itself.

While Rakim can't seem to move off the subject of his own unbelievable defness, the gold-rope duo gets across on **Follow the Leader** on the strength of his dynamic delivery and some of the most original backing tracks around (credit Stevie Blass Griffin). Defying convention, the mix doesn't so much shape the sound around the beat as sink natural-sounding drums into a sonic mid-point, allowing vocals, bass and a variety of other instruments and samples to even things out.

Loaded with Rakim's quiet power, the amazing **Let the Rhythm Hit 'Em** expands and refines the team's style, laying thickly textured tracks—a unique balance of sturdy beats and woozy late-night atmosphere—under increasingly sophisticated raps. The understatement of "In the Ghetto" (not the Elvis song) and "Step Back" make them exceptionally effective; tracks like "Untouchables" and "Run for Cover" raise the energy back up with the duo's usual musical invention. The CD adds the title track's 12-inch remix as a bonus. [rg/i]

ROKY ERICKSON AND THE ALIENS

Roky Erickson and the Aliens (nr/CBS) 1980
The Evil One (415) 1981 [CD] (Pink Dust) 1987 ●
I Think of Demons (nr/Edsel) 1987

ROKY ERICKSON

Roky Erickson EP (Fr. Sponge) 1977
Clear Night for Love EP (Fr. New Rose) 1985 (nr/Fundamental Music) 1988
Don't Slander Me (Pink Dust) 1986 ●
Gremlins Have Pictures (Pink Dust) 1986 (nr/Demon) 1990 ●
The Holiday Inn Tapes (Fr. Fan Club) 1987
Live at the Ritz 1987 (Fr. Fan Club) 1988
Reverend of Karmic Youth (Skyclad) 1990 ●

ROKY ERICKSON AND THE EXPLOSIVES

Casting the Runes (nr/Five Hours Back) 1987

ROKY ERICKSON BAND

Two Headed Dog EP (Fr. Fan Club) 1988

VARIOUS ARTISTS

Where the Pyramid Meets the Eye: A Tribute to Roky Erickson (Sire) 1990 Φ

Roky Erickson established his reputation as a raving looney way back in the '60s as lead singer of Texas' infamous 13th Floor Elevators, whose acid-driven garage mysticism made the group one of the psychedelic era's greatest. Since then, Erickson's sporadic musical career has yielded a slew of often-amazing records that have established the perpetually troubled artist (whose problems with drugs and mental illness have attained near-legendary status) as a formidable cult figure. And while he's regarded by many as a mere curio/novelty, Erickson is in fact a quirky, original talent whose genius lies in an uncanny ability to turn his psychic struggles into compelling music that, at its best, is both profoundly unsettling and strangely accessible.

The Elevators fell apart in the late '60s, when Erickson began a three-year stretch in a state mental institution to avoid criminal prosecution on a drug charge. He didn't return to recording until the second half of the '70s, with a string of one-off singles and the four-song **Sponge** EP (reissued in 1988 as **Two Headed Dog**). Three of the EP's numbers were re-recorded for the 1980 CBS UK LP (the title of which is actually five unpronounceable ideograms). The album is an excellent manifestation of Erickson's post-Elevators persona, expressing his dark dilemmas through creepy horror-movie imagery. Roky sings such offbeat gems as "I Walked with a Zombie" and "Creature with the Atom Brain" in a tremulous voice that insists he's telling the truth—or at least believes he is. Former Creedence Clearwater bassist Stu Cook turned in an excellent production job, bringing the hard electric guitars (and Bill Miller's electric autoharp) into a sharp focus that underscores Roky's excitable state. Erickson and band seem less unstable than the drug-crazed Elevators (best remembered for "You're Gonna Miss Me"), but just barely.

Ditto for **The Evil One**, which takes five tracks from the UK release (overlooking the awesome "Two-Headed Dog") and adds five more, including the ghastly (that's good) "Bloody Hammer." Which LP is better? They're both wonderfully ominous and frightening—splatter-film soundtracks done with real rock'n'roll conviction. The best bet, however, is the Pink Dust CD, which collects the contents of both albums. **I Think of Demons**, created as an expanded reissue of the first LP, is another fine choice, as it contains a dozen of the CD's fifteen songs.

The five songs on **Clear Night**, recorded in Texas with a rudimentary quartet, begin on a note of relative restraint. "You Don't Love Me Yet" is acoustic folk; the title track recalls Creedence's rag-tag balladry. Side Two is a bit wilder, culminating in "Don't Slander Me," an angrily defensive accusatory diatribe. The EP does, however, contain "Starry Eyes," which can only be described as Roky's Buddy Holly tribute.

Don't Slander Me—cut with a quintet that includes assorted ex-Aliens (electric autoharpist Miller among them) and ex-Jefferson Airplane/Hot Tuna bassist Jack Casady—was recorded for (but rejected by) British CBS in the early '80s, but not released until 1986. Although half of the songs appear in different versions on earlier releases (including three on **Clear Night**), it's typically gripping. The inclusion of two Holly-inspired pop tunes makes for a bizarre contrast to "Burn the Flames," a number originally done for the *Return of the Living Dead* soundtrack.

Erickson quit recording again in the mid-'80s, but a steady stream of releases—of varying levels of quality—has persisted. **Gremlins Have Pictures** is an interesting if erratic hodgepodge of tracks ranging from 1975 to 1982, solo and with three different groups (the Explosives, the Aliens and Blieb Alien): some thrilling, some shoddy, all loony. (The CD adds previously released 1980-vintage bonus tracks.)

The Holiday Inn Tapes is simply an atrocity, a pathetic guy in a hotel room fooling around on an acoustic guitar. Even fans shouldn't bother. On the other hand, despite the appalling boot-quality sound of **Live at the Ritz**, this document of an Austin show (February 1987) which begins with "You're Gonna Miss Me" and runs through "Bloody Hammer" with bracing guitar work by Will Sexton is worth hearing, especially for the incidental stage remarks.

Casting the Runes mates Roky's twisted worldview with a hard, crunching band. Recorded on various Texas stages circa '79, it unleashes menacing renditions of such grisly Erickson classics as "Don't Shake Me Lucifer" and "Bloody Hammer," plus a weird version of the mush-pop oldie "I Love How You Love Me." Highly recommended, especially to fans of **The Evil One**. **Reverend of Karmic Youth** is an interesting artifact: six acoustic solo tunes from 1985, plus six live band tracks from **Casting the Runes**.

In 1990, Erickson was arrested in a bizarre mail-fraud mix-up and institutionalized once again. Through the efforts of a longtime fan at the label, this latest round of tribulations inspired the assembly of **Where the Pyramid Meets the Eye**, a benefit disc featuring nineteen covers (22 on the cassette) of assorted Roky compositions, by artists as diverse as ZZ Top, R.E.M., Doug Sahm, Bongwater, Julian Cope, T-Bone Burnett and the Jesus & Mary Chain. It's a mixed bag but, overall, **Pyramid** is remarkably effective. The fact that such intensely personal material can stand up to such a wide variety of interpretations makes it clear that, whatever his personal problems, Erickson is an uncommonly gifted songwriter whose work deserves—but is not likely to find—a wider audience.   [jy/i/hd]

ESG
ESG EP (99) 1981
ESG Says Dance to the Beat of Moody EP (99) 1982
Come Away with ESG (99) 1983
ESG (Pow Wow) 1991

Who would have imagined that four sisters and a pal from the South Bronx would emerge as one of the most dynamic bands that New York could offer at the top of the '80s? (Or that they would pop up again in 1987 . . .) Mixing a solid combination of dub, chant and beat, ESG—simply drums, bass and vocals—virtually stole the cosmic show with their first release, a six-song EP with a live side and a phenomenal studio side recorded under the hand of British producer Martin Hannett.

Their second EP, produced by 99 Records head Ed Bahlman, is not quite as crisp as the debut, but no less enjoyable, a brilliant synthesis of rhythm and restraint. To say the following album stayed in a similar vein and improved little over live shows of the same material would be to damn a fine record with faint praise. ESG offers bouncy funk instead of funk pretensions and elegant simplicity in place of mere primitivism. [jw/mf]

ESSENTIAL LOGIC
Essential Logic EP (nr/Virgin) 1979
Beat Rhythm News (nr/Rough Trade) 1979
LORA LOGIC
Pedigree Charm (nr/Rough Trade) 1982

Essential Logic quickly outlived its usefulness as a vehicle for Lora Logic, once a member of X-Ray Spex, and a most distinctive talent. The original lineup—featured on the band's eponymous four-song debut—includes two guitars, two saxes (including Logic herself) and a clunky rhythm section; a loose but comfortable ensemble. Logic's songwriting had yet to bloom, though her vocal style was already developing.

She was still loopy but lovable on **Beat Rhythm News**, but her singing had become highly stylized with a distinct edge. A tighter rhythm guitarist replaced the uninspired duo of the EP, and Essential Logic soared. The music's vivacity is occasionally undercut by tinny production and a tendency to ramble, and Lora's growth as a writer and performer warranted more versatile backing. The next Logical step: a solo career.

Logic continued to evolve on her first solo outing. Her voice—much better produced—has a slightly softer, jazzy inflection, and her eclectic writing assumes a poppy sheen. Even hitherto impenetrable lyrics reveal a translucent clarity in spots. Businesslike dance rhythms and fewer straying sax excursions take additional steps towards accessibility. **Pedigree Charm** is a delight.

Abandoning rock'n'roll, Logic—along with former bandmate Poly Styrene—wound up becoming a Hare Krishna devotee and playing in a (religious) cult band.   [mf]

EURYTHMICS
In the Garden (nr/RCA) 1981 ●
Sweet Dreams (Are Made of This) (RCA) 1983 ●
Touch (RCA) 1983 ●
Touch Dance (RCA) 1984 ●
1984 (For the Love of Big Brother) (RCA) 1984 ●
Be Yourself Tonight (RCA) 1985 ●
Revenge (RCA) 1986 ●
Savage (RCA) 1987 ●
We Too Are One (Arista) 1989 ●
Greatest Hits (Arista) 1991 ф
DAVE STEWART
Lily Was Here (nr/Anxious) 1990 ●
DAVE STEWART AND THE SPIRITUAL COWBOYS
Dave Stewart and the Spiritual Cowboys (Arista) 1990 ●

Fresh from the unlamented ruins of the Tourists, Annie Lennox and Dave Stewart formed Eurythmics, at first to pursue their love affair with Germanic experimental/electronic music and attempt a translation of it into a peculiarly British form. Co-produced by Conny Plank and featuring an intriguing assortment of musicians—Blondie drummer Clem Burke, members of Can and D.A.F., composer Karlheinz Stockhausen's son Marcus—the alluring debut album (still unreleased in the US a decade later) is filled with lyrical love songs and gently strident social anthems, like "All the Young (People of Today)" and "Your Time Will Come." Empowering it all are Lennox's captivating, flexible but strong vocals and a commitment and humor that turn potentially pretentious material into unaffected, poetic work.

From such humble, non-mainstream beginnings was a new chart-topping, trendsetting group created. **Sweet Dreams (Are Made of This)**—thanks mostly to the monotonic dirge of the same name—took off and lofted the pair into world prominence, a success they maintained on **Touch** by proving themselves capable of enormous stylistic and instrumental variety, as well as exceptional songwriting. From lovely ("Here Comes the Rain Again") to jaunty ("Right by Your Side") to dramatic ("Who's That Girl?") and driving ("The First Cut"), **Touch** is an excellent record filled with invention and chicly styled nouveau pop. To take advantage of sudden global stardom, an album of remixes (four songs with vocals, three of them also presented as instrumentals) by Jellybean Benitez and Francois Kevorkian was issued as **Touch Dance**.

The **1984** album—as the result of a contretemps with the film's director, not exactly the soundtrack but "music derived from Eurythmics' original score"—finds the pair moving further into rhythmic experimentation, as on the crazed cut-up stylings of "Sexcrime" and "Doubleplusgood." A strange but affecting record, although clearly not one intended to be taken as a normal chapter in the group's development.

The hard-edged, relatively low-tech **Be Yourself Tonight** marks a real change in the duo's thinking. Exciting, catchy soul-rock ("Would I Lie to You?"), insipid, aggravating soul-rock ("I Love You Like a Ball and Chain"), two swell duets ("Adrian," with Elvis Costello; "Sisters Are Doin' It for Themselves," with Aretha Franklin), plus five more tracks all have an underlying stylistic consistency. That's a new twist for Eurythmics, but one they seem capable of handling. Retooling into an '80s Motown factory might seem a little selfconscious, but they carry it off with aplomb and even a bit of heart.

Taking an unexpected but worthwhile hell-hath-no-fury detour, the breakup of Lennox's marriage yielded the vituperative lyrics of the blunt and aptly titled **Revenge**. "To run away from you/was all that I could do," from "Thorn in My Side," is only the tip of the impassioned album's iceberg; other songs ("A Little of You," "The Last Time," "Missionary Man") turn a scornful postmortem into deeply felt cries that reverberate in Lennox's remarkable vocal cords. There are draggy spots that overdo the musical sentiment but, by and large, this is one of the pair's best records.

No such luck on the following year's **Savage**, a shoddy mess of scant merit. Where **Revenge** made fine use of a small, crack collection of studio hands to flesh out the material in a variety of luxurious idioms, **Savage** relies on a bed of chilly soundalike computer programs and multi-tracked vocal gimmicks. (Discounting Stewart's guitar work and the all-acoustic "I Need You," only "Wide Eyed Girl" sounds as if human beings played on it. Both add crowd noises, perhaps to underscore the point.) The wooden material has static rhythms, a shortage of melodies and entirely too few hooks; the mostly miserable lyrics suggest continental sophistication and thoughtful emotional reflection but fizzle in a hurried blur of triviality, obscurity and seeming creative apathy.

We Too Are One isn't nearly as bad—electric guitars and a bit of soul (backing vocals are by Charlie Wilson of the Gap Band) provide the humanity missing from **Savage**—but such improvements can't overcome the duo's songwriting fatigue. Bland arrangements of dashed-off melodies and lyrics that are among Eurythmics' worst make this a barely adequate effort. "Don't Ask Me Why" (a return, along with the blunt "You Hurt Me (And I Hate You)," to the subject of postromance recriminations) is solidly catchy, as is the stomping title track, which goes on too long. But when a usually articulate and intelligent band settles for such

simpleminded drivel as "(My My) Baby's Gonna Cry," it's obvious things aren't quite right.

Maybe the problem lies in Stewart's overstuffed calendar. As a songwriter and studio hound, he's undertaken many extracurricular endeavors of late, producing Russian rocker Boris Grebenshikov's awful Anglo-American debut and working on tracks for Brian Setzer, Malcolm McLaren and others. (His mid-'80s production résumé includes Daryl Hall, Tom Petty, Mick Jagger and Bob Dylan.) In 1990, Stewart recorded **Lily Was Here**, a soundtrack album released through his own Anxious label. He also unveiled a cloaked-in-pseudonyms side band. On **Dave Stewart and the Spiritual Cowboys**, an ordinary-sounding guitar-rock LP, he steps into the vocal spotlight with a lot more passion than finesse. As unsubtle and artless a singer as he is a lyricist, Stewart takes embarrassing potshots at assorted targets with all the poetic sophistication of a schoolboy, offering up such idiocy as "King of the Hypocrites" and "Fashion Bomb" ("She's radio active you can see it in her eyes/Radioactive from her hips to her thighs").

[sg/i]

See also *Deutsche Amerikanische Freundschaft, Ramones, Feargal Sharkey, Tourists.*

EVERLAST

Forever Everlasting (Warner Bros.) 1990 ●

A punky white rapper from Ice-T's Rhyme Syndicate, Southern California's Everlast (whose debut preceded Vanilla Ice's by several months) deserves an A for effort, though his skills don't quite match his high spirits. The dude's got the sneer down pat and chatters impressively in doubletime ("Syndicate Soldier")—what he needs now are topics that transcend the usual self-hype. Despite the narrow focus, a couple of killer tracks mark Everlast as a comer: "Fuck Everyone," which carries good-natured belligerence to new artistic heights, and the inspired "I Got the Knack," a riproaring gem that samples "My Sharona." [jy]

EVERYTHING BUT THE GIRL

Eden (nr/Blanco y Negro) 1984 ●
Everything but the Girl (Blanco y Negro-Sire) 1984
Love Not Money (Blanco y Negro-Sire) 1985 ●
Angel EP (nr/Blanco y Negro) 1985
Baby, the Stars Shine Bright (Blanco y Negro-Sire) 1986 ●
Come on Home EP (nr/Blanco y Negro) 1986
Don't Leave Me Behind EP (nr/Blanco y Negro) 1986
Idlewild (Blanco y Negro-Sire) 1988 ●
These Early Days EP (nr/Blanco y Negro) 1988 ●
Driving EP [CD] (nr/Blanco y Negro) 1990 ●
The Language of Life (Atlantic) 1990 ●

TRACEY THORN

A Distant Shore (nr/Cherry Red) 1982 + 1985 ●

BEN WATT AND ROBERT WYATT

Summer into Winter EP (nr/Cherry Red) 1982 ●

BEN WATT

North Marine Drive (nr/Cherry Red) 1983 ●

Individually and as Everything but the Girl, Ben Watt (guitar, keyboards, vocals, songs) and Tracey Thorn (vocals, guitar, songs) have been prominent innovators in England's back-to-jazz neo-pop movement. The popularity of artists like Sade, Swing Out Sister and the Style Council (whose first album featured Thorn and Watt on one song) is due in no small part to the pair's counter-current efforts, helping to lay the critical groundwork for acceptance of this lovely but thoroughly un-rock style.

While also a member of the Marine Girls, Thorn cut **A Distant Shore**, a brief album of nostalgic singer/songwriter modernism with little more than an acoustic guitar for accompaniment. Her somewhat monotonous delivery hampers the effort, but a version of the Velvet Underground's stylistically apropos "Femme Fatale" helps considerably.

Prior to EBTG, Watt had recorded on his own as well as in conjunction with Robert Wyatt. The five-song **Summer into Winter** is a disappointing collaboration; the quietly colorful minimal arrangements of guitar (Watt) and piano (Wyatt) are undercut by Watt's moany lead vocals. It's too bad: Wyatt's voice is much more enjoyable, and might have made something of these vague, atmospheric songs had he done more of the singing. On **North Marine Drive**, a wisp of airy melodicism with only a guest saxophonist joining Watt, the percussionless tracks still manage nicely syncopated, quasi-Latin rhythms; Watt's fine guitar playing and sincerely artless singing make it a quiet pleasure. (One CD contains both records.)

Named after a shop in Hull, Everything but the Girl debuted in January 1982 with a three-song British single that included Cole Porter's "Night and Day." The duo's first album, **Eden**, is a charming, fragile record delicately filled with winsome songs that drift in and out of neo-jazz-pop stylings but are never less than appealing and attractive. Showing enormous growth as a vocalist, Thorn makes the songs memorable even when the music is too low-key to stand out on its own. With harmonies that recall such wonders of the '60s as the Association, understated pop creations prove Everything but the Girl to be an exceptional, unconventional band.

Everything but the Girl, the American version of **Eden**, is a drastically different record, with six substitutions. (The entire second side of the US release is new.) The overall feel of the two albums is similar, but fans should seek out both versions, as there's hardly a dud among the eighteen selections. (The US album isn't on CD, and the British CD offers no extra tracks.)

Love Not Money carries the pair away from jazz and into a pure pop approach that is more accessible and immediately appealing. The album leads off with the alluring "When All's Well" and continues with further literate considerations of growing up and getting along, including "Ugly Little Dreams," which is dedicated to actress Frances Farmer. The US edition adds "Heaven Help Me" and a version of Chrissie Hynde's "Kid."

The **Angel** EP features one affecting song from **Love Not Money**, a version of "Easy as Sin" sung by Watt (instead of Thorn, as it appears on the first US LP), plus two non-album tracks that rank among the duo's finest. "Pigeons in the Attic Room" and "Charmless Callous Ways" sound like demos, Thorn alone with guitar and piano respectively, singing at her most emotionally direct.

The cover of **Baby, the Stars Shine Bright** notes that it was "arranged for orchestra by Ben Watt." Indeed, other than his guitar playing, a prominent rhythm section and a pianist/organist, the musical backing consists of strings, horns and a choir. Fortunately, Thorn's rich voice and the pair's soaringly melodic songs carry it off without losing momentum. The music is neither sappy nor dull; the orchestra's role is supportive without shirking center stage. Like classic Dionne Warwick sides, rock'n'roll energy and excitement is channeled into subtle sophistication that brings the music to life in vivid colors. Pointedly topical lyrics on "Sugar Finney" (for Marilyn Monroe) and "Little Hitler" don't undercut the songs' delicate beauty; other standouts are "Don't Leave Me Behind," "Fighting Talk" and "Cross My Heart."

The **Come on Home** EP features two versions of a sweeping ballad from **Baby, the Stars**, a classic C&W weeper by Thorn called "Draining the Bar" and an ill-advised stab at "I Fall to Pieces." **Don't Leave Me Behind** is another song from the same LP, with B-side covers of Jimmy Webb's "Where's the Playground, Susie" sung by Watt and Bacharach's "Alfie" sung by Thorn.

Taking a turn towards self-contained simplicity, Watt and Thorn recorded **Idlewild** with only a small set of sidemen adding keyboards, bass and horns. Thorn's lyrics have never been this introspective or revealing; the plainly articulated longings and autobiographical expositions resonate through "Oxford Street," "Blue Moon Rose," "Apron Strings" and "Shadow on a Harvest Moon" like a rainy day. With understated, superficially mild-on-arrival music, this is an achingly sad record, filled with quiet grief and deep disappointments. (The British version includes a cover of Danny Whitten's "I Don't Want to Talk About It," which became the duo's biggest UK hit to date—but was left off the US release.)

These Early Days includes a remix of one bittersweet song from **Idlewild** and adds Watt's "Dyed in the Grain," Thorn's "Another Day, Another Dollar" and country star Paul Overstreet's "No Place Like Home."

Thorn and Watt recorded **The Language of Life** in Los Angeles with Tommy LiPuma, known for his slick productions of Miles Davis and George Benson. The sound is a natural evolution of the duo's prior moves towards a classic (i.e., pre-rock) pop presentation. By rejecting it out of hand as a bid for commercial acceptance (which it partly was), lots of people missed the album's strengths, especially the improvement in both partners' voices and songwriting. Granted, some of the songs would have sounded more sincere without the studio glitz and passionless contempo-jazz session players, but Thorn's "Meet Me in the Morning" and Watt's "The Road" (featuring saxman Stan Getz, whose bossa nova work was an early influence on the duo) are keepers that stand up with the pair's best. And the cover of Womack and Womack's "Take Me" hints at what they're aiming for: sophisticated, romantic adult pop.

The **Driving** EP features a "radio edit" of the album's overproduced single plus the umpteenth cover of Tom Waits' "Downtown Train," with Watt handling the lead vocals.   [i/ws]

See also *Grab Grab the Haddock, Marine Girls, Style Council.*

EX

Disturbing Domestic Peace (Hol. Verrecords) 1980
History Is What's Happening (Hol. More DPM) 1982
Dignity of Labour (Hol. VGZ) 1983
Tumult (Hol. FAI) 1983
Gonna Rob the Spermbank EP (Hol. Sneeelleeer) 1983
Blueprints for a Blackout (Hol. Pig Brother Productions)
   1983
Pokkeherrie (Hol. Pockabilly) 1985
1936 (The Spanish Revolution) EP (Hol. Ron Johnson)
   1986
Too Many Cowboys (Mordam) 1987
Live in Wroclaw [tape] (Hol. Red) 1987
Hands Up! You're Free (Hol. Ex) 1988
Aural Guerrilla (Hol. Ex) 1988 (Homestead) 1989
Joggers and Smoggers (Hol. Ex) 1989 ●
Dead Fish EP (Hol. Ex) 1990 ●

VARIOUS ARTISTS

Support the Miners' Strike (Hol. Records Against
   Thaatchism) 1985

This hard-edged Dutch anarcho-punk collective adheres to only the purest ideals in rock music. Since 1980, the Ex has uncorked an endless stream of do-it-themselves vinyl and tapes on a variety of label names (finally settling on Ex Records in '88). Following Crass' example (if not quite that group's sound; the Ex has a cutting Gang of Four rhythmic edge and something of a Fall-like declamatory style), the Ex use their work as a sonic and graphic vehicle to promote a wide range of left-wing socio-political causes. Along with the piercing and articulate punk rock, most of the Ex's albums contain vast amounts of printed material.

Disturbing Domestic Peace includes a bonus live single and an illustrated lyrics booklet. **History Is What's Happening** is a studio rendition of the band's 1981 live set. **Dignity of Labour** is a four-single box that focuses on the decline of a paper mill factory near where some of the Ex were squatting. An illustrated book explaining the issue keeps the songs' political content from being overlooked; instrumentation includes saxophone and marimba.

Jon Langford (Mekons/Three Johns), an occasional figure in the world of Ex, entered the picture as the producer of **Tumult**; he also plays drums on the four-song **Rob the Spermbank** 12-inch. The record's poster announces "hometaping is killing record companies . . . and it's about time."

The Ex employs such musical implements as organ, beer crates and oil barrels on the double **Blueprints for a Blackout** album, further expanding its sonic palette with guest musicians. A poster and info packet about the eviction of a massive Amsterdam squat accompany the LP.

The Ex moved to support striking British coal miners in 1984, organizing a benefit/agit-prop tour and releasing a joint live album with several likeminded bands. **Pokkeherrie** is a collection of new songs the group had performed on an anti-military tour. The double 7-inch of songs from and concerning the Spanish Revolution came with (or vice versa) a 140-page book about that chapter of 1930s anti-fascist history.

The double-LP **Too Many Cowboys**—which was released in the US, complete with a 24-page newspaper—combines live and studio recordings of such no-nonsense songs as "Butter or Bombs," "Olympigs," "Vivisection" and "How Can One Sell the Air." Following a live cassette recorded in Poland, the Ex compiled an album (**Hands Up! You're Free**) of its three John Peel sessions ('83, '85 and '86).

Langford produced **Aural Guerrilla**, an evocative and tightly crimped knot that covers a variety of righteous causes. A bracing blast of barbed wire guitar delivered at reasonable speed with clear (but passionate) vocals, **Aural Guerrilla** is one of the Ex's best; potent highlights include the pro-animal ecology of "Evolution (?)," the anti-rock-star venom of "Meanwhile at McDonna's" and "Welcome to the Asylum," an attack on Holland's shoddy treatment of refugees.

Joggers & Smoggers (the Ex's third double album) reroutes the music from its usual head-on collision and spotlights a few guests, including Sonic Youth guitarists Lee Ranaldo and Thurston Moore, as well as jazz hornmen and a bagpiper. While tracks like "Shopping Street" are brash cacophony, others are far more restrained.

With Langford again co-producing, **Dead Fish** (a 10-inch record plus a 3-inch CD) is one of the Ex's most stirring releases yet, as the group sneers at how the record business has belittled music's significance.

[mg]

(EX)CAT HEADS
See *Cat Heads*.

EXECUTIVE SLACKS

Executive Slacks EP (Red) 1983
You Can't Hum When You're Dead (Fundamental) 1984
Nausea (Fundamental) 1985
Fire and Ice (Fundamental) 1986

FAHRENHEIT 451

House of Morals EP (Active) 1986

Philadelphia's Executive Slacks started out playing a searing combination of electronics, guitar/vocals and percussion. On the trio's first EP, Matt Marello sings with hysterical urgency *and* unnerving calm while spewing white-hot guitar noise out over steady, pulsing Residents-like backing complete with found tape noises. The impact is gratingly industrial but also emotional—it isn't the sheer assault that makes you uneasy, it's the whole demented concoction.

You Can't Hum When You're Dead combines all four tracks from **Executive Slacks** with a subsequent three-song EP. The latter material, produced by ex-Killing Joke bassist Youth (an obvious influence), is more ominously bass-heavy and less scathing—though equally powerful, thanks to screamed vocals and disturbing effects.

Nausea continues in a similar style without any letup. The band and Youth refuse to temper their taste for unsettling din, and "In and Out" ranks with anything by Killing Joke or Chrome for sheer intensity. Elsewhere, Executive Slacks diversifies into other styles and moods, including electronics expert John Young's deft use of hip-hop/dance rhythms, an acoustic guitar tapestry, pulsing metallic percolations and several terrific instrumentals.

The self-produced **Fire and Ice** is the band's most accessible record, dominated by a crucial arrival: percussionist Bobbie Rae. His propulsive style adds a livelier, more human feel to the group's cold, technological framework. While a version of Gary Glitter's "Rock & Roll" is entertaining (if predictable), the more original "Wide Fields" is built around the hook from the Spencer Davis Group's "I'm a Man."

Soon afterward, Marello retired to pursue his art career. Meanwhile, in New Jersey, a band called Fahrenheit 451 were establishing themselves with a somewhat similar, if smoother sound. Their sole release, a four-song EP, melds art-rock guitar, funky bass, Stranglers-like keyboard swells and dominant neo-Latin percussion; Athan Maroulis' charismatic vocals (very Doors/Bauhaus-inspired) top off an interesting record. When Fahrenheit 451 crumbled in '87, Maroulis joined up with Rae and Young, added a guitarist and proceeded as Executive Slacks, evolving into a strangely compelling merger of hard rock and techno-wave, with Maroulis' melodramatics in pleasant contrast to the synthetic drum/keyboard textures, loud heavy metal guitar and Rae's rhythmic pyrotechnics.   [i/gef]

EXPLODING WHITE MICE
In a Nest of Vipers EP (Greasy Pop-Big Time) 1985
Brute Force and Ignorance (Aus. Festival) 1988
Exploding White Mice (Ger. Normal) 1990 ●

Taking their name from *Rock'n'Roll High School* and most of their sound from **Rocket to Russia**, this Adelaide quintet has done its damnedest to be Australia's own Ramones. But while the familiar song skeletons and Paul Gilchrist's Joey-esque delivery are in clear debt to the brudders, the Mice add a distinct garage element (credit Radio Birdman), especially on the early recordings.

The six-song **In a Nest of Vipers** swells with raucous bareback guitar energy and catchy pop-rock tunes. Covering "Pipeline" provides some contrast to the Ramonesy "Burning Red" and a hard-rocking rundown of Bo Diddley's "Let the Kids Dance." While the other originals are fun but forgettable, "Dangerous" caps the EP off with a varied scramble of raunchy guitars. **Brute Force and Ignorance** evolves that hit-and-run freestyle spirit into more of a late-'70s pop-punk sound, replicating the Ramones' light touch with clinging choruses and obvious progressions (as on "Worry About Nothing" and "Bury Me"). Faster cuts ("Uninvited") really spotlight the Mice's adrenaline-soaked sizzle.

The studio side of **Exploding White Mice** contains such memorable tunes as the pogo-speed "Intuition" and the aptly titled "Do the Crunch"; the live side displays more of the Mice's raw power than any of the group's studio work.   [mg]

EXPLOITED
Punks Not Dead (nr/Exploited-Secret) 1981 (nr/Link) 1989 ●
On Stage (nr/Exploited) 1981
Troops of Tomorrow (nr/Secret) 1982 (nr/Link) 1989 ●
Let's Start a War ... Said Maggie One Day (Combat) 1983 ●

Horror Epics (Combat) 1985 ●
Live at the White House (Combat Core) 1985
Totally Exploited (nr/Blashadabee-Dojo) 1986 ●
Jesus Is Dead EP (Combat Core) 1986
Live and Loud!! (nr/Link) 1987
Death Before Dishonour (Rough Justice-Combat) 1987 ●
Punk's Alive (nr/Skunx) 1988
Live Lewd Lust (nr/Grand Slam) 1989 ●

Led by outspoken spike-haired shouter Wattie Buchan, Edinburgh's Exploited are one of the UK's most successful and enduring political thrash bands. Musically harsher, darker and cruder than their '77 forefathers, these gruff yobbos vent unrestrained and bottomless anger against their enemies—the army, warmongers, Margaret Thatcher (pictured on one album cover, cited in the title of another and the subject of assorted songs) and other symbols of government authority. As mainstream-uncommercial as the Exploited are, a huge hardcore audience—in the UK and increasingly in the US—have made Wattie and an ever-shifting set of accomplices highly regarded genre stars.

Although hampered by muffled sound, **Punks Not Dead** is full of angry, gritty anthems of pain and frustration, including "I Believe in Anarchy," "Blown to Bits" and "Royalty." **On Stage** repeats much of the same material but has bootleg-level audio quality, worsened by the clear-vinyl pressing.

Troops of Tomorrow has a crisp, clean guitar sound, and the lyrics are a bit easier to understand, but the improved production doesn't mean the Exploited has gotten slick—the rough and tumble assault is still wild-eyed and unstoppable. The title song was written by the Vibrators; "Sid Vicious Was Innocent" is one of the record's more interesting arguments.

An entirely new lineup—Karl, Wully and Billy—joins Wattie for **Let's Start a War**. The production backslides into the murk a bit, but the band's fervor pushes forward and Wattie's singing is, if such a thing is possible, rawer and less melodic. A variety of tempos offers hope for a brighter future, but there's really nothing new going on here.

The Dracula cover and title of **Horror Epics** suggests a flirtation with the Damned's old horror turf, but the title track veers more towards Black Sabbath, with the rhythm guitars displaced by Willie's thundering drum attack and moaning lead guitar figures; echo on the vocals furthers the comparison to mid-'70s metal. Several other songs are variants on that style; the whole outing benefits from Wattie's growing production prowess. The lengthy numbers are standard Exploited issue, but a tiny hint of experimentalism is creeping in amid the stylistic complacency. The best tune—and certainly one of the band's catchiest ever—is "Maggie," which repeatedly calls the Prime Minister a bad name.

Live at the White House was recorded in Washington, DC, in April 1985 and features a selection of the Exploited's most popular tunes. The four-song **Jesus Is Dead** 12-inch captures yet another lineup with clarity and venom. (Willie's drumming is again a highlight; Nig's spectacular guitar playing is a welcome addition.) For the first time, the Exploited's instruments are clearly articulated and separated in the mix; what a difference real dynamics and seemingly well-rehearsed arrangements make. A solid, fiery punk record with powerful lyrics about a drug bust, televangelism and "Politicians."

Willie and Nig also dominate the fuzzier-sounding **Death Before Dishonour**, in which a slashing metal edge shows the Exploited waffling between forms. Although the music is essentially indistinguishable from any in the band's past, little bits of unexpected business (a fake Reagan speech on "Power Struggle," a brief drum solo on "Police Informer," the female chorus on "Sexual Favours") break up the monotony from time to time.   [cpl/i]

EXPLORERS
The Explorers (nr/Virgin) 1985 ●
MANZANERA & MACKAY
Crack the Whip (Relativity) 1988 ●
Up in Smoke (Relativity) 1989 ●
PLAYERS
Christmas (Rykodisc) 1989 ф

On their own as the Explorers, post-Roxy Musicians Phil Manzanera and Andy Mackay—joined by singer James Wraith and a collection of familiar session cohorts—make polite, sophisticated pop/dance music with no edge. Although superficially not that different from the music Roxy was making towards the end, **The Explorers** is undistinguished, lacking memorable songs and Ferry's unique touch. (Wraith's obvious attempt at imitation on "Venus De Milo" isn't exactly flattery.) Not bad, just not what you'd hope for from artists of this caliber.

Dispensing with the group name, the American **Crack the Whip** retrieves three cuts from **The Explorers**, adding five leftovers from the same '84 sessions and another five dance-conscious tracks of more recent vintage. Manzanera and Mackay do nice work on the mediocre material, but the dominant character here is Wraith. Where he was mildly annoying on the first album, his mannered singing has turned obnoxious—a pompously melodramatic mixture of vocal styles borrowed from Ferry, Erasure and Spandau Ballet.

The following year, the remaining six songs from **The Explorers** were coupled with the same number of new recordings and issued as **Up in Smoke**. With Wraith again being a pompous nuisance. Manzanera and Mackay occasionally chip in with nifty instrumental bits, but the songs and production are so lacking in personality that it's hardly worth the wait.

The Players are a no-tech instrumental band led by Andy Mackay; **Christmas** (executive-produced and "co-presented" by Manzanera, who doesn't play on it) is a delightful folky collection of 33 old-fashioned traditional songs of the season, played with mucho gentle gusto on banjo, fiddle, oboe, clarinet, accordion and acoustic guitar.   [i]

See also *Phil Manzanera, Roxy Music,*

EXTRABALLE
Extraballe EP (Fr. Carrere) 1979
Sales Romances (Fr. CBS) 1980
Extraballe (Fr. CBS) 1981

On their self-titled EP, Extraballe—whose drummer at the time was Michel Peyronel, brother of Heavy Metal Kids/UFO keyboardist Danny—offered high-speed refried punk-a-boogie with hot axework and little else. Thereafter, the band became nothing more than a name

owned by vocalist John Ickx, who wrote the songs. Just about on key, Ickx's French speak-singing covers most typical punk subjects (sex, violence, power, movies) plus a couple of less-likely topics for a young Frenchman. There's potent high-energy accompaniment with lots of organ and guitar vying for domination of the serviceable tunes. (The temporary band for **Sales Romances** included one-time Be-Bop Deluxe *batteur* Simon Fox; Blockhead Davey Payne blew some sax.) Ickx formed a different band for the **Extraballe** album; a pity he couldn't update the sound more.   [jg]

See also *A Split-Second.*

EYELESS IN GAZA
Photographs as Memories (nr/Cherry Red) 1981
Caught in Flux (nr/Cherry Red) 1981
Pale Hands I Loved So Well (Nor. Uniton) 1982
Drumming the Beating Heart (nr/Cherry Red) 1982
Rust Red September (nr/Cherry Red) 1983
Back from the Rains (nr/Cherry Red) 1986 ●
Kodak Ghosts Run Amok (nr/Cherry Red) 1987
Transience Blues (nr/Integrity-Antler) 1989 ●
MARTYN BATES
Letters Written (nr/Cherry Red) 1982
The Return of the Quiet (nr/Cherry Red) 1987 ●
Love Smashed on a Rock (nr/Integrity-Antler) 1988
Letters to a Scattered Family (nr/Integrity-Antler) 1990 ●

Named for Aldous Huxley's ode to pacifist integrity, Eyeless in Gaza consisted of guitarist Martyn Bates and bassist/keyboardist Peter Becker, both credited with voice and instrumentation on the first album, a better-than-decent stab at hook-filled spareness. The tasteful music is marred only occasionally by overly anguished vocals. **Caught in Flux** has a more delicate flavor at first, then rapidly devolves into humpbacked squalor. This one-and-a-half-disc (LP/EP) set shows a hint of progress, with the vocals held in tighter rein. Caught in flux, indeed.

Pale Hands, released only in Norway, is fairly dissolute—a meandering, largely improvisational attempt to make music out of aimless doodles. **Drumming the Beating Heart** (also included in its entirety on the cassette of **Back from the Rains**) finds the duo streamlining their sound to good effect, relying on church organ leads and spontaneous rhythm approaches. If the vocals could be relieved of their melodrama, these fellows might have something here.

Back from the Rains has a charming, Aztec Camera-like beat-pop sound; Bates' vocals aren't quite up to it, but the duo (aided by a drummer and a female backing singer) shows a real facility for shimmering studio arrangements. Just shy of being commercial, this is nonetheless a delight.

After that record, Becker left the group and Bates began a solo career, an idea he had first tested with a pre-Gaza cassette and 1982's 10-inch **Letters Written**. Using strings and a rhythm section on **The Return of the Quiet**, Bates pushes crudely towards airy soul and catchy techno-bop, but the arrangements have an unfinished quality and his unsubtle singing rarely gets in emotional synch with the material. And while the cover of Bacharach/David's "Look of Love" is a nice idea, his execution is agonizing.

Bates' latest effort, handsomely produced by Paul

Sampson (who is best known for his work in and with the Primitives but was actually once Bates' bandmate in the Reluctant Stereotypes), manages to make his voice—showing better control than in the past—more palatable than ever before. With the star handling guitar, harmonica and banjo, a skilled trio (bass, drums, clarinet) helps him realize the songs on the utterly presentable **Letters to a Scattered Family** as textured, shimmering pop and rock full of nuance and character. (The CD adds the entire contents of **The Return of the Quiet**.)

Kodak Ghosts Run Amok, a 1980-'86 singles (and more) compilation, chronicles Eyeless in Gaza's development from idiosyncratic home-brew experimentation through ragged melodicism to full-blown pop. This is really for fans; newcomers are instead recommended to the later, easier-to-like albums. (The double-play cassette appends **Caught in Flux**.) **Transience Blues** is a collection of Eyeless rarities.   [jw/i]

FACE TO FACE

Face to Face (Epic) 1984
Confrontation (Epic) 1985
One Big Day (Mercury) 1988 ●

Depending on where your needle drops on Face to Face's first record, the Boston quintet is either a fascinating blend of hip-hop and rock'n'roll or a noxious pre-fab MTV creation. Four producers worked on the album, yielding both the annoying hit single "10-9-8" and a gripping piece of political consciousness, "Under the Gun," on which Arthur Baker (who produced both tracks) drum-programs and scratch-mixes the band into an exciting new realm. (A subsequent 12-inch further elaborates on "Under the Gun"—fifteen minutes' worth—with two remixes.)

Confrontation was mostly co-produced by Baker and Ed Stasium. Except for the increasing number of ballads, the band rocks enthusiastically, leaning into the rhythmic material. Singer Laurie Sargent remains a strong presence, but the routine presentation and sound make this **Confrontation** too radio-ready to be interesting.

Why Anton Fier would be needed to produce an album that sounds like a tasteful countryfied cross between Scandal and the Motels is a mystery, but that's the story on **One Big Day**. In a further misuse of talent, Syd Straw and Bernie Worrell contribute to the tunefully bland proceedings. [i]

FAD GADGET

See *Frank Tovey.*

FAHRENHEIT 451

See *Executive Slacks.*

JAD FAIR

See *Half Japanese.*

FAIRGROUND ATTRACTION

Perfect EP (nr/RCA) 1988 ●
The First of a Million Kisses (RCA) 1988 ●
Find My Love EP (nr/RCA) 1988 ●
A Smile in a Whisper EP (nr/RCA) 1988 ●
Ay Fond Kiss (nr/RCA) 1990 ●

Scottish vocalist Eddi Reader had sung behind the Gang of Four, Alison Moyet and Eurythmics; joined by guitarist/songwriter Mark Nevin (a onetime sideman of Jane Aire's) and a lightweight rhythm section (Simon Edwards plays an acoustic guitarron in lieu of bass) she led the short-lived Fairground Attraction, a folky star in the UK jazz-pop heavens. **The First of a Million Kisses** is the quartet's only full album, a wonderful, bewitching romance of airy music and Reader's strong, supple voice. From svelte Everything but the Girl-styled elegance ("A Smile in a Whisper") to fuller-figured pop ("Perfect") to Costelloesque folk ("Moon on the Rain") to minimalist Latin-inflected R&B ("Find My Love") to shuffling Dixieland ("Clare"), the catchy songs and intimate performances never fail to charm. (The CD adds two Nevin-penned non-LP songs from the **Perfect** EP, which also boasts an a cappella rendition of "Mystery Train.")

The album was followed by a pair of additional EPs drawn from it; each contains (in some configurations) three non-LP sides. (**A Smile in a Whisper** has the inevitable reading of Patsy Cline's "Walking After Midnight.") After Fairground Attraction broke up in the summer of '89, the group's label assembled **Ay Fond Kiss**, a compilation of B-sides and leftovers titled for a song on the **Find My Love** EP. [i]

See also *Morrissey.*

MARIANNE FAITHFULL

Broken English (Island) 1979 ●
Dangerous Acquaintances (Island) 1981
A Childs Adventure (Island) 1983 ●
Strange Weather (Island) 1987 ●
Blazing Away (Island) 1990 ●

MARK ISHAM/MARIANNE FAITHFULL

Trouble in Mind (Island Visual Arts) 1986

Resuming her recording career after a gap of several years, erstwhile '60s pop singer Marianne Faithfull presents a whole new persona on these intensely individual and powerful albums. Armed with a life-roughened voice filled with suffering and rage, and backed by brilliantly original electro-rock, she grapples with mostly political subjects on **Broken English** and even includes a fascinating interpretation of John Lennon's "Working Class Hero." For **Dangerous Acquaintances**, Faithfull takes a more resigned outlook, and sings of relationships and the passage of time with strength and depth.

Although the music on it is less exemplary, **A Childs Adventure** continues her harrowing voyage. Other than the political commentary of "Ireland," the songs concentrate on personal struggles, with only a glimmer of hope ("Ashes in My Hand") emerging from the otherwise bleak appraisal.

Despite co-billing with composer/horn player Mark Isham, Faithfull merely sings two songs on the **Trouble in Mind** soundtrack album. The cool jazz of the title track for Alan Rudolph's 1986 film offers a foretaste of the direction she took on her next record, **Strange Weather**. Cast as a sophisticated chanteuse (the echoes of Dietrich and Lotte Lenya are duly noted in Terry Southern's liner notes), Faithfull confronts a far-ranging program (blues, swing, folk, Tin Pan Alley) with delicate accompaniment by Lou Reed's sidemen (Fernando Saunders, Robert Quine and J.T. Lewis) as well as Mac Rebbenack, strings and a horn section. An old spiritual ("Sign of Judgment") connects beautifully with Faithfull's emotional conviction; two tunes from the early '30s—"Boulevard of Broken Dreams" and the schmoozy "Penthouse Serenade"—are also rich and wonderful. On the downside, a new version of "As Tears Go By" is mainly academic and her reading of Dylan's "I'll Keep It with Mine" is simply horrible.

Blazing Away is a career retrospective recorded live at St. Anne's Cathedral in Brooklyn. Producer Hal Willner assembled a dream band anchored by longtime Faithfull collaborator Barry Reynolds on guitar; former Lounge Lizards Dougie Bowne (drums) and Marc Ribot (guitar) mesh powerfully with keyboards played by Garth Hudson and Dr. John. Faithfull's vocal interpretations have never been so intelligent or convincing, and she unveils definitive versions of "Working Class Hero," "Strange Weather" and "Sister Morphine" (and another unnecessary recording of "As Tears Go By"). The set includes five songs from **Broken English** and only one mediocre new original, a studio rendition of the country-flavored title track. But on searing new versions of "Ballad of Lucy Jordan" and "Why'd Ya Do It?," Faithfull proves she's a singer for the ages, a Billie Holiday figure for a generation too confused for the blues.   [i/ws]

FAITH NO MORE

We Care a Lot (Mordam) 1985 + 1987
Introduce Yourself (Slash) 1987 ●
The Real Thing (Slash-Reprise) 1989 ●

San Francisco's Faith No More began on the indie scene's Marshall plan, playing a muscular mongrel rock mix containing funk, metal, hip-hop, hardcore and keyboards that punks could easily appreciate. Leading off with the dynamic and inspirational chant/roar of "We Care a Lot," the first album (a Matt Wallace production that was remastered and reissued after the band's second LP) attempts too many things (none, except perhaps "Greed," as memorable as the title track) and lacks the songwriting tools to be really effective, but it does offer a solid dose of street-level guitar power to those revolted by arena bands.

Apparently unconcerned by the danger of seeming like a one-song band, the quintet redid "We Care a Lot" with new topical lyrics for **Introduce Yourself**, a blistering, conceptually refined album built around Jim Martin's well-integrated metal guitar, Mike Bordin's superb drumming and Chuck Mosley's coarse vocals and real-life lyrics. Having located a solid stylistic core, Faith No More's careful digressions into rappish rhythm riot (and other areas) became part of a clear-cut sound, supported by much improved songwriting (like "Introduce Yourself," which namechecks a good chunk of the record industry, and "R'n'R," which is blurted in a hard-rock analogue to Grandmaster Flash's "The Message").

Mosley was sacked in 1988 and replaced by Mike Patton, a quivery young vocalist who'd obviously seen Anthony Kiedis front the Red Hot Chili Peppers more than once. Dispensing with any remaining eccentricities, Faith No More rolled all of its assets (giving new prominence to Roddy Bottum's keyboards) into a tight commercial ball on **The Real Thing**, thereby joining Living Colour as one of the very few electrifying hard-rock bands to remain clearly outside both the metal and pop spheres. Despite Patton's tiresome vocals and the repetitive songs, the record's syncopated street-level power (and the catchy "Epic") hit a nerve, and Faith No More became one of 1990's few credible success stories.   [i]

FALCO

Einzelhaft (A&M) 1982
Junge Roemer (A&M) 1984 ●
3 (A&M) 1986 ●
Emotional (Sire) 1986 ●
Wiener Blut (Sire) 1988 ●

Falco (Johann Hoelcel) is something of a hero in his native Austria; although he sings (in a random pastiche of accented English and German) like an arch, continental smoothie, his shtick is slick, thematically simpleminded chart fare, syncopated and fashionably automated (lots of synth, computerized drums with rototom and cymbal overdubs). The best parts of **Einzelhaft** (co-produced with his songwriting partner, keyboardist Robert Ponger) are tedious rock; the tracks that have earned him international visibility ("Der Kommissar," a US hit when badly covered in English by After the Fire; "Maschine Brennt") are repulsive pseudo-funk with obnoxiously patronizing attempts at African-American lingo, accents and music, sung in a constipated gurgle as appealing as hearing someone vomit outside your window.

On **Junge Roemer**, Ponger's generally lighter touch—leaning towards Philly soul in tone if not content—cuts a lot of the crap to expose a boring collection of tepidly delivered songs. On the other hand, Falco's third LP is a grotesque monstrosity. With two new collaborators replacing Ponger, Falco essays a cultural outreach program with such garishly overproduced, overlong thumpers as "Vienna Calling" (7:40) and "Rock Me Amadeus" (8:20). Each repeats a cloying riff or chorus endlessly while all manner of gimmicky mix tricks (spoken word, scratching, dub echo, sound effects, etc.) attempt to obscure Falco's regurgo blather. Think of an endless loop of Queen's "We Will Rock You" with less melody and you'll get an idea of what a nightmare this is. To cap things off in maximally tasteless fashion, he debases Dylan's "It's All Over Now, Baby Blue" as a sneery lounge singer, complete with spoken asides. What a jerk! (For masochists, **3**—brilliantly mastered, incidentally—runs over 50 minutes, even on vinyl.)

Falco seems a bit of a manipulated wimp on **Emotional**, a record to which he contributed some of the lyrics and none of the music. Producers Rob and Ferdi Bolland are in complete control, writing and playing almost everything except guitars and sax. The (mis-) concept album ranges from ABC-like slick soul to psychopathic shrieking; Falco is as awful as ever, babbling the verbose bilingual lyrics with auto-pilot enthusiasm and the assistance of mega-tracked female backing vocals. The wildly bombastic production and pervasive low-brow mentality here cries out for Jim Steinman to produce Falco's next record.

Thankfully, that didn't come to pass on **Wiener Blut**. The relatively restrained side written and produced by the Bollands dispenses with the kitchen sink, leaving Falco to carry on gurgling over chattering dance tracks that more or less mind their manners. Of course, the material is utterly inane, hitting such lows as ". . . Rides Again" (which begs the how-can-we-miss-you-if-you-won't-go-away? question) and "Garbo" ("a mélange of Aphrodite and Venus"). Falco actually attempts to sing on the album's second side, which takes clumsy aim at soul, power balladry and other uncharacteristic styles, ending with a bizarre sequencer-and-sitar-flavored rendition of Steely Dan's "Do It Again."

[jg/i]

TAV FALCO'S PANTHER BURNS
See *Panther Burns*.

FALL
Live at the Witch Trials (Step Forward-IRS) 1979 ●
Dragnet (nr/Step Forward) 1979 ●
Totale's Turns (It's Now or Never) (nr/Rough Trade) 1980
Grotesque (After the Gramme) (Rough Trade) 1980
Early Years 77–79 (Faulty Products) 1981
Slates EP (Rough Trade) 1981
Live in London, 1980 [tape] (nr/Chaos) 1982
Hex Enduction Hour (nr/Kamera) 1982 ●
Room to Live (nr/Kamera) 1982
A Part of America Therein, 1981 (Cottage) 1982
Perverted by Language (nr/Rough Trade) 1983 ●
Kicker Conspiracy EP (nr/Rough Trade) 1983
Fall in a Hole (NZ Flying Nun) 1983
The Wonderful and Frightening World of the Fall
     (Beggars Banquet-PVC) 1984 ●
Call for Escape Route EP (nr/Beggars Banquet) 1984
Hip Priest and Kamerads (nr/Situation 2) 1985 ●
This Nation's Saving Grace (Beggars Banquet-PVC)
     1985 ●
The Fall EP (PVC) 1986
Bend Sinister (nr/Beggars Banquet) 1986 ●
Domesday Pay-Off (Big Time) 1987
There's a Ghost in My House EP (nr/Beggars Banquet)
     1987
The Peel Sessions EP (nr/Strange Fruit) 1987
The Fall In: Palace of Swords Reversed (Cog
     Sinister-Rough Trade) 1987 ●
The Frenz Experiment (Big Time) 1988 ●
Victoria EP (nr/Beggars Banquet) 1988
I Am Kurious Oranj (Beggars Banquet-RCA) 1988 ●
Jerusalem EP (nr/Beggars Banquet) 1988 ●
Cab It Up/Dead Beat Descendant EP (nr/Beggars
     Banquet) 1989
Seminal Live (Beggars Banquet-RCA) 1989 ●
Extricate (Cog Sinister-Fontana) 1990 ●
Dredger EP (nr/Cog Sinister-Phonogram) 1990
458489 A Sides (Beggars Banquet-RCA) 1990 φ
458489 B Sides (nr/Beggars Banquet) 1990 ●
Shiftwork (nr/Fontana) 1991 ●

Formed in Manchester in 1977, the Fall has attracted a cult following in numerous corners of the globe, but has managed to bend commercial necessities to its own needs and carve no small chart success in the UK. Fall fans are rabid, and the group's influence on likeminded conceptual noisemakers—in England, the US, Iceland, New Zealand and elsewhere—can't be overstated. Led by acid-tongued poet Mark E. Smith, whose caustic lyrics and amelodic vocals provide the Fall's primary features, the band has created a huge body of unique, adventurous and challenging (less so in recent years) rock. From humble experimental beginnings, the Fall has continued to explore and grow stronger over the course of nearly fifteen prolific years, earning a place of real respect in left-of-center musical circles. Whether you enjoy the sounds or not, the Fall has made a crucial difference in modern music, and that counts.

After releasing some singles and contributing two tracks to the watershed **Short Circuit/Live at the Electric Circus** Manchester compilation, the Fall recorded and mixed their debut LP, **Live at the Witch Trials**, in an economical two-day studio session with producer Bob Sargeant, who did nothing (audible) to soften their well-organized dissonance. At once leaning towards punk's directness and charging headlong into poetic pretension, Smith and company (bass, drums, electric piano, guitar) drip sincerity on tracks like "Rebellious Jukebox" and "Crap Rap 2/Like to Blow," occasionally sounding relatively normal amidst the tempest. **Dragnet** followed with a rougher-edged sound, as well as a new lineup. The first album to feature Craig Scanlon's trademark scratchy, dissonant guitar (which has played a major role in the band ever since), **Dragnet** is not one of the Fall's best efforts, but contains at least two classic numbers, "Spectre vs. Rector" and "A Figure Walks."

By the time of their first live album, **Totale's Turns**—recorded in late '79 and early '80—the Fall had consolidated a more commanding style, although it's no easier on the aurals. Jagged, largely recitative and nearly oblivious to musical convention, Smith's witty repartee carries the show as the band lurches and grunts along noisily. Not for neophytes.

Grotesque removes the Fall even further from the world of easy listening. The songs are mostly one-or-two-chord jams played too slowly to be hardcore, but structured similarly. Smith grafts on socio-political lyrics that would be more interesting on paper than accompanied by this one-take-live-in-the-studio atonality.

All of the Fall's pre-LP singles (by a lineup with keyboardist Una Baines and guitarist Martin Bramah, who went off together to form the Blue Orchids) are on one side of **Early Years**; the other collects later 7-inch efforts. One imagines that Public Image listened to the '77 vintage "Repetition" a couple of times before mapping out their first LP.

The 10-inch **Slates** has six tracks with substantially better production than the Fall's preceding ventures; evidence of much greater studio effort abounds. While still not quite Abba-smooth, several numbers, especially "Fit and Working Again" and "Leave the Capitol," are as close to enjoyable, routine (ahem) rock as the Fall had ever come. A solid record of greater potential appeal than just to cultists.

Part of **Hex Enduction Hour** was recorded in Iceland, a nation where the Fall's music had a major cultural impact. An expanded lineup with two drummers turns the sound large and rhythm-conscious; despite a resulting tendency to lumber along at a slow, methodical pace, some of the tracks are intriguingly off the common Fall path. (The German CD edition on the Line label includes some early singles as bonus cuts.)

Room to Live features a sparser, less rhythmic sound than **Hex Enduction Hour**, occasionally returning to **Grotesque**'s flirtation with raw rockabilly. Smith is in top lyrical form, with pungent, satirical views of British life: "Marquis Cha Cha" offers biting commentary on the Falklands War.

Three live Fall albums emerged around this time. **A Part of America Therein** was taped at five gigs on a US tour. The sound quality varies considerably from track to track, but the performances are uniformly strong, particularly the epic "N.W.R.A." Even better, though, is **Fall in a Hole**, a two-disc authorized bootleg released only in New Zealand. Recording quality, execution and song selection (mostly from **Hex** and **Room to Live**) are superb. The **Live in London, 1980** cassette was recorded in front of a none-too-enthusiastic audience at Acklam Hall; it's of dubious legal origin, listing neither songwriting nor publishing credits. Drawing mostly from **Grotesque** and **Slates**, it warrants mention due to sharp performances (except for "Prole Art Threat," which falls apart) and very good sound quality.

The Fall's next studio LP, **Perverted by Language**, marked a brief return to Rough Trade. On the first record with Smith's new American wife Brix as co-guitarist, they chug away with more conviction than ever, particularly on the relentless "Smile" and "Eat Y'self Fitter." Hindsight now shows it to be priming the audience for what was to follow: the John Leckie-produced **Wonderful and Frightening World of the Fall**, easily one of the band's best records. Strengthened by Brix's songwriting and gutsy guitar, the Fall are able to beckon a variety of styles with panache. All nine tracks (eleven on the American release, which adds "C.R.E.E.P." and "No Bulbs," the latter from the subsequent **Call for Escape Route** EP) jump out, highlighted by the fierce "Lay of the Land," "Elves" and the almost Syd Barrett-like "Disney's Dream Debased."

Hip Priest and Kamerads is a compilation of the band's releases on the Kamera label. Except for a live version of "Mere Pseud Mag Ed.," there's nothing otherwise unavailable, but it does offer a good introduction for the uninitiated. The tape and CD have extra tracks.

With what at this point seems like an embarrassment of riches, the Fall unleashed **This Nation's Saving Grace**. Tracks like the (gasp!) synthesized and danceable "L.A." and the contemporaneous 45, "Cruisers Creek," reveal that the Fall is no longer averse to commercial potential, but it's really just a new type of ammo added to the arsenal. "Bombast" builds a guitar din that would make Sonic Youth jealous, while "Paintwork" and "I Am Damo Suzuki" (a song about Can's onetime lead singer) are two of the strangest things they've ever done. The US release substitutes "Cruisers Creek" for "Barmy," which subsequently turned up on the eponymous American EP, alongside four other 45 cuts, like an unlikely cover of Gene Vincent's "Rollin' Dany." (To confuse matters further, Beggars Banquet issued three of the five songs on a 1985 US 12-inch.)

Named for a novel by Vladimir Nabokov, **Bend Sinister** is a rather gloomy, dark sounding record; minor keys and Joy Division-like guitar riffing dominate tracks like "US 80's–90's" and "Gross Chapel—British Grenadiers." But then in the middle of all that is "Shoulder Pads," one of the poppiest, most upbeat songs they've ever done. Multi-instrumentalist Simon Rogers has become the Fall's chief sound-shaper, providing all kinds of odd synths and guitar fills and embellishments. **Domesday Pay-Off**, the equivalent US release to **Bend Sinister**, switches song order a bit and substitutes singles from the same approximate period, such as "Hey! Luciani" and a cover of R. Dean Taylor's "There's a Ghost in My House." The four-song **Peel Sessions** disc (from November 1978) predates the Fall's debut album; two of the numbers are from that LP, the other two are otherwise unreleased. A must for fans.

The Fall In: Palace of Swords Reversed is a compilation of Rough Trade singles, flipsides and LP tracks from 1980 to 1983, released on Smith's own label. **The Frenz Experiment** is an unusual LP—almost a Smith solo—with lower-key backing than usual, and more willfully obscure lyrics than ever, particularly on "Athlete Cured" and the very odd "Oswald Defence Lawyer." Rogers, no longer a fulltime band member, produced and gave it the most detailed sound of any Fall record. Adding to their growing reputation as an able and imaginative cover band, **Frenz** includes a totally delightful version of the Kinks' "Victoria." (The original UK LP includes a bonus single of "Mark'll Sink Us"/"Bremen Nacht Run.")

Recent Fall side projects have established the group in other fields. Smith expanded the idea from the "Hey! Luciani" 45 into a play which ran in London. The Fall wrote the adequate but uneventful vocal music (which the group performed as live accompaniment in Amsterdam, Edinburgh and England, then committed to vinyl as the **I Am Kurious Oranj** album) for *I Am Curious Orange*, a ballet by Michael Clark's experimental dance company. A pair of EPs were drawn from the album: **Jerusalem** (the William Blake song) was released as a boxed pair of 7-inch singles (with a postcard) and as a 3-inch CD, with three more LP tracks, one of them in a drastically altered version. **Cab It Up** (the Mark E. Smith song) comes on a 12-inch with live renditions of "Kurious Oranj" and "Hit the North" and a new song ("Dead Beat Descendant") from the then-imminent **Seminal Live**.

Despite its title, the Fall's 1989 album mixes a side of new material (casual and largely self-indulgent studio efforts) with a dynamic and cavalier side of live oldies, such as "Cruisers Creek," "L.A.," "Pay Your Rates," "2 by 4" and "Victoria." Although hardly an ideal artistic coda, that record proved to be Brix's farewell, thereby ending an extremely productive Fall era. In mid-'89, her marriage to Mark collapsed and she left the group, turning the Adult Net, her side project, into a fulltime endeavor.

The Fall's recovery from their loss was surprisingly quick and complete: by the following year's remarkable **Extricate** (which features Martin Bramah's short return to the fold; he and keyboardist Marcia Schofield left in mid-'90), the only remaining evidence of Brix's existence is in Smith's transparently vindictive lyrics. Production by Smith, Craig Leon, Adrian Sherwood and Coldcut effectively picks up the thread of the Fall's progress with little incident, allowing Smith to unburden himself in extraordinarily fine musical settings. With nothing in common except for the articulate poetic passion, the first four songs—"Sing! Harpy," "I'm Frank," "Bill Is Dead" and the devastating "Black Month Theme Part One"—are among the Fall's best-ever creations. While the rest of **Extricate** (excepting the cool single "Telephone Thing," a Coldcut cover) isn't as potent, the album offers reassuring proof of the Fall's durability and resourcefulness. (The **Dredger** 12-inch contains four post-**Extricate** tracks, none of them entitled "Dredger," and a limited-edition poster.)

Chronicling the Brix years (and serving as something of an extension to **Palace of Swords Reversed**), **458489 A Sides** is, as billed, a compilation of the Fall's singles released between '84 and '89. The seventeen tracks—including such essential items as "Rollin' Dany," "L.A.," "Hey! Luciani," "There's a Ghost in My House" and "Victoria"—follow the band through its pop orientation and subsequent stylistic redeployments. Completing the job, the double-album **458489 B Sides** collects all of the remaining tracks from the same era's singles, including remixes: 31 in all. A major boon to fans who've been stymied by the band's intricate discography.

Fall CDs usually add a few concurrent singles and B-sides; their US LPs usually add the A-side of a single not on the British LP. For instance, 1987's "Hit the North" shows up on the CD of **Frenz** (in the UK, along with four other bonus cuts). **Bend Sinister** adds "Living Too Late" and "Auto-Tech Pilot" on the CD; both of those, plus "Town and Country Hobgoblins," are on the UK cassette. [i/dgs]

See also *Adult Net, Blue Orchids, Marc Riley with the Creepers*.

FALLING JOYS
Omega EP (Aus. Volition) 1989
Wish List (Volition-Nettwerk-IRS) 1990 ●

Clear-voiced singer/songwriter Suzie Higgie gets rich, electric rock backing from her bandmates on **Wish List**, the Sydney quartet's first longplayer. Although Higgie's refined delivery suggests a West Coast Debbie Harry, guitarist Stuart Robertson sounds like a reformed metalhead, cranking up the contrast in a tastefully loud surge. If the band flirts shamelessly with mainstream radio, the album has an undercurrent of recklessness and individuality that shores it up on songs like the barely contained "Shot in Europe," the industrialized "Puppy Drink" and the ominous "Tunnel Vision." The CD adds a bonus track, "Shelter." [i]

FALSE PROPHETS
False Prophets (Alternative Tentacles) 1986
Implosion (Alternative Tentacles) 1987

Don't be thrown by the irreverent religious imagery on **False Prophets**: after they get through "Invokation" and "Seven Deadly Sins," this punk-rocking New York five-piece trains its obviously educated intelligence on more traditional hardcore themes like war, authority, violence and rebellion. The Prophets mediate the punk onslaught with dynamics and tempos that don't all run on overdrive, but there's nothing remarkable about their debut.

Implosion, produced by living legend Giorgio Gomelsky, is light years better, breaking uncharted ground

on three selections with the fourth-dimensional addition of a horn section led by James White. What a concept! Speedcore takes a back seat as False Prophets reveal their expansive and temperate rock imagination, testing varied rough waters with conviction and wild-eyed enthusiasm. Not great, but getting there. [i]

FAMILY CAT
Tell 'Em We're Surfin' (nr/Bad Girl) 1989
Place with a Name EP (nr/Bad Girl) 1990 ●

Following a 1989 debut single entitled "Tom Verlaine," this likably scruffy Cornwall-to-London quintet plays unfussy, mildly psychedelic garage pop with off-kilter lyrics on the catchy and cool eight-song **Tell 'Em We're Surfin'** mini-album. Despite the intimidating threat of a three-man guitar army, the Family Cat is strictly small-scale; while there's a bite to the droney textures, other bands get far more density and aggression from a single strummer.

The subsequent EP smoothes and tightens the Family Cat with four new tunes, including "Place with a Name," a delectable ultra-pop tune with rich harmonies and a scathing noise-guitar solo, and the gently twisted "Theme from 'The Family Cat'." [i]

FAMILY FUN
See *Space Negros*.

MICK FARREN
(Mona) The Carnivorous Circus (nr/Transatlantic) 1970 (nr/Psycho) 1984 ●
Vampires Stole My Lunch Money (nr/Logo) 1978 ●

MICK FARREN & THE DEVIANTS
Screwed Up EP (nr/Stiff) 1977

DEVIANTS
Human Garbage (nr/Psycho) 1984

MICK FARREN & WAYNE KRAMER
Who Shot You Dutch? EP (Spectre) 1987

Mick Farren—music journalist, novelist, vocalist, founding member of the (Social) Deviants and Pink Fairies, Motörhead songwriter, etc.—cut his first solo album with a nascent version of the Fairies immediately upon leaving the Deviants in 1969. He left the spotlight for awhile, but returned in '77 with a four-song 7-inch on Stiff that has its moments but is hardly a milestone.

Released at the height of the punk wave but springing from a much deeper creative well, **Vampires Stole My Lunch Money** is Farren's solo masterwork. With musical assistance from Wilko Johnson, Chrissie Hynde and others, he dishes out a harrowingly honest collection of songs about drinking, dissolution, depression, self-destruction and desperation. About as powerful as rock gets, this nakedly painful LP is most definitely not recommended to sissies, born-again Christians or prohibitionists.

Relocating to New York several years later, Farren pursued a number of musical endeavors with ex-MC5 guitarist Wayne Kramer. In February 1984, joined by ex-Fairies Larry Wallis and Duncan Sanderson and a drummer, the pair did a loose-limbed London gig (billed as the Deviants) at Dingwalls, recorded and released as

Human Garbage. The material mixes selections from **Vampires** ("I Want a Drink" and Frank Zappa's "Trouble Coming Every Day"), Kramer's solo work ("Ramblin' Rose"), Wallis ("Police Car") and similarly casual items like "Screwed Up," "Takin' L.S.D." and "Outrageous Contagious." No points for tightness or tuning, but a neat artifact nonetheless.

Three songs from *The Last Words of Dutch Schultz*, an "R&B musical"—based on death-bed ramblings by the prohibition-era gangster—written and performed by Farren and Kramer, comprise the 1987 12-inch. The powerful title track (sung by Kramer and produced by Don Was) is clever funk-rock rendered giggly by a disco chorus repeating the phrase throughout the number; the others are more theatrical and modestly appealing. [i]

See also *Hawkwind, Motörhead, Social Deviants*.

FAST

For Sale (Recca) 1980
Leather Boys from the Asphalt Jungle (Recca) 1981

Before he moved into oversexed Eurodisco, the late guitarist/songwriter Miki Zone spent a decade, beginning in the early '70s, leading various versions of Brooklyn's own Anglo-pop Fast. A pioneering and exciting force on the Dolls-era club scene and a great example of bootstrapping, the Fast—which included vocalist Paul Zone and, for some years, a third Zone brother—made a handful of ingeniously derivative singles (updating '60s pop-art rock and '70s glam) and self-released an album in 1980. Pulling together tracks from various sessions produced by Ric Ocasek, Richard Gottehrer, Bobby Orlando, Ian North and Zone himself, **For Sale** (the cover a loving parody of **The Who Sell Out**) is a patchy collection of inconsistent sounds and styles, and less than representative of the group's repertoire. It does, however, contain some wonderful tunes, including "Kids Just Wanna Dance," "Boys Will Be Boys" and the winsome "It's Like Love," as well as the quartet's punky interpretation of "These Boots Are Made for Walkin'."

Recorded in one studio effort as a duo of Paul and Miki, **Leather Boys** also fails to convey much of what made the Fast so much fun, but a few good songs (notably "Skinny Kids & Bigger Bullies" and Ian North's "Girls in Gangs") make it a heartwarming souvenir for fans. (Two who remember are Chris Stein and Debbie Harry, who covered Miki's "Comic Books" as a bonus track on **Def Dumb & Blonde**.)

By 1982, the Fast was well past kitschy power pop, and dabbling in dance music with a single containing a simple electro-dance version of the Supremes' "Love Is Like an Itching in My Heart." Subsequently shifting their base of operations abroad, the brothers—playing disco under the name Man to Man—hit the UK charts in late 1986, a victory cut short by Miki's fatal illness a year later. [i]

FASTBACKS

Fastbacks Play Five of Their Favorites EP (No Threes) 1982
Every Day is Saturday EP (No Threes) 1984
... and His Orchestra (PopLlama Products) 1987

Bike-Toy-Clock-Gift [tape] (Bus Stop) 1988
Very, Very Powerful Motor (PopLlama Products) 1990

With future Young Fresh Fellow Kurt Bloch providing the kicky songs and formidable rock'n'roll guitar power, Seattle's Fastbacks made irregular contributions to the world of recorded music throughout the '80s, turning up on numerous compilations and occasionally issuing records of their own. Guitarist Lulu Gargiulo and bassist Kim Warnick play hit-and-miss with the melodies on the casually unpretentious **. . . and His Orchestra**, but everyone winds up sharing a good time anyway. Besides Bloch's charming pop-rock ditties, drummer Richard Stuverud chips in with one number, and the group does an impressive (if incongruous) loud, hard cover of Sweet's "Set Me Free."

Bike-Toy-Clock-Gift is a live album—sixteen tracks from mid-'88—issued only on cassette. Recorded as a trio of Bloch (by then a moonlighting Fellow), Warnick and a different drummer (although Gargiulo puts in several vocal appearances), **Very, Very Powerful Motor** gives Bloch's pop-rooted songs powerhouse rock arrangements that overwhelm some of them; in her rougher vocal moments, Warnick sounds like a more melodically astute Joan Jett. Cool cover: "Apologies" by the Pointed Sticks. [i]

See also *Young Fresh Fellows*.

FAST FLOYD AND THE FAMOUS FIREBIRDS

Devil's Daughter (Kingpin) 1983

Early Mink DeVille sideman Fast Floyd (vocals/guitar) fronts this red-hot San Francisco R&B quintet, breathlessly belting out sizzling numbers (most of them covers) like "You Talk Too Much," "Wish You Would" and "Got the Water Boiling." Floyd's punkabilly whoop—like Tav Falco on steroids or Lux Interior minus the punk kitsch—adds gusto to the frenzied atmosphere; Franco St. Andrew blows a horny enough tenor sax to steam up some windows of his own. Capping off this dynamite blast of retro-styled party rock, the nudie cover shot of '50s sex queen Candy Barr nuzzling up to a phonograph perfectly captures the album's goodnatured sleaze. [i]

FATAL FLOWERS

Fatal Flowers (nr/WEA) 1985
Younger Days (Atlantic) 1986
Johnny D. Is Back! An Album by the Fatal Flowers (Atlantic) 1989 ●
Pleasure Ground (nr/Mercury) 1990 ●

Growing up in Holland must be a strange experience for kids with rock'n'roll dreams. This Amsterdam quartet began blandly enough, playing inoffensive characterless rock on its first two albums, the second of which offers the first glimmer of the group's truly weird (or truly stupid) approach: a punky rendition of "Gimme Some Truth," recorded nearly a decade after Generation X's definitive cover of the John Lennon song.

Produced in Woodstock by Mick Ronson, **Johnny D.** delves deeply into evidently unintended nostalgia: these guys don't seem to realize how dated they sound. (I mean, really, how long has it been since anyone wrote an unironic song entitled "Rock and Roll Star"?) Digging into vintage American rock'n'roll with unself-conscious aplomb, the group relives the fabulous '70s as if "Radar Love" were still in the charts. Perhaps in tribute to the days of stoned-out inanity, the lyrics are utterly ridiculous: "Here's another hippy in smoking/ Thanking all his pimps and more/How he wished he was only joking/But he knows he's just another whore."

Sounding like castaways scavenging through an un-earthed archaeological jukebox and marveling at their ear-opening discoveries, the Fatal Flowers go totally over the top on **Pleasure Ground**, also produced by Ronson. Stumbling across evidence of African-Americans, they go wild covering Arthur Conley's 1968 vintage "Funky Street," complete with wah-wah pedal and dated clichés ("We're grooving in the city/We've got to get down with it"). Elsewhere, the oblivious timewarpers reproduce Kiss-like metal riffs, imitate the J. Geils Band, Bad Company, the Rolling Stones and '70s Pink Floyd, adopt an Arlo Guthrie voice (for "Rage Out") and close the LP with a Bowie-styled cover of Roxy Music's "Both Ends Burning." Amazing. (Memo to the band's lawyer: it's considered poor form to claim writing credit for world-famous songs.)

[i]

FAT BOYS

Fat Boys (Sutra) 1984
The Fat Boys Are Back! (Sutra) 1985
Big & Beautiful (Sutra) 1986
The Best Part of the Fat Boys (Sutra) 1987 ●
Crushin' (Tin Pan Apple-Polydor) 1987 ●
Coming Back Hard Again (Tin Pan Apple-Polydor) 1988 ●
Krush on You (nr/Blatant) 1988 ●
On and On (Tin Pan Apple-Mercury) 1989 ●

In a medium like rap, it helps to have a gimmick, and this Brooklyn trio—originally known as the Disco 3—had several. While most rappers brag about what great lovers they are, Prince Markie Dee (Mark Morales), Buff Love (Darren Robinson) and Kool Rock-ski (Damon Wimbley) brag about what great eaters they are. In this, their claim to originality is undisputed. Gimmick number two is Buff the Human Beat Box (not to be confused with Doug E. Fresh, the self-proclaimed Original Human Beat Box), who uses lips, cheeks and tongue to create a surprisingly varied array of rhythmic noises. The group's raps are also gimmicky, while the well-produced (on the early records, by Kurtis Blow) backing tracks employ full-scale instrumentation and were quick to cross rap with reggae and rock. If the Fat Boys weren't the most talented crew in the business, they were at least consistently good fun.

The Best Part of the Fat Boys is indeed that, as it compiles ten tracks from the first three albums and has everything you'd ever need to hear by them: "Fat Boys," "The Fat Boys Are Back," "All You Can Eat," "Hard Core Reggae," "Sex Machine," etc. The more extensive **Krush on You** repeats seven from **The Best Part** and adds seven more of the same vintage.

Crushin', a mild but winning party collection of mainstream cuts with boundless entertainment spirit and unfailing good humor, has the trio's collaboration with

the Beach Boys ("Wipeout") but few other equally memorable tracks. **Coming Back Hard Again** starts with a rap adaptation of "The Twist" sung by Chubby Checker and includes a funny version of "Louie, Louie" (in which the rappers discuss the song's controversial lyrics) as well as "Are You Ready for Freddy," the theme song for a *Nightmare on Elm Street* film.

Although **On and On** has a few enjoyable numbers (the singsong "If It Ain't One Thing It's Annuddah," f'rinstance), this "rappera"—as horrible as the concept sounds, the out-of-gas trio actually does very little with it—is a boring display of tired clichés and uninspired performances, with none of the cartoony crew's old panache. A futile stab at street credibility, this sorry LP only makes the fading Fat Boys seem hopelessly out of touch. [jl/i]

FATIMA MANSIONS

See *Microdisney*.

SHANE FAUBERT

See *Cheepskates*.

FAUST

Faust (nr/Polydor) 1971 (nr/Recommended) 1979
Faust So Far (nr/Polydor) 1972 (nr/Recommended) 1979
The Faust Tapes (nr/Virgin) 1973 (nr/Recommended) 1979 (Cuneiform) 1990 ●
Faust IV (nr/Virgin) 1973
Munic and Elsewhere (nr/Recommended) 1986
The Last LP (nr/Recommended) 1988

Although Faust was one of the most internationally influential (especially on the noise and industrial generation, starting with Cabaret Voltaire) of the early-'70s German progressive-rock experimenters, the group's work has never been widely known outside of narrow confines. Faust's first album appeared the same year as Kraftwerk's, but the group disbanded two years later without ever enjoying much commercial success (or even international exposure) and has thus become fairly obscure, although its work has been kept in print via reissues.

Released as a dramatic picture disc—an X-ray of a hand embedded in clear vinyl and packaged in a transparent sleeve—**Faust** consists of three long, post-psychedelic jams, each composed of a couple of ideas loosely strung together. The group uses droning fuzz guitar, primitive electronics, silences, piano tinklings, warbled vocals, cabaret accents, tape manipulation and probably at least one kitchen sink. The way Faust throws these elements together suggests dada music for the electronic age.

Faust So Far, the group's best all-around album, is far more tightly structured, boasting actual songs like "It's a Rainy Day, Sunshine Girl" and "Mamie Is Blue," which makes something out of abrasive electronic bursts, wah-wah guitar and minimal vocals. As the album was recorded in 1972, some tracks include twangy distorted guitar/plucky bass jams. Bizarre little experiments pop up between songs: overlays of effects-treated guitars and the like, sort of a German analogue to the Mothers' early sound adventures.

Although it's just a collection of various experiments organized semi-coherently, **The Faust Tapes** is most impressive in terms of sheer sonic invention. You never know what's coming next: an electronic mantra with chanting in a made-up language is followed by a tape collage of radio, kitchen sounds and someone climbing stairs. A moment later, almost-industrial electronics play over a funky rock beat.

Faust IV isn't as consistently innovative as the band's earlier albums, though it still arrived five years ahead of its time. "Krautrock," a parody of longwinded German bands of the era that were heavy on atmosphere and light on content, goes on so long that it winds up indistinguishable from its target.

The two posthumous albums contain odds and ends of notable interest to serious Faust-ians, but novice listeners would be better off sticking with the first four.

[sl]

FEAR
The Record (Slash) 1982
More Beer (Restless) 1985 •

Fear was an early standout on the Los Angeles hardcore scene but quickly grew beyond its boundaries. Skilled, varied, instrumentally confident and inventive, Fear invests **The Record** with searing rock'n'roll and a wild-eyed sense of humor that seems somehow wholesomely good-natured. Lee Ving (who has also pursued a busy and successful acting career) sings like a drunk baseball fan bellowing in the bleachers, roaring like a lout, but completely intelligible, which allows funny—if disturbingly nasty with regard to women and homosexuals—lyrics to rise above the well-ordered din. Guitarist Philo Cramer tosses instrumental cleverness into the material, making Fear something of a cross between the Dictators and Dickies.

Although artistically redundant, **More Beer** is as loud, fast and viciously sarcastic as ever. The sporadic inter-song patter is more amusing than the actual tunes themselves (which are in fact pretty stupid), but there's something pathetically wonderful about Fear, like a dog that you don't really like but keep around anyway because he's so faithful and predictable. (The best Fear on record remains **The Decline of Western Civilization** soundtrack LP, where Ving raises audience baiting to a sidesplitting art and a bandmate coins a new usage for a traditional colloquialism.) [i]

FEARLESS IRANIANS FROM HELL
Fearless Iranians from Hell EP (Boner) 1986
Die for Allah (Boner) 1987
Holy War (Boner) 1988
Foolish Americans (Boner) 1990 •

While some punk bands cover current world affairs—like, say, Iran's Moslem fanaticism—in their topical onslaught, only this powerful San Antonio hardcore outfit can lay claim to an actual Iranian (along with two former Butthole Surfers) in its lineup. The 7-inch EP offers such topical tone poems as "Blow Up the Embassy"; **Die for Allah** (the cover of which represents Ayatollah Khomeini) boasts such blistering speed

tunes as "Life Inside Iran," "Iranians on Bikes," "Die for Allah" and "Chant," which is recited in Farsi.

In danger of running their joke into the desert sand, the Fearless ones broaden their horizons a little on **Holy War**. So while "Faction," the anti-Iraqi "All in a Day's Work," "Kneel to No One" and the title track continue the frenzy of fanatical nationalism (just *how* serious are these guys?), other songs ("Burn the Books," "Dogsperm") hie to more familiar hardcore concerns. In any case, the noisy playing is first-rate punk.

Relegating the late Iranian leader to a dignified back cover portrait but dedicating the album to him, FIFH sharpens their political focus on the metal-geared **Foolish Americans**, attacking Salman Rushdie, George Bush and Americans (for looking down at Iran). [i]

FEAR OF STRANGERS
Fear of Strangers (Faulty Products) 1982
LONESOME VAL
Lonesome Val (Bar/None-Restless) 1990 •

This Albany, New York, quartet was known as the Units until a dispute with the San Francisco band of the same name led to a new handle. **Fear of Strangers** mixes simple, melodic rock with clever topical lyrics (making the group an early entrant in the neo-protest revival), drawing strength from the presence of three songwriters. The music is fresh and catchy if a bit naïve; Val Haynes, a strong, clear-toned vocalist showing traces of Joan Baez amid the rock stylings, provides most of the band's (and album's) character.

Going solo with a mild country twang, Haynes (and Fear of Strangers bassist Steve Cohen) relocated to New York City, where years spent working local clubs brought widespread critical acclaim and, finally, a recording contract. **Lonesome Val** begins with an uplifting, infectious charmer ("To Be Young") and continues with a defiant rocker ("You Won't Say You Love Me"), but the remainder of Haynes's songs plod along slowly and cautiously, lacking the exuberance that would have given them real life. [i]

FEEDTIME
Feedtime (Aus. Aberrant) 1985
Shovel (Aberrant-Rough Trade) 1988
Cooper-S (Aberrant-Rough Trade) 1988 •
Suction (Aberrant-Rough Trade) 1989 •

Descended from pre-hardcore punk and electric blues, this Australian trio offers a fast and loud journey down Tylenol territory, playing it dark, dank, dense and devastatingly simple. "Ha Ha," the first track on **Feedtime**, pulses with deepness, guitar sawing in repetitive circles like the mating call of a didgeridoo, with vocals that are pure low-frequency growl. The grumbled "I've got a Pontiac/gasoline/Pontiac/gasoline" of "Fastbuck" evokes images of Big Black's "Kerosene" with high-intensity drumming and hard, repeating chords. (The guitarist often plays with a bottleneck, which sounds pretty amazing when cranked up to eleven.) An urge to experiment and fuse mismatched genres with each other leads to a stylistic square dance, as blues pairs off with punk and metal meets mantra. Everything is shaken down until it pounds. Even an air of shimmery progressive folk crops up in the vocals of "All Down." Listening to **Feedtime** is like sandblasting your ear canals, but it's worth the agony.

If your tweeters blew out last week, no problem. You won't miss them at all until you get to **Shovel**, where the same pounding sense of repetition slams guitar chords at your face but adds a touch of country warp and twang on the title cut and a crisp upfront drumbeat to the band's repertoire. Like Pere Ubu or Suicide or any number of bands that people didn't know how to appreciate in their time, Feedtime are original, making music that is totally compiled from familiar bits but given enough of a twist to make it the band's own.

Cooper-S applies Feedtime's noisy shredder to cover versions, blessing the Rolling Stones ("Street Fighting Man," "Play with Fire" and two more), Animals ("We've Gotta Get Out of This Place"), Beach Boys ("Fun Fun Fun"), Ramones ("Loudmouth"), Slade ("Hear Me Calling") and others with its tuneless spirited roar, feedback slide experiments and an occasionally untuned bass. Without casting aspersions on Feedtime, it's safe to assume that none of the songs' authors would be able to recognize their handiwork in these rumbling renditions.

Feedtime bid farewell to the world with **Suction**, an all-original swansong that (for more than half the record) runs tidy, occasionally tuneful songs through the usual floor-scraping guitar noise, adding such previously tested accents as horns, harmonica, acoustic guitar and femme vox. (The barking canines on "Drag Your Dog," however, are new.) While the merits of balancing oppression and allure depends on your perspective towards ear abuse, there's no questioning Feedtime's purposeful expression. [e/i]

FEELIES

Crazy Rhythms (Stiff) 1980 (Ger. Line) 1986 (A&M) 1990 •
The Good Earth (Coyote-Twin/Tone) 1986 •
No One Knows EP (Coyote-Twin/Tone) 1986
Only Life (Coyote-A&M) 1988 •
Time for a Witness (Coyote-A&M) 1991 •

TRYPES

The Explorers Hold EP (Coyote) 1984

YUNG WU

Shore Leave (Coyote-Twin/Tone) 1987

SPEED THE PLOUGH

Speed the Plough (Coyote-Twin/Tone) 1989
Wonder Wheel [CD] (East Side Digital) 1991 •

These New Jerseyites are the stuff of legend and cults. Led by guitarists Glenn Mercer and Bill Million (originally featuring future avant-star drummer Andy Fisher, aka Anton Fier), the Feelies dressed like nerdy preppies and paid only passing attention to the conventional demands of rock'n'roll. Even during the original band's period of highest visibility, for example, live dates in New York tended to be infrequent and often fell on holidays.

Crazy Rhythms is far more unequivocal than the group's performances. Mercer and Million draw inspiration from the Byrds, Television and the Velvet Underground, emphasizing the interplay of their electric guitars above all else. The rigid vocals and lyrics take a back seat to the pure textures of the driving rockers and more avant-garde drones. Despite its distinct bloodlessness, **Crazy Rhythms** exudes a principled charm. (A decade later, the album was reissued on CD and cassette, with a newly recorded version of "Paint It, Black" added as an quizzical bonus.)

In the years that followed, the Feelies laid low, but never disbanded, recording and performing around the New York/New Jersey area in various guises and permutations: the Trypes, Willies and Yung Wu. The three bands sound different, although they all play some Feelies songs and share a fascination with layered guitars, drones and the music of Brian Eno and the Velvet Underground.

The seven-person Trypes are the quietest, most introspective of the bunch, and **The Explorers Hold** is a placid, constantly shifting landscape of sounds. The four songs emphasize coloration not beat, yet, for all its subdued calm, there's an explosive tension bubbling underneath the music. The muted guitars threaten—but never give way to—riotous mayhem. Only on the cover of George Harrison's "Love You To" do drummer Stan Demeski's hyperkinetic tom-tom patterns come to the fore, making the Trypes a loud psychedelic folk band. The quieter songs, complete with woodwinds and keyboards, are hauntingly beautiful.

In the mid-'80s, Million and Mercer reactivated the Feelies as a fulltime band with Demeski, bassist Brenda Sauter (also from the Trypes) and percussionist Dave Weckerman. The Feelies finally released their second album, co-produced by Pete Buck, in 1986. **The Good Earth** approaches folk music with its light, airy feel and acoustic guitars, but intensity and obsession lurk near the intricately woven surfaces; slashing leads occasionally pierce the atmospheric tapestry. Million and Mercer display their taut control even as they're strumming away madly in rapturous acceleration; the quiet sections are extraordinarily beautiful. When their voices join for spirited harmonies, you know it was worth the wait. The four-song **No One Knows** is a neat 12-inch sampler joining "The High Road" and "Slipping (Into Something)" from the LP with wonderful covers of the Beatles' "She Said, She Said" and Neil Young's "Sedan Delivery."

Dave Weckerman is the enthusiastically informal lead vocalist and songwriter in Yung Wu—the Feelies augmented by Trypes keyboard player John Baumgartner. **Shore Leave** leans towards acoustic guitars and simplified drumming for a rustic sound that exchanges the Feelies' neurotic suburban intensity for a countryfied gentleness. Influence-revealing covers of Phil Manzanera/Brian Eno ("Big Day"), the Stones ("Child of the Moon") and Neil Young ("Powderfinger") are intriguing but a bit on the plain side.

While preserving the laconic electro-folk drone of **The Good Earth** on **Only Life**, an album of amazingly exacting sound and performances, the Feelies join it with riveting songs of breathless electricity. The first side takes things as they come, gently laying out catchy songs like "Too Much," "Higher Ground" and "The Undertow" to warm the mood with stately-drifting-towards-dull restraint, like an invocation to autumn. But the pace quickens on the second half, as the obsessively brisk "Too Far Gone" and the breakneck "Away"—strong songs given exhilarating performances, and a clear tie to the Feelies' past—lead up to the album's closer, a boiling cover of Lou Reed's "What Goes On" (don't miss Mercer's amazing solo) that overtly renews the band's Velvet Underground links.

Speed the Plough is John Baumgartner's band; Bill Million co-produced **Speed the Plough** and guests on one track. Although STP's hypnotically simple songs strongly resemble the Feelies' work, the six-person lineup (including one other Trype alumnus) plays them on a variety of instruments, subtly supplementing guitar, bass and drums with keyboards, reeds, woodwinds, horns, accordion and more.

Like an uptight square the morning after a drunken orgy, **Time for a Witness** finds the Feelies in a new frame of mind, downplaying crystalline precision and emotional intensity for a fleshed-out sonic reinvention that embraces old Bob Dylan songwriting structures and a trancey Haight-Ashbury acid-rock feeling with free-wheeling enthusiasm rather than anxious determination. Not to overstate it: a casual listener may not notice any drastic change between the albums, but there's definitely a newly relaxed sensibility at work here. Rather than tone things down, the Feelies spread them out, and if the album lacks ferocious intensity or wistful beauty, this resonant and brilliant record is their most richly textured and engrossing work yet.

Turning to another media, the high school reunion scenes in Jonathan Demme's *Something Wild* show the Feelies (credited as the Willies) performing shards of five songs, including "I'm a Believer," "Crazy Rhythms" and "Fame," with tentative Bowiesque lead vocals by Weckerman. [jy/jl/i]

JOHN FELICE & THE LOWDOWNS

See *Real Kids*.

FELT

Crumbling the Antiseptic Beauty EP (nr/Cherry Red) 1981 ●
The Splendour of Fear EP (nr/Cherry Red) 1984 ●
The Strange Idols Pattern and Other Short Stories (nr/Cherry Red) 1984
Ignite the Seven Cannons (nr/Cherry Red) 1985 ●
Ballad of the Band EP (nr/Creation) 1986
Let the Snakes Crinkle Their Heads to Death (nr/Creation) 1986 ●
Rain of Crystal Spires EP (nr/Creation) 1986
Forever Breathes the Lonely Word (nr/Creation) 1986 ●
Poem of the River EP (Creation-Relativity) 1987 ●
The Final Resting of the Ark EP (nr/Creation) 1987
Gold Mine Trash (PVC) 1987 ●
The Pictorial Jackson Review (Creation-Relativity) 1988 ●
Train Above the City (nr/Creation) 1988 ●
Me and a Monkey on the Moon (nr/él-Cherry Red) 1989 ●
Bubblegum Perfume (nr/Creation) 1990 ●

Aided at the outset by a second guitarist, a rhythm section and little more, Birmingham singer/songwriter Lawrence Hayward fashioned a career in homage to Tom Verlaine without once attempting to play his music. On **Crumbling the Antiseptic Beauty**, Felt patterns itself after Television's guitar interplay, with occasional understated vocals that cross Verlaine and

Lou Reed. The instrumental passages are the true high points here, as the guitarists are both melodic and sympathetic to each other. Odd, derivative but exciting and evidently ambitious.

Felt settled down and in on the better-produced **Splendour of Fear** (like the debut, a six-song 12-inch), unwinding the guitars into a gentle mantra-like caress with no sharp corners. Sparingly matched with quiet vocals, the hypnotic melodic drone can sound almost new agey, but the quartet's music is intended to engage, not to lull.

With **The Strange Idols Pattern** (produced by John Leckie), Lawrence and his trio refined Felt into a strikingly attractive sound: clear guitar notes sparkle from every direction in a jewel-like blend that recalls Television without quite imitating it. A nylon-string flamenco piece ("Crucifix Heaven") demonstrates diverse stylistic faculties; the virtuosity of lead guitarist Maurice Deebank—listen to his solo on "Whirlpool Vision of Shame"—is also quite impressive.

Gold Mine Trash is a fascinating developmental chronicle of Felt's Cherry Red years: singles, album tracks and a fine pair of 1984 demos. The LP ends on a pivotal note: "Primitive Painters," an obsessive 1985 British indie-chart hit (with guest vocals by Cocteau Twin Liz Fraser) which incorporates swirling organ for an entirely new effect.

Moving to the Creation label, Felt—by this time a stable quartet including keyboardist Martin Duffy and stalwart drummer Gary Ainge—was enormously productive in 1986, beginning with **Ballad of the Band**. The nearly unlabeled 12-inch—two light-sounding Dylanish songs and two piano pieces—was produced by another Cocteau Twin, Robin Guthrie, and contains the instrumental "Ferdinand Magellan," Lawrence's second tribute to great explorers. ("Vasco de Gama" was on **Strange Idols Pattern**.) The next release, **Let the Snakes Crinkle Their Heads to Death**, is a brief instrumental album that notably lacks a second guitarist. The pleasant but trivial collection consists of ten perky cuts ("Lawrence's songs coloured in by Martin") that rush by in less than nineteen minutes. Although one or two of the simple pieces hold to the group's prior sound, most don't; organ takes a prominent role and there's little of the familiar instrumental blend.

Vocals and another guitarist make a welcome return on **Forever Breathes the Lonely Word**, a finely wrought album with Dylanesque characteristics on which Lawrence sings exactly like Verlaine, adding a nifty Lou Reed imitation on "September Lady" and "Grey Streets." Lyrically, he's in top form, expressing religious doubt in "All the People I Like Are Those That Are Dead" and questioning a lover's fidelity in "Gather Up Your Wings and Fly." Duffy's percolating Hammond organ (no clichéd sounds of the '60s) adds a wonderful component to these songs, especially "Down but Not Yet Out," giving them all new-found energy and texture. Easily Felt's best record to that point, **Forever Breathes the Lonely Word** is unlike anything else in the group's catalogue. The worthy **Rain of Crystal Spires** 12-inch matches a pair of LP tracks with two quick B-sides.

After that, Felt produced a couple of radically different EPs. The six-song **Poem of the River**, produced in the main by Mayo Thompson, makes good use of both organ and piano, turning down the shimmering guitars for a rich instrumental blend that suggests both the Smiths and Aztec Camera. **The Final Resting of the Ark**, produced by Guthrie, is spare and largely acoustic, a forgettably minor outing that has two simple songs with vocals, an unaccompanied Duffy piano piece and two other instrumentals.

With Thomas moving over to lead guitar and a new bassist in the fold, Felt recorded the schizophrenic **Pictorial Jackson Review** "quickly on eight-track." Two of Duffy's jazzy instrumental contemplations (introduced on the preceding EP) fill one side, leaving eight concise Lawrence songs to huddle together on the reverse. Resembling a stripped-down version of **Forever Breathes**, those numbers make Lawrence's Lou Reed fixation abundantly evident: most (not counting the precisely Dylanesque "How Spook Got Her Man" and "Don't Die on My Doorstep," which splices Bob and Lou together) suggest the early Velvet Underground's lighter, melodic side.

Gary Ainge (vibes, drums) and Martin Duffy (piano) are the only Feltists credited on **Train Above the City**, although Lawrence accepts responsibility for titling seven of their eight jazz instrumentals that comprise the record. Sort of a follow-up to **Let the Snakes Crinkle Their Heads to Death**, this is a perfectly fine cocktail-hour detour but, given Lawrence's non-participation, hardly an essential purchase.

Beautifully produced by Adrian Borland, **Me and a Monkey on the Moon** is a full-fledged album of sprightly, unstylized pop songs handsomely performed by Duffy (mostly playing electronic keyboards), Ainge, a bassist and two new guitarists (one of whom adds a neat country steel accent to several cuts). Lawrence's songs are exceptional, revealing autobiographical notes and sensitive contemplations of personal issues. Beyond the album's tender love songs, "Down an August Path" considers mortality and faith; "Budgie Jacket" recalls an episode of child molestation ("He thought that I was a little girl/Because I looked so pretty"), while "Mobile Shack" acknowledges the inspirational power of Television. As it proved to be the band's swansong, **Me and a Monkey on the Moon** ends Felt on a superb high note.

Format complications: a 1988 Creation CD unites **Poem of the River** and **Forever Breathes the Lonely Word**, a 1986 UK Cherry Red CD and cassette joins **Crumbling the Antiseptic Beauty** and **The Splendour of Fear**, the **Strange Idols Pattern** cassette and CD also include **Ignite the Seven Cannons**, **The Pictoral Jackson Review** is likewise joined with **Train Above the City**. The 20-track **Bubblegum Perfume** is a posthumous compilation. [cpl/i]

BRYAN FERRY

These Foolish Things (Atlantic) 1973 ●
Another Time, Another Place (Atlantic) 1974 ●
Let's Stick Together (Atlantic) 1976 ●
Extended Play EP (nr/Island) 1976
In Your Mind (Atlantic) 1977 ●
The Bride Stripped Bare (Atlantic) 1978 ●
Boys and Girls (Warner Bros.) 1985 ●
Windswept EP (nr/EG-Polydor) 1985

Bête Noire (EG-Reprise) 1987 ●
Let's Stick Together EP (nr/EG-Virgin) 1988 ●
The Price of Love EP (nr/EG-Virgin) 1989 ●
He'll Have to Go EP (nr/EG-Virgin) 1989 ●
Bryan Ferry (nr/EG) 1989 φ

BRYAN FERRY/ROXY MUSIC

Street Life: 20 Greatest Hits (nr/EG) 1986 (EG-Reprise) 1989 ●
The Ultimate Collection (nr/EG-Virgin) 1988 ●

Initially braving waves of contemptuous reviews, the voice of Roxy Music began his solo career as an irregular aside, allowing it to become his primary work as Roxy Music faded out of existence in the early '80s. Although hardly the groundbreaking titan he once was, Ferry has had far-reaching stylistic influence; disingenuous claims of total self-invention to the contrary, many nouveau poseurs have let Ferry point the way for them to "be themselves."

A shocking break from Roxy Music's hip glam-rock (with the accent on rock), **These Foolish Things** quickly established the difference between the group's utter originality and Ferry's suavely adult solo interpretations. (For a number of obvious reasons this gap closed over the years to the point of near indistinguishability.) With a backing group that included then-Roxy drummer Paul Thompson as well as future Roxyite Eddie Jobson, Ferry croons his way through such surprising '60s selections as Bob Dylan's "A Hard Rain's A-Gonna Fall," the Beatles' "You Won't See Me" and the Stones' "Sympathy for the Devil." Even years later, this warped '70s jukebox sounds weird but wonderful. **Another Time, Another Place** reprised the exercise, drawing on various epochs for material like "The 'In' Crowd," "You Are My Sunshine," "It Ain't Me Babe" and "Smoke Gets in Your Eyes." Only the title song is an original.

For **Let's Stick Together**, Ferry reached into the vaults and selected five Roxy Music songs (four from the band's first LP) and did something with them: recut the vocals, presented alternate versions or simply re-edited/remixed the tracks. Some of these sound fine, but a funked-up "Re-Make/Re-Model" is too revisionist for words. The record is fleshed out with a brace of neat new covers, including the wonderful title track, "Shame Shame Shame" and the Everly Brothers' "Price of Love." A strange assemblage with some jarring contrasts; still, **Let's Stick Together** has more great tracks than any of Ferry's other solo records. (The CD-3 EP that followed contains four album cuts, including "The Price of Love" and "Shame Shame Shame"; the subsequent 12-inch has two substitutions.)

In Your Mind, produced during a period of Roxy inactivity, is Ferry's first "normal" solo album—all of the material is new and original—but, bereft of a gimmick and lacking the involvement of his usual collaborators, falls short of Ferry's best work. Despite a few good tunes ("This Is Tomorrow," "Tokyo Joe"), the bland sound allows little of Ferry's brilliance to shine through, and the writing is not up to snuff.

Inspired by his broken romance with onetime Roxy LP cover model Jerry Hall, **The Bride Stripped Bare** is Ferry at his most emotionally translucent. The hybrid approach—half new originals, half appropriate revivals—and backing by a new coterie of unstylish

243

session pros (including Waddy Wachtel, Neil Hubbard and Alan Spenner) make it radically different in both construction and sound. Some of the tracks are intensely gripping ("Sign of the Times," Lou Reed's "What Goes On"); others are subtler and less rewarding. A mixed success.

When Roxy Music finally ceased to exist, Ferry's solo career took on new significance. Unfortunately, his own music is not that different from end-time Roxy Music: perfectionist studio technique and seamless production of songs that are at best bland and frequently lifeless. Despite its extraordinarily sleek veneer, **Boys and Girls** (dedicated to Ferry's late father) is so short on tunes that several of the numbers rely on fatiguing one-note vamps to carry them along. Exceptional lyrics might allow one to overlook such inadequacy, but there's nothing much happening on that front, either. It's impossible to dislike the album with any enthusiasm—considerable care, thought and effort obviously went into its creation—still, the lack of even a trace of extremism or subversiveness is unforgivable.

The similarly restrained **Bête Noire** confirms that palatable adult music *is* Ferry's future. That wonderful voice has become the only important ingredient; what he's singing doesn't seem so important anymore. But this record's better melodic development and a wider variety of danceable tempos than on **Boys and Girls** are palpable signs of life; the involvement of ex-Smiths guitarist Johnny Marr as a player and the co-writer of one near-exciting song ("The Right Stuff") is another positive touch. All things considered, "Limbo," "Kiss and Tell" and "Day for Night" are coolly inviting and likable enough, given the diminished expectations one now brings to Bryan Ferry albums.

With no new music forthcoming, Ferry's British label began issuing old/retrospective items. The **Let's Stick Together** EP is available as a remix on CD-3 and CD-5 (with totally different accompanying tracks) as well as 12-inch vinyl (also different); the **Price of Love**, another remix, comes on CD-3 and 12-inch, both with alternate mixes of "Don't Stop the Dance" and two additional items.

Street Life is a poorly annotated two-record career retrospective: twenty songs drawn from Roxy Music as well as solo releases, stretching from "Virginia Plain" to **Boys and Girls**' "Slave to Love." Also combining Roxy and pre-**Bête Noire** Ferry tracks, **Ultimate Collection** adds a new mix of "Let's Stick Together" to a skimpier overlapping selection. The 1989 release entitled **Bryan Ferry** is a boxed set of **These Foolish Things**, **Let's Stick Together** and **Boys and Girls**.

See also *Roxy Music*. [i]

FETCHIN BONES
Cabin Flounder (DB) 1985 ●
Bad Pumpkin (DB-Capitol) 1986
Galaxy 500 (Capitol) 1987 ●
Monster (Capitol) 1989 ●

SKEETERS
Wine, Women and Walleye (DB) 1988 ●

Like the sublimely seedy roadside joints of America's rural South—where you can shoot pool, buy fishing worms and have your lawnmower repaired all in the same room—Fetchin Bones are dedicated to the sort of

unexpected variety that somehow seems to work. On their debut album, the North Carolina quintet peddles an exciting mix of revved-up rock, country twang, folk, blues and swing, driving it all home with unrestrained energy and unpolished charm. The crazed quaver in singer Hope Nicholls' voice provides the heart of the Bones' sound; three songs without her lead vocals are the album's weakest cuts. Producer Don Dixon admirably translates the group's wild-eyed persona to vinyl, but this is a band that must be seen live for a full grasp of their eclectic frenzy. Delightfully different graduates of the R.E.M.-inspired school of Southern pop. (The CD and cassette add three tracks.)

Although docked a few fun points for a lack of focus, **Bad Pumpkin** basically stays the course, with equally direct Dixon production, rough-hewn playing, strong original songs and more inspired Nicholls warbling. Gary White's spicy guitar work and bassist Danna Pentes' violin contributions provide a lot of the instrumental flavor; Marc Mueller keeps things moving along at a brisk pace with lickety-split country drumming.

The self-assured spunk of **Galaxy 500** is immediately evident; a lineup shift (Mueller and White are gone, replaced by Clay Richardson and Errol Stewart) also contributes to the clear and feverish dynamo. The Bones' control is clearly demonstrated by the juxtaposition of the wild'n'funky "Sammy" with the sweeping prettiness of "Steamwhistle." Alternating between a guttural growl, a delicate folk sensibility and a half-dozen other voices, Nicholls is a commanding vocalist; the songs rise and fall strictly on her sing-so. (The CD adds six tracks.)

Monster proved to be Fetchin Bones' last hurrah, and it's a bang-up finale. With Ed Stasium's powerful but disciplined production lending new focus to the band's brashly metallic lurch, **Monster** is simultaneously the Bones' most commercial album *and* their best. Nicholls has never sounded more inspired or possessed, frantically spitting out the likes of "Love Crushin'," "Bonework" and "Say the Word" with a renewed sense of purpose. Indeed, **Monster**'s best moments suggest that, if they'd been inclined to stick around, Fetchin Bones might have carved themselves a niche playing heavy metal for people with a sense of humor. (Following the split, several ex-Bones reorganized as Second Skin.)

On their own, Mueller and White formed the Skeeters with bassist Marco Heeter and issued **Wine, Women and Walleye**, a charmingly ragged rock/pop/folk-rock record produced by Tim Lee. White's Neil Young-ish guitar solos spiff up intriguing material with a smartass streak that surfaces in tunes like "Slummin'" and "Center of the Western Hemisphere." There's even a raving surf-twang instrumental number called "Porno Rock." Neat. [kh/i/hd]

FIELDS OF THE NEPHILIM
Burning the Fields EP (nr/Tower) 1985 (nr/Situation Two) 1987
Returning to Gehenna EP (nr/Jungle) 1986
Dawnrazor (Beggars Banquet-RCA) 1987 ●
The Nephilim (Beggars Banquet-RCA) 1988 ●
Elizium (nr/Beggars Banquet) 1990 ●
Earth Inferno (nr/Beggars Banquet) 1991 ●

Although they hail from Stevenage (a town 30 miles north of London), to judge by their appearance and music, these moody post-goths could have stepped right out of a Sergio Leone spaghetti western, dust flying and spurs clicking. The band's sound is equal parts Sisters of Mercy and Ennio Morricone; dark, deep, smoky vocals coiled around a layered rush of swirling, twanging guitars.

Burning the Fields is a four-track EP; **Returning to Gehenna** mixes then-current singles and B-sides, most of them later appended to the UK CD of the quintet's first full-length album. **Dawnrazor** is an enjoyable creation, with some great songs ("Slowkill," the title track), but the Sisters' influence is so strong that it tends to overshadow the Nephs' unique qualities. (The US version of the LP excises "Reanimator," adding some non-LP British singles, including "Blue Water.")

The Nephilim is a magnum lunge forward to a less derivative, more atmospheric sound. Reminiscent in spots of early Pink Floyd and Joy Division, the harsher-voiced songs are much longer and imbued with a cinematic, soundtrack-like feel, hitting full stride on the solemn epic "Last Exit for the Lost" and the blasting "Chord of Souls."

A 12-inch harbinger of the next album (the CD of which contains it), 1989's ambitious "Psychonaut" is a nine-minute psychedelic wash of icy organ and pulsing beats. Smoother than **The Nephilim**, with no traces of the early western flavor, **Elizium** tantalizes the senses with a headful of dreamlike sounds, coming to a peak in "Wail of Sumer," the best song they've recorded to date. Carl McCoy's singing has mellowed—he sounds like a burnt, brooding Jim Kerr—and the choirlike effects instill a sense of palpable awe. [gef]

FIELD TRIP

Beautiful (Ruby) 1989
Headgear (Slash) 1990 •

It must be tough growing up post-modern in a place called Pleasanton, but these four young Northern Californians don't seem to have been ruined by the experience. On **Beautiful**, singing rites-of-passage originals like "Coming of Age," "No Friends" and "Where Did I Go Wrong?" in a character-filled voice, guitarist/songwriter Jim Galbraith orients the rocking pop band towards Minneapolis, although his mandolin playing and a guest harmonica spot make it clear that Field Trip is headed somewhere else. The record is a bit wet behind the ears, but full of scruffy promise.

Despite the orthodontic cover, **Headgear** is a grown-up album with better material, adult concerns, confident melodic power and a clarified set of influences. Some songs set a course towards the Meat Puppets; elsewhere, the group deftly incorporates country accents with brisk enthusiasm and nifty three-part harmony. With fine playing and tunes that make fast friends on one spin, **Headgear** is a delight. [i]

FIGURES ON A BEACH

Swimming EP (Metro-America) 1983
Standing on Ceremony (I Square-Sire) 1987
Figures on a Beach (I Square-Sire) 1989 •

From the astonishing Rene Magritte-tribute cover photograph to the sparkling music and sound on **Swimming**'s four long songs, this Michigan quartet doesn't skimp or compromise in any regard. Figures on a Beach play complex, serious (but not dour) poetic compositions with intricate instrumental and vocal arrangements that rely mainly on guitars, drums and keyboards. Anthony Kaczynski has a strong, capable voice just on the edge of melodrama; multi-tracking gives him startling creative range. Hard to classify, you might think of this remarkable, unpredictable band as an American (not Americanized) Simple Minds. Don Was produced the Figures' 1984 dance single, "Breathless."

Standing on Ceremony finds the group, expanded to five and relocated to Boston, discouragingly stuck in an art-dance rock ditch. Confident flashes of Simple Minds, Duran Duran, Depeche Mode, Ultravox and their offspring may have been novel and intriguing on a 1983 American indie record, but those same stylistic attributes sound a bit quaint four years later. These guys are obviously skilled and facile, but the boat had already sailed on this record.

While the quintet's stylistic referents are still fairly obvious on **Figures on a Beach**, the confident assertion of the group's flip personality helps set them in a more original context. Rather than rely on swanky execution, some of the hooky songs are angularly offbeat and substantial; Kaczynski's colorful delivery makes good use of the ironically serious lyrics. The only serious drag here is a pounding modern disco version of Bachman-Turner Overdrive's "You Ain't Seen Nothing Yet" that seems tacked on as a commercial afterthought. [i]

FINE YOUNG CANNIBALS

Fine Young Cannibals (IRS) 1985 •
The Raw & the Cooked (IRS) 1989 •
The Raw & the Remix (IRS-MCA) 1990 φ

Factionalism led to the disbandment of the Beat; when the two mainmen became General Public, the others looked set to fade from sight. But the group formed by guitarist Andy Cox and bassist David Steele, joined by fine young vocalist Roland Gift, has proven a commercially propitious venture. **Fine Young Cannibals** approaches modern R&B and soul from a number of fresh rock perspectives, but it's really Gift's Motown-ish, richly emotional vocals that ignite originals like "Johnny Come Home" and "Don't Ask Me to Choose," as well as a rousing cover of Elvis Presley's "Suspicious Minds."

Following that first album, the band turned to film projects. Gift played prominent dramatic roles in 1987's *Sammy and Rosie Get Laid* and 1989's *Scandal*; the entire band contributed an annoying misinterpretation of the Buzzcocks' "Ever Fallen in Love" (later recycled for the band's second album) to *Something Wild*. Meanwhile, as Gift was off making like a movie star, Steele and Cox whipped up a high-tech danceable side project called 2 Men a Drum Machine & a Trumpet, releasing a 1988 IRS 12-inch, "Tired of Getting Pushed Around."

Opening with the distinctive drum/guitar intro of "She Drives Me Crazy," **The Raw & the Cooked** plucked FYC out of the alternative trenches and sent the trio spiralling up the charts. Another crafty salad of pseudo-Motown soul and contemporary dance rock, the album topped the charts, sold more than three million copies and bagged a Grammy nomination. Although the songs are structurally solid and melodically appealing, the arrangements are diabolical, favoring monotonous grooves, with a relentless synthesized drum thwack and robotic guitar scrubbing. Add in the fatigue factor of Gift's mannered Prince-ly falsetto, and **The Raw & the Cooked** starts to grate well before the second song starts. The delightful '60s jump of "Good Thing" and the swoony '50s swing of "Tell Me What" provide respite from the album's tick-tock tempos, but "Ever Fallen in Love" ends it in on a headache high.

No doubt moved by FYC's success as well as the trio's sluggardly production pace, the record company assembled a remix album that offers two versions each of "She Drives Me Crazy," "I'm Not the Man I Used to Be" and "I'm Not Satisfied," as well as solitary danceable overhauls of "Good Thing," "Johnny Come Home" and others. Unlike many such cash-ins, **The Raw & the Remix** offers significant variations on the original tracks, with added raps (by Monie Love on "She Drives Me Crazy") and major stylistic adjustments (Nellee Hooper and Jazzie B put the Soul II Soul stamp on one, "I'm Not the Man I Used to Be," while Smith & Mighty do a dub dissection on another). The CD and cassette add two more, including a "Mayhem Rhythm Remix" of 2 Men's "Tired of Getting Pushed Around." [i]

See also *(English) Beat*.

FINGERPRINTZ
The Very Dab (Virgin Int'l) 1979
Distinguishing Marks (Virgin) 1980
Beat Noir (Stiff) 1981
JACQUI BROOKES
Sob Stories (MCA) 1984

It's difficult to categorize Fingerprintz, which may explain why the group never garnered a large following. The primitively recorded first album occupies a dark, throbbing zone of bobbing pop and wry-to-bizarre lyrics ("Punchy Judy," "Beam Me Up Scotty"). Leader/guitarist Jimme O'Neill's Scottish accent and offbeat songwriting combine to chilling effect on the crime-obsessed narratives "Fingerprince" and "Wet Job"; the former's music also suggests a valid response to reggae/dub influence.

The considerably slicker **Distinguishing Marks**, in contrast, is pure pop in extremis—musically, anyway. The songs hum like a finely tuned motor, with producer Nick Garvey removing any rough sonic edges. Only the relentlessly perverse lyrics betray a refusal to play by the book; O'Neill's disjointed visions are inspired by pulp fiction, police blotters and hospital charts. A catchy collection that all sounds like hit single material.

Beat Noir took yet another 180-degree turn, away from pop and towards a rock/funk fusion. Finally in synch with the times, Fingerprintz delivered a stunning, idiosyncratic package of heavy bass lines, winsome melodies and O'Neill's thematic fetishes (paranoia, frustration). The album was kinky enough to catch on in rock clubs, but too peculiar to reach a broader audience. (The US version deletes two songs.) Drenched in atmosphere, it remains a compelling work.

O'Neill subsequently co-wrote, co-produced and played on an excellent album by singer Jacqui Brookes before launching his new group, the Silencers. Drummer Bogdan Wiczling (no longer dubbed Bob Shilling, as on **The Very Dab**) worked on that record as well, and later toured and recorded with Adam Ant. [si]

See also *Silencers*.

KAREN FINLEY
The Truth Is Hard to Swallow (Pow Wow) 1988

Controversial New York performance artist Finley comes on like a nutty pornographic Mark E. Smith on one side of her album, which puts music of widely varying sorts (raga-rock, semi-industrial funk, hip-hop, African chorale, etc.) under her obsessive sexual rants. ("The Constant State of Desire," a live 1987 recording—before a mildly appreciative audience—of a solo piece, completes the album.) Finley's work is strong stuff of arguable artistic merit, but she's not that far removed from other modern verbal extremists, and there's nothing wrong with her backing tracks. [i]

TIM FINN
Escapade (Oz-A&M) 1983
Big Canoe (nr/Virgin) 1986 (Virgin) 1988 ●
Tim Finn (Capitol) 1989 ●

Singer Tim Finn successfully carved out an identity distinct from his band, Split Enz, with his first solo album, **Escapade**. On his own, he's milder, sweeter and more conventional (though still worth the time). The precedent for **Escapade** can be found in the romantic grandeur of Split Enz's **True Colours**' "I Hope I Never." One track here, the moving "Not for Nothing," is a bona fide lump-in-the-throat masterpiece.

Apparently, the meager sales of **Escapade** were a major setback to Finn's solo career. Released in Europe in '86, **Big Canoe** only came out domestically after brother Neil went big-time with Crowded House—and then as a budget LP. Anyway, it's a middling effort, with overproduction and mega-arrangements (a classic Split Enz weakness) dulling the emotional edge of Finn's bittersweet crooning. He's still boss on "Don't Bury My Heart," a haunting ballad, and the lightheaded rocker "Water into Wine."

No doubt eager to emulate brother Neil's success with Crowded House, Tim next teamed up with the same label and producer (Mitchell Froom). Despite the overly slick presentation, **Tim Finn** sometimes hits the mark, especially on the rowdy "Birds Swim Fish Fly" and "Not Even Close," which turns self-pity into affecting melodrama. What Finn really needs here, though, is an editor/producer willing to pare these smart songs down to essentials, not one who will continue to encourage his weakness for excessive ornamentation.

In late '90, Finn took the plunge and joined Crowded House in time to take an active role in the group's third album. [jy]

See also *Crowded House, Split Enz*.

FIRE ENGINES
Lubricate Your Living Room (nr/Pop: Aural) 1980
Aufgeladen und Bereit für Action und Spass (Fast
America) 1981

WIN

Uhh! Tears Baby (A Trash Icon) (nr/London) 1987
Freaky Trigger (nr/Virgin) 1988 ●

Fire Engines were the most manic of the new Scottish pop crop that surfaced around 1979: primal rock-'n'roll drawing more on raw passion (via guitar din and repetitive noise) than melody or captivating structures. The quartet offered no traditional hooks, just six-string fire and aggressively unpleasant vocals.

The group's two enigmatic albums have a lot of overlap: the American release with the German title adds two of the band's catchier numbers: the punk-country-flavored "Candyskin" (with ridiculously incongruous strings) and "Everythings Roses." It also replaces the tedious "Lubricate Your Living Room Pt. 2" with the more exciting "Meat Whiplash." Using electric guitars without regard to typical pop traditions, the abrasive but ruggedly handsome Fire Engines—a Scottish blend of the Contortions and early Television—will poke and scratch their way into your heart if you let them.

Fire Engines guitarist David Henderson and keyboardist Russell Burn went on to form Win, a subversive sextet that brings an equally iconoclastic set of wonderful ideas to bear on soul-dance-jazz-pop. (Imagine a collaboration between Marc Bolan and Prince for a hint of the possibilities.) Despite a superficially slick and accessible exterior—complete with synthesizers, female backup singers and samples—Win's records are as idiosyncratic and delightfully unsettling in their own way as the old group.   [gf/i]

FIREHOSE

Ragin', Full-On (SST) 1986 ●
if'n (SST) 1987 ●
Sometimes EP (SST) 1988 ●
fROMOHIO (SST) 1989 ●
Flyin' the Flannel (Columbia) 1991 ●

BOOTSTRAPPERS

Bootstrappers (New Alliance) 1989 ●

Born out of tragedy, fIREHOSE began after the 1985 death of Minutemen guitarist D. Boon in a car crash. Knowing there was no way to recapture Boon's burly bluster, bassist Mike Watt and drummer George Hurley didn't try to find someone to fill those iconoclastic shoes. Instead, they recruited another kind of dude entirely in the person of ed fROMOHIO (aka Ed Crawford). A more restrained presence than the raucous Boon, not to mention a prettier singer, Ed settled right into the driver's seat on **Ragin', Full-On**. This bracing LP jumps all over the map, from edgy rockers ("Choose Any Memory") to absorbing mood pieces ("The Candle and the Flame") to acoustic reveries ("This . . ."). First note to last, there's a prickly, intangible integrity to the band that the restless Boon would have admired.

On **if'n**, the Hosers are more self-assured, more articulate and just as freewheeling. Ed really steps out on the propulsive "Anger," an unnerving portrayal of rage, and "For the Singer of REM," a devastating parody of that band. Watt gets his turn at the mic, too, delivering an amusingly disjointed rap (following Minutemen tradition, he calls it a spiel) on "Me & You, Remembering." Unpredictable and unpretentious, fIREHOSE has the exciting aura of a group in constant evolution, willing to follow the muse in any direction whatsoever. First class. The three-track **Sometimes** features two songs recorded for, but not used on, **if'n**.

"I'm reaching out/Hear me spiel and shout," sings Crawford at the start of **fROMOHIO**, fIREHOSE's best, most accessible work yet. There's acoustic folk instrumentals ("Vastopol"), wry Watt spiels ("What Gets Heard"), jittery rockers ("Whisperin' While Hollerin'"), pretty rockers ("Understanding"), jolly sing-alongs ("Liberty for Our Friend"), even a drum solo ("Let the Drummer Have Some"). As usual, listening to fIREHOSE is like hanging out with your best friends, shootin' the breeze and feelin' pretty good.

Watt and Hurley teamed up with avant-garde fave Elliott Sharp for the one-off Bootstrappers. While the rhythm dudes pound away with their usual muscular zest, Sharp tears Hendrixy (and stranger) noises from the guitar (and bass clarinet). No real songs, just lots of jarring sonics.   [jy]

See also *Dos, Minutemen, Elliott Sharp, Sonic Youth*.

FISCHER-Z

Word Salad (UA) 1979 ●
Going Deaf for a Living (UA) 1980 ●
Red Skies Over Paradise (nr/Liberty) 1981 ●
Reveal (nr/Arista) 1988 ●
Fish's Head (nr/Arista) 1989 ●
Going Red for a Salad (The UA Years) (nr/EMI) 1990 ●

JOHN WATTS

One More Twist (nr/EMI) 1982
The Iceberg Model (nr/EMI) 1983

A frequently excellent but widely ignored outfit, Fischer-Z was primarily a vehicle for John Watts, a singer/guitarist/songwriter whose intense vocals and semi-neurotic outlook provided its character. A flair for intricate but accessible arrangements and novel subject matter made Fischer-Z both easy to like and hard to dismiss.

Word Salad, produced by Mike Howlett and recorded as a quartet, displays Watts in the process of searching out an ego, still sharing songwriting credits and vocal chores with the others. It's an impressive debut album, full of great songs, fine musicianship and stylistic variety, all colored by Watts' reedy voice.

With the same personnel and producer, **Going Deaf for a Living** uses a sparer sound, downplaying the keyboards in favor of Cars-like simplicity, best exemplified on "So Long." An odd direction for a second record, but the band's attributes remained unchanged, and it's as good as the first.

Red Skies Over Paradise is a solo album waiting for someone to inform the other members of the group. Watts co-produced, played the keyboards and allowed his songwriting to become entirely self-indulgent. With a serious baritone replacing the plaintive tenor (it's always a bad sign when singers change their voices) and no-nonsense message lyrics, there's a lot wrong with this disappointing album, despite four or five good numbers.

Not surprisingly, Watts then went solo. The material on **One More Twist** is a bit forced and clearly less interesting than his earlier writing, with only a Tom Robinson-sounding single, "One Voice," showing any real signs of life.

After **The Iceberg Model** also failed to ignite his solo career, Watts reassumed the Fischer-Z moniker—without bothering to reform the original band—for **Reveal** and **Fish's Head**. Though these discs hardly amount to a stunning comeback, each contains enough bright moments to suggest that Watts shouldn't be counted out just yet. The cleverly titled **Going Red for a Salad** is an ample condensation of the original band's first three albums, containing about half of each.

[i/hd]

FISH & ROSES
Fish & Roses (Lost-Twin/Tone) 1987
We Are Happy to Serve You (Homestead) 1989

LES BATTERIES
Noisy Champs (Fr. AYAA) 1987

Fish & Roses just may be the friendliest-sounding band that can trace its roots back to NYC's late-'70s no wave scene. Formed in the fall of 1985 by drummer Rick Brown (ex-Information, V-Effect), bassist Sue Garner (ex-Vietnam, Last Round Up) and keyboard player David Sutter, Fish & Roses' decision to eschew guitar gives the material a feel that is both convoluted and light. While the group's sound can be compared to Virginia's Orthotonics or France's Etron Fou, the songs have a political dimension that has more in common with the Minutemen.

Both of Fish & Roses' records are excellent. The full-length **We Are Happy to Serve You** (produced by Thurston Moore) may be a better introduction than the seven-song **Fish & Roses**, since it includes the classic "Hillbilly in a Can" (Georgia-born Garner's best recorded vocal turn) and a wide selection of other postbeat hoot. Those looking for Rick Brown's coolest singing, however, are advised to seek out **Noisy Champs** by Les Batteries, his drum trio with Etron Fou's Guigou Chenevier and Charles Hayward (of Quiet Sun/This Heat fame). On this singular LP, Rick howls a cover of Harry Partch's "The Letter" that is absolutely breathtaking.

[bc]

FISHBONE
Fishbone EP (Columbia) 1985 ●
In Your Face (Columbia) 1986
It's a Wonderful Life (Gonna Have a Good Time) EP
  (Columbia) 1987
Truth and Soul (Columbia) 1988 ●
Ma and Pa EP (nr/Epic) 1989 ●
Bonin' in the Boneyard EP (Columbia) 1990 ●
The Reality of My Surroundings (Columbia) 1991 ●

One of America's greatest and most overlooked bands, this rowdy gang from LA specializes in ska with overtones of go-go, funk and rock. (Imagine George Clinton producing the first Beat LP.) On the **Fishbone** EP, their sense of humor is surpassed only by the six tracks' non-stop hyperkinetic energy. Whether the lyrics are socially relevant ("Another Generation" and especially "Party at Ground Zero") or just plain silly ("Ugly"), the vim and vigor level is maintained. If you can sit still throughout this, you're probably dead.

In Your Face is branded with a then-uncommon "EXPLICIT LYRICS—PARENTAL ADVISORY" warning, but the real warning should be to fans. With David Kahne's inappropriately slick production, the band mellowed out considerably for their debut long-player. Nothing wrong with trying a new direction, but several cuts here are just MOR soul-rock, and that's simply not what this bunch is cut out to play. The lyrics are nowhere, too—the promising title "Post Cold War Politics" is an instrumental. Back to the drawing board.

It's a Wonderful Life, also produced by Kahne, is a Christmas EP that puts a casual ho-ho-ho twist in your stocking. The title tune is actually the least interesting of the four gratuitous charmers; the soulful disenchantment of "Slick Nick, You Devil You" ("Spilling Jack Daniels all over the drapes/Tattoos on his arms and knees/I never thought Santa Claus would be such a sleaze") and the funked-out "Just Call Me Scrooge" are the real winners. A welcome gift to cheer up any celebration.

Shot in the foot by a poor sequencing job and a baffled record company, the brilliant **Truth and Soul** *should* have been Fishbone's breakthrough. While the first side is distinguished only by a scorching metallic cover of Curtis Mayfield's "Freddie's Dead," the second half is a dazzling grand-slam of the band's vibrant stylistic array. From the party anthem "Bonin' in the Boneyard" to the scalding anti-racist "Slow Bus Movin' (Howard Beach Party)," the near-hardcore of "Subliminal Fascism" to the soulful "Ghetto Soundwave" and the acoustic (!) racial-unity ballad "Change," it updates and rivals Sly's finest work.

Abortive sessions produced by the Jungle Brothers figure prominently in the **Bonin'** EP, which couples two radical revisions (one of them completely X-rated) of the two-year-old title track with three insane B-sides.

Over a year in the making (eighteen engineers are credited), the sprawling **Reality of My Surroundings** reprises much of **Truth and Soul**'s spirit and sound, but is far more ambitious in scope and philosophy. Utilising the format of a rap album (lots of mini-songs and chatter between the longer ones), Fishbone tackles even more styles than before: while their characteristic punkfunk-rockska is prominent, the band also explores Sly Stoneland ("Everyday Sunshine"), Funkadelia ("Behavior Control Technician") and even psychedelic territory ("Those Days Are Gone"), finishing the album off with the brilliant "Sunless Saturday," which manages to be the band's most radio-ready single and one of its most poignant lyrics to date ("I see the shards of shattered dreams in my street/I face the morning with my customary sigh"). And although Kahne carries an associate producer credit, most of the production (and all of the songwriting) was done by the band. Once again, they sequenced the best tracks towards the end but, despite the occasional misfire, **Reality** is Fishbone's best and most important album yet.

While the septet's manic stage act belies the members' considerable talents as musicians, Fish (Phillip Fisher) is the group's secret weapon. A soulful blend of Charlie Watts, Keith Moon and assorted great jazz drummers, he's guested on tracks by Little Richard and Bob Dylan. Various 'Bones have stomped, yelled or blown on records by Jane's Addiction, Keith Levene, Thelonious Monster and the Red Hot Chili Peppers.

[dgs/i/ja]

MORGAN FISHER

See *Hybrid Kids*.

FIXX

Shuttered Room (MCA) 1982 •
Reach the Beach (MCA) 1983 •
Phantoms (MCA) 1984 •
Walkabout (MCA) 1986 •
React (MCA) 1987 •
Calm Animals (RCA) 1988 •
Greatest Hits: One Thing Leads to Another (MCA) 1989 •
Ink (Impact-MCA) 1991 φ

Although they sound like a dozen other pretentious synth-heavy atmospheric English dance bands of the early '80s, London's Fixx (originally the Fix), aided immeasurably for a time by producer Rupert Hine's ability to sculpt their mundane songs and uncover marginal tense appeal, have managed to become enormously successful, regularly drawing a couple of irritating hits from each album. **Shuttered Room** offers "Red Skies" and "Stand or Fall"; **Reach the Beach** contains "One Thing Leads to Another" and "Saved by Zero"; **Phantoms** has "Are We Ourselves?" Showing remarkable consistency, they are all equally unpleasant and trivial. (Not too surprisingly, the Fixx's American success has been met by nearly total UK indifference.)

React, a "greatest hits live" package, contains performances, recorded at two late-1986 Canadian shows, of every one of those songs, plus three especially wretched new studio cuts. **One Thing Leads to Another** also includes the original versions of those memorable tunes (except that "Stand or Fall" is live) and more, several in alternate mixes. The rock-oriented **Calm Animals**, the Fixx's first album for a new label, has no songs worth mentioning.

Returning to its former corporate home after a three-year recording hiatus, the Fixx raised guitar's role on **Ink**, managing a fair INXS impression in spots but otherwise doing what the group has always done with no significant evidence of either fatigue or imagination. [i]

FLAG OF CONVENIENCE

Life on the Telephone EP (PVC) 1982

FOC

Should I Ever Go Deaf EP (nr/MCM) 1987
Northwest Skyline (nr/MCM) 1987
War on the Wireless Set (MCM America) 1988
Exiles EP (nr/MCM) 1988

When Pete Shelley disbanded the Buzzcocks in March 1981, guitarist Steve Diggle and drummer John Maher formed Flag of Convenience. Diggle had played the Dave Davies role in the group—writing and singing his two or three songs per LP, getting an occasional A-side, and improving all the while—so it was logical for him to carry on the Buzzcocks' frantic, ambitious pop as Shelley opted for techno-blip dance music. Sadly, they labored long in obscurity, releasing only four singles between 1981 and '86.

Life on the Telephone, a US 12-inch with two versions of the title track and a pair of other songs, is immediately agreeable; the clever parts come into focus after a while.

War on the Wireless Set, which compiles outtakes from '81-'86 (plus one previously released 45, "New House"), is just the kind of hardhitting, ballsy material you'd expect from the people involved. "Heartbreak Story" is a particularly good find, with a martial beat and "Peter Gunn" guitar line. The real killer is "Back of My Mind," one of two tracks here recorded by three-quarters of the Buzzcocks (sans Shelley) for that band's fourth LP, which was scrapped when the band broke up. "Back of My Mind" proves again (as "Harmony in My Head" and "Airwaves Dream" had during the Buzzcocks' existence) that Diggle was really coming into his creative own.

Maher quit around '86, but Diggle carried on under the FOC acronym, releasing **Northwest Skyline** as his first real album. (Maher sits in on three songs.) Though seemingly more cheaply recorded than **War on the Wireless Set**, Diggle himself sounds more committed and more convincing, especially on social-issue lyrics (concerning such topics as racial prejudice and northern England's chronic unemployment). Both "Northwest Skyline" and "Pictures in My Mind" (with Maher's easily identifiable buzzsaw rolls) are especially impressive. (All four songs on **Should I Ever Go Deaf** are repeated on **Northwest Skyline**.)

In 1988, Diggle finally assembled a real, permanent band, including Gary Couzens, founding member of a then-unknown Manchester outfit called Stone Roses (he had left after one single, "So Young"), on second guitar. The resulting **Exiles** EP towers over the rest of FOC's canon. Virtually a Buzzcocks single that never was, "Exiles" flies a "Boredom"-style guitar pattern into a furious verse and a piledriving chorus. A steam-powered hit heard by few, it proved that the writer of "Fast Cars" and "Harmony in My Head" was still capable of greatness. The EP's other three tracks are nearly as good.

Ignored by the press and the public, the frustrated guitarist changed his band's name to Buzzcocks FOC, after a massive Paris concert was unexpectedly advertised under the past/present moniker. When the rechristened group issued a single ("Sunset" b/w the vastly superior "Life with the Lions"), the press stopped ignoring Diggle long enough to howl in predictable outrage. While that led (indirectly) to the 1989 Buzzcocks reunion, it also meant the end of FOC and its finest lineup. On their own, Couzens and drummer Chris Goodwin wasted little time in forming a new group, the High. [jr]

See also *Buzzcocks, High*.

FLAMING LIPS

The Flaming Lips (Lovely Sorts of Death) 1985 (Restless) 1987 •
Hear It Is (Pink Dust) 1986 •
Oh My Gawd!!! ... the Flaming Lips (Restless) 1987 •
Telepathic Surgery (Restless) 1989 •
Unconsciously Screamin' EP (Atavistic) 1990
In a Priest Driven Ambulance (Restless) 1990 •

MERCURY REV

Yerself Is Steam (Rough Trade) 1991 •

The Flaming Lips play around with the same sort of cartoon-psychedelia imagery used by lots of similarly inclined combos, but these disenfranchised Oklahomans (led by songwriter/guitarist Wayne Coyne) possess wit and ingenuity most of the acid-addled competition lacks. From its uniquely disgusting front cover to the brilliant alienation anthem "My Own Planet," **The Flaming Lips** shows considerably more promise than just about anything else in the college-radio underground's drooling-garage-thrash brigade.

Hear It Is fulfills some of that promise. While affectionately borrowing riffs here and there, the Lips (now a trio, with Coyne inheriting vocal duties from his now-departed brother Mark) show real originality, balancing the rockin' grunge of "With You" and "Jesus Shootin' Heroin" with softer acoustic passages. One CD collects the contents of the first two records, adding a version of "Summertime Blues" that's considerably closer to Blue Cheer than Eddie Cochran.

The inventively self-produced **Oh My Gawd!!!** is a surprisingly mature and confident work, with more consistent material and performances. Odes to paranoia ("Everything's Explodin' "), unselfconsciously anachronistic Pink Floydisms ("One Million Billionth of a Millisecond on a Sunday Morning") and moments of genuine sensitivity ("Love Yer Brain"), allow **Oh My Gawd!!!** to transcend the Lips' wacky-cult-band image, marking them as one of the American heartland's brightest—if least likely—new hopes.

Unfortunately, **Telepathic Surgery** is a competent but uninspired time-filler, lacking the manic unpredictability that made its predecessors special. Rather than attempting to reconcile their disparate components into a cohesive style, the Lips stick mainly to a straightforward rockish approach that only serves to make them sound more like everybody else. Curiously, **Telepathic Surgery**'s most exciting numbers (not counting a two-and-a-half minute monologue on UFOs) are the two CD bonus tracks: the frantic "Fryin' Up" and "Hell's Angel's Cracker Factory," a mind-melting 23-minute jam that would do Hawkwind proud.

In a Priest Driven Ambulance is an impressive return to form, with stronger material, committed performances and imaginative production—in short, all the fun and intensity missing from **Telepathic Surgery**. Coyne has developed into a skillful enough songwriter to draw deep emotional truths out of his cartoonish (and sporadically religion-obsessed) lyrical imagery without sacrificing meaning or humor. Similarly, the retooled band (a quartet again, with a new drummer and an added second guitarist) demonstrates new-found finesse, lifting such ravers as "Unconsciously Screamin' " and "Mountain Side" into the stratosphere, and adding an audible sense of discovery to introspective items like "Stand in Line" and "Five Stop Mother Superior Rain." The album ends with a rendition of the Louis Armstrong classic "What a Wonderful World" that's both reverent and playful. (Incidentally, the packaging resorts to an old Phil Spector ruse, listing all of the tracks' running times as 3:26.)

The limited-edition **Unconsciously Screamin'** EP (with a dandy holographic sleeve) teams the title track with three otherwise-unreleased outtakes from the **Ambulance** sessions. Like early pressings of **Oh My Gawd!!!** and **Ambulance**, and the Restless reissue of the debut EP, it's on colored vinyl.

Mercury Rev is a quintet that was formed in Buffalo, NY, prior to guitarist John "Dingus" Donahue's joining the Flaming Lips. (He appears on **Ambulance**, an album co-produced by his Mercury Rev bandmate, bassist Dave Fridmann.) After eighteen months in the Lips, Donahue put Rev back in gear and completed the long-simmering **Yerself Is Steam**. [hd]

FLAMIN GROOVIES

Sneakers EP (Snazz) 1968 (Hol. Skydog) 1975
Supersnazz (Epic) 1969 (nr/Edsel) 1986 (CBS Special Products) 1990 ●
Flamingo (Kama Sutra) 1970 (nr/Big Beat) 1990 ●
Teenage Head (Kama Sutra) 1971 (nr/Dojo) 1990 ●
This Is the Flamin Groovies (Ger. Kama Sutra-Metronome) 1975
Flamingo/Teenage Head (nr/Buddah) 1975
Shake Some Action (Sire) 1976 ●
Still Shakin (Buddah) 1976
Slow Death EP (nr/United Artists) 1976
Flamin' Groovies Now (Sire) 1978
Jumpin' in the Night (Sire) 1979
Flamin' Groovies '68 (Fr. Eva) 1983
Flamin' Groovies '70 (Fr. Eva) 1983
Bucketful of Brains (Voxx) 1983
Slow Death, Live! (Fr. Lolita) 1983
The Gold Star Tapes (Fr. Skydog) 1984
Live at the Whisky A Go-Go '79 (Fr. Lolita) 1985
Roadhouse (nr/Edsel) 1986
One Night Stand (nr/ABC) 1987 ●
Groovies' Greatest Grooves (Sire) 1989 ф
The Rockfield Sessions (Aus. Aim) 1989

Starting out in San Francisco as early as 1965 (predating the Grateful Dead), the Flamin Groovies have always been out of step with the rock world. Ten years before anyone knew about bands releasing their own independent records, the Groovies issued a 10-inch mini-album, **Sneakers**; in the '70s, when that same do-it-yourself spirit was inspiring countless innovative bands to try and challenge the old boundaries, the Groovies retreated to make albums of beat group nostalgia, wearing period clothes and refusing to acknowledge that times had indeed changed.

Always more cult-popular and influential than commercially successful, the Groovies, led by irascible but talented guitarist/singer Cyril Jordan and (until 1971) singer/guitarist Roy A. Loney, always embodied the rebellious, youthful spirit that fueled punk, but held tenuously to their musical roots—'50s American rock-'n'roll and '60s British pop. In effect, they provided inspiration for countless bands (how many covers of "Slow Death" can you name?), and are legendary for good reason.

The Groovies' recording career, generally more exciting on hit-and-run singles than in a sustained album situation, began with the competent amateurism of **Sneakers**—Loney originals played with great energy and a slight psychedelic undercurrent—and continued on their major-label debut, **Supersnazz**, which encompasses a variety of disparate rock'n'roll styles (peaking with killer versions of Little Richard's "The Girl Can't

Help It'' and Eddie Cochran's ''Somethin' Else'') but is more ambitious than impressive. **Flamingo** and **Teenage Head** (years later, the former was reissued as **This Is the Flamin Groovies** in Germany) are the band's strongest early efforts, taking advantage of improved skills and equipment to make loud, brash records in sharp contrast to the era's prevailing bland and puffed-up music.

Following Loney's departure, the Groovies drafted talented guitarist/singer Chris Wilson and began heading in a new direction. The band moved to England, hooked up with the likeminded Dave Edmunds as their producer and, in 1972, recorded the music that would close one phase of the band's career and open the next. Only things didn't exactly work out that way. Later collected as **The Rockfield Sessions** mini-album, those first seven efforts yielded a pair of rock'n'roll singles (including the absolutely classic ''Slow Death'' b/w ''Tallahassie Lassie''), a B-side of Chuck Berry's ''Little Queenie'' and—most importantly—two harbingers of the Groovies' new past that wouldn't surface for four years. When the Groovies finally reemerged with the Edmunds-produced **Shake Some Action** in 1976, it was those two '72 leftovers—''You Tore Me Down'' and the amazing, apocalyptic Byrds-like title track—which most reflected the group's power-pop reorientation.

Still Shakin was rushed out by their old label (Buddah and Kama Sutra being related) as a last chance to cash in, combining tracks from **Flamingo** and **Teenage Head** with a 1971 live-in-the-studio side.

Meanwhile, the Groovies were busy reversing into the future. **Now** and **Jumpin' in the Night** delve further into the past, mixing studiously reproduced British Invasion (and related '60s American) standards with sound-alike originals. While these records are faintly ridiculous and too historically reverent to be taken very seriously, both contain catchy, melodic pop tunes that are impossible to disdain. Besides including the band's fine ''Yeah My Baby,'' **Now** faithfully revisits the Stones (''Paint It, Black,'' ''Blue Turns to Grey''), the Beatles (''There's a Place'') and—perhaps most convincingly—the Byrds (''Feel a Whole Lot Better''). Produced without Edmunds, **Jumpin' in the Night** is less effective, with such inadvisable digressions as Warren Zevon's ''Werewolves of London'' and Bob Dylan's ''Absolutely Sweet Marie'' joining the Beatles (''Please Please Me'') and Byrds (''5D,'' ''It Won't Be Wrong'' and ''Ladyfriend'').

The Groovies didn't issue any new recordings between 1979 and 1987, leading to suspicions that the band had ceased to exist. During that period, however, ongoing European (especially French) interest prompted the release of numerous reissues, compilations and vintage concert material. **Slow Death, Live!** and its equivalent American release, **Bucketful of Brains**, date from a 1971 Fillmore West show; **Roadhouse** is a British repackage combining tracks from the two Kama Sutra albums. **Groovies' Greatest Grooves**, a graphics-encoded 24-track CD, contains most of the non-covers from the band's three Sire albums, as well as five non-originals and some earlier classics, like ''Teenage Head,'' ''Slow Death'' and ''Tallahassee Lassie.''

Although a modest return by any measure, Cyril, bassist George Alexander and three new bandmates did record a new album in 1986: **One Night Stand**, which was done in a single day (two, if you count mixdown) in an Australian studio, sounds live and contains shaggy roadhouse renditions of classic originals (''Shake Some Action,'' ''Slow Death,'' ''Teenage Head'') as well as Paul Revere and the Raiders' ''Kicks,'' the Who's ''Call Me Lightning'' and other covers. If not quite a record to cherish, a reassuring audible reminder that the band lives on—and that Jordan's heart is still in it. [i]

See also *Barracudas, Roy Loney and the Phantom Movers.*

FLAT DUO JETS

In Stereo EP [tape] (Dolphin) 1985
Flat Duo Jets (Dog Gone) 1990
Go Go Harlem Baby (Sky) 1991 ●

Led by good ol' boy Dexter Romweber (guitar-whacking brother of Snatches of Pink drummer Sara Romweber), this smokin' trio (lately a duo) from Chapel Hill, North Carolina, uncorks some of the greasiest, most soulful rockabilly since the real old days. Mixing obscurities with authentic-sounding originals on the eponymous album, Flat Duo Jets avoid the cutesy revivalism of early '80s roots-rock, wringing emotion from the songs instead of championing orthodoxy. The loose, rubbery grooves and Dexter's hillbilly-on-fire vocals have all the immediacy of a late-breaking news flash. Yaa-hoo! [jy]

FLATMATES

Happy All the Time EP (nr/Subway Organisation) 1987
You're Gonna Cry EP (nr/Subway Organisation) 1987
Shimmer EP (nr/Subway Organisation) 1988
Janice Long Session EP (nr/Night Tracks-Strange Fruit) 1988
Heaven Knows EP (nr/Subway Organisation) 1988
Love and Death (The Flatmates 86-89) [CD] (nr/Subway Organisation) 1990 ●

Over the course of four years, England's Flatmates unleashed a series of loudly perfect two-to-three-minute pop blasts, all on singles or four-song 12-inch EPs. That they never made an album is a telling clue to the quartet's aesthetic, favoring the fix of one radio-ready masterpiece over the cumbersome yearly compiling of a ''major'' work. Had the Shangri-Las (perhaps fronted by Nico!) been backed by the Buzzcocks, the Flatmates would have been soulmates.

From the quartet's heart-grabbing first single (''I Could Be in Heaven'') to its exquisite feedback finale (''My Empty Head''), the Flatmates' approach remained consistent, with only a gradual upgrading of sound quality marking the years. How jewels like ''Heaven Knows'' and ''Turning You Blue'' avoided becoming international smashes is beyond comprehension. The 20-track posthumous **Love and Death** CD gathers together most of the band's work, adding a few glittering odds and ends. [sm]

FLESH EATERS

EP (Upsetter) 1979
No Questions Asked (Upsetter) 1980
A Minute to Pray, a Second to Die (Ruby) 1981

Forever Came Today (Ruby) 1982
A Hard Road to Follow (Upsetter) 1983
Greatest Hits—Destroyed by Fire (SST) 1986
Live (Homestead) 1988 ●
Prehistoric Fits Vol. 2 (SST) 1990 ●
Dragstrip Riot (SST) 1991 ●

Young poets on the East Coast were originally attracted to punk by its simplicity, directness and malleability. Most prominently, Patti Smith and Richard Hell found that crudely executed rock'n'roll provided the perfect backdrop for their verbal barrages. Though less celebrated, California's Chris Desjardins made equally ambitious records with a constantly changing set of Flesh Eaters that virtually amounted to a who's who of Los Angeles' new wave notables. Singing in a style akin to Hell's delirious hysterics, Chris D. turns morbid, sensational subjects like murder, vampirism and necrophilia into diverting entertainment through relentlessly intense lyrics. And though their demented tone will drive off most listeners, his albums bear hearing.

Like most visionary types, Mr. D.'s report card was often branded "doesn't work well with groups," which makes it tough for him to maintain a consistent lineup (Plugz guitarist Tito Larriva and then-guitarist Stan Ridgway headed the list of early cohorts). To capture at least a glimpse of said vision, Desjardins finally borrowed an existing band—LA's flower-punk Flyboys—to record the first Flesh Eaters EP. 'Twas a wise choice: the trebly, hyperkinetic playing matches him lunge for lunge on four breathless numbers, including the well-beyond-Costello conflagration "Radio Dies Screaming."

Cramming fourteen tracks into 25 minutes, No Questions Asked uses the simplest punk structures to illustrate such overbearing tales as "Cry Baby Killer" (the name comes from an early Jack Nicholson film), "Suicide Saddle" and "Dynamite Hemorrhage." A formative effort.

By comparison, A Minute to Pray is like seeing Technicolor after a grimy home movie. Partial credit goes to a stellar band that includes the Blasters' Dave Alvin and X's John Doe and D.J. Bonebrake, but primarily it's due to Chris D.'s increased flamboyance. He roars instead of snarling, and his tunes are lively and varied horror-movie stuff. Highlights: "Digging My Grave," "See You in the Boneyard" and "Divine Horseman." For fans of carnival fun houses.

Forever Came Today reverts to a spot about midway between the first two LPs, but it's still riveting. The rudimentary quality of the band matters little when Chris tears into epics of sweaty desperation like "The Wedding Dice" and "Drag My Name in the Mud." A Hard Road to Follow features a revamped lineup and is the closest Chris D. has come to a conventional attack. With the group offering its own warped approximation of hard rock, he chews through a fetid batch of tunes that includes "Life's a Dirty Rat" and the Sam and Dave classic, "I Take What I Want."

Although Desjardins abandoned the Flesh Eaters moniker for his more introspective late-'80s work, the band's rabid followers were left with a variety of compilations. The first SST collection contains relevant tracks from all the albums and adds a few rarities, including the previously unissued "Hard Road to Follow"

and "Lake of Burning Fire" and an alternate version of "Impossible Crime."

While Prehistoric Fits unearths no totally buried treasures, it does dust off a few more early tracks (all previously issued) and makes a nice—if not totally essential—companion piece. Lovingly compiled and packaged with appropriate trashiness, the career-spanning live LP is a welcome document of the thuggish, proto-metal stomp the band (depending on who it included) was so adept at serving up in concert.

Following the Divine Horsemen and the one-off Stone by Stone project, Chris D. reformed the Flesh Eaters in late 1990. In keeping with its title, the sprawling double-LP Dragstrip Riot emphasizes D.'s woozy, pulp-fiction persona-hopping rather than his more fundamentalist santeria-punk ravings. The all-new lineup (especially masterful guitarist Wayne James) proves potent enough to keep pace without clinging to their leader's tornado-swept coattails, whether the context is quietly malicious delta blues ("The Youngest Profession"), Alice Cooper-via-Jim Thompson power-metal ("Sugarhead and Panther Breath") or stripped-down docudrama (the ten-minute title track), not to mention a handful of territory-defining covers (from the Groovies' "Slow Death"—one of the two items deleted from the CD version—to Mott the Hoople's "The Moon Upstairs"). Length alone makes Dragstrip Riot tough to handle in one sitting, but it's hard to imagine taking it off in the middle. [jy/dss]

See also Divine Horsemen.

FLESH FOR LULU

Flesh for Lulu (nr/Polydor) 1984
Blue Sisters Swing EP (nr/Hybrid-Statik) 1985 ●
Big Fun City (Caroline) 1985 ●
Long Live the New Flesh (Beggars Banquet-
　　Hughes-Capitol) 1987 ●
Plastic Fantastic (Beggars Banquet-Hughes-Capitol)
　　1989 ●

The ready adaptability of this Brixton quartet enabled them to rise from the ashes of London's ill-fated Batcave scene—a curious association to begin with, since these mascaraed, leather-clad poseurs are more closely related to old-fashioned rock than gothic grave-robbing. With undisguised superstar aspirations, they signed to Polydor and released two excellent singles ("Restless" and "Subterraneans"). The self-titled album that followed, despite the inclusion of both songs, sinks into the mire, an overlong, overproduced '80s punk take on the Rolling Stones (check the cover of "Jigsaw Puzzle"), a commodity for which there is no pressing demand.

Retreating to the world of independent labels, Flesh for Lulu released the controversial (some deemed the cover art sacrilegious) Blue Sisters Swing EP. An unexpected and most impressive change of course, the five tracks rock with verve and abandon, sometimes approaching heavy metal. Best song title: "I May Have Said You're Beautiful, but You Know I'm Just a Liar."

Big Fun City marks yet another transformation. Though sticking to rock, traces of other musical styles enter the mix: funk, country-western, punk-pop. Still a bunch of vain poseurs, their musical changes don't follow any fashion trends. (The UK CD issue also contains **Blue Sisters Swing**.)

Forever the chameleons, Flesh for Lulu did another about-face on their third album, **Long Live the New Flesh**. This time it's quite clear in which direction the band's course is set—towards popular American acceptance. "I Go Crazy," Flesh for Lulu's contribution to the soundtrack of the John Hughes film *Some Kind of Wonderful*, got a lot of airplay; the entire LP is similarly tailor-made for American radio. "I Go Crazy" (left off the British edition) and "Siamese Twist" are as adventurous as this record gets; the remainder is homogeneous AOR synth/guitar rock.

With **Plastic Fantastic**, another helping of danceable "alternative" rock, glossily enhanced by producer Mark Opitz's decidedly commercial sheen, the group tries yet again to grasp that golden ring. The record starts out strong with the frantic "Decline and Fall" and the heavenly pure pop of "Every Little Word," but is soon overcome by a dark blur of genericism, brightened only momentarily by some laughably lame lyrics and the title track's echoes of "Hot in the City." In fact, beyond its lack of sales, there's little to distinguish this effort from a Billy Idol album.   [ag/db]

FLESHTONES
Up-Front EP (IRS) 1980
Roman Gods (IRS) 1981
Blast Off [tape] (ROIR) 1982 [CD] (Fr. Danceteria) 1990 φ
Hexbreaker! (IRS) 1983
Speed Connection (Fr. IRS) 1985
Speed Connection II (IRS) 1985
Fleshtones vs. Reality (Emergo) 1987 ●
The Fleshtones: Living Legends Series (IRS) 1989 φ
Soul Madrid (Sp. Impossible) 1989

FULL TIME MEN
Fast Is My Name EP (Coyote) 1985
Your Face My Fist (Coyote-Twin/Tone) 1988

PETER ZAREMBA'S LOVE DELEGATION
Spread the Word (Moving Target) 1986

VARIOUS ARTISTS
Time Bomb! The Big Bang Theory (Skyclad) 1988

New York's Fleshtones are caught in the common contradiction of selfconsciously seeking to re-create the unselfconsciousness of '60s rock'n'roll, pre-**Sgt. Pepper** and pre-psychedelia. In other words, they've put a lot of thought and effort into becoming a mindless party band. Although the Fleshtones only occasionally fully capture their high spirits in the studio, the payoff is swell when they do. Nobody else rocks quite like these guys on a good date.

Up-Front's five-song menu includes a fake surf instrumental and a jumped-up account of the Stones' "Play with Fire." Frontman Peter Zaremba's humorously tough approach comes through loud and clear, but the recording's cleanness borders on aridity.

The Fleshtones take a big leap forward on **Roman Gods** by adding new personality and passion to the beat, as witnessed by "I've Gotta Change My Life" and "Let's See the Sun." However, the album's standout underlines the progress remaining to be made elsewhere: "The World Has Changed" crackles like vintage Yardbirds, making ill-advised ventures such as the cover of Lee Dorsey's "Ride Your Pony" seem all the more unfortunate.

Blast Off dates from abortive 1978 sessions for Red Star Records and succeeds beautifully on its own limited terms. It's raw, noisy and incomplete-sounding—just right for debauchery, though unsuitable for careful listening.

Hexbreaker! is the Fleshtones' finest record, an exuberant collection of memorable numbers made even better by brilliant playing and spot-on production by Richard Mazda. "Right Side of a Good Thing," with its hysterical falsetto chorus; "New Scene," a pulsing fuzz-guitar punk raveup; and the shingaling title tune all roll with soul and frolic in the sounds of the '60s without ever losing a grip on the band's own identity. An ultimate '80s garage-rock classic.

The only way to match that achievement was to do it live, smearing as much sweat and personality on the vinyl as possible. It took two attempts: the first **Speed Connection** was issued in France but deemed inferior to the second, which was recorded at a different 1985 Paris show and released in the US and UK. Although technically casual, **Speed Connection II** is a stupendous, old-fashioned warts'n'all concert record, loaded with all the chaos and frantic rock panache the Fleshtones can muster. Especially potent is their brilliant "Kingsmen Like Medley," as well as "Return to the Haunted House" and "Wind Out," the latter featuring guest guitar by Pete Buck of R.E.M.

Buck also collaborated with Fleshtone axeman Keith Streng on the first Full Time Men record, a three-song 12-inch. Although pleasantly unchallenging, the slightly retro-minded countryish pop tunes would have benefited from a more confident vocalist than Streng. Concocting a fuller version of the side band (without further involvement by Buck, although the EP's "I Got Wheels" turns up again), Streng made a full album with three-fourths of the Fleshtones—Gordon Spaeth (sax/harmonica), Bill Milhizer (drums) and Robert Warren (bass)—and a spare guitarist. A busman's holiday of rocking originals and cool covers (by Marvin Gaye *and* the Creation—now that's versatility!) enthusiastically played by a studio full of low-rent superstars, **Your Face My Fist** is as easily enjoyable as it's meant to be.

Undeterred by the outside world's lack of interest, the Fleshtones continue to pursue party nirvana with **Fleshtones vs. Reality**. Typically, the results vary, though the high points are sublime: the snarling prehistoric Kinks guitars of "Way Up Here," the raise-the-dead soul fervor of "Whatever Makes You Happy," a swift remake of "Treat Her Like a Lady" and so on. (The CD adds one track.)

The 20-song **Living Legends** compilation starts with the best tracks from **Up-Front** and **Roman Gods**, adds an odd three-song selection from **Hexbreaker!** and then starts piling on the rarities: the dynamic "American Beat '84" (from the *Bachelor Party* soundtrack), some singles and a pair of previously unissued covers. Rockalicious—but hold on to your copy of **Hexbreaker!** all the same. **Soul Madrid**, a double-live album, was recorded and released in Spain.

Despite relentless good humor, Zaremba's Love Delegation LP (with Streng, a horn section and such guest vocalizers as Barrence Whitfield) illustrates the dangers of unchecked '60s camp revivalism—it sounds more disposable than dynamic. "Turn Me on Again" and Aretha's "Save Me" burn real good, but fluff like "Shama Lama Bing Bang" and a pseudo-heavy remake of Lee Hazelwood's "Some Velvet Morning" (which Thin White Rope does better) are more typical of **Spread the Word**'s dippy spirit.

Time Bomb!, ostensibly a various artists compilation, features variously permutated side projects by Fleshtones and their pals, along with non-LP tracks from the band proper. Love Delegation, Full Time Men, Action Combo, Cryin' Out Loud, Mad Violets and Wild Hyenas all toss in OK cuts, but the disc really catches fire on the Action Dogs' sizzling "I Can't Get Through to You," starring Peter Case, and the mothergroup's "I Was a Teenage Zombie," from the film of the same name. [jy/i]

FLIPPER
Album—Generic Flipper (Subterranean) 1982
Blow'n Chunks [tape] (ROIR) 1984 [CD] (ROIR-Important) 1990 φ
Gone Fishin' (Subterranean) 1984
Public Flipper Limited Live 1980–1985 (Subterranean) 1986
Sex Bomb Baby! (Subterranean) 1988 ●

ANY THREE INITIALS
Ruins of America (Subterranean) 1988

NEGATIVE TREND
We Don't Play, We Riot (Subterranean) 1982

Like a 45 slowed down to sub-LP pace, San Francisco's Flipper delivers a flawless impression of a downed-out hardcore band. The harsh music lumbers and creaks, oozing feedback all the way, while the singer (bassist Will Shatter or bassist—yes, that's right—Bruce Lose) moans and shouts painfully. Flipper could be your car on the verge of a total breakdown or your worst hangover nightmare amped up to brain-splitting volume. And yet, for all the intentional sloppiness and gratuitous noise, not to mention the superficial shock of **Album** tunes like "Life Is Cheap" and "Shed No Tears," Flipper can be uplifting. Underneath the tumult you'll find compassion, idealism and hope, best represented by "Life" ("the only thing worth living for"). That kind of moral statement takes courage.

Blow'n Chunks is a primo live tape of the band onstage in New York, November 1983. Playing all the hits that made them a legend—like "Love Canal" and "Ha Ha Ha"—as well as previewing some songs that made it onto the next LP, the quartet drones along like a factory shutting down for the weekend, a stunning roar of guitar noise and bass pounding that is simply the ultimate loud rock'n'roll imaginable. A real classic album, and the ideal floor-clearer for any club.

Flipper's second studio album, **Gone Fishin'**, makes an ambitious effort to add unexpected sonic components to the din. With vocals taking a clearly predominant role, oddities like clavinet, sax, piano and even open spaces (!?!?) lurk around, while newly sophisti-

cated rhythms (as on the consti/synco-pated "First the Heart") and a relatively restrained mix make Flipper resemble a "normal" band at times. If all you want from Flipper is a visceral thrill, try the live tape; if you want to understand their creative mind, **Gone Fishin'** is the ideal synthesis of sickness and health.

Perhaps sensing that stages held the key to truest Flipperhood, the band's next release was the two-record career-spanning concert compilation, **Public Flipper Limited**. (The PiL parody here is revenge for that group's apparent appropriation of Flipper's generic labelling concept for their 1986 **Album**.) Wrapped in a foldout poster-*cum*-"Flipper on Tour" game, the LP offers a fine selection of tracks, from "Love Canal" to "Sex Bomb" to "Life" to "Flipper Blues." (Locales include San Francisco, New York, Toronto, Washington, DC, and Los Angeles.) The obnoxious onstage patter only adds to the mind-boggling raucous entertainment.

Shatter's death in December 1987 (from a heroin overdose) ended Flipper's on-again-off-again existence once and for all, but didn't stanch the vinyl flow. **Sex Bomb Baby!** compiles all of Flipper's singles (six sides) and tracks from sampler albums, going as far back as the group's 1979 recorded debut on Subterranean's first release, the **SF Underground** collection. The cassette adds three live tracks from the 1980 **Live at Target** compilation; limited quantities of the album contain Bruce Lose's solo single as a bonus.

Any Three Initials, a Shatter side project, was recorded in 1986. Joined by three local musicians (two from the band Bad Posture), Shatter is the lyricist and singer on A3I's **Ruins of America**, a varied album of country music, dirge-rock, PiL-esque anti-pop and other related styles, with subject matter as diverse as meteoric conditions and humanist philosophy. When the going gets rough, the ghost of Flipper rises from the platter; other tracks might be by anybody *but* that group.

Shatter and Flipper drummer Steve DePace were in a pre-Flipper band called Negative Trend, which released the four-song **We Don't Play, We Riot**, recorded in 1978, on Subterranean. [jy/i]

FLOAT UP CP
See *Rip Rig + Panic*.

FLOOR KISS
See *Bush Tetras*.

ROSIE FLORES
See *¡Screamin' Sirens!*

FLOUR
See *Breaking Circus, Rifle Sport*.

KLAUS FLOURIDE
See *Dead Kennedys*.

FLOWERS
See *Icehouse*.

FLOY JOY

Into the Hot (nr/Virgin) 1984
Weak in the Presence of Beauty (nr/Virgin) 1986 •

Don Was produced both of this English dance-music trio's LPs, giving it a full-blown wash of horns, synthesized strings and other high-tech keys to commercial success. On **Into the Hot**, brothers Shaun and Michael Ward (with assistance from Monsieur Was and guests) churn out their music with ease and style, allowing Carroll Thompson's swell, big voice to dominate the record.

Thompson and Shaun Ward subsequently bailed out (resurfacing a few years later in a group called Everyday People) leaving hornman Michael Ward to draft singer Desy Campbell and bassist/drum programmer/co-writer Robert E. Clarke and put together a new all-male Floy Joy. The second LP is more appealing for its material (the title track—which received fine treatment in a 1987 cover by Alison Moyet—is excellent) than its occasionally sterile Was-oriented dance-soul-funk performances. [i]

FLUID

Punch n Judy (Rayon) 1986 •
Clear Black Paper (Sub Pop) 1988 •
Roadmouth (Sub Pop) 1989 •
Glue EP (Sub Pop) 1990 •

Formed from a pair of prominent Denver punk groups, Fluid sets to reviving the Stooges and MC5 (minus the outlook and outrage) and reliving '60s garage-punk and folk-rock on its raunchy-sounding self-produced debut. **Punch n Judy** benefits from the quintet's obvious knowledge of *Creem*'s classics, but the twin-guitar attack and John Robinson's vocals are neither retro-cool nor distinctive, and the haphazard songwriting rarely yields anything memorable.

Adding Grand Funk, the Amboy Dukes and Alice Cooper to its stylistic reference library, Fluid updates punchy riff-based guitar rock with a measured dose of post-punk noise on **Clear Black Paper** (the CD and cassette of which also contain **Punch n Judy**). Caught indecisively between the past and the present, the LP cruises along on a fairly even keel with only limited success. Try as they might, the band's best efforts—simply functional songs like "Cold Outside," "Try, Try, Try" and "It's My Time"—just don't pack enough sonic power to ignite.

Producer Jack Endino fixed that problem on the geometrically more intense **Roadmouth**, sharpening up a wailing knife of dual guitars over which Robinson snarls tensely controlled vocals with real conviction. Besides significantly better playing, Fluid comes up with greatly improved '60s-derived material: "Ode to Miss Lodge," "Twisted & Pissed" and the monumental "Fool's Rule."

The six-song **Glue** (which has **Roadmouth** added to its cassette and CD) cranks the Fluid motor even more. Starting with a spectacular cover of a little-known Troggs' song ("Our Love Will Still Be There") that kicks out the Jams with charging neo-mod catchiness, producer Butch Vig captures up a buzzing punky blitz, pouring flammable Fluid across the entire audio spectrum and igniting it with cool tunes like "Black Glove" and the hooky "Pretty Mouse." [i]

FLUX OF PINK INDIANS

Neu Smell EP (nr/Crass) 1981 (nr/One Little Indian)
1987
Strive to Survive Causing Least Suffering Possible
(nr/Spiderleg) 1982 (nr/One Little Indian) 1987 •
The Fucking Cunts Treat Us Like Pricks (nr/Spiderleg)
1984 (nr/One Little Indian) 1987 •

FLUX

Uncarved Block (nr/One Little Indian) 1986 •

Instead of the near-illiterate (and proud of it) hedonistic roughneckism of some hardcore outfits, this quartet (originally affiliated with the Crass organization and later the proprietor of the commercially potent One Little Indian label) is one of the semi-intellectual, fiercely political bands who use stripped-down guitar punk as the medium for their strong leftist and/or anarchist views. Besides the bracing intensity of their music, Flux has always distinguished itself for impressive packaging standards—**Strive to Survive** boasts a snazzy twelve-page booklet and a dignified gatefold jacket.

The band has a good deal of punchy precision to its crisp drumming and distorto-chord guitar. The catch is that it's all sort of military, as in the way the tuneless vocals resemble the bark of a drill instructor. Like the graphics, these "melodies" and lyrics (not to mention the politics) are all black and white, and aside from the sterility inherent in preaching to the converted, Flux's monochromatic asceticism is ultimately numbing.

The **Neu Smell** reissue—solid rip-snorting protest punk on a stylishly dressed, loud'n'clear 12-inch—puts the three horrible drum-noise'n'screaming tracks from the 1984 "Taking a Liberty" single on the flipside.

Eliminating punk and reducing the political content, Flux's original and often fascinating **Uncarved Block** leans a bit towards the industrial world, alternating muscular mid-tempo rock (which boasts atmosphere and melody for a change) and bizarre free-form ambient improvisations, in which drums pound as instrumental blasts and distorted sound effects leap in and out of the sparse mix. [jg/i]

FLYBOYS

See *Choir Invisible*.

FLYING COLOR

Flying Color (Grifter-Frontier) 1987

HECTOR

Hector (Cryptovision) 1988

Though hardly revivalist, the first LP by this Bay Area quartet abounds with unrepentant Beatlephilia, with generous servings of ringing choruses, exquisite guitar splashes and endearingly ragged harmonies. Sweetly stunning sensitive-but-not-wimpy pop-rock items like "Dear Friend" and "One Saturday" stand out, but Flying Color is equally adept with rock songs ("I'm Your Shadow," "Believe Believe"). Unfortunately, guitarist Richard Chase—author and singer of the memorably melancholic "It Doesn't Matter" and "Bring Back the Rain"—jumped ship shortly after this album was finished, and Flying Color apparently dissolved.

Bassist Hector Penalosa's solo effort—on New York's Cryptovision label, which had released Flying

Color's debut single—includes contributions from Chase and Flying Color drummer John Stuart (who sings lead on one song), but Penalosa handles virtually all of the remaining instruments himself. For the most part, this immensely likable effort offers a less rocking version of Flying Color's sweetly melancholy jangle. But the whooping rocker "Northwest Trip" and the haunting violin-dominated instrumental "Manuela" (both curiously buried on Side Two) indicate that there's more to Hector than just power pop. Here's hoping this departure won't keep Flying Color from fulfilling the promise of this debut. [hd]

FLYING LIZARDS
The Flying Lizards (Virgin) 1979
Fourth Wall (nr/Virgin) 1981
Top Ten (nr/Statik) 1984 ●
DAVID CUNNINGHAM
Grey Scale (nr/Piano) 1980

Led by pianist David Cunningham, the Flying Lizards started as (and largely continued to be) a novelty group that took classic rock songs and reduced them to parody with neo-Kraftwerk synthesizer minimalism and robotic deadpan vocal readings (as epitomized on the eponymous debut album by "Summertime Blues" and "Money"). The serious work shows Cunningham leaning towards the arty high-tech drone of Tangerine Dream, though, and that suffers from comparison with the inspired lunacy of the comedy turns.

Fourth Wall attempts to evolve a happy medium, with helpers including New Yorkers Pat Palladin and Peter Gordon and new-jazz artist Steve Beresford. Cunningham moves uneasily between electro-pop and trance music (as in Steve Reich and Philip Glass). Well-produced and interesting as individual songs, but it fails to jell as an album.

He attempts strictly serious music on **Grey Scale**, improvising on the piano by allowing the course of the music to be altered by random outside events. Though the technique derives from John Cage, the result falls closer to Reich and Terry Riley.

Following a long layoff, the Lizards returned in 1984 with **Top Ten**, another wacky album of demented rock-'n'roll revisionism, this time assaulting the songwriting of Little Richard, Jimi Hendrix, James Brown, Leonard Cohen, Larry Williams and others. Purists and musical conservatives will find this impossible; keep an open mind and forget about the originals, and you'll be amazed at Cunningham's arcane wit and inventive dissection/reconstruction skill. [sg/i]

F MACHINE
See *Simon F.*

FOC
See *Flag of Convenience.*

FOETUS INC.
Sink (Self Immolation-Wax Trax!) 1990 ●

YOU'VE GOT FOETUS ON YOUR BREATH
Deaf (nr/Self Immolation) 1981
Ache (nr/Self Immolation) 1982
SCRAPING FOETUS OFF THE WHEEL
Hole (Self Immolation-ZE-PVC) 1984 ●
Nail (Self Immolation-Some Bizzare-Homestead) 1985 ●
WISEBLOOD
Dirtdish (K.422-Some Bizzare-Relativity) 1986 ●
FOETUS ALL-NUDE REVIEW
Bedrock EP (Self Immolation-Some Bizzare-Relativity) 1987
CLINT RUIN/LYDIA LUNCH
Stinkfist EP (Widowspeak) 1988 ●
FOETUS INTERRUPTUS
Thaw (nr/Self Immolation-Some Bizzare) 1988 ●
Rife (no label) 1989

Thank goodness for rock'n'roll—otherwise, what hope would there be for people like Jim Thirlwell (aka Clint Ruin, Scraping Foetus off the Wheel, Foetus Uber Frisco, Phillip and His Foetus Vibrations, You've Got Foetus on Your Breath, Foetus Art of Terrorism, etc.)? Although enormously talented and possessed of a wide and masterful sonic palette, it's virtually impossible to pin down just what the Australian-born/English-launched New Yorker does. Suffice it to say his projects are all characterized by violence, intensity, irreverence, abrasion, unpredictability and an incredible grasp of music-making's never-ending possibilities to disturb.

The only thing to do with **Hole**, Foetus' first American release, is to jump in and pray you survive. The LP has a little of everything: industrial cacophony ("Clothes Hoist"), high political drama ("I'll Meet You in Poland Baby"), spare crypto-blues ("Sick Man"), demented surf music ("Satan Place"), something sick built on a swing beat ("Water Torture"), the *Batman* theme and lots more. Played at a confusion level that makes Christmas Eve at K-Mart seem placid, the cadences would do Test Dept. proud and the lyrics might upset Frank Zappa. Simply put, you've never heard *anything* like this before. (The album's US edition adds a bonus disc containing all four songs from 1985 12-inch singles by You've Got Foetus on Your Breath and Foetus Uber Frisco plus a rare compilation track.)

Nail is another delicious voyage into Foetus' fevered world. From the soundtrack-styled opening ("Theme from Pigdom Come"), through a generally cinematized concept collection of high-octane rants—sort of Birthday Party with a sense of humor meets latter-day Pink Floyd—Foetus goes about his usual business, layering sound on sound, insult on injury. An apparently nonexistent instrumental entitled "!" is the LP's definitive existential high point, but such vehement audio orgies as "The Throne of Agony" and the '40s-jazzy "Descent into the Inferno" provide plenty clever lyrical competition.

Wiseblood is a duo of Clint Ruin and ex-Swan/producer Roli Mosimann, assisted on **Dirtdish** by Robert Quine, Hahn Rowe of Hugo Largo, Norman Westberg of the Swans and Phoebe Legere. While the pair shares music writing chores (thereby diluting Foetus' awesome power), leaving Ruin in charge of words and vocals ensures that the familiar growled litany of sexually charged insanity will be as damaging to the psyche as ever. (What does "The Fudge Punch" suggest to you?) So if the LP lacks a full load of explosive Foetus audio dynamite, there's more than enough ugliness and venom here to obliterate a roomful of hoodlums.

The title track of **Bedrock** (most assuredly not about Fred and Wilma's hometown) fills one side of the EP and plays at 45 rpm; the four crunching rants on the back run at 33. "Diabolus Musica" and "Shut" are really one slow-starting instrumental that revs up to noise concrète (complete with machine guns, metallic clangs and animal noises) strong enough to peel layers off a boulder at a hundred paces; meanwhile, the vituperative and deliciously vulgar "Bedrock" (and its alternate take, "Bedrock Strip") is a guttural Tom Waits-like swing rap sneered over acoustic bass and bongos. One version adds horns and a backing chorus; both feature an industrial-strength rusty-door guitar solo.

Clint Ruin, Lydia Lunch and a host of celebrity percussion-pounders whip up a rhythm riot on the title track of **Stinkfist** as the happy couple chant the title and make halfhearted sex noises. "Meltdown," the EP's other main track, is a three-part Lunch recital accompanied by a full-scale rock attack and such Ruinous sound effects as car crashes, foghorns and violin scrapings. Unfortunately, nothing in the grooves is half as striking as the record's copulatory cover.

Broiling up an explosive sonic smorgasbord in a free-fire zone, Foetus completely outdoes himself on **Thaw**, an album so intense that it makes his previous platters seem like tune-ups. His arsenal here includes machine guns, clanging industrial percussion, a symphony orchestra and virulent lyrics about suitably violent subject matter spewed out in a voice so shredded it would give Freddy Krueger the willies. Unpredictably amid the successive pin-you-to-the-wall onslaughts, Foetus drops back and whispers a verse or two over acoustic piano and string bass (or, in one case, sitar and tabla). Oppressive in the most rewarding fashion imaginable, **Thaw** (which concludes with the charming "A Prayer for My Death") is the score to a film I would be terrified to see.

Following **Thaw**'s release, Thirlwell formed Foetus Corruptus—borrowing Raymond Watts (of the like-minded Pig) and members of Prong and the Swans—and went off to do a European tour, an event documented on the double-LP **Rife** authorized boot.

The **Sink** compilation (another two-disc set) digs all the way back to the very beginning (1981's "OKFM," by Foetus Under Glass) in its coverage of the madness that is Foetus, compiling twenty (mostly EP) tracks from all phases of his career. While the set contains some rarities and loads of great music, the odd selection logic reproduces nearly all of **Bedrock** and both sides of Foetus Art Terrorism's 1984 single ("Calamity Crush" b/w "Catastrophe Crunch"), the latter of which is merely an instrumental scratch remix. [i]

See also *Lydia Lunch*.

ELLEN FOLEY
Spirit of St. Louis (Cleveland Int'l) 1981

Ellen Foley made other solo albums after gaining fame in the performing company of Meat Loaf, but this one is very different. It was produced by "my boyfriend"—Mick Jones of the Clash—and features his band in toto plus its musical associates (Tymon Dogg, Mickey Gallagher, etc.) as her accompaniment. Additionally, half the songs are new (and otherwise unissued) Strummer/Jones compositions; three others are Dogg's. Coming right after the loose, throwaway feel of **Sandinista!**, Jones did an about-face and created precious arty backing that strains Foley's vocal talent beyond endurance. Her interpretive abilities disappear under the weight of such screamingly pretentious tripe as "The Death of the Psychoanalyst of Salvador Dali." (What books were those boys reading?) A bizarre Clash footnote. [wk/i]

FOLK DEVILS
Fire and Chrome EP (nr/Karbon) 1985
Goodnight Irony (nr/Situation Two) 1987
KING BLANK
Mouth Off EP (nr/Situation Two) 1988
The Real Dirt (nr/Situation Two) 1988 •
IAN LOWERY GROUP
King Blank To (nr/Situation Two) 1989 (Beggars
    Banquet-RCA) 1990 •

Heir to the existential angst of such late-'70s luminaries as John Lydon and Tom Verlaine, England's Ian Lowery (whose first recorded musical strivings were with a late-'70s punk band, the Wall) talk-sings in that wonderfully curdled sneer we've heard a million times before. But few do it as well.

Lowery has had his current moves down pat since the days he fronted the Folk Devils. **Goodnight Irony** reeks with attitude; the band rocks hard and sullen as Lowery grunts, gasps and snarls. Tracks like "Evil Eye," "English Disease" and "Beautiful Monster" would all seem dumb without his theatrical flair.

Going out on his own under the King Blank moniker, Lowery continued his wicked ways on the three-track **Mouth Off**, featuring the input of Screaming Blue Messiahs honcho Bill Carter, who produced and played on one song and co-wrote two. With the Messiahs backing him on the title track, Lowery seems newly dangerous, even throwing in a good imitation of a shivering fit.

Lowery then assembled some sympathetic sidemen and turned King Blank into a real band. Mimicking Dylan's **Bringing It All Back Home** on the cover of **The Real Dirt**, Lowery broadened his range without any reduction in arrogance. Thanks to his versatile sidemen, he's able to touch on rockabilly, woozy ballads, vicious boogie, a chugging throwback to the Velvet Underground ("Uptight"), even bogus country music ("Bulletproof t," as in crucifix). Nasty and delectable.

Renaming King Blank (with only a drummer change) to give himself star billing, the Ian Lowery Group made its debut with an outstanding album. **King Blank To** features harsh, clanging guitars, unpleasantly throbbing beats and an avalanche of knotty, clenched-fist lyrics from the uptight Mr. L. High points: the ominous "A Kind of Loathing" ("The only help that I'd give you is to hand you your pills/And close your eyes when you're gone"), the rollicking "Never Trust Me" ("Crack that bottle Jack and we'll kill this rage in our souls") and other sagas of revenge and regret. [jy]

DREDD FOOLE AND THE DIN

Eat My Dust Cleanse My Soul [tape] (Religious) 1984
(Homestead) 1985
Take off Your Skin (PVC) 1987

Pseudonymous singer Dredd Foole (Dan Ireton) was a longtime friend and musical associate of the Mission of Burma; the Bostonian borrowed that group, redubbed it the Din and had it back him on an early single. Volcano Suns—a Burma offshoot—fulfilled the same role on **Eat My Dust**, originally released on cassette but reissued on vinyl. Recorded live to two-track and including covers of the Doors' "People Are Strange," the Animals' "I'm Crying" and Iggy's "I Got a Right," the LP reveals Foole to be a tuneless bellower; his wobbly marble-mouthisms fit strangely with the skillfully played demi-punk garage music. Enthusiasm may not be a problem, but melody sure is.

Take off Your Skin, which uses the same Din (Peter Prescott, Jon Williams and Jeff Weigand of Volcano Suns, plus guitarist Kenny Chambers, soon to join Bullet LaVolta), manages to make something more listenable out of Ireton's devolved oral emissions. By noising up the music and harnessing a more controlled singing style, the LP hits a workable—almost Crampsian—equilibrium that's plug ugly but bracing in its forceful post-punk courage. [i]

See also *Mission of Burma, Volcano Suns*.

FOOL KILLERS

See *True West*.

FOOLS

Sold Out (EMI America) 1980
Heavy Mental (EMI America) 1981
World Dance Party (PVC) 1985
Wake Up ... It's Alive!!! (PVC) 1988 ●

After an auspiciously flip debut—"Psycho Chicken," the hysterical barnyard parody of Talking Heads' "Psycho Killer"—Boston's Fools proved to be neither funny (intentionally or otherwise) nor musically enthralling on either **Sold Out** or **Heavy Mental**, despite the best efforts of accomplished producers (Pete Solley and Vini Poncia, respectively). After several years of national-scene silence, the Fools returned with **World Dance Party** in 1985, sporting a half-new lineup and a bit of sunny cowpoke vapidity called "Life Sucks . . . Then You Die."

The club-rocking live album, recorded in Boston in early 1987 by the same humorless but competent quartet, includes terrible versions of "Mack the Knife" and "The Sound [sic] of Silence" along with equally enthralling originals, almost none drawn from prior albums. [i]

FOOLS DANCE

See *Cure*.

FOR AGAINST

Echelons (Independent Project) 1987
December (Independent Project) 1988 ●
In the Marshes EP (Independent Project) 1990

For Against are one of the best new American bands of the late '80s, but that's a secret the US new music public has yet to discover, possibly because the trio hails from the unlikely mecca of Lincoln, Nebraska. Although obviously influenced by the UK post-Joy Division sound, For Against add their own distinct ripple; singer Jeffrey Runnings' frantic bass and Greg Hill's charging drums are unusual for such atmospheric music. Yet all through **Echelons**, the echoed sound of guitarist Harry Dingman arouses a berserk fireworks show careening like a thousand power drills. Pin it to the nonstop rhythm section and Runnings' boyishly sweet catchy pop voice, and For Against are a waterfall of sound. When the tempo slows down, they draw you in like a hypnotist, as on the tantalizing six-minute closer, "Broke My Back."

December is a stunner, a high-water mark for UK-inspired American music. Dingman pulls out all the stops for a neo-psychedelic spiderweb of sound. Runnings' bass lines are also more forceful, well supported by Hill's Stewart Copeland-on-speed bashing, a pulsing drive marked by rapid cymbal rolls and floor tom flourishes. There's greater scope, too, from the slow doorbell chime of "The Effect," the moody, emotional collapse of the title track and the brave despair of "The Last Laugh" to the exciting arousal of "Clandestine High Holy" and "Stranded in Greenland." A remarkable and ambitious effort.

In the Marshes is a 10-inch artifact of 1986 demos. Predating both albums, these six tracks bear little relation to their manic pop thrill (especially with Hill supplanted by a no-frills drum machine). Attempting a 4AD-style chamber atmosphere, For Against succeeds only twice, on the bitter "Purgatory Salesman" and the spindly "Amnesia."

Dingman and Hill departed in '89 to form the Millions, while Runnings has switched to guitar and recruited three new For Against members. [jr]

FORGOTTEN REBELS

This Ain't Hollywood ... (Can. Star) 1983
In Love with the System (Can. Star) 1984
The Pride and the Disgrace (Can. Other People's Music) 1985
Surfin' on Heroin (Restless) 1988 ●
(Untitled) (Restless) 1989 ●

CHRIS HOUSTON AND THE SEX MACHINE

Hate Filled Man (Can. Caucasion) 1986

Ridiculous but fun, these Ontario glam punks lead off their first LP with a buzz-saw version of Gary Glitter's "Hello Hello" and then blast a perfect merseybeat melody into the Ramonized present. Elsewhere, they cover "Eve of Destruction," go "Surfin' on Heroin" and vent their frustration about the balance of rock trade in "England Keep Yer Stars." Throughout, singer Mickey DeSadist fights off an overactive echo chamber as the other three Rebels pound out efficient wall-of-guitar punk.

The second LP finds the revamped Rebels in a much more aggressive mood, cursing a lot and resembling Sham 69 on shoutalong choruses like "Bomb the Boats and Feed the Fish" and "In Love with the System." In spots, DeSadist affects an outdated Johnny Rotten voice. The subject matter is similarly well-trod: "Rich and Bored," "Elvis Is Dead," "The Punks Are Alright" (rewriting the Who's "Kids Are Alright"). Also, the playing is fancier, with dynamics and arrangements that often resemble early Clash. It's a weird mixture: pop-punk/straight punk. Not very inventive, but a highly enjoyable throwback.

A new gang of Rebels (DeSadist and guitarist Mike Mirabella are still in charge) cropped up in 1988 with an American album containing all-new recordings of previously released songs. **Surfin' on Heroin** retreads "Bomb the Boats," "Elvis Is Dead," "I'm in Love with the System" and others, adding a couple of topical new compositions (like "A.I.D.S.") for good measure. The vibrant, loud punk-rock sound recalls the Dead Boys or Generation X; low-brow/high-energy songwriting that crosses the Monkees with the Ramones gives the Rebels a solid basis for their polite blow-torch assault. If a total lack of originality can be excused, **Surfin' on Heroin** is a big fun date. But who played the organ?

DeSadist (now spelled DeSadest) is the only original Rebel on (**Untitled**). The material is as derivative and uneven as ever, but a capable new guitarist (Jeffrey Dee) and crisp, roaring sound give the LP a powerful charge. Over the course of this zany set, the quartet delves into Bowiesque glam ("Wild Eyed Darlin' "), gets a good fix on Johnny Thunders ("The Girl Can't Come"), trashes Tommy Roe's "Dizzy" and parodies Johnny Cash in the offensively vulgar "I Gotta Axe." Capping off the silliness is "Science Fiction Double Feature," a dumb name-check of B-movie stars. The (**Untitled**) CD also contains the **Surfin' on Heroin** LP.

Bassist Chris Houston—who went under the name Pogo Aù Go Go on **In Love with the System**—put his own dixieland version of "Surfing on Heroin" on **Hate Filled Man**, a casual solo outing (with a wacky astroturf cover!) that followed his departure from the Rebels. But that song is all that connects the two career phases. Houston exercises his cultural misanthropy in a mixture of rudimentary studio tracks and even simpler solo live performances that have nothing in common with glam punk except the fear of conventionalism. From the woozy blend of trumpet, piano, simple drums and bass on "Ecstasy of Ignorance" to the tremolo electric guitar ravings of "Baby Jesus Looks Like Elvis" to the funky rock of "Negative Groove," Houston demonstrates a quick wit and enough musical skill to make this strange album more than a little entertaining.   [i]

ROBERT FORSTER

See *Go-Betweens*.

FORTUNATE SONS

See *Barracudas*.

45 GRAVE
Sleep in Safety (Enigma) 1983
Autopsy (Restless) 1987 ●
Only the Good Die Young (Restless) 1989 φ
SILVER CHALICE
Evil Birds EP (XES) 1985

CELEBRITY SKIN
Celebrity Skin EP (Triple X) 1990 ●

Los Angeles' 45 Grave were the leaders of the 1981 death-rock explosion that also birthed, among others, Christian Death and **Dance with Me**-era TSOL. The group was a breath of fresh graveyard air and, unlike many serious gloomsters, always kept tongue firmly in cinematic cheek. Playing with punky venom and a slick metallic sound (the goth-horror edge made it an absolutely prescient mix), the fearsome foursome (later a quintet) was led by Phoenix-bred guitarist Paul B. Cutler and his vampiric inamorata, vocalist Mary "Dinah Cancer" Sims, rounded out by ex-Germs drummer Don Bolles and bassist Rob Graves (Ritter), also a member of the Bags and Gun Club.

The legendary "Black Cross"/"Wax" single and three cuts on the seminal **Hell Comes to Your House** compilation inaugurated 45 Grave's career in '81, establishing the blend of Cutler's crisp, offbeat riffing and Cancer's artless, icy shrieks. By the time their first album shambled in, Paul Roessler had joined, adding his effervescent keyboards into the macabre brew. The consistently creepy **Sleep in Safety** contains most of the band's best songs: multi-textured creations like "Insurance from God," "Dream Hits" and "Phantoms" (an '82 single), the catchy "Evil," a delightfully unexpected Ventures-like instrumental ("Surf Bat"), the giddy "45 Grave" theme song and a fist-waving anthem ("Partytime," redone the following year as the B-side to a snazzy version of Alice Cooper's "School's Out").

By '85, Cutler and Cancer had split, effectively ending the band. Cutler went on to a prominent and influential career as a record producer and session player, and joined Dream Syndicate in 1986. **Autopsy** was commissioned to fill in some gray areas, mainly documenting early, punky material: the first single, demo versions of later hits, a hilarious compilation track ("Riboflavin-flavored, Non-carbonated, Polyunsaturated Blood") and nine previously unreleased songs.

Meanwhile, Graves and Bolles formed Silver Chalice with producer/guitarist Geza X; the group also included a guitar-playing songwriter and poppy singer Kim Komet. Despite the name and crypto-metal artwork, the quintet's one EP (released on Geza's label) is surprisingly unthreatening and unpunky, a small-scale rock-pop effort with neither style nor personality.

A few years later, 45 Grave began doing irregular West Coast reunion tours. The full-length **Only the Good Die Young** captures an '88 Hollywood gig with ace sound quality. The invigorated original quartet shreds through all the big numbers and a bevy of entrancing new songs, including "Sorceress," "Akira Raideen," the rib-tickling "Fucked by the Devil" and a surreal version of Dave Brubeck's jazz classic "Take Five" (the jumping-off point for a psychedelicized Cutler solo interlude). Ritter died of an OD in 1990.

Bolles' current outfit, Celebrity Skin, comes on like a high-octane mix of early Cheap Trick, Hanoi Rocks and the Dickies. The three-song (four on CD) **Celebrity Skin** EP offers two doses of humorous hard pop with a snaky glam edge ("Monster" and Abba's reliable "S.O.S.") and a filler metallic instrumental ("Clown Scare"). Nice try.   [i/gef]

See also *D.C.3, Dream Syndicate, Pat Ruthen-Smear, Thelonious Monster*.

FOUNDATION

Voyage (Fartblossom Enterprises) 1986
Tied Up with a Monkey (DSI) 1988

For proof that underground music thrives outside of big cities, consider the Washington, DC, suburb of Reston, Virginia, a planned community originally built by the Mobil Corporation. One of a fine array of young bands that exist there, distinct from their DC peers, Foundation explores a thoughtful punk/rock hybrid with some interesting twists.

Recorded as a quartet, the 23-minute **Voyage** mini-album includes "Winter Vision," an instrumental that treads dangerously close to a '70s wizards and warlocks sound, as well as some above-average rockers ("Halfway to 50," "It's Not as Bad") and the title track, a mixture of pop-punk and new wave cheesiness that is somewhat reminiscent of a certain Psychedelic Furs song. Foundation's bassist, lead guitarist and drummer each share lead vocal duties, sacrificing continuity but adding variety to a set of songs that might otherwise go stale.

After a lineup change, the trio wound up on a Virginia label, which released the remarkably mature **Tied Up with a Monkey**. Intricate punky rockers like "Emo O.D." and "Walking on Stilts" are great tracks, as is the band's theme song, "Foundation." A hardcore sendup ("Must You Keep Us Awake with Your Constant Urinating") and a cover of the Byrds' "The World Turns All Around Her" are also worth hearing.   [icm]

4 SKINS

The Good, the Bad & the 4 Skins (nr/Secret) 1982
A Fistful of 4 Skins (nr/Syndicate) 1983
From Chaos to 1984 (nr/Syndicate) 1984
The Wonderful World of the 4 Skins: The Best of the 4 Skins (nr/Link) 1987
A Few 4 Skins More Volume 1 (nr/Link) 1987
A Few 4 Skins More Volume 2 (nr/Link) 1987
Live and Loud!! (nr/Link) 1989

One of the mainstays of second-wave Brit-punk, London's harsh and serious 4 Skins—not as intense as Crass, but far more earnest than Sham 69—endured major lineup changes (they went through four lead singers including, at one point, the quartet's manager) long enough to record three albums in the early '80s.

The studio side of **The Good, the Bad & the 4 Skins** starts out with a delightful ska-beat tune ("Plastic Gangsters") and then turns angry skinhead generic for shoutalongs like "Justice" and "Yesterdays Heroes." The seven-song live side is equally forbidding (Panther's vocals are especially unpleasant).

With only bassist Hoxton Tom remaining from the first LP, **A Fistful of 4 Skins** moderates a more musical punk sound that makes adequate material (the group's lyrics are actually pretty sharp) easy to take but hard to remember. Packaged in one sleeve, the first two albums were later reissued in toto as **A Few 4 Skins More Volume 1**.

The 4 Skins' last release before splitting in late '84 was the live **From Chaos to 1984**, recorded in a studio before an audience of invited friends. That album comprises one disc of the double **A Few 4 Skins More Volume 2**; the other is a rarities compilation of the group's earliest efforts, B-sides and other obscure ephemera for the hardcore hardcore. The sixteen-track **Wonderful World** retrospective collects up a definitive sampling of singles, album cuts and compilation contributions.   [i]

BRUCE FOXTON

Touch Sensitive (Arista) 1984

Although he was one-third of an ultra-successful band, Foxton had to try and relaunch his career virtually from ground zero after Paul Weller bagged the Jam in 1982. Surprisingly, the bassist's first solo album is quite good, and happily free of any attempt to recapture the sound which made him a star. With a four-man band and a bunch of guests, Foxton sings and plays ten original tunes in a number of styles, from busy dance-rock to wistful big-production pop. Throughout, he adapts his bluff voice as best he can; ingenuous earnestness is a strong suit. The lyrics regularly mention loss, individual responsibility and uncertainty—it's obvious the Jam's end was a traumatic experience—but **Touch Sensitive** is a promising (albeit unsuccessful) new beginning for a sincere, talented performer.   [i]

See also *Jam*.

JOHN FOXX

Metamatic (nr/Metal Beat-Virgin) 1980
John Foxx (Can. Virgin) 1981
The Garden (nr/Metal Beat-Virgin) 1981
The Golden Section (nr/Metal Beat-Virgin) 1983
In Mysterious Ways (nr/Metal Beat-Virgin) 1985 ●

After three albums as lead vocalist, John Foxx (Dennis Leigh) left Ultravox to pursue a solo career. A prime factor in the group's original sound, Foxx was, by extension, a major influence on the new romantic movement that followed in its wake. Fortunately, both Ultravox and Foxx solo continued to make music of quality and distinction.

Metamatic is Foxx's first venture alone into the world of synthesizers, Ultravox's subsequent instrument of choice. In emulation of his own work and Conny Plank's production on Ultravox's **Systems of Romance**, Foxx (aided by another synthesist and a bassist) finds the perfect counterpart for his themes of alienation and dislocation in sterile, minimalist electronic sounds. His vocals are oddly distant, like echoes, but the record has an honesty and directness that are quite affecting. (**John Foxx** is a Canadian compilation that rearranges a number of songs from **Metamatic**.)

The Garden is a lush, thick paean to Foxx's catholicism and the mysticism that has always lurked beneath his austere urbanity. Pastoral in tone, the album flourishes under a denser sound, replete with acoustic instruments that offset the onslaught of synthesizers. Foxx's themes remain the same, which is good, and his songwriting and flair for imagery reach new peaks on masterpieces like "Europe After the Rain" and "Walk Away," which provide melancholic views of familiar, mysterious worlds.

Co-produced by Foxx and Zeus B. Held, **The Golden Section** has a bizarrely Beatlesque sound on several tracks, mildly resembling the Fab Four's late-career psychedelia. Foxx is his usual enigmatic, inventive self, spinning moody creations that neatly sidestep synthesizer clichés; the only flaw is in his dramatic vocals. "Endlessly" (also a single) is the album's clear standout, a magnificent multi-level pop creation that parallels Foxx's former group's development while clearly displaying a character all his own. The cassette version has six extra tracks.

In Mysterious Ways deals largely in romantic clichés (e.g., "Stars on Fire," "This Side of Paradise")—in some cases the title's even the dominant lyric!—and the bombast quotient is sometimes heightened by overuse of female backing vocals (girl-groupy on "Enter the Angel," gospelly on "This Side of Paradise"). But Foxx's earnest, electro-rock casanova charm somehow makes it work. From the dance-rock of "What Kind of Girl" to the **Astral Weeks**-iness of "Morning Glory," the mix may not be all that original, but it's still consistently entertaining.   [sg/i/jg]

See also *Ultravox*.

FRANK CHICKENS

We Are Frank Chickens (nr/Kaz) 1984
The Best of Frank Chickens [CD] (nr/Kaz) 1987 ●
Get Chickenized (nr/Flying Lecords) 1987 ●
Club Monkey (nr/Flying Lecords) 1989 ●

The two Japanese women (Kazuko Hohki, Kazumi Taguchi) who comprise Frank Chickens are both proud of and amused by their country's diverse cultural contributions to the world. On one hand, the debut album pays tribute to Ninja warriors and emotional Enka ballads, but the duo also sings with mock reverence on "Mothra," named for a classic low-budget monster movie. Lyrics and liner notes are both hilarious and/or absurd (see "Shellfish Bamboo"). Musically mixing synth-pop (created in the main by the English writing/production team of Steve Beresford and David Toop) with funk and jazz, the Chickens also incorporate Japanese musical traditions. Very entertaining.

Taguchi became an ex-Chicken and was replaced by Atsuko Kamura prior to **Get Chickenized**. Lyrics are even more preposterously campy than before, this time dealing mostly with observations of, and experiences with, Western culture. "Yellow Toast" concerns being a hip but exploited flavor-of-the-month in England: "You think we are full of Zen/But we prefer lots of yen/We are stupid little Japs/And you are splendid English chaps." Other songs are not as bitter and sarcastic as that, instead addressing subjects ranging from nonsensical Japanese lessons to female wrestling. The premature fifteen-track **Best of Frank Chickens** draws from the debut LP and early 45s.

Always in danger of being viewed strictly as a novelty act, Frank Chickens manage to avoid such trappings by remaining uniquely bizarre. **Club Monkey** tells a story about "Monkey People" who eat dogs as a drug and burn dead bodies so they can revive them as ghosts. After repression by the English squashes these time-honored traditions, they plot a revolution, to be led by a kung fu movie star. Got that? There might be something in there about animal rights; if so, it's a lot more amusing than a similar message from Morrissey. Musically,

the Chickens offer the same oddball mélange as earlier albums, and the lyrics are as farcical as ever.   [dgs]

FRANKIE GOES TO HOLLYWOOD
Welcome to the Pleasuredome (ZTT-Island) 1984 ●
Liverpool (ZTT-Island) 1986 ●
HOLLY JOHNSON
Blast (Uni) 1989 ●
Hollelujah EP (nr/MCA) 1990 ●
Dreams That Money Can't Buy (nr/MCA) 1991 ●
PAUL RUTHERFORD
Oh World (4th & B'way) 1989 ●

In one of rock's most spectacular hypes (certainly the greatest since Malcolm McLaren first perpetrated the Pistols swindle), Frankie Goes to Hollywood—a minor hi-NRG dance outfit with genealogically fascinating origins in the '70s Liverpool scene—became a highly controversial and enormously successful UK chart phenomenon in 1984, thanks to the combined talents of producer Trevor Horn and critic-turned-propagandist Paul Morley, via their ZTT label. The blatant homo-erotica of "Relax" got Frankie banned on English radio while the leather-bar setting of its accompanying video earned them similar turndowns on television. "Two Tribes," an inchoate condemnation of the nuclear threat, complete with thundering dancebeat, continued the band's phenomenal rise. Having reached dizzying heights via what seemed like dozens of remixes of the two songs, all that remained for the icon of a million clever T-shirts was to record an album. And (thanks to the uncredited musical skills of former Ian Dury sidemen, it was later revealed) make one—or, precisely, two—they did.

Welcome to the Pleasuredome has four sides of the Frankies in all their artificial/superficial glory. From the hits (the two pre-LP singles plus "War" and "Welcome to the Pleasuredome") to the pits ("Ferry Cross the Mersey," "Do You Know the Way to San Jose," "The Power of Love"), Frankie say, "We may not be able to do it ourselves, but when you care enough you get the very best to cover for us." A brilliant load of bullshit, served with as much panache—marketing and musical—as the 1980s could muster.

It proved increasingly difficult for the pseudo-group to even appear to work together harmoniously, and the prospects of a second album seemed remote. Nonetheless, **Liverpool** was eventually cobbled together and issued: eight long songs that mimic the sound but possess none of the Oz-like glory that was Frankie. With the golden goose laying nothing but plastic, the group collapsed in 1987.

After surviving an altogether embarrassing legal altercation with his former label, lead singer Holly Johnson began a solo career, issuing the bland-as-beans **Blast** with no residual Frankieness (other than a few vocal gimmicks). Clearly more skilled as a songwriter than he will ever be as a vocalist, Johnson provides himself with goodnatured soul-pop-dance tunes (produced by Dan Hartman and others) but lacks the talent and personality to personalize them on record. If David Bowie ever decides to remake **Young Americans**, he should ask Johnson to return some of these stylistic borrowings. **Hollelujah** contains half a dozen remixes.

Frankie's other vocalist, Paul Rutherford, shaved off his moustache and stepped into the dance club spotlight with a slick series of shallow neo-soul and house singles, some produced/performed by ABC. A compilation of UK hits and more, **Oh World** is a routine dance record that reveals Rutherford to have a personably plain voice and no special aptitude for this sort of music.   [i]

See also *Big in Japan*.

FREAKWATER
See *Eleventh Dream Day*.

FREIHEIT
See *Munchener Freiheit*.

FRENCH, FRITH, KAISER, THOMPSON
See *Henry Kaiser*.

FRANK FRENCH AND KEVN KINNEY
See *Drivin' n' Cryin'*.

DOUG E. FRESH & THE GET FRESH CREW
Oh, My God! (Reality) 1986
The World's Greatest Entertainer (Reality) 1988 φ

Typical of the fast-moving New York rap scene, these two albums by Doug E. Fresh (Davis)—the original human beatbox, and one of the leading young rhymers to pick up from the original old-schoolers like Grandmaster Flash and Kurtis Blow—sound amazingly quaint after only a few years. Far removed from the strong content and intense beats of the Public Enemy/N.W.A. generation, Fresh runs a moderate course, with a bit of reggae toasting, polite tracks and very little attitude. Originally partnered with Ricky Dee (who later went solo as Slick Rick), Fresh—like nearly all MCs until the late '80s—stuck with 12-inch singles, scoring a 1985 international hit with "The Show (Oh, My God)."

Oh, My God! makes good use of live musicians (trumpeter Jimmy Owens, synthesist Bernard Wright, etc.) and contains an anti-abortion number; **The World's Greatest Entertainer** also uses real players (including drummer Charlie Drayton), boasts several tracks co-produced by P.E.'s Bomb Squad and ends with a thoughtful rap about visiting Africa.   [i]

See also *Slick Rick*.

FRESHLY WRAPPED CANDIES
I Like You (T.E.C. Tones-Ralph) 1989 ●

Mental health professionals know that it's healthy to let the child inside you come out and play every now and then. Freshly Wrapped Candies do it in the recording studio. Most of **I Like You** sounds either like a polite juvenile version of the Butthole Surfers or kin-

dergarten teachers on acid; even when the musical style is avant-rock vignettes, it gets topped with nonsense lyrics sung in goofball voices. Most of the songs (ranging from just over ten seconds to almost ten minutes) feature only guitars and vocals, but others actually get their titles from their instrumentation, like "Flute(s)" and "Majestic Popular Keyboarding." (Unfortunately, "Voltage Regulator" doesn't fit into that category.) On the down side, several tracks annoyingly emulate a Walkman with dying batteries. Freshly Wrapped Candies' collective elevator might not make it all the way to the top floor, but they do provide goofy, mildly irritating fun in a nicely art-damaged kind of way. But don't play it for your therapist. (The CD contains seven bonus tracks.)   [dgs]

FREUR
Doot—Doot (Epic) 1983
Get Us Out of Here (nr/CBS) 1985

UNDERWORLD
Underneath the Radar (Sire) 1988 ●
Change the Weather (Sire) 1989 ●

An insular and intentionally remote British art-pop band, Freur was originally identified only by an unpronounceable squiggle rather than a proper name. When the gimmicky hubbub subsided, all that was left for posterity was **Doot—Doot**'s title track, four magnificent minutes of lilting, haunting synthesizer ambience with quirky vocals and choral backing.

Freur faded from sight after a second album met with even less response, but four-fifths of the quintet returned in 1988 as the Underworld, an enigmatic but more commercially geared organization. Rupert Hine's production of **Underneath the Radar** gives it a sturdy dance backbone and the familiar sound of late-'80s British techno-beat; Heaven 17 leaning towards the Thompson Twins. A shade above average with a fair share of ideas and invention, but still nothing to compare with the participants' one extraordinary item.

If singer Karl Hyde were Michael Hutchence, "Change the Weather" would be an INXS single, but the song is not typical of the unchallengingly accessible album named for it. Loudly textured modern rock played on guitars and keyboards, **Change the Weather** has better vocals, more focus and personality (some of it evidently borrowed from more successful groups) than the Underworld's debut. Presentably chart-worthy without being vile—these days, that's quite a feat.   [i]

GAVIN FRIDAY AND THE MAN SEEZER
See *Virgin Prunes*.

FRIGHTWIG
Cat Farm Faboo (Subterranean) 1984
Faster, Frightwig, Kill! Kill! (Caroline) 1986
Phone Sexy EP (Boner) 1990 ●

With songs like "My Crotch Does Not Say Go," "Hot Papa" and "Vagabondage," the women of San Francisco's Frightwig make no bones about their topical focus on **Cat Farm Faboo**. The provocative lyrics' blunt observations on aspects of love would be more worth considering if not for the band's awful noise, a disorganized tumult of screechy vocals and sloppy guitar droning.

Bolstered by a new member and a soft spot for tempo and harmonic coordination, the quartet got Beefheart sideman Eric Drew Feldman to co-produce and contribute a bit of keyboards to **Faster, Frightwig** (the title a nicely ironic poke at filmmaker Russ Meyer). Playing a moderate form of Flipperesque grind-rock with prominent lumbering bass and guitars that sound like they might be on fire, Frightwig puts its satirical outrage (and outrageous satire) to good use in songs like "Punk Rock Jail Bait," "Crazy World" and "American Xpress" (guitarist Susan Miller's bizarre travelogue). Finishing the record on a genuinely tender note, "I Am Here Alone" compresses the band's surging music into a gentle bed of noise, while "Freedom" gets a handsome folky chorus together for a touching gospelly plea.

By the time Redd Kross' McDonald brothers arrived to produce the six-song **Phone Sexy**, Frightwig had become a trio, with only founding bassist/singer Deanna Ashley and guitarist/singer Rebecca Tucker remaining from the previous lineup. (Sister Double Happiness drummer Lynn Perko completes the package.) Kicking out the hard-rock jams with kitschy chanted vocals and guitar feedback on a remake of "American Xpress," Frightwig comes off like Julie Brown doing a heavy metal parody; covering Shonen Knife's "Public Baths" they sound like the Runaways with bigger amplifiers. Is this progress or what? [i]

ROBERT FRIPP

Exposure (EG-Polydor) 1979 (Editions EG) 1985 ●
Under Heavy Manners/God Save the Queen
  (EG-Polydor) 1980
Let the Power Fall (Editions EG) 1981 ●
The League of Gentlemen (EG-Polydor) 1981 + 1985
Network EP (nr/EG) 1985 (EG) 1991 ●

ROBERT FRIPP/THE LEAGUE OF GENTLEMEN

God Save the King (Editions EG) 1985 ●

ROBERT FRIPP AND THE LEAGUE OF CRAFTY GUITARISTS

Live! (Editions EG) 1986 ●

TOYAH & FRIPP

The Lady or the Tiger (Editions EG) 1986 ●

SUNDAY ALL OVER THE WORLD

Kneeling at the Shrine (EG) 1991 ●

In the last half of a seven-year hiatus between King Crimsons, Robert Fripp—self-styled thinking-man's musician and guitarist's guitarist—played axeman/producer to the stars (David Bowie, Peter Gabriel, Blondie, Talking Heads, Brian Eno, Hall and Oates, the Roches) and cut a series of solo LPs reflecting his then-current obsessions.

The loosely autobiographical **Exposure** is the closest Fripp has come to a pop effort, with guest vocals by Gabriel, Daryl Hall, Peter Hammill and Terre Roche. Interlarded with tape-loop guitar episodes and enigmatic spoken-word communiqués from several sources, the record manages to overcome the self-referential preciousness inherent in such an enterprise—but just barely.

Under Heavy Manners/God Save the Queen offers two concepts for the price of one; both, unfortunately, are flops. The first half gets "Frippertronics" off to a bad start with a suite of samey, lackluster performances. It was Eno who showed Fripp this two-tape-recorder strategy that allows accumulation of rich textures. In performance, Fripp would build towering edifices of looped guitar sound and then spin stunning lead solos over them. The loops remained on tape; the solos didn't, thus the best parts of the concerts that produced **God Save the Queen** never made it onto the record. **Under Heavy Manners**, Fripp's first stab at "discotronics" (his version of dance-oriented rock) sounds less austere than impoverished, despite a memorable David Byrne vocal.

The next pair of LPs, continuing Fripp's self-appointed "Drive to 1981," gamely picked up the pieces. **Let the Power Fall** continues the Frippertronics methodology of **God Save the Queen**; although both were recorded during the same 1979 tour, this album's loops provide a far greater wealth of sounds, moods and ideas—Fripp's editing skills evidently having improved with time. However, several bootlegs documenting Frippertronics with the leads intact remain definitive, as much as Fripp may detest them.

Harnessing himself and keyboardist Barry Andrews (ex-XTC) to an adequate rhythm section (that included future Gang of Four bassist Sara Lee), Fripp created the one-shot League of Gentlemen band/tour/LP and firmly claimed his dance-rock territory. A typical League cut took a simple medium-to-fast backbeat over which Fripp and Andrews locked horns, with melodic development emerging slowly, surely, subtly. On the 1980 tour, Fripp played marvelous leads; on the LP (whose cover art is, oddly enough, by Danielle Dax), they are replaced by spoken-word in-jokes. **God Save the King** is a revised, remixed, remastered single-disc distillation of **Under Heavy Manners/God Save the Queen** and **The League of Gentlemen** albums.

In the mid-'80s, Fripp founded a guitar school in West Virginia and set about teaching the instrument to disciples in most extraordinary fashion. The all-acoustic League of Crafty Guitarists (his students) album, conceived as an educational challenge and recorded in concert at George Washington University, features seventeen diligent pupils performing pastoral Fripp instrumentals with delicacy and quiet appeal. (The LP does contain one lengthy and alluring Frippertronics piece for good electric measure.) Without the master on hand, some of Fripp's students also recorded **New Music for Acoustic Guitar Ensemble**, issued on cassette around '89.

Another school project provided the basis for **The Lady or the Tiger**, wherein Fripp's missus, singer/actress Toyah Willcox (who has an extensive record catalogue of her own, beginning in the late '70s), recites Frank R. Stockton's 1882 story (and its sequel, *The Discourager of Hesitancy*) over a mild bed of inconspicuous guitar textures composed by Fripp and performed with the League of Crafty Guitarists. Sunday All Over the World is Fripp's new rock band. [mf/i]

See also *King Crimson, Shriekback*.

FRIPP & ENO

(No Pussyfooting) (Antilles) 1973 (EG) 1981 •
Evening Star (Antilles) 1975 (EG) 1981 •

FRIPP + SUMMERS

I Advance Masked (A&M) 1982
Bewitched (A&M) 1984 •

The two early collaborations between Fripp and ex-Roxy Music muckraker Brian Eno are excursions into effete electronics, with Fripp simply playing his guitar through Eno's synthesizers/tape recorders. The resulting side-long montages of loosely structured sound on the first album are pleasant and recall the work of Terry Riley. **Evening Star** breaks no new ground; it is more a re-exploration of similar terrain.

What did Fripp and Policeman Andy Summers do on their summer vacations? Using a wide harmonic palette, they recorded **I Advance Masked**, a duet LP whose primary mood is tranquility, although Fripp the soloist ultimately reveals himself in ecstatic flights of fancy.

As the sequel proved, however, Andy Summers is no Brian Eno. Given another brief reprieve from producing those lighter-than-air guitar textures for the Police, he thickens the mix with electronic muck, leaving little solo space for himself or Fripp, who co-wrote only half the material on **Bewitched**; the rest is Summers' alone. Maybe they were too busy toying with the synth-pop trappings that dominate the record to bother playing much guitar.   [jw/mf]

See also *Brian Eno, Andy Summers.*

FRED FRITH

Guitar Solos (nr/Caroline) 1974
Gravity (Ralph) 1980 (East Side Digital) 1991 •
Speechless (Ralph) 1981 •
Live in Japan (Jap. Recommended) 1982
Cheap at Half the Price (Ralph) 1983
The Technology of Tears (SST) 1988 •
The Top of His Head (Bel. Crammed) 1990 •
Step Across the Border [CD] (RecRec-East Side Digital) 1990 •
Guitar Solos Complete [CD] (East Side Digital) 1991 •

FRED FRITH ET AL.

Guitar Solos 2 (nr/Caroline) 1976
Guitar Solos 3 (Rift) 1979

If Fred Frith were remembered only for being the guitarist in Henry Cow he would be just another shadowy figure in the history of art-rock. Instead he pursued a unique and influential solo career in the '80s that made its mark on leading avant-gardists worldwide. Frith's sessioneering and collaborative work has figured prominently on records by Material, the Golden Palominos, Brian Eno, John Zorn and others. Massacre, his trio with the Material rhythm section, produced an unforgettably powerful record. His duo, Skeleton Crew, beguiled audiences all over the world. He has played and recorded effectively with Voice of America, compiled three early records of avant-guitar playing (**Guitar Solos 1, 2** and **3; Complete** consists of **1** plus the Frith contributions to **2** and **3**) and recorded duet LPs and live tapes of varying quality with Cow drummer Chris Cutler, saxophonist Lol Coxhill, guitarists Henry Kaiser and Rene Lussier and others.

But Frith's most engaging work was for Ralph, the Residents' label. Structurally, the records resemble Henry Cow's early album in that they, like Frith himself, tend not to stay in one place long enough to try the attention span of neophytes. As such they are perfect vehicles for corrupting straitlaced rock'n'rollers into this world of joyful noise, which can include anything from polytonal polyrhytherama to Eastern European folk tunes to a taped snippet by New York's 13th Street Puerto Rico Summertime Band.

Gravity was recorded with members of several bands, the most substantial contributions coming from Sweden's Zamla and the Maryland-based Muffins (not Martha's). Frith's bass, guitar and violin are prominent, yet merged into a whole that is stronger than its dovetailed parts, all held together by ingenuity and force of will. Yes, "Dancing in the Streets" is a cover of you-know-what.

Speechless continues the process with a greater emphasis on reeds that should give Henry Cow fans a strong sense of déjà vu—yet Cow never did anything this strong. Many of Frith's melodies are influenced by the same strain of European folk music that inspired Béla Bartók. Helping out are Etron Fou Leloublan on one side and Massacre on the other. (Some of the latter's material has turned up, rearranged, on Massacre's album and during Skeleton Crew gigs.) Endlessly fascinating, this is Frith's best solo record.

Cheap at Half the Price marks not one departure but several. For the first time on a solo album, Frith sings. The songs are edgy whimsy squeezed out in a weird high-pitched tone, except "Same Old Me," whose rough lyrics emerge in a tape-slowed drawl over angry riffing. Much of the record, especially instrumental tracks, suffers from an experiment in recording "at home on a 4-track."

For those ready to graduate from the prog-rock safety of the Ralph platters to something harder and weirder, there's **Live in Japan**, which captures Frith's "guitars on the table" approach, concentrating not on standard instruments but on homemade ones that are plucked, raked, abraded and assaulted with a variety of objects. The two discs can be bought separately or together in a black corrugated box containing booklets in English and Japanese. A must for noise fans.

Much of Frith's work in the late '80s was oriented towards film and theater scores. **The Technology of Tears** offers not one but three of Frith's dance-company commissions. Two sides of the double album contain the titular piece, created in 1986 with John Zorn, an occasional scat vocalist and fake-art turntable manipulator Christian Marclay. Although largely a flighty and disjointedly arhythmic effort, parts do coalesce with the arcane logic of Frith's structuralism. The high-strung and disturbing "Jigsaw" (also from '86, with trombonist Jim Staley) and the enticingly diverse episodes of "Propaganda" ('87) each fill a side.

Assembled from enormously varying sources, **Step Across the Border** is a very bizarre version of a film soundtrack. Besides previously unissued live and studio recordings covering a decade, three continents and countless musical variations, the 26 selections include items from Massacre, Skeleton Crew and **Cheap at Half the Price**. As such, this is as much a Frith retrospective as it is a new work. But without the movie to connect the dots, it's impossible to discern what internal logic makes these individually intriguing snippets fit together.

[mf/i]

See also *Golden Palominos, Henry Cow, Henry Kaiser, Material, Skeleton Crew.*

FROGS

The Frogs (Frogs) 1988
It's Only Right and Natural (Homestead) 1989

There is very little, uh, "hard" information available regarding the Frogs. Purported brothers Jimmy and Dennis Fleming were first noted on the "thank you" list for Die Kreuzen's **Cows and Beer** EP back in '82. Since then, the Milwaukee duo has done a lot of home recording, resulting in two LPs. The first is a curiously out-of-time blend of Anglo-clever pop-clichés, heavily referential to Roy Wood and Sparks but with some unusual Christian/smut lyrics tossed into the stew. That few people noted its release is no great surprise.

Then, according to rumor, the Frogs began to send around cassettes of a similarly appointed second LP, backed with some examples of the pair "goofing around." The latter caught the ear of Gerard Cosloy, then head of Homestead Records, and some of the songs were issued as the Frogs' second LP. Declaring themselves leaders of the "Gay Supremacist" movement, the Flemings/Frogs caused a lot of ruckus with their (presumably) tongue in cheek lyrical thrust. Encased in a sleeve showing a little boy wearing a pink triangle badge, songs like "Been a Month Since I Had a Man" and "These Are the Finest Queen Boys (I've Ever Seen)" generated an enormous amount of pissed-off press, but the crazy Tyrannosaurus Rex-like psychedelia and the weird aura created by the lyrics deserve to be heard. "I've Got Drugs (Out of the Mist)" was certainly among 1989's most played songs at this house. Since the release of **It's Only Right and Natural**, the Flemings toured once (with Couch Flambeau's Jay Tiller helping out) but have otherwise been silent. More's the pity.

[bc]

FRONT 242

Geography (Bel. RRE) 1982 (Wax Trax!) 1987 ●
No Comment EP (Wax Trax!) 1987 ●
Official Version (Wax Trax!) 1987 ●
Back Catalogue (Wax Trax!) 1987 φ
Front by Front (Wax Trax!) 1988 ●
Tyranny for You (Epic) 1991 ●

That avant-garde industrial dance music produced by Belgian art terrorists could compete in the 1991 American mainstream says much for the progress of the digital beat through the '80s. While Front 242's early records (best exemplified by their debut album, **Geography**) were firmly rooted in the clinically crisp synthesized sound of Kraftwerk and Cabaret Voltaire, the group's initial approach was no more threatening than Depeche Mode.

When Richard 23 joined founding members Daniel Bressanutti, Patrick Codenys and Jean-Luc De Meyer in 1983, however, Front 242's sound began moving away from alternative pop and into harder, trans-European disco garnished with politically relevant samples. A series of 12-inch singles (later assembled with other '82-

'85 material for **Back Catalogue**) and the six-track mostly instrumental **No Comment** chronicle this progression, but the music remained stark and controlled; it wasn't until **Official Version** that Front 242 truly became a distinctive force.

Ranging from the subliminal pop of "Quite Unusual" through the pummelling industrial dance of "Aggresiva Due," mixing up sub-symphonic instrumentation on "Slaughter" and using sampled bible-thumpers to frightening effect on "Angst," **Official Version** at last captured the band's potential on tape. Having already established a reputation for demonic audio-visual performances, the album helped Front 242 emerge from relative obscurity to become a significant cult force, selling loads of records all over the world.

Front by Front took this confrontational manifesto a logical step further. Images of control, power and war are evident in titles like "Until Death (Us Do Part)" and "Terminal State," and in the frequent use of militaristic beats and samples. But variety again abounds: "First In/First Out" takes their dancefloor obsession closer to the mainstream, while vocal tracks ("Circling Overland" and "Headhunter V 3.0") use dark imagery for commercial gain. (As a single, "Headhunter" became Front's anthem.)

The long wait prior to **Tyranny for You** was marked by one unexceptional single ("Never Stop") and a licensing deal to just the sort of mega-corporation their imagery and music so frequently attacks. But anyone imagining a temperate performance from the band would have been disappointed: released at the start of the Gulf War, **Tyranny**'s edge matches its era. With a fuller sound and less use of straightforward songs, it's a soundtrack to the chaos of a violent world. The "Tragedy for You" single aside, vocals appear sparingly—the chorus of "recession, regression, repression" on "Gripped by Fear" is consciously unnerving—but the hard dance feel is ever present on semi-instrumentals like "Moldavia" and "Neurobashing."

[tf]

See also *Revolting Cocks.*

FUGAZI

Fugazi (Dischord) 1988
Margin Walker EP (Dischord) 1989
13 Songs [CD] (Dischord) 1990 ●
Repeater (Dischord) 1990 ●

As the figurehead and backbone of Washington DC's punk scene throughout the '80s, singer/guitarist Ian MacKaye has led the Teen Idols, Minor Threat, Egg Hunt and Embrace; his latest band (and the city's newest musical legend) is the culmination of it all, a new rock music built on a hardcore foundation.

Fugazi's impressive debut, a seven-song 12-inch, blends an early-DC hardcore sensibility with a mature, objective outlook and crisply produced mid-tempo songs that are dynamic, aggressive and accessible. ("Waiting Room" is an especially catchy shoutalong, with a style of call-and-response vocals that have scant punk precedent.) Both MacKaye and former Rites of Spring vocalist Guy Picciotto have traded their punk anger for an introspective, almost poetic vision, using abstractions in strongly structured compositions like "Bulldog Front" and "Give Me the Cure" (a contemplation on death). The combination of MacKaye's and Picciotto's abilities gives the quartet a rare strength; the two singer/songwriters complement each other perfectly.

Margin Walker—another 12-inch, this one with a deeply distasteful cover photo—illustrates just how far Fugazi's four have come since their hardcore beginnings. The bracing EP oozes confidence—in MacKaye's melodic guitar work, the tight, fluid rhythm section, the incisive lyrics and the sharply arranged vocal exchanges. The songs are great, from the raging title track to the funky Gang of Fourish verses and poppy chorus of "And the Same" to the thickly chorded "Lockdown." Continuing to develop the stylings he began with Minor Threat, MacKaye manages to make the expletives in the vigorously monotonal, part spoken "Promises" sound somewhat eloquent.

Fugazi put the relatively slick sound of **Margin Walker** up on blocks and stripped it down to the bare essentials for the group's first full-length LP. **Repeater** is the blueprint for a post-hardcore world, a stunning and adventurous new stage in Fugazi's development. The title track—indicative of the album at large—offers a more powerful three-minute burst than anything on the first two records, with a dizzying bass line, speedy, powerful drumming and a repetitive squeal that is barely recognizable as guitar. **Repeater**'s only disappointment is its weak lyrics; both MacKaye and Picciotto do a lot of finger-pointing at Joe Average, but the overzealous pontification should not be a distraction from what is otherwise an amazing album.

13 Songs combines **Fugazi** and **Margin Walker** on one CD; the CD of **Repeater** adds the **3 Songs** 7-inch.

[icm/i]

See also *Minor Threat, Pailhead, Rites of Spring.*

FULL FATHOM FIVE

The Cry of a Falling Nation (Link) 1987
4 a.m. (Link) 1988 ●
Multinational Pop Conglomerate (Link) 1989 ●

Proof that serious Midwest post-punk exists outside of the usual locales, this trio from Iowa City, Iowa, (hometown of the wonderful Dangtrippers) builds a vintage Bob Mould wall-of-rhythm-guitar sound and tops it off with winsome Shoesy vocals on **The Cry of a Falling Nation**, a neat declaration of style. Since he hasn't got the pipes to compete straight-on with his own surging guitar power, Boston native Eric Melcher solves the problem (on record, at least) by relaxing and floating above the pop-rooted din. Unfortunately, that makes his clumsy/serious lyrics all too audible.

Despite a general reduction in the sugar content, **4 a.m.** offers pretty much the same thick guitar rock as the first LP. Amid the familiar roar, unwarranted stylistic digressions (like the jazzy piano backing of "The Firing Line") suggest ambitions that may be beyond the band's ken. And what is the inexplicable "Paula's First Piano Recital"—a live instrumental that could be exactly as billed—doing on the album?

With a new face behind the skins and a reaffirmation of the first album's rich, tuneful rock approach, Melcher delivers his best-sounding songs yet on **Multinational Pop Conglomerate**. But one nagging problem remains. To quote from the marvelously catchy "A Little Hope":

"As the world runs the course of entropy/We tend to think that it will all come down next week." Help!

[i]

FULL FORCE

Full Force (Columbia) 1985
Full Force Get Busy 1 Time! (Columbia) 1986
Guess Who's Comin' to the Crib? (Columbia) 1987 ●
Smoove (Columbia) 1989 ●

The six members of Brooklyn's Full Force—three brothers and three others—write, play, sing and produce themselves as well as other artists. In a very short time, boundless energy and a positive outlook have turned Paul Anthony, Bowlegged Lou, B-Fine and their three associates into a remarkably successful full-service hit machine and one of the most influential organizations in "black music."

Full Force first found fame by creating and performing the music for U.T.F.O.'s "Roxanne, Roxanne" smash. They did the same for Lisa Lisa and Cult Jam, yielding huge hits in "I Wonder If I Take You Home," "Head to Toe" and "Lost in Emotion." Their own debut album ties things up in a neat package, with "United," a track that features U.T.F.O., Lisa Lisa with Cult Jam and the Real Roxanne with Howie Tee. It also includes an answer to their own (rhetorical) song, "Girl If You Take Me Home." **Full Force** is nothing but genuine urban contemporary music, a vibrant mix of rap, rhythm, soul and rock.

Get Busy 1 Time! displays the same stylistic dexterity. Whether they're juicing up a mellow soul tune ("Temporary Love Thing," "Body Heavenly") with restrained beatbox percussion, harmonizing over a busy scratch track ("Never Had Another Lover," "So Much"), or showing their affection for Sly Stone ("Old Flames Never Die"), Full Force absorbs and processes various influences into a unique collection of dance sounds.

In a strangely directed crossover bid, the cover of **Guess Who's Comin' to the Crib?** shows a white suburban family breaking out over the Full Force record in the hands of their sunglasses-sporting little girl. Musically, the band is on an energy rush, busying up the tracks with synth horns, complex vocal arrangements and all sorts of percussion action. Downplaying the ballads for a funkier streetwise rhythm sound, Full Force employs dialogue, slang, sound effects and turntable tricks to enliven the dance-ready cuts and provide surprises at every sonic turn. An entertaining record that, cover aside, isn't especially geared to appeal across color (or format: check out "Black Radio") lines.

Smoove is so diverse, accomplished and easily appealing that it doesn't take much imagination to envision Full Force hosting a Saturday night variety show on network television. Besides carefully thanking everybody under the sun, the polite sextet runs a master class in modern African-American music, setting their songs in handsome, lush productions with enough rhythm to move even the most casual listener onto the dancefloor. The program contains rap, soul (a reverent medley of classics from Motown, New York and Philadelphia avoids any single stylistic identification), mild house (with guest vocals by Samantha Fox) and new jack swing, all walking a rare line between street credibility and mainstream accessibility. [tr/i]

See also *UTFO*.

FULL TIME MEN
See *Fleshtones*.

FUN BOY THREE
The Fun Boy Three (Chrysalis) 1982
Waiting (Chrysalis) 1983
The Best of Fun Boy Three (Chrysalis) 1984 ●

It came as quite a surprise when, at the height of the Specials' popularity, vocalists Terry Hall and Neville Staples and rhythm guitarist Lynval Golding broke away to form their own self-contained group, making an off-beat LP that spawned two UK hit singles and took a large step towards injecting an African-based influence into the new pop music vocabulary. On **The Fun Boy Three**, the trio's imaginative use of various conventional and exotic instruments—though the emphasis is on vocals and percussion—is countered by a pervasively dark, pessimistic feel, more so on the US edition, which places most of the brooding stuff on Side Two. Dick Cuthell (horns) and Bananarama, whom the Fun Boys backed in return, occasionally brighten the proceedings.

Waiting, produced by David Byrne, follows that somber avenue much further, using assorted jazzy styles in minor keys to express cynicism in "The More I See (the Less I Believe)," tell a harrowing tale of molestation on "Well Fancy That!" and explode the mythical side of young romance on "The Tunnel of Love." The centerpiece of the album, however, is "Our Lips Are Sealed"—the Go-Go's hit written by Hall and Jane Wiedlin—given a dramatically different reading here, slowed to dirge speed and laden with heavy atmosphere and a resigned feel, yet somehow played with a preter-natural lightness. A remarkable track on a phenomenally powerful album.

The ever-restless Hall left the band in '83 to form another trio, the Colour Field, a move which prompted a concise Fun Boys compilation: nine album selections plus Bananarama's (featuring FB3) "Really Saying Something" and a lazy version of George Gershwin's "Summertime." Hall's bandmates stuck together as Sunday Best, working with ex-Selecter vocalist Pauline Black. [jg/i]

See also *Colour Field, Specials*.

FUNKY KINGS
See *Jules Shear*.

FURYO
See *U.K. Decay*.

FUZZBOX
See *We've Got a Fuzzbox and We're Gonna Use It*.

FUZZTONES
Leave Your Mind at Home (Midnight) 1984
Lysergic Emanations (nr/ABC) 1984 (Pink Dust) 1985

Live in Europe (Ger. Music Maniac) 1987 ●
Nine Months Later EP (Ger. Music Maniac) 1988
Creatures That Time Forgot (Ger. Music Maniac) 1989
  (Skyclad) 1990 ●
In Heat (Beggars Banquet-RCA) 1989 ●
Hurt on Hold EP (nr/Situation Two) 1989
Action EP (nr/Situation Two) 1990 ●

SCREAMIN' JAY HAWKINS AND THE FUZZTONES
Live EP (Midnight) 1984

LINK PROTRUDI AND THE JAYMEN
Drive It Home! (Ger. Music Maniac) 1987
Missing Links (Skyclad) 1989

TINA PEEL
Extra Kicks [tape] (Limp) 1980

New York's garage-rocking Fuzztones—Rudi Protrudi, Deb O'Nair and three lesser-named cohorts—do their wild Crampabilly thing on **Leave Your Mind at Home**, seven numbers recorded live. The sound approaches bootleg quality, but that hardly matters—the shrieks and demented guitar solos here don't exactly call out for laser-level fidelity. Raveup enthusiasm is all that counts, and that's exactly what the record delivers.

Lysergic Emanations is a fab studio LP, released originally in the UK and then, with new graveyard cover art (by Protrudi) and two different tracks, in the States. (It's also available as a pic disc.) The sound is pure '60s garage punk—the Seeds, Chocolate Watch Band, Yardbirds, Animals, ? and the Mysterians, Standells, Shadows of Knight—produced clearly but without any excessive slickness. Absolutely first rate.

In fine early '60s rock'n'blues tradition, the 1984 live EP consists of the Fuzztones backing up veteran grandmaster Screamin' Jay Hawkins on four of his classics, including "I Put a Spell on You" and "Constipation Blues."

Live in Europe is preferable to **Leave Your Mind** in most areas: fidelity, audience participation and song selection are all superior. The only weak link is the band: with the onset of either boredom or laziness, they sleepwalk through this date. The Fuzztones' original lineup fell apart not long after but, as **Creatures That Time Forgot** certifies (in screaming day-glo), not without leaving quite a legacy. Single and compilation tracks are interspersed with demos (neanderthal stomps through "The Witch" and the otherwise unavailable "Fabian Lips" really stimulate the adrenal glands) and deadpan interviews from sources as unlikely as *The Larry King Show* and Finnish radio. Priceless.

Protrudi relocated to Los Angeles and assembled an all-new Fuzztones, largely with fellow New York expatriates. This edition had precious little in common with its antecedent—instead of energized '60s raunch, the emphasis is on sludgy, sub-Steppenwolf biker rock (although, applying a you-can-fool-some-of-the-people-all-of-the-time mentality, the psychedelic trappings remain unchanged). Kindred chameleonic spirit Ian Astbury (who'd soon regress backward to the exact same spot where had Rudi arrived) helped the band procure the record contract that yielded **In Heat**, a jumbled mess of styles that'd fit easily into Astbury's closet.

The few involving moments—the incongruous anti-draft missives "It Came in the Mail" and the self-explanatory "Me Tarzan, You Jane"—date back to the band's first incarnation. Newer Protrudi compositions like "Nine Months Later" and "Hurt on Hold," both of which appear on **In Heat** and their respective EPs, are at once listless and noisily monochromatic (though the **Hurt on Hold** EP boasts a fair rendition of the Troggs' "Can't Control Myself"). **Action**'s four songs further prove the Fuzztones' original reactionary philosophy to have been right on (man).

Between the Fuzztones' East and West Coast eras, Protrudi assembled the Jaymen, a short-lived reverb instrumental trio. With recording quality that would make a bootleg dealer blush, both the full-length German album and the eight-song American mini-LP (no overlap; the latter boasts a nutty live version of "Batman") are the fun-filled results of an informal 1986 session and sound—thanks in no small part to the genuine-article songs and properly reverent originals—like long-lost Link Wray outtakes.

Before the Fuzztones, Rudi and Deb were at the center of Tina Peel, a loosely constructed Harrisburg, Pennsylvania, power-pop troupe that also tangentially involved future actress/Bongwaterite Ann Magnuson. The **Extra Kicks** tape contains perhaps rock's best poodle-in-the-microwave ditty ("Fifi Goes Pop") and a mind-numbing selection of penile paeans—two of which ("Wang It" and "Exception to the Ruler") can also be found on the legendary **You'll Hate This Record** compilation.   [dss/i]

See also *Headless Horsemen*.

F-WORD
Like It or Not Live (Posh Boy) 1978
VARIOUS ARTISTS
Beach Blvd (Posh Boy) 1979
Tooth & Nail (Upsetter) 1980

SLAVES
The Slaves (Happy Hermit-IRS) 1990 ●

Though considered outsiders, F-Word nevertheless bullied their way into the Los Angeles '77 punk scene by virtue of a pummeling, primal sound led by guitarist Dim Wanker and a truly remarkable singer, Rick L. Rick. Playing at hyper tempos long before hardcore (only the Dils were as fast), the quartet never captured its flashpaper assault in the studio, leaving only a live album recorded at San Francisco's Mabuhay Gardens in February '78.

Not only was **Like It or Not Live** the first LP release on the pivotal Posh Boy label, it's the first West Coast punk *album* from an era when most groups stuck to 7-inch singles. Covers of the New York Dolls' "Bad Girl" (great choice, so-so rendition), the Germs' "Shutdown" (before the Germs were a big deal), the Stooges' "No Fun" Pistolized and the Animals' "I'm Crying" prove F-Word's roots-punk credibility, but it's the wild and gutsy originals—the punishing "Do the Nihil" and the equally merciless (in more ways than one) "Hillside Strangler"—that still hold up.

F-Word was short lived, and Rik L. Rik (dropping his c's along the way) latched onto San Francisco's Negative Trend in time for that group's appearance on the seminal LA punk compilation, **Tooth & Nail**. (The five worthy cuts of his that appear on the **Beach Blvd** sampler, although not credited as such, also apparently feature Negative Trend.) In '82, he released a terrific solo single ("Dominique" b/w "Soul Power").

Rik's recent re-emergence, however, is a less pleasant development. The Slaves are strictly sterile classic-rock pap: tired, undemanding, melodramatic hard wank. Not only does **The Slaves** bastardize both songs from his old single, the group's neo-metal version of Joy Division's "Transmission" is appalling. Refuse this refuse.   [jr]

See also *Flipper*.

PETER GABRIEL

Peter Gabriel (Atco) 1977 ●
Peter Gabriel (Atlantic) 1978 ●
Peter Gabriel (Mercury) 1980 ●
Ein Deutsches Album (Ger. Charisma) 1980 (nr/Virgin) 1987 ●
Peter Gabriel (Geffen) 1982 ●
Deutsches Album (Ger. Charisma) 1982 (nr/Virgin) 1987 ●
Peter Gabriel/Peter Gabriel [tape] (nr/Charisma) 1983 ●
Plays Live (Geffen) 1983 ●
Music from the Film *Birdy* (Geffen) 1985 ●
So (Geffen) 1986 ●
Sledgehammer EP (nr/Virgin) 1986
Big Time EP (nr/Charisma) 1987 φ
Passion: Music for The Last Temptation of Christ (Geffen) 1989 ●
Shaking the Tree: Sixteen Golden Greats (Geffen) 1990 φ

VARIOUS ARTISTS

Passion–Sources (Real World-Virgin) 1989 ●

As Genesis' original lead vocalist, Peter Gabriel was the grand old man of the theatrical/commercial wing of the mildly progressive art-rock movement. He abandoned that position in 1975 for a solo career, and has successfully positioned himself as the prototypically individualistic world musician. His work is marked by dark humor, mature intelligence, strong compositional skill and excellent, often innovative use of rhythm and electronics.

Like unnumbered issues of a magazine, his first four albums are titled only with his name, which appears in the same typeface and position on each. (The fourth **Peter Gabriel** was issued as **Security** by his American label, a move Gabriel did not endorse.)

The symphonic pretensions of the first **Peter Gabriel** power a dramatic perception of personal and global apocalypse. Produced by Bob Ezrin, and featuring the playing of Robert Fripp, Tony Levin, Steve Hunter and the London Symphony Orchestra, the album's dark rock songs ("Solsbury Hill," "Modern Love") on Side One are paired with disturbing visions of armageddon ("Slowburn," "Here Comes the Flood") on Side Two, delivered in a wall of sound that fills in every musical corner.

In contrast, the second **Peter Gabriel**, produced in Holland by Fripp, employs the spare and uncluttered sound popularized by the punk movement. (Although you would hardly mistake this for a punk album, Gabriel does neatly display his cognizance and support of what was going on with the song "D.I.Y.") The new method showed Gabriel condensing his songs into tight units linked by themes of paranoia. Freed from the onus of art-rock, Gabriel presents his most obsessive and personal compositions (e.g., "On the Air," "Perspec-

tive"), packets of insight that are misleadingly restrained. (A 1983 British cassette combines the first two records.)

Gabriel returned to a fuller sound on his third album, emphasizing striking electronics developed over unusual rhythms and delivered with seeming desperation. The ballads of social violence and urban fear—including "I Don't Remember" and "Family Snapshot"—feature lyrics and intricate music finally blended (under producer Steve Lillywhite's direction) into perfectly integrated high pop. "Biko," a haunting political anthem about the South African martyr, and the internationalist "Games Without Frontiers" reveal Gabriel's deepening commitment to global issues and social action.

The fourth **Peter Gabriel** refines this, drawing further on exotic rhythms (from Africa, Asia and America) with a musique concrète technique made possible by the Fairlight synthesizer, which allows unlimited manipulation of recorded sounds. Gabriel delivers his examinations of fear and disaster with an oddly paradoxical new emphasis on hope and restraint, displaying his usual fine craft and quality. "Shock the Monkey," "I Have the Touch" and "Kiss of Life" are among the best things he's ever done, combining all of his strengths—lyrical, melodic, structural and experimental—into bracingly original pop music with a solid footing.

Peter Gabriel numbers three and four were both issued (separately) in Germany—and later, on CD only, in the UK—under the name **(Ein) Deutsches Album**, with Gabriel singing all the lyrics in German (as translated by Horst Königstein). Not every song holds up equally well to the linguistic reworking: "Spiel ohne Grenzen" ("Games Without Frontiers") and "Schock den Affen" ("Shock the Monkey"), for example, gain tension and emotional power in German, but the language is too harsh for fragile songs like "Biko" and "Contact."

Three live tracks, recorded in 1979 and 1980, appear on the second edition of the **Bristol Recorder**, a combination album/magazine issued by a small English label in 1981, a forerunner of Gabriel's full-length live album. The two-disc **Plays Live** was recorded in America in 1982 (although some acknowledged "cheating" was later done) and features a good recap of his solo career, relying most heavily on the two most recent records. The four-piece band includes Tony Levin and Larry Fast. (The double-CD contains the entire album; in Britain, fans on a budget could also choose an abbreviated single disc.)

In the mid-'80s, Gabriel began doing film soundtracks. For the *Birdy* score, he wrote new material and adapted previous recordings. Although it's uncommon to hear sustained instrumental work from someone so known for vocal music, the score is audibly identifiable, and provides a fascinating glimpse into his adaptational thinking. A strongly affecting work, a major challenge met admirably with style and character.

So, Gabriel's first new studio album in four years, is another adventurous, varied and striking record, with atypically self-reflective lyrics, some of them clearly demarcating a past-present-future boundary. (The cover portrait also suggests an attitudinal change of some sort.) Gabriel's characteristically sophisticated music touches on funk ("Sledgehammer"), lightly gospel-inflected balladry ("Don't Give Up," with prominent vocals by Kate Bush), folk ("In Your Eyes," with vocal backing by Jim Kerr and others) and catchy dance-rock ("Big Time," featuring Stewart Copeland on drums). The commercial sound and resultant big-time success of the record led to complaints that Gabriel had compromised himself artistically but, on its own merits, So doesn't support such carping.

The **Sledgehammer** 12-inch EP contains a dance mix of the title track, an extended edit of "Biko," the non-LP "Don't Break This Rhythm" and a remix of 1982's "I Have the Touch." The cassette and CD of the **Big Time** EP have different track assortments, but both include three non-LP items.

Beginning in 1982 with his pivotal role in the WOMAD festival and organization, Gabriel has made ethnic world music a major focus of his work. Via the Real World label, he has brought out records by artists from a wide variety of cultures, and his own music has become increasingly intertwined with traditional styles well outside Western forms. In creating the soundtrack for Martin Scorsese's *Last Temptation of Christ*, Gabriel first made field recordings (a selection of which are compiled on **Passion–Sources**) from musicians in such places as Turkey, Senegal, Egypt and Morocco. Those provided the inspiration (and, in some cases, actual material) for his original compositions on the two-record **Passion**. This extraordinary mating of modern and ancient musics unifies an enormous geographic spread into a vaguely Middle Eastern sound that is utterly engrossing in its multitudinous use of instruments and Gabriel's deft manipulation of atmospheric sounds into narrative music of exceptional beauty and drama.

Shaking the Tree edits Gabriel's solo oeuvre to reflect his current concerns. There's only one track from the first album ("Here Comes the Flood" also appears, but in a brand-new acoustic piano rendition) and nothing from the second; other than token choices from **Passion** and Youssou N'Dour's **The Lion** that are unlikely to be on many fans' top-sixteen lists, the material comes entirely from the third and fourth **Peter Gabriel** albums and **So**. Still, the compilation does cover most of the essentials, with only "Contact," "Kiss of Life" and "D.I.Y." standing out as notable omissions.   [sg/i]

DIAMANDA GALAS

The Litanies of Satan (Y) 1982 (Mute-Restless) 1988 •
Diamanda Galas (Metalanguage) 1984
The Divine Punishment (nr/Mute) 1986 (Mute-Restless) 1989
Saint of the Pit (nr/Mute) 1986 (Mute-Restless) 1989
The Divine Punishment & Saint of the Pit [CD] (Mute-Restless) 1988 •
You Must Be Certain of the Devil (Mute-Restless) 1988 •
Masque of the Red Death Trilogy [CD] (Mute-Restless) 1989 •
Plague Mass (Mute) 1991 φ

Radical Southern California avant-garde diva Galas' first record, **The Litanies of Satan**, was not a heavy-metal prayer but rather a vocal adaptation of a poem by Charles Baudelaire. Using many electronic modifications (many learned during her working with such exemplary contemporary composers as Iannis Xenakis), Galas created a disturbing and provocative piece that was almost topped by the composition on the album's second side, the amusingly titled but harrowing "Wild Women with Steak-Knives (The Homicidal Love Song for Solo Scream)"—an endurance-defying unaccompanied stream of hideous vocal noises.

Besides showcasing her astonishing voice and real knowledge of electronic manipulation, the two pieces on **Diamanda Galas** display her social conscience: "Panoptikon" is based on Jeremy Bentham's 1843 proposal for a prison where the inmates could be kept under constant observation by unseen captors, and "Tragouthia Apo to Aima Exoun Fonos" translates from the Greek as "Song from the Blood of Those Murdered."

Desperate times lead to desperate actions. **The Divine Punishment**, **Saint of the Pit** and **You Must Be Certain of the Devil** comprise **Masque of the Red Death**, "the plague mass," Galas' strident but striking response to AIDS, sparked by her brother's 1986 death.

The Divine Punishment is a collection of somehow appropriate Old Testament quotes delivered—in everything from a glass-breaking soprano to an urgent whisper to a depraved shriek to a wicked multi-voiced regurgo rumble—over droning synthesizer music with jarring sonic effects. The more operatic **Saint of the Pit** sets French decadent poetry (by Baudelaire, Nerval and Corbière) into wild vocal excursions, accompanied by keyboards that vary from subtle atmospherics to melodramatic horror-movie organ. Galas' astonishingly varied singing styles and the hypnotic effect of the record's three claustrophobic, obsessive pieces makes **Saint of the Pit** a powerful document of suffering.

Completing the trilogy on a conceptual high note, Galas fills **You Must Be Certain of the Devil** with lyrically specific (mostly) original songs, played with backing musicians. The record gets off to a bracing start with a unique a cappella interpretation of "Swing Low Sweet Chariot" and continues in an unassuming electro-rock vein as Galas warbles, sometimes singing counterpoint with herself in multi-track arrangements, using voice as both a percussion and melodic instrument. The audio intimacy here exaggerates emotional intensity beyond legal limits.

The Divine Punishment and **Saint of the Pit** are contained on one CD; the limited edition two-CD **Masque of the Red Death Trilogy** is a complete set of all three albums.

Plague Mass is a bravura live album recorded in October 1990 at New York's Cathedral of St. John the Divine and includes the recorded premier of "There Are No More Tickets to the Funeral," a new section of the ongoing work.   [gk/i]

GALAXIE 500

Today (Aurora) 1987 (Rough Trade) 1991 ●
On Fire (Rough Trade) 1989 ●
Blue Thunder EP (nr/Rough Trade) 1989 ●
This Is Our Music (Rough Trade) 1990 ●

Jumping off a *Chemical Imbalance* flexidisc, Galaxie 500's singsongy psychedelic "Oblivious" was so sweet and lo-fi that it might have been actual innocence instead of the Velvet Underground's received ghost. **Today**, which features a rendition of Jonathan Richman's "Don't Let Our Youth Go to Waste," confirmed it: this trio (based in New York but formed in Boston; all three are Harvard alumni) may sound as ragged and ambitious as your first guitar plugged into your first amp, but they had a way with dirge and seemed to mean every note. With plaints like "I don't wanna stay at your party/I don't wanna talk with your friends/I don't wanna vote for your president/I just wanna be your tugboat captain," Galaxie 500 made a virtue of lethargy. (The CD adds two.)

On Fire acknowledges a past master of mopery with an unsanctimonious cover of George Harrison's "Isn't It a Pity." This second release shapes out the spaces between Dean Wareham's proto-strum and whine/wail, Naomi Yang's exceptionally melodic bass lines (the band's true emotional center) and Damon Krukowski's economical drumming. Kramer (producer of the band's entire output to date) throws in enough reverb and echo to nearly cover lyrics like "I stood in line and ate my Twinkie" beneath a fuzzy warm sonic blanket. Wareham's lead guitar lines are clearer and more confident here and, with nice touches like saxophone on "Decomposing Trees," the songs are immersion chambers of atmosphere.

This Is Our Music is slicker and features more dynamic crescendos—in places the trio sounds like a treble-free low-tech Feelies—but the melodies aren't as engaging as on the first two discs. For the adventurous, there's a feeling cover of Yoko Ono's "Listen, the Snow Is Falling." The EP reprises "Blue Thunder" from **On Fire** (with a sax part added) and features a powerful cover of New Order's "Ceremony" as well as two other non-LP tracks. [mp]

GAME THEORY

Blaze of Glory (Rational) 1982
Pointed Accounts of People You Know EP (Rational) 1983
Distortion EP (Rational) 1984
Dead Center (Fr. Lolita) 1984
Real Nighttime (Rational-Enigma) 1985
The Big Shot Chronicles (Rational-Enigma) 1986
Lolita Nation (Rational-Enigma) 1987 ●
2 Steps from the Middle Ages (Enigma) 1988 ●
Tinker to Evers to Chance (Rational-Enigma) 1990 φ

VEIL

1000 Dreams Have Told Me (Plastic Medium) 1984

Game Theory is a clean, and for a time, mildly psychedelic, pop band from northern California, which means their departures from conventional meat-and-potatoes reality are more quirky than trippy. Like most over-educated popsters, they tend towards wimpiness—at which times the arcane lyrics don't help—but the hip catchiness of the songs mostly keeps them out of trouble.

With awfully thin sound and more enthusiasm than skill, the young guitar-and-keyboards quartet made its promising debut on the self-released **Blaze of Glory**. Switching drummers, Game Theory then returned with the schizy six-song **Pointed Accounts**. The first side is light; guitarist/singer Scott Miller's songs are slightly off-kilter, with cryptic lines ("She likes metal and glass exact"—huh?), but the hooks make them go down smoothly. Bassist/singer Fred Juhos carries things further out on the second side with two tunes, including "I Wanna Get Hit by a Car." Juhos' vision is darker and somewhat more intriguing, but he isn't Miller's equal as a tunesmith.

The five-song **Distortion**, co-produced by Michael Quercio of the Three O'Clock, is fuller, if not as fresh sounding as the debut. Unfortunately, the more baroque presentation makes Miller's fey falsetto and fragile melodies sound too precious. Pleasant listening, and the good ideas are still there, but it doesn't draw you in. **Dead Center** compiles the two EPs, adding three extra items.

Real Nighttime, the band's second album, was produced by Mitch Easter, with Quercio and others helping out. Miller wrote all the songs, except for a cover of Alex Chilton's Big Star-era "You Can't Have Me." The wispy vocal sound unsurprisingly crosses the Three O'Clock with Let's Active, but the music is tougher and more unpredictable than either influence. Whiny melodica, jagged guitar lines, ominous percussion and noisy sound effects lace through the arrangements, creating an odd but often productive tension. By consciously undercutting power-pop convention, Game Theory steers **Real Nighttime** into uncharted terrain that, for the most part, gives them something to sing about.

Sticking with Easter and paraphrasing John Cheever for its title, **The Big Shot Chronicles** lights the afterburners for aggressively electric pop, louder and more powerful than anything in Game Theory's past. Miller's new lineup without Juhos doesn't fool around, keeping the arrangements relatively unadorned; unfortunately, his fly-away singing (self-described here as a "miserable whine" and later characterized as "my usual obnoxious vocals") can sound silly competing with stacks of highly amplified rock; restrained songs that lean towards acoustic guitars (e.g., "Erica's World," "Where You Going Northern") provide a more conducive setting. With a swell organ hook, the catchy "Crash into June" hits just the right balance and is hummably memorable.

The ambitious and occasionally bizarre two-disc **Lolita Nation** adds synthesizers and assorted crazy noises to an inconsistent set of songs—delivered in unpredictable lengths—and immerses them (especially on Side Three) in tape experimentation, spoken-word bridges and other audio ephemera. This new lineup—a resourcefully vocal quintet, here assisted by longtime band associates—provides variegated support that works wonders some of the time but falls flat in spots. Guitarist Donnette Thayer sings commendable lead on a few tunes, but isn't the strong counterpoint to Miller that would prevent the onset of listening fatigue.

The same five-person Game Theory then returned to power pop earth with an uninterrupted set of discrete songs on **2 Steps from the Middle Ages**. The band's light mélange of wispy vocals, acoustic/electric guitars and gently colorful keyboards makes an unfailingly pleasant (except for the clunky distraction of Gil Ray's drumming) and intelligent—but utterly uninvolving—sound. The bland consistency of both Miller's strained (and hookless) melodies and Easter's uneventful production damns 2 Steps to a familiar monotony.

Along with Miller's amusingly self-deprecating liner notes and substantial samples of every prior Game Theory record (only his songs), the ample 22-cut **Tinker to Evers to Chance** compilation offers charming new recordings (by an ad hoc band) of several old songs—two reclaimed from **Blaze of Glory**—and a remix of **Pointed Accounts**' "Penny, Things Won't."

Prior to joining Game Theory, Donnette Thayer led Sacramento's Veil (not related to the contemporaneous British-based quartet), a slightly tacky melodic rock quartet, whose competent but colorless 1984 LP of her songs was produced by Scott Miller and engineered by former GT drummer Dave Gill. After leaving Game Theory, Thayer joined up with Steve Kilbey of the Church to form Hex. The latest GT lineup features Quercio and ex-Thin White Rope drummer Jozef Becker, Ray having shifted from percussion to guitar and keyboards. [jl/i]

See also *Hex*.

PHIL GAMMAGE

See *Certain General*.

GANG GREEN

Drunk and Disorderly, Boston MA EP (Deluxe) 1986
Another Wasted Night (Taang!) 1986 ●
P.M.R.C. Sucks 12" EP (Taang!) 1987
You Got It (Roadracer) 1987 ●
I81B4U EP (Roadracer) 1988 ●
Older ... (Emergo) 1989 ●
Can't Live Without It (Emergo) 1990 ●

VARIOUS ARTISTS

This Is Boston Not L.A. (Modern Method) 1982

Led by singer/guitarist Chris Doherty, Boston's greatest beer-soaked contribution to the skate-punk genre began as a faster'n'louder hardcore trio, with seven sketchy smears (e.g., "Snob," "Kill a Commie" and "Rabies") averaging under a minute each on a 1982 scene compilation. A breakup (during which Doherty played in Jerry's Kids), lineup changes and a handful of singles and EPs followed, then **Another Wasted Night**. Cogent power and a notable melodic sense marks the quartet as a superior breed of punk. Doherty's Lemmylike shriek is a fiendish attribute, as is Chuck Stilphen's occasional blitzkrieg solos. "Skate to Hell" is a rallying cry for skateboarders; the other originals are convincing thrash. While the decision to cut a slow but incompetently irreverent cover of 'Til Tuesday's "Voices Carry" (complete with synthesizer riff) probably had more to do with local band politics than musical taste, it's still a good giggle. Both the cassette and CD add bonus tracks. (The green-vinyl **P.M.R.C.** EP—which features a priceless cover photo of Doherty and 'Til Tuesday's Aimee Mann together—contains two versions of "Voices Carry," plus "Skate Hate" and "Protect & Serve.")

You Got It finds an overhauled four-piece again celebrating Budweiser and boards with ace playing and a stringent mid-tempo punk sound. (Kudos to lead guitarist Fritz Erickson.) The anthemic "We'll Give It to You" and "Born to Rock" are blistering statements (skatements?) of teen party solidarity; "L.D.S.B." ("let's drink some beer") typifies the band's commitment to hedonistic irresponsibility.

The casual-sounding five-song **I81B4U** offers yet another homage to beer ("Bartender"), its side effects ("Lost Chapter") and sex ("Put Her on Top") all produced with a dull meta-metallic roar by Daniel Rey; meanwhile, a bratty protest against "Rent" returns to the band's punky roots.

Claiming "I'm Still Young" with little conviction, Gang Green skates into a new stage of life on the roaringly dynamic **Older ...** (the punny cover art completes the ellipsis with the inevitable **Budweiser**), a great leap forward by these aging veterans. Driven by the rhythm section's charging gallop, Doherty's frantic shouts and Erickson's full-throttle arena-scale guitar lift the quartet out of small-scale adolescent punk to embrace metal, speed-rock and regular ol' hard rock. While "Church of Fun" and the acoustic/orchestrated power "Ballad," which closes the LP on an absurdly funny note (actually, it's D), restate old values, other songs acknowledge other subject matter.

The louder-than-bombs **Can't Live Without It** (no points for guessing what the title might refer to: these guys have long since raised their obsession with beer to a total lifestyle) was recorded live in London at the beginning of 1990. Covering such classics as "We'll Give It to You," "Voices Carry" and "Rabies" with clear, dynamic sound, the fifteen-track onslaught is a breathless power surge that could probably pulverize concrete. [i]

See also *Jerry's Kids, Mallet-Head*.

GANG OF FOUR

Damaged Goods (nr/Fast Product) 1978
Entertainment! (Warner Bros.) 1979
Gang of Four EP (Warner Bros.) 1980
Solid Gold (Warner Bros.) 1981
Another Day/Another Dollar EP (Warner Bros.) 1982
Songs of the Free (Warner Bros.) 1982
Hard (Warner Bros.) 1983
At the Palace (nr/Phonogram) 1984
The Peel Sessions EP (nr/Strange Fruit) 1986
The Peel Sessions Album (nr/Strange Fruit) 1990 (Strange Fruit-Dutch East India) 1991 ●
A Brief History of the Twentieth Century (Warner Bros.) 1990 φ
Mall (Polydor) 1991 φ

If the Clash were the urban guerrillas of rock'n'roll, Leeds' Gang of Four were its revolutionary theoreticians. The band's bracing funk-rock gained its edge from lyrics that dissect capitalist society with the cool precision of a surgeon's scalpel.

The Gang saw interpersonal relationships—"romance," if you must—as politics in microcosm, a view that gives **Entertainment!** its distinctive tartness. Jon King declaims brittle sentiments with the self-righteous air of someone who couldn't get to first base with his girlfriend the previous evening. The basic backing trio of bassist Dave Allen, drummer Hugo Burnham and guitarist Andy Gill churns up a brutal, nearly unembellished accompaniment on this challenging album debut.

Solid Gold delves further into a quicksand of discontent. More choppy rhythms and pared-down arrangements drive home cries of despair like "Paralysed," "Cheeseburger" and "What We All Want." Not the sort of thing to pack discos, but as compelling as a steamroller.

Songs of the Free is a more upbeat dance of death. With Allen off to form Shriekback, new bassist Sara Lee (fresh out of Fripp's League of Gentlemen) and Joy Yates' backing vocals relieve the gloom of "We Live as We Dream, Alone" and (with typical irony) contribute to the dancefloor success of the anti-militaristic "I Love a Man in a Uniform." King's impassioned delivery, the songs' on-target attacks on society's ills and the band's musical wallop make **Songs of the Free** one of the most stirring, innovative "rock" albums you can find.

Unfortunately, the Gang's next outing exposed an aesthetic about-face of Stalinesque proportions. Inappropriately co-produced by Ron and Howard Albert (Crosby Stills and Nash, Firefall), **Hard** shifts from a political to a personal frame of reference; King drones lyrics against dirge-like music. It might be symbolic of disillusionment. It's certainly a sorry end to the group's career. Drummer Hugo Burnham left months prior to **Hard**'s release (there is no drummer credited on the LP); the Gang pressed on for a bit before disbanding in 1984.

At the Palace (Hollywood's, that is) is a souvenir of the Gang's final tour. With Steve Goulding replacing Burnham (who briefly sat in with ABC before joining Illustrated Man, later becoming Shriekback's manager and then an A&R executive), the album listlessly rehashes better days. Farewell, comrades! (The cassette has two bonus salvos.)

To relieve between-album tension, the band's US label twice released 12-inch EPs consolidating British singles. **Gang of Four** contains "Armalite Rifle" from the band's 1978 **Damaged Goods** three-song debut, a non-LP flipside and both sides of the then-current "Outside the Trains Don't Run on Time" 45 (both later re-recorded for **Solid Gold**). **Another Day/Another Dollar** contains both sides of the "To Hell with Poverty" single and another non-LP flip ("History's Bunk!")—all required listening for fans—plus two live-in-London versions of **Solid Gold** songs that show the Gang's prime-time concert intensity.

Rendering the one-session Peel EP (from January '79) redundant, the eleven-song album (available in the US on CD and cassette as **The Peel Sessions**) offers that artifact as well as return visits to the BBC radio studios from July '79 and March '81. Not quite an alternate greatest hits, the full-length collection nonetheless offers such Gang classics as "To Hell with Poverty," "At Home's He's a Tourist" and "I Found That Essence Rare," all rendered with stiff-backed ferocity.

In 1988, guitarist Andy Gill released a solo single and produced the music for a Derek Jarman film. In 1990, as he and King reunited and began working on a new Gang of Four record (releasing only a single by year's end), the monumental 20-song **Brief History of the Twentieth Century** compilation (with liner notes by Greil Marcus) was issued to indoctrinate a new generation.

The new Gang LP, **Mall**, was well worth the wait. Without trying to jump the bandwagon they helped launch, King and Gill—aided by various rhythm sections and backup singers—get back in the old groove with ease, doing an updated (but not selfconsciously so) version of the band's essence that is as bracingly political and musically potent as ever. The inclusion of a Vietnam War drama ("F.M.U.S.A.") is weird but extremely effective; other songs attack consumer culture and American politics with varying (but generally high) degrees of musical and lyrical success. (The cover of Bob Marley's "Soul Rebel" is white-boy lame.) Sounding in spots like the Clash's funky dance side, **Mall** easily justifies the Gang of Two's return, proof that not all legends should stay out of the action.   [si/i]

See also *Illustrated Man, Shriekback*.

NICK GARVEY
See *Motors*.

GAS
Emotional Warfare (nr/Polydor) 1982
From the Cradle to the Grave (nr/Good Vibrations) 1983

Frequently compared to Elvis Costello, and sometimes even to Graham Parker and the Clash, the Gas were more of the punk-pop-mod school of outfits like the Jam and Chords. **Emotional Warfare**, a ripping pop LP, shows the trio's sharp attack and some of the busiest music this side of the Buzzcocks. "Definitely Is a Lie" and "Losing my Patience" are the kind of aural pummels one never expects from music so catchy; similarly, the band's vitality masked the incredibly bitter lyrics by singer Donnie Burke, an intelligent yet disillusioned and terminally unsatisfied frontman. Imagine someone who'd been left in the lurch by a thousand women and you'd still have trouble imagining Burke's bleak anger. By comparison, the young Costello seems complacent in comparison. **Emotional Warfare** indeed!

The title track of **From the Cradle to the Grave** (which sets the theme for the LP) predates the Godfathers' **Birth, School, Work, Death** by four years, stating almost exactly the same pessimistic outlook on life in Britain. While the battering ram of Burke's rage and despair continues, it's married here to a more somber sound, with pretty piano, light tempos and atmospheric guitar. This soundtrack for a tear-gushing movie of an unhappy life was ignored by the Gas' older fans who preferred their fast and loud origins, and avoided by the post-punk doom and gloom school. The LP faded without much fanfare, as did the band soon thereafter.   [jr]

GAWK
See *Ritual Tension*.

GAYE BYKERS ON ACID
Everythang's Groovy EP (nr/In Tape) 1986
Nosedive Karma EP (nr/In Tape) 1987
Drill Your Own Hole (PFX-Caroline) 1987
The Janice Long Session EP (nr/Night Tracks-Strange Fruit) 1988

Stewed to the Gills .... (Caroline) 1989 ●
Groovedivesoapdisch (nr/Bleed) 1989
Cancer Planet Mission (nr/Naked Brain) 1990 ●
Pernicious Nonsense (nr/Naked Brain) 1991●

Crazy times and the enormous reach of rock'n'roll have made the challenge of turning conscious weirdness into a commercial property increasingly difficult, one that few neophytes are equal to. As arbiters of grebo, the dirty, ugly Bykers, a post-pop-culture quartet from Leicester, cross leather-clad Mad Max apocalyptics with late-'60s London people's-band values to forge a forward-looking/backward-thinking image.

Produced by Jon Langford (Three Johns/Mekons), the 12-inch **Everythang's Groovy** EP is plodding and dull, with unnecessarily silly lyrics that attempt to combine '60s underground memorabilia with punk's aggressive snottiness. A feeble attempt, but the band survived, seemingly propelled by the strength of its name alone.

If **Nosedive Karma** demonstrates a bit of maturity, it brings the band from, say, fourth grade to sixth. The use of sound bites from *Star Trek* throughout the record is one of its more unappealing features; the samples' haphazard placement makes them seem like an end in themselves. "Don't Be Human Eric, Let's Be Frank" stands out as the Bykers' best tune up to this point, a catchy pop-punk ditty that tries to tell a semi-intelligible story with a minimum of nonsensical '60s references. (The first two EPs were later reissued as **Groovedive-soapdisch**.)

Drill Your Own Hole was produced with maximum gimmickry (and, compared to the band's previous work, supreme ability) by Alex Fergusson (ATV/PTV) and includes a cover of a song by radical hippiedom's legendary Edgar Broughton Band. The intentionally chaotic noisy guitar rock (dressed up in wah-wah and moronic solos) shows some improvement in skill and lyrics (which still rely on drug culture jokes); the self-conscious posturing is spottily ear-catching but basically horrible.

Stewed to the Gills suggests that the post-grebo Bykers might have finally learned a lesson; in lieu of TV snippets and antiquated lifestyles, the quartet takes subtle jabs at current pop and underground culture, shrugs off fancy production (Langford again did the honors) and surrenders to sloppy musical technique. The result is one of the most remarkably disjointed mock-concept albums ever, a creation of purposeless nonsense for nonsense's sake, fraught with casual, easily missed microparodies. Bravo.

Come 1990, and the cavalier Bykers seem to care less than ever. In the case of **Cancer Planet Mission**, however, that very lack of forethought produced an uncommonly likable platter of noisy trash. Although you're not likely to find anything useful in its grooves, there's a whole lot of real good nothing going on here. The scattershot mixture of filthy grunge-metal, swampy, reggae-like dub and adrenaline-laced punk is utterly unfathomable; the songs are surrounded with frightening bits of sampled noise (industrial and otherwise), ethnic music, and whatever they could pinch off TV.

The Janice Long Session (recorded in '87) contains radio-broadcast versions of three songs from the first two EPs and one from **Drill Your Own Hole**. [i/icm]

G.B.H.
See *Charged G.B.H.*

GEAR DADDIES
Let's Go Scare Al (Gark) 1988 (Polydor) 1990 ●
Billy's Live Bait (Polydor) 1990 ●

Hailing from Spam-town (Austin, Minnesota, home of Hormel), the Gear Daddies serve up slices of Americana Norman Rockwell forgot to paint. The low-budget **Let's Go Scare Al** showcases singer-guitarist Martin Zellar's somber, country-tinged opus. (Although guitarist Randy Broughten often plays pedal steel and a snippet of a Bob Wills tune finds its uncredited way in, this is definitely a rock band.) Zellar's lyrics are populated with small town folks having trouble coping with life: tear-in-my-beer music without the false sentimentality. These guys would get run out of Nashville on a rail, but they'd probably be welcome in the other Austin.

On **Billy's Live Bait**, the quartet upgrades its sound and rocks more forcefully, with Zellar and Broughten bouncing guitar rhythms off one another. The portraits here are maybe a shade less grim than on **Let's Go Scare Al**, but it's still no laugh-fest. In fact, the album's only real humorous moment—an untitled ditty about a guy who dreams of riding the Zamboni machine used to smooth an ice rink—comes after the supposedly final song. Alas, even that wish goes unfulfilled. [ds]

BOB GELDOF
Deep in the Heart of Nowhere (Atlantic) 1986 ●
Love Like a Rocket EP [CD] (nr/Mercury) 1987 ●
The Vegetarians of Love (Atlantic) 1990 φ
Love or Something EP (nr/Mercury) 1990 ●

In mid-1986, after making enormous efforts on behalf of others, ex-Boomtown Rat Bob Geldof took a few steps in his own behalf, writing an autobiography (*Is That It?*) and signing a solo record deal. Best heard on CD or cassette (the vinyl version has three fewer tracks; others are truncated), **Deep in the Heart of Nowhere** bears the onerous marks of Rupert Hine's tritely commercial overproduction, but also contains some swell tunes and affecting lyrics. "This Is the World Calling" and the outstanding "Pulled Apart by Horses" (amazingly omitted from the vinyl version, but wisely included on the UK **Love Like a Rocket** EP, along with another of the deletions, two mixes of the title song and "This Is the World Calling") both resemble Rat tracks and allude to recent experiences; "In the Pouring Rain" could easily have come from **The Fine Art of Surfacing**. The record contains some true wretchedness (the melodramatically recited "The Beat of the Night") that will confirm skeptics' worst fears about Geldof's ego, but this is by no means a bad showing. Musical supporters here include Dave Stewart, Annie Lennox, Midge Ure, Brian Setzer, Eric Clapton and Alison Moyet.

Four years later, with Hine again producing and ex-Rat Pete Briquette on bass, Geldof adopted a jolly and appealing neo-folk approach for **The Vegetarians of Love**, a casual and light, mostly acoustic, album that gains a mild Irish accent from violin, accordion and pennywhistle. But while the sensitively played music sounds lighthearted, Bob hasn't changed his outspoken and pointed (but amusingly couched and casually conversational) lyrical ways. After ironically listing all the things he doesn't care about in "The Great Song of Indifference," Geldof spends the rest of the album airing his philosophical and emotional angst. "Crucified Me" is a quietly bitter love song; "The Chains of Pain" addresses several world crises with a cry of optimism; "The End of the World" and "Thinking Voyager 2 Type Things" go all existential. "I'm thinking big things," he sings, "I'm thinking about mortality/I'm thinking it's a cheap price that we pay for existence."

The CD edition of the 1990 EP picks the rockingest and poppiest tune (co-written with Dave Stewart) from **Vegetarians** and adds a trio of non-LP cuts, two of which ("Out of Order" and "One of the Girls," played on garage guitar and accordion) are well worth hearing. The four-song 12-inch replaces "One of the Girls" with a remix of "The Great Song of Indifference." [i/pn]

See also *Boomtown Rats*.

GENE LOVES JEZEBEL

Promise (nr/Situation Two) 1983 (Geffen) 1987 ●
Bruises EP (Can. Beggars Banquet-Vertigo) 1983
Immigrant (nr/Beggars Banquet) 1984 (Situation
  Two-Relativity) 1985 ●
Desire EP (Relativity) 1985
Discover (Beggars Banquet-Geffen) 1986 ●
The House of Dolls (Beggars Banquet-Geffen) 1987 ●
Kiss of Life (Beggars Banquet-Geffen) 1990 ●

For most of **Promise**, Welsh twins Jay and Michael Aston generate a powerful, dense sound that falls somewhere between U2, Adam Ant and Public Image: thickly textured guitars coloring a driving beat under aggressively impassioned, generally tuneless vocals that occasionally lapse into YokOnoesque wailing. The songs have a decidedly sexual air, but it's the sheer din—roughly produced but convincing—that makes **Promise** worth repeated listenings. Numbers that don't go for maximum impact peddle a sensitive, spacious attractiveness that suggests considerable range and skill. (**Bruises** is a six-song précis of the album.)

On the enjoyable, atmospheric **Immigrant**, intelligently produced by John Leckie, the Jezebels (acknowledging a five-piece lineup) resemble a pop-sensitized version of Bauhaus, a gritty U2 or a smacked-out Duran Duran. "Always a Flame" is aggro-dance rock with a walloping beat and a real melody; "Shame" has similar attributes, plus a catchy refrain. The US edition of the LP appends **Promise**'s "Bruises," a solid number which brings all of the band's U2 tendencies to the fore. ("Worth Waiting For" is equally Bonoesque.) The **Desire** 12-inch combines two mixes of that song with three album tracks for a dose of Gene Loves Jezebel's best side.

"Desire" also appears on **Discover**, the band's first American major-label release (a development reflecting their burgeoning haircut-based popularity on college radio and in alternative media) and their first to feature veteran London guitarist James Stevenson (Chelsea, Generation X). Beyond "Desire," however, **Discover** wavers from obnoxious (the Lotte Lenya-meets-Bauhaus sound of "Heartache," the annoying push of "Sweetest Thing") to melodious ("Kick" and "A

White Horse," which suggest a mild New Order influence). Throughout, Michael Aston warbles miserably in an unmusical voice which blends the worst excesses of Siouxsie and Bono; it hardly matters how well Gary Lyons' production renders the instrumentation as long as the vocal mic stays on. (The British tape configuration adds eight live tracks recorded in Nottingham in early 1986. Original pressings of the UK album included a bonus disc entitled **Glad to Be Alive** of the same performance.)

A transparent effort to commercialize the Jezebels made **The House of Dolls** their most listenable—that's not to say likable—record yet. Excepting a pair of songs ("The Motion of Love" and "Suspicion") handled by Jimmy Iovine, the LP was produced by Peter Walsh (Simple Minds, China Crisis, Peter Gabriel's live LP), who multi-tracks Aston's vocals (without completely curbing his habit of yelping and wailing unexpectedly) and surrounds them in clearly articulated and tuneful arena guitar rock, leaving the impression that GLJ is on the verge of discovering a most unpleasant hybrid of Van Halen, U2 and a billy goat.

Michael Aston's subsequent departure from the group left Jay in the driver's seat for the slow-moving and uninspired **Kiss of Life**. "Jealousy" and "Evening Star" follow the LA-styled hard-rock path laid down on **The House of Dolls**, but the general tone is far less overbearing this time. ("Tangled Up in You" is virtually a folk song; acoustic guitar is prominent throughout.) Cutting away the bombast, however, reveals insipid lyrics ("Why can't I/see you smile/Just once in a while/Let me see you smile" forms the intellectual body of one seven-minute song), simpleminded musical ideas and a serious shortage of personality. [i]

See also *All About Eve*.

GENERAL PUBLIC
... All the Rage (IRS) 1984 ●
Hand to Mouth (IRS) 1986 ●
RANKING ROGER
Radical Departure (IRS) 1988 ●
DAVE WAKELING
No Warning (IRS) 1991 φ

After terminating the perfect Beat, leader Dave Wakeling and color commentator Ranking Roger (Charlery) stuck together to form General Public, which ultimately involved other 2-Tone veterans. It's hard to hear why the Beat had to die for General Public to live, but evidently the pair felt they needed to leave some people and other career baggage behind. Although an unequal trade, General Public upheld the commitment to excellence that hallmarked the Beat.

Ex-Clashman Mick Jones plays guest guitar on the first LP (although just where on this democratic undertaking is impossible to peg); Aswad's brass section and Gary Barnacle also pitch in. For their part, Wakeling and Roger craft passionate pop, packed with clever tempo shifts, in several styles: a happy Motown bounce ("Tenderness" and the romantic "Never You Done That"), textured drama ("General Public," the political "Burning Bright") and a bluebeat kick ("Where's the Line"). On the negative side, GP engage in annoying verbal play on "Hot You're Cool" and "As a Matter of Fact." Some tracks go on too long and a few of the arrangements are overly busy, but those are small quibbles. **All the Rage** is a rich, mature album filled with intelligence and invention from a band fairly bursting with talent.

The second and final installment in the General Public saga was **Hand to Mouth**, a milder and less striking record. The well-rehearsed lineup of six (augmented by ex-Beatman Saxa, Gaspar Lawal and others) exudes an air of relaxed precision on an easygoing pop program that shows little evidence of creative exertion. Although hardly exceptional, "Too Much or Nothing" is the album's best track; "Faults and All" and "Murder," with snappy horn charts, echo the first record but don't build on it. All in all, the music goes down smoothly enough, but without any lasting impression.

In 1988, with their long partnership at an end, Ranking Roger and Wakeling each set out to launch solo careers. Adding semi-melodic singing to his vocal repertoire, Roger got so far as making **Radical Departure**, a socially conscious but duff album of pop and dance-rock originals that holds little value for fans of his prior endeavors. Wakeling never left the starting gate. Although IRS promised a 1989 release for an album entitled **The Happiest Man in the World**, the record wasn't completed and Wakeling left the music business. But that isn't quite the end of the story. In 1991, the album—or some version thereof—was issued as **No Warning**. [i]

See also *(English) Beat*.

GENERATION X

Generation X (Chrysalis) 1978 ●
Valley of the Dolls (Chrysalis) 1979 ●
Kiss Me Deadly (Chrysalis) 1981 ●
Dancing with Myself EP (nr/Chrysalis) 1981
The Best of Generation X (nr/Chrysalis) 1985

Appearing on the London punk scene shortly after the Sex Pistols, Generation X was an extraordinary but ill-fated outfit that issued five tremendous singles, one classic album and some real dross. It also launched the mega-career of Billy Idol and the ditzy Sigue Sigue Sputnik, developments one must weigh when considering the band's historical significance.

With Idol as the band's voice and image and guitarist Bob "Derwood" Andrews providing its rock power, Generation X broke a lot of punk conventions, and were ultimately ostracized by their peers for refusing to be (or even feign being, as many others did) anti-commercial. Their breakup can be viewed as a parallel to the dispersal of the original punk spirit, although Billy Idol's phoenix-like ascent to world chart domination is equally indicative of the subsequent salability of that ethos.

Following a string of tremendous 45s ("Your Generation," "Wild Youth," "Ready Steady Go"—all included on the US version of the first LP) that crossbred punk insolence with kitschy '60s pop culture to produce catchy, roaring anthems for disaffected youth, Generation X's debut album bore out their promise—not a bum track in the bunch. A commercial streak didn't preclude a punky outlook or closeness to their audience; while the songs don't threaten the established order, they do retain a cocky irreverence that made Generation X more than a latter-day Mott the Hoople. **Generation X**, regardless

of the reputational damage Billy Idol may have subsequently caused, is a classic record. The superior US version deletes "Listen," "The Invisible Man" and "Too Personal"—all fairly unessential—and adds the two single sides ("Wild Youth" and "Your Generation") omitted from the UK album, a definitive John Lennon cover ("Gimme Some Truth") and the amazing pioneering reggae-mix of "Wild Dub."

Valley of the Dolls, produced by Ian Hunter, pales in comparison. Two or three numbers (e.g., "Running with the Boss Sound," "King Rocker") recall the sonic magnificence of the early singles, but the surrounding tracks leave much to be desired. A typical sophomore-record material shortage.

Kiss Me Deadly, recorded after Idol and bassist Tony James (co-writer with Idol of the band's songs) had sacked Andrews and drummer Mark Laff, is a shoddy affair, containing only the wonderful "Dancing with Myself" to recommend it. Their moniker truncated to Gen X, Idol and James employed once and future Clash drummer Terry Chimes and a trio of guitar stars—Steve Jones, John McGeoch and Chelsea's James Stevenson—but the spirit was gone from the music, and the LP is merely a pale shadow of the band's early glories. Indeed, by the time of its release, Idol—under the tutelage of ex-Kiss manager Bill Aucoin—had already declared himself a solo act.

In recapitulating all three records, **The Best Of** catches just about everything worth saving off the second and third albums ("Valley of the Dolls," "Running with the Boss Sound," "King Rocker," "Dancing with Myself") but omits a couple of early masterpieces. For the best of Generation X, you could still do worse than the American **Generation X**. [i]

See also *Billy Idol, Sigue Sigue Sputnik*.

GERMS

(GI) (Slash) 1979
What We Do Is Secret (Slash) 1981
Germicide–Live at the Whisky [tape] (ROIR) 1982
Let the Circle Be Unbroken (Gasatanka) 1985
Lion's Share (Aus. Ghost o'Darb) 1985
Rock n' Rule (XES) 1986

In retrospect, it's easy to dismiss the Germs as the epitome of LA's early identipunk scene. Singer Darby Crash (Paul Beahm) was a barking spikey-haired brat, an alarming adolescent combination of Johnny Rotten's snarling vocal ferocity and Sid Vicious' self-destructive cool. Three years after the band's first live performance (at the Whisky in 1977), Crash died of a drug overdose, reportedly self-inflicted in morbid tribute to Vicious' own fatal OD in 1979.

Germicide, a cassette release of that first show, reinforces that notion. The tape is a raw documentary of spirited incompetence, with Crash ranting through "Sex Boy" and the rather prophetic "Suicide Madness" in a cynical bawl. Behind him, the band plods along with all the cheer of a migraine. A good third of the tape consists of Crash trading obscene insults with the crowd. Also of note: a tortuous disembowelment of the Archies' "Sugar Sugar."

After that, **(GI)** is a revelation, a kinetic outburst of brute punk force. Two years of tightening and a new drummer (Don Bolles, later of 45 Grave) turned the

Germs into a manic punk locomotive, speeding along with Damned intensity in spite of tinny production by Joan Jett. Aside from the overlong live "Shut Down," the songs go by in a breathless rush, fueled by Pat Smear's staccato fuzz guitar and Crash's sometimes confused but often potent punk protest imagery. A key album in the development of American hardcore.

What We Do Is Secret, a posthumous bow to Darby, packages what's left of the Germs' recorded legacy on a 12-inch mini-album. The material includes a 1977 stab at Chuck Berry's "Round and Round" with X drummer D.J. Bonebrake, an outtake from (**GI**) and live tracks recorded in late 1980, shortly before his death. **Lion's Share** is an Australian compilation containing live cuts and assorted rarities.

Recorded under battle conditions by Geza X on a four-track, the fair-sounding **Rock n' Rule** documents a motley but amusing 1979 Christmas party at the Whisky—the noise of flying bottles crashing onstage only adds to the grimy charm. **Let the Circle Be Unbroken** is another document of the band's chaotic concert existence. [df/i]

See also *45 Grave, Pat RuthenSmear*.

GHOST DANCE
See *Sisters of Mercy*.

GIANT SANDWORMS
Will Wallow and Roam After the Ruin EP (Boneless) 1980
GIANT SAND
Valley of Rain (Enigma) 1985
Ballad of a Thin Line Man (nr/Zippo) 1986
Storm (What Goes On) 1988
The Love Songs (Homestead) 1988 ●
Long Stem Rant (Homestead) 1989 ●
Giant Songs: The Best of Giant Sand (nr/Demon) 1989 ●
Giant Sandwich (Homestead) 1989 ●
Swerve [CD] (Amazing Black Sand) 1990 ●
BAND OF BLACKY RANCHETTE
The Band of Blacky Ranchette (Fr. New Rose) 1985 ●
Heartland (nr/Zippo) 1986
Sage Advice (nr/Demon) 1990 ●

Guitarist/singer/pianist Howe Gelb moved from Pennsylvania to Tucson, Arizona, in the late '70s and formed the Giant Sandworms, a quartet preserved on a white-vinyl 7-inch EP: five nifty songs of off-kilter electro-rock that owes rudimentary debts to Roxy Music, Devo and XTC.

Five years of local influence later, only Gelb and three syllables of his band's name remain. Bassist Scott Garber and two drummers (playing on different cuts) join him on **Valley of Rain**, a brash outpouring of dusty Southwestern rock. Gelb's enthusiastic vocals and the charging, well-written music set this apart from other bands of the region (and those from LA who fancy themselves cultural expatriates) who mix cowboys into their music. Green on Red's Chris Cacavas adds piano to one song.

The next Giant Sand incarnation resulted from the departure of one drummer and the arrival of Paula Jean Brown (vocals/guitar), who had served a short tenure (taking Jane Wiedlin's spot) in the Go-Go's. **Ballad of a Thin Line Man** moves in acoustic circles, adding

equal parts of country and bracing Neil Youngesque electricity. Gelb and Brown harmonize richly; his songs about real life with an uncommon outlook just keep getting better. Guests on the LP include Falling James (Leaving Trains), who co-wrote and sings "Last Legs," a smokey piano ballad with an atmospheric '30s feel. A peppy cover of Johnny Thunders' "You Can't Put Your Arms Around a Memory" speeds up the song and adds piano, but keeps its basic sound intact with mangy singing and noisily strummed guitar.

Storm is the best Giant Sand record to that point. Brown moved over to bass, Garber left and Neil Harry joined to play almost imperceptible pedal steel. (Drummer Tom Larkins was still maintaining his concurrent membership in both Giant Sand and Naked Prey.) Crisp production plays up Gelb's guitarings, which sound remarkably like Neil Young at his grungiest; at times, his vocals hit an unnerving Lou Reed plateau. The band is in fine and sophisticated form, mixing up styles with aplomb. Burgh-oriented songs like "Town with Little or No Pity," "Bigger Than That" and "Town Where No Town Belongs" (which opens on the same riff as Cheap Trick's "She's Tight") demonstrate abundant talent and wit, especially in the lyrics department. A distinctive and invigorating album.

The fractious scat-singing of "Almost the Politician's Wife" and the shambling beatnik prose of "Fingernail Moon, Barracuda and Me" are about the only streams-of-outré-consciousness to trickle over the sides of **The Love Songs**' solid, Band-like dam of chunky riffs and churning organ (Gelb and Green on Red's Chris Cacavas switch off on keys). The restraint only intensifies the wallop packed by Gelb's lyrics. "One Man's Woman/No Man's Land" is a litany of betrayal, with Gelb carefully piling on the clichés ("One man's meat is another man's poison . . .") until he delivers the kicker ("One man's woman is . . . another man's woman"). It's positively jolting, as is the medicine-show blues "Wearing the Robes of Bible Black." A misguided Teutonic cover of Leiber and Stoller's "Is That All There Is?" suggests that Gelb has spent entirely too much time in Europe but, digested in its entirety, **The Love Songs** is Giant Sand's most consistent, clear disc. Another significant development is the arrival of drummer John Convertino, who has stuck with Gelb ever since. (Original copies of the LP came with a bonus 7-inch; the CD and cassette add the tracks.)

Long Stem Rant finds both its greatest strength (a contagious, breathless spontaneity) and its greatest weakness (a surfeit of tangled loose ends) in the circumstances of its creation—a sleepless, cathartic one-weekend spurt of near-total improv that followed hot on the heels of Gelb and Brown's divorce. That helps account for the raw emotion that pours from Gelb on "Loving Cup," but the electric intensity that he and Convertino (the entire band here) generate can only be traced to more supernatural sources (and isolation in a windowless barn—pictured on the cover—where it was recorded). Seconds-long stretches of jazzy, freewheeling raves, though often niftily titled ("Patsy Does Dylan," "Lag Craw") add little aesthetically, but do contribute to the you-are-there atmosphere.

Swerve mates the best elements of the last two releases, tempering **Rant**'s scalding emotionalism with more strictly implemented structure. There's a blurry, almost numb feel to the matter-of-fact fatalism of "Can't Find Love" and the mumbling "Sisters & Brothers" (which can easily be traced back to his relationship with Brown), and the mercurial jamfests appear—by dint of title ("Swerver," "Swerving," "Swervette") and sound (a desolately creeping art-blues wave)—to have been hacked from a single piece of rough cloth. The cover of Dylan's "Every Grain of Sand" features backing by Poi Dog Pondering and that other guests include Juliana Hatfield (Blake Babies), Falling James, Steve Wynn and Chris Cacavas.

Folks wanting to test these, er, waters can dip eustachia into two equally worthy pools. **Giant Songs** draws pretty evenly from the first four Giant Sand discs, adding three tracks from **Heartland**. The **Giant Sandwich** CD is a particularly good choice, as it nearly doubles the LPs number of what Gelb's notes call "shy" (read: hard to find) songs and steps rather confidently forward with some previously unheard material, like the very early "Artists" and a very different, starkly emotional reading of "Black Venetian Blind."

The Band of Blacky Ranchette is Gelb's parallel country-western outfit, in which he indulges a passion for Hank Williams and Jimmie Rodgers. Though seldom unauthentic (Gelb's Appalachian roots break the soil of every track), Blacky's eponymous bow is only marginally distinct from Giant Sand. Covers of "Evil" (with manic slide guitar sawing by Rainer Ptacek) and Neil Young's "Revolution Blues" diverge only in Gelb's drawling delivery. **Heartland** is more unique —only the angst-ridden "Roof's on Fire" is the least bit Sand-y—and emphasizes the western half of the C&W equation in its high lonesome duskiness. Gelb's weary weathered croon gives an empathetic kick to the wistful title track and "Moon Over Memphis," and he proves himself a solid roadhouse piano player as well.

Recorded piecemeal over several sessions in '89 and '90, **Sage Advice** further westernizes the sound—a rending version of Waylon Jennings' "Trouble Man" underscores the outlaw feel—by generously slathering Gelb's spooky high-desert ballads with dobro and pedal steel. Blacky sneaks back onto Sand territory again, as well—reinventing **Long Stem Rant**'s "Loving Cup" as a western swing two-step and again as a mournful, Williams-esque croon (the latter retitled "Blanket of Stars"). The CD of **Sage Advice** lassos six of **Heartland**'s best tracks as a bonus. [i/dss]

See also *Low Max*.

ALEX GIBSON
Passionnel EP (Faulty Products) 1981
Suburbia (Enigma) 1984
BPEOPLE
BPeople (Faulty Products) 1981
Petrified Conditions 1979–1981 (Restless) 1986
PASSIONNEL
The Apostle EP (Enigma) 1984
Our Promise (Enigma) 1985

Alex Gibson (vocals, guitar, main songwriter) led LA's BPeople for several years around the turn of the decade. Beginning as the Little Cripples, the quartet (with the ubiquitous Paul Cutler on bass) turned into

BPeople after singer Michael Gira left for New York (forming Circus Mort and then the Swans). The eponymous 1981 eight-song mini-album consists of dark, moody music somewhere between Joy Division and Soft Cell, neither as jarring or desperately distorted as the former, nor as pervasively pop as the latter. On the positive side, there's smart use of sax and organ, but at times the music seems to be pulling in different directions, and poetic license should not be granted for lyrics like "We, they, it, that" (an actual line!).

Petrified Conditions—a full album of original recordings (some, but not all, previously issued on **BPeople** and other vinyl) remixed in 1984-'85 by Gibson and Paul B. Cutler—is a more convincing introduction to BPeople's artsy sophistication. The sonic and stylistic variety is impressive, and Gibson's songwriting displays structural abilities far beyond the punk club milieu in which the band existed. A worthwhile archaeological find.

After BPeople collapsed, Gibson wrote, singlehandedly performed and produced **Passionnel**, an excellent four-song 12-inch of wide-screen rock, made grandiose with timpani and long strains of synthesizer that lurk prominently in the near-background. Very English in sound—like Simple Minds or Ultravox—but not particularly derivative, **Passionnel** is a remarkable achievement for an individual, and a frighteningly good piece of theater in itself.

Not content with the confusion level his career had engendered up to that point, Gibson's next move was to create a band called Passionnel. **The Apostle** (including a surprisingly straight cover of the Beatles' "Glass Onion") offers rhythmic rock of varying intensity, from even-handed ("Make Like You Like It") to intense sheets of dense sound ("Everything Golden"), over which Gibson spills emotional, semi-tuneful vocals. Occasionally chaotic to the point of unpleasantness, elsewhere delicate and pretty, **The Apostle** is striking, but not always for the right reasons.

Gibson scored Penelope Spheeris' punk film, *Suburbia*, the results of which occupy one side of the soundtrack album. Performed with only Passionnel's drummer joining him, the music consists of brief, aggressive rock instrumentals that rely on drums for drive and sharp-edged guitar for flavor. Several pieces sound as if they might have been edited from a long jam session (hard to imagine given the size of the band); other portions create a somber, relaxed mood with synthesizer and piano.

Released under the Passionnel moniker, **Our Promise** pairs the contents of **The Apostle** on one side with five new tracks. Well-crafted, cleanly produced and varied (within Gibson's limited musical field), the songs make some impact but leave only a faint impression. [jg/i]

GIBSON BROS
Build a Raft [tape] (Old Age) 1986
Big Pine Boogie (OKra) 1988 (OKra-Homestead) 1988
Dedicated Fool (Homestead) 1989
The Man Who Loved Couch Dancing (Homestead) 1991 ●
GIBSON BROS/WORKDOGS
Punk Rock Truck Drivin' Song of a Gun (Homestead) 1990

Columbus, Ohio, may not be the crazed rockabilly capital of America, but the Gibson Bros—a noisy minimalist quartet which includes rock-critic-turned-drummer-turned-guitarist-and-singer Don Howland (ex-Great Plains)—are doing their level best to put the town on the map without resorting to B-movie junk culture or hiccups. Although often compared to the Cramps (also from Ohio, as it happens), the Gibsons cast a wider musical net, digging their wildly reverbed guitars, super-simple drumming and Jeff Evans' frantic vocals into obscure blues and hillbilly tunes, gospel classics and derivative originals (where the lyrics can get pretty bizarre), all with equal fervor. Not always focused—or tuned up—enough to be enjoyable, the willfully hapless Gibson Bros are still capable of deep wit and high excitement.

Big Pine Boogie boasts the hysterical mantra of "Bo Diddley Pulled a Boner," while **Dedicated Fool** (on which the group dispenses with bass and has a guest saxman on two songs) has clearer crappy production and reveals a taste for rock'n'roll ("Tight Capris," Elvis Presley's "Trying to Get to You," Alice Cooper's "Caught in a Dream") amid the blues ("No Way to Get Along"), gospel ("Lone Wild Bird") and junkabilly ("Poor White Trash").

The quartet then undertook a joint project with the Workdogs, a skilled Hoboken rhythm section that has recorded on its own and backed Half Japanese, the Velvet Monkeys and others. Drummer Scott Jarvis and bassist-singer-songwriter Rob Kennedy temper the Gibsons into quick semi-respectability, discouraging the excesses of their intentional amateurism in favor of loose-limbed, unfancy country, rock and rockabilly. Gathering up enough eighteen-wheeler songs to justify the album title, the Gibdogs also rev up a version of "Shakin' All Over" and such originals as "Talk Italian to Me." [i]

See also *Great Plains*.

JERRY GIDDENS
See *Walking Wounded*.

BRUCE GILBERT
See *Dome, Wire*.

MICHAEL GIRA
See *Circus Mort, Alex Gibson, Lydia Lunch, Swans*.

GIST
See *Young Marble Giants*.

GIZMOS
The Gizmos EP (Gulcher) 1976
Amerika First EP (Gulcher) 1977
Gizmos World Tour EP (Gulcher) 1978
Never Mind the Sex Pistols Here's the Gizmos EP
　(Gulcher) 1978

DOW JONES & THE INDUSTRIALS/GIZMOS
Hoosier Hysteria (Gulcher) 1980

KENNE HIGHLAND CLAN AND THE EXPLODING PIDGINS
The Kenne Highland Clan and the Exploding Pidgins
　(Stanton Park) 1987
While the serious end of the new wave was busy rewriting the rules of the game, this motley crew of fanzine writers, Marines and Richard Meltzer fans (the label's name is a tribute to his 1972 book) were goofing around the college town of Bloomington, Indiana, issuing records of their silly songs. The music on the EPs (all 7-inch singles, each containing four to seven short tunes like "Pumpin' to Playboy," "Human Garbage Disposal," "Gimme Back My Foreskin" and "Tie Me Up") is fresh-faced fratboy guitar pop going on garage rock, but the alternately obnoxious/funny lyrics are emblematic of the mentality that continues to prevail in much of the alternative rock world. (Incidentally, **World Tour** is "Live—in the studio.")

By the time of the fourth EP (which includes a mistitled cover of the Pistols' "Did You No Wrong"), the Gizmos had undergone a number of lineup changes and were nearing a final incarnation with guitarist/singer Dale Lawrence writing most of the songs. On their side of **Hoosier Hysteria** (shared with another Bloomington quartet), the Gizmos play no-frills rock'n'roll that tears down "Progressive Rock" and pokes tasteless fun at "Dead Astronauts." Closing out with a punked-up version of Al Green's "Take Me to the River" (T. Heads had already been there), the Gizmos bade farewell.

Years later, original Gizmos vocalist Ken Highland (a Marine who had to leave the band when he was stationed in Maryland) returned to vinyl duty in Massachusetts. Singing and playing original retro-garage rockers with shifting sidemen on an album he shares with a related '60sish pop-rock group called the Exploding Pidgins, Highland displays the same unfettered enthusiasm as ever—and a welcome adult mentality. [i]

See also *Crawlspace, Vulgar Boatmen*.

GIZZARDS
See *MX-80 Sound*.

GLASS EYE
Marlo EP (no label) 1985
Huge (Wrestler) 1986
Bent by Nature (Bar/None-Restless) 1988 ●
Christine EP (Bar/None-Restless) 1989
Hello Young Lovers (Bar/None-Restless) 1989 ●
From the very first bars of its six-song debut, Austin's Glass Eye staked out an utterly distinct spot on the cusp of pop and the avant-garde. With edgy vocals over herky-jerky rhythms and, slithering under it all, Brian Beattie's groaning, jazzy fretless bass lines, the quartet's music is sparse, angular and seemingly immune to genre divisions.

Guitarist Kathy McCarty's plaintive vocals wear a bit thin on **Marlo** (Beattie sings one song), but there's already ample evidence of daring songwriting that straddles the line between artiness and genuine fun and emotion. An acoustic piano provides a welcome counterpoint to the plinky electronic keyboards.

Drummer Scott Marcus and keyboardist/singer Stella Weir left after **Huge** and were replaced, respectively, by Dave Cameron and Sheri Lane for the ambitious **Bent by Nature** and **Christine**. Two of the EP tracks are on the album, and all five are on the CD, including the intriguing Latin essay of "Perder la Guerra," the goofy metallic "Ballad of Abraham Lincoln" ("oh, how he hated to shave!") and a cover of Paul Simon's "Cecilia."

In a surprising turn, Marcus and Weir rejoined Glass Eye prior to **Hello Young Lovers**. The reconstituted group's unique sound isn't very different, although richer and more fleshed-out this time. (The democratic songwriting and increased instrumental versatility doesn't hurt any.) Most importantly, Glass Eye continues to come up with lovely melodies, challenging rhythms and affecting lyrics, on stunning tracks like "God Take All" and "The Crooked Place."

Outside the group, McCarty contributed a solo cover of Daniel Johnston's "Living Life" to the 1989 Bar/None sampler, **Time for a Change**. Weir and Marcus also play in a band called Prohibition, while Beattie has produced LPs for the Dead Milkmen and Ed Hall. In late 1990, Glass Eye launched a spoof-metal side project under the name Mönikker. [ws]

GLEAMING SPIRES

Songs of the Spires (Posh Boy) 1981
Life Out on the Lawn EP (Posh Boy) 1982
Walk on Well Lighted Streets (Posh Boy-PVC) 1983
Funk for Children–Party EP (Vodka) 1984
Welcoming a New Ice Age (Tabb) 1985

For much of the '80s, Les Bohem (bass/vocals) and David Kendrick (drums) led a dual existence as members of LA's Gleaming Spires and as the rhythm section of Sparks. Both had been in the punk-oriented Bates Motel; their subsequent work together has taken two divergent paths. The first Spires album is full of catchy, synthesizer-strewn silliness ("Are You Ready for the Sex Girls?," "How to Get Girls Through Hypnotism"), while **Life Out on the Lawn** is more arty and serious, allowing electric guitar and wailing sax to routinize the sound, if not their bizarre outlook. While a somber cover of "Somewhere" (from *West Side Story*) demonstrates a continuing flair for incongruity, this approach is far less entertaining or original than their jollier early work.

As of **Walk on Well Lighted Streets**, the Spires became a quartet and the stylistic influence of their Sparks experience is beginning to show. The lyrics are more bizarre than ever, while the music manages to be simultaneously catchy and quirky, throbbing with drive but punctuated with oddball effects and gimmicky production by Stephen Hague. Best tune: "A Christian Girl's Problems."

Funk for Children consists of four tracks on one side and extended versions of two on the flip. The title tune incorporates a children's chorus and "party" percussion for novelty effect, but is otherwise boring. Two numbers are essentially bubblegum rock-pop—robust and catchy, similar to the Spires' early efforts. The program is rounded out with a Zappa soundalike, "Brain Button." Unfortunately, the remix side features the wrong two songs.

Welcoming a New Ice Age isn't as funny as other Spires' endeavors, but its uncanny resemblance to contemporaneous Sparks records makes one wonder when Russell's voice is going to appear and push Bohem's aside. [i]

See also *Devo, Sparks*.

GLOVE

Blue Sunshine (nr/Wonderland-Polydor) 1983 (Rough Trade) 1990 ●

The band is named after the villain in *Yellow Submarine*, the record after a variety of LSD; the cover is a '60s memorabilia scrapbook. This one-off project by Banshee bassist Steve Severin and Cure leader Robert Smith (at the time also the Banshees guitarist) sounds much like their own bands crossed with the Beatles, circa 1967. The ten pseudo-psychedelic ditties (thirteen on the reissue's CD) show neither participant in top form, although the single "Like an Animal" (with Siouxsie-like guest vocalist Landray) and "Mr. Alphabet Says" do stand out. Not a band to make a career of, but good harmless fun. [dgs]

See also *Cure, Siouxsie and the Banshees*.

CRISPIN HELLION GLOVER

THE BIG PROBLEM ≠ the solution. The Solution = LET IT BE. (Restless) 1989 ●

For a truly bewildering experience, try listening to this indescribable sideshow by actor Crispin Glover (*River's Edge, Back to the Future*). And *try* is the operative word: there's no guaranteeing anyone's ability to endure this entire program of cut-up found stories and neurotic songs. Barnes and Barnes provide the appropriately unsettled music for the album's bizarre musical escapades, which include a multi-part homage to masturbation, Charlie Manson's "Never Say 'Never' to Always" and a tearful version of "These Boots Are Made for Walking." [i]

See also *Barnes & Barnes*.

JEREMY GLUCK WITH NIKKI SUDDEN & ROWLAND S. HOWARD

See *Barracudas*.

GOBBLEHOOF

GobbleHoof EP (New Alliance) 1990

The fact that J Mascis (Dinosaur Jr.) is the drummer on this six-song 12-inch ensures a measure of fanzine-level interest for the Massachusetts group's debut. However, the person who really makes **GobbleHoof** worth hearing is vocalist Charles Nakajima (formerly a bandmate of Mascis' in Dinosaur's hardcore precursor, Deep Wound), less a singer than a dramatic (*not* melodramatic) speaker with a commanding presence. As guitarist Tim Aaron reels off competent postmodern grungerock (complete with wah-wah and all the trimmings), Nakajima recounts his lyrics in a weary, resonant deep voice, occasionally reaching out to embrace melody notes but generally tying the band's sound up in a distinctive, attention-grabbing package. [i]

See also *Dinosaur*.

GO-BETWEENS

Send Me a Lullaby (nr/Rough Trade) 1981
Very Quick on the Eye—Brisbane, 1981 (Aus. Man Made)
  1982
Before Hollywood (nr/Rough Trade) 1983 ●
Springhill Fair (nr/Sire) 1984
Metals and Shells (PVC) 1985
The Able Label Singles EP (nr/Situation Two) 1986
Liberty Belle and the Black Diamond Express (Big Time)
  1986 ●
Tallulah (Big Time) 1987 ●
16 Lovers Lane (Beggars Banquet-Capitol) 1988 ●
1978–1990 (Beggars Banquet-Capitol) 1990 ●

ROBERT FORSTER

Danger in the Past (nr/Beggars Banquet) 1990
  (Beggars-Banquet-RCA) 1991 ●

One of the most critically respected and cultily
adored neo-pop bands to emerge from Australia, Brisbane's Go-Betweens began in 1977 as a Dylan-inflected
duo but had expanded to a more original-sounding trio
by the time **Send Me a Lullaby** was recorded. With
shades of Television and the Cure, the cool but not
chilly LP offers a charming view that isn't overly
pop—no slick gimmickry here—and songs that are more
fascinating lyrically than melodically. Remarkably, the
band's jagged, slightly coarse guitar sound has little
trouble accommodating occasional intrusive blurts of
blank sax noise. **Very Quick on the Eye** is a collection
of outtakes and demos, some of which made it onto
Lullaby.

Before Hollywood is a major improvement—more
tunefulness, stronger harmonies, less stridency—
suggesting R.E.M. and Aztec Camera a bit. The Go-
Betweens, however, are clearly not just like anybody.
Outstanding tracks: ''Two Steps Step Out,'' ''Dusty in
Here'' and the utterly wonderful, airy ''Cattle and
Cane.'' A marvelous, invigorating record.

Four Go-Betweens recorded the more mellifluous
Springhill Fair in France, making it so smooth and
well-ordered that it verges on commercialism. They still
make genteel pop music, but color it with guest keyboards, strings, horns and even (gasp!) synthesizer. Fortunately, the Go-Betweens write such musically
pleasant, lyrically fascinating and intelligent songs that
even creeping complexity and slickness can't seriously
damage their appeal.

Liberty Belle leaves a few more rough edges intact
than its predecessor. The songwriting is again sharp and
the sound nicely augmented with light touches of
strings, vibes, bassoon, accordion and Tracey Thorn's
backing vocals—all without even approaching overproduction. (The CD adds two numbers.) **Metals and
Shells** is a get-acquainted compilation for America,
where the band has yet to break much ground. **The Able
Label Singles** reissues the band's two earliest 45s: ''the
first four songs we ever recorded.''

Tallulah sounds like a stab at creating an essential
yuppie acquisition. There's isn't anything very different
going on, it's just so much more slick and professional
sounding than ever before. Now a five-piece, they've
incorporated a violinist/oboist (!) who adds relatively
little, since they have often thrown in a few odd-
instrument sidemen. Songwriters Grant McLennan and
Robert Forster are not in top form at all, especially

obvious on ''The House That Jack Kerouac Built,'' a
song that ought to be a lot livelier and possess sharper
lyrics if such a venerated name is going to be invoked.
They *will* do better next time.

And better they did. **16 Lovers Lane** proffers ten
bittersweet, smart relationship songs that find Forster
and McLennan at their most lyrically acute. The music
is even more impressive, replacing **Tallulah**'s gloss
with a clean but intimate sound, effectively incorporating Amanda Brown's violin and oboe into the mesh of
Forster and McLennan's intertwined guitars. Amid such
consistent quality, highlights include the single ''Was
There Anything I Could Do?'' and ''You Can't Say No
Forever'' (''My world's tumbling down/Stone by stone
to the ground/Please take out the garbage''). This one
really works.

In early 1990, having reached such a high point, the
Go-Betweens went their separate ways. The posthumous
1978–1990 (two discs on vinyl, one CD) collects album
tracks, singles, a radio session item and one outtake; 22
songs in all. Like any set of this type, the selection is
debatable—the final two albums, for instance, are represented by such weak cuts as, respectively, ''Kerouac''
and ''Streets of Your Town''—but it's still a fitting
farewell to a band that will be missed.

Given the length of time Forster was the Go-
Betweens' main voice, it's easy (if not necessarily fair)
to compare his solo debut, **Danger in the Past**, to the
band's work. There's nothing drastically different in his
songwriting techniques; he still blends lilting melodies
and a relaxed delivery with sweet and sour lyrics. But
here he travels to Berlin, employing Mick Harvey (Nick
Cave's chief Bad Seed and a member of Crime & the
City Solution) as producer, and engaging the services of
Bad Seed/die Haut drummer Thomas Wydler and former
Bad Seed guitarist Hugo Race. Harvey (who also plays
several instruments on the LP) gives Forster a somewhat
more eerie backdrop than he had with the Go-Betweens,
and it brings the darker side of his songs more to the
fore. Although the bands in which Forster and Harvey
began were at the opposite ends of Australia's rock spectrum, their collaboration works surprisingly well.

See also *Hex*. [i/dgs]

VIC GODARD & THE SUBWAY SECT

What's the Matter Boy? (nr/Oddball-MCA) 1980 +
  1982
Songs for Sale (nr/London) 1982
A Retrospective (1977–81) (nr/Rough Trade) 1984

VIC GODARD

T.R.O.U.B.L.E. (Upside) 1986

Although the Subway Sect shared stages with the
Clash, Sex Pistols and Buzzcocks as far back as 1976,
the group's debut vinyl was a 1978 single; their first
longplayer didn't follow until two years later. (The Sect
did record an album in '78 for Clash manager Bernard
Rhodes, but it was never released. As a result, Bristol-
born singer-songwriter-arranger Vic Godard broke up
the band, and original drummer Mark Laff joined Generation X.)

By 1980, the Sect had reformed (at least once).
Several of these early hard guitar-pop incarnations are

chronicled on **A Retrospective**, which consists of two singles and a radio broadcast from '78, a cut from that lost LP plus a 1981 45 side. The evidence is plain that the early Subway Sect had incorporated a strong Buzzcocks influence (plus flashes of Lou Reed and Television), and that Godard was a talented musician slowly fashioning an identity.

By the time they finally got to make an album, the Sect had again been revamped and was serving merely as a backing band for Godard, who had developed into a skillful vocalist with a budding predilection for folky, low-key, non-aggressive—hell, non-rock!—music. Considering the band's background, **What's the Matter Boy?** is a surprising belated debut. The cover is terrible and Rhodes' production is totally flat, but the charming songs' upbeat freshness and originality (start with "Enclave") more than compensates for the flimsy presentation.

The Subway Sect (who transmuted the following year into JoBoxers) may share titular credit with Vic on **Songs for Sale**—a collection of homages to (and one cover of) his idol, Cole Porter—but Godard is entirely in charge. Abandoning rock'n'roll completely, **Songs for Sale** is a wonderful record of concise pop creations delivered in a cool, suave voice. Proving himself a masterful tunesmith and crooner, Godard manages to update 1930s/'40s Tin Pan Alley without resorting to mimicry or selfconsciousness. As produced by Alex Sadkin, the memorable, sturdy tunes sound of the period without being corny. Sure it's a pose, but Godard is evidently sincere in his nostalgic affection, and he makes the music his own with real panache.

Finally emerging as a solo artist, Vic made **T.R.O.U.B.L.E.**, a brasher, more ambitious and almost equally winning swing record with one Porter tune and eleven lively originals. Dance rhythms of the '40s subtly seasoned with horns and a spot of accordion energize the giddy romance of songs like "The Devil's in League with You," "Caribbean Blue" and "Stop That Girl." "Out of Touch," a snazzy guitar instrumental that could have come from a '60s spy flick, is an intriguing change of pace. [i]

GOD BULLIES

Plastic Eye Miracle [tape] (Mad Queen) 1988 (Ger.
  Amphetamine Reptile-Glitterhouse) 1989
Mamawombwomb (Amphetamine Reptile) 1989
Dog Show (Amphetamine Reptile) 1990 ●
Join Satan's Army EP (Amphetamine Reptile) 1990

They cover such songs as Link Wray's "Preacher Man" and Terry Jacks' "Which Way You Goin' Billy." Every other word out of their mouths has to do with god in some shape or form. There are enough sermons embedded between the notes to stock a religious radio station. One song even begins with a sweet little girl singing a hymn. But make no mistake about it: gospel this ain't. The God Bullies are everything Sister Mary Elizabeth warned you about.

Formed in Kalamazoo, Michigan, the God Bullies debuted in 1988 with the single "All I Want Is My Mamma" (a different recording of which appears on **Mamawombwomb**) and followed that with the cassette-only half-live/half-studio **Plastic Eye Miracle** (later vinylized in Germany). Hooking up with Amphet-

amine Reptile, the quartet has proceeded apace, recording songs like "Monster Jesus," "Red Blood" and "Let's Go to Hell" with and without the Jesus Goes to Hell Singers (Mary Kate Murray and Tabatha Predovich).

As the voice of the beast, Mike Hard has learned his lessons well from the Sisters of Mercy: a slow, deep growl interspersed with a glazed-eyed psycho laugh so gleeful and ghoulish that you wonder if it's an act or just the Halidol wearing off. Guitarist (and electronic keyboardist, but fear not: no pseudo strings here) David B. Livingstone works in a harsh and nyarling style on **Mamawombwomb** and in a grungier and scuzzier vein with bassist Mike Corso for **Dog Show**. On the former's "Sex Power Money," the guitar twists like a slug in the garden. In "Follow the Leader," a megaphoned tribute of sorts inspired by Jim Jones, the voice exhorts "All my children, my little sheep, let's go to heaven in a tangled heap" while the guitar squirms in sinew-grunge. Like Foetus, this band revels in badness. Religion and death, murder and death, suicide and death, psychosis and death. It's all locked within the music's hard, guts-über-alles grooves.

The version of "Act of Desire" on **Mamawombwomb** (the song also appears in a live rendition on **Plastic Eye Miracle**) opens with a loop of "Art Linkletter, Art Linkletter" and a repeated "do it now," then proceeds to introduce burbling synthesizers that tweet like the filaments of a 1950s Frankenstein lab, interlaid with soft sirens, followed by television sermonizer Jack Van Impe preaching the evils of rock'n'roll music.

After **Dog Show**, drummer Adam Berg was replaced by Tony Oliveri of the Cows, who made his debut on the double 7-inch **Join Satan's Army** EP: three mutated covers (including Hot Chocolate's "You Sexy Thing") and the metal-parody title track. ['e]

GODFATHERS

Hit by Hit (Link) 1986 ●
Birth, School, Work, Death (Epic) 1988 ●
More Songs About Love and Hate (Epic) 1989 ●
Cause I Said So EP (nr/Epic) 1988 ●
Out on the Floor EP (nr/Epic) 1990 ●
Unreal World (Epic) 1991 φ

Remember Dr. Feelgood? How 'bout Eddie and the Hot Rods? Well, if the white-hot pre-punk R&B/rock'n'roll of those two bands means anything to you, chances are you'll love the early Godfathers—formed by London brothers Peter (vocals) and Chris (bass/vocals) Coyne, initially as the Syd Presley Experience—to death. Not coincidentally, the late Vic Maile (original producer of both the Feelgoods and Hot Rods) was at the helm for the first three Godfathers discs. (He died shortly after the completion of **More Songs**.) With lyrics of working class angst in a Britain where, as Peter Coyne sings in "The Strangest Boy," "My future's past, already gone and been," the Godfathers lay out the worst-case scenario of the Pistols' "No future in England's dream": a landscape of poverty, drugs and desperation. Unlike the punks of yore, though, the Godfathers remain motivated, if only by sexual and material desires and a stubborn streak of self-preservation. Punk meets mod at the bottom of the social barrel.

Hit by Hit presents a band already sporting a remarkably clear vision. Titles like "I Want Everything," "This Damn Nation," "I Want You" and "I'm Unsatisfied," replete with explosive riffing and angry vocals, tell you nearly all you need to know about how the Godfathers saw their lot in Maggie Thatcher's England. A strong cover of John Lennon's "Cold Turkey," and a version of Rolf Harris' "Sun Arise" that makes Alice Cooper's sound sickly round out an essential debut.

Birth, School, Work, Death is even tougher and more focused than **Hit by Hit**. The dynamic title track and "'Cause I Said So" are the high points of a record that just seethes with the anger and aggression that seems to have all but gone out of non-hardcore British post-punk rock.

The fatalistic vision articulated on the song "Birth, School, Work, Death" fully flowers on **More Songs About Love and Hate** (which could just as easily have been titled **More Songs About Resignation and Fate**). Whereas the Godfathers could once sing "I Want Everything," they now realize that dream (such as it was) is behind them. "Life Has Passed Us By" (which ironically offers the music hall ambience of the Stones' **Between the Buttons** and the Small Faces **Ogden's Nut Gone Flake**), "How Low Is Low?," "Those Days Are Over" and "This Is Your Life" (which ends with one guitar chord being hit more than 75 times) are all bleak views of a life where things only get worse. At this point the group seems to live by Pete Townshend's old maxim that great rock'n'roll spells out your troubles, then lets you dance all over them. They certainly offer little hope of any other cure for what ails them.

Although marked by increased allusions to '60s influences, **Unreal World** doesn't get overly retroid (the fab cover of the Creation's "How Does It Feel to Feel" marches the song straight into the '90s). In fact, it's pretty well rooted in the here-and-now, largely due to producer Steve Brown (previously their engineer and mixer, taking over from Maile) and new lead axeman Chris Burrows (replacing Kris Dollimore), who doesn't hesitate to wield wah-wah with a modern flair. Also welcome is the increase in vocal harmonies (especially a high voice/low voice gambit not unlike Squeeze's). End to end, a catchy, rocking album—in fact, if anything, the second half (with gems like "Something About You" and the Beatlesque psychedelic sarcasm of "I Love What's Happening to Me") is better than the first! [ds/jg]

GODFLESH
Godflesh (nr/Silverfish) 1988 (nr/Earache) 1990 (Earache-Combat) 1991 •
Streetcleaner (nr/Earache) 1990 (Earache-Combat) 1991 •
Slavestate EP (Earache-Combat) 1991 •
SWEET TOOTH
Soft White Underbelly EP (nr/Staindrop-Earache) 1990

Ex-Napalm Death guitarist Justin Broadrick formed Godflesh in 1988 upon his departure from Head of David (in which he was the drummer). **Godflesh** is a sonic bulldozer, its ultra-low tunings and distant, disembodied vocals (not unlike **Pornography**-era Cure) creating a bass-heavy lava flow of sound even more engulfing

than early Swans, or Sabbath at half-speed. (Bassist G. Christian Green is said to own Geezer Butler's old amp.) Comprised of a surgically precise drum machine, Head of David-like tornado guitar, bass from another dimension and a mind-melting array of tape loops and effects, the band projects almost no midrange—the high frequencies skitter over the anesthetizing throb of the low. Basically, it's heavy as hell, and there's nothing metal or hardcore about Godflesh except the imagery and the damage.

Streetcleaner is more industrial, more cluttered and even more overwhelmingly powerful and destructive than the debut. Sounds attack from all angles (some cuts include a second guitarist); elements that seemingly have nothing to do with each other frequently run simultaneously. With the exception of the pulsing "Dead Head" (one of four CD bonus tracks), this album jolts where the debut grooved.

In a discographical tangle of singles, EPs and bonus cuts, Godflesh's third phase—basically their version of dance music—gradually coalesced. The first LP's 1990 reissue on Earache includes two brand-new cuts, among them the staggering "Wounds," a dance track so hard that it hurts: this twelve-minute intergalactic shooting gallery of beats and effects wipes the floor with the entire Chicago/Belgium axis (actually, a Godflesh/Al Jourgensen collaboration has been rumored). The four-song **Slavestate** EP finds the band charging full-on into an industrial-dance realm, giving **Streetcleaner**'s lurch-and-crunch the twist of a rhythmic basis. The concurrent "Slateman" single found *that* format mutated into yet another shape, lofting a soaring vocal melody over one of the most pulverising riffs in the band's catalogue.

Sweet Tooth is a side-project trio—Broadrick, Head of David bassist Dave and a hyper-complex drummer named SDK (of Chicago's Slab)—that combines elements of Godflesh and HoD into a wild, almost jazz-like rock unit that thrusts and jolts with more fluidity than (and nearly as much innovation as) its parental units. [ja]

GOD'S LITTLE MONKEYS
New Maps of Hell! (Alias) 1989 •
MALCOLM'S INTERVIEW
Breakfast in Bedlam (nr/Special Delivery) 1987

To compete in the global village, today's self-respecting skiffle group has to have more up its sleeve than an enthusiastic rendition of "Rock Island Line." Besides a strong streak of radical politics, God's Little Monkeys—an acoustic/electric quartet (formerly known as Malcolm's Interview) from York, England—demonstrates a wonderfully broad stylistic reach on the excellent **New Maps of Hell!**, following an old standard like "Pay That Money Down" with the African-styled chanting of "Hangman Botha," and grouping the a cappella folk of "Sea Never Dry" with the Billy Bragg-styled "Where Were You?" and the Poguesy rock of "Tory Heart." Elsewhere, taking good advantage of tradition while ignoring restrictions on what musical regions are open to them, the group delves into rock and other styles, all led by the rich vocals of guitarist Jon Townend and keyboardist Jo Swiss. [i]

GO-GO'S

Beauty and the Beat (IRS) 1981 ●
Vacation (IRS) 1982 ●
Talk Show (IRS) 1984 ●
Go-Go's Greatest (IRS) 1990 φ

HOUSE OF SCHOCK

House of Schock (Capitol) 1988 ●

GRACES

Perfect View (A&M) 1989 ●

The enormous commercial success of **Beauty and the Beat** in America was not only a welcome break-through for new music, but proof that an all-female band could make it big without a man pulling the strings and without resorting to an image grounded in male fantasy, be it sex kitten or tough leatherette. The album mixes honest pop with healthy infusions of rock'n'roll and, besides containing two bona fide hit singles ("We Got the Beat" and "Our Lips Are Sealed"), provides a refreshingly different point of view on some familiar themes ("Lust to Love," "Skidmarks on My Heart").

If not as exuberant or confident as its predecessor, **Vacation** is at least more ambitious. The quintet sounds distinctive and skillful, but the songs generally fall short of the standards set by **Beauty and the Beat**. The exceptions, however, are delightful: the crisp, wistful title track, "I Think It's Me" and the bubbly, modernized girl-group sound of "This Old Feeling."

The third album exchanges the wise punk-pop production hand of Richard Gottehrer for a more challenging experience with Martin Rushent. **Talk Show** attempts a major revamp, turning up the rock energy on all fronts: Gina Schock's drumming receives new prominence in the mix while guitars blaze with added bite. As on the first two LPs, the material includes a few great singles ("Turn to You," "Head Over Heels" and "Yes or No," the last co-written by guitarist Jane Wiedlin with Ron and Russell Mael), plus a lot of forgettable filler. After all that, the first album remains the band's best.

After guitarist Jane Wiedlin left for a solo career, the group pressed on for a while, but disbanded in May 1985 without recording again. Joined by guitarist Charlotte Caffey, Belinda Carlisle made her solo debut the following year.

Drummer Gina Schock took a few years off and then unveiled a short-lived band. Schock sings and co-wrote the songs on **House of Schock** with bassist Vance De-Generes; the backing trio surprisingly includes a drummer who takes her place on half the tracks. Gottehrer's deft production provides a bright, appealing sound, but Schock's limited voice and songs, both equally inoffensive, are easily forgotten.

While the pop world was unwittingly awaiting the multi-platinum arrival of another West Coast female trio, Caffey, Meredith Brooks and Gia Ciambotti formed the Graces, an obviously sound idea ruined by commercial ambition. Rather than let the group find its own use for three complementary voices, executive producer Jimmy Iovine threw an army of producers (including Carlisle's svengali of schlock, Rick Nowels), songwriters and session pros at the project, burying **Perfect View** in a slick but ineffectual wash. If the Graces had any personality, you'd never know it from this bland piece of product.

In 1990, after reuniting for a one-off charity performance, the Go-Go's decided to give it another try. By year's end, an unnecessary compilation—hits, dubious album selections and a worthless new run-through of "Cool Jerk," first covered on **Vacation**—was in the stores and the Go-Go's were on the road again. [ks/i]

See also *Belinda Carlisle, Jane Wiedlin.*

GOLDEN PALOMINOS

The Golden Palominos (OAO-Celluloid) 1983 ●
Visions of Excess (Celluloid) 1985 ●
Blast of Silence (Celluloid) 1986 ●
A Dead Horse (Celluloid) 1989 ●

The Golden Palominos—an above-average avant-funk album—would have been a milestone if it had sounded anything like the Palominos' New York gigs. At one memorable show, the lineup included bandleader Anton Fier (drums), David Moss (drums/noise), Arto Lindsay (guitar/vocals), John Zorn (reeds), Bill Laswell (bass) and Jamaaladeen Tacuma (bass). The double rhythm section packed a wallop in unison, but more often the players broke off into intense and fascinating duets and trios.

On the first record, the Palominos add (Mark Miller, Fred Frith, Nicky Skopelitis) and subtract (most often Tacuma and Moss) players while preserving the basic material, tossing in a couple of new things ("Hot Seat," a song mostly by Miller, and "Cookout," a Fier percussion piece). Those who knew the magic of the Palominos' noise/funk synthesis firsthand will regret Fier's decision to go for the trendier Material sound in his co-production with Laswell. Still, when Lindsay rakes his untuned guitar and lets out a trademark yelp, or Zorn lowers some fragment of a clarinet under water and gurgles with weird ferocity, you know you're hearing a trace—just a trace—of the real thing.

The second phase of Fier's Palomino experiment took an entirely different direction, converting a loose caravan of talent into an unstable side-group which sporadically performs and records in countless permutations and combinations. **Visions of Excess** is a brilliant neo-pop album of tuneful, lyrical songs featuring such luminaries as Michael Stipe, John Lydon, Richard Thompson, Jack Bruce, Chris Stamey, Henry Kaiser and Jody Harris. As producer, drummer and co-writer of the songs, Fier is on stylistically unprecedented ground careerwise, but his control and taste are impeccable. A version of Moby Grape's "Omaha" sung by Stipe is a truly incisive piece of '80s psychedelia (with a crazed Kaiser breakdown solo) that sounds like a pop hit; "(Kind of) True" and "Buenos Aires," both starring talented newcomer Syd Straw, are equally memorable. Lydon's "The Animal Speaks" is, well, what you might expect from him. Just so no one should forget where this project is coming from, the LP closes with an Arto Lindsay extravaganza, "Only One Party." Essentially a revue of 1985's semi-underground stars and sounds, **Visions of Excess** is one disc everyone should own.

Blast of Silence continues the Palominos' singular existence, employing many of the same people as **Excess** (but notably not Stipe or Lydon), while extending the musical family to incorporate Peter Blegvad, Don Dixon, T-Bone Burnett and other meta-stars. The Palominos' previous rotating ensemble work raised expectations of the unexpected, but this plain album has nothing to equal its predecessor's extraordinary content. Except for Straw singing Peter Holsapple's "Diamond," the material isn't especially interesting; the performances are routine and the darkening outlines of a repeatable formula discourage faith in the future of Fier's creative vision and energy.

Fier pretty much ditched the supersession concept for **A Dead Horse**, building this version of the Palominos around a more consistent lineup of Laswell and Skopelitis, with Numbers Band singer/guitarist Robert Kidney (who performed on **Blast of Silence** and wrote "The Animal Speaks" on **Visions of Excess**), ex-Information Society vocalist Amanda Kramer and a few guests, including Bernie Worrell and Mick Taylor. Similarly, the big-rock style of the previous two discs gives way to a calmer, more atmospheric approach. All seven songs are in-house creations (three by Kidney, four by Fier/Skopelitis/Kramer); Kidney's plaintive singing and Kramer's multi-tracked harmonies provide a surprisingly pleasant alternative to playing spot-the-star.

[mf/i/hd]

GONE

"Let's Get Real, Real Gone for a Change" (SST) 1986 •
Gone II—But Never Too Gone! (SST) 1986

Black Flag guitarist Greg Ginn has pursued numerous side projects in recent years. Gone is an instrumental power trio that could use a vocalist as well as more organized power; the first album (named after an Elvis Presley remark) meanders aimlessly like a badly run rehearsal session.

The song-things on **Gone II** (cover artwork by Ginn) are more coherent and tolerable, but still fall short of justifying the band's existence. Riffs with solos make good interludes, but sixteen unengaging pieces in a row do not a good time make. Is the world ready for heavy metal wallpaper? Still, give Andrew Weiss well-earned credit for bitchin bass work. [i]

See also *Henry Rollins*.

GONE FISHIN'

See *Windbreakers*.

GOOD MISSIONARIES

See *Alternative TV*.

GOO GOO DOLLS

Goo Goo Dolls (Mercenary-Celluloid) 1987
Jed (Death-Enigma) 1989 •
Hold Me Up (Metal Blade-Warner Bros.) 1990 φ

Like vintage Replacements (their most obvious influence) or early Cheap Trick, Buffalo, New York's Goo Goo Dolls brandish soaring/searing grunge-garage powerpunkpop. Although recorded two years apart, the trio's first two albums are virtual carbon copies of each other, with flashes of brilliance amid silly covers and scrawny adolescent yapping.

As the Goos tightened up their act, they moved into the raucous stylistic space the 'Mats were abandoning, and the effervescent **Hold Me Up** really delivers the goods, focusing a variety of hard-rocking/good-humored impulses into a solid, distinctive sound all its own. An exhilarating rollercoaster of Ramonesy riffs and insistent hooks, the Goo Goo Dolls write cool originals and make good use of two covers: the Plimsouls' "A Million Miles Away" and Prince's "I Could Never Take the Place of Your Man," a tongue-in-cheek take with guest vocals by Lance Diamond, a schmaltzy crooner (who also contributed his stylings to **Jed**'s crunching rendition of Creedence's "Down on the Corner"). Essential for fans of Cheap Trick and cheap beer.

[ja]

ROBERT GORDON WITH LINK WRAY

Robert Gordon with Link Wray (Private Stock) 1977
Fresh Fish Special (Private Stock) 1978

ROBERT GORDON

Rock Billy Boogie (RCA) 1979
Bad Boy (RCA) 1980
Are You Gonna Be the One (RCA) 1981
Too Fast to Live, Too Young to Die (RCA) 1982
Live at Lone Star (Fr. New Rose) 1989 •
Robert Gordon Is Red Hot [CD] (Ger. Bear Family) 1989 •

Singer Robert Gordon made one of the sharpest *volte-faces* in musical memory when he left New York pseudo-punkers Tuff Darts to reappear as a freeze-dried '50s rocker, complete with sideburns, pompadour, a songbook of Sun Records oldies and authentic guitar icon Link Wray in tow.

Superficial trappings aside, Gordon's strongest asset is his magnificent voice—a clear, clean baritone rarely heard in pop music of any stripe. His debut album, **Robert Gordon with Link Wray**, is suffused with rockabilly material (songs from Carl Perkins, Gene Vincent, Billy Lee Riley and Eddie Cochran), but the accompaniment by the Wildcats is more contemporary, with Wray contributing sizzling guitar licks.

Fresh Fish Special (named after Elvis Presley's haircut in *Jailhouse Rock*—as typical an homage as the use of the Jordanaires) is more of the same, with barely more sophisticated tunes. The odd track here is Bruce Springsteen's "Fire," which was a hit for the Pointer Sisters. Nevertheless, its inclusion proved Gordon didn't need to rely exclusively on nostalgia.

Besides the addition of echo, **Rock Billy Boogie**'s distinction is the replacement of Wray with nimble guitarist Chris Spedding and its inclusion of "Black Slacks," a jivey Gordon signature number. On **Bad Boy**, Gordon seems to be evolving from the '50s into the '60s via schlockier songs (Roy Orbison's "Uptown," Kris Jensen's "Torture").

Gordon's time-traveling into the present continues on **Are You Gonna Be the One**, his most accessible album for those who don't worship at the House of Butchwax. Despite his '50s fixation, Gordon best puts across those songs without a 25-year-old aroma.

Too Fast to Live, Too Young to Die is a compilation of tracks from all the preceding albums except **Bad Boy**, plus a live version of "Black Slacks" and previously unreleased recordings of two Marshall Crenshaw songs.

A more recent concert document, **Live at Lone Star**, finds Gordon running through a classic rock'n'roll program onstage in New York, sharply backed by Spedding, bassist Tony Garnier and drummer Anton Fig. Starting with "The Way I Walk" and running through "Twenty Flight Rock," "Mystery Train," "Black Slacks," "Fire" and ten more, the great-sounding record proves that Robert Gordon is still a master of the form.   [si/i]

GORDONS
Future Shock EP (NZ Flying Nun) 1980 + 1988 ●
The Gordons (NZ Flying Nun) 1982 + 1988 ●
Vol. 2 (NZ Flying Nun) 1984
BAILTER SPACE
Nelsh EP (NZ Flying Nun) 1987
Tanker (NZ Flying Nun) 1988
Grader Spader EP (NZ Flying Nun) 1988
Thermos (NZ Flying Nun) 1990 (Matador) 1991

In 1988, when the Gordons' long out-of-print **Future Shock** EP was re-released on 12-inch to coincide with Bailter Space's emergence, the New Zealand trio was retrospectively praised with frequent comparisons to Sonic Youth. But back in 1980, when the 7-inch first appeared, there simply were no precedents. Renowned locally for punishingly loud and relentless live shows, the Gordons' vinyl matched progressive punk songwriting and aggression with an uncategorizably deliberate yet extreme wall of flailing sheetmetal guitar.

The eponymous seven-song follow-up, recorded and mixed in 22 hours, almost entirely relinquishes the band's punk genetics in favor of spatial control and mood dynamics; still harsh and as heavy as anvil jewelry, the pace is less the point, with jagged chords and evocative song structures edging the vocals into far less prominence. (**The Gordons** CD appends **Future Shock**'s contents.) With simpler riff-plus-chorus constructions elevated mainly by John Halvorsen's manic-depressive guitar-maiming, **Vol. 2** comes surprisingly close to user-friendliness.

In 1987, Halvorsen reunited with the Gordons' other guitarist, Alister Parker, to form Bailter Space, lining up drummer Hamish Kilgour (also concurrently involved in a Clean reunion and backing Chris Knox) as well. With ex-Gordon drummer Brent McLaughlin as engineer, and far more expansive production than the former band, **Nelsh** quite naturally sounds like the Gordons several years on: songs more familiarly structured, vocals still subservient and weak, guitar still inventive (albeit less abrasive), keyboards now filling spaces formerly occupied by feedback and overdrive.

The more confident and considered **Tanker**, an LP of well-constructed songs displaying varied intentions and style, lacks the old recklessness but substitutes a heretofore hidden morose pop skill, as well as vocals no more melodic nor less arresting than those of Ian Curtis. Add a sharpened instrumental prowess—oddly reflective of Sonic Youth (of all things)—and you wind up with an excellent time-capsule condensation of 1988 independent music at its apex. (The spin-off EP is curiously Gordonized, with appropriately B-side material.)

Thermos, with McLaughlin reclaiming drum chores to complete the tail-biting cycle, actually ups both the discordance and pop quotient for, at its frequent best, a monumentally alluring weave of soothing smooth and seething dysphonia.

(A rather dissimilar Boston band calling themselves the Gordons issued an indie album entitled **100 Holidays** in '88, creating some potential confusion for overzealous mail-order consumers.)   [ab]
See also *Clean, Tall Dwarfs*.

MARTIN L. GORE
See *Depeche Mode*.

ROBERT GÖRL
See *Deutsche Amerikanische Freundschaft*.

GOVERNMENT ISSUE
Legless Bull EP (Dischord) 1981
Make an Effort EP (Fountain of Youth) 1982
Boycott Stabb (Dischord-Fountain of Youth) 1983 (Giant) 1988
Joyride (Fountain of Youth) 1984 ●
The Fun Just Never Ends (Fountain of Youth) 1985 ●
Give Us Stabb or Give Us Death EP (Mystic) 1985
Live on Mystic (Mystic) 1985
Government Issue (Fountain of Youth) 1986 (Giant) 1986 ●
You (Giant) 1987 ●
Crash (Giant) 1988 ●
Strange Wine E.P. (Giant) 1988 ●
Joyride/The Fun Just Never Ends [CD] (Giant) 1990 ●
Beyond (Rockville) 1991 ●
VARIOUS ARTISTS
Four Old 7"s on a 12" (Dischord) 1985

One of America's longest-running hardcore shows, Washington DC's Government Issue is a multi-faceted band that has been widely underrated, despite a large and noteworthy catalogue that dates back to 1981. Following an early release on Dischord (the ten-song **Legless Bull** 7-inch, later compiled on **Four Old 7"s**), the band—which initially included bassist Brian Baker, better known as a member of Minor Threat—cut the unprepossessing **Make an Effort**, exhibiting minor flashes of potential brilliance. "No Way Out" and "Twisted Views" are run-of-the-mill quickies, but "Teenager in a Box" is a well-crafted indicator of things to come.

Mainman/vocalist John Stabb Schroeder led a notably diminished Government Issue into a holding pattern on **Boycott Stabb**, sticking close to 'core style in a series of brisk soundalikes, only one (a new version of "Sheer Terror," a song included on both **Legless Bull** and **Make an Effort**) reaching the two-minute mark. Produced by Minor Threat's Ian MacKaye, the record isn't dreadful, it's just generic.

The GIs began to display marked maturity and a bit of stylistic independence on 1984's **Joyride**, loudly co-produced by Baker. With improvements in Tom Lyle's guitar work and Schroeder's singing, and the arrival of Mike Fellows, the quartet's third bassist (and most competent to date), **Joyride** takes a few cautious steps away from hardcore orthodoxy. (Admittedly, the heavy metal insinuations of "Joyride" and "Notch to My Crotch" are not necessarily a step in the right direction.) Odd inclusions: a sludgy but tuneful cover of "These Boots

Are Made for Walkin,'' the second version of "Hall of Fame" (from **Boycott Stabb**) and another (uncredited) version of "Sheer Terror."

With another change of bassist and Baker continuing as co-producer, GI made its last real hardcore record, **The Fun Just Never Ends** (also issued on a joint CD with **Joyride**, adding a live version of "Vanity Fare" as a bonus). Slowed to a solid mid-tempo chug, "Written Word" and "The Next Time" are neat and tuneful class-of-'77 rockers, proof that Government Issue was not just a face in the crowd.

Opening with a thickly melodic hypno-instrumental ("Visions and ?"), **Government Issue** (aka **GI-5**) edges the band away from its roots. The second track, "They Know," uses hardcore as a stepping-off point, and then abandons the format entirely, turning literally post-punk on the next song, "Locked Inside." With Lyle playing keyboards (organ on the backwards "Memories Past"—ha ha) and even electric sitar (on the misbegotten psychedelia of "Last Forever"), the album touches a number of memorably melodic bases, sounding in spots like mid-period Hüsker Dü and/or mid-period Damned. (The CD and cassette add a bonus of—you guessed it—"Sheer Terror.")

Having found its voice, GI (sporting a tremendous new rhythm section) ran with it on the next two albums, both of which are great. Produced by Lyle, **You** is a paragon of pop punk precision, a masterwork of meticulous playing and abundant hooks. Stabb's emergence as an American Dave Vanian of sorts isn't as weird as it sounds, and gangly backing vocals provide flip contrast on catchy songs like "Jaded Eyes" and the Clashy chorus of "Man in a Trap." Special favorites: "Caring Line" and "Where You Live."

The apex of GI's studio career, **Crash** is something of a musical summary of the band's eight-year history. Each track sounds as if it had been assembled on a loom, with fibers of hardcore, punk, pop metal and even early-'80s new wave knitted together. Strong cuts include "Time Will Rearrange," "For Ever" and "Strange Wine."

Strange Wine is a ten-track collection: the titular album cut, new decelerated studio renditions of "I'm James Dean" and "Teenager in a Box" (both from the band's earliest days) and a live retrospective recorded at CBGB in August '87. [icm/i]

See also *Minor Threat*.

HUW GOWER
See *Records*.

GRAB GRAB THE HADDOCK
Three Songs by Grab Grab the Haddock EP (nr/Cherry Red) 1984
Four More Songs by Grab Grab the Haddock EP (nr/Cherry Red) 1985

This terminally cute London quartet with the daft name spun off from the defunct Marine Girls but, unlike former bandmate Tracey Thorn (who went on to form Everything but the Girl), Alice Fox and her crew still hawk the chaotic tunelessness that made the Marine Girls so insufferable.

The first EP has a sparse, almost minimalist feel; even the use of atypical pop instrumentation (maracas, conga drum, cello) does little to alleviate the disjointed clatter. Fox's childlike caterwauling further adds to the annoyance. **Four More** is a slight improvement—clear melodies and a near-logical organization level enhance the tracks. Guitarist/songwriter Lester Noel takes over vocal chores on "Last Fond Goodbye," a bright pop song that provides the 12-inch's only worthwhile interlude. [ag]

See also *Marine Girls*.

GRACE POOL
Grace Pool (Reprise) 1988 ●
Where We Live (Reprise) 1990 φ

Prior to forming the suavely commercial Grace Pool with singer Elly Brown, New York guitarist Bob Riley was the drummer/keyboardist in Rage to Live (Brown guested on the band's first album) and also played in the Love of Life Orchestra. Produced with deft touches of synthesizer ambience and quiet grandeur by Steve Nye (whose work with Japan is duly noted in his efforts here), the quintet's debut is an attractive-going-on-glib haute pop record with catchy songs, fine harmonies and intricately subtle arrangements.

Riley and Brown are the only original Pool-mates in the reconstituted quartet (drummer Frank Vilardi is on the album but not in the band); Riley produced the folkier second album with less sonic flair than Nye. While the sensitively poetic lyrics are easy to overlook in favor of the sweeping melodies, **Where We Live** just isn't as striking or memorable as the debut. [i]

See also *Rage to Live*.

GRACES
See *Go-Go's*.

GRANDMASTER FLASH AND THE FURIOUS FIVE
The Message (Sugar Hill) 1982
Greatest Messages (Sugar Hill) 1983
On the Strength (Elektra) 1988 ●

GRANDMASTER MELLE MEL AND THE FURIOUS FIVE
Work Party (Sugar Hill) 1984
Stepping Off (Sugar Hill) 1985

GRANDMASTER FLASH
They Said It Couldn't Be Done (Elektra) 1985
The Source (Elektra) 1986
Ba-Dop-Boom-Bang (Elektra) 1987 ●

GRANDMASTER FLASH/ THE FURIOUS FIVE/ GRANDMASTER MELLE MEL
The Greatest Hits (Sugar Hill) 1989

Although they were not rap's first stars, Grandmaster Flash's galvanizing 1982 hit "The Message" was the earliest record to demonstrate the form's potential for socio-political commentary and, preceding Run–DMC, initially served to convey rap's excitement to an audience beyond urban blacks. Unfortunately, most of Flash's early raps were of the let's-party-and-tell-our-zodiac-signs variety, with absolutely no consciousness, political or otherwise—good for dancing, but not very stimulating. (Despite his star billing, DJ Flash is not the rapper; lead vocals are by Melle Mel, Rahiem and others. Adding to the credit-where-due confusion, most of the crew's early songwriting and performing was done, in large part, by the Sugar Hill house band.)

Greatest Messages splits the difference between hard-edged social realism and mindless partytime, from "Freedom" (their first hit) and "Flash to the Beat" to "Survival (Message II)" and "New York, New York" (the follow-up to "The Message"). The cassette has two bonus tracks. What the LP doesn't include is Melle Mel's brilliant 1983 anti-cocaine song, "White Lines (Don't Don't Do It)," the music for which, incidentally, was lifted from a Liquid Liquid instrumental.

Following a bitter legal dispute over contracts and ownership of the name, the band split in two: most of the members remained with Grandmaster Flash (Joseph Saddler), dropped the "Furious Five" appellation and signed to Elektra; Melle Mel, who also got to wear the Grandmaster crown, recruited a mostly new FF and stuck with Sugarhill. The former's **They Said It Couldn't Be Done** is a strained effort to diversify and make up for lost time and momentum. There's a rapped-up version of Fats Waller's "The Joint Is Jumpin'," a Run–DMC imitation unoriginally entitled "Rock the House" and two soulful all-singing tunes. Only "Sign of the Times" dips into topicality, employing a sound reminiscent of "White Lines."

The Source, which travels a number of awfully familiar verbal and musical roads, makes a regular point of arguing Flash's significance and supremacy. "Fastest Man Alive," the audio vérité "Street Scene," the hackneyed music-rap marriage of "Style (Peter Gunn Theme)" and the pretend-live "Freelance" make more personal introductions and absurd claims than a convention of used car salesmen. As a routine party record, it fulfills all the minimal obligations; as proof of Flash's creativity and ability to grow with the times, it's a sad example of commercial wheel-spinning.

The word funky gets an aromatically literal interpretation in **Ba-Dop-Boom-Bang**'s "Underarms," an amazingly tasteless put-down about bad smells. Otherwise, the LP avoids **The Source**'s hype to concentrate on praising women ("Them Jeans"), cars ("Big Black Caddy"), parties ("House That Rocked") and self-reliance ("Get Yours"). Interpolations of other people's music, including a lamely belated cover of Queen's "We Will Rock You" with other stuff stitched in, don't prevent **Ba-Dop-Boom-Bang** from being run-of-the-mill.

When members of Grandmaster Flash and the Furious Five—specifically Mele-Mel (new spelling), Scorpio and Cowboy—reunited, the result was the distinctly superior **On the Strength**. The record gets off to a killer start with the streetwise "Gold"; the side ends with "King," a moving gospel-tinged tribute to MLK. (The intervening tracks are routine bragging, with only Flash's deadly turntable work on "Yo Baby" for diversion.) Side Two's bizarre highlight is a rock-rap cover of "Magic Carpet Ride" (shades of "Walk This Way"). Mr. Steppenwolf himself, John Kay, sings it; Flash's gang raps on the chorus and adds a few sections that I don't recall from the twenty-year-old original.

Stepping Off is a compilation; the two-record 1989 **Greatest Hits** contains Sugar Hill-era tracks by all of the original crew's various permutations.   [i]

See also *Duke Bootee*.

DAVE GRANEY
See *Moodists*.

EDDY GRANT

Message Man (nr/Ice) 1977
Walking on Sunshine (Epic) 1979
Love in Exile (nr/Ice) 1980
My Turn to Love You (Epic) 1980
Live at Notting Hill (nr/Ice) 1981 + 1984
Can't Get Enough (nr/Ice) 1981 + 1983
Killer on the Rampage (Ice-Portrait) 1982 ●
Going for Broke (Ice-Portrait) 1984 ●
All the Hits (nr/K-Tel) 1984
Born Tuff (Ice-Portrait) 1986 ●
File Under Rock (nr/Blue Wave-Parlophone) 1988 (Enigma) 1990 ●
Harmless Piece of Fun EP (nr/Blue Wave-Parlophone) 1988 ●
Hits (nr/Starr-Polydor) 1988 ●
Walking on Sunshine: The Very Best of Eddy Grant (nr/Blue Wave-Parlophone) 1989 ●
Barefoot Soldier (Ice-Enigma) 1990 φ

Three expatriate Caribbeans plus two Englishmen equalled the Equals, whose blend of pop-rock, psychedelia, blues, R&B and, of course, a slight Carib accent yielded a wildly diverse and uneven batch of singles and albums in the late '60s. Despite their problems, they amassed a few Top 10 hits, including the oft-revived (most recently by Grant himself) "Baby Come Back," a smash on both sides of the Atlantic in 1968. Several of their other hits now sound like utter tripe, but "Black Skin Blue Eyed Boys" and the LP track "Police on My Back" (covered by the Clash) show just how talented they could be.

The group provided a musical (and music-business) education to its Guyana-born guitarist/chief songwriter/leader (but not lead singer) Eddy Grant, who eventually left to go solo and set up his own record company, Ice. He plays almost everything on his studio albums, except sometimes bass and/or drums, plus horns (when he doesn't use synthesizer instead).

Message Man was a dodgy start, yet Grant immediately began forging his own reggae style ("Jamaican Child") and continued the interracial/cultural theme begun with the Equals ("Cockney Black").

Walking on Sunshine shows his potential in full flower: "Living on the Frontline" is a superb electronic-reggae single, and its remarkable extension into "The Frontline Symphony" on the LP is a lengthy tour de force that features a mock-classical vocal section. The title track and "Say I Love You" (a monster hit in Nigeria) add extra value to an LP already well worth owning.

Love in Exile showcases Grant working in various soul styles (like the Teddy Pendergrass-ish semi-funk of the title track), albeit with his own oddly inflected vocals. "Preaching Genocide" is the one exception, a long mutant calypsoid political chant, but all in all it's only musical water-treading, and inferior. **My Turn to Love You** is the same record with an alternate title and graphics.

The live album is an excellent display of both Grant's talent as a performer and his best solo songs up to that point. It also makes available about half the otherwise rare songs from **Message Man**. Despite the usual live record drawbacks—it needn't have been a double—its best is mighty good.

Can't Get Enough is Grant's "I'm a love man" album, but it's great for what it is, as the catchy numbers take full advantage of Grant's genre-bending and blending. (The reissue adds a nifty instrumental, "Time Warp," that was originally available as the B-side of "Electric Avenue.")

The rock-oriented **Killer on the Rampage** is Grant's most consistent album to date, as well as his biggest commercial success in the US. "Electric Avenue" (the most rock-based track, save for some muscular guitar playing here and there) may prove to be an anthem of classic stature, and cuts like the title track and "I Don't Wanna Dance" demonstrate how Grant's songwriting has matured.

Proof that **Killer** was no fluke: although none of Grant's subsequent albums have high points quite as great as "Electric Avenue," all are quite enjoyable and nearly as varied. **Going for Broke** includes the theme song of the *Romancing the Stone* (only a smidge of which made the film's final cut), the wry Afro-Carib "Political Bassa-Bassa" and some strong rockish tracks. **Born Tuff** has a more varied, less rockified approach and a super title tune that's something of a more confident companion to "Living on the Front Line." If the album—on which Grant performs nearly every note—doesn't begin all that strongly, it does gather steam.

Grant also plays virtually all of **File Under Rock** and **Barefoot Soldier**, both of which maintain the quality level. The former isn't that much rockier than **Going for Broke**, but it does include a tribute to Chuck Berry and a decent remake of "Baby Come Back" (the original still rules, though). **Barefoot Soldier** is stylistically quite varied: Carib-beat, reggae, folk, country-rock (yup) and a bracing protest rocker, "Restless World." Social consciousness is prominent on the LP, which (at least in the US) includes his infectious anti-apartheid tune, "Gimme Hope Jo'Anna," an early-'88 UK hit. If some of the lyrics are obscure or dopey, Grant compensates with his usual charm, sincerity and catchy musical settings.

Harmless Piece of Fun contains "Electric Avenue," "Born Tuff," two swell tracks from **File Under Rock** plus a couple of new items. **Walking on Sunshine** is a pretty good best-of, except that it ignores "Born Tuff." [jg]

GRAPES OF WRATH

The Grapes of Wrath EP (Can. Nettwerk) 1984
September Bowl of Green (Can. Nettwerk) 1985
    (Capitol) 1986
Treehouse (Capitol) 1987 ●
Now and Again (Nettwerk-Capitol) 1989 ●

Playing muscular power pop, this Vancouver trio in its early days alternately resembled Southeastern bands like Let's Active and West Coast folk-rockers like Translator. The impressive four-song EP is a little short on personality but locates a viable commercial midpoint between the radio and the road. Guitarist Kevin Kane is a proficient instrumentalist and a fair vocalist; drummer Chris Hooper indicates his enthusiasm by overplaying.

September Bowl of Green retrieves one fine song ("Misunderstanding," which Chris Stamey might have written) from the EP, but puts different versions of it (and another swell tune, "Love Comes Around") on the album's Canadian and American editions. The latter replaces the original tracks with similar but inferior productions and mixes by Red Rider chief Tom Cochrane. While the Canadian cassette adds bonus tracks, the US LP release deletes a harmonious rendition of the Beatles' "If I Needed Someone."

Cochrane produced all of **Treehouse**, giving Grapes of Wrath a crisp, clear sound, filled with airy guitar picking, subdued if busy drumming and delectable multi-voice arrangements. Neither novel nor progressive, **Treehouse** is simply flawless electric pop written and played with skill and taste.

Adding keyboard player Vincent Jones, Grapes of Wrath became a quartet in time for **Now and Again**, another delectable record. Producer Anton Fier wraps some of the songs in quietly lush orchestrations; while the gamble doesn't pose a grave threat to the band's personality, neither is it distinct improvement. Tunes performed straight are the most easily appealing; keyboards (some played by guest star Chuck Leavell) provide an agreeable extra dimension. Repeating a peculiar (for a band with no country personality, that is) instrumental feature of **Treehouse**, Pete Kleinow adds pedal steel guitar to a few numbers. [i]

GRAVEDIGGER FIVE

All Black and Hairy (Voxx) 1984
The Mirror Cracked (Voxx) 1987

On their first album, this now-defunct San Diego quintet puts down groovy, authentic-sounding (credit the production by label owner Greg Shaw) garage punk with convincing '60s clumsiness and sincerity. Any band that covers a song ("All Black and Hairy") by Screamin' Lord Sutch is already a few rungs up the cool ladder; the Gravediggers further add to the fun with a singer who fairly approximates the legendary T.S. Bonniwell and perfectly evocative arrangements and licks. If **All Black and Hairy** were twenty years old, it would now be a collectors' item.

Perhaps with that future possibility in mind, the first side of **The Mirror Cracked** consists of rehearsals and perfectly serviceable outtakes (mostly covers; one track features Paula Pierce of the Pandoras) from **All Black and Hairy**. The lo-fi live side, from a 1984 gig, repeats three of the same songs, including the title song and the cool prehensile sexism of "Be a Caveman." [i]

GREATER THAN ONE

Dance of the Cowards (nr/Kunst = Kapital) 1988 ●
London (Wax Trax!) 1989 ●
G Force (Wax Trax!) 1989 ●
Index EP (Wax Trax!) 1991 ●

Compared to other industrial dance bands, this London duo (Lee Newman and Michael Wells) is pretty easy on the ears, assembling their version of synth rhythms, found-sound samples and occasional chanted vocals with a reasonably light touch. Not that the four-sided **London** (which expands **Dance of the Cowards** by six tracks) doesn't rattle the walls now and then, but GTO tends to enfold often political (occasionally operatic) real-life samples (the prosaic "Now Is the Time," presented in two mixes here, includes Martin Luther King's "I Have a Dream" speech and calisthenic directions) in a supportive ambient/rhythmic bed rather than jam on the audio vérité just to pump up the tumult.

The duo favors its own voices and stronger beats on **G Force**, but the record is still fairly accessible. GTO isn't exactly bursting with ideas, but their work is not without imagination ("Why Do Men Have Nipples?" snatches some dopey Alaskan TV dating show, surrounding it with snappy synth percolations) or the power to provide diverting entertainment, on or off club floors. [i]

GREAT PLAINS

The Mark, Don & Mel E.P. (New Age) 1983
Born in a Barn (Homestead) 1984
Naked at the Buy, Sell, and Trade (Homestead) 1985
Sum Things Up (Homestead) 1987 ●
Colorized! (nr/Diabolo) 1989

The Midwest not only provides a home to this casually intellectual Columbus, Ohio, quintet, it also informs their post-collegiate cultural outlook. Following the eight-song **Mark, Don & Mel** mini-album (a giddily rudimentary introduction to the band's non-caloric pop), the offhandedly XTC-styled folk-rock of **Born in a Barn** supports witty lyrics about "Lincoln Logs" (ol' Abe's face appears all over the crypto-religious cover), "Rutherford B. Hayes" and the "Columbus Dispatch." Singer/guitarist Ron House's tentative voice lends unavoidable humility to the simply conceived but eminently likable tunes.

Great Plains Naked at the Buy, Sell, and Trade is even better, a wonderful topical romp that knowingly tweaks the underground rock culture ("Letter to a Fanzine"), the king of music television ("Dick Clark") and themselves ("Real Bad," "Origin of My Silly Grin"). Silly but never unserious, Great Plains is a breath of fresh air in the non-mainstream rock scene. Excellent.

Not only does **Sum Things Up** cap things off, it cranks them up, with the loudest production sound the band has ever used. This is a bad thing, as the group's carefree spirit and charming wit wilts in such a brash environment. The punk psychedelia of "The Wind Blows, the Law Breaks" (featuring Mark Wyatt on organ), for instance, is not just clumsy, it's also too far outside the band's frame of reference to be taken seriously; elsewhere, sloppy guitar playing is amplified into hair-raising ineptitude. There may be a few good songs buried underneath the overcharged arrangements, but wearing other people's clothes ill suits the once great Great Plains. (The cassette and CD have two bonus tracks.) **Colorized!** is a compilation. [i]

See also *Gibson Brothers*.

GREAT UNWASHED

See *Clean*.

JOHN GREAVES & PETER BLEGVAD

Kew. Rhone. (nr/Virgin) 1977

JOHN GREAVES

Accident (Europa) 1982

LONGHOUSE

Longhouse (Warner Bros.) 1988 ●

LODGE

Smell of a Friend (Antilles New Directions) 1988 ●

John Greaves (ex-Henry Cow; music, keyboards) and Peter Blegvad (ex-Slapp Happy; lyrics, guitar) essay a jazzy theatricality on **Kew. Rhone.**, a stunning joint endeavor with vocalist Lisa Herman. Featuring a large cast of new music sidepeople, the album is consistently lyrical and lovely, incredibly precise and enduringly intelligent.

On his first solo venture, Greaves encompasses a wide variety of sounds and moods. Some of the instrumentation on **Accident** recalls Henry Cow, and Greaves employs the Cow principle: if a particular sound doesn't pull you in, one on the next cut might, and all the songs are distinct unto themselves, even on first listening. Greaves' singing, however, is too flat and unemotive to sustain interest.

Released just prior to the Lodge album, **Longhouse** (produced by Anton Fier) is a showcase for Herman's original modern-pop stylings. Something of an analogue to Laura Nyro recordings, the LP is finely commercial and supremely tasteful, but not at all adventurous.

Herman guests on **Smell of a Friend**, the only issue so far from the Lodge, an arty and semi-commercial project formed by Greaves with Fier, guitarist Jakko Jakszyk and two Blegvads: Peter and his singing brother Kristoffer. The album brings intriguing ideas and techniques to bear on what—superficially, at least—are straightforward jazzy pop songs, loading them with delicate content. Like a painting whose fascinating details and subtle plans are revealed only upon close examination, **Smell of a Friend** rewards careful listening with a dose of the intelligence that went into crafting it.

See also *Peter Blegvad, Henry Cow*. [mf/i]

GREEN

EP (Gang Green) 1984
Green (Gang Green) 1986 ●
Elaine MacKenzie (Pravda) 1988 ●
White Soul (Hol. Megadisc) 1989 ●
Bittersweet EP (Bel. Megadisc-Play It Again Sam) 1991
White Soul & Bittersweet [CD] (Widely Distributed) 1991 ●

LILACS

The Lilacs Love You! EP (Widely Distributed-Pravda) 1991

Drawing inspiration from the Kinks, Prince, Small Faces and Motown, Chicago's Green revolves around singer/guitarist Jeff Lescher, an ace songwriter able to shift between a stirring pop-rock voice, ear-pinning scream and scarifying gospelly falsetto. On the debut EP (a four-song 7-inch), the trio overcomes rudimentary production values to skirt nostalgia and introduce Lescher's mix of '60s Anglo-melodicism ("Gotta Getta Record Out," "Better Way"), punky rock ("Not Going Down (Anymore)") and soul ("I Don't Wanna Say No"). Amateurish but inspired.

Re-recorded versions of those songs join ten new ones on **Green**, another inadequately produced but patently brilliant collection of weirdly derivative originals played with spirit and innate power. Occasionally pedestrian lyrics (as on "Big in Japan") don't interfere with the amazing rugged pop tunes, a unique and energetic pairing of merseybeat and punk. "She's Not a Little Girl" seemingly takes its chorus straight out of the Hollies songbook; "Technology" employs a catchy Bolanesque bop; "For You" and "Curry Your Favor" are ballads that display a tender, sensitive side. "I Play the Records" introduces the group's Prince influence, while "She, Probably" is achingly beautiful. An independent album that easily surpasses much of the mainstream competition. (The CD adds three bonus tracks.)

Elaine MacKenzie (neat cover painting by Lescher—look for the original textured paper sleeve) unveils a new rhythm section. Bassist Ken Kurson composed and delivers a pair of bilious demi-punk tunes, supplying albumwide backing vox as well; otherwise, the writing and singing is all Lescher's. Courageous ballads about screwed-up romance (including the haunting "She Was My Girl") coexist with Kinksy nostalgia ("Saturday Afternoon," complete with subtle French horn accompaniment), a frantic Princely falsetto raveup ("My Love's on Fire") and the two-speed "Can't Seem to Get It Thru My Head," which somehow nails the Association to the Miracles. Endearingly corny puns and silly concepts demean songs like "Youth in Asia" and "Radio Caroline" but the group's overwhelming spirit and conviction handily saves the day. (The European CD adds both sides of the 1988 **REM** single— "My Tears Are Dry" and "Love on Thin Air"—named in response to R.E.M.'s **Green** album.)

Hooking up with a Dutch label (which issued the band's catalogue on CD), Green—sporting a new drummer—released another great collection of memorable romantic pop songs. **White Soul** (which ironically downplays the group's R&B side) benefits from two significant steps forward: improved production quality and the consistency and maturity of Lescher's songwriting. (No more punny nonsense or obviously derivative tributes.) Subtle emotions and striking melodies fill simply executed gems like "She's Heaven," "Night After Night," "Monique, Monique" and "I Know"; Kurson's boppy "My Sister Jane" is a delightful pop-punk vestige of his hardcore background.

Green's first release with bassist Clay Tomasek (ex-Slammin' Watusis) in the lineup, the ace **Bittersweet** EP consolidates all of Lescher's many stylistic impulses into five fine new songs. The '60s-soul title track gambles with lush strings and horns but laces it all up in a spectacular vocal; "I'll Have Her" is alluring pop; the brutish hard-rock guitars and punky backing cheers of "Maybe You're Right" are topped off with an inveigling Kinksy melody and Gary Numan synth for a really strange effect. Lescher unloads his professional frustrations in "The Record Company Song," a wry torrent of regret ("I'll do anything you ask/My will is broke and

I'm tired and sad") set to an amazingly catchy rock tune. (The belated American release of **White Soul** includes **Bittersweet**.)

The Lilacs, Kurson's post-Green quartet, made its debut in early '91 with a four-song 7-inch of his witty post-adolescent rock and pop originals, produced by Jim Ellison of Material Issue.   [i]

D. GREENFIELD/J.J. BURNEL
See *Stranglers*.

GREEN ON RED
EP (Green on Red) 1981
Green on Red (Down There) 1982 (Enigma) 1984
Gravity Talks (Slash) 1983
Gas Food Lodging (Enigma) 1985 + 1987 ●
No Free Lunch (Mercury) 1985
The Killer Inside Me (Mercury) 1987 ●
Here Come the Snakes (Restless) 1989 ●
Live at the Town and Country Club (nr/China-Polydor) 1989
This Time Around (nr/China) 1989 (China-Polydor) 1990 φ
Scapegoats (nr/China) 1991 ●

CHRIS CACAVAS AND JUNKYARD LOVE
Chris Cacavas and Junkyard Love (Heyday) 1989 ●

JACK WATERSON
Whose Dog? (Heyday) 1988 ●

WILD GAME
Rhythm Roundup (Dangerous Rhythm) 1984

CHUCK PROPHET
Brother Aldo (Fire) 1990 ●

Many of California's psychedelic revival bands originally drew on spacey/chaotic sources like the Velvet Underground, Pink Floyd or classic trance-inducers like the Serpent Power. But early records by the Phoenix, Arizona-born Green on Red alternately recall the fuzzified raunch of the Electric Prunes/Seeds and the merry flower power of the Strawberry Alarm Clock. Filling the seven tracks of **Green on Red** (not actually their debut: *that* was a little-known self-released 1981 red-vinyl 12-inch, with five songs and no overlap) with buzzing guitars, droning organ and pretty melodies, the quartet delivers transcendental lyrics in a monotonic stupor that precisely suggests total pharmaceutical oblivion. Good studio sound helps convey the sincere nostalgia.

Gravity Talks has a simplified and, in one spot, Dylanized feel. (The title track uses chipper organ and reeling vocals to evoke "Most Likely You Go Your Way (And I'll Go Mine).") Elsewhere, Green on Red largely abandons its previous style in favor of unembellished rock and folk-rock. At the LP's relative weirdest, Chris Cacavas' organ-playing sounds like several genres from the '60s, but only mildly; **Gravity Talks** never becomes as intentionally mannered as its predecessor. Unfortunately, Dan Stuart's not much of a singer and his songwriting could likewise be stronger.

Gas Food Lodging introduces guitarist Chuck Prophet IV to the lineup and adopts a full-scale countrified sound, a mangy cowpoke hybrid somewhere between **Pat Garrett**-era Dylan and old Neil Young. Stuart's boozy singing suits the sloppy playing and demi-melodies; the band's comfortable enthusiasm covers a lot of the record's flaws. (Original US copies were pressed on green vinyl and as a 10-inch; the CD adds a track.)

The country-rocking **No Free Lunch** makes it hard to believe that Green on Red was ever remotely connected to psychedelia. At its most effective, the mini-album includes a cover of Willie Nelson's "Funny How Time Slips Away." Otherwise, the band tries far too hard to fit into the boots of hard-drinkin', populist-minded Amuhricuhns for the contents to be taken seriously. The music is adequate (for a loose, amateurish C&W bar band), but the fake accents and predictable lyrical imagery turn this would-be sincerity into a pretentious muddle.

With drummer Keith Mitchell, fresh from work with David Roback and Kendra Smith, joining the lineup, the freeway cowboys oddly add gospelly backup singers to the country-blues-rock mélange on **The Killer Inside Me**, roughly produced by Jim Dickinson. Stuart's raspy whine announces itself as the record's only consistent focal point; alternately overblown and ragtag arrangements don't help selfconscious tunes like "Clarkesville" and "No Man's Land" stand on their own slender merits.

Backed by a local lineup featuring Alex Chilton bassist Rene Coman and co-producer Jim Dickinson, Stuart and Prophet immersed themselves in Memphis ambience to record the loose and likable **Here Come the Snakes**, an overtly Stonesy record that travels the backroads of American music to fine effect. Again switching easily among rock, blues and country idioms, what's left of Green on Red sounds relaxed and confident, a warm and boozy vehicle for Stuart's amusingly wry regrets and social observations. For once, Green on Red has realized its downwardly mobile ambitions.

Getting Glyn Johns to produce **This Time Around**, the Stuart/Prophet duo (backed by Coman, a drummer and an old-fashioned keyboard player) keep messing around in old Stones turf, but the resonant Memphis mood that made sense of the previous LP is in short supply here. Lacking conviction (or at least credibility), the new songs (like the dismal "Pills and Booze"), while of a similar mind, are more by-the-number constructions than emotional outpourings.

Keyboardist Chris Cacavas sings simple, unassuming rock and country-rock originals (with a nifty jazz slant on "Blue River") in a pleasant voice on his fine solo debut, produced by Steve Wynn. Free of his old band's obligation to sound wasted, Cacavas digs into similar roots and comes up with clearheaded, plain-spoken songs about love and loss, leaving out the ambience and attitude in favor of perceptive lyrics and stout melodies. (The CD and cassette add a bonus track.)

Jack Waterson, who was Green on Red's bassist up through **The Killer Inside Me**, also made his solo debut in '89. With primary instrumental backing by a drummer and ex-Long Ryder bassist Tom Stevens (who also played guitar and produced), the acoustic/electric **Whose Dog?** is one of those records that was probably more fun to make than it is to hear. Waterson is neither a talented singer nor a substantial songwriter, and the album is too loosely organized to build on his efforts.

Prior to joining Green on Red, Chuck Prophet had a San Francisco quartet called Wild Game. The seven-song **Rhythm Roundup** is rather a stylistic roundup, with songs that favor early Dexys (with R&B horns and blurted vocals), crisp country (with Nashville guitar), Jam-like Joe Jackson rock and acoustic hootenanny folk. Weird but promising.

Prophet's solo record—slow, sparsely produced swamp/country rock (imagine Johnny Cash, John Hiatt and John Fogerty swapping songs) with snappy guitar frills—is actually a duo effort with singer Stephanie Finch, who provides honeyed balance to Prophet's rough voice. The material on **Brother Aldo** is simple and homey, flimsy but adequate to the pair's approach, which favors mood more than content. [i]

See also *Danny & Dusty, Giant Sandworms, Naked Prey, Opal.*

GREEN RIVER

Come on Down EP (Homestead) 1985
Dry as a Bone EP (Sub Pop) 1987 ●
Rehab Doll (Sub Pop) 1988 ●

More than any other single band, Seattle's Green River (named for a local serial killer) was responsible for the rise of long-haired dudes in Sub Pop T-shirts standing around in clubs, shaking their manes like so many lost Status Quo guitarists. It's tough to hold that existence-as-a-bad-influence against the group though since, in its prime, Green River was a commanding and awesome unit, and one of the first post-punk units to recapitalize the word ROCK. The combination of Mark Arm's full-throated Ig-chunk vocals and the band's powerful downer-punk-blues-shit still sound mighty nice.

Rehab Doll (the CD and cassette of which add **Dry as a Bone**) is the best example of Green River's neck-twitching meta-bunk, and even includes a few guest moans by Sonic Youth's Kim Gordon. The band dissolved when Mr. Arm rejoined original guitarist Steve Turner (who appears on the six-song **Come on Down**) to form Mudhoney. Green River is less formalist and fuzz-specific than Mudhoney, but it's easy to discern the latter's roots on this earlier vinyl scuzz. [bc]

See also *Mother Love Bone, Mudhoney.*

GREGORY'S FUNHOUSE

Obey (Big Chief) 1988 ●

Brooklyn's own Gregory Ambrose Pittman intones rude sexual euphemisms in a stunningly sepulchral bass voice straight out of "The Monster Mash" as his skilled sidemen sling out winningly poppy goth rock (with nods to early Alice Cooper) on this amusing novelty record. Upholding the gimmick through ten tracks—including the wittily dictatorial "I Give It, You Take It" and a leering cover of "Go Away, Little Girl"—while keeping the guitars on a consistent fuzz boil make **Obey** an impressive (and embarrassingly entertaining) oddity.

[i]

CLIVE GREGSON

Strange Persuasions (nr/Demon) 1985 ●
Welcome to the Workhouse (nr/Special Delivery) 1990 ●

CLIVE GREGSON & CHRISTINE COLLISTER

Home and Away [tape] (nr/Eleventh Hour) 1986
(Cooking Vinyl-Flying Fish) 1987 •
Mischief (nr/Special Delivery) 1987 (Rhino) 1988 •
A Change in the Weather (nr/Special Delivery) 1989
(Rhino) 1990 •

Love Is a Strange Hotel (Rhino New Artists) 1990 ϕ

With minimal outside contributions on drums, horns and backing voices, **Strange Persuasions**, the first solo record by former Any Trouble leader Clive Gregson, is a one-man show that plainly lays out its author's heartbreak and pain. In "Summer Rain," a deeply personal stunner actually based on a friend's experiences, the Mancunian singer/guitarist/songwriter/producer questions the wisdom of a court's child-custody decision; elsewhere Gregson limns love lost and mistakes made with self-critical resignation. Over simple music that is attractive and effective, Gregson sings with pride and dignity, making this a deeply moving document of sincere, honest emotions set into song.

Gregson then formed a lasting partnership with Isle of Man-born vocalist Christine Collister, a guest on **Strange Persuasion** who, like Gregson, has toured and recorded with Richard Thompson. The folky **Home and Away**—recorded at a handful of acoustic 1986 gigs and chez Gregson—handsomely blends her deep, strong voice with his on a broad assortment of originals (Any Trouble material like "Northern Soul" and "All the Time in the World," as well as tunes from **Strange Persuasion**) and classics (Merle Haggard's "Mama Tried," Carl Perkins' "Matchbox," Larry Williams' "Slow Down") that is as warmly likable as it is unaffected.

Mischief fits the same heartfelt songwriting and rich singing into full-blown arrangements, many of them tastefully rocked up with drums (by Any Trouble alumnus Martin Hughes) and electric guitars. Gregson's striking melodies and deeply incisive lyrics are more than adequate to the stronger environment; the duo's voices rise to the occasion as well, making **Mischief** an easy record to like (except perhaps by crabby folk purist misled by the pair's habit of performing with just Gregson's acoustic guitar). Highlights: "Everybody Cheats on You," the unflattering "I Specialise," the mournfully romantic "We're Not Over Yet" and the reluctantly happy "This Tender Trap."

Gregson and Collister successfully raised their ambitions and widened their stylistic reach on **A Change in the Weather**, an even better collection of songs and settings. Joining their voices in more intricate harmonies and testing out more complex material, the duo soars through poignant essays on wife abuse ("This Is the Deal"), mortality ("How Weak I Am"), the hollowness of pop stars and culture ("Jumped Up Madam," the CD-bonus "Temporary Sincerity") and overdriven children ("Talent Will Out"). On a lighter note, Gregson reveals an abiding enthusiasm for Elvis Presley with the witty and personal "(Don't Step in) My Blue Suede Shoes," to which Collister adds a rocking rendition of the King's own "Tryin' to Get to You." A tremendous record without one mediocre or ineffectual track.

Rather than build on **A Change in the Weather**, the duo next cut a simple acoustic collection of quiet cover versions with no outside assistance. From the delightfully surprising (10cc's "Things We Do for Love") to the solid (Merle Haggard's "Today I Started Loving You Again," Bruce Springsteen's "One Step Up") and the sappy (Jackson Browne's "For a Dancer"), **Love Is a Strange Hotel** has a quiet, casual charm but not much backbone. Many of the selections are far from standards (Aztec Camera's "How Men Are," Paul Carrack's "Always Better with You," the Boo Hewerdine/Darden Smith title tune), which leaves the unadorned demo-like performances to stand on their own, and they're altogether too unprepossessing for that.

Released earlier in 1990, **Welcome to the Workhouse** provides a fine footnote to Gregson's early career with ten previously unreleased demos and outtakes recorded alone or with simple accompaniment between 1980 and 1985. Any Trouble songs ("I'll Be Your Man") in drastically different form, band versions of "This Tender Trap" and "Standing in Your Shadow" (both now in the duo's repertoire), an acoustic cover of Michael Jackson's "She's Out of My Life" and several otherwise unavailable Gregsongs make this a rich, significant collection.   [i]

See also *Any Trouble*.

GRID

See *Dave Ball*.

GRONG GRONG

See *King Snake Roost*.

GROOVE B CHILL

Starting from Zero (A&M) 1990 •

Moving into the daisy age, other rap crews have begun taking cues from De La Soul and the Jungle Brothers, rejecting pimp/gangster B-boy roles for ingratiating, soul-based middle-class positivity. This intelligent suburban New York trio's debut (two tracks, including the delightful "Top of the Hill," were produced by the genre's acknowledged master, Prince Paul) has some witty samples, a few entertaining bouts of casual group-singing and two good numbers: "Hip Hop Music" (a clear discussion of rap's significance) and "Reminiscin' " (a charming musical memory with non-sampled quotes from Otis Redding, Al Green, the Association). Though clearly promising, **Starting from Zero** hasn't got quite enough personality for serious fun.   [i]

GUADALCANAL DIARY

Watusi Rodeo EP (Entertainment on Disc) 1983
Walking in the Shadow of the Big Man (DB) 1984
(Elektra) 1985 •
Jamboree (Elektra) 1986
2 X 4 (Elektra) 1987 •
Flip-Flop (Elektra) 1989 •

This underappreciated Georgia quartet distinguished itself from any number of smart, tuneful American guitar combos by combining accessible songcraft with provocatively twisted lyrics. Singer/guitarist Murray Attaway's songs reflect a bizarre variety of far-flung interests, from a preoccupation with the supernatural to a fascination with American cultural imperialism; the band delivers them all with rootsy irony.

Conveying a sense of wonder as well as a sense of humor, **Watusi Rodeo**—which doesn't include the song of the same name—is an appealing debut, with four fine, offbeat numbers (most notably "Michael Rockefeller" and "Dead Eyes," both later re-recorded on **Jamboree**) and sturdy playing.

"Watusi Rodeo," a rollicking tale of American cowboys pillaging African wildlife, *does* appear on Guadalcanal's first longplayer, **Walking in the Shadow of the Big Man**. Produced on the cheap by Don Dixon, the album presents rocking explorations of several of Attaway's pet themes: religious fanaticism ("Why Do the Heathen Rage?"), Civil War mythology ("Trail of Tears") and spontaneous human combustion ("Fire from Heaven"). There's also a pair of enjoyable instrumentals, plus an unlikely (though somehow appropriate) rendition of "Kumbayah."

Jamboree, produced by mainstream Southern-rock specialist Rodney Mills (with two additional tracks helmed by Englishman Steve Nye), features upgraded sound quality and contains some fine tunes, but overall the album is more competent than inspired. Standout tracks include "Pray for Rain," "Fear of God" and the title tune, all of which take dark views of religious faith; "Country Club Gun" and "Cattle Prod" (smartass redneck character studies); and "I See Moe," which uses the head Stooge as a metaphor for unchecked personal aggression.

Dixon—and inspiration—returned for the smashing **2 X 4**, on which the group's members dip into their shadowy art-rock pasts (Attaway once fronted a Yes cover band) to finally create music as distinctive as the lyrics. "Litany (Life Goes On)," "Newborn" and "Winds of Change" sport big, ambitious arrangements that suit their subject matter just fine; "Lips of Steel" is an effective stab at space-rock, while "Say Please" and "Let the Big Wheel Roll" make rude cowpunk noise. Perhaps most impressive, however, is "3 AM," Attaway's quietly harrowing account of alcoholism. The CD adds a good cover of the Beatles' "And Your Bird Can Sing."

Flip-Flop, which proved to be Guadalcanal's final album, finds drummer John Poe emerging as a worthy songwriter, supplanting guitarist Jeff Walls as Guadalcanal's auxiliary composer. Poe's moralistic rockers "Pretty Is as Pretty Does" and "The Likes of You" are among **Flip-Flop**'s highlights, alongside Attaway's sardonically wistful "Always Saturday," the psychedelic "Fade Out" and the wacky singalong ". . . Vista."

When last heard from, Attaway was working on a solo album and Poe had joined Love Tractor.   [hd]

GUMBALL

See *B.A.L.L.*

GUN CLUB

Fire of Love (Ruby) 1981 ●
Miami (Animal) 1982
Death Party EP (nr/Animal) 1983 ●
The Las Vegas Story (Animal) 1984

The Birth the Death the Ghost (nr/ABC) 1984 ●
Sex Beat 81 (Fr. Lolita) 1984
Two Sides of the Beast (nr/Dojo) 1985
Danse Kalinda Boom: Live in Pandora's Box (nr/Dojo) 1985
Mother Juno (Fundamental) 1987 ●
Pastoral Hide and Seek (nr/Fire) 1990 ●

JEFFREY LEE PIERCE

Flamingo EP (nr/Statik) 1985
Wildweed (nr/Statik) 1985

Jeffrey Lee Pierce pulled the Gun Club together in LA around his obsession with the blues. But being unseasoned, young, middle-class, white and barely able to play guitar didn't mean he had to be the blues what the Cramps are to rockabilly. For Pierce, the blues is a highly personal medium through which he can (and does) broadcast/exorcise inner demons.

Fire of Love is bona fide mutant blues, with Pierce using the musical structures and lyrical imagery for his own ends. Exciting, intense—even cathartic—and badly (if appropriately) recorded, with a dash of punk leavening, this also has homey and effective touches like bits of violin and slide guitar (by Ward Dotson and Jeffrey Lee). **Miami** expands to include a little folk, country and pop-rock without diluting the strength one whit, not even via harmony vocalizing (by a pseudonymous Debbie Harry, for one). Producer and Animal magnate Chris Stein does procure a clearer sound, although bringing Pierce's generally strong Jim Morrison-styled vocals to the front of the mix does focus attention on his disconcerting tendency to hit notes sharp. (The cassette adds tracks from the **Death Party** EP.)

The next couple of turbulent years yielded little of value. **Death Party** dates from Pierce's 1983 sojourn in New York with a pick-up edition of Gun Club that includes Bush Tetras drummer Dee Pop and guitarist Jim Duckworth from Panther Burns; it's a lackluster episode that can safely be forgotten. The lineup of the first two albums is documented live on the poorly recorded, indifferently performed **Sex Beat 81** LP; the somewhat better live album on ABC—recorded at various LA shows—features a later lineup, with pre-**Fire of Love** guitarist Kid Congo Powers back in the Club following his stint with the Cramps. There's an overlap of five songs; **The Birth** also has several otherwise unreleased numbers.

By **The Las Vegas Story**, the Club was properly reconstituted (notwithstanding a switch of bassists that brought ex-Legal Weapon/future Sister of Mercy Patricia Morrison into the band). Even with the realigned sound and some guest guitar from Blaster Dave Alvin, it's an uneven album. Evidently intended as a snapshot-mosaic portrait of America, with Pierce attempting to carve himself a Morrison/John Fogerty niche, it simply doesn't wash. That's not to say it's bad—just too unfocused and ineffectual for its ambitious goal. (The issue is further confused by opening Side Two with Pharaoh Sanders' "Master Plan" and following it with "My Man Is Gone Now," from *Porgy and Bess*.) Finally, it's instrumentally too sloppy/punky for the Middle America saga it aspires to be. (The cassette has a bonus track: "Secret Fires.")

With that, the Gun Club fell apart again. As a posthumous live record and the two-disc live/studio compilation **Two Sides of the Beast** were released, Pierce made his solo album, **Wildweed**. Although typically erratic and idiosyncratic, it's his best and most fully formed work since **Fire of Love**. Produced in London by Craig Leon, it's crisply played by a good little band, and Pierce helps himself surprisingly well on lead guitar. All nine songs are strong; if at times the lyrics seem offhand, the music backs it up. He has apparently become a consistently worthwhile songwriter; one can only hope that he gets a chance to develop even further. (There's also a bonus 45 which features silliness like a drunken Pierce reciting a strange poem as if he plans to become his generation's William S. Burroughs.)

Pierce then reformed the Gun Club with Powers and a dandy new rhythm section. Produced in Berlin by Robin Guthrie of the Cocteau Twins, **Mother Juno** is one of the band's best LPs yet. "The Breaking Hands" (a single which resembles some of **Wildweed**), is relatively ornate; the rest takes a no-frills approach, sometimes more hard-rock than usual but entirely suited to Pierce's typically grim visions. The album cover painting (by Claus Castenskiold, known for his Fall sleeves) captures the mood: through a car windshield revealing a pair of dice *and* a plastic Jesus, we see a forlorn couple driving through the desert, a booze bottle on its side on the seat between them. The man's face is grim; the woman's got her eyes covered, but can't help peeking. [jg]

See also *Barracudas, Legal Weapon, Pontiac Brothers, Sisters of Mercy.*

GURU JOSH
Infinity (Deconstruction-RCA) 1990 ●

Paul Walden was not the only former rock'n'roll musician to be converted by Britain's dance explosion of the late 1980s. He was, however, one of the first (after Adamski) to recognize the masses swaying to records at all-night raves as a potential audience. Arriving on stage—often uninvited—with portable keyboards and a sax player by the name of Mad Mick, the self-proclaimed Guru quickly became a fixture at such events, noted as much for his audacious behavior as his acid house melodies. With the track "Infinity," separated from other squiggly keyboard instrumentals by dint of its haunting saxophone melodies, he created a dance anthem and a massive hit single. But by the time he could deliver an album of the same name, the scene had slowed down, and the Guru's constant self-promotion had alienated much of his audience. Leaving aside the embarrassing live cover versions of "Louie Louie" and "Popcorn"—which suggest that the performance quality at raves was lower than the audience's drug-colored memories—**Infinity** is a high-quality electro-dance record, full of lush melodies and warm instrumentals. [tf]

GUT BANK
The Dark Ages (Coyote) 1986

Gut Bank was a Hoboken, NJ, quartet whose original lineup included Sonic Youth drummer Bob Bert as its "token male." The band's sole LP (recorded after Bert's departure; the configuration here includes a female drummer and a male rhythm guitarist) was co-produced with Roger Miller and features a combination of neo-noise guitar crunch and songwriting reminiscent of Patti Smith at her most Stones-worshipful. Beyond the fact that **The Dark Ages** is a decent record, the band's straight-ahead, high-energy shows prefigured those of later non-'60sish gal combos like L7, Babes in Toyland et al. Gut Bank were victims of severe anti-female backlash in the fanzine press, but didn't hang around long enough to destroy their detractors. [bc]

GUTTERBOY
See *Kraut.*

GWAR
Hell-O! (Shimmy-Disc) 1988 ●
Scumdogs of the Universe (Metal Blade-Warner Bros.) 1990 φ

To judge Gwar on its musical merits is like judging Kiss by its lyrics or the Butthole Surfers by Gibby's singing ability. To an even greater extent than any of its illegitimate forefathers, songs and musicianship are just one of the many props in the totality of Gwar, the grandest guignol of heavy metal. Claiming to be the spawn of aliens stranded in Antarctica, Gwar (originally a bunch of creative college students from Richmond, Virginia) perform in bizarre papier-mâché variations on suits of armor; their psychotically theatrical show includes mock decapitations, bestiality, gallons of stage blood and a vocalist with a three-foot fake penis.

By any standard, **Hell-O!** is a terrible album—the songwriting, playing and production (a rare sub-par job by Kramer) are below demo quality, and the vocals are nothing but toneless yelling. However, the lyrics are hilarious, and the album boasts some of the funniest liner notes in rock history, a series of conceptual cartoons that includes a photocopy of Picasso's *Guernica* (retitled "Kickasso's Gwar-nica") defaced with Gwar regalia.

Scumdogs of the Universe is a big improvement, elevating Gwar at least to the musical status of an independent-label thrash band. But there is one memorable track, "Horror of Yig," wherein Gwar meets its ideal production team: Hypo Luxa and Hermes Pan (aka Al Jourgensen and Paul Barker of Ministry), who should have done the whole album. [ja]

H H H H H H H

NINA HAGEN BAND
Nina Hagen Band (nr/CBS) 1979 ●
Unbehagen (nr/CBS) 1980
Nina Hagen Band EP (Columbia) 1980
NINA HAGEN
Nunsexmonkrock (Columbia) 1982
Fearless (Columbia) 1983
Nina Hagen in Ekstasy (Columbia) 1985
Punk Wedding EP (Can. Amok) 1988
Nina Hagen (Ger. Mercury) 1989 ●

Although born in East Berlin, one-of-a-kind singer/
songwriter Nina Hagen is restricted by no national
boundaries, working and living in Germany, England
and America. Her radical approach to vocal expression is
consistently bizarre—she runs the gamut from quirky
sing-song (à la Lene Lovich, whose "Lucky Number"
gets a translation/transmutation on **Unbehagen**) to an
anguished howl (much of **Nunsexmonkrock**). Throughout, Hagen projects amazing intensity as well as a consistent and total lack of selfconsciousness in both
delivery and subject matter.

Nina Hagen Band, her first LP, is relatively restrained; all-German vocals mask the subject matter for
non-linguists. (Although "TV-Glotzer" is an adaptation of the Tubes' "White Punks on Dope.") A serviceable rock trio provides generic rock'n'roll backing
which she easily upstages, even without dipping far into
her seemingly bottomless bag of vocal tricks.

Unbehagen is light years better. While the band
(expanded to a much-improved quartet that later recorded on its own as Spliff) offers convincing, precise
modern rock with neat keyboard work, Hagen sings,
screams, growls, whispers and wails her way through
nine gripping tales of decadence. Listening to **Unbehagen** is like stumbling into a monster's lair—feelings
of revulsion and transfixion mingle to make this true
rock-at-the-edge art.

The American **Nina Hagen Band** EP is a 10-inch
with a pair of songs from each of the first two albums,
including both aforementioned cover versions.

Hagen recorded **Nunsexmonkrock** in New York
with a band that includes both Paul Shaffer and Chris
Spedding. To describe it as wild hardly suffices—the
drugs-sex-religion-politics-mystical imagery that spills
out is nearly incomprehensible in its bag-lady solipsism,
but the music and singing combine into an aural bed of
nails that carries stunning impact. It almost doesn't matter that Hagen sticks to English; what counts is the phenomenal vocal drama. Her range seems limitless, and
the countless characters she plays make this fascinating.

Conceptually outdoing herself again, Hagen enlisted
Giorgio Moroder and Keith Forsey to produce **Fearless**
in California; unlike most of their projects, however, the
artist emerges as the dominant force. The album finds
her in a dance frame of mind, singing about club life

("New York New York"), enlisting the Red Hot Chili
Peppers for a rap number ("What It Is"), doing the
funky Hare Krishna ("I Love Paul") and generally acting the warped disco queen while opening her Felix the
Cat bag of voices to roam operatic to munchkin, Grace
Jones to Mr T. It's not clear whether this alliance with
naked commercialism was expected to deliver a hit
record; Hagen's rampant individuality almost precludes
mass comprehension, let alone full-scale popularity.
Nonetheless, **Fearless**—which bears out its title—is
hypnotic and hilarious. One of her best records.

Reflecting Hagen's continuing fascination with Los
Angeles, **Ekstasy** pursues a similar set of mental and
musical notions. "Universal Radio" and "Gods of
Aquarius" are straightforward (well . . .) and catchy
dance rock with (why not?) metaphysical lyrics. "Russian Reggae" (shades of **Unbehagen**'s "African Reggae") and "1985 Ekstasy Drive" are Hagenized metal;
her "Lord's Prayer" adds new meaning to the word
sacrilegious. But then, for different reasons, so do her
versions of "My Way" (take that, Sid Vicious!) and
Norman Greenbaum's "Spirit in the Sky."

Hagen's 1987 marriage to an 18-year-old hardcore
kid inspired her to cut a four-song EP about it the following year. The self-produced **Punk Wedding** giddily
celebrates the event in English, German, rock and punk
variations littered with the sound of wedding bells and
the wedding march. One hopes the couple's happiness is
more enduring than this amusing but trivial effort.

Nina Hagen is another mishmash of kitsch ("Viva
Las Vegas"), '70s rock (Janis Joplin's "Move Over"),
religiosity ("Ave Maria") and original visions
("Michail, Michail (Gorbachev Rap)," "Live on
Mars"). But Zeus B. Held's witless (and, on the oldies,
disastrous) dance production (with incongruous Hendrix quotes) is a straitjacket, and leaves Hagen—who
makes no effort to escape—sounding like a guest singer
on a Grace Jones record. Snore.   [i]

PAUL HAIG
Rhythm of Life (nr/Crépuscule-Island) 1983
Paul Haig EP (Crépuscule-Island) 1984
Swing in '82 (nr/Crépuscule-Island) 1985
The Warp of Pure Fun (nr/Crépuscule-Island) 1985 ●
European Sun: Archive Collection 1982–1987 (Bel.
  Crépuscule) 1988 ●
Paul Haig (nr/Circa-Virgin) 1989 ●
R.O.L. (nr/Circa-Virgin) 1990 ●

For his first album following the dissolution of Scotland's Josef K, singer-guitarist-keyboardist Paul Haig
enlisted some impressive sidemen—including Anton
Fier, Tom Bailey and Bernie Worrell—and producer
Alex Sadkin. A mostly pleasant but unexceptional and
uneven record, the synth-driven tracks on **Rhythm of
Life** variously resemble lighter-hearted versions of New

Order and the Human League. Haig demonstrates a danceable solution that doesn't bang on your head; some of the numbers, however, do drag along tunelessly, replacing invention with mere repetition and nuance with clumsiness. The subsequent American EP offers five-ninths of the album (a wise condensation) as remixed by an obscure New York club DJ. By leaving off a couple of dogs, it makes a better musical introduction.

The Warp of Pure Fun teams him with ex-Associate Alan Rankine for a slicker, more adventurous and entertaining excursion. Haig's not much of a singer—a little dramatic and gruff for the dance-poppish material—but the nimble arrangements and some resilient melodies cover such deficiencies. "The Only Truth" crosses New Order with the Thompson Twins and, like "Love & War," features Bernard Sumner on guitar; "Heaven Help You Now" injects a bit of folk into synth-rock. A triumph of style over substance, but a likable record with some fine moments.

European Sun compiles several of Haig's singles (including his first solo effort, "Running Away") and unreleased recordings from '82 through '87. A near-rockabilly cover of Suicide's "Ghost Rider" is neat, as is "The Executioner," a disturbing collaboration with Cabaret Voltaire. [i]

See also *Josef K.*

HAIRCUT ONE HUNDRED
Pelican West (Arista) 1982 ●
Paint and Paint (nr/Polydor) 1983

NICK HEYWARD
North of a Miracle (Arista) 1983 ●
Postcards from Home (nr/Arista) 1986 ●
I Love You Avenue (nr/Warner Bros.) 1988 (Reprise) 1989 ●

NICK HEYWARD AND HAIRCUT ONE HUNDRED
The Best of Nick Heyward and Haircut One Hundred (nr/Arista) 1989 ●

One of 1982's bright new chart groups, the six energetic young Londoners of Haircut One Hundred created a crisp mixture of melodic pop and African-American and Latin rhythms, seasoned with horns and an occasional dash of jazz. Haircut's funk-oriented songs tend to be a bit samey (placing three of them—"Favourite Shirts," "Lemon Firebrigade" and "Marine Boy"—together on the American version of **Pelican West** doesn't help); their pop songs are more successful. "Love Plus One" and "Fantastic Day" are delightful, near-perfect confections with hooks that will snare even the tone deaf; "Snow Girl" and "Surprise Me Again" run a close second.

Following leader/singer Nick Heyward's departure for a solo career, Haircut promoted percussionist Mark Fox to frontman and recorded the agreeably bland **Paint and Paint**, which reprises **Pelican West**'s chirpy hummability but not its flashes of ironic wit. The group eventually dissolved, and drummer Blair Cunningham went on to stints with the Pretenders and Echo and the Bunnymen.

Heyward, meanwhile, launched his solo career with the pristinely produced (credit Geoff Emerick) **North of a Miracle**, an awesomely pleasant outing that's every-

thing a disposable pop record should be. Filled with layered vocals ("Whistle Down the Wind" sounds remarkably like the Association) and peppy music played by a large collection of studio hands (including Steve Nieve), the album finds Heyward gracefully adopting a more adult persona with no loss in tunefulness.

But there's a line between disposable and useless, and Heyward's technically proficient but emotionally empty **I Love You Avenue** crosses it. With the songs divided into brassy, insubstantial dance-pop and sappy singer-songwriterism, this self-produced disc is sorely lacking in both character and fun. [ks/i/hd]

HALF JAPANESE
Calling All Girls EP (50 Skidillion Watts) 1977
1/2 Gentlemen/Not Beasts (nr/Armageddon) 1980
Loud (nr/Armageddon) 1981
Horrible EP (Press) 1983
Our Solar System (Iridescence) 1984
Sing No Evil (Iridescence) 1984
Music to Strip By (50 Skidillion Watts) 1987 ●
Charmed Life (50 Skidillion Watts) 1988 ●
The Band That Would Be King (50 Skidillion Watts) 1989 ●
We Are They Who Ache with Amorous Love (T.E.C. Tones-Ralph) 1990 ●

HALF JAPANESE/VELVET MONKEYS
Big Big Sun [tape] (K) 1986

JAD FAIR
The Zombies of Mora Tau EP (nr/Armageddon) 1980 (Press) 1982
Everyone Knew ... but Me (Press) 1982 + 1985
Monarchs (Iridescence) 1984
Best Wishes (Iridescence) 1987
Great Expectations (Ger. Bad Alchemy) 1988
Greater Expectations [CD] (Psycho Acoustic Sounds) 1991 ●

JAD FAIR AND KRAMER
Roll Out the Barrel (Shimmy-Disc) 1988 ●
The Sound of Music (Shimmy-Disc) 1990 ●

JAD FAIR AND DANIEL JOHNSTON
Jad Fair and Daniel Johnston (50 Skidillion Watts) 1989 ●

COO COO ROCKIN TIME
Coo Coo Party Time (50 Skidillion Watts) 1990 ●

Within and without Half Japanese, Maryland (by way of San Francisco) genius Jad Fair, America's preeminent and enormously influential idiot savant of revealingly primitivist rock, has built his professionally amateurish career on a uniquely honest and unselfconscious approach to music making. Originally comprising Jad and his brother David (what must mom and dad have thought?), 1/2 Jap's early records were noisy and slapdash; untuned guitars and an uncertain backup band provided minimalist settings from art rock to pre-punk.

The Fairs recorded **Calling All Girls** alone, cramming nine uninhibitedly neurotic songs ("Shy Around Girls," "Dream Date," "The Worst I'd Ever Do") onto a crude and unsettling 7-inch.

Heavy on the percussion and making no claims to melody, **1/2 Gentlemen/Not Beasts** is a three-record boxed set (!) that combines elementary musicianship and electronics with tuneless vocals bursting with angst and ennui. Nods to Devo, the Ramones and Iggy Pop (whose "Fun Time" gets crushed) indicate that the atonal, jagged results are no accident. Many favorite punk tunes are "covered" with surprising results.

Loud expands the music's range, with help from six-part accompaniment, including horns, more guitar and almost avant-garde drumming. The tendency towards jazz doesn't strip Half Japanese of its atavistic charm or chaotic raucousness. **Loud** includes a dirge-like rendition of Jim Morrison's "The Spy."

Horrible, the pair's first release after a long vinyl silence, is a five-song 12-inch obsessed with ghouls and horror movies. "Thing with a Hook" matches the tale of a one-handed insane man-beast "pulling heads off boy/girlfriends down in lover's lane" with truly distressing music; other tracks are about "Vampire" and "Rosemary's Baby." Where the Cramps do this type of cinematic craziness for fun, Half Japanese sounds genuinely tormented.

Music to Strip By, produced (and played on) by Kramer (the Shimmy-Disc mogul who had been a mainstay of Shockability) and pressed on clear red vinyl, is a relatively sophisticated and appealing outing by a full-fledged band that might have actually rehearsed a few times. Working without his brother, Jad is comfortably in control, singing typically strange lyrics in a typically artless voice. "Stripping for Cash" reflects a recent news item; "My Sordid Past" and the countryfied "Ouija Board Summons Satan" scan like what they probably are—lifts from a supermarket tabloid. "Sex at Your Parents' House" would be funnier if it weren't being sung with apparent conviction by an adult. Versions of "La Bamba," Fats Domino's "Blue Monday" and Willie Dixon's "Hidden Charms" add to the stability of this eminently likable 22-song album.

David Fair rejoined the band (which at this point included Don Fleming of Washington DC's Velvet Monkeys, with whom Half Japanese once shared a live cassette release) on **Charmed Life**, contributing lyrics as well as guitar and harmonica. This solidly entertaining record finds a presentably casual form for Jad's wonderful (and not at all creepy) way of looking at life. Gripped in the throes of romance ("I always thought love would change things/And now I know," he sings), Jad gushes about romance, poets and miracles with infectious conviction, making songs like "Penny in the Fountain," "Miracles Happen Every Day" (with fine sax work by John Dreyfuss) and the mildly bitter "One Million Kisses" exemplary outpourings of informed naïveté. (The cassette and CD have ten bonus tracks, bringing the total to 31!)

Besides Fleming (guitar) and producer Kramer (organ, bass), **The Band That Would Be King** gets instrumental contributions from Fred Frith and John Zorn. (No David Fair this time.) Fortunately, all that talent doesn't impede Jad's ability to be himself—he just has to sing a little louder to be heard over the friendly hubbub. Taking on more varied subject matter (which now seems clearly fictionalized and not at all personal) than the rapturous **Charmed Life**, this 30-song collection visits "Daytona Beach," reveals "My Most Embarrassing Moment," delivers the "Curse of the Doll People" and attacks "Ventriloquism Made Easy." A lot of the

songs are fragmentary, and the music—a sloppy mess of guitars, harmonica and saxophones—sounds largely improvised, but a few tunes ("Some Things Last a Long Time," "Postcard from Far Away," etc.) are genuinely delightful.

Compared to **We Are They Who Ache**, however, **The Band That Would Be King** is a mainstream masterpiece. With a rotating stack of fellow noisemakers, Jad manages to deliver some quietly cogent (if unexceptional) performances ("The Titanic," "All of Me," "Three Rings," "Secret" and a few others), but a sizable chunk of the record is unlistenably indulgent nonsense. A couple of thrashy rock covers ("Gloria," "Going Home," "Up and Down") are lost in amateurish overmodulation and should really have stayed in the cassette recorder; other tracks are just noisy improvs in the musical sandbox.

Jad's solo records have generally been weirder than Half Japanese's, but that's a rather rarefied judgment. **Everyone Knew . . . but Me** contains 29 sessions (mostly originals about girls, but two James Brown covers as well) of him whining and vocalizing (singing isn't exactly the word for it), accompanying himself on what sound like pots, pans and guitar. Emerging amid all the painful primitivism, however, is touching defenselessness, a pitiful lack of social abilities and success.

The one-man **Best Wishes**, recorded between 1982 and 1985, is a collection of 42 brief instrumentals, all titled either "O.K." or "A.O.K." Listenable? Yes—in brief spurts, as long as you keep the volume down and don't pay too close attention. Creatively significant? Er, no.

To call Jad's non-solo/non-band efforts "collaborations" would be misleading. He simply proceeds, blinders on, to do his "thing" while his partner du jour scurries to keep up. There's precious little give and take, and therein lies the difficulty with the pair of virtually interchangeable Fair/Kramer outings. As a skilled producer, Kramer contributes plenty of atmosphere, but little (needed) direction. **Roll Out the Barrel** is, by a nose, the better-realized of the two: 24 short tracks (including nine condensed covers from sources as oddly appropriate Bob Dylan, whose "Subterranean Homesick Blues" is turned into an unintelligible B-movie jungle hunt score, and Hoagy Carmichael) that offer up some steep peaks and deep, deep valleys. **Sound of Music** repeats virtually all the above tricks, but dons the sensible shoes of (college) radio-readiness, thereby bulldozing most of the peaks.

The Daniel Johnston disc (which really oughta be subtitled "Dueling Neuroses") is much more gripping, if somewhat painful to endure. The instrumentation on Fair's earlier work may have been amateurish, but the toy piano and de-tuned guitar here is positively novitiate. Johnston bubbles over with the album's best, most hyperactively excited moment ("I Met Roky Erickson"), but the handful of co-written pieces (like the squalling "Frankenstein Conquers the World") occasionally deliver. Most moving though, is the duo's take on Phil Ochs' "Chords of Fame," which has rarely rung truer.

Declaring himself the King of Coo Coo Rockin Time, David Fair takes his solo band out for a spin on **Coo Coo Party Time**, a casual and kooky rock'n'roll record with one foot in the '50s and the other in a typically Fairian can of '80s whimsy. With John Dreyfuss' sax blaring in the foreground, Fair (who wrote all the lyrics and painted the creepy cover) sings about such vintage subjects as "All-Night Drive-In Movie Party," "Rock Me Daddy-O" and "Oldsmobile Girl Magnet 88" and agitates for more good music in "Plenty of Room on the Radio," the anti-CD "Put Records Back in the Record Store" (ironic, considering) and "Coo Coo Record Party Time," which offers this great suggestion: "If you buy a record that you don't like/Don't be upset by that/Just get an iron and heat it up/And iron the record flat/Iron out all the old songs/Until it's smooth again/Then scratch in a new line round and round/With a knife or the point of a pin." [sg/i/dss]

See also *Daniel Johnston, Maureen Tucker, Velvet Monkeys*.

HALF MAN HALF BISCUIT

Back in the D.H.S.S. (nr/Probe Plus) 1985 ●
The Trumpton Riots EP (nr/Probe Plus) 1986 ●
Back Again in the D.H.S.S. (nr/Probe Plus) 1987 ●
The Peel Sessions EP (nr/Strange Fruit) 1988 ●
ACD [CD] (nr/Probe Plus) 1989 ●

This entertaining Liverpool quintet emerged from total obscurity to become a dominant British indie chart regular in the first half of 1986. Playing low-key garage-punk singalong ditties (imagine a cross between Mark Riley and Jonathan Richman), the Biscuits like to name names—songs on **Back in the D.H.S.S.** include "Fuckin' 'ell, It's Fred Titmus," "The Len Ganley Stance" and "99% of Gargoyles Look Like Bob Todd." Throughout, they remain completely unassuming, and exhibit a dry, sarcastic wit. A top-notch debut.

The Trumpton Riots EP is a little heavier—with raw drive and distorted synths, the snarling title cut and "Architecture, Morality, Ted and Alice" are both reminiscent of the early Stranglers. Side Two lightens up with the more hilarious "1966 and All That." Fans should look for the edition which adds a fifth track, "All I Want for Christmas Is a Dukla Prague Away Kit," the best soccer song since the Fall's "Kicker Conspiracy."

Half Man Half Biscuit called it quits in 1987, hence the title of their second album, **Back Again in the D.H.S.S.** (Department of Health and Social Services—where Britons get their unemployment checks). Some of the **Trumpton Riots** cuts are reprised, as is the penchant for titles with real-life stars ("Rod Hull Is Alive—Why?" and "The Bastard Son of Dean Friedman"). The band is a bit tighter this go-around, and has cleaner (but hardly what you'd call glossy) production. The record's highlight is "Dickie Davies Eyes," which contains the inspirational verse, "And all those people who you romantically like to still believe are alive are dead/ So I'll wipe my snot on the arm of your chair/as you put another Roger Dean poster on the wall." No folks, it doesn't get any better than this.

Apparently bored with the dole, HMHB reformed and began playing again in 1990. Along came the **ACD** compilation, seventeen tracks taken from **Back Again** and Peel sessions, plus live versions of material from the first album and **Trumpton Riots**. Catchy, irreverent and always funny (even if their humor is on the level of football hooligans), it's good to have this crew around again. Ever hear a crowd shout "Fuckin' 'ell, it's Fred Titmus!" on cue? [dgs]

JOHN S. HALL

See *King Missile (Dog Fly Religion)*.

MICHAEL HALL

See *Wild Seeds*.

HALO OF FLIES

Garbage Rock! EP (Twin/Tone) 1987
Headburn EP (Amphetamine Reptile) 1987
Garbageburn (nr/What Goes On) 1988
Four from the Bottom [tape] (Amphetamine Reptile) 1988
Singles Going Nowhere (Ger. Amphetamine
   Reptile-Glitterhouse) 1990 ●
Death of a Fly EP (Amphetamine Reptile) 1990
Live EP (Silt Breeze) 1990
Winged EP (Forced Exposure) 1990

Revered and reviled (both, generally, for all the wrong reasons) by post-mods scattered across many lands, this Minneapolis (but don't think that reveals anything) trio has consistently chiseled out the most physically and cerebrally assaultive post-hardcore you'll ever hear. Leader Tom Hazelmyer, who pulled stints in both Otto's Chemical Lounge and the Marines (not a band), has become a counter-counterculture guru of sorts for folks whose righteous disaffection extends to most things "alternative." His persona, aptly self-assessed as "sexist, homophobic, pro-vivisectionist straight-edge litterbug," colors, with varying degrees of irony, virtually all the plentiful releases on his own Amphetamine Reptile label.

Halo of Flies initially doled out tightly wound, intricately improvisational punk rock in impossibly limited editions that believers prize like slivers of the True Cross. Those who missed out can catch up with **Four from the Bottom**, a cassette that compiles the entire contents of the band's four AmRep 7-inches, or the similar **Singles Going Nowhere** (the cover of which is a careful tribute to the Buzzcocks' **Singles Going Steady**), which omits a few of those tracks but adds a two-song salvo (a cover of the Creation's "How Does It Feel to Feel" and the MC5's "I Want You Right Now" retitled "Drunk in Detroit") that hints at Halo's live power. Both are bracing samplers of the band's sub-three-minute virtuosity.

Moving up to 12-inch releases, Halo displays greater savvy in both studio usage and song structure; though the intensity dips just a notch on **Garbage Rock!**, Hazelmyer's spinning, Hendrix-on-Carbona guitar implosions occur regularly enough to sate the feedback-dependent. **Headburn**, however, brings it all together, with disjointed lyrics that have become more violent (apocalyptic, even) in their reflexive response to the outside world. What's more, the rhythm section's brute force can be felt for the first time. Combined in the UK as **Garbageburn**, these two discs provide the easiest entree into an otherwise hermetically sealed universe.

Between breakups, Halo of Flies continues to sporadically disgorge small-scale releases. **Death of a Fly** retreats to basic sonic cruelty, while **Winged** takes a sharp U-turn towards conceptual territory with an all-covers, all-insect bill of fare, highlighted by a version of the Cramps' "Human Fly." It's the live EP, however, that best captures the surly Halo spirit, from the opening

299

"This whole fucking city needs a haircut!" through the screeching coda of "Ballad of Extreme Hate," Hazelmyer and his unit reassert their place as an essential kink in the gears of alternative rock's gravy train.

[dss]

LUCY HAMILTON
See *Lydia Lunch*.

PETER HAMMILL
Nadir's Big Chance (nr/Charisma) 1975 (Blue Plate) 1990 ●

A remark by Johnny Rotten citing Peter Hammill's **Nadir's Big Chance** as an influence cast a brief but bright UK hip-media spotlight on an artist who has otherwise spent most of his long career in the shadows. (Lydon later publicly insulted Hammill—not rotten enough?)

In 1966, while at university in Manchester, the London-born Hammill formed Van der Graaf Generator, a progressive-rock band that had just enough success to remain an active loss-leader for years. Not as hollowly contrived as many likeminded explorers, VdGG's guitar-bass-drums-organ-sax lineup featured no virtuosos. Actually, the band's chief instrument was Hammill's baritone voice, able to swoop into adjacent registers and rasp wickedly like nobody's business. If anything has put people off Hammill, it's been the occasional overkill of his delivery and lyrics, which commonly concern extremists, and the direst contortions into which intellect and emotion can twist each other. He has no compunction about singing from a point of view which he—or we—may only inhabit at a moment of extraordinary emotional duress.

Until the group's demise in 1978, Hammill split his studio time between Van der Graaf (ten LPs) and solo recordings made with some or all of his bandmates. The most influential and best remembered of these is the 1975 LP (Hammill's fifth) for which he assumed the identity of "anarchic" teenager Rikki Nadir. While some tunes and arrangements may be simpler than his usual, none of it's really punk, rather more like **Hunky Dory**, though less image-conscious, much bleaker, more confessional and barely produced at all. A stimulating, affecting record.

Hammill has continued to churn out solo LPs (even to this day with the help of ex-VdGG people, as well as ex-Vibrators guitarist John Ellis). Musically, he has modernized somewhat, but he's still his own unpretentiously pretentious self. Or is that pretentiously unpretentious?

[jg]

HAND OF GLORY
See *LeRoi Brothers*.

HANGMANS BEAUTIFUL DAUGHTERS
Trash Mantra EP (nr/Dreamworld) 1987
The Hangmans Beautiful Daughters (Voxx) 1989

Daniel Treacy of the TV Personalities co-produced, plays keyboards and wrote a few songs for this trippy London quartet (named for a 1968 Incredible String Band album), whose sound isn't as kooky or stylized as his. On the 12-inch EP and the overlapping (all six tracks) album, Emily Brown sings mildly psychedelic '60s pop in a wispy, imperfect-pitch voice as her three bandmates play droney (but brisk) 12-string folk-rock with cute accents like finger cymbals and harpsichord. Things improve a bit when guitarist Gordeen Dawson sings lead on the modish "Something About Today," but the disappointing fact is that the group's image is more colorful than its music.

[i]

HAPPY FLOWERS
Songs for Children EP (Catch Trout) 1985
Now We Are Six EP (Catch Trout) 1986
Making the Bunny Pay (Catch Trout) 1987
My Skin Covers My Body (Homestead) 1987
I Crush Bozo (Homestead) 1988
Oof (Homestead) 1989 ●
Too Many Bunnies (Not Enough Mittens) [CD] (Homestead) 1989 ●
Lasterday I Was Been Bad (Homestead) 1990 ●

LANDLORDS
Hey! Its a Teenage House Party! (Catch Trout) 1985
Our Favorite Songs! EP (Catch Trout) 1987

This Charlottesville, Virginia, duo of Mr. Anus (Charlie Kramer) and Mr. Horribly-Charred-Infant (John Beers) has built a distinctive and unexpectedly productive career out of tuneless sub-garage childhood-trauma rants. The pair's spontaneously composed primal scream tragicomedies recount a litany of prepubescent horrors with an oddly compassionate mix of humor and pathos, adding up to a surprisingly compelling aesthetic that's unlike anything else in underground rock.

Making the Bunny Pay (a 12-inch which compiles the band's two early 7-inch EPs: the three-cut **Songs for Children** and the six-song **Now We Are Six**), **My Skin Covers My Body** and **I Crush Bozo** all effectively evoke a harrowing world of junior angst; titles like "Mom and Dad Like the Baby More Than Me," "I Wet the Bed Again," "All My Toys Hate Me," "There's a Worm in My Hand" and "I Saw My Picture on a Milk Carton" give a good indication of the songs' contents. (And, for those not artistically inclined towards Happy Flowers' jolly preference for indulgent inarticulate rage over traditional musicality, about all the entertainment value they are likely to provide.) These enormously entertaining records are, to put it as mildly as possible, an acquired taste.

Oof covers similar subject matter, but vague hints of accessibility can be heard (if you listen *real* close) creeping into such numbers as "BB Gun" and "There's a Soft Spot on the Baby's Head"; Messrs. Anus and Infant even attempt the blues on "Ain't Got Nothin'." Most shockingly, though, **Oof**'s final track, a cover of Yoko Ono's "Mrs. Lennon," actually conforms to traditional Western notions of melody and song structure. (On CD and cassette, that song is followed by one of the two bonus tracks, "Charlie Said the F-word Again.")

Though it'll still probably sound like a bunch of noise to your mom, **Lasterday I Was Been Bad** ("recorded live in the studio . . . no mixing, no dubbing") makes a few more lurches in the direction of melody, with fairly straightforward covers of Big Star ("Thirteen'') and UFO ("I Don't Want to Share"), hard-rockish originals "Call Me Pudge" and "If This Gun Were Real (I Could Shoot You and Sleep in the Big Bed with Mommy)," and the serenely womblike instrumental "Embryo." Still, "Not a Happy Birthday," "Leave Me Alone" and "I Shouldn't Have Eaten That Stuff" demonstrate that the Flowers haven't yet outgrown their bangin'-and-yellin' stage just yet.

Too Many Bunnies (Not Enough Mittens) is a 26-item CD compilation: LP tracks, singles, outtakes, compilation cuts and "I Crush Bozo," which had appeared as one of two cassette-only bonuses on the album of the same name. (The tape version of **My Skin Covers My Body**—an LP which contains a remake of **Songs for Children**'s "Mom, I Gave the Cat Some Acid"—also has two extra tracks, but neither appears here.)

Before forming Happy Flowers, Kramer (guitar) and Beers (vocals) were half of the Landlords, a freewheeling punk band with an incisive sense of satire but no special musical merits. (Landlords bassist Eddie Jetlag continues to wield his influence, penning liner notes for several Happy Flowers records.) The band's lone album offers intelligently ironic songs about rape, bigotry, kids, suicide and nihilism; the 7-inch EP (recorded after the Flowers were underway) contains nose-thumbing punk-pop covers of "The Night Chicago Died," Leonard Cohen's "Suzanne" and two more. [hd/i]

HAPPY HATE ME NOTS

Scrap EP (Aus. Waterfront) 1987
Out (Waterfront-Rough Trade) 1988 ●

Playing power pop with muscle, this Sydney quartet—sort of a punkier, street-level Hoodoo Gurus—fills **Scrap** with six spunky songs about love and introspection that are both fresh-sounding and high on buoyant energy. Guitarists Paul Berwick and Tim McKay intertwine and interact—one a warm box filled with enough fuzz to choke a lint screen, the other dripping shimmering droplets of clear, clean shine—in "This Is the Wrong World." Horn (on "Go Away"), piano (on "Blue Afternoon") and choral refrains throughout paint the other songs with frown-proof commercialism that never stoops to please.

Berwick's amusedly pessimistic lyrics ("Things Wearing Thin," "Think About Tomorrow," "Modern Times") and strong rock'n'roll vocals give **Out**'s fast-paced and sturdy tunes, occasionally punctuated by a horn section, a Jam-like intensity. Producer Rob Younger (ex-Radio Birdman) captures the live-and-loud sound with all of the quartet's nuance intact, making **Out** a robust demonstration of the Hate Me Nots' amazing ability to give songs a wallop without knocking the pop stuffing out of them.

By the end of '90, the Hate Me Nots had recorded an album's worth of new material, with an eye towards '91 release. ['e/i]

HAPPY MONDAYS

Squirrel and G-Man Twenty Four Hour Party People Plastic Face Carnt Smile (White Out) (nr/Factory) 1987 ●
Bummed (nr/Factory) 1988 (Elektra) 1989 ●
Madchester, Rave On (nr/Factory) 1989 ●

Hallelujah EP (Elektra) 1989 ●
Peel Session EP (nr/Strange Fruit) 1990 (Strange Fruit-Dutch East India) 1991 ●
Pills'n'Thrills and Bellyaches (Elektra) 1990 ●

To call Manchester's Happy Mondays one of the most significant and influential rock groups to emerge in England since the Smiths would not be an indulgence in hyperbole. Together since 1981, the Mondays came to prominence as leaders of the late-'80s British rave scene, a hedonistic party-oriented club culture characterized by its participants' preference for baggy clothes, LSD and the euphoric drug Ecstasy (the E of countless song titles). The Mondays' carefully evolved sound—an odd, trancelike hybrid of '60s flower-power rock, cheesy '70s R&B and '80s acid house, accompanied by the straining, stream-of-unconsciousness words of vocalist Shaun Ryder—became the blueprint for numerous local (later global) imitators. A sextet that includes dancer/drug-tester Bez (Mark Berry), the Mondays are favorites of the British tabloids, which have made much of the members' controlled-substance exploits and generally daft behavior.

Those searching for the key to the Mondays' success won't find it on the bizarrely titled debut, a rather low-key batch of mostly meandering funk tunes, produced with no apparent flourishes by John Cale. Over such transparent and repetitive backing, it's hard not to notice how off-key Ryder's vocals are. Although "Oasis," "24 HR Party People" and "Kuff Dam" are all designed to reflect/support the burgeoning dance phenomenon, the record is no timeless pop classic. One surprise: the gloomy Cure-like intro to "Cob 20."

Martin Hannett (the legendary punk-era producer who died of a heart attack in 1991) stepped in to produce the livelier **Bummed**, the Mondays' pivotal release. (Available in DAT for you techno hounds.) Over liquid, hypnotic grooves supplied by what has become an extremely competent band, Ryder spouts frequently unintelligible lyrics that, by his own admission, don't mean anything but lend the songs a quirky character.

A Vince Clarke remix of **Bummed**'s "Wrote for Luck" appended to the album's CD edition spelled out the discofied direction the band was to take on its next British release, the **Madchester, Rave On** EP, lengthened and issued in the US as **Hallelujah**. Employing no less than four remixers, the seven-track, five-song American edition is a great dance record. Whether it rewards casual listening depends on one's tolerance for lysergically loosened music that quite noticeably, and successfully, sounds a bit off.

Having made a sizable commercial impression in Great Britain, the Mondays then released their bid for world domination. **Pills'n'Thrills and Bellyaches** is a luscious hodgepodge of the dodgiest of post-punk influences—a Labelle quote on "Kinky Afro," the Salsoul string sound on "Dennis and Lois," the "Sweet Jane" references on "Harmony"—all reinforced by the sturdy production of Steve Osborne and Manc DJ Paul Oakenfold. More so than on the other records, Ryder's uncensored rough-hewn lyrics (when understandable) are offhandedly funny, as in the fashion tribute of "Loose Fit."

The **Peel Session** EP, which was recorded in 1989, contains three songs: "Tart Tart," "Mad Cyril" and "Do It Better." [db]

301

PEARL HARBOR AND THE EXPLOSIONS

Pearl Harbor and the Explosions (Warner Bros.) 1980

PEARL HARBOUR

Don't Follow Me, I'm Lost Too (Warner Bros.) 1981
Pearls Galore! (Island) 1984

Pearl Harbor and the Explosions came out of San Francisco's early new wave scene, but their lone album consists of bouncy little pop tunes suitable for FM radio: watered-down soul and funk overtones topped off by Pearl E. Gates' theatrical vocal posturings. Danceably forgettable.

Harbour (dropping Gates and adopting the British spelling) hit her stride as a solo artist on **Don't Follow Me, I'm Lost Too**, a headlong plunge into rockabilly and similarly ancient styles. Smothered by producer Mickey Gallagher in waves of flutter echo, Pearl wails like a demon, obviously happy to have a sympathetic setting. "Fujiyama Mama" and "At the Dentist" rock wildly with old-fashioned panache; "Heaven Is Gonna Be Empty" takes a more countryfied, though equally quaint, approach. This one's a memorable instant party.

A belated follow-up produced by Richard Gottehrer employs twenty musicians—from Ellie Greenwich to Chris Spedding to Masa Hiro Kajiura—for more fun in the old world. Harbour starts off by covering that 1963 Rocky Fellers chestnut, "Killer Joe," and then launches into a program of girl-group soundalikes that quiver with melodic conviction and shake with appropriate, cliché-free backing. Sounding uncannily like Kirsty MacColl in spots, **Pearls Galore!** is a winning collection of tunes by a talented, adaptable vocalist who should be far better known than she is. [jy/i]

See also *Chrome, Henry Kaiser*.

JOHN WESLEY HARDING

It Happened One Night (nr/Demon) 1988 ●
God Made Me Do It: The Christmas EP (Sire-Reprise) 1989 ●
Here Comes the Groom (Sire-Reprise) 1989 ●
The Name Above the Title (Sire-Reprise) 1991 ●

Onto a stage that has already supported three decades of witty and wise topical troubadours strides England's John Wesley Harding (real name: Wesley Harding Stace), well-armed to find a place among the ghosts of Bob Dylan, Phil Ochs, Elvis Costello and Billy Bragg. Wes' folky debut, a friendly but unconvincing acoustic album recorded live in London, offers simple tales about common people and humorously pointed satire. (There's an especially clever number about Live Aid.) He's not a strong melodicist, and his lyrics can be a bit artless, but Harding's voice and personality are disarming, and a few of the songs ("The Devil in Me," "Famous Man," "You and Your Career") are quite pungent.

With three new tunes, a handsome cover of Madonna's "Like a Prayer" and a wacky nine-minute natter between Wes and the inimitable Viv Stanshall, the promising **God Made Me Do It** (the title a lyric from "Here Comes the Groom," included on the EP) indicates what Harding can do in a studio with an ace band (dubbed the Good Liars) that includes ex-Attractions Pete and Bruce Thomas.

Crisply produced by Andy Paley, and reprising several numbers from the live LP, the delightful **Here Comes the Groom** is a fine modern realization of the same honest singing and playing that typified England's pub-rock graduates, informed by a solid knowledge of pop music and its traditions. (In a no-tech variation on spot-that-sample, Wes makes reference to everyone from the Everly Brothers to Steve Miller to Junior Walker to John Otway.) With a load of great (nontopical) songs, the album's only problem is Harding's too-cozy-by-half relationship with the melodies and phrasing of early Elvis Costello.

If Wes spent too much of the last album hanging around Elvis' house picking things up, **The Name Above the Title** simply backs up a truck to the Mac-Manus residence and tries to cart it all away. While Harding doesn't sound as if he's intentionally trying to imitate anybody, there's no getting around the way it comes out. And while he brings plenty of talent and originality (especially the lyrics, which are strictly his own style) to this enjoyable and intelligent party, the frequent resemblance to Costello gives what is in fact a fine album a waxy air of familiarity. [i]

HARD-ONS

Smell My Finger (Aus. Waterhouse) 1986
Hard-Ons (Big Time) 1987
Hot for Your Love, Baby (Aus. Waterfront) 1987
Worst of the Hard-Ons (nr/Vinyl Solution) 1987
Dickcheese (Taang!) 1988 ●
Love Is a Battlefield of Wounded Hearts (Taang!) 1989 ●
Yummy! (Aus. Waterfront) 1990

STUPIDS AND HARD-ONS

No Cheese! (Aus. Waterfront) 1988

Possessing roughly the same obsessions as a B-grade nerd comedy, Australia's premier surf-punks sing about farting, kissing, sex and rejection with various levels of goodnatured crudity. The Sydney trio—Blackie (guitar), Keish (drums/vocals) and Ray (bass/artwork)—has been tooling around since 1980, having a good pubescent laugh and playing some really great tuneful punk rock.

Ray's "granny" drawing on the original Australian issue of **Smell My Finger** was nixed for the US, where the title was changed as well (to **Hard-Ons**). But the songs—from teen angst punk with Descendents-like melodies to more lash'n'thrash like "Dancing Girls"—remained untouched.

More bubblepunk than raw bashing, **Hot for Your Love, Baby** has "I Wanted Everything," in which Keish and crew sound like spoiled schoolkids on a rampage. While the upfront vocals on "Love Song for Cindy" could be an elementary school poetry project, there's catchy redemption in its sophomoric simplicity. The album's British edition (on Vinyl Solution) adds the raveup "All Set to Go."

With between-track vignettes and high-speed slashers like "Fuck Society" and "Yuppies Suck," the heavier-sounding **Dickcheese** thrusts the Hard-Ons towards metal. The vinyl has eighteen tracks; the CD and cassette add three, including a rendition of Kiss' "Rock and Roll All Nite." (**No Cheese!** is an eight-song document of the Hard-Ons' tour with British hardcore humorists, the Stupids.)

Love Is a Battlefield brings the Hard-Ons back to pop punk, though the tunes are generally less memorable than the group's early singles. While some songs seem genuinely romantic (the nifty "I Don't Wanna See You Cry") and others lay belly-up, there's mindless fun in the Satan-shrouded "Kill Your Mum" and the scrubbed-clean "Missing You, Missing Me." The CD adds a bonus bone.

Yummy!'s "Feast on Flesh" revs to hardcore velocity, and a few guitar twists distinguish "Something I Don't Want to Do," but few other tracks stand out as they breeze along. Still, the band's acoustic bludgeoning of "Stairway to Heaven" is carefree, basic and amusing—a fair description of the Hard-Ons as well.

[mg]

HARM FARM
Spawn (Alias) 1990 ●
Nice Job, Einstein (Alias) 1991 ●

Because of their San Francisco home, prominent use of violin and spirited instrumental forays into ethnic territories, Harm Farm has no doubt gotten used to seeing the name Camper Van Beethoven mentioned in the first paragraphs of their clippings. CVB's hijacking of original violinist Morgan Fichter would have doomed lesser bands, but Harm Farm survived, stronger than ever. Drummer Noah Chasin deftly jumped to fiddle, and Melanie Clarin (who played vital roles in the exceptional recorded outputs of both the Cat Heads and Donner Party) stepped in behind the skins. Produced by Henry Kaiser, **Spawn** is Appalachian mountain music on a skewer, waved about in all directions, raising up dust, and spearing bits of whatever it finds. The quartet is at its impressive best on wild twisted-tempo medleys like "Sleep/Señor Tuchus" and "Snapdragons Greeneyedgirl," and at its excusable worst on the intentionally silly (but still fairly irritating) "Clams." Strong debut.

[sm]

See also *Camper Van Beethoven, Cat Heads, Donner Party.*

HARMONY
See *Boogie Down Productions.*

CHARLIE HARPER
See *U.K. Subs.*

JODY HARRIS
It Happened One Night (Press) 1982

JODY HARRIS AND ROBERT QUINE
Escape (Lust/Unlust) 1981

Jody Harris has worked with such New York luminaries as the Raybeats and James White and the Blacks, but remains one of the most underrated guitarists on the scene. His schizophrenic solo album proves him to be an accomplished composer as well, turning his talents toward straight pop ("It Happened One Night"), rockabilly ("I'm After Hours Again"), blues ("You Better Read This Before You Sign") and various forms of jazz, from be-bop to Stephane Grappelli. Harris amply proves that old forms can be given new life, especially with his exquisite, modernistic guitar work.

Along with Robert Quine (Richard Hell's Voidoids, later of Lou Reed's band) Harris made the beautiful **Escape**, which drifts through a plethora of styles—Frippist drone tunes, jazz, country swing—and proves that these two consistently surprising guitarists are even more surprising than suspected. Though hardly rock, **Escape** has a vitality and joy missing in most music today, and so much fun it's sexy. Highly recommended.

[sg]

See also *James Chance, Richard Hell, Raybeats, Lou Reed.*

JOEY HARRIS AND THE SPEEDSTERS
See *Beat Farmers.*

JERRY HARRISON
The Red and the Black (Sire) 1981
Casual Gods (Sire) 1987 ●

JERRY HARRISON: CASUAL GODS
Walk on Water (Fly-Sire) 1990 ●

BONZO GOES TO WASHINGTON
"5 Minutes" EP (Sleeping Bag) 1984

All of the Talking Heads have participated in extracurricular musical activities, and guitarist/keyboardist Harrison is no different—only less successful. Recorded during the band's 1981 sabbatical, **The Red and the Black** continues the pan-ethnic, cross-rhythmic musical explorations of **Remain in Light**—not a surprise, since many of the auxiliary Heads (like Adrian Belew, Bernie Worrell and Nona Hendryx) also appear on Harrison's record. The results are fairly funky, albeit in a relaxed, slow-motion way.

A few years later, Harrison joined bassist Bootsy Collins in a hip-hop groove for the "5 Minutes" 12-inch, a found-sound dance record (in three mixes) that uses Reagan's notorious "We begin bombing . . ." extemporization.

Harrison's second album, **Casual Gods**, leads with its chin: the cover and inner sleeve photos show hordes of poor Brazilians working under horrendous conditions as goldminers. The music, however, is slick rock-funk with lyrics that are serious but not radical. Harrison, who's not a bad singer (his voice sounds a bit like John Cale's), doesn't write songs so much as techno grooves with sketchy melodies; his accomplished cohorts play with chops but little feeling.

With the Heads on indefinite hiatus, Harrison threw himself into **Walk on Water**, earnestly creating a contrasting variety of finely crafted (if a bit clunky) songs: bottom-heavy, soul-tinged rock ("Flying Under Radar"), charming Headsy pop ("Never Let It Slip"), weird Cale-ish dissonance ("The Doctors Lie") and a quiet lullaby ("Sleep Angel"), with a minor smattering of socio-political conscience ("I Cry for Iran," "Cowboy's Got to Go," "Facing the Fire"). Collaborating with the Thompson Twins, Dan Hartman, Bernie Worrell, former Modern Lover bandmate bassist Ernie

303

Brooks and others, Harrison still lacks the adequate musical inspiration and vocal character that would make **Walk on Water** a feat for the ears. [rnp/i]

See also *Talking Heads*.

DEBBIE HARRY
KooKoo (Chrysalis) 1981
Rockbird (Geffen) 1986 ●

DEBORAH HARRY
Def, Dumb & Blonde (Sire-Reprise) 1989 ●

DEBBIE HARRY/BLONDIE
Once More into the Bleach (Chrysalis) 1989 ●
The Complete Picture: The Very Best of Deborah Harry
and Blondie (nr/Chrysalis) 1991 ●

Stepping out of Blondie for her first solo spin, a collaboration with Nile Rodgers and Bernard Edwards of Chic (plus a little help from bandmate Chris Stein), **KooKoo** finds Harry out of her depth. Trying to insert herself into their musical format, she strains for vocal personae (serious romantic and quasi-politically streetwise) to which she is unsuited. About a third of the record is moderately successful infectious funk-pop. For all of its shortcomings, however, the then-controversial pairing with the pre-crossover Chicmen still stands as an example of the adventurous and prescient trailblazing that had typified Harry and Stein within Blondie.

The couple lost the next few years to Stein's extended and debilitating illness, although Harry did contribute a song to the 1985 *Krush Groove* soundtrack and pursue the acting side of her career. Regrettably, **Rockbird**, Harry's first attempt at a real comeback after Stein's recovery, is nearly a cipher. Although nicely produced (by J. Geils Band keyboardist/songwriter Seth Justman), and starting strong with the bouncy "I Want You," the album carries little overall impact. There aren't many catchy tunes; the lyrics are surprisingly flat. "Secret Life" is particularly annoying for announcing a revelation but saying nothing at all. The song that most recalls Blondie's lovable playfulness is "French Kissin'," but Harry had no hand in writing it.

While Harry did little recording over the next few years, fans got a chance to see her in *Hairspray* and on TV's *Wiseguy*, where she portrayed (natch) a rock singer.

Considering how badly *their* career is going, it's ironic that the Thompson Twins wrote and co-produced the best song on **Def, Dumb & Blonde**. "I Want That Man" is a kicky love song with an immediate hook and delightfully flip lyrics. (Their other contribution, "Kiss It Better," is patented TT bounce-pop that Harry coos alluringly.) Otherwise, the surprising reunion with Blondie producer Mike Chapman yields one handy reminder of that band's surging '60s guitar pop ("Maybe for Sure") and a lot of dull stylistic retreads. The CD adds four, including the old-fashioned "Bike Boy" and Harry's crisp rendition of the Fast's kitschy "Comic Books."

Once More into the Bleach is a dance-mix compilation. Besides an assortment of Blondie hits, it features Harry's solo "Rush Rush" (from *Scarface*) plus a handful of tracks from **KooKoo** and **Rockbird**. [jg/i]

See also *Blondie*.

HARRY CREWS
See *Lydia Lunch*.

GRANT HART
2541 EP (SST) 1988 ●
Intolerance (SST) 1989 ●

NOVA MOB
Admiral of the Sea EP (Rough Trade) 1991 ●
The Last Days of Pompeii (Rough Trade) 1991 ●

Popular perceptions of Hüsker Dü's implosion cast Bob Mould as the wounded victim and Grant Hart—drummer, singer, songwriter—as the problem child. Although Mould vented the depths of his disillusion and anger on 1989's **Workbook**, Hart got in the first word on the plucky title track of a 1988 three-song 12-inch, painting the split in terms of a couple's first apartment—the number of which just happened to coincide with the band's office/studio address. (Hart denied that was his intent but few believed him.) In any case, "2541" is a touchingly sad acoustic folk-rock number with a typically catchy melody.

A moving description of Hart's pain as well as an assertion of his survival, **Intolerance**—a simply played one-man-band solo project that avoids familiarity by using '60s-style organ as the most prominent rhythm instrument—deals with more than one traumatic aspect of his life. The obsessively driven (with strings) "Fanfare in D Major (Come, Come)" (remade from the EP, as was "2541," which gets a much rockier arrangement with surprisingly Mouldish vocals) and the shambling (complete with dentist drill) "You're the Victim" are clearly aimed at Mould. In the same vein, the Dylanesque—with wailing harmonica and a killer chorus—"Now That You Know Me" discusses a relationship in vague terms that could apply to the band. But "The Main" is about drug addiction, and the solemn "She Can See the Angeles Coming" recalls the band's manager, Dave Savoy, who committed suicide in 1987.

In late '89, Hart—now sticking to vocals and guitar—formed Nova Mob, a rock trio with a really good bassist and an inferior drummer. (Nova Mob was also the name of an obscure but historically significant late-'70s Liverpool outfit that included Julian Cope, Budgie and Pete Wylie.) Written and performed as a rock opera, **The Last Days of Pompeii** is a weirdly produced (and, for the genre, typically oblique) concept album that is part madness and part fascinating ambition. As a vehicle for quixotic lyrics about ancient history and space exploration, the simple music balances Hart's pop-ulism and sweeping rock ideas with sure strength, if not much ingenuity. (But don't be too surprised if you find yourself idly humming a tune called "Wernher Von Braun.")

Released as a preview of the **Pompeii** LP, **Admiral of the Sea** contains two mixes of its clunky organ-churning title track (a showcase for drummer Michael Crego's shortcomings), a single mix of the catchy "The Last Days of Pompeii," an instrumental mix of a third album track and a live'n'loud "I Just Want to Make to Love to You," recorded in Switzerland. [i]

See also *Hüsker Dü*.

RICHIE HASS & THE BEATNIKS
See *Zoogz Rift*.

JON HASSELL
See *Brian Eno*.

DIE HAUT
Schnelles Leben (Ger. Monogram) 1982
Headless Body in Topless Bar (Ger. What's So Funny
    About) 1988
Die Hard (Ger. What's So Funny About) 1990
DIE HAUT WITH NICK CAVE
Burnin' the Ice (nr/Illuminated) 1983

Rising out of Berlin's post-punk bleakness, die Haut ("the skin") is a largely instrumental quartet with Beefheartian and psychedelic overtones but possessing a disciplined ferocity that yields a strikingly Germanic sound. **Schnelles Leben** is a seven-song, eighteen-minute disc that utilizes terse bass and drum rhythms topped with scratchy guitar work, rarely settling into a tonal center. Five of the tracks are vocal-less and tend to lack development and textural variety. Not so much produced as simply recorded, in many places vocals are conspicuous by their absence.

Die Haut enlisted the services of Birthday Party singer Nick Cave for **Burnin' the Ice** and even gave him co-billing. Cave supplies all vocals and lyrics (for four of the seven cuts), generating an air of leader and backing band. Much of the manic double-guitar work on **Schnelles Leben** turns into psychedelic droning behind Cave's bellowing, but at least the songwriting and production show improvement.

The band wasn't heard from again until 1988's **Headless Body in Topless Bar** (the title courtesy of a legendary *New York Post* headline), an album halved between instrumental and vocal tracks, the latter featuring Cave, Anita Lane and a handful of Bad Seeds (die Haut's drummer, Thomas Wydler, is also in Cave's ensemble). In the band's guest-less work, early influences have been replaced by the distorted metallic guitar (by Jochen Arbeit and Rainer Lingk) riding atop Wydler's adept rhythms. But the results are the same: the work still sounds like unfinished songs and is of minimal interest. The vocal side, however, has more character(s). Cave's contribution is a cover of "Just Dropped In (To See What Condition My Condition Was In)," that laughable 1968 attempt at groovy psychedelia from none other than Kenny Rogers. Bad Seed guitarist Kid Congo Powers is featured on two cuts more similar to die Haut's own work; it sounds as though he's the missing vocalist. Lane's "The Bells Belong to the Ashes" is largely motionless art-noise with lots of timpani (thankfully, she speaks rather than sings). Die Haut knows how to collaborate, but not a whole lot else.
[dgs]

See also *Nick Cave and the Bad Seeds, Lydia Lunch*.

HAVALINAS
The Havalinas (Elektra) 1990 ●

Rejoining another former member of the Rockats (British stand-up bassist Smutty Smith), New York singer/guitarist Tim Scott McConnell ended (or at least shelved) his trend-jumping solo career by forming a tough and dusty California trio with ex-Plugz/Cruzados drummer Chalo Quintana. A selfconscious cowboy rock album played on acoustic instruments, **The Havalinas** (deftly produced by Don Gehman, who does much the same work for John Mellencamp) sets McConnell's any-style-in-a-storm songs into an atmospheric and energetic—but ultimately unconvincing—campfire stew. [i]

See also *Cruzados, Plugz, Rockats, Tim Scott*.

HAVANA 3 A.M.
See *Clash*.

GREG HAWKES
See *Cars*.

HAWKWIND
Hawkwind (UA) 1970 (nr/Sunset) 1975
In Search of Space (UA) 1971 ●
Doremi Fasol Latido (UA) 1972
Space Ritual (UA) 1973
Hall of the Mountain Grill (UA) 1974 ●
Warrior on the Edge of Time (Atco) 1975
Road Hawks (nr/UA) 1976 (nr/Fame) 1984
Astounding Sounds, Amazing Music (nr/Charisma) 1976 ●
Masters of the Universe (nr/UA) 1977 (nr/Fame) 1982 ●
Quark Strangeness and Charm (Sire) 1977 ●
P.X.R.5 (nr/Charisma) 1979 ●
Live '79 (nr/Bronze) 1980
Repeat Performance (nr/Charisma) 1980
Levitation (nr/Charisma) 1980 ●
Sonic Attack (nr/RCA) 1981
Church of Hawkwind (nr/RCA) 1982
Choose Your Masques (nr/RCA) 1982
Hawkwind Friends and Relations, Volume 1 (nr/Flicknife)
    1982 ●
Zones (nr/Flicknife) 1983 ●
Bring Me the Head of Yuri Gagarin (nr/Demi-Monde)
    1983 ●
Independent Days, Volume 1 EP (nr/Flicknife) 1984
Hawkwind Friends and Relations: Twice Upon a Time
    (Volume 2) (nr/Flicknife) 1984 ●
This Is Hawkwind, Do Not Panic (nr/Flicknife) 1984
Hawkwind Friends and Relations, Volume 3 (nr/Flicknife)
    1985 ●
The Chronicle of the Black Sword (nr/Flicknife) 1985 ●
Space Ritual, Volume 2 (nr/APK) 1985 ●
Ridicule (nr/Obsession) 1985 ●
Independent Days, Volume 2 (nr/Flicknife) 1986
Anthology, Volume 1 (nr/Samurai) 1986 ●
Anthology, Volume 2 (nr/Samurai) 1986 ●
Anthology, Volume 3 (nr/Samurai) 1986 ●
Quark Strangeness and Charm/P.X.R.5 [tape]
    (nr/Charisma) 1986
The Collection (nr/Castle Comm.) 1986 ●
Live 1970–1973 (nr/Dojo) 1986 ●
Angels of Death (nr/RCA) 1986
Out & Intake (nr/Flicknife) 1987 ●
Early Daze (nr/Thunderbolt) 1987 ●
British Tribal Music (nr/Start) 1987 ●
The Official Picture Log Book (nr/Flicknife) 1987

Live Chronicles (GWR-Profile) 1988
Levitation/Live '79 (nr/Castle Comm.) 1988 •
The Xenon Codex (GWR-Enigma) 1988 •
The Text of Festival (nr/Thunderbolt) 1988 •
Spirit of the Age [CD] (nr/Virgin) 1988 •
Zones/Stonehenge [CD] (nr/Flicknife) 1988 •
The Best of Hawkwind, Friends & Relations [CD]
   (nr/Flicknife) 1988 •
Night of the Hawk (nr/Power House) 1989 •
Stasis (The U.A. Years) (nr/EMI) 1990 •
Acid Daze Volume 1 (nr/Receiver) 1990 •
Acid Daze Volume 2 (nr/Receiver) 1990 •
Acid Daze Volume 3 (nr/Receiver) 1990 •
Space Bandits (GWR-Roadracer) 1990 •
Palace Springs (Roadracer) 1991 •

HAWKLORDS
25 Years On (nr/Charisma) 1978 + 1982 •

HAWKWIND ZOO
EP (nr/Flicknife) 1981

VARIOUS ARTISTS
Greasy Truckers Party (nr/UA) 1972
Revelations (Glastonbury Fayre) (nr/Revelation) 1972
Travellers Aid Trust (nr/Flicknife) 1988 •

DAVE BROCK
Earthed to the Ground (nr/Flicknife) 1984 •

DAVE BROCK AND THE AGENTS OF CHAOS
The Agents of Chaos (nr/Flicknife) 1988 •

ROBERT CALVERT
Captain Lockheed and the Starfighters (nr/UA) 1974 •
Lucky Leif and the Long Ships (nr/UA) 1975 (nr/Beat
   Goes On) 1987 •
Freq EP (nr/Flicknife) 1984
Test-Tube Conceived (nr/Demi-Monde) 1986 •
Hype (nr/See for Miles) 1989 •
Live at the Queen Elizabeth Hall (nr/Clear) 1989

LLOYD LANGTON GROUP
Outside the Law (nr/Flicknife) 1983
Night Air (nr/Flicknife) 1985
Time Space and Lloyd Langton Group (GWR-Restless)
   1988

HUW LLOYD-LANGTON
Like an Arrow (nr/Gas) 1986

MELODIC ENERGY COMMISSION
Stranger in Mystery (Can. Energy) 1979

STEVE SWINDELLS
Fresh Blood (Atco) 1980
Messages (nr/RCA) 1981

NIK TURNER
Sphynx Xitintoday (nr/Charisma) 1978

Hawkwind's influence has been extensive, if often indirect and, when acknowledged at all, done so grudgingly. The group's faults (most notably a chronic tendency towards excess) have generally been over-criticized to the exclusion of its virtues: that gargantuan and impenetrable pre-metal/hardcore drone, those great riffs, that inexorable drive to destinations unknown. Unfashionable in Britain for most of its existence and unknown outside of a cult following in the US, Hawkwind has often been judged offensive merely for existing. If that isn't pure punk . . .

Through a checkered twenty-years-plus history, Hawkwind has been ruled either by a dictator under the guise of near anarchy or by a purported leader with no control at all. Whichever it be, Dave Brock has been the lineup's only constant through 40 or so personnel changes. A busker who did a stint in the Dharma Blues Band (preserved on anthologies of early British blues), he formed Group X—which became Hawkwind Zoo and then Hawkwind—in London in 1969. Since then, Brock has written and sung the great majority of the material and played most of the guitar, not to mention a fair amount of synthesizer.

Hawkwind's first album is an unexciting hodge-podge of street folk/blues, riff-rock and electronics, with Nik Turner's sax and flute thrown in. The LP's indulgent improvisations fit in with the band's rebellious hippie image, as evinced by their early drug busts and indefatigable benefit-playing, which initially got them positive attention in the alternative culture media. Stacia, a voluptuous (and frequently topless) dancer who joined in 1971, also drew attention to the group and probably had some influence on it; she eventually got a full vote in Hawkwind affairs.

Despite its intricate, attractive unfolding sleeve (designed by the late Barney Bubbles), **In Search of Space** is pretty lukewarm; the sole song of canonical note here is "Master of the Universe." Most important, though, the aforementioned musical elements, along with a more explicit science-fiction orientation, can now be heard as a stylistic blend, integrating Turner, electronics gremlin Dik Mik and newly added synthesizer player Del Dettmar. Some of the electro-noise/saxoid drone bears a strange resemblance to subsequent mid-song blasts by early Roxy Music, whose own electronics specialist Eno had resided, like Dik Mik, in London's funky Ladbroke Grove.

Doremi Fasol Latido is Hawkwind's first strong album. The band's intensity was lifted a notch or two by the manic hyper-drive of new bassist and occasional guitarist Ian "Lemmy" Kilmister, who had played in '60s beat group the Rockin' Vicars and horrible drummerless psychedelicians Sam Gopal. Also, Robert Calvert, who'd drifted into the group's periphery, began to shape its mythology, writing and declaiming some of its lyrics, just as Turner's own writing was starting to emerge.

Earlier the same year, Hawkwind had played at a London benefit concert for the Greasy Truckers, an alternative music organization. The subsequent double live album included a full side of Hawkwind but, more significantly, an *outtake* from it, the queerly poppy space-chug "Silver Machine." Penned by Brock (under his then-wife's name), it was released as a single and became Hawkwind's only UK hit—a huge one, which didn't appear on LP until years later. That success financed the tour chronicled on **Space Ritual**. The double live LP (from London and Liverpool) includes versions of "Master of the Universe" and two-thirds of **Doremi**'s songs (although two had chunks cut out); the new material included Calvert and Brock's synth-embroidered recitations of scary scenarios (e.g., the armageddon classic "Sonic Attack") penned by Calvert and their new buddy, noted sci-fi novelist Michael Moorcock. The LP is solid to super, and not as longwinded as you might imagine.

Dik Mik departed before **Hall of the Mountain Grill** and was replaced by violin-wielding keyboardist Simon House; Calvert left to do his solo albums. By **Warrior on the Edge of Time**, Dettmar had gone too, and Alan Powell picked up the slack for injured drummer Simon King, subsequently playing alongside him. House added formal musical knowledge and skill for a fuller, often more melodious brew. The actual sound of the discs was also clearer, which pointed up the anarchy of the droning psychedelic raveups.

Hall of the Mountain Grill's highlights include the rampaging "Psychedelic Warlords (Disappear in Smoke)" and Lemmy's bleak "Lost Johnny" (co-written by Mick Farren). **Warrior on the Edge of Time** has four tracks co-written by Moorcock, who makes a murky, overly echoed thespian debut on two of them. It also sports Brock's own rocking pseudo-mythology ("Magnu") and a quiet, thoughtful tune ("The Demented Man"), as well as "Kings of Speed," released as a single. The latter's B-side was "Motorhead"; Lemmy took that name for the band he formed after being sacked from Hawkwind following a 1974 on-tour Canadian drug bust. (Although it ceased to exist in reality, the Lemmy lineup resurfaced in fiction as the protagonists—dubbed the Hawklords, led by "Baron Brock"—in a trilogy of books by Moorcock and Michael Butterworth.)

By that point, Hawkwind had achieved all it ever would, in terms of trailblazing; since then, it's all been refinements, variations, even regurgitations. This isn't to say none of the subsequent albums are any good, just not particularly original, and move in a more normal direction. When the band switched UK labels from UA to Charisma, UA decided to do some summing up. **Road Hawks** is a fine retrospective, and includes "Silver Machine"; **Masters of the Universe** is a strong secondary collection.

Astounding Sounds noticeably backed off from the heaviness of the Lemmy era. His replacement, Paul Rudolph (ex-Pink Fairies), had lots of zip, just no overkill. Meanwhile, Calvert had returned, more fully part of the band than ever. Almost every cut is quite good but too long by half, except for the single "Kerb Crawler," which is sharp and to the point. More internal problems: Turner was asked to leave; Rudolph and Powell, allegedly engaging in power play tactics, got the boot.

So next came—what else?—one of Hawkwind's best, most pop-oriented albums. **Quark Strangeness and Charm** features tuff tracks like "Hassan I Sahba" (clever mating of Hawkwind's patented drone with Middle Eastern music) and the delightfully rollicking (!) title tune.

P.X.R.5 contains some gems'n'junk cut in '77 and '78, including three previously unreleased live tracks and two cuts with Brock playing everything but drums. House departed to play with Bowie's touring band, and the Hawks' subsequent US trek so depressed Brock that he quit and sold his guitar. He soon joined up with the Sonic Assassins (with whom Hawkwind had done a one-off gig in '77): Calvert, songwriting bassist Harvey Bainbridge and drummer Martin Griffin. With the addition of keyboardist Steve Swindells (ex-String Driven Thing/Pilot), Hawkwind was reconstituted . . . sort of.

For legal reasons, and to reflect a new direction, the group was christened the Hawklords. Fliply futuristic in

lyrical slant, and more succinct and modern (almost—gasp—new wave) in sonic approach, **25 Years On** is immediately likable and catchy, if surprisingly lightweight. (King and House made contributions in the LP's early stages.) But the 'Lords started playing the old songs live and blessed the release of **P.X.R.5**; soon they transmuted back into Hawkwind and signed to Bronze. (**Repeat Performance** is a fine distillation of the Charisma era, although it omits "Hassan I Sahba.")

After **Live '79**, Swindells left to make his solo LPs, become an outspoken member of the gay musical community and turn into a hotshot club DJ. Tim Blake (ex-Gong) joined in his stead, while Griffin was replaced by Ginger Baker (!). None of this, however, could compensate for the loss of Calvert (back to his solo career); **Levitation** is bland and tame, its main grit supplied by newly returned guitarist Huw Lloyd-Langton, who'd left Hawkwind after cutting the very first album a decade earlier! (**Levitation** and **Live '79** were later paired and reissued jointly in all three formats.)

Griffin returned to replace Baker, and Bainbridge and Brock took up the keyboard slack for the departed Blake as the band moved over to RCA. Actually, as they started to do **Sonic Attack**—somewhat of a return to the earlier Hawkstyle and less playful lyrical stance—Griffin came down with German measles, and the other three started in on the very electronic **Church of Hawkwind** LP. In any case, the net impression left by the three RCA albums is of a hard, heavy and humorless band, but one often capable of being grimly evocative; the generous **Angels of Death** compilation is an apt summary.

At this point, the band began a prolific association with the Flicknife label. The union's first issue—the Hawkwind Zoo EP—contains an alternate version of "Hurry Sundown" (presumably recorded *before* the first album), a live "Kings of Speed" and the early (and surprisingly erotic) "Sweet Mistress of Pain." The 12-inches that followed—some with newly recorded material (e.g., "Night of the Hawks," with Lemmy guesting)—were later collected on two volumes of **Independent Days**.

The three **Friends and Relations** discs consist of outtakes, concert recordings, demos, side projects, related bands, etc. **Volume 1** has live Hawkwind, Hawklords and Sonic Assassins ('77 and '78), plus studio sides by Hawkwind, Nik Turner's Inner City Unit and Michael Moorcock's Deep Fix, but the series goes downhill from there. (**Volume 3** is absolutely bottom-of-the-barrel scrapings.) The best two-thirds of all three is crammed onto the 1988 CD, **The Best of Hawkwind, Friends and Relations**.

Zones is a punchy live LP featuring the pre- and post-RCA lineups (including Nik Turner, who rejoined in '82); **This Is Hawkwind, Do Not Panic**, recorded live at Stonehenge in the summer of '84 (with a bonus 12-inch), shares its title with the band biography published around the same time. (On CD, **Zones** is piggy-backed with an album's worth of live cuts from Stonehenge.)

In '85, after some realignment, Hawkwind endeavored to make its first all-new LP in three years. With Turner reforming Inner City Unit, Bainbridge took on keys and synth exclusively, while singing/writing bassist Allan Davey and drummer Danny Thompson (son of the same-named Pentangle bassist) completed the lineup. With Moorcock's help (but not actual participation), **The Chronicle of the Black Sword** successfully adapted his popular Elric sword-and-sorcery sagas, possibly the band's most disciplined, ambitious undertaking yet. Even better is **Live Chronicles** (from the '85 tour), which includes versions of most of that record, numbers from the RCA years and even "Magnu" and "Master of the Universe." Hawkwind could still smash and slash.

With two rhythm sections (Davey/Thompson and Bainbridge/Griffin) sharing the work, **Out & Intake** is dominated by songs spotlighting band members other than Brock—including, on two, Nik Turner in a guest role. Some of the material is new, some old but not the work of these musicians (like the two Calvert numbers). Hodgepodgey but good.

The next year, using Motörhead producer Guy Bidmead, Hawkwind came up with **The Xenon Codex**, an entertaining romp through familiar territory with some enjoyable twists, like the "Magical Mystery Tour"-ish vocals and cinematic sweep of the "Neon Skyline/Lost Chronicles" medley, and the comedic hijinks of "Good Evening."

The (Hawk)winds of change swept through once again. Lloyd-Langton went off to follow his own muse (such as it was/is), Thompson gave way to Richard Chadwick, and a young ex-schoolteacher (?!) named Bridgett Wishart stepped in as lead and harmony vocalist (and onstage mime). The results, on **Space Bandits**, are intriguing but uneven. Tuneful female vocals make a neat change on "Images," which otherwise has all the earmarks of a typical Hawks hyperdrive romp (i.e., overlong but enjoyable); "Black Elk Speaks" features a Native American declaiming the words of the 19th-century Sioux prophet; half of Side Two offers unsettling atmospherics and uneasy dreams. Prodigal son Simon House is a welcome musical presence throughout, but for personal reasons did not continue with the group after the recording.

As for the rest of the Hawkwind albums listed above, they are almost all live recordings, like **Bring Me the Head of Yuri Gagarin** and **Early Daze**, both tapes from the personal collection of **In Search of Space**-era bassist Dave Anderson, and **Ridicule**, also from the same time frame. Likewise, **Text of Festival** is a double album, with both the expected songs and side-long jams. For what it's worth, the (not scrupulously labelled) **Anthology** series later came out as the **Acid Daze** series which, in CD form, is on two discs.

The Official Picture Log Book is vinyl picture discs of **Chronicle**, **Out & Intake** and **Do Not Panic**, plus an interview disc, badge and poster. **The Collection** is a best-of that doesn't contains the "hits" in their original versions. ("Silver Machine" is the only one explicitly marked live, but most of it is.) The studio material includes two old blues standards, done straight. A couple of tracks seem like arbitrarily edited jams; in fact, there are a surprising number of awkward moments (tracks starting by fading in, abrupt edits, etc.). All the same, much of it is really pretty good.

In the solo album department, there's Brock's batch of demos, **Earthed to the Ground**, "recorded at home while waiting for Hawkwind to get going again." The writing and playing are pretty thin, although the odd

number like "Green Finned Demon" suggests it would've been worth an EP.

Much better is **The Agents of Chaos**, which is evidently just him (guitars and synths) with the limited assistance of someone named Crum (four pseudo-Terry Riley/new agey instrumentals credited to Crum are not great recommendations). It's safe to say that the best of **Agents** has been done better with Hawkwind, but if you have all the other studio albums (heh, heh) and are just dying for another, help yourself. (Flicknife combined the two Brock solos on one compact disc.)

Calvert's **Captain Lockheed** is a deluxe concept album dramatizing the true story of an airplane disastrously modified into an unstable, unsafe machine (aka the Widow Maker). The project is ambitiously outfitted with Rudolph, Lemmy, King, Dettmar, Turner, Brock, plus Eno (!) and—reading dialogue, yet—Viv Stanshall and Jim Capaldi, all overseen by Roy Thomas Baker. Despite some decent tracks, the talk segments are just plain awkward, and make it impossible for the songs to sustain a flow.

Another Calvert concept album, **Lucky Leif** argues that the Vikings really discovered America. Is this trip necessary? Some of it's just plain silly. Produced by Eno, music dominated by Rudolph, with House and Turner along for the ride. Other participants: Winkie Brian Turrington, Roxy bassist Sal Maida and Moorcock on banjo.

Freq is Calvert's industrial record, in a sense. Five of the six tracks (played on guitar and synths by him and two cohorts) relate to the workplace; the other is about a bomb squad. Kernels of good ideas/images abound, but the only one that's well and fully realized is "All the Machines Are Quiet," a song about being on strike. The weirdness ante is upped by the inclusion of union-related conversations and speeches scattered throughout the album. Calvert suffered a heart attack and died at the age of 43 in the summer of 1988.

The best of the solos is Swindells' **Fresh Blood**. It's just him (producing, too), with Lloyd-Langton, King and ex-Van der Graaf Generator bassist Nic Potter. It sounds like Thin Lizzy meets Graham Parker with a rocket up his ass. Narsty. Roger Daltrey sang Swindells' "Bitter and Twisted" in the soundtrack of his film, *McVicar*.

As for Del Dettmar, he resurfaced in the Vancouver area in the Melodic Energy Commission, making new age music before there was such a thing, and cosmic hippy-dippy mystic electronic folk. Blech.

Believe it or not, the **Travellers Aid** double LP, cut at various late-'80s free festivals in Great Britain, isn't a load of crap. Despite the billing, not much of it is Hawkwind, though: one and a half okay tracks, plus one great one by Agents of Chaos. Nik Turner brings up the rear with a crowd sing-along of "Silver Machine." In between is very promising punky hard-rock to a ska beat by Culture Shock, Tubilah Dogs (Hawkwind-*cum*-Blue Öyster Cult that kind of works), some variable but amusing punk (Hippy Slags, Screech Rock), two decent-to-good reggae bands (Israel Movement and Rhythmites) and some goofballs (2000 D.S., Radio Magnolia and Ozric Tentacles), some of which is gruesomely interesting.   [jg]

See also *Inner City Unit, Motörhead*.

BONNIE HAYES WITH THE WILD COMBO

Good Clean Fun (Slash) 1982
Brave New Girl (Bondage) 1984

BONNIE HAYES

Bonnie Hayes (Chrysalis) 1987 ●

Originally known around San Francisco as the Punts, singer Bonnie Hayes and her backing trio take the grossly overused pure pop formula and actually manage to turn it interesting again on **Good Clean Fun**. She follows in the tradition of early Blondie and the Go-Go's by making bright, simple melodies hop and skip incessantly. Hayes and crew avoid the monotony that sometimes plagues their counterparts by downplaying the preciousness and incorporating a wide variety of influences, including jazz and R&B.

Hayes' 1987 major-label album employs a larger backing band and a brand-name producer (Stewart Levine), but nothing can stop the vim and infectious enthusiasm of this adorable one-woman pop dynamo. Hayes writes mature songs about romance from a gingerly hopeful, self-reliant standpoint and performs them with pristine, airy simplicity that at one point ("The Real Thing") precisely resembles Todd Rundgren at his most joyfully upbeat. [jy/i]

HAYSI FANTAYZEE

Battle Hymns for Children Singing (RCA) 1983

Battle Hymns is one of the most willfully annoying records of all time. With Paul Caplin pulling the strings, singing characters Jeremiah Healy and Kate Garner spew out juvenile nonsense lyrics attached to bouncy dance rock, tricked out with gimmicky production to make it reach maximum quirky obnoxiousness. A few tracks (like the McLarenesque square-dance rocker "Shiny Shiny" and the Bow Wow Wow-like "More Money") are fine for *very* occasional listening, but enduring this entire album in one sitting is like having painful dentistry performed by an overbearing three-year-old. Garner made some solo records after the London group evaporated; Healy has done some remixes (including the Clash) and recorded for Boy George's label as the Ezee Posse. [i]

OFRA HAZA

Yemenite Songs (nr/Globestyle) 1985 ●
Fifty Gates of Wisdom (Shanachie) 1987 ●
Shaday (Sire) 1988 ●
Desert Wind (Sire-Warner Bros.) 1989 ●

Whether or not music is indeed the universal language, the fact is that if you slap on a contemporary dance beat, people will buy just about anything, no matter how exotic its origins. Such is the case with Yemenite singer Ofra Haza, who funked up ancient Hebrew music and became the international darling of folks who would never bother to borrow an ethnic record from the public library.

After her sinuous singing was sampled by Coldcut onto a remix of Eric B. and Rakim's "Paid in Full" and from there onto M/A/R/R/S' "Pump Up the Volume" in 1987, Haza—a huge pop star at home in Israel—gave a

rethink to three selections from her traditional-minded **Yemenite Songs** (issued in the US as **Fifty Gates of Wisdom**) and rocked them into the late 20th century on her next album. Bits of **Shaday** (mostly done with British producer Wally Brill) are intriguing blends of strange and familiar sounds (a bit reminiscent in approach to Monsoon), but most of the LP is horrible globopop disco (in English) that could almost be mistaken for Gloria Estefan.

With production by Arif Mardin and Thomas Dolby (as well as Haza and her longtime collaborator/manager, Bezalel Aloni), Haza settled down on **Desert Wind**, forging a subtler, more organic hybrid. Making a self-conscious effort to maintain a connection to her musical roots while reaching out for mainstream appeal, Haza locates a fascinating midpoint between the Middle East and the Midwest on "Ya Ba Ye," "I Want to Fly" and "Da'Asa"; elsewhere, she drops instrumental and vocal accents into otherwise characterless concoctions and, on two tracks, succumbs to Dolby's high-tech irrelevancy. [i]

HEAD

A Snog on the Rocks (nr/Demon) 1987 ●
Tales of Ordinary Madness (nr/Virgin) 1988 ●
Intoxicator (nr/Virgin) 1989 ●

Led by Gareth Sager (ex-Pop Group/Rip Rig + Panic/Float Up CP) and featuring guitarist Nick Sheppard (a onetime Cortina who played in the Clash's miserable afterlife), this loopy Bristol rock quintet—a casually clever in-joke that's not hard to share—has a jolly old time on its first album, indulging in fake sea chanteys and traditional folk songs, sending up Elvis Presley and making mincemeat of assorted rock (i)conventions. Clevedon Pier's commanding Iggy-like voice and the band's ever-changing musical approach makes **A Snog on the Rocks** as unpredictable as a Three Johns record, but a lot easier on the ears.

The stronger **Tales of Ordinary Madness** (on which the slightly refigured group uses an entirely different set of pseudonyms) turns Head's light on rambunctious, occasionally panoramic rock (with horns and piano as well as load guitar and mighty rhythms), taking in quite a bit of stylistic ground. The funky "Get Fishy," which sounds like Foetus getting busy with the J. Geils Band, follows the brassy theatricality of "Machete Vendetta"; complete with strings, the jazzed-out "1000 Hangovers Later" evokes swanky nightclub dissolution with a distinct Nick Cave bent, while "32a" gives an **Exile on Main Street** treatment to the subject of jukebox addiction. Crazy, and loads of fun.

Co-produced by Michael Jonzun (brother of New Kids on the Block svengali Maurice Starr), Head's rock, funk and soul are disappointingly unambitious—even sappy—on **Intoxicator**, a flat-sounding album that displays no more than a glimmer ("Under the Influence of Books") of the previous records' feverish invention, humor or radicalism. Pier's dramatic voice gives the songs most of their character; otherwise, both the material and presentation (with the exception, on both fronts, of the brisk Sager-produced pop of "B'Goode or Be Gone") are entirely lusterless. [i]

See also *Rip Rig + Panic*.

JOWE HEAD

See *Swell Maps*.

(THEE) HEADCOATS

See *Thee Mighty Caesars*.

HEADLESS HORSEMEN

Can't Help but Shake (Resonance) 1987
Gotta Be Cool EP (Resonance) 1988

CHRIS SUCH AND HIS SAVAGES

EP (Chaos) 1989

The Fuzztones (as they existed in NYC) were '60s garage snazz with a smirk. The Tryfles were the same, but with reverence. When the two split and melded, the resultant Headless Horsemen began to rebuild a lost past somewhere between the Flamin Groovies and Easybeats. Initially a trio overly inclined towards acne-era Who, by the time they hit vinyl, the re-aligned Horsemen foursome had invented a more stylistically singular pop music, spanning quiet introspection to hyperkinetic blueball odes. Echoing Green in their Kinksian romanticism of lust and longing, the Horsemen also shuffled frontmen and moonlighted occasionally as Chris Such and the Savages (incisive Anglo-rock esoterica name), playing spirited covers of familiar beat rockers. Interestingly, the Such EP was recorded and mixed in stereo, then folded into mono by an overzealous label owner striving for "authenticity," accounting for some odd sound levels. The Headless Horsemen disbanded as the decade turned. [ab]

See also *Fuzztones*.

HEAD OF DAVID

Dogbreath EP (nr/Blast First) 1986
LP (nr/Blast First) 1986
CD [CD] (nr/Blast First) 1986 ●
The Saveana Mixes EP (nr/Blast First) 1987
Dustbowl (Blast First-Dutch East India) 1988 ●
White Elephant (nr/Blast First) 1989 ●

Progenitors of Britain's extremist grindcore scene, Head of David (who hail from the industrial backwater of Dudley, near the Birmingham birthplace of Black Sabbath) may not have been the first band to blur the line between industrial music and grunge metal, but one need look no further than their calculated, incessant pounding to witness its near obliteration. The virulent sterility of **Dogbreath** suggests what Big Black might have sounded like had Steve Albini been obsessed by Black Sabbath's **Paranoid**: an overwrought guitar barrage and sinister, neanderthal machine rhythms (best put to use on a faithfully compulsive cover of Suicide's "Rocket USA").

LP (digital copies, which include **Dogbreath**'s four tracks, are appropriately dubbed **CD**) is at once more minimalist and more selfconsciously anti-emotional. It's blessedly easy, though, to ignore such stunted, sub-Sonic Youth lyrical fixations as "Joyride Burning X" and "Snuff Rider MC" since the dense, omnivorous metalslide sweeps up the lot with fascinating, twisted grace. Producer John Fryer extracts more surprises from the band's hermetic sound on the **Saveana Mixes** EP, including some noirish ambience on "Adrenicide."

By **Dustbowl**, Head of David had removed most of the electro-shock trappings (except for the devastatingly powerful rhythm machine) in order to be cast as tequila-swiggin', Harley-ridin' zombies from the Planet Hopper . . . Dennis, that is. While the psychotic Americana overkill quickly surpasses mere laughability on its way up the scale from *Police Academy* to (Monty Python's) Killing Joke, Head of David pull off the stiff-limbed metal swagger with all the necessary thuggishness. Once again, production (this time by Albini in the wiry flesh) saves the day by submerging most of the verbiage. After **Dustbowl**, drummer/singer Justin Broadrick (who had been serving concurrently as the guitarist in Napalm Death) left to form the even *more* abrasive Godflesh. Head of David pressed on as a three-piece, but hadn't issued any new material by the end of 1990.

White Elephant's eight tracks are drawn from a pair of John Peel radio sessions (1986 and '87). [dss]

See also *Godflesh, Napalm Death*.

TOPPER HEADON

See *Clash*.

HEARTBREAKERS

L.A.M.F. (nr/Track) 1977 (nr/Jungle) 1984 ●
Live at Max's Kansas City (Max's Kansas City) 1979
D.T.K.—Live at the Speakeasy (nr/Jungle) 1982

JOHNNY THUNDERS & THE HEARTBREAKERS

L.A.M.F. Revisited (nr/Jungle) 1984
D.T.K L.A.M.F. (nr/Jungle) 1984 φ
Live at the Lyceum Ballroom 1984 (nr/ABC) 1984
(nr/Receiver) 1990 ●

The New York club circuit's first supergroup, the Heartbreakers originally (circa 1975) consisted of ex-NY Dolls Johnny Thunders (Genzale) and Jerry Nolan, ex-Television bassist Richard Hell and ex-nothing guitarist Walter Lure. Hell quit to go solo and was replaced (in only the most technical sense) by Billy Rath; the band moved to England and recorded a technically disappointing debut LP, **L.A.M.F.**, for Track Records. The irony of that label's name was not lost on Heartbreakers fans, who suspected that the group's move to Britain was motivated primarily by the UK's heroin-maintenance program. So feeble was the album's mix that drummer Jerry Nolan actually quit over it, though the material itself shows the band to be masters of the stripped-down, souped-up arrangement later copied by many punk groups.

The Heartbreakers subsequently returned to New York, where they performed an endless succession of "farewell" gigs with various pickup drummers, most often Ty Styx. One of these shows was preserved for the **Live at Max's** LP, an ultimate party record—loud and sloppy with lots of dirty talk—and probably the best official document of any local band of the era.

In 1982, a 1977 London performance was sprung from the vaults and released as **D.T.K.—Live at the Speakeasy**. Recorded with Nolan, it presents the darker side of the ambience that pervades the **Live at Max's** set, if only because the band has a more secure drummer. Clearly the Johnny Thunders show, the LP exposes some incredibly sloppy playing, self-righteous audience baiting and a few devolved lyrics (like a reworking of

310

"Can't Keep My Eyes on You" into "Can't keep my cock in you.")

Another live release—this one from a March '84 show at London's Lyceum—turned up a few years later, showing how far the Heartbreakers had come and how little they had changed. The program is a full-fledged Thunders retrospective: the Dolls' "Personality Crisis," the Heartbreakers' "Born To(o) Lo(o)se," his solo "So Alone" and a couple of chestnuts (like "Pipeline" and "Do You Love Me?") from his youth. The show is hot and reasonably coherent, with fine singing by JT and Lure; clear production helps immeasurably.

In 1984, Thunders (assisted by Tony James) remixed **L.A.M.F.** to repair its miserable sound, and the Heartbreakers' lone studio album was given a much improved and much-needed second life as **L.A.M.F. Revisited**. The same label later paired the remixed record with the Speakeasy live album, dubbing this maximum punk package **D.T.K L.A.M.F.**

The Heartbreakers played a reunion show in New York in late '90; Thunders died in April 1991. [jw/i]

See also *Richard Hell, New York Dolls, Sex Pistols, Television, Johnny Thunders*.

HEART THROBS

Cleopatra Grip (Elektra) 1990 ●

Playing gutsy girls'n'guitars rock-pop, the Heart Throbs—a quintet from Reading, England—have a nifty melodic sound that ages the Primitives from adolescence into young-adulthood. The Heart Throbs win brownie points by resisting the temptation to add what would be trendy but superfluous J&M Chain-styled noise. Guitarist Rose Carlotti (augmented by her bass-playing sister, Rachel) gives the songs a strong vocal personality; the band's three male members underpin the dynamic, full-bodied arrangements with a mid-Atlantic stylistic accent that occasionally recalls Holly and the Italians. Richly produced by Gil Norton, about half of **Cleopatra Grip** is as good as any likeminded group around (we're talking total decimation of Transvision Vamp, Voice of the Beehive, Darling Buds, etc.). "Tossed Away," "Dreamtime" and "Here I Hide" all show a real intuitive sense for what makes a good pop tune memorable. But not all of the songs hit the same sublime nirvana; while the band puts on a bold face for this debut album, too often they sound like they haven't got a clue what to do. And someone really needs to help these guys with lyrics, which run from fine to completely awful. [i]

HEAVEN 17

Penthouse and Pavement (nr/B.E.F.-Virgin) 1981 ●
Heaven 17 (Arista) 1982
The Luxury Gap (Virgin-Arista) 1983 ●
How Men Are (Virgin-Arista) 1984 ●
Endless (nr/Virgin) 1986 φ
Pleasure One (Virgin) 1986 ●
Teddy Bear, Duke & Psycho (nr/Virgin) 1988
   (Virgin-Caroline) 1989 ●

After disproving all accusations of synthesizers as limited vehicles of expression, the British Electric Foundation—a multifarious offshoot of the Human League—got their Heaven 17 alter-ego underway with

Penthouse and Pavement. Lyrically, the album ranges from silly to exciting; musically, it's an almost flawless blend of funk and electronics, highlighted by the pressurized new-dance fever of "(We Don't Need This) Fascist Groove Thang."

The American **Heaven 17** release deletes three tracks from **Penthouse and Pavement** and replaces them with the top-notch pop soul of "Let Me Go" and "Who Will Stop the Rain," both from the UK edition of **The Luxury Gap**. (The American release of *that* album swapped them for two of the three tracks omitted from **Heaven 17**.) In all of its incarnations, **The Luxury Gap** contains "Crushed by the Wheels of Industry," "Temptation" and "We Live So Fast," all stellar examples of Heaven 17's chartbound craftsmanship: catchy, toe-tapping dance-pop with horns, guitars and an orchestra providing musical depth behind Ian Craig Marsh and Martyn Ware's synthesizers. Glenn Gregory's gruff vocals aren't immediately mellifluous, but they suit the material and ambience perfectly.

With B.E.F. the Concept falling onto the scrapheap of progress, Heaven 17 (named for an LP cover pictured in *A Clockwork Orange*) made a third album, graced with another awful cover painting. **How Men Are** features an expanding cast of musicians and concomitant sprawl—"And That's No Lie" runs over ten tedious minutes! The LP has a few lively cuts—"This Is Mine" and "Sunset Now" in particular—but is otherwise overblown, indulgent and excessive.

Endless is a poshly packaged, limited-edition, career-spanning retrospective issued originally on cassette but later offered on CD. Besides such essentials as "(We Don't Need This) Fascist Groove Thang," "Crushed by the Wheels of Industry," "Let Me Go" and "We Live So Fast," the collection includes a "Heaven 17 Megamix" medley and an alternate version of "Let's All Make a Bomb" (from either the first or second album, depending on your national orientation). The tape has four additional selections, including "Play to Win" and a new recording of "Song with No Name."

Pleasure One, recorded in various studios over a seventeen-month (hmmm . . .) span, uses scads of guest musicians and vocalists to flesh out an accessible collection of upbeat dance numbers held to almost reasonable song lengths. (Interestingly, at this juncture, the stylistic gap between Heaven 17 and the Human League has never been narrower.) "Contenders," "Trouble" and "Free" are the strongest tracks.

Incapable of any further innovation, and with the novelty of soul-styled electronic dance music having long since worn off, Heaven 17 (like their former mates in Human League) reached the late '80s lacking a strong identity: too many bands sound like this now. Despite the trio's efforts to tart things up with incongruity (heavy rock guitar, Barry White mush, pseudo-jazz, wailing blues harp), **Teddy Bear, Duke & Psycho** keeps returning to the chattering funky bounce and schmaltzy strings of every other H17 record. When Gregory isn't crooning arch love songs, the lyrics moralize about television, self-reliance, personal freedom and war. Hey everybody, let's party like it's 1984! [sg/i]

See also *British Electric Foundation, Human League*.

HECTOR
See *Flying Color*.

RICHARD HELL & THE VOIDOIDS
Richard Hell EP (Ork) 1976
Blank Generation (Sire) 1977 + 1990 ●
Richard Hell/Neon Boys EP (Shake) 1980
Destiny Street (Red Star) 1982 (nr/ID) 1988 ●
Funhunt [tape] (ROIR) 1990

RICHARD HELL
R.I.P. [tape] (ROIR) 1984 [CD] (ROIR-Important) 1990 φ

With his fierce poetic nihilism, Richard Hell embodied and helped set the initial style for '70s punk rock. He founded the Neon Boys with Tom Verlaine in 1971; several years later, they changed the name to Television. He co-founded the Heartbreakers with Johnny Thunders, thereby injecting a poetic intelligence into mindless self-destruction, and went solo as a venerable figure before most future new wave stars had even formed a band. Malcolm McLaren used Hell's mode of dress as the prototype for punk style.

Employing the double guitar threat of Ivan Julian and Robert Quine (later a Lou Reed sideman) and drummer Marc Bell (a former member of the horrifying Dust who departed to become Marky Ramone for several years), Hell formed the Voidoids, whose unwavering individualism kept the group out of the big time while producing a demanding and impressive corpus of work. "I was saying let me out of here before I was even born," opens Hell's masterpiece, "(I Belong to the) Blank Generation," on the 7-inch **Richard Hell** EP, which also includes "Another World" and "You Gotta Lose."

That lyric sums up Hell's attitude, which he expanded and perfected on **Blank Generation** with a new version of the title track and such powerful statements as "Love Comes in Spurts" (an old tune the Heartbreakers recycled into "One Track Mind") and "New Pleasure." The album combines manic William Burroughs-influenced poetry and raw-edged music for the best rock presentation of nihilism and existential angst ever. Hell's voice, fluctuating from groan to shriek, is more impassioned and expressive than a legion of Top 40 singers. (Besides solid liner notes, the 1990 CD adds two tracks—"I'm Your Man," a non-LP B-side from '79, and "All the Way," a Sinatra cover done for the *Smithereens* soundtrack—and substitutes an inferior alternate version of "Down at the Rock and Roll Club.")

After a gap of three years (during which Hell issued only one single, produced by Nick Lowe), the 7-inch **Richard Hell/Neon Boys** appeared, featuring grimly touching songs by the modern Voidoids on one side and old demos by the Neon Boys on the other.

Destiny Street shows a more contemplative Hell, with even sharper imagery and guitar work (again courtesy of the stunning and underrated Robert Quine) and expressively painted poetry. Supported by Fred Maher's crisp drumming and produced with little fanfare by Alan Betrock, Hell offers a second version of "The Kid with the Replaceable Head" (first heard on the '78 Lowe-helmed single), "Destiny Street" and covers of Them's "I Can Only Give You Everything" (okay), the Kinks' "I Gotta Move" (good) and Dylan's "Going Going

Gone" (great). Ruthless yet touchingly romantic, Richard Hell may be rock's last real visionary.

A résumé of Hell's post-Television decade, from his 1975 days with the Heartbreakers through 1984 sessions in New Orleans, **R.I.P.** is inevitably his least polished and most inconsistent work, which may be why it sums up his style so well. Neither as mannered as his first LP nor as professional as his second, this collection showcases his most uninhibited singing on retreads, live takes and previously unissued material. The liner notes (signed with the artist's real name—Lester Meyers) describe the tape as Richard Hell's swansong, but he did begin playing out again, with a short-lived new band, a few months after its release.

Despite shitty sound quality, the live performances (from '78, '79 and '85) on **Funhunt** are totally worth hearing and occasionally extraordinary. Three different sets of Voidoids (including an otherwise undocumented lineup with Jody Harris and Anton Fier) follow Hell through enthusiastic renditions of his own best tunes and such surprising borrowings as the Stones' "I'm Free" and Jimi Hendrix's "Crosstown Traffic." [sg/mf/i]

See also *Heartbreakers, Robert Quine, Ramones, Lou Reed, Television*.

HELLMENN
Herbal Lunacy EP (Aus. Waterfront) 1987
Bastard Sons of 10,000 Maniacs EP (Aus. Waterfront) 1988
Mourning of the Earth (Aus. Waterfront) 1990

Early on, these representatives of the rowdy Sydney surf-punk crowd showed only glimmerings of ability that might lift them above the garage-grunge mass—and oh, those inane lyrics! On the LP, a lot of the audible words are still dopey (one decent set are borrowed from someone else's poem). Yet the band also shows some real melodic strength as they add folk-rock and other musical elements to their now-potent noise-rock. Too bad screamer Ben Brown can't sing; the more demanding the song, the worse he sounds. [jg]

HELMET
See *Band of Susans*.

NONA HENDRYX
Nona (RCA) 1983
The Art of Defense (RCA) 1984
The Heat (RCA) 1985
Female Trouble (EMI America) 1987 ●
SkinDiver (Private Music) 1989 ●

Following a mainstream hard-rock solo album in the '70s, ex-Labelle singer Hendryx upped her hipness quotient considerably in the '80s. Co-produced by Material, **Nona** features an all-star cast of Talking Heads and Go-Go's, as well as Laurie Anderson, Nile Rodgers, Jamaaladeen Tacuma and Sly Dunbar. The dance-funk is, unfortunately, more stimulating on paper than disc; Hendryx is a powerful singer and there are some slick production moves, but the tunes (with the exception of the memorable "Keep It Confidential") are too shapeless to be gripping.

On **The Art of Defense**, again teamed with Material (as well as much of the preceding LP's cast, plus Afrika

Bambaataa and Eddie Martinez), Hendryx sings seven long songs *about* passion *with* passion, obliterating any possible emotional impact with numbing one-note, one-beat repetition. Technically excellent and funky as hell, the album is also boring beyond words.

Produced in large part by Bernard Edwards and Arthur Baker, **The Heat** is a lot better. The songs—more melody, less bombast—take maximum advantage of the musical interplay possible with electronic percussion and studio wizardry. Hendryx evidently still believes that any line worth singing is worth singing half a dozen times, but the well-arranged, muscular backing tracks keep moving, so things don't wind down—even when she drills a lyric into the ground. "If Looks Could Kill (D.O.A.)" is a return to her soul roots; Keith Richards guests on "Rock This House," providing trademark rhythm riffing that fits just right.

Sounding in spots very much like Peter Gabriel's **So** album, **Female Trouble**—dedicated to Winnie Mandela—is another unpredictable jumble of styles (synth-dance, rock, Prince-like funk, etc.), songwriters, producers (mainly Hendryx, Dan Hartman and the System) and guest musicians. Hendryx's irrepressible full-throttle approach makes this an invigorating blast, a tough-minded party record about sex *and* sexual politics.

After four studio free-for-alls, Hendryx finally grabbed the reins of creative responsibility on **Skin-Diver**, making a concerted effort to focus her music in one direction for a change. Co-producing with Private Music boss (and Tangerine Dream-er) Peter Baumann, Hendryx wrote the material, played synthesizer and did all the drum programs. Following the Gabrielesque path introduced on **Female Trouble**, the songs on this restrained, atmospheric and frequently alluring album float along as if in a dream state; dispensing with the kinetic power and diversity of Hendryx's previous LPs, the masterful **SkinDiver** reveals substantially more personal artistry.   [i]

JOE HENRY

Talk of Heaven (Profile) 1986
Murder of Crows (Coyote-A&M) 1989 ●
Shuffletown (Coyote-A&M) 1990 φ

While there has been substantial support for modern folk music at the grass-roots level, singer/songwriters who aren't folkies and don't play any identifiable brand of rock or pop are still something of an anomaly in the post-punk world. Produced by Anton Fier and backed by a bunch of old-time rock stars (ex-Rolling Stone Mick Taylor, ex-Allman Brother Chuck Leavell), singer/guitarist Henry makes an intelligent but characterless showing on **Murder of Crows**, a record whose solid material and styleless performances are as unassailable as they are unmemorable.

Produced by T-Bone Burnett and recorded live-to-two-track in a brief studio session with more sympathetic players, the acoustic **Shuffletown** is immeasurably better, a poetic statement whose evocative power and casual instrumental excellence recalls prime Van Morrison. Henry proves himself here to be a real singer, filling his plain voice with confident power and conveying the haunted power of someone who truly feels his lyrics.   [i]

HENRY COW

Legend (Virgin) 1973 (Red) 1979 [CD] (East Side Digital) 1991 ●
Unrest (nr/Virgin) 1974 (Red) 1974 [CD] (East Side Digital) 1991 ●
Concerts (nr/Caroline) 1976
Western Culture (nr/Broadcast) 1979 (nr/Recommended) 1980 ●

SLAPP HAPPY/HENRY COW

Desperate Straights (nr/Virgin) 1975 (nr/Recommended) 1982
In Praise of Learning (nr/Virgin) 1975 (Red) 1979 [CD] (East Side Digital) 1991 ●

ART BEARS

Hopes and Fears (Random Radar) 1978
Winter Songs (Ralph) 1979
The World as It Is Today (nr/Re) 1981
Winter Songs/The World as It Is Today [CD] (nr/Recommended) 1987 ●

FRED FRITH/CHRIS CUTLER

Live in Prague and Washington (nr/Re) 1983
Live in Moscow, Prague and Washington [CD] (nr/Recommended) 1990 ●

NEWS FROM BABEL

Sirens and Silences/Work Resumed on the Tower (nr/Re) 1984 ●
Letters Home (nr/Re) 1986 ●

DAGMAR KRAUSE

Supply & Demand (Hannibal) 1986 ●
Tank Battles (nr/Antilles New Directions) 1988 ●

Lumpy Gravy-era Zappa, free jazz, early King Crimson, serial music—Henry Cow (the group's name is a truncation of American composer Henry Cowell) brought all of these influences to bear on its early music. Coming together at Cambridge University, these talented British composers/multi-instrumentalists (foremost among them guitarist/violinist Fred Frith, who has since become a new music capo in New York, and drummer/noisemaker Chris Cutler, who has a sound like no other percussionist in rock) could seem at times less a rock band than a contemporary chamber ensemble.

The group's first LP, known as **Legend** in the UK and just **Henry Cow** in the States, is an admirable if somewhat impersonal and occasionally thin statement of purpose. Skillfully arranged and very well played, it nevertheless at times displays an awkward rigidity when it means to be bitingly austere. Humor, such as it is, shows up only in the titles ("Teenbeat" and "Nirvana for Mice"). And Geoff Leigh's anemic sax playing—when he tries to really "blow," you feel like calling an ambulance—gives the record an overly attenuated feel. (The ESD CD of **Legend** has two extra tracks.)

The first side of **Unrest**, where Leigh is replaced by bassoon/oboe player Lindsay Cooper, is a substantial improvement, and contains some of the most full-bodied music Cow ever put on record. Cooper's sound steers the group away from the American jazz influence and grounds it more solidly in European art music, where a better time is had by all. The band's unique wit and invention are on full display here, from the audacious Yardbirds deconstruction ("Bittern Storm Over Ulm") to the somber starkness of "Ruins." Side Two presents the band's first (unfortunate) foray into the realm of musique concrète and, while not entirely worthless, isn't nearly as compelling as the three superior compositions that comprise Side One. (The ESD CD adds two bonus outtakes from the same sessions.)

While Henry Cow really had nothing in common with Slapp Happy (other than an utter lack of commercial recognition and some related hipness in certain circles), the two bands—both then signed to Virgin—joined forces. Dialectical Marxists that they were, the Cow people figured that a merger with their dissimilar labelmates would create a unique synthesis. (Or so they told the music press at the time—insiders suggest that the band really just wanted to poach vocalist Dagmar Krause). The union's first fruit, the predominantly Happy **Desperate Straights**, is a hit-and-miss affair that boasts some really stunning high points, including the brooding "Bad Alchemy" (the first collaboration between Slapp Happy guitarist Peter Blegvad and then-Cow bassist John Greaves; their subsequent work together has also been outstanding).

Cow dominated **In Praise of Learning**, which initially seems like another great A-side/lousy B-side deal, but proves far more problematic than that. The first side contains just two cuts: Anthony Moore/Peter Blegvad's "War," which melds music worthy of Kurt Weill to some witty, bitter Blegvad mythologizing, and Cow keyboardist Tim Hodgkinson's "Living in the Heart of the Beast," a musical magnificence nearly sunk by its lyrics. It's not that the political analysis is way off base, but concepts this cerebral defy the anthemic spirit the band so clearly wants to evoke. Nice try, but basically a longwinded preach to the most likely converted. The otherwise excellent "Beautiful as the Moon–Terrible as an Army with Banners" (sandwiched between two dull "free" pieces) suffers from pretty much the same problem. (The ESD CD has an added track.)

That much-vaunted Marxist synthesis failed to materialize; instead, the tensions among the various players broke up Slapp Happy, and Henry Cow ended up with Krause after all. This Cow lineup would not endure, but survived long enough to perform the gigs that make up the **Concerts** double LP. Side One is a beautifully rendered song cycle, framed by "Beautiful as the Moon" and featuring a couple of previously unrecorded numbers; Side Two features Robert Wyatt dueting with Krause on "Bad Alchemy" and his own "Little Red Riding Hood Hits the Road," as well as an unessential rendition of **Unrest**'s "Ruins"; the second disc contains group improvs of varying success. This was effectively the last of Henry Cow; while the band regrouped in 1978 (sans Dagmar) to record the superb **Western Culture**—its most chamber-like effort ever, comprising two side-long instrumental compositions by Cooper and Hodgkinson—the band's days as a performing unit were through.

Cutler, Frith and Krause continued to record as the Art Bears. More song-based than Henry Cow ever was, the Art Bears melded Cow's leftist politics with a personal sense of despair that deepened over the span of three albums—pretty impressive considering that **Hopes and Fears**' first song is Brecht/Eisler's "On Suicide." All three records are bracing, involving, original works; Frith's composing is trenchant in any number of song idioms, and lyricist Cutler is equally effective at oblique poeticizing (many of **Winter Songs**' lyrics are allegories based on friezes in the Amiens Cathedral) and direct observation (**The World as It Is Today** is a plainspoken depiction of the nightmare of capitalism). The instrumentation and production—often involving backwards and off-speed recording, both Frith and Cutler intent on exploiting the possibilities of the studio as a compositional tool—are first rate.

When Frith (by this point residing in New York) decided to concentrate on his Stateside musical activities, Cutler and Krause enlisted two instrumentalists—Lindsay Cooper (who also took over composing chores) and harpist/accordionist Zeena Parkins—to form News from Babel. Even more introspective than the Art Bears, News from Babel's songs tackled modern alienation from a dour, skewed angle but occasionally let in a glimmer of hope; witness **Work Resumed on the Tower**'s "Anno Mirabilis." Robert Wyatt's vocals dominate the band's second album, **Letters Home**. Both records are worthy efforts, but since Cooper isn't as much of a sonic adventurer as Frith, they lack the edgy daring of the Art Bears' best.

In the mid-to-late '80s, Krause recorded albums of songs by two composers some believe she was born to sing—Brecht/Weill (**Supply & Demand**) and Hanns Eisler (**Tank Battles**). Hodgkinson and Cooper have released solo LPs (much of the latter's work has been in film soundtracks), and Cooper and Cutler spent time in David Thomas' band. The seemingly inexhaustible Cutler has also been running the exemplary, adventurous Recommended label (which put out a nifty, noisy set of Frith/Cutler improvs in 1983, later reissuing it on CD with a lengthy 1989 performance recorded in the Soviet Union) since the late '70s; he wound up in Pere Ubu when that band relaunched itself in 1987. [gk]

See also *Peter Blegvad, Fred Frith, John Greaves, Material, Anthony More, Skeleton Crew, David Thomas*.

HERRERA & THE HANDOUTS
See *Cheepskates*.

HE SAID
See *Dome*.

HETCH HETCHY
See *Oh-OK*.

BOO HEWERDINE AND DARDEN SMITH
See *Bible*.

HEX
Hex (First Warning) 1989 (First Warning-Rykodisc) 1990 ●
Vast Halos (First Warning-Rykodisc) 1990 ●

JACK FROST
Jack Frost (Arista) 1991 ●

Evidently unable to sate his creative impulses with the Church and his solo career, the multi-talented Steve Kilbey formed a side group with Donnette Thayer, late of Game Theory. On **Hex**, he uses modest portions of guitar, keyboards and percussion to sketch out light, ambient backing for her airy vocal excursions. Poised dangerously close to the brink of arty/poetic vagueness, the duo manages to stay on terra firma for most of the record, holding track lengths to sustainable limits and structuring material so that it flows rather than drifts.

Recorded with a drummer, **Vast Halos** takes an entirely different approach: full-bodied arrangements of clear-cut songs with layers of Thayer's multi-tracked harmonies. More accessible but less distinctive than the first album, **Vast Halos** resembles a toned-down Church record with a different singer as well as a suave (post-paisley?) successor to California flower-pop.

With one side group underway, Kilbey launched another, with Grant McLennan, late of the Go-Betweens. Joined by a drummer and string and horn players, the two share vocals, guitar and bass (overachiever Kilbey also plays keyboards and drums) on **Jack Frost**, a fine collection of collaborative originals that don't so much add their individual styles as cross them in various ways, from acoustic duo folk ("Civil War Lament," "Thought That I Was Over You") to suave and moody electro-pop ("Threshold") to noise-flecked rock ("Every Hour God Sends") to eerie atmospherics ("Number Eleven"). The CD adds a song.   [i]

See also *Church, Game Theory, Go-Betweens.*

RICHARD X. HEYMAN
Actual Size EP (N.R. World) 1986
Living Room!! (N.R. World) 1988 (Cypress) 1990 ●
Hey Man! (Sire-Warner Bros.) 1991 φ

With some assistance, multi-talented New York power-popper Heyman does it all—vocals, guitars, keyboards, drums, etc.—on his six-song EP and sparkling debut album (an impressive 8-track home-brew job which was remixed and slightly resequenced for reissue with a new cover). Despite the closeted solo environment, Heyman's music—a smoothly accomplished and undated collection of tuneful styles—is warmly realized in well-written songs filled with subtlety (like the typewriter on "Local Paper") rather than eccentricity.   [i]

NICK HEYWARD
See *Haircut One Hundred.*

JOHN HIATT
Hangin' Around the Observatory (Epic) 1974 ●
Overcoats (Epic) 1975
Slug Line (MCA) 1979
Two Bit Monsters (MCA) 1980
All of a Sudden (Geffen) 1982
Riding with the King (Geffen) 1983 + 1989
Warming Up to the Ice Age (Geffen) 1985 + 1989
Bring the Family (A&M) 1987 ●
Slow Turning (A&M) 1988 ●
Y'All Caught? The Ones That Got Away 1979–1985 (Geffen) 1989 ●
Stolen Moments (A&M) 1990 ●

After recording an unnoticed pair of promising but stylistically confused Nashville country-soul-rock-gospel-singer-songwriter albums—**Hangin' Around the Observatory** (really good) and **Overcoats** (a bit bland), which tip a hat to everyone from Bob Dylan to Al Green, Leon Russell to Billy Joel—Indiana's John Hiatt exploded onto the new wave scene in 1979, a fiercely original soul-inflected rock character likened to Elvis Costello, Graham Parker and Joe Jackson, but wholly his own man. Despite their underwhelming commercial success, all of his albums testify to an exceptional talent, both as a much-covered songwriter and as an intense, emotional performer.

Slug Line is Hiatt's rawest and most powerful LP, with appropriately rudimentary production highlighting dynamic playing on a full set of angry songs. Drawing with genuine conviction on both reggae and fiery R&B styles, Hiatt invests "Madonna Road," "You're My Love Interest," "The Negroes Were Dancing" and other tracks with bitterness, insightful intelligence and occasional tenderness, making it a stunning work by an exciting artist.

Two Bit Monsters essentially repeats **Slug Line**'s style, but with less bite. Several tunes ("Back to Normal," "Good Girl, Bad World," "String Pull Job") are comparably impressive, but the album is less focused and nearly haphazard. Hiatt's venom sears through, but it's not his best work.

Tony Visconti produced **All of a Sudden**, sympathetically if incongruously displaying the songs in a complex, highly arranged setting that works to good advantage most of the time. Amid a nod to rockabilly ("Doll Hospital") and a dose of Motown ("Getting Excited"), excellent songs like "Something Happens" and "I Look for Love" get filtered once through Hiatt's expanding musical sensibilities and then through Visconti's synth-rocking Bowieness, making it a strange collision of seemingly irreconcilable styles.

Hiatt's bumpy career subsequently brought him into contact with Nick Lowe and Lowe's manager, Jake Riviera. The former produced and led the backing band on one side of **Riding with the King**; the latter loaned an eye-popping motorcycle for the front cover photo. The record's other side was produced by Scott Matthews and Ron Nagle; Matthews and Hiatt are the only musicians on those tracks. Although it may be down to the allotment of material, Lowe comes up the loser; on his side, Hiatt affects a languid swamp sound that doesn't convey much excitement. He comes alive only for such Matthews/Nagle-produced tracks as "Death by Misadventure," "Say It with Flowers" and "I Don't Even Try," prime songs given modest but appealing treatment.

Veteran mush-rock producer Norbert Putnam got the nod for **Warming Up to the Ice Age**. On the first track, "The Usual," he smothers Hiatt in raucous heavy metal guitars and arena-scale drums; fortunately, that's not the only sound on this weird record, which also contains a great soul duet with Elvis Costello ("Living a Little, Laughing a Little"), an emotion-laden ballad ("When We Ran") and other typically on-the-mark slices of Hiatt's cynical viewpoint ("She Said the Same Things to Me," "Number One Honest Game"). The mix is consistently too rock-oriented—these aren't dance tracks, for crying out loud!—but Hiatt's subtle vocals keep things in balance. (Footnote: "The Usual" resurfaced a few years later, sung by Bob Dylan and rocker Fiona in the movie *Hearts of Fire.*)

Hiatt's career was going nowhere fast and his personal life was no picnic, either. Luckily, for his next outing (and label), Hiatt hit on a far more rewarding format. Alone in an LA studio for four days with just Lowe, guitarist Ry Cooder (with whom Hiatt has often played), veteran session drummer Jim Keltner and a hands-off producer, he cut an extraordinary album of uncommon simplicity and candor. Ruggedly real and honest in extremis, **Bring the Family** has bottomless emotional depth and sonic spaces the size of sinkholes. The well-played music only serves to focus attention on that gritty, passionate voice, serving up new melodies and words reflecting the maturation and authority Hiatt's hard travelling has earned him.

An attempt to recapture that magic with the same four collaborators ran aground over business deals, and the album was instead recorded with David Lindley, Dave Mattacks and John Doe. Upon completion, however, that record was scrapped and the process recommenced with producer Glyn Johns and Hiatt's road band, the Goners, plus some guests. The rustic **Slow Turning** has some of **Family**'s sonic attributes (if not its exciting immediacy), with the bonus of Hiatt's increasingly confident and optimistic outlook. The parental warmth of "Georgia Rae" and "Slow Turning" offsets the lonely uncertainty of the gospellish "Is Anybody There?" and the stormy love in "Feels Like Rain," while the joyous liberation of "Drive South" is tempered by the suicidal mundanity of "Ride Along." Utterly likable but lacking emotional starch, **Slow Turning** is an uneven ride that could use more gas and colorful scenery.

Again produced by Johns, **Stolen Moments** electrifies Hiatt in more ways than one. Tastefully fired-up arrangements match Hiatt's exuberance, the perfect complement to his articulate songs' deepening insights about such familiar topics as faith, family and self-awareness. Finally accepting peace and happiness as a wonderful gift, Hiatt puts on a powerfully melodic variety show here, sending pop songs ("Child of the Wild Blue Yonder," "Real Fine Love") soaring, gently wah-wahing life into a romantic Philly soul tune ("Bring Back Your Love to Me"), rocking out (the riff in "The Rest of the Dream" is lifted from AC/DC's "You Shook Me All Night Long") and, surprisingly, paying repeated homage to Bob Dylan. Rewriting "Every Grain of Sand" in the haunting "Through Your Hands" and echoing "Girl from the North Country" in the somber "Thirty Years of Tears," Hiatt makes fine and fair use of a few pages from the Dylan's songbook.

Released four years after his departure from Geffen Records, **Y'All Caught** reviews Hiatt's work on that label as well as his earlier two-album MCA career. A concise refresher course for those arriving late in the story, **Y'All Caught** is organized stylistically in a partially successful bid to downplay the lurching album-to-album inconsistency. [i]

SARA HICKMAN

Equal Scary People (Four Dots) 1989 (Elektra) 1989 ●
Shortstop (Elektra) 1990 ●

An endless stream of competent singer/songwriters have emerged in the acoustic-guitar backwash of Suzanne Vega and Tracy Chapman, but very few have the versatile artistry of Sara Hickman. This North Carolina-born Texan has a marvelous voice—at once sweet and sexy—that can gently croon a folk lullabye and hold its own in a polite rock'n'roll arrangement. With winning songs that are emotionally resonant and a little loopy, **Equal Scary People** (initially issued by a Texas indie) is an album that easily stands out in a soundalike crowd. Cool enough to make peace with James Brown in a solemn, bluesy upended version of "This Is a Man's World" and unselfconscious enough to write a soppy "Song for My Father," Hickman takes some chances on her first LP and comes through with the warm intimacy of an old friend.

David Kershenbaum's overzealous adult-contemporary production on **Shortstop** seems designed to cast Hickman as a young Joni Mitchell. (Denny Fongheiser's big-beat drumming and Larry Klein's fretless bass clichés are particularly annoying.) Hickman's willing participation, especially on the jazzy "I Couldn't Help Myself," in this sleek commercial effort is disappointing in light of her first album's easygoing openness, but she rises to the challenge with exquisite vocal control and clever, inventive songs on such diverse topics as Salvador Dali, American hostages, sisterly love and the foibles of male sexuality. [i]

HICKOIDS

We're in It for the Corn (Toxic Shock) 1987 + 1988
Hard Corn EP (Toxic Shock) 1988
Waltz a Crossdress Texas (Toxic Shock) 1989

Cure the Butthole Surfers' hallucinatory madness but not their Texas junk-culture mentality or careening noise. Add country-western rhythms and some revved-up guitar licks, and that pretty much describes Austin's zealous Hickoids, America's only hard-corn (white thrash?) band. Whether they're adding lyrics to a familiar TV theme ("Williamanza") or delivering a cruel ode to one-armed farmers ("O.A.F. Anthem"), the band's colorful guitar work, four-on-the-floor punk overdrive and depraved sense of humor ("Animal Husbandry" mates man and cow) make **We're in It for the Corn** a raucous and funny souvenir of the Lone Star state. (The cassette adds four bonus cuts.)

Following the 7-inch **Hard Corn** EP (two originals and two freewheeling covers: "Corn Foo Fighting" and Jackson Browne's "Take It Easy"), the Hickoids ease up on the punk for more of a Tex-Mex/country flavor on the relatively slick second album, **Waltz a Crossdress Texas**. Using steel guitar, piano, trumpet and (yes!) flugelhorn, well-played jokes about transvestites, beer, sex and trucks are loaded with local color and the Hickoids' winningly sociopathic outlook. [i]

HIGH

Somewhere Soon (London) 1990 φ

Formed by ex-Stone Roses guitarist Andy Couzens and drummer Chris Goodwin (both ex-Flag of Convenience), this Manchester-area quartet plays effortlessly appealing modern atmos-pop (y'know—ringing guitars, acoustic piano, breathy vocals and a little bit of cello when it fits the mood) of no great consequence. Signed after one gig, the High don't do anything wrong on their relaxed and pleasant album, but that's about the strongest praise they deserve.   [i]

See also *Flag of Convenience*.

KENNE HIGHLAND CLAN

See *Gizmos*.

HOLGER HILLER

A Bunch of Foulness in the Pit (nr/Cherry Red) 1984
Hyperprism (Jap. Wave) 1985
Oben im Eck (nr/Mute) 1986 ●

Virtually the only English on Hiller's first album (released originally by the German Ata Tak label) is the translated title; otherwise, you're on your linguistic own. Hardly the horrorshow the billing might have you imagine, the former Palais Schaumburg member conveys bemusement and tension rather than squalor or desperation, using overlaid (and not always musically related) instrumental lines (mostly keyboards and, if my dictionary guessed correctly, percussion), detached vocals, plus found sounds and assorted blips and squeaks. While the effect is not exactly pleasant—although a few songs, notably "Jonny (du Lump)," are—it is riveting, and Hiller is masterly at aurally painting a scene in living color.

Hiller's collaborators on **Oben im Eck**, a revised version of **Hyperprism** (retitled for a track which appears on it in two versions), include keyboardist Izumi Kobayashi and vocalist Kaori Kano, as well as Billy Mackenzie (Associates). Sampling keyboards have opened new creative worlds for sonic experimentalists like Hiller, allowing him to electronically manipulate sounds that were not so long ago uncontrollable and available only on tape. Although parts of the LP have an offbeat Japanese flavor, sections that are noisy or childlike take a much more neo-European approach, suggesting such sonic adventurers as Foetus or Renaldo and the Loaf. Ostensibly a set of songs, the album's rambling and colorful collections of sounds have little cohesion; even the multilingual lyrics (one song's written by Tom Verlaine) add scant structure to this dadaist picnic. [i]

HILT

See *Skinny Puppy*.

PETER HIMMELMAN

This Father's Day (Orange) 1986 (Island) 1986
Gematria (Island) 1987 ●
Synesthesia (Island) 1989 ●
From Strength to Strength (Epic) 1991 ●

SUSSMAN LAWRENCE

Hail to the Modern Hero! (Bigger Than Life) 1980
    (Regency) 1980
Pop City (Orange) 1984

Minneapolis quintet Sussman Lawrence works very hard to sound like early Elvis Costello on their first outing, although singer/guitarist Peter Himmelman's vocals tend to favor Phil Lynott more. The songs, which are clearly derivative of Costello and Joe Jackson, are still sharp enough to be entertaining. Absurdist pop cul-

ture lyrics add some originality; smart playing and solid production also give this dubious venture its limited validity.

Pop City—a double-album with 21 songs in a number of styles—is far less imitative and proves this likable band to be highly skilled and creative, smoothly skipping across genres (often several times per song) to play everything—jazz-R&B-rock-pop—with abundant good spirits and a commitment to nothing but making simply enjoyable music. (Only reservation: some of the lyrics are clumsy and/or trite.)

Sussman Lawrence vanished when Himmelman opted to continue his career under his own name—remarkably, the other four band members remained as his sidemen. **This Father's Day**, a doleful and sensitive singer/songwriter record (with some polite rock arrangements) dedicated to Himmelman's late father, was originally released on the band's label. After a video (for "Eleventh Confession") became an MTV hit, Island reissued it. Free of the imitative amateurness of early efforts, Himmelman's love, passion and intelligence come to the fore in a strong display of craft and talent.

Gematria, recorded in just three days, is an uplifting explosion of joyful ensemble playing that shows how tight and sympathetic these guys are. Himmelman's lower-case lyrics are fairly meaningless (and worse, pretentious in spots) but his music has spirit, power and clarity that far outweigh such concerns.

Himmelman's religious orthodoxy doesn't intrude on **Synesthesia**, but a growing resemblance to Billy Joel (plus frequently colorless songwriting and production) is more than enough to curdle the album. Between dull electric raveups and oh-so-sensitive semi-acoustic efforts, only such tastefully full-bodied ensemble efforts as "A Million Sides" and "Surrender" have the right type and amount of starch to endow the songs with melodic power. (The CD and cassette have three bonus tracks.)   [i]

HINDU LOVE GODS

See *R.E.M.*

HIS NAME IS ALIVE

Livonia (4AD) 1990 ●

Having successfully tested its American scouting skills on Boston (home of Throwing Muses and the Pixies), London's 4AD label ventured to Michigan and signed this curious studio creation, whose album is named for its hometown. Crystal-voiced singers Karin Oliver and Angie Carozzo deliver the lyrics over Warren Defever's simple and semi-formed constructs of guitar, bass and noises that owe debts to Fripp/Eno drones and anyone that ever fooled around with a reel-to-reel tape deck. Somewhere between Hugo Largo's stately restraint and rankly amateurish diddlings (frequently a mix of the two, occasionally just the latter), **Livonia** is an artistic mountain that didn't need climbing. The women's voices are far more attractive than anything in Defever's small bag of tricks, but neither side of this equation would stand on its own. If the two pieces don't really go together in any organic way, each at least offers the other an uncommon way to make an impression. Making this whole thing seem just a bit weirder, Defever is a member of Elvis Hitler's raunchy rock band, the drummer of which guests here.   [i]

See also *Elvis Hitler*.

ROBYN HITCHCOCK

Black Snake Diamond Röle (nr/Armageddon) 1981
(Glass Fish-Relativity) 1986 ●
Groovy Decay (nr/Albion) 1982 ●
I Often Dream of Trains (nr/Midnight Music) 1984 (Glass
Fish-Relativity) 1986 ●
Exploding in Silence EP (Relativity) 1986 ●
Groovy Decoy (Glass Fish-Relativity) 1986 ●
Invisible Hitchcock (Glass Fish-Relativity) 1986 ●
Eye (Twin/Tone) 1990 ●

ROBYN HITCHCOCK AND THE EGYPTIANS

Fegmania! (Slash) 1985 ●
Gotta Let This Hen Out! (Relativity) 1985 ●
Element of Light (Glass Fish-Relativity) 1986 ●
Globe of Frogs (A&M) 1988 ●
Queen Elvis (A&M) 1989 ●

Robyn Hitchcock's entire body of work—both as leader of the Soft Boys and as a solo performer—remains one of the great undiscovered treasures of modern pop music. Psychedelic pop of the '60s provides the touchstone for his melodic, emotional compositions, but Hitchcock blends his own ideas with those of John Lennon, Syd Barrett, Captain Beefheart, the Doors and Byrds to create music that advances the tradition rather than merely recapitulating it.

Black Snake Diamond Röle, his first solo salvo, opens with two jaunty music-hall ditties but quickly descends to Hitchcock's typical deranged concerns. He offers a sardonic knock at authority in "Do Policemen Sing?" (which features a chorus like a frenzied hail of blows) and a melodic, cracked-crystal ballad, "Acid Bird," whose mood and production could stand proud next to "Eight Miles High." Alternate takes on emotion—"Meat" (all brash) and "Love" (all heart)—finish off each side.

Groovy Decay, produced by Steve Hillage, has a smoother sound that somewhat undermines the dark emotion and irony that are Hitchcock's greatest strengths. Still, great songs gleam through the mix. "Fifty Two Stations" stunningly captures the alternation of rage, resignation and hope that follows the failure of love, while "St. Petersburg" views only the black side. "Grooving on an Inner Plane" blends an arch rap-styled vocal into a fluid groove (Sara Lee is the album's bassist) with stirring results. In a surprising move four years later, Hitchcock did it his way by putting out the revisionist **Groovy Decoy**. With almost an identical set of songs, the entirely reordered **Decoy** uses only four of **Decay**'s recordings, substituting simple but effective demos produced (and played on) by onetime Soft Boys bassist Matthew Seligman for the rest. The results are a bit rudimentary next to the original release, but Hitchcock fans will want to hear both.

After nearly two years of self-imposed retirement, Hitchcock returned in 1984 with a surprising, mostly acoustic album, **I Often Dream of Trains**. Performing nearly all the instruments and vocals himself, he echoed the solo work of his models—Barrett in the amiably slapdash production and Lennon on an aching ballad, "Flavour of Night." The album features Hitchcock's usual balance of bitterness and weirdness in unusual settings, rounded off with piano nocturnes at the start and finish. Two bizarre a cappella close-harmony essays—"Uncorrected Personality Traits" (about difficult children when they grow up) and "Furry Green Atom Bowl" (about life's biological processes)—make this one of the stranger outings in a career dedicated to strangeness.

Fegmania!, which features several old Soft Boy cronies in a new band, the Egyptians, shows Hitchcock polishing the best aspects of his craft to a new sheen, achieving a mature merger of lyric with melody (particularly on the morbidly catchy "My Wife & My Dead Wife" and the beautiful emotional study, "Glass") which sacrifices none of the urgency that brings his best songs to life. He has also continued to hone his sound, adding instruments to create a rich, ringing production that highlights his superb guitar textures and Andy Metcalfe's moody bass lines amid a variety of settings.

Gotta Let This Hen Out! is an essential live album recorded April '85 at London's Marquee. Sampling all of his prior albums for items like "Brenda's Iron Sledge," "Heaven," "My Wife and My Dead Wife," and tossing in the acerbic "Listening to the Higsons" (a non-LP single that contains the live album's title, borrowed from a Higsons song), Hitchcock and the three Egyptians—Metcalfe, Morris Windsor and Roger Jackson—do a fine job of putting the songs across in crisp, energetic fashion. A great introduction for neophytes and a treat for fans. (**Exploding in Silence**, available on picture disc, contains six live cuts, only half of them from the album.)

Except for a creeping trace of self-conscious weirdness-for-its-own-sake in the lyrics, the exceptionally melodic **Element of Light** is another terrific addition to Hitchcock's oeuvre. The descending drama of "If You Were a Priest," the arcing delicacy of "Winchester" and "Airscape," as well as the moody restraint of "Raymond Chandler Evening" put the well-rehearsed Egyptians (especially Metcalfe on fretless bass) to fine use, while still leaving Hitchcock's plain but appealing voice a clear field in which to operate. Most of the record is unmistakably Hitchcock, although it does include two eerie Lennon re-creations: "Somewhere Apart" and "Ted, Woody and Junior."

Recycling a Soft Boys LP title, **Invisible Hitchcock** is a compilation of assorted outtakes dating from 1981-'85. A few songs (like "Grooving on an Inner Plane") had previously surfaced in different versions, but most are heard here for the first time. The simple recording quality and mostly non-electric performances with various assortments of sidemen are entirely adequate, if not strictly consistent. **Invisible** may not be crucial but it is certainly illuminating, and a handful of rough gems ("All I Wanna Do Is Fall in Love," "Trash," "Give Me a Spanner, Ralph," "I Got a Message for You") make it a worthwhile purchase.

Thanks to the power of college radio and the music press, Hitchcock's growing popularity brought him a contract with A&M, which released his American major-label debut. Unfortunately, Hitchcock's obscurely lucid liner notes on **Globe of Frogs** are more fascinating than the album, which neglects tuneful songwriting in favor of big beat exercises that would mask insubstantial content with busy production. "Flesh Number One (Beatle Dennis)" and "Chinese Bones"—beautiful pop confections featuring R.E.M. guitarist Pete Buck—keep things from sinking, but "Balloon Man" and the title track, while both likably silly, underscore Hitchcock's annoying tendency to be selfconsciously absurdist.

Queen Elvis is the nadir of Hitchcock's by now substantial body of work. The song structures are overly familiar, the weirdness seems forced and, worst of all, the emotions don't seem real. He seems to have tapped out the veins he'd mined so rewardingly for more than a decade.

Eye is Hitchcock's finest release since the first explosion of his post-Soft Boys career. Like **I Often Dream of Trains**, this is a predominantly acoustic solo effort on which he casts off the influence of bandmates and producers to create a work of astonishing delicacy, beauty, honesty and power. As if to underscore the improvement, "Queen Elvis" is easily superior to anything on the LP with which it shares only a title. "Linctus House" is a gorgeous meditation on flagging love with the achingly drawn-out chorus "I don't care anymore." "Executioner" teases the entrails of another failed romance ("I know how Judas felt/But he got paid"). But the record opens with the jaunty proclamation "I'm in love with a beautiful girl," so maybe things aren't so bad after all. In any case, **Eye** finds Hitchcock still playing complex guitar figures, bending song structures and laying bare his emotions as no one has since Barrett recorded his dementia-in-progress.   [mp/i]

See also *Soft Boys*.

ELVIS HITLER

Disgraceland (Wanghead) 1987 (Restless) 1988 ●
Hellbilly (Restless) 1989 ●

As any good marketing executive will tell you, one key to successfully introducing a new product is an effectively descriptive name. So when a young singer/guitarist decides to call himself Elvis Hitler, he'd better not be counting on a career in new age harpsichord music, knowhutImean? Fortunately, this fiery Michigan 'billyrocker can handle the handle, as he and three rugged sidemen (one of whom moonlights as His Name Is Alive) roar through familiar-sounding originals that cross the Cramps, Mojo Nixon and the Stray Cats. **Disgraceland** has such convincingly obvious anthems to delinquency as "Hot Rod to Hell" and "Live Fast, Die Young" as well as the dubiously topical "Rocking Over Russia" and a few numbers about another feller named Elvis. But the album's ingenious highlight is "Green Haze (Pt. I & II)," a demento hybrid in which EH sings the *Green Acres* theme over "Purple Haze."

Hellbilly is louder and harder, a less stylized but still exciting dish of overamped guitars, raw vocals and drummer Damian Lang's swampy backbeat. Besides covering "Ballad of the Green Berets" and borrowing "(Ghost) Riders in the Sky" (for "Showdown"), little Elvis pokes fun at glam-rockers ("Hang 'Em High"), car-nuts ("Gear Jammin' Hero" and "Crush, Kill, De-

stroy"), saving his least judgmental sentiments for vampires and other horror-movie monsters.   [i]

See also *His Name Is Alive*.

HITMEN

Aim for the Feet (Columbia) 1980
Torn Together (Columbia) 1981

London's Hitmen—not the unrelated Australian group, a contemporaneous outgrowth of Radio Birdman—debuted with a DIY debut single ("She's All Mine" b/w "Slay Me with Your 45") of razor-sharp rhythm'n'pop which meshed terse but tasty guitar and keyboards over snappy bass and drums, topped by Ben Watkins' Graham Parker-*cum*-David Bowie vocals. Yet on **Aim for the Feet**, re-recorded versions of those songs fall flat; it takes repeated listenings to discover that they—along with a passel of other tunes as good and better—have fallen victim to colorless, punchless production.

With producer Rhett Davies at the helm on **Torn Together**, the quartet fares far better, crafting a succession of cleverly arranged and smartly played hooks that grow more impressive (not to mention catchier) with each hearing. The format incorporates more modern, Ultravoxian elements while avoiding the inherent pitfalls—until Side Two, that is, which is alternately arty and bathetic instead of hewing to the earlier, earthier approach.

Ex-Hitmen guitarist Pete Glenister later turned up recording and touring with Bojangles, Terence Trent D'Arby's band.   [jg]

See also *Youth & Ben Watkins*.

SUSANNA HOFFS

See *Bangles*.

MYRA HOLDER

Four Mile Road (Coyote) 1989 ●

One of the few expatriates of the late-'70s Winston-Salem, North Carolina pop scene who *never* played in or produced the dB's or Let's Active, New York singer/guitarist Myra Holder got help from some of her old crowd on this Chris Stamey-produced solo debut. (Faye Hunter, Mitch Easter and brother Gene Holder all put in brief appearances.) Other than one spunky track recorded in 1981, **Four Mile Road** offers nicely sung adult pop and rock—folky enough in spots to resemble 10,000 Maniacs a bit—that avoids obvious stylization in favor of unadorned purity and easy allure. Besides such creditable originals as "Rosa" and "Billy," Holder includes reverent covers of Roy Orbison ("It's Over") and Alex Chilton ("Blue Moon").   [i]

HOLIDAY

See *Oh-OK*.

JOOLS HOLLAND

Jools Holland and His Millionaires (IRS) 1981
Jools Holland Meets Rock'a'Boogie Billy (IRS) 1984
World of His Own (IRS) 1990 ●

This flamboyant pianist—a cigar-chomping hustler able to energize even the most blasé audience—provided much of the zest on Squeeze's first three albums. For his solo debut, Jools adopted a less contemporary stance, playing old-fashioned bar-room romps with energy and panache. Produced by Glyn Johns, the record contains one classic oldie ("Bumble Boogie") and rollicking originals, some co-written with Chris Difford.

Leaving his Millionaires behind, **Rock'a'Boogie Billy** reunites Holland with once-and-future Squeeze drummer Gilson Lavis; otherwise, the self-produced album was recorded solo "at the back room of Holland's home (which accounts for the authentic sound)." The eight tracks, including four Difford collaborations and the old "Flip, Flop & Fly," offer more rustic uptempo friskiness soaked with American barrelhouse and ragtime atmosphere—imagine a young Jerry Lee Lewis in prime condition with no religious hangups. Turn it up and hoist a few!

When Squeeze reformed in 1985, Holland was back in the piano seat, and stayed through the group's '89 tour documented on **A Round and a Bout**. With instrumental assists from his ex-bandmates and numerous other artisans, **World of His Own** provides an impressive sampling of Holland's various talents. There's Squeezy synth-pop, plenty of boogie-woogie, some horn-fed R&B, even a New Orleans-*cum*-ska version of the Lee Dorsey-Allen Toussaint classic "Holy Cow." To top it off, Holland throws in a bizarre but captivating modern instrumental number featuring keyboards, pedal steel and harp (the stringed kind). Really wild, Jools! Unlike Holland's past albums, which always had something of a novelty feel, **World of His Own** is serious fun, and by far his best solo record yet.   [i/ds]

See also *Squeeze*.

HOLLY AND THE ITALIANS
The Right to Be Italian (Virgin-Epic) 1981
HOLLY BETH VINCENT
Holly and the Italians (Virgin-Epic) 1982

Chicago-born singer/guitarist Holly B. Vincent formed her band in Los Angeles, but it took a 1979 move to England to secure a recording deal. An early single released there ("Tell That Girl to Shut Up") established her tough pop-rock style and briefly captured the full attention of the British press and public. The band's sole album was hindered by numerous problems (like firing the producer halfway through and starting from scratch with another, losing the drummer in midstream and having to find a replacement) and wasn't finished until over a year later, but it was well worth the wait. Richard Gottehrer's production fits the melodic rock songs perfectly, melding the hybrid LA/London sound—with glimpses of the Ramones, Blondie and Cheap Trick—into a powerful and original creation. The songs (mostly Vincent's) concern troubled romance, successful romance, teenage rebellion and kitsch culture; her convincing delivery gives them import, and the catchy phrases and solid rock foundation make it a masterful record by an important young talent.

The Right to Be Italian wasn't a commercial success and Holly broke up the band, opting instead for a solo career. Her stunning LP, produced by Mike Thorne, has a misleading title and bears little resemblance to its predecessor. **Holly and the Italians** plays

up her voice and songs, providing ample room for far-reaching emotional expression; the striking, atmospheric music is based on violin and keyboards as much as guitar. (The American release has one different cut and much better sequencing.) Although Vincent took some flak for recording a totally overhauled version of the Buffalo Springfield's "For What It's Worth," she does manage to make something new and different out of the well-known tune. Elsewhere, sensitive, moody originals like "Samurai and Courtesan" and "Uptown" contrast with upbeat rockers like "We Danced" and "Honalu," all displaying a unique viewpoint in subtly evocative lyrics. Even more than its predecessor, this is an incredible album by an enormously gifted singer, writer and performer.

Vincent has not made a record under her own name since, although she did duet with Joey Ramone on a 45 of "I Got You Babe" and served a brief, unrecorded stint in the Waitresses. In 1988, Britain's Transvision Vamp made a run at international stardom with "Tell That Girl to Shut Up."   [i]

See also *Eastern Bloc*.

ROBERT HOLMES
See *Red Guitars*.

PETER HOLSAPPLE & CHRIS STAMEY
See *dB's*.

HOLY COW
Call It What You Will (Head Chunk) 1986
Suggested Reading/Apocalypse Cow (Head Chunk) 1988

New England's Holy Cow are merchants of the macabre, partaking equally of the dark intensity of Bauhaus and the bleak, forceful pound of the Swans. Though mohawked lead vocalist Chris Means occasionally sounds a bit too much like Peter Murphy for comfort, he is able to conjure up a seething well of rage, nausea and utter dislocation, rendered with such authority that it can't help but work. The band takes the best elements of the gothic and industrial-noise genres, yet belongs wholly to neither—theirs is an older, weirder tradition harking back to prime local/literary inspiration H.P. Lovecraft.

Call It What You Will is a patchwork affair, jumping from an avant-garde experiment to the Christian Death-like crawl of "Ichorous Pus" and metal-machine mantra of "Work" to the punkishly brisk "Black & White" and the gruesomely catchy "Lady Cadava." On "Noises," a pulsing, strumming, neo-acoustic gloom-pop number, all the vocals save for the chorus are backwards.

By its sophomore effort, Holy Cow had turned meaner and harder, grabbing onto a pretty original (but definitely not pretty) and far more unified sound. The record is broken up into thematic halves. Each of the four songs (not counting a closing instrumental) on the Suggested Reading side puts a favorite horror short story to hyper-distorted bass riffs. The results: frighteningly good songs like the ferocious, bone-chilling "Rep Fuck" (inspired by Stephen King's *Gramma*). The album's slightly less gripping flipside, Apocalypse Cow, is a live document, highlighted by an intense medley of their own "God" and "39 Lashes" (from *Jesus Christ Superstar*).　　　　　　　　　　　　　　　　[gef]

HOLY ROLLERS
The Origami Sessions EP (Dischord) 1990
As Is (Dischord) 1990

There may be an awful record on the Dischord label, but I've yet to hear it. Like such labelmates as Fugazi, Washington DC's Holy Rollers combine the hardness of punk with the melodicism of pop to create sparklingly listenable songs that pound and pummel while making you feel good, too.

Besides bassist Joe Aronstamn and guitarist Marc Lambiotte, Maria Jones rounds out the trio with loud, clear drumming that can be fast and hard, or click and clatter in palpitating textures (as in "Freedom Asking" or the percussion-dominated "Head On"). Throughout **As Is** she shifts seamlessly from one feeling and intensity to another; she's not just adequate, she's good. (Like her bandmates, she sings lead and backup.)

Most of the songs on the loud and crisp **As Is** are full-speed ahead, but the band's not above a little acoustic country style balladeering in "Johnny Greed." Like the poppier side of the Seattle bands, they play with dynamics; even when things ease down, high-energy intensity is never more than a few seconds away. Just when you think "Greed" is gonna wimp away like a Simon & Garfunkel oldie, it bursts into a screaming shriek of guitar fury. "Ode to Sabine County," meanwhile, could be the political side of the Minutemen reincarnated, with its chanted vocals and alternately pulsing and racing guitars. (**The Origami Sessions** is a four-track LP preview.)　　　　　　　　　　　　['e]

HONEYMOON KILLERS
Honeymoon Killers from Mars (Fur) 1984
Love American Style (Fur) 1985
Let It Breed (Fur) 1986
Turn Me On EP (Buy Our) 1988
Take It Off! EP (Buy Our) 1989 ●

Calling the Honeymoon Killers' debut disc a bad album is about as informative as calling **Catch a Fire** a reggae record: it's just a generic description. This New York four-piece (not to be confused with a Belgian band named after the same 1970 psychotronic cinema classic) is firmly rooted in the aesthetics of the splatter drive-in, where badness is just the starting point. The fake voodoo music, recorded in "four track horror fidelity," is abrasive and primitive—like the Cramps with its noncommercial instincts and an even sicker sense of humor. More a curio than anything anyone would ever want to listen to, **Honeymoon Killers from Mars** is at least an entertaining curio. Think of it as aural pain in the service of black humor. Or think of it as obnoxious incompetence—you'll be neither alone nor unjustified. But miss it, and you'll never get to hear the world's worst version of "Who Do You Love."

After half of the band split, guitarist Jerry Teel and bassist Lisa recruited drummer Sally for **Love American Style**, another crunching descent into lighthearted sonic warfare, recorded at CBGB in such a way as to suggest the sound of a bottomless pit. The squeals, screams, beats and roars hung on vari-speed rockabilly that strolls around like a dissipated hog caller don't always engage, but it's perfect accompaniment for latenight movie viewing with the TV sound off. And miss the ultimate garage grunge version of "Batman" at your peril.

Let It Breed ends with a version of the Blue Öyster Cult's "Godzilla" that right in with the album's horror motif. "Day of the Dead" eulogizes that classic cinematic series; "Brain Dead Bird Brain" suggests a future project for some current film student to contemplate. Trimming the musical insanity a tad without giving up any of their intensity, the Killers try a few numbers that are relatively straightforward. Investing more in vocals, the women chime in with Jerry for a neat X/Cramps-like effect; they also exchange bass and drum chores on the brief "Zoo Train."

The Killers expanded to a quartet with the addition of guitarist Cristina (ex-Pussy Galore) and became an even noisier proposition, as evidenced on **Turn Me On**. Songs like "Choppin' Mall" (basically a reworking of the pre-Who High Numbers' already derivative "I'm the Face"), "Octopussy," "Flophausen" and "Fingerlickin' Spring Chicken" demonstrate abundant junkcinema wit; the music shows continued development and structural strength.

Within **Take It Off!**'s day-glo sleeve (in itself a radical time-frame jolt for these orthodox back-to-thestone-agers), the Killers dole out six more glistening slabs from their well-stocked abbatoir. Back to being a trio (those members *do* seem to disappear rather quickly), the group struts its primordial stuff on "I'm Glad My Baby's Gone" and six tantalizingly trashy minutes of "The Sexorcist." Talk about your drive-in massacres!　　　　　　　　　　　　　　　　[jl/i/dss]

See also *Pussy Galore*.

HOODOO GURUS
Stoneage Romeos (Big Time-A&M) 1983 ●
Mars Needs Guitars! (Big Time-Elektra) 1985 ●
Blow Your Cool! (Big Time-Elektra) 1987 ●
Magnum Cum Louder (RCA) 1989 ●
Kinky (RCA) 1991 ●

Australia has produced few bands as crazily entertaining as Sydney's Hoodoo Gurus, whose roots intersect with the early Scientists. Who else would dedicate their debut album to, among other pop culture giants, American TV sitcom stars Larry Storch and Arnold Ziffel? That their music is an invigorating combination of cow-punk, garage-rock and demi-psychedelia only makes it better fun. "(Let's All) Turn On" is as good as any Lyres song; "In the Echo Chamber" has the mad abandon of prime Cramps; "I Want You Back" is winsome teen-angst power pop with a deadly hook; "I Was a Kamikaze Pilot" resembles the Fleshtones and displays a brilliant sense of absurd humor. (Think about that title again . . .) **Stoneage Romeos** is a great record.

Mars Needs Guitars! boasts a hip title, spiffy cover art, characteristically kitschy thank-yous and a top-notch opening tune in "Bittersweet." But while the band's spirit is as willing as ever, an ill-considered mix and

321

several clumsy arrangements hamper the rough'n'ready delivery, losing the melodies in the impressive raveup playing. Such promising numbers as the title track, "Like Wow–Wipeout" and the countryfied "Hayride to Hell" don't come off the way they should; the Gurus can definitely make better albums than this.

The improved **Blow Your Cool!** still isn't quite it, despite lively electric sound, plenty of offhand wit, crisp, energetic playing and hardy melodies. Increased emphasis on vocal harmonies distinguishes Side One; backup by the Bangles, blending nicely with songwriter Dave Faulkner's appealing voice on "What's My Scene" and "Good Times," helps put those tunes over the top. The fine "I Was the One" takes a similar tack without them. Lest anyone misjudge the Gurus' intentions, the record quickly turns (and stays) a lot tougher. Wild geographically minded cave stompers like "Where Nowhere Is," "Hell for Leather," "In the Middle of the Land" and "On My Street" are happily hard-nosed and noisy; "Party Machine," which closes the LP, is virtually a tribute to the Fleshtones.

Patient fans were finally rewarded bigtime with the spiffy **Magnum Cum Louder**, a confident, catchy collection that cuts the stylistic affectations to focus all of the group's strengths on songs that stick. The classic power-pop trick of mixing acoustic and electric rhythm guitars enlivens the album, especially "Come Anytime," an unbelievably catchy blast of layered vocals, guitars and handclaps that springs from the same well as "I Want You Back." Elsewhere, Brad Shepherd unleashes a firestorm of raucous guitar energy, slamming out AC/DC riffrock in "Axegrinder," raving up "I Don't Know Anything" and, for contrast, adding atmospheric, barely controlled feedback to the haunting, stately "Shadow Me." [i]

See also *Scientists*.

PETER HOPE & RICHARD KIRK

See *Cabaret Voltaire*.

BRENT HOSIER

See *Plan 9*.

HOTHOUSE FLOWERS

People (London) 1988 ●
Home (London) 1990 φ

How one feels about Hothouse Flowers depends very much on one's attitude towards (and tolerance for) bombast. The five members of this Dublin group are all talented musicians; vocalist/keyboardist Liam Ó Maonlai has a fine voice and sings from the heart. But there's a tendency to bludgeon virtually every song to death, slowly building each up to a gut-wrenching climax, with Ó Maonlai singing for his life as the piano pounds and the backing voices wail. To some listeners this may spell S-O-U-L, but others will beg for R-E-L-I-E-F. That said, many Bruce Springsteen and Joe Cocker fans (to name just two popular bombast-kings) will probably find this just what the doctor ordered.

People is the shorter of the two albums, and earns some additional points for the songs "I'm Sorry," (which contains a rare bit of humor) and "Don't Go." **Home** features guest appearances by Steve Nieve and Daniel Lanois, and contains a version of Johnny Nash's pop-reggae classic "I Can See Clearly Now" that'll blow your socks off. [ds]

HOUSEMARTINS

Flag Day EP (nr/Go! Discs) 1985
Sheep EP (nr/Go! Discs) 1986
Happy Hour EP (nr/Go! Discs) 1986
London 0 Hull 4 (Go! Discs-Elektra) 1986 ●
Think for a Minute EP (nr/Go! Discs) 1986
Caravan of Love EP (nr/Go! Discs) 1986
The People Who Grinned Themselves to Death (Go! Discs-Elektra) 1987 ●
There Is Always Something There to Remind Me EP (nr/Go! Discs) 1988 ●
Now That's What I Call Quite Good! (nr/Go! Discs) 1988 ●

As the cover of their first EP boasts, this quartet from Hull (actually, only drummer Hugh Whittaker is from the city; the rest wound up there for various reasons) are quite good, creating distinctive, finely crafted pop songs. **Flag Day** is an outstanding debut, four polished tunes that are memorable and intelligent. No fey pop wimps here. The melancholy title track laments the economic deterioration of Great Britain; the punchy and percussive "Stand at Ease" offers an unusual view of militarism. "You" is bright, bouncy pop with spectacular harmonies; "Coal Train to Hatfield Main" is a country stomp. Paul Heaton's vocals shine throughout, providing an integral part of the Housemartins' overall charm.

They followed with **Sheep**: three fine pop songs plus an extraordinary a cappella cover of Curtis Mayfield's uplifting "People Get Ready" and a choir-filled gospel song. As the sleeve states, "The Housemartins are my bestest band." **Happy Hour** propelled the Housemartins headfirst into the top of the UK charts (no mean feat for a band on an independent label) and earned them an American record contract. Exuberant guitar pop at its best, the title song is a humorous dig at the yuppie lifestyle.

After **Happy Hour** came a brilliant debut album. **London 0 Hull 4** (a play on an age-old soccer rivalry), a dozen perfect pop jewels (including "Sheep" and "Flag Day"), firmly established the band's position as crown princes of the three-minute pop classic. From the lusty bounce of "Happy Hour" to the gospel tones of "Lean on Me," the Housemartins are lyrically literate and musically precise.

Think for a Minute continues the band's ascent to stardom. Five flawless tracks, including the title song (remixed from **London 0 Hull 4**) and a delightful excursion into rap music entitled "Rap Around the Clock."

Caravan of Love (the title track is an Isley/Jasper/ Isley song) confirms the quartet's spiritual side and aptitude for gospel stylings with five songs of praise done a cappella. Considering Heaton's voice, this is as natural and comfortable an inclination as their usual pop trappings.

Personnel and musical changes marred the band's second album, **The People Who Grinned Themselves to Death**. Heaton's lyrics, once pointed and exact, have become obtuse and, in some instances ("Me and the

Farmer," "I Can't Put My Finger on It"), downright inane. The title track, "You Better Be Doubtful" and the solemn "Johannesburg" provide some good moments, but the majority of songs lack the immediate impact of previous Housemartins records. (The LP's US version contains a bonus 45 of "Caravan of Love" b/w "The Day I Met Jesus.") It's clear from this album the band's pop throne might be in jeopardy—a supposition turned fact when they disbanded months after its release.

The Housemartins' final UK single, "There Is Always Something There to Remind Me" (*not* the Bacharach/David tune), is included on **Now That's What I Call Quite Good!**, a posthumous double album whose 24 tracks—hits, album material, B-sides, radio sessions and unreleased songs—span the band's entire career. Though **London 0 Hull 4** remains the essential Housemartins disc to own, **Now That's What I Call Quite Good** offers a fine overview.   [ag/hd]

See also *Beats International, Beautiful South*.

HOUSE OF FREAKS
Monkey on a Chain Gang (Rhino) 1987 ●
Tantilla (Rhino) 1989 ●
All My Friends EP (Rhino) 1989 ●

Anyone skeptical of a two-piece rock'n'roll band should immediately check out Virginia-to-California transplants Bryan Harvey and Johnny Hott. What makes House of Freaks work is not the novelty of the guitar 'n'drums lineup, but Harvey's guitar and vocals, which jump out at you with all urgency and stripped-down emotionalism. Furthermore, Hott's industrial-strength drumming and Harvey's terrific songs that draw on American folklore and mythology from the days of the slave trade up through the atomic era make for a winning combination of punch and intelligence. The **Monkey on a Chain Gang** CD adds two bonus tracks.

Produced by John Leckie, the masterful **Tantilla** is liberally sprinkled with lyrical expressions of the Freaks' Southern (and religious) heritage. Over memorably original music that smolders with repressed passion and explodes in gloriously liberated choruses, Harvey castigates the memory of Jim Crow racism ("White Folk's Blood"), summons up the Civil War ("Big Houses"), questions religious faith ("The Righteous Will Fall," "I Want Answers") and ruminates on his roots ("Family Tree"). The duo's unabashed rock edge invests the catchy folk melodies with sturdy power; a piano/organ-playing guest adds a bit of subtle texture to the band's ample resources. Absolutely first-rate.

Little on the six-song **All My Friends**, however, comes close. Guest horns (a nice touch) don't make up for the listless material's tossed-off melodies or stylistic dilettantism; the lyrics (about pop star reality and armageddon) have scant cultural resonance. "Pass Me the Gun," a dissonant and downcast effort that sounds like a **Tantilla** outtake is the record's only bright spot.

     [ds/i]

HOUSE OF LOVE
The House of Love (Creation-Relativity) 1988 ●
The House of Love (Ger. Creation-Rough Trade) 1988 ●
The House of Love (Fontana-PolyGram) 1990 ●

A Spy in the House of Love (nr/Fontana) 1990 (Fontana) 1991 ●

The Smiths' massive success rewrote the rules for British indie bands, laying a perilous path for artists whose non-mainstream musical ideas masked serious commercial aspirations. For a group like London's House of Love, the realities of building substantial popularity on the Creation label into full-fledged pop stardom proved disastrous, and nearly ended its career after one album.

Originally a quintet with three guitarists, House of Love caught England's attention with its third single, the insidious Jesus & Mary Chain-meets-the-Left Banke three-chord pop of "Christine," later the leadoff track of the quartet's (typically) untitled debut album (the cover pictures two band members). While the self-produced music on this effectively uncomplicated LP explores some of the same stately and weird '60s elevations as the psychedelic Rolling Stones and the Bunnymen, singer/guitarist Guy Chadwick's reassuring deadpan also conjures up Velvet Underground tension and occasionally dips into a quixotic Robyn Hitchcock drone. "Road" accentuates a nifty up-and-down guitar line; the vacuous "Love in a Car" echoes away into oblivion with grace and beauty.

After **The House of Love** became a sizable UK hit, the band signed to PolyGram and spent the better part of two years making a follow-up. The second untitled album (generally known abroad as **Fontana**) was recorded, scrapped and redone, ultimately employing four different producers in four separate bouts of recording. Lead guitarist Terry Bickers quit amid the turmoil in early '90, and hasn't been adequately replaced since. Despite its painful creation, the album (butterfly cover) proves to be surprisingly well crafted and consistently great, easily bettering the debut.

Built around a sharp new version of "Shine On" (the band's first single, from 1987), **The House of Love** has a placid atmosphere that keeps the songs' edgy mood from being immediately apparent. Having endured artistic crisis, the House of Love now has the dexterity to bring off the crackling "Hannah" and "I Don't Know Why I Love You" as well as the temerity to attempt the quiet tribute of "Beatles and the Stones." Meanwhile, "In a Room" and "32nd Floor" slither menacingly, little eruptions shimmering up from the depths.

The German compilation collects up early singles, offering a primitive but more exciting view of the band's beginnings than the debut album. If nothing else, it's worth owning for two fantastic (and otherwise rare) B-sides: "Plastic" and the ebullient "Nothing to Me."

Far less compelling is the later compilation, known as **A Spy in the House of Love** because of the Anäis Nin novel prominently displayed on the cover. A fourteen-track patchwork of three unreleased leftovers from the abandoned second album and outtakes that were subsequently used as B-sides, it's not hard to understand why these efforts were deemed inadequate or relegated to supporting roles. Nevertheless, it is an economical purchase for fans who may have missed some of the preceding year's multi-format singles.   [jr]

HOUSE OF SCHOCK
See *Go-Go's*.

CHRIS HOUSTON AND THE SEX MACHINE

See *Forgotten Rebels*.

PENELOPE HOUSTON

See *Avengers*.

ROWLAND S. HOWARD

See *Barracudas, Birthday Party, Crime and the City Solution, Lydia Lunch, Nikki Sudden, These Immortal Souls*.

HOWARD & TIM'S PAID VACATION

See *Windbreakers*.

H.P. ZINKER

... And There Was Light EP (Matador) 1989
Beyond It All (Roughneck-Fire) 1990 φ
The Sunshine (Roughneck-Fire) 1991 ●

Raised and originally based in Innsbruck, Austria, Hans Platzgumer and Frank Puempel had toured Europe with several bands (and managed prolific recording careers as precocious teens) before relocating to New York in mid-'89 as H.P. Zinker. Produced by Wharton Tiers and recorded with a drum machine, ... **And There Was Light** opens with a cover of Led Zeppelin's "Dancing Days"; from there, the weird original material fuses metal with classical, punk, jazz, folk and noise. The rumblin' rockers and intricate, intriguing soundscapes would be a lot easier to take seriously in a voice that didn't so unmistakably recall Elmer Fudd; still, the songwriting and imagination resonate long after the initial laughter.

Beyond It All adds drummer Dave Wasik and shows dramatic improvement on all fronts. The power-trio format enables Zinker to create looming, pristine riffs (not unlike Dinosaur Jr.) amid the neo-classicism, shades of Sabbath and balls-out rock. Lengthy instrumental passages make for some startling updates on early-'70s progressive but, unlike the icons of that genre, Zinker seldom wanders into excess or incoherence. Platzgumer no longer sounds even remotely like a cartoon, and the lyrics ("Some of the triangles have four sides/And some have five/And some of them have five raised to the fifth power of sides") are likewise no joke.   [ja]

H.R.

See *Bad Brains*.

HUANG CHUNG

See *Wang Chung*.

HUDSON-STYRENE

See *Paul Marotta*.

HUGO LARGO

Drum (Relativity) 1987 (Opal-Warner Bros.) 1988 ●
Mettle (Opal-Warner Bros.) 1989 ●

Responding to the predominance of noisemongers on the New York downtown hipster scene, rock critic-turned-Glenn Branca sideman Tim Sommer took a turn for the ethereally haunting and formed Hugo Largo: two bassists, an electric violinist and indescribable vocalist Mimi Goese. **Drum**, a sublime seven-song mini-album produced in part by Michael Stipe, builds a remarkable bridge between new age airiness and sturdy new wave experimentation. While Goese's voice dives and glides as if airborne, the three instruments (plus a touch of guitar) play at a measured tempo that belies their power; lyrics are diverted into evocative, mesmerizing sounds. Although the originals are substantially engaging, an almost unrecognizable rendition of Ray Davies' "Fancy" provides a beautiful highlight. (The 1988 reissue on Brian Eno's label is remixed and contains two additional tracks.)

With violinist Hahn Rowe stepping forward as chief producer, **Mettle** has a clearer, more vibrant sound. As the group serves up memorable melodies on pieces like "Turtle Song" and "Hot Day," Goese executes daring vocal feats. Like the debut, **Mettle** builds to a dramatic climax near the end with "Nevermind." After Hugo Largo played its last gig in the summer of 1989, the foursome scattered into assorted projects and careers, although a new incarnation of the group surfaced two years later.   [i/ws]

HULA

Cut from Inside (nr/Red Rhino) 1983
Murmur (nr/Red Rhino) 1984
1,000 Hours (nr/Red Rhino) 1986
Shadowland (nr/Red Rhino) 1986
Voice (nr/Red Rhino) 1986
Cut Me Loose EP (nr/Red Rhino) 1987
Threshold (Red Rhino-Fundamental) 1987 ●
VC1 EP (Wax Trax!) 1988

JOHN AVERY

Jessica in the Room of Lights (nr/Technical) 1986

Formed in Sheffield by guitarist/tape manipulator Ron Wright, Hula furrowed a techno-industrial-multimedia path unmistakably influenced by Cabaret Voltaire (whose Stephen Mallinder produced their first single), yet fused with their own esoteric impulses into a unique strain of future-shock rock. Hula undercut its cluttered rhythms and flanged, ranting vocals with seriously funky bass and a disorienting melodic undertow; the media-overload of their live shows (employing at least a dozen film projectors) combined with the pulverizing music to build a mindbomb of epic proportions. Throughout its career, Hula released its best work on 45s, keeping LPs more deliberately experimental.

Cut from Inside and **Murmur** veer between funk, tribal, jazz-ish territory and noise; although the band's fascination with media sometimes led it down aural blind alleys of tape-loops and grating noise, the hypno-ambient grooves of "Tear-Up" and "Mother Courage" are both timely and prescient.

By 1985, however, serious self-indulgence began to creep in. The two-record **1,000 Hours** combines a thin-sounding live LP with a side each of more singles-oriented material and ominous, ambient drone. Likewise, **Shadowland**—a mostly improvised soundtrack to an art exhibit—is meandering and badly recorded drivel. **Voice**, which includes three songs produced by Mute supremo Daniel Miller, is relatively coherent and accessible, yet ironically less interesting. It does, however, contain one ace dance track ("Poison").

The excellent **Threshold** singles compilation is by far Hula's best release; it's also the only one that consists predominantly of the throbbing, brutal techno-funk upon which the band built its reputation. The CD and cassette tack on three extra cuts.

Following the 1988 demise of Red Rhino, Hula (by then just Wright and bassist John Avery) disappeared from view. The band's last release (its first on Wax Trax!) was a dreary "dance" version of Hendrix's "Voodoo Chile," aptly subtitled "Very slight return."

Avery's LP contains quiet, ambient instrumentals in an Eno/Bowie/Sylvian vein—hypnotic, cold atmospheres that would have made an excellent soundtrack to a Wim Wenders film. [ja]

HUMAN HANDS
Hereafter (Nate Starkman & Son) 1988

This turn-of-the-decade LA quintet featured such future stars of the California underground as drummer Dennis Duck (Dream Syndicate), guitarist Juan Gomez (Romans) and keyboardist Bill Noland (Wall of Voodoo). Although Human Hands never recorded an album proper, a limited-edition (and now hopelessly rare) two-disc demos/live compilation was issued by Independent Projects in 1982, later followed by a posthumous retrospective. Assembling Human Hands' few singles, compilation contributions and a few items from the first LP, **Hereafter** is an intriguing document of an ambitious outfit with lots of good ideas and uncommon influences. Pleasantly comparable in spots to pop groups like the Monochrome Set or Yachts, but also capable of disturbing art/jazz angles and fringey experiments (like Duck's percussion/found-sound/tape manipulation piece, "In the Heart of China"), Human Hands are not the missing link or anything. But **Hereafter** does add a neat paragraph to West Coast rock history. [i]

See also *Dream Syndicate, Wall of Voodoo*.

HUMAN LEAGUE
Dignity of Labour Pts. 1–4 EP (nr/Fast Product) 1979
Reproduction (nr/Virgin) 1979 (Virgin) 1988 ●
Travelogue (Virgin Int'l) 1980 (Virgin) 1988 ●
Dare (A&M) 1981 ●
Fascination! EP (A&M) 1983
Hysteria (A&M) 1984 ●
Crash (Virgin-A&M) 1986 ●
Greatest Hits (Virgin-A&M) 1988 ●
Romantic? (Virgin-A&M) 1990 ●

LEAGUE UNLIMITED ORCHESTRA
Love and Dancing (A&M) 1982 ●

PHILIP OAKEY & GIORGIO MORODER
Philip Oakey & Giorgio Moroder (Virgin-A&M) 1985 ●

LOOT!
Loot! (nr/Homa) 1990

It took a near-fatal lineup overhaul, two developmental albums and a fortuitous partnership with the right producer to put the Human League in a position to create the record that would make them, for a time, the unchallenged world champs of synthesizer pop. Interestingly, the group that topped the charts in 1982 with "Don't You Want Me" bears almost no resemblance to the dour trio that recorded "Being Boiled" for Fast Product in 1978.

The first two albums were the work of Sheffield's Phil Oakey, Ian Craig Marsh, Martyn Ware (all synth/vocals) and Philip Adrian Wright, who handled visual chores. **Reproduction** suffers from a simplistic approach—high-tech primitivism—given added monotony by Oakey's frequently deadpan vocals. Amid all the glum sonic novelties (like "You've Lost That Loving Feeling"), the atmospheric "Morale" and the surprisingly poppy "Empire State Human" indicated promise for the future and brought the League—at a time when such a notion seemed farfetched—some success on the British charts.

Travelogue is much better, broadening the palette to include a wide variety of subtle synthesizer shadings, from the arcane to the sublime, and introducing vastly improved material. Lyrical subjects concern science-fiction and kitsch culture. Although still emotionally ambivalent, **Travelogue** is warmer and more fun than its predecessor, and suggested a direction for the band to pursue.

And pursue it they did. After a schism sent Marsh and Ware off as the British Electric Foundation, Oakey and Wright revamped the Human League with four new members (Ian Burden, Susanne Sulley, Joanne Catherall and ex-Rezillo guitarist Jo Callis) and a rededication to danceable pop music. That intent, along with producer Martin Rushent—whose skills dovetailed with almost all of the band's shortcomings (almost all—there's no cure for Oakey's crooning)—ultimately led to such interplanetary hits as "Don't You Want Me" and "Love Action (I Believe in Love)." The irresistible mix of state-of-the-art technology and old-fashioned pop-single formulae set millions of toes tapping, although the **Dare** LP contains much headier and heavier stuff as well. With incredible ambience and subtle tension, "Seconds"—about the Kennedy assassination—is, in fact, the LP's unheralded best track. A great record, and not just for its popular songs.

The trailblazing (for white rockers, that is) remix album, **Love and Dancing**, pays titular homage of sorts to Barry White and contains Rushent's revamped versions of seven cuts from **Dare**, plus one extra tune. Some of the record bears listening to; other parts, however, are either repetitively dull or noisily annoying.

Subsequently proven incapable of delivering a timely follow-up to sustain their new-found megastardom, the Human League had to make do with stopgap singles, two of which were compiled on the **Fascination!** EP. "Mirror Man" is pedestrian but catchy; "(Keep Feeling) Fascination" (which appears here in its original form and an extended remix), however, is ruined by awful sick-cow vibrato on the synthetic horns.

Three years after **Dare**, following a pitched battle with their commercial insecurities, the League finally came up with **Hysteria**. Following a traumatic split with Rushent, the band itself produced the LP with Chris Thomas and Hugh Padgham, wisely omitting the prior

45s in favor of new songs, some of which are quite good. Stretching styles to encompass a subtler, tender side, the ballads ("Louise," "Life on Your Own") provide the record's most engaging moments, although they exacerbate Oakey's vocal limitations. Taking an ill-advised political turn, "The Lebanon" offers simpleminded drama with a pop hook; "Don't You Know I Want You" is an almost-clever attempt to acknowledge and recycle the sound (and title) of their biggest hit.

During another Human League hibernation, Oakey collaborated with Giorgio Moroder, first on a song for the *Electric Dreams* film soundtrack, then continued the partnership for a joint album. Giorgio wrote the music and produced; Phil added lyrics and sang; Arthur Barrow and Richie Zito provided the backing tracks on, respectively, synth and guitar. With a bouncy, upbeat sound, it's an unchallenging bit of fun that could easily be mistaken for a jollified League record were it not for Moroder's lighthanded, deft arrangements and percolating tunes. "Good-bye Bad Times" and a reprise of "Together in Electric Dreams" stand out, but the rest is almost as immediately enjoyable.

In a desperate maneuver to locate a functional musical personality, the Human League enlisted the stunningly successful pop-funk team of Jimmy Jam and Terry Lewis to produce and co-write the absurdly misbegotten **Crash**. The imprudent collaboration produced a collection of musical nightmares: preening soul ballads ("Human," "Love Is All That Matters") that Oakey isn't up to singing, fraudulent funk workouts ("Swang," "Jam," "I Need Your Loving") that only underscore the band's emotional sterility and inadequate dance-rock ("Money," "Love on the Run") that trails the field's cutting edge by a few years. Like the cover's intentionally out-of-focus photograph, this halfhearted effort falls well short of nominal quality standards.

When another couple of years had passed without productive noise from the League's camp, **Greatest Hits** arrived to keep the band's name in circulation. This non-chronological assembly of a dozen singles, from 1978's "Being Boiled" through 1986's "Human," is not a very compelling reminder of why anyone ever took this music seriously. Although bits and pieces stand up to the test of a few years' time, the cream of this crop is more like crap. (The American edition deletes "Together in Electric Dreams.")

Disproving rumors of non-existence, a five-piece Human League (Oakey, Catherall and Sulley, joined by recent arrivals on guitar and keyboards) resurfaced with the labored and dull **Romantic?** in 1990. Half a dozen producers (including the long-missing Martin Rushent) vainly try to breathe life into the weak songs, even adding a few house elements in hopes of helping the once-futurist group catch up with the present.

After leaving the League, Callis formed a group called SWALK; Loot! is Ian Burden's new band.   [i]

See also *British Electric Foundation, Heaven 17, Shake*.

HUMAN SEXUAL RESPONSE
Figure 14 (Eat-Passport) 1980
In a Roman Mood (Passport) 1981

A most promising (but ultimately unsuccessful) band from Boston, the seven-person HSR (including four vocalists!) explored sexual identities, both physical and mental, on **Figure 14**, as on the wonderful "What Does Sex Mean to Me?" Elsewhere, there's a healthy irreverence towards the famous and the neurotic, with sex never quite out of the picture. Leanings in the direction of art rock, led by singer Larry Bangor's Tom Verlaine-style vocals, occasionally get HSR in trouble, coming off too cute.

In a Roman Mood is darker and more oblique than **Figure 14**, showcasing the band's growing lyrical complexity regarding human beings and what they expect from each other. Again their nervous rhythms—over an entire LP—don't produce anything outstanding. Human Sexual Response makes background music for difficult relationships.

The band broke up in 1982 and spawned several offshoots. A reunion show took place on Halloween 1984.   [gk]

See also *Zulus*.

HUMAN SWITCHBOARD
The Human Switchboard EP (Under the Rug) 1977
Human Switchboard Live (no label) 1980
Who's Landing in My Hangar? (Faulty Products) 1981
Coffee Break [tape] (ROIR) 1982
BOB PFEIFER
After Words (Passport) 1987 ●
MYRNA
Human Touch EP (OKra) 1989

Transplant the early Velvet Underground to the late '70s, trade that band's kinkier concerns for conventional male-female issues, and you've got Kent, Ohio's Human Switchboard in a nutshell. Repeated disclaimers aside, leader Bob Pfeifer sings in a dry, ironic style suggestive of young Lou Reed, while Myrna Marcarian's wobbly organ-playing adds an amateurish tint that evokes **White Light/White Heat**.

The Human Switchboard debuted with a junky-sounding 7-inch (mixed by Pere Ubu's David Thomas) whose four songs clearly (if ineptly) demonstrate the two sides of the trio's sound. "Distemper" and "Shake It, Boys" are straight garage rock, while "San Francisco Nights" is a total Lou Reed imitation.

On the Switchboard's sole studio album, **Who's Landing in My Hangar?**, Pfeifer creates a neurotic, high-strung persona that makes for gripping listening. Two uptempo cuts ("Book on Looks" and "(I Used to) Believe in You") celebrate the ups and downs of romance, while the LP's high point, "Refrigerator Door," carefully weaves an intriguing web of personal details. It all seems embarrassingly confessional, which is a pretty neat trick.

The Switchboard's other two releases are live recordings that overlap material extensively with **Hangar**; both are interesting, if redundant. The 1980 disc, an authorized bootleg, features Marcarian's haunting rendition of "Downtown." **Coffee Break** is from a November 1981 Cleveland radio broadcast.

Time mellows even a sourpuss like Pfeifer, it seems. Without the Switchboard behind him (though ex-members of the defunct group appear on **After Words**), he's looser, more willing to play off the rhythms, which themselves are less constricted than before. Pfeifer's still got an obvious affinity for Lou Reed's plain-spoken approach to interpersonal tales, offering diary-like accounts in "She Always Smiled" and "I'm Better for You." In "Knock-Knock," he finally succumbs to the urge to do a straight Reed imitation. Otherwise, worthwhile.

Myrna Marcarian's solo EP may leave folks wishing she'd stepped out sooner. Apart from a track in a Switchboard vein that finds her sounding unpleasantly like Stevie Nicks, she successfully tackles some tough, driving rockers here, assisted by nimble guitarist Jack Johnson and ex-Switchboard drummer Ron Metz.

[i/jy]

HUMMINGBIRDS

loveBUZZ (rooArt-PolyGram) 1990 φ

Australia's Hummingbirds play an agreeable form of brisk guitar-band pop that's hypnotic in small doses, but soporific at full-CD (55 minutes) length. With classicist Mitch Easter producing, the Sydney quartet's debut emphasizes a ringing blend of male and female three-part harmonies, generating a sweet, airy vibe with unabashed guitar energy. While toned-down efforts like "Everything You Said" (which resembles a juiceless Primitives) occasionally threaten preciousness, the rhythm section kicks hard enough in songs like "Blush," "Word Gets Around" and "Get on Down" to keep the record in a good gear. [jy]

IAN HUNTER

Short Back n' Sides (Chrysalis) 1981

Ian Hunter emerged as an early patron saint of punk—quite a feat considering that the movement was allegedly based on the rejection of his generation of old wave musicians. Hunter's popularity with the young rebels stemmed primarily from his salad years as leader of Mott the Hoople and was based on attitude as much as music. In the late '60s and early '70s, Hunter and band were down-to-earth, streetwise blokes who voiced a sense of disillusionment and failure instead of indulging in the fantasy and self-aggrandizement typical of so many big-league rockers. Punks of the later '70s saw themselves as fighting against the same climate of unreality and vanity.

Specifics: Beginning with Mott's debut, **Mott the Hoople**, you can hear the tight, driving guitar of Mick Ralphs, later appropriated in whole by the Clash, Pistols and, most pointedly, Generation X. **Mott**'s "Violence" and **The Hoople**'s "Crash Street Kids" both forecast with uncanny accuracy the emergence of a new generation of disaffected, angry kids. Hunter produced Gen X's second LP, **Valley of the Dolls**. The late Guy Stevens, who pulled Mott together and produced their first four LPs, produced the Clash's **London Calling**.

Mick Jones joined with long-time Hunter-mate Mick Ronson to produce Ian's sixth solo effort, **Short Back n' Sides**, an ambitious, unfocused LP with a Clash-

family guest list that covers more styles than a single record should. Still, Hunter continues to be the straight-shooter that originally endeared him to his "kids."

[jy]

HUNTERS & COLLECTORS

Hunters & Collectors (Aus. White Label) 1982
Hunters & Collectors (Oz-A&M) 1983
Fireman's Curse (nr/Virgin) 1983
The Jaws of Life (Slash) 1984
Way to Go Out (Aus. White Label) 1985
Human Frailty (IRS) 1986 ●
Living Daylight EP (IRS) 1987 ●
What's a Few Men (Aus. White Label) 1987 ●
Fate (IRS) 1988 ●
Ghost Nation (Atlantic) 1990 ●
Collected Works (IRS) 1990 φ

At the outset, Melbourne's Hunters & Collectors offered an Australian response to the Fall: an unremittingly bleak and powerful ensemble capable of horrendous noise, gripping drama and slithery funk. They do all three on both eponymous albums, which are almost entirely different records. The Australian release is a self-produced double-album with only three tracks common to the UK/US single disc of the same name, which Mike Howlett produced. (And remixed "Talking to a Stranger.") Utterly oblique lyrics (and a credit to the band as a whole for "lyrics, music, artwork, management") typify this enigmatic album. Fans of challenging, noisy rock and rhythm should enjoy, if not understand, this; real enthusiasts would do well to seek out both versions.

It took a while to locate another American label courageous enough to take the band on, but eventually Slash saw their way clear to releasing **The Jaws of Life**, recorded in Germany with Conny Plank. Thanks to normal cover info, it becomes possible to compliment bassist John Archer and drummer Doug Falconer for their dominant rhythm work, suggest that guitarist Mark Seymour let someone else attempt to sing next time and praise keyboard player Geoff Crosby for the nifty cover assemblage. **Way to Go Out** is a live album recorded in Melbourne in the summer of '84.

Human Frailty was the band's long-delayed IRS debut (a 1983 deal with the label had fallen through at the eleventh hour). One immediately notices the more mainstream sound—or at least as close as they can get to one and still retain some of their trademarks. The unorthodox horn section (trumpet, trombone and French horn) plays conventional parts, and there's a lot more in the way of background vocals. Fans of the band's early work simply won't believe that several cuts, especially the Top 40-flavored "Throw Your Arms Around Me," are actually the work of the band credited on the album cover. While **Human Frailty** doesn't lack in quality per se, Hunters & Collectors have certainly done more interesting music than this.

"Inside a Fireball," which opens the five-track **Living Daylight** EP (a three-songer back home), indicates that all is well; while not as art-noisy as early work, the record at least has the punch and bite its predecessor lacks. It also contains remixed versions of "The Slab" and "Carry Me" from **The Jaws of Life**. (The entire

327

EP is appended to the American **Human Frailty** CD.)

Fate (originally released in Australia as **What's a Few Men**) is accessible, has a nice clear, guitar-driven sound and its share of catchy hooks; nothing to alienate the casual listener. What sets the group apart here is Seymour's vivid word pictures and urgent delivery. His vocals have improved a lot over the years; on **Fate** he sounds like he's wound pretty tight, but never resorts to histrionics. Highlights: the semi-hit "Back on the Breadline" and the haunting, anti-militaristic CD-only "What's a Few Men?," an account of an Aussie fighting for the British army. Although almost undetectable, there are thirteen (!) guest artists augmenting the seven-piece band.

Ghost Nation is more relaxed; acoustic and slide guitars figure prominently and several tracks feature somewhat awkward background vocals (some supplied by Crowded House leader Neil Finn). But with only a few exceptions (the plaintive "Lazy Summer Day," "The Way You Live"), no songs really stand out. "Running Water," a fearful view of the environmental future, sounds an awful lot like Midnight Oil, and this band has never had to imitate anyone before. Hunters & Collectors just don't stand out the way they once did.

Barring the obligatory "Talking to a Stranger," **Collected Works** only acknowledges material recorded during the band's IRS era. Considering how much their sound has changed, the sixteen-track collection doesn't serve any valuable purpose. A real Hunters & Collectors compilation would have to go back further than this.

See also *Deadly Hume*.   [i/dgs]

BILL HURLEY WITH JOHNNY GUITAR
See *Inmates*.

HÜSKER DÜ
Land Speed Record (New Alliance) 1981 (SST) 1987 ●
Everything Falls Apart (Reflex) 1982
Metal Circus (Reflex-SST) 1983 ●
Zen Arcade (SST) 1984 ●
New Day Rising (SST) 1985 ●
Flip Your Wig (SST) 1985 ●
Candy Apple Grey (Warner Bros.) 1986 ●
Sorry Somehow EP (nr/Warner Bros.) 1986
Warehouse: Songs and Stories (Warner Bros.) 1987 ●

Hüsker Dü emerged from the punk rock scene; vast improvements in songwriting over the years may have changed the shape of their music, but they never lost their firm attachment to bracing, loud guitar rock. Although failing to achieve the mainstream success of R.E.M. or even the Replacements, the often exhilarating Minneapolis trio was hugely popular and influential (and has grown legendary) in certain circles, maintaining its vision, integrity and dedication to independent music to the end. With Bob Mould's impassioned talk-shout-singing and masterful guitar overlaid with feedback and amplifier distortion, Greg Norton's straight-ahead driving bass and Grant Hart's only slightly less demented singing and excessive drumming, the Hüskers piled on the pop hooks in their songs to the point of explosion, creating a startling rush of momentum.

The live **Land Speed Record** is basically a tour document from a year in which they covered a lot of land and took a lot of speed—a cheap recording that only hints at any juice the performance may have contained. In those days, the group was naturally sloppy, and this disc captures the mess but not the overkill power.

Everything Falls Apart, in fact, puts everything back together. While the band hadn't totally mastered the studio, this is a great improvement over the live record. And it offers the first taste of pop-oriented things to come: a cover of Donovan's "Sunshine Superman."

Metal Circus marks a giant leap forward. With this brief seven-song disc, Hüsker Dü began to reach for a broader audience. The often misconstrued title refers not to heavy metal (an area of exploration for many hardcore bands), but to the flat gray solidity of alloys, which fairly describes the record. **Metal Circus** is a collection of anthems, slow and fast, with twisted, abrasive guitar licks and twisted lyrics. The rousing Mission of Burma-ish "It's Not Funny Anymore" is the most potent track, but "Diane" is the most haunting, a Hart-penned power dirge about rape and murder. When he screams the title over and over, it sounds like "dying." A monster song from a heavy record.

After **Metal Circus**, Hüsker Dü released a 7-inch statement of purpose, the totally gonzoid cover of "Eight Miles High." The single brings together Mould's love of jangly '60s pop with the band's adrenaline charge. Punk covers of '60s songs generally devolve into camp, but this one retains the flavor of the original without compromising the sonic blitz.

Zen Arcade, an ambitious double-record concept album about the strange adventures of a kid leaving home, covers more ground than Greyhound and is successful a surprisingly high percentage of the time. The band plays acoustic, psychedelic and unabashedly poppy songs; when it's good, the material is among their best. A straight rocker, "Turn on the News," deserves to be a classic. Unfortunately, there's also some over-reaching and self-indulgent dross, possibly related to the one-take production technique. As on **Sandinista!**, it isn't really filler; still, backwards tape loops and extended drones dilute the effect.

By contrast, **New Day Rising** is as tight as a duck's behind, and that's waterproof. The band flails the hell out of the kind of loping melodies currently ringing out of the New South. The album is LOUD, intense, funny, accessible and downright catchy. From the opening cut, in which Mould just screams "new day rising" over and over above a rising tide of triumphant sound, to the elliptical closer, "Plans I Make," they do the Dü with nary a false step. Seldom have hooks been this powerful, nor full-throttle punk this melodic.

The Hüskers' final SST release, **Flip Your Wig**, is positively brilliant—fourteen unforgettable pop tunes played like armageddon were nigh. The production is taut and claustrophobic, pushing the busy, anechoic drums right into your head, competing with Mould's precise stun-assault guitar wash and vocals. Besides the compressed, efficient Top 40 sound of "Makes No Sense at All" (one of 1985's best 45s), the LP boasts such classic fare as the loving, fragile "Green Eyes," the boppy, bubblegummy "Hate Paper Doll" and the somberly psychedelic (complete with backwards guitar) of "Don't Know Yet," which closes things out in appropriately enigmatic fashion.

Following the Replacements to Warner Bros., Hüsker Dü self-produced **Candy Apple Grey** with an equally unselfconscious lack of commercial consideration, sacrificing nary a drop of energy nor an ounce of spirit. (They did, however, cut back to a mere ten songs.) Too many cuts start with the same brief Hartbeat, but the charged, varied music and never-better reflective, adult lyrics on Mould's six compositions provide a seductive wallop. "Sorry Somehow" (with surprising Deep Purple organ), "Don't Want to Know If You Are Lonely" and "Dead Set on Destruction" are typically staggering rock numbers; "I Don't Know for Sure" sounds good but resembles "Makes No Sense at All" a tad too much. Two all-acoustic numbers ("Too Far Down" and "Hardly Getting Over It") demonstrate the band's flexibility and a casual disregard for punk convention. While more diverse, **Candy Apple Grey** ultimately falls a bit short of **Flip Your Wig** in intensity and impact.

The British **Sorry Somehow** 12-inch contains "All This I've Done for You" (also from **Candy Apple Grey**), acoustic live versions of one track each from the previous two albums and "Fattie," an all-noise studio recording. The same year, American Warners issued a 12-inch of "Don't Want to Know if You Are Lonely" with a terrible live "Helter Skelter" and a numbingly repetitive eight-minute studio track ("All Work and No Play") on the flipside.

It took wrangling with (and concessions to) Warner Bros., but the group was able to prevail and release the ambitious two-disc **Warehouse: Songs and Stories**, on which Hart and Mould co-produced and evenly split the songwriting. Neither sprawling nor start-to-finish essential, this twenty-song collection breaks no new ground and is short on variety but still quite enjoyable—the thick sound is in itself sensually satisfying. With fine tracks strewn randomly throughout, the album's strongest side is its third (with the hypnotically swirling "It's Not Peculiar," the folky "No Reservations" and the late-'60sish "Tell You Why Tomorrow")); other notable cuts are "She Floated Away," a rocking sea chantey, "Standing in the Rain" and "Ice Cold Ice."

Hart quit or was fired in December 1987, and Hüsker Dü broke up shortly thereafter. [jl/i]

See also *Grant Hart, Bob Mould*.

PARTHENON HUXLEY
Sunny Nights (Columbia) 1988 ●

Not his real name; the Parthenon bit may be a tip of the hat to his high school days in Greece. On this debut LP, Huxley engages in thoughtful whimsy ("Between the sacred and the profane/Runs a crooked yellow line/you dance around from lane to lane . . ."). The music is power pop that's equally skewed, though not equally effective; its cleverness tends to overpower melodies that seem to deserve better. (He co-produced with David Kahne.) Promising all the same. [jg]

HUXTON CREEPERS
12 Days to Paris (Big Time) 1986
Keep to the Beat (Big Time-Polydor) 1988 ●

This quartet from Melbourne, Australia, plays gritty Stonesish rock and harmony-laden Byrdsy folk-rock on their first American LP, which might easily be mistaken for the work of an American "heartland" band. The Huxton Creepers could use a more mellifluous singer than Rob Craw—gruffness when he strains is a problem—but his guitar interplay with Paul Thomas, supported by a fluid, strong rhythm section, makes **12 Days** an unfailingly engaging record. Guest Hammond work (on one song—a second, indicated on the back cover, was somehow omitted from the US LP!) by ex-Procol Harum organist Chris Copping is more eyebrow-raising than ear-opening.

The follow-up is an equally inoffensive collection, highlighted by the high-spirited and eminently catchy "Rack My Brains" and "Visually." Craw's vocals tend to venture into perilous adenoidalism, but the rest of the band is still sharp, the material fresh. Though these two albums are hardly essential, Huxton Creepers traffic in the kind of commercial rock that has made stars out of lesser (and less-talented) mortals. [i/db]

HYBRID KIDS
Hybrid Kids (nr/Cherry Red) 1979
Claws (nr/Cherry Red) 1980
VARIOUS ARTISTS
Miniatures (nr/Pipe-Cherry Red) 1980
MORGAN FISHER
Ivories (nr/Strike Back) 1985

What happens when Jah Wobble meets country clods the Wurzels for a raveup on Kate Bush's greatest hit? You get Jah Wurzel's version of "Wuthering Heights," zonked-out reggae with quizzical vocals in a back-country accent, that's what. Actually, this is Morgan Fisher, ex-Mott the Hoople keyboardist, pretending (with a dab of help from uncredited friends—he himself is billed as "producer/director") to be a baker's dozen different acts having a go at their fave tunes. What purports to be British Standard Unit takes a pretty amusing off-the-wall industrial-synth whack at "D'Ya Think I'm Sexy," but most of the rest of **Hybrid Kids** tends to be gratuitously high in the ozone, or tediously puerile (or both). Nice version of Sun Ra's "Enlightment" [*sic*], allegedly by Combo Satori, all the same.

Miniatures, conceived, compiled and edited by Fisher, is a widely variegated collection: 51 tracks (of no more than a minute apiece) by just as many artists. (No relation to the Residents' **Commercial Album** of the same year, which Fisher first learned of when he invited the Residents to chip in a track; they medley "We're a Happy Family" with "Bali Ha'i.") Fred Frith encapsulates the history of Henry Cow in one minute; Andy Partridge encapsulates the history of rock'n'roll in twenty seconds; Neil Innes strums as his five-year-old son sings and drums "Cum on Feel the Noize"; Quentin Crisp rants about the evils of music; artist Ralph Steadman (also responsible for the LP cover) plaintively sings John Donne. Trivial, indulgent, amusing and educational. [jg]

PAUL HYDE AND THE PAYOLAS
See *Payolas*.

HYPNOLOVEWHEEL

Turn! Turn! Burn! (Fabian Aural Products) 1988
Candy Mantra (Fabian Aural Products) 1990 ●
Space Mountain (Alias) 1991 ●

A fine quartet originally from Long Island, Hypnolovewheel carry a kinda avant-garage ethos into all sorts of unexpected places. Refusing to be pinned down to any one stylistic board, the group wiggles around through a wide array of psychedelic pop, punk and garage-mush puddles. That they're able to do so without seeming like a bunch of lost ponies is testament to their ability to create a genuinely cordial mix of low-ball guitar-rant and tossed-off melodic hooks. (Hypnolovewheel's music bears textural similarities to the Embarrassment.) When they come up with something that's potentially too catchy, Dave Ramirez and Steve Hunkins bury it under a small load of six-string noise.

As a tendency to write funny lyrics has been tempered with age, all of the band's records are easily commendable to hepsters and squares alike. Nice, a-generic, non-flash all-purpose pop-noise is a too rare commodity these days. [bc]

HYPNOTICS

See *Thee Hypnotics*.

HYPSTRZ

Hypstrz Live EP (Bogus-Twin/Tone) 1979
Hypstrization! (Voxx) 1980

MIGHTY MOFOS

The Mighty E.P. (Midnight) 1986
Sho' Hard! (Treehouse) 1988

Although barely considered worth a footnote today (cross-reference under "singleminded" and "energy OD"), the Hypstrz were nevertheless radical in their own special time and place, blasting through '60s garagemania in late-'70s Minneapolis, purposefully stamping their frantic rifferama into countless pubescent brains, personalizing punk in a subversively idiosyncratic (and decidedly *song*-oriented) manner, thereby paving the way for the Twin City sound of the early '80s.

Voxx quickly followed up the manic four-song 7-inch debut on Bogus with a full album of live Hypstrz (fifteen stripped-down classics: "96 Tears," "Slow Death," "Midnight Hour," "Riot on Sunset Strip," etc.). That no-studios policy was wisely upheld on Midnight's live EP six years later but sadly ignored by Treehouse, which plopped the retitled band of Batsons (Ernie and Billy; guitars and vocals respectively) plus new rhythm section in a salon de recording with brand-name indie producer Lou Giordano to "polish" their now (nominally) original songs. Onstage, the Mofos roared as unrestrainedly as their predecessors, but on **Sho' Hard!**, the fury is reeled in to showcase mediocre songwriting and recycled formulaic garage pop. Tellingly, the standout track is an MC5 cover. (The cassette contains extra tracks.) [ab]

ICE CUBE

See *N.W.A.*

ICEHOUSE

Icehouse (Chrysalis) 1981 ●
Primitive Man (Chrysalis) 1982 ●
Fresco EP (Chrysalis) 1983
Sidewalk (Chrysalis) 1984 ●
Measure for Measure (Chrysalis) 1986 ●
Man of Colours (Chrysalis) 1987 ●
Great Southern Land (Chrysalis) 1989 ●

FLOWERS

Icehouse (Aus. Regular) 1980

For the record, Icehouse began as Flowers. For its first US/UK album, the Sydney, Australia band renamed itself after the title of the Flowers LP, subtracted one cut, remixed and resequenced it. Icehouse's debut LP effectively mates emotional tension with the streamlined efficiency of modern synthesizer outfits. "Icehouse" and "Can't Help Myself," in particular, exploit the contrast between smooth surfaces and frontman Iva Davies' anxious singing. Despite inconsistent material, this is a promising start.

Unfortunately, Davies let it all go to his head on **Primitive Man**, hiding the underrated band and declaring allegiance to empty stylishness. By emphasizing the elegance in his artful compositions and restricting his passions to poses, Davies ends up with slick, pretty product that neither demands nor encourages listener involvement. (It does, however, contain the global hit single, "Hey Little Girl," a remarkable Roxy Music simulation.)

That song, two others from **Primitive Man**, plus two new tracks of forgettable roaring rock comprise the **Fresco** EP, evidently issued to capitalize on the band's sudden commercial emergence.

Sidewalk is a tedious two-voiced exercise: fake Bryan Ferry (hey—doing it once may be cute, but two albums in a row is lame!) and histrionic guitar rock; occasionally the two are blended together in a misbegotten vision of Roxy Metal. Melt this sucker down.

While retaining the mannered Ferry imitation in spots, **Measure for Measure** adds an equally artificial version of David Bowie (circa **Lodger**) and drops **Sidewalk**'s over-energized sandtrap. "No Promises" is the atmospheric pop hit (one of three cuts on which ex-Japan drummer Steve Jansen plays; Eno receives an all-LP credit for backing vocals, treated piano and keyboards), but other songs are more memorable. (Most are less.) Smooth, crafty and pointless.

The unfocused but blatantly commercial **Man of Colours** tries a little of this (ersatz Roxy, imitation Bowie) and a little of that (semi-fake Hall and Oates, a halfhearted stab at Billy Idol's neighborhood). Davies' voice briefly resembles Barry Manilow's on the mega-hit single, "Crazy" (which also appears in two needless bonus remixes on the CD), a hollow slab of romantic melodrama. Oates co-wrote and sings on "Electric Blue," which sounds like an INXS discard.

Great Southern Land is a ten-song compilation named for the song Icehouse contributed to the *Young Einstein* soundtrack; the CD and cassette add a dance mix of "No Promises." [jy/i]

ICE-T

Rhyme Pays (Sire) 1987 ●
Power (Sire) 1988 ●
The Iceberg/Freedom of Speech ... Just Watch What You
Say (Sire) 1989 ●
O.G. Original Gangster (Sire-Warner Bros.) 1991 ◌

One of the earliest and most convincing indications that Los Angeles wasn't going to sit out the East Coast hip-hop revolution, rapper Ice-T quickly proved the equal of any New York MC. On **Rhyme Pays**, working over energetic tracks programmed and produced by Afrika Islam, Ice (who had already made his film debut in 1984's *Breakin'*) puts a little flair into the presentation, using a toaster singsong, other vocal styles and assorted theatrical gimmicks to make detailed tales of sex, parties, wealth, criminal activity and jail more absorbing and distinguished than they might otherwise be. A strong debut but, in retrospect, hardly the peak of his career. (And the mix stinks: his voice is way too low.)

Ice-T made great strides on **Power**, a dynamic and confident shift into solidly delivered ambivalently positive messages built on his unassailable street cred. (Acknowledging mixed loyalties, Ice-T allows "I'm not here to tell ya right or wrong/I don't know which side of the law you belong.") So if there's no clear-cut moral in the violent first-person criminality of "Drama" or "High Rollers," Ice-T does stop short of endorsing the gangster life. His sex rap ("Girls L.G.B.N.A.F.") pulls no punches but doesn't get abusive and does recommend safe sex; the anti-dope "I'm Your Pusher" proffers music in place of drugs, folding in Curtis Mayfield's original "Pusher Man" for added impact.

Responding to the climate of censorship by attacking it *and* defying it, Ice-T made the hard and intense **Iceberg**, a great-sounding but disturbingly confused mixture of right-on politics and repulsive vulgarity. "I'm a pimp and a player and a hustler and kinda a mack and a poet," he raps in "The Iceberg," the crude spew that follows the amazing "Shut Up, Be Happy," in which Jello Biafra declaims martial law edicts over the ominous toll of "Black Sabbath." Similarly, while Ice-T attacks ignorance, sexism and drug addiction (in the powerfully atmospheric "You Played Yourself") and attacks the narrowmindedness of radio programmers and governmental complicity in narcotics ("This One's for Me"), the amoral gangster rap of

"Peel Their Caps Back" and the grisly sonic joke of "Black'n'Decker"—overtly posed as an ironic comment about the violence in Ice's lyrics—take the opposite stance. [i]

See also *Jello Biafra*.

ICICLE WORKS

Icicle Works (Arista) 1984 ●
The Small Price of a Bicycle (Chrysalis) 1985 ●
Seven Singles Deep (nr/Beggars Banquet) 1986 ●
Understanding Jane (nr/Beggars Banquet) 1986
Who Do You Want for Your Love? EP (nr/Beggars Banquet) 1986
Up Here in the North of England EP (nr/Situation Two) 1986
If You Want to Defeat Your Enemy Sing His Song (Beggars Banquet-RCA) 1987 ●
Numb EP (nr/Beggars Banquet) 1988 ●
Blind (Beggars Banquet-RCA) 1988 ●
Little Girl Lost EP (nr/Beggars Banquet) 1988 ●
Motorcycle Rider EP (nr/Works-Epic) 1990 ●
Permanent Damage (nr/Epic) 1990 ●
Melanie Still Hurts EP (nr/Epic) 1990 ●

"Whisper to a Scream (Birds Fly)," which leads off this Liverpool trio's debut album, is a brilliant pop single filled with sparkling guitars, a hook-laden chorus and Chris Sharrock's surprisingly powerful, creative drumming. Unfortunately, nothing else on the LP is nearly as good. It's typical. Icicle Works' prolific career has been extremely inconsistent, with only brief flashes of similar inspired creativity.

The Small Price of a Bicycle has its moments of listenable (if ponderous) guitar-pop, but is marred by singer/guitarist Robert Ian McNabb's self-important lyrics and weak melodies.

As six of its seven songs also appear on the band's first two albums, **Seven Singles Deep** is an unessential compilation of two years' worth of A-sides. (The cassette, however, adds seven bonus tracks.)

In a pivotal year for the group, Icicle Works issued three new singles: "Understanding Jane" is the band's best-ever song, a terse and spunky piece of singalong rock. "Who Do You Want for Your Love?" is fine, unassuming pop, but "Up Here in the North of England," McNabb's verbose contemplation on the cultural gaps between English regions, is bad, verbose pomp. While all three songs turned up on the next album, the 12-inch EPs are worth investigating for their non-LP tracks. **Understanding Jane** has three live versions of **Bicycle** songs; **Who Do You Want for Your Love?** has a good live "Understanding Jane" and not-so-good live covers of the Clash ("Should I Stay or Should I Go") and the Doors ("Roadhouse Blues"); **Up Here in the North of England** has stately, occasionally handsome studio covers (with clarinet and saxophone) of songs by Robert Wyatt, the Band and Spirit.

His regrettable vocal resemblance to Neil Diamond and Anthony Newley notwithstanding, McNabb sounds confident and mature on **If You Want to Defeat Your Enemy**, an album of increased sophistication and ambition, skillfully produced by Ian Broudie. The quality of "Understanding Jane" and "Who Do You Want for Your Love?" is made even more conspicuous by the leaden tracks which surround them. (For casual sleeve

scanners who may recognize the titles, "When You Were Mine" and "Walking with a Mountain" are not covers.) The tape adds two; the CD four.

All but one-quarter ("Whipping Boy") of the 12-inch/CD **Numb** EP turned up on the terrible **Blind**, a mixed-up mainstream mush of loud rock, quiet soul and gutless funk. If there were any worthwhile songs, the stylistic blur wouldn't be a problem, but the variety does nothing to sell the weak material. (The only semi-good song, "High Time," is also on **Numb**.) The **Little Girl Lost** EP adds a second album track and two new items, only one of which (the folky "One Time") is noteworthy. [i]

BILLY IDOL

Don't Stop EP (Chrysalis) 1981 ●
Billy Idol (Chrysalis) 1982 ●
Rebel Yell (Chrysalis) 1983 ●
Whiplash Smile (Chrysalis) 1986 ●
Vital Idol (nr/Chrysalis) 1986 (Chrysalis) 1987 ●
Idol Songs: 11 of the Best (nr/Chrysalis) 1988 ●
Charmed Life (Chrysalis) 1990 ●

STEVE STEVENS ATOMIC PLAYBOYS

Steve Stevens Atomic Playboys (Warner Bros.) 1989 ●

After Generation X's demise, Billy Idol packed his bags and moved to New York, got himself managed by former Kiss svengali Bill Aucoin and began recording with local players and producer/drummer Keith Forsey (Giorgio Moroder's protégé). The first results of that union—a four-song EP—had only an awkward but entertaining cover of "Mony Mony" and a phenomenal five-minute edit of Gen X's "Dancing with Myself" to recommend it. (Interestingly, the belated CD credits the track to "Billy Idol with Generation X.")

Billy Idol and a series of generally noxious videos made the former William Broad a huge star while providing erstwhile fans of his original band with an ideological dilemma: was he new wave's ultimate Frankenstein mutation or an arena-metal fraud trading on his now-dubious punk roots? In any case, the record—a marriage of Moroder's trademark *Midnight Express* sequencer sound and a throbbing rock beat—proved to be a lode of memorable hits ("White Wedding," "Hot in the City," "Love Calling"). Steve Stevens' caricatured Ronson/Thunders guitar wildness noisily matches Idol's macho postures and sneering vocals; the powerfully built modern rock band has subtlety *and* near-metal strength. An album to despise while you hum along.

With only writing partner Stevens held over from the first record, Idol kept the same producer and formula on **Rebel Yell**, another collection of hits that run hot ("Rebel Yell," "Blue Highway"), cool ("Eyes Without a Face," "Catch My Fall") and both ("Flesh for Fantasy"). Refined and carefully groomed for platinum success, it's an undeniably good rock'n'roll record that is also reprehensible for its phoniness and calculation.

Whiplash Smile repeats the recipe: Forsey, Stevens and a duotone program of hard/soft songs. Characteristically, the staggering guitar riffarola of "Worlds Forgotten Boy" runs directly into the engagingly modest, sweet-voiced technobilly of "To Be a Lover." The problem here is that there's no wind in Idol's sails: he takes it easy and relies too heavily on his partner's pyrotechnics. Unlike Idol's previous records, his vocals here lack the gism that made his hits soar with enthusiasm and energy. With second-rate material (the notable "To Be a Lover" is a non-original) and Idol out of contention, Stevens easily steals the spotlight; all of the record's best moments are his.

Naturally, that was a cue the partnership was over. The guitarist went off and eventually made a terrible every-style-imaginable solo album with a shrill metal singer. Except for a shallow interest in the blues, Stevens' axework here reveals nothing new; a carbon-copy rendition of the Sweet's "Action" is about as clever as Atomic Playboys gets.

The release of Charmed Life was delayed and nearly overshadowed by Idol's serious motorcycle crash in February 1990. Haunted by the ghost of Jim Morrison (a crummy version of "L.A. Woman" is only the most overt evidence of Idol's interest in the Doors), the Forsey-produced record has less blazing guitar than usual, reaching for a charged atmosphere rather than hooks and explosive rock power. But since the songs are deadly dull, the absence of instrumental diversion makes them seem endless. Even Billy's 'billy cover—Jody Reynolds 1958 "Endless Sleep"—sacrifices momentum for mood and winds up flat. The only tunes that work are an unpretentious three-chord singalong ("Love Unchained") and "Cradle of Love," a simple, restrained rock'n'roll single that seethes with echo and passion.

Available in the UK for two years before its American release, Vital Idol is a remixed greatest hits LP: extended versions of such Idolisms as "White Wedding," "Mony Mony," "Catch My Fall," "Dancing with Myself" and "Flesh for Fantasy." With a lot of material overlap, Idol Songs is simply a collection of hit singles in their original versions.   [i]

See also Generation X.

IGGY AND THE STOOGES
See Stooges.

ILLUSTRATED MAN
Illustrated Man EP (Capitol) 1984

I'm not sure if I-Man's brief and miserable existence quite qualified it as a supergroup: Hugo Burnham (ex-Gang of Four), Roger Mason (a Gary Numan sideman), Rob Dean (ex-Japan) and Australian singer/bassist Philip Foxman. I hope not, because this overbearing, overproduced, soul-free dance-funk hardly reflects well on any of the participants. Actually, if they had lost Foxman—his voice was the band's worst feature—Illustrated Man might have had a future. Instead, this is just corporate bandwagon-jumping of no merit.   [i]

See also Gang of Four, Japan.

INCA BABIES
The Big Jugular EP (nr/Black Lagoon) 1984
Rumble (nr/Black Lagoon) 1985
Surfin' in Locustland EP (nr/Black Lagoon) 1985
This Train (nr/Black Lagoon) 1986
Opium Den (Black Lagoon-Fundamental) 1987
Evil Hour (Communion) 1988 ●

There's not much to say about early releases by Manchester's Inca Babies beyond noting that the band makes every conceivable effort to be the Birthday Party. Each member emulates his BP counterpart, but the Inca Babies lack the original's power and completely miss the dark humor. Even the song titles on the early records have a familiar ring: "16 Tons of Fink," "Cactus Mouth Informer," "Luecotomy Meat Boss." Real tribute-band stuff.

Adding a member for Opium Den, Inca Babies toned down the Birthday Party-isms and enhanced their presentation with raw psychedelia and some dirty (if dilettantish) country-blues. Lead singer Harry S combines his Nick Cave imitation with a gratuitous and phony Southern accent (the American South, that is). Still, Opium Den shows that the band is capable of producing work with their own signature on it, or at least drawing from more than one influence. (But the inclusion of lyrics is an ill-advised move.)

The next year, the Babies came up with Evil Hour, a solid piece of work following in its predecessor's style. They're not re-inventing the wheel here, but they have developed into their own band. Although tempos occasionally approach hardcore velocity on Side Two (usually at the expense of hooks), there are actually melodies you might find yourself humming later on, lots of nifty organ washes (courtesy of Clint Boon of Inspiral Carpets) and really nice clear-but-raw sound. And by now I believe that Harry just happens to sound like Nick Cave.   [dgs]

INCORPORATED THANG BAND
See George Clinton.

INDIGO GIRLS
Indigo Girls EP (Indigo) 1986
Strange Fire (Indigo) 1987 (Epic) 1989 ●
Indigo Girls (Epic) 1989 ●
Nomads-Indians-Saints (Epic) 1990 ●

Graduates of Atlanta's folk scene, Indigo Girls' basic formula is simple: two women, two voices, two guitars. With strong harmonies that mix folk influences and church choir cadences, the duo's albums build from the contrasting sensibilities of Amy Ray, whose lyrics and delivery have a jagged rock-conscious emotional edge, and the more sweet-toned and sentimental Emily Saliers. The songs are non-narratives that use religious and naturalist metaphors to describe personal struggle; beneath the language and shirt-sleeve sincerity (both of which have taken flak for being overly precious), the Girls are about the strain of self-understanding and the yearning for love as an absolute.

Although it sounds like it was recorded in a closet, the debut EP has some bright moments, such as "Lifeblood," with its rich pop melody and boost of percussion, and "Finlandia," an a cappella hymn with flawlessly pitched vocals. Strange Fire is also spotty: the slow ballads just sound sleepy, and moments of crucial intensity come off more like Judy Blume novels. But the title track shows just how much Ray and Saliers can accomplish on their own: a single strum of Ray's guitar feels as big as a decade, and the interplay of voices and guitars creates rhythmic balance and a beautiful dynamic. "Crazy Game," "Make It Easier" and the mandolin-accompanied "I Don't Wanna Know" are also standouts.

Despite the move to a major label, the differences between **Strange Fire** and **Indigo Girls** are subtle. Together with producer Scott Litt, Ray and Saliers take a few more chances with embellishments—members of Hothouse Flowers help out on two tracks (including the single "Closer to Fine"), and a Michael Stipe-less R.E.M. backs Ray on the country-rockish "Tried to Be True." Stipe delivers a beautiful backing vocal on "Kid Fears," a cutting chronicle of lost innocence. But the pair's indelible harmonies remain at the forefront; having learned to better manipulate and regulate their emotionalism, Saliers and Ray make **Indigo Girls** their most consistent work.

By **Nomads-Indians-Saints**, the Girls are getting too good at their own formula. Instead of strategic dynamics, they settle for straightforward folk-rock, and about half the album feels redundant. However, Ray's "Welcome Me" is as lonely as a walk down a deserted street, while Saliers' melody in "Watershed" offers a more cheerful antidote. [kss]

INDIVIDUALS
Aquamarine EP (Infidelity) 1981
Fields (Plexus) 1982

This New York quartet bears some resemblance to bands like the (early) dB's, whose Gene Holder produced both records; musically, however, the Individuals' arty pretentiousness makes them sound like a poor copy of the Cure or a less aggressive Gang of Four. **Aquamarine**'s five numbers are spartan in both arrangement and melody. Despite characteristically sprightly guitars and simple drum figures, style supplants substance, and there's nothing much lurking behind the hip artifice.

Fields has more fully realized sound, with good vocal harmonies and studio effects; still, the songs are unmemorable and the performances rather tepid. The one number that does stand out, "Dancing with My Eighty Wives," is rather senseless, but mixes real songwriting acumen with an interesting arrangement—and a definite group identity for a change.

Individuals guitarist/singer Glenn Morrow followed his muse into Rage to Live; Janet (bass/vocals) and Doug (drums) Wygal formed a band that bears their surname; guitarist Jon Klages went on to play solo and with Richard Lloyd. [i]

See also *Rage to Live, Wygals*.

IN EXCELSIS
See *U.K. Decay*.

INFORMATION SOCIETY
Information Society (Tommy Boy-Reprise) 1988 •
Hack (Tommy Boy-Reprise) 1990 •

A chilling illustration of the danger of technology falling into the wrong hands, the Minneapolis-bred Information Society dresses up inane techno-disco tunes in post-industrialist clichés, funk/hip-hop pretensions and found-sound actualities. On the Fred Maher-produced first album, the quartet plays shallow and

poorly sung electro-pop—a lighter variation on Ministry's early records—that takes its cues from Kraftwerk, OMD, Giorgio Moroder and the Human League. (The CD is graphics-encoded.)

With Amanda Kramer gone from the group, the remaining three—Kurt Valaquen, Paul Robb and James Cassidy—go seriously over the top on **Hack**, a sonic collage that attempts to make some statement about modern techno-culture by surrounding (and invades) ten remarkably stupid (and melodically similar) songs with scratched-in cut-ups, TV bites, phone calls, instrumentals and other trivia. As the cover art warns, **Hack** isn't art—merely the noise of boys with toys. [i]

See also *Golden Palominos*.

INMATES
First Offence (Radar-Polydor) 1979
Shot in the Dark (Polydor) 1980
True Live Stories (Fr. Lolita) 1984
Five (Fr. Lolita) 1984
Fast Forward (nr/Sonet) 1989 •

BILL HURLEY WITH JOHNNY GUITAR
Double Agent (nr/Demon) 1985

Britain's Inmates had a big American radio hit in 1979 with a cover of the Standells' "Dirty Water"; overall, their records sound like a cross between early Stones and early Dave Edmunds. Drawing on realistic-sounding originals plus well-chosen oldies, the Inmates don't offer anything new, but make good, primal rock-'n'roll. **First Offence** contains "Dirty Water" as well as Jimmy McCracklin's "The Walk" and Don Covay's "Three Time Loser" (one of several tracks employing the Rumour brass section). Thanks, no doubt, to common icons, there are audible similarities to everyone from Creedence Clearwater to Robert Gordon.

Adding a permanent drummer to the lineup, the Inmates made **Shot in the Dark**, dredging up the old Jagger/Richards gem, "So Much in Love," the Music Machine's "Talk Talk" and some real obscurities. Fun, but too faceless to make any difference.

Singer Bill Hurley went off to form a group called the Big Heat, and the Inmates pressed on for a while with original Eddie and the Hot Rods vocalist Barrie Masters. The 1984 live album reprises both the Inmates' best-known tracks ("Dirty Water," "The Walk") and the early Hot Rods' (Bob Seger's "Get Out of Denver"), adding the Doors' "Love Me Two Times" and some originals.

After the Big Heat cooled down, Hurley made a solo album in collaboration with ex-Count Bishops axeman Johnny Guitar. A little of this (R&B, soul) and that (sentimental country), the solid but plain **Double Agent** features contributions from Inmates guitarist Peter Gunn.

Hurley and the other original Inmates reconvened in the late '80s and recorded **Fast Forward** with the band's old producer, Vic Maile, shortly before his death. [i]

INNER CITY UNIT
Pass Out (nr/Riddle) 1980
The Maximum Effect (nr/Avatar) 1981
Punkadelic (nr/Flicknife) 1982

The Presidents Tapes (nr/Flicknife) 1985
New Anatomy (nr/Demi-Monde) 1985

If you can accept the notion that Hawkwind was the original punk-psychedelic-heavy-metal-dada fusion band, then it makes perfect sense that saxophonist Nik Turner should lead the humorous Inner City Unit, a devolving London five-piece whose music is so far over the edge that it almost defies comprehension. Taking mind-expanding drugs is theoretically essential to appreciation here, but the frantic and funny rock-with-horns of "Watching the Grass Grow," "Space Invaders" and "Cars Eat with Autoface" (all on **Pass Out** and, in alternate versions, on **Punkadelic**) update the Hawkwind legend with style and energy that anyone can enjoy. Had the Bonzo Dog Band spent the '70s attending muddy rock festivals, this might have been the outcome.

The first side of **Punkadelic** dredges up different takes of four **Pass Out** songs; the album (subtitled "Revaulting from the volts") also contains five previously unreleased compositions, including the band's earliest explorations, the wacky "God Disco" and "Disco Tango." In a gambit truly worthy of old hippies, "Bildeborg" has two bandmembers singing different lyrics and melodies in the left and right channels.

ICU pokes gentle fun at Turner's back pages on **The Presidents Tapes**, an amusing but somewhat disappointing album. Singing topical songs like "World of LSD," "Big Foot" and "Stonehenge Who Knows?" the group uses organ, flute and production effects to evoke the period. Despite the flashes of satirical inspiration, too many normal-sounding tracks and a shortage of left-field sax noise keep **The Presidents Tapes** from being a revelation. [i]

See also *Hawkwind*.

INNOCENCE MISSION

The Innocence Mission (A&M) 1989 ●

On paper, this tasteful Pennsylvania quartet has it all: a distinctive singer in keyboardist Karen Peris, well-crafted arty folk-pop songs with intelligent, substantial lyrics, delicately skillful musicianship. On record, however, the Innocence Mission sounds like a once-sprightly group that's had the life washed out of it. Lacking the resonant eccentricities of 10,000 Maniacs or the artistic depth of the Cocteau Twins, this polished veneer of adult refinement is much easier to admire than enjoy. [i]

INSPIRAL CARPETS

Plane Crash EP (nr/Playtime) 1988
Trainsurfing EP (nr/Cow) 1989
Joe EP (nr/Cow) 1989
The Peel Sessions EP (nr/Strange Fruit) 1989 (Strange
    Fruit-Dutch East India) 1991 ●
Cool as **** EP (Cow-Rough Trade) 1990 φ
Life (Cow-Mute-Elektra) 1990 ●
Island Head EP (nr/Cow-Mute) 1990 ●
She Comes in the Fall EP (nr/Cow-Mute) 1990 ●
The Beast Inside (Cow-Mute-Elektra) 1991 φ

Emerging on the Manchester scene alongside Happy Mondays and Stone Roses, Inspiral Carpets' notable innovation in the retro-groove psychedelipop stakes is

Clint Boon's vintage organ sound. Ironically, an all-American idiom that wouldn't get any likeminded Stateside band out of the garage has made the Inspirals a major chart attraction in contemporary England. The quintet goes so far as to pay its respects with a brisk cover of "96 Tears" on the five-song **Plane Crash** EP (produced by ex-Chameleon Dave Fielding), otherwise relying on its own simple creations, which are precisely tailored for the Inspirals' thickly surging rock.

The four new tunes on **Trainsurfing** hint at the band's biggest shortcoming: shallow and ineffectual songwriting (by Boon and guitarist Graham Lambert). "Butterfly" and "Causeway" are adequate fodder for the band's narrow range of sensuous textures but are way too flimsy to hold up on their own merits. Although the title track of **Joe** (by which time Tom Hingley had taken over the vocals from original singer Stephen Holt; bassist Martin Walsh had replaced David Swift) is forgettably lame, the flipside of the EP introduces two of the band's few good songs: the Doors meet the Electric Prunes in the droney "Directing Traffic," while San Francisco acid-rock gets a colorful revisit in "Commercial Rain." Recorded immediately after the **Joe** sessions, the four-track **Peel** EP includes "Directing Traffic" and a terrible organ-colored rendition of the Stones' "Gimme Shelter," as well as Hingley's first recorded swipe at **Plane Crash**'s "Keep the Circle Around."

Cool as ** (the title is a sanitization of the Cow label's T-shirt parody on a British milk-ad slogan) weakly introduced Inspiral Carpets to America with a compilation of "Joe," a subsequent B-side and all three tracks from the "Find Out Why" single, including the numbing sixteen-minute "Plane Crash" jam (not to be found on the EP of the same name). Wow, man—this shit is groovy!

By the time Inspiral Carpets got around to recording a full album, their international discography was hopelessly out of synch. As a result, the American version of **Life** omits "Besides Me" to add an overzealous remake of "Commercial Rain," two items from the three-song **Island Head** EP and another song from those sessions. The resulting sixteen-track extravaganza is way too much of an occasionally good thing, surrounding appealing songs like the sturdily melodic "This Is How It Feels," the Stranglersish "Song for a Family," the poppy "Move" and a new unimproved version of "Directing Traffik" with far too many inferior soundalikes. [i]

INTELLIGENT HOODLUM

The Intelligent Hoodlum (A&M) 1990 ●

On the best moments of his debut album, the Intelligent Hoodlum (aka Tragedy aka Percy Chapman) raps passionately about the lousy state of the world. Backed by hard, unadorned beats from ace producer Marley Marl, he leads a furious chant against racism in "No Justice, No Peace" and bristles with righteous anger on "Black and Proud." He still sounds like a kid, which gives even venomous diatribes like "Arrest the President" an appealing fresh edge. Elsewhere, though the man resorts to predictable bragging and party-down topics, the aggressive tracks continue to crackle. [jy]

INTERSTELLAR VILLAINS

See *Scientists*.

IN THE NURSERY

Temper EP (nr/Sweatbox) 1985
Twins (nr/Sweatbox) 1986 ●
Köda (Wax Trax!) 1988 ●
Counterpoint (Wax Trax!) 1989 ●
L'esprit (Wax Trax!) 1990 ●

Originally a fraternal duo of Klive and Nigel Humberstone, Sheffield's In the Nursery added a drummer and a female singer to further explore its bizarre brief: complex military-industrial music with classical pretensions. The band's early efforts—a number of 12-inch singles, EPs and the **Twins** album, all of which are represented on the **Counterpoint** compilation—range from restrained atmospherics (the breaking waves and gothic organ of 1985's "Arm Me Audacity" resemble soundtrack music for *Dark Shadows*) to brutal assemblies of martial beats, obscure vocals, synthesized accents and strings (as on **Temper**'s shrieking "Breach Birth" and **Twins**' title track). Meanwhile, bowed electric bass provides striking counterpoint to the tingly strings in 1987's "Blind Me," an unsettling mix of cries and spoken dialogue. (The **Counterpoint** CD adds an alternate mix of "Breach Birth" and two more tantrums from **Temper**.)

Except for the scarcity of vocals, the ambitious **Köda** would be best described as operatic. Mainly using classical instrumental sounds and percussion, the stirring record glides smoothly from moody film music to marchable stridency, all of it seemingly designed to accompany—or evoke—theatrical action. If Art of Noise scored a German war epic, this might be the result.

Lifting **Köda**'s portentous military cloud, the Humberstones turned over a romantic leaf on **L'esprit**, a graceful album of surprising gentleness that conjures up balletic images. Vocals play a significant role for the first time: "Sesudient," "Retaliation" and "The Pearl" all float on Dolores Marguerite C.'s whispery French crooning; "To the Faithful" opens the record with the brothers' surprisingly pleasant pop tones. Besides occasional somber passages, **L'esprit** does roll out the timpani and rat-a-tat-tat snare drum in "Träumerei," but the dramatic intrusion only serves to heighten the album's serene impact.   [i]

INXS

INXS (Aus. Deluxe) 1980 (Atco) 1984 ●
Underneath the Colours (Aus. Deluxe) 1981 (Atco) 1984 ●
Shabooh Shoobah (Atco) 1982 ●
Inxsive (Aus. Deluxe) 1982 ●
Dekadance EP (Atco) 1983
The Swing (Atco) 1984 ●
Listen Like Thieves (Atlantic) 1985 ●
Kick (Atlantic) 1987 ●
X (Atlantic) 1990 ●

VARIOUS ARTISTS

Dogs in Space (Atlantic) 1987

MAX Q

Max Q (Atlantic) 1989 ●

It took these six Australians (three of them brothers) from Sydney a long time to develop into something America wanted to hear; **INXS** is dull rock that sounds like a less musical Joe Jackson or a no-soul Graham Parker. **Underneath the Colours**—like its predecessor, issued in the US only after the band had become successful—has much better audio quality (although no one bothered to integrate the drums into the mix) and shifts the focus among keyboards, sax and guitar in a vain effort to vitalize the underwhelming songs.

Shabooh Shoobah, with good loud production by Mark Opitz (and one Farriss brother mysteriously missing from the credits), was the first INXS album to be released in the US and UK. Despite major strides in several areas, on the whole it's still not a happening record. A few outstanding numbers do display growth in personality and style: "The One Thing" sews a bunch of riffs together into an energetic, dense fabric, while "Soul Mistake" generates a foreboding mood and "Don't Change" gets up a good head of textured rock steam.

Following an Australian label change, the group's previous record company issued **Inxsive**, a compilation that includes outtakes and obscurities as well as hits.

Four songs from **Shabooh Shoobah** (three extended remixes plus a wholly new version of a fourth) comprise the club-oriented **Dekadance** EP. If not specifically better, the six-minute edit of "The One Thing" is certainly longer.

The Swing proved to be the first INXS LP of any real significance, moving the group clearly into the mainstream of modern dance-rock with the inclusion of the suavely insistent "Original Sin," produced by Nile Rodgers. (The record was otherwise done under the direction of Nick Launay.) "Burn for You" is another highlight, using a female backing chorus to affect an amusing resemblance to Roxy Music. On the other hand, "I Send a Message" finally reveals INXS' enormous potential to annoy: a basically tuneless song synth-funked into repetitive and grating obnoxiousness. Elsewhere, **The Swing** offers strong beats, mannered vocals and a unified, au courant sound.

Produced by Chris Thomas, **Listen Like Thieves** is crisp, lively rock with as little vocal posturing as Michael Hutchence seems capable of, and substantial aggressive guitar work where required. The title tune, "What You Need" and "This Time" all have solid melodies, strong rhythms and decisive hooks. "Shine Like It Does" attempts to generate a folk-rock sensibility with moderate success; other tracks are, at worst, negligible.

With Hutchence launching an acting career (in *Dogs in Space*) and emerging as a pin-up sex god for teenagers, INXS made the completely vapid **Kick**, again using Thomas to dress up the mediocre material. (Needless to add, it became their biggest seller, shifting upwards of four million copies.) The inappropriate and unconvincing meta-political consciousness of a few lyrics doesn't improve what is essentially tuneless video-dance-rock; the contrived poses on the sleeve indicate what really makes INXS run. Ludicrous soul pretensions only underscore just how phony INXS is. **Kick** does contain one consolation: a plodding version of the Aussie-punk classic, "The Loved One," originally recorded in the late '60s by Melbourne's groovy Loved Ones and first covered by INXS on a 1981 single.

While the band took a three-year break from recording, Hutchence did a side project, singing, co-writing and co-producing an album with Ollie Olsen (ex-Whirlywirld), a patron saint of Australia's rock underground. Their joint approach gives **Max Q** a bit of a Midnight Oil feel, with more politics and a rougher rock sound than INXS. The use of synthesizers and strings keeps **Max Q** from being exactly earthy, but the record's got a certain energy and forthrightness that makes it an intriguing superstar aside.

That indulgence over, Hutchence got down to platinum tacks with his usual crew and made the dire **X** (no, it's not their tenth album). Weak hooks jammed roughly into weaker (and obviously self-derivative) songs, melodies that go absolutely nowhere, well-intentioned lyrics of stunning vacuity and an absurd funk-groove-and-harmonica single ("Suicide Blonde") that crosses U2 and Blondie—those are **X**'s good points. The only member of the group who comes off well here is bassist Garry Gary Beers, and he's stuck on the same old riffs. Compared to this halfbaked exercise, INXS's previous records now seem more like profound artistic achievements. [i]

See also *Whirlywirld*.

IPPU-DO
Normal (Jap. Epic-Sony) 1979
Real (Jap. Epic-Sony) 1980
Radio Fantasy (nr/Epic) 1981
Lunatic Menu (nr/Epic) 1982
Some-Times (Jap. Epic-Sony) 1982
Live and Zen (Jap. Epic-Sony) 1985

MASAMI TSUCHIYA
Rice Music (nr/Epic) 1982

Led by androgynous, Bowiesque guitarist Masami Tsuchiya, this Japanese trio stepped into the commercial void created by Yellow Magic Orchestra's decreased group activity. It's hard to make out what the songs are really about since most have only a chorus or bridge in English, but the lyrics seem simpleminded enough —themes of romantic fantasy, travel and technology evidently dominate. Tsuchiya's voice is high but gutsy and always in control (even when yelling)—he's got his shtick down pat, and his guitar playing fits. Ippu-Do alternates between modernized arrangements of '50s and early '60s vocal pop-rock melodies and steaming, heart-pounding rock'n'roll, sometimes in the same song. They also use reggae syncopation and synthesizers, so all bases are covered—except originality. (**Lunatic Menu** and **Some-Times** are anthologies of the other LPs.)

It sounds like these fellas, especially Tsuchiya, possess the ability to go further but just aren't sure how. Tsuchiya gives it a try on his solo LP with lots of help from YMO's Ryuichi Sakamoto, though several tracks include members of Japan (the band) and Bill Nelson on e-bow guitar. Most successful when he tries to mildly funkify Japanese music, with further cross-fertilization, Tsuchiya could be a real innovator.

By 1985's live album, Ippu-Do was just a duo, aided by two ex-members of Japan (with whom Tsuchiya toured and recorded) plus English bass ace Percy Jones.

Despite its recent vintage, the album portrays the band treading musical water with jagged, arty treatments of old material (the group's and Tsuchiya's), plus a version of the Zombies' "Time of the Season." Despite stylistic growth, Ippu-Do needs new—not old—content to make it meaningful. [jg]

See also *Japan*.

GREGORY ISAACS
In Person (nr/Trojan) 1975 + 1983
All I Have Is Love (nr/Trojan) 1976 (nr/Tad's) 1983
The Best of Gregory Isaacs Vol. 1 (Jam. GG) 1977
Cool Ruler (nr/Front Line) 1978
Soon Forward (nr/Front Line) 1979
Showcase EP (Jam. Taxi) 1980
The Lonely Lover (nr/Pre) 1980 ●
Extra Classic (Shanachie) 1981
The Best of Gregory Isaacs Vol. 2 (Jam. GG) 1981
The Early Years (nr/Trojan) 1981 ●
More Gregory (Mango) 1981 ●
The Sensational Gregory Isaacs (nr/Vista) 1982
Lover's Rock (nr/Pre) 1982
Mr. Isaacs (Shanachie) 1982 ●
Night Nurse (Mango) 1982 ●
Crucial Cuts (nr/Virgin) 1983
Out Deh! (Mango) 1983 ●
Reggae Greats (Live) (Mango) 1984 ●
Live at the Academy Brixton (nr/Rough Trade) 1984 ●
Private Beach Party (RAS) 1985 ●
Easy (nr/Tad's) 1985
Watchman of the City (Rohit) 1987 ●
Victim (nr/C&E) 1987 ●
Sly and Robbie Presents Gregory Isaacs (RAS) 1988 ●
Red Rose for Gregory (RAS) 1988 ●
I.O.U. (RAS) 1989 ●
Slum (In Dub) (nr/Burning Sounds) 1989
My Number One (Heartbeat) 1990 ●
Call Me Collect (RAS) 1990 ●
Cool Ruler/Soon Forward (Front Line) 1990 φ
Once Ago (Front Line) 1990 φ
Dancing Floor (Heartbeat) 1990 ●
Come Again Dub [tape] (ROIR) 1991
Love Is Overdue (nr/Network) 1991 ●

GREGORY ISAACS AND DENNIS BROWN
Two Bad Superstars (nr/Burning Sounds) 1984
Judge Not (Greensleeves) 1984 ●
No Contest (Music Works) 1989 ●

The Cool Ruler, Gregory Isaacs, is one of the best-loved and most durable reggae singers. Highly prolific (he writes nearly all his material) and business-savvy (he runs his own Jamaican label, African Museum), Isaacs' voice is still the key to his success. His delivery is marked by a combination of ice and fire rare even among soul singers—an urgent longing, tempered with cool control. Although comparable to a Jamaican Al Green or Marvin Gaye, Isaacs is a completely unique stylist. His repertoire is equal parts lovers rock and Rasta protest; the link is his seductive delivery. Whether he's urging romance or reform, the call to action will give you goosebumps.

Like many popular reggae performers, however,

Isaacs' recording career is a confusing jumble. His early work involved a number of producers. **Sensational**, for instance, has one side produced by Rupie Edwards and one by Ossie Hibbert, resulting in a mix of hits ("Black and White," "Mr. Know It All") and duds. **Extra Classic** compiles his work with Pete Weston and Lee Perry, as well as his first self-produced sessions. While also spotty, the record offers early proof of Isaacs' authority and strength as a songwriter.

Isaacs' career began to move under the guidance of producer Alvin Ranglin. Their collaboration is chronicled on the two excellent **Best Of** collections. Though available only as Jamaican imports, these consistently strong LPs are worth finding, and crucial for fans. Another Ranglin/Isaacs session, **In Person** (which includes the UK hit, "Love Is Overdue") is available on Trojan, along with an LP produced by Sidney Crooks, **All I Have Is Love**. Both are of mixed quality, but Trojan took the best from each and combined them with a third batch (produced by Winston "Niney" Holness) for **The Early Years**, good all the way through.

For his next career phase, Isaacs chose to produce himself. Despite weak covers of the Temptations' "Get Ready" and Billy & Vera's "Storybook Children," **Mr. Isaacs** has bold, assured singing and at least one classic, "Slave Master."

Virgin's Front Line label then released two inconsistent albums, subsequently culling the best tracks for an edition of the **Crucial Cuts** series; still, it's pretty weak. The outstanding **Soon Forward**, however, launched his collaboration with Sly Dunbar and Robbie Shakespeare. The title song of that record also appears on the **Showcase** EP, released on Sly and Robbie's Taxi label, which adds a version of Bob Marley's "Slave Driver." Although tight and lively from start to finish, the record allows Isaacs' personality to be somewhat overshadowed by the duo's fine playing. Besides his work with Sly and Robbie, Isaacs began an association with Roots Radics, another fine Jamaican session band, that would last several LPs.

The Lonely Lover and **More Gregory** contain his finest middle-period work. Both feature excellent backing (divided between the Radics and Dunbar/Shakespeare) and a steady stream of high-quality material. Best of all, Isaacs is singing at the peak of his form. **More**, in particular, firmly establishes his lover-boy persona in an easygoing groove that lasts for all ten cuts. **Once Ago** pairs the two records on CD and cassette.

In contrast, Isaacs' work on Island is marred by inconsistency. Both **Night Nurse** and **Out Deh!** boast first-rate singing and playing (by Roots Radics), but the material is erratic, frequently weak—more a series of gestures than songs. To compensate, perhaps, two live albums were released around the same time. The song selection—an essential greatest hits—is similar on both, but the Brixton set has the edge, featuring a horn section and a more enthusiastic performance.

A short period of inactivity was broken in 1985 by the release of **Private Beach Party**. In a clear effort to lighten the load, Isaacs enlisted the help of an outside producer, Augustus Clarke, and several songwriters. The result is his best album in years—a fresh, diverse package.

Easy maintains his rule; the sensual crooning is as lilting and refreshing as a cold mint julep on a Caribbean beach. In "Cool Ruler Come Again," Gregory announces that "he was only taking a nap." Both the title track and "Love Is Overdue" are absolute Gregory.

Isaacs remained prolific, recording LPs of his own material with a variety of producers for a few small labels. While none of these mid-'80s releases are particularly distinct, each of them demonstrates nicely how Isaacs' smooth and sexy formula is as dependable as Smokey Robinson's, and how his professionalism and talent have withstood the test of time.

Isaacs had a big late-'80s hit with "Rumours," which then turned up on **Red Rose for Gregory**. This is the lonely lover of days gone by, complete with his famous sexy moans and mannerisms. From the title track to the evocative "Teacher's Plight" to "Rough Neck" (on which he's joined by the Mighty Diamonds), Gregory is in his glory.

Isaacs' next huge hit was "Big All Around," another in a series of collaborations with Dennis Brown. The pair included that song on their joint **No Contest**, a mixture of solo performances and duos. Their sensual voices, with rootical foundations in Gussie Clarke's state-of-the-art production, makes this album a must. "Easy Life" and "Jealousy" are crucial combination tracks. The earlier **Judge Not** only pairs Isaacs and Brown vinylistically: each man keeps to his own side of the platter. Lacking the collaborative fire of **No Contest**, it's rather boring.

My Number One is a compilation. **Come Again Dub** is the companion to **Call Me Collect**.   [bk/aw]

CHRIS ISAAK

Silvertone (Warner Bros.) 1985 ●
Chris Isaak (Warner Bros.) 1987 ●
Heart Shaped World (Reprise) 1989 ●

The look of a sensitive young Elvis . . . moody, atmospheric tunes . . . sweet, brooding vocals . . . heaps of twangy guitar. Chris Isaak has his shtick down cold, that's for sure. Happily, this retro package offers more than selfconscious imagery. At his best, Isaak summons up the deep hurt of classic blues or the soaring spirits of footloose rockabilly. On **Silvertone**, consult the swinging "Livin' for Your Lover" or "Western Stars," a lazy, loping piece of sagebrush hokum. On **Chris Isaak**, try the quietly menacing "You Owe Me Some Kind of Love" or "Blue Hotel," the woeful sound of a tortured soul crying for help. No wonder Isaak's been compared to Roy Orbison.

Heart Shaped World has more of the wonderful same, from the high and lonesome "I'm Not Waiting" to the slo-mo "Blue Spanish Sky" to "Wrong to Love You," a quietly driving tale of romantic woe. Upon release, this entrancing LP inspired the same chart action as its predecessors (i.e., none). But wonders never cease: After a walk-on in Jonathan Demme's *Married to the Mob*, Isaak contributed the gorgeously despondent "Wicked Game," one of **World**'s finest moments, to the soundtrack of David Lynch's *Wild at Heart*. By early '91, the boy had himself a bona fide hit.   [jy]

MARK ISHAM

See *Marianne Faithfull*.

ISM

A Diet for the Worms (S.I.N.) 1983
Constantinople EP (Broken) 1985
I Think I Love You (The Hits That Missed 1982–1989)
[CD] (no label) 1990 ●

A Diet for the Worms is hysterically funny New York hardcore with a tasteless baby-being-delivered cover and gutbusting numbers like "Shitlist," "Vegetarian at a Barbeque," "Life Ain't No Bowl of Brady Bunch" and the classic "John Hinckley Jr. (What Has Jodie Done to You?)." The band (not to be confused with a similarly named Elliott Sharp outfit) plays at easily followable speed and has a reasonably articulate bellower in Jism, who gives the longwinded lyrics (mostly his) appropriate exercise. A good, scatological laugh for the vulgar at heart.

On **Constantinople**, Jism and his band connect with their roots, slam-dunking songs by the Residents *and* the Fugs with reverent but rowdy enthusiasm. Rather than hardcore, Ism here plays restrained rock with piano and relative subtlety. Judging by this EP, Ism is developing a novel time warp, mixing various breeds of outrage into a hybrid all its own.

The post-**Constantinople** tracks (several of them previously unissued) on the self-issued **I Think I Love You** retrospective confirm Ism's singularity, but the (intentionally) unfinished sound of the vaguely pomp-rock "Excerpt from Sermon for the Watchdog" and instrumental "Theme" cushions their force a little too much. Far better are items reclaimed from the band's many compilation contributions (notably Jism's ode to political activism, "Nixon Now More Than Ever") and the long-lost first single, a Flipper-gum version of the Partridge Family "classic" that gives the collection its title—not to mention the inspiration for the jocularly offensive cover. [i/dss]

IT BITES

The Big Lad in the Windmill (Virgin-Geffen) 1986 ●
Once Around the World (nr/Virgin) 1988 ●
Once Around the World EP (Virgin-Geffen) 1988 ●
Eat Me in St. Louis (Virgin-Geffen) 1989 ●
Sister Sarah EP [CD] (nr/Virgin) 1989 ●

Hailing from Cumbria, a remote northern county of England, It Bites plays energetic, carefully produced (by Alan Shacklock) chart-pop that adds considerable offbeat spunk to the easy-listening sounds of peppy outfits like Haircut One Hundred. **The Big Lad in the Windmill** has the merry attitude (if not the extraordinary talent) of early 10cc: unexpected styles and noises abound in a shiny rush of giddy melodicism. While hardly groundbreaking, this provincial quartet is agreeably paranormal. (In a taste of things to come, the album was resequenced for US release.)

Cutting three tracks from the Steve Hillage-produced sophomore album, It Bites' American label issued the five-song **Once Around the World**, a showcase for the once-offbeat band's new sound: blandly energetic and annoying dance-rock that apparently takes its cues from Genesis.

Eat Me in St. Louis further complicates the international discography. Rather than issue the band's heavy and boring third album (loudly produced by Mack) intact, Geffen combined half of it with two tracks each from **The Big Lad** and the **Once Around the World** EP. **Sister Sarah** is a 3-inch CD of an album track with three B-sides. [i]

IT'S IMMATERIAL

It's Immaterial EP (nr/Ark) 1985
Life's Hard and Then You Die (Siren-Virgin-A&M) 1986 ●
Song (nr/Siren-Virgin) 1990 ●

More bizarreness from the Liverpool art college set. In this case, the Manchester duo of John Campbell and Jarvis Whitehead plus myriad friends (including the Christians, whose Henry Priestman was an Itsy in the group's early days). On **Life's Hard**, It's Immaterial cooks up a fascinating musical hybrid that touches variously on synth-pop, atmospheric art-rock, recitation and a unique brand of English country music. It may remind you of early OMD, Pete Townshend, Talking Heads, even Ronnie Lane's late-'70s gypsy-rock aggregation Slim Chance—which is to say there's a lot going on in this mix. The only thing missing is an identity.

That identity finally turned up four years later on **Song**, an ironic title for an album that's more a collection of stories put to music than actual songs. (There's not a chorus anywhere to be found.) Whitehead's tracks—flowing, repetitive patterns, mainly based around piano—function as a soundtrack for Campbell's lyrics, which he both sings and speaks in a pleasant but limited voice. The effect is often hypnotic—something like Philip Glass meets Marc Almond—but unless you're drawn in by the words, you may find the going a bit tedious. This is music best listened to when distractions are at a minimum; don't expect to hear it in dance clubs. [ds]

See also *Christians*.

DEBORA IYALL

See *Romeo Void*.

J J J J J J J J J

JACK FROST

See *Hex*.

JACKOFFICERS

See *Butthole Surfers*.

JACK RUBIES

Fascinatin' Vacation (TVT) 1989 ●
See the Money in My Smile (TVT) 1990 ●

Everyone views romance in their own way, but Ian Wright, the singer of London's Jack Rubies, has a very strange way of expressing affection. On the first song of the quintet's debut, he offers "to be hung, drawn and quartered" to "Be with You"; in "You're So Wild," after describing the "spontaneous combustion . . . in my heart," he admits to being "overcome . . . when you stuck out your tongue at that man." The band's unassuming acoustic/electric music—a pleasant pop style of no special character—isn't nearly as colorful, but does provides a hospitable enough atmosphere for the offbeat musings.

More diverse and complex arrangements on the Pat Collier-produced follow-up decrease the prominence of Wright's frank Lloyd Cole-ish vocals in favor of raising the band's overall personality profile. A substantial and thoughtful album, with bits of western country flavor, **See the Money in My Smile** could be the prelude to something great. [i]

JACKS

See *Beat Farmers*.

JOE JACKSON

Look Sharp! (A&M) 1979 ●
I'm the Man (A&M) 1979 ●
The Harder They Come EP (nr/A&M) 1980
Beat Crazy (A&M) 1980 ●
Jumpin' Jive (A&M) 1981 ●
Night and Day (A&M) 1982 ●
The Real Men EP (Hol. A&M) 1982
Mike's Murder (A&M) 1983
Body and Soul (A&M) 1984 ●
Big World (A&M) 1986 ●
Will Power (A&M) 1987 (A&M-Mobile Fidelity) 1988 ●
Live 1980/86 (A&M) 1988 ●
Tucker (A&M) 1988 ●
Blaze of Glory (A&M) 1989 ●
Stepping Out: The Very Best of Joe Jackson (nr/A&M) 1990 ●
Laughter & Lust (Virgin) 1991 φ

What songs! What hair(line)! What shoes! **Look Sharp!** sounded as striking as its cover photo looked, and Joe Jackson was unduly anointed a member—

alongside Graham Parker and Elvis Costello—of England's angry young troubadours club. (Ironically, Jackson was the first of the three to really sell records in America, largely due to the wry "Is She Really Going Out with Him?," which was a hit single.) Smart but minus Elvis' overt intellectualism or artiness, or Parker's great white soul man pose, Jackson's songs mixed cheek, edge and a self-deprecating wit that set him apart from his more serious peers. Maybe all the lyrics don't sound as clever now as they seemed back then, but stuff like "Happy Loving Couples" and "Pretty Girls" took the pulse of post-adolescent heebie-jeebies, and kicked a little butt, too.

Much of the material on the follow-up, **I'm the Man**, dates from/is an extension of **Look Sharp!**, though several songs up the bile quotient, notably "On Your Radio" and "Don't Wanna Be Like That." The revved-up lyrics are balanced by catchy high-speed pop-rock (as on the title tune and "Get That Girl") and that affecting approximation of genius, "It's Different for Girls." The LP may lack the crispness and consistent impact of its predecessor, but it's a strong and enduring platter.

That Jackson was seeking an alternative to the fast-paced rock'n'roll of his first two albums was signaled by **The Harder They Come** EP (a straight reggae reading of the Jimmy Cliff song, plus two Jackson originals) and then trumpeted in no uncertain terms by **Beat Crazy**, his final LP with his original tight-knit band. Jackson put it bluntly in the liner notes: "This album represents a desperate attempt to make some sense of Rock and Roll. Deep in our hearts, we knew it was doomed to failure. The question remains: Why did we try?" The attempt seems less desperate than just plain confused, and its failure makes the LP the least satisfying of his initial salvo.

With the Joe Jackson Band dissolved, Joe took a musical detour, recording **Jumpin' Jive**, a tribute to Louis Jordan: cool jazz vocals over mock big-band swing. Obviously enjoying himself (for once), Jackson romps his way through "Is You Is or Is You Ain't My Baby" and related gems from the Louis Jordan/Cab Calloway school of hepness. Jackson's production is warm and loving, and though **Jumpin' Jive** was a clear respite from the official progress of his music, the album is enormous fun and holds up.

Night and Day proved to be Jackson's most successful outing since **Look Sharp!**, although the urban/Latin flavor bears not the slightest resemblance to the white-hot sound of his early days. The Latin rhythms seem somehow less honest even than the buoyant bop of **Jumpin' Jive**, yet Jackson is obviously sincere. **The Real Men** EP is "Real Man" from **Night and Day** plus three more from the LP with vocals in Spanish.

Jackson's next departure—an intended film soundtrack—proved to be something of an embarrassment.

Months after the **Mike's Murder** album (billed as music from the film) appeared, the James Bridges picture still hadn't, and rumors circulated over which problems were causing the delay; while the decision not to use Jackson's music was one of them, that could hardly have been the prime problem. Regardless, it's Jackson at his least assured, and the most notable item is "Memphis," whose organ line and rhythm are lifted straight from the Spencer Davis Group's "Gimme Some Lovin'."

Jackson survived that debacle to make **Body and Soul**, an ambitious attempt to simplify and repersonalize the recording process as much as possible. With a distant, light sound—quite in contrast to the stuffy closeness of most contemporary records—and '50s jazz stylings tinged by an ongoing affection for Latin music, the record has plenty of atmosphere, and contains some of his strongest, most mature songwriting. Unlike his previous time-tunnel trip, **Body and Soul** eschews period re-creation (except on the cover) in favor of a wistful ambience indicative of Jackson's distaste for much modern music.

The three-sided **Big World** was recorded live directly to a digital stereo master with a small band at a three-day New York concert engagement staged especially for that purpose in January 1986. With no postproduction tinkering of any sort, the fifteen new songs—some about current world political affairs, others about societal issues—are reproduced on two discs as accurately as possible. Stylistically, **Big World** is a return to stripped-down, lightly seasoned jazzy rock. A little self-important (the rampantly multi-lingual booklet smacks of grandstanding) and creatively inconsistent, but an impressively ambitious effort.

Redolent with unrestrained pomposity, the ironically titled **Will Power** is an instrumental album that mixes Jackson's least interesting film-score composition style with the "overture for two pianos" which turned into the title track. The type-free cover and the inside photo of the suffering artist, sitting dejectedly alone in a huge studio, merely indicate the imagined depths of this trivial self-indulgence. While Jackson may be impressed by his ability to convince an orchestra to play his melodramatically panoramic music, it's unlikely anyone else will find this exercise especially rewarding.

The conceptually masterful live album is divided into four different creative eras; each side presents a different incarnation of the Joe Jackson Experience. Side One, recorded in Manchester and Holland in 1980, features material from the first three albums, played with his original backing trio. Side Two (1983), recorded with a keyboard-laden quintet in Sydney, Australia, is billed as "The Night and Day Tour" but contains only "Cancer" from that album. Instead, it draws further from the same three records, offering the second (this time a cappella) rendition of "Is She Really Going Out with Him?" on the LP. Side Three (1984), recorded in Sydney and Melbourne during the horn-heavy "Body and Soul Tour," again includes that song, only this time in an acoustic version; Side Four (1986) hails from Canada and Japan and features a straight electric rock quartet doing selections (including "Breaking Us in Two," "It's Different for Girls" and "Jumpin' Jive") from various albums.

Comparing **Mike's Murder** with **Tucker** shows that Jackson learned not to make the same mistake twice. Although the latter picture was a commercial flop, it was a Francis Ford Coppola flop, and at least had some artistic raison d'être. To his credit, Jackson's music is of a piece with the project's high quality: a cinematic use of '40s-style jazz, with a spot of artistic license, allowing for a few anachronistic styles and production techniques. But it's deftly crafted, credible stuff—there's even an apparent nod to Thelonious Monk—that creates its moods well.

Blaze of Glory is a concept album that's not a concept album. You can imagine him saying, "On *this* concept album, every song can stand on its own," a self-defeating approach that virtually defies the realization of any overriding plan. Still, the idea—a rock'n' roller of Jackson's generation followed from frustrated childhood to chastened but wistful adulthood—is not so fancy that it really needs much elucidation. Indeed, the songs can stand alone, and most are unquestionably cogent and catchy (faves include "Nineteen Forever" and "The Human Touch"). In the process, Jackson answers the **Beat Crazy** question: rock may no longer be his message, but it still can be a swell medium. [jw/i/jg]

JACOBITES
See *Nikki Sudden*.

JAH LION
See *Lee Perry*.

JAM
In the City (Polydor) 1977 ●
This Is the Modern World (Polydor) 1977 ●
All Mod Cons (Polydor) 1978 ●
Setting Sons (Polydor) 1979 ●
Sound Affects (Polydor) 1980 ●
The Jam EP (Polydor) 1982
The Gift (Polydor) 1982 ●
The Bitterest Pill EP (Polydor) 1982
Beat Surrender EP (Polydor) 1982
Dig the New Breed (Polydor) 1982 ●
Snap! (Polydor) 1983
All Mod Cons/Setting Sons [tape] (nr/Polydor) 1983
Sound Affects/The Gift [tape] (nr/Polydor) 1983
Compact Snap! [CD] (Polydor) 1984 ●
The Peel Session (nr/Strange Fruit) 1990 ●

How ironic that the band from the class of '77 that seemed to stand least for the tenets of punk at the outset should wind up the one that remained truest to them over the long haul. The Jam's refusal to compromise their ideals and integrity during a six-year career tends to polarize reactions to them. In the end, once-common complaints about unoriginality and Paul Weller's lack of vocal prowess are overshadowed by their accomplishments as songwriters, musicians and commentators, but mostly by the Jam's living proof that a band's commercial success need not divorce it utterly from its fans *or* sense of purpose. The trio's parting at the end of 1982 can be looked at as symbolic of victory (a courageous decision not to become pointless dinosaurs in the UK, where they were virtually superstars) or failure (they were never able to achieve more than modest success in America, despite plenty of effort on the part of both the

Jam and their label) or just as an indication that Weller's ever-changing moods had led him away from the Jam's rock'n'soul aesthetic towards more "stylish" pursuits. Regardless, the Jam left behind a recorded legacy as important as any the new wave produced.

Black mohair suits, smart white shirts, skinny ties, stylish razor-cut hair, Rickenbacker guitars—on **In the City** the Jam were the new mods, emerging from a sea of spiky-haired leather-and-chain-clad punks. They may have looked different, but their energy level gave no ground, as Weller's jagged, choppy double-tracked guitar led the attack over Bruce Foxton's busy, melodic bass lines and Rick Buckler's stiff-backed drumming. The songs themselves are as taut and well manicured as the group, but match the explosiveness and attitude of the punks easily enough to establish an indisputable kinship to bands like the Sex Pistols and Clash. (It was no surprise when the Pistols swiped the riff for "Holidays in the Sun" from Weller's "In the City.")

If the songs and playing of **In the City** are derivative—especially of **The Who Sings My Generation** and '60s Motown—there's no arguing that the Jam was speaking to a generation for whom it was all new. Also, the main points—youth regaining pop culture from the grasp of conservative people with old-fashioned ideas, the individual vs. the crowd—were well taken by the group's growing British following.

This Is the Modern World, recorded just months after **In the City** was released, is a cleaner-produced version of its predecessor, breaking little new ground. The songs themselves are hit-and-miss, with "The Modern World," "Standards" and "All Around the World" (a brilliant single added to the US version of the LP) the obvious standouts.

Since they had by then spawned dozens of neo-mod soundalikes, the Jam needed a change of direction, and on **All Mod Cons**, Weller rose to the challenge. Prior inconsistency is replaced by an album that explores new avenues with almost complete success, while never straying too far from the band's roots. Weller's writing showed him to have blossomed into a major-league tunesmith, as well as a lyricist possessing a keen eye for detail and a refreshing sense of the vagaries of his own position. While retaining a great deal of the Who influence, the Jam also began to incorporate other sources. (Especially Ray Davies, which resulted not only in a hit version of the Kinks' "David Watts" but also in the biting social commentary of "Mr. Clean.") "In the Crowd" gives Weller a chance to open up as a guitarist and proves that he's more than just a Townshend copyist. **All Mod Cons** is a brilliant record.

Setting Sons takes five songs from a scrapped concept album about three friends who meet after much of England has been destroyed by atomic war and combines them with four even bleaker tracks, then lightens up by ending the LP with a version of the uplifting "Heatwave." The album is the Jam's most somber—not that any of their records are big on humor—but it is also their most effective. Weller's songs stick, and the beauty of his melodies provides stark contrast to the blackness of his lyrical vision.

Perhaps as a conscious change from the heaviness of **Setting Sons**, **Sound Affects** is more danceable and, for the most part, less pointed, although songs like "That's Entertainment" are hardly cheerful. The rage is still

there, but it's channeled into fiery playing and singing, loosening up somewhat on the lyrics.

The Jam EP—five songs previously released on singles—served mostly as an interim measure between LPs, but includes essential tracks—"Absolute Beginners," "Funeral Pyre"—as well as the Who's arcane "Disguises."

The Gift explores a lot of new territory on songs like "Trans-Global Express" and "Precious," where a strong funk/Latin rhythm fueled by loads of percussion is heavily in evidence. The album takes a lot of chances and doesn't always succeed; some of the rhythmic experiments sound forced, others fall victim to overly dense, ponderous production. **The Gift** has its moments—notably "Happy Together," "Ghosts" and the Motownish "Town Called Malice." It also offers some evidence as to why Weller may have felt the band had exhausted its possibilities.

The Bitterest Pill (named for an emotional song with one of Weller's best vocals) shows the band forging still further into the realm of R&B. Although not recorded as such, the five tracks form a cohesive work.

Beat Surrender, containing the Jam's last studio work together, was released as a British double-45 and an American 12-inch. The driving title track is absolutely smashing, and the four accompanying tracks are swell as well, including a lively rendition of Curtis Mayfield's "Move on Up." The record is additionally noteworthy for its audible indications of Weller's subsequent direction with the Style Council.

Dig the New Breed, issued after the band's split had been announced, is an honest, retrospective live album (complete with bum notes) recorded at gigs during various stages of the Jam's career—a powerful parting shot. **Snap!** is an awesome two-disc career compilation (including a remixed "Funeral Pyre" and a demo version of "That's Entertainment") which was later abridged and issued on CD as **Compact Snap!**

Recorded in April '77, **The Peel Session** contains versions of three songs from the group's debut album, plus the title track of the then-yet-to-be-released **This Is the Modern World**, that are barely distinguishable from the originals, save for the fact that these sound about a thousand times better. A worthwhile investment for real fans.

In the Jam's wake, Weller formed the Style Council with ex-Merton Parka keyboardist Mick Talbot. Foxton launched a short-lived solo career. Buckler formed Time (UK) with ex-Tom Robinson Band guitarist Danny Kustow and issued a handful of singles in the mid-'80s.

See also *Bruce Foxton, Style Council*.   [ds/i]

JAMES
Village Fire EP (nr/Factory) 1985
Stutter (Blanco y Negro-Sire) 1986
Strip-mine (Blanco y Negro-Sire) 1988 ●
One Man Clapping (nr/One Man-Rough Trade) 1989 ●
Gold Mother (Fontana) 1990 φ

Manchester's winsome and demure James proffer a folksy, intricate version of pop with top-notch percussion and vocals that range from baritone to falsetto, often in the same verse. **Village Fire** collects five tracks from the band's first two singles, presenting a diverse range: from folk enhanced with numerous layers of acoustic guitar to revved-up funk and keen-edged punk.

Stutter, produced by Lenny Kaye, proved to be a rather surprising first album for the quartet. Unlike the singles, the LP adheres to one particular style of music—loud semi-acoustic folk. Tim Booth's vocals lurch around poorly arranged songs that are not all that memorable; gaining focus has inadvertently obscured some of James' strengths. Potential for greatness exists in several tracks—the accelerating "Skullduggery," "So Many Ways," "Why So Close" (an amazing remix from **Village Fire**) and "Just Hip"—but the album fails to realize it.

Fortunately, **Strip-mine** sets things to right. Crystalline production by Hugh Jones makes the most of the band's alluring and intelligent folk-pop. ("Charlie Dance," "Ya Ho" and "Stripmining" are highlights.) Gavan Whelan's uncommon around-the-beat drumming and Booth's imaginative vocals outline the songs, leaving guitarist Larry Gott (doubling on keyboards and flute) to delicately paint them in with bright colors. Where James dragged its heels on **Stutter**, the frequently delightful **Strip-mine** kicks them up in the air, as if an artistic weight had been lifted.

Booth's onstage emergence as a theatrical Morrissey wannabe ruins the live **One Man Clapping**, recorded in Bath at the end of 1988. While the other three, augmented by a keyboard player, rough up the songs (only two come from **Strip-Mine**; three are from **Stutter**) with cavalier enthusiasm, Booth puts on an insufferable demonstration that overwhelms the music's subtlety and underscores the pretentiousness of his lyrics. (The CD and cassette add a track.)

Marking a switch in Manchester style loyalties from the Smiths to house-pop, **Gold Mother** introduced the new James, a grandiosely dramatic seven-piece (Whelan is gone; the lineup now includes a trumpeter and violinist) playing long, instrumentally overloaded poetic rock epics. (Comparisons to the early Waterboys are not unwarranted.) Booth's lyrics have never been this self-important—preaching revolution in "Government Walls," damning religion in "God Only Knows," slagging off a woman in "How Was It for You" and enigmatically celebrating childbirth in the title track—but he winds up sounding foolish rather than fiery. Inspiral Carpets provide backing vocals on "Gold Mother." [ag/i]

BRIAN JAMES

See *Damned, Lords of the New Church*.

JAMS

See *Justified Ancients of Mu Mu*.

JANE'S ADDICTION

Janes Addiction (Triple X) 1987 ●
Nothing's Shocking (Warner Bros.) 1988 ●
Ritual de lo Habitual (Warner Bros.) 1990 ●

PSI COM

Worktape 1 [tape] (Right Brain) 1984
Psi-Com EP (Mohini) 1985

These obnoxious Los Angeles glam-punk poseurs recorded most of their debut album (pressed on clear vinyl) live, onstage at the Roxy in Hollywood. Perry Farrell sings in an aggressive womanly warble as his three bandmates pound out competent but unoriginal post-'70s rock. "My Time" and the dramatic "Jane Says," both played with acoustic guitar, show the group capable of moderate musical achievement, but most of the record—especially "Sympathy" (for the Devil) and Lou Reed's "Rock 'n' Roll"—sounds like the work of an incompetent Aerosmith cover band. And Farrell's effete habit of interjecting the word "motherfucker" merely frosts the album's maggotry.

As guitarist David Navarro and the lumbering rhythm section work themselves into a dull sub-Led Zeppelin metallic stupor on the rambling **Nothing's Shocking**, Farrell's double-tracked screech delivers smugly self-obsessed lyrics—repeating favorite lines over and over—as if his idiotic free-form musings were somehow significant. A new version of "Jane Says" allows Farrell to give the two-chord song an even more mannered vocal performance; the rest of the amorphously tuneless material runs either hot ("Had a Dad") or cool ("Summertime Rolls"), with a laughably crude funk-rhythm detour ("Idiots Rule"). Farrell's skillful front-cover sculpture of two nude women—joined at the shoulder and hip—with pierced nipples and their heads ablaze is the album's only effective piece of artistic creativity.

Pulling himself further into a private world of self-congratulatory decadence (the inclusion of a methadone bottle on the back cover's *botanica* shelf is bad news, whatever the intention), Farrell fills the absurd **Ritual de lo Habitual** with pretentiously irrational ravings that, when they manage to coagulate into coherence, describe the joys of shoplifting ("Been Caught Stealing," the pathetic bleat of a spoiled rich asshole that inexplicably begins with barking dogs), masochism ("Ain't No Right"), his supposed solidarity with black people ("No One's Leaving") and a nebulous eleven-minute opus about a ménage à trois ("Three Days"). The band's swirling demi-metal—still limited by Navarro's inadequacy as a guitar hero—is loudly functional, but Farrell's expanding ego and detachment make the album unbearable. (Because of the front cover sculpture's graphic sexuality, **Ritual** was also released in an alternate sleeve that simply offers the text of the First Amendment.)

Although no one in the pre-Jane's Addiction Psi Com is identified by name, it's impossible to miss Farrell's unmistakable Siouxsie-like warble amid the swirling, atmospheric rock, a proficiently transparent imitation of the Banshees and Cure. After undergoing some lineup shifts, the group finally splintered when the guitarist and drummer became Hare Krishnas. Post-EP bassist Dino Paredes subsequently formed Red Temple Spirits. [i]

JAPAN

Adolescent Sex (Ariola-Hansa) 1978 ●
Obscure Alternatives (Ariola-Hansa) 1978 ●
Quiet Life (nr/Ariola-Hansa) 1979 (nr/Fame) 1982 ●
Gentlemen Take Polaroids (nr/Virgin) 1980 ●
Tin Drum (nr/Virgin) 1981 ●
Assemblage (nr/Hansa) 1981 (nr/Fame) 1985
Japan (Virgin-Epic) 1982
Adolescent Sex/Obscure Alternatives [tape]
    (nr/Ariola-Hansa) 1983

Oil on Canvas (nr/Virgin) 1983 ●
Exorcising Ghosts (nr/Virgin) 1984 ●
A Souvenir from Japan (nr/Ariola-Hansa) 1989 ●

MICK KARN
Titles (nr/Virgin) 1982 (Blue Plate) 1990 ●
Dreams of Reason Produce Monsters (nr/Virgin) 1987 ●

JANSEN/BARBIERI
Worlds in a Small Room (nr/Virgin) 1986 ●

DOLPHIN BROTHERS
Shining EP (nr/Virgin) 1987
Catch the Fall (nr/Virgin) 1987 ●
Second Sight EP (nr/Virgin) 1987

RAIN TREE CROW
Rain Tree Crow [CD] (Virgin) 1991 ●

In one of rock's most remarkable examples of bootstrapping, South London's Japan pulled themselves up from lowly beginnings as a ludicrously overdressed glam-punk-pose band who (badly) emulated the New York Dolls and Alice Cooper to finish, five years later, as one of England's most sophisticated art-rock outfits, earning the respect of their peers and branching out into such fields as sculpture and photography.

Adolescent Sex introduces Japan in all its guitar-rock misery, playing such Bowie-influenced tripe as "Wish You Were Black" with less style than a sense of urgency. Obscure Alternatives adds more keyboards but still relies on Rob Dean's buzzing guitars and David Sylvian's sneery vocals for its sound. (Ill-advised digressions into reggae and funk are strictly dilettante poses.) The songs are fairly unmelodic, the production nondescript. With a quick listen, you might mistake this for a junior-league Stones imitation.

Japan entered the modern world with Quiet Life. The choice of producer John Punter—who had worked with Roxy Music and Bryan Ferry—was significant, as the band's sights had shifted from gutter-glam to elegant decadence. A cover of the Velvet Underground's "All Tomorrow's Parties" allows Japan—and especially Sylvian, sporting a totally revised singing voice—to show off their new suave reserve, relying on sequencers, Mick Karn's proto-funk basswork and generally understated aplomb. Around this time, Japan also released a marvelous non-LP single of Smokey Robinson's "I Second That Emotion."

On the excellent Gentlemen Take Polaroids, Sylvian's debonair Ferryisms—more shyly quiet than dissipated—are met by Karn's astonishing fretless bass work, Richard Barbieri's wide-ranging keyboard work (incorporating Asian and other traditions) and Steve Jansen's inventive drumming. (Jansen is Sylvian's brother; their family name is Batt.) The technically exquisite and musically adventurous sound is loaded with atmosphere, yet displays a very light touch. Sylvian's songs are, however, very hard to hold, as many lack a backbone and waft along with little evident structure.

Tin Drum presents Japan at peak form, playing subtle creations with intricate rhythms and tightly controlled dynamics. Spare but strong drumming (abetted by Karn's rubbery bass) provides needed propulsion, and the breadth of influences—from Middle Eastern to funk—color the music a number of fascinating shades. Having almost totally escaped pop constraints, Japan's sound here—except for a few tunes (especially

"Ghosts") that strongly resemble latter-day Roxy Music—is a willowy fabric of interwoven threads.

Assemblage is a collection of songs from the band's pre-Virgin period, including "Adolescent Sex," "Quiet Life," "I Second That Emotion" and "All Tomorrow's Parties." (The cassette version adds remixes, an extra studio track and three otherwise unreleased live recordings. Years later, the same album—expanded by two extra Obscure Alternatives tracks—was issued as A Souvenir from Japan.) In a new effort to interest America, Epic issued Japan, which is actually Tin Drum minus two tracks, plus three from Gentlemen Take Polaroids.

Oil on Canvas is a crystalline live set featuring Ippu-Do guitarist Masami Tsuchiya as an adjunct member. The two records offer a good cross-section of the band's repertoire, adding some previously unrecorded ambient doodling. When Japan's long-rumored dissolution finally came to pass, Virgin issued Exorcising Ghosts, a two-record anthology of their later work.

While the band still appeared to be an ongoing proposition, Karn (real name: Anthony Michaelides) recorded Titles, essentially a showcase for his proficient bass stylings and ability to play a multitude of woodwinds and keyboards. Featuring such guests as Jansen, Barbieri and Ricky Wilde (!), it's all very impressive but rather vague and pointless.

After Japan, Karn did lots of session work, formed the short-lived Dalis Car with Peter Murphy of Bauhaus and then made a second solo album. Dreams of Reason Produce Monsters, a collaboration with Jansen that features Sylvian's Ferryesque vocals on two songs, is another tastefully appointed, highly accomplished waste of time. Orchestral arrangements and a choir don't make the slow-moving instrumentals any more involving. Meanwhile, all the textural achievement buries the two exceedingly Japan-ese songs in the sonic wash.

After releasing an album under their own names, Jansen and Barbieri became the Dolphin Brothers; their guest-filled Catch the Fall, and the two EPs drawn from it, follow in Japan's delicate footsteps, but take a simpler, less distant path and stop to rock out a bit now and again. Between Jansen's singing (a weak imitation of his former bandmate's) and the duo's lackluster songwriting (the pretentious lyrics are a bigger problem than the vague melodies), Catch the Fall is a needless footnote to Japan's fine career.

After six years of scattered and sporadic collaborations, the four key members of Japan temporarily united to record a one-off album during 1989 and early '90, releasing it—after almost a year of titular consideration—under the name Rain Tree Crow. With the majority of the LP "written as a result of group improvisations" (a neat trick in eight studios spread across Europe), Rain Tree Crow is split almost evenly between soundscapes and more conventional "songs." Although employing some outside musicians (including Nelson and guitarist Phil Palmer), the album doesn't sound drastically different from any of their previous work together, but successfully revives Japan's late-period neo-tribal rhythms and vaguely Asian feel. Some of the looser instrumentals recall Sylvian's excesses in that realm, but the lovely "Blackwater" and "Cries and Whispers" inhabit ballad territory, while the oddly urgent neo-fusion of "Blackcrow Hits Shoe Shine City" breaks unfamiliar ground. Perfect for late-night ambience.   [i/ja]

See also *Illustrated Man, Ippu-Do, Peter Murphy, Ryuichi Sakamoto, David Sylvian.*

JASON AND THE SCORCHERS
Reckless Country Soul EP (Praxis) 1982
Fervor EP (Praxis) 1983 (EMI America) 1984
Lost & Found (EMI America) 1985
Still Standing (EMI America) 1986 ●
Thunder and Fire (A&M) 1989 ●

In 1981, as the legend goes, Jason Ringenberg left his daddy's Illinois hog farm for the bright lights of Nashville and promptly stumbled upon guitarist Warner Hodges and bassist Jeff Johnson in a gutter. With drummer Perry Baggs, they became Jason and the Nashville Scorchers, and recorded a bunch of tunes on a 4-track during a drunken night in the studio. The resulting **Reckless Country Soul** EP, a 7-inch released by a local indie label, is rough-hewn and half-realized, but enough to help the band earn a rep as the best country-metal-thrash band in the state of Tennessee.

Rigorous touring and a rep for wild shows helped spread the Scorchers' noisy mutant gospel. They play tighter and nastier on the 12-inch **Fervor**, displaying Ringenberg's knack for clever songwriting. The band signed to a major label, dropped Nashville from their name, and saw their second EP reissued with the addition of a smoking version of Bob Dylan's "Absolutely Sweet Marie."

Lost & Found puts the Scorchers in the forefront of an ever-growing country-punk genre, only they've got the roots others lack: Hodges' folks toured with Johnny Cash, Baggs' dad sang gospel and Johnson was reared in the Blue Ridge Mountains. More than just a pedigree to brag about, the band's genuine hick beginnings make them a lot less inhibited and more apt to cross from cool to corny, punk to heavy metal without fretting much about it. There's great tension between Ringenberg's two sides—bible-quoting, straitlaced country boy and yelping, flailing, demon-possessed madman—and the cigarette-chomping, white-noise-mongering Hodges. On **Lost & Found**, Jason and the Scorchers burn like nothing since General Sherman's troops marched through Georgia.

Still Standing was produced by Tom Werman (Cheap Trick, Mötley Crüe, Poison), who captured the Scorchers' melodic power without overdoing it or pushing any obvious commercial concessions down their throats. The folky "Good Things Come to Those Who Wait" and the equally optimistic "Crashin' Down" are as pretty, memorable and uplifting as anything they've done; "Shotgun Blues" and "Ghost Town" give Hodges plenty of encouragement to unleash his wildest electric dreams. A charging cover of "19th Nervous Breakdown" acknowledges the band's clear debt to the Stones and proves that Jason and the boys know just how to treat a piece of classic rock.

By the time the Scorchers delivered their long-come (and long-gone: they broke up soon afterwards) third album, the group was sporting a second guitarist and a new bassist. Rather than successfully integrating the group's stylistic impulses, **Thunder and Fire** divides them into reheated rockers that short the Scorchers' per-

sonality and semi-acoustic country numbers that seem out of place. With Jason's good-ol'-boy voice undercutting Hodges' raucous guitar fury (and vice versa), only "Bible and a Gun" (co-written by Steve Earle), Phil Ochs' propulsive "My Kingdom for a Car" and the bluesy "Away from You" mix up a truly potent blend.   [ep/i]

JAYHAWKS
The Jayhawks (Bunkhouse) 1986
Blue Earth (Twin/Tone) 1989 ●

Numerous young American bands have attempted to recapture the soulful spirit of country-rock as pioneered by Gram Parsons, but few have come as close to getting it right as the Jayhawks. Where similarly inclined combos have used the sound as little more than a stylistic affectation, this Minneapolis quartet captures Parson's sense of fatalistic moralism, remaining scrupulously faithful to their musical sources yet never seeming contrived—despite the fact that frontman Mark Olson's Midwestern drawl is often a dead ringer for GP's, and his songs cover similar emotional ground.

The Jayhawks is an auspicious debut; the band stakes out its derivative style with so much spirit that it almost sounds original. The playing (particularly guitarist Gary Louris) is clean and economical; the material is largely uptempo and lighthearted. The regretful "The Liquor Store Came First" gives a hint of the increased emotional depth to come.

Though it's largely a piecemeal assemblage of tracks recorded as demos by a then-unstable lineup, **Blue Earth** is a mature, cohesive work that certifies the Jayhawks' significance. Olson's material is more skillful and streamlined than before, and the band plays with a thoughtful restraint that intensifies the emotional gravity of such numbers as "Two Angels" and "Commonplace Streets," and the humor of "Red Firecracker" and "Dead End Angel."   [hd]

JAZZ BUTCHER
A Bath in Bacon (nr/Glass) 1982 ●
A Scandal in Bohemia (nr/Glass) 1984 ●
The Gift of Music (nr/Glass) 1984 ●
Sex and Travel (nr/Glass) 1985 ●
Bloody Nonsense (Big Time) 1986 ●
Big Questions (The Gift of Music Vol. 2) (nr/Glass) 1987 ●
Fishcotheque (Creation-Relativity) 1988 ●
Spooky (Can. Creation-Mercury) 1988 ●
Big Planet Scarey Planet (Genius) 1989 ●
Cult of the Basement (Rough Trade) 1990 ●
Edward's Closet (nr/Creation) 1991 ●

JAZZ BUTCHER AND HIS SIKKORSKIS FROM HELL
Hamburg (Ger. Rebel) 1985
Hard EP (nr/Glass) 1986

JAZZ BUTCHER VS. MAX EIDER
Conspiracy EP (nr/Glass) 1986

JAZZ BUTCHER CONSPIRACY
Distressed Gentlefolk (Big Time) 1986 ●

MAX EIDER
The Best Kisser in the World (Big Time) 1987 ●

In ten years, the Jazz Butcher has undergone more transformations than most bands do in several lifetimes. Led by the Jazz Butcher (aka Butch; in truth, Pat Fish) himself, it is, regardless of incarnation, his lyrical witticisms and humorous critiques around which the group's music revolves.

The debut LP, **A Bath in Bacon**, is for all intents and purposes a one-man show. Butch plays a startling array of instruments, from guitar to xylophone, and employs a legion of session musicians to help create an album that encompasses an awesome variety of styles. Good ideas abound in songs like "Love Zombie," "Sex Engine Thing" and "Gray Flannelette"; there's just some uncertainty as to where they're going.

The second album was recorded by a stable quartet that included ex-Bauhaus bassist David J. Almost exclusively in a folky pop-punk format, the songs are better-developed and reach logical conclusions. Among the gems are a hysterical anti-macho anthem "Real Men" ("Some things never change/Notice how they never sit together on buses?") and "Southern Mark Smith."

The Gift of Music is a collection of single sides, an excellent package that affirms the band's folk-punk commitment. Of special note is an early up-tempo version of "Southern Mark Smith" and the pop gospel "Rain."

Sex and Travel is the Jazz Butcher's crowning achievement. The eight near-perfect tracks run the gamut from funk to folk to country-western and punk. Butch's lyrics aim high; subject matter, more than anything else, determines the style of each song. "President Reagan's Birthday Present" addresses the problems of America, Russia and nuclear arms with a healthy chunk of dance funk. "Holiday" uses a typewriter backing track and cabaret stylings to make light of the staid British persona; the frantic adrenaline punk of "Red Pets" tackles preconceptions about Russians ("Everyone says they lift weights/Except for me, I think they're great"). All this, plus two great pop tunes: "Big Saturday" and "Only a Rumour." (One CD joins **Sex and Travel** with **A Scandal in Bohemia**.)

With a new bassist replacing David J (off to rejoin his old bandmates in Love and Rockets), the rechristened Jazz Butcher and His Sikkorskis from Hell issued the live **Hamburg** LP and an EP, **Hard**, which picks up where **Sex and Travel** left off, adding blues and merseybeat to the seemingly bottomless bag of musical tricks. **Bloody Nonsense** is an American collection that includes some of the above-mentioned tracks.

Leaving the rest of the band by the wayside, Butch and guitarist Max Eider then released a four-song 12-inch, **Conspiracy**. The best things on it are the title track, a clever play on rap music, and the hilarious homage "Peter Lorre."

With Butch and Max as the nucleus, a newly formed Jazz Butcher Conspiracy recorded **Distressed Gentlefolk**. A Jazz Butcher record by any other name, this album reveals the usual diversity—folk ("Still in the Kitchen"), funk ("Big Bad Thing"), country-western ("Falling in Love") and pop ("Angels," "Nothing Special")—as well as Butch's ever-incisive wit, which is in rare form on the track "Domestic Animal."

Shortly after **Distressed Gentlefolk**, Eider resigned his Butchership for a solo career. **Best Kisser in the World** is a beautifully romantic record consisting of soft

rock ballads and jazzy torch songs. Max's vocals replicate Butch's almost exactly; only lyrical content provides a decisive difference. If the Jazz Butcher has a sane and serious alter-ego, Max Eider is he.

In 1988, a two-person Jazz Butcher (Butch and Kizzy O'Callaghan) released the fifth proper LP, **Fishcotheque**, proving the Butcher to be as resilient as he is prolific. Reorganization has had no effect whatsoever on Butch's abilities, and this record rivals **Sex and Travel** in its brilliance. "Next Move Sideways," "Living in a Village" and "Chickentown" are sterling.

Big Questions is an assortment of tracks (including "Groovin' in a Bus Lane," "Rebecca Wants Her Bike Back" and "Olof Palme") drawn from previous releases by the Jazz Butcher, Sikkorskis from Hell, Jazz Butcher vs. Max Eider and the Jazz Butcher Conspiracy. Limited quantities of the original pressing contained a live 7-inch EP.

As Butch insists in his liner notes, **Spooky** "is not an LP; it is a single and a radio session nailed together for your amusement." A smoky cover of the titular Classics IV hit and an extended version of **Fishcotheque**'s silly chicken rap "The Best Way" highlight the new stuff, and the Montreal radio broadcast sounds quite all right.

By **Big Planet Scarey Planet**, Butch had acquired a fairly steady group of sidemen, losing not a morsel of his keen wit or musical individuality. He even reveals a renewed vitriolic vigor in "Bicycle Kid" (a hilarious tale of working-class juvenile delinquency) and "Do the Bubonic Plague" (a lethal dance craze). Sharply observant and masterfully executed, this is a record from one band that has well earned its reputation for eclecticism. Sheer entertainment.

Cult of the Basement opens with an instrumental that sounds like the Ventures performing at a Greek wedding. A Mediterranean refrain wafts through the rest of the LP, subtly linking the thirteen cuts into what is as close to a "concept" album as the Jazz Butcher is likely to make. (What the concept might be, however, is anyone's guess.) Nevertheless, on "The Onion Field" Butch manages to flawlessly replicate Nick Cave's stripped-down gothic atmospherics. And faced with song titles like "Daycare Nation" and "Turtle Bait" and a sweet lullaby called "Fertiliser," one can only smile and enjoy. If the wild psychedelic raveup of "Panic in Room 109" is totally incongruous, it's also perfectly in synch with the rest of this wonderful collection.

Edward's Closet is an unessential compilation containing "Spooky" and an assortment of album tracks from 1987-'90.   [ag/db]

See also *Love and Rockets*.

JAZZY 5
See *Afrika Bambaataa*.

JAZZY JEFF
On Fire (Jive) 1985

The original Jazzy Jeff offers solid rap action with a strong, clear delivery, significantly cliché-reduced rhymes and a variety of socially responsible concerns on his debut album, **On Fire**. He warns about "King Heroin (Don't Mess with Heroin)," shows a real soft spot for "My Mother (Yes I Love Her)" and asks the DJ to "Mix So I Can Go Crazy" and "Rock It (Rock It)." Electric guitar, inventive percussion and clever mix gimmickry (by Bryan "Chuck" New and Phil Nicholas of the Willesden Dodgers) give this a fairly familiar sound, but Jazzy Jeff is an above-average rapper.   [tr]

(D.J.) JAZZY JEFF & THE FRESH PRINCE

Rock the House (Word Up-Jive) 1987 + 1988 ●
He's the D.J., I'm the Rapper (Jive) 1988 ●
And in This Corner . . . (Jive) 1989 ●

Although both use the same handle, the same producer and are (were) both on the Jive label, the Jazzy Jeff (Townes) turntable master who is teamed up with Will Smith (aka the Fresh Prince, star of stage and sitcom) is entirely different from the earlier rapper named Jazzy Jeff. However it came to pass, the upshot is that these mega-successful clean-cut young men from Philadelphia—purveyors of mild-mannered middle-class rap—are the ones people know.

Amid routine boasts and human beat box exhibitions, **Rock the House** introduces the 17-year-old Smith's friendly singsong delivery and engagingly hapless persona on the PG-rated story, "Just One of Those Days" (an approach later developed by Young MC). The album's only similar track, "Girls Ain't Nothing but Trouble," is a gentle gender gripe that samples the *I Dream of Jeannie* theme and earns a rebuke from female rapper Ice Cream Tee elsewhere on the LP. (**Rock the House**'s reissue replaces the original hit single version of "Girls" with an extended remix.)

Sensing the correct path to lasting fame and fortune, the duo and their associates consigned most of the traditional hip-hop on **He's the D.J.** (which sold several million copies) to a bonus disc of scratch tracks (plus a truly cruddy live performance from 1986). That left the main album to showcase their unabashed suburban preppiedom and bubblegum stylings in lighthearted raps like "Parents Just Don't Understand" (a comic complaint about middle-class fashion oppression), "Charlie Mack–The First Out the Limo" and "A Nightmare on My Street," which weaves a personal tale around Freddy Krueger, complete with audio bites from *A Nightmare on Elm Street.*

Except for a couple of obligatory boasts and tributes, the dapper duo severed its vestigial ties to street-level rap (the closest the Fresh Prince—on his way to TV stardom—comes to sounding tough is an acknowledged joke) on the third album, turning instead to broadly accessible pop entertainment. With intricately arranged musical tracks surrounding the beat, **And in This Corner . . .** delivers a witty and winning collection of engaging stories in which the cocky rapper keeps getting clobbered—by a boxer ("I Think I Can Beat Mike Tyson"), a thief ("Who Stole My Car?"), a crooked travel agent ("Everything That Glitters (Ain't Always Gold)") and even the supernatural ("Then She Bit Me").   [i]

JEAN PAUL SARTRE EXPERIENCE

The Jean Paul Sartre Experience EP (NZ Flying Nun) 1986

Love Songs (NZ Flying Nun) 1987
Love Songs (Communion) 1988 ●
The Size of Food (Communion) 1989 ●

Mankind may be condemned to experience the limitations of its own will with nothing beyond nothingness staring down from the sky but, as long as a copy of a Jean Paul Sartre Experience record exists, there will always be something out there . . . for your stereo. There will be gentle and warm guitar chords, boy-next-door vocals and delicately produced melodies. The JPSE may be nothing more than a simple janglepop band but they're one of the globe's best.

Born in a suburb of Christchurch, New Zealand in 1984, the Jean Paul Sartre Experience paid for the recording of the first EP with a government grant, yet the sounds of their shoestring put slick megabudget crap to shame. On "Fish in the Sea," an ounce of water sloshes from one tiny cup to another as a tingling triangle plings delicately. A hand knocking on a block of wood punctuates "Walking Wild in Your Firetime" like a tom-tom in a hazy beatnik coffee house, as a soft voice sings "I've got weapons and I've got hope and I've got guns and I've got rope . . . and I don't know what I feel" before xylophone tangs out a repeat of the tune. The result is plain-wrap majesty: simple, uncluttered, satisfying.

Their quartet's second vinyl outing isn't as good: too many **Love Songs** sound the same. The album concentrates on song-craft rather than texture, making the lightweight nature of their genre very obvious. From the whisper-breath blues of "All the Way Down" through the sweet-soul-tinged "Let There Be Love" and on to the herky-jerky sparse funk of "Crap Rap," Sartre wind their way through eight songs about relationships and one staggering pop song about rain.

The US album of the same name is actually the first EP plus four of the tracks (six on the CD) from the original **Love Songs**. It would have been nice if the funk and wiggle-guitar of "Let That Good Thing Grow" could have been included in place of the slow, sleepy harmonies of "Grey Parade," but otherwise this US album is truly the best-of. Highly recommended.

The Size of Food is larger in scope, expanding upon the band's wild fluctuations between atmosphere, irritation and pure pop. The economical arrangements highlight the hazily wafting melodies that swirl around the basic rock format, creating remarkably different settings for the kaleidoscopic variety of the songs, from shimmering pop to hazy psychedelia and hypnotic ambience. Essential.   ['e/ja]

MARC JEFFREY/PLAYTIME
See *Certain General*.

JELLYBEAN
Wotupski!?! EP (EMI America) 1984
Just Visiting This Planet (Chrysalis) 1987 ●
Rocks the House! (Chrysalis) 1988 ●
Spillin' the Beans (Atlantic) 1991 φ

New York mixer/producer (Madonna, Jocelyn Brown, Hall & Oates, etc.) John "Jellybean" Benitez stepped out under his own name for the first time on the five-song **Wotupski!?!** mini-album. The only problem is he doesn't play or sing on it. Nor did he write any of the material. Benitez did, however, produce it, bringing together such powerful friends as Nile Rodgers, Madonna, John Robie and Dan Hartman to create one long instrumental and a batch of dance numbers. Best track: an otherwise unrecorded Madonna composition, "Sidewalk Talk."

Three years later, the Great Delegator returned to the creative world with a full-length hands-off album, **Just Visiting This Planet**. Besides producing and some arranging, just what did the diminutive doyen get saddled with this time? Drum programming on seven of the eight light and infectious dance songs, background vocals on three, synthesizers on two; he actually takes credit for writing one. As strange an approach as Jellybean takes, he certainly can't be faulted for assembling a spectacular cast and assigning the lead vocals to a talented trio: Adele Bertei, Elisa Fiorillo and Steven Danté. Leave your brain at the door and get down!

Following the credo that a mixer mixes, Jellybean then mixed himself up a an extended compilation of songs from his two albums and released the results—including two versions of "The Real Thing" and six minutes of "Sidewalk Talk"—as **Jellybean Rocks the House!**

The all-new **Spillin' the Beans** introduces the latest trio of vocal debutantes; the CD has four bonus 12-inch mixes.   [i]

See also *Adele Bertei*.

JELLYFISH
Bellybutton (Charisma) 1990 φ
BEATNIK BEACH
At the Zulu Pool (Industrial) 1987
Beatnik Beach (Atlantic) 1988 ●

In one of the rare second chances afforded a band by the record industry, San Francisco drummer/singer Andy Sturmer and keyboardist Roger Manning (not the folkie) survived the failure of Beatnik Beach (a forgettable pop-rock quartet whose one boring indie album—shorn of five tracks and bolstered by four better new songs for its retitled major-label reissue—makes half-baked attempts at wit while managing to sound like a younger Supertramp) to reinvent themselves as Jellyfish and fake their way into retro-'60s psychedelic success. Marketing is a wonderful thing, baby.

If not for the band's outrageous junk-store clothes and the album's spectacular art direction, it's unlikely many would have taken **Bellybutton**—an occasionally catchy but more often dull amalgam of pop songs blithely stitched together from bits of the Beatles (**Abbey Road**-era), Beach Boys, Cheap Trick and (most of all) Squeeze—as anything of stylistic note. Despite the presentation, the record isn't even faintly psychedelic; considered apart from the image, **Bellybutton** is too transparently derivative (and lacking inspiration) to merit any serious attention.   [i]

JERRY'S KIDS
Is This My World (X-Claim) 1983 (Ger. Taangl-Funhouse) 1987 ●
Kill Kill Kill (Taang!) 1989 ●

VARIOUS ARTISTS
This Is Boston Not L.A. (Modern Method) 1982

Boston cranked up its loudest hardcore bellow in the early '80s with the likes of Gang Green, SS Decontrol, the F.U.'s and Jerry's Kids, one of the early pioneers of metal-meets-hardcore thrash. The Kids pummel with spearing guitars, grinding rhythms and hammering vocals.

Jerry's Kids first made their presence known in the seven minutes it took them to blast out six songs on the **This Is Boston Not L.A.** scene compilation. With shrieks of "help me!" and "let me out!," "Desperate" simulates a shackled soul struggling to break free, while "Pressure" slows and speeds to searing effect.

With guitarist Chris Doherty of the temporarily defunct Gang Green in the lineup (Kids drummer Brian Betzger joined Gang Green when Doherty restarted it), bassist Rick Jones replaced his brother Bryan on vocals for **Is This My World**, which reveals more complexity and packs more impact than the first set. (Their parents reportedly forbid Bryan to perform live after he broke his leg at a gig.) The virulent intensity of songs like "Cracks in the Wall," "No Time," "Lost" and "Is This My World" makes the album a hardcore classic.

After a couple of years off, a revised Jerry's Kids (still fronted by Rick Jones and guitarist Bob Cenci) returned in 1986, but didn't release anything new for several years. The new Kids harness some of the original blurring speed on solid crunchers like "Fire," "Bad Trip" and "Back Off," but there's a weightier demi-metal bottom to most of **Kill Kill Kill**. While the LP generally delivers tight, driving mature rock power, "Breathe and Fuck" trudges in relatively lead boots. Meanwhile, the pulsing "Satan's Toy" summons up a religious demon or two with subliminal speech and an evangelical preacher. (The CD includes both albums.)

See also *Gang Green*.   [mg]

JESTERS OF DESTINY
See *Jeff Dahl Group*.

JESUS AND MARY CHAIN
Just Like Honey EP (nr/Blanco y Negro) 1985
Psychocandy (Reprise) 1985 ●
Some Candy Talking EP (nr/Blanco y Negro) 1986
April Skies EP (nr/Blanco y Negro) 1987
Happy When It Rains EP (nr/Blanco y Negro) 1987 ●
Darklands EP (nr/Blanco y Negro) 1987 ●
Darklands (Blanco y Negro-Warner Bros.) 1987 ●
Sidewalking EP (Blanco y Negro-Warner Bros.) 1988
Barbed Wire Kisses (Blanco y Negro-Warner Bros.) 1988 ●
Blues from a Gun EP (nr/Blanco y Negro) 1989 ●
Automatic (Blanco y Negro-Warner Bros.) 1989 ●
Head On EP (nr/Blanco y Negro) 1989 ●
Rollercoaster EP (nr/Blanco y Negro) 1990 ●

By blithely combining power-pop melodies with industrial-strength guitar noise and lowbrow lyrical perversity, the Jesus and Mary Chain—Glasgow brothers Jim and William Reid, bassist Douglas Hart and rotating drummers—created a sound that can't quite be described as new, but does stand miles apart from anything that's been done before. If nothing else, what the Reids dredged up from the Velvet Underground has inspired endless imitation.

Awash in feedback and fuzz, tunes and drones, wit and vulgarity, **Psychocandy** is the quintessentially tense, claustrophobic soundtrack to these pressurized, multiphasic times—easy listening for troubled teens. The band's three exceptional pre-LP singles ("Never Understand," "You Trip Me Up," "Just Like Honey") are only the most immediately striking of the fourteen cuts; such others as "Inside Me," "Cut Dead" and "Sowing Seeds" further illustrate the group's variety, imagination and ability to enthrall. (The American CD helpfully appends the post-LP single, "Some Candy Talking.")

Typical of the Reids' determined anti-conformism, **Darklands** all but eliminates the characteristic crazed sound of the first LP, leaving skeletal guitar-pop songs—menacingly restrained and drenched in echo—colored only occasionally with familiar washes of fuzz guitar. Displaying a notable mid-'60s Dylan influence (check the verses of "Deep One Perfect Morning") and delivering their best song yet, "Happy When It Rains," the album predictably put off fickle fans and critics disappointed by the stylistic regression. Nonetheless, "April Skies," "Down on Me," "Darklands," "Nine Million Rainy Days" and "Fall" ("I'm as dead as a Christmas tree . . . ") stand proudly as exceptional and truly original pop fare for the '80s. (Incidentally, for a thoughtful if hyperbolic analysis of the band's early stages, read John Robertson's 1988 biography.)

One of J&M's fetishes is to release singles in as many different formats as possible. As a result, there are numerous 12-inch and 10-inch EPs, double-pack 7-inch singles and CD EPs (some of which are listed above) which add live tracks, acoustic demos, remixes, outtakes and other ephemera. A batch of those, with the addition of a cool T. Rexy new single, "Sidewalking," comprise **Barbed Wire Kisses (B-sides and More)**: sixteen (twenty on the CD and cassette) arcane tales from the Chain's darkside. Not a cohesive album and far from consistently excellent, it offers a helpful recapitulation of what the group does in its spare time. Targets include the Beach Boys (the demented slaughter of "Kill Surf City" *and* a semi-reverent version of "Surfin USA") and Bo Diddley (a devolved rendition of "Who Do You Love" and, on the tape/CD, a similar-sounding tribute, "Bo Diddley Is Jesus"). Not a quick fix for fanatics lacking a complete collection, **Barbed Wire Kisses** merely points the direction in which the obscurities lie.

The devastating Dylanized T. Rexisms of "Blues from a Gun" (the 12-inch EP adds three non-LP tracks, two of which—including the killer surf dementia of "Penetration," unrelated to any other song by that name—also appear on the CD-3, rounded out with a lovely near-acoustic version of Smokey Robinson's "My Girl") previewed **Automatic**, a lazy but entertaining album the Reids recorded with no assistance other than a live drummer on one song. (The mindless synth-drums are one of the record's main problems.) No longer in search of—or shying away from—the ultimate guitar distortion, the Reids hold to a loud down-the-middle sound over which Jim can sing what have become fairly predictable lyrics. Still, their incisive pop sense makes "Blues from a Gun," the Lou Reedish

"Halfway to Crazy" and another irresistible single, "Head On," which sticks a venerable rock'n'roll riff into a song that seems to allow a bit of warped positivism into the band's perverse fantasies of self-degradation: "I'm taking myself to the dirty part of town/Where all my troubles can't be found." (The CD adds an acoustic/strings version of "Drop" sung by William and a pointless dance/noise instrumental, "Sunray.")

The CD-3 of the **Head On** EP (a three-song 12-inch) has a remix of the acoustic "Drop" (without the strings) and two non-LP tracks: "In the Black" and "Break Me Down." (The "Head On" 7-inch was issued in four different sleeves, with four different B-sides.)

Despite a concerted effort to ruin Leonard Cohen's "Tower of Song," the only good thing on the **Rollercoaster** EP is "Lowlife," a buzzing tune with a new (for the Chain) chord progression and loads of tremolo guitar noise; the by-the-numbers "Rollercoaster" has half a hook and way too much echo.   [i]

See also *John Moore and the Expressway, Primal Scream.*

JESUS JONES

Liquidizer (nr/Food) 1989 (Food-SBK) 1990 ●
Live EP (Food-SBK) 1990 φ
Right Here, Right Now EP (nr/Food) 1990 ●
Doubt (Food-SBK) 1991 φ

Led by Drano-gargling vocalist/guitarist Jesus H. Jones (Mike Edwards), this scruffy English quintet that owes a major stylistic debt to Pop Will Eat Itself made quite an initial splash, playing busy, sample-heavy dance rock. Producer Craig Leon helps load the grooves of **Liquidizer** with constant activity: ringing telephones, sirens, meaty power chords, squealy feedback and insistent disco drum beats. That the album is—with one exception, a sluggish redo of Crazyhead's "I Don't Want That Kind of Love"—basically a set of variations on one brilliant song ("Move Mountains") shouldn't discourage potential disciples. Judicious CD track programming is recommended.

Live captures the band in Chicago, performing four songs from the debut (including, of course, "Move Mountains") and a new one, "Barry D. Is Next to Cleanliness," a profane sample-thon. The *very* vocal audience adds to the fun.

Doubt avoids the debut's repetitiveness, but it doesn't lack any of the hyperactive rhythms. Edwards (also the band's songwriter) apparently took criticisms of **Liquidizer** to heart, and endeavored to mix things up a bit. He sprinkles superb, shuffling dance rock ("International Bright Young Thing," "Right Here, Right Now") with slower, more thoughtful morsels (most notably the XTC-echoing "Welcome Back Victoria") and one exceptionally grating noisefest ("Stripped"). The American edition contains one track ("Are You Satisfied") not included on the UK album.   [db]

JESUS LIZARD

Pure EP (Touch and Go) 1989 ●
Head (Touch and Go) 1990 ●
Goat (Touch and Go) 1991 ●

Following Scratch Acid, bassist David Wm. Sims went off to play in Steve Albini's Rapeman and then rejoined singer (er . . .) David Yow in the Jesus Lizard, a Chicago-based group (originally using a drum machine but later incorporating a human skinbeater) co-produced by Albini. With exceptional guitar playing by Duane Denison, the barbed five-song **Pure** drifts towards the windy city's relentless industro-drive without relinquishing any of Yow's ability to terrify. (And if you can't find a trace of Neil Sedaka in the carefully credited "Breaking Up Is Hard to Do" instrumental, you're not alone.)

Distorted vocals and masterfully controlled arrangements introduce new realms of dramatic power to the Jesus Lizard experience on the full-length **Head**. In "If You Had Lips" and "Waxeater," the group hangs sharp objects and crude lyrics from rising and falling riffs; lightening the instrumental assault in "Pastoral" squeezes maximum benefit from Yow's conscientiously off-key crooning; key changes in the instrumental "Tight 'n Shiny" cap off this impressive and abrasive sophistication program. (The **Head** CD also contains **Pure**.)   [i]

See also *Phantom 309, Rapeman, Scratch Acid*.

JET BLACK BERRIES
Sundown on Venus (Pink Dust) 1984
Desperate Fires (Pink Dust) 1986
Animal Necessity (Restless) 1988

NEW MATH
They Walk Among You EP (415) 1982
Gardens (Brain Eater) 1984

Under their original New Math handle this ominously entertaining five-man psychedelic outfit from Rochester, New York is alternately dirgelike and urgent on **They Walk Among You**, a five-song 12-inch that delivers ponderously intoned poetic lyrics over thick rock backing. Heavyweight bass and drums support reasonably normal guitar and pulsing organ for a complex blend of sounds that defies easy description. "Invocation" pays stately homage to the devil and would probably impress Roky Erickson; the magnificent title track recalls (if no one else does) Atomic Rooster's "Death Walks Behind You."

Gardens offers seven new imprecations and tales of madness. The music is grander, more open and less malevolent; New Math reins in the rhythmic power a wee bit and moves Mark Schwarz's organ drone and Kevin Patrick's lead vocals to the fore. The effect may not be the one desired, however, as the band sounds more accessible but less striking this way. Still, it's the work of a talented, unique group with sicko ideas.

Without undergoing any personnel changes, the quintet became the Jet Black Berries and issued **Sundown on Venus**, an offbeat concept album that almost carries off an attempt to meld two familiar cultural idioms, science-fiction and westerns. The music is polite California cowpunk (think Green on Red or Dream Syndicate, occasionally colored by faint synth noises); the lyrics describe showdowns between bad hombres and masked men in space suits. (A brief run-through of Ersel Hickey's obscure classic "Bluebirds" neither aids nor impedes the effort.) Unfortunately, the Berries don't bother to develop their imaginative notion musically,

letting what might have been a fascinating record drift into mediocrity. (The cassette release adds six bonus tracks—also included as a one-sided disc in original pressings of the LP—of similar rock, a surprising slice of Gary Glitter singalong pop, the old group's dirge-pound rock and even another version of "They Walk Among You.")

Produced with likable simplicity and directness, **Desperate Fires** is a taut album of western-leaning rock-pop that hardly resembles the group's early work, but makes a convincing case for the validity of this new direction. Patrick's voice suits the material; unassuming songs like "Kid Alaska," "The Flesh Element" and the rockabilly "Sweet Revenge" pack a wicked kick.

Animal Necessity continues the Berries' (now a sextet) appealing casual affair with musical styles of the American Southwest. Fans of Green on Red, Giant Sand and Naked Prey should especially appreciate the album's dusty melodies, snappy country drumming and roughly strummed electric guitars. Guitarist Gary Trainer and drummer Roy Stein (whose songwriting is developing nicely) both contribute plainspoken tunes with occasionally offbeat lyrics.   [i]

JFA
Blatant Localism EP (Placebo) 1981 •
Valley of the Yakes (Placebo) 1983 •
JFA (Placebo) 1984 •
Mad Garden EP (Placebo) 1984 •
Live (Placebo) 1985 •
Nowhere Blossoms (Placebo) 1988 •

These Phoenix, Arizona skate-punks—the name was originally an acronym for Jodie Foster's Army—are major figures on the Southwest hardcore scene. Besides touring extensively and releasing lots of records, their Placebo label is the most active outlet in the area, and has issued discs by a number of cool underground bands.

Blatant Localism is a 7-inch whose six songs race along cohesively at warp speed with vocals that mostly defy comprehension. There's an eponymous number explaining the group's name, a relatively prolix exposition on "Beach Blanket Bong-Out" and a four-second display of counting. **Valley of the Yakes** stretches fifteen songs out to fill a 12-inch, slowing things down in spots, but not doing much to increase vocal articulation. Still, a crisp, well-played slice of hardcore with real drive and commitment, plus two great, normal-sounding, reverb-splattered surf-guitar instrumentals: "Walk Don't Run" and "Baja." (One CD contains both records.)

JFA exposes increased sophistication and wit, starting with a backwards snippet called "Deltitnu" and continuing by tempering the thrash with variety, understatement and other interesting digressions. In a fit of major cleverness, JFA crash the Ventures into the Dead Kennedys for "Pipetruck" and cover both David Bowie and George Clinton during the course of the album. (JFA's funky-butt turn on the latter's "Standin on the Verge" is nifty.) A bit unfocused, but much more than a simple hardcore record. Standout track: "The Day Walt Disney Died." (The CD also includes the **Mad Garden** EP that followed **JFA**.)

Mad Garden, a four-song 12-inch with a wrestling cover and a new bassist in the lineup, encompasses more-or-less straight speedrock plus one milder (non-surf) instrumental with singer Brian adding keyboards. The live album was recorded in 1984, at gigs in New York and Pittsburgh.

Adding acoustic guitar, more keyboards (piano/organ) and pacifistic lyrics, JFA (with old bassist Mike C. back in the fold) grew up on **Nowhere Blossoms**, an album of tight, occasionally pretty rock that rarely cruises anywhere near punk power. As excellent as the music is, the lower noise threshold leaves the rough, tune-shy vocals glaringly inadequate. (He does fine on a completely straight horn-based rendition of James Brown's "I Feel Good," however.) Proving they haven't outgrown their bratty sense of humor, JFA includes a complete (and great) rendition of the classic "Signifyn' Monkey" sung a cappella by some old man on a Chicago street corner. [i]

JIMMY K
See *Johnny Thunders*.

JING
See *Shirts*.

RICHARD JOBSON
The Ballad of Etiquette (nr/Cocteau) 1981
An Afternoon in Company (Bel. Crépuscule) 1982
Ten Thirty on a Summer Night (Bel. Crépuscule) 1983
The Right Man (Bel. Crépuscule) 1986
16 Years of Alcohol (Bel. Crépuscule) 1987
Badman (nr/Parlophone) 1988 ●

ARMOURY SHOW
Waiting for the Floods (EMI America) 1985

It's nice to see musicians with the courage of their convictions. After turning the Skids into a joke with his absurd pretensions, Richard Jobson—on his way to a career as a television host—effetely pursued poetry and preciousness, allying himself with assorted artsy types. Meanwhile, his onetime bandmate Stuart Adamson got on with Big Country, turning the Skids' anthemic Scottishness into a salable guitar-rock commodity.

Released the same year as the Skids ended, Jobson's first solo album, **The Ballad of Etiquette**, was a collaboration with Virginia Astley, John McGeoch and someone named Josephine. The LP, released on Bill Nelson's Cocteau label, consists of the would-be poet's recitations over lovely music, some of it adapted from pieces by Debussy and Britten. Piano, clarinet, flute, sax and guitar provide a much more enticing component than Jobson's unpleasantly accented readings.

Alternating spoken passages and artless singing, and playing piano and guitar, Jobson (with such sitting-room associates as pianist Cecile Bruynoghe, reedman Steven Brown, Blaine Reininger, Astley and Durutti Columnist Vini Reilly) fills the two discs of **The Right Man** with the audio equivalent of an especially boring and pretentious *Masterpiece Theatre*. To be fair, the dramatic story ("Ten Thirty on a Summer Night") that fills Side Four is engrossing, and the music is lovely, but beware of ex-punks reciting lines like "In Aragon I lost a love/The Pyrenees so high above/To England hailed away from Spain/I promise you I am happy to be here again."

Issued as a record with an illustrated booklet containing exactly the same text, **16 Years of Alcohol** is a spoken-word autobiographical memoir in seventeen parts, occasionally accompanied by glimmers of keyboard music. The writing is incisive and captivating, but the presentation is perplexing: it's not something anyone would listen to twice, and who would bother reading this were it not included with an album?

Amid all this serious art, Jobson took some time to join with Russell Webb (ex-Skids), John McGeoch and John Doyle (both ex-Magazine) to form the short-lived Armoury Show, a band whose resemblance to Big Country didn't escape notice. **Waiting for the Floods** is not a bad album, it's just a shame Jobson had to take such a long way 'round to get back to where he started.

See also *Skids*. [i]

JODY GRIND
One Man's Trash Is Another Man's Treasure (Safety Net-DB) 1990 ●

The Jody Grind's debut album caught on with the college-rock audience, but just about the only style this Atlanta trio doesn't touch is rock'n'roll. Displaying the well-oiled versatility of a lounge act and a healthy reverence for schmaltz, the Jody Grind (unintentionally borrowing its name from a late-'60s British group) skips from Duke Ellington to country-western to flamenco to demented delta blues to Burt Bacharach and the Gershwins at the drop of a high hat. Evenly split between covers ("Peter Gunn," "Wishin' and Hopin'," "It Ain't Necessarily So") and originals like the hilariously morbid "Death of Zorba," **One Man's Trash** resembles a cabaret revue more than a cohesive album, but singer Kelly Hogan Murray's captivating melodramatics steady even the most outrageous stylistic takeoffs. (The CD adds one song.) [kss]

DAVID JOHANSEN
David Johansen (Blue Sky) 1978
In Style (Blue Sky) 1979
Here Comes the Night (Blue Sky) 1981
Live It Up (Blue Sky) 1982
Sweet Revenge (Passport) 1984 ●
Crucial Music: The David Johansen Collection (CBS Special Products-Relativity) 1990 φ

BUSTER POINDEXTER
Buster Poindexter (RCA) 1987 ●
Buster Goes Berserk (RCA) 1989 ●

Having escaped his magnificently sordid reputation as the decadent voice and face of the New York Dolls, singer David Johansen managed to earn himself a place in mainstream rock circles. While keeping a firm grip on the musical values that originally inspired the Dolls, Johansen crafted a uniquely urban style that suits his rough-throated singing as well as his Lower East Side personality.

David Jo's solo debut was a very successful launch, containing most of the songs for which he came to be known. "Funky but Chic," "Donna," "Frenchette" and "Cool Metro" (three of which were co-written by ex-bandmate Syl Sylvain) are played in grand post-CBGB fashion by some of the Bowery's best vets. Better than bar-band but decidedly unslick, **David Johansen** perfectly transforms an insolent punk into a rock'n'roll adult.

Without destroying his urban soul, **In Style** makes an effort to clean and dress up Johansen's sound. Adding synthesized strings and horns, attempting overambitious stylistic experiments and relying on decidedly sophomore-slump material, **In Style**'s two good tracks ("She" and "Melody") are lost in the morass. The failure of **In Style** undoubtedly inspired the misdirected **Here Comes the Night**, an ill-conceived stab at making Johansen simultaneously into a heavy metal shouter and a sensitive, poetic artist. A lot of very talented people had their hands in this project, but weak songs and the lack of cohesion make it a disaster.

Fortunately, **Live It Up** put Johansen's career right back on course. With his longstanding reputation as a great performer and empirical evidence of a well-received live promotional-only record made for radio in 1978, it was a judicious tactic to cut a live album for regular release. Benefiting from carefully chosen classic tunes and Johansen's extraordinary skill as a song interpreter, **Live It Up** is a great party record by a great singer. Johansen comes alive!

Relieved of his CBS-affiliated record contract, Johansen concentrated on performing (appearing regularly in New York as his suave alter-ego, Buster Poindexter) for over a year before returning to the vinyl jungle with **Sweet Revenge**. Sharing the bulk of the songwriting and production with keyboard player Joe Delia and joined in a half-dozen studios by a large collection of sidemen, Johansen disconnects from the R&B rootsiness that, to some extent at least, had always characterized his work, replacing it with strong, synth-heavy rock that would be regrettable were it not for distinctive vocals and witty songwriting. Some of the record flops, but "Heard the News," complete with ersatz Spanish newscaster, blends Latin American political commentary with one of the catchiest melodies of his career. "King of Babylon" is a clever novelty item.

Crucial Music is a well-chosen, if rather skimpy, ten-track sampler drawn from the Blue Sky albums, with an unsurprising focus: six songs come off the first LP, although several are actually from the live record.

Johansen finally hit the big time when he allowed his part-time persona, adult jazz/blues smoothie Buster Poindexter (also the longtime name of his music publishing company), to take over his career. Aided by a New York club residency and regular television appearances (on *Saturday Night Live*), Buster's debut album with the horn-heavy non-rock Banshees of Blue (led by Joe Delia) did the trick. The generally lighthearted romp through cabaret and swing styles of the '30s and '40s recalls both Spike Jones and Cab Calloway, blending sweet nostalgia with gruff crooning. Given the inconsistent, scattershot program (a schmaltzy ballad, one terrible rocker, another cover of "House of the Rising Sun" done as a torch song, a few other misdirected duds), the choice of a sprightly pre-lambada soca number, "Hot Hot Hot," as a single was a stroke of genius: it did the chart trick and guaranteed Buster's continued existence.

Buster Goes Berserk more or less repeats its predecessor's formula, but with less quirkiness and more party-animal posturing. On the album's only two original tunes, Johansen attempts to bridge the gap between the Buster persona and his "real" self, but not enough to keep the album from sounding amiably redundant.

[i/hd]

JOHN AND MARY

See *10,000 Maniacs.*

EVAN JOHNS AND HIS H-BOMBS

Giddy Up Girl EP (Deco) 1980
Rollin' Through the Night (Alternative Tentacles) 1986
Evan Johns and the H-Bombs (Jungle) 1986
Bombs Away (Speedo-Rykodisc) 1989 ●
Please Mr. Santa Claus [CD] (Rykodisc) 1990 ●
Rockit Fuel Only! (Rykodisc) 1991 φ

Jerry Lee Lewis worshiper (who claims to have blown his hero off the stage on a good night!) and certified lunatic of the geetar, Evan Johns simply personifies the most incendiary and rebellious elements of rock'n'roll. A teenaged Virginia hellion who apprenticed in the DC bar circuit under the legendary Danny Gatton, Johns formed the H-Bombs in 1979 and made the reelin' rockabilly 10-inch **Giddy Up Girl** in 1980. The four songs are roughly recorded, but blueprint the searing six-string mayhem that has marked Johns' best work.

It wasn't until a move to Austin, a stint with the LeRoi Brothers and a Grammy nomination for his featured participation in the **Big Guitars from Texas Trash Twang and Thunder** compilation LP that Johns' name began to spread across the land he'd already crisscrossed time and time again. **Rollin' Through the Night**, a 1982 session unreleased until Jello Biafra came across it four years later, is the pinnacle by which Johns—and any other purveyors of roots-surf-guitar-billy-boogie—must forever be measured. With second guitarist Mark Korpi's taut speed runs setting the pace, EJ provides fireworks galore on cuts like "Madhouse," "Sugar Cookie" and "Do the Dootz." Put this album on a 90-minute cassette with **The Best of ZZ Top** and drive till you die happy.

Released the same year, **Evan Johns and the H-Bombs** gathers three years of scattered sessions for a predictably less-focused set, highlighting Johns' love of Tex-Mex, blues and country, as well as head-stompin' rock.

The H-Bombs backed Eugene Chadbourne on the berserk, twisted **Vermin of the Blues** before making the relatively polished and consistently superb **Bombs Away**. Producer (and erstwhile Springsteen sideman) Gary Tallent manages to squeeze the band into a clear, vibrant framework without obliterating the trademark hog-wild spirit of Johns' best outings. The seasonal and primarily instrumental **Please Mr. Santa Claus** is a holiday postcard that features a polka, the fiddle-fueled "Little Cajun Drummer Boy," a raging "Telstar" and plenty of free-style pickin' throughout.

Rockit Fuel Only!, while allowing for the broad stylistic whims of its creator (like a surprising compassionate piano ballad, "Prove It to Each Other"), also rocks harder than anything since **Rollin' Through the**

Night. "Juvenile Delinquent," "Boogie Disease" and "Little Scene Setter" are among the rip-it-up corkers that keep Evan Johns among rock'n'roll's guitar elite. [sm]

See also *Eugene Chadbourne, LeRoi Brothers*.

HOLLY JOHNSON

See *Frankie Goes to Hollywood*.

LINTON KWESI JOHNSON

Forces of Victory (Mango) 1979 ●
Bass Culture (Mango) 1980 ●
LKJ in Dub (nr/Island) 1980
Making History (Mango) 1984
Reggae Greats (Mango) 1984 ●
In Concert with the Dub Band (Shanachie) 1985 ●
Tings an' Times (Shanachie) 1991 ●

POET AND THE ROOTS

Dread Beat an' Blood (Heartbeat) 1978 (Front Line) 1990 ●

Poet and social critic (as the name Poet and the Roots suggests) Linton Kwesi Johnson—born in Jamaica, raised in London—helped bridge the gap between reggae and punk, infusing the music with powerful political content and an urge for freedom rooted in his experience as a black man living in Brixton.

Dread Beat an' Blood was a call to arms, a dark commemoration of police harassment and social repression of blacks told in a forceful but strangely spiteless manner. Speaking his poems over absolutely flawless throbbing reggae, Johnson uses the patois of the streets to speak to his audience, calling for brotherhood and vigilance. The clean, supple, vibrant music and incisive, pointed words make it a powerful and memorable political statement. Highly recommended. (The 1990 reissue—no vinyl—contains two extra tracks.)

Forces of Victory continues Johnson's call to action. Again supported by feverish reggae, Johnson's voice gains greater range and expressiveness while his poetry speaks of dire truths, and sounds increasingly complex, compact and expert. Muscular, dramatic stuff.

Bass Culture expands Johnson's style, including more humor and even a shy, touching love song. The music is sparer and more coherent, and Dennis Bovell's co-production slickens the sound just enough to remove its rough edges. Johnson is no less determined on his political numbers, but it's nice to know there are other things on his mind as well.

LKJ in Dub is a tribute to Bovell's engineering talents; while it has little to do with the Linton Kwesi Johnson canon, it's an interesting and successful example of dub technique.

During a four-year sabbatical, Johnson worked as a journalist. He then reunited with Bovell for **Making History**, a "comeback" album as vital as any they had made together.

The two-disc **In Concert** documents Johnson's strength and onstage presence. Though hardly perfunctory (the performances are all first-rate), it's still a greatest-hits-live package, and shouldn't deter listeners from acquiring any or all of the studio LPs. **Reggae Greats** is a compilation.

Seven years after **Making History**, Johnson repeated the feat with the all-new **Tings an' Times**, an upbeat but stringently critical album that is at once traditional and modern. Backed by Bovell and a collection of ace players (including a violinist!), LKJ considers "Di Good Life" as well as "Di Anfinish Revalueshan," attempting to make—as he discusses in the first track—"Sense outa Nansense." [sg/bk/i]

MATT JOHNSON

See *The The*.

JESSE JOHNSON'S REVUE

Jesse Johnson's Revue (A&M) 1985 ●

JESSE JOHNSON

Shockadelica (A&M) 1986 ●
Every Shade of Love (A&M) 1988 ●

Former Time guitarist Johnson reckons himself another pretender to Prince's throne. His first solo album, **Jesse Johnson's Revue**, reeks of conscious imitation, from the chronic pink color scheme to the band's carefully shaped mustaches. The self-produced music likewise favors a mixture of his former band and Prince's **Purple Rain**; not unpleasant, occasionally catchy ("I Want My Girl"), but no threat to the reigning monarch.

Although Prince's influence is still evident on **Shockadelica** (check "A Better Way"), Johnson's obvious talent and stylistic dexterity diminishes the significance of such comparisons. The accomplishment of leading a ten-piece band (seven instrumentalists and two female vocalists) and ending up with clear, well-organized sound is impressive in and of itself. The LP features a funky duet with Sly Stone ("Crazay") and a diverse, appealing set of danceable songs with a surprising ending: Johnson sings a message of hope on the touching "Black in America," accompanied only by acoustic guitars, synthetic strings and a small chorus.

Dispensing with his band (a drummer, saxophonist and female vocalist are credited) for a harder-edged solo effort, Johnson uses **Every Shade of Love** to show off his Hendrix-influenced guitar work. The eight tracks revolve around skittish strumming as much as surging keyboards, and those tracks that dig bottomless holes with endless one-chord vamps lose listener interest in short order. The delightful title tune and "I'm Just Wanting You" are notable exceptions. [i]

See also *Time*.

DANIEL JOHNSTON

Songs of Pain [tape] (Stress) 1980
Don't Be Scared [tape] (Stress) 1982
The What of Whom [tape] (Stress) 1982
Yip/Jump Music [tape] (Stress) 1983 (Homestead) 1989
Hi, How Are You [tape] (Stress) 1983 (Homestead) 1988
Retired Boxer [tape] (Stress) 1984
Respect [tape] (Stress) 1985
Continued Story [tape] (Stress) 1985
Live at SXSW [tape] (Stress) 1990
1990 (Shimmy-Disc) 1990 ●

JAD FAIR AND DANIEL JOHNSTON

Jad Fair and Daniel Johnston (50 Skidillion Watts) 1989 ●

Troubled enough to be institutionalized and talented enough to be taken seriously, this West Virginian (who has lived since 1984 in Austin, Texas) has written and recorded—solo, in the most primitive lo-fi circumstances imaginable, accompanying his vulnerably boyish voice with piano and, on occasion, chord organ, guitar, even old jazz records—a vast and remarkable body of songs. Often disturbing, nearly pathetic, sometimes beautiful, Johnston's music is at once freakshow exploitation and fringe-weird genius, an uncomfortable but extraordinary mixture of art and madness. Although influential fans and national exposure on MTV's *Cutting Edge* show helped make Johnston a full-fledged cult figure in 1985, incarceration (at the end of '86 and again in '88) has made his "career" intermittent and unpredictable.

Johnston began his haphazard and bizarre musical trek by self-releasing a series of homemade tapes. Played simply but skillfully on piano, **Songs of Pain**—jolly-sounding outpourings of deep alienation ("Grievances," "Joy Without Pleasure," "Like a Monkey in a Zoo") and misbegotten romance ("An Idiot's End," "Urge"), as well as an expression of religious faith—is lucid and stunningly incisive, casually cogent and artistically invigorating. On the other hand, **Don't Be Scared** is inconsistent and disjointed, with really muddy sound, but there are some really good songs (like the Neil Young-y "Evening Stars"). As musically accomplished and clear as **Songs of Pain** but significantly more revealingly confessional, **The What of Whom** is quietly harrowing, a riveting collection that cuts to the quick, plaintive cries for help set in gracefully tender melodies accompanied by piano.

Johnston first reached vinyl with Homestead's 1988 reissue of **Hi, How Are You**. Despite the muffled sound and toy instruments, there's no mistaking the inspired wit and riveting honesty. "Big Business Monkey" attacks an employer with venom and clever rhymes; "I'll Never Marry," "Walking the Cow" and "She Called Pest Control" allude to romantic problems. While "Hey Joe" rewrites "Hey Jude," the anguished autobiographical complaints of "Keep Punching Joe" is ingenuously sung over a big-band swing record.

The two-record **Yip/Jump Music** is more consistent in sound and style, performed almost entirely on chord organ and less motivated by anger. The lyrics offer enthusiastic elegies to "The Beatles," "God" and "Casper the Friendly Ghost" while exploring personal issues in "Sorry Entertainer," "I Live for Love" and "I Remember Painfully," but the album's standout is "King Kong," an extended and erudite a cappella plot summary and analysis.

Continuing his tape-capades, Johnston next released **Retired Boxer**, an uneven but generally high-quality nine-song set that includes a reminiscence about Daniel by an unidentified acquaintance, a Christmas greeting and the moving "I'll Do Anything but Break Dance for Ya, Darling." Johnston's piano playing on this cassette is among his best ever.

Respect is a very strong effort, an eighteen-song extravaganza that contains the remorseful "An Angel

Cry," a solemn cover of the once-goofy "A Little Bit of Soap," the winsomely winning "I Know What I Want" and the poorly recorded but sharply worded "Just Like a Widow." Besides "Go" and the laughably speeded-up "Fast Go," there's "Dream," a marvelous piece of spoken-word prose, a grimly offbeat interpretation of "Heartbreak Hotel" and much more. Brilliant.

Recorded as badly as possible, the electric Texas Instruments back Johnston on five **Continued Story** tracks (including a "Cadillac Ranch" parody entitled "Funeral Home"); Bill Anderson and Rick Morgan each contribute to a tune or two as well. Played on two guitars, "Ain't No Woman Gonna Make a George Jones Outta Me" is a left-field winner, as is Johnston's measured piano version of "I Saw Her Standing There," the rocking "Ghost of Our Love" and "Girls." There's more disposable nonsense than usual, but not enough to outweigh the good stuff. The bootleg-quality **Live at SXSW** (the title refers to the annual South by Southwest music-biz convention) finds Daniel and his acoustic guitar enthusiastically performing with strength and confidence at three Austin venues: an auditorium and two record stores. The delightful ten-song program includes "Casper," two versions each of "Silly Love" and "Do You Really Love Me."

Following a joint album with Jad Fair (who, in comparison to Johnston, seems about as weird as an insurance salesman), Daniel made **1990**, which consists of four live tracks (from 1988) and a half-dozen professional studio recordings, one with instrumental assists from drummer Steve Shelley and guitarist Lee Ranaldo of Sonic Youth. (Producer Kramer plays on the magnificent "Some Things Last a Long Time," a bewitching song co-written with Fair.) Clear sound, well-recorded piano and a touch of echo on the vocals don't damage Johnston's basic virtues, but neither do they make these songs—most of which are strongly religious—any more widely palatable than they would have been on a two-dollar cassette. If the eccentricities of Johnston's damaged mind aren't an impediment to enjoyment, sound quality is certainly not an issue. [i]

See also *Half Japanese, Texas Instruments*.

FREEDY JOHNSTON

The Trouble Tree (Bar/None-Restless) 1990 ●

With an artless, slightly strangled voice and melodic rock/country songs that show plenty of promise but could use a lot more development and meatier presentation than they receive here, Kansas-to-Hoboken singer/guitarist Johnston makes an indifferent debut on **The Trouble Tree**, produced by Chris Butler. Played at various volume levels (all without much color) by a rudimentary acoustic/electric trio, Johnston's naïve, emotive writing conveys simple, painfully honest ideas with no hint of mystery. [i]

JOINED AT THE HEAD

See *Controlled Bleeding*.

JON & THE NIGHTRIDERS

Surf Beat '80 (Voxx) 1980
Recorded Live at Hollywood's Famous Whisky A Go-Go (Voxx) 1981

Splashback! EP (Invasion) 1982
Charge of the Nightriders (Enigma) 1983
Stampede!! (Norton) 1990

Although probably still in nursery school when guitar instrumentals filled the American record charts, twang-bar king John Blair and his three cohorts brilliantly re-create the innocence and excitement of that long-lost genre. With resplendent, ringing tones, vibrato and mountains of reverb, **Surf Beat '80** pays homage with fourteen numbers, including a few soundalike originals and a selection of covers that proves the band's dedication to—and familiarity with—their forebears. All of the tracks sound the same, but that's the idea. Great!

The live LP reprises some of the studio record's items, but incorporates new material and spot-on renditions of additional classics like "Pipeline" and "Hawaii Five-O." **Splashback!**, produced by the legendary Shel Talmy (to no particular effect, other than perhaps spiritual), features a six-minute medley that touches on eleven instantly recognizable melodies in one seamless nostalgia romp. **Charge of the Nightriders** is a compilation.

Self-billed as "America's No. 9 Surfing Band," the unshakably orthodox Nightriders reclaimed their piece of the beach on the self-produced **Stampede!!**, another cleanly played, reverb-soaked collection of standards ("Wild Weekend"), originals ("Beneath the Reef," "Storm Dancer") and obscurities ("Minor Chaos," "The Breeze and I"), some goosed by George White's period sax work.

As if any further proof of scholarship in his chosen field were needed, Blair put down his guitar long enough to assemble *The Illustrated Discography of Surf Music (1961-1965)*.   [i]

GRACE JONES

Portfolio (Island) 1977 ●
Fame (Island) 1978
Muse (Island) 1979
Warm Leatherette (Island) 1980 ●
Nightclubbing (Island) 1981 ●
Living My Life (Island) 1982 ●
Island Life (Island) 1985 ●
Slave to the Rhythm (Manhattan Island) 1985 ●
Inside Story (Manhattan) 1986 ●
Bulletproof Heart (Capitol) 1989 ●

At the outset of her singing career, model-*cum*-actress Grace Jones was a musical product in the truest sense of the word, more or less invented by artist Jean-Paul Goude. When new wave became the dance-club staple around the turn of the decade, this glamorous disco diva sailed into the genre on an airbrush jetstream, performing slickly produced covers of mainstream modern material borrowed from Chrissie Hynde, Bryan Ferry et al., while mixing in a safe dose of thumped-up funk.

Warm Leatherette (named for the Normal's pioneering 1978 new wave electro single, which she has the guts and insight to cover) was the first Jones disc to embrace this formula; **Nightclubbing** followed suit, utilizing songs by Iggy and Sting. The balance of this LP features a slightly more fluid vocal style than the monotone that rules the previous album.

Living My Life shows Grace maturing, escaping the restrictive machinations that had controlled her. The material allows more personality to show through, and songs like "My Jamaican Guy" and "Nipple to the Bottle" show the Sly-and-Robbie reggae rhythm team to be more into the music at this point. **Island Life** recaps her career to that point, compiling such tracks as "La Vie en Rose," "Pull Up to the Bumper" and "Love Is the Drug," adding "Slave to the Rhythm," a new single taken from a subsequent album which was released almost immediately thereafter.

Some bizarre business dealings must have led to the one-off alliance of Island and Manhattan Records to jointly issue **Slave to the Rhythm**. Trevor Horn produced this outrageous, astonishing so-called biography, including inter-track recitations, recollections and interview bites and creating theatrically massive orchestrations. The songs—written by a collective of Horn, Bruce Woolley and others—aren't intrinsically strong or interesting, but the ZTT Big Beat Colossus does such a job filling the grooves with beats, strings, horns, vocals, keyboards and god knows what else that the material counts for relatively little. But by the same token, Grace's vocal contribution to this audio love fest seems disconcertingly expendable.

Returning to the real world for a relatively routine (but still Grace-ious) outing, Jones wrote **Inside Story** with Bruce Woolley and produced it with Nile Rodgers; her collaborators also played most of the LP's music. The lyrics contemplate such offbeat-going-on-dada topics as "Hollywood Liar," "Victor Should Have Been a Jazz Musician" and "Chan Hitchhikes to Shanghai," while the music dully retreads various familiar late-'80s high-tech sounds. Grace's voice is fine, but this is not one of her more invigorating records.

Continuing on a path back to dull rhythmic functionality, Jones attempts a surrender to the hit parade on **Bulletproof Heart**, employing David Cole and Robert Clivilles, the crass slicksters behind Seduction and C+C Music Factory, on three tracks. Her songwriting (in collaboration with co-producer Chris Stanley) has never been worse ("Crack Attack" sounds like the work of a gradeschooler ordered to write a poem against drugs); her awkward delivery only makes this bad scene worse.   [jw/i]

HOWARD JONES

Human's Lib (Elektra) 1984 ●
The 12-Inch Album (nr/WEA) 1984 ●
Dream into Action (Elektra) 1985 ●
Action Replay EP (Elektra) 1986
One to One (Elektra) 1986 ●
Cross That Line (Elektra) 1989 ●

Starting out as something of an '80s answer to early Marc Bolan, Howard Jones is a well-scrubbed ex-hippie embracing humanist principles and possessing acute pop sensibilities. Times being what they are, he doesn't play acoustic guitar with a bongo drummer on the side, he controls an array of sophisticated electronic keyboards, singing earnest, reflective lyrics of personal awareness and individualist philosophy. **Human's Lib**, produced mainly by Rupert Hine, boasts a few warm techno-pop standouts—"New Song," "Pearl in the Shell" and

"What Is Love?"—which stop just short of over-perkiness or saccharine platitudes.

Dream into Action, which employs more outside musicians (horns, vocalists, a cellist) to vary the sound, serves up another dose of engaging nouveau-pop ("Things Can Only Get Better," "Life in One Day," "Like to Get to Know You Well"). The album does, unfortunately, contain an extremely duff howler, "Bounce Right Back." **The 12-Inch Album** compiles six hits in their remixed forms.

Taking advantage of Jones' massive American popularity, Elektra issued **Action Replay**, a collection of five alternate versions and remixes of songs from **Dream into Action** and other sources, plus the previously unreleased "Always Asking Questions."

For **One to One**, producer Arif Mardin put Jones in the studio with a full complement of backup musicians, thereby focusing attention on him as writer/singer. The conservative cover portrait reflects an overall stylistic retrenchment: the once-colorful elf has become part of a mainstream adult pop machine. He hasn't sold out—nothing about Jones was ever that outré to begin with—but the shift leaves the soul-inflected **One to One** noticeably short on twink and charm.

Jones attempts to engage his musical gears more aggressively on the heavyhearted **Cross That Line** and partially succeeds. Besides the familiar HoJo bounce of "Everlasting Love," the mostly self-produced album stretches to encompass a solo piano piece, funky dance tunes with horns, a waltz played on Fairlight strings, new age ambience, a blast of raunchy electric guitar and other stylistic digressions. While the melancholy lyrics about a troubled relationship coming to a disappointing end give the record emotional gravity, the same seriousness prevents the music from reaching escape velocity. Impressive in its ambitious stylistic variety, **Cross That Line** is an aimless adventure with only a few gripping chapters. [i]

MARTI JONES
Unsophisticated Time (A&M) 1985
Match Game (A&M) 1986 ●
Used Guitars (A&M) 1988 ●
Any Kind of Lie (RCA) 1990 ●

COLOR ME GONE
Color Me Gone EP (A&M) 1984

Color Me Gone's one EP introduced a nice, reedy vocalist in guitar-playing Marti Jones; rich arrangements and clear production allowed her to draw everything out of the six agreeable songs. Without really holding to any one style, the Ohio quartet flirts with radio rock, neo-ethnic Americana, country (in that mode, the downcast "Hurtin' You" is the best thing here) and '60sish folk-rock, winding up pleasant but unmemorable.

Jones' solo debut—brilliantly produced by future husband Don Dixon, who also plays most of the instruments on it—draws strength from a very astute selection of tunes. She covers songs by the dB's, Bongos, Costello and Dixon in a clear voice on this delightfully unprepossessing album.

Match Game follows roughly the same pattern, adding songs by David Bowie ("Soul Love"), Marshall Crenshaw ("Whenever You're on My Mind") and Free ("Soon I Will Be Gone") to the prior album's returning writing collective. Given a comfortable setting by Dixon's sparkling studio work, Marti shines on tracks played by such prestigious supporters as Crenshaw, Mitch Easter, Richard Barone, Gary Barnacle, Paul Carrack, T-Bone Burnett and Darlene Love.

Boding well for an autonomous future, Don'n'Marti co-wrote three songs for the third chapter in a by-now-familiar, but no less enjoyable, book. **Used Guitars** gets major contributions from Crenshaw and Janis Ian (!), adding songs by John Hiatt ("The Real One," "If I Can Love Somebody") and Graham Parker ("You Can't Take Love for Granted"), plus instrumental assists by the Woods, Easter and the Uptown Horns. Ian's "Ruby" stretches Jones into smoky piano balladry that's a bit out of keeping with the sprightly pop elsewhere, but might be the key to long-overdue commercial success.

Any Kind of Lie raises the stakes in a tasteful but determined effort to make Marti a star. Using a stable band and only two outside writing submissions (Clive Gregson's "Second Choice" and Loudon Wainwright's "Old Friend"), Dixon loads the songs up with every time-tested trick in the pop-country-rock singer/songwriter manual, making for a carefully arranged record that tries to consolidate a wide range of successful stylistic referents, from Suzanne Vega to Linda Ronstadt to Bonnie Raitt. A fine album to be sure, but it's unsettling to hear this down-home gal turned out in such cosmopolitan duds. [i]

See also *Don Dixon*.

STEVE JONES
Mercy (Gold Mountain-MCA) 1987 ●
Fire and Gasoline (Gold Mountain-MCA) 1989 ●

The ex-Pistol guitarist, known for his chunky chords and rough'n'randy attitude, caught followers off guard with **Mercy**, a solo debut that allows low-key, sentimental moments—like the title track, the hopelessly sappy "Love Letters" and others—to mingle with the rock numbers. Although Jones is no vocalist, he gamely sing-speaks his way through the record, assisted only by two drummers and a pair of keyboardists. "Drugs Suck" is a terrible track that reveals a healthy attitude; **Mercy** isn't Jones' best post-Pistols work, but it's by no means his worst.

That onus falls on **Fire and Gasoline**. An unforgivable plodding replay of the Pistols' "Did You No Wrong" shrieked by W. Axl Rose and Ian Astbury (also the album's co-producer and songwriting collaborator) reduces Jones to auto-cannibalism; the rest of this serviceable but unnecessary record either emulates the Cult or settles into self-parody. Ironically, Cult guitarist Billy Duffy upstages Jones on "Get Ready" with an electrifying solo. [i]

See also *Duran Duran, Iggy Pop, Professionals, Sex Pistols*.

JONES VERY
See *Articles of Faith*.

JOOLZ
Never Never Land (nr/Abstract) 1985
Hex (nr/EMI) 1987 (nr/Anagram) 1990 ●

Bold, beautiful and British, modern-day poet Joolz is one of a kind. Though her main arena is literature (publishing two fine books), she has made a number of records of considerable potency and vision. Following a couple of singles on which she was backed by Jah Wobble's funkisms, **Never Never Land** is an unaccompanied album of spoken-word poetry, delivered in a style that owes something to John Cooper Clarke. Joolz relays essential thoughts on the bewildering facets of small-town life in Bradford, captures the attitudes and vernacular of UK culture, celebrates love and freedom, and rages at injustice, hypocrisy and betrayal in pieces that are by turns observational, defiant, romantic, satirical and touching. The live closer—a passionate, anti-nuke call-to-arms ("Jerusalem")—strikes a particularly fierce nerve.

The even better **Hex** adopts a more ambitious tack, with help from singer/guitarist Slade the Leveller and drummer Rob Heaton, both of New Model Army. (Joolz has managed the band and painted its record covers.) The pair provides a sympathetic musical backdrop for her resonant poems (some, like the upbeat "Protection," cross the line to become actual songs). In particular, the moving "Requiem" is beautifully bittersweet; "House of Dreams" is nearly as good. Throughout, the diverse music is exemplary, from pulsing rock'n'roll and synthesizer tapestries to more atmospheric, soundtrack-like compositions. (The Anagram CD adds three single sides also done with New Model Army.)   [gef]

See also *New Model Army*.

JOSEF K

The Only Fun in Town (nr/Postcard) 1981 (Bel. Play It
    Again Sam) 1990 ●
Heaven Sent EP (nr/Supreme Int'l Editions) 1987
Young and Stupid/Endless Soul (nr/Supreme Int'l Editions)
    1987 (Bel. Play It Again Sam) 1990 ●

A leading light in Scotland's neo-pop revival, Josef K attempted an uneasy marriage of pop form and psychedelic sensibilities on a string of melancholic singles, all contained on their one original album. Singer Paul Haig is the only member identified by name, and his presence is certainly the strongest here. There is a fragility in Josef K's gentle but foreboding work, produced in darkest wall-of-molasses sound, that suggests an intensity of thought comparable to Joy Division's. (Some of Haig's subsequent solo work sounds a lot like New Order.) But the album—which was first recorded in 1980, scrapped and then redone with largely different material from scratch the following year—never reaches the level of animation found in the singles, and it was neither surprising nor inappropriate when the group broke up shortly after its release. Dank but intriguing.

Heaven Sent and **Young and Stupid/Endless Soul** are both posthumous affairs, consisting of singles, outtakes, demos and John Peel sessions. Ironically, these two records contain the band's best material. "Heaven Sent," "Radio Drill Time" and "Heart of Song" are nothing short of pure pop brilliance, surprisingly unaffected by the passage of time. Josef K were the definitive Scottish neo-pop masters, and their legacy lives on in many of the groups currently emerging from that land.   [sg/ag]

See also *Paul Haig*.

JOY DIVISION

An Ideal for Living EP (nr/Enigma) 1978 (nr/Anonymous)
    1978
Unknown Pleasures (Factory) 1979 (Qwest) 1989 ●
Closer (Factory) 1980 (Qwest) 1989 ●
Still (nr/Factory) 1981 (Qwest) 1991 ●
The Peel Sessions EP (nr/Strange Fruit) 1986 ●
The Peel Sessions EP (nr/Strange Fruit) 1987 ●
Substance (Qwest) 1988 ●
The Peel Sessions Album (nr/Strange Fruit) 1990 ●

VARIOUS ARTISTS

Something About Joy Division (It. Vox Pop) 1990

Emerging from the industrial desolation of Manchester and originally known as Warsaw, Joy Division expressed, in uncompromising terms, the angst of the great wrong place in which we live, and their updating/refinement of the oppressive weight of heavy metal music combined with singer Ian Curtis' tormented lyrics and Martin Hannett's crystalline production to make a qualitative leap onto totally original ground. The band came to an end when Curtis hung himself—hours before they were to leave on their first American tour, thus (though it may be cynical to say so) proving the strength of his convictions. The surviving trio, with one new member, continued, finding far greater commercial success as New Order.

Following the self-release of the 7-inch **An Ideal for Living**, a skillful but rather unexceptional quartet of Bowie-influenced guitar punk songs, Joy Division did tracks for a local compilation and then signed with the incipient Factory label. (Three of these early tracks, as well as other rarities, can be found on the **Substance** compilation.)

Unknown Pleasures contrasts the message of decay and bemused acceptance of life's paradoxes with the energy and excitement of a band set loose in a studio for the first time. The tension of originality constrained by inadequate instrumental skills—simple synthesizers and guitar set against the Peter Hook/Stephen Morris rhythm section's more obvious punk roots—gives the record a powerfully immediate air; Hannett glazes the chilling, despondent music (including the classic "She's Lost Control") with a Teutonic sheen, fusing medium and message into a dark, holistic brilliance. The grim songs are punctuated by the sounds of ambulance sirens and breaking glass, picturing a world speeding towards incomprehensible chaos. Very highly recommended.

With group and producer gaining confidence and ambition, **Closer** sounds emptier and more distant, with occasional use of strangely distorted synthesizer and jagged shards of guitar, both played by Bernard Albrecht (aka Dicken aka Sumner). Meanwhile, a dislocated Curtis meanders through a world that has robbed him of joy and hope. From the blunt anomie of "Isolation" to the accusatory chorus of the martial-beat "A Means to an End" to the somber piano-based "The Eternal," Curtis' commanding vocals dominate the record. On **Closer**, refinement of the Joy Division ethos produces a purgatory of sound and words. A stunning, deeply personal album.

More than a year after Curtis' suicide (in May 1980, immediately prior to the release of both **Closer** and the band's single best-known song, "Love Will Tear Us Apart"), Joy Division's outtakes were gathered (along with a few previously issued rarities) on one disc of the two-record **Still**. (The second record documents the group's final concert.) Besides four previously unissued tracks from the **Unknown Pleasures** sessions, **Still** contains a long, enthusiastic (but carefully controlled) rendition of the obviously influential Velvet Underground's "Sister Ray," also recorded live. One of the most notable aspects of the album's engrossing concert half is the inclusion of "Ceremony," a then-new song that would provide the bridge between Joy Division and New Order as the latter's first single. As a compilation, **Still** lacks the coherent intensity of the other two albums, but features a good representation of the various facets of Joy Division's intimate, desperate music.

Both of Joy Division's John Peel sessions (January 1979 and November 1979) were issued on four-song EPs and later compiled onto an album. Since both contain material the group had not yet recorded, these artifacts are of immense interest. The first previews "Transmission" and "She's Lost Control," while the second boasts a brilliant rendition of "Love Will Tear Us Apart" and a foretaste of "Twenty Four Hours."

Also of enormous historical value is the **Substance** CD (also available, in the UK, on DAT), which includes a seven-track "appendix" to the vinyl album's ten songs. This posthumous antidote to Joy Division's willful obscurity draws almost nothing from the band's two albums, instead focusing on singles, rarities and the band's early contributions to Factory and Fast label compilations. Although annoyingly unannotated, **Substance** offers both non-LP classics ("Transmission," "Love Will Tear Us Apart") and high-quality esoterica (like "Atmosphere," a gently oppressive number first issued on a French flexi-disc).

Although there aren't any household names on it (judging by the accented English, a lot of them may be Italian), the tribute album is quite wonderful, an imaginative (and refreshingly un-derivative) assortment of interpretations that preserve Joy Division's dark mood in settings that range from gentle piano ballads ("Love Will Tear Us Apart" performed by the Carnival of Fools) and mild acid-pop (Allison Run's "Ceremony") to the manic guitar storm of "Atmosphere" played by Hitchcock's Scream. The only thing missing is P.J. Proby's legendary version of "Love Will Tear Us Apart": "Why's the room so gol-darned cold?" [sg/i]

See also *New Order*.

BRUCE JOYNER
See *Unknowns*.

PHIL JUDD
See *Swingers*.

JULES AND THE POLAR BEARS
See *Jules Shear*.

JULUKA
See *Johnny Clegg & Savuka*.

SYLVIA JUNCOSA
See *SWA, To Damascus*.

JUNGLE BROTHERS
Straight Out the Jungle (Idlers-Warlock-Gee St.) 1988 ●
Done by the Forces of Nature (Warner Bros.) 1989 ●

Along with their friends De La Soul and A Tribe Called Quest, New York's Jungle Brothers helped liberate rap from the stereotype of the macho aggressor. Like the original JB—James Brown—these JBs are versatile, upbeat and relentlessly funky. **Straight Out the Jungle** boasts an abundance of loose, swinging jams, including the cheerfully lewd "Jimbrowski," social commentary inspired by Marvin Gaye's "What's Going On" and "I'll House You," an exuberant blend of hip-hop and house.

Done by the Forces of Nature vaults the Jungle Brothers into the major leagues with a heap of soulful energy and some of the warmest, most personable raps on the planet. Anybody who can resist the propulsive momentum of "Beyond This World" and "What 'U' Waitin '4'?" probably didn't have a pulse to quicken. [jy]

JUNKYARD
See *Dag Nasty*.

JUSTIFIED ANCIENTS OF MU MU
1987 (What the Fuck's Going On?) (nr/KLF Comm.) 1987
1987 The JAMS 45 Edits EP (nr/KLF Comm.) 1987
Who Killed the JAMS? (nr/KLF Comm.) 1988
Shag Times EP (nr/KLF Comm.) 1989 ●
The History of the JAMS a.k.a. the Timelords (TVT) 1989 ●
DISCO 2000
"I Gotta" (nr/KLF Comm.) 1987
"One Love Nation" (nr/KLF Comm.) 1988
"Uptight" (nr/KLF Comm.) 1989
KLF
The What Time Is Love Story (nr/KLF Comm.) 1990 ●
Chill Out (nr/KLF Comm.) 1990 (Wax Trax!) 1991 ●
The White Room (Arista) 1991 φ
BILL DRUMMOND
The Man (nr/Creation) 1987 (Bar/None-Restless) 1989 ●
ORB
A Huge Ever Growing Pulsating Brain That Rules from the Centre of the Ultraworld EP (nr/Wau! Mr Modo) 1989
Adventures Beyond the Ultraworld (Mercury) 1991 φ
SPACE
Space (nr/Space-KLF Comm.) 1990 ●

With synthesizers, sampling and the dominance of dance helping to pry the skeletal fingers of basic values—old-farty things like melody, lyrics and originality—from their traditional vise grip on popular music, the world is wide open for such high-concept jokers as Bill Drummond. Although America has largely been spared his mischievous machinations, the UK has been Drummond's lab, a proving ground for a series of colorful sonic marketing experiments, one of which topped the singles charts in 1988.

Born in Scotland but arriving in the music biz via the 1977 Liverpool scene, Drummond was a founding member of Big in Japan, launched the Zoo label with Dave Balfe and then became the manager of Echo and the Bunnymen and the Teardrop Explodes. (He was largely responsible for some of the more outlandish escapades of the former and was celebrated in song by Julian Cope of the latter.) Later, as an A&R man, he worked with Youth's wretched Brilliant, a mid-'80s group whose lasting cultural significance amounts to its inclusion of ex-Zodiac Mindwarp keyboardist/guitarist Jimmy Cauty, with whom Drummond concocted the Justified Ancients of Mu Mu (JAMS) and launched a label, Kopyright Liberation Front (KLF).

Rapping and shouting inspired nonsense in exaggerated Scottish accents over a diverse collection of stolen artifacts (from Queen to Led Zeppelin to Dave Brubeck), the JAMS—billing themselves as King Boy D and Rockman—pasted together the energetic **1987**, a loopy dance album that isn't unlike a lot of sampled records, but proceeds from an entirely different cultural understanding. As the JAMS neglected to obtain any clearances, however, the LP was promptly sued out of circulation by Abba's attorneys. (After its commercial withdrawal and destruction, a re-edited **1987** EP—with all of the illicit borrowings unceremoniously deleted—was offered to consumers in exchange for their original copies of what had become, in a stroke, an unbelievably valuable collector's item.)

Who Killed the JAMS? offers more of the same post-hip-hop fun, pumping up Eurobeat with bites from your favorite records—Hendrix's "Foxey Lady," Sly Stone's "Dance to the Music," etc.—thrown in wholesale. At times using relevant sound bites to answer a spoken remark (as in Dickie Goodman cut-in records), the LP merrily pisses on itself but reveals a viciously self-serving and proto-racist outlook in "King Boy's Dream," a short rap delivered over an insane hacking-cough-and-finger-pop percussion track: "I ain't no B-boy/I hate that shit/Those golden chains and Def Jam hype." In other words, it's okay for me to copy the work (both conceptually and literally) of African-Americans, but don't mix *me* up with that culture.

The History of the JAMS expands the six-track **Shag Times** compilation by two items. Both versions contain three of the group's 1987 singles (the non-Beatlesque "All You Need Is Love," the Houstonized "Whitney Joins the JAMS" and the Petula Clark-based gospel "Downtown") plus "Don't Take Five (Take What You Want)" from the first LP and two cuts ("Candyman" and the Sly-stolen "Burn the Bastards," retitled "Burn the Beat" on the US record) from the second. To that, **History** adds "Porpoise Song" (a Donna Summer jam from **Who Killed the JAMS?**) and "Doctorin' the Tardis," a genuine (if inexplicable) UK summer-of-'88 chart-topper—the title and lyrics refer to the *Doctor Who* TV program—stitched together from glam-rock classics by Gary Glitter and the Sweet and released under the Timelords pseudonym. Typical of the duo's penchant for self-amusement, they celebrated their victory with a DIY book entitled *The Manual (How to Have a Number One the Easy Way)*.

Abandoning one guise (but retaining Disco 2000, the entity responsible for an entertaining 1989 45 of Stevie Wonder's "Uptight" that sounds like Bananarama on a rap tip), Drummond and Cauty became the KLF and released—in numerous mixes—a fairly straightforward house record, "What Time Is Love?" Elevating what is barely a song to absurd heights, **The What Time Is Love Story** is ostensibly a collection of "cover versions and soundalikes." In the meantime, the KLF had already moved away from such thumping and kineticism and were claiming preeminence in the absurdly named ambient house field with **Chill Out**, a 50-minute snooze of slowly alternating organ chords over which Fleetwood Mac, radio news reports, Elvis Presley, a steel guitar (etc.) are gently laid. Sounding like nothing so much as an accidental recording of 1970 Pink Floyd sessions during which all the participants have either left or fallen asleep, it's a dull joke with no punchline, and lacks any trace of original musical merit.

Continuing to explore spacey trance music, Cauty formed the Orb, a side band with Alex Patterson, and began recording an Orb album. The duo managed to release one excellently titled crap EP before splitting; the disc (billed as "ambient house for the E generation") contains one endless side-long mixture of water noises and some incidental bits of Minnie Riperton's "Lovin' You" (damn, wish I still had my Tangerine Dream LPs!) and two shorter versions thereof, both with prominent drum beats. (After the Orb partnership ended, Cauty reportedly erased Patterson's tracks and finished the work-in-progress on his own, releasing it under the Space moniker.)

On a completely different note, Drummond's solo album is a tastefully understated country-rock collection of original songs with backing from, among others, nearly all of the Triffids and the Voice of the Beehive. Although the Man's vocals and melodic sense both fall somewhat short of good, his confidence and clever lyrical wit makes a good go of the sarcastic "Julian Cope Is Dead" (a very belated answer to Cope's "Bill Drummond Said"), "Ballad for a Sex God" and the pseudo-sappy autobiography of "I Believe in Rock & Roll." In addition, the exuberant "I'm the King of Joy" puts a Scottish accent to Jonathan Richman-like folk pop and winds up the album's easy highlight.   [i]

See also *Big in Japan, Julian Cope, Zodiac Mindwarp and the Love Reaction, Youth & Ben Watkins*.

K K K K K K K

HENRY KAISER

Studio Solo (Metalanguage) 1981
It's a Wonderful Life (Metalanguage) 1984
Marrying for Money (Ger. Minor Music) 1986
Devil in the Drain (SST) 1987
Those Who Know History Are Doomed to Repeat It (SST) 1988 ●
Re-Marrying for Money (SST) 1988 ɸ
Hope You Like Our New Direction (Reckless) 1991 ●

HENRY KAISER BAND

Heart's Desire (Reckless) 1990 ●

FRED FRITH & HENRY KAISER

With Friends Like These (Metalanguage) 1979
Who Needs Enemies? (Metalanguage) 1983
With Enemies Like These, Who Needs Friends? [CD] (SST) 1987 ●

FRENCH, FRITH, KAISER, THOMPSON

Live, Love, Larf & Loaf (Rhino) 1987 ●
Invisible Means (Windham Hill) 1990 ●

CRAZY BACKWARDS ALPHABET

Crazy Backwards Alphabet (SST) 1987

HENRY KAISER AND SERGEI KURIOKHIN

Popular Science (Rykodisc) 1989 ɸ

If you're in the market for a brilliant postmodern guitar hero, you could do a whole lot worse than Henry Kaiser. This Bay Area diver/filmmaker/musician has appeared on more than 50 records since the early '70s, ranging from total improvisations to jazz to experimental and progressive rock. While augmenting his flawless techniques with a wide array of electronic effects, Kaiser has familiarized himself with the ethnic musics of Southeast Asia, India and Japan, yet recently cited Jerry Garcia as a personal guitar fave.

Studio Solo and **It's a Wonderful Life** are solo LPs that find Kaiser building dazzling architechtonic solos, from ghostly and ghastly textures to cartoonlike goofs to disjointed bluegrass, blues and jazz constructions. The key to Kaiser's strategy is never to play the same thing twice, making his records and solos endlessly listenable.

Kaiser adds a Synclavier to the mix on **Devil in the Drain**, allowing him to record impossible lines and create otherworldly textures. The title track is built around a hilarious text by children's writer Daniel Pinkwater.

Kaiser wails in a power-trio format on **Re-Marrying for Money** (an expanded reissue of the German **Marrying for Money**), where he's supported by Hilary (bass) and John (drums) Hanes (who were once the mainstays of Pearl Harbor and the Explosions), both subsequently of the Henry Kaiser Band. John Abercrombie, Bruce Anderson (of MX-80 Sound) and Glenn Phillips join them for a series of improvised electrified raveups (including Cream's "I'm So Glad").

Kaiser returns to his roots on **Those Who Know History**, which includes a side-long version of the Grateful Dead classic "Dark Star" (integrating other Dead hits) as well as "Ode to Billie Joe" and the theme from *The Andy Griffith Show*. But this record doesn't hold a candle to the Henry Kaiser Band's live gigs. A particularly exceptional night (actually, two) is documented on **Heart's Desire**, a program made up mainly of covers that stretch from the Band to Stockhausen. Bruce Anderson and original Dead keyboardist Tom Constanten help make this one of the greatest and hippest live bands you never heard. (The CD has fewer selections than the double album, but each contains some different renditions of the same songs.)

With Enemies Like These, Who Needs Friends? contains heretofore unreleased improvised live performances by Kaiser and former Henry Cow guitarist Fred Frith, along with some gems from their two previous duo albums. The two plonk, bang and drone around on guitars, keyboards, violin and a particularly volatile (electronic) set of Linndrums. Equally loose and difficult are the duets with Russian Synclavierist Sergei Kuriokhin on **Popular Science**. Kaiser gooses the Synclavier himself on this disc, which is divided pretty equally into duets and solo excursions.

Kaiser revisits '70s progressive rock on **Crazy Backwards Alphabet**, his not-entirely successful link-up with amazing drummer John French (formerly Drumbo of Captain Beefheart's Magic Band), the hockey-influenced Swedish drummer/vocalist Michael Maksymenko and ex-Dixie Dregs bassist Andy West. Gnarly instrumentals are unfortunately forced to share space with distracting vocals.

Live, Love, Larf & Loaf is a much more pleasant supergrouping in which Kaiser, French and Frith (on bass) are joined by British folk-rock guitar wiz Richard Thompson. The LP combines excellent post-Beefheart compositions by French with Thompson's acid-etched Anglo-mysticism and a remarkable Okinawan pop song, "Hai Sai Oji-San." This is eclecticism at its finest. Unfortunately, the second episode, **Invisible Means**, sounds incomplete, like a joke that doesn't come off. (Although, considering the releasing label, perhaps it did.) Far from unlistenable, with the odd magnificent moment, the record is just spotty.   [rg]

See also *Fred Frith*.

HARRY KAKOULLI

See *Squeeze*.

360

BIG DADDY KANE

Long Live the Kane (Cold Chillin'-Warner Bros.) 1988 ●
It's a Big Daddy Thing (Cold Chillin'-Reprise) 1989 ●
Taste of Chocolate (Cold Chillin'-Reprise) 1990 ●

A pivotal figure in one sphere of the mid-'80s rap scene, Brooklyn's Big Daddy Kane (Antonio Hardy) is the quintessential smooth operator, an influential party MC (and would-be '70s soul crooner) with a convincing hard-edged style and an inconsistent, occasionally dismal, lyrical outlook. Produced by Marley Marl, **Long Live the Kane** lists the gold-wearing ladykiller's many talents and achievements with more skill than wit and includes an entertaining goof with longtime associate Biz Markie as well as an ill-advised stab at singing ("The Day You're Mine"). Showing a taste for topicality, Kane delves into Muslim Afrocentricity in "Word to the Mother(land)" and paints a utopian fantasy (in "I'll Take You There") where crime, welfare and crack are unknown, but "fresh Gucci wear is only $5.99!"

Announcing "I Get the Job Done," Kane demonstrates his fiery power on the masterful **It's a Big Daddy Thing**. When he's not engaging in raw boasts and putdowns (some of which recycle rhymes from the first LP), Kane's raps attack racism and self-destruction, promote pride and celebrate the next generation (in the reggae-styled "Children R the Future"). The smug playboy jive of "On the Move" is easy to ignore, but the crude sex tales of "Pimpin' Ain't Easy" (complete with a gratuitous expression of anti-gay hatred) is a pernicious development in Kane's repertoire.

Taking advantage of stardom's perks, Kane built some inter-generational bridges on **Taste of Chocolate**. Barry White ("All of Me") and Rudy Ray Moore ("Big Daddy vs. Dolemite") guest on the mellow-sounding LP, an intelligently mature triumph which switches easily from sex-machine egotism and gauzy romantic soul to incisively astute and realistic street politics (like "Dance with the Devil" and the surprisingly poppy "Who Am I," co-written and rapped with Gamilah Shabazz). Typical of Kane's newly raised consciousness, "No Damn Good" *sounds* misogynist, but only disses women who don't respect themselves. [i]

MICK KARN

See *Japan, Peter Murphy*.

EDWARD KA-SPEL

See *Legendary Pink Dots, Skinny Puppy*.

KATRINA AND THE WAVES

Walking on Sunshine (Can. Attic) 1983
Katrina and the Waves 2 (Can. Attic) 1984
Katrina and the Waves (Capitol) 1985 ●
Waves (Capitol) 1985 ●
Break of Hearts (SBK) 1989 ●

KIMBERLEY REW

The Bible of Bop (Press) 1982

WAVES

Shock Horror! (nr/Aftermath) 1983

Like ex-bandmate Robyn Hitchcock, Kimberley Rew survived the end of the Soft Boys to take further forays into melodious '60s folk-rock and psychedelia, as the eight tracks (seven previously released) on his 1982 solo release prove. Working with the dB's, ex-Soft Boys and a new group called the Waves, Rew doesn't pursue weirdness as avidly as Hitchcock does, but the singer/guitarist/keyboardist has a neat winner with **The Bible of Bop**.

Rew and the Waves subsequently became a fulltime proposition, a sympathetic and commercially potent outlet for his ace songwriting. The Anglo-American quartet's other major asset is singer/guitarist Katrina Leskanich, a Kansas native with a strong, flexible voice equally suited for full-tilt pop harmonies and belt-it-out rock'n'roll. The band melds a diverse collection of styles, personalities and ethnic backgrounds.

The low-budget **Shock Horror!** contains early versions of eight songs, only a few of which have since surfaced on the band's albums. "Strolling on Air," cut with a former bassist, is an especially rich find; the other tunes (except for an MC5-ish raver, "Atomic Rock-'n'Roll") are typically engaging but not particularly well recorded. Interesting and certainly no embarrassment.

Walking on Sunshine contains such absolutely brilliant songs as "Going Down to Liverpool" (cleverly covered by the Bangles, who could spot a tune worth singing) and the infectious title track. Guarantee: hear this record once and you'll find yourself humming at least one track from it a week later. It flows magnificently from start to end, and subsumes individual accomplishments into a true group effort. A greatest hits album the first time out.

KATW 2 takes a harder-rocking bent, downplaying the tunefulness slightly to highlight jumping numbers like "She Likes to Groove," the nutty "Maniac House" and a powerful, Janis Joplin-like blues, "Cry for Me." Pointing up the band's only weakness, the lyrics to "Mexico" (written by bassist Vince de la Cruz) don't achieve much in the way of profundity; the soaring vocals and ethnic-flavored simplicity, however, make that a strictly academic problem. Other great tracks: "Red Wine and Whisky" and "The Game of Love." Not as glorious as the debut, but a boss record nonetheless.

Katrina and the Waves consists entirely of songs from the first two albums, but they've all been re-recorded or remixed. In most cases, it's an improvement, exposing untapped realms of both pop and power, but the second "Going Down to Liverpool" obliterates the atmosphere and the hooky melody of the original in an absurdly overheated arrangement. With that one caveat, **Katrina and the Waves** is otherwise a delight.

Evidencing mild signs of commercial selfconsciousness, **Waves** isn't as charming, although several of the tunes boast all the attributes that make the band so appealing. Foamy Hammond organ, prominent in spots, matches Leskanich's newly soul-ized singing to push the group towards a Stax sound. Although the songs (only two of them by Rew, previously the band's main writer) aren't as memorable, they're solid enough to make this a reasonably pleasing record.

Break of Hearts is a horrendously wrongheaded comeback bid that shows the Waves to be utterly oblivious to their own strengths. With the exceptions of the peppy Tex-Mex-style "Rock'n'Roll Girl" and the Cheap Trickish pop-metal "Rock Myself to Sleep," it's bland, overprocessed commercial slop, with Katrina (who sports a metal-chick makeover on the album cover) shrilly belting over characterless backing tracks. And the Waves have no one but themselves to blame for this disaster, since they get the production credit.

See also *Soft Boys*.　　　　　　　　　　　　　[i/hd]

KATYDIDS
Katydids (Reprise) 1990 ●

As produced by Nick Lowe, this London quintet's fine debut mixes its pop metaphors and age sensibilities in generally delightful fashion. The perky adolescent songs ("Stop Start," "Heavy Weather Traffic," "Lights Out (Read My Lips)," "Dr. Rey") layer American-born Susie Hug's pretty voice (with harmonies by co-writer/guitarist Adam Seymour, a veteran jingle singer; the pair met at a Big Bam Boo session) into Banglesque allure over the band's tastefully brisk backing. When the group delves into more mature rock ("Miss Misery"), folk-rock ("Chains of Devotion") and country ("What Will the Angels Say?," its melody evidently cribbed from early Elvis Costello), however, she sings with less of an edge.　　　　　　　　　　[i]

IAN KEAREY + GERARD LANGLEY
See *Blue Aeroplanes*.

TOMMY KEENE
Strange Alliance (Avenue) 1982
Back Again (Try ...) EP (Dolphin) 1984
Places That Are Gone EP (Dolphin) 1984
Songs from the Film (Geffen) 1986
Run Now EP (Geffen) 1986
Based on Happy Times (Geffen) 1989 ●

As the jacket blurb on **Strange Alliance** attests, Keene's music does bear some superficial resemblance to the Only Ones and early U2, though without their depth or charisma. (Audible influences also include the Beatles and the Byrds.) The first album contains eight immediately likable, if melancholic, tunes, every one a winner. (A later pressing adds a subsequent single.) Keene's reedy voice, chiming, arpeggiated guitar chords and occasional piano make for a lightweight but appealing blend. On all of the records through **Run Now**, two of Keene's former bandmates from Washington, DC's Razz accompany him on bass and drums.

Back Again (Try ...) offers two cool covers, recorded live at the Rat in Boston, and two studio originals. Roxy Music's "All I Want Is You"—why didn't anyone think of doing that sooner?—and the Stones' "When the Whip Comes Down" show Keene's rock-'n'roll abilities, while the title track and "Safe in the Light" are in more of a Tom Petty power pop vein, and quite striking at that. **Places That Are Gone** mixes five originals with Alex Chilton's "Hey! Little Child." All of the memorable melodies are underscored by strong vocal harmonies, yet the delivery retains a gutsy, even abrasive, edge.

Finally signed to a major label, Keene hooked up

with producer Geoff Emerick (Badfinger, Split Enz, Nick Heyward) to make **Songs from the Film**, a further refinement of his virtues with occasionally more substantial lyrics. The standout is a different version of "Places That Are Gone," but the new compositions are good and sturdy in their own right. The sole non-original is a weirdly "normal" version of Lou Reed's "Kill Your Sons."

Run Now adds another enjoyable chapter to the Keene canon, despite the occasional unease in what he says and the way that he says it ("I Don't Feel Right at All"). The closest to a dud is the commercial title track, which is not offensive, just inconsequential. (That number was produced by Bob Clearmountain; the rest was overseen by the team of T-Bone Burnett and Don Dixon.) The EP's closer is a good live version of "Kill Your Sons."

The growing tension and melancholy in Keene's lyrics belies the melodic power and contagiously confident sound of **Based on Happy Times**, an excellent, overcast album that alternately resembles **Pleased to Meet Me**-era Replacements and the darker side of Let's Active. Keene's songwriting (with some assistance from Jules Shear) has never been better; the playing and production (by bassist Joe Hardy, drummer John Hampton and Keene) is spot-on, except for the strings that intrude in several arrangements. Pete Buck guests on a pair of tunes, including the record's sole stinker: an unpleasantly bluesy cover of the Beach Boys' "Our Car Club."
　　　　　　　　　　　　　　　　　　　　　　[jg/i]

KIRK KELLY
Go Man Go (SST) 1988 ●

Affected enough to drop his g's but too selfconscious to omit the resulting apostrophes in his liner notes, earnest neo-folkie Kirk Kelly gives his Robert Zimmerman fixation (with a side order, on "Heroes of Tomorrow," of Phil Ochs) a full airing on **Go Man Go**. This solipsistic one-man (two, if you count producer Brian Ritchie's bass contribution to one song) acoustic album is so derivative of **Bob Dylan** (etc.) that maybe A.J. Weberman should consider rooting through Kelly's trash.　　　　　　　　　　　　　　　　　　　[i]

PAUL KELLY AND THE DOTS
Talk (Aus. Mushroom) 1981
Manila (Aus. Mushroom) 1982
PAUL KELLY
Post (Aus. White Label) 1985
PAUL KELLY & THE MESSENGERS
Gossip (Aus. Mushroom) 1987 (A&M) 1987 ●
Under the Sun (A&M) 1988 ●
So Much Water So Close to Home (A&M) 1989 ●

After releasing three Australian albums in the early '80s, Adelaide's Paul Kelly put together a quartet called the Coloured Girls (wisely billed as the Messengers in the US; the international dichotomy was later resolved by dumping the original moniker entirely). Originally a 24-song double album back home, **Gossip** arrived in America as a fifteen-track single disc (the CD has two more). In any case, the LP reveals Kelly to be an expressive if limited singer and an extraordinary song-writer, with an especially keen eye for lyrical detail and a wide-ranging catalogue of musical influences in his stylistic arsenal. Perhaps the best comparison is to early Graham Parker, although Kelly leans more towards folk, blues and some pop in place of Parker's preference for country and R&B. **Gossip** has plenty of local color, but the pain at the root of most of these songs is universal.

Under the Sun rocks a bit harder, though its production is equally lean and minimal. What stands out are the songs, beautifully realized stories put to record. Kelly's got the rare ability to introduce detailed characters and substantial scenarios in three minutes. Check out "To Her Door," "Don't Stand So Close to the Window" (or, for that matter, any track here) for proof. (Again, the US and Australian editions differ.)

Kelly recorded his next album in America, working with R.E.M. producer Scott Litt. **So Much Water So Close to Home** (the title comes from a Raymond Carver short story that Kelly condenses into the album's most chilling song) finds the singer/guitarist at his most subdued and thoughtful, although "Sweet Guy" and "No You" are two of his most vicious rockers yet. It's the first album he's done that's "produced" in any sense (he even allows a bit of reverb on some of his vocals), and also his least Australian, although "Pigeon/Jundamurra" is based on the true story of an Aboriginal freedom fighter. [ds]

KLARK KENT

See *Stewart Copeland*.

JACK KETCH AND THE CROWMEN

See *Thee Mighty Caesars*.

KID CREOLE AND THE COCONUTS

Off the Coast of Me (ZE) 1980
Fresh Fruit in Foreign Places (ZE-Sire) 1981
Wise Guy (ZE-Sire) 1982
Tropical Gangsters (nr/ZE-Island) 1982 ●
Doppelganger (ZE-Sire) 1983
Cre-Ole: The Best of Kid Creole and the Coconuts
(nr/ZE-Island) 1984 + 1990 ●
In Praise of Older Women and Other Crimes (Sire) 1985
I, Too, Have Seen the Woods (Sire) 1987 ●
Private Waters in the Great Divide (Columbia) 1990 φ

COCONUTS

Don't Take My Coconuts (EMI America) 1983

COATI MUNDI

The Former Twelve Year Old Genius (nr/Virgin) 1983

In an interview, black Bronxite August "Kid Creole" Darnell—writer, singer, producer—once alluded to not being able to play reggae as well as Bob Marley or salsa as well as Tito Puente, but possibly being able to combine the two styles better than anyone else. Darnell's internationalist fusion was one of the freshest new sounds of the '80s, drawing together strains of Latin, reggae, calypso, disco, rap and rock into a unique

sound. Add to his vision and smarts an amiable partner in "Sugar Coated" Andy Hernandez (aka Coati Mundi), the singing/dancing Coconuts and a medley of talented sidepeople, and you have one of the most formidable bands around.

Off the Coast of Me introduces Darnell and company's unusual sound (more Latin-tinged here than on later records). Although the material isn't strong enough to make this more than adequate, its uniqueness and danceability, along with the Kid's occasionally risqué wordplay, are enough to suggest the band's potential.

Launching a conceptual album trilogy, **Fresh Fruit in Foreign Places** stands as Kid Creole's tour de force, a musical odyssey in which the Kid and the Coconuts set off from New York in search of the elusive Mimi. The flavor of the music changes with each stop on the journey, providing a perfect setting for the band to display its mastery of intercontinental bop. Each cut is an adventure, and the album works as well as any rock concept LP. A major achievement.

After the perfect realization of **Fresh Fruit**, nearly anything would have been a letdown. **Wise Guy** (entitled **Tropical Gangsters** outside the US) follows the concept, but much more loosely. The material is far less adventurous, with **Fresh Fruit**'s wonderful diversity toned down in favor of a straighter dance music approach. As a commercial move it worked, at least in Europe, where two tracks ("Stool Pigeon" and "I'm a Wonderful Thing, Baby") became hit singles and elevated Darnell to stardom.

Doppelganger is posited as the continuation of "the saga." In this installment, the Kid is cloned by King Nignat's evil scientist. The songs don't all move the story along in narrative fashion—they sound more like the disjunct score of a Broadway musical—but that's fine, since each stands as a marvelous example of Darnell's multifarious brilliance. Mixing '40s be-bop with Carib-beat, reggae, country, funk, salsa and something like highlife, the record sparkles with a cover of "If You Wanna Be Happy" (a 1966 American hit for the Jimmy Castor bunch as "Hey Leroy") as well as such original frolics as "The Lifeboat Party" and "Bongo Eddie's Lament." Sung partially in Spanish, "Survivors" laments the death of rockers from Frankie Lymon to Sid Vicious.

In Praise of Older Women, while less spectacular, is still another (ca)rousing success, a collection of wittily written, sublimely arranged, energetically performed songs. "Endicott" (cleverly verbose), "Caroline Was a Drop-Out" (a nasty character study), "Particul'y Int'rested" (exaggerated, showy torch song)—to name but three—all reflect the Kid's wonderful attitude and outlook. With Coati Mundi and the Coconuts, plus a stageful of sidemen, King ("self-appointed in Feb. this year") Creole demonstrates his stylistic transcendence by making every track different but identifiable; no longer a mere genre dabbler, he's developed the Kid Creole format.

On **I, Too, Have Seen the Woods**, Darnell seems to be treading water a bit within that format. Although he introduces female singer Haitia Fuller to share lead vocals with him, her overall impact is fairly negligible. As always, there are some very good tunes (especially "Dancin' at the Bains Douches" and "Call It a Day"); Darnell's words are typically clever and insightful. On the whole, though, the music seems less innovative, succumbing to repetition of previously charted lands. (Hernandez's "El Hijo" is a near carbon-copy of his 1980 dance hit "Me No Pop I.") Good, but hardly top-notch.

Showing tons more imagination and inspiration, Darnell bounced back to full artistic strength with the marvelously entertaining **Private Waters in the Great Divide**, a diverse party of singular wit and intelligence. While the lyrics of songs like "(No More) Casual Sex" and "He's Takin' the Rap" demonstrate an awareness of changing times, the music still comes in time-warped from a tropical dance-happy era somewhere around 1940; the only track that even acknowledges rap bends it all out of shape. (How many other hip dance records released in 1990 can claim such stylistic nonconformity?) There is a reggae-styled love song, however, a surf-pop harmony exhibition and "Lambada," the intent and irony of which is unclear. Mundi is only a minor player here (Darnell acknowledges his departure in the self-referential "Funky Audrey and the Coconut Rag," which Hernandez co-wrote), but the Coconuts are in full effect, providing a campy foil in such fizzy delights as "Laughing with Our Backs Against the Wall" and "Funky Audrey." Not a bad banana in this bunch.

The UK-only **Cre-Ole** compilation includes all the band's 1981-'83 British hits (and then some), with such classic Darnellisms as "Stool Pigeon," "I'm a Wonderful Thing, Baby" and "Annie, I'm Not Your Daddy," as well as "Me No Pop I."

The Coconuts' solo album, produced by Darnell to resemble a stage revue (complete with crowd sounds and stage introductions), is rife with innuendo and apparent internecine squabbling. Despite the billing, Darnell sings the introductory title track *without* the three ladies; the inclusion of "If I Only Had a Brain" (from *Wizard of Oz*) might be someone's idea of an editorial comment. Otherwise, it's a typically rich, clever dance-funk-Carib-salsa-tango stew, and the Coconuts' smooth harmony vocals are as appealing as ever.

Coati Mundi has done some odd musical projects in his time (including a production job for Germany's Palais Schaumburg!), and the singing vibraphone/keyboard player's solo album is no less idiosyncratic in lyrical outlook. In addition to the clever title reference to Stevie Wonder, the irrepressibly funny Hernandez also parodies "Grand Master Flush and the Fluffy Five" and "Kurtis Bluff" on the rap jape "Everybody's on an Ego Trip." While the album cleverly—and occasionally buoyantly—mixes soul, salsa and disco, it also suffers from Hernandez's simply trying too hard.   [ds/i/jy]

KID FROST
Hispanic Causing Panic (Virgin) 1990 ●

The Chicano hip-hop translation by Kid Frost (Arturo Molina Jr.) involves more than dropping Spanish. Although some of the tracks on **Hispanic Causing Panic** are nearly generic, the LA rapper brings his own positive cultural identity to such outstanding tracks as "La Raza," "Hold Your Own," "In the City" and "Homicide." Using a perilous bass-heavy sound and sparing percussion accents (with such added ingredients as sax, metal guitar and harmonica), Kid

Frost cuts a distinctive figure, making **Hispanic** not just a fine album, but a significant cultural development.   [i]

KID 'N PLAY
2 Hype (Select) 1988 ●
Kid 'n Play's Funhouse (Select) 1990 ●
VARIOUS ARTISTS
House Party Soundtrack (Motown) 1990 ●

Along with DJ Jazzy Jeff and the Fresh Prince, New York's Kid 'n Play are among the best of the lite rappers, middle-class performers whose pursuit of pop stardom doesn't preclude exciting grooves. Christopher Reid (Kid)—he of the towering fade—and Christopher Martin (Play) concentrate on shameless self-promotion, but brag with such frisky good humor that it's hard to object. And the quick interplay of these two wise guys simulates a live feel missing from much contemporary rap. **2 Hype** features the snappy "Rollin' with Kid 'n Play" and "Undercover," a cheatin' morality tale guest-starring the Real Roxanne. **Funhouse** has the explosive "Energy," perhaps the guys' best yet, and the title track, also spotlighted in their delightful feature film *House Party*. The soundtrack includes boss tracks by Public Enemy ("Can't Do Nuttin' for Ya Man"), L.L. Cool J, Full Force and other fine folks.   [jy]

STEVE KILBEY
See *Church, Hex.*

KILBURN AND THE HIGH ROADS
Handsome (nr/Dawn) 1975 (nr/Pye) 1977 (nr/Sequel) 1990 ●
Wotabunch! (nr/Warner Bros.) 1978
Upminster Kids (nr/PRT) 1983

Although new wave was still two years away, the London music scene of 1975 wasn't all Queen and the Rolling Stones; pub-rock bands were making fresh and exciting music, laying the groundwork for more radical outfits to follow. Some included musicians whose skills came in very handy when the dam broke in 1977; Kilburn and the High Roads, named after a highway sign, included Ian Dury, saxman Davey Payne (a future Blockhead) and Keith Lucas, who changed his name to Nick Cash and helped found the group 999. During a commercially frustrating career that lasted from 1970 to 1976, the Kilburns were cult-popular and influential. Their records serve as neat reminders of a wonderful band.

An album cut in 1974 was shelved due to record company politics; the band's debut was in fact their second recording. (That first LP, **Wotabunch!**, was dredged up and finally released once Dury's solo career took off.) The subsequently recorded **Handsome** contains much of the same material (co-written by Dury with pianist Russell Hardy) that the group had used the first time. Got that?

Handsome is musically low-key, featuring Dury's clever Cockney wordplay and a bit of high-powered blowing from Payne, but it leans overly towards understatement, touching on rockin' '50s styles and dapper '40s lounge subtlety to make it a generally debonair record not above some raving. **Upminster Kids** is a reissue of **Handsome** with several tracks deleted.   [i]

See also *Ian Dury, 999*.

KILKENNY CATS
Hands Down (Coyote-Twin/Tone) 1986
Hammer EP (Texas Hotel) 1988

The ascendancy of R.E.M. created a major band boom in Athens, Georgia, but some of the resulting combos would have been best left within the privacy of the members' imaginations. Kilkenny Cats, for example, put their R.E.M. influences to good use on the A-side of a 1984 single, "Attractive Figure," where singer Tom Cheek's highly derivative mumbling was interspersed with a buzzy guitar melody. **Hands Down** attempted to incorporate a metal feel, but the quintet's two guitars are about as thick as paper; the bigger problem is that Cheek seems to be laboring under the art-hippie assumption that a bunch of unconnected images strung together makes a song. Even the album's prettiest moment, "Morning Song," is simply R.E.M.'s "Gardening at Night" twelve hours later. The six-song **Hammer** EP, performed by a one-guitarist quartet, is marginally less tedious.   [kss]

KILLDOZER
Intellectuals Are the Shoeshine Boys of the Ruling Elite
    (Bone Air) 1984 (Bone Air-Touch and Go) 1989 ●
Snakeboy (Touch and Go) 1985 ●
Burl EP (Touch and Go) 1986
Little Baby Buntin' (Touch and Go) 1987 ●
12 Point Buck (Touch and Go) 1988 ●
For Ladies Only (Touch and Go) 1989 + 1990 ●

This Madison, Wisconsin trio would have you believe that they're truly moonshine-swilling, small mammal-torturing dudes who do a whole lot more than just *kiss* their cousins—and they back it up with one of the most twisted (not to mention influential) sounds since the days of field recording. Imagine the most primitive country blues you've heard impaled on shards of Birthday Party distortion. Sure, they're hicks from the wrong side of the tracks—in one of the few American burgs to have fallen under Socialist rule this half-century. The resultant (uneasy) mix of brawn and brains makes Killdozer as likely to quote Ed Gein as Voltaire—and do both with a smirk.

Intellectuals owes quite a bit to the shadowy swamp tales of Creedence Clearwater Revival (more than just the cover of "Run Through the Jungle"); singer/bassist Michael Gerald's spookily incisive, virulent invective is riveting. When he's picking at his own psychic scabs (as on "A Man's Gotta Be a Man to Be a Man"), it's hard not to shudder with empathy. When he's tugging at someone else's, though, the desire to slap him is overwhelming. Fortunately, the former situation prevails by a large measure. Key line: "If there's one thing in this world I cannot understand, it's that there's so many things I cannot understand."

Snakeboy all but bursts with those things. In an abdomen-emptying growl midway between Howlin'

Wolf and Leonard Cohen, Gerald bellows tense monologues from radically diverse points of view; children being torn away from dead mothers give way to swaggering sex prowlers (like the, er, protagonist or "King of Sex"). The album's crawling trek through the lives of folks who could never have been contenders (and know it) is reminiscent of prime Cave, but the everpresent danger of seeming overwrought is neatly avoided by secreting a laugh—in this case a parodic version of Neil Young's "Cinnamon Girl"—in some dark corner. On **Burl**, which is otherwise loaded with electro-shock folk songs all about murder, deception and plagues in the best pre-Woody Guthrie tradition, the gut-buster is, coincidentally, again a cover (Jessi Colter's "I'm Not Lisa").

Little Baby Buntin' (which might as well be subtitled **More Songs About Building Collapses and Castration**) travels much the same terrain, only at much slower speed. That's a plus, because Killdozer is more effective when lumbering along slowly enough to make novices check the power supply. With Bill Hobson's fractured guitar barrages bisecting Gerald's fat, anaconda-like basslines, **12 Point Buck** is the best sounding Killdozer record. The shtick, however, has seen better days.

Issued as a boxed set of singles before being reincarnated as an LP, **For Ladies Only** collects Killdozer's agribusiness/performance-art interpretations of a passel of **Have a Nice Day**-quality (if not exactly era) Top 40 hits (including "American Pie" *and* "Hush") in much the same way a thoughtless child would collect butterflies—swooping down and pinning their flapping wings, allowing the hapless victims to tear themselves apart. Versions of "Funk #49" (James Gang), "Good Lovin' Gone Bad" (Bad Company) and even "One Tin Soldier" (from *Billy Jack*) are neither pisstakes nor homages; these guys don't hate or love the songs, they simply act as though they'd written 'em. **Intellectuals** and **Snakeboy** are packaged on one CD; **Buntin'** and **12 Point Buck** are on another.   [dss]

KILLDOZER 85
See *Sharky's Machine*.

KILLING JOKE
Almost Red EP (nr/Malicious Damage) 1979 (nr/Island)
    1981 (EG) 1990 ●
Killing Joke (EG) 1980 ●
what's THIS for . . . ! (EG) 1981 ●
Revelations (Malicious Damage-EG) 1982 ●
Birds of a Feather EP (Malicious Damage-EG) 1982
"Ha" EP (Malicious Damage-EG) 1982
Fire Dances (EG) 1983 ●
Night Time (EG) 1985 ●
Brighter Than a Thousand Suns (EG-Virgin) 1986 ●
Outside the Gate (EG) 1988 ●
The Courtald Talks (Invisible) 1989
An Incomplete Collection (EG) 1990 ●
Extremities, Dirt & Various Repressed Emotions (Noise
    Int'l-RCA) 1990 ●

London's Killing Joke are practitioners of intellectual dance-thrash-rock with a penchant for apocalypse.

Originally something like Birthday Party but more restrained and rhythmic, singer/keyboardist Jaz Coleman, bassist Youth (Martin Glover), guitarist Geordie and drummer Paul Ferguson launched the tumultuous group on its voyage through intense, angry records of striking strength and fringe weirdness.

Killing Joke is an imaginative interface between heavy metal and new wave. With a few synthesizer incursions, the music fields a basic guitar/bass/drums attack, filtered through distortion and tone modulation. Pounding and pulsating at breakneck speed with occasional funk or reggae overtones, the songs ("Wardance," "Tomorrow's World," "Bloodsport") are coldly compelling doomsday anthems.

what's THIS for . . . ! brings funk to ambient music, implying feeling sublimated in a chaotic world. The retreat from empathy and communication doesn't prevent inventive guitar work that hides steady, rhythmic alterations against repetitious, thumping drums—the postmodern dance. (The first two albums were later paired on a double-play cassette.)

Revelations returns to the brutal stride of **Killing Joke**, racing atonally towards total collapse, social and otherwise. Conny Plank's co-production hinders the sound, trying to normalize the enchanting wrongness of the group. Perhaps expecting the end of the world, Coleman and Geordie vanished to Iceland before the album was released and worked with bands there, notably Theyr.

Birds of a Feather, the first release after the band's traumatic reorganization, showcases a more accessible Killing Joke, less shrill and more tuneful, yet retaining all of the manic depression. The 10-inch **"Ha"** was recorded live in Toronto, proving that this is a trend, not a fluke. Both boast excellent production by Plank and the band. (A cassette joining **"Ha"** and **Fire Dances** was later issued.)

Fire Dances continues in this manner, but with further sonic refinement. "Rejuvenation," "Frenzy" and "Feast of Blaze" all rank with Killing Joke's very best; **Fire Dances** is a frighteningly solid album. After a sabbatical of nearly two years, **Night Time** was released in 1985. Still concentrating on sharpening their overbearing presence by incorporating some space amidst the fury, it contains "Love Like Blood," their catchiest number (and biggest UK hit single) yet.

Following another two-year layoff, Killing Joke returned in 1987 with **Brighter Than a Thousand Suns**, toning down the trademark guitar thunder in favor of synths, a big dancefloor beat and more of the melodicism explored on "Love Like Blood." Fans of the easy nihilism of their earlier efforts will have to be patient and attentive for this one. "Sanity" is a great single; several other cuts are just as good. Although more palatable than ever, the album still packs too much of a wallop to warrant any real sell-out accusations.

The same cannot be said for the abominable **Outside the Gate**, an obvious attempt at slick commerciality and the Joke's only disposable joke. Gaudy keyboard arrangements swamp the atypically anemic guitar, energy is non-existent and Coleman's lyrical frothings on bombast like "America" seem forced. The band wisely broke up.

When Killing Joke reformed over a year later, there was renewed resolve to recapture the old formula. New drummer Martin Atkins (PiL/Brian Brain/Ministry) provided a visceral shot in the arm, and a 1989 US tour proved they could still write and play new songs as arresting and aggressive as the early classics.

Released on Atkins' label, **The Courtald Talks** is a lecture given by Jaz and Geordie, a spoken-word aside while the next studio album was gestating. Bassist Paul Raven, who'd replaced Youth after **Revelations**, rejoined just in time for **Extremities, Dirt & Various Repressed Emotions**, a whopper of a comeback. Easily one of Killing Joke's finest LPs, it has all the intoxicating intensity and righteous fury absent from **Outside the Gate**, mated with a modern, Ministry-like feel. The throbbing juggernaut "Money Is Not Our God" and scalding pound of "The Beautiful Dead" are only the tip of a tightly composed musical iceberg, primed by Atkins' powerful drum work and Geordie's scorchingly obtuse chording.

An Incomplete Collection is a boxed set of **Killing Joke, what's THIS for . . . !, Revelations, Fire Dances** and **Night Time**. [sg/dgs/gef]

See also *Youth & Ben Watkins*.

KING

Steps in Time (Epic) 1984
Bitter Sweet (Epic) 1985 ●
The 12" Tape [tape] (nr/CBS) 1986

PAUL KING

Joy (Epic) 1987 ●

From the ashes of promising rock-ska band the Reluctant Stereotypes, Coventry singer Paul King decided to go for the gold ring with a crass chart-geared quartet he thoughtfully named after himself. Launched in 1983, the colorfully uniformed King (the group) served a noxious, unmelodic pseudo-funk concoction that got an inexplicably favorable response: "Love & Pride" and "Won't You Hold My Hand Now" became hits. Produced (and drummed on) by Richard James Burgess, **Steps in Time** is filled with alarmingly stupid lyrics, fickle stylistic dabbling, arena-rock attributes and art-school pretensions. Awful.

Bitter Sweet is precisely more of the same. (In fact, the American edition includes "Won't You Hold My Hand Now" for the second time!) Ex-Member Adrian Lillywhite plays the drums, resulting in some improvement in that area, but King (the singer)'s overbearing, tuneless vocals still dominate the band's unpleasant sound. The best thing about this LP is its lyric sheet, which offers no end of unintended giggles. (The 1986 cassette EP collects the 12-inch mixes of King's five best-known singles.)

King's solo career began with **Joy**, an all-American mock-white-soul album masterminded by one of the acknowledged titans of that dubious genre, Dan Hartman. Dispensing with glam-pop gimmickry, Hartman produced the record with commercial savvy, giving prominent roles to the Uptown Horns and session singers. King wisely curbs his past excesses and gets by on what he has: a mediocre but well-controlled sub-Paul Young voice. The songs are nothing, but at least they're not annoying. [i]

See also *Reluctant Stereotypes*.

DEE DEE KING

See *Ramones*.

KING BLANK

See *Folk Devils*.

KING CRIMSON

Discipline (Warner Bros.) 1981 ●
Beat (Warner Bros.) 1982 ●
Three of a Perfect Pair (Warner Bros.) 1984 ●
The Compact King Crimson (EG) 1987 ●

Centered around guitarist extraordinaire Robert Fripp, King Crimson was a seminal band of our time. Formed originally in 1969, the band had, from the outset, pivotal influence on both heavy metal and art-rock. The ever-principled Fripp refused to let Crimson become a dinosaur and broke up the band in 1974, retreating from the tour-album-tour grind to do solo and session work as a self-styled "mobile compact unit." One of his endeavors, the dance-rock oriented League of Gentlemen, spurred Fripp to reincarnate King Crimson at the start of the 1980s. Consisting of guitarist/vocalist Adrian Belew, Chapman Stick/bassist Tony Levin and drummer Bill Bruford (the only pre-split vet other than Fripp), the current (at least recent) Crimson is a cutting-edge patchwork of modern influences: dance music, art-rock, mysticism, minimalism.

Discipline introduces the new cast of characters and displays their attempt at cerebral dance rock; Fripp is at least as interested in touching the mind as the heart. Not really songs, these pieces are unfolding musical sculptures, played with precision and rare imagination, a mostly successful synthesis of ambition, simplicity and Kraftwerkian clarity.

Beat achieves Fripp's long-sought union of mind, soul and body, centering around the anniversary of Jack Kerouac's *On the Road*. An ode to the beat generation, the album elucidates Crimson's past and purpose, melding Frippertronic tape techniques in equal partnership with Belew's manic physicality. Picking up foreign rhythms and electronic overdubs, the players push their instruments into a new form, akin to fusion and art-rock, but miles beyond either, and beyond description as well.

Three of a Perfect Pair is the most disjunct album in recent memory, from a band that prided itself on carefully matched contradictions. The Left Side sports four of Adrian Belew's poorer songs and a self-derivative instrumental; the flip is nearly all-instrumental, nearly free-form, nearly brilliant. As a bonus, the LP ends with "Larks' Tongues in Aspic Part III," the last in a distinguished series of rhythmically skewed tours de force. Apparently the Frippressive "discipline" that forged the critically acclaimed pop/art synthesis of the first two latter-day Crimson albums is not a permanent condition.

The Compact King Crimson mixes tracks by the group's final incarnation and items from the original band's earliest albums. [sg/mf]

See also *Adrian Belew, Robert Fripp, Fripp & Eno*.

KING KURT

Ooh Wallah Wallah (nr/Stiff) 1983
Road to Rack & Ruin (Ralph) 1985

Second Album (nr/Stiff) 1986
Last Will and Testicle (GWR-Restless) 1988
Live and Rockin' (nr/Link) 1989
Destination Demoland (nr/Link) 1990

This bunch of British goofballs (originally known as Rockin' Kurt and the Sour Krauts) picks up where novelty songs like "Stranded in the Jungle" and "Alley Oop" left off. They mix big-band R&B-flavored rockabilly with a crazed, comic book mentality and lots of drums. Dave Edmunds produced the boisterous debut LP, which raucously proffers such non-classics as "Bo Diddley Goes East" and "Destination Zulu Land." A bit too formulaic for mega-fun, but a good smirky laugh nonetheless.

KK's **Second Album**, known semi-officially as **Big Cock** (thanks to the monstrous rooster on the cover), is great, a wildly out-of-control ride through a half-dozen areas of lighthearted rock'n'roll fun. Side One kicks off with an energetic, distinguished version of Eddie Cochran's "Nervous Breakdown" and ends with an uncredited voice that sounds suspiciously like Nigel Planer (Neil of *The Young Ones*) lost in a jazzy novelty number called "Billy." "Horatio" recalls the inimitable Tenpole Tudor; "Pumpin' Pistons" leers like a drunk in a strip joint; the horrific thought of there being a "Momma Kurt" is enough to power this greasy R&B number along. (The disc was released in both black and red vinyl; the tape has two extra tunes.)

Road to Rack & Ruin is an American mini-album culled from tracks on the first LP plus a couple that wound up on the second; **Live and Rockin'** is a concert document from Japan. [i]

KING MISSILE (DOG FLY RELIGION)

Fluting on the Hump (Shimmy-Disc) 1987 ●
They (Shimmy-Disc) 1988 ●

KING MISSILE

Mystical Shit (Shimmy-Disc) 1990 ●
The Way to Salvation (Atlantic) 1991 φ

DOGBOWL

Tit! (An Opera) (Shimmy-Disc) 1989
Cyclops Nuclear Submarine Captain (Shimmy-Disc) 1991

JOHN S. HALL & KRAMER

Real Men (Shimmy-Disc) 1991 ●

Underappreciated and understated metaphysical comedy music comes in strange forms. This is one of them. With words by singer John S. Hall and music by guitarist Dogbowl, beefed up by Kramer's production and auxiliary musicianship, New York's King Missile (Dog Fly Religion) produced two uneven yet insinuating records of bellicose nubbins concerning the secret guilts and torments of modern lowlife scum. On the original band's two albums, Hall's black humor meshes nicely with Dogbowl's more romantic inclinations; when the latter departed, he took the parenthetical portion of the moniker with him. (Both LPs are contained on a single cassette; the **They** CD adds two bonus tracks to the basic 20-song menu.)

Post-partum, Dogbowl cranked out **Tit! (An Opera)**, an ambitiously skanky (although decidedly non-operatic) collection of scratchy, wistful love ditties that ooze by on a tide of guitar, cello, organ and Hawaiian lap steel. Kramer produced and performs on **Tit!**, but not on **Mystical Shit**, where Hall steps to the fore, joined by frequent Bongwater guitarist Dave Rick and When People Were Shorter multi-instrumentalist Chris Xefos. The revamped King Missile sounds more focused than before, with the humor coming off as conceptual rather than jokey. And Hall has a new-found penchant for monologuish material such as "Gary & Melissa" (detailing a couple's sexual explorations) and "Jesus Was Way Cool." (The **Tit!** cassette contains seven bonus tracks; the **Mystical Shit** CD contains **Fluting on the Hump**.) [rg]

KING SNAKE ROOST

From Barbarism to Christian Manhood (Aus. Aberrant) 1987 (Aberrant-Amphetamine Reptile) 1989
Things That Play Themselves (Aus. Aberrant) 1988 (Aberrant-Amphetamine Reptile) 1989
Ground into the Dirt (Aberrant-Amphetamine Reptile) 1990 ●

GRONG GRONG

Grong Grong (Alternative Tentacles) 1985

Delta blues, as interpreted by disaffected urban bookworms, has to be post-punk's most over-explored, under-realized vein. Partly because they harbor no fantasies about bein' down in the swamp, moonshine bottle in hand, and partly because they go after riffs like a pit bull after a mailman, Sydney, Australia's King Snake Roost waste no time in making believers out of casual listeners.

On the 1987 debut, the fat, wriggling basslines of Michael Raymond (since departed) are impaled on rusty skeins of Charles Tolnay's thug-jazz guitar. A feverish disc indeed. The follow-up leans more towards the modern world, with nods to pre-**Modern Dance** Ubu (in the bleating "Fried") and a long-overdue tribute to the Legendary Stardust Cowboy ("The Ledge Does Vegas"). About the only misstep was not corrallin' the Ledge for a guest shot.

Recorded Stateside with dairyland production legend Butch Vig, **Ground into the Dirt** proffers a sound at once burlier and more graceful, not unlike Killdozer fused with Funkadelic. Even with all four members sharing writing chores, there's a frightening degree of singleminded aberrance—from singer Peter Hill's bizarro haikus ("I Am Hog" in its entirety: "Call me hog. I am hog. Curly tail. I am hog.") to bassist David Quinn's malevolent, Burroughs-like cut-ups ("Travel Was a Meat Thing"). Start here and work backwards.

Tolnay previously led Grong Grong, where his fine abstract-expressionist guitar mist was subordinate to a series of overly pious Birthday Party eulogies like "Poor Herb" and "Louise the Fly." Too bad. [dss]

KINGS OF WYOMING

Kings of Wyoming (Community 3) 1989

Comely if amateurish, this New York trio led by Community 3 prexy/producer Albert Garzon (guitar, piano, vocals, production) plays gentle folk-pop that goes one for eight on the group's brief album. Singing lead (with Garzon's harmonies adding a warm undercurrent) on "Janelle," bassist Cathy Crane's pretty high voice focuses the rudimentary arrangement and covers the un-

exceptional playing. The remaining tracks, however, suffer to varying degrees from her uncertain pitch and/or Garzon's plain voice. [i]

KING SWAMP

King Swamp (nr/Virgin) 1988 (Virgin) 1989 ●
Wiseblood (Virgin) 1990 ◊

Here's a sad tale of promise quickly squandered. Featuring bass-ace-turned-top-producer Dave Allen (Gang of Four, Shriekback) and fronted by wailin' Walter Wray, King Swamp debuted with a brawny, exciting set of anthemic rockers like "Man Behind the Gun," "Is This Love?" and "Year Zero." If the potential for arena-rock bombast seems high, **King Swamp** is too much fun to worry about it. By **Wiseblood**, however, all of the worst tendencies in the band (reduced from a quintet to a trio, still starring Allen) come to the fore. Undistinguished, crass material would be tiring enough, but Wray bellows with the obnoxious panache of Roger Daltrey at his most operatic. Sad. [jy]

See also *Shriekback*.

KING TEE

Act a Fool (Capitol) 1988 ●
At Your Own Risk (Capitol) 1990 ●

The detailed playboy's-night-out tale, set over a pair of sampled guitar chords and a James Brown shout, that opens Compton rapper King Tee's first LP pretty much pegs the lifestyle to a (sorry) T. Nothing else on **Act a Fool**—which includes an informal rank session, "Baggin' on Moms," an influenza sound-effects joke called "I Got a Cold" and a serious ode to "Guitar Playin' "—comes close, but producer D.J. Pooh makes his mark with tracks that are effectively spare *and* musical.

Tee wastes most of the harder-sounding **At Your Own Risk** alternately vamping and rambling through loose, barely structured rhymes that go nowhere slowly. (People with nothing to say probably shouldn't make rap records.) When he finally fixes on a subject, it's screwin' his friend's wife (in "Skanless"). Besides the impressive commentary of "Time to Get Out," a serious and well-stated message to gang members and black youth, the album's only original idea is "Diss You," a boring rap that makes its bed on the Stones' "Miss You." ("Do Your Thing," meanwhile, bites "Satisfaction" as an unnamed Valley dude praises Tee for "crossing over into rock'n'roll, man!") At your own risk. [i]

KEVN KINNEY

See *Drivin' n' Cryin'*.

RICHARD H. KIRK

See *Cabaret Voltaire*.

KITCHENS OF DISTINCTION

Elephantine EP (nr/One Little Indian) 1989 ●
Love Is Hell (nr/One Little Indian) 1989 (One Little Indian-Rough Trade) 1990 ●
Strange Free World (One Little Indian-A&M) 1991 ◊

On its first album, this London trio plays seriously dramatic, intensely human music dominated by Julian Swales' delayed, swirling, lost-in-space guitar. It cascades from every direction, an otherworldly out-of-body experience. While the material is first-rate (see "Prize" and "The 3rd Time We Opened the Capsule," as well as the sparkling "In a Cave"), it's that guitar—seemingly five guitars in one—that probes new depths, twinkling, glistening, ravishing. One doesn't so much listen to such a dreamy, echoing, caressing LP as absorb it; from start to finish, **Love Is Hell** flows like syrup on pancakes. The US CD and cassette tack on the earlier UK "Elephantine" single and its three B-sides.   [jr]

KLF
See *Justified Ancients of Mu Mu*.

KMFDM
What Do You Know, Deutschland (Ger. Skysaw) 1986 ●
Don't Blow Your Top (Wax Trax!) 1988 ●
UAIOE (Wax Trax!) 1989 ●
Naïve (Wax Trax!) 1990 ●

This Hamburg quartet (later a trio) began by providing soundtracks for friends' performance art in Paris, and their music has maintained a certain pan-European cinematic quality ever since. Often tagged as an industrial band, KMFDM (whose acronym is most frequently explained as Kein Mitleid Für Die Mehrheit, which translates as "no pity for the majority") do indeed produce dark, throbbing post-modern noise. But they also toy with heavy metal, disco and hip-hop—often within the same song.

Their debut album gathers up early singles under the title of its strongest track. A grim dance beat interspersed with samples concerning US foreign policy—"America is here to stay," the German audience is told—the cut displays KMFDM's political awareness and fondness for found sound, although the sampling would ease its way out of the group's music along with the disappearance of its only British-born member. Other numbers are reminiscent of the The in sheer intensity; a few sparse dance tracks fill out the program.

Hauling in Adrian Sherwood to produce most of **Don't Blow Your Top** yielded obvious results: a simpler, slower and more stripped-down record, verging on dub as much as on harsh rock. Most of the relatively spare tracks push the synthesized rhythms right up front, adding electronic accents, occasional vocals and found-sound ephemera almost as afterthoughts. With the arched eyebrow of dubious tourists visiting America for the first time, "What a Race" satirically samples sports commentators; the frequent use of TV bites preserves the same sense of cultural bewilderment.

UAIOE finds KMFDM embracing rap to excellent effect on cuts like "Ganja Rock" and "Murder," the latter an exemplary marriage of industrial and hip-hop. Elsewhere, the group either rocks out like metal maniacs, or just hammers home an intensive dance beat: what **UAIOE** lacks in cohesion it makes up for in inspiration.

Following two aggressive singles—the morbid "Virus" and the excellent guitar-driven "Godlike," a dif-

ferent version of which appears on the CD—**Naïve** adds female singers for the title track's warped disco, funk riffs for "Piggybank" and a wider use of German vocals. KMFDM's most accomplished release to date, **Naïve** benefits from full sound and attention to the beat.   [tf]

KNITTERS
See *X*.

KNOX
See *U.K. Subs, Vibrators*.

CHRIS KNOX
See *Tall Dwarfs*.

RONALD KOAL AND THE TRILLIONAIRES
Ronald Koal and the Trillionaires (No Other) 1982
DRAGSTERS
Stoked (Great Jones) 1989 ●
RONALD KOAL BAND
White Light (Watertower) 1991 φ

On their 1982 album, the Trillionaires—a semi-modern Ohio rock quintet—come on like a kitschy Suburbs. Koal has one of those melodramatic Anthony Newley-type voices, but doesn't sound selfconscious about it; the songs are cinematic and campy, with subject matter like "Check the Attic" and "Beast in the Cellar." The '60sish "(Theme from) Girl World" achieves the same B-movie effect without words.

Years later, two of the Trillionaires (not including Koal) resurfaced in New York's Dragsters, a quartet dedicated to twang-and-sax beach instrumentals but open to the occasional vocal by guitarist Todd Novak. **Stoked** soaks in the exact same cars-sun-surf-film nostalgia as every other album by bands that pray to Dick Dale and Duane Eddy, but the harmony-filled Beach Boys sound of "Waikiki" and P.F. Sloan's "Anywhere the Girls Are" wisely add a musical dimension that prevents the surrounding tracks from sliding into twistable tedium.   [i]

KOMMUNITY FK
The Vision and the Voice (Independent Project) 1983
Close One Sad Eye (Independent Project) 1985
SATIVA LUVBOX
No Sleep for the Evil (Splatco) 1989

Kommunity FK arose from the LA avant-garde gloom scene with a sound somewhere between Joy Division, Christian Death and Savage Republic. **The Vision and the Voice** is an excellent album, starting with its Boschian cover art depicting naked figures cavorting and fornicating around a giant red penis. Patrick Mata's clear, soaring vocals nicely match his minimalist guitar work. The trio isn't afraid to try different ideas—from primitive art-punk with ominous synthesizer effects through dense, doomy punk noise and blur-thrash to neo-industrial experiments resembling a milder Neubauten. Gripping, lurking bass comes to the fore on "Unknown to You" and the circular, rhythmic "We Will Not Fall."

The band split and reformed repeatedly, keeping Mata and drummer Matt Chaikin as the only constants. One stable stretch in 1984 allowed the creation of the similarly satisfying **Close One Sad Eye**, released late in '85. The rough, punk/industrial edges had been smoothed out to a Comsat Angels/Tuxedomoon sheen, and the Joy Division influence (especially on the dramatic drone of "Junkies" and the "Love Will Tear Us Apart"-ish "Trollops") is noticeably greater. A full-time keyboardist integrates synth into the compositions, and Mata's vocals are far more theatrical and dynamic. The haunting "Something Inside Me Has Died" is not only the standout track on the LP, but one of the finest gothic anthems by any American group. (In 1990, both albums were scheduled to be issued on CD by Dali/Chameleon.)

Mata spent the latter half of the '80s alternating between England, where he formed bands with bassists Cam Campbell (of Andi Sex-Gang notoriety) and Eddie Branch (ex-UK Decay/Furyo), and Los Angeles, where he continued to shuffle ineffectual KFK lineups and work with other groups, but Sativa Luvbox is the only project of his to actually result in a record so far.

[gef]

KONK

Konk Party EP (nr/Rough Trade) 1982 (Celluloid) 1983 ●
Yo (nr/Crépuscule-Island) 1983 ●
Konk Jams (Dog Brothers) 1988 ●

Slick and supple New York big-band funk: Konk's seven-piece lineup includes three horn players and a vocalist who doubles on conga drum. The sound leans Latinward, with scads of percussion and sharp arrangements, plus some subtle dub effects thrown in for good measure. Clocking in at over 23 minutes, the four songs on the **Konk Party** EP are indeed for partying, and best heard on a mammoth boombox.

Konk laid low for a while, resurfacing with the inclusion of "Love Attack" on the soundtrack (and album) of *Bright Lights, Big City*. (Konk had in a sense launched its film career several years earlier when trumpet player Richard Edson—who had been the original drummer in Sonic Youth—started acting in pictures like *Stranger Than Paradise* and *Platoon*.)

Konk Jams is a collection of extended remixes (some with vocals) that downplay the funk and the brass for a powerful reliance on rhythm and amusing audio gimmickry.

[i]

KOOL G RAP & DJ POLO

Road to the Riches (Cold Chillin'-Warner Bros.) 1989 ●
Wanted: Dead or Alive (Cold Chillin'-Warner Bros.) 1990 ●

Produced and co-written by Marley Marl, **Road to the Riches** is a perfectly adequate but hardly distinguished-sounding vehicle for New York rhymer Kool G (Nathaniel Wilson). Unfortunately, the young MC's routine raps about women, words and wealth—delivered with an in-your-face lisp—defuse the tracks' potential.

Like a lot of young hustlers hustled into debuts they weren't prepared for, Kool G made a much more impressive showing on his stronger second go-'round. The LP leads off on a powerful note with the memorably grim reality check of "Streets of New York," an insinuating, mellow groove with a hip sax'n'piano arrangement. What follows is a violent police drama ("Wanted: Dead or Alive") produced at high anxiety by Eric B, and an entertaining all-star anti-racism jam with Big Daddy Kane and Biz Markie. But the LP isn't all dope: the rough language and crude promises of "Talk Like Sex" and "Death Wish" are vile, some of the tracks are conceptually weak and G's speech impediment undercuts his delivery.

[i]

KOOL MOE DEE

Kool Moe Dee (Rooftop-Jive) 1986 ●
How Ya Like Me Now (Rooftop-Jive) 1987 ●
Knowledge Is King (Jive-RCA) 1989 ●
African Pride EP (Jive) 1990 ●
Funke, Funke Wisdom (Jive) 1991 ●

Using a stone-cold serious tone that does not encourage disagreement, popular New York rapper Kool Moe Dee (Mohandas Dewese), a former third of the Treacherous Three, puts his positive social messages plus the usual braggadocio to medium-weight rhythm tracks, many of them enhanced by loping synth-bass lines, electronic horns and other musical ingredients. The versatile vocalist's records earn their mainstream appeal by tempering the music and taking a firm stand against violence and sexual irresponsibility.

The first album's "Go See the Doctor" offers a slangy but detailed warning about venereal disease; "Little Jon" characterizes a young hoodlum as a loser not a hero; "Monster Crack" warns kids against messing with drugs.

How Ya Like Me Now experiments with one-chord funk vamps instead of mere beats, and quotes James Brown, Paul Simon and others. But the raps aren't as captivating as before, and the cuts tend to drag. "No Respect," recited to an adaptation of Aretha's "Respect," tells a powerful cautionary tale of a street hustler's downfall and joins the self-serving title tune as a highlight.

Back in control with another masterful blend of uplifting rhymes, inventive music and no-nonsense delivery, Moe Dee pushes his don't-steal-it/earn-it philosophy in the appealing **Knowledge Is King**, announcing "I Go to Work" over a dramatic brassy film noir track, defending his bachelorhood in "They Want Money," prizing intelligent women in "All Night Long" and promoting education the title track. "Pump Your Fist" wraps up the album in a wide-ranging discussion of racism, history and contemporary urban life.

The **African Pride** 12-inch contains three mixes of "God Made Me Funky," a remix of "Knowledge Is King" and two other tracks.

[i]

PETER KOPPES

See *Church*.

KRAFTWERK

Kraftwerk 1 (Ger. Philips) 1971
Kraftwerk 2 (Ger. Philips) 1972
Kraftwerk (nr/Vertigo) 1972
Ralf and Florian (Vertigo) 1973
Autobahn (Vertigo) 1974 (Warner Bros.) 1984 (Elektra)
    1988 ●
Radio Activity (Capitol) 1975 ●
Exceller 8 (nr/Vertigo) 1975
Trans-Europe Express (Capitol) 1977 ●
The Man Machine (Capitol) 1978 ●
Elektro Kinetik (nr/Vertigo) 1981
Computer World (Warner Bros.) 1981 (Elektra) 1988 ●
Techno Pop EP (nr/EMI) 1983
Electric Cafe (Warner Bros.) 1986 (Elektra) 1988 ●
The Mix (Elektra) 1991 ●

Kraftwerk (German for "power station") began in the electronic metal trend that erupted in Germany in the early 1970s. Although quiet in recent years, the four-piece synthesizer group showed amazing resiliency for more than fifteen years, tightening its electro-pop formula to fit smoothly into art-rock and, later, disco. Kraftwerk essentially created the sonic blueprint from which the British new romantic and techno-pop movements arose, and provided the essential technology for much of hip-hop.

Autobahn is built around an epic version of the title track, a bizarre hit single that broke the band as a commercial property in numerous countries. Enchanting in its simplicity, hypnotic in its construction, the song introduces the repetition typical of all Kraftwerk music, but the record's other pieces are less inspired synthesizer noodling.

Radio Activity coincided with a change of image that sliced away beards and hair and converted Kraftwerk from aging hippies into modern sonic engineers; greater use of repetition and purposeful self-limitation is evident, though there is no breakthrough.

The robotic **Trans-Europe Express** placed mechanistic aspects of the music up front, in a brilliant epiphany of style. Rhythms and themes recur throughout, with little emotion expressed in the vocals; lyrics emphasize the dehumanization suggested by the production and delivery. Recommended.

The Man Machine further builds on the developments of **Trans-Europe Express**, with the one humanizing effect—background music—yielding to *Star Wars* noises. More work with manipulated vocals—especially on the title track and "We Are the Robots"—takes the automaton stance to the limit. Despite the science fiction themes and heavy musical repetition, the album has inventive, catchy compositions and an eerie warmth. Highly recommended.

Computer World broke years of silence, bringing Kraftwerk into a world that had largely embraced and vindicated their social and musical visions. Technically advanced machinery yields sharper, brighter music, but otherwise Kraftwerk haven't tampered with their style, except to shift their thematic content from science-fiction to industrial documentary. Excellent synthesizer pop.

The musics Kraftwerk helped launch—British post-rock industrial sounds and rhythm-is-everything dance grooves—come full circle on Side One of the long-awaited **Electric Cafe**. The virtually interchangeable "Technopop" and "Musique Non-Stop" take sparse, simple, unvarying percussion tracks and add bits of treated vocals, synthetic noises and quasi-instrumental effects. On the reverse are three straightforward (albeit numbingly repetitive) songs that use actual melodies, singing and lyrics. While the second side is certainly listenable, even Kraftwerk fans will find this brief album disappointingly short on ideas and content.

There are German-language versions of many, if not all, of Kraftwerk's albums. There have also been several compilations released in the UK. In 1988, the group signed with Elektra, which reissued some of their catalogue. **The Mix** is a drastically remixed best-of.

[sg/i]

KRAMER

See *Carney-Hild-Kramer, Half Japanese, King Missile (Dog Fly Religion)*.

WAYNE KRAMER

See *Mick Farren, MC5, Johnny Thunders*.

DAGMAR KRAUSE

See *Henry Cow*.

KRAUT

An Adjustment to Society (Cabbage) 1983
Whetting the Scythe (Cabbage) 1984
Night of Rage (New Red Archives) 1989
The Movie [CD] (New Red Archives) 1990 ●

GUTTERBOY

Gutterboy (DGC) 1990 ●

One of New York's most deserving punk legends, Kraut made their live debut opening for the Clash in 1981 and went on to play a big part in the city's burgeoning hardcore scene. On its first album, the quartet throws off awesomely dense but distinct slabs of post-Pistols/Clash guitar chords while galloping along at a good clip. Although genuine ex-Pistol Steve Jones played guitar on three songs ("Onward," "Sell Out" and "Kill for Cash"), the spotlight remains firmly fixed on Doug Holland, one of punk's best-ever string smashers. The urban reality/armageddon lyrics are only a bit above the usual monosyllabic protest, but no matter. (Jones also performed with the band on occasion, and a version of the Pistols' "Bodies" appears on the Kraut live compilation, **Night of Rage**.)

Whetting the Scythe, a brief nine-song album, finds Kraut abandoning punk for tasteful demi-metal, using doubled guitar leads and charging, articulated power at more moderate tempos. It's a partially successful variant, easier to follow than hyperdrive punk. Kraut has the chops, the intelligence and (occasionally) the songs to make something really unique.

After doing some unfinished sessions, Holland left to become a Cro-Mag and was replaced by Chris Smith (ex-Battalion of Saints). The new lineup completed three of those hard-rock items in '85, but Smith drowned and Kraut threw in the towel. Singer Davy Gunner and drummer Johnny Feedback (under the names Dito and Johnny Koncz) went on to form Gutterboy. **The Movie**, a 27-track CD, combines the three previously unreleased tracks with both studio albums in their entirety.

An attempt to glorify punk ruggedness as stylish tough-guy sexuality (undershirt chic!), Gutterboy is a remarkably contrived quartet produced to sound like a street-level cross between Bruce Springsteen and U2. With Dito getting outside songwriting assists (probably on lyrics, which are well-suited to the group's mission), the material is obvious but entertaining; the foursome's playing is as exciting and credible as their carefully manicured looks.   [jg/i]

See also *Cro-Mags*.

LENNY KRAVITZ
Let Love Rule (Virgin) 1989 ●
Mama Said (Virgin) 1991 φ

Like some musical castaway wandering back into civilization two decades after Woodstock, this young do-it-yourselfer, who was barely born when the flower-power hippie/soul era of his imaginings ended, sings drippy idealistic songs about love and harmony to simple feel-good music that rolls baroque Beatle pop, Joe Cocker gospel and Sly Stone soul—all with Billy Preston's effusiveness—into a mock nostalgic trip for those too young to have any actual memories. A reasonably good singer who plays guitar, drums and keyboards on the vintage-sounding **Let Love Rule**, Kravitz is emotionally insufferable, whether testifying to the uncontrollable joys of love ("I Built This Garden for Us"), whipping up a fraternal frenzy in the title track or delivering an obnoxiously effete condemnation of racism ("Mr. Cab Driver").   [i]

KRYST THE CONQUEROR
See *Misfits*.

K-SOLO
See *EPMD*.

ED KUEPPER
See *Laughing Clowns, Saints*.

KUKL
See *Sugarcubes*.

SERGEI KURIOKHIN
See *Henry Kaiser*.

KURSAAL FLYERS
Chocs Away (nr/UK) 1975
The Great Artiste (nr/UK) 1975
Golden Mile (nr/CBS) 1976
Five Live Kursaals! (nr/CBS) 1977
In for a Spin: The Best of the Kursaal Flyers (nr/Edsel) 1985 ●
A Former Tour de Force Is Forced to Tour (nr/Waterfront) 1988 ●

This seminal pub-rock outfit is more of interest for what the individuals did after the group split than for the band's own recordings. Drummer Will Birch went on to found the Records (with guitarist John Wicks, briefly a Kursaal at the end of the band's first go-round) and produce records for various people. Graeme Douglas, whom Wicks replaced, joined Eddie and the Hot Rods, and wrote their best songs.

The Kursaals' first two LPs are thinly produced countryish rock'n'roll, bolstered considerably by Birch's witty lyrics. **The Great Artiste** does contain what may be the earliest recorded cover of a Nick Lowe composition, "Television," later done to better effect by Dave Edmunds.

With Mike Batt producing, the group tried something completely different on **Golden Mile**, an eclectic musical travelogue through rock'n'roll's root styles from swing to Spector to ska to '60s pop-rock. The album is a little-known treasure, similar in concept to the Turtles' equally ignored and enjoyable **Battle of the Bands**.

By the time of **Five Live**, the Kursaals had almost totally weeded out their country strain and, showing the influence of the punk revolution going on around them, got into music with a more driving beat. The band's last hurrah, the "Television Generation" single, is great, proof positive that the band had seen the new light. What else could they do but break up?

And what else could they do after releasing **In for a Spin**—a best-of featuring nine cuts from the first three albums, "Television Generation" and five unreleased tracks (including one later recorded by Birch's next group, the Records)—but reunite for another album?

Tour de Force—an all-new studio album by the reformed group—sounds like a record the Kursaals might have made in 1978 had they stayed together. With only a song titled "Pre-Madonna" as a token gesture to topicality, the LP melds all the best elements of what the group initially had to offer. Good to see that ten years haven't affected these guys a bit, or dulled Birch's way with words; he remains one of the most disarmingly clever lyricists this side of Nick Lowe.   [ds]

See also *Eddie and the Hot Rods, Records*.

DAVE KUSWORTH
See *Nikki Sudden*.

FELA ANIKULAPO KUTI
Fela's London Scene (nr/EMI) 1970
Fela Ransome-Kuti and Africa '70 with Ginger Baker: Live! (Signpost) 1972 ●
Gentlemen (nr/Creole) 1979
Everything Scatter (nr/Creole) 1979
Black-President (Capitol) 1981
Original Sufferhead (Capitol) 1982
Army Arrangement (Remix) (Celluloid) 1985 ●
Shuffering and Shmiling (Celluloid) 1985 ●
Army Arrangement (Celluloid) 1985 ●
No Agreement (Celluloid) 1985
Upside Down (Celluloid) 1986 ●
2,000 Black (Celluloid) 1986
Mr. Follow Follow (Celluloid) 1986
Volume One and Two (Celluloid) 1987
Teacher Don't Teach Me Nonsense (Mercury) 1987 ●
Overtake Don Overtake Overtake (Shanachie) 1990 φ
The Best of Fela (Oceana-Celluloid) 1990 ●

FELA AND AFRIKA 70
Shakara (nr/EMI) 1972
Zombie (Mercury) 1977 (Celluloid) 1985 ●

FELA ANIKULAPO KUTI AND EGYPT 80
Live in Amsterdam (Capitol) 1984
Beasts of No Nation (Shanachie) 1989 ●

FELA ANIKULAPO KUTI AND ROY AYERS
Music of Many Colours (Celluloid) 1986 ●

One of the world's true musical revolutionaries, Fela Ransome-Kuti's life and work embody most of the contradictions inherent in any major collusion of Western and African styles of thought and art. Born in Lagos, Nigeria in 1938 to an affluent Christian family and educated in London, Fela was just another minor highlife bandleader until he received funk's call via Sierra Leonese James Brown-imitator Geraldo Pino in 1966. By weaving funk rhythms into highlife, Fela developed Afrobeat, a mesmerizingly potent style he has spent years refining.

Most of Fela's recorded pieces take up to an entire side of an LP, beginning slowly, with a lengthy electric piano and/or saxophone introduction (Fela plays both instruments) before breaking into exuberant horn fanfares, followed by call-and-response vocals between Fela and chorus and interlocking polyrhythmic percussion patterns.

During a 1968 Los Angeles stint with his group Koola Lobitas, Fela was introduced to American black radical politics. Fela's stock rose considerably when EMI released **Fela's London Scene** in 1970, leading to a friendship and collaboration with ex-Cream drummer Ginger Baker. (Their **Live!** album provides a fairly tame example.) Nigerian authorities tormented the bandleader after his triumphant return from London in the early '70s, for as Fela's fame grew, so did his influence. (Fortunately, Kuti's name translates as "He who emanates greatness, who has death inside his quiver and who cannot be killed by human entity.") Castigatory songs about government corruption (on **Black-President**'s "I.T.T. (International Thief Thief),)" military fascism ("Zombie," on the album of the same name) and national apathy ("Army Arrangement," ditto), sung by a rich marijuana smoker with a couple of dozen wives who isolated himself in a concrete fortress called the Shrine, challenged the local authorities in a manner they couldn't ignore.

Since 1974, Fela has been arrested several times for various crimes; during a particularly vigorous 1981 crackdown, a beating by soldiers left him temporarily incapable of playing saxophone. His most recent incarceration came in 1984, on the eve of his first major American tour. Arrested on a trumped-up money-smuggling rap, he was released from his five-year sentence after two years, thanks to intercession by Amnesty International.

Celluloid began re-releasing some of Fela's many records in 1985. **Upside Down** dates from 1976; **No Agreement** from 1977. But the most controversial of these was Bill Laswell's remix of **Army Arrangement**, on which he added tracks by keyboardist Bernie Worrell, drummer Sly Dunbar and talking drummer Aïyb Dieng. This reportedly displeased Fela greatly, and one need only compare the remix with the rough yet stirring original to understand why. Roy Ayers joins Fela on **Music of Many Colors** (originally released on Phonodisk in 1980), eliciting the vibraphonist's meatiest playing ever. **Zombie** is one of the classics of the Celluloid batch.

PolyGram cashed in on Fela's successful and long-delayed 1987 American tour by releasing one of his hits from the show, **Teacher Don't Teach Me Nonsense**. The wild master hadn't lost his chops. **Beasts of No Nation** is a fine example of vintage Fela, while **O.D.O.O.** is simply spectacular. With compact disc technology catching up to Fela's long-form Afrobeat creations, the two half-hour compositions that comprise the disc provide ample room for ensemble workouts, saxophone solos, high guitar stepping, polyrhythmic noodling and call-and-response groovulation. Indeed, Fela even reprises his classic "Zombie" in the middle of the title track. [rg]

KWAMÉ FEATURING A NEW BEGINNING
The Boy Genius (Atlantic) 1989 ●

KWAMÉ AND A NEW BEGINNING
A Day in the Life: A Pokadelick Adventure (Atlantic) 1990 ●

With one foot in the old school (courtesy of producer Hurby "Luv Bug" Azor) and an easy feel for daisy-age soul-pop, this bright young New York rapper—whose middle-class values aren't so different from the overtly Afrocentric Native Tongue crew—brings a neat nerdy element to his first album. On **The Boy Genius**, Kwamé (Holland) comes off as the lovestruck overachiever next door, a goodnatured and upbeat rhymer with inventive ideas, lightweight beats and easy charm.

A Day in the Life is even better, a colorful and musically diverse self-willed world of polka-dots in the freewheeling "Bone Age." Although posited as a concept album about the high-schooler's quotidian existence, the record largely relies on phone messages to connect some of the oh-so-vaguely related autobiographical tales and boasts. If **A Day in the Life** isn't all it's cracked up to be, Kwamé's youthful exuberance and imaginative tracks still make it uncommonly entertaining. [pn]

L L L L L L L L

LACH

Contender (Gold Castle) 1991 φ

As a pivotal figure in getting the New York anti-folk scene up and running, singer/guitarist/pianist Lach was evidently too busy being an impresario to make a record until most of his friends had taken their vinyl shots. **Contender** has no problem dispensing with acoustic guitar formalism; as produced by Tom Goodkind of the Washington Squares, the album employs a nimble rhythm section and mild electric backing, giving the central acoustic strums a rich and strong setting. ("Hard Time" and "Steven Said" break on through to overt rock.) Lach hasn't got much of a voice, and his tunes don't exactly send you home humming, but he's an enthusiastic character who brings more imagination to faux-folk than many of his better known peers. Best song: "The Edie Effect," a wry attack on Warholian poseurs.   [i]

LADYSMITH BLACK MAMBAZO

Induku Zethu (Shanachie) 1984 ●
Ulwandle Oluncgwele (Shanachie) 1985 ●
Inala (Shanachie) 1986 ●
Shaka Zulu (Warner Bros.) 1987 ●
Umthombo Wamanzi (Shanachie) 1988 ●
Journey of Dreams (Warner Bros.) 1988 ●
Two Worlds One Heart (Warner Bros.) 1990 ●
Classic Tracks (Shanachie) 1990 φ

Led by Joseph Shabalala—who formed the ten-man group almost 30 years ago and has been recording with it for two decades—Ladysmith Black Mambazo is one of South Africa's most popular ensembles. For sheer vocal ecstasy, few organizations can equal its lush, comforting and sophisticated choral harmonies sung in the open *mbube* style. Simultaneously sorrowful and optimistic, the music originated in South African dormitories housing immigrant workers who'd left their townships and families for employment in the area's diamond and gold mines.

Mbube is characterized by a cappella harmonies and short phrases, either sung in unison or against an overlapping call-and-response pattern. Reflecting on matters both familial and spiritual, the music is tied closely to the group's Zulu culture. They generally sing in Zulu; the occasional English-language songs are a pleasant shock.

Noted ethno-music appropriator Paul Simon got wind of Ladysmith Black Mambazo and, despite the African National Congress' cultural boycott of South Africa, recorded part of **Graceland** with them in Johannesburg and London. (He also featured the group on two subsequent tours and produced **Shaka Zulu.**) All that American attention led to the group's remarkable

commercial exploitation by 7-Up, which adapted "Beautiful Rain" from that album for a TV spot.

On **Umthombo Wamanzi**, Mambazo changes its strategy slightly, emphasizing ensemble work rather than call-and-response structures or a leader singing over backing voices; this accentuates their irregular punctuations and stop-start rhythms. As with previous records, it provides an almost overwhelming atmosphere of emotional power and grace. The unadorned human voice has rarely sounded so godlike.

Shabalala and Mambazo pay tribute to Paul Simon, Miriam Makeba, Hugh Masekela and god (although not exactly in that order) on **Journey of Dreams**, ending the record with a lovely gentle rendition (in English) of "Amazing Grace" that features Simon.

Taking the regrettably inevitable step into fusion, Mambazo recorded some of **Two Worlds One Heart** with musical backing. At the mixture's mildest point, Mambazo sings the handsome "Rejoice" over traditional instruments with no harm done. But Shabalala's duet with American gospel star Marvin Winans (which employs synthesizers) is an incongruity next to the group's unaccompanied efforts, and the funk track co-written and co-produced by George Clinton makes it sound as if Mambazo were merely sampled into the mix—an undesirable effect considering whose album it is.

Although consistent enough to sound like it was recorded in one go, **Classic Tracks** is a compilation of tracks from the group's first two dozen or so albums. As annoying as the lack of annotation may be, there's no faulting the music, which is unfailingly magical.

[rg/i]

LAIBACH

Through the Occupied Netherlands [tape] (Hol. Staal)
    1984
Laibach (Yugoslavian Skuc) 1985
Rekapitulation 1980-84 (Ger. Walter Ulbricht) 1985 ●
Nova Akropola (nr/Cherry Red) 1985 (Wax Trax!)
    1986 ●
Baptism (Ger. Walter Ulbricht) 1986 ●
Opus Dei (Mute-Wax Trax!) 1987 ●
Panorama/Die Liebe EP (Wax Trax!) 1987
Let It Be (Mute-Enigma) 1988 ●
Sympathy for the Devil EP (Mute-Restless) 1988 ●
Macbeth (Mute-Restless) 1990 ●

Formed in 1979 in Ljubljana, the capital of the Yugoslavian republic of Slovenia, Laibach (the city's German name) set out to revitalize Slovenian culture and create a mythic persona through careful manipulation of the group's image. As much theater as music, Laibach often used to appear in the uniforms of the Nazis who occupied Ljubljana during WW II, and has made a point, on record, of highlighting the connection between Western rock and capitalism.

The double-album boxed-set **Rekapitulation** summarizes Laibach's first four years of recording and contains some of the band's most innovative material: strange mixtures of rock, jazz, disco and ambience with occasional Wagnerian overtones. Sieved through an Eastern European consciousness, this combination provides unique flavors, ranging from astonishing beauty to totalitarian menace.

Though released in 1985, most of the material on **Laibach** was recorded years earlier and is also contained on **Rekapitulation**. The poorly recorded **Through Occupied Europe** offers two live performances, adding little to the studio versions of material also found on **Rekapitulation**.

By the time Laibach recorded **Nova Akropola**, the band had picked up a following in Western Europe and received a lot of attention in the music press. **Nova Akropola** is a more sophisticated undertaking than earlier efforts, furthering the group's music and concept. Wagnerian horns sound over the surging beats of science fiction armies, while singer Milan Fras growls lyrics in a gravely basso. Two songs use nationalistic speeches by Marshal Tito as lyrics; while the intent is ironic, not the faintest smile is discernible.

Baptism, a second double set, is the soundtrack to a play done with the theater branch of the New Slovenian Art movement, of which Laibach is a part. The album uses tape loops, beats, horns and chants and is far more atmospheric than the group's more pop-oriented work. With the exception of half a side that sounds to be an "appropriation" of an old, scratchy opera record, this is excellent, innovative music.

Four of **Baptism**'s shorter, livelier tracks are appended to the CD of **Opus Dei**, at the time, Laibach's poppiest and most conceptually ambitious record. It contains fascist-tinged covers of Queen's "One Vision" and the Eurodisco hit "Life Is Life," sung in German with grandiose horns and a marching beat. (**Panorama/Die Liebe** is a 12-inch containing two tracks from **Nova Akropola** and two other items.)

Laibach has always maintained that Western pop music is nothing more than capitalism, that rock stars should be viewed as successful businessmen and that concerts are akin to political rallies for canned rebellion. After **Opus Dei**, the group took the logical—albeit radical—step of attacking pop icons by parodying them. Laibach's version of **Let It Be** (an LP the group considers the Beatles' worst) realizes the entire album (minus the title track) as melodramatic drinking and fighting songs, with horns, synthesized strings and military beats. The female choir version of "Across the Universe," deadpan with faint Slovenian accents and tinkling harpsichord, is at once hilarious, chilling and beautiful. The similarly conceived **Sympathy for the Devil** locks onto that one song, reinterpreting it six times (which is at least two too many), as disco, rock, acid house, etc., including one merciless send-up of its pretensions to evil.

Perhaps realizing that they had painted their pop efforts into a corner, Laibach's next release was an amazing soundtrack to New Slovenian Art's version of *Macbeth*. Combining the better attributes of **Baptism**

with a sense of restraint and atmosphere not heard since the early days, **Macbeth** is one of their best albums yet.

[sl]

LA MUERTE

And the Mystery Goes On EP (Bel. Soundwork) 1985
Peep Show EP (Bel. Soundwork) 1986
Every Soul by Sin Oppressed (nr/Big Disk) 1987
Scorpio Rising EP (Bel. Sex Wax) 1988
Death Race 2000 (Play It Again Sam) 1989 ●
Experiment in Terror (Bel. Play It Again Sam) 1990
Kustom Kar Kompetition (Play It Again Sam-Caroline) 1991 ●

In the wake of the Birthday Party came a worldwide wave of psychoswampabilly rockers who took that band's manic-depressive bluesrock and turned it into a music genre. Belgium's La Muerte was one of those bands. With growling, howling French and English vocals, stop/start frenzy and a guitar that at times does nothing more than squeal with feedback shavings, **And the Mystery Goes On** out-Parties the Birthday Party, delivering a four-song gothic dose of angst and aggression. The entire lyrics of the fierce "Massacre" are "whooaaah" and "suffering," voiced in a deviled frenzy of a howl over a hard-crunched drum pound and feedback shivers of guitar; the outstanding "Blues, Heaven or Hell" veers from tense to burning through a dark, crawling labyrinth.

There's not much difference between **Mystery** and the five-song **Peep Show**. The latter contains a swamp-beat re-arrangement of Syd Barrett's "Lucifer Sam" that squiggles with warped guitar, tweets off into space-rock territory and climaxes with a feedback crescendo; there's also a phone sex tape, "Blues, Heaven or Hell" and two new BP-styled tracks.

Every Soul by Sin Oppressed finds La Muerte capable of far greater intricacy, incorporating harmonica, acoustic guitar and a more slowly woven web of tension in "The Rope's Around Your Neck" and "Mannish Boy." "So Bad" crosses into psychobilly, while "You're Not an Angel" continues their parallel development with Nick Cave's work, sounding like a companion piece to "From Her to Eternity."

The four tracks on **Scorpio Rising** take four different directions. The title tune introduces sampling and dialogue cut-ups in a collage of air raid control room talk, newscasts, TV/movie bites and laugh boxes, all slathered over a slowly shifting base of feedback. The percussion in "Lost My Mind" sounds like a bullet doing a tap-dance; the monster growl screams could pass for demonic possession at your next exorcism. "Shoot in Your Back" (which also turns up on **Death Race 2000**) continues to reflect Cave's influence, while "Hellfire" is a foray into a loud psychedelia.

La Muerte's first American release, **Death Race 2000**, has harder and sparser percussion; guitar chords are grungier, even metallic at times. The faintly post-industrial production style occasionally obscures the Cave/BP influence, but the monster scream hasn't changed a bit. Imagine away the beat on "Ecoute Cette Priere," and you've got the same dark bluesy undulations as ever.

['e]

LANDLORDS

See *Happy Flowers*.

ANITA LANE

See *Nick Cave*.

MARK LANEGAN

See *Screaming Trees*.

CLIVE LANGER AND THE BOXES

I Want the Whole World EP (nr/Radar) 1979
Splash (nr/F-Beat) 1980
Hope, Honour, Love (nr/Demon) 1988

The big disappointment of Clive Langer's solo career is that he doesn't give it top priority. Presumably freed from financial pressures by co-producing numerous hit records for Madness, Dexys and others, the talented singer/guitarist—judging by his lack of "product"—seems to take only passing interest in making records of his own.

As chief songwriter for the late Deaf School, Langer successfully mated the music hall tradition with highly melodic rock'n'roll, topped off with anxious lyrics about modern-day pressures—i.e., a cross between the Kinks and Roxy Music. His solo works are more personal, and lean decidedly to the Ray Davies school, partly because Langer's weary singing has a similar charm.

The five tunes on **I Want the Whole World** are nearly perfect vignettes of anger, tenderness and regret, performed with casual ingenuousness. Though less effective, **Splash** has its moments, including the charming "Had a Nice Night" and the embarrassingly abject "Splash (A Tear Goes Rolling Down)." Elvis Costello produced two of the tracks.

Hope, Honour, Love summarizes the album and the EP, adding "Even Though" from a subsequent single. Clive Langer seems like a guy you wouldn't mind inviting to your house for dinner. [jy]

See also *Deaf School*.

GERARD LANGLEY + IAN KEAREY

See *Blue Aeroplanes*.

LAQUAN

Notes of a Native Son (4th & B'way) 1990 ●

With a live band and backing singers on every track, this precocious Los Angeles teenager's debut album (produced by Bell Biv Devoe studio associates Richard Wolf and Bret Mazur) has the panoramic sound of big-league soul, an exceptionally posh musical setting for real hip-hop. Looking beyond that stylistic innovation, Laquan's an extremely articulate rapper who goes easy on the clichés and slang to deliver a serious god-praising black-pride message with grace and dignity—but he has too little style to fully electrify the handsome grooves. [i]

LARD

The Power of Lard EP (Alternative Tentacles) 1988 ●
The Last Temptation of Reid (Alternative Tentacles) 1990 ●

Jello Biafra brings his voice, record label and sense of humor to the Lard party; guitarist Al Jourgensen and bassist Paul Barker (both of Ministry) whip up a batch of pounding semi-industrialized rock with drummer Jeff Ward. A casual and exciting bit of supergrouping, **The Power of Lard** (a three-song 12-inch) demonstrates the fun potential in this seemingly unlikely alliance.

The excellent full-length album (no duplication) standardizes the Lard concept, resolving itself into a more-or-less even mix of the Dead Kennedys and Ministry. (And is thus equally recommendable to fans of both.) Loopy topical lyrics lighten the driving music's dominance-and-submission power; a martial-beat cover of "They're Coming to Take Me Away" merrily confirms the project's open-ended aesthetic. [i]

See also *Jello Biafra, Dead Kennedys, Ministry, Revolting Cocks*.

LA'S

The La's (nr/Go! Discs) 1990 (Go! Discs-London) 1991 ●

One of the few new British pop groups to evince the influence of '60s beat, rather than psychedelia or punk, this distinctive Liverpool quartet—which favors acoustic guitars and folky harmonies but delivers taut electric rock as well—echoes groups like the Hollies, Searchers and Beatles on its fine debut album, produced by Steve Lillywhite. Singer Lee Mavers writes profoundly tuneful songs with thoughtful words and sings them with a skilled mixture of pop allure ("There She Goes" is a falsetto gem) and pub-band sturdiness ("Failure" is an odd bit of garage punk). Beyond melodic assets, the La's—who, to their credit, never employ contemporary dance beats here—make good use of rhythm as well. "Liberty Ship" has the seafaring tempo to match its lyrical metaphor, while "Way Out" pairs a measured drum/rhythm guitar beat with double-time lead figures and "Freedom Song" uses the oompah swing of a Kurt Weill number. Very impressive. [i]

LAST

L.A. Explosion! (Bomp!) 1979
Fade to Black EP (Bomp!) 1982
Painting Smiles on a Dead Man (Fr. Lolita) 1983
Confession (SST) 1988 ●
Awakening (SST) 1989 ●

Although heavily indebted to the sounds of the '60s (they touch freely on surf-rock, psychedelia, folk-rock, etc.) Los Angeles' Last—formed in 1976 and led by three Nolte brothers—play with modern-day punk intensity. **L.A. Explosion!** is a near-perfect debut, marred only by flat production. The performances are stunning, with Vitus Mataré's authentic Vox/Farfisa organ riffs adding color to the melodic guitar leads and Joe Nolte's distinctive vocals. Every track holds up, especially the hypnotic rocker "She Don't Know Why I'm Here" and a surf-inspired ode to lost youth, "Every Summer Day."

The 12-inch **Fade to Black** EP shows that the Last are indeed a group worth taking seriously. The four tracks are darker and moodier, yet the melodies are so enticing it's a crime this stuff can't find a commercial opening.

Amidst personnel changes, and facing an uncertain future, the Last released a French-only second album. **Painting Smiles on a Dead Man** is another winner, moving the organ up front and showcasing vocals that are at once more confident and demanding. Although one of Los Angeles' most gifted groups, the Last split up in 1985.

A new Last—Joe and Mike Nolte, plus three newcomers—resurfaced unexpectedly in 1988 with a neat album produced by All leader Bill Stevenson. (David Nolte—now in Wednesday Week—had been in a very early version of the Descendents, Stevenson's group.) Energized '60s power pop remains the Last's stock in trade, and they've lost none of their pep or melodiousness. The Noltes' new songs have a resigned, cynical edge ("And They Laugh," "Going Gone," "Everywhere You Turn"), but the music belies that with ringing Byrdsy guitars, mild keyboards and appealing harmonies.

Again produced by Stevenson, **Awakening** makes no stylistic changes in composition but benefits from a toughened attack. Giving clear play to the band's dual affinities for punk and paisley pop, the crisply tuneful album ranges from souped-up covers of the Beatles ("She Loves You") and the Shirelles ("Baby It's You") to a great ballad/rocker "You," the Farfisa-heavy pop of "Book of Life" and the intense "Garden Grow," punctuated by Dave Nazworthy's furious snare rolls. (Both Mataré and David Nolte make cameo appearances.)

Footnotes: Alex Gibson designed the sleeve of a 1978 Last single. Mataré has become a well-known LA record producer (Divine Weeks, Angst, Leaving Trains, etc.) and co-founded Trotsky Icepick. Drummer Dave Nazworthy splits his time between the Last and the Chemical People. In 1988, the Last ended a curious habit of not playing outside California, an isolationist (lazy?) policy that had been in force for fourteen years. [cpl/i/jr]

See also *All, Chemical People, Trotsky Icepick.*

BILL LASWELL
Baselines (Celluloid-Elektra-Musician) 1983 ●
Hear No Evil (Venture-Virgin) 1988 ●

PRAXIS
Praxis EP (Celluloid) 1984

Erstwhile Material mainman Laswell released his first solo album right around the time people began to realize that his talents extend beyond excellent bass playing into the conceptual stratosphere. **Baselines'** gut-bucket funk foundation and experienced experimentalism provide a convincing résumé for his subsequent work as producer to the stars (Mick Jagger, Yellowman, Herbie Hancock, Motörhead, Afrika Bambaataa, etc.). Guests here include fellow Materialists Michael Beinhorn (a frequent co-writer on the LP) and Martin Bisi, percussionist Ronald Shannon Jackson, the ubiquitous Fred Frith and avant-noisemaster extraordinaire David Moss.

Following group albums with Massacre and duo recordings with John Zorn and bass saxist Peter Brotzmann (as well as **Praxis**, a bass-and-drum-machine outing that unites the avant-garde Laswell with the hip-hop Laswell in an admirable experiment that doesn't quite jell), Laswell essayed another disc under his own name in 1988. Joined by violinist Shankar, guitarist Nicky Skopelitis and a small group of equally sophisticated players, he wrote and produced **Hear No Evil**, an album of hauntingly beautiful instrumentals with resonances of exotic cultures adding depth to the simple compositions. Lovely. [mf/i/gk]

See also *Golden Palominos, Material.*

LAUGHING CLOWNS
Laughing Clowns EP (Aus. Missing Link) 1979
Sometimes ... the Fire Dance EP (Aus. Prince Melon) 1980
3 EP (Aus. Prince Melon) 1981
Mr. Uddich Schmuddich Goes to Town (Aus. Prince Melon) 1982
Laughing Clowns (nr/Red Flame) 1982
Laughter Around the Table (nr/Red Flame) 1983
Law of Nature (nr/Hot) 1984
History of Rock n' Roll Volume One (Aus. Hot) 1985
Ghosts of an Ideal Wife (Aus. Hot) 1985

ED KUEPPER
Electrical Storm (Aus. Hot) 1986
Rooms of the Magnificent (nr/Hot) 1987
Not a Soul Around EP (nr/Hot) 1987
Everybody's Got To (Aus. True Tone) 1988 (True Tone-Capitol) 1989 ●
Happy as Hell EP (Aus. True Tone) 1989

TODAY WONDER
Today Wonder (Ger. Rattlesnake) 1990 ●

After the Saints broke up in 1978 (and before Chris Bailey started the group up again) guitarist/songwriter Ed Kuepper returned to Sydney to form a band with a couple of early Saints alumni. The resulting quintet, dubbed the Laughing Clowns, included sax and electric piano and was topped off with Kuepper's odd voice: he's a slightly lower-pitched, nasal and nastier Robert Smith, limited in range, but a commanding presence.

The Clowns' strange but remarkably bracing debut EP features piano that both meshes its timbral resonance with Kuepper's guitar chording and co-states the melodies with the sax, as well as—at one point—providing an unnervingly calm anchor while the drums run wild. The romantic and musical clichés of supper-club/movie jazz go berserk in an astonishingly eloquent yet intense statement of disillusionment and frustration.

Oddly enough, the manic energy and tunefulness seemed to dissipate—over the course of two additional EPs—in favor of despair, ennui, cynicism (or just sarcasm?) and decidedly less lustrous music, in both text and texture. The addition of a trumpeter on **3** does provide a spark, only to be neutralized by satirically discordant riffing. By this point, the moments of musical anarchy seem less passionate than perverse.

On **Mr. Uddich Schmuddich Goes to Town**, a shift in the lineup brought in a new saxman and bassist (playing acoustic stand-up) and dropped the pianist. The tracks are more succinct, and the overall impression is that of consolidation and retrenchment.

The Red Flame **Laughing Clowns** is a compilation that includes both Prince Melon EPs plus three tracks from the album.

By **Laughter Around the Table**, the Clowns' sound had coalesced into something resembling the Cure gone avant-jazz. The sax playing states melody lines and provides some credible solos, but the overall effect, with one exception, is too willfully abrasive and reaches beyond its musical grasp, especially the drumming.

The arrangements on **Law of Nature** continue to step on Kuepper's melodies—they're never harmonically brought out to their fullest. Also, the occasional awkwardness or disjointedness of his bitter lyrics is unintentionally emphasized by this kind of non-production, a frustrating undercutting of Kuepper's compositional efforts.

By the time they cut **History of Rock n' Roll Volume One**, though, all the gears meshed. The Clowns turn out music perversely unillustrative of the title, but with its own dark force and rich, occasionally abrasive textures: swaggering, punching horns, sedate, melodic piano, scratchy, tinny guitar and sliding, stretching acoustic bass, all underpinned by frenetic but authoritative drums. Bravo!

Unfortunately, that apotheosis didn't last. **Ghosts** is more controlled than **Law of Nature**, clarity-wise as well as compositionally, but as before it's awkward; the lapses of the drums and sax seem unnecessarily (if unintentionally) overemphasized. The songs seem to be making gestures in the direction of more "normal" structure and style without any commitment to that (or any other) direction.

Gone solo, Kuepper grasped some key elements of the later Clowns sound (notably the use of horns to voice songs' signature riffs) but otherwise opted to skin it back to much more conventional and accessible folk-rock on **Electrical Storm**. **Rooms of the Magnificent** took this to another level, displaying much musical variety, even within the same number: "Show Pony" is a quiet, folkish tune which adds horns, which gives way to "Suzie Q"-ish riffing that becomes a coda nearly as long as the song, as guitars and piano flail away like the end of "Layla" gone angry. "Also Sprach the King of Euro-Disco" mates a faintly "Zarathustroid" chord sequence, a James Bondish guitar lick, cool female backing voices, and a killer horn riff.

All of this supports lyrics which twist clichés, making them sardonic (or flat-out bizarre) via voice-tone, juxtaposition or both. The album should have gotten him more attention in America, and it did: Capitol picked up **Everybody's Got To**, although nothing came of it, commercially speaking. Too bad—it's a further refinement of the distinctively blended arrangements of the previous two albums: intelligent, infectious rock-'n'roll that, without being at all avant, sounds like nobody else. (**Not a Soul Around** takes its title track from **Everybody's Got To**, adding two from **Rooms** and the title track of **Electric Storm**.)

With his career going absolutely nowhere, Kuepper dropped everyone in his band except drummer Mark Dawson, became Today Wonder and cut an acoustic folk LP that includes "If I Were a Carpenter." Has he lost it? Well, no. "Carpenter" ain't so hot, but most of the rest (including treatments of two other chestnuts, "I'd Rather Be the Devil" and "Hey Gyp") is. It's impressive to hear how full acoustic guitars, drums, a cardboard box and a little echo can sound; Kuepper's voice (in a slightly lower register here) is even better than before. Inspirational love song opening: "I've designs on you that come from dirty books." [jg]

See also *Saints*.

LAUGHING HYENAS
Come Down to the Merry Go Round EP (Touch and Go) 1987
You Can't Pray a Lie (Touch and Go) 1989 ●
Life of Crime (Touch and Go) 1990 ●

While three-fourths of this Ann Arbor, Michigan group lays down routine post-punk rock with steady, measured beats (Jim Kimball is a fine drummer) and serious guitar aggression by Larissa Strickland, frontman John Brannon unleashes intelligently irascible/creepy lyrics in a merciless animal shriek that will have you instinctively swallowing to check if *your* throat hurts.

The six-song 12-inch EP, produced (as were the next two records) by Butch Vig, lays out the Hyenas' basic plan, but there isn't enough equilibrium between the understated music and the overdone vocals to be convincing. Bits work, but Brannon's full-throttle efforts leave his bandmates in the dust.

You Can't Pray a Lie gets the balance right. Strickland's charged contributions (it sounds like she's been listening to her Rapeman records) give the singer a high-intensity run for his money. Ironically, while the challenge inspires Brannon to greater feats of frenzy, his roars—mixed to a nearly equal footing with the music—become easier to endure, if not exactly enjoy.

Continuing to organize its four-wheel drive into real forward motion, the Laughing Hyenas lash out with unified vehemence on **Life of Crime**, honoring the spiritual memory of those legendary Ann Arbor forefathers, the Stooges. While the music heats up, Brannon cools down a bit here and there, showing signs that he could yet become an effective rock growler rather than a fringe-weird screamer. (Both eight-song albums are contained on a single CD.) [i]

PETER LAUGHNER
Peter Laughner (Koolie) 1982
ROCKET FROM THE TOMBS
Life Stinks (Jack Slack) 1990

As chronicler of—and prime mover in—the groundbreaking Cleveland underground scene of the early '70s, Peter Laughner (who died in 1977) galvanized one of the most disparate collections of musicians imaginable into a potent and influential (if ultimately short-lived) force. While crediting his prescience, his eulogists all too often ignore the sheer quality of Laughner's own original musical talent. Though Lou Reed was his major influence (particularly as a vocalist), Laughner's work can scarcely be narrowcast as simply tributary. The posthumous album (gleaned from demos and a brace of live shows) reveals a folkier side; nods to Ramblin' Jack Elliott (on "Rag Baby") and Richard Thompson (the melancholy "Baudelaire") don't obscure the true, life-affirming essence of an original.

Rocket from the Tombs, alternately "led" by Laughner, David Thomas (later of Pere Ubu) and/or Stiv Bators (then merely the ex-lead singer of Youngstown glitter-bozos Mother Goose), kept the flames of Detroit stun-rock raging through the early '70s. **Life Stinks**, culled from a local radio broadcast, showcases the band at its best, melding searing shock guitar (by Laughner and Gene O'Connor, who later copped the nom de punque Cheetah Chrome) with spaced-out Germanic doodle on tracks like "30 Seconds Over Tokyo," "Life Stinks" (both Laughner compositions that would grace the Ubu catalogue) and "Ain't It Fun" (a future Dead Boys staple). The lovingly, exhaustively annotated set (which comes with a bonus 7-inch featuring "Transfusion" co-written by Laughner and his ex-wife, Cleveland poet/musician Charlotte Pressler) also includes a bevy of lesser-known tracks that attest to the band's intuitive futurism. Anyone attempting to divine the roots of punk will certainly have their rod set awhirl here.   [dss]

See also *Dead Boys, Pere Ubu.*

CYNDI LAUPER

She's So Unusual (Portrait) 1984 ●
True Colors (Portrait) 1986 ●
A Night to Remember (Epic) 1989 ●

She's So Unusual certainly didn't sound like a multi-platinum record on first listen, but that just goes to show you. Originally recognized as the only memorable member of New York's unlamented Blue Angel, Lauper's big voice grew to scarifying proportions under the sympathetic production of Rick Chertoff, supported by the able playing of Eric Bazilian and Rob Hyman, leaders of Philadelphia's then-obscure Hooters. Lauper's songwriting was just getting started, so the album draws on outside material—a potentially disastrous minefield—which proved superb, from the Brains' "Money Changes Everything" (much better in Lauper's live 45 version than on the album's somewhat turgid rendition) to Prince's unforgettable "When You Were Mine" and, of course, Robert Hazard's "Girls Just Want to Have Fun." With talent, easy confidence and self-deflating humor, the colorful Lauper won countless hearts, injecting warmth and graciousness into the mega-pop world.

Two years later, the inevitable letdown of **True Colors** is fairly serious as Lauper, who co-produced and co-wrote most of the material, takes bad spills on both fronts. While "Maybe He'll Know" and "True Colors" are wholeheartedly wonderful, "Change of Heart" and a cover of Marvin Gaye's "What's Going On" are sabotaged by overzealousness (especially the bombastic drumming) on the former and blandness on the latter. Considering what a unique and remarkable singer Lauper is, the squandering of her gifts on this uninspired, halfbaked throwaway is tragic.

Seemingly with nowhere to go but up, Lauper then made—after a lengthy delay during which the record was advertised in *Billboard* as **Kindred Spirit**—a record that is even worse. Reeking of commercial trepidation, **A Night to Remember** showcases a no-two-the-same set of vocal guises in service of mediocre,

often bizarre material by various hits-for-hire songwriters. "My First Night Without You" recaptures some of Lauper's brassy allure, but an artist whose initial popularity sprang from her charmingly casual aplomb shouldn't sound this anxious. Scratchy snippets of imitation Appalachian folk, coy novelties ("Like a Cat," "Insecurious"), a Joan Armatrading soundalike, a melodramatic Spectorish torch song—it's all here, and none of it works.   [i]

See also *Blue Angel.*

LAVA HAY

Lava Hay (Nettwerk-Polydor) 1990 φ

On its American debut, this Toronto duo sounds like half the Bangles. Steve Berlin's hack-in-a-coffee-house rock production (lose the flute, guys) lays too heavy a burden on Michèle Gould and Suzanne Little, who write nice but unspectacular folk-pop romances and sing them with liquid, uplifting harmonies. Lava Hay is certainly talented, but **Lava Hay** doesn't have the magic (or even the hooks) to be anything more than a passing warm breeze.   [i]

LAWNDALE

Beyond Barbecue (SST) 1986
Sasquatch Rock (SST) 1987 ●

As part of an effort to change its image and expand its scope beyond the confines of punk, SST signed this surf-guitar quartet from Lawndale (the Southern California town where the label is based) and released two albums of winning twang. Staking a claim on '60s West Coast beach instrumentals, Lawndale plays original compositions (plus occasional offbeat borrowings, like "Interstellar Caravan," credited to Pink Floyd *and* Duke Ellington) with unaffected enthusiasm and spunk. The only indication of the band's '80s orientation is song titles like "The Story of Vanna White," "The Days of Pup & Taco," "March of the Melted Army Men" and "Sasquatch Rock."

The second album has a less-specific period feel and exchanges Mosrite clarity for ambitious clutter (adding fuzzbox, harmonica and even a fleeting "Robert Plant vocal" on "Take Five," which quotes "Whole Lotta Love"), but both promise a refreshing dip into delightful, if well-charted, waters.   [i]

LAWSON SQUARE INFIRMARY

See *Triffids.*

LAZY COWGIRLS

Lazy Cowgirls (Restless) 1985
Tapping the Source (Bomp!) 1987
Third Time's The Charm (Aus. Grown Up Wrong) 1988
Radio Cowgirl (Sympathy for the Record Industry) 1989
How It Looks: How It Is (Sympathy for the Record Industry) 1990

By the time a pair of ne'er-do-well Hoosier punks rechristened themselves Axl and Izzy and headed west to the promised land, the core of Vincennes, Indiana's Lazy Cowgirls had already blazed that trail, absorbing many of the same substances (both aurally and otherwise) while retaining the ingrained grittiness and knee-jerk bad attitude that marks 'em as true punks. The quartet's self-titled debut is a near-perfect crystallization of everything that was right about pre-Anglomaniac punk: the Dictators' fuck-'em-if-they-can't-take-a-joke mentality, the Dolls' loving R&B butchery and (most importantly) the Ramones' strum *und* bang "subtlety." On the first Cowgirls album, "Time" and "Drugs" are especially Brudda-like in their eloquently monosyllabic exploration of said subjects.

Realizing that a repeat performance might brand them as nostalgists, combined with a bit of bonding with speed-poet auteur Chris D., the Cowgirls were pushed to create their masterwork—the amphetaminized **Tapping the Source**. The bitterness that lurks just beneath Allen Clark's hyperspeed Sandy Nelson beats makes songs like "Heartache" and "Goddamn Bottle" (perhaps the finest cry-in-your-suds punk tune ever) truly affecting. This no-hope factory-town blues just can't be learned; the Cowgirls are steeped in it.

Third Time's the Charm (which features a sidesplitting side-long interview with the band) is a bit flat but, even when the music veers towards standard hardcore structures, there's layers of subtext (about only the most pressing subjects, of course: liquor, cheatin' and the Christianization of Larry Flynt).

Radio Cowgirl, which documents one of the band's legendary excessive live sets (minus the sorely missed visual aspect of the diminutive and balding dervish frontman Pat Todd), boasts chafing-at-the-bit covers of the Saints' "Know Your Product" and the Ramones' "Carbona Not Glue." It's also notable as the first release on Sympathy for the Record Industry, a prolific label that repeatedly attests to the huge impact Todd and company have had on their city's punk scene.

Alleged to be the band's swansong, **How It Looks** never downshifts from overdrive, but the wheels are often left spinning. Generic blitzkrieg bops like "Teenage Frankenstein" and "Sex Kittens Compare Scratches" are conceptually hackneyed and musically shopworn. Then again, Todd's sneering delivery alone can carry hate missives like the title track and the very Pagans-like "D.I.E. in Indiana." If they've indeed ridden into the smog-shrouded sunset for the last time, the Lazy Cowgirls have left quite a legacy—and staked a pretty secure claim to being the Last True Punk Rock Band. [dss]

LEAD INTO GOLD
See *Ministry*.

LEAGUE OF CRAFTY GUITARISTS
See *Robert Fripp*.

LEAGUE OF GENTLEMEN
See *Robert Fripp*.

LEAGUE UNLIMITED ORCHESTRA
See *Human League*.

PAUL LEARY
See *Butthole Surfers*.

LEAVING TRAINS
Well Down Blue Highway (Bemisbrain-Enigma) 1984
Kill Tunes (SST) 1986 ●
Fuck (SST) 1987 ●
Transportational D. Vices (SST) 1989 ●
Sleeping Underwater Survivors (SST) 1991 ●

Co-produced by Rain Parader David Roback and featuring a guest drummer from Gun Club and a keyboard player from Green on Red, **Well Down Blue Highway** makes it clear that Leaving Trains, a Pacific Palisades trio, is well-connected in the California nuevorock/folk/blues community. Unlike many new bands, they don't sound like R.E.M. and are neither psychedelic, country nor otherwise '60s-derived, which makes **Well Down Blue Highway** individual, but hard to characterize. Falling James' introspective songs and unaffected, clumsy vocals form the basis of the sound and personality, eschewing complexity, hooks and smoothness in favor of dry, blunt rock'n'roll.

With **Kill Tunes**, the Trains opt for a bopping punk edge. The LP is particularly inspired by the early Saints ("Private Affair" from **Eternally Yours** is covered) and manages to continuously shift gears, from shitkicking 4/4 like "She's Looking at You" and "Black" to lighter ballads ("Light Rain" and "Kinette"), with an appropriate mixture of humor ("A Drunker Version of You" is a blast), anger, sadness and restlessness.

Fuck debuts a new lineup with Falling James (Moreland) as the quartet's only holdover and is even more of a slam-bang affair. The songs come in one-minute blasts like "How Can I Explode?"—no frills, just start 'em up and let 'er rip. **Fuck**'s overall manic tone makes it half the album **Kill Tunes** is, but so long as you can get mounted on this wild bronco, it's an exciting ride. Afterwards, the LP winds up with a nine-and-a-half-minute dirge called "What the President Meant to Say," offering listeners plenty of time to recuperate.

Transportational D. Vices is so similar that it might as well be titled **Fuck II**. Again characterized by blink-and-you'll-miss-'em 4/4 blowouts and James' so-spontaneous-they-must-be-one-take vocals, the Trains nevertheless integrate a bluesy skanker ("Dude the Cat") and two driving, cool rockers ("Any Old Time" and "You're Never Gonna Love Me Anymore") that would do **Kill Tunes** justice. There's also a striking rendition of the Urinals' (later known as 100 Flowers) anti-pop obscurity, "Black Hole." Fun from start to finish.

One of America's most reliable, simple, high-octane rock'n'roll bands with chops, attitude and commitment to chaos, Leaving Trains released a new album, **Sleeping Underwater Survivors**, in early '91 and reportedly have another LP in the can. Stay tuned. [i/jr]

KEITH LEBLANC
See *Tackhead*.

JACK LEE
See *Nerves*.

TIM LEE

See *Windbreakers*.

LEGAL WEAPON

No Sorrow EP (Arsenal) 1981 (Triple X) 1991 ●
Death of Innocence (Arsenal) 1982 (Triple X) 1991 ●
Your Weapon (Arsenal) 1982 (Triple X) 1991 ●
Interior Hearts (Arsenal) 1986 (Triple X) 1991 ●
Life Sentence to Love (MCA) 1988

No Sorrow—five slices of catchy rock in an early X/Avengers mode—documents the earliest version of this Southern California punk outfit, when it contained bassist Patricia Morrison, late of the Bags. With Morrison headed off to a more visible career with Gun Club and Sisters of Mercy, however, **Death of Innocence** catapulted Legal Weapon into greatness, and is one of the last decade's most underrated punk albums. From start to finish it goes all-out, song after darkly astringent song. Brian Hansen's loud, Ramones-meet-Stones guitar riffs mesh with dynamic rhythm playing; Kat Arthur possesses a wonderfully sensual whiskey voice, like a hardcore Janis Joplin. From galvanizing rockers like "Daddy's Gone Mad," "Waiting in Line," "War Babies" and a redone "No Sorrow" to the anti-incest drama of "Don't Pretend" and the superb, disillusioned title track, the material is tightly arranged and powerful, replete with gritty hooks and complex, semi-metallic twists. Members of the Adolescents help out on bass and rhythm guitar.

Wasting no time, Legal Weapon quickly whipped out the nearly-as-amazing **Your Weapon**, packaged in an elaborate fold-out poster. While not quite as consistent, it has basically the same sound as its predecessor, but with meatier production and a solid, fulltime rhythm section. Arthur once again pushes the material—especially the epic ballad "Only Lost Today" and the bluesy-punk anthem, "Equalizer"—to compelling heights. On "The Stare," the raw mix of lust and vulnerability in her voice is a revelation.

Legal Weapon signed to a major label around 1984 and began recording an album. But the project fizzled and **Interior Hearts**—a likable but disappointing LP, with thin sound and more of a country/blues flavor (again, like then-current X)—appeared on their own label instead.

That record is a gem compared to **Life Sentence to Love**, which totally blows. Having finally done the big time deal, Legal Weapon serve up a keyboard-laden cross between Heart and the Cult over which Arthur tries to emote. Re-recorded versions of "Interior Hearts" and "Tears of Steel" from the previous album are not improvements; the old spark and power are nowhere to be found. A life sentence to oblivion is more like it. [gef]

See also *Gun Club, Sisters of Mercy*.

LEGENDARY PINK DOTS

Chemical Playschool [tape] (nr/Mirrodot) 1981
Kleine Krieg [tape] (nr/Mirrodot) 1981
Brighter Now (Bel. Terminal Kaleidoscope-Play It Again Sam) 1982 ●
Curse (Bel. Terminal Kaleidoscope-Play It Again Sam) 1983 ●

Faces in the Fire (Bel. Terminal Kaleidoscope-Play It Again Sam) 1984 ●
The Tower (Bel. Terminal Kaleidoscope-Play It Again Sam) 1984 ●
Greeting 9 (It. Materiali Sonori) 1984
The Lovers (Hol. Ding Dong) 1985
Asylum (Bel. Play It Again Sam) 1985 ●
Curious Guy EP (Bel. Play It Again Sam) 1986
Island of Jewels (Bel. Play It Again Sam) 1987 ●
Stone Circles: A Legendary Pink Dots Anthology (Play It Again Sam) 1987 ●
Any Day Now (Play It Again Sam) 1987 ●
The Golden Age (Play It Again Sam) 1988 ●
Legendary Pink Box (Bel. Play It Again Sam) 1989
The Crushed Velvet Apocalypse (Play It Again Sam) 1990 ●
The Maria Dimension (Play It Again Sam-Caroline) 1991 ●

EDWARD KA-SPEL

Laugh China Doll (Hol. Torso) 1984 (nr/Play It Again Sam) 1989 ●
Eyes! China Doll (Hol. Scarface) 1985
Cheykk, China Doll (Hol. Torso) 1986
Perhaps We'll Only See a Thin Blue Line (nr/Play It Again Sam) 1989

TEAR GARDEN

Tired Eyes Slowly Burning (Can. Nettwerk) 1987 (Nettwerk-Capitol) 1990 ●

Formed in London around 1980, the Legendary Pink Dots relocated to Amsterdam in the middle of the decade, using that city as the basis for an enormously productive and diverse career that—despite clear crypto-pop accessibility amid occasionally excessive psychedelic exotica—has remained well below commercial radar. Proceeding out of a hodgepodge of gloomy/fringey/hippie antecedents—Joy Division, Syd Barrett, Faust, etc.—but adding a classical sensibility, involuted mythology, found-sound sampling weirdness, plus all sorts of stylistic cross-mingling and experimentation, Edward Ka-Spel (vocals, lyrics, keyboards), Phil Knights (aka The Silver Man; keyboards) and a shifting collection of associates have turned the Legendary Pink Dots into an open-ended adventure. Although certainly prone to enigmatic risk-taking, the enormously resourceful LPD is a mellifluous and dynamically restrained proposition: this is one dip into the rock netherworld that won't send you running for cover. The lyrics, however—a disturbing onslaught of doom, violence and apocalypse—are a different story.

After years of Europe-only releases, the Dots issued the **Stone Circles** compilation, an introductory essay of selected album tracks and one new track. With the ice thus melted, all of the group's subsequent albums have been issued Stateside (save for the limited-edition **Legendary Pink Box** set: three albums' worth of rarities, unreleased items, alternate versions and compilation contributions).

Opening with a majestic church organ that suddenly goes all wobbly, **Any Day Now** is a lovely album of songs with strong (dare it be said—catchy?) melodies and a blend of electro-pop and classical arrangements. Ka-Spel's preternaturally calm multi-tracked singing helps focus the diverse instrumentation, which includes violin, horns and harmonium; real-world sound effects add a strong dramatic element.

Lyrically, **The Golden Age** is a concept drama about a psychopath stalking his former lover, a model (?) who taunts him from the TV screen and magazine pages. The chilly and suavely spare continental music—imagine a dessicated version of the Pet Shop Boys—does little to distract from Ka-Spel's nearly dissolute delivery, which wavers in and out of Gary Numanesque melodrama. Elegantly, deceptively powerful.

Several tracks on **The Crushed Velvet Apocalypse**—a pleasant but creatively anemic outing—interrupt scenes of pastoral musical beauty with musique concrète noises; "The Green Gang" runs sitar/tabla meanderings into twittering flutes and winds up building a quietly disturbing skein of motorway noise. "The Death of Jack the Ripper"—an artfully lurid, slow-paced horror tale accompanied by the electronic sound of water dripping—comes as a grisly jolt on an album that begins with "I Love You in Your Tragic Beauty," an affectingly sad acoustic-guitar-plus-accordion pop song that strongly suggests the TV Personalities, and ends with the offbeat but enticing "New Tomorrow."

The Dots expend more effort on **The Maria Dimension**, a highly imaginative but relatively straightforward (for this decidedly bent group) and consistently engrossing collection that romps ambitiously—and, more often than not, successfully—through colorful '60sish psychedelia, electronics, disconcerting sound effects and baroque pop. A most entertaining and stimulating trip.

Besides making a handful of solo albums, the prolific Ka-Spel collaborated with members of Skinny Puppy on the Tear Garden album. [i]

See also *Skinny Puppy*.

RAY LEMA
See *Stewart Copeland*.

LEMONHEADS
Laughing All the Way to the Cleaners EP (Huh-Bag) 1986
Hate Your Friends (Taang!) 1987
Creator (Taang!) 1988
Create Your Friends [CD] (Taang!) 1989 ●
Lick (Taang!) 1989 ●
Lovey (Atlantic) 1990 ●
Favorite Spanish Dishes EP [CD] (Atlantic) 1991 ●

Boston's Lemonheads must have great record collections. Throughout a five-year (and counting) career fraught with lineup upheavals, the core (until 1990) of bassist Jesse Peretz and guitarists/singers/drummers Evan Dando and Ben Deily seemed able to absorb loads of different rocks (punk-, hard-, even folk-) and toss off nugget after nugget of pure pop.

The brief introductory 7-inch contains four raw and restless poppy punk songs, three of which eventually turned up on later albums. With tuneless hardcore tantrums, noisy guitar raunch *and* pristine power pop, **Hate Your Friends** is a jarring and frustrating debut LP whose jewels ("Second Chance," "Don't Tell Yourself It's OK," "Uhhh" and the remarkable Saints soundalike "Fed Up") luckily manage to outweigh the dross.

As the young quartet continued to do its growing up in public, **Creator** has more ambitious arrangements, and the influence of such bands as Mission of Burma

and the dB's can be sensed in songs like "Clang Bang Clang" (later redone, on **Lovey**, as "Left for Dead") and "Take Her Down." Unfortunately, a couple of pretty numbers are marred by wretched Hallmark-card sentiments. One neat surprise: a fairly reverent cover of Kiss' old "Plaster Caster." (Both albums were later combined on the **Create Your Friends** CD.)

In 1989, the same year Dando served as the Blake Babies' bassist, the Lemonheads gained some notoriety with a bracing, off-the-cuff version of Suzanne Vega's "Luka." That track (and, on the CD, an effective electrified stab at Patsy Cline's "Strange") highlight the schizophrenic **Lick**, which counters almost every clever move (like the appropriation of the *All in the Family* theme on "7 Powers") with a misguided dead end (like the trite "Anyway").

(The Lemonheads had a 1990 UK hit with another cover version, Mike Nesmith's "Different Drum." That track, and its two Dando-penned B-sides, were later issued Stateside on **Favorite Spanish Dishes**, a five-song CD with tributes to the Misfits and New Kids on the Block.)

With the departure of Deily, Dando—for years the group's creative force and chief songwriter—stepped to the fore. While the move to a major label thankfully did nothing to undercut the Lemonheads, Dando's sensitive side is very much in evidence on **Lovey**. The R.E.M.-ish "Half the Time," BÖC-ish "(The) Door" and Gram Parsons' "Brass Buttons" reveal a punk kid almost all grown up, with no qualms about expressing his perhaps unfashionable faves/influences. Dando's lyrical preoccupations may seem a little strange at times: he quotes (and discusses) Charlie Manson on "Ballarat," offers an ode to pot on the wah-wah workout "Li'l Seed" and embraces true mundanity in "Stove," a song about getting rid of one. The sole Lemonhead remaining after a post-LP split, Dando reportedly performed much of **Lovey** himself. If so, that's quite an achievement, as it's a fine, varied collection. [db]

See also *Blake Babies*.

LEN BRIGHT COMBO
See *Wreckless Eric*.

LEONARDS
The Leonards (Rock Ranch) 1988

Considering the mediocrities that constantly get signed out of the Hollywood club scene, it's amazing that a band like the Leonards can deliver a red-hot seven-cut indie album like this and still be ignored by the majors. **The Leonards** contains nothing but searing, sneering garage rock'n'roll—'60s in construction, '80s in energy. The band has no pose to sell, just good tunes executed with verve and skill. Guess that explains it.

[ds]

LEOPARDS
Kansas City Slickers (Moon) 1977
Magic Still Exists (Voxx) 1988

On first listen, you'd swear that the 1977 indie album from Kansas City, Kansas is **Muswell Hillbillies**-era Kinks—and on second and third listen, as well. This talented foursome not only perfectly re-creates the

Kinks' klassic sound (complete with a spot-on Ray Davies vocal impression by main Leopard Dennis Pash), they also turn out originals that subtly rewrite various Kinks tunes without ever resorting to obvious lifts. Genius.

By the time the Leopards got around to releasing another album more than a decade later, the Kinks had a lower profile than ever, which makes **Magic Still Exists** a most welcome arrival. On its opening track, the hyper "Block Party," the band threatens to stake out a style of its own; after that, Pash and friends get back to business, sounding as wonderfully Kinky as ever. Here's hoping they do it again in 1999.   [i/hd]

LEROI BROTHERS
Check This Action (Jungle) 1983 (nr/Demon) 1984
Forget About the Danger Think of the Fun EP (Columbia) 1984
Lucky Lucky Me (Profile) 1985
Protection from Enemies (nr/Demon) 1985
Open All Night (Profile) 1986 •
Viva Leroi (Fr. New Rose) 1989 •

BALLAD SHAMBLES
Ballad Shambles EP (Skyclad) 1988

HAND OF GLORY
Far from Kith and Kin (Skyclad) 1990 •
Here Be Serpents (Skreamin' Skull-Skyclad) 1991 •

It goes without saying that no one in Austin, Texas' LeRoi Brothers is named LeRoi. Debuting on the unpretentious **Check This Action** as a trio (singer/guitarists Steve Doerr and Don Leady and drummer Mike Buck) plus a guest bassist, the LeRois set to rocking without ado, reeling off energetically unreconstructed rock'n'roll/R&B covers (plus a few originals that don't slow down the party one bit) in an unmistakable Southwestern accent. Nothing fancy at all, just solidly American music given a sweaty workout.

Adding singer Joe Doerr and a permanent bassist, and recutting "Ain't I'm a Dog" (dig that syntax!) from the first LP, the LeRois entered the big leagues with six greasy slices of fun, **Forget About the Danger**. Burning with the hellfire spirit of Jerry Lee Lewis (only lacking his pumping piano), songs like "Treat Her Right" and "D.W.I." state the band's case with conviction and maximum excitement.

With Evan Johns replacing guitarist Don Leady (who went on to form the Tail Gators), **Lucky Lucky Me** is even better—a full menu of high-energy tunes played for keeps. "Fight Fire with Fire," the zydeco-tinged "The Back Door" and a quick history lesson, "Elvis in the Army," are among the highlights. (**Protection from Enemies** is the same album with an alternate title, cover and song sequence.)

The following year, a four-man lineup (Joe Doerr is gone; Johns has returned to his own career, replaced by Rick Rawls) led by Steve Doerr and Mike Buck whipped off the seemingly effortless **Open All Night**, a splendid slice of tasty archetypal Texas R&B that shimmies and howls with understated eloquence from start to finish. (Actually, "Ballad of the LeRoi Brothers," the mock-serious cowboy ballad which closes the album, isn't that great.) Fans of Dave Edmunds are strongly advised not to miss this one.

Dispensing with the traditional electric grit, **Viva Leroi** finds the quartet in a slower and gentler mood (read duller) than usual, playing Buddy Holly-styled Texas pop, Doug Sahm-speed rock, country and a little lightweight N'Orleans gumbo with so little pep and zest that it sounds as if someone's baby might be asleep in the next room. (When new bassist Speedy Sparks sings a song that complains about music being too loud, you know things have gone very wrong.) The record gets interesting (not exciting, mind you) when the idioms bump into each other, as in "Mambo Leroi," which feeds Rawls' Nashville-styled picking into Doerr's pumping accordion, but otherwise this is pretty tepid.

Joe Doerr's Ballad Shambles is a similar (but less rootsy or stylish) quartet. Although hot guitarist Michael Maye (ex-H-Bombs) is the band's main songwriter, the 12-inch EP—which is okay, but no big deal—contains two Joe Doerr tunes and one by his brother Steve. Following that band, Joe formed the far superior Hand of Glory, a diverse and exciting quartet which includes guitarist Bill Anderson (a B.S. holdover) and bassist Tim Swingle (ex-Doctor's Mob). Mixing up cowboy rock, blues, Doorsy atmospherics and more with confidence and creativity, Hand of Glory is a strikingly potent band. Rey Washam (ex-Scratch Acid/Rapeman) is the drummer and co-producer on the fine **Here Be Serpents**.   [i]

See also *Evan Johns and His H-Bombs*.

LET'S ACTIVE
Afoot EP (IRS) 1983 •
Cypress (IRS) 1984 •
Big Plans for Everybody (IRS) 1986 •
Every Dog Has His Day (IRS) 1988 •

Cursed by chronic cuteness, North Carolina's Let's Active is probably the most misunderstood of the South's new pop bands. Though dogged by a rosy-cheeked nicest-guys-of-wimp-pop image, they can be downright moody. Led by *wunderkind* producer/multi-instrumentalist Mitch Easter, the trio began in 1981, but emerged nationally in the wake of R.E.M., whose first two discs Easter co-produced in his now-fabled Drive-In garage studio. Joining that band's label, Let's Active released a six-song EP, **Afoot**, bringing new meaning to such overused pop adjectives as crisp, bright and ringing. All the songs, even those with melancholy lyrics, emerged hook-filled, boppy and ultra-hummable.

But things were not as they seemed. Although perceived as the engineer of the now-sound-of-today in American guitar pop, Easter's own tastes were running towards the electronic gadgetry of techno-rock. Also, his two original partners—bassist Faye Hunter and drummer Sara Romweber—were viewed as sidepeople, notwithstanding Easter's egalitarian efforts to counter that impression. In real life, the trio were not just simple, cheerful popsters. Both Easter's love of "sounds" and the band's inner conflicts were explored on **Cypress**, making it deeper and more enduring, though not as immediately winning as **Afoot**. Denser, rambling textural pieces—some wistful, even angry—came to the fore. Few records sound so multi-dimensional, and Let's Active has, for that reason, been tagged psychedelic—they make sounds you can almost touch. (In 1989, IRS released a single CD of **Afoot** plus **Cypress**.)

Both Romweber and Hunter subsequently left the band. Easter did shows with other players (including Windbreaker Tim Lee), recording **Big Plans for Everybody** piecemeal with four people, including Hunter and two permanent associates: Angie Carlson (the future Mrs. Easter; guitar, keyboards) and Eric Marshall (drums). Far less twinky and hardly cute, **Big Plans** is disturbingly downcast, a doleful version of pop music that isn't about sad things, but still leaves you feeling that way. The album connects emotionally, with offbeat songs that really make an impression.

Adding bassist John Heames and a few dBs of electric power, **Every Dog Has His Day** effectively combines Easter's homey studio approach with co-producer John Leckie's chartworthy British experience. From the blazing-guitars title track and the stomping romance of "Sweepstakes Winner" to the overtly Beatlesque "Mr. Fool," the best songs (most of them on Side One; "I Feel Funny" dominates the flip) are classic Easter: unsettled emotional lyrics and eccentric pop melodies that have him straining on vocal tiptoes to reach the hard bits.   [ep/i]

See also *Snatches of Pink, Sneakers, Windbreakers*.

KEITH LEVENE

2011—Back Too Black EP (Iridescence) 1987
Keith Levene's Violent Opposition EP (Taang!) 1987
Keith Levene's Violent Opposition (Taang!) 1989 [CD]
  (Rykodisc) 1989 ●

Best known for his five-year stint in Public Image Ltd. (ending in 1983 when he was wiped off the finished mix of **This Is What You Want**, resulting in his dubiously legal release of an alternate edition, **Commercial Zone**), guitarist Levene was also an original member of the Clash, but left after a handful of gigs. He also played with Ken Lockie in Cowboys International.

As a solo artist, Levene hasn't done much recording in recent years, but his meager output has managed to create an involved little discography anyway. The first EP consists of simple instrumentals—played on guitar, bass, Fairlight and rhythm machines—in reggae, funk and industrial veins. The four-song second EP, with members of the Red Hot Chili Peppers, Fishbone and Thelonious Monster supporting, contains another dub instrumental (with sax) as well as a pointless copycat version of Hendrix's "If 6 Was 9" (which Rykodisc issued on a 3-inch CD).

The confusingly titled 1989 album (released simultaneously on tape and vinyl by Taang! and on CD by Ryko) combines the two EPs, adding a trivial ska cover and a razor-edge version of John Lennon's "Cold Turkey."   [i]

See also *Public Image Ltd., Jah Wobble*.

LEVI AND THE ROCKATS

See *Rockats*.

GRAHAM LEWIS

See *Dome, Wire*.

LIFE IN A BLENDER

Welcome to the Jelly Days (Fake Doom) 1988

A textbook example of contemporary New Jersey college pop, Life in a Blender brings ample musical (not vocal) skills to witty material on its friendly and lightweight album, nicely produced by ex-Waitress Chris Butler. Don Ralph's nerdy singing (and the occasional embarrassingly adolescent sex lyric) gives the enterprise a certain humility it doesn't really need; his five bandmates' economically neat playing (especially Jon Gregg's crisp guitar work) is hardly ivory tower stuff. On those tracks where Ralph hits his stride and gets a good grip on the melody, **Welcome to the Jelly Days** is quite enjoyable; the annoyingly amateurish episodes undercut the pleasure but don't ruin the record.   [i]

LIGHTNING

Lightning Strike (RCA) 1988 ●

If you've worn out your early Clash records and still can't get enough of the fiery mid-speed sound of '78 Anglopunk, try this enthusiastically derivative London quintet for a good second-hand dose of intelligent and tuneful rock. Adding echoes of various new wave legends, updated lyrics, skillful playing and a bit of hip-hop iconography, Lightning succeeds in reliving a great era with conviction and credibility. The CD adds one track.   [i]

LIGHTNING SEEDS

Cloudcuckooland (nr/Ghetto) 1989 (MCA) 1990 ●

Rock criticism isn't the only refuge for failed musicians: many successful record producers harbor dreams of making their mark on the other side of the studio glass as well. Starting in the '70s, Ian Broudie played guitar in various pivotal Liverpool bands (Big in Japan, Opium Eaters, Original Mirrors) before becoming a prosperous knob-twiddler with Echo and the Bunnymen, the Fall, Icicle Works, etc. In this new phase of his career, Broudie *is* the Lightning Seeds, crafting likable, occasionally spectacular (e.g., "Pure") pop songs with finely modulated arrangements that use new instruments to honor old values. **Cloudcuckooland**'s slick amalgam of familiar styles (the obvious borrowings aren't enough to be annoying) can turn a bit glib, but Broudie's artlessly adequate voice (like Neil Tennant's, but with more melody and less attitude) puts an end to that, making the record's tone as friendly as a puppy. (The CD and cassette add "Frenzy.")   [i]

See also *Big in Japan, Original Mirrors*.

LILACS

See *Green*.

LILAC TIME

The Lilac Time (nr/Swordfish) 1987 (Mercury) 1988 ●
Paradise Circus (Fontana) 1989 ●
& Love for All (Fontana) 1990 φ

Abandoning his solo career and discarding the Tin Tin moniker once and for all, Birmingham singer/songwriter Stephen Duffy formed a band with his brother Nick and a rhythm section. Although the group's idiom is rustic folk-pop rather than catchy dance music, the unfailingly delightful Lilac Time displays the same perfectionist craftsmanship Duffy brought to his solo work.

The Lilac Time is an unprepossessing gem, a collection of jaunty love songs, small-town contemplations and skeptical bits of philosophy brought to life with simple delicacy on acoustic guitar, mandolin, piano, harmonica and beautiful harmonies. (The two CD bonus tracks are "Railway Bazaar" and the elegiac "Gone for a Burton," about the late actor.)

A country-western influence complicates Duffy's romantic songwriting on **Paradise Circus**, an attractive but less glorious album that fits the same folky instrumentation (plus accordion) into fuller, smoother arrangements with horn and string accents. Highlights: "American Eyes," "If the Stars Shine Tonight" and "The Girl Who Waves at Trains."

Half-produced by Andy Partridge (Duffy collaborated with John Leckie on the rest), **& Love for All** brings XTC's involuted art-rock arranging style to bear on Duffy's far less intricate tunes. Although electrifying the Lilac Time (the LP uses plenty of piano played by Billy Bragg sidewoman Cara Tivey and acoustic guitar, but Partridge's tracks rock at about the same level as **Skylarking**) is an iffy proposition, songs like "Fields," the nostalgic "All for Love & Love for All" (which incorporates the Beatles in both lyrics and music), "The Laundry" and the brilliantly XTC-ish "It'll End in Tears (I Won't Cry)" work out fine. But that leaves the less dynamic performances sounding flat. Sometimes you just can't win. [i]

See also *Stephen Duffy*.

LIME SPIDERS

Slave Girl EP (Big Time) 1985
Weirdo Libido EP (Aus. Virgin) 1987
The Cave Comes Alive! (Virgin) 1987 ●
Headcleaner (Aus. Virgin) 1988 φ
Volatile (Caroline) 1988 ●
Beethoven's Fist (nr/Fun After All) 1990 ●

The excellent retro-rock that fills the Lime Spiders' aptly titled **Cave Comes Alive!** album gleefully plunders various '60s punk vaults. Rather than imitating any specific genre, this quartet from Sydney, Australia synthesizes an original version of that musical era with searing guitars, Tony Bambach's exceptional bass work, occasional churning organ, raveup drumming and Mick Blood's hardy singing. Sketchy but unaffected production allows the group to color their songs (plus a swell cover of Cream's "NSU" and a couple of more obscure non-originals) in different shades of black leather, day-glo green and deep purple.

Slave Girl is a compilation of the band's first two Australian 45s: a 1983 double 7-inch and "Slave Girl"/ "Beyond the Fringe." **Headcleaner** is a sixteen-track compilation.

The Spiders' second album is well played but miserably plain, utterly lacking **The Cave**'s colorful personality. With dumb lyrics and pedestrian hard-rock that is less inspired by the past than mired in it, **Volatile** does have a few stick-to-your-ribs tunes ("The Other Side of You," the CD-only "Jagged Edge"), but is otherwise old-fashioned in the worst possible way. A needless dance mix of the dismal title track is among the three CD bonuses. [tr]

ERIK LINDGREN

See *Birdsongs of the Mesozoic, Space Negros*.

ARTO LINDSAY/AMBITIOUS LOVERS

Envy (Editions EG) 1984 ●

AMBITIOUS LOVERS

Greed (Virgin) 1988 ●
Lust (Elektra) 1991 φ

PETER SCHERER/ARTO LINDSAY

Pretty Ugly [CD] (Bel. Made to Measure) 1990 ●

Lindsay, an American who grew up in Brazil, came to New York in the mid-'70s intent on becoming an artist. Only later did he adopt music as his medium and develop a unique percussive style of singing and playing guitar—generally around the beat, seldom on it—and no melodies, thank you. His guitar is untuned; his voice strains to deliver its quota of sounds. (Lindsay's two main vocal influences are James Brown and the sound of people screwing.) In assembling the Ambitious Lovers, Lindsay balances the electronic expertise of Peter Scherer with Brazilian percussionists and injects himself as the catalyst, with help from Mark Miller of the Toy Killers.

On **Envy**, Lindsay and five Lovers recapitulate his career—the tight, anti-melodic structures of DNA, the charging funk-noise of the Golden Palominos—yet deliver something new as well. "Let's Be Adult" is an unabashed dancefloor move and, on "Dora," Lindsay turns crooner, caressing a soulful melody anyone could hum. The catch is that it's in Portuguese—oh, that Arto! Lindsay's words are tantalizingly oblique, but there's nothing oblique about his record's lusty cry for recognition.

The Ambitious Lovers then settled down to a duo of Lindsay and keyboardist Scherer, although John Zorn, Vernon Reid, Naná Vasconcelos and others make contributions to **Greed**. Still frequently spattered with nutty noises, the album is surprisingly accessible; Arto's singing (again in English and Portuguese) rarely requires listener indulgence. So if "King" contains some impressive chicken squawk guitar and a houseful of Latin percussion instruments, the song itself is reasonably mainstream. Whether **Greed** is viewed as a commercial compromise or a more subtly subversive undertaking than the first LP, the mixture of normalcy and extremism gives it fascinating dynamic tension.

Pretty Ugly consists of ballet and theater commissions Scherer and Lindsay undertook between the first two Ambitious Lovers LPs. Mostly instrumental, the disc offers a tonic to those who deemed **Greed** too mainstream. This sonic feast, including the 26-minute title cut, brims with jarring sounds and rhythms but it coheres just as well—and as unexpectedly—as late DNA material.

Still reflecting a strong Brazilian influence, the Lovers' next album, **Lust**, ventures even further into commercial realms than **Greed**, eschewing the short, quirky song fragments that were dotted among the more accessible numbers on the previous album and going for an overall smoother feel. The group remains artistically uncompromised, however; one might say that Scherer and Lindsay are as mersh as they wanna be. And as funky, too: the group's cover of Jorge Ben's classic "Umbabarauma" is an irresistible dancefloor workout. **Lust** has enough of that unique Lindsay guitar squeal to keep the old-timers interested, but traditionalists might be disappointed that Arto's turning into an out-and-out crooner—and a damn good one at that. His lyrics, almost exclusively dealing with romance and sexuality, remain as peculiarly trenchant as ever—in that department, he's a postmodern Cole Porter. With all that going for it, plus the always innovative and intriguing sonic textures Scherer so effortlessly weaves, **Lust** is another solid and dazzling work in the Ambitious Lovers' canon. But what happens when they run out of deadly sins? [mf/i/gk]

See also *DNA, Golden Palominos, Lounge Lizards, Love of Life Orchestra*.

LIQUID LIQUID

Liquid Liquid EP (99) 1981
Successive Reflexes EP (99) 1981
Optimo EP (99) 1983

Along with labelmates ESG, Liquid Liquid exemplified the minimalist funk movement that swept New York's music underground in 1981. The band's impressive five-song debut (one side recorded live) fuses metalphones with congas, marimba and other percussive gadgetry to create hypnotic urban-tribal funk. Except for the vocals, that goal is realized. **Successive Reflexes** also works, although full-scale production values alter the previously skeletal sound.

Optimo—four more songs on another 12-inch—continues the rhythmic intensity, and is specially notable for "Cavern," an insidious and lengthy bass/drums groove that was later adopted as the musical basis for Grandmaster Flash & Melle Mel's "White Lines (Don't Don't Do It)." [gf/i]

LIVE SKULL

Live Skull EP (Massive) 1984 ●
Bringing Home the Bait (Homestead) 1985
Cloud One (Homestead) 1986
Don't Get Any on You (Homestead) 1987
Dusted (Homestead) 1987 ●
Snuffer EP (Caroline) 1988 ●
Positraction (Caroline) 1989 ●

Droning and dragging rusty guitar streaks and deep stormy basslines as dark as bus exhaust, Live Skull combine great grating sheets of guitar shimmer with deliberately monotonous vocals to create swirling intense tunes that you couldn't hum if a loaded gun were aimed at your head. As part of the same New York avant-noisy scene that spawned Sonic Youth, Lydia Lunch and the Swans, Live Skull records come complete with creepy lyrics, circular melodies and nod-out drum beats designed to lull you into their macabre world.

The quartet plays slow, grinding hypno-rock on **Live Skull**; there *are* vocals buried in the mix but you won't notice them much. The relentless wash of semi-organized guitar noise is clearly the band's focal point. The promising **Bringing Home the Bait** features livelier tempos; some tracks move along at a good tear. Guitar textures vary from an atonal din to Killing Joke-style ringing quasi-metal; parts of "Skin Job" sound exactly like Hüsker Dü. Newly prominent vocals, whether by bassist Marnie Greenholz or guitarists Mark C. and Tom Paine, are all appropriately snarly.

Recorded by the same lineup (as usual, working with producer Martin Bisi), **Cloud One** is quite similar to **Bringing Home the Bait**, although a temperate mood, increasing tightness and undercurrents of mutant pop melody (in the title track, for instance) hold the promise of more widely accessible artistic realms in the group's future.

The live Live Skull album, **Don't Get Any on You**, was recorded at CBGB in New York at the end of 1986 and contains brutal dominance-and-feedback renditions of "Skin Job" and "Sparky" (from **Bait**), "I'll Break You" and "The Loved One" (from **Cloud One**), several previews of the upcoming **Dusted** (including "Debbie's Headache") and Curtis Mayfield's "Pusherman" (Live Skull had previously issued their studio version of the song on a 12-inch single) and others. The cassette adds "Brains Big Enough," a live track recorded "somewhere in Europe."

Bostonian Thalia Zedek—who had previously exercised her rant'n'roll vocals in Uzi and, before that, Dangerous Birds—joined Live Skull in time for **Dusted**. With her tuneless intensity giving the band a solid kick back towards anarchic clamor, the album returns to deliberate noise storms, now with the added benefit of maddeningly repetitive singing. Make no mistake: Zedek's the perfect sparkplug for Live Skull, but one really has to be in a certain frame of mind (or on a loud subway train) to appreciate such baleful cacophony. (The CD and cassette add a bonus track.)

Zedek's stylistic integration into the group's music is much better on **Snuffer**. (All six songs possess one-word titles like "Was," "Step" and "Straw.") Besides sinking her deep into the mix along with the other loud instruments, the effectively textured record benefits from a variety of tempos and the complex, interwoven guitar figures. Far more listenable than **Dusted**, **Snuffer** focuses the band's power enough to give it impact.

Sonda Andersson (ex-Rat At Rat R) replaced Greenholz on **Positraction**, an occasionally excessive but generally likable song-oriented record that strips back the noise to reveal succinct and dynamic rock with atmosphere and distortion. Mark C. and Tom Paine have become extremely adept at building interconnected guitar lines, and Zedek's strength has been channeled, at least part of the way, into emotional expression of such hardhearted sentiments as "Anger is a crowbar that you must learn to fight for." The material isn't especially noteworthy but, as an indication that Live Skull is willing to come into the sonic open, **Positraction** is a most welcome development. (The CD appends **Snuffer**.)

See also *Of Cabbages and Kings*. ['e/dgs/i]

LIVE WIRE

Pick It Up (A&M) 1979
No Fright (A&M) 1980
Changes Made (A&M) 1981

After Advertising's demise, guitarist/producer Simon Boswell joined singer/guitarist Mike Edwards' talented London pub band. Live Wire had already released **Pick It Up** (which resembles Kilburn and the High

Roads, or early Dire Straits without the flashy guitar work) when Boswell arrived. Replacing a guitarist named Chris Cutler (not the Henry Cow drummer), he also became the quartet's producer, introducing a slicker, more commercial sound. **No Fright** has no stylistic connection with Boswell's previous band, but it's a worthy companion to other modest pub-veteran documents.

Boswell wields far more audible influence on the charmingly popped-up **Changes Made**, eclipsing Edwards' Knopfleresque rock songs with his own delightful "Don't Look Now" and the collaborative "Child's Eye," which suggest a gutsier version of the Records.

See also *Advertising*.   [i]

LIVING COLOUR
Vivid (Epic) 1988 ●
Time's Up (Epic) 1990 ●
Biscuits EP (Epic) 1991 φ

Led by guitarist and chief composer Vernon Reid (also a music critic and co-founder of the Black Rock Coalition, a New York organization of African-American bands), Living Colour promises more than it delivers on **Vivid**. Because the quartet doesn't match stupid preconceptions about the kind of music people of color should and shouldn't play, the record raised many a bigoted eyebrow. But such issues aside, this is fairly routine hard-rock, loudly produced by Ed Stasium. (Ironically, one of the LP's few funky moments is contained in a version of Talking Heads' "Memories Can't Wait.") But if **Vivid** is lacking in the catchy tune/riff department, at least the topical lyrics are substantial ("Cult of Personality," "Open Letter (To a Landlord)"), occasionally using ironic humor to make a point ("No I'm not gonna rob/beat/rape you, so why you want to give me that funny vibe?"). Reid's guitar cuts loose just once (très flash, though); Mick Jagger's guest production of two tracks makes no audible difference.

With a two-million seller and a tour opening for the Stones behind them, Living Colour (again working with Stasium) made **Time's Up** from a position of considerable strength. When Reid vents his spleen on the coronation of Elvis Presley (in "Elvis Is Dead"), he can now get Little Richard to add his thoughts on the subject. Ambitiously throwing jazzy designs into occasionally thrashy blitzkriegs, the guitarist has plenty of room to peal off dizzying riffs (but no way to avoid speedrock's usual hollowness). In addition, the album has a stronger Afrocentric consciousness than the first, most bluntly in "Pride" ("Don't ask me why I play this music/It's my culture, so naturally I use it"). But the band has more (or less) to say on **Time's Up**: the catchy "Type" offers terminology rather than philosophy, "New Jack Theme" is a nonjudgmental observation and the funky "Under Cover of Darkness" (written by singer Corey Glover) is personal, not political.

At this point, armed with talent and fame, Living Colour seems poised between merely recycling a standard musical form as a vehicle for addressing African-American concerns and pioneering a new style built on the members' rich cross-cultural awareness. If the band can make that transition, the next Living Colour album could be a major event.   [jg/i]

L.L. COOL J
Radio (Def Jam-Columbia) 1985 ●
Bigger and Deffer (Def Jam-Columbia) 1987 ●
Walking with a Panther (Def Jam-Columbia) 1989 ●
Mama Said Knock You Out (Def Jam-Columbia) 1990 ●

Following his electrifying appearance in *Krush Groove* (the film that essentially chronicles the birth of the Def Jam label and the launch of the Fat Boys), New York rapper L(adies) L(ove) Cool J(ames Todd Smith) released **Radio**, a great full-length album ("reduced by Rick Rubin") that promptly went gold. From the monster boombox on the cover to grooves like "I Can't Live Without My Radio" and "You Can't Dance," L.L. touches all the right cultural totems, delivering his sharp-tongued lines with adolescent urgency and a deliciously snotty attitude. The rhythm tracks are stripped-down and aggressive; raps on familiar subjects sidestep clichés and are clever enough to warrant repeated listening.

The double-platinum success of L.L.'s second album (billed as **BAD**) proves that Rubin is unnecessary to his continuing popularity. Released in clean and dirty versions, **Bigger and Deffer** draws on redoubtable innovation to diversify itself out of the basic rap mold. L.L. waxes nostalgic on "Go Cut Creator Go" (which uses Chuck Berry guitar edits), and "The Do Wop," an imaginative '50s/'80s hybrid. "I Need Love" is a touchingly romantic ballad with smoothly melodic instrumental backing; "Ahh, Let's Get Ill" makes considerable use of a backing chorus to set off the rapid-fire rhymes. Meanwhile, back at the same-old-thing ranch, "I'm Bad" picks up on a piece of "The Theme from *Shaft*," "Kanday" touches on classic James Brown and "Get Down" throws the kitchen sink into the hyperactive mix.

While L.L. the producer comes through with inventive tracks (who else could get away with using the *Cheers* theme?) on **Walking with a Panther**, L.L. the rapper is treading water. Granted, his boasts, romantic entreaties and dynamic delivery put most MCs in the ground, but "Jingling Baby," "I'm That Type of Guy" and "Big Ole Butt"—standard sentiments given above-average settings—are pretty much all there is to recommend this lightweight album.

Cars and girls still dominate L.L.'s world on **Mama Said Knock You Out**, but a harder sound (courtesy of producer Marley Marl) and a more aggressive attitude put back some of the intensity and personality that were in short supply the last time out. Besides revisiting his old neighborhood ("Farmers Blvd.") and doing a remix of "Jingling Baby," L.L. describes his ideal woman ("Around the Way Girl"), works his come-on charm ("Mr. Good Bar"), shows off his mobile home ("The Boomin' System") and delivers a standard-issue positive message ("The Power of God"). Except for an annoying habit of repeating phrases over and over (as on the powerful title track), the smooth seducer uses his best moves to get the job done.   [i]

BILL LLOYD
Feeling the Elephant (Throbbing Lobster) 1987 (DB) 1990 ●

Although best known as half of the country duo Foster & Lloyd (whose hip sensibilities are reflected in

387

albums with titles like **Faster & Llouder**), singer/guitarist Bill Lloyd started out as a power-popper. This lovely album consists of song demos he recorded in Nashville between 1983 and 1986. Even fans of F&L's exuberant Everly Brothers-influenced grooves will be unprepared for the rich sounds within: Lloyd displays a heavy Alex Chilton influence as he serves up lush melodies embellished by crisp guitars, topped with sardonic vocals you'd swear were lifted from a Big Star or dB's album. Highlights: the woozy psychedelia of "Everything's Closing Down," the melancholy "Lisa Anne" ("I've got a hole in my life the size of your apartment") and "All at Once You Unzipped," a vicious rocker. Country's gain was clearly rock'n'roll's loss. (The two editions have completely different artwork; the second is remastered.) [jy]

RICHARD LLOYD
Alchemy (Elektra) 1979
Field of Fire (Mistlur-Moving Target) 1985 ●
Real Time (Celluloid) 1987 ●

The former Television guitarist's first solo album is a gem. Assisted by assorted New York scene veterans, Lloyd spins a beautiful, understated web that proves him to be a successful songwriter, a limited but engaging vocalist and a relaxed team player who never hogs the spotlight. The material (especially the wonderful title track and a brilliant ballad, "Misty Eyes") pursues the melodic, sensitive side of late-period Television, ceding all the rough edges and manic intensity to Tom Verlaine.

Six years and several lifetimes later, Lloyd returned from oblivion with an all-new album, recorded in Stockholm with local musicians and first released by a Swedish label. **Field of Fire** is another direct hit: loud, energetic rock with sturdy melodies, intelligent lyrics and confident playing. In spots, Lloyd's singing is too raw-throated to be pleasant, but the material holds up regardless, and the fine guitar work is a fair trade-off. **Field of Fire** bears no resemblance whatsoever to **Alchemy**, but is just as enjoyable.

Lloyd recorded the live **Real Time** album in the comfort of TV's old haunt, CBGB, with a bass/drums/guitar trio. The song selection draws from both solo records, adding a few new numbers—adapting the resultant diversity without incident—and dredging up "Fire Engine" for a bracing opening salvo. Clear production highlights Lloyd's upbeat and articulate singing as well as the thoughtful and passionate guitar work. (With the inclusion of three extra songs at the end, the CD runs almost an hour.) [i]

See also *Television*.

ROBERT LLOYD
See *Nightingales*.

HUW LLOYD-LANGTON
See *Hawkwind*.

LMNOP
LMNOP [tape] (Baby Sue) 1982 + 1984
LMNOP LMNOP [tape] (Baby Sue) 1984

LMNO3 [tape] (Baby Sue) 1985
Elemen Opee Elpee (Baby Sue) 1986
Pony [tape] (Baby Sue) 1988 (Fr. New Rose) 1988
Numbles (Fr. New Rose) 1989 ●

One-man Atlanta power pop auteur Stephen Fievet (aka Don W. Seven) *is* LMNOP, although the drummer of a performing lineup did help on **Elemen Opee Elpee**. (Two non-participants are also pictured for confusion's sake.) The ambitious twinkster, who also draws and publishes a quarterly *Baby Sue* magazine and numerous pamphlets, writes stupendous melodies with substantial lyrics and sturdy hooks, and loads up the perky arrangements with rich guitar tracks, adorable vocal harmonies and febrile invention. Except for an occasional descent into corny puns or gratuitous vulgarity (**LMNO3**'s "Sitting on Uranus" scores in both departments), LMNOP/Fievet offers quintessential alternative pop packed with intelligence and enthusiasm.

The first cassette offers early versions of songs (e.g., "Breakfast Cereal," "Hide in Fiction's Hands," "Sandwich Time for the Smaller Children") Fievet re-recorded for inclusion on **Elemen Opee Elpee** and **Pony**. Despite rudimentary sound quality (drums especially suffer), it's a fine starting point.

Following two more cassette albums, LMNOP finally reached vinyl. The unfailingly perky **Elemen Opee Elpee** contains charming and provocative contemplations on mendacity ("Please Believe Me"), conformity ("The Big Ride"), world peace ("Breakfast Cereal") and the study of anthropology ("Comparitive [sic] Analysis"), all sparked by crisp production and flawless playing. Anyone fond of Shoes, Advertising, Milk'n'Cookies, Sneakers, Three O'Clock, etc. should find the record a most agreeable treat.

Leading off with the brilliant "Idea," the **Pony** tape (issued on vinyl only in France) contains such idiosyncratic outpourings as "Suggestion for Rock Culture in the 90s" and "Automobile History." Not all the songs are of the same quality as on the first vinyl album, but fans won't be disappointed.

LMNOP's darker side (no secret to readers of the deeply disconcerting *Baby Sue*) surfaces in the lyrics of the excellent **Numbles**, whose perky melodies and simple guitar-rock arrangements sound as jolly as ever. As Fievet's delightful voice leads the way, you may find yourself humming to such provocative lines as "You're getting headaches so much of the time/Your memory has run dry and darkness is all you feel" or "How can you take what you've heard and reverse?/I never thought bad could get worse." With nine of the best tracks from **Pony** and **Elemen Opee Elpee** added as a bonus, the **Numbles** CD is an essential LMNOP purchase. [i]

LODGE
See *John Greaves*.

LORA LOGIC
See *Essential Logic*.

LONE JUSTICE
Lone Justice (Geffen) 1985 ●
Shelter (Geffen) 1986 ●

MARIA MCKEE

Maria McKee (Geffen) 1989 ●

It isn't that Lone Justice's first album is bad (it's not), but the ballyhoo that preceded the LA quartet's debut raised expectations that these frisky countryfied rock tunes (Linda Ronstadt on speed, perhaps, or Dolly Parton backed by the Blasters) couldn't possibly satisfy. Maria McKee is an impressive young singer—an energetic, throaty powerhouse with a Southern twang and a slight Patsy Cline catch—and the band is solid enough, but **Lone Justice**, produced by Jimmy Iovine, doesn't come anywhere near extraordinary. Chief songwriter McKee's "A Good Heart," ridden to the top of the British charts in late 1985 by Feargal Sharkey, is far more memorable than anything she penned for her own first record.

Little Steven (a guest on the first album) co-produced **Shelter** with Iovine and Lone Justice, helping the almost-entirely overhauled group (here a loud, vibrant sextet with ex-Patti Smith Grouper Bruce Brody on keyboards) to nail down a dynamic sound that's something like the articulate passion of an old Van Morrison record, pumped up by McKee's gospelly fervor and walloping modern drums. Van Zandt also co-wrote some of the songs, which are far more subtle than before. The first album's religious content is supplanted here by heartfelt emotions about love, faith and morality. Without burying her beliefs, McKee universalizes them in ways that don't require listeners to share anything beyond humanity and sensitivity.

On her solo debut, McKee's voice and songwriting have matured and strengthened, and she sings out like she's got one night onstage in a two-bit bar to prove herself. Unfortunately, Mitchell Froom's production is overbearing, and the endless parade of guest musicians (Richard Thompson, guitarist Marc Ribot, Waterboys fiddler Steve Wickham, drummer Jim Keltner) eventually drains some of the album's personality. Still, "Panic Beach" and "Am I the Only One (Who's Ever Felt This Way?)" are vivid narratives told with literary precision, and when McKee revs into a twangy stomp (like the CD-only "Drinkin' in My Sunday Dress") she's pretty darn irresistible.   [i/kss]

See also *X*.

LONESOME VAL

See *Fear of Strangers*.

ROY LONEY AND THE PHANTOM MOVERS

Out After Dark (Solid Smoke) 1979
Phantom Tracks (Solid Smoke) 1980
Contents Under Pressure (War Bride) 1981
Having a Rock'n'Roll Party (War Bride) 1982
Fast & Loose (Double Dare) 1983
The Scientific Bombs Away!!! (Aus. Aim) 1988
   (Norton) 1989

Singer/guitarist Roy Loney assembled the Phantom Movers after splitting from the Flamin' Groovies in 1975. While the Groovies without Loney turned to merseybeat, Byrds covers and other '60s soundalikes, **Out After Dark** finds him rekindling the pure American rock'n'roll spirit that originally inspired the band. Abet-ted by two ex-Groovies (drummer Danny Mihm and guitarist James Ferrell), Loney excels at straightforward, unsophisticated party music made strictly for fun.

Phantom Tracks consists of smokin' live tracks and new studio cuts that aren't terribly different from the material on **Out After Dark**. The only change worth noting is that about half of the **Phantom Tracks** are out-and-out rockabilly; **Out After Dark**, while rooted in rockabilly, is contemporary-sounding rock'n'roll.

Contents Under Pressure, recorded after both Mihm and Ferrell had left (the former to launch the similarly unreconstructed Kingsnakes in Europe), goes off in a number of directions: Yardbirds-type raveups, rockabilly, ska, heavy metal and even corporate mush. A total failure.

As the name implies, **Having a Rock'n'Roll Party** is a return to what Loney does best, and the results are a big improvement over the previous outing. The band even dips into the Groovies' catalogue for "Gonna Rock Tonight" and "Dr. Boogie." Also released in France, **Fast & Loose** features various lineups (Mihm is back) and includes a version of the Groovies' "Teenage Head."

After another long absence, Loney returned in 1988 with his best record yet, **The Scientific Bombs Away!!!**. What stands out in this jolt of pure manic rock'n'roll is the uniformly strong material and performances, from the hiccupped neo-rockabilly of "Bad News Travels Fast," "Bip Bop Boom" and "Boy, Man!" to the modern rock'n'roll of "Ruin Your Shoes," "Your Best Friend's Number" and "Nobody." There's even c-razy novelty numbers like "Here Comes Curly" and "Nervous Slim," the latter omitted from the album's American release. Not for normals, to be sure, these songs will make you laugh while they rock the socks off your feet.   [ds]

See also *Flamin Groovies*.

LONGHOUSE

See *John Greaves*.

LONG RYDERS

10–5–60 EP (PVC) 1983 ●
Native Sons (Frontier) 1984 ●
State of Our Union (Island) 1985
Two Fisted Tales (Island) 1987 ●
Metallic B.O. [tape] (Long Ryders Fan Club) 1989 [CD]
   (nr/Overground) 1990 φ

TOM STEVENS

Points of View EP (Pulse) 1982

Born in the South but assembled in California, the Long Ryders (who broke up around the end of 1987) color mild '60s revivalism with country stylings (steel guitar, autoharp, mandolin, etc.) on the five-song **10–5–60** EP, produced by Earle Mankey. Pleasant but too easygoing to be earthshaking, Kentucky native Sid Griffin (vocals, assorted stringed instruments) and his three bandmates took care of that business on **Native Sons**, a stirring dose of memorable and unpretentious country-rock that incorporates **Highway 61** Dylan, paisley pop, Kingston Trio balladry and wild rock'n'roll. A guest vocal appearance by Gene Clark legitimizes the Long Ryders' spiritual update of the Byrds' pioneering hybrid. (Griffin made a specific literary statement on behalf of his roots in 1985, when he edited/wrote a biography of Gram Parsons.)

State of Our Union is a big disappointment, an occasionally corny collection of weak melodies, inane lyrics and misguided arrangements. The Ryders seem to have been fooled by their own image. "Looking for Lewis and Clark" is sung in a pathetically bad monotone; other tunes that attempt to align the band with American populist sentiment are only slightly better. Produced in England by Will Birch, it sounds good in spots, but heavyhandedness is clearly no asset.

The Long Ryders found solid footing again with the less selfconscious **Two Fisted Tales**, an enjoyable album nicely produced in a variety of appealing styles by Ed Stasium. The writing is back up to snuff and the natural-sounding presentation makes the group's ethical culture far more palatable. One-song studio visits each by the Bangles and David Hidalgo of Los Lobos are unobtrusive but unneeded—these boys can handle the job nicely by themselves.

Metallic B.O., a spirited cassette-only hodgepodge of live covers, interview snippets and general fooling around, was assembled posthumously by the Long Ryders' fan club (and subsequently issued in abbreviated CD form by a British label). With energetically sloppy renditions of tunes by everybody from Dylan to Public Image Ltd. (not to mention a dandy version of Michael Jackson's "Billie Jean"), it's a fine epitaph, outlining the Ryders' historical pedigree and distilling the punky edge that rarely made it onto their studio recordings.

On his early solo EP, bassist Tom Stevens (joined by two sidemen) plays guitar and sings half a dozen original melodic pop songs that wouldn't fit the band's format but are quite appealing on their own.   [i/hd]

See also *Danny & Dusty*.

LOOP

16 Dreams EP (nr/Head) 1987
Spinning EP (nr/Head) 1987
Heaven's End (nr/Head) 1987 •
Collision EP (nr/Chapter 22) 1988
The World in Your Eyes (nr/Head) 1988
Fade Out (nr/Chapter 22) 1988 (Rough Trade) 1989 •
Eternal–The Singles 1988 (nr/Chapter 22) 1989
A Gilded Eternity (Beggars Banquet-RCA) 1990 •

Frequently likened to Spacemen 3 for their aggressive approach to trance creation, Croydon's Loop create pulsating, nearly impenetrable pieces that are often lunkheaded in their maximal approach to minimalism. (Imagine all the "NO"'s trumpeted on the sleeve of **Metal Machine Music**—panning, phasing, instruments—replaced by "MORE PLEASE!" and you'll begin to get the drift.) But more often, the shadowy quartet is just plain dogged in its pursuit of The Holy Riff; locating said icon, Loop clamps down hard, wielding minor chords like marrow forks, greedily digging out sustenance with all the insane energy of the Stooges, tempered by the fanatical symmetry of German experimenters like Can and Faust.

The germ of that fusion is evident on Loop's first two EPs. Setting the tone, the rudimentary drumming of Bex (the wife of group leader Robert, who like the rest of the band, goes to great pains to hide his surname—in

this case, it's Hampson) brings back fond memories of Teenage Jesus and the Jerks' Bradley Field. (The contents of those two discs, plus an enveloping, drugged-out version of Suicide's "Rocket USA," were repackaged as **The World in Your Eyes**.) **Collision** cut back on the cocooning tendencies; Loop covers the Pop Group's lurching "Thief of Fire," adding brass knuckles to the original's sinewy threat. Released a bit too close to the band's similarly titled album for comfort, **Eternal** is a pairing of **Collision** and "Black Sun," a late-'88 single.

A few lineup changes (and plenty of new effects boxes) later, Loop unleashed the head-nodder's paradise of **Heaven's End**, a mini-album unsettling enough to suit those who keep their noses in the ether and feet planted firmly in the gutter. **Fade Out** heightens the menace a notch. With Robert's husky whisper mixed low, songs like "Black Sun" and "This Is Where You End" would *sound* like odes to Baal even if they were about girls on the beach.

A Gilded Eternity seems like the apex of Loop's trance-essential meditation phase. Cursory listens might leave the impression that not much actually happens in any of these lengthy songs, but concentration reveals catalytic conversions aplenty—from ambient violence to Detroit-drawn thrash. Given the maelstrom they cut a swath through, enervating tests of dub technique are fascinating, perhaps pointing the band in a less static (but no less hypnotic) direction.   [dss]

LOOT!
See *Human League*.

LORDS OF THE NEW CHURCH

Lords of the New Church (IRS) 1982 •
Is Nothing Sacred? (IRS) 1983 •
The Method to Our Madness (IRS) 1984 •
Killer Lords (IRS) 1985
Live at the Spit (nr/Illegal) 1988

BRIAN JAMES
Brian James (Fr. New Rose) 1990 •

Formed by ex-Dead Boy Stiv Bator (following a solo turn and the developmental Wanderers, which must be where he temporarily parked the "s" from his surname) with ex-Damned/Tanz der Youth guitarist Brian James, ex-Sham 69/Wanderers bassist Dave Tregunna and ex-Barracudas drummer Nick Turner, the Lords emerged with a fully realized debut album that draws on their individual and collective strengths. Dense and powerful, with Bator's sneering whine setting the tone and attitude, the Lords combine '60s punk with '80s apocalyptics to create an original sound that updates the Stooges for a post-punk world. Only a few awful, indulgent lyrics (one song attempts a tribute to the New York Dolls by merely stringing song titles together) detract from the record's intense dark power. Highlights: "New Church," "Russian Roulette," "Open Your Eyes." Cool cover: Balloon Farm's "Question of Temperature."

Live at the Spit is a 1982 Boston radio broadcast from the band's first American tour. Sounding more like friendly punks than nascent goth-rockers, the quartet delivers basic live versions of nearly the entire first album, punctuated by Stiv's crudely didactic stage patter. Curious how long ago 1982 was? By way of introducing "Russian Roulette," Stiv announces "The other day we played a really strange game. We passed around six girls and one of them had the clap."

In place of the first LP's claustrophobic, murky production, **Is Nothing Sacred?** substitutes a livelier, crisper swirl; keyboards and horns contrast the band's throaty roar. Thus armed, the Lords unfortunately ran out of material after the first song. Following the excellent "Dance with Me," the album rolls straight down the songwriting slope, stopping off only briefly to ram through the Grass Roots' venerable "Live for Today" to no audible end. As a soundtrack for a gothic punk horror movie, the Lords' second album gets the ambience right, but that's all.

The third outing hits a fair compromise, modulating both the volume and the velocity to lighten the mood and cut the stylishness. As a result, **The Method to Our Madness** resembles a cross between **Raw Power** and **Rebel Yell**. It's the band's least distinctive—but most popular-sounding—record, with "Murder Style," "Method to My Madness" (featuring a funny spoken interjection by IRS owner Miles Copeland) and a pretty ballad, "When Blood Runs Cold," to recommend it. By sacrificing their mystery and danger, the Lords of the New Church are revealed as nice guys after all.

The **Killer Lords** compilation includes not only remixes of essential album tracks but a hysterically nasty mugging of Madonna's "Like a Virgin," a solid and straight reading of John Fogerty's "Hey Tonight," and ex-Advert Tim Smith's duff but amusing "Lord's Prayer."

Putting the Lords on ice in the mid-'80s, James wound up back in the Damned for a spell and then released his first (!) solo album—a miserably pedestrian hard-rock LP (à la Steve Jones' post-Professionals efforts) with only occasional evidence of James' past adventures, if not achievements—in 1990. That same year, it was reported that Bators was forming a band with Dee Dee Ramone and ex-Godfathers guitarist Kris Dollimore. Before anything could come of that alliance, however, Bators was struck by a car in Paris in June '90 and died of his injuries.   [i]

See also *Stiv Bators.*

LORRIES

See *Red Lorry Yellow Lorry.*

LOS LOBOS

... and a time to dance (Slash) 1983
How Will the Wolf Survive? (Slash-Warner Bros.) 1984 ●
By the Light of the Moon (Slash-Warner Bros.) 1987 ●
La Pistola y el Corazón (Slash-Warner Bros.) 1988 ●
The Neighborhood (Slash-Warner Bros.) 1990 ●

VARIOUS ARTISTS

La Bamba (Slash-Warner Bros.) 1987 ●

Lacking serious competition and buoyed by the enormous success of *La Bamba*, Los Lobos are *the* Mexican-American rock band; it wouldn't matter if there were contenders for that honor, however—these four East Los Angelenos (plus ex-Blaster saxman Steve Berlin, who joined in time for the second Slash record)

are peerless masters of their music and a whole lot more. They smoothly incorporate vastly divergent styles—early rock'n'roll, jazz, rockabilly, *norteño*, blues, R&B, Tex-Mex folk music—into a colorful patchwork. The group had self-released an album (**Just Another Band from East L.A.**) in the late '70s, but only came to national attention when the seven-song **and a time to dance** appeared in '83. From a sharp cover of Ritchie Valens' "Come On, Let's Go" to the infectious, accordion-powered "Let's Say Goodnight," singer/guitarist David Hidalgo leads a spicy romp (in two languages) back and forth across musical borders few can traverse with such ease.

How Will the Wolf Survive? is an occasionally more serious venture, delving into heavy blues ("Don't Worry Baby") and tender social commentary ("Will the Wolf Survive?," subsequently a country hit for Waylon Jennings) as well as finding time for a jolly square dance ("Corrida #1") and an airy instrumental ("Lil' King of Everything"). Hidalgo's plaintive tenor and the group's subtlety and skill make the album immediately likable; depth and variety ensure its enduring pleasure.

Poised on the brink of major stardom, Los Lobos stopped to make a limp mainstream album, **By the Light of the Moon**. Under the usually reliable production direction of T-Bone Burnett, the maturing band sheds its richly complex musical personality for a hodgepodge of assimilationist easy-listening crap and ill-advised stylistic dilettantism. "Prenda del Alma," a traditional Spanish ballad, seems horribly out of place; the gritty "Shakin' Shakin' Shakes," co-written by T-Bone and guitarist Cesar Rosas, belongs on a Blasters record; "Set Me Free (Rosa Lee)" is a brassy mess with synth drums. Only "My Baby's Gone," a fine Chicago blues, suggests life in the grooves, but it's not enough to salvage the record.

The obvious choice to re-create the music for *La Bamba*, a moronic bio-pic about Ritchie Valens' brief life and career, Los Lobos faithfully and enthusiastically recorded the highlights of his slim repertoire and vaulted into the pop stratosphere. The skidillion-selling **La Bamba** soundtrack album contains their renditions of "La Bamba," "Come On, Let's Go," "We Belong Together," "Donna," and four more; Brian Setzer (aping Eddie Cochran) and Marshall Crenshaw (finally succumbing to the temptation to play Buddy Holly) each contribute a track as well.

After that massive success, Los Lobos (consigning Berlin to a minimal role) returned to far more substantial music, and a different sort of nostalgia, by making a consciously uncommercial (at least for the American pop audience) acoustic album in Spanish. Recorded and mixed in five days, the brief **La Pistola y el Corazón** wraps the band's warm and enthusiastic embrace around traditional Mexican *canciones* and suitable originals. Except for Hidalgo's sickly violin playing on the instrumental "(Sonajas) Mañanitas Michoacanas," **La Pistola** is as delightful to hear as it must have been therapeutic to record.

Thusly recharged, Los Lobos made an about face and wanged out **The Neighborhood**, an amazingly varied and great rock'n'roll record free of any Latin flavor whatsoever. Aided by John Hiatt, Levon Helm and Jim Keltner, the quintet laces into a blistering boogie snake

("I Walk Alone"), a swampy Little Feat-styled rocker ("Down on the Riverbed"), a pulsing Chicago blues co-written by the legendary Willie Dixon ("I Can't Understand"), a twisting oldie (Jimmy McCracklin's "Georgia Slop") and a twisting original ("Jenny's Got a Pony"). They also downshift effectively for semi-acoustic love songs ("Emily," "Take My Hand"), a tender lullaby ("Little John of God") and a visit to Johnny Cash country ("Deep Dark Hole"). Exciting, evocative and highly satisfying.   [i]

LOUNGE LIZARDS
The Lounge Lizards (EG) 1981 ●
Live from the Drunken Boat (Europa) 1983
Live 79/81 [tape] (ROIR) 1985 [CD] (Fr. Danceteria) 1990 φ
Big Heart Live in Tokyo (Island) 1986
No Pain for Cakes (Island) 1987 ●
Voice of Chunk (Jap. Agharta) 1989 (Verabra) 1989 φ

TEO MACERO/LONDON PHILHARMONIC ORCHESTRA/LOUNGE LIZARDS
Fusion (Europa) 1984

EVAN LURIE
Happy? Here? Now? (Bel. Crépuscule) 1985
Pieces for Bandoneon (Bel. Crépuscule) 1989 ●
Selling Water by the Side of the River (Island) 1990 φ

JOHN LURIE
Stranger Than Paradise (Enigma) 1986 ●
Down by Law (Intuition-Capitol) 1988 ●
Mystery Train (RCA) 1989 ●

Despite some interesting personnel in their initial lineup and a memorable debut album, New York's Lounge Lizards will never be remembered as anything more than an interesting footnote in rock's history. This has less to do with the "fake jazz" label they took for themselves than with the purely social nature of their rock connection: they played jazz-as-exotica to a hip downtown rock-club audience.

Nonetheless, **The Lounge Lizards** remains a minor masterpiece for the way it remains true to its Monk-derived jazz (including two covers of Thelonious Sphere himself) by subverting it still further with Arto Lindsay's atonal guitar playing. Whatever Lindsay may lack as a conventional guitarist, he makes up with an innate rhythmic savvy that never fails to entertain and engage. Ex-Feelies drummer Anton Fier, as a rock player learning the jazz ropes, approaches his kit a bit cerebrally, but ironic detachment was never far from the Lizards' agenda. Saxman John Lurie's compositions here turn out to have been his best, alternating a loving, melodic lilt with film noirish exhilaration.

By the time of **Live from the Drunken Boat**, the Lurie brothers (John and pianist Evan) were playing with a different and less interesting band; the results are slight and forgettable. (Lindsay and Fier went on to lead myriad projects, including, respectively and most notably, the Ambitious Lovers and the Golden Palominos.)

The Lizards joined their producer, Teo Macero (veteran producer/arranger of many a distinguished jazz record), as he indulged his post-romantic orchestral fantasies with the London Philharmonic on **Fusion**, an uninteresting '50s "third stream" symphonic jazz composition.

The **Live 79/81** cassette (later issued on CD as well) features sharp performances from New York (including their first gig), Cleveland, London and Berlin. The core of the debut lineup (the Luries, Fier and bassist Steve Piccolo) remains intact, but two other guitarists besides Lindsay divvy up the tracks. Nine originals, plus covers of Thelonious Monk's "Epistrophy" and Earle Hagen's classic "Harlem Nocturne."

John Lurie went on to star in and score Jim Jarmusch's film Stranger Than Paradise, the album of which devotes a side to an unrelated Lurie dance piece called "The Resurrection of Albert Ayler." His next multi-media collaboration with Jarmusch was Down by Law: Lurie co-starred in the picture and composed the score. **Down by Law** contains his soundtrack music for that film—played by most of the Lounge Lizards and even alumnus Lindsay—as well as music done for a Betty Gordon film entitled Variety. Although he didn't appear in the movie, Lurie also composed music for Jarmusch's next picture, Mystery Train, the soundtrack LP of which is largely made up of appropriate vintage rock'n'roll and R&B numbers.

Evan's first solo piano album, **Happy? Here? Now?**, exhibits an introspective sensitivity not always prevalent in the ensemble's work, but that's not to say it's any less stimulating or intense. While "Tesla's Pigeons" has the power and fury of a piano version of Stravinsky as performed by Birdsongs of the Mesozoic, "Suite from Punch" has such a diversity of feeling, it could easily be the accompaniment to a silent film.

In mid-'86, a new incarnation of the Lounge Lizards—the Luries bolstered by another saxophonist (Roy Nathanson) and a trombonist (Curtis Fowlkes), plus a rhythm section and guitarist Marc Ribot—signed to Island. While the one-show **Live in Tokyo** continues in the Lizards' almost-jazz tradition, the in-studio **No Pain for Cakes** opens up their frame of reference to include influences like Erik Satie and Kurt Weill. And the group breaks the word barrier with John Lurie's distinctive voice on "Bob and Nico" and the anecdotal "Where Were You."

The most novel aspect of **Voice of Chunk** is non-musical: the album was sold by mail-order only. The multi-part compositions are surprisingly humorless, and sound at least as indebted to early-'70s "progressive" rock as to jazz, fake or otherwise. The band's swaggering vocal chorus on Evan Lurie's jaunty "Tarantella" doesn't quite right the emotional balance.

"Tarantella" also turns up, sans vocals, on Evan's own **Selling Water by the Side of the River**. His group features Jill Jaffe's violin and Alfredo Pedernera's bandoneon (button accordion), lending quite an ocean-voyage-salon air to the tango-tinted tunes. The dark, wistful modalities and harmonies make the album more compelling than a mere exercise in good neighbor policy.   [mf/dgs/rs/si]

See also Golden Palominos, Arto Lindsay, Marc Ribot.

BUDDY LOVE
See Alan Milman Sect.

MONIE LOVE

Down to Earth (Eternal-Warner Bros.) 1990 ●

Having made spotlight-grabbing cameos with Queen Latifah, De La Soul, the Jungle Brothers and Fine Young Cannibals, this unaccented London-born rapper (Simone Johnson) leapfrogged to the top echelons of female MCs with a brilliant album of her own. **Down to Earth** follows Latifah's example in mixing up soul, hip-hop and house in a tumult of musical variety all bound together by staunchly independent—and charmingly blunt—feminist lyrics. Love's prickly charisma and sharp wit fills "Monie in the Middle" (an insidiously catchy putdown tale of high school romance and one of three tracks produced by FYC's Andy Cox and David Steele) and the autobiographical "Don't Funk wid the Mo."

One of Love's main topics is the mistreatment of women, and quite a few tracks—"Pups Lickin' Bone," "It's a Shame (My Sister)," "R U Single," "I Do as I Please" and "Just Don't Give a Damn"—are powerful assertions of women's rights and the need for self-respect in a hostile environment. Except for an over-the-top attack on pork ("Swiney Swiney") and the irritable tone that occasionally creeps into Monie's singsong delivery (the repeated "move, damn it!" command of "Ring My Bell" really grates), **Down to Earth** is a spectacular debut. (The British vinyl release initially included a bonus EP of additional material.)   [i]

LOVE AND ROCKETS

Seventh Dream of Teenage Heaven (nr/Beggars Banquet) 1985 (Beggars Banquet-RCA) 1988 ●
Express (Beggars Banquet-Big Time) 1986 ●
Earth-Sun-Moon (Beggars Banquet-Big Time) 1987 ●
Love and Rockets (Beggars Banquet-RCA) 1989 ●

DAVID J

Etiquette of Violence (nr/Situation Two) 1983 ●
Crocodile Tears and the Velvet Cosh (nr/Glass) 1985 ●
David J on Glass (nr/Glass) 1986 ●
Songs from Another Season (Beggars Banquet-RCA) 1990 ●

DANIEL ASH

Coming Down (Beggars Banquet-RCA) 1991 ●

From near oblivion to solid stardom, Love and Rockets is the group that refused to die. Named after the Hernandez brothers' underground comic, Love and Rockets reunited three-fourths of Bauhaus, which had broken up in 1983. First, drummer Kevin Haskins joined guitarist Daniel Ash's side-project-turned-serious Tones on Tail, which folded a year later. Then, David J—following his stint with the Jazz Butcher—joined them in an aborted attempt to reform Bauhaus. When that was kiboshed by Peter Murphy, the three transmuted into Love and Rockets, with Ash and J splitting the vocals and songwriting.

Murphy's absence allows his three former bandmates to avoid any trace of his poseur pretensions on **Seventh Dream of Teenage Heaven**, an odd, unnervingly varied album. There's folk-rock, funk, ominous rock and a number that resembles the Moody Blues crossed with Bow Wow Wow—a huge, boomy drum sound smothered in close harmony vocals and what

sounds to be a mellotron. "Saudade," a similar (albeit instrumental) piece, blends aspects of New Order and the Dream Academy. The faintly Beatlesque, pretty "Haunted When the Minutes Drag" suggests an '80s take on Donovan in a droney acoustic mode. Neat record—wonder what it all means. (The British CD adds three tracks.) The belated American issue adds "Inside the Outside" and a remix of "Dog-End of a Day Gone By." In Canada, the record includes a version of the Temptations' "Ball of Confusion" and several other remixes.

There's less stylistic dilettantism on the fine **Express**, although disparate variety is still among the trio's hallmarks. To wit, "All in My Mind" appears on one side as evanescent folk-rock and on the other as a dirgey sigh with echoed snare drum accents. "Kundalini Express" updates the old train gambit with modern ideas; "Yin and Yang the Flower Pot Man" puts another Moody Bluesy melody to a galloping beat; "Love Me" has dubwise backing and whispered vocals. Love and Rockets seem to be charting out their terrain ever more clearly, concentrating on genres that work for them. (The US edition adds "Ball of Confusion.")

After two good records, Love and Rockets began lurching this way and that as Ash and J began asserting themselves individually, writing and singing their own lyrics in rarely intersecting styles. The self-produced **Earth-Sun-Moon** is an enigmatic bummer, a dull and often murky digression that buries its few promising ideas in echo and overdubbed guitar tracks. Ash comes up with flaky lyrics and flaky stylistic ideas; J's work is less weird, but no more effective. (He's responsible for the album's funniest track: the Jethro Tull parody "No New Tale to Tell.") **Earth-Sun-Moon** has the earmarks of a record cut reluctantly and/or without benefit of ideas. A shame. (The CD adds a "slow version" of the LP's lead-off track, "Mirror People.")

Those who bought **Love and Rockets** on the strength of its coolly atmospheric Top 20 single (the faintly '50sish "So Alive") may have been surprised by the rest of the bizarre distortion-heavy album. Ash has obviously been listening to a lot of Jesus and Mary Chain records (check out "No Big Deal" and "Motorcycle"); J seems to be entranced by the magic of vocal processing and string arrangements. Track by track, **Love and Rockets** is flimsy fun; considering it as some unified artistic effort, however, is utterly impossible.

David J's first solo record is an indulgent one-man affair with lots of acoustic guitar, a little electronic percussion and occasional keyboards; while some of the songs have amusingly cinematic lyrics ("Joe Orton's Wedding," "With the Indians Permanent"), the music is trivial and the presentation underwhelming. **Crocodile Tears** is much better, an enjoyable singer-songwriter collection with simply effective and varied arrangements (acoustic guitar, string bass, occasional drums, sax accents) and well-developed songs with good melodies and substantial lyrics that strain the limits of poetic unpretentiousness but more often wind up involving than off-putting. Not all of it works, but the title track is fine and a self-examination entitled "Too Clever by Half" is thoughtfully perceptive. "Stop This City" paints an urban landscape with care and precision; with guest flute by the Jazz Butcher, the fantasy romance of the mildly Dylanesque "Justine" is a treat.

Elsewhere, however, the influence of Zim overpowers J's good sense.

David J on Glass is a messy and eclectic collection of little merit. The lyrics are ill-considered and overdone; the uneven material includes inferior examples of the previous LP's faux-folk ("The Conjurers Hand"), effective rockers ("The Promised Land"), an atrocious piano-and-strings homage to Kurt Weill ("This Vicious Cabaret"), a Clock DVA cover ("4 Hours") and a solo acoustic demo of "Crocodile Tears and the Velvet Cosh."

The band kept him busy for several years, and J didn't make another solo album until 1990. **Songs from Another Season** follows nicely from **Crocodile Tears** with accomplished and attractive light folky pop somewhere around Lloyd Cole or the Waterboys. With sax and Max (Eider, ex-Jazz Butcher) helping out, this is an enjoyable and—in light of L&R's gross unpredictability—reassuringly low-key album.

Coming Down, Ash's solo debut, takes off in a bunch of different directions—from sedate cocktail swing to low-key salsa (!) to somber atmospherics to jittering dance noise—most fairly understated, several reflecting the Reidian thrall in which he lately seems to be gripped. Joined by singer Natacha Atlas and Haskins (doing a lot of the drum programming), Ash comes off as flaky as his band, with effective originals ("Coming Down Fast" and the pseudo-Velvet "Not So Fast" could easily be L&R tracks) and such bizarre detours as a nearly subliminal "Day Tripper" cover.   [i]

See also *Bauhaus, Tones on Tail*.

LOVE CLUB
Lime Twigs and Treachery (Popular Metaphysics-MCA) 1990 φ

A skilled diva with a closetful of unappetizing voices, Deborah Borchers is the raison d'être for this San Francisco quartet, which delivers her theatrical adventures and the pretentious lyrics as an updated variation on new romantic dance-rock. While Borchers' diversity suggests Danielle Dax or Nina Hagen, what little appeal her strident dramatics hold is drowned out by the band's overheated guitar arrangements. Ambitious but confused, Love Club possess substantial skills, but no idea how to make a record for anyone but themselves.   [pn]

LOVELIES
See *Bush Tetras*.

DAMIEN LOVELOCK
See *Celibate Rifles*.

LOVE OF LIFE ORCHESTRA
Extended Niceties EP (Infidelity) 1980
Geneva (Infidelity) 1980

Love of Life Orchestra was created by Peter Gordon (sax, keyboards, composition) and David Van Tieghem, a talented, smart-aleck avant-garde percussionist with ties to new music composer Steve Reich. Both have gone on to greater fame as elder statesmen of the down-town music scene in New York, but these early works stand as an important developmental chapter.

Extended Niceties debuted LOLO's avant-disco in fine form. "Beginning of the Heartbreak"/"Don't, Don't" is quite powerful, pushed along by a vividly colored piano and the distinctive, kinetic rhythm guitars of guests Arto Lindsay and David Byrne.

Geneva succumbs to blandness as Lindsay and Byrne are supplanted by less-inspired fulltimers and Gordon attempts to spread his clichéd writing over a longplayer. Exceptions: "Revolution Is Personal" and "Lament," which offers the rarity of a truly interesting drum solo.   [mf]

See also *David Van Tieghem*.

LOVE TRACTOR
Love Tractor (DB) 1982
Around the Bend (DB) 1983
'Til the Cows Come Home EP (DB-Landslide) 1984
Wheel of Pleasure (nr/Armageddon) 1985
Double Play [tape] (DB) 1986
This Ain't No Outerspace Ship (Big Time) 1987 ●
Themes from Venus (DB) 1989 ●

Athens, Georgia's Love Tractor started out playing instrumental rock'n'roll, with reference points in the non-vocal golden rock era of two decades ago. Unlike the Raybeats, they're not so style-conscious, so you get far fewer sly references to the Ventures and other camp heroes, and more outright flirtation with fusion and cocktail lounge muzaks. Though the material is inconsistent, **Love Tractor** never lacks poise.

The quartet exhibits new polish on **Around the Bend**, seeking to avoid stagnation by adding vocals on a few tracks. Not very memorable ones, though. The diverting **'Til the Cows Come Home** EP fails to answer questions about Tractor's future path, since it's a compilation of odds and ends. **Wheel of Pleasure** is likewise a sampler of the group's work, assembled for the English market. (In 1986, **Love Tractor** and **Around the Bend** were joined on one cassette and issued as **Double Play**.)

Produced (and played on) by ex-Raybeat Pat Irwin, **Outerspace Ship** sees the lads plunging wholeheartedly into vocals, with chirpy singing (led by guitarist Michael Richmond) that's a natural extension of their twinkly guitars. Breezy rockers like "Beatle Boots" and "Cartoon Kiddies" are charming enough, but such ephemera ultimately seems like a dubious achievement. When it's done, you'll feel like you've pigged out on cotton candy. Weird cover: a semi-funky take on the Gap Band's "Party Train."

Featuring a typically crisp Mitch Easter production job, **Themes from Venus** continues in the direction of **Outerspace**, with even more sunny, forgettable vocals. Richmond resembles a less nutty Robyn Hitchcock (not that we needed one) this time. The lightweight instrumental "Nova Express" inspires fond memories of the band's early days, when Love Tractor was more distinctive. The CD adds two.   [jy]

LENE LOVICH
Stateless (Stiff-Epic) 1979 ●
Flex (Stiff-Epic) 1980 ●

New Toy EP (Stiff-Epic) 1981
No-Man's-Land (Stiff-Epic) 1982
The Stiff Years: Volume One (nr/Great Expectations) 1990
March (Pathfinder) 1990 Φ

Lene Lovich helped pave the way for female vocalists to use as many vocal eccentricities as their male counterparts, to be unafraid to play a solo instrument (Lovich's is sax), and—as important as anything else—to feel free to adopt and project personae that are obviously feminine yet not socially stereotyped.

During her erratic and sporadic career, the Detroit native has made a batch of good tracks, but has yet to deliver an entire satisfying LP. This seems to stem from the fact that she and husband-guitarist-songwriting partner Les Chappell are not exactly prolific; even with choice selection of other people's material (including songs given to her expressly by Thomas Dolby and Fingerprintz's Jimme O'Neill) she has released only four full albums in twelve years.

Stateless, her debut LP, sports a pair of great singles: "Lucky Number" and "Say When." But despite her distinctive chirp'n'yodel vocals, the keyboard-dominated arrangements and the blend of great old American pop-rock with spooky occult and Balkan overtones, she needed more consistent material. Better production also might have helped; the US version has a reshuffled song order, a different cover and a much-needed remix.

Flex has a more modern studio sound and uses synthesizers, adding more varied vocal colors (and emphasizing the distinctive deep male backing voices). The songs are more consistent, yet the standouts, original and otherwise, don't quite match those on **Stateless**. The expansion of Lovich's religio-mystical worldview partially compensates.

New Toy, a foretaste of **No-Man's-Land**, is a single expanded to EP length; only the title track is truly worthy of any attention. Surprisingly, although two of the songs appear in slightly altered versions on the subsequent LP, "New Toy" itself doesn't. Lacking it, **No-Man's-Land** is another half-good LP, with Lovich's appropriation of "It's You, Only You" (from Holland's Meteors) again demonstrating her ability to bring out melody and create her own airy, eerie atmosphere.

The long-awaited **March** is a mixed blessing, but it's a welcome arrival all the same. While only "Wonderland" (the single) really jumps out, most of the album is pretty enjoyable. For every mannerism that seems a bit too cutesy or affected, there's another couple of moves that'll make you sit up straight in admiration. (One exception is "Shadow Walk," on which Chappell's grave enunciations of the title sound dangerously like frog croaks—or belches.) But for a spot of bass and percussion, Lovich and Chappell wrote, produced and played it all themselves. [jg]

NICK LOWE
Jesus of Cool (nr/Radar) 1978 (nr/Demon) 1989 ●
Pure Pop for Now People (Columbia) 1978 ●
Labour of Lust (Columbia) 1979 ●
Nick the Knife (Columbia) 1982 ●
The Abominable Showman (Columbia) 1983 ●

16 All-Time Lowes (nr/Demon) 1984 ●
Nicks Knack (nr/Demon) 1986 ●
Pinker and Prouder Than Previous (Columbia) 1988 ●
Basher: The Best of Nick Lowe (Columbia) 1989 ●
Party of One (Reprise) 1990 ●

NICK LOWE AND HIS COWBOY OUTFIT
Nick Lowe and His Cowboy Outfit (Columbia) 1984 ●
The Rose of England (Columbia) 1985 ●

Once a teen dream with London-area pop group Kippington Lodge then a pub-rocker with Brinsley Schwarz, Nick Lowe burst into new wave as a pop mastermind who could give you anything you wanted, and to heck with social significance. The cover of his first solo album graphically displays his kaleidoscopic versatility in six different poses/personae, all fairly sleazy. Lowe's tunes, though, are invariably well crafted, charming (within a '60s pop context) and offbeat enough to hold attention.

For its US release, the wildly diverse **Jesus of Cool** was retitled **Pure Pop for Now People** by corporate wimps (a copout that continued on the 1990 Columbia CD). Besides a well-scrambled track order, **Pure Pop** substitutes the smooth "They Called It Rock" for **Jesus**' stompy "Shake and Pop" (in fact, the same song with a different arrangement) and adds "Rollers Show," a parodic tribute to the Bay City Rollers. The US album also inserts Lowe's studio recording of "Heart of the City" (the B-side of Stiff's first-ever release) in place of the searing live version on the British record. (The same live recording, but with a Dave Edmunds vocal replacing Lowe's, appears on Edmunds' **Tracks on Wax 4**.)

Labour of Lust is a calmer collection, sticking mostly to medium-tempo rockers played by the dependable Rockpile (Lowe, Edmunds, drummer Terry Williams and guitarist Billy Bremner). Instead of stylistic variety, Lowe concentrates on love songs, both silly ("Switch Board Susan," "American Squirm") and sincere ("Without Love," "You Make Me"). The album also contains his first (and so far only) US hit single, "Cruel to Be Kind."

Following **Labour of Lust**, Lowe put his solo career on hold to assist Edmunds and play in Rockpile. He resumed with **Nick the Knife**, not surprisingly filled with more foot-tapping love songs. His emotional palette had broadened to include unhappy ("My Heart Hurts," "Too Many Teardrops," "Raining Raining") as well as happy ("Queen of Sheba," "Couldn't Love You (Any More Than I Do)") subject matter. And of course there are the obvious musical/lyrical borrowings Lowe-watchers enjoy getting incensed about.

The Abominable Showman is fast out of the starting gate with "We Want Action" and "Raging Eyes." After that, Lowe turns surprisingly serious on tracks like "Time Wounds All Heels" and "Wish You Were Here." The album closes on a curious (for Lowe) note: "How Do You Talk to an Angel" even has strings.

He returned to form on **Nick Lowe and His Cowboy Outfit** (which actually features almost the same band as on the preceding album). Once again, Nick essays a variety of pop styles, from Tex-Mex ("Half a Boy and Half a Man") to '50s instrumental ("Awesome"). Don't take the LP title too seriously; on a good day, Lowe takes nothing seriously.

Maintaining the same lineup but cobbling together a far better set of tunes, Lowe made **The Rose of England** with a lot more evident effort. While the variety is impressive, the lack of consistent quality mainly comes down to specific songs. Winners: Costello's "Indoor Fireworks" (predating its appearance on **King of America**), John Hiatt's "She Don't Love Nobody" and Lowe's own "Lucky Dog," "The Rose of England" and "(Hope to God) I'm Right." A new treatment of "I Knew the Bride," produced by and performed with Huey Lewis and band, is unsettlingly anxious but reasonably entertaining; a few other items are throwaways or sappy ballads. Overall, however, **The Rose of England** offers some of the deepest, most reassuring music Lowe's done in ages.

16 All-Time Lowes is a compilation of his early solo work, from "So It Goes" and "Heart of the City" through "When I Write the Book." Of special interest: precise musician credits for each track. Statisticians (and those who feel Lowe's quality level has been steadily waning) should note that almost half of these songs appeared on his first album. **Nicks Knack** is a complementary collection of another sixteen tracks, including Rockpile's "Now and Always," a rare B-side ("Basing Street") and a balanced selection of mostly second-string material from Lowe's pre-Cowboy Outfit albums. While the American release of the 25 (or 27)-song **Basher**—the third Lowe anthology to date—is understandable since the first two never came out in the States, its British issue (with track differences in all three formats) is utterly inexplicable. Nitpickers' treat: the American sleeve inadvertently refers to the first album as **Jesus of Cool**.

Pinker and Prouder Than Previous was recorded in pieces during 1986 and '87 in London and Texas, with a host of old friends, including Paul Carrack, Terry Williams, Martin Belmont and John Hiatt. (Lowe had been instrumental in Hiatt's 1987 "comeback" album, **Bring the Family**.) He even made up with Edmunds, who produced one song. Reclaiming the straightforward one-take-sound R&B/pop magic he has imparted to many protégés, Lowe comes out pub-rocking here, positively glowing with casual aplomb. Besides the familiar helpings of spicy rock'n'roll and smooth pop, he dishes out a bit of greasy roadhouse R&B, some maudlin but touching balladeering, even spots of cajun and demi-reggae, without a hint of selfconsciousness or effort. (Echoes of Rockpile are everywhere.) Minor criticisms: the sequencing doesn't really work, the abrupt fades are disconcerting and a few of the tunes (like Graham Parker's "Black Lincoln Continental") don't rate.

After a solo tour with Elvis Costello, Lowe followed his friend to a new label, and got Edmunds to produce **Party of One**, a likable but shallow return to simple songs and flash-free presentation. Carrack, Edmunds, Ry Cooder and Jim Keltner give standard-issue Lowe-isms like "You Got the Look I Like" and "Who Was That Man" their easygoing all, picking up more or less where Rockpile left off. Had Basher expended a bit more effort in the songwriting stage, the conducive atmosphere provided here would have made **Party of One** as good as fans wanted it to be. Instead, there's only the brilliant "(I Want to Build a) Jumbo Ark," the quietly soulful "What's Shakin' on the Hill" and the lyrically

clever "All Men Are Liars" to demonstrate Lowe's ability to find new pearls in such old oysters.   [si/i]
See also *Dave Edmunds, Rockpile*.

IAN LOWERY GROUP
See *Folk Devils*.

LOWLIFE
Rain EP (nr/Nightshift) 1985
Permanent Sleep (nr/Nightshift) 1986
Diminuendo (nr/Nightshift) 1987
Swirl, It Swings EP (nr/Nightshift) 1987
From a Scream to a Whisper (nr/Nightshift) 1989
Godhead (nr/Nightshift) 1989

After leaving the Cocteau Twins in 1983, bassist Will Heggie formed this quartet and continued playing atmospheric Scottish indie-pop, albeit in a somewhat darker hue. The **Rain** EP sets ringing, occasionally clashing guitars and echoey deadpan vocals into long, rhythmically charged songs (some in a minor key) whose deep and dramatic vocals (by Craig Lorentson) contain a solemn trace of Joy Division.

Permanent Sleep delves deeper into instrumental and vocal textures, with layers of strummed and picked guitar and slippery bass chords (shades of New Order) dominating the sound. Despite Lowlife's concentration on ambience, the affecting "Wild Swan" is a lovely song, punctuated by repeated guitar triplets fluttering overhead.

The aptly titled and excellent **Diminuendo** reduces Lowlife's volume by stripping the arrangements of their thickening ingredients, leaving only the bass, simple drums and frugal bits of guitar and keyboards to support the increasingly ambitious and musical vocals. (The octave-jumping falsetto in "Big Uncle Ugliness" and commanding power of "Licking Ones Eyes" are indicative of his expanding stylistic range.) While opening up the sound does wonders for some songs (including "From Side to Side," "Wonders Will Never Cease" and "Tongue Tied and Twisted," which *really* sounds like a New Order track), the results can also be too dreamy, leaving tracks lusterless.

The four disappointing new songs on **Swirl, It Swings** sound like outtakes from **Diminuendo**, only with feeble drumming and grandiose vocals. Named for a phrase scratched into one of **Diminuendo**'s run-off grooves, **From a Scream to a Whisper** is a 1985-'88 compilation containing most of the 1987 EP plus several tracks from each of the three prior records.

Succumbing to the excesses of Lorentson's newly dramatized vocal style, **Godhead** also marks a partial return to the early records' busy instrumentation. While understandably moving to erase the New Order comparisons, the misnamed **Godhead** lacks the emotional drive that sparks all of Lowlife's other albums and winds up labored and dull, a collection of unaffecting songs that plod—even at brisk tempos.   [i]

LOW MAX
Low Max EP (Ger. Glitterhouse) 1988 (Skyclad) 1989
Spitzbube (Ger. Houses in Motion) 1990 (Skyclad) 1991 ●

Singer/guitarist Ricky Gelb—younger brother of Giant Sand man Howe Gelb (who drew the front cover of

Low Max)—leads this Tucson, Arizona group, playing dryly dramatic Southwestern rock in the wake of bands like Green on Red and True West. Low Max's six-song debut has a few rough spots (like pitch and tunings) that need work, but it gets enough juice from Gelb's affecting vocals and sturdy songs (not to mention Johnny Macarchick's energetic guitar strivings) to make its mark.

Rolling more acoustic guitar into the mix, **Spitzbube** has a loose, folky feel—a bit Dylanesque in spots—that doesn't always encourage Gelb's best singing or Macarchick's most purposeful playing. Still, the rambly and reflective songs make their points with plenty of personality. Dan Stuart of Green on Red guest-sings on "You Used My Name"; Howe Gelb plays keyboards on "Don't Know Why." [i]

LOW MEATO
Low Meato (Ger. Pigs Ear) 1989

If there's a way to offend even the hardiest sexual sensibilities, this talented but tasteless New York trio knows it. Bassist Felix Sebacious and guitarist Thruster H.W. share the humorous vocals on such blatant indelicacies as "Ben Wa Balls," "Penis Power" and "Easy Girl" (turning responsibly serious on "AIDS Hymn," which consists of one repeated line—"Stop fucking around/Find the cure for AIDS"), while playing skin-tight power rock with punk, glam-pop, Cheap Trick and metal overtones. If their lyrics weren't so conscientiously offensive, Low Meato would be totally cool. [i]

LUBRICATED GOAT
Lubricated Goat Plays the Devil's Music (Aus. Black Eye) 1987 (Amphetamine Reptile) 1989
Paddock of Love (Aus. Black Eye) 1988 (Amphetamine Reptile) 1989
Schadenfreude EP (Aus. Black Eye) 1989
Psychedelicatessen (Amphetamine Reptile) 1990 ●

Some of the crudest sounds from Australia's belly have been belched up by Lubricated Goat, a band which features two former members of Salamander Jim. Since getting underway in early '86, Goatees have slipped in and out and back in again, though the groans, gristle and guttural grunts of Stu Spasm (as well as the backdrop of bleating horns and discordant guitars) have held steady.

Despite ten-cent production and an organization level that makes playtime in kindergarten seem like a crack marching band, **The Devil's Music** offers the Goat's most inventive montage of styles and instrumentation; beneath the recurring sodomite/fatality themes and Spasm's occasional possessed rants smolders a weird core of blues and jazz inspiration. "Goats and the Men Who Ride Them," one of several instrumentals, could serve as a striptease for strangling hyenas; overlooking the titles, other vocal-less tracks that could be film scores include "Frotting with Ennio" (a disturbed children's movie, perhaps), "Nervequake" (slapstick) and "Anal Injury" (silent comedy).

Paddock of Love emits similar primal sentiments (with an emphasis on cannibalism), but at less obtuse angles. The Goat forfeits the spontaneity and creativity of the first album in favor of cohesion. Still, there are plenty of fun-filled moments of tightly wound psychotic gumbo: "Funeral on a Spit," "Promised Land" and "He Moves in Mysterious Ways."

The **Schadenfreude** EP winds and meanders in dissembled repetition, lacking humor and direction, though the accelerator motion and skidding distortion of "Magumbo Head" does briefly relieve the monotony.

The guitar-rock sound may hardly reflect it, but the Goat on **Psychedelicatessen** includes sampler wrangler Lachlan McLeod (also ex-Salamander); Spasm and longtime drummer Martin Bland both take credit for synths as well. (The lineup is completed by a guitar/sax player.) Abandoning the overt dementia of previous records, Spasm here relaxes into a more integrated, spoken pitch, and the tightened-up band drives the songs along with brain-driller riffs, as on the seasick humor of "Stroke," the insidious crawl of "Spoil the Atmosphere" and the flat-out instrumental mania of "Never Know What Hit You." [mg]

See also *Beasts of Bourbon*.

LUDICHRIST
Off the Board [tape] (CBGB) 1986
Immaculate Deception (Combat Core) 1986
Powertrip (Combat) 1988

SCATTERBRAIN
Here Comes Trouble (In-Effect) 1990 ●

New York's Ludichrist takes a mix-and-match approach to hardcore and speed metal on its first studio album, **Immaculate Deception**. Singer Tommy Christ keeps pace easily as the skillful band abruptly shifts gears from storming punk to careening rock in topical (frequently irreligious) tunes like "Big Business," "God Is Everywhere," "Tylenol," "Mengele" and a tuneless speeding rendition of "Last Train to Clarkesville." (Agnostic Fronters, Crumbsuckers and others guest.)

Christ and guitarist Glenn Cummings are the only holdovers from the first album on **Powertrip**, a competently generic thrash-metal assault whose best feature is its sporadically inventive lyrics. Dispensing with the theological references, the quintet comes up with a science-fiction defense of rock'n'roll ("Zad") and various complaints about workaday life.

Chucking the problematic band name and sonic orthodoxy, Christ, Cummings and guitarist Paul Nieder got themselves a new rhythm section and escaped the metal ghetto by becoming Scatterbrain. A well-rounded program with deftly modulated rhythms and carefully controlled stun strength, **Here Comes Trouble** touches up the Beastie Boys ("Earache My Eye" is a bratty gang rap), the Chili Peppers ("That's That" runs a popping bass line under horns and chanted vocals) and Mozart (Nieder does a classic Brian May overdub job on "Sonata #3"), kicking ass with humor ("Don't Call Me Dude") as well as seriousness ("Goodbye Freedom, Hello Mom"). Power plus invention makes Scatterbrain a bright band. [i]

LUNACHICKS
Lunachicks EP (nr/Blast First-Mute) 1989 ●
Babysitters on Acid (nr/Blast First) 1990 ●

Stepping into the garbage-rock wrestling ring with a four-song EP (issued on two 7-inch singles in a gatefold sleeve; the CD came later), New York's five Lunachicks strut their overdrive guitar noise in such witless sloptunes as "Sugar Luv," "Jan Brady" and "Makin' It (With Other Species)." The thrashy music's not half bad, but Theo Kogan's vocals—at best she resembles comedian Judy Tenuta channeling the devil—are terrible.

The album reprises those three songs and adds nine more crudities (like "Octopussy" and the mild novelty fun of "Babysitters on Acid") in the same vein. Producer Wharton Tiers wisely sharpens up the instrumental assault in the direction of old MC5 and sinks the improved Kogan halfway into the mix, but the Lunachicks can't seem to make up their mind if they want to be the Plasmatics, the Ramones or Killer ("Teenage Enema Nurses in Bondage") Pussy.   [i]

LYDIA LUNCH
Queen of Siam (ZE) 1980 (Widowspeak) 1985 ●
13.13 (Ruby) 1982 (Widowspeak) 1988 ●
The Agony Is the Ecstacy EP (nr/4AD) 1982
In Limbo EP (nr/Doublevision) 1984 (Widowspeak) 1986
The Uncensored Lydia Lunch [tape] (Widowspeak) 1985 φ
Hysterie (nr/Widowspeak) 1986 (CD Presents) 1986 ●
Honeymoon in Red (Widowspeak) 1987 ●
Drowning in Limbo [CD] (Widowspeak) 1989 ●
Oral Fixation (Widowspeak) 1989 ●

LYDIA LUNCH/MICHAEL GIRA
Hard Rock [tape] (Ecstatic Peace) 1984

LYDIA LUNCH AND LUCY HAMILTON
The Drowning of Lucy Hamilton EP (Widowspeak) 1985

CLINT RUIN/LYDIA LUNCH
Stinkfist EP (Widowspeak) 1988 ●

LYDIA LUNCH/THURSTON MOORE
The Crumb EP (Widowspeak) 1988 ●

HARRY CREWS
Naked in Garden Hills (Widowspeak) 1989 ●

Lydia Lunch's career since deep-sixing Teenage Jesus and the Jerks has been an unpredictable path governed by boredom, sarcasm, romance, perversity and whatever musicians or collaborators are convenient at the time. Queen of Siam proves, at the very least, that she can do more than just scream (although her version of the Classics IV hit, "Spooky," shows she ain't exactly Beverly Sills, either). Half of the album consists of muted, somber variations on her Teenage Jesus fear-and-suffering dirges, but the real surprises are songs like "Lady Scarface," in which the big band arrangements (by Flintstones-theme composer Billy Ver Planck) turn Lunch's wry asides into a Billie Holiday nightmare.

On the heels of Queen of Siam's release, Lunch formed 8 Eyed Spy with ex-Contortions bassist George Scott, ex-Jerk Jim Sclavunos on drums, guitarist Michael Paumgardhen and saxophonist/guitarist Pat Irwin, who had worked on Lunch's solo album. The lifespan of the group set a pattern for Lydia's ventures:

assemble a band, work with it for a while, disband it when she got "bored"; six months later some vinyl would appear. (One conglomeration, an alleged blues abortion called the Devil Dogs, didn't last long enough to be documented.)

13.13, concocted with a trio of ex-Weirdos, was hypothetically an attempt at new psychedelia; actually it revived the grind-and-caterwaul of Teenage Jesus as filtered through Metal Box-era PiL, all deviant guitar and rolling rhythms. Like her previous stuff, it manages to be simultaneously fascinating and annoying.

Lunch hung out in Europe for a while with Nick Cave and the Birthday Party, a sympathetic association reflected in a number of recordings. The Agony Is the Ecstacy (a record she splits with the Party) captures an impromptu London gig featuring Banshees bassist Steve Severin on feedback guitar and is easily one of the most extreme Lunches to date. On the other hand, a 12-inch single done with Party guitarist Rowland S. Howard of "Some Velvet Morning" (an old Lee Hazelwood song—Nancy Sinatra has been a longtime touchstone for Lydia) recalls the softer moments of Queen of Siam.

In Limbo is a six-track disc with an all-star supporting crew that includes Thurston Moore of Sonic Youth and former Contortion/Bush Tetra Pat Place. With snail's-pace tempos, Moore's shards of acrid, harsh guitar and Lunch's trademark ululations, it's typically rough going, but recommended for anyone who has trouble contending with an entire album's worth of her clamor.

The Drowning of Lucy Hamilton is the soundtrack to a film (The Right Side of My Brain) starring Jim (Foetus) Thirlwell and Henry Rollins. Lucy Hamilton herself is actually Lydia's collaborator on the record, which consists of eerie instrumentals orchestrated with piano, honking bass clarinet (both played by Hamilton) and guitars that sound like they're being played with ice picks and hedge clippers. Something rather different for Lunch, and less like background music than most soundtracks. Drowning in Limbo, as might be surmised, is the CD pairing of that record with In Limbo.

Having successfully launched the Widowspeak label, Lunch used it to release Hysterie, an ambitious ten-year two-disc career-spanning compilation, starting with Teenage Jesus, recapitulating 8 Eyed Spy and the little-known Beirut Slump, and winding up with three recent collaborations (Die Haut, a pre-These Immortal Souls group and something called Sort Sol).

Honeymoon in Red was recorded with members of the Birthday Party, Thurston Moore and Genevieve McGuckin (now in These Immortal Souls) in 1982 and '83, and was originally going to be a Birthday Party album. When that band split up, the record was shelved. After several years' worth of tinkering, it was finally remixed by Clint (Foetus) Ruin and released on Lydia's label. (The only BPers whose names appear on the record are Rowland Howard and the late Tracy Pew; Nick Cave and Harvey are credited pseudonymously.) Lunch and the Party are/were obvious soulmates, but her input here is too often predominant; her penchant for slow tempos dilutes the band's brutal strength. Not a great album by any means, but of definite interest to fans of those involved. The CD adds "This Velvet Morning" from the Lunch/Howard single.

Although her world view hasn't changed, **Stinkfist**—a collaboration with Clint Ruin—could be the first joint effort she doesn't dominate; most of the EP's tracks are primarily instrumental, as Foetus speeds things along with a thunder-drum/noise guitar assault akin to his solo work. But even these two can't make this much noise without a little help; guests include ex-Red Hot Chili Pepper Cliff Martinez and ex-X D.J. Bonebrake pounding on things. Lots of noise and energy but nothing new, especially for the already Foetus-ized.

The Crumb EP is credited to Lunch, Thurston Moore and the Honeymoon in Red Orchestra, which consists of Lunch, Moore, Thirlwell and Howard. It's not on your local soft-rock station's playlist, nor is it perfect for the office. Moore shares vocals, and the sound is a fairly predictable, semi-defined sonic crunch. (**The Crumb** is included on the **Stinkfist** CD.)

In recent years, Lunch has occasionally foregone musical accompaniment entirely and chosen to share her muse via the spoken word. **The Uncensored** tape is in this format, as are **Hard Rock** (done with lead Swan Michael Gira) and **Oral Fixation**. The last-named captures a full-length solo rap at the Detroit Institute of Art from January 1988. As venomous as her song lyrics can get, this format allows her to take a giant step further. Sometimes clever, frequently condescending and always relentless, she spits out her observations about sex, death, middle class values, etc. with plenty of nihilistic passion, but never offers any reference point: everything in the world just plain sucks. Lunch never runs out of things to say, but as a speaker she is less an original artist than a type. The **Oral Fixation** CD also includes **The Uncensored**.

Harry Crews is a Southern novelist and professor whose name and work supply the inspiration for a band Lunch formed with Sonic Youth bassist Kim Gordon and a drummer. (The trio toured Europe in September '88.) **Naked in Garden Hills**, recorded live in London and Vienna, is not unlike previous Sonic Lunches, but with quicker tempos than Lydia's usual and a bit more noise than either might employ without this symbiotic provocation. "The Gospel Singer" is especially interesting, with a hard bluesy backing to almost rapped vocals.

Besides her recording career, Lunch has appeared in underground films and collaborated with Exene Cervenka (of X) on a book of poetry. Throughout, she continues to project the most negative charisma since Johnny Rotten.   [rnp/dgs]

See also *Birthday Party, 8 Eyed Spy, Einstürzende Neubauten, Foetus Inc., No Trend, Teenage Jesus and the Jerks.*

EVAN, JOHN LURIE

See *Lounge Lizards.*

LURKERS

Fulham Fallout (nr/Beggars Banquet) 1978 ●
God's Lonely Men (nr/Beggars Banquet) 1979
Greatest Hit: Last Will and Testament (nr/Beggars Banquet) 1980 ●

Final Vinyl EP (nr/Clay) 1983
Wild Times Again (Ger. Weserlabel) 1988
King of the Mountain (nr/Link) 1989
Live and Loud!! (nr/Link) 1989
This Dirty Town (nr/Clay) 1990

PETE STRIDE/JOHN PLAIN

New Guitars in Town (nr/Beggars Banquet) 1980

Despite the occasional glimmer of greatness, the Lurkers were never much more than a lightweight, second-string suburban London punk band, playing simple numbers in a plodding manner over repetitive drum figures. The tantalizing bits suggested a much better band lurking (sorry) inside; the post-split record by southpaw guitarist Pete Stride and part-time Lurker Honest John Plain (otherwise in the Boys) proves that the group was not without talent, but simply lacked the ability to express itself successfully.

Fulham Fallout has the advantage of crystal-clear sound (thanks to producer Mick Glossop) and a few impressive songs ("Ain't Got a Clue," "Shadow"), but suffers from tedium and general punky cloddishness. **God's Lonely Men** seems to employ only one beat; the overbearing rhythm section's dense, muffled pounding gives the record an air of mock metal. Two poppier tracks hint at better things ahead musically, but time had run out for the Lurkers.

Greatest Hit gathers up twelve numbers from the two LPs and adds a half-dozen single sides. Surprisingly enough, it's much better than either of the preceding albums, and has enough fun times to make it a worthwhile investment in low-brow punk. Not essential, but good enough.

The relationship between the Boys and the Lurkers began sometime before the latter broke up—guitarist Honest John Plain appears on two of the **Greatest Hit** tracks, including one called "New Guitar in Town"—so it took only a melding of the two bands to provide backing for the collaborative effort by Stride and Plain. **New Guitars in Town** starts off with a Spectoresque version of Sonny Bono's "Laugh at Me" (also recorded by Mott the Hoople) and gets better from there. Rather than a flashy collection of solos as the title suggests, the two stringleaders show off their singing and songwriting more than guitar pyrotechnics, which remain decidedly in the background. All in all, a delicious collection of rollicking pop-rock, played with spit and spirit.

After a short non-existence, Stride, bassist Nigel Moore and drummer Dan Tozer reformed the Lurkers with a different singer and began releasing new singles inna old punk style. **This Dirty Town** (named for the reincarnated quartet's 1982 debut) collects up—for better and worse—all of the band's tracks (A's, B's and EP) from this era, demonstrating both a shameless connection to slowed-down Clash/Pistols punk and a little stylistic progress (note the keyboards and dub mixing on "Lets Dance Now"). As ever, the Lurkers rise above their chosen genre, but not enough to escape it.

In early 1989, again swapping singers (this time for Arturo Bassick, who had been the Lurkers' bassist at one early point), the Lurkers cut the crisply melodic **King of the Mountain**, an ace mini-album that compares very favorably to vintage Ramones. Judging by "Barbara Blue" and the weirdly topical "Going Monkee Again (Hey Hey Hey)," the third time may be lucky for the Lurkers. The live album, recorded later in '89, is also loads of casual fun, energetically recapitulating the band's career in nineteen merry selections, from "Ain't Got a Clue" to "Barbara Blue."   [i]

See also *Boys*.

LUSH

Scar EP (nr/4AD) 1989 ●
Mad Love EP (nr/4AD) 1990 ●
Gala (4AD-Reprise) 1990 ●

Bowing with the six-song **Scar**, this winsome young London noise-pop quartet combines guitarist Miki Berenyi's wispy voice with wanton semi-freakout playing. Although some songs are not as tuneful as they might be (Lush stands well left of the Primitives), memorable items like the thick "Scarlet" and the float-away "Etheriel"—both co-written by Berenyi and guitarist Emma Anderson—arrange the band's basic components with naïve ingenuity.

Cocteau Twin Robin Guthrie produced the four-song **Mad Love**, giving the band a more intricately textured sound (turning up the distorted rhythm guitars, for one thing) that only half suits Lush's skills and style. While Berenyi makes the most of "De-Luxe" and "Thoughtforms" (on which she sounds like Kirsty MacColl fronting the Cocteaus), Chris Acland's busy drumming isn't a beneficial contribution.

Besides compiling the EPs in their entirety, **Gala** adds two more Guthrie collaborations (a nifty cover of Abba's obscure "Hey Hey Helen" and a much lighter second version of "Scarlet"), plus three subsequent tracks produced by Tim Friese-Greene, who mistakenly divides Lush's music into distinct segments of guitar craziness and overly restrained pop orderliness.   [i]

LUXURIA

See *Howard Devoto*.

LYRES

The Lyres EP (Ace of Hearts) 1981
On Fyre (Ace of Hearts) 1984 ●
Someone Who'll Treat You Right Now EP (Fr. New Rose) 1985
The Box Set (Fr. New Rose) 1986
Lyres Lyres (Ace of Hearts) 1986 ●
Live at Cantones! (Pryct) 1987
A Promise Is a Promise (Ace of Hearts) 1988 ●
Live (Sp. Impossible) 1989
Live 1983: Let's Have a Party!! (Pryct) 1989

After the demise of DMZ—one of Boston's most exciting retro-rock-punk bands—singer/organist Jeff "Mono Mann" Conolly assembled the Lyres to play authentic '60s garage music in the '80s. Once an imitator of his heroes, Conolly's talent and devotion made him nearly their equal, and the Lyres' four-song debut (a 12-inch EP also known as **Buried Alive**, after its lead track) showcases a tough, spirited brand of rock'n'roll that sets the standard to which all other contemporary nostalgic grungophiles must be compared.

On Fyre is simply the genre's apotheosis, an articulate explosion of colorful organ playing, surging guitars and precisely inexact singing. Drawing on just the right selection of songwriters (Ray and Dave Davies each get tapped once; another esoteric cover revives a song originally recorded by ex-Beatle drummer Pete Best) and adding his own brilliant creations (especially the urgent "Help You Ann," powered by phenomenal tremolo guitar), Conolly leads the Lyres on a nostalgic trip that is utterly relevant to the here and now. The CD, issued several years later, adds eight bonus tunes.

(The Lyres' French label, which had already issued the band's debut EP and album, put out a four-song 12-inch in 1985 and then repackaged all three items in a limited-edition hot-pink box the following year.)

A few moments into the excellent **Lyres Lyres**, Conolly quotes the riff from the Grass Roots' "Let's Live for Today" in "Not Looking Back." There aren't any further citations of that caliber, but the entire record rocks with a mixture of Animalized R&B, touching and melodic barrelhouse pop and raving old-style punk. Danny McCormack's guitar work is spectacular; Conolly's voice has never sounded better. Among the covers this time are a pair by veteran Dutch rocker Wally Tax, an idol of Conolly's; other selections may be even less familiar to loyal Casey Kasem fans.

Live at Cantones! is a compilation of live cuts (dating from 1979-'81) that suffers from inconsistent, often inadequate, sound quality but has such cool tunes as "Let's Talk About Girls," "She Pays the Rent" and—of course—"Louie Louie." **Let's Have a Party!!** is much better, a single live-in-the-studio radio broadcast from March 1983. Conolly is in fine form, singing and organ-izing the Lyres through an informal history of '50s and '60s garage rock, from Elvis Presley/Wanda Jackson's "Let's Have a Party" to the Human Beinz's "Nobody but Me." Although still far from exemplary audio fidelity (and slightly out of tune in spots), this is a fine showing by the very best.

Never the most prolific group, the Lyres let two years elapse before releasing a third studio album. Just prior to **A Promise Is a Promise**, recorded by the Lyres' thirteenth incarnation (according to Pete Frame's detailed family tree on the gatefold), a three-song 12-inch surfaced, containing "Here's a Heart," a neat merseybeat oldie featuring Stiv Bators, and "Touch," recorded in Holland with Tax. Both of those appear on the flatly recorded LP, which marks a real departure for the group. "Every Man for Himself" flirts with funk; "Feel Good" is a soulful rocker with a vocal that resembles Percy Faith; "Worried About Nothing" has the rueful tone of acoustic Neil Young. Dispensing with most of the dated stylization for about as modern a sound as a group with prominent Vox organ can get, the energy-spewing album drags in spots but blasts off in others. The CD and cassette add seven uneven live tracks. Clearly captured in a Dutch radio studio, the Lyres sound a lot like the Small Faces on "She Pays the Rent" and the LP's "She's Got Eyes That Tell Lies"; five additional tracks (including "Help You Ann"), however, come from some other concert source and are pretty crappy. (Collectors note: the Canadian vinyl edition has the extra material on a bonus disc and uses the US back cover on the front.)   [cpl/i]

See also *DMZ, Barrence Whitfield and the Savages*.

M M M M M M

M

New York*London*Paris*Munich (Sire) 1979
The Official Secrets Act (Sire) 1980
Famous Last Words (Sire) 1982
High Life Music EP (nr/Swahili-Albion) 1983
Boogie with a Suitcase (nr/Freestyle) 1989 ●
Walking on the Water (nr/Fuego) 1989 ●

M (Robin Scott) may stand in Top 40 history as a glorious one-hit wonder but, oh, what a hit! Easily the highlight of his first LP, "Pop Muzik" combines the moronic appeal of a brilliant semi-electronic novelty record with the sturdy danceability of a hot disco mix. Give this Englishman (with assists by Wally Badarou and Julian Scott) credit for partially paving the way for hip-hop and modern electro-pop in one fell swoop. Other cuts on the LP, such as "Cowboys and Indians" and "That's the Way the Money Goes," are just as silly but less immediate, leaving the listener free to observe how much Scott can sing like Bowie.

He shifted gears on **The Official Secrets Act**, playing superficial foolishness against an underlying current of fear; "Join the Party," "Working for the Corporation," "Your Country Needs You" and "Official Secrets" conjure up murky images of a threatening world. Scott clearly derives pleasure from inventing unexpected melodies and bending his tunes with quirky production touches.

Scott confirmed his status as a doodler on **Famous Last Words**: no two tunes are alike. Everything's a little odd, but never unpleasantly so. In short, this third LP possesses only the limited value of cleverness in a vacuum. One longs for less calculation, and references beyond the studio.

In 1981, Scott collaborated on an album with Yellow Magic Orchestra keyboardist Ryuichi Sakamoto. In 1989, "Pop Muzik" was re-released as a CD single to, in Scott's words, "celebrate ten years of obscurity."

See also *Ryuichi Sakamoto*.   [jy]

SIPHO MABUSE

Sipho Mabuse (Virgin) 1987 ●
Chant of the Marching (Earthworks-Virgin) 1989 ●

British new wave pioneer Martin Rushent co-produced and remixed veteran Soweto singer/drummer Mabuse's first American album, recorded in both Johannesburg and London. Mabuse sings mostly in English on the strongly westernized songs, which blend African percussion styles and sounds with rock guitar, popping fretless bass, funk horns and other dance-ready attributes. "Shikisha" and "Ti Nyanga (African Doctor)" both feature backing by a female vocal group and are the most colorfully appealing tracks here; "Burn Out" (previously issued in the US as a 12-inch from a 1985 import LP), with no African character whatever, is just plain terrible.

The sunny **Chant of the Marching**, recorded in Brussels, is an uplifting mainstream album with fewer commercial concessions than its predecessor. (The American-soul styled "Celebration" sounds like a sincere embrace rather than a forced attempt to imitate.) Over a blend of spirited backup singers, neat hornwork (by Hugh Masekela and others) and percussion (used in more of a musical than rhythmic role), Mabuse confidently sings his forthright (bilingual) lyrics about the townships, Mandela and resistance in a handsome, almost unaccented voice. Miriam Makeba duets with Mabuse on one song.   [i]

KIRSTY MACCOLL

Desperate Character (nr/Polydor) 1981
Kite (nr/Virgin) 1989 (Charisma) 1990 ●
Free World EP (nr/Virgin) 1989 ●
Days EP (nr/Virgin) 1989 ●
Don't Come the Cowboy with Me Sonny Jim! EP
  (nr/Virgin) 1990 ●
Electric Landlady (Charisma) 1991 ●

Daughter of the late folk-music giant Ewan MacColl, singer/songwriter Kirsty cut a great two-sided 45 for Stiff ("They Don't Know"—later an international hit for Tracey Ullman—b/w "Turn My Motor On") that went nowhere, but she scored two years later on the UK charts with the twangy "There's a Guy Works Down the Chip Shop Swears He's Elvis" (included in two versions on **Desperate Character**). For MacColl's first album, ace sidemen Billy Bremner, Lew Lewis and Gavin Povey helped her whip up a lively rock-country-pop stew that could be a female-led Rockpile. Nary a bad track in the bunch.

A second LP (recorded around '82 with bassist Pino Palladino) was completed but rejected by her label and went unreleased. In 1984, MacColl married producer Steve Lillywhite (whom she met at the sessions for Simple Minds' **Sparkle in the Rain**) and they collaborated on a single of Billy Bragg's "A New England," drastically overhauling the spare tune into a hitbound pop extravaganza.

In 1989, MacColl interrupted her successful career as a backing vocalist (her extensive credits include both the Pogues and the Rolling Stones) to make the Lillywhite-produced **Kite**, a mature and substantial contrast of sweet sounds and strong words. Writing sturdy, wisely provocative songs on her own and with the album's two main guitarists—Johnny Marr (ex-Smiths) and Pete Glenister (ex-Hitmen)—MacColl mixes a variety of full-bodied pop styles with some country ("Don't Come the Cowboy with Me Sonny Jim!"), adding a film noir story sung in French, a pair of wonderful covers (the Kinks' "Days" and the Smiths' "You Just Haven't Earned It Yet Baby") and pointed attacks on both Margaret Thatcher and shallow pop stars. Alluring layers of marvelous vocals and MacColl's colorful no-nonsense personality make **Kite** an utter delight.

In the UK, where the album's "Complainte pour Ste. Catherine" and "You Just Haven't Earned It Yet Baby" were CD-only bonus tracks, those songs also surfaced on the four-song CD-3s of, respectively, **Don't Come the Cowboy with Me Sonny Jim!** and **Free World**. The **Days** EP contains three non-LP tracks, including a handsome rendition of the old country standard "Please Help Me I'm Falling." [i]

See also *Pogues*.

ANDY MACKAY

See *Explorers, Roxy Music*.

MADBALL

See *Agnostic Front*.

MADNESS

One Step Beyond ... (Sire) 1979 ●
Work Rest & Play EP (nr/Stiff) 1980
Absolutely (Sire) 1980 ●
7 (nr/Stiff) 1981 (nr/Virgin) 1988 ●
Complete Madness (nr/Stiff) 1982 (nr/Virgin) 1986 ●
Madness Present the Rise and Fall (nr/Stiff) 1982
 (nr/Virgin) 1988 ●
Madness (Geffen) 1983
Keep Moving (Geffen) 1984 ●
Mad Not Mad (Geffen) 1985 ●
Utter Madness (nr/Zarjazz) 1986 ●
The Peel Sessions EP (nr/Strange Fruit) 1986 ●

THE MADNESS

The Madness (nr/Virgin) 1988 ●
I Pronounce You EP (nr/Virgin) 1988 ●

NUTTY BOYS

Crunch! (nr/Street Link) 1990 ●

The world needs more bands like Madness. One of the original London perpetrators of the ska revival, they grew from a silly novelty group into full-scale international superstars, beloved by seemingly everyone in Europe, from tot to pensioner. Though diversity in contemporary music is generally laudable, the factionalism it sometimes engenders isn't; Madness' ability to appeal to different audiences suggests that pop needn't always polarize listeners into incompatible camps.

Produced by Clive Langer and Alan Winstanley, Madness' records tend to sound the same, which testifies more to their lighthearted, bubbly style of execution than any actual uniformity of material. The band's inspirations originally came (less later on) primarily from ska and the music hall—i.e., sing-along music—though you're likely to find classic rock'n'roll, Arabic overtones, utterly insipid jokes, easy-listening pop, incisive observations on society (not unlike Ray Davies) and just about everything else.

Highlights of **One Step Beyond** include the titular instrumental, "Night Boat to Cairo," "Chipmunks Are Go!" and Prince Buster's "Madness." (The subsequent **Work Rest & Play** 7-inch EP has four cuts, including "Night Boat.") **Absolutely** features the giddy "Baggy Trousers" and "Return of the Los Palmas 7." **7** con-

tains "Grey Day," an uncharacteristically somber ballad, and "The Opium Eaters," a tinkly movie-music instrumental.

Complete Madness is highly recommended because it collects the band's many hits, but in reality any Madness LP guarantees lively and—dare it be said?—wholesome fun.

Displaying added maturity and creative breadth, **The Rise and Fall** is another fine crowd-pleaser, with such likable fare as "Tomorrow's Just Another Day" and "Our House," a virtual sociology primer on English family life.

The nutty boys finally did themselves a favor and signed in the US with Geffen Records, who managed to scare up a hit single for the band in the form of "Our House." That track is also included on **Madness**, a compilation of previously released UK tracks dating back to 1979. (**Madness** contains about half of **The Rise and Fall** in addition to oldies like "Night Boat to Cairo" and the tender "It Must Be Love.") Good stuff.

What followed was a period of tumult: Madness left Stiff, keyboardist Mike Barson left Madness and the band set up their own Zarjazz label. **Keep Moving**, their final LP as a septet, offers a full platter of typically tuneful, thoughtful, lightweight pop songs covering familiar ground, musically and lyrically. "Wings of a Dove" incorporates a gospel choir; "Michael Caine" uses a cute pop-culture gimmick to sell an otherwise weak number. The growing vocal skills of Carl Smyth (aka Chas Smash) and Graham (Suggs) McPherson have made them the band's most recognizable trait; the others' seemingly effortless playing is easy to take for granted.

Although it has its moments, **Mad Not Mad** is an uneasy, odd record, sounding a bit like Bryan Ferry in more than one spot ("Yesterday's Men," "Coldest Day"), offering a quizzical look at America ("Uncle Sam") and covering Scritti Politti's beautiful "Sweetest Girl" with little élan. With Barson gone, keyboards are played by Steve Nieve and Roy Davies; a lot of guest musicians add strings, horns and backing vocals. Not unpleasant, but unsettlingly out of the Madness mainstream.

Having achieved far more success in eight years than these north Londoners ever imagined, Madness announced its breakup in September 1986. But late '87 brought the return of a slimmed-down band rechristened *The* Madness and early '88 saw the release of a self-titled new album. Further than ever from their ska roots, the semi-reunited group (McPherson, Chris Foreman, Lee Thompson and Carl Smyth, with help from, among others, Specials leader Jerry Dammers and Attractions Nieve and Bruce Thomas) comes up with low-key, almost dour adult techno-pop that, like **Mad Not Mad**, gains in force with repeat listenings. The CD includes four extra tracks.

Following the dismal failure of **The Madness** (it spent one week in the British Top 100), Foreman (guitars, keyboards, programming) and Thompson (sax and, after a fashion, vocals) alone had the stamina to continue. The duo adopted Madness' old nickname, the Nutty Boys, and made a new album on their own. The self-produced **Crunch!** upholds the old group's standards of pop craftsmanship, returning to ska beats (not

402

the full 2 Tone environment) with only slightly less imagination and a bit more casual aplomb. (The CD adds two.)

Following the original Madness' breakup, another compilation appeared. **Utter Madness** contains all of the band's UK hits ("Wings of a Dove," "Our House," "Michael Caine") from 1982 to 1986. The CD adds "Seven Year Scratch (Hits Megamix)." The John Peel EP dates from the first year of Madness, 1979.

[jy/i/hd]

MADONNA

Madonna (Sire) 1983 ●
Like a Virgin (Sire) 1985 ●
True Blue (Sire) 1986 ●
Who's That Girl (Sire) 1987 ●
You Can Dance (Sire) 1987 ●
Like a Prayer (Sire) 1989 ●
I'm Breathless (Sire) 1990 ●
The Immaculate Collection (Sire) 1990 ●

Forget for a moment, if you can, all the personality, press and image that attends these albums and consider their contents. The first (reissued in the UK with an alternate cover as **The First Album**) consolidates simpleminded singles ("Lucky Star," "Borderline," "Holiday") and five other lengthy numbers for a bouncy program of dance music that owes a lot to the remnants of disco. The album is a bit slick; Madonna's lack of a discernible style keeps it from being a creatively significant debut. Three producers (Reggie Lucas, Jellybean Benitez and Mark Kamins) give her different sonic settings, but in every case the beat and the voice—alternately soulful and coquettish—are the focal points.

Like a Virgin (a British reissue adds the alluring "Into the Groove," recorded for the soundtrack of Madonna the Actor's film debut, *Desperately Seeking Susan*) is a far more impressive affair, a full-blown self-invention that covers all the bases and made Ms. Ciccone a culture-rending global star. Nile Rodgers' outrageous production packs the songs with hooks and gimmicks, finishing each off with a fine sonic shine. "Material Girl," "Like a Virgin," "Over and Over," "Dress You Up" and others all served to build her character, fill dancefloors and remain in pop fans' memories indefinitely. (Incidentally, Madonna the Songwriter was barely involved in composing the tunes: the dreaded Billy Steinberg/Tom Kelly hook factory, for instance, whipped up the image-building "Like a Virgin" all by themselves.) Regardless of opinions about Madonna the Star, **Like a Virgin** is a first-rate record.

True Blue, on the other hand, isn't very good at all. Mega-successful, yes, but the clichéd electro-dance production (Madonna, Patrick Leonard and Stephen Bray) and half-baked songwriting keep it from serious creative contention. Madonna sings up a storm, but her dedication to musical variety makes for hit-or-miss records, and **True Blue** rarely connects. Only "Open Your Heart," with an unforgettably hooky chorus, the atmospheric "Live to Tell," on which she resembles Joni Mitchell, and the corny '50s-like title track are any

good. Maudlin rubbish ("Papa Don't Preach"), mindless dancearama ("Where's the Party") and an embarrassingly amateurish cinematic salute ("White Heat") are among the album's missteps.

Who's That Girl, although virtually billed as such, isn't a Madonna album. The soundtrack of her best-forgotten 1987 film contains tracks by Coati Mundi, Scritti Politti, Club Nouveau and others; Madonna contributes a quartet of new tunes, although only the delightful "Who's That Girl" is worth hearing.

Flexing her dance-club muscles, Madonna then issued **You Can Dance**, a career-spanning retrospective of various producers' mundane remixes. "Holiday," "Everybody," "Physical Attraction," "Over and Over," "Into the Groove" and "Where's the Party" all get the treatment; the record also contains "Spotlight," a previously unissued throwaway. The CD adds three more remixes for a full program of moving and (into the) grooving.

Fully anointed as the decade's biggest and most influential female pop star, Madonna demonstrated her ability to craft flawless and hollow product on **Like a Prayer**, an album/event pretentious enough to be bathed in the scent of church incense and conscientious enough to include serious information about AIDS on a small insert. Musically, the record (written and produced by Madonna in collaboration with, individually, Patrick Leonard, Prince and Stephen Bray) has something for everybody, especially dancers: high drama ("Like a Prayer"), pseudo-Motown ("Express Yourself") and bouncy '50s pop ("Cherish"). But while Madonna is busy cashing in with those catchy hits (and a Prince tune, "Love Song," that never gets off the ground), she also devotes much of the record to personal exorcisms that would be stronger if her voice bore even a trace of conviction. The grand ballad "Promise to Try" is a farewell to her late mother; "Oh Father" offers a lot of blame and a bit of forgiveness to her dad; "Till Death Do Us Part" is a bitter kiss-off to her ex-husband. Enigmatically, the album's closing track, "Act of Contrition," is a wild psychedelic joke that conflates religion and squalling guitar noise to no appreciable effect.

That **I'm Breathless** (subtitled "Music from and Inspired by the Film *Dick Tracy*") is a bad record probably goes without saying, but it's still a surprise to hear how grotesque the results of Madonna's theatrical aspirations are. Using a frightening closetful of unsuitable voices (leave Carmen Miranda alone!), Madonna sings three of the great Stephen Sondheim's worst toss-offs and a bunch of inept genre imitations, culminating in a smugly crude spanking number, "Hanky Panky." The record's only notable track, "Vogue," is just an empty shell of a song, style sans substance. Madonna may have the power to do anything she cares to, but this record demonstrates that she doesn't have the talent to get away with it. (In the next test of her abilities, Madonna wound up 1990 with the controversial "Justify My Love" single/video/sample.)

While omitting such huge charters as "Dress You Up" and "True Blue," **The Immaculate Collection** rounds up fifteen of Madonna's smashes, from 1983's "Holiday" through 1990's "Vogue," adding two new tunes: "Justify My Love" and "Rescue Me." [i]

MAD PROFESSOR

See *Lee Perry, Ruts.*

MAGAZINE

Real Life (Virgin) 1978 (Blue Plate) 1991 ●
Secondhand Daylight (Virgin) 1979 (Blue Plate) 1991 ●
The Correct Use of Soap (Virgin) 1980 (Blue Plate) 1991 ●
Sweetheart Contract EP (nr/Virgin) 1980
Play. (IRS) 1980 ●
Magic, Murder and the Weather (IRS) 1981 ●
After the Fact. (nr/Virgin) 1982 (IRS) 1982 ●
Rays & Hail 1978–1981 [CD] (Virgin) 1987 ●
Scree: Rarities 1978-1981 [CD] (nr/Virgin) 1990 (Blue Plate) 1991 ●

Singer/writer Howard Devoto left the Buzzcocks in an effort to move beyond punk and power pop and take rock music to new levels of complexity and sophistication without losing the recently regained energy of the form. To this end, he formed Magazine with then-unknowns John McGeoch (guitar/sax), Barry Adamson (bass), Dave Formula (keyboards) and drummer Martin Jackson (replaced after just one LP). They advanced a music of many styles and moods with lyrics full of obfuscation and a lush, many-faceted sound, still maintaining the rudimentary passion au courant in the music of 1978. Devoto disbanded Magazine in 1981 to pursue a solo career.

Produced by John Leckie, **Real Life** sports an eerie Grand Guignol sound throughout its nine punchy pop tunes, including the Devoto/Shelley-composed hit, "Shot by Both Sides." Adamson's driving bass and Formula's electronics dominate the presentation, while Devoto paints a deranged world of betrayal and suspicion, mixing urban alienation with such material as Tibetan mysticism and the Kennedy assassination. But beneath the dark veneer is humor and top-notch music.

Secondhand Daylight, produced by Colin Thurston, benefits from the change in drummers—John Doyle's style is more fluid and less chunky than his predecessor. Devoto's simplified lyrics focus on insurmountable emotional distances between people, aurally realized with dislocated, keyboard-heavy music.

The Correct Use of Soap is more upbeat, returning to **Real Life**'s popness (without the manic depression), and shows Magazine to be a mature and cohesive band. The mix adds an element of funk, and Devoto reveals a Costello-like flair for playful lyrics. The album uses some of Magazine's best songs, including "Sweetheart Contract," "Philadelphia" and "A Song from Under the Floorboards." Highly recommended. (The subsequent 12-inch appends three 1980 live performances from Manchester—including "Shot by Both Sides" and "Twenty Years Ago"—to the title track.)

Play. records a 1980 Australian concert, but a great performance is marred by production that distances Devoto's vocals from the music. Although guitarist Robin Simon, John McGeoch's replacement, fails to integrate fully, the band is relaxed and in control, and the album continues in **Soap**'s joyously sardonic vein. "Give Me Everything" and "Twenty Years Ago," both otherwise non-LP, are included.

Magic, Murder and the Weather is controlled by Dave Formula's keyboards, with Devoto taking a turn for the grotesque, as on the casual ditty called "The Honeymoon Killers." The prevalent moods are sarcasm and resignation, making Devoto's decision to break up the band almost simultaneously with the record's release no great surprise.

The posthumous **After the Fact.** collection was released in two drastically different forms, with only five tracks in common. The British edition (green cover) contains an obvious trio of singles and seven album tracks—a nice retrospective, but nothing extraordinary. The American version (red cover) contains B-sides ("My Mind Ain't So Open," a 1978 item incorrectly noted as having been released in 1977, "Goldfinger," "I Love You, You Big Dummy," "TV Baby" and "The Book") as well as some of the same album extractions. **Rays & Hail**, a CD-only retrospective which almost completely absorbs the prior UK compilation, draws on all of the band's albums, adding the original single version of "Shot by Both Sides." In a final stroke that makes every last bit of Magazine's catalogue widely available, **Scree**—a carefully annotated collection of B-sides (and non-LP A-sides) that repeats ten songs from the American **After the Fact.** and complements **Rays & Hail**—was released. [sg/i]

See also *Barry Adamason, Buzzcocks, Nick Cave and the Bad Seeds, Howard Devoto, Richard Jobson, Visage.*

MAGNOLIAS

Concrete Pillbox (Twin/Tone) 1986
For Rent (Twin/Tone) 1988 ●
Dime Store Dream (Twin/Tone) 1989 ●

TOADSTOOL

The Sun Highway (Twin/Tone) 1990

Like a Frankenstein monster assembled to synthesize the sounds of Minneapolis, this young quartet spews back aspects of their hometown's Replacements, Soul Asylum and Hüsker Dü with gusto on **Concrete Pillbox**, which they co-produced with Grant Hart. (Note the familiar drum sound.) Some of weedy singer/rhythm guitarist John Freeman's songs show real melodic and structural promise; a bit of power pop (and a faint Cheap Trick influence) emerges in the group's aggressive playing.

Replacements soundman Monty Wilkes co-produced **For Rent**, a looser, better-developed collection that features a new bassist and a snare-happy mix. Roaring out of the starting gate with "Walk a Circle," "Glory Hop" and "Goodbye for Now," the Mags shed imitation (save an abiding Buzzcocks influence) for a loud, textured personality they can call their own. Over catchy riffs that put a nifty twist into the hard-driving songs, Freeman's voice registers aggression in both hoarse rage and quiet poise. A very promising sophomore LP.

Recording the inconclusive **Dime Store Dream** in Prince's Paisley Park Studios didn't make the Magnolias funky, but it did give them a raging guitar sound. A busy new drummer and producer Jim Rondinelli's overheated mix interfere with the group's small-scale charm, but some cool songs ("Flowin' Thru," "Don't See That Girl," the pseudo-Replacements "Coming on Too

Strong," "In My Nightmare") do cut through. While Freeman's singing gives the album its reassuring consistency, bits of vocal syncopation add an intriguing new dimension.

Concrete Pillbox bassist John Joyce later formed Toadstool with guitarist Brad White and a drummer. Co-produced by Dave Pirner of Soul Asylum, **The Sun Highway** is a promising but underdeveloped debut that frequently obscures great lyrics and intriguing ideas (the jazz horns and folk forays, f'rinstance) in an amorphous blur of loose'n'noisy post-punk.   [i]

FRED MAHER
See *Material, Robert Quine.*

MALCOLM'S INTERVIEW
See *God's Little Monkeys.*

MALLET-HEAD
Mallet-Head (Old Nick-Frontier) 1988 ●
Yeah Yeah Yeah (Frontier-BMG) 1990 ●

Leaving Boston skatepunks Gang Green to their stylistic waffle, guitarist Chuck Stilphen and his bass-wielding brother Glen took a decisive step across the metal line and formed Mallet-Head with singer Morgan Keating and a drummer. Buoyed by Chuck's effective production and the occasionally clever lyrics ("It Was a Blasphemy, Was It a Blast for You?"), **Mallet-Head** is crisp and economical speed metal that makes its entrance with a brief dub reggae instrumental. (The cassette adds two bonus tracks.)

Changing drummers, Mallet-Head slowed the pace and thickened up the instrumental tone to become bullshitless Cult-like hard-rockers on the solidly enjoyable **Yeah Yeah Yeah**. Keating's commanding vocals fit the part, and Stilphen's guitar work is strictly '70s raunch, not '80s hot-finger blur. Packing memorable melody hooks into straightforward numbers like "One Good Reason" and "Rolling Thunder," the quartet captures the old bands' surging spirit as much as their exciting sound. I wonder if they know "Nantucket Sleighride" . . .   [i]
See also *Gang Green.*

STEPHEN MALLINDER
See *Cabaret Voltaire.*

MANITOBA'S WILD KINGDOM
... And You? (Popular Metaphysics-MCA) 1990 ●

Where the Dictators shouldered heavy metal as a means to commercialize their punky pop, Wild Kingdom—reuniting that legendary New York band's vocalist Handsome Dick Manitoba, songwriter/bassist Andy Shernoff and super-guitarist Ross the Boss (a genuine metal star in his post-Dics career with Manowar)—does exactly the opposite. Injecting wit, economy, intelligence and classic pop structure into heavyweight rock power, the brief but utterly satisfying . . . **And You?** is metal for those allergic to the form and a substantial post-punk treat for those partial to attitude-heavy Velvet Underground acolytes. Reviving the Dictators' old "New York, New York" and adding nine equally

potent new tunes (many taking a chillingly older'n'wiser cautionary approach to drug-abuse and other self-indulgence), the LP is a fun-filled blast of riffs and roars that rocks like crazy, a credible continuation of the Dictators' ethos in a contempo setting.   [i]
See also *Dictators.*

MAN-KA-ZAM
See *Alan Milman Sect.*

EARLE MANKEY
Real World EP (Happy Hermit) 1985

Between studio stints with Dream 6 and his brother Jim's Concrete Blonde, ex-Sparks guitarist-turned-producer Earle Mankey—who launched his solo career with a nifty 1978 single ("Mau Mau" b/w "Crazy") and an overlapping 1981 EP—issued the six-song **Real World**. Johnette N. "designed" the cover (the art is an adorable primitive portrait of the artist by his son) and, along with brother Jim, "yells" on one track. "Bigger Than Life" has tongue-in-cheek Nick Lowe charm and harmonies Brian Wilson might enjoy; otherwise **Real World** passes by quickly and uneventfully.   [i]
See also *Sparks.*

BARBARA MANNING
Lately I Keep Scissors (Heyday) 1988 ●
One Perfect Green Blanket EP (Heyday) 1991 ●

WORLD OF POOH
Land of Thirst (NufSed) 1989

On her solo debut, **Lately I Keep Scissors**, SF Bay Area singer/songwriter Barbara Manning—once bassist/vocalist in Chico's under-recorded 28th Day—produces starkly pretty folk-pop ("Never Park," "Scissors") and grungier rock ("Make It Go Away," "Something You've Got") with help from members of various San Francisco combos (Flying Color, Donner Party, Cat Heads). The album's deceptively simple music (with Ms. M. contributing cello, guitar and bass to the effort) is an apt reflection of Manning's unpretentiously personal songwriting, an uneasy balance of calm and tumult. (But what does one make of a musical fan letter to "Mark E. Smith & Brix"?) The album's CD version includes a stack of bonus tracks, which were also released separately on vinyl as **One Perfect Green Blanket**.

The World of Pooh has Manning playing bass and sharing vocal and songwriting duties with guitarist Brandan Kearney (a drummer rounds out the lineup). The music on **Land of Thirst** is considerably nastier than on Manning's solo record, but both writers' material—including a rougher-edged remake of "Scissors"—is well-crafted enough that the approach works.   [hd]

ROGER MANNING
Roger Manning (SST) 1988 ●

The problem with most of New York's "anti-folk" acousticians is that they can't shake Bob Dylan out of their Woody Guthrie fantasies. Wrapping themselves in the poverty and left-wing politics of classic troubadours, their rock roots make them selfconscious, overly aware and ambitious: stylemongering stars-in-training rather than hard-traveling truth-is-its-own-reward balladeers. That's not to say the genre hasn't unearthed talented artists and worthwhile records, merely that the price of honesty has gone up over the years.

On his engaging first album, Manning strums a simple guitar and sings intelligent, occasionally annoying, lyrics in a weedy tenor. While covering all the obligatory self-referential scene bases (Michelle Shocked, Cindy Lee Berryhill and Woody Guthrie all get namechecks), he spends a lot of time rambling ("The Hitch-Hikers' Blues," "The Airport Blues," "The Sicilian Train Blues") and singing about women. So what else is new? More interesting than entertaining, **Roger Manning** offers a clear lesson in the neo-folk form's strengths and contradictions. [i]

MANO NEGRA
Puta's Fever (Virgin) 1990 •

Reasonably but incompletely described as the French Pogues, the zany eight-man Mano Negra throw together a frenzied ragout of multinationalism on **Puta's Fever**, a record—sung in English, Spanish, French and Arabic—in which rock, funk, reggae, folk, flamenco, zouk, salsa, gospel, jazz and numerous other pancultural idioms collide in an exhilarating rush of hyperkinetic merriment. Forget the boring Gipsy Kings—Mano Negra is a band Jerry Lewis fans can really understand! With lyrics that are just as conventional as the music, guitarist/singer Manu Chao's well-crafted songs switch settings—continents, even—as if it were the most natural thing for them to do. Hearing the album for the first time is to enter a dizzying carousel of colorful sounds that are impossible to grasp; becoming intimate with **Puta's Fever** is to really feel its indescribable pleasures. [i]

MAN SIZED ACTION
Claustrophobia (Reflex) 1983
Five Story Garage (Reflex) 1984

To be the coolest band in Minneapolis nowadays you need a little more vision and talent than the gallant Man Sized Action could muster. But to be a cool band anywhere, all you need is this unpretentious lot's commitment to a few good ideas. Man Sized Action opened up punk structures with distorted, ringing guitar, some off-kilter rhythms and emotionally *sung* lyrics. Like Hüsker Dü, they applied a neanderthal, propulsive attack to fundamentally poppy songs.

The lo-fi **Claustrophobia**, produced by Hüsker Düde Bob Mould, sets up powerful grooves, but never escapes its murky dynamic. Particularly on "My Life," Tippy's singing wall of guitar and Kelly Linehan's supporting bass hint at the band's ability to create beautifully textured sounds without sacrificing power or bracing crudeness.

Five Story Garage adds better production, better songs and a second guitarist. The quintet generates a surge of momentum that threatens to explode its punky pop hooks, making the album fast, powerful and surprisingly accessible. [jl]

ZEKE MANYIKA
See *Orange Juice*.

PHIL MANZANERA
Diamond Head (Atco) 1975 (EG) 1990 •
K-Scope (EG-Polydor) 1978 (EG) 1982 •
Primitive Guitars (Editions EG) 1982 •
Guitarissimo 75–82 (EG) 1987 •
Southern Cross (nr/Expression) 1990 •

QUIET SUN
Mainstream (Antilles) 1975

PHIL MANZANERA/801
801 Live (EG-Polydor) 1976 (EG) 1982 •
Listen Now (nr/Polydor) 1977 (EG) 1982 •

WETTON/MANZANERA
Wetton/Manzanera (Geffen) 1987

Although not quite the founding guitarist in Roxy Music, Phil Manzanera was one of its three enduring pillars, and his radical instrumental approaches were as much a part of the band's early stylistic groundbreaking as Bryan Ferry's equally unprecedented vocals.

Before joining Roxy (as sound mixer; he took over on guitar in early '72), the debonair Briton who was raised in Latin America spent a couple of years in Quiet Sun, a progressive outfit that had broken up but reformed temporarily in 1975 to cut a debut album. **Mainstream** is a jazzy, Soft Machine-like outing enlivened by Manzanera's distortion-crazed solos and slices of other bizarreness (thanks, in part, to Eno's participation) cutting through the sophisticated instrumental arrangements. Best song title: "Mummy was an asteroid, daddy was a small non-stick kitchen utensil." The following year, drummer Charles Hayward went on to form This Heat.

Prior to the Quiet Sun reunion, Manzanera stepped out of Roxy for his pleasurable solo debut, the look-what-I-can-do **Diamond Head**. Joining him on this exploration of diverse styles are Roxy cohorts (Eno, Paul Thompson, Andy Mackay, John Wetton, Eddie Jobson), Quiet Sun (the whole group on one track) and the redoubtable Robert Wyatt, who sings lead—in Spanish—on "Frontera." Manzanera scarcely opens his mouth on the half-instrumental record, leaving Eno the mic for the wonderful "Big Day" and "Miss Shapiro," both of which strongly resemble **Here Come the Warm Jets**.

Manzanera's next significant side project (neglecting, of course, his contributions to records by Nico, Eno, Ferry, John Cale, Mackay, Split Enz and others) was 801. Originally assembled to play a handful of concerts during a period of Roxy inactivity in 1976, the first 801 consisted of Manzanera, Eno, Quiet Sun bassist Bill MacCormick, drummer Simon Phillips and two others. Recorded in London, **801 Live** draws material from **Diamond Head**, **Here Come the Warm Jets** and **Mainstream**, adding the Beatles' "Tomorrow Never Knows" and the Kinks' "You Really Got Me." A spectacular example of cross-culturalization that should be of serious interest to Roxy fans.

Two years later, a studio album, employing almost the entire performing cast and then some, returned 801 to life. **Listen Now** consists of new Manzanera compositions and is actually not unlike a solo record, but his partnership with MacCormick justifies the group designation. Unfortunately, much of the record is conservative and dull, an overly smooth and sophisticated collection (maybe it's Kevin Godley's influence) that rarely ignites. The long pieces—mostly vocalized by Simon Ainley and a collection of backup singers—are radio-ready but barely sentient.

During another Roxy hiatus, Manzanera created the livelier solo-billed **K-Scope** in collaboration with many of 801's players. Clever lyrics sung by Tim Finn (ex-Split Enz) and saxes by Mel Collins (ex-King Crimson) are matched by Manzanera's invigorated (and invigorating) guitar work and Phillips' kinetic drumming. There's calm restraint (like "Cuban Crisis" and the endless "Walking Through Heaven's Door") amid the rock drive and dance-happy energy, but that contrast only gives the delightful record even deeper appeal.

To celebrate his tenth anniversary as a professional musician, Manzanera released **Primitive Guitars**, a solo instrumental album that shows numerous sides of his virtuosity. Guided by chronological and geographical themes that defy instant comprehension, the album stretches the sound of guitar all over the map (much of it to Latin lands) in a challenging zigzag of styles and approaches. Except for one bass part, Phil plays everything on the LP, which suffers not a jot by the isolation. As a fascinating self-defined retrospective of Manzanera's musical development, **Primitive Guitars** may be lost on some of his followers, while certainly connecting with others.

The lengthy (over 54 minutes on vinyl!) **Guitarissimo** "collocation" organizes tracks from Manzanera's solo records and both 801 outings into four thematic sections. Careful annotation and thoughtful sequencing make up for the compromised sonic quality, but the CD (with four bonus tracks) is an altogether better value.

Proving that even unassailably tasteful artists can take a dive, Manzanera made an unfortunate album with onetime bandmate John Wetton, following the latter's superstar sojourn in Asia. **Wetton/Manzanera** is depressing commercial tripe seemingly geared to relaunch Wetton's career from Asia's coattails. Strangely, "Keep on Loving Yourself" is about self-respect, something this project pointedly lacks.

Manzanera's Latin heritage gets strong play on **Southern Cross**, a record with a lot of taste and seasoning but no strong flavor. Surrounding a glitzy guitar-and-horns rendition of "Guantamera" (ably sung by Ana Maria Velez, one of the album's three lead vocalists; Tim Finn is another), the original material is bland, with political-minded lyrics ("Dr Fidel," "A Million Reasons Why") that are too clumsy and vague to make any point. In fact, the most eloquent track on the album is the dreamy and steamy titular instrumental, performed by Manzanera and Brazilian percussionist Basco De Oliviera.   [i]

See also *Explorers, Roxy Music, This Heat.*

THOMAS MAPFUMO AND THE ACID BAND
The Chimurenga Singles 1976–1980 (Shanachie) 1984 ●

THOMAS MAPFUMO AND THE BLACKS UNLIMITED
Gwindingwi Rine Shumba (nr/Earthworks) 1980 + 1986
Ndangariro EP (nr/Earthworks) 1983 (Carthage) 1984 ●
Mabasa (nr/Earthworks) 1984
Mr. Music (nr/Earthworks) 1985

Chimurenga for Justice (Shanachie) 1986
Corruption (Mango) 1989 ●
Chamunorwa (Mango) 1991 ●

From nightclub singer to political firebrand, Thomas Mapfumo's career has elevated him to near-sainthood in his native Zimbabwe. **The Chimurenga Singles**, recorded with the Acid (as in bitter) Band, carries an interesting disclaimer: "The quality of these tracks leaves much to be desired, but remember they were made under war conditions." Influenced by Voice of Zimbabwe radio broadcasts, Mapfumo participated in the country's liberation struggle, and was jailed for his troubles. The singles deal in political innuendo and are sung in the native Shona language. The sound is rushed, as if time were of the essence; as the cymbals hyperventilate and the guitars skitter along (in plinking imitation of the thumb piano), Mapfumo sings serious and subtle songs of revolution.

Some of the six long tracks on **Ndangariro** (which postdate the material compiled on **The Chimurenga Singles** and Zimbabwe's independence) resemble Mapfumo's early work, but others foretell his calmer artistic future. His later recordings are more languid and even include some love songs. The grooves are lazier, but the guitar retains a rapid-fire hunt-and-peck quality. The wonderful **Chimurenga for Justice**, for instance, blends a surprisingly uninflected loping reggae beat with a peppy African sound and even an American soul-influenced approach on half a dozen richly performed songs about struggle and praise. Trumpets and two female vocalists provide sweet counterpoint to Mapfumo's husky singing.

Delivered with the same heavenly allure by pretty backing vocals, crisp horns and gently rolling tempos, the songs on **Corruption** grapple with troubles aplenty. The English-language title track chants "something for something/nothing for nothing" in criticizing the misuse of power; "Shabeen" chastises men led astray by alcohol and hookers; "Kupera Kwevhanu" concerns the travails endured by Mozambique. Were more of the lyrics in English, accepting the stark contrast of content and presentation might be more challenging; as it stands, however, basking in the sounds of Mapfumo's marvelous music is no chore at all.   [rg/i]

MARC AND THE MAMBAS
See *Marc Almond.*

MARCH VIOLETS
Religious as Hell EP (nr/Merciful Release) 1982
Natural History (nr/Rebirth) 1984
Electric Shades (Relativity) 1985

The March Violets began in 1981 as one of Leeds' four famous drum machine bands, alongside the Sisters of Mercy, Three Johns and Red Lorry Yellow Lorry. The Violets favored stark, primitive rhythm-box beats (as did the others), overlaid by Loz Elliott's heavy bass throb and Tom Ashton's inventively droning guitar (reminiscent of Magazine's John McGeoch). What set this quartet apart was the unique interplay (à la X or the Airplane) between the two complementary lead vocalists—big, bearded Simon Denbigh and enigmatic Rosie Garland. His dark, commanding intonations intertwined with her eerie soprano wailing, imbuing the simplistic material with a strident, almost dissonant mystery.

Before a schism with Andrew Eldritch led the Violets to start their own Rebirth label, they were on the Sisters' label, Merciful Release, starting with **Religious as Hell**, an establishing 7-inch. **Natural History** collects the band's early work, including the EP (save for the odd "Bon Bon Babies"), three follow-up 45s (the brilliant "Grooving in Green," "Crow Baby" and the insistent '84 dancefloor hit, "Snake Dance") and such rarities as the searing "Radiant Boys" (copping the riff from the Cure's "Object") and mesmerizing "Undertow." Though not a discrete album, **Natural History** flows magnificently.

By "Snake Dance," Garland had departed, replaced by the more upbeat Cleo Murray. The lineup held for the subsequent "Walk into the Sun" but, as 1985 dawned, Denbigh was squeezed out of the band (he immediately formed Batfish Boys). The first post-Denbigh 45 (the misnamed "Deep") laid bare the Violets' weakened condition. **Electric Shades**, the band's second compilation album, assembles the entire contents of the three later singles: "Snake Dance," "Walk into the Sun" and "Deep." With the dissipation of the band's intensity, Cleo's thin, pretty lead vocals simply don't carry the new material. The Violets continued to surrender to conventionality, obtaining a real drummer and crassly exploiting Cleo's beauty. After contributing two items (including an amazingly catchy rendition of the Rolling Stones' "Miss Amanda Jones") to 1987's **Some Kind of Wonderful** soundtrack, the March Violets faded away. [gef]

See also *Batfish Boys*.

A.C. MARIAS

One of Our Girls (Has Gone Missing) (Mute-Restless) 1989 ●

When not working behind the camera as a successful video clip director, Angela Conway steps up to the mic and assumes the identity of cool chanteuse A.C. Marias. On her quietly atmospheric records, she receives writing and production assistance from Wire guitarist Bruce Gilbert, as well as former Fad Gadget sideman-turned-bigtime-producer John Fryer. The somnolent first side of **One of Our Girls**—a sheer pastel curtain of arty guitar figures, light synth strains, and dry, wispy vocals that never quite achieves song-ness—floats by uneventfully. Fortunately, the rest of the record has more structural starch, and Marias' dance through an evanescent field of gentle art-rock has moments of real allure. [i]

MARINE GIRLS

Beach Party (nr/Whaam!) 1981 (nr/Cherry Red) 1987 ●
Lazy Ways (nr/Cherry Red) 1983 ●

Except for flashes of vocal strength ("He Got the Girl" is pretty impressive) from future Everything but the Girl woman Tracey Thorn, the Marine Girls' minimalist debut—released on the TV Personalities' label—is a sorry attempt at writing and performing offbeat romantic pop. Between Thorn's hapless guitar playing—supported by bits of percussion, Jane Fox's

marginally better bass work and occasional seagull sounds—and the quartet's two inept singers (one of whom, Alice Fox, would go on to form Grab Grab the Haddock), **Beach Party** is a winceable soiree worth missing.

Produced by Stuart Moxham (Young Marble Giants/Gist), **Lazy Ways** is a lot better, although still not a complete treat. Besides an overall improvement in songwriting, Thorn's jazzy playing is vastly improved. With the first album's most egregious tune-mangler gone, Jane Fox's uneven singing has become the trio's weakest link, and she dooms a good chunk of the album to the wrong side of competence. (**Lazy Ways** and **Beach Party** were later combined on a single cassette and CD.) [i]

See also *Everything but the Girl, Grab Grab the Haddock*.

MARLEY MARL

In Control Volume 1 (Cold Chillin'-Warner Bros.) 1988 ●

As many mainstream rappers—from Heavy D. and Biz Markie to Big Daddy Kane and Roxanne Shanté—already know, having producer Marley Marl (also a New York radio DJ) in control means great backing tracks. Keeping his own voice off the mic, Marl's album is a collection of collaborations with various MCs, including all of the above, M.C. Shan, the up-and-coming Master Ace and others. For all its diversity, **In Control** gives too much play to second-string rhymers, leaving the LP's few highlights (such as the Biz twigging Barry Manilow in "We Write the Songs" and Shanté playing cute word games in "Wack Itt") adrift in a sea of verbal boreplay. [i]

BOB MARLEY & THE WAILERS

Natty Dread (Island) 1975 (Tuff Gong) 1990 ●
Live! (Island) 1975 (Tuff Gong) 1990 ●
Rastaman Vibration (Island) 1976 (Tuff Gong) 1990 ●
Exodus (Island) 1977 (Tuff Gong) 1990 ●
Kaya (Island) 1978 (Tuff Gong) 1990 ●
Babylon by Bus (Island) 1978 (Tuff Gong) 1990 ●
Survival (Island) 1979 (Tuff Gong) 1990 ●
Uprising (Island) 1980 (Tuff Gong) 1990 ●
Confrontation (Island) 1983 (Tuff Gong) 1990 ●
Legend: The Best of Bob Marley and the Wailers (Island) 1984 (Tuff Gong) 1990 ●
Rebel Music (Island) 1986 (Tuff Gong) 1990 ●
Talkin' Blues (Tuff Gong) 1991 ●

WAILERS

Catch a Fire (Island) 1973 (Tuff Gong) 1990 ●
Burnin' (Island) 1973 (Tuff Gong) 1990 ●

It is safe to say that the world would be a very different—and vastly poorer—place were it not for Bob Marley. Carrying the homegrown sounds of a small Caribbean island to Europe, Africa and America, he is directly responsible for a rhythm and a style that has moved millions and influenced every form of popular music for the past two decades. By exploding Eurocentric myths about the vitality and value of cultures beyond the borders of Britain and the US, he encouraged widespread cultural curiosity, as well as sparking the rediscovery of their heritage by countless people of color. And by building his art on a platform of esoteric religious faith and progressive Third World politics, Marley demonstrated a rare degree of defiance and courage for a global celebrity, and that has made him an enduring political/cultural hero to many.

In the early '60s, the Wailin' Wailers—basically Marley, Neville Livingstone (aka Bunny Wailer) and Peter MacKintosh (later Tosh)—were Jamaica's leading ska band, taking their cues from American R&B as much as an indigenous form called mento. (The group's early work can be heard on numerous anthologies, including 1990's **The Birth of a Legend**.) They disbanded in 1966, and Marley moved to Delaware, but returned home in 1967, reunited the old group and began fitting together the pieces of what would come to be known as reggae: a rhythmic style that was then gaining popularity in Jamaica, belief in Ras Tafari and its attendant effects (marijuana use, dreadlocks, language, politics, etc.) and a bottom-heavy production sound learned from producer Lee Perry and his studio's mighty rhythm section (bassist Aston "Family Man" Barrett and his drummer brother Carlton, both of whom became Wailers).

By the early '70s, the reggae revolution was in full swing in Jamaica, and the timely interest of Island Records was all it took to introduce this local phenomenon to the rest of the world. While awfully mild-sounding now, **Catch a Fire** (originally issued in a gimmicky flip-top cigarette lighter sleeve) delivered a stunning blast of warm tropical air and eloquent political reality amid the giddy glam-rock of 1972 England. "Concrete Jungle" and "Stir It Up" (an international hit for Johnny Nash around the same time) proved Marley to be an extremely gifted songwriter; Tosh's "400 Years" showed that there was more to the quintet than its charismatic lead singer. (Besides changing the cover art, later editions of the album began crediting it to Bob Marley and the Wailers.)

Released the same year, **Burnin'**—the final record by the original lineup—has a funkier sound and two genuine classics: "Get Up, Stand Up" and "I Shot the Sheriff." As watered down as his interpretation of the song is, Eric Clapton's 1974 hit cover of the latter actually helped bring reggae to the attention of those who hadn't yet met the real thing.

With Tosh and Wailer gone, Marley brought in guitarist Al Anderson, a keyboard player and a female backing trio (the I-Threes: Judy Mowatt, Rita Marley and Marcia Griffiths) to make **Natty Dread**. Completely in charge and growing in confidence, Marley demonstrates the diversity in his music and the seriousness of his message with such memorable songs as the tender "No Woman, No Cry," "Revolution" and "Lively Up Yourself," an old Wailers' tune given an updated arrangement.

Recorded onstage in London in July 1975, **Live!** (aka **Live at the Lyceum**) draws six of its seven numbers from the preceding two albums, thereby summarizing and expanding upon his international career to that point. More so than in their studio versions, the songs ring with emotional power in these concert renditions, allowing listeners to join Marley in his life-affirming celebration.

Although not released until 1991, **Talkin' Blues** contains intriguing rarities from this era: seven live tracks from a 1973 California radio broadcast (with Tosh but not Livingstone on hand), a second version of "I Shot the Sheriff" from the London gigs recorded for **Live!** and three outtakes from the **Natty Dread** sessions. While gratuitous, the brief interview bites that alternate with these extraordinary performances are not particularly disruptive to the record's flow.

Stylistically, **Rastaman Vibration** builds on **Live at the Lyceum**'s loose-limbed atmosphere. A ten-person group lays down bubbling riddims covering reggaecentricity ("Positive Vibration," "Roots, Rock, Reggae") and pointed demands for justice ("Johnny Was" and "War," its lyrics taken from a 1968 speech by Ras Tafari himself, Haile Selassie).

Marley's first release after being wounded in a December 1976 assassination attempt is a handsomely delivered but firmly stated outpouring of politics and religion. Although **Exodus** offers upbeat optimism in "Jamming," "One Love/People Get Ready" and the title track, it also contains imprecations against "Guiltiness" and "The Heathen." Still capable of bringing things down to an individual level, "Waiting in Vain" is one of Marley's most touching love songs. Besides making good use of horns, the Wailers benefit here from an adjusted lineup that includes guitarist Junior (Julian) Marvin.

A lyric in the first song on the understated but enticing **Kaya** aptly describes the record: "We're taking it easy/We taking it slow." At the outset, the lighter sounds and personal lyrics that fill the sunny grooves skirt the big issues for joyful celebrations ("Kaya") and gentle romance ("Is This Love"). But the mood slides straight downhill, from "She's Gone" to "Crisis," culminating in the fatalistic spiritualism of "Time Will Tell."

The Wailers' 1978 tour was chronicled in **Babylon by Bus**, a double live album (originally released in a nifty die-cut sleeve) recorded at various European venues. Another flawless Island-spanning recap of hits given new resonance onstage, the program includes elongated renditions of "Positive Vibration," "Stir It Up," "Jamming," "Is This Love?" and many more.

Al Anderson, who had returned to the group in time for **Babylon by Bus**, again shares leads with Marvin on **Survival**, a politically significant album in which Marley dedicates himself to Third World solidarity. "Africa Unite," "Zimbabwe," "One Drop" and "Top Rankin' " all preach an international message and reflect Marley's growing stature.

The last album Marley recorded before his death in 1981, caps his career by touching on many diverse elements with his most profoundly beautiful music. From the hauntingly political lament of "Redemption Song" to the irresistible surge of "Could You Be Loved" and the praises of "Forever Loving Jah," **Uprising** comes straight from Marley's soul.

The posthumous **Confrontation**—which contains the excellent and pointed "Buffalo Soldier" and other worthwhile tracks without quite adding up to a real album—is in fact an uneven collection of outtakes and tracks that had not previously been released outside of Jamaica.

Legend is a unassailable one-disc compilation of the best-loved tracks from Marley's Island catalogue; **Rebel Music** attends to the political side of his oeuvre, both celebrating and ghettoizing it.

A complete discography of the Wailers would include countless other compilations of various eras, solo albums by Wailer, Tosh (who, like Carlton Barrett, was murdered in 1987) and others, as well as releases by the alumni who began using the Wailers name again in the late '80s.   [i]

See also *Alpha Blondy, Judy Mowatt.*

ZIGGY MARLEY AND THE MELODY MAKERS
See *Melody Makers.*

PAUL MAROTTA
Agit-Prop Piano (Do Speak) 1983
STYRENES
Girl Crazy (Mustard) 1982
HUDSON-STYRENE
A Monster and the Devil (Tinnitus) 1989

On his solo album, Marotta—a very early leading light in the Cleveland underground scene with such bands as the Poli Styrene Jass Band, which also contained future Pere Ubuites Anton Fier and Jim Jones—plays acoustic piano in a thickly overlapping, improvised mesh of ambient sound that can be considered either as serious avant-garde music or a hypnotic drone for trancing out. The two long pieces, much like Glenn Branca's work on guitars, go nowhere, but do something aurally seductive while getting there.

As a fascinating retrospective of a weird old band, the Styrenes' album (Marotta produced, co-wrote, sings and plays piano, guitar and bass with longtime cohort guitarist Jamie Klimek and others) is worth seeking out for its odd combination of styles and sounds. Best of all, it contains the crazed 1975 "Drano in Your Veins," one of America's first independent-label new wave records.

Marotta wrote and organized the brassy noir jazz/ rock for **A Monster and the Devil**, providing a textured and kinetic bed for vocalist Mike Hudson (of Cleveland's legendary Pagans) to rhythmically riff seedy hard-edged stories about drug abusers and assorted losers. Hudson's casual conviction and Marotta's inventive instrumentation gives the mix of words and music a dramatic energy that's utterly riveting. Recommended to fans of Bukowski and Selby.   [i]

MARS
The Mars EP (Infidelity) 1980
78 (Widowspeak) 1986
VARIOUS ARTISTS
No New York (Antilles) 1978
John Gavanti (Hyrax) 1981

"Your hair on cars/your arms detach/your eyes fly by/your torso in wax." With those immortal words Mars caterwauled into the hearts of noise lovers everywhere, marking the quartet's four-song appearance on **No New York** with an absolutely total lack of musical ability. (All the other bands on the Eno-produced compilation contained at least one member who could play in the traditional sense.) A bunch of New York art types who formed a band when that was considered a cool New York art type thing to do, Mars was pretty impressive if for nothing else than singleness of purpose. Often

sounding like a screeching subway car driven by a jabbering, convulsive castrato, Mars' constantly revulsed stance made the rest of **No New York**'s I-hate-sex crowd seem like a bunch of rank sensualists by comparison. Arto Lindsay recorded a 1978 CBGB set that comprises the 1980 12-inch EP; a few years later, Jim (Foetus) Thirlwell compiled and remixed the **No New York** tracks, all but one song from the EP and the group's single. The resultant **78** is all the Mars you need.

Around the turn of the decade, Mars leader Sumner Crane corralled a bunch of cohorts (including DNA drummer Ikue Mori) and recorded **John Gavanti**, a no wave adaptation of—get this—**Don Giovanni**. Some have called this the most unlistenable record ever made, and that's a fine invitation indeed.   [gk]

CARL MARSH
See *Shriekback.*

MARTHA AND THE MUFFINS
Metro Music (Virgin Int'l) 1980
Trance and Dance (nr/DinDisc) 1980
This Is the Ice Age (nr/DinDisc) 1981
Danseparc (RCA) 1982
Faraway in Time [CD] (nr/Virgin) 1988 ●
M + M
Mystery Walk (RCA) 1984
The World Is a Ball (Can. Current) 1985

Martha and the Muffins were originally clever amateurs who had fun fooling around with music in Toronto. However, the subtly catchy "Echo Beach" made them chart stars in the UK and brought their days of leisure to an abrupt halt. A minor miracle of this slick age, **Metro Music** captures a mild-mannered, unpretentious group at its most charming, before stress and self-consciousness took their toll. Vocalist Martha Johnson has a sometimes awkward but always personable style of singing on "Echo Beach," "Indecision" and "Paint by Number Heart"; it's as if she walked into a studio to tell what happened to her that day rather than to perform. Sax player Andy Haas adds jazzier, more exotic flavorings (à la Roxy Music's Andy Mackay), while a confident rhythm section preserves the hard foundation. Some might call **Metro Music** wimpy, but a more sensitive observer would judge it the result of introverts trying to rock, and—on their own terms—succeeding handily.

The more mature **Trance and Dance** treads less appealing waters. The title track and "Was Ezo" retain the haunting quality of "Echo Beach," but other songs seem a little glib and too willing to be cute. Martha and the Muffins sound as if they're having less fun than before; second vocalist Martha Ladly (composer of "Was Ezo") left the group after this LP.

The band painted itself into a corner with **This Is the Ice Age**. "Women Around the World at Work," a catchy stab at mainstream pop-singledom, lacks the innocence that was their strong point. Much of the LP suffers from arid artiness—they're too cool for pop but can't settle comfortably into another groove. Sax player Andy Haas left after this LP.

Thus reduced to a quartet, Martha and the Muffins ventured down funky Broadway on **Danseparc**, adding a throbbing beat to the blend. As a detour, the title track is fine, and the guest sax provides a bit of continuity, but in other spots, Johnson's self-important singing grates and Mark Gane's overdrive guitar can't overcome the repetitious, overbearing pounding. The tunes that have a jazzy pop sensibility are good, but the battle between humming and bumping is clearly lost to the forces of motion. On a positive note, the album ends with a beautifully textured languid instrumental, "Whatever Happened to Radio Valve Road?"

Mystery Walk presents the penultimately reductive group of Martha and Mark—billed as M+M—paradoxically playing prosaic social-conscience funk on "Black Stations/White Stations" and rediscovering delicate, attractive melodicism (best exemplified by "Cooling the Medium"). Throughout, the record mixes a less-aggressive intellectual dancefloor sound and enticingly atmospheric, jazz-tinged pop. An excellent return to form.

Unfortunately, the competent but aimless **World Is a Ball** provides a rather chilly denouement to the band's career, emphasizing the portentousness of the Muffins' less-memorable work with nary a trace of the playfulness that made the original band fun. Only on the dancey "Song in My Head" do Johnson and Gane lighten up enough for the music to live up to the album's title.

A substantial sampler but by no means a definitive retrospective, the CD-only **Faraway in Time** compilation contains the entire **Metro Music** album plus selected tracks from **Trance and Dance** and **This Is the Ice Age**. [jy/i/hd]

See also *Crash Vegas*.

MARTINI RANCH

Holy Cow (Sire) 1988 ●

California musician Andrew Todd and Texas-born actor/filmmaker Bill Paxton (director of Barnes & Barnes' classic "Fish Heads" video) comprise Martini Ranch, a wickedly inventive, visually oriented pop-culture nuthouse of a band based in Los Angeles. **Holy Cow** variously resembles the B-52's (whose Cindy Wilson guests here), Devo (Mark Mothersbaugh and Alan Myers contribute vocally and instrumentally; Bob Casale produced one song) and Oingo Boingo. Judge Reinhold whistles on one tune; Bud Cort vocalizes on another. Kinetic, silly, intelligent and infectious. [i]

MARY MY HOPE

Museum (Silvertone-RCA) 1989 ●
Suicide Kings EP (Silvertone-RCA) 1989 ●

On the flawed and unfocused **Museum**, Atlanta's Mary My Hope simply tried to do and be too much, as shades of the Beatles, Doors, Pink Floyd, Bauhaus, R.E.M. and U2 flit through the overly ambitious songs, resulting in two killer tracks ("Suicide King" and "Communion"), several near-misses and several clunkers. Producer Hugh Jones does little to help untangle this intriguing but frustrating mess, which is not entirely unlike R.E.M.'s **Fables of the Reconstruction**—another album made by a quartet of Georgia boys out of their element in the UK.

Oddly, the five-song **Suicide Kings** shreds Museum and would have made a staggering debut. The album's two best cuts are combined with one shimmering new song and powerfully live "No remix no overdubs so it goes" renditions of two of the album's near-misses. It sheds a whole new light on the band, who produced the three new tracks themselves, thank you very much.

Vocalist James Vincent Hall left in 1990; Mary My Hope is carrying on with a replacement. [ja]

MARY'S DANISH

There Goes the Wondertruck ... (Chameleon) 1989 ●
Experience (Chameleon) 1990 φ

Inspired by fellow Los Angelenos X, this spunky sextet—which includes ex-Three O'Clock guitarist Louis Gutierrez in a subordinate role—takes tart, twangy vocal harmonies and sets 'em to a tough beat. Mary's Danish isn't nearly as demanding, however—shouters Julie Ritter and Gretchen Seager don't strive for the desperate intensity that came so easily to Exene and John Doe, while high-powered numbers like "Blue Stockings" and "Don't Crash the Car Tonight" have the accessibility of classic pop, something X always found elusive. **Wondertruck** has these and other cool cuts, including "Can I Have a Smoke, Dude?" and "Mary Had a Bar."

The spirited but mostly superfluous **Experience** features six live songs (five from the LP), plus a chaotic Dave Jerden-produced studio cover of Hendrix's "Foxey Lady," complete with grating horn section (!?!). [jy]

MASSACRE

See *Fred Frith, Material*.

MASTER ACE

Take a Look Around (Cold Chillin'-Reprise) 1990 ●

Decent enough to single out an 8th-grade English teacher as a positive influence, Brooklyn rapper Master Ace uses a set of fine Marley Marl tracks to deliver an optimistic uplift-the-race middle-class message on his highly impressive debut. Educational without being didactic, the imaginative young MC runs down a new program that shrugs off crass materialism and self-indulgent boasting without sounding sappy. **Take a Look Around** mixes things up effectively, partying with a better-known labelmate on "Me and the Biz" while innovatively adopting a fictional persona to convey a powerful sense of African-American despair in "The Other Side of Town" and ruing the B-boy errors of his youth in "Movin' On." With talent to spare, Master Ace is a man to watch. [i]

MASTERS OF CEREMONY

See *Brand Nubian*.

MASTERS OF REALITY

Masters of Reality (Def American) 1988 (Delicious Vinyl) 1990 ●

Hailing from Syracuse, New York, this unapologetically nonphotogenic quintet, led by singer/guitarist Chris Goss, kicked around NYC for some time before

411

catching the metallic ears of producer-guru and Def American honcho Rick Rubin. The result? One of the heaviest, most inventive hard rock records of the '80s, a heady amalgam of dripping Cream-style blues-blasting, mystical (and occasionally drug-related) lyrics and Zeppelinesque whomp. Among the album's many highlights is "The Candy Song," a crunching slab of riff-rock that showcases Goss' unusually smooth and supple pipes. Unfortunately, the Poison-fed MTV generation didn't get with this startling alternative.

In an unusual move, two powerful fans—Matt Dike and Michael Ross—decided the album needed a second shot, and arranged to reissue it (with an altered running order and one new track, "Doraldina's Prophesies," replacing "Sleep Walkin'," now CD-only) on their label, Delicious Vinyl. Meanwhile, the group underwent a notable lineup change, replacing axeman Tim Harrington with prolific producer-guitarist Daniel Rey and drummer Vinnie Ludovico with legendary Samuel Beckett lookalike Ginger Baker.   [db]

See also *Shrapnel*.

JAMES MASTRO
See *Bongos*.

MATCHING MOLE
See *Robert Wyatt*.

MATERIAL
Temporary Music 1 EP (Zu) 1979 (nr/Red Music) 1979
Temporary Music 2 EP (nr/Red Music) 1981
Temporary Music (Fr. Celluloid) 1981 ●
American Songs EP (Hol. Red Music) 1981
Busting Out EP (ZE-Island) 1981
Memory Serves (Celluloid-Elektra-Musician) 1981 ●
One Down (Celluloid-Elektra) 1982 ●
Red Tracks (Red) 1986
Seven Souls (Virgin) 1989 φ

MASSACRE
Killing Time (OAO-Celluloid) 1982 ●

NICKY SKOPELITIS
Next to Nothing [CD] (Venture-Virgin) 1989 ●

Originally formed to back Daevid Allen when the erstwhile Gong leader first toured the US, Material began as a small core of New York-based musicians around which an endless string of interesting one-shot gigging and recording bands formed. Bassist/producer Bill Laswell alone continues to use the Material name, but the original triumvirate with Michael Beinhorn (synthesizer, tapes, vocals) and Fred Maher (drums) made a virtue of eclecticism, effectively blending funk, rock, experimentalism and jazz into a subtle, credible fusion music all their own.

Not that they managed it right away. **Temporary Music 1**, produced by Giorgio Gomelsky, shows a promising progressive-rock band toying with funk and quickly miring itself in extraneous noise. But the funk-rock fusion takes hold on the sequel, as Stockhausen (figuratively) meets Moroder, and that approach didn't let them down thereafter. The **Temporary Music** album reissues the two EPs on one disc, as does **Red Tracks**.

American Songs, which features an intriguing appearance by guitarist Robert Quine on two new items, is just interesting enough not to be expendable.

Memory Serves is Material's most jazz-tinged album, with its complement of prominent jazz players on cut after relentless cut. Guitarist Fred Frith is also featured, starting an intermittently ongoing alliance. The procession of textures is dazzling, the funk cuts like a knife and the hornwork is disciplined within tight structures. As "black" classical and dance music refined with a rock sensibility, **Memory Serves** is a highly original crossover.

One Down extends the experiment to urban pop music with almost equal success, aided by Nile Rodgers, Nona Hendryx, Frith, Oliver Lake and many others. However, it lacks the edge of **Memory Serves**, and Maher's departure is probably the reason. Saxophonist Archie Shepp, black-power spokesman and angry young man of '60s jazz, puts in a politically interesting but musically low-key appearance on Hugh Hopper's "Memories."

In 1982, Laswell, Maher and Frith combined as Massacre, a radical power trio. The distinctively skewed melodies of **Killing Time**'s composed half—mostly on the first side, a brilliant procession of techniques and ideas—bear the Frith hallmark. Propelled by the virtuoso rhythm section, Frith plays with unprecedented urgency—no cold cerebration here. The improvisations are tough and sinewy too, benefiting from Frith's experience in Henry Cow. Highlights: the bouncy title cut and "Corridor," a manic exercise in machine-gun feedback.

By the late '80s, with Beinhorn and Maher long gone (both to producing, although Maher plays with Scritti Politti and has drummed on plenty of records, most memorably Lou Reed's **New York**), there was no longer any discernible difference between Material and Laswell solo. Still, after the commercial failure of Laswell's not-new-age-but-an-incredible-simulation-of-it **Hear No Evil** (which probably flopped because it betrayed more active intelligence than its target audience wants to know about), he adopted the Material name for **Seven Souls**, a great record that's as much a masterpiece of sheer calculation as it is art. (Laswell is nothing if not an extremely canny operator.)

Having worked with William S. Burroughs on Laurie Anderson's **Mister Heartbreak**, Laswell here has the author read from his novel *The Western Lands* over tracks that span a wide area of world music turf, mixed with licks and samples deployed with Laswell's usual taste, innovation and economy. The percussion, courtesy of Sly Dunbar and Aïyb Dieng, is consistently brilliant. At times the music is restive, creating very delicate atmospheres; Burroughs' voice and text add appropriate notes of doom. That aside, **Seven Souls** is clearly designed to be new age music for hipsters.

Around the same time as **Seven Souls**, guitarist Skopelitis—a longtime Laswell crony who has joined the bassist on most of the projects he's undertaken since 1982, including all of the Golden Palominos records—released his first solo LP, **Next to Nothing**. With Laswell, Ginger Baker (drums), Fred Frith (violin), Simon Shaheen (violin, oud) and Dieng (percussion), it's similar in texture to **Seven Souls**, albeit without the spoken-word content. Along with that record and Baker's excellent, Laswell-produced **Middle Passage**, **Next to Nothing** forms something of a triptych, and an exemplary one at that. [mf/gk]

See also *Afrika Bambaataa, Fred Frith, Golden Palominos, Nona Hendryx, Bill Laswell, Robert Quine, Scritti Politti*.

MATERIAL ISSUE
Material Issue EP (Big Block-Landmind) 1987
International Pop Overthrow (Mercury) 1991 •

Fans of early Cheap Trick, Tom Petty and Big Star were known to weep tears of joy upon first hearing Material Issue's independently released debut EP (a six-song 12-inch), co-produced with Jeff Murphy of Shoes. Centered around the talents of vocalist/songwriter/guitarist Jim Ellison (a brief, early member of Green), the Chicago trio was playing unashamed Beatle/Byrdsy power pop when it was decidedly unfashionable, and each of the six songs is its own distinct three-minute thrill.

Material Issue continued to record with Murphy, completing **International Pop Overthrow** before signing to a major label. One of the best power pop albums in recent memory, this gem contains no less than four songs with girls' names in the titles. Although Ellison's occasional inclination towards quantity over quality makes some of the fourteen tracks less memorable than others, "Valerie Loves Me," "Renee Remains the Same," "This Far Before" and "Very First Lie" are should-be singles of the first order. And this is only album number one. [ja]

MAX Q
See *INXS*.

MAZZY STAR
See *Opal*.

SCOTT MCCAUGHEY
See *Young Fresh Fellows*.

MCCLUSKEY BROTHERS
See *Bluebells*.

IAN MCCULLOCH
See *Echo & the Bunnymen*.

MC5
Kick Out the Jams (Elektra) 1969 + 1983
Back in the USA (Atlantic) 1970
High Time (Atlantic) 1971
Babes in Arms [tape] (ROIR) 1983 [CD] (Fr. Danceteria) 1990 φ
Do It (Fr. Revenge) 1987 •
Live Detroit 68/69 (Fr. Revenge) 1988 •

Formed in and around John Sinclair's White Panther Party, the Motor City 5's enduring relevance lies less in the Detroit quintet's music (the in-concert **Kick Out the Jams** sounds closer to early-'70s heavy metal than anything else) and more in the political attitudes behind that music; "Kick Out the Jams" and "Motor City Is Burn-

ing" are obvious harbingers of "Anarchy in the UK." Unfortunately for the 5, their utopian beliefs didn't translate to vinyl with the intensity of, say, the first Clash album. Led by Rob Tyner's rabble-rousing vocals and the twin guitar assault of Wayne Kramer and Fred "Sonic" Smith, **Kick Out the Jams** has plenty of high-energy rock, with science-fiction noise ("Rocket Reducer No. 62" and "Starship," co-credited to Sun Ra) thrown in for class. But would the revolution be recorded by Elektra?

Evidently not. The next MC5 album, produced by Jon Landau (prior to his more financially rewarding alliance with Bruce Springsteen), finds them downplaying the rabble-rousing in favor of claustrophobically taut and blisteringly electric sub-three-minute odes to "High School," "Teenage Lust" and "Shakin' Street" ("where all the kids meet"). The LP also contains performances of "Tutti Frutti" and the Chuck Berry title cut, with its refrain of "I'm so glad I'm living in the USA." Sarcasm? A timely return to the roots? Probably both. At least the concise songs are easier to like than the first LP's hippie-era sprawl.

Having lost their audience between the first two albums, the MC5 felt free to put down the best playing of their recording career on the totally ignored **High Time**. Song lengths are back up, but the band stretches out comfortably on "Sister Anne," "Over and Over" and the jazzy "Skunk (Sonically Speaking)." Did the MC5's circular saga prove the invincibility of pure pop? In any case, their records and legend remain an oft-cited influence on the nose-thumbing irreverence and chaotic energy of punk groups.

Babes in Arms is a belated appendix to the band's catalogue. It consists of early 45 sides done for indie labels, alternate takes and remixes (some scarcely different from the originals) from the three original albums, plus one otherwise unreleased cut.

Like the Stooges and other groups, numerous live concert albums of the MC5 have been issued. Amid a rash of obvious bootlegs, the two French releases at least appear to be legal issues. **Do It** is a muddy sounding radio broadcast from '71 well-played renditions of eight songs, including "19th Nervous Breakdown," "Tutti Frutti" and John Lee Hooker's "Motor City Is Burning" alongside "Kick Out the Jams" and "Looking at You." But beware of the utterly unlistenable pink-vinyl **Live Detroit**, an inaudible mush of muffled noise. [si/i]

See also *Mick Farren, New Order, Patti Smith, Sonic's Rendezvous Band, Johnny Thunders, Was (Not Was)*.

M.C. HAMMER
Feel My Power (Bustin') 1987
Let's Get It Started (Capitol) 1988 •
Please Hammer Don't Hurt 'Em (Capitol) 1990 •

The Oakland rapper with the soul of an ad man, M.C. Hammer dominated the record charts in 1990 with his second album. (Actually his second-and-a-half: the self-released **Feel My Power** was given four new tracks and reissued as **Let's Get It Started**.) Far less talented as a musician (his dancing skills are exceptional) than he is as a salesman, Hammer's primary influence would appear to be Madison Avenue. His records use familiar songs to establish audience rapport, adding on simple, repeated catch phrases that people can easily remember when it comes time to make consumer decisions. It was only a matter of weeks before the title of the ubiquitous "U Can't Touch This" (to the music of Rick James' "Superfreak") entered the vernacular. Still, it's hard to give critical credence to a mediocre MC who pretty much borrows classical songs whole, tacks on a modern beat and substitutes his own clumsy vocals. Unless we're talking the art of the deal, Hammer's no artist.

Besides duffing up BB King, P-Funk, Rick James and Queen, **Let's Get It Started** has the moderately exciting "They Put Me in the Mix" and a lot of boring boasts. **Please Hammer** takes commercial advantage of Prince ("Pray," "She's Soft and Wet"), Marvin Gaye ("Help the Children"), the Chi-Lites ("Have You Seen Her") and others. Beyond the intrinsic worthlessness of Hammer's own records, his crossover success—which helped make rap the dominant sound entering the '90s—opened the door to an even shallower purveyor of recycled rhyming, Vanilla Ice. What's next? [i]

KRIS MCKAY
See *Wild Seeds*.

MARIA MCKEE
See *Lone Justice*.

MALCOLM MCLAREN
Duck Rock (Island) 1983 ●
D'ya Like Scratchin' EP (Island) 1984
Fans (Island) 1984 ●
Swamp Thing (Island) 1985

MALCOLM MCLAREN AND THE BOOTZILLA ORCHESTRA
Waltz Darling (Epic) 1989 ●

MALCOLM MCLAREN PRESENTS THE WORLD FAMOUS SUPREME TEAM SHOW
Round the Outside! Round the Outside! (Virgin) 1990 ◊

Besides being an imperialistic cultural plunderer (a non-judgmental designation), Malcolm McLaren is one of rock's true visionaries. His role in the formation and promotion of the Sex Pistols has been construed as everything from inspired instigator to Machiavellian manipulator, and his solo career has been as righteously criticized as it's been influential. The ever-provocative McLaren tends to bring out the moral indignation in people.

It's hard to say just what McLaren does as an artist. He's more an assembler than a creator, piecing together artifacts from various musical cultures in such a way that, at the end of the day, his own input seems invisible. And yet his perspective as hip outsider has continued to provide a link between his Anglo-American audience and Third World forms. If McLaren's a musical tourist, these records are his home movies.

Duck Rock, produced by Trevor Horn and featuring the rapping World's [*sic*] Famous Supreme Team, is a vanguard album in the new music/rap crossover movement. (The Keith Haring artwork is equally au courant.)

It offers vignettes of hip-hop, Appalachian music (McLaren shows no real racial preference in his thievery), African music and *merengue*. Instead of assimilating the forms and reconstructing them, McLaren puts his actual source material on vinyl (and then his name to it). The most striking cut, "Buffalo Gals," sets a square dance call over a hip-hop scratch track. **D'ya Like Scratchin'** plucks three songs from the album and funks with the mix, adding two versions of a new tune as well.

Never one to stand still, McLaren succeeds against all odds in combining hip-hop with opera on **Fans**. As unlikely a synthesis as this is, McLaren mainly uses opera for its recitative form and story lines (namely *Carmen*, *Madam Butterfly* and *Turandot*) and, damn it, the thing works more often than not.

The aptly named **Swamp Thing** is a murky and bizarre creature grown during various sessions between '82 and '84. The title track perverts "Wild Thing" into a nightmarish but enjoyable mess. "Duck Rock Cheer" is so unlike the original that you'd never connect the two, save for minor overlapping of mix components; "Duck Rockers/Promises" sounds only slightly more familiar. "Buffalo Love" has even less to do with "Buffalo Gals," offering instead a smooth disco creation breathily sung by an unidentified woman. "B.I. Bikki" combines McLarenize exercise exhortations with opera and all sorts of extraneous rubbish; "Eiffel Tower" turns the old Bow Wow Wow song inside out to interesting effect. As aggravating as he often is, McLaren's work is invariably fascinating and provocative.

McLaren foists another demented but entertaining musical hybrid on the world in **Waltz Darling**. Hooking muscular rock-funk—starring Bootsy Collins and Jeff Beck—together with a classical orchestral, McLaren comes up with what, at times, resembles an electrified version of Gilbert and Sullivan. He tops this weird blend off with a variety of female vocalists (the artist himself speaks lyrics on a couple of numbers), swanky dance lyrics and up-to-date production techniques. Unfortunately, the record wanders casually around its concept—too many tracks are merely standard dance-club fare with lush flourishes, hardly a novelty—but the instrumental "House of the Blue Danube" and "Algernon's Simply Awfully Good at Algebra," co-written by Dave Stewart, are pretty amusing.

Tempted by yet another stylistic fad he could attempt to corrupt, McLaren reunited with the World Famous Supreme Team—his hip-hop compadres on **Duck Rock**—and threw together a hip-house stew sampling (intellectually, not electronically) both Shakespeare and opera for a dance record whose bizarre conception is designed to be easily overlooked in the appropriate environment. (I mean, really, who cares if the chant over a techno-dance groove is "Diva opera house" rather than "Love to love you baby"?) Perhaps angling for greater historical recognition (or just recycling an asset whose time hasn't yet passed), McLaren includes an updated remix of "Buffalo Gals." [jl/i]

See also *Bow Wow Wow, New York Dolls, Sex Pistols*.

MC LYTE
Lyte as a Rock (First Priority Music-Atlantic) 1988 ●
Eyes on This (First Priority Music-Atlantic) 1989 ●

This sassy young rapper from Brooklyn—no-nonsense star of hip-hop's burgeoning distaff side—waxes funny, moral and toughly self-reliant on the musically inventive and entertaining **Lyte as a Rock**. Not only is her assessment of the sexual battlefield a refreshing change of pace, the chip on Lyte's shoulder yields hysterical and vicious putdowns. Aided by sharp production, minor appropriations from Ray Charles, Helen Reddy and the Four Seasons, Lyte fills her first LP with a number of strong cuts, like the introductory "Lyte vs. Vanna White" and the hit "I Cram to Understand U."

In one of the most intriguing cross-cultural moments of 1988, Lyte appeared in the video for Sinéad O'Connor's "I Want Your (Hands on Me)." Unfortunately, **Eyes on This** doesn't show any such imagination: Lyte revisits the same 'hood as her debut, in good-sounding but tired expressions of singleminded self-obsession and rhyming supremacy like "I Am the Lyte" (produced by future Brand Nubian Grand Puba Maxwell, who also collaborated on "Funky Song"), "Slave 2 the Rhythm" and "Throwin' Words at U." The album's only flight of fancy is "Cappucino," an intriguing but undeveloped visit to the afterlife.   [i/tr]

See also *Audio Two*.

MC 900 FT JESUS WITH DJ ZERO
MC 900 Ft Jesus with DJ Zero EP (Can. Nettwerk) 1989 ●
Hell with the Lid Off (Nettwerk-IRS) 1990 ●

With his long legs firmly straddling danceable hip-hop and found-sound industrialism, Dallas' MC 900 Ft Jesus (Mark Griffin) uses beats, samples and scratches to support his distorted (non-rap) narratives that proceed ironically from a supermarket tabloid view of life and religion. While using far too many sound bites from Public Enemy, the rudimentary EP previews the album's "Too Bad" and "Shut Up," joining them with a pair of retitled remixes.

Since the basic format is too uninvolving to sustain an entire LP, **Hell with the Lid Off** makes a greater stylistic effort, embracing funk ("Truth Is Out of Style"), warm soul ("Spaceman") and pulsing techno-beat ("UFO's Are Real"). Although diverting in small doses (more suited for club play), MC 900 Ft Jesus makes shaggy dog music—colorfully convoluted but lacking a punchline.   [i]

M.C. SHAN
Down by Law (Cold Chillin'-Warner Bros.) 1987
Born to Be Wild (Cold Chillin'-Warner Bros.) 1988 ●
Play It Again, Shan (Cold Chillin'-Warner Bros.) 1990 ●

Unstylish but top-notch, Queens free-styler Shawn Moltke supposedly got his career break in 1983 when the future chairman of Cold Chillin' caught him attempting to steal his car. (Having Marley Marl for a cousin probably helped a little, too.) With Marl's minimalist production and Shan's dynamic B-boy raps, the fine **Down by Law** includes an amateurish pre-LP single, "The Bridge" (about the Queensbridge housing project), as well as the anti-crack "Jane, Stop This Crazy Thing!" and the classic bad-girl story of "Project 'ho."

Leading off the ambitiously sampled **Born to Be Wild** with "I Pioneered This" (actually, he tempers the claim in the lyrics), Shan doesn't cope very well with sonic competition, coming through best on the relatively spare cuts, like the historical "They Used to Do It Out in the Park" and the autobiographical "Back to the Basics" ("One day when me and Marley Marl was playing in a ditch/We made this jam that we knew was slamming/Someday it would make us rich"). Answering John Kay in the title track is a neat idea that fails; the sax line running through "Words of a Freestyle" effectively draws attention away from the words.

Moving out from under Marl's production umbrella, Shan swapped his Kangol hat and Puma sweats for a swanky white suit and an adult outlook on the moderately dull **Play It Again**. In good-sounding tracks that seem to go on forever, Shan attacks police injustice ("Time for Us to Defend Ourselves"), expounds on musical theory ("It Ain't a Hip Hop Record"), disses dope pushers with help from Richard Pryor ("Death Was Quite a Surprise"), quotes Fats Waller ("It Don't Mean a Thing") and even sings one ("I Want to Thank You").   [i]

MC TUNES
See *808 State*.

MDC
Millions of Dead Cops (R Radical) 1982 ●
Multi-Death Corporation EP (R Radical) 1983
Smoke Signals (R Radical) 1986
Millions of Damn Christians: This Blood's for You (R
   Radical-Boner) 1987 ●
More Dead Cops 1981–1987 (R Radical-Boner) 1988 ●
Metal Devil Cokes (Boner) 1989 ●
Elvis—In the Rheinland (Ger. Destiny) 1989 ●

Originally launched in Austin, Texas around 1980, this explosive political hardcore quartet (aka Multi-Death Corporation, Millions of Dead Children and Millions of Damn Christians) has long been based in San Francisco. Precise breakneck rock makes **Millions of Dead Cops** a powerful means by which to deliver messages like "John Wayne Was a Nazi" (originally recorded and released on 45 when MDC was known as the Stains) and "I Hate Work." Best title: "Corporate Deathburger." After the first pressing sold out, the LP was remastered and reissued, ultimately joining **More Dead Cops** on CD.

Smoke Signals offers a more mature lyrical stance and challenging post-hardcore arrangements, which organize thrash sounds into a tightly structured musical framework. New arrival Gordon Fraser's throaty guitar and the deft rhythm section set the scene for Dave Dictor's clearly enunciated soapbox announcements like "No More Cops," "South Africa Is Free," "Missile Destroyed Civilization" and the vegetarian "Country Squawk." Turning to cultural concerns, MDC also offers the flavorful "Tofutti," the sarcastic "Skateboards to Hell" and "King of Thrash." An exceptionally good record.

Turning non-'core, **This Blood's for You** starts out as an attack on religion, but quickly broadens the free-fire zone to include merciless indictments of Reagan

("Bye Bye Ronnie," "Guns for Nicaragua," "Who's the Terrorist Now"), bureaucrats ("Henry Kissmyassinger," Cream's "Politician"), agricultural imperialism ("Chock Full of Shit"), intolerant punks ("S.K.I.N.H.E.A.D.") and junkies ("Your Death Wish Is Sick"). The music is likewise expansive: MDC uses acoustic guitar, melody, guitar solos and other good things. A fine development from a deeply committed and talented quartet.

More Dead Cops 1981–1987 is a rarities retrospective, including both sides of the band's debut single ("John Wayne Was a Nazi" b/w "Born to Die"), the four-song **Multi-Death Corporation** EP, the three-song **Chicken Squawk** EP, two compilation tracks (including "Pay to Come Along," an attack on the Bad Brains) and two unreleased covers ("Born Under a Bad Sign" and "Spanish Castle Magic") from '87.

Despite one simple acoustic number ("Acid Reindeer") and a country stomp ("Ain't It Funny"), **Metal Devil Cokes** returns MDC's thrash power, with excellent playing and production. New guitarist Eric Calhoun contributes effectively to the tight electric roar, but Dictor's delivery and the band's humorous polemics are still the primary element in MDC's personality. Actually, the radical content here is significantly toned down, with songs like "I'm a Knucklehead" and "White Men in Suits" (not to mention a straight punk cover of "Love Potion No. 9") that avoid any specific finger-pointing or protesting. The complete cooking instructions of "Tofu Spaghetti" make for one funny song, while a new use for nursery rhymes ("Three Blind Mice") and the revised lyrics of "Deep in the Heart of (Racist Amerikkka)" prove that political rock doesn't have to be grim or boring.

Elvis–In the Rheinland, recorded live in Berlin in November 1988, finds the quartet ripping through a great-sounding 24-song career retrospective, plus a restrained rendition of Michelle Shocked's "Fogtown" (a song which they also play on her second album).   [i]

See also *Michelle Shocked*.

MEAT BEAT MANIFESTO

Storm the Studio (Wax Trax!) 1989 ●
Armed Audio Warfare (Wax Trax!) 1990 ●
99% (Play It Again Sam-Mute-Elektra) 1990 φ

Much has been made of the fact that two members of Meat Beat Manifesto—dancer/choreographer Marcus Adams and costume/set designer Craig Morrison—have no musical input. But the group's commitment to the visual aspect of its stage presentation shouldn't create the impression that the audio side can't stand up on its own. In fact, the sounds (produced mainly by Jack Dangers with Jonny Stephens) have consistently merged hip-hop rhythms with industrial overtones and a myriad of samples to devastating effect.

A series of UK 12-inches put Meat Beat Manifesto on the map, only to have a fire at the group's London headquarters destroy its debut album. (A collection of early mixes and unreleased tracks later emerged as the frequently rewarding **Armed Audio Warfare**.)

Four 12-inch tracks were then disassembled and (to borrow a title) re-animated in four different versions apiece for the double album **Storm the Studio**. Meat Beat stretch the concept of the remix further than most,

and few of the tracks on this violent sonic assault sound like any of the others. Taking the groundbreaking electronic grooves of Throbbing Gristle and Cabaret Voltaire as their base, toughening them up enormously and occasionally adding vitriolic stream-of-consciousness raps makes for uneasy but rewarding listening.

With **99%**, Meat Beat readjusted their focus, maintaining the industrial aspect but tidying things up and making use of house grooves. Very little of the musical content (apart from Dangers' raps) is actually recorded by the group, but the enormous range of sampled voices, TV themes and pop cuttings lead to a bizarre and fascinating clash of styles on instrumentals like "Hello Teenage America" and "Hallucination Generation."

[tf]

MEATMEN

Blood Sausage EP (Touch and Go) 1982
Crippled Children Suck EP (Touch and Go) 1982
We're the Meatmen ... and You Suck! (Touch and Go) 1983
War of the Superbikes (Homestead) 1985 ●
Rock'n'Roll Juggernaut (Caroline) 1986
We're the Meatmen ... and You Still Suck!!! (Caroline) 1989
Crippled Children Suck (Touch and Go) 1990
Stud Powercock: The Touch and Go Years [CD] (Touch and Go) 1991 ●

TESCO VEE

Dutch Hercules EP (Touch and Go) 1984

Obnoxious, crude, offensive, blasphemous, tiresome and funny—the Meatmen are one band you'd never be able to explain to your parents (or even the vast majority of your peers). The rude punk parodists from Michigan heard on the infamous **Blood Sausage** and **Crippled Children Suck** 7-inches stomped on the sensitive issues of society with a coarseness that makes dead baby jokes seem like church fare. If there were some reference points—something the Meatmen *did* care about—the gratuitous and tedious irreverence might have had some real shock value.

We're the Meatmen . . . and You Suck! (initially pressed on white vinyl) runs aground in a sea of unoriginality. The puerile forays into morbidity ("One Down Three to Go," about the Beatles), homophobia ("Tooling for Anus"), misogyny ("I'm Glad I'm Not a Girl") and racism ("Blow Me Jah") are too familiar and predictable to be outrageous. A little more wit would have made the Meatmen a more engaging (if despicable) cartoon. One side of the album is live; the other is a reissue/remix of **Blood Sausage**.

The original Meatmen dissolved when singer/schoolteacher Tesco Vee moved to Washington DC, but his resulting itchiness bore fruit in the form of a solo record. Aided by guitarists Lyle Preslar and Brian Baker of Minor Threat (both of whom subsequently helped Vee form a new, improved Meatmen) and produced by Minor Threat's Ian MacKaye, **Dutch Hercules** stands on more solid musical ground. Apparently mellowing with age, Vee limits the objects of his attacks to lesbians, blacks, post-punkers and rock stars. The satire works better because he offers himself as an object of parody. The only useless cut is a side-long disco perversion ("Crapper's Delight").

With the new five-jerk lineup, **War of the Super-bikes** focuses and refines the Meatmen's miserable charm, retooling the punk onslaught into a strong, sharp-edged rock sound and presenting a mixed material grill, from utterly inoffensiveness (the great title track and "Abba God and Me") to typical juvenalia (the flamen-coed "Kisses in the Sunset," "Cadaver Class" and a cover of the Pagans' "What's This Shit Called Love," which opens as a demented Elvis parody). Just what the doctor ordered! Bonus: spoken-word tripe hidden at the end of each side.

James Cooper replaced Baker (off to start Dag Nasty) on **Rock'n'Roll Juggernaut**, leaving the Meatmen a musically undistinguished rock machine, playing tight but plain guitar raunch. Amid bursts of worthless comedy shtick, Vee's lyrics keep the faith, leering salaciously while attacking foreigners ("French People Suck," "Dichstrudel"), American proles ("True Grit") and health nuts ("Nature Boy") with the unenthusiastic knee-jerk bravado of morons yelling out car windows at women to impress their friends. Yawn.

We're the Meatmen . . . and You Still Suck!!!, recorded at two dates on the '88 farewell tour, finds the crew raging through songs from every previous platter and the Vee EP, plus an exuberant Sweet ("Rebel Rowser" [*sic*]) cover. The funniest item—besides Tesco's between-song raps—is "Camel Jockeys Suck," completing the "Suck" trilogy (all set to the same tune). On the debit side, final guitarist Stuart Casson's generic metallicisms are simply no match for Baker's fantastic lead work, thus the **Superbikes** songs—the heart of the set—are a step down from the studio versions. (It's a shame that with all the live Meatmen material left to posterity, the superior '85 gig lineup remains undocumented.)

The **Crippled Children Suck** album contains the entire **Crippled Children** EP, a **Blood Sausage** out-take, a fair set of '81 demos, one live track from '82 (the notorious, never-before-released "TSOL Are Sissies") and three live cuts from '84 (the updated "Becoming a Gay Man" is a must-hear). **Stud Powercock**, as its subtitle makes clear, collects every track on the Touch and Go releases (even **Dutch Hercules** and this new compilation) on one CD, making it a definitive retrospective of the band's original Midwest existence. See also *Dag Nasty, Minor Threat*.   [jl/i/gef]

MEAT PUPPETS

In a Car EP (World Imitation) 1981 (SST) 1985 ●
Meat Puppets (Thermidor-SST) 1982 ●
Meat Puppets II (SST) 1983 ●
Up on the Sun (SST) 1985 ●
Out My Way EP (SST) 1986 ●
Mirage (SST) 1987 ●
Huevos (SST) 1987 ●
Monsters (SST) 1989 ●
No Strings Attached (SST) 1990 ●

This Phoenix, Arizona trio has made a career out of defying expectations. The two Kirkwood brothers, Curt (guitar/vocals) and Cris (bass/vocals), along with drummer Derrick Bostrom, made their debut with **In a Car**, a locally released 7-inch—five songs in five minutes—of shrieking thrash-punk and unrealized avant-guitar ambitions. The Puppets' first album (a full-length disc that

spins at 45 rpm) similarly mixes intriguing instrumental experimentation—and, significantly, a bit of restrained country—into sloppy blurs of noisy punk-rock.

On **Meat Puppets II**, however, they made the first of many shifts—into radical country-punk. The album offers a startlingly strong set of stylistic contrasts—loud and soft, fast and slow—all supporting moving, poetic lyrics. The songs are melodic and memorable; Curt's high'n'lonesome singing is made even more effective by its uninhibited shoddiness. One of the best albums ever to blend Joe Strummer with Hank Williams, **Meat Puppets II** avoids clichés of any sort in its brilliant evocation of the wide open world of the Southwest. Make no mistake—this is not a hardcore album with some corny twang, it's a fully realized work in a unique hybrid style.

Up on the Sun removes the Puppets further from punk, but doesn't adequately replace the rock'n'roll energy. Curt's growing mastery of delicate guitar weaves—an Arizona answer to Jerry Garcia, perhaps—provides the Puppets' new focus; the hoedown coda of "Enchanted Pork Fist" owes as much to modern jazz as cowboy rock. The title track is a lovely, contemplative folk song with an airy vocal and a skipping guitar riff that repeats throughout. In a lighter moment, Curt and Cris whistle their way through "Maiden's Milk"; waxing serious, "Creator" offers a poetic contemplation on god and nature.

The Puppets sound far more involved and enthused on the superior six-track **Out My Way**, again quite unlike anything in their prior repertoire. An utterly crazed raveup of "Good Golly Miss Molly" merely caps off an ineffable, diverse collection of occasionally funky, occasionally psychedelic, occasionally country-fied rock tunes.

Mirage harks back to the sonic translucence of **Up on the Sun**, forcing Bostrom's muscular drumming to find a way to maintain its reserve while kicking up a subtle storm. Curt's intricate finger-picking and plectrum work leads the relaxed stroll on "Mirage," "Leaves," "Get on Down" and "I Am a Machine." The bluegrass-styled "Confusion Fog" shows a different side of the Pups, as does the rocking "Liquefied," an incongruous souvenir of the band's early sound with acid-trip lyrics and distorted rhythm guitar. The only discordant ingredient on this technically accomplished record is Curt's uncertain, often cringeably tuneless singing.

As legend has it, the genesis of **Huevos** began with a magazine interview in which Curt announced his adoration of ZZ Top guitarist Billy Gibbons. Gibbons' reply sent Kirkwood into a writing frenzy, and the album—which begins with the Top soundalike "Paradise"—was recorded in one marathon 72-hour stretch. The mildly commercialized sound (read: rhythm guitar, sweet melodies and a thick Les Paul tone) led hardline fans to call it a sellout, but that's hardly the case. In this generally upbeat outing, the only discouraging words can be heard in "Dry Rain" and the self-deprecating "I Can't Be Counted On." Otherwise, Curt celebrates "Fruit," "Sexy Music" and even "Bad Love." Except for the out-there-with-the-cacti vocals, **Huevos** is quite fine.

Saving most of his liquid lead runs for showy instrumental passages, Curt again plays a lot of rhythm

417

guitar on **Monsters**, a heavier, more traditional-minded rock album than usual. Beyond "Attacked by Monsters," however, the colorless and repetitive songs aren't very appealing, and the sound—which alternates between the band's late-'80s clarity and a murky sonic swamp—doesn't do much for them. (Ironically, the vocals here are fairly presentable.) Not among the Puppets' best.

The generously endowed **No Strings Attached** recapitulates the Meat Puppets' career to date with two dozen chronological selections—from the first EP through **Monsters**. [i]

MEGADETH

Killing Is My Business . . . and Business Is Good! (Combat) 1985 ●
Peace Sells . . . but Who's Buying? (Combat-Capitol) 1986 ●
So Far, So Good . . . So What! (Capitol) 1988 ●
Rust in Peace (Combat-Capitol) 1990 ●

After leaving Metallica, guitarist/songwriter Dave Mustaine formed Megadeth to better realize his vision of a band that would play a faster, louder and more intricate brand of metal with far more realistic and relevant lyrics (when you can make them out) than the usual metal macho bravado.

The quartet's first album meets most of those goals. The precise, complex (but clearly articulated) hyperspeed guitar power almost sails into jazz waters; Mustaine's rock vocals dispense with typical tremulous screeching for listenable roughness. Only the lyrics are business as usual: even an overhaul of "These Boots Are Made for Walking" adds vulgarity to maximize headbanger appeal. Other songs—about death, sex and religion—witlessly tread well-worn ground. Still, Megadeth's galloping high-tech sound (check "Rattlehead" and "Mechanix")—soon to influence numerous young rock/metal bands—is clearly taking shape.

Peace Sells continues Megadeth's macabre assault on the senses. Like a metal version of Dante's Inferno, the LP offers various visions of hell on earth—murder, adultery, alienation, imprisonment and (d)evil cults. Quite frankly, the music's scarier than the lyrics, since Mustaine's strangled vocals are barely audible in the mix; the music, on the other hand, hurtles forward with undeniable and relentless power. Oldsters will be left stunned by the incredible version of Willie Dixon's (via Beck and Stewart) "I Ain't Superstitious," rewritten in trademark Megadeth style.

Recorded with a new guitarist and drummer, **So Far, So Good . . . So What!** includes a tribute to Metallica's late bassist Cliff Burton ("In My Darkest Hour"), a driving-while-drunk song ("502"), an instrumental that starts acoustic before hitting typical Mega-drive ("Into the Lungs of Hell"), an unnecessary (and lyrically inaccurate) cover of "Anarchy in the UK" with ex-Pistol Steve Jones in tow and the obligatory PMRC putdown ("Hook in Mouth"). Though Mustaine's vocals are improving and the new guys fit in fine, it's a bit of a letdown after **Peace Sells**.

After a layoff prompted by Mustaine's growing drug dependence (and subsequent abatement thereof), plus more conflict within the band, **Rust in Peace** was recorded with yet another new guitarist and drummer. The change is for the better, especially Nick Menza's supple drumming, which elevates the band to a new plateau, on which they swing (!) as never before. It's also the group's best album sonically, even if Mustaine's lyrics (nearly all about war or his former habit) and his still-improving-but-not-quite-there vocals could both use a dose of clarity at times. Musically, though, Megadeth's at the top of its game right now. [ds]

See also *Metallica*.

MEKONS

The Quality of Mercy Is Not Strnen (nr/Virgin) 1979 (Blue Plate) 1990 ●
Devils Rats and Piggies a Special Message from Godzilla (nr/Red Rhino) 1980
It Falleth Like Gentle Rain from Heaven—The Mekons Story (nr/CNT Productions) 1982
The English Dancing Master EP (nr/CNT Productions) 1983
Fear and Whiskey (nr/Sin) 1985
Crime and Punishment EP (nr/Sin) 1986
The Edge of the World (nr/Sin) 1986
Slightly South of the Border EP (nr/Sin) 1986
Honky Tonkin' (Sin-Twin/Tone) 1987
New York [tape] (ROIR) 1987 [CD] (ROIR-Important) 1990 ф
So Good It Hurts (Twin/Tone) 1988 ●
Original Sin [CD] (Twin/Tone) 1989 ●
Dream and Lie of . . . EP (nr/Blast First) 1989 ●
The Mekons Rock'n'Roll (Twin/Tone-A&M) 1989 ●
F.U.N. '90 EP (Twin/Tone-A&M) 1990 ф
The Curse of the Mekons (nr/Blast First) 1991 ●

SALLY TIMMS AND THE DRIFTING COWGIRLS

This House Is a House of Trouble EP (nr/T.I.M.) 1987
Butcher's Boy EP (nr/T.I.M.) 1987
Somebody's Rocking My Dreamboat (nr/T.I.M.) 1988

VARIOUS ARTISTS

Fast Product—Mutant Pop (PVC) 1980
'Til Things Are Brighter . . . (Red Rhino-Fundamental) 1988 ●

Although formed in the punk era, and—like another Leeds band of similar vintage, the Gang of Four—originally known for abrasive guitar funk more concerned with content and politics than commercial niceties or style, the Mekons (not to be confused with the Manchester Mekon, a minor class-of-'77 outfit) covered a lot of ground in the '80s, and have grown into one of the most venerable and entertaining post-punk institutions. Ring-led by singer/guitarist/producer/etc. Jon Langford (also one of the Three Johns, and a major force/influence in underground and indie-rock circles), the Mekons have held true to the same precepts they started with, but have wisely moved with the times in a number of significant ways.

The first album—a major landmark erected by one of the few late-'70s British bands that didn't want to be either the Sex Pistols or the Clash—suffers from the screamed vocals, which obscure both the music and the left-wing lyrics: minimalism is one thing, but rank amateurism another. (The CD reissue adds a half-dozen single sides from '79 and '80.)

On the second album (more commonly known as **The Mekons**), the group moves into danceable synth-

418

pop, with protest lyrics attacking bourgeois culture, the army and hollow lives. **The Mekons Story** is a retrospective album of old tracks and outtakes, punctuated by inter-track narration. Ending the first chapter in a long story, the Mekons ceased performing in 1981 and cut back on recording work after that 1982 release, although a core trio of Langford, guitarist Tom Greenhalgh and bassist/guitarist Kevin Lycett kept the band in occasional vinyl circulation.

A large new incarnation returned the Mekons to prominence and much international critical adulation in 1985 with **Fear and Whiskey**, a ragged album with sturdily memorable tunes that mix equal parts of electrified rustic country dance music and cow-rock. Fiddle, piano and harmonica join the guitars and drums for a sound that is reasonably comparable to a less loopy, more rocking version of John Otway. Sin's label design mimics Sun's; the sounds are likewise Americanized and, characteristically for the new Mekons, a cover of Hank Williams' "Lost Highway" closes the LP on an appropriate note. Nothing (well, only some things, perhaps) could be further from the Mekons' early noise days. **Crime and Punishment** offers four songs (including the Robyn Hitchcock-like "Chop That Child in Half" and Merle Haggard's "Deep End") from a John Peel session.

Following the four-song 10-inch **Slightly South of the Border**, **Honky Tonkin'** (named for the Hank Williams lyric quoted on the back cover) finds a cast of dozens (actually one dozen) working its way stylistically towards the Pogues' drunkenly revisionist folk-fundamentalism. A case of the sillies ("Sympathy for the Mekons") competes with responsible topicality (a remake of the band's old "Trimdon Grange Explosion," "Kidnapped," "If They Hang You," which eulogizes Dashiell Hammett for refusing to name names at the HUAC hearings) and conspicuous literacy ("Hole in the Ground," "Charlie Cake Park"). The notes for each song cite relevant books, movies or artworks for those undaunted by intellectualism. The genially appealing music, a well-organized wash of fiddles, accordion, guitars and simple drums, makes few demands but keeps the folky standards high.

US tours by the octet in 1986 and 1987 yielded the live tracks (and assorted audio ephemera, like commentary on various subjects by band members) compiled on **New York**. The material is mostly drawn from recent albums, although a version of the Band's "The Shape I'm In" and a handful of otherwise unreleased items are also included. Motley but charming, it's a casually enlightening trek.

So Good It Hurts has its share of fiddle tunes but also expands the band's stylistic repertoire to embrace reggae, straight rock and calypso. The results suggest certain portions of the Clash's later career, as well as the Boomtown Rats and other musical adventurers. The slickest, most accessible album in the Mekons' long career, it holds fast to a politely delivered but tough-minded political consciousness (Richard Nixon is mentioned in more than one song), pausing to include the Stones' "Heart of Stone." Although unsettling in its normalcy, **So Good It Hurts** is a stimulating new chapter in this unfinished saga.

Original Sin is a remastered CD of **Fear and Whiskey** plus the whole **Slightly South** EP, three-quarters of

Crime and Punishment and one song each from **The English Dancing Master** and **Edge of the World**. A handy sampler of the band's mid-'80s work.

The Mekons Rock'n'Roll is an unexpected development at this stage of the game: a punk-rock concept album filled with eloquence and passion. The subject, as announced in the title, is here in all its sordid glory, from lines about "Eric Burdon stunned in Mississippi on the Animals' U.S. tour" (from "Amnesia") to a dig at Bono ("the Dublin messiah scattering crumbs," in "Blow Your Tuneless Trumpet") and the grim morality tale of "Cocaine Lil." It's a tough, dark album that includes five of the best songs the band has ever written, plus some half-baked ideas mired in mud and feedback. (Released as "a preview of **Rock'n'Roll**," the four-song **Dream and Lie of . . .** EP is of interest only for "Heaven and Back," one of the two tracks (the other is "Ring o' Roses") left off the album's American edition.)

The Curse of the Mekons is another leap forward for the band, extending the worldbeat forays of **So Good It Hurts**, the surprising techno-dance experiments of **F.U.N. '90** (a four-song response to acid-house that covers songs by the Band and Kevin Coyne and includes a track co-written with Lester Bangs) and the attack of **Rock'n'Roll** into the group's most melodic collection to date. Among the highlights are two numbers sung by the bell-toned Timms: the eerie "German for Secrets" and a straight cover of "Wild and Blue" by Nashville star John Anderson. The sound is all over the place, from the Stonesy-Cajun hook of the title song to the metallic anthem "Authority" to the plodding reggae of "100%," complete with banjo, accordion and mariachi horns. Elsewhere, dubby psychedelia, drum machines, treated vocals, sound effects and spacey synths add colorful scenery to this bizarre sonic odyssey.

Sometime lead singer Sally Timms' solo releases distance her impressively from the Mekons camp (although she's backed by three members of the band on the album). "Horses" and the countryish "Chained to the Anchor of Love" on **Somebody's Rocking My Dreamboat** could be stray Mekons tracks, but the rest stakes out very different ground, a more mainstream, electronic-based rock over which her cool, clear voice soars. Occasionally clunky but worth seeking out. The title track of the three-song **This House** is a duet with Marc Almond, while the four-song **Butcher's Boy** includes a version of "Long Black Veil."

'Til Things Are Brighter is an uneven AIDS-benefit album of Johnny Cash covers, with the Mekons backing folks like Almond, Michelle Shocked, Pete Shelley, Stephen Mallinder of Cabaret Voltaire and sometime Mekon/Notting Hillbilly Brendan Croker. The Mekons themselves do "Folsom Prison Blues" and Timms contributes "Cry, Cry Cry." [gf/i/ws]

See also *Three Johns*.

MELLOW MAN ACE
Escape from Havana (Capitol) 1989 ●

Despite clever production by the Dust Brothers, Def Jef and others, most of this romantic LA rapper's first album—even with the novelty of four tracks in Spanish ("Rap Guanco," "Mas Pingon," "En la Casa," "Enquentren Amor")—is by-the-numbers dull. But when he drops a clever bilingual rap over Santana's "Evil Ways" (in the delightful "Mentirosa"), running suspicious rhymes around a deceitful girlfriend, Ace (alongside Kid Frost) suggests the unique possibilities of Latin-American hip-hop, both in terms of rhymes and music.   [i]

MELODIC ENERGY COMMISSION

See *Hawkwind*.

MS. MELODIE

See *Boogie Down Productions*.

MELODY MAKERS

Play the Game Right (EMI) 1985 ●

ZIGGY MARLEY AND THE MELODY MAKERS

Hey World! (EMI) 1986 ●
Conscious Party (Virgin) 1988 ●
Time Has Come: The Best of Ziggy Marley and the
    Melody Makers (EMI Manhattan) 1988 ●
One Bright Day (Virgin) 1989 ●
Jahmekya (Virgin) 1991 ɸ

While still in their teens, Ziggy (David) Marley and the Melody Makers reached a level of international stardom known by very few other reggae acts. This is partly due to genes—Ziggy resembles his late father and, more significantly, sounds uncannily like him. Such instant identification has enabled the group (which includes three other Marley progeny) to easily step into the commercial vacuum left by the elder Marley's death.

The Grammy-nominated **Play the Game Right**, which utilizes a traditional Wailers-like sound—complete with horns—and includes a song ("Children Playing in the Streets") the elder Marley had written for them, is attractive and surprisingly accomplished in light of the group's tender years.

The wonderful **Hey World!** shows the Melody Makers coming into their own, bending delightfully light reggae grooves to new stylistic ends. "Give a Little Love" is a soulful party track; "Lord We a Come" has an amazing gospelly African folk feel; Ziggy's vocals in "Police Brutality" stick on good funk grunts for emphasis.

Released several months after **Conscious Party** (the group's first album for a new label), the **Time Has Come** compilation (hardly a best-of, but that's the record biz for you) selects five numbers from each of the band's two EMI albums, adding a pair of 1984 tracks.

Symbolically *and* literally, the Melody Makers represent reggae's new generation. **Conscious Party** bears this out, from its aura of optimism (in songs like "Tomorrow People," "New Love" and "We Propose") to its thoroughly modern sound. Produced by Talking Heads Chris Frantz and Tina Weymouth, and featuring a superb crew of international backup musicians, the record is smart and professional—like the Heads and more consistent than either Tom Tom Club LP. If the kids' songwriting doesn't compare with Dad's, it's at least competent and promising. The LP isn't at all rootsy, but it's fresh, appealing and sincere: reggae for the Benetton generation.

Ziggy's talents really blossomed on **One Bright Day**, which he co-produced with Frantz, Weymouth and Glenn Rosenstein. Downplaying Rasta culture even more than before, the freedom-minded album uses the band's catchiest songs to promote the power and universality of music. With explicit lyrics and stylistic demonstrations, the Melody Makers express their solidarity with the South African struggle as well as black culture in America and elsewhere. Although reggae purists have all but disavowed the group, "Black My Story (Not History)," "One Bright Day" and "Look Who's Dancing" are nearly magical in their delightful blending of slick dance pop and roots rock.   [bk/i]

MELVINS

Gluey Porch Treatments (Alchemy) 1987 ●
Ozma (Boner) 1989 ●
Bullhead (Boner) 1991 ●

Formed in Aberdeen, Washington, this trio led by Buzz Osbourne (guitar, vocals) pounds out an unpredictable, unsteady, confusing sort of metal, an ominously heavy Black Sabbath rumble—without the screechy vocals, guitar solos or dumb-ass lyrics. Songs stop and start, bash and crash on **Gluey Porch Treatments**, an album of measured, careening noise in which uneven, unexpected tempo changes make dancing absolutely out of the question.

With longtime bassist Matt Lukin opting to stay in Washington and join Mudhoney, the Melvins relocated to San Francisco in 1988 and got themselves a new bassist named Lori. Better production makes **Ozma** a more consistently listenable longplayer, although such maximum heaviosity without any of the related trappings probably inhibits the Melvins' appeal among headbangers of either persuasion. **Ozma**'s main strength lies in Osbourne's tortured lyrics, and his ability to turn such disjointed nihilistic poetry into songs. (The cassette includes an extra song; the CD includes **Gluey Porch Treatments**.)   [icm/i]

See also *Mudhoney*.

MEMBERS

At the Chelsea Nightclub (Virgin Int'l) 1979 (Blue Plate)
    1991 ●
1980—The Choice Is Yours (nr/Virgin) 1980 (Blue Plate)
    1991 ●
Radio EP (Arista) 1982
Uprhythm, Downbeat (Arista) 1982
Going West (nr/Albion) 1983

At the Chelsea Nightclub finds the Members using punk as a jumping-off point, but that doesn't tell the whole musical story. Incipient instrumental smarts and simple tunes nailed down by infectious, above-average riffs countered the rough-edged delivery and Nicky Tesco's one-o'-the-lads vocals. The themes—mainly variations on the suburban kid in the city getting streetwise fast—are framed in mischievous yet endearing (even corny) humor. The album's added bonus is that it contains one of the first, and even now best, white punk ventures into reggae (including, on the US pressing, the subsequent "Offshore Banking Business" single). Thoroughly entertaining.

The second album, however, signaled the advent of a downswing from which the band never really recovered. The material seems thin—a cover of ex-Pink Fairy Larry Wallis' "Police Car" is far and away the most memorable track—and any spark and grit the band might have mustered is sterilized by Rupert Hine's production. (The first LP was produced by Steve, the brother of the Members' drummer, Adrian Lillywhite.)

Working with Martin Rushent, the Members' comeback—after a layoff which some mistook for a breakup—sounded for real, first on the teaser EP (one extra track on the US version) and then more substantially on **Uprhythm, Downbeat**. Besides the crisp, full sound, the quintet had grown to a septet with a pair of horns, and the music integrated funk and rap in addition to reggae. No longer humorous, lyrics instead alternate social critiques/rallying cries with personal traumas, at which they prove less adept, but the music is more powerful and danceable than ever. Inspired touch: reggaefication of Kraftwerk's "The Model." (**Uprhythm, Downbeat** was later released in the UK as **Going West**. The cassette version has extra tracks.)   [jg]

See also *King*.

MEMBRANES

Muscles EP (nr/Rondelet) 1982
Pin Stripe Hype EP (nr/Rondelet) 1982
Crack House EP (nr/Criminal Damage) 1983
Death to Trad Rock EP (nr/Criminal Damage) 1985
The Gift of Life (nr/Creation) 1985
Giant (nr/Constrictor) 1986
Everything's Brilliant EP (nr/In Tape) 1986
Songs of Love and Fury (Homestead) 1986
Time-Warp 1991 (Long Live Trad Rock) EP (Homestead) 1987
Back Catalogue: Peter Sellers Versus the Virgin Mary (nr/Vinyl Drip) 1987
Kiss Ass Godhead (Homestead) 1988
To Slay the Rock Pig (nr/Vinyl Drip) 1989 ●

Stalwarts of the British independent scene, Blackpool's Membranes have essayed numerous styles with countless lineups. They began as a quirky, not-too-loud quartet, playing simple tunes with offbeat lyrics and melodica for unexpected coloration. **Back Catalogue**, issued on the band's own Vinyl Drip label, reprises fifteen early efforts, including a rare 1980 flexi-disc, the contents of two four-song EPs (the 12-inch **Muscles**, **Pin Stripe Hype**) and three re-recordings of the same material. The six-song **Crack House**, done as a bass/guitar/drums trio, finds the Membranes nearing their creative peak, shooting out jagged, tense jazz-tinged punk—ugly, abrasive, ambitious and gripping—as well as more accessible droney rock.

Death to Trad Rock builds the guitar chaos to an unnerving plateau on four lengthy songs that also feature bassist John Robb's manic vocals and, on "Myths and Legends," a guest violinist. With Robb switching over to guitar, however, **The Gift of Life** sails right over the edge in a tumult of screaming, banging and incoherent music. The goofy "I Am Fisheye" chant offers a briefly amusing alternative, but this seemingly tossed-off album deserves tossing. Jon (Three Johns/Mekons) Langford adds guitar on the title track; a saxophonist only adds to the din. **Giant** is a compilation.

Produced by Langford, the **"Everything's Brilliant"** 12-inch (two versions plus three B-sides) returns the Membranes to the realm of responsible musicmaking, moving a clear, gothic drum sound and give-a-shit sloppy vocals to the fore and relegating guitars to a subsidiary role at non-distorto volume levels. **Songs of Love and Fury**, with another new bassist and Nick Brown (a guest contributor soon to become a permanent member) adding guitar and violin, takes a further step backwards, almost eliminating electric guitars entirely. Not that far in sound from the band's earliest work, songs like "Kennedy '63," "Day My Universe Changed" and "Phoney T.V. Repairman" mix a flat, trippy '60s approach with the lyrical attitude of Mark E. Smith. A little hard to fathom at first, **Love and Fury**—the band's first US release—reveals itself gradually to be one of the Membranes' best records.

Time-Warp is entirely different, a highly produced and carefully performed collection of six folk-rock originals that sound like something the Animals might have done after "Sky Pilot." Synthesizers, drum programs and sound effects add to the bewildering fray. Robb's vocals are reverbed and mixed into a semblance of melodiousness; while not a great record, it certainly is an unexpected one. Incidentally, artist Simon Clegg deserves kudos for his unfailingly brilliant artwork on all of the Membranes' covers and sleeves.

Steve Albini co-produced **Kiss Ass Godhead** with the Membranes; songs like "Bulbous Love Child," "Long Live the Hooligan!" and "Cheap Male Aggression" are as chaotically loud and abrasive as one could reasonably expect from such a dangerous combination.

Sticking to the loose and rugged, the Membranes made **To Slay the Rock Pig** with producer Steve Mack, pouring typically grouchy and unselfconsciously outrageous (and remorselessly misspelled) lyrics like "A Missive from Couch Potatoe Command," "Tuff Veggie Agro" and "Life, Death and the Scarey Bits Inbetween" into a poorly mixed cauldron of guitar, bass and drums. Not a good place to first meet the Membranes, but a conducive enough environment to maintain an ongoing relationship.   [i]

MEN & VOLTS

Rhythms & Blues EP (Eat) 1982
*Hootersville (Eat) 1983
Tramps in Bloom (Fr. New Rose) 1984 (Iridescence) 1985
The Mule (Shimmy-Disc) 1987 ●
Stay in Touch (Shimmy-Disc) 1989 ●
Cheer Up (50 Skidillion Watts) 1990 ●

With the arcane musical instincts of Captain Beefheart and the dada poetic mindset of Tom Waits, the well-educated Men & Volts (based in the Boston area, although mainstay/lyricist David Greenberger lives in upstate NY) debuted with the challenging and bizarre **Rhythms & Blues**. Employing horns and difficult tempos, the quartet offers the same four songs—including "Rotten Truth," a disturbing number superficially about cats—pressed on both sides.

***Hootersville** (the cover is a map detail; the asterisk marks a locale) is a very full album bursting with unpredictable music that veers from complex and noisy to charmingly rustic and even pastoral. The lyrics on songs like "Pickwick Papers," "Big Ball of String" and "No Shower No Shave" similarly traverse a wide range of topics and are often amusingly absurdist. Stimulating and entertaining.

Dropping the brass and revealing a new folk-based orientation, **Tramps in Bloom** keeps the guitar-built music rudimentary, allowing simply witty paeans to "New York," "Someone Else's Money" and "The History of the Moon" to speak for themselves. At times sounding like the Band, elsewhere resembling the Grateful Dead, Men & Volts make no effort to dress up their artless songs, and it's just as well. Remaining offhandedly unprofessional (not unaccomplished) is no mean feat.

Sounding even more like the Dead, **The Mule** has cloudy sound (so much for direct mastering to metal), noticeably more ambitious arrangements (although nothing you'd call fancy) and serious, sensitive evocations of loneliness ("Records Go 'Round"), aging ("You and Me, Pushin' Up Daisies") and several intriguing characters ("The Loveless," "One Holiday Too Many"). Not a spectacular record, but one with old-fashioned attributes that won't leave you wondering where to park your brain. **The Mule** was later included on the CD and cassette of the band's next album.   [i]

MENTAL AS ANYTHING

Mental as Anything Play at Your Party EP (Aus. Regular) 1978
Get Wet (Aus. Regular) 1979
Mental as Anything (nr/Regular-Virgin) 1980
Expresso Bongo (Aus. Regular) 1980
Cats and Dogs (Aus. Regular) 1981
If You Leave Me, Can I Come Too? (A&M) 1982
Creatures of Leisure (Oz-A&M) 1983
Fundamental (Columbia) 1986 ●
Mouth to Mouth (Columbia) 1988 ●
Cyclone Raymond (Columbia) 1989 ●

MARTIN PLAZA

Plaza Suite (Aus. CBS) 1986

A kind of Australian Rockpile with a case of the vaudeville giggles, Sydney's Mental as Anything first surfaced Down Under in 1978 with an EP containing a sly, skiffle-like drinking song called "The Nips Are Getting Bigger" (featured on **Get Wet**, **Mental as Anything**—the equivalent UK release—and the US debut **If You Leave Me**) which accurately summarizes their pub-rock earthiness and randy humor. **Get Wet** is certainly a good-natured introduction to a band unafraid to write a love song to a foreign country based on travel ads ("Egypt") or pitch a cheesy instrumental bit with Sam the Sham organ as a "Possible Theme for a Future TV Drama Series."

Combining a song from **Get Wet** and the best of the Australian-only **Cats and Dogs**, the Anglo-American compilation **If You Leave Me, Can I Come Too?** is more of the same—the band's (un)usual mix of cheek and underlying lyrical sincerity captured in the poignant "Mr. Normal" drawl of singer/guitarist Martin Plaza. The album also features a track produced by Elvis Costello ("I Didn't Mean to Be Mean") in which the rest of the band—guitarist Reg Mombassa, organist Greedy Smith, bassist Peter O'Doherty and drummer Wayne Delisle—work up a good Attractions-like head of steam.

Creatures of Leisure reveals an overwhelmingly downcast band, singing wistful lyrics about romantic discord ("Bitter to Swallow," "Float Away") and a general lack of gumption ("Nothing's Going Right Today," "Spirit Got Lost"). Even the music is depressed, playing in the same countryish style with barely a trace of enthusiasm. These boys are down, and can't help but lay their burden down in the grooves. Without wallowing in self-pity or indulging in any overt declarations of misery, **Creatures of Leisure** is an enormously sad record.

A much better frame of mind prevails on **Fundamental**. Songs like "I Just Wanna Be Happy" and "Live It Up" offer optimistic lyrics about getting past hard times and bad feelings. Other subjects temper that attitude: in "Hold On," O'Doherty admits a case of the guilts about a ladyfriend, while Plaza marvels about public transportation in "Bus Ride." As produced by Richard Gottehrer, the Mentals' music has hit a certain stride that discourages zaniness (a shame), but their sound—still an Australian answer to Nick Lowe—is never less than bouncily appealing.

The emotional barometer holds steady on **Mouth to Mouth**, another Gottehrer production. Employing plain and pleasant music that could use a bit of a recharge, Plaza delivers harsh words to an ex in "Don't Tell Me Now" and "Thinking Out Loud"; Smith welcomes an old friend in "My Door Is Always Open to You" and offers a hopeful suggestion (in the very Nick Lowe-ish "Let's Go to Paradise"). O'Doherty expresses his pleasure about an ongoing relationship in "I'm Glad." There isn't an unlikable moment anywhere on the record, but the Mentals seem in danger of drifting into musical senility unless they find some collective personality and start showing a little more enthusiasm.

Some people just don't heed the warning signs of encroaching blandness. **Cyclone Raymond** is completely boring, a collection of tepid love songs that couldn't possibly please anyone other than a soft-rock radio programmer anxious to fill air time with anything inoffensively presentable. O'Doherty's chugging "Baby You're Wild" and the Everlyesque "Love Comes Running" show faint glimmers of life (if not wit), something which can't even be said of a rote Chuck Berry exercise reclaimed from the *Young Einstein* soundtrack.

Using a lot of modern-sounding electronic keyboards and saxophone in addition to guitars, Plaza's solo album has adequate energy, a few dance rhythms and a shortage of substantial, memorable material. And covering "Concrete and Clay" (following some sort of titular theme, two of **Plaza Suite**'s originals are entitled "Bats and Balls" and "Chalk and Cheese") in synth strings does nothing to improve a bad situation.   [df/i]

MEN THEY COULDN'T HANG

Night of a Thousand Candles (nr/Imp-Demon) 1985 ●
Greenback Dollar EP (nr/Demon) 1986
How Green Is the Valley (nr/MCA) 1986 ●
Waiting for Bonaparte (nr/Magnet) 1988 ●
Silvertown (Silvertone) 1989 ●
The Domino Club (Silvertone) 1990 ●

This English quintet acquired its name when original bassist Shanne Bradley nicked it from her former Nips bandmate, Shane MacGowan, who had it in mind for his own combo—which instead became the Pogues. Playing whistles, mandolin, bouzouki (with guests adding fiddle, accordion, etc.), the Men sail a musical sea that is not that far removed from the early work of their better-known contemporaries. Pogue Philip Chevron produced part of **Night of a Thousand Candles**, which includes "The Green Fields of France" (written by Australian folk singer Eric Bogle, also covered by the Pogues). Despite the similarities (is it merely coincidence that both bands formed with female bassists who didn't stay long?), the Men They Couldn't Hang have nonetheless carved out a distinctive, rocking identity all their own, with dual lead vocals and original songs (mostly by singer Phil "Swill" Odgers and guitarist Paul Simmonds) that combine folky humanism and an earthy working-class sensibility.

The basic approach hasn't varied much over the years. **Night of a Thousand Candles** (the six songs on the **Greenback Dollar** 12-inch, including the titular Hoyt Axton classic and "Rawhide," are appended to the CD and cassette editions) displays the band at its pub-bred rootsiest, racing through tunes with uninhibited enthusiasm. From there, the band filled out its delivery and improved its songwriting, reached a pinnacle of sorts on the smoothly realized **Silvertown**, a rich folk-rock brew of topical numbers about actress Frances Farmer ("Lobotomy Gets 'em Home!"), capitalist paternalism ("Company Town") and the Channel tunnel ("Rain, Steam & Speed"), with a woebegone tale of European travel ("A Place in the Sun") and similarly romantic adventures.

Produced by Pat Collier, **The Domino Club** is a bit too slick for its own good, with inconsistent material (Simmonds is the main contributor) and plain, uninspired performances.   [hd/i]

See also *Pogues*.

MEN WITHOUT HATS

Folk of the 80's EP (Can. Trend) 1980 (Stiff) 1981
The Safety Dance (nr/Statik) 1982 ●
Rhythm of Youth (Backstreet-MCA) 1982 ●
Folk of the 80's (Part III) (MCA) 1984 ●
Pop Goes the World (Mercury) 1987 ●
The Adventures of Women & Men Without Hate in the
    21st Century (Mercury) 1989 ●

From an almost-unknown Stiff EP to a million-selling debut album, Montreal's Men Without Hats made their incredible one-step ascent without drastically revising their sound. Although **Folk of the 80's** is somewhat rudimentary, Ivan Doroschuk's remarkably obnoxious singing is already in full flower, and the songs display his characteristically skewed lyrical perceptions and aggressively bouncy tunes.

Reprising the EP's "Antarctica" while adding an unlikely and aggravating hit single ("The Safety Dance") and the eminently likable "I Got the Message," **Rhythm of Youth**—roughly the same record as **The Safety Dance**—is slicker but otherwise pretty similar to the band's first release in every aspect save sales volume. Ivan's yelping and theatrical bellowing cries out for the swift application of duct tape to his mouth; still, the band's earnest individuality makes the album hard to truly dislike. The 1984 follow-up leaves the formula unchanged; songs like "Where Do the Boys

Go?" and "Messiahs Die Young" are sprightly and entertaining. But other parts drag mercilessly as Ivan's inflated self-image is delivered pompously to vinyl.

Chastened by the second album's commercial disappointment, Ivan took a lengthy powder, returning three years later with the best single of his career, "Pop Goes the World," done for the soundtrack of *Date with an Angel*. Unfortunately, the rest of what surrounds that insidious techno-pop ditty on **Pop Goes the World** is only pleasantly dull. But give the group—now an artificial quartet of Ivan, his brother Stefan "in the guise of Johnny the guitarist," a bassist named Jenny and noncorporeal drummer J. Bonhomme—the odd guest of the week award for getting Jethro Tull leader Ian Anderson to add a spot of flute to one song.

Yawn went the world, but that didn't stop the Doroschuks from returning two years later with another modestly appealing album. None of the brothers' diverse originals on **21st Century** are as insidiously clever as Abba's "S.O.S." (which they cover here), but Ivan's toned-down singing (on one quiet love song he threatens to turn into Leonard Cohen) and well-crafted, lyrically intriguing numbers about romance, the environment, sexism, the rock'n'roll game do make some of the material fetching. The record ends with "21st Century Safety Dance," a throbbing demi-industrial instrumental with assorted audio snippets (of the relevant King Crimson and MWH songs, a child's voice, TV news, etc.) thrown in.   [i]

MERCURY REV
See *Flaming Lips*.

MERCY SEAT
See *Violent Femmes*.

MERTON PARKAS

Face in the Crowd (nr/Beggars Banquet) 1979 ●
The Singles EP (nr/Beggars Banquet) 1983

If the Merton Parkas had called their LP **Just Another Face in the Neo-Mod Crowd**, no review of it would be needed. This utterly unmemorable group had nondescript vocals, tame playing (guitar and piano so polite as to be biteless even at high volume) and dull songs (a cover of "Tears of a Clown" not excepted). They do deserve two points for the name, a pun combining the band's London neighborhood and the essential outer garment of Mod garb. Ha, ha. The group finally earned posthumous notoriety when keyboardist Mick Talbot became Paul Weller's partner in the Style Council.   [jg]

See also *Dexy's Midnight Runners, Style Council*.

METALLICA

Kill 'Em All (Megaforce) 1983 (Elektra) 1987 ●
Ride the Lightning (Megaforce) 1984 (Megaforce-Elektra)
    1984 ●
Whiplash EP (Megaforce) 1985
Master of Puppets (Elektra) 1986 ●
The $5.98 E.P. Garage Days Re-Revisited EP (Elektra)
    1987 ●
... And Justice for All (Elektra) 1988 ●
The Good, the Bad and the Live (nr/Vertigo) 1990

One of the most important and influential new rock bands to emerge in the 1980s, California's uncompromising Metallica rose from humble origins to influence the attitudes of a generation, its bone-crunching grooves and punkish fuck-that-shit ideology providing the backdrop to contemporary teenage wasteland.

Formed in 1981 by Danish drummer/tennis pro Lars Ulrich and skatepunk guitarist James Hetfield, the band originally included guitarist Dave Mustaine, who split to form Megadeth just days before **Kill 'Em All** was recorded in mid-'83. Combining Ulrich's love for Eurometal (everything from Motörhead to Jethro Tull) with Hetfield's Misfits worship, the album shrugged off many of metal's traditional sonic clichés, retaining only the power, velocity and blazing guitars. Bracingly unusual (although hardly radical), tracks like "The Four Horsemen" show off lead guitarist Kirk Hammett's technical prowess as well as the mighty Cliff Burton/Lars Ulrich rhythm section. (The 1987 reissue adds a bruising pair of then-obscure metal covers—dubbed "Garage Days Revisited"—from the European B-side of "Creeping Death.")

Ride the Lightning found the band's sound taking on a life of its own. Hetfield's lyrics and strained vocals had scarcely improved, but the pulverizing crunch-grooves—most effective on the awesome "For Whom the Bell Tolls"—unleash primal instincts and are essential lessons in the science of the riff. The limited production and weaker songs detract but don't keep this album from milestone status.

The **Whiplash** EP includes a "neck-brace" remix of the title track and two live cuts.

Releasing its trump card at the ideal moment turned Metallica into superstars almost overnight. Despite mainstream radio's general boycott of uncommercial metal, **Master of Puppets**, universally acknowledged as the band's creative peak, roared into the Top 30 on the strength of constant touring and a rabid underground buzz. Multi-tracked harmony solos, tautly controlled rhythms and simple vocal arrangements make songs about insanity ("Welcome Home (Sanitarium)" and "The Things That Should Not Be"), the futility of war ("Disposable Heroes") and cocaine addiction ("Master of Puppets") burn white-hot with excitement.

Metallica's future was cast in doubt in September 1986 when a bus crash in Sweden killed Burton. But they recruited new bassist Jason Newsted and returned in late '87 with **The $5.98 E.P. Garage Days Re-Revisited**, an intriguingly conceived package of five cover versions recorded casually in LA during rehearsal jams. The bands favored with Metallicazation include Budgie, Killing Joke and the Misfits. Despite the fascinating selection, however, the hurried execution and "not very" production reduce everything to soundalike dullness.

After beginning sessions for its fourth LP with Guns n' Roses producer Mike Clink, the band recalled the producer of its prior two albums and completed the sprawling **. . . And Justice for All** way behind schedule. The album that finally emerged runs over 65 minutes, which, considering the contents, is about 25 too many. An ultra-dry mix and endless directionless riffage make it cold and static; although "Blackened" and "Dyers Eve" are relatively brief (i.e., less than seven minutes) blasts of speed, and the chilling "One" (ba-

sically a third rewrite of **Ride the Lightning**'s "Fade to Black") yielded an unlikely hit single, metal's most underground band had become perilously bloated.

A limited edition boxed set of six 12-inches, **The Good, the Bad and the Live**, reconfigures almost all of Metallica's singles and non-LP material: along with six new live cuts, it includes most of the **Whiplash** EP and both **Garage Days** collections, plus the Budgie and DiamondHead covers from the B-side of "Harvester of Sorrow." [i/rj/ja]

See also *Megadeth*.

METAL MIKE

See *Angry Samoans*.

M.I.A./GENOCIDE
Last Rites for M.I.A. and Genocide (Smoke 7) 1981
M.I.A.
Murder in a Foreign Place (Alternative Tentacles) 1984
Notes from the Underground (National Trust) 1985
After the Fact (Flipside) 1987

Although Las Vegas may be an entertainment capital, its gambling tourists typically prefer Wayne Newton or Bill Cosby to the Sex Pistols. As a result, Vegas' only great punk band gave up before their career could get off the ground. Were it not for their half of a posthumous release, the prematurely titled **Last Rites**, M.I.A. would have remained an unknown, gifted punk band. **Last Rites** sold well, especially after its outstanding opener, "Tell Me Why" (not the Beatles' tune), was included on **American Youth Report**, an excellent West Coast punk/hardcore compilation. Finding themselves wanted, M.I.A. reunited for good, relocating to the more supportive Southern California punk community.

Last Rites contains a side each by M.I.A. and New Jersey's Genocide. (The less said about *them* the better.) Although M.I.A. come across as naïve, uncomplicated, almost willfully unimaginative 1-2-3-4-off-we-go punk, the record drips with the excitement that many such records of that time had. The roaring guitar sounds like a Marshall amp on twelve and the hooks are as instant as oatmeal—just add *steaming* water. Mike Conley's singing is unusually clear, easy to decipher and pop-melodic. The subject of "Gas Crisis" may be out of date, but on the pulverizing two-chord verse of "I Hate Hippies," Conley's ironic tongue is so far in his cheek it's almost coming out his ear: "Cause they're dumb/I'm smart/They're weak/I'm strong/I'm right/And they're fucking wrong." Hilarious!

The songs on **Murder in a Foreign Place** aren't overly political; the music resembles early Brit-punk (Generation X, Sham 69) in spots. By tempering fierce enthusiasm with clear organization (although the mix buries Conley), relatively leisurely tempos and musical coherence, M.I.A. rises well above the crowd.

The much-improved **Notes from the Underground** leaves hardcore behind for a pretty fair Damned/TSOL-influenced punk LP with occasional acoustic guitar and even sax (on an anti-apartheid song). The hooks are occasionally a little too obvious, but "Another Day," "Write Myself a Letter" and "Shadows of My Life" are first-rate punk-pop. Nick Adams' wall of guitar dominates each of the ten tracks.

After the Fact is one of the best US punk records of the late '80s, mostly because it mixes in many post-punk influences and innovates where other punks cling to tradition. The two guitars rarely play similar parts, there are dynamics and mood settings, contemplative sound ("Whisper in the Wind") and even a Killing Jokey tribal backbeat ("When It's Over"). The production on **After the Fact** is far superior to M.I.A.'s past efforts, with real bottom, kick, drive and guts. Just check out the cover of "California Dreaming" or the effortless "Edge of Forever" for proof that punk can be a fresh aural pleasure, even at this late date.

M.I.A. ultimately paid the same price that the original TSOL and Effigies did when they went against the grain and tried to take punk to its next step: they split up in early 1988. [jr]

See also *Big Drill Car*.

MICKEY AND THE MILKSHAKES
See *Pop Rivits*.

MICRODISNEY
Everybody's Fantastic (nr/Rough Trade) 1983
We Hate You South African Bastards! EP (nr/Rough Trade) 1984
Microdisney in the World EP (nr/Rough Trade) 1985
The Clock Comes Down the Stairs (Big Time) 1985
Crooked Mile (Virgin) 1986 ●
39 Minutes (nr/Virgin) 1988 ●
Gale Force Wind EP (nr/Virgin) 1988 ●
The Peel Sessions Album (nr/Strange Fruit) 1989 ●

FATIMA MANSIONS
Against Nature (nr/Kitchenware) 1989
Viva Dead Ponies (nr/Kitchenware) 1990
    (Radioactive-MCA) 1991 ●

SEAN O'HAGAN
High Llamas (nr/Demon) 1990 ●

Originally a duo from Cork, Ireland, Microdisney combine heavily orchestrated smooth pop with potent songwriting. A sublimely seductive paradox, the music goes down easy but invariably returns to haunt the intellect. After moving to London and recruiting three more members, Cathal Coughlan (vocals/lyrics) and Sean O'Hagan (guitar/music) recorded **Everybody's Fantastic**, thirteen gently atmospheric songs that touch the heart and the mind with resonant guitar and Coughlan's passionate brogue. Starkly romantic ("Dolly," "I'll Be a Gentleman") and ardently political ("Come on Over and Cry," "Before the Famine"), the record commands attention.

Virtually nonexistent commercial response to their first LP prompted the release of **We Hate You South African Bastards!**, a mini-album compilation of early singles and demos recorded as a duo that assured Microdisney's survival while making an unequivocal statement against apartheid. Their next release was a four-song 12-inch of new material, **In the World**.

The Clock Comes Down the Stairs suffers from improved production: Coughlan's vocals, curiously relieved of their Irish accent, are set deep within a mix of overwhelming instrumentation. "Birthday Girl,"

"Horse Overboard" and "Past" are pleasant enough, but verge on a generic sound. Gone are Coughlan's heartfelt protests and O'Hagan's sharp melodic chords, making this complacent background muzak—a far cry from the compelling impact of **We Hate You**. (The tape has five extra songs.)

The drawbacks so prevalent on **The Clock Comes Down the Stairs** reassert themselves on **Crooked Mile**. Lenny Kaye's lush production renders this LP as nothing more than a collection of languid, dismissible pop symphonies. One exception, however, is the passionate "Give Me All of Your Clothes"—the first possible sign that Microdisney may be getting just a bit tired of churning out useless fodder.

39 Minutes, which actually clocks in at just under 38, restores the group's sense of purpose, balancing the slick production of recent efforts with a slightly more aggressive attack and Coughlan's sharpest lyrics in ages. While songs like "Singer's Hampstead Home," "Ambulance for One" and "Gale Force Wind" promised much for Microdisney's future, **39 Minutes** proved to be the band's last hurrah.

On the two albums by his new group, the Fatima Mansions (of which he appears to be the only actual member), Coughlan tosses aside polite notions of mainstream pop music in favor of a staggeringly eclectic, uncompromisingly leftist mélange of airy melodicism and frenzied house-inspired dance noise. His conceptual range is particularly impressive on the epic **Viva Dead Ponies**, whose imposing sound palette shouldn't distract from such inspired compositions as "White Knuckle Express" and "Look What I Stole for Us, Darling."

O'Hagan's solo disc is a tasteful and tuneful singer-songwriter effort; short on surprises but long on low-key pleasure. [ag/hd]

MICRONOTZ
See *Mortal Micronotz*.

MIDNIGHT OIL
Midnight Oil (Aus. Powderworks) 1978 (Columbia) 1990 ●
Head Injuries (Aus. Powderworks) 1979 (Columbia) 1990 ●
Bird Noises EP (Aus. Powderworks) 1980 (Columbia) 1990 ●
Place Without a Postcard (Aus. CBS) 1981 (Columbia) 1990 ●
10,9,8,7,6,5,4,3,2,1 (Columbia) 1983 ●
Red Sails in the Sunset (Columbia) 1985 ●
Species Deceases EP (Aus. CBS) 1985 (Columbia) 1990 ●
Diesel and Dust (Columbia) 1987 ●
Blue Sky Mining (Columbia) 1990 ●

A quintet that originally found a following in the rowdy surf crowd frequenting Sydney-area bars, Australia's Midnight Oil went on to become an international phenomenon, and its music grew far beyond its hard-rock roots. But that categorization never quite fit in the first place; hearing their watershed **10,9,8,7,6,5,4,3,2,1** and then reviewing their previous output, the natural query of "how did they make that leap" becomes "what took them so long?"

Oil's iconoclasm is the primary answer. Lead singer Peter Garrett both symbolizes and embodies it: well over six feet tall and bald as a cue ball, he gave up a law career to sing rock'n'roll. His angst/anger-ridden vocals have nothing in common with the standard styles of hard-rock singers, nor do the band's lyrics (chiefly by drummer Rob Hirst) share any of the genre's fixation on refried love themes. The songs are frequently political, yet just as often are couched in extremely personal terms, be they about romance (rarely), self-doubt, hopes and fears and so on. And despite its share of semi-normal hard-rock, complete with blistering guitar solos, the eponymous debut album also includes strange notions about chord progressions and arrangements that would eventually flower: "Dust" is a bluesy riff stated on two basses an octave apart, backed by organ and drums.

No doubt the Oils' insistence on intra-band democracy and doing things their own way was why they refused a major-league deal for five years. Unfortunately, that also meant a lack of money for studio experimentation, and most of their independent-label work sounds like demos, lacking the firm command of a proper producer.

It may also have retarded the band in working out the complexities of songs and arrangements, including adapting the music to odd lyrical meter (or vice versa). **Head Injuries** makes some progress on that front, and the songwriting—still largely done by various teams in the group—seems to have matured. A clutch of songs are able to transcend the limitations of their presentation, assisted by Garrett's impassioned vocals and the group's overall intensity. What at first seem to be arranging gaffes eventually take on an air of almost integral idiosyncrasy. The four-song **Bird Noises** EP continues that development and also features an anomalous but delightful Shadows-like instrumental, "Wedding Cake Island." (The 1990 reissues of Oil's early records and the 1985 EP are all CD/cassette; no domestic vinyl exists.)

Place Without a Postcard should've been a brilliant breakthrough; instead, it's muscle-bound, all worked up and uncertain where to go first. The few simple strokes are the most effective—in fact, "Someone Else to Blame" is a cracker—but most of it's at war with itself. Also, the sound achieved with veteran producer Glyn Johns in England is demo-thin. But the experimentation yielded valuable lessons, and James Moginie, the group's most prolific composer, also began to jell his distinctive guitar sound, as well as creatively exploring keyboards. The stage was set for the group's international introduction.

The strong political views expressed on **10,9,8,7,6,5,4,3,2,1** may have been a sticking point outside the band's homeland, but they're frequently more personally expressed than, say, the Clash's and, when not, they're more articulate. Increased use of synthesizer handsomely complements the quintet's most cohesive songwriting and arranging; while no two tracks are more than vaguely similar, they're all completely unified. Some credit must also go to Nick Launay (co-producer, with the band), who obtained a crisp, if slightly odd, sound. Although much of Side Two is more thoughtful and less visceral than Side One, overall the album is a masterpiece, from the desperate hopefulness of "Outside World" to the controlled hysteria/rifferama of "Only the Strong" to the danceable fist-shaker, "Power and the Passion."

On **Red Sails in the Sunset** (again with Launay), the Oils indulge in too much experimentation at once (though more successfully than **Place Without a Postcard**). The LP opens with two relatively simple tracks, "When the Generals Talk" (more clichéd than the band's usual political statements, but a stirring mix of hard rock and—new for the Oils—funk) and "Best of Both Worlds," one of their best straight-ahead rockers ever. From there on, excessive musical complexity, plus some topics that are simply beyond the ken of non-Australians, make it heavy going. Some tracks (notably "Sleep" and "Minutes to Midnight") do unfold eventually, but others remain steadfastly impenetrable.

Evidently inspired by the 40th anniversary of the bombing of Hiroshima, Midnight Oil recorded **Species Deceases**, four survival-of-humanity tracks cut virtually live in the studio (co-produced by Francois Kervorkian). Solid and heartfelt, but no lyrical or musical revelations.

Diesel and Dust doesn't reach the highs of **10,9,8**, but it is consistently powerful and compelling. The production (the band with Warne Livesey) is snappier than ever, and the passion for the issues comes across loud and clear. Actually, the passion comes through regardless of the issues; few Americans who made "Beds Are Burning" the Oils' first US hit single had any idea it was about Aboriginal land rights. **Diesel** is a consolidation of strengths, and isn't even beyond a bit of recycling, but the results can be impressive (as on "Bullroarer," which partially reprocesses **Red Sails'** "Sleep"). And it's hard to fault such dandy goods as "The Dead Heart," sung from an Aborigine's point of view.

Blue Sky Mining continues the disappointing trend of decreasing musical inspiration. It's like **Species Deceases** with more production (Livesey and the Oils again); not without its fine points, and occasionally as lyrically on-the-mark as ever (e.g., the title track), but the melodies, most of the messages and the general excitement level just aren't the band's best. If the Oils weren't so eminently capable of greatness, an album this good would seem quite impressive.   [jg]

MIGHTY CAESARS
See *Thee Mighty Caesars*.

MIGHTY LEMON DROPS
Happy Head (Sire) 1986 ●
Out of Hand (Sire) 1987 ●
Janice Long Session EP (nr/Nighttracks-Strange Fruit) 1987
World Without End (Sire-Reprise) 1988 ●
Fall Down (Like the Rain) EP (nr/Blue Guitar) 1988 ●
Laughter (Sire-Reprise) 1989 ●
Sound ... (Sire-Reprise) 1991 ф

Imagine the neo-psychedelia of early Echo & the Bunnymen played with a jangling Rickenbacker as the lead instrument and a less mannered (and less interesting) vocalist and you're on your way to sussing the sound of **Happy Head**. That's not to take anything away from the intensity and dynamic mood shifts the

Midlands-bred quartet (initially known as the Sherbert Monsters) can achieve, but it's hard to hear the album without making the connection. That said, there's at least a side's worth of first-rate songs here, and the uncluttered, stripped-down approach is distinctive enough to recommend it to anyone who likes this sort of thing.

Out of Hand, an eight-cut hodgepodge comprising energetic but unrevelatory live versions of three of **Happy Head**'s better songs and some new studio cuts that add string synthesizers and Eastern flavoring (shades of the Bunnymen, circa "The Cutter"!) to the brew, is for fans only. It has the feel of "product" put out to coincide with a tour or something. (The **Happy Head** CD also contains **Out of Hand**.)

Produced by Tim Palmer, **World Without End** shows the group matured beyond obvious comparisons. The sound is fuller and warmer than before, the arrangements more sophisticated; if not riveting, singer Paul Marsh at least sounds confident. The only downside is the loss of some of **Happy Head**'s manic energy. The CD adds "Shine"; the subsequent EP draws its title track from the album.

With the departure of bassist Tony Linehan (co-writer of all the group's material) during the recording of **Laughter** (he appears on two cuts), guitarist David Newton—who founded the band after leaving the Wild Flowers—became the group's lone songwriter. Judging from **Laughter**, he's up to the task, since the material here is among the band's best—shimmering guitar pop with stick-to-you choruses. The Lemon Drops experiment with more complex vocal arrangements to good effect, but it's Newton's guitar work that really shines—he manages to say something different on each song, while staying true to the band's tight ensemble sound. Superb. (The CD adds "Rumbletrain?," a British B-side.) [ds]

See also *Wild Flowers*.

MIGHTY MOFOS

See *Hypstrz*.

MIGHTY SQUIRRELS

See *Young Fresh Fellows*.

MIGHTY WAH!

See *Wah!*.

MILKSHAKES

See *Pop Rivits*.

DANIEL MILLER

See *Silicon Teens*.

ROGER MILLER

No Man Is Hurting Me (Ace of Hearts) 1986
The Big Industry (Ace of Hearts) 1987 + 1988
Oh. guitars, etc ... (Forced Exposure) 1988
Roger Miller Presents Xylyl and A Woman in Half (New Alliance) 1991 ●

NO MAN IS ROGER MILLER

Win! Instantly! (SST) 1989 ●

NO MAN/NO MAN'S BAND

Damage the Enemy (New Alliance) 1989

NO MAN

Whamon Express (SST) 1990 ●

As Boston's preeminent new wave sonic experimenter, Roger Miller (guitar, piano, vocals) led Mission of Burma and, later, Birdsongs of the Mesozoic, provocative groups that tested various musical possibilities from a progressive rock-derived context. Beginning with the Maximum Electric Piano examinations of **No Man Is Hurting Me**'s second side, Miller's solo career has been equally exploratory. The five pieces (all instrumental, save for a dramatic reading of Lewis Carroll's *Jabberwocky*) apply Frippertronic tape-loop technique to a prepared (with things like clips, bolts and combs put on the strings) keyboard, generating fascinating ambient textures and pulsing rhythms from a single performance. The remainder of the album is formless and flakier, stretching from a delightful clarinet-damage rock rendition of the other Roger Miller's "King of the Road" to haphazard kinetic noodling on assorted instruments.

The Big Industry ambitiously incorporates Maximum Electric Piano into vocal music, underpinning semi-melodic art-tunes like "Portrait of a Mechanical Dog" and an atonal free-for-all cover of Jimi Hendrix's "Manic Depression" with intriguing contrivances that blend noise (hammers, sampled egg beater, etc.) and music in a challenging tension of nice and rough. Occasionally off-putting but more frequently impressive.

Miller's home-brew album of guitar experiments, **Oh. guitars, etc . . .** , uses avant-garde compositional tricks, improvisation, conceptual gimmicks (like a nine-minute feedback symphony), tape manipulations ("The Fun World Reductions" is merely an old Burma recording run at extremely high speed) and noises. More irritating than significant, this is an audio scratch pad with few worthwhile notes.

The far more accessible **Win! Instantly!** (recorded with chord bassist Russ Smith) productively returns Miller (aka No Man) to song form. Although **Win!**'s din can get awfully loud, clearly defined structures that allow plenty of room for Miller's unique keyboard approach and strange percussion samples invigorate this fine record. Operating on numerous sonic levels at once, songs like "Renegades," "No Man's Landing" and Burma's "This Is Not a Photograph" resemble a collaboration between XTC and Test Dept. under the direction of Brian Eno.

The No Man (Miller alone on vocals and guitar, with sampled rhythm accompaniment) side of **Damage the Enemy** is wonderful, an energetic and well-sung set of textured rock tunes with crazy noises. The No Man's Band (a keyboardless improv trio with Smith and a percussionist) side takes more listener effort, although the occasionally humorous pieces (the found-implement noises suggest Spike Jones rather than any contemporary artistes) are a far cry from the ear-pinning misery of other unplanned ensembles. (And Miller's trumpet work is a revelation.)

Proceeding from the previous LP's No Man efforts, **Whamon Express** is a surprisingly straightforward guitar-plus-keyboards rock/pop record with the usual sonic ephemera reduced to a mere industrial accent. Joined by a singing percussionist, Miller redoes "Red Ants IV" (from **No Man Is Hurting Me**) on guitar and the brief "You S.O.B." (from **Oh.**), covers "The Man Who Sold the World" without incident and antes up nine good-to-great new originals, some of which could easily pass for Burma tunes. [i]

See also *Birdsongs of the Mesozoic, Mission of Burma*.

ALAN MILMAN SECT
EP (Britz) 1977
MAN-KA-ZAM
EP (Britz) 1978
BUDDY LOVE
Buddy Love (Davco) 1983
DUCK AND THE PONDS
Lost World (nr/Big Beat) 1988

Shifting musical styles the way some people change addresses, singer/songwriter Alan Milman first surfaced on New York's Long Island in 1977, with a 7-inch EP of tossed-off punk-rock jokes. Dropping the beat-era name for the modernized Man-ka-zam handle, Milman and guitarist Doug Khazzam returned a year later with another 7-inch: four derivative new wave tunes (including "Spankathon" and "Surf Rhapsody"). That was Milman's last vinyl for a while.

Opting for a lower-profile role as a songwriter, co-producer and backing vocalist, Milman let the pseudonymous Buddy Love (Khazzam, using a name borrowed from Jerry Lewis' *Nutty Professor* alter-ego) sing lead and play guitar on the exceptional **Buddy Love**, a charming and memorable pop/rock collection that knowingly mines a wide variety of sources, from '50s rockabilly to '60s Britbeat to '70s glam. Besides covering Gary Glitter ("Rock n' Roll"), Gene Vincent ("Who Slapped John?") and Buddy Holly ("Rave On") with straightforward skill, the quartet delivers sparkling pop originals like the ultra-catchy "Liar," "Why Can't We Make Believe We're in Love?" and "Dead Ringer." Virtually unknown, but great.

Five years later, Milman popped up in the garage-rocking Duck and the Ponds, where his tuneless shout (not for nothing is he billed as Howlin Alan Milman) suits such generic stompers as "Wanna Ruin Ya" and "Wild About You." The noisy and echo-laden **Lost World** isn't bad (in fact, the poppish "Wrong" and "On the Corner Again" are pretty neat), but—other than having convinced a British tabloid of their kidnapping by space aliens, who ostensibly helped write the album's songs—the trio hasn't got any distinguishing characteristics. [i]

TED MILTON
See *Blurt*.

ZODIAC MINDWARP AND THE LOVE REACTION
High Priest of Love (nr/Food) 1986 ●
Tattooed Beat Messiah (Vertigo) 1988 ●

Perhaps hoping to repeat the career feat of ex-*Smash Hits* editor-*cum*-Pet Shop Boy Neil Tennant, onetime *Flexipop!* magazine art director Mark Manning adopted the grungelicious psychedelic motor-thug persona of Zodiac Mindwarp, concocted a ridiculous story about being from another planet, assembled a backing band with names like Slam Thunderhide, Trash D Garbage and Cobalt Stargazer, and set about to test the gullibility of the pop world with a great single called "Prime Mover." Brilliantly produced by Liverpool coolsters Dave Balfe (ex-Teardrop Explodes) and future KLF/JAMS mastermind Bill Drummond, the band's sole US LP, **Tattooed Beat Messiah**, crosses AC/DC with T. Rex: a back-straightening, breath-taking guitar assault, intentionally low-brow wiseacre lyrics and chanted choruses that demand enthusiastic attention. The melodic headbanging metal power could give Motörhead, Judas Priest or Van Halen a youthful run for their money; one can savor the selfconscious stupidity of songs like "Backseat Education" and "Let's Break the Law" either as sophisticated parody or the real thing. After leaving the Love Reaction, bassist Kid Chaos (aka Haggis) played in the Cult. [i]

See also *Cult, Justified Ancients of Mu Mu*.

MINIMAL COMPACT
Minimal Compact EP (Bel. Crammed Discs) 1981
One by One (Bel. Crammed Discs) 1983
Deadly Weapons (Bel. Crammed Discs) 1984 ●
The Next One Is Real EP (Crammed Discs-Wax Trax!) 1984 ●
Raging Souls (Bel. Crammed Discs) 1986 ●
Lowlands Flight (Bel. Made to Measure) 1987 ●
The Figure One Cuts (Bel. Crammed Discs) 1987 ●
One Plus One by One [CD] (Bel. Crammed Discs) 1988 ●
Live (Bel. Crammed Discs) 1988 ●

Not so much a rock band as a pan-cultural chamber ensemble with rock instrumentation, the members of Minimal Compact are (mostly) Israelis who didn't see much of a future in their homeland, emigrated to France and signed with Belgium's Crammed Discs. Their music is tasteful and intelligent but avoids selfconscious artsiness, and they've worked with some connoisseur favorites: Tuxedomoon's Peter Principle, Wire's Colin Newman (who's married to the group's Malka Spigel) and John Fryer (who's worked with the Cocteau Twins) have all produced them. They served as Newman's backup band on his **Commercial Suicide** LP; some of their sleeves were designed by Eno collaborator Russell Mills. Minimal Compact's records consistently display an ability to switch gears between atmospheric, British-style art-rock, Middle Eastern-flavored folk and Beatlesque pop, while also retaining the ability to rock out with a danceable beat.

Minimal Compact's first (and, so far, only) American release was an expanded EP. **The Next One Is Real** contains five songs (including two mixes of the title track) and is a relatively commercial effort, containing hard funk played masterfully by a band whose usual approach is considerably gentler. Both **Lowlands Flight** (part of Crammed's Made to Measure series, written in part for a Dutch dance troupe) and **The Figure One Cuts** show quieter moments and greater versatility; those familiar with **Commercial Suicide** will recognize the guitar textures and delicate arrangements that gave that LP its unique sound. Minimal Compact may be very refined and mature, but they're never boring. [dgs]

MINISTRY
Cold Life EP (Wax Trax!) 1981
With Sympathy (Arista) 1983 ●
Work for Love (nr/Arista) 1983
'Twitch' (Sire) 1986 + 1990 ●
Twelve Inch Singles 1981–1984 (Wax Trax!) 1987 ϕ
The Land of Rape and Honey (Sire) 1988 ●
The Mind Is a Terrible Thing to Taste (Sire) 1989 ●
In Case You Didn't Feel Like Showing Up (Live) EP (Sire) 1990 ϕ

LEAD INTO GOLD
Age of Reason (Wax Trax!) 1990 ●

Although Cuban-born singer/writer/producer/keyboard player Alain Jourgensen launched Chicago's Ministry as an obnoxiously collegiate modern-dance alliance, he didn't leave it there, and wound up at the epicenter of an extremist cult of industrial noisemakers, madly ripping up rock's floorboards with an intensity rarely heard outside of nuclear test sites. But it took a while to get from point A to point B.

Ministry debuted in 1981 with an EP built around the cloddish "Cold Life." (That song and "Cold Life Dub" both appear, along with three other long tracks and their remixes, on the half-good/half-bad developmental **Twelve Inch Singles** compilation.) Signing to a major label, the group—here consisting of Alain Jourgensen and drummer Stephen George, with session guests—made the similar-sounding **With Sympathy**, co-produced by Ian Taylor and Psychedelic Fur Vince Ely. (The British edition, **Work for Love**, resequences the record and replaces one track.) A sophomoric dose of yuppie-funk, the LP is filled with brutish singing and scanty, derivative ideas stretched by numbing repetition beyond any reasonable limits of listenability. Most heinously, "I Wanted to Tell Her" (a finished version of the **Cold Life** EP's vocal-less "Primental") chants the title lyric like a litany, as does "Work for Love," which adds moronic lyrics to the numbing two-chord vamp.

Fortunately, that was the end of Ministry's polite attempts at dance-floor accessibility. Produced by Adrian Sherwood, **'Twitch'** is a far different beast, and the first steps into a murky swamp that subsumes Jourgensen's distorted, nearly spoken vocals within a pounding electronic rhythm onslaught, with found-sound tape bits and barrages of scratch-mix noise effects. Although much of this unsuccessful experiment throbs along dully, with haphazard intersections of good new ideas and bad old ideas, the militaristic "All Day Remix" (an inter-album single that appears in a better mix on **Twelve Inch**) offers a cogent demonstration of the direction Jourgensen is headed.

Ministry's arrival in **The Land of Rape and Honey** is heralded by "Stigmata," a queasy synth riff and a blood-curdling shriek. Co-produced by Jourgensen (in the guise of Hypo Luxa) and his lone bandmate, bassist/keyboardist Paul Barker (aka Hermes Pan), the album steps off the ledge of rock convention for an unnervingly powerful sonic assault. Thundering drums (by guest

Minister William Rieflin) underpin distorted layers of guitars, keyboards, tapes and effects, with Jourgensen's deranged vocals frantically competing to be heard. Hard to understand, but impossible to ignore, **The Land of Rape and Honey** is an efficiently ferocious and frightening comment on the modern world.

The Mind Is a Terrible Thing to Taste—on which Jourgensen began listing his given name as Alien—compresses that explosive energy into a tightly wound punk-influenced guitar attack that threatens to skitter off the turntable. Such focus leaves the album a bit less chaotically unpredictable than its predecessor, but no less obsessive in its diabolical power. When Jourgensen chants the title of "Breathe" over and over in a commanding roar, obedience seems like the safest course. Chris Connelly (of Fini Tribe and the Revolting Cocks, one of Ministry's many side projects) sings lead on "Cannibal Song" and "Never Believe."

Six songs with a running time exceeding 40 minutes, the live EP is a speaker-shredding souvenir of Ministry's '89-'90 North American tour, a memorable extravaganza that saw as many as nine musicians—including Martin (Brian Brain) Atkins and Skinny Puppy's Nivek Ogre—onstage at one time. Storming through a devastating précis of the two previous LPs, this incarnation of Ministry is a punishing beast, thrashing in incomprehensible fury to a runaway piledriver beat. Brutally oppressive but irresistibly fascinating.

Lead into Gold is Paul Barker's solo project, a needless opportunity for him to write, perform and sing his own material electronically, with only a guest guitarist chucking in chords here and there. Wrapped in a nifty embossed cover, **Age of Reason** puts grimly pretentious lyrics (a random couplet: "Covered in mud for glory/ Belies our sense of fun") to plodding songs which Barker sings in an artless voice. The Eno-oriented "Faster Than Light" (also available on a three-song 12-inch entitled **Chicks & Speed: Futurism**) is the closest thing to a real song you'd want to hear twice.

See also *Lard, Pailhead, Revolting Cocks*. [i]

MINISTRY OF LOVE
See *Red Temple Spirits*.

MINK DEVILLE
Mink DeVille (Capitol) 1977 ●
Return to Magenta (Capitol) 1978
Le Chat Bleu (Capitol) 1980
Coup de Grâce (Atlantic) 1981
Savoir Faire (Capitol) 1981 ●
Where Angels Fear to Tread (Atlantic) 1983
Sportin' Life (Atlantic) 1985 ●
Cabretta (nr/Razor) 1987

WILLY DEVILLE
Miracle (A&M) 1987 ●
Victory Mixture (Orleans) 1990 ●

Around 1976-'77, Willy DeVille and pals could, on a good night, be the coolest cats on the New York underground scene, despite occasional stylistic sidetracking. After being "discovered," producer Jack Nitzsche got them on the lean, tough R&B beam for a first LP that sweats and smokes through and through as a classic of such fully and lovingly assimilated music should.

Unfortunately, **Return to Magenta** is more of the same but less; on the first LP, the cover of Moon Martin's "Cadillac Walk" was one of many highlights, but here Martin's inferior "Rolene" is pretty much it. **Le Chat Bleu**'s arrival was welcome mainly because it ended Willy's prolonged absence from recording, but it confirmed that stagnation had set in. The band was, by then, a couple of Minks plus sessionmen; it seemed Willy was looking to become the soul crooner of his dreams without providing the songs to fuel ours (despite some collaborative songwriting with Doc Pomus, hitsmith for Joe Turner, Dion, the Drifters, etc.). **Savoir Faire** collects tracks from those three albums.

Evidence that DeVille had lost touch with the trash/sleaze aesthetic (not to mention Louie X. Erlanger's lowdown guitar) is even plainer on **Coup de Grâce**. Despite a new, young band and a reunion with Nitzsche (Mink saxist Steve Douglas had produced the third LP), the magic is still largely absent. Tracks like "Maybe Tomorrow" offer traces of the old bite almost as a concession.

Where Angels Fear to Tread, produced by the hit-making team of Ron and Howard Albert (who ruined a Gang of Four album that same year), is a fine record of new DeVille originals, starting with the soulful and sweet "Each Word's a Beat of My Heart." This uncluttered and uncomplicated tribute to DeVille's forebears—Sam Cooke, Phil Spector, the Drifters, Joe Tex, James Brown—also includes forays into Spanish Harlem and other wondrously nostalgic time warps. DeVille's songwriting and singing have returned to top strength, and the record burns with sincerity and warmth. Simply, elegantly excellent.

Sportin' Life maintains those standards with a set of brand-new oldies that effortlessly transport you back to the era of sweet soul music. "Something Beautiful Dying" (note the Righteous Brothers reference) is tenderly melancholic; "Little by Little" tries barrelhouse rockabilly; "Italian Shoes" is classic bad dude strutting. Apt production and a sharp backing band make this first rate.

Inexplicably selected to write and sing the theme song for *The Princess Bride*, DeVille astonishingly earned an Academy Award nomination for "Storybook Love," the schmaltzy cut that ends **Miracle**. While the pale and inconsistent record is nowhere near Willy's best work, his seasoned voice is as strong and colorful as ever. The snappy "Angel Eyes," romantic "Nightfalls" and Van Morrison's "Could You Would You?" are among the album's merits. Mark Knopfler, who played all the guitar here, produced the LP cleanly but without color, forgetting the smoky ambience essential to DeVille's music.

Victory Mixture finds Willy living in the Big Easy, making music with Dr. John, Allen Toussaint and other local legends. [jg/i]

See also *Fast Floyd and the Famous Firebirds*.

LIZA MINNELLI

See *Pet Shop Boys*.

MINNY POPS

Drastic Measures, Drastic Movement (Hol. Plurex) 1979 + 1982
Sparks in a Dark Room (Bel. Factory Benelux) 1982

SMALTS

Werktitels EP (Hol. Plurex) 1982

POSTE RESTANTE

Poste Restante (Hol. Plurex) 1983

Even in 1979, Minny Pops didn't seem drastic in the purest sense but rather deliberately, almost clinically extreme. The Dutch foursome's most salient characteristic on record is dissonance, even sheer noise—valid artistic devices in the proper hands, but it takes vision and inspiration, of which the Pops seem to possess little. Whether they're having a go at industrial clang or setting pop clichés and oldies in jarringly alien musical contexts, even their best comes up short of what others (e.g., Throbbing Gristle, Half Japanese) have achieved in the same area. No doubt they've applied themselves diligently to make this music, but the net result lacks spark and invention. Minny Pops' first LP, released on the band's Plurex label, Holland's most important and active indie, was reissued in 1982 with the addition of a bonus 45.

Glimmerings of something better flicker on the Smalts EP. The syncopated percussion and keyboards/synth noises, including an arresting accordion/harmonium-type sound, are like a soundtrack in search of a movie, but effective within its limits. Smalts was, in fact, two members of Minny Pops exploring new avenues in preparation for creating the musical setting for a stage production entitled *Poste Restante*. The resulting LP of that name involved the whole band, plus others; although they didn't write all the material, Minny Pops perform everything except some vocals (mostly declaimed, not sung). Out of context, and entirely in Dutch, whatever meaning it has is limited to the vaguely unified feel and the knowledge that it's ostensibly a drama about travel. [jg]

MINOR THREAT

Minor Threat EP (Dischord) 1981
In My Eyes EP (Dischord) 1981
Out of Step (Dischord) 1983
Minor Threat (Dischord) 1984
Complete [CD] (Dischord) 1988 •

EMBRACE

Embrace (Dischord) 1987

TEEN IDLES

Minor Disturbance EP (Dischord) 1981

VARIOUS ARTISTS

Four Old 7"s on a 12" (Dischord) 1985

As the seminal hardcore band of our nation's capital, Minor Threat played fast, impassioned music that defined the genre while never succumbing to its shortcomings. The quartet had both a sense of melody and a sense of purpose. "Straight Edge" was among the first hardcore songs to call for abstinence from drugs and booze, and the band's self-titled theme song acknowledged both the aspirations and realities of political punk rock.

The posthumous **Minor Threat** compiles the band's two initial 7-inch EPs, released on the group's own label. The twelve selections effectively define the city's hardcore sound, with a powerhouse adrenalized rush and Ian MacKaye's explosive and articulate vocals. "Filler," "I Don't Wanna Hear It" and "Minor Threat" are some of *the* classics of the genre; if you haven't heard them, you have never—repeat, never—heard hardcore. One of the most intense, ungodly-force-of-technology records ever launched.

Out of Step, the group's only true LP, shows Minor Threat coming out of adolescence and slowing down to merely quick tempos where they have more room to move. If less a direct rush than the early EPs, the trade-off is a good one: dynamics and crashing hooks come to the fore, replacing the old burn with a punk musician-ship up there with only the Ruts (a prime influence) for crack precision. **Out of Step** is a whale of an LP, one that made their ensuing demise (the pressures of being the most revered and hardline message-oriented hard-core band taking its toll) that much more of a tragedy. Not surprisingly, nothing has come close to matching their ability, drive and emotional level since. (**Complete** compiles the band's entire recorded career into one handy CD. Look no further!)

Sometime after Minor Threat's 1983 breakup, MacKaye joined forces with the three musicians from another recently disbanded DC hardcore band, Faith (ironically, Faith's singer was Alex MacKaye, so he was effectively replacing his younger brother!), to form Embrace. After a brief existence, Embrace also disap-peared seemingly without a trace. A 1987 LP of their 1985 recordings was released, making it apparent that the group should have stuck around a bit longer. If not equal to Minor Threat's one-of-a-kind sonic excellence, Embrace are strong and muscular, an effective backdrop for MacKaye's lead vocals. The confrontational lyricist rages through "Money" and "No More Pain" like a hellfire preacher, condemning a corrupt and greedy cul-ture. Overenunciating, shouting, cajoling and scream-ing at the top of his lungs, this is an impressive performance by a seemingly possessed man, transform-ing an okay mid-tempo punk LP into a great one.

MacKaye subsequently reunited with Minor Threat drummer Jeff Nelson for one terrific single as Egg Hunt and then formed Fugazi with old Rites of Spring leader Guy Picciotto. (He also records occasionally with Min-istry's Al Jourgensen as Pailhead.) Nelson joined up with Senator Flux for a while; bassist-*cum*-guitarist Brian Baker (ex-Government Issue) spent time in the Meatmen and Dag Nasty and can now be found in the metallic Junkyard.

The Teen Idles were MacKaye and Nelson's original group, prior to Minor Threat. **Minor Disturbance**, also a 7-inch EP, was the very first Dischord release, and served as a blueprint for the DC hardcore scene. Inter-estingly, MacKaye doesn't sing lead (he was the bassist and main songwriter) on these seven songs of typical punk-teen ennui and self-determination (plus one inau-dible live cut). Structurally, the music is basic punk on its way to becoming hardcore, dominated by singer Nathan Strejcek's (later of Youth Brigade) youthful blare and MacKaye's catchy bass riffs. The lyrics to "Deadhead" ("Driving that train high on cocaine/The music is really lousy, the fans are a pain/Troubles be-

hind, troubles ahead/The only good deadhead is one that's dead") are as funny today as when the teenaged MacKaye wrote them. **Minor Disturbance** was later reissued on the **Four Old 7″s** album with other Dischord EPs by S.O.A., Youth Brigade and Government Issue.

[jl/jr/gef]

See also *Dag Nasty, Fugazi, Government Issue, Meatmen, Misfits, Pailhead.*

MINUTEMEN

Paranoid Time EP (SST) 1980 ●
The Punch Line (SST) 1981
Bean-Spill EP (Thermidor) 1982
What Makes a Man Start Fires? (SST) 1983
Buzz or Howl Under the Influence of Heat (SST) 1983
Double Nickels on the Dime (SST) 1984 ●
The Politics of Time (New Alliance) 1984
Tour-Spiel EP (Reflex) 1985
... Just a Minute Men (Virgin Vinyl) 1985
My First Bells 1980–1983 [tape] (SST) 1985
Project: Mersh EP (SST) 1985
3-Way Tie (for Last) (SST) 1985 ●
Ballot Result (SST) 1987 ●
Post-Mersh, Vol. 1 [CD] (SST) 1987 ●
Post-Mersh, Vol. 2 [CD] (SST) 1987 ●
Post-Mersh, Vol. 3 [CD] (SST) 1989 ●

MINUTEFLAG

Minuteflag EP (SST) 1986

San Pedro, California's greatest musical export clearly understood the concept of brevity. The trio's albums and EPs pack an astonishing number of songs, most of which (on the early releases, at least) clock in at under a minute. In that brief time, they took apart rock, jazz and funk and put the pieces back together in a jagged collage. Although the Minutemen refused to write verses and choruses, based on their belief that rock'n'roll as we know it is a lethargic dinosaur, each of their songs is a satisfying composition.

The Minutemen saga began in 1980 as a four-piece called the Reactionaries that played regular-length songs. Later that year, they slimmed down (numerically speaking) and adopted their new name and radical modus operandi. They stuck to that twisted idea of dada with a groove until the end, and with one out-of-chronology exception, their records kept getting more ambitious *and* better.

The 7-inch **Paranoid Time** EP offers dogmatic pol-itics redeemed by idiosyncratic Wire-type songs. Kicked along by drummer George Hurley, each abbreviated blurt of rhythm serves as a backdrop for the rants of bassist Mike Watt and guitarist D. Boon. The best is the apocalyptic "Paranoid Chant," in which Boon screams, "I don't even worry about crime anymore."

The Punch Line is more complex, musically and lyrically. The band loosens up with more funk, off-kilter rhythms and enigmatic twists in which songs seem to fall apart but don't quite. As proof of the musicians' seriousness, the 12-inch 45 includes an insert entitled *Fundamentals of Design*, which waxes philosophic about "The Order of Harmony," "The Order of Bal-ance" and "The Order of Rhythm." Actually, the record is evidence enough, as it reveals three imagina-tive musicians capable of playing music that holds together without a center. A subsequent 7-inch, **Bean-Spill**, contains five songs (total running time: six minutes) and a vulgar genitalia drawing by Raymond Pettibone on the label, over the legend "(We need the money)."

What Makes a Man Start Fires? throws jazz and blues elements into the blender, and features the Minutemen's first semi-dramatic song ending—that is, the first on which they do something other than just stop playing. The songs tend towards near-epic length—only one of eighteen is under a minute. On this album, the Minutemen show their instrumental depth, shifting effortlessly from one fragmentary clash of styles to another. On the trio's most poetic record, the eight-song **Buzz or Howl**, they don't try to make the pieces add up, crafting the loosest improvisations over which Boon and (on one song) Watt scream their lyrics.

Double Nickels on the Dime slaps 45 numbers onto four sides of vinyl. The unifying concept is driving in a car, but the record is really held together by the band's unflagging commitment to idiosyncrasy. The quirky songs are about Michael Jackson, Minutemen history, WW III and virtually everything else under the sun. Each is different and somehow good. With this much room to work, the Minutemen don't attempt to bludgeon listeners with lyrics, and deliver terse gems like "If we heard mortar shells we'd cuss more in our songs and cut down the guitar solos."

As if their abundant output left unjustifiable gaps, the trio issued **The Politics of Time**, a collection of unused tracks that vary widely in recording and performance quality. The 7-inch **Tour-Spiel**—drawn from a live-in-the-studio performance done for a Tucson radio broadcast—offers the trio's takes on Van Halen ("Ain't Talkin' 'Bout Love"), Blue Öyster Cult ("The Red & the Black"), Creedence ("Green River") and the Meat Puppets ("Lost"). Like all of the group's records no matter what shape they take, this sounds above all like the Minutemen. (In a weird footnote, the Arizona DJ who organized the 1984 session took umbrage at its appearance on **Tour-Spiel** and released the entire broadcast as **Just a Minute Men**, defending his dubious action in the album's self-righteous liner notes.)

My First Bells is a retrospective cassette: 62 cuts, including the group's first two albums and EPs, plus singles and compilation contributions from the same era. Essential.

Project: Mersh (the title is a sardonic reference to commercialism—"I got it! We'll have them write hit songs," says Boon's cover painting) consists of six lengthy tracks, including Watt's autobiographical "Tour-Spiel" as well as the endlessly looped, psychedelicized "More Spiel" and a cover of Steppenwolf's "Hey Lawdy Mama." Half employ guest trumpet; one even has synth. Typically brilliant and intelligent? Yes. Better presented and more accessible? Somewhat. A compromise of any sort? Hardly. A fine record.

Taking time out from both bands' busy schedules, the Minutemen and Black Flag recorded a one-day-studio-party EP in March 1985 under the spliced name of Minuteflag. In an odd tontine, the participants reportedly agreed not to issue the results until at least one of the bands had broken up. They could have waited: the four rambling song-jams are long on bonhomie but short on cohesion. **Minuteflag** is an ill-advised outing that

was undoubtedly fun to record but unwise to release.

3-Way Tie (for Last) ironically appeared the same week (in December 1985) Boon's tragic death in an Arizona car crash ended the Minutemen. Indicating now-moot artistic independence or divergence, the sides are marked "D." and "Mike." Boon's collection combines three of his tunes (including the gripping Vietnam veteran tribute, "The Price of Paradise," and a Nicaragua protest, "The Big Stick") with straight readings of the Meat Puppets' "Lost" (again) and John Fogerty's "Have You Ever Seen the Rain," plus a composition by Watt and then-Black Flag bassist Kira. Watt's more diverse ten-track side has two by Boon, a spoken word piece named "Spoken Word Piece," four more co-written with Kira, Roky Erickson's "Bermuda" and another killer take on the Cult's "The Red & the Black."

The Minutemen had included a mail-in ballot with **3-Way Tie**, offering fans the opportunity to select their favorite songs for inclusion on a planned triple-live set. The idea was to do all of the selections in concert for the mooted album, provisionally titled **Three Dudes, Six Sides, Half Studio, Half Live**. Despite Boon's death, the votes were tabulated and the **Ballot Result** was assembled from extant material and released anyway. Drawing on various radio broadcasts, audience and board performance tapes, studio outtakes and rehearsals (with three LP tracks serving as needed ringers), the two discs bulge with almost three dozen representations of the group's best-loved material. The audio quality varies, but the trio's vitality and invention never waver. A fine epilogue.

With the exception of **Double Nickels** and the unauthorized live album, the three **Post-Mersh** CDs contain the Minutemen's entire oeuvre up through **Project Mersh**. **Vol. 1** combines **The Punch Line** and **What Makes a Man Start Fires**. The second volume pairs **Buzz or Howl** and **Project Mersh**. Collecting the rest, **Vol. 3** has **Paranoid Time**, 1981's three-song "Joy" single, **Bean-Spill**, **The Politics of Time** and **Tour-Spiel**.

Following Boon's death, Watt and Hurley formed fIREHOSE with singer/guitarist Ed Crawford, a Minutemen fan who badgered them into starting a new group.   [jl/i]

See also *Dos, fIREHOSE, Saccharine Trust*.

MIRACLE LEGION

A Simple Thing [tape] (Incas) 1984
The Backyard EP (Incas) 1984 (Rough Trade) 1987
Surprise Surprise Surprise (Rough Trade) 1987
Glad (Rough Trade) 1988
Me and Mr. Ray (Rough Trade) 1989 ●

Criticized for their uncanny resemblance to R.E.M., Connecticut's Miracle Legion cannot be so easily dismissed as rote imitators. There's no denying the obvious similarities (vocals and guitar); thanks to musical creativity, however, Miracle Legion manages to stake out their own territory.

Savvy production techniques and aggressive playing make **The Backyard** a landmark. Mark Mulcahy's whining vocals tend to grate after a few listens, but not enough to sully the sheer brilliance of the title track, "Stephen Are You There," "Closer to the Wall" and

"Butterflies." **Surprise Surprise Surprise** lacks the honest abandon of **The Backyard**, an essential ingredient to Miracle Legion's appeal. In spite of improved musicianship and vocals, it's a disappointment.

The new studio work on **Glad** (a side of the LP was recorded live in New York with a one-song guest appearance by the entirety of Pere Ubu!) is a welcome relief from the restraint of **Surprise**. The three songs literally bristle with renewed heartfelt emotion, and the formerly enigmatic lyrics now conjure up a vast array of crystalline images on "A Heart Disease Called Love" and "Hey, Lucky."

Down to a duo, Miracle Legion returned with the bittersweet **Me and Mr. Ray**. By now Mulcahy and guitarist Ray Neal have honed their music into a warm, deep folk-rock. Like the late Byrds, it's akin to old-time acoustic country in spirit more than sound. There's nothing ironic or post-modern or even rocking here, just sad, lovely melodies and words that seem to carry the weight of humanity. Even the upbeat love songs ("You're the Õne Lee" and "Even Better") are tinged with doubt and loss. This is an album that grows on the listener slowly and nourishes the soul.   [ag/ws]

MIRACLE ROOM

Miracle Room [tape] (Miracle Room) 1988
Miracle Room EP (Bar/None-Restless) 1990

Jazzy, rocky improv groups with homemade instruments were a dime a dozen in New York in 1988, but Miracle Room muscled most of the others aside with refreshing energy, wit, melody and try-anything attitude. The group's cassette debut, recorded live in both its birthplace (Austin) and adopted home (New York) was quite a revelation, as guitarist Stephen Marsh chants or bullhorns funny, enigmatic lyrics over Hendrixy feedback squalls and rhythms that can only be described as tribal. (One delay-soaked track from the tape, "Open Heart," later appeared on the first **Live at the Knitting Factory** compilation.)

The trio (later a quartet) puts on a live show that is nearly as entertaining visually as sonically. They take circular saws to large metal appliances and pound the hell out of 55-gallon drums, like a jollier, funkier Einstürzende Neubauten loose in Pee-wee's Playhouse. Miracle Room's first studio attempt, a four-track 12-inch, suffers a bit from strained seriousness, but the band's way with a clanging groove is intact on "These Are My Friends." Meanwhile, the eerie "Untitled" sounds like **Music for Films** played backwards in a wind-tunnel with several species of small furry animals.   [ws]

MIRACLE WORKERS

Miracle Workers EP (Moxie) 1983
1000 Micrograms of the Miracle Workers EP (Sounds
    Interesting) 1984
Inside Out (Voxx) 1985
Live at the Forum (Ger. Glitterhouse) 1988
Overdose (Ger. Love's Simple Dreams) 1988 ●
Primary Domain (Ger. Glitterhouse) 1989
Moxie's Revenge (Get Hip) 1990 ●
Roll Out the Red Carpet (Triple X) 1991 ●

As the Pacific Northwest entry in garage-rock's second coming, Portland, Oregon's Miracle Workers looked no further than their own backyard for initial inspiration. Rather than the more psychedelic meanderings of their peers, the original five-piece lineup stomped and snarled through layers of fuzz much like local deities the Sonics and the Wailers. Both of the Miracle Workers' early EPs boast a heartening percentage of originals—not a majority, mind you, but they *were* playing to an audience that considered the use of strings manufactured after '66 heretical—that easily outstrip the group's covers in both songwriting and energy. Tracks from each (as well as a slew of previously unreleased treasures) are collected on **Moxie's Revenge**.

A little more reserved on its 1985 full-length bow, the quintet still scores big, keeping the songs short, the guitars distorted and Gerry Mohr's snotty adolescent blurt mixed high. Voxx supremo Greg Shaw's production, while not state-of-the-art (even by these standards) is more sympathetic than their earlier, lower-budget efforts.

As the '80s drew to a close, the Miracle Workers stepped outside their garage (minus a member), checked their watches not once but twice and stepped firmly forward . . . into the '70s. **Overdose** (recorded in Berlin, though the band is now based in LA) is just that: a sensory overload of attitude-laden rock somewhere between early Flamin Groovies (whose "Teenage Head" gets a speedy snarl-through) and the MC5 (who are no doubt curious as to why no one asked permission to borrow "Kick Out the Jams" for the feral "Rock'n'Roll Revolution in the Streets Part 2"). Guitarist Matt Rogers' judicious use of feedback augments the new material much more effectively; Mohr's grown some as well. **Live at the Forum** scrapes away what little veneer of subtlety finds its way into the group's studio work; the Iggy/Stooges' atmosphere is so overpowering you can practically smell the peanut butter! A little time-warped, perhaps, but just plain warped enough to be worth hearing.   [dss]

MISFITS

Bullet EP (Plan 9) 1978
Beware EP (nr/Cherry Red) 1979
Walk Among Us (Ruby) 1982 + 1988 ●
Evilive EP (Plan 9) 1982
Earth A.D./Wolfsblood (Plan 9) 1983
Earth A.D./Die Die My Darling [tape] (Plan 9) 1984
Legacy of Brutality (Plan 9-Caroline) 1985 ●
Misfits (Plan 9-Caroline) 1986 ●
Evilive (Plan 9-Caroline) 1987

SAMHAIN

Initium (Plan 9) 1984 (Plan 9-Caroline) 1986 ●
Unholy Passion EP (Plan 9) 1985 (Plan 9-Caroline)
    1986 ●
November-Coming-Fire (Plan 9-Caroline) 1986 ●
Final Descent (Plan 9-Caroline) 1990 φ

KRYST THE CONQUEROR

Deliver Us from Evil EP (Cyclopean) 1989 ●

Although considered part of the hardcore scene, New Jersey's Misfits date back to the first CBGB and London punk surge. Drawing their sound from the Ramones and the Damned, and their look from horror movies and Kiss, the Misfits began by releasing a string of 7-inches on their Plan 9 label. Two of these—the superb **Bullet** EP and the subsequent "Horror Business" single—are compiled on the English **Beware** EP (along with the legendary melodic outtake "Last Caress") and epitomize what made the Misfits great: a combination of hooky power-chording, weird horrific lyrics and singer Glenn Danzig's distinctive basso roar. (For a musical genre in which tone and articulation don't count for much, Danzig's power and control are awesome.)

After years as a strictly underground force, the Misfits seized on hardcore and grafted horror-punk onto slam-thrash. As a result, **Walk Among Us** practically wallows in psychotronic shock imagery, imbuing many of the band's anthems—including "Astro Zombies," "Skulls," "Vampira" and "Mommy, Can I Go Out and Kill Tonight?"—with a new-found intensity and larger-than-life touch of evil. Years of solid songwriting effort paid off, making this classic album as strong as it is consistent. (As a posthumous Misfits cult grew to gigantic proportions during the later half of the decade, goaded by the avid endorsement of bands like Metallica, **Walk Among Us** became one of punk's most feverishly sought-after albums.)

The **Evilive** 7-inch EP (later expanded and reissued as a full-length album) catches the Misfits on rare good 1981 nights in New York and San Francisco, playing material drawn mostly from **Walk Among Us**. One cut includes guest vocals by Henry Rollins.

Earth A.D./Wolfsblood is an unfortunate step in the wrong direction—a misguided attempt to conform to hardcore convention. California's legendary Spot produced; while his monochromatic technique served other groups well, it negated many of the Misfits' strengths. Danzig's voice is downplayed, and the faster, stiffer beat robs the songs of their innate tunefulness. Good tracks like "Blood Feast" and "Green Hell" aside (the latter, along with "Last Caress," was covered by Metallica on **Garage Days Re-Revisited**), **Earth A.D.** remains a disappointing finale. (A later German edition adds the terrific "Die Die My Darling"; an American cassette issue appends that single and its two B-sides.)

Legacy of Brutality is a posthumous collection of outtakes and alternate versions, a good chunk of them from the '78 session that produced **Bullet**. It also contains a band take on "Who Killed Marilyn," Danzig's 1981 solo debut. Though uneven at points, **Legacy** does preserve some of the Misfits' finest moments, such as "Angelfuck" and "She." Originally CD-only, then reissued on vinyl and cassette, **Misfits** is a 20-cut retrospective that includes remixes, alternate takes and one jarring edit that cuts out the second half of "Teenagers from Mars"/"Children in Heat."

After the Misfits ended, Danzig wasted no time in forming Samhain with drummer-turned-bassist Eerie Von. **Initium** took a few smart steps back to the singer's punk roots, mixing in some metal and gloom rock influences and using far more mature and disturbing horror lyrics. This wholly enjoyable LP offers a memorable selection of material, including the band's invigorating signature tune ("Samhain"), a choppy arrangement of "Horror Business" (every Samhain release featured an updated 'Fits tune) and "Archangel" (originally written for the Damned's Dave Vanian). As the residue of an early lineup, Lyle Preslar (ex-Minor Threat) adds some

sparse guitar, but the LP is basically Danzig's affair.

The **Unholy Passion** EP, a token gothic record, would have succeeded if not for the abysmal production. Still, the dark urgency of the pulsing title track, "Moribund" and "The Hungry End"—laced with new guitarist Pete "Damien" Marshall's droning leads—is hard to resist. (**Initium**'s CD and tape release include a remix of **Unholy Passion**'s five tracks and the previously unreleased "Misery Tomb.")

The transitional **November-Coming-Fire** has some of Samhain's most intriguingly arranged songs, most notably the atmospheric ballad "To Walk the Night." The heavier, more metallic music (exemplified by the crunching "Mother of Mercy") and lyrical development (the horror angle is out, pagan religion is in) helped pave Samhain's evolution into Danzig. **Final Descent** ties up the loose ends from this period, combining a splendid five-song session from '87 with Danzig guitarist John Christ (the hypnotic, rolling "Lords of the Left Hand" is the highlight of these previously unreleased cuts) and what sounds like the same set of **Unholy Passion** remixes to reach album length.

In an attempt to exploit their cult fame among the thrash generation, surnameless ex-Misfit brothers Jerry (bass) and Doyle (guitar), always the band's live albatross, formed a dopey metal act, Kryst the Conqueror. On **Deliver Us from Evil**, a self-released five-song EP, the brothers are aided by an anonymous singer and Skid Row guitarist Dave Sabo. [rnp/dgs/gef]

See also *Danzig, Undead*.

MISSING FOUNDATION

Missing Foundation (Purge/Sound League) 1987
(Restless) 1990 ●
1933 (Purge/Sound League) 1988 (Restless) 1990 ●
Demise (Humanity) 1989 (Restless) 1990 ●
Ignore the White Culture (Restless) 1990 ф

Notorious for a highly visible graffiti campaign (the upturned martini glass logo, accompanied by cryptic sloganeering), violently destructive confrontational live appearances and a television newscaster who accused them of fomenting a 1988 riot in Tompkins Square Park, New York's mysterious Missing Foundation has also made records that preach what the anarchist band practices.

Cacophonous and incoherent, **Missing Foundation** has near-random bits of guitar and bass amid the garbage din of junkyard thrashing. Quite unlike the industrial orchestrations of early Test Dept., Missing Foundation doesn't whack at things in any discernible pattern. They simply pound whatever's handy to create chunks of screaming noise-vérité, capture some of it on tape and slap on a title. (In that department, at least, they're pretty traditional.)

There's a shred more structure to the tracks on **1933**, but the LP still amounts to the kind of sonic brutality sentient people try to avoid, rather than consume. (I mean, honestly, when was the last time you turned off the stereo and opened your window so you could enjoy the sound of jack hammers and garbage trucks more clearly?) **Demise** opens with the chaotic sounds of a riot in progress and includes relative restraint (hissed, rather than shrieked, vocals; room between the clangs), live concert recordings and, for the first time, a comprehensible bit of prose ("Surround the White House!" in "Pistol Archive").

Ignore the White Culture makes some minor accommodations with the real world, printing the harsh lyrics (the use of any lyrics at all is a big step here) and reducing the magnitude and the randomness of the din to a sort of atmospheric accompaniment for Peter Missing's apocalyptic pronouncements. A few tracks actually resemble music, but just barely. [i]

MISSING PERSONS
Missing Persons EP (Capitol) 1982
Spring Session M (Capitol) 1982
Rhyme & Reason (Capitol) 1984
Color in Your Life (Capitol) 1986
The Best of Missing Persons (Capitol) 1987 •

DALE
Riot in English (Paisley Park) 1988 •

Notwithstanding singer Dale Bozzio's outrageous auto-sexploitation and the overall commercial-record-industry-hype packaging that permeated the group, Missing Persons were one positive manifestation of the '80s accommodation between new and old in rock. Designed to shift product but retaining high musical standards and an adventurous outlook, Missing Persons fell between genres, simultaneously offending and intriguing intelligent sensibilities.

Originally built on the core of Bozzio, her then husband—drummer/keyboardist Terry (once a Zappa employee and a member of would-be supergroup U.K.)—plus ex-Zappa guitarist Warren Cuccurullo, Missing Persons changed their name from U.S. Drag and were given a boost by producer Ken Scott who recorded and released their debut EP; it became a hit when picked up by Capitol. In the latter form, it contained both "Words" and "Destination Unknown," idiosyncratic songs that also turned up on the first LP.

Spring Session M (an anagram of the band's name) is slick, clever modern rock, using synthesizers and guitars in a hybrid style that came to be very familiar in the '80s. What sets Missing Persons apart from other state-of-the-arters, however, is Bozzio's non-clichéd singing—tough/smart with a bemused, occasionally philosophical outlook, and a characteristic hiccup hitch that recalls Lene Lovich's early vocal gymnastics. Especially impressive for a debut album, Bozzio's voice exudes confidence to spare and enough personality to invest the band's novel tunes with an appropriate attitude as required.

Continue to suspend your disbelief for a few lines more: although it takes a while to become accustomed, **Rhyme & Reason** is an equally fine record. The lyrics of "Give," in what weirdly became a minor pop music trend, amount to an ethical exhortation to selflessness, attached to dynamic rock backing. Elsewhere, "Right Now" and "Surrender Your Heart" address romance with a little sensitivity, attractive melodies and sophisticated, full-blooded instrumentation. Bozzio sings with less affectation but consistent skill and subtlety. At its worst, the album offers appealing vacuity. Ignore the trappings and enjoy the music.

Bernard Edwards produced **Color in Your Life**, pumping up the volume with horns and funk rhythms on the Motown-based "Flash of Love" and "I Can't Think

About Dancin'," one of the few rock songs ever to use the word "pretentious." Elsewhere, the dancebeat of "Boy I Say to You" sells this once-provocative band extremely short. While the inviting title track could fit on any of the band's albums, the cloying keyboards and messy arrangements here compete with Bozzio's vocals to no one's benefit. The misconceived stylistic overhaul proved a total disaster; despite a couple of worthwhile tunes, this LP is a must to avoid.

With that, Missing Persons split up, something Dale and Terry had already done. Capitol issued a comprehensive retrospective, Cuccurullo joined Duran Duran and Dale signed on the dotted line with Prince's label. Her first solo record is a joint project with producer Robert Brookins, who wrote most of the songs and played drums and keyboards on a lot of them. Although Prince's instrumental sound permeates the LP, it is nowhere so evident as on his contribution, "So Strong." The commercial dance music on **Riot in English** plays up the flexibility of Dale's voice, but the pre-fab cookie-cutter material and arrangements come as quite a disappointment after the stylistic invention of her former group.

Since Missing Persons, bassist/keyboardist Patrick O'Hearn (another Zappa alumnus and member of the 1980 Group 87 with Mark Isham and Terry Bozzio) has been making nicely textured instrumental albums for Private Music. [i]

See also *Duran Duran.*

MISSION (UK)
Gods Own Medicine (Mercury) 1986 •
The First Chapter (Mercury) 1987 •
Children (Mercury) 1988 •
Beyond the Pale EP (nr/Mercury) 1988 •
Carved in Sand (Mercury) 1990 φ
Grains of Sand (Mercury) 1990 φ

Leeds natives Wayne Hussey (guitar, vox) and Craig Adams (bass) left the gothic Sisters of Mercy (Hussey had also been in Dead or Alive) to form their own group, the Mission. (The American "UK" was appended because a Philadelphia R&B band was already using the name.) Joined by ex-Red Lorry Yellow Lorry drummer Mick Brown and a guitarist drafted from Artery, the group planted one foot in the British neo-hippie camp and another in the land of pompous goth-metal stupidity.

The dull and insipid guitar/keyboard/string bombast of **Gods Own Medicine** proceeds from a horrible amalgam of Led Zeppelin, Yes and Echo & the Bunnymen. Several tracks were huge British hits, but listening to the LP fails to reveal any exceptional qualities "Garden of Delight" or "Stay with Me" might have that would explain their popularity. Hussey's ponderous and toneless intonation ruins the songs' scant intrinsic merit; thick-sounding production (by Tim Palmer and the band) finishes the job. The CD has two extra cuts.

As if anyone cared, an odds-and-nods collection was issued to bring listeners up to date with non-LP items. **The First Chapter**, which is actually less of an audio trial than **Gods Own Medicine**, presents the Mission's debut 45, "Serpents Kiss," as well as an extended remix of "Garden of Delight" and unwarranted covers—"Tomorrow Never Knows" (Beatles), "Wishing

435

Well'' (Free), ''Dancing Barefoot'' (Patti Smith) and ''Like a Hurricane'' (Neil Young)—that only point up the band's songwriting incapacity. Despite the borrowed title, ''Over the Hills and Far Away'' is an original.

John Paul Jones evidently didn't hold that bit of pilferage against the Mission: he produced the semi-listenable **Children**. Hussey's pseudo-poetic lyrics are pure middle-brow malarkey and his singing is still a problem, but the measured music benefits from the organization and air of Jones' firm dynamic grip, economically applied guitar lines and occasionally neat fripperies, like the sitar on ''Beyond the Pale.'' Although not recommended, not altogether horrible. The **Beyond the Pale** EP surrounds **Children**'s lead-off song with ''Love Me to Death'' from **Gods Own Medicine** and a couple of non-LP tracks.

With Led Zep out of the Mission's system, the group reenlisted Tim Palmer to produce **Carved in Sand**, which doesn't sound very different from its predecessor. Hussey's melodramatic voice, precious/dumb lyrics—although the portrait of child abuse in ''Amelia'' is an exception, ''Grapes of Wrath'' piles on the heartland clichés and the iteration of beliefs in ''Lovely'' merely inverts John Lennon's ''God''—and the band's unimaginative music (another use of sitar?) weigh down the meandering, incoherent effort. The one flash of life—a striking guitar riff that opens ''Hungry as the Hunter''—is quickly buried in a swirling sea of pompous noise.

Other than ''Hands Across the Ocean,'' a fine new track (gulp—did I say that?) produced by Andy Partridge of XTC, **Grains of Sand** consists of outtakes, covers, B-sides and a remix from **Carved in Sand**. As big a thrill as this release may be to Missionaries, drivel like ''Mercenary'' could easily have remained in the can. And why record a lovely song like the Kinks' ''Mr. Pleasant'' if you're only going to sound obnoxiously condescending about it? [i]

See also *Dead or Alive, Sisters of Mercy*.

MISSION OF BURMA

Signals, Calls, and Marches EP (Ace of Hearts) 1981
VS. (Ace of Hearts) 1982
The Horrible Truth About Burma (Ace of Hearts) 1985
Mission of Burma EP (Taang!) 1987 ●
Forget (Taang!) 1987 ●
Mission of Burma [CD] (Rykodisc) 1988 ●
Let There Be Burma (Hol. Taang!-Emergo) 1990 ●

During its existence, Boston's Mission of Burma was one of the most important American bands surviving outside the major-label record industry. Their thrilling and challenging vocal rock is both intellectually and emotionally engaging. Staking out bracing post-pop guitar turf with hard edges and sharp corners, Burma's records never leave melody or structure behind; they just meander around it sometimes.

The debut EP has two sides (musically speaking): aggressive/strident in some spots, inviting/attractive elsewhere. Standing out among the six tracks is one tremendous song, ''That's When I Reach for My Revolver,'' as well as a powerful but pretty instrumental, ''All World Cowboy Romance.''

VS. is more unremittingly intense, a loud, vibrant assault that never becomes unpleasant. While the lineup (guitar, bass, drums, tape manipulation) doesn't inherently stake out any original stylistic ground, Burma never proffers clichés; every track has individual character. On first listen, these records sound very British; on further investigation, they're all American.

Because of hearing problems caused by the astonishingly loud band, guitarist Roger Miller left Burma, turned to piano and devoted himself to Birdsongs of the Mesozoic, taking time out to make solo records as well. Tapeman Martin Swope joined him in Birdsongs. Drummer Peter Prescott formed Volcano Suns who, as the pseudonymous Din, have also backed Dredd Foole on two albums.

On record, at least, the Mission of Burma saga was far from over. The posthumous **Horrible Truth** compiles live performances from four US cities in the band's final (1983) tour. Besides a merciless rendition of the Stooges' ''1970'' and nine dynamic minutes of Pere Ubu's ''Heart of Darkness,'' the album offers eight originals in several stylistic veins. Some of the tracks are intense and captivating, while others are sloppy, lacking the focused punch of their best work.

The all-fun **Mission of Burma** EP consists of five loud studio cuts, produced by either Lou Giordano or Peter Dayton between '79 and '82. (Two songs overlap the live LP.) ''Peking Spring'' is an obsessive dark mantra with cool choral chanting; the title track builds a powerful drone over a bewildering drum pattern; ''Dumbells,'' although not much of a song, has an amazing overdriven guitar sound. (The cassette and CD both contain five bonus cuts.)

Forget is an unannotated (but the inclusion of 1980's ''Forget'' suggests the vintage) album of previously unreleased songs, given basic studio treatment (rehearsals?). Obviously not the band's premier material nor ideal recording circumstances, the loud and muscular songs seem undeveloped, samey. The most exciting moments are breaks in which Miller and Swope work their rowdy magic. Fans won't be disappointed—these are by no means trivial scraps—but the preceding EP seems to have contained the band's best outtakes.

The 80-minute-plus CD-only compilation entitled **Mission of Burma** consists of **Signals, Calls, and Marches** and **VS.** in their entirety, plus two tracks from **Horrible Truth**, two single sides (''Academy Fight Song'' and ''OK/No Way'') and two previously unreleased items. For another listen to the band's ephemera, the two-record **Let There Be Burma** reissues **Forget** and the eponymous Taang! EP in its expanded form, adding alternate (but not very different) takes of ''This Is Not a Photograph'' from the 1981 EP and ''Einstein's Day'' from **VS.** [i]

See also *Birdsongs of the Mesozoic, Dredd Foole and the Din, Roger Miller, Space Negros, Volcano Suns*.

MR. PARTRIDGE

See *XTC*.

MR. T EXPERIENCE

Everybody's Entitled to Their Own Opinion (Disorder) 1986
Night Shift at the Thrill Factory (Rough Trade) 1988

Big Black Bugs Bleed Blue Blood (Rough Trade) 1989
Making Things with Light (Lookout!) 1990

On the face of things, little has changed for the Mr. T Experience over the years. They switched bass players midway. Otherwise, the two guitars, bass and drums lineup has steadfastly blared punk rock peppered with wit and melody for five solid years of minimal financial reward and maximal rock'n'roll respect. The self-released **Everybody's Entitled to Their Own Opinion** gained the Berkeley, California band immediate notoriety for its careening take on the Monkees' "Pleasant Valley Sunday" and the singalong cult classics "Danny Partridge" (commemorating Bonaduce's cocaine bust) and "I'm in Love with Paula Pierce" (a lustful ode to the Pandoras' lead sex-slave). Although overlooked in the excitement, the album also contains some terrific songs of pain, anger and confusion ("Sheep," "Disconnection," "Scientific").

Night Shift at the Thrill Factory, produced by Celibate Rifle Kent Steedman, sticks to the same formula, with Herman's Hermits' "No Milk Today" getting the full-on treatment, an over-the-top surf instrumental ("Skatin' Cows"), manic slabs of sarcastic hilarity like "Velveeta" and "What Is Punk?" (a fantasy about the group appearing on *Donahue*) and an incredible rapid-fire philosophical essay, "The History of the Concept of the Soul."

The seven-song **Big Black Bugs Bleed Blue Blood** toys ambiguously with the band's Ramones fixation ("End of the Ramones"), pays tribute to Berkeley's all-ages punk palace "Gilman Street" and tears up Sesame Street with "Up and Down" (also covered by Donner Party). The long, touching slice-of-life "Song About a Girl Who Went Shopping" showcases main songwriter Dr. Frank's observant eye (name one other song that details the purchase of a Lurkers single!) and storytelling sense.

Producer Kevin Army (who has recorded all of the band's efforts but **Night Shift**) deserves credit for the success of **Making Things with Light**, as it is the most powerful-sounding Mr. T disc yet, with strong material to match. (Amazingly, half of the album was recorded as demos.) Frank and co-conspirator Jon von (guitar, vocals) again celebrate girls—good, bad and sad—somehow working way in thermodynamics, Latin benedictions, *sturm und drang* and Rachel Sweet's "What's in the Cuckoo Clock." Genius.   [sm]

M+M

See *Martha and the Muffins*.

MOCK TURTLES

Turtle Soup (nr/Imaginary) 1990 (Relativity) 1991 ●
87-90 (nr/Imaginary) 1991 ●

Having appeared on nearly every Imaginary tribute LP, offering their interpretations of songs by Beefheart, Barrett, Hendrix, the Byrds, Kinks and others, Manchester's otherwise little-known Mock Turtles defy all reasonable expectations on their debut album by performing original material in a semi-consistent style. Not that the quintet isn't entirely derivative of numerous '60s/'70s art-pop icons, but it's reassuring to see them expend a little creative effort for a change. When not

indulging in obvious affectations, **Turtle Soup** is an above-average retro album: polite guitar/keyboards arrangements of nicely melodic tunes sung with attractive softness, all bathed in a light psychedelic glow. The second LP is a compilation of the Mock Turtles' EPs and tributes.   [i]

MODERN ENGLISH

Mesh & Lace (nr/4AD) 1981
After the Snow (Sire) 1982 ●
Life in the Gladhouse EP (nr/4AD) 1982
Gathering Dust EP (nr/4AD) 1983
Ricochet Days (Sire) 1984
Stop Start (Sire) 1986 ●
Pillow Lips (TVT) 1990 ●

Colchester's Modern English (originally formed as the Lepers) undertook a drastic change of direction after its debut, an oppressively pretentious load of monotonous droning and shouting by a precious art band. **After the Snow**, on the other hand, is a flawed but rewarding batch of hard-edged, melodic dance songs, a style to which the group subsequently adhered. Instead of the muddy production that favored only the drummer on **Mesh & Lace**, the second record has both sparkling sound and overtly normal musical intentions. If nothing else on **After the Snow** is as striking as the wonderful "I Melt with You," it's still a fine album. (Besides the **After the Snow** track for which it's titled, the four-song **Life in the Gladhouse** 12-inch contains three non-LP songs.)

Ricochet Days, an attempt to reconcile the band's abiding commitment to free artistic expression with the lure of growing American stardom, is rather equivocal, offering several finely wrought slices of catchiness ("Hands Across the Sea," "Rainbow's End") as well as slightly more obscure efforts. Greater intricacy nicely tints all the material; pristine production by longstanding collaborator Hugh Jones adds to their appeal. Still, Modern English remains precariously perched on a fence between making a musical statement and aiming for commercial easy street. That decision can't be postponed indefinitely.

With the release of **Stop Start**, it's obvious which way Modern English is leaning. It may be a bit early to write them off as boring has-been sell-outs, but they're not headed anywhere particularly challenging. Bad sign: the refrain of "Ink and Paper," co-written by erstwhile Rubinoo (!) Tommy Dunbar, is too reminiscent of "Born to Run" to be a coincidence. With nowhere left to turn, the group sat out the remainder of the decade.

An inferior new version of "I Melt with You" is the red radio carpet on which **Pillow Lips** returns Modern English (three-fourths of the **Stop Start** lineup) to action—as if anyone had noticed their absence. The diverse record contains some easy-to-like bounce-pop ("Beauty," "Care About You") but other tracks either drift along listlessly (like the enervated title tune) or sag under clichéd lyrics ("Life's Rich Tapestry"—now there's a novel idea) and equally unimaginative melodies.

The five non-LP tracks from Modern English's pre-pop era ('80-'81) gathered on the 12-inch **Gathering Dust** are atmospheric, dense, aggressive and abrasive.

See also *This Mortal Coil*.   [i]

MODERN LOVERS

See *Jonathan Richman and the Modern Lovers*.

MOFUNGO

Elementary Particles EP (Living Legends) 1980
End of the World [tape] (Mofungo) 1982
Out of Line (Zoar) 1983
Frederick Douglass (Coyote-Twin/Tone) 1985
Messenger Dogs of the Gods (Lost-Twin/Tone) 1986
End of the World, Part 2 (Lost-Twin/Tone) 1987
Bugged (SST) 1988 ●
Work (SST) 1989 ●

Mofungo's frayed vocals, twitchy rhythms and snarling saxes are an acquired taste but, on **Out of Line**, the quartet—formed from the ashes of New York no wavers Blinding Headache—does an excellent job of preventing discordance from descending to chaos. The urgent attack of "Wage Slave," "FBI Informer (He Sold His Soul)" and others never lacks the credibility that eludes many fancier bands. Hard on the nerves, though.

Frederick Douglass furthers Mofungo's drive into annoyingly random sounds and pointedly political lyrics. Willie Klein's guitars and producer Elliott Sharp's occasional sax contributions wander off in the most haphazard directions; the rhythm section isn't exactly session-level tight, but at least bassist Robert Sietsema and alternating drummers Phil Dray and Chris Nelson keep a semblance of the beat going between them. Unlistenable.

Dray's departure (and vocalist Heather Drake's temporary arrival) prior to **Messenger Dogs of the Gods** was accompanied, evidently, by a total sonic rethink, leaving Mofungo a rhythmically loaded, occasionally jagged, folk-rock group. Sharp, now a full bandmember, still blows wall-rattling sax and triples on guitar and keyboards. Palatable, even pretty in spots, the album includes such American classics as "Big Rock Candy Mountain" and Woody Guthrie's "Deportee" alongside original instrumentals and topical songs like "Johnny Didn't Come Marching Home," "The Typist's Plea" and "George Washington Carver/Sojourner Truth." Humorless but estimably well intentioned.

While the uncommon blend of folk, jazz and rock on **End of the World, Part 2** shows steps in the right direction (Sharp finally seems to be bowing to the chromatic scale here), Mofungo's lyrics are getting so didactic that they require a helpful paragraph of footnotes (about aircraft, a remark made by Baby Doc Duvalier, etc.) on the back cover. The varied and intricate music is a lot better than the wavery sub-Tom Verlaine vocals, but this album is still only for intelligent listeners with the patience to survive the band's unpolished and prickly exterior.

With dated lyrics about Judge Bork and Oliver North, and a Sietsema essay explaining such irrelevancies as the band's fear of aluminum and annoyance (now there's a gutsy political stance) at Cardinal O'Connor, **Bugged** is still Mofungo's most appealing and accessible record, a tuneful and tight set of real songs built more on collective chord progressions than anarchic instrumental assemblies. Actually, when Sharp wraps his lips around a reed and sets off for the moon at the start of Face 2, the momentary chaos is bracing but welcome amid the pleasant rock and old-time folk surroundings.

Work thankfully omits the monograph, but that's the best thing about this lyrically conceptual collection of labor songs. In a total rejection of **Bugged**'s listener-friendliness, **Work** returns to unmelodic noise mode with lunging hunks of discontinuity, pointless rhythm shifts, atonal vocals and cacophonous bits of sonic ephemera running roughshod through the tracks. Although covers of Sonny Boy Williamson, Blind Alfred Reed and the Minutemen provide brief oases of musical reason, **Work** is a chore to avoid.   [jy/i]

See also *Elliott Sharp, The Scene Is Now*.

MOMUS

Circus Maximus (nr/él-Cherry Red) 1986 ●
Nicky EP (nr/él-Cherry Red) 1986 ●
The Poison Boyfriend (nr/Creation) 1987
Tender Pervert (nr/Creation) 1988 ●
Don't Stop the Night (nr/Creation) 1989 ●
Monsters of Love—Singles 1985-90 (nr/Creation) 1990 ●

On first listen, the early recordings of Briton Nicholas Currie (aka Momus) suggest some sort of unholy alliance between Donovan and Morrissey. Both literate and literary, Currie is an erudite singer/songwriter of striking originality who merges European music-hall tradition with more conventional new-agey folk and synth disco; call it "fop" music. Like Woody Allen, Currie is obsessed with sex and death and, on record, gives these preoccupations clever, deadpan twists.

The cover of **Circus Maximus** depicts Currie as the Roman soldier St. Sebastian, eight arrows piercing his body. Inside, the majority of songs riff on Biblical themes, with titles like "The Lesson of Sodom (According to Lot)" and "King Solomon's Song and Mine." But far from being Christian contemporary, this is compelling secular pop with enticing narratives, sung by a young man with a remarkably soothing voice. Acoustic guitar predominates, accented by snatches of violin, flute, even harpsichord—all of which serves to make the initially daunting, wordy songs extremely palatable.

The momentum of **Circus Maximus** was interrupted by **Nicky**, a three-song Jacques Brel tribute which features the agonizingly maudlin "Don't Leave" and "See a Friend in Tears," a spare-sounding soporific that would seem more at home on a This Mortal Coil album. (This EP is included on the CD of **Circus Maximus**.)

On **The Poison Boyfriend**, Currie dispenses with the religious imagery and enlists a backup band, while taking a less studied approach to consistently ace material. His bayonet wit is most apparent on the comically torchy "Sex for the Disabled"; even Barry White's not safe as Currie delivers a horny faux-soul sex rap with everything but the heavy breathing.

Tender Pervert is a more synthetic-sounding disc that relies heavily on sequencers and other gewgaws in addition to the lightly strummed guitars. Luckily, the technology fails to overpower the songs, which are among Currie's sexiest, funniest and most human. In between toying with New Order-like disco and electronic R&B, he constructs a couple of wrenching acoustic ballads (including the great "Right Hand Heart") that would likely turn the most hardened non-romantic into a quivering tower of jello.

Inexplicably including a remake of "Right Hand Heart" that unsuccessfully attempts to turn the song into a *Fat Albert*-style (!) rap track, the weird **Don't Stop the Night** is an unsubtle indulgence with wretched Eurodisco production that drains the lifeblood from fairly interesting, sexually explicit songs. Some are spared, however, including "The Guitar Lesson," a peculiar, gauzy bit of jailbait erotica. In all, a surprisingly wrongheaded experiment, much of which would've sounded stale a decade earlier.

Creation wisely followed up this disc with a singles retrospective that's obviously the perfect starting place for those wishing to immerse themselves in Momus' adventurous oeuvre. (The title track of the previous LP appears here in a startlingly different—and infinitely more listenable—form, as "Ballad of the Barrel Organist.") Although impatient listeners may find much of this mellow to the point of catatonia, the elegant songcraft reveals a true poet at work.   [db]

MONKS OF DOOM
See *Camper Van Beethoven, Ophelias*.

MONOCHROME SET
Strange Boutique (DinDisc) 1980 ●
Love Zombies (nr/DinDisc) 1980 ●
Eligible Bachelors (nr/Cherry Red) 1982
Volume, Contrast, Brilliance (nr/Cherry Red) 1983
Jacob's Ladder EP (nr/Blanco y Negro) 1985
The Lost Weekend (nr/Blanco y Negro) 1985
Fin (nr/él-Cherry Red) 1986
Colour Transmission [CD] (Virgin) 1988 ●
Westminster Affair (nr/él-Cherry Red) 1988 ●
Dante's Casino (nr/Vinyl Japan) 1990 ●

Beginning with a series of arty rock singles, this amusingly suave and sarcastic London quartet fronted by Bid (vocals), Lester Square (guitar) and Andy Warren (bass)—all of whom had played with Adam Ant in obscure early bands—took a sharp sardonic swing towards lightweight pop when they reached album format. Aided by producer Bob Sargeant on keyboards, the Set mixes uncommon source material (polkas, etc.) into cabaret material (à la **Village Green** Kinks) on **Strange Boutique**. Fortunately, the highly controlled results are untainted by seriousness; even without much to say, the arch Set says it well.

Love Zombies expands the cabaret stylings while limiting the bizarre material, producing a smoother and more accessible sound. The melodies are stronger, and Bid's vocals are brought up to spotlight lyrics that take sharp, light jabs at emotional traps and social mores.

With a new drummer in the lineup, **Eligible Bachelors** strips the music down to essential elements—clean, bouncy melodies and gently satirical verse, performed with deceptive facility. Songs like "March of the Eligible Bachelors," "The Jet Set Junta" and "The Great Barrier Riff" typify the band's wittily intelligent verse.

Another lineup revision ensued, making Bid and bassist Warren the only remaining original members. Leading off with the suave pop of "Jacob's Ladder," **The Lost Weekend** has such a light touch that it threatens to float away. Nostalgic recollections from the '30s,

'50s and '60s color most of the songs, variously suggesting "When I'm 64" crossed with recent XTC and a bikini beach movie soundtrack. Clever and entertaining, although only the second side is truly compelling.

Volume, Contrast, Brilliance compiles early singles and significant album tracks. **Fin** is a compilation of live recordings dating from 1979 to 1985. Although presented as a supposed French film soundtrack, the strangely compiled **Westminster Affair** (with four repeats from **Volume, Contrast, Brilliance**) actually contains half of **Eligible Bachelors**, a song from **The Lost Weekend** and some singles; the CD appends four more. **Colour Transmission** is a straight one-disc repackage of **Strange Boutique** plus **Love Zombies**.

Augmented by a keyboard-playing second guitarist, the original core trio reunited around the end of the decade and recorded the all-new **Dante's Casino** with a guest drummer. Still sounding very much like XTC's upper-class city cousins, the Monochrome Set picks up the reins of attractive pop oddity with ease, filling the LP with such typically airy and clever charmers as "Bella Morte," "Hate Male" and "House of God," which bizarrely borrows a melody from Slade's "Gudbuy t'Jane" and sets it to an acid-house beat.   [sg/i]

MONSOON
Third Eye (nr/Mobile Suit Corp.) 1983 (nr/Great
    Expectations) 1989 ●
SHEILA CHANDRA
Out on My Own (nr/Indipop) 1984 ●

Monsoon was a left-field pop concept, but one that worked marvelously. British producer/songwriter/instrumentalists Steve Coe and Martin Smith create (with some outside assistance, mostly on percussion) raga-rock along the lines of George Harrison's Beatle excursions ("Within You, Without You," especially), which Anglo-Indian actress Sheila Chandra delivers in a very lovely voice. The alternately languid and kinetic songs (English lyrics and pop structures, hybrid instrumentation)—"Wings of the Dawn (Prem Kavita)" and "Shakti (The Meaning of Within)" are two highlights—meld intriguing sounds to memorable melodies, making **Third Eye** a wondrous, if gimmicky, pop achievement.

Following Monsoon's lone album, Chandra continued working with Coe and Smith as a solo artist. While the trio's formula is not all that different, **Out on My Own** is a bit of a disappointment, upping the songs' pop structures and ambient possibilities, consigning the previously strong Indian character to an accent rather than an element of its style. The title track is quite nice and only the miserable "All You Want Is More" and the recited "Unchanged Malady" fall below pleasant, but the rest is rarely invigorating or memorable.

Chandra released additional albums, all of which were recently made available on CD by a Swedish label.   [i]

MOODISTS
Engine Shudder (nr/Red Flame) 1983
Thirsty's Calling (nr/Red Flame) 1984
Double Life EP (nr/Red Flame) 1985

DAVE GRANEY WITH THE CORAL SNAKES

At His Stone Beach EP (nr/Fire) 1988 ●

DAVE GRANEY WITH THE WHITE BUFFALOES

My Life on the Plains (Fire) 1989 ●
Codine EP (Fire) 1990 ●

Originally from Australia, the Moodists are graduates of the thump'n'grind school of gothic punk. Combining dense metallic bass and razor-sharp guitar riffs with singer Dave Graney's demonic growl, the band is capable of a most unholy din. Although dark and ominous, the music can at times be surprisingly melodic.

The seven-song **Engine Shudder** is not the Moodists at their most effective. The tracks are devoid of coherence and slip readily into redundancy. Only "Gone Dead" hints at a promising future, thanks to Graney's layered vocals and Chris Walsh's bass work.

Thirsty's Calling is a remarkable improvement. The addition of a second discordant guitar and judicious production makes this music for nightmares. Setting vocals and guitars further back in the mix, the rhythm section comes into its own on "That's Frankie's Negative" and the standout, "Machine Machine." Grimly primal, this music breathes life into pop's forbidding alter-ego, a region where many dare to tread and few prove this successful.

The Moodists' reign of terror continues on the six-song EP. Bass and voice are up-front this time, giving the tracks full-bodied menace. "Double Life," "Six Dead Birds" and "Can't Lose Her" are wonderfully desperate songs and by far the Moodists' best to date. Following the EP, the band underwent personnel and label changes, returning in '86 with the "Justice and Money Too" single—light, bluesy pop augmented with strings and piano. They may have lost their venom, but not the ability to craft stunning tunes.

Like the band's late work, Graney's post-Moodists output ditches the aggression and concentrates on tasteful, literate songcraft. **At His Stone Beach** finds Graney (backed by a group that includes ex-Orange Juice/Aztec Camera guitarist Malcolm Ross and Moodists drummer Clare Moore) making the most of his limited but expressive voice on four impressively crafted new tunes.

My Life on the Plains is a resounding fulfillment of the promise hinted at on the preceding EP (the contents of which are included as bonus tracks on the album's CD). The fascination with frontier Americana suggested by the cover motif is reflected in haunting originals like "I'll Set the Scene" and "Robert Ford on the Stage," as well as thoughtful reworkings of songs by Gene Clark, Gram Parsons and Fred Neil. There's also a spooky version of "The Streets of Laredo." With a new combo that reunites the Moodists' rhythm section, the music is supple and textured, providing a perfect vehicle for Graney's increasingly accomplished writing and singing.

The **Codine** EP is five tracks from a live-in-the-studio Australian radio broadcast—the Buffy Sainte-Marie title tune, the trad folk standard "Jack of Diamonds" and three from Graney's solo records. With **My Life on the Plains**' pianist traded in for a pedal-steel player, it's a worthy addendum to the album.

[ag/hd]

JOHN MOORE AND THE EXPRESSWAY

Expressway Rising (Polydor) 1989 ●

JOHN MOORE

Distortion (nr/Polydor) 1990 (Polydor) 1991 ●

Singer/guitarist John Moore briefly drummed (and played guitar) in the Jesus and Mary Chain, but that experience—other than some familiar beats and occasional bolts of noisy guitar—barely informs his inexplicably overlooked solo debut, a dandy one-man-band project. Solid pop songwriting skills (some of his tunes reuse classic chord progressions to good effect) combined with a surprising Billy Idolish voice and charged but simple rock arrangements make for memorable tunes like "Friends," "Back to Stay," the Ramonesy "Good Times" and the shoulda-been-a-hit "Something About You Girl." The album's unfinished demo-like sound is part of its unassuming charm. (The CD and cassette have two bonus tracks, including the loudly countryfied "Live from Death Row.")

With producer Andy Wallace and a batch of sidemen (including horns and, on "Soul for Rent," strings), Moore turns all-pro on his slick and slightly serious second album which, other than the vocals, scarcely resembles **Expressway Rising** at all. Beyond suggesting that **Distortion** (at least some parts of it) is a record Billy Idol would be proud of if he weren't so lost in his own superstar hype, it's hard to tell what Moore's up to, as the unstylized rock—interrupted by minor artistic pretenses—doesn't seem headed anywhere. There's likable stuff here (like "Mean Streak," "Put Up or Shut Up") and plenty of contrast (from the gentle "Summer Song" to the mega-noisy "Heart of Darkness"), but **Distortion** sacrifices too much of Moore's earthy appeal in a concerted push for commercial credibility. The CD's highlight is a seven-minute bonus of "On Broadway," which gives spoken-word/found-sound drama to an effective treatment of the Drifters' soul classic. [i]

R. STEVIE MOORE

Phonography (Vital) 1976 (HP Music) 1978
Four from Phonography (HP Music) 1978
Stance EP (HP Music) 1978
Delicate Tension (HP Music) 1978
Everything You Always Wanted to Know About R. Stevie Moore but Were Afraid to Ask (Fr. New Rose) 1984
What's the Point?!! (Cuneiform) 1984
Verve (nr/Hamster) 1985
Glad Music (Fr. New Rose) 1986
R. Stevie Moore (1952-19??) (nr/Cordelia) 1987
Teenage Spectacular (Fr. New Rose) 1987
Warning: R. Stevie Moore (Fr. New Rose) 1988
Has-Beens and Never-Weres (nr/Heliotrope) 1990
Greatesttits [CD] (Fr. Fan Club) 1990 ●

The son of a top Nashville session bassist, R. Stevie Moore began doing his own one-man home recordings in the early '70s. Over the course of years spent perfecting his technical and conceptual skills, Moore's individualistic, wry pop and musique concrète excursions have developed into an awesome—and seemingly bottomless—world of talent just waiting to be unleashed on the masses. In recent years, Moore (now living in New Jersey) has self-released dozens of cassettes of his work via mail order; the two 1984 albums partly draw their contents from those tapes. Suffice to say, if you like what you hear on the discs, there's plenty more of equal quality where that came from.

Phonography (issued twice with different artwork) consists of his very early efforts, done between 1974 and 1976. Some of it is fairly rudimentary, but the Bonzo Dog Band-like "Goodbye Piano" displays Moore's incipient brilliance, and a massed-guitars rendition of the *Andy Griffith Show* theme is classic.

Stance is a three-song 12-inch, running time around fifteen minutes. Recorded in '76 and '77, top-to-bottom improvement is obvious, from the moody, mostly instrumental "Ist or Mas"—an interpretation of awakening (theme for a ballet perhaps?)—to "Manufacturers," a rollicking jazzy rocker.

Delicate Tension is excellent: great songs of astonishing variety, all tied together by his idiosyncratic, gentle perceptions of life and smooth, versatile voice. There are hints of Zappa, Rundgren, Townshend, McCartney and countless others; Moore's limitations, if indeed he has any, have yet to be encountered.

Moore's tape club's issue is staggering in sheer volume, variety and consistency of quality. (His catalogue includes well over 150 titles!) More like eclectic radio shows than straight collections of music, he includes anything and everything on the tapes, and they collectively provide an in-depth self-portrait of a truly prodigious talent.

Everything You Always Wanted to Know is a two-record compilation of tracks—with historical liner notes (in English) purportedly by Robert Christgau—sampling a decade's worth of discs and tapes with originals, covers ("Mama Weer All Crazee Now," "Chantilly Lace"), strange experiments and sublime successes. Although disjointed in spite of Moore's skillful efforts to compile it in some rational fashion, the album provides proof positive of the man's remarkable gift to do virtually any type of music and do it extremely well.

More concise and better conceived, the American one-disc **What's the Point?!!** provides an ideal introduction to Moore, with such gems as "Part of the Problem," "Puttin' Up the Groceries," "Bloody Knuckles" and "World's Fair." (The last three also appear on **Everything**.)

Released by a small UK label, the erratic but gem-strewn **Verve** compilation (early-'80s tracks—including an in-concert live recording from '83—chosen by the artist) quickly became a rarity; **Glad Music**, a proper studio album recorded in late 1985, reprises "Part of the Problem" and adds a dozen more examples of Moore at the top of his creative powers. There's real C&W played with mock-seriousness ("I Love You So Much It Hurts"), an unnervingly precise synth-flavored version of the Association's "Along Comes Mary" and witty, hand-clapping rock'n'roll ("Shakin' in the Sixties"). Delightful!

(1952-19??) is yet another career-spanning compilation, this one a hodgepodge assembly of 21 tracks from as early as 1973 and as late as 1986, with stops along the way for "Delicate Tension," "Goodbye Piano" and "Satisfaction." Some of the items are tossed-off fragments, others excellent achievements with full-fledged arrangements in a wide variety of styles. The

punky "Jesus Rocks" ('78) and the reflectively acoustic "Back in Time" ('86) are among the album's previously unvinylized treasures.

Teenage Spectacular includes covers of Dr. Hook ("The Cover of 'Rolling Stone'," half of it performed a cappella) and Dr. Dylan (the anti-boxing classic "Who Killed Davey Moore?" given an ironically upbeat folk reading) amidst the original pop musings, witty balladeering and brief mind-altering tape experiments ("Non Sequitur I–V"). The simple musical constructions on guitars, keyboards and drums reveal traces of Moore's many influences—from the Beatles to Todd Rundgren to the Bonzo Dog Band to XTC and back again—and huge chunks of his monumental creative grasp. "On the Spot" is satiric big band bar-room sleaze in the key of G sharp; "Blues for Cathy Taylor" is a delightful love song of a different sort; "Baby on Board" castigates childless drivers with those yellow stickers on their car windows.

A collection of recent ('86-'87) home and studio productions, **Warning** includes remakes of several RSM oldies (e.g., "Manufacturers") as well as a rendition of the Beatles' "Getting Better." **Has-Beens and Never-Weres** samples a decade of Moore music, beginning in the mid-'70s and including a tribute to the Residents, "What's the Point?" (not from the album of the that name) and a song entitled "Bonus Track (LP Only)."

Building on **Everything You Always Wanted to Know**, the CD-only **Greatesttits** is a monumental 24-track retrospective of Moore's most appealing pop originals ("Why Can't I Write a Hit?," "Debbie," "U R True") and covers ("Chantilly Lace," "Along Comes Mary," "Cover of 'Rolling Stone' ")—a perfect introduction to his wonderful world. The American record industry's failure to recognize and promote the unique gifts of this giant talent is a case of criminal neglect.

[i]

ANTHONY MORE

Pieces from the Cloudland Ballroom (Ger. Polydor) 1971
Secrets of the Blue Bag (Ger. Polydor) 1972
Reed, Whistle and Sticks (Ger. Polydor) 1972
Out (nr/Virgin) 1976
Flying Doesn't Help (nr/Quango) 1979
World Service (nr/Do It) 1981
The Only Choice (nr/Parlophone) 1984

Anthony More (né Moore) was a founding member of progressive trio Slapp Happy in the early '70s; following that band's merger with Henry Cow and subsequent dissolution, More went his own way, continuing his solo career at erratic intervals. Although he hasn't released a record under his own name since 1984 (he does pop up as a producer now and again, especially in and around the Golden Palominos camp), More's last three releases are stunning. As an artist, he's a highly idiosyncratic innovator who combines art and rock into a far-reaching, weird and wonderful set of styles, from the atonal to the hook-laden. More imparts all his songs with a nonconformist's perspective that defies easy comprehension.

Flying Doesn't Help displays More's melodic stance, with such beautiful and haunting creations as "Judy Get Down" and "Lucia"; his wit surfaces in sardonic pieces like "Caught Being in Love" and "Girl It's Your Time." Building dense sonic forests filled with jagged splinters and dry, incongruously delicate vocals, the results fall somewhere between Peter Gabriel, John Cale, David Bowie and Kevin Ayers. An extraordinary record that reveals itself a little further each time it's played.

World Service (which, unlike **Flying**, offers musician credits) takes a decidedly less attractive route, better displaying the anti-music aspect of More's work; dour singing and bitter lyrics make it a challenging record that's as brilliant but not as easily enjoyed as the first. "Broke'n Idle," despite glum intent, contains the record's strongest melody. In contrast, "Fat Fly" is unrelentingly bleak; the light relief is provided by atonal background guitar. **World Service** isn't unpleasant; rather, it explores different ground with the same caustic eye and inventive mind.

With ex-Fingerprintz guitarist Jimme O'Neill in tow and Dagmar Krause providing backing vocals, More lightens the mood considerably on **The Only Choice**. He incorporates African rhythms on a few cuts, found sounds on others, and presents a lyrical mix of wry observations on ills of the modern world ("Industrial Drums," "Find One Voice") plus fascinating outlooks on communication and relationships (and not simply romantic ones). The often-understated music is consistently likable but a bit less invigorating than his best. Nonetheless, More's varied talents, craft and incisiveness combine to make it a rewarding album.   [i]

See also *Peter Blegvad, Henry Cow*.

MORELLS

Shake and Push (Borrowed) 1982 (East Side Digital) 1990 ●

SKELETONS

Rockin' Bones (nr/Next Big Thing) 1987
In the Flesh! (nr/Next Big Thing) 1988 [CD] (nr/Demon) 1990 ●

How's this for an intriguing assortment of musicians: a middle-aged couple (he, once of Arthur "Sweet Soul Music" Conley's band, on bass and guitar; she on keyboards; both sing), a phenomenal guitarist who'd be stiff competition for Dave Edmunds and Brian Setzer if he were based in a city larger than Springfield, Missouri and—on occasional sax—a fellow whose main occupation is producing unconventional country star Boxcar Willie. Guitarist D. Clinton Thompson and bassist Lou Whitney (producer of the first Del-Lords LP) have been together in a variety of lineups; the former's superb "Driving Guitars" 45 rescued a swell Ventures tune from obscurity. In the Skeletons and Original Symptoms, the pair has mined the vaults of rock, R&B and country arcana for some ought-to-have-been classics and the inspiration to pen their own instant winners.

The Morells can easily slay most revivalist bands, and **Shake and Push** proves it with a casualness that's all the more ingratiating. A dozen bars into the second track, if you ain't slobbering on the LP jacket wondering where you're gonna find a dee-luxe greaseburger place like "Red's," then you just ain't American. (The 1990 reissue adds two outtakes from the original album sessions and in-depth liner notes by Dave Fricke.)

The Skeletons consist of Thompson and Whitney

with a different drummer and keyboard player. **Rockin' Bones** compiles the entire contents of the band's original three pre-Morells singles (from '79-'80), adding three tunes cut after the Skeletons were revived in the mid-'80s. The album, which is simply delightful from start to finish, takes an automotive angle, with Whitney's flawless "Trans Am" and covers like "Gas Money" and the instrumental "B/Gas Accord." If Johnny Otis' "Crazy Country Hop" and Whitney's Presleyesque "Tell Her I'm Gone" break the topical mold, they do nothing to interrupt the magical mood.

Adding a second keyboard player, the Skeletons made an all-new (recording-wise, that is) album, reducing the overt nostalgia in favor of a more integrated old-fashioned sound that brings a wider collection of influences into the studio. But forward progress for such a backwards-looking band isn't such a swell idea. Besides covers of Sonny Bono's "Laugh at Me" and the Flying Burrito Brothers' "Older Guys," **In the Flesh!** contains one of the Del-Lords' lesser creations ("I Play the Drums"), the sappy "For Every Heart" and a brief "Take Me Out to the Ball Game." The playing's great and the spirit never falters, but this accomplished collection doesn't have enough of what makes **Rockin' Bones** so downright upright. The Demon CD contains both Skeletons LPs in their entirety.   [jg/i]

SCOTT MORGAN BAND

See *Sonic's Rendezvous Band*.

GIORGIO MORODER & PHILIP OAKEY

See *Human League*.

MORRISSEY

Viva Hate (Sire-Reprise) 1988 ●
Bona Drag (Sire-Reprise) 1990 φ
Kill Uncle (Sire-Reprise) 1991 φ

Having killed off the much beloved Smiths, Morrissey carried the hopes of countless fans into his solo career, but rewarded them with **Viva Hate**, a bland album that provides striking proof of how special and irreplaceable his partnership with Johnny Marr was. Joined by guitarist Vini Reilly (Durutti Column) and bassist/co-writer Stephen Street (producer of some Smiths records) as well as a drummer and string section, Morrissey brings his usual lyrical angst and wobbly singsong to the project, but the colorless music offers nothing beyond smoothly orchestrated static. The minimally arranged and epic-length "Late Night, Maudlin Street" is the closest thing to a good track, but it's too simple by half. "Suedehead" attempts to mimic the Smiths with moderate selfconscious success, but little inherent creativity. **Viva Hate** drops Morrissey from masterful pop star to bland solo artist in one easy step. The tape and CD add "Hairdresser on Fire."

Like his former band, Morrissey releases singles as frequently as other pop stars make hotel reservations; in the two album-less years following **Viva Hate**, he produced enough new tracks to necessitate the **Bona Drag** A's and B's compilation. Repeating two tracks ("Suedehead" and "Everyday Is Like Sunday") that were 45s taken from the previous LP, **Bona Drag** adds the fruits of Morrissey's work with Clive Langer and Alan Winstanley (the Madness-inflected "Piccadilly Palare," the danceably dense "November Spawned a Monster," the bluesy "Yes, I Am Blind") as well as Street productions like the absolutely ace "Interesting Drug" (on which Morrissey and Kirsty MacColl harmonize over music played by all the ex-Smiths save Marr) and the lushly orchestrated "Hairdresser on Fire." By and large, this fine collection puts Morrissey back on track, with varied music that supports his unique lyrical vision as well as the Smiths ever did.

Morrissey evidently liked the Langer/Winstanley tracks enough to have them produce all of **Kill Uncle**. Although the unnervingly posh commercial presentation boldly takes Morrissey places he's never been before (leading off with the hideously mainstream "Our Frank" and the string-laden "Asian Rut" seems like a tactical goof), his songwriting collaboration with Mark Nevin (the ex-Fairground Attraction guitarist also plays on the LP) seems to have finally solved the Marr problem; **Kill Uncle** contains some of Morrissey's best songs ever. ("Driving Your Girlfriend Home," "Sing Your Life" and "King Leer" are highlights.) For their part, Langer and Winstanley leave enough idiosyncrasies amid the radio-ready fabrications to make this surprising-sounding record a subtle and substantial success. [i]

See also *Smiths*.

MORTAL MICRONOTZ

The Mortal Micronotz (Fresh Sounds) 1982
Live Recording of the Video Soundtrack EP (Fresh Sounds) 1984
MICRONOTZ

Smash! (Fresh Sounds) 1983
The Beast That Devoured Itself (Fresh Sounds) 1985
40 Fingers (Homestead) 1986

This quartet—teenagers at the outset, their minds filled with the world—must have felt constricted in the confines of Lawrence, Kansas. The sound on the Mortal Micronotz album is a little tinny, but these guys have your standard '70s Ameri-punk moves down cold—sort of a sub-Dead Boys, but tighter. Dean Lubensky is actually an okay singer, making the adolescent alienation lyrics sound more believable than they read. He also handles lyrics given to the band by homeboy William S. Burroughs with similar aplomb. Added treat: a good noisy version of "Let It All Hang Out," which the Hombres first released when these guys were still in diapers.

Their name truncated and Burroughs nowhere in sight, the Micronotz show no sign of losing any of their rock'n'roll energy on **Smash!**, a 45 rpm album that includes Iggy's "I Got a Right" plus seven originals. Lubensky's vocals are mighty rough, John Harper's guitar playing pretty swift and the song subjects a bit more mature; a convincing record with a personality (of sorts) all its own. Production could have been a lot clearer, though.

The band's next release (under the old name) was a 7-inch EP containing five live renditions. Lubensky then left and was replaced by Jay Hauptli in time for **The Beast That Devoured Itself**, another raggedly entertaining punked-out collection that generally rises above all of the genre's typical limitations.

The bracingly good **40 Fingers** is a triumphant stylistic distillation, a powerful and varied dose of mature post-thrash intelligence that in spots resembles Hüsker Dü. Without losing any of their adolescent strength, the Micronotz play better than ever, and Hauptli's coarse vocals have gained a melodic validity, vastly improved by Harper's harmonies. (At times they sound a tad like the Ramones.) A cover of Simon & Garfunkel's "Scarborough Fair" serves as a showcase for the band's newfound abilities. [jg/i]

MOTHER LOVE BONE

Shine EP (Stardog-PolyGram) 1989 ●
Apple (Polydor) 1990 ф

With one pair of Green River refugees off to form Mudhoney, another two ex-members of that seminal Seattle crew—guitarist Stone Gossard and bassist Jess Ament—launched their own hoary '70s hard-rock band, Mother Love Bone. With another guitarist, a drummer and singer Andrew Wood (formerly of Malfunkshun), MLB made its debut on **Shine**, an EP whose five songs shrug off both common tendencies—Zeppelin and motorsludge—of the New Pacific Northwest in favor of a crisp rip that favors Free, Aerosmith and other blues-based bands of the very early '70s. Rather than wallowing in wah-wah and stun volume, the quintet demonstrates noteworthy songwriting facility, the wisdom to tone things down and open the sound up, and a real three-dimensionality to the presentation.

With a major-label deal and an extremely promising future, Wood died of an overdose in March '90, casting an enormous pall over the release of the band's completed first album. Produced by Terry Date, **Apple** focuses all of Mother Love Bone's assets into a potent rock rush, making it everything a Guns n' Roses LP should be—but with better vocals and worse guitar.

See also *Temple of the Dog*. [i]

MARK MOTHERSBAUGH

See *Devo*.

MOTOR BOYS MOTOR

Motor Boys Motor (nr/Albion) 1982

Strange sense of humor: the cover and enclosed poster is a freak-show photo of a black man's face with lots of little snakes coming out of his mouth. The foursome (two guitars, bass, drums) do a song called "Here Comes the Flintstones." They should have done the show's actual theme—this ditty ain't happening. Nothing much here is, despite the energetic punk-*cum*-boogie musical mode and Beefheartian overtones. Interesting, but doesn't come near justifying its existence. (Half of MBM later organized the Screaming Blue Messiahs and put a song called "I Wanna Be a Flintstone" on their second album.)

See also *Screaming Blue Messiahs*. [jg]

MOTORCYCLE BOY

See *Shop Assistants*.

MOTÖRHEAD

Motörhead (nr/Chiswick) 1977 (nr/Big Beat) 1978
(Roadracer Revisited) 1990 ●
Overkill (nr/Bronze) 1979 (Profile) 1988 ●
Bomber (nr/Bronze) 1979 (Profile) 1988 ●
On Parole (nr/Liberty) 1979 (nr/Fame) 1982 (EMI
America) 1987 ●
Motörhead EP (nr/Big Beat) 1980
The Golden Years EP (nr/Bronze) 1980
Ace of Spades (Mercury) 1980 (Profile) 1988 ●
No Sleep 'til Hammersmith (Mercury) 1981 (Profile)
1988 ●
Iron Fist (Mercury) 1982 (Roadracer Revisited) 1990 ●
Stand by Your Man EP (nr/Bronze) 1982
What's Words Worth? (nr/Big Beat) 1983
Another Perfect Day (Mercury) 1983 ●
No Remorse (Bronze) 1984 (Roadracer Revisited) 1990 ●
Anthology (nr/Raw Power) 1985 ●
Born to Lose (nr/Dojo) 1985
Orgasmatron (GWR-Profile) 1986 ●
Rock 'n' Roll (GWR-Profile) 1987 ●
EP [CD] (nr/Special Edition) 1988 ●
Another Perfect Day/Overkill (nr/Castle Comm.) 1988 ●
No Sleep at All (GWR-Enigma) 1988 ●
Blitzkrieg on Birmingham '77 (nr/Receiver) 1989 ●
Dirty Love (nr/Receiver) 1989 ●
The Best of & the Rest of Motörhead Live (nr/Action
Replay) 1990 ф
Welcome to the Bear Trap (nr/Castle Comm.) 1990 ●
Bomber/Ace of Spades (nr/Castle Comm.) 1990 ●
Lock Up Your Daughters (nr/Receiver) 1990 ●
The Birthday Party (GWR-Enigma) 1990 ф
From the Vaults (nr/Sequel) 1990 ●
1916 (WTG) 1991 ●
Meltdown (nr/Castle Comm.) 1991 ●

MOTÖRHEAD AND GIRLSCHOOL

St. Valentine's Day Massacre EP (nr/Bronze) 1980

VARIOUS ARTISTS

Eat the Rich (Filmtrax-GWR) 1987

WURZEL

Bess EP (nr/GWR) 1987

PHILTHY PHIL AND FAST EDDIE

Naughty Old Santa's Christmas Classics (nr/Receiver)
1989

The early pigeonholing of Motörhead as punks may
have stemmed from their loud'n'fast playing, their
leather jackets, engagements opening for the Damned
and their early releases on a UK indie label, but then, as
now, the band was engaged in its own hard-rockin'
rebellion—slashing guitar, flailing drums and Lemmy
playing bass like a lead and rhythm instrument, singing
as though he were in the process of being strangled.
Inspired moronism? You bet, just like "Louie, Louie,"
which the band covered for a minor hit in 1978!

Motörhead's very existence opposed the safe, sterile, flabby ritual "heavy music" had become (not to
mention the rest of what had been passing for rock-
'n'roll), and prefigured the new wave of rawer British
metal bands (Iron Maiden, Saxon et al.) in the early
'80s, not to mention the thrash bands of recent years.
All told, Motörhead's primal urgency clearly recalled

their spiritual forebears: the Amboy Dukes/Bob Seger
System/MC5 Detroit axis.

After being fired from Hawkwind, bassist Ian
"Lemmy" Kilmister hooked up with two ex-Pink Fairies
(also Hawkwind chums): Larry Wallis and Lucas Fox.
Producer Dave Edmunds allegedly fled their recording
session, covering his ears; Fox was dumped and his
replacement, Phil "Philthy Animal" Taylor, overdubbed some of the drum parts. UA let Motörhead's
contract expire, and didn't see fit to release the results
until 1980 (as On Parole). In any case, Lemmy sought
to beef up the sound by bringing in guitarist "Fast"
Eddie Clarke (like Jimi Hendrix, a former employee of
Curtis Knight), at which point Wallis took a powder.

In their second attempt at a debut album, Speedy
Keen (ex-Thunderclap Newman), who'd mis-mixed the
Heartbreakers' L.A.M.F. LP, successfully captured
Motörhead's sturm und klang. Cut after cut, it's phe-
nomenal: remakes of Hawkwind's "Motörhead" and
"Lost Johnny" (the latter co-written by Mick Farren),
"White Line Fever," "Iron Horse/Born to Lose" and
more, all with a force and fury unequalled until the 1981
live LP. A 1980 12-inch of outtakes from those
Chiswick sessions features Wallis' "On Parole," Mo-
törhead's "Beer Drinkers & Hell Raisers" and oldies by
John Mayall and ZZ Top. (The belated American reissue of Motörhead appends the entire four-song EP as
well as the band's first B-side, the Pink Fairies' "City
Kids.") Released in '83, the live What's Words
Worth? revealed the band in an early '78 show—
uneven, although some of the cover tunes, like "Leavin'
Here" and "Train Kept a-Rollin' " strike some pretty
good sparks.

Moving from Chiswick to Bronze, and from Keen to
ex-Stones producer Jimmy Miller, the trio put out a trio
of solid LPs, each with its own merits and classic cuts.
Overkill's title track, "Stay Clean" and that ultimate
putdown, "No Class," are balanced by the atypically
slow, deliberate "Capricorn." Bomber has its title track
and "Dead Men Tell No Tales" as highlights. Ace of
Spades also has a great title track and "(We Are) The
Road Crew." Vic Maile produced the last of those LPs,
achieving more sonic fullness and texture than Miller
had, though Overkill's material is the best of the three.

In a collaboration alternately referred to as Motor-
school and Headgirl, Motörhead and labelmates Girlschool ganged up on the 1959 Johnny Kidd & the Pirates
hit "Please Don't Touch" (with a flipside containing
each group murdering a fave song by the other, the
single was packaged on 7-inch and 10-inch as the St.
Valentine's Day Massacre EP) and had a hit. Then the
live No Sleep went into the UK album charts at number
one: Maile's super production job balances ambience
and clarity. It was all any Motörfan could've asked.

Fast Eddie ran the console for Iron Fist, with the
help of engineer Will Reid Dick. The results are relatively lackluster, in material as well as sound. (The
1990 reissue adds "Remember Me, I'm Gone.") Eddie
was not happy with the direction of the band, and while
the others were busy combining with the Plasmatics as
they had with Girlschool (less successful artistically and
commercially, on Tammy Wynette's "Stand by Your
Man"), he decided to split and form the bluesy, Zep-ish
Fastway. Ex-Thin Lizzy guitarist Brian Robertson im-

mediately replaced him. **Another Perfect Day** was a good change of pace. Considering how unsuited Robertson figured to be, it works surprisingly well. But it just wasn't Motörhead, and after a tour-shortening illness, he left.

No sooner was he replaced by two unknowns, Phil Campbell and Mick "Wurzel" Burston, than Taylor decided he wanted out, too. In stepped Pete Gill (ex-Saxon, and before that the Glitter Band, as in Gary!). The next release, **No Remorse**, was no stopgap, though. They didn't get the rights to the Chiswick tracks, but otherwise the two-record set is a model best-of collection: a wise, balanced choice of LP and EP cuts, non-LP single sides, four smokin' new numbers, annotation (and commentary by Lemmy) on all tracks, complete lyrics, a smart, detailed band history (by *Kerrang!*'s Malcolm Dome) and some cute pics. It does include "Please Don't Touch," "Louie, Louie," "Leaving Here" (the best version of the *five* the band has cut over the years, from the snappy **Golden Years** live EP) and that instant classic, "Killed by Death." ("If you squeeze my lizard, I'll put my snake on you.") Sheer Shakespeare in a Chevy. (The 1990 American CD omits "Louie, Louie," "Leaving Here" and the original liner notes, but the cassette has two tracks entitled "Under the Knife" from the initial Wurzel/Campbell sessions.)

The next year, Raw Power licensed enough tracks from Bronze to make up a second two-LP retrospective, **Anthology**, suitable for those whose only previous purchase was **No Remorse** (although five tracks do overlap). **Born to Lose** is a substantial compilation of tracks from **On Parole** and **Motörhead**, plus alternate takes of "White Line Fever" and "Leaving Here" that had been issued only as part of a Stiff boxed set.

Orgasmatron was produced by Bill Laswell with Jason Corsaro. Laswell's involvement got lots of critics to pay attention, and they got to hear a decent Motörhead record—including classic "Doctor Rock"—but hardly their best. On the LP's opener ("Deaf Forever") and closer ("Orgasmatron") the sound is a striking juggernaut but, generally, it seems a bit sonically squashed.

The very next LP, **Rock 'n' Roll**, produced by the band and Guy Bidmead (who'd engineered **Orgasmatron**), has more sonic depth, a bit of slide guitar and backing-vocal *harmonies*! Also Phil Taylor, who had a change of heart and was allowed to step back in after Gill departed. Better than **Orgasmatron**, though not quite top-notch, it also includes "Eat the Rich," done for the film of the same name in which Lemmy has—gasp!—an acting role. (Aside from the title tune, the soundtrack LP consists of previously released material plus non-Motörhead scoring.)

Wurzel's EP is not bad: a "Sleepwalk"-esque instrumental, a Jeff Beck-ish hyper-waltz and a couple of Motörhead Jr.-type numbers.

Next, some reassessment and watershedding. **No Sleep at All** (live at a Finnish festival) combines top-notch playing and crappy sound, especially compared to the much hotter **Hammersmith**. That's sonically, though, not performance-wise. Campbell and Wurzel outplay Clarke on their version of "Ace of Spades," and their much-longer "Overkill" brims with pyrotechnics. On the rest (all post-Clarke material), it's doubly

a shame the sound is muffled, since these takes out-rock almost every studio version (not true of **Hammersmith**). The CD adds two cuts.

Blitzkrieg on Birmingham (early '77, pretty raw) and **Lock Up Your Daughters** (mid-'77, much smarter) are live LPs of virtually the same vintage and material as **What's Words Worth?** (early '78). **Welcome to the Bear Trap** is a double-LP's worth of Bronze tracks, mainly the same as previously compiled. **Dirty Love** consists of **Ace of Spades** rehearsal tapes. The rough versions of six tracks (one not even listed on the cover or the disc label!), plus a B-side of the same vintage, offer little creative insight; of four rejected/unfinished numbers (for which Clarke—source of the tapes—claims sole writing credit), only one is worthy of notice.

The Birthday Party—an album Motörhead tried to block the release of no less than three times—is the soundtrack of the band's 1985 tenth anniversary concert video. The sound is crisper than on the other live LPs, but you can't hear any bass drum, which makes Pete Gill sound even worse (compared to Philthy) than he actually is. Plus, some of the songs are played too fast, which further undercuts him. A few tracks are quite good and the twin guitars smoke throughout, but Clarke's shadow looms large, as eleven of the twelve songs date from his tenure (five from **Ace** alone). The CD adds three, one a show-closing "Motörhead" with past and present bandmembers onstage.

From the Vaults is an unessential but good collection for fans who only have the albums: all four (live) tracks of the **Golden Years** EP (okay); assorted B-sides (mostly quite good); "Bomber" by Girlschool from the **St. Valentine's** EP; "Masterplan" by Motörhead, "No Class" by the Plasmatics and "Stand by Your Man" by Wendy O. and Lemmy from the notorious '82 maxi-single (amusing); and a fun, Quo-ish cut by the Young & Moody Band (Quo roadie Bob Young and ex-Whitesnake guitarist Mick Moody, plus Lemmy, Cozy Powell and—yes—the Nolan Sisters).

The all-new **1916** album was more than worth the long wait. For once able to take time and care in the studio, and armed with their best set of songs since **Ace** (or even **Overkill**), Motörhead delivers an aggressive firestorm (check "The One to Sing the Blues") with the huge and harsh sound the band always needed but never previously achieved—kudos to producers Pete Solley and (for three tracks) Ed Stasium. Unexpected stylistic variations abound: a weird and sophisticated soundscape ("Nightmare/The Dreamtime"); Motörmetal à la Chuck Berry ("Going to Brazil"); a tongue-in-cheek boogie-paean to Los Angeles ("Angel City"); a 1:25 tribute to the Ramones ("Ramones"); a *ballad* blending slamming chords and churning solos with vocal harmonies, synth-strings and credible romantic (!) lyrics ("Love Me Forever"). Lemmy quietly closes the LP with "1916," sung from the perspective of a young soldier dying in WW I. The startling diversity and mastery of this album brings Motörhead to a new level.

Meltdown is an excellent, well-balanced boxed set (three CDs or five LPs) compilation that includes a solid selection from the band's live and studio albums. [jg]

See also *Mick Farren, Hawkwind, Social Deviants*.

445

MOTORS

Motors 1 (Virgin) 1977 (Blue Plate) 1991 •
Approved by the Motors (Virgin) 1978 (Blue Plate)
  1991 •
Tenement Steps (Virgin) 1980
Greatest Hit (nr/Virgin) 1981

NICK GARVEY

Blue Skies (nr/Virgin) 1982

Formed by two ex-members of Ducks Deluxe (singers/songwriters/multi-instrumentalists Andy Mc-Master and Nick Garvey) plus two younger pub vets (Bram Tchaikovsky and Ricky Slaughter), the Motors seemed like a hit machine from the outset. On record, they made grandiose rock-pop—wide-screen, brilliantly arranged and energetically performed—drawing on their longtime experience and solid talents.

Motors 1, produced by future metal maven Robert John Lange, is a fresh, exciting record, solidly rooted in electric guitars but light-years more subtle and three-dimensional than the rock'n'roll retreads the band's members had been playing prior to the Motors. While the six-minute "Dancing the Night Away" is an engrossing and muscular lead-off track, nothing else that follows it on the album is quite as striking. **Approved By** is a better effort, containing the fruits of the Motors' attack on the singles chart ("Airport" and "Forget About You" both went Top 20 in the UK) and exhibiting all of the band's strengths: catchy melodies, inventive arrangements and exciting, energetic use of rock instrumentation.

The Motors effectively disbanded after the second album. Garvey and McMaster continued working together using the group name, eventually engaging Jimmy Iovine to produce their next album in New York. **Tenement Steps**, the unfortunate result of far too much time spent in the studio, is an appalling, overblown mess, reeking of self-indulgence and artistic confusion. The chorus of the best-known track, "Love and Loneliness," sounds exactly like Steve Stills' "Love the One You're With"—and that's as good as the record gets.

Greatest Hit has all of the above-mentioned songs as well as the rest of the Motors' best work. Neophytes would do well to start (and end) here.

On his solo album, guitarist/bassist/producer Garvey demonstrates the versatility of his voice (clear tenor, hoarse baritone, agile falsetto). But he's even more adroit at the mixing console, able to whip up tuneful, ringing Spector/Springsteen pop melodrama and make lush, spacious pop-rock out of the riff from "Willie and the Hand Jive." He also throws a curve or two, like the clever, 10cc-ish "(Think) Tough" or the semi-parodic Squeeze-*cum*-Bowie of "Skin." But even the support by members of the Motors/Tyla/Bram Tchaikovsky axis and his own genuine likability can't save this record when Garvey descends into schlocky, banal romanticism.   [i/jg]

See also *Ducks Deluxe, Bram Tchaikovsky.*

BOB MOULD

Workbook (Virgin) 1989 •
Black Sheets of Rain (Virgin) 1990 •

The miserable implosion of Hüsker Dü left guitarist/singer Bob Mould embittered and saddened, but buoyed by the promise of a new beginning. Launching his solo career, Mould confounded audience expectations by choosing not to paint his unhappiness in walls of guitar fury. Instead, he delivered the haunted majesty of **Workbook**, a largely acoustic account of his emotional condition that uses soaring melodies and richly harmonic vocal and instrumental textures to maturely convey the subtleties and depth of his mood. Bookended by a pastoral instrumental and a paint-peeling feedback frenzy, Mould shrugs off any imagined stylistic restrictions and—backed by drummer Anton Fier (Golden Palominos et al.), bassist Tony Maimone (Pere Ubu) and cellist Jane Scarpantoni (Tiny Lights)—crafts beautiful documents of profound passion that both sigh and roar with equal sensitivity. Highlights: "See a Little Light," "Wishing Well," "Poison Years" and "Dreaming, I Am."

The ex-punk took a lot of predictable flak for going soft, and moved back into the noise tunnel for his second album, the subject of which is a different personal loss: the heartbreaking end of a love affair. As deeply felt as it might be for Mould (the scathing lyrics attest to that), **Black Sheets of Rain** has less power and poignancy—not in the clunky material, the generally unmodulated performances or the strange-sounding production, which suppresses the vocals, squishes the crudely overlaid roar of guitars into a thin blur and makes Fier's busy drumming the focus of the mix. Besides sounding like they're all playing in different studios, Mould, Fier and Maimone wrestle too many of the songs into the same neo-Dü shape. "It's Too Late" has a great pop melody but lyrics that actually mention the word "fluorocarbons." Otherwise, a few hard-hitting songs ("Disappointed," "Stop Your Crying" and "Out of Your Life") that connect intermittently and the touching acoustic melancholy of "The Last Night" help prevent the disappointing **Black Sheets of Rain** from being a total washout.   [i]

See also *Hüsker Dü.*

MOVEMENT EX

Movement Ex (Columbia) 1990 •

Armed with the myopic self-confidence of flaming youth and the unfamiliar language of a sectarian religious cult, Lord Mustafa Hasan Ma'd, the lyrical/rapping half of LA's teenaged Movement Ex (DJ King Born Khaaliq provides the backing tracks, which are complex, heavy with effective samples and really exciting, if overloaded with high-pitched scratches), runs down the obscure look-what-you-made-us-do Five-Percent Nation of Islam perspective on a litany of serious subjects (global politics, guns, ecology, history, sexually transmitted diseases, drugs, etc.). The duo's album sounds great—the fully modern Movement Ex is unquestionably talented—but the militant anti-white fingerpointing, conspiracy theories and other dubious assertions make it impossible not to choose up sides on intellectual, rather than artistic, grounds. Fascinating if not exactly fun, **Movement Ex** presents listeners with a grave political and cultural challenge.   [i]

MOVING TARGETS

Burning in Water (Taang!) 1986 •
Brave Noise (Taang!) 1989 •

Moving Targets came blasting out of a Boston scene at a time when most Boston hardcore and punk outfits were going metal. The big guitar detonations were actually closer to Squirrel Bait and, to a lesser extent, Hüsker Dü, with more precise control than those bands ever attempted. **Burning in Water** is a gaping piece of power-trio battery, an intense wall-of-sound fireball married to rapid (not thrash) tempos, developed melodies and the sort of kick associated with, say, early D.O.A. What the record lacks in variety, it makes up for with convincing material and relentless determination.

The band's future looked grim after guitarist/singer Ken Chambers enlisted in Bullet LaVolta, but he has managed to split his time between the two groups and was present when Moving Targets (sporting a new bassist) reappeared three years later with the equally formidable **Brave Noise**. While the pace is still fast, the songs have been slowed down just enough to allow the trio to flex an even heavier strong-arm sound. The songwriting may not be as consistent, but Chambers' guitar playing is even more pulverizing, using dim-and-flare dynamics to set up—and knock down—listeners. (Both records are on one CD.) [jr]

See also *Bullet LaVolta*.

JUDY MOWATT

Black Woman (Island) 1980 (Shanachie) 1983 ●
Only a Woman (Shanachie) 1982 ●
Working Wonders (Shanachie) 1985 ●
Love Is Overdue (Shanachie) 1987 ●

Partly because Rastafarianism is intrinsically patriarchal, the number of important women reggae performers can still be counted in single digits. Singing behind Bob Marley, the I-Threes (Marcia Griffiths, Rita Marley and Judy Mowatt) were, for a long time, the only visible female presence in roots music. While they've all enjoyed successful solo careers, Mowatt has made the most significant strides, writing and producing her own material.

On **Black Woman**, she covers three Wailers songs and dedicates an original to Marley. The album amply displays her talents as a composer as well as performer, and brought her international acclaim. The quiet militancy of **Only a Woman** is offset by an engaging vocal style—strong and clean—that recalls American R&B. By the time **Working Wonders** was released, she was being called the queen of reggae by the press. Featuring a variety of producers and material, the LP suffers from its crossover efforts, but Mowatt's singing is more assured than ever.

By contrast, **Love Is Overdue** is nearly ruined by Mowatt's attempt to reach the mainstream. Produced by TSOP alumnus Dexter Wansel, Side One's first four tracks (including covers of "Try a Little Tenderness" and UB40's "Sing Our Own Song") are lightweight pop-soul, bland and forgettable. Luckily, Mowatt salvages the rest of the LP by singing, writing and producing the sprightly reggae she does best. [bk]

ALISON MOYET

Alf (Columbia) 1984 ●
Raindancing (Columbia) 1987 ●
Alf/Raindancing [CD] (nr/CBS) 1988 ●
Hoodoo (Columbia) 1991 ●

Alison Moyet's soulful vocals were the best thing about Yazoo (Yaz in the States), her odd but successful partnership with ex-Depeche Moder Vince Clarke. He went on to form Erasure; she launched a commercially rewarding mainstream solo career. On **Alf**, her amazing pipes are supported by smooth synth-and-drums dance music created by full-service producers Tony Swain and Steve Jolley, who co-wrote the material and played on it as well. Moyet's consistently great singing and her producers' impersonal backing leave songwriting the only variable, and that's unfortunately what it is. Other than "All Cried Out," the coyly tasteless "Love Resurrection" and Lamont Dozier's magnificent "Invisible," there aren't many tunes in the winning column. What made Yazoo work was great writing; judging by **Alf**, maybe Moyet's symbiotic partnership with Clarke wasn't such a weird idea after all.

Producer Jimmy Iovine stayed out of the other aspects of the creative process on **Raindancing**, leaving Moyet to take greater responsibility for the material. Although sincere enough, her lyrics about romantic challenges don't amount to much; the mostly collaborative music is plain but sturdy, allowing Moyet's rich voice to do the work. Standouts are "Glorious Love," "Is This Love?" and Floy Joy's wonderful "Weak in the Presence of Beauty." The low point is the stiflingly schmaltzy "Sleep Like Breathing." [i]

See also *Yazoo*.

MUD BOY & THE NEUTRONS

See *Panther Burns*.

MUDHONEY

Superfuzz Bigmuff EP (Sub Pop) 1988 ●
Mudhoney (Sub Pop) 1989 ●
Boiled Beef & Rotting Teeth EP [CD] (nr/Sub Pop-Tupelo) 1990 ●
Every Good Boy Deserves Fudge (Sub Pop) 1991) ●

Alongside Soundgarden, Seattle's Mudhoney are kings of the Pacific noise-west frontier, playing unceremonious, nonspecific '70s-based hard rock with an '80s attitude. Formed by ex-members of Green River (singer Mark Arm and original guitarist Steve Turner) and the Melvins (bassist Matt Lukin) and their respective distortion pedals, the quartet made a loud but colorless debut on the six-song **Superfuzz Bigmuff**, getting up a good, semi-tight head of steam (including loads of wah-wah, slide and feedback) but—with the partial exception of the frantically sung "In 'n' Out of Grace"— not finding any effective stylistic application for it.

Thanks to terse, cut-to-the-chase songs, **Mudhoney** offers a punkier view of the band, a roaring garagey behemoth that, in spots, owes quite a bit to Blue Cheer (circa "Summertime Blues"—check "Get into Yours" for details) and rolls out a good number (like "You Got It") now and again. Over the course of an entire album, however, Mudhoney hasn't got the songwriting substance to justify its noise. Neither strictly derivative nor in any sense original, **Mudhoney** is merely a generic mediocrity.

Assembled for the overseas market, **Boiled Beef & Rotting Teeth** contains a 1988 compilation LP contribution and two singles—five songs in all, including an alternate version of **Mudhoney**'s "You Got It (Keep It Outta My Face)." [i]

See also *Green River, Melvins*.

MUNCHENER FREIHEIT

Umsteiger (Ger. CBS) 1982
Licht (Ger. CBS) 1983
Herzschlag Einter Stadt (Ger. CBS) 1984
Von Anfang An (Ger. CBS) 1986
Traumziel (Ger. CBS) 1986

FREIHEIT

Romancing in the Dark (Ger. CBS) 1987
Fantasy (nr/CBS) 1988 (WTG) 1989 ●
Kissed You in the Rain EP (nr/CBS) 1989 ●

Munchener Freiheit (Munich Freedom) started as a two-guitar quartet on **Umsteiger** (**Transfer**). Displaying a definite knack for power pop with exceedingly good Beatlesque harmonies, they also go in for some tracks with slightly eccentric arrangements. At points they reach genuine offbeatness, fitting for a band led by an ex-member of fringe space rockers Amon Duül II, namely singing guitarist Stefan Zauner. It's a bit of an unsatisfying mix, but the high points are, well, kind of like eating Ring Dings: empty calories, but awfully tasty. (Despite Zauner's Anglo-pop voice, the record's all in German, including a version of Dylan's "It's All Over Now, Baby Blue.")

They subsequently jettisoned the musical weirdness altogether. On **Licht**, with Zauner moving over to keyboards, the overall sound is more commercial and pop-oriented. That it comes shrink-wrapped with a combination sweat-band/visor (!) should suggest the record's intended appeal. Again, there's the same kind of swell pop-rock, but some veers dangerously close to pap.

By **Herzschlag Einer Stadt**, possibly the group's best album, the lineup had stabilized as a quintet with two keyboardists including Zauner, by then primarily the singer (and, teamed with guitarist Aron Strobel, chief songwriter). He'd also been the producer, with former bassist Freddie Erdmann but, starting with **Herzschlag**, the records were overseen by Armand Volker. This proved to be a formula for success—the quintet are now quite big pop stars—but the slickness that went into it became increasingly annoying. (Here, it's just insidiously ingratiating.)

Von Anfang An (**From the Beginning On**) conveniently summed up Munchener Freiheit's output for their hit parade fans, with non-LP single tracks and the most commercial (not necessarily the best) of the previous LPs, including live, alternate and remixed versions. **Traumziel** has a surprisingly mature sound and, while some of it lapses into blandness, the rest is enjoyable ear candy. Curiously dropping the first half of their name, Freiheit issued **Traumziel** in an English-language version, **Romancing in the Dark**, with three remakes from previous LPs slotted in. **Traumziel** actually hangs together better, and understanding the lyrics hardly makes a big difference.

By **Fantasie**, the gradual stylistic modernization (adding in dance-rock elements and so on) had coun-terbalanced most of the original charm—even of Zauner's voice. The record still has worthwhile moments, but it's mostly dull. For international consumption, the lyrics were translated into English (or, as on at least some of the tracks, rewritten). "Keeping the Dream Alive" (a softer, fluffier, longer version of "So Lang' Man Traume Noch Leben Kann") leads off the LP, instead of ending it. Yawn. [jg]

COATI MUNDI

See *Kid Creole and the Coconuts*.

PETER MURPHY

Should the World Fail to Fall Apart (nr/Beggars Banquet) 1986 ●
Love Hysteria (Beggars Banquet-RCA) 1988 ●
Deep (Beggars Banquet-RCA) 1990 ●

DALIS CAR

The Waking Hour (nr/Paradox-Beggars Banquet) 1984 ●

After leaving Bauhaus, singer Peter Murphy joined Mick Karn (ex-Japan) and a no-name drummer to form Dalis Car, whose one album mixed Japan's sensuous sound with Bauhaus' obsequious lyrical constructs. As a mellifluous noise, **The Waking Hour** is fine, if a bit heavy on the bass; dig any deeper, however, and what you get is a hollow attempt to create art without any redeeming artistry.

Moving on to a solo career, Murphy made his debut with **Should the World Fail to Fall Apart**. Guitarist/keyboard player Howard Hughes co-wrote and co-produced this dreamy, mildly experimental effort that makes good use of modest understatement. If Murphy could remove the melodrama from his delivery, a lot of the songs might have been quite nice. But even at low volume and languorous tempo, he can't shake the old goth theatrics out of his voice. He almost pulls it off in "Canvas Beauty," an appealing wash of fretless bass and synthetic horns, but winds up doing a frightening vocal imitation of mid-period Moody Blues. And that's as good as it gets. Covering Magazine's "The Light Pours Out of Me" and Pere Ubu's "Final Solution" probably seemed like good, culturally resonant ideas at the time, but the awkward results are far from impressive.

Keyboardist Paul Statham co-wrote **Love Hysteria**, an album on which Murphy's commanding baritone contrasts with brittle, airy music built on a dual fixation with **Lodger**-era Bowie and the group Japan. (At its most commercial, however, the record resembles the Fixx.) Regardless of stylistic intent, the pompous pseudo-babble lyrics and keyboardist/guitarist Simon Rogers' horrible production (the sound has almost no bottom) makes this of interest only to implacable Bauhaus fanatics.

Having covered "Funtime" (from **The Idiot**) on **Love Hysteria**, Murphy added an ominous Iggy Pop impression to his colorful repertoire on **Deep**. Using the same crowd—Statham, Rogers, bassist Eddie Branch, guitarist Peter Bonas—as the previous album, Murphy shifted into simple dance-rock, extrapolating what Bowie might sound like fronting, say, Modern English. Actually, **Deep** isn't bad—multi-tracking the vocals and swamping them in thick pop instrumentation softens

Murphy's voice (whose control has clearly improved) to the point of easy listening. Where **Deep** sinks is in the songwriting: amid the few nicely rounded melodies are dead serious songs with titles like "The Line Between the Devil's Teeth (And That Which Cannot Be Repeat!)" and "Marlene Dietrich's Favourite Poem." (One bonus track on the CD and cassette.)   [i]

See also *Bauhaus*.

MURPHY'S LAW
Murphy's Law (Rock Hotel-Profile) 1986
Back with a Bong! (Profile) 1989 ●

These popular skate punks from Astoria, Queens take a wisely unserious approach to thrash on their fine debut album. The quartet varies the tempos every which way—the LP only intermittently utilizes hardcore burn velocity—holding fast to a rollicking punk spirit without conforming to its stylistic regulations. The clearly produced record's title track has a winning "arf-arf" chorus; "Sit Home & Rot" addresses the urgent topic of couch potatodom without apology; other numbers ratify such essential life functions as "Crucial Bar-B-Q," "Fun" and "Beer." Throughout, the violent energy, good playing and Jimmy Gestapo's spirited vocals make **Murphy's Law** (on green vinyl no less) a near-brilliant mistake.

Back with a Bong! repeats the feat, adding simple horn charts to songs about eating, drinking, dental health, buying/smoking dope and patriotism. (Does this actually make youth culture sense?) The mixture of brass and thrash is more surprising than effective—except on a clumsy stab at ska, where the combination sounds awful—but the quartet's refusal to leave punk alone just might lead somewhere amazing one of these days. (Judging by "Bong," reggae is not their wisest path.)   [i]

PAULINE MURRAY
See *Penetration*.

JUNIOR MURVIN
Police and Thieves (Mango) 1977

Not to be confused with Wailers guitarist Junior *Marvin*, Murvin is the possessor of a fabulous falsetto. (In the late '60s he did reggae covers of Curtis Mayfield tunes and was known as Junior Soul.) In 1976, after some success writing for others, he teamed with legendary producer Lee Perry and delivered "Police and Thieves," an instant classic with phenomenal impact in both Jamaica and England (it came as a timely remark on increased racial tensions in both nations). As an added intercultural bonus, the song's appropriately rebellious lyrics offered the Clash a convenient way to make an early reggae statement on their first LP.

Murvin's original is worth every bit of applause it's gotten. The cool, understated presentation contradicts the mood of the lyrics, but lends them an underlying tension unattainable by histrionics (which, by contrast, gives extra weight to the more dramatic middle eight). As for the rest of the album, other than the excellent,

more groove-minded "Roots Train," it's a swell voice and righteous riddims buoying plain songs. Murvin never did really capitalize on his big success.   [jg]

See also *Lee Perry*.

MUSIC REVELATION ENSEMBLE
See *James Blood Ulmer*.

MUSSOLINI HEADKICK
Themes for Violent Retribution (World Domination-Wax Trax!) 1989 ●
Blood on the Flag (World Domination-Caroline) 1990 ●

Those generally intimidated by industrialists' relentless amelodic pounding may find this Belgian-American group's debut easier to face: the most off-putting thing about **Themes for Violent Retribution** is the (antifascist) cover's swastika. While this part-time party starring Luc Van Acker (of Revolting Cocks) and singer/keyboard manipulator John Butcher (of King Butcher) does employ the form's standard tools—stern beats, found sounds and distorted chants—MH keeps things reasonably musical with an undercurrent of techno-dance conservatism and, on Side B, actual songs with verses, choruses and rough melodies.

The harsher **Blood on the Flag**, again produced by Van Acker, delves more deeply into the punishing power of electronic percussion and chaotic noise, as Butcher angrily shouts his military-minded political lyrics in topical songs like "Kabul," "Homeland" and "War Drum." With the exception of two near-songs ("Cracking Up" and "Holy War"), the shards of musical intelligence here crop up only as accents, playing a similar role to the audio vérité sound bites.   [i]

See also *Revolting Cocks, Luc Van Acker*.

MUTABARUKA
Check It (Alligator) 1983
Outcry (Shanachie) 1984 ●
The Mystery Unfolds (Shanachie) 1986 ●
Any Which Way ... Freedom (Shanachie) 1989 ●
Blakk wi Blak ... K ... K ... (Shanachie) 1991 ●

VARIOUS ARTISTS
Word Soun' 'ave Power (Heartbeat) 1983
Dub Poets Dub (Heartbeat) 1983

As a dub poet, Mutabaruka (born in Jamaica as Allan Hope) inevitably inspires comparisons to Linton Kwesi Johnson, but where LKJ's poems are often ironic and his delivery knife sharp, Mutabaruka's work is more direct, thick with dread. Unlike Dennis Bovell's gorgeous formal arrangements on Johnson's LPs, Mutabaruka is more spontaneous. His poems dictate the musical direction—the rhythms jerk the band along. Suffice to say both artists derive from the same traditions of Jamaican poetry and music; if you like one, chances are you'll like the other.

Mutabaruka's first two albums are equally strong. **Check It**, a bold debut, contains three early singles: "Naw Give Up," "Everytime I Hear de Soun'" and "Hard Time Loving." **Outcry** continues the poet's verbal attack, while showing the influence of his dramatic concert appearances. (He performs in manacles.) Music and lyrics sound more linked than on the prior LP, and the band seems to be working with the poet rather than just backing him up.

On his third release, **The Mystery Unfolds**, Mutabaruka's lyrics are presented in a variety of musical settings. The LP is assured and versatile, an ambitious mixed bag with a cappella tracks, full-scale arrangements, audio effects and special guest vocalists (including Marcia Griffiths and Ini Kamose). While widening the performer's range, **The Mystery Unfolds** broadened his appeal as well. Indeed, "Dis Poem" enjoyed some popularity in NYC dance clubs, sampled in with house music.

"By the ballot or the bullet, by the Bible or the gun, any which way freedom must come!" On **Any Which Way . . . Freedom**, the revolutionary dub poet returns, stronger and more outspoken than ever; humor, anger and love mingle with political analysis as the music and words twist, turn, jump and soar to create message music for listening, dancing and serious contemplation. The title track samples *My Fair Lady*'s "I Could Have Danced All Night," while "Revenge" employs South African *mbaqanga* music.

Mutabaruka has also produced other West Indian poets, with two significant compilations (**Word Soun' 'ave Power** and **Woman Talk**) to his credit. The first also spawned the excellent **Dub Poets Dub**, a companion LP of instrumental tracks. [bk/aw]

MX-80 SOUND
EP (BRBQ) 1976 (Gulcher) 1977
Hard Attack (nr/Island) 1977
Out of the Tunnel (Ralph) 1980
Crowd Control (Ralph) 1981
MX-80
Existential Lover [tape] (Quadruped) 1987
Das Love Boat (A&R) 1990

BRUCE ANDERSON
Brutality I . . . America/Iran [tape] (Quadruped) 1987
Brutality II . . . Israel/Palestine [tape] (Quadruped) 1988

O-TYPE
O-Type [tape] (Quadruped) 1986
Darling [tape] (Quadruped) 1988

GIZZARDS
Unicork [tape] (Quadruped) 1985
Humdinger [tape] (Quadruped) 1986
Sgt. Peppersteak [tape] (Quadruped) 1988
Where Good Friends Meet EP (Quadruped) 1989

This weird post-metal art band originally from Bloomington, Indiana (from the same scene that spawned the goofy Gizmos) centers their sound around Bruce Anderson's slashing, trebly guitar riffing and Rich Stim's deadpan, often indecipherable, mumble. As a five-piece (with two drummers), they twice released a 7-inch EP (subtitled "Hard Pop from the Hoosiers") on local labels, impressing Island Records enough to sign them. But the resulting **Hard Attack** never came out in the States and attracted little attention aside from some critical raves. A move to San Francisco (shedding one drummer in the process) brought them to the attention of that city's Ralph Records, home of the Residents and other offbeat types.

Out of the Tunnel may well be MX-80's high-tide

mark, particularly on the concurrent single, "Someday We'll Be King" b/w "White Night"; on these two sides, their formula of convoluted, breakneck melodies, cross-fed musical genres and Anderson's white-hot soloing nears critical mass.

Crowd Control doesn't quite reach the same lofty heights. With more strict adherence to "metal" (in the Blue Öyster Cult sense) form, the songs here merely replace much of the white-hot intensity of **Tunnel** with volume. The results range from epiphany ("Obsession: Devotion" and "Face of the Earth") to nails-against-chalkboard (like a take on the theme from Brian DePalma's *Sisters*). A litigation-enforced five-year hiatus followed; while the band never technically split (note the plethora of pseudonymous releases), they did a pretty convincing disappearing act. When the curtain lifted again, a chopped and channeled leaner MX-80 was revealed.

Existential Lover is a step back from overkill's precipice; a biting and nasty artifact that simmers constantly with the psychotic abandon that spewed irregularly from earlier efforts. The filmic bent is still there on "Monster from Japan" and "Orson," and Stim's deadpan drawl recalls a non-homogenized Stan Ridgway in its seamy travel guide monotone. A real edge-of-your-seat listen.

Das Love Boat (perhaps the first all-instrumental album to sport a parental advisory) is an exhaustively complete retrospective, encompassing material from all the band's releases, plus early ('75-'78) live tracks. The package is topped off with a brace of newly recorded jazzy efforts, the best of which is the rasping title track.

Anderson's solo tapes are essential for those with a passion for volume-intensive but fluid guitar improv; imagine a cross between Sonny Sharrock and a bad-mood Robert Fripp. The first tape borrows a few MX-80 themes, but expands on them enough that you'll barely notice. **Israel: Palestine** is a touch harsher and more claustrophobic in tone. Bracing stuff.

O-Type was the moniker Anderson and MX-80's extraordinary bassist Dale Sophiea used to create theme music for a Ralph film (the theme to which crops up on **Das Love Boat**) and sporadically revived to churn out doom-laden, Germanic power-rock that's not all that far removed from an axe-wielding Suicide—especially Anderson's impassioned vocals. **Darling** is the pick of that litter. The Gizzards (identified as "the weak, separated Siamese twins of three MX-80 members"—geddit?) offer a few more laffs, though not nearly as many as **Sgt. Peppersteak**'s title would suggest. Over the course of these releases, the mood has become decidedly more bleak (and MX-80-ish), peaking with **Peppersteak**'s martial, creepy "Straight Line" and "Trailer Park."

Members of MX-80 also back Stim's singing wife, Angel Corpus-Christi, on her releases, discs that meld Patti Smith-poesy with fringey no wave. If ever a band realized the potential of pre-punk "underground" noise rock, MX-80 is it. [rnp/dss]

MY BLOODY VALENTINE
This Is Your Bloody Valentine EP (nr/Tycoon) 1985 (Ger. Dossier) 1988
Geek EP (nr/Fever) 1986

The New Record by My Bloody Valentine EP
   (nr/Kaleidoscope Sound) 1986
Sunny Sundae Smile EP (nr/Lazy) 1987
Strawberry Wine EP (nr/Lazy) 1987
Ecstasy EP (nr/Lazy) 1987
My Bloody Valentine Isn't Anything (Creation-Relativity)
   1988 ●
Feed Me with Your Kiss EP (nr/Creation) 1988
You Made Me Realise EP (nr/Creation) 1988
Ecstasy and Strawberry Wine [CD] (nr/Lazy) 1989 ●
Glider EP (nr/Creation) 1989 (Sire) 1990 ●
Tremolo (nr/Creation) 1990 (Sire-Warner Bros.) 1991 ●

Formed in Dublin in 1983, the dauntingly prolific My Bloody Valentine quickly became a cornerstone of a loose, largely media-built coalition of independent-label bands playing aggressive (and aggressively opaque) pop music that stood in direct opposition to both "rockism" and the twee bedsit romanticism of the pallid anti-rockists.

The first recordings capture a band in step with the times, but perhaps a bit too eager to get into the studio. **This Is Your Bloody Valentine** (recorded, incidentally, in Berlin) displays graveyard roots, style-hopping from campy (almost Batcave) Doors-isms like "The Love Gang" and "Don't Cramp My Style" to the Cramps to funereal spelunking in Nick's Cave. The only thing missing is originality. **Geek** is pretty much a carbon copy, largely because of David Conway's *basso profundo* (occasionally *ridiculoso*) croon, but **The New Record** uses a broader palette: the breathy "Lovelee Sweet Darlene" is outright childlike in its innocence.

By this time, My Bloody Valentine had begun construction on a wall of sound/noise (depending on your perspective) that's often likened to the Jesus and Mary Chain's. But where the Reids sequester themselves in a forbidding cage of hardened steel, MBV beckon from behind a glistening, almost transparent curtain of the thinnest gold leaf. This approach became all the more tantalizing when Conway left after **Sunny Sundae Smile** (notable for the silliest song ever about blow-up-doll love) and took most of the stormclouds with him. **Strawberry Wine** retreats almost completely from gloom, as the quartet instead immerses itself in West Coast psychedelia (Arthur Lee looms large over the wispy melody of "Can I Touch You?").

Ecstasy (paired on CD with **Strawberry Wine**) ups the dissonance factor a bit, and by relegating the shared vocals of new member Bilinda Butcher and Kevin Shields (both also play guitar) to the status of just another instrument, simultaneously increases the level of mystery—appropriate, considering the general Creation-band tendency to elevate sound qua sound over individual songs. There are certainly some of the latter on the band's first bona fide longplayer, **Isn't Anything**. Most, it seems, revolve around, er, non-mainstream sexuality (check out "Cigarette in Your Bed"—only on the British edition—for some strange kicks); all ride waves of languid "glide guitar" (the band's phrase) to almost narcotic effect. Trivia buffs should note My Bloody Valentine's appropriation of Public Enemy's "Security of the First World" riff—a full two years before Madonna's "Justify My Love."

Perhaps as a byproduct of a less hectic schedule, **Feed Me** and **You Made Me Realise** (not its real name: the four-song 12-inch that features that tune actually has no title) are at once as resolute and disparate as any consecutive releases in the band's considerable catalogue: the Butcher-sung tracks throb with subdued thriller soundtrack tension, while "You Made Me Realise" strips down to skeletal riff-rock basics for an X-like hootenanny.

Glider, on the other hand, is a wholehearted embrace of stasis, not at all a bad thing, given the band's extraordinary ability to arrive without travelling. The best track, "Soon," all but entirely dispenses with frills like choruses and chord progressions, opting instead for seven minutes of mesmerizing swells and contractions.

[dss]

MY DAD IS DEAD

My Dad Is Dead ... and He's Not Gonna Take It
   Anymore (St. Valentine) 1986 (Ger. Houses in
   Motion) 1990
Peace, Love and Murder (Birth) 1987
Let's Skip the Details (Homestead) 1988 ●
The Best Defense (Homestead) 1989
The Taller You Are, the Shorter You Get (Homestead)
   1989 ●
Shine EP (Scat) 1990

Under his open-to-misinterpretation nom de disc My Dad Is Dead, Cleveland singer/writer/one-man-band Mark Edwards makes music whose appeal lies largely in its matter-of-fact handling of deep personal traumas. As comforting as they are harrowing, Edwards' records have grown steadily in fluency and confidence.

My Dad Is Dead, most of whose songs were indeed inspired by the loss of Edwards' father, is a compelling, hypnotic debut that ranges from thrashy aggression ("Black Cloud") to supple melodicism ("Talk to the Weatherman") to industrial gloom ("Say Goodbye"). The unifying thread is the downbeat lyrics; the sole weak link is Edwards' flat singing, which improved on subsequent releases.

Peace, Love and Murder and **Let's Skip the Details** show considerable growth, both lyrically and musically. The instrumental attack has greater bite, and the latter disc finds Edwards applying subtler melodic devices (on tracks like "Lay Down the Law" and "Boiling Over") without sacrificing the music's original tension. **The Best Defense** is an assemblage of tracks from an unreleased EP, outtakes from **Let's Skip the Details** and some 4-track home recordings; though not as essential as its predecessor, it has some fine moments, including three surprisingly harmonious instrumentals.

The Taller You Are, the Shorter You Get (a double LP) is simultaneously Edwards' most ambitious effort and his most accessible. The expanded format allows for some longer experimental tracks, most of which work out quite nicely; there's even an almost-danceable instrumental, "Meep Meep." Elsewhere, Edwards veers relatively close to the musical mainstream (hard rock on "Too Far Gone," acoustic folk-rock on "Nothing Special") with considerable success. His lyrics, meanwhile, have grown less morose and more philosophical, and he sings them with new-found expressiveness.

Shine is a double 7-inch recorded with the rhythm

section of Cleveland's Prison Shake: four new songs and four rocked-up remakes of previously released material. [hd]

MY LIFE WITH THE THRILL KILL KULT

I See Good Spirits and I See Bad Spirits (Wax Trax!) 1988 ●
Kooler Than Jesus (Wax Trax!) 1990 φ
Confessions of a Knife ... (Wax Trax!) 1990 ●

There's house music, and then there's Amityville Horror music. But this pseudonymous conglomerate of sample masters and programmers—Groovy Mann (Frank Nardiello, vocals), Buzz McCoy (Marston Daley, keyboards/bass) and Buck Ryder (Thomas Lockyear, keyboards/percussion)—wasn't so great at saying *get out!* right off the bat. On **Good Spirits**, dialogue

samples (mostly dealing with that pop icon, Satan) and silly vocals aside, Thrill Kill Kult veers between sounding like a stripped-down Tangerine Dream and an overtly discofied . . . Tangerine Dream. Which is not to say it's a bad record.

Kooler Than Jesus, named for a 1989 12-inch single, is a CD/cassette compilation of the group's non-LP work to date.

Confessions of a Knife synthesizes the dance smarts of "Kooler Than Jesus" with the first album's sample-happy excesses. To boot, there are touches of metal and world music and constant evocations of bad trips and gory scares. Perfect background music for an evening of acid, speed and Herschell Gordon Lewis movies. [gk]

MYRNA

See *Human Switchboard*.

NAKED PREY

Naked Prey (Down There-Enigma) 1984
Under the Blue Marlin (Frontier) 1986
40 Miles from Nowhere (Frontier) 1987
Kill the Messenger (Fundamental) 1990 ●

Van Christian was at one time Green on Red's drummer; back home in Tucson, Arizona, he switched to vocals and guitar and formed Naked Prey. The quartet plays rough-edged country rock with similarities to Green on Red (as well as Dream Syndicate and others in the California/Arizona axis). Although the seven-song debut's powerful sound is strictly modern, some of David Seger's sociopathic guitar solos recall acid-drenched summer of love shows at the Fillmore. An unassuming, occasionally exciting record.

With a new drummer, label and producer (Paul B. Cutler), Naked Prey revved up their folk-distorto-rock on **Under the Blue Marlin**. Christian's colorful singing and Seger's guitar work remain the group's virtues, as Prey's songs don't make much of an impression. (A Stooges cover is both helpful and indicative of the band's own failings.)

The same problem plagues the thematically linked **40 Miles from Nowhere**: despite killer guitar (including slide) and relentless energy, unimaginative melodies and lyrics derail the effort. (Christian's deteriorating voice is another trouble spot.) Still, a pair of covers—Jagger/Richards' "Silver Train" and a funereal version of "Wichita Lineman" (get the drift?)—proves what these boys might do with substantial material. **Kill the Messenger** is a live album recorded in Tucson in 1988.

[i]

NAKED RAYGUN

Basement Screams EP (Ruthless) 1983
Throb Throb (Homestead) 1985 ●
All Rise (Homestead) 1986 ●
Jettison (Caroline) 1988 ●
Understand? (Caroline) 1989 ●
Raygun ... Naked Raygun (Caroline) 1990 ●

PEGBOY

Three-Chord Monte EP (1/4 Stick-Touch and Go) 1990

Chicago's Naked Raygun is one of the encouraging new punk bands that bloomed in the Midwest long after thrash had apparently isolated the punk aesthetic in its own circumscribed ghetto, where it would never again challenge the musical values of regular folk. Lump the longer-running Raygun in with Hüsker Dü, Man Sized Action, Big Black and Breaking Circus and you'll be oversimplifying, but you'll have your finger on an early-'80s movement of sorts. All of these bands expanded the boundaries and cast aside some of the trappings of punk to bring it back into contact with the mainstream. If none of them ever attained huge success, at least all

appealed to adventurous people who don't have mohawks.

Naked Raygun (like most of the other bands mentioned) has an unabashed love for the naïve arty experimentation of Wire and the Buzzcocks. **Basement Screams** is a hodgepodge of underproduced, underconceived songs with a lot of Misfits-type paramilitary chanting; energetic and articulate but not directly compelling. **Throb Throb**'s songs are much better, its drive more urgent and John Haggerty's piercing guitar lines a sonically expansive, sharp force. Even at low volume, the album is loud. The best track, "I Don't Know," is a grippingly melodic art-punk anthem that turns on singer/plumber Jeff Pezzati's anti-idol wail, "What poor gods we do make." A potent, impressive album.

All Rise keeps up the all-out assault level, with dynamic co-production by Iain Burgess making the guitars roar with speaker-shredding distortion. Pezzati's subtly vindictive lyrics (e.g., "Mr. Gridlock" and "The Strip") voice their critiques in an oblique, ironic fashion generally outside the capabilities of punk auteurs. **All Rise** may be a bit short on melodies (something hinted at in "Knock Me Down"), but Raygun is obviously getting better all the time.

Raygun continue to achieve excellence on their third LP, **Jettison**. Quite different from previous releases, the music's considerably slower speed (only the most notable change) gives almost breathtaking impact to the already forceful sound. "Hammer Head," "Soldier's Requiem," "When the Walls Come Down" and the utterly brilliant "Walk in Cold" are staggering in their intensity. The CD adds four songs: three live cuts and "Vanilla Blue," originally issued as a single.

Understand? finds the band at peak power, delivering its best collection of songs to date. Continuing a trend begun on **Jettison**, all four members contribute more or less equally to the songwriting, resulting in a compelling array of martial chants and supercharged rockers. With one exception (the overtly geopolitical "Hips Swingin' "), the lyrics all stick to the theme of personal politics as filtered through macho adventure comics.

John Haggerty then left to form Pegboy, creating a void in the band which new guitarist Bill Stephens doesn't adequately fill on **Raygun . . . Naked Raygun**. A disappointing album full of pretentious cyberpunk lyrics and half-baked ideas (isn't it a little late for skateboard songs?), some cuts add insult to injury with muddy, almost demo-quality production. Stephens lacks the chops to step into Haggerty's combat boots, but he is the author of the disc's best song, "The Promise," an aggressive shot of melodic punk that does the band's class of '77 forebears proud. Though hardly a total disaster, **Raygun** is a definite misstep from a band that has done much better.

As for Haggerty's new endeavor, Raygun's loss is Pegboy's gain. On the introductory 12-inch, Haggerty, his drummer brother Joe and a couple of ex-Bhopal Stiffs race through four blistering doses of melodic punk reminiscent of, well, Naked Raygun and Bhopal Stiffs. A nice job, but the gooey, introspective lyrics could use some work.   [jl/ag/db]

NAPALM DEATH

Scum (nr/Earache) 1987 ●
From Enslavement to Obliteration (nr/Earache) 1988 ●
The Peel Sessions EP (nr/Strange Fruit) 1989 ●
Napalm Death EP (nr/Rise Above) 1989
Mentally Murdered EP (nr/Earache) 1989 ●
Harmony Corruption (Earache-Combat) 1990 ●
The Peel Sessions (Strange Fruit-Dutch East India) 1991 φ
Mass-Appeal Madness EP (Earache-Combat) 1991 ●

NAPALM DEATH/S.O.B.

EP (Jap. Sound of Burial) 1989

PAINKILLER

The Guts of a Virgin (Earache-Combat) 1991 ●

Just as they missed the boat with rap, the champions of "alternative" music refused to acknowledge a new alternative several years later when it arose from the English hinterlands in the form of grindcore, a virulent mutation of the most extreme elements of hardcore, metal and industrial. This blurred sonic cesspool just might be the death of traditional music: in its purest form, grind's 5-to-50-second blasts of time-defying beats, hyper-distorted guitars and unintelligible growls and shrieks contain no verses, choruses or anything nice at all, just exploding bites of encapsulated hate and rage.

Formed around 1981, vaguely in line with the British hardcore and Crass-related tribes, Napalm Death made its vinyl debut on the third **Bullshit Detector** sampler. Crass' influence is clear in both **Scum**'s structureless metal-core blur and its cover art. Although the album's 28 tracks were recorded in two sessions eight months apart (with different lineups, to boot: guitarist Justin Broadrick left after the first to form Head of David and, later, Godflesh; he was replaced by Bill Steer of Carcass), the songs are indistinguishable to all but the most carefully attuned ears; Lee Dorrian's larynx-shredding nightmares of a contaminated world explode on impact with the sonic holocaust. Several tracks are under five seconds; "You Suffer (But Why?)" actually reaches the one-second mark.

Grindcore quickly outgrew its "extreme hardcore" parentage in virtually every category except intelligibility. **From Enslavement to Obliteration** lengthens the songs but maintains a superhuman intensity level, with a distinct early-Swans influence adding an even more sadistic twist. The scathing lyrics attack a mind-boggling array of topics. ("Cock Rock Alienation" quotes Rudimentary Peni and contains the priceless lines, "Who cares if they've got no brains/Give us tits and tools/We love it when you feed us shit.") First pressings came with a five-song bonus EP; **Scum** and four from the EP are included on the 54-track **From Enslavement** CD.

Enslavement rallied the likeminded bands that had

arisen in England, Europe and Japan into a full-fledged international grind movement. John Zorn championed the band Stateside, forming a Napalm-ish "jazzcore" outfit called Naked City with Boredoms vocalist Yamatsuko Eye. (Zorn and Napalm drummer Mick Harris later recorded the Painkiller album, **The Guts of a Virgin**, with Bill Laswell.)

The **Mentally Murdered** EP presents a more articulate (yet no less savage) sound, its advanced and better-structured songs suggesting a promising new direction, putting a thrash metal tinge where its predecessor's industrial accent had been. **Napalm Death** is a hopelessly rare 7-inch recorded live on the band's European tour in November '88; the apparently titleless Japanese EP offers six rough but otherwise unissued tracks plus a half-dozen cuts by a local outfit. Cut in '87 and '88, **The Peel Sessions** crams a total of 26 songs (including several rarities) into a mind-melting 21 minutes: an awesomely brutal listening experience.

In mid-'89, vocalist Lee Dorrian and guitarist Bill Steer left. Dorrian went on to form Cathedral, positively the slowest, lowest-tuned band ever; Steer opted to concentrate fulltime on Carcass. Napalm Death's remaining half quickly recruited vocalist Barney Greenway (ex-Benediction) and two new guitarists, thrash metalers who helped remake Napalm in their own style: first-class, but no longer innovative. **Harmony Corruption** concentrates the metallic elements of **Mentally Murdered**; lightning-fast drums, buzzsaw riffs and Greenway's wolfman vocals push the band firmly into Slayer territory. Initial British vinyl copies came with a live LP that includes an awesome cover of Godflesh's "Avalanche Master Song." The British CD adds a bonus studio cut and the entire **Mentally Murdered** EP (also available on its own CD); the American CD only includes the studio track, "Hiding Behind."

Mass-Appeal Madness, a raw-in-the-studio rapid-fire romp through two new cuts and new versions of two older songs, finds the band in much looser form than on **Harmony Corruption** and promisingly suggests a return to their trademark sound, high-pitched screams and all. The American edition adds two non-LP tracks of **Harmony Corruption** vintage, as well as the **Mentally Murdered** EP.   [ja]

See also *Carcass, Godflesh, Head of David.*

NAZ NOMAD & THE NIGHTMARES

See *Damned.*

NEATS

The monkey's head in the corner of the room. (Ace of Hearts) 1982
Neats (Ace of Hearts) 1983
Crash at Crush (Coyote-Twin/Tone) 1987
Blues End Blue (Coyote-Twin/Tone) 1989 ●

Boston's Neats started out playing unselfconscious nouveau folk-rock. Sidestepping nostalgia, the quartet's simple, low-key style would sound perfect in the discothèque scene of some '60s Sunset Strip teen-scene movie, but there is also something clearly modern in the straightforward guitar/bass/drums blend. Eric Martin's dramatic voice gives the seven tunes on the 1982 **Monkey's Head** mini-album their strength. Although the material is serviceable, none of it is striking; a really memorable number would have made this a great debut.

Neats sports an extraordinary white and black pop/op-art cover and nine new tunes, but little evidence of development other than the addition of organ (which makes them resemble a droning California paisley neo-psychedelic band). The album has good, dense sound and solidly mesmerizing, if rushed, playing, but lacks the exemplary songs (or even findable melodies) to give it shape or form.

With the lineup intact but for a new bassist, the Neats that returned to vinyl four years later were a much different proposition. Led by the song "Big Loud Sound" and a raunchy remake of "Monkey's Head," the pounding big-beat swamp-rock comes as a shock from this once modestly amplified group. Raspy guitar distortion (intentional and otherwise—shitty production adds to the fuzziness) dominates, as Martin gallantly vies for attention over Phil Caruso's thick six-string roar. While bluesy passages suggest a cross between Creedence and old Gun Club, other cuts take an aboveground rock'n'roll approach. (Throughout, Terry Hanley recalls the Cramps with mongoloid tom-tom drumming.) **Crash at Crush** doesn't quite work, but it's a promising enough experiment.

Blues End Blue (originally announced as **Dig Deeper**) refines the Neats' gonzo approach with bracing power and reasonably clear sound. Shifting between measured R&B and charging rock'n'roll (nothing too swampy this time), the Neats take standard bar-band conventions and crank them up to eleven, steering clear of California-band metalisms or mainstream rock success by keeping things raw-sounding and checking any potential bombast at the studio door. The songs aren't all strong enough to handle such rough treatment, and the relentless blare gets wearing—the piano-led power ballad, "Time Is a Lie," arrives to provide contrast a track or two late—but, in small doses, **Blues End Blue** is a blast. [i]

NECESSARIES
Big Sky (nr/Sire) 1981
Event Horizon (nr/Sire) 1982

These two albums are almost the same; the original release was withdrawn, given a partial overhaul, a new title and a relaunch. Although the band was from New York, and included ex-Modern Lover bassist Ernie Brooks, both LPs are UK-only. (Chris Spedding was a member, but had split by the time of these recordings.)

The Necessaries' high-power pop puts the best attributes of rock (crazed, distorted guitars, loud drums) to the service of melodious, intelligent songwriting. Like the early Motors or Records, the Necessaries start with catchy, solid tunes and then give 'em full electric treatment. Rough but sensitive, **Big Sky/Event Horizon** is an impressive outing from a criminally neglected band.

Brooks went on to play with numerous bands around New York; keyboardist Arthur Russell became a radically original new music cellist; singer/guitarist Ed Tomney wound up in Rage to Live; drummer Jesse Chamberlain (ex-Red Crayola) worked with Spedding and others. [i]

See also *Rage to Live*.

NECROS
Necros EP (Dischord-Touch and Go) 1981
Conquest for Death (Touch and Go) 1983
Tangled Up (Restless) 1987 ●
Live or Else (Medusa) 1989 φ

NECROS/WHITE FLAG
Jail Jello EP (Gasatanka) 1986

This Ohio punk quartet's crunching thrash metal is devastating—and not just in its speed and power, although those qualities are present in brutal abundance. The tough part about listening to the Necros is the awkward, ungainly chord sequences they drag you through. As soon as they gather a head of steam, the band dives into a deliberate tune-defeating change for the mosh section. But the harsh result keeps a fresh edge on the energy, preventing the thrash from blurring into generic noise. Although **Conquest for Death** is pigeonhole hardcore, the Necros have enough creative verve and imagination to make it exciting. (The earlier EP—nine surprisingly clear-sounding pre-hardcore punk slices on a 7-inch 45—shows a young early lineup, including Touch and Go's Corey Rusk on bass, to be starting out with a commitment to song structure and careful playing.)

Tangled Up comes wrapped in a spiffy Big Daddy Roth cover painting of Rat Fink; the Necros (only two original members remain) temper their hardcore instincts for bristling, burly guitar rock—an easily accessible and likable punk sound. There are still a few obligatory mosh parts so skins know where to change their mode of dance, but, for the most part, songs blaze straight through without a breather. Stalwart Barry Henssler sings routine lyrics in a strong and listenable voice against the answering refrains as Andy Wendler's power chords sizzle with distortion in a frenzy of well-focused energy. (Credit the band and their manager for the noteworthy production.)

The joint EP with White Flag contains three songs by each, recorded in support of Dead Kennedys leader Jello Biafra during his censorship-related legal troubles. [jl/i]

NEGATIVE TREND
See *Flipper*.

NEGATIVLAND
Negativland (Seeland) 1980
Points (Seeland) 1981
A Big 10-8 Place (Seeland) 1983
Jamcon '84 [tape] (Seeland) 1984
Escape from Noise (SST) 1987 ●
Helter Stupid (SST) 1989 ●
Pastor Dick [tape] SST 1989
The Weatherman [tape] (SST) 1989

One member of California's Negativland works in a day-care center; another writes computer programs. That pretty well sums up the group's conceptual spectrum. Negativland raids the sonic junkyards of suburban culture to create disjointed, pointedly inorganic aural sculptures that seem to start where John Cage left off. They frequently juice up the found sounds with keyboards and percussion, but that only serves to emphasize the tenuous nature of that crazy stuff we like to call pop music.

Negativland, each copy of which is uniquely and attractively packaged with a different kind of wallpaper, isn't really music and it isn't merely sound effects. Lots of different things blip by, while voices allude to subjects that one never really gets a grip on. Evocative yet very elusive.

Points adds more music to the mix. Beginning in rather a childish mood, it turns increasingly darker and more despairing, finally fading out into a monotonous industrial hum.

A **Big 10-8 Place** is a musical exploration of the band's Contra Costa County home (just over the hills from Berkeley). As much a loving tribute as a scathing indictment of suburbia's soulless façade, the record is a richly detailed, remarkably complex combination of the inorganic (electronics and industrial atmospherics) and the human (voices discuss whatever).

Escape from Noise attempts to answer a musical question—"Is there any escape from noise?"—*and* parody a perfect pop product. Amid a wide variety of sonic constructions and actual songs, you'll find "Christianity Is Stupid" (allegedly the impetus for Minnesota teenager David Brom's familicide), a little girl with hiccups singing "Over the Rainbow," and calculatedly negligible guest appearances by Jello Biafra, Jerry Garcia, the Residents, Fred Frith and Mark Mothersbaugh.

A weird practical joke involving the aforementioned murder becomes the convoluted source material for the side-long title track on **Helter Stupid**, the band's disturbing masterpiece about media manipulation.

Negativland has also released a series of cassettes culled from the band's ongoing weekly free-form radio show, *Over the Edge*. **Pastor Dick** offers absolution on a budget, while **The Weatherman** tries to drag listeners out of their closets. Innovative and loose—the way radio oughta be. [rg]

NEGAZIONE
... Lo Spiritio Continua ... (Mordam) 1986

You want to hear hardcore blurted in Italian by a singer named Zazzo? This quartet from Turin has the crashing sound of high-speed American punk down cold, and lyrics like "Non sprecare parole e sorrisi per me/Io conosco giá la fine del libro" (which, judging by the English translation provided, are surprisingly articulate for the genre). Hey, it works for opera . . . [i]

LES NEGRESSES VERTES
Mlah (Sire-Warner Bros.) 1989 ●

Impossible to categorize (forget that Gallic Pogues nonsense), this bizarre eight-man group indulges the typically French fascination for exoticism without giving up any native ground. The instrumentation on **Mlah**—mostly acoustic guitars, accordion, horns, Spanish-and-African flavored percussion—is in the tradition of Parisian buskers, but the sound isn't. Heady,

invigorating and often dark, it's perfect existentialist-basement-café music for the more worldbeat minded; while some of the songs tend to be arch, others (like "Orane") evoke wonderful, one-of-a-kind moods and images. [gk]

NEIGHBORHOODS
Fire Is Coming (Mustang) 1984
... the high hard one ... (Restless) 1986
Reptile Men (Emergo) 1987
Hoodwinked (Emergo) 1990 ●
The Neighborhoods (Third Stone-Atlantic) 1991 φ

This veteran Boston trio's appeal is immediate: they sound good. Nothing fancy or intricate, just good tunes, good vocals, good rock'n'roll drive and feel. Leader David Minehan (guitars, singing, songs) ain't exactly a lyrical Einstein, but he's no stoop either.

The group started out playing strong power pop (a 1980 single, "Prettiest Girl," remains a local classic) in the wake of British neo-mods. The eight-song **Fire Is Coming** is a get-your-feet-wet proposition, relative to the albums; a likable pointer to the future. The production is a bit thin, but you can tell what the horns on the very first track (ambitious idea) were meant to sound like. The cover of "If I Had a Hammer" was a great idea, enthusiastically (if unimaginatively) executed.

The first two full-length LPs show maturation; both are full of instantly memorable tunes, though the earlier outing still has some sincere but clichéd lyrics. The production on **high hard one** is plain but crisp; **Reptile Men**'s sound is fuller and punchier. The Who influence (the EP's horns were a hint) is more early Who on **hard one**, middle Who on **Reptile Men** (the silly part is the use of "Tommy" and "Pure and Easy" as song titles, but the rest reflects an unslavish **Who's Next** influence). Solid rock'n'roll.

The trio virtually goes arena-rock on **Hoodwinked** (later revised and reissued as **The Neighborhoods**), co-produced by Aerosmith guitarist Brad Whitford. But the 'Hoods avoid the posturing and overstatement that normally goes with the territory, and the songs are consistently decent. (Notable exceptions: Minehan's paean to Evel Knievel and a pointless rehash of Cheap Trick's "Southern Girls," minus piano and the panache.) Unfortunately, the band's identity has all but vanished into this punchy yet slick conventionality. [jg]

BILL NELSON
Northern Dream (nr/Smile) 1971 (nr/Butt) 1981
Quit Dreaming and Get on the Beam (nr/Mercury) 1981 (nr/Cocteau) 1985 (Cocteau-Enigma) 1989 ●
Sounding the Ritual Echo (nr/Mercury) 1981 (nr/Cocteau) 1985 (Cocteau-Enigma) 1989 ●
Das Kabinett (The Cabinet of Dr. Caligari) (nr/Cocteau) 1981 ●
The Love That Whirls (Diary of a Thinking Heart) (PVC) 1982 (Cocteau-Enigma) 1989 ●
La Belle et la Bête (PVC) 1982
Flaming Desire and Other Passions EP (PVC) 1982
Chimera EP (nr/Mercury) 1983 (nr/Cocteau) 1987 ●
Savage Gestures for Charms Sake (nr/Cocteau) 1983 (Cocteau-Enigma) 1989 ●
Vistamix (Portrait) 1984 [CD] (Epic) 1991 ●

Trial by Intimacy (The Book of Splendours) (nr/Cocteau) 1984

A Catalogue of Obsessions (nr/Cocteau) 1984 (Cocteau-Enigma) 1989 ●

The Summer of God's Piano (nr/Cocteau) 1984 (Cocteau-Enigma) 1989 ●

2fold Aspect of Everything (nr/Cocteau) 1984 (Cocteau-Enigma) 1989 ●

Das Kabinett/La Belle et la Bête (nr/Cocteau) 1985 (Cocteau-Enigma) 1989 ф

Getting the Holy Ghost Across (nr/Portrait) 1986 ●

On a Blue Wing (Portrait) 1986

Chamber of Dreams (nr/Cocteau) 1986 (Cocteau-Enigma) 1989 ●

Map of Dreams (nr/Cocteau) 1987 (Cocteau-Enigma) 1989 ●

Chance Encounters in the Garden of Lights (nr/Cocteau) 1987 (Cocteau-Enigma) 1988 ●

Life in Your Hands EP (nr/Cocteau) 1988 ●

The Strangest Things Sampler (Cocteau-Enigma) 1989 ф

Pavillions of the Heart and Soul (Cocteau-Enigma) 1989 ф

Simplex (Cocteau-Enigma) 1989 ●

Duplex (nr/Cocteau) 1989 ●

Demonstrations of Affection (nr/Cocteau) 1989 ф

Luminous (nr/Imaginary) 1991 ●

BILL NELSON'S RED NOISE

Sound-on-Sound (Harvest) 1979 (Cocteau-Enigma) 1985 ●

Revolt into Style EP (nr/Cocteau) 1983

BILL NELSON'S ORCHESTRA ARCANA

Iconography (nr/Cocteau) 1986 (Cocteau-Enigma) 1989 ●

Optimism (Cocteau-Enigma) 1988 ●

From hippie folk singer to awesome rock guitarist to high-tech art-adventurer to unstoppable instrumental noodler, Bill Nelson's musical career, now spanning two decades, has consistently shown style, character and exemplary attention to quality—as well as unrestrained indulgent excess. Beginning with a homemade solo album released by a local Yorkshire record store through a six-album stint leading the hard-rocking but intelligent Be-Bop Deluxe then the short-lived experimental Red Noise and finally as a wholly independent solo act (again), Nelson has made lots of brilliant music, and has also worked with some of the most interesting purveyors of modern sounds, producing and playing on numerous records.

Northern Dream is a lovely amateur work, mixing some electric lead guitar with a melodic folk sense— sort of early Neil Young with an English accent. Very impressive, given the circumstances, and not without genuine merit. **Northern Dream** led to the glam-inflected Be-Bop Deluxe and a major-label contract; that band succumbed to audience expectations and business problems, becoming an unfortunate symbol of guitar showboating and retarded creative development.

Nelson launched Red Noise after the dissolution of Be-Bop, which had forced him into the confining role of guitar pyrotechnician. Retaining Be-Bop's keyboard player but outlawing guitar solos, Nelson attacked the future with gusto, drawing together lyrical modernism and subtly infiltrated synthetic sounds. Only the songs

are the weak link—despite good ideas, some are half-formed and not up to his usual standards. **Sound-on-Sound** has its moments, but is essentially a work in progress.

Also in progress during Red Noise's brief existence was Nelson's solo work. Although not issued until 1981, **Quit Dreaming and Get on the Beam** was recorded, piecemeal, at various times and places in early 1979. Unaccompanied save for his brother Ian on sax (and all of Red Noise on one cut), Nelson relieved the selfconsciousness of Red Noise's technocracy with more varied subjects and styles. There are more keyboards, but his avoidance of guitar is less forced, and there's even an old-fashioned solo on one number. Although a little disjointed, **Quit Dreaming** is a mature record of real substance and style. Included in the first ten thousand copies was a bonus LP, **Sounding the Ritual Echo (Atmospheres for Dreaming)**, which consists of synthesizer/tape instrumental fragments; interesting if unfocused. The fifteen pieces sound like audio sketches for later works.

Das Kabinett (The Cabinet of Doctor Caligari) was written and recorded as the score for a stage presentation by the Yorkshire Actors Company. Released on Nelson's own label, the record consists of eighteen instrumental pieces, each designed to accompany a particular scene in the story. Although musically stunning, it's a hard concept for rock fans used to song structure (and words) to grasp.

The Love That Whirls—which also included a bonus record, **La Belle et la Bête (Beauty and the Beast)**, the score for another dramatic production by the same company—was Nelson's finest work to that point. Preponderantly synthesized and showcasing great songs, it finds him dabbling in a variety of styles—Oriental, techno-pop, dance rock, artsy—all with confidence and success. His most accessible work outside of Be-Bop, it was Nelson's long-overdue breakthrough, opening many eyes and ears to his talents. (**Das Kabinett** and **La Belle et la Bête** were reissued in 1985 as a double-album set and in '89 as a single CD or cassette.)

The 12-inch **Flaming Desire** EP consists of an extended version of the title song (an LP track) and five leftovers from the **Love That Whirls** sessions, some also available on UK 45s.

Chimera is an important release, documenting Nelson's acknowledged influence by Japan's Yellow Magic Orchestra, most notably drummer Yukihiro Takahashi, who plays on four of the six tracks. Also joining the previously hermetic artist is (the group) Japan's bassist, Mick Karn, and others, invigorating dynamic tracks like "Acceleration" and "Glow World." Again playing a lot of guitar, Nelson is in fine form, singing better than ever and writing strong, fascinating songs in a number of different modes. (All of **Chimera** wound up on the American **Vistamix**, joined by four prior creations, including "Flaming Desire" and "Empire of the Senses.")

Nelson's next major new album was **Getting the Holy Ghost Across** (revised, resequenced and issued in the US as **On a Blue Wing**), ten fully produced numbers ranging in length from under one minute to nearly nine. The sound is vintage Nelson—percolating rhythms, layered synths and guitars, Iain Denby's prominent bass, passionately cool vocals—and the songs are warmly accessible, with tasteful lyrics and likable melodies; the wiggly synths and hornwork on "Heart and Soul" even forge a faint link to funk. Nelson's songwriting no longer explores new ground, but he continues to mine the same field with success. Perhaps to mark the time since Be-Bop, "The Hidden Flame" throws a fiery guitar solo amid the keyboards.

Savage Gestures for Charms Sake is a lovely but unessential collection of one-man studio instrumentals. The sumptuously packaged **Trial by Intimacy** is a boxed set containing four individually titled records (**The Summer of God's Piano**, also released on its own, **A Catalogue of Obsessions, Pavillions of the Heart and Soul, Chamber of Dreams**), all previously unreleased solo instrumentals: ambient pieces, improvisations, experiments, incidental mood music and odds and ends. Over time, all four of the albums saw individual release, at least on tape and compact disc.

The **2fold Aspect of Everything** is a two-disc (**Eaux d'Artifice** and **Confessions of a Four-Track Mind**) compilation of obscurities: B-sides, remixes, demos and other non-LP matter.

Although Orchestra Arcana is still a strictly one-man Nelson project, the specific idea is to weave doodly instrumentals around found-sound spoken-word matter (or vice versa). **Iconography** and the dance-beat **Optimism** are both fine in their way, but their existence suggests that Bill's been spending too much time watching old movies on the tube.

Created as the soundtrack for a 1987 British television series (talk about finding the right man for a job!), **Map of Dreams** is a collection of cogent pieces that mix ambience and rhythm into nicely affecting soundscapes that are vaguely scientific in tone.

Nelson made another monumental addition to his canon in 1988 with **Chance Encounters in the Garden of Lights**, a huge set of meditative instrumentals on two discs, **The Book of Inward Conversation** and **The Angel at the Western Window**: 41 short pieces in all. You want more? Get the cassette (49 selections) or the jumbo double CD (63 items!).

The deluge continues. For a modest review of Nelson's activities since 1979, **The Strangest Things** dips into the solo records, Red Noise and Orchestra Arcana. Something of a best-of package, **Duplex** contains one disc of vocal recordings (things like "Acceleration," "Do You Dream in Colour," "Contemplation," etc.) and a platter of instrumentals that includes a few previously unreleased items. **Demonstrations of Affection** is a box containing four CDs and a T-shirt.   [i]

See also *A Flock of Seagulls, Ippu-Do, Skids, Yukihiro Takahashi*.

NENA

Nena (Ger. CBS) 1983
? (Fragezeichen) (Ger. CBS) 1984 ●
99 Luftballons (Epic) 1984 ●
It's All in the Game (Epic) 1985

STRIPES

The Stripes (Ger. CBS) 1980

German pop sensation Nena hit it big internationally in 1984 with the nuclear protest of "99 Luftballons." Boasting the attractive voice of Gabriela "Nena"

Kerner and a jolly modern sound, the Berlin group's catchy songs tend towards bubblegum simplicity, but are undeniably engaging, whether sung in English or German. **Nena**, the band's monolingual homeland debut, contains "99 Luftballons" as well as the equally wonderful "Nur Geträumt" and "Leuchtturm" ("Lighthouse"), all melodic and bouncy hits that mix rock strength with pure pop arrangements. However, the record is inconsistent, and has a lot of draggy songs that don't make any lasting impression.

While it still presents a few sprightly pop delights ("Rette Mich," the Abba-esque "Küss Mich Wach"), Nena's second album (whose parenthetical title means, reasonably enough, **Question Mark**) moves the band closer to universal easy-listening mush and sub-Blondie demi-disco. (David Sanborn blows some treacly sax on two songs; the pseudo-Africanisms of "Das Land der Elefanten" make Toto's efforts in this department seem almost credible.)

The band's first Anglo-American release, **99 Luftballons**, was stitched together half-and-half from the two German LPs. **Nena** provided "99 Red Balloons" (as well as the German-language original), "Leuchtturm," "Kino" (a song about the movies) and "Nur Geträumt," smoothly converted into "Just a Dream." The second album contributed "Rette Mich," "? (Fragezeichen)," "Das Land der Elefanten," "Unerkannt Durchs Märchenland," "Ich Häng' an Dir" and "Lass Mich Dein Pirat Sein," the last two translated into English as "Hangin' on You" and "Let Me Be Your Pirate."

Although no serious stylistic changes were made in the interim, **It's All in the Game** (sung entirely in English, translated by Canada's Lisa Dalbello, who also does backing vocals on the record) is fairly irrelevant, lacking any great songs that would enliven this forgettable collection. Sanborn makes another guest appearance; the record's general resemblance to mid-period Abba—five years after the fact—may explain why it was Nena's last. (Not for nothing is the final song is entitled "Auf Wiedersehen.")

Kerner's pre-Nena band, Stripes, played post-Blondie rock of the most rudimentary variety. **The Stripes** tells virtually the same joke thirteen times with only minor variations—notwithstanding the two American-written tunes, one by Hall and Oates, no less.   [i/jg]

NEON JUDGEMENT

1981–1984 (Hol. Scarface) 1985
MBIH! EP (Bel. Anything But) 1985
Mafu Cage (Bel. Play It Again Sam) 1986 ●
First Judgements (Bel. Play It Again Sam) 1987 ●
Horny as Hell (Play It Again Sam) 1987 ●
General Pain & Major Disease (Play It Again Sam) 1989 ●
Blood & Thunder (Play It Again Sam) 1989 ●
The Insult (Bel. Play It Again Sam) 1990

Another beneficiary of the Brussels-to-Chicago pipeline, this durable Belgian electro/industro band made its trans-Atlantic debut with **Horny as Hell**, a mechanical-sounding drone of cold rhythms, warm keyboards, barbed guitars and chanted English vocals. Although sex—overeager rather than crude—runs through the entire album, the unappealing music is strictly geared for robot nookie.

General Pain & Major Disease, a refresher course in early Neon Judgement, compiles singles from the very beginning (the live "Factory Walk") up through the present (a 12-inch version of **Horny as Hell**'s "Miss Brown"). The non-chronological retrospective reveals Neon Judgement as having begun as an aseptically rhythmatized electro-thud product of British new wave synthesists—from the grim Joy Division school and the dopey Gary Numan pop-hook division. While later tracks introduce noise effects and more accomplished instrumentation, the band's unadventurous essence has remained pretty consistent.

The trio brings ambitious new elements (like chipmunky disco vocals and a harmonica player!) into play on **Blood & Thunder**, but the metronomic music is too monotonous for the effort to make any significant difference. Clear, occasionally interesting English lyrics are a help, but the numbness of songs built on one note and an unvarying tempo is just too big an obstacle to overcome with irrelevant window dressing.   [i]

NERVES
Nerves EP (Nerves) 1976
The Nerves (Fr. Offence) 1986
JACK LEE
Jack Lee's Greatest Hits Vol. 1 (Maiden America) 1981

The Nerves were seminal new wave power-popsters, a fertile California trio of drummer Paul Collins, bassist Peter Case and guitarist Jack Lee. All three sang and wrote cool songs, recycling '60s AM radio fare with the awareness, energy and excitement of the punk underground's earliest stirrings. Lee turned out concise and catchy heartbreak tunes like "Hanging on the Telephone"; Case leaned to garagey merseybeat rockers like "When You Find Out"; Collins split the difference, penning ambitious melodic rockers like "Working Too Hard." All three of those songs appeared on the self-released 7-inch EP, and again on the musically impressive retrospective, an affordable and convenient compilation of the Nerves' hopelessly rare records.

Going their own ways in '78, Collins formed the Beat (and promptly re-recorded "Working Too Hard") and Case launched the Plimsouls. That left Lee to bask alone in the glory and riches of Blondie's (British) hit with his "Hanging on the Telephone." A few years later, in the hopes of parlaying that big score into a solid songwriting career, Lee released a musical résumé of his best work, including four Nerves-era numbers. (Those early tunes are, for the most part, better than the later efforts showcased here.) Case, Collins, the Rubber City Rebels (who had recorded a great cover of his "Paper Dolls") and others provide rocking instrumental and vocal support, but Lee never again reached the big-time. Don't wait up for **Vol. 2**.   [i]

See also *Beat, Peter Case, Plimsouls*.

NEUROTICS
See *Newtown Neurotics*.

NEW AGE STEPPERS
New Age Steppers (nr/On-U Sound) 1980 (nr/Statik) 1982
Action Battlefield (nr/On-U Sound-Statik) 1981
Crucial 90 [tape] (nr/Statik) 1981
Threat to Creation (nr/Cherry Red) 1981
Foundation Steppers (nr/On-U Sound) 1983
Victory Horns (nr/On-U Sound) 1983
DUB SYNDICATE
One Way System [tape] (ROIR) 1983
Tunes from the Missing Channel (On-U Sound) 1985
Pounding System (On-U Sound) 1988
Classic Selection Vol. 1 [CD] (On-U Sound) 1989 ●
Strike the Balance (nr/On-U Sound) 1990 ●

British producer Adrian Sherwood is the only constant in the New Age Steppers, an ever-changing jam session that has included members of the Slits, Public Image, Rip Rig + Panic, Raincoats and the Pop Group. The records are a wild melting pot of synthesized post-rock and reggae, transmuted through dub studio techniques. In practical terms, that amounts to variations on a theme or, more accurately, a rhythm. Everything is built on top of a slow, steady reggae pulse, but what's heaped on varies from electronic no wave noise to pretty, melodic singing. It's weird, but occasionally very nice, and consistently unpredictable.

New Age Steppers varies widely, from entrancing to repulsive, with lots of synthesizer babble and overlong dub mixes. A few of the songs stand out, but it's an effect they're reaching for, not hit singles, so you take the whole package, not bits and pieces. Intriguing, if not entirely successful.

Action Battlefield (repackaged, along with the first LP, on the cassette-only **Crucial 90**) is much better—more organized and song-oriented. Ari of the Slits sings lead on all the tracks; her voice, while not exactly pleasant, adds a comforting personality and continuity. Not as weird or chaotic as its predecessor, **Action Battlefield** is strange but appealing.

Which is not true of **Threat to Creation**, recorded jointly with reggae band Creation Rebel. The LP has almost no vocals, little structure and no discernible direction. When it doesn't consist of understated meanderings, it's self-indulgent art-noise that could please only the most indiscriminate fan. Keith Levine [sic] performs half of the guitar chores.

Between that chapter of his career and the widespread launch of the more generally known Tackhead, Sherwood ran/produced the loosely constituted Dub Syndicate. The ad hoc cast on the **One Way System** compilation cassette includes members of Aswad, Roots Radics and Creation Rebel; the languid, instrumental reggae is more repetitive and unnaturally elongated than invigorating. **Tunes from the Missing Channel**, released on Sherwood's own On-U Sound label, has Levene and others providing fodder for his wild studio assemblies.   [i]

See also *Tackhead*.

NEW CHRISTS
Detritus EP (What Goes On) 1987
Divine Rites (Aus. Citadel) 1988
Distemper (Aus. Citadel) 1989 ●

ROB YOUNGER AND THE RIFLES

Rob and the Rifles EP (Ger. Compassion Explosion!) 1989

Rob Younger, who cut his teeth in Australia's seminal pre-Pistols punk combo Radio Birdman, is probably more responsible than anyone (aside, perhaps, from Iggy himself) for promulgating the aggro-heavy Stoogian feel that imbues so many Down Underground bands. With his Sydney-based New Christs, Younger has continued to serve notice as to who, exactly, are the punks and who is the godfather.

Detritus culls four tracks from the band's second and third singles. (The first, a 1981 threat entitled "Face a New God," remains uncompiled.) Considering the lack of lineup consistency (no fewer than three axemen—Screaming Tribesman Chris Mazuak [*sic*], Celibate Rifle Kent Steedman and Lime Spider Richard Jakimyszyn—take turns cranking it to eleven), there's a magnificently undiluted attitude in both the Dee-troit non-stops ("No Next Time," "Sun God") and the less mannered brooders ("Born Out of Time"). **Divine Rites**, also assembled from 7-inch tracks, boasts a solidified cast, including the underrated ex-Barracudas bassist Jim Dickson, and an exponentially less derivative palette. While there are some lighter moments (the mutant surf ditty "You'll Never Catch My Wave" isn't all that far from the Hoodoo Gurus), Younger's developing a bitter, morbid vision not unlike **Fear**-era John Cale. The triad of "Dropping Like Flies," "Addiction" and "Dead Girl" makes for a particularly harrowing close.

The sudden mid-screech start of "No Way on Earth" sets the dark, brooding tone for **Distemper**, and the apocalyptic tone carries through the crashing "There's No Time," the piano-drizzled "Burning of Rome" and the discordant fairground wheeze "Circus of Sour"—making the disc nothing short of a 40-minute call to emotional jihad.

Recorded live in Germany, the four-song **Rob and the Rifles** EP sees both Younger and the (Celibate) Rifles in peak form, with Steedman wrenching some lovingly crazed leads from the bones of such chestnuts as "She's So Fine" and "Shakin' All Over." The fi is surprisingly hi, considering the dubious origins; Younger's limber yowl is far looser than the studio environment had previously allowed. Rockin'! [dss]

See also *Celibate Rifles, Radio Birdman.*

NEW DUNCAN IMPERIALS

See *Service.*

NEW FAST AUTOMATIC DAFFODILS

Pigeonhole (nr/Play It Again Sam) 1990 (Mute) 1991 ●

From Manchester, with attitude: the New FADs' percussionable dance-groove songs may share little with that city's retro-pop ravers (the quartet owes more to Manchester's late-'70s funk scene), but willful insufferability (a 1989 12-inch was entitled **Music Is Shit**; the band's lyrics are pretentious nonsense) makes them just as big a pain in the ass. Waffling between serious old-fashioned bass-driven dance rock (à la Konk or Liquid Liquid) diminished by lousy sub-John Cale vocals and meandering bits that could charitably be explained as experiments, **Pigeonhole** squanders the FADs' solid and effective rhythmic drive on a hill of arty beans. [i]

COLIN NEWMAN

A-Z (nr/Beggars Banquet) 1980 ●
provisionally entitled the singing fish (nr/4AD) 1981 ●
Not to (nr/4AD) 1982 ●
Commercial Suicide (Crammed Discs-Enigma) 1986 ●
It Seems (Crammed Discs-Restless) 1988 ●

A-Z was actually meant to be Wire's fourth album, but the band's record company didn't see it that way. So it became a Newman solo LP, demonstrating that he was indeed the prime creative force in the group, but also suggesting that perhaps ex-partners Lewis and Gilbert might have stemmed the excesses of producer Mike Thorne, who (as he'd done with Wire) both runs the console and adds keyboards. On **A-Z**, he helps create spacious, sensuous soundscapes, but often overcrowds them with keyboards. Newman delivers his oblique lyrics with a strangely detached urgency; the overall effect at times suggests being drugged and locked in a room with an inquisitor shouting senseless questions. **A-Z**'s triumph is that it shows how even simple pop-rock devices can be rearranged and/or modified to devastating effect. (The CD adds five tracks.)

Newman experiments on **the singing fish** by building up textures and melodies with an interesting assortment of instruments (all played and produced by him) in a dozen different ways ("Fish 1," etc.). It isn't the tuneless or monotonous "art" you'd expect from this sort of no-vocals venture either—it's thinking man's muzak which, unlike ambient Eno-isms, doesn't dissipate before your ears upon careful attention. Newman is at once more clinical *and* more playful than ever before.

Not to is a return to the instrumental format of **A-Z**, with a significant change: Thorne is absent. Wire drummer Robert Gotobed and Desmond Simmons remain (with Simmons' guitar/arranging role expanding) and Simon Gillham picks up the bass, giving it an identity of its own. Wire and **A-Z** leftovers are interspersed between newer songs, and the feeling suggests what post-**Pink Flag** Wire might have been without Thorne: minimalist threads rather than sheets of sound; thorny, sometimes atonal, dissonant and rhythmically disjointed, but somehow more personally engaging. Newman himself seems vulnerable—bitter, wistful, showing less lyrical self-assurance, like Ray Davies' art-rock cousin. (In 1988, UK 4AD issued a CD containing both **Not to** and **the singing fish**, adding a bonus CD single to initial quantities.)

That vulnerability is again exposed on **Commercial Suicide**. ("I'm still here, waiting for mercy," he sings.) As potent a creator as Newman is, he seems to function best with outside creative input and tension in the situation. That's ideally been provided by Lewis and Gilbert and, to lesser extents, Thorne and Simmons. Malka Spigel (Newman's wife) and Sean Bonnar of Minimal Compact individually co-wrote four of the nine tracks, which aren't quite up to snuff. It's more than worthwhile—quiet, thoughtful, delicate, artistic, melancholic, hopeful—but lacks the edge that makes Newman so effective in the reformed Wire, even on that group's dreamy **A Bell Is a Cup**.

It Seems is by the same crew, plus engineer/musician/co-producer Gilles Martin, with guest appearances by Gotobed and several horn and reed players. The fuller, more expressive arrangements and general honing of focus suggest they've gotten to know each other better, and it is a distinct improvement. Much of the LP is as conventional and "normal" (in terms of musical and lyrical structure) as Newman's ever been, and as pretty. It still could be more consistent and, although Bonnar and Spigel between them co-write half the ten tracks, the best two are by Newman alone. If you like his other work, you won't want to miss either of these recent discs. [jg]

See also *Minimal Compact, Wire*.

NEW MATH

See *Jet Black Berries*.

NEW MODEL ARMY

Vengeance (nr/Abstract) 1984
No Rest for the Wicked (Capitol) 1985 ●
Better Than Them EP (nr/EMI) 1985
The Ghost of Cain (Capitol) 1986 ●
New Model Army (Capitol) 1987
Vengeance/The Independent Story (nr/Abstract) 1987
    (JCI) 1988 φ
Radio Sessions 83–84 (nr/Abstract) 1988 ●
Thunder and Consolation (Capitol) 1989 ●
Impurity (nr/EMI) 1990 ● ⁄

A trio vigorously lauded by supporters as the new Clash, New Model Army are long on principle and maintain a fervent, unyielding political stance. Taking their primary inspiration from early punk roots (though less abrasive and more melodic), NMA breathe life into the genre, providing a most effective medium for singer/guitarist Slade the Leveller (Justin Sullivan) to deliver his charged messages. The eight angry, vehement cuts on **Vengeance** rely equally on Stuart Morrow's acrobatic bass lines and Slade's accusatory Cockney rants. Although the intensity wanes towards the end, it's an arresting debut.

Morrow left prior to the release of **No Rest for the Wicked**. Despite his presence on it, the LP lacks the determined ferocity of its predecessor. Some potentially great songs ("My Country," "Grandmother's Footsteps," "No Rest") are forceful enough to have belonged on **Vengeance**; other tracks swap enthusiasm for overindulgence and suffer as a result. "Better Than Them," a surprising acoustic foray, meanders interminably; the preachy "Shot 18" is simply ridiculous. Without appropriate musical backing, Slade's harsh protests lose their impact, leaning dangerously towards hollow sloganeering.

The **Better Than Them** EP—a double-pack 45 of the LP track plus three new items—ventures deeper into acoustic territory and shows the Army at ease in these surroundings, but sacrifices the remainder of their vitality in the process. The new songs have the heartfelt honesty that was becoming questionable on **No Rest for the Wicked**.

The Ghost of Cain presents a revitalized (remobilized?) New Model Army, due in large part to the international success of the protectionist single "51st State," which the album contains. Stabilizing as a three-piece unit has refueled the fires of the group's convictions, and this is a most welcome return to form. **New Model Army** is a stay-the-course sidestep, with three studio tracks ("White Coats" is the standout) and four live cuts ("51st State" is most notable).

Adding a palpable sense of urgency to already strong songs, **Radio Sessions '83-'84** provides energetic alternate versions of twelve NMA faves crisply captured live on the radio. **Vengeance/The Independent Story** appends eight early single sides and a pair of radio takes to the band's first LP. A must for completists, the disc puts the spotlight on Morrow's driving lead bass, which at times suggests the early Cure.

A mere decade after forming, New Model Army finally released its masterpiece, **Thunder and Consolation**. The guidance of mainstream producer Tom Dowd on a half-dozen tracks and the occasional presence of a violin have done nothing to quell the fury of these electric-folk heroes. In fact, Dowd's sumptuous touches on the epic "Green and Grey" add immeasurable drama to Slade's passionate, opaque lyricism. The songs, on the whole, are the most personal the band has ever recorded—especially the searing "Inheritance," on which Slade manages to not sound foolish chanting a bitter message to his parents over a stark drum track. The CD adds five songs, including **New Model Army**'s three studio tracks and the haunting, heartfelt "Nothing Touches."

On **Impurity**, NMA retains the previous LP's expressive fiddle, but drops its cinemascopic grandeur, returning instead to the unadorned precision and economy of earlier releases. With new bassist Peter Nelson (ex-Brotherhood of Lizards) in tow, the Army metes out a few of its more forthright football-style chants ("Lust for Power," "Get Me Out") and some gentler moments ("Space," "Marrakesh") that strike like a gruffer Billy Bragg. The guys even exhibit an admirable levelheadedness on the sharp, direct "Bury the Hatchet," which offers a neat response to the themes of retribution that made **The Ghost of Cain** too much like a vigilante's call to arms. All in all, **Impurity** exemplifies a fervent, trend-bucking band that has remained true to its original goals. [ag/db]

See also *Joolz*.

NEW MUSIK

Straight Lines EP (Epic) 1980
From A to B (nr/GTO) 1980
Anywhere (nr/GTO) 1981
Sanctuary (Epic) 1981
Warp (nr/Epic) 1982

New Musik's Tony Mansfield (writer, producer, vocalist, keyboardist, guitarist) has never been overly enamored of trendy trappings of music or image, which is why his band, never fashionable, had only minor UK hits. (As a freelance producer, however, Mansfield has had no such trouble.) Nonetheless, in attempting to recast and/or rediscover pop-rock through modern technology, New Musik helped launch the style as a commercial force in America, where its debut single, "Straight Lines"—predating Gary Numan's US hit with "Cars"—nearly crossed over from the dance clubs to the mass market as an import. (The 10-inch EP also includes its follow-up and both B-sides.)

New Musik's full but spacious sound is immediately appealing: vocals, acoustic guitars, synths and other keyboards ply melodious ditties impeccably deployed and ingeniously enhanced at the mixing console. What's most telling about this new musik is that it's sensuous but not sensual, energetic but not violent, calling up a sort of bittersweet, melancholic feeling, but never redolent of the gloom-doom syndrome. Which makes the band either a breath of fresh air or an overly polite and sterile waste of time.

Yet, surprisingly enough, the lyrics are almost all about loneliness, alienation and humanity's inability to cope with the modern world—but worded simply, and exclusively in terms of ideals (safety, identity, luxury), abstractions (lines, numbers, motion) and/or metaphors (often to do with the ocean and travel). Though hardly immortal poesy, when put in context by the music, core phrases can be most evocative.

From A to B contains three strong singles (one, "This World of Water," is brilliant) unmatched by those on **Anywhere**, but otherwise there's little difference in quality or style between the two. **Sanctuary** takes the best of both, making it a near-apotheosis of ear candy. **Warp**, however, sounds transitional: band involvement in the studio had apparently increased, adding a new rhythmic component with no effective niche. More acute (and pessimistic) lyrics are accompanied by a paucity of new melodic ideas.

Mansfield's subsequent life as a pop producer yielded hits for Naked Eyes, the B-52's, Captain Sensible and others.   [jg]

NEW ORDER
Movement (Factory) 1981 ●
1981–1982 EP (Factory) 1982
Power, Corruption and Lies (Factory) 1983 (Qwest)
   1985 ●
Low-life (Qwest) 1985 ●
Brotherhood (Qwest) 1986 ●
The Peel Sessions EP (nr/Strange Fruit) 1986 ●
Substance (Qwest) 1987 ●
The Peel Sessions EP (nr/Strange Fruit) 1987 ●
Technique (Qwest) 1989 ●
The Peel Sessions Album (nr/Strange Fruit) 1990 ●

VARIOUS ARTISTS
Salvation! (Giant) 1988 ●

REVENGE
One True Passion (Capitol) 1990 ●

ELECTRONIC
Electronic (Warner Bros.) 1991 ϕ

Following the bizarre 1980 death of Ian Curtis and the remarkable success of "Love Will Tear Us Apart," guitarist/singer Bernard Sumner and the two other remaining members of Joy Division transmuted into New Order, adding guitar/synth player Gillian Gilbert before recording **Movement**. Largely accomplishing what Joy Division set out to do, New Order has sold millions of records and earned boundless critical enthusiasm playing a heady and uncompromising mix of dreamy meanderings and unforgettable techno-dance music, taking off from that memorable swan song, alleviating some of Curtis' lyrical suffering while retaining the depth and unique musical personality he outlined.

Movement, produced by Martin Hannett, wisely sidesteps the Joy Division comparisons by downplaying the vocals and emphasizing electronics; it may lack the former band's sheer sharpness of vision, but maintains a fascination with decay and paradox, showcasing excellent guitar and synthesizer work.

The **1981–1982** EP consists of five songs taken from British 45s, and presents New Order's pop-styled work, especially the magnificent "Temptation" and "Procession." Coincidentally, New Order was already showing remarkable facility for making uncommon—but highly popular—singles, issuing a huge UK smash, "Blue Monday." (Long unavailable on album, the song was later added to the cassette version of **Power, Corruption and Lies**. In 1988, the song was newly remixed and successfully reissued on 12-inch in America.)

New Order's second album is a masterpiece, from the cryptic (but decipherable if you work hard at it) artwork to the eight lengthy tracks of state-of-the-creative-art electronic dance music. Blending moody strains of pseudo-strings with seemingly misplaced guitar bits and coldly kinetic rhythms, plus artless but engaging vocals and syncopated effects, deceptively simple tracks like "Age of Consent" and "Leave Me Alone" convey intense sensations that you can't easily shake. An emotionally and physically moving record by one of the era's most important bands. The CD adds two tracks.

Oddly enough, New Order was formally introduced to America through the auspices of Quincy Jones, whose Qwest label put out **Low-life** and reissued **Power, Corruption and Lies**. One of the finest LPs of 1985, **Low-life** starts out with an ironic folk-form ballad, "Love Vigilantes," that is utterly unlike anything the band has ever tried but scores brilliantly. "The Perfect Kiss" is very poppy, with lush synth strains and perfectly inappropriate froglike (!) sound effects. The other six tracks are almost as appealing, tentatively exploring other stylistic areas without abandoning the essence of New Order's format.

The lightheaded and seemingly half-hearted **Brotherhood** retreads the characteristic sound of **Low-life** but largely lacks the first-rate songwriting that gives purpose and significance to the proficient synthesizer/guitar musical machine. Only "Weirdo," the downcast "All Day Long" and the magnificent "Bizarre Love Triangle" intertwine the delicately rising and falling electrobeat tides with melodies that fix themselves firmly in your head; the rest shimmer with the same near-folk veneer but are just not as memorable.

Fashioning their own version of a career retrospective, the enigmatic and retiring quartet gathered six years' worth of 12-inch singles (some appearing in special new mixes) on two vinyl discs under the title **Substance**. If one needs a reminder of New Order's unique genius, this album (also available on DAT) has it all: "Blue Monday," "Perfect Kiss," "Shellshock," "Confusion," "Bizarre Love Triangle" and seven more. (The double-CD issue boasts a dozen B-sides as a bonus and extremely harsh sound as a problem.)

Along with "Touched by the Hand of God" (also on the "Blue Monday 1988" remix 12-inch), New Order contributed four instrumentals ("Salvation Theme" is quite nice) to the soundtrack album of *Salvation!*, Beth B's scathing satire about televangelism in which Exene Cervenka made her dramatic film debut.

Technique, New Order's first new album in more than two years, contains a sonic postcard from Ibiza, the Spanish island where the momentary dance-music fad known as Balearic beat flashed amid the first flowerings of acid house. While half of the songs go the crazy rhythms route (synthetic bongos pitter-patter throughout "Round & Round"; the thundering "Fine Time" throws electronic sheep into the mix; with blips and percussive blasts, the powerful "Mr. Disco" hammers a beat into a dreamy song), other numbers mine the group's pop side. In "All the Way," Sumner encourages self-reliance over a tart blend of acoustic guitars and Peter Hook's thrusting bass; the ripping electric leads and martial drumming that cut through "Run" leave the summery tune sounding like Donovan fronting the Jesus and Mary Chain. Adding new ingredients to a familiar recipe makes **Technique** most effective. (Also available on DAT.)

New Order then retreated into solo projects. Sumner and guitarist Johnny Marr, initially in collaboration with Pet Shop Boy Neil Tennant, formed Electronic, issuing a single in 1990 and an album in mid-'91. **Electronic** is a strange melding of styles, an entertaining electro-pop dance record with guitar, blipping sequencers and a strong Tennant vocal/keyboards influence. (He sings two cuts.) With Marr's creative role not strikingly evident, Electronic sounds like New Order—complete with Sumner's distinctive voice and rhythmic patterns—on holiday in a parallel universe controlled by the Pet Shop Boys.

For his part, Hook assembled a trio called Revenge and whipped out the wretched **One True Passion**. (The title apparently refers to buxom leather-clad women.) Restyling New Order's formula with a thicker, warmer sound and second-rate vocals, the oversexed Revenge could almost be a tribute band, if not an especially good one. New Order's flimsy lyrics are one thing, but Hook's macho black leather bluster is aggressively dumb. "Kiss the chrome/Why am I alone?" Gee, I can't imagine.

New Order's first **Peel Sessions** 12-inch (the initial release in the UK series) was recorded in June 1982 and contains four songs; the second hails from January 1981. Both are combined on the 1990 LP.   [sg/i]

See also *Paul Haig, Joy Division*.

NEW ORDER
The New Order (Fr. Isadora) 1977
NEW RACE
The First and the Last (nr/Statik) 1983 •
DESTROY ALL MONSTERS/ SONIC'S RENDEZVOUS BAND
Ron Asheton/Sonic's Rendezvous Band (Fr. Revenge) 1987

Early American punk fanzines had little to write about, which is probably why New Order (the first/ American one) got a lot of press. But just because the group featured Ron Asheton (ex-Stooges guitarist), Scott Thurston (ex-Stooges keyboardist and future Motel) and Dennis Thompson (ex-MC5 drummer) didn't mean its music had to be worthwhile. **The New Order** is full of misplaced guitar breaks, heavy metal sludge and little or no passion. Some things look great on paper, but on vinyl this one stinks.

New Race, a 1981 one-Australian-tour aggregate of Asheton, Thompson and three former members of seminal Sydney punk band Radio Birdman (including guitarist Deniz Tek—who grew up in Ann Arbor, Michigan—and singer Rob Younger), fares a lot better on **The First and the Last**, an album recorded live and then improved in the studio by an added guitarist on two numbers and a backing vocalist on three. Production, sound and playing are all real good (except for the intros and the applause, you may not think it's a concert album at all) and the energy level is impressive. The material includes the MC5's "Looking at You" (given a blistering seven-minutes-plus raveup), several Birdman tracks and one (ugh!) topical number, "November 22, 1963," written by Asheton and Niagara, his singing bandmate in Destroy All Monsters. **The First and the Last**, while not an essential historic document, remains a powerfully charged rock'n'roll album with some searing moments.

The joint album melds four songs originally issued by Ron Asheton's band, Destroy All Monsters, on singles around 1978-9 with a side of ex-MC5er Fred Sonic Smith's band, which includes ex-Stooge drummer Scott Asheton.   [cpl/i]

See also *MC5, Radio Birdman, Sonic's Rendezvous Band, Stooges*.

NEWS FROM BABEL
See *Henry Cow*.

NEWTOWN NEUROTICS
Beggars Can Be Choosers (nr/Razor) 1983
NEUROTICS
Repercussions (nr/Jungle) 1986
Is Your Washroom Breeding Bolsheviks (nr/Jungle) 1988
Never Thought EP (nr/Jungle) 1988
45 Revolutions a Minute: Singles 1979–1984 (nr/Jungle) 1990
NEUROTICS ET AL.
Kickstarting a Backfiring Nation (nr/Jungle) 1987

The Newtown Neurotics began in the late '70s in Harlow (just north of London) as a brave trio who still thought punk could be something other than a spent force. Singer/guitarist Steve Drewett must have been inspired by early punk's willingness to discuss politics, as his socialist-flavored lyrics—never overbearing—have been grouped with those of Easterhouse, Billy Bragg, Three Johns and Housemartins.

For rockin' humdingers influenced by a synthesis of everything cool in early punk—Ramones to the Clash to mid-period Undertones—**Beggars Can Be Choosers** is a blast from the past, punk with extraordinary get-up-and-go that's both fun-sounding and sharp-edged. Drewett's social commentary is at its best, from the "sexual double standards" in "No Respect" to his version of the Members' "Solitary Confinement," redone with a clever twist as "Living with Unemployment." Punk-reggae is even handled competently on "Newtown People."

By '86, the Neurotics had dropped their Newtown and had come up with a different sound. The (mostly) moderate tempos, restrained guitar and other refinements (such as the addition of blaring Stax horns) on the engaging **Repercussions** showed the Neurotics could broaden their appeal without changing their message. "This Fragile Life" condemns the Falklands War through the story of a young woman widowed by it; "(Fanatical) Sects" takes the piss out of religious extremists. But the bulk of the record concerns the families of striking miners, to whom the LP is dedicated.

Is Your Washroom Breeding Bolsheviks continues this progress. The rock-soul-mod hybrid has advanced to a point where the Neurotics sometimes sound like a Motown group, with more wild brass and keyboards. (Ex-Member Chris Payne chips in.) "An Inch Away," a breathless number about women victimized by domestic violence, shows that Drewett can still pair sadness and hard-pop with great success; "Local News" proves they can also crank up the attack on demand.

The brilliant-sounding **Kickstarting a Backfiring Nation** was recorded live—with no overdubs—in the studio before an audience. Selections draw from the first two LPs, plus the Flamin Groovies' "Shake Some Action" redone as "Take Strike Action," again for the miners. The record also contains poetic contributions, recorded live the same evening, by Atilla the Stockbroker, the Big J, Porky the Poet and Peter Campbell. Their rants identify them as offspring of John Cooper Clarke; the subject matter is entirely commensurate with the Neurotics' and fills out this fine package. (The LP was released on a joint cassette with **Repercussions**.)

The **Never Thought** 12-inch contains five live tracks on the flipside.

The group soldiered on bravely until October '88 when bassist Colin Dredd developed pleurisy and had to quit. The Neurotics got a friend to play bass, and did a string of three-hour farewell shows, performing every song they'd ever released! **45 Revolutions a Minute: Singles 1979–1984** compiles the group's 45s (A- and B-sides), none of which had previously appeared on album. These tracks are among the band's most humorous (e.g., "Where Are You When I Need You," an ode to a disappearing penis; "Licensing Hours," a dig at Britain's pub curfew) and most angrily political ("Kick Out the Tories," "Mindless Violence," "When the Oil Runs Out"). Although one single is omitted— "Blitzkrieg Bob" (with original lyrics about bombing raids) and its two flip sides, a remake of an earlier track and another Ramones cover—**45 Revolutions** substitutes two previously unissued outtakes. An excellent collection. As the sleeve notes, "File under good pop on bad budgets."

Drewett and Mac have since formed the Unstoppable Beat, mating the Neurotics' guitar pulse with more reggae and African flavors. [jr]

NEW YORK DOLLS

New York Dolls (Mercury) 1973 ●
In Too Much Too Soon (Mercury) 1974 ●

New York Dolls (Mercury) 1977
Lipstick Killers [tape] (ROIR) 1981 [CD] (ROIR-Important) 1990 φ
Red Patent Leather (Fr. Fan Club) 1984 ●
Best of the New York Dolls (nr/Mercury) 1985
Night of the Living Dolls (Mercury) 1986
Personality Crisis EP (nr/Kamera) 1986

DAVID & SYLVAIN
Tokyo Dolls Live! (Fr. Fan Club) 1986

THE ORIGINAL PISTOLS/NEW YORK DOLLS
After the Storm (nr/Receiver) 1985 ●

The New York Dolls had the style, attitude, rawness and audacity to reinterpret the notion of punk as it had existed in the '60s and to create a decidedly '70s over-the-edge new reality prior to punk. Although they made only two proper albums and were a meaningless relic by the time the Sex Pistols played their first gig, the Dolls singlehandedly began the local New York scene that later spawned the Ramones, Blondie, Television, Talking Heads and others. A classic case of the whole being greater than the sum of its parts, the Dolls were much more than just a band. Their audiences emulated them and formed groups. Detractors' venom inspired countless teenage rebels. Their signing to a major label set an example of commercial feasibility; their subsequent failure to shift product turned the record industry anti-punk for years.

After building a reputation on seedy late-night New York stages, the Dolls' awful magnetism netted them a label contract. Todd Rundgren took the production reins, and delivered a great-sounding document with all the chaos intact. A genuine rock classic, **New York Dolls** contains "Personality Crisis," "Looking for a Kiss," "Trash" and other wondrous slices of gutter poetry punctuated by David Jo Hansen's slangy howl and Johnny Thunders' sneering guitar. No home should be without one.

The legendary Shadow Morton produced the second album; though the results don't match Rundgren's, the Dolls come roaring through nonetheless. There are fewer originals, but the songs they covered have never been the same. "Stranded in the Jungle," "Showdown," "Bad Detective" and "Don't Start Me Talking," reflecting the band's live repertoire at the time, affirm the Dolls' R&B roots.

Thunders and (with a newly spelled surname) Johansen (and, for a while, guitarist Syl Sylvain) proceeded in opposite directions and had polar but equally noted solo careers; bassist Artie Kane and drummer Jerry Nolan went through various local bands before disappearing entirely. In 1977, Mercury repackaged both original Dolls albums together with new artwork and liner notes by Tony Parsons.

Except for the appearance of original drummer Billy Murcia (whose overdose death in London, noted in Bowie's "Time," considerably helped build the Dolls' legend), the cassette-only collection of 1972 demos released as **Lipstick Killers** is of archival value only, underscoring the enormity of Rundgren's accomplishment on the first record.

More archaeology: **Red Patent Leather** captures the fading Dolls on a New York stage in 1975 during a brief era when a pre-Pistols Malcolm McLaren managed them. The set includes a bunch of otherwise unvinylized numbers (e.g., "Daddy Rolling Stone," "Something Else," "Pirate Love") but is not exactly a peak performance. The Johansen/Sylvain record, recorded a few months later in Tokyo on a post-breakup contractual obligations tour, is a bootleg-quality live album by the remains of the band (Thunders and Kane are absent; Tony Machine is on Nolan's stool). Strangely, the cover design of this blue-vinyl item makes an unabashed bid to be mistaken for a David Sylvian release.

Indicative of the Dolls' enduring relevance to young people, both English and American Mercury issued compilation albums in the '80s. **Night of the Living Dolls** manages to uncover a heretofore unreleased take of Shadow Morton's "Give Her a Great Big Kiss," a tune the Dolls used to play. The Dolls' side of **After the Storm** contains killer '72 demos (not the ones on **Lipstick Killers**) of "Personality Crisis," "Looking for a Kiss," "Bad Girl" and "Subway Train."   [i]

See also *Heartbreakers, David Johansen, Sylvain Sylvain, Johnny Thunders*.

NICE STRONG ARM

Reality Bath (Homestead) 1987
Mind Furnace (Homestead) 1988 ●
Cloud Machine EP (Homestead) 1989
Stress City (Homestead) 1990 ●

Originally from the Austin scene that spawned such kindred spirits as the Butthole Surfers and Scratch Acid, this NYC trio crafts a so(m)ber mixture of Brit gloom (Joy Division, Bauhaus) and New York guitar screech (Sonic Youth, Swans). While its work has been spotty, Nice Strong Arm has never been less than intriguing.

Initially distinguished by a propulsive two-drummer lineup (only captured on the first LP), NSA's debut is shot through with an art-rock sensibility that cushions the entropic din. From guitarist Kevin Thomson and bassist Jason Asnes' brooding vocals to the grim, almost directionless songs, the record is all about hurt and despair. "Date of Birth" and "Minds Lie" have bite, but a more focused look into the abyss would be welcome. (The **Reality Bath** cassette adds a bonus track.)

Mind Furnace is a far more subdued effort, angst-ridden and often beautiful. The intricate song structures (that don't grab immediately but reward upon further examination) and downbeat lyrics detailing domestic decay comprise the bulk of a record that always seems on the verge of bursting through its self-imposed restraints. Highlights: the gripping "Swingset" and frightening "Faucet Head."

Cloud Machine pairs two new studio tracks (including a bright, metallic funk instrumental called "Cop Show") with two songs cut live at CBGB. **Stress City** is an extremely forceful (read: LOUD) and rhythmically sophisticated record that fairly approximates what Nice Strong Arm can do live. The songs' excessive verbiage does, upon closer inspection, resemble bad collegiate poetry, but the requisite dank imagery colors such skewed funkers as "Desert Beauty Bloom" and "Neighborhood Voyeur." The stirring sound of collapse.   [db]

NICO

Chelsea Girl (Verve) 1967 ●
The Marble Index (Elektra) 1969 ●
Desertshore (Reprise) 1971
The End ... (Island) 1974
Drama of Exile (nr/Aura) 1981 (Ger.Line) 1988
Do or Die! Nico—in Europe—1982 Diary [tape] (ROIR) 1982
The Blue Angel (nr/Aura) 1985 ●
Behind the Iron Curtain (nr/Dojo) 1986 ●
Live in Tokyo (nr/Dojo) 1986 ●
Live Heroes (Performance) 1986 ●
The Peel Sessions EP (nr/Strange Fruit) 1988 ●
Hanging Gardens (Restless) 1990 φ

NICO + THE FACTION

Camera Obscura (Beggars Banquet-PVC) 1985 ●

KEVIN AYERS—JOHN CALE—ENO—NICO

June 1, 1974 (Island) 1974 ●

A fashion model and bit player in Fellini's *La Dolce Vita*, the German-born Nico (Christa Paffgen) was plunged into the maelstrom of rock when Andy Warhol introduced her to the Velvet Underground, which she then joined. **Chelsea Girl**, her maiden voyage on a solo musical career, is of interest mainly for its links to the band Nico had just left. Five songs were written (but not recorded) by Velvet Undergrounders; three others were written or co-written by a very young Jackson Browne. The material, however, is sabotaged by tepid arrangements and weak production. Highlight: the hypnotic "It Was a Pleasure Then," on which Nico's sepulchral voice is accompanied only by feedback guitar, undoubtedly played by Lou Reed.

The Marble Index was a substantial improvement. Arranger John Cale took Nico's disturbing poetry and set it to even more disturbing music; the result is one of the scariest records ever made. Unlike **Chelsea Girl**, in which Nico tried to adapt to an outmoded chanteuse tradition, **The Marble Index** blasts her off to her own universe. Regardless of whether more credit is due her or Cale, the album is powerfully effective.

The Nico-Cale collaboration continued on **Desertshore**. Here the disjunctive imagery is set to slightly less gothic arrangements than before, proving Nico's chanting (she doesn't "sing" any more than she writes "songs") can be as chilling a cappella as it is accompanied by a horror-movie soundtrack. (The **Peel Sessions** EP dates from early '71.)

Three years later, she and Cale turned up with Roxy Music guitarist Phil Manzanera and Brian Eno on synthesizer for **The End . . .** The title track is the Doors epic, which Nico had also just previously recorded on the all-star **June 1, 1974** album. With one exception, the rest of **The End** is original material, putting the emphasis on Nico's voice and eerie, foot-pumped harmonium rather than on distracting sound effects. The exception, "Das Lied der Deutschen" (or "Deutschland über Alles"), is enough to make you run out and buy war bonds.

After a lengthy recording hiatus, Nico re-emerged without Cale but with a conventional rock band on **Drama of Exile**. This jarring blend hurts everyone involved; adding insult to injury, bassist/producer Philippe Quilichini filters Nico's voice for a tinny effect.

Her psychotic writing is still fascinating, and certainly preferable to aimless versions of Lou Reed's "Waiting for the Man" and David Bowie's "Heroes."

Joined by two sidemen and Cale as producer, Nico made the odd but exciting **Camera Obscura** in 1985. This modernization program includes both the nearly vocal-less title track's meandering semi-random improvisation and an attractively somber version of "My Funny Valentine," with stops in between for fascinating blends of Nico's unique singing and post-noise industrial music. **Camera Obscura** raises Nico's artistic average this decade to a respectable 50 percent.

Do or Die!, recorded live throughout Europe with various bands (including the Blue Orchids) backing her, is a lengthy sampler of Nico's work minus the production flourishes of her studio albums. The fascinating and innately bizarre **Live Heroes** mini-album draws on some of the same shows—adding two tracks done with the Invisible Girls—for "My Funny Valentine," "Heroes" and five others. Another concert set, the two-LP **Iron Curtain** was recorded in 1985 in Warsaw, Budapest and Prague with a band that included Eric Random. **The Blue Angel** is a retrospective compilation of solo and Velvet Underground material.

Nico died in July 1988 on the island of Ibiza, suffering a cerebral hemmorhage in a bicycle spill. The posthumous **Hanging Gardens** contains her last recordings—six powerfully somber processions, tastefully produced and evocatively sung—as well as two heretofore unreleased 1982 tracks (the full-blown "Vegas" and the spare "The Line") and **Drama of Exile**'s version of "I'm Waiting for the Man." [si/i]

See also *Velvet Underground*.

STEVE NIEVE
Theme Music from Outline of a Hairdo EP (nr/F-Beat) 1980
Keyboard Jungle (nr/Demon) 1983 ●
Playboy (nr/Demon) 1987

Keyboardist Steve Nieve first stepped out of Elvis Costello's Attractions for a 7-inch EP of four brief, relatively straightforward piano (plus tasteful electronic accents) instrumentals, ostensibly (but not really) drawn from a film soundtrack. If not for titles like "Sparrow Crap" and "Page 1 of a Dead Girl's Diary," no one would blindly attribute these efforts with a rock musician. Likewise, **Keyboard Jungle** is a cute set of miniatures crafted at the keyboard of a Steinway: fake film and classical music, none of it taken (or given) particularly seriously. Quite agreeable.

The cover of **Playboy** shows Nieve, dressed to the nines, looking a bit like Bryan Ferry; the solo acoustic piano record mixes suave originals with uniquely conceived versions of standards, just like Ferry's first solo efforts. The material in receipt here of Nieve's straight-faced (and, therefore, hysterically funny) cocktail-lounge treatment includes Sting's derivative and trivial "Russians," Bowie's overwrought "Life on Mars," 10cc's weepy "I'm Not in Love" and the Specials' nearly tuneless "Ghost Town." (X and Wham! also get their comeuppance in Nieve's graceful hands.) The eleven other short pieces display the artist's wit, compositional talent and instrumental agility. [jy/i]

See also *Elvis Costello*.

NIGHTINGALES
The Nightingales EP (nr/Cherry Red) 1982
Pigs on Purpose (nr/Cherry Red) 1982
Hysterics (nr/Ink-Red Flame) 1983
The Crunch EP (nr/Vindaloo) 1984
Just a Job (nr/Vindaloo) 1984
In the Good Old Country Way (nr/Vindaloo) 1986
The Peel Sessions EP (nr/Strange Fruit) 1988

ROBERT LLOYD
Me and My Mouth (nr/Virgin) 1990 ●

Trebly guitar scrubs and busy drumming, both at a hyper pace, support Robert Lloyd's snide, self-mocking, self-pitying, annoyed, despairing, sarcastically scathing and generally intelligent (if not always intelligible) tirades. (Dry wit, too.) The boy from Birmingham has a lot of mind to give the world a piece of. (Prior to the Nightingales, Lloyd led the late-'70s punk Prefects; he later organized the Vindaloo label.)

On the Nightingales' first EP, the melodies are memorably minimal, and the playing seems just a touch out of control. **Pigs on Purpose** shows a bit more instrumental skill (despite bad mastering) and an increased variety of tempos and textures. The Fall would seem to be a major influence, not only in the abrasive, paradoxically unobtrusive guitar work but Lloyd's singing/ranting, which owes something to Mark E. Smith's vocal and lyrical style.

Hysterics marks a label change and much improved production; tone colors are expanded with the use of banjo, trombone and viola. The Nightingales also demonstrate a greater assortment of styles: bass parts borrowed from reggae, an inside-out Bo Diddley beat on "Ponces All" and a flirtation with country-western in "The Happy Medium." **The Crunch** features the contrast of tightly controlled chaos *and* some of Lloyd's more melodic vocals. Released during a period of numerous personnel shifts (they were briefly a sextet), the Nightingales manage to avoid sounding transitional; there's plenty of drive and power on these tracks. Highly recommended.

In the Good Old Country Way wisely isn't an attempt to make a straightforward country album. Many bands lacking a real identity might make such an error, but the 'Gales are able to embellish their own sound with country and bluegrass elements. Lyrics are more smart-ass than ever (see "Part Time Moral England" and "I Spit in Your Gravy"); the playing gets downright hot on "The Headache Collector." Highly recommended, even—or maybe especially—for those who hate country-western.

Just a Job is a compilation of **The Crunch**, non-LP singles and a track from **Hysterics**.

Busy running Vindaloo, Lloyd took four years after the Nightingales' demise to release his solo debut on another label. **Me and My Mouth** is a far cry from any Mark E. Smith comparisons; producer Craig Leon (who worked on the Fall's **Extricate**) gives the LP such a huge, glossy sound that it could pass for a Todd Rundgren job. If all of the songs were as strong as "Cheap as Sin" or "Something Nice," the disc could survive, but this simply isn't the right setting for Lloyd's talents. While he glibly shifts gears between R&B and C&W in completely pedestrian fashion, the production shines it all up so much that it might as well be ska and be-bop. Guests include Attractions Steve Nieve and Pete Thomas along with ex-Aztec Camera/Smiths guitarist Craig Gannon, but to little avail. "The Part of the Anchor," recorded in 1987 for a John Peel session, is easily the highlight—the only cut to approach the raw urgency of the 'Gales or Lloyd's lyrical potential. Better luck next time. [jg/dgs]

NIHILISTICS

Nihilistics EP (Visionary) 1982
Nihilistics (Brain Eater) 1983
Bad ... Dirty ... Hate (Visionary) 1989
Fuck the Human Race (Visionary) 1990

Nihilistics are a stupid, obnoxious hardcore band from Long Island, New York. Their lyrics are predictable banalities and their attitudinizing is irritating. That's the bad news. The good news is that the **Nihilistics** album is pretty good (even if the preceding five-song 7-inch is much better). However full of it their ideas may be, the band members at least believe in them, and advance them with all the passion of the errantly self-righteous. Emotional commitment does count for something, even if that commitment is to a credo like "Take it from me man . . . fuck the human race." People hate hardcore precisely for stuff like this, but the Nihilistics go far enough to almost make it work.

After a five-year hiatus, the original lineup scraped off the cobwebs and exhumed the band's corpse, ready to pour some corrosive spit from the original punk bucket on the positive 'core and straight-edge generation. The message on **Bad . . . Dirty . . . Hate** (as opposed to good clean fun) is that life and people suck. In a few cases, singer Ron Rancid manages to tweeze a slender path between sincerely deranged hatred and absurdly grotesque humor; meanwhile, guitarist Ajax Lepinski slices through the din on "Story Box" and "Punisher." Returning more to the age of punk rather than hardcore, the Nihilistics keep the emphasis on attitude and hybrid tempos, not speed and tightness. "Sub-liminal," "Big Fun" and "The Good Life" all prove the band's competent musicianship while promoting its demented viewpoint.

Besides the grungy "Sorry Hairy Tail" and the rockabilly bass-lined "Vexation," **Fuck the Human Race** (stickered in stores as **Feed the Human Race**) includes between-song antics like Rancid's crank calls to a morgue (his day job). Not as generally gripping as the previous LP, but still entertaining. [jl/mg]

NILS

Sell Out Young! EP (Can. Psyche Industry) 1985
The Nils EP (Can. Siegfried) 1986
The Nils (Rock Hotel-Profile) 1987 ●

Inspired into existence by the Sex Pistols, this young Montreal guitar quartet, led by brothers Alex and Carlos Soria, plays energetic and competent punkergized rock with rich vocals on their Chris Spedding-produced debut album. (Ivan Doroschuk of Men Without Hats financed and produced the first Canadian EP; the second was actually recorded earlier but went unreleased until 1986.

The Nils is only a semi-official title; the record is also known as **The Red EP**.)

The Nils album has the same kind of fearless commercial sensibility and melodic intuition as 1978 Generation X or 1987 Soul Asylum: songs like "When the Love Puts on a Sad Face," "Bandito Callin' " and the Hüsker Dü-like "Young Man in Transit" don't reach those bands' heights but show just as much effort and ingenuous spirit. [i]

NINE BELOW ZERO

Live at the Marquee (nr/A&M) 1980
Don't Point Your Finger (A&M) 1981
Third Degree (nr/A&M) 1982
Live at the Venue (nr/Receiver) 1989 ●

The underrated Nine Below Zero started out as a cautious but promising London R&B cover band but progressed to fresh, confident originals by the time they broke up in 1982. Releasing a live album as a debut is a mite unusual, but **Live at the Marquee** clearly captures NBZ's early tightness and enthusiasm. The material—mostly such old tunes as the Four Tops' "I Can't Help Myself" and Sam the Sham's "Woolly Bully"—get powerful readings here. **Don't Point Your Finger**, produced by old pro Glyn Johns, is a transitional album. Though the majority of songs are originals, most written by singer/guitarist Dennis Greaves, they sound authentically old.

Nine Below Zero updated its sound on **Third Degree** with wonderful results. Greaves successfully cross-cuts his beloved R&B roots with elements of traditional rock-'n'roll, pop and even a touch of reggae ("Easy Street SE 17"), all infused with a healthy shot of punky energy ("Eleven Plus Eleven," "Tearful Eye," "True Love Is a Crime" and the terrific "Wipe Away Your Kiss").

The second live album, released nearly a decade after it was recorded, is fast, hard and taut, with Mark Feltham's harp playing providing a strong blast of Chicago blues in the band's originals and solid covers of "I've Got My Mojo Working," "Keep on Knocking," "Homework" and "Just a Little Bit." The set isn't very different from the one on the first album, but this music is more than durable enough to withstand repeated use.

See also *Truth*. [ks/i]

NINE INCH NAILS

Pretty Hate Machine (TVT) 1989 ●

Cleveland singer/synthetic noise wiz Trent Reznor is yet another tortured soul with a whole lexicon of Excedrin headache beats stored on floppy disc. As Nine Inch Nails, this junior industrialist takes out his anxiety and despair on the rest of the world. But while the tracks are springier and less stringent than on other likeminded hammer parties, the vocals carry very little in terms of threat. Reznor is talented, though, and many instrumental segments on **Pretty Hate Machine** (co-produced with, variously, Flood, Adrian Sherwood, John Fryer and Keith LeBlanc) are intriguing indeed. If he wasn't trying so hard to sound like Skinny Puppy and Ministry, he could make really effective records of his own. [gk]

999

999 (nr/UA) 1978 (Fr. Fan Club) 1987 ●
Separates (nr/UA) 1978 (Fr. Fan Club) 1987
High Energy Plan (PVC) 1979
The Biggest Prize in Sport (Polydor) 1980
The Biggest Tour in Sport EP (Polydor) 1980
Singles Album (nr/UA) 1980
Concrete (Polydor) 1981
13th Floor Madness (nr/Albion) 1983
Greatest Hits (nr/Albion) 1984
Face to Face (nr/Labritain) 1985
In Case of Emergency (nr/Dojo) 1986
Lust Power and Money (nr/ABC) 1987 ●
Live and Loud!! (nr/Link) 1989
The Cellblock Tapes (nr/Link) 1990

Despite a large recorded output and an avoidance of typecasting, London's 999 never amounted to anything more than an undistinguished and dispensable band of moderate ability. Variously posing as mutant bubble-gum, rocky art-school cleverness, hard R&B rock and quirky pop, 999's problem has always been a lack of adequate talent to invest their music with real originality; to be fair, they *have* managed a few good sides along the way and also deserve credit for endurance and persistence.

999 introduced the band, dressed in kicky, colorful clothes and working with pop producer Andy Arthurs, yet it's not a pop album. The music is harmless but charmless, although the vocals are occasionally winning, as on "Me and My Desire" and the whiny "Emergency." The CD adds three bonus tracks.

For their second effort, 999 enlisted soon-to-be-a-superstar producer Martin Rushent, and **Separates** does have a lot more going for it. The band's playing is harder and tighter, with better focus, although the semi-hit "Homicide" benefits more from a clever arrangement than intrinsic quality. Other good tunes include the taut "Feelin' Alright with the Crew" and an all-out rocker, "High Energy Plan." Still minor, but improving. (**High Energy Plan** is an American revision, with two tracks deleted and two 45 cuts added.)

The Biggest Prize in Sport teamed 999 (temporarily a five-piece, having added a second drummer to aid the injured Pablo Labritain) with producer Vic Maile, resulting in a disc that is trebly and lifeless, except for the poppy title track, which sounds like a Cockney Ramones.

Hoping to stir up some domestic interest, 999's American record company issued a six-song mini-album, **The Biggest Tour in Sport**, recorded live in 1980 in the States. The sound's good and hot; selections include "Homicide," "Emergency" and "Feelin' Alright with the Crew."

Not to be outdone, their English label whipped up a collection—in chronological order—of 999's singles, starting with "I'm Alive" (1977) and running through "Waiting" (1978), including both sides of each—fifteen tracks in all. If you need to find out about 999, **Singles Album** is the record to have, containing all their essential (i.e., good) material.

Concrete could almost be mistaken for an Inmates record, thanks to two pointless covers ("Li'l Red Riding Hood," "Fortune Teller") and a mundane, characterless guitar-rock sound.

13th Floor Madness was slagged off in the press as

soft disco, but the self-released **Face to Face** is a pleasant surprise, offering melodic rock with a certain charm (despite occasional gaffes and lapses of wit). The band's original lineup, still together after all these years, is not exactly getting better by leaps and bounds, but the songs here are their most likable in a long time—a few could even be characterized as memorable—and bits of invention keep them moving along.

Following another compilation (**In Case of Emergency**), 999 released **Lust Power and Money**, an all-new live-in-London album recorded in April 1987. The band's lineup is essentially intact (only the bassist is new); the program includes the ancient ("Hit Me," "Homicide," "Feelin' Alright with the Crew") and the relatively recent ("White Trash" and "Lust Power and Money"). The performance is dull but the sound is good. (One hopes there was more audience present than what's audible.)

As hard as it might be to believe that an audience exists for such a thing, **The Cellblock Tapes** is an out-of-the-vaults album containing eight vintage live tracks and seven old demos.   [i]

See also *Kilburn and the High Roads*.

NINE POUND HAMMER

The Mud, the Blood, and the Beers (Wanghead) 1989

A trailer-park sensibility, genuine Kentucky accents and racing Ramonesy punk make this rowdy Lexington quartet a smoke-belching blast of fun. I won't use derogatory expressions like "white trash" and "redneck" (the group will: "Redneck Romance" is one of the best tracks), but these guys have enough low-culture resonance (not to mention mechanical skills) to become the kings of drive-in rock'n'roll. And if Nine Pound Hammer sounds like a four-headed Mojo Nixon, it should be noted that their "Bye Bye, Glen Frey" predates his "Don Henley Must Die" by a year.   [i]

9353

To Whom It May Consume (R+B) 1984
We Are Absolutely Sure There Is No God (Fountain of Youth) 1985

With hardcore just as stagnant in Washington DC as it was everywhere else in 1984, the appearance of 9353 came as quite a jolt. Although the band wasn't first-rate—Jason Carmer's delay-driven guitar serves as only a decorative ornament, and the rhythm section is rarely more than competent—**To Whom It May Consume** is surprisingly good, psychotic punk psychedelia (with a twist of good-humored evil) highlighted by Bruce Merkle's astounding vocal range, which can shift from a deep drawl to a convincing Ethel Merman warble in a flash.

We Are Absolutely Sure There Is No God was released at the end of 1985, after the short-lived band's breakup. Merkle continues to display his bag of tricks, never once treating any of his many voices with seriousness or respect. The album does not contain as many memorable songs as the first, but try "American Schizo," "Evil Teen Facility Yard" and "Who Does What and Why."   [icm]

NIPS 'N' NIPPLE ERECTORS

See *Pogues*.

NIRVANA

Bleach (Sub Pop) 1988 ●
Blew EP (Ger. Sub Pop-Glitterhouse) 1989 ●

Nirvana was formed in 1986 by vocalist/guitarist Kurdt Kobain and bassist Chris Novoselic in Aberdeen, Washington, home of legendary quaalude-metal titans the Melvins, whose drummer played on the band's 1987 demo. After a brilliant debut single (a snarling cover of the Shocking Blue's "Love Buzz," included on the first album), **Bleach** elevated Nirvana to major hip-press status, as Kobain's sandpaper growl and roaring guitar propelled amazing hard-rock hooks. His taut, jagged songs contain elements of the Seattle sound but show a rare sophistication.

The **Blew** EP combines two album tracks with two new songs, the slow-grinding "Been a Son" and the bruising "Stain." [ja]

NITECAPS

Go to the Line (Sire) 1982

Spearheaded by erstwhile Voidoid (known then as X-sessive) Jahn Xavier, the Nitecaps—a multi-racial quartet including New York Dolls roadie/bassist Peter Jordan—were sort of an American counterpart to Graham Parker's Rumour. On **Go to the Line**, with the fab Uptown Horns and production by Langer and Winstanley, the babyfaced Xavier reveals himself to be not only a mean guitarist, but a throaty growler with a voice that crosses Joe Jackson and Otis Redding. R&B like this rarely sounds so strong or credible. The only misstep is a Zombies/Easybeats medley; the rest (originals, aside from one arcane oldie) is solid, foot-stompin' fun. Nitecaps guitarist Al Maddy later joined the Dots.

In 1990, several Nitecaps resurfaced as Jahn Xavier and the Preachers. [jg]

See also *Dots, Richard Hell & the Voidoids*.

NITS

The Nits (Hol. Scramble) 1978
Tent (Hol. Epic) 1979 ●
New Flat (Hol. CBS) 1980 ●
Work (Hol. CBS) 1981 ●
Omsk (Hol. CBS) 1983 ●
Kilo EP (Hol. CBS) 1983 ●
Adieu, Sweet Bahnhof (Hol. CBS) 1984 ●
Henk (Hol. CBS) 1986 ●
In the Dutch Mountains (Hol. CBS) 1987 (nr/CBS) 1988 ●
Hat EP (Hol. CBS) 1988
Urk (Hol. CBS) 1989 ●
Giant Normal Dwarf (Hol. CBS) 1990 ●

R.J. STIPS

U.P. (Hol. CBS) 1981 ●

The obvious derivativeness on the Nits' early albums could have been written off as cut-rate local filtration/reassembly of the real thing from Britain and America (Beatles, Talking Heads, etc.). In retrospect, however, those records can be seen as learning experiences of a world-class band now deserving international attention.

Evidently a thousand or so copies of an LP entitled

The Nits were pressed prior to their CBS signing, an achievement apparently best forgotten. That's only marginally less true of their first three CBS outings. Comparisons to tongue-in-cheek pop synthesists like 10cc and fellow Dutchmen Gruppo Sportivo immediately come to mind, but leave the Nits on the short end of the stick—too cute, not clever enough by half and too sterile, especially on **Tent**. Arty touches provide welcome contrasts here and there on **New Flat**, and a melody or two does catch the ear. **Work** attempts to up the Serious Artistic Expression ante, but the music rarely can carry the lyrical weight. Still, at points on both **New Flat** and **Work**, Hans Hofstede reveals a growing aptitude for creating little emotional postcards.

Omsk and **Kilo** show the Nits beginning to find their voices; it must be at least partly attributed to the arrival of keyboardist Robert Jan Stips. Previously known for his work with Golden Earring and for producing Gruppo Sportivo albums, he oversaw part of **Tent** and all of **New Flat**. His own LP is a curious blend of pop-rock and jazz syncopations, in a unique style that starts out intriguing but turns irritating. All the same, he does bolster the Nits' brighter, poppier side and shades the darker, moodier aspect most often explored by Hofstede. On **Omsk** and **Kilo**, Hofstede unveils a mild resemblance to Elvis Costello (but dreamier, more vulnerable, less venomous); Stips' dominant keyboards make for settings that are affecting, even haunting.

Adieu, Sweet Bahnhof reflects the group's odd international sensibility. None of the Nits' lyrics have ever been in Dutch; a song on the LP which refers to Holland is sung half in English, half in Turkish. Is there some national inferiority complex at work here? In any case, the record is more musically confident and aggressive, yet less affecting, than its immediate predecessors. There are still clumsy phrasings and syntactical mistakes (in songs by Stips and Michiel Peters, not Hofstede), which would be more easily forgiven/ignored if the melodies were stronger. This album seems to be a move sideways, a retrenchment, a sort of public ironing out of the kinks, though the really good tracks (like those featuring Hofstede's Lennonish Costelloisms) do make it a respectable opus.

Henk is another story altogether. Firstly, there's the mystery of the title (weirder since Hofstede changed his name from Hans to Henk after the **Work** LP). Peters is gone. Hofstede now writes all the lyrics, while he, Stips and agile drummer Rob Kloet share equal credit for the music. Other than a spot of banjo (!) and one track's worth of guitar, there are no fretted instruments to be heard—it's all voices, keyboards and drums. And it's great—oddball pop-rock of the first order. The imaginative range of electronic sounds and textures can be breathtaking, as on "Cabins" and "Under a Canoe." The melodies are attractive. The words are often abstract but always evocative. The Nits now sound like . . . the Nits. (The **Henk** CD also contains **Kilo**.)

In the Dutch Mountains—the title track inspired by Cees Nooteboom's acclaimed quasi-fantasy novel—is also impressive. The Nits again sound like the Nits, but substantially different Nits. Intended to resemble a live show, it was recorded "in their own rehearsal room, an old gym in Amsterdam . . . straight to two-track digital tape with no dubbing or mixing after the actual recording." New bassist Joke Geraets plays only a stand-up acoustic; Hofstede's back to playing guitar. The occasional guests are three female backing vocalists and a steel guitar player. Hofstede's lyrical approach is—as on **Henk**—offbeat, but also consistently personal (even at one point confessional). Surreal juxtapositions of prosaic imagery suggest travels through his dreams. The cleverly contrapuntal music and rhythms use a tonal/timbral palette that is more subdued (yet equally effective in its way) than **Henk**. And this is nearly a live album! Brilliant.

The **Hat** mini-album (six tracks, 25 minutes) refines the earlier "emotional postcard" approach, with the theme of loneliness—romantic, spiritual, physical—getting a real workout. It's quite enjoyable, the unified sound not unlike **Omsk** or **Kilo**, yet sonically lighter and simpler.

Soon after, the Nits recorded a double live album, **Urk**. The selection of 29 songs (over two hours) samples every record from **Work** on, with **Dutch Mountains** getting the most emphasis, followed by **Henk**, **Omsk** and **Hat**; a strong, well-blended assortment. Carps: While several songs from weaker records seem more impressive than before, some better numbers are a little less so. In addition, a couple of theatrical songs geared for the stage lose something without the visual component. Still, it's an enjoyable overview as delectable as the original albums.

Geraets had departed by **Giant Normal Dwarf**, and the LP is all Stips' keyboards, Kloets' drums and Hofstede's voice(s). Even more explicitly than **Dutch Mountains**, the record concentrates on dreams, fantasies and childlike visions. With less energy and more reserve, it's not as immediately imposing as **Dutch Mountains** or **Henk**, but is still an attractive, wistful, sometimes disturbing album, engagingly capturing the internal logic of dreams and translating complex emotional states into songs. And it's darned pretty, too! [jg]

NITZER EBB

Isn't It Funny How Your Body Works EP (nr/Power of Voice Comm.) 1985
That Total Age (Mute-Geffen) 1987 ●
Belief (Mute-Geffen) 1988 ●
So Bright So Strong (Ger. Upfront) 1988 ●
Showtime (Mute-Geffen) 1990 ●

With its aggressive music and Teutonic name, casual listeners may assume Nitzer Ebb to be of German origin when, in fact, the trio is from the tranquil English town of Chelmsford. Nonetheless, this is one angst-ridden band: seizing on simple catchphrases (shouted more often than sung or rapped), minimal synthesized hooklines and pounding, cathartic beats, the songs on **That Total Age** are industrial-strength anthems. "Join in the Chant" became a bizarre early favorite of British acid house fans (its references to "muscle and hate" having little to do with peace and love), and equally intense songs such as "Let Your Body Learn" and "Murderous" are heard more on alternative dancefloors now than at the time of their release. For such a challenging combination of anger and rhythm, and without a dull moment, **That Total Age** is a monumental album.

Armed with that highly identifiable sound, Nitzer

Ebb has repeated it again and again; the songs on **Belief** could easily be substituted for those on the first album. In noteworthy cuts like the pulsating "Control I'm Here," "Blood Money" and "Hearts and Minds," Nitzer Ebb's lyrics hone in on basic emotions and issues of power and lust. There is no sense of advancement or development on **Belief**; arguably none is required.

A German label collected the group's first singles (including four versions of "Warsaw Ghetto," a song from **That Total Age**) for the **So Bright So Strong** compilation. The four tracks from the 1985 12-inch debut are notable for being more melodic and faster than what would become the archetypal Nitzer Ebb sound; even more unusual—given that Nitzer Ebb artwork tends to be as minimal and clinical as the music itself—the record contains photos of what was then a trio (now pared down to the duo of vocalist Douglas McCarthy and musician Bon Harris).

Showtime finds the group trying to diversify with little success: the electronic blues of "Nobody Knows" is messy, and attempts at melodic vocals only emphasize McCarthy's weakness as a singer. There are strong moments—the single "Lightning Man," with its incessant keyboard refrain, and the jaunty "Fun to Be Had"—but this isn't their strongest opus. Not so ironically, it proved a quick seller; touring stadiums with Depeche Mode made Nitzer Ebb the underground name to drop at the start of the new decade. [tf]

MOJO NIXON AND SKID ROPER

Mojo Nixon and Skid Roper (RBI-Enigma) 1985 (IRS) 1991 ●
Frenzy (Restless) 1986 (IRS) 1991 ●
Get Out of My Way! (Restless) 1986 (IRS) 1991 ●
Bo-Day-Shus!!! (Enigma) 1987 (IRS) 1991 ●
Root Hog or Die (Enigma) 1989 (IRS) 1991 ●
Unlimited Everything (nr/Enigma) 1990 ●

MOJO NIXON
Otis (Enigma) 1990 (IRS) 1991 φ

SKID ROPER AND THE WHIRLIN SPURS
Trails Plowed Under (Triple X) 1989 ●
Lydias Cafe (Triple X) 1991 ●

You figure it out. Mojo Nixon and sidekick Skid Roper first gained attention with a delicate love-letter ditty to then-MTV VJ Martha Quinn subtly entitled "Stuffin' Martha's Muffin." In addition to bluntly proclaiming his desire to get intimate with the perky Ms. Q, the call-and-response vocals in the bridge take on the whole institution: "MTV/get away from me . . . I say, Music Television/should be covered in jism." Several years later, there's Mojo doing spots on MTV, talking about post-punk philosophers while hanging from a jungle gym and serving as a roving reporter on the beach for Spring Break.

Sold out? Quite the opposite. **Mojo Nixon and Skid Roper** is a bit on the tame side—songs with titles like "Jesus at McDonalds" and "Art Fag Shuffle" should be great, but are merely clever. Mojo finds his true voice on **Frenzy**. The musical accompaniment to Nixon's often hysterical socio-political commentary is mostly a frisky down-home mixture of blues, R&B and rockabilly. Roper's contributions consist of things like washboard, harmonica, mandolin, etc. Besides "Stuffin' Martha's Muffin," **Frenzy** offers Nixon's appraisal of such topics as gigging ("Where the Hell's My Money"), fatherhood ("I'm Living with the Three-Foot Anti-Christ") and savings & loans ("I Hate Banks"). Add to that his hilarious checkout line tabloid spoof, "The Amazing Bigfoot Diet," and a fleeting harmonica-driven version of "In-a-Gadda-Da-Vida," and this LP should appeal to anyone with a funny bone.

Get Out of My Way! is a seven-track mini-LP (issued, at one point, on clear vinyl) reprising "Stuffin' " and "Jesus at McDonald's," plus a few of Mojo's very own Christmas songs. All of these tracks are included on the **Frenzy** CD.

Bo-Day-Shus!!! is every bit as big a hoot, with the epic "Elvis Is Everywhere" (finally revealing the identity of the much-feared anti-Elvis—sure to be a Trivial Pursuit question to some future generation) and a topical ode to the just-say-no crowd, "I Ain't Gonna Piss in No Jar." Other little slices of Americana include "B.B.Q.U.S.A.," "Wash No Dishes No More" and "I'm Gonna Dig Up Howlin' Wolf." Folks, Nixon is the man this country needs—Mojo ain't no Dick. (CD bonus cuts: "Don't Want No Foo-Foo Haircut on My Head" and "The Story of One Chord.")

Jim Dickenson's [*sic*] production and a few extra sidemen makes **Root Hog or Die** relatively fancy (for Nixon and Roper, that is). Mojo kicks things off with the hilarious one-two pop-iconography punch of "Debbie Gibson Is Pregnant with My Two-Headed Love Child" and "(619) 239-KING" (a plea to locate Elvis who is, as we all know, everywhere) and follows it with a patriotic rendition of "This Land Is Your Land" that devolves into a convincing pitch for that imaginary trash heaven, Mojo World. The record sags a bit after that, although Skid's "Tennessee Jive" serves up a sweet bit of Rockpilish rock and the Mojo sexuality rears its ugly head in "She's Vibrator Dependent" and the funky "Louisiana Liplock."

Skimming the scunge off the top of the Mojo and Skid oeuvre, the **Unlimited Everything** compilation condenses the best of the duo's four albums together for a brainbusting dose of raucous pop culturecide from the best in the business. (Kids, don't attempt to sing these songs at home. These men are professionals.)

Parting company with Mojo, Skid formed a rocking cowboy/country band and launched his solo career with an amiable album of (mostly) romantic (mostly) originals. Jayne Robson's vocals, harmonizing nicely with Skid's, help the agreeable **Trails Plowed Under** drift along, a twang in its heart and nothing much on its mind. (The ironic "Please Forgive Me" is one clever exception.) Lacking his ex-partner's demented imagination, Roper's more modest talents as a frontman and songwriter make the album easy to hear but hard to remember. (The CD adds two bonus tracks.)

Old producer pal Dickinson helped Mojo assemble the ultimate trailer-park-rock studio band for his solo debut. As John Doe (bass; X), Country Dick Montana (drums; Beat Farmers), Bill Davis (guitar; Dash Rip Rock) and Eric Ambel (guitar; Del-Lords) launch **Otis** into a solidly musical orbit, Mojo adjusts himself to such skilled company and straddles their sonic missile, ranting and raving about the legal profession ("Destroy All Lawyers"), ex-Eagles ("Don Henley Must Die,"

complete with a relevant guitar quote), politics (the funky "Put a Sex Mo-Sheen in the White House"), celebrity teeth ("Shane's Dentist") and pomposity (the Stonesy "Ain't High Falutin' "). With the exception of an unironic ballad bad enough to hopefully discourage any such missteps in the future, **Otis** is maximum Mojo.

[dgs/i]

NO DIRECTION

No Direction (No Direction) 1984
Becoming Obsession (No Direction) 1986
The No Direction Tapes (No Direction) 1988

On what has to be the first independent album ever released by a Sioux Falls, South Dakota punk band, No Direction plays earnest political protest numbers with a lot more spirit than technique. Far removed from any stylistic trendiness (or, for that matter, pop musical trends of any sort), this trio gains strength from its basic simplicity. The sixteen songs on **No Direction** have energy but a spare sound with open spaces that would benefit enormously from bigger amps and a skilled producer.

Except for horribly mis-EQ'd sound that entirely ignores the audio spectrum's bottom half, **Becoming Obsession** (recorded in 1984) demonstrates an enormous amount of growth: guitarist Rick Smith works complex jagged figures around singer Rich Show's busybody bass (at least what can be heard of it) and Charles Luden's understated drumming. Without suggesting that it sounds dated, the trio's drivingly hypnotic swirls here recall '78/'79-vintage Cure or Gang of Four, with a bit of Joy Division in the rhythm section. Really cool.

Presented in unedited form—complete with false starts, unstructured jams, etc.—the album is positively amazing, easily comparable to the work of any other post-punk band around. Displaying exceptional trio skill (Show's vocals, having acquired a Bonoesque emotional range, are also drastically better), the thickened attack turns rich and catchy melodic rock songs like "Rise Up," the touching "Letter to Jeffrey" and the evocative "Michael Nydelski" into storms of harmonics and rhythm that are equally powerful on conscious and subliminal levels. A reverent cover of Joy Division's "Transmission" may be a bit too tributary, and "Dark Basement" more or less reinvents U2 (clearly the strongest influence here) in an unpretentious American mold, but "Life Is a Crisis" switches through something resembling the Minutemen's sideways funk, some unmistakable Who quotes and a U2-ish charge within a few seconds. That the tracks were recorded virtually live suggests what an awesome unit these guys had become; few local indie bands sound as ready to play for 50,000 people as this. Or not. No Direction broke up in 1989. [i]

NO MAN

See *Roger Miller*.

NOMEANSNO

Mama (Can. no label) 1984
Sex Mad (Can. Psyche Industry) 1986 (Alternative Tentacles) 1987

The Day Everything Became Nothing EP (Alternative
    Tentacles) 1988
Small Parts Isolated and Destroyed (Alternative Tentacles)
    1988
The Day Everything Became Isolated and Destroyed [CD]
    (Alternative Tentacles) 1988 ●
Wrong (Alternative Tentacles) 1989 ●

Emerging from a basement in Victoria, British Columbia, brothers Rob (bass, vocals, guitar) and John (drums, vocals, keyboards) Wright began NoMeansNo's strange recording career with **Mama**, a self-released album of selfconsciously warped lyrics ("We Are the Chopped," "My Roomate Is Turning into a Monster") and semi-melodic music that asserts its angular divergence from the norm politely, more jazzy Devo than anti-chromatic noise.

But that was just the first step. On **Sex Mad** (the American edition was revised from its original Canadian release), NoMeansNo pours out punky collegiate weirdness with some of the same slash'n'burn egghead energy as Couch Flambeau. Songs like "Self Pity" and "Dead Bob," not to mention an appropriately titled instrumental ("Obsessed"), revel in conscientious bizarritude and a feverish demi-musical attack.

The Day Everything Became Nothing—a six-song 12-inch—offers more dadaesque invention with concertedly intense and pointed music. The unstructured prose of the title track is supported by pounding drums alternating with bursts of guitar noise; "Beauty and the Beast" syncopates the rhythms for a disorienting effect that suggests funk and negates it in the same line. Impressive.

Small Parts Isolated and Destroyed focuses the band's anomie into fairly presentable form, modulating the carefully arranged muscular rock and punk into a tense knot of energy with fewer jagged points and rough edges than usual. John's syncopated drumming and Rob's noisy guitar solos provide most of the record's appeal; the frequent rhythm shifts are unsettling. (**Small Parts** later joined its immediate predecessor on a power-packed CD entitled **The Day Everything Became Isolated and Destroyed**.)

Wrong puts an angry amphetamine charge to **Small Parts**' precision, sending NoMeansNo into clamorous, roaring overdrive that, in its most organized portions, approaches thrash jazz. The lyrics don't bother with longwinded expressions of sensitive emotions: the complete libretto of "Brainless Wonder" (albeit not typical) is "I need lunch/Feed me now/I need lunch/Where's my break?!!!" The album's occasional descents into mere punk are more often than not disappointingly plain, but tracks like "The End of All Things" and "Big Dick" are bracingly original and utterly invigorating. (The CD and cassette add two.)   [i]
See also *Jello Biafra*.

NON
See *Boyd Rice*.

NO TREND
Teen Love EP (No Trend) 1983
Too Many Humans (No Trend) 1984
A Dozen Dead Roses (No Trend) 1985

Heart of Darkness EP (Widowspeak) 1985
When Death Won't Solve Your Problems (Widowspeak)
    1986
Tritonian Nash—Vegas Polyester Complex (Touch and Go)
    1986

No Trend clunked around Washington DC in the '80s, releasing a number of wildly inconsistent records in the process. The **Teen Love** EP, a fun four-song 12-inch, has the off-kilter and terrific "Mass Sterilization Caused by Venereal Disease," a Flipperesque pandemonium feast punctuated by the simple lyrics of the title. What follows is the bumbling "Die," a song not all that dissimilar from PiL's "Death Disco." The flipside contains the lengthy, snidely vituperative "Teen Love."

After that promising beginning, **Too Many Humans** succumbs to abject hero worship, as the group kneels before Public Image's **Metal Box** altar. Toss in Flipper, Alien Sex Fiend and, in one case, Negativland and you've got No Trend's recipe here. The Flipperish songs include heavily reverbed vocals (just like Flipper), and the PiL-isms feature blatant Levene and Lydon imitations—albeit pretty good ones. Think about the original combos real hard and you won't need to hear this record.

Lydia Lunch made a guest appearance on **A Dozen Dead Roses** and then joined forces with the group for a 10-inch EP, **Heart of Darkness**. Her label, Widowspeak, also released a No Trend compilation, **When Death Won't Solve Your Problems**. All of which led up to **Tritonian Nash**, a thoroughly amazing chunk of plastic crammed full of surprises, including a horn section, bells, a cellist, guitarists who don't want to be Keith Levene and a sorely needed sense of humor. Start to finish, **Tritonian Nash** is a nearly indescribable aural romp of punk, funk and pop, with dashes of lounge music and some dreadful country twinges. Find this record and buy it.   [icm]
See also *Lydia Lunch*.

NOVA MOB
See *Grant Hart*.

NOYES BROTHERS
See *Spherical Objects*.

GARY NUMAN
The Pleasure Principle (Atco) 1979 ●
Telekon (Atco) 1980 ●
Living Ornaments '79 (nr/Beggars Banquet) 1981
Living Ornaments '80 (nr/Beggars Banquet) 1981
Dance (Atco) 1981 ●
I, Assassin (Atco) 1982 ●
New Man Numan: The Best of Gary Numan (nr/TV)
    1982
Warriors (nr/Beggars Banquet) 1983 ●
Berserker (nr/Numa) 1984
White Noise—Live (nr/Numa) 1985
The Fury (nr/Numa) 1985 ●
Strange Charm (nr/Numa) 1986 ●
Exhibition (nr/Beggars Banquet) 1987 ●
Metal Rhythm (nr/Illegal) 1988 ●
New Anger (IRS) 1989 ●

Selection EP [CD] (nr/Beggars Banquet) 1989 ●
The Skin Mechanic (IRS) 1989 ●
The Collection (nr/Castle Comm.) 1989 ●
Outland (IRS) 1991 φ

TUBEWAY ARMY
Tubeway Army (nr/Beggars Banquet) 1978 (nr/Fame)
1983 ●
First Album (Atco) 1981
The Peel Sessions EP (nr/Strange Fruit) 1987

GARY NUMAN & TUBEWAY ARMY
Replicas (Atco) 1979 ●
The Plan 1978 (nr/Beggars Banquet) 1984 ●
The Peel Sessions Album (nr/Strange Fruit) 1989 ●

RADIO HEART FEATURING GARY NUMAN
Radio Heart (nr/NBR) 1987 ●

SHARPE AND NUMAN
Automatic (nr/Polydor) 1989 ●

DRAMATIS
For Future Reference (nr/Rocket) 1981

Gary Numan (Webb) originally rose to UK prominence in 1979 with a frigid synthesizer dance hit, "Are 'Friends' Electric?" His basic sound—subsequently very influential in the dance music and new romantic spheres—began with precise, antiseptic synth handling much of the instrumental work, topped off with lobotomized deadpan vocals singing science-fiction lyrics.

His first album, **Tubeway Army** (released in America three years later as **First Album**) features primitive electronics and production that show some flair, though guitars dominate and compositions are locked into the three-minute post-punk structure. Shifting the band's billing, **Replicas**, on which synth emerges as the dominant instrument, includes "Are 'Friends' Electric?" and reached the top of the British charts. A composite of material from J.G. Ballard novels, Germanic iciness and '60s pop, the album forged a style that was stunningly new at the time but now sounds hopelessly dated.

The Pleasure Principle, Numan's first release under his own name, contains the international hit "Cars" and continued Numan's maturing love affair with the synthesizer. His interest in technology showed itself to be increasing in both the lyrics and the music. **Telekon** brought guitar noticeably back into the mix. The songs raised Numan's despondent romanticism to new heights (depths?), permeated by doom and synthetic syncopation.

Living Ornaments '79 and **Living Ornaments '80**, each of which documents a London gig from the specified year, were issued separately as well as in a special boxed set. (All three were, by plan, quickly deleted.) Performances give energy to the songs, and Numan's live voice is frequently more impassioned than his studio persona's. The 1979 LP features synthesizer pyrotechnics by Ultravox's Billy Currie that are unmatched on the 1980 recording.

Dance was Numan's first outing following the disbanding of his backup group and his retirement from touring. It exposes a flair for ironic lyrics and a most undanceable set of dance tunes, downplaying the beat and showing new interest in melodics. Unfortunately, **I,**

Assassin suggests that Numan had hit a stylistic quandary, as it tended back towards the sound of his hits but—in the wake of new fashions—without any sense of contemporary style. Whereas **Pleasure Principle** was the vanguard of the future, **I, Assassin** borders on nostalgia.

Numan's former backing group became Dramatis, and tried a little of everything—mock symphonics, electro-disco, mainstream pop—on the mistitled **For Future Reference**. Predictably, the only track worth a toss is the one on which Numan adds his deadpan signature to an otherwise faceless outfit.

Subsequently stumped for a way to revive his flagging career, Numan made the roundly dismissed, almost laughable **Warriors**. He was much better served by the TV best-of and, surprisingly, a collection of presynthesizer riff-rockers dating from 1978. The dozen previously unreleased guitar-based demos on **The Plan** are punky but clear and nonaggressive, providing an unassuming setting for Gazza's characteristically robotic voice and ridiculous lyrics, free of the formulaic setting that typified his early hits, some of which clearly had their beginnings in this material. (Three of the songs were re-recorded with keyboards for **Tubeway Army**.) Funny stuff that holds up quite well and proves he hasn't always been a bozo.

Numan then began issuing albums and singles on his own Numa label, feeding faithful UK fans, who responded by sending every new item briefly into the lower ends of the charts. He began an occasional collaboration with Shakatak keyboardist Bill Sharpe, producing a neat 1985 single ("Change Your Mind") and an album four years later.

Abiding interest in Numan's back catalogue prompted the 1987 release of a comprehensive two-disc, 25-cut (studio and live) career summary, **Exhibition**. (**Selection** offers a sampling of classics from the anthology, including an impressive Zeus B. Held overhaul of "Cars," "Down in the Park," "We Are Glass" and three others. The unrelated **Collection** is also a two-record compilation; there's some overlap with **Exhibition**, but the focus is on familiar LP tracks rather than hit singles.)

In an unsuccessful bid to move his career out of its rut, Numan got a new record deal and made **Metal Rhythm** (released in the US, with two swapped tracks and a remix, as **New Anger**). Except for soulful female backing vocals and technical improvements that bring them into line with contemporary electro-dance sound (if not style—Numan's hip-hop era has yet to begin), Numan's new songs are indistinguishable from his old ones. (And the attempted appropriation of David Byrne's Talking Heads voice is no benefit.)

Recorded live at one London show in September 1988, **The Skin Mechanic** adds another concert album to Numan's catalogue with a program of hits (including the umpteenth "Down in the Park" and "Cars" as well as "New Anger" and 1986's "I Can't Stop") played with an eight-piece band.

Beggars Banquet has issued many of Numan's original albums on twofer CDs, pairing **The Plan** with **Replicas**, **Tubeway Army** with **Dance**, **Pleasure Principle** with **Warriors** and **Telekon** with **I, Assassin**. Completists may also feel compelled to shell out for **The Peel Sessions** EP, three Tubeway Army songs ("Me I

Disconnect from You," "Down in the Park" and "I Nearly Married a Human") recorded in January 1979, or the superseding **Peel Sessions Album**, which adds a second batch, four post-Army efforts recorded eight months later. [sg/i]

NUNS

The Nuns (Posh Boy-Bomp!) 1980
Rumania (PVC) 1986

For a brief moment in the late '70s, it seemed as if the Nuns might be the catalyst for a successful new wave/punk scene in San Francisco. Their early days earned media praise and they owned a rabid local cult following, but time quickly passed them by. Aggressive musicianship and demanding vocals—especially Jennifer Miro's ice-cold, intense singing—make the first album (which the group had to reform to record) well worth hearing. Lyrically, the Nuns spoke to the decadent side of life as well as anyone, with such tales as "Wild," "Child Molester" and "Suicide Child."

The Nuns inexplicably reformed again, with much the same lineup, for another, more innocuous, album six years later. Miro and Jeff Olener share the vocals on **Rumania**, a sophisticated dance record that generally resembles a tasteful version of the group Berlin. Although he's evidently serious, Olener's idiotic melodramatics suggest Fred Schneider as a sarcastic lounge sleaze, while the far more talented Miro melds nicely with the lightweight synthesizer concoctions. Enjoy her solo turns here, but ignore the rest. [cpl/i]

See also *Rank and File*.

NURSE WITH WOUND

Chance Meeting of a Sewing Machine and an Umbrella on a Dissecting Table (nr/United Dairies) 1979 ●
To the Quiet Men from a Tiny Girl (nr/United Dairies) 1980 ●
Merzbild Schwet (nr/United Dairies) 1980 ●
Insect and Individual Silenced (nr/United Dairies) 1981
Homotopy to Marie (nr/United Dairies) 1982
Ostranenie 1913 (nr/Third Mind) 1983
Gyllensköld, Gijerstam and I at Rydberg's EP (Bel. Laylah) 1983
Brained by Falling Masonry EP (Bel. Laylah) 1984
Sylvie and Babs Hi-Fi Companion (Bel. Laylah) 1985 ●
Automating Vol. 1 (nr/United Dairies) 1986
Spiral Insana (Hol. Torso) 1987
Drunk with the Old Man of the Mountains (nr/United Dairies) 1987
Alas the Madonna Does Not Function EP (nr/United Dairies) 1988
Soliloquy for Lilith (nr/Idle Hole) 1988
Automating Vol. 2 (nr/United Dairies) 1988
Present the Sisters of Pataphysics (nr/Idle Hole) 1988
A Sucked Orange (nr/United Dairies) 1989 ●
Cooloorta Moon EP (nr/Idle Hole) 1989
Gyllensköld/Brained (Bel. Laylah) 1989 ●
Soliloquy for Lilith Parts 5/6 (nr/Idle Hole) 1989
Psilotripitaka [CD] (nr/United Dairies) 1990 ●

NURSE WITH WOUND/ORGANUM

A Missing Sense (nr/United Dairies) 1986

NURSE WITH WOUND/CURRENT 93

Nylon Coverin' Body Smotherin' [tape] (nr/United Dairies) 1988

As a testament to the random disorder and beauty of life, London's Nurse with Wound (Steve Stapleton) functioned outside the normal musical channels for a decade, experimenting with tape collages of disjointed phrases, improvised music, electronics and found sounds on a series of intriguing, provocative, humorous and frequently entertaining self-released records. Between 1978 and 1988, Stapleton collaborated with such likeminded sonic adventurers as David Tibet of Current 93 and Tony Wakeford of Sol Invictus to produce a prodigious body of work that embraces surrealism in both content and graphics.

NWW's debut, **Chance Meeting** (originally issued in an edition of 500), welds introverted, spacey guitar to converging hemispheres of intergalactic blips. Then, like much of the band's music, it veers into sketchy doodles: between intermittent lulls of humming and buzzing, there are bursts of frenzied screeching, torture chamber screams, piano scales, women speaking French, etc.

To the Quiet Men from a Tiny Girl resembles a nest of vibrating insects, with clinking chains, someone practicing saxophone, an operatic soprano and other voices. "Ostranenie" suggests a house of a hundred rooms—with a different noise in each.

Merzbild Schwet is as challenging as a Buñuel film, with repeated lines (like "We have fallen silent . . . lost the power of speech . . . our heads are empty . . .") as women laugh and sing. Other ingredients: clanking, ripping velcro, angry voices and something like a sick elephant honking.

Those first three albums were later reissued in a CD boxed set (**Psilotripitaka**), which also includes **Ladies Home Tickler**, another bizarre cut-up collage: snippets of sappy tunes, electrical noises and taunting laughter. **Present the Sisters of Pataphysics** compiles passages from the first three LPs.

The avant drippings on **Sylvie and Babs**—the most guest-laden NWW effort, with dozens of contributors as opposed to the usual one or two—include more laughter and repetition of the word "pardon." The two **Automating** albums collect material from the many compilations to which Nurse with Wound has contributed. Slices of show tunes, repetitive background beats and advice like "Never eat anything bigger than your head" are sprinkled throughout. **Volume II** addresses the hierarchy of biological existence; one segment could be the soundtrack for a science fiction feature about giant rampaging tarantulas.

A pair of 12-inch EPs paired as an album, **Gyllensköld** bristles the coarsest of hairs with scratching and horror dungeon screams while **Brained** adds the demonic voice of Clint Ruin yet contains a movement that could accompany an underwater Cousteau documentary.

A Sucked Orange offers 20 experimental vignettes, many of which justify their titles: the scraping murmur of "Flea Bite," the repetitive clank of utensils beneath a spoken loop of "It ain't necessarily so" on "It Just Ain't So," the catchy ditty plinked out on "This Piano Can't Think."

Soliloquy for Lilith is Stapleton's surprising chef d'oeuvre, a three-album box of contemplative, atmospheric experiments employing treatments of a stringed instrument of his own invention.

Over time, however, the group's usual organized chaos gained a certain predictability. At the end of 1988, Stapleton retired to a farm in Ireland and Nurse with Wound ended.   [mg]

See also *Current 93*.

NUTTY BOYS
See *Madness*.

N.W.A
N.W.A. and the Posse (Macola) 1987
Straight Outta Compton (Ruthless-Priority) 1988 ●
100 Miles and Runnin' EP (Ruthless-Priority) 1990 ●
Niggaz4Life (Ruthless-Priority) 1991 ●

EAZY-E
Eazy-Duz-It (Ruthless-Priority) 1988 ●

ARABIAN PRINCE
Brother Arab (Orpheus) 1989 ●

THE D.O.C.
No One Can Do It Better (Ruthless-Atlantic) 1989 ●

ICE CUBE
AmeriKKKa's Most Wanted (Priority) 1990 ●
Kill at Will (Priority) 1990 ●

Like any grassroots movement, the hard end of rap music attracts a diversity of views and motives. Where Public Enemy brings some intellectual analysis to its militant demands for African-American justice, N.W.A. (Niggas With Attitude) give voice to urban alienation and black rage, offering an unpoliticized expression of their own lives and fantasies. By offering a vast audience of disaffected young people an unvarnished and inherently glamorized version of brutal street life, this potent crew from Compton (south of central Los Angeles) has managed to sell loads of records, pique governmental interest and raise disturbing issues about the reality quotient in rhymes about violence, misogyny and sociopathic behavior.

N.W.A. and the Posse is a loose and funky warm-up, showcasing the young crew—Eazy-E, Ice Cube, Arabian Prince, M.C. Ren, etc.—in various permutations rapping about cars, girls and booze over Dr. Dre's on-the-money Cali-style backing tracks. Although much of the record is strictly for fun ("Drink It Up" is a goofy party number sung to the tune of "Twist and Shout"; "Fat Girl" tells a dumb story about an overzealous, overweight gal), Eazy-E's autobiographical "Boyz-n-the Hood" and the nonjudgmental "Dope Man" aptly demonstrate the group's tougher side. Although delivered as a TV joke, "Panic Zone" elevates Compton to a mythological domain over which N.W.A. prevails.

Beginning with the classic "Crazy motherfucker named Ice Cube/From the gang called Niggas With Attitude," the blistering **Straight Outta Compton** defines gangsta style, laying down a shockingly fearless tough-guy line, demanding respect and threatening violence at every turn. "Do I look like a motherfucking role model?," asks Ice Cube in "Gangsta Gangsta": "To a kid looking up to me life ain't nothin but bitches and money." (His nearly upstanding "Express Yourself," however, confuses matters completely.) The controversial "__ tha Police," a mock trial of the boys in blue, promises armed resistance to unwarranted hassles, underscoring the point with the sound of gunshots. Whether this hyper-drama is meant to be taken seriously or not, the distinction—created by first-person delivery of realistic tales that shift without blinking from hustling women at parties to shooting people for fun—is obviously lost on some listeners.

Exploiting their notoriety as FBI-certified outlaws, N.W.A—no longer numbering Ice Cube in the posse—rap a high-tension action adventure on the title track of **100 Miles and Runnin'**, which also includes "Sa Prize (Part 2)," a crudely theatrical continuation of "__ tha Police." But any hope of a political consciousness taking hold is dashed by "Just Don't Bite It," a detailed discussion of fellatio, and the pointlessness of the record's two other cuts.

On his own album, Eazy-E (Eric Wright) reveals himself to be a surprisingly ineffectual rapper, an unconvincing hothead and would-be sex machine who sounds like the victim of peer pressure. **Eazy-Duz-It** demonstrates E's ready willingness to restrain himself (something that has evidently never occurred to Ice Cube) and make commercial concessions (Cube's got him beat there, with an absurd cable-TV beer ad that rhymes "malt liquor" and "makes your jimmy thicker"). Eazy's weedy voice suits meaningless tripe like "We Want Eazy," "Radio" and "I'mma Break It Down" on the cleaned-up side, but he sounds forced and fake on the nasty discussions of crime ("Nobody Move," a rap over Yellowman's toast of the same name) and sex ("Still Talkin'," which contains such charming remarks as "I might be a woman-beater but I'm not a pussy-eater") that fill the album's Street Side.

With one memorably bad pun ("She's Got a Big Posse," a dating nightmare) the understated **Brother Arab** is a nonconfrontational album with a couple of positive doses of reality ("Let the Good Times Roll (Nickel Bag)," "It's a Dope Thang") amid the macho sex and party rhymes. While Arabian Prince has distinctive beats and a quiet authority to his voice, he isn't an inventive enough rhymer, and his LP is easy to overlook.

The D.O.C., another member of the N.W.A. family, released only one album before his rhyming career was derailed in a near-fatal car crash, but it's a good one. Sharply produced (using live musicians as well as transistor beats) by Dr. Dre, **No One Can Do It Better**—with guest spots by the entire clan, from Eazy-E and Ice Cube to Michel'le—is a symphony of scratching and party funk that avoids politics to make a more general cultural statement.

Quitting N.W.A after a management dispute, Ice Cube (Oshea Jackson) hooked up with Public Enemy and the Bomb Squad and went solo, playing his viciously coldhearted punk role to the hilt on **AmeriKKKa's Most Wanted**. Overdoing it on every level—attitude, misogyny, gunplay, crude sexuality and language—the brilliantly produced record is unarguably powerful and frequently incisive in its venomous stabs at various targets (taking as many haphazard pot shots as **Fear of a Black Planet**) and expressions of incoherent rage. But the victimization of women and the glorification of violence makes this platinum-selling outpouring of profound sociopathy a deeply unsettling cultural achievement.

Kill at Will consists of two LP remixes and four new tracks, including the lighthearted "Jackin' for Beats" (which bites EPMD, PE, Digital Underground, L.L. Cool J and other peers) and the devastating "Dead Homiez," solemnly contemplating the murder of a friend over an evocative mix of horn, guitar and piano.

[i]

JUDY NYLON AND CRUCIAL
Pal Judy (nr/On-U Sound) 1982 [tape] (ROIR) 1990
SNATCH
Snatch EP (nr/Fetish) 1980
Snatch (nr/Pandemonium) 1983

Abandoning New York for London, no-wave singer Judy Nylon teamed with Pat Palladin to form Snatch, ultimately making the German-inspired sound collage "R.A.F." with Brian Eno, which appeared on the B-side of his "King's Lead Hat" 45. The **Snatch** EP features Nylon and Palladin teaming up for a pseudo-Tom Waits blues drone called "Shopping for Clothes" and the softly electronic ballad, "Joey," as well as "Red Army," which imitates the technique and style of "R.A.F." Clever and inventive, the work has gentle strength, bitter humor and a thoroughly jaundiced worldview.

Pal Judy, which she co-produced with Adrian Sherwood, grafts Snatch's blues poetics and electronic compositional structures onto fairly straightforward rock music. The result—a moody, adeptly created and performed record suggestive of Patti Smith—smacks of modernized cocktail-lounge music (in the best tradition of that genre). Nylon's originals are acrid and funny in their scope, but the record is stolen by her laconic, opiated rendition of "Jailhouse Rock." [sg]

See also *Johnny Thunders*.

PHILIP OAKEY & GIORGIO MORODER

See *Human League*.

EBENEZER OBEY

Je Ka Jo (nr/Virgin) 1983
Miliki Plus (nr/Virgin) 1983
Juju Jubilee (Shanachie) 1985 ●
Get Yer Jujus Out (Rykodisc) 1989 ф

Along with King Sunny Adé, Chief Commander Ebenezer Obey dominates the juju music genre, that beautiful, spiritual and eminently danceable combination of traditional chants, hymns, highlife, rock and country-western. An easy way to think of juju is as inverted Western pop: interlocking guitars function as rhythm instruments while numerous drummers take on the melodic responsibilities. Born in Western Nigeria in 1942, Obey joined his first professional band, the Fatai Rolling Dollars, in 1958. By 1963 he had formed his own group, and has since released over 90 singles and albums.

Obey calls his personal style the *miliki* (enjoyment) sound. Beginning where noted juju entertainer I.K. Diaro left off, Obey has drawn in such Western elements as multiple guitars and a Hawaiian steel guitar soloist, adding them to the traditional rhythmic fundament. Songs tend to reflect Obey's strong Christian beliefs as well as the common problems (often economic) of everyday life.

No record could do justice to the endlessly intense melodic and rhythmic variations heard during one of Obey's all-night concerts. (His touring band is fifteen members strong.) Most juju albums contain side-long songs, but even those rarely put across the scope of a single number. **Je Ka Jo** and **Miliki Plus** are similar to Obey's many Nigerian records; **Jubilee** is a sampler package—edited versions of eight tunes—that displays Obey's progression from grassroots juju to ever-more-sophisticated compositions. Unfortunately, it suffers from a severe case of enjoyment interruptus.

Recorded onstage in exotic Seattle (1987) with his Inter-Reformers Band, **Get Yer Jujus Out** delivers the live goods, as Obey weaves a sinuous spell for nearly 70 minutes. Featuring nine songs from his scores of Nigerian records, the music rolls with a hipshaking pan-African lilt informed by the guitar styles of *soukous*, highlife and, of course, juju.   [rg]

RIC OCASEK

See *Cars*.

OCEAN BLUE

The Ocean Blue (Sire-Reprise) 1989 ●

Despite echoes of Echo and the Bunnymen, Ultravox and other post-Roxy Britons, this tasteful and skilled quartet actually hails from central Pennsylvania. Energetically playing pristine art-pop of varying character (although some of the tracks are rather styleless), the Ocean Blue comes up with a few winners on the second side of its Mark Opitz-produced debut, but is otherwise too mild-mannered to matter. The group obviously has all the necessary artistic tools in hand, but will need a stronger vision to create a really striking record.   [i]

SINÉAD O'CONNOR

The Lion and the Cobra (Ensign-Chrysalis) 1987 ●
I Do Not Want What I Haven't Got (Ensign-Chrysalis) 1990 ●

It's been a while since a newcomer burst onto the scene with quite as much impact as this amazingly talented young Dubliner. With masterful ability to switch gears between the delicate and the pompous or the direct and the ambiguous, O'Connor piles bits of hard rock, funk, '70s-style spaciness and Celtic traditionalism into her self-produced debut album. Delivering deliberately vague lyrics that manage to at least *sound* poetic, O'Connor wails, shrieks, whispers, croons, snarls and bellows with the skill and confidence of a veteran. Although **The Lion and the Cobra** doesn't display much sophistication in the way of musical skills—the songs are pretty basic—her creativity and expressiveness are quite impressive. It wouldn't hurt if she did lighten up a bit, but it's rare to hear such a young artist (20 when the LP was recorded) so clearly in control; if the six-and-a-half-minute "Troy" sounds slow and laborious, she probably wanted it that way.

As grand an artistic and commercial success as the debut was, O'Connor was just warming up. **I Do Not Want What I Haven't Got**, again self-produced, dwarfs its predecessor in terms of creative ambition and achievement. Amazingly, this harrowingly personal testament to the tumult in her life sold two million copies in its first month of release, largely on the strength of Prince's "Nothing Compares 2 U," ironically one of the record's weakest efforts. Again refusing to be typecast, O'Connor makes a warm orchestral bed for "Three Babies," delivers the otherwise a cappella "I Am Stretched on Your Grave" over a clattering hip-hop beat, conjures up catchy pop-rock for "The Emperor's New Clothes," gathers thickly chugging electric guitars for "Jump in the River" and sings "Black Boys on Mopeds"—a topical indictment of English hypocrisy—as acoustic folk. But such diversity is no impediment to the album's overall impact. Unified by the razor-sharp intensity of her lyrics and the staggering power of her vocals, **I Do Not Want What I Haven't Got** is an absolute masterpiece.   [dgs/i]

See also *U2*.

477

OF CABBAGES AND KINGS

Of Cabbages and Kings (Purge/Sound League) 1987
Face (Purge/Sound League) 1988
Basic Pain Basic Pleasure (Triple X) 1990

Evolved from early-'80s Chicago-to-New York transplants the Bag People (whose one undistributed 45 was seemingly pressed solely for the jukebox at their local Brooklyn bar), guitarist Carolyn Master reassembled Of Cabbages and Kings in 1985 from parts scattered to Swans, Foetus, Glenn Branca, etc. Playing only sporadically due to their outside commitments, they gradually coalesced into a focused unit, although Ted Parsons bailed out after the second record (for his full-time group Prong) to be replaced by ex-Live Skull/Ruin drummer Rich Hutchins (also now departed); Diane Wlezien, still a Chi-based blues chanteuse, remains a cameo vocalist both live and on record. Effectively, the core of OCAK is the duo of Master and bassist/singer Algis Kizys (a Swan and sometime Branca associate) plus a drummer.

Decidedly unprolific and rare to perform, OCAK's highly visceral attack is founded on a vivid technical mastery owing little to the commonly revered tenets of speed and/or flash, instead conjuring a brutal, primal power and intensity virtually unmatched in modern music, with Kizys' bone-rattling semi-chorded playing rendering most contemporary rhythms effete, even as Master's guitar shards swirl about the edges like razors in a tornado.

Of Cabbages and Kings delivers a dizzying panorama of dark surrealistic desire and fear—both in sound and lyric—the latter including a soundtracked snippet of Baudelaire. The seven-song **Face** delves deeper into the group's grueling, obsessive world, stretching the music into less predictable shapes and ingesting piano and accordion while reintroducing Master as a vocalist. Comparatively quiet in spots but no less redolent of dis/unease, it (like the first record) includes radical updates of Bag People material, reinterpreted in Cabbage style as paranoid introspection, more like the ruminations of a self-loathing rape victim than the simpleminded lurid voyeurism so common in deathmetal and elsewhere. Two of the eight songs on **Basic Pain Basic Pleasure** were previously issued on a 45 and a compilation; what the album lacks in length it more than makes up in breadth, offering the band's crispest (if not most physically imposing) production and arrangements, as well as increased variety of approach. Hutchins is neither as creative nor as aggressively captivating a drummer as Parsons, but songs like the moody, guitarless "Crawl Again" illustrate yet more facets of a band too facilely dismissed as "mere" New York noisemongers.   [ab]

See also *Live Skull, Swans*.

SEAN O'HAGAN

See *Microdisney*.

OH-OK

Wow Mini Album EP (DB) 1982
Furthermore What EP (DB) 1983

BUZZ OF DELIGHT

Sound Castles EP (DB) 1984

HOLIDAY

Hello EP (Nightshade) 1987

HETCH HETCHY

Make Djibouti EP (Texas Hotel) 1988
Swollen (Texas Hotel) 1990

After hearing so many art bands buried in their own sense of self-importance, it's refreshing to bask in the modesty of Athens' Oh-OK. Like R.E.M. (with whom they share a family tie), this humble group put their elliptical ideas over as much by being good guys as anything else.

Oh-OK was a guitarless trio on the 7-inch **Wow**, offering four clever and tuneful songs that get their drive from Lynda (sister of Michael) Stipe's pumping bass and their charm from Linda Hopper's breathy singing: a delightful mix of Pylon and the female side of the B-52's.

With a new drummer and guitarist Matthew Sweet joining Hopper and Stipe, **Furthermore What** (a six-song 12-inch, co-produced by Mitch Easter) has dreamy melodies, oblique lyrics, ringing guitars—it *is* the New South, after all—and quirky, minimalist arrangements that hover just outside the pop realm. This kind of undersell rarely ascends to greatness, but Oh-OK is a distinctly fresh pleasure.

Following Oh-OK, Sweet formed the Buzz of Delight, a sugary pop duo, with original Oh-OK drummer David Pierce. The six finely wrought tunes on **Sound Castles** capture the essence of airy Southern power-pop and are ultimately delightful.

Hopper, meanwhile, formed Holiday with Lynn Blakey (also a singer/guitarist/songwriter) and a rhythm section. Recorded in 1985, the 12-inch **Hello** makes good use of the women's vocal interplay on five light and sprightly songs that have an appealingly casual sense of accomplishment. (More recently, Hopper has been fronting a new quartet that changed its name from Homemade Sister to Swell.)

Although her name is Lynda L. Limner, the Hetch Hetchy singer with a sometimes harsh loud-soft-loud style is the selfsame Stipe sister. (Michael produced the trio's six-song debut.) From the lightly laughing clarinet that opens "Retarded Camel" through chunks of darkly deep guitar and lots of smooth new music electronic keyboards, the melodic group—named after a valley in Yosemite National Park—creates the kind of lightly arty pop-rock that college radio eats for breakfast, lunch and dessert.

With production by Hugo Largo's Tim Sommer, Hetch Hetchy—now a duo of Limner (vocals, bass, guitar and keyboards) and Jay Totty (bass and guitar), assisted by local singers and players—moves into tastefully restrained atmospheric vagueness on **Swollen**. Some of the songs use drums and a few ("Satanette," "Retsina," "Mother's Drum") actually have decisive melodies but, for the most part, this is sub-Largo background music in need of a spine.   [jl/'e/i]

See also *Matthew Sweet*.

OINGO BOINGO

Oingo Boingo EP (IRS) 1980
Only a Lad (A&M) 1981 ●
Nothing to Fear (A&M) 1982 ●
Good for Your Soul (A&M) 1983 ●

478

Dead Man's Party (MCA) 1985 ●
Boi-ngo (MCA) 1987 ●
Boingo Alive: Celebration of a Decade 1979-1988
    (MCA) 1988 ●
Skeletons in the Closet: The Best of Oingo-Boingo (A&M)
    1989 ●
Dark at the End of the Tunnel (MCA) 1990 ●

DANNY ELFMAN
So-lo (MCA) 1984 ●
Music for a Darkened Theatre (MCA) 1990 ●

This eight-piece LA outfit (with a three-man horn section) started out trying to be a West Coast answer to XTC and Devo, but suffered from studied wackiness/quirkiness and managed to hide solid cleverness behind overproduction and hamminess. While frontman Danny Elfman has emerged as the king of the soundtracks, Oingo Boingo has pretty much continued to ply their rather pointless trade with little modification.

The EP, all 10 inches of it, is the band's most succinct engagement. The four cuts belie the size of the lineup—a trio might have made these long slices of mild perversity. The album that followed, however, plays up OB's flaws, letting contrived bits diminish the impact of demi-clever lyrics and thoroughly competent music. The only track that stands out is "On the Outside," and it succeeds because it sounds normal. Despite obvious talent, **Only a Lad** is a waste.

Taking a turn towards synth-funk (as either a commercial ploy or an amused art statement), **Nothing to Fear** is more likable, yet still sounds phony. A couple of the tunes, especially the title cut, are forceful enough to be exciting. When not pushing pressurized dance rock, Oingo Boingo revert to their previously established lighter style, and the horns play it subtle rather than brassy. Better, but still a derivative disappointment.

Electronic music veteran Robert Margouleff produced **Good for Your Soul** and trimmed some of the usual excess, giving Oingo Boingo a streamlined and powerfully driven attack. The timely "Wake Up (It's 1984)" and "Who Do You Want to Be" are among the most invigorating and engaging things the band has ever done. There's still significant quantities of chaff, but on this outing the wise-guy dance-rock largely works.

Singer, chief songwriter and Oingo Boingo leader Danny Elfman made **So-lo** with five members of the band, but it offers a slightly different, more synthesized outlook. "Gratitude" is a brilliant construct combining Elfman's best melody and absurd vocals in one wacky tour de force; other tracks (a ballad, a raveup, etc.) are more like Oingo Boingo's work. Displaying Wall of Voodoo B-movie aspirations, Elfman unfortunately lacks the focus or vision to counteract his grandiose, theatrical instincts.

Dispersing rumors of nonexistence, Oingo Boingo returned with their least obnoxious record yet. **Dead Man's Party** benefits from one captivating soundtrack single ("Weird Science") and a couple of other strong songs (including "Stay," a soulful "Help Me" and the Akron-oriented title track).

Did Spike Jones mix **Boi-ngo** or what? Instruments fly out of the speakers at crazy angles as if this were a stereo effects demonstration record. The absurdly busy arrangements make the songs take a back seat to the studio showboating as each guitar chord, horn toot and drum beat calls attention to itself. Elfman is really in control here, and his mastery of this hyperkinetic niche (at times it sounds like two coordinated recordings being played simultaneously) is an awesome individual accomplishment. The LP jitterbugs, bounces and slides from start to finish, leaving listeners either happily exhausted or utterly exasperated.

With Elfman's career as a composer of film and television scores in superstar overdrive (the **Music for a Darkened Theatre** compilation—orchestral excerpts from *Batman*, *Dick Tracy*, *Scrooged*, *The Simpsons* and many more—provides a summary of his soundtrack albums that no one need actually hear), he still finds time to fit the band into his schedule. And Boingo—with just two personnel changes in eleven years—just keeps on keeping on, issuing a double-live set (recorded, without the distraction of an audience, in a Hollywood rehearsal studio), a straightforward studio retrospective of the band's A&M era and **Dark at the End of the Tunnel**, an all-new LP of Elfman originals which won't surprise anyone at all familiar with the group's past work. [i]

OLD SKULL
Get Outta School (Restless) 1989 ●

Billed as the youngest punk band in the world, these noisy Wisconsin tykes (two Toulon brothers and a non-fraternal drummer whose dad is in the Tar Babies) make a godawful calamity on **Get Outta School**, screaming and ripping through fifteen semi-coherent noisefests that are amusingly bad but still hard to believe as the work of nine-year-olds. With daddy Toulon (who has some connection to Missing Foundation) co-producing, these precocious skate-rockers switch from dead serious ("Homeless," "AIDS") to silly ("Hot Dog Hell") in a flash, sounding like nothing so much as a pre-teen birthday party spiked with Jolt cola and amplifiers. [i]

100 FLOWERS
100 Flowers (Happy Squid) 1983
Drawing Fire EP (Happy Squid) 1984
100 Years of Pulchritude [CD] (Happy Squid-Rhino)
    1990 ●

You wouldn't know it to listen to their records, but West Los Angeles' 100 Flowers started as a joke, a black-humored parody of the punk scene. As the Urinals, they recorded a pair of 1979 7-inch EPs and a single for Happy Squid, then got serious, changed their name and got *real* serious. In their second incarnation, the trio played arty, poetic music that is kinetic in spite of occasional murkiness.

100 Flowers owes a mild debt to the Fall, although its more melodic guitar sound is all-American. Dispensing with such concepts as verses and choruses, the trio favors subterranean funk grooves and drones; the effect is impressive if limited, and wears thin over the record's course. The five-song **Drawing Fire** EP benefits from stronger material. With songs that build but never cop out with climaxes and releases, this is how R.E.M. might have sounded as a punk band.

Neatly recapitulating 100 Flowers' entire existence, the 28-track **100 Years of Pulchritude** combines the album, EP, both sides of a 1982 single and three compilation contributions. Two previously unreleased cuts offer a bonus to real fans. [jl/i]

See also *Trotsky Icepick*.

101ERS

Elgin Avenue Breakdown (nr/Andalucia) 1981

Before there was a Clash, Joe Strummer was in a gritty, R&B-styled London pub band. The 101ers broke up after a short career, issuing only one incredible 45, "Keys to Your Heart" (an alternative version of which is included here), while in business. Released five years after the fact, **Elgin Avenue Breakdown** combines three 1975-'76 demo sessions and a live performance captured on cassette. It's an essential artifact for Clash-ologists, spreading hints of things to come all over the place. As an energetic slice of simple, raucous rock'n-'roll, it's worth every penny as well. [i]

See also *Clash*.

ONLY ONES

The Only Ones (nr/CBS) 1978
Even Serpents Shine (nr/CBS) 1979
Special View (Epic) 1979 ●
Baby's Got a Gun (Epic) 1980
Remains (Fr. Closer) 1984 ●
Alone in the Night (nr/Dojo) 1986
Live (Skyclad) 1989 ●
The Peel Sessions Album (nr/Strange Fruit) 1989 ●

ENGLAND'S GLORY

Legendary Lost Recordings (Skyclad) 1989 ●

Led by singer/songwriter Peter Perrett, England's Only Ones combined the energy of the punk movement and a more traditional sense of rock craft, with Perrett singing his goodnatured tortured-romantic lyrics in a distinctive (and not unpleasant) whine. The quartet's mix of youthful spunk and seasoned experience (drummer Mike Kellie was a member of Spooky Tooth and bassist Alan Mair's résumé stretched back to the early '60s) helped gain the Only Ones quick prominence, but only one song—the much-covered "Another Girl, Another Planet"—earned the highly touted group any lasting acclaim.

The Only Ones (which includes that stupendous number) is the best of the three original albums. Perrett's languid vocals and songs provide the character and focus, while the band's skills carry it off handsomely. **Even Serpents Shine** varies little from its predecessor and contains some captivating material, but lacks anything as great as "Another Girl, Another Planet." **Special View** picks tracks off both albums and adds the two sides of the band's self-released 1977 debut single for an introductory lesson in the Only Ones' early oeuvre.

Although finally realizing simultaneous release in the US and the UK with the Colin Thurston-produced **Baby's Got a Gun**, the Only Ones' commercial success was still too slight to sustain them, and they called it quits in 1981. The group's cult status has grown steadily ever since, as evidenced (or at least encouraged) by a stream of posthumous releases. **Remains** and **Alone in the Night** are decent collections of non-album material.

The songs on **Live** predate the CBS albums, and show the band to have been firmly in musical control even at that early juncture. **The Peel Sessions Album** compiles sixteen BBC recordings from 1977 to '80, and is actually a stronger representation of the Only Ones' gifts than any of the band's studio albums.

The England's Glory disc offers ten 1973 demos by Perrett's pre-Only Ones combo (including future Squeeze bassist Harry Kakoulli) and demonstrates nascent talent as well as an overriding Lou Reed fixation. Two of the songs, "City of Fun" and "Peter and the Pets," later showed up on the Only Ones' first LP. [i/hd]

OPAL

Northern Line EP (nr/One Big Guitar) 1985
Happy Nightmare Baby (SST) 1987 ●
Early Recordings (Rough Trade) 1989 φ

MAZZY STAR

She Hangs Brightly (Rough Trade) 1990 ●

KENDRA SMITH/DAVID ROBACK/KEITH MITCHELL

Fell from the Sun EP (Serpent-Enigma) 1984

After he left the Rain Parade, guitarist David Roback and ex-Dream Syndicate bassist Kendra Smith formed a quartet known as Clay Allison (obscurely named after a character in a TV movie) with drummer Keith Mitchell and guitarist Juan Gomez. The group issued a single, but dropped a member and shed the moniker before adding two new songs to flesh out **Fell from the Sun**. On it, Smith's vocals perfectly meld with the subtle mood music—a pleasant drone with translucent elegance that resembles the Velvet Underground at their most restrained. Lovely and touching.

Renaming themselves Opal, the group issued a three-song 12-inch that continues in the same vein. "Northern Line" and "Empty Bottles" are gorgeous acoustic folk-blues, while the B-side, "Soul Giver" (which also turns up on **Happy Nightmare Baby**), is eight-and-a-half minutes of spacey organ and feedback guitar.

Opal clung to neo-psychedelia, even after many of its original Los Angeles scene compatriots had moved on to other fads. **Happy Nightmare Baby** has its share of nostalgic organ-colored drone contemplations, but adds an unexpected and amusing item to the repertoire: a stripped-down T. Rex imitation ("Rocket Machine") that drifts towards Television. Criticisms: Smith's laconic singing can become arduous, some of the instrumental work is self-indulgent nonsense and the pace is too slow. Qualities: the songs are there, the ambience is affecting and the performances offer enough texture and dynamics to make Opal's debut album ultimately satisfying.

Smith exited the group in the middle of the **Happy Nightmare** tour, and the posthumous **Early Recordings** gathers outtakes, all four **Fell from the Sun** tracks, plus "Northern Line" and "Empty Bottles." Draining away much of **Happy Nightmare**'s pseudo-mystical fiddle-faddle, **Early Recordings** concentrates on Opal's acoustic side; the spare production adds a chilling closeness to Smith's vocals, and Roback's guitar noodlings feel loose and uncontrived. The previously unissued tracks, especially "Empty Box Blues" and "My Only Friend," have a casual, unrestrained grace. The CD appends "Hear the Wind Blow."

A few years later, Roback joined up with LA singer Hope Sandoval, formerly of an acoustic duo (Going Home) whose unreleased album Roback had produced. Like Smith, Sandoval has a smooth, passionless voice, but she also has a disarming childlike quality that's almost ghostly. Other than that, differences between Opal and Mazzy Star are minor. Roback shifts between acoustic folk and electric psych-outs while Sandoval rambles, waiflike, about love, highways and sailboats.   [i/kss]

See also *Dream Syndicate, Rain Parade*.

OPHELIAS

The Ophelias (Strange Weekend) 1987
Oriental Head (Rough Trade) 1988
The Big O (Rough Trade) 1989

This San Francisco quartet sings/chants theatrical lyrics over colorfully dramatic rock—like Oingo Boingo but more inclined to genuine offbeatness and exciting music—on **The Ophelias**, an accomplished if not entirely appealing debut. "Mr. Rabbit," an old children's folk song given a charming update, is the album's high point; elsewhere, Leslie Medford (vocals, guitar, trumpet, harmonica, recorder) tries too hard to sell his songs, obscuring whatever lies beneath all the multi-tracked play-acting. And using dialogue from *Hamlet* is just a little pretentious, n'est-ce pas?

Besides unveiling a half-new lineup that includes guitarist David Immerglück (also of the Monks of Doom), **Oriental Head** displays a mildly psychedelicized rethink and a Zappaesque goof-jazz influence. Medford's still on his Shakespearian kick (the LP leads off with "Midsummernight's Scene," a number credited to Marc Bolan), but tones down the delivery to improve songs rather than suffocate them. Unpredictable, uneven and occasionally fascinating, **Oriental Head** is filled with ideas, some of which actually make weird sense.

Issued in a circular sleeve, **The Big O**—easily the Ophelias' best effort yet—irons the group's music into an effectively derivative set of '60s folk-rock/acid-garage/rock idioms. Using other songwriters besides Medford helps, as some of the record's most entertaining tunes ("Leah Hirsig," for instance) aren't his. Typical of the escapade's goodnatured foolishness are "Lawrence of Euphoria" (sung like a Bonzo Dog Band outtake), a cover of the Nervous Breakdown's crude proto-punk "I Dig Your Mind" and an inexplicable T. Rex parody, "When Winter Comes."   [i]

See also *Camper Van Beethoven*.

O-POSITIVE

Only Breathing EP (Throbbing Lobster) 1985
Cloud Factory EP (Link) 1987 ●
toyboatToyBoatTOYBOAT (Epic) 1990 ●

Although some may view Boston's O Positive as nothing more than generic college-radio pop, the Boston group's talent and potential exceed that of many similar bands. Unfortunately, the quintet has yet to make the most of its abilities on record.

Only Breathing is a promising debut. Drummer Alex Lob and bassist David Ingham unite to form a monstrously strong rhythmic backbone, upon which guitarist/singer Dave Herlihy drapes his clumsy but earnest lyrics about self-preservation in the face of obsession and unrequited love. Although this is thematic terrain which has been crossed a million times, Herlihy displays an Andy Partridge-like penchant for clever wordplay, some of which works nicely.

Released two years later, **Cloud Factory** is a horrible sophomore effort. Murky sound negates the rhythm section; Herlihy's lyrics and delivery are also gutterballs, an apparent attempt to emulate Michael "This doesn't make much sense but it sure does sound intellectual" Stipe stylings. Add in a shameful overdependence on guitar effects, and this is one bad record. (Perhaps for comparison purposes, the CD and cassette include **Only Breathing**.)

toyboatToyBoatTOYBOAT, the band's major label debut (and its first full-length album), combines the first record's best attributes with some of the second's shortcomings. The results—which often waver between R.E.M. imitations and U2 guitar quotes (with one laughably bad Wilson Pickett rewrite)—are generally pleasantly listenable, if nothing more. The rhythm section is as complex and appealing as before, and Herlihy's guitar work and lyrics show improvement, but this innocuous LP is, at best, distinctly short on character.   [icm]

ORANGE JUICE

You Can't Hide Your Love Forever (nr/Polydor) 1982
Rip It Up (nr/Polydor) 1982 ●
Texas Fever EP (nr/Polydor) 1984
The Orange Juice (nr/Polydor) 1984
In a Nutshell (nr/Polydor) 1985

ZEKE MANYIKA

Call and Response (nr/Polydor) 1985
Mastercrime (nr/Some Bizzare-Parlophone) 1989 ●

EDWYN COLLINS

Hope and Despair (nr/Demon) 1989 ●
Hellbent on Compromise (nr/Demon) 1990 ●

Glasgow's insufferably coy Orange Juice, de facto leaders of the Scottish neo-pop revolution, typified a UK trend towards clean, innocent looks that unfortunately spilled over into the music. Emphasizing their "unspoiled" raggedness, the band began with clumsy tunes about insecurity and romantic rejection; singer Edwyn Collins mumbles and croons like a slowed-down Ray Davies. **You Can't Hide Your Love Forever** is supposed to be charming, but isn't.

Surprisingly, **Rip It Up** (not named after the Little Richard tune) explores the first album's ingenuousness in greater depth with thought-provoking results. Though young love remains the theme, tension has replaced cuteness; on the title track, "Louise Louise" and others, Collins responds angrily to being treated like a chump. He's still a bit of a narcissistic vocalist, but **Rip It Up**'s more realistic approach is appealing and rewarding.

Escalating musical differences and other internal conflicts caused the band to split prior to the release of **Texas Fever**, leaving Collins and drummer Zeke Manyika to carry on as a duo. Salvaged from the original band's final sessions, the **Texas Fever** EP (produced by Dennis Bovell) further refines the standards set on **Rip It Up**. There's an implicit Western theme, but most of the songs have a quirky, exotic Afro-funk feel, fleshed out with stellar guitar work by Collins and Malcolm Ross (later of Aztec Camera). Their talents make "Punch Drunk," "A Place in My Heart" and "A Sad Lament" memorable.

Collins and Manyika again teamed up with Bovell for **The Orange Juice**, which contains some of Collins' strongest songs: the sadly biographical "Lean Period," the melodically haunting "What Presence?!" and "Artisans," a garage-styled raveup.

Embittered by commercial failure, Orange Juice called it quits. **In a Nutshell** is a posthumous compilation that contains the band's very best, from the early days on Postcard ("Falling and Laughing," "Poor Old Soul") through the last days on Polydor (tracks from the third LP).

Collins and Manyika continue to be musically active. Turning again to Bovell as producer and bassist, Collins made a spectacular solo debut with **Hope and Despair**, a debonair but rocking album of strongly worded downcast contemplations delivered in a commanding deep voice over varied music that rings and resonates with exceptional songwriting craft. Aztec Camera's Roddy Frame is one of the luminary sidemen; the CD and cassette add the title track as a bonus.

[jy/ag]

ORB

See *Justified Ancients of Mu Mu*.

WILLIAM ORBIT
Orbit (IRS) 1987 ●
Strange Cargo (IRS No Speak) 1988 ●
Strange Cargo 2 (IRS No Speak) 1991 φ
TORCH SONG
Wish Thing (IRS) 1984
Exhibit A (IRS) 1987
BASSOMATIC
Set the Controls for the Heart of the Bass (nr/Virgin) 1990
(Virgin) 1991 ●

Torch Song debuted as a trio on **Wish Thing**, an ethereal set of instrumentally subtle synth-dance tracks, given most of their character by Laurie Mayer's delicate voice and the gimmicky production. "Don't Look Now" and "Sweet Thing" are appealing, airy concoctions; a demento version of "Ode to Billy Joe" seems calculated to shock and/or offend but is nonetheless amusing. Intriguing.

Three years later, reduced to a duo, Torch Song ("featuring William Orbit") issued a second record consisting of four cuts (including "Don't Look Now" and "Sweet Thing") remixed from **Wish Thing**, plus five new ones that also benefit from Mayer's wan singing. Inconclusive but equally appealing, **Exhibit A** has another weird cover version: an atmospheric deconstruction of Blind Faith's "Can't Find My Way Home."

Multi-instrumentalist Orbit (real name: Wainwright) then dropped the Torch Song name, found a new singing partner in Peta Nikolich and recorded **Orbit**. (Mayer is still his co-writer, but she performs on only one song.)

A disappointingly conservative—except for the mock-Spanish horns—cover of the Psychedelic Furs' "Love My Way" leads off the album, and things never get much more adventurous than that. Despite an assortment of genres, most of the music is short on individual character; Nikolich is a capable singer without enough personality to carry the weight. "Feel Like Jumping," a mildly revisionist reggae cover (Jackie Mittoo), is the weak album's lively highlight.

Building on his soundtrack work, Orbit released **Strange Cargo**, a one-man-band collection of unrelated instrumental pieces recorded between 1984 and 1987. Mostly urgent and kinetic, with colorful sound effects, the unresolved semi-songs are mood-heavy and suggest a number of visual idioms, including action-adventure, comedy, espionage and mystery.

In recent years, Orbit has become an extremely successful remixer, with credits that include Madonna, Prince and the Cure. In early 1991, however, he released a second instrumental album, **Strange Cargo 2**.

Bassomatic is Orbit's dance band with singer Sharon Musgrave, a DJ and a percussionist.   [i]

ORCHESTRA ARCANA
See *Bill Nelson*.

ORCHESTRAL MANOEUVRES IN THE DARK
Orchestral Manoeuvres in the Dark (nr/DinDisc) 1980
(Virgin) 1987 ●
Organisation (nr/DinDisc) 1980 (Virgin) 1987 ●
O.M.D. (Virgin-Epic) 1981
Architecture & Morality (Virgin-Epic) 1981 ●
Dazzle Ships (Virgin-Epic) 1983 ●
Junk Culture (Virgin-A&M) 1984 ●
Crush (Virgin-A&M) 1985 ●
The Pacific Age (Virgin-A&M) 1986 ●
Shame EP (nr/Virgin) 1987 ●
The Best of OMD (Virgin-A&M) 1988 ●
Sugar Tax (Virgin) 1991 ●

Moving from electronic tape experiments to highly polished synthesizer pop and beyond, Liverpudlians Andy McCluskey (bass/vocals/keyboards) and synthesist Paul Humphreys (with other fulltime members, including—very significantly—a corporeal acoustic drummer) are among the most successful practitioners of electro-pop, as first demonstrated by a delightful string of singles. Abandoning their formula after two albums, however, OMD proved capable of far more ambitious creations not tied to the apron strings of technology.

Orchestral Manoeuvres in the Dark exhibits stylish electro-pop comparable to Ultravox. Aided by Dalek I's Andy Gill, McCluskey and Humphreys build the songs up from computer-generated rhythms and, while the album does not create any new forms, it polishes the synthesizer song into a full-bodied medium. Thanks to a knack for melodies and hooks, notable attractions are the catchy "Electricity" and "Messages."

Organisation (which originally included an excellent bonus single of early tape experiments and live tracks) introduces drummer Malcolm Holmes and ethereal synthesizer techniques that suit the depressive sub-

482

ject matter of "Enola Gay" and the like. It also pays attention to ensure variation in the tunes, a problem that mars the first LP. With nods to John Foxx and David Bowie, OMD overlays melodies to dramatic effect; the performances are excellent.

O.M.D. is an American compilation of songs from the two British albums, including both catchy OMD standards, "Enola Gay" and "Electricity." Recommended.

Architecture & Morality struggles with new techniques, and includes two magnificent, ethereal hit singles: "Souvenir" and "Joan of Arc." OMD is again experimenting with sound and much of the album sounds more naturalistic than electronic. An intriguing and highly inventive use of the technology.

The conceptual **Dazzle Ships** overreaches by a mile, succumbing to excessive found-tape gimmickry in lieu of adequate songwriting. It does contain the striking "Genetic Engineering" (which integrates a Speak and Spell toy to make a point) and "Radio Waves," as well as some amazing sounds and a powerful atmosphere to recommend it. Impressive but not satisfying.

Junk Culture is much stronger, pulling away further from sparkling pop while retaining smart melodies in far denser and newly dance-based styles. "Tesla Girls" employs scratch production to great effect while fixing on science as a clever lyrical base (shades of Sparks); the rhythm-heavy "Locomotion" and the more fanciful "Talking Loud and Clear" are likewise ace tracks.

Despite its easygoing ambience and a shortage of really memorable songs, **Crush**—OMD's least stylized, most mainstream album—isn't half-bad. "So in Love" and "Secret" are the obvious romantic singles, but the record has more serious moments as well: the topical "88 Seconds in Greensboro," "Women III" (an ambiguous consideration of feminism) and "Bloc Bloc Bloc," wherein McCluskey sings some truly stupid lyrics with only a trace of embarrassment.

OMD's international commercial breakthrough began with **Crush** but exploded when "If You Leave," a dull ballad from the *Pretty in Pink* soundtrack, became a Top 10 American single. That song was thankfully omitted from OMD's subsequent album, **The Pacific Age**, but so was anything that might have prevented the record from being dull, ponderous and self-important. (Typical of the band's well-meaning missteps is "Southern," an instrumental bed over which excerpts of Martin Luther King speeches are played.) OMD's expansion from a duo to a sextet—the three recent additions play horns, guitars and more keyboards—has cost the group focus and clarity, its singleminded creative vision. Except for the smoothly contrived hit "(Forever) Live and Die" and the catchy "We Love You," this dilettantish mess is less a set of songs than a meaningless collection of sounds. Re-recorded and released on an EP, "Shame" was combined with a couple of other **Pacific Age** tracks and the 10-inch edit of "Messages."

The Best of OMD is the ideal remedy for **The Pacific Age**. After a concise recapitulation of the band's artistic development—via fourteen A-sides, from clever synth-based pop ("Electricity," "Enola Gay," "Souvenir") to well-realized audio experiments ("Tesla Girls," "Locomotion") to increasingly bland chart fodder ("So in Love," "If You Leave")—it ends with a promisingly pert new single, "Dreaming." (The CD adds two bonus 12-inch versions of "We Love You" and "La Femme Accident.")

Returning from a lengthy absence, OMD—no longer including Humphreys—issued **Sugar Tax**, its first new album in five years, in June 1991. [sg/i]

ORDINAIRES

The Ordinaires (Ger. Dossier) 1985 (Bar/None-Restless) 1990 ●
One (Bar/None) 1989 ●

Like many of the all-instrumental big-band ensembles on New York's semi-underground scene (er . . .), the Ordinaires' debut album was originally released only in Germany. On it, nine men and women—covering guitars, horns, woodwinds, strings and percussion—make a totally unique and marvelous sound, combining styles and eras with equanimity. Polytonality rules here with a twisted but firm hand, guiding the convoluted pieces through strident (never discordant) passages filled with sharp turns, sudden volume shifts and abrupt tempo changes. Advanced without being obnoxiously arty, this is an album to curl your hair and spark your imagination. (The 1990 reissue, despite incorrect sleeve and label copy that omits any mention of "The Last Song," does contain the entire original record, as well as a bonus version of the Stones' "She's Like a Rainbow" from the same sessions.)

The equally delightful **One** is alternately swinging and funky, at its best suggestive of Henry Cow with a highly developed sense of humor (one number is titled "The Dance of the Coco Crispies"). The group's rhythmic command remains incredible, and its eclecticism comes off as honest and modest, not ostentatious. The album ends with a wry but powerful rendition of Led Zeppelin's "Kashmir," which earned the group some attention outside of its usual circles. The Ordinaires disbanded in April '91. [i/gk]

ORIGINAL MIRRORS

Original Mirrors (Arista) 1980
Heart-Twango & Raw-Beat (nr/Mercury) 1981

After Deaf School bit the dust, that band's Steve Allen, a strong crooner in the Bryan Ferry mold, started his own Liverpool band with ex-Big in Japan guitarist Ian Broudie (who would go on to be a successful producer and leader of the Lightning Seeds) and three others. It didn't work out well at all. The Original Mirrors seemed entranced by the kind of pop-opera bombast that characterized Deaf School at its worst; self-discipline was never a high priority. For every rockin' moment that crystallizes passion into something comprehensible, there are ten others of sprawling excess. [jy]

See also *Deaf School, Lightning Seeds*.

ORIGINAL SINS

Big Soul (Bar/None) 1987
The Hardest Way (Psonik) 1989 ●
Party's Over (Aus. Dog Meat) 1990
Self Destruct (Psonik-Skyclad) 1990 ●

Big Soul is an instant classic, contemporary garage grunge stripped of nostalgia and ready for consumption. Led by diminutive howler J.T. (John Terlesky), the

Bethlehem, Pennsylvania quartet avoids the easy cover route to re-create the down and dirty excitement of the Standells and the Seeds on "Not Gonna Be All Right" and "Can't Feel a Thing," with Dan McKinney's cheesy organ adding the appropriate icing. Less aggressive tunes—like "Why Don't You Smile, Joan?"—maintain the no-nonsense spirit, peeling away tough posturing to get at searing emotions that are never far from the surface.

Kicking off with the selfconscious "Heard It All Before," **The Hardest Way** ("All distortion purely intentional") demonstrates the Sins' marvelous ability to synthesize an original sound—less stylized than the Lyres'—from now-standard ingredients. Rather than quote punk scripture in an attempt to turn back the calendar, the album seems like the logical result of an anachronistic environment. J.T.'s storming guitar roar and McKinney's chunky organ-izing provide a tersely exciting bed for lyrics that—other than a few happy love songs—resound with alienation ("Don't Fit In," "Out of My Mind"), dejection ("Rather Be Sad," "Can't Get Over You") and negativity ("I Can't Say," "End of the World").

Four of the eight songs on the Australian **Party's Over** are first-rate bonus tracks from **The Hardest Way** CD and cassette (which also contain an alternate version of the album's title track); three more are developmentally significant outtakes from the same sessions. Most pointedly, "That's All There Is" whips up a psychedelic guitar frenzy as J.T. shrieks blunt sex'n'drugs lyrics. A remix of the band's 1986 Bar/None single, "Just 14," winds up this particular party.

After the modest and concise garage freakouts of the first two albums, **Self Destruct** (dedicated to, among others, "everyone who knows anger can be fun") delivers a surprising level of domineering intensity, beginning with the cover photo of J.T. with a grin on his face and a pistol held to his head. The new-sound Sins are a snarling psychedelic powerhouse, a thickly seething cauldron of hyperactive feedback and wah-wah, rabid vocals, galloping rhythms and lyrics about drugs and sex. Some of the longer songs (the teetering-on-the-brink "Black Hole" runs past eight minutes) spend too much time on instrumental workouts, but **Self Destruct** captures acid-rock's disorienting chaos with a visceral impact few other bands can touch. The two CD/cassette bonuses are from a 1990 single.   [jy/i]

BEN ORR
See *Cars*.

OTTO'S CHEMICAL LOUNGE
See *Blue Hippos*.

JOHN OTWAY & WILD WILLY BARRETT
John Otway & Wild Willy Barrett (nr/Extracked) 1977
(nr/Polydor) 1977
Deep & Meaningless (nr/Polydor) 1978
Way & Bar (nr/Polydor) 1980
I Did It Otway EP (Stiff America) 1981
I Did It Otway (Can. Stiff Canada) 1981

Gone with the Bin: The Best of Otway & Barrett
(nr/Polydor) 1981
12 Stitch EP (nr/Empire) 1982

JOHN OTWAY
Where Did I Go Right? (nr/Polydor) 1979
Deep Thought (Stiff) 1980
All Balls & No Willy (nr/Empire) 1982
John Otway's Gleatest Hits (nr/Strike Back) 1986
Cor Baby, That's Really Me! [CD] (nr/Strike Back) 1990 ●

WILD WILLY BARRETT
Krazy Kong Album (nr/Black Eyes) 1981
Organic Bondage (nr/Galvanised) 1986

This charming nutter from Aylesbury (40 miles northwest of London), best heard in the company of his multi-instrumental sidekick/musical interpreter Barrett, is tough to evaluate on vinyl. Unpredictable, ingenious, inconsistent, unselfconscious, totally unafraid of making a fool of himself, Otway is capable of extraordinary quality swings. Since so much of what he's about just doesn't translate to disc, seeing him is nearly essential, and enhances listening to even the relatively duff tracks.

Otway renders covers—from "Green Green Grass of Home" to Alfred Noyes' "The Highwayman" to "You Ain't Seen Nothing Yet"—with daffily inspired abandon. He writes hysterically infectious ditties ("Really Free," "Louisa on a Horse," "Baby's in the Club") and likably sentimental tunes ("Montreal," "Geneve"), though these can be a little drippy. There's little pattern for rule-of-thumb judgment, save that Barrett-less he comes off bland (**Where Did I Go Right?**, which boasts "The Highwayman" and the poignant "Frightened and Scared," as well as the guitar playing of Ollie Halsall and keyboardist Morgan Fisher) or energetic but less effective (**All Balls & No Willy**, which has such tender romantic odes as "Montreal" and "Middle of the Winter").

The most consistent records are the first album (in part produced by Pete Townshend) and **Way & Bar** (or **Deep Thought**, which is half the latter plus assorted cuts). The **Gone with the Bin** compilation is a neat if incomplete summation of Otway's haphazard repertoire, drawn (with the exception of "I Did It Otway," a Barrett guitar instrumental in which someone—hmm, wonder who?—methodically destroys the instrument on mic) from the duo's first three albums and Otway's **Where Did I Go Right?**.

The six-song **I Did It Otway** EP mixes the A-sides from Otway's first three Stiff singles ("Green Green Grass of Home," "Turning Point" and the hysterical "Headbutts") with three LP tracks: "Running from the Law" (from **Deep and Meaningless**), "The Highwayman" and "I Did It Otway." The expanded Canadian equivalent (in a red, rather than green, cover) of **I Did It Otway** adds two tracks from the first album, one from the second and "Makes Good Music" from **Where Did I Go Right?**

The penultimate collection of Otway new and old is available on the recent **Gleatest Hits** album. (The title is a cheap Japanese dialect joke.) The record trundles out familiar favorites ("Really Free," "Headbutts," "Beware of the Flowers Cause I'm Sure They're Gonna Get You, Yeah" and "Green Green Grass of Home") as well as other fine LP tracks ("Middle of Winter," "Montreal") and an uproarious version of Bachman-

Turner Overdrive's "You Ain't Seen Nothing Yet" from a 1982 B-side.

After years of successfully avoiding Otway (and releasing solo records now and again), Barrett was cajoled into an abortive 1987 reunion that lasted long enough to record part of an album that was to be called **The Wimp and the Wild**. (What actually surfaced was a single, "The Last of the Mohicans.") In 1990, Otway penned an amazingly detailed and humble third-person autobiography (*Cor Baby, That's Really Me!*) and assembled a spectacular 21-track career retrospective (solo and duo) under the same title. Billed as "The CD of the Book," **Cor Baby** has classics ("Louisa on a Horse," "Headbutts," "Green Green Grass of Home," "Really Free," etc.), rarities (the staggering orchestral version of "Geneve," a live version of "Racing Cars" from a '77 promo LP), an unreleased 1972 version of "Misty Mountain" produced by Townshend and—bringing the story up to date—"The Last of the Mohicans." [jg/i]

O-TYPE

See *MX-80 Sound*.

OUR DAUGHTERS WEDDING

Digital Cowboy EP (EMI America) 1981
Moving Windows (EMI America) 1982

This snappy San Francisco-relocated-to-New York electro-pop trio's 1980 indie single "Lawnchairs" became a dancefloor favorite, combining a good beat and a catchy hook with absurdist lyrics of bemused paranoia ("Lawnchairs are everywhere"). Unfortunately, the five-song **Digital Cowboy**, produced by Colin Thurston, makes the mistake of redoing "Lawnchairs" with a real drummer (and not just any real drummer, but Simon Phillips) and badly rephrased vocals.

Before retiring into the annals of one-hit-wonderdom, ODW made a full-length album, managing to fit two memorable tunes ("She Was Someone" and "Elevate Her") amid the rudimentary dance-pop.
[rnp/i]

OUTSETS

Outsets EP (Plexus) 1983

Led by guitarist Ivan Julian (ex-Richard Hell's Voidoids and later briefly in Shriekback), this trio's six-song EP is a clear and strong exercise—half funky-butt dance grooves, half slow rockers—with particularly interesting axework and a lot of spunk. The four songs produced by Garland Jeffreys aren't brilliant, but Julian's singing and playing provide them with a distinctive and attractive flavor. [i]

See also *Bush Tetras, Richard Hell & the Voidoids*.

OUTTA PLACE

We're Outta Place (Midnight) 1984
Outta Too! (Midnight) 1987

Of NYC's short-lived but plentiful litter of garage revivalists, this quintet was the last to form, the first to reach vinyl and probably the only ones young enough not to have been around for the real thing. On their debut, "New York's own cave teens" display plenty of raunch, ripping through seven songs in the most distorted mono imaginable, with cheesy two-finger organ bleats and Mike Chandler's epileptic-fit shrieks. They also display plenty of chutzpah; changing two words of the Chöb's garage classic "We're Pretty Quick" gets Chandler a writing credit and the band a titular theme song.

Begun in '84, **Outta Too!** was completed and issued three years after the volatile band's demise. Chandler, who had left to front the even more over-the-top Raunch Hands agreed to a sodden evening of vocal sessions and presto! it's 1984 (or was that 1966?) all over again. Outta Place bassist Jordan Tarlow is currently in the Fuzztones, and drummer Andrea Matthews plays with '70s monsters Freaks. [dss]

See also *Fuzztones, Raunch Hands*.

OYSTERS

Green Eggs and Ham (Taang!) 1985

Imagine for a moment what the Replacements would sound like nowadays if Bob Stinson were still in the band, and Paul Westerberg had increased his drinking tenfold. They might sound a bit like the Oysters, a Boston-based one-album cult wonder. **Green Eggs and Ham** is a delightful alcohol-soaked platter; a mesh of sloppy playing, incompetent production and slobbering vocals that makes the same sort of effort to blend pop-punk with other styles as **Hootenanny**. Entirely free of seriousness, each song hits the devil-may-care punk-rock bullseye. Toe-tappers like "Reeperbahn" and "Headhunter" are enough to gouge a special memory groove, but the confessional "On Special"—extolling the virtues of a local chainstore—is singularly entertaining. [icm]

P P P P P P P P

AUGUSTUS PABLO

This Is Augustus Pablo (Jam. Tropical) 1973
Ital Dub (nr/Trojan) 1975
King Tubbys Meets Rockers Uptown (Jam. Clocktower)
 1976 (Message) 1984 ●
Original Rockers (nr/Greensleeves) 1979 (Message)
 1982 ●
Africa Must Be Free Dub (RAS) 1979
Rockers Meets King Tubby in a Firehouse (Shanachie)
 1981 ●
East of the River Nile (Message) 1981 ●
Earth's Rightful Ruler (Message) 1983 ●
Thriller (nr/Vista Sounds) 1983 (nr/Echo) 1985
King David's Melody (Alligator) 1983
Rising Sun (Message) 1986 ●
Rebel Rock Reggae (Heartbeat) 1986 ●
Rockers Come East (Message) 1987 ●
Eastman Dub (RAS) 1988 ●
Presents Rockers Story (RAS) 1989
Blowing with the Wind (Shanachie) 1990 ●
Presents Rockers International Showcase (Rykodisc)
 1991 φ

A true reggae original, dubmaster Augustus Pablo is as closely identified with his instrument—the melodica—as most jazz musicians are with theirs. Pablo (Horace Swaby) was a Kingston pianist when he borrowed a melodica; the simple instrument's unusual sound caught the ears of local record producers, who hired him to give their dub treatments some exotic color. Soon he was composing, arranging and producing his own instrumental tracks; now the reedy, vaguely Middle Eastern sound of Pablo's melodica is immediately recognizable, a plaintive cry in the dub landscape.

Like his music, Augustus Pablo has always been in a class by himself. His music is a sensory stimulation interlude, evoking different moods as it carries the listener to other lands and other times. Pablo's deep spirituality and carefully guarded public image only add to his mystique.

Pablo's earliest available recordings are mainly session work. Both **Ital Dub** and **King Tubbys Meets Rockers Uptown** (widely considered a dub classic) are as much showcases for King Tubby's mixing as for Pablo's playing. His own debut, **This Is Augustus Pablo** (later reissued as **Rebel Rock Reggae**), is much better, distinguished by strong presence and lively playing. So is **Original Rockers**, a collection of singles he doctored. The selection is diverse, and Pablo's production (particularly the drum sound) is bright and snappy. For the uninitiated, either of these two offers a perfect starting point.

His recent work is, to some extent, of a piece, with little variety and few distinguishing characteristics. **Africa Must Be Free Dub** is an adequate companion to an LP made by singer Hugh Mundell, a young Pablo protégé who was murdered. **Rockers Meets King Tubby**

in a Firehouse, while compelling, features less melodica than usual. **East of the River Nile** is quintessential Pablo, and perhaps his most consistent LP. **Earth's Rightful Ruler** includes a real rarity—a vocal—along with a new version of Pablo's first record, "Java." **King David's Melody**, a singles collection, has the evenness of sound and style of an album. It's a bit sleepy, but lovely all the same.

Pablo's '86 release, **Rising Sun**, marked a change in direction. Mixed by Scientist, the overall sound is less distinctive than Pablo's other work. Many of the tunes are uptempo and disappointing, even though some of the playing—particularly on "Pipers of Zion"—is superb.

But it proved to be a transitional album rather than a glimpse of things to come. On **Rockers Come East**, Pablo returns to the dreamy sound that is his trademark, using lots of synthesizer bits to supplement his melodica. The synthetics are subtle, however, so the dub remains warm and compelling. More richly textured than ever, the music on the LP ranks with Pablo's best, and shows the maestro to be at the top of his form.

Like Sugar Minott (with his Youth Promotion label), Pablo has always provided a forum for ghetto youth to explore and express their musical talents; his Rockers label has become a training ground for up-and-coming artists. **Rockers Story**, the fifth collection of Pablo's various protégés, is a mixed bag of Pablo's own material, singers such as Delroy Williams and Barry Reid, U-Roy-style DJs (e.g., Dillinger and Ras Bull) and such groups as Tetrack and the Rockers Allstars.

Eastman Dub is actually the dub version of the Tetrack album **Let's Get Started**, a classic example of Pablo's exotic and meditative melodies, not to mention his renowned melodica playing. The subtleties and colorations that a wind instrument can express are elevated to an almost ethereal quality in Pablo's music.

[bk/aw]

PAGANS

The Pagans (Terminal) 1983
Buried Alive (Treehouse) 1986
Live—The Godlike Power of the Pagans (Treehouse) 1987
Street Where Nobody Lives (Resonance) 1989 ●

While Pere Ubu and other Ohio cousins were offering only cerebral dissonance, the 1977 punk explosion visited Cleveland in the form of the Pagans. Picking up where the departed (for NYC) Dead Boys left off, the Pagans were younger and, if not as snotty, better in other ways. Led by raspy-voiced Mike Hudson, this slam-dunk garage quartet produced a small stack of classic singles: "Not Now No Way," "Street Where Nobody Lives" and "What's This Shit Called Love" (later covered by the Meatmen) are all down and dirty, glorious three-chord excursions into the filth and the fury.

The Pagans broke up in late '79 without ever issuing an album. The band's first longplayer was the result of a 1983 reunion gig (only Hudson and guitarist Tommy Gunn are holdovers from the old days), pressed as a limited-edition (500 copies) live LP. The sound quality of **The Pagans** isn't horrible and the rawness is true to the band's essential spirit, but the performances of the group's best tunes are sorely deficient.

Buried Alive compiles seven of the Pagans' eight original single sides, adding ten outtakes of the same late-'70s vintage, including the grubbiest version of Jagger/Richards' "Heart of Stone" imaginable. The Pagans' unrefined attitude saturates the entire first-rate collection.

Buried Alive sparked more reunions and a spate of touring. One such gig—a November 1986 date at Minneapolis' 7th St. Entry—resulted in a second concert LP. With six new songs (like "She's a Cadaver and I Gotta Have Her"), **Live–The Godlike Power of the Pagans** is far better than the '83 live disc (original bassist Tim Allee is back in the lineup), but still doesn't reach the godlike power of the band's studio work.

Street Where Nobody Lives mostly rehashes the same recordings as **Buried Alive**—odd, since the latter is still widely available. In November 1989, the Pagans opened for the reunited Buzzcocks in Cleveland. [jr]

See also *Paul Marotta*.

PAILHEAD

Trait EP (Wax Trax!) 1988 ●

Although not quite the cultural turning point of Run–DMC's collaboration with Aerosmith, Pailhead's two records (1988's "I Will Refuse" and **Trait**) do mark an historic genre conjunction. By the late '80s, hardcore and industrial were ripe for merger, and two preeminent icons—Ian MacKaye (frenetic vocalist of Minor Threat and Fugazi) and Ministry's Al Jourgensen/Paul Barker axis—were ready to make the move.

"I Will Refuse" (included, with its flipside, on the **Trait** CD) is positively explosive, repeatedly escalating from funk-industrial verses to a screamingly defiant hardcore-tempo chorus with thrashing guitars. The more seamless mixture of **Trait**'s four songs integrate the passion and three-chord thrust of punk with advanced electronics, a sound subsequently employed by Ministry and Lard, the Jourgensen/Barker collaboration with another hardcore legend, Jello Biafra. [gef]

See also *Fugazi, Lard, Ministry, Minor Threat, Revolting Cocks*.

PAINKILLER

See *Napalm Death*.

PAINTED WILLIE

Mind Bowling (SST) 1985
Live from Van Nuys EP (SST) 1986
Upsidedowntown (SST) 1987
Relics (SST) 1988

More noisy guitar excitement from SST: this non-punky Los Angeles trio shows a certain wit and lyrical perception on **Mind Bowling**. Although the music sounds like a sanitized junior version of Motörhead, songs about Chia Pets, sex without love and an obscure monkey species share an uncommon view of the world that elevates the tiresome vamps a bit. The inclusion of the classic "Little Red Book" only points up the band's lack of songwriting aptitude.

The energetic live mini-album features that song plus "Cover Girl" from **Mind Bowling**; there's the next-LP preview of "Upside Down Town" plus three other "tunes." These guys (especially guitarist Vic Makauskas) can play well enough, but their material lacks melody, focus and structure—once again, Burt Bacharach steals their thunder without even showing up!

Upsidedowntown has spiffy cover art and more taut riff-rock songs, this time on such less intriguing topics as "My Seed," "Personality and Style" (thirteen minutes of it!) and "Totem Pole." The playing keeps getting stronger, but the Willies should put out an APB for a songwriter.

Relics is a compilation of outtakes and leftovers, dating back to the band's prehistory. [i]

PALE SAINTS

Barging into the Presence of God EP (nr/4AD) 1989 ●
The Comforts of Madness (nr/4AD) 1990 ●
Half-Life EP (nr/4AD) 1990

Along with London's Lush, this Leeds trio is the closest thing to a "normal" British guitar pop group on 4AD. Pale Saints do have the label's familiar etherealism (some songs on **The Comforts of Madness**—like "A Deep Sleep for Steven"—even approximate the Cocteau Twins' trancescapes), and each track features long, languid instrumental passages. But the hooks keep coming, amid an alternation of slower pop numbers ("Sea of Sound," "Little Hammer" and "Sight of You," which first appeared as the A-side of the **Barging into the Presence of God** 12-inch) and rapid, powerful clankers, an odd mix of piston power and floating vocals. The faster selection ("Language of Flowers," "True Coming Dream" and the closing "Time Thief") offer strongly contrasting emotions and undeniably catchy tunes. Using triple-time tempo for the chorus, a cover of Opal's "Fell from the Sun" completely bowls over the original, taking off in directions Opal's foggy murk never intimated. A remarkable, ear-catching debut.

After Gil Norton and John Fryer's inspired work on the LP, Pale Saints chose Wedding Present producer Chris Allison to record the four-song **Half-Life** EP, with less impressive results. Although Allison leaves them sounding like a less scratchy Wedding Present, the record is not without merit: "Baby Maker" features little slugs of psychedelic guitar and more swooning vocals, while "A Revelation" applies the group's curious penchant for gear-switching. As a particularly unsettling bonus, the 12-inch EP contains an untitled and unlisted horror-scream track that only plays if you pick up the needle and reposition it. [jr]

PATTI PALLADIN

See *Judy Nylon and Crucial, Johnny Thunders*.

ROBERT PALMER

Sneakin' Sally Through the Alley (Island) 1974 ●
Pressure Drop (Island) 1976 ●
Some People Can Do What They Like (Island) 1976 ●
Double Fun (Island) 1978 ●
Secrets (Island) 1979 ●
Clues (Island) 1980 ●
Maybe It's Live (Island) 1982
Pride (Island) 1983 ●
Riptide (Island) 1985 ●
Heavy Nova (EMI Manhattan) 1988 ●
"Addictions" Volume 1 (Island) 1989 ●
Don't Explain (EMI) 1990 φ

It's not surprising that this stylish rock dilettante—whose '70s dabblings included excursions into R&B, funk, reggae and Little Feat-backed rock'n'roll—should catch up with post-punk in the '80s. What is remarkable is that on **Clues** he manages to come up with two tracks as sublime as "Johnny and Mary" and "Looking for Clues," which are heady, intricate and danceable at the same time. Also commendable is the job he does on a couple of collaborations with Gary Numan, injecting more life into them than one would think possible. Still, **Clues** retains an irritating stylistic disparity (heavy metal track/Beatles cover), as if Palmer were afraid his going wholeheartedly into anything new might alienate his audience.

Two years on, Palmer's dilemma is even more apparent on **Maybe It's Live**, a sidestep tentative down to its title and half-live/half-studio format. Combining inferior concert versions of old material, blah new stuff and another collaboration with Numan, the LP continues Palmer's indecisive course.

Without any big-name collaborators, Palmer again delivers a weirdly mixed bag on **Pride**, venturing into electro-disco with the herky-jerky, overbearing "You Are in My System," while affecting a charming calypso flavor in other spots. There's also a reprise of the unsettling undercurrents of "Johnny and Mary" on "Want You More." Palmer's voice is such that the less he tries, the better he sounds: when the going gets hot, his singing becomes overwhelming and irritating.

Palmer's next move was into the vile but hit-bound Power Station, a temporary all-star band with two Durannies, produced by Bernard Edwards. When the group opted to tour, however, Palmer bailed out, retaining Edwards and Tony Thompson from the brief collaboration to finish **Riptide**, a bombastic funk record with such tripe as "Addicted to Love," a song whose main value lies in its parody potential.

Can an album get any more eclectic than **Heavy Nova**? From the trashy (and awful) pop hit "Simply Irresistible" to the reggae-cajun fusion of "Change His Ways" (a bizarre song that, amazingly, works), the Peggy Lee ballad "It Could Happen to You," Brazilian, African, funk, metal . . . every record ever recorded all on one disc! It's nice to see that Palmer is so open-minded, but if an LP is meant to suit or promote a particular mood, this one's just too hectic.

Compared to **Heavy Nova**, the **"Addictions" Volume I** best-of plays like a concept album. (In his excellent sleeve notes Palmer mentions the care he took in programming it.) There are only three pre-1980 cuts here and none from before '78. As an overview of post-

punk Palmer (through **Heavy Nova**), it's all there—the good and the bad.

More strange fusions abound on **Don't Explain**. Palmer rocks hard (with guitarists Steve Stevens and Eddie "Rock Box" Martinez) on one number; sings pop on the next; then soca, a cappella, etc. No doubt pleased by "It Could Happen to You" and the other softer moments on **Heavy Nova**, he devotes the last seven songs of this double-album-length disc to string-laden torch songs of the type Billy Holiday sang late in her life (though only the title track is actually hers), a couple of Brazilian-influenced pieces and a rollicking Mose Allison cover. When he covers Mose, he sounds like Mose; when he covers Otis Redding and Marvin Gaye elsewhere on this LP, he takes on their inflections. Whatever the setting, Palmer plops down and makes himself comfortable. People used to call David Bowie rock's great chameleon, but it's hard to imagine any commercial music fan, regardless of personal taste, not finding something to like (and hate) on any of Palmer's recent records.   [ds/i]

See also *Power Station*.

PANDORAS

The Pandoras EP (Moxie) 1984
It's About Time (Voxx) 1984 ●
Stop Pretending (Rhino) 1986
Rock Hard EP (Restless) 1988 ●
Live Nymphomania (Restless) 1989 φ

The unashamedly '60s-obsessed Pandoras (led by singer/writer/guitarist Paula Pierce) are revivalists in the best sense of the word, recapturing the gleeful amateurism of vintage garage-punk-pop while adding their own cheerfully slutty persona to the mix. Following an energetically amateurish 7-inch EP, the LA band made its longplaying debut on **It's About Time** (produced by Greg Shaw), which makes a virtue of its shoestring primitivism. With some crackerjack tunes awash in Pierce's fuzztones and Gwynne Kelly's appropriately trashy organ, it's as good a '60s punk record as any contemporary combo is likely to make. (The Voxx/East Side Digital CD adds five bonus tracks, including three songs from the EP.)

Pierce ditched the rest of the band soon after the debut LP (though the other three original members continued performing under the Pandoras name for a while) and recorded **Stop Pretending** with a new lineup. While maintaining the '60s fixation and playing up the brash-hussy stance, **Stop Pretending** features stronger playing and a harder-rocking edge (there's no reason why "In and Out of My Life (In a Day)" shouldn't have been a hit), suggesting that the Pandoras aren't as hopelessly mired in historical fetishism as one might assume.

Although the Pandoras were signed to Elektra and recorded an album (entitled **Come Inside**), the band and label went their separate ways and the LP was scrapped. Instead, the Pandoras issued **Rock Hard**, five blaring rock songs of horny raunch—with titles like "Six Times a Day," "Craving" and "He's Coming"—and one strongly suggestive pop song. Judging by this unseemly musical and lyrical display, Pierce has just discovered masturbation, her G spot or the Runaways. Unless five women in leather singing about sex with the crotch-grabbing delicacy of dockhands sounds like a cheap thrill, avoid being slimed by this embarrassing adolescent tripe.

Demonstrating that **Rock Hard** was no one-disc stand, the Pandoras recycle four of its songs (alongside others in the same vein) on **Nymphomania**, a hopeless live set recorded in Dallas. Pierce's voice is totally unsuited to such loud rock; her uncertain grip on melody and sloppy, out-of-tune guitar work (not to mention drummer Sheri Kaplan's lame thumping) make listening to this quite a chore. Most significant liner note thank you: "to my human sexuality teacher & classmates." Just what *are* they teaching in school these days?

[hd/i]

PANKOW
Freedom for the Slaves EP (Wax Trax!) 1988 ●
Gisela (Wax Trax!) 1989 ●
Pankow Show You Their Dongs EP (Wax Trax!) 1990 ●
Omne Anima Triste Post Coitum [tape] (ROIR) 1991

One is naturally wary when Italians and Germans get together, and at least some of this caution is justified by Pankow, which uses Florence as its operational base. Multi-instrumentalist (okay, sample-meister) Maurizio Fasolo and singer Alex Spalck form the core of this intermittently interesting and conscientiously provocative group that gets Adrian Sherwood to do a lot of its mixes. Always sonically engaging, Pankow goes wrong whenever Spalck opens his mouth. You can laugh at the nihilism of Revolting Cocks (indeed, that's probably the point), but with Pankow you can only roll your eyes and hope for the vocals to end.

The six-song **Freedom for the Slaves** boasts a cut called "Art & Madness" (yeesh!) as well as a cover of the Normal's classic "Warm Leatherette." The beats are loud and nasty, and the accompanying noises crunch in all the right places.

Although it was actually released in a 100-copy edition with a gold-embossed slab of marble for a cover, the more commonly circulated edition of **Gisela** merely has a particularly creepy sleeve illustration. In any case, it contains another swipe at "Warm Leatherette," which sounds like a nightmare concocted by *Saturday Night Live*'s Hans and Franz. Although it rocks, "Me & My Ding Dong" is basically an industrial-noise take on Chuck Berry's "My Ding-a-ling." (Which is to say unessential.) "I shall die in mediocrity," Spalck sings on "Germany Is Burning" (from **Pankow Show You Their Dongs**, the 12-inch/CD version of "Me & My Ding Dong"); speaking as someone whose favorite Pankow cut is the CD's instrumental remix of that song, I don't doubt it.

The 1991 cassette (the title of which translates as **All Animals (Are Sad After Coitus)** is a live compilation from a recent tour.

[gk]

See also *Ben Vaughn Combo*.

(TAV FALCO'S) PANTHER BURNS
Behind the Magnolia Curtain (Rough Trade) 1981 (Fr. Fan Club) 1988 ●

Blow Your Top EP (Animal) 1982 ●?
Now! [tape] (Frenzi) 1984
Sugar Ditch Revisited EP (Frenzi) 1985 ●
Shake Rag EP (Fr. New Rose) 1986 ●
The World We Knew (Fr. New Rose) 1987 ●
Red Devil (Fr. New Rose) 1988 ●
10th Anniversary Live LP: Midnight in Memphis (Fr. New Rose) 1989 ●
Return of the Blue Panther (Triple X) 1990 φ

MUD BOY & THE NEUTRONS
Known Felons in Drag (Fr. New Rose) 1986

JAMES LUTHER DICKINSON
Delta Experimental Projects Compilation Volume 2: Spring Poems (Fr. Fan Club) 1990

For folks who prize unspoiled simplicity in rock-'n'roll (and especially in rockabilly), Tav Falco's Panther Burns may be the ultimate band. On the early records, his voice drenched in echo, Falco goes through a familiar repertoire of Presley-derived whoops, mutters and coos, while an amateurish backing ensemble that often includes Alex Chilton grinds away laboriously like high-school rockers struggling through their first rehearsal. The deliberately slowed-down tempo and brazen sloppiness invest **Behind the Magnolia Curtain** with an intriguing conceptual purity, but the rawness turns prolonged exposure into a painful experience.

The four songs on **Blow Your Top** provide more of the same frayed recklessness. But thanks to cleaner sound and playing that verges on being professional, this set almost has commercial potential. (See "Love Is My Business" for proof.) There's still plenty of ground separating Falco's sweaty hysteria and the well-oiled appeal of the Stray Cats, though.

Falco recorded **Sugar Ditch Revisited** at Sam Phillips' Memphis studio with "Lx" Chilton and a few other Panther Burnsmen; the six tracks are well played, well sung, well recorded, under control and somewhat underwhelming. The countrybilly spirit and sincerity is there, but the performances start and stop without ever really heating up, and the absence of chaos leaves the simple (if esoterically sourced) material to stand alone, which—until the frisky finale, "Tina, the Go Go Queen"—it doesn't do all that well.

The **Now!** cassette, issued by Falco on his own label, contains seven numbers (including ten minutes of "Jump Suit") taped absolutely live in Memphis in 1984. New Rose subsequently included that material as a bonus disc in original pressings of the killer 12-inch **Shake Rag** E.P.: studio recordings with Jim Dickinson that include one original (the stomping "Cuban Rebel Girl," also on the live tape/disc) and three typically swell obscurities.

Chilton's revitalized production and playing on **The World We Knew** helps make it one of Falco's all-time best showings. Using a rotating collection of sidemen, the carefully annotated songs—a scholarly combination of R&B, Sun rockabilly, blues and other wondrous musical inventions ("desert skulk fugue; decorticated cycle tune; the Stuttgart, Arkansas sound," to quote the liner notes)—get a thorough and affectionate workout that remains surehanded without ever slipping down off the rustic funk meter. (There are no originals on this non-didactic history course.) All concerned sounds as though

489

they're having a blast, and that feeling comes right through the speakers. The CD adds **Shake Rag**.

The 10-inch **Red Devil** signals a measured return to the uncontrolled wildness of early Panther Burns' records. Falco lays some truly soulful hollerin' over noisy electric guitars and a thumping backbeat on tracks produced individually (not to mention artlessly) by Chilton, Dickinson and others. **Red Devil**—ten songs and an abundance of hellacious energy—features esoterica by Chuck Berry, Lee Hazelwood and others, adding the songwriting talents of Dickinson and even Tav himself to the party. (The French CD also contains **Sugar Ditch Revisited**.)

The tenth anniversary album—a two-disc live-in-Memphis (February '89) extravaganza with Chilton, Dickinson, other alumni and assorted guests—confidently covers a broad variety of vintage material, from "It's Only Make Believe" to "Goldfinger" to "Train Kept a-Rollin'," but generally lacks the fiery excitement of Panther Burns' fringey best. The years have evidently been too kind to Falco: the former rockabilly loony has become—of all things—an accomplished entertainer. (Could his small role in *Great Balls of Fire* have anything to do with such a shocking transformation?) Despite a few flat notes, an out-of-tune guitar and some offbeat song introductions, the performances are kind of colorless—calm and controlled where they should be frantic.

Not to worry. **Return of the Blue Panther** is wonderfully crappy-sounding, an edgy three-day session in reverb-land as raw as you please. (In keeping with the music's fast'n'loose spirit, the sleeve has its share of mistakes.) Considerately performing material people outside of swap meets are likely to have heard, Falco rips through a fine R&B-oriented program that includes "Rock Me, Baby," "Got Love If You Want It" and "I Got a Woman." Falco's back!

Mud Boy & the Neutrons are Dickinson's band. **Known Felons** is Elmore James and Sleepy John Estes, Chuck Berry and Bo Diddley ᴐ cranked out by white Memphis boys in the late '80s. Considerably more rigid and fratlike than Tav's excursions into like territory, Mud Boy could be NRBQ's little cousins with twice the reverence and half the talent. **Spring Poems**, the second volume in a Memphis compilation series helmed by Dickinson, unexpectedly offers him solo for ambience with a paucity of songs, perhaps effective in their intent as soundtracks but fairly pointless on album. [jy/tr/ab]

See also *Alex Chilton*.

PARIS
The Devil Made Me Do It (Scarface-Tommy Boy) 1990 ●

Under the dual banners of the Black Panther Party and the Nation of Islam (a contradiction in terms that evidently eludes him), this devastating young MC's debut is the most politically potent radical rap record yet. (That Paris' self-produced backing tracks are diverse, imaginative and burningly intense only adds to the record's heavy impact.) Stepping away from Public Enemy's scattershot militancy, **The Devil Made Me Do It** expands on the ruthless rhymes—rooted in the Panthers' revolutionary nationalism ("Brutal," a non-vinyl bonus track, offers a concise history of the African-American struggle) and Muslim faith—with archival sound bites

and carefully detailed written descriptions of pivotal historical figures, from Nat Turner to Huey P. Newton. (Indicative of Paris' truth-bending divided loyalties, the liner notes attribute the murder of Malcolm X to "an agent of the U.S. government.") Whether you agree with his opinions or not, Paris is a bold and important new spokesman. [i]

GRAHAM PARKER
Howlin Wind (Mercury) 1976 ●
Heat Treatment (Mercury) 1976 ●
Another Grey Area (Arista) 1982 ●
The Real Macaw (Arista) 1983
Anger: Classic Performances (Arista) 1985
The Mona Lisa's Sister (RCA) 1988 ●
Live! Alone in America (RCA) 1989 ●
Human Soul (RCA) 1989 ●
Struck by Lightning (RCA) 1991 φ

GRAHAM PARKER AND THE RUMOUR
Stick to Me (Mercury) 1977 ●
The Pink Parker EP (Mercury) 1977
The Parkerilla (Mercury) 1978
Squeezing Out Sparks (Arista) 1979 ●
The Up Escalator (Stiff-Arista) 1980 ●
High Times (nr/Vertigo) 1980
It Don't Mean a Thing If It Ain't Got That Swing (nr/Philips) 1984
Pourin' It All Out: The Mercury Years (Mercury) 1986

GRAHAM PARKER AND THE SHOT
Steady Nerves (Elektra) 1985 ●

Before Elvis Costello and Joe Jackson, there was Graham Parker, redefining the singer/songwriter category for mid-'70s rock'n'roll audiences suspicious of the James Taylors and Carly Simons. With his raspy, Van Morrison-influenced vocals and soul-on-fire tunes, this diminutive Englishman burst on the scene just before the punk explosion and showed how to make music personal without sacrificing power.

Produced by Nick Lowe, **Howlin Wind** is a classic debut album, full of fresh ideas fleshed out with ragged enthusiasm. Parker acknowledges his roots throughout, singing original R&B boppers ("White Honey" and "Lady Doctor") with sly wit and masterfully reconstructing rockabilly on the angry "Back to Schooldays," complete with guest twangin' by Dave Edmunds (who later recorded the song himself on **Get It**). Evidencing an equally powerful sensitive side, Parker checks in with the reflective "Between You and Me" and "Don't Ask Me Questions," the latter a chilling wail of anguish.

On **Howlin Wind** (and all subsequent LPs through **The Up Escalator**), Parker received formidable backing from the Rumour: Brinsley Schwarz (guitar) and Bob Andrews (keyboards), both ex-Brinsley Schwarz band members; Martin Belmont (guitar), ex-Ducks Deluxe; Stephen Goulding (drums) and Andrew Bodnar (bass), both ex-Bontemps Roulez. Often compared to Dylan's erstwhile '60s cohorts, the Rumour displays the same self-assurance and finesse as the Band, but rocks harder. Despite a checkered recording career on its own, the Rumour was always a stellar support group.

Although produced by Robert John Lange, **Heat Treatment** is essentially a punchier continuation of **Howlin Wind**. For spirited soul, there's "Hotel Chambermaid" and "Back Door Love." Parker's serious tunes are also more intense: "Turned Up Too Late" delivers a devastating romantic rejection; the anthemic "Fools' Gold," one of his finest achievements, affirms the need to search for the best, however elusive—it's unaffected and inspiring.

The Pink Parker, an EP pressed on colored vinyl, combines non-LP studio renditions of the Trammps' "Hold Back the Night" and a Parker original with hot live versions of "White Honey" and "Soul Shoes."

With the vastly improved music scene as a catalyst, Parker evidently felt the need to assert himself more strongly on **Stick to Me**, but the resulting overstatement and stylistic diversity couldn't be contained comfortably on one LP. Nonetheless, taken individually, many tracks are undeniably compelling. The title cut is Parker's soaring declaration of dedication in the face of a hostile world; he unleashes exhilarating nastiness in Ann Peebles' "I'm Gonna Tear Your Playhouse Down." But one need only look at Side Two to sense the confusion: it begins and ends with raucous throwaways designed to compensate for the massive epics in the center. No amount of party fun, however, could clear the air after the overblown theatrics of the seven-minute "Heat in Harlem." Parker is sabotaged by his own indecision.

In classic contract-fulfilling tradition, Parker cranked out a two-record set, **The Parkerilla**: three live sides plus a second studio version of "Don't Ask Me Questions." Adequate but musically unnecessary, it did the legal trick, and Parker was free to switch to a different American label. The sour-grapes "Mercury Poisoning" (1979) was his first release on Arista, which declined to put its name to the promo-only gray 12-inch one-sided single.

Squeezing Out Sparks resolved Parker's stylistic dilemma. It's his toughest, leanest and most lyrically sophisticated LP; in a way a sad loss of innocence. Eschewing the lighter soul elements of his earlier work, Parker adopts a harsh, nearly humorless tone that suggests cynicism instead of anger. (Regardless, critics generally loved it and sales were decidedly improved over previous efforts.) "Discovering Japan" and "Nobody Hurts You" are sizzling, passionate rockers; for better or worse, the album's centerpiece (echoing the album title's judgmental metaphor) is "You Can't Be Too Strong," an anti-abortion ballad full of disturbing imagery and emphatic phrasing. In his eagerness to forge a coherent style, Parker neglects to vary the emotional tone. (A novel 1979 promo album—live versions of every **Sparks** song in the same running order as on the studio version, plus two other live cuts—was issued to radio as **Live Sparks**, further strengthening the band's concert reputation.)

Parker somehow lost his sense of purpose on **The Up Escalator**. Although retaining the intense, driven approach of **Squeezing Out Sparks**, the material on this album falls short, possessing fury without context, which results in unsatisfying overkill. Individually, "No Holding Back," "Devil's Sidewalk" and "Love Without Greed" crackle nicely; collectively, they produce a hollow roar. Those looking to assign blame will notice the increasing influence of the king of rock melodrama,

Bruce Springsteen, who even joins in vocally on the bloated "Endless Night." Also, the departure of Bob Andrews must have added to the changing situation.

The rest of the Rumour followed Andrews through the exit prior to **Another Grey Area**, which actually constitutes a minor comeback, avoiding the noisier extremes of **The Up Escalator**. A band of New York session musicians provides precise though unspectacular accompaniment; Parker co-produced with Jack Douglas. Interestingly, the harder-rocking tracks are the least effective: "Big Fat Zero" and "You Hit the Spot" seem little more than halfhearted gestures. In contrast, ballads like "Temporary Beauty," "Dark Side of the Bright Lights" and "Crying for Attention" have a graceful and unforced ring of sincerity never before heard on a Parker LP. Though **Another Grey Area** seldom overwhelms, it does indicate that, after six studio albums, Parker is still willing to take chances.

The Real Macaw, however, is a chance he probably shouldn't have taken. Songs like "You Can't Take Love for Granted" and "Life Gets Better" reach Parker's required level of intensity, but the production and playing do not. Producer David Kershenbaum gives Parker the kind of sparse, colorless setting that has its uses for Joe Jackson; the musicianship is unnecessarily understated. The end product: a disc that is watered down and should have been harder.

Steady Nerves rights the balance, blending the pop veneer of **The Real Macaw** with a tougher band attack for a bracing series of characteristically pithy performances, from the cheerfully raunchy "When You Do That to Me" to the gorgeously romantic "Wake Up (Next to You)" to "Break Them Down," a classic Parker fist-waver. A solid album that bodes well. (The CD has an extra song, "Too Much Time to Think.")

Parker soon left Elektra and, following an abortive alliance with Atlantic that didn't result in any releases, signed to RCA and, three years after **Steady Nerves**, came up with **The Mona Lisa's Sister**. Getting excellent backing from the extraordinary Schwarz (who co-produced with Parker), Bodnar, ex-Rockpile drummer Terry Williams and keyboardist James Hallawell, Parker engages his sharp tongue and sketchy melodicism for another collection of smooth songs that has its ups ("OK Hieronymous") and downs ("Get Started. Start a Fire"). Brittle sound tends to undercut Parker's soulful strut (especially on "I'm Just Your Man" and a lovely reading of Sam Cooke's "Cupid"); "The Girl Isn't Ready" and "Don't Let It Break You Down," however, gain edgy tension from the same audio characteristic. Although not among his best, **The Mona Lisa's Sister** confirms Parker's continued artistic vitality.

The only thing Parker's solo live album (recorded in Philadelphia, October 1988) confirms is that he really does need accompaniment to put his songs across. Naked renditions of classic material ("White Honey," "Gypsy Blood," "Back to Schooldays," "Protection," "You Can't Be Too Strong") are blunt but lifeless; of the provocative new songs, only the blistering "Soul Corruption" is strong enough to rise above the demo-like presentation.

Fronting a band composed of Schwarz, Bodnar and Steve Nieve and Pete Thomas from the Attractions, Parker bounced back with **Human Soul**, an exceptionally fine album of memorable, mature songs. With nods to ska, brassy soul and swinging rock, romance dominates the first side. The sturdy "My Love's Strong," sexy "Call Me Your Doctor" and the familial "Big Man on Paper" all reveal Parker's gravity and sensitivity. The second half of the record is supposedly a thematic whole, but all that amounts to is that individually noteworthy songs run into each other with crude transitional logic. Never mind. With abundant energy and imagination, Parker addresses topics familiar (imperialism, the record industry's torment of a certain self-important genius), unexpected (AIDS misinformation) and downright oblique ("Sugar Gives You Energy"). Thoughtful, tuneful and altogether extraordinary.

Taking a step back from **Human Soul**'s commercial-minded intensity and intricacy, **Struck by Lightning** is rustic and mostly acoustic, with Parker's lonesome harmonica underscoring the Dylanesque leanings. The six-minute rant ("She Wants So Many Things") that opens the sprawling hour-long LP paints Parker in the worst possible light—as a guy you've just met who goes off on a creepy and endless tirade about someone you don't know—but the song is merely misplaced, and the record quickly finds more solid footing. Although Parker devotes himself to intimate, personal lyrics rather than music here, the tunes—played by Andrew Bodnar, Pete Thomas and guests, with Parker handling all the guitar work—are typically sturdy, graceful and occasionally ("The Kid with the Butterfly Net," "That's Where She Ends Up," "A Brand New Book," "Children and Dogs") memorable. As usual, GP leads with his chin, blurting out lines that either miss by a mile (try to find the music in a refrain that goes "Pull your skin like wrapping paper round my heart") or hit their mark with heat-seeking accuracy ("Some believe in a heaven up above/With a God that forgives all with His great love/Well I forgive you if you forgive me hey!/Who needs the third party anyway?").

High Times and **Pourin' It All Out** are, respectively, English and American greatest hits packages of songs cut with the Rumour. **It Don't Mean a Thing** is a mix of early album tracks and singles; **Anger** collects tunes from Parker's Arista albums.   [jy/i]

See also *Rumour*.

PASSIONNEL

See *Alex Gibson*.

PASSIONS

Michael & Miranda (nr/Fiction) 1980
Thirty Thousand Feet Over China (nr/Polydor) 1981
Sanctuary (nr/Polydor) 1982
Passion Plays (nr/Polydor) 1985

As introduced on **Michael & Miranda**, the Passions (most of whom had been in a London punk band called the Derelicts) appeared to be part of the post-punk movement. The record is characterized by spare arrangements, stark vocals and fairly unmelodic—though lyrically interesting—songs. Subjects like unhappy love ("Oh No, It's You") and frustrated attempts at relationships and communication ("Palava"), along with "Obsession," "Suspicion," fear ("Man on the Tube") and neuroses ("Absentee"), make the world of **Michael & Miranda** a particularly anxious one.

Thirty Thousand Feet Over China is less bleak, though still tainted with anger, deceit and suspicion. With a new producer, Nigel Gray, and a new bass player, the quartet sounds smoother and more melodic (as on "Someone Special," "Runaway" and the nicely poppy "Bachelor Girls"). Lyrics are as sharp and offbeat as ever—check the clever, almost tongue-in-cheek "I'm in Love with a German Film Star."

Between **Thirty Thousand Feet** and **Sanctuary**, the Passions released a single, "Africa Mine," arguably their best song. A pretty, haunting, bitter and impassioned condemnation of colonialist exploitation, it could really be applied to greed by any name. "Africa Mine" foreshadowed the sound of **Sanctuary**, which is smooth without being bland, sophisticated without being smug, and pretty without being soppy. Barbara Gogan shows growing confidence as a singer; her new expressiveness and the addition of a synthesizer serve to fill in and soften what used to be rough edges. The soaring title track is especially memorable.

Footnotes: Barbara Gogan's sister Susan, who had been in the Derelicts but not the Passions, was the mastermind of a bizarre 1980 record under the name pragVEC. Before the Passions, guitarist Clive Timperley had been in the 101ers. In the late '80s, Barbara Gogan turned up in New York, playing a lot of the Passions' old songs as a solo performer.   [ks/i]

PASTELS

Up for a Bit with the Pastels (Glass-Big Time) 1987 ●
Comin' Through EP (nr/Glass) 1987
Suck on the Pastels (nr/Creation) 1988 ●
Sittin' Pretty (Homestead) 1989 ●

Thoroughly wistful and eternally childlike, Glasgow's Pastels exemplify a much maligned style of UK music for a time referred to as "anorak pop." Characterized by an amateurish devotion to '60s pop conventions and wide-eyed naïveté, the sound is as lovable as it is easily copied. The Pastels have the distinction of being more influential than imitative, and are one of the better outfits working in this well-trod arena.

Produced by John Rivers, the Pastels' album debut, **Up for a Bit**, followed a five-year string of wonderful singles. Ten polished guitar tracks stamped with Jonathan Richman-worshiper Stephen McRobbie's nearly atonal vocals, the LP falls just short of fulfilling the 45s' promise, and overproduction is the culprit. "Crawl Babies," "Automatically Yours" and "I'm Alright with You" are winning tracks; checking the excesses, however, would have made this a much better album.

Comin' Through restores many of the rough edges lost on the LP, giving the four tracks a refreshing boldness. The rockabilly-laced "Sit on It Mother" is the fiercest this band is likely to get and displays the intuitive versatility that separates the Pastels from the rest of the anorak pack.

In 1987, the band re-signed with Creation just long enough to compile some singles and radio sessions into **Suck on the Pastels**.

While there's nothing new in **Sittin' Pretty**'s off-key awkwardness and gawky grooves (for the first time, the Pastels sound like they're consciously trying to sound like themselves), this outing from the monsters of twee is not without its gems, especially the cute but noisy "Baby, You're Just You" and the revamped "Sit on It Mother." (Richard Mazda produced.)

Deliberately amateur and willfully obscure in that distinctively Scottish manner, the Pastels are notorious for cutting multiple versions of the same songs: if you include radio sessions, there are as many as five different renditions of some early tunes. Stephen's label, 53rd & 3rd, has been almost as influential as the Pastels, releasing records by the Vaselines, Pooh Sticks, Shop Assistants and Beat Happening. [ag/ja]

JEAN-FRANCOIS PAUVROS
See *Blurt*.

PAYOLA$
Introducing Payolas EP (IRS) 1980
In a Place Like This (IRS) 1981
No Stranger to Danger (A&M) 1982
Hammer on a Drum (A&M) 1983
PAUL HYDE AND THE PAYOLAS
Here's the World for Ya (A&M) 1985
ROCK AND HYDE
Under the Volcano (Capitol) 1987 ●

Vancouver, British Columbia was the site of one of Canada's most volatile early punk explosions, but only a couple of bands managed to spread their fame much beyond the city limits. The Payolas were one of those, and temporarily managed to retain some of the scene's fire after signing to an American label.

The gatefold 7-inch EP—four songs, two of them redone for the first album—records an early four-piece lineup, produced by guitarist Bob Rock to sound like a high-voltage cross between the New York Dolls, the Clash and the Ramones.

An impressive debut, **In a Place Like This** is political (but not preachy), offering sophisticated punk with reggae seasoning, which makes it again reminiscent of the Clash without being derivative. Musical variety, lyrical quality and youthful power add to the album's strong impact.

No Stranger to Danger, expertly produced by Mick Ronson (who had not previously distinguished himself in that role), shows enormous progress—from an able but inexperienced adolescent band to a skilled and creative heir to Mott the Hoople. (If that connection doesn't register, consider that Ronson was a late member of Mott and subsequently worked extensively with Ian Hunter.) The judicious addition of contemporary keyboards, vastly improved singing and a more-melody/less-thrash outlook make every track a treat. In a nice touch, it's dedicated to the late Alex Harvey.

Sticking with Ronno, **Hammer on a Drum** takes a large step away from the youth and energy of the band's beginnings. Singer Paul Hyde selectively affects a near-perfect vocal imitation of Ian Hunter (who also appears on the record, furthering the Mott relationship). It's slick and engaging, but sorely lacking in believable personality. It may not be fair to expect any group to remain true to its (perceived) principles, but getting this fogeyish so fast is neither commendable nor flattering.

Here's the World for Ya, produced by big-time mainstreamer David Foster, is even worse. Typical of this boring and bland synth-rock record, the band is careful to thank members of Rush and Loverboy.

Ditching the band name, Rock (guitar, keyboards and bass) and Hyde (vocals, guitar), joined by ex-Payola Chris Taylor (drums, keyboards) and several other part-timers, returned with an excellent duo album. Spanning a number of styles—all of which show imagination, pop and rock smarts and enthusiasm—the album is adult and intelligent. One of those rare multi-faceted records that reveals itself differently each time, **Under the Volcano** more than makes up for the long dry spell.

Rock has since gone on to become a very successful producer, working with the Cult, Metallica and other hard-rock bands. [i]

PEDALJETS
Today Today (Twilight) 1988 ●
Pedaljets (Communion) 1989 ●

This nifty Kansas alterno-pop trio lays noisy rock energy and unmitigated passion into melodies strong enough to withstand rough handling. Singer/guitarist Mike Allmayer does a really good job on both, giving **Today Today** an intriguing sound—Byrdslike harmonies and punky Replacements rawness—that works just as well (albeit differently) at high and low volumes.

The addition of a second guitarist and more stylistic variation complicates things a bit on the ambitious but uncompelling **Pedaljets**. Stretching out and opening up his songwriting, Allmayer decompresses the first album's tersely surging pop with empty spaces, slower rhythms and acoustic guitars; the results are enjoyable but not as distinctive. Had the group not made **Today Today** this record would have been a credible starting point. As a developmental step, however, **Pedaljets** is a disappointing step in the wrong direction. (The CD adds two songs.) [i]

PEGBOY
See *Naked Raygun*.

PENETRATION
Moving Targets (nr/Virgin) 1978 ●
Coming Up for Air (Virgin Int'l) 1979
Race Against Time (nr/Clifdayn) 1979
PAULINE MURRAY AND THE INVISIBLE GIRLS
Pauline Murray and the Invisible Girls (nr/Illusive) 1980
Searching for Heaven EP (nr/Illusive) 1981
PAULINE MURRAY
Hong Kong EP (nr/Polestar) 1987
Storm Clouds (nr/Cat and Mouse) 1989 ●

Originally inspired into existence by Patti Smith and the Sex Pistols, Penetration emerged from northern England (Durham, near Newcastle) in 1977 with a great punk single, "Don't Dictate." Led by singer Pauline Murray, the band's brash amateurism had been converted into competent musicianship by the time of **Moving Targets**, released at first on glow-in-the-dark gimmick vinyl that was far noisier than illuminating. Playing mostly originals (written by Murray in collaboration with bandmates), but including Smith's "Free

Money" and the Buzzcocks' "Nostalgia," Penetration's debut LP mixes expansive creations and direct punk-outs, all done with flair and originality. Unlike other LPs by young bands of this era, **Moving Targets** still sounds surprisingly fresh. (The belated CD issue adds five tracks, including "Don't Dictate" and its B-side, 1978's "Fire Squad" and *its* B-side, and the flip of the album's incisive "Life's a Gamble.")

Coming Up for Air, produced poorly by Steve Lillywhite, isn't nearly as good, despite some swell tracks. Where the first record was almost consistently exciting, only "Shout Above the Noise," "On Reflection" and "Lifeline" have the same melodic, dramatic intensity. The band had evidently run out of good songs, and the muffled sound only exacerbates the mishmash.

An officially sanctioned bootleg, **Race Against Time**, joins a side of demos with a side of live performance. The studio work predates the band's album sessions and is pretty boring; the live material, recorded in Newcastle mostly in 1979, is energetic and well played.

After Penetration, Murray joined forces with producer Martin Hannett's occasional agglomeration, the Invisible Girls; the 1980 incarnation that backed Murray on an LP included Buzzcocks drummer John Maher and future Sisters of Mercy/Mission guitarist Wayne Hussey. The eponymous album's subtle pop is closer in spirit and execution to British folk-rock than to the Beatles or Sex Pistols. Murray's singing is too bright and lively to handle the more downbeat material, but the band's ability to pattern exciting sounds around her brings out the inherent passion in her voice, and the soft but dense rock creates a mood of chilling agitation.

Searching for Heaven repeats the album's accomplishments but digresses on "Animal Crazy," which introduces a dislocated disco beat that turns it into an interesting dance music variant.

Between 1981 and '89, Murray struck out on her own and managed some wonderful singles like "New Age" and a striking chamber treatment of Alex Chilton's "Holocaust." **Storm Clouds** compiles the best of those efforts and the **Hong Kong** EP, adding some newer tracks as well. While more consistent and more thoroughly listenable than any of Penetration's albums or the Invisible Girls record, it's also lighter and breezier. Like Poly Styrene's later solo work, Murray sounds hushed, introspective and quiet, a marked contrast to her full-throated Penetration histrionics. The soothing vocals combine with sparkling textures; Murray is inclined to make modest pop gems that succeed with understatement. Investigate completely, then head backwards. [i/sg/jr]

PERE UBU

The Modern Dance (Blank) 1978 (Rough Trade) 1981 ●
Datapanik in the Year Zero EP (nr/Radar) 1978
Dub Housing (Chrysalis) 1978 (Rough Trade) ●
New Picnic Time (Rough Trade) 1979 ●
The Art of Walking (Rough Trade) 1981 ●
390 Degrees of Simulated Stereo (Rough Trade) 1981 ●
Song of the Bailing Man (Rough Trade) 1982 ●
Terminal Tower: An Archival Collection (Twin/Tone) 1985 ●
The Tenement Year (Enigma-Mercury) 1988 ●

One Man Drives While the Other Man Screams (Rough Trade) 1989 ●
Cloudland (Fontana) 1989 ●
Worlds in Collision (Fontana) 1991 φ

In its first incarnation, Cleveland's Pere Ubu—a crucial pioneer in the American underground—combined disorienting, often dissonant, rock and urban blues in a stunningly original and outlandish mix, but never lost an urgent, joyous party atmosphere. Lead singer David Thomas' plebeian warble, the band's most noticeable sonic feature, colors all of Ubu's proceedings in a bizarre light; casual listeners might, as a result, overlook the powerful, polished musicianship. One of the most innovative American musical forces, Pere Ubu is to Devo what Arnold Schoenberg was to Irving Berlin.

The Modern Dance includes two songs remade from early 45s that Pere Ubu had released on its Hearthan label (when Thomas was calling himself Crocus Behemoth and the late Peter Laughner was one of the sextet's guitarists and main songwriters). Focusing on themes of alienation and adolescent angst, the album cuts a precarious middle ground between art-rock and Midwestern garage pop. The British **Datapanik in the Year Zero** catching-up compilation is more successful, collecting five of the original Hearthan tracks, including the dynamic, paranoiac "30 Seconds Over Tokyo." Dark, challenging material.

Dub Housing takes a quantum leap in production and material. Tom Herman's eerie guitar and Allen Ravenstine's keyboard work rivets Thomas' otherworldly vocals to a dark vision at once surreal and lodged in claustrophobic real life. Ubu's music is uncompromising and its songwriting solid, especially on the obsessive drone, "Codex."

Ubu shifted towards brighter, more open sound and a deformed blues ethic on **New Picnic Time**. Still bearing an air of disaster, Thomas' lyrics develop story-songs that increasingly focus on common elements of everyday life, drawing more in line with his strong religious (Jehovah's Witness) beliefs. A bizarre album that is more than a little reminiscent of Captain Beefheart. In 1979, Herman left and Red Crayola guitarist/leader Mayo Thompson joined.

The Art of Walking evinces increasing interest in developing the band's musical range, and tends towards ambient use of sound to create new aural landscapes, as well as more creative use of dissonance.

Ubu's first live album, **390 Degrees of Simulated Stereo**, takes an overview of the band's development through a collection of live recordings from Cleveland, London and Brussels, featuring the group's best songs from the 1976-9 era, including "30 Seconds Over Tokyo," "My Dark Ages" and "Heart of Darkness."

With Thompson's expanding influence and the replacement of drummer Scott Krauss by Anton Fier, Pere Ubu firmly entered the art-rock fold on **Song of the Bailing Man**. With clean production (by Adam Kidron) and spare sound, Pere Ubu abandoned the chaotic inspiration that charged its earlier work, substituting an unaccustomed and incongruous restraint. After finishing the album, Ubu decided to disband, allowing Thomas to concentrate on his solo career.

Terminal Tower is, as billed, an archival collection with lyrics and abundant liner notes. Many of these

494

eleven essential Ubu tracks—from "Heart of Darkness" and "Final Solution" to "Not Happy" and "Lonesome Cowboy Dave"—are otherwise hard to find; two are alternate mixes.

Pere Ubu formally reformed in late 1987, but all that actually meant was a name change and inclusion of Scott Krauss in the lineup of Thomas' most recent solo support band, the Wooden Birds. In July 1988, Thomas, Krauss, bassist Tony Maimone, synthesist Allen Ravenstine, drummer Chris Cutler and guitarist Jim Jones released Ubu's first new LP in six years. Although not entirely successful (two drummers is one too many; Ravenstine's noise doodles now seem extraneous and dated), **The Tenement Year** builds a solid rock structure around Thomas' whimsical fascinations, putting restless instrumental curiosity to work in a mix of mild noise ("George Had a Hat") and moderate accessibility ("We Have the Technology").

One Man Drives While the Other Man Screams, the long-delayed second Ubu tour document, offers thirteen tracks recorded in London (1978, with Tom Herman), Cleveland (1980, with Mayo Thompson) and Germany (1981, ditto). Drawing a lot of its material from **Dub Housing** ("Navvy," "Ubu Dance Party," "Codex," etc.), the record has a relaxed feel and (on CD, at least) extremely clear sound.

Using **The Tenement Year**'s prettier tunes as a rough sketch, Ubu put itself in producer Stephen Hague's competent hands for half of **Cloudland** and delivered a big surprise: wonderful pop. Jettisoning such inconvenient sonic baggage as vocal disharmony, chaos and electronic graffiti, the album offers an ingenious subversion of classic Top 40 as run through Ubu's unique wringer. While "Breath" and "Race the Sun" appropriate simple chord structures from such familiar sources as Buddy Holly pop and surf-rock, unlikely bridges, tantalizing lyrics and Thomas' moderate warble make them modern and magical. "Waiting for Mary" and "Bus Called Happiness" (Hague's other efforts) are even better, matching catchy choruses to adventurous verse arrangements. On his tracks, longtime Ubu studio chum Paul Hamann helps steer the group back into temperate weirdness, resulting in a demento version of "Sloop John B" that surfaces in "Nevada!" and the recitation and sickly chanting of "Flat." As unpalatable as this open-armed album may be to fans of challenging music, **Cloudland** is quite obviously a masterpiece.

[sg/i]

See also *Peter Laughner, Paul Marotta, Bob Mould, Red Crayola, David Thomas, Tripod Jimmie.*

PERFECT DISASTER

Perfect Disaster (Fr. Kampa) 1985 (nr/Glass) 1987 (Fire) 1991 ●
Hey Hey Hey EP (nr/Glass) 1987
T.V. (Girl on Fire) EP (nr/Fire) 1988
Asylum Road (Genius-Rough Trade) 1988 ●
Up (nr/Fire) 1989 (Fire) 1990 ●
Mood Elevators EP (nr/Fire) 1989
Rise EP (nr/Fire) 1989
Heaven Scent (nr/Fire) 1990 (Fire) 1991 ●

Singer/guitarist Phil Parfitt and guitarist Dan Cross have been the only constants in this fascinating and prolific English band's intricate genealogy. (Part of an early incarnation transmuted into Fields of the Nephilim; ex-bassist Josephine Wiggs is now a Breeder.) Typified by constant artistic tension and a habit of shifting direction as frequently as possible, the Perfect Disaster is a strange bird, but one worth keeping an ear on.

The restrained and debonair (but far from slick) suave-pop on **Perfect Disaster** gently builds alluring, occasionally rocking (with a bit of sax and even feedback), arrangements around Parfitt's deep, character-laden voice. With a cover of Lou Reed's "Over You" to underscore affection for the Velvets' pretty side and such tunefully neurotic Parfitt originals as "What's Happening to Me" and "Hiding from Frank," this stylessly inventive collection—easily commendable to fans of Aztec Camera—is a most auspicious debut.

Two of the four new songs (including a weird Vietnam-war number entitled "The Night Belongs to Charlie" that later turned up, in a different recording, on **Asylum Road**) on the 1987 12-inch firm up the Perfect Disaster's pop backbone with more guitar intensity; the other two keep things light and airy. After previewing another album track—this one with Wiggs' cello and string bass providing an eerie aura—on the **T.V. (Girl on Fire)** EP, the band released its second LP, **Asylum Road**. A shifting sky of cloudy moods, the songs run from somber ("All the Stars") to rushing enthusiasm ("The Crack Up") to Velvety drone ("In Conference Again"), all punched up by Cross' incisively diverse guitar work. In a typical contradiction of sound and content, "What's the Use of Trying?" voices disgust over a delightful pop melody.

The band brought its stylistic approach more in line with Parfitt's increasingly bitter and cynical lyrics on **Up**, kicking up a bracing Velvets-derived noise. (Although, of course, one segment of a lengthy three-parter named "Down" is a mock-baroque cello/acoustic guitar instrumental.) While the rhythm section sets a driving "Sister Ray" backbeat in motion, Cross goes to town, overlaying distortion, feedback, toggle-switching, noise-rock aggression and all the other good things he could only hint at on prior records. (On the few quiet songs—like "It Doesn't Matter" and "Go Away"—he satisfies himself with veiled threats.) For his part, Parfitt unveils a suitably roughened-up voice on the louder tunes.

From there, it was only a small step to the strong Madchester-oriented rock of "Mood Elevators" (available in two versions, plus a pair of non-LP songs, on a 12-inch) and the nearly Jesus & Mary Chain pop roar of the wonderful "Rise." All three additional tracks on the **Rise** EP—a fragile lullaby entitled "Lee" plus '89 live versions of **Up**'s "B52" (thirteen minutes' worth) and an early single—reappear on the **Heaven Scent** CD as bonuses, along with the weaker mix of "Mood Elevators" from the preceding EP.

Other than "Rise," which opens it, the kicky "Takin' Over" and the dramatic "Sooner or Later," the other two-thirds of **Heaven Scent** (Wiggs' last stand with the band) are claustrophobically subdued, deeply personal songs ("Father," "Little Sister (If Ever Days)," "Where Will You Go with Me") given sleepy, intimate performances. Even the songs with loud guitar bits (e.g., "Wires" and "It's Gonna Come to You") are played at such a woozy tempo and with so much sonic room that an occasional bit of window-rattling doesn't really upset the gentle mood. [i]

See also *Breeders*.

LEE "SCRATCH" PERRY (AND THE UPSETTERS)

Super Ape (Mango) 1976
Roast Fish Collie Weed and Corn Bread (Jam. Upsetters) 1976
Cloak and Dagger (Hol. Black Art) 1979 (nr/Anachron) 1990
Scratch on the Wire (nr/Island) 1979
The Return of Pipecock Jackxon (Hol. Black Art) 1980
The Upsetter Collection (nr/Trojan) 1981 ●
Scratch and Co.: Chapter One (Jam. Clocktower) 1982
Mystic Miracle Star (Heartbeat) 1982
History, Mystery and Prophecy (Mango) 1984
Reggae Greats (Mango) 1984 ●
The Upsetter Box (nr/Trojan) 1985 ●
Battle of Armagideon (Millionaire Liquidator) (nr/Trojan) 1986 ●
Some of the Best (Heartbeat) 1986 ●
Time Boom X De Devil Dead (nr/On-U Sound) 1987 ●
Satan Kicked the Bucket (Bullwackies) 1988 (Rohit) 1990 ●
All the Hits (Rohit) 1989 ●
Chicken Scratch (Heartbeat) 1989 ●
Build the Ark (nr/Trojan) 1990 ●
From the Secret Laboratory (Mango) 1990 ●
Message from Yard (Rohit) 1990 φ
Lee Scratch Perry Meets Bullwackie in Satan's Dub [tape] (ROIR) 1990
Lord God Muzick (Heartbeat) 1991 ●

LEE PERRY AND FRIENDS

Give Me Power (nr/Trojan) 1988 ●
Open the Gate (nr/Trojan) 1989 ●
Shocks of Mighty 1969–1974 (nr/Attack) 1989 ●
Public Jestering (nr/Attack) 1990 ●

JAH LION

Colombia Colly (Mango) 1976

LEE "SCRATCH" PERRY & MAD PROFESSOR

Mystic Warrior (RAS) 1989 ●
Mystic Warrior Dub (Jam. Ariwa) 1989 [tape] (ROIR) 1990

UPSETTERS

Version Like Rain (nr/Trojan) 1990

VARIOUS ARTISTS

Heart of the Ark Vols. 1 & 2 (nr/Seven Leaves) 1982
Megaton Dub Vols. 1 & 2 (nr/Seven Leaves) 1982

Certainly eccentric, possibly mad (even his record company bio acknowledges it!), Lee "Scratch" Perry is reggae's most influential producer, with a career that spans the entire history of the music. He started at Coxsone Dodd's Studio One label, first as a talent scout, then as producer. Moving on to other labels, he recorded hit after hit for Jamaican artists, assembling the original Wailers and producing their earliest—some say best—tracks. Perry has also done extensive solo work, composing, arranging and singing his own records.

With the help of a studio band, the Upsetters (named for one of his aliases), Perry has forged a style that's idiosyncratic and revolutionary—full of shifting, echoey rhythms and weird sound effects. His characteristic sound is unique—extended grooves layered like fog, with odd vocals and percussion shimmering in the dense mist.

Perry became an Island house producer in the '70s and a major influence on new wave bands with an affinity for reggae. (The Clash covered "Police and Thieves," a tune he co-wrote with Junior Murvin, on their first LP; Perry later did some production for the band.)

Perry's early work as both producer and performer is well chronicled. **Some of the Best** contains many fine recordings, including "People Funny Boy" and others that make plain American R&B's essential link to reggae. **The Upsetter Collection** has "Return of Django," a UK hit, and the Gatherers' "Words of My Mouth," the rhythm track of which Perry has used again and again. **Chapter One** features a dub of Junior Byles' "Curly Locks," Ricky and Bunny's "Bush Wed Corn Trash" and others co-produced with Brad Osbourne. All three compilations are lively, vital and consistent.

Perry's Island releases are also notable. **Colombia Colly** (billing him as Jah Lion) is one of the best, showing him in stylistic transition and getting weirder, with a cover of Peggy Lee's "Fever" and one cut that features a creaking door. **Super Ape**, from the same year, is more conventional, a dub LP that emphasizes the Upsetters' playing. Perry's personality is evident, though subdued. The number of engineers credited on **History, Mystery and Prophecy**, Perry's last Island LP, suggests the label might have been attempting to smooth out the roughness. The sound is too clean, static and unexciting.

Perry's Island years also yielded two almost identical compilations—**Scratch on the Wire** and **Reggae Greats**. Both feature Junior Murvin's "Police and Thieves," as well as his own "Roast Fish and Cornbread" and "Soul Fire" (from the brilliant Jamaican-only **Roast Fish Collie Weed and Corn Bread** LP), but neither is essential.

His other LPs vary in quality. **The Return of Pipecock Jackxon** derives from Dutch sessions during which Perry reportedly experimented with LSD and destroyed the studio. Needless to say, it's brilliant. So is **Mystic Miracle Star**, which he made with the Majestics. Surprisingly straightforward, with few sound effects, it's still filled with his characteristic production signatures. Less impressive are the two so-so volumes of **Heart of the Ark** (compilations of Perry-produced singers); worse, the two **Megaton Dub** volumes are so lackluster that one authority wondered in print whether Perry had actually produced them.

Two notable '85 releases: on "Judgment in a Babylon," a startling Jamaican 12-inch, Perry accuses Island Records boss Chris Blackwell of being a vampire who killed Bob Marley. Although libelous and crazy, it must be heard. In a more historical vein, **The Upsetter Box** makes three classic out-of-print LPs (**African Blood**, **Rhythm Shower** and **Double 7**) available again. Pricey but worthwhile, the set features appearances by U-Roy, I-Roy and others, and marks Perry's return to Trojan. His next release for the label, **Battle of Arma-**

gideon, is a collection of new tracks recorded in London. A return to form of sorts, the LP is full of his characteristically dense production (which sounds thoroughly contemporary) and lots of cryptic, stream-of-consciousness lyrics. (On one song, "I Am a Madman," he even celebrates his lunatic persona.) Perry's time in London also resulted in **Time Boom X De Devil Dead**, a collaboration with British dubmeister Adrian Sherwood. Influenced by Perry in the past, co-producer Sherwood provides a steadying hand, so the music is consistent, even if Perry's personality—he does all the singing—seems restrained. While perhaps lacking the eccentric edge of Perry's own work, the LP is still weird and wonderful, a sample of some of the best avant-garde groove music being made today.

In 1988, Trojan released **Give Me Power**, another compilation of tracks Perry wrote and produced for other artists. Superbly sequenced and annotated, it's one of the best and most representative collections of the producer's past work. Don't miss it.

Produced by Coxsone Dodd during Perry's 1964-'66 heyday, most of the tracks on **Chicken Scratch** have been unavailable for over 20 years, and some are previously unreleased. All of the cuts are performed by the peerless Skatalites, and many include the female vocals of either the Soulettes (Rita Marley's first group) or the Dynamites. This is Lee Perry in his pre-Upsetter days, before his artistically and commercially fruitful collaboration with the Wailers. Songs like "Man to Man" (featuring Marley, Tosh and Bunny Wailer), "Cruma," "Takcoo," "Roast Duck" and the title track (which provided one of Perry's many aliases) make **Chicken Scratch** a time capsule of Jamaica's ska era.

Way beyond weirdness, the world of Lee "Scratch" Perry is one where people wear umbrellas on their heads, where the bass is the place, where space constantly shifts, where age does not whither, where reason sleeps and the dub quivers, and where avant-garde sonic formalism and mindless fun are bedmates. The madman who for years has continually pushed the frontiers of dub with his heavy sounds, surprising tricks and unorthodox methods, currently resides on a mountaintop in Switzerland. And he keeps making records, seemingly more than ever.

From the Secret Laboratory is Perry's second co-production with Adrian Sherwood. The Dub Syndicate and Jamaica's veteran Roots Radics underpin Perry's free-form word associations and social commentaries on "Secret Laboratory (Scientific Dancehall)," "You Thought I Was Dead" and the crowning "Seven Devils Dead."

With such signature tunes as "Run for Cover" and "Water Pump," **All the Hits** covers Perry's rock steady-era work.

Mystic Warrior, the collaboration between reggae's preeminent techno-wiz geniuses, doubles your madmen-*cum*-musical visionaries pleasure. The Mad Professor (Neal Fraser) is a Guyana-born producer-engineer who rules over the cutting edge of Britain's avant-garde reggae scene and runs the Ariwa Sounds label. **Mystic Warrior** is an awesomely imaginative display of effects and far-ranging musical references.

Trojan Records has mined Perry's incredible back-log of hard-to-find '70s productions with three recent compilations: **Version Like Rain** is a brilliant collection of sixteen tracks taken from three popular Upsetter rhythms, while the three-LP/two-CD **Build the Ark** box set features eighteen mid-'70s tracks (and their dubs): Scratch at his production peak. [bk/aw]

See also *Junior Murvin*.

MARK PERRY

See *Alternative TV*.

PET SHOP BOYS

Please (EMI America) 1986 ●
Disco (EMI America) 1986 ●
Pet Shop Boys, actually. (EMI Manhattan) 1987 + 1988 ●
Introspective (EMI Manhattan) 1988 ●
Behavior (EMI) 1990 ●

LIZA MINNELLI

Results (Epic) 1989 ●

Pet Shop Boys, the London duo of ex-*Smash Hits* journalist Neil Tennant and electro-musician Chris Lowe, have made an enormously successful career by applying intentionally provocative intellectual pretension and philosophical self-indulgence to au courant dance music. **Please** is a slick set of anonymous easy-listening disco tracks, brilliantly, soullessly produced (mostly by Stephen Hague), with ridiculous, overbearingly smug lyrics recited by Tennant, who speak-sings suspiciously like a young Al Stewart. The in-joke references and self-amused esoterica strewn throughout songs like "West End Girls" and "Opportunities (Let's Make Lots of Money)" should have precluded their general popularity, but evidently the laxative-smooth synth backing has utilitarian value for clubgoers. Ghastly, depressing and offensive.

The **Disco** remix album employs an assortment of American dubmen (Shep Pettibone, Arthur Baker, the Latin Rascals and others) for extended versions of those two songs, plus "In the Night" (the B-side of "Opportunities") and other selections from **Please**: the dreamy "Love Comes Quickly" (botched by the incongruous ticking sequencers) and the sarcastic "Suburbia," subtitled here "The Full Horror" and loaded with barking dogs and other ambient ephemera. A crackling snare drum on "West End Girls" is likewise an extraneous annoyance. While it's nice that the pair can acknowledge the crassness of their motives, how much better does that make the music sound?

Virtually a sonic translation of the ambivalent cynical fiction of writers like Jay McInerney and Bret Easton Ellis that became popular around the same time, the uncertain attitudinal incoherence of **Please** is traded for a decisive formula on **actually**, a crafty album of naked '80s yuppiedom (or, of course, a scathing indictment thereof) with songs like "Shopping" and "Rent" offering incisive social satire (or merely basking in the fruits of stardom). To be fair, the duo's melodic sense shows remarkable improvement, and the well-arranged record (entirely programmed on Fairlight synthesizer) draws as much from **Abbey Road** as Kraftwerk. Tennant's voice has lost none of its creepy unctuousness and songs like the abominable "One More Chance" are virtual rewrites of past hits. But "It's a Sin" has a

497

brilliant refrain, and Dusty Springfield's guest vocals on "What Have I Done to Deserve This?" salvage that tune handily. In early 1988, **actually** was reissued in the US with a second disc containing two versions of "Always on My Mind" (the Willie Nelson hit) and "Do I Have To?"

The following year, the Pet Shop Boys wrote, "performed" and produced the magnificent "Nothing Has Been Proved" for Springfield to sing on the *Scandal* soundtrack. The pair played much the same role on Liza Minnelli's ungodly **Results**. Co-producing the record with their frequent studio collaborator, Julian Mendelsohn, the Pet Shop Boys did a lot of the programming and wrote most of the material, leaving Liza to emote absurdly over coy and starkly inappropriate songs like "Don't Drop Bombs" and "I Want You Now." (Actually, a schmaltzy remake of "Rent" doesn't come off too badly.) Slathering strings (arranged by Art of Noisette Anne Dudley and *Twin Peaks* composer Angelo Badalamenti) on top of pulsing synthesizers creates the superficial impression of a sympathetic environment for the melodramatic chanteuse, but the vast stylistic gap between singer and songs makes the record comical.

The boring and redundant **Introspective** jams six songs (four of them also issued as singles) into 48 minutes, largely dispensing with such needless formalities as melody in favor of protracted pre-mixed dance grooves. "Always on My Mind" makes a repeat appearance in a nine-minute house version; "Left to My Own Devices," which employs an orchestra, is yet another of Tennant's droll and insufferable diary entries; "Domino Dancing" deftly inserts a salsa breakdown into the middle of a standard mid-tempo concoction.

Where **Introspective** revealed absolutely nothing about the men behind the smug facade, "Being Boring," the first song on **Behavior**, is downright generous in its reflective view of the band's shifting existence *and* the decimation wrought by AIDS. Co-produced by Harold Faltermeyer, the album returns to the lush and tuneful musicality of **actually**, with Tennant *singing* lyrics that are, for a change, not simply irritating. While "How You Can Expect to Be Taken Seriously?" provocatively addresses an unnamed pop star, "Jealousy" and "So Hard"—both touching breakup songs—and the new-love "Nervously" prove that Tennant can actually manage emotional conviction in his lyrics and delivery. Opening the Pet Shop door to a bit of equally unfamiliar musical styles, Johnny Marr is one of two guest guitarists.   [i]

See also *New Order*.

BOB PFEIFER

See *Human Switchboard*.

P-FUNK ALL-STARS

See *George Clinton*.

PHANTOM, ROCKER & SLICK

See *Stray Cats*.

PHANTOM 309

A Sinister Alphabet (Tupelo) 1989 ●

With cover art and lettering by Edward Gorey (uncle of bassist Mac McNeilly, who left P309 to become the drummer in Jesus Lizard) and production by Jon Langford (Mekons/Three Johns), all this erstwhile trio—self-billed as the biggest band in Picayune, Mississippi—had to do was show up on its first record to make its small cultural impact. A dish of gutter-level grungeabilly and cohesively crude rock noise distinguished by guitarist John Forbes' devilish growl, **A Sinister Alphabet** simmers with backwoods weirdness and domineering intensity. There may not be much difference between songs like "Beaver Hollow Turnaround," "Slowboat to China" and "Janitor to the Stars," but Phantom 309's demento racket easily slinks below such petty criticisms.

See also *Jesus Lizard*.   [i]

PHANTOM TOLLBOOTH

Phantom Tollbooth EP (Homestead) 1986
One-Way Conversation (Homestead) 1987 ●
Power Toy (Homestead) 1988 ●
Daylight in the Quiet Zone EP (Homestead) 1990

Some of those prone to facile analogies have compared this latter-day power trio led by guitarist Dave Rick (an early member of Yo La Tengo and a frequent participant in Bongwater and B.A.L.L. before joining King Missile fulltime in 1990) to Hüsker Dü and the Minutemen, but New York's Phantom Tollbooth was more like a thrash-inflected version of Fred Frith's Massacre than anything else. (In all fairness, the inclusion of an original song entitled "Flip Your Wig" on **Phantom Tollbooth** didn't help matters.) Various art-rock influences—quick tempo shifts, the occasional jazzy swing and the use of noise as a genuine musical element (rather than a cheap way to telegraph rage or intensity)—gave these guys away.

That said, it must be added that Tollbooth's addition of vocals to its heady and complex clamor wasn't always the greatest thing for the music. **One-Way Conversation** and **Power Toy** (which has a pretty funny version of Heart's "Barracuda" and two bonus tracks on CD) contain the band's best, most focused work, a striking synthesis of the art-rock that so clearly influenced its song structures and the frenzied attack of hardcore.   [gk]

BINKY PHILIPS

Binky Philips EP (Caroline) 1987

Sixteen years after his band, the Planets, first opened for the New York Dolls, this Manhattan scene veteran finally made his first record. Whew! Amazingly, he seems none the worse for wear. The five songs cut live at CBGB sound pretty darned fresh: an infectiously rockin' plea for peace (between lovers? friends? countries?), a power pop love song (slight but durable), a nasty slice of early Elvis Costello-meets-Pete Townshend (or, how to say goodbye to an ex-lover with no physical violence but still be guilty of assault and battery), a regretful farewell that's sort of a wailin' hard-rock hoedown and a sardonic expression—in loud, modern guitar-funkatiousness—of the hoary dictum, "Nothing's Free." It all hangs together by virtue of Philips' strong guitar playing and savvy (if a bit hoarse) vocals, and the tight, punchy rhythms of his cohorts, ex-Gang of Four/League of Gentlemen bassist Sara Lee and drummer Mick Leyland. [tr]

PHILTHY PHIL AND FAST EDDIE

See *Motörhead*.

PHRANC

Folksinger (Rhino) 1985 (Island) 1990 ●
I Enjoy Being a Girl (Island) 1989 ●
Positively Phranc (Island) 1991 φ

Looking like a buzz-cut Matt Dillon on the cover of her first album, California's Phranc—a veteran of such punk bands as Nervous Gender and Catholic Discipline—is an otherwise tradition-minded descendant of such '60s protest singers as Bob Dylan, Phil Ochs, Joan Baez and Tom Paxton. Phranc's topical songs, performed with simple beauty on acoustic guitar, address various subjects and personalities of current interest, from women athletes to Marvel's Pope comic book to "Female Mudwrestling" to Los Angeles' celebrity coroner, Thomas Noguchi. Taking one too many cues from Dylan, there's an unnecessary reading of his chilling "Lonesome Death of Hattie Carroll" and several overly similar originals. Phranc's not a timeless melodicist, but her wry lyrical observations and attractive singing make **Folksinger** a fine effort. The 1990 reissue adds "Everywhere I Go (I Hear the Go-Go's)."

Phranc can barely suppress the giggles as she croons the absurdly outdated Rodgers and Hammerstein song—several layers of gay and feminist irony here—for which she named her second album. **I Enjoy Being a Girl**, produced by Violent Femme Victor DeLorenzo, has incidental instrumental accompaniment on a few jazzy numbers but is otherwise another one-woman/one-guitar show. Phranc's concerns here are white guilt ("Bloodbath"), the trendiness of acoustic performers ("Folksinger"), family (the tender "Myriam and Esther"), pets (the winsome "Rodeo Parakeet"), mindless emblem wearing (the clumsily righteous "Take off Your Swastika") and a tennis heroine ("M-A-R-T-I-N-A"). Ace. [i]

PIANOSAURUS

Live at the Speakeasy NYC [tape] 1985
Live at Folk City [tape] 1985
Groovy Neighborhood (Rounder) 1987 ●
Back to School (unreleased)

High concept on a low budget: New York-region trio Pianosaurus plays Alex Garvin's charmingly light-hearted pop songs entirely on toy instruments for a tikki-takki effect that only adds to their winsome adorability. Plinking away on itsy-bitsy pianos, cheapie organs, kiddie guitars, baby drum kits and plastic horns with sincerity and enthusiasm, Pianosaurus proves that big-people equipment isn't necessary for big-people music. (**Groovy Neighborhood**'s renditions of Chuck Berry's "Memphis" and John Lee Hooker's "Dimples" indicate that the gambit can work on well-known songs without any diminution of delight.) Peter Holsapple of the dB's produced this warm and wonderful debut.

In 1988, Pianosaurus appeared in Francis Ford Coppola's segment of the *New York Stories*, and on the accompanying soundtrack, playing the title song of their second album in a version produced by Chris Butler. Then things went awry. With the **Back to School** album in the can, Garvin skipped town, apparently following in the emotional footprints of his musical influences, Brian Wilson and Alex Chilton. Rounder decided against releasing the record.

It's a shame the LP has yet to see the light of day. Pianosaurus' lost album shows the group growing up without straying far from the debut's ingenuous urban-pastoral whimsy. Still performed exclusively on toys, the sophomore effort finds Garvin's bandmates playing greater roles. Drummer Steve Dansiger and keyboardist Bianca "Flystrip" Miller join in on tasty harmonies throughout, lending depth to the sound; each gets a lead vocal. [i/ws]

CHARLIE PICKETT AND THE EGGS

Live at the Button (Open) 1982 (Safety Net) 1988
Cowboy Junkie Au-Go-Go EP (Open) 1984 (Safety Net) 1988 ●

CHARLIE PICKETT

Route 33 (Twin/Tone) 1986

CHARLIE PICKETT & THE MC3

The Wilderness (Safety Net) 1988 ●

Pickett may have led *the* new wave bar band; on the Eggs' records, these Floridians throw original tunes in with covers of wildly varying notoriety, shake it all up and pour out fiery stuff. That Pickett's own tunes often compare favorably to those he chooses to cover makes their scarcity on the live LP disappointing, and using three tunes by the Pirates (during and after Johnny Kidd) and three written or adopted by the Flamin Groovies on one album is a bit much, even if Pickett's slide work and the nasty ensemble nearly makes numbers like "Slow Death" sound newly minted. (Other borrowings come from Manfred Mann and Lou Reed.)

For their long-awaited second vinyl outing, the Eggs took to the studio and cut five songs, including the great Miami localisms of "Overtown" and "Marlboro Town," a dopey "Louie Louie" adaptation that was a local hit two decades ago for its author, Charlie's cousin Mark Markham. (Markham also penned "If This Is Love, Can I Get My Money Back?" which is included on the live LP and was also recorded and issued as a 1982 Pickett single.) Even without the special charge they get onstage, the Eggs reel off true-blue high-energy rockers, further establishing guitarist John Salton as a first-rate student of Thunders, Fogerty and Sky Saxon (not to mention a dead-great slide player). It's hard to believe this band isn't as big a global legend as it deserves to be.

Eggless, but joined by such sympathetic grunge talents as ex-Panther Burns guitarist Jim Duckworth and Maureen Tucker, Charlie is still burning with unquenchable rock'n'roll fire on **Route 33**. The material is almost entirely Pickett's; Minneapolis legend Chris Osgood produced it to resemble an old Stones album from a real ethnic American perspective. A little bit blues, a little bit country, but strictly bullshit-free, the album is a straightforward electric charge from a real heartlands original.

The Wilderness finds Pickett howling and rocking at top form with a new backing band. The Magic City (Miami, that is) Three includes ex-Egg Salton, whose blistering blues-based guitar excitement provides fiery encouragement for Pickett's plain and emotional singing which, at times, recalls Neil Young's mournful country wail. Covers of a twelve-bar blues and a gospel song, both penned by Son House, and an electrifying new rendition of "If This Is Love" settle in nicely alongside such new originals as "Religion or Pleasure" and the cowboy saga, "Destry Rides Again."

The CD of **The Wilderness** contains **Cowboy Junkie Au-Go-Go**. That record was also re-released in an expanded edition that appends the contents of Pickett's first two singles and a track from a compilation cassette.   [jg/i]

JEFFREY LEE PIERCE
See *Gun Club*.

PIG
A Poke in the Eye ... with a Sharp Stick (Wax Trax!) 1988 ●

Although he subsequently got Jim (Foetus) Thirwell to produce a 12-inch single, Raymond (Pig) Watts managed to record the exceedingly Foetuslike **Poke in the Eye** with just a bunch of German guitarists and percussionists. A powerfully bestial singer with an outraged lyrical view ("Scumsberg," "It Toll for Thee (Pigbreath)," "Shit for Brains") and a good sense of rhythm, Pig also has a surprising lighter side that nearly derails the record. But when Watts revs up a thundering herd of angry noise, Pig can be a real party animal. [i]

See also *Foetus Inc*.

PIGBAG
Dr. Heckle and Mr. Jive (Stiff) 1982
Lend an Ear (nr/Y) 1983
Pigbag Live (nr/Y) 1983
Favourite Things (nr/Y) 1983
Discology: The Best of Pigbag [CD] (nr/Kaz) 1987 ●

Bristol's Pigbag was an instrumental sextet with a four-piece brass-and-reed section. The music they played—mostly uptempo, Latin-tinged jazz-funk—was good fun for the length of a 1981 single, and "Papa's Got a Brand New Pigbag" was duly a big dancefloor hit. Stretched out over an album, though, the band's writing limitations become stultifyingly clear.

Dr. Heckle and Mr. Jive contains three variations on the "Papa" formula and a couple of slower cuts that reveal a band with plenty of technical know-how and nothing to say. Following a second studio album and a poorly received live set, Pigbag called it a day. **Favourite Things** and the CD-only **Discology** are retrospectives, the latter containing "Papa's Got a Brand New Pigbag" in both its album and 12-inch remix versions.   [si]

PINK CADILLAC
See *Treat Her Right*.

PINK FAIRIES
See *Social Deviants*.

PINK MILITARY
Blood and Lipstick EP (nr/Eric's) 1979
Do Animals Believe in God? (nr/Eric's) 1980

PINK INDUSTRY
Forty-Five EP (nr/Zulu) 1982
Low Technology (nr/Zulu) 1983
Who Told You, You Were Naked (nr/Zulu) 1983
New Beginnings (nr/Zulu) 1985
Pink Industry (nr/Cathexis) 1988

With many of her early Liverpool compatriots on their way to worldwide fame and fortune, singer Jayne Casey formed Pink Military after the short-lived but seminal Big in Japan folded in 1978. Pink Military's one album, recorded after two years and numerous lineup changes, is an eclectically derivative (yet amusing) hodgepodge that is neither stunningly original nor disgustingly clichéd.

After Pink Military ended, Casey joined up with bassist/keyboardist Ambrose Reynolds (a onetime member of Frankie Goes to Hollywood), adding a guitarist after the first album, and continued to evade commercial success as Pink Industry. Inhabiting and exploring an original world of sound and vision, Pink Industry sounded something like Siouxsie Sioux fronting Japan, using bits of guitar, bass, drums, electronics and found audio to weave a fascinating soft cushion for Casey's plain vocals. As the trio progressed (Casey's vocals on the later records are a big improvement), their efforts turned more towards alluringly textured layers of electronics, making the group's end all the more regrettable.

Pink Industry, released during a surprising spurt of UK interest in the by-then-defunct band, is a fine condensation of the three albums that adds a pair of alternate versions, a remix of "What I Wouldn't Give" and the otherwise unissued "Cruel Garden."   [sg/i]

See also *Big in Japan*.

PIXIES
Come on Pilgrim (nr/4AD) 1987 (4AD-Rough Trade) 1988 ●
Surfer Rosa (4AD-Rough Trade) 1988 ●
Gigantic EP (nr/4AD) 1988 ●
Doolittle (4AD-Elektra) 1989 ●
Monkey Gone to Heaven EP (4AD-Elektra) 1989 ●
Here Comes Your Man EP (4AD-Elektra) 1989 ●
Bossanova (4AD-Elektra) 1990 ●

With so much of what was once the rock underground drifting towards shamefaced respectability and mainstream acceptance, the Pixies reclaimed the land of the disfranchised with a lively, thoughtful new outlook and unique sounds for these disturbing times. As a result, the quartet quickly became the darlings of college radio and have grown into major stars for those who no longer believe in R.E.M.

The Pixies hail from such diverse locales as Ohio, the Philippines, California and Boston, where the group assembled in 1986. Following Throwing Muses onto

Britain's 4AD label, they debuted with **Come on Pilgrim**, an eight-song explosion (recorded, roughly, as a demo) of gritty art passion: strummed and scratched acoustic and electric guitars, vocals sung and shrieked in English and Spanish, rhythms that race, rest and drift. The fuzzy chaos alternates noisy pop melodicism with primal anarchy; fervid singer Black (Charles) Francis' lyrics, when audible, skew towards surprising, occasionally shocking terrain. Difficult and intriguing.

Ex-rock crit/Big Black mainman (not yet established as a bigtime underground studio maven) Steve Albini produced **Surfer Rosa**, giving the Pixies a virulent, slashing guitar sound and organizing drummer David Lovering and bassist Mrs. John Murphy (Kim Deal) into a stronger, surer rhythm unit. A sturdy grasp on melody and the importance of good—not necessarily pleasant—vocals (Francis and Murphy) make songs like "Bone Machine," "Gigantic," "Vamos" (reprised from **Pilgrim**) and the crazed B-52's noise parody of "Tony's Theme" into gripping rock that equally invites dancing and bewildered headshaking. (The CD of **Surfer Rosa** includes **Come on Pilgrim**.)

Taking the spotlight off Francis, the **Gigantic** 12-inch features Deal singing on all four of its tracks: superior remakes (produced by Gil Norton) of the title tune and "River Euphrates" (another **Surfer Rosa** number) and exciting live renditions of "Vamos" and "Heaven," a brief song borrowed from the *Eraserhead* soundtrack.

Doolittle is the apotheosis of the Pixies' art, a tension-filled blend of abrasion and balm that shifts uneasily between the freakout horror of "Debaser," the catchy pop of "Here Comes Your Man," the punky roar of "Crackity Jones," the melodic surf-noise of "Wave of Mutilation" and the unnerving calm of "Monkey Gone to Heaven" (which even incorporates a string quartet). Norton's production helps rein in Francis' excessive tendencies (not that he doesn't still manage some merciless shrieking) and harnesses Joey Santiago's guitar to striking effect. Overall, fine songwriting and clearly articulated performances demonstrate the band's visionary self-awareness.

The **Monkey** EP has three non-LP studio tracks: two variations on a theme ("Manta Ray" and "Dancing the Manta Ray") and the silly "Weird at My School." **Here Comes Your Man** has a really slow live rendition of "Wave of Mutilation" as well as "Into the White" and "Bailey's Walk," half-assed studio productions that sound like abandoned song demos.

Whether the result of too much praise and power or merely a creative drought, **Bossanova** is a major drag, a bad-sounding record with little variety or invention, few good songs (the lyrics are especially trivial) and an annoying atmosphere of smug indifference. Reasonably well-crafted tracks like "Velouria," "The Happening," "Blown Away" and "Allison," all of which would have been fine secondary items on **Doolittle**, are hardly adequate to carry an album on their own, and the rest of **Bossanova** offers them neither support nor competition. See also *Breeders*. [i]

HONEST JOHN PLAIN

See *Boys, Lurkers*.

PLAN B

Plan B EP (Ger. Wall City) 1985
Three Songs by Plan B EP (Ger. Wall City) 1986
Fortune Favors Fools (Ger. Wall City) 1986
The Greenhouse Effect (RCA) 1990 ●

Fervent young Germans with a love for English-speaking bands, Plan B have emerged from the shadows of heavies like U2 and the Clash to become solid rockers in their own right. The quintet's debut EP is marked by good intentions and an obvious delight at being able to create a ruckus: "Gimme the Reason" is a fine, foot-stomping shoutalong.

The **Three Songs** EP (recorded as a four-piece) has the same mixture of grit and grandiosity that made **London Calling** so electrifying. If these guys are simply following Strummer and crew, they're doing a damn fine job of it.

Fortune Favors Fools boasts a five-man lineup and a full complement of ingredients: insistent vocals à la Midnight Oil's Peter Garrett, edgy guitars and crackin' drums. "Stop These Men," "House of Decline" and others resonate with the inflamed passions unleashed in the quest for a meaningful existence. When they sing "It's the sound of us/Trying to break free" in "Plan B," it's hard not to cheer 'em on.

Bolstered by increased confidence and, for the first time, slick, professional production (by Pat Collier), Plan B became an impressive rockin' machine on **The Greenhouse Effect**, the quartet's first Stateside release. Still in dogged pursuit of truth, justice and electric epiphanies, they fight the cool fight on "Mad World," "The Day to Be Jesus," "Devil's Train," etc. Comparisons no longer apply. [jy]

PLANET WILSON

See *Red Guitars*.

PLAN 9

Frustration (Voxx) 1982 ●
Dealing with the Dead (Midnight) 1984
Plan 9 (Fr. New Rose) 1984
I've Just Killed a Man I Don't Want to See Any Meat (Midnight) 1985
Keep Your Cool and Read the Rules (Pink Dust) 1985 ●
Anytime Anyplace Anywhere EP (Pink Dust) 1986
Sea Hunt (Enigma) 1987 ●
Ham and Sam Jammin' (Restless) 1989 ●

BRIAN T. & PLAN 9
"Hideaway" EP (Midnight) 1984

BRENT HOSIER
The Secret That Lies (Fr. New Rose) 1987

Outside of its art college, Rhode Island hasn't exactly been a storehouse for modern rock music. But the state has a group to be proud of in Plan 9, whose **Frustration** is exciting garage psychedelia. The swirling, mesmerizing effect of four (!) guitars recalls the best of the late '60s and gives able support to Eric Stumpo's emotional vocals. There are no original songs here, just covers of period gems like Them's "I Can Only Give You Everything."

The French-only **Plan 9** is an assortment of 1981-'84 studio recordings (plus a live cut) by various lineups, including a poppy five-piece fronted by singer/ guitarist Brian Thomas. (Three songs—two of which overlap the LP—by that formulation also appear on the "Hideaway" maxi-single.) Surprisingly, these recordings manage to hang together as an album.

Dealing with the Dead features eight originals, played with a '60s sound so convincing you'll swear you can smell incense burning. Stumpo's vocals are great, a whiny growl cross-breeding Michael J. Pollard and John Kay; the massed guitars and Deborah DeMarco's atmospheric keyboards increase the sense of déjà entendu even further. Far more convincing than a lot of other similar-minded outfits, Plan 9 knows just how to launch a magic carpet ride to the center of your mind. Diabolical.

I've Just Killed a Man is a steamy live album recorded as a six-piece in Boston, Washington, DC, New Haven and back home in Providence. A trio of ace covers, including the MC5's "Looking at You," and a guest appearance by head Lyre Jeff Conolly on "I'm Gone" add extra excitement to the spirited fun.

Keep Your Cool covers lots of stylistic ground, including the film noir ambience of "Street of Painted Lips" sung by DeMarco, an unclassifiable rollicking instrumental ("King 9 Will Not Return") and various stripes of '60s rock, running the stylistic gamut from Spirit to Steppenwolf. Although some are a little undeveloped, the band's songs are solid; the two covers are righteously arcane.

Anytime Anyplace Anywhere is a five-song EP of new material, including the title tune and "Green Animals."

A revised seven-person lineup on **Sea Hunt** cuts the guitar army down to three and adds a female sax player. The LP removes Plan 9 from revivalism, leaving in the resulting vacuum a rather plain-sounding rock band with a predilection for guitar solos. **Sea Hunt** is by no means bad, but the lack of focus creates an imbalance that Stumpo's unexciting originals don't resolve. The dreamy title track drifts along aimlessly for almost fourteen instrumental minutes; it's followed by the Ramonesque eleven-second "Human Mertzes." Faced with a choice of the lady or the tiger, Plan 9 fluffs it.

Eric, Debora and the rhythm section from **Sea Hunt** drafted a cool new lead singer named Pip and made **Ham and Sam Jammin'** as an economical quintet. Although the band's direction hasn't really changed, the elimination of two guitarists leaves DeMarco's colorful keyboards room to stretch out and be noticed; a guest violinist provides a provocative alternative to Stumpo's fevered riffing on most of the songs. Overall, **Ham and Sam** is better than **Sea Hunt**, although still nowhere as wacky or enjoyable as the band's early work.

Virginian singer/guitarist Hosier was in Plan 9 briefly (he appears on half of **Keep Your Cool**); his intriguing and not overly stylized psychpunk solo album is a weird blend of David Bowie's Anthony Newley vocal period, a variety of players' brisk guitar work and colorful songs inspired by exploitation films. [cpl/i]

PLASMATICS

New Hope for the Wretched (Stiff America) 1980
Beyond the Valley of 1984 (Stiff America) 1981 ●

Metal Priestess EP (Stiff America) 1981 ●
Coup d'État (Capitol) 1982

WENDY O. WILLIAMS

W.O.W. (Passport) 1984
Kommander of Kaos (Gigasaurus) 1986
Maggots: The Record (Profile) 1987

ULTRAFLY AND THE HOMETOWN GIRLS

Deffest! and Baddest! (Defest Disc-Profile) 1988

New Hope for the Wretched, "produced" by Jimmy Miller, represents the Plasmatics' first stage— mere artless gimmickry—as conceived by the group's manager and lyricist, ex-porn entrepreneur Rod Swenson. Former sex-show queen Wendy O. Williams hoarsely talks/shouts/heavy-breathes lyrics jumbling the psychotronic film aesthetic (sex, violence, gratuitous grotesqueries) accompanied by a band playing with no subtlety whatever at punk speed and volume, reprising the "best" bits of the 'Matics' preceding proto-hardcore indie singles (e.g., Williams buzzsawing a guitar in half). Entertaining for its sheer crassness perhaps, though hardly listenable.

Beyond the Valley of 1984, though, *is* quite listenable, if only intermittently memorable. Swenson's lyrics aspire to nightmares of apocalypse and superhuman lust and degradation. The music is likewise heavier, but clearer and not without flashes of finesse: punchy drums (courtesy of guest Neal Smith, once in Alice Cooper), good guitar squeals from Swenson's main writing collaborator, Richie Stotts, and even a culture-shock backing-vocals appearance by the girl-group Angels. (The CD, released many moons later on the PVC label, appends **Metal Priestess**.)

Metal Priestess—25 minutes at a sub-LP price—is the best buy of the lot: smokin' live versions of two of **Beyond**'s best, not to mention proof that Williams can sweetly carry a tune, as grim as it is ("Lunacy"). Co-produced by Dan Hartman (!) and Swenson, it captures the band in mid-transition to metal; part of that change included the departure (early in the project) of Beauvoir for his solo and production career.

Wendy kicks off the awkwardly metallicized **Coup d'État** with some superhuman screaming (a compliment, really!), but it's downhill from there. While Side A's simpleminded messages—"Put Your Love in Me," "Stop" ("the rape of the earth"), etc.—are capped by an adequate take on Motörhead's "No Class," the lyrics on the backside echo the fever-dreams of **Beyond** and **Priestess**, but less compellingly.

When Stotts left (to form the Richie Stotts Experience and King Flux, which also included Marc Bell between stints in the Ramones) it was decided to drop the Plasmatics name. In came Michael Ray to play flashy licks, and Williams' transformation to metal priestess was complete. With writing and performing help from Kiss bandmates, Gene Simmons produced **W.O.W.**, on which Wendy sounds like a hoarse Joan Jett doing Kiss outtakes.

K.O.K. is modestly successful speedy metal and speedmetal, but the sex-goddess role-playing (Motörhead's "Jailbait," "Bad Girl," "F**k That Booty") falls as flat as ever; Williams' voice has always been too tough for that. Her singing is much more suited to the apocalyptic world-domination concept album that followed. **Maggots** isn't all that bad, but how much attention can *you* focus on a subject that gross?

Deffest! and Baddest! is (gulp) Wendy O's *rap* album. [jg]

See also *Jean Beauvoir, Motörhead.*

PLASTIC BERTRAND

Plastic Bertrand AN1 (nr/Sire) 1978
Ça Plane pour Moi (Sire) 1978
J'te Fais un Plan (Bel. RKM) 1979
L'Album (Can. Attic) 1980
Grands Succès/Greatest Hits (Can. Attic) 1981
Plastiquez Vos Baffles (Can. Attic) 1982

One of the first punk gag records and still one of the greatest, "Ça Plane pour Moi" was a major European hit in late '77 and early '78, launching the career of blond Belgian pretty boy Roger Jouret, aka Plastic Bertrand. Scuttlebutt at the time claimed Bertrand was the invention of some anonymous French studio pranksters; in fact, Jouret had already played drums in an earlier Belgian punk trio called Hubble Bubble (whose one LP was notable for a trashy cover of the Kinks' "I'm Not Like Everybody Else"). Together with producer/songwriter Lou Deprijck, he created the persona of Plastic Bertrand, a jolly satire on the safety-pin image and jackhammer crunch of punk.

"Ça Plane pour Moi" ("This Life's for Me") is truly great dumbness—Bertrand singing verbose, seemingly nonsensical French lyrics over a classic three-chord Ramones roar with Spectorish saxes and a winning falsetto "oooh-weee-oooh" on the chorus. **Ça Plane pour Moi** (the US title of **Plastic Bertrand AN1**, released first in Belgium, then in England) also contains more of the hilarious same—a spirited remake of the Small Faces' "Sha La La La Lee" and "Wha! Wha!," wherein Bertrand does barnyard animal imitations.

J'te Fais un Plan has two limp reggae entries actually recorded in Jamaica (the title song and "Hit 78") and a sugary-sweet ballad ("Affection") dedicated to Jonathan Richman. More interesting is the ten-minute electro-disco "Tout Petit la Planète," a blatant Kraftwerk cop tarted up with a nagging hook and a rich synthesizer sound—predating by two years the synth-pop confections of the Human League and OMD.

L'Album is for the true P-Bert devotee, its more tightly formulaic new wave pop distinguished only by a catchy vanilla-funk rap track, "Stop ou Encore," which bears a passing similarity to Blondie's "Rapture." **Greatest Hits** collects his big European successes, adding a pair of live tracks. [df]

PLASTICLAND

Pop! Op Drops EP (Scadillac) 1982
Color Appreciation (Fr. Lolita) 1984
Plasticland (Pink Dust) 1985
Wonder Wonderful Wonderland (Pink Dust) 1985 ●
Salon (Pink Dust) 1987 ●
Confetti (Midnight) 1990
Let's Play Pollyanna EP (Ger. Repulsion) 1990 ●

Following several 7-inch EPs and 45s on their own label, this time-warped psychedelic quartet from Milwaukee (the successor to a legendary band called Arous-ing Polaris) began issuing wonderful albums of original acid-paisley retro-rock.

Except for two track substitutions, the pink-vinyl **Plasticland** is the same LP as the French **Color Appreciation**; both contain all four songs from **Pop! Op Drops**. Adding two bonus cuts, the cassette of **Plasticland** contains the whole kit and kaboodle: seventeen slices of droning delight, including a Pretty Things tune and such evocative band creations as "Euphoric Trapdoor Shoes," "Rattail Comb" and "Driving Accident Prone." **Wonder Wonderful Wonderland** features such giddy items as "Grassland of Reeds and Things," "Processes of the Silverness" and "Fairytale Hysteria." Charming, whimsical, stylish, exciting, witty and utterly entertaining.

Salon puts an even less selfconscious twist on things (although the faint British component in Glenn Rehse's accent argues against that) and displays an easy command of swinging London art-school power pop psychedelia. Armed with a mellotron and other relevant instruments, Plasticland shoots delicious flashes of Manfred Mann, frilly-shirt-era Who and Stones, Yardbirds and **Magical Mystery Tour** into their creations, making **Salon** an incisive nostalgia exercise that transcends its basis to stand on its own merits. A remarkably good time.

Confetti presents songs from all of the band's albums (plus a game stab at a section of George Harrison's **Wonderwall** soundtrack) in churning, stripped-down live versions that attest to the fundamental strength of Plasticland's uncanny melodic sense. Despite inconsistent production, the **Let's Play Pollyanna** EP (three tracks on 12-inch, four on CD) is a welcome return to the studio, with a rockingly memorable title track (also available in a live rendition on **Confetti**) and some enjoyably experimental B-sides. [i/hd]

See also *Social Deviants.*

PLASTICS

Welcome Plastics (Jap. Invitation) 1979 ●
Origato (Jap. Invitation) 1980
Welcome Plastics (nr/Island) 1981
Plastics (Island) 1981

HAJIME TACHIBANA

H (Jap. Yen-Alfa) 1982
Hm (Ralph) 1984
Mr. Techie & Miss Kipple (Jap. Alfa) 1984
Taiyo-Sun (Jap. School) 1986

Those who have only experienced Plastics through their lone Western album release—the English **Welcome** and its American equivalent, **Plastics**, an Alex Sadkin-dulled production of inferior remakes of material from the band's first two albums—are missing out on the Japanese quintet's best work.

The original Japanese albums—**Welcome Plastics** and **Origato**—are marvelous and well worth finding for fans of extreme kitsch and quirk. Sung in English by Toshio Nakanishi and Chica Sato, the Plastics' ultraperky art-pop (played on guitar and synth) takes its cues from American culture of the '60s as portrayed by the B-52's and Devo. Jumpy and clever, nervous and zany, the group takes Western ideals of technology and commercialism and makes catchy Asian sport of them. The first album's song titles say it all: "Digital Watch,"

"Too Much Information," "Robot," "I Am Plastic," "Top Secret Man." (There's also a silly cover of "Last Train to Clarksville"; **Origato** includes the Plastics' rendition of "Eight Days a Week.") A great, cool, original band that might just as well be from Mars.

Following Plastics' breakup at the end of 1981, Tachibana put down his guitar in favor of exploring jazz sax, resulting in **H**, a diverting album which is wacky but not silly—his commitment to this musical path is no less sincere for its synthesis with what he helped develop in Plastics.

On **Hm**, his saxisms are a touch artier and less light-heartedly playful, but it's still a fun record. Primitive drums (or were they copped from a '40s B-movie conga line production number?) are often used to underpin "outside" jazz sax charts and solos, interlarded with quieter numbers minus bass and drums in which pretty melodies are stated. Odd but ingratiating.

With Yukihiro Takahashi producing and supplying occasional drums, the synth-oriented **Mr. Techie & Miss Kipple** just doesn't make it. The menu: a James Brown tribute that goes on too long, oddball instrumentals (including one Tachibana wrote with Devo's Mark Mothersbaugh) that are interesting at best and irritating at worst, a stiff Plastics rehash and a poker-faced hymn professing "No Disappointment in Jesus" (delivered in a low and slurry half-speed voice). Weird yet uninvolving. [i/jg]

PLAYHOUSE

Gazebo Princess (Twin/Tone) 1987

Soul Asylum's Dave Pirner co-produced **Gazebo Princess**, this uncommon Minneapolis trio's rawboned mini-album debut. Skittish, disorienting syncopation supports guitarist Eric Haugesag's distorted power-'n'jazz chords and throaty vocals in a punk-folk-jazz hybrid that derives equally from Killing Joke, the Minutemen and Love. Melodic but no less challenging than the flintier tracks that surround them, "My Eyes" and "Rule No. 1" are standouts that indicate the extent of Playhouse's potential. [i]

MARTIN PLAZA

See *Mental as Anything*.

PLIMSOULS

Zero Hour EP (Beat) 1980
The Plimsouls (Planet) 1981
Everywhere at Once (Geffen) 1983
One Night in America (Fr. Fan Club) 1988 ●

LA's Plimsouls were one of numerous bands which were sucked up by record-label power pop madness in the Knack's wake. Following a short independent recording career, they signed a big deal and made one fine LP that didn't sell. That was very nearly the end of that.

Heaps of promise are already evident on the cheap-sounding **Zero Hour** 12-inch EP. Fronted by sharp-voiced Peter Case (formerly Paul Collins' bandmate in the Nerves), the Plimsouls toss out enough cutting harmonies and nifty guitar licks to recall **Beatles VI**, although their spirit is totally fresh and beyond nostalgia, the aggression modern.

That promise is fulfilled on **The Plimsouls**, the band's first major-label LP, which trims only the raggedest edges to showcase vibrant, hummable tunes like "Now." The Plimsouls' affection for '60s soul also gets a tumble via the use of a horn section and a hot cover of "Mini-Skirt Minnie."

The band's relationship with Planet soured soon after the LP stiffed, and the Plimsouls left the label to make a wonderful independent 12-inch called "A Million Miles Away." In a show of enormous resilience (both commercial and individual), the Plimsouls subsequently joined the Geffen roster and produced **Everywhere at Once**, re-recording that memorable single alongside a batch of similarly strong new ones, all bubbling with undiminished fire and melody. Lyrics, however, show signs of frustration: "How Long Will It Take?," "My Life Ain't Easy," "Play the Breaks." But the Plimsouls were never to hit the big time, and soon faded away.

The posthumously released **One Night in America** captures a live set from 1981, mixing original tunes with some fine vintage covers. Recorded during the Plimsouls' cocky, hard-rocking prime, it's a fitting epitaph for an underappreciated band. [jy/i/hd]

See also *Peter Case, dB's, Walking Wounded*.

PLUGZ

Electrify Me (Plugz) 1979 (Enigma) 1990 ●
Better Luck (Fatima) 1981 (Enigma) 1990 ●

SNAKE FARM

What Kind of Dreams Are These (Fr. New Rose) 1989 ●

Featuring guitarist/singer Tito Larriva (later in the Cruzados) and drummer Chalo Quintana (most recently of the Havalinas), this early LA new wave band play sharp and punky rock'n'roll with a strong sense of pop structure on the varied **Electrify Me**. The title track is mildly reggaefied; there's also a pre-Los Lobos cover (in Spanish) of "La Bamba" and some folky detours, but the band never strays too far from an essentially unadventurous core.

The more mainstream **Better Luck** ups the Plugz's folk and country sides for a blend of Rank and File (another ex-punk outfit whom they predated) and Tom Petty, displaying a promising rock talent enervated to the point of tedium. (The Plugz subsequently contributed three very divergent songs to the *Repo Man* soundtrack.)

Years after the Plugz folded, bassist Barry McBride resurfaced as a guitarist leading an atmospheric cowboy band of no fixed lineup. Snake Farm's album is crisp and taut, resonant Southwestern rock played with unadorned skill and conviction. Given eloquent instrumental support—Dave Alvin and Billy Bremner each make one-song cameos—McBride's vocals and playing are quite effective, but his often ungainly lyrics need help.

See also *Cruzados, Havalinas*. [tr]

POET AND THE ROOTS

See *Linton Kwesi Johnson*.

POGUES

Red Roses for Me (nr/Stiff) 1984 (Stiff-Enigma) 1986 ●
Rum Sodomy & the Lash (Stiff-MCA) 1985 ●
Poguetry in Motion EP (Stiff-MCA) 1986
If I Should Fall from Grace with God (Island) 1987 ●
Peace and Love (Island) 1989 ●
Misty Morning, Albert Bridge EP (nr/WEA) 1989 ●
Yeah Yeah Yeah Yeah EP (Island) 1990 ●
Hell's Ditch (Island) 1990 ●

NIPS 'N' NIPPLE ERECTORS

Bops, Babes, Booze & Bovver (nr/Big Beat) 1987

VARIOUS ARTISTS

Straight to Hell (Hell-Enigma) 1987 ●

The London-based Pogues (originally known as Pogue Mahone—Gaelic for "kiss my ass") are a motley Anglo-Irish agglomeration (at last count an eight-piece) of erstwhile punk rockers—as a young raver, singer/songwriter Shane MacGowan was in the late if unlamented Nipple Erectors (later the Nips), a frisky Ted-style punkabilly-*cum*-beat quartet memorialized a decade after the fact in the eight-song **Bops, Babes, Booze & Bovver** retrospective; guitarist Philip Chevron led Dublin's estimable Radiators from Space, also in the late '70s—and knockabout folkies. Their repertoire mixes traditional Irish, English and Australian folk songs with an increasing majority of MacGowan's stylistically antiquated originals. Although early supporters of the group conveniently overlooked the existence of genuine folk artists in Great Britain who play traditional music with more knowledge and credibility, the Pogues have managed to transcend such beginnings to hone themselves into a unique and original creation.

The first two albums are exploratory, but both have their fine moments. Concertina, banjo, pipes, guitar, bass, minimal drums, mandolin and the like in the hands of post-rock rebels make for an intriguing blend of old-fashioned and newfangled. Recorded as a drape-jacketed six-piece, **Red Roses for Me** (the American cassette of which adds three cuts) mixes traditional balladry ("Poor Paddy," "Greenland Whale Fisheries") with Shane's derivative but promising creations ("Boys from the County Hell," "Dark Streets of London").

Red Roses' rudimentary acoustic instrumentation gave way to relative sophistication on the more varied **Rum Sodomy & the Lash** (produced by Elvis Costello), which evidences growing stylistic ambition as well. MacGowan, a besotted Tom Waits-like figure with an obvious Brendan Behan/James Joyce jones, shows increased confidence and talent as a songwriter on numbers like "The Old Main Drag" and "A Pair of Brown Eyes," notable examples of his gritty, realistic tales of life's urban downside.

Miles better than either of those, however, is **Poguetry in Motion**: an EP of three new MacGowan songs and a reel. Mixing zydeco with Gaelic soul, "London Girl" is a rousing singalong, an urban travelogue that sounds like the hit of Kevin Rowland's dreams; "A Rainy Night in Soho" plays a hauntingly beautiful Van Morrison-like waltz on piano, with tasteful horns and strings; "The Body of an American" is a drinking song that most closely resembles the Pogues' primal busker sound, with uilleann pipes, martial drums and jolly tin whistle.

Along with Costello and Joe Strummer, the Pogues fell in with director Alex Cox, contributing a pair of tracks to *Sid & Nancy*, appearing in the motley *Straight to Hell* and providing the bulk of its soundtrack. Surrounded by contributions by the (Declan) MacManus Gang, Strummer and others, the Pogues offer atmospheric Latinisms like "Rabinga" and Ennio Morricone's "The Good, the Bad and the Ugly," as well as more European creations like "If I Should Fall from Grace with God" (a preview of their next album) and the traditional "Danny Boy," recorded as a reunion with ex-bassist Cait O'Riordan.

If I Should Fall from Grace with God is an exciting, strong album that opens new vistas for the Pogues. Almost all of the material is by the band; amidst winningly unreconstructed folk designs ("The Broad Majestic Shannon," "Medley," the title tune) is a jazz/swing instrumental ("Metropolis") and the oddly accented "Turkish Song of the Damned." But the record's easy standout is another example of the melancholic urban balladeering introduced on **Poguetry in Motion**: "Fairytale of New York," a fragile piano-and-strings lullaby with guest vocals by Kirsty MacColl, wife of the album's producer, Steve Lillywhite, and daughter of folk titan Ewan MacColl, whose songs the Pogues have covered.

What were merely digressions on **If I Should Fall** form the stylistic basis of **Peace and Love**, an amazing album (also produced by Lillywhite) that redefines the Pogues and demonstrates the enormous breadth of talent the eight men possess. Kicking off with a blistering big-band instrumental ("Gridlock") and then careening joyously into one of MacGowan's finest folk-rock creations ("White City"), the record is a marvel of rich playing, resonant emotions, sturdy melodies and low tales. In this varied effort, mandolinist Terry Woods offers a fiery acoustic calumny against Oliver Cromwell in "Young Ned of the Hill"; Chevron contributes the rollicking New Orleans-accented "Blue Heaven"; banjo-player Jem Finer chips in with the dramatic "Night Train to Lorca" and a wistful waltz ("Misty Morning, Albert Bridge"). Meanwhile, MacGowan tops things off with "Boat Train," an engrossing recollection of a drunken voyage, the American-conscious "Cotton Fields" and "London You're a Lady," ending the album in an orchestral flourish. (The **Misty Morning** EP offers three album tracks—one in a surprising dub mix—and Finer's "Train of Love.")

Although the excellent stomping and lusty R&B single "Yeah Yeah Yeah Yeah" was released in 1988, a 12-inch EP built around it—adding a rambunctious banjofied rendition of "Honky Tonk Woman" [*sic*] and a pair of Irish folk songs (one a Pogues original) performed with the Dubliners (the two bands had previously teamed up on a 1987 single)—suddenly appeared in 1990.

Joe Strummer produced **Hell's Ditch**, a casually organized musical voyage that spends far too much of its time in Spain and the Mediterranean. While keeping the music close to home, MacGowan drops eight place names in the first three songs (two of which—"The Ghost of a Smile" and "The Sunnyside of the Street"—are positively wonderful examples of Poguetry) but that's only an orientation session. Once the Pogue ship sets sail, he turns cinematic, spinning spaghetti western yarns ("Hell's Ditch," "Lorca's Novena") with sinuous Middle Eastern accents. Before finishing (with an African-styled chant no less), the Pogues try out cocktail jazz (complete with piano and harp), insert what sounds like a Semitic dance melody into Finer's "The Wake of the Medusa" and manage a convincing early-'70s Dylan impression in "5 Green Queens & Jean." Track by track, there's some fine stuff here, but Strummer's casual production and the album's maddening stylistic hopscotch make it, overall, a frustrating exercise. See also *Men They Couldn't Hang*. [i]

POI DOG PONDERING

Poi Dog Pondering EP (Texas Hotel) 1988
Circle Around the Sun EP (Texas Hotel) 1989
Poi Dog Pondering (Texas Hotel-Columbia) 1989 ●
Wishing Like a Mountain and Thinking Like the Sea (Texas Hotel-Columbia) 1990 ●
Fruitless (Texas Hotel-Columbia) 1990 ●

As noted by Robert Downey (Sr.) in *Putney Swope*, you've got to know the rules before you can break the rules. That axiom certainly applies in the world of "alternative" rock, where bands with big dreams must be colorfully offbeat, but not too weird for radio. As such, Poi Dog Pondering—a modern jug band formed on the streets of Waikiki but based in Austin, Texas—is a record industry fantasy, a lovable mongrel bred of gentle folk-rock exotica with richly diverse influences and enough built-in mystique and credibility to last a career. Led by singer/guitarist Frank Orrall, the large ensemble made a delightful debut on **Poi Dog Pondering**, performing whimsically bright pop songs (like "Living with the Dreaming Body") on a shifting brew of accordion, banjo, horns, fiddle, percussion, acoustic guitar, etc. Despite the potential for instrumental calamity, Poi manages to keep their sound light, leaving plenty of room in the varied arrangements. If Poi were a restaurant, it would be an urban fern bar with a kooky international menu, efficiently run by the children of hippies.

Haunted around the edges by encroaching preciousness and more overt stylistic expeditions (the tenor guitar swing of "Aloha Honolulu," for instance), **Circle Around the Sun** allows for a stronger rock sound ("Wood Guitar" has a crisp backbeat and amplifiers) to shift the stylistic balance a bit. The songs are okay, but the partial loss of innocence is disturbing. (Upon signing the group, Columbia combined the two EPs and reissued them as **Poi Dog Pondering**, using the front cover art of the first.)

Poi took a step closer towards adult contemporary acceptance on **Wishing Like a Mountain**, locating a tropical folk-rock headquarters from which to make assorted folk and country sorties, traveling outside national borders to embrace Latin and African styles. The songs are unfailingly pleasant and occasionally wonderful, but the selfconscious granola consciousness of Orrall's lyrics and the slickening sound of inspired amateurism on its way to becoming selfconscious multicultural calculation weighs down the record, punching holes in the group's easy allure. Just where does genuine diversity end and insufferable dilettantism begin? Even if Poi has the decency to acknowledge the designs of "The Ancient Egyptians," crafting a song in the style

of Jonathan Richman seems like a condescending academic exercise. (The CD adds two bonus songs, "Big Beautiful Spoon" and "Sugarbush Cushman.")

The **Fruitless** mini-album is a patchwork assortment: three live cuts, a remix from **Wishing**, covers of New Order ("Love Vigilantes," given the folk treatment it so obviously merits) and Canned Heat ("Going Up the Country"), plus "I Had to Tell You," Poi's acoustic contribution to the Roky Erickson tribute LP.
[i]

BUSTER POINDEXTER

See *David Johansen*.

POISON GIRLS

Hex (Xntrix-Small Wonder) 1979
Chappaquiddick Bridge (nr/Crass) 1980
Total Exposure (nr/Xntrix) 1981
Where's the Pleasure (nr/Xntrix) 1982
I'm Not a Real Woman EP (nr/Xntrix) 1983
7 Year Scratch (nr/Xntrix) 1984
Songs of Praise (CD Presents) 1985

The Poison Girls—a wise post-adolescent poet/singer/guitarist who wittily calls herself Vi Subversa plus a male backing band—are politicized musical agitators employing rock (minimalist at the start but improving steadily to the point of sophisticated diversity later on) as their means for registering social and sexual protest. Lyrics are clever and subtle, making points with intelligence rather than sloganeering.

Produced by Crass drummer Penny Rimbaud and featuring guest vocals by that band's Eve Libertine, **Hex** makes no grand statements (even the frantic "Bremen Song" doesn't really say anything cogent). Instead, Vi's lyrics deal cleverly with sex roles and existential personal issues. What is normal? Do we really need doctors? Is romance political? The guitar-based music is really good—nothing fancy, but subtle and effective on its own terms.

The music isn't much more raucous on **Chappaquiddick Bridge** (also produced by Rimbaud), but the lyrics (and Subversa's angry singing) are far more bilious. From the bluntly titled "Statement" (a humanist manifesto delivered via a bonus flexi-disc) to the sexual analysis of "Good Time (I Didn't Know Sartre Played Piano)" and the duck-for-cover "Underbitch," the prose is substantial (if unfocused) and Subversa's theatrical delivery sells it even when the words don't amount to much.

Some of the songs on the live (in Edinburgh, mid-'81) **Total Exposure**—pressed on clear vinyl and fitted in a transparent plastic sleeve—come from the first two LPs, but there's new material as well. It's an exciting document, but the studio albums offer an easier entry point to the Poison Girls' music, thanks to a somewhat varied approach that doesn't carry over in concert.

With their musical skills much improved, **Where's the Pleasure** balances intellectual integrity with audio listenability and achieves a measure of success on musical merit alone. Largely ignoring the governmental politics of the first two studio discs, **Where's the Pleasure** deals almost solely with sexual matters, using refined music and crystal-clear vocals. Subversa's weary, whisky-and-tobacco-stained voice is a husky but serviceable instrument that perfectly suits the material and lends a tragic, poetic air to the record.

Even more accessible is the wonderful **I'm Not a Real Woman** EP—four varied songs that utterly abandon punk for a rock-cabaret sound, Celtic folk singing and poetic recitation. At her funniest, Subversa employs a Noel Coward-like delivery to offer her sharp feminist lyrics.

Songs of Praise is even more skillful and attractive. Having long since proven herself a talented and unique singer, Vi is in fine voice; the band stretches further into areas of sublime, suave rock and funk scarcely imaginable at the group's outset. Lyrics are likewise subtler and more intriguing, setting this album somewhere between Marianne Faithfull, John Cale and Ian Dury.   [i]

POLECATS

Polecats Are Go! (nr/Vertigo) 1981
Make a Circuit with Me (Mercury) 1983
Cult Heroes (nr/Nervous) 1984
Live and Rockin' (nr/Link) 1989
The Polecats Won't Die! (nr/Vinyl Japan) 1989

This young, stylish London trio (plus a drummer) dropped out of the spotlight after releasing **Polecats Are Go!**, a gem of a rockabilly revival album. Producer Dave Edmunds applies the same polish he brought to the Stray Cats, and these 'Cats truly sparkle. Piano, saxophone and careful vocal harmonies ice the usual neo-rockabilly cake of trebly guitars, acoustic bass and driving drums. A bizarrely conceived stab at David Bowie's "John, I'm Only Dancing" doesn't quite come off; otherwise, this mix of oldies and originals parties like crazy.

The Polecats' American label passed on releasing the band's original LP, and instead patched together a seven-cut disc from singles (the glossy title track, a version of T. Rex's "Jeepster" and the aforementioned Bowie tune) and album tracks.

The original trio (plus a different drummer) reaffirmed its continued retro-rock existence in 1989 with a live mini-album (seven okay cuts, including "Blue Jean Bop" and "Rock Billy Boogie") and a new studio set. Despite a garish cartoon cover which reflects the development of a garage-trash/rock'n'roll side, the snappy rockabilly cuts on **Won't Die** are even more traditional than the group's initial pop efforts. (No more glam-rock covers: the handful of old tunes here are strictly Eddie Cochran et al.) The revival fad may have ended, but the Polecats rock on.   [si/i]

POLICE

Outlandos d'Amour (A&M) 1978 ●
Reggatta de Blanc (A&M) 1979 ●
Zenyatta Mondatta (A&M) 1980 ●
Ghost in the Machine (A&M) 1981 ●
Synchronicity (A&M) 1983 (A&M-Mobile Fidelity) ●
Every Breath You Take/The Singles (A&M) 1986 ●
Compact Hits EP [CD] (nr/A&M) 1988 ●

VARIOUS ARTISTS

Brimstone & Treacle (A&M) 1982 ●

Though neither bassist/singer Sting nor veteran guitarist Andy Summers would have gone in this direction

individually, they became intrinsic to ex-Curved Air drummer Stewart Copeland's notion of being new wavers in 1977, when it was still pretty new. As a band, the three (Summers having replaced original guitarist Henri Padovani after one single) worked in earnest to stake out their own musical turf, even probing a few of rock's boundaries. Their considerable abilities eventually yielded the Police sound: rock and reggae interlocked in proportions varying from number to number, further spiced with musical influences like Summers' quasi-classical harmonic overtones and Sting's reggae-into-jazz vocalisms.

Outlandos d'Amour is the brisk, brash initial Police barrage of bright, featherweight tunes (like "Roxanne," "Born in the 50's," "Can't Stand Losing You") and deceptively clever riffs and rhythms. It's pithy, infectious and seductive, sometimes all at once. Only a silly joke in dubious taste and Sting's pair of "let's own up" diatribes are irksome, but those can be ignored—musically, they aren't bad anyway.

Sting came up short of material on **Reggatta de Blanc** and only one of Copeland's attempts at taking up the slack is truly spot-on, funny and catchy. All the same, "Message in a Bottle" is an all-around gem, and if Sting's other material isn't stellar, the performances are: effective vocal emoting and instrumentally sparkling tours de force like the title track (which also shows the virtue of space in music). The sound was further enhanced for **Zenyatta Mondatta**, and that same instrumental excellence brightens much of the record, but *too* much of the album relies on just that. The more direct cuts are too cute for words (hence "De Do Do Do . . .") but, like bubblegum (the music and the candy), they stick to you.

Ghost in the Machine was critically considered the milestone marking the threesome's arrival as Major Artistes, but this critic begs to differ. Aside from a half-step forward (mainly Sting's sexual experimentation) the record shows the Police taking several giant leaps in the direction of the rock mainstream at the expense of at least half the songs (which are, in and of themselves, okay to pretty good).

Synchronicity (or at least "Every Breath You Take") pitched the Police into the ranks of commercial rock superstars, but most of the record simply can't be taken seriously by anyone but a chowderhead and/or indiscriminate fan. The "humor" is flat, the "experiments" with jazz shadings and electronic touches more yawn-provoking than mood-evoking; in the end, it seems just an overgrown platinum molehill. Sting's "love me—I'm the sexy, intellectual and vulnerable man of the '80s" off-the-record image is hard to divorce from his songs, especially when he whines about being the "King of Pain." And Iron Maiden has churned out epics as gripping as "Synchronicity II." The Police have clearly become the bloated dinosaur they once complained about. But "Every Breath You Take" *is* every bit a classic, a surf-music rhythm line utterly transmogrified, relentlessly driving Sting's declaration of love-hate-obsession. So skip the LP and get the 45, which even edits out the song's draggier bits. (The posthumous singles compilation named for that huge hit features a dozen Police standards, including a 1986 remake of "Don't Stand So Close to Me" in lieu of the 1980 original. The British **Compact Hits** CD-5 contains four songs drawn from the first three albums.)

As a movie, *Brimstone and Treacle* has lots of mystical mood, with Sting effective as a rogue busy smudging the line between good and evil. The soundtrack album consists of one Go-Go's track, a Squeeze item, two choral pieces and some miscellaneous music by Sting, with and without his two compatriots, successful only on the evocative title instrumental and the band's resurrection (from Sting's early days in Last Exit) of the smoldering "I Burn for You."   [jg]

See also *Stewart Copeland, Fripp & Eno, Sting, Andy Summers.*

POLYPHONIC SIZE

Live for Each Moment/Vivre pour Chaque Instant (Fr. New Rose) 1982
Mother's Little Helper EP (Enigma) 1982
Walking Everywhere (Fr. New Rose) 1984
The Overnight Day (Fr. New Rose) 1987

Polyphonic Size is Belgian; their first album was produced by Strangler Jean-Jacques Burnel, who also contributed bass and vocals. Unlike Burnel's other work outside the Stranglers (his first solo LP, production for Japan's Lizard), this effort has none of his usual aggression. Instead he delicately captures Polyphonic Size's lovely synthesizer art-pop. Sung primarily in French by a man and a woman backed by simple (not rudimentary—carefully constructed and subtle) electronics, this resembles Orchestral Manoeuvres' lighter work. Excepting some perky numbers that lean towards Japanese synthesists like Plastics, a low-key approach—gentle, almost tender singing and languid tempos—makes **Live for Each Moment** as relaxing as a hot bath, but without the ennui, thanks to a resolute commitment to pop song structures. A very pretty record.

The **Mother's Little Helper** 12-inch singles assemblage has five tracks, including a humorous electronic reinterpretation (not unlike the Flying Lizards) of the Rolling Stones classic after which it is named.

A new four-piece lineup, working with producer Nigel Gray (Police, Siouxsie and the Banshees) on **Walking Everywhere** and **The Overnight Day**, has kept Polyphonic Size moving towards mild, commercialized pop fare—a less quirky Plastic Bertrand or perhaps a Flemish answer to Nena. The wispy male and female vocals (in French and lightly accented English) and the understated music keep the records unfailingly pleasant, but a shade too skimpy on character to make Polyphonic Size a bigger international commercial property.   [i]

POLYROCK

Polyrock (RCA) 1980
Changing Hearts (RCA) 1981
Above the Fruited Plain EP (PVC) 1982
No Love Lost [tape] (ROIR) 1986

Formed in 1978, Polyrock was one of New York's first groups to explore post-disco/new-sensibility dance music. The sextet led by ex-Model Citizens singer/guitarist Billy Robertson gained unquestionable artistic credibility through the patronage of Philip Glass, who (with Kurt Munkacsi) produced and played on their two original albums. The first combines minimalist repetition with electro-pop and smart, aware songs, then strips it all down to skin and bone for extremely singleminded dance music. Fascinating in its extremity.

Changing Hearts follows the same basic pattern but loosens up the sound, occasionally breaking away from austere dance music for a taste of straightforward pop, including a reworking of the Beatles' "Rain." Otherwise, Billy and Tommy Robertson write some of the most vulnerable songs this side of David Byrne, with solid (if lean) performances and production.

Following Tommy's departure (which left Polyrock a notably improved five-piece), his brother produced **Above the Fruited Plain**, five tracks with more character and melody than any of the group's previous releases. **No Love Lost** is a posthumous collection of 1980 and 1983 live performances, plus unreleased studio demos done as recently as 1984.   [sg/i]

POMPEII 99

See *Christian Death.*

PONTIAC BROTHERS

Big Black River (Fr. Lolita) 1985
Doll Hut (Frontier) 1985
Fiesta en la Biblioteca (Frontier) 1986
Be Married Song EP (Frontier) 1987
Johnson (Frontier) 1988 ●

Even their record company describes the Pontiac Brothers as Stones-influenced, a rare case of restraint in advertising. The Orange County, California band has never denied it; indeed, they originally got together in 1983 to play Stones tunes. (Guitarist Ward Dotson had previously been a mainstay in the Gun Club; the other Brothers are California scene veterans with numerous credits, including the Middle Class.)

Big Black River, their first album, was released only in France, which might reinforce prejudices about French taste in rock. Singer Matt Simon pushes his Mick Jagger impression beyond what it's worth; the original songs are uninspired pastiches of the Rolling Stones and '60s punk in general; the production can charitably be called shitty.

Using a new rhythm guitarist, the Pontiacs recorded a third of **Big Black River** for **Doll Hut**. Their US debut has a more polished sound, though still decidedly Jagged vocals. The new Dotson/Simon material shows promise: "Out in the Rain" sets a poignantly wasted lyric against well-juggled musical clichés, while "Keep the Promise"—with acoustic guitar, a first—is passionate if murky. (The cassette reflects the band's fondness for performing vintage covers by including a version of the MC5's "Tonight.")

Simon finally downplayed his Jagger tendencies on **Fiesta en la Biblioteca**, also the first Pontiac Brothers album as a quartet. There's some welcome variety in tempos, arrangements and sentiments. (The cassette adds a Bad Company song, "Movin' On.") The album's wistful "Be Married Song"—a rare Dotson lead vocal—was redone in an electric arrangement on a 12-inch EP, which also contains "Doll Hut" (from **Fiesta**), the fine non-LP "Brenda's Mom" and a bracing rendition of AC/DC's "Dirty Deeds (Done Dirt Cheap)."

The Pontiacs' chef d'oeuvre, **Johnson**, starts with a roar ("Ain't What I Call Home") and scarcely lets up in intensity. The inevitable Stones substratum remains—guest pianist Ian McLagan adds British authenticity—but the band has grown its own shaggy personality. Replacements fans will enjoy the frustrated vitriol of "Creep" (another Dotson vocal) and "Real Job," which Simon delivers in a Westerbergian howl. (The cassette and CD add Paul McCartney's "Magneto and Titanium Man.") Identifying with the underdog without getting misty-eyed about it, the Pontiac Brothers are ragged but right.

After that triumph went unnoticed by the masses, the Pontiac Brothers parted company. Ward Dotson moved to New York, formed a new band and also joined the retro-pop Pussywillows.   [si]

See also *Clawhammer, Gun Club, Pussywillows*.

POOH STICKS

Alan McGee EP (nr/Fierce) 1988 ●
The Pooh Sticks EP (nr/Fierce) 1988
Orgasm (nr/53rd & 3rd) 1988 ●
Trade Mark of Quality (nr/Fierce) 1989 ●
Formula One Generation (Sympathy for the Record
    Industry) 1990

On the whole, British pop music has always taken itself far too seriously, and no less so since the trad-busting original '77 wave. Consequently, aberrations as polar as Half Man Half Biscuit, Sigue Sigue Sputnik and Zodiac Mindwarp (to name three at random) have all based careers on taking the piss out of pop iconography. Likewise, some of the anorak and twee pop stylists of the late '80s (like edgy gentlepunks the Pastels) invested netherness with genuine wit and value. But it took Wales' Pooh Sticks (aided and abetted by the open-minded Fierce Records) to perform the ultimate inbreeding of pure pop and pure cynicism. Brilliantly derivative and deliriously infectious, the quartet's debut P (half an LP—the flipside is a scratched-in-vinyl stick figure portrait of the band) gathers four of the five songs from their **Alan McGee** boxed set of one-sided singles (later on CD), adding a prior 45 for a first-rate collection of bare-bones pop with magnificently minimal barbed hooks. Characteristically, the record's sole cover (the 1910 Fruitgum Company's "1,2,3 Red Light") is by far the least catchy and invigorating thing on it.

Creating a sea of "product," the Pooh Sticks continued to release a string of limited edition singles, picture discs, flexies and a side-project (Dumb Angels, with a one-song Brian Wilson tribute 45). **Orgasm** is ostensibly an official low-budget bootleg taken from one of the band's rare live gigs (six shows in three years), mixing familiar songs with new faves, nearly every one as sharp and kinetic as on the first P. (The CD includes ten additional unreleased songs from October 1988.) Also live, also a borderline bootleg, **Trade Mark of Quality** has excellent sound, great playing, good songs, okay crowd interaction and absolutely none of the wicked spark that ignites their best recordings. On the other hand, the band's first proper studio album, **Formula**, is sublimely poppy in the classical sense, the dark satire and deep appreciation of precedents combining to create an inspired if imperfect LP by the most selfconscious, referential and *knowing* band in post-punk pop.   [ab]

POOPSHOVEL

Opus Lengthemus (Community 3) 1989 ●
I came, I saw, I had a hotdog (Community 3) 1991 ●

If not for the bizarre lyrics (in songs like "Young People in Love Are Hardly Ever Hungry," the cautionary "African Bees" or the womb-delivered "Earliness Factor"), singer Bill Crawford's unpredictable jazz trumpet interpolations would be this raucous Madison, Wisconsin, quartet's strangest feature. As it is, **Opus Lengthemus** rambles imaginatively and excitingly through wicked noise-punk, understated rock-pop and crude fusion, all united under the band's oblique world-view. A bit sophomoric at times, but otherwise smart and involving.   [i]

POOR RIGHTEOUS TEACHERS

Holy Intellect (Profile) 1990 ●

Wise Intelligent, Culture Freedom and Father Shaheed—the three Trenton, New Jersey rappers known as Poor Righteous Teachers—are members of the Islamic Five-Percent Nation, and **Holy Intellect** is littered with the sect's phraseology and philosophy. On a strictly sonic level, the album is funky and inviting, with soulful tracks, skilled warm-voiced rapping and a bit of romantic crooning (on "Shakiyla"), but the lyrics' religious content is as boring and irrelevant to non-believers as it was when born-again rockers—from Little Richard and Wanda Jackson through George Harrison and Cat Stevens—started sharing their personal faith on record. The fact that PRT's moralistic views involve issues of racial superiority (not strongly pushed here) further complicates matters, limiting the trio's audience to a very select segment of the hip-hop audience.   [i]

POP

The Pop (Automatic) 1977
Go! (Arista) 1979
Hearts and Knives EP (Rhino) 1981

DAVID SWANSON

Reclamation (RCA) 1990 ●

Essentially a routine hard-rock/power pop outfit, this LA group acquired hipness through an actively pro-local scene stance as well as attitudes shared with more overtly rebellious colleagues. Their DIY debut LP shows them equally adept at pounding out fierce rockers and lovingly constructing softer, more melodic tracks, with occasionally eccentric production touches, linking both in the anthemic "Down on the Boulevard." As good as the Raspberries' **Starting Over** but more urgent, and less studiedly nostalgic or obviously derivative.

Produced by Earle Mankey, **Go!** shows how the band moved with the times, modifying British modern pop notions to suit themselves. Not quite as humor-conscious (for better and worse) as XTC, the Pop employs a strangely detached intensity that gives a fillip to each track. There isn't any one brilliant number (although "Under the Microscope" comes close), yet **Go!** is entertaining straight through.

Two years later, without the guitar and arranging talents of Tim McGovern (who had joined the pre-stardom Motels) or the support of a major label, the remaining foursome sound somewhat chastened for not having played it safer—and they do. The six-song **Hearts and Knives** presents a blander version of their former selves: pleasant, lightweight originals and a lame Stones cover that's limply out of character.

Towards the end of the '80s, singer/guitarist Roger Prescott surfaced in a band called Train Wreck Ghosts, which he formed with ex-Plimsouls guitarist Eddie Munoz following the latter's brief stint in the dB's. He and Munoz then hired on to the Walking Wounded, and appeared on one of that group's records before continuing their Texas-based band. The Pop's other frontman, David Swanson, reappeared in 1990 with a dull album of awkwardly sung heartland rock.   [jg/i]

See also *Walking Wounded*.

IGGY POP

The Idiot (RCA) 1977 (Virgin) 1990 ●
Lust for Life (RCA) 1977 (Virgin) 1990 ●
TV Eye Live (RCA) 1978
New Values (Arista) 1979
Soldier (Arista) 1980
Party (Arista) 1981 ●
Zombie Birdhouse (Animal) 1982
I Got a Right (Invasion) 1983 (Enigma) 1985
Choice Cuts (RCA) 1984
Blah-Blah-Blah (A&M) 1986 ●
I Got a Right (Fr. Revenge) 1987
Compact Hits EP [CD] (nr/A&M) 1988 ●
Instinct (A&M) 1988 ●
Livin' on the Edge of the Night EP [CD] (nr/Virgin) 1990 ●
Brick by Brick (Virgin) 1990 ●

Iggy Pop (James Jewel Osterberg) embodied everything punk stood for when it exploded in England in the mid-'70s, but he had begun performing in Middle America nearly a *decade* earlier. Moving into the '90s, he is still a vital and active performer, serving up much the same arrogant honesty that first put him in the punk pantheon.

After the Stooges ended, Iggy resurfaced as a solo artist, under the influence of David Bowie, **The Idiot**'s producer and co-writer. Instead of flailing all over the place, Iggy conserves his energy on numbers like the surprisingly funky "Sister Midnight" and the menacing "Funtime." The album's tone is generally subdued ("Baby," "Nightclubbing," "Dum Dum Boys"), lumbering along in medium gear. It's disturbingly effective, but of mixed parentage.

Iggy reasserted himself on the rapid follow-up, **Lust for Life**. More upbeat than its predecessor (just check the smiling cover snap), the album swaggers along to Iggy's confident delivery of the title track, "Success," the powerful "Turn Blue" and other self-analytic tunes. The music is Bowie's, and Jim Morrison's unmistakable influence is noticeable on a few vocals, but the clear-eyed vision is Iggy's own.

The dreadful **TV Eye Live** was a contract-breaker and sounds like it. Half of the tracks—recorded on 1977 US tours—include Bowie on keyboards. Those sound bad; the others sound worse. Iggy is uninspired throughout. Forget this quickie.

Reuniting with Stooges guitarist James Williamson, Iggy signed to Arista and released **New Values**, a nononsense collection of hard rockers. His increasingly sophisticated lyrics abound in mordant humor ("I'm Bored," "Five Foot One," "New Values"). **Soldier** features a supergroup of sorts (Glen Matlock, Ivan Kral, Steve New, Barry Andrews, Klaus Kruger) riffing along to Iggy's mostly bitter rants. **Party** continues in this vein, vacillating between self-deprecation ("Eggs on Plate") and obnoxiousness ("Rock and Roll Party," "Sincerity," etc.). Two non-original oldies—"Sea of Love" and "Time Won't Let Me"—also get perfunctory treatment.

After the aesthetic dead-end of the Arista albums, the Chris Stein-produced and released **Zombie Birdhouse** marks a welcome shift in strategy. No longer singing so much as rap-chanting, Iggy turns surprisingly cerebral for a crazy blend of sociological ("The Villagers") and philosophical ("Eat or Be Eaten") discourse, pseudo-folk ("The Ballad of Cookie McBride") and topical documentary ("Watching the News"). Spare musical accompaniment underscores the album's ascetic nature. He's come a long way since the Stooges, but **Zombie Birdhouse** reveals that Iggy is far from reaching the end of his creative tether.

Following Bowie's 1983 hit version of the pair's collaborative "China Girl" (originally from **The Idiot**), Iggy's two RCA albums were culled for the hoped-for-fast-buck **Choice Cuts**, the cover of which helpfully notes the inclusion of that song and prominently mentions Bowie's songwriting and production credits.

Their creative partnership thus re-established, Iggy took some time off before recording **Blah-Blah-Blah** in Switzerland with Bowie. The individual musical changes both have undergone (with further diversion by the considerable involvement of ex-Pistol Steve Jones) make it a strange and sometimes mainstream-sounding maelstrom of styles, but the lyrics—thoughtful personal reflections on various topics—provide at least intellectual cohesiveness. The commanding "Cry for Love," "Fire Girl," "Winners and Losers" and a wonderful cover of '50s Australian rocker Johnny O'Keefe's "Real Wild Child (Wild One)" are more than worthy of Iggy's ready-to-wear legend. (The UK CD EP merely contains four selections from **Blah-Blah-Blah**.)

Bill Laswell produced **Instinct**, a straightforward rock record that sags under a cloddish rhythm section and Jones' unmodulated, unimaginative guitar work. Although Iggy's unshakeable stylishness and some impressively dramatic vocalizations (especially on "Lowdown" and "Cold Metal") keep the LP out of the worthless-oldtimers-why-bother dumper, he's hovering dangerously close to artistic vacuity here.

After signing Iggy, Virgin (UK) issued the foursong **Livin' on the Edge of the Night** EP, joining the new song with "China Girl," "Nightclubbing" and "The Passenger"—songs from **The Idiot** and **Lust for Life**, crucial Pop albums the label had licensed and reissued.

Evidently, the change of corporate scenery did Iggy a world of good: **Brick by Brick** is his strongest, most rewarding (not to mention commercially presentable) album in a decade. Taking a firm and creative role in the project, producer Don Was deftly helps organize a stellar lineup of session players into sympathetic backing for surprisingly accomplished songwriting. As huge a disaster as the record could have been, the bizarre mix of LA studio hacks (like David Lindley and Waddy

Wachtel), groovy session pros (bassist Charley Drayton, drummer Kenny Aronoff), John Hiatt, members of Guns n' Roses and Kate Pierson of the B-52's works like a charm, rising and falling in synch with Iggy's shifting stylistic moods. Going from strength to strength, **Brick by Brick** rocks ("Home," "I Won't Crap Out," "Butt Town"), rolls ("Pussy Power"), slithers ("Something Wild"), cruises ("Main Street Eyes," "The Undefeated"—now there's an apt epitaph), dances around ("Candy") and even takes a gentle romantic breather ("Moonlight Lady"). [si/i]

See also *New Order, Stooges*.

POPEALOPES

An Adder's Tale (Skyclad) 1988
Kerosene (Skyclad) 1990 ●

With two albums produced by Russ Tolman, this Davis, California quartet isn't defying any laws of logic by bearing a certain stylistic resemblance to True West (not to mention the pride of Davis, Thin White Rope). The popeAlopes' quirky pop rhythms and trancey psychedelic flavors (the latter especially on a noisy cover of the Stones' "2000 Light Years from Home") provide **An Adder's Tale** with some personality; otherwise, the band's western-flavored guitar rock runs a bit on the generic side.

It's probably not due to the change in bassists, but the confident **Kerosene** is much better, a striking-sounding wash of layered guitar and Steven Dueker's quietly haggard vocals. While the heavy atmospherics overcome songwriting deficiencies, the popeAlopes spin echoes of U2, R.E.M. and the Psych Furs into the stew, making **Kerosene** a dose of the right medicine. [i]

POP GROUP

Y (nr/Radar) 1979
For How Much Longer Do We Tolerate Mass Murder? (Y-Rough Trade) 1980
We Are Time (nr/Y-Rough Trade) 1980

These abrasive, militant British punks rage against racism, oppression, hunger and anything else that's a world problem; as usual, there's no solution, only anger. The seminal Bristol band synthesizes Beefheartian structures and tribal dance beats to create a didactic soundtrack that barely lets you breathe. Their two primary albums are alternately brilliant and intolerable, with exhortatory songs like "Feed the Hungry," "Rob a Bank" and "Communicate." **We Are Time** collects outtakes, live tracks and other assorted items.

Despite the limitations of their own records, the Pop Group made their influence strongly felt, both as credible rock minimalists ahead of their time and via the members' subsequent musical ventures. Bassist Simon Underwood helped found Pigbag; multi-instrumentalist Gareth Sager formed Rip Rig + Panic; singer Mark Stewart is well known under his own name. [gf]

See also *Pigbag, Rip Rig + Panic, Mark Stewart and the Maffia*.

POP RIVITS

Pop Rivits EP (nr/Hypocrite) 1979
The Pop Rivits Greatest Hits (nr/Hypocrite) 1979
Empty Sounds from Anarchy Ranch (nr/Hypocrite) 1979

Fun in the U.K. (Jim's) 1987
The Original First Album (nr/Hangman) 1989
Live in Germany '79 (nr/Hangman) 1990

MICKEY AND THE MILKSHAKES

Talking 'Bout Milkshakes (nr/Milkshakes) 1981

THE(E) MILKSHAKES

14 Rhythm & Beat Greats (nr/Milkshakes) 1982 (nr/Big Beat) 1983
After School Session (nr/Upright) 1983 (nr/Hangman) 1988
The Milkshakes IV: The Men with the Golden Guitars (nr/Milkshakes) 1983
Brand New Cadillac EP (nr/Big Beat) 1983
Showcase (Brain Eater) 1984
The Milkshakes Sing and Play 20 Rock and Roll Hits of the 50's and 60's (nr/Big Beat) 1984
The Milkshakes in Germany (Ger. Wall City) 1984
Nothing Can Stop These Men (nr/Milkshakes) 1984
Ambassadors of Love EP (nr/Big Beat) 1984
Thee Knights of Trashe (nr/Milkshakes) 1984
They Came They Saw They Conquered (Pink Dust-Enigma) 1984
The 107 Tapes (nr/Media Burn) 1986
The Milkshakes' Revenge! (nr/Hangman) 1987
Live from Chatham (nr/Hangman) 1987
19th Nervous Shakedown [CD] (nr/Big Beat) 1990 ●

MILKSHAKES/PRISONERS

The Last Night at the M.I.C. (nr/Empire) 1985
Thee Milkshakes vs the Prisoners (nr/Media Burn) 1985

1979: The Pop Rivits, a Canterbury group of devoted acolytes to punk's gritty DIY ethos, release **Greatest Hits**, home-recorded and enclosed in handmade sleeves (later repressed in printed covers; later still retitled for its Hangman reissue). A more mod-oriented and less reserved TV Personalities or Desperate Bicycles, the Rivits retrospectively fit neatly in with the sloppy, violent pop noisemeisters of the era, endearingly careless (though even the best songs leave mere flesh wounds as opposed to the scars inflicted by their more prominent contemporaries).

Empty Sounds from Anarchy Ranch consolidates the band's sound into a tamer, more controlled—albeit equally ill-tempered—punk stew. While **Fun in the U.K.** is a compilation drawn somewhat randomly from both LPs, **Live in Germany '79** simultaneously nods deeper to their UK punk basis and points up their obvious (again in retrospect) trash '60s roots and attitudes—all recorded in glorious monoloudarama.

1981: **Talking 'Bout Milkshakes**, the debut LP by Chatham's Mickey and the Milkshakes, limps into stores. "Mickey" is guitarist M. Hampshire; he and bassist Banana Bertie (both former Pop Rivits roadies) had formed the band to do opening slots at Rivits gigs but recombined with two of their former employers—Rivits drummer Bruce Brand and guitarist Billy Childish—when the headliners split. Discovering a chemistry (particularly in the Hampshire/Childish tagteam), they sat back and calmly began writing and performing a song every other minute. But only when fueled by excessive alcohol. Meaning only 22-1/2 hours a day.

1982: With ex-Rivit Russ Wilkins replacing Bertie on bass, **14 Rhythm & Beat Greats** (recorded in Germany on borrowed money) showcases a band more in

511

dynamic control and confident of their direction. Distinct echoes of the Kinks and assorted forgotten US garages begin to reverberate in the vinyl canyons.

1983: **After School Session** offers a somewhat tempered 'Shakes, playing familiar covers (like Bo Diddley's "Cadillac" and "I Can Tell") and chummy originals with all the verve but none of the previous grit. **The Milkshakes IV** is an instrumental album that calculatedly sidesteps their "career," consisting instead of Link Wray-influenced dark chord/riff-rockers.

1984: Having hit their stride (and quickly surpassing it), the Milkshakes finagled the same-day release in March of four different albums in three separate countries. **Showcase**, the US debut, pits a pair of unreleased tunes against a dozen more culled from prior LPs. **In Germany** is a rowdy and stylistic representative collection of new originals. **Nothing Can Stop These Men** is a less rambunctious variation of same, while **20 Rock and Roll Hits of the 50's & 60's** consists of common classics ("Peggy Sue," "Hippy Hippy Shake," "Money," etc.) and is a considerably less essential shot of partytude. **Brand New Cadillac** and **Ambassadors of Love** are both four-song 7-inches.

Although not issued until 1987, **The Milkshakes' Revenge!** (or "The Legendary Missing 9th Album") was the next to be recorded. Rather low-key and well-mannered, its greatest notoriety is as the debut release on Billy Childish's Hangman Records & Books label.

With an extra "e" in their article and the ouster of Russ Wilkins (to be replaced by John Agnew), things are definitely on the upswing, with countless compilation appearances as well as a prominent lip-synch role in a garage rockumentary for British television. **They Came They Saw They Conquered** rocks as blearily and singlemindedly as anything preceding, but **Thee Knights of Trashe** really ignites where they previously only sizzled, with great songs (including an alternate version of the excellent "Out of Control," written for the TV documentary), confident (if basic) playing and enormously complementary raw—yet detailed—production. Unfortunately it's the last Milkshakes album proper, their tenth (eight all-original) in three years. The posthumous **107 Tapes**—sleeved in a monumental interview—contains one LP of blisteringly ragged, painfully overdriven '81 demos with the Prisoners' bassist on loan and a disc of '83 live-in-Germany drunken mayhem. If not quite the Milkshakes' recorded apex, this package may nonetheless be the band's most representative document.

Live from Chatham is cleaner and warmer, like your fondest bootleg tape, while **Last Night at the M.I.C.** is uncontrolled hysteria. **Thee Milkshakes vs the Prisoners** (recorded live in the studio) is pure libido on parade, and one of the band's vinyl peaks. **19th Nervous Shakedown** is a CD-only compilation and so far the only Milkshakes available to the post vinyl/tape generation.   [ab]

See also *Delmonas, Prisoners, Thee Mighty Caesars*.

POP WILL EAT ITSELF

Poppiecock EP (nr/Chapter 22) 1986
Poppiecock (nr/Chapter 22) 1986
The Covers EP EP (nr/Chapter 22) 1987
Box Frenzy (Rough Trade) 1987 ●
Now For a Feast! (Rough Trade) 1988 ●
Can U Dig It EP (nr/RCA) 1989 ●
This Is the Day ... This Is the Hour ... This Is *This!* (RCA) 1989 ●
Cure for Sanity (RCA) 1991 ϕ

In the grand British tradition of selling a band on self-hype and a look—with the music added on as an afterthought—Pop Will Eat Itself became the guiding lights of England's "grebo" (slimy-looking lowlifes playing retrograde raunch) movement of 1986-'87, probably because nobody else wanted the dirty job. Hailing from Stourbridge (a city near Birmingham), PWEI has so far made a career out of hopping on the latest musical bandwagon (so long as it doesn't require dressing up or sounding like Duran Duran). What the Poppies lack in originality, they more than compensate for it with good dirty fun.

The ten cuts (expanding a previous five-song EP of the same name) of hooliganism on **Poppiecock** owe more than a little to early Damned records (not to mention several pints of lager). Just draw a mental picture of longhairs in torn jeans thrashing away on guitars, playing songs with titles like "The Black Country Chainstore Massacreee," "There's a Psychopath in My Soup" and the seminal "Oh Grebo I Think I Love You" and you'll have a fairly accurate synopsis.

The Covers EP is just that—four good, raunchy raveups of an interesting selection of tunes, highlighted by Sigue Sigue Sputnik's "Love Missile F1-11" (vastly superior to both the original and the second take on **Box Frenzy**) and Hawkwind's "Orgone Accumulator." **Box Frenzy**, their first US release, goes for both of 1987's top trends, hip-hop and sampling. This time around, the Poppies are basically a British answer to the Beastie Boys—their rapping is laughably awkward but they do get the self-promotion part down just fine. The sampling is funny, too, with everyone from L.L. Cool J to Nat King Cole making unauthorized guest appearances. The approach on **Poppiecock** seems more up their alley, but **Box Frenzy** is still a good time.

Now For a Feast! compiles **Poppiecock**, three covers and the "Sweet Sweet Pie" 45 for a solid pre-**Frenzy** recapitulation. (The cassette adds two for a fuller course.)

The Poppies' mastery of hip-hop hooliganism reaches its apogee on the brilliant Flood-produced **This Is the Day**, an aurally exciting sonic collage informed by a pronounced affection for Alan Moore's groundbreaking comic books and *Blade Runner*'s sci-fi nihilism. The amazing single, "Can U Dig It?" (the Poppies' answer to the Psychedelic Furs' "We Love You," itself a catalog of cool), can be found here, as can "Def. Con. One.," which samples Siouxsie Sioux, the Beastie Boys and Rod Serling, ripping off both the Stooges and Lipps, Inc. in a seamless dadaist stew. Bright, vital and bitingly funny (check out the scratch-mix ode to a felonious James Brown), this record teems with invention.

Cure for Sanity is **This Is the Day** minus the jokes. Not content with being the Beastie Boys' retarded cousins, the Poppies decide to get serious and come down heavy on the KKK, scary air travel and censorship. That's not necessarily a bad thing, and some of the beats still pack a wallop (especially on "Dance of the Mad

Bastards" and "Lived in Splendour: Died in Chaos"), but the absurd sloganeering is tiresome. One anomaly: the beatific electropop "X Y & Zee," a splendid extended remix of which appears on the CD.   [dgs/db]

POSIES
Failure [tape] (23 Records) 1988 (PopLlama Products) 1988 ●
Dear 23 (DGC) 1990 ●

Bucking Seattle's prevailing grunge-noise-metal trend, singing guitarists Jonathan Auer and Kenneth Stringfellow have devoted themselves to '60s-influenced Anglo-pop and the music's primary American interpretation by Big Star. The duo's fine first album (originally self-released on cassette) would have been just another skillful neo-merseybeat retread (albeit with odd daily-life lyrics about such things as waiting in line and scheduling household chores) were it not for the magic that occurs when the two Posies harmonize, a blend that is remarkably similar to the joyous sound of Allan Clarke and Graham Nash in the original Hollies. Despite a few notable missteps, **Failure** is quite a successful debut.

Having moved to a major label, enlisted a rhythm section and gotten John Leckie in to produce, the Posies confidently play to their Holliesque strengths while also consciously working against type on the marvelous **Dear 23**. Sticking offbeat lyrics into irresistible melodic power, "My Big Mouth" opens the record in a crisp wash of acoustic strums and a jazzy falsetto chorus; "Golden Blunders" puts a strong rhythmic charge under a cautionary bit of advice about adulthood. While the vintage-sounding "Apology" and "Any Other Way" can only offer illusions of familiarity, the heavy harmony rock of "Help Yourself" and the epic "Flood of Sunshine" (which winds in an awesome spiraling guitar solo) underscore the Posies' thoroughly modern versatility.   [i]

POSITIVE NOISE
Heart of Darkness (nr/Statik) 1981
Change of Heart (Statik-Sire) 1982
Distant Fires (nr/Statik) 1985

The title of Positive Noise's second album signifies the drastic change that took place after the group's debut LP as a result of the departure of Ross Middleton, the band's singer/leader/lyricist who left in mid-1981 to form Leisure Process with saxophonist Gary Barnacle. The Scottish band began as a five-piece (including two other Middleton brothers who stuck it out to the end) and in late 1980 recorded **Heart of Darkness**, which is pretty dire—a badly produced mishmash of art-funk, Skids-like cheering, PiL noise and assorted pretentious nonsense. It suffers from indecisive direction as much as a lack of originality.

For **Change of Heart**, guitarist Russell Blackstock also assumed the vocal chores, and Positive Noise transmuted into a slick electronic dance machine, churning out precise rhythms with anxious, semi-melodic vocals. Gone is the audio clumsiness and uncertain footing of the first LP; Positive Noise's niche is definitely in club music.

Produced by Dave Allen, **Distant Fires** finds the quintet trying to balance techno-dance sterility and coarse melodic pop. While the continued use of synthesizer leaves some of the uneven material sounding like a credible alternative to Human League or junior-league Ultravox, sturdy guitar-based arrangements and Blackstock's rough singing make the soaring "When Lightning Strikes" (originally issued as a 1983 single) and "A Million Miles Away" distinctive and memorable.   [i]

ROBERT POSS
See *Band of Susans*.

POSTER CHILDREN
Toreador Squat [tape] (Poster Children) 1988
Flower Power (Limited Potential) 1989 ●

This Champaign, Illinois, quartet plays loud, punky guitar-rock. The bass is mushed into the guitar, which in turn drenches the voice; the drums are machine-gun popcorn underneath. The writing is slightly influenced by late-'70s Britwave (a smidge of Buzzcocks here, a dab of Jam), plus a soupçon of the poppier side of Television, but those are all influences, not derivations. **Toreador Squat** is a raw, basic, set-length cassette for admirers of their live shows.

Flower Power, half produced in 1988 by Iain Burgess and the rest in '89 by Steve Albini, displays two different approaches. The earlier sessions are more or less straightforward songs; the later yielded a more fragmented, impression-oriented effect which stretches words out over the thundering music. Both work, and though neither is fully realized, guitar-sound lovers will enjoy this even before the songs start to kick in. The CD and cassette have six worthwhile bonus tracks, making (gulp) vinyl the least worthy choice.   [jg]

POSTE RESTANTE
See *Minny Pops*.

POWER STATION
The Power Station (Capitol) 1985 ●

This short-lived supergroup (whose name would be "Kraftwerk" in German) agglomerates Andy and John Taylor—then the guitar/bass axis of Duran Duran—with ex-Chic drummer Tony Thompson and singer Robert Palmer. (Plus Bernard Edwards as producer.) On paper, a promising idea—especially in light of the Durannies' funk pretensions and Simon Le Bon's vocal inadequacies—but, on vinyl, a miserable, boring explosion of overbearing drums pounding (you thought the drums were mixed high on **Let's Dance**?) through tuneless, formless "songs." While Power Station's slickly functional dance-funk is just minor on the softer numbers, the ultimate realization of the concept, "Some Like It Hot," offers a numbingly industrial take on electro-funk made truly execrable by Palmer's contemptible singing. But that's *nothing* compared to the excruciating jam/destruction of Marc Bolan's classic "Bang a Gong (Get It On)," matching an appalling lack of originality with utter disdain for and desecration of the song's melody, tempo and boppy charm. Repugnant.

When the band that swore it would not tour hit the road, it was without Palmer, replaced for disputed reasons by the even-less-talented Michael Des Barres, adding another chapter to his Chequered Past.   [i]

See also *Duran Duran, Robert Palmer*.

POWERTRIP

See *Jeff Dahl Group*.

PRAXIS

See *Bill Laswell*.

PRECIOUS WAX DRIPPINGS

Ain't We a Wishin' Bunch EP (Fat Bat-Landmind) 1987
Rayon EP (Pravda) 1988
After History (Amoeba) 1990 ●

Playing with the breathless enthusiasm (and some of the velocity) of a young band told their studio time is nearly up, Chicago's Precious Wax Drippings give the six ruggedly melodic numbers on the **Wishin' Bunch** 12-inch a real charge, firing up the richly distorted twin-guitar attack to devastating effect. While the jumpin' cuts (especially "Prayers" and "Soulbait") also benefit from unfancy mean-it vocals, the racing instrumental "Big Cheese" reveals chordal ingenuity and sharp interplay by the unpretentious quartet.

Heralded by an incongruous bagpipe chant, the more confident 7-inch **Rayon** offers up four cool new songs in a full-bodied Anglo-rock vein that owes something to the Small Faces (via the Rich Kids).

After History is divided into Industrial and Sexual sides, but that distinction doesn't begin to cover the boldly diverse collection of styles the group attempts on this ambitious longplayer. Sure, "Brontosaurus" (not the Move song) moderately acknowledges Ministry, but the same side also includes the gentle, pretty pop of "Steeptime." The flip, meanwhile, has a remake of "Rayon" as well as some sizzling punky funk ("Break Down"), thrashy rock ("This Year") and mildly countryfied rock ("Bob," with piano and a buzzing guitar undercurrent). Throughout, the group uses simple guitar-bass-drums resources to craft memorable songs, continually revealing imaginative twists. Fascinating.   [i]

PREFAB SPROUT

Prefab Sprout EP (nr/Kitchenware) 1983
Swoon (Kitchenware-Epic) 1984 ●
Steve McQueen (nr/Kitchenware) 1985 ●
Two Wheels Good (Kitchenware-Epic) 1985 ●
From Langley Park to Memphis (Kitchenware-Epic) 1988 ●
Swoon/Steve McQueen [CD] (nr/CBS) 1988 ●
Protest Songs (nr/Kitchenware-CBS) 1989 ●
Jordan: The Comeback (Kitchenware-Epic) 1990 ●
Machine Gun Ibiza EP (Kitchenware-Epic) 1990 ●
Jordan: The EP EP (nr/Kitchenware-CBS) 1990 ●

Smart and sophisticated garden-pop-jazz. Imagine Aztec Camera meets Steely Dan with absurdist lyrical inventions and close-formation female backing vocals—that's Prefab Sprout, the unique creation of Newcastle singer/songwriter Paddy McAloon. Performed as a trio joined by a guest drummer, the debut EP and **Swoon** (no overlapping tracks) reveal a unique and ingenious wit—the album's "Cue Fanfare" is about chess champ Bobby Fischer—supported by light and mellifluous music in a number of refined styles. Remarkable and enticing.

Steve McQueen (issued in the US as **Two Wheels Good**) was produced with a fine hand by Thomas Dolby, who also plays on it as the group's fifth member. (Drummer Neal Conti had signed on fulltime, making the Prefabs a standing quartet.) A significant advancement over **Swoon**, the adult gossamer pop includes the remarkably airy "When Love Breaks Down" (guest produced by Phil Thornally, indicating the band's strong stylistic backbone), the obscure but lovely "Appetite" and the mesmerizing "Goodbye Lucille #1." "Blueberry Pies" sounds like a lost Sade tune; "Horsin' Around" is as cavalier as its title. Brilliant!

On the airy **Langley Park to Memphis**, the quartet gets minor assistance from Pete Townshend (inaudible acoustic guitar on one track), Stevie Wonder and a gospel group; Dolby produced and played keyboards on four tracks. Notwithstanding one energized exception ("The Golden Calf," which bizarrely resembles Cheap Trick), the easy listening lounge music—deco-era strings, movie-music horns, stage-whisper vocals, restrained tempos—is boring and uninvolving, burying McAloon's offbeat lyrics in too deeply mellow an audio disguise.

After that loss of stylistic footing, it took the band a while to regroup—a situation effectively camouflaged by the belated official release of **Protest Songs**, an oft-bootlegged collection that was actually recorded on the heels of **Steve McQueen**, and suffers from that proximity. There's a cavernous emptiness beneath the gossamer surface of unfinished-sounding songs like "A Life of Surprises" and the blue-contact-lensed soul of "Wicked Things" that's all the more frustrating when you can hear the germs of so many squandered ideas.

Dolby's return helps insure that not a drop of **Jordan: The Comeback**'s considerable inspiration is wasted. With atmospheric worries out of mind, McAloon is free to rush headlong, through the doors of the Brill Building, across the Great White Way, into the arms of his muse. Echoes of Sondheim and Jimmy Webb resonate throughout the joyfully faux samba of "Carnival 2000" and the eerily precise Swede-pop of "The Ice Maiden," but that's not the real story here. The scoop is that Prefab Sprout has revived the concept album by crafting an interlocking sequence of concept mini-albums. Roughly half of **Jordan**'s nineteen (!) tracks fall into two tightly laced suites that pursue McAloon's dual obsessions; religion and celebrity (or, more specifically, God and Elvis). The latter supplies two of **Jordan**'s most moving songs ("Jesse James Bolero" and "Jesse James Symphony"), while the former gets the best line ("One of the Broken"'s salutory "Hi, this is God here," and an open letter of apology from Lucifer: the breathless "Michael"). Remarkably dense, intensely rewarding listening. The related American EP joins the album's souled-out "Machine Gun Ibiza" with three non-LP tracks.   [i/dss]

PRESSURE BOYS

Jump! Jump! Jump! EP (A-Root-Da-Doot-Doo) 1983
Rangledoon EP (A-Root-Da-Doot-Doo) 1984
Hell Tape [tape] (ARDDD) 1986
Krandlebanum Monumentus (AR3D) 1987

Chalk up another one for Mitch Easter, who co-produced **Jump! Jump! Jump!** at his world-famous Drive-In Studio. Given his background, one might expect power pop, but North Carolina's P-Boys instead deliver hot'n'sweaty horn-inflected ska-beat rock. The sextet's gangbusting, headlong enthusiasm recalls the early Specials (without the accents or trebly sound) but songs like "Tina Goes to the Supermarket" undercut any seriousness that might have been intended. Easter acquits himself admirably on this atypical production fare, making a record likely to pump your speakers free of their cabinets.

Produced by Don Dixon, the four songs on **Rangledoon** (a 12-inch with entirely blank grooves on one side) are even more ambitious and better realized than the first album. By toning things down stylistically, the group reveals more conceptual depth, applying its brassy assets with intuitive imagination. "Where the Cowboys Went," for instance, makes effective use of spoken narration, while the brisk "Policemen (In My Neighbor's Yard)," complete with gunshots, executes tricky musical turns on a dime. Excellent.

Besides the entirety of **Rangledoon** and four of the six tracks from **Jump! Jump! Jump!**, the cassette-only **Hell Tape** has an early four-song demo (including alternate versions of the two first-EP omissions) and three tracks recorded for (but unused on) the band's subsequent album. Despite the varied studio circumstances and personnel, **Hell** is an entirely enjoyable collection of pep and pop.

Krandlebanum Monumentus contains a second rendition of "Tina" as well as such offbeat weirdditties as "Terrible Brain," "Trombonehead" and "A Chew and a Swallow." Three horns still lead the kinetic attack, but the Pressuremen no longer hie to bluebeat, choosing a straighter rock direction (a bit like Oingo Boingo) that proves their tightness but leaves less of a lasting impression. [i]

PRESSURE COMPANY

See *Cabaret Voltaire*.

PRETENDERS

Pretenders (Real-Sire) 1980 ●
Extended Play EP (Real-Sire) 1981
Pretenders II (Real-Sire) 1981 ●
Learning to Crawl (Real-Sire) 1984 ●
Get Close (Real-Sire) 1986 ●
The Singles (Real-Sire) 1987 ●
Packed! (Sire) 1990 ●

Although bands fronted by ex-music critics have generally been doomed to culty oblivion, the Pretenders—formed in London by Ohio-born Chrissie Hynde—became huge around the world. Surviving the tragic deaths of guitarist James Honeyman Scott in 1982 and bassist Pete Farndon (after leaving the group) a year later, Hynde has pressed on, overcoming disaster with incredible strength and resilience. At this point, the Pre-tenders seem capable of existing and succeeding as long as Hynde cares to exercise her unique talents as a songwriter and vocalist.

After several brilliant singles (starting with an unforgettable Nick Lowe-produced Kinks cover, "Stop Your Sobbing"), the long-awaited **Pretenders** (produced by Chris Thomas) proved that the 45s were only the beginning. The band's several strengths—Hynde's husky voice and sexually forthright persona, drummer Martin Chambers' intricately syncopated (but never effete) rock rhythms, Honeyman Scott's blazing, inventive guitar work—give numbers like "Tattooed Love Boys," "Mystery Achievement," "Kid," "Brass in Pocket" and "Stop Your Sobbing" (the last three were pre-LP singles) instantly identifiable character and obvious rock excitement.

Mind-boggling success caught the Pretenders short of material, and producing a follow-up proved no small challenge. Eighteen months of touring left little time for writing or recording; the stopgap EP compiles both sides of two singles and a live version of "Precious." The record's fine as a placeholder, but was rendered redundant when both A-sides turned up on the second album.

Pretenders II would have been a real stiff, creatively speaking, were it not for those selfsame 45 cuts ("Message of Love" and "Talk of the Town"), the latter being one of the best things the band has ever done. Only a handful of the other ten tunes match the first album's quality, with selfconsciousness and repetition marring Hynde's writing and performance. An air of uncertainty—whether to play up the overstated arena-scaled side or explore restrained ballads and more complex, subtle arrangements—stymied them, and resulted in a confusion of conflicting directions. (Cassette collectors may be interested in a US tape pairing of the first two albums.)

Scott's death and Farndon's departure, coupled with Hynde's pregnancy, kept the band out of action for most of 1982. They released only one 45: "Back on the Chain Gang" b/w "My City Was Gone," with Billy Bremner guesting on guitar and future Big Countryman Tony Butler on bass. The band's output the following year also amounted to one fine single, the wistful, sentimental "2000 Miles."

Rather than the rattled, self-pitying record many expected, **Learning to Crawl** was a remarkable return to prime form. A revitalized Hynde and Chambers lead two new Pretenders through a collection of characteristic songs, including all three aforementioned single sides and such new grippers as "Middle of the Road" and "Time the Avenger," which are equal to anything she had previously written or recorded. The only thing lacking is Chambers' percussive complexity, replaced here by sturdy beats that are nothing special. But free of the misjudgment that ankled the second album, Hynde and the Pretenders again display mettle and talent.

Unrelated to the music, but typical of the inescapable private life drama that seems intrinsic to the band, Hynde then took time off to marry Simple Minds' singer Jim Kerr and tend to two children, forcing another long wait between records. When the Pretenders returned to action in 1986 with the disappointing **Get Close**, Chambers (and everyone else, save for guitarist Robbie McIntosh) was gone, although he does appear on an ill-advised cover of Jimi Hendrix's "Room Full of

Mirrors.'' The new lineup includes ex-Haircut One Hundred drummer Blair Cunningham, but the record relies on session players (including Bernie Worrell, Carlos Alomar and Simon Phillips) and contains only two sentimental love songs (''Don't Get Me Wrong'' and ''My Baby'') and Meg Keene's haunting ballad (''Hymn to Her'')—all released as singles—to recommend it.

That trio of songs, plus a dozen more classics and near-greats, comprise what is unquestionably the best Pretenders album of all. One can overlook **The Singles'** shockingly shoddy packaging; this is a true best-of career distillation (all the A-sides from 1979 to 1986) with one bonus track: Hynde's winning duet with UB40 on a reggaefied ''I Got You Babe.''

Although Hynde sags dangerously close to self-parody on Side 2 of **Packed!**, her amazing voice does manage to breathe a little life into the Pretenders' stiffening body. Subtle production (plus keyboards) by Mitchell Froom and skilled studio work by Cunningham, Bremner and others free Hynde to give the songs her all. Unfortunately, many of the melodies are rewrites; worse, the lyrics lack focus and intensity. Even when narrating the end of her marriage, Hynde's pain is reduced to bland phrases and simple clichés. Other than a dreamy cover of Hendrix's ''May This Be Love,'' the album's most affecting tunes—''Let's Make a Pact'' and ''When Will I See You'' (co-written by Johnny Marr)—find their strength in emotional maturity, expressing love without resorting to bravado. [i]

ANDY PRIEBOY
See *Wall of Voodoo*.

PRIMAL SCREAM
Sonic Flower Groove (nr/Elevation) 1987
Primal Scream (nr/Creation) 1989 ●
Loaded EP (nr/Creation) 1990
Come Together EP (Sire) 1990 ●

Scotland's Primal Scream made its live public debut in Glasgow in late '84, a show at which singer Bobby Gillespie also made his first appearance as the Jesus and Mary Chain's style-over-competence drummer. Signed to Creation, Primal Scream released a couple of singles on Creation over the next two years, but the band took a back seat to Gillespie's other career. When John Moore replaced him in the Chain's drum slot in early '86, Gillespie finally turned his full attention to his own band.

Primal Scream's influences are a hip mix not unlike the Chain's: Stones, a dash of psychedelic Beatles, MC5, Velvets, etc. Yet instead of, say, adopting a couple of salient characteristics of one of those bands, exaggerating them, and adding a personal imprint (as the J&M Chain did with the Velvets, Primal Scream seek a more careful blend, with little to add of their own. The result: the Chain have an easily identifiable sound; Primal Scream doesn't. It does, however, use lots of little bits nicked from various sources. At best, Primal Scream records are pleasant but no-stick.

The band evidently felt that 1987's **Sonic Flower Groove** was enough of a mistake to try to scrap it (unsuccessfully). If they felt **Primal Scream** redressed their self-grievances, they should've thought twice.

About a third sounds good, the slow stuff drags under its own weight and none of it has much (of its own) to say. ''You're Just Dead Skin to Me'' is a striking title, but it's just another distraction that overshadows the song itself (all too easy anyway)—the band's problem in a nutshell.

Come Together (**Loaded** plus two versions of the subsequent single, ''Come Together,'' and two additional mixes of ''Loaded'') is worse. The title track makes a big deal out of essentially reusing people's lyrics. Lyrically, ''Loaded'' (as in ''let's get . . .'') takes off from lines in Peter Fonda's '60s biker pic *The Wild Angels* (repeatedly sampled into the track), while musically it reworks ''Sympathy for the Devil'' with a slower, funkier (dance) beat. Also included: a cut from **Primal Scream** and an okay live version of the MC5's old ''Ramblin' Rose.'' [jg]

PRIME MOVERS
See *Prisoners*.

PRIMITIVES
Thru the Flowers EP (nr/Lazy) 1986
Lovely (RCA) 1988 + 1988 ●
Out of Reach EP (nr/RCA) 1988 ●
Secrets EP (nr/RCA) 1989 ●
Pure (RCA) 1989 ●
Lazy 86-88 (nr/Lazy) 1989 ●

Coventry's Primitives are one of best results of a British pop genre that first gained notoriety around 1986, in the wake of the Jesus and Mary Chain (but with a backwards nod to early Blondie). Characterized by self-consciously naïve vocals and distorto-guitar backing tracks that pay tribute to the '60s while reveling in post-punk insouciance, such efforts can either be utterly charming or noxiously grating. Thanks to excellent songwriting and the enchanting vocals of Tracy Tracy (guitarist/songwriter Paul Court sings the occasional tune as well), the Primitives have made some sparkling catchy bubblegum gems. Unfortunately, the young quartet peaked early and has been sagging downhill ever since.

The most memorable tracks on the wonderful **Lovely** reprise material from the group's early UK singles. (The American edition was reissued with the post-LP ''Way Behind Me,'' also included on **Pure**). Produced by Paul Sampson (later the group's bassist), **Lovely** runs through a variety of musical formats—from abject California bubblegum pop (''Thru the Flowers,'' the ultimate ''Crash,'' ''Stop Killing Me'') to early Blondiepunk (''Nothing Left'') and '60's mock-Indian psychedelia (''Shadow''). An ingenious and tune-crazy album of instantly accessible pop standards.

The two inter-album EPs contain some interesting non-LP material. The **Out of Reach** 12-inch plucks four songs from **Lovely** and adds live takes of ''Crash'' and ''Really Stupid.'' **Secrets**, a two-song preview of **Pure**, adds the song's demo and a non-LP bonus.

Pure has its charms, but this attempt to fancy things up in the face of inconsistent material leaves it no match for the first LP. Bookended by the rushing ''Secrets'' and the gently swaying ''Summer Rain,'' fine songs like ''Outside,'' ''Lonely Streets'' and the spectacular ''Way

Behind Me'' all unearth delightful new ingredients with which to modulate the group's stylistic approach. Amusing little guitar references to the Who, Status Quo and Sonny and Cher add to the fun. But other songs are halfbaked or dull, pale rewrites of prior tunes. Slathering echo on the vocals in an obvious homage to the J&M Chain (''All the Way Down'') is a bad idea, as is the mild infusion of Manchester house rhythm in the clunky ''Sick of It.'' (The British album has two songs not on the American; the British CD further adds an alternate version of ''All the Way Down'' and ''I Almost Touched You'' from the **Secrets** EP.)

Compiling the Primitives' first four releases, **Lazy 86-88** includes the miserably primitive **Thru the Flowers** debut EP and the title track's vastly superior remake, two additional three-song singles (''Really Stupid'' and ''Stop Killing Me,'' both with neat non-LP tunes) and a rare alternate version of ''Shadow'' from a limited-edition give-away 45. [ag/i]

PRIMITIVE SOULS

See *Real Kids*.

PRIMITONS

Primitons (Throbbing Lobster) 1985
Happy All the Time (What Goes On) 1987

The two prime movers in Birmingham's Primitons are drummer/accordionist Leif Bondarenko and singer/guitarist/organist Mots Roden, a Swede who somehow wound up living in Alabama. Following a long stint in Jim Bob and the Leisure Suits (a promising but gimmicky local adaptation of new wave), the pair formed the all-pop Primitons with singer/guitarist Brad Dorset and non-performing lyricist Stephanie Truelove Wright.

Joined by a guest vocalist, the trio recorded a sturdy and attractive seven-song debut, produced with Mitch Easter. **Primitons** is a pop record, but with the same sort of gravity and lyrical depth as the Windbreakers. ''All My Friends'' offers a rich R.E.M.-influenced rush; ''She Sleeps'' puts a gothic tale of death and grieving to simple music strengthened by high, lonesome singing; ''You'll Never Know'' is an ominous whisper about nuclear destruction.

Bassist Don Tinsley replaced Dorset; the trio (plus Wright) issued an ambitious and spectacular Anglo-pop 12-inch, ''Don't Go Away,'' which covers the Left Banke's ''Something on My Mind'' as one of its two B-sides. **Happy All the Time**, which boasts ''Don't Go Away'' and other similarly well-executed numbers, is a winning collection and shows what a fine band the Primitons are. Layers of guitars and vocals are the main ingredients; subtlety and diversity are a bonus; talented songwriting and offbeat lyrics provide the solid foundation. Tim Lee guests. [i]

PRIMUS

Suck on This (Prawn Song) 1989 (Caroline) 1990 ●
Frizzle Fry (Caroline) 1990 ●
Sailing the Seas of Cheese (Interscope) 1991 φ

Although Primus is one of numerous metal-funk outfits to emerge from the Bay Area in the late '80s, what sets this trio apart is bassist Les Claypool's distinctive reedy vocals, the band's herky-jerky rhythms and the stop-and-go song structures (perfect for moshing!).

Recorded live in early '89, **Suck on This** (first released on Primus' own label, then reissued after **Frizzle Fry**) offers a decent introduction to the band, capturing its manic energy, if not the intricacies and vocal firepower subsequently displayed in the studio. (The two records have five songs in common.)

Although by no means excessively produced, the improved sound quality and the chance to overdub an extra guitar part or two to heighten the abrasive textures of the songs make **Frizzle Fry** a far more definitive artistic statement. Claypool is an impressive lyricist (maybe the genre's best), whether he's writing morning-after streams-of-consciousness (''Harold of the Rocks,'' ''Groundhog's Day'') or spinning cautionary political/environmental tales à la the Mothers' **We're Only in It for the Money** (''Too Many Puppies,'' ''Pudding Time,'' ''Sathington Willoughby''). Having established such a unique sound and vision, all Primus has to do now is build and expand on it. [ds]

PRINCE

For You (Warner Bros.) 1978 ●
Prince (Warner Bros.) 1979 ●
Dirty Mind (Warner Bros.) 1980 ●
Controversy (Warner Bros.) 1981 ●
1999 (Warner Bros.) 1982 ●
Sign "o" the Times (Paisley Park) 1987 ●
The Black Album (unreleased) ●
Lovesexy (Paisley Park) 1988 ●
Batman (Warner Bros.) 1989 ●
The Scandalous Sex Suite EP (Warner Bros.) 1989 ●

PRINCE AND THE REVOLUTION

Purple Rain (Warner Bros.) 1984 ●
Around the World in a Day (Paisley Park) 1985 ●
Parade (Paisley Park) 1986 ●

PRINCE ET AL.

Music from Graffiti Bridge (Paisley Park-Warner Bros.) 1990 ●

Prince's impact on the direction and sound of '80s pop music can't be overstated. By the mid-'70s, race segregation had become nearly as rigid a musical barrier as it was at the outset of rock'n'roll in the '50s, but Prince's brilliant stylistic cross-fertilization has been a major agent in its slow dissolution. He continually demonstrates a phenomenal grasp of forms, styles and production techniques, and he has the ability to create stunning syntheses of them. True, he's shown a lyrical penchant for excessive and/or tasteless sexuality, but he's also responsible for some of the most playful, open and un-hung-up sexiness in pop music. Prince is the biggest figure in '80s pop music whom musicians at opposite ends of the rock and soul spectrum will admit liking and paying attention to.

The upstart 19-year-old's first album, **For You**, operates within the conventions of soul music—even of disco—without sounding like a tired string of clichés or succumbing to corporate overkill. The assertive sexuality (e.g., ''Soft and Wet'') isn't the LP's big surprise, which he saves for last—something like a cross between MFSB and the Delfonics trying to condense the Cream songbook into one number. **Prince**'s soul is also slick, its rock less crunchy. His libido advertisements range from mock-coy to wham-bam, from straightforward to confusing ("I wanna be your lover . . . your brother . . . your mother and your sister too") to confused ("It's mainly a physical thing . . . [but] I think it's love"). **Prince** is a bit more entertaining than **For You**, but both are a touch too clinical.

Dirty Mind and **Controversy** began to attract the attention of the rock crowd. To oversimplify, the two LPs blend Blondie, Bootsy and Blowfly; while other artists bared their souls, Prince preferred to bare his genitals. Ultimately, **Dirty Mind** comes off as a flawed triumph, **Controversy** as a miscalculation. The former's crotch-mindedness is offset by ingenuous ingenuity. The sly lyrics, good tunes, strong production and his super falsetto all make for a winning combination; a song like "When You Were Mine" (later covered to great effect by Cyndi Lauper) declared that he was a tunesmith to be reckoned with. **Controversy**, though, shows too much flash with too little substance—Prince is straining too hard for approval from his new audience and the touch-all-bases agenda yields "Ronnie, Talk to Russia," "Annie Christian" and "Jack U Off," all on one LP side.

The largely dance-oriented **1999**, however, is his first real tour de force. Prince exercises even greater skill than before, and when he couples that with some restraint, the results are incredibly gratifying. (The first side alone has three of his best-ever cuts: "1999," "Little Red Corvette" and "Delirious.") Gratuitous sexuality and stylistic indulgences that overstretch tracks make the double-album set less than an unmitigated success; all the same, sometimes his talent is so dazzling that you don't notice (or care about) his excesses. (As a result of single-disc time constraints, the **1999** CD was originally issued without "D.M.S.R.," a defect finally rectified in 1990.)

Purple Rain is the first Prince album to use a band in the studio, and his first movie music; however much those factors influenced the outcome, it also clearly topped its predecessors. Superior focus and control enable him to move effortlessly from the party-down ebullience of "Let's Go Crazy" to the spare, delicate anguish of "When Doves Cry" to the commandingly Hendrixian guitar balladry of the title track.

From back-to-back killers, though, he went to back-to-back turkeys: **Around the World in a Day** and **Parade**. But no matter what he gets into on these records, each has at least one ace track and another just a notch below. Prince's father helped him write three of the tunes on **Around the World**, but don't blame Dad— the blatherings on sex and religion, and the neo-psychedelic/flower-power tripe in which it's couched, are all Prince's doing. All the same, "Raspberry Beret" is an uncanny recycling of the Small Faces and the bouncy "Pop Life" (which allegedly incorporates a tape of the crowd that booed him offstage when he opened for the Stones) offers politely witty lyrics. **Parade**'s strangeness isn't as bad as the worst of **World**, though it's a wonder the soundtrack of Prince's laughably bad second film, *Under the Cherry Moon*, was any good at all. Some of it is weird—stripped-down funk that just doesn't work—but the spartan "Kiss" is an instant classic. Right on its heels comes "Anotherloverholenyo-

head," which isn't—*can't* be—as good, but is still pretty stimulating.

The time for the Revolution had evidently come and gone, so Prince decided to strike out on his own again. The split was apparently amicable; Wendy and Lisa (guitar, keyboards, vocals) appear on his next LP (while also making one of their own). **Sign "o" the Times** is a two-disc bag of goodies, filled with different flavors and colors. The title track is the most minimal of his minimalist singles (even compared to "Kiss"), an off-beat reality-minded protest record that's hardly there. It shouldn't work, but it does, like crazy. Sheena Easton and Sheila E. join in for "U Got the Look," a throw-back to the "old" Prince sound and over-the-top sexual aggression ("let's get to rammin' ") and a strong track in spite of itself. Otherwise, there's some of everything—rap, funk, pop, James Brown tributes, rock'n'roll, etc. Highlights include "If I Was Your Girlfriend," which redefines a relationship in a surprisingly mature way; "Strange Relationship," a nonplused admission of emotional sado-masochism; and the sleeper ending Side Three, "I Could Never Take the Place of Your Man," a "When You Were Mine" melody with an older and wiser message. A double album eminently worthy of the vinyl.

Ostensibly in a disagreement with Warner Bros. over release scheduling, Prince withdrew a completed record known as **The Black Album**, which wound up widely bootlegged on cassette, vinyl and CD. It's not a great album, but it's pretty damned neat. Except for the pretty (X-rated) ballad, "When 2 R in Love," each track offers a slightly different kind of (usually scatological) funk. The sneer of "Le Grind," a leering call to orgy to the beat, is grating but, like the rest, is so well done it succeeds anyway. "Bob George" is fabulously nasty, off-the-wall black (in many senses) humor; "2 Nigs United 4 West Compton" is a tribute (?!?) of sorts to guys like Jimmy Smith and Brother Jack McDuff; "Cincy C" is a hot, sexy groove. Lots of synthetic sounds, not the least of which is the obvious electronic alteration of Prince's voice. This LP would've received no airplay, but it's a gas.

Prince must have known **The Black Album** wouldn't really pass muster at the label: he already had **Lovesexy** ready. (Its cover caused a different retail furor.) With backing by the group Madhouse (minus its drummer, replaced by Sheila E.), it's a fine record. "Alphabet St." brightly continues that minimalist single string. "Anna Stesia" is a wonderfully weird intertwining of love, sex and religion that works where it failed before; the title track is a funny/affecting affirmation of real and exciting romance that *doesn't* have to be immediately consummated (even though "race cars burn rubber in my pants"!). The only song carried over from **The Black Album** is "When 2 R in Love." Prince was on a roll, and the sky seemed the limit. Then came *Batman*.

Like the movie itself, the lines that open **Batman** the album ("I've seen the future and it will be/I've seen the future and it works") are incomplete, unsatisfying and say less than meets the eye. The film may not have been a total bust, but it had too little substance to live up to its hype. The album is equally deficient, and Prince acting out some of the parts in song, trying to take them even further, simply doesn't make it. (Caught up in the

Batman hype wind, the record did return Prince to the top of the charts.) "The Future" and "Batdance" have moments, but the best bit is still the chorus chanting "Batman!" in emulation of Neal Hefti's '60s TV theme. (A special edition of the CD—packaged in a can—was issued commercially.)

"Scandalous" didn't live up to its title in the 6:15 **Batman** version; neither do its equally (over)long reworkings, "The Crime," "The Passion" and "The Rapture" on **The Scandalous Sex Suite** EP. Prince adds bedroom dialogue with actress Kim Basinger (the couple allegedly had an affair), more "sexy" whimpering from the original (which may not actually be Basinger) and instrumental excess (including heavy guitar). Also included: a non-LP track ("Sex") and **Lovesexy**'s "When 2 R in Love."

The soundtrack to Prince's flop movie *Graffiti Bridge* is nowhere near as disappointing, but neither can it stand up to very many of his other albums. Prince shares the spotlight here: although he had a hand in producing and writing everything and played and sang most of it, three of the seventeen tracks are performed by the Time (Prince joins the Time on another); there's a collaboration with George Clinton and lead vocals by Mavis Staples and (on the hit "Round and Round") young Tevin Campbell. The musical mix is a virtue, but the writing is too rarely impressive or memorable, much of it retreading ground he's already crossed with far more style and grace. Two of the best tracks are the rock'n'rolly opener ("Can't Stop This Feeling I Got") and the sing-along title tune. Time for a rethink? [jg]

See also *Andre Cymone, Morris Day, Jesse Johnson's Revue, Time, Wendy and Lisa.*

PRINCESS TINYMEAT

See *Virgin Prunes.*

PETER PRINCIPLE

See *Tuxedomoon.*

PRISONERS

A Taste of Pink! (nr/Own-Up) 1982
Thewisermiserdemelza (nr/Big Beat) 1983 ●
Revenge of the Prisoners (Pink Dust) 1984
The Last Fourfathers (nr/Own-Up) 1985
Whenever I'm Gone EP (nr/54321 Countdown) 1986
In from the Cold (nr/54321 Countdown) 1986
Rare & Unissued (nr/Hangman) 1988

PRISONERS/MILKSHAKES

The Last Night at the M.I.C. (nr/Empire) 1985
Thee Milkshakes vs the Prisoners (nr/Media Burn) 1985

PRIME MOVERS

Sins of the Fourfathers (nr/Cyanide) 1989 (Ger. Universe) 1989

JAMES TAYLOR QUARTET

Wait a Minute (nr/Urban-Polydor) 1988 ●
Get Organised (nr/Polydor) 1989 ●
Do Your Own Thing (nr/Polydor) 1990 ●

Lesser-known purveyors of the "Medway Delta" sound, Graham Day's Prisoners/Prime Movers, alongside Billy Childish's myriad combos, butted their way into prominence through sheer persistence in the '80s

Chatham (the city between London and Canterbury where the Medway River meets the North Sea) chapter of the Great Garage R&R Manifesto. Less spontaneous than Mr. C and considerably more of a popsmith (in the Jeff Conolly sense), Day's songs are uniformly well crafted, with fully dynamic backing as opposed to Billy's headlong drunken bashing. The sixteen-hours-in-a-studio extravaganza **A Taste of Pink!** comes closest to a melding of the two Medway styles, both raw/immediate and hooky/heady.

Thewisermiserdemelza hones the Prisoners' unique blitz, emphasizing Jamie Taylor's atmospheric trashpop organ and Day's appealingly raspy vocals. (The 1990 CD issue adds an EP and a 7-inch for an hour of fun.) **Revenge of the Prisoners** pulls the best tracks off **Wiser**, adding 7-inch and unreleased songs for the apex of studio Prisonhood. **The Last Fourfathers** (back on their own label) sounds dangerously like Deep Purple just prior to metal ascension: humor withdrawn, keys all broody rather than bracing, the overall tone quite serious and enervated.

Briefly signed to the renamed and fading remnants of the Stiff empire, the Prisoners cut a niftily retro EP (**Whenever I'm Gone**) and then made their last studio album, **In from the Cold**, a dreadful kitchen-sink mess that sounds, by turns, like everyone except the Prisoners. **Rare & Unissued** rebalances the scales a bit, with several songs rescued from the last LP but done in more traditional Prisoner style, surrounded by noise and trash and ephemera. Recorded in January and September of '84, both of the live LPs shared with The(e) Milkshakes echo the snot, raunch, abandon and crisp sonics (snort) of **Got Live If You Want It**.

Subsequent to his term as pseudonymous drummer for Thee Mighty Caesars, Graham Day once more allowed his own undiluted musical vision full vent with the Prime Movers (not to be confused with imbecilic West Coast synthsters of the same name, nor Boston's amazing late-'80s amphetamine acidheads), playing garage Hendrixia backed by the Prisoners' bassist and the drummer from the Daggermen (short-lived little-brother Medway band with Prisoners/Milkshakes ties), both of whom had also been in the original James Taylor Quartet, the '60sish all-instrumental combo led by Prisoners organist James Taylor.

Sins of the Fourfathers, originally released as a return-to-basics early-Prisoner-style LP, was quickly remixed with the added keys of Graham's new wife Fay Day (formerly Fay Fife of the Revillos/Rezillos, aka Fay Hallam of the excellent beat-soul combo Makin' Time) and re-released in Germany.   [ab]

See also *Pop Rivits, Thee Mighty Caesars.*

PROCLAIMERS

This Is the Story (Chrysalis) 1987
Sunshine on Leith (Chrysalis) 1988 ●
King of the Road EP (nr/Chrysalis) 1990 ●

One of the neo-folk movement's most rewarding eruptions is the Proclaimers, a pair of sharp-tongued Scottish twins (Craig and Charlie Reid) who not only acknowledge their thick accents, they sing about 'em (in "Throw the 'R' Away"), strumming acoustic guitars and tapping on bongos for accompaniment. Oldtimers will be forgiven for thinking the duo sounds like Lonnie

Donegan, the Glaswegian superstar whose skiffle records served to popularize American folk music in the UK three decades ago. By telling it straight and artlessly, **This Is the Story** stands out, embracing and updating ancient traditions without phony posing. Those who like Billy Bragg's sound but find his politics an impediment are recommended to the Proclaimers for a largely non-topical dose of similarly spare melodicism.

The upscale production of **Sunshine on Leith** adds a full complement of sidemen (including LP producer Pete Wingfield and a couple of Fairport Convention veterans) and a certain gloss, but only succeeds in making the duo's second record even more delightful than the first. On their way to becoming Scotland's very own Everly Brothers, the Reids deliver another batch of lyrically clever and extraordinarily tuneful songs. Coping handsomely with the fuller sound, their harmonizing voices and the tastefully electrified arrangements combine into a rich brand of folk-rock loaded with pop hooks.

King of the Road is a four-cut EP which contains the duo's amusingly pointless version of the Roger Miller song.   [i]

PROFESSIONALS

I Didn't See It Coming (nr/Virgin) 1981

Following the breakup of the Sex Pistols, Paul Cook and Steve Jones—aka the Professionals—stuck together, finishing some final tracks under the Pistols' name, backing people like Joan Jett and Johnny Thunders and doing lots of production work. **I Didn't See It Coming**, however, is their only joint post-Pistols album. With Paul Meyers (bass) and Ray McVeigh (guitar), the trademark Cook/Jones rock crunch stretches over wide terrain, on songs that are neither trusty punk oldies nor retreads thereof. The album's not consistently good, but "The Magnificent" (a song seemingly aimed at John Lydon, complete with parodic Public Image guitar), "Payola" and the anthemic "Kick Down the Doors" are among the tracks that bear repeated spins.

Cook and Jones can be seen in several movies, including the Pistols' *Great Rock'n'Roll Swindle* and *Ladies and Gentlemen, the Fabulous Stains*. Jones went on to record a solo album and work with Iggy Pop, Andy Taylor and others; Cook wound up in a band called Chiefs of Relief.   [i]

See also *Chiefs of Relief, Steve Jones, Sex Pistols*.

PROFESSOR GRIFF AND THE LAST ASIATIC DISCIPLES

See *Public Enemy*.

PRONG

Primitive Origins (Mr. Bear) 1987
Force Fed (nr/Spigot) 1988 (In-Effect) 1989 ●
Beg to Differ (Epic) 1990 ●
The Peel Sessions EP (nr/Strange Fruit) 1990 (Strange
  Fruit-Dutch East India) 1991 ●

Whether they're metal or not, this underground-spawned, speedcore-trained New York trio produces some of the most brutally assaultive power rock around. Little surprise, considering the group's bloodlines trace back to such eustachia-batterers as Damage and the Swans.

Although Prong's debut generated loads of critical enthusiasm, it'd be hard to finger the record in a lineup of East Coast speedmetal; an annoying reliance on change-on-a-dime tempos keeps the lyrical street-smarts from sinking in. **Force Fed** is a far less hysterical showcase for the group's considerable chops. The control displayed on "Look Up at the Sun" and (on the US version) the grinding "Bought and Sold" is heartening. A pair of creepy-crawly instrumentals ("It's Been Decided" and "The Coliseum") that are equal parts muscle-flex and mind-control set the stage for Prong's major label bow.

Oddly enough, **Beg to Differ** is a lot more radical than either of Prong's indie discs. Delivering violent minimalist lyrics in a drill-sergeant bark over stark backdrops, the LP has the feel of a post-nuke documentary. The pointillist precision of ex-Swan Ted Parson's drumming leaves plenty of room for guitarist/singer Tommy Victor and bassist/singer Mike Kirkland's shared death dance. (The CD adds a nice live version of Chrome's "Third from the Sun.")

Recorded in January 1989, the Peel EP offers commanding high-voltage renditions of "Defiant," "Decay," "Senseless Abuse" and "In My Veins." [dss]

See also *Of Cabbages and Kings, Swans*.

PROOF OF UTAH

A Dog, a Dodo, and a Fool (Smiley Turtle) 1985
It Doesn't Matter Much (Smiley Turtle) 1986
The Belly's Virginal Polylips [tape] (Smiley Turtle) 1986
Happy to Be Here (Ger. No Man's Land-Recommended)
  1988
Out of Order (Smiley Turtle) 1989
Free and Female (Ger. No Man's Land-Recommended)
  1990

Originally from Bowling Green, Ohio and now based in Champaign, Illinois, Proof of Utah has no Utah connection at all. The name's just a phrase co-founder Louie Simon overheard in a conversation—but what kind of conversation was that? The band's records are left-field in much the same way: musical and lyrical banalities transformed via unexpected juxtapositions into deliciously deadpan whimsy. To liken them to Frank Zappa, Captain Beefheart, the Residents, Brian Eno, Talking Heads and Devo is an ultimately misguided impulse, and the bases for such comparisons are mostly pretty general: POU use (or subvert) a variety of musical styles, and seek out strange sonic textures. They incorporate radio snippets (or simulations thereof); recite, or talk-sing, in homely (sometimes funny) voices; their lyrics are nothing if not off-the-wall.

Simon (voice, drums, tapes) and co-conspirator Mike Brosco (aka Bosco: voice, guitar, bass, synths, tapes) were, with some guests invited at the last minute, the group on POU's debut album, a consciously eclectic collection of styles somewhat primitively performed. Starting with the second album, Brosco and Simon acquired three sidemen, contributing sax, keyboards, harmonica, etc.

Each side of **It Doesn't Matter Much** starts with a dopey, seemingly mundane ditty that's just a little bit off. Then things get weird. There's tuneful guitar rock with oblique lyrics, a bizarre tone poem, an offbeat jazz tune. It's all pretty goofy yet ingratiating; even amid some of the silliest bits, striking sounds and lyrical images emerge. **Happy to Be Here** is a tad more varied, and the weird stuff is definitely weirder. Some of it isn't all that odd: an ode to corn dogs ("On a Stick") is a rockin' little hoedown. But then "The Wedding Song" alternates wacky rapid-fire verses with mutant dance-rock, and the sax-laden "Mamba" has four different tempos ("movements"?) in succession; its "lyrics" are a guest couple speaking in foreign languages.

Out of Order is the rockiest album, especially the first side; new listeners may find this the most accessible. It's pure coincidence that several of its tracks are among the band's best: the rocking lope and curiously evocative nonsense lyrics of "The Pointed Lady" and the dense, tense, intense rock of "Mr. Summer."

Free and Female returns to the antic assortment, though it also has some rockin' sides. "Death of Italian Acrobats" intones typically skew(er)ed POU lyrics over Big Brother's "Combination of the Two" as interpreted by the Banana Splits on drugs; "Forks or Blades" is a boogyin' little commentary of sorts on the state of radio. But it also includes a self-parodic quasi-jazz "tribute" to John Coltrane's "A Love Supreme" ("I Love Ice Cream").

Despite their intellectual leanings and occasional concerns about the dark side of human relations, POU albums possess an innocent, almost childlike sense of wonder and even happiness (irreducible to some pat intellectual formulation). Each has so much going on that it takes more than a few listenings to catch it all. **Happy to Be Here**, **Out of Order** and **Free and Female** are all highly recommended to listeners with a sense of adventure, but virtually any POU is worthwhile. (One possible exception is **The Belly's Virginal Polylips**, which consists of live stuff, outtakes and fragments, none of which exactly deserves to be on an album.) [jg]

PROPAGANDA
Propaganda's Secret Wish (ZTT-Island) 1985 ●
Wishful Thinking (nr/ZTT-Island) 1985
1234 (Charisma) 1990 φ

CLAUDIA BRÜCKEN
Love: And a Million Other Things (nr/Island) 1991 ●

On their first album, Propaganda—two men and two women—play intricate, almost orchestral synth-based rock of little inherent excitement. As encouraged by Trevor Horn and Paul Morley, each divergent track is a huge stylized production number, but none offers much in the way of listening pleasure. The German band's character—when any is present—derives mainly from gimmickry (gory English S&M lyrics on "Duel," Art of Noise-styled mix hysterics on the song's invigorating instrumental version, "Jewel"). **Secret Wish** includes contributions from Steve Howe, David Sylvian, Glenn Gregory and others, not that you'd notice them without reading the credits. **Wishful Thinking** contains remixes and reworkings of previously released material.

The Propaganda on **1234** is a drastically different outfit—only keyboard player Michael Mertens remains from the original lineup, although two ex-members do make guest contributions. Playing intelligent and slick

but rarely exciting music that varies electronically between mainstream Anglo-soul and mainstream dance-rock, the new quartet now features British vocalist Betsi Miller and Simple Minds' old rhythm section (Derek Forbes and Brian McGee).

Original Propaganda vocalist Claudia Brücken issued her first solo album in early '91. [tr]

CHUCK PROPHET
See *Green on Red*.

LINK PROTRUDI AND THE JAYMEN
See *Fuzztones*.

PRUNES
See *Virgin Prunes*.

PSEUDO ECHO
Pseudo Echo (EMI America) 1984
Love an Adventure (RCA) 1987 ●
Long Plays 83-87 (Aus. EMI) 1987
Race (RCA) 1989 ●

The distance between Australia and the world's musical capitals occasionally leads to lame time-zone wrinkles like Pseudo Echo, a Melbourne quartet whose functional dance-rock sound (on **Pseudo Echo**) would have fit nicely alongside Duran Duran or other emergent hair-synth-guitar bands a few years earlier. The Pseuds' weird move was hitching their wagon to turn-of-the-decade disco, cutting a pablumized Sparks-like version of "Funkytown" in 1987. (For what it's worth, that goofy hybrid appears on **Love an Adventure**.)

John Punter produced the first album (entitled **Autumnal Park** outside of the US), setting the vapid and repetitive songs in a posh blend of sounds traceable to Duran Duran and Ultravox. (Although the catchy hook of "Listening" actually owes more to Men Without Hats.)

Having undergone a major personnel shift and a radical image change (out went the lipstick and stupid haircuts, on went the leather jackets and casually rumpled look), Pseudo Echo re-recorded three of the first LP's songs with lots more percussion for the dance-oriented **Love an Adventure**, a slicker and less overtly stylized album that still has no reason to exist.

Co-produced by Julian Mendelsohn and singer Brian Canham, **Race** (another image change: long hair/serious expressions) drops the synthesizers and crashing beats to play melodic hard-rock with blustery Eddie Van Halen-imitation solos. Having discovered three styles to which they can't make any contribution, Pseudo Echo should really consider going away. [i]

PSI COM
See *Jane's Addiction*.

PSYCHEDELIC FURS
The Psychedelic Furs (Columbia) 1980 ●
Talk Talk Talk (Columbia) 1981 ●
Forever Now (Columbia) 1982 ●

Mirror Moves (Columbia) 1984 ●
12" Tape EP [tape] (nr/CBS) 1986
Midnight to Midnight (Columbia) 1987 ●
All That Money Wants EP (nr/CBS) 1988 ●
All of This and Nothing (Columbia) 1988 ●
Book of Days (Columbia) 1989 ●
Crucial Music: The Psychedelic Furs Collection [CD] (CBS
    Special Products-Relativity) 1989 ●

The Furs, whose lineup has varied substantially around a core of three (singer Richard Butler, his bassist brother Tim and guitarist John Ashton), came onto the London scene well after the initial punk explosion, but debuted with an album that mixed a drone-laden wall of noise (two guitars, sax and/or keyboards) and an odd adaptation of the quieter Bowie **Low**-style sound over which Butler rasped his lyrics in a bored, asthmatic drawl. While the record sounds great in the blur of history, at the time it was belated and too stylistically derivative not to seem redundant.

Talk Talk Talk, produced by Steve Lillywhite, displays surprising melodiousness in a newly crystallized style that amalgamates the Velvet Underground, **Highway 61**-era Dylan and even **Revolver**-era Beatles, all given a fresh face and a driving beat. The wall of noise is sculpted to bring the components into sharp relief; Butler tosses off memorable imagery with mock-casual aplomb. The catchy opening track, "Pretty in Pink," served as the titular inspiration for a 1986 film and soundtrack album of the same name.

Butler writes to his strengths on **Forever Now**. Though the Furs had lost two key members, the others' increased sophistication—shored up by wisely chosen session help (somber cello, horns, Flo & Eddie)—is orchestrated by Todd Rundgren in a major production coup, best exemplified by the brilliant single, "Love My Way."

In collaboration with producer/pro tem drummer Keith Forsey (filling in for the departed Vince Ely), the Furs turned decisively commercial on **Mirror Moves**, which is distinguished by a full side of memorable rockers written and played in the group's by-now-inimitable style. "The Ghost in You," "Here Come Cowboys," "Heaven" and "Heartbeat" may not be profound or timeless, but they do show perspicacity and exceptionally well-ordered playing and production. (Prior to the next album's release, a UK cassette appeared, compiling five singles including "The Ghost in You," "Love My Way" and "Pretty in Pink.")

Midnight to Midnight gets off to a fine start with "Heartbreak Beat," a deceptively restrained rocker whose lyrics reflect Butler's relocation to New York, but then founders amid listenable but low-impact songs. Sparked by semi-member Mars Williams' metropolitan brass, Chris Kimsey's production tightens the Furs into a muscular, focused unit, making the shallow material accessible by shortchanging the band's stylish personality. The reliable "new music" hit machine is running on empty here.

Amid a long period of inactivity, the Furs finally released a new single ("All That Money Wants") in mid-'88. A few months later that song appeared on **All of This and Nothing**, a career review that wisely reaches beyond the familiar to include equally significant material like "President Gas" and "Imitation of Christ." **Crucial Music**, prepared without the band's

involvement, repeats "Heaven" and "Heartbreak Beat" and adds eight other worthy selections ("Sleep Comes Down," "She Is Mine" and "Here Come Cowboys") from the catalogue.

With Vince Ely back on the drum throne, David Allen co-producing and no horn players in attendance, **Book of Days** repudiates **Midnight to Midnight** without advancing a completely viable alternative. In place of posh, uptempo slickness, **Book of Days** substitutes a simple, slow-moving guitar roar; if the songs were any good, the album might have been great. But after a powerful beginning ("Shine"), monotony sets in, a richly textured roar that goes nowhere beneath Butler's weary vocals. Two notable exceptions are the single "House," which has a real melody and pulsing energy, and "Torch," a melancholy lament effectively performed on acoustic guitar and cello.

Note: The first three LPs have different track sequences in their US and UK releases. Also, two tracks were substituted for a controversial cut on the first LP and one was altered and retitled on the third. The **12" Tape** is, reasonably enough, a cassette containing the 12-inch mixes of five familiar singles, including "Pretty in Pink," "Love My Way" and "Heaven." [jg/i]

PSYCHEFUNKAPUS
Psychefunkapus (Atlantic) 1990 ●

As the name suggests, this Bay Area quintet offers up equal doses of '60s psychedelia and Chili Peppers-influenced hyper-funk. Basically a metallic power trio with two lead singers, Psychefunkapus shows a lot of promise on its debut album, despite a damaging tendency to over-freneticize. Still, there's a kind of silly charm at work here: "We Are the Young," for example, comes off as a well-meaning update of The Monkees' theme ethics, set to the groove of Spencer Davis' "I'm a Man," while other tracks walk an uneasy line between '60s optimism and '80s street reality. The message: it ain't easy growing up these days. The cure: turn up the volume and get down with the funk. [ds]

PSYCHIC TV
Force the Hand of Chance (nr/Some Bizzare) 1982
Dreams Less Sweet (nr/Some Bizzare) 1983
N.Y. Scum Haters (nr/Temple) 1984
25 December 1984—A Pagan Day (nr/Temple) 1985
Those Who Do Not (Ice. Gramm) 1985
Themes (nr/Temple) 1985
Themes II (nr/Temple) 1985
Mouth of the Night (nr/Temple) 1985
Live in Tokyo (nr/Temple) 1986
Live in Paris (nr/Temple) 1986
Live in Heaven (nr/Temple) 1987
Live in Reykjavik (nr/Temple) 1987
Live en Suisse (nr/Temple) 1987
Live in Glasgow (nr/Temple) 1987
Live in Gottingen (nr/Temple) 1987
Live in Toronto (nr/Temple) 1987
Themes III (nr/Temple) 1987
The Yellow Album (nr/Temple) 1988
Live at Mardi Gras (nr/Temple) 1988
Jack the Tab: Acid Tablets Volume One (nr/Castalia)
    1988

Allegory and Self (Revolver-Fundamental) 1988 ●
Live at thee Circus (nr/Temple) 1988
Tekno Acid Beat (nr/Temple) 1989 ●
Tekno Acid Beat Vol. 2 (nr/Temple) 1989 ●
Live at thee Ritz (nr/Temple) 1989
Kondole/Copycat (nr/Temple) 1989 ●
Live at thee Pyramid NYC 1988 (nr/Temple) 1989
Towards thee Infinite Beat (Wax Trax!) 1990 ●
Beyond thee Infinite Beat (Wax Trax!) 1990 ●

PSYCHIC TV/Z'EV
Berlin Atonal Vol. 1 (Ger. Atonal) 1984

PSYCHIC TV/LA LOORA
Berlin Atonal Vol. 2 (Ger. Atonal) 1984

An album that appears to be devoted to an obscure faith known as "The Temple ov Psychick Youth" might be accepted on face value—after all, various cults have produced albums of devotional music to spread their gospel among rock fans. However, when the musicians behind the project are the former leader of Throbbing Gristle—merry prankster Genesis P-Orridge—and one-time Alternative TV-er Alex Fergusson (joined by Peter Christopherson, also a TG co-conspirator) it becomes much harder to judge where religious sincerity ends and elaborate put-on begins. (With hindsight, the notion that overzealous conceptual shenanigans can spiral out of anybody's control offers a third alternative.) Adding to the confusion, Stevo, who runs Some Bizzare (the label that originally abetted the group), is quoted on the back cover of their first album: "A naïve person can open his eyes in life, but someone with his eyes open can never end up naïve." Just who's kidding who here?

Force the Hand of Chance, regardless of its sincerity or utter lack thereof, is an amazing package: two records (one purported to be the partial soundtrack of a four-hour videocassette), a poster/booklet, pictured costumes, symbology and mail-order merchandise offerings. Musically, the main disc is a weird assortment of quiet ballads, screeching white noise, simple pop and more, with lyrics by P-Orridge that drift over terrain not all in keeping with the mystical concept. At times, form far outweighs function and some songs become merely effect without substance; others stand up nicely on their own regardless of the accompanying baggage. The adjunct record, **Psychick TV Themes**, uses real and imagined ethnic instruments from various exotic cultures to produce instrumentals that range from crazed to cool, intense to ephemeral—something like Eno's ambience filtered through a Spike Jones sensibility.

Dreams Less Sweet is another remarkable record, no less appealing for its equally abundant bizarrity. From the avant-pop of "Hymn 23" or "White Nights" to pan-ethnic soundscapes and soundtracks that employ everything from English horn to Tibetan thighbone (as well as a lot of found sounds), PTV display an ineffable mastery of avant-garde dadaism as well as traditional musicmaking. Like tuning into a radio station overrun by university-educated acid-freaks, **Dreams Less Sweet** provides a thoroughly unpredictable and unsettling, yet profound, experience. The LP originally contained a bonus 12-inch entitled **The Full Pack**. (The cover photograph, while seemingly innocuous, is an astonishingly vulgar visual double entendre. Shades of **Lovesexy**.)

PTV has since continued to release disturbing live albums, featuring different lineups around the P-Orridge-Christopherson-Fergusson core. **Berlin Atonal Vol. 1**, recorded at a festival in December 1983, matches a grisly side of speaker-shredding, grinding, excruciating chaos by PTV with a side by American percussionist Z'ev. The limited edition **N.Y. Scum Haters**—an all-PTV onslaught, captured at New York's Danceteria in November 1983—is better organized and recorded, more varied and sporadically more musical. There's still a lot of fearsome noise, but there's also some respite from the mania. **Berlin Atonal Vol. 2** is shared with a band called La Loora; **Those Who Do Not** is a double-LP live in Iceland. Extending the group's influence into other artistic endeavors, PTV was commissioned to score a ballet, a work which became **Mouth of the Night**.

As strange as it may seem, PTV hit the UK charts in early '86 with a catchy pop single ("Godstar") about Brian Jones; that song was later remixed and included on the group's first-ever American release, **Allegory and Self**, joined by a typical PTV assortment of delicate tapestries and unsettling madness. In the meantime, PTV had begun releasing a series of 23 albums—all concert recordings, titled after the venue's locale—on the 23rd of each month. Squeezing out fourteen British LPs (either some not listed above or somebody has the dates wrong) in eighteen months got the group into the *Guinness Book of World Records*, but Genesis—himself no stranger to hallucinogens—had already turned his attentions to the burgeoning acid house dance scene, finding in the smiley-face warehouse-raves Ecstasy environment the perfect vehicle for his subversive socio-musical plots and semiotic fascinations.

Under the PTV banner and a variety of pseudonyms (including Jack the Tab, a collaboration with journalist Richard Norris and ex-Soft Cell synthesist Dave Ball) used to create all-PTV pseudo-compilation albums, Genesis became a major underground force on the UK dance scene. **Towards thee Infinite Beat** conveys some of what he's been up to: a few songs (like "S.M.I.L.E." and "I.C. Water") co-written by guitarist Fred Giannelli, but mostly varispeed grooves of bass and percussion lightly layered with guitar, keyboards and other instrumental touches as well as non-singing vocals and found-sound debris. Even on the sketchiest constructions, Genesis' demented imagination fills the tracks with enough action to keep them from being totally tedious. **Beyond thee Infinite Beat**, the associated remix record, delves deeper into house with extended—in some cases overhauled and retitled—deconstructions of a half-dozen tracks.   [i]

See also *Dave Ball, Throbbing Gristle*.

PUBLIC ENEMY
Yo! Bum Rush the Show (Def Jam-Columbia) 1987 ●
It Takes a Nation of Millions to Hold Us Back (Def Jam-Columbia) 1988 ●
Fear of a Black Planet (Def Jam-Columbia) 1990 ●

PROFESSOR GRIFF AND THE LAST ASIATIC DISCIPLES
Pawns in the Game (Skyywalker) 1990 (Luke) 1991 ●

Just as sages of the hippie era discovered that a shared musical culture had created a longhaired nation of millions, someone was bound to recognize the political potential of rap for African-American youth in the '80s. That person turned out to be Carlton Ridenhour, a college student from New York's "Strong" (Long) Island. Taking the handle Chuck D, the self-styled lyrical terrorist formed Public Enemy as a militant mouthpiece for an abstractly violent form of black nationalism that owes its aggressive stance (if nothing in the way of a cogent vision) to the Black Panthers. Unlike other educational rappers (most notably Boogie Down Productions), PE is big on image and attitude and, as a result, has caused almost endless controversy in the music community. But as a role model for disaffected B-boys, Chuck D is the articulate embodiment of their frustration and rage. He also happens to be, hands-down, the strongest, most exciting MC ever to rock a microphone.

With PE's characteristic bracing, bustling sound, **Yo! Bum Rush the Show** (produced by Hank Shocklee, Bill Stephney and others) is a brilliant combination of white-hot, hard-edged guitar (largely supplied by Vernon Reid) and odd, off-kilter samples of all descriptions, topped with in-your-face raps by Chuck D and his comical foil, Flavor Flav (William Drayton). Considering what an impact the record had upon its release, it's surprising how few of the tracks actually evince any political perspective whatsoever (even "Public Enemy No. 1" and the provocatively titled "Miuzi Weighs a Ton" are standard DJ boasts; "You're Gonna Get Yours" is about a car). But amid such wheel-spinning, "Rightstarter (Message to a Black Man)" and "Timebomb" reveal the stirrings of an incisive thinker with something much more potent on his mind.

It Takes a Nation of Millions to Hold Us Back— the cover of which pictures Chuck and Flav in a prison cell, under the group's gunsight logo—delivers on **Bum Rush the Show**'s promise with a blistering collection of raps that makes that first album seem like a practice run. "Don't Believe the Hype," "Bring the Noise," "Prophets of Rage," "Rebel Without a Pause," "Party for Your Right to Fight" and others make masterful use of knowledge and language, firing off topical salvos in a dozen directions, dropping names from Marcus Garvey to Minister Farrakhan, J. Edgar Hoover to Margaret Thatcher. While the record's titanic musical power is undeniable, its content polarized listeners, making this one of the first pop albums in history to elevate politics to a crucial aesthetic criterion.

Before PE could make another album, a very public ruckus broke out over crudely absurd anti-Semitic assertions made by Professor Griff (Richard Griffin), the group's minister of ignorance, in a newspaper interview. Attempting to salvage the situation, Chuck D cut Griff loose in June of '89, then dissolved the group—briefly. When PE returned to action, Griff was (temporarily, as it developed) back in the lineup. In January '90, a couple of lines in a pointed new single about the band's troubles ("Welcome to the Terrordome") fanned the embers back into flames, setting the stage for **Fear of a Black Planet**'s release a few months later.

Produced by Shocklee's peerless Bomb Squad, PE's third album is a masterpiece of art and articulation, a roaring subway train of rhythmic noise over which Chuck and Flav (aided, news-style, by relevant spoken-word bites and guests) deliver harangues flowing from a chaotic but rising Afrocentric consciousness. Beyond "Fight the Power"—a spectacular call to arms initially recorded for Spike Lee's *Do the Right Thing*—**Black Planet**'s power is in its topical specificity. "Burn Hollywood Burn" attacks racism in the movies; "911 Is a Joke" takes a potshot at the efficiency of emergency services; "Pollywanacraka" dissects black sexism. "Who Stole the Soul" and "Revolutionary Generation" complain, respectively, about the mistreatment of culture icons and women. (While PE has transcended common rap attitudes about women, homosexuality still gets the shaft on "Meet the G That Killed Me.")

After leaving Public Enemy for good, Griff made a solo album that has all the charm and musical appeal of a religious fanatic ranting to an audience of disciples. Although the strong rhythm tracks are gripping, **Pawns in the Game** isn't about entertainment. In one typical example of the outlandish remarks Griff's bizarre beliefs about science, history and world events lead him to make, he describes the Universal Product Code as "an anti-Christ mechanism." [dgs/i]

PUBLIC IMAGE LTD.

Public Image (nr/Virgin) 1978 ●
Metal Box (nr/Virgin) 1979 ●
Second Edition (Island) 1980 ●
Paris au Printemps (nr/Virgin) 1980 ●
The Flowers of Romance (Warner Bros.) 1981 ●
Live in Tokyo (nr/Virgin) 1983 (Elektra) 1986 ●
This Is What You Want ... This Is What You Get (Elektra) 1984
Commercial Zone (PiL) 1984
Album (Elektra) 1986
Cassette [tape] (Elektra) 1986
Compact Disc [CD] (Elektra) 1986 ●
Happy? (Virgin) 1987 ●
9 (Virgin) 1989 ●
The Greatest Hits, So Far (Virgin) 1990 Φ

The Sex Pistols were a tough act to follow, even for Johnny Rotten. After that band's entropic dissolution, Rotten reclaimed his civilian surname, Lydon, and started Public Image Ltd., supposedly more a way of life than a mere band, "rock" or otherwise.

The first of PiL's many lineups featured Keith Levene (guitar), Jah Wobble (bass) and Jim Walker (drums). The group's opening salvo, **Public Image** (aka **First Issue**, thanks to the album's arch magazine-cover design) couldn't seem to make up its mind between more-or-less straight rock (the unnaturally likable guitar drive of "Public Image") and musical endurance tests. "Annalisa" could be a Led Zeppelin backing track, but other cuts ("Theme," "Fodderstompf") are excruciating and/or self-indulgent. Lydon knew he wanted to annoy, but was still working out the best way to do it.

He hit the green on **Metal Box**, a brilliant statement from original packaging—three 12-inch 45s in an embossed circular tin—to performance. Jah Wobble's overpowering bass sets up throbbing lines around which Keith Levene's guitar and keyboards flick in and out. Lydon wails, chants and moans impressionistic lyrics. A disturbing and captivating milestone. The limited-edition **Metal Box** wasn't cheap to produce, and so the music was reissued as **Second Edition**: two LPs in a gatefold sleeve. **Second Edition** benefits from printed lyrics and funhouse photos, but has inferior sound—this is *tactile* music—and a running order that makes less sense. (**Metal Box** came full conceptual circle in 1990 when it was issued as a single CD in a five-inch tin.)

The live **Paris au Printemps** (**Paris in the Spring**) offers no new material, and may even have been released primarily to stifle a bootleg from the same concert. The band plays well, with drummer Martin Atkins—later a solo artist under the name Brian Brain—more noticeable than on **Metal Box**. But the Parisian audience is barely perceptible. All cover type (title, songs, etc.) is in French. Get the joke?

PiL shows a healthy desire not to repeat itself on **The Flowers of Romance**. With Wobble gone, Lydon relies on other resources; compared to this, **Metal Box** could be played in supermarkets. Lacking a bass, the "band" centers its "songs" around drum patterns and little else. Lydon's romantic imagery dabbles in ghostly apparitions ("Under the House") and Middle East chic ("Four Enclosed Walls"). He also serves up customary rants against hangers-on ("Banging the Door"), women ("Track 8") and Britain ("Go Back," "Francis Massacre"). But the music is so severe as to lend credence to a record executive's statement that **The Flowers of Romance** is one of the most uncommercial records ever made—at least within a "pop" context.

Never a comradely bunch, PiL seemed to unravel beyond repair when Levene left in 1983. But the band had just scored a surprise comeback demi-hit with "(This Is Not a) Love Song," so Lydon rounded up some unknown New Jersey accompanists and went to Japan. Only two of the ten tracks on **Live in Tokyo** are new songs; the faceless recruits are shoved in the back of the sonic mix; the album stretches about 45 minutes of material over two 12-inch 45s without **Metal Box**'s punch. Forget this one.

PiL had started work on **This Is What You Want** before Levene's departure. His guitar parts were wiped off the finished product, leaving them spiked only by Lydon's glum caterwauling. Levene saw to the release of his own version of the session tapes under the name **Commercial Zone**; the music here is considerably more interesting—perhaps even lively. By taking PiL seriously as a career, Lydon committed heresy against punk anomie. But at least he's still excruciating.

The same can't be said for the eminently listenable **Album** (or **Cassette** or **Compact Disc**, depending on your format of choice), which is either the worst sell-out of Lydon's career or the first popular-oriented PiL album ever. Dispensing with noise, free-form aggression and anti-music production, a stack of uncredited musicians play powerful, highly organized, prickly but accessible rock (and, on the brilliant "Rise," demi-pop) while Lydon masterfully bleats in near-tuneful harmony on top. The studio sound (courtesy Lydon and Bill Laswell) is live and virile; the seven tersely named songs ("FFF," "Home," "Ease") are as intelligent and captivating as any in PiL's past. **Album**. Great.

Happy? (co-produced by Gary Langan), hindered only by not-quite-as-good material, continues PiL's productive gambit of playing self-amused footsie with the rock audience. Despite conscious concessions to formal structures and traditions, the record maintains an unbending undercurrent of off-center subversion, manifested in skewed melodies, bizarrely contrapuntal instrumental figures and dub-styled percussion. Joined by a wonderful, tight band—guitarists Lu Edmonds (ex-Damned, etc.) and John McGeoch (ex-Magazine, Siouxsie and the Banshees, Armoury Show), drummer Bruce Smith (Rip Rig + Panic, Float Up CP) and New York bassist Allan Dias—Lydon (or Rotten, depending on his fluctuating preference) is in peak form, creating captivating dance rock ("Seattle," "Hard Times," "The Body," "Fat Chance Hotel") that holds back the bile and intentional aggravation in favor of first-rate musicianship and invention.

If **Album** and **Happy?** were accommodating, the sound of **9** is downright loveydovey. Under the production guidance of Stephen Hague and Eric Thorngren, a four-piece PiL (Edmonds co-wrote the songs but doesn't play on the record) magically channels Lydon's irascible iconoclasm into prickly minor-key rock'n'roll songs that meet timorous listeners more than halfway. In spots, thick layers of guitar, keyboards, close-formation female backing vocals, strings and horns challenge the supremacy of Lydon's declamatory howls, but he rises from the hubbub with wavery aplomb. It may be difficult to take Lydon seriously when he describes himself romantically as a "Warrior," but there's no questioning his sincerity in the venomous "Disappointed." From the electronic dance gimmickry of "Just Like a Woman" (no, not that one) to the galloping, Gang of Four blueprint of "Same Old Story," **9**'s shifting balance of content and presentation makes it a great record.

Following the PiL safari through an unassailable selection of thirteen songs (representing every studio album), **The Greatest Hits, So Far** telescopes a decade of thrashing about in the post-punk underbrush into a spectacular hour of power. Five remixes actually improve the material. The only extraneous item here is "Don't Ask Me," a crappy-sounding song that surprisingly preaches environmental responsibility.   [si/i]

See also *Afrika Bambaataa, Brian Brain, Keith Levene, Sex Pistols, Jah Wobble*.

PURPLE HELMETS
See *Stranglers*.

PURPLE OUTSIDE
See *Screaming Trees*.

PURPLE TOADS
See *Durango 95*.

PURRKUR PILLNIKK
Tilf EP (Ice. Gramm) 1981
Ekki enn (Ice. Gramm) 1981
Googooplex (Ice. Gramm) 1982
No Time to Think EP (Ice. Gramm) 1982
Maskínan (Ice. Gramm) 1983

A quartet of bratty minimalists featuring future Sugarcubes Einar Örn (vocals) and Bragi Olafsson (bass),

Purrkur Pillnikk was the most successful band formed in the early-'80s days of Iceland's post-punk revolution. Although together for only seventeen months, the group recorded lots of material, hit the Icelandic Top 10 with its first album and even toured England with the Fall, their most obvious musical influence.

There's more spit than wit on the teenage group's early releases. The 1981 debut, a ten-song 7-inch released on Gramm (a label co-founded by Einar), was recorded less than a month after the group was formed and sounds it. **Ekki enn** is a distinct improvement; Einar's robust haranguing (a kind of Arctic Circle version of Mark E. Smith) is underscored with pithy, scrappy guitar riffs that rarely outstay their **Pink Flag**-style welcome, although the songs—all seventeen of 'em—do blur together after awhile.

On **Googooplex** (issued as a pair of 12-inch 45s), Purrkur Pillnikk finally hits its musical stride, fortifying that spiky riffing with catchy, angular melodies and locomotive improvising. Einar even sings, after a fashion, in spots. Unfortunately, following a second 7-inch EP (with English lyrics) a few months later, the group broke up. The posthumous **Maskínan** is a ragged-but-righteous live album that captures both the spirit of the band and the Icelandic scene which it helped create.   [df]

See also *Sugarcubes*.

JIMMY PURSEY
Imagination Camouflage (nr/Polydor) 1980
Alien Orphan (nr/Epic) 1982
JAMES T. PURSEY
Revenge Is Not the Password (nr/Turbo) 1983
The Lord Divides (nr/Eskimo Green) 1983

As a solo artist, the earnest Sham 69 mouthpiece took a turn for the artier, leaving behind some of his plain-spoken charm as well as much of his punky obstreperousness in favor of more emotional and creative depth and range. Slide guitar, sax and even synthesizers broaden the instrumental palette of **Imagination Camouflage**; while none of the songs are excellent, they're almost all good. (Renegades from Generation X aided in composition and performance.)

Unfortunately, **Alien Orphan** goes almost too far. Leaving behind the stagey rock of its predecessor for a goulash of electro-rock-funk-jazz often held together by fluid, graceful bass riffing (guitar and keyboard are used only as embroidery), Pursey seems to have forgotten the notion of songs as songs, not elaborate aural concoctions. Still, it's swell background music—a meticulously constructed soundscape—and other than the parts that *do* try to be poignant or obvious, most of it does connect eventually, one way or another.

Revenge is similarly varied in its stylistic concept: eight spare semi-songs that wander off in different directions as if the idea of consistency had never occurred to the artist. Pursey is not the cleverest lyricist or suavest composer in the world, but his heart has always been in the right place and it's hard to denigrate sincerity. Although the album doesn't hold up at all, a few of Pursey's unpredictable forays are odd enough to work.

See also *Sham 69*.   [jg/i]

PUSSY GALORE
Feel Good About Your Body EP (Shove) 1985
Groovy Hate Fuck (Shove) 1986
Exiles on Main Street [tape] 1986
1 Yr. Live [tape] 1986
Pussy Gold 5000 EP (Buy Our) 1987
Right Now! (Caroline) 1987 ●
Groovy Hate Fuck (nr/Vinyl Drip) 1987
Sugarshit Sharp EP (Caroline) 1988
Dial M for Motherfucker (Caroline) 1989 ●
Historia de la Musica Rock (Caroline) 1990 ●
BOSS HOG
Drinkin' Lechin' & Lyin' EP (Amphetamine Reptile) 1989
Cold Hands (Amphetamine Reptile) 1990 ●

The aesthetic dilemma presented by intentionally offensive and/or consciously anti-musical groups is probably best settled by a critical rumble in the alley. There's certainly no rational way to discuss the potential merits of a record like this Washington, DC aim-to-offend quartet's four-song 7-inch debut (**Feel Good About Your Body**) or the eight-song 12-inch **Groovy Hate Fuck**, a raucous one-take no-rehearsal guitar-army tossoff. Setting the question of their atrocious non-musicianship aside, puerile compositions like "Teen Pussy Power," "Cunt Tease" and "Dead Meat" are nothing more than smears of self-satisfied juvenilia. You're *supposed* to be repulsed by Pussy Galore, but that certainly doesn't make this pathetic effluvia worth hearing. Cheap thrills for vulgar sissies.

Relocating to New York and adding a fifth member, Jon Spencer and his crew issued two limited-edition cassettes at the end of 1986: an infamous home-brew version of **Exile on Main Street** (in its entirety) and a live set called **1 Yr. Live**.

With ex-Sonic Youth drummer-turned-metalpounder Bob Bert in the lineup along with stalwarts Julia Cafritz (guitar, vocals), Neil Hagerty (guitar, vocals, organ) and Cristina (Martinez; guitar, organ), the five-song **Pussy Gold 5000** 12-inch displays improved—not good, but better—playing and sound. On the studio tracks, that is. The live "No Count" is as wretched as ever. It's still trash, but not quite as rank as before.

Following further personnel changes (Cristina defected to the Honeymoon Killers), Pussy Galore wound up a quartet: three guitarists (they've never had a bassist) and Bert. The full-length **Right Now!** album, coproduced (without credit) by the group, Steve Albini and Kramer, contains nineteen songs of almost interesting garage raunch. The LP brings Pussy Galore into the realm of artistic consideration but reveals them as a fairly bad noise band. (The CD adds six previously released tracks.) The 1987 **Groovy Hate Fuck** album—released on the Membranes' Vinyl Drip label—is a compilation of the first three records.

Sugarshit Sharp continues Pussy Galore's journey further into the realm of Art; the A-side is a lengthy, sample-ridden cover of Einstürzende Neubaten's "Yu Gung," the most entertaining portions of which are the repeated interpolations of Public Enemy's Flavor Flav saying "Don't believe the hype." Indeed. Side Two contains five grunge tunes of a somewhat higher grade than usual.

The cover art of **Dial M for Motherfucker** looks

like it comes straight from a '70s exploitation flick (an idea that would find its ultimate realization with the Velvet Monkeys' **Rake**, which features Cafritz); the album's sound is more flagrantly pretentious noise than fake garage. As the product of honest bourgeois artistry rather than arch posturing, it's the band's best album. Standouts include the lurching "Understand Me" and the one-joke "Dick Johnson." The CD includes the five songs from the B-side of **Sugarshit Sharp**.

On the other hand, cover art triumphs over content in **Historia de la Musica Rock**, an album done up to look precisely like one of those ultra-cheap Spanish "classic rock" compilations. (The cover photo is atrocious; the liner notes are all in Spanish; the list of other artists in "the series" includes the Rolling Stones, Blodwyn Pig, Murphy's Law and the Cro-Mags.) The record itself—more under-rehearsed ersatz grunge played by a trio of Spencer, Hagerty and Bert—is only intermittently entertaining.

The loosely configured Boss Hog features Spencer, ex-Galore guitarist Kurt Wolf, Jerry Teel of the Honeymoon Killers, Cristina (making her most notable contribution as the records' sexy cover model) and a revolving cast of friends. Produced by Albini, the six-cut 12-inch debut is casual good-natured sex noise with better songs than Pussy Galore can usually muster and better sound than the Honeymoon Killers generally allow, but the offspring definitely favors Spencer's side of the family. The full-length **Cold Hands** moves a bit closer towards the establishment of a Boss Hog audio personality—a louder, more aggressive effort, with grungier, bottom-heavy sound and songs ("Gerard," "Eddy," "Pop Catastrophe") that lurch and groan under the strain of thick rhythm-driven performances.

[i/gk]

See also *Honeymoon Killers, Velvet Monkeys*.

PUSSYWILLOWS

Spring Fever! (Telstar) 1988

New York's Pussywillows have an obvious mania for '60s girl groups like the Shangri-Las—the seven songs on their brief debut (recorded before the band had ever performed live) mix Lisa, Lisa and Elinor's heavily reverbed three-part harmonies with surfy guitar power-pop. All the tracks are covers, borrowed from such relevant obscuros as the Coupons, the Cinderellas and the Short-Cuts. Although some of the lead vocals are shaky and the concept is shamelessly derivative, **Spring Fever!** is nonetheless a goodnatured homage. [kss]

PYLON

Gyrate (DB) 1980
Pylon!! EP (nr/Armageddon) 1980
Chomp (DB) 1983
Hits (DB) 1989 φ
Chain (Sky) 1990 ●

One of the new South's most revered and influential bands, this Athens, Georgia quartet came on like a cross between the B-52's and Gang of Four. Atop thin, almost brittle metallic guitar, muscular bass and no-nonsense drums—which all mesh into stark but inviting dance rhythms—Vanessa Briscoe artlessly shouts/talks/gargles celebrations of life and innocent warnings/wonderings about restrictions on freedom. Though limited in material—the first two records contain about four really good songs all told; the rest are merely okay or repetitive—Pylon is fraught with possibilities for development. The 10-inch **Pylon!!** EP has two of their best, including the dance-club staple, "Cool."

Promise notwithstanding, **Chomp** (produced by Chris Stamey and Gene Holder, both then-dB's) was the quartet's swansong. More ambitious in scope, the record incorporates a psychedelic drone in spots; Pylon sometimes sounds less anxious and strident than before. The album includes both melodic (!) sides of a great preceding single ("Crazy" b/w "M-Train") and other cool slices ("Beep," "Gyrate") of floor-shaking art.

After a half-decade of inaction, the original Pylon reunited and played a mid-'88 show in preparation for a full-fledged resurgence. **Hits**, a 20-track compilation of nearly all their work to date (including both sides of the 1979 "Cool" b/w "Dub" single), cleared the decks with digital sound and set the stage for the band's first new album in seven years.

While retaining the band's traditional bite, **Chain** gets more melody and texture from Briscoe-Hay's singing and Randy Bewley's sharp guitar jabs. The rhythm section cedes not an inch of dancefloor, but very few of the new songs build obsessively on a single chord. (Actually, three seems to be the optimum chord quantity here.) As a result, "Look Alive," "There It Is," "This/That," "Crunch" and others are memorable for more inviting reasons than the old band's tense sonic harangues. If maturity has softened Pylon's edge somewhat, **Chain** is still a strong link (sorry) to the past.

[jg/i]

Q Q Q Q Q Q

Q-FEEL

Q-Feel (Jive) 1983 + 1989

These tiresomely upbeat British techno-poppers recall the giddy chirp of Pilot, getting down to their appointed dance-music chores with mucho polish and absolutely no soul. The popular club single contained here, "Dancing in Heaven (Orbital Be-Bop)," is a descendant of "Pop Muzik," lacking only that song's charm and originality. [i]

Q-TIPS

See *Paul Young*.

QUANDO QUANGO

Pigs + Battleships (nr/Factory) 1985

A masterful assortment of big-beat grooves helped make this Anglo-Dutch quartet popular on dancefloors (if not record stores) on both sides of the Atlantic. Latin and jazz-tinged funk shares the spotlight with reggaefied disco; orchestration is primarily busy percussion beneath bass, keyboards and horns, with mostly tuneless, chanted vocals of lyrics that aren't exactly poetry. Playing and production are uniformly sharp, but Quando Quango was best served by 12-inch dance mixes; an entire LP's worth becomes redundant and forgettable. [dgs]

QUEEN LATIFAH

All Hail the Queen (Tommy Boy) 1989 ●

The talented herald of a welcome new feminist consciousness in hip-hop, New Jersey's dynamic Queen Latifah (Dana Owens) shakes off years of whore-bitch-victim dogma with pride and power, demonstrating that African-American women can redefine roles just by grabbing a mic and refusing to play boys' games. Latifah's first album—a masterful and original collaboration with producer DJ Mark the 45 King and such family friends as De La Soul, Monie Love and Stetsasonic's Daddy-O—is loaded with memorable tracks in a variety of styles: horn-buttered soul ("Dance for Me," "Ladies First"), dub ("The Pros"), high-energy dance ("Come into My House"), Native Tongue hip-pop ("Mama Gave Birth to the Soul Children") and more. (The CD contains three remixes of album tracks.) [i]

QUICK

Mondo Deco (Mercury) 1976
Alpha/Beta EP (Quick Fan Club) 1978

After losing his grip on the Runaways, Kim Fowley discovered the Young Republicans, five male Californians (including drummer Danny Benair) he rechristened the Quick. They aspired to be an adolescent version of Sparks, playing melodic, Anglophilic tunes verging on bubblegum (like, but not as good as, Milk 'n' Cookies). Guitarist/songwriter Steven Hufsteter was pretty much the man in charge, and his limited talents shunted the Quick into a fairly tight mold; **Mondo Deco** is now more of an amusing artifact than it seemed at the time.

Alpha/Beta, a 10-inch souvenir of the group's unsuccessful attempt to court Elektra Records in 1977, came out early the following year through the band's fan club and showed they could draw on far more power than had previously been indicated. They're still basically Anglo/effete but, even on a version of "Somewhere Over the Rainbow," the Quick could manage real punch. [i/jg]

See also *Cruzados, Three O'Clock*.

QUIET SUN

See *Phil Manzanera*.

ROBERT QUINE/FRED MAHER

Basic (Editions EG) 1984 ●

New York guitar master Quine (Voidoids/Lou Reed) and ex-Material drummer Maher recorded a mesmerizing no-frills celebration of the sound of the electric guitar. Over the pro forma mechanized rhythm patterns suggested by the title, the pair lay down their riffs and then Quine embroiders them—magically. Don't look for memorable tunes or even clever tricks—this is a player's album, amazingly pure, though not so simple. [mf]

See also *Jody Harris and Robert Quine, Richard Hell, Lou Reed*.

RADIATORS FROM SPACE
TV Tube Heart (nr/Chiswick) 1977 ●
RADIATORS
Ghostown (nr/Chiswick) 1979 + 1989 ●

London independent label Chiswick discovered these early Irish punk frontiersmen in Dublin; although never a commercial success, the Radiators from Space were a wonderful find. Their recording career, which actually predated the debut vinyl of such first wavers as the Clash and Elvis Costello, evinces talent and intelligence far beyond many of the forgotten bands of that generation.

TV Tube Heart may not have been revolutionary, but energetic delivery of clever and melodic songs about such soon-to-become-hackneyed topics as the music press and club denizens make it a much better survivor of its era than many now hopelessly dated artifacts. From the outset, Radiators from Space showed themselves to be a better breed of punk.

Ghostown, produced by Tony Visconti, is nearly a power pop record with some unsettling flaws damaging another batch of good tunes. One item is almost identical to later Boomtown Rats (although who recorded it first is unclear); there's also a trite '50s homage that seems out of place. **Ghostown** does have its moments, though, and several tracks have the same wonderful feel as the second Fingerprintz LP. Obviously a band with great untapped potential, the Radiators were a surprisingly sophisticated bunch whose records are worth hearing. (The reissue has new artwork, a different track sequence and two cuts from a 1988 reunion.)

In 1985, singer/guitarist Philip Chevron surfaced in association with Elvis Costello as a producer and performer; he then joined the Pogues.   [i]

See also *Pogues*.

RADIO BIRDMAN
Burn My Eye EP (Aus. Trafalgar) 1976
Radios Appear (Aus. Trafalgar) 1977 (Sire) 1978
Living Eyes (Aus. WEA) 1981
More Fun! EP (Aus. WEA) 1988
Under the Ashes (Aus. WEA) 1988 ●
NEW RACE
The First and the Last (nr/Statik) 1982
VISITORS
The Visitors EP (Aus. Citadel) 1982
The Visitors (Aus. Citadel) 1982
DENIZ TEK
Orphan Tracks (Aus. Citadel) 1982 ●

Longtime cult darlings well on their way to becoming one of Australian rock's most enduring legends, Sydney's Radio Birdman sprang from a primordial stew comprised of the Doors, Stooges, MC5 and Blue Öyster Cult. The sextet's 7-inch **Burn My Eye** melded bits from each of those bands and, in so doing, became a durable archetype for the musical explosion that was about to occur. With twangy, reverberated guitar fleshed out by a barrelhouse piano, Rob Younger's commanding vocals and guitarist Deniz Tek's wandering leads, the EP's "Burn My Eye," "Smith and Wesson Blues" and "I-94" are positively revered by fans of the Aussie underground; the fourth ("Snake") is merely terrific.

Like many primal punks in '77 and '78, Radio Birdman was quick to acknowledge and indulge its stylistic ancestry; **Radios Appear** opens with a rendition of the Stooges' "TV Eye." (Born in Ann Arbor, Michigan, Tek played a crucial role in bringing the radical fruits of the American Midwest to Australia when he emigrated there in the early '70s.) While "Anglo Girl Desire" and the raucous Detroit tribute "Do the Pop" flirt with the punk upsurge occurring half a world away, the lengthy "Man with the Golden Helmet" sounds genuinely like 1970 vintage, finding the conceptual spot where the Doors and the Stooges intersected. "Descent into the Maelstrom" incorporates a bit of surf music, "Love Kills" is distressingly dreamy and "New Race," Birdman's rallying cry (dig those "Yeh-Hup!" chants), closes the album.

The Saints opened the world's eyes to Australian punk in late '76, and that group's American label went looking in Sydney and Melbourne to see if there were any more like them back home. Sire wound up issuing an overhauled version of **Radios Appear** with a totally different cover. The international edition retained some of the original's songs—some intact and some re-recorded—and added a chunk of new material, including the phenomenal "Aloha Steve & Danno" (an unapologetic *Hawaii Five-O* swipe coupled with a go-nowhere-life-in-front-of-the-TV narrative by Younger), as well as a hot cover of the 13th Floor Elevators' "You're Gonna Miss Me" and "Hit Them Again," a track co-written by Tek and Stooges guitarist Ron Asheton. The revised edition is a bit more aggressive than the original, but retains the same musical sensibilities.

Hard on the heels of their first (and only) worldwide release, Radio Birdman shut themselves up in a Welsh studio and concocted a fine sounding stack of tracks, **Living Eyes**. Australian fans got to sample the band's clearest recording yet—three years after it was finished. Birdman had broken up one tour after the LP's completion, scattering its members around Australia to go forth and multiply (band-wise), bolstering the country's already thriving underground with numerous new groups. (Canadian-born guitarist Chris Masuak went on to the Screaming Tribesmen. Bassist Warwick Gilbert joined the Lime Spiders.)

Living Eyes is a bit more somber and pensive than its predecessor. Tek coaxes some thoroughly frightening notes from his guitar, and Younger's lyrics conjure up clammy, sweat-soaked images of a world in flames.

There's a flipside, however, on the beachy bubblegum pop of "More Fun" and "Do the Movin' Change." (The LP also contains credible re-recordings of three **Burn My Eye** tracks.) Radio Birdman breathed its last with "Hanging On," three-and-a-half minutes of dense rock'n'roll history.

In 1981, Tek, Younger and Gilbert reunited to form the short-lived (one Australian tour) New Race with Ron Asheton and former MC5 drummer Dennis Thompson. **The First and the Last** is an impressive live record that includes searing renditions of the 5's "Looking at You," several Birdman tracks (including "Love Kills" and "Breaks My Heart") and some new originals. The crisp live mix and some deft studio tinkering make this a walloping good platter.

Younger went on to form the New Christs; Tek was part of the Visitors and had a brief solo career before becoming a flight surgeon in the US Navy. The Visitors, a short-lived project that also included Birdman drummer Ron Keeley, released an album in '82 (previewed on a four-song EP) of semi-memorable tracks (like "Euro Girls") that depart from the pair's past work to focus on an overtly '60s-style Lyres sound that relies heavily on Farfisa-style organ and B-movie kitsch.

Collected from a number of studio sessions, Tek's solo LP (**Orphan Tracks**) largely resembles Birdman's output, sans the intensity and keyboards. On many of the cuts, Tek's vocals are nearly identical to Younger's.

Although it contains only four songs (two drawn from **Living Eyes**), the extremely belated **More Fun!** is the definitive live Birdman record (there are scads of bootlegs as well). **Under the Ashes** is a boxed set (available on multi-disc vinyl or double-CD) of the band's entire legit catalogue: both editions of **Radios Appear**, **Living Eyes**, **Burn My Eye** (here a 12-inch), **More Fun**, a remix of the 1978 "Aloha Steve & Dan-no" single and the New Race album, **The First and the Last**.   [icm]

See also *Lime Spiders, New Christs, New Order, Screaming Tribesmen*.

RADIO STARS

Songs for Swinging Lovers (nr/Chiswick) 1977
The Holiday Album (nr/Chiswick) 1978
Two Minutes, Mister Smith (nr/Moonlight) 1982

Britain's Radio Stars generally had more good ideas than they knew what to do with. On their two original albums they play fast-moving pop/rock with heavy overtones and a penchant for bizarre lyrical matter. On **Songs for Swinging Lovers** (even the cover is a poorly executed great idea), they come on like a 1977 version of singer Andy Ellison's legendary '60s psychedelic pop outfit, John's Children; faster and louder, but still decidedly off-center. Bassist/producer Martin Gordon, fresh from a stint in Sparks (a band many compared to John's Children), supplies the odd ditties, covering such topics as rotting corpses, rapists and macaroni'n'mice casseroles. He even adds a jingle for the group's label, "Buy Chiswick Records." If Gordon's way with a tune were always up to his words, the band might have lived up to its name. But the quality of the material is too inconsistent to sustain interest for a whole album—there's too much dull, repetitive riffing.

The Holiday Album suffers from much the same

malady as its predecessor: too many throwaways. For that reason, **Two Minutes, Mister Smith**, a posthumous compilation of singles and choice album tracks, is *the* Radio Stars album to own. The group's heights were almost all achieved on singles, especially the brilliant "From a Rabbit," a kitchen-sink pop production number of the highest order, included here.   [ds]

RAGE TO LIVE

Rage to Live (Bar/None) 1986
Blame the Victims (Bar/None) 1990 •

JONATHAN BOROFSKY/ED TOMNEY

The Radical Songbirds of Islam [tape] (ROIR) 1987

The dissolution of New York's Individuals produced a number of positive developments. Doug and Janet Wygal formed a group (under their family name) which later included ex-dB Gene Holder; Glenn Morrow launched Bar/None Records (which brought out fine records by They Might Be Giants and others) and formed Rage to Live with ex-Necessaries leader Ed Tomney. Morrow's limited voice proves no serious impediment to enjoyment of the first album's well-written, exuberantly played melodies. Almost a sampler of New York/Hoboken styles, Morrow's songs lean from mild soul to twangy cow-pop to a Marshall Crenshaw-like gossamer; the quartet plays 'em clean and sweet.

A crude and careless electric cover of Crosby, Stills and Nash's "Suite Judy Blue Eyes" sets the general energy level but not the quality range for **Blame the Victims**, another fine set built on conscientious variety. With a few nods to the first record's polite pop, Rage to Live plays it a little harder and rougher this time. Besides the gently alluring "Deep Blue Sea," the countryish "Divorcee" and the Dylanesque "Again & Again," there's gritty Gang of Four-ish funk ("Sexy #'79"), taut garage rock ("Fireman"), parodic Led Zeppelin quotes ("Joker's Punch") and richly tuneful heartland rock ("My Heroine"). The CD includes eight songs from the first album.

Tomney's side project with conceptual artist Jonathan Borofsky, which involves computer-directed tape manipulation of Borofsky's vocals, is an intriguing but ultimately tedious ambient experiment that sounds like a cellist practicing random notes.   [i]

See also *Grace Pool, Individuals, Necessaries*.

RAGING SLAB

Assmaster (Buy Our) 1987
Raging Slab (RCA) 1989 •

Imagine the thundering '70s sludge that would erupt from a Cuisinart containing Grand Funk Railroad, Blue Öyster Cult, Kiss and Molly Hatchet. That Raging Slab—a New York quintet led by two Washington DC escapees with roots in hardcore and art-funk and bottleneck guitarist Elyse Steinman—can make all this retro nonsense sound relevant today is no small achievement, but frequent dips into the speedmetal jug help.

Despite an ultra-trebly mix that levels the sonic abilities of a high-tech stereo system with those of an AM portable, **Assmaster** cranks. Slab's molten fusion of chicken-fried metal and meaty '70s power rock is exciting as hell, and singer/guitarist Gregory Strzempka's lyrics—chock full of transparent double entendres and celebrations of chemical recreation—are never less than prurient. The record is even packaged with its own nifty comic book.

Besides much better songwriting, the band's self-titled major-label debut greatly benefits from Daniel Rey's muscular production. "Don't Dog Me," "Joy Ride" and "Bent for Silver" steamroll past with all the force of a fleet of monster trucks, while "Sorry's All I Got" possesses the kind of big fat hook .38 Special used to ride up the charts. All in all, **Raging Slab** is a wonderful reminder that not all guilty pleasures come from Sweden.   [db]

RAHEEM

The Vigilante (Rap-a-Lot-A&M) 1988 ●

Signed to the majors in the record industry's mad rush to get hip-hop of any sort onto the roster, this Houston rapper (a labelmate of the Ghetto Boys) came up with a great-sounding album that didn't have a commercial prayer. Under Raheem's raps—a mix of mack/gangster crap and less outrageous boasting—the tracks break out into reggae ("Punks Give Me Respect"), hard soul ("Dance Floor") and hard rock ("Shotgun"). In the most intriguing innovation, "Freak to Me" nearly dispenses with drum/bass beats for an effective rhythmic keyboard/turntable pulse. (The CD adds one.) [i]

RAILROAD JERK

Railroad Jerk (Matador) 1990 ●

By dragging Lower East Side New York scum-rock on a *Christmas Carol* jaunt with the ghost of the Gun Club, this scaly foursome rocks in a hellhound-on-your-tail world all its own. Led by Marcellus Hall (guitar, vocals, harmonica) and Chris Mueller (guitar, vocals), Railroad Jerk takes Led Zeppelin's worst mistreatment of the blues and crosses it with a simpler, more spirited (but ironically lighter) swamp sensibility. Stopping well short of Crampsian luridity, this casual and freewheeling album offers a powerful contrast of dark personality and knotty melodicism; a fascinating Northern realization of Southern roots music that exists outside of specific time and place.   [dss/i]

RAILWAY CHILDREN

Reunion Wilderness (nr/Factory) 1987 (Virgin) 1987 ●
Recurrence (Virgin) 1988 ●
Native Place (Virgin) 1990 φ

Named after a 1971 film, this young light Anglo-pop quartet from Wigan (near Manchester) sounds like any number of other northern groups, from the Smiths to James to Aztec Camera. Somehow, the group wound up on the usually adventurous Factory, releasing the singles compiled on the **Reunion Wilderness** mini-album (expanded by two tracks for American release). Gary Newby's attractive voice is the band's only notable asset; otherwise this exercise in ringing electric guitars and briskly strummed acoustics is entirely routine.

With two real producers (Jamie Lane and Bruce Lampcov) working the board, Railway Children show a little more stylistic breadth on **Recurrence**, but Newby's songs have yet to demonstrate any special strength

or character that would elevate the records beyond mere pleasantness. (And his voice doesn't sound as richly expressive as it did the first time out.)

The overbearing **Native Place** adds synthesized keyboards, sampled drums, loud guitars and other rock attributes to a new batch of tunes. No longer an unassuming pop group, the Railway Children are growing into dance-oriented chart hacks. "You're young/ And it feels all wrong/To be someone you're not." Exactly.   [i]

RAINCOATS

The Raincoats (nr/Rough Trade) 1979
Odyshape (Rough Trade) 1981
The Kitchen Tapes [tape] (ROIR) 1983
Animal Rhapsody EP (nr/Rough Trade) 1983
Moving (nr/Rough Trade) 1984

The Raincoats introduced four English women parked on the fringes of conventional pop music. Or are they just an avant-garde edition of the Roches? The harmonies are there and the lyrics are esoteric and philosophical, eschewing predictable sentiments, but the music comes together only in spurts. A cover version of "Lola" plays havoc with that song's gender enigma. The rest of the songs just play havoc.

On **Odyshape**, the scope of the band's sound expands; the mingling of snappy acoustic and jangly electric guitars provides saner contrast to the violin shrieks. There's even a poignant song about a girl who's "Only Loved at Night." But the Raincoats are still no easy listen.

The Kitchen Tapes captures a December 1982 New York show, on which the Raincoats are supported by three demi-monde musicians. The playing, while still a bit low on the virtuosity index, shows refinement and development. In spots, the Raincoats spin a shimmery curtain of lovely sound; elsewhere, pan-cultural percussion supports fascinating vocal arrangements. But their potential for cacophony (better organized than before, but boisterous nonetheless) will keep you alternately straining to hear and jamming your fingers in your ears. **Moving** reprises some of the material from the live cassette; the four-song **Animal Rhapsody** EP in turn reprises two from the LP.   [gf/i]

RAIN PARADE

Emergency Third Rail Power Trip (Enigma) 1983 ●
Explosions in the Glass Palace EP (Enigma) 1984 ●
Beyond the Sunset (Restless) 1985
Crashing Dream (Island) 1986

VIVA SATURN

Viva Saturn EP (Heyday) 1988

VARIOUS ARTISTS

Rainy Day (Serpent-Enigma) 1984 (Serpent-Rough Trade) 1989 ●

Like most of the bands implicated in the West Coast psychedelic revival (the paisley underground, if you will), Rain Parade has a better ear for style than for substance. Most of the genre's bands tend to make very deft, subtle music but have nothing to say; Rain Parade at least knows the nuances of form better than anyone else. And if the Velvet Underground-meets-the Lemon

Pipers pop sound tells more about who they like than who they are, at least the Paraders have good taste.

Emergency Third Rail Power Trip is a gentle record with neatly crafted songs and mildly trippy textures. However, the retreat into style discourages listener identification and, while the songs make good background music, as foreground they're a snore. **Explosions in the Glass Palace** is a somewhat misleading title: there are, in fact, no explosions on this five-song EP. But the sound is filled out and less generic. The record has a dreamlike quality—where the band once sounded lethargic, it now waxes hypnotic. The psychedelic touches, rather than offering a running historical narrative filled with inside jokes, give the pop structures some depth. Not a glandular jolt, but a nice quiet listen. (**Explosions** is included on the **Emergency Third Rail** CD.)

The live-in-Japan **Beyond the Sunset** (originally released in Japan as **Behind the Sunset**—that's geography for you), which introduces a new drummer as well as a replacement for guitarist David Roback, is a mite redundant—five songs are from the two previous discs, with three more originals and covers of Television and Green on Red—but not badly executed.

Crashing Dream, Rain Parade's major label debut, has one simply beautiful song ("Depending on You"). Another ("Mystic Green") sounds uncannily like the Records, while "Don't Feel Bad" hybridizes two Beatles songs (you figure out which ones). The album is attractive but flimsy—competent technique in search of a spine and a direction. In other words, it sounds like the work of a band on the verge of breaking up—which, in fact, Rain Parade did not long after the album's release.

With David Roback off leading, in turn, Opal and Mazzy Star, his bass-playing brother (joined by another Rain Parade alumnus, guitarist John Thoman, and several sidemen) reemerged at the helm of Viva Saturn. The eponymous five-song 12-inch—a relaxed, wistful and intermittently rocking disc—finds him mining familiar musical territory in an unselfconscious continuation of his former band's good work.

While the Rain Parade was still a going concern, David Roback organized and produced **Rainy Day**, a heartfelt but uneven paisley underground supersession, with members of the Bangles, Three O'Clock, Dream Syndicate and Rain Parade covering their fave tunes by the Velvets, Bob Dylan, Alex Chilton, Jimi Hendrix, Who, Beach Boys, etc. The simple arrangements and enthusiastic readings are fine-to-sublime, but the casual vocal performances are occasionally one-take second-rate.

As a bizarre but not entirely inappropriate postscript, Rain Parade guitarist Matt Piucci went on to record an album with Neil Young's sometime band, Crazy Horse. See also *Opal, Windbreakers*.   [jl/i/hd]

RAIN TREE CROW
See *Japan*.

RAMONES
Ramones (Sire) 1976 ●
Leave Home (Sire) 1977 ●
Rocket to Russia (Sire) 1977

Road to Ruin (Sire) 1978
It's Alive (nr/Sire) 1979
End of the Century (Sire) 1980
Pleasant Dreams (Sire) 1981
Subterranean Jungle (Sire) 1983
Too Tough to Die (Sire) 1984
Animal Boy (Sire) 1986
Halfway to Sanity (Sire) 1987 ●
Ramones Mania (Sire) 1988 ●
Brain Drain (Sire) 1989 ●
End of the Decade (nr/Beggars Banquet) 1990
All the Stuff (And More) Volume One (Sire) 1990 φ

VARIOUS ARTISTS
Rock'n'Roll High School (Sire) 1979 ●

DEE DEE KING
"Funky Man" (Rock Hotel) 1987
Standing in the Spotlight (Sire) 1989 ●

With just four chords and one manic tempo, New York's Ramones blasted open the clogged arteries of mid-'70s rock, reanimating the music. Their genius was to recapture the short/simple aesthetic from which pop had strayed, adding a caustic sense of trash-culture humor and minimalist rhythm guitar sound. The result not only spearheaded the original new wave/punk movement, but also drew the blueprint for subsequent hardcore punk bands, most of whom unfortunately neglected the essential pop element.

Ramones almost defies critical comment. The fourteen songs, averaging barely over two minutes each, start and stop like a lurching assembly line. Joey Ramone's monotone is the perfect complement to Johnny and Dee Dee's precise guitar/bass pulse. Since the no-frills production sacrifices clarity for impact, printed lyrics on the inner sleeve help even as they mock another pretentious convention—although the four-or-five-line texts of "Now I Wanna Sniff Some Glue," "I Don't Wanna Walk Around with You" and "Loudmouth" are an anti-art of their own. Like all cultural watersheds, **Ramones** was embraced by a discerning few and slagged off as a bad joke by the uncomprehending majority. It is now inarguably a classic.

The slightly glossier **Leave Home** is cut from the same cloth: another Ramones' dozen (fourteen hits) and under a half-hour in length. The band's warped Top 40 aspirations emerge on "I Remember You" and "Swallow My Pride," sandwiched between such anthems as "Gimme Gimme Shock Treatment" and "Pinhead." Like "Let's Dance" on **Ramones**, "California Sun" relates the band to the pandemic moronity that has always informed the best rock'n'roll.

Rocket to Russia is the culmination of the Ramones' primal approach. Virtually all fourteen tracks (including ideally chosen golden oldies "Do You Wanna Dance?" and "Surfin' Bird") are well-honed in execution, arrangement and songwriting wit. Clean production streamlines toe-tappers like "Cretin Hop," "Teenage Lobotomy" and "Rockaway Beach," and emphasizes Joey's increasingly expressive singing on two ballads, "I Don't Care" and "I Wanna Be Well." The LP also contains the Ramones' naïve first attempt at a hit single, "Sheena Is a Punk Rocker."

"Sheena" only scraped the charts, and drummer Tommy Ramone (né Erdelyi) left, to be replaced by ex-Voidoid (and ex-Dust!) Marky Ramone (né Marc

Bell). The Ramones had spewed out well over 40 tracks (including a couple of B-sides) inside of two years. They next emerged with **Road to Ruin**, an understandably downbeat collection. Desperate to join the mainstream, the band lengthened its material, even breaking the three-minute barrier on "I Wanted Everything" and "Questioningly," a touching love song. Despite the perky "I Wanna Be Sedated," pretty "Don't Come Close" and oldie "Needles and Pins," **Road to Ruin** is a bit lackluster; earlier raveups, unlike "I'm Against It" and "Go Mental," never sounded forced. A rethink seemed in order.

Meanwhile, the band lent their musical and dramatic talents to the movie *Rock'n'Roll High School*. The soundtrack album includes two new compositions (one the theme song), an eleven-minute live medley of previously recorded tunes, plus the Ramones backing the Paley Brothers ("C'mon Let's Go") and co-star P.J. Soles (on a different version of "Rock'n'Roll High School"). Appropriate songs by various artists fill out the record. Anyone whose appetite for live Ramones was whetted by the film soundtrack should seek out **It's Alive**, a two-disc London concert recording (with Tommy drumming) that pretty much reprises their first three albums.

End of the Century features intimidating production by the legendary Phil Spector. The band responds with a good brace of songs whose polish and (relative) wordiness show them outgrowing punk. Dubious bonus: Joey warbling "Baby, I Love You." On the Graham Gouldman-produced **Pleasant Dreams**, the Ramones move away from their pioneering minimalism into heavy metal territory, although distinctive lyrics proved they hadn't lost their grasp of teenage angst.

Subterranean Jungle put the Ramones back to where they once belonged: junky '60s pop adjusted for current tastes. That means not only a couple of acid-age oldies ("Time Has Come Today," "Little Bit o' Soul") but original tunes with male protagonists hung up on girls and themselves. It also means easing off the breakneck rhythm that was once Ramones dogma. **Subterranean Jungle** is an underrated item in the band's canon.

On **Too Tough to Die**—with Richie Ramone (Reinhardt) as the new drummer and Tommy Erdelyi returning as co-producer—the Ramones got serious about stealing back some thunder from the hardcore punk scene they'd inspired. The sound is more ferocious than ever, and they dip back into quick-hit song lengths. Some by-now predictable macho sentiments (the title track, "I'm Not Afraid of Life") are offset by the token dose of sensitivity ("Howling at the Moon," guest-produced by Eurythmician Dave Stewart). But the Eddie Cochranesque "No Go" that closes the album shows they haven't lost their sense of humor.

The Ramones' big release in, what was for them, an otherwise quiet 1985 was "Bonzo Goes to Bitburg," a topical UK 45 assailing Ronald Reagan for the itinerary of his German vacation. That song, retitled "My Brain Is Hanging Upside Down," turned up on **Animal Boy**. Produced by ex-Plasmatic Jean Beauvoir, the Ramones resemble a straight rock band as never before (mostly in the drum sound and articulated rhythm guitar). The animal-theme record has typically entertaining entries (Richie's "Somebody Put Something in My Drink," a

wistful ballad called "She Belongs to Me," the hopefully anthemic "Something to Believe In"); Dee Dee (the LP's main songwriter) affects a quasi-British accent to sing "Love Kills," a Pistols-styled tribute to Sid'n'Nancy that wasn't used in Alex Cox's film. Meanwhile, the nostalgically terse "Eat That Rat" is the Ramones' closest brush with punk in eons.

The years of stylistic foundering ended on **Halfway to Sanity**, a confident-sounding dose of Ramones fundamentalism. The dozen cuts mix basic guitar riffs ("I Know Better Now," "Bop 'Til You Drop") and effervescent pop ("Go Lil' Camaro Go," with guest vocals by Debbie Harry, "A Real Cool Time"), adding some of the most intriguingly thoughtful lyrics ("I Wanna Live," "Garden of Serenity") in the band's career. This encouraging return to near-top form also benefits from gutsy rock production by the band and guitarist Daniel Rey. (The UK CD adds the bubblegum classic "Indian Giver" and "Life Goes On.") Upon the album's release, Richie quit over a salary dispute and Marc Bell reclaimed the drummer's seat.

The **Ramones Mania** compilation packs in 30 digitally remastered cuts (some of the tracks sound ace; others don't fare so well), adding detailed annotation and Billy Altman's voluminous liner notes. Although the song selection is straightforward, the running order is entirely non-chronological; a British B-side ("Indian Giver"), a previously unvinylized movie mix of "Rock-'n'Roll High School" and a couple of 45 versions make it mildly attractive to collectors. Despite such dubious inclusions as "Commando," "Wart Hog" and "Momma's Boy," **Ramones Mania** isn't a bad textbook for Ramones 101.

Besides a T-shirt and poster, the luxurious limited edition (2,500) boxed set entitled **End of the Decade** contains half a dozen UK 12-inch singles (with some B-side rarities), dating from 1984-'87. A strange era to cover in such an expensive package.

The uneven quality of **Brain Drain**—produced with no special character by Bill Laswell—is most easily understood in light of Dee Dee's subsequent departure from the band. Clinging together in an uneasy alliance, the Ramones here sound aimless and diffuse on all but a few tracks. So while the album sinks to the grumbly "Don't Bust My Chops," it also rises to deliver the anthemic inspirational message of "I Believe in Miracles," the clumsy but convincing "Pet Sematary" (indulging Stephen King's rock music fandom for a horror film theme), and the poignant if unseasonal "Merry Christmas (I Don't Want to Fight Tonight)." Like a shopworn ghost, the band's negligible cover of "Palisades Park" punkifies a pop classic (well, a familiar pop oldie) with little of the bratty hubris that once invigorated such endeavors.

Dee Dee has tried to go solo twice (so far) with no success. Redubbing himself Dee Dee King, the goofy bassist made an inexcusably stupid rap-rock 12-inch ("Funky Man") in 1987, and then released an entire album just months prior to **Brain Drain**. And he *still* went ahead and left the group. **Standing in the Spotlight** finds him talking over music, but it's hardly a rap record; Dee Dee's nerdy sense of rhythm, inane good-time lyrics and la-de-da delivery make it a laughable disaster. The slickness of the Daniel Rey-produced/played tracks—a variety show of rock, oldies and pop idioms (with minor assists from Debbie Harry and others)—only underscores the star's awfulness. Most embarrassing are two surprising stabs at autobiography: the schmaltzy "Baby Doll" and the (hypothetically) bilingual "German Kid," which contains the eminently mortal "It's pretty cool to be half German."

All the Stuff (And More) Volume One looks like another greatest hits compilation, but is actually the one-CD/cassette pairing of **Ramones** and **Leave Home**, combined with two previously unreleased demos, a 1977 B-side ("Babysitter") and a live pairing of "California Sun" with "I Don't Wanna Walk Around with You." Piling 33 of these terse explosions of punk-pop genius onto one non-stop program makes for an avalanche of fun. [si/i]

See also *Holly and the Italians, Rattlers.*

RANDY RAMPAGE
See *D.O.A.*

LEE RANALDO
See *Sonic Youth.*

RANK AND FILE
Sundown (Slash-Warner Bros.) 1982
Long Gone Dead (Slash-Warner Bros.) 1984
Rank and File (Rhino) 1987 ●

Rank and File first came together in Austin, Texas, although three of its four original members were Californians who had played in San Diego's Dils and San Francisco's Nuns. The distance from those early punk outfits is more than geographical: Rank and File was formed to play delicately crafted cowboy rock. (Imagine if Marshall Crenshaw had been raised on a straight diet of Hank Williams.) David Kahne's production of **Sundown** gives a squeaky clean sound to the tuneful and tasty pop numbers, which also benefit from pretty harmonies and confident playing. Effortlessly enjoyable.

But, alas, too good to last. **Long Gone Dead** retains only half the band—brothers Chip and Tony Kinman (the main creative force on **Sundown**, writing almost all the songs)—joined by such temps as Tom Petty drummer Stan Lynch. It's hard to pin down the problem: **Long Gone Dead** has all the right ingredients but only a skimpy bit of **Sundown**'s evocative magnificence. Perhaps it's Jeff Eyrich's production, which is fussier than Kahne's and partially obscures the Kinmans' melody-laden writing and rich vocals. Lacking the first LP's lost and lonesome prairie feel, **Long Gone Dead** is appealing but disappointing.

Hanging onto **Long Gone Dead** guitarist Jeff Ross, the Kinmans added a permanent drummer and kept going, but didn't release another album for three years. The loud run-of-the-mill rock production on **Rank and File** doesn't totally obscure the melodies and Tony's fine voice, but the band's wandering personality all but evaporates in the guitar solos, bass riffs and overeager drumming. [i]

See also *Blackbird, Dils, True Believers.*

ALAN RANKINE
See *Associates.*

RANKING ROGER
See *(English) Beat, General Public.*

RAPED
Pretty Paedophiles EP (nr/Parole) 1977

CUDDLY TOYS
Guillotine Theatre (nr/Fresh) 1981
Trials and Crosses (nr/Fresh) 1982

As (lower) class-of-'77 punks, these London buttheads released a 7-inch EP of sub-Clash pop aggression which included their idiotic but hardly shocking 1:20 theme song, "Raped." Along with a name change to Cuddly Toys, the quartet dyed their hair, donned androgynous threads and began playing Bowie-style glam-rock. Despite an auspicious debut 45 (covering "Madman," the only song ever co-written by Bowie and Marc Bolan), their first album is merely a pathetic attempt to clone **Ziggy Stardust**; lacking anything original or clever to add, it's a total flop. **Trials and Crosses**, by a revamped lineup (retaining only singer Sean Purcell), tries to be more modern by adding early-'80s rhythms and keyboards, but comes up similarly devoid of creativity and substance. [i]

RAPEMAN
Budd EP (Touch and Go) 1988 ●
Two Nuns and a Pack Mule (Touch and Go) 1989 ●

Between the dissolution of Big Black and his career as a noise-loving record producer, Chicago's Steve Albini led this steel-edged thrash trio, whose crudely provocative name (borrowed from a Japanese comic character) contributed to the brevity of its existence. Three of the four songs on the **Budd** 12-inch were recorded live and loose, an unfocused batch of impressive shards that doesn't make a convincing introduction to the group.

Two Nuns and a Pack Mule (which, like **Budd**, has a nifty die-cut cover) fits Albini's distinctive melt-down guitar and shriek vocals into rough song forms outlined by the ex-Scratch Acid rhythm section of David Wm. Sims (bass) and Rey Washam (drums). Whether paraphrasing Sonic Youth ("Kim Gordon's Panties"), dismantling '70s rock ("Radar Love Lizard"), slowly discussing sex scenarios ("Trouser Minnow") or revving up ambiguously intended furiosities ("Hated Chinee"), Rapeman spits out sparks with the conviction of Albini's acerbic intelligence. (Both records are on a single CD.) [i]

See also *Big Black, Jesus Lizard.*

RAS MICHAEL
See *Bad Brains.*

RAT AT RAT R

Rock & Roll Is Dead, Long Live Rat At Rat R (Neutral) 1985
Stainless Steel/Free Dope for Cops & Kids EP (Purge/Sound League) 1988
Rat at Rat R (Sound League) 1991

Rat At Rat R (you figure out the anagram, sport) was one of the brighter lights of the NYC noise-groove scene back in '83. Originally hailing from Philadelphia, the quartet was formed in '81 by poet/guitarist Victor Poison-tête, and reassembled on the Lower East Side a year or so later. Their craven guitar-crack, female bass player (Glenn Branca's cousin, Sonda Andersson), and shouty-dunty approach to tunerism soon put them in the company of Live Skull, Swans and Sonic Youth. At the time, Rat At Rat R was probably the most trad-sounding of these combos, but the group imploded before garnering much positive notice outside its neighborhood. The records combine swinging, fucked-up guitar rock with neo-artsy mouth action. [bc]

RATIONAL YOUTH

Cold War Night Life (Can. YUL) 1982
Rational Youth EP (Can. Capitol) 1983
Heredity (Capitol) 1985

Although the Montreal synthesizer trio occasionally lapses into lyrical pomposity, for the most part, Rational Youth serves up fresh sounds and workable songs that show lots of promise. A bit like early Human League but better-natured, Cold War Night Life is a well-produced LP from talented technicians with minds *and* hearts.

Rational Youth added a drummer and exchanged another member by the time of the major-label EP, a slick and poppy five-song 12-inch that includes a remake of the first LP's "Just a Sound in the Night" and two previews (the OMD-derived "In Your Eyes" and "Holiday in Bangkok") of the second album.

With an altogether different lineup (singer/synthesist Tracy Howe is the only holdover; ex-Klaatu guitarist Dee Long is his main collaborator), Heredity blends in more guitar for increased commercial appeal, but maintains a certain down-to-earth spunkiness that distinguishes Rational Youth from other post-Duran tech-pop bands. Flash of fame footnote: the group was later featured—on the soundtrack and in a concert scene—in an early Kiefer Sutherland movie called *Crazy Moon*. [i]

RATTLERS

Rattled! (PVC) 1985

Led by Joey Ramone's soundalike younger brother Mickey Leigh, New York's Rattlers take a less stylized but equally sincere approach to essential '60s pop on Rattled!, a swell LP of zesty originals and cool covers partially produced by ex-Ramone Tommy Erdelyi. The quartet uses a touch of keyboards and neat vocal harmonies to dress up simply drawn tunes like the melodic "I Won't Be Your Victim," the beat-era "Pure + Simple" and imaginary monster-movie theme song "On the Beach." An ace version of the Nightcrawlers' classic "Little Black Egg" is worth the price of admission, but the rest of the LP won't disappoint either. [i]

See also *Lester Bangs*.

RAUNCH HANDS

El Rauncho Grande EP (Relativity) 1985
Learn to Whap-a-Dang with the Raunch Hands (Relativity) 1986
Payday (Crypt) 1989
Have a Swig (Crypt) 1990

In their mid-'80s heyday (such as it was), New York's Raunch Hands were retro-rock representatives of that presumed golden age of sleaze, the mid-'50s to mid-'60s. Thus El Rauncho Grande offers neo-rockabilly, neo-R&B and even neo-Mex, all filtered through the band's beer-heightened (lowered?) sensibilities. Learn to Whap-a-Dang is less quaint than the EP, and its denser band sound helps the Raunch Hands barrel through their own R&B: Raucous & Bawdy. Mike Chandler isn't much of a singer, but attitude counts for a lot here, and guitarist Mike Tchang's occasional sax is a definite plus. Too bad their originals (about half of each record) can't match the '50s obscurities for sheer mindlessness—not counting Whap-a-Dang's "Kangaroo Juice," an "original" stolen from Eddie Cochran.

On following recordings the band increased its songwriting contributions, with mixed results. The last thing the Raunch Hands' chosen genre needs is ambition, and Payday sometimes chokes on it; thus "Detox Moon," an over-five-minute (!!) wino response to the Stones' "Moonlight Mile." The schoolyard couplets of "Bottle-Now!" (in praise of cheap booze) and immature humor of "Hare-Raisin' " (in praise of the Raunch Hands' hapless career) prove that less is definitely more.

Which may be why Have a Swig is under a half-hour long. Highlights here include a lascivious stomp, "Everybody Loves Yo' Mama," and the less-than-existential "Naked, Naked, Naked." More power to these guys, whose gutter-view perspective has undeniable aroma and charm. [si]

See also *Outta Place*.

RAVE-UPS

Class Tramp EP (Fun Stuff) 1984
Town + Country (Fun Stuff) 1985
The Book of Your Regrets (Epic) 1988 •
Chance (Epic) 1990 •

At the time they were being touted as the next big thing to erupt from the LA club scene, the Rave-Ups were working in the mailroom and warehouse of A&M Records. Although launched by singer/guitarist Jimmer Podrasky in Pittsburgh, the group on the 1984 EP was a quartet he assembled in California. Class Tramp is a mighty impressive debut: a hook-laden six-song rocking pop collection that reveals Podrasky as an inventive, commercially minded songwriter with a wealth of ideas and a fresh lyrical perspective. Richly multi-tracked guitars, crisp rhythms and easy-to-like vocals buttress original tunes that deftly sidestep power pop and other pigeonholes.

Podrasky and drummer Timothy Jimenez acquired a new bassist and guitarist before recording the refined *and* ruralized Town + Country, a good (not great) record that gives away some of the EP's '60sish pluck to take an energetic crack at unstylized Southwestern twang and winds up sounding a shade or two less distinguished than before. Pedal-steel master Sneaky Pete Kleinow plays on two tracks. The record still manages a fair amount of variety: "Remember (Newman's Love-song)" is almost a bluegrass breakdown done as a rock song, while "Positively Lost Me" (one of two songs the band performed on camera for *Pretty in Pink*; A&M graciously left the tunes off the soundtrack LP) tells of a broken relationship with only a mild country touch. The lighthearted Beach Boys car-song parody of "In My Gremlin" harks back to **Class Tramp**; Dylan's "You Ain't Goin' Nowhere" becomes an uptempo rocker.

The Rave-Ups had legal problems getting off Fun Stuff and couldn't find the record industry's on-ramp for a long while. Three years passed before Epic issued **The Book of Your Regrets**, a downcast but determined effort. Guitarist Terry Wilson takes a more prominent role here, co-writing most of the material with Podrasky and expanding his instrumental contribution to include mandolin, keyboards and harmonica. While retaining a glimmer of the previous LP's country inflection, this well-produced (by David Leonard) record leans towards the textured, harmony-laden sound of West Coasters like Translator, Peter Case and Wire Train. Consistently invigorating and remarkably original, **The Book of Your Regrets** signals the Rave-Ups' unyielding vitality and creative resources.

The uneven **Chance** (named after Podrasky's infant son, whose photograph appears on the album cover) repaints the previous album's strong western folk-rock sound with a mild '60s psychedelic overcoat and a more optimistic view of life. Despite occasional clunkiness in the writing and performances, **Chance** has the surging "She Says (Come Around)," the Televisionesque "Hamlet Meets John Doe," the rip-snorting "The Best I Can't" and a few other songs with equally oblique titles to recommend it. [i]

RAW POWER

Screams from the Gutter (Toxic Shock) 1985
Wop Hour EP (Toxic Shock) 1986
After Your Brain (Toxic Shock) 1987

In an interesting bit of Euro-American hardcore fraternity, the debut album by this Italian punk band—five guys from Reggio—was recorded in Indiana and issued by a California label. On **Screams from the Gutter**, Raw Power plays genre creations like "Hate," "Nihilist," "Bastard" and "My Boss" with fiery punk venom, helpfully singing them in English. (The cassette adds the contents of **Wop Hour**, a subsequent four-song 7-inch.)

After Your Brain offers far better production and more instrumental refinement, but Raw Power still burns up the grooves on thirteen new cuts like "You Are Fired," "We Shall Overcome," "Shut Up" and "What For." Mauro's careful diction makes him clearer and more understandable than many American vocalists; the two guitarists (one of them a new arrival in the band) work hard to avoid sounding routine. A powerful piece of work. [i]

RAYBEATS

Roping Wild Bears EP (nr/Don't Fall off the Mountain)
 1981

Guitar Beat (PVC) 1981
It's Only a Movie! (Shanachie) 1983

DANNY AMIS

Whiplash! EP (Coyote) 1983

With so many late-'70s musicians possessing a strong sense of rock'n'roll history in addition to their overriding interest in style, the emergence of groups like the instrumental Raybeats was inevitable. Pat Irwin, Jody Harris and Don Christensen, refugees from the New York City no wave avant-garde, had been in such outfits as the Contortions and 8 Eyed Spy. Together (with a procession of bassists including, on **Guitar Beat**, Minneapolis' Danny Amis), they made frothy rock dance pieces, recalling the tightly structured formats of the Ventures, Duane Eddy and the Shadows. The simple melodies are defined by sparkling guitars, junky organ and wailing sax—a golden opportunity for most educated bands to condescend. But the Raybeats never did. They obviously enjoyed what they were playing, and that made their records absolutely kinetic.

The **Wild Bears** EP offers four songs (including the Shadows' "Rise and Fall of Flingel Bunt") on a 12-inch. The UK and US versions of the peppy **Guitar Beat**, ably produced by Martin Rushent, differ by two tracks. **It's Only a Movie!** introduces electronic instruments (and ceramic destruction on "Doin' the Dishes") to remind listeners of the band's actual time frame, but also includes appropriately dated covers: Henry Mancini's "Banzai Pipeline" and Booker T's "Jelly Bread."

Amis' Overtones made one wonderful surf-rock single ("Red Checker Wagon") for Twin/Tone before he headed out East to join the Raybeats. After leaving the group, Amis continued to explore '60s guitar instrumentals on his own, recording the five evocative Mitch Easter-produced twangers that comprise the 12-inch **Whiplash!**. [jy/i]

See also *Jody Harris, Romeo Void*.

RAYMEN

Going Down to Death Valley (Ger. Rebel) 1985
Desert Drive (Ger. Rebel) 1986
Tonight the Raymen: From the Trashcan to the Ballroom
 (Blue Turtle) 1988

Imagine a band playing Cramps-type stuff, somewhere out in the heartland. Now imagine that heartland's in Germany, and you'll have some idea of how bizarre the Raymen are. The guitar-bass-drums-singer dementobilly combo hails from Dortmund, which has been described as Deutschland's Gary, Indiana; maybe they're not as inspired as the Cramps or Shockabilly, but fun anyhow.

The first LP is charmingly wacked-out and trashy. One leader of the hit parade is "I'm a Hillbilly Werewolf," which Hank Ray sings with as much sincerity as anyone could muster for such a song. (His heavily echoed baritone typically hits the right notes at least two-thirds of the time.) The title track is the Raymen's idea of traditional cowboy country music (where they're usually most effective) and includes suitably strange slide guitar. Axeman Martin Toulouse uses feedback, slide, fuzzbox and twang-bar to excellent noisemaking effect throughout the LP (if anything, not often enough). A so-horrible-it's-grand rendition of "Locomotion" completes the picture.

Desert Drive isn't as good. The new rhythm section is an improvement, but the material doesn't hold up. Toulouse puts down his slide and doesn't go wild as often. Ray is most fun when he's frantically stuttering and echoing every word into complete unintelligibility, which doesn't happen much here.

The third album continues both trends. There's more music (seventeen tracks on two 45 rpm discs) but less frenzy from Ray and less craziness from Toulouse (if it's he—guitar is credited to Junior Ray). When he does let it all hang out, as on "Saturn Doll," it sounds like it could well be our man. There's still some of the crew's trademark wigginess, but only on half the tracks; they do, however, take the time to bludgeon the Contours' "Do You Love Me" into complete submission.   [jg]

REAL KIDS
Real Kids (Red Star) 1978 (Norton) 1991
Outta Place (Star-Rhythm) 1982
All Kindsa Jerks Live (Fr. New Rose) 1983
Hit You Hard (Fr. New Rose) 1983

TAXI BOYS
Taxi Boys EP (Star-Rhythm) 1981
Taxi Boys EP (Bomp!) 1981

REAL KIDS/TAXI BOYS
Girls! Girls! Girls! (Fr. Lolita) 1983

PRIMITIVE SOULS
Primitive Souls EP (Aus. Grown Up Wrong!) 1987

JOHN FELICE & THE
LOWDOWNS
Nothing Pretty (Ace of Hearts) 1988 ●
The Real Kids were one of Boston's earliest new wave bands; their debut album is full of dynamite tracks that take the trashier aspect of the Rolling Stones and couple it with the high-power guitar approach of the Ramones. Frontman (and onetime Modern Lover) John Felice not only provides tough guitar and distinctive lead vocals, he has a knack for writing clear, infectious melodies. Spin "All Kindsa Girls," "She's Alright" or "My Baby's Book" for proof.

Poor sales of the Real Kids' first LP led Felice to become a Ramones roadie, but he subsequently returned to Boston and formed the Taxi Boys, whose two EPs (each with a different lineup) carry on the Real Kids tradition with high-energy '60s garage-band rock. The production of the records might be crude, but Felice is in fine form on both. (The Bomp! release is a 12-inch, the earlier one a 7-inch pressed on pink vinyl.)

Reactivating the Real Kids with a new and improved lineup, Felice then made the dandy Outta Place. Harder yet still pop-oriented, with stellar production by Andy Paley, the record is strengthened by consistently good material and plenty of rock'n'roll spirit. After releasing the album in France, New Rose kept the Real Kids' recording career going, issuing another sharp studio LP, Hit You Hard, and the live-in-Paris All Kindsa Jerks Live, which recaps Felice's song catalogue onstage with fiery enthusiasm. The Lolita release is a Real Kids/Taxi Boys compilation.

Ex-Real Kids Alpo Paulino (bass) and Billy Borgioli (guitar) lead the Primitive Souls, whose 12-inch— two originals by each—follows the righteous path of bar-band pop'n'roll with tuneful flair and serious skill. (For the record, Paulino has the better singing voice and slightly catchier songs.)

After five years of national invisibility, Felice returned, unrepentant and embittered, with a rocking new trio and the Nothing Pretty album. Although his casual writing and punchy guitar playing is in fine shape, uncertain singing undercuts the songs' impact; Felice's attitude is, like his voice, a little worse for wear. The title track rues the loss of innocence; "I'll Never Sing That Song Again" describes a view of life as a musician that is both cynical and poignant; "Nowadaze Kids" tells the other side of the story, castigating modern audiences for lacking the rock'n'roll spirit that inspires him. Fans who fear that he's becoming too disgusted to carry on should take note of the LP's final cut, "Can't Play It Safe."   [cpl/i]

REAL ROXANNE
The Real Roxanne (Select) 1988 ●
Like the endless claims to popular pizzeria names— Manhattan currently boasts eleven "Original Ray's"— this young New Yorker was one contender in the 1984 "Roxanne, Roxanne" fracas, which boiled down to a two-for-all with Roxanne Shanté. By the time either woman released an album, however, there couldn't have been any less interest in the object of UTFO's romantic frustration. Nonetheless, with fine sample-heavy old-school production by the likes of Jam Master Jay and Howie Tee, The Real Roxanne is irascible nasty-girl fun, a salty set of boasts, putdowns and don't-mess-wid-the-Ro' antagonism.   [i]
See also UTFO.

RECKLESS SLEEPERS
See Jules Shear.

RECOIL
See Depeche Mode.

RECORDS
Shades in Bed (nr/Virgin) 1979
The Records (Virgin) 1979
Crashes (Virgin) 1980
Music on Both Sides (Virgin Int'l) 1982
A Sunny Afternoon in Waterloo (nr/Waterfront) 1988 ●
Smashes, Crashes and Near Misses [CD] (nr/Virgin) 1988 ●
Paying for the Summer of Love (Skyclad) 1990 ●

HUW GOWER
Guitarophilia EP (X-Disque) 1984

JUDE COLE
Jude Cole (Warner Bros.) 1987 ●
A View from 3rd Street (Reprise) 1990 ●
Like the Motors, the Records were reborn pub-rockers, who made a giant leap into the present by leaving their history behind and starting afresh with finely honed pop craftsmanship and the full-scale record company support they had never previously enjoyed. While the Motors went for grandiose production numbers, the Records—led by ex-Kursaal Flyer drummer/songwriter Will Birch—made sharp, tuneful confections that of-

fered maximum hooks-per-groove in a classic Anglo-pop style not unlike the Hollies, with similarly brilliant harmonies and ringing guitars.

Shades in Bed (resequenced, retitled **The Records** and dressed in a completely different cover for America) is a wonderful LP, featuring song after song of pure pop with clever lyrics and winning melodies. Almost every track could have been a single; "Starry Eyes" and "Teenarama" were actually released, which left "Girls That Don't Exist," "Affection Rejected" and "Girl" as untested chart material. The English album included a bonus 12-inch, **High Heels** (an untitled 7-inch in the US), of the Records doing four classic tracks, including the Kinks' "See My Friends" and Spirit's "1984."

Crashes, produced mainly by Craig Leon, showcased a revised lineup, Jude Cole having taken Huw Gower's guitar slot. (Gower resurfaced a continent away in David Johansen's band around 1982.) Nothing here can match the first LP's charm except for two tracks produced by Mick Glossop—"Man with a Girl Proof Heart," written while Birch was still in the Kursaals, and "Hearts in Her Eyes," which was done better by the Searchers later that year. At best a weak rehash of the first LP, **Crashes** is passable, but hardly a great follow-up.

After a two-year recording gap, **Music on Both Sides** introduced a new five-piece lineup, with guitarist Dave Whelan and singer Chris Gent joining the surviving core of Birch, bassist Phil Brown and guitarist John Wicks. Birch produced this muddled but generally pleasant album, which sounds like **Rubber Soul** with a crappy rock singer. Not a great parting shot, although less annoyingly precious than their early work.

Gower's solo EP is pretty much in the Records' vein: well-crafted, unprepossessing rock-pop, but without their often-cloying preciousness. An earnest enough performer, the left-handed guitarist is a limited songwriter and not much of a singer; the EP's best track is a fascinating cover of Graeme Douglas' brilliant "Do Anything You Wanna Do," originally recorded by Eddie and the Hot Rods.

Unexpectedly, the late-'80s saw a sudden resurgence of Records records. (The original group even got back together long enough to cut a version of Brian Wilson's "Darlin'," for 1990's **Smiles, Vibes, & Harmony** tribute record.) **A Sunny Afternoon in Waterloo**—the fruits of a one-day '78 songwriting demo session—finds the Records playing simple, hard-driving Rockpilish rock'n'roll, reportedly in the hopes of selling some songs Birch had written with Dr. Feelgood, then enjoying large UK success, in mind. Although the effort was commercially unsuccessful, the loss was all Dr. F's, as the music is brilliant, a taut mixture of strong melodies and amusing lyrics about loving, drinking and driving.

Another set of demos—recorded during '78 as preparation for the Records' first album—comprise the bulk of the white-vinyl **Paying for the Summer of Love**. All but two of **Shades in Bed**'s songs appear in raw—but perfectly presentable, and not drastically different—form here, alongside self-produced renditions of other early tracks ("Hearts in Her Eyes," B-sides like "Wives and Mothers of Tomorrow" and "Held Up High," and "If I Write Your Number in My Book," written for, but unrecorded by, Rachel Sweet). A delightful companion piece.

Although by no means definitive, **Smashes, Crashes and Near Misses** is a carefully annotated 20-song compilation containing about half each of the first two albums, a modest three-song reminder of the third, a couple of B-sides ("Held Up High" and "Paint Her Face") and previously unreleased outtakes of "I Don't Remember Your Name" and "The Same Mistakes" (two songs that appear on **Crashes**). In a case of rarer isn't necessarily better, the CD ends with a previously unreleased Mick Glossop-produced version of "Rock and Roll Love Letter" that isn't nearly as good as the band's 1979 single of the song.

Jude Cole, the Illinois guitarist/singer who replaced Gower for **Crashes**, had shaken off any vestiges of the Records' joyful power pop by the time he made his own slickly commercial heartland-rock albums.   [i]

See also *Kursaal Flyers*.

RED BOX
The Circle & the Square (Sire) 1986 ●

This fascinating London twosome takes an offbeat and rewarding direction on their first album, folding American Indian (covering Buffy Sainte-Marie in the process) and other ethnic folk influences into sophisticated modern pop creations for an unpredictable and indescribable pan-ethnic mélange. Unlike arid studio-based partnerships, Simon Toulson Clarke (vocals, acoustic guitar) and Julian Close (programming, flute, sax) make warm and varied music, much of it employing a vocal chorus which adds African color. The evocative lyrics bring a global political intelligence to the songs, making them not only appealing but affecting as well. Something like a less stern Peter Gabriel LP, this imaginative and engaging record is simply astonishing.
          [i]

RED CRAYOLA
Parable of Arable Land (Int'l Artists) 1967 + 1980
　　(nr/Radar) 1978
God Bless the Red Crayola and All Who Sail on Her (Int'l
　　Artists) 1968 + 1980 (nr/Radar) 1979
Soldier-Talk (nr/Radar) 1979
Three Songs on a Trip to the United States
　　(nr/Recommended) 1984
Parable of Arable Land/God Bless the Red Crayola [CD]
　　(nr/Charly) 1990 ●

ART & LANGUAGE AND THE RED CRAYOLA
Corrected Slogans (Music Language) 1976
　　(nr/Recommended) 1982
Kangaroo? (Rough Trade) 1981
Black Snakes (Sw. Rec-Rec) 1983

MAYO THOMPSON
Corky's Debt to His Father (nr/Glass) 1986

Red Crayola first surfaced on Texas' International Artists label during the psychedelic '60s. Charter member Mayo Thompson (guitar, vocals) would remain the group's mainstay throughout its checkered career, but the lineup that recorded 1967's **Parable of Arable Land** contained someone whose fame would not be in music: drummer Frederick Barthelme (younger brother of postmodern master Donald Barthelme), a widely acclaimed avatar of the "dirty realist" school of American fiction. Barthelme quit the group after that one album, but he and Thompson have remained close, and the writer contributed cover photos to **Three Songs**.

The first two Red Crayola records couldn't be more different. **Parable of Arable Land** is vintage psychedelia that boasts a more engaged intelligence than most of the era's aural acid baths, and its excellent songs ("Hurricane Fighter Plane" obviously influenced Pere Ubu's sound; Spacemen 3 later covered "Transparent Radiation") are punctuated by "Free Form Freak Outs," random noise excursions by a large group of Texas hippies. **God Bless the Red Crayola** is a considerably more subdued but equally eccentric effort, with an emphasis on very brief, acoustic-based numbers; "Ravi Shankar: Parachutist" and "Tina's Gone to Have a Baby" are among its memorable titles. (Galaxie 500 covered the LP's "Victory Garden" on a 1990 single.)

Red Crayola then faded into limbo until turning up to do sessions in 1976 with the Art & Language organization, which yielded the demos collected on **Corrected Slogans**; the album parallels somewhat the serious/silly music of Robert Wyatt. Largely acoustic in nature, **Corrected Slogans** has extremely simple songs, operatic vocals and complex lyrics that are satirical and/or political.

Exhilarated by the critical success of Pere Ubu's dada punk, Radar Records reissued **Parable of Arable Land** in 1978 and **God Bless** in 1979. Mayo Thompson and New York drummer Jesse Chamberlain reformed Red Crayola to make **Soldier-Talk**, aided by Lora Logic and the entirety of Pere Ubu (which Thompson later joined). Uniting Red Crayola's flower-power garage music with modernistic, fragmented arrangements and a fierce, broken beat, the album centers on cynical military themes. A challenging work.

Reuniting Red Crayola with Art & Language, **Kangaroo?** tones down the chaos for a musical discussion of Soviet Communist ideals and history, including the gentle, poignant instrumental, "1917." More in the style of avant-garde theater music than rock, the LP is like Brecht out of Vivian Stanshall, with impressive results. **Black Snakes** has more of Thompson's dramatic vocals and features Ubu's Allen Ravenstine on sax and synth. The cornerstone tracks are "The Sloths," a peculiar rewrite of a James Thurber short story (*The Unicorn in the Garden*), the puerile "Ratman, the Weightwatcher" and "A Portrait of V.I. Lenin in the Style of Jackson Pollock."

Three Songs on a Trip to the United States is packaged as an EP, but it's practically album length; the A-side contains the three songs themselves, while the flip is a generous chunk from a German concert featuring the stripped-down lineup of Thompson, drummer Chamberlain and synthesist Ravenstine. Both sides find the Crayola back in the sometimes crazed, sometimes obtuse psychedelic mode of the band's first Radar 7-inch, "Wives in Orbit." (The live side contains a reading of that tune that's even more frenzied than the original.) The studio side is frustratingly murky. As intriguing as it would be to hear what the Texas-born expatriate has to say about a visit to the country he left, it's impossible to make out much more than a phrase here and there. Still, it's a safe guess that "California

Girl" isn't a song of praise; nor, for that matter, is "Monster." Pretty slamming stuff nonetheless and, like the rest of the Crayola's oeuvre, a genuine mind trip in almost every sense of the term.   [sg/i/gk]

See also *Pere Ubu*.

RED CROSS
Red Cross EP (Posh Boy) 1980
Born Innocent (Smoke 7) 1982

REDD KROSS
Teen Babes from Monsanto (Gasatanka) 1984
Born Innocent (Frontier) 1986 ●
Neurotica (Big Time) 1987 ●
Third Eye (Atlantic) 1990 φ

VARIOUS ARTISTS
The Siren (Posh Boy) 1980
Desperate Teenage Lovedolls (Gasatanka) 1984
Lovedolls Superstar (SST) 1986

TATER TOTZ
Alien Sleestacks from Brazil (Gasatanka-Giant) 1988
Sgt. Shonen's Exploding Plastic Eastman Band Request
Mono! Stereo (Gasatanka-Giant) 1989 ●

ANARCHY 6
Hardcore Lives! (Gasatanka-Giant) 1988

Originally known as the Tourists, Red Cross was formed in Hawthorne, California (home of the Beach Boys) by brothers Steven and Jeff McDonald and high school chums Ron Reyes (later of Black Flag) and Greg Hetson (a future Circle Jerk). Through various lineups, adventures and setbacks, the McDonalds have kept their group going and growing, turning Redd Kross into the bemused focus of an increasing national cult.

Red Cross' recorded debut (later reissued as a standalone 12-inch EP) was on **The Siren**, a three-band sampler LP. Although bassist Steven was barely 13 at the time, the six tracks sound surprisingly self-assured. The culturally resonant snot-punk-rock-pop selections include "Annette's Got the Hits" (which became an LA radio staple), "I Hate My School" and the B-52's-ish "Standing in Front of Poseur."

After Hetson and Reyes left, the McDonalds formed a new band and released 1982's **Born Innocent**, subsequently re-released under their post-legal-intervention name. The LP celebrates such wonderful pop anti-idols as "Linda Blair," "Charlie" (Manson) and Patty Hearst; although unmentioned on the sleeve and label (for fear he would come after them for royalties) the LP actually includes a cover of Manson's "Cease to Exist." The muddy sound and sloppy, uninspired playing make **Born Innocent** dull in spots, but guitarist Jeff's wild-eyed singing and the overall junk-is-good aesthetic make it a record of—and for—its time.

Ex-Black Flag singer Dez Cadena had already come and gone through Redd Kross by the time Geza X produced the seven-song **Teen Babes from Monsanto**. Running strictly on wicked irreverence, the McDonalds and drummer Dave Peterson turn the spotlight on various musical victims, and the Redd Kross living jukebox bangs out loud and convincing covers of Kiss ("Deuce"), the Stones ("Citadel"), Stooges ("Ann"), Bowie ("Savior Machine") and others, leaving "Linda Blair 1984" the sole original. A record of the ultimate bratty garage band in its element.

With Redd Kross providing most of the music, the McDonalds appeared in *Desperate Teenage Lovedolls*, a no-budget Super-8 psychotronic Z-movie made by LA scenesters. The soundtrack album—tracks by Black Flag and a few minor bands, as well as various interlocking permutations of Redd Kross and White Flag—is well-produced and, for the most part, a real offhand treat. With Redd Kross backing their then-manager, Joanna Spockolla McDonald (we're all McDonalds in this life), "Legend" is typical of the rocking pop that keeps the record hopping. Redd Kross offered the same service for the soundtrack album of the sequel, *Lovedolls Superstar*, which includes a brilliant rendition of "Sunshine Day," a *Brady Bunch* chestnut.

Drummer Roy McDonald (no relation) and guitarist Robert Hecker fill out the lineup card on **Neurotica**, the band's national underground breakout record. The LP reclaims "Ballad of a Love Doll" from the first film's score and adds such fuzzed-out folk-pop acid trips as "Peach Kelli Pop," "Janus, Jeanie, and George Harrison," "Frosted Flake" and "Ghandi Is Dead (I'm the Cartoon Man)." With harmony-heavy arrangements that occasionally suggest Shoes, Redd Kross has never sounded better—a full-fledged, mind-boggling outing that confirms their potential and makes the next record something to anticipate. (The CD appends "Tatum O'Tot," a hint of things to come.)

Following the failure of Big Time, Redd Kross didn't make another album under its own name for three years. But that's not to say the McDonalds didn't stay busy. Joined by various collaborators—including Special Guest Tater Danny Bonaduce (David Cassidy's kid brother on *The Partridge Family*; now a successful disc jockey) and such Accessory Tots as Michael Quercio of the Three O'Clock—Steve and Jeff launched the ridiculously parodic Tater Totz with **Alien Sleestacks from Brazil**. Besides perpetrating such atrocities as "Give Peace a Chance," "I've Just Seen a Face," "Sing This All Together," "We Will Rock You" and "Tomorrow Never Knows," the record offers a vicious, seemingly endless version of Yoko Ono's "Don't Worry Kyoko."

The second Tater Totz album—a much more accomplished effort—again focuses on the extended Beatles family, beginning with covers of "Rain" (sung by Shonen Knife) and "Strawberry Fields Forever," but spiraling off into Lennon's "The Luck of the Irish" and "Instant Karma!," McCartney's "Lovely Linda" and a batch of Ono compositions. In an audacious bit of genetic engineering, Queen's "Bohemian Rhapsody" gets jammed together with Ono's "Who Has Seen the Rain," proving that the line between tribute and satire can sometimes be imperceptible. Ex-Runaway Cherie Currie, ex-Germ Pat RuthenSmear, members of Frightwig, the Pandoras, Celebrity Skin and others contribute to the madness. (The CD, LP and cassette all have slightly different tracks.)

In another side project, the McDonalds and several associates run punk through an ironic blender as Anarchy 6 on **Hardcore Lives!**, a fast'n'sloppy guitar-rock onslaught—starring Steven and "executive produced" by Jeff—that sounds like a cross between Suicidal Tendencies and Black Flag but lampoons the form and its followers in such lyrics as "Skate and Destroy," "Unite & Fight," "Drugs Aren't Great" and "Old Punks." It's hard to gauge who the audience for this is: those

inclined to buy a record that looks and sounds so punk are unlikely to enjoy (or even get) the joke, and vice versa. Maybe that's the point.

With Hecker still abetting the brothers, **Third Eye**, Redd Kross' major-label debut—and the long-awaited follow-up to **Neurotica**—is a partially successful attempt to go straight (or at least straighter) for mass-market consumption. Much of the band's trademark wackiness is gone—channeled into the Tater Totz, perhaps?—replaced by disciplined musicianship, streamlined songwriting and radio-savvy production. Strangely, **Third Eye**'s accessible pop-rock songs ("The Faith Healer," "Bubblegum Factory," "I Don't Know How to Be Your Friend," "Love Is Not Love") are pretty good, while scattered attempts to fuse the new slicked-up sound with the humor of earlier efforts—like "Elephant Flares" and "1976" (which revisits the dreaded decade with incisive passing tributes to Kiss, Cheap Trick and Elton John)—sound forced. Whether the world needs another accessible pop-rock band more than it needs iconoclastic pop-culture satirists is certainly open to question, but there's no denying that Redd Kross has made the transition to big-league recordmaking with more skill than most. [i/hd]

See also *Sky Saxon*.

RED GUITARS
Slow to Fade (nr/Self Drive) 1984 ●
Tales of the Expected (nr/Virgin) 1986 ●

PLANET WILSON
In the Best of All Possible Worlds (nr/Virgin) 1988 ●
Not Drowning but Waving (nr/Records of Achievement) 1989 ●

ROBERT HOLMES
Age of Swing (nr/Virgin) 1989 ●

On their first major-label album, Hull's Red Guitars sound briefly like Cockney Rebel (from whom they borrow the refrain of "Sweetwater Ranch"), as well as Lloyd Cole, Bowie, Aztec Camera and Dream Academy. The quintet's light songs are pretty flimsy; guitarist Robert Holmes' vocals are likewise second-rate. While delicate and varied, arrangements and production alone can't make up for **Tales of the Expected**'s inherent lack of raison d'être.

With two LPs behind them, the Red Guitars split. Holmes went solo, while bassist Lou Howard and guitarist/vocalist Hallam Lewis got themselves a drummer and formed the Planet Wilson. **In the Best of All Possible Worlds** is a strange record, a percussion-accented (but not dance-oriented) collection on which the three bandmembers occasionally seem to be playing different songs. With some of XTC's jagged rhythmic intricacy and a bit of the early Police's spare improvisation, the Planet Wilson's first LP imaginatively tests out an assortment of unfamiliar stylistic approaches, none of which really connects. Lewis' songs, lyrics and vocals are obviously all reaching for something, but it's impossible to discern just where he's heading. (The CD adds two tracks.)

Not Drowning but Waving (a phrase already in service as the name of an Australian band) doesn't shy away from discordant strangeness, but the indie-label album with a fancy die-cut sleeve is generally more focused and consistent-sounding than its predecessor. That's not to call it enjoyable: this is uncommon pop music with claws. Songs twist and turn and go all funny when they should be coalescing into accessible form; instruments shift from playing nice to spinning off the scale. The Planet Wilson is an exotic and intriguing place to visit, but I sure wouldn't live there.

Holmes' **Age of Swing** consists of handsome, unpretentiously sophisticated modern pop with solid melodic appeal. While lacking any distinctive artistic personality, the savvy songs (the title track is especially fine) are timelessly mainstream without being overly bland. Holmes (who also co-produced) has blossomed into a strong, plain singer with an unnerving current of Neil Diamond drama (check "American Lullaby"). The CD adds a pair of dull tracks co-produced by Ian Priestman, the album's main guitarist. [i]

RED HOT CHILI PEPPERS
The Red Hot Chili Peppers (Enigma-EMI America) 1984 ●
Freaky Styley (Enigma-EMI America) 1985 ●
The Uplift Mofo Party Plan (EMI Manhattan) 1987 ●
The Abbey Road E.P. EP (EMI Manhattan) 1988 ●
Mother's Milk (EMI) 1989+1990 ●

Pioneers of the thrashy rock-funk hybrid that has lately come into vogue, this awesomely powerful California quartet—distinguished by Anthony Kiedis' out-there vocals and the maniacally possessed basswork of Flea (Michael Balzary)—melds floor-shaking rhythm-'n'roll to wickedly clever songs like "True Men Don't Kill Coyotes," "Baby Appeal" and "Get Up and Jump" on their debut album. The Chili Peppers, who aren't above a little self-obsessed boasting or earnest political protest, play a thoroughly entertaining mutation of George Clinton, Was (Not Was), Peter Wolf, Sly Stone, Kurtis Blow, Sonic Youth and Wall of Voodoo. Move it, but make sure you pay attention at the same time!

Founding guitarist Hillel Slovak, who had missed the Peppers' debut LP during a stint with What Is This, returned to the fold in time for the second outing. Sagely engaging Clinton—a sympathetic soul, both musically and mentally—to produce, the Peppers made **Freaky Styley** more outrageous but easier to swallow as utilitarian dance-rock as well. A version of Sly Stone's "If You Want Me to Stay" shows they can play it straight; "Yertle the Turtle," based on Dr. Seuss, proves their unhinged sensibilities remain in full force. Other bits of rhythmicized doggerel ("Catholic School Girls Rule," "Thirty Dirty Birds," "Blackeyed Blonde") keep tongue in cheek and mind in the gutter. **Freaky Styley** is a ton of raunchy, funky fun.

Bob Dylan's "Subterranean Homesick Blues" gets a weirdly re-tempoed electro-rap overhaul on **The Uplift Mofo Party Plan**, a busy, casual-sounding album that divides rock and funk down the middle. On some guitar-heavy tracks ("No Chump Love Sucker," "Fight Like a Brave," "Me and My Friends"), Flea's popping bass is the only connection with the group's characteristic sound; elsewhere, familiarly repetitive rhythm grooves reaffirm the Peppers' primal commitment to butt-shaking. In "Organic Anti-Beat Box Band," the self-described Fax City 4 issue their offbeat statement of (cross) purpose: "We represent the Hollywood kids . . .

you just might slam dance." Bonus warning to prudes everywhere: "Special Secret Song Inside" is better known as "Party on Your Pussy."

Fans won't need the four previously released album cuts that comprise the four-song **Abbey Road** 12-inch, but the nude tribute cover is positively priceless. Sock it to 'em, Peppers!

Sobered by Slovak's fatal OD in June 1988, the Chili Pepper regrouped with guitarist John Frusciante and drummer Chad Smith to score their commercial breakthrough with **Mother's Milk**, a hard-driven funky concoction again produced by Michael Beinhorn and dedicated to their late guitarist. Fired by the band's relentless intensity, the cautionary anti-drug strength of "Knock Me Down" and "Taste the Pain" somehow fits in with the wanton sexuality of "Sexy Mexican Maid." In the album's best mix of song and performance, Flea's mindfuck bass work pushes the band through an overpowering version of Stevie Wonder's "Higher Ground." [i]

See also *What Is This*.

RED LORRY YELLOW LORRY
This Today EP (nr/Red Rhino) 1984
Talk About the Weather (nr/Red Rhino) 1985
Paint Your Wagon (nr/Red Rhino) 1986 ●
Smashed Hits (Red Rhino-Fundamental) 1987 ●
Nothing Wrong (Beggars Banquet-RCA) 1988 ●
Blow (Beggars Banquet-RCA) 1989 ●

LORRIES
Crawling Mantra EP (Homestead) 1987

If you loved Joy Division, you'll like Red Lorry Yellow Lorry, who similarly inhabit a bleak world in which swirling guitar figures and pretentious, gloomy lyrics are the only comforts. While Joy Division was the unchallenged champ of these nether regions, Leeds' Lorries work the territory with enough savvy and intelligence (not to mention a cool suppressed-acid-rock guitar sound) to make it work. **Talk About the Weather** ultimately succumbs to its own murky tunelessness, but not without a fight.

After that LP, they recorded a great single, "Chance." With distorted organ drone and a rushed tempo, it sounded as if the band had located its own true voice. However, **Paint Your Wagon** borrows enough from Ian Curtis and Joy Division that you'd think it had been released by Factory (c. 1981), especially on cuts like "Head All Fire" and "Save My Soul." A disappointing follow-up to such a promising debut.

The back cover of the **Smashed Hits** singles compilation is covered with flattering bits from newspaper clippings, and the tracks really do live up to most of the praise. Most of the band's finest moments are included, such as "Hollow Eyes," "Generation" and "Chance." The guitar work is so good that it covers up the weak points, especially the vocal Curtisisms and the kickless, rudimentary rhythm section. (The CD adds two tracks.) They've changed their name back and forth between Red Lorry Yellow Lorry and the Lorries a few times recently, releasing one mini-LP (**Crawling Mantra**) as the latter.

Nothing Wrong is marked and almost marred by an unshifting swarm of buzzing guitar noise with just enough off-kilter harmonies to break up the drone. A developing melodic flair is apparent, but none of the material ranks with the band's best, and Chris Reed's bleak lyrics are straight out of an Existentialism 101 textbook. "Only Dreaming (Wide Awake)" is the most diverting effort, with an acoustic guitar intro and outro, a bass riveting enough to please J.J. Burnel and even a tambourine in the chorus; only Reed's deep bellowing prevents it from being a genuine pop song (maybe that's the idea).

Blow sports Ecstasy/rave cover art (after the Lorries' usual black, gray and brown, bright colors are a breakthrough). Half-jumping on the acid house bandwagon, **Blow** takes the band a giant step forward in terms of melodicism and diversity of sound. Staying clear of the old monochromatic wall of noise, the production gives them plenty of punch and much more warmth; the space between instruments (more keyboards and background vocals this time) helps clarify the sound more than ever before. The Joy Division comparisons can finally be put to rest. [jl/dgs]

RED NOISE
See *Bill Nelson*.

RED TEMPLE SPIRITS
Dancing to Restore an Eclipsed Moon (Nate Starkman & Son) 1988 ●
"If tomorrow I were leaving for Lhasa, I wouldn't stay a minute more ... " (Nate Starkman & Son) 1989 ●

MINISTRY OF LOVE
Wide Awake and Dreaming EP (Underworld) 1987

Los Angeles quartet Red Temple Spirits skillfully mix tribal post-punk influences—mid-period Cure, Savage Republic, early (Death) Cult—with a loving dose of lysergic psychedelia (Syd Barrett and Roky Erickson are particular touchstones). Bassist Dino Paredes and guitarist Dallas Taylor coax entrancing drones and pulses from their instruments with judicious use of echo and other effects, whi'- shamanistic frontman William Faircloth (a colorful immigrant from Britain's original '60s psychedelic movement) delves into mysticism (Native American on the first album, Tibetan on the second) with a grace and passion rarely seen before.

Dancing to Restore an Eclipsed Moon is an astonishing debut. The luxurious packaging (double LP/single CD) mirrors the care put into the music, which tastefully incorporates flutes, bells and natural sounds (water, birds) to create a heady atmosphere of ritualistic ecstasy. Short catchy compositions like "Dark Spirits" and "Dreamings Ending" alternate with several long and complex pieces.

The follow-up album is far more direct, both in the melodic music and the lyrics, which turn towards external/environmental stimuli. As crystallized by the gorgeous "Dive in Deep" and an incandescent cover of Pink Floyd's "Set the Controls for the Heart of the Sun," the theme of hope for the magic and beauty of life in the face of despair remains.

Prior to the Spirits, Faircloth lent his vocal ululations to the similarly psychedelic Ministry of Love, a trio that included guitar wiz Mark Nine. Although lacking the Red Temple Spirits' brilliant chemistry, there are some great moments on the five-track EP, including

"Living in the Moment" (a showcase for Nine's e-bow mastery) and Faircloth's touching ballad, "You're Not on Your Own." [gef]

See also *Jane's Addiction*.

REDUCERS
The Reducers (Rave On) 1984
Let's Go! (Rave On) 1984
Cruise to Nowhere (Rave On) 1985

Quick—name a great band from Connecticut. Well, you need be stumped no longer. Just keep the Reducers in mind. This New London quartet has absorbed all sorts of styles—from Chuck Berry to Anglo-pop, glam-rock to punk—and returns them all in a solid hybrid of tunes, blazing guitars and speedy tempos. On **The Reducers**, they sing of "Black Plastic Shoes," "Better Homes and Gardens" and "Information Overload," painting a picture of alienation in the boonies ("Out of Step"). Polite but energetic, **The Reducers** introduces a band with ideas and spunk.

The title track on the better-produced **Let's Go!** is a great number about getting out, with a catchy, urgent chorus; the rest of the LP (which includes a raving cover of the beat classic "Hippy Hippy Shake") is equally enthusiastic and has more acute lyrics. (On "Bums (I Used to Know)" they play a churning R&B vamp while chiding themselves for "this honky imitation of the blues.") The Reducers may not be fashionable—no synthesizers or even cowpunk aspirations—but they have the spirit and the sense to keep changing and working. Their albums have an integrity and sincerity that more than compensates for any lack of stylishness. [i]

LOU REED
Lou Reed (RCA) 1972
Transformer (RCA) 1972 + 1981 ●
Berlin (RCA) 1973 + 1981 ●
Rock n Roll Animal (RCA) 1974 + 1981 ●
Sally Can't Dance (RCA) 1974 ●
Lou Reed Live (RCA) 1975 + 1981 ●
Metal Machine Music: The Amine B Ring (RCA) 1975 + 1991 ●
Coney Island Baby (RCA) 1976 + 1980 ●
Rock and Roll Heart (Arista) 1976
Walk on the Wild Side: The Best of Lou Reed (RCA) 1977 + 1988 ●
Street Hassle (Arista) 1978
Live Take No Prisoners (Arista) 1978
The Bells (Arista) 1979
Growing Up in Public (Arista) 1980
Rock and Roll Diary 1967–1980 (Arista) 1980
The Blue Mask (RCA) 1982
I Can't Stand It (nr/RCA) 1982
Legendary Hearts (RCA) 1983 ●
Live in Italy (nr/RCA) 1984
New Sensations (RCA) 1984 ●
City Lights: Classic Performances (Arista) 1985
Mistrial (RCA) 1986 ●
New York (Sire) 1989 ●
Retro (nr/RCA) 1989 ●

LOU REED/JOHN CALE
Songs for Drella (Sire-Warner Bros.) 1990 ●

Since he formed the Velvet Underground in 1966, Lou Reed's career has spanned several major rock upheavals, but he has always managed to be a leader not a follower, despite an iconoclastic resistance to fashion. A highly principled free-thinker, Reed has provided inspiration, direction and songs for bands with a taste for the seamier side of the rock sensibility.

Reed's influence began with the Velvet Underground's predilection for forbidden fruit—drugs, bizarre sex, suicide—in its lyrics, and raging electric chaos in its music. How could punk (much less the Jesus and Mary Chain) have ever occurred without "Sister Ray" or "Heroin" as touchstones? In his solo work, Reed has casually strayed far into heavy metal territory and experimental noise, as well as restrained, seemingly normal rock, but always with a rebellious attitude, probing honesty and unselfconscious abandon. He has always managed to remain relevant, serving as a guide for all sorts of unconventional music makers.

Lou Reed, recorded in England with session players like Steve Howe and Rick Wakeman (both of Yes!), includes previously unreleased Velvet Underground material (some of which turned up much later on **VU**) and the first incarnation of "Berlin." Effortlessly alternating nihilism with ironic wistfulness, the music is surprisingly lean and no-nonsense, getting Reed's solo career off the ground with a flourish.

The existence of a glam-rock New York café society in the early '70s led to an alliance between Reed and David Bowie, who co-produced **Transformer** with his then-sideman, Mick Ronson. Joining the legion of androgynous glam-rockers, Reed penned "Walk on the Wild Side," a chronicle of the Warhol crowd that—issued as a single—became a genuine subversive hit (and, many years later, a television jingle!). Although **Transformer**'s music is a bit too campy, the LP is nonetheless a classic.

Fresh from his work with Alice Cooper, Bob Ezrin produced **Berlin**, using such players as Jack Bruce and Steve Winwood. While lyrically intense and haunting, the music is understated, almost plain. But Reed's tragic tales—like "Caroline Says" and "Sad Song"—pack an intense emotional charge. **Berlin**, in spite of itself, is one of his best, although not recommended for depressives or would-be suicides.

Rock n Roll Animal captures Reed onstage in New York with an unbelievably bombastic heavy metal band powered by guitarists Steve Hunter and Dick Wagner. Playing a collection of elongated hits ("Sweet Jane," "Rock'n'Roll," "Heroin") at stun volume, Reed proves he can sound as neanderthal as any arena band of the day, but his songs and singing make it powerful.

Sally Can't Dance attempts a mainstream sound with boring songs that lack fire; although a commercial success, it's one of Reed's most forgettable efforts, marking the beginning of a bad period in his career. To mark time, his next release was **Lou Reed Live** (more **Rock n Roll Animal**), followed by the truly deviant **Metal Machine Music**, four sides of unlistenable noise (a description, not a value judgment) that angered and disappointed all but the most devout Reed fans. If he was simply looking to goad people and puncture perceptions, **Metal Machine Music** was a rousing success.

Coney Island Baby and **Rock and Roll Heart** proffer the same unambitious restraint as **Sally Can't Dance**; the new wrinkle is Reed's revelatory lyrics. After years of describing a depraved life-style with a hint of defensive pride, Reed began to open up and admit personal pain and doubts. A new creative vista mired in a musical rut.

Street Hassle shows Reed somewhat revitalized—or at least moved to action—by the onslaught of his young punk apostles. More aggressive sound and new-found vocal strength power songs like "Real Good Time Together" and the scathing "I Wanna Be Black." The band is exciting, and every path pursued bears fruit.

Another live album, **Take No Prisoners**—recorded at New York's Bottom Line—gives Reed a chance to try his hand at being a standup comedian. The four sides include only two or three songs each: the no-name band vamps endlessly as Reed banters with the crowd, offering sharp opinions and cutting comments on a variety of subjects. Although not a great musical accomplishment, it's one of the funniest and most entertaining live albums of all time.

Reed continues to expose his sensitive side on **The Bells** and **Growing Up in Public**, using driving rock and delicate melodicism to back thoughtful lyrics and impassioned singing. A triumphant success, **The Blue Mask** uses almost no instrumental overdubs to get a spontaneous feel from a basic backing trio (including ex-Richard Hell guitarist Robert Quine) and features some of Reed's strongest writing in years. The portraits he paints are miserable characters living outside society; it's not clear whether or not they're fictional.

Reed found new acclaim with the band he enlisted for **The Blue Mask**; adding drummer Fred Maher to the core of Quine and bassist Fernando Saunders completed a perfect touring/recording unit that Reed lost no time in exploiting. **Legendary Hearts** could just as well have been credited to the Lou Reed Band—every song is fully developed and confidently delivered in a manner suggesting a tight, well-rehearsed unit. It ranks with any Reed record all the way back to the Velvets in substance and stands out as his strongest work in style, using the group as a powerful lens that magnifies his themes and obsessions down to the finest detail. Picking an ideal moment to sum up his career to date, Reed recorded **Live in Italy** with the same band—two albums of material divided almost evenly between Velvets-era songs and solo work.

For his next record, Reed decided to play all the guitar himself, yet **New Sensations** is anything but self-indulgent. Forsaking the two-guitar sound just throws Saunders' distinctive fretless bass playing and Reed's spare arrangements into higher relief, and they merit the attention—as do the songs, which prove that a middle-aged rock songwriter can have plenty to offer.

Mistrial is an essentially styleless observation of the times in which we live, simply played as variable-strength rock with Lou on guitar and Saunders (with a little outside assistance, including a live drummer on those tracks that don't employ all-electronic percussion) doing the rest. Reed's 1986 concerns are television ("Video Violence"), the state of world affairs ("The Original Wrapper," in which a credible funk track sets the stage for Reed to demonstrate his abilities as an urban contemporary wordsmith), emotional violence ("Don't Hurt a Woman," "Spit It Out") and personal realities ("Mama's Got a Lover" and the moving, memorably beautiful pair that close the album: "I Remember You" and "Tell It to Your Heart"). Although many of the melodies are too spare and casual to endure, lyrics are obviously what's important here; by this point, Reed's albums have a higher purpose than mere toe-tapping or bus-stop humming.

After taking a couple of years off to read newspapers, Reed reared back and fired his most ambitious verbal salvo, coalescing years of simmering outrage and frustration into **New York**, a tumultuous and frequently stunning outpouring of articulate commentary about the state of life in the big city—and beyond. For an hour, drummer Fred Maher, second guitarist Mike Rathke and bassist Rob Wasserman eloquently follow Reed as he talk-sings about crack addicts, child abusers, welfare hotels, racism, AIDS and much more, finishing things off with a gentle remembrance of the late Andy Warhol ("Dime Store Mystery"). As clunky as some of its modest songs and ambitious lyrics may be, this unlikely sounding masterpiece is among Reed's strongest, most durable albums. (The CD is graphics-encoded with the album's lyrics in five languages for those few who own the necessary equipment.)

Reed's next project was a sentimental collaboration with old VU bandmate John Cale on a love letter to mentor and friend Andy Warhol. **Songs for Drella**, presented as a chronological progression of fictitious biographical (and autobiographical) songs, is utterly fascinating for its personal reminiscences, but doesn't have much integrity as an album. Cale and Reed share the vocals, attempting to make music out of distinctly unmusical prose; the dashed-off backing on guitar, keyboards and viola is equally artless. Rather than attempt to make a record, Cale and Reed would have done better to write **A Book for Drella**. (The record was initially available as a limited edition CD with a velvet cover and an insert book.)

Walk on the Wild Side, **Rock and Roll Diary**, **I Can't Stand It**, **City Lights** and **Retro** are all compilations—the first of his RCA albums and the second (which has excellent liner notes by Ellen Willis) mixing Velvet Underground material (almost two sides' worth) with a spotty bunch of tracks from both RCA and Arista records. **City Lights** draws only from the Arista releases; **Retro** is all RCA, with four tracks each from **Transformer** and **Berlin**, one from **New Sensations** and a spotty sampling of the intervening years. There are other English and continental retrospectives as well.

See also *John Cale, Fernando Saunders*. [i/mf]

JUNIOR REID
See *Black Uhuru*.

VINI REILLY
See *Durutti Column*.

BLAINE L. REININGER
See *Tuxedomoon*.

REIVERS
See *Zeitgeist*.

RELUCTANT STEREOTYPES
The Label (nr/WEA) 1980

This Birmingham outfit—whose main men were future pop star Paul King and future Primitive/producer Paul Sampson—played likable reggaefied rock/pop much like another band of the same city and era, the Beat. Similarities include pointed-but-subtle lyrics that avoid clichés while covering political topics, prominent horn work, boppy dance rhythms and high musical standards. Differences include a more free-form, less-soulful approach and stricter adherence to reggae rhythms on most tunes. Comparisons aside, **The Label** is an ace record by a skillful, inventive band. [i]

See also *Eyeless in Gaza, King, Primitives*.

R.E.M.
Chronic Town EP (IRS) 1982 ●
Murmur (IRS) 1983 ●
Reckoning (IRS) 1984 ●
Fables of the Reconstruction (IRS) 1985 ●
Lifes Rich Pageant (IRS) 1986 ●
Dead Letter Office (IRS) 1987 ●
Document (IRS) 1987 ●
Eponymous (IRS) 1988 ●
Green (Warner Bros.) 1988 ●
Out of Time (Warner Bros.) 1991 ●

HINDU LOVE GODS
Hindu Love Gods (Giant-Reprise) 1990 ●

Who would ever have expected an American musical revolution to be launched from Athens, Georgia? R.E.M.'s rough-hewn guitar pop, introduced in 1981 by a stunning independent single ("Radio Free Europe"), has put them in the vanguard of a wide-reaching musical movement that relies on homegrown, populist rootsiness rather than any transatlantic inspiration. Blending Pete Buck's Byrdsian guitar playing with Michael Stipe's hazy, sometimes melancholic (but never miserable) vocals and impressionistic lyrics, plus a strong, supple rhythm section (Bill Berry and Mike Mills), R.E.M. plays memorable songs with unprepossessing simplicity and emotional depth. As hip acceptance has given way to full-fledged stardom, R.E.M. has grown less exciting but remained intelligent and committed to artistic expression (not only theirs).

The five-song **Chronic Town** EP, co-produced by Mitch Easter, continues the sound (if not all the rushed excitement) of the single, and boasts the remarkable "1,000,000" and the equally memorable "Carnival of Sorts (Box Cars)."

Murmur is a masterpiece, containing all the essential components of truly great serious pop music. On "Catapult," "Pilgrimage" and a reprise of "Radio Free Europe," Stipe inscrutably (but evocatively) mumbles his vocals with unmistakable passion, while the band spins haunting webs of guitar rock that are heavy with atmosphere. A completely satisfying collection, **Murmur** served as a guidepost for many of the bands who chose to follow R.E.M. back to the New South for inspiration.

Doomed to disappoint by comparison to the debut, **Reckoning** is not quite as consistent, although it contains enough equally great music to maintain R.E.M.'s reputation for excellence. "Harborcoat," "So. Central

Rain (I'm Sorry)," "(Don't Go Back to) Rockville" and "Pretty Persuasion" are all wonderful, and display not only clearer production (Easter and Don Dixon) but a less hurried pace and more articulate singing.

Fables of the Reconstruction (aka **Reconstruction of the Fables**), produced in London by Joe Boyd, finds R.E.M. largely neglecting catchy melodicism and driving rhythms for reflective, languidly meandering numbers that lack focal points and seem to start and finish with the structured inexorability of a light switch. A number of the songs are flat-out boring, and the album in toto is vague and colorless, although not entirely bland. "Can't Get There from Here," "Driver 8" and the raucous "Auctioneer (Another Engine)" do have familiar R.E.M. attributes.

A shortage of rewarding musical ideas and an air of flagging enthusiasm on the politically minded and far too restrained **Lifes Rich Pageant** makes it a remote and generally ignorable chapter in R.E.M.'s inexorable march towards the big time. Excepting a totally ace cover of the Clique's psychedelic obscurity, "Superman," sung in a delicious near-whine by Mike Mills, the rushed "Hyena" and the languid "Fall on Me," the record is instrumentally dull and almost entirely uninvolving.

With Stipe opting for a brave new world of enunciation on **Document**, Scott Litt's dynamic co-production pushes the songs back into the world of the living, with a bright, loud sound and an infusion of much-needed rock energy. Without sacrificing sensitivity, Buck plays up a storm, pushed into high gear by Berry's walloping big beat. The entire first side is brilliant, from the maniacally intense "Finest Worksong" to the stomping horn-flecked nostalgia of "Exhuming McCarthy," a goofball cover of Wire's "Strange" and the wordily name-dropping nonsense of "It's the End of the World as We Know It (And I Feel Fine)." The back of the LP is half as good, which is to say the sound is swell but the songs aren't. Nonetheless, millions misunderstood the stinging irony of "The One I Love" and made it a huge hit single.

Dead Letter Office, a curious and amusing B-sides/rarities collection, reveals R.E.M.'s proclivity for recording covers (it contains material by Pylon, Roger Miller, the Velvet Underground and Aerosmith) and a goofy sense of humor not often heard on their albums. Buck's liner notes explain the origins of all fifteen outtakes, pisstakes and oddities, including "Walter's Theme," written to be a restaurant commercial. The CD has a bonus: the contents of **Chronic Town**.

Raising their commercial sights in a way the faithful never imagined possible, R.E.M. then left IRS for the greener pastures of Warner Bros., prompting the release of a greatest hits package. **Eponymous** (now there's a band that knows its rock criticism) is a nearly straightforward compilation, except that it omits some crucial songs and has the original independent 45 version of "Radio Free Europe," an unused vocal take on "Gardening at Night" (from **Chronic Town**), an alternate mix of "Finest Worksong" and "Romance," a soundtrack contribution not previously on an R.E.M. record.

The quartet's arrival into the global pop stakes, **Green**, is a great, artistically mature record with more good songs than any prior R.E.M. album. Dropping the familiar jangle pop and crisp rhythms, the band finds a characteristic compromise with modern rock (although several numbers are entirely acoustic) that grants the lyrics and melodies precedence over immediately recognizable presentation. Indeed, Stipe's voice is the only familiar R.E.M. feature on the catchy "Stand," the U2-ish "Orange Crush" and the measured droney roughness of "Turn You Inside Out." Buck's diverse playing has never sounded better, and piano provides him with an effective complement. "Pop Song 89"—a witty reflection on stardom's social complications—and the old-fashioned "World Leader Pretend" flesh out a brilliant collection.

Opening the stylistic doors to keyboards, strings and horns, R.E.M. challenged audience expectations a little with the ambitious but uneven **Out of Time**, a generally entertaining collection of obliquely romantic (as opposed to obliquely political) songs given diverse arrangements that aren't as far outside the band's usual parameters as they might at first seem. Familiarly constructed songs like "Radio Song" (with a guest appearance by KRS-One), "Losing My Religion," "Shiny Happy People" (with Kate Pierson chiming in) and "Half a World Away" effectively progress from **Green**'s forthright presentation, while others sacrifice the band's artistic edge for the sake of flaccid conceptual meandering. "Low" sounds like a second-rate demo plus cello; "Endgame" is a baroque instrumental with Mike Mills and Michael Stipe combining on wordless pseudo-Beach Boys harmonies. Having toured extensively with the band, Peter Holsapple contributes bass or guitar to half the songs.

Hindu Love Gods, the belated issue of a 1987 studio get-together in which Buck, Mills and Berry backed singer/guitarist Warren Zevon on a well-chosen program of blues classics (with a terrible Prince cover thrown in for bad measure). Disregarding the album's general merits, it has little specific value for R.E.M. fans. The characterless playing is standard bar-band issue, and not especially adept at that: unable to locate a groove, Bill Berry clanks along haplessly throughout the LP. Thanks to the folks involved, however, this redundant exercise is the ideal modern blues album for people who bought the Robert Johnson reissue and never played it. [i]

See also *Fleshtones*.

RENALDO AND THE LOAF

Songs for Swinging Larvae (Ralph) 1979
Arabic Yodelling (Ralph) 1983
Streve and Sneff [tape] (Ralph) 1984
Olleh Olleh Rotcod (nr/Rotcod) 1985
The Elbow Is Taboo (Ralph) 1987

RESIDENTS & RENALDO AND THE LOAF

Title in Limbo (Ralph) 1983

Only the Residents' label would deign to sign a duo as deeply weird as Renaldo and the Loaf—in real life two Englishmen named David Janssen and Brian Poole (the latter *not* of '60s swingers the Tremeloes). Their bizarre studio-doctored vocals, cut-and-paste arrangements, jerky robot rhythms and alien instrumentation (among the pair's noisemakers: scalpel, metal comb, hacksaw blade, pickle jar, biscuit tins) suggest that Renaldo and the Loaf was evolved in the Residents' image. Unfortunately, **Songs for Swinging Larvae** has all the madness and none of the coherence of the Residents' nutty concepts, its offbeat wit stampeded instead by rampant disorienting eclecticism. Guaranteed to clear the room of your choice.

Arabic Yodelling is roughly more of the same, a collection of Rube Goldberg home-brewed insanity recorded over a two-year period. A bit less weird for weird's sake (although hardly in danger of mass appeal), it keeps the blindly whimsical faith the Residents themselves were in the process of outgrowing. **Title in Limbo**, the group's joint effort with their American soul brothers, however, is not at all enticing. **Streve and Sneff** is an American reissue of a pre-**Larvae** cassette the band had previously distributed on their own.

The general worldwide overuse of electronic sampling instruments may partially explain the delightful alternate-reality sound of **The Elbow Is Taboo**; then again, perhaps Renaldo and the Loaf have simply advanced past musical infantilism. The songs are indeed songs; they may contain obscure, unexpected sounds and bizarre vocals, but little of it seriously impedes the spare, charming folksiness. "A Street Called Straight," a most agreeable mélange, employs dulcimer and bouzouki as well as a keyboard; the title track shuffles along on a devolved reggae beat with mandolin as a prime instrument; the vocal-less "Dance for Somnambulists" mixes in glockenspiel and guitars. Crazy, man, crazy! [df/i]

RENEGADE SOUNDWAVE

Biting My Nails EP (Mute-Enigma) 1988
Soundclash (Mute-Enigma) 1989 φ
RSW in Dub (Mute-Elektra) 1990 φ

Originating as DJs and warehouse party promoters, the three members of Renegade Soundwave have always shown as much enthusiasm for dance beats and studio gimmickry as for actual songs. A home in the multi-ethnic west London enclave of Ladbroke Grove has also instilled in them the love of reggae and dub that is evident from the 1986 debut "Cocaine Sex" (included, along with its successor, "Kray Twins," on the American **Biting My Nails** 12-inch) through to the club-oriented **RSW in Dub** album. Along the way, a more conventional use of vocals, guitars and dance breaks has yielded two crossover UK hit singles: "Biting My Nails" and "Probably a Robbery" (both on **Soundclash**).

All of which gives Renegade Soundwave an identity crisis. Unsure whether to produce rock songs, dance anthems or dub jams, they experiment with each on **Soundclash** (the CD of which contains two bonus tracks) and just come across confused. On **RSW in Dub**, which contains mostly new and totally revamped material, they do away with the vocals but still zigzag between industrial house and dub reggae. Like many products of the dancefloor, Renegade Soundwave can be inspired when working with 12-inch singles (the trio's remixes for other bands, from Inspiral Carpets to Nitzer Ebb, are easily identifiable by the dominance of bass and percussive rhythm over melody). But they have yet to demonstrate such mastery on their albums. [tf]

REPLACEMENTS

Sorry Ma, Forgot to Take Out the Trash (Twin/Tone) 1981 ●
The Replacements Stink EP (Twin/Tone) 1982 + 1986 ●
Hootenanny (Twin/Tone) 1983 ●
Let It Be (Twin/Tone) 1984 ●
The Shit Hits the Fans [tape] (Twin/Tone) 1985
Tim (Sire) 1985 ●
Boink!! (nr/Glass) 1986
Pleased to Meet Me (Sire) 1987 ●
Don't Tell a Soul (Sire-Reprise) 1989 ●
All Shook Down (Sire-Reprise) 1990 φ

For a time the world's best rock'n'roll band—proof that those who missed the '60s could still build something great on the crass and hollow corpse of '70s music—Minneapolis' Replacements began as juvenile punks whose give-a-shit attitude masked the seeds of singer/guitarist/songwriter Paul Westerberg's self-destructive genius for injecting sensitivity into flat-out chaos. When it all clicked—volume, rawness, speed (pace *and* ingested substances), energy and passion—the Mats (short for Placemats) teetered drunkenly at the brink of the abyss and recklessly cracked jokes about it. Onstage and on vinyl, nothing could compare with their unpredictable excitement. But over the years, the onset of maturity and a reasonable desire for self-preservation caused Westerberg to draw the group back to the point where the latest album has almost none of the old fire.

The original foursome got written off a lot as sloppy, but only by those who chose not to see beyond the confusion. Chris Mars drummed as one possessed; spoiled teen Tommy Stinson (twelve when the band started) thumped a mean bassline; buffoonish guitarist Bob Stinson might wear a dress (or less) onstage but could alternate between ripping metal leads and achingly tender melody lines that come from his heart (if not his brain). And Paul Westerberg—too terrified to sing his soft songs—hid behind the band's noise. The Mats were one of those classic rock'n'roll combos whose music, looks and personalities fit together perfectly, the stuff of which legends are made.

The musical evidence of their creative importance was there on the first album, eighteen songs following the usual loud/fast/cynical rules with titles like "Shutup," "Kick Your Door Down," "I Hate Music" and "Shiftless When Idle." But a slow, bluesy ode to J. Thunders, "Johnny's Gonna Die," showed depth beyond their years. The **Stink** EP—initially issued in a white hand-rubberstamped sleeve—went for pure driving thrash and produced some gems, including "Dope Smokin Moron," "Kids Don't Follow" and "God Damn Job." But it landed them in the hardcore bins, even though the music and lyrics are much sharper than most, mixing equal parts arrogance and self-deprecating humor.

When **Hootenanny** combined blues, power pop, folk, country, straight-ahead rock, surf (or, more accurately, ski) and punk in a way few hardcore bands could even imagine, people started taking notice. **Stink**'s "Fuck School" gave way to "Color Me Impressed," a wise and soaring rock number about getting drunk and being bored by trendinistas that sounded pretty incongruous next to "Run It," a paean to beating red lights. Amid the roaring power of "Take Me Down to the Hospital" and the wacky Beatlesque collage of "Mr.

Whirly," Westerberg reached into his bag of solo heart-stoppers for a naked (yet never sappy) confession of loneliness, "Within Your Reach."

With **Let It Be**, the Mats became "stars," at least on the independent club/college radio circuit. The LP is more focused than anything else they'd done, boldly carrying out what they'd only tried on **Hootenanny**. They blended rock-pop and country shuffle on "I Will Dare," covered Kiss' "Black Diamond" and raved-up on novelty rockers like the lyrical vérité of "Tommy Gets His Tonsils Out" and "Gary's Got a Boner." Westerberg's knowledge of loneliness ("Sixteen Blue," "Answering Machine") gave way to total emptiness on the harrowing "Unsatisfied."

Critics trampled each other in a rush to claim discovery rights, Sire signed them and Twin/Tone celebrated with a cassette-only live tape—stolen from some kid bootlegging an Oklahoma show—which showed the feckless Mats at their most messed-up, playing (at least starting to play) a motley collection of their favorite covers, from R.E.M. to the Stones, Thin Lizzy to X.

The Replacements made the transition to major-labeldom with their artistic integrity intact. Ex-Ramone Tommy Erdelyi produced **Tim**, retaining all of the band's raggedness and devil-may-care spirit. Westerberg's tunes here are among his best ever, from a melancholy bar ballad ("Here Comes a Regular") to an obnoxiously mean-spirited anti-stewardess slur, "Waitress in the Sky." His raging insecurity shines through on "Hold My Life" ("because I just might lose it . . . ") and the anthemic "Bastards of Young." "Left of the Dial" celebrates alternative radio, while "Kiss Me on the Bus" considers the romantic possibilities of public transportation. A stupendous record.

Boink!! is an eight-song UK condensation of the band's pre-**Let It Be** catalogue, with the added bonus of an otherwise unreleased Alex Chilton-produced cut, "Nowhere Is My Home."

When it became apparent that Bob Stinson was in danger of succumbing permanently to the band's treacherous lifestyle, the Mats fired him and proceeded to record the incredible **Pleased to Meet Me** as a trio. With Jim Dickinson producing and Westerberg doing all the guitar work, the group stirred up another batch of their finest brew: virile, witty rockers ("Valentine," "Red Red Wine," "I.O.U."), tender ballads ("Nightclub Jitters," "Skyway"). There's a rollicking number about "Alex Chilton," a bizarre but fabulous stab at commercial radio acceptance ("Can't Hardly Wait") in which the Memphis Horns echo a deliciously nagging guitar riff over a wicked backbeat, and "The Ledge," a tense suicide vignette musically rewritten from **Hootenanny**'s "Willpower." On tour following the LP's release, the group unveiled a new guitarist, Slim Dunlap (ex-Curtiss A), and a far less obstreperous attitude.

Whether **Don't Tell a Soul** is a strong album with a few clunkers or a weak album with some great songs, the Mats' previous glories tinge the record with disappointment. (Initial impressions were strictly the latter; the record's better qualities have emerged over time.) Westerberg's arrival in adulthood has softened his outlook (while increasing his disillusionment) and reduced his desire to play blaringly loud, wild rock. But as his passions have cooled, his lyrical concerns have grown increasingly private; the songs are as strong and artistic as ever, but somehow less compelling. Arrangements which favor acoustic guitars, layers of harmony vocals and keyboards undercut the band's standard attack; Mars is consigned to keep the backbeat with a criminal minimum of rhythmic variation. "Achin' to Be," a gentle country love song, and the stately minor-key "Darlin' One" are extremely effective, as are "I'll Be You," the soaring "We'll Inherit the Earth" and "Anywhere's Better Than Here." But there's still an unsettling aloofness to the record. Rather than the previous album's reach-out-and-grab-someone impact, **Don't Tell a Soul** is merely an uneven collection of songs.

Compared to the stultifying **All Shook Down**, however, **Don't Tell a Soul** is positively blistering. A band album in name only, Westerberg used session players (including the three other Replacements) to craft lightweight songs that resemble the Replacements, but lack fire, content, imagination and tension. Considering the Mats' past achievements, the vocal duet with Concrete Blonde's Johnette Napolitano on "My Little Problem" is a fairly lame excuse for rock'n'roll. ("Bent Out of Shape" is the album's sole working burner, although the Stonesy "Happy Town" comes close.) While the acoustic "Sadly Beautiful" (with viola by John Cale) demonstrates how to find intensity in tranquility, the album—even a piano-based pitch for sobriety entitled "The Last"—fails to perform that feat twice. Oh momma, can this really be the end?

For Chris Mars, it was. He quit in November 1990. With a new drummer, the group hit the road soon after, playing mostly recent material to extremely favorable notices.   [ep/i]

REPTILE
Ivar Bongo EP (Bad Taste) 1989
Fame and Fossils (Bad Taste) 1990 ●

Oh, those wacky Icelanders! Related to the Sugarcubes through keyboardist Magga Örnólfsdottir (who left in '88, prior to Reptile's album, but appears on the four-song EP), this Reykjavik quintet makes its full-length debut with a charming hubbub of marimba, banjo, violin and sax, as well as guitar, bass and drums. **Fame and Fossils** fuses a version of the Sugarcubes' bizarre theatrics (I wouldn't attempt to grasp the logic of songs like "Gun Fun," "Candyflos War" or "What Are You Up To," in which giggling Magga Stina requests the song's object to "Hit me on the forehead") to an Ordinaire-y mad-jazz orientation, coming up with a dizzying pastiche that would be equally at home in a Spike Jones tribute show or an avant-garde multi-media performance.   [i]

See also *Sugarcubes*.

RESIDENTS
Meet the Residents (Ralph) 1974 + 1977 + 1985 ●
The Residents Present the Third Reich 'n Roll (Ralph) 1975 + 1979 ●
Fingerprince (Ralph) 1976 ●
Duck Stab EP (Ralph) 1978 + 1987
Duck Stab/Buster & Glen (Ralph) 1978 ●
Not Available (Ralph) 1978 ●
Eskimo (Ralph) 1979 ●
Nibbles (nr/Virgin) 1979

Diskomo/Goosebump EP (Ralph) 1980 ●
The Residents Commercial Album (Ralph) 1980 ● /
Mark of the Mole (Ralph) 1981 ●
The Tunes of Two Cities (Ralph) 1982 ●
Intermission EP (Ralph) 1982
The Residents' Mole Show (no label) 1983
Residue of the Residents (Ralph) 1983
George & James (Ralph) 1984
Whatever Happened to Vileness Fats? (Ralph) 1984
Assorted Secrets [tape] (Ralph) 1984
The Census Taker (Episode) 1985
The Big Bubble (Black Shroud-Ralph) 1985 ●
PAL TV LP (nr/Doublevision) 1985
Heaven? [CD] (Rykodisc) 1986 ●
Hell! [CD] (Rykodisc) 1986 ●
Stars & Hank Forever (Ralph) 1986 ●
13th Anniversary Show—Live in Japan (Ralph) 1986
Hit the Road Jack EP (Ralph) 1987
The Mole Show Live in Holland [CD] (Hol. Torso) 1987
    (East Side Digital) 1988 ●
God in Three Persons (Rykodisc) 1988 ●
God in 3 Persons: Original Soundtrack Recording
    (Rykodisc) 1988 ●
The King and Eye (Enigma) 1989 ●
Buckaroo Blues & Black Barry [tape] (Ralph Special
    Products) 1989
Stranger Than Supper (UWEB Special Products) 1990 ●
Cube-E Live in Holland (Enigma) 1990 ●
Freak Show (Official Product) 1991 ●

RESIDENTS & RENALDO AND THE LOAF

Title in Limbo (Ralph) 1983

What's a Resident? Epithets abound, but anent actual identities, anyone who knows ain't talking. Transplanted cinéastes—so the story goes—from Shreveport, Louisiana to the San Francisco area who also dabble in musical experiments, the foursome (trio? duo?) has woven a remarkable cloak of secrecy. Aside from the avowed purpose of avoiding misleading and potentially divisive individual credits, this creates an attention-getting mystique which, when the limited speculation on same has been exhausted, leaves absolutely nothing to contemplate but the music itself.

The Residents led Ralph Records from cottage industry to self-sufficient label, able to sell artistically ambitious oeuvres without selling themselves out. They're also paradigmatic of limited technical and compositional ability, marshalled, along with wit and imagination, in the service of works seeking to trample sacrosanct icons and rock's boundaries.

It's evidently not in them to write distinctive melodies that don't sound utterly bizarre. When they try, the results invariably sound like someone else's—albeit distinctly distorted or perverted—which is probably one reason why the dissection and reassembly of various bits of rock tradition has been one of their fortes since early on. Also, the Residents' approach owes great debts to the early groundbreaking of both Frank Zappa and Captain Beefheart. (It was at one time rumored that the storied N. Senada, a poet/saxist who allegedly collaborated with the Residents during his brief sojourn in the Bay Area, was actually Beefheart.) All that said, the Residents are superior synthesists, and the derivations

of their work can't deny the entertainingly provocative nature of their best achievements.

The first four efforts by the then-unnamed group were album-length tapes, including one which was sent (with no name on it) to a record company in the hopes of a deal and sent back to the quartet's return address, care of "Residents." Hence the moniker.

N. Senada's contribution, the concept of phonetic (re)organization, was adapted by the Residents on their first vinyl releases, the 1972 double-45 set **Santa Dog** and the 1974 debut album, **Meet the Residents**. **Santa Dog**'s four intriguing but inchoate expressions of Residency include weird manipulations of verbal as well as musical logic, de(con)struction of familiar (in this case, Yuletide) songs and the formulation of their own "instant standard" ("Fire," aka "Santa Dog," remade in 1978 and again in 1990). The album does likewise but more so, in quality as well as quantity, alternately a sophomoric giggle and a striking, off-the-wall twist of musical mind. The Residents had arrived, but weren't yet sure quite where they were. (The LP's cover, which snidely uses the graphics of **Meet the Beatles** in order to trash the Fab Four, was allegedly the subject of legal threats; the album was re-released in '77 with a tamer jacket and improved sound. Issued on CD in the late '80s—as were most of the group's early records—by East Side Digital, it adds the **Santa Dog** tracks and reverts to the original cover design.)

On **The Residents Present the Third Reich 'n Roll** the band transforms hooky bits from '60s Top 40 hits into two ridiculous, funny, scary and just plain jaw-dropping-weird side-long suites, "Swastikas on Parade" and "Hitler Was a Vegetarian," intended as "revenge" for the brainwashing of American youth into acceptance of rock's trivialization (or something like that). The LP was reissued with partially censored graphics in '79 (the original cover showed a carrot-toting Nazi officer bearing a distinct resemblance to Dick Clark) and on CD in '87, with the addition of two brilliant early 45s (and their B-sides): "Satisfaction," which makes Devo's subsequent try sound like the 1910 Fruitgum Co., and the Beatles perversion, "Beyond the Valley of a Day in the Life." (Again, the CD graphics return the lurid originals.)

In 1976, the band recorded **Tourniquet of Roses**, but since it supposedly would have taken up three sides, Ralph subtracted one side and released the rest as **Fingerprince**. The four excised songs were later released as the extremely limited edition **Babyfingers** EP, but reinstated (in the approximate middle of the program!) on the CD. (Technically speaking, the whole thing could have fit on one vinyl disc, albeit with reduced audio fidelity; alternately, they could have removed less than sixteen minutes' worth.) The need isn't clearly programmatic either; a little instant myth-making? At any rate, while **Fingerprince** (like the first album) contrasts a batch of brief tracks with one lengthy piece (the "ballet" "Six Things to a Cycle"), the band had shifted into a higher gear: imagine Frank Zappa meeting Steely Dan in a very avant mood, with the results then processed through a computer programmed by a paranoid schizophrenic with a sense of humor. This also applies fairly well to the **Babyfinger** tracks, which include the eight-minute "mini-opera" "Walter Westinghouse." (The late Snakefinger, whose outrageous guitar graced their early tapes and "Satisfaction," guests.)

Duck Stab was originally released as a 7-inch EP—the group at its most consistently accessible—but was enlarged to album size by the **Buster & Glen** half (also succinctly catchy and humorous). Noteworthy here is the dominance of songs with vocals, and the emergence of the distinctive voice of a Resident who eventually became the group's *only* voice. A 1987 reissue of the album dropped **Buster and Glen** from the title; the CD of the same name appends **Goosebump** (the B-side suite of the **Diskomo** 12-inch) and a swell lyric book.

Duck Stab was evidently cut as a lightweight diversion from the sessions for the more crucial conceptual masterwork, **Eskimo**. That project may have gotten out of control, since its release was postponed a year. Instead, out popped **Not Available**, supposedly recorded just after **Meet the Residents**—and, according to "the theory of obscurity," never intended for release. Hooey? If new, it's the culmination of various ideas the band had cultivated; if genuinely old, a lasting influence on Residentalia to come. I'd say the latter, since most everything said to have been recorded after it seems more refined in execution, if not so grand in sweep. Can you imagine a vast epic in five sections told with the recitative cadence of nursery rhymes (a Residents vocal trademark) but sounding as though played by E.T. and family? (The **Not Available** CD adds five tracks from **Title in Limbo**, the Residents' collaboration with Renaldo and the Loaf.)

With help from ex-Mothers keyboardist Don Preston and drummer Chris Cutler (of Henry Cow/Art Bears fame), **Eskimo**'s broad, electronically spacey sonic contours form a backdrop for what the Residents would have you believe is a re-creation of Eskimo life and culture (instrumental, but with printed narration on the jacket to explain the "stories.") It's brilliant and—yep—chilling, a most (but not totally) serious undertaking, evocative if not quite authentic. Some of its sections were reprogrammed as "Diskomo" and coupled on a 12-inch EP with a toyful look in on Mother Goose. The **Eskimo** CD appends the Residents' four contributions to Ralph's 1979 **Subterranean Modern** compilation.

They then cut an LP of 40 one-minute songs, with some celebrity helpers (Fred Frith is credited; Lene Lovich and XTC's Andy Partridge, among others, aren't). The rationale: a Top 40 song is just a minute of essence repeated three times and a commercial jingle is a minute long; ergo, "jingles are the music of America," and **The Residents Commercial Album** is an alternative Top 40. Cute idea for a minute but not enough justification for this gimmicky exercise. Many of the tracks boil down to a few seconds of "essence" repeated for a minute. Yet with the CD, programmability—even random shuffle sort—can bring out the gems and make it all sound better. Plus, the CD has bonus tracks: four from **Residue**, two great cover-version 45s ("Hit the Road Jack" and "This Is a Man's Man's Man's World" [*sic*]) and four more one-minute cuts: two excellent, one sowhat and one an okay take on the Ramones' "We're a Happy Family" done for Morgan Fisher's more imaginative brevity challenge, **Miniatures**.

The Mole trilogy began auspiciously with **Mark of the Mole**, a murkily limned, yet engrossing story of the Moles, forced out of their home into sharing one with the Chubs, and the ensuing conflict between the "underground" and slick complacency. A thin story, but musically harrowing. Unfortunately, **The Tunes of Two Cities** suggested that the Residents had painted themselves into a corner. The narrative isn't advanced and, although its context is fleshed out, it's simply not enough. The Residents seek to convey the cultural contrast in musical terms, alternating the Moles' abrasive, industrial grind with the Chubs' offbeat yet unctuous cocktail jazz. Neither the device nor its execution, notwithstanding some swell sax by Norman Salant and guitar by Snakefinger, can justify the whole album—not by Residential standards, anyway. (The **Tunes** CD adds three outtakes, again inserted in the middle of the program.)

The Residents' camp was in disarray. Despite the temporary acquisition of hotshot LA management, the Residents began to reel, first from internal dissension and later from desertions by members of the Ralph brain trust.

The 1983 **Mole Show** LP is the Residents' own authorized bootleg of the show's groundbreaking presentation at LA's Roxy Theatre in late '82. The band then proceeded to tour Europe, and released a second album, from an '83 performance in Holland. Both present **Mark of the Mole** surprisingly well, with the benefit of Penn Jillette (a longtime fan and friend) providing periodic narration to clarify the story. Although the performances are basically the same, the later one is a little tighter and has clearer sound. (The early one does have an amusing Jillette ad lib, during a staged argument with the band: "I don't care who you are, you sing like Gomer Pyle.") All the same, the Residents' charming way of squirming out of having presented an unfinished work is still an evasion. **Intermission** is exactly as billed—"extraneous" music from the show—and the first Residents record unable to stand on its own. (**Intermission** later became a bonus add-on to the CD of **Mark of the Mole**.)

Residue collects Resident leftovers, rarities and unreleased versions. It, too, sidesteps the Mole issue, but is at least exciting and entertaining (if a bit uneven and unintegrated), relying notably on the group's patented warpage of rock clichés. That's more than can be said of their collaboration with likeminded English weirdos Renaldo and the Loaf. Just who's at fault isn't clear (it can't all be Renaldo), but the record is far less than the sum of its parts. Only one track ("Monkey & Bunny") is truly worthy of the Residents; the rest deserves to be forgotten.

Not content with one incomplete ambitious venture, the Residents then launched another: the American Composer Series, an attempt to lionize their favorite songwriters by interpreting their work. The first volume of the projected sixteen-year (!) undertaking, **George & James**, matches up a side each of George Gershwin and James Brown (live at the Apollo, no less—with crowd sounds) and is an excellent, typically bizarre success. **Stars & Hank**, the series' second volume, has some worthwhile material, but isn't up to the creative level of **George & James**. Its examination of Hank Williams on Side One is hit (amusing) and miss (silly); the flip's fun-house-mirror treatment of John Philip Sousa's marches could've been done as effectively in a third of the time. That's a case of the format dictating the execution, something they'd wisely never allowed to happen before.

Soundtrack albums—one of a Residents short film ('84) and the other of a Hollywood feature ('85)—are hardly the records you'd expect to offer hope for a bright Residential future, but that's just what they do. The long-rumored *Vileness Fats* was intended to be a full-length music video back in 1972 (!), but was later abandoned. It's hard to believe the music was recorded that long ago; the songs may date from then, but the recordings on **Whatever Happened to Vileness Fats?** sound of more recent vintage. And it's a good, if not major, addition to the group's canon. Even better is the certifiably recent **The Census Taker**, which subverts more soundtrack music genres than you can shake a stick at in brilliant Residential fashion. Could this be the band's mode of entry into the real world?

Next came **The Big Bubble**. The contradictory "Part Four of the Mole Trilogy" self-description suggests that the Residents don't know how to kill off the monster they've created. That much of the album within an album *is* entertaining is besides the point. We've mainly heard this before, and positing it as the politically charged record by the miscegenated offspring of Moles and Chubs doesn't justify its billing. The Unfab Four (or Three, or—by now most likely—Two) are doing too much tail-chasing.

The neat **Live in Japan** (October 1985, in Tokyo, with Snakefinger along for the ride) draws on diverse corners of the group's output, from the '84 single of James Brown's "Man's World" (*not* on **George and James**) all the way back to "Smelly Tongues" from their very first LP. They do two songs from their collaborations with Snakefinger, and even the one decent number from their ill-begotten hook-up with Renaldo and the Loaf. Several tracks from **The Commercial Album** are exhumed and reworked with great success.

"Hit the Road Jack," the Percy Mayfield classic popularized by Ray Charles, gets an uncharacteristically accessible Residential once-over in a "special almost dance mix" on a 12-inch that also contains one track each from three recent albums.

The ambitious **God in Three Persons** is an hour-long scenario of Anyresident's personal journey to awareness of the balance and relativity of maleness and femaleness, pain and pleasure, reality and illusion. (Did anyone mention that pesky old Mole trilogy?) It begins with "song stylist" Laurie Amat singing the album's credits, including an abridged music publishing ID, and proceeds to tell its story via singing and (rhymed) narration over surprisingly simple, straightforward keyboard accompaniment. (Just *how* simple can be judged by a listen to the **Soundtrack**'s remixed and re-edited versions of most of **God**'s backing tracks: this music can't stand alone any more than **Intermission**.) The remarkable candor with which the piece addresses lust—we're talking blunt and uninhibited here—is yet another of the record's atypical attributes. The narrative is sometimes didactic, sometimes awkward and sometimes confusing, but impressive in spite of it. After being issued initially on CD, **God in Three Persons** was made available as a two-LP set.

Perhaps chastened by the Mole mess, the band plotted another tripartite project, but instead of trumpeting something they might not deliver, they just went ahead and did it. First they debuted "Buckaroo Blues" and "Black Barry" as sister pieces in the summer of '89 at New York's Lincoln Center, and then they added "The King and Eye" to form "Cube-E" that fall, honing the show in subsequent European and US tours. (The **Buckaroo Blues & Black Barry** cassette is a live recording from San Francisco, September 1989.) These full-fledged multi-media presentations included dancers, costumes, backdrops and props. Although occasionally flat and/or bewildering, the overall impression was stunning. Here at last was the Residents' history of American pop music in three "E-Z" steps: cowboy music, black slave and reconstruction music, and Elvis (the King . . . but of *what*?). This was a refinement of Residential modus and a new level of artistic achievement.

It comes across on the records, too, even without benefit of the visual aspect. Reconsidering familiar western idioms, the Residents fashion them into weirdly alien—yet more universal—epics of love and desperation. Stereotypical images are turned inside out to provide disturbing angles on the African-American slave and post-slave experience. Using just some narration and a batch of Presley hits reinterpreted Residents-style, **The King and Eye** (a studio recording with more material than was used onstage or, consequently, included on the live **Cube-E** album) incisively portrays Elvis' life and work as a misguided abandonment of innocence in favor of a sad yet comedic Oedipal journey. This is the near-perfection of (some of) what they started two decades ago with **Santa Dog**. Bringing an utterly unique perspective to an utterly unique icon, the Residents delivered a masterpiece, possibly their most successful work yet.

The UK-only **PAL TV** offers excerpts from **Vileness Fats** and selections from a Dutch performance of the Mole show. **Heaven?** and **Hell!**, two lengthy CD-only compilations, offer plenty of good music, but no rhyme or reason in the selection other than a general division into "beautiful" (**Heaven?**) and "ugly" (**Hell!**). A random-selection CD player equipped with a complete Residents catalogue could have done just as good a job choosing material as these discs do.

Two compilations eminently worthy of attention are **Assorted Secrets** and **Stranger Than Supper**. One side of the former is an early (spring '82) live Mole show; the other contains two live-in-the-studio sessions of songs they rarely (if ever) played onstage, including material from **Duck Stab/Buster & Glen**, **Not Available** (!) and **Tunes from Two Cities**.

A rare public/commercial release by the band's UWEB (Uncle Willie's Eyeball Buddies) fan club—which has, since 1988, issued a bunch of otherwise unavailable Residentalia, including a studio recording of **Buckaroo Blues** and a four-version **Santa Dog** CD—**Stranger Than Supper** offers a tasty sampling of what lies beyond. There's an early-'90 performance of "Teddy Bear" (a song also done for **The King and Eye**) from David Sanborn's *Night Music* (where the group shared the stage with Conway Twitty), a fine squint at "Oh Susannah" that didn't make it into "Buckaroo Blues," a great New Year's Eve serenade and an eleven-and-a-half-minute medley of "Land of 1000 Dances"/

"Double Shot of My Baby's Love," which includes the riff that later became a major motif in **God in Three Persons** (plus a chunk of the narration, too). Real good stuff; it will make you want to join UWEB.

Even prior to their *Night Music* appearance, the Residents reached network television, through a likely door—the one that leads into *Pee-wee's Playhouse*. Following artist Gary Panter (who used to do Ralph record covers) into his nutty corner of the CBS Saturday morning lineup, the Residents supplied the music for the infamous *Zizzybalubah* episode. On another media front, the group has frequently appeared as guest protagonists in *Those Annoying Post Bros.* and *Savage Henry*, two comic book series by Matt Howarth, creator of the Mole trilogy mini-comics.   [jg]

See also *Hybrid Kids, Snakefinger*.

MARTIN REV
Martin Rev EP (Infidelity) 1980
Clouds of Glory (Fr. New Rose) 1985

The keyboard half of pioneering New York psychoelectronic duo Suicide proves only slightly more melodic on his eccentric eponymous solo outing—all keyboards and rhythm machines, with only the occasional grunting vocal. The rich layering of synthesizer effects—at least compared to the brute minimalism of Suicide—is close to the articulate electronic orchestration of the Ric Ocasek-produced **Suicide** album (also released in 1980). The simple floating melody and disco rhythm-box ping of "Mari" also suggest the mantric pop quality of Suicide's near-hit 12-inch single, "Dream Baby Dream." More typical of **Martin Rev**, though, is the hellish pumping of "Nineteen 86" and "Jomo"'s industrial racket; the only thing missing is Suicide singer Alan Vega's mad bark.

Half a decade later, Rev returned with the likeminded **Clouds of Glory**, pressed on red vinyl. Musical styles may have finally caught up with this minimalist electro-rhythm pioneer, but he sticks resolutely true to course here, dispensing with vocals and layering weird sound effects over sturdy sequencer lines. The gently attractive "Whisper" would have made a very pretty song were Rev to give it lyrics.   [df/i]

See also *Suicide*.

REVENGE
See *New Order*.

REVERB MOTHERFUCKERS
Route 666 (Race Age) 1988
Twelve Swinging Signs of the Zodiac (Rave) 1989 ●

It's hard not to be leery of any band that defines itself as a purveyor of New York Scum Rock, as these gents do on the cover of their second LP. (Stuff like that always makes me think of those hideous "punk fashion" window displays Macy's had around '77. Anybody who'd wear a $400 leather jacket with the word "PUNK" spelled out in studs across the back would just have to be an asshole, y'know?)

Anyway, the Reverb Motherfuckers combine the funny-punk tendencies of some NYC-area hardcore bands with genuinely screwy guitar-smoked huzz. Imagine a version of Shockabilly in which both Chadbourne

and Kramer were still into Zappa and downs. Cross that horrible result with Adrenalin O.D. and you've got something similar to these guys' lesser stuff. RMF does have its moments, however, and there's no denying that **Route 666**'s silkscreened cover was one of the decade's best.   [bc]

REVILLOS
See *Rezillos*.

REVOLTING COCKS
Big Sexy Land (Wax Trax!) 1986 ●
You Goddamned Son of a Bitch (Wax Trax!) 1988 ●
Beers, Steers + Queers (Wax Trax!) 1990 ●
CHRIS CONNELLY
Whiplash Boychild (Wax Trax!) 1991 ●

PiL mixed disco beats with arty noise on **Metal Box**, taking a cue from Can, whose drummer (Jaki Liebezeit) made that band's most far-flung journeys swing. Revolting Cocks—a highly productive collaboration between Chicago powerhouse Al Jourgensen (Ministry, etc.), Belgian producer/musician Luc Van Acker and Scotland's Chris Connelly (his semi-industrial dancerock group, Fini Tribe, once recorded a Can song), with contributions from assorted other brothers-in-noise, including Jeff Ward of Lard—initially followed those early PiL efforts, rather than the dozens of industrial dance outfits that sprang up in Europe throughout the '80s. Deliberately and unapologetically abrasive (the vocals are invariably Brillo-throated), Revolting Cocks are a big heap of snarling, ugly fun.

With Richard 23 of Front 242 joining the basic RevCo pair, **Big Sexy Land** is diverting but unremarkable; nearly all of the material on it receives an unexpected charge on the charmingly titled double-live set **You Goddamned Son of a Bitch**. Cut at one Chicago show in September 1987 with a cast that includes Ministry's Paul Barker (who co-produced) and William Rieflin, the LP benefits from refined technical abilities and the almost palpable hostility the band radiates to its audience—and vice versa.

Employing the same quintet lineup as on the live record, **Beers, Steers + Queers** is, to a point, RevCo's tour de force. The title cut makes the most of the complex interaction of a set of very stiff rhythms, the base provided by a looped turntable scratch that's sure to send your roommate off the roof. The monolithic "Get Down" is highlighted by an honest-to-god guitar solo that recalls both prime Lou Reed and prime Tom Verlaine. Alas, "(Let's Talk) Physical," a seven-minute CD "bonus" reduced from the album's "(Let's Get) Physical," simply loops someone screaming the word "physical," and is meant to send *you* off the roof.

By the time of Connelly's solo album, the Scottish native had moved to Chicago and become a permanent member of both Ministry and RevCo. Building on the musical breadth of Fini Tribe, **Whiplash Boychild** is an amazing stylistic mixture of late-'70s Bowie and Iggy (accent on the former; the lead-off track could almost be an outtake from **Heroes**). Connelly makes the most of his deep, resonant voice, surrounding it with alternately muscular and atmospherically restrained rock music (although one hearty cabaret song is performed with just piano) of real power and subtlety. Very impressive.

[gk/i]

See also *Front 242, Ministry, Luc Van Acker*.

KIMBERLEY REW

See *Katrina and the Waves*.

REZILLOS

Can't Stand the Rezillos (Sire) 1978
Mission Accomplished ... but the Beat Goes On (nr/Sire) 1979

REVILLOS

Rev Up (nr/Snatzo-DinDisc) 1980
Attack! (nr/Superville) 1983

Scotland's Rezillos were a blast of fresh air compared to the more serious bands of new wave's first charge. The ex-art students were partial to an overhauled '60s look (e.g., foil mini-skirts, pop-art fabrics) and songs with titles like "Flying Saucer Attack" and "Top of the Pops." **Can't Stand the Rezillos** is an action-packed document of their pop/camp approach. Thrashings of the Dave Clark 5's "Glad All Over" and Gerry & the Pacemakers' "I Like It" surround "(My Baby Does) Good Sculptures," a typically loopy original.

The band flew apart not long after their album debut, leaving the live **Mission Accomplished** as an unsatisfactory memorial. Besides duplicating six tunes from **Can't Stand**, the record is plagued by near-bootleg-quality sound. Otherwise the performance is a raveup from start to finish, with five new originals and versions of the Kinks' "I Need You," Cannibal & the Headhunters' "Land of 1,000 Dances" and even Sweet's "Ballroom Blitz."

Fortunately, singers Fay Fife (real name: Sheilagh Hynde) and Eugene Reynolds regrouped with new musicians as the Revillos, and took the Rezillos' promise even further. **Rev Up** is filled with pastiches of '60s genres—"Bobby Come Back to Me," "On the Beach," "Secret of the Shadow," "Motorbike Beat"—and the obligatory non-originals—"Cool Jerk," "Hungry for Love," "Hippy Hippy Sheik" [*sic*]. The only foul touch is retitling the Rock-a-Teens' "Woo-Hoo" as "Yeah Yeah" and pawning it off as an original. But **Rev Up** is hilarious.

Attack!, the band's long-playing swansong, shows signs of strain. Some tunes ("Sputnick Kiss," "Man Attack!," "Your Baby's Gone") are as delightful as ever; others ("Mad from Birth to Death," the instrumental "Man Hunt") are decidedly slight. If there's another non-original besides the Exciters' "Tell Him," it's virtually indistinguishable from the rest, not only because of stylistic similarity but by the lack of songwriter credits anywhere on the album. For sheer sustained obsession with a Toontown '60s approach, though, the Rezillos deserve a tinfoil merit badge. [si]

See also *Prisoners, Shake*.

MARC RIBOT

Rootless Cosmopolitans (Island) 1990 φ

In the past few years, guitarist Ribot (who got his start in the Real Tones, a pickup band that backed NYC-visiting soul singers, including Wilson Pickett) has racked up an impressive résumé, working with talents as diverse as Tom Waits, Elvis Costello, John Zorn, Marianne Faithful and the Lounge Lizards. He's also a charter member of the Hal Willner rep company, having played on, among other things, the producer's spoken-word-and-music projects with Allen Ginsberg and William S. Burroughs.

Ribot's album (named for his band; the phrase is from a Ginsberg poem, out of Joseph Goebbels) is a pretty enjoyable hybrid of "free" styles that has a distinctly Beefheartian air at times, particularly when Ribot's alternately fluid and jagged playing goes one-on-one with Don Byron's bass clarinet. While it would be easy to live without the arch spoken vocal on an otherwise inventive cover of Hendrix's "The Wind Cries Mary," the guitar-only deconstruction of "While My Guitar Gently Weeps" is right on the money. **Rootless Cosmopolitans** isn't a life-changer but, as avant-garde ear candy goes, it's unusually chewy. [gk]

See also *Lounge Lizards*.

BOYD RICE

Boyd Rice (nr/Mute) 1981

NON

Physical Evidence (nr/Mute) 1982
Blood & Flame (nr/Mute) 1987 ●

BOYD RICE/FRANK TOVEY

Easy Listening for the Hard of Hearing (nr/Mute) 1984

BOYD RICE AND FRIENDS

Music, Martinis and Misanthropy (nr/Bad) 1990 ●

The first album by California conceptualist Boyd Rice (one of the first avant-garde "musicians" to use turntables as a creative tool) offers no information beyond the artist's name (embossed on the all-black cover), that it was recorded in the mid-'70s and is "playable at any speed." The droning noise slices, which are not audibly ascribable to any specific instruments, seem to consist of short tape loops layered over one another to create repetitive but varying textures (like Frippertronics, but without the guitar) that slow down and speed up on their own. Unlistenable.

Having thus cleared the decks of past achievements, Rice (aka Non) released **Physical Evidence**, a collection of more recent pieces, some of them recorded live. Armed with the deadpan conceptual humor of individual titles (my favorite is "(Theme from) Dark Shadows," the writing of which is, astonishingly, credited to someone other than Rice), the fifteen jarring loops and layers of shapeless (but uniformly unpleasant) noise that comprise **Blood & Flame** make it a sound effects record for the deeply disturbed.

Easy Listening, while fairly routine for the eccentric Rice, takes Frank Tovey—aka Fad Gadget, himself no stranger to found sounds—off on a conceptual trip far from his usual recording format. "All sounds either collected or generated ... by non-musical appliances"—in other words, this ain't music at all, but rather repetitive, rhythmically ordered noises, mostly on the order of church bells and other things that can be struck. Not all that radical and not in the slightest bit charming, the LP (recorded in 1981) is structurally impressive but aggravating in the extreme. [i]

RICH KIDS

Ghosts of Princes in Towers (nr/EMI) 1978 (nr/Fame)
1983

After being squeezed out of the Sex Pistols, bassist/singer Glen Matlock formed the Rich Kids with guitarist Midge Ure and drummer Rusty Egan (both of whom later collaborated on Visage, with Ure eventually going on to join Ultravox), plus one Steve New. During their tempestuous year-long alliance, the Rich Kids managed only one album, ludicrously misproduced into a muffled mess by Mick Ronson. Despite abysmal sound, the band's talent emerges, and **Ghosts** is an extraordinary album of daring experimental rock/pop that has two utterly brilliant pieces (the title track and "Marching Men") plus a few others nearly as good. While the predominant guitar work is occasionally mundane, there are enough novel ideas and convincing songs to make this uniquely flavored project survive the audio bloodbath and emerge victorious.   [i]

See also *Doll by Doll, Sex Pistols, Ultravox, Visage.*

JONATHAN RICHMAN AND THE MODERN LOVERS

Jonathan Richman & the Modern Lovers (Beserkley) 1977
(Beserkley-Rhino) 1986 ●
Rock'n'Roll with the Modern Lovers (Beserkley) 1977
(Beserkley-Rhino) 1986 ●
Back in Your Life (Beserkley) 1979 (Beserkley-Rhino)
1986 ●
The Jonathan Richman Songbook (nr/Beserkley) 1980
Jonathan Sings! (Sire) 1983
Rockin' and Romance (Twin/Tone) 1985
It's Time for Jonathan Richman and the Modern Lovers
(Upside) 1986 ●
Modern Lovers 88 (Rounder) 1987 ●
The Beserkley Years: The Best of Jonathan Richman and
the Modern Lovers [CD] (Beserkley-Rhino) 1987 ●
23 Great Recordings by Jonathan Richman and the
Modern Lovers [CD] (nr/Beserkley-Essential-Castle
Comm.) 1990 ●

MODERN LOVERS

The Modern Lovers (Beserkley) 1976 (Beserkley-Rhino)
1986 ●
Live (Beserkley) 1977 ●
The Original Modern Lovers (Bomp!) 1981

JONATHAN RICHMAN

Jonathan Richman (Rounder) 1989 ●
Jonathan Goes Country (Rounder) 1990 ●

At the outset of his career, Jonathan Richman was considered a radical trailblazer, precociously exploring minimalist rock years before such behavior became popular (or even acceptable). Not only was his unique approach enormously influential on later bands, early members of the Modern Lovers went on to become successful in such groups as Talking Heads and the Cars. Over the course of his recordings, however, Richman's predilection for childlike whimsy replaced the angst-ridden emotionalism of his first songs, and he eventually lost his flock by refusing to remain the same character he had been a decade earlier.

The first Modern Lovers album was cobbled together by Beserkley supremo Matthew King Kaufman from demos, the bulk of which had been produced by John Cale in 1971 when it looked as if the band would be signed to Warner Bros. Despite the fragmentary nature of its parts, **The Modern Lovers** is surprisingly coherent and contains all of Richman's classic creations: "Roadrunner," "Pablo Picasso," "Girl Friend," "She Cracked," etc. The stark, simple performances highlight an adenoidal New England voice that lacks everything technical but nothing emotional. One of the truly great art-rock albums of all time.

Although released shortly after **The Modern Lovers, Jonathan Richman & the Modern Lovers** was recorded five years later with a totally different band, and has little in common with the first LP. Not realizing the time frame, many people took this as a sign of artistic inconsistency, and were put off by such silliness as "Abominable Snowman in the Market" and "Hey There Little Insect." The record is, in fact, pretty great, blending guilelessness with such heart-wrenching pieces of honesty as "Important in Your Life." Enough of Richman's early approach carries over to temper the giddy romps, and it's a thoroughly charming, low-key album.

Rock'n'Roll takes Richman even further away from seriousness. Mixing traditional folk songs and lullabies with originals that would do Mister Rogers proud ("Ice Cream Man," "Rockin' Rockin' Leprechaun"), the ironically titled album stretched the ability of his adult fans to join in the fun. Abiding wittiness—like "Dodge Veg-O-Matic"—hedges the album's stylistic bet, but many were left wondering just where Richman was heading.

Live, recorded in England, is full of the flakiest songs in his repertoire—featherweight and best suited for very young people. **The Jonathan Richman Songbook** is a compilation, as is **The Beserkley Years**, a fine CD-only collection of eighteen classic tracks, both studio and live. The unrelated UK-only **23 Great Recordings** is an even bigger anthology covering basically the same '70s material.

Back in Your Life was recorded (after a long layoff) with two different bands, the regular Modern Lovers and a vocals/string bass/glockenspiel ensemble. The songs—which include five uniquely appropriate cover versions—are totally over the top, as fanciful and ridiculous as possible. There's nothing remotely connected to the original Modern Lovers' rock'n'roll work; comparisons to Groucho Marx's musical ventures are more relevant. Impossible to hate, this record merely defies honest enthusiasm.

Four years later, the same is fortunately not the case on **Jonathan Sings!**, a wonderful LP showcasing a fully revitalized Richman with an altogether new outlook. Audibly bursting with love, Richman eloquently (in his own ingenuously clumsy way) sings of "That Summer Feeling," exclaims "You're the One for Me" and rejoices at having "Somebody to Hold Me." Elsewhere, he defends the innate wisdom of infants in "Not Yet Three," offers a new look at world travel ("Give Paris One More Chance") and even extols the joys of "This Kind of Music." The new Modern Lovers—two women and three men—have a strong but understated presence that keeps Richman exciting without getting in his way. Simply put, **Jonathan Sings!** is one of the most uplifting albums in memory, and Richman's best since his debut.

Jonathan's stayed on the right track (with an exception) ever since, issuing one charming album after the next. **Rockin' and Romance** (retaining two Modern Lovers from **Sings**) is a spartan, casually produced (to the point of sonic obscurity) affair, but songs about "The Beach," "Vincent Van Gogh" (number two in Richman's Great Painters series), baseball ("Walter Johnson," "The Fenway"), travel ("Down in Bermuda") and other winning topics are all filled with his remarkable wit and intelligence. Who else could write a paean to bluejeans that discusses the relative merits of various brands without being mistaken for a commercial? Slight demerits for the shoddy sound quality, but no complaints whatsoever about the music.

It's Time For reunites Richman with erstwhile Modern Lover guitarist Asa Brebner. The audio fidelity is better; an accordionist, producer Andy Paley's guitar work and Richman's sax tooting make for an unusual, busier-than-ordinary (relatively speaking) rock sound. "Yo Jo Jo" is a crazed instrumental raveup, the most electric thing he's done in this decade. Richman's lyrical concerns are more general than in the recent past: for every "Double Chocolate Malted" (which has a strangely cranky tone to it) or "Corner Store," there are two songs (e.g., "It's You," "When I Dance," "Just About Seventeen," "This Love of Mine") that are less specific and to a degree less captivating. A confusing (or is that confused?) album, **It's Time For** has the aura of a transitional project.

Never fear. Accompanied by a second guitarist and a drummer, Richman grabbed his oft-neglected saxophone and cut the magical **Modern Lovers 88**, an all-too-brief set of semi-electric rock tunes that hark back in composition and presentation to **Jonathan Richman & the Modern Lovers**. The woolly "Dancin Late at Night" and the romantic "Gail Loves Me" display a budding Holly orientation that bears more exploration; "New Kind of Neighborhood" resembles Dion; "California Desert Party," "Everything's Gotta Be Right" and "Circle I" (a delightful ode to vegetables) convert the essential ingredients of '50s R&B into airy but exciting dance-rock as only the Modern Lovers can.

As the title intimates, **Jonathan Richman** continues its predecessor's minimalist direction, presenting the artist accompanied only by his guitar and percussive footstomps (though an unobtrusive rhythm section pops up on two songs). The solo thing doesn't work as well on record as it does live, and the material's a bit spotty (three out of twelve tracks are instrumental covers of pop standards, one is sung in French and another in Spanish), but **Jonathan Richman** is not without its charms. Check out "Closer," "Fender Stratocaster" and "I Eat with Gusto, Damn! You Bet," a spoken-word verse defending Jojo's sloppy table manners.

In contrast, **Jonathan Goes Country** finds the singer backed by a full band of seasoned studio pros, led by producers Lou Whitney and D. Clinton Thompson (of Morells/Skeletons fame), with ingratiating results. The program is a mixture of well-chosen covers, reworkings of previously recorded Richman tunes and a few swell new originals. Rather than sounding like a gimmicky affectation, the album's faux-Nashville arrangements prove to be a perfect vehicle for Jonathan's bucolic sincerity.

The demos dredged up for **The Original Modern Lovers** date from 1973 and were produced by Kim Fowley. The LP includes two versions of "Roadrunner," plus "Astral Plane," "Girlfren" and "She Cracked," as well as some otherwise unrecorded numbers. Despite thin sound it offers slightly different approaches from what surfaced on the first album. Shoddy but relevant. [i/hd]

See also *Cars, Necessaries, Real Kids, Talking Heads*.

RIDE

Ride EP (nr/Creation) 1990 ●
Play EP (nr/Creation) 1990 ●
Smile (Sire-Reprise) 1990 ϕ
Fall EP (nr/Creation) 1990 ●
Nowhere (Sire-Reprise) 1990 ϕ

Inspired by the Manchester rave scene, this young quartet from the English university city of Oxford finished art college and began laying washes of guitar damage and catchy echoed vocals over shuffling dance beats. The tentative first EP leads off with an original entitled "Chelsea Girl" and follows it with three similar long noise-pop songs, the best of which is "Close My Eyes." The more distinctive **Play** has a louder, harder sound (converting the previous record's jagged squalls into a continuous thick gauze) and, on the exemplary "Like a Daydream," rich folk-rock harmonies. (As Ride's introduction to America, **Smile** combines the two EPs—which contain too much filler to make a strong album—on a single disc under a new title.)

Focusing on the band's vocal side but also displaying its extended dance groovability, Ride's first real album—produced with an annoyingly conscientious lack of sonic clarity—is indistinct and frequently dull, a collection of unmemorable songs given ineffectually stylized atmospheric performances on acoustic and electric instruments. While too many of **Nowhere**'s bland tunes drag along at a lazy clip, turning up the pep-o-meter doesn't ensure any significant improvement. With the exception of the tuneful tremolo surge of "Polar Bear," the hypnotic "Vapour Trail" and the winsome "Taste," **Nowhere** is no big deal. [i]

STAN RIDGWAY

The Big Heat EP (nr/Illegal) 1985
The Big Heat (IRS) 1986
Mosquitos (Geffen) 1989 ●
Partyball (Geffen) 1991 ●

It's no coincidence that the lyrics on **The Big Heat** album (the EP is a pre-LP teaser) are printed on the inner sleeve in prose format; ex-Wall of Voodoo singer Ridgway's a pulp novelist at heart. Proffered with his exaggerated side-of-the-mouth delivery and instrumentation that reaches for maximum film noir ambience, the songs recount amazing stories of crime, war and bizarre characters in uncommon and highly engaging fashion. **The Big Heat** is a rare record—one that will have you as interested in the lyrical action as its substantial musical attributes.

If anything, Ridgway outdoes himself on **Mosquitos**, a record so chock full of atmosphere that it's nearly visual. As before, Ridgway is more of a narrator than a singer, and he shows his skill as a song- and story-writer on nearly every cut. If **The Big Heat** was film noir, **Mosquitos** is *The Last Picture Show*. Another essential album.   [i/ds]

See also *Wall of Voodoo*.

RIFLE SPORT
Voice of Reason (Reflex) 1983
Complex EP (Ruthless) 1985
White (Ruthless) 1987 ●
Live at the Entry, Dead at the Exit (Ruthless) 1989
Primo (Big Money-Ruthless) 1991 ●

FLOUR
Flour (Touch and Go) 1988 ●
Luv 713 (Touch and Go) 1990 ●
Machinery Hill (Touch and Go) 1991 ●

Rifle Sport are central members of Minneapolis/St. Paul's "third wave." After the Suicide Commandos/Suburbs in the mid-'70s, and the Hüskers/Replacements at the beginning of the '80s, along came bands like Soul Asylum, Man Sized Action and Otto's Chemical Lounge. These combos bloomed roughly around the time of the worldwide hardcore explosion, but none of them were the least bit doctrinaire. Rifle Sport drew on some of the "post-punk" Angloisms that colored the sound of certain Chicago groups emerging in the same period, and the band has always valued structural tension over compositional speed. The lineup has been stable for almost a decade, and in that time the quartet's sound has evolved into uniquely propulsive, but somehow low-key, guitar rock. The lyrics are sometimes opaquely personal, and the songs are more circularly mopey than ecstatically expanding.

Describing Rifle Sport as a younger version of Mission of Burma without the underlying Stooges-worship may have a bit of truth to it; the band's records document its progress and evolution in a laudable and noisy fashion. Fans of edge-heavy shuffling should find them quite winning; newcomers should start with the most recent wax and work backwards.

Bassist Pete (Flour) Conway—also a longtime member of Breaking Circus—has cut several solo discs (the first two are on one CD) that are grungier one-man-shows. The sound is reminiscent of that Big Black/Helios Creed wall-of-shit approach, crossed with Eno's early pop-whuzz. Both **Flour** and **Luv 713** are pleasant pieces of atmospheric blanket-snuff, even if live shows in support of them have been a tad weak.   [bc]

See also *Breaking Circus*.

ZOOGZ RIFT
Idiots on the Miniature Golf Course (Snout) 1979 (SST) 1987
Amputees in Limbo [tape] (Snout) 1982 (SST) 1987
Music Sucks [tape] (Snout) 1982
Can You Smell My Genitals from Where You're Standing? [tape] (Snout) 1983
None of Your Damn Business! [tape] (Snout) 1983
The Diseased Confessions of Moamo Milkman [tape] (Snout) 1984
Ipecac (Azra) 1984 (SST) 1987
Interim Resurgence (Snout) 1985 (SST) 1987
Amputees in Limbo, Deluxe European Edition (nr/Cordelia) 1985

Island of Living Puke (SST) 1986
Looser Than Clams ... A Historical Retrospective (SST) 1986
Water (SST) 1987
Water II: At Safe Distance (SST) 1987
Son of Puke [tape] (SST) 1987
Nonentity (Water III: Fan Black Dada) (SST) 1988 ●
Murdering Hell's Happy Cretins (SST) 1989 ●
Torment (SST) 1989 ●
War Zone (Ger. Musical Tragedies) 1990
Europe 1990 (Ger. Musical Tragedies) 1990

ZOOGZ RIFT & MARC MYLAR
Nutritionally Sound [CD] (Trigon) 1990 ●

RICHIE HASS & THE BEATNIKS
Drummers' Hall of Fame [tape] 1985

SCOTT COLBY
Slide of Hand (SST) 1987

As imaginative and stimulating as he is irritating and vitriolic, California's Zoogz Rift (Robert Pawlikowski) is an iconoclastic original, a reactionary whose paranoia has too frequently detracted from his music's experimental pizzazz and considerable exotic charm. This might be explained by what were, for a long time, his primary intellectual inspirations: Salvador Dali's dadaist strategies and Ayn Rand's objective realism. The singer/guitarist is (too) often compared musically to Frank Zappa and Captain Beefheart; while this may have applied to his earlier recordings, the past few years have found Rift toiling prolifically in a fertile field all his own. And lest casual observers be intimidated by his scatology and other intentional offenses to good taste and community standards, let it be stated clearly that Rift is not some talentless asshole making noise for an audience of one. Although they are wildly uneven, many of his records are genuinely good.

Idiots on the Miniature Golf Course features the Micro Mastodons, a band which includes songwriter/drummer Richie Hass, a longtime Rift associate. Dedicated to Don Van Vliet, this collection of private surrealistic humor, overambitiously complex writing and selfconsciously zany performances sets the tone for much of what was to follow. Another featured player on this collection is guitarist John Trubee, who has stuck it out with Rift on and off over the years, and is infamous in his own right for the classic novelty single, "A Blind Man's Penis." (The **Idiots** cassette adds "I Wanna Dismember You Just the Way You Are" and "Lovely Girl."

Over the next three years, Rift issued five cassette-only albums. While SST later reissued one of them on vinyl and tape, the remaining four were left to obscurity. **Amputees in Limbo** and **Ipecac** form a paranoid pair whose emotional timbre is evident in titles like "My Daddy Works for the Secret Marines," "Art Band" ("You're nothing but a fart band"), "I Was the Only Boy at the Teen Girls Slumber Party" and "You Fucked Up." Rift's Amazing Shitheads, his band at the time, was an uncompromising group of competent ya-hoos in acerbic synch with their leader. (The original issue of **Ipecac** is a picture disc. There's an extra track on the **Ipecac** tape. Likewise, the SST cassette of **Amputees** adds an alternate version of "Eyes of Bodhidharma" and another bonus.)

Rift began to lighten up slightly on **Interim Resur-**

gence and the charmingly titled **Island of Living Puke**. Cosmic etherea ("X-Ray Girls") and amusing self-analysis ("Nightclub Sequence") share space with his usual spleen ventilation.

Looser Than Clams is an, ahem, "greatest hits" LP that served as an intermission prior to Rift's H2O trilogy. By **Water**, his musical talents had far surpassed his ranting, although his misanthropy continues unabated. **Water II** is tighter yet, with synthesizers and samplers coming to the fore. The off-kilter instrumentals on **Nonentity** show off his idiosyncratic guitar playing to fine advantage and allow the group to simmer eccentrically in the breeze. (The CD and cassette add three tracks.)

While preparing and releasing the Water trilogy, Rift stuck together **Son of Puke**, a patience-defying cassette mixing samples from his collection of spoken-word ephemera and instrumental bits—a few guitar chords here, some $40 Casio keyboard plinks there—all seemingly at random. It's occasionally fun but not easy to endure for the full 45 minutes. If Rift's liner notes are to be believed, the cassette's flip side—a female vocal group carefully singing Beatles songs to the accompaniment of two jazzy electric guitarists (except for the full-scale sonic hell of "Revolution No. 9")—is by the unknown Transients and comes from a tape he discovered in a garbage bin. Hmmm . . .

Divided into a live-in-Holland side and a dead-in-Los Angeles side, **Murdering Hell's Happy Cretins**—a pivotal album on which Rift renounces his adherence to dada—is an absolutely delightful mixture of Zoogz's personable stage presence (the guy can really sing!) and some fine (mostly instrumental) studio work. The title track puts jolly music to one of his patented (and amusing) rants; the demento "One of Us" features Hass' wild vibraphone riffing.

Recorded a few months prior to **Hell's Happy Cretins**' studio side, **Torment** is an all-new record that marks the reappearance of saxophonist Marc Mylar (absent since **Water**). While the cassette adds three songs, the CD packs in an entire unreleased album entitled **United We Fall**.

Given his ongoing difficulties with the American record industry, Rift has recently had to look overseas to maintain the flow of his massive output to vinyl. The weak **War Zone** (subtitled **Music for Obnoxious Yuppie Scum**) consists of the 20-minute "Kasaba Kabeza (Drop the Facades)" instrumental suite (whose final movement is dubbed "Pharquar Resolvo Kaputo Solo Resolvo Redundo Bono Honko"—an entirely apt description for this tedious horns'n'noise workout) and a side of shorter items, including a viciously funny Traveling Wilburys' spoof, "You Can Count on Us."

Unlike the ambitious sextet Rift led on the '88 tour preserved on **Hell's Happy Cretins**, he is joined only by a post-Hass rhythm section and keyboardist Jonathan "Mako" Sharkey on **Europe 1990**. This compendium of performances from Switzerland, Germany, Austria and Holland has a disconcerting undercurrent of tension and harsh sound, but does review an impressive range of material and gives Zoogz a chance to spotlight some extremely inventive guitar work.

A lot of the two-man **Nutritionally Sound** project consists of barely structured high-tech studio dabbling,

nicely recorded sounds (including keyboards, horns, guitar, percussion, spoken and/or found vocals) that don't coalesce into any clear-cut musical form. Several of the things that most resemble songs (a nearly straight rendition of "I'm Telling You Now" with a twisted guitar solo, "Get Up offa That Thing," "All Bets Are Off") are, in fact, songs; a lot of what surrounds them, however, is just self-indulgent hooey.

Slide guitarist Scott Colby (who has also accompanied Henry Kaiser) was a frequent member of the Rift entourage up through 1986 or so, and his old trail boss returned the favor by producing **Slide of Hand**. This adventurous instrumental album sets Colby's bottleneck loose in a studio with such sidemen as Kaiser, John French and Willie Lapin (also a Rift vet). Since Colby doesn't come at slide guitar from a blues angle, his playing is fairly uncommon; the album is more or less jazz played like rock. [rg/i]

See also *John Trubee*.

WILL RIGBY

See *dB's*.

MARC RILEY WITH THE CREEPERS

Creeping at Maida Vale EP (nr/In Tape) 1984
Cull (nr/In Tape) 1984
Gross Out (nr/In Tape) 1984
Shadow Figure EP (nr/In Tape) 1984
Fancy Meeting God! (nr/In Tape) 1985
Four A's from Maida Vale EP (nr/In Tape) 1985
Warts 'n' All (nr/In Tape) 1985

CREEPERS

Miserable Sinners (In Tape-Last Time Round) 1986
Rock'n'Roll Liquorice Flavour (Red Rhino-Fundamental) 1987 ●
Sleeper: A Retrospective (nr/Bleed) 1989

Guitarist/keyboardist Riley was booted out of the Fall in 1982, reportedly over an unseemly penchant for pop. His prolific output as a solo artist and bandleader, however, only slightly warrants such categorization. Although Riley shares his former group's taste for deadpan vocals and distorted guitar and keyboard sounds, freed of Mark E. Smith's clutches he exhibits more melodic, structured songwriting and has one foot firmly rooted in the garage punk tradition.

All three EPs are taken from sessions for John Peel's radio program and feature one of Riley's favorite lyrical gambits—taking the piss out of other groups. **Creeping at Maida Vale** is a great little record, with four strong songs, including "Location Bangladesh," a clever stab at bands who travel the world for exotic video locales. **Four A's**, equally enjoyable, contains "Bard of Woking," aimed at the people's-poet pretensions of one Style Councillor. The **Cull** compilation fills one side with **Creeping** and the other with reprises of prior, vaguely Velvets-ish singles.

Gross Out, while not breaking any new musical ground, does contain one of Riley's finest moments, "Gross." **Fancy Meeting God!** is an energetic, sometimes catchy and often hilarious LP, which unfortunately loses a little zip towards the end. Had it been

556

edited together with **Gross Out**'s highlights, the sum would have been much greater than the parts.

Warts 'n' All is a fun greatest-hits run-through recorded live in Amsterdam. As entertaining for Riley's between-song banter as it is for great songs (including Eno's pre-ambience "Baby's on Fire"), it can serve as a very good introduction to the uninitiated.

Miserable Sinners and **Rock'n'Roll Liquorice Flavour** both drop Riley's name (even though he's still obviously the leader) and employ Mekon/Three John Jon Langford in the producer's chair. It is on these two LPs that the Creepers are at their peak. The sound on **Miserable Sinners** is a dense swirl of guitars, but the real change is in the lyrical approach, which has gone from satiric fun-making to introspective and self-referencing. "I strive to be original/have my own sound/I don't run my VU records/into the ground," sings Riley.

Liquorice Flavour follows suit with clever but serious self-examination, again tipping a hat to influences (and including a brilliant cover of the Pretty Things' '64 classic, "Rosalyn"). The Tom Waits-like piano ballad "Sweet Retreat" states "You don't have to listen to **Swordfishtrombone** [*sic*] . . . but it helps." The LP has a down-home feel—not unlike the Mekons—on several tracks, giving it more textural and stylistic variety than its predecessors. (The artsy, spoken "Derbyshire" almost sounds like Sonic Youth.) It's only reasonable that the group should dissolve after releasing their finest record.

Unfortunately, precious little has been heard from Riley since the breakup, although he did contribute to the 1988 Johnny Cash tribute, **'Til Things Are Brighter**, playing with his Mekon pals. The following year, **Sleeper: A Retrospective** was released, a four-sided, history-spanning collection reprising material from all the studio records save one (**Fancy Meeting God!**). With such highlights as all of **Shadow Figure**, three of the **Four A's** and about half each of the final two albums, **Sleeper** is a very useful sampler, and an effective demonstration of Riley and company's musical development. Now if he'd only get back to work.

See also *Fall*.   [dgs]

PENNY RIMBAUD & EVE LIBERTINE
See *Crass*.

RINGLING SISTERS
See *¡Screamin' Sirens!*

RIP RIG + PANIC
God (nr/Uh Huh-Virgin) 1981
I Am Cold (nr/Virgin) 1982
Attitude (nr/Virgin) 1983
FLOAT UP CP
Kill Me in the Morning (Upside) 1985
MARK SPRINGER
Piano (nr/Illuminated) 1984

One of the Pop Group's numerous offshoots, Rip Rig + Panic was a jazz-funk fusion band that left art-punk behind musically but retained a similarly irreverent sensibility. Named after a Roland Kirk LP, the band appropriately featured saxophone/piano free-for-alls. They were not as anarchic as their jazz inspirations, though; repetitive bass licks (Sean Oliver) and stable percussion (Bruce Smith) are great aids for more centrist listeners.

The band's most appealing aspect is its high-spiritedness. Beyond absurd titles, Rip Rig + Panic leaps around stylistically from (short) track to track. Tranquil piano (Mark Springer) solos and silly chats provide respite from screeching sax (Gareth Sager), Arabic and Far Eastern touches and hard-edged vocals (a very young Neneh Cherry and, on **God**, ex-Slit Ari Upp). **Attitude**, the band's most accessible album, comes closest to normal songs, while maintaining a zany eclecticism. Far from forbidding, Rip Rig + Panic keeps the show rolling with deft musicianship and oddball humor.

In late 1983, Rip Rig + Panic reorganized as Float Up CP; Sager (playing guitar and keyboards) and Oliver co-produced the sextet's sole album. The material on **Kill Me in the Morning** is straightforward funk/soul/jazz, with the rough edges left intact in just the right places. But this outing lacks the diversity of the previous band's work, and Cherry is its only star: she sings up a storm, even when the sexual metaphors ("Chemically Wet," "Joy's Address") get a bit trite. The band chugs along behind her with energy and panache, but there's nothing unique or catchy enough on **Kill Me in the Morning** to make a lasting impression.

Springer made a solo record. Cherry went on to huge stardom under her own name. Sager formed Head. Oliver, who co-wrote a 1987 hit ("Wishing Well") and did sessions for Terence Trent D'Arby, died of sickle cell anemia in March 1990.   [si/dgs]

See also *Neneh Cherry, Head, Pop Group*.

RITES OF SPRING
Rites of Spring (Dischord) 1985
All Through a Life EP (Dischord) 1987

Led by singer/lyricist Guy Picciotto, Washington DC's Rites of Spring—which broke up in '87, leaving him to help found Fugazi—was an extraordinary punk band. Part of a dubious emo-core (emotionally charged hardcore) mini-movement, the quartet enveloped articulate sentiments in a relentless rush of rhythm and melody that was simultaneously pulverizing and delicate. **Rites of Spring** is a staggeringly great record, with excellent sound, crisp playing and evocative songs.

Unfortunately, while Rites of Spring plays with the same force and vigor on the four-song **All Through a Life** 7-inch, the mix reduces the band's blasts to artsy whimpers. Where the lyrics were formerly reflective and personal, here they're intimate nonsense.   [icm]

See also *Fugazi*.

BRIAN RITCHIE
See *Violent Femmes*.

RITUAL
See *Cult*.

RITUAL TENSION

I Live Here (Sacrifice) 1986
I Live Here/Hotel California (Sacrifice) 1987 φ
The Blood of the Kid (CBGB-Celluloid) 1987 ●
Expelled (Safe House) 1991 ●

MARC SLOAN

Yeow (Little Animal) 1985

GAWK

Lure of the Oxowl [tape] (Sacrifice) 1989

I Live Here is a challenging debut from a band that was somewhat overlooked in the rush to gush over such New York noise scene contemporaries as Sonic Youth, Live Skull and Swans. The links are there, both stylistic and genealogical (Ritual Tension's vocalist drummed on Greed and Holy Money), but this quartet writhes to its own noisemaker. On the best material (like the gripping "Tightrope" and the scathing "Social Climber"), Ivan Nahem offers an alienated, surreal persona, his voice a cool monotone rising to a frantic bray, while his brother Andrew spews piercing, Rowland S. Howardian drone-guitar. The rhythms are unpredictable and convoluted; Ubuesque arrangements play havoc with traditional songcraft. (The tape and CD mix in the three songs from a subsequent EP, including a totally out-there devolution of the Eagles' "Hotel California.")

Live at CBGB, The Blood of the Kid presents Ritual Tension in a most conducive atmosphere. More intense than on I Live Here, the band presents some great new material, like the throbbing "New Super," the tempestuous "Devil Dog" and a primer of paranoia, "Oh I See."

Ritual Tension has been an on-again, off-again proposition the last few years. Recorded in 1988, the excellently self-produced Expelled is the finest display yet of the band's offbeat musicianship. The dissonance is so vibrantly arranged and performed that it actually becomes catchy.

Bassist Marc Sloan has kept himself busy during Tension downtime with a multitude of projects, including a stint in the False Prophets. While the solo Yeow predates Ritual Tension, Lure of the Oxowl finds him collaborating with Reed Ghazala under the Gawk moniker. The all-instrumental cassette ranges from ambient classical to avant-rock, played on Sloan's usual bass-with-effects and such instruments as kalimba, bamboo flute, ravanastron, er hu, cello and "electronic insects."

See also Swans. [gef]

DARREN ROBBINS

Darren Robbins Steals Your Girlfriend [CD] (Like) 1988 ●

Chicago singer/songwriter Darren Robbins (no relation)—with production, playing and songwriting assistance by Graham Walker (and, in a lesser capacity, the two other Elvis Brothers)—makes a sterling debut with this sprightly collection of pure-pop/rock tunes. Robbins has a versatile voice and an engaging lightweight musical personality; making the most of simple ingredients and crude facilities, he comes up with a high percentage of winners here, including drummer Brad Steakley's sardonic "Get Out of My Life (I Can Mess It Up Myself)," Walker's magical "Try for a Miracle" and Robbins' own plaintive "Fire from a Stone" and "Travel Long My Wanderin' Heart." As much a show-

case for the star's solid skills as a tantalizing indication of what the Elvis Brothers could be doing if they were still making records, Steals Your Girlfriend is a nifty delight. [i]

See also Elvis Brothers.

TOM ROBINSON BAND

Power in the Darkness (Harvest) 1978
TRB Two (Harvest) 1979
Tom Robinson Band (nr/EMI) 1981 (nr/Fame) 1982

TOM ROBINSON

North by Northwest (IRS) 1982 ●
Cabaret '79 (nr/Panic) 1982 ●
Atmospherics EP (nr/Panic) 1983
Hope and Glory (Geffen) 1984
Still Loving You (nr/Castaway) 1986 ●
Midnight at the Fringe (nr/Dojo) 1987 ●
The Collection 1977–1987 (nr/EMI) 1987 ●
Back in the Old Country (nr/Connoisseur Collection) 1989 ●
Last Tango (Ger. Line) 1989 ●

SECTOR 27

Sector 27 (IRS) 1980

TOM ROBINSON & JAKKO M. JAKSZYK

We Never Had It So Good (Fr. Musidisc) 1990 ●

In 1975, Tom Robinson escaped from the ashes of Cafe Society, a London folkiepop outfit produced by Ray Davies, to become a highly visible rock bandleader, championing various radical causes through music. Signed to EMI in the wake of that label's disastrous liaison with the Sex Pistols, Robinson's avowed homosexuality and uncompromising political stance made him an extremely controversial figure. Luckily, a brilliant (and surprisingly non-topical) first single, "2-4-6-8 Motorway," and a riveting album made the band internationally successful, affording the singing bassist the opportunity to be a real rock activist—spearheading Rock Against Racism—rather than merely a complainer. But a myopic outlook and limited musical range drew Robinson into a morass of sloganeering and overbearing self-righteousness that forced a major career rethink after only two LPs.

Power in the Darkness contains track after track of impassioned, heartfelt political anger, funneled through articulate lyrics and Danny Kustow's roaring guitar figures. The memorable songs seethe with honest conviction and convert rock energy into anthemic power. (The American release originally contained a bonus seven-song disc, compiling live tracks from an English EP and both sides of the "Motorway" single.)

TRB Two was produced by Todd Rundgren and basically encores the style and content of its predecessor, but with a more mainstream sound and fewer rough edges (not really an improvement). Robinson's alternate approach—slower numbers played at a bouncy shuffle perfect for in-concert singalongs—does improve with Todd's treatment. This brace of polemics isn't as striking as Robinson's first, but fans of Power in the Darkness won't find anything obviously missing here (except perhaps drummer Dolph Taylor and keyboardist Mark Ambler, who had both been replaced). Tom Robinson Band is a compilation.

After the TRB collapsed, Robinson formed Sector 27 and refocused his efforts on personal relationships rather than politics. With a new lineup—notably including a bassist, which allowed Robinson to concentrate on singing—the restrained album has some winning songs, although none with the same immediacy as before.

Recorded in Hamburg with only producer Richard Mazda and a drummer, **North by Northwest** is a mature and subtle album. Featuring material co-written with Peter Gabriel and a cover of a Lewis Furey song, Robinson explores various sophisticated settings and succeeds in making a pleasantly slight record, marred only by an agonized (and agonizing) song of love lost, "Now Martin's Gone."

Cabaret '79 is a live recording made shortly after the original TRB's dissolution; it includes Robinson's confrontational signature tune, "Glad to Be Gay," as well as a reading of Noel Coward's "Mad About the Boy," which resulted in some legal problems between Robinson and Coward's estate. **The Collection** is a useful compilation (with liner notes by the artist) of the band's best tracks, drawing on singles and EPs for items like "Don't Take No for an Answer," "Glad to Be Gay" and "Motorway."

Turning over a new page, Robinson then began a successful era of plainly commercial rock, captured on the **Atmospherics** EP (parts of which were incorporated onto the subsequent LP) and **Hope and Glory**. He's certainly capable of writing and recording skillfully routine music; it just doesn't make for very interesting listening: "War Baby" and a terrible version of Steely Dan's "Rikki Don't Lose That Number" were inexplicable hits. Robinson's sincerity and commitment are obvious, but mediocre singing and bland arrangements keep **Hope and Glory** from being anything but ordinary.

Robinson has continued making records with no notable commercial (or critical) success ever since. **Last Tango** is a live album. [i]

ROCK AND HYDE
See *Payolas*.

ROCKATS
Live at the Ritz (Island) 1981
Make That Move EP (RCA) 1983
LEVI AND THE ROCKATS
At the Louisiana Hayride (Posh Boy) 1981
LEVI
The Fun Sessions EP (PVC) 1983

The Rockats, hybrid English/American rockabilly specialists, were formed by singer Levi Dexter, whose appreciation of '50s American rock infused the band with a real traditionalist ethic. They made only one record together before splintering; bassist Smutty Smiff subsequently kept the Rockats' name alive. **Louisiana Hayride**, recorded live in Shreveport, Louisiana in 1979, bristles with feeling but lacks something in recording quality, especially as regards the mix. And if there was an audience at that gig, no one bothered telling them to clap.

Live at the Ritz, cut in New York over a year later, is a much slicker affair—a premonition of the Stray Cats

but without a magnetic personality like Brian Setzer. With Levi gone and a new lineup in place, the playing's fine, the sound quality is great and the tunes all sound like Johnny Cash should be singing 'em. (One of the new members—guitarist Tim Scott—went on to a solo career and later formed the Havalinas.)

Make That Move, with a new guitarist and drummer in the quintet, attempts to effect a stylistic escape. Produced by Mike Thorne, one side isn't rockabilly at all; keyboards are used to build an energetic but characterless soup. On the flip, the overbearing "Go Cat Wild" contains more drums than all of the Stray Cats' records put together. Only the title song and "Never So Clever" recapture the band's original sound with a glimmer of the old spirit.

Dexter, for his part, sticks to the straight and narrow on **The Fun Sessions**. Sharing production with Richard Gottehrer and employing a basic 'billy trio, he hiccups his way through five cool tracks exploding with understated energy. Not innovative by any means, but his earnest copies beat the Rockats' boring originals any day. [i]

See also *Havalinas, Tim Scott*.

ROCKET FROM THE TOMBS
See *Peter Laughner*.

ROCKPILE
Seconds of Pleasure (Columbia) 1980 ●

Rockpile, the top-rank rock'n'roll group Nick Lowe and Dave Edmunds formed in the late '70s, played on solo records by both men and backed each on tours. A year before breaking up, the quartet—which also included drummer Terry Williams and guitarist Billy Bremner—had its sole moment in the vinyl spotlight, and came up with an album that is every bit as exhilarating as anything either Lowe or Edmunds has done on his own. Obvious influences on **Seconds of Pleasure** include the Everly Brothers ("Now and Always") and Chuck Berry (his own "Oh What a Thrill"); the blues "A Knife and a Fork" and the medium-tempo "When I Write the Book" are rare respites. Besides everything else, the album has the extra bonus of guitarist Billy Bremner singing the rollickin' "Heart" and Rockin' Sidney's "You Ain't Nothin' but Fine." Throughout, the band delivers the hard-partying, good-time music we've come to expect from Lowe and Edmunds. Initial copies of the LP included a 7-inch single, **Nick Lowe & Dave Edmunds Sing the Everly Brothers**, with renditions of "Take a Message to Mary," "When Will I Be Loved" and two more classics—all later appended to the CD. [si]

See also *Billy Bremner, Dave Edmunds, Nick Lowe*.

PAUL ROESSLER
See *D.C.3.*

HENRY ROLLINS
Hot Animal Machine (Texas Hotel) 1987 ●
Big Ugly Mouth (Texas Hotel) 1987
Sweat Box (Texas Hotel) 1989

HENRIETTA COLLINS AND THE WIFEBEATING CHILDHATERS

Drive by Shooting EP (Texas Hotel) 1987 ●

HENRY ROLLINS/GORE

Live (Hol. Eksakt) 1987

ROLLINS BAND

Life Time (Texas Hotel) 1988 ●
Do It (Texas Hotel) 1988 ●
Hard Volume (Texas Hotel) 1989 ●
Turned On (1/4 Stick-Touch and Go) 1990 ●

WARTIME

Fast Food for Thought EP (Chrysalis) 1990 ●

Since the dissolution of Black Flag in 1986, singer/lyricist Henry Rollins has pursued a dual existence as a published poet (by the time Black Flag broke up, he was already a seasoned veteran of the spoken-word tour circuit) and leader of his own hardnosed band, producing powerful, driven rock as a platform for his ferocious vocals.

With cover art by Mark Mothersbaugh, Rollins' first solo effort, **Hot Animal Machine** (recorded in the UK in late '86) gets off to an explosive start with "Black and White" before sailing into a paranoia-tinged trio ("Followed Around," "Lost and Found," "There's a Man Outside") that keeps up the frenzied pace. The LP occasionally lapses into silliness ("A Man and a Woman," the bluesy, cliché-riddled "Crazy Lover"), but provides some neat covers (Suicide's "Ghost Rider" and the Velvet Underground's "Move Right In").

Recorded during the **Hot Animal Machine** sessions and inexplicably credited to Henrietta Collins and the Wifebeating Childhaters (band members are rechristened with female monikers; Henry Rollins gets guest billing), **Drive by Shooting** kicks off with the title track, a novelty number about Los Angeles gang warfare replete with surf/car song appropriations (guitar line courtesy of "Wipeout"). The EP also boasts a solid rendition of Wire's "Ex Lion Tamer" and a pretty funny (albeit tasteless) send-up of Queen's "We Will Rock You" called "I Have Come To Kill You." To prove his fallibility, Rollins includes two total throwaways: "Hey Henrietta" and "Men Are Pigs." (One CD combines the EP with **Hot Animal Machine**, adding a previously unreleased live track.)

The spoken-word **Big Ugly Mouth** was culled from various 1987 speaking engagements around the country. In an uncharacteristic display of humility and sensitivity, Rollins discourses on a variety of subjects, including social and racial injustice, child abuse and sexual harassment. In a more humorous vein, he tackles masturbation, birthdays and advertising—just for starters. **Sweat Box** is more poetry from the mouth of Rollins—three albums' worth.

Recorded at Toronto's El Mocambo club in May '87, Rollins shares the **Live** album with a side of performances by Dutch thrash-rock trio Gore. Testing out the newly formed Rollins Band—guitarist Chris Haskett of the previous lineup plus a rhythm section drawn, oddly enough, from ex-Black Flag bandmate Greg Ginn's Gone—Henry runs roughly through material from **Hot Animal Machine** and a preview of the as-yet-unrecorded "What Am I Doing Here?" While not

the most effective setting, the tracks are strong and well-played.

Alienation is the unifying lyrical theme on **Life Time**, the first studio album by the still-running Rollins Band. "Burned Beyond Recognition," "What Am I Doing Here?" and "There's Nothing Like Finding Someone When You're Lonely to Make You Want to Be All Alone" all get the point across. (A typical lyric: "I hate the world that I think hates me/Punch holes in the wall you know that hurts me/I feel dark and cold and alone, it burns me/Wish someone would come and touch me.") Musically, it's Rollins' most adventurous project. Without compromising the band's sheer force, straightforward rock stylings give way to more experimental song structures, jazz-inflected bass lines and tricky time changes. (The CD adds four live tracks recorded in Belgium.)

While the live side (recorded later in '87 in Holland) of **Do It** is pretty similar in content and delivery (not sound: this is much clearer) to Rollins Band's side of **Live**, the album's three studio tracks (produced by Rollins' DC homeboy, Ian MacKaye) are killer. Starting with a powerful version of the Pink Fairies' classic urge to action "Do It," there are two other covers: "Move Right In" (incorporating "In-a-Gadda-Da-Vida") and Richard Berry's R&B-styled "Next Time," both benefiting from Rollins' dramatic vocals and Haskett's overdrive guitar.

Rollins is in an existential funk on the seven-song **Hard Volume**, announcing (in "What Have I Got") that "I've got a wantless need . . . I am a clenched fist/Looking for a wall to kiss" and discovering (in "Down and Away") that "I am the last place that I want to be." Oddly, the rest of the band seems unaffected by any such feelings of angst, and the music—a well-organized rock juggernaut—thunders along as if all were well in the world.

Documenting the group's 1989 European tour, **Turned On** catches a November show in Vienna, a lengthy set that includes material from **Hot Animal Machine** up through **Hard Volume**, including another version of "Do It." Rollins is his usual balls-to-the-wall self, and Haskett is in rare form, spewing out sizzling solos that carom around various '70s hard-rock styles.

Wartime is a vaguely political side project by Rollins and Rollins Band bassist Andrew Weiss. The latter produced and played the music (an overpowering grungeheap of percussion, distorto guitar, samples and blustery fuzz bass) over which Henry delivers his demands for freedom, peace and truth. **Fast Food for Thought** includes four originals and a cover of the Grateful Dead's "Franklin's Tower." [rj/i]

See also *Black Flag, S.O.A.*

ROMANTICS

The Romantics (Nemperor) 1980 ●
National Breakout (Nemperor) 1980
Strictly Personal (Nemperor) 1981
In Heat (Nemperor) 1983 ●
Rhythm Romance (Nemperor) 1985 ●
What I Like About You (And Other Romantic Hits) (Epic Associated) 1990 φ

560

ROMANTICS AND FRIENDS
Midwest Pop Explosion! (Quark) 1980

Once upon a time, Detroit's Romantics were the band the Knack always wanted to be, hammering out a few essential chords while the singer wailed out inconsequential lyrics about girls. They played fast, loose and tough but, unlike the Knack, weren't obnoxious. This is the kind of band that would have been happy jamming to "Louie, Louie" or "La Bamba" all night if they hadn't been able to devise their own alternatives.

The Romantics' 1980 debut and **National Breakout** capture that era beautifully. Silly red leather suits notwithstanding, **The Romantics** shows the boys at their most raucous, crashing through "What I Like About You" (their best-ever track, sung by drummer Jimmy Marinos) and other dance-floor pips. The optimistically titled second LP continues in the "Twist and Shout" vein, highlighted by "Tomboy" and "Stone Pony." (Besides tracks by Stiv Bators, Nikki & the Corvettes and the Singles, **Midwest Pop Explosion!** contains both sides of the Romantics' 1978 Bomp! single and two other pre-'80 efforts.)

Strictly Personal, the panicky response to disappointing sales, finds the Romantics switching from powerful pop to soulless arena-rock. All broad, exaggerated gestures and no charm. Sad. **In Heat** wiped away the tears, elevating the band into the Top 10 with the execrable "Talking in Your Sleep" and the far more likable "One in a Million." Having hit the heights, Marinos left the group; the others hung in to make **Rhythm Romance**, another likably dumb batch of pop songs culminating in a credibly rootsy version of "Poison Ivy."

The 1990 compilation brings together the quartet's two hits, the title track and seven additional album selections, paying special attention to **In Heat**. Adding a deeply weird commercial postscript to the Romantics' career, "What I Like About You" wound up being used in a Bud Light TV spot. Is that post-punk or what? [jy/i]

ROMEO VOID
Its a Condition (415) 1981
Never Say Never (415-Columbia) 1982
Benefactor (415-Columbia) 1982
Instincts (415-Columbia) 1984

DEBORA IYALL
Strange Language (415-Columbia) 1986

Walloping big-beat riffs with snaky sax and darkly intelligent lyrics characterize this San Francisco area dance/think combo. Native American artist-and-poet-turned-vocalist Debora Iyall uses her smoky, conversational voice to wax reflective on love and lust in these modern times; consistent with the band's name, she sings not only of situations where love is absent, but also of when it *should* be absent.

Its a Condition introduced Romeo Void's unique blend of jazz, funk, rock and confrontational poetry in its formative stages, the music a bit tentative and unfocused, especially in contrast with Iyall's hard-edged lyrics. **Never Say Never**, a four-song EP co-produced by Ric Ocasek, gained the group significant airplay and

sales, leading to the link between San Francisco independent 415 and the CBS megalith. It's consequently no surprise that a truncated version of "Never Say Never" opens up **Benefactor**; as it turns out, that song proved to be more of a stylistic mold than might be considered healthy.

The most fully realized record of the bunch, **Instincts** boasts David Kahne's rich, full-blooded production, top-notch playing and reprises of various stylistic avenues. "Just Too Easy" resembles "Never Say Never" and pairs Ben Bossi's ace sax work with Iyall's sardonic, spoken monologue; "A Girl in Trouble (Is a Temporary Thing)" touches a poppier, more melodic side; "Six Days and One" reverts to a spare, mainly rhythmic approach. Mixing strength with beauty, Romeo Void makes very special dance music for the mind.

A strange blend of unlikely people creating rather unsurprising music, Iyall's solo album was produced by Pat Irwin, once a Lydia Lunch collaborator in 8 Eyed Spy and later a Raybeat. The cast includes Irwin (clarinet, sax, guitar, synth), Richard Sohl (pianist in the original Patti Smith Group) and others; Ben Bossi (sax) and Aaron Smith (drums) of Romeo Void also participate. Iyall obviously takes her poetry seriously; unfortunately, Irwin (co-writer of six tunes here) leads the musicians through underwhelming, blandly faceless rock backing that pointedly lacks Romeo Void's atmospherics. [rnp/i]

SKID ROPER AND THE WHIRLIN SPURS
See *Mojo Nixon and Skid Roper*.

ROSA LUXEMBURG
Puri Puri (Jap. School) 1986 ●
II (Jap. Midi) 1986 ●

Why this excitable Japanese art-rock dance quartet named itself after a historically significant German Marxist is a mystery, but it would seem from the group's first two albums that David Byrne is probably their philosopher of choice. The tightly strung but casually offbeat **Puri Puri** lays scratchy guitars and giddily enthusiastic vocals into jittery rhythms that alternately suggest Talking Heads, the Suburbs and early B-52's. Despite the Japanese lyrics, horn/percussion accents, tropical/Latin influences and the band's non-stop exuberance all help translate this diverse platter of fun into a universal language.

Rosa L. relaxes a little on the wonderful **II**, focusing all of its energies into ensuring that no two songs sound anything alike. The album leads off with a twisted ska number and then shifts into a raving R&B rocker that features a wall-climbing guitar solo. From there, anything goes: Sly Stone boom-laka-laka-lakas, garage rock, wailing harmonica, California surf-pop, an acoustic guitar tune that revs into a major workout, a choral song accompanied by electronic sound effects, etc. Wheee! If the words on **II** are half as inventively weird as the music, I'm dying to know what they mean. [i]

KRISTI ROSE AND THE MIDNIGHT WALKERS

Some People (Rounder) 1986 ●

High-voltage country-western rock from New York: powerhouse singer Rose, backed by a loud trio that boasts ex-Television bassist Fred Smith, belts out twangy Nashville-styled originals and a couple of classics on this energetic debut. Rose's bracing voice takes after Wanda Jackson and is the most notable ingredient here; the Midnight Walkers wander between polite country backing and near-punk aggression. The Uptown Horns help out on a couple of tracks.   [i]

MICHAEL ROSE

See *Black Uhuru*.

DAVID ROTER METHOD

Bambo (Unknown Tongue) 1987
Beauty of the Island (Unknown Tongue) 1989

A friend of—and occasional songwriting collaborator with—the Blue Öyster Cult and Del-Lords and other vaguely related New York-area outfits (erstwhile rock crit Richard Meltzer being the spiritual center of this family), David Roter brings an artless voice and the soul of a standup comedian to incisively funny moderate-rent records that alternate topical satire and personal complaints. After making a minor cult-single splash with 1979's "I Think I Slept with Jackie Kennedy Last Night," Roter cut two albums with skilled small-scale rock-pop accompaniment by assorted Cult-ists and Del-Lords, as well as musical associates of David Johansen.

Bambo has amusingly irreverent biographies of Sonny Liston, Mussolini and Joan Crawford (a song first recorded by the Cult), a wry love letter to an ex-wife and the titular epic in which forest creatures turn the tables and go ballistic against hunters. **Beauty of the Island** repeats "My Ex-Wife," "Sonny Liston" and "Adopt Me" (co-scribed by Meltzer), appending some clever current-events reports on the Big Apple ("New York, New York," "Beauty of the Island").   [i]

See also *Del-Lords*.

ROTTERS

Presumed Dead—In Japan (Baka) 1989

Blindly idolizing the Sex Pistols et al., Santa Barbara's Rotters knowingly baited the censors in 1978 with their first 45, "Sit on My Face Stevie Nix" b/w "Amputee," which garnered considerable press when it was instantly banned from LA record stores and radio. One of the most slavishly imitative tributes to pure '77 UK punk ever recorded in America, the record features faux-Brit vocalist Nigel Nitro (Mike Rogers) singing "Sit on my faiiice"/"I dowanna be no amputeeyuh." The Rotters broke up in 1980 but got back together a few years later; 1984 compilation tracks and an unreleased EP of the time evinced no softening of subject matter ("I wanna fuck a new wave slut"/"My penis hurts"). The new lineup was no more nor less contemporaneously punk than the last, although guitarist Phester Swollen (Tom Chartier) had obviously learned a trick or nine in the interim, exploding forth with manic fills and electrocution leads betwixt the music's rote hardcorisms.

Absent for another five years, the newest Rotters resurfaced, bearing a debut LP that—a full decade after the first single—includes numerous songs from the band's beginnings. Recorded live-to-4-track in Japan (where the band had reassembled with a local drummer), **Presumed Dead** is, oddly, even *more* garagey and sloppy than the early stuff, showcasing a band as carelessly noisy and artlessly annoyed as any in the original (new) wave, elevated by guitar playing so rampant and excessive as to virtually reinvent heavy metal. A classic.   [ab]

MIKEL ROUSE

See *Tirez Tirez, Tuxedomoon*.

KEVIN ROWLAND

See *Dexy's Midnight Runners*.

ROXY MUSIC

Roxy Music (Reprise) 1972 (Atco) 1977 (EG-Reprise) 1989 ●
For Your Pleasure ... (Warner Bros.) 1973 (Atco) 1977 (EG-Reprise) 1989 ●
Stranded (Atco) 1973 (EG-Reprise) 1989 ●
Country Life (Atco) 1974 (EG-Reprise) 1989 ●
Siren (Atco) 1975 (EG-Reprise) 1989 ●
Viva! (Atco) 1976 (EG-Reprise) 1989 ●
Greatest Hits (Atco) 1977 ●
Manifesto (Atco) 1979 (EG-Reprise) 1989 ●
Flesh + Blood (Atco) 1980 (EG-Reprise) 1989 ●
The First Seven Albums (nr/EG-Polydor) 1981
Avalon (Warner Bros.) 1982 ●
The High Road EP (Warner Bros.) 1983
The Atlantic Years 1973–1980 (Atco) 1983 ●
The Early Years (nr/EG) 1989 ɸ
The Later Years (nr/EG) 1989 ɸ
Heart Still Beating (EG-Reprise) 1990 ɸ

ROXY MUSIC/BRYAN FERRY

Street Life: 20 Greatest Hits (nr/EG) 1986 (EG-Reprise) 1989 ●
The Ultimate Collection (nr/EG-Virgin) 1988 ●

ANDY MACKAY

In Search of Eddie Riff (nr/Island) 1974
Resolving Contradictions (nr/Bronze) 1978

Arguably the most influential rock group of the '70s, Roxy Music's impact has only grown in the years since the punk return-to-the-basics ethos gave way to a growing interest in high style, fashion and musical sophistication. The "new romantic" movement and the synth fops would have had no historical traditions to follow were it not for the pioneering efforts of Bryan Ferry, Brian Eno, Phil Manzanera, Andy Mackay, Paul Thompson and their various cohorts. Even though Roxy Music grew pale and timid in its later years, the recorded work (not to mention the countless side projects in which the various members have participated) stands as a seminal wellspring of nonconformity and successful art-pop experimentation.

With the release of their first LP (produced by King Crimson lyricist Pete Sinfield after the departure of original Roxy guitarist Davy O'List, formerly of the Nice), the fledgling sextet revolutionized rock—trashing concepts of melodic conservatism, ignoring the prevalence of blues-based and otherwise derivative idioms and denying the need for technical virtuosity, either vocally or instrumentally. The flamboyantly bedecked poseurs presaged such low couture iconoclasts as the New York Dolls and all the glamsters who followed; the music mixed all sorts of elements into a newly filtered original sound that set the stylish pace. The tracks—Ferry-penned fantasies like "Re-make/Re-model," "2 H.B.," "If There Is Something" and the group's monumental debut, "Virginia Plain" (a 45 not on the original album, but added to later editions)—are at once amateurish and highly developed, brilliant blunders that took some acclimation to fully appreciate. As much as the music, the album's kitsch graphics were also widely imitated.

For Your Pleasure, another enduring classic (with the second of Roxy's many bassists), refines and magnifies Roxy's style with equally amazing material: "Do the Strand," "Editions of You" (the album's punchy rock single), "In Every Dream Home a Heartache" and the obsessive nine-minutes-plus "Bogus Man."

Brian Eno departed after the second album, and ex-Curved Air violinist/keyboardist Eddie Jobson (a session man on Ferry's solo debut earlier that same year) joined, either precipitating or merely participating in the successful stylistic downshift of **Stranded**. Without Eno's "treatments," the third album (produced by Chris Thomas) has more subtle sound, favoring piano and restrained, stately songs such as the haunting "A Song for Europe" (one of two songs co-written by Manzanera), "Just Like You," "Psalm" and the second segment of "Mother of Pearl." Demonstrating the group's continuing ability to rock, "Serenade" and "Amazona" do it with dignity, while only the beginning of "Mother of Pearl" and the whirlingly chaotic "Street Life" dances around the maniac fringe.

Roxy's best LP, **Country Life**, ran into trouble over its revealing cover photo—some American copies were shrink-wrapped in opaque green plastic; later the artwork was changed to remove the bra'n'panties-clad models and leave only the foliage. Regardless, the ten tracks—a smooth integration of the band's divergent stylistic designs—are exemplary and of consistent strength, making it a virtual greatest-hits album of new material. Highlights: "All I Want Is You," "Out of the Blue," "The Thrill of It All," "A Really Good Time," "Three and Nine," "Prairie Rose."

Reuniting with Chris Thomas, Roxy made the disappointingly dull **Siren** (with Jerry Hall crawling on the cover), closing the studio book on their first era. The record contains some great tracks ("Love Is the Drug," "Both Ends Burning," "Sentimental Fool"), but an overabundance of forgettable numbers substantially diminishes its value. Roxy then went on sabbatical, with only the one-disc live document (the Eno-free **Viva!**, recorded in '73, '74 and '75 with three different bassists and a fine selection of songs given decisive, powerful performances) and the absolutely essential **Greatest Hits** collection issued during the two-year gap.

In 1978, Ferry, Manzanera and Mackay reactivated Roxy Music, making three more group albums with various temporary sidemen. But it was never the same. Cooling down from where **Siren** left off, Roxy Music had become—whether through maturation, skill or fatigue—a pale, genteel imitation of its old self. Al-

though there are a few brilliant (at least presentable) tracks on each album, the lack of conviction and adventurous spirit makes all three less than compelling for fans of the group's early work. Fortunately, these records neither embarrass nor contradict the Roxy legacy; this period (subsequently proving to be the group's last and, in America at least, most successful) is separate and, though not equal, at least estimable.

The self-produced **Manifesto** has "Dance Away," "Still Falls the Rain" and "Angel Eyes" to recommend it, but is still easy to live without. The inferior **Flesh + Blood** (Roxy's first album without Paul Thompson, who resurfaced years later in, of all places, Concrete Blonde) is more like a Ferry solo record, with session men playing humorless covers of "In the Midnight Hour" and "Eight Miles High." Even the best originals are unoriginal and fainthearted: the Cars-ish (now there's irony for you) "Over You," the schmaltzy (but catchy) "Oh Yeah" and the funky "Same Old Scene."

Regaining its self-esteem if not its power, Roxy made **Avalon** more like **Manifesto**, a careful blend of air and beat that amounts to a sparkling if meaningless dance record for would-be sophisticates. Unassailably well made and even occasionally engaging, the worst that can be said of songs like "More Than This," "The Space Between," "Avalon," "Take a Chance with Me" and "The Main Thing" is that they're too quiet and that the lyrics lack bite. Those who came upon Roxy late probably reckon it's their best album.

An otherwise needless compilation, **The Atlantic Years**, skims the cream from **Manifesto** and **Flesh + Blood** onto one disc, adding two earlier cuts (also on **Greatest Hits**).

In 1981, all of Roxy Music's studio albums to that point—seven in all—were repackaged as a boxed set; add in **Avalon**, and you've got the works. **The Early Years** and **The Later Years** also box six of the original albums: the first three in one, and the last three in other. (What would be wrong with a complete reissue package for once?) The two-record **Street Life** and the overlapping single-disc **Ultimate Collection** each mix tracks from the group and Ferry's solo career.

The High Road, a 12-inch ostensibly recorded live in Glasgow, offers an odd four-song program and a running time of nearly half an hour, as a ten-person lineup walks through Neil Young's "Like a Hurricane," John Lennon's "Jealous Guy" and two Ferry tunes. The playing is, of course, great and the sound magnificent—only the band's crucial personality is absent. Exactly the same can be said of **Heart Still Beating**, recorded in France at a massive open-air concert in mid-1982. (In fact, given the amazing similarity of the EP's four songs to their performances on the album, it seems very likely that **The High Road** actually hails from the French date.) Notwithstanding Manzanera's searing work (especially on "Out of the Blue" and his own "Impossible Guitar" instrumental) and Ferry's suave showboating, this one is mostly for **Avalon** fans.

Roxy Music ceased to exist after 1983. Ferry resumed his solo work with a new album in mid-'85; Manzanera and Mackay formed a new trio called the Explorers and have worked on numerous other projects.

As big a long-term disappointment as Ferry's and Manzanera's extra-Roxy careers have been, Andy Mackay's individual efforts reached the blandness plateau way ahead of the pack. His mildly diverting first showcase, **In Search of Eddie Riff** is a mostly instrumental outing enlivened only by a sweaty saxual interpretation of Richard Wagner's "Ride of the Valkyries" and several more-traditional covers. Otherwise, it's merely a display of his technical abilities.

His next big project was to write and produce two albums' worth of pop music for *Rock Follies*, a neat '70s British TV show about a female singing trio. They're neat, but clearly work for hire. By the time of the Asian-oriented **Resolving Contradictions**, Mackay had banished any trace of wit: the record is a snooze. However, on a literary front, Mackay wrote a useful 1981 text (*Electronic Music*) on the development of electronic music. [i]

See also *Concrete Blonde, Brian Eno, Explorers, Bryan Ferry, Phil Manzanera, Yukihiro Takahashi*.

ROYAL COURT OF CHINA
Off the Beat'n Path (Desperation) 1986
The Royal Court of China (A&M) 1987 ●
Geared & Primed (A&M) 1989 ●

SHAKERS
Living in the Shadow of a Spirit EP (Carlyle) 1988

Nashville's Royal Court of China (formerly known as the Enemy) play it hot and sloppy on their independent-label debut, a vivacious seven-song minialbum that fills out Joe Blanton's songs with swirls of wild-eyed guitar to counterbalance his dramatic singing. The quartet's ripping cover of the Yardbirds' "Heart Full of Soul" indicates one influence on their garage-rocking Southeastern pop, but it's only one of several. A fine informal introduction to a promising band with a cool sound.

As if the group's meaningless name weren't misleading enough, the artwork on their 1987 album furthers the stylistic obfuscation. **The Royal Court of China** shows impressive instrumental and studio facility, but cuts back on the youthful energy a tad too much. While there's no shortage of melodies or guitars, some of the songs fade towards repetitive anonymity, veering into an undistinguished Byrds-country sound. The Royal Court may have escaped the bar band wilderness for a brighter, smoother future, but they need to find something more compelling to replace the immediacy they've lost.

The blustery hard rock on the Vic Maile-produced **Geared & Primed** wasn't quite what I had in mind. With a new guitar player and bassist, the RCC became a fairly convincing dirtbag band, but Blanton's hoarse shout doesn't cut the mustard and the songs are a hair too complex to suit such rugged treatment.

Rather than follow the Royal Court down the Marshall stack route, the two defectors got themselves a female vocalist, formed the folky Shakers and released a four-song 12-inch, **Living in the Shadow of a Spirit**, on a local Nashville label. [i]

ROYAL CRESCENT MOB
Land of Sugar EP (No Other) 1986
Omerta (Moving Target-Celluloid) 1987 ●
Something New, Old and Borrowed (Moving
     Target-Celluloid) 1988 ●

Spin the World (Sire) 1989 ●
Midnight Rose's (Sire-Warner Bros.) 1991 φ

This quartet from Columbus, Ohio takes punk-funk to its logical extreme, combining a strongarm/goodfoot rhythm section with a guitarist (by the name of B) weaned on both James Brown and the Stooges, and a passionate harmonica-blowing singer (David Ellison). The results are pretty excellent: the casual vamps display an irreverent sense of humor and rock like crazy, drawing on two lifetimes of musical tradition for a blast of unstereotyped dance noise. The poorly recorded but enthusiastic six-song **Land of Sugar** (with an early drummer) contains both the original version of RCM's quintessential original ("Get on the Bus," a goofy lyrical sensibility applied to a sloppy funk workout) and a characteristic disco cover (the Ohio Players' "Love Rollercoaster").

Omerta boasts a brilliant rendition of "Get on the Bus," covers of the OPs ("Fire") and James Brown ("Payback") and a bunch of ass-shaking originals that either rock tight or fall apart with equal panache.

Something New, Old and Borrowed (aka **S.N.O.B.**) reprises **Land of Sugar** in its entirety, adding five ostensibly live performances (including Led Zep's "Immigrant Song" and a straight rocker called "Marv Diamond") and two new studio recordings ("Happy at Home" is a classic).

Reaching the majors, the Mob tightened its instrumental wig and reduced funk to a smaller component of its personality, making **Spin the World** good and credible, but only as far as it goes. Co-produced with ferociously hot sound by Richard Gottehrer, the album has unprecedented variety, from mighty hip-hop ("Big Show") to thrusting dance power (the zany "Silver Street") to '60sish rock'n'roll ("Stock Car Race") to annoying jazzy doodles ("Corporation Enema"). All in all, the Mob survives the big-league transition adequately (the lyrics are especially cool) but the group could have made more of the opportunity. In a strange bit of in-state cultural poaching, "5 More Minutes" borrows its hook from Jo Jo Gunne's "60 Minutes to Go."

While **Midnight Rose's** still shows some versatility in the stylistic bullpen, the album downplays the funk even further and aims for a more integrated rock-with-a-beat sound, concentrating the Mob's efforts on songwriting more than showboating. The results are uneven, although never less than entertaining; the record is good fun, if not quite an intense treat. Whether Ellison is telling a sorry story of justice miscarried ("Big Mistake"), painting a sympathetic portrait of yuppiedom ("Pretty Good Life") or ruminating on a damaged proboscis ("Drunkard's Nose"), Mr. B (as he's billed here) colors the songs in with cogent flashes of aptly aimed guitar as the rhythm section sets the rhythmic clock in motion. [i]

ROYAL MACADAMIANS
Experiments in Terror (Island) 1990 ●

DAVITT SIGERSON
Falling in Love Again (ZE-Island) 1984

Prior to becoming the president of Polydor Records in 1991, music critic/record producer Davitt Sigerson had an occasional career as a songwriter and singer. Six years after making a lyrically clever but musically bland solo album scorched with his unpleasantly raspy vocals, Sigerson formed a quartet with keyboardist Bob Thiele Jr. (a sideman on **Falling in Love Again**) and created an arty and idiosyncratic mixture of jazz-and-funk-inflected tunes given a surrealistic spin. **Experiments in Terror** is a descriptive mind-movie soundtrack with cryptic vocal passages in place of character dialogue. The electronic music and disembodied texts are reminiscent of Will Powers, but the Macadamians stimulate a wider variety of moods, using source material as far-ranging as George Jackson's *Soledad Brother* prison memoir. A concentration camp and the twisted, oppressive minds that run it—clinically described in the lyrics of "Arbeit Macht Frei"—are echoed in the pounding drums, crunching guitar and distorted solos. Intriguing and provocative. [i/rs]

RUBBER RODEO

Rubber Rodeo EP (Eat) 1982
Scenic Views (Mercury) 1984 ●
Heartbreak Highway (Mercury) 1986

Armed with the slogan "It don't mean a thang if it ain't got that twang" inscribed in the vinyl, the six-song **Rubber Rodeo** 12-inch helped announce/advance the development of country-punk. The band hailed from Rhode Island, but that didn't stop it from dressing in Nashville finery and forging a fun and different mix with synthesizer, fiddle, organ and pedal steel guitar. While the originals (especially "How the West Was Won") are bouncily tuneful and heartfelt, a cover version of Dolly Parton's "Jolene" comes off a bit like Heart without the arena pomp.

Following a three-song 12-inch most notable for its inclusion of the theme from "The Good, the Bad and the Ugly," Rubber Rodeo misplaced its personality and emerged on **Scenic Views** playing disappointingly plain dance-rock, the mild pedal steel coloration notwithstanding. Only the vocals—by Trish Milliken and Bob Holmes, sometimes together—serve to distinguish the group at all. "The Hardest Thing," which most recalls the band's early Great Plains ambience, is the LP's strongest song.

Heartbreak Highway (produced by Ken Scott) is much better, but still leaves one wishing the band's records were more colorful and gimmicky. Rubber Rodeo's urban cowpoke image remains stronger than its musical personality here, although some of the songs (the title track, "Maybe Next Year," a radical cover of Fred Neil's grotesquely sappy "Everybody's Talkin' " and an instrumental called "The Civil War") have a redeemingly jaunty air of good-humored kitsch. [i]

RUDIMENTARY PENI

Rudimentary Peni EP (nr/Outer Himalayan) 1981
Farce EP (nr/Crass) 1982
Death Church (nr/Corpus Christi) 1983
The EPs of RP (nr/Corpus Christi) c. 1987
Cacophony (nr/Outer Himalayan) 1988

This London hardcore trio from the Crass family always stood apart from the generic anarchist legions, more like a UK counterpart to the Minutemen. The eponymous 7-inch EP is rough going, as the band is tight but tuneless; Nick Blinko's screeching vocals obscure heartfelt lyrics skewering complacency. A bit of rhythmic variety suggested promise, however, and the second EP benefits from better production, fascinating sleeve artwork and some mini-masterworks of alienated vitriol. Both were later paired and reissued as **The EPs of RP**.

Things come together on **Death Church**, with venomous lyrics ripping through loud and clear (as they should, given titles like "Vampire State Building" and "Alice Crucifies the Paedophiles"). While the songs are not exactly hook-laden, this is quite melodic for the genre. Tempos run from moderate metal through Pistolian thrash to hyperdrive blur. An intelligent, exciting and highly recommended album.

Bassist Grant Brand's long but successful battle with cancer meant hibernation for Peni during the mid-'80s. By the end of the decade, however, the trio was back with a radical piece of work. **Cacophony** features a staggering 54 songs (the first album had a mere 20) in about 45 minutes, many only a few seconds long. The trend towards melodicism continues (brief fragments like "The Old Man Is Not So Terribly Misanthropic" are quite catchy), though they remain as cagey, intense and weird as ever. The lyrics abandon politics, dwelling almost wholly on the life, death and work of horror writer H.P. Lovecraft. Peni spin surreal rants like "Nightgaunts" in a sort of obsessive tribute, interspersed with rugose instrumentals such as "Sunset for the Lords of Venus." With Blinko's vocals frequently Darth Vaderized by a harmonizer, the album's sensibility comes close to Monty Python's black humor—"New England Tombstone Inscriptions" runs off a morbid litany of same, while "A Great Gnashing of Teeth" is exactly that. **Cacophony** is one of the strangest albums ever made—a **Trout Mask Replica** for the hardcore age—but the rewards of close attention are ample. [dgs/gef]

CLINT RUIN

See *Foetus Inc.*

RUMOUR

Max (Mercury) 1977
Frogs Sprouts Clogs and Krauts (Arista) 1979
Purity of Essence (Hannibal) 1980

It's tempting to compare the Rumour's relationship with Graham Parker to the Band's with Bob Dylan. Highly respected but unsuccessful bar band (Brinsley Schwarz and Ducks Deluxe versus the Hawks) hooks up with talented singer/songwriter (Parker versus Dylan) to create some of the decade's best music ('70s versus '60s). Of course Parker is not Dylan, and **Max**, the Rumour's first LP on their own, is not **Big Pink**, although they would obviously have loved it to be. Often enough, the Rumour (Brinsley Schwarz, Bob Andrews, Martin Belmont, Andrew Bodnar, Steve Goulding) captures the *sound* of the Band, minus Robertson's lyrical profundity. What's really strange is that the Rumour is far more natural and interesting as a minor-league Band (on great tracks like "Hard Enough to Show," Nick Lowe's "Mess with Love" and a sublime Band-like arrangement of Duke Ellington's standard "Do Nothing

'Till You Hear from Me'') than when attempting to forge their own identity on the subsequent albums. **Max** may not be terribly original but it is utterly enjoyable.

Frogs, on the other hand, seems to be an attempt to recast the Rumour in a vein that conforms more with Stiff's offbeat image. As a clever pop-oriented band, the Rumour succeeds mainly in *sounding* stiff, with only a couple of songs (''Emotional Traffic,'' ''All Fall Down'') standing out from other failed experiments.

Purity of Essence succeeds in recapturing some of the looseness of **Max**. The band had been reduced to a quartet with the departure of Bob Andrews, whose voice—the group's best—and keyboards are missed. Even so, the album has its moments, although they mostly come on non-original material. While lacking a real frontman and strong material of its own, the Rumour is talented enough to make enjoyable (if not hit) records.   [ds]

See also *Graham Parker*.

RUNAWAYS
The Runaways (Mercury) 1976
Queens of Noise (Mercury) 1977
Live in Japan (nr/Mercury) 1977
Waitin' for the Night (Mercury) 1977
And Now ... the Runaways (nr/Cherry Red) 1979
Flaming Schoolgirls (nr/Cherry Red) 1980
Little Lost Girls (Rhino) 1981
The Best of the Runaways (Mercury) 1982 ●
I Love Playing with Fire (nr/Laker-Cherry Red) 1982

Opinion is still divided on the Runaways' place in the musical universe. To many, they were the first all-girl (instrument-playing) rock band to matter, spiritual godmothers to the Go-Go's and Bangles, and seminal punk rockers to boot. Others see them as nothing more than a pre-packaged peepshow whose heavy metal-*cum*-glitter approach was dated from the very start.

Here are the facts: LA teenagers Joan Jett (whose love of T. Rex and Suzi Quatro inspired her to learn guitar) and drummer Sandy West decided to form a band with encouragement (and eventual management) from Kim Fowley. The band that recorded **The Runaways** was a combination of raw garage-band playing and brassy, high-school-bad-girl sexuality typified by their unofficial anthem, ''Cherry Bomb.''

By the time **Queens of Noise** (a decided improvement over the debut) was released, trouble was fomenting; although Cherie Currie was the ''official'' lead singer, Jett wound up taking the microphone on six of the ten songs. Things came to a head when, after a tour of Japan (documented on the **Live in Japan** album), Currie and bassist Jackie Fox quit the band. Vicki Blue was hired as a new bassist, and Jett took over the reins for good.

Except in Japan, the Runaways never made any real commercial inroads. Many saw them as inept puppets—merely another Fowley hype—and refused to take the music seriously. **Waitin' for the Night** did nothing to alter that. The album came out just as modern-day punk was emerging, and Jett (if not the rest of the band) readily latched onto the scene to the extent that Steve Jones of the Sex Pistols contributed one song (''Black Leather'') to **And Now . . . The Runaways**. But West

and guitarist Lita Ford wanted to go in a more heavy metal direction, and the album would prove to be their last.

Posthumous notes: **Flaming Schoolgirls** is a sub-standard odds and ends compilation of live tracks and studio outtakes, while **Little Lost Girls** is actually **And Now . . . The Runaways** re-released as a picture disc. **The Best of the Runaways** and **I Love Playing with Fire** are further recaps of various material. As for the band members, Lita Ford has become a huge metal star under her own name; Laurie McAllister (who held down the bass spot in the band's waning months) ended up in another all-girl Fowley project, the Orchids. After several film roles and failed attempts at making it both as a solo act and with her sister Marie, Currie married Toto guitarist Steve Lukather. And we all know where Joan Jett's love of rock'n'roll got her.   [rnp]

RUN–DMC
Run–DMC (Profile) 1984 ●
King of Rock (Profile) 1985 ●
Raising Hell (Profile) 1986 ●
Tougher Than Leather (Profile) 1988 ●
Back from Hell (Profile) 1990 ●

AFROS
Kickin' Afrolistics (JMJ-RAL-Columbia) 1990 ●

Besides all its other accomplishments, this trio from Hollis, Queens was the first to succeed in doing what no other black artist (with the exception of Grandmaster Flash, briefly) had done before: make white people listen to rap in large numbers. After building a core hip-hop audience via several smart and witty singles (''Sucker M.C.'s'' and ''It's Like That''), Run–DMC made ''Rock Box'' (included on the first album), a bold step that lifted them into a league all their own. Melding a simple bass riff to the thunderous rhythm tracks that provided the entire accompaniment for their early raps, the song's coup de grâce is blazing rock guitar, played by Eddie Martinez (for a while an adjunct member of Blondie). The perfect combination—verbal acuity and theatrical drama matched by an inexorable pounding beat *and* the power of electric guitar—made the single huge, setting the stage for a whole meeting of the races that has helped chip away the barriers that kept ''black music'' and ''white music'' segregated all through the '70s.

Run–DMC contains all the early hits and is an utterly essential record. Even though the repetitious rhythms get tiring if you're not in the dancing mood, the funny, perceptive interwoven raps remain captivating centers of attention. **King of Rock** takes some chances—like a reggae/rap blend long before such things were common—while repeating the functional formula of ''Rock Box'' on the title track, which simply inverts the riff and recasts the rap. Without peer in pop hip-hop, Run (Joseph Simmons), DMC (Darryl McDaniels) and DJ/musician (and later rapper) Jam Master Jay (Jason Mizell) demonstrated enormous potential, and this was only the beginning.

Co-producers Russell Simmons and Rick Rubin add characteristic rock-funk touches to **Raising Hell**—like the ''My Sharona'' riff in the Beastie Boyish ''It's Tricky'' and the chart-topping hybrid cover of Aerosmith's rap-like "Walk This Way" (with Steve Tyler and Joe Perry contributing). On the downside, most of the rhymes are nothing special, making the commendable racial consciousness of "Proud to Be Black" stand in strong contrast to the litany of typical "I'm Run/He's DMC" business, the commercial culturalisms contained in "My Adidas" and the predictable words of "Dumb Girl." Overly spartan backing—simple beats (some of which actually sound man-made) and Jay's percussive turntable action—hurt some of the tracks (especially since the group has proven itself equal to more active and complex arrangements). More familiar than inherently exciting, **Raising Hell** could still use some more heat. Regardless, the record sold millions, elevating Run–DMC (alongside L.L. Cool J and the Beastie Boys) to the top echelons of the pop world.

Preceding (if scantily related to) the film for which it's named, **Tougher Than Leather** is much better, a self-assured three-dimensional superstar record with a dense, rock-influenced sound that's become as distinguishable as the crew's trademark verbal jousting. Sampling classic records and building original songs around them, the trio grabs the Monkees' "Mary, Mary" and turns it into a hysterical putdown, while the Temptations' "Papa Was a Rollin' Stone" becomes "Papa Crazy," the same paternal disenchantment given a modern chop job. (Bites of James Brown, Malcolm X, Led Zep—even old Run–DMC—crop up as well.) At the record's strangest, Run, DMC and Jay (affecting snooty accents) rap over a mock-Dixieland band. Throughout, the witty writing, deft delivery and riotously crowded production make **Tougher Than Leather** a progressive and peerless statement of the art that neither excludes nor panders to any audience segment.

Facing potential obsolescence—due to rap's massive popularity, the platinum proliferation of softheaded rappers unworthy of lacing the trio's Adidas and the raised ante of sex and language—the once-lighthearted Run–DMC aggressively (a little *too* aggressively) reinvented itself as a serious organization on **Back from Hell**, a tough, rugged album that holds its own against the crew's onetime disciples. With a new emphasis on solo vocal performances (by all three) and few of the band's familiar sonic traits, the largely self-produced record bears little resemblance to Run–DMC's prior works, but the up-to-date tracks are no less dynamic or effective for it. With power and intelligence (not to mention plenty of swear words), the deadly "Pause," "Word Is Born," "Back from Hell," "The Ave." and "Kick the Frama Lama Lama" all speak bluntly and sharply to the black community about social problems. For contrast, the sexy "Bob Your Head," "Party Time" and D's silly reggae-rhythm fragment "P Upon a Tree" keep things from getting too heavy.

While raising his creative profile within Run–DMC, Jason Mizell has also begun doing side projects on his own JMJ label. The Afros' album, which he co-wrote, co-produced and does a bit of vocalizing on, is a frivolous, overlong rap/soul romp (partly delivered in a theatrical pimp whine) through a jokey world of women and hairdos—or, in the record's vernacular, "hoes and fros." Thin humor doesn't excuse the exaggerated misogyny; the promising idea of lampooning '70s culture in rap evaporates early on, and **Kickin' Afrolistics**

(which occasionally veers selfconsciously towards Digital Underground before taking an incongruous Public Enemy-style turn on "Federal Offense") winds up annoying or dull more often than funny.   [i]

RUN WESTY RUN
Hardly Not Even (SST) 1988 ●
Run Westy Run (SST) 1988 ●
Green Cat Island (Twin/Tone) 1990 ●

Stylistically dissimilar to all of Minneapolis' other post-punk guitar bands, Run Westy Run restlessly ambles down its own path, casually playing around the edges of noisy blues, dissonant rock, chunky funk and twisted country. Despite frequent displays of substantial imagination, it took the energetic quintet a while to distill a personality from those bright ideas.

Produced by Pete Buck and Grant Hart (with no audible debt to either R.E.M. or Hüsker Dü), **Hardly Not Even** is mostly a showcase for Kirk Johnson's literate lyrics and dramatic vocals, plus the band's complementary guitarists. Repeatedly shifting rhythmic and loudness gears, the songs are gutsy but tuneless, with too many one-chord vamps blunting the better efforts.

The first half of the self-produced **Run Westy Run** shows another side of the Westies: clearer, lighterweight sound and melodic, folk-inflected songs, played in a warm-rush haze with woozy gang vocals. On the muddy flipside, the group indulges a fondness for early-'70s slop-rock, riffing up a Stoogey storm of thick guitar drive and even making up their own Led Zep song ("Gee").

With time out for a pair of folky lullabies ("Kiss the Night," "So Long") and a couple of other exceptions, the excellent **Green Cat Island** (co-produced by Buck again) organizes memorable rock tunes around the band's dynamic gods-of-thunder citations. Guitarists Terry Fisher (billed here as Terrance James) and Kyle (Jay) Johnson repeatedly whip off exciting vintage tributes to Aerosmith, the Stones and others, driving taut modern songs that finally get to the core of Run Westy Run's talents.   [i]

PAT RUTHENSMEAR
Pat RuthenSmear (SST) 1988
DEATH FOLK
Deathfolk (New Alliance) 1990

In a strange case of artistic abdication, ex-Germs (and occasional Tater Tot) guitarist Pat RuthenSmear (in punk's heyday, his surname was simply Smear) composed virtually all the music and sings (with a pronounced lisp and almost no melodic sense) lead on his eclectic solo album—but only co-wrote two lyrics, one of them retrieved from his late bandmate, Darby Crash. Working with DC3 keyboardist Paul Roessler, a drummer and a few guests, RuthenSmear takes an unpredictable and frequently enjoyable weird romp (showcasing a variety of accomplished guitar styles) through Cheap Trick rock-pop, swinging nightclub jazz, Barrett-like acoustic songs, even psychedelic dance-rock.

RuthenSmear and guitarist Gary Jacoby of Celebrity Skin go the Chad & Jeremy acoustic route on the casual and enthusiastic **Deathfolk**, jointly singing and strumming an amusing mixture of adolescent humor ("Monkey Brains," "Rad Man"), rude sex ("Yellow 1," "Typical Girl") and the only appropriate Queen song ("'39"). The last three numbers (loud punk, a jokey pirate rendition of Jacques Brel's "Amsterdam" and a bass'n'drums workout with haunted house vocals) ruin the mood, but the rest of the record is good for a tuneful laugh or two. [i]

See also *45 Grave, Germs*.

PAUL RUTHERFORD
See *Frankie Goes to Hollywood*.

RUTS
The Crack (Virgin Int'l) 1979 (nr/Virgin) 1988 (Blue Plate) 1991 ●
Grin & Bear It (nr/Virgin) 1980
The Peel Sessions EP (nr/Strange Fruit) 1986
The Ruts Live (nr/Dojo) 1987
Live and Loud!! (nr/Link) 1987
You Gotta Get Out of It (nr/Virgin) 1987 ●
The Peel Sessions Album (nr/Strange Fruit) 1990 ●

RUTS D.C.
Animal Now (nr/Virgin) 1981
Rhythm Collision (nr/Bohemian) 1982

RUTS DC AND THE MAD PROFESSOR
Rhythm Collision Dub Vol. 1 [tape] (ROIR) 1987

On **The Crack**, the Ruts meld the Pistols' instrumental attack with leader Malcolm Owen's Strummeresque bellow; while less inspired than either of those bands, the Ruts started out with far more finesse (including nimble bass). True to their early association with reggae collective Misty in Roots (sponsor of their first 45), the Ruts often incorporated reggae riffs—adeptly, not heavy-handedly and without missing a single roughshod 4/4 stride. Simple, straightforward political lyrics are heartfelt but not strident.

The late-'80 **Grin & Bear It** compilation is odds-'n'sods and sounds it, but the LP does contain an assortment of minor gems (including their pre-Virgin debut 45, live sides, etc.), highlighted by brilliant career-high-point single "Staring at the Rude Boys." In short, a fitting tribute (as intended) to Owen, dead of an OD four months previously.

As Ruts D.C. (for da capo) the remaining three made saxist/keyboardist Gary Barnacle a full member. On **Animal Now**, personal themes of self-doubt and angst ("Despondency," anyone?) get equal airing with the usual attacks on hypocrisy and social manipulation. It's often gripping, but undercut by a tendency to infuse intrusive jazz-funk touches.

Minus Barnacle (who departed for session work and Leisure Process), the trio—along with the Mad Professor, a British reggae producer—cut **Rhythm Collision**, an LP of funk-inflected reggae in ready-made dub form, akin in concept to Dennis Bovell's **I Wah Dub**. It's a sharp, sometimes powerful, sometimes catchy piece of work, with saxist Dave Winthrop (ex-Secret Affair) and one Mitt (harmonica) supplying additional shades to the dark-hued mood. In 1987, the long-deleted record was reissued on cassette, with a credit that played up the reggae connection, as **Rhythm Collision Dub Vol. 1**.

Although Ruts D.C. stopped working in 1983, archival releases keep on appearing. Joy Division and the Ruts were BBC DJ John Peel's two favorite bands, so it's fitting they've both been remembered in the **Peel Sessions** EP series. The Ruts' artifact from May 1979 unfortunately doesn't debut any long-lost material, and the versions sound too similar to the tracks on **The Crack** to get worked up about it, but it nevertheless documents a great band.

The Ruts Live and **Live and Loud!!**, on the other hand, fail to document anything. Though both are legal releases, they sound like bootlegs; the muddy audio falls far short of capturing what was an explosive live band. In particular, **Live and Loud** gets the concert right, but used the wrong tape: the live track recorded at the Marquee on the UK edition of **The Crack** sounds great, but the same concert, as presented here, is of dodgy quality. Until a true live artifact can be excavated and released, these two are for scholars only.

While filled with inarguably great music, the CD-only **You Gotta Get Out of It**, is one screwed-up package. The material (all of **The Crack** plus half of **Grin and Bear It**) is haphazardly intermingled, "West One" (the band's epic swan song) is twice listed as "West On" and the notes confuse the two LP titles, incorrectly identifying the tracks' original sources. Bizarrely, the same label that released the Ruts' albums in the first place is responsible for this inexcusable mess. Perhaps to correct its folly, Virgin later issued a proper CD of **The Crack** with the original sleeve artwork, following its twelve songs with the three B-sides (including the Damned-inspired "I Ain't Sofisticated") omitted from **Grin & Bear It**.

The Peel Sessions Album renders the series' EP obsolete, adding two sessions of far more archival merit that offer genuinely different views of familiar songs. The "Savage Circle" here blisters with a more staccato attack; "Dope for Guns" is far faster and meaner; "In a Rut" gets entirely new treatment. A sterling document of the second punk wave's most explosive band, one still admired and influential—Fugazi, Dag Nasty and the Effigies all do covers. [jg/jr]

568

SACCHARINE TRUST

Paganicons (SST) 1981
Surviving You, Always (SST) 1984
Worldbroken (SST) 1985
The Sacramental Element [tape] (SST) 1986
We Became Snakes (SST) 1986
Past Lives (SST) 1989 ●

JACK BREWER BAND

Rockin' Ethereal (New Alliance) 1990 ●

Too early to be post-hardcore but too uncommon for any simple classification, this Southern California quartet doesn't try to create a blizzard of noise—they go at it more artfully, but with equally ear-wrenching results. On **Paganicons**, singer Joaquin Milhouse Brewer tunelessly barks lyrics (as in "We Don't Need Freedom" and "A Human Certainty") that aren't bad in a pretentious mock-intellectual vein; the music is loudly abrasive, but with spaces and dynamics largely uncommon to the genre.

From Brewer's back cover credit of "vocals and sermons" to his complex, provocative lyrics (despite numerous misspellings on the lyric sheet), Saccharine Trust—guitarist Joe Baiza plus a new rhythm section—takes an abrupt religious turn on **Surviving You, Always**. "Yhwh on Acid," "Lot's Seed," "Remnants" and "Our Discovery" all contain biblical imagery and religious references, but in a context that obscures and reorients the themes well beyond easy recognition and comprehension. Musically, Sac Trust uses the punk idiom like avant-jazz, liberating the vocals to function semi-independently as blurt poetry, while the band goes through tight formation riffs that are carefully structured but not really within traditional song form. Sophisticated, and engrossing once you get past the daunting attack. (The first two albums were later joined as **The Sacramental Element** cassette.)

Proceeding further into the experimental realms generally reserved for the "new music" folks, Saccharine Trust attempted something *really* unusual with **Worldbroken**. The LP was not only recorded live, it was improvised on the spot! Joined by ex-Minutemen bassist Mike Watt, Brewer and two surviving sidemen rise to the challenge, producing a loose but controlled-sounding jam record (no punks here) that reveals its total extemporaneousness only in the rambling narrative of Brewer's lyrics.

On the jazzy **We Became Snakes**, a five-piece lineup (with sax and a new bassist) returns to the old-fashioned way: write 'em, rehearse 'em and *then* record 'em. Watt produced the record, which again reflects Brewer's religious fixation. The sonic formula includes syncopated rhythm vamps, lots of riffy solos on sax and guitar and dramatic vocal recitations. Imaginative and far-reaching, if not exactly enjoyable or accessible.

Over the course of 75 gripping minutes (gleaned from a vault stocked with seven years' worth of live tapes made by machines of wildly differing audio quality), **Past Lives** paints a slightly more complete (if less stark) picture of Saccharine Trust's awesome live capabilities as both inward-looking improvisers and kick-out-the-jams shamen. Quick cuts between the two facets that also crisscross chronological "order" create some jarring juxtapositions, but that's probably the idea. Only one song is repeated from **Worldbroken**; the seven tracks that are otherwise unavailable include one rare glimpse of the band, (spiritual) lampshades on heads, ripping through Black Flag's "Six Pack."

Freed from freedom's shackles, Brewer created a brooding, cohesive solo album of surprisingly concise, typically dark guitar rock. Though he's still as obsessive/compulsive as anyone tilling rock-poetry's increasingly infertile soil, Brewer seems to have toned down his more hysterical Elmer Gantry approach—even when petitioning the Lord. You'll only wince once (upon hearing the cover of the Doors' "Peace Frog," a reprise from **Past Lives**) over the course of the many listens you'll need—and want—to breathe in this essence rare. [i/dss]

See also *Joe Baiza & the Universal Congress Of, Slovenly.*

SADE

Diamond Life (Portrait) 1984 ●
Promise (Portrait) 1985 ●
Stronger Than Pride (Epic) 1988 ●

The '80s British trend towards mild jazz/Latin-inflected pop music (Carmel, Everything but the Girl) found its first globally successful proponent in Sade. A stunningly beautiful Nigerian raised in England, Sade Adu writes (the lyrics are hers alone, the music mostly co-written with Stuart Matthewman, the sax/guitar player in her trio) and performs mellifluous, thoughtful tunes with aplomb and jazz leanings that seem to derive from a wholly different era. Despite the music's obvious stylization, Sade's almost colorless voice exudes little personality; her strength is a cool timbre that conveys dispassionate wisdom.

Somehow avoiding both nostalgia and schmaltz, **Diamond Life** is an anomaly: nothing about it would turn off Andy Williams fans, but selfconsciousness legitimizes it to a rock audience. "Hang on to Your Love," "Sally," "Smooth Operator" and "Your Love Is King" are the standouts, evoking chic nightclub society of the '60s. (In fact, the first of those tracks includes the very noticeable sound of glasses clinking.) The perfect soundtrack to your Laurence Harvey dreams, and a very alluring pop record.

Promise is slightly drier and less cozy, but the nine songs are every bit as good. Economical arrangements make each carefully placed rim shot and guitar twang count on such excellent songs as "Is It a Crime" and "Sweetest Taboo." (In England, a dual CD of the first two albums was released.)

On the other hand, weak material, pale singing and Sade's effete production/arranging leave **Stronger Than Pride** well off the mark, a dignified but slack collection of adult love songs with little of the fashionable élan that invigorated her first two albums.   [i]

SAD LOVERS AND GIANTS

Epic Garden Music (nr/Midnight Music) 1982 ●
Feeding the Flame (nr/Midnight Music) 1983 ●
In the Breeze (nr/Midnight Music) 1984
Total Sound (nr/Midnight Music) 1986
The Mirror Test (nr/Midnight Music) 1987 ●
Cow Boys EP (nr/Midnight Music) 1988
Les Annes Vertes (nr/Midnight Music) 1988

This quintet, which originally came from Watford—near London, but evidently insulated from that city's turbulent trendiness—resembles a cross between R.E.M. and a garage-spawned analogue of **Dark Side of the Moon**. Tristan Garel-Funk plays jangly guitar, almost all of it arpeggio chorded (à la Byrds/Searchers), and David Woods adds texture and melody with sax and keyboards, eventually growing more sophisticated in sound and shading, if not technique. The songs canter at new wave uptempo or a more brooding mid-speed, but the music is moody and contemplative. Vocals by one Garce Allard aren't trendily emotive, instead possessing the kind of quiet gravity that makes overstatement unnecessary, even with lyrics of hurt or anger.

While **Epic Garden Music** is pretty much what its self-satiric title suggests, it also boasts several excellent crystallizations of the group's style. **Feeding the Flame**, after an abrasive opening, is much quieter, a less immediate and ultimately more distressing record. (Both CDs contain numerous bonus tracks.)

The group dissolved around the end of '83, but resumed activity in 1985. Before the release of any new material, however, a pair of artifacts from the original lineup appeared. **In the Breeze** contains alternate versions of some tracks (several are from a John Peel session) plus a few unreleased rough gems; it's almost as essential as the first LP, although the three songs the two discs share are presented in earlier, rawer takes here. The seven-song **Total Sound** is a mini-album recorded live in Holland for a radio broadcast.

On **The Mirror Test**, Allard and original drummer Nigel Pollard are joined by a completely new guitar/bass/keyboards axis, not to mention new songwriting partners for Allard. Sad Lovers are a smoother crew this time around and, although the LP does resemble the band's previous sound, the music is pleasant without being quite so memorable; the lyrics are generally less poignant. Yet, as with all of their records, each listening reveals more. (The CD has a revised sequence and four bonus tracks.)

The **Cow Boys** EP contains remixes of two early singles (1982's "Lost in a Moment" and 1983's "Cow Boys"), a live version of another oldie and a song lyrically overhauled from **The Mirror Test**.   [jg]

GREG SAGE
See *Wipers*.

SAINTS
(I'm) Stranded (Sire) 1977 ●
Eternally Yours (Sire) 1978 ●
Prehistoric Sounds (nr/Harvest) 1978 ●
Paralytic Tonight Dublin Tomorrow EP (Fr. New Rose) 1979 ●
Prehistoric Songs (Fr. Harvest) 1981 ●
The Monkey Puzzle (Fr. New Rose) 1981 ●
Out in the Jungle ... (nr/Flicknife) 1982 ●
A Little Madness to Be Free (Fr. New Rose) 1984 ●
Live in a Mud Hut (Fr. New Rose) 1985 ●
Best of the Saints (nr/Razor) 1986 ●
All Fools Day (TVT) 1987 ●
Prodigal Son (TVT) 1988 ●
Scarce Saints (Aus. Raven) 1989 ●
Box Set (Aus. Mushroom) 1989
The New Rose Years (Fr. Fan Club) 1989 ●
Songs of Salvation 1976–1988 (Aus. Raven) 1991 ●

CHRIS BAILEY
Casablanca (Fr. New Rose) 1983 ●
What We Did on Our Holidays (Fr. New Rose) 1984 ●

Every decade's snotty kids are the same, as Brisbane, Australia's Saints handily prove. These punks emerged in '77 with a raw, driving sound recalling the Pretty Things of more than a decade earlier. On **(I'm) Stranded**, Chris Bailey sings with the same irritable snarl that band's Phil May had back when he was considered competition for Mick Jagger. The rest of the Saints (guitarist Ed Kuepper, drummer Ivor Hay and bassist Kym Bradshaw) respond in kind, issuing sheets of rough, gray rock'n'roll noise, including the title track, a pioneering international punk hit.

Eternally Yours refines the attack without diminishing the impact, boasting tighter playing and even a horn section. Highlights include the cynical outburst of "Know Your Product" and "Run Down," the kind of putdown bands like this have to do well to maintain credibility. With consistency and tasteful variety (handling sharp acoustic ballads as well as the standard burners), the LP is deservedly regarded as a punk classic, and even yielded a UK Top 40 single, the searing "This Perfect Day."

On **Prehistoric Sounds**, the Saints abandoned punk (for good) in favor of a brooding, bluesy, R&B-flavored style they've been expanding on since, best characterized by the melancholy and hypnotic "All Times Through Paradise." Though a bit of a downer compared to the meteoric energy of the first two LPs, and containing claustrophobic bits of paranoia like "Brisbane (Security City)," a succinct condemnation of boringtown inertia, and "The Prisoner," the album has a strange, soothing effect. Unfortunately, it was the last LP by the original lineup.

Chris Bailey re-emerged in 1979 with an all-new band of Saints, and debuted the group on the Frenchonly **Paralytic Tonight Dublin Tomorrow** EP, the first-ever release on the now mighty New Rose label. There's hornwork on several of the five tracks, but the rip-roaring energy drive finds these Saints working into something like punked-up Chicago blues.

Prehistoric Songs collects highlights from the preceding albums, along with various singles. Hearing a bunch of their ragged cover versions in succession can be unsettling, but it's also thrilling, in a sick way, to witness "River Deep, Mountain High," "Kissin' Cousins," "Lipstick on Your Collar" and Otis Redding's "Security" being put through the meatgrinder. Not for the fainthearted or tradition-minded.

The Monkey Puzzle continues to develop the new Saints' tone. Although this lineup is not nearly so abrasive as the original band, the devotion to rootsy no-nonsense rock'n'roll remains undiminished. See the buoyant cover of "Dizzy Miss Lizzy" for details. (The CD appends **Paralytic Tonight**.)

Out in the Jungle finds Bailey at his most polished, handling brooding ballads and horn-laden rockers with impressive aplomb. Although still a superlative growler, much of the exhilarating edge of previous Saints classics has been unduly muted by professionalism. Brian James, then in the Lords of the New Church, guests on guitar.

Bailey recorded his first solo album, **Casablanca**, in Paris; accompanying himself only on simple guitar (acoustic/electric, double-tracked in spots), he sings like a folk/blues troubadour. The songs are mixed in quality—from a straight reading of Jimmy Reed's "(Take Out Some) Insurance on Me" to the pretty "Wait Till Tomorrow"—and, lacking domineering rock power to drive them, have a tendency to drift a bit. Nonetheless, some of the songs are quite strong, and gain urgency from the stark presentation.

What We Did on Our Holidays followed: half acoustic solo, half backed by a full band. With the exception of one original ("Wait Till Tomorrow" again, retitled "Ghost Ships"), this album is all covers: folk/blues on the acoustic side and Sam Cooke, Marvin Gaye, Wilson Pickett, etc. on the electric side. A good workout for Bailey's rich voice, which is obviously growing deeper with age. (The CD adds eight of **Casablanca**'s twelve songs.)

Bursting with fresh enthusiasm, Bailey then reassembled the Saints, and made two studio albums that are the crowning achievement of a long career. **A Little Madness to Be Free** reveals him to be a consummate arranger, as violins, cellos, trumpets, you-name-it fill the record without cluttering up the sound. "Ghost Ships," "Down the Drain" and "The Hour" are lush, yet powerfully dramatic.

All Fools Day, the Saints' first US release in nine years, is more of the same formula, only even better. Recorded at Rockfield Studios in Wales with Hugh Jones producing, the LP even features the return of original drummer Ivor Hay and a batch of the strongest Saints material ever, particularly on Side One. With more strings, horns and soul/blues influences than ever, it's a brilliant and inspired work.

After two phenomenal albums in a row, **Prodigal Son** is a bit of a step back, although Bailey's singing and a batch of characteristically good songs make it worth a good listen. With a variety of alumni on hand, the backing is familiar and simple, approximating past successes on the best tracks ("Grain of Sand," "Before Hollywood" and "Fire and Brimstone"). But two substitutions on the US edition (an ill-advised new record-

ing of "Ghost Ships" and a dull cover of the Easybeats' "Music Goes Round My Head" done for the *Young Einstein* soundtrack) and lackluster commercial production (by Bailey and Brian McGee) drag the LP down enough to make it the least significant in the group's large catalogue.

Live in a Mud Hut is an official bootleg of sorts, taken from a 1984 European tour. The recording quality is fair, but the LP is best avoided by all but fans who already own the studio versions. The performances range from flat to buzzed, but the biggest problem is the lack of a horn section or any other embellishments. (**Live in a Mud Hut** is appended to the CD of **A Little Madness to Be Free**.)

Best of the Saints is hardly a best-of at all, as its track selection almost mirrors that of the previous greatest hits anthology, **Prehistoric Songs**. However, as the early Saints LPs are largely out of print, it can serve as a useful introduction.

Likewise, Side One of **Scarce Saints** isn't scarce, merely a reprise of much of the same early material as **Prehistoric Songs** and **Best of the Saints**. Side Two, however, is a 1981 live set from London's Dingwalls, presumably by the lineup that made **Monkey Puzzle**. Despite a preponderance of punk standards, the tracks showcase the group's later rock'n'roll side, and is much better than **Live in a Mud Hut**. The final track is a '77 recording from a Sydney gig, a razor-sharp runthrough of "Nights in Venice."

The New Rose Years is an appealing sampler covering 1980-'84, the years when a lot of early fans lost touch with the band. The overall quality is excellent, and offers an effective précis of the three superb albums and one EP from which it was primarily culled. (There's a smattering of tracks from **Live in a Mud Hut**, singles, etc.) The CD adds five more tracks from related sources.

If your pockets are deep and your Saints collection lacking, the Australian boxed set offers a tidy vinyl package with a tempting lure for even the most diligent collectors: the eight studio albums (including, oddly, the American version of **Prodigal Son**, which was subsequently released in Australia), **Scarce Saints** and a disc of post-'85 outtakes that are not otherwise available. [jy/i/jr]

See also *Laughing Clowns*.

ST. VITUS DANCE
See *Echo & the Bunnymen*.

RYUICHI SAKAMOTO
Thousand Knives of Ryuichi Sakamoto (Jap. Alfa) 1978
  (Hol. Plurex) 1982 ●
B-2 Unit (nr/Alfa-Island) 1980 ●
Merry Christmas, Mr. Lawrence (MCA) 1983
Illustrated Musical Encyclopaedia (Jap. School-Midi) 1984
  (nr/10) 1986 ●
Esperanto (Jap. School-Midi) 1985 ●
Miraiha Yaro (Jap. School-Midi) 1985 ●
Adventures of Chatran (Jap. School-Midi) 1986 ●
Media Bahn Live (Jap. School-Midi) 1986 ●
Koneko Monogatari (Jap. School-Midi) 1986

Aile de Honneamise—Royal Space Force (Jap.
    School-Midi) 1987 ●
Neo Geo (Epic) 1988 ●
Coda (Jap. Midi) 1988 ●
Risky EP [CD] (Jap. CBS-Sony) 1988 ●
Playing the Orchestra [CD] (Virgin) 1989 ●
A Handmaid's Tale (GNP Crescendo) 1989 ●
Beauty (Virgin) 1990 ●
The Sheltering Sky (Virgin Movie Music) 1991 φ

RIUICHI SAKAMOTO FEATURING ROBIN SCOTT

Left Handed Dream (Epic) 1981 ●
The Arrangement (Jap. Alfa) 1990 ●

VARIOUS ARTISTS

Piano One (Private Music) 1986 ●

RYUICHI SAKAMOTO, DAVID BYRNE AND CONG SU

The Last Emperor (Virgin Movie Music) 1988 ●

Keyboardist Sakamoto did his first session work during his post-graduate studies of electronic and ethnic music at the University of Art of Tokyo in the mid-'70s. He continued after getting an MFA and, in 1978, released his first solo album, **Thousand Knives**. Presaging his work with Yellow Magic Orchestra (which he formed later that year), the record consists of electronic disco, commendably quirky for the time it was recorded but now largely dated, with some unnecessary guitar soloing—the chief guest performance on the disc, since almost everything else was played by Sakamoto. Only surreal environment-conjuring on one track and musical cross-pollination on another hint at the avant-garde and world music aspects of Sakamoto's later work.

While with YMO, he made **B-2 Unit** with the help of British reggae musician/producer Dennis Bovell and XTC's Andy Partridge. Though not throwing up as many sparks with them as might have been expected—what might he do with Bovell now?—it clearly shows him to be an adventuresome oddball rather than a trendy studio hack.

On 1981's **Left Handed Dream**, Sakamoto effectively draws out and integrates his collaborators (Robin "M" Scott and Adrian Belew, as well as both YMO cohorts), who in turn get the best out of him. The LP varies from slippery, fractured funk to a duel between a grim, darkly atmospheric drone and assorted percussion; it consistently scintillates, though sometimes in a curiously offhand way. (In 1990, **The Arrangement** reissued the tracks featuring Scott—about half the album—plus several more, evidently outtakes of the original session.)

Merry Christmas, Mr. Lawrence is the soundtrack to a film starring Tom Conti, David Bowie and Sakamoto, who performed the entire evocative synth score alone (save a vocal of dubious worth by David Sylvian in an alternative version of the main theme). He more recently acted in *The Last Emperor* (1987), also contributing half of the suitably atmospheric soundtrack album. (The score won an Oscar.) The disc's only memorable music is Sakamoto's main theme (with its surprisingly European feel), which he explores through much of his side.

Both films' music appeared later in other forms. **Coda** reprises the first seven tracks of **Mr. Lawrence**, while **Playing the Orchestra** is a live symphonic rendering of music from *The Last Emperor*, followed by an equally in-depth investigation of about a third of *Mr. Lawrence*, capped by the restatement of the *Last Emperor* theme. Lovely, warm, spacious and extremely tough to obtain: a limited-edition CD release in a gorgeous decorated box, with a bonus CD-3 featuring a trio of non-movie tracks.

Esperanto is an abridged version of Sakamoto's end of a dance performance collaboration with New York choreographer Melissa Fenley. **Adventures of Chatran** and **Koneko Monogatari** are also movie scores, the latter for one of Japan's biggest-ever box-office flicks; **Honneamise** is his score for an animated sci-fi film. **Piano One** consists of solo acoustic piano pieces by four artists, including Sakamoto and Eddie Jobson.

Illustrated Musical Encyclopedia (originally released in 1984 in Japan, as **Ongakuzukan**) opens with "Field Work," a low-key dance-rock joint venture with Thomas Dolby that was also released as a single; it's immediately likable but unrelated to the feel of the rest of the record. The LP's title states an idea Sakamoto has toyed with since **Thousand Knives**: combining pieces of Eastern and Western musics so they're not readily identifiable yet complement each other as part of an organic whole. He sometimes crosses the line into pretentious piano muzak when meddling with European "classical" music, but it's a mostly worthwhile attempt, if it does require patience to absorb the subtler angles. (He explores all this more ambitiously—and successfully—on **Neo Geo**.)

Three tracks on **Miraiha Yaro** (aka **Futurista**) have conventional melodies—almost reminiscent of TV themes—but tricked up with oddball, loud and/or abrasive synth arrangements (as if to counterweight the tunes' prettiness). "Milan 1909" is an electronic curator's narration on the Futurist art movement, over restrained keyboard; "Verso lo schermo" is electro-disco-*cum*-opera, with Italian lyrics; "Water Is Life" is a wall of music chopped up and distorted, along with a voice slowed to a deep slur. Helpers include vocalist Bernard Fowler, guitarist Arto Lindsay, Sakamoto's wife Akiko Yano (some Japanese lyrics) and saxist Maceo Parker (of James Brown fame). Not as engaging as it is impressive, but almost. **Media Bahn** is a double live LP of a subsequent tour in support of the album; Sakamoto is aided by Fowler and percussionist David Van Tieghem.

Neo Geo is Sakamoto's biggest all-star affair, boasting Van Tieghem, drumming by jazz star Tony Williams and reggae heavyweight Sly Dunbar, bassists Bootsy Collins and Bill Laswell (also Sakamoto's co-producer/ writing partner here) and, on one track, a strangely simpatico Iggy Pop vocalizing his own thoughtfully dramatic lyrics. Sakamoto spends the rest of the album carrying forth the **Illustrated Musical Encyclopedia** experiments, which get most exciting when he tries weird intertwinings of Japanese music and rock/funk. The LP's highlights are among Sakamoto's best work. (**Risky** is a CD-V of five **Neo Geo** tunes, four of which have visual contents for those equipped with videodisc players.)

With **Beauty**, Sakamoto really becomes the Quincy Jones of alternative music. His all-star cast includes Arto Lindsay (no guitar, only vocals and poem reading), Robbie Robertson (Sakamoto co-wrote songs for

Robertson's second solo LP), Sly Dunbar and—would you believe—Brian Wilson singing backup to Robert Wyatt's lead on the Stones' "We Love You"? Although more exciting on paper than it turns out to be in the grooves, that's not so bad a thing. About the only celebrity who retains much identity here is Youssou N'Dour, with various vocal embellishments and a lead vocal on "Diabaram" (which he co-wrote); otherwise it's Sakamoto's show (he even sings lead in English for the first time) as he deftly injects Japanese, Arabic, Indian and African elements into western pop musics. It's not as exciting—or as decisively successful—as **Neo Geo**, but its sophisticated synthesis is both pleasant and A-for-effort admirable.

A Handmaid's Tale and *The Sheltering Sky* are both critically and commercially unsuccessful movie adaptations of well-received novels, the former by Margaret Atwood and the latter by Paul Bowles; Sakamoto did the scores for both. For the latter, his compositions—mostly played by the London Royal Philharmonic Orchestra—are somewhat repetitive but evocative, with a main theme vaguely reminiscent of his *Last Emperor* theme. Half of **The Sheltering Sky** album has little or nothing to do with Sakamoto: three tracks are by composer Richard Horowitz and there are several striking samples of North African music and a couple of period pieces.

See also *Yellow Magic Orchestra*.   [jg]

SALAMANDER JIM
See *Beasts of Bourbon*.

WALTER SALAS-HUMARA
See *Silos*.

SALEM 66
Salem 66 EP (Homestead) 1984
A Ripping Spin (Homestead) 1985
Frequency and Urgency (Homestead) 1986
Your Soul Is Mine, Fork It Over [CD] (Homestead) 1987 ●
Natural Disasters, National Treasures (Homestead) 1988 ●
Down the Primrose Path (Homestead) 1990 ●

Led by two Massachusetts singer/songwriters, Salem 66 plays generally delicate electric guitar music that embraces folk more than rock traditions. The trio's six-song debut EP—produced by Neighborhoods guitarist David Minehan—has plenty of poetic ambience and some surprisingly complex arrangements, but consistent jangly-trebly sound makes it hard to stay engrossed, and occasional bum notes also interrupt the mood. Guitarist Judy Grunwald and bassist Beth Kaplan both sing, but their voices don't harmonize all that well. Needs work.

With the arrival of a new guitarist, the Salems became a quartet for **A Ripping Spin**, a full-length LP also produced by Minehan. The songs and playing are better, but the vocals are still hit-and-miss. Kaplan takes an indecisive approach to the issue; Grunwald's gurgly warble can also be a trial. The brief "Fragile" shows their potential, but other tunes are less mellifluous.

A guitarist switch brought Stephen Smith into the lineup for **Frequency and Urgency**, which resulted in noticeably improved music on the Ethan James-produced album. With stronger, more assured playing, the simple pop-rock provides a firm basis for the alternating 50-50 mix of sensitive, occasionally offbeat tunes written and sung individually by Grunwald and Kaplan. The latter's lighter tone and smoother delivery is generally more attractive here, but neither is remotely qualified to be a lead singer.

Your Soul Is Mine, Fork It Over is a CD-only compilation—seventeen selections from the first three records plus "Across the Sea," a 1984 single.

Taking another instrumental step forward, **Natural Disasters, National Treasures** finds Kaplan and Grunwald ably supported by a different guitarist and a new drummer. The Salems' productive relationship with James results in the most accomplished and appealing sound of their career; amazingly, Kaplan's vocals are nicely Bangleish and Grunwald's are slowly approaching adequacy as well. (Caveat to Eddy Grant fans: the "Electric Avenue" here is a different song entirely.)

Stylistic tensions surface on **Down the Primrose Path**. Amid some of their most unpalatably pretentious lyrics in years, surprisingly loud arrangements all but overwhelm Kaplan and drive Grunwald to sing worse than usual. A few songs (the inquisitive "Bell Jar" and "Primrose Path," for instance) are treated gently, but the band's overriding readiness to rock this time out leaves them sounding wan and stranded.   [i]

KIM SALMON AND THE SURREALISTS
See *Scientists*.

SALVATION ARMY
See *Three O'Clock*.

SAMHAIN
See *Misfits*.

SATIVA LUVBOX
See *Kommunity FK*.

FERNANDO SAUNDERS
Cashmere Dreams (Grudge) 1989 ●

A pair of Saunders' past employers—Marianne Faithfull and Lou Reed, who also co-wrote a song—offer generous endorsements on the back cover of the bassist's solo debut (no word from Jeff Beck or John McLaughlin, however), but that doesn't make this bland record sound any better. Saunders has a nice enough voice and acquits himself on a number of instruments (the main assists are from a drummer, synthesists and hornmen), but the material and performances are about as deep and exciting as Toto—who actually collaborated on two tunes.   [i]

JIM SAUTER, DON DIETRICK, THURSTON MOORE
See *Sonic Youth*.

573

SAVAGE REPUBLIC

Tragic Figures (Independent Project) 1982 + 1987 ●
Trudge EP (Bel. Play It Again Sam) 1985
Ceremonial (Independent Project) 1985 ●
Live Trek 1985–1986 (Nate Starkman & Son) 1987
Jamahiriya (Fundamental Music) 1988 ●
Customs (Fundamental) 1989 ●
Live in Europe 1988 (Bel. Fundamental) 1990 ●

17 PYGMIES

Hatikva EP (Resistance) 1983 (It. Viva) 1988
Jedda by the Sea (Resistance) 1984
Captured in Ice (Resistance) 1985
Welcome (Great Jones-Island) 1988 ●

Originally named Africa Corps, Los Angeles' Savage Republic got its start at UCLA, where Jeff Long, Bruce Licher, Mark Erskine and Jackson Del Rey (Philip Drucker) were attending school. The twin-bass lineup (plus some outside assistance) yielded an arty, industrial ensemble which serenaded cement walls with lightly droning grates of monotone guitar, exotic percussion and noisy, ranted vocals. The band changed their name to avoid confusion with the East Coast Afrika Korps (and the implied affiliation with the Nazipunk fad of the time) a week before releasing their debut album, **Tragic Figures**. (Their records' unique graphic look was the result of a school project that gave Licher access to an antique letterpress.)

A combination of industrial drone with deep machine-like swaths of dragging bass, Halloween horror-movie screams and some of the most delightfully tribal and tropical percussion found on disc, **Tragic Figures** also introduced a touch of Arabic cat slink that would show up more prominently in later work. When keyboardist Robert Loveless joined, the quintet's sound turned from frantically abrasive to almost meditatively cool.

Drucker and Loveless launched a side band, 17 Pygmies, to delve into lighter, more melodic music than Savage Republic. Retaining the group's tribal percussion and Arabic feel, they added electronic keyboards for **Hatikva**, an EP which crosses Emerson, Lake & Palmer's "The Sheriff," a spaghetti western soundtrack and a Caribbean rhythm fest. Only a thousand copies were originally pressed, but it was reissued by an Italian label.

In the midst of recording a second album at the end of 1983, Savage Republic split up; Drucker and Loveless, under the 17 Pygmies name, completed the record, which was released as **Jedda by the Sea**. The Pygmies went on to record **Captured in Ice**, an even more pop-oriented album which features lilting electronic keyboards, clearly sung female vocals, new wave "oooohh-oooohh"'s, sometimes crisp, dance-club drumming and synthesizers.

Licher and Erskine reformed Savage Republic. The ambient, almost meditative **Trudge** EP came out in Europe only. A crawling, building excursion into the avant Arabic surf textures the band had been exploring live, it lopes through a kind of Western movie soundtrack with some limited vocalizations but no lyrics. The abrasive edge that was engraved in the music from their industrial days is gone, leaving only the racing adrenaline that accompanied it, the clank and clatter of clay-pot percussion accents. At times, there's a processional maj-

esty that hints at what Savage Republic's completion of the **Jedda** tracks might have sounded like.

Almost the same week as **Trudge** was released, the Republic came out with **Ceremonial** in the US. With Loveless back in the band (here a sextet), the album showcases a pop and melodic side with gentle male and Pygmies-like female vocals and only a hint of the Savage's banana Republic feel. There are even keyboards, mandolin, wind chimes and a dulcimer hidden in the (almost) lush and relaxed grooves. (**Tragic Figures** and **Ceremonial** were later issued on one CD.)

Live Trek (1985–1986) is most like **Trudge** in texture, reworking the material from their earliest industrial days to excise the abrasion. It would make a good introduction for anyone who has not heard the band.

Jamahiriya continues to fuse their past into their future with a sound that reflects and melds all of their evolutions onto one disc. Jackson Del Rey is back in the lineup, but Loveless is gone. The CD version of the disc includes three instrumental remixes of vocal album tracks.

Meanwhile, 17 Pygmies—now a Drucker/Loveless trio with singing poet Louise Bialik—signed to a major label and released **Welcome**, a ambitiously complex mixture of music and theater (by guest speaker Charles Schneider), assembled into a diverting program loaded to the teeth with provocative ideas and sounds.

Recorded as a quintet, Savage Republic's latest studio LP undertakes another fascinating cultural expedition, with mixed results. In an audio analogue to visiting six countries in three days, **Customs** juxtaposes polite Arabic and Greek influences—mostly expressed through the use of ethnic instruments, although "Song for Adonis" really sounds the Mediterranean part—with merciless noise ("Rapeman's First EP" matches the funny title with an appropriately violent sonic physic) and found-sound ambience. Overall, **Customs** (I think we're talking border checkpoints, not habits here) is a dizzying blur, but not an unpleasant trip.   ['e/i]

SKY SAXON

Sunlight & the New Seeds (Expression) 1976
Stars New Seeds Live at the Orpheum Theatre (Sunbow) 1977
In Love with Life (Expression) 1978
Lovers Cosmic Voyage (Golden Flash) 1978
Bad Part of Town (Fr. Eva) 1982
New Fruit from Old Seeds: The Rare Sky Saxon Volume One (Archive Int'l Productions) 1983
Starry Ride (nr/Psycho) 1984
Masters of Psychedelia (Fr. New Rose) 1985

SKY "SUNLIGHT" SAXON AND PURPLE ELECTRICITY

Private Party (Voxx) 1986

SKY "SUNLIGHT" SAXON AND FIREWALL

A Groovy Thing (Fr. New Rose) 1986
Destiny's Children (PVC) 1986
... In Search of Brighter Colors (Fr. New Rose) 1988
World Fantastic (Skyclad) 1988

If Henry Rollins incarnates all the smoldering hatred and intensity of familyman Charlie Manson, then Sky Saxon—the legendary leader of LA's protopunk

Seeds—is a self-made construct of all the qualities Rollins discarded: drug-addled, hippie mystical, stuck in the '60s, inconsistent and unfocused. The above discography is a necessarily abbreviated listing of Saxon's activities and does not include most of the countless (and endless) cult chants from his days as a late-'70s Hawaiian guru (pressed in editions of as few as two, some on 8-track tape only) or cult-refugee material (the Alright Family Band).

New Fruit is exactly what the subtitle claims: a collections of obscurities beginning with the squeaky-clean (ex-Little Rascal Darla Hood was part of the original entourage) doo-wop-derived '62-'63 teen pop of Little Richard Marsh, including a song with the Rivingtons on backing vocals. Missing his debut single, the sole AIP volume is nonetheless a more complete version of the Eva retrospective, skirting the familiar late-'60s Seeds years (with one '67 selection) and interview recorded in distant shoebox mono from a live broadcast, through to the '70s Seeds—not appreciably different in content or approach from the '60s version (albeit angrier and heavier on a pair of raging punk ravers)—until the final two tracks, when suddenly they kick into wah-wah overdrive and unexpectedly veer into sheetmetal blues (as practiced by Frijid Pink or the Frost). Fade out the '70s.

Fade in the '80s, with Sky now on Psycho, the foremost British acid-casualty label, sandwiched between Deviants reissues and Crystalized Movements freakouts. Joined by a stellar cast culled from Iron Butterfly, Fraternity of Man and Steppenwolf (the latter represented by Mars Bonfire), **Starry Ride** reaches into Sky's head and pulls out a set of genuine plums: sharp if formulaic Seedspunk framing a worldview no less oblique than Roky Erickson's, as illustrated most emphatically on the side-long "24 Hour Rocker," a minor riff-plus-variations repeated live beneath scream-of-consciousness ranting and rave.

A Groovy Thing documents his studio excursions in LA under the "Firewall" moniker, with sidemen moonlighting from the Dream Syndicate, Plimsouls and Droogs, all Phil Spectorized (by co-producer "Marcus Tybalt," longtime Jekyll to Saxon's Hyde) for maximum sonic dressing, minimal riffing and left-field vocalizing (the Seeds legacy). **Destiny's Children** puts the same songs in a new order (with inferior artwork), while **In Search of Brighter Colors** updates Saxony to a less anxious, more moody plane befitting California's then-crumbling garage scene, closer aurally to the Seeds than anything since 1971. Goofily poppy, it hit the US racks as **World Fantastic**, minus the lesser songs and joined by a number of unreleased crosseyed neo-classics dredged from Sky's days amidst the California underworld.

Voxx caught the rebounding Sky on a four-song 1986 7-inch shared with soothing/scathing psych punks SS-20, whom the aging guru had first augmented/sabotaged (according to one's point of view) onstage during his unexpected resurgence in Hollywood in the early '80s, when he would climb up unannounced to join every single band of the then-popular garage contingent spearheaded by Greg Shaw's Voxx label and Cavern Club. Originally a kick, it quickly became a drag to the young Beatle-booted hipsters, and a band called Purple Electricity was cooked up as a stake

through Sky's hollow heart. Featuring the McDonald brothers from Redd Kross and Primate Brian Corrigan on drums, the intent was to daze and confuse Mr. Saxon, as well as any sycophants still blindly following. Drawing heavily from familiar '70s metal tunes, the blatantly unrehearsed music of the March '86 show documented on **Private Party** is matched with a disconnected and distracted Sky, recorded in glorious walkmanorama. Just to cap off this travesty, all of the songs—including indisputable covers—are credited to SS Saxon.   [ab]

See also *Red Cross*.

SCATTERBRAIN
See *Ludichrist*.

SCENE IS NOW
See *The Scene Is Now*.

PETER SCHERER
See *Arto Lindsay/Ambitious Lovers*.

PETER SCHILLING
Major Tom (Coming Home) EP (Elektra) 1983
Error in the System (Elektra) 1983
Things to Come (Elektra) 1985
The Different Story (World of Lust and Crime) (Elektra) 1989 ●

Back when German music was affectionately referred to as "krautrock," it seemed as if spacey progressive experimentalism was the only kind of music Teutonic youth could play. Since that era, the nation's stylistic scope has widened considerably and been exported to global popularity as well. So there's something nostalgic and heartwarming about the sci-fidom of Peter Schilling's left-field hit single, "Major Tom (Coming Home)," which essentially copies the story of David Bowie's "Space Oddity" into a modern electro-pop setting. The 12-inch offers the single four ways: English, German, instrumental and an eight-minute John Luongo remix. The song sounds best *auf deutsch*.

Error in the System contains "Major Tom (Coming Home)" sung in English, a plodding instrumental called "Major Tom Part II" and a German version of "Silent Night, Holy Night" (with new lyrics), as well as fake reggae and a bunch of needless "Major Tom" soundalikes. Throughout, Schilling's almost accentless multi-tracked vocals are blandly sweet, and the metronome-powered electro-bubblegum is pleasant if shallow. A full album of this synthetic weightlessness is more than enough; briefer doses aren't at all painful.

Things to Come proves the narrow limits of Schilling's appeal. At best, a few songs echo his hit; otherwise, it's a tedious and unoriginal bore. If that much repetition wasn't enough, eight tracks from **Error in the System** and **Things to Come** were later recombined (with the addition of one new song) to form **The Different Story**.   [i]

FRED SCHNEIDER & THE SHAKE SOCIETY
See *B-52's*.

SCHNELL FENSTER

See *Swingers*.

SCHOOLLY D

Schoolly-D (Schoolly-D) 1986
Saturday Night!—The Album (Schoolly-D) 1987 (Jive)
  1987
The Adventures of Schoolly-D [CD] (Rykodisc) 1987 •
Smoke Some Kill (Jive) 1988 •
Am I Black Enough for You? (Jive-RCA) 1989 •

One of the earliest and most influential proponents of gangster rap, Philadelphia's Schoolly D (Jesse Weaver) has built a career on dispassionate reports from the grittier side of inner-city life. As troubling as the entertainment value of rhymes that discuss gun possession, drug use and street violence without any negative context (or clear-cut fictionalization) may be, Schoolly argues that people take his lyrics too seriously. (After NWA semi-politicized the issue, it took the Geto Boys to rekindle the debate over the way such raps are meant and perceived.) In any case, the uncompromising rapper offers a deromanticized streetwise corollary of urban-reality filmmaking.

Ably supported by his sidekick DJ Code Money's uncomplicated rhythm tracks, Schoolly began by releasing a pair of albums on his own label. **Schoolly-D** contains "PSK—What Does It Mean?" (Parkside Killers, a local gang), "Gucci Time" and "I Don't Like Rock-'n'Roll," a scratch-happy warning to long-haired freaks: "be on your guard." The more ambitious and unsettling **Saturday Night!** has "We Get Ill" (the Beastie Boys were allegedly greatly influenced by seeing Schoolly perform), "Do It Do It" (complete with children's chorus singing "Who's afraid of the big bad wolf?"), "It's Krack" and the title track. After Jive picked up on Schoolly, the label reissued **Saturday Night!**, with three extra tracks: "Housing the Joint" (which quotes Sly Stone), "Parkside 5-2" and "Dis Groove Is Bad." **The Adventures of Schoolly-D** combines the contents of both records (in their original configurations) and adds an extra cut.

Schoolly's arrival on a major label (or maybe it's just the handsome back-cover photo) shifts the context of his raps, removing their intimidating credibility and leaving a lot of empty-sounding big talk instead. Without the aura of reality, **Smoke Some Kill** lacks emotional impact; Schoolly's not the most dynamic MC here, and the repetitiveness of his simple beats and samples does nothing to charge up the record. Despite a lot of cussing and such cold topics as "Smoke Some Kill," "Mr. Big Dick" and "Same White Bitch (Got You Strung Out on Cane)," **Smoke Some Kill** is no heavy scene.

Shifting his image from street crime to black power, Schoolly gets back in the groove on **Am I Black Enough for You?**, a loud and proud album of slamming tracks that use spoken word bites (political speeches, *Star Trek* dialogue, Richard Pryor crack-horror routines) to indicate new political consciousness. Actually, the record doesn't wind up saying much of anything (a lot of the tracks are routine boasts, and Schoolly's old nastiness resurfaces in "Pussy Ain't Nothin' "), but the fact that he's moving in such a positive direction (check

the inspirational chant of "Get Off Your Ass and Get Involved" or the Afrocentricity of "Black Jesus") on this strong album is encouraging and exciting. [i]

SCHRAMMS

See *Yo La Tengo*.

BRINSLEY SCHWARZ

Brinsley Schwarz (Capitol) 1970
Despite It All (Capitol) 1970
Silver Pistol (UA) 1972 (nr/Edsel) 1986 •
Nervous on the Road (UA) 1972
Please Don't Ever Change (nr/UA) 1973 (nr/Edsel)
  1987 •
Original Golden Greats (nr/UA) 1974
The New Favourites of Brinsley Schwarz (nr/UA) 1974
Fifteen Thoughts of Brinsley Schwarz (nr/UA) 1978
Brinsley Schwarz (Capitol) 1978
It's All Over Now (nr/Charly) 1988 •

VARIOUS ARTISTS

Greasy Truckers Party (nr/UA) 1972

Many pub-rock bands of the early '70s served as launching pads for English musicians whose fame and fortune increased enormously with the advent of new wave. Along with Ducks Deluxe, Brinsley Schwarz easily takes the cake as a hotbed of talents just waiting for the right moment to burst forth. Although largely unheralded (and commercially ignored) at the time, its five members—Nick Lowe, Ian Gomm, Brinsley Schwarz, Bob Andrews and Billy Rankin—have surely proven their skill and importance many times over since the band dissolved in 1975.

Lowe's solo career and membership in Rockpile, not to mention his voluminous production credits, have made him a constant presence, a revered elder in the Church of Cool. Gomm's solo albums are more in keeping with the Brinsleys' laid-back, easy-listening countryfied pop. Confirmed sidemen Schwarz and Andrews both served in the Rumour (with and without Graham Parker) and have each produced and played alongside many other spotlight stars as well. Rankin played in a band called Tiger and has drummed on loads of records by likeminded rockers. (He and Schwarz also joined future Rumour member Martin Belmont in the last incarnation of Ducks Deluxe.)

The music on Brinsley Schwarz's albums seems at once totally removed and perfectly in keeping with the individuals' later escapades; little hints of the future keep cropping up amid the genial, American-flavored rock and mild pop. Dave Edmunds later recorded "Ju Ju Man" (a cover included on **Silver Pistol**) on **Get It**, backed by Lowe, Rankin and Andrews. The first appearance of Lowe's "(What's So Funny 'Bout) Peace, Love and Understanding" is on **New Favourites**; it's since become a classic item in Elvis Costello's repertoire. Lowe's brush with American chart success, "Cruel to Be Kind," was co-written with Gomm and doesn't sound very different from some of the Brinsleys' richer pop numbers. Much of the Rumour's crisp Van Morrison swing is present in tracks like "Surrender to the Rhythm" (**Nervous on the Road**). You get the point.

In a nutshell, while some of the music on these albums is either dull or wimpy beyond belief—and check those embarrassing hippie pictures!—they contain enough wonderful stuff to make Brinsley Schwarz's records well worth discovering. Of discographical interest: the first two LPs are also available as an American twin set (**Brinsley Schwarz**) released in 1978. **Original Golden Greats** and **Fifteen Thoughts** (kudos to the latter's Maoist art direction) are compilations of tracks from the band's entire career; there's some duplication, but both have gems not otherwise found on any album. Brinsley Schwarz also contributed five cuts to the 1972 live compilation, **Greasy Truckers Party**.

[i]

See also *Ducks Deluxe, Nick Lowe, Graham Parker, Rockpile, Rumour*.

SCIENTISTS

Scientists EP (Aus. White Rider) 1979
The Scientists (Aus. YPRX) 1981
Blood Red River EP (nr/Au-go-go) 1983
This Heart Doesn't Run on Blood, This Heart Doesn't Run on Love EP (nr/Au-go-go) 1984
Demolition Derby (Bel. Soundwork) 1985
Atom Bomb Baby (nr/Au-go-go) 1985
You Get What You Deserve (nr/Karbon) 1985
Heading for a Trauma (nr/Au-go-go) 1985
Rubber Never Sleeps [tape] (Aus. Au-go-go) 1985
Weird Love (Big Time) 1986
The Human Jukebox (nr/Karbon) 1987
The Sweet Corn Sessions EP (Aus. Timberyard) 1989
A Pox on You EP (Sp. Munster) 1989
Pissed on Another Planet EP (Aus. Timberyard) 1990

KIM SALMON AND THE SURREALISTS

Hit Me with the Surreal Feel (Aus. Black Eye) 1988
Just Because You Can't See It ... Doesn't Mean It Isn't There ... (Aus. Black Eye) 1989 ●

INTERSTELLAR VILLAINS

Right Out in the Lobster Quadrille EP (Aus. Timberyard) 1989

Perth, Australia; May 1978. An unrecorded band named the Invaders (which included bassist Boris Sujdovic, guitarist Rod Radalj, and guitarist/lead vocalist Kim Salmon) joins forces with drummer James Baker, changes their name to the Scientists and releases "Frantic Romantic," a bright little pop single. A four-track EP and a delightfully gritty LP of hard pop follow. But music life in Perth (on the far west coast of Australia, 2,500 miles of outback away from anyplace else) becomes frustrating. Baker leaves for Sydney where he meets up with fellow Perth renegade Dave Faulkner (who had been in a band named the Gurus and was then in an unnamed ensemble with fellow Perth-escapee Radalj). Baker joins the new Faulkner/Radalj group and they name it Le Hoodoo Gurus.

September 1981: Salmon also gives up on Perth and relocates to Sydney, where he and Sujdovic create a new Scientists with a manic swamp-grunge sound. Full of dirty feedback and great swaths of nod-out guitar, **Blood Red River** (one of several Scientists records to be issued by Au-go-go in the UK as well as in Australia) pays homage to Suicide with pounding basslines and echo-chamber-overkill vocals, while hinting at the hypnotic fusion of '60s hookah smoke and screechingly overheated guitar that bubbles through **This Heart Doesn't Run on Blood** and on into **Weird Love** to become the Scientists sound. From screaming blues-rooted mania laid over repeating circles of bass and twists of cacophony lead guitar, through the frenetic Cramps-meet-Birthday Party dirges of the Belgian-only **Demolition Derby**, each release nudges the band's sound a step further through a path of deep, dark, nod-out blasts until 1984 when, ever in search of someplace else, the Scientists left Australia for London, where their story begins to fall apart.

Except for **Atom Bomb Baby** (a mighty collection of blistering rockers recorded in London in late '84) and the very Crampsy "You Only Live Twice" single (a cover of the James Bond theme), the next three Scientists releases are mostly archive material. **You Get What You Deserve** combines the seven-song **Atom Bomb Baby** and **Demolition Derby** with the B-side from "You Only Live Twice" as a bonus cut. **Heading for a Trauma** has four new songs but is otherwise a compilation of pre-**Blood** singles, a radio session and the **Demolition Derby** tracks (again). The tape-only **Rubber Never Sleeps** digs even further into the vaults to include live material from two of the Scientists' pre-Hoodoo Gurus lineups, as well as 1982-'83 live tracks.

Although the poundingly intense **Weird Love** (the only Scientists record released in the US)—with the exception of the earlier "You Only Live Twice"—newly recorded in London (February 1986) with producer Richard Mazda, it again portrays the band's music as history by consisting entirely of old material, including such tracks as "Demolition Derby," "Atom Bomb Baby" and "Nitro" (originally on **This Heart**).

By **The Human Jukebox**, only guitarists Salmon and Tony Thewlis remained from the Australian band. A dreary album lacking the searing frenzy that gave the Scientists their impact, **Jukebox**'s repetition comes off as industrial rather than mesmerizing; Salmon's vocals are flat and droney as if he'd taken lessons from a reject from Lou Reed High.

In 1989, the "Frantic Romantic" single and the 1979 EP recorded in Perth's Sweet Corn Studios were compiled and reissued as the **Sweet Corn Sessions**, a six-track EP. That same material was later reissued again with different artwork as **Pissed on Another Planet**, taking its name from one of the cuts.

Despite the Scientists' demise, the band's archives continue to be raided. In 1989, the Spanish fanzine *La Herenica* issued a four-track EP featuring alternate versions of "Swampland," "Nitro," "Solid Gold Hell" and "A Pox on You" along with its 72-page all-Scientists issue.

Since the Scientists, Salmon and his new band, the Surrealists, have been churning out wild and frenzied rock music: untamed, primal and filled with frenzy. Like the Scientists, the new group uses the mantra of repetition to suck listeners into its groove. Sometimes it's a nightmare; other times (as in **Just Because**'s cover version of "Je t'Aime") it's just a wet dream. But the music is always imbued with a fine and tortured spirit. Alternately funky and bluesy/rootsy but always based on the scrapes and squeals and manipulations of hard, electric guitar, the records are, above all, rock'n'roll. (Not content to limit his creativity to just one group or perspective at a time, Salmon has more recently released a solo single, "Lightning Scary" that couples '60s AM radio-style pop with rap.)

Following the Scientists, Tony Thewlis assembled the Interstellar Villains, whose 12-inch EP (**Right Out in the Lobster Quadrille**) is a psychocandied fusion between pop and pound. More twisted than the mid-'80s paisley but not a self-indulgent space-rock ramble either, Lobster grafts American roots rock to British production styles, putting its pop proclivities across in a more cleanly textured surface than American garage bands working the same tradition, but with more guts than the glossier Brits.   ['e]

See also *Beasts of Bourbon, Hoodoo Gurus.*

ROBIN SCOTT

See *M, Ryuichi Sakamoto.*

TIM SCOTT

Swear EP (Sire) 1983
The High Lonesome Sound (Geffen) 1987 ●

Ex-Rockat guitarist Scott pounds out some of the dumbest dance-rock ever on the five-song **Swear**, produced by Richard Gottehrer. Joined by ex-Holly and the Italians bassist Mark Sidgwick and future Beat Rodeo drummer Lewis King (with one guest vocal by Jane Wiedlin), Scott's inadequacy as a singer and writer are made abundantly clear on the moronic title song and "Good as Gold"; elsewhere, he's just a bland and forgettable rocker.

So much for stylistic consistency: **The High Lonesome Sound** is unconvincing predigested commercial country and cowpunk. Mitchell Froom produced and played the keyboards; Elvis Presley sideman Jerry Scheff is the bassist; David Hidalgo of Los Lobos adds accordion and backup vocals; the redoubtable James Burton even takes a nice dobro solo on "Release." Give Scott points for improved vocals and bland inoffensiveness, but that's about all.   [i]

See also *Havalinas, Rockats.*

SCRAPING FOETUS OFF THE WHEEL

See *Foetus Inc.*

SCRATCH ACID

Scratch Acid (Rabid Cat) 1984
Just Keep Eating. (Rabid Cat) 1986
Berserker EP (Touch and Go) 1987

This potent Austin, Texas quartet started out with a remarkably unsettling outlook and wound up—at least the members did following the band's dissolution—playing a crucial role in the development of late-'80s noise rock that has taken deep root in the industrialized Midwest. The eight intense songs on **Scratch Acid** live up to their abrasive promise, powerfully and painfully muscling around just on the edge of listenability, with only sometime-Big Boy Rey Washam's strong drumming to anchor walls of guitar noise and (ex-Toxic Shock) David Yow's hysterical shriek-singing. In spots, relative restraint and organization prevail, and the record succeeds in conveying something; elsewhere, an overdose of PiL/Birthday Party takes hold and you get nothing but chaotic, raw angst that is simply no fun at all. Some of the inspired lyrics ("Cannibal," "Monsters") are classic *Mondo Cane* material, but a more palatable sonic setting would have increased their impact.

Without sacrificing a jot of their psycho weirdness, Scratch Acid show a mite more focus and control on the full-length **Just Keep Eating.** The music is just as virulent and loud, but Yow's increased effort to be understood gives an extra kick to the demented lyrics of songs like "Eyeball," "Unlike a Baptist" and "Crazy Dan," the longwinded chronicle of a crazed murderer. Fun stuff!

Lacking the far-reaching conceptual imagination of the Butthole Surfers, Scratch Acid keep the presentation simple while reaching deep into the lyrical cesspool on the **Berserker** EP's six well-produced songs. Yow's raging, hysterical delivery goes nicely with the punk wash of "Mary Had a Little Drug Problem" and a perverted character study called "Moron's Moron," but the words are their most amusing element. Likewise, the festering dermal ugliness of "Skin Drips" (accompanied by a bluesy swing) and the ironic near-hardcore of "This Is Bliss" do their best work on the lyric sheet. Throughout the 12-inch EP, debauchery, vulgarity and viciousness intertwine for a truly seedy experience. [i]

See also *Jesus Lizard, Rapeman.*

SCRAWL

Plus, Also, Too (No Other) 1987 (Rough Trade) 1989
He's Drunk (Rough Trade) 1988 ●
Smallmouth (Rough Trade) 1990 ●

Columbus, Ohio's Scrawl show more enthusiasm than skill on **Plus, Also, Too**, a sloppy, occasionally strident indie-pop record in line with the trio's name. Although her aggressive guitar work is dandy, Marcy Mays' uncertain singing (joined in disharmony by bassist Sue Harshe) isn't equally beneficial to Scrawl's rugged melodicism, cutting sidelong through songs rather than moving them along. There's promise in the grooves, but the vocals just don't cut it. (Besides reissuing the album, Rough Trade later stuck, appended, attached **Plus, Also, To** on the CD of **He's Drunk.**)

Strings of cryptic fragments serve as the intriguing lyrics on **He Drunk**, a more proficient and varied follow-up. The songs are neat (besides their originals, Scrawl demolish and then rebuild the Hombres' garage-rock classic, "Let It All Hang Out," and give Felice and Boudleaux Bryant's "Rocky Top" a politely quiet reading); the instrumental work is generally solid. But while Mays and Harshe both show improvement, their voices still don't blend together very well at all.

Producer Gary Smith, who worked wonders for the Blake Babies and has done records with Throwing Muses and other neo-pop ensembles, reigned in Scrawl's discordant excesses on **Smallmouth**, drawing out the sturdy melodies with presentably confident vocals. Tidying up the sound might have removed the jagged corners that make Scrawl invigorating, but the trio (especially Mays' intense guitar strikes) skillfully holds its own, making songs like "Charles," "Tell You What" and "Time to Come Clean" both bracing and appealing. Evidently responding to the song's feminist content, Scrawl ends **Smallmouth** with a pretty piano-based cover of Eurythmics' ironic "I Need You." [i]

SCREAMING BLUE MESSIAHS
Good and Gone EP (nr/Big Beat) 1984
Twin Cadillac Valentine EP (nr/WEA) 1985
Gun-shy (Elektra) 1986 ●
The Peel Sessions EP (nr/Strange Fruit) 1987
Bikini Red (Elektra) 1987 ●
Totally Religious (Elektra) 1989 ●

One part Scottish, two parts English, this fierce trio (led by two ex-members of Motor Boys Motor) is well-named. Not averse to howling until blue in the face, they could very well be the prophesied saviors of static '80s pop. The Messiahs take their jaundiced love of Americana and render it into an unrecognizable hybrid of psychobilly, R&B, garage grunge and lethal punk energy.

Blistering would be a euphemistic description for **Good and Gone**: singer/songwriter/guitarist Bill Carter shrieks and wails his way through these six tracks in a merciless attack. The crudely worded "Someone To Talk To" (supposedly culled from a Marine drill chant), "Happy Home" and a cover of Hank Williams' "You're Gonna Change" give the Messiahs a roguish sort of appeal. Daring, foolhardy and just plain good fun. (The Peel EP dates from July of that same year and captures the band in its primal glory. Tracks include a trio of songs from **Good and Gone** and "Let's Go Down to the Woods," later included on **Gun-Shy**.)

On the title track of **Twin Cadillac Valentine**, the jagged edges have been smoothed down and the tune wanders amid sterile production. The three other tracks are raucous live versions of previously issued songs and provide the EP's only real signs of life.

Gun-shy contains "Twin Cadillac Valentine" and generally suffers from the same restraint. Occasional glimpses of the old form seep through, but never gain the momentum needed to sustain the effort. (Vic Maile and Howard Gray produced separately.)

Overproduction couldn't restrain a band this volatile, and **Bikini Red** is the triumphant outcome. An American tour after the release of **Gun-shy** apparently intensified the trio's love of America, because it's a consistently recurring theme throughout this entire album, produced by Vic Maile. The title song, "I Wanna Be a Flintstone," "I Can Speak American," "Jesus Chrysler Drives a Dodge" and "55–The Law" all derive from singularly American ideals and are the strongest tracks on this LP. **Bikini Red** is a joyous powder keg of a record that makes the transgressions on **Gun-shy** easy to forgive.

While **Totally Religious** lacks the eloquent fury of the Messiahs' best, it's not for lack of trying. Carter and crew still crash and burn, but the results are often tired, verging on generic. Great titles like "Four Engines Burning (Over the USA)," "All Gassed Up," "Watusi Wedding," etc. don't deliver on their promise. [ag/jy]

See also *Motor Boys Motor*.

SCREAMING TREES
Other Worlds EP [tape] (Velvetone) 1985 (SST) 1988
Clairvoyance (Velvetone) 1986 ●
Even If and Especially When (SST) 1987 ●
Invisible Lantern (SST) 1988 ●
Buzz Factory (SST) 1989 ●
Time Speaks Her Golden Tongue EP (Sub Pop) 1990
Something About Today EP (Epic) 1990 ●
Uncle Anesthesia (Epic) 1991 ●

BEAT HAPPENING/ SCREAMING TREES
Beat Happening/Screaming Trees EP (K-Homestead) 1988

MARK LANEGAN
The Winding Sheet (Sub Pop) 1990 ●

PURPLE OUTSIDE
Mystery Lane (New Alliance) 1990 ●

SOLOMON GRUNDY
Solomon Grundy (New Alliance) 1990 ●

Hailing from the town of Ellensburg, Washington, Screaming Trees use psychedelia not as a stylistic affectation, but as a jumping-off point for more personal existential explorations. The quartet specializes in droning melodic rock tunes spotlighting Mark Lanegan's portentous vocals and Gary Lee Conner's inventively primitive guitar work and thoughtful, vivid lyrics.

The early efforts (**Other Worlds** and **Clairvoyance**) have their impressive moments, but mainly show the quartet grasping for a distinctive style. The Trees master that style—an imposing mix of post-punk aggression and post-hippie mysticism—on the SST albums, and each of the three discs is well worth hearing. **Even If and Especially When** has a slight edge thanks to the inclusion of the Trees' most infectious song, "Transfiguration."

Despite inappropriate mainstream hard rock production (by Seattle metal guy Terry Date and Soundgarden frontman Chris Cornell) that saps much of the band's sonic forcefulness, **Uncle Anesthesia** isn't the big-league disaster one might have predicted for these indie stars. Several attempts at diversification—like the near-power pop "Bed of Roses" and the doom-metal title track—are quite successful, but Lanegan sounds uncomfortably like Ian Astbury on "Caught Between." Three of the four songs on the **Something About You** EP ended up on **Uncle Anesthesia**.

The Trees celebrated their ascension to major-labeldom with the release of extracurricular projects by three of the band's four members (the fourth, drummer Mark Pickerel, quit the band after playing on **Uncle Anesthesia**).

Lanegan's **The Winding Sheet** is something of a revelation. The pensive cover pic gives a good indication of the album's contents: quietly intense and obviously personal songs, most of them sung over spare instrumental backup. Lanegan uses his dark, brooding voice to good effect here; the lengthy title track is particularly impressive.

Gary Lee Conner manages to sound remarkably like the Trees for about half of the Purple Outside LP, on which he sings and plays everything but the drums; the rest is mainly soft, acoustic-based pop. His brother,

Trees bassist Van Conner, leads the four-man Solomon Grundy, whose album consists mostly of solid if unexceptional thrashy rock. [hd]

See also *Beat Happening*.

SCREAMING TRIBESMEN

EP (Aus. no label) 1982
Move a Little Closer EP (What Goes On) 1984
Date with a Vampyre EP (What Goes On) 1985
Top of the Town EP (Aus. Rattlesnake) 1986
Bones + Flowers (Aus. Survival) 1987 (Rykodisc) 1988 ●
Take Cover EP (Aus. Survival) 1989

There's nothing tribal about the sound of these Aussies, and they don't scream either. Their music is full of pop-song harmonies, including "oohh" and "ahh" background singing, jangle chords and repeated refrains. From beginnings as a post-Ramones punky ensemble (on the first four-track EP), they've gone through an assortment of members and sonic textures but all of their releases have been exercises in good old pop-rock. **Move a Little Closer**, a compilation of the band's first two Australian singles ("Igloo" and "A Stand Alone") could easily mix and match with a stack of mod-revival albums, while the squealier and grungier guitar chords of **Date with a Vampyre** (also four songs) nudge their sound closer to garage territory.

Top of the Town contains six songs by a new lineup that reveals an ongoing transition towards more mainstream pop-rock. "You Better Run" is the most impressive track, and a fair precursor to the excellent **Bones + Flowers**. The album launches the Tribesmen into a new international league, offering richly played rock-melody songwriting (by ex-Radio Birdman guitarist/pianist/producer Chris "Klondike" Masuak and singer/guitarist Mick Medew) that's got all the needed attributes for major stardom. Standouts: a new version of "Igloo," the wittily '60sish "Our Time at Last," the peppy Anglo-popping "Dream Away" and the Rockpiling "Living Vampire." The CD has two bonus tracks.

Despite the album's appeal and high commercial prospects, nothing much came of **Bones + Flowers**. By the time of the disappointing 1989 12-inch (five songs, including covers of Lou Reed and the Dictators), Medew was the only member remaining from the LP's lineup. ['e/i]

¡SCREAMIN' SIRENS!

¡Fiesta! (Enigma) 1984

ROSIE FLORES

Rosie Flores (Reprise) 1987

SCREAMING SIRENS

Voodoo (Restless) 1990 φ

RINGLING SISTERS

60 Watt Reality (A&M) 1990 φ

Ah, the wonders of showbiz. As lead guitarist and singer for the ¡Screamin' Sirens!, Rosie Flores (previously of San Diego's Rosie and the Screamers) performed her share of perky throwaway power pop, the kind of junk that fairly exploded out of the woodwork in the wake of Blondie's late-'70s success. At other times, the four Sirens served up transparently fake country-

rock or the entertaining bogus funk of "Mr. T Luv Boogie."

Lo and behold, three years after the halfhearted ¡Fiesta!, Flores turned up as a "real" country artist, doing that old Bakersfield boogie on a fine solo album produced by Pete Anderson of Dwight Yoakam fame. Billy Bremner is her guitarist; Los Lobos' David Hidalgo contributes rippling accordion on "Midnight to Moonlight," a Flores tune first heard on ¡Fiesta!.

With only vocalist/songwriter Pleasant Gehman and bassist Miiko Watanabe returning from the first album, a new set of Sirens made the personality-free **Voodoo**, a stinky, poorly sung collection of coy songs about sex and romance.

The Ringling Sisters—a sextet whose first album is a diverse jazz/folk/rock/country collection produced by Lou Adler—includes Gehman and Annette Zilinskas (Bangles/Blood on the Saddle). With amusing spoken interludes and uneven songwriting on a broad variety of topics, **60 Watt Reality** is an intriguing, odd and occasionally stimulating LP. Best tracks: "Way Out West" and "Kimberly Rose," both of which have lyrics by Gehman and music by guitarist/bassist Gary Eaton. [jy/i]

SCREECHING WEASEL

Screeching Weasel (Underdog) 1987
Boogadaboogadaboogada! (Roadkill) 1989

Playing skillful unstylized punk with goofy suburban lyrics, this funny Chicago-area quartet makes no bones about its likes and dislikes on **Screeching Weasel**, a 27-song debut. Besides covering the Oscar Mayer weiner theme, singing odes to cows and convenience stores, vocalist/punkzine columnist Ben Weasel leads his group in terse attacks on TV talk-show hosts, California and assorted cultural archetypes ("Clean-Cut Asshole," "Jockpunk," "Hardcore Hippie," "Liar"). The Weasel may sound generic, but there's a superior intelligence at work here.

The shredded-speaker guitar sound of **Boogadaboogadaboogada!** is a shame, as the witty group moves into more tuneful, better structured songs without sacrificing any of its incendiary punk energy. Stomping merrily through pop culture, romance and reality, the songs spit on Led Zeppelin, politics, police, paper boys and psychotherapy, stopping to cover Del Shannon ("Runaway"), quote "Wipeout" (in "This Ain't Hawaii") and send a mash note to Madonna and Sandra Bernhard. [i]

SCRITTI POLITTI

4 A-Sides EP (nr/St. Pancras-Rough Trade) 1979
Works in Progress EP (nr/St. Pancras-Rough Trade) 1979
Songs to Remember (nr/Rough Trade) 1982 ●
Cupid & Psyche 85 (Warner Bros.) 1985 ●
Provision (Warner Bros.) 1988 ●

Originally an arty conceptual trio from Leeds, Scritti Politti underwent a number of drastic developmental changes on the way to becoming, ultimately, a slick vehicle for Welsh-born singer Green Gartside. By the time Scritti Politti released its long-awaited first album in 1982, Green had pulled the band from its early experiments (on the **A-Sides** EP and the Peel session released as **Works in Progress**) through a phase of alluring synth-pop and into a souled-out revamp of early T. Rex, minus Bolan's unique sword-and-sorcery outlook. **Songs to Remember** is an unassumingly warm and charming set, with boppy beats, quirky tunes and abundant catchy goodwill. While Green's obvious songwriting mastery and affecting voice make every song appealing, a few—"Asylums in Jerusalem," "Faithless" and "The Sweetest Girl"—are absolutely wonderful.

Subsequently shedding the pretense of a band, Green moved himself to New York, where he turned to high-sheen soul music as his life's work. With venerable producer Arif Mardin, Material drummer Fred Maher and other heavyweights, the entirety of Green's output for the following two years was a 1984 12-inch, which nonetheless established him as a brilliant (if unprolific) pop craftsman. "Wood Beez (Pray Like Aretha Franklin)" and "Absolute" are stunning, traditional musical values given up-to-date modern stylings.

Green consolidated his triumph by including both songs on **Cupid & Psyche 85**, only the second Scritti Politti album in six years. Recorded and produced in the main with Maher and keyboardist David Gamson but featuring numerous other musicians, the painstakingly well-crafted record is unfailingly pleasant. Nonetheless, only "The Word Girl" approaches the engaging excellence of the two singles.

Three years later, Gartside, Gamson and Maher finished **Provision**, another meticulous studio exercise that takes a lighthanded approach to bouncy pop soul. Loads of backing singers do their best not to upstage Gartside's wispy voice, but the cushiony cloak of suavely boring, repetitive material is all it takes to thwart his reedy efforts. In a brief break from the album's numbing reliance on electronic technology, Miles Davis drops in to contribute a thin-sounding trumpet solo to "Oh Patti (Don't Feel Sorry for Loverboy)." The CD adds two extra tracks. [jw/i]

SCRUFFY THE CAT
High Octane Revival EP (Relativity) 1986
Tiny Days (Relativity) 1987 ●
Boom Boom Boom Bingo EP (Relativity) 1987
Moons of Jupiter (Relativity) 1988 ●

This Boston combo plays good-natured countryish rock with a romantic streak—sometimes a bit too ephemeral for its own good, but always unpretentiously enjoyable. Frontman Charlie Chesterman sings the surprisingly witty lyrics (all five Scruffys write) in an earnestly bemused drawl, and the band plays in an amiably rollicking—if not particularly individual—style that's well-suited to their modest musical goals.

Both the six-song **High Octane Revival** (produced by Dave Minehan of the Neighborhoods) and **Tiny Days** (produced by ex-Waitress Chris Butler) are consistent funfests, with such winning numbers as the former's "Tiger, Tiger" and "40 Days & 40 Nights" and the latter's "Shadow Boy" and "My Fate Was Sealed with a Kiss." Multi-instrumentalist Stona Fitch left after **Tiny Days**, but the loss isn't evident on the inconclusive **Boom Boom Boom Bingo**, two new studio tracks (including the wonderful busted-heart kiss-off "You Dirty

Rat") plus three live tunes, among them a decent cover of Del Shannon's "Runaway."

Produced by Jim Dickinson, the band's final album, **Moons of Jupiter**, is characteristically well-played and typically tuneful, but with a poignant sense of melancholy that suffuses even cheery-sounding numbers like "Capital Moonlight," "I Do" and "Betty Drops In." A bittersweet farewell.

Scruffy the Cat did make one more vinyl appearance with "Love Song #9," one side of a joint single with the Young Fresh Fellows, on the Cruddy Record Dealership (i.e., PopLlama Products) label. [hd]

SECRET AFFAIR
Glory Boys (Sire) 1979
Behind Closed Doors (Sire) 1980
Business as Usual (nr/I Spy-Arista) 1982
The Peel Sessions EP (nr/Strange Fruit) 1988

Secret Affair were the mod revival's top dogs because they forged a distinctive sound that didn't simply pick up where the Jam (or Who) left off. Ian Page's mellifluous vocals and Dave Cairns' plangent guitars spearheaded the band's enthusiastic drive, hampered only by occasionally stiff drumming; the consistently above-average tunes of **Glory Boys** get an extra fillip by the sporadic addition of horns. What grates, though, is the pushy, overstated rhetoric, especially in light of the would-be movement's brief, faddish existence.

The instrumental attack on **Behind Closed Doors** is tighter and the lyrics—though still pretentious—arty on a more personal level. At least half of the songs are excellent. By the time of **Business as Usual**, though, the Affair was a big fish in an evaporated neo-mod pond. The group could hardly maintain its self-important image, and with it went the creative spark. The album, while smoother than ever before, is as journeyman-like as its title suggests. [jg]

SECTOR 27
See *Tom Robinson Band*.

JONATHAN SEGEL
See *Camper Van Beethoven*.

SELECTER
Too Much Pressure (Chrysalis) 1980
Celebrate the Bullet (Chrysalis) 1981
Selected Selecter Selections (Chrysalis) 1989 φ

The Selecter—an interracial, multinational seven-piece—emerged from the same Coventry scene that gave birth to the Specials; founder Neol Davis was in on the creation of 2-Tone, the label which in turn ignited the entire neo-ska movement in England. The company's first release was a Specials 45; its flipside was an instrumental credited to and entitled "The Selecter" which had, in fact, been recorded by Davis and Specials drummer John Bradbury some months earlier. When the A-side became a hit, interest in the Selecter also grew, and Davis was obliged to recruit musicians and start up the group. With the gifted Pauline Black handling most of the lead vocals, the Selecter sounded like no other band in the genre; they employed the same upbeat rhythms, but added a much poppier and individual touch, much of it due to Black's style and influence.

Too Much Pressure is bursting with great songs like "On My Radio," "Three Minute Hero," "Time Hard" and the title track. Davis wrote much of the material, but contributions from other sources—within and without the lineup—add further variety. As the playing hops along, with a horn section added in spots, Pauline Black, shining with enormous vocal talent, continually provides the spark.

Celebrate the Bullet has little of the first LP's brilliance; although the performances don't lack anything tangible, the songwriting is vastly less inspired and none of the anti-trendy cleverness so vital to the previous album's uniqueness can be discerned. The Selecter dissolved soon after; Black did several solo singles and some acting.

Lacking both rarities and liner notes, **Selected Selecter Selections** contains, more or less, the nine best songs from the first LP and the five best from the second. [i]

SEMANTICS

See *Elliott Sharp*.

SENDERS

Seven Song Super Single (Max's Kansas City) 1980
Do the Sender Thing (Midnight) 1989

BACKBONES

The Backbones (Midnight) 1986

Although the '70s Senders never broke out of the New York club circuit, the unreconstructed rock'n'roll quartet left behind the **Seven Song Super Single** as a delightful, all too brief, memento. The rambunctious blend of originals and oldies (Little Richard, Howlin' Wolf et al.) disproves the conventional wisdom that classicism has to be stuffy; the energy level here matches that of the Ramones in their prime. Bands will continue in R&B and rockabilly no matter what the wave, but few will match the verve of the Senders.

In the mid-'80s, Senders singer Philippe Marcade led the Backbones, using a saxophone player to spice up rough'n'ready soul covers (Ike Turner, Chips Moman, Jerry Ragovoy) and exciting '60s-styled rock originals on the powerpacked album, which captures the music's feel as well as its sound.

A few years later, the Senders—three old members plus a new bassist—reconvened. Recorded live at CBGB in August 1988, **Do the Sender Thing** is a tight, driving rock'n'roll/blues record (kudos to guitarist Wild Bill Thompson) in the Dr. Feelgood/Little Bob Story vein. Only problem: the performances are much hotter than the sound. [jy/i]

WILL SERGEANT

See *Echo & the Bunnymen*.

SERVICE

Zebu EP (Pravda) 1985
America's Newest Hitmakers (Pravda) 1986

George's Duty-Free Goulash (Pravda) 1987
In Nonsense Is Strength (Pravda) 1988
Head vs Wall (Pravda) 1990 ●

NEW DUNCAN IMPERIALS

Hanky Panky Parley Voo! (Pravda) 1990 ϕ

Chicago's Service made its longplaying vinyl debut—following a couple of cassette-only releases and a four-song EP—as a guitar'n'keyboards quintet (guests add sax, trombone, tuba and fiddle), armed with wry material about such topics as sobriety ("Straight Song") and marriage ("Ring Gets Tighter"), all skillfully delivered in modest pop-rock-country arrangements topped off by David Briggs' sardonic voice.

The blue-vinyl **George's Duty-Free Goulash**, released in a clear plastic cover with a "Basic Side" and a "Bonus Side," is rushed in tempo and semi-punky in tone. Indicative of the Service's open-ended stylistic view, "Defeated" runs together a new wavey melody, skating rink organ and the lonesome wail of harmonica; "You'll Come Back," however, is swanky cocktail piano jazz. Somehow, the strong melodies and textures hold it all together.

Several Servicemen stayed home when the group began work on its next album. The excellent **In Nonsense Is Strength** finds the group reduced to a quartet, with guitarist/songwriter Rick Mosher and keyboardist Kenn Goodman (proprietor of the Pravda label) sharing the vocals. The resulting album of passionate post-garagepunk (plus organ and tuba) has great material and dynamic performances that pour on the electric energy but never get out of control. At times ("If You Will, I Will") resembling the Replacements, elsewhere ("Honesty Defends") following an unselfconscious '60s path, **Nonsense** is anything but. (The cassette contains a bonus track.)

Recorded during another lineup change, the lighter-sounding **Head vs Wall** features no less than four separate bassists (the former, the future and two fill-ins) and Mosher's Westerbergian melodies. Besides the serious pop/rock goods, **Head vs Wall** features a remake of "El Amigo" (from **George's Duty Free Goulash**) and a '70s-styled hard-rocker entitled "Hogfat" ("because it sounds like Foghat, that's why").

With the Service dropping humor from its standard repertoire, the task of acting stupid falls to the band's entertaining three-man alter-ego, the New Duncan Imperials. Using a mixture of rudimentary country rock, simplified Cheap Trick and similar energetic guitar vehicles, the rambunctious 23-song **Hanky Panky Parley Voo!** offers cheap jokes ("I'm Schizophrenic (No I'm Not)," "Born to Be Hit"), scattershot satire ("Jimi Page Loves Country"), covers of Buck Owens, Hank Williams *and* Hasil Adkins, trashy romance ("6-Pack of Love") and celebrations of essential products ("Jägermeister" and "Velour!"). As serious as a warm seltzer bottle, but a whole lot safer for the stereo. [i]

BRIAN SETZER

See *Stray Cats*.

SEVEN SIMONS

Clockwork (Dog Gone) 1988

Gently defying the predictability of jangle-pop quartets from Georgia, Athens' Seven Simons (who lost an early drummer to Drivin' n' Cryin') have enough original ideas about guitar texture, melody, vocal stylings and drumming to lift **Clockwork** well above the ranks of genredom, lacking only the sense of mystery that might ensure high scene credibility. From decisive tom-tom power to a modest backbeat, Mike Zwecker kicks the beat with subtle variety; guitarist/songwriter Keith Joyner likewise shifts from near-gothic pinging density to simple folk-rock strums. With the added benefits of Nat Webb's engaging vocals, the open-faced **Clockwork** is just like every other New South debut album—only better.   [i]

17 PYGMIES
See *Savage Republic*.

SEVERED HEADS
Blubberknife [tape] (Aus. Terse Tapes) 1983
Since the Accident (nr/Ink) 1983 (Can. Nettwerk) 1989 ●
Dead Eyes Opened EP (Can. Nettwerk) 1985 (Nettwerk) 1990 ●
City Slab Horror (nr/Ink) 1985 (Can. Nettwerk) 1989 (Nettwerk) 1990 ●
Clifford Darling, Please Don't Live in the Past (nr/Ink) 1985 ●
Come Visit the Big Bigot (Can. Nettwerk) 1986 (Nettwerk) 1990 ●
Bad Mood Guy (Can. Nettwerk) 1987 ●
Bulkhead (Can. Nettwerk) 1988 (Nettwerk) 1990 ●
Rotund for Success (Nettwerk) 1989 ●

This cheerfully obscure Australian chaos group manipulates tapes, found sounds and assorted electronic gear—essentially any audio source that isn't quite a traditional musical implement—to squeak and plunk out synthetically rhythmatized fogs of craziness. Not really a noise machine, Severed Heads generally stays on the safe side of unpleasant, but sometimes sacrifices accessibility in a jumble of competing sounds.

Starting out on their own Terse Tapes label in 1980, Severed Heads—at the time Garry Bradbury, Paul Von Deering and Tom Ellard, collectively credited with tape recorders, drum programming, sequencers, turntables, televisions, etc., plus a guitar player and sporadic guest vocals—hooked up with England's Ink Records and made its longplaying European debut with **Since the Accident**, an alternately entertaining and irritating experimental patchwork of kitchen-sink sonics that occasionally reveals a strong Eno influence. **City Slab Horror** is more accomplished and conceptually conventional ("4.W.D." is dissonant electro-pop with a proper melody and lyrics), although the audio ingredients that layer songs like the onomatopoeic "Spitoon Thud" and the maddening "Bladders of One Thousand Bedouin" are still drawn from a uniquely bizarre world. Belatedly released on individual CDs, **Since the Accident** and **City Slab Horror** comprise a retrospective set that divvies up the tracks from **Blubberknife**, an intermittently worthwhile but more often underwhelming exploratory effort that uses synthesizers and spoken-word vocals.

Clifford Darling is a double album of early outtakes, dating from 1979 to 1983.

The **Dead Eyes Opened** EP consists of remixes of the title track (a 1983 UK single), "Petrol" (a 1985 single) and "We Have Come to Bless This House," along with two new songs. (All five tracks later appeared as bonuses on the **Big Bigot** CD.)

Come Visit the Big Bigot reveals development of a strong and cogent (treated) vocal electro-pop sensibility amid more familiar hubbub that might have been created by Martians armed only with Eno's **Here Come the Warm Jets** and Orchestral Manoeuvres' first LP for templates. At the record's high point—"Phantasized Persecutory Breast"—the Heads (Ellard, videosynthesist (?) Stephen Jones, drum/computer programmer Obereta Kvojin and Topsy Ke-Evil, credited with "choir control") build an oddly shaped sound castle of conflicting rhythms, left-field effects, amusingly treated vocals and crisply pinging sequencers. Stimulating if you don't get too involved.

Bad Mood Guy continues to reduce the polyphasia, centering the tracks with stable tempos and reasonably sturdy song structures, keeping the distracting gimmicks back in the mix until needed. Something like lightweight Cabaret Voltaire or a hyperactive DJ collective spinning five records simultaneously, this Severed Heads outing draws within spitting distance of conventional music.

Bulkhead is a handy ten-song compilation: tracks from the four preceding albums plus a few non-LP cuts. The American CD adds a remix of "Greater Reward," a 1988 single (subsequently included on **Rotund for Success**) that opens the collection.

Reduced to a duo of Ellard and Jones but bolstered by sampling technology, Severed Heads jettisoned willful weirdness and moved into politely presentable synth-dance-rock on **Rotund for Success**, an unnervingly plain-sounding and faintly dated record that could almost be by Blancmange. Ellard's lyrical sensibility is typically off-kilter and flashes of a twisted mind do erupt now and again in the mix, but the diminution of musical disturbance and the elimination of the band's creative challenge is most disturbing.   [i]

SEX CLARK FIVE
Strum & Drum! (Records to Russia) 1987
Battle of Sex Clark Five (Bloodmoney) 1989 ●
Ketchup If You Can EP (Records to Russia) 1991

Natives of a state not widely known for its post-punk underground, Huntsville, Alabama's Sex Clark Five probably get a lot of suspicious questions about their name which, of course, has nothing whatsoever to do with the collegiate quartet's deft music: light, faintly Celtic folk-pop with literate, sometimes political (and not sexual politics, either) lyrics and serviceable artless vocals by guitarist/songwriter James Butler and bassist Joy Johnson. Despite some halfbaked material, weak drumming and the everpresent danger of earnestness about to turn precious, **Battle** is full of likable, economical ditties like "Girl I Like," "Liberate Tibet" and the succinctly self-explanatory "Ballad of Sex Clark Five."

The 7-inch EP (on red vinyl) has four new songs

that—with the chaotic title track's exception—neatly fall into the Windbreakers' realm of deep Southern pop. [i]

SEX GANG CHILDREN

Naked [tape] (nr/Sex) 1982
Beasts EP (nr/Illuminated) 1982
Sebastiane EP (nr/Illuminated) 1983
Song and Legend (nr/Illuminated) 1983 (nr/Dojo) 1986 ●
Beasts (nr/Illuminated) 1983 (nr/Dojo) 1986
Sex Gang Children (nr/Sex) 1983 (nr/Arkham House-Jungle) 1987
Ecstasy and Vendetta Over New York [tape] (ROIR) 1984
Re-enter the Abyss (The 1985 Remixes) (nr/Dojo) 1985 ●
Nightland (Performance USA 83) (nr/Arkham House-Jungle) 1986

ANDI SEX-GANG

Ida-ho EP (nr/Illuminated) 1985
Blind! (nr/Illuminated) 1985
Arco Valley (nr/Jungle) 1989 ●

DIRTY ROSEANNE

Dirty Roseanne EP (It. D.E.A.) 1986

London's fervent Sex Gang Children were all the rage of the English underground in 1982-'83, spearheading the positive-punk movement which mixed the raw energy and commitment of punk rock with the dark theatrics of goth. Sex Gang's individual parts resemble a mélange of the Banshees, T. Rex, Bowie, UK Decay, Sex Pistols and Adam and the Ants, yet the whole really resembles none of the above. Dave Roberts' droning, spiny bass work is the music's dominant feature of the music (practically a lead instrument), battling with Andi Sex-Gang's androgynous, high-pitched vocals, Terry Macleay's scratchy/chiming guitar overlays and Rob Stroud's tribal drum patterns. Like many enthralling substances, their music—with its breathtaking shifts in tempo and mood—can be hard to digest at first, but there's addiction in its opulent din.

The **Beasts** EP, weakly produced by UK Subs guitarist Nicky Garratt, still manages to engrave the band's doomy energy on wax through such anthems as "Sense of Elation" and "Cannibal Queen." The LP of the same name is a compilation, adding several later singles, B-sides (including the entire **Sebastiane** EP) and dub mixes.

Song and Legend is a landmark in gothic/postpunk, holding forth with an unequalled baroque fury. While the title epic and "Shout and Scream" epitomize the band's out-of-the-galaxy song structures, "Sebastiane" 's swooping strings flirt with classical motifs and the tom-tom mantra "Draconian Dream" has the aura of ancient folk musics. Andi's unique lyrics jumble up obscure historical references, political anomie, sexual/religious imagery and more. Producer Tony James smothers everything (especially a remake of "Cannibal Queen") in tons of echo, giving the album a haunting, catacomb sheen. (James also explored the band's taste for dub, creating spacey B-side remixes and ambient/experimental flotsam used as segues and codas.)

Sex Gang Children's well-deserved rep as a killer live band spurred the release of numerous live albums and tapes. **Naked** is one rare cassette worth searching out. Though the sound quality is mediocre, the buzzed performance is from the band's very early pre-**Beasts** days, and two otherwise-unreleased tracks ("Soldier" and "People with Dirty Faces") are well worth a listen. The eponymous live album, also released on the band's label, is a slightly muddy set recorded at London's Lyceum (plus several tracks from a gig in Glasgow) during a spring '83 tour.

Ecstasy and Vendetta over New York, a cassette recorded at the Peppermint Lounge in December '83, documents the Sex Gang's overture to America. The sound is loud and crisp, capturing the regal excitement of the group at their musical and popular peak. **Nightland** is also from the same tour (though not the same gigs). The two albums are fairly interchangeable, with the cassette offering more songs and better audio quality. Both boast terrific performances of Edith Piaf's "Les Amants d'un Jour," the haunting single, "Mauritia Mayer," and three new tunes, not to mention acrobatic drum work by Raymondo, late of the Death Cult. (The two bands had swapped drummers.)

Dave Roberts left shortly thereafter (later performing with Christian Death and recording as Car Crash International), replaced by the even more talented Cam Campbell. Subsequent record releases used Andi's name, with the band credited as the Quick Gas Gang. Their first issue was a studio 45 of "Les Amants," followed by an album. **Blind!** is the most fully realized Sex Gang work, dominated by Campbell's gliding, intricate bass lines and Andi's heightened sense of ornate melody. From excellent studio versions of songs debuted on **Ecstasy** through the funky burlesque of "Ida-Ho" and two touching ballads ("Last Chants for the Slow Dance" and a rendition of the Poison Girls' "I've Done It All Before"), **Blind!** is brilliant, lushly layered and grandiose. Highly recommended.

The Quick Gas Gang soon evaporated, leaving Andi in limbo. **Re-Enter the Abyss**, a shoddy piece of hack work, didn't help matters. A selection of the Sex Gang's best material is subjected to totally unnecessary—and for the most part, ludicrously out of balance—remixes. Skip it.

A holiday in Italy spawned **Dirty Roseanne**; the four-song EP finds Andi and keyboardist Piero Ballegi experimenting with more offbeat styles, from classic Elton John/Marc Bolan-style British pop with soul strings on "Search Your Soul" to the deft balladry of "Nebulous Canaan." In 1987 Andi issued a three-song EP ("The Naked & the Dead") from the soundtrack to '85 horror flick *Phenomena* (released in America as *Creepers*, minus the Andi tracks).

Andi's impressive comeback, **Arco Valley**, was produced by onetime guitar hero Mick Ronson (who also plays on it). Even if he hasn't messed with makeup in fifteen years, the former Spider from Mars adds (at least spiritually) to the glam feel that pervades this diverse album. The bopping numbers that sound uncannily like prime T. Rex ("7 Ways to Kill a Man") are loads of fun. While some of the attempts at dance-pop ("Rock Revolution") are too cloying, measured, melodic creations ("Belgique Blue") in the **Blind!** mold are to be savored. And what would a Sexgang album be without another version of "Les Amants"? [gef]

SEX PISTOLS

Spunk (nr/Blank) 1977
Never Mind the Bollocks, Here's the Sex Pistols (Warner Bros.) 1977 ●
The Great Rock'n'Roll Swindle (nr/Virgin) 1979 ●
Some Product Carri On (nr/Virgin) 1979
Flogging a Dead Horse (nr/Virgin) 1980 ●
The Heyday [tape] (nr/Factory) 1980
The Mini Album EP (nr/Chaos) 1985 (Restless) 1988 ●
The Original Pistols Live (nr/Receiver) 1985 ●
Live Worldwide (nr/Konexion) 1985
Best of the Sex Pistols Live (nr/Bondage) 1985
Anarchy in the UK Live (nr/UK) 1985
Where Were You in '77 (nr/77) 1985
Power of the Pistols (nr/77) 1985
We Have Cum for Your Children (Wanted: The Goodman Tapes) (Skyclad) 1988 ●
Better Live Than Dead (Restless) 1988 ●
The Swindle Continues (Restless) 1988 ●
Anarchy Worldwide (nr/Specific) 1988 ●
Cash for Chaos EP (nr/Specific) 1988 ●
Pirates of Destiny (I Swirled) 1989 ●
The Mini Album Plus [CD] (nr/Chaos) 1989 ●
Live and Loud!! (nr/Link) 1989 ●
No Future U.K? (nr/Receiver) 1989 ●
Live at Chelmsford Top Security Prison (Restless) 1990 ●

THE ORIGINAL PISTOLS/NEW YORK DOLLS

After the Storm (nr/Receiver) 1985 ●

SID VICIOUS

Sid Sings (nr/Virgin) 1979 ●
Love Kills NYC (nr/Konexion) 1985

Although their importance—both to the direction of contemporary music and more generally to pop culture—can hardly be overstated, the Sex Pistols did not make their stand primarily on albums. In fact, the massive discography notwithstanding, the Pistols made only one actual studio album during their fourteen-month existence (November 1976 to January 1978). In a textbook McLuhanesque example of the media being the message, the quartet's impact did not result from vast commercial success; against the general rock tide, most of their revolutionary work was released on 7-inch singles.

Fulfilling an essential and immaculate role as martyrs on the new wave altar by logically self-destructing (and politely waiting until no one was paying much attention before descending into typical wasted rockstardom) rather than falling prey to standard rock'n'roll conventions, the Pistols and manager/provocateur Malcolm McLaren challenged every aspect and precept of modern music-making, thereby inspiring countless groups to follow their cue onto stages around the world. A confrontational, nihilistic public image and rabidly nihilistic socio-political lyrics set the tone that continues to guide punk bands. On top of everything, the Pistols made totally unassailable and essential electric music that has stood the test of time, and sounds just as exciting and powerful today as it did way back when.

Populated by such classics as "Anarchy in the UK," "God Save the Queen," "Pretty Vacant" and "No Feelings," **Never Mind the Bollocks, Here's the Sex Pistols** is an epiphany. Prototypical punk without compromise, it includes almost everything you need to hear by the Sex Pistols. Oddly, at the time of its release, the LP was a disappointment in light of sky-high expectations. Four of the tracks had already been released as singles; many others had circulated on well-known album-in-progress bootlegs, like **Spunk**. Now, of course, as the best recorded evidence of the Pistols' existence, it almost defies criticism. Paul Cook, Steve Jones, Johnny Rotten (Lydon) and Sid Vicious (plus Glen Matlock, the original musical architect and songwriter, who was sacked early on, allegedly for liking the Beatles) combined to produce a unique moment in rock history and **Bollocks** is the evidence. (The American release adds "Sub-Mission," changes the track sequence and alters the artwork; the 1985 British CD also contains the extra track.)

The Great Rock'n'Roll Swindle, the soundtrack to the band's amazing bio-pic posthumously banged together into semi-coherent form by Julien Temple from a number of aborted film projects, exists in three forms: a one-disc album of highlights and two slightly different full-length two-record collections. In any case, it's a semi-connected batch of songs by various bands (not just the Pistols) that's just full of surprises, fun and strange goings-on. There are regular Pistols tracks—some with vocals by Sid, Steve Jones and Eddie Tudorpole taking the departed and uncooperative Rotten's place—as well as live performances, studio outtakes, symphonic renditions, a surprisingly great disco medley, McLaren's first vocal foray and much more. A bit lighthearted (and lightheaded), but with loads of sharp music. The single-record extract has most of the prime material, but either full dose is highly recommended. (The CD contains the whole shebang.)

Some Product Carri On is for diehards only, scraping the barrel for radio interviews and commercials—audio vérité for idiots whose interest in the Pistols has more to do with sociopathic fascination than pop culture. However gratuitous and unnecessary as it may be, the album shows careful assembly and is wickedly funny in spots—good for one embarrassing listen then straight into the trash compactor.

While **Some Product** is completely expendable, **Flogging a Dead Horse**—wretched back-cover scatology aside—provides the commendable service of compiling seven ace 45s (both sides of each) into one handy Pistols primer. From "Anarchy in the UK" to "The Great Rock'n'Roll Swindle," all of their greatest moments are delivered. If you don't have a complete set, this record catches you right up; for newcomers, the LP is a must-have. **The Heyday** is a cassette-only collection of interviews with Lydon, Cook, Jones and Vicious.

In 1985, a flood of new Sex Pistols records—legal, dubious and plainly unauthorized—began appearing. **The Mini Album** (issued in the US three years later and then expanded in the UK and re-released as the CD-only **Mini Album Plus**) consists of a half-dozen early album outtakes (July '76, with Matlock), probably from the same studio supply as those issued on **Spunk**. **The Original Pistols Live**, with liner notes by producer Dave Goodman, records a 1976 gig with moderate fidelity and a lively mix. **Live Worldwide** is a compendium of a dozen cuts from various shows. **Cash for**

Chaos and **Anarchy Worldwide** are mixtures of live takes and studio outtakes. The Pistols' side of **After the Storm** contains four muddy live cuts—"Anarchy," "Pretty Vacant," "Liar" and "New York"—from a '76 gig at Burton-upon-Trent.

For those interested in bootleg-quality concert material from unspecified shows, **Live and Loud!!** reproduces almost the entire first album (although it omits "Sub-Mission" and "Liar" and includes "I Wanna Be Me" and "Belsen Was a Gas") in what sounds like a surprisingly cogent and well-played single show. (The CD adds a bonus track.)

The low-fi/high-energy **Better Live Than Dead** documents another pre-Sid concert with selections from the Pistols' non-original repertoire—"Substitute," "Stepping Stone," "No Fun"—alongside their own classics. Fascinating and reasonably well-mastered, **We Have Cum for Your Children** is a motley but meaningful packet of oddities and endities: the notorious "Filth and the Fury" Bill Grundy television interview (1 December 1976), radio spots, live and for-broadcast recordings and an intriguing assortment of studio rehearsals and outtakes. Although it contains "Pretty Vacant," "Submission," "EMI" (mistitled, perhaps intentionally, "Unlimited Supply") in versions that are, or at least closely resemble, the ones on **Spunk**, the LP's main value lies in clear recordings of the otherwise unissued "Suburban Kid" (just a variation on "Satellite," the B-side of "Holidays in the Sun"), "Revolution in the Classroom" (with vocals that sound more like a bad imitation of Rotten than the real thing) and Cook'n'Jones' "Here We Go Again."

Jointly billed to the Sex Pistols and Ex-Pistols, **The Swindle Continues** is a similar (and overlapping) studio compilation with a side of first-album rehearsals, demos and outtakes (with one actual B-side, "No Fun," stuck in as a ringer) and a side of post-split items, mostly by Cook and Jones. There's the fabulous "Silly Thing" (a '79 Pistols B-side with Jones doing lead vocals), an absurd acoustic version of "Anarchy in the UK" from a French single, a hysterical disco-mix medley-of-hits called "Sex on 45" and much less. The sound is a shade below good and the total lack of credits an annoyance, but the LP title precludes any such carping. Ever had the feeling you've been conned?

An entertaining soundtrack to a nonexistent scrapbook, the haphazardly edited **Pirates of Destiny** jumps from interview bites to live Sid-era tracks and studio outtakes (but who really cares about an unused backing track for "Pretty Vacant"?), with an Australian LP ad, the otherwise unissued "Schools Are Prisons" (a different song from "Revolution in the Classroom," with a truly Rotten vocal) and a classic pox-on-punk speech by a London government official for good measure. Most of Side Two is given over to "alternate mixes" of **Swindle**'s live-in-the-studio covers ("Substitute," "Roadrunner," "Whatcha' Gonna Do About It?," etc.) that sound like they were recorded on a cheap cassette machine during a rehearsal.

No Future U.K? ("released with kind permission of Glen Matlock, Steve Jones and Paul Cook") consists of late-'76 demos and outtakes of the Pistols' original repertoire: most of **Bollocks** and the preceding singles. The sound quality is better than the slow, rudimentary performances, few of which have the electric juice the songs ultimately received. "No Feelings" is striking, as are one of the two renditions of "Anarchy" (the other is appallingly weak), "No Fun" and a take on "Liar" that sounds more like Generation X.

Had Matlock's 1990 autobiography, *I Was a Teenage Sex Pistol*, not confirmed the fact that the Pistols did indeed play a 1976 prison gig, few would have believed that **Live at the Chelmsford Top Security Prison** wasn't just a sensationalist fraud. Indeed, the crowd noises are obviously fake. Adding to the album's suspect nature, "producer" Dave Goodman's liner note recollection of the gig mentions that the band opened with "Anarchy"—but the song appears next to last on the record. Regardless of its source(s), the album—a rare coincidence of great playing and pretty clear sound (save for Rotten's singing, which comes and goes in the mix)—is one of the better post-Pistols items to surface.

Sid's post-Pistols album is a classic piece of campy horribleness, a miserable-sounding live record of one of his New York rent-party gigs. The doomed bassist teams here with ex-Doll Jerry Nolan's band, the Idols, for a pathetic performance of punk standards that's depressing and morbid. **Love Kills NYC** is a similar record, issued during the Pistols unexpected vinyl onslaught. There have been others.   [i]

See also *Chequered Past, Chiefs of Relief, Steve Jones, Malcolm McLaren, Public Image Ltd., Professionals, Rich Kids*.

S'EXPRESS
Original Soundtrack (Rhythm King-Capitol) 1989 ●
Intercourse (Sire) 1991 ɸ

Trained neither as a musician or producer, Mark Moore was instead a young DJ deeply involved in Britain's dance scene. In the spring of 1988, his aggressively erotic British No. 1 hit "Theme from S'Express," along with debut hits by Bomb the Bass and Coldcut, opened the doors for a whole legion of young DJs to not just play, but provide, the music for the forthcoming acid house explosion.

Much of **Original Soundtrack**—a remarkably self-assured debut—harks back to '70s disco, as titles like "Superfly Guy" and "Pimps, Pushers, Prostitutes" would indicate. It could be argued that S'Express has little relevance to the history of rock'n'roll, but it can't be denied that the group played a major role in diverting a nation's youth away from guitar-driven songs and towards beat-heavy dance collages.   [tf]

LAKIM SHABAZZ
Pure Righteousness (Tuff City) 1988
The Lost Tribe of Shabazz (Tuff City) 1990 ●

Despite his extreme Five-Percent Nation (of Islam) militancy, this dynamic young Afrocentrist—ably produced by DJ Mark the 45 King (Queen Latifah, etc.)—takes surprisingly little advantage of his first vinyl platform, spending nearly the entire record on crisply delivered but politically insignificant boasts and messages about the importance of knowledge. The Newark, New Jersey native does drop a little obscure racial science here and there, praising Allah and namechecking Minister Farrakhan, but the album is hardly likely to send moderates running for the hills.

On the other hand, **The Lost Tribe** is largely given over to critical analyses of African-American oppression and discourses on Five-Percent history and religious theory. Ignoring the ethical contradictions in such tracks as the rational "Need Some Lovin' " and the violently uncharitable "When You See a Devil Smash Him," Shabazz—author of a most untypical rap to "Ladies"—seems like a serious young professor who hasn't quite mastered his lessons.   [i]

SHAGGS

Philosophy of the World (Third World) 1969 (Red
    Rooster-Rounder) 1980 ●
Shaggs' Own Thing (Red Rooster-Rounder) 1982

There's always room for dada in rock, and New Hampshire's three Wiggins sisters virtually define ingenuous amateurism on their first album, a home-brew oddity originally released in 1969. This startling treatise tears down every skill-related barrier that generally precludes musically unskilled children from making records and boasts that perennial candidate for worst song of all time, "My Pal Foot Foot." **Philosophy of the World** is truly inspired awfulness: incompetent drumming totally unrelated to the song under attack, two not-quite-tuned guitars and clumsy vocals offering Hallmark card platitudes. In toto, a triumph!

After reissuing the first album, NRBQ's Red Rooster label saw to the Shaggs' creation of another batch of tunes, this time making a concerted effort to achieve a semblance of musical acceptability. To that end, another Wiggins was brought in to play bass, the selection of material encompasses some non-originals, and both the sound and playing is several hundred times improved. (The benchmark is a swell remake of "My Pal Foot Foot.") **Shaggs' Own Thing** gives up a lot in terms of ear-wrenching misery, achieving instead a simple Jonathan Richman-like sweetness—a piece of true rock primitivism.   [i]

SHAKE

Shake EP (nr/Sire) 1979

SWALK

The Way We Were EP (nr/Disposable) 1985

When the Rezillos split into vocal and instrumental factions, the latter became Shake. A trio led by guitarist Jo Callis (who'd penned 90 percent of the Rezillos' originals), and later including Troy Tate, Shake overreacted to their ex-bandmates' frivolity by playing their loud'n'fastisms deadpan on this 10-inch. Second mistake: Callis let the other two write. Third mistake: dull sound. Smart move: breaking up. Smarter move (for Callis): joining the Human League.

SWALK, a quartet featuring Callis after his superstardom sojourn in Human League plus the Rezillos/Shake's old drummer, wanted to revive glitter-rock really badly—and did so, really badly. In all fairness, "No Shame" is goodish Gary Glitterism, but doesn't justify the rest of the ordeal (or a "dub" version, either).   [jg]

SHAKERS

See *Royal Court of China*.

ROBBIE SHAKESPEARE

See *Sly & Robbie*.

SHAKESPEAR'S SISTER

See *Bananarama*.

SHAMEN

Young 'Till Yesterday EP (nr/Moksha) 1986
Drop (Communion) 1987 ●
What's Going Down? EP (Moksha-Communion) 1988 ●
Strange Day Dreams (It. Moksha-Materiali Sonori) 1988
In Gorbachev We Trust (nr/Moksha-Demon) 1989 ●
Phorward EP (nr/Moksha) 1989 ●
En-Tact (nr/One Little Indian) 1990 ●

Forerunners (and side-runners) of the acid-house movement, Aberdeen's neo-psychedelic Shamen trip back to the spacey side of 1967 British rock with scrappy production, tremolo guitars, whining mellotrons and echoed vocals, suggesting 1967 Who, 1968 Pink Floyd, the Move, Tomorrow and others without specifically quoting anyone. Except for a few songs that lean towards less colorful folk-rock and aren't as bewitching, **Drop** is adventurous and entertaining stuff that easily outclasses most neo-psychedelic wannabes with abundant invention and élan. In a brilliant piece of unintentional subversion, a Scottish brewery—completely missing the song's lyrical intent—chose the LP's "Happy Days" (an ironic protest against the Falklands War) for use in a massive TV ad campaign. The US edition of **Drop** removes "Do What You Will" and "The Other Side," adding "Strange Days Dream."

Undoubtedly affected by the late-'80s doings in Manchester, the Shamen adopted a stronger rhythmic stance on **What's Going Down?** With a nod to hip-hop electronics, the group builds a devastating beat under the Carnaby Street vocals and squiggly guitar noise of "Christopher Mayhew Says," while "Knature of a Girl" adopts the now-standard stutter shuffle of countless rave records, and "Shitting on Britain" finds an exciting midpoint. Rounding off the 12-inch, there's the boring title song, a crazed cover of the 13th Floor Elevators' (by way of Television) "Fire Engine" and a remake of "Happy Days."

The Italian-only **Strange Day Dreams** compilation is brilliant, offering a complete view of the group's best work. The program includes **Drop**'s "Something About You" and "Do What You Will," a live "Strange Days Dream," retitled remixes of two **What's Going Down?** cuts (one augmented, the other dismantled), "Fire Engine," three atmospheric Syd Barrett covers (two of them from the 1986 EP, which also contained a pair of **Drop** previews and the original "Strange Days Dream") and "Grim Reaper of Love." Especially in light of the Shamen's disappointing subsequent adventures, this is the LP to own.

Following many of their English psychedelic counterparts from A(cid) to E(cstasy)—a name mentioned more than once on the album—the Shamen reoriented themselves to play simplified dance rock on the pointedly political but boringly de-Shamenized **In Gorbachev We Trust**. (The cover shot of the Soviet leader in a crown of thorns is genius.) "Adam Strange" and, to a lesser degree, "Raspberry Infundibulum" stick to

587

the band's familiar backwards-guitar rock guns, but the rest of the sparsely furnished album (including an unrecognizable house cover of the Monkees' "Sweet Young Thing") amounts to electronic percussion, bass, vocals, spoken word actualities and sound effects. Deconstructing the music allows lyrics to come through clearly, however, and that's a boon, especially on the anti-nuclear "War Prayer." (The CD and cassette have extra tracks.)

The 10-inch **Phorward** (initially packaged with a bonus 7-inch) completes the Shamen's devolution: the six new songs are stark, monotonous clatters of synth drums and chanted vocals . . . music for leaving the room. [i]

SHAM 69

Tell Us the Truth (Sire) 1978
That's Life (nr/Polydor) 1978
The Adventures of Hersham Boys (nr/Polydor) 1979
The Game (nr/Polydor) 1980
The First, Best and Last (nr/Polydor) 1980
Angels with Dirty Faces: The Best of Sham 69
 (nr/Receiver) 1986
Live and Loud!! (nr/Link) 1987
Live and Loud!! Volume 2 (nr/Link) 1988
Volunteer (nr/Legacy) 1988 ●
That's Live EP (nr/Skunx) 1988 ●
The Best of & the Rest of Sham 69 Live (nr/Receiver)
 1989 ●
The Complete Sham 69 Live (nr/Castle Classics) 1989 ●
Tell Us the Truth/That's Life (nr/Receiver) 1989
The Adventures of Hersham Boys/The Game (nr/Receiver)
 1989
Sham's Last Stand (nr/Link) 1989 ●
Live at the Roxy (nr/Receiver) 1990 ●

The archetypal working class ramalama dole-queue band, deliverers of socio-political bromides over blazing guitars, Sham 69 (the name, and the band, came from Hersham, a town on London's southern fringes) had a bad case of arrested development. Their populist slogans were ultimately chanted like football cheers and taken seriously only by the enormous British Sham army. Arguably their best single, "Hurry Up Harry" is about the importance of "going down 'a pub." Lead singer/lyricist Jimmy Pursey was earnest enough, and the band simple and basic: although their records are of no lasting import, Sham became the most popular UK punk band of their time, scoring five Top 20 singles.

The first LP sidesteps the issue of decent production by having one side with none at all and the other recorded live. The sound, oddly enough, isn't so much derived from the Clash and Pistols as it is from the Dolls, Heartbreakers and Ramones. (It's hard to judge how much of that is by design and how much is due to sheer incompetence.) More than any of those, Pursey's Cockney yelling tabbed him as the Anykid who could, but it's also true that almost any kid could have written the LP in his sleep.

That's Life offers more of the same, while enlarging on an idea heard briefly on **Tell Us the Truth**: inserting narrative slice-of-life dialogues (kid vs. parents, boy and girl, boy and girl's boyfriend, etc.) between songs. All told, a funny punk LP which features "Hurry Up Harry" and the anthemic "Angels with Dirty Faces," both hit singles.

Pursey worked up some "poetic" lyrics for **Hersham Boys**; this, plus the increased use of keyboards (played by Pursey's co-producer, Peter Wilson) meant that Sham was nearing the stage of early Boomtown Rats, complete with a surprising cover of the Yardbirds' classic "You're a Better Man Than I." A break with the punk scene, but no less aggressive than usual. (Although it wasn't issued in the States, American Polydor imported the LP and distributed a few copies as if it were a domestic release.)

By **The Game**, Sham's playing and lyrics had sharpened to the point of respectability, with the strongest material (the single "Give the Dog a Bone" in particular) of all their LPs. However, having perfected their narrow craft, there was nothing to do but disband, which they did soon after. The **First, Best and Last** compilation does include some non-LP singles (but not their first, from '77, on Step Forward) plus a limited-edition bonus live EP.

Live and Loud!!, a scorching live album recorded in 1979 and released eight years later, dwarfs Sham's studio catalog. Featuring their best, most mature (**Hersham Boys/The Game**) lineup, the LP is an ideal distillation of material from the first three albums, played with fire and confidence. It's odd that the truly essential Sham LP—their finest moment and the only record that could put to rest their reputation as a sloppy, by-the-numbers punk circus—would emerge so late in the game.

Immense UK sales of **Live and Loud!!** led to **Volume 2** (though redundant, it's more of the same quality; **That's Live** is a five-song live EP on a subsidiary of the same label) and the 1987 reformation of the group. Unfortunately, their two singles, **Volunteer** LP and a brief, aborted '88 US tour (they'd snuck over to play without work permits) reveal that the new Sham is nothing like the old: Pursey and original guitarist Dave Parsons attempt a fifth-rate Beastie Boys rap/metal/boogie-down trip. While there's something to be said for resurrected groups who don't simply trade in nostalgia, Sham '88 is totally banal and contemptible.

Besides a straightforward hits compilation (**Angels with Dirty Faces**), late-'70s Sham artifacts continue to surface. A document of the band's 1979 farewell gig at London's Rainbow, **Sham's Last Stand** rehashes the same material as its two predecessors. Although not as good as the first **Live and Loud!!**, it's an emotional, last-chance gas. (The CD adds bonus tracks.)

Live at the Roxy is one concert record too many. Though not as embarrassingly awful as the Buzzcocks' **Live at the Roxy**, neither is it any good. Worse, it's the same old songs with an original '77 lineup far inferior to the later Shams of the Link live albums. What's more, the live side of **Tell Us the Truth** (featuring the same musicians) blows this away. Only those with real time to kill will make it to the ill-advised cover of "Day Tripper." Boring and unnecessary.

In 1989, Receiver repackaged Sham's first four LPs as two double (vinyl!) albums. [jg/jr]

See also *Angelic Upstarts, Cockney Rejects, Jimmy Pursey, Wanderers*.

SHANGO

See *Afrika Bambaataa*.

ROXANNE SHANTÉ

Bad Sister (Cold Chillin'-Reprise) 1989 ●

At 14, pioneering female rapper Roxanne Shanté (Lolita Gooden of Queens, New York) earned her stage name and no small reputation by recording "Roxanne's Revenge" in response to UTFO's "Roxanne, Roxanne." A few singles followed, but it was five years before she cut a debut album. Produced by Marley Marl, **Bad Sister** includes remixes of the singles "Have a Nice Day," "Wack Itt" and "Go on Girl," balancing slow-grooving, almost mellow raps with tougher, faster ones. Shanté has a cute, coy voice that takes on an authoritative edge when she kicks into high gear. "Independent Woman," a lecture aimed at young mothers, is the album's only serious side; Shanté's at her best delivering lurid details of her encounters with men ("Knockin' Hiney," "Feelin' Kinda Horny") and other women rappers, whom she puts to shame in the title track.   [kss]

See also *UTFO*.

FEARGAL SHARKEY

Feargal Sharkey (Virgin-A&M) 1985 ●
Wish (Virgin) 1988 ●
Song from the Mardi Gras (nr/Virgin) 1991 ●

Following a slow start—three singles, only one of which ("Never Never," with Vince Clarke's Assembly) was any good—Sharkey's ascent from ex-Undertone to chart-topping singing sensation was accomplished with relative alacrity, thanks in large part to producer Dave Stewart of Eurythmics. Sharkey's first solo album is an uneasy pairing of his distinctive vocals and tame, mainstreamed arrangements of material from diverse sources. "A Good Heart" (written, but unrecorded, by Maria McKee) is a sturdy piece of slightly soulful pop; "You Little Thief" (by Benmont Tench of Tom Petty's band) is similarly memorable. "Love and Hate" resembles late-period Undertones, while the Sharkey version of the venerable "It's All Over Now" is simply a mistake.

Sharkey takes another giant step away from his past with **Wish**. The high-gloss West Coast album—production, guitar and keyboards by Danny Kortchmar; songs mostly co-written with Kootch, Waddy Wachtel and Mark Goldenberg—has characterless backing tracks that could serve any number of lame singers. The stark contrast of Sharkey's strange voice with such bland commercialism results in a listenable soul-pop-rock record with only one strong character trait. A guest turn by Keith Richards on Tench's "More Love" is wasted; except for the rousing "Out of My System," the routinely romantic songs, while competent, are entirely forgettable.   [i]

See also *Undertones*.

SHARKY'S MACHINE

Let's Be Friends (Shimmy-Disc) 1987

KILLDOZER 85

There's No Mistaking Quality (Lucha Libre) 1984

Born as an odd post-hardcore band named Killdozer 85, this NYC quartet changed its name to Sharky's Machine after Wisconsin's Killdozer signed to Touch and Go. **There's No Mistaking Quality** has a decent amount of guitar-slurping (in an amped-up Gun Club style), but the rhythmic base is too frequently reliant on hardcore's polka-born time keeping.

Let's Be Friends is a much more interesting effort. The rhythms are a lot more open, the guitar heads into the kind of heat-shimmering overload associated with James Williamson's work, and the songs seem much more cohesively screwy. Without abandoning some of hardcore's more goofball tactics, Sharky's Machine managed to create a kind of noisy street rock that was both mesmerizingly complex (in a vaguely dumb way) and unlike anybody else working the same crowded genre.   [bc]

ELLIOTT SHARP

Hara (Zoar) 1977
Resonance (Zoar) 1979
Rhythms and Blues (Zoar) 1980
ISM (Zoar) 1981
I/S/M:R (Zoar) 1982
Nots (nr/Glass) 1982
(T)here (Zoar) 1983
Live in Tokyo [tape] (Zoar) 1985
Virtual Stance (Ger. Dossier) 1986
In the Land of the Yahoos (SST) 1987 ●

ELLIOTT SHARP/SOLDIER STRING QUARTET

Tessalation Row (SST) 1987 ●
Hammer, Anvil, Stirrup [CD] (SST) 1989 ●

ELLIOTT SHARP/CARBON

Carbon (Atonal) 1984
Marco Polo's Argali/Carbon: Six Songs (Ger. Dossier) 1985
Fractal (Ger. Dossier) 1986
Larynx (SST) 1988 ●
Monster Curve [CD] (SST) 1989 ●
Datacide (Enemy) 1990

SEMANTICS

Semantics (Rift) 1985
Bone of Contention (SST) 1987 ●

In addition to his own prolific work, New York multi-instrumentalist/composer Elliott Sharp has played with, among many others, the Hi Sheriffs of Blue, Mofungo, The Scene Is Now, members of fIREHOSE (as the Bootstrappers), John Zorn and Wayne Horvitz. Although Sharp writes jarring, heavily rhythmic music using tunings and rhythms based on number systems and other schemes normally associated with contemporary classical music, there's nothing at all classical about his pounding guitar and bass rhythms or screeching bass clarinet and tenor and soprano sax. Due to its abrasive edges and sheer strangeness, Sharp's music is, for many, an unacquirable taste.

Sharp recorded **Hara**, a series of duets with guitarist and flutist Dave Fulton, largely to facilitate getting gigs. On **Rhythms and Blues**, he offers a version of R&B on electric and acoustic guitars, clarinet and saxes. (**T)here** consists of one solo side recorded live in Prague; the reverse features trumpeter Lesli Dalaba and percussionist Charles Noyes.

Both Dalaba and Noyes play in Carbon (a loose and shifting group of musicians Sharp uses to play his ensemble pieces); **Carbon** is a clear example of how Sharp organizes his music around rhythm, with melody taking a subordinate role. Most of the tracks feature Sharp on guitar, sax or clarinet, cranking out spiky rhythms while drummers pound bass drum, congas and tom-toms. Sometimes Sharp growls too. An exotic sound, straight from downtown New York.

Although Carbon is credited on **Marco Polo's Argali/Carbon: Six Songs**, the annotation never makes it clear just what that means in terms of personnel. In any case, the side with six songs is strong stuff. With Sharp's rhythmic reed work, plenty of percussion and strange sounds from his invented instruments, the tracks clank along on the edge of chaos, but never succumb to it. "Marco Polo," a side-long piece based on a number series, has some excellent moments, but, despite great trombone work by Jim Staley, gets a bit tedious over the course of 20 minutes.

Fractal is one of Sharp's strongest works, six shorter pieces and the long "Not-Yet-Time," which features some great rhythmic guitar work. It also showcases one of Sharp's gambits—using his hands to beat out quick harmonic patterns on a bass neck, as if it were a drum. The rhythms and textures play off each other beautifully, the whip-saw guitar and thick percussion offset by bass harmonics that sound like bells ringing. (**Monster Curve** is a CD-only compilation of tracks from the first three Carbon albums.)

Sharp also experiments with computers and sampling technology, and uses both extensively on **Virtual Stance**. The extended title track is composed of samples, some of which are fascinating and/or amusing, some of which are not. The rest of the record consists of briefer pieces: half sound like the previous two albums, while the others are slower and more textured.

In the Land of the Yahoos is Sharp's self-described pop album, meaning that he and others sing, his guitar and bass are toned down and the percussion is almost normal. An amazing LP with more variety than many of his others, it explores numerous textures and moods, dishes out surprises at every turn and displays a witty sense of humor.

Around the same time as **Yahoos**, Sharp turned his attentions to a new format of music, and began composing for an amplified string quartet, namely violinist David Soldier and his group. The shrill, rapid sawings of **Tessalation Row** (a thirteen-minute title piece plus four shorter works) make Bartók seem like a valium addict. (With the addition of two extensive—and stylistically consistent—new pieces, **Tessalation Row** was reissued on CD as **Hammer, Anvil, Stirrup**.) Although Sharp generally uses similar rhythms and tunings as on his rock albums, one movement mostly consists of the instruments' bodies being used for percussion.

Thanks to his increased skill at writing for ensembles, **Larynx** is Sharp's best album with Carbon. As much jazz as rock, somehow it's neither. Constructed in six sections with five interludes, the titular piece runs over both sides of the record. Four drummers play on the opening and closing sections; the Soldier String

Quartet, Jim Staley and others combine to create an amazing array of textures and rhythms. But the most inspired playing comes from Sharp himself. For the last ten minutes he pounds red-hot rhythms on bass and guitar fretboards, accompanied by frenzied drumming and dissonant violin. Awesome.

Datacide combines **Fractal**'s instrumentation with the shorter framework and polished production of **Land of the Yahoos**, with positive results.

Semantics is a rock/jazz power trio with drummer Samm Bennett (who sometimes plays with Carbon) and saxophonist Ned Rothenberg. The group's phenomenal debut meshes Rothenberg's rhythmic, interweaving sax lines with Sharp's forceful bass and guitar. The more chaotic and noisy **Bone of Contention** generally eschews the song structures of **Semantics** and is more on the jazz, if not the free jazz, side of the band's stylistic fusion. [sl]

See also *fIREHOSE, Mofungo, The Scene Is Now.*

JULES SHEAR
Watch Dog (EMI America) 1983
Jules EP (EMI America) 1983
The Eternal Return (EMI America) 1985
Demo-itis (Enigma) 1987
The Third Party (IRS) 1989 ●

FUNKY KINGS
Funky Kings (Arista) 1976

JULES AND THE POLAR BEARS
Got No Breeding (Columbia) 1978 ●
Fenĕtĭks (Columbia) 1979

RECKLESS SLEEPERS
Big Boss Sounds (IRS) 1988 ●

Despite his unbeatable songwriting talents, pop stardom has proven elusive for Jules Shear. His two songs are the highlights of the Funky Kings album, but the rest of the LP is forgettable laid-back California rock.

The two Polar Bears albums are gems; Shear's breathless vocals and the cascading lyrics are perfectly matched with the rollicking playing of his three bandmates (including future star-producer/keyboardist Stephen Hague). Both albums were commercial duds, however, and a third album (**Bad for Business**) was rejected by the group's label and was never released.

Shear's first two solo LPs contain some of his finest songs, including "All Through the Night" and "If She Knew What She Wants" (Top 40 hits for, respectively, Cyndi Lauper and the Bangles). **Watch Dog** suffers from a smothering Todd Rundgren production job, but **The Eternal Return**—co-produced by Shear and Bill Drescher—is a complete delight. (The **Jules** EP contains two mixes of the non-LP "When Love Surges" and a four-song condensation of **Watch Dog**.)

As the name implies, **Demo-itis** is a collection of song demos, half recorded by Shear at home on 8-track and the rest recorded with various musicians in a full-fledged studio situation. Despite the rough edges, it's fascinating to hear these familiar songs in their early stages. **Demo-itis** has spontaneity and enthusiasm not heard on any of Shear's other albums.

Reckless Sleepers brought a collaboration with three new bandmates on the music (Shear still writes all

590

the lyrics), but it's hard to discern any substantial creative change as a result. **The Third Party** is an interesting experiment with solo vocals by Shear and guitar accompaniment by Marty Willson-Piper of the Church. The songs are as well-crafted as ever, but a certain monotony results from Shear's unmelodic singing style (never his strongest asset) and the unvarying guitar arrangements. Providing the guitar chords along with the lyrics is a nice touch, though.   [sk]

See also *'Til Tuesday*.

STEPHEN SHEEHAN

See *Digital Sex*.

PETE SHELLEY

Sky Yen (nr/Groovy) 1979
Homosapien (Genetic-Arista) 1982
XL1 (Genetic-Arista) 1983
Heaven and the Sea (Mercury) 1986 ●

As creative linchpin of the Buzzcocks, Pete Shelley perfected a pop style based on intellectualizing his emotional responses, often to humorous effect. But, as with the group, he is strongest making singles, apparently hard-pressed to sustain his energy throughout an entire album.

Shelley's first solo LP, **Sky Yen**, was actually recorded in 1974, long before the Buzzcocks, and demonstrates an early interest in Germanic electronic music. An exercise in simpleminded drone electronics conducted on a single oscillator rather than full-fledged electronic instruments, the album is a collectors' item of minor interest.

The post-Buzzcocks **Homosapien**, including the hit single of the same name, is a dance album in which Shelley takes the reins and eliminates guitars and drums as the axis of his songs. The turn to electronics doesn't signal a surrender to them, though; the songs, not the technique, remain paramount. Shelley seems to draw influence from a wide group of sources (such as the Doors and Marc Bolan), and the album cleverly sidesteps the trap of monotony that sometimes afflicted the Buzzcocks. (The US version latter replaces "Pusher Man," "It's Hard Enough Knowing" and "Keats' Song" with "Love in Vain," "Witness the Change" and "In Love with Somebody Else.")

Shelley reintroduces guitar on **XL1** and downplays the electronics to create more direct, urgent dance music. "Telephone Operator" is the equal of "Homosapien," and the LP contains other solid examples of clear-headed songwriting—"If You Ask Me (I Won't Say No)" and "You Know Better Than I Know," for instance—that allow strong rhythms to predominate without obscuring the abundant musicality. The American cassette adds remixes of "Homosapien" and another song; the English tape tacks on an extra LP's worth.

Heaven and the Sea serves up more of Shelley's reflective soul-searching, but without much relish. Except for the percussion-laden "No Moon," the songs are fairly routine, and Stephen Hague's mundane production does little to distinguish them.   [sg/i]

See also *Buzzcocks*.

SHELLEYAN ORPHAN

Helleborine (Rough Trade-Columbia) 1987 ●
Century Flower (Rough Trade-Columbia) 1989 ●

Bournemouth's Shelleyan Orphan, the poetic singer/songwriter duo of Caroline Crawley and Jemaur Tayle, make use of a number of guests for **Helleborine**, mostly playing woodwinds and orchestral strings (members of Kate Bush's band provide some bass and drums). Instead of trying to create make-believe classical music, however, the group plays pastoral folk-pop, using the winds and strings for parts that would normally be handled by standard rock instruments. Although **Helleborine** ultimately succumbs to its own preciousness, it is refreshing in small doses.

More blood flows through the group's veins on **Century Flower**, produced by Dave Allen. The opening "Shatter" has a string quartet intro, but with pounding drums; a rather gritty sax eventually joins the fun. Electric guitars even work their way onto the LP, and Crawley's vocals turn far more passionate than on the debut. (Tayle sings mostly harmonies, and his voice is on the slight side.) **Century Flower** doesn't exactly kick butt, but it does move along nicely with well-written songs. Everything but the Girl's art-school cousins?   [dgs]

ADRIAN SHERWOOD

See *New Age Steppers, Tackhead*.

SHINEHEAD

Rough and Rugged (African Love Music) 1986
Unity (African Love-Elektra) 1988 ●
The Real Rock (African Love-Elektra) 1990 ●

Born in Jamaica, Shinehead (Edmund Carl Aiken) grew up in the Bronx, combining his two cultural heritages to become one of the first roots-rock-rappers. As a member of the early-'80s African Love Soundsystem, he surprised New Yorkers with his wacky, superb lyrical content and performance. Now signed to a major label, he has thus far endured the transition from turntable jamming to full-fledged concert tours without any compromise in his quirky vision of reality.

Shinehead's first album, released on producer Claude Evans' label, showcases a talented young rapper versatile enough to mix his musical metaphors into reggae rap ("Rough & Rugged"), American soul ("Good Love Tonight") and hybrid NYC-JA MC-style (the reggae-biographical "Hello Y'All"). From socially conscious lyrics ("Who the Cap Fits") to outright comedy, **Rough and Rugged** is a brilliant LP with something for everyone.

New York's raggamuffin roughneck continues to mix yankee hip-hop and yardee MC on **Unity** (which includes remixes of tracks like "Know How Fe Chat," "Hello Y'All" and "Who the Cap Fits" from the first album). With Run–DMC's Jam Master Jay producing three cuts (the "Come Together" Beatles rewrite of "Unity," the Sam Cooke-styled "Chain Gang" and "Truth"), and members of Roots Radics laying down musical rhythms, Shinehead rocks the house from Jamaica, Queens to Kingston, Jamaica.

The music on **The Real Rock** is more sophisticated in terms of technology and styling, but the songs are hit-and-miss. In the winning column, Shinehead does an impressive reworked version of Sly Stone's "Family Affair," flashes his rapid-fire lyrical style (as well as his sense of humor) on "Cigarette Breath," clings to his Jamaican birthright with "Musical Madness," delivers an inspiring sermon in "Strive" and lands a dose of reality on the title track. [aw]

SHIRTS
The Shirts (Capitol) 1978
Street Light Shine (Capitol) 1979
Inner Sleeve (Capitol) 1980

JING/CHEMICAL WEDDING
Off the Board [tape] (CBGB) 1987

JING
Jing (Three Cherries) 1989

Six Brooklynites known as the Shirts were playing Top 40 covers in local bars until they happened onto the Bowery club circuit in 1975. Abandoning the boroughs for a career in Manhattan with original material, the Shirts became a popular (if unhip) fixture on the burgeoning New York new wave scene, and went on to make three albums of totally bland hoping-for-the-mainstream rock. Singer Annie Golden went on to success as a singer/actress—in the movie of *Hair*, with a solo single in 1984 and on Broadway—but the Shirts are little more than a dull memory. Each of the albums has an enjoyable song or two, but there's nothing remarkable about any of them.

A decade later, Shirts guitarist/vocalist Artie La Monica (now calling himself Arthur Jing) turned up back on CBGB's stage, filling one side of a live cassette with his solo debut. Supported by a skilled quartet and bearing traces of Elvis Costello, Bob Dylan and Dion in his voice, Jing makes a credible, well-recorded showing. Four of the same songs turn up again on the eponymous studio album, a not unpleasant anachronism that has its roots in '70s new wave, Brill Building pop and the same mixture of '60s rock and soul that informed Springsteen's early records. Golden guests on three tracks. [i]

SHOCKABILLY
The Dawn of Shockabilly EP (nr/Rough Trade) 1982
    (Shimmy-Disc) 1988
Earth vs. Shockabilly (nr/Rough Trade) 1983
    (Shimmy-Disc) 1988
Greatest Hits EP (Red) 1983
Colosseum (nr/Rough Trade) 1984
Vietnam (Fundamental Music) 1984
Heaven (Fundamental Music) 1985
The Ghost of Shockabilly [CD] (Shimmy-Disc) 1989 ●
Vietnam/Heaven (Shimmy-Disc) 1990 φ
Live ... Just Beautiful (Shimmy-Disc) 1990 ●

Crazed rockabilly-tinged remakes of "Psychotic Reaction" and two Yardbirds classics isn't a bad idea, especially if gonzo guitar and drums like those on **The Dawn of Shockabilly** are brought to bear on 'em. Taking the same tack on "A Hard Day's Night" and a country oldie, adding silly organ also makes a funny kind of sense. But guitarist Eugene Chadbourne's nonsense vocals (stupidly muffled, or in silly cartoon character styles, with at least two or three different voices

per track) ruin the whole thing. Eugene shouldn't be careful with his axe, but with his mouth.

Greatest Hits takes one track each from the two preceding English records and adds a quartet of stunning live cuts, including the amphetaminized "Bluegrass Breakdown" and a nearly unrecognizable version of the Doors' "People Are Strange." **The Ghost of Shockabilly** CD combines **Earth** and **Colosseum**, the album on which the writing team of Chadbourne and Mark Kramer (bass/organ/production) began to flourish, with the Kramer musically embellishing Eugene's political and instrumental rants, parodies and white-trash obsessions. (The Shimmy-Disc cassette of **Earth** contains **The Dawn of Shockabilly**.)

Vietnam is a relatively grand affair, with a huge tour-diary poster and material by Arthur Lee, John Fogerty, John Lee Hooker and the Beatles mercilessly savaged by Chadbourne, Kramer and drummer David Licht.

Heaven takes the terrible trio further into the realms of the truly weird. Only three covers (Bolan, Lennon and a mystery), but such inspired originals as Eugene's "How Can You Kill Me, I'm Already Dead" and "She Was a Living Breathing Piece of Dirt" more than make up the difference. On that (bum) note, Shockabilly ceased to exist. (Shimmy-Disc later paired **Vietnam** and **Heaven** on CD and cassette.)

The posthumous live CD, **Just Beautiful**, is a generous 27-track plunge into the group's hyperkinetic non-stop electric vaudeville: Chadbourne wreaks havoc on an electrified rake and birdcage while Kramer and mutant-percussionist Licht fall apart in the background. Almost entirely comprised of covers, the CD includes five remixed tracks from **Dawn of Shockabilly** sutured in the middle. The cassette version has a dozen live tracks (from '84 and '85), the entire **Colosseum** LP and the five **Dawn** remixes.

Occasionally listenable, often more stupid than funny, Shockabilly was, if nothing else, absolutely unique. [jg/i/rg]

See also *Bongwater, Carney-Hild-Kramer, Eugene Chadbourne*.

MICHELLE SHOCKED
The Texas Campfire Tapes (Cooking Vinyl) 1986
    (Mercury) 1988 ●
Short Sharp Shocked (Mercury) 1988 ●
Anchorage EP (nr/London) 1988 ●
If Love Was a Train EP (nr/London) 1989 ●
Captain Swing (Mercury) 1989 ●

In the interests of critical fair play, let it be acknowledged that Bob Dylan also changed his name, invented (or at least outrageously embellished) his personal mythology and slyly claimed an entirely fictitious folk rootsiness with all the guile of film star. Since Michelle Shocked is no Bob Dylan, her ability to pull off the same charade only proves that you *can* fool some of the people all of the time. That's not to say she's not talented but, as a well-rounded pop star, her strained efforts at self-promotion and political action are dubiously credible and unforgivably distasteful in light of her pretensions of unpretentiousness.

Recorded live at a folk festival on a portable tape machine (not exactly a field recording but close enough to seem legitimately earthy), **The Texas Campfire Tapes**—complete with the post-production sound of chirping crickets—made the Dallas-born Shocked the darling of the British folk scene. An uncertain but ambitious singer whose style is woven of jazz, blues and rock'n'roll as much as folk, she comes off as a talented amateur with modestly appealing songs and the hint of substantial potential.

Parlaying UK success into an American record deal (which led to the **Campfire Tapes**' domestic issue), Shocked made her first studio album with guitarist Pete Anderson (Dwight Yoakam's producer), who provided a crisp, tasteful Nashville country bed for some of her songs. While maintaining a tenuous connection to acoustic folk with the winsome "Memories of East Texas" and Jean Ritchie's "The L + N Don't Stop Here Anymore" (the outraged protest lyrics of "Graffiti Limbo" don't quite achieve the desired effect), Shocked otherwise favors full-bodied arrangements. Hence the uptight R&B sound of "If Love Was a Train" and the glib singer/songwriter pop treatment of "Anchorage," a wonderful and affecting correspondence between old friends. And though you wouldn't know it from the jacket or label, Shocked even rocks out punkwise, joining ex-Texas politicos MDC for a hard-rocking rendition of the first album's "Fogtown." (It's the eleventh song, right after "Black Widow.")

If **Short Sharp Shocked** was a surprising follow-up to **The Texas Campfire Tapes**, the slick **Captain Swing** came as a real shocker. Anderson leads a band of session men in a modern evocation of '40s jazz (with horns, piano and strings) reminiscent of certain Joni Mitchell records. As a songwriter, Shocked isn't yet equipped to pull off an entire album in this style (indeed, she has to recycle one first-album tune to make ten tracks, most of which are insubstantial love songs), and her voice isn't quite up to the challenge, either.   [i]

SHOES

Un dans Versailles (no label) 1975
Black Vinyl Shoes (Black Vinyl) 1977 (PVC) 1978
Present Tense (Elektra) 1979
Tongue Twister (Elektra) 1981
Boomerang (Elektra) 1982 (Black Vinyl) 1990 ●
Silhouette (nr/Demon) 1984 (Black Vinyl) 1991 ●
Shoes Best (Black Vinyl) 1987 φ
Present Tense/Tongue Twister [CD] (Black Vinyl) 1988 ●
Stolen Wishes (Black Vinyl) 1989 φ

This brilliant power pop outfit from Zion, Illinois began by recording at home on a 4-track, which resulted in a self-released LP that attracted national attention and (eventually) a major-label contract. John and Jeff Murphy, Gary Klebe and drummer Skip Meyer blend electric guitar—loud, distorted and multi-tracked—with breathy, winsome vocals to create melodic rock made most impressive by the strength of three equally talented singer/songwriters.

Black Vinyl Shoes was recorded in a living room; the intricately layered guitars and vocals make that hard to believe. The songs, telling tender tales of failed romance, are catchy and instantly likable. The band also put the record in an impressive package and distributed it as a vinyl demo; in fact, it's one of the finest home-brewed releases ever, and is a much more valid piece of

music than many productions by well-known bands with far greater technical resources. After the small initial pressing sold out, the album was licensed to PVC and reissued with wholly different artwork.

Black Vinyl is actually not Shoes' first album. A prior longplayer was recorded by the Murphy brothers with a previous drummer and privately issued in a minute pressing quantity. Charming but a bit rough, it sounds like a less-developed attempt at what was to come. Shoes also recorded—but never released—an album's worth of excellent tunes in 1976 under the working title **Bazooka**.

After signing to Elektra, Shoes recorded **Present Tense** in a full-scale English 24-track studio with a professional producer, but ended up sounding pretty much the same as before, only with much greater audio fidelity. Given the chance to experiment and open up their sound, Shoes opted to hold fast—lots of vocals, lots of melody, lots of fuzzed-out guitars. Another triumphant LP that probably could have been made at home without losing any appreciable amount of charm or appeal—it's Shoes' talent, not studio technology, that matters here.

Tongue Twister successfully maintains the quality level of **Present Tense**, but Shoes are clearly standing still creatively. Their style is honed as far as it's going to go, and they're sticking with it. **Boomerang**, recorded near the band's home base without a strong outside producer, suffers from inconsistent song quality and an overanxious feeling, no doubt brought on by the band's failure to catch on commercially. (Early pressings of **Boomerang** included a 12-inch EP, **Shoes on Ice**, recorded live at the Zion Ice Arena in 1981, offering six of the band's best tunes as proof of their ability to play them in public.)

Parting company with their label, Shoes retired to the studio they had built in Illinois and continued writing and recording. A trio of Murphy, Murphy and Klebe made the next Shoes album, **Silhouette**, released only in Europe via various licensing arrangements. The sound (incorporating more keyboards and subtler dabs of guitar) is typically exquisite, and the songs—four by each member—are fine examples of the band's seemingly effortless pop suss. A fine, relaxed return that reasserts Shoes' considerable talent.

Reacquiring the rights to their three Elektra albums, Shoes issued **Shoes Best**, a 22-song non-chronological retrospective of album tracks that includes one live cut from **On Ice** and one new tune. (P.S. I wrote the liner notes.) Continuing the reissue program, **Present Tense** and **Tongue Twister** were joined on a single CD while the entire **Shoes on Ice** was appended to **Boomerang**.

Stolen Wishes, the trio's first new album in five years (and the inspiration for an unprecedented bicoastal tour in mid-'90), has all the hallmarks of Shoes' best work, plus synthesizer dressing on several of the irresistibly catchy tunes. Strident electronic percussion provides a strange contrast to the heavenly harmonies in "Feel the Way That I Do," while mock horns add a handsome texture to the glorious guitar pop of "Let It Go" and imitation strings quietly shade in "Love Does." The introduction of new elements into the group's exceedingly consistent sound is overdue, but Shoes' warm songs would be better served by real instruments rather than obviously fake simulations. Standouts: "Your Devotion," "Inside of You," the **Help!**-

styled "She's Not the Same," the dour "Torn in Two" and "Love Is Like a Bullet," the song previewed on **Shoes Best**.   [i]

SHONEN KNIFE
Burning Farm (Jap. Zero) 1983 (K) 1985
Yama No Attchan (Jap. Zero) 1984
Pretty Little Baka Guy (Jap. Zero) 1986
Shonen Knife (Gasatanka-Giant) 1990 ●
Pretty Little Baka Guy + Live in Japan (Gasatanka-
    Rockville) 1990 ●

VARIOUS ARTISTS
Every Band Has a Shonen Knife Who Loves Them
    (Gasatanka-Giant) 1989 ●

It is tempting—though not quite accurate—to call this female trio the Japanese Shaggs. While every bit as winsomely adorable and unaffectedly strange as the Wiggins sisters, Shonen Knife brings more competence to their instruments (i.e., they get by, if barely) and a very real appreciation and grasp for goofy pop song structure (as opposed to the accidental unorthodoxy that endeared the Shaggs to Ornette Coleman fans). Finally, the Knife revels in modern Japanese obsessions with commercial/pop culture and cuteness (inclinations that allow adult women to carry Hello Kitty lunch boxes to work and while away time in discos playing rock/scissors/paper). Knife song titles include "Ice Cream City," "Flying Jelly Attack" and "Tortoise Brand Pot Scrubbing Cleaner's Theme" (a would-be jingle).

Heard by Western ears, the observations and credos uttered by guitarist Naoko Yamano and bassist Michie Nakatani (the group is rounded out by Naoko's sister Atsuko on drums) are alternately amusing and disturbing: "I like public baths" is a scream, but "I wanna be/Twist Barbie" says perhaps more than they intend to about the way Japanese women are conditioned to see themselves. The trio's songs are all ridiculously catchy (and vice versa), betraying the dual influences of the Ramones and the Beatles; almost all of them, collected from Japanese EPs and LPs, are contained on the two Gasatanka albums. (The American issue of **Pretty Little Baka Guy** contains a five-song 1990 concert performance; the CD and cassette replace three vinyl tracks with live efforts from 1982.) K's cassette-only edition of **Burning Farm** adds three songs from a Japanese compilation.

Spearheaded by the lads in Redd Kross (who have involved the Knife in Tater Totz projects and have a song entitled "Shonen Knife" on **Third Eye**), the trio has gained huge cult status in Los Angeles (a 1990 gig there was a major hip-scene event), prompting a local label to assemble a tribute album (**Every Band Has a Shonen Knife Who Loves Them**), wherein many of the band's more memorable themes are given a full-blown treatment that makes you appreciate their innocent ingenuity all the more. Christmas' brilliant cover of "Ice Cream City" is better than any of the band's recent original output, Sonic Youth's version of "Burning Farm" is sexy sinister, and there's much, much more. The single-album, double-album and CD versions all annoyingly delete and/or add tracks; you'll have to locate the double-vinyl edition to hear this book's editor (as a member of Pippi Eats Cherries) play guitar on "One Day at the Factory."   [gk]

SHOP ASSISTANTS
Shop Assistants EP (nr/Subway Organisation) 1985
Safety Net EP (nr/53rd & 3rd) 1986
Shop Assistants (nr/Blue Guitar-Chrysalis) 1986
Here It Comes EP (nr/Avalanche) 1990
Big E Power EP (nr/Avalanche) 1990 ●

MOTORCYCLE BOY
Trying to Be Kind EP (nr/Blue Guitar-Chrysalis) 1989
Scarlet (nr/Blue Guitar-Chrysalis) 1989 ●

Along with the Jesus and Mary Chain, Edinburgh's Shop Assistants are part of a trend away from the terribly twee pop coming out of Scotland in the early '80s. Four lasses and a lad (including two drummers), the Shop Assistants are raw, catchy and utterly without pretense. Their first two EPs combine some of J&M's white-noise pop with Buzzcocks-influenced buoyancy, and—when necessary—tuneful delicacy (see **Safety Net**'s "Somewhere in China"). The four-song debut is promising; **Safety Net** is nothing short of brilliant.

The band's first album reprises two songs from each of the preceding releases; while it's by no means a bad record, there aren't any ideas on it that weren't already covered on the EPs. **Shop Assistants** is good, straightforward, tuneful rock'n'roll (and a real good party album), but too many of the tracks blend into one another.

In 1987, lead singer Alex (a woman) split to form the extremely similar Motorcycle Boy (not to be confused with the American band of the same name).

The Shop Assistants reconvened in 1989 as a four piece, but not without playing some musical chairs. Former bassist Sarah took over lead vocals, one drummer left, one took over bass duties and another arrived, leaving only guitarist David staying put (still no surnames). Despite all the changes, **Here It Comes**'s title track pretty much picks up where the band left off, although without the old feedback blur. A cover of Half Japanese's "Too Much Adrenalin" is great retro raunch, as is the concluding "Look Out." **Big E Power** (these Ecstasy references are getting out of hand) is more tuneful, even if the airy-voiced Sarah sounds almost intimidated in her starring role. The title song is included twice, once as a bootleg-quality live "big flares mix" recorded in Manchester; the atonal jam would do the Velvets proud. A cover of the Beatles' "She Said She Said" is, strangely enough, not credited as such. The Shop Assistants won't change anyone's life, but it's nice to have them back.   [dgs]

SHRAPNEL
Shrapnel EP (Elektra) 1984

One of the lesser lights of New York's new wave club scene, Shrapnel was a young quintet of pop-conscious metal-heads who began playing out around 1977 and clung on long enough to make this five-song 12-inch, distinguished mainly for an entertaining cover of Gary Glitter's "Didn't Know I Loved You" ("Till I Saw You Rock-n-Roll)" and a pair of tracks nicely produced by sometime Psychedelic Fur Vince Ely. The most notable thing about Shrapnel, however, was the subsequent career of guitarist Daniel Rey as a producer and player with the Ramones, Manitoba's Wild Kingdom and Masters of Reality.   [i]

SHRIEKBACK

Tench EP (Y America) 1982
Care (Warner Bros.) 1983
Jam Science (nr/Arista) 1984
Knowledge, Power, Truth and Sex EP (Ger. Arista) 1984
The Best of Shriekback: The Infinite (nr/Kaz) 1985 ●
Oil and Gold (Island) 1985 ●
Big Night Music (Island) 1986 ●
The Best of Shriekback Volume Two: Evolution (nr/Kaz) 1988 ●
Go Bang! (Island) 1988 ●
The Peel Sessions EP (nr/Strange Fruit) 1988
The Dancing Years (Island) 1990 φ

CARL MARSH

Too Much Fun (nr/Polydor) 1989 ●

Barry Andrews was a founder of XTC and later the organist in Robert Fripp's League of Gentlemen. David Allen was coincidentally replaced in Gang of Four by League bassist Sara Lee. Together with guitarist/vocalist Carl Marsh and a drum machine, Andrews and Allen formed Shriekback, a cagey dance band with solid rhythms and insidiously weird vocals. The playing is top-notch, a slithering swamp snake that oozes cool malevolence on **Tench**'s six tracks. Shriekback abounds in originality and creativity, if not warmth. Despite changes in personnel, Andrews has remained the band's core, preserving its spirit of prickly iconoclasm and imaginative exploration.

Care is an intelligent, well-produced, spirited debut, demonstrating what every XTC fan knew all along—Andrews is one of rock's most original and musical keyboard players. Over Allen's slinky, oblique bass lines, he provides subtle shadings and clever doodles that move in and out of the mix, making this perfect for both dancing and scrutiny. Most bands with this much talent would be content to showcase their chops, but Shriekback can write a good song, too, especially the haunting "Lined Up," a unique funk concoction that sets an impossible standard for inferior but like-minded bands.

Jam Science doesn't quite match **Care** for sheer invention, but is nonetheless a solid, confident LP. More prominent use of drum machines, female backing vocals and string synths give the record a slick Euro-disco feel. (Released by UK Arista, this LP should not be confused with an unauthorized release of the same name on Dutch Y, which contains most of the same songs but in unfinished form. The German EP, with four of the proper album's tracks, is legit.)

Oil and Gold goes for a much harder sound, with booming, sometimes overpowering guitar and drums (most evident on "Nemesis," a big club hit and the only pop song ever to make good lyrical use of the word "parthenogenesis") When they lean toward the more ethereal colors found on **Care**, the results are pretty boring ("This Big Hush," "Faded Flowers"). After the LP was released, Marsh left the group, and was replaced, for one American tour, by former Voidoid guitarist Ivan Julian.

The garrulous liner notes on the next album explain it in some detail. "Shriekback celebrate the blessed dark—the place where they were always most at home. Songs to sing in your sleep . . . the shape and rhythm of two different kind of nights—nights of heat and weird-

ness . . . and nights incandescent with moonlight and dreams. **Big Night Music** is entirely free of digital heartbeats of every kind.'' Except for a few familiar-sounding entries, this radical departure resembles nothing in the Shriekback's previous repertoire and thus requires a real commitment to get over the shock of hearing evanescent continental delicacy and understated piano music instead of pounding dance-rock bizarritude. But do it—your efforts will be well rewarded with beauty, grace and originality. After the album, Dave Allen left to form King Swamp, making Andrews the only remaining original member.

The Infinite, the first of two British compilations, offers a solid introduction to the band's early period, excerpting **Tench** and **Care**, plus some other things. **Evolution**, the second volume, is more eclectic, containing tracks from **Oil and Gold**, **Jam Science**, 12-inch versions of three singles and another song from **Care**.

With guest star Doug Wimbish (Tackhead, etc.) playing a lot of the bass, Andrews and stalwart drummer Martyn Barker—joined by guitarist Mike Cozzi, who first appeared on **Big Night Music**, and two backup singers—returned to musical daylight on **Go Bang!**, a winning LP produced by Richard James Burgess. While the ominous undercurrent in Andrews' voice remains one of the band's best features, the kinetic arrangements (including electronic horns) are almost playful, largely picking up where **Oil and Gold** left off.

Shriekback disbanded in mid-1989. Martyn Barker followed Allen into King Swamp, Cozzi joined the Andrew Ridgeley Band and Andrews formed Illuminati. The final release from Shriekback—**The Dancing Years**—is a start-to-finish career retrospective that contains the songs you'd expect, but not in overly familiar form. Other than one new song ("White Out"), the album consists of four re-recordings (including a radically revamped "My Spine (Is the Bass Line)" and "Deeply Lined Up," which has a little something, but not much, to do with "Lined Up"), two live renditions (four on the CD) and three remixes, leaving only "Everything That Rises (Must Converge)" and "Shark Walk" untouched from their original album versions. More an intriguing coda than a convenient summary, **The Dancing Years** bids farewell on a typically offbeat and atmospherically entrancing note. [i/dgs]

See also *Robert Fripp, Gang of Four, King Swamp, XTC.*

JANE SIBERRY

Jane Siberry (Can. Street) 1981 (East Side Digital) 1991 ●
No Borders Here (Open Air) 1983 ●
The Speckless Sky (Duke Street-Open Air) 1985 (Duke Street-Warner Bros.) 1988 ●
The Walking (Duke Street-Reprise) 1987 ●
Bound by the Beauty (Duke Street-Reprise) 1989 ●

This thrush-voiced Canadian has inspired comparisons with female artistes as diverse as Kate Bush, the Roches and Laurie Anderson, but Siberry is a refreshing original, combining the best aspects of singer-songwriterism and art-pop to produce music that's both artful and fun. Her eponymous debut album (reissued a decade later with upgraded packaging) finds the artist's playful humanist worldview and predilection for inventive, wide-ranging arrangements already firmly in place on smartly observed material that's by turns humorous ("Marco Polo") and darkly atmospheric ("The Strange Well"), with quietly effective arrangements that focus firmly on Siberry's delicate, yet sturdy, vocals.

On the more elaborate **No Borders Here**, her witty, literate compositions are well-served by imaginative, near-cinematic arrangements and production, most notably on the brilliant mini-opera "Mimi on the Beach." The subsequent **Speckless Sky** is even better, with impressive numbers like "One More Colour," "Vladimir, Vladimir" and "Map of the World (Part II)" effectively blending the epic and the intimate.

The Walking is airier and more abstract, with fewer obvious melodies and lyrical hooks, but it's a quietly rewarding album that shows growth and new confidence (e.g., "The White Tent the Raft," "Lena Is a White Table"). In contrast, **Bound by the Beauty** is relatively earthy and direct. The title song, "Everything Reminds Me of My Dog" and "The Life Is the Red Wagon" are among Siberry's friendliest and most inviting efforts to date, while "Half Angel Half Eagle" and "La Jalouse" hint at darker emotional territory.   [hd]

SICK OF IT ALL

Blood, Sweat, and No Tears (In-Effect) 1989 ●
We Stand Alone EP (In-Effect) 1991

Without bringing anything new to the form, this dynamic New York hardcore quartet rips through familiar fast/mosh/shout/chant maneuvers with explosive power and remarkable tightness on the clearly articulated debut. Other than a guest introduction by KRS-One, there are no surprises in the no-nonsense thrash of angry songs like "World Full of Hate," "Disillusion," "Pushed too Far" and "My Revenge."

Returning with a new rhythm section, guitarist Pete Koller and his singer brother Lou introduced their 'core rhythms to a buzzing metallic environment on the studio side of the brief **We Stand Alone** mini-album. Besides covering Minor Threat's "Betray," speaking out against senseless violence ("What's Goin' On") and defiantly standing up to false friends ("We Stand Alone"), the band fills out the 7-inch record (and tape) with savage live performances of four songs from the first LP.   [i]

FRANK SIDEBOTTOM

Frank's Firm Favorites EP (nr/Regal Zonophone) 1985
Oh Blimey It's Christmas EP (nr/Regal Zonophone) 1985
Sci-Fi EP (Oh Supermum) EP (nr/Regal Zonophone) 1986
Christmas Is Really Fantastic EP (nr/In Tape) 1986
Frank Sidebottom Salutes the Magic of Freddie Mercury
    and Queen and also Kylie Minogue (you know, ...
    her off "Neighbours") (nr/In Tape) 1987 + 1988
Timperley EP (nr/In Tape) 1987
5:9:88 (nr/In Tape) 1988
13:9:88 (nr/In Tape) 1989
Medium Play (nr/In Tape) 1990

At first glance, Frank Sidebottom is just an idiotic soccer fan from Timperley (a town just outside Manchester) who performs inanely nasal renditions of popular songs—accompanying himself in various musical modes, from rock to acoustic piano to a rinkydink synthesizer approximation of '20s ragtime—while wearing an enormous painted papier-mâché head. But what Chris Sievey (former leader of the equally prolific punk-era Freshies) has done as Frank Sidebottom is so completely over the top, so singlemindedly weird, funny and charming that one has to marvel at the wit and intensity with which he pursues his bewildering career. As British as a sixpence and as mad as a hatter, this tireless and hilarious character offers the world (or at least the hardy members of his fan club) a much-needed blast of self-indulgent fun. And unlike so many rude, crude and lewd performers, he always remembers to say "Thank you" at the end of each song.

After outlining the parameters of his parodic career with three self-released EPs that include, respectively, covers (of the Sex Pistols, Police, Queen, etc.), holiday originals (like "Christmas in Australia") and space-themed oddities (including the Bonzo Dog Band's "Urban Spaceman" as well as the "Fireball X15 Theme"), Frank hooked up with In Tape and delivered **Christmas Is Really Fantastic**. Besides the inspirational title track, the EP (in its expanded 12-inch form) includes a medley of seasonals, an absurd oompah version of Roy Wood's "I Would It Could Be Christmas Everyday" and "Mull of Timperley," which allows Frank to advance his own geocentric worldview *and* twig Paul McCartney at the same time. Troublesome puppet sidekick Little Frank even gets a turn, closing the record with the punk-rocking "Football Is Really Fantastic."

Pictured on the cover of **The Magic of Freddie Mercury and Queen** (a 1987 7-inch expanded to foot-long form with extra tracks the following year) with a mustache and detached mic stand, surrounded by a constellation of Kylie Minogue faces clipped from newspapers, Frank croons "I Should Be So Lucky" and reads "Love Poem for Kylie" ("Oh Kylie Kylie Kylie, as a person you are ace/Oh Minogue Minogue Minogue, let's run away to space/I'll build a dream house next to yours, with Australian cheap labor/And you can be the girl next door, and I can be your neighbor"). The rest of the record consists of goofy Queen covers and adaptations, including "We Will Rock You," "Frank Gordon," "I Am the Champion" and "Everybody Sings Queen," which strings together the band's song titles. Fantastic.

Timperley is a conceptual tour de farce, a delicately delicious romp through the Kinks ("Timperley Sunset," with all-new regional lyrics), Bruce Springsteen ("Born in Timperley," which helps explain the town's fantastic-ness: it has two post boxes!), the Troggs ("J'Taime Wild Thing in Timperley") and—for all of 27 seconds—the Monkees ("Next Train to Timperley"). As usual, Frank and Little Frank squabble about this and that between tracks.

The original concept behind **5:9:88** and **13:9:88** was to make and release the two albums a week apart, but that's not exactly how things worked out. The first, a double-LP (and somewhat revised cassette), did appear on schedule in September 1988: nearly two hours of music and chat (the two Franks engage in a lot of the latter; "The Tomb of Maurice Karmen" is sort of a homemade radio play, an echoey little excursion ("The Tomb of Maurice Kamen") which yields such useful information as the ancient Egyptian derivation of the word "formica") that runs the top-to-bottom gamut from '60s nostalgia ("It Was Nearly 20 Years Ago To-day"), a jolly sea chantey ("Fantastic Sea Shanty") and the incisively Floydian "First Puppet on the Moon" to some total time-wasters.

The second half of Frank's week didn't go so well; his follow-up extravaganza ran into legal difficulties regarding Little Frank's Christmas parody of the Beastie Boys' "Fight for Your Right" and wasn't issued until the following April. Presented as a holiday trip (by train, of course), **13:9:88** begins on a merry note with the singalong "Blackpool Fool." But it quickly develops, however, that Frank has neither enough songs for an album (a problem Little Frank repeatedly mentions, much to big Frank's vexation and depression) nor a train ticket. Although Frank does make it to Blackpool, he really doesn't really have any songs, and this winds up being a largely non-musical vacation of radio-play nonsense that ends on a classical note with "18:22:88 Overture."

The 10-inch/ten-song **Medium Play** has no overriding concept, but this more-wonderful-than-not hodgepodge includes really fantastic interpretations of songs by Elvis Presley and the Beach Boys, Little Frank's "Tummy" rock opera and a sketchy guest rendition (on guitar and sloperatic tenor) of Duran Duran's "Planet Earth" by some dolt who belches at the end. Alongside a spiffy upending of "Twist 'n' Shout," **MP**'s highlight is "Timperley Blues" (apologies to Eddie Cochran), which contains the following profound exchange between the artist and his sidekick (prompted by Little Frank's having fetched a pizza instead of the visa Frank wanted): "You stupid, stupid, stupid, stupid puppet." "I'd like to help you Frank, but I'm cardboard." If that makes you smile, Frank Sidebottom's your man.   [i]

DAVITT SIGERSON

See *Royal Macadamians*.

SIGUE SIGUE SPUTNIK

Flaunt It (Manhattan) 1986 ●
Dress for Excess (nr/Parlophone) 1988 (EMI) 1989 ●
The First Generation (nr/Jungle) 1990 [tape] (ROIR) 1991 ●

In this cynical and suspicious era, criminals—including politicians, preachers, murderers and swindlers of all persuasions—have found it easy to get away with the most outrageous transgressions by being upfront about their sins. Nothing succeeds these days like the profession of sincerity: most people, it seems, prefer a known felon to a possible liar. No matter how indefensible one's actions may be, a confident pre-emptive announcement or tearful apology evidently wipes away all evil.

Spurred no doubt by former Generation X bandmate Billy Idol's solo stardom (and possibly the successful no-music-necessary starmaking machinery of Frankie Goes to Hollywood), bassist/producer Tony James formed this colorful and sweeping multi-media hype as a post-everything adaptation of Malcolm McLaren's great rock'n'roll swindle. But instead of trying to manipulate the record industry and music-consuming public with cagey behind-the-scenes machinations, Sigue Sigue Sputnik confronted the challenge with total frankness, blithely acknowledging the naked crassness of their intentions. The sextet proved exceedingly adept at outrageous style-mongering, attracting press coverage (much of it highly unfavorable), self-marketing and favorable deal-making. Creating and selling records, however, was another matter.

Prior to the release of **Flaunt It**, SSS debuted with a three-version 12-inch of "Love Missile F1-11"—a ticking bass sequencer with a simple vocal, shards of guitar and piles of unpredictable sound effects, goosed with wild production tricks into a mixed trashcan of trivia that's amusing enough but bears only the scantiest relationship to music. The album, also produced by Giorgio Moroder, proffers another version of "Love Missile," following it with an utterly useless program of near-identical assemblages and other likeminded tripe that attempts to replicate the T. Rex glam-pop atmosphere with meaningless slogans and ultra-simple hooks. (Besides the obvious Bolanisms, SSS tangentially acknowledges a massive debt to Suicide with occasional cries of "Rocket USA," not-so-cleverly disguised as "Rock It Miss USA.") Despite spectacular Japanese-styled art and the distinction of being the first rock record to contain paid audio advertisements, **Flaunt It** doesn't got it.

The notation "This time it's music" on the front cover of **Dress for Excess** is almost touching, but hardly supported by the repetitive trivia contained in the grooves. Dispensing with sponsorship and toning down the samples (except on "Hey Jayne Mansfield Superstar!," which *has* to be a first LP outtake, "Super Crook Blues" and the armageddon fantasy, "M*A*D"), Sigue Sigue roots around its songwriting closet in search of something worthwhile to dress up, but what gets simple '50s-by-way-of-guitars'n'synths treatment here is totally worthless and forgettable. (There isn't even an attempt at originality in "Rio Rocks!," which puts cribbed lyrics to "La Bamba.")

The utterly redundant **First Generation** retrieves the complete **Flaunt It** 4-track demos (essentially the same LP, with wicked amounts of echo and none of the sonic window dressing, plus "Jayne Mansfield") and sticks on three 1990 recordings and a limp live rendition of "Rebel Rebel." At that point, neck-deep in a rising sewer, James went off and joined the Sisters of Mercy.

See also *Generation X, Sisters of Mercy*.   [i]

SILENCERS

A Letter from St. Paul (RCA) 1987 ●
A Blues for Buddha (nr/RCA) 1988 (RCA) 1989 ●
Dance to the Holy Man (RCA) 1991 ●

You can't keep a good Scot out of the recording studio. After his commercially frustrating experience with Fingerprintz, Jimme O'Neill reunited with guitarist Cha Burns, formed the Silencers and went further—commercially—than his old group ever did. Not that this band purveys pop pastry: **A Letter from St. Paul** addresses neuroses both personal and political, set to churning guitar-based rhythms. The music's hypnotic, the lyrics compelling. "We decided we wanted to write only about serious subjects without sounding anxious," O'Neill said. Without sounding derivative of U2, the Silencers appeal to the same psychological demographic—only minus the naïveté.

The single "Painted Moon" did much to boost the Silencers' debut album. Unfortunately, history didn't repeat with the succeeding **A Blues for Buddha**. When an album's most commercial track—pushed briefly as a single—is called "Razor Blades of Love," you're not exactly thinking multi-platinum. Despite the band's sparkling sound, O'Neill's voice and lyrics convey an unrelieved sense of doom. Apocalyptic imagery abounds, and the album winds down until left with an acoustic guitar and a drum. The music is less carefully composed than before—second-album syndrome? But the pervasive gloom is what makes **A Blues for Buddha** so enervating.   [si]

See also *Fingerprintz*.

SILENT RUNNING

Emotional Warfare (EMI America) 1984
Walk on Fire (Atlantic) 1987 ●
Deep (Atlantic) 1989 ●

If Belfast bands are generally esteemed for their passionate intensity, someone forgot to tell Silent Running. **Emotional Warfare** (released abroad as **Shades of Liberty**) contains slick humdrum dance-rock with only Peter Gamble's Bonoesque bellow to suggest—if not generate—any enthusiasm. The pounding "Emotional Warfare" is as good as it gets, and that's not very. The eager-for-airplay **Walk on Fire** reduces Silent Running to a quartet (the keyboardist left) and comes on like a dull hybrid of the Fixx and Bad Company.

Recorded by a drummerless trio, **Deep** is the best of a sorry bunch. The first two tracks on each side are invigorating blasts of determined and confident-sounding U2-conscious 4/4 guitar rock, but elsewhere the record runs aground on Bryan Adams' soundalikes and metalhead power ballads.   [i]

SILICON TEENS

Music for Parties (Sire) 1980

Whether people realize it or not, Daniel Miller has probably been as responsible as anybody (save Robert Moog) for the rise of synthesizers in modern rock, via his Mute Records, a groundbreaking single (as the Normal) and production work for Depeche Mode and many others. The illusory Silicon Teens (despite the personnel list on the sleeve) is a pseudonymous Miller studio project, offering fourteen percolating synth versions (with vocals) of such rock'n'roll classics as "Memphis, Tennessee," "Judy in Disguise," "You Really Got Me"—you get the idea. There are several originals as well, but the title says it best: a good time is guaranteed for all. The approach here is more conservative and reverent than the prior more devolutionary Flying Lizards, but the two concepts are not that far apart.   [i]

SILOS

About Her Steps. (Record Collect) 1985 ●
Cuba (Record Collect) 1987 ●
Tennessee Fire EP (Record Collect) 1987
The Silos (RCA) 1990 ●

WALTER SALAS-HUMARA

Lagartija (Record Collect) 1988 ●

This New York combo's style is basically an idiosyncratic urban-bohemian variation on country-rock, with sly melodies, deceptively simple lyrics and the attractively laconic vocals of up-from-Florida frontmen Walter Salas-Humara (founder of the Vulgar Boatmen) and Bob Rupe (formerly one of the Bobs, who released a pair of neat records on Safety Net). The eight short songs that comprise **About Her Steps.** have a laid-back charm, with the jangly "Shine It Down," the steel-guitar-drenched "4 Wanted Signs" and the slow, haunting "Start the Clock" standing out.

Cuba forges a more distinctive band personality on tracks as diverse as the incendiary "Tennessee Fire," the poignant "She Lives Up the Street," the jauntily hippieish "Mary's Getting Married" and the regretful, acoustic "Going Round." This last song makes good use of a string quartet; the rest of **Cuba** finds Mary Rowell's violin emerging as an integral element in the Silos' sound. The **Tennessee Fire** 12-inch contains the album versions of the title track and "Start the Clock," plus two previously unreleased and unremarkable numbers.

Salas-Humara's well-crafted and appealing solo album (which doesn't sound very different from the group's work), **Lagartija**, has contributions from Rupe and includes "About Her Steps." and "Cuba," neither of which (despite their familiar titles) have been released by the Silos. (The CD adds two songs.)

The Silos' major-label debut doesn't deviate substantially from the group's indie efforts, maintaining the earlier discs' live-in-the-studio feel and confidently unflashy instrumental attack. Rather than exploit their natural accessibility to maximize their commercial potential, Rupe and Salas-Humara seem to be taking pains to maintain the songs' scaled-down ramshackle charm, avoiding obvious hooks or gimmicks. The pair gives equal play to rockers ("Caroline," "I'm Over You," "Don't Talk That Way") and quieter tunes ("Commodore Peter," "The Only Story I Tell," "Picture of Helen"), and make like a sleepy Sam & Dave on the horn-laden "Maybe Everything."   [hd]

See also *Bobs, Vulgar Boatmen*.

JIMMY SILVA

See *Young Fresh Fellows*.

SILVER CHALICE

See *45 Grave*.

SIMON F

Gun (Chrysalis) 1986
Never Never Land (Reprise) 1987 ●

F MACHINE

Here Comes the 21st Century (Reprise) 1989 ●

Singing keyboardist Simon F was half of a mid-'80s British flop-in-the-pan called Intaferon; ex-partner Simon G is one of the guitarists on his first solo album. **Gun** takes its best shot right at the start, leading off with a histrionic version of the Hoodoo Gurus' indestructible "I Want You Back" complete with a blinding Steve Stevens solo, and heads downhill from there. Despite an annoying synthesizer squeal, the mock-Bowie pop of

"Baby Pain" isn't bad; everything else on this half-baked, unoriginal synth-dance LP is.

Never Never Land begins with "New York Girl," which blends ticking sequencers, surging guitar chords and a wall of backing vocals: the resemblance to Billy Idol's early records is unmistakable. But so is the marked difference in vocalists. Elsewhere, Simon fails to lay a glove on funk, botches the Beach Boy allusion on "American Dream," makes assorted absurd lyrical assertions and generally bores his way through two sides of an insipid attempt to squeeze talent out of recording studio walls.

Corralling a guitarist, drummer and keyboard player, F formed F Machine and set about imitating his Idol in earnest. On **Here Comes the 21st Century** (the cover of which charmingly pictures a dozen infamous murderers, from Hitler to David "Son of Sam" Berkowitz: is there a rock'n'roll message here?) he assembles an overproduced collection of riffs learned from **Rebel Yell**, this asshole nonchalantly endorses rape and drug abuse, complains about "Too Many White People" ("Gonna get a gun, gonna kill me some/Won't that be a lot of fun") and sings lines like "I want to raise my fist/To my sexy terrorist/Escape from Czechoslovakia/Make love in the back of her daddy's car" as if such wanton stupidity actually means something.   [i]

SIMPLE MINDS

Life in a Day (PVC) 1979 (Virgin) 1987 ●
Real to Real Cacophony (nr/Arista) 1980 (nr/Virgin)
    1982 (Virgin) 1988 ●
Empires and Dance (nr/Arista) 1980 (nr/Virgin) 1982 ●
Sons and Fascination/Sister Feelings Call (nr/Virgin)
    1981 ●
Celebration (nr/Arista) 1982 (nr/Virgin) 1982 ●
Themes for Great Cities (Stiff) 1982
New Gold Dream (81-82-83-84) (Virgin-A&M) 1982 ●
Sparkle in the Rain (Virgin-A&M) 1984 ●
Once Upon a Time (Virgin-A&M) 1985 ●
Sister Feelings Call (Virgin) 1987
Live in the City of Light (Virgin-A&M) 1987 ●
Street Fighting Years (Virgin-A&M) 1989 ●
Themes Vol. 1: March 79–April 82 [CD] (nr/Virgin)
    1990 ●
Themes Vol. 2: August 82–April 85 [CD] (nr/Virgin)
    1990 ●
Themes Vol. 3: September 85–June 87 [CD] (nr/Virgin)
    1990 ●
Themes Vol. 4: February 89–May 90 [CD] (nr/Virgin)
    1990 ●
Real Life (Virgin-A&M) 1991 φ

Scotland's Simple Minds once took a lot of (mostly) undeserved criticism for being arty and pretentious, but in the early days, their mix of serious/philosophical lyrics with danceable rhythms supporting oblique musical structures did make them something of an acquired taste. Often dense, occasionally discordant and gloomy, Simple Minds' music also stretches to commercial pop, an area they pursued with increasing enthusiasm and success in the '80s.

Life in a Day largely recalls Roxy Music, but also touches lightly on several forms, including pop, psychedelia and an adventurous tense/terse style they explored on subsequent albums. "Sad Affair" is modish; "All for You" has disturbing overtones of the Doors and early Jefferson Airplane; "No Cure" sounds like the Buzzcocks-meet-the-Who; "Chelsea Girl" is delightful '60s pop, complete with full orchestration.

With **Real to Real Cacophony**, the band lives up (or down) to the album's clever title. Excepting a couple of standouts like "Carnival (Shelter in a Suitcase)" and the haunting instrumental "Film Theme" (Simple Minds are one of the few bands that can and do create worthwhile instrumentals with real skill), **Real to Real Cacophony** is just like the band in the title song; "Real to real cacophony/Echo, echo on endlessly."

As soon as the needle sets down on **Empires and Dance**'s "I Travel," it's obvious that Simple Minds have reorganized and changed direction; while not completely successful, the album is extremely atmospheric and promising, including some good dance tunes and a few more quasi-psychedelic ones ("Kant-Kino" and "Room"). **Celebration** is a compilation of tracks from the first three LPs.

Two discrete albums originally released as one packaged work, then reissued separately (the latter several times), **Sons and Fascination/Sister Feelings Call** is Simple Minds' first really good record. While still experimental, the group sounds more comfortable in the semi-funky, semi-dancey, semi-electronic groove introduced on **Empires and Dance**. "The American," "20th Century Promised Land" and "Love Song" are all top-drawer examples of modern dance music; "Theme for Great Cities" is another fine instrumental.

Picking up its title from that composition, **Themes for Great Cities** (subtitled "Definitive Collection 79–81") takes the best material from albums not then released in America—**Real to Real Cacophony**, **Empires and Dance** and **Sons and Fascination/Sister Feelings Call**—and presents the band much more strongly than the individual records originally did. (One notable omission: "20th Century Promised Land.")

Opening the band's commercially rewarding phase, **New Gold Dream (81-82-83-84)** takes another great step forward. The songs are stronger and the sound shows a definite thawing, mellowing trend, yet retains its majestic power. "Promised You a Miracle" (a soulful and dramatic dance tune), "Glittering Prize" (a warm, pretty ballad) and the panoramic title track stand out. A memorable, mature record marked by compassion and sensitivity. Drummer Brian McGee had departed, and was replaced on the LP by three different players, one of whom—Mel Gaynor—wound up joining the band.

Working with producer Steve Lillywhite, **Sparkle in the Rain** is another fine, affecting record with textured, intricate rhythmic rock and Jim Kerr's personable singing. Simple Minds sound firmly in control of their sound, equally capable of grand gestures and subtle nuance. The first side is great, featuring four of their best songs: "Speed Your Love to Me," "Book of Brilliant Things," "Up on the Catwalk" and "Waterfront." The flipside is less exhilarating, but does include a cover of Lou Reed's "Street Hassle."

At this point, Simple Minds' story gets complicated. Jim Kerr married Chrissie Hynde in 1984. The following year, the band had its first chart-topping hit with

"Don't You (Forget About Me)," done for the soundtrack of *The Breakfast Club*. Bassist Derek Forbes was replaced by John Giblin. They appeared at Live Aid. Jim and Chrissie had a baby. And Simple Minds sold themselves out on their first post-stardom LP.

Produced by Jimmy Iovine and Bob Clearmountain, **Once Upon a Time** is appalling, a perversion of the group's sound specifically—and most unpleasantly—geared for American radio. While Kerr still has enough self-respect to not repeat the band's hit with a soundalike, tracks like "Sanctify Yourself," "Alive and Kicking" and "Oh Jungleland" (great title) are surprisingly wretched, transparent stabs at Album Rock Radio that bear only passing resemblance to Simple Minds' prior work. In the passage from arty obscurity to arty success, Simple Minds lost their balance forever.

The sumptuous and sonically excellent live double album was recorded in Paris in 1986, a triumphant celebration of the band's enormous success. Augmented by a backing vocalist, percussionist, violinist and computer programmer, Simple Minds play the recent hits, reaching back before **New Gold Dream** only once—in a three-song medley on Side Four that runs together "Love Song," Little Steven's "Sun City" and Sly and the Family Stone's "Dance to the Music."

Street Fighting Years reveals Kerr neck-deep in moral righteousness, writing and performing self-important songs about Third World struggles (the title track is in memory of Victor Jara) with much the same messianic bombast as U2, substituting Sting-like pretense for Bonoesque passion. Co-produced by Trevor Horn, the album—which goes so far as to include an utterly redundant seven-and-a-half-minute remake of Peter Gabriel's majestic "Biko," complete with bagpipes—sounds spectacular, a complex wash of rhythms (Manu Katché joins Mel Gaynor in the twin-drummer attack), guitars, keyboards and strings. It's a technical achievement to be sure, but rock music on such an operatic scale isn't exactly entertaining, and the record seems distant and unapproachable. Lou Reed guest-sings on "This Is Your Land"; African percussionists add social credibility. (The CD contains a bonus, "When Spirits Rise.")

Each of the four **Themes** sets—an ingenious package that folds out to reveal a cross of five CDs—compiles the contents of the band's 12-inch singles from a different era.   [ks/i]

See also *Propaganda*.

SIOUXSIE AND THE BANSHEES

The Scream (Polydor) 1978 (Geffen) 1984 ●
Join Hands (nr/Polydor) 1979 (Geffen) 1984 ●
Kaleidoscope (PVC) 1980 (Geffen) 1984 ●
Juju (PVC) 1981 (Geffen) 1984 ●
Arabian Knights EP (PVC) 1981
Once Upon a Time/The Singles (PVC) 1981 (Geffen) 1984 ●
A Kiss in the Dreamhouse (nr/Polydor) 1982 (Geffen) 1984 ●
Nocturne (Geffen) 1983 ●
Hyaena (Geffen) 1984 ●
The Thorn EP (nr/Wonderland-Polydor) 1984
Cities in Dust EP (Geffen) 1985
Tinderbox (Geffen) 1986 ●

Through the Looking Glass (Geffen) 1987 ●
The Peel Sessions EP (nr/Strange Fruit) 1987 ●
Peepshow (Geffen) 1988 ●
The Peel Sessions EP (nr/Strange Fruit) 1988 ●
The Peel Sessions (Strange Fruit-Dutch East India Trading) 1991 φ
Superstition (Geffen) 1991 ●

In 1976, Siouxsie Sioux (née Susan Dallion) and Steve Severin were part of the clique of steady Sex Pistols fans known as the Bromley Contingent. As Siouxsie and the Banshees, the nascent punk rock stars debuted at the 100 Club's legendary 1976 punk festival; aided by future Ant guitarist Marco Pirroni and the unknown Sid Vicious on drums, the motley crew bashed through a lengthy free-form rendition of "The Lord's Prayer," stopping only when they became bored.

From such uncertain beginnings, Siouxsie and the Banshees quickly evolved into a highly popular band, regularly appearing on the British charts despite the group's brooding, abrasive style. **The Scream** capsulized the first-generation sound of the Banshees: Siouxsie's icy, sometimes tuneless wail swooping over the metal-shard roar of John McKay's guitar and the brutish rhythms of bassist Severin and drummer Kenny Morris. The songs are relentlessly grim, albeit often sardonic (as in "Carcass" and their version of the Beatles' "Helter Skelter"). In a bit of artistic tampering, the American label included the almost upbeat "Hong Kong Garden" (a pre-LP 45 that punched its way into the UK Top 10), beginning the album with an unintended stylistic departure.

The Scream seems positively cheerful in light of its follow-up, **Join Hands**, a plodding, depressive album notable only for the commission of the band's "Lord's Prayer" butchery to vinyl. Two days into a tour to promote the album, Morris and McKay abruptly walked out; the Banshees drafted guitarist Robert Smith from opening act the Cure and ex-Big in Japan/Slits drummer Budgie and completed their concert schedule. Budgie subsequently signed on as a permanent Banshee and the group proceeded to record **Kaleidoscope** without a guitarist to call their own. (Guest stars John McGeoch of Magazine and ex-Pistol Steve Jones alternated guitar duties on the LP.) **Kaleidoscope** marked a bilateral move away from the group's original wall of noise; many of the songs are softer and more melodic (e.g., "Happy House" and the flower-powery "Christine"), and there is an increased use of framing concepts ("Red Light" is built around the whirr-click of a camera autowinder). After McGeoch signed on permanently, they toured America for the first time.

Finally a full-fledged band again, the Banshees released the strong and satisfying **Juju**. Siouxsie's voice had developed into a surprisingly subtle instrument, and the technical prowess brought by Budgie and McGeoch brought power and complexity to songs like "Spellbound" and "Arabian Knights."

Also released in 1981, **Once Upon a Time** assembled all of the band's singles (including the otherwise non-LP "Staircase (Mystery)" and "Israel") on one record. The American **Arabian Knights** EP reprises the contents of a British 12-inch plus one extra tune.

A Kiss in the Dreamhouse finds the Banshees veering back into the more experimental terrain of **Kaleidoscope**, letting their jarring, near-pop style pass through some pretty strange permutations (like the deviant neo-bop of "Cocoon" and the medieval recorder stylings of "Green Fingers.") McGeoch fell ill, sat out the next tour (replaced by Smith) and decided not to rejoin the band.

Nocturne is a two-LP live set recorded (with no overdubs) at a pair of Royal Albert Hall shows in late 1983. Smith is the featured guitarist on a full-course selection from the band's repertoire, stretching back to "Switch," "Helter Skelter" and "Israel," but also drawing heavily from Dreamhouse. Awesome.

With Smith still in the lineup, Hyaena starts off with the utterly magnificent "Dazzle," a haunting blend of industrial-strength drumming and symphonic backing, with some of Siouxsie's best singing ever. The album is much more melodic, light and inviting than any of the band's others, going so far as to touch on an earlier extra-curricular excursion into jazzy stylings ("Take Me Back") and allowing piano to dominate "Swimming Horses." The Beatles' "Dear Prudence," a big 1983 hit single for the Banshees, also helps leaven the traditional dark intensity.

Smith was subsequently forced to flee, as being a fulltime member of two major groups had taken its toll on his health. Former Clock DVA guitarist John Carruthers replaced him. Already maintaining a rather low 1985 profile, the Banshees were set back a bit further when Siouxsie broke her kneecap during a show.

At a point where some were ready to write the band off as aging, lazy veterans, they came back in early '86 with Tinderbox, one of their strongest LPs in years. Carruthers fits in well, his rich playing stylistically similar to both Smith's and McGeoch's; the rhythm section is as steady as ever. The big plus is punk's original princess herself—Siouxsie's voice has never been so warm and tuneful as it is on tracks like "The Sweetest Chill," "Cannons" and the great single, "Cities in Dust." (Geffen's 12-inch contains a remix, an edit and two non-LP cuts. The album's British CD adds five extra cuts.)

Through the Looking Glass—an eclectic and uneven but generally entertaining album of covers—works best on the numbers which receive the most radical revamps. Crisp hornwork and a no-nonsense vocal performance focus Iggy's "The Passenger"; orchestral lushness and rock power beautify "This Wheel's on Fire." Kraftwerk's spare "Hall of Mirrors" is converted into an alluring dance drone; "Trust in Me," originally sung by a snake in Disney's Jungle Book, becomes a delirious tropical seduction. But seemingly arbitrary—mostly symbolic—choices of oldies by the Doors, Roxy Music, Sparks, John Cale and Television receive little creative comment and fall flat.

Following the Looking Glass sessions, Carruthers left and was replaced by keyboardist/cellist Martin McCarrick and ex-Specimen guitarist Jon Klein. Although Peepshow begins with an incongruous dive into techie dance music (the jokey "Peek-a-Boo"), most of this finely wrought album confidently presents the band's chilly rock persona in a more familiar setting. The haunting "Carousel" draws quietly from the band's own Kurt Weill songbook; "Turn to Stone" heightens the drama with a mild Latin flavor; "The Killing Jar" suggests Echo and the Bunnymen in more than title. In an amusingly camp turn, "Burn-Up" takes an extremely

loose poke at country music, adding a harmonica solo for effect. Overall, the writing could be more durable, but the delicate understatement of Peepshow is reassuring evidence of the group's continued ambition and enthusiasm.

The two Peel Session EPs (later joined as an album and issued in the US on CD and cassette with new artwork as The Peel Sessions) date from November '77 and February '78. Although the later set still finds the group months away from recording its first album, the six songs that later appeared on The Scream (the other two—"Love in a Void" and "Hong Kong Garden"—became singles) receive strong, almost fully developed performances, distinguished by exceptionally good vocals and Kenny Morris' thundering drum anchor.

See also Creatures, Glove. [rnp/i/tr]

SISTER DOUBLE HAPPINESS
See Dicks.

SISTER RAY
Coming to Terms EP (Sad) 1985
Sister Ray Live [tape] (KX4) 1986
Random Violence (Hol. Resonance) 1987
No Way to Express (Resonance) 1989 ●
To Spite My Face (Resonance) 1990 ●

Except for the name, this crude garage band from Youngstown, Ohio owes little to the Velvet Underground. In fact, Sister Ray doesn't seem nearly selfconscious enough about their proletarian retro-rock to want to shoulder such heavy cultural baggage. On Random Violence, guitarists Mark Hanley and Greg Cadman rip up the floorboards with old-fashioned Midwest moxie while Sam D'Angelo has the right idea (if not the right voice) for sneery, snarly punk. (The album contains four tracks from pre-LP singles, including the four-song 7-inch Coming to Terms.)

Dropping Cadman to become a quartet, Sister Ray fills the self-produced No Way to Express with no-nonsense music and all-nonsense lyrics (like "Beef Pud," "Sex," "I Don't Want Your Sex," "Sick of Skulls," etc.). Whether these guys reckon they're capturing the '60s rebel zeitgeist or just don't know any better, such juvenile expressions of hostility just don't cut it. (The CD includes eight tracks from Random Violence.)

Sam D'Angelo and his bass-playing brother Joe get up to their old lyrical tricks on To Spite My Face, penning obvious putdowns ("Piss Off and Die"), obvious grossouts ("Worms," "Doctor #9") and original songs that use classic titles. (They recycled "A Day in the Life" on No Way to Express; this go-round includes "One Step Beyond" and "20th Century Boy.") While the energetic record has blisteringly loud sound and some stupendous Hanley guitar work, a total lack of style and atmosphere dooms Sister Ray's artless simplicity to sub-generic mediocrity. [i]

SISTERS OF MERCY
Alice EP (Brain Eater) 1982
The Reptile House EP (Brain Eater) 1983
Body and Soul EP (Merciful Release) 1984
First and Last and Always (Elektra) 1985 ●

601

Floodland (Elektra) 1987 ●
Dominion EP (nr/Merciful Release) 1988 ●
Vision Thing (Merciful Release-Elektra) 1990 ●

SISTERHOOD
Gift EP (nr/Merciful Release) 1986 ●

GHOST DANCE
River of No Return EP (nr/Karbon) 1986
Heart Full of Soul EP (nr/Karbon) 1986
Stop the World (nr/Chrysalis) 1989 ●

The Sisters of Mercy, an originally all-male Leeds group named after an order of cut-the-crap Catholic nuns, began by playing what they jokingly called heavy metal, which it sort of was; an odd (but prescient) feat, considering that the band's "drummer" was Doktor Avalanche, a rhythm generator. Andrew Eldritch has always been the band's focus: chief lyricist, co-producer of virtually every track (briefly at first with Psychedelic Fur John Ashton, then with Dave Allen of Associates/Cure fame), graphics designer and lead singer, in a deep, aptly gothic voice.

Although their pre-LP body of work amounted to several albums' worth of tracks, only two of the songs ultimately turned up on **First and Last and Always**. As with most of their early work, the 12-inch **Alice** EP (particularly its excellent title track) suffers from sub-par sound. The sound got better and the group's identity began to come into its own by **Reptile House**; with the issue of the brilliant "Temple of Love" single, the Sisters extended their reach to include danceable doom-rock.

The first album finally attained the group's long-sought clarity and sophistication and is nearly sublime in its pristine bleakness. (Well, Side One anyway; the flipside ain't too poor, neither.) Somewhat distanced from the original metal idea, incorporation of power-poppish guitars and dancey rhythms does nothing to place the Sisters within either category; their sonic integrity somehow remains intact. Eldritch's vocals—Jim Morrison meets David Bowie, slowed down to half-speed—are as gloriously gloomy as ever.

While advancing an anti-fashionist philosophy, Eldritch had nonetheless cultivated a posture for the band. A live German bootleg gives some indication of where he's coming from: mainly reworkings of oldies, the Sisters draw on the canons of Dolly Parton and Hot Chocolate as well as the Stooges and Stones. Regrettably, the other members of the group became, as Eldritch (only partly tongue-in-cheek) put it, "distorted little creatures with black teeth . . . set on making a career." Guitarist Wayne Hussey (who'd come to the Sisters from an early edition of Dead or Alive) and bassist Craig Adams formed the pose-heavy Mission (UK). Co-founding guitarist Gary Marx went on to form Ghost Dance with ex-Skeletal Family vocalist Anne-Marie.

There was in fact some legal wrangling over the split, making it uncertain who had the legal rights to the band's name. While this was being sorted out, Eldritch cut the **Gift** EP as the Sisterhood. He doesn't sing on it (presumably also for litigial reasons), but substituted tape collages and speaking by other folks, including Alan Vega. Not too hummable, but effective in conveying some serious concerns, notably the sinister dehumanization inherent in acts of terrorism.

Ex-Legal Weapon/Gun Club bassist Patricia Morri-son, who'd guested on **Gift**, became Eldritch's only fellow Sister (so to speak) when the legal coast was clear. Eldritch had written the material for **First and Last and Always** half with Hussey and half with Marx; could he equal that alone?

He came through on **Floodland** as though he'd been writing every song by himself since the beginning. American producer/songwriter Jim Steinman oversaw two key tracks, "This Corrosion" and "Dominion," and that worked out fine too, yielding great Sisterly Grand Guignol rock. The rest is not as theatrical but, overall, it's a richer LP than the first, the tracks more maturely constructed and the lyrics more engrossing, loaded with nuance in the juxtaposition of terse, concrete observations and poetic, abstract feelings. (The CD adds two.) **Dominion** is an album track, two okay instrumentals and a strong version of Hot Chocolate's "Emma," which the old Sisters used to play onstage.

By **Vision Thing**, Tony James (ex-Generation X/Sigue Sigue Sputnik) had replaced Morrison on bass; the group had added guitarists Andreas Bruhn (who co-wrote three tracks) and Tim Bricheno (ex-All About Eve, a band with ties to the Mission). The full-bodied guitar sound is further augmented by guest axeman John Perry (ex-Only Ones)—but it's not overkill, it's all for the sake of texture and feel. Eldritch displays increased maturity and control even as he delegates more responsibility: the sound is terrific, the music is track-for-track more consistent than before and the lyrics more evocative. Eldritch's almost overwhelming sourness and dark visions are tempered by a mordant wit that cuts too sharply to dismiss, even when it occasionally sounds clever with a capital C. Varied (a couple of ballads and "More," a "Gimme Shelter"-ish collaboration with Jim Steinman) and visceral, engaging on several levels.

[jg]

See also *All About Eve, Gun Club, Legal Weapon, Mission (UK)*.

SKEETERS
See *Fetchin Bones*.

SKELETON CREW
Learn to Talk (Rift) 1984 ●
The Country of Blinds (Rift) 1986 ●

TOM CORA
Live at the Western Front (Ger. Recommended) 1987

Its three-man lineup quickly trimmed to a less-extravagant two, Skeleton Crew regaled audiences in America, Europe and Japan with a unique and functional mix of rhythmically twisted rock, electric and acoustic noise, wittily interpolated taped voice fragments and "fake folk music." Most of the latter had a distinctly East European flavor, though one New York gig consisted entirely of folk music from around the world. Guitarist Fred Frith alternated conventional and homemade guitars, six-string bass, violin and keyboards while occasionally singing in a high-pitched voice. Tom Cora busied himself on cello as well as four-string bass and devices; both worked kickdrums with their feet as their fingers flew. They had enough material for maybe three good albums, but the fine **Learn to Talk** and **Country of Blinds** (on which the Crew expanded to include singer/keyboardist/harpist Zeena Parkins) will serve for posterity. Both albums are available on a single CD. [mf]

See also *Fred Frith*.

SKELETONS

See *Morells*.

SKIDS

Wide Open EP (nr/Virgin) 1978
Scared to Dance (Virgin Int'l) 1979 (Blue Plate) 1991 ●
Days in Europa (nr/Virgin) 1979
The Absolute Game (nr/Virgin) 1980
Joy (nr/Virgin) 1981
Fanfare (nr/Virgin) 1982
Dunfermline [CD] (Virgin) 1987 ●

The Skids' rise and fall revolved around Richard Jobson—singer, writer, creative dilettante. Emerging from Scotland as a promising punkish quartet playing literate and challenging rock music with anthemic proclivities, under Jobson's leadership the Skids became more and more pretentious and less and less a band, finally evaporating into the mist after a miserable fourth LP, recorded as a duo. The first three albums, however, offer a precious body of inspiring and unique rock'n'roll with obvious Scottish blood. In hindsight, it's easy to see what role guitarist Stuart Adamson (now a star in his own right with Big Country) played in defining the Skids' sound.

Wide Open, a four-song 12-inch on red vinyl, contains two inspired successes in "The Saints Are Coming" and "Of One Skin," both of which also appear on the similarly excellent **Scared to Dance**. Using loud guitar and semi-martial drumming for its basis, Jobson's hearty singing sounds like an 18th century general leading his merry troops down from the hills into glorious battle. Two other standouts on the LP ("Into the Valley" and "Hope and Glory") maintain the style but are different enough to keep things exciting. (The US release on Virgin substitutes two tracks and has an altered song order.)

Bill Nelson produced the Skids' (with a new drummer and bassist) second album, **Days in Europa**, but the match-up proved problematic. In polishing and refining the band's sound even a little, he smoothed off the vital edge. There's less gusto in the grooves, although some songs (like "Working for the Yankee Dollar," "Charade" and "Animation") shine through regardless.

While the lineup remained stable for **The Absolute Game**, a new producer took over the helm. Mick Glossop did a good job presenting Jobson's widening vision amidst semi-grandiose arrangements, but the blooming Jobson ego had led the band a long way from its early forthrightness. Parts of **The Absolute Game** are just arty pretense, but the inclusion of substantial, engaging material makes it a reasonable addition to the collection. **Strength Through Joy**, a bonus album of finished studio outtakes, came with early pressings—interesting, but not essential.

After a few more changes in the lineup, only Jobson and bassist-*cum*-multi-instrumentalist Russell Webb remained Skids. Joined by an all-star guest cast of ten,

they made **Joy**, a failed concept album about Scotland. To call it bad is curt but realistic.

Fanfare, released after the sinking group finally (mercifully) ceased, is an excellent compilation of singles and album tracks that serves as the perfect introduction to the Skids' magic. Six years later, the **Dunfermline** CD appeared, reprising **Fanfare** (though deleting one cut) and adding seven more, only one ("Scared to Dance") of which is truly consequential.

Afterlife: Adamson formed Big Country and furthered the Skids' pan-ethnic experimentation in service of arena metal; Jobson, in between albums of pretentious poesy, formed the Armoury Show and briefly followed his former bandmate back into the rock'n'roll fray. [i]

See also *Big Country, Richard Jobson, Zones*.

SKIN

See *Swans*.

SKINNY PUPPY

Remission EP (Can. Nettwerk) 1984 (Nettwerk) 1990 ●
Bites (Can. Nettwerk) 1985 (Nettwerk) 1990 ●
Mind: The Perpetual Intercourse (Nettwerk-Capitol) 1986 ●
Cleanse Fold and Manipulate (Nettwerk-Capitol) 1987 ●
VIVIsectVI (Nettwerk-Capitol) 1988 ●
Rabies (Nettwerk-Capitol) 1989 ●
Twelve Inch Anthology (Can. Nettwerk) 1990 ●
Too Dark Park (Nettwerk-Capitol) 1990 ●

HILT

Call the Ambulance Before I Hurt Myself (Can. Nettwerk) 1989 (Nettwerk) 1990 ●

TEAR GARDEN

Tired Eyes Slowly Burning (Can. Nettwerk) 1987 (Nettwerk) 1990 ●

One of the most interesting bands to come from north of the border in quite a while, Vancouver's Skinny Puppy was formed by multi-instrumentalist cEVIN Key (that's how he spells it) and singer/lyricist Nivek Ogre (Kevin Ogilvie, who is *not* related to Puppy producer Dave Ogilvie). They have produced a large body of dark electronic music, drawing on such obvious influences as Cabaret Voltaire, Chrome, Suicide and Throbbing Gristle. Orchestration is predominantly distorted, the vocals are non-melodic and the group makes very creative use of synths and tapes. The only problem is that Skinny Puppy has often worked harder at creating a mood or a sound than writing songs and has, at times, borrowed just a little too freely from favorite bands.

There isn't much evident progress from **Bites** to **Mind: The Perpetual Intercourse**; both are filled with mildly gloomy but danceable tracks, virtually indistinguishable (instrumentally and vocally) from early Cabaret Voltaire. Production is a little better (at least the sound is a bit clearer) on **Mind**. The **Bites** CD also includes all the cuts from the prior **Remission** EP.

Having appeared on four **Mind** tracks, Dwayne Goettel (electronics/sampling) became a fulltime Puppy and helped open up the sound on **Cleanse Fold and Manipulate**, a finely honed album which, unfortunately, reveals precious few new musical ideas. Likewise, the lyric sheet contains no surprises—just your basic foreboding visions of a skewered world. Skinny Puppy (who are outspoken anti-vivisectionists) may not be quite as evil or demented as they seem to fancy themselves, but **Cleanse Fold and Manipulate** does show promise.

VIVIsectVI brings SP's views on sociopolitical matters (both human and non-human) to the forefront of their work with more conviction than ever. The cover art consists of overlaid (animal?) X-rays; tracks like "Human Disease (S.K.U.M.M.)," "Testure," "Hospital Waste" and others decry brutality against the planet and all of its inhabitants. "VX Gas Attack" (recorded in 1988) goes after Iraq long before George Bush chose up sides. The sound is bigger (especially the percussion), filled in with robotic bass lines and effective sampling.

The Puppies are joined on **Rabies** by Ministry/etc.'s Al Jourgensen, who provides guitar, vocal and production assistance. Although he adds some blood and guts with quasi-metal guitar, it's not enough to distinguish the LP from previous efforts. Each track varies in rhythm and tempo but, with the exception of the two shortest cuts, they all have the same feel. Minor keys, electro-beats, distorted, otherworldly voices (from tapes and band members)—so what else is new?

Too Dark Park continues in much the same mode, this time with a dense, bottom-heavy—almost symphonic—sound. The lyrics offer frightful visions of a diseased, decayed planet (apparently that's what the awful, high-school-space-cadet-style cover art is trying to convey, but the lyrics do a much better job). The overall result is pure claustrophobia—no breathing room.

12 Inch Anthology culls the A- and B-sides from four 12-inches released between 1985 and 1989. Most of the ten tracks (including two versions of "Stairs and Flowers") are non-LP, making **Anthology** important for completists, but it offers nothing out of the ordinary, save for a hint of humor: the old Bugs Bunny cartoon with the evil scientist and the monster is sampled on "Deep Down Trauma Hounds."

The Tear Garden is Key's side project with Edward Ka-Spel of the Legendary Pink Dots. While Ogilvie and Key performed most of the studio chores on **Tired Eyes Slowly Burning**, the latter co-wrote the material with Ka-Spel, creating an album that is much more sparse, clean and melodic than most Puppy work. Ka-Spel's English-accented vocals (he sounds something like Marc Almond or Syd Barrett) and the two sides' obvious musical differences make this an interesting diversion, and one that Skinny Puppy would do well to pursue further on their own.

Following Jourgensen's lead in side-project overkill, Skinny Puppy is also behind Hilt, which includes Alan Nelson (a '70s punk-rock bandmate of Key's and a longtime Puppy associate). With Key handling production (and members of Caterwaul and the Sons of Freedom making guest appearances), Nelson's thrashy contributions make **Call the Ambulance** rock out a bit more, but the basic ingredients of Puppydom are pretty much intact. "Baby Fly Away" has a sung (and almost catchy) melody and "Down on Mommys Farm" moves along at a busy, breakneck tempo; there are moments of lighter, warmer production than SP records. Still, Hilt is no major breakaway. (The CD adds five.) [dgs]

SKIN YARD

Skin Yard (C/Z) 1986 ●
Hallowed Ground (Toxic Shock) 1988
Fist Sized Chunks (Cruz) 1990 ●
1000 Smiling Knuckles (Cruz) 1991 ●

JACK ENDINO

Angle of Attack (Bobok) 1990

Stuck between rock and an art place, this Seattle contingent—led by guitarist Jack Endino, whose pivotal role as the Sub Pop scene's leading producer has overshadowed his musical efforts—has borne the bridesmaid's mantle for years as others have taken turns on the city's Next Big Thing pedestal. It's hard to see why: Skin Yard is every bit as powerful (and dopey and ponderous) as anyone tilling the Northwest passage.

Positively glacial in both temperature and speed, the self-titled debut should appeal to fans of, say, Swans or Saint Vitus, but more ambulatory types may have difficulty weathering a side. (Just for laughs, the CD adds five tracks.) **Hallowed Ground** boasts more structure, and a drummer who can marshal the music along more effectively. Endino's great wall of wail buckles and lurches when pummeled by Daniel House's steamrolling bass. The rough'n'tumble interplay works best on the swirling "In the Blackhouse" and "G.O.D." Elsewhere (and more frustratingly on **Fist Sized Chunks**), singer Ben McMillan bears an uncanny vocal resemblance to Dick Smothers attempting to imitate Jack Bruce—pristine, but laden with melodrama.

Endino's solo outing is far more compelling, with a wide swath of humor ("Naive Bid for HM Stardom #2"), a good understanding of atmospherics ("Create What You Fear") and, most importantly, a strict avoidance of solo guitar excess. [dss]

NICKY SKOPELITIS

See *Material*.

SKUNK

Last American Virgin (Twin/Tone) 1989

Once you get past the initial resemblance to Soul Asylum, this guitar-mad young New Jersey quartet's first record reveals an amazingly diverse blend of styles and influences on their way to becoming a clearly defined Skunk sound. "(There'll Be Other Girls) Hoss," for instance, runs a Duane Allman solo into the middle of storming post-punk with uncommon chords and dangerous time shifts. With a range that covers hardcore to sweet balladry, not everything on **Last American Virgin** works equally well, but it's an enormously impressive and promising debut. [i]

SLAMMIN' WATUSIS

Slammin' Watusis (Epic) 1988 ●
Kings of Noise (Epic) 1989 ●

And slam they do! When this breathless Midwestern quintet thanks the Damned in the liner notes, they aren't kidding: their rip-snorting platter has the careening, free-for-all edge of those zany punk pioneers. It's buzzy fun with a message: "Won't Sell Out" champions integrity, while "It's Alright to Show You CARE" proves the Watusis aren't blank generation poseurs. Special kudos to Fast Frank Raven's sizzlin' sax.

Despite the title, **Kings of Noise** flirts with more mainstream approaches, as bluesy rockers ("She's a Rocker"), towering pop epics ("Hush") and gothic pseudo-metal ("Eight Ball") attempt to broaden the group's appeal. Those tracks are good enough, but they don't provide the sheer exhilaration of the gonzo stuff. Happily, "Madness & Mania" and "Everytown" prove the lads can still get nutso when inclined.   [jy]

See also *Green*.

SLAM SLAM
See *Style Council*.

SLAPP HAPPY
See *Peter Blegvad, Henry Cow*.

SLAUGHTER & THE DOGS
Do It Dog Style (nr/Decca) 1978 (nr/Damaged Goods) 1989
Live Slaughter Rabid Dogs (nr/Rabid) 1979
Live at the Factory (nr/Thrush) 1981
Rabid Dogs (nr/Receiver) 1989
The Slaughterhouse Tapes (nr/Link) 1989

SLAUGHTER
Bite Back (DJM) 1980

This Manchester punk group's classic "Cranked Up Really High" was the first 45 released by that city's pioneering independent label, Rabid Records; Slaughter and the Dogs regularly gigged at London's famed Roxy Club. (They appear in the punk documentary Don Letts filmed there.) About as talented as others in the second tier of '77 punk (Adverts, Eater, Lurkers, etc.), this lot had enough juice to get through a neat string of poppy punk singles and one fine album.

Do It Dog Style, day-glo cover and all, is exciting, energetic rock'n'roll heavily indebted to the New York Dolls and Damned. Besides the band's singles—"Dame to Blame," "Quick Joey Small" (an incisive bubble-gum cover with guest guitar by Mick Ronson) and the pulsating "Where Have All the Boot Boys Gone" (though not "Cranked" or "You're Ready Now")—the album includes de rigueur covers of "I'm Waiting for the Man" (fair) and the Dolls' "Who Are the Mystery Girls" (wonderful), the latter also featuring Ronson. Simple, hooky songwriting plus Wayne Barrett's endearingly zesty vocals helped distinguish the Dogs from lesser genre fare.

The band split, leaving guitarist Mike Rossi, bassist Howard Bates and future Cult axeman Billy Duffy to form the Studio Sweethearts. Slaughter reunited in late '79, replacing Barrett with ex-Nosebleeds shouter Eddie Garrity (aka Ed Banger) in time for **Bite Back**, a nothing bland of guitar-rock noise produced by ex-Mott the Hoople drummer Dale Griffin. Garrity makes a good try, but he simply isn't as effective as Barrett. The group quit for good in '81.

Live at the Factory (later reissued as **Rabid Dogs**) is a posthumously released concert disc (with Barrett) that contains renditions of the band's singles and flip-sides, as well as superior early versions of four **Bite Back** tunes. Unlike the band, however, the sound quality is quite awful. A later three-song EP, mislabeled "Live in 77," documents the same show's encore: "Cranked Up Really High," "Boot Boys" and the boppy "Twist and Turn."

The Slaughterhouse Tapes is a belated scrapbook of outtakes, demos, live tracks and an interview, with studio versions of "Twist and Turn" and "White Light White Heat" to recommend it. The sound quality is flat and weak, but the music's not. It's reassuring to hear such unpretentious sincerity and hooky tunes from a band that's all but forgotten.   [i/gef]

SLAVES
See *F-Word*.

SLAYER
Show No Mercy (Metal Blade) 1983 ●
Hell Awaits (Metal Blade) 1985 ●
Live Undead (Metal Blade) 1985 ●
Reign in Blood (Def Jam-Geffen) 1986 ●
South of Heaven (Def Jam-Geffen) 1988 ●
Seasons in the Abyss (Def American) 1990 ●

"Bones and blood lie on the ground/Rotten limbs lie dead/Decapitated bodies found/On my wall: your head!" Whether you find these lyrics brilliant, hilarious, moronic, repulsive or genuinely evil (or all of the above) is a nearly foolproof indication of how you'll feel about Slayer. A more hateful breed than homeboys Metallica or Megadeth, Slayer was formed in Orange County, California in 1982 from hardcore and metal roots.

Slayer hadn't ventured far from the garage before making its vinyl debut on Metal Blade's **Metal Massacre III** (Metallica and Voivod also debuted on the compilation series), and **Show No Mercy** followed soon after. While rockers from Robert Johnson to Venom had flirted vaguely with the forked one down below, Slayer took the "evil" image to realms of hitherto-unimagined overkill. Musically, the band combined the speed and power of hardcore with ultra-graphic takes on Black Sabbath's lurching riffs and lyrical subject matter. Although the production is hardly pristine, Slayer's first two albums are unquestionably among the most threatening music of their time; in coming years bands would fuse that approach with that of another extremely threatening (if completely different) American band: the Swans. (The **Show No Mercy** CD adds a three-song 1984 EP, **Haunting the Chapel**; the **Live Undead** CD adds several songs but this badly recorded '84 concert document still isn't worth owning.)

The unlikely figure of producer Rick Rubin then entered the picture. Although known at that point only for his pioneering work in rap, Rubin had long been sampling old metal albums, and co-produced Run–DMC's duet with Aerosmith ("Walk This Way"). Applying his lean, less-is-more production technique to Slayer's blistering aural apocalypse, **Reign in Blood** wields a punch, clarity and sense of doom rivalled only by Sabbath and Metallica's best. Variations on the word "death" appear in the lyrics no less than 56 times, and between "Angel of Death" (a revoltingly graphic song about Joseph Mengele) and "Jesus Saves," the album manages to offend all denominations. ("Angel of Death" 's refrain was sampled to staggering effect on Public Enemy's "She Watch Channel Zero?!," arguably the best-ever fusion of rap and metal.) A surgically precise hit-and-run attack that lasts all of 26 minutes, **Reign in Blood** is almost universally regarded as the ultimate speedmetal LP.

Slayer's cover of "In-a-Gadda-Da-Vida" on the **Less Than Zero** soundtrack was an indicator of things to come. Having established a reputation as the fastest and most extreme band in the world, Slayer did the only thing possible: they slowed down. **South of Heaven**'s sound is even leaner, with Dave Lombardo's astonishingly innovative drumming providing an intricate framework for the sharp, angular riffs and piercing leads. Most impressively, this album grooves from end to end, and vocalist/bassist Tom Araya truly comes into his own, lofting haunting melodic refrains as well as his trademark volatile spew. The lyrics confront such real-life topics as mass-murderers, abortion and yet more Nazis. **Seasons in the Abyss** basically fuses its two predecessors, exploring little new territory and even repeating ideas from older songs. That said, it's still a scorcher.

While Slayer is constantly forced into the same we're-not-advocating-it-we're-just-writing-about-it corner that bedevils gangsta rappers, they continue to fill arenas with many of the same kids who idolize an equally threatening cultural icon: Freddy Krueger.   [ja]

SLEEP CHAMBER

Speak in Tongues EP (Inner-X) 1982
Speak in Tongues [tape] (Inner-X) 1982
Sleep Chamber (Inner-X) 1984
Trance [tape] (Inner-X) 1985
Submit to Desire (Inner-X) 1985
Best ov the Rest [tape] (Inner-X) 1986
Sexmagick Ritual (Austrian Trinity) 1987
Babylon EP (Inner-X) 1987
Spellbondage (Inner-X) 1987
Sacred And Surreal (Austrian Trinity) 1988
Sins ov Obsession (Ger. Fünfundvierzig) 1988 ●
Satanic Sanction (It. Musica Maxima Magnetica) 1988 ●
Sharp Spikes & Spurs (Inner-X) 1989
Stop Being Silly, and Go to Sleep [tape] (Inner-X) 1990
Sleep, or Forever Hold Your Piece (Inner-X) 1990 ●
Hotpants & Wet Panties EP (Inner-X) 1990
Sirkle Zero (It. Musica Maxima Magnetica) 1990 φ

If ever there was a group obsessed with obsessions, Sleep Chamber is it. This Boston outfit (basically the warlockish John ZeWizz aided by constantly shifting personnel) makes ritualistic industrial music that works on both a shock imagery level and on a more intellectual erotic/occult plateau. ZeWizz is mind-bogglingly prolific, having independently unleashed (in the US, Germany, Austria and Italy) over ten albums, several EPs and 45s, almost 20 cassette-only releases (only some of which are listed here) and a batch of long-form videos (many of which correspond to the records) in under a decade.

The heavy S&M content and explicit graphics (**Submit to Desire**'s negative-exposure lesbian scene cover is a classic) have gotten Sleep Chamber banned and/or

ignored—which is a shame. Not all that chaotic, the group's unique sound is more trancelike: ZeWizz's ultra-deadpan declarations, minimal electronic pulsebeats, eerie basslines, sparse synth/violin/guitar and occasional samples all serve to induce a heightened mood (sexual or otherwise). The main body of Sleep Chamber's work divides into "song"-oriented albums and dense, mostly instrumental works (**Satanic Sanction**, **Sexmagick Ritual**) reminiscent of Nurse with Wound and Current 93.

Released amid a steady stream of cassettes that began in 1982 and continued unabated through 1985, the eponymous 1984 vinyl album is primitive and distant. **Submit to Desire** is the band's most notorious (and intriguing) record so far, containing the anthemic "Fetish" and "Oral Maze," a tribute to cunnilingus. **Spellbondage** is very similar and almost as good (the prizes being the unnerving "Kiss the Whip" and another erotic epic, "Odoratus Sexualis"), while the four-song **Babylon** EP contains the exhilarating synth-pump of "Babes ov Babylon."

Two years in the making, **Sleep, or Forever Hold Your Piece** beefs up the drum machine and guitar overlays, giving Sleep Chamber a more accessible sound, comparable to Skinny Puppy. A cover of Magazine's "The Light Pours Out of Me" fits smoothly into the record's aesthetic; "A Synthetic Woman" is a remake of a track from **Speak in Tongues**; "A Better Way" rides on a sample from Led Zep's "Immigrant Song." Nine short fragments, called "Verbum Sapienti," fill in the grooves between each track.

The early **Speak in Tongues** tape is quite different from the vinyl EP of the same name. **Sharp Spikes & Spurs**, recorded live in Boston in 1989 (and much longer in its cassette/video form), finds Sleep Chamber exuding songs from the previous albums and the then-unfinished **Sleep**. **Sins ov Obsession** is a compilation of odds and ends, including a remix of the band's smart cover of "Warm Leatherette" and three outtakes: two instrumentals and a naughty ditty, "The Mistress." **Sacred and Surreal** combines three tracks (and an outtake) from **Sleep Chamber** with a **Submit** outtake and two 1983 instrumentals. In a gimmick copied from Throbbing Gristle, **Best ov the Rest** is a limited edition set of twelve otherwise unreleased live tapes packaged in a suitcase.   [gef]

SLICKEE BOYS

Hot and Cool EP (Dacoit) 1976
Separated Vegetables (Dacoit) 1977 (Limp) 1980
Mersey, Mersey Me EP (Limp) 1978
Third EP (Limp) 1979
Here to Stay (Ger. Line) 1982 ●
Cybernetic Dreams of Pi (Twin/Tone) 1983
Uh Oh ... No Breaks! (Twin/Tone) 1985
Fashionably Late (Fr. New Rose) 1988 ●
Live at Last (Giant) 1989 ●

DATE BAIT

I Split on Your Grave (Fr. New Rose) 1990

Led by guitarists Kim Kane and Marshall Keith, Washington, DC's Slickee Boys have been scene stalwarts for a decade and a half; through a series of lineups they developed from a punky rock'n'roll band with an affection for classic English forebears into a far more individualistic and distinctly American band with their own ideas. Featuring the vocal stylings of Martha Hull (replaced by Mark Noone shortly thereafter), the five-song **Hot and Cool** 7-inch antes up one Kane original and covers like "Brand New Cadillac" and the Yardbirds' "Psycho Daisies." **Mersey, Mersey Me** has Kane's inspiring "Put a Bullet Thru the Jukebox" as well as the Slickees' fervent cover of the Grass Roots' "Let's Live for Today." **Third** contains almost all originals, including Noone's brisk "Gotta Tell Me Why."

The German **Here to Stay** compilation recapitulates the contents of those three EPs and a pair of contemporaneous singles, adding the unreleased "Kids" as a bonus. Guileless, earnest, occasionally embarrassing, bizarre in its selection of covers (Talking Heads?), often exciting in its basic enthusiasm, **Here to Stay** is an unprepossessing, entertaining collection of homemade records by a developing band.

On **Cybernetic Dreams of Pi** the Slickee Boys play brawny, good-natured power pop. Songs like "When I Go to the Beach" (jolly surf parody), "Pushin' My Luck" and a breezy version of Status Quo's ancient "Pictures of Matchstick Men" may be a bit glib, but are loads of fun nonetheless. **Uh Oh . . . No Breaks!** finds the quintet plundering their own vaults to re-record their best material. No matter: all thirteen tracks display the same vim and charm of **Cybernetic Dreams** and scads more skill and smarts. Melodies, hooks and energy to spare, variety and clever lyrics—these boys may not be the *dernier mot*, but they *are* worthwhile.

Twelve years on, the Slickee Boys are still going strong, even if they again have to go abroad to get a record released. **Fashionably Late** is another winner—the rock'n'rolling spunk of the original Flamin Groovies crossed with the seasoned flair and solidity of the Fabulous Thunderbirds. Although a bit less varied than usual (Side 1 concentrates on driving music; Side 2 is lighter and more melodic), this is another easy-to-like outing from a natural energy resource that will, thank goodness, never be fashionable.

The Slickee Boys' live LP, recorded in France in mid-'88, finds the quintet energetically running through a retrospective program of going-stale tunes dating as far back as 1979. Tight and proficient but routine-sounding on the first side, things start heating up on the flip ("The Brain That Refused to Die," "When I Go to the Beach," "Jailbait Janet," "This Party Sucks," etc.), which kicks out the jams with fierce dispatch. Kane then left the group.

Date Bait, his new combo, takes two steps from the Slickee Boys' grinning groove, spiking its punch with sparring wah-wahs and snaky leads, emerging as a punkier and more angular purveyor of the same '60s clichés. While unquestionably heartfelt and occasionally compelling, the overall impression is that of a band nurtured on the Cramps' lesser material now flirting goodnaturedly with the trendily popular proto-metal of '70 Detroit. Covers: Troggs, Syndicats, Gary Glitter (?), Dictators . . . Stooges . . .   [i/jy/ab]

See also *Afrika Korps*.

SLICK RICK
The Great Adventures of Slick Rick (Def Jam-Columbia) 1989 ●

Living up to his nickname by having his gold-selling album zip up the charts, "Slick" Ricky Walters' career made an equally precipitous descent the following year, when a shooting incident landed the London-born Bronx MC (onetime partner of Doug E. Fresh) in jail, facing an attempted murder rap. For what it's worth, **The Great Adventures**—superbly co-produced by Jam Master Jay, Hank Shocklee, Eric Sadler and Walters himself—is an exceptionally effective bad-guy record, offering the vulgar misogyny of "Treat Her Like a Prostitute" and similarly reprehensible notions delivered with all the gentle sensitivity of letters to the editor of *Hustler*. To be fair, some of the cliché-light rhymes are fairly innocuous: indeed, the reggae-styled "Hey Young World" takes a warm, positive stand. Rick's delivery—a self-amused singsong that resembles Shock-G of Digital Underground—is also excellent, making both his idiotic mentality and his sorry fate that much more regrettable.   [i]

See also *Doug E. Fresh*.

SLINT
Tweez (Jennifer Hartman) 1989
Spiderland (Touch and Go) 1991 ●

Despite a great name, the indie-scene cred of being a Squirrel Bait offshoot and the sonic potential of Steve Albini as their producer, this Louisville, Kentucky noise-guitar quartet hasn't got much to say for itself on its first record. Employing a nifty variety of great guitar tones (from bandsaw to breezy) and songs cutely named for the members' parents and dog, the brief and roomy **Tweez** consists of simple, repetitive riffs over which more guitar, ambient sounds and a few spoken or shouted words occasionally intrude. Essentially a warm-up that never gets around to anything (let's be fair: "Pat" is *almost* a song), it's hard to imagine why these unformed scraps (recorded in '87) were released, or precisely what merit Slint imagines they have.   [i]

See also *Breeders, Squirrel Bait*.

SLITS
Cut (Antilles) 1979 ●
Retrospective (nr/Y-Rough Trade) 1980
Return of the Giant Slits (nr/CBS) 1981
The Peel Sessions EP (nr/Strange Fruit) 1987
The Peel Sessions (nr/Strange Fruit) 1989 ●

Lurching into existence during the original 1977 explosion of pre-commercial London punk, the all-female Slits wrested the anyone-can-make-a-band-so-why-not-do-it-yourself ethos away from the traditionally no-women-allowed rock brotherhood and unselfconsciously paraded their stunningly amateur rock noise with support from bands like the Clash. While on the road as part of a punk package tour, the Slits were immortalized in all their primitive glory in *The Punk Rock Movie*. Looking back at the group's tentative beginnings now, it's clear that while the Slits may have been truly awful, they weren't much worse than many of their male contemporaries, and undoubtedly a damn sight better and smarter than some.

It was probably fortunate, however, that several years elapsed before the Slits got around to recording a debut album; by the time they reached the studio, Viv

Albertine, Ari Upp and Tessa, joined by drummer Budgie (later of Siouxsie and the Banshees) had become reasonably competent players. Spare and rudimentary, but bursting with novel ideas and rampant originality, **Cut**—brilliantly produced by Dennis Bovell—forges a powerful white-reggae hybrid that serves as a solid underpinning for Ari Upp's wobbly, semi-melodic vocals.

Retrospective (so-called; the LP actually has no title) is a coverless authorized bootleg consisting of early (pre-reggae) studio doodles and live tracks that should really have stayed in the can (or wherever).

Return of the Giant Slits, released originally with a bonus 45 featuring an extra track and an interview with the band (both appended to the cassette version) turned towards African, rather than Jamaican rhythms, and attempted to make the Slits slightly more commercially accessible.

The **Peel Sessions** EP dates from September 1977 and includes "Vindictive" as well as three previews of **Cut** material; the second release combines that session with a second—three more future album tracks, ending up with a bunch of random radio noise—recorded in April '78. The bracing performances have their own scratchy power, but the main value of these recordings is as further proof of the role Bovell (and time and practice) played in making the Slits a really appealing musical proposition. [i]

See also *New Age Steppers, Siouxsie and the Banshees.*

MARC SLOAN

See *Ritual Tension.*

SLOPPY SECONDS

The First Seven Inches EP (Alternative Testicles) 1987
Destroyed (Toxic Shock) 1989

Playing unassailable melody punk (New York Dolls meet the Ramones, c. 1977), this tight and talented Indianapolis junk-culture quartet has the intelligence to sing "I Don't Wanna Be a Homosexual" (the first track on **Destroyed**, and not one of those recycled from the four-song EP) without a trace of homophobia and the psychotronic skill to build a catchy surfpunk song out of 1964's *Horror of Party Beach*. When Sloppy Seconds visit the video store—to borrow dialogue from John Waters' *Female Trouble* or rue the removal of Traci Lords from the porno shelves—these gulcher hounds really get on to something. However, too many of the songs, despite their sturdy musical merits, are just simple Ramones derivatives ("Janie Is a Nazi," "Time Bomb," "I Want 'Em Dead") and don't offer the same degree of fun. [i]

SLOVENLY

After the Original Style (New Alliance) 1985
Thinking of Empire (SST) 1986
Riposte (SST) 1987 ●
We Shoot for the Moon (SST) 1989 ●

Originally known as Slovenly Peter, this San Francisco sextet—whose drummer, Rob Holzman, was a 1981 member of Saccharine Trust—is actually quite fastidious in its work, disregarding conservative musical convention to play down-to-earth semi-avant art-rock.

After the Original Style is crude and cheap-sounding; Steve Anderson's grad-student singing suit the pointy instrumental excursions (slide and regular guitars and keyboards, plus bits of violin, sax and clarinet), but it doesn't make for an especially enticing sonic package.

Better produced and less prone to scurrying too far out on dangerous limbs, **Thinking of Empire** reveals a stronger and more accessible Slovenly proffering weirdly highbrow lyrics that sound like fragments overheard in a pretentious restaurant: "My sly deluded optimism/The oversight of treachery and all its entailments." Or "I feel and find realness amid dysfunctions/ And the poverty of reverting to the norm." What would Little Richard say?

A five-man Slovenly took a wisely tempered path that led to easy appeal on **Riposte**, subtitled (**A Little Resolve**). An involving and invigorating dose of offbeat words and (mostly) melodious guitar music that fully serve each other, the band's easiest-to-like record offers stimulating coffee-house rock that doesn't dare you to hate it.

By **We Shoot for the Moon** (the CD of which adds an unnecessary 20-minute tape-splice song cycle-*cum*-free-form improvisation, "Things Fall Apart"), the quintet is cruising on potent creative juice, smoothly spewing out adventurous and energetic jazz-rock, making ambitious art-noise/found-sound experiments and nicely covering Neil Young's "Don't Cry No Tears" and the Blue Orchids' "A Year with No Head." The lyrics are still pretty annoying, but Slovenly's music—even at its fringiest—is as enjoyable as ever. [i]

SLY & ROBBIE ET AL.

Sly and Robbie Present Taxi (Mango) 1981
The Sixties, Seventies + Eighties=Taxi (Mango) 1981
Raiders of the Lost Dub (Mango) 1981
Crucial Reggae Driven by Sly & Robbie (Mango) 1982 ●
A Dub Experience (Mango) 1985
Reggae Greats (Mango) 1985
Language Barrier (Island) 1985 ●
Taxi Fare (Heartbeat) 1986 ●
Rhythm Killers (Island) 1987 ●
A Dub Extravaganza (nr/CSA) 1987 ●
The Summit (RAS) 1988 ●
Silent Assassin (Island) 1989 ●

TAXI GANG FEATURING SLY AND ROBBIE

The Sting (Moving Target-Celluloid) 1986 ●
Taxi Connection Live in London (Mango) 1986
Electro-Reggae Vol. 1 (Mango) 1986
Two Rhythms Clash (RAS) 1990

SLY DUNBAR

Simple Slyman (nr/Front Line) 1976
Sly, Slick & Wicked (nr/Front Line) 1977
Sly-go-ville (Mango) 1982

The cornerstone of contemporary roots, the nonpareil rhythm section of Sly Dunbar and Robbie Shakespeare has probably played on more reggae records than anyone else. Musical partners for many years beginning in various Jamaican studio bands, the pair founded Taxi—a production company and label that worked with many top Jamaican vocalists, including Gregory Isaacs and Black Uhuru—in the late '70s. The Taxi sound was characterized by Robbie's clean, monolithic bass lines and Sly's tasteful use of syndrums, decorating the reggae backbeat with state-of-the-art zing. The team went on to produce and play with such artists as Grace Jones, Joan Armatrading, Bob Dylan and Ian Dury. Their trademark high-tech style has become familiar (some say tired), but their modern treatments have been a significant factor in reggae's development and popularity.

Many of their own albums are surprisingly unexciting. Sly's solo records sound like dry runs, uneventful groove collections (**Sly-go-ville** does have one Delroy Wilson vocal). **Sixties, Seventies + Eighties** is not much better. Their reworkings of past and present hits (including "El Pussy Cat Ska") demonstrate why they don't sing more often. Worse still is **The Sting**, a collection of uninspired dance tracks and reggaefied versions of "Peter Gunn," "The Entertainer" and "The Good, the Bad and the Ugly," each more dreadful than the last. Their most consistently listenable instrumental LP is probably **The Summit**, where the duo (joined by a piano player) pump out a variety of straightforward yet highly textured rhythms.

Two other releases that bear their names are actually departures, experiments in crossover. **Language Barrier**, a superstar fusion jam produced by Bill Laswell, features everyone from Afrika Bambaataa to Bob Dylan; danceable enough, but hardly related to reggae. **Rhythm Killers** is the same idea, but more successful. Featuring covers of the Ohio Players' "Fire" and the Pointer Sisters' "Yes We Can Can," the LP is an unbroken song cycle, a seamless series of rap, funk, rock and reggae grooves. Again produced by Laswell, the session features Bootsy Collins, Henry Threadgill and many others; Shinehead vocalizes on "Boops! (Here to Go)." It's heavy-bottomed from start to finish, and interesting to boot.

In general, Sly and Robbie are most enjoyable on the various Taxi compilations, which also feature vocals. **Crucial Reggae**, which has the Mighty Diamonds' original "Pass the Kouchie," is not quite as good as **Sly and Robbie Present Taxi**, but both are fine introductions to the duo's playing and the Taxi roster of singers. (The British and American editions of the latter differ slightly.) Similarly, **A Dub Experience** (released in the **Reggae Greats** series) and **Raiders of the Lost Dub** are remix collections of backing tracks originally done for Black Uhuru, Burning Spear, Dennis Brown and others. Both are supersonic headcharges with an eerily haunting edge and should not be missed.

Less crucial are **Taxi Fare**, a largely instrumental collection of B-sides, and **Taxi Connection Live in London**. The concert LP, featuring songs by Ini Kamoze, Yellowman and Half Pint, conveys the drama and full sound of the all-star revue, but the performances are uneven.

Giving heavy bipartite endorsement to the rap-reggae fusion, KRS-One (of Boogie Down Productions) produced **Silent Assassin**, an ambitious undertaking with vocals by KRS, Queen Latifah, Young MC and others. "Dance Hall" is a lively and bouncy single; "Party Together" makes ingenious use of the Turtles' "Happy Together"; Latifah rules the mic on "Woman for the Job"; the CD-only "It's Me" samples Tenor Saw's "Ring the Alarm" with lyrics over a beatbox rhythm. While there are many old-time reggae rhythms

sprinkled and weaved into the songs, one of the album's strongest tracks—"Under Arrest," a heavy story about an innocent man—includes no reggae.

No matter what mega stars and adventurous styles they may dally with, the Riddim Twins always return to their roots. Originally issued on their own Jamaican label, Taxi, **Two Rhythms Clash** is an authentic dancehall collection of singers and rhythms. In addition to some killer instrumentals by the producers themselves, there's music from Half Pint ("Cost of Living"), Little John ("Champion Bubbler") and, most impressively, Third World's Cat Coore ("Mello Cello"). [bk/aw]

SMACK
Ao Vivo No Mosh (Braz. Baratos Afins) 1985

Into a slightly postdated style blended from turn-of-the-decade new wave funk and jagged-edge guitar pop (imagine a jittery Gang of Four singing more melodically in Portuguese) this Brazilian quartet acknowledges its own culture with an occasional tropical dance rhythm. Despite the language barrier, **Ao Vivo No Mosh**'s excitingly adrenalized playing, tuneful vocals and simply effective drumming make it something Northern Hemisphere post-punks would have no trouble understanding. [i]

SMALTS
See *Minny Pops*.

PATTI SMITH
Horses (Arista) 1975 ●
Dream of Life (Arista) 1988 ●
PATTI SMITH GROUP
Radio Ethiopia (Arista) 1976 ●
Easter (Arista) 1978 ●
Wave (Arista) 1979 ●

Chicago native Patti Smith was already an established poet and playwright on the New York underground literary scene when she expanded her repertoire to include rock criticism (her work appeared in *Creem*, *Crawdaddy* and *Rolling Stone*) and public performance, first reading her poetry and then singing with minimalist musical accompaniment provided by Lenny Kaye, veteran rock writer and would-be guitarist. Sharing Tom Verlaine's fascination with 19th-century decadent literati (like Rimbaud, Baudelaire and Verlaine), Smith drifted into the New York rock underground. Backed by Kaye and pianist Richard Sohl, she a striking single ("Piss Factory") on a private label long before such efforts were commonplace. By the time Smith signed to Arista in 1975, Ivan Kral had joined her group, sharing guitar and bass chores with Kaye, and drummer Jay Dee Daugherty had been lured away from Lance Loud's Mumps.

Horses, produced by John Cale, broke a lot of stylistic ground, thanks to Smith's wild singing and disconcerting lyrics, but it also showcased inspired amateurism in the playing and an emotional intensity that recalled the Velvet Underground at its most powerful. Too idiosyncratic to be generally influential, **Horses** is a brilliant explosion of talent by a challenging, unique artist pioneering a sound not yet fashionable or, by general standards, even acceptable.

With **Radio Ethiopia**, the Patti Smith Group made an effort to drop **Horses**' clumsiness in favor of a more refined, organic sound and grander artistic pretensions. Smith plays a lot of guitar on the album, and producer Jack Douglas renders the proceedings with great seriousness. Tracks like "Ask the Angels" and "Pumping (My Heart)" have a nearly routine rock sound, made special largely by Smith's untrained but expressive voice and, of course, her highly individual songwriting.

Bruce Brody replaced Sohl for **Easter**, and Jimmy Iovine produced the album, which contains the band's big hit single, "Because the Night," co-written by Bruce Springsteen. Having proven that they could play as well as most bands, the PSG set out to make something of their sound; Iovine did a fine job. By this point a much more mature singer, Smith sounds confident and striking and the band keeps pace.

After the success of **Easter**, Smith stumbled on **Wave**, evidently the victim of overconfidence. Todd Rundgren's production is inappropriate and Smith's lyrics are preciously self-indulgent; although songs like "Dancing Barefoot" and "Frederick" are accessible and memorable, much of the record is unfocused and halfbaked, frequently insufferable. A misguided cover of the Byrds' "So You Want to Be (A Rock 'n' Roll Star)" rings phony and selfconscious.

Smith then took an extended career breather; she bailed out, moved to Detroit, married ex-MC5/Sonic's Rendezvous Band guitarist Fred Smith and raised a family. The Smiths stayed far from the spotlight for nearly a decade, not releasing a new album until the summer of 1988. Like a lot of cherished fantasies, the reality of **Dream of Life** is a big disappointment. Although Smith reassembled the troops—Daugherty and Sohl (who died of heart failure in June 1990) joined Fred Smith and a few others—and wrote all the songs with her husband (who co-produced with Jimmy Iovine), you can take the record off after the uplifting opener, "People Have the Power." That fine single, which bears a passing resemblance to Starship, is the only sign of life on this bland effort. While an older and wiser Smith does her legend no serious damage here, the optimistic **Dream of Life** adds precious little to it. [i]

SMITHEREENS

Girls About Town EP (D-Tone) 1982
Beauty and Sadness EP (Little Ricky) 1983 (Enigma) 1988 ●
Especially for You (Enigma) 1987 ●
The Smithereens Live EP (Restless) 1987 φ
Green Thoughts (Enigma-Capitol) 1988 ●
11 (Enigma-Capitol) 1989 ●

You like pop music? You want to hear three potential number one singles played as if the future of the world depended on making them impossibly winsome, memorable and rapturous without sacrificing any rock-'n'roll energy or guts? Then get **Beauty and Sadness**, a 12-inch EP by New Jersey's Smithereens. Singer/guitarist Pat DiNizio knows exactly what it takes to write great pop songs, and his three bandmates prove they know what to do with 'em on "Beauty and Sadness," "Some Other Guy" and "Tracey's World." As a bonus, they rock'n'bop on "Much Too Much" and

reprise the title tune as an instrumental. Top-notch. (The 1988 reissue is remixed but otherwise identical.) **Girls About Town** is a charming but rudimentary four-song concept single, including three originals with "girl" in the title and a cover of the Beach Boys' "Girl Don't Tell Me."

After signing to Enigma, the Smithereens wound up getting a song ("Blood and Roses") on a film soundtrack. The picture was a flop, but the tune garnered airplay and brought the Smithereens national attention. Their Don Dixon-produced album, **Especially for You**, benefited from the exposure and momentum, and wound up a successful chart happening. Fortunately, it's also a wonderful record, an unfancy set of memorable songs—"Alone at Midnight," "Strangers When We Meet," "Time and Time Again"—that reflect both DiNizio's sour view of romance and the quartet's sincere fandom for a number of great bands of the '60s—the Beatles, Searchers, Who and Kinks. (Suzanne Vega, with whom DiNizio had worked in an office, guests on "In a Lonely Place.")

The Smithereens was recorded live in New York City in late '86. The six selections (a perfect cover of the Who's "The Seeker" joins the group's own tunes) is flawless, the performance crisp and exciting. Smithereens drummer Dennis Diken's witty and informative liner notes are likewise exemplary.

Green Thoughts (the titular reference is to jealousy) neatly dodges the sophomore jinx, delivering another set of terrific DiNizio songs, played with the same unpretentious guitar-driven excellence. "House We Used to Live In," "Drown in My Own Tears," the countryish "Something New" and the paranoid (and proud of it) title track are especially good, but the entire record is instantly likable and hard to shake. Producer Don Dixon and Del Shannon are among the small group of guests.

Terse, tuneful and towering, **11**—excellently produced by Ed Stasium with unmistakable evidence of his Living Colour work—adds considerable rock crunch to the guitar sound, while allowing DiNizio's vocals (getting attractive support from Belinda Carlisle, the Honeys and others) to float gently above the fray. With typically great songs ("Yesterday Girl," "Baby Be Good," "A Girl Like You"), this contains some of the loudest power pop ever, erasing the Beatlesque genre's nostalgia with fully modern intensity. Neatly balancing the muscle with a quartet of quieter numbers (the baroque, Left Banke-styled "Blue Period," quaintly complete with cello and harpsichord, "Cut Flowers," "Kiss Your Tears Away" and "Maria Elena," an engaging tribute to Buddy Holly's widow), **11** is easily the Smithereens' best album. [i]

See also *Young Fresh Fellows*.

SMITHS

The Smiths (Rough Trade-Sire) 1984 ●
Hatful of Hollow (nr/Rough Trade) 1984 ●
Meat Is Murder (Rough Trade-Sire) 1985 ●
The Queen Is Dead (Rough Trade-Sire) 1986 ●
The World Won't Listen (nr/Rough Trade) 1987 ●
Louder Than Bombs (Rough Trade-Sire) 1987 ●
Strangeways, Here We Come (Rough Trade-Sire) 1987 ●

Rank (Rough Trade-Sire) 1988 ●
The Peel Sessions EP (nr/Strange Fruit) 1988 (Strange
    Fruit-Dutch East India) 1991 ●

You'd be perfectly within your rights to hate the Smiths. No other pop music act since Jonathan Richman ever raised blatant self-absorption to such a high level. The Smiths' ability to turn shameless solipsism into incalculable stardom, however, was their entirely unique accomplishment. With remarkable consistency and integrity, Mancunian singer/lyricist (Stephen) Morrissey and company proudly represent the traditional values of selfishness, self-pity and the unbearable anguish of love. His melancholy romantic sensibility makes Elizabeth Barrett Browning sound like Nelson Algren.

The key to the Smiths' enormous success (in addition to sixteen UK hit singles, all seven of the quartet's albums went Top 10 there) was that the no-nonsense band—under the direction of brilliant guitarist/songwriter Johnny Marr—offset Morrissey's flightiness with bright and catchy music. Supported by a deft rhythm section, Marr's spare, hooky guitar created a seriously compelling underground (i.e., self-defined and uninfluenced by the existing commercial order) pop sound with a simplicity more telling than all of the singer's unwanted confessions.

The Smiths boasts ten near-perfect tunes (the US edition adds an eleventh, "This Charming Man"), over which Morrissey sings—in his wavery, defenseless voice—about the bittersweet agonies of coming out of the closet. He overindulges to the point of sounding almost like a parody of a lounge singer, but goes far enough to make it more daring than forced. With lines alternately funny ("Hand in glove/The sun shines out of our behinds") and clunky ("Does the body rule the mind/Or does the mind rule the body/I dunno"), the album dares you to resist it and then makes it very difficult to do so.

The UK-only **Hatful of Hollow** is a generous sixteen-track collection of singles and radio sessions which doubles **The Smiths**' best cuts and betters its lesser material. It also adds the tremolo-crazy single "How Soon Is Now?," which takes the heaviest art-rock dance groove since U2's "Pride (In the Name of Love)" and throws the lines "I am the son/and the heir/Of a shyness that is criminally vulgar" in its path. Quite a formidable obstacle, but the groove wins out. The Smiths in a nutshell.

Meat Is Murder is both less frilly and less appealing than prior efforts. Morrissey is nearly as dry as the rest of the band, and the whole thing sounds two-dimensional. And while anyone at all disposed towards tragic romanticism can accept some of his indulgences in that direction, who can forgive the vegetarian self-righteousness of the title track? (The US edition adds "How Soon Is Now?" to the program.)

The most dangerous gift for the chronically self-obsessed is a devoted audience, and **The Queen Is Dead** shows just how far Morrissey could take his outrageous neurotic fantasies. "Never Had No One Ever" is ostensibly a paean to virginal celibacy; "Frankly, Mr. Shankly" questions the benefits of stardom; "Bigmouth Strikes Again" (which goes out on a limb to claim " . . . now I know how Joan of Arc felt"), "There Is a Light That Never Goes Out" and "The Boy with the

Thorn in His Side" obliquely address an assortment of insecurities. The band is typically astute and subtle, although Marr's guitar playing takes a relatively inconspicuous lead role.

The World Won't Listen, the Smiths' second compilation, contains singles (A's and B's) and obscurities from 1985-'86, including "That Joke Isn't Funny Anymore," "Shakespeare's Sister," "Shoplifters of the World Unite" and "Panic." The album contains one otherwise-unreleased item, "You Just Haven't Earned It Yet, Baby" (later covered to good effect by Kirsty MacColl on her **Kite** album).

The American-only **Louder Than Bombs** two-record set contains many of the same tracks (deleting those which appeared on **The Queen Is Dead** and two others) as **The World Won't Listen**, adding album tracks and single sides dating as far back as 1983. The album contains such Smiths essentials as "Hand in Glove," "Heaven Knows I'm Miserable Now," "William, It Was Really Nothing" and "Please Please Please Let Me Get What I Want." Five numbers feature ex-Aztec Camera/Bluebells guitarist Craig Gannon, who was briefly a Smith; "Ask" has backing vocals by MacColl. Amazingly, the band's stylistic consistency and musical excellence never falter, leaving the impression that these two dozen songs could have been recorded in one lengthy session. Remarkable.

Marr and Morrissey parted company in late 1987, putting the Smiths to rest with a disappointing final album, **Strangeways, Here We Come**. In spots, Marr's guitar takes a harder tone than ever before. Drummer Mike Joyce and bassist Andy Rourke also come on stronger than usual; strings and saxophone contribute to the crowded melodic din. Morrissey's lyrics are half-baked and more artless than usual, turning especially irksome when they substitute naked anger and disgust ("Paint a Vulgar Picture," "Unhappy Birthday") for clever snideness. The delicate "Girlfriend in a Coma" and the shimmering "Stop Me if You Think You've Heard This One Before" are the album's best tracks, and they aren't exceptional additions to the canon.

The live **Rank** album (recorded in London in October '86) closes the book on the Smiths' extraordinary career with a hastily paced program of songs drawn largely from **The Queen Is Dead** and that year's singles. While the band (augmented by Gannon) sounds great, Morrissey's singing is uneven, and the song selection leaves much to be desired.

The Peel Sessions EP—reissued on cassette and CD in the US with a different cover and a singular title—is a more exciting semi-live souvenir, containing seriously energetic 1983 versions of "What Difference Does It Make," "Handsome Devil" and two others. Unfortunately for fans, "Reel Around the Fountain" is the only cut not already released on **Hatful of Hollow**.

While Marr went off to record with Bryan Ferry, Paul McCartney, Talking Heads, Kirsty MacColl and others before joining the The, Morrissey prudently launched a solo career.   [i]

See also *Morrissey, New Order, The The*.

T.V. SMITH'S EXPLORERS
The Last Words of the Great Explorer (Epic) 1981

T.V. SMITH

Channel 5 (nr/Expulsion) 1983

Tim Smith was the leader of the punk-era Adverts, who clung on long enough to make two albums in the '70s. After they expired, Smith formed the Explorers—originally a trio, but expanded to a five-piece (including an ex-Doctors of Madness bassist) by the time of the album. A far cry from the Adverts' stripped-down guitar drone, **The Last Words** uses synthesizer and slick musicianship to mold an engaging dance program that benefits from Smith's strong voice and inventive songwriting. There are touches of Sparks, the Only Ones, new romantics and others; a great record from a gifted performer.

Channel 5 finds Smith going it alone on a tiny indie label, with only ex-Adverts keyboard player Tim Cross, a bassist and a drum machine helping out. The LP reverts to Smith's earlier no-nonsense, no-frills sound (if not exactly Adverts-styled punk), with his guitar leading the charge. A pleasant little record with strong songs, clever production and Smith's burgeoning social conscience ("On Your Video," "War Fever"). Sharp lyrics make the spry "A Token of My Love" the best track on this entertaining (if sobering) record.   [i/jr]

See also *Adverts*.

SNAKE FARM

See *Plugz*.

SNAKEFINGER

Chewing Hides the Sound (Ralph) 1980
Greener Postures (Ralph) 1981
Manual of Errors (Ralph) 1982 ●
Against the Grain (Ralph) 1983
Snakefinger: The CD Collection [CD] (East Side Digital) 1988 ●

SNAKEFINGER'S VESTAL VIRGINS

Live in Chicago [tape] (Ralph) 1986
Night of Desirable Objects (Ralph) 1986 ●

Although his musical career began in the early '60s and he recorded two albums in the early '70s with pub-rockers Chilli Willi and the Red Hot Peppers, guitarist Phil "Snakefinger" Lithman is best known for his association with the Residents and his resultant Ralph Records solo career. On songs like "Sinister Exaggerator" and their savage reworking of "Satisfaction," Snakefinger's deranged slidework and upside-down solos—trickily playing the wrong notes in the right places—adds an immediately recognizable deviant edge. He died of a heart ailment in July 1987; the work he left behind typifies both imagination and technical excellence.

Snakefinger's solo debut outing was "The Spot," a cutely weird little 1978 single that ended up on **Against the Grain**. But his first two albums pointed up Snakey's major weakness as a solo artist: even with copious musical and technical input from the Residents (who co-wrote and co-produced both), he just isn't that weird (for a Ralph act, that is). Skeletal arrangements and over-reliance on clichéd rhythm-box beats don't help, either. Nonetheless, when released as singles, a track from each—"Man in the Dark Sedan" and Kraftwerk's "The Model"—became modest (but deserving) underground hits.

Around the time of **Greener Postures**, Snakefinger hit the club circuit with a backing band variously known as Bast and the Dead Residents. The presence of steady company (including Beefheart alumnus—and future Pere Ubuite—Eric Drew Feldman) makes **Manual of Errors** an improved listening experience; juxtaposed against (relatively) straight rock backing, Snakefinger's innate weirdness comes across as even more subversive.

Against the Grain is a thoughtful compilation of his Ralph work to date, providing the perfect entry to this unique guitarist's demi-warped world. Everything you'd want to hear is here—from "The Spot" through "Beatnik Party"—plus a great unreleased track, "I Love You Too Much to Respect You."

Armed with his new backing group, the Vestal Virgins (again led by keyboardist Feldman), Snakefinger recorded **Night of Desirable Objects** and the cassette-only **Live in Chicago**, which have no songs in common. The excellently produced record is quite good, comprising complex jazz instrumentals, a believable English fiddle ballad, unadorned a cappella gospel and typical (for Snakey) originals like "There's No Justice in Life" (which might serve as a blueprint for Oingo Boingo) and the organic "I Gave Myself to You." The live tape gives up something in audio sophistication and audio variety, but offers showy and extended new versions of such oldies as "Save Me from Dali," "Beatnik Party," "The Model" and Ennio Morricone's "Magic and Ecstasy."

The posthumous **CD Collection** comprises **Chewing Hides the Sound** (minus two songs), **Greener Postures** (minus one) and both sides of his 1978 single, "The Spot" b/w "Smelly Tongues."   [rnp/i]

See also *Residents*.

SNATCH

See *Judy Nylon*.

SNATCHES OF PINK

Send in the Clowns (Dog Gone) 1987
Dead Men (Dog Gone) 1989 ●

They're from Chapel Hill, North Carolina. Sara Romweber (ex-Let's Active) plays drums. They're on a label run by R.E.M. manager Jefferson Holt. Think you've got 'em pegged? Wrong! This loud trio is a tasty blend of Stones raunch and punk insistence, well-crafted tunes delivered with jackhammer finesse. Singer Andy McMillan is a young good-old-boy with an aching twang stuck in his throat, spurred to spill his guts by Michael Rank's barbed guitars. Need a party starter? Try "Ones with the Black" on **Send in the Clowns**. A good'un.

The Snatches up the grunge level dramatically on **Dead Men**, creating the thrilling sound of chaos in the key of E. With Rank assuming lead vocal duties from Andy McMillan (now the full-fledged bassist), the trio imitates a big-time boogie band debilitated by bad drugs. With urgent performances and a thoroughly muddy mix, the rockers seem like the prelude to world destruction, while the ballads suggest a last desperate cry for help. In other words, highly cool.   [jy]

See also *Let's Active*.

SNEAKERS

Sneakers EP (Carnivorous) 1976
In the Red (Car) 1978

U.S. SECRET SERVICE

U.S. Secret Service EP (Moonlight) 1980

The 7-inch **Sneakers** EP—six quirky power pop originals engineered by Don Dixon—marked the first vinyl appearance of a seminal but little-heard band containing North Carolina rock scene VIPs Chris Stamey, Will Rigby and Mitch Easter (a guest contributor). To get the folklore out of the way, Stamey and Rigby founded the dB's; Stamey went on to a solo career; Dixon became a busy producer and solo artist; Easter is also a well-known producer, fronts Let's Active and operates Mitch's Drive-In Studio, one of the breeding labs for new American rock. The record itself has such lyrically anxious Stamey-penned elements of the legend as "Love's Like a Cuban Crisis," "Condition Red" and "On the Brink."

The 12-inch **In the Red**, made after Stamey had relocated to New York, was really an extended family reunion in which Stamey and Easter combine their Angloid pop/rock with brooding quasi-baroque clavinet, the saunter of a Parisian *boulevardier*, even some avant-gardish desperation, all with an air of sophistication received in innocence. Besides a cover of Bo Diddley's "Roadrunner," the record features five songs penned individually by Stamey ("The Perfect Stranger," "What I Dig") and Easter ("Decline and Fall," "Quelle Folie") and a brief noir instrumental.

Secret Service includes ex-Sneakers bassist Robert Keely plus other North Carolina pals who stayed put. The Dixon-produced record sounds more pro than Sneakers ever did and consequently lacks most of that band's ingratiating twinkiness. The 12-inch includes one goody ("Backseat Sinner") and three other tunes that are only fair. Easter guests on acoustic guitar.   [jg/i]

See also *dB's, Let's Active, Chris Stamey.*

SNEETCHES

Lights Out! with the Sneetches (nr/Kaleidoscope Sounds) 1988 (Alias) 1991 ●
Sometimes That's All We Have (Alias) 1989 ●
Slow (Alias) 1990 ●

This San Francisco-based Anglo-American quartet matches the heady artfulness of the Zombies with the giddy exuberance of the Partridge Family. Demos made as a fledgling three-piece found their way to a UK label, which proudly released the eight songs as **Lights Out!** The rudimentary recording quality only adds to the fresh, unpretentious appeal of beat numbers like "I Need Someone" and pretty, atmospheric tracks like "Lorelei." (The belated—and expanded—American issue adds three songs from a 1989 single, four new tracks and a Raspberries cover recorded in collaboration with Shoes.)

Sometimes That's All We Have delivers what **Lights Out!** only promised. Behind the engaging, sunny choruses and bouncy lovescapes lies a healthy dose of Syd Barrett-sized neuroses. The LP is bursting with brilliant production and arranging ideas: the piano and hand-clap break in the rocking "Nowhere at All," the worn-vinyl intro to "Another Shitty Day," pedal steel and

finger-snapping on "Don't Turn Back," the almost campy ooh-la-la-la's of "In a Perfect Place." The songs by bassist Mike Levy and guitarist Matt Carges float right into your subconscious, and the band displays its muscle when you least expect it.

The addition of a second Englishman, ex-Stingrays bassist Alec Palao (dapper drummer Daniel Swan cut his teeth with the Cortinas), allowed Levy to move to guitar and gave the Sneetches a new forcefulness on the 1989 12-inch "Please Don't Break My Heart," which also includes a fired-up dash through the Monochrome Set's "He's Frank." The comparatively raw nature of that teaser, plus inspired live shows riddled with Buzzcocks or Wire raveups, hardly prepared fans for **Slow**, a sparse, yet somehow dreamier and darker vision of Sneetches-brand popedelia. "Heloise" and "Broke Up in My Hands" are among the bongo-driven favorites on this lovely and unusual no-fixed-decade release.   [sm]

SNIVELLING SHITS

I Can't Come (nr/Damaged Goods) 1989

The hazard of anyone-can-do-it musical movements is what might get dragged in. Fortunately, the jokey Snivelling Shits—two London rock critics (singer Giovanni Dadomo and guitarist Dave Fudger) and such musician friends as Steve Nicol of the Hot Rods and bassist Steve Lillywhite—were sharply skilled at smuttily satirizing the sounds of '77. As anthologized in this archival colored-vinyl document, the band's brief recording career (eight whole tracks, including the viciously irreverent "isgodaman?," originally released on a Beggars Banquet compilation LP under the name Arthur Comics?) included incisive swipes at the Sex Pistols, John Cooper Clarke ("I Wanna Be Your Biro") and the Velvet Underground. That's history for you.
[i]

SIGMUND SNOPEK III

See *Violent Femmes.*

SNUFF

Snuffsaidbutgorblimeyguvstonemeifhedidn'tthrowawobbler-chachachachachachachachachachachachachayou'regoing-homeinacosmicambience (Workers Playtime-Rough Trade) 1990 ●

Taking its cue from such fellow Brits as the UK Subs and such US brethren as the Descendents, Snuff plays speedy raveups bursting with frenetic drumming and sing-songy choruses ("Some-How" and "Not Listening," in particular, stand out) on its marvelously titled debut (generally referred to as **Snuff Said**). Uncluttered production and the band's unbridled enthusiasm and complete lack of pretension (no "society sucks" songs here) do much to move Snuff way ahead in the hardcore sweepstakes. And dig the raucous cover of "Purple Haze," which resourcefully appropriates guest vocals from Jimi himself. The CD adds six cuts to an already worthy collection.   [db]

S.O.A.

No Policy EP (Dischord) 1981

VARIOUS ARTISTS

Four Old 7"s on a 12" (Dischord) 1985

While working at an ice cream parlor in his native Washington DC, the teenage Henry Rollins (né Henry Garfield) got out his aggressions by singing for local hardcore pioneers S.O.A. (State Of Alert), which existed from October 1980 until July 1981, when Rollins joined Black Flag. The group's posthumous 7-inch EP (later reissued on a compilation with three other early Dischord 45s) offers ten very brief blasts of abrasive hardcore, primed by talented guitarist Michael Hampton's wall of riffing and Henry's fierce bark. **No Policy** is a most effective nervous system stimulant, and the songs are over before they have a chance to get tiresome. Years away from developing into his trademark tortured psychological introspections, Rollins' lyrics call for just violence ("Gonna Have to Fight") and explore familiar punk complaints: anti-drugs ("Lost in Space"), anti-romance ("Girl Problems") and anti-police ("Public Defender"). Interestingly, Hampton and post-EP drummer Ivor Hanson wound up working (together) in Alec MacKaye's Faith and Ian MacKaye's Embrace.   [gef]

See also *Henry Rollins*.

SOCIAL DEVIANTS

Ptoof (nr/Underground Impressarios) 1967 (nr/Decca)
    1969 (nr/Psycho) 1983

DEVIANTS

Disposable (nr/Stable) 1968 (Sire-London) 1969
Deviants #3 (Sire-London) 1969 (nr/Transatlantic-
    Demon) 1989
Human Garbage (nr/Psycho) 1984

MICK FARREN & THE DEVIANTS

Screwed Up EP (nr/Stiff) 1977

TWINK

Think Pink (nr/Polydor) 1970
Mr. Rainbow (nr/Twink) 1990

TWINK WITH PLASTICLAND

You Need a Fairy Godmother (Midnight) 1989

PINK FAIRIES

Never Never Land (nr/Polydor) 1971
What a Bunch of Sweeties (nr/Polydor) 1972
Kings of Oblivion (Polydor) 1973
Flashback: Pink Fairies (nr/Polydor) 1975
Live at the Roundhouse (nr/Big Beat) 1982
Kill 'Em & Eat 'Em (nr/Demon) 1987 (Skyclad) 1989 •

VARIOUS ARTISTS

Revelations (Glastonbury Fayre) (nr/Revelation) 1972

Although the two nations' social climates were significantly different, British youth culture of the late '60s provided the same fertile environment for the blending of radical politics, recreational drug use and rock'n'roll as America did. If the Deviants were less incendiary (both in outlook and sound) than the MC5, the loose London group was every bit as subversive, and played a crucial historical role by transmuting into the Pink Fairies and launching the genealogical and stylistic process that, alongside Hawkwind and a few other hippie hordes, kept the countercultural spirit alive in British rock'n'roll through the early '70s. In a very real sense, the Deviants—singly and collectively—played a not insignificant role in godfathering the punk era.

Founded and fronted by singer/writer Mick Farren, the Social Deviants—later just the Deviants—made three bizarre albums in two years before caving in, as such chemically polluted anti-authoritarian enterprises were wont to do, leaving behind such anthems as "Let's Loot the Supermarket," "Slum Lord" (both on the goodnaturedly weird **Disposable**) and "The People Suite" ("We are the people who pervert your children . . . we are beyond rehabilitation . . . ") and "Metamorphosis Exploration" (from the harder-rocking *and* spacier **#3**).

After the Deviants folded in 1969, Farren recorded a solo album with a short-lived Pink Fairies that featured drummer/singer Twink (John Alder, a veteran of the Pretty Things who had a momentary band with Syd Barrett that actually performed in public in 1972). When the first Pink Fairies fell apart, Twink assembled a second version with the other three ex-Deviants and recorded **Never Never Land**, performing two songs from it on an apocalyptic side of **Revelations**, the Glastonbury Fayre festival live triple-album: a terse "Do It" (later covered by Rollins Band) and 20 minutes of "Uncle Harry's Last Freak-Out." Twink then flew the coop, leaving Duncan Sanderson (bass/vocals), Paul Rudolph (guitar/vocals) and Russell Hunter (drums) to carry the Fairies flag.

Despite a fair measure of artistic confusion and the lack of a real vocalist, **What a Bunch of Sweeties** is an offbeat and occasionally exciting, but now totally dated, guitar-rock (plus drum solo) record. Things really got good, however, when Rudolph was replaced by Larry Wallis (a veteran of both the jazzy Blodwyn Pig and the nearly metal UFO). With Wallis singing, playing ingenious guitar and doing nearly all the songwriting (in one case, collaborating with Farren), the resulting **Kings of Oblivion** is absolutely amazing, a thunderous jolt of electricity with monumental melodies and bizarre sideways lyrics like "I Wish I Was a Girl," the drugged-out "When's the Fun Begin?" and "City Kids." Still brilliant sounding after two decades, **Kings** is a widely unknown masterpiece that stands on its own but also set the stage for Motörhead, which Wallis and Hawkwind refugee Lemmy initially formed in 1975.

Flashback is a compilation of studio tracks; although not released until '82, **Live at the Roundhouse** (which includes renditions of "City Kids," "Uncle Harry's Last Freak-Out" and "Waiting for the Man," among others) was recorded in 1975 by a Fairies reunion that featured Twink, Rudolph, Wallis, Hunter and Sanderson.

The Deviants and Pink Fairies names have been used for various one-offs over the years: **Human Garbage**, for instance, is a 1984 live recording by Farren, Wallis and Sanderson. The '77 Mick Farren & the Deviants EP is a raunchy-sounding 7-inch that includes a fun new version of "Let's Loot the Supermarket" and three other tracks, produced by Wallis and performed with Rudolph and guitarist Andy Colqhoun (then of Warsaw Pakt).

Colqhoun and Wallis—as well as Twink, Hunter and Sanderson—are all on the recent Fairies reunion album, **Kill 'Em & Eat 'Em**. Although there's no problem with the straightforward rock music, the quintet's attempt to recapture and reglamorize the past in songs like "Taking LSD" and "White Girls on Amphetamine" is a serious drag.

As one step in Twink's late-'80s reactivation, he cut the inexcusably dull **You Need a Fairy Godmother** mini-album live in a Chicago club, blandly backed—on a far-ranging selection of career oldies (including the Pretty Things' "Alexander," the Pink Fairies' "Do It" and a 1978 solo tune, "Psychedelic Punkaroo") and one terrible newie ("Seize the Time")—by Plasticland. Brad Warner of Dimentia 13 guests on one of the seven tracks; Twink plays drums on another, leaving lead vocals to P-land's Glenn Rehse.   [i]

See also *Bevis Frond, Mick Farren, Hawkwind, Motörhead, Plasticland.*

SOCIAL DISTORTION

Mommy's Little Monster (13th Floor) 1983 (Triple X) 1990 ●
Prison Bound (Restless) 1988 ●
Social Distortion (Epic) 1990 ●
Story of My Life..and other stories EP [CD] (Epic) 1990 ●

Formed around the turn of the decade by singer/guitarist Mike Ness, Social Distortion established itself as a top-rank Southern California punk group in 1982 with the "1945" 45. In an era known more for West Coast hardcore (Black Flag, TSOL, Circle Jerks, Fear), this Fullerton band covered the Stones (the B-side is a *red*-hot "Under My Thumb") and Creedence in their live shows. **Mommy's Little Monster** is a near-perfect example of melodious, riffing punk, just oozing rock-'n'roll suss. From the piledriving opener ("I Just Want to Give You the Creeps") to the swaggering "It Wasn't a Pretty Picture" to "Another State of Mind," **Monster** is a two-guitar punk-pop classic. (The CD adds "Under My Thumb" and another early track.)

Five years later, Social Distortion were among the last practitioners of this form, and **Prison Bound** adds a new twist. Acoustic guitars abound and Ness has obviously been listening to Johnny Cash; at least half of the LP is tinged with a country feel. "Indulgence" and "Like an Outlaw" (with cowboy yells and snapping whips) are like parts of a soundtrack for a heroic but sad Western we'll never see; there's also another Stones cover, "Backstreet Girl." Although **Prison Bound** lacks the all-out dynamics of **Monster** (credit the loss of original bassist Brent Liles and singing drummer Derrick O'Brien), it's still a maturely paced, knowing follow-up, and not just for punks.

With Social Distortion signing to a major label, many might have expected the group's third LP to ease up on the intensity. Instead, the quartet returns to the debut LP's guitar assault on such burners as the opening "So Far Away," and "She's a Knockout." The rootsy leanings of **Prison Bound** are still present, but far more restrained; Johnny Cash's "Ring of Fire" gets a back-to-basics reading. The rhythm section (including ex-Lewd drummer Chris Reece) finally jells, and Dave Jerden's production is just right, a striking backdrop for Ness' great vocals. This veteran punk band not only stuck to its rock'n'roll guns in a higher-stakes outing, but reached a measure of mainstream acceptance in the process. Shocking.

The **Story of My Life** EP combines the single version of that album track with two bracing live cuts ("1945" and "Mommy's Little Monster") and a pair of newly recorded covers: Willie Dixon's "Pretty Thing" and rockabilly legend Ersel Hickey's "Shame on Me."   [jr]

SOFT BOYS

Wading Through a Ventilator EP (nr/Raw) 1978 (nr/De Lorean) 1984 ●
A Can of Bees (nr/Two Crabs) 1979 (nr/Aura) 1980 (nr/Two Crabs) 1984 ●
Underwater Moonlight (nr/Armageddon) 1980 (nr/Glass Fish) 1990 ●
Two Halves for the Price of One (nr/Armageddon) 1981 (nr/Glass Fish) 1990
Invisible Hits (nr/Midnight Music) 1983 ●
Live at the Portland Arms [tape] (nr/Midnight Music) 1983 (nr/Glass Fish) 1987

From Cambridge they came, in 1976: a brilliant songwriter leading a two-guitar band that revered the Byrds, the Beatles and, most of all, Syd Barrett's Pink Floyd. Some called it the start of a psychedelic revival; the Soft Boys' verve and wild-eyed sincerity made it more of a post-psychedelic awakening.

Wading Through a Ventilator shows a promising weirdness that sets it apart from what most everyone else was doing in 1977, but reveals singer/guitarist Robyn Hitchcock as a still-embryonic songwriter. He got off a few good ones on **A Can of Bees**, by which time guitarist Kimberly Rew had joined the band, but the rest declines disappointingly into grating medium-metal power pop. (The album's second reissue is somewhat revised from the original, adding "Anglepoise Lamp" from a 1978 single and other tracks.)

That same year (1979), the Soft Boys recorded an uncharacteristic all-acoustic live tape—later sold by mail to buyers of **Invisible Hits** as **Live at the Portland Arms** and subsequently reissued and generally distributed on disc—which contains the most bizarre assortment of cover versions imaginable. But then cover versions were always one of the band's strong suits, from Hitchcock's intense reading of John Lennon's "Cold Turkey" on **Can of Bees** to his hilarious ravings on **Portland Arms**' "That's When Your Heartaches Begin." Also of historic interest are two Syd Barrett numbers: "Vegetable Man" on a British maxi-single (also included on the Canadian Attic issue of **Underwater Moonlight**) and "Astronomy Domine" on **Two Halves for the Price of One**. That album *is* actually two, with individually titled sides and cover art: **Lope at the Hive** was recorded at London's Hope and Anchor, while **Only the Stones Remain** contains otherwise unreleased oddities mixed in both chronology and quality.

The core of the Soft Boys canon, however, are **Invisible Hits** (actually recorded in '78 and '79) and **Underwater Moonlight**. Some form of insanity prevented the timely release of the former; it shows Hitchcock at his best—maturely immature and crazily serious—as he races from hearty lust ("Let Me Put It Next to You") to vulnerable harangue ("Empty Girl," "Blues in the Dark"). Few other albums capture the humor, pathos, anger and grotesquerie of man/woman so well.

Underwater Moonlight is one of the new wave's finest half-dozen albums and unquestionably its most unjustly underrated one. "I Wanna Destroy You" is a rant against war and intolerance; "Insanely Jealous" builds to a frenzy—twice; "I Got the Hots" contains some of the funniest erotic lines ever written. This album has everything—melody, power, wit, laughs and heart, not to mention a great guitar sound.

Hitchcock remains one of the '80s most unique songwriters. He later reunited with the original Soft Boys rhythm section of Andy Metcalfe (also in the reformed Squeeze) and Morris Windsor for some of his solo recordings; Rew went on to form Katrina and the Waves. [mf]

See also *Robyn Hitchcock, Katrina and the Waves*.

SOFT CELL

Mutant Moments EP (nr/Big Frock) 1980
Non-Stop Erotic Cabaret (Sire) 1981 ●
Non-Stop Ecstatic Dancing EP (Sire) 1982
The Art of Falling Apart (Sire) 1983
Soul Inside EP (Sire) 1983
This Last Night in Sodom (Sire) 1984 ●
The Singles 1981–1985 (nr/Some Bizzare) 1986 ●

Singer Marc Almond and keyboardist David Ball performed a minor miracle in 1981, taking an obscure soul song and turning it into a most atypical synthesizer tune, coming up in the process with a worldwide smash hit that rode *Billboard*'s chart for almost a year. "Tainted Love" (written by Ed Cobb but known in its version by Gloria Jones) is as passionate and desperately sleazy as Kraftwerk is cool and clean. The Almond/Ball originals on **Non-Stop Erotic Cabaret** don't always cut so deeply, but all offer nice, decadent fun. Among them: "Sex Dwarf," highlighted by a nagging synthesizer riff, and "Say Hello, Wave Goodbye," blatant though stirring sentimentality. Almond's breathy, insinuating vocals and Ball's surprisingly varied electronic and acoustic keyboards (kudos to producer Mike Thorne) never stand pat.

Non-Stop Ecstatic Dancing, half an hour (six tracks) of dance mixes, intends primarily to divert and manages to overcome its basic filler role. Highlights include a languid version of "Where Did Our Love Go?" and the unforgettably neurotic "Insecure . . . Me?"

It's too bad Almond and Ball didn't part ways before descending into the embarrassing self-parody of **The Art of Falling Apart**. With Ball's keyboards growing progressively cooler, Almond tries ever more desperately to invoke a sleazy atmosphere and just ends up sounding silly. The nadir—indeed, the worst Soft Cell effort of all time—is the pitiful ten-minute Jimi Hendrix medley of "Hey Joe," "Purple Haze" and "Voodoo Chile (Slight Return)" that comes on a bonus 12-inch 45. It's like a five-year-old trying to read Shakespeare. **Soul Inside** is a collection of odds and ends, including a version of "You Only Live Twice (007 Theme)," two remixes and a live radio session. **This Last Night in Sodom** contains further fruitless flailing, as titles like "The Best Way to Kill" and "Mr. Self Destruct" attest. [jy]

See also *Marc Almond, Dave Ball*.

SOLDIER STRING QUARTET

See *Elliott Sharp*.

SOLOMON GRUNDY

See *Screaming Trees*.

JIMMY SOMERVILLE

See *Bronski Beat, Communards*.

SOMETHING HAPPENS

I Know Ray Harman EP (nr/Virgin) 1988
Been There, Seen That, Done That (nr/Virgin) 1988 ●
Stuck Together with God's Glue (Charisma) 1990 φ

This Dublin quartet plays straightforward guitar-based pop-rock, refreshingly free of the '60s trappings or indie-dance copycatism of many likeminded UK and Irish contemporaries.

Arguments over the mix on the Tommy Erdelyi-produced debut album precipitated the release of a six-song live set recorded before a crowd of the converted. As it previews a couple of songs from the then-imminent **Been There**, the EP (named for the group's lead guitarist) is not mandatory, but it is fun.

Been There was finally released at the end of '88, remixed and containing two Vic Maile-produced tracks in place of three deletions. Unspectacularly pleasant, it announces a band that could well become a huge commercial property. The fact that Tom Dunne's vocals often bear an uncanny resemblance to Bono doesn't hurt the group's chances.

Stuck Together with God's Glue is much more assured, boasting a varied selection of songs and tougher production by Ed Stasium. With a catchy chorus and comically awkward syntax, "Hello, Hello, Hello, Hello, Hello, (Petrol)" is a certified shoulda-been hit; the sumptuously melancholy "Kill the Roses" takes things in a more textured, moody direction. Good show. [db]

SONIC'S RENDEZVOUS BAND/ DESTROY ALL MONSTERS

Ron Asheton/Sonic's Rendezvous Band (Fr. Revenge) 1987

SONIC'S RENDEZVOUS BAND

Strikes Like Lightning (Black Adder) 1989

SCOTT MORGAN BAND

Rock Action (Fr. Revenge) 1990

By virtue of who they were, Sonic's Rendezvous were legendary long before anyone outside their hometown ever heard them, The veritable Detroit-scene supergroup consisted of Scott Morgan (ex-Rationals), Gary Rasmussen (the Up), Scott Asheton (Stooges) and Fred Sonic Smith (MC5). Officially, the band's recorded output consists of a single song, the long-rare mono/stereo 45 "City Slang." Unofficially, they made a pointed resurgence in the mid-'80s Michigan-worship years, first on a 1985 self-titled bootleg (a lo-fi dub of the original 45, followed by lower-fi live cuts that fail to disguise the fact that, yeah, SRB *were* worth the hoopla all along).

The split LP with Ron Asheton's Destroy All Monsters again resurrects "City Slang" from the 45 (also reissued elsewhere on a facsimile bootleg single), but with clean, sharp sound, as mean as the original. The side also includes a studio instrumental that was obviously intended for vocals and suffers for their absence, and a pair of live tunes on a par with the prior LP. An '89 bootleg (**Strikes Like Lightning**) culled from numerous '78-'79 gigs varies in sound quality, but the songs and performances are inarguably the best yet, with a fury and interplay only hinted at on the earlier material.

Nearly a decade later, Scott Morgan resurfaced with a somewhat well-received local 45 of Seger/Springsteen commercialism, on which the band consists of SRB minus Sonic (by then Mr. Patti Smith, with his wife's awful comeback LP in the offing). The subsequent **Rock Action** follows tradition by beginning with the 45 A-side (closing with its flip), spending the time between touring through Detroit soul of the sort associated with Mitch Ryder. Thankfully, flamboyant hack vocalist Kathy Deschaine (the fourth bandmember, the fifth wheel) is relegated to a minor role; nevertheless, the LP elicits a dulled demo feel, lacking the kinetic electricity conjured by the former band even on the crummiest archival bootlegs. [ab]

SONIC YOUTH
Sonic Youth EP (Neutral) 1982 (SST) 1987 ●
Confusion Is Sex (Neutral) 1983 (SST) 1987 ●
Kill Yr. Idols EP (Ger. Zensor) 1983
Sonic Death: Sonic Youth Live [tape] (Ecstatic Peace) 1984 (SST) 1988 φ
Bad Moon Rising (Homestead) 1985 ●
Death Valley 69 EP (Homestead) 1985
EVOL (SST) 1986 ●
Sister (SST) 1987 ●
Master Dik EP (SST) 1988 ●
Daydream Nation (Blast First-Enigma) 1988 ●
Daydream Nation EP [CD] (Blast First-Enigma) 1988 ●
Goo (DGC) 1990 ●

LEE RANALDO
From Here to Infinity (SST) 1987 ●

CICCONE YOUTH
The Whitey Album EP [CD] (Blast First) 1988 ●
The Whitey Album (Blast First) 1989 ●

JIM SAUTER, DON DIETRICK, THURSTON MOORE
Barefoot in the Head (Forced Exposure) 1990

BEWITCHED
Brain Eater (No. 6) 1990

Latter-day rock'n'roll revolutionaries have shown a marked tendency towards swift burnout. They reveal their raw vision to the world, but the world, being the philistine place that it is, turns away; the musicians move on. Sonic Youth, unlike so many of the noise bands that formed in New York at the beginning of the '80s, has had the fortitude to hold on long enough to develop its ideas well beyond the original stances. As a result, the quartet has gotten better and better, moving

from cacophony to chilling beauty, arising from the underground to become its emissaries to the real rock world.

The five-song debut EP proves that a reliance on artsy posturing can get boring in an awful hurry. Rigidly defined beats (by original drummer Richard Edson, simultaneously a trumpet player in Konk and later strictly an actor) and disembodied poetic vocals (alternately by guitarist Thurston Moore and bassist Kim Gordon) eviscerate Sonic Youth's principal weapon—jangling, ringing, dissonant guitar noise. This disc is no fun.

With Bob Bert taking over the drum duties, **Confusion Is Sex** gives the guitars freer rein, and the result is a happily anarchic and intense mess. The tortuous "(She's in a) Bad Mood" captures its subject matter like few songs before it, and a crude cover of Iggy's "I Wanna Be Your Dog" proves that the artistes can rock. The record alternates between pulse and drone; its quiet spaces quickly get cluttered with weirdly tuned percussive guitars, often bowed or struck with drumsticks.

Kill Yr. Idols reprises two tunes from **Confusion Is Sex** and adds three similarly twisted tracks. Like **Confusion**, the EP is dark and haunting, particularly on "Early American," where the guitars ring like macabre bells.

Sonic Death, a live compilation of the band's formative years (1981 to '83), offers little song structure, primitive playing, poor sound quality and worse editing. In other words, it effectively documents the noisy breech birth of a legend.

Bad Moon Rising brings Sonic Youth into the light, and shows an enormous developmental leap. The sounds are still harsh—feedback, distortion and dissonance—but the group uses them to create a variety of effects and moods. Like many records made in 1984 and 1985, the album is a statement about America and, while avoiding the ennoblement of the mythological common man, does capture both the beauty and creepiness of the frontier west of the Bowery. The song "Death Valley 69," written and recorded with Lydia Lunch, sounds like X on a bad trip, and puts the band's screaming guitars into a straight rocker. The rest of the disc is more painterly and less propulsive; Sonic Youth gets its explosiveness from the quiet sections, where interwoven guitar parts hint at jarring disorder. The **Death Valley 69** EP, its title track a reprise from the LP, also culls one track each from the previous three discs, adding the heretofore unissued anarchy of "Satan Is Boring."

Steve Shelley then replaced Bert, who went on to play with Pussy Galore and later formed a band called Bewitched. The material on **EVOL** is presented in more basic song structures, giving Sonic Youth more accessibility and versatility than ever before without diluting its brutal strength one iota. The band's command of its resources is so great that rackety shards of atonal guitars can sound almost catchy on tracks like "Green Light." Meanwhile, "Shadow of a Doubt" and the end of "Expressway to Yr Skull" (listed on the back cover as "Madonna, Sean and Me") both take raw, jagged sounds and blend them into a peaceful stillness. **EVOL** is a very impressive album wherein Sonic Youth makes the step from great noise band to great band. The CD adds a cover of Kim Fowley's "Bubblegum" that also appears on the three-song 12-inch of **EVOL**'s "Starpower."

EVOL was a tough act to follow, but **Sister** proves well up to the task. Reportedly recorded on all vacuum tube equipment (mixing board and all), the album has a very warm, immediate feel, and the tonalities aren't so strange as to alienate the general public. Not that it's all polished up—far from it—but the emphasis is more on rocking out than on demonic guitar tunings or defining East Village art. Sonic Youth is simply one of the very best American bands of the decade. The CD adds the powerful and haunted "Master-Dik," with guest guitar licks by J. Mascis of Dinosaur Jr.

"Master-Dik" was subsequently recycled as the title track of a bizarre 12-inch that calls itself a single but contains (on the flip) a straight cover of "Beat on the Brat," an impromptu live swipe at "Ticket to Ride," radio interview bites and assorted musical and found-sound rubbish, all haphazardly strung together in a day-in-the-life side of Sonic stupidity.

The productive stirrings of artistic self-discovery on **EVOL** and **Sister** flowered on the double-album **Daydream Nation**, a full-blown and carefully sustained masterpiece that funnels all of the band's past textural explorations and instrumental resources into a staggeringly original and accessible record charged with cultural atmosphere. While putting hummable tunes and easily grasped guitar hooks into songs like "Teen Age Riot," "Silver Rocket," "Total Trash" and "Kissability," the group continues to throw off electric sparks in frenzies of urban noise. **Daydream Nation** is a completely satisfying blend of invitation and threat. (The CD EP is merely a four-song sampler of the LP that edits "Teen Age Riot" down from its original length.)

Finally signing to a major label, the underground superstars couldn't avoid the predictable backlash, but there's nothing about **Goo** that suggests sellout. (Indeed, the use of a typically crude and stupid Raymond Pettibon cover is a clear and pretentious nose-thumb at the overground.) Unfortunately, there's also very little about the record that suggests effort, imagination or inspiration. In a pre-emptive strike at the critics, the quartet seemingly overcompensated, removing most of the previous album's progress in favor of self-amused we-can-get-away-with-it nonsense, flat material and lazy playing.

Thurston's "Dirty Boots" is a dandy opener, but sounds like a **Daydream Nation** leftover. Things run straight downhill from there. In "Tunic," Gordon inexplicably sings lyrics about Karen Carpenter that are only five or six years past their potential morbid kitsch prime; in "Kool Thing," she numbly repeats 1990's most overused catchphrase—"I don't think so"—a bunch of times before holding an absurd aren't-we-totally-def conversation with Public Enemy leader Chuck D. **Goo** repeatedly strains to be the coolest shit and fails miserably.

Guitarist Lee Ranaldo's solo outing, **From Here to Infinity** is a challenging adventure in listening. Sonically akin to **Metal Machine Music**, with plenty of fuzzy drones and repetitious sounds of various descriptions, each short track (most under a minute) ends with a lock groove (the cassette version achieves the same effect by inserting extended pauses between numbers), so they can actually be very long tracks if you want. The sleeve explains that the record, pressed on grey marble vinyl, is a variable-speed 45. Difficult but rewarding.

Ciccone Youth, Sonic Youth's parodic side project with Mike Watt of fIREHOSE, issued a three-song single in 1986, a four-song sampler CD and, after numerous delays, a full LP in January 1989. Besides twigging Madonna in covers of "Burnin' Up" (included only in its pre-single Watt solo demo form) and the 45's "Into the Groove(y)," and offering an obnoxious version of Robert Palmer's "Addicted to Love," **The Whitey Album**—a blithering collection of pointless self-indulgent instrumentals, fake hip-hop and spoken/manipulated ephemera—has absolutely nothing to recommend it.

Barefoot in the Head, Moore's record with the two-man sax section of a band called Borbetomagus, takes an absolutely unendurable swipe at improvised free jazz, resulting in a crude and cacophonous collection of bleats, honks and guitar slashes that seems faintly funny when it isn't simply ear-splitting. [jl/dgs/i]

See also *Gut Bank, Konk, Lydia Lunch, Pussy Galore*.

SONS OF FREEDOM

Sons of Freedom (Slash) 1988 ●

From Vancouver with power: this exciting quartet plays bracing, thoughtful hard-rock with strong melodies and a dynamic rhythmic foundation. Not as metallic or intense as labelmates Faith No More, the Sons concentrate on good songs and hypnotic funk grooves that occasionally (mis)lead them into resembling the Cult. A fury of surging runs and lunging chords, bassist Don Binns dominates the sound, giving singer Jim Newton and Don Harrison—busy building an impressive dual-guitar forcefield—a real run for their place in the mix. Although the album's power (captured cleanly by producer Matt Wallace) makes it consistently striking, **Sons of Freedom**'s best songs (e.g., "Mona Lisa," "The Criminal" and "Fuck the System," whose melody is very nearly a quote from *Hair*'s "Aquarius") are totally cool. [i]

SOUL ASYLUM

Say What You Will ... (Twin/Tone) 1984
Made to Be Broken (Twin/Tone) 1986 ●
Time's Incinerator [tape] (Twin/Tone) 1986
While You Were Out (Twin/Tone) 1986 ●
Hang Time (Twin/Tone-A&M) 1988 ●
Clam Dip & Other Delights EP (nr/What Goes On) 1988
 (Twin/Tone) 1989 ●
Say What You Will, Clarence ... Karl Sold the Truck [CD]
 (Twin/Tone) 1989 ●
Soul Asylum and the Horse They Rode in On
 (Twin/Tone-A&M) 1990 ●

Emerging from the Minneapolis hardcore circuit (where the young quartet was originally known as Loud Fast Rules), Soul Asylum quickly set about earning a spot in the same league as that city's two leading ex-punk outfits, the Replacements and Hüsker Dü. **Say What You Will**, produced by the latter's Bob Mould, ends their punk phase and introduces an awareness of country music and a nascent aptitude for difficult rhythms and deft vocal interplay. Dave Pirner's hoarse singing leaves something to be desired here, but the indication that he possesses real songwriting talent—

especially in the wry, often self-deprecatingly depressive lyrics—is encouraging. (In 1989, **Say What You Will** was reissued on CD with the inclusion of five tracks recorded for, but left off, the original album. What's more, the version of "Black and Blue" on **Clarence** is not from the LP, but a neat 1981 memento of Loud Fast Rules' first session.)

The confident, emotionally compressed sound and material on **Made to Be Broken** is light years better: rich dual vocals by guitarists Pirner and Dan Murphy, supported by young new arrival Grant Young's precise, varied drumming and a wash of loudly but subtly interwoven guitars make the tuneful power of "Tied to the Tracks," "Ship of Fools," the countryish "Made to Be Broken" and "New Feelings" staggeringly original and memorable. Additionally, "Never Really Been" reveals the group's ability to convey the same wit and energy on touching (mostly) acoustic guitar ballads; Murphy displays his own songwriting ability on "Can't Go Back." The onomatopoetic "Whoa!" explodes in a breathtaking syncopated fury of incoherent shrieking and stands as one of Soul Asylum's funniest, most accomplished adventures. An astonishing, original and durable record that states the band's case most convincingly.

One highlight of **Time's Incinerator**—a tape-only compilation of 1980-'86 outtakes (including the first album's five missing songs), covers, concert cuts and other nonsense—is a live version of James Brown's "Hot Pants" sung by bassist Karl Mueller. Otherwise, there are a few ace studio tracks, a lot of justifiable discards and some wild bits of onstage craziness. Unessential, but a worthwhile place-keeper between albums.

While You Were Out (Sides 5 and 6 in the band's consecutively numbered oeuvre) is a disappointment that doesn't do the songs adequate justice. Chris Osgood's production is messy and uneven; the performances sound hurried and the arrangements unfinished. As evidenced on "Carry On," "No Man's Land," "The Judge," "Closer to the Stars"—complex songs filled with melody, energy and intelligence—Pirner's writing (not to mention vocals) just keeps getting better. Murphy's "Miracle Mile" is also a highlight, but the delivery here lacks the clarity and elaboration the material deserves.

A pact between A&M and Twin/Tone landed the band in a New York studio, making **Hang Time** with the production team of Ed Stasium (Ramones, Julian Cope, Living Colour, etc.) and Lenny Kaye (James, Suzanne Vega). Bolstered by unprecedented sonic excellence and the luxury of time to flesh out and refine their material, Soul Asylum entered the big leagues with a riff-rocking bang. The first two tracks—"Down on Up to Me" and "Little Too Clean"—surprisingly suggest a regression to the '70s chart fare of their youth, but the record abruptly rights itself with the throaty roar of "Sometime to Return" and doesn't again falter. Highlights of a consistently impressive platter are "Ode," "Marionette," Murphy's "Cartoon" (containing such typically succinct lines as "if you're cryin' in your beer you're gonna drown"), the poignant "Endless Farewell" (a wistful ballad on which Pirner plays piano) and the explosively Clashlike "Standing in the Doorway." (That song's 12-inch is worth seeking out for the "James at 16" live medley on the flip: thirteen diverse covers in just over eleven minutes.) The **Hang Time** CD adds "Put the Bone In," a rude canine double entendre which the group learned, amazingly enough, from the B-side of Terry Jacks' 1974 MOR hit, "Seasons in the Sun."

The six-song **Clam Dip** EP—whose cover shot of a nude Mueller up to his waist in party food spoofs an old Herb Alpert album sleeve—was scheduled to precede **Hang Time** (hence the latter's numbering as sides 9 and 10), but didn't. The enjoyable mixture of cover versions (Janis Joplin-by-way-of-Slade's "Move Over," Foreigner's "Juke Box Hero" and "Chains," a terrific Minneapolis new wave obscurity) and originals (including a topical labor song, "P-9," written and first recorded to benefit a striking local) first surfaced on an English label. By the time it was released Stateside, two of the covers ("Chains" remains) were removed, replaced by two weird SA tunes: the horror-movie "Artificial Heart" and a raving funkfest, "Take It to the Groove."

Steve Jordan (the drummer who collaborated on Keith Richards' solo LP) produced **And the Horse They Rode in On**, exchanging **Hang Time**'s sharply focused studio finesse for a rawer, live sound. (Jordan, ironically, isn't as considerate of Young's superb playing as Stasium and Kaye were, and the album's drum tone is rather tin-canny.) Delicate applications of guitar effects, melodica (on Murphy's chantey-like "Gullible's Travels"), even choral bells (on Pirner's affecting piano lament, the romantic "We 3") give the honest performances extra appeal; the brilliant and varied material does the rest. With a chanted refrain and anti-suicide lyrics that acknowledge Cheap Trick, "Easy Street" is an instant SA anthem; "Veil of Tears," "Be on Your Way," "Grounded" and "Nice Guys (Don't Get Paid)," a bizarre but moral crime fantasy, are all further proof of Pirner's unpretentious songwriting genius and the band's remarkable ability to roar and sigh at the same time. A tremendous record. (Collectors' note: tape, vinyl and CD all have related but different cover art.) [i]

SOULED AMERICAN

Fe (Rough Trade) 1988 ●
Flubber (Rough Trade) 1989 ●
Around the Horn (Rough Trade) 1990 ●

Heavy and heartfelt country'n'strychnine from this hard-touring Chicago quartet. Closer to Neil and Graham than Lefty and George, Souled American specializes in low-key grooves that gurgle and bounce with songwriter Joe Adducci's reggae-style lead bass, Jamey Barnard's slapping New Orleans-style drums and Scott Tuma's shimmering rhythm guitar, which sounds like pedal steel but isn't.

Sporting the heaviest drawls in all god's country, Adducci and co-writer/vocalist Chris Grigoroff pen original material that sounds like long-lost traditional laments. The first side of **Fe** (group code for "feel") focuses on an imagined rural present, while the flip dishes out a world of hurt. The group masterfully cranks up to speed on **Flubber**, adding a swampy undercurrent to a thick mix of inscrutable deep-South fantasizing. "Marleyphine Hank" swirls country into dub, while covers of John Fahey ("Cupa Cowfee") and, on the

CD, John Prine ("The Torch Singer") lend serious roots credence, if any were needed.

Souled Am's guitarists evoke lazy New Orleans brass-band grooves on the more musically ambitious **Around the Horn**. While the album includes a song written by Joe's C&W-singing mom Vicki ("I Keep Holding Back the Tears"), "Six Feet of Snow," by Lowell George and Keith Godchaux, heads the band in a southerly psychedelic direction. [rg]

SOULSONIC FORCE

See *Afrika Bambaataa*.

SOUL II SOUL

Club Classics Vol. One (nr/10-Virgin) 1988 ●
Keep on Movin' (10-Virgin) 1988 ●
Vol II-1990-A New Decade (10-Virgin) 1990 ●

CARON WHEELER

UK Blak (EMI) 1990 ●

"A happy face, a thumpin' bass, for a lovin' race." Such is the credo of Jazzie B (Beresford Romeo), radio/club-DJ-turned-record-producer-*cum*-cultural entrepreneur. Never actually a group, Soul II Soul began as a floating dance happening in East London, where DJ Jazzie B played an eclectic mix of the music he loved best—hip-hop, Philly soul, dub, house and more. In the studio with collaborator/programmer Nellee Hooper and a host of players and singers, he created a sound and a shuffling beat that mixed elements of all these styles; the resultant singles, including the undeniable "Keep on Movin'," caused enough of a stir in England that it was not too much of a stretch to entitle the album that compiled them **Club Classics Vol. One**. (Lacking that buzz in the States, the album was released here as **Keep on Movin'**.)

Given the hype that accompanied its trans-Atlantic arrival, the album is shockingly spotty: one cut is repeated twice in a row, the second time featuring an execrable Jazzie B rap. ("Conscious people tend to dance" he portentously intones in a James Earl Jones-goes-dread voice.) The wonderful "Back to Life" is included only in an a cappella version. Still, the overall sound of Soul II Soul, while hardly original, is quite refreshing, a soulful and equally au courant alternative to hip-hop.

In the meantime, singer Caron Wheeler, the featured vocalist on "Keep on Movin' " and "Back to Life," announced that she was embarking on a solo career. Some expressed doubt that Jazzie B could put over Soul II Soul without Wheeler's exceptionally warm and clear voice. But while she is missed, **Vol. II-1990-A New Decade** is actually a more consistent and cohesive album than the first. Claiming no instant classics but offering no filler either, it's enjoyable from drop to stop, and Jazzie B keeps his little happy raps bearably brief, couching them inside songs rather than making entire cuts of them.

Wheeler's solo debut, **UK Blak**, presents yet another mixed bag. Boasting nine (!) different co-producers, the album is eminently listenable—a groove that hardly ever lets up—but very few songs make a real strong impression. The title cut is great, tackling the ambitious topic of cultural assimilation, and Wheeler's

songwriter paints her as intelligent and goodhearted. But talk about mixed messages—one minute she's staking feminist ground for her autonomous existence, and the next she's telling a lover that "I am honored to be your lady." Please, nobody introduce her to Stephen Stills. [gk]

SOUND

Jeopardy (nr/Korova) 1980
Live Instinct EP (Hol. WEA) 1981
From the Lions Mouth (nr/Korova) 1981
All Fall Down (nr/Korova) 1982
Shock of Daylight EP (A&M) 1984
Heads and Hearts (nr/Statik) 1985
In the Hothouse (nr/Statik) 1985
Heads and Hearts and Hothouse and Shock of Daylight [CD] (nr/Statik) 1986 ●
Thunder Up (Can. Nettwerk) 1987 ●

ADRIAN BORLAND AND THE CITIZENS

Alexandria (Bel. Play It Again Sam) 1989

It's hard to understand why this London quartet never found commercial success. At their best, the Sound's excellent neo-pop bears favorable comparison to the Psychedelic Furs and Echo and the Bunnymen. **Jeopardy** has a stark, beautiful quality, with the material given direct exposure rather than a production bath. Adrian Borland's vocals are sincere and gripping; the musical attack is both subtle and aggressive.

The inconsequential **Live Instinct** contains four songs recorded onstage in London, including renditions of the band's 1979 debut single ("Cold Beat") and a few **Jeopardy** songs. The recorded performances add little to the studio versions.

From the Lions Mouth builds on **Jeopardy**'s firm foundation with a fuller sound that faintly recalls U2. Produced by Hugh Jones (around the same time he did Echo's **Heaven Up Here**), it's bright, dramatic and sometimes ("Fire," "Sense of Purpose," "Winning") powerful. A riveting LP—the group's best.

Pushed by their label to sound more commercial, **All Fall Down** is the defiant reply—a stark, barren landscape of harsh tones and dark passages. The black, clashing music makes the challenging LP an acquired taste, an ambitious, admirable exploration of the downside; not surprisingly, the record company sent the band packing.

Shock of Daylight—a six-song mini-album produced by Pat Collier—is a strong return, building melodic, dramatic songs on a gutsy bass/drums drive, overlaying guitar, keyboards and even brass to create an attractively textured and varied sound. **Heads and Hearts** is even better, a quilt of bright colors woven with simple care. Though it lacks the knockout punch they'd shown in the past ("Winning" or **Shock of Daylight**'s "Golden Soldiers," for example), the record's modesty and continuous flow make it a thoroughly engaging listen, a memorable LP whose sum is greater than its parts.

In the Hothouse is a double live thriller from London's Marquee, with all the claustrophobic ambience of the club's packed space coming through on the recording. Live records this immediate sounding are hard to find. With the bulk of the material chosen from **Heads and Hearts** and **Lions Mouth**, this is a superb introduction for the curious.

Thunder Up is a middle ground between **All Fall Down**'s emotional warfare and the later, more sensuous pop. Punching right in with one of their most exciting tracks ("Acceleration Group"), the LP is a rollercoaster ride through desolation ("Shot Up and Shut Down"), titillation ("Kinetic"), cynicism ("Prove Me Wrong") and profound beauty ("You've Got a Way"). Though the contrast can be jarring, unpredictability is a strength, and this is a bold up/down, hot/cold, built-up/knocked-down record most bands would not attempt. It was to be their last such uncompromising work; the group finally called it quits in early '88.

Borland's subsequent solo career got off to a good start with **Alexandria**, as he brings a variety of moods to the alternately austere, sensuous and lighthearted pop, revealing a mild Velvet Underground influence. More swimming strings and tasteful background horns add to the overall warmth of this acoustic-based, romantic LP. "Light the Sky" and "Beneath the Big Wheel" pair somber detachment with graceful chord changes; elsewhere, the deeply moving, strings-to-the-fore "Rogue Beauty" shows Borland still capable of dramatic flourish.   [cpl/i/jr]

SOUND BARRIER

See *Tot Taylor and His Orchestra*.

SOUNDGARDEN

Screaming Life EP (Sub Pop) 1987
Fopp EP (Sub Pop) 1988
Ultramega OK (SST) 1988 ●
Louder Than Love (A&M) 1989 ●
Screaming Life/Fopp [CD] (Sub Pop) 1990 ●

Just when you though the '70s were over . . . along comes Seattle's Soundgarden, spearheading the Northwest's revival of that non-metal rock gulch between late-'60s innovation and late-'70s rebellion, years in which groups like Grand Funk, Led Zep and Mountain—shirtless men singing about shirtless women—dominated, erecting monuments to indiscriminate penile guitar worship with endless wank'em-crank'em solos. Remember those good old days? Well, they're back, and Soundgarden's reliving'em.

The accomplished six-song **Screaming Life** EP introduces Chris Cornell's Robert Plantish vocals, Kim Thayil's turgid guitar talents, Hiro Yamamoto's rubbery bass action and Matt Cameron's steady-as-she-goes drumming. While the music is happily unspecific in its derivation—the assimilation of both classic rock riffs and punk noise ("Entering" specifically quotes Bauhaus) keep things interesting—it's impossible to overlook the absurdity of Cornell's unabashed Percy tribute. (The **Screaming Life** encompasses the **Fopp** EP: three live tracks, including a remake of Green River's "Swallow My Pride," and a pointless dub mix of the titular Ohio Players cover, complete with apocalyptic found-sound drama.)

After signing to A&M, Soundgarden released an album through SST as part of the large label's plan to build a new rock/metal dynasty from the ground up.

Although still mired in the '70s, **Ultramega OK** is noticeably better than **Screaming Life**, with less selfconscious posturing and more evidence of an emerging personality. Cornell has reduced (without actually eliminating) his reliance on Plant clichés, but the traces of Ozzy Osbourne caterwauling in his voice are not a good omen. These guys can sure play, but an inadequate comprehension of what constitutes songs (a subject their archetypes, for all their failings, always understood) leaves Soundgarden in an unhealthy nudge-nudge-wink-wink relationship with the past, attempting to get by with references (the inclusion of Howlin' Wolf's "Smokestack Lightning"—just the sort of cover Led Zep would have done—is emblematic of their historical shorthand) rather than original material of real merit.

A sloppy, disorganized murk of dull sound (credit co-producer Terry Date, who seems to have captured only the slackest performances) and plodding songs which could be covers of Led Zep discards, **Louder Than Love** is a most ineffectual major-label debut. Thayil throws out licks haphazardly, whether they fit or not; the rhythm section does nothing beyond (more or less) keeping the beat; Cornell is in strong form but back to his old fringed-leather tricks. Even when songs begin to hit their stride with a workable groove or a pattern that moves, they fall apart on the bridge (or vice versa). A rewrite of the descending riff from "Dazed and Confused" with Jeff Beck fillips, "Uncovered" is the closest the record comes to finding and sticking with an idea that works; the chords of "Big Dumb Sex" hold together, but the lyrics are unendurably stupid. The '70s might not have been so bad after all . . .   [i]

See also *Temple of the Dog*.

SOUP DRAGONS

Hang-Ten! EP (nr/Raw TV Products) 1986
Hang-Ten! (Sire) 1987
This Is Our Art (Sire) 1988 ●
Lovegod (Big Life-PolyGram) 1990 ●

This young Scottish foursome garnered a lot of initial interest because of their striking musical resemblance to the Buzzcocks. Singer Sean Dickson's falsetto whine, in front of the speedy grind of his and Jim McCulloch's guitars, made the Soup Dragons the very reincarnation of those punk-pop pioneers. An admirable point of reference, to say the least.

The four-song **Hang-Ten!** EP followed two well-received UK singles. The blistering title track can be aptly described as punk-surf-pop—the Beach Boys sifted through the Buzzcocks, if you will. The other songs run about the same speed, and are just as outstanding.

The American **Hang-Ten!** album collects the UK EP, three songs from a previous single ("Whole Wide World"), and three songs from a later single ("Head Gone Astray"). All reaffirm the band's reverence for the Buzzcocks tradition.

This Is Our Art (subtitled **Useless, boring, impotent, elitist and very, very beautiful.**) is a shock. The new-sound Soup Dragons are devoid of any Buzzcocks references, mutating instead into a bizarre assortment of styles: '60's garage psychedelia ("Great Empty Space"), hard rock (the Black Sabbath-sounding "Passion Protein") and Scottish funk ("King of the Castle''), to mention just a few. It's an amazing range, yet there's something insincere about these songs, which seemingly don't know when to end.

For **Lovegod**, the Soup Dragons' second proper album, the group abandoned any punk edge they may have once had and embraced young Britain's burgeoning Ecstasy-fueled trippy dance culture. This redirection paid off, as the funky, anthemic cover of the Rolling Stones' "I'm Free" (featuring guest toasting by Black Uhuru's Junior Reid) became a hit both in England and the States. With its odd, house-influenced rhythms and Dickson's obviously mind-expanded lyrics dominating all the other tracks, the record is nothing if not consistent. As such, it's also deeply repetitive. In small, er, doses, though, percolating ditties like "Backwards Dog" and "Kiss the Gun" are primo dancefloor fodder. (The CD adds a dub mix of the title track and the "Crotch Deep Trash" single.)   [ag/db]

SOUTHERN DEATH CULT
See *Cult*.

SPACE
See *Justified Ancients of Mu Mu*.

SPACEMEN 3
Sound of Confusion (nr/Glass) 1986 (nr/Fire) 1989 ●
The Perfect Prescription (nr/Glass) 1987 (Genius) 1988 ●
Transparent Radiation EP (nr/Glass) 1987
Performance (nr/Glass) 1988 (nr/Fire) 1988 ●
Playing with Fire (nr/Fire) 1989 (Bomp!) 1989 ●
Spacemen 3 EP (nr/Fire) 1989
Taking Drugs to Make Music to Take Drugs To (Father Yod Production) 1990
Recurring (Dedicated-RCA) 1991 ●

SONIC BOOM
Spectrum (nr/Silvertone) 1990 ●

To bake a mind-altering cake nowadays, you've got to smash a few sugarcubes. Unlike bands who get all cutesy with the pop trappings of '60s acid-rock, Spacemen 3 are content to let the music be its own hallucinogen. At the outset, their records lay down a droning thick-pile carpet of overdriven guitar and mongoloid drumming; later on, they began exploring the equally unsettling powers of more tranquil waters. Not as self-consciously arty as Sonic Youth or as decisively melodic as the Jesus and Mary Chain, Spacemen 3 follow both stylistic poles of the Velvet Underground with more wholehearted enthusiasm than most of the group's self-appointed apostles.

Recorded as a quartet (including, for once, an on-board drummer), **Sound of Confusion** brings the psychedelic sound of Rugby (an industrial city near Birmingham) to bear on a mixture of bizarre covers (Glen Campbell's "Mary Anne," Iggy Pop's "Little Doll," the 13th Floor Elevators' "Rollercoaster") and originals that all sound exactly the same. Except for the clever pun of "Hey Man" (sung as if it were the homonymic gospel assent) and the bonus dynamics of "2.35," the album roars along on the precipice of monotony, with only the frequent appearance of vocals to ensure listener consciousness.

The Perfect Prescription finds Jason Pierce (guitar, organ, vocals), Sonic Boom (guitar, organ, vocals) and Pete Bassman (bass) abruptly reducing the dosage with lots of sonic space, varied instrumentation (acoustic guitar, violins, horns, keyboards) and very little percussion. Although things heat up towards the end, much of the album—like its quietly contemplative string-driven centerpiece, a cover of Red Crayola's "Transparent Radiation"—is pretty and evocative, but hardly engrossing. (The Glass cassette adds 40 minutes of bonus material, including an endless version of "Rollercoaster" and a lengthy reworking of "Starship," a Sun Ra adaptation from the first MC5 album; the Fire CD tacks on two bonus B-sides.) **Transparent Radiation** contains two different renditions of the title track, a distended version of the album's placid "Ecstasy Symphony," "Starship" and one other item to counter the band's tender tendencies.

Performance, recorded semi-loud and live in Amsterdam before—judging by the meager applause—an audience of three, introduces a new song ("Come Together," a blatant lift of the Who's "I Can See for Miles"), recycles favorite covers ("Mary Anne," "Rollercoaster," "Starship") and puts forth three other songs, including "Take Me to the Other Side" and "Walkin' with Jesus," respectively the darker and lighter sides (and two of the best songs) from **The Perfect Prescription**.

Playing with Fire is the trio's crowning achievement, a perfectly integrated mixture of trippy pop, spaced-out poetry, acoustic romance and mind-boggling guitar devastation. The album starts out gentle ("Honey"), turns explosive ("Revolution") and then settles into an obsessive drone (the tributary "Suicide") that dominates Side 2. Throughout, the Spacemen exhibit solid songwriting and careful control of their art, modulating the album's mood ring with the ease of experienced navigators. (The American vinyl edition is on colored wax; the British CD adds two live cuts. Additionally, two thousand copies of **Spacemen 3**, an untitled 12-inch—stock number THREEBIE 3—containing 1988 live versions of "Revolution," "Suicide" and "Repeater," plus the uneventful drone-strumental "Live Intro Theme (Xtacy)," were distributed free to purchasers of the British album.)

As legally dubious as its title suggests, **Taking Drugs**, a document of the quartet's prehistory (early 1986), resembles the first album (with which it overlaps three songs) except in the degree of sonic intensity and the sound quality. Besides songs that found their way intact onto S3 LPs, this neat artifact includes a developmental version of "Walkin' with Jesus" entitled "Sound of Confusion" and the second album's "Come Down Easy," poppy proof that the group was capable of restraint from the very beginning.

With S3 nearing collapse (Jason Pierce launched his own band, Spiritualized, in mid-1990, with an enjoyably grandiose rendition of Chip Taylor's "Anyway That You Want Me," a '66 hit for the Troggs), Sonic Boom (Peter Kember; on the first Spacemen LP he was billed as Peter Gunn) made **Spectrum**, an album more noteworthy for its ambitious adjustable op-art sleeve than its content. With playing assists from Jason as well as the Jazz Butcher and members of the Perfect Disaster, Sonic stays inside the one-chord amelodic vamps of Spacemen country, tightening the stylistic bond to Suicide by covering the duo's "Rock'n'Roll (Is Killing My Life)." But the album has a serious lack of vitality. Where Sonic ought to rev things up (a few real songs would have been nice), he turns nearly subliminal, and the instrumental portion of the doomy "If I Should Die," which closes the album, floats away on strains of lighter-than-air atmosphere. (A 10-inch bonus record entitled **Octaves and Tremelos** was offered by mail to purchasers of **Spectrum**.)

Surprising fans who assumed they would never work together again, Jason and Sonic did reunite for another album. The buzzing guitars and shy organ that drone gently through "Why Couldn't I See?"—the second song on the narcotically relaxed **Recurring**—amount to sitar-free raga-rock, laying a poppy (poppie?) bed for the vibratoed and reverbed wispy vocals. Otherwise offering an undated adaptation of '60s folky acid-rock with elements of the Beatles, Stones and others, the lullingly pleasant album—one of the most subtly retro-styled records of the current English scene—contains both sides of the Spacemen's 1989 UK single ("Hyp-notized" b/w "Just to See You Smile"), an incongru-ous sequencer-driven dance track ("Big City"), an ominous bluesy cover of Mudhoney's "When Tomor-row Hits" and such future flashbacks as "Set Me Free/I Got the Key," the "Hang on Sloopy"-derived "I Love You" and "Feel So Sad."   [i]

See also *Darkside*.

SPACE NEGROS

Maximum Contrast from Moment to Moment EP (Sounds Interesting) 1979
The Space Negros Go Commercial EP (Arf Arf) 1980 + 1984
Have a Lousy Xmas EP (Jingle Jungle-Arf Arf) 1981
The Space Negros Do Generic Ethnic Muzak Versions of All Your Favorite Underground Punk/Psychedelic Songs from the Sixties (Arf Arf) 1987

FAMILY FUN

Record (Eat) 1981

Before there was a Mission of Burma, two of its future founders played in this minor Boston group, alongside keyboardist/producer Erik Lindgren, a future member of Birdsongs of the Mesozoic. The 7-inch **Maximum Contrast** contains six offbeat offerings of experimental synth'n'tape tricks.

That same year, the original Space Negros fell apart; **Go Commercial** (shades of the Residents), another 7-inch with eight songs, is actually a Lindgren solo record. His upbeat pop songs—sort of a synth-happy R. Stevie Moore—are witty and sophisticated. The B-side includes a cover of the Yardbirds' "Happenings Ten Years Time Ago." The 1980 rendition of that classic took a Kraftwerkian electro-pop approach; the record's 1984 reissue replaced it with a heavy metal guitar version. **Have a Lousy Xmas** offers a topical foursome of laughable ill cheer originals (e.g., "Jingle Hell") played by Lindgren with Space Negro alumnus Roger Miller and others.

The windily titled album, recorded between 1981 and 1985 with a large number of instrumental contrib-utors, consists entirely of exotically idiomatic (raga, bluegrass, Balkan, etc.) easy-listening instrumental in-terpretations of songs originally popularized by such venerable musical organizations as the Seeds, Who, Easybeats, Balloon Farm, Smoke, 13th Floor Elevators, Hotlegs and Tomorrow. Not as conceptually explosive as the Residents, perhaps, but delightful.

Flipper may have a gripe against Public Image for lifting their concept of a generic record sleeve, but Fam-ily Fun—a Lindgren-led quartet—has them both beat. The cover of their 1981 EP (one side of four electro-pop tunes with Sara Goodman providing folkie vocals over the slightly off-kilter backing and a side of instrumental "EZ Listening Music") mimics the no-name products in grocery stores by carrying only the word "RECORD" stenciled over "Net Wt. 4.9 Oz. (45 RPM.) 135 g."
                                                                  [i]

See also *Birdsongs of the Mesozoic, Mission of Burma*.

SPANDAU BALLET

Journeys to Glory (Chrysalis) 1981 ●
Diamond (Chrysalis) 1982 ●
True (Chrysalis) 1983 ●
Parade (Reformation-Chrysalis) 1984 ●
The Singles Collection (Chrysalis) 1985 ●
The 12-Inch Mixes (nr/Reformation-Chrysalis) 1986 ●
Through the Barricades (Epic) 1986 ●
Heart Like a Sky (nr/Reformation-CBS) 1989 ●

Viewed at the start by some as adventurous and trendsetting, the ludicrous garb and chic disco of Lon-don's Spandau Ballet were both dubious new wave de-velopments, but spawned much replication. Head poseur Tony Hadley and his four cohorts (including songwriting guitarist Gary Kemp) found success with a heavily rhythmic brand of distant funk-rock dolled up with synthesizers and stentorian singing. Produced by Richard James Burgess, **Journeys to Glory** contains one great dance hit (actually, one tightly compressed riff: "To Cut a Long Story Short," their first single) and a batch of variations thereon. With the addition of horns and other reformulated moves, **Diamond**—issued in the UK as a set of four 12-inch singles as well as a regular single album—also produced a few more estimable Brit-ish chart smashes ("Chant No. 1," "Paint Me Down"). Possessing only limited talent themselves, Spandau opened the floodgates to a wave of superior electro-dance bands who had little trouble creatively eclipsing them.

Spandau then abandoned synthesizers and high-tension funk for schmaltzy pop with soul pretensions. Working with the production team of Tony Swain and Steve Jolley, the fivesome cut **True** and **Parade**, the first yielding several attractive blends of energy, mel-ody, warmth and stylishness ("Communication," "Lifeline") as well as some of the sappiest MOR in memory ("True," which became a global hit). Gener-ally less wimped-out, **Parade** nonetheless continues the bland chart fare, with the stylistic divergence best rep-resented by "Revenge for Love" (good) and "Only When You Leave" (egregiously mellow).

During legal tumult between Spandau and Chrys-alis, the label issued a collection of the band's singles, followed by a UK-only compilation of extended re-mixes.

The wretched **Through the Barricades** dumps the Perry Como snooze for an overheated American album-rock sound that echoes Eric Carmen, REO Speedwagon (or is it Styx?) and Billy Joel. Gary Langan's co-production (with the group) has all the earmarks of a desperate last-ditch grab at reclaiming US airplay. Kemp's songs are worthless; the echo on Hadley's melodramatic warbling (backed in maximally clichéd fashion by a female trio) only makes the whole affair more laughable.

With the cinematically inclined Kemp brothers getting good notices for their work in *The Krays*, Spandau's days may be numbered. But the group (no longer meriting American release—is that any way to treat a Top 5 act six years later?) hasn't given up yet. A characterless nothing whose blandly antiseptic soul, rock and funk stylings sound like an amalgam of VH-1's worst mushmongers, **Heart Like a Sky**'s main entertainment value lies in the clumsy syntax of Kemp's greeting-card sentiments. (At random: "Two young babes in a foreign land/Draw no milk from the dusty sand/Close their eyes from the night so cold/Feel the love in their mothers [*sic*] hold.") Say goodnight, boys.

[i]

SPARKS

Halfnelson (Bearsville) 1971
Sparks (Bearsville) 1971
A Woofer in Tweeter's Clothing (Bearsville) 1972
Kimono My House (Island) 1974
Propaganda (Island) 1974
Indiscreet (Island) 1975
Two Originals of Sparks (nr/Bearsville) 1976
Big Beat (Columbia) 1976
Introducing Sparks (Columbia) 1977
No. 1 in Heaven (Elektra) 1979
Best of Sparks (nr/Island) 1979
Terminal Jive (nr/Virgin) 1979
Whomp That Sucker (Why-Fi-RCA) 1981
The History of Sparks (Fr. Underdog) 1981
Angst in My Pants (Atlantic) 1982
Sparks in Outer Space (Atlantic) 1983
Pulling Rabbits Out of a Hat (Atlantic) 1984
Music That You Can Dance To (Curb-MCA) 1986 ●
Interior Design (Fine Art-Rhino) 1988 ●
Mael Intuition: The Best of Sparks 1974-1976 [CD]
  (nr/Island) 1990 ●
Profile: The Ultimate Sparks Collection (Rhino) 1991 φ

Ron and Russell Mael—two enormously talented wiseacres from Los Angeles—have influenced numerous bands through their own records and outside projects; it's possible to trace many contemporary musical trends back to the pair's prescient and trailblazing efforts. Although their lengthy recording career has the consistency of chunky peanut butter, some of their albums are truly wonderful in a number of stylistic modes. Sparks remain unpredictably capable of greatness each time they enter the studio.

As an art-rock quintet called Halfnelson, Sparks made their earliest, misanthropic efforts to appeal to the neurotic nouveau pop segment of 1971 America via a debut album produced by Todd Rundgren. First released as **Halfnelson** (by Halfnelson), it was promptly withdrawn, repackaged and reissued as **Sparks** (by Sparks). That original band—sort of Marlene Dietrich meets the Stooges—included Earle Mankey, who went on to be-

come a producer (and recording artist) of some note, and his brother Jim, who later formed the chartbound Concrete Blonde. The album is a subtle and brilliant exposition of unique talent, displaying the Maels' remarkable facility for bizarre, dadaist lyrics and Russell's scarifying falsetto. The triumphant **A Woofer in Tweeter's Clothing** refined, energized and improved on the first LP; it's a demented blueprint of incomprehensible weirdness. Many hated them, few heard them, but none who did forgot them on the basis of this utterly individual effort. (Although not issued there at the time, the first two LPs were packaged together and reissued in Britain after the group's success.)

Moving to London and recruiting an all-new set of sidemen, keyboardist Ron and singer Russell hooked up with producer Muff Winwood and made a series of singles (many included on the first two Island albums) that turned them into enormously popular glam-pop teen idols. Mixing prolix and profoundly funny wordplay with killer hooks and a solid guitar-and-piano-based sound, Sparks were the forerunners (and, to some extent, instigators) of the skinny tie Anglo-pop revival that swept America a few years later. Two brilliant albums (**Kimono My House** and **Propaganda**) worked that irresistible formula, but the gimmickry wore thin; **Indiscreet**, produced pompously by Tony Visconti, has some terribly boring, unbelievably overblown numbers amidst the succinct pop smashes. Sparks were outgrowing bubblegum.

Their lock on the top of Britain's charts ended, the Maels fired their band and returned to America to begin a very bad career patch, starting with **Big Beat**. They benefit from a bit of leftover momentum (and perhaps material) from their previous work, but it's basically a poor homecoming. (The band for this record included head Tuff Dart Jeff Salen on guitar, ex-Milk 'n' Cookies bassist Sal Maida and drummer Hilly Michaels.) The far worse **Introducing**, recorded with LA session men, is Sparks' creative nadir.

The group's complex saga then began to involve Giorgio Moroder, who produced **No. 1 in Heaven**, converting the one-time pure-guitar-poppers into a driving Euro-disco synthesizer machine, pounding out repetitive drum-laden dance grooves. Only semi-successful, musically speaking, it does deserve credit for predating the entry of countless other rock groups onto the high-tech dance-floor. **Terminal Jive**, the only Sparks album not released in the US, tempers the funk but suffers a serious personality loss, the result of the Maels' co-writing too much of the material with others.

Leaving the disco behind, Sparks next began an alliance with a Moroder associate, German producer Mack. They recorded **Whomp That Sucker** in Munich with their first steady band since **Indiscreet**: David Kendrick, Leslie Bohem and Bob Haag (who also work on their own as Gleaming Spires). The songs reclaim some of Sparks' early pop wit, but with new maturity and dignity. A definite improvement, it's still a transitional record, leading the Maels out of the creative woods with some ace numbers, but they're still not at peak power.

Angst in My Pants, however, is that promise fulfilled, a top-notch collection of tunes with offbeat humor, winning melodies and excellent arrangements, displaying the benefits of touring with a band. It's the first new Sparks album that belongs alongside **Woofer**

and **Kimono**. The self-produced **In Outer Space** features Jane Wiedlin (then in the Go-Go's) duetting with Russell on two songs, and is a mixed creative success due to songs that drag and a shortage of stunning lyrics. The equally inconclusive **Pulling Rabbits Out of a Hat**, produced by Ian Little, has better material, less personality and only a few outstanding tracks. Perhaps tiring of unrewarded cleverness, the album's most durable effort is "With All My Might," a syrupy ballad distinguished by its plainspoken emotionalism.

Hooking up with yet another record label (but keeping the band intact), Sparks next made **Music That You Can Dance To**, an aggressively loud high-energy dance record—dynamic keyboards, mock-symphonic arrangements and Bohem's bass play a large part—that has its moments (the title track, "Change," "The Scene") and its mistakes (a painful version of Stevie Wonder's "Fingertips"). Clever lyrics help, as does the Maels' inventive self-production. (In an outrageous attempt to mislead, Curb's 1990 CD reissue of the album is titled **The Best of Sparks: Music That You Can Dance To**.)

The patchy **Interior Design** was recorded in Russell's home studio with just a keyboard player and a guitarist, making it the first bandless outing since **Terminal Jive**. Despite a few good songs ("The Toughest Girl in Town," the dance-happy "So Important"), reliance on synthesizers leaves the album sounding choppy and monochromatic. The CD adds three songs: "Madonna," "Big Brass Ring" and "So Important."

The 1979 British compilation has the group's six hits (1974-'75) and another half-dozen tracks from the same era. Besides reprising half of **Terminal Jive**, the '81 French compilation includes three songs from **No. 1 in Heaven**, two each from **Woofer** and **Whomp That Sucker**, and the first LP's "Wonder Girl."

At 20 tracks, **Mael Intuition** is less a compilation of Sparks' three Island albums than a listener's digest of them. Still, the choice of omissions is not without flaws: "Talent Is an Asset"? "Who Don't Like Kids"? "How Are You Getting Home?"? This is a good introduction, but it's no substitute for the original albums (nor a good excuse for their unavailability on CD). **Profile** is a career-spanning two-disc/two-cassette compilation of album tracks plus a few rarities. The CD configuration has eight bonus tunes.   [i]

See also *Concrete Blonde, Gleaming Spires, Earle Mankey, Telex*.

SPEAR OF DESTINY

Grapes of Wrath (nr/Burning Rome-Epic) 1983
One Eyed Jacks (nr/Burning Rome-Epic) 1984
World Service (nr/Burning Rome-Epic) 1985
Outland (Virgin) 1987 ●
The Epic Years (nr/Epic) 1987 ●
The Price You Pay (nr/Virgin) 1988 ●
Radio Radio EP [CD] (nr/Virgin) 1988 ●

CRAZY PINK REVOLVERS

First Down! (nr/Chainsaw) 1987
Timeless Smiles EP (nr/ABC) 1987
At the Rivers Edge (nr/ABC) 1988 ●

Following the stormy existence of Theatre of Hate, singer/guitarist Kirk Brandon and bassist Stan Stammers launched Spear of Destiny. **Grapes of Wrath**, produced by Nick Launay, unveils a straightforward guitar/bass/

drums quartet; Andy Mackay-like saxophone work provides the sole distinguishing tonal component. Brandon's songs are a drag—spare, dirgey things with hopeless quasi-Scottish melodies and self-important, insignificant lyrics. Slight Nick Cave tendencies don't add enough extremism to salvage these effortlessly ignorable tracks.

One Eyed Jacks introduces a different, larger lineup (including ex-Tom Robinson Band drummer Dolph Taylor; the superior results lean alternately towards Big Country and Adam Ant. A basically inept vocalist with nothing in the way of a natural instrument, Brandon sings everything like he's rousing the troops for a final assault, a tactic that overpowers the flimsy tunes. Lacking a feel for full-blown majesty (like Richard Jobson), he's too zealous for his own good.

Co-produced by SOD and Rusty Egan, **World Service** is again hindered by Brandon's horrifically bad singing. He repeatedly misses notes on "Rocket Ship" and makes the lyrics on "Come Back" sound almost unpronounceable. The operatic melody of the title track exposes all of his aural inadequacies at once. With that, Brandon discharged his band, signed to Virgin and went right on doing what he's always done.

On the occasion of the band's departure from the label, **The Epic Years**—unceremoniously dumped on the market right on top of SOD's new LP—cherry-picks the first three albums, including five songs that were minor UK hits as singles.

Outland, which unites Brandon with ex-Ant guitarist Marco Peroni [*sic*], the Barnacle brothers rhythm section and producer Zeus B. Held, isn't a bad record. The advent of goth-metal groups like the Cult, Sisters of Mercy and the Mission makes marble-mouthed Brandon seem far less offensive in context; perhaps he's also improved a bit. (Naaah.) While nowhere near a desert island disc, **Outland** is a reasonable current example of rough'n'ready semi-political rock by a sincere, if limited, individual. (The UK CD and cassette add five bonus tracks, most of them alternate mixes of LP tracks.)

Brandon maintains his never-say-die romantic punk ethos on **The Price You Pay**, an album that brought him a UK Top 40 with "So in Love with You." (The CD adds two.) **Radio Radio**—a 3-inch CD produced by Alan Shacklock and packaged in a black matte tin—consists of the titular album track and three soundalike B-sides.

Following his departure from SOD, bassist Stan Stammers formed Crazy Pink Revolvers.   [i]

SPECIALS

The Specials (2-Tone-Chrysalis) 1979 ●
More Specials (2-Tone-Chrysalis) 1980 ●
Ghost Town EP (2-Tone-Chrysalis) 1981
The Peel Sessions EP (nr/Strange Fruit) 1987
The Singles Collection (Chrysalis) 1991 φ

SPECIAL A.K.A.

The Special A.K.A. Live! EP (nr/2-Tone) 1980
In the Studio (2-Tone-Chrysalis) 1984 ●

STAN CAMPBELL

Stan Campbell (Elektra) 1987 ●

Coventry's Specials spearheaded the British ska revival in 1979, with leader/keyboard player Jerry

Dammers also serving as head of 2-Tone, the band's trendsetting label, which altered pop culture by releasing records by Madness, the Beat, Selecter and Bodysnatchers.

Produced by Elvis Costello, the Specials' debut LP also boasted the assistance of an elder statesman of bluebeat, trombonist Rico Rodriguez, an original member of Jamaica's Skatalites. With the double lead vocals of Terry Hall and Neville Staples, guitarists Lynval Golding and Roddy Radiation, and an impeccable rhythm section composed of John Bradbury and Sir Horace Gentleman, the Specials were widely acclaimed as the most exciting band to emerge in 1979, and their impact continued well into the '80s.

The Specials contains such classic 2-Tone (as the sound came to be called) numbers as "Doesn't Make It Alright," "Too Much Too Young," "A Message to You Rudy" and (on the American edition) the hit single "Gangsters." Mixing socially and politically aware lyrics with infectious dance rhythms, **The Specials** served as a virtual blueprint for many bands to follow. A few months later, under the full Special A.K.A. handle, the band released a hot 7-inch EP—recorded live in London and Coventry—that includes "The Guns of Navarone" (a Skatalites classic in the previous decade) and a sidelong medley of covers dubbed "Skinhead Symphony."

Unfortunately, their momentum foundered with the release of **More Specials**. The group abandoned the fresh sound of their debut in favor of a more turgid experimental approach. (**More** does, however, contain some prime material: "Enjoy Yourself" and, in the US, "Rat Race.") Rumors of internal strife abounded, and though the Specials managed to release the angry **Ghost Town** 12-inch—which went straight to number one in riot-torn Britain—the original band soon succumbed to infighting. Hall, Staples and Golding split off to form the Fun Boy Three, and other members drifted off as well.

By then it was clear that the Specials name was merely a vehicle for whatever Dammers would do, but it was three reportedly arduous years before he completed the "group" 's third album, pointedly titled **In the Studio**. Working with several steady associates (notably vocalists Stan Campbell and ex-Bodysnatcher Rhoda Dakar, in addition to loyal drummer John Bradbury) plus a large pool of sessioneers, Dammers filled the album with disarmingly varied, largely unstylized (nothing you would really call ska) essays on serious political topics ("Racist Friend," "Free Nelson Mandela," "Alcohol") leavened by the lighthearted "(What I Like Most About You Is Your) Girlfriend." Striking but troubled, the music's easygoing bounce belies the overweening polemicism.

The Peel session, from May 1979, includes live runthroughs of "Gangsters," "Too Much Too Young," "Concrete Jungle" and "Monkey Man" by the original band. **The Singles Collection** has the three tracks from the **Ghost Town** EP, two live cuts from the '80 EP, some non-LP single sides and a lot of redundancy: album tracks that were issued as 45s.

In 1987, ex-Special Campbell released a bland soul/reggae-flavored commercial solo album. A vocal resemblance to Michael McDonald of the Doobie Brothers is only one of Stan's problems; his dull originals and underdone cover versions ("Don't Let Me Be Misunderstood," "Crawfish" and "Strange Fruit") are the others.   [jw/i]

See also *Colour Field, Fun Boy Three, Selecter*.

CHRIS SPEDDING

Chris Spedding (nr/RAK) 1976 ●
Hurt (nr/RAK) 1977 ●
Guitar Graffiti (nr/RAK) 1978 (Fr. Fan Club) 1989 ●
I'm Not Like Everybody Else (nr/RAK) 1980 (Fr. Fan Club) 1989 ●
Friday the 13th (Passport) 1981
Mean and Moody (nr/See for Miles) 1985
Enemy Within (Fr. New Rose) 1986 ●
Cafe Days (Fr. New Rose) 1990 ●

One of Britain's top session guitarists of the '70s (even participating in records by the furry Wombles!), Chris Spedding has had a truly aberrant solo career. A veteran of numerous outfits starting in the '60s, Spedding made several LPs under his own name before joining Andy Fraser's post-Free band, Sharks, who made two hard-rocking LPs in 1973 and '74. (Spedding also played on one of Sharks vocalist Snips' subsequent solo outings.) After that band split, Spedding released a succession of LPs that combine exquisite rock guitar with lackluster vocals and songs so vapid as to be virtually nonexistent. (On a 1970 Japanese release, he dispensed with vocals entirely.) The highlight of **Chris Spedding** is a novelty item called "Guitar Jamboree" which features Spedding aping various guitar heroes in a show of chameleonlike virtuosity.

We pick up the story later in 1976, however, when Spedding teamed up with the then-unrecorded Vibrators for a great single, "Pogo Dancing," the first punk dance record. **Hurt**, Spedding's next LP, is a more solid follow-up, thanks to Chris Thomas' crisp production. The material is generally better, and there's one outstanding number, the ominous "Lone Rider."

Guitar Graffiti finds Spedding meandering again, producing a crass attempt to cash in on his new wave credibility (legitimately established through his seminal alliances with the Sex Pistols and the Cramps, for whom he produced demos, and the Vibrators). The worthwhile track is "Hey, Miss Betty," the only one produced by Thomas; the song is a rocking homage to '50s bondage queen Betty Page.

In 1979, Spedding surprised everyone by joining the Necessaries, a New York band that included former Modern Lover Ernie Brooks. Though he kept a low profile—refusing featured billing within the group—the combination of his dark pop ditties and leader Ed Tomney's preppie sensibility never melded. Spedding added brilliant leads to Tomney's material, but his songwriting still lacked coherency, and in some instances he abandoned guitar for keyboards. Spedding split without fanfare after less than a year (he was gone by the time the Necessaries made their LP in 1981), returning to England to record **I'm Not Like Everybody Else**, an album of his Necessaries-era material.

Friday the 13th is a live set on which Spedding is joined by former Sharks/occasional Talking Head bassist Busta Cherry Jones and New York drummer Tony Machine. Featuring a selection of songs from all the above-listed albums, **Friday the 13th** was released primarily as an ersatz retrospective of his RAK material. Showing off Spedding's guitar work in the context of some extended soloing, it's the best of the lot.

Spedding does a fairly good Dave Edmunds turn on **Enemy Within**, mixing a few rock'n'roll classics ("Love's Made a Fool of You," "Shakin' All Over") with unprepossessing originals, filling them all with twangy guitar work and serviceable vocals that somehow resemble Mark Knopfler. "Hologram," co-written with Marshall Crenshaw, is a highlight of this likable record.   [tr/i]

See also *Necessaries, Vibrators*.

SPEED THE PLOUGH

See *Feelies*.

SPHERICAL OBJECTS

Past and Parcel (nr/Object Music) 1978
Elliptical Optimism (nr/Object Music) 1979
Further Ellipses (nr/Object Music) 1980
No Man's Land (nr/Object Music) 1981

NOYES BROTHERS

Sheep from Goats (nr/Object Music) 1980

Manchester's Spherical Objects were led by Steve Solamar, a terrible singer with an intensely personal viewpoint. His songs concern typical subject matter, but utter lack of selfconsciousness invests his writing with more openness and introspection than you're probably hoping to hear.

The five Objects of **Past and Parcel** play simple rock that's lightweight but pleasant; Solamar's overbearing vocals spoil it. **Elliptical Optimism** has the same lineup and a more textured sound, featuring organ (prominently) and trumpet (occasionally). The songs are instrumentally inventive, while the vocals are less abrasive but no more interesting.

Further Ellipses takes a danceable turn, playing it smooth and rhythmic with more horns and synthesizer and less guitar. Solamar's singing continues to resemble David Thomas' but sounds too forced to be believably weird. The musical development is impressive, the songs are good, but the same old problem persists.

No Man's Land, which announces itself to be the final Spherical Objects album, has a different lineup from the previous three and sounds it. Gone are the keyboards and horns, replaced by rudimentary guitar/bass/drums plus patches of Solamar's wailing harmonica. There are some very pretty songs that are slowed down to add emotion, but overall the initial impression isn't as strong as **Further Ellipses**. A strange way to go out, **No Man's Land** is a record that slowly reveals itself to be quite lovely in spots.

With the help of Manchester indie scene fixture Steve Miro, Solamar managed to dam his stream-of-consciousness long enough to allow for the collection of the Noyes Brothers' atypically unrevealing double-LP set. More experimental than the Objects' concurrent work, **Sheep from Goats** owes more than a little to German groups like Can. While a few of the redundant, largely free-from instrumentals could easily be dispensed with, there are moments worth remembering,

from the amusing (an apparent Fall parody dubbed "Bo Scat Um I.D.") to the lovely (the side-long instrumental "It Seemed Like a Good Idea at the Time") to the freakishly prescient (an excursion into what sounds like modern-day computer-enhanced hip-hop christened "Byte to Beat").   [i/dss]

SPIZZ ET AL.

See *Athletico Spizz 80*.

SPLIT ENZ

Mental Notes (Aus. Mushroom) 1975
Mental Notes (Chrysalis) 1976
Dizrythmia (Chrysalis) 1977
Frenzy (Aus. Mushroom) 1979 (A&M) 1982
The Beginning of the Enz (Aus. Mushroom) 1979
True Colours (A&M) 1980 ●
Waiata (A&M) 1981
The Beginning of the Enz (nr/Chrysalis) 1981
Time and Tide (A&M) 1982
Enz of an Era—Greatest Hits 1975–1982 (Aus. A&M) 1982
Conflicting Emotions (A&M) 1983 ●
See Ya Round (Aus. Mushroom) 1984
The Living Enz (Aus. Mushroom) 1985
History Never Repeats: The Best of Split Enz (A&M) 1987 ●

New Zealand's Split Enz began their recording career in pleasantly uncommercial fashion, writing gently eccentric tunes that echoed the softer side of **Foxtrot**-era Genesis. A compilation of demos, Mushroom's **The Beginning of the Enz** chronicles those earliest days and finds Tim Finn's bittersweet singing style starting to work its magic.

For **Mental Notes**—their first proper album—the Enz took shape as a sprawling seven-piece, including spoons player Noel Crombie. They had grown overtly weird and flamboyant, with many tunes resembling little, distorted symphonies. The effects don't always work, simply because flakiness carried past a certain point can't be taken seriously on any level. The Genesis parallel holds here as well.

By the time Roxy Music's Phil Manzanera produced the second **Mental Notes**, the Enz were ready for the world beyond. Bizarre carnival costumes and distorted upsweep hairdos served as colorful attention-grabbers. Tim Finn's wistful voice adds a sweet patina to disoriented and lyrically offbeat outings like "Stranger Than Fiction" and the morbid "The Woman Who Loves You."

Dizrythmia made a distinct lurch towards the mainstream, thanks primarily to the departure of co-leader/guitarist Phil Judd, replaced by Tim's brother Neil. With Tim in full command, the melodically intricate material went from coldly weird to genuinely appealing, even cute. Highlights: the dizzy "Bold as Brass" and "Crosswords," at once bristling and ornate.

The second LP to be called **Beginning of the Enz** is a distillation of tracks from Chrysalis' **Mental Notes** and **Dizrythmia**.

Financial woes subsequently forced the band to work on a diminished budget. With Neil Finn contributing songs and vocals as well as guitar, the Enz cut **Frenzy**, poppier still and less elusive than before. It's hampered by cheap sound, but "I See Red" is a delightfully tuneful whirlwind, and "Mind Over Matter" re-creates the warmly majestic quality of the best of **Dizrythmia**. The US/UK version of the LP differs from Mushroom's by half.

The Enz staged a full assault on America with **True Colours**. They had become a cuddly pop band with sweet vocals, crackerjack melodies and hardly any strangeness. Fortunately, the material is genuinely first-rate, including the bouncily contagious "I Got You" and "I Hope I Never," a plainly melodramatic number suitable for Barbra Streisand. (As a marketing ploy, the LP was pressed on laser-etched plastic and packaged in variously colored covers.)

Although **Waiata** (issued in Australia under the Aborigine title **Corroboree**) has gorgeously haunting tracks like "Iris" and "History Never Repeats," as well as adorable ones like "Clumsy," there's a hint of blandness around the edges. The Enz show no desire to surprise here, and seem on the verge of becoming a hipper Bee Gees.

Happily, **Time and Tide** restores the passion, adding a new sense of wonder to the palatable melodies. "Dirty Creature" (of habit), "Hello Sandy Allen" and "Make Sense of It" all merit inclusion in the Enz hall of fame, blending a gentle beauty with vaguely unsettling otherworldliness.

Conflicting Emotions is effectively the band's swan song, and it's hard to imagine a grander exit. Keeping the ethereal melodies intact, the Enz finally build up the physical side of the music to equal strength. The playing is tough and direct like never before; "Bullet Brain and Cactus Head," "I Wake Up Every Night" and others drive hard without obscuring the wholesome moralism of the lyrics. The message? Try to lead a good life. Who could quarrel with that?

The final Enz studio LP, **See Ya Round** is an unusually mild affair, hard to remember once it's over. However, it's of historical note as Neil Finn's warmup for his massive success with Crowded House. Big bro' Tim has flown the coop, leaving Neil in charge, with a golden opportunity to make his own mistakes and get the art affectations out of his system once and for all. Which he apparently did: compare the pale version of "I Walk Away" here with the full-bodied reading on the first Crowded House LP.

The Living Enz is a decent two-disc live set from a band not widely known for its stage performances. **History Never Repeats**, a lovingly assembled posthumous compilation, has swell liner notes by Cary Darling and Tim Finn and contains such Enz necessities as "I See Red," "History Never Repeats," "I Got You" and "I Hope I Never." Split Enz reunited briefly in 1989 and played an old-time's-sake show in New Zealand. [jy]

See also *Crowded House, Tim Finn, Swingers*.

SPLODGENESSABOUNDS

Splodgenessabounds (nr/Deram) 1981
In Search of Seven Golden Gussets (nr/Razor) 1982
Live and Loud!! (nr/Link) 1988

Drummer-turned-singer Max Splodge led this fiercely tasteless London joke which actually scored a couple of UK hits in 1980. The rest of the crew on the eponymous debut sports names like Miles Runt Flat and Pat Thetic Von Dale Chiptooth Noble. The record includes an order form for such delectables as "moulded bum logo badge" and is generally concerned with various bodily functions and scatological maladies (not to be confused with scat melodies!), with only the scantest trace of humor. Except for some clever song titles, this is utterly worthless tripe.

Splodge has stayed around the scene, joining the Angelic Upstarts (!) in the late '80s while keeping the Splodgenessabounds concept alive. The supposedly live album—recorded by a quartet in front of an obviously fake throng of cheering thousands—has some mildly funny stuff ("I Fell in Love with a Female Plumber from Harlesden NW10") amid the predictably inexcusable rubbish ("Michael Booth's Talking Bum," "Crabs," etc.). [i]

See also *Angelic Upstarts*.

SPOOKS
See *Curtiss A.*

MARK SPRINGER
See *Rip Rig + Panic*.

SQUALLS
Rebel Shoes (Dog Gone) 1987
No Time (Dog Gone) 1988

Although the Squalls aren't exactly immune to the Athens environment, the eclectic Georgian sextet is too unaffectedly artless in its polite pop-folk-rock to strongly resemble any of their musical neighbors. **Rebel Shoes** is earnestly bland, a colorless ice-breaker of no special merit; the engaging **No Time** has more energy, skilled musical variety and hooky melodic strength. (If only singer Bob Hay's voice didn't occasionally make the group sound like Dire Straits . . .) A Squalls style is emerging, but it's not there yet. [i]

SQUEEZE
(U.K.) Squeeze (A&M) 1978 ●
Cool for Cats (A&M) 1979 ●
6 Squeeze Songs Crammed into One Ten-Inch Record EP (A&M) 1979
Argybargy (A&M) 1980 ●
East Side Story (A&M) 1981 ●
Sweets from a Stranger (A&M) 1982 ●
Singles—45's and Under (A&M) 1982 ●
Cosi Fan Tutti Frutti (A&M) 1985 ●
Babylon and On (A&M) 1987 ●
Frank (A&M) 1989 ●
A Round and a Bout (Deptford Fun City-IRS) 1990 φ

HARRY KAKOULLI
Even When I'm Not (nr/Oval) 1981

DIFFORD & TILBROOK
Difford & Tilbrook (A&M) 1984 ●

Squeeze's songwriting team of Glenn Tilbrook (melody) and Chris Difford (words) has been compared favorably to Lennon and McCartney; that's not only a reflection of their abilities but also an indication of how little real craftsmanship is found in rock'n'roll these days. Like their supposed models, Difford and Tilbrook are blessed with enormous talent which has often enabled them to get by on less than full expense of effort. What has often passed for ingenuity in Squeeze has, in fact, been little more than glibness.

A classic premature debut, **Squeeze** finds the five lads barreling through inconsistent material, a situation exacerbated by John Cale's cluttered production. However, "Take Me I'm Yours" and "Bang Bang" (both produced by the band) show spirit and potential.

Squeeze entered adolescence with **Cool for Cats**. Primary vocalist Tilbrook, a sweet triller, and the gruffer Difford show greater confidence at the mic; together, they create arresting, odd harmonies to go with their bent pop tunes. Wonderful cuts abound, including "Slap & Tickle," a sleazy synth rocker, "Cool for Cats," a modern pub-rock romp, and the cinematically inspired "Up the Junction," three minutes of working-class heartbreak that outdoes McCartney for pathos. **6 Squeeze Songs**, a well-chosen mini-greatest hits, was an effort to establish the band in the US.

Squeeze grew up on **Argybargy**. Tilbrook and Difford had found their style and were settling into it, creating finely etched pop music with increasing intricacy. "If I Didn't Love You" is wryly awkward; "Farfisa Beat," is a delightful throwaway; "Pulling Mussels (from the Shell)" teaches a herky-jerky lesson in catchy cleverness. Any lack of commitment is outweighed by the witty humor, variety and freshness of the material. Holland then left and was replaced by Paul Carrack.

If the Beatles parallel holds, **East Side Story** is Squeeze's **White Album**. Produced by Elvis Costello and Roger Bechirian (apart from one cut by Dave Edmunds), the jumble of fourteen songs touches on everything from soul to country to psychedelia. Each tune qualifies individually as a glittering little gem, but the album lacks coherence; still, it's a dazzling tour de force. Highlights include Carrack's vocal showcase ("Tempted"), "Someone Else's Heart," a Difford excursion into sentiment that recalls the Zombies, "Mumbo Jumbo," reflecting Costello's influence, "Messed Around" (a slick piece of fake rockabilly) and the winsome "Is That Love."

Don Snow replaced Carrack as the band pulled back slightly from the elaborate excesses of **East Side Story** for **Sweets from a Stranger**, without any loss of class. "When the Hangover Strikes" conducts a leisurely trip into Cole Porter land, while "I've Returned" soars on the strength of an exuberant Tilbrook vocal and ringing guitars. But again, the record has little coherence or musical vision.

Squeeze concentrated on making albums rather than singles after **Cool for Cats**, so **Singles—45's and Under**, a compilation released soon after the announcement of the band's dissolution, serves little purpose, pleasant though it may be. As the band's selection of which LP tracks to release as 45s often seemed totally arbitrary, there's no sense of occasion. Even "Annie Get Your Gun," the one new track, isn't great.

As it was their decision to disband Squeeze and continue writing and performing together, Difford and Tilbrook surprised no one by releasing an album that, except for being funkier and even more boring, basically sounds no different from the band's lesser efforts. Joined by the rest of a Squeezelike lineup (drums/bass/keyboards) plus occasional horns and strings, the dull duo try to come on like Hall and Oates, but lack the cynical instincts to make a slick veneer interesting. "Action Speaks Faster," "Love's Crashing Waves" and "Picking Up the Pieces" are merely turgid, overproduced and lifelessly smooth.

After two years of unsatisfying divorce, Tilbrook and Difford reconvened Squeeze with original pianoman Jools (now Julian) Holland, drummer Gilson Lavis and a new bassist, Keith Wilkinson (ex-Nasty Pop). But things didn't fall into place. The Laurie Latham-produced **Cosi Fan Tutti Frutti** is a bland collection that generally repeats the **Difford & Tilbrook** laxo-soul approach to much the same (non-)effect. The utterly depressive "Last Time Forever," while sonically impressive, is a regrettably somber development for this once-giddy band.

The new Squeeze—including second keyboardist Andy Metcalfe (simultaneously serving as Robyn Hitchcock's bassist)—righted itself on **Babylon and On**, a confident and likable return to the band's pre-breakup sound and form. "Tough Love," "Footprints" and especially "The Prisoner" affirm Squeeze's aptitude for agreeable pop. However, dubious stabs at soul and funk (like "Hourglass" and the annoying "853-5937") fall flat, and Tilbrook's sitar playing on the insipid "Some Americans" is downright absurd.

The tragically overlooked **Frank** completed Squeeze's rehabilitation, bringing the group full circle to a modernized version of jaunty pub rock. Relocating its original magic with memorably inventive material and spirited delivery, Squeeze here seems exuberantly youthful, as if music-making had suddenly become fun again. From giddy celebrations of new romance ("If It's Love," "Peyton Place") to sardonic views of emotional wreckage ("Slaughtered, Gutted and Heartbroken," "Rose I Said"), the songs surge with wit and melodic magic. (And who else would write a truly sensitive song about melancholy and menstruation?) Co-produced by Tilbrook and Eric Thorngren, **Frank** has a relaxed, live-in-the-studio sound that makes it intimate and inviting. Easily Squeeze's best since **Argybargy**.

The same enthusiasm flows in **A Round and a Bout**, recorded live at a pair of English dates in January '90. Matt Irving (keyboards, accordion) joins the Hollandaised lineup for an utterly delightful career summary, including four numbers from **Frank**. The brisk, no-nonsense performances work wonders, recharging everything on the program. Proof that miracles do happen: an upbeat overhaul turns the plodding "Black Coffee in Bed" into a marvelous jolt of pop soul. Even the audience-participation "If It's Love" sounds like fun.

Following his involuntary departure (after **Cool for Cats**), original bassist Harry Kakoulli recorded a like-minded set of dignified pop tunes. **Even When I'm Not** is an adequate record, although his compositions lack the clarity and crackle that typify Difford and Tilbrook's best work.   [jy/i]

See also *Paul Carrack, Jools Holland*.

SQUIRREL BAIT

Squirrel Bait (Homestead) 1985 ●
Skag Heaven (Homestead) 1987 ●

The only precedent most critics could find for the manic, crackling, power-pop destruction of Louisville, Kentucky's Squirrel Bait was Hüsker Dü, and that myopic, ignorant comparison may unfortunately be the main way the band's music is remembered. But singer Peter Searcy's anguished delivery was like a frightened Paul Westerberg, ten years younger (and twice as animal brutish), on eighteen cups of coffee—the terrified scream of a boy being chased by an axe-murderer. With a total lack of refinement or restraint, David Grubbs and Brian McMahan's distorted guitars threatened to blow the felt right out of your speakers. An immense sonic overload with monster hooks.

The self-titled debut may be a bit too thrashy for those unused to such fast speeds, but "Sun God" into "When I Fall" pack a total power wallop. The far better, more mid-tempo **Skag Heaven** manages to keep this intensity and great songs coming throughout, right from the opening shocker "Kid Dynamite." An eye-opening, blasting, sweaty, over-the-edge satori not for the timid. Unfortunately, the group packed it in before its release (the members scattered to various colleges and launched other musical ventures), thereby diminishing **Skag Heaven**'s impact and relegating Squirrel Bait to the little-known root of a burgeoning indie-band family tree. (Both records are available on a single compact disc.) [jr]

See also *Bastro, Big Wheel, Bitch Magnet, Slint.*

SQUIRRELS GROUP
See *Young Fresh Fellows.*

SS DECONTROL
The Kids Will Have Their Say! EP (XClaim!) 1982
Get It Away (XClaim!) 1983
SSD
How We Rock (Modern Method) 1984
Break It Up (Homestead) 1985

Boston's SS Decontrol was, to some minds, the most important New England hardcore band of the early '80s. With its now quaint cover shot of shiny-headed little punks charging the Massachusetts State House and such blistering, simple rockers as "How Much Art," **The Kids Will Have Their Say** was a pivotal event in Boston hardcore history.

Likewise, **Get It Away** helped define the city's straight-edge movement and remains a definitive hardcore classic. Seven quick songs on a 12-inch leave plenty of spare vinyl, but the impact couldn't possibly be any greater. From the opening "Glue," in which vocalist Springa addresses the need to hold together the straight-edge coalition, to the EP's closer, a cover of the Buzzcocks' "No Reply," guitarists Alan Barile and Francois Levesque tear open a sonic hole with a devastating metal-on-metal grind. With some predictable but astounding amateur musicianship on "Forced Down Your Throat," and "Nothing Done," as well as a fleeting flirtation with dub in "Get It Away" and "Under the Influence," SS Decontrol hit its enduring hardcore peak.

The following year, SS Decontrol (now billed merely as SSD) became one of the pioneers in the now-common shift from hardcore to thrash-metal. While the cover of **How We Rock** features gothic lettering and a glossy gold backing, it's not that bad a record, a consciously brainier variation on hard-rock traditions. **How We Rock** was, at the time, slagged by hardcore purists, but it stands as a crucial step in the evolution of underground rock.

Break It Up, the quintet's first full-length LP (and their last recording) was again trashed in some quarters for its metallic strivings, but curious rock students would do well to give it another spin. Considered from a post-Seattle vantage point, **Break It Up** couldn't possibly be considered heavy metal. (For one thing, it's not nearly heavy enough.) Springa's Noddy Holder rasp and the band's melodic guitar rock may have even less to do with punk than metal (except for Levesque's flashy solos), but it should be noted that this convincing take on '70s Brit-rock predates those bands commonly credited with that particular archaeological dig. [icm/i]

STAINS
Stains (SST) 1983

More than one turn-of-the-decade punk band—including the Austin, Texas group that became MDC—called itself the Stains, but the Latin-American LA quartet that issued an album (recorded in 1981) on SST is remembered as an early and skilled pioneer of hardcore's metal developments. A heavier and humorless mid-speed variation on early Black Flag, the accomplished and well-produced (by Spot) **Stains** has standard punk attributes but breaks the rules: guitarist Robert Becerra doesn't just play chords in lockstep with the bass, rather he works in and around the patterns and takes occasional brief solos.

A decade later, the Stains—who had evidently broken up for a number of years—resurfaced on the LA club scene playing heavy metal. [i]

CHRIS STAMEY
It's a Wonderful Life (DB) 1983
Instant Excitement EP (Coyote) 1984
It's Alright (Coyote-A&M) 1987 ●
CHRIS STAMEY GROUP
Christmas Time (Coyote) 1986

One of the guiding lights of the Southeast's nouveau-pop explosion, Chris Stamey led North Carolina's pioneering Sneakers before moving to New York, recording ultra-pop records on his own label, playing with Alex Chilton and forming the dB's. Recorded while Stamey was still in that band, **It's a Wonderful Life** (subtitled, on the back cover in reverse type, "It's a Miserable Life") takes him far afield from the offbeat Big Star sound for which he is best known. Joined by longstanding compatriots Ted Lyons and Mitch Easter, Stamey plays mesmerizingly moody and somber tunes ("Winter of Love," "Depth of Field," "Oh Yeah!") and aggressive demi-pop ("Never Enters My Mind"). Elsewhere, he warps the lyrics of "Tobacco Road" over a nearly all-drums background ("Get a Job"), offers cynical humor about urban life in a jarring, percussive setting ("Brush Fire in Hoboken") and plays a quiet piano piece with tape effects (the aptly named "Still Life #3"). The only relatively straightforward pop song is the bitter "Face of the Crowd." Overall, a strange and unsettling album, filled with fascinating adventures and subcurrents of profound unhappiness.

Opting out of the dB's on the eve of the group's first American album, Stamey instead made his own **Instant Excitement**, an odd but more upbeat hodgepodge which encompasses a homely reading of John Lennon's "Instant Karma," an idyllic love song ("When We're Alone"), a frisky country-rocker and an instrumental opus, "Ghost Story." Produced by Don Dixon, the songs are somewhat more typical of Stamey's original outlook and played with little attempt to impose a style in the studio. Eclectic and a little casually underbaked, but likable and, in spots, utterly touching.

The delightful **Christmas Time** mini-album introduces Stamey's new combo (actually the same people credited on **Instant Excitement**) and marks a brief reunion with the dB's. The original songs are all seasonal: "The Only Law That Santa Claus Understood," "You're What I Want (For Christmas)," "Snow Is Falling," even a new acoustic version of the unexpectedly appropriate "It's a Wonderful Life." The attractive title track sounds a lot like Brian Wilson's reflective mode.

Stamey recorded and toured extensively with the Golden Palominos and then settled down to make **It's Alright**—the most emotionally lucid pop-rock album of his career—with a snazzy collection of old and new friends. Alex Chilton, Richard Lloyd, Anton Fier, Mitch Easter, Faye Hunter, Bernie Worrell and Marshall Crenshaw are among the players. The songs vary from boppy ("Cara Lee") to somber ("The Seduction") to loud ("Incredible Happiness") to idyllic ("27 Years in a Single Day") but Stamey's dry, plaintive voice invests it all equally with peerless sincerity and familiar melodic appeal.

Stamey played second guitar behind Bob Mould on the latter's first-LP tour in 1989; two years later, Stamey teamed up with ex-bandmate Peter Holsapple and made an excellent duo album.   [i]

See also *dB's*, *Sneakers*.

STARJETS
Starjets (Portrait) 1979

Spunky if unoriginal, this Belfast quartet showed some promise, but not enough to really count. The album consists of simple punky rock, with added melody and restraint (plus some clever touches, like Beach Boys harmonies), but not as poppy as the Undertones. The lyrics rerun predictable subject matter—school, camaraderie, war, stardom—and the music's not strong enough to divert on its own merits. Likable but lost. Some Starjets later wound up in the Adventures.   [i]

See also *Adventures*.

STEEL POLE BATH TUB
Butterfly Love (Boner) 1989 ●
Lurch EP (Boner) 1990 ●
Tulip (Boner) 1991 ●

Given the shared cultural experiences of the twenty-something generation, a noisy power trio that puts a picture of Marcia Brady on the cover of its mighty debut album could be accused of demographic pandering. Fortunately, Steel Pole Bath Tub—born in Montana, based

in San Francisco and including a drummer with roots in the primordial stew that belched forth Seattle's current longhairs—thrashes about with enough unrestrained fervor and animal lust on **Butterfly Love** to attract an audience that probably kicked in their TV screens at an early age. SPBT stretches out on the less-appealing **Lurch** (also included on the **Butterfly Love** CD), reveling in frantic guitar noise for its own sake and demolishing several of the songs with long patches of fairly pointless feedback cacophony.   [i]

STEEL PULSE
Handsworth Revolution (Mango) 1978 ●
Tribute to the Martyrs (Mango) 1979 ●
Caught You (nr/Mango) 1980 ●
Reggae Fever (Mango) 1980 ●
True Democracy (Elektra) 1982 ●
Reggae Sunsplash '81 (Elektra) 1982
Earth Crisis (Elektra) 1983 ●
Reggae Greats (Mango) 1984 ●
Babylon the Bandit (Elektra) 1986 ●
State of ... Emergency (Loot-MCA) 1988 ●

In the mid-'70s, this young English sextet from Birmingham—inspired into existence by Bob Marley's **Catch a Fire**—found an affinity with the righteous rebellion of white new wavers and built its early reputation largely by touring British punk venues (as documented on live anthology records from Manchester's Electric Circus and London's Hope and Anchor). Steel Pulse's crossover appeal derives in large part from its young, modern thoughtfulness, but even more so from the group's incredible strength as one of the world's very best self-contained reggae units.

Steel Pulse's virtues include a gorgeous, multi-textured musical palette (especially on the first album and much of **Caught You**), intelligent lyrics (most notably on **Handsworth Revolution**, but also on **Tribute to the Martyrs**), a wondrous, sinuously propulsive beat and sweet lead vocals by Selwyn "Bumbo" Brown, who also has a nice quasi-scat style. Criticisms: the music, while always ear-enriching and heartfelt, lacks consistently memorable tunes. An increasing tendency towards preachy, trite lyrics on **Caught You** (retitled **Reggae Fever** in America) is a disappointment, since songwriting guitarist David Hinds has already shown he can do better.

If **Caught You** is Steel Pulse at its most pop-oriented, **True Democracy** has the band reaching for the most common denominator. Steel Pulse's best falls between the two extremes. Which brings us to **Earth Crisis**, where tasty use of synth and sharp production make it their finest, most consistent album since **Tribute to the Martyrs**. As for the documentary festival album, **Reggae Sunsplash '81**, Steel Pulse has an entire side, but never quite shakes a frustrating stiffness and artificiality. Pass it up. **Reggae Greats** is a compilation.

With the release of **Babylon the Bandit**, however, it was clear that the band's professed ideals were no longer jibing with their attempts to crack the (American) market. Protest lyrics swathed in slick, upwardly mobile production were pretty hard to take seriously, and the LP sank like a stone.

The group then left Elektra and, three years later, returned on MCA with **State of Emergency**. Although still fairly hi-tech, the LP isn't as aggressively slick as its predecessor, and is saved by the determined performances of uneven songs. The fiery energy that marked the group's early work still manages to come through. [jg/bk]

STEEL TIPS
Steel Tips EP (Red) 1981

Universally ignored and/or abhorred during their existence, Steel Tips were one of the few punk bands in the late '70s to wallow in and lionize actual street-level violence, as opposed to costumes and makeup. At a time when sado shock was an easily marketable commodity, this New York group trafficked in genuine physical assault, attacking their jaded tuff punk audiences. Spiralling away from the 1978 debut 45, ''Krazy Baby'' b/w ''96 Tears'' (featuring soon-to-be-infamous art and battery confrontational geek Joe Coleman on his sole recorded vocal with the group; he was generally relegated to support antagonist behind prime antagonist Tom O'Leary), the group dropped the goofy quirk of that 45 and by the '81 EP (which included a bonus 45) was playing a thicker, superficially meaner and more accomplished new wave thrum. Frontman O'Leary, a sociopathic biker with little but contempt for the thrill-seeking crowds, played the clubs like Godzilla played Tokyo; unfortunately neither he nor his band had the slightest inkling how to translate their stomp and slash into musical terms, and left behind a musical legacy no more enduring than Tuff Darts or the Shirts. [ab]

MARTIN STEPHENSON & THE DAINTIES
Boat to Bolivia (nr/Kitchenware-London) 1986 ●
Gladsome Humour & Blue (nr/Kitchenware-London) 1988 (Kitchenware-London-Capitol) 1989 ●
Salutation Road (Kitchenware-London-Capitol) 1990 ●

Those old enough to remember Donovan's late-'60s albums, on which he combined strains of folk, rock, blues and wispy jazz with sincere, unpretentious singing, have a good reference point for Martin Stephenson and the Dainties.

Hailing from a small town outside of Newcastle (which he reputedly never left until he was 27), singer/guitarist Stephenson is a performer of extraordinary warmth and depth whose major strength is his gift for understatement. On **Boat to Bolivia**, he's presented in a variety of settings—from reggae to ragtime—and seems entirely at ease in all of them. At a time when music is thoroughly dominated by urban and suburban voices, many of Stephenson's songs offer a refreshing rural perspective.

Gladsome Humour & Blue tones down the stylistic eclecticism of **Bolivia** in favor of a darker, even more introspective approach, with strings and acoustic instruments at the forefront on most tracks. This is Stephenson's least immediate, most subtle album, though many of the songs project an almost religious intensity. Not light listening, but rewarding. (The American **Gladsome** is a double-vinyl/single-CD-or-cassette package that includes **Boat to Bolivia** in its entirety.)

Teamed up with American producer Pete Anderson (Dwight Yoakam, Michelle Shocked), Stephenson's

outlook is considerably brighter—often downright celebratory—on **Salutation Road**. Anderson puts him in more of a rock setting than on either previous album, spicing things up with horns and background vocalists on many of the tracks—but never to the detriment of the star, who responds with some of his best performances yet. A lovely record. [ds]

STEPPES
The Steppes (Mystic) 1984
Drop of the Creature (Voxx) 1987
Stewdio (Voxx) 1988
Tourists from Timenotyet (nr/Bam Caruso) 1988
Enquire Within (Voxx) 1989
Harps & Hammers (Voxx) 1990

Though they apparently have a substantial cult following in Europe, the Steppes remain inexplicably obscure in the States. A shame, since this far-flung quartet (singer/songwriters John and David Fallon reside in Ireland; the American rhythm section lives in Oregon and San Francisco) is easily one of the best and most distinctive combos of the current neo-psychedelic crop, combining a subtly baroque musical sensibility with an ability to pull off ambitiously original arrangements and production ideas. The Steppes capture the essence of vintage psychedelia without sounding pretentious or unduly derivative.

The band's albums have steadily grown more accomplished and impressive, from the friendly acoustic stylings of the limited-edition eight-song debut to the multi-textured mini-epics of their more recent efforts. **Stewdio**, **Enquire Within** and **Harps & Hammers** are all mesmerizing, extraordinarily realized works whose inventive musical settings belie their low-budget origins. **Tourists from Timenotyet** combines tracks from **Drop of the Creature** and **Stewdio**. [hd]

STETSASONIC
On Fire (Tommy Boy) 1986
Sally EP (Tommy Boy) 1988
In Full Gear (Tommy Boy) 1988 ●
Blood, Sweat & No Tears (Tommy Boy) 1991 ●

A fine example of rap's producer-oriented developmental process, Brooklyn's Stetsasonic began as a trio of rappers (Daddy-O, Delite and Fruitkwan), a keyboardist/drummer/scratcher (DBC) and two mixers (Prince Paul and Wise). The sound of **On Fire** is hard and spare: one-at-a-time raps over rhythm tracks (including human beat box noises) with sporadic bits of music added. Topics are likewise familiar (''My Rhyme,'' ''Faye,'' ''Bust That Groove''), but Stetsasonic has a decisive sound that takes full advantage of the varied voices.

Prince Paul (Huston) subsequently emerged as a talented and successful second-generation producer, working with Queen Latifah, De La Soul, 3rd Bass and others. Meanwhile, Daddy-O, Wise and DBC all gained enough studio skills to produce tracks for the diverse and marvelously entertaining **In Full Gear**.

As a precursor to Stet's second coming, the **Sally** 12-inch contains two versions of the title tune (which faintly resembles—without quoting—Wilson Pickett and Sly Stone) and three mixes of ''DBC Let the Music

Play," which surprisingly almost uses a rock drumbeat for its bed. The album itself adds a customized version of the Floaters' 1977 soul classic, "Float On" (with labelmates the Force M.D.'s guesting), a bottom-heavy lesson in musical geography ("Miami Bass") and a dozen more entertaining mixtures of genial hip-hop, '70s soul, amusing raps and other expressions of the group's fertile imagination.

Despite the liner notes' dubious claim that "Stetsasonic is the one and only Hip Hop Band and the future of soul music," there's no argument that the ambitious **Blood, Sweat & No Tears** is extraordinary, an engaging state-of-the-art album seamlessly loaded with diverse music, thoughtful and/or amusing raps and more friendly family atmosphere than an Italian wedding. With positive power and enough production and rhyming talent for three groups, the six-man crew (now including a fulltime drummer) covers a wide range of topics—from politics ("Free South Africa," "Corporate America"), social issues ("Ghetto Is the World") and autobiography ("To Whom It May Concern," "The Hip Hop Band," "Heaven Help the MF's") to peers ("Uda Man," "Do You Remember This"), a favorite fan ("Speaking of a Girl Named Suzy") and parties ("So Let the Fun Begin"). Marvelous. [i]

STEVE STEVENS ATOMIC PLAYBOYS
See *Billy Idol.*

TOM STEVENS
See *Long Ryders.*

DAVE STEWART
See *Eurythmics.*

MARK STEWART AND THE MAFFIA
Learning to Cope with Cowardice (nr/Plexus) 1983
MARK STEWART
As the Veneer of Democracy Starts to Fade (nr/Mute) 1985 ●
Mark Stewart + Maffia (Upside) 1986 ●
Mark Stewart (nr/Mute) 1987 ●
Metatron (Mute-Restless) 1990 φ

Teamed with dubmeister Adrian Sherwood and his Tackhead associates (Keith LeBlanc, Doug Wimbish and Skip McDonald), ex-Pop Grouper Stewart produces what could best be described as avant-garde reggae on **Learning to Cope with Cowardice.** Making a wide left turn past Sly and Robbie, the disc is dark and forbidding, with a plethora of ghostly, off-center sounds floating in and out of nowhere, rarely paying heed to musical convention. At times, things get gimmicky enough to resemble a demo disc for effects units, but **Cowardice** is a rewarding album with political consciousness.

Stewart's convictions push further to the fore on his second album. **As the Veneer of Democracy Starts to Fade** abandons reggae for a disorienting marriage of big-beat drums and dissonant electronics that is not unlike early Cabaret Voltaire. Several tracks feature taped

authoritarian voices that you probably thought only existed in your nightmares.

Mark Stewart + Maffia, Stewart's first US release, is a compilation culled from those first two LPs (plus one non-LP cut), and is well worth it for those who don't have the imports. Stewart's next LP, simply titled **Mark Stewart** (although the same Mafia—note the new spelling—members are present), pushes funk and stripped-down metal; while Stewart and Sherwood's aural experiments work well in this context, running out of ideas doesn't deter them from letting a track go on for seven or eight minutes. The lyrics are uncharacteristically innocuous—some are even kind of smug. The CD contains a bunch of extra remixes of cuts that were already too long. Stewart is a very talented artist who should be mandatory listening for anyone who thinks using synthesizers only means sounding like the Human League, but those wishing to sample his work should go for the US compilation and leave this one alone.

By contrast, **Metatron** has a much warmer, more immediate feel, and the band really gets a chance to explode. The sparing and effective use of electronics leaves plenty of room for crunching guitar cascades atop a megabeat rhythm section. Stewart's lyrical visions have shifted from revolutionary politics to paranoia about late-20th-century life: "These Things Happen" is his response to a bloodthirsty "human time bomb . . . an accident waiting to happen." Musical ideas are still more or less at a premium, as riffs are prolonged ad nauseum and passed off as complete songs. The CD adds an instrumental version of the opening "Hysteria," which sounds an awful lot like Black Sabbath's "Iron Man." [dgs]

See also *Pop Group, Tackhead.*

STIFF LITTLE FINGERS
Inflammable Material (Rough Trade) 1979 (Restless Retro) 1990 ●
Nobody's Heroes (Chrysalis) 1980 (Restless Retro) 1990 ●
Hanx! (Chrysalis) 1980 (Restless Retro) 1990 ●
Go for It (Chrysalis) 1981 (Restless Retro) 1990 ●
Now Then . . . (nr/Chrysalis) 1982
All the Best (nr/Chrysalis) 1983 ●
The Peel Sessions EP (nr/Strange Fruit) 1986 ●
Live and Loud!! (nr/Link) 1988 ●
No Sleep 'Til Belfast EP (nr/Skunx) 1988
No Sleep 'Til Belfast (nr/Kaz) 1988 φ
See You Up There! (Caroline) 1989 ●
The Last Time EP (nr/Link) 1989
The Peel Sessions Album (nr/Strange Fruit) 1990 ●

Belfast's Stiff Little Fingers began as four exciting (if narrow-minded) sloganeers, led by raw-voiced singer/guitarist Jake Burns. SLF's debut (the Rough Trade label's first LP release) includes such classic protest punk as "Suspect Device," "Alternative Ulster" and "Wasted Life." The LP is generally regarded as a classic punk LP; its UK chart success was the spark that set off a second wave of new bands like the Ruts and Undertones.

By **Nobody's Heroes,** they had changed labels, acquired a new drummer (Jim Reilly) and developed a bit more subtlety in the music and lyrics. (Contravening punk's push for DIY autonomy, most of SLF's lyrics were written by Gordon Ogilvie, a journalist who later became their manager.) The title track and "Gotta Getaway" are the highlights, but "Wait and See" audaciously thumbs a collective nose at the band's detractors; a roughed-up version of the Specials' "Doesn't Make It Alright" showed SLF to be developing interests outside punk's limits. Although slicker, more sedate and half as fiery as **Inflammable Material**, it's a solid LP. A live set, **Hanx!**, served as a premature greatest hits collection, containing powerful renditions of their best material in a well-recorded concert environment, before an enthusiastic audience.

Go for It broke Stiff Little Fingers' mold, and they emerged a much different sounding band. Burns' voice is smoother and less anguished; the music, while no less energetic or committed, is more diverse and sophisticated. The title track, a memorable martial guitar instrumental, shows how far they'd come, bearing scant resemblance to their early rabble-rousing roughness. Other numbers draw on reggae stylings for variety; "Silver Lining" even utilizes prominent brass.

Now Then, their least popular but most lasting LP, continues the exploration of more accessible musical turf and is full of solid rock songs that pair energy and melody with clever guitar play. With new drummer Dolph Taylor (ex-Tom Robinson Band) in the lineup, SLF sounds better than ever. Their political consciousness remains undiminished, but subtler and stronger lyrics effectively replace inchoate rage with on-target criticism.

Following the group's dissolution, the two-LP singles compilation **All the Best** appeared, containing 30 tracks that chronologically review their progress from raw rage to sharp power-pop. Burns later released several solo singles.

Five years later, SLF unexpectedly reformed for two UK tours (December '87 and March '88). The crowd's excited roar is the real star of **Live and Loud!!**, a double LP from a December London gig. After a house-on-fire version of "Alternative Ulster," SLF proves sloppier and slower than when they left off, and the choice of material clearly aims to please, with not one selection from **Now Then**. Nevertheless, the LP documents a triumphant, if brief, comeback of a once-great band ironically at the height of its popularity. (Link licensed **Live and Loud!!** to Kaz, which issued it on CD and cassette as **No Sleep 'Til Belfast**, also the title of a four-song live EP on a Link subsidiary; Link then brought out a competing CD of its own, identical except for the deletion of "The Only One.")

The band was unhappy with the live LP and released a far better one (See You Up There!), recorded on St. Patrick's Day '88 at London's Brixton Academy. Since the track listings are—with some notable differences—very similar, it's obviously meant to replace **Live and Loud!!** and, on sound quality, there's no contest. Not to be outdone, Link turned around and issued a live 12-inch (**The Last Time**) of three more songs from the earlier gig, including the intentionally awful Stones cover of the record's title. This appears to have been the last shot in the war of live records—for now.

The Peel Sessions album replaces the '86 Peel EP, as it combines all four songs from it with sessions from '78, '79 and '80. The versions are, in general, rawer than the familiar recordings of the same songs. In par-

ticular, second-album songs recorded first-album style are truly ear-opening, most notably an embittered, enraged "Fly the Flag" that is clearly superior to the **Nobody's Heroes** version. What's more, the early "Nobody's Hero" has slightly different lyrics.   [i/jr]

STING

The Dream of the Blue Turtles (A&M) 1985 (A&M-Mobile Fidelity) 1989 ●
Bring on the Night (A&M) 1986 ●
... Nothing Like the Sun (A&M) 1987 ●
... Nada Como el Sol EP (A&M) 1988 ●
The Soul Cages (A&M) 1991 ●

In 1985, with the Police on hiatus and heading for an unannounced *fin*, Sting produced a multi-platinum solo debut, **The Dream of the Blue Turtles**. Enlisting a seasoned collection of top-notch American players (Branford Marsalis, Omar Hakim, Kenny Kirkland and Darryl Jones), Sting attempted to distance himself from the common vulgarity of mere rock music by introducing jazz trappings to a new set of songs, including "If You Love Somebody Set Them Free," "Love Is the Seventh Wave," "Fortress Around Your Heart" and the unbelievably stupid "Russians." Despite the illustrious company and his switch from bass to guitar, Sting alone is little different than Sting in the Police: smug and pretentious. And his like-it-or-not voice is still his voice.

The four sides of **Bring on the Night**—recorded at several 1985 European concerts with the same sidemen—prove Sting can pull it off live. Mainly drawing on Blue Turtles, the LP also revamps old Police songs (e.g., "Driven to Tears," "I Burn for You," "Demolition Man"), giving them airy refinement and a measured gait. The sound quality is spectacular, the instrumental arrangements and performances unassailably accomplished but dull. Sting's liner notes even reveal a glimmer of self-effacing humility.

The same can't be said for the effete intellectual masturbation of **Nothing Like the Sun**. Even as the nouveau sophisticate sings "History Will Teach Us Nothing," his pedantic instincts and bulging ego inform the lyrics at every turn with political dilettantism, literary namedropping and prolix pseudo-profundities. Aided by a new batch of virtuosos and famous guests (Andy Summers, Gil Evans, Eric Clapton, Mark Knopfler and Rubén Blades, credited on one track with "Spanish"), Sting stretches a dozen delicate songs over two short discs, coming down off his high horse long enough to show Jimi Hendrix aficionados a numbingly dull way to perform "Little Wing." A tedious, bankrupt and vacuous cavern of a record.

For some reason (condescension? avarice? arrogance? practice?), Sting cut Spanish-language versions of "Little Wing," "We'll Be Together," "They Dance Alone" and "Fragile" (also in Portuguese) and released the five as **Nada Como el Sol**, thereby allowing a sizable portion of the non-English-speaking world to join the rest of us in wondering just what he's prattling on about.

Putting down his guitar and global pretensions, Sting made his next album more personal and reflective, alternating obvious pop singles ("All This Time" sounds like the Police performing a Paul Simon song; "Why Should I Cry for You?" is an elegantly atmospheric ballad; the romantic title track touches old Police ground with new sophistication) and expansive theatrical meanderings ("Island of Souls," "Mad About You," "The Wild Wild Sea") that are individually handsome but cry out for a context which the album fails to provide. With repeated references to his late father, **The Soul Cages**—antiseptically produced with Hugh Padgham—has solemn emotional resonance and a settled maturity unheard in Sting's previous work, but the attempt to reconcile lofty artistic ambitions and demographic commercial desires casts a pall over the entire undertaking. [i]

See also *Police*.

R.J. STIPS

See *Nits*.

STONE BY STONE W/ CHRIS D

See *Divine Horsemen*.

STONE ROSES

Stone Roses (Silvertone) 1989 + 1989 ●

Manchester's Stone Roses began around 1980 as a Clash-inspired punk band called the Patrol. Joining the neo-mod scene, the group changed its name to English Rose (after the Jam song); by '85 it had become Stone Roses, playing atmospheric guitar rock like the Chameleons. After two early singles, producer John Leckie arrived, and he helped the group combine its magnetic, charming pop with the dramatic and pulsing heights of post-punk rock. The result was a nearly flawless debut LP, released in May 1989, that launched a stylistic craze centered in Manchester.

With all the hype and hysteria, it's easy to overlook what a solid and enduring record **Stone Roses** is. With his inventive ringing sound, guitarist John Squire seems destined to be the next Johnny Marr. Drummer Reni is likewise extraordinary, giving otherwise usual pop tunes an exciting kick. But it's the songs, and Leckie's thick, molten production, that hit home. Slowly building towards quick bursts of fire, the opening "I Wanna Be Adored" sets the tone, echoed in the equally incredible "Made of Stone." "She Bangs the Drums" is brawling pop, while "Elephant Stone" (a Peter Hook-produced single that was added to the album's US edition) percolates New Order-style. Best of all, the powerpacked closer, "I Am the Resurrection," slams incessantly for the better part of four minutes, only to switch seamlessly into an overloaded funk groove with wild drumming and squealing peals of guitar feedback.

Stone Roses' fame (if not success: several of the groups that followed in their wake have become much bigger stars) has seemingly held them back. Only two new singles appeared (the first, "Fool's Gold," was added to a second US version of the album) in the eighteen months following the album's release. [jr]

STOOGES

The Stooges (Elektra) 1969 + 1977 + 1982 ●
Fun House (Elektra) 1970 + 1977 + 1982 ●
No Fun (nr/Elektra) 1980
Rubber Legs (Fr. Fan Club) 1987 ●

What You Gonna Do EP (Fr. Revenge) 1988
Live 1971 (Fr. Starfighter) 1988
My Girl Hates My Heroin (Fr. Revenge) 1989 ●

IGGY AND THE STOOGES

Raw Power (Columbia) 1973 + 1981 ●
Metallic K.O. (Import) 1976
I'm Sick of You EP (Bomp!) 1977
(I Got) Nothing EP (Skydog) 1978 ●
I'm Sick of You (Ger. Line) 1981 + 1987 ●
Iggy & the Stooges (no label) c. 1987 ●
Death Trip EP (Fr. Revenge) 1987
Pure Lust EP (Fr. Revenge) 1987 ●
Raw Power EP (Fr. Revenge) 1987 ●
Gimme Danger EP (Fr. Revenge) 1987 ●
She Creatures of Hollywood Hills EP (Fr. Revenge) 1988 ●
The Stooges (Fr. Revenge) 1988
Metallic 2xKO (Fr. Skydog) 1988 ●
Raw Stooges Vol I (Ger. Electric) 1988
Raw Stooges Vol II EP (Ger. Electric) 1988
Search and Destroy—Raw Mixes Vol III (Curtis) 1989
Iggy and the Stooges (Fr. Revenge) 1991

IGGY POP

I Got a Right (Invasion) 1983 (Enigma) 1985
I Got a Right (Fr. Revenge) 1987

IGGY POP & JAMES WILLIAMSON

Jesus Loves the Stooges EP (Bomp!) 1977
Kill City (Bomp!) 1978 ●

VARIOUS ARTISTS

Hard to Beat (Aus. Au-go-go) 1988

The Stooges, the debut LP by Iggy Pop's self-willed band—which at the time also included guitarist Ron Asheton, drummer Scott Asheton and bassist Dave Alexander—sounds like nothing else released in 1969. Moronic lyrics and three-chord "tunes" clearly anticipate the lowest-common-denominator populism of '70s punk. Tempos are a bit draggy, but all the ingredients for what followed are present. One of the most superficially artless records ever made.

By contrast, **Fun House** knowingly sucks the listener into its raucous vortex. This ingeniously constructed album starts out menacingly ("Down on the Street") and builds relentlessly to its apocalyptic conclusion ("L.A. Blues"). Iggy's singing—much more expressive than on **The Stooges**—veers from sullen petulance to primal scream on songs of adolescent solipsism. **Fun House** comes as close as any one record ever will to encapsulating what rock is, was and always will be about. Inspired touch: Steven Mackay's saxophone. (**No Fun**, appearing between reissues of the two original Stooges albums, consists of tracks from both.)

Raw Power is another masterpiece, featuring the stinging lead guitar of James Williamson in a reorganized Stooges. (Ron Asheton had switched to bass to replace Dave Alexander.) With Williamson as co-author, Iggy's songs are more musical (i.e., a sense of structure emerged) in their sex-and-death conflation ("Gimme Danger," "Death Trip"). The title track and "Search and Destroy" are only two of **Raw Power**'s tunes to achieve classic status for staring into the abyss, guitar in hand. Heavy metal in every sense, the album marked the end of the Stooges as a band concept—Iggy

635

hereafter received solo billing—and, effectively, the first stage of Iggy's career.

Setting the tone for the vinyl deluge that would follow a decade later, **Metallic K.O.** is a semi-notorious, semi-legal document of the Stooges' final concert; at the Michigan Palace, Detroit, January 1974. The band staggers towards entropy as Iggy maliciously baits the crowd, which responds in kind. There are only six songs, but more than your money's worth of bile. Highlight: a version of "Louie Louie" you've never heard before.

Kill City was salvaged from the period between the Stooges' breakup and Iggy's Bowie-inspired redemption. The songs plod, the sound is bad and the vocals—recorded on weekend leaves from the hospital where Iggy was residing at the time—are buried. The strung-out music has a morbid voyeuristic appeal if you enjoy wallowing in other people's degradation; otherwise, avoid this nasty stuff. After **Kill City** had gone out of print, the German **I'm Sick of You** album collected tracks from it, along with the '77 "I Got a Right" single and two Bomp! EPs (**I'm Sick of You** and **Jesus Loves the Stooges**) of rough but intense and worthwhile demos. The 1983 **I Got a Right** (and the French variation thereon) is drawn from the same pool of material, containing an entire side of **Kill City**; the subsequent **Pure Lust** offers four of the same tracks in mixes ranging from identical to wildly divergent.

In late '87, a groundswell of interest in the Stooges (fueled in no small part by the increasingly prominent and numerous Australian bands playing in Detroit-influenced post-Radio Birdman/New Race style), resulted not only in one of the first single-artist tribute projects—**Hard to Beat**, a double LP of mostly over-reverent Iggyness—but the beginning of a spate of reissues, predominantly from renamed French labels previously notorious for questionably legal '60s reissues at the height of the mid-'80s garage revival.

Rubber Legs offers six '73-'74 rehearsal tracks, including "Cry for Me." Although a bit heavy on the keyboards (as are many of the "rehearsal" tapes to follow onto vinyl), the sound is good, revealing Iggy at his rawest and most powerful along with James Williamson in all his glory on such new songs as "Head On" and "Cock in My Pocket."

My Girl Hates My Heroin is one of the best of the lot. Although mostly familiar '73 rehearsal material (with the guitars are turned up and the keyboards turned down), there are a few surprises, and a studio mix of "Death Trip" that is unquestionably one of the most violent recordings ever made.

Iggy & the Stooges consists half of earlier, lower-fi studio run-throughs, three songs of which were previously unreleased in any (nominally) legit form, though "She Creatures of the Hollywood Hills" (already familiar to **Hard to Beat** owners, thanks to the version by the unimaginatively named Raw Power) has since turned up several times on bootlegs. The three songs that comprise the other side of **Iggy & the Stooges** are moderate quality live-at-the-Whiskey versions of by-now-familiar tracks. (The same recording of "Open Up and Bleed" also showed up, with far hotter mastering, on **She Creatures**, backing a weird and spicy para-funk rendition of the title track.) **What You Gonna Do** again excerpts the same show with a fairly rote take on "Gim-

m(i)e Danger," along with a minutiae-filled Ron Asheton radio interview and the obscure title song, horrendously recorded in '68 but undeniable testimony to the fury of the band even in its formative stages. For wealthy novices, five of the Revenge titles—**Pure Lust**, **Raw Power**, **Gimme Danger** (also available as a picture disc), **She Creatures of Hollywood Hills** and **What You Gonna Do**—were offered in a limited edition boxed set simply titled **The Stooges**.

Live 1971 (with the same excellent cover photo as **What You Gonna Do**) presents the Stooges' least documented and, to many, most intriguing phase (along with the Hawaiian guitar lineup, of course): the brief period from late-'70 to mid-'71 when Asheton and James Williamson dualed (dueled) on guitar. Unfortunately, the sound quality is by far the worst of all the recent records; muted, mushy and moribund. For collectors only.

Metallic 2xKO, the two-disc reissue of **Metallic K.O.**, adds two previously unreleased songs (plus the previously bootlegged "Heavy Liquid"), and a brief a cappella poetic recitation of "I Wanna Be Your Dog"), supposedly from the same final gig (though exact dates of certain tracks on both versions of the LP are questionable). There's also a somewhat less biting/baiting chunk of interaction with the juiced-up audience and an unpolished, extended demo of "I Got Nothin' " (later/previously on **Kill City**). Besides the title track (also said to be from that same final show at the Palace), **Gimme Danger** offers a considerably crisper sounding if less urgent additional cut as well as the first third of "Open Up and Bleed," backed by a bizarrely hybridized "Heavy Liquid (part one)"/"I Got Nothin' " and—oddest of all—Iggy and James (unaccompanied), paying musical tribute to James Brown.

Presumably from the same goof session come an Iggy/Williamson duet on "Purple Haze" and "I'm Waiting for My Man" (on the French **Raw Power**), "I'm a Man" and a percussed, drawn-out version of Dylan's "Ballad of Hollis Brown" (on **Death Trip**). With several duplications from previous titles, **Raw Power** and **Death Trip** are disorganized hodgepodges that mix tasty radio ads in with backing tracks lifted from the original lost **Raw Power** mixes,

The first two volumes of **Raw Stooges** offer some of the weirdest Stoogerama yet. Purportedly cheap pre-Elektra studio recordings of the songs soon to become the band's first two LPs (with a stray treat or two thrown in), the basic sound is incredibly harsh and direct, not nearly so developed or wickedly insinuating as **Funhouse**, yet unnervingly affecting on an even more immediate basis. The truly weird thing is how the mix in places simulates sound leakage/print-through bleeding from one groove to the next, creating weird guitar echoes and premonitory vocals throughout the set. Amazing stuff, but it's like listening to a live show with one ear in the first row and another behind the outfield scoreboard. When the elements hit an uneasy balance, as on "Real Cool Time" and "Little Doll," this is some of the very best Stooge music on record. When they clash, it still ain't too shabby, either. Volume III, the pic disc **Search and Destroy**, combines the famous suppressed mixes from **Raw Power** (as radio broadcast in a then-current promotion) with remixed and alleged CBS outtakes that ought to sound awfully familiar by now to anyone stouthearted or singleminded enough to have waded completely through the preceding.   [si/i/ab]

See also *Iggy Pop, Sonic's Rendezvous Band*.

STOP THE VIOLENCE MOVEMENT
See *Boogie Down Productions*.

STRAITJACKET FITS
Life in One Chord EP (NZ Flying Nun) 1987
Hail (NZ Flying Nun) 1988 (Flying Nun-Rough Trade) 1990 ●
Missing from Melt EP [CD] (Flying Nun-Arista) 1991 ●
Melt (Flying Nun-Arista) 1991 ●

Pretty-pop New Zealand outfits like Chills, Clean and Bats get more attention, but Auckland's Straitjacket Fits are the most intense and versatile group on Flying Nun's extraordinary roster. Where some of the other bands work in a narrow scope, the Fits alternate subtlety and hell-raising, displaying muscle here, dexterity there and quiet longings everywhere. Hooks abound, and the vocals (by guitarists Shayne Carter and Andrew Brough) are pretty yet masculine. The debut EP showcases all these strengths, with the nicely strummed "All That That Brings" contrasting the paranoid "She Speeds" and the caterwauling waltz-time "Dialing a Prayer."

The original New Zealand edition of **Hail** contains ten new songs; the American deletes four, replacing them with the contents of **Life in One Chord**. On the common tracks, **Hail** blasts off in fuzzy, distorted Mission of Burma-like power-rhythmed guitar buzz ("Life in One Chord"—*not* from the EP—is downright fierce). But there are plenty of softer touches, including a moody cover of Leonard Cohen's "So Long Marianne," the ghostly organ on "Grate" and the gentle ebb of "This Taste Delight" and "Fabulous Things." Those impressed by the American **Hail** are well advised to seek out the import so as not to miss the scintillating "Take from the Years," "Telling Tales," "Dead Heat" and "Only You Knew."   [jr]

RICHARD STRANGE
The Live Rise of Richard Strange (ZE-PVC) 1980
The Phenomenal Rise of Richard Strange (nr/Virgin) 1981

RICHARD STRANGE AND THE ENGINE ROOM
Going–Gone (Ger. Side) 1987 (nr/Nightshift) 1988 ●

This former Doctor of Madness made two albums of a thematic work similar in concept to the rise and fall of a demagogue chronicled by the Kinks in **Preservation Act 2**, but less meticulously plotted and more thoughtful in content. Only the vocals on **Live Rise** were recorded onstage at Hurrah in New York; the backing tracks had been cut previously and played back for the performance.

Aside from the obvious sound/production quality upgrade, the second (all-studio) version drops three numbers and adds five to flesh out the concept, and sports

beefier back-up (stronger guitar plus some super sax work courtesy of ex-Secret Affair Dave Winthrop). Strange emerges as a significant artist in the vein of Ziggy-era Bowie, but tougher and minus the androgyny.

The record that marked Strange's return after a number of years is more than welcome, and more than worthwhile. Originally issued in Germany and then remixed and released by a Scottish label, **Going–Gone** was evidently recorded over quite some time in half a dozen studios; five of the ten tracks were produced by Dave Allen (Cure, Sisters of Mercy, etc.). Keyboardist James T. Ford co-wrote all but two tracks, co-produced (with Strange) a pair and handled "electronic hardware" on all but one. The 53 minutes of music ranges from mid-Eastern intrigue ("Damascus") to Poe-ish theatrics ("Fall of the House of 'U' ") to sentimental pop ("Dominoes") to ominous, churning dance-rock ("Fear Is the Engine"). The inner sleeve bears, with no elaboration, the legend "recalled to life." No kidding.   [jg]

STRANGE CRUISE
See *Visage*.

STRANGLERS
IV Rattus Norvegicus (A&M) 1977 (nr/Fame) 1982 ●
No More Heroes (A&M) 1977 (nr/Fame) 1987 ●
The Stranglers EP (A&M) 1977
Black and White (A&M) 1978 ●
The Stranglers EP (Jap. UA) 1979
Live (X Cert) (nr/UA) 1979 ●
The Raven (nr/UA) 1979 (EMI America) 1985 ●
Don't Bring Harry EP (nr/UA) 1979
IV (IRS) 1980 ●
The Meninblack (Stiff) 1981 (nr/Fame) 1988 ●
La Folie (nr/Liberty) 1981 (nr/Fame) 1983 ●
The Collection 1977–1982 (nr/Liberty) 1982 (nr/Fame) 1989 ●
Feline (Epic) 1982 ●
Great Lost (Jap. UA) 1983
Great Lost Continued (Jap. UA) 1983
Aural Sculpture (Epic) 1984 ●
Off the Beaten Track (nr/Liberty) 1986
Dreamtime (Epic) 1987 ●
All Day and All of the Night EP (nr/Epic) 1987 ●
All Live and All of the Night (Epic) 1988 ●
Rarities (nr/Liberty) 1988 ●
The Evening Show Sessions (nr/Nighttracks-Strange Fruit) 1989 ●
Singles (The UA Years) (nr/Liberty) 1989 ●
10 (Epic) 1990 ●
Greatest Hits 1977–1990 (nr/Epic) 1990 (Epic) 1991 ●

HUGH CORNWELL + ROBERT WILLIAMS
Nosferatu (nr/Liberty) 1979

J.J. BURNEL
Euroman Cometh (nr/UA) 1979 (nr/Mau Mau) 1987
Un Jour Parfait (Fr. CBS) 1989 ●

D. GREENFIELD & J.J. BURNEL
Fire & Water (Ecoutez Vos Murs) (nr/Epic) 1983

HUGH CORNWELL

Wolf (Virgin) 1988 ●
Another Kind of Love EP (nr/Virgin) 1988 ●

PURPLE HELMETS

Ride Again (Fr. New Rose) 1988
Rise Again (nr/él-Anagram) 1989 ●

Formed in 1975, the Stranglers became enormously popular in Britain and Europe when they burst on the scene in 1977 with one of the first new wave albums, preceding both the Clash and the Sex Pistols to the shops by several months.

The first album was produced by Martin Rushent (who continued to work with them through 1979's live LP). **Rattus Norvegicus** includes both sides of the awesome debut single, "London Lady" and "(Get a) Grip (on Yourself)," as well as other blunt gonad-grabbers like "Hanging Around" and "Sometimes." The violently emotional lyrics and bitterly spat vocals are supported by Jean-Jacques Burnel's almost impossibly deep-throated bass grunts and Hugh Cornwell's slashing guitar, with contrasting jolly organ sounds by Dave Greenfield providing the only relief from otherwise relentless aggression. A great album. The UK edition initially included a free single, "Choosey Suzie" b/w "Peasant in the Big Shitty."

No More Heroes continues in the same vein, but drops whatever hint of restraint may have been in force the first time around. Rude words and adult themes abound, with no punches pulled, from the blatant sexism of "Bring on the Nubiles" to the sarcastic attack on racism ("I Feel Like a Wog") to the suicide of a friend ("Dagenham Dave"). Despite the increased virulence, the music is even better than on the debut, introducing pop stylings that would later become a more common aspect of the Stranglers' character. **No More Heroes** is easily their best album.

The Stranglers' American label then put out a colored-vinyl 7-inch, with "(Get a) Grip" and "Hanging Around" from the first album, "Something Better Change" (from the second) and that killer songs equally powerful UK B-side, "Straighten Out."

Tricked out with gray-swirl vinyl and a limited edition bonus 45 (three tunes, including a wonderful gruff version of "Walk on By"), **Black and White** lacks only good songs. Except for "Nice 'n' Sleazy," most of the tracks are merely inferior rehashes of earlier work, making the LP easily forgettable. (The subsequent British CD incorporates the single's contents.)

Four gigs in '77 and '78 provided the basis for **Live (X Cert)**. The material is all familiar, but the high-tension ambience and some choice bits of Cornwell-vs.-the-audience banter make it an effective dual-function live/greatest hits album. (The CD appends two cuts.)

Borrowing an old packaging gimmick from the Rolling Stones, original copies of **The Raven** sported a 3-D cover panel. Inside, a political consciousness (first unveiled on **Black and White**) flowered, permeating songs like "Nuclear Device," "Shah Shah a Go Go" and "Genetix." Freed from the relative mundanity of exploring interpersonal relationships, the basis of most of the Stranglers' previous lyrics, **The Raven** adopts a global perspective, including the scathing put-down entitled "Dead Loss Angeles." Meanwhile, "Duchess" pioneered a surprising new direction—catchy, level-headed melodic pop totally outside the group's general sound.

Released near the end of 1979, the mixed-menu **Don't Bring Harry** 7-inch EP (wrapped in a delightfully morbid seasonal sleeve) combines one song from **The Raven**, a track from Cornwell + Williams' **Nosferatu** album and live Stranglers' performances of two songs, including one from Burnel's **Euroman Cometh**.

Having lacked an American label for two years, the Stranglers signed with IRS, who assembled **IV**, a mongrel consisting of half of **The Raven** and some non-LP singles, plus one totally new track, "Vietnamerica." As a bonus, the album included a four-song 7-inch similar to **Don't Bring Harry**: an actual track from **Euroman Cometh**, a different Cornwell/Williams selection, "Straighten Out" and "Choosey Suzie," from the UK first album's free 45.

The Meninblack—previewed on **The Raven** (and **IV**) by a song of that name—is a hypothetical soundtrack/concept album concerning aliens with godlike powers that is essentially an attack on organized religion. There's a fair amount of non-vocal instrumental content, lots of synthesizers and other keyboards, tricky special effects and little of the Stranglers' usual thrust. Although radically different, **Meninblack** is a departure for nowhere. (The CD adds two.)

Without abandoning their melodic pop explorations, the Stranglers returned to topicality and forthrightness on their next LP. **La Folie** offers a striking juxtaposition of attractive backing and scathing lyrics. Subtle, effective, mature and energetic–but no outstanding songs.

Following a change in British labels, a catalogue compilation called **The Collection** appeared in 1982, including almost everything you'd want from the preceding albums, plus a couple of bonus single sides. A great introduction for neophytes and a record that should be of interest to anyone not owning absolutely everything the band has done.

A worldwide deal with Epic allowed the Stranglers to free themselves of past musical baggage and gave them a consistent American release schedule. The first fruit of that arrangement, **Feline**, is restrained and dignified, but also lackluster and boring. (The US edition adds the appropriately low-key 1981 single, "Golden Brown," which had also appeared on **La Folie**.)

Aural Sculpture is far better, containing several strong tracks: "Skin Deep," melodic rippling-organ pop that recalls "Duchess," and "Ice Queen," a simple-minded allusion to cinematic irony that has lots of neat hooks and a pleasing chorus, punctuated by brassy brass. Additionally, "Uptown" melds powerful acoustic guitar to a fractured melody and comes out like a Pete Shelley song that wasn't. Although not fully satisfying, **Aural Sculpture** has enough quality merchandise to make it a worthwhile purchase.

Another byproduct of their label switch was **Off the Beaten Track**, a thirteen-track compilation of pre-Epic B-sides and non-LP A's. Although a lot of what's on **Rarities** really isn't that obscure, it does delve into the recesses of the Stranglers' enormous discography enough things most collections will be missing that it's a worthwhile investment (especially the CD, which has half a dozen bonus tracks) for serious enthusiasts. The two-disc **Singles** covers the band's early years (1977-'82) with all the A-sides (and a few of the B-sides) from

"(Get a) Grip (on Yourself)" to "Strange Little Girl."

The Stranglers' steady march towards total blandness continues on **Dreamtime**, an unfocused time-filler that randomly touches areas that resemble Ultravox, Fleetwood Mac, Shoes, Glenn Miller and Johnny Cash, all with little enthusiasm. Accomplished but bereft of ideas or concept, **Dreamtime** is a soporific, characterless nightmare. There's hardly an identifiable trace of the once-great band in these grooves.

The subsequent live album—recorded at three gigs in 1985 and 1987—underscores the Stranglers' paradox. Despite their recent wimpo work, onstage—banging out such classics as "London Lady," "Nice 'n' Sleazy" and "No More Heroes" with a horn section—they can convincingly revive the grungy electric power we used to know and love. The lengthy **All Live** draws heavily from recent albums; fortunately, these concert renditions improve on the songs, providing them with a little context. (Still, the notion of the Stranglers performing with acoustic guitars is not easy to accept.) Capping things off is a hearty but economical UK-hit-single studio version of the Kinks' song which the LP title paraphrases. (The CD version of the **All Day and All of the Night** EP adds a remix, two live tracks and something called "Viva Vlad.")

Although Roy Thomas Baker produced the rock-'n'rolly **10** (indeed the band's tenth studio LP), things didn't turn out all that bad. As horrifying as it is to hear this once-dynamic group reduced to covering "96 Tears" (and then penning a tune called "Too Many Teardrops" on top of it), the originals that otherwise comprise the record are pretty lively ("Sweet Smell of Success," "Someone Like You"). Except on "Man of the Earth" and "Out of My Mind," where he sounds like Robyn Hitchcock, Cornwell applies traces of the group's old rugged personality to simple pop melodies, as Greenfield stacks on colorful keyboard fills and a three-man horn section chips in occasionally. (Burnel is utterly out of the picture, stylistically speaking: he sings a couple of songs, but anyone could have played these bass parts.) With that album out of the way, Cornwell left the group in August 1990.

There's something to be said for **Greatest Hits 1977–1990**—namely, it's the first bona fide Stranglers compilation to be issued in the US. Otherwise, it half overlaps the **Singles** collection, proceeding from the often brilliant UA years into the paltry Epic era, as the group succumbed to commercial temptation with its rote covers and boring originals. Still, the liner notes are good and the selection of singles—at least a third of them solidly great—is evenhanded enough to make it a fair starting point for new arrivals.

Solo work: Burnel's gravel-bottom bass and guttural vocals played a crucial role on the group's early, maximum-aggression records. For his own 1979 album, Burnel made a self-indulgent political statement, complete with historical maps, slogans and polemic songs like "Euromess" and "Deutschland Nicht über Alles." Using a rhythm box and playing almost all the instruments himself, Burnel invests the pedantic **Euroman Cometh** with neither musical direction nor engaging ideas, making it about as much fun as sitting through a lecture.

Teaming with bandmate Dave Greenfield, Burnel then made an album that "forms the musical basis for the film 'Ecoutez Vos Murs' by Vincent Coudanne." **Fire & Water** takes two approaches—typical soundtrack ambience, relying on doomy keyboard effects, and songs, some with vocals. "Rain & Dole & Tea" is sung in Phil Spector fashion by a multi-tracked female vocalist; "Nuclear Power (Yes Please)" actually quotes Albert Einstein in a remarkably clumsy science lesson; "Detective Privée" is a sensuously murmured French number. It's not heinously awful, but few are likely to give it repeated spins.

For *his* first extracurricular outing, Cornwell co-wrote, co-produced and co-performed an album with American drummer (and former Captain Beefheart sideman) Robert Williams. The collaborative compositions on **Nosferatu** offer substantive lyrics, but the atonal performances sound even more dour than the early Stranglers. Two members of Devo put in guest appearances, and there are some Devo-like effects worked in but, if not for an incongruous cover of Cream's "White Room," there wouldn't be any light relief at all. While it's nice that the pair (with some assistance from Ian Underwood) has the instrumental prowess to do it all themselves, **Nosferatu** requires more from the listener than it deserves (or returns).

Nine years later, Cornwell took a dull stab at playing lightweight dance-pop outside the Stranglers' sphere with **Wolf**. (Langer and Winstanley garishly co-produced two songs, which don't work at all.) Other than affording Hugh the audibly meaningless opportunity to play keyboards, escape his usual company and fool around in the studio with the likes of Jools Holland and ex-Tears for Fears drummer Manny Elias, **Wolf** stakes out no significant musical terrain and contains nothing the Stranglers couldn't have done just as well. (The EP adds three non-LP tracks to the album's lead-off song.) In retrospect, maybe he was just checking to see that he could make a solo go of it.

Whether the result of, or the impetus for, the Stranglers' penchant for covering rock'n'roll standards (or just an indication of artistic burnout), Burnel and Greenfield launched a just-for-kicks sideband with Stranglers' saxman Alex Gifford, ex-Vibrators guitarist John Ellis and Manny Elias. On two similarly titled but totally different albums, the Purple Helmets (nice name . . .) do nothing but relive the songs of their misspent youth. Whether they're playing "Woolly Bully," "I Can't Explain," "Over Under Sideways Down" and "Not Fade Away" (on the live **Ride Again**) or "She's Not There," "Money" and "First I Look at the Purse" (on **Rise Again**, a slightly more accomplished studio concoction), the Helmets approach their chosen jukebox classics with the enthusiasm of teenagers and the skill of seasoned professionals.   [i]

See also *Polyphonic Size.*

SYD STRAW

Surprise (Virgin) 1989 ●

As an unknown, Straw—one of very few vocalists to whom the description "honey-throated" can be accurately applied—swiped the spotlight on the Golden Palominos' **Visions of Excess** from the likes of Michael Stipe, Jack Bruce and John Lydon. On **Blast of Silence** she provided grace notes to an otherwise confused product. Her self-produced solo debut, **Surprise**, boasts a guest list that suggests a hipper version of the bloated superstar processions Peter Asher used to assemble for James Taylor and Linda Ronstadt. As a result, inveterate family-tree makers now have a way to connect ex-Slapp Happy keyboardist Anthony Moore and Tom Petty sideman Benmont Tench—they're both here.

While never less than enjoyable listening, **Surprise** often falls victim to the diffusion that invariably attends Big International Productions. It's slackly paced, and some of the songwriting doesn't do her justice—the nonsensical, wanting-to-mean-something obscurities of "Future 40's (String of Pearls)" are obviously co-writer Stipe's, but they're annoying if you pay attention to them. On the other hand, Straw sometimes goes over the top when a lighter touch is called for—the gallows-humor wordplay of "Sphinx" would be better served by offhanded irony than belting. Still, when she hits it just right, as on Peter Holsapple's "Think Too Hard," she's absolutely undeniable. [gk]

See also *Golden Palominos*.

STRAWBERRY ZOTS

Cars, Flowers, Telephones (Acid Test) 1989 (RCA) 1990 ●

Despite the colorful name and day-glo artwork, smattering of righteous covers and the fact that the Albuquerque quintet originally self-released it, **Cars, Flowers, Telephones** has almost none of the cool character one usually expects from retro-psychedelicatelics. (Little wonder the LP was reissued by a major label and promoted as part of the imitation-Redd Kross '60s revival.) Evidently inspired by no one so much as Paul Revere and the Raiders, the Zots play pleasant collegiate power pop, like Blotto without the overt satire, and mild-mannered '60s-styled rock, using organ, wah-wah guitar and songs by the Troggs, Electric Prunes, etc. in a halfhearted stab at elusive cultural resonance. Feh. [i]

STRAY CATS

Stray Cats (nr/Arista) 1981
Gonna Ball (nr/Arista) 1981
Built for Speed (EMI America) 1982 ●
Rant n' Rave with the Stray Cats (EMI America) 1983
Rock Therapy (EMI America) 1986 ●
Blast Off! (EMI) 1989 ●
Rock This Town: Best of the Stray Cats (EMI) 1990 φ

PHANTOM, ROCKER & SLICK

Phantom, Rocker & Slick (EMI America) 1985
Cover Girl (EMI America) 1986

BRIAN SETZER

The Knife Feels Like Justice (EMI America) 1986 ●
Live Nude Guitars (EMI Manhattan) 1988 ●

Disenchanted with modern new wave, Brian Setzer bagged his trendy New York group, the Bloodless Pharaohs, to form a rockabilly trio and abandon Long Island for London. There, the Stray Cats wowed 'em with exotic American appeal, spearheading a rockabilly revival that naturally became absorbed into new wave. Is there a moral here?

Unlike some neo-rockabillies, the Stray Cats don't care about painstaking reconstructions of moldy old recordings. They diddle around with non-originals, while Setzer's own early songs tackle topical events ("Storm the Embassy," "Rumble in Brighton"). Setzer's extended guitar soloing sometimes seems descended from jazz rather than rockabilly, but there's no faulting his skill or the group's spirit.

Gonna Ball, released about nine months after **Stray Cats**, finds the band moving into R&B turf. Musical veterans like Ian Stewart and Lee Allen help fill out the sound; a strong producer, like Dave Edmunds on the first album, would have helped even more. Setzer is a better guitarist than singer, and some of **Gonna Ball**'s songs resemble the music rockabilly was revolting against.

Combining the best of both British albums and adding one new cut, **Built for Speed** is a good introduction to the band. The US, generally not known for humoring nostalgic musical throwbacks, sent it into the Top 5. The Stray Cats must have been doing something right.

If chart success is the yardstick, they continued to do that something on **Rant n' Rave**, the trio's first identical and simultaneous US/UK release, and also their last record together. Again produced by Dave Edmunds, the effervescent rock'n'roll teen rebellion of "(She's) Sexy + 17" leads the stylistic parade (with one exception—the beautiful soul ballad, "I Won't Stand in Your Way," with vocal backing by Fourteen Karat Soul) and the rest of the record falls neatly in line, recalling Eddie Cochran, Carl Perkins and the whole rockabilly-into-early-rock'n'roll era. Sure it's formulaic and derivative as hell, but timelessly enthralling and truly entertaining as well.

The Stray Cats broke up in late 1984. While his bandmates teamed up with guitarist Earl Slick and issued a run-of-the-mill rock album the following year, Brian Setzer worked with Robert Plant in the Honey Drippers and then released **The Knife Feels Like Justice**, a strong, varied LP that further illustrates his multi-dimensional talent. The record encompasses unembellished frontier rock ("The Knife Feels Like Justice"), wistful balladry ("Boulevard of Broken Dreams"), Cochranesque rock'n'roll ("Radiation Ranch"), soulful power pop (the autobiographical "Chains Around Your Heart"), rock bluegrass ("Barbwire Fence") and lots more. With tasteful restraint, Setzer checks his wilder instincts, avoiding showy guitar work, verbal grandstanding or self-parody; maturity and subtlety are the album's two most unexpected and welcome qualities.

In 1986, Phantom and Rocker made **Cover Girl**, an improved—credit producer Pete Solley and generally better original material—but equally pointless and bland second album with Slick. Then, prompted by a contract they wanted out of, the threesome cut a Stray Cats reunion LP, **Rock Therapy**, and redeemed themselves handily. With Setzer back at their helm, the rhythm section sounds good as new; amazingly, the fine record picks up exactly where **Rant n' Rave** left off. Setzer's old-fashioned originals blend seamlessly with fine borrowings from appropriate sources (Buddy Holly, Chuck Berry, Gene Vincent, Charlie Feathers) and contributions from his bandmates. (The only misstep is "Broken Man," a clumsy stab at bluegrass.) The spare self-production gives the record a comfortably loose feel; the exuberant air of playing for fun, free of commercial considerations, adds a magical dimension.

Where Setzer's first solo album was nearly eloquent in its artistry, **Live Nude Guitars**—produced in pieces by Dave Stewart, Chris Thomas and others—finds B.S. in frantic commercial overdrive, foolishly aping Billy Idol and the Romantics, mucking about in inappropriate settings and self-parodic clichés ("Rockability"?) and—now this is serious—reducing Eddie Cochran's classic "Nervous Breakdown" to modern triviality. The songs are crap, the performances routine and colorless. When Stewart begins laying on the synthetic horns and driving female backing vocals at the beginning of Side Two, you know it's time to get off this ride. (But if you stick around, you get to hear Setzer's Mark Knopfler guitar imitation in the heinous "Love Is Repaid by Love Alone.")

The Stray Cats' next album is no great shakes, but at least **Blast Off!** (well-oiled to run smooth by producer Dave Edmunds) offers a modest and pleasingly simple-minded dose of the trio's standard-issue rockabilly froth. Redundant in the extreme but no less enjoyable for it, these ten slices of slap'n'wiggle rewrite the group's canon (actually, "Gene and Eddie" is stitched together from the Vincent and Cochran songbooks) with no innovation but as much enthusiasm as ever.

The don't-bother-it's-just-some-old group ten-track **Rock This Town** compilation starts with "Rock This Town" (the trio's first US hit) and ends with "Runaway Boys" (the Cats' first UK hit, two years earlier). In between, the obvious tunes ("Stray Cat Strut," "(She's) Sexy + 17," "I Won't Stand in Your Way") join some lesser-known LP cuts ("Bring It Back Again," "Look at That Cadillac," "Gene and Eddie"), with nothing at all from **Rock Therapy**. Gone, cat, gone. [si/i]

PETE STRIDE/JOHN PLAIN

See *Lurkers*.

STRIPES

See *Nena*.

JOE STRUMMER

Walker (Virgin Movie Music) 1987 ●
Earthquake Weather (Epic) 1989 ●
Gangsterville EP (nr/Epic) 1989 ●
Island Hopping EP (nr/Epic) 1989 ●

VARIOUS ARTISTS

Permanent Record (Epic) 1988 ●

Having discovered that the Clash without Mick Jones was not a viable proposition, and that Big Audio Dynamite wasn't big enough for the both of them, Joe Strummer turned instead to film. In 1986, Strummer began working for director Alex Cox, creating "Love Kills" (the theme song for *Sid & Nancy*), starring in *Straight to Hell* (1987) and contributing to its soundtrack.

Strummer also did a credible job scoring and producing the mock-Latin music for Cox's *Walker*. Strummer sings the narrative "Unknown Immortal" and "Tennessee Rain" in likably rustic folk fashion, adding mostly spare, relaxing acoustic instrumentals that use *guitarron*, marimba, horns and piano to evoke the film's Central American locale.

Expanding his horizons beyond director Cox, Strummer worked on the soundtrack of *Permanent Record*, a 1988 flick about teen suicide. One side of the LP features an assortment of bands (Stranglers, Godfathers, Lou Reed), while Strummer & the Latino Rockabilly War (a small band including ex-Circle Jerk guitarist Zander Schloss, who also played on **Walker**) complete the disc with four energetic vocal songs (funk/folk-rock/R&B) and an instrumental theme. The old Clashman hasn't lost his touch.

In 1989, after a large (and surprisingly effective) role in Jim Jarmusch's *Mystery Train*, Strummer gathered up Schloss and a rhythm section and took an all-music break to record **Earthquake Weather**. Although the complex lyrics are jam-packed with intriguing names and places (some explained in a glossary on the inner sleeve) from the cultural kitbag of Strummer's intelligence, the easygoing earthy music is simply lackluster. Strummer's flat self-production and the band's consciously casual approach squash any traces of life out of the songs, making this boring exercise sound like **The Basement Tapes** or **Pat Garrett** outtakes. Sloppy stabs at rock (and one Princely funk tossoff) are equally unconvincing. Both of the four-song EPs built around ordinary album tracks contain non-LP material. [i]

See also *Clash*.

STUMP

Mud on a Colon EP (nr/Ron Johnson) 1985
Quirk Out EP (nr/Stuff) 1986
The Peel Sessions EP (nr/Strange Fruit) 1987
A Fierce Pancake (Ensign-Chrysalis) 1988 ●

This wacky British quartet plays Beefheart-inspired avant-pop with goodnaturedly surreal lyrics. The low-budget **Mud on a Colon** is shambolic and unfocused, with little to distinguish it from scads of less-talented UK indie combos. But the subsequent **Quirk Out**, smartly produced by Hugh Jones, is a delight, channeling the band's boundless energy into a more disciplined and rewarding direction. Highlights include the hiccupy Yank-bashing caricature "Buffalo," the quasi-vulgar litany-of-bodily-functions "Everything in Its Place" and the uncharacteristically melodic, introspective "Our Fathers."

A Fierce Pancake (the US version reprises "Buffalo") strips away still more surface kookiness, revealing some memorable melodies and genuinely inventive instrumental work (particularly from guitarist Chris Salmon). And, while vocalist Mick Lynch's absurdist lyrics are as full of puns and non sequiturs as ever, they're also cogent statements—as in "Chaos," which bemoans Britain's sinking-ship economy via a metaphorical sea chantey, and "Bone," which builds a convincing case against human evolution.

"Buffalo" also appears, in a January 1986 live version, on **The Peel Sessions** EP, along with three other tunes. [hd]

STYLE COUNCIL

A Paris EP (nr/Polydor) 1983
Introducing the Style Council EP (Polydor) 1983 ●
Café Bleu (nr/Polydor) 1984 ●
My Ever Changing Moods (Geffen) 1984

SLAM SLAM

After six years spent growing up in public with the Jam, Paul Weller felt the need to function within a more relaxed, less restrictive framework. That in mind, he enlisted the services of former Merton Parkas/Dexys keyboard player Mick Talbot to form the Style Council, with all other needed instruments to be supplied by guests. Promising that the band would be nothing if not unpredictable, the duo then proceeded to issue a single, "Speak Like a Child," that sounded much like where the Jam left off. Another single, the funky "Money-Go-Round," preceded the four-song **A Paris** EP, the sleeve of which shows the pair carefully posed with the Eiffel Tower in the background, looking like a Giorgio Armani ad. Highlighted by the catchy "Long Hot Summer," the material is light, breezy summertime soul, owing as much to Weller's pretensions of some sort of continental flair as it does to obvious referents like Curtis Mayfield.

The American **Introducing the Style Council** combined both singles with the contents of the UK EP, although some of the numbers were remixed. Not released in England, it sold better there as an import than it did in the country of its issue.

Café Bleu and **My Ever Changing Moods** are equivalent LPs with slightly different tracks. (The resequenced US version replaces two minor cuts with the UK hit, "A Solid Bond in Your Heart.") A scrambled assortment of soul, be-bop, cocktail jazz, rap and whatever else Weller could think of, it's simply too schizophrenic to be a good album, although it does show integrity—this band is unlikely to be guided by public demand. "Headstart for Happiness" and "The Paris Match" (this time featuring Everything but the Girl) are improved versions of previously released material; "My Ever Changing Moods" gave Weller the first US Top 30 single of his career.

The Style Council's second album was also released in alternate trans-Atlantic forms. **Internationalists** has a different cover than **Our Favourite Shop** and omits the latter's title song. Though still rather varied, the album is much more coherent than its predecessor. There are still clinkers: "The Stand Up Comic's Instructions" is clever but awkward, and the rhumba-shuffle of "All Gone Away" would sound at home in a dentist's office. However, tracks like "Walls Come Tumbling Down!," "Come to Milton Keynes" and "Boy Who Cried Wolf" more than tip the scales in the record's favor. As ever, it's undeniable that Weller means every word, but the continuing trend towards a crystalline, antiseptic sound is unfortunate.

It was obvious that the *Absolute Beginners* film was not going to be released without a contribution from Weller, so the band rewrote "With Everything to Lose" from the second album (itself already a direct lift from "Long Hot Summer") and came up with "Have You Ever Had It Blue." Shortly thereafter, the Style Council issued a live album, **Home & Abroad**, a squeaky-clean, all-too-accurate collection of songs drawn from both albums as well as singles. (The UK CD adds two tracks.) Considering that the Style Council often put live version on their flipsides (see **The Lodgers** EP), this set seems to be mostly for those who absolutely must own everything Weller puts his name to.

By the time **The Cost of Loving** was released, both Weller's demi-god status in Britain and the Style Council's significance had plunged. The LP—originally issued in limited UK quantities as a set of two 12-inch 45s—is nothing more than a collection of redundant, forgettable jazz/soul trifles, played very professionally but bloodlessly, with arrangements that resemble Chicago (the band) more than anything else. The first album of Weller's career to fall completely on its face comes after a lengthy drought of particularly meritorious undertakings. Ousted by Morrissey as young England's favorite male pop icon, his creativity seems to be waning. Can a Jam reunion be far off?

Maybe not, but the Style Council's adjournment was certainly due. The trio (by this point, singer Dee C. Lee, the talented Mrs. Weller, was counted officially in the lineup) stuck together long enough to make **Confessions of a Pop Group**, a presentable outing with some of the irascible songwriter's grouchiest and most dispirited lyrics. Weller's general disgust at everything in sight is vitriolic and undisguised: the record's very first sound is a toilet flushing. Ending the LP's brassy soul-funk-pop portion, the nine-minute-plus title track (which bears a frightening stylistic resemblance to Tears for Fears' third album) offers a vindictive, disillusioned dismissal of modern England: "Cheap and tacky bullshit land/Told when to sit don't know where you stand/Too busy recreating the past/To live in the future." The rest of the long record is given over to "The Piano Paintings," a collection of jazzy songs with fancy vocal arrangements (the Swingle Singers guest on "The Story of Someones Shoe") and lots of work for Talbot's magic fingers. Capping things off with a grandly thumbed nose, the LP ends with a glibly pretentious ten-minute orchestral suite (complete with harp!) whose coda is a doo-wop chorus.

The Singular Adventures is a nearly complete UK singles recap, from 1983's "Speak Like a Child" through "Life at a Top Peoples Health Farm" (from **Confessions**). By scraping away the band's many indulgences and self-amused digressions, the cogent fourteen-track set (sixteen on tape/CD) winds up being an ideal souvenir, a stylish scrapbook loaded with great songs. By early '90, Weller was off to form the Paul Weller Movement. Dee C. Lee was fronting a band called Slam Slam (hubby co-wrote and co-produced most of the album). Can a Jam reunion be far off?

See also *Jam*. [dgs/i]

POLY STYRENE

See *X-Ray Spex*.

STYRENES

See *Paul Marotta*.

SUBHUMANS

The Day the Country Died (nr/Spiderleg) 1982
Time Flies . . . but Aeroplanes Crash (nr/Bluurg) 1983
From the Cradle to the Grave (nr/Bluurg) 1984
Worlds Apart (nr/Bluurg) 1985
EP-LP (nr/Bluurg) 1986
29:29 Split Vision (nr/Bluurg) 1987

CULTURE SHOCK

Go Wild! (nr/Bluurg) 1987
Onwards & Upwards (nr/Bluurg) 1988
All the Time! (nr/Bluurg) 1989

CITIZEN FISH

Free Souls in a Trapped Environment (nr/Bluurg) 1990

Unrelated to Vancouver's D.O.A.-related Subhumans, these lower-income types from England's Southwest corner were one of the original UK hardcore bands, carving a distinct niche directly between Pistol-punk and the subsequent iconoclastic thrash of Rudimentary Peni. Borrowing the aggression, belligerent tunefulness, social conscience and sneering vocal atonality of the former, they magnified each by a factor of three, releasing a series of increasingly impressive 7-inches (later gathered as **EP-LP**), culminating in **The Day the Country Died**, a deliciously dated quasi-classic of second-generation British punk.

Assiduously documenting their career with self-released and shoddily recorded live cassettes, the Subhumans' next "professional" release was the eight-song, 45 rpm **Time Flies**. Pointedly poking and stretching in odd directions, alternating moody doubletracked vocals or solo piano accompaniment with driving live numbers, it was a more than appropriate intro to **Cradle**—possibly the first post-hardcore opera. Somewhat akin to the Pretty Things' epic **SF Sorrow** but pared down and compressed to a single unbroken side, the increased variegation in the music (while fascinating on LP) signalled an inevitable disunion, rendering **Worlds Apart** a sardonic title for their last full-length outing. The Subhumans' most diverse LP interpolates echoic post-punk, pseudo-reggae, rote rock and ruttish roll. **Split Vision** offers their final eight tracks, actually recorded *after* the breakup.

Vocalist Dick Lukas formed Culture Shock, sounding in every way like the Subhumans, but with less angry verve and considerably more of a ska/reggae bias. That band's bassist then rejoined the Subhumans drummer and—after a false start—guitarist, with Lukas helming the resultant Citizen Fish.   [ab]

SUBURBAN NIGHTMARE

See *Dwarves*.

SUBURBS

The Suburbs EP (Twin/Tone) 1978
In Combo (Twin/Tone) 1980
Credit in Heaven (Twin/Tone) 1981
Dream Hog EP (Twin/Tone) 1982 (Mercury) 1983
Love Is the Law (Mercury) 1983
Suburbs (A&M) 1986

One of Minneapolis' major musical resources, the Suburbs maintained the same lineup from their vinyl debut (and the first single on the extraordinary Twin/Tone label), via a 1978 nine-song 7-inch red vinyl EP of above-average punkish rock'n'roll, to the band's 1987 dissolution.

With their first album, the Suburbs began displaying signs of incipient greatness; singer Beej Chaney's ominous, neurotic calm providing perfect counterpoint for the band's enthusiastic playing; guitarist B.C. Allen adding tension with scrabbly rhythm and violent lead. The songs unpredictably explore real-world subjects like "Hobnobbin with the Executives" and "Cig Machine."

After demonstrating what they could do on **In Combo**, the Suburbs proved how well they could do it with the double-album, **Credit in Heaven**, a slickly delivered opus that refines the band's approach and fairly bubbles over with creative concepts, great playing and bizarre songs. The Chaney comparisons to Bryan Ferry—cool in the eye of the storm—are amplified by his blasé delivery, but the music—powered by Hugo Klaers' ultra-busy drumming—is something else, blending cool funk with nervous disco and jazzy aplomb. A highly recommended stunner, regardless of religious persuasion.

Things heated up for the Suburbs in '82, when they started attracting significant club play for a 12-inch of the song "Waiting." They included that track on the **Dream Hog** EP (in original and extended remix form), along with two sharp new white-funk tunes (one of them about dance music) plus a restrained near-ballad. When they signed to Mercury, the label reissued it before sending the 'Burbs into the studio to cut a new album.

The result of that maneuver, **Love Is the Law**, is easily their best vinyl chapter, a powerful and personality-laden set of songs that incorporate more rock than usual, as well as horns and some of their most offbeat lyrics ever. "Rattle My Bones" is brilliantly demento bebop; the superb "Love Is the Law" has the most memorable hook in the repertoire; "Hell A" took one of its verses from a Los Angeles phone booth scrawl. **Love Is the Law** is a great, great album.

Making the probably inevitable Prince connection via the production guidance of Robert Brent (better known as Revolution drummer Bobby Z), the Suburbs came roaring back three long years later with another powerful record, albeit one whose character is less firmly held in its musical approach than its lyrics. Gone is the antsy, skittish urgency of yore; **Suburbs** is utterly listenable (but not overwhelmingly unique), with equally subtle nods to both the band's traditional crypto-funk and Prince's happy-feet dance rock. Thankfully, Chaney and keyboardist Chan Poling's nastily humorous lyrics—notably on "Every Night's a Friday Night" (. . . in hell), "America Sings the Blues" and "Superlove"—are as clever as ever.

That, unfortunately, was the end of the Suburbs, although they did release a 12-inch single ("Little Man's Gonna Fall" b/w "Don't Do Me Any Favors") on a local independent label the following year.   [i]

SUBWAY SECT

See *Vic Godard & the Subway Sect*.

CHRIS SUCH AND HIS SAVAGES

See *Headless Horsemen*.

NIKKI SUDDEN

Waiting on Egypt (nr/Abstract) 1982 + 1986
The Bible Belt (nr/Flicknife) 1983

NIKKI SUDDEN & DAVE KUSWORTH: JACOBITES

Jacobites (nr/Glass) 1984 ●
Shame for the Angels EP (nr/Glass) 1985
Robespierre's Velvet Basement (nr/Glass) 1985 ●
Pin Your Heart to Me EP (nr/Glass) 1985
Lost in a Sea of Scarves (Ger. What's So Funny About) 1985
When the Rain Comes EP (nr/Glass) 1986
The Ragged School (Twin/Tone) 1986
Fortune of Fame (nr/Glass) 1988 ●

NIKKI SUDDEN AND THE JACOBITES

Texas (nr/Creation) 1986
The Last Bandit EP (nr/Creation) 1986
Dead Men Tell No Tales (nr/Creation) 1987 ●

NIKKI SUDDEN & ROWLAND S. HOWARD

Kiss You Kidnapped Charabanc (Creation-Relativity) 1987 ●

NIKKI SUDDEN AND THE FRENCH REVOLUTION

Groove (nr/Creation) 1989 (Giant) 1990 ●
Back to the Coast (nr/Creation) 1990 (Rockville) 1991 ●

DAVE KUSWORTH

The Bounty Hunters (Swordfish-Texas Hotel) 1987

BOUNTY HUNTERS

Threads: A Tear Stained Scar (nr/Creation) 1989 (Giant) 1990 ●

After dissolving Swell Maps, singer/guitarist/former rock scribe Nikki Sudden released two solo albums, **Waiting on Egypt** and **The Bible Belt**, which basically offered more of what that band had been doing. But then he formed the Jacobites—a core trio of Sudden, guitarist/singer Dave Kusworth and ex-Swell Maps drummer Epic Soundtracks (Sudden's brother), plus assorted friends—and began to sing an altogether different tune. With Kusworth co-writing the songs, Sudden promptly rid himself of all references to his previous career.

The Jacobites' records all have a similar woozily romantic format: seductive strummed acoustic guitar, a thumping, muffled rhythm section and Sudden's whining, Dylanesque vocals. (Imagine a folky Johnny Thunders growing up in the English countryside and learning to play guitar by listening to "Knockin' on Heaven's Door" with a bottle by his side.) The group pillages idols like the Stones, Neil Young and Dylan with such loving devotion—as on "Fortune of Fame," "Where Rivers End" (both on **Robespierre's Velvet Basement**)

and others—that their motives transcend any appearance of carbon-copy revivalism.

The duo made only two full albums, all recorded during '84 and '85. **Lost in a Sea of Scarves** contains outtakes from **Robespierre's Velvet Basement**, which was to have been a double album. **The Ragged School**, a consistently strong twelve-song American condensation of the UK albums, shares only three tracks with the carefully annotated and sounding-better-with-age nineteen-song **Fortune of Fame** (subtitled **Big Hits and Stereo Landings**) retrospective.

Parting company with Kusworth and switching to Creation (but retaining the band name), Sudden released **Texas**, relying on his brother and bassist Duncan Sibbald for primary assistance. A violinist and ex-Birthday Party guitarist Rowland S. Howard make notable appearances, giving Sudden's languid, atmospheric Southwesternisms the extra color they need to prevent sameness. (Two notable style-busting exceptions are the Velvetsy "Glass Eye" and "Such a Little Girl," both winning piles of melodic distortion.) **The Last Bandit** EP pairs two album tracks with two others.

A month after finishing **Texas**, Sudden returned to the studio and began work on the spare **Dead Men Tell No Tales**, which has almost no percussion and very little accompaniment of any sort for his guitar, bouzouki and dulcimer strumming. Howard and Sibbald again put in appearances and the cover still credits the Jacobites, but it's basically a solo album—and an underwhelming one at that. Only "Girl with the Wooden Leg" makes a powerful impression, as Howard's crazed guitar noises contrast with Sudden's maudlin balladeering.

Howard takes a more prominent role on **Kiss You Kidnapped Charabanc**, another largely drum-free record that drifts along aimlessly at quarter-speed. Nikki does the singing and Rowland provides most of the instrumentation; the duo split the songwriting.

Judging by **Groove**'s posturing, halfhearted distorto-blues core, it's clear that Sudden continues to suffer from delusions of Keith Richardsdom. Unfortunately, his *true* roots show through on "See My Rider," an ostensibly rough-hewn blues that's so fey you just *know* he's singing about how many scarves his touring contract requires concert promoters to provide. (**Groove**, or at least some form of it, was originally released—reportedly without authorization—by the Italian Crazy Mannequin label, which titled it **Crown of Thorns**.)

The uneven and poorly organized **Back to the Coast** has a few really good tracks (like the Howard collaboration "Crossroads," Robert Johnson as heard by Nick Cave) in which Sudden makes a concerted artistic effort and manages to roll his pretensions into a convincing ball of transcendent rock'n'roll, but it also contains whatever else he had lying around: further lazy designs clipped from the usual cloth (where have I heard "The Last Bandit" before?), a total toss-off (the acoustic "Flower Bed Romance") and "In Your Life," a shitty-sounding slice of '60s retro-organ punkedelia that sounds like an outtake from someone else's album.

Kusworth lay low a while after leaving the Jacobites in mid-'86, spending his time recording a solo album (also credited to the Bounty Hunters, the quartet he leads) which was released the following year. Marriage is on Dave's mind on **The Bounty Hunters**, as several of the songs—which interlock to form a long, vague romantic narrative—make reference to weddings, rings, wives and other such symptoms of betrothal. Showing an affinity for the folky side of Johnny Thunders, Kusworth's thin voice is no dynamic instrument, but it serves the material, as do the energetic arrangements of acoustic guitar and electric rock rhythms.

Threads furthers Kusworth's quest for beauty in the underbelly. With the addition of a bevy of pastoral instruments (ranging from pocket trumpet to harpsichord), much of the material is redolent of that particular time in late-'60s/early-'70s Britain when debauchery gave way to rusticity (à la **Led Zep II** crossed with Blind Faith). Then again, the volume-heavy stuff could pass for Black Crowes outtakes, so go figure. [ag/i/dss]

See also *Swell Maps.*

SUGARCUBES
Life's Too Good (Elektra) 1988 ●
Coldsweat EP (Elektra) 1988 ●
Motorcrash EP (Elektra) 1988 φ
Here Today, Tomorrow Next Week! (Elektra) 1989 ●
Regina EP (Elektra) 1989 φ
Illur Arfur! (nr/One Little Indian) 1989
Box of 12-inch singles (nr/One Little Indian) 1990
Box of 7-inch singles (nr/One Little Indian) 1990
Box of 6 CDs [CD] (nr/One Little Indian) 1990 ●

KUKL
The Eye (nr/Crass) 1984
Holidays in Europe (The Naughty Nought) (nr/Crass) 1986

Not since the Jesus and Mary Chain made their initial assault a few years back has a band come out of nowhere to generate as much excitement and acclaim as Iceland's Sugarcubes. Drumming (by Siggi Baldursson) and guitar work point to such influences as Joy Division and Siouxsie and the Banshees and, in more delicate moments (such as "Birthday," their debut single), bits of the Cocteau Twins. They also make very interesting use of an electronically mutated trumpet and sound effects. But the Sugarcubes' main instrument is the amazing voice of lead singer Björk Gudmundsdottir, an elfin character whose range of pitch is only surpassed by her range of emotions: one moment she's a little girl soprano, the very next she's growling like a crazed animal about to go for the kill. Singer/trumpeter Einar Örn handles some of the vocals with awkwardly accented English, but Björk's background vocals usually steal the show on those tracks.

What she sings is noteworthy as well: Freud would have a field day with the childhood/sexual metaphors of the lyrics, most of which are more interesting than those from bands whose first language is English. **Life's Too Good** is no letdown from the initial 45s (both are on the LP), with eleven cuts that retain a signature sound but avoid redundancy. Iceland is a country whose little-known rock scene has produced a number of rather interesting, if not earth-shattering bands. This one is the real thing. ("Birthday" and "Cold Sweat" were also issued as CD singles with numerous B-sides. The CD of the album adds six extra tracks—some sung in Icelandic—including an incredible alternate version of "Deus.")

Matching up to the debut proved a difficult chal-

lenge for the Sugarcubes on their second album. **Here Today, Tomorrow Next Week!** has a more mainstream sound, fewer memorable songs, blander lyrics and entirely too much of Örn's overly affected, annoying vocals. There are still special touches no other band could offer, and tracks like "Regina," "Eat the Menu" and "Nail" stand out, but there's nothing here that makes one sit up and take notice the way **Life's Too Good** did (and does). For a more provocative experience, try the album's alternative version, **Illur Arfur!** ("evil inheritance"), issued abroad under the band's native name, Sykurmolarnir. The tracks are identical, but sung in Icelandic (although lyrics and titles are provided in English). The **Here Today** CD adds three cuts, one a dumb spaghetti western reworking of "Cold Sweat" entitled "Hot Meat."

Most Sugarcubes singles have been issued on CDs with non-LP and/or Icelandic-language tracks or alternate versions (it's always nice to see non-English speaking bands who don't ignore their own tongue.) For hardcore 'Cubes collectors, several years' worth of now-deleted singles are available in boxes, available as 7-inch and 12-inch vinyl as well as CD. The 12s and CDs are loaded with extra goodies including remixes, live takes and non-LP tracks (such as original Christmas songs).

Prehistory: In the early '80s, a band from Reykjavik's bourgeoning scene—Purrkur Pillnikk—supported the Fall on the latter's Icelandic tour (during which time most of **Hex Enduction Hour** was recorded), sporting a similarly anarchic, jagged sound. Einar Örn handled Pillnikk's lead vocals with Bragi Olafsson on bass. When that band ended, Örn met up with Björk and formed Kukl (sometimes K.U.K.L.), joined on the second LP by drummer Sigtryggur Baldursson, formerly of Theyr.

The Eye is a dark, almost Teutonic excursion into rock chamber music; the sound is somewhat subdued, dominated by lots of woodwinds (played by Björk), bells and other pitched percussion, Einar's trumpet and heavily treated guitar. Lyrics tend towards the morbid. **Holidays in Europe** lies between the experimentalism of its predecessor and the off-center pop the 'Cubes would later become known for. (When Kukl broke up, Björk, Einar, Olafsson and Baldursson formed the Sugarcubes with guitarist Thor Eldon; Reptile keyboardist Margaret Ornolfsdottir joined after **Life's Too Good.**) All of the pre-Sugarcubes catalogue is recommended for fans of the band and/or experimental rock (who don't mind doing some serious record hunting). [dgs]

See also *Purrkur Pillnikk, Reptile, Tappi Tíkarrass, Theyr.*

SUICIDAL TENDENCIES
Suicidal Tendencies (Frontier) 1983 ●
Join the Army (Caroline) 1987 ●
How Will I Laugh Tomorrow … When I Can't Even Smile Today (Epic) 1988 ●
Controlled by Hatred/Feel Like Shit … Deja Vu (Epic) 1989 ●
Lights … Camera … Revolution (Epic) 1990 ●

Every once in a while, a band previously lost in genre mire emerges from the crowd ineffably different and better than the competition. Suicidal Tendencies—a

Venice, California quartet once voted both Worst Band and Best New Band by the readers of *Flipside* magazine—could have been just another hardcore band, but they're not. The first LP benefits enormously from clear production (by Glen E. Friedman), tight, careful playing—fast and blurry in spots, but never indistinct—and singer/lyricist Mike Muir, whose intelligence and forceful personality invest songs like "Fascist Pig" and "Suicide's an Alternative" with wit and wisdom. Suicidal Tendencies' other strength is a facility for sudden tempo shifts, a gambit best used on the great "Institutionalized," a half-sung, half-recited alienation number which powerfully encapsulates all the punk sociology of *Repo Man* and *Suburbia* in four minutes. Don't miss this one.

After the first album sold unbelievable quantities for an independent release, Suicidal Tendencies took a lot of time organizing a new lineup and recording a second next record. Following the general hardcore drift towards metal, Muir, stalwart bassist/co-writer Louiche Mayorga and two new bandmembers straddle styles on the Motörhead-ish **Join the Army**, embracing ominous war-pigs power and blistering crap-guitar solos, but cutting it with sudden shifts into hyperspeed (or halfspeed for moshing), punk vocals and a continuing dedication to skate-punk culture. The sound isn't great, but the playing and energy, plus Muir's exceptionally strong singing, makes the LP worthy of the band's exalted status.

Sharpening the band's music into an articulate speedcore rocket, Muir and a new set of sidemen reached the major leagues with **How Will I Laugh Tomorrow**, a powerful and intelligent outpouring of alienation, self-examination and identification with the band and its attendant culture. Mike Clark (Muir's songwriting partner) and Rocky George keep the guitar pressure up, while Muir delivers his reflective lyrics with typical authority. The first side is especially great, a breathless series of well-constructed explosions, from "Trip at the Brain" and "Pledge Your Allegiance" through the title track and "The Miracle," a denunciation of idealism. The flip kicks off with a galloping instrumental ("Surf and Slam") and includes the tuneful and catchy "One Too Many Times." An uncommon example of what can happen to speedmetal when it's approached with imagination and originality.

The 1989 **Controlled by Hatred** has two non-LP edits of the previous LP's title track plus seven new songs in an unchecked metallic vein. Lacking the band's usual precision and clarity, thick-sounding tracks like "Master of No Mercy" and the death-metal clichés of "Waking the Dead" wind up blurry and indistinct, with Muir's vocals stubbornly battling the dense noise.

Cogently observing that "I'd rather feel like shit than be full of shit," Muir roars like a wounded animal on **Lights . . . Camera . . . Revolution**, an electric storm so loud and bracing that tracks seem to echo over the silence after they end. As if **Controlled by Hatred** hadn't happened, the band whips up a deafening guitar frenzy (turning quiet for the beginning of "Alone" and switching to funk for the first part of "Lovely"). Muir covers his standard alienation-nonconformity-loneliness topics with typical intensity, adding vague thoughts about political action (in "Give It Revolution," he as-

serts that "The greatest weapon of the fascist/Is the tolerance of the pacifist"), the atmosphere of violence ("Disco's Out, Murder's In") and televangelism ("Send Me Your Money"). [i]

SUICIDE

Suicide (Red Star) 1977 + 1981 (nr/Demon) 1986
24 Minutes Over Brussels (nr/Bronze) 1978
1/2 Alive [tape] (ROIR) 1981
Ghost Riders [tape] (ROIR) 1986 [CD] (Fr. Danceteria) 1990 φ
A Way of Life (nr/Chapter 22) 1988 (Wax Trax!) 1989 ●

ALAN VEGA AND MARTIN REV

Suicide (ZE) 1980 ●

A mainstay of the New York rock underground since the early 1970s (thereby prefiguring Soft Cell and all the other synth-based duos as well as an entire subsequent generation of droney noisemongers), Suicide mixed Alan Vega's blues-styled vocals and Marty Rev's synthesizer (originally a broken-down Farfisa organ they couldn't afford to repair). Escaping the dingy clubs of Manhattan, Suicide went on to cause riots in Europe while on tour supporting Elvis Costello and later provided the soundtrack for Werner Fassbinder's film *In a Year with 13 Moons*. Often confrontational in nature, they always provoked extreme reactions by producing a unique, obsessively American electronic music of enormous and enduring influence.

Suicide (1977) is a nearly perfect relic of mid-'70s Manhattan attitudes, a portrait of society grinding down to self-destruction. Rev's powerful minimalist repetition catapults Vega's pained and constantly cracking voice through indictments of Vietnam mentality ("Ghost Rider"), broken romance ("Cheree," "Girl") and holocausts both public and personal ("Rocket USA," "Frankie Teardrop"). Stolid and restrained, the record simmers with repressed emotion and excellent, unusual performances. Four years later, the LP was reissued with "I Remember," "Keep Your Dreams" and "96 Tears" added, as well as a flexi-disc of Suicide live in Brussels, taken from a 1978 authorized live bootleg. Recommended, though clearly not for everyone.

Suicide (1980), the confusingly titled Vega/Rev LP, was produced by Ric Ocasek, who smoothed the sound out to an almost socially acceptable level. (These same sessions produced the duo's zenith, 1980's anthemic "Dream Baby Dream," issued as a 12-inch single.) Rev's use of electronics had grown more subtle and complex, while Vega's vocals seem tethered and uneasy. "Harlem," a stunning mélange of urban despair and tortured musicianship, is the album's most affecting number.

The tape-only **Half-Alive** pairs one side of live material and one side of studio outtakes. Released soon after Suicide's dissolution, it offers no breakthroughs, but stands simply as a tribute to a fine, underrated band. The live side demonstrates how much fun Suicide was in concert, despite sloppiness and Vega's antagonism towards audiences. **Ghost Riders**, another live cassette, chronicles the pair's 1981 tenth anniversary gig in Minneapolis with clear sound and a convincing performance.

Long after bands they inspired had achieved commercial rewards Suicide never enjoyed, Rev and Vega reunited to reclaim their dominion with **A Way of Life**. Putting Ocasek back in the producer's chair, Rev and Vega barely acknowledge their disciples' innovations, and do what they've always done together: spin atmospheric tales with throbbing sequencers and dramatic Morrisonesque vocals. No catchy hooks, no high-energy disco rhythms, no old soul covers—just Suicide, polished but uncompromised. "Jukebox Baby 96" neatly bridges the pair's past adventures, while "Wild in Blue" offers a pounding reminder of industrial dance music's pre-Ministry beginnings.   [sg/i]

See also *Martin Rev, Alan Vega*.

ANDY SUMMERS

XYZ (MCA) 1987 ●
Mysterious Barricades (Private Music) 1988 ●
The Golden Wire (Private Music) 1989 ●
Charming Snakes (Private Music) 1990 φ

As the Police's mostly mute guitarist, Summers—whose long and winding career stretches back to 1963 and includes stints in both the Soft Machine and the Animals, not to mention sessions for Neil Sedaka—was recognized as one of rock's most versatile and venerated sidemen. Additionally, he asserted his independence by cutting two artsy instrumental records with Robert Fripp. But whatever could have possessed him—hubris? jealousy? a bet?—to write lyrics and *sing* on a solo album? **XYZ**'s laughable first line: "Some sex can be better when it's on the phone." Summers' froggy, unmusical croak overshadows his extraordinary musicianship, making him sound far less talented than we know him to be.

Prudently, there's no singing on **Mysterious Barricades**, an attractive wash of sonic wallpaper that continues Summers' tastefully productive partnership with keyboardist and co-producer David Hentschel. Working with no outside assistance, the duo weaves translucent new age instrumentals that fade in and fade out without incident, a technically flawless reverie.

Besides scoring 1989's *Weekend at Bernie's*, Summers expanded his artistic horizons with **The Golden Wire**, another co-production with Henstschel that uses a variety of musicians (on keyboards, horns, bass, drums and woodwinds) for much-needed rhythmic muscle and textural variety. One track has a guest vocalist; Summers breaks tradition to play a bit of banjo on another.

See also *Fripp & Eno, Police*.   [i]

SUN AND THE MOON

See *Chameleons (UK)*.

SUN CITY GIRLS

Sun City Girls (Placebo) 1984
Midnight Cowboys from Ipanema [tape] (Breakfast Without Meat) 1986
Grotto of Miracles (Placebo) 1986
Horse Cock Phepner (Placebo) 1987
Torch of the Mystics (Majorca) 1990

They may not be girls, but this elusive trio does live in a place known as Sun City, Arizona. (It's a bit northwest of Phoenix.) Like the Meat Puppets, they seem to have been out in the heat too long. Their hallucinatory debut album contains seventeen sketchy tracks (including "Your Bible Set off My Smoke Alarm") that range from nerve-wracking noise instrumentals to avant-jazz horn fantasies to actual songs with lyrics and seemingly conscious arrangements. "Uncle Jim" offers a ranting monologue with jazz guitar and sax; "My Painted Tomb" is a raga with toy piano; "Metaphors in a Mixmaster" presents free-form guitar improvisation. Bewildering, aggravating and intriguing.

Grotto of Miracles continues the group's unconventional adventures, carrying them out of the noise ghetto into the realm of airy guitar instrumentals favored by the Puppets: well-rehearsed Wes Montgomery threads and textures. (The Girls, however, don't evince any particular taste for local stylistic traditions.) The demented lyrical concepts and offbeat musical accessories (trumpet, cello, antelope bells, chimes, temple blocks, etc.) preclude any overall resemblance between the two groups, but openminded fans of the Puppets should find things of interest here. **Grotto of Miracles** is an ethnic stew that shows enormous creative growth.

After that relatively restrained album, it's back to perverse wild-eyed politicized insanity on **Horse Cock Phepner**. Forget jazzy guitar breakdowns, this record concentrates on tuneless chants and foul-mouthed expositions, performed over backing that varies from promising acoustic folk to conscientiously ugly noise. The maniacally vulgar "Nancy Reagan" is spoken over tribal chanting and drumming; Tuli Kupferberg's "C.I.A. Man" (with new lyrics by the SCG) uses only monotonic piano and a simple drum beat for accompaniment; the lengthy "Without Compare" is a collection of simultaneous conversations, a grisly refrain, a speech about history, an all-play-at-once bridge, a news report and a chaotic fade. Yeuch! Amid such delicacies (and worse—trust me), "Esta Susan en Casa?" provides the neatest alternative: a brief but convincing flash of rock salsa.   [i]

SUNDAY ALL OVER THE WORLD

See *Robert Fripp*.

SUNDAYS

Reading, Writing and Arithmetic (Rough Trade-DGC) 1990 ●

Proffering a lighter-than-air mixture of the Cocteau Twins, Smiths and Everything but the Girl, the Sundays burst on the British scene in a shimmer of catchy pop and Harriet Wheeler's enchanting little-girl voice. David Gavurin builds subtle tension into wonderful tunes like "Can't Be Sure" and "Hideous Towns" by picking out trancey guitar figures in songs that cry out for a satisfying strum. Elsewhere, minor-key contemplations ("My Finest Hour") evoke a rainy afternoon feel with poetic skill. Unlike other semi-acoustic bands of this ilk, the London-based quartet has energy to spare, exploding into uplifting sweeps of melodic joy ("Skin & Bones," "I Won"), getting faintly funky ("A Certain Someone"), even raising a good cloud of mild U2-tinged guitar smoke now and again. As frosting on this brilliant debut, the band's lyrics are bizarre fragments of opaque introspection that reveal themselves slowly in Wheeler's uncommon phrasing.   [i]

SURF TRIO
Almost Summer (Voxx) 1986
Safari in a Living Graveyard (Moxie) 1988 (Can. Star) 1989

The Surf Trio thank their idols—Link Wray, Jon and the Nightriders, Brian Wilson, the Ventures and the Ramones—for inspiration on **Almost Summer**, and those names go a long way towards describing the Portland, Oregon quartet's joyful sound. Facility for Ramonesy '60s melody-punk, surf-twang, beach pop and garage-rock makes each track in this sampler of delightful retro styles a different kind of magic. Exemplary and refreshing.

The second waxing is equally great, with such resonant originals as "Hang Ten," "Go, Go, Go," "My Real World" and "Girl with No Name," all written by bassist/singer Jeff Martin or guitarist/singer Ron Kleim. The album's only disappointment is an inconsiderately rushed cover of Bobby Fuller's classic "Let Her Dance."   [i]

SUSSMAN LAWRENCE
See *Peter Himmelman*.

BOBBY SUTLIFF
See *Windbreakers*.

SWA
Your Future if You Have One (SST) 1985
Sex Dr. (SST) 1986
XCIII (SST) 1987
Evolution 85–87 [CD] (SST) 1988 ●
Winter (SST) 1989 ●

Damaged-era Black Flag bassist Dukowski now leads this LA power-rock quartet which unselfconsciously draws on the sound of the '70s for likable, if unchallenging, original mainstreamisms that stop well short of metal. Former Flagmate Greg Ginn produced the hard-driving, intelligent debut album which revolves around Merrill Ward, a singer who can really project. **Sex Dr.** refines the concept on a batch of new tunes, penned mostly by Ward. The lyrics are generally presentable without saying much; tight group playing lends the music—which favors Steppenwolf a bit—conviction and dignity.

Replacing guitarist Richard Ford with Sylvia Juncosa (who simultaneously led her own band, To Damascus), SWA took a radically different route on the third LP, exchanging the precisely focused rock for a noisier, chaotic smear of aggression. Despite spots of MC5-ish excitement ("Optimist," for instance), **XCIII** is a disappointment, with SWA's best feature—Ward's voice—partially blunted by Dukowski's blurry production and Juncosa's ceaseless garbage riffing.

Following **Evolution**, an unnecessary eighteen-song/70-minute CD condensation of the first three albums, SWA found itself a new guitar player (Juncosa had begun her solo career in earnest) and regained its

focus on the heavy-duty **Winter**. A lot of the demi-metal fire (new axeman Phil Van Duyne is from the Black Sabbath bore-a-hole-in-your-skull school) is lost in the cloth-eared production, but Ward gets the tritely bombastic lyrics across with more clarity than they deserve.   [i]

See also *Descendents, To Damascus*.

SWALK
See *Shake*.

SWAMP OAF
See *Bags*.

SWANS
Swans EP 1982 (Young God) 1990 ●
Filth (Neutral) 1983 (Young God) 1990 ●
Cop (nr/K.422) 1984 ●
Swans EP (Homestead) 1985
Greed (PVC) 1986
Holy Money (PVC) 1986 ●
Children of God (Caroline) 1987 ●
Love Will Tear Us Apart EP (Caroline) 1988
Feel Good Now (nr/Product Inc.) 1988
The Burning World (Uni-MCA) 1989 ●
Anonymous Bodies in an Empty Room (no label) 1990
White Light from the Mouth of Infinity (Young God) 1991 ф

SKIN
Blood, Women, Roses (nr/Product Inc.) 1987 ●
Shame, Humility, Revenge (nr/Product Inc.) 1988
The World of Skin (Product Inc.) 1988 ●

WORLD OF SKIN
Ten Songs for Another World (Young God) 1990 ●

Play the Velvet Underground's "Sister Ray" at half-speed—go ahead, do it—and you've got Swans plus a sense of humor and the possibility that, if you just adjust the speed control, everything will get good. Take away the sense of humor and the speed control, and you've got Swans. In all probability, you've also got either a high threshold for crunching pain or a splitting headache. Well, that's Swans: downtown New York arties, friends of the infinitely more imaginative Sonic Youth. Swans trudge through dragging tempos, 2/2 meters and low frequency mush, all the while howling about alienation and despair. Listening to their records isn't like banging your head against a wall; it's like banging your head against the side of a swimming pool—underwater.

Filth is all that it promises to be: squalor without catharsis. The group is so conceptually strapped to its sludge m.o. that this album is actually more formulaic than any Top 40 band. (The **Filth** CD contains the first EP as well.)

Cop features new album and song titles, a new label, a trimmed-down lineup and new cover art. What it lacks are new ideas. *Boom*. Crunch. *Boom*. Crunch. Where Sonic Youth makes great music that's painful to listen to, Swans offer pain without reason. But things got better.

The 1985 EP featuring "Raping a Slave" offers few changes in the actual sounds the band incorporates, but makes things more interesting by using them in previously unexplored ways. A marked improvement over previous discs, and a good lead-in to **Greed**, where everything finally jells. New weapons are added to the Swans' arsenal, along with a variety of seemingly inconceivable approaches: the harrowing "Fool" is almost all piano and (sung!) vocals; several songs feature female background singers (serving more as an instrument than harmony). The closing "Money Is Flesh" has a two-note trumpet part played ad nauseum. Each track is a complete work in itself, enthralling and narcotizing.

Holy Money is more or less a twin to **Greed**, virtually identical in cover art and musical approach (the two LPs sandwich a great single, "Time Is Money (Bastard)"). Instrumentation is back to basic guitar, bass and drums, but the introduction of female vocalist Jarboe on "You Need Me" provides an effective counterpoint to leader Michael Gira's basso profundo. The lineup was in a state of flux; eight different performers appear on this album.

Children of God is Swans' finest moment, a diverse double album of pure, primitive, naked emotion. Some cuts simply pound the listener into submission, but others (generally those sung by Jarboe), are delicate, gentle ballads, finally providing a reference point for the more thunderous numbers. The lyrics deal with religious obsession, submission and suffering—they are stated simply yet remain open to all sorts of interpretations. A unique and powerful vision.

After releasing a farethewell-to-the-past live album (**Feel Good Now**), the Swans entered a new and more accessible career phase with a pair of slickly listenable but utterly useless covers of Joy Division's "Love Will Tear Us Apart" (apparently in a cynical bid to get college radio play) on a 1988 EP that also contains alternate versions of two **Children of God** tracks. The group then signed to a major label and teamed up with producer/bassist Bill Laswell. Perhaps the best Leonard Cohen record he never made, **The Burning World** benefits a great deal from the world-music instrumentation and structural abilities Laswell brings to it. The arrangements are uniformly strong, the gentler sounds don't strike one as a compromise and the cover of Blind Faith's "Can't Find My Way Home" is both apt and surprising. A nice one that's almost as haunting as it wants to be.

Skin is a spinoff band of Gira and Jarboe. The duo's first release, **Blood, Women, Roses**, is an LP dominated by Jarboe's avant-garde torch songs. The overall tone is one of quiet passion, with mostly acoustic instruments, but the occasional drum thunder will remind the listener of just who these folks are. Highlights include the mostly vocal and percussion "Come Out" and an impressive reading of Gershwin's "The Man I Love." Swans, yes, but they'll always be one of rock's ugliest ducklings.

Following a second sortie (**Shame, Humility, Revenge**), Skin combined both of its records (minus a few tracks) and reissued them as **The World of Skin**. Around 1990, Skin *became* the World of Skin; with **Ten Songs for Another World** (released on a label Gira created to release new product and reissue old Swans material), they effectively close whatever gap existed between it and the Swans. As varied as **The Burning World**, the album features some amusing psychedelic

touches, as well as a nice-try cover of Nick Drake's "Black Eyed Dog." Pere Ubu bassist Tony Maimone and Mary My Hope guitarist Clinton Steele guest on the LP which, for all its dour subject matter, comes off lighter and less would-be monolithic than anything Gira and Jarboe have previously done.

Anonymous Bodies in an Empty Room is a live (presumably authorized) bootleg of **Burning World** material and two new songs. [jl/dgs/gk]

See also *Circus Mort, Lydia Lunch, Of Cabbages and Kings, Prong, Ritual Tension*.

DAVID SWANSON
See *Pop*.

MATTHEW SWEET
Inside (Columbia) 1986
Earth (A&M) 1989 ●

Interesting list of musical connections for the ex-Oh-OK guitarist's solo debut, produced in NYC, Boston, London and LA by Stephen Hague, Scott Litt, Don Dixon, David Kahne and Dave Allen, among others. The Nebraskan native co-wrote three songs with Pal Shazar (ex-Slow Children) plus one each with Jules Shear and Adele Bertei; performers include Aimee Mann ('Til Tuesday), John McGeoch (Magazine, Banshees), two Bangles, Jody Harris, Mike Campbell (Petty's Heartbreakers), Valerie Simpson (Ashford and . . .), Bernie Worrell, Chris Stamey, Fred Maher and Anton Fier—again, among others. (Sweet was part of a 1987 Golden Palominos mini-tour.)

For all of this impressive name-dropping, Sweet plays nearly everything himself on two tracks, and manages to maintain a consistent feel throughout **Inside**, which is a bit like R.E.M. and early dB's doing sincere power-pop with keyboards. While most of Side Two is simply good, four of the five tracks on Side One are excellent.

Recording **Earth** in Los Angeles, Sweet diluted his England-via-Georgia sound with a dose of SoCal laid-backism. (Ironically, most of the participants are from the East Coast, mainly New York.) Dave Allen and Fred Maher co-produced with Sweet; Kate Pierson of the B-52's and Trip Shakespeare chip in backing vocals, while mucho guitar is supplied by Richard Lloyd, Robert Quine and Gary Lucas (ex-Beefheart). The album overdoses on pleasantness at moderate tempos—please, get obtrusive already! (A snappy rocker on Side Two is merely an aberration.) Not bad, but a disappointment after the promise of **Inside**. [jg]

See also *Lloyd Cole and the Commotions, Oh-OK*.

RACHEL SWEET
Fool Around (Stiff-Columbia) 1978
Protect the Innocent (Stiff-Columbia) 1980
... And Then He Kissed Me (Columbia) 1981
Blame It on Love (Columbia) 1982

The proverbial little girl with the big voice, Rachel Sweet burst out of Akron, Ohio in her early teens under the watchful eye of producer Liam Sternberg. An integral component (along with Lene Lovich) of the second Stiff Records signing blitz, Sweet recorded an impressive debut on which Sternberg figured prominently as both writer and producer. In its original English release, **Fool Around** is a great-sounding record that has Sweet voicing Sternberg's vision of the hip girl-child. The American version—remixed, re-ordered and with two different tracks—has less verve.

Protect the Innocent shows Sweet forsaking Sternberg's new wave-*cum*-country sensibility, muddling about in search of a focal point. Dolled up in black leather and singing songs that run the gamut from Lou Reed's "New Age" to Elvis' "Baby, Let's Play House" to the Damned's "New Rose," Sweet seems the victim of somebody's half-assed marketing goof.

And Then He Kissed Me is Sweet's third horse change in the middle of a career busy going nowhere, a Spectorish stab at MOR rock. Devoid of the freshness that was her most obvious asset, the LP contains her first genuine American hit, "Everlasting Love," a duet with teen dream Rex Smith.

Blame It on Love shows signs of revitalization. Though it sounds Tom Petty-influenced, Sweet wrote the entire album's worth of catchy material. She may never regain the youthful charm of her debut LP, but at least this LP shows her regaining control over her musical direction.

The diminutive powerhouse was not again heard from until early 1988, when John Waters tapped her to record the title song of his film, *Hairspray*. Sweet entered the TV world in '89 with a daily show on cable's Comedy Channel and wound up (reportedly) as the voice of Barbie on a Saturday morning cartoon.   [jw/i]

SWEET TOOTH
See *Godflesh*.

SWELL MAPS
A Trip to Marineville (nr/Rather-Rough Trade) 1979
 (nr/Mute) 1989 ●
Jane from Occupied Europe (nr/Rather-Rough Trade)
 1980 (nr/Mute) 1989 ●
Whatever Happens Next ... (nr/Rather-Rough Trade)
 1981
Collision Time (nr/Rather-Rough Trade) 1982
Train Out of It (nr/Antar) 1987
Collision Time Revisited (Mute-Restless) 1989 ●

JOWE HEAD
Pincer Movement (nr/Armageddon) 1981
Strawberry Deutschmark (Ger. Constrictor) 1986
The Jowe Head Personal Organizer (Ger. Constrictor)
 1989

In existence for most of the '70s, England's Swell Maps proved that a group of intelligent, fearless, versatile people can record five LPs and produce little of any lasting value. Though promising at the outset, Swell Maps (from a town outside Birmingham) succumbed to preciousness and self-indulgence with depressing speed. Significantly, however, three of the Maps' four mainstays—Jowe Head (bass / vocals) and brothers Nikki Sudden (guitar/vocals) and Epic Soundtracks (drums/keyboards)—have continued to be major figures on the international independent music scene.

A Trip to Marineville, released with a bonus four-song EP, finds our embryonic cartographers dabbling in Pistols-styled punk and more experimental noise-making, using unorthodox implements. Despite their energy and tenacious desire to produce something new, the package simply does not contain enough ideas that work. The following **Jane from Occupied Europe** shows the band's confidence waxing while its will to organize wanes. Since it's the *desire* to organize sound that fills the gap left when avant-gardists throw the rules away, this proved to be Swell Maps' undoing.

By the time of the interminable two-record **Whatever Happens Next**, mainly a collection of homemade cassette demos dating back to 1974, Swell Maps were rambling and floundering. **Collision Time** consists of about half of **Jane from Occupied Europe** plus an assortment of singles and other album cuts. The group broke up in 1980.

Following Nikki Sudden's success in the Jacobites, a posthumous compilation of singles and outtakes, **Train Out of It**, was issued. Two years later, as the group's first two LPs were reissued, **Collision Time Revisited**, a 27-song retrospective of rarities, singles, album tracks and unreleased efforts (with brief adulatory liner notes from Sonic Youth's Thurston Moore) appeared, putting a final cap on the Maps.

Besides playing in the Television Personalities and the Palookas, Jowe Head has made a couple of solo albums. **Personal Organizer** sounds like a low-budget Captain Sensible record, with casual, accented vocals (in a nice, deep voice) and casual, accented music. Head draws on cabaret pop, '60s cinema, dinky electronics, industrial noise and his own multicultural imagination to put together weirditties like "Sudden Showe," "Lolita" and "Nebelwerfer," a gloomy German-language number that quotes disco lyrics.   [mf/i]

See also *Barracudas, Crime and the City Solution, Nikki Sudden*.

SWIMMING POOL Q'S
The Deep End (DB) 1981
The Swimming Pool Q's (A&M) 1984
Blue Tomorrow (A&M) 1986
The Firing Squad for God EP (DB) 1987
World War Two Point Five (DB-Capitol) 1989 ●
ANNE RICHMOND BOSTON
The Big House of Time (DB) 1990 ●

While the snappy first album by Atlanta's Swimming Pool Q's generally follows the Athens sound—a singular fusion of collegiate-ham artiness and post-punk desperation—the Q's add a few interesting wrinkles of their own. "Big Fat Tractor" favors "Rock Lobster" whimsicality, but "Rat Bait" is an exhilarating chip off Captain Beefheart's block with jarring rhythms and growling guitar. In "Stick in My Hand," the Q's apply a heavy blues throb and aggro-folk vocal harmonies (guitarist/songwriter Jeff Calder and organist Anne Richmond Boston) to a story of Southern religious fanaticism. What's more, they have a great sense of black humor, like the comic masochism of "I Like to Take Orders from You."

The Q's play it more seriously on their second album, blending intelligent, evocative lyrics with a roaring folk-into-rock sound. When Boston sings "The Bells Ring," you feel like you're on the Trailways bus with her, escaping from romance, with a walkman turned up full-blast. When Calder sings "Pull Back My Spring," you can tangibly sense the tension. Armed with excellent, semi-regional songs and great flexibility in arranging and singing them, the quintet fills the LP with honest, heartfelt music that has inherent strength not reliant on volume or dance beats.

Blue Tomorrow is even better, evidencing the band's growing confidence and burgeoning songwriting skill. Mike Howlett's production finesse adds the audio definition and power their records previously lacked; the Q's take the opportunity to stretch their stylistic range further afield than ever before. Boston's vocals are exquisite—Linda Ronstadt meets Wanda Jackson and Sandy Denny—and songs like "Now I'm Talking About Now," "Pretty on the Inside" and "More Than One Heaven" show them off to best effect. (For aficionados, a brand new version of "Big Fat Tractor" demonstrates how far they've traveled since that first LP.)

Back on DB Records, the Q's next issued a rocking, Cheap Trickish single, "The Firing Squad for God," joined on a 12-inch by four diverse items recorded between 1982 and '86. Although she designed the cover (and plays pedal steel on "Working in the Nut Plant," the oldest track), Boston is gone from the band, leaving a stronger but less sensitive quartet.

"The Firing Squad for God" is included as one of two bonus tracks on the CD version of the unjustly neglected **World War Two Point Five**. Even without Boston (who nonetheless designed the swell cover), it's a fine record—an audacious song cycle outlining the spiritual downslide of post-WW II America. With equal proportions of humor ("The Lord of Wiggling," "Sweet Reward") and sadness ("1943 A.D.," "The Common Years," "More Often Than Never"), the songs convey a tragic sense of loss, and mark Calder as an increasingly accomplished tunesmith and conceptualist. Additionally, the underrated Bob Elsey's guitar work is more inventive than ever.

The Q's toured in 1989 with Windbreaker Tim Lee standing in for longtime bassist J.E. Garnett, who'd left to join a reformed Atlanta Rhythm Section (!). More recently, Calder has been dividing his musical attentions between the Q's and the Supreme Court, a collaboration with veteran avant-guitarist Glenn Phillips (an occasional Q's guest).

Meanwhile, Boston returned from self-imposed musical exile with **The Big House of Time**, a strong solo effort that reveals her as a mature, confident pop stylist. In addition to tuneful new songs by her ex-Coolie husband Rob Gal (who also co-produced and played guitar) and a new Calder tune, Boston breathes life into familiar material by John Sebastian, John Hiatt and Neil Young. [df/i/hd]

STEVE SWINDELLS
See *Hawkwind*.

SWINGERS
Picking Up Strangers (Aus. Mushroom) 1982
Counting the Beat (Backstreet) 1982

VARIOUS ARTISTS
Starstruck (A&M) 1983
PHIL JUDD
Private Lives (Aus. Mushroom) 1983
The Swinger EP (MCA) 1983
SCHNELL FENSTER
The Sound of Trees (Atlantic) 1990 φ

Leading the three-man Swingers up from Down Under, ex-Split Enz guitarist/composer Phil Judd rejected his earlier, convoluted melodicism for a still-quirky but more compact, abrasive approach, with phenomenal results. Judd's eccentric mental mixmaster spews out the clichés of mid-'60s Anglo-rock (Beatles, Stones, Who, Kinks) wackily updated, unreal and askew. His Dave Davies-as-young-schizo vocals (often abetted by gibberish falsettos) deliver lyrics almost too rock-songbanal to believe, surrounded by twangy guitars that resemble so many layers of electrified rubber bands. (The band performed selections from both of their LPs in the 1982 movie *Starstruck*, the soundtrack album of which contains Swingers tracks not found on **Counting the Beat**.)

Following the Swingers, Judd made a solo album, the Australian-only **Private Lives**, partially produced by Al Kooper. Although the cover is nicely surreal, the American EP that draws five songs from it shows no audible vestiges of his once-eccentric outlook, instead offering forgettable missives from the mainstream. Ironically, the album's six superior tracks—deemed unfit for American consumption (and co-produced by Judd)—reveal that the old goofball still has a few aces up his sleeve.

A bunch of years later, Judd made an unexpected and quite welcome return as the leader of Schnell Fenster (huh?), a quartet that includes old Enz-mates Nigel Griggs (bass) and Noel Crombie (drums). This overlooked gem finds Mr. J as appealingly warped as ever, playing the excitable boy to the hilt on askew anthems and fractured funk. Spooky, funny and haunting.

See also *Split Enz*. [tr/jy]

SWING OUT SISTER
It's Better to Travel (Mercury) 1987 ●
Another Non-Stop Sister (Jap. Mercury) 1987 ●
Kaleidoscope World (Fontana) 1989 ●

Quite unlike most of the groups emerging from Manchester in the late '80s, Swing Out Sister follow the path of such neo-smoothies as Everything but the Girl and Sade: jazzy, horn-colored pop that puts an '80s techno veneer to the smoky aroma of late-'50s nightclubs. The first album introduces the trio: Martin Jackson (Magazine's original drummer and a later member of the Chameleons), keyboardist Andy Connell (formerly of A Certain Ratio) and Corrine Drewery (ex-Working Week). Drewery's cool, dry vocals perfectly suit such appealing, uptempo creations as "Breakout," "Fooled by a Smile" and "Twilight World." Unfortunately, the songwriting is inconsistent: if all the material were of the same quality, **It's Better to Travel** would be an out-and-out joy. (**Another Non-Stop Sister** matches three new tunes with five remixed album tracks.)

Recording the second album as a duo (although Jackson did some drum programming, he's out of the band), Connell and Drewery revealed their Jimmy Webb jones. Interestingly, while they got the real McCoy in to arrange and conduct the orchestra for two songs, those aren't the tracks that most resemble the 5th Dimension or "MacArthur Park." ("You on My Mind" wins that award; Webb's work on "Precious Words" sounds more like Burt Bacharach.) By employing Webb's approach but cutting down the syrupy excess, Swing Out Sister reinterpret a corner of '60s pop without any sour aftertaste. Indicating one stylistic formula SOS should abandon, "Waiting Game" mixes elec-tronic dance percussion with strings. The arrangement ill suits Drewery's voice—despite a passing visual re-semblance, Lisa Stansfield she's not.   [i]

SWOLLEN MONKEYS
After Birth of the Cool (Cachalot) 1981

Every rock generation has its hip hornmen. As an outgrowth of Ohio's Tin Huey/Waitresses axis, the Swollen Monkeys (which featured Ralph Carney of the Hueys and Mars Williams, later of the Psychedelic Furs, as well as future Shimmy-Disc supremo Mark Kramer on "noisy tape loops") brought an anarchic new wave sensibility to horn-happy Spike Jones-influenced toot-ing. Produced by Hal Willner, **After Birth of the Cool** is a three-ring circus of kinetic instrumentals and loopy vocal songs, more silly than serious and plenty fun. If They Might Be Giants had been around a few years earlier, the Swollen Monkeys would have definitely been their horn section.   [i]

SYLVAIN SYLVAIN
Sylvain Sylvain (RCA) 1979
'78 Criminals (Fr. Fan Club) 1985

SYL SYLVAIN AND THE TEARDROPS
Syl Sylvain and the Teardrops (RCA) 1981

To hear Syl Sylvain nowadays, you'd never guess he was once a member of the dreaded, subversive New York Dolls. For one thing, he's an absolutely winsome singer, the perfect punk-with-a-heart-of-gold who seems to be striking an "aw, shucks!" pose at the mic. For another, his records are glistening, rocking pop with no hard edges, plenty of ingratiating melodies and lots of pizzazz. One of the fun things about Syl is trying to spot all the elements his eclecticism has absorbed. Over the course of these two LPs, he borrows from salsa, Tom Petty, Phil Spector, Gary Lewis and the Playboys and many more.

Sylvain's solo debut features the breathless "14th Street Beat," an ode to the Big Apple; the better-focused follow-up (with different musical associates) heightens the romantic angle with such tunes as "I Can't Forget Tomorrow," "Just One Kiss" and "It's Love." Pure charm.

'**78 Criminals** is a compilation of singles Sylvain did with various bands, including the Criminals, follow-ing the Dolls' collapse.   [jy]

DAVID SYLVIAN
Brilliant Trees (nr/Virgin) 1984 ●
Alchemy—An Index of Possibilities [tape] (nr/Virgin) 1985
Words with the Shaman EP (nr/Virgin) 1985 ●
Gone to Earth (Virgin) 1986 ●
Secrets of the Beehive (Virgin) 1987 ●
Weatherbox [CD] (Virgin) 1989 ●

DAVID SYLVIAN AND HOLGER CZUKAY
Plight & Premonition (Venture-Virgin) 1988 ●
Flux + Mutability [CD] (Venture-Virgin) 1989 ●

Unfairly characterized as a poseur since his earliest days with Japan, David Sylvian's obtusely alluring mu-sic and muse rendered him one of the most distinctive and influential artists of the '80s. Besides his own work, Sylvian has collaborated extensively with escapees from the rock world (Ryuichi Sakamoto, Holger Czukay, Robert Fripp, Bill Nelson) as well as jazz figures (in-cluding horn players Jon Hassell, Kenny Wheeler and Mark Isham).

Sylvian's solo career began shortly before Japan split in '82, when he released the first of two singles with Sakamoto (the second, 1983's "Forbidden Co-lours," was part of the soundtrack for the dreary Merry Christmas Mr. Lawrence) very much in the late-Japan style. With assistance from former bandmates Steve Jan-sen (Sylvian's brother; the family name is Batt) and Richard Barbieri, **Brilliant Trees** expands and refines that approach; contributions from Czukay, Sakamoto and Hassell emphasize Sylvian's growing immersion in jazz and more esoteric musics, most successfully on "The Ink in the Well" and the less structured second side.

Sylvian then embarked upon a perplexingly compli-cated multimedia project. He made a Japanese video documentary called Preparations for a Journey (from which a 20-minute short entitled Steel Cathedrals was released) based on an exhibit of his photographs (later assembled into a lavishly-packaged book, Perspectives); the video's ephemeral (some might say near-comatose) ambient music was issued as a cassette (**Alchemy–An Index of Possibilities**), extracts of which became an EP (**Words with the Shaman**). Now that's maximizing creative effort.

The ambitious double-LP **Gone to Earth** marks a more substantial departure in technique. Although Jan-sen and Barbieri participate, Sylvian pursues a sparser, more natural setting, as the strong presence of Fripp, Nelson and Wheeler moves the music further and fur-ther out. While some parts are sharply and jarringly defined, others are like **Music for Airports in Antarc-tica**. The first disc contains relatively conventional songs, contrasting the jazzy "Taking the Veil" with the languid drift of "Before the Bullfight," the grating Fripp-onance of the title track with the almost schmaltzy "Silver Moon" and "Laughter & Forgetting"—by far the most conventional "love" songs he's ever released. The second disc, which consists entirely of lulling, of-ten rhythmless instrumentals, could safely be titled **Gone to Sleep**.

While pursuing a more jazz-oriented and acoustic-based direction with notable contributions from Saka-moto and Isham, **Secrets of the Beehive** is significantly more accessible (reaching the VH-1 audience, "Orpheus" became a near hit). Abandoning its predecessor's spaciness, the simpler format still manages to cover nearly as much territory.

Sylvian's two albums with Czukay feature other members of Can (as well as Markus Stockhausen) and contain long, lulling instrumentals—not unlike extensions of **Gone to Earth** and **Secrets of the Beehive**.

The subtitles of the two pieces on **Flux + Mutability**—"A big, bright, colourful world" and "A new beginning is in the offing"—fairly reflect their music.

Weatherbox is a lavishly packaged five-CD set that contains **Brilliant Trees**, an expanded **Alchemy**, **Gone to Earth** and **Secrets of the Beehive**, as well as an extensive and carefully detailed booklet. [i/ja]

See also *Can, Japan, Ryuichi Sakamoto.*

HAJIME TACHIBANA

See *Plastics*.

TACKHEAD

Friendly as a Hand Grenade (TVT) 1989 ●
Strange Things (SBK) 1990 ●

KEITH LEBLANC

"No Sell Out" (Tommy Boy) 1983
Major Malfunction (World) 1986
Stranger Than Fiction (Nettwerk-Enigma) 1989 ●

GARY CLAIL'S TACKHEAD SOUND SYSTEM

Tackhead Tape Time (Nettwerk-Capitol) 1987 ●

GARY CLAIL & ON-U SOUND SYSTEM

End of the Century Party (nr/On-U Sound) 1989 ●

GARY CLAIL

The Emotional Hooligan (nr/Perfecto) 1991 ●

The winding path of the Tackhead collective can be a confusing—if musically fascinating—adventure for even its most ardent followers. The concept originated when the members of New Jersey disco/rap label Sugar Hill's house band—Keith LeBlanc (drums, percussion, keyboards), Doug Wimbish (bass) and Skip McDonald (guitar)—collided with British dub producer Adrian Sherwood. Besides going on to work with Mark Stewart and releasing singles as Fats Comet, the collaboration's first longplaying venture into the world of overturned rhythms, deconstructed tunes and rearranged found sound was released as **Major Malfunction** under Keith LeBlanc's name, presumably because the drummer had already stirred much interest with his provocative cut-up dance hit of Malcolm X speeches, "No Sell Out," and a similarly conceived tribute to England's striking miners.

Enter Gary Clail, an unconventional British MC who specialized in adding twisted vocals from the mixing board during Tackhead's live shows. **Tackhead Tape Time** is effectively the group's second LP, with Clail rapping and chanting semi-political rants through what sounds like a megaphone. Abrasive beats, funky guitars and the frequent use of sampled speeches (Margaret Thatcher is a perennial Tackhead favorite) make for a mind-bending/butt-moving experience.

Stranger Than Fiction is again credited only to LeBlanc, but Wimbish and McDonald make frequent appearances, Clail pops up once, and Sherwood co-produced. Clearly political without ever being overtly so, the album is never less than intriguing, ranging from the pure rhythmic repetition of "Einstein" to the jazz feel of "Count This" and the eerie ambience of "Men in Capsules."

Adding Bernard Fowler as lead singer, Tackhead attempted to solidify into a proper group with its "debut" album, **Friendly as a Hand Grenade**. Opening and closing with the jaunty "Ska Trek," living up to the title of "Demolition House" and pursuing the by-now-familiar sardonic comments on the military with the infectious "Airborne Ranger," **Friendly** indeed finds Tackhead at its most coherent.

Strange Things did indeed happen on the way to a major deal. After years of tantalizing avant-garde sounds, Tackhead launched themselves wholeheartedly into the mainstream and completely lost their sense of purpose. As angry black rockers, they aren't close to Living Colour; as funky cynics, they are leagues behind Was (Not Was). As electronic experimentalists, they are not a patch on their former selves.

Gary Clail, meanwhile, remained back in Britain; while he continues to draw from the Tackhead talent pool, his vision is thankfully much clearer. **End of the Century Party** is dub-heavy, a white reggae record that uses vocal samples, football chants, rap and narration. Clail may be politically obsessed, but he is only occasionally dogmatic. His vegetarian rap "Beef," which reconstructs a famed Public Enemy phrase, was subsequently revamped to launch a new British record label (Perfecto) and became a minor hit.   [tf]

See also *New Age Steppers, Mark Stewart and the Maffia*.

TAD

God's Balls (Sub Pop) 1989
Salt Lick (Sub Pop) 1990 ●
8-Way Santa (Sub Pop) 1991 + 1991 ●

Hey, they laughed at Leslie West, too! If you're gonna wallow in the loud dumb excesses of '70s hard rock, this slow-moving Seattle quartet—led by large-and-in-charge guitarist/growler/namesake/Idaho native Tad Doyle—gets up as good a head of steam as anyone, and with better focus and more gumption than most. **God's Balls** (70 percent of which is bonusized on **Salt Lick** CD and cassette) defines the band's face-in-the-mud perspective in songs like "Satan's Chainsaw," "Behemoth," "Nipple Belt" (something mass murderer Ed Gein actually owned) and "Boiler Room" (source of the LP's title) backing up Doyle's rugged vocals with serious sludge-guitar riff/feedback power.

Steve Albini produced **Salt Lick**, a dose of angry saw-toothed intensity that recasts Tad as a far noisier behemoth. In "Wood Goblins," Kurt Danielson's speeding bass sounds like a radioactive rubber band; throughout the seven tracks, Doyle and Gary Thorstensen peel off splintery guitar sounds that deserve the word "metal" more than any deathmongering glam-pussies.

8-Way Santa was withdrawn and reissued with a

new cover after one of the two unwitting cover stars took exception to seeing her photo on the sleeve. [pn]

TAIRRIE B
The Power of a Woman (Comptown-MCA) 1990 ●

With a guest endorsement by Eazy-E and production on two tracks by Schoolly D, California's hip-hop blonde Madonna busts her tough-girl rhymes in an ineffectual little voice, but with a lot of heart. Armed with an uncommon persona—rejecting the culture's usual sex roles to be one of the boys who knows she's a woman—Tairrie B (it's pronounced Terry) almost gets over on sheer attitude (check "Ruthless Bitch" and "Murder She Wrote," both of which are really cool tracks), but she's doesn't quite have the juice to make most of her claims sound convincing.   [i]

YUKIHIRO TAKAHASHI
Saravah! (Jap. Toshiba-EMI) 1977 (Jap. Seven Seas)
    c. 1989 ●
Neuromantic (Alfa) 1981
Murdered by the Music (nr/Statik) 1982
What, Me Worry? (nr/Alfa) 1982
What, Me Worry? EP (Jap. Yen-Alfa) 1982
Time and Place (Jap. Yen-Alfa) 1983
Wild & Moody (nr/Cocteau) 1985
Poisson d'Avril (Jap. Yen-Alfa) 1985
The Brand New Day (Jap. Alfa) 1985 ●
Broadcast from Heaven (Jap. EMI) 1990 ●

BEATNIKS
The Beatniks (nr/Statik) 1982

The outside projects of Yellow Magic Orchestra drummer/vocalist Takahashi (not to mention his colleague, Ryuichi Sakamoto) suggest that there was something amiss with the band's format during its existence; his solo work is far more amusing, even when the other members are involved. (They contributed half an album's worth to his solo LPs and play on lots more; Sakamoto even appears on the pre-YMO **Saravah!** LP.)

Takahashi's albums are far less programmatic and predictable than YMO's. He'll go from a reggae-style version of "Stop in the Name of Love" to a new-romantic soap opera to tongue-in-cheek pop powered by galloping synths to poignant soul-searching to a loopy update of Duane Eddy guitar instrumentals. He gives prominence to guitar (mostly played by YMO pal Kenji Omura, although Bill Nelson's e-bow graces much of **What, Me Worry?** and Phil Manzanera, bringing fellow Roxy Musician Andy Mackay along for the ride with sax and oboe, is on much of **Neuromantic**).

The two 1982 albums are pleasant surprises, with playing and material that's at once aggressive and arty. **Murdered by the Music** (from 1980 but unreleased in the West for two years) is the more goofy and eclectic. The **What, Me Worry?** EP features three tracks from the LP of the same name—one with Japanese lyrics this time—plus another bright original and a sprightly cover of an old German tune.

Selecting those songs that best combine melody and muscle, **Time and Place** is a strong live set mostly interpreting Takahashi's previous repertoire but also adding some new things (plus a version of Bacharach/David's "The April Fools"). The band giving it all a

unified feel is keyboardist Keiichi Suzuki, Bill Nelson, Hajime Tachibana (ex-Plastics) and drummer David Palmer. Interestingly, Takahashi doesn't drum—he sings, plays keyboards and guitar.

Wild & Moody is an LP of pretty songs—mainly romantic, though a little lyrically offbeat—dressed (but not tarted up) in electro-dance clothing. Nothing awesome, but nearly all of it delightful.

Poisson d'Avril (the French idiom meaning April Fools) is the soundtrack of a film starring Takahashi. (A large poster of "Yuki" is included.) He was apparently seized by an urge to *become* Burt Bacharach; a surprisingly large amount of it is movie music, in the style of "sophisticated" '60s romantic comedy. Enh. The best of it is represented on **The Brand New Day**, a fairly representative survey of his Alfa material (i.e. **Neuromantic** through **Poisson**).

The Beatniks, a duo of Takahashi and Suzuki, split all the playing (including some twittery synth) and singing on **The Beatniks**. Suzuki's vocals are better than Takahashi's (which often resemble overly echoed mumbling). The lyrics, most in English and the rest in French, are moodier and less cogent than those on Yuki's solo LPs. Overall, a lukewarm effort.   [jg]

TALKING HEADS
Talking Heads: 77 (Sire) 1977 ●
More Songs About Buildings and Food (Sire) 1978 ●
Fear of Music (Sire) 1979 ●
Remain in Light (Sire) 1980 ●
The Name of This Band Is Talking Heads (Sire) 1982 ●
Speaking in Tongues (Sire) 1983 ●
Stop Making Sense (Sire) 1984 ●
Little Creatures (Sire) 1985 ●
True Stories (Sire) 1986 ●
Naked (Sire) 1988 ●

Talking Heads—three conservative-looking refugees from the Rhode Island School of Design—first appeared on the New York Bowery circuit in mid-1975, playing on a CBGB bill headlined by the Ramones. From the outset, it was clear that, although the Heads shared an attitude and commitment to self-expression with the other bands then on the New York scene, they were charting a course all their own. That individuality, coupled with a strong adventurous streak, has resulted in both critical and commercial success for their group albums and some spin-off projects as well.

Led by the impossibly high-strung David Byrne (who has mellowed somewhat over the years), his neurotic but insightful perceptions focus the group's sensibility. The core of Talking Heads additionally consists of bassist Tina Weymouth, drummer Chris Frantz (now her husband) and ex-Modern Lover keyboardist/guitarist Jerry Harrison, who joined the trio in time for their first album. Together, and enlarged at times by temporary adjunct members, the Heads have produced intellectual dance music and artistic pop of different sorts, finding numerous rewarding levels on which to function.

Talking Heads: 77 is an astonishing debut with uncomplicated, almost low-key music supporting tense, bizarre lyrics, sung by Byrne in a wavering voice. He sounds downright uncomfortable admitting rather than proclaiming the words, but that only adds to the edgy appeal of such songs as "The Book I Read," "Psycho Killer" and "Uh-Oh, Love Comes to Town."

The Heads began a relationship with Brian Eno on their second album, essentially taking him on as a temporary fifth member. On **More Songs About Buildings and Food** (and the two succeeding LPs), they worked a sonic overhaul, at first adding elements to the basic framework and then ultimately subsuming the foundation into a wholly new approach. Here, the use of acoustic and electronic percussion fills previous spaces; the inclusion of Al Green's "Take Me to the River" indicated the band's deep interest in "black music" and provided them with their first glimpse of Top 40 popularity. The material isn't as startlingly fresh or satisfying as on the first LP, but some of the tracks work fine. (The first two albums were later joined on one cassette.)

The collaboration with Eno shifted into high gear on **Fear of Music**, moving rhythm to the front on "I Zimbra," and foreshadowing the band's new direction. It's a tentative step—most of the album sounds like a refinement of **More Songs**—but it draws still further away from their spartan origins.

Remain in Light incorporates various outside players (Adrian Belew, Nona Hendryx, a horn section) and makes a fully realized Great Step Forward. Funk and African influences meet electronics and selfconscious intellectual artiness to produce intricate, occasionally stunning tapestries that almost abandon song structure but do make a new kind of sense. "Once in a Lifetime" and "Houses in Motion" are among the group's finest achievements, and the relationship with Eno seems at its peak. But trouble was apparently brewing, and the Heads spent the next year pursuing solo projects, leaving the band on hold and revoking Eno's guest membership.

The Name of This Band is a two-record live album which showcases the group's best material and recapitulates the stages in its development to that point. Sides One (1977) and Two (1979) feature the basic quartet in the early days; Sides Three and Four (1980 and 1981) chronicle the augmented lineup, with Belew, Hendryx, Bernie Worrell, Busta Jones and others adding a brilliant funky flavor. The Heads' second concert record is **Stop Making Sense**, the one-disc soundtrack to Jonathan Demme's acclaimed concert film of the same name. Not only are the performances uniformly excellent, but the selection—from "Psycho Killer" to "Once in a Lifetime" to "Burning Down the House"—again neatly recaps the various periods of their career in a concise, cohesive setting.

Speaking in Tongues, a perfectly realized synthesis of budding pop instincts, powerful atmospherics and solid dance tunes, contains some of the Heads' best work, exemplified by "Burning Down the House" and "Girlfriend Is Better." Having experimented with communal music-making, the Heads reclaimed their tight control; while there are numerous guest players, it is the Heads' album all the way. Uncovering new areas of ambition, the group commissioned noted modern artist Robert Rauschenberg to design a novel plastic package for the record (also issued with a Byrne painting on a more traditional sleeve.)

Nine simple songs played with relative restraint and the fewest sidemen they've employed in a long time, **Little Creatures** is ostensibly the Heads' back-to-the-minimalist-roots rock'n'roll album, an escape from pan-culturalism and artistic grandiosity. (It's not.) Byrne's songs are as straightforward and non-Headsy as he can make them; considerations of mundane topics (sex, babies, television) join his typically oblique character studies and essays on being and nothingness. Were the flimsy songs sturdier, the album might have been more creatively successful; as realized, **Little Creatures** merely sounds careless and insignificant. "Road to Nowhere" and "Walk It Down" are the winners in a weak crop.

Although released in conjunction with Byrne's film of the same name, **True Stories** is not its soundtrack, but rather a new Heads LP. Again artfully exploring the complexities of modern culture in the superficially simple context of unembellished pop music, renaissance genius Byrne selfconsciously masks his awesome sophistication to sing *seemingly* (or so one is expected to understand) trivial ditties. Some are likable ("Love for Sale" and "Wild Wild Life," for instance) enough, but the conceptual attitude that attends its creation makes respecting **True Stories** impossible. Unfortunate though it may be, Talking Heads—with far-flung experimentation and groundbreaking originality under its collective belt—can't possibly sell conviction when slumming in the mundane world of tunesmiths and working musicians.

After two records of jus'-us-rock-folks, the courageous exploration (or overwhelming pretension, as you will) of **Naked**, recorded in Paris with Steve Lillywhite, seems reassuringly honest. Each song augments the quartet with numerous classy session players in varying combinations: ex-Smiths guitarist Johnny Marr, reggae keyboardist Wally Badarou, Pogue accordionist James Fearnley, saxophonist Lenny Pickett, etc. Horns and mountains of percussion filter a full set of oblique Byrnisms into merrily danceable exotica that's not as challenging as it is uninvolving. The CD adds "Bill"; three tracks appear in longer versions than on the vinyl LP. What's more, the CD is "graphics-ready," meaning that those in possession of the needed equipment—a CD player with a graphics output and a not-then-available decoder ($500 or so)—can watch the lyrics and real-time instrument list on a television screen while listening. [i]

See also *David Byrne, Jerry Harrison, Tom Tom Club.*

TALK TALK

Talk Talk EP (EMI America) 1982
The Party's Over (EMI America) 1982 ●
It's My Life (EMI America) 1984 ●
It's My Mix EP (It. EMI) 1984
The Colour of Spring (EMI America) 1986 ●
Spirit of Eden (EMI Manhattan) 1988 ●
Natural History: The Very Best of Talk Talk (EMI) 1990 φ
History Revisited: The Remixes (EMI) 1991 φ

Talk Talk's first album is slick, professional and lifeless, sounding as though it were programmed by British record company execs to be a synth-rock Foreigner. The London group earned some early comparisons to Duran Duran thanks to their double name, producer (Colin Thurston) and similarly superficial veneer. (The two young bands even toured England together in 1982.) But Talk Talk lacked Duran's panache. Songs by singer/keyboard player Mark Hollis (younger brother of producer Ed Hollis) are full of melodramatic angst and amateurish lyrics; his epic delivery is suitable but not overly appealing. In a cross-genre footnote, the album's best song ("Talk Talk," co-written by the two Hollises) had previously been recorded by Mark's 1977 mod-punk band, the Reaction, for Beggars Banquet's **Streets** compilation. (The **Talk Talk** EP previews **The Party's Over** with four selections from it.)

Things took a turn for the better on **It's My Life**, although Talk Talk still hadn't become an essential component of modern culture. While the title song wins the 1984 Roxy Music soundalike award, other synth-powered dance tracks like "Dum Dum Girl" reveal Hollis to be a truly mixed-up vocalist. Still, the band's creative future looked promising.

Bad bet. Except for "Life's What You Make It" and a gritty guitar solo on "I Don't Believe in You," the first side of **The Colour of Spring** is gruelingly slow and soporific; Side Two is sporadically more energetic, but the languid pacing still makes it an endurance challenge. Producer Tim Friese-Greene collaborated with Hollis on both material and keyboards.

Spirit of Eden continues the trio's perverse slide towards silent inertia. The album's six long tracks—which seem to begin and end at random—drift along at near-subliminal volume, with very little song structure and almost no audible signs of life. Tasteful understatement is one thing, but the delicate shadings—a choir, horns, reeds and Hollis' ginger singing—in this musical cipher don't even create any tangible atmosphere.

Given Talk Talk's patchy career, a retrospective may not be the wisest move, but record companies will be record companies. **Natural History** combines four tracks from **The Colour of Spring**, three from **It's My Life**, two each from **The Party's Over** and **Spirit of Eden**, adding the non-LP 1983 single, "My Foolish Friend." (That last song also appears on **It's My Mix**, a six-track collection of remixed singles.) The **Natural History** CD adds live versions of "Life's What You Make It" and "Tomorrow's Started." **History Revisited** is an album of remixes.   [ks/i]

TALL DWARFS

Three Songs EP (NZ Furtive) 1981 (NZ Flying Nun) 1985
Louis Likes His Daily Dip EP (NZ Flying Nun) 1982
Canned Music (NZ Flying Nun) 1983
Slugbucket Hairybreath Monster EP (NZ Flying Nun) 1984
That's the Short and Long of It (NZ Flying Nun) 1985
Throw a Sickie (NZ Flying Nun) 1986
Hello Cruel World (nr/Flying Nun) 1987 (Homestead) 1988 ●
Dogma EP (NZ Flying Nun) 1987

CHRIS KNOX

Songs for Cleaning Guppies (NZ Flying Nun) 1983
Monk III-AD 1987 [tape] (NZ Walking Monk) 1987
Not Given Lightly/Guppiplus (NZ Flying Nun) 1989
Seizure (NZ Flying Nun) 1989 + 1990
Song for 1990 + Other Songs (NZ Flying Nun) 1990

TOY LOVE

Toy Love (NZ WEA) 1980

Snow White had it easy. She only had to deal with seven little men who whistled while they worked. New Zealand's Tall Dwarfs not only whistle, they jingle, jangle, gurgle, grumble, grunt, sputter, bang on tables and guitars, play crumhorn, clarinet, clavinet, spoons and shake an angry bee-colony's worth of tambourine. Worse yet, as many as three times the population of White's house turn up for recording sessions: "Nothing's Going to Happen" (from **Three Songs**, later collected on **Hello Cruel World**, a sampler of the band's first four releases) features 20 different players on everything from bagpipes to *cabasa* (a Cuban percussion instrument).

The core of the group is Alex Bathgate and Chris Knox, formerly of seminal Auckland band Toy Love. The inspiration for Tall Dwarfs comes from somewhere between the alienated dementia of the Beatles' "Blue Jay Way" and comic horror movies on late-night TV. The Dwarfs could almost be accused of having a Simon & Garfunkel fixation for all the melodic acoustic guitars used in their early work, but then out spills a mangled masterpiece (such as "Paul's Place" from **Louis Likes His Daily Dip**) where tremolo overkill and Knox's simple, clear singing suggest a lovesick Irishman trapped in a bagpipe. No matter how pretty, the Dwarfs' music is always strange.

Tall Dwarfs don't have a drummer, so they use creative repetition of all sorts to provide a percussive element, from **Canned Music**'s pitterpat pawbeats and growling monster groans (which appear in "Turning Brown, and Torn in Two") through the harsh guitar saws and scat singing loops of "The Brain That Wouldn't Die" (on **Slugbucket Hairybreath Monster**, also later appearing on **Hello Cruel World**).

Most of the group's material was recorded on Knox's home Teac with neither EQ nor expensive microphones. This is strictly primitive DIY psychedelicacies with great green gobs of greasy grimy talent and monstrously surreal cover art (drawn by Knox) to match.

That same spirit of home taperism shows up most prominently when Knox is on his own. All he's got is a shy and fragile voice and two hands that can start a multi-track tape machine, tap impatiently on the table or strum an acoustic guitar. His earliest solo songs are short (few exceed three minutes, most run around or under two), sensitive and bittersweet. On **Songs for Cleaning Guppies**, "Sand Fly" has two voices whispering and humming against each other like a medieval madrigal harmony, while "Jesus Loves You" is an arty Chipmunk answer to "They're Coming to Take Me Away" and bears no resemblance to any hymn by the same title. "The thing that you call hope is just a legal form of dope that makes you happy," Knox recites as a pulse of music is played backward over two layers of recitational vocals, one at double speed, the other flatly half-whispered. Only 300 copies of **Songs for Cleaning Guppies** were pressed, but material from it resurfaced on **Guppiplus**, a companion disc to the **Seizure** album.

The multi-faceted **Seizure** (issued twice: the original cover shows Knox in zombie make-up, the second has only utilitarian yellow and black stripes) is sonically indistinguishable from a Tall Dwarfs album. It's got the Dwarfs' highly imaginative percussion and the same delightfully fuzzed-under sense of noise. It palpitates on

657

"Wanna!!," a track that could be named "Rock & Roll Part 3" for its textural similarities to a Gary Glitter song. **Seizure** also continues Knox's fascination with gentle acoustic balladeering, as on the percussionless "And I Will Cry," where his voice is multi-tracked into a warm boy-next-door lead against a sweetly soured chorus of higher harmonies. Some of **Seizure** is a cappella ("Voyeur"); at other times the sea of grunge is deep enough to drown in.

At the time of **Seizure**'s release, Knox remixed its "Not Given Lightly" for a 12-inch single (**Not Given Lightly/Guppiplus**), the B-side of which contains ten rarities: **Guppies** tracks, "Indigestion" (a recitation done for a compilation) and "Wanna Die with You" (a love song of sorts) from **Monk III**, a 24-song cassette assembled from '83 and '84 works.

The 10-inch **Song for 1990** couples the gentle sparseness of Knox's early ballad-oriented work with more confident singing and better production to give his very simple voice'n'guitar songs greater richness and substance. While "Haze" is texturally akin to the Beatles' "Blackbird," the title cut, a sarcastic bit of patriotic cheerleading for New Zealand's 1990 sesquicentennial, highlights the nation's problems with typical humble humor. Fans of such homey balladeers as Daniel Johnston or Mark Edwards (My Dad is Dead) are likely to enjoy Knox's surprisingly feminist views on love, life and the unreality of everything.

Toy Love's lone album is a deceptively cheerful-sounding collection that falls somewhere between power pop and new wave. Despite efforts to minimize it, the nonconformist spark that would later make the Tall Dwarfs so appealing surfaces in songs like "Frogs," a twisted little horror story of fuzz-guitar racings and keyboard blurts interlaid with a whistle-while-you-work chorus, a cappella "Exodus" theme and sound effects (squeeze toys, coughs, objects falling to the floor, a grumbled voice) in dizzying array. The country-bouncing "Bride of Frankenstein" is a wiggling guitar ditty full of yee-haws (delivered incongruously in New Zealand accents); "Who's at the Bottom of Your Swimming Pool?" lists dead rock stars and popular music magazines of the time to make an anti-rock-culture statement. An interesting artifact, but strictly developmental.   ['e]

See also *Bats*.

TAPPI TÍKARRASS

Miranda (Ice. Gramm) 1983

The band's name is Icelandic for "Witch's Kiss Ass," but its main claim to fame is petite wailer Björk Gudmundsdottir (later of the Sugarcubes), who was the lead singer and a founding member of this appealing but limited Reykjavik quartet. Björk was only in her mid-teens when Tappi Tíkarrass released their sole LP (a six-track 12-inch had appeared in '82). But the erotic intensity of her delivery belies her years, and she revels in the operatic zigzagging—from spookhouse cooing to hellish growling and skyscraping whoops—that has distinguished her work in the 'Cubes. Indeed, her performances here generally eclipse the music, which is haunting but melodically parched gloom-beat of the early Cure/Banshees variety.   [df]

See also *Sugarcubes*.

TAR

Handsome EP (Amphetamine Reptile) 1989
Roundhouse (Amphetamine Reptile) 1990 ●

Beneath a thick molten stew, Chicago's Tar spews lurching tunes that hover and circle with frozen precision. Drawing several of its members from hardcore outfit Blatant Dissent, the quartet has remnants of riled frenzy, but Tar builds its music at slower speeds. Even when the watts start flowing hard and heavy, Tar stays well within song form, favoring a solid and dense post-punk rock sound that's a lot more generally accessible than, say, Wreck or any of the Big Black soundalikes.

On the six-song **Handsome** (produced separately by Steve Albini and Iain Burgess), Tar's assault stresses churning guitars and chunky rhythms, occasionally doffing a cap to '70s rock, elsewhere raving with post-punk intensity. On some of the jolt'n'burn songs (particularly the spiraling standout, "Mumper") singer/guitarist John Mohr wails with an urgency that suggests Jeff Pezzati of Naked Raygun. But in "Static" and the screaming "Mel's" (remade from an '88 single) he establishes an anguished voice all his own.

Roundhouse tones down the pace but maintains the power and intensity. Burgess frames Mohr's vocals rather than burying them (one of **Handsome**'s weaknesses), revealing desperation in place of stifled anger. Though not as wind-whipped as the EP, songs like "Glass Grief" and "Les Paul Worries" showcase Tar's agitated electric aggression.   [mg/i]

TAR BABIES

Face the Music EP (Bone Air) 1982
Respect Your Nightmares (Bone Air-Paradise) 1985
Fried Milk (SST) 1987
No Contest (SST) 1988 ●
Honey Bubble (SST) 1989 ●

From the ashes of Midwest proto skate-thrashers Mecht Mensch came the Tar Babies. But these Madison, Wisconsin kids quickly outgrew the hardcore pee-wee straitjacket in which they'd been born. As far back as **Face the Music**, Bucky Pope's guitar displayed a unique, lunging hard-psych quality that separated the Tar Babies from their brethren. With the eight-song **Respect Your Nightmares**, the band began to insert choppy, neo-funk highlights into their primal psych-punk trash (like a thinner version of Texas' Big Boys, or the Minutemen), and that pointed them off in a whole new direction.

Although there are interludes of stoned scutter-pluck reminiscent of the Meat Puppets' work at the time, **Fried Milk** is most notable for the overtness of its funk underpinnings. (People inclined to dance have been known to do so whilst this album plays.) Beginning with **No Contest**, they began adding horns and a techno-bup filigree that isn't supremely appealing and tends to swamp Pope's guitar (still the Tar Babies' central shaft). Live shows provided evidence that the band was still capable of mind-blowing groove-excess, but their discs are less successful than the funkadelic shit they seem to be trying to emulate. Which isn't to say that a George Clinton/Bucky Pope/Bootsy Collins/Sonny Sharrock/Sonny Murray collaboration shouldn't be scheduled promptly.   [bc]

TROY TATE

Ticket to the Dark (nr/Sire) 1984
Liberty (nr/Sire) 1985

Armed with an impressive résumé (the Index, Shake, The Teardrop Explodes, Fashion) dating back to '77, singer/guitarist Troy Tate made his solo debut with the assistance of an eclectic set of musicians, including David Balfe, Nicky Holland, Virginia Astley and Woodentop Rolo McGinty. Tate uses his attractively husky voice and substantial songwriting skill—as well as deft electronic effects and complex arrangements—to put across ten melodic songs that approach modern pop from several different directions. "Safety Net," "Love Is . . ." and "Thomas" are the most memorable tracks on **Ticket to the Dark**, but most of the album is well worth hearing. An exceptionally good record.

Simply played by an unfamous guitar-bass-drums trio and produced with equally effective restraint, **Liberty** focuses attention on Tate's best asset, his handsome crooning. Although this sophomore LP doesn't have enough great songs ("Sorrow," "God's Puppet" and "Tomorrow I'll Be Gone" are the highlights), the stylistic consistency and Tate's engaging personality keep **Liberty** appealing. Stranger-than-fiction art note: the squiggly face drawn on the back cover bears a striking resemblance to Bart Simpson, who hadn't yet been introduced to the world.   [i]

TATER TOTZ

See *Red Cross.*

TAXI BOYS

See *Real Kids.*

TAXI GANG

See *Sly & Robbie.*

ANDY TAYLOR

See *Duran Duran.*

JAMES TAYLOR QUARTET

See *Prisoners.*

TOT TAYLOR AND HIS ORCHESTRA

The Girl with Everything EP (nr/GTO) 1981
Playtime (nr/Easy Listeners) 1981 (nr/London Popular Arts) 1988 ●

TOT TAYLOR

The Inside Story (nr/Easy Listeners) 1984 (nr/London Popular Arts) 1988 ●
Box-Office Poison (nr/London Popular Arts) 1986 ●
Arise, Sir Tot EP (nr/London Popular Arts) 1986
Jumble Soul (nr/London Popular Arts) 1986
My Blue Period (nr/London Popular Arts) 1987 ●
Menswear (nr/London Popular Arts) 1987
Scrapbook (nr/London Popular Arts) 1988

SOUND BARRIER

The Suburbia Suite (nr/Compact Organization) 1984

Tot Taylor is a Brit-popper who loves Tin Pan Alley. After EMI adjudged his band Advertising (pop-rock plus punky perspiration) to be a non-starter, Taylor convinced another commercial powerhouse to take him on but, after three 45s, GTO decided it had been a big mistake. By then, he'd discovered Mari Wilson (who'd also signed to GTO) and Virna Lindt; when he and Mari were dumped, Taylor launched his own empire, the Compact Organization. (GTO, meanwhile, has long since gone out of business.)

Tot had recorded **Playtime** for GTO, and arranged to take all sixteen tracks of it with him. The usual rhythm section (including the odd bit of dribbly synth) is frequently augmented by horns and strings. What saves Taylor from seeming an insufferable twit for presuming to emulate Porter, Gershwin, Rodgers and Hart, Kern, etc. is his cleverly unassuming and self-parodic word-play. Sometimes he spouts gloriously goofy rock ("I Wanna Play the Drums Tonight"—Kevin Ayers meets Sparks), but he also slips in observations on the grayness of the modern day-to-day—we *are* all "Living in Legoland"—for effective commentary.

The Inside Story (which Taylor pretty much plays all himself) is another delightful grab-bag; less playing time than **Playtime**, but otherwise nearly its equal. Taylor's flaky charm is even equal to his choice of Porter's "All of You" as an album-closer, in a treatment which sounds sincere and true to the original song.

Tot next composed a whole instrumental LP, **The Suburbia Suite**, for the Sound Barrier, and penned Slim Gaillard's number (plus some incidental music) for the film *Absolute Beginners*. Then he cut three new albums in two years! Regrettably, none of them are up to his first two. Sometimes he tries too hard to be witty; other times, songs or arrangements go on too long.

Box Office Poison might appear more impressive if it not for its illustrious predecessors. In fact its musical execution is, if anything, more facile. "Arise, Sir Tot" gently deflates his own delusions of grandeur; "Australia" is a longing toast to a place we haven't destroyed—yet; "Spoil Her" is romantic strategy that's only partly tongue-in-cheek. (The **Arise** EP is a 12-inch with four of the LP tracks on it.)

Recorded with lots of instrumental assistants, **My Blue Period** is Tot's jazz record; Aluminum Pan Alley. The aptly named "The Wrong Idea," a strained attempt at cleverness, gets things off on the wrong foot. "The Compromising Life" is a much better notion, and its swell mute trumpet work is a well-executed example of the LP's stylistic intentions. Additionally, "A Girl Did This" ranks with his best, but **Period** just isn't consistent.

On **Menswear**, Tot went to the other extreme for a DIY approach in his modest home studio. Lyrically and arrangement-wise, he regains top form (sixteen tight little vignettes) but, melodically, his catchiness quotient is still not one hundred percent. When he's on, however, the LP ranges from good ("Trouble in Store," as in department store) to brilliant ("Waiting for My Egg," a procrastination anthem).

Jumble Soul is a fourteen-cut best-of, collecting some of the first three LPs plus some unalbumized 45s (including the two non-LP GTO A-sides), the title track of **The Girl with Everything** (the 7-inch EP also contains "Modern Wife" from **Playtime** and instrumental soundtrack music looking for a film). **Scrapbook** is a limited-edition boxed set for the true Totfan: two albums, a 10-inch EP of previously unreleased tracks, a four-song 7-inch of new tunes, a cassette of radio interviews and more. Whew! [jg]

See also *Advertising*.

BRAM TCHAIKOVSKY

Strange Man, Changed Man (Polydor) 1979
The Russians Are Coming (nr/Radar) 1980
Pressure (Polydor) 1980
Funland (Arista) 1981

Bram Tchaikovsky was a group as well as Peter Brammell's nom de rock, but it was the lack of a similarly strong second creative force to him in the band that proved to be its undoing. The ex-Motors guitarist/bassist/vocalist had the talent to make his band work for a while, but couldn't maintain its quality alone.

Strange Man, Changed Man sounds fresh and punky (if rather trebly)—an energetic mixture of the Byrds, Springsteen and, not surprisingly, the Motors. (Nick Garvey, one of Bram's ex-bandmates, co-produced.) The LP includes three fine singles ("Girl of My Dreams," "I'm the One That's Leaving," "Sarah Smiles"); the rest of the material has also worn remarkably well.

Expanding from a trio to a quartet and doing the production themselves, Bram (the band) came up with a sophomore effort (**The Russians Are Coming**, retitled **Pressure** for the cold-war-minded USA) that improves the sound but has far less consistent songs, with writing divided among various combinations of the members.

Subsequent personnel shifts left Bram (the man) with neither satisfactory writing partners nor an alternate (or harmony) vocalist to shore up his own shortcomings. An attempt to pursue several ill-advised directions makes **Funland** (production again by Garvey) lifeless. The only times Bram's tepid vocals cut loose are on the oft-covered "Breaking Down the Walls of Heartache" and an old Motors B-side, "Soul Surrender," recorded as an afterthought by Bram, Garvey and deputized drummer Hilly Michaels. [jg]

See also *Motors*.

TEARDROPS

Final Vinyl (nr/Illuminated) 1980

Buzzcocks bassist Steve Garvey was a Teardrop; the rest of this Manchester outfit had ties to the Fall and other local legends. **Final Vinyl** is very inconsistent—too much mucking about in the studio ruins the decent tracks with spurious talking and noises—but there is some fine music here that hovers between the Buzzcocks and the Sex Pistols. [i]

TEAR GARDEN

See *Skinny Puppy*.

TEARS FOR FEARS

The Hurting (Mercury) 1983 ●
Songs from the Big Chair (Mercury) 1985 ●
The Seeds of Love (Fontana) 1989 ●

OLETA ADAMS

Circle of One (Fontana) 1990 φ

One of the '80s' most astonishing debuts, **The Hurting** introduces Tears for Fears—Roland Orzabal (vocals, guitar, keyboards) and Curt Smith (bass, vocals, keyboards)—and their intensely dour, introspective worldview. Grounded in Janovian primal scream theory and other aspects of modern psychology, Orzabal's songs discuss only somber topics of deep pain and sorrow. Like their titles ("The Hurting," "Mad World," "Start of the Breakdown," "Watch Me Bleed"), the lyrics are more often depressed than angry. Odd fare for hit records with teenybop appeal to be sure, but occasionally anxious vocals and the eclectic, often remarkable music belie the dark thoughts being conveyed. It's disconcerting to find yourself humming along with such misery, but **The Hurting** is an excellent, mature record.

Over two years in the making, **Songs from the Big Chair** finds Tears for Fears less miserable, more capable of expressing anger and well on their way to major stardom. (The LP ultimately sold nine million copies worldwide.) "Head Over Heels" (grand pop), "Everybody Wants to Rule the World" (haunting pop) and "Shout" (measured, gruff rock)—all co-written by Orzabal with others in the group—are the best three out of eight. The music is more ambitious and sophisticated, allowing a few numbers to go on too long without generating much impact, but the strong entrants are top-notch.

Emboldened by success and growing fanatical in his perfectionism, Orzabal (emerging as the group's creative heavyweight) saw **The Seeds of Love** through a ten-month false start, two changes of producers (TFF ended up doing it themselves with engineer Dave Bascombe) and painstaking byte-by-byte computer manipulation of the music. Rivaling Tom Scholz for the Guinness studio slowpoke record, he and Smith spent a fortune fussing over eight tracks in earnest for seventeen months. Eventually, they completed an album, a suite-like assortment of songs that—with the exception of the immediately delightful Beatles tribute, "Sowing the Seeds of Love"—are almost impenetrable in their delicate complexity and maddening density. Although she appears only on "Woman in Chains" and "Badman's Song," American vocalist/pianist Oleta Adams steals the show by injecting some soul into these absurdly overintellectualized exercises.

Returning the favor, Orzabal co-produced and played on **Circle of One**, fitting Adams' mature songs (mainstream pop soul originals with a theatrical bent and stirring lyrics of womanly self-determination) into tasteful arrangements that highlight the rich warmth of her voice. [i]

TENDER FURY

See *True Sounds of Liberty*.

TEENAGE FANCLUB

A Catholic Education (Matador) 1990 ●

If Sonic Youth had spent more time listening to Neil Young as kids, they might resemble this unpretentiously shaggy Glasgow quintet, which fishes memorable hooks and involving melodies out of lazy, thick pools of overdriven guitar rock. Relaxed and rough, **A Catholic Education** has a wonderfully informal feel, surprisingly clear vocals, cool lyrics and simple chord-based songs (like the solemn "Everything Flows," the peppy "Critical Mass" and the anthemic "Eternal Light") that ably withstand repeated hearings. [i]

TEENAGE HEAD(S)

Teenage Head (Can. IGM) 1979 (Can. Other Peoples
    Music-Goon Island) 1981
Frantic City (Can. Attic) 1980
Some Kinda Fun (Can. Attic) 1982
Tornado EP (MCA) 1983
Endless Party (Can. Ready) 1984
Trouble in the Jungle (Can. Warpt) 1986
Electric Guitar (Can. Fringe Product) 1988 •

Fronted by singer Frankie Venom, this hard-rockin' quartet from Toronto owes more than its name to the Flamin Groovies—the records are full of non-stop crazed rock'n'roll songs about cars, parties, girls, booze and general wanton fun, all imbued with the original Groovies' unreconstructed spirit. With nods to Eddie Cochran, Chuck Berry, Gene Vincent and other pioneers, Teenage Head races along, Gordie Lewis' guitar blazing, through numbers like "Ain't Got No Sense" and "Kissin' the Carpet" (both on **Teenage Head**, which was remixed and reissued), "Disgusteen" (**Frantic City**) and "Teenage Beer Drinking Party" (**Some Kinda Fun**). If they were smarter and more sarcastic, T. Head might have more in common with the old Dictators; as it stands, their sound, while hardly original, is perfect for parties held in gymnasiums. The first three records aren't hip, but they are solid, sweaty and convincingly salacious.

Given a pluralizing, name-sanitizing "s," the group lowered its hysteria level on the six-song **Tornado**, an ill-advised stab at maturity and commercial hard-rock acceptability. Snore. **Endless Party** is a live greatest-hits rundown recorded on New Year's Eve 1983.

Fortunately, the story doesn't end there. Safely removed from the Lower Fifty's crass influence, the quartet reclaimed both its spelling and sense of fun on the nifty **Trouble in the Jungle**. Covering Bobby Fuller, Eddie Cochran and Elvis Presley amid a variety of equally gonzo originals, the band shifts gears easily from lightly played rockabilly pop to electric punk—sometimes in the same song.

Electric Guitar has only one non-original, but self-propulsion does nothing to impede the versatile fun. "She Rips My Lips," "Can't Stop Shakin' " and "Full-Time Fool" are all vintage-flavor rockers, crisply delivered with chops and spirit; "Your Sister Used to Love Me" makes a cool milkshake of Dave Rave's relaxed surf vocals and Lewis' sizzling punk chords; "You're the One I'm Crazy For" is a spectacular Ramones imitation. **Electric Guitar** is convincing proof that a neat and clean garage can still rock. (Daniel Lanois plays guitar on two tracks.) [i]

TEENAGE JESUS AND THE JERKS

Teenage Jesus and the Jerks EP (Lust/Unlust) 1979
VARIOUS ARTISTS
No New York (Antilles) 1978

LYDIA LUNCH

Hysterie (nr/Widowspeak) 1986 (CD Presents) 1986 •

Teenage Jesus pushed the anything-goes/anyone-can-do-it philosophy of punk about as far as it would stretch without breaking. Formed in 1976 by onetime CBGB waitress Lydia Lunch and saxophone/conflict artist James Chance, TJ & the Jerks went beyond minimalism and atonality into what Lunch proudly called "aural terror"; the band cranked up a musical death knell over which she screamed her lyrics of fear, pain and unpleasantness. After Chance quit to form the equally abrasive but funkier Contortions, the Jerks soldiered on as a trio, leaving their sonic bloodbaths on the **No New York** anthology and the two Bob Quine-produced singles ("Orphans" and "Baby Doll") preserved on the 12-inch pink vinyl 1979 EP. (The group also issued a three-song 12-inch on ZE.) Lydia ranks as one of the most creatively untalented guitarists of all time; her blistering walls of noise, while completely lacking in melody or taste, possess an unremitting atavistic ferocity. Never a band to waste the audience's time, Teenage Jesus specialized in 20-second songs and ten-minute sets (which some witnesses still considered about nine minutes too long.)

The double-album **Hysterie** compilation contains an entire side of Teenage Jesus & the Jerks: a ten-track onslaught that pretty much recapitulates the group's oeuvre, some of it in glorious live-at-CBGB sound. Lunch went on to numerous other bands and musical alliances. Drummer Bradley Field popped up briefly as a bongo player for the Contortions; bassist Jim Sclavunos became the *drummer* in two of Lydia's subsequent bands, Beirut Slump and 8 Eyed Spy. [rnp]

See also *James Chance, 8 Eyed Spy, Lydia Lunch*.

TEEN IDLES

See *Minor Threat*.

DENIZ TEK

See *Radio Birdman*.

TELESCOPES

7th # Disaster EP (nr/Cheree) 1989
The Perfect Needle EP (nr/What Goes On) 1989
Taste (nr/What Goes On) 1989
To Kill a Slow Girl Walking EP (nr/What Goes On) 1989
Trade Mark of Quality (nr/Fierce) 1990 •
The Telescopes EP (nr/Creation) 1990
Everso EP (nr/Creation) 1990
Celeste EP (nr/Creation) 1991

Violently coupling '60s punk with a Jesus and Mary howl, Burton-upon-Trent's Telescopes originally got on the map via their debut single (presaged by a live flexi). While the title tune of **7th # Disaster** only improves on the quintet's formula, the other three tracks slither tentacles into neighboring pies, demonstrating, in particular, a decidedly un-Dinosaur(Jr)-like grasp of strum/shriek dynamics. **Perfect Needle** goes one rung further up the ladder of iconoclasm, adding violins and slow seething tunes to the distortion, resulting in music that is no more complicated nor any less aggressive than the Stooges, yet sounds like nobody but the Telescopes.

Taste reprises "Perfect Needle" from the EP, mating it with a set ranging from gentle fury to frantic abandon. The band's control of aural mania and anger is impeccable (credit due debut-till-death producer Richard Formby), but precious little of the actual *material* equals preceding or subsequent EPs.

To Kill a Slow Girl Walking adds nothing to the canon save a few trumpet bleats—and more highly memorable tuneage. **Trade Mark of Quality** is essentially an upper-end bootleggish bit of live mayhem in the dodgy Fierce-label series also covering Spacemen 3 and the Pooh Sticks, interesting only in its glimpse of the band sans studio augmentation. While the muted live buzz is unquestionably less invigorating than their "crafted" material, the 'Scopes do manage to kick out several flavors of jam for a tense and tasty megadecibel, megadrenaline rush.

Sidestepping onto Creation, the group's next record ups the pop content two notches while decreasing the pain quotient to the same degree, allowing nuances previously buried in feedback to surface. **Everso** subtracts all remaining scree for a brief garage psych outing that could have graced their first two records if they'd had greater control—and politer manners—back then. Proceeding from there, the dull and faceless **Celeste** totally drops the band's personality and is sonically unidentifiable as the Telescopes. [ab]

TELEVISION

Marquee Moon (Elektra) 1977 ●
Adventure (Elektra) 1978 ●
The Blow-Up [tape] (ROIR) 1982 [CD] (Fr. Danceteria) 1990 ◊

Live, they were the ultimate garage band with pretensions—Television's influences were Coltrane and Dylan as well as Roky Erickson—but on record they achieved a polish that added genuine strength. The group evolved from the Neon Boys and initially consisted of Tom Verlaine (guitar/vocals), Richard Lloyd (guitar), Billy Ficca (drums) and Richard Hell (bass). Hell left to form the Heartbreakers with Johnny Thunders, and ex-Blondie bassist Fred Smith took over his slot. Thus constituted (and significantly reduced in fringe aggression), Television recorded "Little Johnny Jewel," a privately pressed single which many regard as a turning point for the whole New York scene.

TV signed to Elektra and released **Marquee Moon** in 1977. A tendency to "jam" onstage caused detractors (and, paradoxically, British fans) to refer to them as the Grateful Dead of punk, but it was the distinctive two-guitar interplay (along with Verlaine's nails-on-chalkboard vocals) that set them apart. Verlaine's staccato singing in songs like "Prove It" and "Friction" is impressive, and the long workout on the title track showed a willingness to break away from the solidifying traditions of their more selfconscious contemporaries.

Adventure was, contrary to its title, smoother and more controlled than its predecessor, but did not want for good material. "Glory," "Foxhole" and the beautiful "Days" showed the band to have a firm grip on their songwriting. Television lasted about another year before splintering. A posthumous tape-only compilation

of live performances shows the band's rawer side and includes such concert cover staples as "Knockin' on Heaven's Door," "Satisfaction" and the 13th Floor Elevators' classic "Fire Engine" (listed as "The Blow Up" and credited to Verlaine, though the song is mentioned by its true name and source in the liner notes). Verlaine and Lloyd have both pursued solo careers; Ficca became a Waitress. Richard Hell released records and fronted bands under his own name after leaving the Heartbreakers. [jw]

See also *Heartbreakers, Richard Hell, Richard Lloyd, Kristi Rose and the Midnight Walkers, Tom Verlaine, Waitresses, Washington Squares.*

TELEVISION PERSONALITIES

Where's Bill Grundy Now? EP (no label) 1978 (Rough Trade) 1979
... And Don't the Kids Just Love It (nr/Rough Trade) 1980
Mummy Your Not Watching Me (nr/Whaam!) 1981 (nr/Dreamworld) 1987
They Could Have Been Bigger Than the Beatles (nr/Whaam!) 1982 (nr/Dreamworld) 1986
Then God Snaps His Fingers (nr/Whaam!) 1983
The Painted Word (nr/Illuminated) 1984
Chocolat-Art (Ger. Pastell) 1985
Privilege (Fire) 1989 ●
Salvador Dali's Garden Party EP (nr/Fire) 1989

Drawing inspiration from '60s British pop and psychedelia, London's Television Personalities—led by Daniel Treacy, with schoolmate Edward Ball (also the man of the Times, to whom he became singly loyal in the early '80s) and Joe Foster (later of Slaughter Joe)—are a haphazard and amateurish band whose records offer no slick musicianship but loads of brilliantly adapted pop-art weirdness. They started out wide-eyed and Jonathan Richman-like but evolved into (and beyond) rambling, jagged space noise and various stripes of time-warped psychedelia.

Ball and Treacy began casually, recording singles together as the Television Personalities, O Level and Teenage Filmstars; Foster contributed to the vinyl minideluge as the Missing Scientists. Showing a healthy awareness for 1978's here-and-now, they released **Where's Bill Grundy Now?**, a 7-inch EP also known as **Part Time Punks** (after another of its four songs).

The TVPs (for this project, Treacy, Ball and a drummer) made their longplaying debut with **And Don't the Kids Just Love It**, an altogether charming and guileless version of Carnaby Street pop given a modern neurotic outlook. The cover sets the period with a collage that fits together John Steed of *The Avengers* and Twiggy. From a Kinksish tale of boyish admiration ("Geoffrey Ingram") to the lyrically acute "I Know Where Syd Barrett Lives," simply and softly played guitars, bass and drums support coy vocals sung in Treacy's adenoidal accent. Haunting melodies and abundant wit make the record bizarre but wonderful, far more eccentric and original than the solemn neo-mod rehashers of the same era.

Ball and Treacy then formed the Whaam! label, later renamed Dreamworld after George Michael's people took an interest. In between Times sessions (which generally included Treacy), the TVPs moved from succinct pop art and flower power to trippy psychedelia on **Mummy Your Not Watching Me**, a mixture of keyboards and low-budget studio effects. Although some of the songs follow the first album's art-school template ("Painting by Numbers" and "Lichtenstein Painting"), others meander through mild mind expansion, in homage to Barrett and other acid-rockers. The standout in this vein is "David Hockney's Diaries," which also demonstrates the problems inherent in adorableness trying to be spacey. The shoebox production removes any grandiosity that may have been intended, and what's left sounds mixed up and silly. If it weren't for the redeeming pop tunes, **Mummy** would have been a real disappointment.

Released concurrently with the announcement of the band's dissolution (actually, Ball and Treacy merely parted ways for a while; the TVPs continued apace), **They Could Have Been Bigger Than the Beatles** includes reprises of previously recorded songs as well as a pair of prime numbers—"Painter Man" and "Making Time"—by the '60s ultra-mod Creation, which receive affectionate and respectful (if incompetent) treatment. The album offers sixteen tracks of should-have-been-good nostalgic art-rock, but sacrifices a lot of charm with an overly heavy guitar sound. Best cut: "The Boy in the Paisley Shirt."

The Painted Word lists a four-man lineup and actually features a group photo (albeit a dark, fuzzy one) on the front cover. Musically, the TVPs have drifted off into spare, droning psychedelia and ultra-restrained rock that's hauntingly beautiful, like the most delicate moments of the Velvet Underground. While less resonantly topical than before (save for "Back to Vietnam"), the all-original songs effectively convey a melancholic sense of futility, even when superficially addressing relatively jolly topics. Highlighted by "Stop and Smell the Roses" and "Someone to Share My Life With," **The Painted Word** is surprisingly serious and altogether excellent.

Chocolat-Art (sarcastically subtitled "A Special Tribute to James Last") was recorded live as a trio in Germany (1984), and features simple but effective performances of such TVP classics as "Silly Girl," "I Know Where Syd Barrett Lives" (appending "I know where Paul Weller lives—'cause he's a hippie, too") and the stupendous "Look Back in Anger." The band's isn't always in tune, but you know they mean well.

Recorded as a trio with ex-Swell Maps bassist Jowe Head and drummer Jeffrey Bloom (both also participants in Slaughter Joe), the very wonderful **Privilege** only improves on **The Painted Word** with better songs, production, singing and playing. Sounding in spots very much like Pete Shelley (especially on "Sometimes I Think You Know Me Better Than I Know Myself"), Treacy is a bad-mood-guy here (witness "All My Dreams Are Dead," "This Time There's No Happy Ending" and "Sad Mona Lisa"), but he does brighten long enough for the pop-art happening of "Salvador Dali's Garden Party" (which winsomely lists all the posh celebrities in attendance). The music is brilliant—characteristically direct songs dressed up with just the right amount of keyboards—and Treacy's voice is as boyishly engaging as ever. [i]

See also *Times*.

TELEX

Looking for Saint Tropez (nr/Sire) 1979
Neurovision (Sire) 1980
Sex (PVC) 1981
Birds and Bees (nr/Interdisc) 1982
Looney Tunes (Atlantic) 1988 ●

This Belgian synth trio—specializing in suave Eurodisco—is at once a bland dance machine and a reasonably clever techno-pop team. Deadly slow adaptations (with artificial-sounding processed vocals) of "Rock Around the Clock" and Plastic Bertrand's "Ça Plane pour Moi" make **Looking for Saint Tropez** amusingly noteworthy; the originals, while faster, are mundane and one-dimensional.

Neurovision takes the same approach, giving Sly Stone's "Dance to the Music" the full Telex treatment amid another batch of boring originals. (If the group's use of synthesizers weren't as dull as technically possible, their records might be a lot better.) **Sex** adds a novel element by employing Ron and Russell Mael as lyricists; the collaboration resembles Sparks' work with Giorgio Moroder in form, if not content. Unfortunately, Telex's languid creations lack the spunk to keep up with the warped wordplay of "Sigmund Freud's Party," "Exercise Is Good for You" and "Carbon Copy." (**Birds and Bees** replaces three of **Sex**'s tracks with subsequent singles.)

Whatever Telex did during its '80s vacation, **Looney Tunes** is a significantly different kettle of ducks. Treading a jokey electronic path somewhere between Art of Noise, Kraftwerk and Yello, the trio concocts simple dance grooves with absurd chanted lyrics and then starts emptying its bag of sound effects, chucking in everything but you know what. Ironically, "Spike Jones"—named for someone to whom the group obviously owes a conceptual debt here—is one of the flimsy album's least inspired collages. [i]

TEMPLE OF THE DOG

Temple of the Dog (A&M) 1991 ●

Yet another twist in the incestuous Seattle scene, **Temple of the Dog** was recorded over weekends in the fall of 1990 by vocalist Chris Cornell and drummer Matt Cameron of Soundgarden with the surviving members of Mother Love Bone. Meant as a tribute to the late Andrew Wood, the album is as good as anything either band has produced. The Temple has a rootsy side that Soundgarden doesn't touch; freed from his confining lovegodhead image, Cornell *sings* instead of shrieking, and exposes more sides of his musical talent than past work ever suggested. Sympathetic but laden with some harsh drug imagery, **Temple of the Dog** manages to address its difficult subject without getting corny or tasteless. [ja]

See also *Mother Love Bone, Soundgarden*.

TENPOLE TUDOR

Eddie Old Bob Dick and Gary (Stiff) 1981
Let the Four Winds Blow (Stiff) 1981
Swords of a Thousand Men (Can. Stiff) 1981

This wonderful, over-the-top crew of rowdies is led by the inimitable Edward Tudor-Pole, whose wobbly vocals lend the proper air of debauchery to the band's hard-driving arias. **Eddie Old Bob Dick and Gary** contains such classy trash as "Wunderbar," "3 Bells in a Row" and "Swords of a Thousand Men," replete with bizarre concepts, catchy melodies and loopy singing. The great tracks co-exist with some real dogs, but when Tenpole Tudor are on the mark, their good humor and rock energy are undeniably infectious.

Let the Four Winds Blow takes the band (up or down isn't an issue) to a new plateau, working flippant pseudo-country ("Throwing My Baby Out with the Bathwater"), mock-funk ("Local Animal"), even ersatz ballroom schmaltzola ("Tonight Is the Night"). The Canadian-only **Swords of a Thousand Men** picks the best tracks from both LPs and wraps them in the artwork from the second. Not for the uptight or supercilious, but John Otway fans will understand.

Sir Edward then abandoned his fulltime singing career for a series of blindingly funny cameos in such films as *The Great Rock'n'Roll Swindle* (in which he sings "Who Killed Bambi?" into a vacuum cleaner handle), *Sid & Nancy* (a great bit as a hotel clerk), *Walker* (a rare dramatic role), *Absolute Beginners* and *Straight to Hell*. He has also done London theater.   [i]

10,000 MANIACS
Human Conflict Number Five EP (Mark) 1982 (Christian Burial Music-Press) 1984
Secrets of the I Ching (Christian Burial Music) 1983 (Christian Burial Music-Press) 1983
The Wishing Chair (Elektra) 1985 ●
In My Tribe (Elektra) 1987 ●
Blind Man's Zoo (Elektra) 1989 ●
Hope Chest (Elektra) 1990 φ

JOHN AND MARY
Victory Gardens (Rykodisc) 1991 φ

Hailing from Jamestown in provincial upstate New York, 10,000 Maniacs play deceptively challenging new pop music with rustic folky underpinnings. On the early records, singer Natalie Merchant's innocent voice skips lightly over gentle melodies while her five cohorts provide unobtrusive reggae-folk-pop backing. But on closer inspection, all is not so cozy. Warped guitars slice in and out, and Merchant's fragmented lyrics gently evoke images of a decaying society bent on violent self-destruction.

The five-song **Human Conflict Number Five** EP is simple and a little underbaked, but does introduce the Maniacs' early trademarks: Merchant's voice, strong, soaring melodies and, on a couple of numbers, lilting Caribbean grooves. **Secrets of the I Ching** offers a much stronger creative vision; the lyrics serve up tastes of Latin and Spanish, and the music ranges from screeching noise over a pop hook to almost psychedelic power calypso. Both records present difficult ideas without compromise in a most palatable manner.

(A remixed and resequenced compilation of the two records—omitting only one version of "Tension," a song done on both—was issued in 1990. Besides its value for making these rarities widely available with fine sound and informative liner notes, **Hope Chest** is an elementary but thoroughly credible record that blends nicely with the band's recent efforts.)

The Maniacs' major label debut codified their sound as never before, essentially dispensing with everything except for neo-traditional electric folk. Although comparisons to Fairport Convention (Joe Boyd produced **The Wishing Chair**) are somewhat valid, the Maniacs' sensibility and cultural references are totally different: small-town Americana isn't rural Great Britain. Merchant's reflective, impressionist lyrics and clear, powerful singing shine on new songs like "Can't Ignore the Train" and new versions of three tunes from **Secrets of the I Ching**. Honest, intelligent and enthralling.

Peter Asher's slick production of **In My Tribe**, the band's first release as a quintet (following the departure of guitarist John Lombardo), is initially bland and off-putting, but the songs' emotional depth and Merchant's awe-inspiring voice ultimately overcome the record's dispiriting homogeneity. The realistic view of child abuse in "What's the Matter Here?" is as troubling as Suzanne Vega's "Luka"; "Cherry Tree" addresses illiteracy with poignant understanding; the cautionary "Gun Shy" is spoken directly at a brother who has newly become a soldier. For contrast, the delighted family vignette of "My Sister Rose" shares joy for its own sake and the cover of Cat Stevens' "Peace Train" offers a utopian alternative to Merchant's more realistic originals. (After Stevens joined other Moslems in calling for the violent death of novelist Salman Rushdie, the group moved to have "Peace Train" removed from the album, but their record company demurred.)

Although the Maniacs' music—no longer prominently folk-oriented—seems mired in a glib soft-rock rut, **Blind Man's Zoo**'s literate, sturdy songs again rise through the bloodless presentation. "Eat for Two" contemplates motherhood with skepticism; "Trouble Me" addresses an elderly relative with compassion; "Hateful Hate" attacks colonialism in Africa; "You Happy Puppet" enigmatically condemns a willing victim of manipulation. Stimulating rather than overtly exciting, **Blind Man's Zoo** is nonetheless effective in its own way.

Victory Gardens is John Lombardo's first album with singer/violinist/co-writer Mary Ramsey. Maniacs guitarist Robert Buck and drummer Jerome Augustyniak—as well as unrelated oldtimers Ronnie Lane, Augie Meyers and Joey Molland—guest on the collection of pristine electro-folk originals whose designs are familiar but nonetheless appealing.   [jl/i]

TERRY, BLAIR AND ANOUCHKA
See *Colour Field.*

TEST DEPT.
Beating the Retreat (nr/Some Bizzare) 1984 ●
The Unacceptable Face of Freedom (nr/Ministry of Power-Some Bizzare) 1986 ●
A Good Night Out (Ministry of Power-Some Bizzare-Relativity) 1987 ●
Terra Firma (Play It Again Sam USA) 1988 ●
Materia Prima (nr/Department One) 1990

TEST DEPT. AND THE SOUTH WALES STRIKING MINERS CHOIR
Shoulder to Shoulder (nr/Some Bizzare) 1985

TEST DEPT./BRITH GOF

Gododdin (nr/Ministry of Power) 1989 ●

Like that other notable contemporary band of philosophical noisemakers, Einstürzende Neubauten, Test Dept. originally eschewed all musical tradition to play stunning ultra-percussion with an industrial bent. Like their Teutonic soul brothers, this enigmatic British organization uses large metallic objects and power tools to add stark modern realism to the drum overload, but also brings more structure and rhythm to the assault.

Beating the Retreat—two 12-inch EPs comprising a single-length album—adds occasional vocal effects (not singing) that do little to vary the din, which is simply awesome in its intensity and singlemindedness. But several startling tracks take a wholly different approach, offering sparse ambient sound and effects that blithely incorporate real instruments like cello and harp. **Shoulder to Shoulder**, proving the band's political commitment and activism, gives half of its running time to the 90-member Welsh choir. In one truly strange exercise, the two seemingly unconnectable forces collaborate on a track.

The Unacceptable Face of Freedom, with an unwieldy fold-out cover Hawkwind would be proud of, is a powerful record, both in its potent musical attack and ongoing political convictions. Real drums seem to have replaced most of the steel-bashing, and the instrumentation also includes Fairlight-built orchestras, taped voices (speaking and singing), sequencers and bagpipes. Observations about the state of British life are angrier than ever—"Statement" features a miner giving a firsthand account of picket-line police brutality, while recurring military themes in the music drive the point home even harder.

A Good Night Out continues their forceful manifesto, although the execution has progressed from the tribal pounding of early work to ambitious performance art. Much of the LP was recorded live in London and Amsterdam in what was, judging by the cover photo, a huge multi-media extravaganza—some sort of Marxist military opera. Lyrics which continue to spew bitter, sarcastic and intelligent tirades against the domestic policies of the British Empire are more powerful than ever. Pretentious perhaps, but **A Good Night Out** also shows Test Dept.'s abiding commitment to their beliefs—social, political and artistic.

The only information given on the cover of **Terra Firma** is a brief libretto for each of the five tracks (which range from five to fourteen minutes each). Try "While the melancholy piper Alistair pipes a lament, the lovely Nadka grieves" on for size. No, you haven't picked up a Russian novel by mistake. The stories all lead to a concluding call for all world citizens to unite on firm ground (hence the title). The omnipresent drums shape four of the five cuts (the one exception being the inadvisably sung "Dark Eyes"), with other instrumentation—pianos, tapes, horns, (other peoples') voices, etc.—providing each with a distinctive signature. Another ambitious effort that only Test Dept. could have undertaken.

Gododdin is the result of another collaboration, this time with Brith Gof, a Welsh theater group, and some of the lyrics and liner notes are in that beautiful and unusual language. The performance from which the album developed is based on an epic Welsh poem, and was originally staged in an abandoned car factory in Cardiff. (It was later performed in Hamburg, Germany with sponsorship from Mobil and Philip Morris; a rather ironic capitalist twist.) Despite the militaristic theme, the music is more haunting and less bombastic than **A Good Night Out**. A chilling work.

The live **Materia Prima**, recorded around Europe between 1986 and 1989, contains much of the same material as **The Unacceptable Face of Freedom**.

[i/dgs]

TEX AND THE HORSEHEADS

Tex and the Horseheads (Bemisbrain-Enigma) 1984
Life's So Cool (Enigma) 1985
Tot Ziens: Live in Holland (Hol. Enigma) 1986

One of the wilder exponents of cow-punk, Tex and the Horseheads are spiritual kin to the Gun Club. And while they lean toward a very punky image (lead singer Texacala Jones dresses like a female Stiv Bator; on the first album, the bassist's name is Smog Vomit and the drummer is Rock Vodka), their playing is fairly coherent. Mixing mutant blues (even a cover of Jimmy Reed's "Big Boss Man") into the first album's punk-country-rock blender, Tex and the Horseheads have a convincingly strong sound, but are a few pints short on material.

John Doe produced the much-better **Life's So Cool**, an uncontrolled blues-rock riot that recalls **Exile on Main Street**. It starts with an uncredited quote from the old instrumental "Cat's Squirrel" (see Jethro Tull's first LP for corroboration) and then goes on to such topics as drinking, fornication and legal tangles in songs that are substantial and thoughtfully developed. Texacala's singing shows great improvement; exciting guitarist Mike Martt and bassist J. Gregory Boaz also pitch in complementary vocals. A very impressive showing with enough bite and spit to satisfy anyone.

Thanks to poor sound and undistinguished playing, the Dutch concert documented in **Tot Ziens** is an incoherent blur of guitar noise and hard-to-hear vocals. Mostly recapping the band's two studio records (new tunes include "Cutie Rudy," "Go West" and Oscar Brown Jr.'s "Snake"), this live record adds nothing to the originals beyond Jones' scurrilous stage comments. See also *Divine Horsemen*. [i]

TEXAS

Southside (Mercury) 1989 ●

Defying all the generic stereotypes of contemporary Scottish rock, this Glasgow quartet (whose bassist, John McElhone, was an Altered Image) plays decidedly American heartland folk-rock with inflections of country and gospel. Singer/guitarist Sharleen Spiteri has a strong, handsome voice (with no discernible accent), and the band provides crisp, agile guitar backing. But the songs—mostly Spiteri/McElhone collaborations—are bland archetypal rewrites with more commercial than artistic value. And not to get jingoist about it, the Scottish perspective adds nothing to already well-explored territory. [i]

TEXAS INSTRUMENTS

iMore Texas Instruments! EP (Longhead) 1985
The Texas Instruments (Rabid Cat) 1987

665

Sun Tunnels (Rabid Cat) 1988
Crammed into Infinity (Rockville) 1991 •

One of the advantages of growing up musical in Texas is that you can play cowboy rock without getting all stupid and selfconscious about it. Austin's Texas Instruments don't waste a lot of time or fuss detailing their stylistic concepts, the unpretentious trio just gets on with it, delivering crisp post-punk songs in a distinctly regional dialect. Over a simple Southwestern backbeat, Dave Woody drops an occasional ZZ Top lick into his barbed wire guitar playing, the backbone of lyrically substantial, reasonably tuneful material.

Following a four-song 12-inch and a stint backing Daniel Johnston on his **Continued Story** cassette, TI made its unassumingly strong longplaying debut on **The Texas Instruments**, an album of good songs (like the garagey "Prussian Blue") and energetic arrangements that stay loud without turning abrasive. Besides putting an infrequent Dylan inflection in its own songs, the trio covers Woody Guthrie's "Do Re Mi" and gives "A Hard Rain's a-Gonna Fall" an effective rattlesnake boogie bite.

Double-dipping into the Dylan catalogue, the more temperate **Sun Tunnels** (again produced by Spot) includes a rendition of "You Ain't Going Nowhere" and an amusingly derivative original entitled "Watch'n It All Go Down." While only "Little Black Sunrise" goes so far as to be acoustic folk, the LP is a lot less aggressive overall, with impressive sophistication (especially rhythmic) that, on some of the harder numbers, owes a clear stylistic debt to the Minutemen. An exciting step down a promising path.   [i]

See also *Daniel Johnston*.

THAT PETROL EMOTION

Manic Pop Thrill (nr/Demon) 1986 •
Babble (Polydor) 1987 •
The Peel Sessions EP (nr/Strange Fruit) 1987 •
Live (Mansfield) 1988
End of the Millennium Psychosis Blues (Virgin) 1988 •
Peel Sessions Album (nr/Strange Fruit) 1989 •
Chemicrazy (Virgin) 1990 •
Sensitize EP (nr/Virgin) 1990 •

The talented O'Neill brothers left the ashes of the peerless Undertones behind with few prospects for their musical future. While Feargal Sharkey began his transformation into a boring California pop chanteur, they lay low, quietly scorning the business that had shattered their teenage dreams. After several false starts, they returned, with an excellent new quintet that built on past accomplishments without revisiting them. Damian O'Neill took up bass for the Petrols; big brother Seán (previously known as John) and Derry homeboy Reámann O'Gormáin play guitar; drummer Ciaran McLaughlin and Seattle singer Steve Mack complete the band, which is politically aware, occasionally abrasive and devoutly independent.

Manic Pop Thrill is an apt title for the angry, articulate rock melodies that span the continuum from sweet balladry to PiL/Fall-like noise. Mack is a fine, controlled shouter in the Keith Relf/Steve Marriott tradition; the band's combination of slide guitars, Bo Did-

dley beats, wild harmonica wailing and raveup energy recalls the early Stones, Yardbirds and Velvet Underground. The utter lack of nostalgia or revivalism here suggests that, even with all the crap that masquerades as music nowadays, some things about rock'n'roll will never die. (The CD adds four tracks.)

Produced by ex-Swan Roli Mosimann, **Babble** puts the issues—mostly concerning religion and Irish nationalism—right up front: "Creeping to the Cross," "Big Decision," "Swamp," "Chester Burnette" and others unleash the group's vehemence and informed radical commentary. Since the lyrics aren't very specific and the singleminded music is ruggedly invigorating, agreement isn't a prerequisite to appreciation. The Petrols could benefit from a little more stylistic consistency (everybody writes, often in very different directions), but the melding of real-life anger with germane musical passion gives **Babble** a visceral quality that is impossible to ignore.

The June 1985 performances on the Peel EP predate the band's first album; songs include "V2," "Can't Stop," "Lettuce" and "Blind Spot." The full-length Peel album pairs that session with a second recorded later the same year. Recorded in Los Angeles, the nifty but questionable 1988 **Live** mini-album (seemingly a boot, but openly distributed through legitimate channels) has covers of Neil Young's "Cinnamon Girl" and Pere Ubu's "Non Alignment Pact" alongside five of the band's own tunes, from the pre-**Pop Thrill** "V2" to the then-new "Here It Is . . . Take It!"

While some of the more restrained material on the stylistically scattered **End of the Millennium Psychosis Blues** (again produced by Rosimann) is underwhelming, tracks like "Sooner or Later," "Tension," "Here It Is . . . Take It!" and "Groove Check"—on which the band's Celtic funk-rock, complete with horns, is in full effect—are gripping. As the music shifts gears to suit their tone, the lyrics run alternately bleak, resigned and angry (a few of them, in keeping with the militant liner notes, specifically topical, the rest more generally directed). When it all clicks, the band's charging sound and fiery ideas combine to make a powerful artistic statement.

Shortly after the album's release, Seán O'Neill chose family life over the rock'n'roll jungle, and left the band. Damian returned to guitar, McLaughlin emerged as the leading songwriter and the Petrols drafted a new bassist, John Marchini, who made his debut on the Scott Litt-produced **Chemicrazy**. Given all the changes, it's surprising that the album sounds anything at all like its predecessors; unfortunately what remains in the absence of Seán's disconsolate moodiness and Mosimann's loud impudence is crisply presentable but emotionally defused, lyrically inadequate and blandly commercialized. While the cool "Scum Surfin' " proves that there is life after the end of the millennium, **Chemicrazy** is a dose of the wrong medicine.

Built around an album track and the non-LP "Chemicrazy," the **Sensitize** EP is a multi-format extravaganza, available (besides two two-track single configurations and a three-song 12-inch) as a CD and, with different tracks, a 10-inch vinyl platter in a box with a poster.   [i]

See also *Undertones*.

666

THEE HEADCOATS

See *Thee Mighty Caesars.*

THEE HYPNOTICS

Live'r Than God! (Sub Pop) 1989 ●
Come Down Heavy (Beggars Banquet-RCA) 1990 ●

Assembling a host of 1967 psychedelic fuzz-guitar stars—Blue Cheer, Cream, Jimi Hendrix, etc.—as primary influences, adding a bit of Pretty Things/Rolling Stones ambience and jamming on a frenzied Stooges/MC5 drive, this London quartet handily re-creates the pre-Zeppelin era with more flair than most. Singer James Jones knows all the right moves, as does guitarist Ray Hanson, who pulls off the neat trick of overdubbing several different specific styles in a single song. Combining four live tracks from a UK EP of the same name and four studio tracks from a pair of British singles, the American **Live'r Than God!** album is a swirling carpet ride of electrifying nostalgia, effectively digested and powerfully delivered. Lacking overdubs, the energetic concert side sounds rather thin and monochromatic, but such studio creations as "Soul Trader" and "Earth Blues" are mighty potent.

Just as the '60s greats gave way (commercially speaking) to junkyard knockoffs like Grand Funk Railroad, so Thee Hypnotics moved the wrong way forward on their first full-length studio LP. Abandoning the claustrophobic atmosphere and excitement of their initial pose, they opted for a bombastic and hollow '70s arena-rock sound—incorporating funk-metal and Cultish raunch—that frighteningly recalls such turn-of-the-decade nightmares as Bloodstone and Rhinoceros. **Come Down Heavy** is, pardon the cheap joke, a heavy comedown.   [i]

THEE MIGHTY CAESARS

Thee Mighty Caesars (nr/Milkshakes) 1985
Beware the Ides of March (nr/Big Beat) 1985
Little by Little EP (nr/Media Burn) 1986
Thee Caesars of Trash (nr/Milkshakes) 1986
Acropolis Now (nr/Milkshakes) 1986
Live in Rome (nr/Big Beat) 1987
Wiseblood (nr/Ambassador) 1987 (nr/Hangman) 1989
Don't Give Any Dinner to Henry Chinaski (nr/Hangman) 1987
Punk Rock Showcase (nr/Hangman) 1987
Thusly, Thee Mighty Caesars English Punk Rock Explosion (Crypt) 1988
John Lennon's Corpse Revisited (Crypt) 1989
Surely They Were the Sons of God (Crypt) 1990

(THEE/WILD) BILLY CHILDISH

I've Got Everything Indeed (nr/Hangman) 1987
The 1982 Cassetes (nr/Hangman) 1987
"i remember ... " (nr/Hangman) 1987
Poems of Laughter and Violence (nr/Hangman) 1988
50 Albums Great (nr/Hangman) 1991

WILD BILLY CHILDISH AND BIG RUSS WILKINS

Laughing Gravy (nr/Empire) 1987

BILLY CHILDISH AND SEXTON MING

Which Dead Donkey Daddy? (nr/Hangman) 1987
Plump Prizes and Little Gems (nr/Hangman) 1987
Ypres 1917 Overture (Verdun Ossuary) (nr/Hangman) 1987

JACK KETCH AND THE CROWMEN

Brimfull of Hate (nr/Hangman) 1988

WILD BILLY CHILDISH AND THE BLACKHANDS

Play: Capt'n Calypso's Hoodoo Party (nr/Hangman) 1988

WILD BILLY CHILDISH AND THE NATURAL BORN LOVERS

Long Legged Baby (nr/Hangman) 1989

THEE HEADCOATS

Headcoats Down! (nr/Hangman) 1989
The Earls of Suavedom (Crypt) 1990
The Kids Are All Square–This Is Hip! (nr/Hangman) 1990
Beach Bums Must Die (Crypt) 1990
Heavens to Murgatroyd, Even! It's Thee Headcoats! (Already) (Sub Pop) 1990 ●

Noted painter/woodcut artist Bill Hamper considers music a sideline, a hobby. But don't tell that to record producer Rollin Slim, or music historian/art director William Loveday (or his colleague, Chatham Jack), Jack Ketch or . . . Billy Childish. Idiosyncratic dyslexic poet of discontent and disgruntlement, Hamper organized a mutually hateful bunch into the Medway (named for a British river) poets, elevating them into the public eye and even putting the runts on vinyl before their acknowledged distaste for one another melted the union.

In addition to publishing booklets by assorted members of the Medway cartel, Billy's Hangman imprint has released a library of several dozen volumes of his own introspective/socially accusatory poems and lyrics, plus LPs by various friends and co-conspirators, as well as Link Wray and Billy's own manifold incarnations. Challenging the accepted corporate policy of attempting to sell 50,000 copies of one LP, the Childish strategy calls for absolute immediacy and absence of polish, constant inspiration (if not innovation) and the release on vinyl—in limited numbers for a decidedly limited (if insatiable and growing) audience—virtually every musical spark, no matter how bright or dull. In other words, 1,000 copies each of 50 different LPs.

Following his stints in the Pop Rivits and the Milkshakes, Billy briefly retreated to svengali status in the Delmonas, but quickly hopped back into the spotlight, and the attendant machiavellian control that had helped drive his partner M. Hampshire from the Milkshakes. As heard on its first 45 and LP, the Mighty Caesars consist of the final 'Shakes lineup minus Mickey, and sound predictably like the former band, if a bit more ragged and amped up, with one guitar substituting for two. **Beware the Ides of March** introduces new drummer Del (aka Graham Day of Medway stalwarts the Prisoners/Prime Movers) for a slightly more reserved and crafted set of idiopathic beat punk, with the best track excerpted for the **Little by Little** EP. The next two albums only hone their spew, with more of a garage pop underpinning; **Acropolis Now** adds Fay (organ, vocals) from Makin' Time and Sarah from the Delmonas.

Live in Rome isn't; reprising past Mighty Caesars' highlights alongside covers of the Damned, Pistols and Chuck Berry, the exuberant crowd is dubbed in, the spontaneous banter a boozy prank. **Wiseblood** (released on Wreckless Eric's label) is rougher (à la the debut), whereas **Henry Chinaski** (subtitled "Early Demonstration Recordings") offers some of their loosest and least solicitous performances of material (both familiar and unreleased) from several periods.

Punk Rock Showcase collects fourteen tracks from previous LPs, some of them duplicated on **Thusly, Thee Mighty Caesars English Punk Rock Explosion**, their US debut, which contains only one new item. **John Lennon's Corpse Revisited** (with a **Sgt. Pepper** "tribute" cover) is all new, all loud, all lewd, all rowdy—a rampant romp of unhinged punk trash. **Surely They Were the Sons of God** is yet another compilation, and the last Mighty Caesars release to date, with bassist John Agnew discovering a more lucrative career as soundman for the James Taylor Quartet, while "Del" busies himself with the Prime Movers.

Respecting the Caesars' reputation, Billy retired the name until such time as the band (which all insist has not broken up) finds time to once again play together. In the meantime, Billy has focused on various solo projects, duo projects, one-off projects and the ongoing nonspecific project known as Thee Headcoats. **I've Got Everything Indeed** is pure solo mono blues and rhythm, roll'n'rock in the tradition of Jimmy Reed, but reduced to absolute raw essentials. **The 1982 Cassetes** [sic] has far more of a demo feel, with painfully ragged tunes more in an acoustic blues vein; the home-recording hiss and screwy levels contribute to the maniacally insular feel, making it perhaps the most *personal* Childish LP to date, hence the "Warning! You most likely won't like this record . . . " **i remember** fits stylistically (if not chronologically) between these two LPs, riding the Medway rails between rural Mississippi and the urbanized Chicago sound.

Poems of Laughter and Violence is Billy in even more reduced terms, reading his often vitriolic prose alone into a microphone, accompanied only by the sound of pages being turned and liquid being guzzled. Still, this is as possessed and incensed, as *naked* an LP as any punk classic.

The 10-inch **Laughing Gravy** reunites Billy with Milkshake/Rivit Russ, again bowing to the blues muse for a mostly relaxed, mostly acoustic set of tunes celebrating Delta traditions.

Which Dead Donkey Daddy? pairs Billy with Medway poet Sexton Ming (likeminded and similarly dyslexic leader of Auntie Vegetable and the Mindreaders and solo artist; B. Childish makes major contributions as musician and vocalist on both of his Hangman LPs), mixing elements of forgotten blues with bleary Beefheartian subversive art, plus two parts all things nonpop and four parts uncaring self-indulgence, with just a niggle of music off in the distance. **Plump Prizes and Little Gems** is a goofily selfconscious distillation of same, while **Ypres 1917 Overture** is so perpendicular as to be virtually unfathomable in its mute alleyway operatics to all but its two principals, intent on condemning all war via the microcosm of Verdun.

Elsewhere in history, incompetent British executioner Jack Ketch frequently watched his charges die of strangulation rather than snapped necks and, on at least one occasion, abandoned his beheading axe for a knife after several unsuccessful blows. Reincarnated as a Billy Childish pseudonym (with Bruce Brand and Banana Bertie, for an original Milkshakes reunion minus Mickey Hampshire), the rock on **Brimfull of Hate** is punk with darkly arty tendencies, riff-simple but psychotically unblinking and devoid of roll.

The Blackhands coalesced after Nicaragua's Bluefield Express declined Billy's offer of a UK release on Hangman, prompting him to record his own out-of-tune New Orleans-*cum*-reggae version. Returning to the blues, **Long Legged Baby** deposits Billy in front of Sexton Ming and Big Russ for a minor run through familiar territory.

Which brings us to Thee Headcoats. Originally Billy Childish, Bruce Brand and either Alan Crockford (of the Prisoners) or John Agnew, the band's first LP is like a more assured Mighty Caesars, with punkier punk, trashier trash and a major dollop of solid unadulterated country blues. **The Earls of Suavedom** is a more obvious LP that echoes past glories, but it is far overshadowed by **The Kids Are All Square**, which branches into new pop directions. The resurrected Delmonas are here redubbed Thee Headcoatees, and new bassist Ollie Dollar has joined the revolving lineup. Catchy as poison ivy, the uniformly excellent tunes fall into any number of styles, not just the same old blueprints. **Beach Bums**, an augmented compilation, eschews any stylistic escapades for a pure garage LP, including several remakes with new titles and lyrics (in accepted blues tradition). **Heavens to Murgatroyd** (its CD "mastered directly from vinyl") bows in both directions, including new pop wonders alongside updated versions of their own and others' songs.

Released early in '91, Childish's **50 Albums Great** (his fiftieth LP only by creative arithmetic) consists mostly of "hits" from various post-Milkshakes phases of his career, plus several new tracks and a Billie Holiday cover, all played raw and solo with and without guitar. Not his best.

In Billy's words: "Half the songs I steal ideas direct, the other half indirect, which is true of everyone. Sometimes I have an idea of my own . . . " [ab]

See also *Delmonas, Pop Rivits, Prisoners*.

THEE MILKSHAKES

See *Pop Rivits*.

THELONIOUS MONSTER

Baby . . . You're Bumming My Life Out in a Supreme
   Fashion (Epitaph) 1986
Next Saturday Afternoon (Relativity) 1987 ●
Stormy Weather (Relativity) 1989 ●

Thelonious Monster built its rep on the LA club scene by playing lurching, shambolic club sets (featuring a seven-man, four-guitar lineup), but the thinly produced **Baby . . . You're Bumming My Life Out in a Supreme Fashion** does little to capture the wacked-out appeal of the Monster's live act. What you get instead is a half-assed grab-bag of styles, some of them effective and others just plain lazy, unified by self-indulgent down-in-the-gutter lyrics and frontman Bob Forrest's whiny personality.

Next Saturday Afternoon is a bit closer to conventional rock'n'roll and is the better for it, unveiling heretofore hidden strengths. The band, now pared down to a quintet (including Weirdos guitarist Dix Denney and 45 Grave bassist Rob Graves) has discovered melody, producing musically and lyrically impressive material like "Next," "Anymore" and "Walk on Water."

The John Doe-produced **Stormy Weather** (the CD includes all of **Next Saturday Afternoon**) continues the trend towards musical and lyrical discipline, with surprisingly graceful stabs at topical folk-rock on "Lena Horne Still Sings Stormy Weather" and "Sammy Hagar Weekend," not to mention straightforward (and successful) readings of Tracy Chapman's "For My Lover" and Blind Lemon Jefferson's "See That My Grave Is Kept Clean." [hd]

THE PURSUIT OF HAPPINESS
Love Junk (Chrysalis) 1988 ●
One-Sided Story (Chrysalis) 1990 φ

The first LP from this Canadian quintet seemed like a godsend to many aging rock fans; **Love Junk** combines grown-up irony with obsessive adolescent lust, setting it all in a convincing, energetic hard rock-pop crunch. Lead singer/songwriter/guitarist Moe Berg's lyrics are simultaneously literate, wise, poignant and irremediably horny. The key cut on the LP is the wry "I'm an Adult Now," but that's just for starters; **Love Junk** is delightful and surprising from beginning to end. Berg's chord changes and structure bear the unmistakable influence of Todd Rundgren, who proved a most simpatico producer as well.

One-Sided Story is as disastrous an example of the sophomore jinx as has been heard in modern rock. Berg's observations and plaints on **Love Junk** could evoke any number of complex responses; here he sounds slack and whiny. His once daring wit is now received in the worst way. On the opening track, when he compares his girlfriend's amatory technique to "greasy fried noodles", well, it doesn't take a genius to guess the hungry-an-hour-later punchline. The music isn't nearly as inventive or memorable, and Rundgren's production, so apt on **Love Junk**, is raw to the extreme. The band deserves to bounce back though, and Berg is too talented to leave it at this. [gk]

THE SCENE IS NOW
Burn All Your Records (Lost) 1985
Total Jive (Lost-Twin/Tone) 1986
Tonight We Ride (Lost-Twin/Tone) 1988

Over a half-decade of existence, this fluid-membership gaggle of NYC bohos has developed from a marginally less political arm of Mofungo's Marxist art-terrorism into a sometimes downright goofy jug band for post-mod beatniks. **Burn All Your Records** might be rough terrain for diehard capitalists to navigate, but the bracing orchestration—employing more than two dozen noise-things—makes for a fascinating, if occasionally difficult, listen.

Total Jive accentuates the contributions of Mofungo's Chris Nelson (and, to a lesser extent, Elliott Sharp) and takes a more easygoing approach to both music and subject matter—at times it's almost mellow, man! With ex-dB's drummer Will Rigby and Pere Ubu bassist Tony Maimone joining the Scene, **Tonight We Ride** continues this progression, with Nelson blowing some surprisingly swinging trombone on the good-timey "Midnight Broil," while the entire ensemble locks into a low-key, Grateful Dead-like groove on "California," originally performed by second wave Lower East Side noisemongers I Ride the Bus. [dss]

See also *Mofungo*.

THESE IMMORTAL SOULS
Get Lost (Don't Lie!) (SST) 1987

The members of this band have been around the block a few times. First there was the Birthday Party, from the ashes of which arose Crime and the City Solution with ex-Birthday Party guitarist Rowland S. Howard. After two years and three releases, Howard had his differences with singer Simon Bonney and left, taking his bass-playing brother Harry and drummer Epic Soundtracks (ex-Swell Maps/Jacobites) with him. Adding keyboardist Genevieve McGuckin, he formed These Immortal Souls in 1987.

Get Lost (Don't Lie!) is a 30-minute mini-LP that works as well as, if not better than, any Crime and the City Solution record. Howard can't really sing much, but this doesn't require him to: the shady lyricism which underlies all seven tracks would lose its color if sung by someone more conscious of pitch than self. McGuckin has listened to plenty of Ray Manzarek; Soundtracks turns in brilliant performances. Most of the guitar work is acoustic strumming, although Howard does allow himself to cut loose on "'Blood and Sand' She Said." A very impressive marriage of splendor and squalor. [dgs]

See also *Birthday Party, Crime and the City Solution*.

THE TEARDROP EXPLODES
Kilimanjaro (Mercury) 1980 (Skyclad) 1988
    (Fontana-PolyGram) 1990 ●
Wilder (Mercury) 1981 (Skyclad) 1988
    (Fontana-PolyGram) 1990 ●
You Disappear from View EP (nr/Phonogram) 1983
Everybody Wants to Shag ... The Teardrop Explodes [CD]
    (Fontana) 1990 ●
Piano (nr/Document) 1990

Charming despite frequent bouts of pretentiousness, singer/songwriter Julian Cope (once in a crypto-band called the Crucial Three with future-Echo icon Ian McCulloch and future-Wah! man Pete Wylie) led Liverpool's great psychedelic hope, The Teardrop Explodes, through two albums before moving on—in the midst of an aborted third—to a solo career. Cope's influences include everyone from Scott Walker to the Doors to Tim Buckley, but Teardrop's sound was better than the sum of its parts. The group's problem was Cope's scattershot approach—his songs are filled with too many amorphous, meaningless and just plain silly images—and his unanswered need for a good editor. Excesses notwithstanding, the Teardrops created some of the era's most exciting music, exerting considerable influence on succeeding generations—Morrissey and the Inspiral Carpets being just two examples of those so influenced.

Kilimanjaro is the more focused of the two albums; next to it, **Wilder** sounds like a debut, as whatever restraining influence the band had on Cope was removed, leaving him to write all of the songs unaided. (The original US and UK editions had different sequences and two different cuts each. The UK album was later reissued with a different cover and the addition of "Reward"; the Skyclad version uses the reissue's cover but the American track listing. The 1990 model reverts to the original cover but keeps the UK reissue's track listing. Lost in the shuffle is the excellent "Suffocate.") In any form, it's a lush, mesmerizing, appealing album, whose only problem (other than the lyrics) is that the songs—most of which have a childlike, dreamy quality—tend to float together with little individual character. But the ones that do stand out are terrific: "Poppies in the Field," "Treason," "Reward" and "When I Dream," the last providing a brush with American radio success.

While better-defined musically, **Wilder** is more confused lyrically, though still infused with the band's unique atmosphere. Cope's flat voice serves to provide instrumental-like color, especially on "Bent Out of Shape," "Seven Views of Jerusalem" and "The Culture Bunker." The US and UK editions had the same track listing but different sequences and covers; Skyclad again reissued the American edition and Fontana the British.

The band split up in mid-'82 during the sessions for its third LP, four songs from which were released on **You Disappear from View**. The EP also includes both the original recording (on the double 7-inch) and a newly recorded string-quartet version (on the 12-inch) of "Suffocate."

The four basic **Disappear** tracks (including a more finished-sounding recording of "The In-Psychlopaedia") join seven others for **Everybody Wants to Shag**, a Cry of Love-style paste-up of the unfinished third LP that finds the dissolving unit as adventurous and powerful as ever. Mixing experimental material with more familiar brass-speckled pop (as well as early versions of two songs that found their way onto Cope's brilliant 1984 solo debut, **World Shut Your Mouth**), the album tacks on an earlier, brilliantly psychotic B-side ("Strange House in the Snow") but again no "Suffocate."

Piano compiles the band's complete pre-**Kilimanjaro** discography (three singles and three compilation tracks). While the first two 45s are weak enough to make one wonder what all the fuss was about, the alternate versions of "Books" and especially "When I Dream" cast a charming new light on the songs. Best of the rare material is the slinking "Camera Camera" and the paranoid "Kwalo Kawlinsky's Lullaby," basically a rhythmless interstellar dub of "Sleeping Gas."

With an album's worth of B-sides and at least two Peel sessions still awaiting circulation, the final chapter in the Teardrop/Cope reissue saga has yet to be heard. [ks/ja]

See also *Julian Cope, Troy Tate*.

THE THE

Soul Mining (nr/Some Bizzare) 1983 (Epic) 1984 ●
Infected (Epic) 1986 ●
Soul Mining/Infected [CD] (nr/Epic) 1988 ●
Mind Bomb (Epic) 1989 ●

MATT JOHNSON

Burning Blue Soul (nr/4AD) 1981 + 1984

In 1981, London singer/guitarist Matt Johnson (a) recorded an EP as a member of the Gadgets, a hapless Bowie-oriented art-rock band in which he played a subordinate guitar role (and later none at all: the group continued on through the '80s, long after he had bowed out) (b) recorded an untitled electro-weird song for the seminal **Some Bizzare Album** compilation as the The (here a duo; a four-man lineup had issued a 1980 single on 4AD) and (c) released a sparsely arranged (read: unfinished-sounding, with percussion sorely missing) one-man-band solo album of intermittently appealing pop songs and meandering tape-collage instrumentals that revealed some intriguingly offbeat ideas (and had two songs produced by Dome) but didn't exactly establish him as a major new talent. Will the real Matt Johnson please stand up?

Apparently not. Although he has since used the The handle exclusively, Johnson's career has been nothing if not unpredictable, running from the pretty commercial dance-pop of **Soul Mining** to the harsh political realities of **Mind Bomb**.

Following **Burning Blue Soul**, Johnson recorded tracks for an LP (**The Pornography of Despair**) in a similar solo vein; it was scrapped, although some of the tracks were released on singles and others turned up as bonus cuts included with initial British pressings of **Soul Mining** (two on a 12-inch with "Perfect," a song done for, but originally omitted from, **Soul Mining**; five on cassette). The fully produced **Soul Mining** locates a warm and attractive medium for the The in fine songs like "Uncertain Smile," "Perfect" (added to the American edition of the album) and "This Is the Day," although Johnson's eerie vocal resemblance to Ian Anderson of Jethro Tull is a distraction. Elsewhere, though, Johnson's adventurous streak—and what sounds like the spiritual influence of Foetus—results in some weird and not altogether entertaining digressions. (A different version of "Perfect"—with David Johansen on harmonica—was released as a single.)

Three years later, Johnson returned with the ambitious and sophisticated **Infected**. The eight metaphorical songs—addressing sexual, social and political issues—use a studio full of notable musicians (Neneh Cherry, Roli Mosimann, Zeke Manyika, Anne Dudley and others) for a wide range of new sounds, some far more energetic than the The's previous work. So while "Heartland" recalls the low-key ambience of **Soul Mining**, the title track is pounding dance music, with big drums and broad-brush production; "Twilight of a Champion" is '40sish jazz noir that again suggests Foetus. Overall, however, it's surprisingly uninviting. While Johnson strains to say something important on **Infected**, he fails to connect on a most basic musical level. (While the world patiently awaited the The's new album, British Epic issued a joint CD of **Soul Mining** and **Infected**.)

With ex-Smiths guitarist Johnny Marr a full-fledged bandmember (along with drummer David Palmer and bassist James Eller), Johnson elevated his conceptual sights on **Mind Bomb**, a musically ambitious album that contemplates war, god, truth and sex to the tune of a bluesy, sample-accented soundscape that *really* suggests Foetus on valium. Although the whole album is powerful and provocative, the unforgettable "Armageddon Days Are Here (Again)" demonstrates an insightful acuity about religion's rising role in political conflicts. [i]

THEY MIGHT BE GIANTS
They Might Be Giants [tape] (TMB Music) 1985
They Might Be Giants (Bar/None) 1986 ●
Don't Let's Start EP (Bar/None) 1987 ●
(She Was a) Hotel Detective EP (Bar/None) 1988 ●
Lincoln (Bar/None-Restless) 1988 ●
They'll Need a Crane EP (Bar/None-Restless) 1989 ●
Don't Let's Start (nr/One Little Indian) 1989 ●
Flood (Elektra) 1990 ●
Birdhouse in Your Soul EP (nr/Elektra) 1990 ●
Istanbul (Not Constantinople) EP [CD] (Elektra) 1990 ●

Imagine, if you will, a modern all-pop update of Spike Jones and the Bonzo Dog Band crossed with the Mothers of Invention, Residents, XTC, Stackridge, Tom Lehrer and R. Stevie Moore. Contemplate the idea of a NYC-based duo with a highly sophisticated sense of absurd humor which writes, sings and plays guitar, accordion and keyboards. John Flansburgh and John Linnell—They Might Be Giants—might in fact be geniuses; their debut album is one of the greatest musical things ever, a diabolically clever and wildly eclectic collection of fully realized masterpieces that could not possibly fail to entertain even the fussiest, hardest-hearted idiot. Literate, accomplished, bursting with ideas, hooks, puns, dadaist absurdities and other neat tricks, TMBG are almost beyond belief. By conservative estimate, roughly fifteen of the first album's nineteen tracks (a revised version of the rare self-released cassette LP, subtracting eight items and adding four) are brilliant.

The 12-inch (and 3-inch CD) **Don't Let's Start** EP takes a remix of a **They Might Be Giants** highlight and appends the mild peer fun of "We're the Replacements," "The Famous Polka" (uncelebrated, but deserving of recognition) and "When It Rains It Snows," a first-cassette song omitted from the album. The title track of **Hotel Detective** is another LP cut, also remixed; the foot-long EP also contains three swell new songs ("Kiss Me, Son of God," "For Science" and "Mr. Klaw"), another deleted oldie ("The Biggest One") plus a bewildering phone conversation *about* the group.

Lincoln maintains the duo's baffling level of invention while raising the musical complexity, electricity, energy level and stylistic variety. Playing mix'n'match with their instruments, idioms and influences on eighteen songs, the Giants hit a few clinkers but also come up with such enduring gems as "Ana Ng," "Purple Toupee," "They'll Need a Crane," "Cowtown," "Piece of Dirt," "Shoehorn with Teeth," "Kiss Me, Son of God" (rearranged from the EP version) and

"Snowball in Hell." Plucking intricate wordplay and uncommon melodies from some private creative ether, the pair magically continues to explore a part of the musical continuum no one else can locate.

The three no-big-deal newcomers that join the title tune on **They'll Need a Crane** also appear on **Don't Let's Start**, a British rarities compilation. So do the bonus songs from the **Don't Let's Start** and **Hotel Detective** EPs (as well as remixes of the lead tracks) and other non-LP matter, like "Hey, Mr. DJ, I Thought You Said We Had a Deal" and an irritating instrumental rendition of "The Lady Is a Tramp."

Moving to a major label for **Flood** brought the two Johns a vastly expanded audience as well as the predictable (and utterly undeserved) critical backlash. Another deft pogo dance on the tightrope between whimsy and self-amusement, **Flood** is an avalanche of bizarre ideas made mighty by the duo's gyroscopic sense of what makes a pop tune click. With improved production resources (Clive Langer and Alan Winstanley did an ace job producing four tracks; the band did the rest), the Giants sound better than ever; the material is equally top-notch. "Birdhouse in Your Soul" anthropomorphizes a nightlight; "We Want a Rock" tries to sell the idea of fake foreheads; "Particle Man" is a science lesson set to an oompah beat; the Farfisa-rock "Twisting" mentions the dB's and Young Fresh Fellows in lyrics about a spiteful ex-girlfriend. In a sudden and surprisingly serious turn, Flansburgh excoriates a bigoted jerk in "Your Racist Friend," a righteous song which does just borrow its title from the Specials' "Racist Friend."

The **Birdhouse in Your Soul** EP adds "Hot Cha" and "Hearing Aid" (both from **Flood**) as well as an amusing tune ("Ant") about nighttime paranoia. "Ant" also appears on the American **Istanbul (Not Constantinople)** EP, joining that uproarious geopolitical lesson (written, in what can only be called proto-Giants style, by Jimmy Kennedy and Nat Simon in 1954), a droll lecture on the subject of President "James K. Polk," a brief soul goof called "Stormy Pinkness" and a wild intercultural hip-hop mix (by Daddy-O of Stetsasonic) that turns the title track inside out. [i]

THEYR
Pagad i hel (Ice. S6) 1980
Utfrymi EP (Ice. Eskvimó) 1981
Idur til Fóta EP (Ice. Eskvimó) 1981
Mjötvidur Maer (Ice. Eskvimó) 1982
As Above (Enigma) 1982
The Fourth Reich EP (nr/Shout) 1982
Lunaire EP (Ice. Gramm) 1983

While Theyr—an English approximation of untranslatable Icelandic characters—reportedly means "thaw," it took a while for this pioneering Reykjavik band, featuring soon-to-be Sugarcubes drummer Sigtryggur Baldursson, to get any heat going on record. The debut, **Pagad i hel**, is little more than lukewarm jazz-rock fusion with a few damp detours into new wave-ish boogie and vanilla reggae. In a word, unlistenable.

Two years (and two singles; the latter is a sharply compelling four-song 10-inch) later, Theyr was a much different—and far more compelling—band. On **Mjötvi-**

dur Maer and its revised English-language counterpart, **As Above**, they kick out the punk-funk jams in the serrated, apocalyptic style of the Fall and Killing Joke. The dark, droney guitar work also shows strong traces of Bauhaus and Joy Division, while there's more than a hint of the Residents' art-rock terrorism in the weirdly distorted, declamatory vocals and idiosyncratic songwriting. The English lyrics on **As Above** are the only bringdown—earnest but overwrought tripe, most of which is thankfully obscured by the band's inspired musical turbulence.

Theyr never lived up to its obvious promise. **The Fourth Reich** is a fine four-track EP released shortly before the group broke up in 1983. (A three-cut swansong, "Lunaire," ended the story; three tracks recorded with Jaz Coleman of Killing Joke remain unreleased.) Baldursson then joined the notorious Kukl, which eventually mutated into the Sugarcubes.   [df]

See also *Sugarcubes*.

TH'INBRED

A Family Affair (Toxic Shock) 1986
Kissin' Cousins (Toxic Shock) 1988
Family Pack [tape] (Toxic Shock) c. 1988

BILLY ATWELL

Ferret in a China Shop ... (Bobok) 1988

Despite an image that screams it-came-from-the-swamp psychobilly, the West Virginia quartet's two albums consist of topical songs and instrumentals played in a disciplined form of sharply thrashed jazz-rock which can turn tight melodic corners on a screeching dime and make abrupt rhythm shifts amid a hailstorm of free-fire guitar power. Very much in a Minutemen/Blind Idiot God vein, **A Family Affair** and **Kissin' Cousins** (matched on the **Family Pack** cassette) find the sharp-witted anarchists angrily attacking Christianity, Satanism, hardcore ideologues, apathy, American policy, etc. and backing it up with crisply organized noise.

After Th'Inbred folded at the end of '87 (prior to **Kissin' Cousins'** release), drummer Billy Atwell worked on his solo album between stints with the Rhythm Pigs, who disbanded the following year. On **Ferret in a China Shop**, an impressively skilled and surprising refutation of punk, Atwell ably demonstrates what he can do with guitar, bass, keyboards and ambience instead of speed and volume. But the meandering instrumental sketches are pointless, and the fusion-rock songs bear a disturbing resemblance to junior-league Police. Atwell has the tools to go it alone, but this album doesn't explain why he should.   [i]

THIN WHITE ROPE

Exploring the Axis (Frontier) 1985 ●
Moonhead (Frontier) 1987 ●
Bottom Feeders EP (nr/Zippo) 1987 ●
In the Spanish Cave (Frontier) 1988 ●
Red Sun EP (nr/Demon) 1988
Sack Full of Silver (Frontier-RCA) 1990 ●
Squatter's Rights EP (nr/Frontier-Real Time) 1991

Psychedelia has nothing to do with the '60s or day-glo trousers. It is music of an altered state, and nobody sees the world with a more altered perspective than Guy Kyser of Davis, California's Thin White Rope. He sings like the leader of the Twilight Zone house band. With a high, tangled voice that quavers between the band's sinewy slithering guitars, he has an exotic clip to his inflection that sometimes chops phrases into stabbing bits.

Thin White Rope exists in the same general Western-roots-influenced-rock genre as Green on Red or True West. On **Exploring the Axis**, that shows up in clean, slippery touches of country guitar work and fuzzy little edges of deeper and darker chords. "Disney Girl" lopes along with Jozef Becker's laid-back drum pulse as squealy shivers of feedback slip between the smooth flows of the melody. "Down in the Desert" marches off the disc with a martial beat and bopping intensity. Throughout the LP, Becker's drumming speeds up to heighten tension but softens when the guitars or lyrics change mood. Laid between his constant changes and the warmth of Rope's guitar (Kyser and Roger Kunkel), the twisted tales almost seem to make sense. (The cassette adds a bonus track, "Macy's Window," which was later included on **Bottom Feeders**. The CD adds two more, including a live radio take on Suicide's "Rocket USA.")

Thin White Rope is also mantra-minded, setting up a groove and driving down it until their amps threaten to smoke. That love of repetitive textures fueled by subtle changes begins to show up in **Moonhead**, giving it a smoother and more unified sound. The guitar interplay strongly suggests Television.

On **Spanish Cave**, the hoedown rhythms and acoustic-sounding bass of "Mr. Limpet" and the Dylan-meets-Roky Erickson narrative of "Ahr-Skidar" prove Rope aren't just country wannabes, but a band of the country. (The US and UK CDs are different. The American adds one bonus track, "Munich Eunich"; the British appends the entire subsequent **Bottom Feeders** EP as well.)

Thin White Rope is also dedicated to rock'n'roll. The **Bottom Feeders** EP (four originals and two cover versions) puts all the dark, bluesy guitar and frog-throated vocal delivery a raunch hand could want in Jimmy Reed's "Ain't That Loving You Baby"; later on, their textures collide with a jackhammer in the loud and searing rendition of "Rocket USA" from the **Axis** CD. (The EP's version of **Axis**'s "Atomic Imagery," however, is different.)

After becoming the first American indie band to tour the Soviet Union in December 1988, TWR released **Red Sun**, an EP which reprises the most powerful song off **Spanish Cave**. That track is joined by an even more chilling acoustic demo of the song with an entirely different lyrics. Four affectionate cover tunes round out this pure-pleasure EP: Gene Pitney's "Town Without Pity," Marty Robbins' "They're Hanging Me Tonight," the Lee Hazelwood/Nancy Sinatra classic "Some Velvet Morning" and the instrumental "Man with the Golden Gun," all rearranged for maximum scary impact and country heart.

With the major-label release of **Sack Full of Silver**, Thin White Rope staked a claim as one of America's most original guitar bands. It all comes together here: Kyser's lyrics and vocals have never been so direct and shattering ("Sometimes I make burns on my arms/

'Cause it moves that feeling from my heart to my arms''), while a widened instrumental palette fleshes out the group's sound. Best of all, the arrangements break new ground on the cusp of improvisation and extended-form composition, moving from delicate acoustic sketches to howling feedback sculptures. Sound like art rock? TWR obliges the comparisons with a goofy cover of 1969's "Yoo Do Right" by Can—which turns out to be the most primal, simpleminded thing on the album. This is the sound of a truly great American rock band in its prime.

Squatter's Rights is a six-song EP of cover versions, only some of which have previously been issued on tribute albums. [e/ws]

3RD BASS
The Cactus Album (Def Jam-Columbia) 1989 ●
The Cactus Revisited (Def Jam-Columbia) 1990 φ
Derelicts of Dialect (RAL- Def Jam-Columbia) 1991 ●

Two years before the talentless Vanilla Ice's watered-down pop-hop and bogus claims of street credibility made him the sorry-ass superstar of white rap, New York City's 3rd Bass—MC Serch (Michael Berrin), Prime Minister Pete Nice (Pete Nash) and DJ Richie Rich—had already demolished the fantasy (a clear corollary to the blacks-can't-rock prejudice faced by Living Colour) that race should be a decisive factor in determining musical style. A brilliant pastiche of musical samples, ingenious on-target raps and found-sound junk-culture humor, **The Cactus** (produced variously by Sam Sever, most of Public Enemy's Bomb Squad and Prince Paul) established 3rd Bass as both legit and talented. From the hysterical putdowns of "The Gas Face" (a mark of disapproval which quickly gained widespread acceptance) to the heavy chronological drama of "Steppin' to the A.M." to the autobiographical "Product of the Environment" and "Sons of 3rd Bass" (whose bite of Blood, Sweat and Tears' "Spinning Wheel" wasn't well-received in some circles) to the title track's coy sexuality to Serch's goofy Louis Armstrong imitation of "Flippin' off the Wall like Lucy Ball," **The Cactus** careens wildly from solid to stupid, but hits the target often enough to be thoroughly enjoyable.

With their first album reaching gold-level sales, 3rd Bass issued a remix record, overhauling (in one case updating) the lyrics and/or sound of six **Cactus** tracks (including all four singles drawn from it: "The Gas Face," "Brooklyn-Queens," "Steppin' to the A.M." and "Product of the Environment"), plus the last-named's B-side, "3 Strikes 5000." Rather than just recycle old material while working on a follow-up, **Revisited** has substantial merit as both an extension and a summary of **The Cactus**. [i]

13 ENGINES
Before Our Time (Nocturnal) 1987
Byram Lake Blues (Nocturnal) 1989
A Blur to Me Now (SBK) 1991 φ

This Toronto quartet plays loud rock-pop with greater artistic ambitions than most such bands, both in the literate lyrics and the broadly dynamic instrumental designs. While singer John Critchley (guitar, key-

boards) and guitarist Mike Robbins write dramatic songs that cry out for intricate wide-screen arrangements, the group's reliance on simple rock tools creates an exciting tension between grand imagination and restrictive execution. (Fortunately, 13 Engines play well enough to keep the material from sounding shortchanged.) If **Before Our Time** has a slight edge over the Neil Young-inflected **Byram Lake Blues**, it's in the debut's unselfconscious sense of exploration and discovery, but both albums are well worth hearing. [i]

THIRTEEN NIGHTMARES
Shitride (Pravda) 1990

While reviving the ethos of a '60s new-left stereotype—white guilt, inchoate rage, the romance of poverty and misery—in its lyrics, this striking quartet from Lincoln, Nebraska slams three generations—the MC5, Cheap Trick and Soul Asylum—of Midwest rock into each other on the powerful **Shitride**. Great tunes, loose'n'lively hair-raising electric music and guitarist Greggory-David Cosgrove's ripping vocals load the album with bracing energy and an extraordinary balance of rawness and subtlety. Except for occasionally insufferable lyrics (the title track is a whiny complaint about the rock'n'roll life that goes so far as to gripe about bartenders who withhold free drinks; "E.C" expresses solidarity for Eldridge Cleaver with the line "It's a white man's world for everybody but you and me"—yeah, right), this is an extremely cool record. [i]

THIS HEAT
This Heat (nr/Piano) 1979 (nr/Recommended) 1983
Deceit (nr/Rough Trade) 1981 (nr/These) 1988
This Heat with Mario Boyer Diekuuroh [tape] (Fr. Tago Mago) 1982
The Peel Sessions EP (nr/Strange Fruit) 1988

In 1976, Charles Hayward of Gong (and Phil Manzanera's Quiet Sun) joined with Charles Bullen and Gareth Williams to form This Heat. Though arising from art-rock and the British school of fusion jazz, This Heat quickly developed into an experimental band largely dependent on tape loops and production tricks.

This Heat covers two years of the band's history, with both live and studio cuts. They use guitar, clarinet, drums and keyboards, permuted with loops, phasing and overdubs, breaking down patterns into only faintly connected musical moments that include artificial skips and looped end-grooves. Though insolent and withdrawn, the music is adventurous and, in its own peculiar way, engrossing. The punnily titled **Deceit** is more coherent and raucous, yet avoids the dismal drones and cacophony of other "experimental" groups. Free of clichés, the music blends politics and intelligence, steering clear of artifice and trendiness. Austere, brilliant and indescribable.

This Heat with Mario Boyer Diekuuroh, which compiles tapes from 1977/8, features studio sessions with the Ghanian drummer who greatly influenced their perceptions of rhythm.

Renamed Camberwell Now, the group has continued to release albums on the Swiss Recommended label; in the late '80s, Hayward issued a solo album. [sg]

THIS MORTAL COIL

It'll End in Tears (4AD-Valentino) 1984 ●
Filigree and Shadow (nr/4AD) 1986 ●
Blood (nr/4AD) 1991 ●

Not so much a band as a hip British studio party, This Mortal Coil combines the prodigious talents of members of the Cocteau Twins, Modern English, Dead Can Dance, Xmal Deutschland and others in the 4AD label stable to produce atmospheric vignettes, drawing material from such diverse sources as Alex Chilton, Tim Buckley and Colin Newman as well as penning new songs. **It'll End in Tears** mixes a few instrumentals with lush vocal performances; though all rather agreeable, most of it wouldn't disturb a sleeping infant.

Filigree & Shadow is a double album, with most of the work being done by various members of Dif Juz, the Wolfgang Press and Simon Raymonde of the Cocteau Twins. Once again, it neither rocks nor rolls. Tender, light piano and string arrangements predominate; the second side is half over before any drums enter the picture. With very few exceptions (including Wire and Talking Heads covers), this is the aural equivalent of herbal tea and would probably bore your grandparents.

[dgs/i]

DAVID THOMAS AND THE PEDESTRIANS

The Sound of the Sand and Other Songs of the
 Pedestrians (Rough Trade) 1981
Vocal Performances EP (nr/Rough Trade) 1982
Variations on a Theme (Sixth Int'l) 1983
More Places Forever (Twin/Tone) 1985

DAVID THOMAS & HIS LEGS
Winter Comes Home (nr/Re) 1982

DAVID THOMAS AND THE WOODEN BIRDS
Monster Walks the Winter Lake (Twin/Tone) 1985 ●
Blame the Messenger (Twin/Tone) 1987

A song stylist in the truest sense of the word, David Thomas is one of rock's few *truly* one-of-a-kind artists. But the Pere Ubu vocalist's first solo album came as something of a surprise. His lyrics and unusual compositions bring strangeness out of the mundane—imparting magic to everyday objects and activities—aided by an eclectic bunch: Richard Thompson, Anton Fier, Chris Cutler, Eddie Thornton, Philip Moxham and others. Each demonstrates hitherto unimagined aspects of their talents, and Thomas' otherworldly voice—animal noises transmuted into human speech—has never been more expressive. A high point of Thomas' avant-garde folk-blues-jazz-rock cultural reach.

Variations on a Theme, which prominently features Richard Thompson, again mixes a bit of everything—including country, jazz and blues—into Thomas' own unique style. Only two tracks on this musically sedate, almost "normal"-sounding record recall Pere Ubu's general looniness. Throughout, Thomas demonstrates genuine fascination with his subject matter, as well as an invariably novel perspective. A good follow-up, and one indicative of enormous artistic reach.

Winter Comes Home—which gives front cover billing to ex-Henry Cows Cutler and Lindsay Cooper—mixes intellectual stand-up comedy with winning performances, all recorded live in Munich in 1982. Cooper's bassoon perfectly suits Thomas' tastefully strident vocal excursions. Most notable is the title track, essentially a shaggy-dog story.

Thomas reunited with Ubu bassist Tony Maimone for **More Places Forever**. Along with Cutler's drums and Cooper's one-woman woodwind section, Thomas has all the backdrop he needs to gather us into his little world and cast his spell. He displays his love for things like insects and sunshine, and in "New Broom" follows some dust on its journey. Ubu fans finally get to hear the track for which **Song of the Bailing Man** was titled.

The new band (re)assembled for **Monster Walks the Winter Lake** is almost an Ubu reunion, with Maimone joined by Allen Ravenstine on synths and Paul Hamann producing. The low-key music moves more slowly than usual, with cello and strangely played accordion often the predominant instruments; the increasingly philosophical lyrics containing recurring monster metaphors. The four-part eleven-minute title track is a real treat.

Blame the Messenger was recorded with much the same lineup that reformed Pere Ubu. One listen confirms that they must have been itching to get back together; the sound and arrangements are more a throwback to the band's earlier recordings than any of Thomas' previous solo work, thanks especially to Ravenstine's electronic keyboards. The lyrical fascination this time is mostly with nature, particularly ironic when juxtaposed with such beautifully unnatural sounds. A great record.

[sg/dgs]

See also *Pere Ubu*.

PAT THOMAS
See *Absolute Grey*.

MARC ANTHONY THOMPSON
Marc Anthony Thompson (Warner Bros.) 1984
Watts and Paris (Reprise-Warner Bros.) 1989 ●

On his debut LP, this hard-to-categorize maverick—born in Panama, raised in California—makes slick, soulful pop music that manages to be subtle *and* edgy. Thompson gives free reign to his poised, slightly gritty voice in a variety of settings, from cool struttin' ("So Fine") to moody romance ("Love Cools Down") to after-hours elegance ("Coffee").

Five years later, **Watts and Paris** sports a nastier, more percussive edge, with in-your-face singing and dense, oddball arrangements obviously inspired by Prince. Don't miss the murky "Monkeytime," a startling attack on Paul Simon ("I taped the black man so let me be/South Africa been so good to me"), the hard funk of "In Time" and the screaming "I Never Promised." Tough and compelling, Thompson is a widely undiscovered talent on a major label.

[jy]

MAYO THOMPSON
See *Red Crayola*.

THOMPSON TWINS

A Product of ... (nr/T) 1981 (nr/Fame) 1983
Set (nr/T) 1982 (nr/Fame) 1984
In the Name of Love (Arista) 1982 ●
A Product of ... /Set [tape] (nr/T) 1983
Quick Step & Side Kick (nr/Arista) 1983 ●
Side Kicks (Arista) 1983 ●
Into the Gap (Arista) 1984 ●
Here's to Future Days (Arista) 1985 ●
Close to the Bone (Arista) 1987 ●
The Richard Skinner Sessions EP (nr/Nighttracks-Strange
　　Fruit) 1987
Greatest Mixes: The Best of Thompson Twins (Arista)
　　1988 ●
Big Trash (Red Eye-Warner Bros.) 1989 ●

The name notwithstanding, there are no twins and no Thompsons in this globally successful modern pop band. Once an obscure, loose collection of as many as seven Sheffield-to-London players led by singer/synthesist/songwriter Tom Bailey, the Twins pared down to just Bailey, New Zealander Alannah Currie and Joe Leeway and became one of the world's leading purveyors of occasionally adventurous, invariably danceable modern chart fare.

All six musicians credited on **A Product of . . .** manage to play some percussion in addition to their primary instruments—sax, guitar, keyboards, etc. The cleverness and variety of the tracks, however, eliminate any potential monotony that might have resulted from the heavy reliance on rhythm. And although the music is designed to incite maximum motion, there isn't one track that skimps on lyrical, melodic or structural depth. The album isn't uniformly wonderful, but the textures and sounds make it pleasurable and energizing. (The 1987 Richard Skinner radio session was recorded at this early stage of the band's career.)

Set adds one member (bassist Matthew Seligman) but is otherwise not very different—in cast or content—from its predecessor. Exemplified by such great numbers as "In the Name of Love" and "Bouncing," Bailey and his cohorts prove that it is possible to make totally listenable dance music that doesn't beg suspension of critical faculties. Producer Steve Lillywhite and Thomas Dolby also pitch in, making **Set** a very nice record. (The Thompsons' first exposure in America came via **In the Name of Love**, which consists of two tracks from the first LP and eight from the second.)

Building on the popular dance sound of "In the Name of Love" (in fact, deftly quoting it on the first track, "Love on Your Side"), the three Twins emerged mature, motivated and commercially focused on their third album, **Quick Step & Side Kick**. Demonstrating varied and skilled songwriting and extraordinary self-contained music-making—the trio plays almost everything you hear on keyboards—the album bounces from start to finish, but no two tracks have much in common other than a good mood and a strong beat. (The American label perversely altered the title and rearranged the tracks a tad. The British cassette includes a bonus side of remixes.)

Consolidating their stardom, **Into the Gap** is a virtual new greatest hits album, containing "Hold Me Now," "Doctor Doctor," "You Take Me Up" and "Sister of Mercy," which were all radio, chart and club

staples for many months. The Twins' strength is their avoidance of repetition; the songs vary widely in tempo, style, instrumentation, subject matter and vocal arrangements. (All three sing.)

By **Here's to Future Days**, co-produced by Bailey and Nile Rodgers, the hit machine was starting to run on a cracked wheel. "Lay Your Hands on Me" is brilliant, but "Don't Mess with Doctor Dream" is boring. "King for a Day" is cute but overly familiar; "Tokyo" is corny. And who needed to hear a new version of the Beatles' "Revolution"? With all its ups and downs, **Future Days** is not significantly inferior to the Twins' best albums, but it lacks their freshness and vitality.

In April 1986, at the end of a six-month world tour, Joe Leeway left the band, reportedly to go solo, although the results have yet to surface. (He did front a band for one song in the 1989 film Slaves of New York, however.) Finally reduced to the titular duo, Bailey and Currie carried on, releasing the modest and, for the most part, likable **Close to the Bone**, produced by Rupert Hine. Currie's lyrics (Bailey wrote the music) take a surprisingly reflective approach here, suggesting doubt and anxiety instead of the usual oblique contemplations. "Gold Fever" bitterly attacks someone (wonder who?) for greed, saying "Now it bothers me to think that I used to call you a friend." While spottily derivative (mostly of their own work, but "Long Goodbye" could easily be mistaken for Sting) and notably lacking the group's characteristic energy and rhythmic magic, the record proves that the Thompson factory can turn out quality merchandise even when the creative thinkers are napping.

The Twins left Arista, and the label issued a hits-heavy remix album—eight elongated dance versions more suited to the clubs where they originated than to a home stereo. Bailey and Currie took some time off from the Twins (writing and producing songs for Debbie Harry and Jerry Harrison), but their creative batteries didn't quite get recharged. Intended as an amused comment on junk culture, **Big Trash** is an uninspired waste of time and plastic, a lame pairing of grade-school rhymes and bland music that is, at best, self-imitative. Reduced to simplemindedness ("Kiss your wife goodbye/'Cos you know it's time to die/There are bombers in the sky"), the once-clever Twins sleepwalk through such nonsense as "Sugar Daddy," "T.V. On" and "Salvador Dali's Car" with no apparent effort or conviction. [i]

TRACEY THORN
See Everything but the Girl.

THRASHING DOVES
Bedrock Vice (A&M) 1987 ●
Trouble in the Home (A&M) 1989 ●

Another bunch of informed modern pop stylists, London's Thrashing Doves mix and match their varied stylistic borrowings on **Bedrock Vice**. "Beautiful Imbalance" takes spectacular chart-ready flight; otherwise, Ken Foreman's vocals merely echo Tom Verlaine, Lloyd Cole and Violent Femme Gordon Gano in songs that often seem transparent attempts at imitating various

Bob Dylan eras. Colorful but meaningless. Producers on the proficient quartet's minor album include Chris Thomas and Jimmy Iovine.

The restlessly diverse **Trouble in the Home** isn't any more original, but at least it has more vitality and some different second-hand arrows in the callow quiver. ("Another Deadly Sunset," for instance, draws from the T. Rex bop book.) But the music is still wholly lacking in purpose and conviction, and the lyrics' cagey religious references are too coy by half. [i]

THREE JOHNS

Men Like Monkeys EP (nr/CNT Productions) 1983
A.W.O.L. EP (nr/CNT Productions) 1983
Some History EP (nr/Abstract) 1983
Do the Square Thing EP (nr/Abstract) 1984
Atom Drum Bop (nr/Abstract) 1984
Death of the European EP (nr/Abstract) 1985
Brainbox (He's a Brainbox) EP (nr/Abstract) 1985
The World by Storm (nr/Abstract) 1986
Live in Chicago (Last Time Round) 1986 ●
Demonocracy: The Singles 1982–1986 (nr/Abstract) 1986
Never and Always EP (nr/Abstract) 1987
Deathrocker Scrapbook [tape] (ROIR) 1988
The Death of Everything (Caroline) 1988 ●
Eat Your Sons (nr/Tupelo) 1990 ●

This casual Leeds trio—Jon Langford (guitar; also in the Mekons), John Hyatt (vocals, lyrics) and John Brennan (bass)—began by specializing in discordant socio-political guitar punk with trembling falsetto vocals; their career-long use of a rhythm machine rather than a live drummer has lent a unique tension to the group's sound. **Some History** compiles two singles (from 1982 and 1983) on one 12-inch, and is very much indicative of the trio's approach. Save for a surfacing maniacal edge, **Men Like Monkeys** and **A.W.O.L.** stake out more of the same turf. Hyatt's whining vocals would grate in large doses, but brevity—four songs each—keeps these two records from becoming downright annoying.

The Johns plunge headfirst into dance-rock on **Do the Square Thing**. Lyrically oblique and riddled with innuendo, the title track is, for these thrashers, an extraordinarily slick piece of extended dancefloor fodder. Surprisingly, it makes a stronger impression than their usual dirges.

Characteristics that might be tiresome if abused are kept judiciously in check on the Johns' first LP, **Atom Drum Bop**. The vocals don't wander unnecessarily, guitar lines are blindingly sharp and melodic and the production is crystalline. "Teenage Nightingales to Wax," "Firepits," "Do Not Cross the Line" and the odd ballad, "No Place," all help make this the trio's most fully realized endeavor.

The two succeeding four-song EPs both show continued growth towards tuneful pop. Without losing any of their bite, the A-sides offer incisive comments on some pretty heady subject matter: America's destructive influence on continental heritage ("Death of the European") and yuppiesque self-centered apathy ("Brainbox"). The B-sides are more jagged, and just as strong.

The World by Storm, released with a limited edi-

tion 7-inch live EP, is highly recommended. The Johns have honed their craft to seeming perfection: it will be difficult for them to improve on tunes like "King Car," "Torches of Liberty," "Demon Drink" and the pre-LP single, "Sold Down the River."

Langford's commitment to the Mekons, as well as his high demand as a producer, temporarily put the Three Johns on hold. But that didn't stop the group from releasing records. **Demonocracy** is a highly recommended compilation of singles and LP tracks. The equally enlightening **Live in Chicago**—the Johns' first American release—dates from June 1985 and contains renditions (some of them already issued on the **World by Storm** bonus EP) of such material as "Teenage Nightingales to Wax," "Death of the European," "AWOL" and "The World of the Workers," as well as a brief (and uncredited) version of Madonna's "Like a Virgin." **Deathrocker Scrapbook** is accurately described on the cassette insert as "some great fun and games recorded by a very informal Three Johns during the 1980's." A mad dash through the Johns' back pages—live appearances, outtakes, rehearsals, acoustic one-offs, etc.—captures the three in the extremely entertaining act of being themselves. Highlights: "Conversations with Freud" and "Cheap Computer."

Although the sleeve credits utterly bollix up which cuts are from where, half of **The Death of Everything** was recorded live in Leeds at the beginning of '88. The rest of the tracks—including the Adrian Sherwood-produced pre-LP single, "Never and Always" (a straightforward hard-rock song that sounds like PiL)—are recent/new studio efforts. Although the Johns' range now includes thundering Glitter-rock ("Spin Me Round"), droning Fallish poetry ("The King Is Dead (Four Words Too Long)") and a neat Captain Beefheart cover, this diverse album is a bit short of the band's familiar ingenuity and fire. [ag/i]

THREE O'CLOCK

Baroque Hoedown EP (Frontier) 1982 ●
Sixteen Tambourines (Frontier) 1983 ●
Arrive Without Travelling (IRS) 1985
Ever After (IRS) 1986 ●
Vermillion (Paisley Park) 1988 ●

SALVATION ARMY

The Salvation Army (Frontier) 1982

BEFOUR THREE O'CLOCK

Befour Three O'Clock (Frontier) 1985

One of the brightest lights of new American pop psychedelia, LA's Salvation Army debuted with an album that was liable to inspire young bands all around the world to join in the fun. The trio's melodies have the ethereal quality of a young Syd Barrett; the music is a blend of all the most colorful '60s sounds, showing the influence of such groups as the Byrds, Move, Hollies, Music Machine and others.

Following legal action by the real Salvation Army (concerns over musical competition?), the group changed its name to the Three O'Clock. (Three years later, Frontier cleverly repackaged the original album as **Befour Three O'Clock**.) The five songs on **Baroque**

Hoedown have poppier vocals and equally engaging music. The addition of ex-Quick/Weirdos drummer Danny Benair also brought the quartet a harder edge. Don't miss their cover of the Easybeats' "Sorry."

Sixteen Tambourines is even better—an incredible full-length collection of chiming, memorable power pop tunes played and sung as if each track were likely to get played on every radio station coast-to-coast. Slick and inventive production by Earle Mankey delivers the songs (most co-written by guitarist Louis Gutierrez and bassist Michael Quercio) in utterly engaging style. Best numbers: "On My Own," "Jet Fighter," "And So We Run." Absolutely charming and remarkably memorable. (The CD includes **Baroque Hoedown**.)

In 1985, the Three O'Clock signed to IRS and released their second album. **Arrive Without Travelling** isn't quite as delightfully twinky as its predecessor, but it does contain enough characteristically lightheaded material ("Her Head's Revolving," "Simon in the Park") to maintain the group's standing as preeminent paisley popsters.

Ever After saw Gutierrez exit the group (he's now in Louis and Clark), to be replaced by Steven Altenberg without any major changes in the group's sound or direction. Shortly after its release, the group parted ways with IRS, spent some time in legal limbo and then signed to Paisley Park. Apparently, Prince had heard and liked them (not too surprising, since **Around the World in a Day** draws on many of the same influences as Three O'Clock's records), though they'd never actually met. With Jason Falkner replacing Altenberg and Ian Ritchie producing, the group recorded **Vermillion**, their most interesting and varied album to date, which includes Prince's (sorry, Joey Coco's) "Neon Telephone"—just right for them—a lead vocal apiece by Falkner and keyboardist Mike Mariano (both great) and Quercio's six-minute ballad, "Through the Sleepy Town." Three O'Clock broke up later that year.   [cpl/i/ds]

See also *Mary's Danish*.

THROBBING GRISTLE

Second Annual Report (nr/Industrial) 1978 (nr/Fetish) 1979 (nr/Mute) 1983
D.o.A. (nr/Industrial) 1979 (nr/Fetish) 1981 (nr/Mute) 1983
Twenty Jazz Funk Greats (nr/Industrial) 1979 (nr/Fetish) 1981 (nr/Mute) 1983
Heathen Earth (nr/Industrial) 1979 (nr/Fetish) 1981 (nr/Mute) 1983
Throbbing Gristle's Greatest Hits (Rough Trade) 1980
Funeral in Berlin (Ger. Zensor) 1981
24 Hours [tape] (nr/Industrial) 1981
Mission of Dead Souls (nr/Fetish) 1981 (nr/Mute) 1983
Five Albums (nr/Fetish) 1982
Thee Psychick Sacrifice (nr/Illuminated) 1982 (nr/Dojo) 1986
Editions Frankfurt–Berlin (nr/Illuminated) 1983
Once Upon a Time (Live at the Lyceum) (nr/Casual Abandon) 1983 (nr/Obsession) 1990 ●
In the Shadow of the Sun (nr/Illuminated) 1984
Live at Heaven [tape] (nr/Rough Trade) c. 1985
TG CD1 [CD] (nr/Mute) 1986 ●

Raised on William S. Burroughs and Philip K. Dick, and inhabiting a science-fiction-now world of industrial

depression, Britain's prolific Throbbing Gristle produced some of the most confrontational and unpleasantly fascinating music of recent years, ostensibly as a means to radicalize the listener into abandoning bourgeois romanticism for a realistic view of life.

Second Annual Report (the quartet's first release) uses mournful synthesizer drones to paint a grimly powerful vision of post-industrial, mid-depression England.

D.o.A. is brighter in tone and more polished in technique. Less cohesive than the previous album, **D.o.A.** places greater emphasis on live material, found tapes and individual productions by separate members of the band. The music is aggressively anti-melodic, but the spirit is powerful and the surprises plentiful. Recommended for the strong.

Twenty Jazz Funk Greats breaks away from **D.o.A.**'s stark bleakness in an attempted truce between the group's radical attitudes and pop music, removing the cutting edge from their calculated chaos but offering more accessibility.

Heathen Earth is a return to form, adding savagery to the mix, expanding TG leader Genesis P-Orridge's obsession with the profane juxtaposition of everyday symbols and motifs. The music is clean, vicious, sharp and occasionally displays the band's transition to energetic, if still outré, rock.

Greatest Hits, subtitled "Entertainment Through Pain" (an apt description of the band's approach), collects material from the first four albums. Recommended for a solid overview.

Funeral in Berlin and **Mission of Dead Souls** are live albums. The first features all previously unreleased material; the latter is a recording of the band's final show in San Francisco. Those who desire a lot more Throbbing Gristle live should check out **24 Hours**, a collection of two dozen C-60 cassettes packed in a suitcase and containing most of the group's live shows. (Rough Trade reportedly also offered a suitcase set of 33 tapes around the same time. Did anyone actually buy one of these?) In 1983, however, Rough Trade bowed to public pressure and made those 33 cassettes available individually. **Five Albums** is more reasonably sized, a boxed set reissuing all the albums that had previously been on Fetish.

Although the group has been defunct now for years and its members (P-Orridge, Chris Carter, Cosey Fanni Tutti, Peter Christopherson) scattered into the similarly uncommon Chris and Cosey, Psychic TV and Coil, new TG records—most of them live (how can there be anything left?)—are still being released, many only on cassette. **TG CD1**, however, contains 42 minutes of previously unissued instrumental studio dribblings from early '79, with reflective '86 liner commentary by the participants.   [sg/i]

See also *Chris and Cosey, Coil, Psychic TV*.

THROWING MUSES

Throwing Muses EP (Throwing Muses) 1984
Throwing Muses [tape] (Throwing Muses) 1985
Throwing Muses (nr/4AD) 1986 ●
Chains Changed EP (nr/4AD) 1987
The Fat Skier (Sire) 1987
House Tornado (Sire) 1989 ●
Hunkpapa (Sire) 1989 ●

Dizzy EP (nr/4AD) 1989 ●
The Real Ramona (Sire) 1991 ●

If for no other reason, this Boston-based quartet has its reserved seat in music history for being the first American band signed to the British 4AD label. An eclectic blend of jerky guitar pop and songwriter Kristin Hersh's unpredictably eccentric vocals, the early work by Throwing Muses bears no resemblance to any other group or artist in recent memory.

The group's first two untitled releases are fairly obscure: a commonly bootlegged five-song 7-inch EP that features an early bassist and a self-released 1985 cassette that contains most of the songs that would comprise the band's first album (plus one that wouldn't get redone until **The Fat Skier**).

Produced by up-and-coming studio star Gil Norton, **Throwing Muses** (the LP) is startling; attribute the uniqueness to Hersh's remarkable singing on "Hate My Way," "Green" and "America (She Can't Say No)." Truly one of a kind. With fewer twists and turns than the album's songs, the four-track **Chains Changed** (with one lead vocal by Tanya Donelly, the group's junior guitar-playing songwriter) somehow has even more impact.

College radio airplay and critical acclaim prompted Sire to sign Throwing Muses and release **The Fat Skier**: six songs on one side and a nearly nine-minute seventh ("Soul Soldier") on the flip. With onetime Violent Femmes producer Mark Van Hecke behind the board, the music appears to be verging on the formulaic; the record is considerably less striking than the band's prior output. It's still distinctive, but an injection of fresh ideas at this point wouldn't hurt. But **House Tornado** only amplifies the problems of **The Fat Skier**: with a minimum of musical variety, songs run into one another. What was, upon inception, avant-garde has become static and predictable.

David Narcizo's stiff drumming sets the tone for **Hunkpapa**, a chilly and dull record that could be by any number of contempo jangle-pop bands. Along with the uneventful material, Hersh's voice, no longer possessing any strong character, is ineffectual and a bit strident at times; the rote guitar backdrop doesn't pick up the slack. Of Donelly's two tunes, "Angel" is actually tuneful and appealing; the other merely provides a bit of light variety.

The four-song **Dizzy** EP (built around a **Hunkpapa** track) also contains the non-LP "Santa Claus" and compelling 1988 live recordings of "Downtown" (from **House Tornado**) and the frenetic "Mania" (from **Hunkpapa**).

Produced by Dennis Herring, **The Real Ramona** introduces new bassist Fred Abong; the reinvigorated Muses seem comfortably settled into a functional sound, taking few chances but getting the job done with confidence, enthusiasm and none of **Hunkpapa**'s bland aloofness. Hersh's songwriting is solid if not spectacular; Donelly contributes two, including the gentle power-punk of "Not Too Soon." [ag/i]

See also *Breeders*.

THUG

See *Beasts of Bourbon*.

LES THUGS

Frenetic Dancing (Fr. Cougnaf Movement) 1985
Radical Hysterie (Fr. Closer) 1986 (Gr. Dikeoma Diavasis) 1989
Electric Troubles EP (nr/Vinyl Solution) 1987
Dirty White Race (nr/Vinyl Solution) 1988
Electric Troubles (Sub Pop) 1989
Still Hungry (nr/Decoy) 1989

To say that France is not known for cutting-edge rock is akin to noting that elephants don't generally travel in Subarus. The French love synthesizers. They also love '50s music, like basic rock'n'roll, rockabilly and R&B. While les Thugs are French (from Angiers, to be exact), this is one elephant of a band. They sing mostly in English, sometimes in what they call yoghurt (meaningless syllables that only *sound* like English) with pleasantly curly French accents, and play a twin-guitar assault with nary a synth or slap bass in sight. A punk band in the earliest sense of the word, les Thugs' records are a pre-hardcore blast of pop-rooted pounding, from the same school as the Buzzcocks.

Formed in 1984 from the ashes of a new wave band called Dazibo, les Thugs debuted with **Frenetic Dancing**, a four-track 7-inch (later remastered and reissued as a two-song single). Following the relatively primitive **Radical Hysterie**, the band made **Electric Troubles**, an EP that comes as close to perfection as a record can. Hard without being metallic, packed with a knock-over energy punch, it's fueled by guitars that saw and scrape, deliberately undermixed harmonic singing and pacing that won't quit. "Dead Dreams" opens with a native American recording that crossfades into an Arabic slink of fuzz guitar, then explodes in frenzy. "Bulgarian Blues" gallops with shaking percussion that sounds like a train.

Though not reaching the same heights, **Dirty White Race** still blows most other vinyl halfway to Jupiter. It's mixed slightly brighter, takes its guitar playing a bit more seriously (including some isolated barf-awful metal clichés) and makes fine use of dynamics. "Hedgehogs" particularly plays with the loud and soft buttons, simmering down with an angelic choir of background vocals while an accompanying guitar slinks in hard peals of chime before the band gears up for a recharged sonic assault. The American **Electric Troubles** album combines **Dirty White Race** and the **Electric Troubles** EP.

The Iain Burgess/Tim Lewis-recorded **Still Hungry** is les Thugs' most sophisticated production, but that doesn't mean more than a slight detour in getting their energy down your ear canals. With les Thugs' records, you can't lose. ['e]

JOHNNY THUNDERS

So Alone (nr/Real) 1978
In Cold Blood (Fr. New Rose) 1983 ●
Diary of a Lover EP (PVC) 1983
New Too Much Junkie Business [tape] (ROIR) 1983 [CD] (ROIR-Important) 1990 φ
Hurt Me (Fr. New Rose) 1984 ●
Que Sera, Sera (nr/Jungle) 1985 ●
Stations of the Cross [tape] (ROIR) 1987 [CD] (ROIR-Important) 1990 φ
Bootlegging the Bootleggers (nr/Jungle) 1990 ●

JIMMY K
Trouble Traveller (Jap. Meldac) 1986 ●
JOHNNY THUNDERS & PATTI PALLADIN
Copy Cats (Restless) 1988 ●
JOHNNY THUNDERS & WAYNE KRAMER
Gang War (Zodiac-DeMilo) 1990 ●

For his first solo LP, the legendary New York Dolls/ Heartbreakers guitarist enlisted the aid of ex-Pistols Paul Cook and Steve Jones, some of the Hot Rods, the Only Ones and even old-timers Steve Marriott and Phil Lynott. Choosing material representative of all his prior musical phases, and aided immeasurably by co-producer Steve Lillywhite, Thunders turns in reasonably strong performances, perfectly employing his gutter guitar and New York sneer in a number of (musical) veins, including greasy R&B and a tender ballad. Not since the Dolls' two records has he sounded so lucid and involved—**So Alone** is Johnny Thunders at his best.

Thunders didn't release anything else under his own name for five years after that. The LP-plus-EP **In Cold Blood** returned him to the racks, combining five newly recorded studio tracks—with just a drummer and guitarist Walter Lure—that don't amount to much with a poor live Boston show taped in 1982. (**Diary of a Lover** consists of those studio cuts plus a subsequent item.) At **Cold Blood**'s best, Thunders pounds out a stinging "Green Onions" that suggests his guitar skills aren't gone yet.

Narrated in New Yawkese by the artist, **New Too Much Junkie Business** offers live, demo and live-in-the-studio recordings from 1982, co-produced by Jimmy Miller, with a variety of players helping out on renditions of everything from the Dolls' "Jet Boy" and "Great Big Kiss" to a Gang War track and numbers that overlap **Diary of a Lover**. Most notable is "Sad Vacation," a tribute to Sid Vicious. That song also appears on the French-only **Hurt Me**, alongside "Eve of Destruction," "It Ain't Me Babe" and renditions of some of Thunders' best songs. (The **Hurt Me** CD contains five bonus tracks.)

Que Sera, Sera boasts a batch of solid new songs, a solid rhythm section (Keith Yon and Tony St. Helene), an illustrious cast of guest stars and a surprisingly easygoing, clearheaded outlook. Variety is a watchword, as Stonesy pseudo-reggae ("Cool Operator"), sneering sexist raunch ("Little Bit of Whore"), restrained reality ("Short Lives," wherein JT denounces the live-fast-die-young credo), familiar Dollsy bebop ("Tie Me Up" and "Endless Party," co-written with David Johansen) and a hot uptempo instrumental ("Billy Boy") mix gaily. In fact, the most wasted thing about this LP is the unnecessary cover shot of Thunders looking like the not-so-living dead.

Punk filmmaker Lech Kowalski shot and recorded a pair of 1982 Mudd Club shows to use in his junkie portrait feature (*Gringo*) but didn't, so the music for an hour of them wound up on **Stations of the Cross**. Backed by Lure and drummer Jerry Nolan, plus someone identified only as Talarico, a reasonably cogent JT runs through such songs as "So Alone," "In Cold

Blood," "Chinese Rocks" and "Too Much Junkie Business," punctuating the lively performances with typically hysterical inter-song patter. Before ending, the tape takes an odd detour: a hotel room conversation, participants unknown, followed by a solo acoustic number.

JT the DJ returns—in assorted goofy voices—to introduce the songs on **Bootlegging the Bootleggers**, an uneven (and that's not just the widely varying sound quality) compilation of 1985-'89 live recordings, ostensibly drawn from assorted unauthorized albums. The old, borrowed and sloppy song selection—including "Personality Crisis," "In Cold Blood," "Sad Vacation," "As Tears Go By" and Dylan's "Joey" (the last three performed acoustic)—is great, but this isn't the ultimate concert document Thunders' solo career still deserves. (Note the editing boo-boo that swaps the spoken introductions for "Pipeline" and "Wipeout," both identified correctly on the sleeve.)

Thunders co-wrote, produced and played guitar on the bizarre **Trouble Traveller**, surrounding young Japanese singer/guitarist Jimmy K(urata) with such Anglo-American luminaries as Jerry Nolan, Glen Matlock, Pete Thomas, John "Irish" Earle, Martin Belmont and Bob Andrews. The modestly talented Kurata is totally out of his league here. Faced with crisp, energetic rock-'n'roll tracks—nothing extraordinary, just top-notch Thunders issue—his echo-drenched vocals (in Japanese and imperfect English—Eddie Cochran's "Nervous Breakdown" merits especially bad pronunciation) are hopelessly lame.

Copy Cats—an accomplished joint effort with ex-Snatch vocalist Pat Palladin (who also produced the LP) and a bunch of their friends—contains swell studio covers of songs by Dion, the Seeds, Shirelles, Elvis Presley, Chambers Brothers, Screaming Jay Hawkins and Shangri-Las, among others. Sharing the spotlight for once, Thunders contributes solid musicianship, imaginative (occasionally poignant) performances and an overriding sense of well-behaved fun. Two songs (Mickey & Sylvia's "Love Is Strange" and "Let Me Entertain You") from the original UK album were deleted for the American version, which also has a different track sequence.

Another era, another partnership: the half-studio/half-live **Gang War** LP documents Thunders' nearly forgotten 1980-vintage sideband with ex-MC5 guitarist Wayne Kramer. Totally crap sound ruins the concert portion (mostly covers), and the studio sessions are nearly as bad. Obviously not taken from first (or even third) generation masters, there are a few significant songs ("Crime of the Century," "M.I.A."), a couple of trivial ones and the rest is vocal-less jams or incomplete backing tracks. If the original tapes could be located, there'd be a great single in here. As it stands, however, **Gang War** is a total waste.

Thunders died in New Orleans in April 1991.   [i]

See also *Heartbreakers, New York Dolls*.

'TIL TUESDAY
Voices Carry (Epic) 1985 ●
Welcome Home (Epic) 1986 ●
Everything's Different Now (Epic) 1988 ●

Boston's underground scene has spawned some excellent, adventurous bands, but 'Til Tuesday is not one of them. "Voices Carry," the quartet's one mega-hit, is a catchy (if lyrically clumsy) song that utilizes the full extent of ex-Young Snakes singer/bassist Aimee Mann's limited vocal capabilities; the rest of the band's Mike Thorne-produced debut album is surprisingly unstylish, bland and unengaging.

Armed with a Chrissie Hynde-like warble and another clutch of slow-going sensitive torch-rockers, Mann and her three bandmates issued a soundalike follow-up, produced by Rhett Davies. Although the dynamically mixed sound is technically flawless, the playing is dull and there aren't many melodies you're likely to remember. (The soaring "On Sunday" comes close.) Mann's uncertain singing and the earnest collegiate pretentiousness of her lyrics make it hard to imagine just what kind of a home would welcome 'Til Tuesday.

The fascinating results of life intruding on art, **Everything's Different Now** considers a sad affair from two separate angles: during and after. The Jules Shear-penned title track expresses his joy at falling in love with Mann; "(Believed You Were) Lucky" puts her thoughts on their parting to *his* music. Romantic disappointment and loss dominate the album, through such heartfelt songs as " 'J' for Jules," "How Can You Give Up?" and "The Other End (of the Telescope)," the last written and sung with Elvis Costello. The music (again produced by Davies) takes a polite back seat, supporting Mann's controlled and sincere vocals without attracting attention. [i]

TIMBUK 3

Greetings from Timbuk 3 (IRS) 1986 ●
Eden Alley (IRS) 1988 ●
Edge of Allegiance (IRS) 1989 ●

Pat and Barbara K. MacDonald are best known for their much-misunderstood fluke hit "The Future's So Bright, I Gotta Wear Shades," and for eschewing backup musicians in favor of overdubs on record and pre-recorded rhythm tapes live. But the Austin-based couple is more noteworthy for Pat's songwriting talent than for the mere novelty of their minimalist lineup. Unlike the deceptively breezy "Shades," MacDonald generally writes sardonic slices of life; his pessimism is consistently redeemed by unflagging humanity and perfectly complemented by the pair's drawling, deadpan harmonies. Despite (or because of) a fondness for mechanical percussion, the music has a homey ambience that balances frequent lyrical archness.

Greetings, surely one of the darkest albums ever to have yielded a hit single, collects some rueful snapshots of Americana ("Life Is Hard," "Just Another Movie") alongside enjoyable lighter fare ("Facts About Cats," "Hairstyles and Attitudes") with impressive results. **Eden Alley** trades much of that album's country twang for a more varied recording approach (e.g., "Sample the Dog" does just that). Stylistic eclecticism comes in handy on Pat's mini-morality-plays (the title track, "Dance Fever," "Rev. Jack & His Roamin' Cadillac Church"). Barbara, meanwhile, shines on her two featured cuts, "Welcome to the Human Race" and "Easy."

Edge of Allegiance (co-produced by drummer De-

nardo Coleman, Ornette's son) is yet another small triumph of sane, thoughtful songcraft. The chipper "National Holiday" provides a facetiously optimistic opening to an album that paints a bemused but bleak view of an America ruled by economic inequity ("Dirty Dirty Rice"), environmental horror ("Acid Rain") and an atrophied democratic process ("Count to Ten"). [hd]

TIME

The Time (Warner Bros.) 1981 ●
What Time Is It? (Warner Bros.) 1982 ●
Ice Cream Castle (Warner Bros.) 1984 ●
Pandemonium (Paisley Park-Reprise) 1990 ●

Prince's first major male extracurricular effort, Minneapolis' six-man Time was an exceptionally fertile launching pad for several careers. Vocalist Morris Day walked away with the *Purple Rain* film and did well as a solo artist. Jesse Johnson went on to emulate Prince not only with soundalike records but by mentoring a number of other acts as well. Jimmy Jam and Terry Lewis became an awesomely successful writing-production team, scoring hits for/with Janet Jackson, Patti Austin, the S.O.S. Band, Force M.D.'s, Human League and many others.

The group's three original albums alternate between straight, infectious dance-funk tunes and extended jams punctuated by all sorts of silly business. Day's personality informs all the tracks, filling them with sharp-dressed sex-machine jive, but occasionally allowing a glimpse of the self-effacing chump who realizes that having an onstage valet (Jerome Benton) to hold the mirror for on-site preening is a satire on just that smugness.

Although **What Time Is It?** boasts "777-9311" and the pose-heavy "Gigolos Get Lonely Too," **Ice Cream Castle** is the best of the three, a six-track party that includes the signature dance groove, "Jungle Love," which the Time performed in a memorable *Purple Rain* club sequence. But loving is the Time's speciality, and **Ice Cream Castle** lays it on in "If the Kid Can't Make You Come" and "My Drawers." To cap off this divergent LP, the title tune is fine bubblegum funk-pop.

In 1990, a much-ballyhooed reunion brought the entire group back together, somehow coordinating these stars' broadly developed talents into a solidly entertaining record of new material that is unmistakably Time-like. Faced with the challenge of getting all those little time-release pills back in the capsule, **Pandemonium** comes through like a breeze, fitting Day's beseechingly egotistical humor, patented Jam/Lewis dance grooves and Johnson's psychedelic funk guitar back together as if nothing had happened. [i]

See also *Morris Day, Jesse Johnson's Revue.*

TIMES

Pop Goes Art! (nr/Whaam!) 1982 (nr/Artpop!) 1983 ●
This Is London (nr/Artpop!) 1983
I Helped Patrick McGoohan Escape EP (nr/Artpop!) 1983
Hello Europe (nr/Artpop!) 1984
Blue Period (nr/Artpop!) 1985
Boys About Town EP (nr/Artpop!) 1985
Go! With the Times (Ger. Pastell) 1985

Up Against It (nr/Artpop!) 1986
Times T.V. EP (nr/Fire) 1986
Enjoy the Times (nr/Artpop!) 1986
Beat Torture (nr/Creation) 1988 ●
E for Edward (nr/Creation) 1989 ●
Et Dieu Créa la Femme (nr/Creation) 1990 ●

Led by singer/songwriter Edward Ball (original co-conspirator in the Television Personalities and numerous related endeavors under such names as O Level, Teenage Filmstars, etc.), these psychedelic poseurs set out to recapture the lightweight pop sounds of swinging England (circa 1967). If you don't mind that the Times are totally derivative and enjoy the style they lift, the group's early records are a seamlessly integrated genre heist, superb examples of successful nostalgia.

The low-budget **Pop Goes Art!** includes the marvelously kitsch "I Helped Patrick McGoohan Escape" (a song the group has repeatedly re-recorded) as well as appropriately devised creations like "Biff! Bang! Pow!" and the title track. (Despite its belated German-only release, **Go! With the Times** was actually recorded in 1980, prior to **Pop Goes Art!**.)

With tunes like "Goodbye Piccadilly" and "The Chimes of Big Ben," **This Is London** offers convincing evidence that the paisley-colored '60s are back. But the Times aren't totally unconnected to the present: the pointed lyrics of "Whatever Happened to Thamesbeat" offer lucid insight into the neo-mod revival.

After reading British playwright Joe Orton's work, Ball wrote a song based on (and titled after) *Up Against It*, a screenplay commissioned and discarded by the Beatles. That song turned up on the six-song **Patrick McGoohan** EP, along with a new version of the title track and the "Danger Man Theme."

The following year, Ball and Tony Conway of Mood Six wrote and attempted to mount a one-act theatrical condensation of *Up Against It*; in 1985, they co-directed a complete stage production of Orton's script, incorporating original songs Ball had written for it. Those were then issued as **Up Against It**, a studio LP of discrete power pop tunes that sound very noticeably like various well-known artists, including the Jam, Beatles and Bowie. As the songs are linked in a narrative logic that wants for an explanatory script, it's an okay album but not one of the Times' best. (Other than Ball's claim that Joseph Papp's people pinched the idea from him, this project is musically and practically unrelated to the subsequent off-Broadway musical of the same name, scored by Todd Rundgren.)

On the Times' first Creation LP, Ball is joined by Jowe Head (ex-Swell Map/occasional TVP) and two members of Biff Bang Pow!, including Creation boss Alan McGee. (Ball also plays in that group on occasion.) No longer beholden to any specific era and a lot less innocent-sounding than the group's old records, **Beat Torture** is an uneven mixture of light pop, moderate rock and heavy psychedelia. While "Department Store," the old-fashioned "It Had to Happen" and the strange "How to Start Your Own Country" are notable, too much of the record is halfbaked and disposable.

E for Edward is a Ball solo album in all but name. Although the set-up encourages too many wispy acoustic numbers of little effect, solitude seems to agree with him. Highlights of this simple but skillfully produced LP include the contemporary scene tableau of

"Manchester," the witty T. Rex pisstake of "Catherine Wheel" and the wry cinematic parody of "French Film Blurred." In keeping with the album's drug-oriented title, the record closes with "Acid Angel of Ecstasy," a character study hissed over oscillating tremolo guitar. From there, it was only a drop, trip and a thump to the Love Corporation, a nom-de-dance under which Ball released a 1990 acid-house EP. [i]

See also *Biff Bang Pow!*, *Television Personalities*.

TIME ZONE
See *Afrika Bambaataa*.

SALLY TIMMS AND THE DRIFTING COWGIRLS
See *Mekons*.

TINA PEEL
See *Fuzztones*.

TIN HUEY
Contents Dislodged During Shipment (Warner Bros.) 1979

This sextet of eccentrics from Akron, Ohio were more eclectic and musicianly than their local colleagues. The Hueys' stunning should-have-been-a-hit version of the Monkees' "I'm a Believer" (included on the album) was inspired by Robert Wyatt's re-arrangement, and the band owes a nod to Frank Zappa as well. Yet their blend of blues, jazz and progressive rock is hilariously unique, offering up a warped vision of Middle America. For Tin Huey, "weekends in my Lay-zee Boy" (from "Hump Day") might be punctuated by the discovery of a car filled with doll heads ("Puppet Wipes"); a surreal "Chinese Circus" comes to town; they even admit to fantasies of technological megalomania ("I Could Rule the World If I Could Only Get the Parts"—later the title of a mini-LP by the Waitresses).

After Tin Huey's artistically fruitful (but commercially hopeless) one-album career ended, various members went on to pursue other projects, the most notable of which are guitarist Chris Butler's creation, the Waitresses, and multi-horn wizard Ralph Carney's Swollen Monkeys. [jg]

See also *Carney-Hild-Kramer*, *Swollen Monkeys*, *Waitresses*.

TIN MACHINE
See *David Bowie*.

TIN TIN
See *Stephen Duffy*.

TINY LIGHTS
Prayer for the Halcyon Fear (Uriel) 1986 (Absolute A Go Go) 1990 ●
Hazel's Wreath (Gaia) 1988 ●
Hot Chocolate Massage (Absolute A Go Go) 1990 ●

While the brand of fragile, childlike folk-pop embraced by this New Jersey quintet has led many a sincere young combo down the garden path of pretension and preciousness, Tiny Lights possesses the talent and personality to execute the style with just the right blend of innocence and smarts, as well as a minimum of self-consciousness. In addition to a fulltime cellist (the much-borrowed Jane Scarpantoni) and a rhythm section that doubles on horns, the lineup boasts a distinctive frontwoman in singer/violinist Donna Croughn, who collaborates on the band's songwriting with guitarist John Hamilton.

Prayer for the Halcyon Fear is a delightful debut, alternately delicate ("Flowers Through the Air," "Blue Dot Cleanser") and rocking ("Zippity-Do-Dah," "Chesterfield Gorge"), with a mildly psychedelic sense of play that sets the band apart. (Inexplicably, this unpretentious, accessible record was issued in the UK by Psychic TV's Temple label.)

Hazel's Wreath lacks its predecessor's giddy sense of discovery, but is a solid mix of solemnity and abandon (often within the same song, as on "Grown-up Fish" and "The Bridge"). Following **Hazel's Wreath**, Tiny Lights recorded a third album, **Know It You Love**, but Gaia folded before issuing it.

The band recut two of the unreleased album's songs for the wonderful **Hot Chocolate Massage**, obviously the work of a mature, confident group that's eclectic yet consistently focused, romantic without being sappy. The combination of lilting pastoral tunes ("Moonwhite Day," "Big Straw Hat") and heavier numbers ("Wave," "After All") once again proves that sincerity needn't be dull. [hd]

TIREZ TIREZ
Etudes (nr/Object Music) 1980 (nr/Aura) 1981
Story of the Year (Bel. Crépuscule) 1983
Social Responsibility (Primitive Man) 1987 ●
Against All Flags (Primitive Man) 1988 ●
MIKEL ROUSE BROKEN CONSORT
Jade Tiger (Bel. Crépuscule) 1983
A Walk in the Woods (Bel. Made to Measure) 1985
   (Club Soda) 1985 ●
A Lincoln Portrait (Cuneiform) 1988
MIKEL ROUSE
Quorom (Club Soda) 1984
BLAINE L. REININGER/ MIKEL ROUSE
Colorado Suite EP (Bel. Made to Measure) 1984 ●

The French *nom* to the contrary, Mikel Rouse originally formed his trio in Kansas City, relocating it to New York in 1979. As a singer, Rouse shows promise, but **Etudes** borrows far too much from early Talking Heads to be accused of originality and is rhythmically monotonous to boot. Following a Belgian LP release, Tirez Tirez released a 12-inch on Sire before finding an American label to put out the group's third album.

Except for bass (credit James Bergman), Rouse sings and plays (keyboards, guitars, drum programs) **Social Responsibility** singlehandedly; he wrote all nine songs and co-produced it as well. Not surprisingly, there's a certain sluggish insularity to the music, an audible lack of human interaction. But when Rouse's over-educated structuralism succumbs to the uplifting pop momentum, Tirez makes for attractive, intelligent listening.

Against All Flags is the first Tirez Tirez record to feature a full band, and the difference in feel (not to mention the filled-out sound) is immediately apparent. Rouse's writing here shows as much heart as craft, and the result is a batch of very engaging tunes that are still compositionally rigorous. A great pop record.

Rouse also records with a forward-thinking chamber quartet, Broken Consort. **Jade Tiger** shares definite affinities with the work of Steve Reich, and features a snappy but mellifluous soprano sax sound that has unfortunately been appropriated by the new age crowd. Succeeding Broken Consort records—**A Walk in the Woods** and **A Lincoln Portrait**—find Rouse growing bolder and more intricate in his compositions. While he's a composer of undeniable and substantial gifts, his work has gotten lost in the crossdrifts of contemporary classical music, not really bare-boned enough to be called minimal and too easy on the ears to attract the attention of the academic crowd. (Initially released by Belgium's Crammed Discs as part of its Made to Measure series, **A Walk in the Woods** was joined on CD with **Colorado Suite**, Rouse's joint album with Tuxedomoon violinist Blaine L. Reininger.)

Released under his own name on his own Club Soda label, **Quorum** is an interesting but extremely dry solo composition for Linndrum. [jy/i/gk]

See also *Tuxedomoon*.

TOADSTOOL
See *Magnolias*.

TOAD THE WET SPROCKET
Bread and Circus (Abe's-Columbia) 1989 ●
Pale (Abe's-Columbia) 1990 ●

Accidentally caught in the nets of a major label trawling the alternative (aka college-radio) waters for hip credibility and the next R.E.M., this mild Santa Barbara, California quartet plays perfectly competent pop without a shred of personality. Except for the silly name (borrowed from a Monty Python sketch) and a close demographic resemblance to their target audience of bright white suburban middle-class kids, Toad the Wet Sprocket is as countercultural as skim milk, and every drop as exciting. **Bread and Circus** reveals guitarist Glen Phillips' passing vocal similarity to Elton John; when bassist Dean Dinning joins in to harmonize, the dread ghost of California lite-rock lurks in the grooves.

With producer Marvin Etzioni adding a mature sheen and semi-acoustic restraint, **Pale** turns bland pop into dire singer/songwriter tepidity, underscoring the gravity of the marketers' miscalculation. Anyone who finds this stimulating needs to get out more. [i]

TO DAMASCUS
Succumb (Ringent) 1986
Come to Your Senses (Ringent-Restless) 1987
SYLVIA JUNCOSA
Nature (SST) 1988 ●
One Thing (Nate Starkman & Son-Fundamental) 1989

Originally a keyboardist, LA's Sylvia Juncosa switched to guitar and formed To Damascus after leaving Leaving Trains and touring with Kendra Smith and David Roback in Clay Allison. (She also concurrently played guitar in SWA.) **Succumb**, her trio's ragged first album, contains undistinguished post-punk. Juncosa's a carefree, marble-mouthed singer and a solid rhythm guitarist but a sloppy soloist with few original ideas; the rhythm section does its part adequately, but no more.

The lyrics on **Come to Your Senses** indicate Juncosa's evocative talent for expressing alienation and disaffection in unusual ways; her organ and piano contributions leaven the much-improved hyperactive guitar smears (if not her dubious singing). The inclusion of acoustic creations with strings and things offer helpful variety but are also limited in appeal by wobbly vocals. A creative focal point and stronger songwriting would have helped, as Ethan James' co-production fills the LP with layers of energizing aggression that are left hanging like burning wallpaper.

With a new bassist and drummer in tow, Juncosa initiated her solo career with **Nature**, a relatively accomplished guitar demonstration, covering everything from waves of psychedelic noise to gentle acoustic fingerpicking. It's interesting to watch this burgeoning fret technician find her feet as well as her chops: "Lick My Pussy, Eddie Van Halen" makes it clear that today's guitar hero doesn't need a penis to have balls. She should really refrain from singing, however: her uncertain Onoesque warble does nothing to improve the instrumental showcases.

A change of producers and sidemen on the thick-sounding **One Thing** gives Juncosa new-found stylistic focus and brings her a step closer to metal. But unfailingly horrid vocals undercut the music's larger-than-life potential. Her instrumental skills steadily improving, Juncosa desperately needs to hitch her britches to a band with a real singer and a more talented songwriter. [i]

See also *SWA*.

TODAY WONDER

See *Laughing Clowns*.

TOKEN ENTRY

Ready or Not Here We Come EP (Turnstyle Tunes) 1985
From Beneath the Streets (Positive Force) 1987
Jaybird (Hawker) 1988 ●
The Weight of the World (Emergo) 1990 ф

Formed in 1980 as Gilligan's Revenge and renamed in 1984, Queens' Token Entry has survived a number of lineup changes (drummer Ernie Parada is the only remaining original member) to become one of New York City's most versatile and respected skatepunk groups. With vocalist Anthony Comunale (now fronting Killing Time), the quartet released the 7-inch **Ready or Not** EP in '86: all four tracks resurfaced on the first LP, but with Timmy Chunks snagging the mic. Despite Tim's off-key moments, his exuberance propels the band, especially on "Look Around," "Over You" and "The Edge." Between bullets of unrefined energy lurks a sense of melody, streaks of tempo changes and guitarist Mickey Neal's metallic twist.

Produced by Bad Brains guitarist Dr. Know (Gary Miller), **Jaybird** anchors the Token Entry rhythm section and inflates the overall sound. Most of the highlights are on Side One: the raging opener ("The Fire"), the infectious chants on "The Bright Side" and the guitars that spiral through "The Whip." The flipside glides into a more basic rock groove with some psychedelics on "Pink Things" and the CD bonus track, an off-the-cuff cover of "Born to Be Wild." Sticking with Dr. Know but debuting a new bassist and a different guitar player, **Weight of the World** adds a bit of Chili Peppers thrash-funk to Token Entry's expanding stylistic repertoire. [mg]

RUSS TOLMAN

Totem Poles and Glory Holes (Down There-Restless) 1986
Down in Earthquake Town (nr/Demon) 1988 (Skyclad)
  1989 ●

RUSS TOLMAN AND THE TOTEM POLEMEN

Goodbye Joe (Skyclad) 1990 ●

The (intentionally?) shoddy self-production on former True West leader Tolman's eccentric solo debut covers up any of the guitarist's potential vocal inadequacies in a blur of flat, boomy sound; there's enough echo on the rhythm section to fill the Grand Canyon. (Maybe that's where this was recorded.) Fortunately, Tolman's spirit and songwriting aptitude are strong even if the audio is weak—cheap bootleg ambience only adds to the outlaw fun.

On **Down in Earthquake Town**, Tolman takes the opposite extreme: such production frills as horns, girl-group singers, accordion and mandolin give the songs buoyancy and lightness. Tolman's voice is thin and twangy, like a Fender Telecaster. With songs about "Vegas," "Palm Tree Land" and other scenes from the West Coast underbelly, **Earthquake Town** has a kind of slouchy sleaziness, songs of slot machines and crumbling relationships.

Goodbye Joe falls somewhere between its predecessors, more polished than **Totem Poles** but packing more of a rock wallop than **Earthquake Town**. Tolman finally seems to have settled into a solo persona—a slightly nostalgic, world-weary Everyguy who's willing to let dreams and reminiscences serve as his adventures. The imagery of bends in the road and rainbows mined for pots of gold may not be new, but Tolman gives them resonance and authenticity. [i/kss]

See also *True West*.

ED TOMNEY/JONATHAN BOROFSKY

See *Rage to Live*.

TOM TOM CLUB

Tom Tom Club (Sire) 1981 ●
Close to the Bone (Sire) 1983
Boom Boom Chi Boom Boom (nr/Fontana) 1988 (Sire)
  1989 ●

Tom Tom Club provides light refreshment for Talking Heads Tina Weymouth (bass) and her husband Chris Frantz (drums). Although their friend-filled albums ap-

683

pear during lulls in Heads activity, the first gained its own momentum with two popular dance tracks: "Wordy Rappinghood" and "Genius of Love." Weymouth and her three sisters' airy vocals sound delightfully innocent over steady but unthreatening rhythm. **Close to the Bone** continues in the same whimsical and sensitive vein (e.g., "Pleasure of Love"). Both records skirt cloyingness, saved by the Tom Tommers' selfconsciousness.

Two of the four Weymouth sisters dropped out after **Close to the Bone**, leaving a less distinctive vocal signature. Beware the British version of **Boom Boom Chi Boom Boom**; the band obviously did, replacing four of its ten songs for the domestic release. The new tracks, all during the first half, build up a serious power surge without sacrificing danceability. (One of these, "I Confess," is a total overhaul of "Mighty Teardrop" from the British album.) So if you're denied the chance to hear Frantz declaim Bob Dylan's "She Belongs to Me," you still get the drummer's audacious "Challenge of the Love Warriors"—heavy breathing looped with percussion—and all the Talking Heads plus Lou Reed performing the latter's "Femme Fatale." The track-switching had no effect on **Boom Boom Chi Boom Boom**'s US success (minimal), but considerably improved an album that, like its predecessors, is as much fun for as deep as you care to listen. (The US CD adds one bonus track.)   [si]

See also *Talking Heads*.

TONE-LŌC

Lōc-ed After Dark (Delicious Vinyl-Island) 1989 ●

Never underestimate the power of a solid left hook or the importance of a good corner man: the nagging guitar figures in "Wild Thing" (sampled from Eddie Van Halen) and "Funky Cold Medina" (both co-written by Marvin Young, aka Young MC) helped make the unmistakable hoarse voice of LA's likable Tone-Lōc (Tony Smith) a radio staple in 1989 and **Lōc-ed After Dark** the second rap album (after the Beastie Boys) to top the pop charts. The LP has both of the hits (including an unexpurgated "Wild Thing"), an ode to pot ("Cheeba Cheeba") and more of the same lighthearted party fun, all delivered with Lōc's engaging good humor.   [i]

TONES ON TAIL

Tones on Tail EP (nr/4AD) 1982
Burning Skies EP (nr/Situation Two) 1983
'Pop' (nr/Beggars Banquet) 1984 (Beggars Banquet-PVC) 1986 ●
Tones on Tail (nr/Situation Two) 1985
Night Music [CD] (Beggars Banquet-PVC) 1987 ●
Tones on Tail (Beggars Banquet-RCA) 1990 Φ

Originally formed in 1981 as a duo of Bauhaus guitarist Daniel Ash and Bauhaus roadie-turned-bassist Glenn Campling, Tones on Tail was a generally interesting, shortlived experiment in various styles. When the parent group called it a day in 1983, Ash chose to make this modest side project a going concern, and Bauhaus drummer Kevin Haskins hopped aboard to make it a fulltime trio.

Tones on Tail, a full-length album stitched together from the band's first three records—the initial self-titled EP, "There's Only One" 45 and the **Burning Skies EP** (Haskins' ToT debut)—careens from languid, whispered rock to jumpy light funk to spare atmospheric soundtracks, and offers very little songwriting content, merely scanty ideas in service of largely pointless studio fiddling.

But while **'Pop'**—the trio's only actual album—reveals some draggy recidivist Bauhaus tendencies, it also has real songs of modern music that show taste, delicacy and moderate imagination. "Lions," for instance, roams an attractively light synth-samba range while proffering lyrics like "Lions always hit the heights/'Cause to kill it's always the easy way out." Say what? The multi-movement "Real Life" blends acoustic guitar picking with hushed vocals, angry lyrics and weird sound effects—neo-Yes? (The US version is revised, with the replacement of three tracks by subsequent singles, including "Go!," a B-side that took off in American clubs, and "Christian Says.")

Ash became unsatisfied with Campling, however, and after a US tour in the fall of '84, Tones on Tail was shelved. At this point, on the heels of erstwhile Bauhaus bassist David J.'s departure from the Jazz Butcher and the utter failure of Peter Murphy's experiment with Dalis Car, a full-scale Bauhaus reunion was planned. When Murphy backed out, the three remaining members decided to continue under the name Love and Rockets.

With the admonition "don't rock—wobble," the 72-minute **Night Music** CD compiles sixteen previously released items, including most of **'Pop'**, half of **Tones on Tail**, the wonderfully bent dance kineticism of "Go!" and a horrible, bootleg-quality live "Heartbreak Hotel." Three years later, the same basic assortment of tracks was repackaged, under the weary title of—you guessed it—**Tones on Tail**. This latest compilation (seventeen tracks on CD; the cassette adds "Rain," "A Bigger Splash" and "Means of Escape") gets the slight nod over **Night Music**, as it has some different tracks (replacing "Heartbreak Hotel" with the stellar single "Performance" and adding two others) and liner notes instead of a lyric booklet.   [i/gef]

See also *Bauhaus, Love and Rockets*.

WINSTON TONG

See *Tuxedomoon*.

TOO MUCH JOY

Green Eggs and Crack (Stonegarden) 1987
Son of Sam I Am (Alias) 1988 (Alias-Giant-Warner Bros.) 1990 ●
Cereal Killers (Alias-Giant-Warner Bros.) 1991 Φ

Bands comprised of young suburban smartalecks are frequently too clever by half, tripping over themselves in endless demonstrations of irony. This flip quartet from Scarsdale, New York, however, is just clever enough. Playing charming, melodic guitar rock (developing a surprising hip-hop consciousness along the way), TMJ carefully navigates the funny-rock straits between making jokes and being one, occasionally showing flashes of inspiration.

Despite inconsistent production, the unassuming **Green Eggs and Crack** (assembled from four years' worth of sessions) is a neat little pop record. In a personable boy-next-door voice, Tim Quirk sings entertaining wry odes to "James Dean's Jacket," bogus cartography ("Map Like Mine"), romance ("Bored with Love") and malt liquor ("No Beer") that are each worth a smile or three.

Sharpening both instrumental skills and songwriting wit, TMJ hit their stride on **Son of Sam I Am**, an accomplished rock album that mixes silly history lessons ("My Past Lives," "1964"), snotty social (un-) consciousness ("Making Fun of Bums") and a poke at fallen rock idols ("Hugo!") with an impressive melodic rewrite of L.L. Cool J's "That's a Lie" that elevates dishonesty to an art. The 1990 CD/cassette reissue substitutes a remix of "That's a Lie," removes the borrowed Bozo intro to "Clowns" and adds two: a cover of Terry Jacks' "Seasons in the Sun" and a tribute to the Mekons.

Produced by Paul Fox (who did XTC's **Oranges & Lemons**), **Cereal Killers** organizes TMJ's maturing humor and instrumental skills into presentable catchy college rock. Whether griping goodnaturedly about the unfair seductive advantage of Britons ("Long Haired Guys from England"), recounting a sorry vacation story ("Thanksgiving in Reno") or revisiting a favorite topic ("King of Beers," sure to become a frat-house classic), the band's puppy-dog personality makes **Cereal Killers** a lightweight smileathon.   [i]

TOO $HORT

Life Is … Too $hort (Dangerous Music-RCA) 1988 ●
Born to Mack (Dangerous Music-Jive) 1989 ●
Short Dog's in the House (Dangerous Music-Jive) 1990 ●

Without suggesting that he's emblematic of California's early slow-to-grow rap scene, Oakland's Too $hort (Todd Shaw) is a jimmy-come-lately cliché of routine beats and halfhearted generic sex'n'gold rhymes. While half of the debut is harmless/worthless autobiography, playboy tracks like "Pimp the Ho" and "CussWords" (on the X-rated side of **Life Is …**) are crude and stupid.

Born to Mack has slightly better tracks (thanks in part to a scratch DJ on the job), but nothing more intellectually stimulating to offer than jailbait troubles (in "Little Girls") and the ever-willing big-booty fantasies of "Freaky Tales" (essentially a nasty hip-hop answer to the Nails' "88 Lines About 44 Women").

Too $hort wised up a bit on the third album, keeping his hot dog zipped up (except in the dubious joke of "Pimpology") to reveal a solid social conscience, repeatedly attacking crack (especially in "The Ghetto," a mushy soul track ruined by an absurdly sung refrain) and making a clever statement against censorship in "Ain't Nothin' but a Word to Me," a two-team performance with Ice Cube that intentionally obliterates the pair's stream of profanity with maddening beeps.   [i]

TOP JIMMY & THE RHYTHM PIGS

Pigus Drunkus Maximus (Down There-Restless) 1987

Chris Morris' LP liner notes characterize Top Jimmy as a legendary live attraction in Los Angeles, a true-blue white bluesman with a wide, star-studded following. (Van Halen wrote and recorded a song about him on **1984**.) Regardless of where the burly singer and his crackerjack band (unrelated to the Texas Rhythm Pigs) come from, it's easy enough to hear where they're going—straight into the history books, for playing blues and old-fashioned rock'n'roll with more electric panache and gusto than almost anyone else currently on the scene. Covering Merle Haggard, Bob Dylan, Willie Dixon and Jimi Hendrix with unwavering comprehension and equally enthusiastic sweaty abandon, these no-shit bar-busters turn their debut LP into a resounding lesson on how it's s'posed to be done. Steve Berlin produced and plays sax; guest star Don Bonebrake (of X) does most of the drumming.   [i]

TORCH SONG

See *William Orbit*.

TOURÉ KUNDA

Touré Kunda (Fr. Celluloid) 1981 (Celluloid) 1987 ●
Ém'ma Africa (Les Frères Griots) (Fr. Celluloid) 1982
    (Celluloid) 1987 ●
Amadou-Tilo (Celluloid) 1984
Casamance au Clair de Lune (Celluloid) 1984 ●
Live Paris–Ziguinchor (Celluloid) 1984 ●
Natalia (Celluloid) 1985 ●
81/82 [CD] (Celluloid) 1986 ●
83/84 [CD] (Celluloid) 1986 ●
Karadindi (Celluloid) 1988 ●

The international appeal of Senegal's Touré brothers—Ismaila, Sixu Tidiane and Ousmane—must be attributed in large part to their soothingly mellifluous voices, tones that wash over the listener like warm milk. Of course, their sultry and tasteful integration of Afro-urban and Western dance music have something to do with it too. Like traditional griot songs (they themselves belong to the artisan class), many of their lyrics consist of simple reflections on nature and family life. But after first performing on such traditional instruments as balafon and kora, they gradually integrated electric guitars and keyboards into their arrangements.

Their first album, **Touré Kunda**, contains beautiful melodies over reggae and Arabic rhythms, along with unobtrusive hints of rock music. **Ém'ma Africa**, featuring the music of Sixu and Ismaila, has a notable Jamaican influence.

Amadou-Tilo memorializes Amadou Touré, who died (reportedly from exhaustion) in 1983. The group next recorded an acoustic album of traditional songs, **Casamance au Clair de Lune**, before going high-tech (with Fairlight synthesizers!) under the sway of producer Bill Laswell and his studio regulars (including former Parliament keyboardist Bernie Worrell, guitarist Nicky Skopelitis and drummer Aïyb Dieng) on **Natalia**. The live album, recorded at various dates in Western Africa around the end of 1983, includes sparkling performances of songs from **Amadou-Tilo**, as well as earlier albums. The Tourés are backed by a female singer and six musicians, playing keyboards, sax, flute, guitar, bass and drums. **81/82** and **83/84** are compilations.   [rg/i]

685

TOURISTS

The Tourists (nr/Logo) 1979
Reality Effect (nr/Logo) 1979 (Epic) 1979
Luminous Basement (Epic) 1980
Tourists (nr/RCA Int'l) 1981
Should Have Been Greatest Hits (Epic) 1984 ●

In light of Dave Stewart and Annie Lennox's subsequent work as Eurythmics, the Tourists were remarkably low on vitality and originality, content to rehash '60s American acid and folk-rock. Symptomatic of the quintet's shortcomings, the crowning achievement of their three albums was a dull remake of Dusty Springfield's "I Only Want to Be with You."

Lennox, who later proved to be a far more expressive vocalist, here sings with strength but no character; duets with guitarist Peet Coombes (the band's primary songwriter) resemble the Jefferson Airplane. Elsewhere, the group recalls It's a Beautiful Day, the Byrds, Mamas and Papas, the Who and others. The Tourists were so busy aping others that if they had had a personality to call their own, they probably wouldn't have known what to do with it. It's a shame, because some bands have successfully absorbed and adapted these same musical prototypes with much greater élan. At their best, the Tourists could only imitate. (Proof that derivation never ends, **The Tourists'** mod-pop "Blind Among the Flowers" could be the stylistic blueprint for the Primitives.)

The US version of **Reality Effect** is actually a mixture of the band's first two British releases. **Tourists** (1981) and **Should Have Been Greatest Hits** are compilations.   [i]

See also *Eurythmics*.

FRANK TOVEY

Snakes & Ladders (Mute-Sire) 1986 ●
The Fad Gadget Singles (Mute-Sire) 1986 ●
Civilian (Mute-Restless) 1988 ●
Tyranny and the Hired Hand (Mute-Restless) 1989 ●

FRANK TOVEY & THE PYROS

Grand Union (Mute) 1991 φ

FAD GADGET

Fireside Favourites (nr/Mute) 1980
Incontinent (nr/Mute) 1981
Under the Flag (nr/Mute) 1982
Gag (nr/Mute) 1984

The enigmatic Frank Tovey (formerly known as Fad Gadget) is a creative and unpredictable writer, singer and performer whose records all differ considerably from each other; he's an acquired taste with little consistency. After an eerie second 45 ("Ricky's Hand," on which Mute head Daniel Miller contributes synthesizer and Fad plays a "Black and Decker V8 double speed electric drill"), he released **Fireside Favourites**, an album that closely resembles early Human League. Except for the title track, which bounces along cheerfully, the basic mixture is dour vocals, heavy, repetitive bass lines, solid drums and odd noises. Tacky tunes like "Coitus Interruptus" only cheapen the proceedings.

Incontinent, which pursues the grubbier side of Fad Gadgetry, employs more instrumental variety and better production. Forgetting tripe like "Swallow It" and the charming title tune, some of this is interesting enough, but none is really involving; overall, the self-indulgent album rambles incoherently.

Taking a major leap towards lyrical and musical maturity, **Under the Flag** joins pristine production quality with a no-nonsense synth drive that could pass for dance music, and shows absorption of a mild soul influence. (Then-labelmate Alison Moyet sings on a few tracks and even adds saxophone to one.) The funky approach gives Tovey a direct and accessible sound, but that's not necessarily an accomplishment—it's hard to avoid the feeling that he's slumming in such relatively commercial seas.

By the time of his first American release, Tovey had retired his alter-ego. The lively dance-rock—solid beats, strong synth lines, spurious electronic noises and occasional guitar solos and funk bass—on **Snakes & Ladders** alternately suggests contemporaneous Wire and Human League, but Tovey can hardly be accused of imitating anyone. His sense of humor makes "Collapsing New People" (retrieved from the British-only **Gag**) a satiric treat; "Luxury" and the poetic but dull "Small World" display an unexpectedly serious and mature side.

The Fad Gadget Singles offers eleven peeks at Tovey's past, from his overlong and rudimentary 1979 debut ("Back to Nature" b/w "The Box") and "Ricky's Hand" to 1984's "Collapsing New People." Most of these tracks are available on albums, and none are particularly essential, but new fans may find it an agreeable means to sample and catch up on his import-only releases.

Hardened by its grim indictments of political strife, violence and modern urban life, **Civilian** sends Tovey to an adventurous land wherein percussion and triggered electronic soundmakers take the lead. Interestingly, rather than underscore the album's focus on (generally not dance-oriented) rhythm, the mix allows vocals and the scanty melody instruments a fair chance to compete. If not for Tovey's firm grip on song structure, this radical record might have turned into an endurance test. As it is, **Civilian** poses its intriguing challenge without discouraging participation.

Never one to repeat himself, Tovey next corralled a bunch of acoustic musicians and turned his attentions to American labor ballads. Despite the anomaly of an electronic baby strumming politely in the folk woods, the delightful **Tyranny and the Hired Hand** is successful on its own terms. Tovey's courageous defiance of stylistic preconceptions may not have aided his commercial career any, but he deserves credit for exceedingly fine taste in both material ("Sixteen Tons," "Joe Hill," "Pastures of Plenty," "North Country Blues") and execution.   [i]

See also *Boyd Rice*.

TOYAH & FRIPP

See *Robert Fripp*.

TOY LOVE

See *Tall Dwarfs*.

TRAGICALLY HIP

The Tragically Hip (MCA) 1987
Up to Here (MCA) 1989 ●
Road Apples (MCA) 1991 φ

An effective blend of garage angst, country spirit and jangle-pop uplift, this badly named quintet from Kingston, Ontario made its just-left-of-center Canadian debut on an independent mini-album, later given an American release. Confident and well-articulated, "Small Town Bringdown" and "Evelyn" are sturdy and catchy pop-rock, the unchallenging sort of quality material that makes a Thursday night bar band worth sticking around to hear.

The full-length **Up to Here** is bigger and harder, sacrificing some of the melodic appeal for stiff-backed guitar power and pretty routine heartland rock. As a result, Gordon Downie wraps his pipes—a powerful, quivery mixture of Michael Hutchence and John Cougar Mellencamp—around songs with interesting lyrics that are more geared to arenas than taverns.

Produced by Don Smith, the bluesy **Road Apples** integrates the band's upwardly mobile aspirations and down-home roots with a bit more subtlety and conviction. The record is strictly commercial but frequently credible, with a smoky atmosphere and a funky swing that makes tracks like "Twist My Arm" and "Bring It All Back" (which has a killer guitar solo that sounds like Neil Young working the wah-wah pedal) uncommonly tasty. [i]

TRAGIC MULATTO

Judo for the Blind (Alternative Tentacles) 1984
Locos por el Sexo (Alternative Tentacles) 1987 ●
Hot Man Pussy (Alternative Tentacles) 1989 ●
Chartreuse Toulouse (Alternative Tentacles) 1990

If you aren't totally repelled by the first album's title or indescribably grotesque cover painting, you may find yourself enthralled by Tragic Mulatto's bizarre musical universe. The five members—whose names are given as Fluffy, Blossom, Flossy, Sweetums and A Piece of Eczema—collectively sing and play bass, drums, trumpet and sax. Produced with little sonic élan by Dead Kennedy bassist Klaus Flouride, parts sound like jazzy Flipper; an ominous rock rumble with jagged horn noise and dramatic vocals. Some numbers are faster and well-organized to the point where they resemble a '40s big band on bad drugs; others could be an incompetent jazz combo vainly tuning up while someone soundchecks the microphones.

A suspiciously rechristened quartet (Reverend Elvister Shanksly, Flatula Lee Roth, Jazzbo Smith and Richard Skidmark) turned up for the salacious second LP (pointedly numbered VIRUS 69), a wild honking noise party that includes such brilliantly titled scatological creations as "Swineherd in the Tenderloin," "Underwear Maintenance" (a detailed paean to menstruation) and a sex manual titled "Twerpenstein." Strangely, the music is really good, with enough structural backbone to give the songs non-satirical legitimacy. Flatula the female vocalist (who triples on sax and tuba) is wonderful, and the taste-is-no-obstacle lyrics are funnier than a poke in the eye with a sharp stick. Fans of the vulgar but hysterical could do worse than to bathe in this delectable cesspool.

Hot Man Pussy presents a disheveled roar of improvisational guitar-and-sax noise over which Fistula (for it is she) and the Rev. E. Shanksley bellow songs like "She's a Ho," "My Name Is Not O'Neill" and the

outstanding *Blue Velvet*-quoting "Mr. Cheese." The incoherent blur of feedback and neck-wringing gets fairly numbing, but two digressions—the tuba'n'banjo closer ("The Sheriff of Weed") and Fistula's operatic vocal on "Hardcore Bigot Scum Get Stabbed"—provide welcome breaks in the action. (The CD also contains **Locos por el Sexo.**)

A well-rehearsed cover of Slade's "I Don't Mind" (with mondo guitar and a bit of tuba) gets **Chartreuse Toulouse** off to an excellent start, and the album rarely loses momentum from there, although the shrill "My Mother" and the lengthy and monotonous "Scabs on Lori's Arm" are hazards to avoid. The solidly constructed (and, except for "Bathroom at Amelia's," conceptually tamer) songs, Flatula's down-to-business Grace Slick-style singing and the quintet's ability to follow a musical road map through a squealing storm of six-string horror (shifting into acoustic gear on a couple of folky tracks!) make this psychedelic trip one of Tragic Mulatto's great adventures. [i]

TRANSLATOR

Heartbeats and Triggers (415-Columbia) 1982
No Time Like Now (415-Columbia) 1983
Translator (415-Columbia) 1985
Evening of the Harvest (415-Columbia) 1986
Everywhere That I'm Not—A Retrospective (415-Columbia) 1986

Formed in Los Angeles in 1979, this talented quartet really got rolling after moving to San Francisco. Translator's music encompasses elements of traditional folk-rock, adding modern sounds, novel ideas and cool deadpan pop—simply put, diversity makes Translator fine and often fascinating. Singing guitarists Steve Barton and Robert Darlington have a wide stylistic arsenal and each has the ability to write varied songs of quality and endurance. **Heartbeats and Triggers**, produced by David Kahne, is a great debut album with very few weak tracks.

No Time Like Now contains another batch of melodic and rocking tunes played with ringing guitars and attractive harmonies; unfortunately, a lot of the songs don't wash. While "Un-Alone," "Break Down Barriers" and the title track keep the musical faith, "L.A., L.A." is a trite, gimmicky digression and "I Hear You Follow" is too reserved. Others are equally unprepossessing or simply plain. Stick with the first album.

Translator, produced by Ed Stasium, is for the most part a return to form. "Gravity" is as good as anything they've done; other tunes maintain a tasteful, invigorating blend of vocals, rhythm guitars and intelligent songwriting. The biggest problem here is time: for a third album, they're not really going anywhere new creatively, and commercial success still seems well over the horizon.

Perhaps that frustration explains the radically different album that followed: the one-take guitar rock on **Evening of the Harvest** scarcely resembles prior Translator music. To be fair, this isn't your average numb-skull arena rubbish, but the muscle comes as an unwelcome shock. Each track includes (individually credited) guitar riffing, but most retain a trace of the band's melodicism amid the audio clutter.

Translator broke up in '86. The career-summing

Everywhere That I'm Not draws from all four albums, adding one otherwise non-LP bonus: a version of Jefferson Airplane's "Today." The track selection isn't ideal, but it's a fair representation of this special group's work.   [i]

TRANSVISION VAMP
Pop Art (Uni) 1988 ●
Velveteen (MCA) 1989 ●
Little Magnets vs. the Bubble of Babble (MCA) 1991 ●

Anyone harboring the illusion that American teenagers have worse taste than their British counterparts have only to note that this pathetic glam-pop band reached the UK Top 5 with its first album and topped the charts there with its second. The less offensive of the two, **Pop Art** is a flimsy but tuneful put-up job built around singer Wendy James' weak voice and petulant pout. Besides a lame rendition of Holly Vincent's "Tell That Girl to Shut Up," the quintet makes a charmlessly selfconscious stab at rockabilly (Sigue Sigue style), attempts to ape T. Rex, Blondie and the Primitives and generally does some of the things worthless bands with no imagination are known for.

Again jointly produced by Duncan Bridgeman and Zeus B. Held, **Velveteen**—which announces itself as "Born to Be Sold"—sheds any pretense of pop innocence and relies on crude-sounding programmed keyboards and deeply unoriginal music. (In the most obvious instance, "Baby I Don't Care" is "Hang on Sloopy" with different words.) James' dissolute voice is already shot to hell, and the album should be an embarrassment to all concerned.   [i]

TRASH CAN SINATRAS
Cake (Go! Discs-London) 1990 φ

Proudly reclaiming the joyous pop sound of such early-'80s Postcard bands as the Bluebells, Orange Juice and Aztec Camera, this young Scottish quintet parlays a rush of ringing guitars and rich broguish harmonies into an exceptionally good debut album. Roger Bechirian and John Leckie each produced tracks on the pristine-sounding **Cake**, adding an occasional light brush of cool jazz to the folky spines of the band's witty and agile tunes. While there might be a tad too much Morrissey in "The Best Man's Fall," songs like "Obscurity Knocks," "Only Tongue Can Tell" and "Thrupenny Tears" are calling cards of a bright new talent.   [i]

TREAT HER RIGHT
Treat Her Right (Soul Selects) 1986 (RCA) 1988 ●
Tied to the Tracks (RCA) 1989 ●

PINK CADILLAC
Pink Cadillac EP (Alpha-Media) 1983

Not quite a blues band, not exactly swamp trash and too stylized for basic rock'n'roll, this Massachusetts quartet (which features David Champagne, formerly of Shane Champagne, a Rumour-like outfit which issued several singles around the turn of the decade, and Pink Cadillac, a sharp rockabilly-*cum*-rock'n'roll trio) uses guitar, slide guitar, harmonica, ultra-simple drumming and exotic taste in cover versions to come up with a hybrid that bears equally faint similarity to Creedence

Clearwater and the Violent Femmes. Before ending with a James Blood Ulmer (!) number, **Treat Her Right** explores some intriguing terrain of its own, hindered only by lyrics that rely on tough-guy clichés and get a bit dumb in spots.

Produced by Don Gehman, the stylish and self-assured **Tied to the Tracks** gives Captain Beefheart's "Hit a Man" the Treat Her Right treatment and surrounds it with strong and memorable originals individually written and sung by Champagne ("Picture of the Future") and Mark Sandman ("Marie," "Junkyard"), all given added juice by Jim Fitting's wailing harp work.
[i]

TREES
Sleep Convention (MCA) 1982

A one-man synth army from San Diego, California, Dane Conover (here dubbed Trees) offers a wonderful collection of modern musical ideas and clever tunes that efficiently combine up-to-date electronics with old-fashioned rock instruments, tossing in inventive production and intelligent, provocative lyrics. **Sleep Convention** is a stunning debut which shows remarkable originality and talent. That this record died the commercial death is not just incomprehensible, it's criminal.
[i]

TREPONEM PAL
Treponem Pal (RC-Roadracer) 1989 ●
Aggravation (RC-Roadracer) 1991 ●

Treponem Pal *hates* you. And your mother, your family and, from the sounds of it, everyone and everything else as well. Hatched in a country with a weak rock history, Treponem Pal formed in Paris in 1986, taking their name from a syphilis virus. While the quartet's brutal sound is rooted in the bludgeoning, beyond-metal grind of early Head of David, Voivod and Gore, singer Marco Neves (who says, in his best broken English, that "musically we enter in the person we hate") has a terrifyingly distinctive slasher-movie rasp and spews some of the most aggressive lyrics you'll encounter anywhere: a track on the first album (produced by Franz Treichler of the Young Gods) is called "Soft Mouth Vagina."

Aggravation offers an even more deeply distilled breed of hate, honed by an improved five-piece lineup and sharper production by Roli Mosimann (Swans, That Petrol Emotion, etc.). Once again, the band ventures deep into the heart of darkness and emerges, dripping blood and guts, wielding an evil grin and some horrible medieval torture device, harnessing the essence of fear and loathing with a power comparable to a Butthole Surfers live show. To underscore the album's ambience, a jolting cover of Kraftwerk's "Radioactivity" actually adds *warmth*.   [ja]

TRIFFIDS
Treeless Plain (nr/Hot-Rough Trade) 1983
Raining Pleasure (nr/Hot-Rough Trade) 1984
Field of Glass (nr/Hot-Rough Trade) 1985
Love in Bright Landscapes (Hol. Hot-Megadisc) 1986
Born Sandy Devotional (Hot-Rough Trade) 1986

In the Pines (nr/Hot-Rough Trade) 1986
The Peel Sessions EP (nr/Strange Fruit) 1987
Calenture (Island) 1987 ●
Holy Water EP (nr/Island) 1988 ●
The Black Swan (nr/Island) 1989 ●
Goodbye Little Boy EP (nr/Island) 1989 ●
Falling Over You EP (nr/Island) 1989 ●
Live Stockholm (Swed. MNW) 1990 ●

LAWSON SQUARE INFIRMARY

Lawson Square Infirmary EP (Aus. Hot) 1984

Although based in London since 1984, this quintet originally hails from Perth, Australia. Their musical influences, however, are strictly American. Occasionally augmenting standard rock instrumentation with strings, trumpet and pedal steel, the Triffids manage a spacious country blues-meets-Television sound.

Raining Pleasure is a lightweight, lilting album with some nice songs and more-than-competent playing, but self-righteous lyrics decrying promiscuity and alcohol are pretty much ruinous. The preachy "Property Is Condemned" is almost worthy of a TV evangelist's seal of approval.

Treeless Plain and **Field of Glass** both have more bite—"My Baby Thinks She's a Train" (from the former) sounds like the best song Tom Verlaine never wrote. (Singer/songwriter David McComb's voice bears similarity to both Verlaine and Jim Morrison.) Most of the Triffids' best early material is on **Love in Bright Landscapes**, a Dutch compilation.

Gil Norton's production on **Born Sandy Devotional** is bigger and denser than that on prior releases; while it sounds just fine and is a natural progression, one wishes that McComb's maturing songwriting talents would be allowed to stand on their own a bit more. But on the other hand, it's kind of difficult for a six-piece band (with additional backing on strings, keyboards, vibes and vocals) to be minimalist.

In the Pines strips things back down; it was recorded on an 8-track in a wool-shearing shed in the Aussie outback on a tiny budget, most of which went for beer, wine and vodka. A lot of it sounds as though it was done live, and such immediacy suits the Triffids well.

On **Calenture**, the band's US/major-label debut, McComb's sensitive, personal visions are again all but obscured by Norton's big league gloss; this time the band's personality barely surfaces. There are plenty of good songs here, mind you, they're just hidden.

The **Holy Water** EP combines the title tracks from **Calenture** and **Raining Pleasure** with "Red Pony" from **Treeless Plain** and the band's cover of the Beatles' "Good Morning Good Morning" from the **Sgt. Pepper Knew My Father** benefit album.

The **Black Swan** finds the Triffids scrambling to come up with something new. The first side dabbles in country, nightclub jazz, off-center doo-wop, strangely arranged funk and even pseudo-rap ("Falling Over You," also the title cut of an EP). Arrangements are jammed with incongruous drum machines, bouzouki, operatic background vocals and electric cello (?). Side Two starts off with "The Clown Prince," which attempts to combine flamenco and French café accordion music. Who told them to try so hard? Just sounding like

the Triffids should suffice. Despite quality material, **The Black Swan** ends up drowning in its own excesses. The live LP is a career-spanner: a dozen songs recorded in Sweden in 1989.

Completists will want the **Peel Sessions** EP: three songs from May 1985. True fans should also be on the lookout for the Triffids' pseudonymous releases under the name Lawson Square Infirmary. The 1984 12-inch is a bouncy visit to informal jug-band music: six enticing original folk songs winningly performed with low-key rustic rambunctiousness. [dgs/i]

TRIO

Trio (nr/Mobile Suit Corporation) 1982
Live im Frühjahr 82 [tape] (Ger. Mercury) 1982
Trio EP (Mercury) 1982
Trio and Error (Mercury) 1983
Bye Bye (Ger. Mercury) 1983 ●

Originally issued in Germany in 1981, Trio's Klaus Voorman-produced debut album was updated to include their European million-seller, "Da Da Da ich lieb dich nicht du liebst mich nicht aha aha aha." (With the lyrics redone in English, the song was popular in dance clubs outside Germany as well.) Compared to the rest of the album, though, the minimalist hit sounds nearly symphonic; **Trio** is basically guitar and drums behind monotonal (but bilingual) vocals. Lyrics are obsessed with lousy relationships and steeped in black humor—sometimes just blackness without the humor. But the band's brutally primitive sound announces itself first.

The cassette-only **Live im Frühjahr 82** essentially reprises the album, emphasizing guitar for a hot sound, and includes between-song raps *auf deutsch*. The 12-inch **Trio** EP consists of five tracks from the album of the same name (including six-plus minutes of the English-language "Da Da Da") plus a later single, "Anna."

After that tentative step, Trio's American label took the plunge with **Trio and Error**, which *also* includes "Da Da Da"; the new material—almost all in English—is a little more musical and only a little less downbeat. But the naïveté is charming.

With **Bye Bye**, Trio departed roughly the same as they entered: simple, witty and sarcastic in two languages. A '50s revivalist spirit informs the crazed guitar work of "Ich lieb den Rock'n'Roll" and a constipated "Tutti Frutti"; for those with longer memories, Trio thoughtfully includes an (almost) reverent version of "Tooralooralooraloo." Full-scale production on "Out in the Streets" renders it the most routine-sounding track Trio ever recorded; others (e.g., the catchy "Immer Noch Einmal") are as deliciously spartan as ever.

[si/i]

TRIPOD JIMMIE

Long Walk off a Short Pier (Do Speak) 1982
A Warning to All Strangers (All Ball) 1986

Tripod Jimmie, an Erie, Pennsylvania trio starring ex-Pere Ubu guitarist Tom Herman, inhabits a world of hypertense vocals and simple, rough, aggressive rock noise—an underground '80s revision of the power trio concept. Recorded "live on the shore of Lake Erie,"

Long Walk's eleven numbers display traces of Television, Ubu and Talking Heads—all essentially similarly minded organizations. Powerful and disquieting.

With better production and playing, **A Warning to All Strangers** organizes the trio's music into a concise attack that occasionally resembles the Minutemen. As diverse as it is emotionally intense, this anxiety-ridden collection (song titles are given under the heading "List of Worries") lurches from a barking contest to a James Brown funk breakdown to gibberish without skipping a groove. Over the rhythm section's propulsive chug, Herman's thrusting guitar chords and edgily confident shout-singing emboldens the bizarrely fascinating lyrics, making Tripod Jimmie's concerns seem very real and urgent.   [i]

See also *Pere Ubu*.

TRIP SHAKESPEARE

Applehead Man (Gark) 1988 (Clean) 1988
Are You Shakespearienced? (Gark) 1988 (Clean) 1989 ●
The Crane EP (A&M) 1990
Across the Universe (A&M) 1990 ●

This Minnesota combo mines an eclectic strain of rustic folk-pop, with an energetically quirky sound that's bohemian without being cutesy. **Applehead Man** is a spunky debut, with stylishly visceral lyrics and inventive melodies. Though the band—here a trio—doesn't yet possess the expertise to do full justice to Matt Wilson's surprisingly sophisticated compositions, the songs make it clear that this is a combo to watch.

Are You Shakespearienced? shows increased depth and a more distinctive musical voice. With upgraded production and the addition of Wilson's brother Dan as second guitarist, Trip developed an approach that's both far-reaching and personal; ditto for their odd, homespun harmonies.

Across the Universe is a too-rare example of an indie act benefiting musically from major-label treatment. With Fred Maher co-producing, the quartet tightens its sound while maintaining its identity. A new version of "Pearle," originally recorded on **Applehead Man**, demonstrates how much Trip has grown; the playing is more confident and interactive than ever, with an increased rock edge that doesn't detract from the gentle charm of "Turtledove," "Gone, Gone, Gone," "Snow Days" (sung by bassist John Munson) and "The Crane." "The Crane" was also featured on an EP released prior to **Across the Universe**, along with three dandy live versions of older Trip tunes.   [hd]

TRISOMIE 21

Million Lights (Play It Again Sam) 1987 ●
Works (Play It Again Sam) 1989 ●
T21 Plays the Pictures (Play It Again Sam) 1990 ●

Although Trisomie 21 (whose lineup includes a full member credited with "advice and assistance") has an extensive back catalogue of records at home, America has only recently begun enjoying the French quartet's unsettling mutation of lush techno-pop with industrial dance ingredients. Alternating discrete songs with bilingual semi-tuneless vocals and Hervé Lomprez's intriguing instrumentals, **Million Lights** is a continually shifting soundscape, combining keyboards, guitar, percussion, sound effects and other elements in a nicely moderated loud/soft pleasant/disturbing environment that never turns sonically hostile.

Works, however, is a hapless stab at suave continental electro-pop (including, in "The Missing Piece," a futile attempt to copy New Order), an awful album that downplays the group's adventurous side to showcase Philippe Lomprez's inept crooning, a laughable approximation of Maurice Chevalier imitating Bryan Ferry. Besides a tendency to drift along aimlessly, like Pink Floyd at its most dissolute, the spare and delicately atmospheric **Plays the Pictures**—a concept album based around movies and their music—searches out surprising contrasts through frequent use of incongruous samples.   [i]

TROTSKY ICEPICK

Poison Summer (Old Scratch) 1986 (SST) 1990 ●
Baby (SST) 1988 ●
Trotsky Icepick Presents Danny and the Doorknobs in
    'Poison Summer' (SST) 1989
El Kabong (SST) 1989 ●

DANNY AND THE DOORKNOBS

Poison Summer (Old Scratch) 1985

Formed by the unification of two talented veterans of the LA indie-rock scene—ex-100 Flowers guitarist/singer Kjehl Johansen and ex-Last keyboardist/guitarist/singer Vitus Mataré—Trotsky Icepick began life as a trio (with ex-Last drummer John Frank), striking a workable stylistic compromise between the two fraternal bands. Rather than just play airy/edgy pop (friendlier than 100 Flowers and more modern than the Last), the group hit on a Big Concept: keep the same title for every album, and change the band name instead!

Recorded two years prior to its 1985 release, Danny and the Doorknobs' clear-vinyl **Poison Summer** is a neat little pop record—underproduced and haphazard, perhaps, but sprinkled with good songs (like the title track) and skillfully varied arrangements. (Granted a more explanatory title, this debut was later overhauled—replacing several tracks with vintage outtakes—remixed and reissued in an inferior sleeve as **Trotsky Icepick Presents Danny and the Doorknobs in 'Poison Summer'**.)

The second **Poison Summer**, an entirely different 1986 LP credited from the get-go to Trotsky Icepick, was recorded as a quartet in which the arrival of a keyboardist allowed Mataré to concentrate on guitar. Harmony vocals and improvements on every front—studio sound, twin-guitar arrangements, melodies, lyrics—make the LP a treat, a crisply uncommercial demonstration of unstylized pop with intelligently offbeat lyrics.

Abandoning the name game and dispensing with keyboards entirely, Mataré and Johansen then drafted two new bandmates—ex-Leaving Trains drummer Jason Kahn and ex-Last bassist/guitarist John Rosewell—for **Baby**, a louder, thicker rock album of tuneful songs about hated crooners ("Bury Manilow"), lost loves ("Mar Vista Bus Stop," the fingerpicked folk of "Robitussin Rag") and the evils of advertising ("Don't Buy It").

Upon Kahn's departure (to join the Universal Congress Of), the Trotskys absorbed another Last alumnus (drummer Hunter Crowley, a sorry substitute) and another 100 Flowers alumnus (singer John Talley-Jones, a solid asset). Thus constituted, the quintet made **El Kabong**, a well-integrated blend of fascinating lyrics and intricately textured catchy guitar rock. Besides a cover of Magazine's "The Light Pours Out of Me," TI takes another swipe at rampant consumerism ("The Conveniences of Life") and explores bizarre corners of the imagination in weird character studies. (The CD has three bonus tracks.)   [i]

See also *Last, 100 Flowers*.

TROUBLE FUNK

Drop the Bomb (Sugar Hill) 1982
In Times of Trouble (D.E.T.T.) 1983
Saturday Night. Live! from Washington DC (Island) 1985
Trouble Over Here Trouble Over There (Island) 1987 ●

Trouble Funk belongs to Washington DC's go-go scene. Go-go is a throwback to percussive, endless-groove funk that sacrifices structure, production and slickness for loose feeling and community involvement. The bands—basically fluid rhythm sections with a few added frills—do their thing while the musicians and audience yell a whole lot of nonsense (like "Let's get small, y'all" or "Drop the bomb!") The funk is solidly Southern, with a strong James Brown flavor and tons of sloppy percussion. In no other North American music does the cowbell play such a major role.

Chuck Brown, father of go-go, developed it from drum breakdowns which he used in clubs to link Top 40 covers. Not surprisingly, he found people were grooving more on these bridges than the songs. Go-go has grown concurrently (though not as popularly) with hip-hop, and offers a spirited group alternative to beatbox isolationism. The unsophisticated grooves began to break out nationwide in '85, and Trouble Funk were quickly established as one of the genre's leaders. (They were, however, eclipsed in 1988, when E.U. had a huge smash with "Da'Butt," a number originally created for Spike Lee's *School Daze*.)

Drop the Bomb is a seminal go-go album because it was released by Sugar Hill, home of the uptown rap set. Virtually all prior go-go releases were on Washington's local T.T.E.D. (aka D.E.T.T.) label. Bronx DJs used to find the discs and soak the labels off to keep audiences (and competitors) from learning what they were playing; **Drop the Bomb** gave everyone a chance to get go-go. It also produced two classic tracks: the title tune and the monster 12-inch, "Hey Fellas." Both are wet, sticky and great for dancing. Spin them and you're part of the party.

In Times of Trouble is like two separate albums. The two sides of studio material have nowhere near the juice of the debut. The other two contain long live jams that sum up the scene. The band maintains a low-tech groove, and the four lead singers move the jam along with a lot of assistance from the crowd. It's not like the Godfather of Soul's side-long live medleys because Trouble Funk doesn't do songs: just a hot bottom, some rolling percussion, a couple of tag phrases and a lot of audience participation. The ultimate funk spirit of these sides is intoxicating. **Saturday Night** continues the fun with six long, generic demi-instrumentals (and a couple of shorter shards) wisely cut live in front of an enthusiastically cooperative crowd. Cue it up and move!

The title of **Trouble Over Here** is prophetic, as T-Funk rides off the rails in a fit of misguided stylistic ambition. With production and performing assistance by Bootsy Collins and Kurtis Blow, the studio grooves are gussied up in defiance of the band's traditional limber unpretentiousness. The familiarly mobilizing rumble'n-'shuffle bottom is intact, but the attempt to turn the grooves into songs busies up the business and blunts the infectious impact.   [jl/i]

JOHN TRUBEE AND THE UGLY JANITORS OF AMERICA

The Communists Are Coming to Kill Us! (Enigma) 1984
The Deserts of Utah [tape] (Space & Time) 1985
Naked Teenage Girls from Outer Space (Restless) 1985
Strange Hippie Sex Carnival (Ger. Musical Tragedies) 1990

Best known for his inspired 1984 novelty single "A Blind Man's Penis"—a deranged spume of dada vulgarity given an inanely straight country-western reading by one of those songs-from-your-lyrics mail-order companies—guitarist/keyboardist John Van Zelm Trubee, a frequent Zoogz Rift associate, has assembled several albums of his crank phone calls, puerile rants, rude noises and misanthropically deranged musical efforts. **The Communists Are Coming to Kill Us!**, which collects up odds and ends dating from the mid-'70s through the mid-'80s, is intermittently listenable but more frequently an offensive embarrassment.

Well on the way to working out his juvenile fixations, Trubee comes nearly correct on **Naked Teenage Girls from Outer Space**, a relatively serious jazz/rock horns'n'guitars album with perfectly reasonable—actually quite attractive—instrumentals and a few songs which manage to avoid such previously typical subject matter as genitalia and regurgitation. Even one raucous noisefest makes some artistic sense. If not for the inclusion of a couple of obnoxious telephone pranks, Trubee's creepy past would seem to be entirely behind him.   [i]

See also *Zoogz Rift*.

TRUE BELIEVERS

True Believers (Rounder-EMI America) 1986

Rank and File grad Alejandro Escovedo (guitar/vocals) and his brother Javier (guitar/vocals) spearheaded this unjustly overlooked band and album—a bristling brew of big-beat rock, rockabilly-influenced rhythms and sweaty ol' noise. The stomping "Hard Road," sexy "So Blue About You" and the country tang of "We're Wrong" deliver what they promise, meaning cathartic rock'n'roll that doesn't insult your intelligence. Jim Dickinson (Replacements, Panther Burns) produced.   [jy]

See also *Rank and File*.

TRUE SOUNDS OF LIBERTY (TSOL)

T.S.O.L. EP (Posh Boy) 1981
Dance with Me (Frontier) 1981
Beneath the Shadows (Alternative Tentacles) 1982
   (Restless) 1989 ●

Change Today? (Enigma) 1984 ●
Revenge (Enigma) 1986 ●
Thoughts of Yesterday 1981–1982 (Posh Boy) 1987 ●
Hit and Run (Enigma) 1987 ●
TSOL Live (Restless) 1988 φ
Strange Love (Enigma) 1990 φ

CATHEDRAL OF TEARS
Cathedral of Tears EP (Enigma) 1984

TENDER FURY
Tender Fury (Posh Boy) 1988 ●
Garden of Evil (Triple X) 1990 ●

True Sounds of Liberty exploded out of Long Beach in 1978 to become one of Southern California's premier hardcore bands. Their first vinyl foray is a tough, politically inspired five-song EP that bristles with excitement. Ron Emory's thrashing guitar provides a steady foundation for vocalist Jack Greggors, credited on the sleeve with "mouth and other organs." These fine songs, like "Abolish Government/Silent Majority," are super hot.

Moving from Posh Boy to Frontier, TSOL made other changes as well. For one thing, Greggors changed his name to Alex Morgon; more importantly, the group abandoned politics to join the trendy horror/shock-rock movement. Along with a cover depicting the grim reaper in a boneyard, the lyrical themes of **Dance with Me** are largely those of B-movie scare flicks, and nearly as much fun. While other bands have proven useless at this genre, TSOL succeed because their brutal, razor-edge sound keeps its musical conviction, regardless of the subject matter.

Volatility is a TSOL hallmark. **Beneath the Shadows** introduces a third label, an added keyboard player and a new drummer (plus a "new" vocalist named Jack Delauge taking over for Morgon). Oh, and they also sound totally different. Dropping any remaining connection with hardcore, this newly refined approach takes the group on a neo-psychedelic trip, but with bonus amounts of rock drive and character. A great record from an always surprising band.

Singer Jack Takeyourpick selected another surname (Loyd) and joined Cathedral of Tears, which issued a weirdly commercial six-song mini-album—raunchy guitars, synthesizers and a danceable resemblance to both the Cult and Dead or Alive.

The aptly named **Change Today?** unveils another stage in TSOL's ongoing impermanence: a new label and two new members. Stalwart guitarist Ron Emory and bassist Mike Roche are joined by Joe Wood (guitar/vocals) and Mitch Dean (drums). Fielding a whomping near-punk rock sound, the foursome is aggressive, coherent and lucid, singing shapeless, insubstantial songs that pack a sonic wallop if nothing else. Not a bad record, but not a primo effort.

Remarkably retaining both lineup and label, TSOL issued **Revenge**, a powerful LP that shows the group still vital and active. The mixture of Alice Cooper/Golden Earring-styled '70s arena rock and traditional LA punk (with a dollop of X-into-the Doors on the title track) could have soared with better (or at least more consistent) material, but there's nothing wrong with the self-assured, energetic performances. (Incidentally, **Revenge** includes a new song entitled "Change Today.")

Thoughts of Yesterday—a reissue of the first EP

with the added bonus of 1982's terrific genre-defying **Weathered Statues** 7-inch EP and a speedier alternate version of **Dance with Me**'s "Peace Thru Power"—is an essential document of a once-great band. Just try to keep from laughing at the embarrassingly fawning liner notes from label head Robbie Fields. (A bunch of tracks from punkrockers Pariah fill out the CD.)

By **Hit and Run**, TSOL's mutation from hardcore standard-bearers through progressive new wavers into tattooed blues-metal boys was complete, resulting in a record of rote fist-punchers, vigorously delivered but tired-sounding all the same. On **TSOL Live** (recorded at a California date in January '88), the band sloughs off a full set of **Change Today**-forward originals as well as who-cares covers of "All Along the Watchtower" and "Roadhouse Blues." Well-recorded, but pretty tepid.

Emory left the group during the recording of **Strange Love**, and Roche took a walk on the eve of its release, leaving TSOL with no original members. This John Jansen production is a joke—lame minor-league metal replete with stock leather'n'love clichés and sluggish playing.

In the late '80s, original TSOL mouthpiece (now billed as Jack Grisham) and skins-pounder Todd Barnes reappeared with a metal-gilded project of their own, Tender Fury. The eponymous debut (produced by Bad Religion guitarist Brett Gurewitz) is thin-sounding punky (but definitely *not* punk) rock, augmented on some fairly hooky tunes by Daniel Root's incendiary riffing and Barnes' solid drumming. In all, a not-bad effort that will come as a surprise to punkers who never thought they'd be hearing West Coast hardcore legend Grisham croon the word "baby."

Barnes and bassist Robbie Allen are conspicuously absent from **Garden of Evil**, Tender Fury's awful follow-up, produced by Hunt Sales. Half-written songs and Grisham's annoyingly hyperdramatic vocals sink this effort, though the title track is a catchy chunk of no-brainer hard-rock.   [cpl/i/db]

TRUE WEST
True West EP (Bring Out Your Dead) 1983
Hollywood Holiday (Fr. New Rose) 1983 ●
Drifters (PVC) 1984 ●
Hand of Fate (CD Presents) 1986
West Side Story (Skyclad) 1989
TV Western EP (Skyclad) 1990
Best Western EP [CD] (Skyclad) 1990 ●

FOOL KILLERS
Out of State Plates (Mad Rover) 1989 ●

True West may have been part of California's psychedelic underground, but the Davis quintet definitely had a sound and style all its own. Drawing inspiration from Syd Barrett (the band's first release was a single of his "Lucifer Sam," reprised on the EP) and Roky Erickson, they played a frenetic, dense drone with crazed guitars and dramatic vocals.

Co-produced by guitarist Russ Tolman and Dream Syndicate's Steve Wynn, **True West** is a rough, marvelous record—five slices of chaos that kick out nostalgia in favor of powerful rock with a dark, threatening ambience. Echo-laden sound gives tunes like "Hollywood Holiday" and "Steps to the Door" an unsettling noise/chaos level that considerably heightens their tension. **Hollywood Holiday** contains the entire EP plus three more-sophisticated tracks subsequently recorded with a new rhythm section. (New Rose later included **Hollywood Holiday** on its CD of **Drifters**.)

Drummer Jozef Becker left to rejoin Thin White Rope; True West recorded the **Drifters** album with his not-so-good replacement. The nine new songs (reprising "And Then the Rain" from the French LP) showcase Gavin Blair's vocals as much as Tolman's inventive, original guitar work. A strikingly good record that escapes the strictures of neo-psychedelia by incorporating folk-rock ambience, **Drifters** retains just enough raw-edged aggression to keep things from getting unacceptably melodious. "Look Around" is the clear standout, but other numbers—"Shot You Down" and "Hold On," for instance—also marry engaging sound and arrangements to solid songwriting.

After losing Tolman (and with him their edge), True West pressed on as a quartet. Despite compensatory efforts—the countryish **Hand of Fate** receives valuable guitar assistance from Matt Piucci (Rain Parade) and Chuck Prophet (Green on Red)—Tolman's departure had a major negative impact on True West. The record is by no means bad, just colorless. A careful, nostalgic cover of the Yardbirds' "Happenings Ten Years' Time Ago" lacks the energy surge needed to justify the effort.

True West broke up in 1987; **West Side Story** is a posthumous patchwork of previously unreleased studio efforts and medium-fi live performances, including fiery run-throughs of "Hollywood Holiday" and the Stooges' "1969." While there are a few finds ("Free Men Own Guns") among the outtakes, the generally disappointing material and inadequate sound quality make this a meager career appendix.

On the other hand, the 1983 demos (produced, with clear stylistic impact, by Tom Verlaine) that are on the **Best Western** CD are among the band's most striking work: an intense, lead-guitar-spiked pre-**Drifters** version of "Look Around," a clearer second rendition of **Hollywood Holiday**'s "Throw Away the Key" (with Becker turning in drastically improved drumming) and a fine studio take of **West Side Story**'s "Burn the Roses." The vinyl-only **TV Western** (any puns left?) pairs some of those tracks with an exciting trio of live items from 1985.

Singer Gavin Blair and guitarist Richard McGrath remained together after True West and became Fool Killers. **Out of State Plates** adds a country undercurrent, a Stonesy side and occasional acoustic instrumentation to the remnants of True West's measured drama, but winds up slow-moving and dull, with only a handful of lively tunes to brighten the ride. [i]

See also *Russ Tolman*.

TRUTH
Five Live EP (nr/IRS) 1984
Playground (IRS) 1985
Weapons of Love (IRS) 1987 ●
Jump (IRS) 1989 ●

Leaving behind the constricted scope of Nine Below Zero's skinny-tie R&B revivalism, singer/guitarist Dennis Greaves formed the Truth and proceeded to follow the Style Council's lead in updating '60s soul (Hammond organ, doo-wop vocal backing, shingaling rhythms) for an audience unlikely to know or care that much about the originals. After the introductory **Five Live** EP, **Playground** is a fine album of intelligent, tasteful originals played with real character and a minimum of selfconsciousness. Of special note: "Exception of Love," "I'm in Tune" (an exciting raveup) and the title track, a straight rocker.

Weapons of Love finds Greaves suffering from burgeoning Robert Palmer delusions and transparent commercial aspirations. The bombastic album veers wildly from one dodgy style (INXS, U2, etc.) to another, with nary a glimmer of originality or dignity. This is the Truth, eh?

If you can get past the spot-on Bryan Adams imitation and the cliché-addled lyrics, **Jump** isn't that bad an exemplar of easy listening commercial rock. Avoid the bombastic version of Argent's "God Gave Rock & Roll to You" (wasn't '70s radio great?); most of Greaves' originals would sound fine coming out of a car radio.

See also *Nine Below Zero*. [i]

TRYPES
See *Feelies*.

MASAMI TSUCHIYA
See *Ippu-Do*.

TUBEWAY ARMY
See *Gary Numan*.

MAUREEN TUCKER
Playin' Possum (Trash) 1981
MOE TUCKER
MoeJadKateBarry EP (50 Skidillion Watts) 1987
Life in Exile After Abdication (50 Skidillion Watts) 1989 ●

In 1981, original Velvet Underground drummer Maureen (Moe) Tucker released a one-woman album on her own Trash Records. The frantic guitar playing and cluttered sound on **Playin' Possum** could have come straight from sessions for the first Velvets album, if you can imagine that band playing "Slippin' and Slidin'," "Bo Diddley" and other oldies.

Tucker subsequently joined forces with a label run by rich'n'famous rock dilettante Penn Jillette and Florida's hardworking Velvet Underground Appreciation Society. Motley as hell but reeking with credibility and unpolished spirit, the wonderful **MoeJadKateBarry** EP (pressed on red vinyl) was recorded in six hours in a garage (how's that for poetic justice). Jad Fair (vocals) of Half Japanese and two young locals (on bass and guitar) join in for the 1986 date; the five songs cover VU obscurities ("Guess I'm Falling in Love," "Hey, Mr. Rain," "Why Don't You Smile Now"), a Jimmy Reed blues ("Baby What You Want Me to Do") and an impromptu instrumental, "Jad Is a Fink." In her own simple way, Tucker has kept the Velvets' legacy alive better than anyone else.

With the involvement of Lou Reed, Jad Fair, Daniel Johnston and Sonic Youth making it an historically significant reunion, as well as a profound inter-generational meeting of prophet and disciple, Tucker's loose and unpredictable **Life in Exile** offers a little of everything, all performed and recorded with ramshackle casualness. There's wall-rattling noise, acoustic folk (''Goodnight Irene''), rock'n'roll (a five-minute return visit to ''Bo Diddley'' with Sonic Youth's rhythm section), even a whispery version of Reed's ''Pale Blue Eyes.'' Tucker's charmingly amateurish originals include a droning guitar/piano tribute to Andy Warhol. (A subsequent three-song single combines an album track and two outtakes from the sessions.) [si/i]

See also *Half Japanese, Velvet Underground.*

TUFF DARTS

Tuff Darts! (Sire) 1978

New York's Tuff Darts will probably be best remembered (if at all) as a résumé item for Robert Gordon, who was the glam-punk band's original singer in 1976. Although he did record as a Dart on the **Live at CBGB's** compilation, Gordon was long gone by the time the band made an album of its own two years later. (The band was on hold for part of that time while guitarist/leader Jeff Salen played with Sparks.)

The Darts—a junior-league rock band with a penchant for gangster clothes—had a total of two good songs, both of which are included on the LP. Otherwise, the record ranges from simply bad to truly wretched, as on the moronic ''(Your Love Is Like) Nuclear Waste.''

See also *Robert Gordon.* [i]

NIK TURNER

See *Hawkwind.*

TUXEDOMOON

No Tears EP (Time Release) 1978 (nr/CramBoy) 1985
Scream with a View EP (nr/Pre) 1979 (Bel. CramBoy) 1985
Half Mute (Ralph) 1980 (nr/CramBoy) 1985 ●
Desire (Ralph) 1981 (nr/CramBoy) 1985 ●
Divine (nr/Operation Twilight) 1982
A Thousand Lives by Picture (Ralph) 1983
Holy Wars (Restless) 1985 ●
Ship of Fools (Restless) 1986
You (nr/CramBoy) 1987 ●
Pinheads on the Move (nr/CramBoy) 1987 ●
Suite en Sous-Sol–Time to Lose (Bel. Crammed Discs) 1987 ●
The Ghost Sonata (Bel. Crépuscule) 1991 ●

BLAINE L. REININGER/MIKEL ROUSE

Colorado Suite EP (Bel. Made to Measure) 1984 ●

BLAINE L. REININGER

Instrumentals 1982–86 (nr/Interior) 1987
Byzantium (Bel. Crépuscule) 1987
Live in Brussels 82-86 (Bel. Crépuscule) 1987 ●
Broken Fingers (Bel. Crépuscule) 1988 ●
Book of Hours (Bel. Crépuscule) 1989 ●
expatriate journals (Giant) 1989 ●

PETER PRINCIPLE

Sedimental Journey (Bel. Made to Measure) 1985 ●
Tone Poems (Bel. Made to Measure) 1988 ●

WINSTON TONG

Theoretically Chinese (Bel. Crépuscule) 1985 ●

Pioneers in performance-oriented synthesizer music, Tuxedomoon started out in San Francisco at the very beginning of that city's punk upsurge. The mercurial aggregate of musicians and artists later relocated to Belgium and became a leading light in the international post-rock avant-garde. Sidestepping the mistakes of many early synthesizer bands, Tuxmoon leavened their attack with sax and violin and were quick to integrate electronic percussion as a true substitute for real drums.

Prior to their Ralph records, Tuxedomoon had released singles and EPs on their own label. **No Tears**, a four-cut EP, is an early new wave DIY effort, which sounds coyly dated but still exciting at the time of its reissue seven years later. It was immediately obvious that Tuxedomoon was a step apart from many other bands of the era. Winston Tong had been a mime, and brought a theatrical approach to singing; plenty of synths and electronic percussion (when they were still called rhythm boxes) dominate, violin gets some use and two of the songs exceed the five-minute mark. The succeeding **Scream with a View** (also four songs) is noticeably more art-damaged; itemization of instrumentation cites parallel thirds guitar, vocal concept, six-part doo-wahs and CB interference. In retrospect, this release makes obvious the direction in which they were headed.

Half Mute is a balanced assemblage of pop (''What Use?''), futuristic chamber music (''Tritone'') and impressionistic sound collages (''James Whale''). **Desire** is a generally unsatisfying follow-up, save for a sneaky parody of ''Holiday for Strings'' entitled ''Holiday for Plywood.'' **Divine**, the score for a Maurice Béjart ballet, jettisons the synth beat that makes their best work so attractive. **A Thousand Lives by Picture** is a compilation of tracks previously issued on Ralph.

By the time of **Ship of Fools**, only Principle and singer/multi-instrumentalist Steven Brown remained from the original lineup. Trading in clever humor for selfconscious artsiness (always just beneath the surface anyway), the LP falls flat on its face, especially on the second side, where the band proffers ''pieces'' rather than songs; titles include ''A Piano Solo,'' ''Lowlands Tone Poem'' and ''Music for Piano + Guitar.'' Flirting with both light jazz and 20th-century classical styles without getting much of a grip on either, the music is about as creative as the nomenclature.

You is a squeaky-clean, virtually bloodless record of meandering jazz-rock fusion with lots of mellow trumpet and sax riffs. Yuck. In ''Never Ending Story,'' we're told ''This is only the beginning of a long story that will take many more songs to tell.'' I'm not sure if I've heard it before, but I'll stop you anyway. Side Two introduces a *Twilight Zone*-style three-part yarn spoken with minimalist backing. Skip it.

Pinheads on the Move is a two-disc compilation dating all the way back to the band's California beginnings (the title song was their first 45) and contains singles, B-sides, rehearsals, live tracks and jingles for radio programs. Most of the material and performances date from 1977-'79, and the lengthy liner notes (an excerpt from an Italian book about the band) provide an intensive history lesson.

Tuxedomoon continues to eschew the commercial

success they likely could achieve; meanwhile, the members have undertaken many outside projects. Violinist Blaine L. Reininger, Tuxmoon's co-founder, recorded **Colorado Suite** with Mikel Rouse of Tirez Tirez in 1984 as part of Crammed's Made to Measure series. The four-track, 28-minute mini-LP of a performance piece is similar to Philip Glass in its bright timbre and repetitive motifs but lacks Glass' technique of introducing changes so subtly that they're barely noticeable. This suite goes for a little while on one riff, then another similar one, then another and so on, often with Reininger's violin counterpoint dominating. Not a winner.

Reininger's **Live In Brussels 82-86** contains defensive, condescending liner notes and credits him with vocals, violin, keyboards, Captain Beefheart impersonations and snide comments. Okay. The sound—a well-played synthesized mélange, not dissimilar to early electro-pop à la Ultravox—only gets to be rough going when the vocals turn overly pretentious.

Book of Hours is an intelligent collection of songs driven by synths and guitars, but Reininger's full-of-himself voice cancels out much of what's in the plus column. An ill-advised cover of Marty Robbins' "El Paso" sounds more like a Las Vegas arrangement, and there are too many cuts with plodding tempos. Steve Brown of Tuxmoon guests.

expatriate journals is a compilation of this prolific artist's work, some of it good ("Birthday Song"), some of it weak ("El Paso" again), some of it indicative of a taste for Eurochic ("A Cafe au Lait for Mr. MXYZPTLK" and "Ralf and Florian Go Hawaiian," a song about half of Kraftwerk on holiday). Overall, an admirable showcase for Reininger's versatility.

About half of **Sedimental Journey**, bassist Peter Principle's first solo record (also from the Made to Measure collection), is a video film soundtrack. The one-man show is stylistically similar to the off-center pop of the first two Tuxedomoon albums—lots of mild synth dissonance with found voices drifting around. Agreeable enough, but nothing the band hasn't already accomplished.

Tong's solo album, **Theoretically Chinese**, features an all-star cast, including New Order's Steve Morris, ex-Magazine keyboardist Dave Formula, Jah Wobble, A Certain Ratio's Simon Topping; then-Associate Alan Rankine produced. Although literary name-dropping under the guise of inspiration is a little annoying, working with a different cast suits Tong well. The LP combines artsy dance cuts with deliberate electronic tone poems; although Tong is sometimes strangely buried in the mix, he seems in control of the proceedings. A Eurodance version of Marianne Faithful's "Broken English" concludes the album. [rnp/dgs]

See also *Tirez Tirez*.

24-7 SPYZ

Harder Than You (In-Effect) 1989 ●
Gumbo Millennium (In-Effect) 1990 ●

Although largely hidden in the sudden explosion of late-'80s thrash-funk combos, this exceptional New York quartet is virtually everything Living Colour would be if Vernon Reid weren't such an overachieving technician and Corey Glover didn't take himself so seriously. Jimi Hazel can play guitar in a variety of speed-metal, jazzbuster and post-funk styles, but spends his time contributing to the songs rather than trying to escape them with flash solos; the rhythm section moves easily from junior-gods-of-thunder to thumb-popping bass and irresistible sacroiliac adjustments. Capping it all off, singer Peter Fluid sings his lyrical mixture of African-American culture, cogent politics and punky stupidity with confidence and power.

Harder Than You is a mighty and confident debut that unabashedly pays loving respect to an influential relative ("Grandma Dynamite"), covers Black Uhuru without making a big fuss ("Sponji Reggae"), gets dumb and dirty ("New Drug"), offers a striking condemnation of the anti-democratic violence in Haiti ("Ballots Not Bullets") and rocks from wall to wall.

Employing an uninhibited stylistic palette that seems to reflect whatever springs into the Spyz's collective consciousness at any given moment, **Gumbo Millennium** winds up retreating to opposite corners of relatively serious hard-rock (still with pungent political/personal lyrics, but now employing a thick, hardened metal-*cum*-hardcore sound) and flaky digressions that don't really add up to an album. Individual tracks—like the cool fusion groove of "Dude U Knew," the ska-beat "Culo Posse" and the throbbing world report of "We'll Have Power"—are fine, but the band needs a strong outside force to focus it all into a cohesive package. Fluid and drummer Anthony Johnson left at the end of '90 and were replaced by, respectively, Jeff Broadnax and Joel Maitoza. [i]

27 VARIOUS

Hi. (Susstones) 1987
Yes, Indeed (Susstones) 1989
Approximately (Clean-Twin/Tone) 1990 ●

Debuting as a flip pop-rock duo, Minneapolis' 27 Various used the magic of overdubbing to assemble a complete guitar-band sound on the amateurishly inventive **Hi.** Clever songs (the vituperative "Principal Percival" and "Temperamental Artist," the trippy "Venetian Blinds"), nice instrumental touches and a variety of styles (including droney mod psychedelia and **Something Else**-era Kinks) suggest witty possibilities but don't quite add up.

Jettisoning the first album's topical humor and haphazard approaches, singer-guitarist-songwriter Ed Ackerson and drummer Jed Mayer drafted two new members and planted their feet firmly in the '60s on the well-produced **Yes, Indeed**. With songs like "Feedtime for Martin" and "Stick It in and Bake It," the mild-mannered quartet's accomplished mix of lightweight garage psychedelia and offbeat Anglo-pop avoids overt nostalgia in favor of more intriguingly idiosyncratic designs.

Slimming down to a trio, 27 Various came into its own on **Approximately**, an ace collection of striking songs and confident performances. Most of the tracks aren't any more derivative than the Byrdsy connotation of 12-string guitars on "I Feel Damage(d)" and "Like the Poison." But "You Look a Treat" revisits the lighter side of **Their Satanic Majesties Request** with flair, and "The Things I Wasn't Supposed to See" takes off from a couple of Beatles songs, including "She Said She Said." More than the sum of its borrowings, **Approximately** knows better than to dwell entirely in the past.   [i]

23 SKIDOO

Seven Songs EP (nr/Fetish) 1982 (nr/Illuminated) 1985
Tearing Up the Plans EP (nr/Pineapple-Fetish) 1982
The Culling Is Coming (nr/Operation Twilight) 1983 (Bel. Laylah) 1988
Urban Gamelan (nr/Illuminated) 1984
Just Like Everybody (nr/Bleeding Chin) 1986

One of England's most daringly experimental post-punk bands, 23 Skidoo are friendly with the members of Cabaret Voltaire; the two outfits once entertained thoughts of merging. But while 23 Skidoo's early avant-dancefloor style was similar to the Cabs', they've always maintained a closer link to both free-form improvisation and non-Western idioms, especially in their later work.

Seven Songs (which lists eight tracks, has nine and was reissued with twelve) is a near-brilliant fusion of funk, tape tricks and African percussion. The band switches gears effortlessly between different-yet-accessible dance tracks like "Vegas el Bandito," the ethnomusicology of "Quiet Pillage" and sound collages ("Mary's Operation"). **Tearing Up the Plans** continues in much the same vein.

On **The Culling Is Coming**, 23 Skidoo gets too obscure for its own good. The first side, recorded live at the WOMAD Festival, is a mish-mash of tape loops, random percussion and primitive horn honks which sound like dying animals and add up to third-rate Stockhausen. Side Two utilizes Balinese gamelans (tuned gongs of a sort) and sounds better thought-out. **Urban Gamelan** is a stronger album, livelier and less esoteric. As the title implies, real gamelans aren't used, but glass jugs and carbon-dioxide cylinders are. 23 Skidoo will never enjoy wide-scale popularity, but they are an earnest, disciplined band which makes uncompromising music. **Just Like Everybody** is a compilation.   [dgs]
See also *Current 93*.

22-PISTEPIRKKO

The Kings of Hong Kong (Fin. Pygmi) 1987
Bare Bone Nest (nr/Spirit-Sonet) 1990

Since debuting with a 1985 single, this trio from Finland ("22-ladybug") has taken American country, blues and psychedelia as leaping-off points to much stranger experimentation. The first album is mostly infectious garage pop powered by a roller-rink Farfisa organ, except for "Don't Try to Tease Me," which re-imagines Hank Williams with a weird accent and bizarre production values. Frontman P.K. Keränen sings bad English in one of the most endearingly odd voices this side of Daniel Johnston.

Bare Bone Nest finds the band moving into surreal fractured-blues territory where Giant Sand and Captain Beefheart might be neighbors. "Shot Bayou" is a haunting nocturne with a slide guitar and waves breaking on a beach; "Round Table Blues" layers traffic sounds, tablas and a sampled Armenian *duduk* over an acoustic Bo Diddley jangle before segueing into a dusty Texas

two-step; if that's not enough, the closing track is an extended feedback opera that purports to tell a birds-versus-bulldozers environmental story. Intoxicating and well worth seeking out.   [ws]

TWINK

See *Bevis Frond, Social Deviants*.

TWISTED ROOTS

See *D.C.3*.

2 LIVE CREW

The 2 Live Crew Is What We Are (Luke Skyywalker) 1986 (Luke) 1989 + 1991 ●
Move Somethin' (Luke Skyywalker) 1987 (Luke) 1989 + 1991 ●
As Nasty as They Wanna Be (Luke Skyywalker) 1989 (Luke) 1989 ●
As Clean as They Wanna Be (Luke Skyywalker) 1989 (Luke) 1989 + 1991 ●
Live in Concert (Effect) 1990 ●

LUTHER CAMPBELL FEATURING THE 2 LIVE CREW

Banned in the U.S.A. (Luke-Atlantic) 1990 ●

As the catalyst for a terrifying governmental attempt to censor ostensibly obscene musical expression—making it a crime in some districts to tell a dirty story with a beat—Luther Campbell, leader of the 2 Live Crew and owner of Luke (formerly Luke Skyywalker) Records, has followed Larry Flynt into the free-speech history books as another crude sleazemonger of trivial artistic merit whose prosecution nonetheless threatens basic constitutional freedoms. What Miami's 2 Live Crew does is hardly new (check old party records by Blowfly or Redd Foxx for historical precedents), but rap's enormous word-of-mouth audience turned what should have remained a fringe novelty for *Hustler* readers into a massively popular (and, unfortunately, influential) pop phenomenon. Coupled with Southern fear of a black planet, that was all it took to bring the 2 Live Crew into the crosshairs of a hysterical judiciary, resulting in the group's third album being outlawed in some counties of Southeastern Florida in June 1990.

The Crew's amateurish first album sets the basic parameters: simple boomin' tracks (the Miami sound generally uses ultra-deep synth bass as the rhythmic foundation) with scratches, obvious samples and energetic dance-party rhymes, several of which crudely discuss the group's hobby (e.g., "We Want Some P--sy!!").

Besides his improving production skills, Campbell's serious marketing savvy emerged on **Move Somethin'**, the first 2 Live Crew record to be released in both clean and dirty versions. Brother Marquis and Fresh Kid Ice make a game effort to make the expurgated version work (actually, the rewriting isn't noticeably awkward), but it winds up being a party without a bottle opener.

An emboldened and meaner-sounding Crew reached its dubious apex on the overwhelming **As Nasty as They Wanna Be** double-album and its expurgated single-album extract, **As Clean as They Wanna Be**. Although the notorious "Me So Horny"—a catchy sexcapade built around a hooker's line bitten from *Full Metal Jacket*—is fairly innocuous, other numbers like "Put Her in the Buck" and "The Fuck Shop" (which uses guitar lines from Guns n' Roses as well as the Music Explosion) are as obsessively animalistic as the most violent porno movie. That people enjoy such nauseating garbage is a really sad comment on the state of American culture. **Clean** adds a goofy frat-styled parody of Roy Orbison's "Pretty Woman" and manages to do an occasionally clever job of sanitizing "Me So Horny" and reworking tracks like "The Funk Shop." Still, the songs are about what they're about, and the euphemisms leave little doubt as to what's not being said.

With official attacks on **Nasty** turning the 2 Live Crew into a cause célèbre, the unrepentant group revamped Bruce Springsteen's "Born in the U.S.A." with specifically topical lyrics and used it as the lead-off track of **Banned in the U.S.A.**, which brought Luke under Atlantic's distribution wing. Otherwise, the album jumps back and forth between raps about the legal battle (with relevant audio actualities and fictional narration) and the Crew's traditional paeans to bodies and boning. A very strange blend but, under such weird circumstances, probably as logical as they're gonna be.

The live album—apparently the first-ever full-length rap concert LP—is a poorly recorded cattle call, in which Luke and the boys deliver a selection of their crudest sex raps (plus a couple of previously unrecorded sure-to-be-classics) to an enthusiastic Phoenix crowd. (Interesting choice of venue.) Regardless of the band's ultimate place in history, the sound of an audience cheering "Head! Booty! Cock!" is unquestionably a cultural low.   [i]

TWO NICE GIRLS

2 Nice Girls (Rough Trade) 1989 ●
Like a Version EP (Rough Trade) 1990 ●
Chloe Liked Olivia (Rough Trade) 1991 ●

Two Nice Girls began in 1985 as the duo of Gretchen Phillips (vocals/guitar) and Laurie Freelove (vocals/guitar). Joined by Kathy Korniloff (vocals/bass/guitar), they won Austin's "Sweet Jane" contest with a gorgeous, meditative version that interpolated Joan Armatrading's "Love and Affection" into the Lou Reed classic.

That medley appears on the trio's delightful debut album, along with a tasteful cover of Jane Siberry's "Follow Me" and a batch of fine Phillips and Freelove originals. The Girls' uncategorizable sound draws on folk, rock, bluegrass, cajun and jazz, all woven together with great warmth and virtuosity. (The sleeve credits D. Boon and Nina Simone as inspirations, along with the Shaggs, Slits and Throwing Muses.) But the group's primary appeal lies in its angelic harmonies, wry humor and durable songwriting.

Freelove, who had written two of the album's highlights ("Looking Out" and "Heaven on Earth"), left the group for a solo career shortly after its release. With two new members, Two Nice Girls made **Like a Version**, an EP which reprises the album's hilarious send-up of heterosexuality, "I Spent My Last $10.00 (On Birth Control & Beer)" ("My life was so much simpler/when I was sober and queer"), and adds five covers: from Sonic Youth's "Cotton Crown" to the Carpenters' "Top of the World." Repeating the "Sweet Jane (With Affection)" trick, the Girls graft Donna Summer to Bad Company in "I Feel (Like Makin') Love."

Chloe Liked Olivia, the new lineup's first full-length album, takes a bold but wobbly commercial step towards mainstream acceptability. By and large, the group's ambitious adventures into rock production don't work. While Korniloff's folky-pop "Eleven" and "Rational Heart" receive subtle and sympathetic treatment, some of Phillips' material goes very wrong. "For the Inauguration" is a clumsy political song that actually employs a Bush impersonator; slathering electric guitar on the lovely "Princess of Power" shows a lapse of both taste and artistic logic. New Girls Meg Hentges and Pam Barger both make positive songwriting contributions, but having four lead vocalists in the group may not be such a wise idea.   [ws/i]

SEAN TYLA GANG

Yachtless (Beserkley) 1977 ●
Moonproof (Beserkley) 1978 ●

SEAN TYLA

Just Popped Out (Polydor) 1980

From seminal pub-rock bandleader (Ducks Deluxe) to early Stiff signee (his "Texas Chainsaw Massacre Boogie" was the label's fourth release) to the Tyla Gang and a solo career, guitarist Sean Tyla's been around. His three albums (the first two with a steady band of pub compadres) are hard-rocking and honest but not thrilling, despite good playing and Tyla's sincere hoarse vocals. **Yachtless** is the raunchy one, full of lead guitar and aggressive drumming. **Moonproof** takes a subtler attack, introducing acoustic guitar and a more American sound, but no energy loss. **Just Popped Out**, which employs an amazing cast of pub-rock characters (including former members of Ace, Bees Make Honey, Ducks Deluxe, Chilli Willi and the Red Hot Peppers and Man) not to mention Joan Jett and Kenny Laguna, offers bitter, depressed songs given the best studio treatment of Tyla's career. Comparisons to Bob Seger's gritty rock don't exactly say it, but both have a commitment to personal vision and unfancy, straightforward music.   [i]

See also *Ducks Deluxe*.

UB40

Signing Off (nr/Graduate) 1980 •
Present Arms (nr/DEP Int'l) 1981 + 1985 •
Present Arms in Dub (nr/DEP Int'l) 1981 + 1985
The Singles Album (nr/Graduate) 1982
UB44 (nr/DEP Int'l) 1982 •
Live (nr/DEP Int'l) 1983 •
1980–83 (A&M) 1983 •
Labour of Love (A&M) 1983 •
Geffery Morgan (A&M) 1984 •
The UB40 File (nr/Graduate) 1985 •
Baggariddim (nr/DEP Int'l) 1985 •
Little Baggariddim EP (A&M) 1985 •
Rat in the Kitchen (DEP Int'l-Virgin-A&M) 1986 •
UB40 CCCP–Live in Moscow (A&M) 1987 •
The Best of UB40 Volume One (nr/DEP Int'l) 1987 •
UB40 (DEP Int'l-A&M) 1988 •
Labour of Love II (Virgin) 1989 •

This eight-man integrated reggae outfit from Birmingham built its huge following on an independent label (the band's own DEP International) with non-Rastafarian lyrics concerning social issues—not unlike what many new wave bands addressed—and an ineffable pop sensibility. From the get-go, UB40's music has held appeal far beyond the specialized market; they are the most commercially successful self-contained reggae band in the world. Quietly percolating grooves garnished with sultry horn lines and centered around Ali Campbell's cool, Stevie Wonderesque crooning (with and without sweet harmonies) give UB40 an instantly identifiable sound—or formula, as you will.

On the early albums, even the best of the uneven songwriting—as catchy as it does get—sounds samey and is dominated by the group's style. Contrary to the lyrics' urgency, the music suggests that even when "The Earth Dies Screaming," we'll hear it calmly sipping tea in a hot tub. In the early days, the band's tunesmithing seemed to rise to the occasion only for singles (and often, surprisingly, for B-sides).

The Singles Album is UB40's best English-only LP, even though over half of it had already appeared on **Signing Off**. (For the quantity-minded, the latter does include a bonus disc with another 21 minutes of music.) As a matter of fact, any non-fan possessing a couple of UB 45s might hesitate before buying an album by the group.

Present Arms is notable for more prominent use of toasting (which continued on **UB44**) and little else, aside from two solid singles. **Present Arms in Dub**, though, thoughtfully attempts an alternative to the usual dub style, which is generally just vocal-less electronic fiddling of greatly variable quality. Here, UB40 drastically changed the face of its music to the point where some songs are hardly recognizable; it's nearly as though the material were written explicitly for dub treatment. A for effort.

UB44, in addition to minor alterations (more Latin percussion, sparingly applied gurgling synth), displays wider lyrical range and increased verbal acuity, but the only truly striking tune is, naturally, a single ("So Here I Am"). It's not that UB40 have little to offer; it's just that their singles are the brightest spots cut from the same relatively unvarying cloth.

The group's first live album was recorded on tour in Ireland in 1982 and features such tunes as "Food for Thought," "Tyler" and "One in Ten."

In an effort to export some of UB40's success to the States, the group's American label issued **1980–83**, a selection of tracks from **UB44**, **Present Arms** and early singles. Not a bad set, but not the introduction America wanted to hear. What finally did the trick was a novelty of sorts, but one that sidestepped the band's shortcomings as songwriters. **Labour of Love** is an LP of cover versions, drawing on reggae (and reggaefied) hits from a number of diverse authors: Neil Diamond ("Red Red Wine"), Jimmy Cliff ("Many Rivers to Cross"), Delroy Wilson ("Johnny Too Bad") and others. The resultant variety and melodic quality make the album easily and enduringly enjoyable, a rich mine of superbly played, loving tributes.

The entirely new original material of **Geffery Morgan** shows a vastly more creative UB40 at work. Inventive production, intriguing rock rhythms, powerful and memorable songwriting and new outlooks all combine to make it a great record that remains rooted in reggae but is much more diverse than the form generally allows. "Riddle Me" and "If It Happens Again" are ace reggae/rock hybrids; "Nkomo a Go Go," with a propulsive dance-rock beat and wailing saxophone, shows the full range of UB40's development. A very impressive step forward from a band who already know the formula for success.

The UB40 File is a repackage of **Signing Off**, with a second disc consisting of all the singles the band cut that year. (It doesn't require a detective to realize that it merely reissues—and not for the first time—everything on their original label.) Unnecessary, except for completists.

Baggariddim consists of three new recordings (the catchy "Don't Break My Heart," "Mi Spliff" and a charmingly reggaefied "I Got You Babe" sung with Chrissie Hynde) on an EP plus a seven-song album of dub mixes—with guest toasters—from **Labour of Love** and **Geffery Morgan**. The one-disc **Little Baggariddim** offers the three new items, plus "I Got You Babe" dub and two additional numbers.

Rat in the Kitchen is another spectacularly accomplished collection of originals that makes clear the maturity of UB40's songwriting. Lyrics concern employment and poverty; "Sing Our Own Song" vaguely discusses apartheid. (The LP includes postcards for protesting to P.W. Botha and contributing to Amnesty International.) Although no tracks particularly stand out, **Rat in the Kitchen** bops from start to finish with infectious warmth and top-notch musicianship.

Live in Moscow, a single disc recorded during a historic 1986 Russian tour, draws from various periods in the band's career and includes "If It Happens Again," "Don't Break My Heart," "Cherry Oh Baby," "Johnny Too Bad" and "Please Don't Make Me Cry." The performances are lively, but thin, barely adequate sound makes it more a milestone in UB40's history than an important contribution to it. **The Best of UB40 Volume One** compiles fourteen British hits; the CD adds four bonus tracks.

Tragedy struck UB40 in November 1987, when bassist Earl Falconer drove his car into a Birmingham factory wall, killing his brother Ray, the band's co-producer. Although he was eventually sentenced to prison for causing a death by reckless driving, he was back in the group for the recording of **UB40**, a lightweight, restrained new album. "Come Out to Play," "Breakfast in Bed" (another guest vocal by Hynde), the solemn "I Would Do For You" and "Matter of Time" make the most of catchy pop choruses, leaving the remaining material to just throb along pleasantly.

Moviemakers do it, so why not musicians? The sequel to the massively successful **Labour of Love** (which finally reached platinum status in America five years after its release) contains UB40's interpretations of reggae-identified R&B classics by Al Green, the Chi-Lites, the Miracles, John Holt and others. Although **II** is less convincing and harder to fit into UB40's commercial and creative arc than the first covers album, several tunes—especially "Here I Am (Come and Take Me)" and "The Way You Do the Things You Do"—ably locate that magical blend of song and style.   [jg/i]

See also *Pretenders*.

U.K. DECAY
The Black EP (nr/Plastic) 1979
For Madmen Only (nr/Fresh) 1981
Rising from the Dread EP (nr/Corpus Christi) 1982
A Night for Celebration [tape] (nr/Decay) 1983

FURYO
Furyo EP (nr/Anagram) 1983

IN EXCELSIS
Carnival of Damocles EP (nr/Jungle) 1983
Ladder of Lust EP (nr/Jungle) 1984

Theatrical post-punks with an unfortunately short lifespan, U.K. Decay provided a crucial bridge between such art-gloom bands as Bauhaus, PiL, Theatre of Hate and Killing Joke and the anarchy-punk camp led by Crass, Rudimentary Peni and Flux of Pink Indians. Quite unlike the politico/nasty-thrash image suggested by their name, U.K. Decay had a classical bent, both in frontman Abbo's theatrical intonations (think Shakespearian) and the complex, almost stately modalities of the music.

The Black EP captures the band in an early, somewhat immature state. The four tracks are far more traditional (not to mention humorous) punk constructions than their later, highly serious work. On **For Madmen Only**, the band's sole album, Steve Spon's five-string guitar produces a lucid, biting wash of sound—akin to

John McKay's work on the first two Banshees albums—mated to Steve Harle's tribal drum patterns. (Although he does play on some songs, bassist Martyn "Segovia" Smith died before the LP was completed.) No matter how ambitious or full of portent the group gets, the record remains invigorating; driving and angular, and an inestimable influence on the '82 positive punk movement (Sex Gang Children, Southern Death Cult, etc.).

Rising from the Dread is a creative apex. The sidelong "Werewolf" boasts ingenious hair-raising sonic effects, while the other three cuts (especially "Testament") are nearly as good. U.K. Decay went out in style with an explosive series of final concerts in December of 1982.

Three-fourths of the group appeared on **The Whip** compilation as Slave Drive, then soldiered on under the name Furyo the following year (with former Gene Loves Jezebel guitarist Albie De Luca in Spon's place), attempting even weightier and more baroque compositions.

Spon formed the sub-par In Excelsis, joined by two ex-members of Ritual. Though clearly reminiscent of both parent groups, In Excelsis possessed neither the cool intensity and compositional mastery of the former nor the raw potential of the latter. A few clever touches (like the bell motif in **Ladder of Lust**'s "Bonanza") aside, the band proved a dead end.   [gef]

See also *Cult*.

U.K. SUBS
Another Kind of Blues (nr/Gem) 1979
Live Kicks (nr/Stiff) 1980
Brand New Age (nr/Gem) 1980
Crash Course (nr/Gem) 1980
Diminished Responsibility (nr/Gem) 1981
Endangered Species (nr/NEMS) 1982 (nr/Link) 1990
Best Of (1977–1981) (nr/Abstract) 1982
Flood of Lies (nr/Scarlet-Fall Out) 1983
Demonstration Tapes (nr/Konexion) 1984
Subs Standard (nr/Dojo) 1985
Gross-Out USA (nr/Fall Out) 1985
Huntington Beach (nr/UK Subs) 1986 (nr/Revolver) 1990
In Action—Tenth Anniversary (nr/Fall Out) 1986 ●
Left for Dead: Alive in Holland '86 [tape] (ROIR) 1986
Raw Material (nr/Killerwatt) 1986
A.W.O.L. (New Red Archives) 1987
Japan Today (Restless) 1988
Killing Time (nr/Fall Out) 1989 ●
Greatest Hits (Live in Paris) (nr/Released Emotions) 1990

CHARLIE HARPER
Stolen Property (nr/Flicknife) 1982

URBAN DOGS
Urban Dogs (nr/Fall Out) 1983
No Pedigree (nr/Flicknife) 1985

Alongside their contemporaries, London's never-say-die U.K. Subs' 1977-vintage punk sounds old-fashioned, yet Nicky Garratt's wall-of-sound rhythm guitar and Charlie Harper's chanted/sung vocals make for highly enjoyable charged rock'n'rage. Maybe it's the familiarity of their style that makes the quartet more listenable than, say, the early Exploited; whatever the case, the Subs play high-energy, fast-paced rock with a social conscience, and that keeps them one of England's most successful punk outfits.

Brand New Age finds the Subs bemoaning alienation in the modern world (on the title track) and singing their signature tune, "Emotional Blackmail," twice. **Diminished Responsibility** confronts such issues as racism, rioting, gangsters, Paris, prison and urban decay. Harper's songwriting (in collaboration with various members of the band) shows lyrical growth—he's quite capable of incisive lines and spot-on humor—on **Endangered Species**, a fact he almost acknowledges on "Sensitive Boys"; elsewhere, the bleak terrain is littered with better-expressed and subtler observations about the world's ills. Best tune: the touching "Fear of Girls."

Flood of Lies showcases a new lineup and has a great political cartoon of Maggie Thatcher on the cover; the songs are once again more aggressive ("Violent Revolution," "Soldiers of Fortune"), but there's room for some humor as well ("Revenge of the Jelly Devils"). **Gross-Out USA**, the Subs' second live album (after **Crash Course**), recapitulates the band's career in fine raucous form with sixteen songs offered start-to-finish, just as they happened. **Left for Dead** does the same feat, adding to the Subs' live album legacy with a tape-only release, recorded with yet another lineup in Holland. The 23 songs overlap only a half-dozen with **Gross-Out**; the performance is typically incendiary and the recording quality not half bad.

Japan Today is the Subs' tenth studio album (but who's counting?), a more controlled and musical assault than usual, recorded by Harper and five sidemen, including ex-Vibrator guitarist Knox and bassman Flea from the Chili Peppers. The sound is a bit '70s hard rock, the lyrical stance broader and less clichéd as well. An improvement, but not exactly a high point in contemporary rock'n'roll.

In mid-'88, Harper and Garratt reunited (the last UK Subs album they had done together was **Endangered Species**) in New York to record the likable **Killing Time**, a crisply produced example of moderate Clash-styled guitar rock with some workable melodies and lyrics that don't take a very strong stand on cars, cities and women. Although the solemn piano/acoustic guitar tribute to Nico that ends the LP is a nice idea poorly executed, the record's overall lack of consistency—Harper shares lead vocals with Garratt and bassist Alvin Gibbs, and all three contribute to the uneven song collection—is its major flaw. (The CD adds three outtakes from the sessions.)

Harper's first solo effort is worth checking out. Unlike the Subs' all-original music, **Stolen Property** oddly consists of traditional garage band standards, such as "Pills," "Louie, Louie," "Hey Joe" and "Waiting for My Man."

On **Urban Dogs**, the not-so-super session of Harper and Knox (plus a rhythm section) plays highly charged riotpunk that sounds like a cross between early Stranglers, early Pistols and early Stooges. Alongside Knox originals (including the Vibrators' classic "Into the Future," here retitled "Sex Kick") and a couple of Harper's own raunchy numbers, there are covers of Iggy's "I Wanna Be Your Dog" and the Dolls' "Human Being," the latter complete with soundalike Thunders licks. The raunch, spirit and electricity run high from start to finish, making **Urban Dogs** everything a great punk record should be.

Harper, Knox and a drummer called Turkey made the turkey called **No Pedigree** with Anthony Thistlethwaite (of the Waterboys) adding a little sax. Unlike the Dogs' first outing, this one is, for the most part, lame and uninspired, a plodding mush of (presumably) originals and such covers as "Monster Mash," Marc Bolan's "Children of the Revolution" and the Fugs' "Slum Goddess." The only track of real note is John Lennon's "Cold Turkey," sung by two women dubbed the Raspberry Tarts. [cpl/i]

JAMES BLOOD ULMER

Tales of Captain Black (Artists House) 1979
Are You Glad to Be in America? (nr/Rough Trade) 1980
(Artists House) 1981
Free Lancing (Columbia) 1981
Black Rock (Columbia) 1982
Odyssey (Columbia) 1983
Part Time (nr/Rough Trade) 1984
Got Something Good for You (Ger. Moers Music) 1986
Phalanx (Ger. Moers Music) 1986
Live at the Caravan of Dreams (Caravan of Dreams) 1987
America—Do You Remember the Love? (Blue Note) 1987 ●
Original Phalanx (Ger. Moers Music) 1989

MUSIC REVELATION ENSEMBLE

No Wave (Ger. Moers Music) 1980

Called the most innovative electric guitarist since Jimi Hendrix, James Blood Ulmer is certainly worthy of that challenge. Joined by mentor Ornette Coleman, Ulmer introduced many to the avant-garde concept of harmolodics with the release of **Tales of Captain Black**, eight songs of hot funk and boiling rhythms. The production is somewhat flat and Coleman upstages him, but it's still an eye-opening debut.

The exceptionally fine **Are You Glad to Be in America?** features Ulmer's first vocal efforts and reveals a staggering understanding of the roots of jazz, dance music, Eastern polyrhythms and harmolodic textures in a lively sound mix. Without Coleman, Blood works with fabled electric bassist Amin Ali and the stunning sax combo of David Murray (tenor) and Oliver Lake (alto); the music fairly crackles.

No Wave is an experimental album recorded with the Music Revelation Ensemble (Ali, Murray, Lake and Ronald Shannon Jackson on drums). It's Ulmer's most inaccessible work and his least focused.

Free Lancing and **Black Rock** are technical masterpieces, making up in precision what they lack in emotion (as compared to **Are You Glad to Be in America?**). Working to expand his audience, Ulmer concentrates more on electric guitar flash, and actual melodies can be discerned from the improvised song structures (improvisation being one of the keys to harmolodics).

Odyssey takes Ulmer in a novel direction: working with just a drummer (Warren Benbow) and violinist (Charles Burnham), he builds mesmerizing but patchy fabrics of busy guitar, traversing kinetic jazz, blues, pop and rock idioms with relaxed power. Singing in an engaging rustic blues voice, Ulmer essays extremely traditional song forms. ("Little Red House" and "Are

You Glad to Be in America?'' sound like Taj Mahal.) Matching the cheery cover photo, this is easily his most accessible, commercial and likable record.

Following a number of European releases (including the live-in-Switzerland **Part Time**) and **Caravan of Dreams**, an American live album recorded with Burnham, Benbow and Ali, Ulmer joined forces with bassist/co-producer Bill Laswell and Ronald Shannon Jackson (plus Nicky Skopelitis and Bernard Fowler) to make another marvelous vocal record, **America—Do You Remember the Love?**, that has even more to offer a mainstream audience than **Odyssey**. Half incisive instrumentals and half songs that skip extensive soloing in favor of a group approach with nearly constant vocals, the album unifies Ulmer's many musical abilities into a unique, mesmerizing style. Unfairly characterized as jazz by its nonetheless welcome release on Blue Note, this message of discouraged but hopeful patriotism instead offers extraordinarily adventurous pop for thinking people with soul. [gf/i]

ULTRA VIVID SCENE
She Screamed EP (nr/4AD) 1988 ●
Ultra Vivid Scene (4AD-Rough Trade) 1988 ●
Mercy Seat EP (nr/4AD) 1989
Staring at the Sun EP (4AD-Columbia) 1990 ●
Joy 1967–1990 (4AD-Columbia) 1990 ●
Special One EP (4AD-Columbia) 1990 ●

Listen past the pretty facade of Ultra Vivid Scene to the barely suppressed screams within, and you'll find an admirably subversive mind at work. Whether performing techno-pop, ambient soundscapes or Patsy Cline covers, UVS wields the same breathless, desperate menace.

For all its attempts to be perceived as a band, UVS is still essentially Kurt Ralske, a musical prodigy of sorts from Long Island who grew up on jazz and classical music. After quitting the Berklee School of Music at 17, he bought a guitar and began playing in rock, hardcore and jazz bands, moving to London with a group called Crash (which soon did). He then formed the first incarnation of UVS and hung out with members of the Jesus & Mary Chain, My Bloody Valentine and Loop before returning to New York and signing with 4AD.

Ralske created the elaborate **Ultra Vivid Scene** entirely by himself, offering a disturbingly intimate glimpse into his evidently tortured soul as well as his considerable musical talents. The bittersweet juxtapositions—a beautiful melody with S&M lyrics, a bouncy pop song driven by hyper-distorted guitar—create a tension that jangles even the album's most sedate songs. Anguished yet never overbearing, soothing without turning complacent, it's one of 1988's best.

She Screamed joins the album cut with a lazy cover of Patsy Cline's ''Walkin' After Midnight'' and two brooding originals, while a new version of **Mercy Seat** transforms that song into a towering, majestic tour de force; combined with the LP version, the stalking ''H Like in Heaven'' and a cover of Buffy Sainte-Marie's ''Codine,'' it makes for a devastating EP.

Joy 1967–1990 hones Ralske's pop sensibility to a surgically precise point, Hugh Jones' radio-oriented production reducing his quiet Bolanesque lisp to a whisper. It's a far more straightforward pop album than the debut (and much less disturbing), although ''Praise the Low'' breaks formation with a beautifully ambient neo-Celtic arrangement. The **Staring at the Sun** EP previewed two album tracks with a new version of ''Crash'' and a lilting cover of Goffin/Mann's ''Something Better,'' both of which rival anything on **Joy**.

Those who feared that Ralske had replaced angst with joy were relieved by the B-sides on **Special One** (the album's ''hit single,'' which shamelessly lifts the melody from Alex Chilton's ''September Gurls''), revealing exactly the progress the album lacked. Sampling two of rap's most commonly employed drum beats (''Funky Drummer'' and ''When the Levee Breaks'') on ''Kind of a Drag'' and a radically different version of **Joy**'s ''Lightning,'' Ralske integrates songs so atypical to the genre that the genericized beats work brilliantly to his advantage. [ja]

ULTRAVOX
Ultravox! (Island) 1977
Ha!Ha!Ha! (nr/Island) 1977
Systems of Romance (Antilles) 1978
Live Retro EP (nr/Island) 1978
Three into One (Antilles) 1980 ●
Vienna (Chrysalis) 1980 ●
Rage in Eden (Chrysalis) 1981 ●
New Europeans (Jap. Chrysalis) 1981
Mini-LP EP (Aus. Festival) 1981
Quartet (Chrysalis) 1982 ●
Monument—The Soundtrack EP (nr/Chrysalis) 1983 ●
Lament (Chrysalis) 1984 ●
The Collection (Chrysalis) 1984 ●
U-Vox (nr/Chrysalis) 1986 (Chrysalis) 1990 ●
The Peel Sessions EP (nr/Strange Fruit) 1988

MIDGE URE
The Gift (Chrysalis) 1985 ●
Answers to Nothing (Chrysalis) 1988 ●

BILLY CURRIE
Transportation (IRS No Speak) 1988 ●
Stand Up and Walk [tape] (nr/Hot Food Music) 1990

Originally lost in the gap between glam-rock and punk, Ultravox became prime movers of the electro-pop and new romantic movements when they combined synthesizer with the direct and danceable pop music of the new wave.

Ultravox!—produced by Brian Eno, Steve Lillywhite and the group—marries the flamboyance of poseurdom to the cold minimalism of Kraftwerk, with more than a touch of punk's roughness. John Foxx's voice is typically distant, singing lyrics that contain jumbled images expressing passive dislocation (a popular Ultravox theme). While synthesizers are in short supply, the budding Ultravox style can be noted in ''Dangerous Rhythm,'' the oddly passionate ''I Want to Be a Machine'' and the classic ''My Sex.''

Ha!Ha!Ha! comes closer to the spirit of punk, filled with tight, straightforward rockers outlining a spirit of alienation and life free of love, companionship and comprehension. Billy Currie plays stunning electric violin and, on the climactic ''Hiroshima Mon Amour,'' introduces full-force synthesizer into Ultravox's music, delineating the boundary between past and future. Recommended.

Systems of Romance, produced by Conny Plank, fuses the band's pop vision with spare, crystalline electronic sound. Focused both lyrically and musically on the fragmentation of experience, the album weaves a sinuous existential mood that suggests dreams and autumn nights. Highly recommended.

Vienna, also produced by Plank, was marked by the departure of Foxx and guitarist Robin Simon (who had replaced founding member Stevie Shears after the second LP); Scottish vocalist/guitarist (ex-Slik/Rich Kids) Midge Ure filled out the new lineup and took over the group. Ultravox's recast sound included a more symphonic use of synthesizer, layered in deep swells for new heights of sonic density. **Vienna** includes Ultravox's best hits: "All Stood Still," "Sleepwalk," "Passing Strangers" and the title track. The new approach proved highly satisfying and successful, spawning a horde of less-inspired imitators collectively referred to as new romantics.

Noting **Vienna**'s success, Island/Antilles issued **Three into One**, a compilation of songs drawn from the first three albums, including "My Sex" and "Hiroshima Mon Amour."

Rage in Eden, Ultravox's last outing with Plank, finds Ure sliding into operatic vocals and pretentious lyrics, but the music—again displaying complex synthesizer patterns—is superb, with Currie, Ure, bassist Chris Cross and drummer Warren Cann blending brilliantly.

New Europeans is a Japanese compilation of B-sides from the **Vienna** and **Rage in Eden** period, added to A-sides "The Voice" and "New Europeans." Though the flipsides are hardly top-notch, they are interesting, and the mastering/pressing provides exceptional audio quality.

The Australian **Mini-LP** combines two rare tracks from an early flexi-disc ("Quirks" and "Modern Love") with the contents of **Live Retro**, an excellent 7-inch concert EP originally released in 1978. (The **Peel Sessions** EP, recorded in November 1977, chronicles the same era.)

Quartet continues in much the same vein as **Rage in Eden**, but producer George Martin thins out the sound too much, reducing the band to a subordinate role as backing for Ure, whose lyrics are infused with religious overtones. Clear but unsatisfying.

Ultravox self-produced **Lament**, proving themselves quite capable of working without outside supervision. The album contains two of their finest singles, "One Small Day" and "Dancing with Tears in My Eyes," amidst a host of other suave and personable excursions. **Lament** further elevates Ultravox's reputation as one of the few groups to capably incorporate synthesizers and other modern conveniences into a truly unique sound.

The six-song **Monument** also serves as the soundtrack to a concert videocassette of the same name. **The Collection** is a remarkable compilation of the band's post-Foxx/post-Island singles (1980-'84): fourteen cuts, including "Sleepwalk," "We Came to Dance," "All Stood Still" and "One Small Day," all stellar examples of craft and creativity. Not a bad introduction to the group's post-Island work.

Except for a slightly increased guitar focus and the large proportion of instrumentals, Ure's one-man solo album (with a little assistance, mostly on bass and vocals) sounds enough like Ultravox in spots to unsettle his bandmates—it could easily be mistaken for a group effort. (Although few would believe *they* would attempt a laid-back cover of Jethro Tull's "Living in the Past"— downright bizarre, but not as awful as you might imagine.) "If I Was" has a nice refrain but trite lyrics— Ure's uncertainty quickly becomes aggravating—and goes on too long. If nothing else, this mix of familiar synth-rock and adventurous instrumentals showed how Ure would survive the end of Ultravox; perhaps **The Gift** hastened that eventuality.

Warren Cann quit in mid-'86 and has not been heard from since; the three remaining members deputized Big Country drummer Mark Brzezicki to finish the competent but unassuming **U-Vox** album. All their fire and personality seems to have evaporated. Ure's singing has never been so restrained; the bland overall sound (punctuated with brass on two big production numbers) bears only occasional resemblance to their past work, yet offers nothing especially new to replace it. "Follow Your Heart" is about as good as it gets; in an odd detour, "All Fall Down" is a folky anti-war drinking song with accompaniment by the Chieftains.

Ultravox broke up in mid-'87, freeing Ure to complete his second solo album. Quite different from the group's work, **Answers to Nothing** has lots of lead guitar and puts a surprising emphasis on hyperactive bass guitar (Mick Karn, Level 42 thumbster Mark King and Steve Brzezicki do the honors; Mark Brzezicki is the album's drummer). With the exception of "Dear God" and other simple songs, Ure downplays Ultravox's reliance on synthesizers, avoiding extended keyboard chords and artificial sounds. The guest appearance by Kate Bush is more than symbolic of Ure's new aesthetic: **Answers to Nothing** is a relatively cerebral journey (ignore Ure's overly earnest lyrics) that pursues painterly audio art rather than pop hooks or dance rhythms.

Currie's first record—an instrumental collaboration with Yes/Asia guitarist Steve Howe—finds the keyboard/viola player mutely ambling through songlike compositions that aren't that far removed from Ultravox, although the overambitious title track is a notable exception. Lacking a structural backbone, the aimless and fragmentary "Transportation" is mostly an opportunity for Howe to show off some of his stringed instrument collection. [sg/i]

See also *John Foxx, Gary Numan, Visage*.

UNCLE TUPELO

No Depression (Rockville) 1990 ●

Coming as close as any recent band has to translating the spirit of American folk music into the rock idiom, this St. Louis threesome plies its tales of tribulation and remorse in a style that combines an acute understanding of country-music dynamics with punky power-trio punch. Thus, the band's judicious use of mandolin, banjo and pedal steel guitar doesn't detract from the thrashy appeal of noisy cuts like "Graveyard Shift" and "Before I Break." Meanwhile, the impressive original "Whiskey Bottle," a CD-only cover of Leadbelly's

"John Hardy" and the title track (a '30s Carter family gospel tune) demonstrate surprising melodic subtlety that should serve Uncle Tupelo well in the future.

[hd]

UNDEAD

Nine Toes Later EP (Stiff) 1982
Never Say Die! (Ger. Rebel) 1986
Act Your Rage (Post Mortem) 1989

Guitarist Bobby Steele quit the Misfits in 1980 and formed the Undead, a trio that cut Stiff's very last US release. (Its title refers to the accident that left Steele with a pronounced limp.) **Never Say Die!** combines the EP with two subsequent independent singles into a solid mini-LP (eight songs in under nineteen minutes). It's gritty, rocking, catchy and angry but, like the title track, often shows a positive attitude. With a settled lineup, the Undead might have made a super live record; these documents are just as good.

An insert in **Never Say Die!** claimed the Undead were already in the studio recording **Act Your Rage**, but it took three years to finish. While Steele's relish for performing is consistent, the sound, music and lyrics are pretty uneven, and the best isn't exactly riveting. Even "Put Your Clothes Back On" (the LP's best title and premise) gets an A for inspiration and a C for execution. See also *Misfits*.

[jg]

UNDERTONES

Teenage Kicks EP (nr/Good Vibrations) 1978
The Undertones (Sire) 1979 ●
Hypnotised (Sire) 1980
Positive Touch (Harvest) 1981
The Love Parade EP (nr/Ardeck) 1982
The Sin of Pride (nr/Ardeck) 1983
All Wrapped Up (Ardeck-Capitol) 1983
Cher o' Bowlies (nr/EMI) 1986 ●
The Peel Sessions EP (nr/Strange Fruit) 1986 ●
The Peel Sessions Album (nr/Strange Fruit) 1989 ●

The best band ever to come from Northern Ireland, the Undertones took a youthful adoration for the glam-rock era and gave it the stripped-down simplicity and energy of punk to create truly wonderful albums of pop/rock (and, towards the end, soul) with a difference. Their body of work reveals rapid creative growth; each album clearly shows a different stage in their development. The group's 1983 demise, as unavoidable as it was disappointing, resulted from a lack of sustained commercial success and the inability to shake the public's first impression of them as an Irish Ramones.

Very young Derrymen when they began in 1976, the Undertones started out writing simple, fetching melodies with lyrics about teenagehood and playing them fast and raw on basic guitars, bass and drums. With Feargal Sharkey's unique, piercing tenor out front, songs on the first album ("Jimmy Jimmy," "Here Comes the Summer," "Girls Don't Like It") are spare and efficient pop gems that are as infectious as measles, suggesting a bridge between teenybop and punk. (The US edition—wrapped in completely different color Xerox artwork—adds the crucial "Teenage Kicks" and "Get Over You" from the band's first two 7-inches; a limited-edition English 10-inch released at the same time combined those two tracks plus a pair from the LP.)

The Undertones broadened their scope for **Hypnotised**, making the sound clearer and more instrumentally distinct while offering uniquely cast lyrics telling stories and describing characters with impressive skill. Outstanding tracks include "My Perfect Cousin," the delicate "Wednesday Week" and the gently self-mocking "More Songs About Chocolate and Girls." Of the four original albums, **Hypnotised** has the best balance of sophistication and innocence.

Positive Touch introduces well-placed horns and piano (by Paul Carrack) to the sound and explores much more ambitious ground, in reflection of the band's personal and musical maturation. While the songs are not all immediately catchy, they are ultimately rewarding, displaying numerous new sides and levels to the Undertones. An enormous artistic achievement for a band that had been playing rudimentary four-chord riff numbers a scant two years earlier.

The Love Parade EP—actually a 12-inch single with four songs on the B-side—includes three otherwise unavailable live recordings tied together with weird noises and unfathomable dialogue. Most importantly at the time, it showed the band to be newly focused on '60s soul psychedelia.

Perhaps overly stung by their commercial problems, the Undertones made their final album with more ambition than concentration. **The Sin of Pride** has its brilliant moments—the soulful "Got to Have You Back" (a soul cover), "Bye Bye Baby Blue," "Love Parade," "Chain of Love"—but the fear of being thought of as an immature pop band drives them into low-key excursions that drift away tunelessly, and overactive horn charts bury the band's instrumental personality. Also, the sound quality is disturbingly distant.

The English version of **All Wrapped Up**, the Undertones' posthumous singles collection, has two discs and features all thirteen of their A-sides plus seventeen flips—30 magnificent cuts in all. From the entire four-song **Teenage Kicks** EP right up through "Chain of Love," it's a stirring reminder of what a truly marvelous band they were. The American version has the same gross cover photo (a female model dressed only in cured meats) but eliminates one disc and sixteen of the B-sides. **Cher o' Bowlies**, subtitled "The Pick of the Undertones," is another compilation with some overlap, but rather than concentrating on 45s, the selection of album tracks portrays the group differently.

The Peel BBC radio EP, produced by Bob Sargeant in January 1979, offers sloppy but wonderful live versions of "Here Comes the Summer," "Family Entertainment" and two others. Combining that quartet of tracks with repeat visits in January '80 and November '82, **The Peel Sessions Album** amounts to a definitive live retrospective, following the Undertones from what the liner notes refer to as their "callow, endearingly goofy period" through their more proficient prime ("What's with Terry," Gary Glitter's "Rock n' Roll" with a nifty T. Rex coda) to a resourceful horn-free preview of the final album ("The Sin of Pride," "Untouchable," "Luxury").

After the Undertones ended, Feargal Sharkey made one great 1983 single ("Never Never") with Vince Clarke's otherwise stillborn Assembly and then a not-

so-great solo 45 ("Listen to Your Father") for Madness' Zarjazz label the following year. After a third one-off single produced by Queen drummer Roger Taylor, he linked up with Eurythmic Dave Stewart and got his briefly successful solo career underway with "A Good Heart." The O'Neill brothers formed That Petrol Emotion; the rhythm section left the music biz.   [i]
See also *Feargal Sharkey, That Petrol Emotion.*

UNDERWORLD
See *Freur.*

UNION CARBIDE PRODUCTIONS
In the Air Tonight (Swed. Radium 226.05) 1987 (Skyclad) 1989 ●
Financially Dissatisfied Philosophically Trying (Radium 226.05-Skyclad) 1989 ●
From Influence to Ignorance (Swed. Radium 226.05) 1991

Iggy Pop has always insisted that the Stooges were really a free-jazz band in rock drag. If you accept that, then you'll likely find Sweden's Union Carbide Productions to be the best—or at least the most authentic—band mining the Dee-troit vein of sonic scrunge. The first album's top tracks ("Financial Declaration," "Cartoon Animal") could play hide'n'seek on any late-'60s Michigan compilation tape you'd care to make, while the furthest out (like the epic "Down on the Beach") owe more to Sun Ra. By adding howling horns (two members double on sax) and a non-traditional rhythm section that rarely functions as just a timekeeper to the wah-wah heavy rock on **In the Air Tonight**, UCP neatly sidesteps any charges of revivalism.

Financially Dissatisfied sees the quintet spackling yet more tiles—both breathtaking (haunting, spare piano) and grimace-inducing (cheesy sitar)—into the gonzo mosaic. There's also a little, um, post-structuralism creeping into songs like "Another Rock-'n'Roll Statement" and "San Francisco Boogie," but Ebbot Lundberg's Drano-gargling vocals keep 'em firmly earthbound.   [dss]

UNITY 2
What Is It, Yo?! (Reprise) 1990 ●
VARIOUS ARTISTS
Funky Reggae Crew: Strictly Hip-Hop Reggae Fusion (Warner Bros.) 1989 ●

With the empowering rise of rap, New York has again become a potent conduit for Third World culture to inseminate the pop world. Making explicit the perfectly logical combination of reggae toasting and its American derivative, this duo of Sean "Cavo" Dinsmore and Lionel "Nene" Bernard (both former members of the Toasters, a prolific New York ska crew) and their band play raggamuffin hip-hop, a kinetic mix of upbeat styles that jumps easily from saxophone-driven ska to dub to turntable scratching. Although a bit glib and weak in spots (Dinsmore's not much of an MC), the diverse and imaginative **What Is It, Yo?!** attempts to answer the question with a marvelous bluebeat-plus original ("Shirlee") and an assortment of easily enjoyable hybrids.

"Shirlee" got its first airing on the **Funky Reggae**

Crew compilation, which also includes tracks by Queen Latifah and Daddy-O, Mikey Dread (co-produced by KRS-One) and Tippa Irie.   [i]

UNIVERSAL CONGRESS OF
See *Joe Baiza & the Universal Congress Of*

UNKNOWNS
Dream Sequence EP (Bompl-Sire) 1981
The Unknowns (Invasion) 1982
BRUCE JOYNER AND THE PLANTATIONS
Way Down South (Invasion) 1983
Slave of Emotion (Fr. Closer) 1985
Swimming with Friends (Fr.Closer) 1986
Hot Georgia Nights (Fr. New Rose) 1987 ●
The Outtake Collection 1978—88 (Fr. Fan Club) 1989
BRUCE JOYNER & THE TINGLERS
Beyond the Dark (Fr. New Rose) 1990 ●

Liam Sternberg, Ohio's answer to Phil Spector, produced the six tracks for **Dream Sequence** "in an aircraft hangar." The Unknowns play pure '60s garage rock with Mosrite guitars (displayed and mentioned on the cover for added authenticity), heaps of echo and tremolo, and incorporate various period genres (surf music, Creedence swamp choogle, psychedelia, punk) into their songs. Where **Dream Sequence** is slick but boring, **The Unknowns** shows them in greater command of their musical vocabulary and adds traces of the Animals, Yardbirds, Blues Project and the Doors to spice things up considerably. A rendition of Buddy Holly's "Rave On" ties up a neat package of heavily stylized nostalgia.

After the Unknowns, singer Bruce Joyner formed the Plantations. **Way Down South** abandons the literal aspects of the Unknowns' nostalgia for a more direct, unassuming sound that is still colored by weedy organ and other '60s affectations. Some of the fourteen varied numbers are catchy and well-constructed; others drag. (Appearances aside, none of the music and only the occasional lyric is particularly reflective of the land below the Mason-Dixon line.) Joyner is moderately talented but needs stronger collaborators.

A few years later, a new set of Plantations (guitarist Dave Greene being the only holdover) joined Joyner for the seven-song **Swimming with Friends**, which also features guest shots by Steve Wynn, John Doe, Ray Manzarek, Stan Ridgway and Sky Saxon. As lively and exciting as a wax museum, the music is formally psychedelic in nostalgic intent, but stultifyingly bland and made worse by Joyner's vocals, which remain characterless despite liberal amounts of echo. The lurid lyrics to songs like "Deep Green Water" and "The Darkside of Your Brain" are right on the money, but nothing in the grooves fulfills the titles' atmospheric promise.   [i]

UNREST
Tink of S.E. (Teen Beat) 1987
Malcolm X Park (Caroline) 1988
Kustom Karnal Blackxploitation (Caroline) 1990

Unrest is an exquisitely versatile and eclectic band from Washington DC whose one constant is vocalist Mark Robinson. Named after Henry Cow's second LP, the group formed during the heyday of Washington's hardcore scene, but Unrest's early recordings are far stranger and much more varied than anything their contemporaries produced. **Tink of S.E.** is far too scattered to lend itself to easy categorization, but it joins recombo-trash moves (truly fucked-up covers of both "Wild Thing" and "21st Century Schizoid Man") with the sort of intensely personal insanity that rarely gets further than an isolated cassette recorder in some miserable sap's bedroom. Each of the first album's covers were individually crafted (by a host of local artists), and the results are possessed of extremely good vibes.

Malcolm X Park follows in its predecessor's footsteps, veering through songs as disparate as "Lucifer Rising" (which sounds like a sputter-punk update of some lost Swell Maps tune) and a balls-up cover of Kiss' "Strutter." Recorded by the ubiquitous Mark Kramer, it didn't even suffer much from the unpleasant sheen that "real" studios give many underground bands. The third LP is a similarly mixed bag; the fact that it's less aggressively "out" than its predecessors led some jerks to decry it as a loss. Wise old owls realized that Unrest was merely twisting the throat of sounds more mainstream than those they'd throttled previously. What they'll do next is anyone's guess. [bc]

UNTAMED YOUTH
Some Kinda Fun!! (Norton) 1988
More Gone Gassers from the Untamed Youth!!! (Norton) 1990

From the clothes they sport and the cars they drive to the design of their record jackets and the music inside—yeah, from any angle but that of real time, the Untamed Youth are a '60s band. In an era of drum machines, Fairlights and Exposé, many might find the concept of a hotrod/surf combo from Columbia, Missouri to be frivolous or downright silly. But the fact is this hearse-driven quartet has made two LPs unrivaled in recent memory for pure dancing and drinking enjoyment. Authentic co-production by Billy Miller (Zantees/Kicks/Norton) and Andy Shernoff (Dictators/Manitoba's Wild Kingdom) captures the supercharged atmosphere created whenever the Untamed Youth fill a teen club or tavern. Why debate the modern relevance of motorbikes, girls, guitars, Pabst Blue Ribbon, bikinis, and Elly May Clampett? Their praises may have been sung before, but rarely so eloquently. [sm]

UNTOUCHABLES
Live and Let Dance EP (Twist-Enigma) 1984
Wild Child (Stiff-MCA) 1985
Dance Party EP (Stiff-MCA) 1986
Agent 00 Soul (Twist-Restless) 1989 ●
A Decade of Dance (Restless) 1990 φ

There were other R&B-*cum*-ska outfits on the LA scene at the time, but it was only the worthy Untouchables who caught Stiff's attention and wound up with a label deal on both sides of the Atlantic. **Live and Let Dance** introduced the band's energetic dance attack with a half-dozen exciting numbers, starting with the unfor-

gettably catchy "Free Yourself." (One listen and you'll swear you heard it on a 1980 2-Tone single.) The 12-inch also presents solid reggae and ska in the UB40 mold; the live take of "(I'm Not Your) Stepping Stone," however, asserts real individuality.

Reprising "Free Yourself," **Wild Child** surrounds it with ten other strong items, including the similarly effective title track, a cool version of "I Spy (for the FBI)"—an obscurity also recorded by John Hiatt—produced by Jerry Dammers, a slice of straight rap-funk ("Freak in the Streets") and a synth-tinged rock tune ("Lovers Again"). Stewart Levine's production could be more full-bodied, but the sextet's enthusiasm and precision keep things rocking from start to finish.

With no new material forthcoming, a 12-inch compilation EP was released. **Dance Party** contains four remixed album tracks, including "Freak in the Street" (by Don and David Was) and "Free Yourself," a tune from the first EP and a new live funk workout.

Agent 00 Soul (titled for the Edwin Starr oldie, which the group covers blandly) reveals the Untouchables to be suffering from multiple personality disorder. On some songs they're a brassy soul revue putting hip-hop moves to Rick James sex-funk, elsewhere, they're a rocked-up reggae band. On the ska beat, there's a snappy translation of the Coasters' "Under the Boardwalk" and an inferior rewrite of "Free Yourself." Only one of the originals (the '60sish "Shama Lama," buried in the middle of the second side) is really good; while **Agent 00 Soul** has its moments, the album doesn't hang together at all. (The CD adds three bonus tracks.) [i]

UPSETTERS
See *Lee Perry*.

URBAN DANCE SQUAD
Mental Floss for the Globe (Hol. Ariola) 1989 (Arista) 1990 ●

Only in the Netherlands: This vibrant pan-cultural quintet was formed in Amsterdam in 1987, by a rapper (who speaks both Dutch and Brooklynese), a bassist from the former Dutch colony of Surinam and three Dutchmen. Atop the rapping, funk bass, power chords and acoustic slide, DJ DNA adds the same wild-card element to Urban Dance Squad that Brian Eno provided in the original Roxy Music: the band never knows if it's going to be accompanied by Mongolian desert music, Benny Goodman or Chuck D. And although UDS comes from a country not widely regarded for its rock heritage, these seasoned musicians have played with everyone from Jah Wobble to Rufus Thomas. And, like Fishbone and the Chili Peppers, UDS never forgets to have fun.

For all its semiotic world-unity rap-rock possibilities, **Mental Floss for the Globe** has brilliant flashes but captures only some of the band's potential. While rapper Rudeboy scatters the occasional profundity amid weird slang, the band veers between stomping funk-rock and swampier bluesy grooves, letting the DJ have his day on "God Blasts the Queen" and the throbbing "Struggle for Jive," one of the most successful fusions of power-riffs and techno-dance yet.

In a bizarre discographical twist, no less than four different versions of **Mental Floss for the Globe** exist.

The album was originally released independently in a limited pressing, licensed to Ariola in Holland and Europe, and eventually Arista in the States—replacing copyright-offending samples (including Hendrix, the Stones and Captain Beefheart) on each edition. The American version adds two hot European B-sides and drops the inane "Hitchhike H.D." [ja]

URBAN DOGS
See *U.K. Subs.*

MIDGE URE
See *Ultravox.*

URGE OVERKILL
Strange, I . . . EP (Ruthless) 1986
Jesus Urge Superstar (Touch and Go) 1989 ●
Americruiser (Touch and Go) 1990 ●
Supersonic Storybook (Touch and Go) 1991 ●

With a great cartoon cover and hypnospiral label, the first 12-inch from this Chicago trio looks a lot better than it sounds. The five numbers have just enough pop backbone to hold together as songs, but they're played with the abrasive thrashings of a Small Black wannabe and produced with every imaginable sonic shortcoming. Yuch.

Jesus Urge Superstar is a little better, but the band's intriguing junk-culture pretensions are still buried too deeply within the haphazard Cheap Trick-as-guitar-throttling-noise-punks attack to make any impression. With an unpredictable mix that moves the vocals all over the place (pushing them way up front on "Dubbledead" and nearly losing them entirely amid the stun-guitar chaos of "Last Train to Heaven") and the band's undefined stylistic personality, such promising titles as "The Polaroid Doll," "Dump Dump Dump" and "Eggs"—despite occasional clever bits—go right down the tubes.

With clear production (finally) by Butch Vig, **Americruiser**—the CD of which includes the previous LP as a bonus of sorts—makes further improvements, bringing the group's sound into focus and toning down the Overkill overdrive to give the self-amused songs (which aren't half bad) a chance. That's not to say **Americruiser**'s a great LP—it ain't even close, and some of it is downright awful—but at least Urge Overkill has found the on-ramp to music that may yet amount to something. [i]

U-ROY
Version Galore (nr/Trojan) c. 1973 (nr/Front Line) 1978
U-Roy (nr/Trojan) 1974
Dread in a Babylon (Virgin) 1975 + 1983 (Virgin Front Line) 1990 ●
Natty Rebel (nr/Virgin) 1976 + 1983
Rasta Ambassador (nr/Virgin) 1977
Jah Son of Africa (Jam. Live & Love) 1977 (nr/Front Line) 1979
With Words of Wisdom (nr/Front Line) 1979
Crucial Cuts (nr/Virgin) 1983
Music Addict (RAS) 1987 ●
Line Up and Come (Tappa) 1987

With a Flick of My Musical Wrist (nr/Trojan) 1988
Version of Wisdom (Virgin Front Line) 1990 φ

Just as dub reggae anticipated funk and rock remixes, toasters—chanting reggae DJs—prefigured rap. U-Roy (Ewart Beckford) was one of Jamaica's first DJs to graduate from sound systems to chart success in the late '60s. (Indeed, for several weeks early in 1970, he had three records—"Wear You to the Ball," "Wake the Town" and "Rule the Nation"—atop the charts on Jamaica's two radio stations.) His signature style is plain and direct: he shrieks and chants over the instrumental tracks of other hits, interrupting and talking back to the vocals. When he first appeared, such musical antics were unprecedented on record, and he became an immediate sensation. While it can't be said that U-Roy invented toasting, he's considered the style's godfather, and an inarguable reggae pioneer.

Because U-Roy isn't very active, his records drift in and out of print. **Version Galore**, which collects many of his first hits, is a must, although far from definitive. Most of his available LPs, in fact, date from the mid-'70s, when he was signed to Virgin and produced by Tony Robinson. Both **Dread in a Babylon** and **Natty Rebel** are excellent samplings of U-Roy's forceful toasting, though the sound and production are smoother, less offbeat and startling than his early work. (**Dread** has the slight edge for featuring the wonderful "Runaway Girl" and "Chalice in the Palace.") **Crucial Cuts** combines some early items with tracks from **Rasta Ambassador** for an odd combination of old and new styles (some hits are re-recordings) that is inconsistent but serviceable. **With a Flick of My Musical Wrist** is a compilation of DJ music (by U-Roy and others) from the early '70s.

U-Roy quietly resurfaced in 1987 with **Music Addict**, a collection of contemporary tracks produced with Prince Jazzbo. The LP finds him in fine form, toasting with authority and ease, and it compares favorably with much of his older work. The song "Jah, Jah Call You" reaffirms U-Roy's Rasta faith and reinforces the many positive messages he's delivered. Ironically, the record got lost in the flood of releases by younger and hipper DJs—U-Roy's musical descendants—and attracted little attention. **Line Up and Come**, produced and arranged by Tappa Zukie, surfaced around the same time as **Music Addict**. While there are some good tracks, this weak LP lacks U-Roy's usual punch and spice.

Version of Wisdom is an essential 20-track compilation of two landmark U-Roy albums, **Version Galore** and **With Words of Wisdom** (aka **U-Roy**), showcasing him at his creative peak in the '70s. Concise highlights (only one track exceeds three minutes) of this R&B-flavored cornucopia include "Your Ace from Outer Space," "Rule the Nation," "Version Galore," "True Confession," "Words of Wisdom" and John Holt's "Tide Is High." [bk/aw/i]

U.S. SECRET SERVICE
See *Sneakers.*

UT
UT Live [tape] (nr/Out) 1981
UT EP (nr/Out) 1984

Conviction (nr/Out) 1986 (nr/Out-Blast First) 1987
Early Live Life (nr/Out-Blast First) 1987
In Gut's House (Blast First) 1988 ●
Griller (nr/Blast First) 1989 ●

UT was formed in NYC at the tail end of 1978, after Nina Canal abandoned Robin Crutchfield's band, Dark Day. Together with Jacqui Ham and Sally Young, Canal produced rattling trio noise that was akin to that of other second generation no wavers like Information. Swapping instruments after each song, UT were more interesting to watch than many of their kith, and their sound started coming together pretty quickly. Lust/Unlust Records held a release party for their debut single in '80, but the company folded before the disc hit the streets; soon after, UT packed up and moved to London.

There they remain, enjoying a certain amount of success. The eponymous 1984 EP captures them in their original raw state. **Conviction** is more produced, padding some of the band's acerbic edge with a near-goth gauze. **Early Live Life**, recorded at various shows in New York and England between '79 and '85, offers a nice assortment of rackety guitar numbers and documents a brief quartet lineup. It's really only with **In Gut's House**, however, that UT's recording attempts have been completely successful. This one's nearly as winning a balance of pop-conscious song-structuring and outright-croak as Sonic Youth's **EVOL**-period. Relatively unknown in the States, UT seems to have splintered some time after the Steve Albini-produced **Griller**. Which is a drag. They deserved far more hep attention than they got.   [bc]

See also *DNA*.

UTFO

"Beats and Rhymes" (Select) 1984
"Roxanne, Roxanne" (Select) 1984
U.T.F.O. (Select) 1985
Skeezer Pleezer (Select) 1986
Lethal (Select) 1987
Doin' It! (Select) 1989 ●
Bag It and Bone It (Jive-RCA) 1990 ●

DOCTOR ICE

The Mic Stalker (Jive) 1989 ●

For a brief period in late winter 1984/5, you couldn't leave your house or turn on your radio in New York without hearing some rapper going on about a girl named Roxanne. There was "Roxanne's Revenge," "The Real Roxanne," "Roxanne You're Through," "Roxanne's Mother," "Roxanne's Brother," "Roxanne's Doctor"—even "Roxanne's a Man." Demonstrating the volatility of the dance music market, Roxanne replaced "y'all" as the word most frequently used in raps, and the term quickly passed into urban slang for an unaccommodating woman. Credit for this fad goes to Brooklyn's UTFO (Untouchable Force Organization), the trio who started it all with "Roxanne, Roxanne," a playful poke at a good-looking girl with the temerity to resist their suave attentions.

From the beginning, Doctor Ice, the Kangol Kid and the Educated Rapper (later joined by Mix-Master Ice) led a charmed life. After winning a break-dancing contest, they went on a European tour with Whodini and ultimately found themselves on the *Phil Donahue Show*, which led to an invite to Dustin Hoffman's daughter's birthday party. Before things could get any weirder, they released a 12-inch of the sharp and fast "Beats and Rhymes," oddly, a better rap than its follow-up, "Roxanne, Roxanne" (both cuts were included on the band's first album, along with "The Real Roxanne" and "Calling Her a Crab," subtitled "Roxanne Part 2"). The latter's lyrics aren't exceptionally clever, but UTFO created such strong personae for themselves and the stuck-up Ms. R., while isolating such a familiar problem (girl says no), that teenagers identified with them in a singular way. What the record may have lacked in raw power, it made up for in character.

The Roxanne fad ended, leaving the talented UTFO at mortal levels of popularity. The Educated Rapper sat out **Skeezer Pleezer**, but that didn't stop the group (produced, as ever, by Full Force) from making major artistic strides or finding new subject matter. "Where Did You Go?" and "The House Will Rock" combine rap and soulful crooning, while "We Work Hard" (a lecture on the subject of rap) has a solid funk track. The sob story of "Bad Luck Barry" is pretty funny, and chants its refrain over harpsichord!

Restored to full four-man strength, a more adult UTFO came back harder on **Lethal**, a sharp-sounding record with a couple of good ideas but not much lyrical imagination. Dabbling in gangster rap and performing a cross-cultural mating ritual with Anthrax (on the anti-drug title track), the crew demonstrates a desire to try new things, but otherwise this is just a trip to the old neighborhood. The record's low point finds UTFO crooning "Pull your panties down/All I want to do/Is put my unh-unh-unh in you." Smooth.

As steady as UTFO's musical progression has been, the band's rhymes have been headed in the opposite direction. **Doin' It!** puts more excitement and musical action than ever in the grooves (the samples are really cool, and the raps are delivered with skill and authority), but UTFO comes on too rude ("Battle of the Sexes") and too egotistical ("Cold Abrasive," "My Cut's Correct," etc.) to be enjoyable.

Staying under the Full Force umbrella, Doctor Ice's commercially minded solo debut offers a boring litany of product citations and crypto-medical boasting, occasionally delivered inna toasting style with a Jamaican accent. The woozy anachronistic soul sound of the old "Love Jones" and the album's reggae borrowings (Yellowman might want to know about "Nobody Move," credited to Doctor Ice and Full Force) give **The Mic Stalker** its only workable personality: the straight rap tracks are solidly redundant.   [jl/i]

See also *Full Force, Real Roxanne, Roxanne Shanté*.

U2

Boy (Island) 1980 ●
October (Island) 1981 ●
War (Island) 1983 ●
Under a Blood Red Sky (Island) 1983 ●
The Unforgettable Fire (Island) 1984 ●
Wide Awake in America EP (Island) 1985 ●
The Joshua Tree (Island) 1987 ●
Rattle and Hum (Island) 1988 ●

EDGE WITH MICHAEL BROOK

Captive (Virgin) 1987 ●

With a unique, passionate sound, strongly individual lyrics and youthful guilelessness, Dublin's U2 made a big splash quickly. The quartet had released a few praiseworthy singles before **Boy** introduced them to the world at large, via such songs as "I Will Follow," "An Cat Dubh" and "Into the Heart." Powerful and emotional, singer Bono (Paul Hewson) mixes a blend of rock, Gaelic and operatic styles with the occasional yowl or yodel to lead the band's attack; guitarist Dave "the Edge" Evans largely shuns chords in favor of brilliant lead or arpeggio figures that propel and color the songs. Drummer Larry Mullen Jr. and bassist Adam Clayton provide a driving and solid (but sensitive) foundation, completing **Boy**'s musical package, delivered to disc with great skill and invention by producer Steve Lillywhite. An unquestionable masterpiece, **Boy** has a strength, beauty and character that is hard to believe on a debut album made by teenagers. (Note to novice collectors: the US and UK covers are entirely different.)

Although it might have been unreasonable to expect U2 to remain pure and ingenuous indefinitely, **October** seems a bit overblown and oblique by comparison. Already showing signs of becoming a bit of a sensitive *auteur*, Bono's lyrics abandon "Stories for Boys" and adopt "Stranger in a Strange Land." Lillywhite, meanwhile, embellishes the magnificent and direct rock power with found-sound gimmicks, piano and abundantly atmospheric sensuality. **October** does have significant virtues: "Gloria," "I Fall Down" and "Is That All?" rank with the group's best work, and several others fall just short, mostly the result of incomplete songwriting efforts. But, in totality, not a great record.

War, on the other hand, *is* tremendous—an emotional, affecting collection of honest love songs ("Two Hearts Beat as One," "Drowning Man") and political protest ("Sunday Bloody Sunday," "Seconds," "The Refugee") given complex and varied, but unfailingly powerful, treatments. The mix is uncomfortably skewed—towards the drums and, on "New Year's Day," bass—but judicious addition of violin and trumpet supports, rather than detracts from, the band's fire. (Bizarre casting note: the LP's backing vocals are by Kid Creole's Coconuts.)

Taking advantage of U2's growing rep as a commanding live act, **Under a Blood Red Sky** presents them on American and German stages, playing eight dynamic numbers drawn from all three albums, with awesome strength and clarity. Although billed as a mini-LP, the running time exceeds 32 minutes.

Abandoning Steve Lillywhite in the hopes of exploring new audio terrain, U2 made an unusual selection of producer and recorded **The Unforgettable Fire** with Brian Eno and his Canadian collaborator, Daniel Lanois. While the record's lyrical theme—largely a commemoration of Martin Luther King Jr., freedom and individual heroism in general—is both commendable and occasionally articulate, the record's success as an ambitious piece of pop music is more mixed, hitting highs—"Pride (in the Name of Love)," "A Sort of Homecoming," "Wire," the title tune (all on the first side)—as well as an embarrassing low—"Elvis Presley and America." U2's predicament is that their strength is their strength, and the more complex their aspirations, the harder to convey their passion.

One doesn't ordinarily expect to encounter an epiph-

any on a budget-priced disc of outtakes and ephemera, but **Wide Awake in America**'s absolutely mesmerizing eight-minute live version of "Bad" is among U2's finest recordings, and sent me scurrying back to **The Unforgettable Fire** to hear what else I might have missed. Besides another live track, the EP also contains two worthy-of-release studio cuts: "Three Sunrises" and "Love Comes Tumbling." Even when these guys don't put their best forward, what they've got is still pretty amazing.

The Joshua Tree (again produced, but with less personality this time, by Eno and Lanois) helped elevate U2 into the commercial stratosphere, making them one of rock's all-time biggest—and least creatively compromised—money machines. (Whatever the shortcomings of their records, pandering is not one of them.) The LP begins magnificently, with three classic tracks ("Where the Streets Have No Name," "I Still Haven't Found What I'm Looking For" and "With or Without You") that perfectly crystallize U2's majestic essence. Each of the songs is filled with atmosphere, power, melody, instrumental invention *and* rock drive, yet they are all strikingly different. From there, the album turns oddly inconsistent. "Bullet the Blue Sky" shows the danger of listening to too many Doors records; the semi-acoustic "Running to Stand Still" has mood but no presence; "In God's Country" puts the pieces together just right, with a haunting, countryish refrain; the jaunty "Trip Through Your Wires" is weird but intriguing; "One Tree Hill" sounds like a good track but collapses under Bono's Daltreyesque bellowing and Edge's distorto guitar; "Mothers of the Disappeared," while intellectually commendable, lacks a cogent musical framework. Not as good as it was popular, **The Joshua Tree** indicates both U2's strengths and weaknesses.

The delicate balance with which U2 had maintained its artistic equilibrium throughout the group's dizzying ascent crumbled all over *Rattle and Hum*, a dismaying tour film shot by director Phil Joanou in 1987. More than anything, the documentary finds the messianic Bono—no longer remotely capable of expressing anything subtle, honest or believable—awash in overwrought self-importance, a superstar painfully conscious of his position and power. From the egotistical introduction ("This is a song Charles Manson stole from the Beatles—we're stealing it back") to a hideous rendition of "Helter Skelter" through his disconcertingly authoritarian delivery of "Pride (In the Name of Love)," the half-live/half-studio soundtrack album's concert tracks convey more of Bono's burgeoning demagoguery than the band's thrilling live power. And after the bracingly direct "Desire," a catchy horn-charged tribute to Billie Holiday ("Angel of Harlem") and a bizarre collaboration with B.B. King ("When Love Comes to Town"), the new songs are not very good.

The Edge wrote the score for political kidnapping film *Captive*, playing and co-producing it with Michael Brook. The instrumental pieces—a variety of understated acoustic guitar/piano excursions and gripping synthesizer/electric guitar adventures—may not be extraordinary (despite the cool guitar work), but the LP earned enduring significance for featuring the album debut of Sinéad O'Connor, who sings "Heroine (Theme from *Captive*)." [i]

See also *Jah Wobble*.

V V V V V V

LUC VAN ACKER

Luc Van Acker (Wax Trax!) 1986
Heart and Soul EP (Wax Trax!) 1986

Belgium's Van Acker (a member of both the Revolting Cocks and Mussolini Headkick, leader of the short-lived 3 Angry Poles, etc.) is one of the few members of the Chicago/Brussels industrial axis willing to display a gentle side. The cover of his first solo album (aka **The Ship**) shows him smoothly decked out like a character from Fassbinder's *Querelle*, and the grooves inside match the image—suave, continental, but slightly off-kilter Eurodisco with a certain quaint regard for listenability. Contributors include Anna Domino and Blaine Reininger.

The 12-inch EP is a compilation of two Belgian singles, including a remix of the album's "Heart and Soul." [gk]

See also *Mussolini Headkick, Revolting Cocks*.

VANILLA ICE

To the Extreme (Ultrax-SBK) 1990 φ
Extremely Live (Ultrax-SBK) 1991 φ

No sooner had MC Hammer released his grip on the album chart's top spot then this joker came along, jet propelled by a catchy pop single, "Ice Ice Baby," built on the bass and piano intro of Queen and David Bowie's "Under Pressure." Playing both sides of the racial fence with a dual (and equally unreal) image of street tough and non-threatening all-American, this third-rate rapper reached an absurd level of popularity, a phenomenon that mainly serves to underscore the primacy of marketing and prejudice in current music.

To the Extreme isn't totally wretched (not that it's good, but there *are* worse hip-hop LPs to be had), and "Ice Ice Baby" has the notable pop attributes of modulated chords and a real chorus (Ice isn't the first rapper to make that move, but it is a significant and valid crossover maneuver that bears further exploration). On the other hand, the notion that this is PG-rated pap for teenyboppers is completely unsubstantiated by the sex and guns lyrics; the charge that Ice has watered down the essence of rap to make it palatable to a non-black audience would seem to be the result of simple lameness more than conscious stylistic moderation. [i]

DAVID VAN TIEGHEM

These Things Happen (Warner Bros.) 1984
Safety in Numbers (Private Music) 1987 ●
Strange Cargo (Private Music) 1989 ●

In her bid to become the leading terpsichorean patron of avant-rock music, choreographer Twyla Tharp followed projects with David Byrne and Glenn Branca by commissioning a score from Van Tieghem, a multi-instrumentalist mainly known as a drummer in the Love of Life Orchestra and other New York experimental ensembles. Working with many local luminaries, Van Tieghem's music for *Fait Accompli* (released as **These Things Happen**) covers a wide range of styles, from African-tinged rhythms to obscure pop. The interpolation of extraneous bits of found sounds (news, animal noises, etc.) keeps things going when the music threatens to drag, which—given its subordinate role as accompanying earwork—it frequently does.

Excerpts from two subsequent ballet scores and another theatrical project appear on **Safety in Numbers**, as well as a pair of trans-Pacific computer collaborations with Ryuichi Sakamoto. Ultra-modern electronic equipment and ancient acoustic instruments blend harmoniously into an unidentifiable but fascinating sonic stew that favors percussion sounds more than rhythmic adventurism. Much of the album is spare and open, a well-ordered and dynamic backdrop for dances—and dreams.

Van Tieghem's unexpected (and surprisingly attractive, in a cool, Enoesque fashion) vocal performance on "Volcano Diving" is in keeping with the warm allure of **Strange Cargo**. Co-produced with Laurie Anderson collaborator Roma Baran and others, the record is lively and upbeat, evading wallpaper ambience with invention and enthusiasm. [i]

BEN VAUGHN COMBO

The Many Moods of Ben Vaughn (Fever-Restless) 1986
Beautiful Thing (Restless) 1987 ●

BEN VAUGHN

Ben Vaughn Blows Your Mind (Restless) 1988 ●
Dressed in Black (Enigma) 1990 φ

Having outgrown Philadelphia's punk scene, Ben Vaughn's first claim to national fame came when two influential recording artists covered his songs. The Morells put "The Man Who Has Everything" on their 1982 LP, and Marshall Crenshaw did the brilliant "I'm Sorry (But So Is Brenda Lee)" on **Downtown**. For Vaughn, that was enough to get him a record deal.

Although his own sleepy acoustic/country rendition of "I'm Sorry" is a letdown, the rest of **Many Moods** is entertaining no-frills rock'n'roll, with clever lyrics, clever titles and catchy tunes. Besides penning romantic ditties, Vaughn pokes fun at the tyranny of trendies ("Wrong Haircut," "I Dig Your Wig") and defines down-to-earth suburbanism ("Lookin' for a 7-11," "M-M-Motor Vehicle") with implicit satire of statemate Springsteen's epochal bombast. A trio (bass, drums, accordion) provides raucous support for Vaughn's unstylized vocals and guitar.

Beautiful Thing has a fresh, easygoing feel, but too much restraint can be dangerous: halfway through the first side, this mild record threatens to slide right off the turntable. (Flat-sounding production, sorely deficient in highs and lows, exaggerates that impression.) The LP's other shortcomings are its lack of funny titles ("Jerry Lewis in France" is as good as it gets), the paucity of overtly clever lyrics (two exceptions being "Shingaling with Me" and "Big House with a Yard") and a decided shortage of raveups (a crazed polka called "Gimmie, Gimmie, Gimmie" and the peppy guitar instrumental "Desert Boots" notwithstanding).

Opting for the Combo-free life, Vaughn nonetheless made **Blows Your Mind** with instrumental and vocal contributions from his former bandmates. Where the last record's lack of energy was a drag, this one has the creative spine and sprightly production to low-key its way into the pop pleasuredome, somewhere between Jonathan Richman and Yo La Tengo. The relaxed love songs (like "She's Your Problem Now") are delightful; the vintage-styled rockers ("Darlene," the gentle instrumental "El Rambler Dorado") are lively without getting out of hand. (The CD adds three songs.)

Vaughn undertook a four-date tour of East Germany—reportedly backed by the group Pankow, although that's hard to envision—in December 1989 before releasing the star-studded **Dressed in Black**, whose cover, for reasons unknown, pictures Vaughn in blackface. The strongly played rock record features John Hiatt, Marshall Crenshaw, Alex Chilton, Peter Holsapple and Gordon Gano (playing violin on a slow acoustic ballad called "New Wave Dancing"). Although he runs out of wit too early to keep the record afloat, Vaughn does manage to rip through the cool title track and a great version of his old "Man Who Has Everything." After that, it's down to a Velvet Underground quote at the beginning of "Cashier Girl" (an old idea that didn't merit a return visit) and a faintly amusing ode to facial hair ("Growin' a Beard"). [i]

TESCO VEE

See *Meatmen*.

ALAN VEGA

Alan Vega (ZE-PVC) 1980
Collision Drive (ZE-Celluloid) 1981
Saturn Strip (ZE-Elektra) 1983
Just a Million Dreams (ZE-Elektra) 1985
Vega [CD] (Fr. Celluloid) 1989 ●
Deuce Avenue (Fr. Musidisc) 1990 ●

As the vocal half of Suicide, singer Alan Vega was an infuriating electronic shaman. On his own, he creates seductive, '50s-inspired music that succeeds with or without rockabilly revivals. **Alan Vega**'s impact is the result of its spare instrumentation—just the singer plus Phil Hawk on guitar and drums—and deceptively simple songs. "Jukebox Babe" transcends a stuttering lyric and solitary riff to engulf its idiom and then the universe. "Lonely" should be the last word (or moan) on that subject. The rest of the album is similarly zen-like, and no less enjoyable for it.

The self-produced **Collision Drive** has a three-piece band and broader musical range. Besides the droning rock'n'roll of "Magdalena 82" and "Magdalena 83," "Outlaw" flirts with heavy metal rhythms and textures; "Viet Vet" is an extended narrative reminiscent of the Doors. Vega's moody lyricism has the poet's touch—

sometimes heavy-handed but always his own. This recycling is creative.

Continuing Ric Ocasek's association with Suicide, the tall Car produced Vega's third solo album, which mostly abandons the simplicity of his early work in favor of propulsive keyboard-dominated drone-rock played by Ocasek and a variety of sidemen, including Ministry and the Cars' Greg Hawkes. Vega mumbles like an inarticulate offspring of Lou Reed and Jim Morrison, but **Saturn Strip** covers a lot of ground. "Video Babe" reasserts his atmospheric rockabilly sensibility (recall "Jukebox Babe") but with very modern accessories, while an offhand cover of Hot Chocolate's "Every 1's a Winner" closes the LP on an enigmatic, inconclusive note.

Just a Million Dreams finds Vega acquiescing in an almost routine rock milieu, produced in the main by Chris Lord-Alge. Alan's not exactly Mr. Mister, but the backing tracks are so filled with typical synth sounds, electronic rhythms and sizzling lead guitar that they provide little or no musical excitement to stimulate vocal hysteria. In fact, it's difficult at times to believe that this bland singer is actually Vega.

Despite a new collaborator, the self-produced **Deuce Avenue** reveals Vega deeply out of touch with musical reality—his own or anyone else's. Over Liz Lamere's "drums and machines"—impotent and dull backing electronic keyboard tracks rooted in hip-hop style—Vega offhandedly runs down shambling and pale imitations of his potent art-rock raps, expending no effort and making no impression. (Instead of doing anything that might have inspired Vega to better performances, Ric Ocasek helped with the crappy cover art.) **Vega** is a compilation. [si/i]

See also *Suicide*.

SUZANNE VEGA

Suzanne Vega (A&M) 1985 ●
Marlene on the Wall EP (nr/A&M) 1986
Left of Center EP (nr/A&M) 1986 ●
Solitude Standing (A&M) 1987 ●
Compact Hits EP [CD] (nr/A&M) 1988 ●
Days of Open Hand (A&M) 1990 ●

Like Patti Smith a decade earlier, Suzanne Vega was selected from an "underground" New York scene—in this case, the post-rock neo-folk crowd that outgrew new wave for acoustic guitars and sensitively poetic lyrics—and elevated to preeminent status with a major label record deal. Singing in a cool, wispy voice, Vega resembles a mix of Joni Mitchell, Laurie Anderson and Tim Buckley. Producers Lenny Kaye and Steve Addabbo assembled a number of studio players to support Vega in discreet, restrained fashion on her first album; the unobtrusive backing presents her songs clearly and pleasingly. With memorable material and little preciousness or obfuscation, **Suzanne Vega** introduces a talented melodicist with plenty of potential for development.

Whatever its other merits, **Solitude Standing** will always be known as the album containing the enormous hit single, "Luka." Vega's offbeat first-person tale of a child-abuse victim is doubly disturbing, both for its chilling lyrics and her unclear motivation and intent. Captured with exquisitely clear sound, Vega's subtle and inventive quartet provides texture, dynamics and context for the wan tales of urban alienation, preventing her unchanging voice—soft, dry, seductive—from unduly homogenizing the sound. (Three years after **Solitude Standing**'s release, a British production group called DNA stuck an acid house rhythm track under Vega's vocals from the album's "Tom's Diner" and wound up moving Vega—unexpectedly but not, as it turned out, unhappily—into the charts and onto the world's dancefloors.)

The **Compact Hits** mini-compilation puts "Luka," "Neighborhood Girls," "The Queen and the Soldier" and "Left of Center" (a fine track done for the **Pretty in Pink** soundtrack but not on any Vega LP) on a British CD.

Gaining confidence as a performer and as a pop star, Vega handily co-produced **Days of Open Hand** with her synthesizer player, Anton Sanko. The increasingly courageous songwriter tackles a variety of subjects here, from the mundanity of voting ("Institution Green") to an artfully simple and emotionally frank account of visiting a gravely ill loved one in the hospital ("Fifty-Fifty Chance"). With an uplifting catchy pop song ("Book of Dreams") and a handful of less immediate but equally engrossing tales, **Days of Open Hand** is a wholly successful declaration of independence.   [i]

VEIL
Surrender (nr/Clay) 1985

Bryan Gregory's post-Cramps project, the aptly titled Beast, were nothing like his old group, instead attempting a gothic sound comparable to mid-period Siouxsie and the Banshees. Their three early-'80s 45s were of mixed quality, and Gregory soon dropped back into obscurity. His three bandmates, however, moved to the UK and forged ahead as the Veil, releasing an underrated album of dark poptones like "Manikin," "Twist" (both singles) and "Love in a Dying World" (a Beast remake). Vocalist Andrella's wispy voice and quasi-Egyptian shtick manage to charm even when some of the material does not.   [gef]

VEIL
See *Game Theory*.

VELVET MONKEYS
Everything Is Right [tape] (Monkey Business) 1981
Future (Fountain of Youth) 1983
Rotting Corpse au Go-Go (Shimmy-Disc) 1989 ●
Rake (Rough Trade) 1990 ●

HALF JAPANESE/VELVET MONKEYS
Big Big Sun [tape] (K) 1986

One of the simpler pleasures of the noisy-post-new-wave thang, the Velvet Monkeys don't attach any highbrow pretensions to their love of cheesy pop clamor. Whatever irony their work possesses is strictly an afterthought. In the band's earliest incarnation, leader Don Fleming (vocals/guitar) wrote songs with time-honored trash themes ("Let's go to the drive-in tonight") and the Washington DC group played them with the requisite amounts of enthusiasm and Farfisa. Subsequent al-

liances with Half Japanese brought out the avant-gardisms, but nothing serious enough to catch the attention of highbrow critics, and more power to the Monkeys for that.

The 1989 **Rotting Corpse** compilation gathers the band's previous high points (1980-'84) into one convenient package. When the Velvet Monkeys broke up, Fleming and drummer Jay Spiegel moved to New York and formed B.A.L.L.; when *that* group ended, they reformed the Velvet Monkeys, enlisting such new pals as J Mascis (Dinosaur Jr.), Thurston Moore (Sonic Youth) and Julia Cafritz (ex-Pussy Galore) for the fake-'70s exploitation "soundtrack" **Rake**. Given Fleming's new residence and acquaintances, the album is predictably more grungy and smartass than previous Monkeys records, but an enjoyable kick nonetheless.   [gk]

See also *B.A.L.L., Half Japanese*.

VELVET UNDERGROUND
The Velvet Underground & Nico (Verve) 1967 + 1985 ●
White Light/White Heat (Verve) 1967 + 1985 ●
The Velvet Underground (MGM) 1969 (Verve) 1985 ●
Loaded (Cotillion) 1970 ●
Live at Max's Kansas City (Cotillion) 1972 ●
Lou Reed and the Velvet Underground (Pride) 1973
Squeeze (nr/Polydor) 1973
1969 Velvet Underground Live with Lou Reed (Mercury) 1974 ●
VU (Verve-PolyGram) 1985 ●
Velvet Underground (nr/Polydor) 1986
Another View (Verve-PolyGram) 1986 ●
The Best of the Velvet Underground (Verve-PolyGram) 1989 φ

VARIOUS ARTISTS
Heaven and Hell Volume One (Communion) 1990 ●
Heaven and Hell Vol. 2 (nr/Imaginary) 1991 ●

The Velvet Underground marked a turning point in rock history. After the release of **The Velvet Underground & Nico**, knowing the power of which it was capable, the music could never be as innocent, as unselfconscious as before. The band's first album may have come on a bit cute with its Andy Warhol-designed banana cover—indeed, patron Warhol's name (he also "produced") was splashed around like a talisman—but singer/guitarist Lou Reed's tough songs and the band's equally tough playing owed nothing to anybody. In perverse subject matter ("Heroin," "Venus in Furs"), deceptively simple musical forms and anarchic jamming, the Velvets displayed the rebellious traits new wave bands would pick up on ten years later. Singer Nico's four vocals provide textural context and breathing space between Reed's darker visions.

With Nico gone, **White Light/White Heat** is almost unbearably intense. John Cale recites a gruesome little story ("The Gift") over steamy accompaniment, and Reed sings the praises of methamphetamines (the title track)—and that's the light entertainment. The second side consists of extended, feedback-wailing guitar solos ("I Heard Her Call My Name") and graphic porno-junkie tales (seventeen minutes of "Sister Ray"). The album is as morally black as its cover.

Something had to change, and when the Velvet Underground next surfaced, they sounded like a different band. Cale's departure (replaced by multi-instrumentalist Doug Yule) might have played a part, but remaining *auteur* Reed has since shown himself capable of wide mood swings. The music on **The Velvet Underground** is quiet, melodic, gentle even when it turns up the juice ("What Goes On," "Beginning to See the Light") and—who would have believed it?—moving ("Jesus," "I'm Set Free"). Only "The Murder Mystery," with its double-tracked chatter, is guilty of self-indulgence.

Lou Reed and the Velvet Underground is a bargain-bin compilation of the first three LPs.

The group started on a fourth, unreleased album before switching record companies. Sixteen years later, songs from those sessions finally surfaced officially on **VU**. They show the Velvet Underground stoking the rock'n'roll fire that blazed forth on **Loaded**: "Foggy Notion" is a timeless raveup of classical simplicity (though typically kinky subject matter). Reed recycled half of **VU**'s material on his early solo albums, but it's charming to hear them played forcefully by a functioning band.

By 1970, the Velvet Underground was into a wholesome overdrive. **Loaded** may have seemed superficial in comparison to the preceding albums, but it does include Reed's twin anthems, "Sweet Jane" and "Rock & Roll." Personality conflicts, however, resulted in his leaving the group before the record's release; Yule took some of the vocals and most of the credit. **Loaded**'s sweetness-and-light music was the Velvets' death throes.

With its creative force gone, the band shuffled along for two more years and even released a British album, **Squeeze**, with no original members. For new doses of the real thing, fans had to be content with live recordings of past glories. **Live at Max's Kansas City** is a low-fi document of the Velvets' last hurrah in the Big Apple. The band—Reed, Sterling Morrison and two Yules—is tight but mellow; three of the four songs taken from the first album were originally sung by Nico.

The two-record **1969** (from assorted late-'69 shows in Texas and San Francisco) is more interesting in its extended view of the group and choice of material. As on the Max's LP, the post-Cale band is generally relaxed—a far cry from the musical entropy of the first two albums. The Velvet Underground got its groundbreaking out of the way early. (When it arrived on CD in 1988, the album had inexplicably been separated into two individual volumes. Take your pick.)

In 1986, British Polydor released **Velvet Underground**, a five-album boxed set of the first three original LPs, **VU** and a bonus record of nine previously unavailable tracks, including an early "Rock and Roll," an instrumental "Guess I'm Falling in Love," a studio take of "We're Gonna Have a Real Good Time Together" and two versions of "Hey Mr. Rain." Sensibly, **Another View** was also issued separately.

Having issued the three original albums and **VU** on CD in 1985, PolyGram assembled a chronological one-disc studio career summation, **The Best of the Velvet Underground** (subtitled **Words and Music of Lou Reed**). What you get is half the first LP, the title track of the second, three each from the third and **VU**, and **Loaded**'s obvious pair. A neat introduction, but a skimpy one.

With an entire generation of Velvets-worshipping noisemongers to choose from, the first ten contributors to what is threatened as an ongoing tribute-album series to the band are far from the most obvious. Nirvana, Buffalo Tom and Screaming Trees do the homeland honors on **Heaven and Hell Volume One**, leaving Ride, James (who deserve to be smacked for turning "Sunday Morning" into a song title medley), Wedding Present, Telescopes and Motorcycle Boy to interpret such classics as "Candy Says," "Run, Run, Run" and "She's My Best Friend" with varying degrees of sonic and cultural distortion.   [si/i]

See also *John Cale, Nico, Lou Reed, Maureen Tucker*.

TOM VERLAINE

Tom Verlaine (Elektra) 1979
Dreamtime (Warner Bros.) 1981
Words from the Front (Warner Bros.) 1982 ●
Cover (Warner Bros.) 1984 ●
Flash Light (IRS) 1987 ●
The Wonder (nr/Fontana) 1990 ●

Television was the satisfying result of a clash between two disparate styles. Leader Tom Verlaine was the dreamer, playing sinuous guitar and singing in the strangled, intense voice of a young poet. Guitarist Richard Lloyd and the rhythm section of Billy Ficca and Fred Smith tended more to classic, bash-it-out rock-'n'roll. When Verlaine went solo, many assumed he'd simply float off into the ozone.

Surprisingly, he managed to preserve Television's delicate balance and even add new elements on his first solo LP. Two tortured, driving mini-epics—"The Grip of Love" and "Breakin' in My Heart," a classic from the old group's live sets—blend flesh and spirit perfectly. The vividly desperate "Kingdom Come" has the honor of being covered by David Bowie on **Scary Monsters**—how's that for an endorsement? There's even a playful nonsense song, "Yonki Time," indicating Verlaine is using his freedom to grow.

Alas, with **Dreamtime**, Verlaine narrows his scope, seeming to retreat into the isolation of the familiar. There are taut, anxious tunes ("Down on the Farm"), lilting ones ("Without a Word") and an abundance of exquisite guitar licks, but it's too predictable. A performer who trades in passion can't afford *not* to surprise.

Words from the Front shows more daring, although—like its predecessor—it suffers from inconsistent material. "Postcard from Waterloo" proves that Verlaine can be as romantic as Barry Manilow without sacrificing keenness. "Days on the Mountain" provides perhaps the ultimate in lightheaded ecstasy, with his fluttering guitar skillfully imitating the ascension into heaven.

In some ways, **Cover** constitutes a return to the style of Verlaine's first LP. The songs are short and to the point, without the sometimes florid expansiveness of his previous two efforts. On the other hand, brevity doesn't discourage Verlaine from floating into the ozone—he just does it quicker. For every "Lindi-Lu," a fine jerky rocker, there's two like "Swim," a gentle evocation of airheadedness.

Co-producing **Flash Light** with Fred Smith, Verlaine achieves an energetic rock sound that exudes new realms of self-confidence. Meanwhile, his poetry remains characteristically brilliant. In "The Scientist Writes a Letter," a song taking precisely that form, he writes, "It's funny how attractive indifference can be/My sense of failure . . . it's not so important/ Electricity means so much more to me." As Verlaine has developed and refined his music over the years, his urgent vocals and guitar playing (especially on "Cry Mercy Judge") still carry the stylistically hallmarks of his old band.

Verlaine and Smith continue their subversive tryst with contemporary rock on **The Wonder**, concocting muscular, superficially routine arrangements in which familiar lines of wiggly guitar and other unsettling dramatics drift in and out of range. The surprisingly cozy tone of Verlaine's self-amused vocals put his mildly offbeat lyrics in an entirely new context; combined with the music's dynamic tension, mixed signals make **The Wonder** an intriguing, multifaceted experience.   [jy/rj/i]

See also *Television*.

VERLAINES

Ten O'Clock in the Afternoon EP (NZ Flying Nun) 1984
Hallelujah All the Way Home (NZ Flying Nun) 1985
   (Homestead) 1989 ●
Juvenilia (Homestead) 1987
Bird-Dog (NZ Flying Nun) 1987 (Homestead) 1988 ●
Some Disenchanted Evening (Flying Nun-Homestead)
   1990 ●

Named after the French symbolist poet and fronted by a classical music student, the Verlaines are based in Dunedin, New Zealand, the same hometown as the Chills and the Clean. From the band's first single, "Death and the Maiden" (inspired by an Edvard Munch painting), through their recent releases, poetry and high art have had a large impact on singer/songwriter/multi-instrumentalist Graeme Downes' approach to rock music. Besides his anguished, mournful voice, the trio's sound is characterized by furious electric guitar strumming and deft time shifts.

The first Anglo-American release, **Juvenilia**, is a compilation that offers an excellent overview of the band's early career. Combining the six-song **Ten O'Clock in the Afternoon** EP, "Death and the Maiden" and three songs from a Dunedin scene compilation, this stunning anthology has a punkish immediacy and an almost pastoral freshness. Downes' tales of drunkards, romantics and kids on the dole are punctuated by feisty drumming and such instrumental flourishes as oboe and carnival organ.

Hallelujah All the Way Home is the group's attempt at stylistic definition and refinement. Although ambitious and pretentious (lyrics harp on the antiquated concept of the artist as exile), the album is nevertheless grounded in Downes' exquisite and inventive sense of melody. **Bird-Dog** is a stronger, more realized effort. Augmenting their sound with horns, strings and piano, the Verlaines craft a truly memorable album that builds from delicate, hushed ballads to explosive rock'n'roll burlesque. "C.D. Jimmy Jazz and Me," "Slow Sad Love Song" and "Just Mum" are standouts, but each track seems to surpass the one before it.

Lacking the exhilarating richness and devastating melancholy of **Bird-Dog**, **Some Disenchanted Evening**

is more restrained and a bit less confident. "Jesus What a Jerk" and "The Funniest Thing" are straightforward guitar-pop—solid and listenable, but without the spark of unpredictability that elevated the band's early work. The album's coda, a piano ballad styled after Randy Newman, is actually the collection's crowning achievement; harnessing a dapper melody to a bitterly sardonic lyric about failure, it reveals new-found subtlety and clarity in Downes' writing.   [kss]

VIBRATING EGG

Come on in Here If You Want To EP (Dog Gone) 1988

A 12-inch of five cool covers by an unknown band on an indie label would normally rate little notice, but Georgia's Vibrating Egg has more than just the good sense to dedicate its record to Leonard Cohen and Viv Stanshall. Raoul Duplott, the unsteady vocalist on these amiable renditions of Procol Harum's "Whiter Shade of Pale," Roky Erickson's "Bermuda," an old spiritual and two of Alice Cooper's finest, is none other than Jefferson Holt, manager of R.E.M. and founder of the Dog Gone label, surrounded by a host of pseudonymous players. (Hmm . . .) Good fun, but Holt had best keep his day job.   [i]

VIBRATORS

Pure Mania (Columbia) 1976 ●
V2 (nr/Epic) 1978
Batteries Included (nr/CBS) 1980
Guilty (nr/Anagram) 1983
Alaska 127 (nr/Ram) 1984
Fifth Amendment (nr/Ram) 1985
Live (nr/FM-Revolver) 1986
Recharged (nr/FM-Revolver) 1988
Meltdown (nr/FM-Revolver) 1988 ●
Disco in Moscow EP (nr/FM-Revolver) 1988
Vicious Circle (nr/FM-Revolver) 1989 ●
Volume 10 (nr/FM-Revolver) 1990 ●

KNOX

Plutonium Express (nr/Razor) 1983

Like the Stranglers, the Vibrators were considerably older than the other bands comprising the London punk scene in 1977. A rudimentary quartet with a knack for insidiously catchy songs, the Vibrators—after a brief alliance with Chris Spedding, whom they backed on the first punk novelty record, "Pogo Dancing"—established themselves with a stream of clever pop singles that captured the minimalist energy (minus the inchoate anger) of their peers.

Pure Mania—with its soon-to-be-a-cliché color-Xerox artwork cover—is a treasure trove of memorable ditties that strip down pop in a parallel to the Ramones' streamlining of it. A brilliant record, cheerful in a loopy way and filled with great fragmentary tunes and innocuously threatening lyrics.

Recorded in Berlin (briefly the band's adopted home base), **V2** features new bassist Gary Tibbs (later a Roxy Musician and Ant) and a more ambitious agenda. While some of the material is not that different from the debut LP, **V2** is pretentious and overblown, following too many different cul-de-sacs to hang together.

Although trends quickly passed them by, the Vibrators trundled on until 1980. When they split up, CBS issued the **Batteries Included** retrospective, with such classic tunes as "Judy Says" and "Yeah Yeah Yeah." Compiling the best tracks from the first two LPs and adding a couple of other treats, it's an essential souvenir of the class of '77.

The original Vibrators (Knox, Eddie, Pat Collier and John Ellis) reformed two years later and issued **Guilty**, an okay diversion highlighted by the name-dropping title song and a remake of "Baby, Baby," the Vibes' classic '77 single. Though lacking the debut's full-throttle punk rush, **Guilty** nonetheless entertains by sheer force of its elemental melodic tracks.

That same year saw the release of a solo LP by singer and chief songwriter Knox. (He has also recorded, with Charlie Harper of the U.K. Subs, as the Urban Dogs.) Unspectacular in all departments, **Plutonium Express**' banal contents are telegraphed by such song titles as "Goin' Uptown" and "Love Is Burning."

Alaska 127, named after bassist/producer Collier's recording studio, is the band's best post-reunion LP. The opener, a furious rewrite of "I Fought the Law" called "Amphetamine Blue," sets the pace for the eleven songs that follow, all either likable lightweight pop or kick-ass hard rock.

The excitement began to wane by **Fifth Amendment**, which finds the group plugging away at midtempo rock with no distinguishing marks. Collier departed soon after to concentrate more on his bigtime career as a producer (Katrina and the Waves, House of Love, Soup Dragons, etc.), but did pop back around to remix and edit the band's live album. (His replacement was engineer/soundman Noel Thompson.) Plucking songs from all the previous LPs save for **Guilty**, **Live** shrewdly concentrates on older, greatest-hits material. And while the performances are quite good, you get the feeling these guys don't really have their hearts in it anymore. Thompson and guitarist Ellis left after **Live** (Ellis turned up in the 1991 edition of the Stranglers), and the band played on with two new members.

Despite the optimistic title, **Recharged** makes it clear the Vibrators have long since run their course. Hacking out simplistic good-timey rockers centered on stale lines like "Heart of the city/Beneath the neon light," they create something that's not totally awful but still a major drag in comparison to the good old days. **Volume 10** is a slight improvement, thanks to virtuoso show-offy lead work from yet another new guitarist, Nigel Bennett, and some tasty sax. [i/db]

See also *U.K. Subs*.

SID VICIOUS

See *Sex Pistols*.

HOLLY BETH VINCENT

See *Holly and the Italians*.

VIOLENT FEMMES

Violent Femmes (Slash) 1983 ●
Hallowed Ground (Slash) 1984 ●
The Blind Leading the Naked (Slash-Warner Bros.)
　1986 ●
3 (Slash-Warner Bros.) 1989 ●
Why Do Birds Sing? (Slash-Reprise) 1991 φ

MERCY SEAT

The Mercy Seat (Slash) 1987

BRIAN RITCHIE

The Blend (SST) 1987 ●
Sonic Temple & Court of Babylon (SST) 1989 ●
I See a Noise (Dali-Chameleon) 1990 φ

VICTOR DE LORENZO

Peter Corey Sent Me (Dali-Chameleon) 1991 φ

SIGMUND SNOPEK III

WisconsInsane (Dali-Chameleon) 1987 ●

The Violent Femmes burst out of Milwaukee, Wisconsin in the early '80s, a remarkably original trio playing acoustic instruments and singing intense, personal songs with remarkable candor and love. Initially resembling a punk version of the Modern Lovers, the Femmes—Gordon Gano (vocals, guitar, songs), Brian Ritchie (bass) and Victor De Lorenzo (drums)—have grown more uncommon over the years, fixing a flexible style that resembles no other band.

On the skeletal first album, Gano's articulate passion and lyrical maladjustment combine with the charged (but not very loud) playing to convey an incredible sense of desperation and rage. "Blister in the Sun" and "Kiss Off" are typical of the anger seething in the grooves, while "Gone Daddy Gone" and "Please Do Not Go" show a more upbeat side still rooted in extreme individuality and super-ego. The disc's best couplet: "Why can't I get just one fuck?/Guess it's got something to do with luck." (There are two bonus tracks on the CD.)

Hallowed Ground takes a much different approach, displaying Gano's religious fervor and connecting with traditional American folk music. The cast includes a banjo picker and autoharp strummer, as well as a horn'n'clarinet section; the material encompasses tragic balladry ("Country Death Song"), old-timey spirituals ("Jesus Walking on the Water," "It's Gonna Rain"), mild be-bop ("Sweet Misery Blues") and demented jazz-funk ("Black Girls"). Not as pointed as the first album, it nonetheless showcases an inquisitive band deeply committed to self-expression, regardless of the consequences.

The third LP was produced by Talking Head Jerry Harrison with conscious mainstreaming intent. Of course, the Femmes at their most commercial are still pretty radical, although "I Held Her in My Arms" does sound unnervingly like Bruce Springsteen. As if to prove their orneriness, a vituperative attack on "Old Mother Reagan" and the similarly anti-authoritarian "No Killing" demonstrate an undying rebellious spirit. But it's another type of spirit that invests the bluesy "Faith" and the Stonesy "Love & Me Make Three," keeping god in the grooves alongside Marc Bolan, who gets worked over with a misbegotten Headish version of "Children of the Revolution." The Velvet Underground fares better on "Good Friend," a Femmes original that uncannily echoes Lou Reed.

The Mercy Seat is an energetically electric album by Gano's all-gospel side group. Backing big-voiced (but mini-skirted) singer Zena Von Heppinstall in a lineup with a bassist and drummer, he plays guitar and joins the choruses of such numbers as "I Am a Pilgrim" and "I Don't Need Nobody Else (but Jesus)."

De Lorenzo co-produced and, with Ritchie, provided most of the instrumental backing on **WisconsIn-sane**, a loopy extravaganza from singing dairy state keyboardist/flautist Sigmund Snopek III. (Snopek's previous albums—solo and with his eponymous group, going back to the late '70s—were subsequently reissued by his new label.) While their contributions to such serio-comical Midwest maunderings as "The Rose of Wisconsin," "Thank God This Isn't Cleveland" and "I'm So Tired of Singing About the Sky" tend to be lost in the slick production, the LP is a cute theatrical diversion.

Snopek returned the favor by playing keyboards on **3**, the Femmes' first new LP in three years. Settled into a comfortable creative torpor, the trio revisits familiar terrain with easy confidence and very little evident artistic ambition or effort: the loudly electric arrangement of "Fool in the Full Moon" is about the extent of the record's adventures. (The swaying jazzy feel of "Outside the Palace" and the rock beat of the vengeful "Mother of a Girl" make them **3**'s only memorable tunes.) Gano's songwriting and delivery have their usual odd character and some of the old passion, but the Femmes don't seem to be making much progress or impact in any direction here.

Ritchie's solo debut ("dedicated to Sun Ra, Son House and my son Silas") shows off his diverse musical interests, from topical blues to avant-garde exotica and beyond. Joined by various players, he sings and handles guitar, banjo, flute, recorder, accordion and other instruments, leaving most of the bass chores to Cynthia Bartell of Têtes Noires. (He and De Lorenzo had earlier produced her group's **Clay Foot Gods** LP.) Not all of the excursions work equally well, but **The Blend** certainly proves that Ritchie's talents extend far beyond his role in the Femmes.

Using a wide variety of instruments (from conch and ocarina to bass flute, baritone sax, Arabic tabla and kalimba), Ritchie and his four talented sidemen still manage to sound entirely organic—even a little plain—on **Sonic Temple & Court of Babylon**. While the folky music has a nice rustic feel, Ritchie's lyrics are far less friendly. In an artless but adequate voice, he fires off splenetic attacks on Christianity, American mores, capitalism and someone who deceived him, taking time to praise Sun Ra and marvel at life within some Arabic castle. (Imagine the arguments he and Gano must have . . .)

With the countryfied sarcasm of "Religion Ruined My Life" and the Middle Easternisms of "2 Tongues, 2 Minds," **I See a Noise** repeats two of Ritchie's previous themes, but he applies far more wit, humor and imagination this time. Playing down-to-earth music—an acoustic and electric mix with easy, direct appeal—he offers wry and funny (often autobiographical) commentary on such topics as death, babies and Ernest Hemingway. Easily the best of Ritchie's three albums.

The last Femme to strike out on his own, Victor De Lorenzo sings (sort of), drums, percusses and, for one song, plays guitar and keyboards on **Peter Corey Sent Me**, an intriguing and thoughtfully artistic effort that resembles the Bonzo Dog Band in dada spirit, if not humor. No two tracks are alike (except perhaps in their literate, idiosyncratic lyrics and eloquently understated execution); the stylistic compote of country, noir jazz, spoken musical comedy, 12-bar African chanting, folk, Talking Headsy rock, continental balladry, etc. unfolds to reveal many delightful surprises. [i]

VIPERS
Outta the Nest! (PVC) 1984
How About Somemore? (Midnight) 1988
Not So Pretty . . . Not So New [tape] (Midnight) 1988
Nest in Peace (Skyclad) 1989

Rather than discuss the relevance or validity of the entire garage-rock-*cum*-psychedelic revival—bands who dress up like 1967 and play tambourines and fuzzed guitar—I'll just note that New York's Vipers were one of the leading lights of said movement. Suffice to say **Outta the Nest** sounds precisely like your (best/worst) memories of mid-'60s American rock, from the Seeds to the Standells to the Shadows of Knight. The Vipers write good tunes that sound properly dated and play them with equally stylized vim. The production could be better, but that's the idea. As they sing in the lead-off track, "Nothing's from Today." (Five years later, a remixed, remastered and expanded—by two LP tracks, plus a bonus 7-inch of two more—edition of the Vipers' first album was issued, in a new sleeve and on white vinyl, as **Nest in Peace**.)

In the meantime, a new lineup—retaining only guitarist David Mann and singer Jonithan Weiss—made an all-original-material second album, which was released in a limited edition with a bonus three-song EP and quickly reissued with a different cover. Taking its cues from both the Yardbirds and the Raiders and making blatant derivation sound like the latest invention, **How About Somemore?** is every bit as cool as **Nest**, with the added benefit of far better production. **Not So Pretty . . . Not So New**, a 20-track cassette of previously unreleased demos and outtakes dating from 1981 to 1985, has mediocre sound quality but loads of otherwise unavailable Vipers originals. [i]

VIRGIN PRUNES
A New Form of Beauty 2 EP (nr/Rough Trade) 1981
A New Form of Beauty 3 EP (nr/Rough Trade) 1981
A New Form of Beauty 4 "Din Glorious" [tape] (Rough Trade) 1982
A New Form of Beauty 1–4 (It. Rough Trade) 1982
. . . If I Die, I Die (nr/Rough Trade) 1982 (Rough Trade) 1990 ●
Heresie (Fr. L'Invitation au Suicide) 1982 (Fr. Baby-New Rose) 1987
Over the Rainbow (Fr. Baby-New Rose) 1985 ●
The Moon Looked Down and Laughed (Touch and Go) 1986 ●
The Hidden Lie (Live in Paris 6/6/86) (Fr. Baby-New Rose) 1986 ●

PRUNES
Lite Fantastik (Fr. Baby-New Rose) 1988
Nada (Fr. Baby-New Rose) 1989

GAVIN FRIDAY AND THE MAN SEEZER
Each Man Kills the Thing He Loves (Island) 1989 ●

PRINCESS TINYMEAT
Herstory (nr/Rough Trade) 1987

Dublin weirdoes with androgynous names and a predilection for semi-melodic rock and conceptual lyrics, the Virgin Prunes (one of whom, original guitarist Dik Evans, is the Edge's brother) released two intriguing 45s before embarking on the ambitious "A New Form of Beauty" project (the concept being the beauty of being different—and by metaphor, sounding different). Following a 7-inch (part 1), the 10-inch **A New Form of Beauty 2** contains two ominously dark and abrasive assaults (including incestuous classic "Come to Daddy") plus a quieter abrasive doodle; the 12-inch **Beauty 3** pairs a frightening occult opus "Beast (Seven Bastard Suck)" with a three-tune suite, "The Slow Children." The **"Din Glorious"** cassette features highlights from a Dublin gallery performance, mixing early PiL-style semi-songs from the three previous EPs and all sorts of taped sounds to very unsettling effect. The Italian **A New Form of Beauty 1–4** lays out the entire series on two albums, making it easier to grasp the gist of the concept.

Produced by Colin Newman, **If I Die** offers hard-edged but delicate pop ("Ballad of the Man") and anthemic post-punk ("Walls of Jericho") contrasting challenging, longwinded opuses with skewed, angular instrumentation and ponderous vocal recitations ("Baudachong," "Caucasian Walk"). A complex band of many minds (not to mention three lead vocalists), the Prunes stake out unique ground, straddling art and mundanity with style and skill. Difficult but fascinating. The CD adds an '82 goth-dance single, "Pagan Lovesong."

Commissioned to create a work based around the theme of insanity, the Prunes came up with **Heresie**, a boxed set of two 10-inches. One disc shows the more experimental side of the band, varying from the dense, neo-industrial "Rhetoric" to a sing-song ditty ("Down the Memory Lane"); the other disc contains an excellent five-song set taped live in Paris. **Over the Rainbow** is an odds-and-ends compilation of previously unreleased and rare/compilation tracks up to 1983, highlighted by the awesome "Red Nettle" (which consists of a majestic, sampled chord movement repeated for two minutes). The CD version includes all of **Heresie**.

The Moon Looked Down and Laughed, produced rather unimaginatively by Dave Ball (ex-Soft Cell), is an unpalatable mishmash of Bowiesque glitter and music-hall camp. Gavin Friday's vocals are overwrought; several songs plod along painfully, going nowhere and taking forever to get there. Jim (Foetus) Thirlwell guests to little effect.

A chasm soon grew between main singer Friday, who wished to explore more romantic cabaret music, and bassist Strongman and drummer-turned-guitarist Mary, who just wanted to be a rock band. Both sides got their wishes when the Virgin Prunes called it a day in mid-'86. **The Hidden Lie** is an unnecessary posthumous live album, although it does contain a large percentage of otherwise unissued material. Strongman and Mary continued to release records under the truncated Prunes moniker, but with little success and limited artistic viability.

Friday went down a much different road. After taking a breather to paint, open a nightclub, record a 12-inch single of the Stones' "You Can't Always Get What You Want" with buddy Simon Carmody and explore his new roots (the cabaret tradition of Brel, Piaf and Brecht/Weill), he began an extremely promising solo career. Taking cues from Tom Waits, the mercurial crooner and his piano sidekick the Man Seezer came up with **Each Man Kills the Thing He Loves**. Producer Hal Willner gets the most out of the skilled ensemble (which includes guitarist Marc Ribot, bassist Fernando Saunders and drummer Michael Blair), the lush, timeless songs and Friday's voice which, finally given the spotlight denied him by the democratic Prunes, has never revealed so much emotion. A highly recommended album with passion and drama to spare.

Going by the name Princess Tinymeat, early Virgin Prunes transvestite drummer Haa Lacka Bintii has made a number of singles, collected on the **Herstory** album, that rival his former band in the weirdness department.
[i/dgs/gef]

VISAGE
Visage (Polydor) 1980 ●
The Anvil (Polydor) 1982 ●
Fade to Grey—The Singles Collection (Polydor) 1983
Visage/The Anvil [tape] (nr/Polydor) 1983
Beat Boy (Polydor) 1984 ●

STRANGE CRUISE
Strange Cruise (nr/EMI) 1986

Formed around cult-figure fop Steve Strange (Harrington), Visage began as a part-time group uniting the formidable talents of Ultravox's Midge Ure and Billy Currie, Dave Formula and John McGeoch (both then in Magazine) and ex-Rich Kid drummer Rusty Egan for the ultimate in dance-oriented new romanticism. **Visage** is filled with rich humor and sound puns in addition to solid musicianship on guitars and synthesizers; how could anyone not crack a smile over the Ennio Morricone-styled homage to Clint Eastwood, "Malpaso Man," or the self-mocking "Visa-age"? Added to the humor, the fine music automatically deflates Strange's colorful pretensions.

Unfortunately, those pretensions dominate **The Anvil**, wherein Strange attempts to wring every mannered drop of angst and meaning out of his lyrics and vocals. Luckily, the rest of Visage perform as strongly as ever, although in a far darker mood than before.

Continuing their dance-geared version of Heaven 17-styled electro-funk, **Beat Boy** finds Visage (comprising, this time, Strange and Egan joined by the Barnacle brothers and Andy Barnett) readier to rock, using plentiful guitar on the endless title track (and elsewhere) to color the inexorable rhythms and repetitious, vapid lyrics. The songs are incredibly (and annoyingly, if you're paying attention) long, but there are still eight of 'em, with a total party time of over 45 minutes.

Fade to Grey is the most concise proof of Visage's merit, compiling nine catchy slices of dance-rock (two remixed for the occasion) and an otherwise unreleased (and utterly unnecessary) cover of Zager & Evans' "In the Year 2525." "Pleasure Boys," "We Move" and "Night Train" are among the best efforts, showing that conciseness can surely be an asset.

When last heard of, Strange had formed Strange Cruise with Wendy Wu, ex-lead singer of the Photos, and released an eponymous album. [sg/i]

See also *Magazine, Rich Kids, Ultravox*.

VISITORS

See *Radio Birdman*.

VIVA SATURN

See *Rain Parade*.

VOICE FARM

The World We Live In (Optional) 1982
Voice Farm (Ralph) 1987
Bigger Cooler Weirder (Morgan Creek) 1991 ●

On **The World We Live In**, San Francisco's Voice Farm was a trio—two guys who appear on the front cover dressed only in their underpants, and a less-exposed female—employing synthesizers, vocals and acoustic percussion to weave moody instrumentals, some of which are paired with incisive, intelligent (and, in one case, horrifying) lyrics. The band's dynamic range, from hauntingly beautiful to startlingly intense, and stylistic variety—encompassing movie-music vagueness, machine noise and disco bump, as well as direct song forms—surpasses many other all-electronic bands, and makes this a totally fascinating album with nary a dull moment. Producer David Kahne did his usual ace job, and whoever thought of covering the Jaynetts' venerable "Sally Go Round the Roses" also deserves a compliment.

The radically different **Voice Farm** finds the group reduced to its core: Myke Reilly (keyboards/percussion/voices) and Charly Brown (vocals/keyboards). Aided by an assortment of backing singers and a guitarist, the two are firmly in vocal/song mode, pairing their rhythmic sonic adventures with witty, pointedly satirical lyrics about intriguingly offbeat modern subjects. (A relatively straight cover of the Supremes' "Nowhere to Run" doesn't add anything to the song or the record.) The accomplished assemblages overlay the dance beats with synthesized effects, found sounds, spoken-word tape manipulation and other ear-catching ephemera for a diverting album that has more club-play potential than home turntable longevity. [i]

VOICE OF THE BEEHIVE

Just a City EP (nr/Food) 1987
I Say Nothing EP (nr/London) 1987 + 1988 ●
Let It Bee (London) 1988 ●

Built around American singing sisters Tracey Bryn and Melissa Brooke, London's Voice of the Beehive is a delightful clash of two sensibilities: California girl-bop and English buzz-pop. With the exception of two tracks, the material on the two UK EPs is repeated on the band's sole album; throughout **Let It Bee**, principal songwriter Bryn throws together catchy guitar tunes that are at once ditzy, raunchy and ironic. She's shameless enough to add a misogynist twist to the "Beat of Love" ("There are all kinds of ways to get banged"), but she's also willing to show some vulnerability ("Sorrow Floats"). In the Beehive's lexicon of love, girls are bitches, boys are cruel and everyone's a fool: "Trust Me" is, in fact, a warning. Bryn's fascination seems to be the flipside of good times—life isn't a party, it's the slightly drunk and miserable walk home alone afterwards. [kss]

VOIVOD

War and Pain (Metal Blade) 1984 ●
RRRÖÖÖAAARRR (Noise Int'l-Combat) 1986 ●
Thrashing Rage EP (Noise Int'l-Combat) 1986
Killing Technology (Noise Int'l-Combat) 1987 ●
Dimension Hatrüss (Noise Int'l) 1988 ●
Nothingface (Mechanic-MCA) 1989 ●

Montréal's Voivod is a thrilling anomaly, staking out a unique terrain on the postmodern frontier. While often classified as metal, what this group of French Canadian weirdoes does is better described as dark progressive rock with a strain of conceptual sci-fi.

Beginning the band's album-by-album concept—the adventures of a futuristic warrior entity called the Voivod—**War and Pain** is a crude, careening blast of youthful energy, post-apocalyptic Mad Maxisms and prickly power-thrash reminiscent of Motörhead. Exciting tracks like "Voivod" and "Black City" possess a raw, neo-bluesy quality that overcomes the poor production quality.

RRRÖÖÖAAARRR takes Voivod's original style to its logical extreme/dead end, offering a homogeneous wall of cathartic riffing and Denis "Snake" Belanger's most tortured vocal articulations. While "Korgüll the Exterminator" is convoluted enough to be memorable, the rest of the album's white-noise metal is a blur that leaves no substantial impression. A change was both imminent and necessary. (The picture-disc EP consists of four tracks from the album.)

Killing Technology brought Voivod into maturity. Soaking up disparate influences (especially progressive/psychedelic rockers like Pink Floyd and Van der Graaf Generator and post-punk/industrialists like Killing Joke and Einstürzende Neubauten), Voivod formed a fresh, dissonant sound, merging metal's power with these other genres' experimental imperatives, and doing it better than anyone since Chrome. Like the Voivod himself (who, at this point, ventures into the unknown vastness of space), the album reveals a band making a successful, brave transition from primitivism to futurism. The CD and cassette include two bonus tracks.

Each subsequent release has exponentially continued this upward climb in quality and imagination. **Dimension Hatrüss** conceptually capsulizes the rise and fall of an alien universe, primed by complex songs that flirt with melody yet retain all of Voivod's previous energy. With the appearance of electronics and Snake's new-found singing abilities, this is an excellent album.

Nothingface is Voivod's most interesting achievement to date, showcasing a full-blown melodic sensibility, vibrant production, the integration of sampling technology, guitarist Denis "Piggy" D'Amour's increasing stature as the Robert Fripp of alternative metal and a stunning rendition of Syd Barrett's "Astronomy Domine." The haunting "Missing Sequences" is only one of many high-quality songs, all mated to the band's most serious (subjects range from ecology and alchemy to existentialism) and deftly composed lyrics yet. [gef]

VOLCANO SUNS

The Bright Orange Years (Homestead) 1985
All-Night Lotus Party (Homestead) 1986
Bumper Crop (Homestead) 1987 ●
Farced (SST) 1988 ●

Thing of Beauty (SST) 1989 •
Career in Rock (1/4 Stick-Touch and Go) 1991

When Mission of Burma ended in 1983 only drummer Peter Prescott continued to play loud rock music. On **The Bright Orange Years**, his trio with bassist Jeff Weigand and guitarist Jon Williams takes energetic folk-rock with sturdy Midwest melodies and overplays it into a punky mixture of Cheap Trick and Hüsker Dü. The record's sound could be sharper, but there's no mistaking the talent in songs like "Jak," "Balancing Act" and "Cornfield," which pitches a noise piano solo into the mixture.

The ghost of Burma looms in Williams' mindblow guitar on **All-Night Lotus Party**, a less tuneful album (credit Prescott's reduced music-writing role) that is still pretty rewarding. The Suns reach into new regions with "Cans," a crypto-rockabilly raveup; "Walk Around," a Ramonesy punk rush; "Sounds Like Bucks," a distorted crypto-ballad; and "Dot on the Map," a Wall of Voodoo-styled slice of Americana gone off the deep end.

Prescott reclaimed creative control on the Suns' third album, which also unveiled a new incarnation of the trio. (Williams and Weigand left in March '87.) Although lyrics continue to reflect **Lotus Party**'s fascination with the social and cultural mundanities of rural life, **Bumper Crop** more closely resembles the first LP in song, sound and style.

Adding trumpet, found-sound samples and guest contributions of sitar, violin and cello to the trio's bag of tricks, the uneven **Farced** has more instrumental depth, if not artistic subtlety, than the previous records, and even fits an industrial-strength noise assault ("Belly Full of Lead") into the usual roaring post-pop. But the band's melodic sense comes and goes; too many of the songs dissolve into a cacophonous blur.

David Kleiler, a guest on **Farced**, became the Suns' cool new guitarist (and astute songwriter) on the extremely consistent—in both style and quality—four-sided **Thing of Beauty**. Recommitting itself to wall-shaking tuneful overdrive, the trio antes up nineteen fine new numbers (with clearly audible clever lyrics) plus a great cover of Eno's "Needles in the Camel's Eye" that both credits and honors an obvious inspiration. [i]

See also *Big Dipper, Dredd Foole and the Din*.

VOX POP

See *Jeff Dahl Group*.

VULGAR BOATMEN

You and Your Sister (Record Collect) 1989 •

When an unpretentious band happens along with so much talent, it makes you wonder why those who have to mask their inabilities behind style and gimmicks even bother. Formed in the early '80s by future Silos founder Walter Salas-Humara, this pop quintet—based either in Gainesville, Florida or Bloomington, Indiana—was strictly a local Florida phenomenon (circulated on a pair of cassette albums) until Salas-Humara returned to produce (and guest on) **You and Your Sister**, a wonderful album which brought the group's semi-acoustic magic to national attention. Robert Ray and Dale Lawrence (a veteran of the Gizmos) write remarkably catchy and intelligent songs in a number of mildly inflected accents, performing them all with unadorned eloquence—and a touch of obsession—on guitar and accordion, with a polite backbeat to push them along. Buddy Holly would have been proud. [i]

See also *Gizmos, Silos*.

WAH!

Nah = Poo—The Art of Bluff (nr/Eternal) 1981
The Maverick Years '80–'81 (nr/Wonderful World) 1982

MIGHTY WAH!

Hope EP (nr/Eternal) 1983
Come Back EP (nr/Eternal-Beggars Banquet) 1984
A Word to the Wise Guy (nr/Eternal-Beggars Banquet) 1984 •
Weekends EP (nr/Eternal-Beggars Banquet) 1984
The Way We Wah! (nr/WEA) 1984
The Peel Sessions EP (nr/Strange Fruit) 1987

PETE WYLIE

Sinful (Virgin) 1987 •

One of the most significant and underappreciated groups of the punk-era Liverpool scene, Wah! (and titular variations thereon) functions as a vehicle for extrovert Pete Wylie. On **Nah = Poo**, Wah! sounds like Emerson, Lake and Palmer with hipper (though equally flamboyant) arrangements. Wylie sings melodramatically on stirring but superficial material like "The Death of Wah!" and "Seven Minutes to Midnight." The man may (as he intimates) be a fraud, but at least he's an entertaining one.

A Word to the Wise Guy—a full album and a bonus 12-inch—contains more of Wylie's flighty excursions into soul, pop, funk and anything else he happens across. Although not very consistent, it's an unpredictable and generally likable collection. **Come Back** has two versions of that ace track (also on the LP) plus a couple of other items. **Weekends** contains an alternate version of that album track as well as a demo for it and two other odds and ends from Wylie's sprawling career.

The Way We Wah! is a retrospective of Wylie's single successes, from "Hope," "The Story of the Blues" and "The Seven Thousand Names of Wah!" to his reading of Johnny Thunders' poignant "You Can't Put Your Arms Around a Memory."

Wylie's first-ever American release, the delightful and commercial **Sinful** drops the Wah! front and finally acknowledges his solo-ness. He takes credit for vocals, guitar, harmonica and "odd bits"; the only other contributor listed is vocalist Josie Jones. Colorful widescreen production (suggestive of the Motors a bit) frames the peppy melodies ("Break Out the Banners," "If I Love You," the memorable title tune) and unpredictable lyrics ("Train to Piranhaville"), making the ambitious **Sinful** a rewarding, fully realized effort reflecting Wylie's unique perception of pop music and the world.

The Peel Sessions contains four Wah! songs, recorded live for British radio in August 1984.   [jy/i]

WAILERS

See *Alpha Blondy, Bob Marley.*

WAITRESSES

Wasn't Tomorrow Wonderful? (ZE-Polydor) 1982
I Could Rule the World If I Could Only Get the Parts EP (ZE-Polydor) 1982
Make the Weather EP (nr/Polydor) 1983
Bruiseology (Polydor) 1983
The Best of the Waitresses (Polydor) 1990 ɸ

Ohio composer/guitarist Chris Butler invented the Waitresses; fellow Akronite Patty Donahue gave the group/idea its voice. From an original germinal joke (before Butler's spell in the more avant-garde Tin Huey) and an appearance on a local Ohio compilation LP, the Waitresses grew into a well-known New York-based sextet (including ex-Television drummer Billy Ficca) churning out danceably funky pop tunes spiked with a few twists (not the least of which is Mars Williams' searing and satirical sax). Furthermore, Donahue's persona—she doesn't sing so much as carry a simultaneous conversation and tune—developed into the archetypal young, white, middle-class woman trying to sort out her identity while beset with standard societal conditioning on one hand and specious, voguish "alternatives" (the Sexual Revolution, the Me Generation) on the other. The Waitresses' combination of musical aplomb and lyrical acuity makes the first LP at once funny, sad and universally true.

The American **I Could Rule the World** EP contains a TV sitcom theme ("Square Pegs"), a wonderful Yuletide rap track ("Christmas Wrapping"), a live-for-TV take of an old Hueys-era Butler tune and more. The related English release, **Make the Weather**, is somewhat different, most notably lacking "Christmas Wrapping."

Bruiseology was recorded amidst serious personnel tension. (Donahue subsequently quit, was briefly replaced by Holly Vincent, but later rejoined.) Although Butler penned another batch of witty and wise songs about the exigencies of modern womanhood—perhaps less pointed, but not far removed from those on the first LP—and the playing and production are fine, the formula doesn't wear all that well.   [jg]

See also *Swollen Monkeys.*

TOM WAITS

Closing Time (Asylum) 1973
The Heart of Saturday Night (Asylum) 1974 •
Nighthawks at the Diner (Asylum) 1975 •
Small Change (Asylum) 1976 •
Foreign Affairs (Asylum) 1977 •
Blue Valentine (Asylum) 1978 •
Heartattack and Vine (Asylum) 1980
Bounced Checks (Ger. Asylum) 1981
Swordfishtrombones (Island) 1983 •
Rain Dogs (Island) 1985 •
Anthology of Tom Waits (Asylum) 1985 •

Franks Wild Years (Island) 1987 •
Big Time (Island) 1988 •

Armed with one of the most distinctive voices in popular music—a gravely, smoke-scratched rasp that crosses Joe Cocker and Louis Armstrong at the end of a particularly bad bender—Tom Waits has spent the past two decades writing and performing some of the most fascinating and creatively stimulating music around. Bringing acute intelligence to a seemingly casual (and dissolute) sensibility, Waits' lyrics read as if they were written in some eerie collaboration with the likes of (depending on the LP) Mickey Spillane, Charles Bukowski or Captain Beefheart.

Waits' career generically divides into two periods: the melodic, barroom jazz-poet sound of his Asylum years (1973-'80), and the harmonic dissonance of his Island releases, beginning in 1983. But within such parameters, Waits has repeatedly changed direction and kept things interesting.

The debut, **Closing Time**, shows the young Californian at his least confident and most vulnerable, searching for a sound but having his work whitewashed by Jerry Yester's formulaic production. While his artistry and originality are evident in such emotive tracks as "I Hope That I Don't Fall in Love with You" and "Martha," the album is polluted by attempts to shoehorn Waits into a bland singer/songwriter mold. Overburdened by acoustic guitars and occasional backing singers, the songs don't focus enough on Tom's expressive lyrics or vocal talents.

The similar **Heart of Saturday Night** is entertaining, but relatively faceless. As with **Closing Time**, the material Waits sings straight melts into the mush of mid-'70s AOR. Nevertheless, the album bears the first hints of the highly stylized, jazzy, after-hours persona that would become Waits' trademark (shaped, in part, by producer Bones Howe—Waits' collaborator for the remainder of his Asylum stay). "Diamonds on My Windshield" is the first good example of Waits' narrative-lyric technique, backed only by an upright bass and high-hat/snare combo. The moving title track reveals a more emotive and intimate side—one that would prove equally significant during his Asylum years.

The double-live **Nighthawks at the Diner** is the quintessential pre-'80s Waits LP, portraying him as a hep and humorous sleazy nightclub act playing the fictional Rafael's Silver Cloud Lounge. The small-audience intimacy and Howe's sparing production are key factors in the LP's success. From the introspective, metaphorical "Emotional Weather Report" to the bachelor anthem "Better Off Without a Wife," Waits sells this show on sheer character. Milking his rapport with the audience for all it's worth, he throws out one-liners and local cultural references like a hip Henny Youngman. As it established a solid identity, **Nighthawks** was a turning point in Waits' career, and a good place for neophytes to begin.

Small Change and **Foreign Affairs** are, overall, his strongest Asylum releases. Both sessions were recorded and mixed live in the studio—complete with orchestra—and possess the perfect balance of compositional maturity and production expertise, allowing the strings' lush romanticism to augment the songs rather than overshadow them. **Small Change** contains his most fervent tracks ("The Piano Has Been Drinking (Not Me)" and

"Tom Traubert's Blues"), as well as "Step Right Up," a jumpy ode to snake-oil salesmen everywhere.

Foreign Affairs tugs on the heartstrings with the piano-bar ballad "Muriel" and the music-box beauty of "A Sight for Sore Eyes"; the scat-like "Barber Shop" complements the circus-barker call of "Step Right Up." Best of all, however, is "I Never Talk to Strangers," a duet with Bette Midler; "Burma-Shave," a tale of unfulfilled dreams, comes in a close second.

Blue Valentine, while a satisfying enough album, seems a bit short on originality when set in career context. Side One, for instance, reads like a Waits how-to manual: one part strings ("Somewhere"), one part jazz poetry ("Red Shoes by the Drugstore"), one part piano ballad ("Christmas Card from a Hooker in Minneapolis"), one part colorful narrative ("Romeo Is Bleeding"), and one part sultry blues ("$29.00"). Side Two is more of the same.

Heartattack and Vine is the bluesiest of Waits' albums, highlighted by the Chicago-electric sound of the instrumental "In Shades" and the killer Hammond organ sound that runs throughout. A bit of this blues touches several of the other tracks (most notably the title cut and "Downtown"), reprising an infrequently used ingredient in Waits' now-consistent recipe. Also contributing to the LP's power are the raucous "'Til the Money Runs Out" and the tender "Jersey Girl" (far better than Springsteen's subsequent cover).

Bounced Checks is a German compilation that overlooks **Closing Time** but does contain some previously unreleased tracks, including "Mr. Henry," alternate versions of "Jersey Girl" and **Blue Valentine**'s "Whistlin' Past the Graveyard" and an amusing spoken version of "The Piano Has Been Drinking" which, recorded live in Dublin, might as well be a different song. With the subsequent release of **Anthology**, **Bounced Checks**' enduring value is in its unreleased material rather than as an Asylum collection.

Released after a long hiatus during which he changed labels, the self-produced **Swordfishtrombones** transforms Waits from a bourbon-drenched barfly to an autonomous and eccentric ringmaster. Gone are the romantic piano ballads and jazz trios, replaced by adventurous arrangements of creepy marimba rhythms, pleasing dissonance and creative absurdity. The album's anthem is undoubtedly "16 Shells from a Thirty-Ought-Six" in all its twisted glory; "Frank's Wild Years" and "Down, Down, Down" are also prime cuts.

Rain Dogs is Waits' best Island release; it picks up the previous LP's trail but is consistently more intoxicating. Working with the finest musicians he's ever assembled (plus guest appearances by, among others, the Uptown Horns, Keith Richards and Tony Levin), it's highly percussive, laced with quirky guitar and garnished with unusual brass. Such diverse cuts as "Cemetery Polka" (with Farfisa, trombone and parade drum), "Blind Love," (virtually a country cover of "Jersey Girl," complete with fiddle and Keith Richards' twanging) and "Jockey Full of Bourbon" (a conga-driven rhumba) give it a wonderful sense of schizophrenia.

Anthology is an excellent sampler of Waits' Asylum years: thirteen of the best tracks from every album except **Nighthawks**.

Franks Wild Years ("Un Operachi Romantico in Two Acts") formed the basis for a stage show that

720

toured traditional theatrical venues in 1988. In small ways, the album harks back to **Rain Dogs** ("Hang on St. Christopher," for instance, is akin to that album's "Clap Hands"), but in a real sense it's entirely different from any of Waits' previous work. Most importantly, it succeeds as a concept album about a character who escapes from "Rainville" to travel the world, seeing Vegas, New York and parts unknown. Waits' idiosyncratic production employs vocal treatments, chameleonizing his already unmistakable voice into assorted colors and textures.

The soundtrack for the documentary film of the same name, **Big Time** draws most of its songs from **Rain Dogs** and **Franks Wild Years**. It also includes "Red Shoes" (an adaptation of the similarly named track on **Blue Valentine**) and two new cuts: "Falling Down" and "Strange Weather." As no other such collection exists, **Big Time** is, in a sense, a compilation, but the versions on it are so different from their studio equivalents that it's more like an adjunct to the three preceding albums.

In recent years, Waits has done quite a bit of acting, appearing in *The Cotton Club* (1984), *Down by Law* (1986), *Candy Mountain* (1987) and other films. [rs]

DAVE WAKELING

See *(English) Beat, General Public.*

WALKABOUTS

The Walkabouts EP [tape] (Necessity) 1984
22 Disasters EP (Necessity) 1985
See Beautiful Rattlesnake Gardens (PopLlama Products) 1987
Cataract (Sub Pop) 1989 ●
Rag & Bone EP (Sub Pop) 1990 ●

This talented Seattle-area combo produces smart, no-nonsense folk-rock. **22 Disasters** and **See Beautiful Rattlesnake Gardens** belie their low-budget origins thanks to pointed songwriting, focused instrumental performances and Chris Eckman and Carla Torgerson's committed vocals, which energize such impressive tunes as "Laughingstock" and "Jumping Off."

The group's two Sub Pop releases (collected on a single CD) feature upgraded production and more confident playing. The full-length **Cataract** resonates with rueful Americana on such tracks as "Whiskey XXX," "Hell's Soup Kitchen" and "Long Black Veil" (not the traditional song), marking the Walkabouts as a distinctive band with loads of potential. The six-song **Rag & Bone** adds a keyboard player to the original four-person lineup, and makes good use of the expanded cast with consistently imaginative arrangements, from the honky-tonking of "The Anvil Song" to the acoustic hush of "Medicine Hat." [hd]

TODD WALKER

See *Defenestration.*

WALKINGSEEDS

Skullfuck (nr/Probe) 1987
Upwind of Disaster, Downwind of Atonement (Communion) 1989 ●
Shaved Beatnik EP (nr/Glass) 1989
Sensory Deprivation Chamber Quartet EP (nr/Glass) 1989
Bad Orb..Whirling Ball (Shimmy-Disc) 1990 ●

Led by singer Frank Martin and guitarist Robert Parker, Liverpool's Walkingseeds bring mischievous intelligence and a taste for the underside of '60s pop culture to their wanton psychedelic guitar throttles. The first album offers a noisy listen-in to the band's learning process; **Upwind of Disaster**, while still enthusiastically sloppy and prone to bum notes, proffers conceptually witty songs ("Imperious, Vain, Selfish and Wilful" [sic], "Louie, Louie, Louie," "28IF," named for a license plate pictured on the **Abbey Road** cover—now is that groovy or what?) that make strange sense and production by Kramer that keeps the roar boiling (boar roiling?). If the band's sound falls somewhere between Motörhead and the Quicksilver Messenger Service, that's seems just about where it seems headed. (The CD adds two, including a cover of the Blue Öyster Cult's "Transmaniacon MC.")

While the title track of the four-song **Shaved Beatnik** 12-inch embraces Seedsy American retropsychepunk to good effect, the quartet's endless version of Cream's "Sunshine of Your Love," "New! Improved! Blue Cheer" and "Dirty Water (From a Dirty Pond)" all come rocking out of a grungier garage. Skip this one.

With production and playing by the Bevis Frond, the Walkingseeds again run haphazardly hot and cold on **Sensory Deprivation Chamber Quartet** (aka the **Dwarf LP**), an intermittently entertaining ("People of the World Rise Up and Die," a tuneful slice of political nonsense, is the best track) mini-album that contrasts acoustic guitars with tube-blowing overdrive, crude pop with brain-burrowing crunch.

Bad Orb..Whirling Ball ties up all the stylistic loose ends, hitting a noisy but clear nostalgic acid-rock stride with strong material like "Gates of Freedom," "Broken Cup," "Caged Beatnik" and the Beatles' "She Said She Said," which easily endures the rough handling. Kramer's incisive production here keeps the level of Parker's guitar distortion inside functional limits; Martin's singing is likewise less ragged—and thus more enjoyable—than usual. Except for the needless repetition encouraged by excessive song lengths, **Bad Orb** is a really good disc. [i]

WALKING WOUNDED

Walking Wounded (Stonegarden) 1986 ●
The New West (Chameleon) 1987 ●
Raging Winds of Time (Chameleon) 1989 ●
Hard Times (Doctor Dream) 1991 ●

JERRY GIDDENS

Livin' Ain't Easy (Mountain Railroad) 1989 ●

If you can get past the bombastic self-importance and drama in Jerry Giddens' voice, the rich Western folk-rock originals on the studio side of Walking Wounded's debut album are catchy, crafty and well-played. Recorded in a Hollywood club as a percussionless trio, the acoustic live side—which repeats three of the flip's studio songs and adds four more—is entirely dominated by Giddens' overzealous delivery.

Formalizing a four-man selection from the small pool that played on the first LP, Walking Wounded sounds solidly commercial but less striking on **The New West**. Giddens' singing isn't quite as pushy, but the material and electric arrangements aren't as memorable, so the overall progress is slight. The LP includes one song redone from **Walking Wounded**, the CD appends the whole thing.

Raging Winds of Time unveils a potent new lineup, including guitarists Eddie Munoz (ex-Plimsouls) and Roger Prescott (ex-Pop), in between stints together as Train Wreck Ghosts; Chalo Quintana (Havalinas) is the LP's drummer. The tastefully charged music is quite good; unfortunately, Giddens is still the singer (although he has improved a lot) and grimly earnest songwriter (his topic here is poverty and gang violence), a concentration of creative power which restricts his talented bandmates to supporting roles.   [i]

See also *Havalinas, Plimsouls, Pop*.

WALL OF VOODOO

Wall of Voodoo EP (Index-IRS) 1980
Dark Continent (IRS) 1981
Call of the West (IRS) 1982 ●
Granma's House (nr/IRS) 1984
Seven Days in Sammystown (IRS) 1985
Happy Planet (IRS) 1987 ●
The Ugly Americans in Australia* (IRS) 1988 ●

ANDY PRIEBOY

... Upon My Wicked Son (Doctor Dream) 1990 ●
Montezuma Was a Man of Faith EP (Doctor Dream) 1991 ●

Los Angeles' Wall of Voodoo makes junk music that can be extremely entertaining as long as you don't expect too much from it. Working in the same general cinematic groove as Devo, only taking their cues from Westerns and film noir rather than science fiction, Voodoo generate a stiff (though human) sound that furnishes a vivid backdrop to Stanard Ridgway's semi-catatonic vocals. Poised uneasily between machine music and rock'n'roll, Wall of Voodoo embodies the conflict between old and new for the serious-minded: classy Halloween music that's scary, but pleasantly so.

The four-song EP includes a wacked-out version of Johnny Cash's "Ring of Fire." The band displays more polish on **Dark Continent**, with tunes like "Back in Flesh" and "Full of Tension" benefiting from colorfully morose guitar and keyboards.

Call of the West's execution is livelier and more articulate, but just as spooky. It contains the now-classic "Mexican Radio," which crystallizes the band's loopy approach in one memorable number.

Ridgway left Wall of Voodoo in 1983 for a solo career; the band decided to replace him and continue. The 1984 compilation album, **Granma's House**, contains all of Voodoo's best tracks, from "Ring of Fire" to "Mexican Radio."

Unveiling new singer Andy Prieboy and a new drummer (Joe Nanini had departed in the interim), Wall of Voodoo returned to action with **Seven Days in Sammystown**, their first new album in three years. Ridg-

way's absence forced a major rethink of the band's sound and purpose; the record is adequate, but somewhat short of character and thus uncompelling. "Far Side of Crazy" (ostensibly about John Hinckley, Jr.) and a dirgey cover of the old mining song "Dark as the Dungeon" are quite good, but the rest falls short. And Prieboy's failed attempt to mimic Ridgway (on "Big City") is a major faux pas.

The vanishing Devo left a wide open field of informed weirdness, but a uniformly costumed Voodoo failed to make anything more of the opportunity. **Happy Planet** reveals an intact sense of humor left dangling by an utter lack of demented invention. The band works over the Beach Boys' "Do It Again," converting it to their idiom but adding nothing substantial which would make it worth hearing; the rest of the album likewise takes aim at assorted cultural artifacts but lacks the requisite inspired oddness to make the songs truly original.

The Ugly Americans in Australia* is a rambunctious live disc recorded in Melbourne and (here's where the asterisk comes in) Bullhead City, Arizona. Stripped of studio comforts, the quartet (plus keyboard guest) gamely confronts old material like "Far Side of Crazy," "Mexican Radio" and "Ring of Fire" and introduces several newies. (The cassette and CD add "The Grass Is Greener" and "Pretty Boy Floyd.")

Prieboy's solo album starts off with a witless but powerful rendition of Canned Heat's classic "On the Road Again" (hence the LP title) but then sticks to smart, full-bodied rock with Devoesque accents and offcenter lyrics for a while. (The low point comes early on, with "Tomorrow Wendy," a totally stupid number about mortality sung with Johnette Napolitano of Concrete Blonde. Not surprisingly, she liked the song enough to cover it on her band's **Bloodletting**.) From there, things spin further out, as Prieboy (whose personal stylistic orientation seems more Oingo Boingo than Wall of Voodoo) kicks out the conceptual jams with macho jive ("Man Talk") set to dramatic round'em-up/move-'em-out music, cocktail party chatter over a driving piano line on "The New York Debut of an L.A. Artist (Jazz Crowd)" and, on one of two CD-only tracks, an operatic extravaganza entitled "Maybe That's Not Her Head." Strange but entertaining. The EP contains three non-LP tracks, including a duet with Napolitano on "Whole Lotta Love."   [jy/i]

See also *Human Hands, Stan Ridgway*.

WANDERERS

Only Lovers Left Alive (nr/Polydor) 1981

This brief liaison between members of Sham 69 and ex-Dead Boy Stiv Bators set the stage for the subsequent Lords of the New Church, and resulted in one album. Although begun as a Sham 69 record (with Bators replacing singer Jimmy Pursey), contracts prevented its release as such; under the Wanderers name, it attracted almost no attention.

It deserved a better fate. Presenting legible rock with a strong political bent, **Only Lovers Left Alive** brings together loads of influences that had never been present in either faction's background, and synthesizes a varied, well-produced angry assault that's more radical in stance than music. In any case, the album is noteworthy for including a courageous rockified version of "The Times They Are A-Changin'." [i]

See also *Dead Boys, Lords of the New Church, Sham 69*.

WANG CHUNG
Points on the Curve (Geffen) 1984 ●
To Live and Die in L.A. (Geffen) 1985 ●
Mosaic (Geffen) 1986 ●
The Warmer Side of Cool (Geffen) 1989 ●

HUANG CHUNG
Huang Chung (Arista) 1982

Despite the exotic name, this posh British band plays familiar post-Ultravox pop—with saxophone instead of keyboards and less of a heavy dance beat—on **Huang Chung**. The talented and proficient quartet lacks only an identity and the first-rate songs that might have made it memorable.

Points on the Curve unveils several major changes, including the new spelling, a different label and a slimmed-down trio lineup (no more sax), now focused on singer Jack Hues. "Dance Hall Days" has dumb lyrics but a good rhythmic sound and a strong hook; "Wait" has dumb, awkward lyrics ("evidently/there's a difficulty") but a clever arrangement with synthesized strings and chimes for punctuation. Elsewhere, they essay dance-funk and Foreigner-like pomposity. Having banished its facelessness, Wang Chung is revealed in all its mediocrity.

And then there were two. Drummer Darren Costin formed a band called Heroes which released an LP (**Here We Are**) in 1987. The remaining members of Wang Chung (Hues and multi-instrumentalist Nick Feldman), meanwhile, wrote and recorded the soundtrack for the movie *To Live and Die in L.A.*—a good title song plus lots of expendable atmospheric instrumentals.

That same slender lineup, aided by drummer/producer Peter Wolf, a horn section and a stack of backup singers, created **Mosaic**, another stylish and trivial synth-dance (plus the horrific ballad "Betrayal") pursuit which happened to contain one catchy and clever number, "Let's Go," and the monster hit single/video clip "Everybody Have Fun Tonight." (Which Tom Jones reportedly sang in his act for a while, changing the lyrics to "Everyone Tom Jones tonight!")

After a long vacation, Wolf shifted to keyboards and produced **The Warmer Side of Cool**, a smoothly bland collection of relatively restrained retreads (a little Police, a lot of Wang Chung) that can't muster a single track as irritatingly catchy as "Everybody Have Fun Tonight." Although Feldman's lyrics make Hues' sound positively brilliant, neither man has anything of substantial artistic value to offer. Only two songs—"Praying to a New God" and "What's So Bad About Feeling Good?"—are worth a fig, so you can safely turn the record off after eight minutes without missing much. I can't imagine why anyone would actually want to own this. [i]

WARSAW PAKT
Needle Time! (nr/Island) 1977

Out of London's exploding early punk scene came this novelty—an album that reached local shops *within 24 hours of the start of its recording!* The band wasn't anything extraordinary—just amateur working class thrash'n'bash—but the speedy creation of the record made quite a stir for a few moments. The record came packed in a mailing envelope covered with stickers and rubber stamps; the insert sheet includes a complete log of the 21 hours it took to finish. Bizarre. [i]

See also *Social Deviants*.

WARTIME
See *Henry Rollins*.

WASHINGTON SQUARES
Washington Squares (Gold Castle) 1987 ●
Fair and Square (Gold Castle) 1989 ●

Outfitted with uniform berets, conservative suits, black sunglasses and acoustic guitars, these three New Yorkers escaped a post-punk background (ex-rock crit Lauren Agnelli's former band was Nervus Rex; Tom Goodkind's varied career on the local scene included such '70s bands as U.S. Ape; Bruce Jay Paskow was in the Invaders) the to shoulder the untendered responsibility of being the nouveau in-crowd's answer to Peter, Paul & Mary.

Despite the inexcusably pretentious folk-beatnik pose, the band's evident sincerity and their attractive harmonies give the first album its own inherent validity. But the lyrics are simpleminded, and the trio's treatment of two traditional songs isn't very nice. Ex-Television drummer Billy Ficca and producer Mitch Easter (on piano) help out.

Winningly produced by Steven Soles, **Fair and Square** pushes the Squares further towards a musical personality they can legitimately claim as their own. Alongside well-chosen and adequately performed covers of Leonard Cohen and Hoyt Axton (the classic "Greenback Dollar"), some of the originals are quite good. "Join Together" is a rousing populist anthem that should have circulated in the '60s; "The Other Side of Sin" rediscovers folk-rock with reedy innocence and a voice that frighteningly resembles Freddie Mercury in spots. But when the pose dominates, as in a precious tribute to Neal Casady, the whole thing goes out the window. (And why dredge up Quicksilver Messenger Service's wretched "Pride of Man"?) [i]

WAS (NOT WAS)
Was (Not Was) (ZE-Island) 1981 ●
Born to Laugh at Tornadoes (ZE-Geffen) 1983 ●
What Up, Dog? (Chrysalis) 1988 ●
Are You Okay? (Chrysalis) 1990 φ

Shattering the imaginary divisions between "black music" and "white music," Detroiters David (Weiss; sax, flute, keyboards, vocals) and Don (Fagenson; bass, keyboards, guitar) Was use undated soul and funk as a flexible backdrop for their alternately serious and sarcastic commentary. The historical problem with a lot of dance music has been its rabid dissociation from intellect; more than almost any other group, Was (Not Was) obliterates that gap. The first album's material, while drawing on such familiar sources as Grace Jones and Stevie Wonder, blends in enough humor and cleverness to make virtually every song an original gem, including the disco hits "Out Come the Freaks" and "Tell Me That I'm Dreaming" (which includes mutilated found vocals by Ronald Reagan). The remarkable cast of players is a disparate mix of rock and funk: among the many contributors are Wayne Kramer (ex-MC5), Larry Fratangelo (P-Funk), Bruce Nazarian (Brownsville Station) and Frank McCullers (Wild Cherry).

Born to Laugh at Tornadoes is a conceptual tour de force, a cavalcade of incongruous guest vocalists. Among the stars on parade: Ozzy Osbourne, Mel Tormé, Mitch Ryder and Doug Fieger of the Knack. Also in attendance: Wayne Kramer, Marshall Crenshaw, Vinnie Vincent and many others. The Was Bros. originals typically mix wiseacre/devolution lyrics with muscular soul-funk-rock, making the album enjoyable on at least three levels—powerful dance music, cleverly worded smart-aleckdom and super-session bizarreness.

Kings of cross-fertilization, Was (Not Was) have worked with an eclectic variety of artists; mostly on his own, Don Was has produced Bonnie Raitt, the B-52's, Bob Dylan and Iggy Pop. In the late '80s, they put their own group back in gear, reuniting with singers Sweet Pea Atkinson and Sir Harry Bowens and a stack of sympathetic sidemen to implement their imaginative vision of dance music. Beginning with "Somewhere in America There's a Street Named After My Dad," which has a relaxed Steely Dan feel, and ending with the mondo bizarro "Dad I'm in Jail," which owes more to the Butthole Surfers, **What Up, Dog?** encompasses the broad stylistic palette of the pair's past experiments and proceeds outward from there. Among the highlights: a lively overhaul of "Out Come the Freaks" with new lyrics, the hysterical "Earth to Doris," the poshly soulful "Love Can Be Bad Luck," an "Under the Boardwalk" rewrite co-penned by David Was and Elvis Costello and the funky paleontology of "Walk the Dinosaur." The resequenced CD also boasts a cushy ballad sung by Frank Sinatra Jr., a crisp cover of Otis Redding's "I Can't Turn You Loose" and two others.

Are You Okay? puts musical innovation on the back burner to concentrate on offbeat lyrics ("In K Mart Wardrobe," "I Blew Up the United States," "Elvis' Rolls Royce") and an endless stream of guest vocalists—Leonard Cohen, Syd Straw, Iggy Pop, the Roches and rapper G Love E, who puts his stamp on an otherwise straight (albeit updated) cover of the Temptations' "Papa Was a Rolling Stone." David Was' numb delivery of the spoken "I Feel Better Than James Brown" puts a bizarre twist on the sarcastic lyrics. Despite the album's narrower stylistic focus, **Are You Okay?** again demonstrates how dance music can be enormous, captivating fun, even for confirmed couch potatoes.   [sg/i]

WATERBOYS

A Girl Called Johnny EP (nr/Chicken Jazz) 1982
December EP (nr/Ensign) 1983
The Waterboys EP (Ensign-Island) 1983

The Waterboys (nr/Ensign) 1983 (Ensign-Chrysalis) 1986 ●
A Pagan Place (Ensign-Island) 1984 (Ensign-Chrysalis) 1987 ●
This Is the Sea (Island) 1985 (Ensign-Chrysalis) 1987 ●
Fisherman's Blues (Ensign-Chrysalis) 1988 ●
Room to Roam (Ensign-Chrysalis) 1990 ●
The Best of the Waterboys '81-'90 (Ensign-Chrysalis) 1991 φ

Edinburgh-born singer/guitarist/pianist Mike Scott formed the Waterboys in London, singing bombastic folky rock derived in equal parts from U2, Bruce Springsteen and Bob Dylan. On **The Waterboys** (and its five-song American condensation, later supplanted by a belated issue of the entire LP), Scott, saxophonist Anthony Thistlethwaite, an organist and various rhythm players squeeze every ounce of drama into his preciously poetic lyrics and pseudo-epic melodies. Enough of a selfconsciously sensitive artiste to confuse extended song length and artistic depth, Scott comes off as a modestly talented blowhard.

Having reused three of the eight songs (including the Rupert Hine-produced "A Girl Called Johnny") from the early EPs on **The Waterboys**, two more (including the torturous I-read-a-book-so-now-I-understand-history "Red Army Blues"—all eight minutes of it!) were recycled on the wretched **A Pagan Place**, a horrific realization of Scott's grandiose vision. With Welsh keyboardist Karl Wallinger and a drummer joining the Scott/Thistlethwaite nucleus, the Waterboys overlay mountains of acoustic guitars, horns and vocals to build majestically Spectoresque sand castles ("Church Not Made with Hands," "A Pagan Place") that are as flimsy as Scott's sophomoric lyrics. If Jimmy Webb had happened into the studio, an ultimate remake of "MacArthur Park" would have been inevitable. (Incidentally, one of the record's backup singers is Eddi Reader, later the voice of Fairground Attraction.)

An overambitious variety of production styles—piano-based simplicity on "Spirit," vocal gimmicks and "Penny Lane" horns on "The Whole of the Moon," the **Pagan Place**-styled title track and the insufferable amped-up guitar rock of "Don't Bang the Drum" and "Be My Enemy"—leaves **This Is the Sea** an unfocused mess. Scott's melodic sense (if not his lyrics) is actually improving, although habitual overstatement makes it hard to notice.

Wallinger went off to form World Party and Scott (who had sung "Old England is dying" on **This Is the Sea**) moved to Ireland and formed a new band with Thistlethwaite (now playing more mandolin than sax). In a remarkable case of self-willed ethnic transubstantiation, **Fisherman's Blues** (which ironically includes the song "World Party") unveiled the Waterboys Mark II, a neo-traditional Irish folk-rock group. Without raising questions as to Scott's sincerity, entitlement or motivation, wholesale appropriation of a cultural that still has genuine practitioners remains a fairly dubious (albeit not unknown) basis for a band. Where the Pogues concocted an original identity from old ingredients, the Waterboys merely copy what they've heard. But in fairness, the album is entirely bad: the Van Morrison-stylings are superficially attractive, and rollicking songs like "And a Bang on the Ear," "Has Anybody Here

Seen Hank?'' and ''When Will Be Married?'' make fine use of the folk idiom. The Waterboys don't bring much originality to this music, but they imitate it well enough to get by. (The CD adds a pair of acoustic instrumentals featuring Steve Wickham on fiddle.)

Scott's identification with Ireland gets even more intense on **Room to Roam**, a sprightly mixture of fiddle, tin whistle, accordion, mandolin. With appropriately rustic melodies and dreamy, romantic subject matter, the Waterboys strive desperately to be a youthful pop version of the Chieftains. Scott pledges his troth to the Emerald Isle in ''Islandman'' (one of the album's two incongruous electric rockers; there's also a swanky ballroom ballad) and celebrates the town in which the LP was recorded. Okay, okay, we believe you! But the album's best track is a straight rendition of the genuinely traditional ''Raggle Taggle Gypsy,'' an exercise which underscores the shortcomings in Scott's own songwriting and the overall redundancy of the group. **Room to Roam**—fiddle tunes notwithstanding—misses the point of folk music by a country mile.   [i]

See also *World Party*.

JACK WATERSON
See *Green on Red*.

BEN WATT
See *Everything but the Girl*.

JOHN WATTS
See *Fischer-Z*.

WAVES
See *Katrina and the Waves*.

WAXING POETICS
Hermitage (Emergo) 1987
Manakin Moon (Emergo) 1988 ●
Bed Time Story (Emergo) 1990 ●

On its first album, this sturdy power pop quartet from Norfolk, Virginia had the benefit of co-production by Mitch Easter and R.E.M.'s Mike Mills (who also contributes piano on one song). Keeping things plain and simple, **Hermitage** eschews any strong personality or overt influences to walk a unpretentiously straightforward line through the tuneful New South.

Exchanging the casual clothes of the first album's portraits for more formal black leather jackets, the Poetics also hardened their musical stance on the nicely varied and spunky **Manakin Moon**. The songs are still tuneful, but lyrics about death and ghosts are matched by a semi-tough heartland rock sound with strong rhythms and gritty guitar. Displaying a propensity for offbeat covers, the Poetics take on Eno's ''Needles in the Camel's Eye'' and give it a credibly understated reading. (The CD adds a bonus track.)

A deep and unsettling investigation of the Poetics' maturing musical obsessions, **Bed Time Story** ambitiously plunges into atmospheric tough-edged rock-'n'roll and country. From such moody/edgy originals as ''The Attic or the Underground'' to an ominous version

of Wreckless Eric's ''Semaphore Signals,'' this provocative record is unlikely to help anyone sleep easier. The House of Freaks help out on ''Jet Black Plastic Pistol''; the CD adds a live recording of ''The Train Kept a-Rollin'.''   [i]

WE ARE GOING TO EAT YOU
I Wish I Knew EP (nr/All the Madmen) 1987
Everywhen (TVT) 1989 ●

Pure pop lives in the luscious textures of this snazzy London quartet. Despite the stupid name, We Are Going to Eat You have a magic formula, blending Julie Sorrel's cool, heavenly voice, Paul Harding's bracing guitar chords and catchy, other-worldly tunes, largely written by drummer Chris Knowles, once the only male in a pop-punk band called Hagar the Womb. While the 12-inch EP is decent enough, **Everywhen** is a gas, with ''If You Believe,'' ''Glory'' and ''Each Life a Mystery'' achieving a state of three-minute grace. File with Buzzcocks, Primitives, Darling Buds.   [jy]

WEATHERMEN
Ten Deadly Kisses (nr/Play It Again Sam) 1987 ●
The Black Album According to the Weathermen (Play It Again Sam) 1988 ●
Beyond the Beyond (Bel. Play It Again Sam) 1990 (Mute) 1991 φ

Besides being one of the few contemporary techno-dance bands to draw its primary synthetic inspiration from Kraftwerk, this hybrid California/European duo is nearly alone in bringing an easy sense of humor to what is, at least in a sense, industrial music. With samples and repetitive rhythmatics connecting the Weathermen to far more abrasive club fiends, the clever and ingratiating **Ten Deadly Kisses** blends light, repetitive blip-rock and loopy lyrics into a meeting between Yello pop (less the continental snootiness) and Wall of Voodoo. Neat stuff.

The Black Album is heavier, harder and crazier, a rock record played on synthesizers that produce dinky-bop squiggles as well as more aggressively weird noises. In place of the first LP's monotonous grooves, the music here moves around a lot, while the vocals run from a quietly kinky socio-sexual conversation between ''Barbie and Ken'' to the melodramatic sci-fi nightmare of ''Twisting Doorknob'' to the ominous whisper of ''Punishment Park.'' Lurid fun that never stops grinning, **The Black Album** offers solace to those looking for new thrills now that Devo is out of the running.

Miles better than either of those, however, **Beyond the Beyond** is a hard-driving and penetrating critique of contemporary America with the engrossing qualities of a short-story collection and the humor of an underground comic. Whether attacking mindless culture (''Custom Brain''), American adventurism abroad (''Heatseeker'') or televangelism (''Freedom or Slavery''), the Weathermen make their points with accuracy and abundant wit; when they shift their sights to tell odd little stories of personal degradation (''Such a Beautiful City,'' ''California or Bust,'' ''Muzak''), the panoply of pop culture reference points makes them even more entertaining.   [i]

WEATHER PROPHETS

Almost Prayed EP (nr/Creation) 1986
Why Does the Rain EP (nr/Elevation-WEA) 1987
Mayflower (nr/Elevation-WEA) 1987
Judges, Juries & Horsemen (Creation-Relativity) 1988 ●
Hollow Heart EP (nr/Creation) 1988
Temperance Hotel ... (nr/Creation) 1989 (Giant) 1990 ●

As a vehicle for singer/guitarist Peter Astor, the Weather Prophets of the four-song **Almost Prayed** 12-inch were proponents of ultra-mild pop, exceedingly pleasant trifles with provocatively off-center lyrics. Lenny Kaye's production on **Mayflower**, the quartet's longplaying debut, put some starch in the Prophets' sound, bringing the rhythm section into play but keeping things tastefully light and, if anything, faintly countryish. Astor's singing is likewise more forthcoming, but **Mayflower**—and **Why Does the Rain** (a 12-inch containing an LP track, a sloppy BBC session version of "Mayflower" and a cool instrumental, "Annalea")—is still a few volts short of captivating. Only "Naked as the Day You Were Born," an organ-based three-chord number that seems to be straining towards a minor freakout, hints that the band would not always be limited to such politeness.

Dropping guitarist Oisin Little from the lineup (although he still plays on half the tracks), the Weather Prophets made the uneven Astor-produced second album as a rocking trio. Despite a few individual exceptions (like the sublimely emotional "Born Inbetween" and the hip distorto-pop of "Hollow Heart"), **Judges, Juries & Horsemen** is a meandering and uninvolving indulgence in need of clear direction. One interesting item is the intense '60sish "Thursday Seems a Year Ago," in which bassist Greenwood Goulding's organ work clearly prefigures Inspiral Carpets et al.

Temperance Hotel collects up some of the Prophets' best scraps: a half-dozen charming BBC radio session tracks from 1986, four B-sides (including "Chinese Cadillac"), two demos (one a nifty version of the gospel "I Saw the Light") and both sides of a bizarre single ("Odds & Ends" b/w "Stepping Lightly on the Ancient Path") that was included in early UK copies of **Judges, Juries & Horsemen**. Not only is this compilation as enjoyable as either of the band's proper albums, it's no more stylistically disparate than the second. (The CD adds a pair of 1989 live recordings: "Hollow Heart" and "Chinese Cadillac.")   [i]

WEDDING PRESENT

The Peel Session EP (nr/Strange Fruit) 1986 ●
George Best (nr/Reception) 1987 ●
Ukrainski Vistupi v Johna Peela (nr/Reception) 1988
    (nr/RCA) 1989 ●
Tommy (nr/Reception) 1988 ●
Why Are You Being So Reasonable Now? EP
    (nr/Reception) 1988 ●
Janice Long Evening Show EP (nr/Night Tracks-Strange
    Fruit) 1988 ●
Kennedy EP (nr/RCA) 1989
Bizarro (nr/RCA) 1989 (RCA) 1990 ●
Brassneck EP (nr/RCA) 1990
Corduroy EP (nr/RCA) 1990

When the Smiths stepped down as England's reigning indie-pop superstars in 1987, Leeds' Wedding Present—led by semi-insufferable/semi-witty singer/songwriter David Gedge—was conveniently poised to fill the vast cultural void that created with a carefully cultivated package of music and attitude, a balance of arrogance and insouciance, archness and populism, art and artlessness. The quartet's initial work—catchy, rushed, loud guitar pop singles reeking of the Smiths, New Order and Joy Division—could not have been more certain to win the hearts and minds of self-obsessed sensitivos lost in a collegiate world of romance and books if a computer had swallowed up a decade's worth of classic records and spewed the best bits back onto tape. In a sense, the Wedding Present represents the last hurrah of the new wave, the ultimate sublimation of independence for commerce.

All that said, however, the Wedding Present *have* made some eminently likable records, displayed an inordinately good sense of humor and generally managed their career with wonderfully mischievous unpredictability.

After releasing a boisterous **Peel Session** EP (recorded in February '86), the Wedding Present named its first album—for no discernible reason—after soccer star George Best, who appears on the cover. With guitarist Pete Solowka strumming away as if his right hand were on fire and the unfussy rhythm section keeping energetic pace, Gedge delivers his offbeat flurries of small-scale perception ("Everyone Thinks He Looks Daft," "It's What You Want That Matters," "My Favourite Dress," "Shatner") in an artless semi-singing voice that, while unlike Morrissey's (especially in the avoidance of moaning), is similarly idiosyncratic and cavalier with regard to melody.

Inspired by Solowka's father and employing a guest vocalist/balalaika player and a mandolinist, the group then took a detour into traditional Ukrainian folk music (including "Those Were the Days," a 1968 hit for Mary Hopkin) on the **Ukrainski Vistupi v Johna Peela** LP. It's sort of fun in a let's-go-exploring sense, but the augmentation as well as the material makes it difficult to consider as part of the band's oeuvre, and the intent—genuine or simply willful—is equally hard to pin down.

The archly titled **Tommy** summarizes the band's first two years, with singles ("This Boy Can Wait," "Once More," the pre-LP version of "My Favourite Dress") and radio sessions from '85 and '86. The Janice Long radio session was recorded two months after the Peel tracks, some of which also appear on **Tommy**.

The between-albums EP of "Why Are You Being So Reasonable Now?" contains a French variation on the title track, an acoustic version of **George Best**'s "Give My Love to Kevin," the group's contribution ("Getting Better") to **Sgt. Pepper Knew My Father** and another non-LP track.

It took American noise producer Steve Albini (whose four tracks were issued in the UK as **Brassneck** and added to the American CD and cassette of the otherwise uneventful **Bizarro**, a mature effort that sorely lacks **George Best**'s breathless rush) to push the Wedding Present off its increasingly precious perch. While Gedge's offhand ruminations are still delivered in something of Ian Curtis-fan-next-door voice, the sound of Solowka burning out amplifiers presents an exciting distraction and is far more enjoyable than his usual cloying jangle. **Kennedy** is a 12-inch that surrounds the title tune (a Madchester-styled **Bizarro** preview) with three non-LP cuts.   [i]

WEEKEND

See *Young Marble Giants*.

WEEN

God Ween Satan—The Oneness (Twin/Tone) 1990 ●

The things nerdy misanthropes do when they think no one's listening. Kicking off their why-stop-at-fifteen-tracks-when-there's-still-tape-left? debut double-album with a shrieking diatribe entitled "You Fucked Up," New Hope, PA's Dean and Gene Ween (aka Mickey Melchiondo and Aaron Freeman) play around in a dada sandbox of made-up voices and devolved musical idioms for more than an hour. Fortunately, the duo's silly sonic supermarket isn't all crude, cacophonous or sophomoric: poorly disguised musical skills and a sharp sense of parodic humor make **God Ween Satan** (produced by Andrew Weiss of Rollins Band) an entertaining, if unpredictable, shaggy dog story that can go from delightful genius to infuriating annoyance in seconds. From the remorseless munchkin dink-pop of "Don't Laugh (I Love You)" to a funky cover of Prince's "Shockadelica," a two-line demento jazz-blues ("I Gots a Weasel") to overweight Hawkwind metal ("Mushroom Festival in Hell"), breezy reggae ("Nicole") to fake flamenco ("El Camino"), the Ween'll-eat-anything ethos confronts an enormous agenda and comes up a winner. There's even a Beastie Boys send-up ("Old Queen Cole") and an incisive nineteen-second Springsteen parody ("Old Man Thunder"). Give up? Just holler Ween!   [i]

WEIRDOS

Who? What? When? Where? Why? EP (Bomp!) 1979
Action Design EP (Rhino) 1980
Condor (Frontier) 1990 ●
Weird World 1977-1981 Time Capsule Volume One
   (Frontier) 1991 ●

The Weirdos were arguably the first and best entrant in late-'70s Los Angeles punk. The crunching powerhouse wallop of "Destroy All Music" (the band's first 45) and the incendiary "(We've Got the) Neutron Bomb"—a classic US punk singles—provided a convincing reply to those who dismissed the efforts of Southern California youth in 1977. Unfortunately, the quintet splintered before the Weirdos began making longer records, leaving the Denney brothers (singer John and guitarist Dix) and guitarist Cliff Roman to carry on, employing various sidemen with stellar but less poignant results.

With ex-Quick (later Three O'Clock, etc.) drummer Danny Benair, the six-song **Who? What? When? Where? Why?** is an appealing blend of punk, psychobilly (a bizarre cover of Hank Mizzel's '50s obscurity, "Jungle Rock") and gonzo rock with unsettling lyrics.

Action Design adds only four selections to the Weirdos' oeuvre (including a pedestrian rendition of the Doors' "Break on Through"), but "The Hideout" finds the Denneys at their most sinister, offering a lowriders'

invitation to dark places. The silly "Helium Bar" is a frantically irreverent pogothon.

Although the Weirdos split soon after, the group never completely vanished. They did reunion shows throughout the '80s and made semi-regular home recordings. In '88, the Denneys formally relaunched the Weirdos. The all-new **Condor** features original drummer Nickey Beat (Alexander) and Cliff Roman in a part-time role, playing a bit of synthesizer and sharing bass chores with Flea (on loan from the Red Hot Chili Peppers). This inconsistent LP suffers from the long layoff, but the old flair for mildly subversive rock surfaces on such head-rushing hyper-punk zaniness as "Cyclops Helicopter" and the more conventional "Shining Silver Light."

Weird World is a compilation of early 45s, demos and other unreleased items.   [jr]

See also *Lydia Lunch, Thelonious Monster*.

WENDY AND LISA

Wendy and Lisa (Columbia) 1987 ●
Fruit at the Bottom (Columbia) 1989 ●
Eroica (Virgin) 1990 φ

On their maiden voyage away from former führer Prince, ex-Revolution guitarist Wendy Melvoin and keyboard player Lisa Coleman delivered a generous helping of smooth, likable tunes. The lyrical department is a little shakier, sometimes veering into bathos—"The Life," "Song About" (guess who). But the compositions show flashes of harmonic and structural daring, and there's no faulting Wendy and Lisa's chops: they play almost all the instruments. Respectable, if not Revolutionary.

Succeeding albums have shown Wendy and Lisa to be musically restless. **Fruit at the Bottom** is a virtual song cycle about falling in, out of and again in, love. Holding to that theme, the lyrics are almost simplistic, and the danceable pop-funk has little of the musically progressive tendencies of the pair's debut. The fearlessly and humorously titled **Eroica**, on the third hand, dives into a rococo whirlpool of textures, with deeper lyrics to match. Dense sonic layering and impressionistic imagery exude a '60s-revivalist fragrance; the ambiguous emotions the words call up are less bound to stylistic convention. And Wendy and Lisa still play almost all the instruments. More than respectable.   [si]

See also *Prince*.

WEST INDIA COMPANY

See *Blancmange*.

JOHN WETTON

See *Phil Manzanera, Roxy Music*.

WE'VE GOT A FUZZBOX AND WE'RE GONNA USE IT

We've Got a Fuzzbox and We're Gonna Use It EP
   (nr/Vindaloo) 1986
Bostin' Steve Austin (nr/Vindaloo-WEA) 1986 ●

FUZZBOX

We've Got a Fuzzbox and We're Gonna Use It!!
   (Vindaloo-Geffen) 1986

International Rescue EP (nr/WEA) 1989 •
Big Bang! (Geffen) 1989 •

These four young misses from Birmingham took over-the-top hairdos, colorful clothes and a devil-may-care amateurish attitude straight into the British Top 30 with their five-song debut EP. (All of the songs are one side of a 12-inch; the flip uses the vinyl only as a medium for scratched-in portraits of the group.) Proud of their lack of instrumental prowess (rightly so—it's a main part of their appeal), WGAFAWGUI simultaneously exploits and satirizes the prurient tabloid mentality on great cuts like "X X Sex" and "She." And isn't "Aaarrrggghhh!!!" a totally inspired title? Musically, the songs are built around rudimentary drums and guitar (yes, they do use their fuzzbox), occasional bass and unbridled enthusiasm. A real breath of fresh air.

The quartet's splendid name was truncated to just Fuzzbox for the retitled American release of **Bostin'** **Steve Austin**, which actually has music on both sides. Along with two songs redone from the EP, the well-played record includes the world's worst version of Norman Greenbaum's "Spirit in the Sky" and a bunch of new originals that waffle between Banglish girl-group harmony pop ("What's the Point," "Love Is the Slug," "You Got Me") and chanted dancebeats. In a far more professional setting, Jo's distorto guitar drones along nicely at varying levels; arrangements also feature sax and keyboards. "Preconceptions," which might have been a poppy X-Ray Spex number, ends the album on a bewildering note, instructing listeners to "pay less attention to the packaging and listen to the voice!"

After proving that they could adapt their bubblepunk to major-league record-making without sacrificing their inspired-amateur spirit, the quartet made an abrupt about-face on **Big Bang!**, which recasts Fuzzbox as a slick dance-pop vocal group, with the spotlight on budding sex symbol Vickie. Though the album's smooth, heavily programmed sound (no musician credits, but the women apparently did little or no playing) seems a complete repudiation of Fuzzbox's DIY roots, "Pink Sunshine," "Fast Forward Futurama" and "International Rescue" (all co-written by Liam Sternberg) are big, brassy fun nonetheless, and demonstrate scads more personality and humor than most commercial girly-pop. Still, it's sad to hear Fuzzbox go straight—though a remake of Yoko Ono's "Walking on Thin Ice" demonstrates a few remaining quirks.   [dgs/i/hd]

WHAT IS THIS

Squeezed EP (San Andreas) 1984
What Is This (MCA) 1985
3 Out of 5 Live EP (MCA) 1985

Wild, muscular rock-funk with a demented outlook, LA's What Is This bears more than a passing resemblance to the Red Hot Chili Peppers, but that's no mystery—guitarist Hillel Slovak formed What Is This after leaving the Peppers, whom he rejoined after making **Squeezed**. Chris Hutchinson and Jack Irons (who later played briefly with Redd Kross) ride a fearsome rhythm behemoth, and Alain Johannes and Slovak both provide offbeat songs ("Mind My Have Still I" isn't even the weirdest), unnervingly mental vocals and psycho guitar licks, making **Squeezed** a gut'n'butt-shaking experience you won't soon forget.

Cut as a Slovak-free trio, **What Is This** (produced by Todd Rundgren) is a less invigorating move towards the rhythmic rock mainstream. Some of the excitement remains, but not enough. The subsequent EP adds live versions of three numbers to a pair of album cuts.   [i]
See also *Red Hot Chili Peppers*.

CARON WHEELER

See *Soul II Soul*.

WHEN PEOPLE WERE SHORTER AND LIVED NEAR THE WATER

When People Were Shorter and Lived Near the Water EP (Trace Elements) 1987
Uncle Ben EP (Shimmy-Disc) 1988
Bobby (Shimmy-Disc) 1989 •

Not quite an artsy avant-garde ensemble and not exactly a wacky party band, this Brooklyn sextet—led by singer Kim Rancourt—specializes in anarchic trashings of pop marginalia. The group's first two releases—both four-song 7-inch EPs—consist of enjoyable if somewhat aimless cover-version deviltry. The first features a hopped-up rendition of Ray Davies' "Dandy" (a hit for Herman's Hermits) as well as a rock adaptation of the Gettysburg Address (!). **Uncle Ben** takes similar swipes at Herb Alpert, the Singing Nun, Eric Burdon and the Buoys; on the last two (Burdon's psychedelic non-classic "A Girl Names Sandoz" and the Rupert Holmes-penned Top 40 cannibalism epic, "Timothy"), WPWS&LNTW finally work up enough musical steam to endow their output with something more substantial than theoretical interest.

Bobby, the band's first full-length album, is a collection of fifteen Bobby Goldsboro covers, many of them unrecognizable as such in these interpretations. Depending on your frame of reference, it's either a deeply ambivalent treatise on the duality of popular culture or a colossal in-joke by artsy bohos with too much free time on their hands. **Bobby** isn't exactly an affectionate tribute, but it's not a complete joke, either. (The **Bobby** cassette includes the contents of **Uncle Ben**; the CD adds two more tracks to that pairing.)

In late 1990, Shimmy-Disc's planned release of the band's **Porgy**—an album of tunes from *Porgy and Bess*—was temporarily held up due to legal objections by the Gershwin estate and was not issued until mid-'91.   [hd]

WHIRLWIND

Blowin' Up a Storm (nr/Chiswick) 1977
Midnight Blue (nr/Chiswick) 1980

This London quartet (named after a Charlie Rich Sun recording) was one of the first English rockabilly bands to emerge at a time when the music press was looking for the "next big thing" after punk. On its debut, **Blowin' Up a Storm**, Whirlwind—whether by design or simply limited competence—offers up a bare-bones style, with little or no concession to the advancement in recording quality since the originals. The instrumentation is semi-traditional (one lead guitar, one muted-bass-strings rhythm guitar, electric bass and snare drum) and was recorded with no overdubbing, resulting in a sound that can charitably be called thin.

While painstakingly trying to recapture the simplicity of early rockabilly recordings, Whirlwind never manages to re-create the frenzied, fiery abandon that is really what it was all about.

Midnight Blue, recorded over two years later, shows the group past its hang-ups about purity: the sound is filled-out, the drummer plays an entire kit (albeit with amazing clumsiness at times) and pedal-steel guitar even finds its way onto one track. While an improvement over the first LP, **Midnight Blue** still fails to present any clear reason why anybody would want to listen to it, when both the originals and far more imaginative updates like the Stray Cats are available.

A decade later, singer Nigel Dixon unexpectedly popped up as the vocalist for Paul Simonon new band, Havana 3 A.M.   [ds]

See also *Clash*.

WHIRLYWIRLD

Whirlywirld EP (Aus. Missing Link) 1980

On their four-song 12-inch (original copies of which included a bonus 45), Whirlywirld combines guitar, bass, drums and electronics—not synthesizers—to make lots of staccato noise over which Ian "Ollie" Olsen can dispense his own brand of doom and gloom. This sort of amelodic anger has to be compelling to succeed, but Whirlywirld aren't and don't. Surprisingly, when the pioneering Melbourne quartet (considered locally to be Australia's home-spun Suicide) gets relatively conventional on the final track, the savagery of their ska styling does indeed make you sit up and take note.

Keyboardist Olsen, whose pre-Whirlywirld band also boasted future Birthday Party guitarist Rowland S. Howard, scored and served as musical director of the 1987 film *Dogs in Space*, which starred INXS singer Michael Hutchence. A reformed Whirlywirld contributed two songs to the soundtrack, one with Hutchence as their vocalist. Hutchence and Olsen subsequently launched a side project called Max Q.   [jg/i]

See also *INXS*.

JAMES WHITE

See *James Chance*.

WHITE ZOMBIE

Psycho-head Blowout (Silent Explosion) 1986
Soul-Crusher (Silent Explosion) 1987 (Caroline) 1988
Make Them Die Slowly (Caroline) 1989 ●
"God of Thunder" EP (Caroline) 1989

These trashy troglodytes began life as a high-density cross between the Birthday Party and Black Sabbath, just one of the noisy grunge-rock outfits common around New York in the late '80s. But then the quartet's brutish strain of lysergic madness bloomed into something far more distinctive.

Although the dank **Psycho-head Blowout** EP evinces some potential, the album isn't gripping enough to truly terrify. On **Soul-Crusher**, however, corrosive monstrosities with titles like "Ratmouth," "Drowning the Colossus" and "Scum-Kill" cower in your subconscious, pounding for release. A vague scent of the blues permeates Tom Five's dissonant guitar scrawl, while Rob Straker sings like he has razor-sharpened tonsils

—a strangled off-key yowl to rival the young Foetus or Nick Cave. In addition, his bizarre, stream-of-consciousness lyrics (a sample: "Ze wheels o' fire/a doubleman defier/a motor and I/regenerate I am your final Pompeii/o' etched in acid/like a shack of hate") are the work of a finely demented mind.

Make Them Die Slowly is markedly different from its predecessor. New guitarist John Ricci, who left shortly thereafter, dispenses with Five's squealing Beefheartisms in favor of ominous, stripped-down riffing, like the mosh segments of Slayer songs. Sean Yseult's bass throb is nearly inaudible, weakened by Bill Laswell's trebly production, but the songs deliver the goods, especially the almost funky "Disaster Blaster" and the viciously inexorable "Acid Flesh."

The "God of Thunder" 12-inch more than makes up for the LP's production inadequacies. Capturing the full grotty fury of their live gigs, the three Daniel Rey-produced tunes (a great Kiss cover, an improved remake of "Disaster Blaster" and one ace new cut) scour the pants off their other recordings. And the liberal use of samples (from *Phantasm*, porn flicks and **Kiss Alive**) points White Zombie in a colorful new direction.   [gef]

BARRENCE WHITFIELD AND THE SAVAGES

Barrence Whitfield and the Savages (Mamou) 1984 ●
Dig Yourself (Rounder) 1985
Call of the Wild EP (nr/Rounder Europa-Demon) 1987
Ow! Ow! Ow! (Rounder) 1987 ●
Live Emulsified (Rounder) 1989 ●
Let's Lose It (Fr. New Rose) 1990 ●

The music young New Jersey native Barry White had in mind was entirely different from the bass soul cooing of his namesake so, when the Boston University student decided to shout gutbucket R&B with a swinging band, he became Barrence Whitfield. On the spectacular first album, backed by a frisky quartet of young, greasy roadhouse rockers (including a couple of ex-Lyres), he stakes his reverent claim to the priceless hipshake legacy of Screaming Jay Hawkins and other venerable titans of primal rock'n'roll. Whitfield is a tremendous vocalist with a bloodcurdling falsetto, the enthusiasm of a drunk amateur and the easy control of a seasoned pro. The Savages—especially saxman Steve LaGrega—keep pace on wacky old numbers like "Bip Bop Bip," "Mama Get the Hammer" and "Georgia Slop," contributing likely originals to this raw adventure that hardly seems like it was recorded in 1984.

The brief but exhilarating **Dig Yourself** adds a little surface sheen and showband politesse to the proceedings, but still contains a weekend's worth of sweaty, sexy excitement. "Juicy Fruit," "Geronimo's Rock" and "Breadbox" fit all the pieces together in a sweet frenzy, but the remaining tracks are almost as good.

Whitfield recorded **Call of the Wild**, a six-song 12-inch released only in the UK, with an entirely new set of Savages, revamping the sound with piano and organ as well as a slicker, steadier rhythm section. Not as wildly thrilling as either previous record, this takes a tamer posture and reduces the fun accordingly: Ben Vaughn's bluesy but lightweight "Apology Line" indicates Whitfield's moderate direction here. The American **Ow! Ow!**

Ow! album expands the EP with four more tracks recorded around the same time. It's likable enough—this man can *sing*—but seriously short in the funkalicious spirit that makes the earlier ones so precious.

Some, but not all, of Whitfield's old fervor is back on **Live Emulsified**, an enjoyable—though only occasionally inspired—approximation of a Savages club set, recorded with some of the same sidemen in California and Texas at the end of 1987 and the beginning of '88. With a broad selection of tunes—including a bunch not previously vinylized—this may not be the great live album that Whitfield's doubtless got in him, but there are plenty of worse ways to spend 45 minutes. (The CD and cassette contain three bonus tracks.)   [i/hd]

WHODINI
Whodini (Jive) 1983
Escape (Jive) 1984 ●
Back in Black (Jive) 1986 ●
Open Sesame (Jive) 1987 ●
Greatest Hits (Jive) 1990 ●
Bag-A-Trix (MCA) 1991 ф

This trio (originally a two-man crew) from Brooklyn does something very original and exciting within the context of rap, blending in wit and variety to make entertaining records. On their debut, Jalil Hutchins and Ecstacy (John Fletcher) worked with three different producers—Thomas Dolby, Conny Plank and the Willesden Dodgers—to come up with an '80s version of "Monster Mash" ("The Haunted House of Rock"), two bouncy history-of-rap/rap-is-good numbers ("Magic's Wand" and "Rap Machine") plus a couple of alternate versions and three more cuts. Although the moderate-tempo big-beat gets a bit numbing, the pair's sharp lyrics and straightforward delivery, plus countless bits of electronic flotsam and jetsam prevent serious tedium.

Escape brought Whodini under the talented studio wing of Run–DMC co-producer Larry Smith, who created a smooth, semi-spare sound and did a lot of the writing as well. With fewer quirky synthesizer accents, the action centers on raps about the urban nightmare ("Escape (I Need a Break)"), failed romance ("Friends") and New York's 24-hour lifestyle ("Freaks Come Out at Night"), as well as other more egocentric topics. Airy without being simple, **Escape** is appealing and innovative.

With Grandmaster Dee (celebrated on an **Escape** song) officially expanding Whodini to a threesome, **Back in Black** is a blunter record, with less reliance on fancy production and more concentration on varied, organic arrangements. However, while Whodini's music has gotten noticeably stronger, their lyrics are stagnant: all eight cuts cover familiar rap ground with no special outlook and only intermittent cleverness.

The centerpiece of the lively **Open Sesame** teams the trio with the original bad girl of rap, Millie Jackson. (A pre-LP 12-inch offers six different mixes of "Be Yourself," a busy statement against mindless conformity, a message which is reprised, after a fashion, on the LP's "For the Body.") Elsewhere along this moralistic ride, Whodini praises mom ("Early Mother's Day Card"), recommends lusty human devotion as an alternative to drugs ("Hooked on You") and touts personal responsibility ("You Brought It on Yourself"). Behind the board, Smith touches on all of hip-hop's current sonic trendsetters, from L.L. Cool J to Full Force to Rick Rubin to Run—DMC, making **Open Sesame** an exciting sampler of rap styles. Whodini may not have a sound of their own, but they synthesize with flair.   [i]

WIDE BOY AWAKE
Wide Boy Awake EP (RCA) 1983

Ex-Ant bassist Kevin Mooney formed and led London's Wide Boy Awake, an exciting interracial quartet which only released some singles, the first two of which were collected on this eponymous American 12-inch. Hard to classify, the Wide Boys offer clever wordplay and a preponderant funk beat on "Slang Teacher," while square-dancing into wonderful country-tinged pop for "Bona Venture." Elsewhere, they try scratch cajun and dance-rock.   [i]

See also *Adam and the Ants*.

JANE WIEDLIN
Jane Wiedlin (IRS) 1985 ●
Fur (EMI Manhattan) 1988 ●
Tangled (EMI) 1990 ●

Free of the Go-Go's, guitarist/singer/songwriter Wiedlin's first record is stylistically eclectic to a fault, and stresses goody-goody lyrical concerns too bluntly. But it's also substantial, attractive and joyously reflects her new-found artistic freedom. "Blue Kiss" is an adorable love lament; "Somebody's Going to Get into This House" is sturdy dance-rock. "Where We Can Go" could have been done by her former band, while the moody "Modern Romance" would better suit the Motels. Wiedlin isn't the world's strongest vocalist, but her enthusiasm and sincerity largely compensate.

With perky synth-pop production by Stephen Hague (ex-Naked Eye Rob Fisher played and programmed the keyboards), the similarly diverse **Fur** moves Wiedlin into a slickly modern mainstream, relying on her sweet, vulnerable voice to balance the impersonal arrangements. Wiedlin's aspirations to be a junior dance diva (on the pro-animal title song) and suave ballad crooner (on "The End of Love," "Whatever It Takes") are still futile; the album's only winners are bouncy fizz-pop: "Inside a Dream," "Rush Hour" and "Give!"

In 1989, Wiedlin made an adorable screen appearance as Joan of Arc in *Bill & Ted's Excellent Adventure* and then cut her third album. **Tangled** is an unsubtle attempt to make a woman—artistically speaking—of her, with an unclothed cover photograph, lusty lyrics (on the idiotic title track and "World on Fire") and loudly generic rock backing. Wiedlin's desire to shake her innocent little-girl image is understandable, but she sounds adrift and embarrassed on this charmless record.

See also *Go-Go's*.   [i]

WILD BILLY CHILDISH
See *Thee Mighty Caesars*.

WILD FLOWERS

The Joy of It All (nr/Reflex) 1984
Dust (Big Time) 1987
Sometime Soon (Slash) 1988 ●
Take Me for a Ride EP (nr/Chapter 22) 1988
Tales Like These (Slash) 1990 ●

A guitar band from the English Midlands, the Wild Flowers mate the Ramones' breakneck speed and Television's guitar interplay with Echo & the Bunnymen's intensity and attack on **The Joy of It All**. Poorly recorded for a tiny label, the album disappeared quickly as, so it seemed, did the band when founding guitarist-songwriter Dave Newton left to start the Mighty Lemon Drops.

Replacing Newton with David Atherton, the quartet recorded a couple of singles during '86; adding three more tracks, that made **Dust**. With the exception of "A Kind of Kingdom" (which Hugh Jones produced), the recordings are again pretty awful, but the band's energy can't be denied. While the guitars play off each other with reckless abandon, Mark Alexander's bass darts in and out between them. Television is still the best reference point, especially as singer Neil Cook tends to shamelessly ape Tom Verlaine.

Sometime Soon is the Wild Flowers' first fully realized album, and it's intense from start to finish. The songs are virtually all vitriolic putdowns of the girl who left the guy behind, and Cook's vocals are so filled with bile you can almost picture the veins popping out of his neck as he sings them. The guitars bark, bite, scratch and yell at a furious pace. Angry music, ideal for people nursing a deep hurt.

The **Take Me for a Ride** EP features two very different versions of one of **Sometime Soon**'s less caustic numbers (one all electric, the other featuring an acoustic lead) plus three non-LP cuts more in keeping with the album's nasty tone.

Tales Like These was recorded in California with Matt Wallace, who'd just finished the Replacements' **Don't Tell a Soul**. Perhaps, like the Mats, the Wild Flowers felt the need to slow down a bit; musically it's far more varied than **Sometime Soon**. But the subject matter hasn't changed much: either these guys really know how to hold a grudge or they're doormats for a whole procession of hellish women. Let's hope they work it out before things get too ugly. [ds]

See also *Mighty Lemon Drops*.

WILD GAME

See *Green on Red*.

WILD SEEDS

Live Is Grand (Life in Soul City) EP (Aznut) 1984
Brave Clean + Reverent (Jungle) 1986
Mud, Lies + Shame (Jungle) 1987 (Passport) 1988 ●

MICHAEL HALL

Quarter to Three (Record Collect) 1990

KRIS MCKAY

What Love Endures (Arista) 1990 ●

Austin, Texas' Wild Seeds had an immensely likable, tough and twangy guitar-pop sound, but the heart and soul of the band was Michael Hall's songwriting. A former music journalist, Hall took the rock'n'roll ethic of good times, lonesome trains and love gone wrong and spun it into lusciously twisted personal narratives inscribed with poetic literacy. Throughout the Wild Seeds' albums and into his solo work, Hall has cultivated the persona of an Everyman befuddled by an America gone sour; he's constantly searching for truth, justice, a wife and two kids, yet he's repeatedly thwarted by forces bigger than himself.

The first EP is a mere skeleton, with weak jangly guitars and ragged performances muffling the tunes. Hall returned with an entirely new lineup for **Brave Clean + Reverent**, an album so monstrously well-crafted, well-written, well-played and just plain good-feeling that it may make you wonder why you've ever settled for less. "Sharlene" is a raucous, Springsteen-style rocker about a girlfriend who just happens to be a transvestite ("my baby walks like a queen"); "A Girl Can Tell" exposes the lies in a relationship. "Shake This World," the album's closer, best sums up Hall's hopes and fears: "Now I did shake this world like a man shakes a tree/But the leaves came tumbling down and buried me."

Mud, Lies + Shame applies slightly slicker roadhouse production to another smart and elegant collection of songs. "Debi Came Back" and "You Will Be Married to a Jealous Man" make excellent use of Hall's trademark romantic irony, and "I'm Sorry, I Can't Rock You All Night Long" is as feisty as its title. But there's a feeling of forced democracy going on, and the album peters out towards the end; when second vocalist Kris McKay takes the reins for the closer, "All This Time," her affected country belting undercuts the aw-shucks endearment of Hall's singing.

After the Wild Seeds broke up, Arista groomed McKay as something of a folk-rock interpreter, but **What Love Endures** is weighed down by Barry Beckett's faceless AOR-lite production and an indistinct batch of songs (a cover of Billie Holiday's "Don't Explain" notwithstanding). Hall, meanwhile, hooked up with Walter Salas-Humara of the Silos, who coproduced **Quarter to Three**. Hall's songwriting is as strong as ever (especially "Congratulations" and "Roll Around Heaven This Way"), but the restrained acoustic arrangements occasionally prevent the songs from building to the emotional peaks the Wild Seeds so masterfully reached. While it's hard to argue with a guy who can turn out a line like "I want to wake at dawn, long after our best years are gone," Hall sounds as tired as an old man, as though he has finally allowed his disappointments to get the best of him. [kss]

WILD SWANS

The Peel Sessions EP (nr/Strange Fruit) 1986
Bringing Home the Ashes (Sire-Reprise) 1988 ●
Space Flower (Sire-Reprise) 1990 ●

Led by onetime Teardrop Explodes organist Paul Simpson, Liverpool's Wild Swans had already existed, broken up (leaving a Zoo single and a posthumously released 1982 radio broadcast), spent four years in limbo and then reformed by the time of its first album. Behind Simpson's splendid deep voice, the trio plays derivative suave-pop on **Bringing Home the Ashes**, artfully mixing up a blend of the The, the Smiths, Echo & the Bunnymen, Aztec Camera and others that's enticing— but unsatisfying.

With producer Ian Broudie playing guitar and organ and two guests from the Icicle Works (guitarist Ian McNabb and drummer Chris Sharrock), Simpson and stalwart bassist Joe Fearon turn mildly psychedelic on **Space Flower**. Flavorfully titled songs like "Vanilla Melange," "Chocolate Bubblegum," "Tangerine Temple" and "Melting Blue Delicious" aren't nearly as colorful as they sound, but Broudie helps give the neo-retro rock-pop a handsomely textured identity the Wild Swans—evidently destined for very modest cultural significance—can call their own. [i]

SCOTT WILK + THE WALLS
Scott Wilk + the Walls (Warner Bros.) 1980
BONE SYMPHONY
Bone Symphony EP (Capitol) 1983

Encountering the line between artistic influence and stylistic plagiarism, Scott Wilk grabbed a copy of Elvis Costello's **Armed Forces** and blithely pushed ahead. Parts of his record are uncannily accurate impressions; the cover design and group photo do nothing to reduce the Costello/Attractions allusion. Funny thing, though— the album is really good! If you can ignore its derivative raison d'être, you'll find powerful, well-crafted songs, impressive playing and production and an overriding sense of cohesion. An unexpected but disconcerting thrill.

With two new bandmates, Wilk switched to techno-dance in Bone Symphony, whose lame five-song EP mixes the sounds of Devo, Oingo Boingo and Ultravox without distinction. [i]

WILL AND THE BUSHMEN
Gawk (Mustang) 1987
Will and the Bushmen (SBK) 1989 ●

Formed in Mobile, Alabama, but later based in Nashville, this nifty pop quartet did two inspired things on its first album: write a tributary bio-song entitled "Neil Young" (they had already eulogized Alex Chilton on a pre-LP B-side) and get Mississippi's Tim Lee and Randy Everett to co-produce three tracks. Otherwise, the modest **Gawk**—in the Windbreakers' style, but not as moody or as instrumentally accomplished— merely has great tunes, excellent harmony vocals (by guitarists/songwriters Will Kimbrough and Sam Baylor) and a solid dollop of the innocent spunk that greases the wheels of young talent.

Although there's nothing wrong with **Will and the Bushmen**, there's nothing really right about the band's major-league debut, either. Most noticeable on remakes of the three best songs from **Gawk**, producer Richard Gottehrer fits the group's music into the tasteful kind of arrangement that—like a tomboy in her first dress— gently discourages youthful ebullience. [i]

LUCINDA WILLIAMS
Ramblin' on My Mind (Folkways) 1979
 (Folkways-Smithsonian-Rounder) 1991 ●

Happy Woman Blues (Folkways) 1980
 (Folkways-Smithsonian-Rounder) 1991 ●
Lucinda Williams (Rough Trade) 1988 ●
Passionate Kisses EP (Rough Trade) 1989 ●

Louisiana-born Lucinda Williams sings poignant songs in a rich, world-weary voice, drawing on blues, folk, country and rock, but resisting all pigeonholes. Her first two albums went largely unnoticed, but have been reissued in light of her growing notoriety. **Ramblin' on My Mind** is a warm, lively album of blues, gospel and folk covers, including three Robert Johnson songs. (The album title was shortened to **Ramblin'** for its 1991 re-release; a cassette edition available from Folkways in the intervening years was named **Ramblin' Early Blues**.)

While **Ramblin'** shows off Williams' affecting vocals and her roots—from the bayou to the church choir to the Opry—the more rock-oriented **Happy Woman Blues** proves her to be an evocative song-crafter akin to Gram Parsons and Emmylou Harris. Smoke-stained bars, open roads and a heart that never learns are well-worn subjects, but Williams rewrites them in a way that is both contemporary and uncynical.

Williams later recorded for CBS, which decided she wasn't marketably country or rock enough and dropped her. She continued touring, honing a collection of songs that became **Lucinda Williams**. Her second debut is a near-perfect album of originals (plus a wrenching version of a Howlin' Wolf number) played with a band led by guitarist/co-producer Gurf Morlix. This is an unflinching self-portrait of a woman with mythic powers to remake herself and the world ("Changed the Locks"), to sketch working-class portraits worthy of Tobias Wolff ("The Night's Too Long") and to let her hair down for a zydeco romp ("Crescent City"). But mostly she's a lover; "Side of the Road" (a poetic declaration of independence within a committed relationship) and the meditative and erotic "Like a Rose" are both especially moving.

Passionate Kisses reprises that catchy, earnest plea for happiness from the album and adds tracks from her lean years: three songs recorded live at an LA radio station plus an '83 demo featuring Taj Mahal on guitar and harp. Not a place to begin, but a between-albums snack for fans. [ws]

ROBERT WILLIAMS
See *Stranglers*.

VICTORIA WILLIAMS
Happy Come Home (Geffen) 1987
Swing the Statue! (Rough Trade) 1990 ●

By virtue of her now-ended marriage to singer Peter Case and other friends in high musical places, Victoria Williams' career has been a bit suspect in some quarters. She is, however, a deeply talented (if erratic) songwriter and possessor of a most distinctive voice. On **Happy Come Home**, producers Anton Fier and Stephen Soles make the mistake of burying Williams in a massive studio effort; Williams sounds like an avalanche survivor, vainly trying to climb out from under sitars, drum machines and horn sections. The pair's only stroke of insight was hiring Van Dyke Parks to do string arrangements on three songs—the album's best, especially the charming fairy tale, "TC." Parks and Williams are kindred souls: childlike, fanciful and impatient with pop formats. With luck, they'll work together again.

Co-produced by Michael Blair (percussionist and multi-instrumentalist with Tom Waits and Elvis Costello), **Swing the Statue!** is a vast improvement. Williams sounds like she's in control here. Her often-remarkable lyrics can be heard this time, and her rangy voice—an intoxicating blend of little-girl breathiness and old-lady crackle and wisdom that is definitely an acquired taste—is well out in front. (As is her idiosyncratic Christianity, in the gospel-country "Holy Spirit.") There are a few annoying moments, like the cutesy "Wobbling" (about a baby bird) and the repetitious, screechy "On Time." But songs like "Tarbelly and Featherfoot," with its haunting piano refrain, the wry, chilling "Summer of Drugs" and the moving "I Can't Cry Hard Enough" triumphantly unveil Williams' personal vision. [ws]

WENDY O. WILLIAMS
See *Plasmatics*.

JAMES WILLIAMSON
See *Iggy Pop, Stooges*.

MARTY WILLSON-PIPER
See *Church*.

WIN
See *Fire Engines*.

WIND
Where It's at with the Wind (Cheft) 1982
Guest of the Staphs EP (Cheft) 1984
Living in a New World (Midnight) 1986

Playing exuberant power-pop with abundant talent and a solid grounding in '60s AM radio—from merseybeat to folk-rock to summery soul—this Miami trio made a wonderful debut with the winningly unpolished **Where It's At**. The marvelous fourteen-song collection of beguiling originals not only re-creates the sound of a simpler time, but captures the giddy innocence of musical self-discovery, as if this were all new.

The Wind then relocated north to Queens, New York, stopping in North Carolina long enough to have Mitch Easter co-produce the six-song **Guest of the Staphs** at his studio. Although the charming rush of cluttered, busy arrangements and overstuffed lyrics occasionally resembles Let's Active or the dB's—especially when the rhythms turn off the main road and the guitars and vocals go on a harmonic rampage—"Delaware 89763" is a '60s raveup in the style of early Manfred Mann.

Fronting a new four-piece lineup, songwriters Lane Steinberg (vocals/guitar) and Steven Katz (vocals/bass/keyboards) mix XTC, the Lovin' Spoonful, British Invasion bands and numerous other classic antecedents on the self-produced **Living in a New World**, an ambitious but lighthearted pop gem of great songs, witty (occasionally funny) lyrics and pretty harmonies.   [i]

WINDBREAKERS
Meet the Windbreakers EP (Big Monkey) 1982
Any Monkey with a Typewriter EP (Big Monkey) 1983
Terminal (Homestead) 1985
Disciples of Agriculture (Fr. Closer) 1985
Run (DB) 1986
A Different Sort ... (DB) 1987
At Home with Bobby and Tim (DB) 1989 ●
Electric Landlady (DB) 1991 ●

HOWARD & TIM'S PAID VACATION
I Never Met a Girl I Didn't Like (Midnight) 1985

GONE FISHIN': MATT PIUCCI & TIM LEE
Can't Get Lost When You're Goin' Nowhere (Restless) 1986

BOBBY SUTLIFF
Another Jangly Mess EP (nr/Tambourine) 1986
Only Ghosts Remain (PVC) 1987 ●

TIM LEE
What Time Will Tell (Coyote-Twin/Tone) 1988 ●

Mississippi singer/guitarists Tim Lee and Bobby Sutliff gave their band a terrible name (one hopes the reference is to jackets . . .), but they do bring something distinctly unique to the power pop genre, reflecting more of an American than English influence with strange melodic turns and a ragged Southern vocal style. Following the group's introductory salvo, a 1982 debut 7-inch on their own label, Mitch Easter produced **Any Monkey with a Typewriter**, assisting the trio instrumentally as well. (Richard Barone of the Bongos also appears on the record.) The six-song 12-inch is amateurish but well worth hearing.

Recorded as a duo with help from Easter and others, **Terminal** is a brilliant raw pop-rock-folk record with insidious melodies, fuzzed-out guitars and bristly lyrics, all delivered with unselfconscious sincerity. An appropriately atmospheric version of Television's "Glory"—produced by and played with the Rain Parade—led to Lee's side projects with Parader Matt Piucci (as Gone Fishin'). (A planned outing with another Rain Parader, Steven Roback—announced as Distant Cousins—didn't actually take place.)

The engaging **Run** is another collaboration with Easter, who had by then become a virtual (non-writing) bandmember, and longtime associate Randy Everett. A bit less quirky than prior releases, the electrically energized pop could have been mixed more evenly, but that's not a major distraction. Although the coolest song concept is Lee's anxiety-ridden "Braver on the Telephone," Sutliff's "Visa Cards and Antique Mirrors" runs a close second.

Sutliff and Lee then went their separate ways, leaving the latter—no sign of Easter this time—alone to make the final Windbreakers' LP, which he co-produced with Everett. **A Different Sort** offers another striking set of unsettling lyrics, powerful, inventive playing and production, and emotional singing. From the bells on "Knowing Me" through the affecting piano on "We Never Understand" to the pained roughness of "Forget Again," Lee demonstrates his multifarious talents and abundant creativity.

The French-only **Disciples** recaps the Windbreakers' career up through **Terminal**.

The low-budget Paid Vacation LP Lee cut in 1985 with Howard Wuelfing (an ex-Slickee Boy bassist who led the Washington-area Nurses in the late '70s and then worked with Half Japanese) offers sketchy previews of three Windbreakers' songs: "Run" (from **Run**) and "Fit In" and "Forget Again" (from **A Different Sort**). Besides a cover (Tommy Hoehn and Alex Chilton's "She Might Look My Way"), the LP also contains Wuelfing singing his own originals, one of which ("The Week You Were Mine") is quite lovely. Unfortunately, muffled sound and indifferent performances limit the value of this seven-song artifact.

Lee and Piucci recorded the unexciting Gone Fishin' LP together in Mississippi in February 1986. While the arrangements mix things up effectively, the pair co-wrote only two tracks—the rest are individual efforts. The creative collaboration is unproductive: meandering acoustic doodles with electric guitar overdubs, poorly sung rock tunes and dusty pop songs that suffer from the incompatibility of their voices. The nerdy organ on the joint "Lift It Up" suggests a possibly functional period approach that is otherwise ignored on the LP.

Sutliff's first post-Windbreakers record is a wryly titled British 12-inch magically produced at the Drive-In by Easter, who also plays drums and some guitar. (On his own, Sutliff recorded one cut in Jackson, Mississippi with Tim Lee and a rhythm section.) His pretty voice, piercing guitar solos, understated keyboards and Beatlesque pure-pop sensibility combine to make **Another Jangly Mess** a state-of-the-art exposition on the genre. The equally spectacular **Only Ghosts Remain** repeats the EP's five songs and adds six more (including a spiffy cover of Richard Thompson's "Small Town Romance") of equal quality, four of which employ Wuelfing as bassist.

Left to his own devices on **What Time Will Tell** (relativity speaking: members of Let's Active, the Bongos and the Wygals all lend a hand), Lee comes up with another winner. His first actual solo album, produced by dB-turned-Wygal Gene Holder, offers sparkling, occasionally beautiful guitar pop and richly resonant lyrics about romance and life (mentioning religion a bunch of times) in the South. Trimming his tendency to experiment, Lee plays his songs (and one by Faye Hunter) with straightforward arrangements and evident craft.

Sutliff and Lee reunited in 1989 to tour and record the self-produced **At Home with Bobby and Tim**, a solid and confident album as comfortable-sounding as its title. Although their relationship-oriented lyrics run the emotional gamut from "Just Fine" to "Ill at Ease," the pair—backed by a crisp rhythm section and keyboardist Mark Wyatt (on loan from Great Plains)—easily blend songs, winsome vocals and guitar parts like they'd never been apart. Highlights: the hostile "On the Wire," the Feelies-ish "Down to It" and the folksy "Closer to Home." (The **At Home** CD also contains **Terminal**.)

Like a pair of old Stratocasters, the Windbreakers'

sound continues to gain richness and roundness with time. Produced by Russ Tolman, **Electric Landlady** has some of the duo's most immediate and resonant creations, played and sung with rare pop insight. Closing a circle of sorts, the Windbreakers do a new version of Sutliff's "The Devil and the Sea," a song which Tolman recorded on his '90 LP.   [i]

WIPERS
Is This Real? (Park Ave.) 1979
Youth of America EP (Park Avenue) 1981 (Restless) 1990 •
Over the Edge (Brain Eater) 1983 (Restless) 1987
Wipers (Enigma) 1985
Land of the Lost (Restless) 1986
Follow Blind (Restless) 1987 •
The Circle (Restless) 1988 •
The Best of Wipers and Greg Sage (Restless) 1990 •

GREG SAGE
Straight Ahead (Enigma) 1985

Led by singer/guitarist Greg Sage, Portland, Oregon's Wipers began as a trio playing heavy rock that flirted with hardcore. The first LP is kind of primitive, allowing high velocity and volume to obscure (but not hide) a competent collection of songs with introspective and intelligent lyrics. Raw and abrasive, but well above the usual.

Youth of America, a six-song album with a transitional lineup, shows refinement and bears some resemblance to early Stranglers but for Sage's weird guitar work on some long instrumental bridges. The title track, a ten-and-a-half-minute monster, is worth noting: a simple, repetitive, colossal anthem, then (as now) the ultimate Wipers' effort.

Over the Edge is as appealing, with some of Sage's most memorable songs. The thick title track, the simmering "Doom Town" and the roaring "So Young" define the Wipers' sound—dense and methodical chunky aggression with heavy, cloudy guitar so full it gains a Hendrix-like flavor. The LP also includes the zippy "Romeo," which adds a weird country twang.

Sage recorded his solo album as a fundraiser of sorts while looking for a new label for the band. When Enigma picked up the Wipers, the label released **Straight Ahead** as well. Side One sounds much like the group, but Side Two is just Sage and his guitar making atmospheric space pieces—haunting and strange consciousness-expansion compositions like "Astro Cloud." The therapeutic music is so ethereal that it's over before you notice it. An unexpected, intriguing work.

Wipers is a live album which highlights a 1984 tour and includes three excellent tracks never recorded in the studio, ending with the epic "Youth of America." The sound is honest, the playing true.

Land of the Lost, the Wipers' first new album in three years, shows they didn't get rusty. "Way of Love" and "Nothing Left to Lose" add a certain spark to the charging rockers fed by Sage's fire-breathing guitar. "Just Say," on the other hand, glides on a pretty, lilting guitar line like a quiet waterfall. A strong return.

Follow Blind backsteps a bit, with more hypnotic guitar riffing and much more challenging bass parts. Perhaps the first "moody" Wipers LP, Brad Davidson's prominent bass sets up subconscious undercurrents—in much the way Joy Division once did—for Sage to sing over. "Any Time You Find" is what you might get if you plugged Sage's solo atmospherics into the Wipers' repetitive style. Yet another quality LP from one of America's best-kept secrets.

The sixth and final Wipers studio album sounds familiar enough to seem like business as usual, but this is one band that went down fighting. The scorching opener ("I Want a Way") and the tumultuous title track are typically exciting rockers, but the LP also includes one of their rare pop songs, the excellent "Time Marches On." Even more breathtaking, **The Circle**'s last three tracks are unlike anything in the group's past: the somber, slow shudder of "Goodbye Again" flows into the surprisingly tender "Be There" and then into the beautiful closer, "Blue & Red." With that unexpectedly introspective tear, the Wipers' long career ended.

Sage compiled the 1990 retrospective and, like many artists, favors his more recent albums. While nearly half of the tracks (thirteen on LP, sixteen on tape and CD) are from **Land of the Lost** and **Follow Blind**, there's only one item from the seminal **Youth of America**. (The complete exclusion of the first LP is due to litigation.) But Sage's sequencing is excellent, and he's included rarities like the blistering '78 debut single ("Better off Dead") a long-forgotten compilation track (from Sage's **Trap Sampler**) and other goodies. If not a definitive history, **The Best of Wipers and Greg Sage** is nevertheless a perfect introduction to one of America's best independent-label bands.   [i/jr]

WIRE

Pink Flag (Harvest) 1977 (Restless Retro) 1989 ●
Chairs Missing (nr/Harvest) 1978 (Restless Retro) 1989 ●
154 (Automatic-Warner Bros.) 1979 (Restless Retro) 1989 ●
EP (nr/Rough Trade) 1980
Document and Eyewitness (nr/Rough Trade) 1981 (Mute) 1991 ●
And Here It Is ... Again ... Wire (nr/Sneaky Pete) 1984
Wire Play Pop (nr/Pink) 1986
Snakedrill EP (nr/Mute) 1986 (Mute-Enigma) 1987 ●
The Ideal Copy (Mute-Enigma) 1987 ●
Ahead EP (Mute-Enigma) 1987 ●
The Peel Sessions EP (nr/Strange Fruit) 1987
A Bell Is a Cup Until It Is Struck (Mute-Enigma) 1988 ●
Kidney Bingos EP (Mute-Restless) 1988 ●
Silk Skin Paws EP (nr/Mute) 1988 (Mute-Restless) 1989 ●
It's Beginning to and Back Again (Mute-Enigma) 1989 ●
The Peel Sessions Album (nr/Strange Fruit) 1989 (Strange Fruit-Dutch East India) 1991 ●
On Returning (1977–1979) (Restless Retro) 1989 ●
Manscape (Mute-Enigma) 1990 φ
Life in the Manscape EP (Mute-Enigma) 1990 ●

In the beginning, this self-taught South London quartet were as much atavistic thrashers as many other bands of the time, yet they quickly honed a genuinely expressive, "minimalist" style that made them one of the most influential bands of the class of '77, profoundly touching such descendants as R.E.M., the Minutemen, Big Black and Sonic Youth. The 21 tracks of **Pink Flag** show Wire still in the process of arriving at an identity—disjointed, angry, defiantly odd. Abrupt, too: as bassist

Graham Lewis described their attitude to song length, "When the text ran out, it stopped." (This worked to chilling effect with the harrowing narrative of "Reuters.") Yet this primitive approach didn't prevent Wire from including two conventionally tuneful rockers ("Mannequin" and "Ex Lion Tamer") as well as what just might be the prettiest song by any (so-called) punk band, "Fragile." (Since Wire will not play such old stuff themselves, a New York area band named Ex Lion Tamer faithfully reproduced the LP's songs onstage as Wire's chosen opening act on their 1987 US tour.)

In January 1978, shortly after the release of Wire's first album, the group recorded a John Peel session, which was issued almost a decade later. The selections include "106 Beats That" from **Pink Flag**, "Practice Make Perfect" and "I Am the Fly" from **Chairs Missing** plus the non-LP "Culture Vultures." The subsequent **Peel** album adds the results of a repeat visit in September '78, previewing tracks from **154**; and September '79.

Chairs Missing is more mature than **Pink Flag**, moving decisively beyond any simple punk pigeonhole with much greater scope. As on its predecessor, amid the anger of "Being Sucked in Again," the bile of "I Am the Fly," the neurotic anxiety of "Too Late," even the ironic detachment of "French Film Blurred," sat the pretty if abstruse "Outdoor Miner."

On **154**, producer Mike Thorne became more integral than on the first two LPs, acting almost as a fifth member, using keyboards and studio technique to contour the sound. That was Wire's development—stylized and smoothed out—although still dissonant; more abstract and detached, with the venom and sardonicism more subtly conveyed. Thus refined, this brilliant groundbreaking band adjudged their experiment complete and broke up, with guitarist Bruce Gilbert and bassist/vocalist Graham Lewis creating Dome and vocalist/guitarist Colin Newman pursuing a solo career.

The 1980 EP is a bizarre 45 rpm 12-inch: one side is titled "Crazy About Love," but the anxiety (among other things) conveyed over a haunting, repeated riff *for more than fifteen minutes* suggests something other than the usual meaning of the phrase. The flip is a powerhouse remake of the single "Our Swimmer" plus "Catapult 30" (strange, pulsing doings).

Document and Eyewitness, two live discs (one full-length, the other an eight-song quickie which plays at 45 rpm), owes its raunchy sound as much to Wire's disdain of musical niceties as to dodgy recording. Audience sounds and other incidental noise are left in; for aficionados only. **And Here It Is . . . Again . . . Wire** is a career retrospective containing singles, album tracks and live cuts. **Wire Play Pop** likewise compiles seven old tracks, but limits its scope to Wire's extraordinary, trailblazing A-sides, including "Dot Dash," "I Am the Fly," "Mannequin" and "1-2-X-U."

In 1986, seemingly out of nowhere (well, Mute UK, anyway) popped the **Snakedrill** EP. These were indeed new tracks, but the portent was mixed; the two on the A-side ("A Serious of Snakes" and "Drill") are engrossing, dangerous music, while the pair on the back are interesting without being eyebrow-raising impressive. If they'd gotten back together, they must have felt they had something new to say. But did they? **The Ideal Copy** declared Wire was plugged in again, for real. It's a varied bill of fare, in some ways resembling a more mature **Chairs Missing**, with highlights ranging from the breezily melodic, rhythmically busy "Ahead" to the slow, relentlessly fearsome "Feed Me" (an awesome Graham Lewis vocal) to the topical funk (!) of "Ambitious." Perhaps it's not brilliant—maybe "merely" excellent?

The **Ahead** EP contains two remixes of that track, plus three live cuts, two previously unreleased, including the strange a cappella "Vivid Riot of Red." Those three live (from Berlin) cuts, as well as the entirety of **Snakedrill**, are appended to the CD and cassette of **The Ideal Copy**.

In a sense, **A Bell Is a Cup** is to **The Ideal Copy** what **154** was to **Chairs Missing**—a stylized set of dreamscapes and consciousness streams (though it's not as musically sedate as Newman's own **Commercial Suicide**). Some of it has extensive lyrical wordplay, with the accent on *play* (a new attitude for Wire that Newman developed on his own **singing fish** LP); a prime example is "Kidney Bingos," which also happens to be one of the most melodious tracks Wire's ever recorded. Other tracks offer vignettes, yet the subjectivity of view, with its associative images, is continually emphasized. It's arguably Wire's most ruminative album, and while immersion in it won't, as "Silk Skin Paws" suggests, "wring your senses"—that's more a job for **Chairs Missing**—it will twirl your lobes a time or two. An album to live with. (The five-song **Kidney Bingos** EP includes live-in-London takes of "Drill" and "Over Theirs," as well as two versions of the brooding, intense "Pieta," which deserved to be on the LP but would not quite have fit in.) The **Bell** CD adds the four extra items from **Kidney Bingos**, which is also available on a separate 3-inch CD.

The **Silk Skin Paws** EP consists of three numbers from **Bell Is a Cup** in remixed or alternate versions plus the otherwise unreleased "German Shepherds."

Various releases made 1989 a big year for re-evaluating Wire's work. **On Returning** is a 31-track redaction (22 on LP and cassette) of the group's EMI years; while the selections are arguable, a dilettante would prefer one of the previous collections and a fan would own the original albums. (**On Returning** does include the non-LP singles "Dot Dash" and "A Question of Degree.") The live-in-the-studio **Peel** LP includes three sessions' worth: early '78 (one track from the first LP, two from the second and the otherwise unreleased "Culture Vultures"), late '78 (four tracks from **154**) and late '79 ("Crazy About Love"). Interesting but not essential.

It's Beginning to and Back Again (aka **IBTABA**) began as live recordings (from Chicago and Portugal), but the tracks were subsequently rebuilt almost totally in the studio. Whatever was intended at the outset, all that's left from the original live takes on some of the tracks is room ambience! Five songs from **Bell** and **Copy** (plus the non-LP B-side "German Shepherds") are all notably improved here, with more authority, punch, breadth—you name it. The other four songs—including the single, "Eardrum Buzz," which appears in two different versions—are also excellent.

As **Pink Flag** was the band's perverse take on punk, **Manscape** is its subversion of alternative dance-rock. Busy syncopated rhythms amid synthetic keyboards—

sometimes providing strings and horns—predominate. Lewis takes a more active role in singing, yet that doesn't mean an escalation of sonic abrasiveness. While the textures are fairly conventional, they're still unsettling enough to accompany Lewis' ire ("I'm going to torch it with you on the top"); elsewhere, a subdued mood suffuses uneasy lullabies with Newman's thoughtful, but often stark, lyrical fragments. "To the third rate butcher's dance-hall mix . . . I'll say goodbye," indeed. (The EP contains three mixes of "Manscape" and two non-LP tracks (one good, one so-so).

Wire's first three albums have been reissued on CDs, all with extra tracks. **Pink Flag** adds "Options R," a non-LP B-side, while **Chairs Missing** has two non-LP Bs ("Go Ahead" and "Former Airline") plus the classic menacingly jaunty non-LP A-side, "Question of Degree." **154** has four otherwise unalbumized tracks: "Song 1," "Get Down 1 & 2," "Let's Panic Later" and "Small Electric Piece."

Drummer Robert Gotobed left the band following **Manscape**; the remaining three continued on as WIR.

[jg]

See also *Dome, A.C. Marias, Colin Newman*.

WIRE TRAIN

In a Chamber (415-Columbia) 1983
Between Two Words (415-Columbia) 1985
Ten Women (415-Columbia) 1987 ●
Wire Train (MCA) 1990 ●

Like former 415 labelmates Translator, San Francisco's Wire Train plays exceptional, character-filled modern folk-pop, using strong songwriting as a basis. (The two groups also shared producer David Kahne, whose brilliant efforts contributed greatly to both's records.) Wire Train achieves its style with a full-blooded guitar attack, echoey vocals and strong, rushed drumming. **In a Chamber** has wonderful, memorable tracks like "Chamber of Hellos" and "I'll Do You"; lesser creations at least *sound* just as good. A great debut album.

Between Two Words, despite Kahne's absence and a version of Dylan's "God on Our Side" that unintentionally trivializes its earnest concerns, is equally memorable. Not all of the songs work, but those that do— "Last Perfect Thing," "Skills of Summer," "Love, Love"—exhibit folk-derived melodic beauty and an uneasy emotional perspective that is not easily ignored. The writing/singing/guitar-playing duo of Kevin Hunter and Kurt Herr doesn't display a lot of range or depth, but gives the group an unmistakable, invariably pleasing identity.

Herr was replaced prior to **Ten Women** and his absence from the record is immediately evident. While the crystalline pop production and Hunter's sandy voice give the record a familiar patina, the slower-paced songs are pretty but routine. Where the band once soared on rich guitar interplay, Wire Train here lacks character and conviction.

The sudden arrival of a new album in 1990 ended whatever-happened-to speculation as the same quartet, assisted by Pettymen Benmont Tench and Mike Campbell and others, returned with **Wire Train**. Hunter's Southwestern Dylan affectations predominate: at the low point, "Oh Me Oh My" fits an obnoxious vocal imitation into "Rainy Day Women"-style carousing and pointedly includes "Is it rolling, Bob?" However, "Simply Racing" is a Stonesy chugalug and the record's most striking song ("Should She Cry?," a catchy breath of pop air) owes no stylistic debt outside the band's own past.   [i]

WISEBLOOD
See *Foetus Inc.*

BOB WISEMAN
See *Blue Rodeo.*

WITCH TRIALS
See *Dead Kennedys.*

JAH WOBBLE
The Legend Lives On ... Jah Wobble in "Betrayal" (nr/Virgin) 1980 (Blue Plate) 1990 ●
V.I.E.P. EP (nr/Virgin) 1980
Jah Wobble's Bedroom Album (nr/Lago) 1983
Tradewinds (nr/Lago) 1986

DON LETTS, STRATETIME KEITH, STEEL LEG, JAH WOBBLE
Steel Leg v the Electric Dread EP (nr/Virgin) 1978

JAH WOBBLE, JAKI LIEBEZEIT AND HOLGER CZUKAY
How Much Are They EP (nr/Island) 1981

JAH WOBBLE + ANIMAL
A Long, Long Way EP (nr/Island) 1982

JAH WOBBLE—THE EDGE— HOLGER CZUKAY
Snake Charmer EP (Island) 1983

JAH WOBBLE & OLLIE MARLAND
Neon Moon (nr/Island) 1985

After falling out with John Lydon and Keith Levene, bassist Jah Wobble (John Wardle) left Public Image Ltd. and launched an on-again-off-again solo/collaborative career. He also played in a group called the Human Condition and did a brief stint as a London taxi driver.

Wobble's anti-musical playfulness on **The Legend Lives On** is matched only by his horrid vocals. But then again, that's the appeal: the return to the DIY, no-rules punk tradition. Wobble accentuates his reggae pretensions, fiddles with electronics and overdubbing and plays shadowy, threatening bass. If nothing else, Wobble has anti-style.

V.I.E.P., which sounds like outtakes from the album sessions, reprises the LP's "Blueberry Hill." Twice. "Sea Side Special" is notable for its professionalism and use of brass. But the EP is for completists only.

Far more indicative of Wobble's real talent is the four-song 12-inch made with Can-men Jaki Liebezeit and Holger Czukay in 1981. Manifesting a dour modern landscape, Wobble's bass buttresses the dark tunes with style and precision that balance his earlier solipsistic

sloppiness. Freed from ego, Wobble teeters at last towards art.

Unlike previous Wobble projects, **A Long, Long Way** is sweetly pop-like, treading on Joy Division territory (with assistance from guitarist Dave "Animal" Maltby). Especially interesting is "Romany Trail," which mixes "Peter Gunn" jazz with modern sensibilities. Top-notch.

The Bedroom Album was recorded alone—you guessed it—in the master's chamber, with Animal providing the only outside contact. A cross between a legit solo studio job and the kind of one-man-band who plays on street corners, the LP finds Wobble building unstable and atmospheric polyrhythmic instrumentals over which he intones ponderous lyrics with only the barest glimpses of melody or meter. The lengthy record requires a lot of patience, but is not without undercurrents of charm or appeal.

In collaboration with producer Francois Kevorkian, Czukay, Liebezeit, Animal and U2's guitar star (among others—Wobble certainly appears to make friends easily), he pounds out far slicker dance-rock on **Snake Charmer**, but it's all for naught, as the record is overstaffed and overstuffed, mixing repetitive rhythms with extraneous sounds to achieve audible boredom.

Wobble's 1978 pre-PiL 12-inch with Keith Levene, filmmaker (and future Big Audio Dynamite member) Don Letts and someone called Steel Leg is a bizarre assemblage of dub reggae and noisome doom-funk that has Levene playing drums and guitar while Wobble adds bass, synth and vocals. Whew!   [sg/i]

See also *Public Image Ltd.*

WOLFGANG PRESS
The Burden of Mules (nr/4AD) 1983
Scarecrow EP (nr/4AD) 1984
Water EP (nr/4AD) 1985
Sweatbox EP (nr/4AD) 1985
The Legendary Wolfgang Press & Other Tall Stories (nr/4AD) 1985 ●
Standing Up Straight (nr/4AD) 1986 ●
Big Sex EP (nr/4AD) 1987
Bird Wood Cage (4AD-Rough Trade) 1988 ●
Kansas EP (4AD-Rough Trade) 1989

Ever-changing and always challenging, London's Wolfgang Press is one of the most enigmatic groups on a generally enigmatic label. Known better for their stylish Alberto Ricci record covers than their music, the trio comprises Michael Allen (vocals/bass) and Mark Cox (keyboards)—both of whom had been in Rema Rema with Adam Ant collaborator Marco Pirroni before transmuting into a pre-Press quartet called Mass which released a 1980 single on 4AD—and Andrew Gray (drums).

The Burden of Mules is dark and cacophonous, an angry, intense slab of post-punk gloom that is best left to its own (de)vices. **Scarecrow**, however, makes the most of the band's better attributes with spotless production by Cocteau Twin Robin Guthrie. Allen's almost-spoken, heavily accented vocals sputter through a mix of up-front bass, rhythm guitar, synthesizers and creative percussion. Some dreary moments remain, but a send-up of Otis Redding's "Respect" reflects the lightened mood.

Water continues the band's evolution, but in a totally different direction. Over minimalist backing, Allen's vocals turn baladeerish: Frank Sinatra sifted through Joy Division. A track called "My Way" is curiously reminiscent of Burt Bacharach.

Continuing to work with Guthrie, the Wolfgang Press sounds fully mature and more musically adept than ever ·on Sweatbox. The EP strengthens and confirms their fundamental approach: the deconstruction and reconstruction of pop conventions in their own image. Put through the Wolfgang Press breakdown process, Neil Young's "Heart of Gold" becomes "Heart of Stone," in effect creating an original. Sweatbox also establishes the group's mastery of moving instrumentals. The Legendary Wolfgang Press compiles the three EPs onto one disc, with some songs remixed and/or edited from their original form.

Musically, Standing Up Straight is as challenging and inventive as the band's other work, adding industrial and classical instrumentation to the creative arsenal. "Dig a Hole," "Hammer the Halo" and "Rotten Fodder" are the best the Wolfgang Press has to offer—dark and thoroughly uncompromising—on a record which is not for the easily intimidated. Also of interest is the enclosed lyric sheet, a multi-fold affair in which lyrics are presented as artistic design elements.

The Wolfgang Press continue to astound and delight on the Big Sex EP, four tracks that clearly demonstrate just what it is that makes this band so special. "The Wedding" is weighty and primal; "The Great Leveller" is desperate, insistent and the closest the Press will likely come to a real pop tune. The oppressive "That Heat" has wonderful blasts of distorted guitar throughout; "God's Number" is virtually all drums, with the novelty of female soul backing vocals. Daring music for daring times.

Bird Wood Cage maintains the trio's habit of inserting fascinating bits of business into superficially forbidding songs. Allen's highly strung dramatic vocals (a gruffer Nick Cave, perhaps) and the measured tracks' plodding, trancey construction may discourage easy access to the Wolfgang Press' world, but the band's thickly laid atmosphere envelops all sorts of effective ingredients: female backing vocals on "King of Soul," wah-wah guitar on "Kansas," dub reggae effects on "Hang on Me (For Papa)." Making the most of understatement, the Wolfgang Press fills Bird Wood Cage with intrigue.

Mixing up geo-political concerns on the Cyrillic-titled Kansas EP, the Wolfgang Press begins "Assassination K./Kanserous" with a banjo picking out "Yellow Rose of Texas" and then proceeds into a pastiche of spoken-word tapes about JFK before opening into a remix of the Talking Headsy track (from Bird Wood Cage) for which it's named. The EP's two other songs pursue a more muscular sound than usual; "Twister" takes its cues from Suicide.   [ag/tr]

WONDER STUFF

The Eight Legged Groove Machine (Polydor) 1988 ●
Hup (Polydor) 1989 ●

Arrogance and mean-spiritedness are not two traits you'd normally offer as key ingredients for a successful pop band. But then, most pop bands don't have half as many hooks as this Birmingham foursome. With its clever self-explanatory title and crisp production (by ex-Vibrator Pat Collier), The Eight Legged Groove Machine is a fine showcase for the Stuffies' memorable British punk-pop, which is stylistically not all that far removed from Collier's old band. The record's fourteen nuggets (each clocking in at under three minutes) offer ingratiating melodies and, on such tracks as "It's Yer Money I'm After, Baby," "Give, Give, Give Me More, More, More" and "Unbearable," some of the most comically selfish and snotty lyrics you're likely to encounter. The CD and cassette add four tracks, including the essential "Astley in the Noose," a death wish dedicated to one of the '80s most plastic pop-singing icons.

Again produced by Collier, Hup finds the Wonder Stuff getting serious and attempting to diversify stylistically, incorporating psychedelia ("Let's Be Other People"), acoustic folk ("Unfaithful"), bluegrass ("Golden Green"), even a spot-on PiL soundalike ("Good Night Though") into its ever-pissed-off repertoire. Although commendably ambitious, Hup lacks the peppy charm of the debut and contains some cloying filler.

When last heard from (on the 1990 "Circlesquare" single), the Stuffies were heading in another direction altogether, successfully embracing the fashionable Manchester trance-dance corps. Go figure.   [db]

WOODENTOPS

Straight Eight Bushwaker EP (Hol. Megadisc) 1986
Well Well Well ... (Upside) 1986 ●
Giant (Rough Trade-Columbia) 1986 ●
Hypno-Beat (Upside) 1987 ●
Wooden Foot Cops on the Highway (Rough Trade-
     Columbia) 1988 ●

In this era of retro-rock, revivals and ripoffs, it's not easy to find truly innovative pop music. That's what makes this quintet from Peckham so special—they literally defy categorization. Led by the exuberant Rolo McGinty, the Woodentops employ only the barest of essentials—vocals, keyboards, acoustic guitars, bass and rudimentary drums.

The first two records chronicle a string of five brilliant singles. The Dutch EP collects six tracks. "Move Me," like many of the Woodentops' songs, builds to a manic crescendo before collapsing into a wall of sound; "Well Well Well" is held together with skittering drums and pulsating keyboard chords; "It Will Come" rushes along in a flurry of guitar, piano and good-natured mayhem. The Woodentops tend to throw caution to the wind on their B-sides, and the three here explore all sorts of new territory. Well Well Well adds two more B-sides (from 12-inch singles) and substitutes a longer version of "Well Well Well" that has incredible keyboard and drum breaks. (When that record was subsequently issued on CD, it was retitled The Unabridged Singles Collection.)

The Woodentops' long-awaited debut album proved to be more than worth the wait. Giant is a bright handful of pop gems hallmarked with the band's special sound. They've filled out musically with the addition of trumpet, marimba, strings and accordion, and the songs are more structured. But that in no way detracts from their originality. You're not likely to hear more innovative pop than "Hear Me James," "Love Affair with Everyday Livin' " or "Travelling Man." An incredible first album.

Recorded in Los Angeles at the end of 1986, **Hypno-Beat** draws its material from singles and **Giant** and reveals that the Woodentops play three times as fast onstage as they do in the studio. You'll work up a sweat just listening to this. The CD adds the contents of **Straight Eight Bushwaker**; the cassette also contains an extra pair of live recordings.

Wooden Foot Cops on the Highway finds the band suffering a bit from a lack of fresh ideas and the loss of keyboard player Alice Thompson. Some good songs appear (e.g., "In a Dream" and "What You Give Out"), but there is little distinction between this album and **Giant**. Some bands survive for years (even decades) by making the same album over and over; the Woodentops deserve a better fate.   [ag]

WORKDOGS
See *Gibson Bros.*

WORLD DOMINATION ENTERPRISES
Let's Play Domination (Product Inc.-Caroline) 1988 ●
Dub Domination (nr/Product Inc.) 1988
Love from Lead City (nr/Product Inc.) 1989
012
Let's Get Professional (nr/Flicknife) 1984

The disturbing noise/chaos level achieved by this angular Ladbroke Grove (London) trio—formed by singer/guitarist Keith Dobson after the dissolution of his previous band, 012—is indeed something marvelous. The astonishing high-pressure racket of **Let's Play Domination**'s opening salvo ("Message for You People") may send you rushing to the turntable to see if your stylus is accidentally gouging a hole in the platter. Besides sturdily unsettling originals, the album—clearly a stiff-upper-lip cousin to Big Black, Birthday Party and other punishing pain-inflicters—includes a relatively straight rendition of L.L. Cool J's "I Can't Live Without My Radio" as well as deranged interpretations of Lipps, Inc.'s "Funkytown" and a U-Roy number. As Dobson layers on the scathing, slithery guitar and sings in a plain, serviceable voice, the rhythm section lurches and pounds in a tight phalanx; producer Dave Allen captures the entire meltdown with thrilling clarity.

Judging by their 12-inch singles, all of which contain alternate mixes, WDE is big on remixes, which makes the release of **Dub Domination**—eight album tracks given studio massages—no big surprise. **Love from Lead City**, packaged to look like a bootleg, with no information or credits, is a crude live record (with no hint of an audience's presence) that features spare but crushing renditions of such headbutts as "Funkytown," "Message for You People" and the political "Asbestos Lead Asbestos," a song originally from 012's album.   [i]

WORLD OF POOH
See *Barbara Manning.*

WORLD OF SKIN
See *Swans.*

WORLD PARTY
Private Revolution (Chrysalis) 1986 ●
Goodbye Jumbo (Ensign-Chrysalis) 1990 ●

For all intents and purposes, Wales' Karl Wallinger *is* World Party on **Private Revolution**, which he recorded at home after leaving the Waterboys. (World Party, the group, thus far seems to be only a touring band.) He sings, plays guitars, keyboards and uses samples to create a refreshingly unique musical backdrop that probably owes more to the psychedelic-era Beatles than any one other source, yet never actually sounds like them. The music, in fact, serves like a kind of free-flowing pop soundtrack to Wallinger's lyrics—a hybrid of '60s-hippie and '80s-new-age ideas about ecology and self-knowledge. (Though, thankfully, they're not quite as silly as that sounds.) Highlights include a terrific cover of Dylan's "All I Really Want to Do," and a cameo by Sinéad O'Connor. Leave your cynicism at the door and you may find yourself trading in your black leather jacket for love beads. In a word: groovy.

While **Goodbye Jumbo** doesn't have the seamless flow of **Private Revolution**, it does have a handful of great songs, especially the single "Way Down Now" and "Put the Message in the Box." You won't think of the Beatles so much here as you will the Stones and Van Morrison, particularly when Wallinger repeats lines over and over à la Vanbo on a bunch of the tunes. And who do you think of when you hear a title like "Sweet Soul Dream"? (Sinéad guests on that song, while Wire Train's Jeff Trott adds slide to three others.)   [ds]

See also *Waterboys.*

BERNIE WORRELL
Funk of Ages (Gramavision) 1990 ●

P-Funk keyboardist and composer Worrell's synthesizer basslines helped redefine modern funk, a fact that wasn't lost on the legions of stiff new wave white boys suddenly possessed by the need to get down. Hence, when David Byrne fell under that compulsion in the early '80, he enrolled Worrell in the extended Talking Heads family. Stints with the Golden Palominos followed, and Worrell even became a Pretender for one LP.

Funk of Ages finds him in a rare spotlight, jamming with Maceo Parker and Bootsy Collins, calling on the many friends he made during years of session work: Sly and Robbie, Keith Richards, Chris Spedding, Vernon Reid and Jerry Harrison are only part of the all-star cast. And because the man's a genius, the result sounds like an exuberant, no-holds-barred funk party rather than another tired supersession. At its best, the songwriting has real bite; at the least it carries a strong groove. Things falter a bit when Byrne, as affected as he's ever been, turns up. Other than that, **Funk of Ages** lives up to its title. As revolutionary as Worrell's work has been (and continues to be), the borderline-goofy, uniquely P-Funkitized party atmosphere that it evokes is something you don't hear much of these days.   [gk]

WRECK

Wreck EP (Play It Again Sam USA) 1989
Soul Train (Play It Again Sam USA) 1990 ●

This Chicago-based trio of Milwaukee natives (including Die Kreuzen vet Keith Brammer on bass) slams harsh guitar power into abrupt Minutemen-styled material on its first two records, creating a hectic rush of jagged electricity within sturdy song structures.

A lot less brutal than other current Steve Albini protégés, Wreck doesn't make much of a case for itself on the rather generic-sounding four-song 12-inch. With bracing covers of both the Fall (a great version of "Various Times") and the Sensational Alex Harvey Band (an okay rendition of "Ribs and Balls"), **Soul Train** covers more ground and demonstrates real growth potential. Shouter/guitarist Dean Schlabowske is a commanding frontman, but the lumbering rhythm section's struggle to find its rightful place in the songs occasionally frustrates his efforts.   [i]

WRECKLESS ERIC

Wreckless Eric (nr/Stiff) 1978
The Wonderful World of Wreckless Eric (nr/Stiff) 1978
The Whole Wide World (Stiff) 1979
Big Smash! (Stiff-Epic) 1980
The Peel Sessions EP (nr/Strange Fruit) 1988
Le Beat Group Électrique (Fr. New Rose) 1989
At the Shop! EP (Fr. New Rose) 1990 ●

CAPTAINS OF INDUSTRY

A Roomful of Monkeys (nr/Go! Discs) 1985

LEN BRIGHT COMBO

The Len Bright Combo Present the Len Bright Combo by
the Len Bright Combo (nr/Empire) 1986
Combo Time! (nr/Ambassador) 1986

On the front of his first LP, the grinning "Wreckless" Eric Goulden wears a badge proclaiming "I'm a mess," and a drop of the needle on the disc confirms it. Led by producer Larry Wallis (himself an ex-Pink Fairy), a motley crew whose previous employers include Ronnie Lane, Marc Bolan and Ian Dury slosh together some mangy guitars, slurpy sax and cheesy organ to surround the strangled, semi-sodden vocals of this lovable scruffy runt from Brighton. All too often, though, catching the bits of perception and knowing desperation requires clearing the sonic mud, not to mention deciphering Eric's drawl.

All, that is, except on the brilliant "Whole Wide World," produced and mostly played by Nick Lowe. As if noticing that Lowe's well-defined pop sense seemed to bring out Eric's best, a series of producers then tried to clean up and dress up his sound. The next album's roster was only slightly less rag-tag (Hollywood Brats holdovers and ex-Man man Malcolm Morley), helmed by Pete Solley. This time, though, a balance was obtained between Eric's innate looseness and the clarity and sheer musicality needed to adequately present his tunes. As a result, **The Wonderful World** is a rollicking good time propelled by Eric's trademark guitar chug.

No hits were forthcoming, though, and Stiff apparently decided to clean Eric's act up further, as is evident from the new-material first half of the double set, **Big**

Smash!. Fresh faces in the band (who also collaborated with him on songwriting) and decidedly more commercial-minded production unfortunately seemed to have sanded off all of the Wreckless edges. (The standout tune, "Good Conversation," is one he wrote alone; it's also the nastiest.)

Clearly establishing his merits once and for all, the other half of **Big Smash** is an irreproachable distillation of the first two LPs and a batch of singles. That disc had previously been issued separately in the US as **The Whole Wide World**, indicating—even to those who might have otherwise dismissed him—Eric's surprising resonance, not to mention his squandered and/or squelched potential. (For collectors of odd discs, the first LP was also issued as a brown-vinyl 10-inch, with two songs fewer.)

Dropping the "Wreckless" and reverting to his given name, Goulden returned in 1985 as leader of Captains of Industry, a trio including ex-Blockhead bassist Norman Watt-Roy. The group's sole release, **A Roomful of Monkeys** (guest-starring Mickey Gallagher, another ex-Blockhead, whose roller-rink organ is actually the most prominent instrument on many tracks), makes it clear that his five-year absence did nothing to dull Eric's spirit or his talent. Considering that Goulden produced himself, it's a surprisingly disciplined effort, mixing the craftsmanship of **Big Smash** with the spontaneity of earlier efforts. With songs that are as pungent as ever (including the uncharacteristically serious reggae-tinged "Food Factory"), Eric sings them confidently (and in tune!). A resounding comeback by an estimable talent; why it wasn't greeted as such by the British public remains a mystery.

Noting that professionalism didn't get him anything but good marks, Eric went low-fi again, fronting the three-man Len Bright Combo (no one named Len Bright is involved; the other two members are ex-Milkshakes) on two wonderful albums, giving swell tunes like "You're Gonna Screw My Head Off" and "Someone Must've Nailed Us Together" cleanly played garage-raveup treatment that suits them as well as the pop arrangements on **A Roomful of Monkeys**.

Though Captains of Industry and the Len Bright Combo demonstrated that Eric had finally gained enough self-control to hone his raw talent into consistently satisfying music without putting himself at the mercy of unsympathetic producers, his subsequent releases make it clear that this was just a phase. Reverting to the Wreckless moniker, Goulden teamed with a French rhythm section to record **Le Beat Group Électrique**, a casually delivered set that—despite its title—is the most minimalist and least-rocking studio disc in his catalogue. Though it lacks the musical cohesion of the preceding group efforts, it's a charming little reminder that Eric can still sound like a mess when he's in the mood. The brief "Fuck by Fuck" could be interpreted as misogynistic, but it's more likely that Eric's just trying to be annoying.

The six-song **At the Shop!** is even more spare, with Eric and three barely audible French sidemen performing live at New Rose's record store in Paris. (Actually, the solo acoustic rendition of "Semaphore Signals," as well as the two similarly realized CD bonus tracks—"Depression (Version Francaise)" and "Boney

Maronie"—were "found in the warehouse.") Eric's liner notes indicate that he's finished trying to tailor his music to suit mainstream recording standards. An enjoyable keepsake to be sure, but Goulden's sloppiness-for-its-own-sake ethos does not bode well for his artistic future. [jg/hd]

WURZEL

See *Motörhead*.

ROBERT WYATT

The End of an Ear (Columbia) 1971 (nr/CBS) 1980
Rock Bottom (Virgin) 1974 (Blue Plate) 1990 ●
Ruth Is Stranger Than Richard (Virgin) 1975 (Blue Plate) 1990 ●
Rock Bottom/Ruth Is Stranger Than Richard (nr/Virgin) 1981
Robert Wyatt (It. Rough Trade) 1981
Nothing Can Stop Us (nr/Rough Trade) 1981 (Gramavision) 1986 ●
The Animals Film (nr/Rough Trade) 1982
Work in Progress EP (nr/Rough Trade) 1984
1982–1984 (Rough Trade) 1984
I'm a Believer EP (nr/Virgin) 1984
Old Rottenhat (Gramavision) 1985 ●
The Peel Sessions EP (nr/Strange Fruit) 1987
Compilation (Gramavision) 1990 φ

MATCHING MOLE

Matching Mole (nr/CBS) 1972
Matching Mole's Little Red Record (Columbia) 1973

Having first come to prominence as founding drummer/vocalist with Canterbury's Soft Machine, Bristol-born Robert Wyatt is one of the English art-schools' most notable (and best-loved) musical alumni, retaining that genre's spirit of musical adventurousness without indulging in the bloated pretensions that sidetracked many of his contemporaries. In the unselfconscious experimentalism of his post-Softs work, and in the political commitment of his more recent material, Wyatt has served as an inspiration for a new generation of socially conscious British artists.

End of an Ear, Wyatt's first solo LP, was recorded right before he left Soft Machine and basically continues in that group's freewheeling avant-jazz spirit. Wordless scat-sung originals are bookended by two lengthy versions of Gil Evans' "Las Vegas Tango."

The four-man Matching Mole—the name is a phonetic adaptation of the French translation of "soft machine"—recorded two albums of meandering (and occasionally charming) pieces, mostly instrumentals. The spotty **Matching Mole** is mainly a Wyatt showcase; the more driving **Little Red Record** (produced by Robert Fripp) is a collective effort, but both are weighed down with the sort of aimless noodling that helped give progressive rock a bad name.

Following a crippling fall that left him permanently wheelchair-bound, Wyatt recorded **Rock Bottom**, produced by Pink Floyd's Nick Mason, and the self-produced **Ruth Is Stranger Than Richard**. Both records are idiosyncratic, mixing woozy experimentation ("Little Red Riding Hood Hit the Road," which appears in two utterly different versions on **Rock Bot-**

tom, and **Ruth**'s "Muddy Mouse," a collaboration with Fred Frith) with charmingly pastoral nursery rhymes ("Sea Song," "Alifib," both from **Rock Bottom**). **Ruth** is the better focused of the two, and includes the remarkable "Team Spirit," which hints at the political outlook that dominates Wyatt's later work. **I'm a Believer** and the live **Peel Sessions** also contain material from this period; both feature Wyatt's droll non-LP reading of the Monkees' Neil Diamond-penned classic.

Wyatt lay low for the remainder of the '70s, finally reemerging at the turn of the decade with a series of four audacious Rough Trade singles. Those eight sides (two of which are performed by artists other than Wyatt) are collected on the Italian **Robert Wyatt**, and form the basis of **Nothing Can Stop Us**. Though basically a compilation with only one original composition, **Nothing Can Stop Us** is a cohesive and incredibly moving statement, with Wyatt's fragile, plaintive vocals breathing new life (and political content) into material as diverse as Chic's "At Last I Am Free," the obscure American gospel tune "Stalin Wasn't Stallin'," the folk song "Caimanera" (aka "Guantanamera") and the disquieting lynch-mob protest "Strange Fruit" (most associated with Billie Holiday). Though Wyatt personally adheres to a fairly ruthless strain of Stalinism, you'd never know it from the compassion and empathy that radiate from every groove of this record.

Nothing Can Stop Us was subsequently re-released with the significant inclusion of the Elvis Costello/Clive Langer-penned "Shipbuilding" (produced by Costello, Langer and Alan Winstanley), as subtle and insightful an anti-war song as anyone's ever written. The album's US version, released in 1986, ditches the poet Peter Blackman's reading of his "Stalingrad" and adds "Shipbuilding," plus its British 12-inch B-sides (interpretations of Thelonious Monk's "Round Midnight" and Eubie Blake's "Memories of You") and cover art.

The Animals Film contains Wyatt's appropriately harsh instrumental score for a harrowing documentary chronicling institutionalized human cruelty. The four-song **Work in Progress** is similar in approach to **Nothing Can Stop Us**, with a reworking of Peter Gabriel's "Biko" and Spanish-language folk songs by Victor Jara and Pablo Milanes. The American **1982–1984** combines the contents of **Work in Progress** and the British "Shipbuilding" 12-inch.

The completely self-penned **Old Rottenhat** is a perceptive, beautifully performed and ultimately bleak view of ongoing political struggle, more specific than **Nothing Can Stop Us** but equally emotive. Though many of Wyatt's lyrics veer towards the doctrinaire, his singing is as quietly passionate as ever. (The 1990 **Compilation** is merely a CD/cassette pairing of **Old Rottenhat** and **Nothing Can Stop Us**.)

The **Peel Sessions** EP was recorded in September 1974 and contains "Soup Song," "Sea Song," "Alifib" and "I'm a Believer." [hd]

See also *Everything but the Girl*.

WYGALS

Honyocks in the Whithersoever (Rough Trade) 1989 ●

Though this New York combo has been around in one form or another since the mid-'80s, it took leader

Janet Wygal and her drummer brother Doug (both ex-Individuals) four years to release an album under the family name. By that time, ex-dB Gene Holder (who had produced both of the Individuals' releases), had joined as guitarist/producer, helping to refine the band's once-sprawling sound into a refreshingly nonformulaic brand of guitar-based art-pop that's aurally attractive but never sappy. On **Honyocks in the Whithersoever**, tracks like "Eat a Horse," "Creature Comforts" and "Slap Me Like a Wave" balance Janet's mischievous wordplay and offhandedly impassioned vocals with inventively layered melodies that even sound good back-

wards (as on the title track). A fine record by an under-recorded band. [hd]

See also *Individuals*.

PETE WYLIE

See *Wah!*.

STEVE WYNN

See *Dream Syndicate*.

X X X X X X X

X
Los Angeles (Slash) 1980 ●
Wild Gift (Slash) 1981 ●
Under the Big Black Sun (Elektra) 1982 ●
More Fun in the New World (Elektra) 1983 ●
Ain't Love Grand (Elektra) 1985 ●
See How We Are (Elektra) 1987 ●
Live at the Whisky A Go-Go on the Fabulous Sunset Strip
    (Elektra) 1988 ●

KNITTERS
Poor Little Critter on the Road (Slash) 1985

EXENE CERVENKA + WANDA COLEMAN
Twin Sisters (Freeway) 1985

EXENE CERVENKA
Old Wives' Tales (Rhino) 1989 ●
Running Sacred (Rhino New Artists) 1990 ●

JOHN DOE
Meet John Doe (DGC) 1990 ●

Named after the band's hometown, X's debut album is identifiable as a forerunner of hardcore; the simple, unrestrained energy often threatens to crush the "realistic" tunes ("Sex and Dying in High Society," "Nausea," etc.), but never does. Certainly, the elements that give X their majesty on later LPs are already present: Billy Zoom's vibrant rockabilly/Chuck Berry guitar licks, D.J. Bonebrake's thundering drums and arresting vocal harmonies by Exene Cervenka and bassist John Doe, strongly reminiscent of early Jefferson Airplane. Doors organist Ray Manzarek produced the first four albums; on **Los Angeles**, the band saluted him by covering "Soul Kitchen."

Wild Gift constitutes a great leap forward, bringing **Los Angeles**' action blur into sharp focus. Zoom's ingeniously simple guitar transcends its influences, and the Doe/Exene harmonies attain a knifelike sharpness. Also, their songs are frequently as incisive as their voices: "We're Desperate," "In This House That I Call Home" and "White Girl," a spooky ballad, ambitiously peer into unglamorous realities without either diminishing or inflating their subjects. **Wild Gift** was such a success as an independent label release that the band's jump to a big company (where greater success has ironically eluded them) was practically inevitable. (In 1988, the first two X albums were issued on a single Slash CD.)

Though **Under the Big Black Sun** primarily refines the techniques of **Wild Gift**, it's no disappointment. Bonebrake's drums just get harder and harder, while Doe and Cervenka continue to expand their prowess as singers and songwriters. "Motel Room in My Bed" revives the sleaze motif of earlier LPs; "The Have Nots" skillfully separates compassion from mawkishness.

The problematic **More Fun in the New World** is the work of a band filled with energy and ideas, but unsure how to apply them. As a result, this thoroughly respectable LP is too much like **Big Black Sun** to be fully satisfying. Sizzling tracks such as "Make the Music Go Bang" and "I Must Not Think Bad Thoughts" would have worked fine on that previous disc, which is a bad sign for a band accustomed to growing by leaps and bounds. In "True Love Pt. #2," X wonders about its own relationship to American mainstream music without arriving at a clear answer. After the LP, they attempted to make contact with Top 40 by covering "Wild Thing" and fell flat.

An album by the Knitters—a part-time, mostly acoustic band consisting of X (minus Billy Zoom), Blaster Dave Alvin and a stand-up bassist—proved to be a glimpse into the future when, in early '86, Zoom left X to form his own band and Alvin gave up the Blasters (at least temporarily) to replace him. **Critter on the Road** records a sincere but futile attempt to imitate several varieties of folk and country music, from traditional to swing. The material mixes cleverly cliché-laden originals (and an acoustified version of "The New World" for anyone who didn't realize what a weak song it is) with Merle Haggard and Leadbelly covers; Doe/Exene's wistful "Love Shack" is the record's standout.

Ain't Love Grand, the original lineup's final album together, is a hot (if styleless) rock'n'roll record that cuts the crap to bang out unprepossessing raveups like "Burning House of Love." On most songs, lead vocals are taken by Exene or Doe alone; the partial elimination of their harmonies is a distinct improvement, as is Michael Wagener's loud, gimmick-free production style. The biggest boner here, a misbegotten amateurish cover of the Small Faces' "All or Nothing," indicates that X—or at least some portion thereof—has never had a clue about rock music's heritage.

X rebounded from the loss of guitarist Billy Zoom with a vengeance on **See How We Are**. Dumping Wagener's metal flourishes for the less flashy approach of producer Alvin Clark, this polished platter cooks wickedly on desperate rockers like the lead-off "I'm Lost" then tugs at the heartstrings with "You," an old-fashioned love lament even non-fans should appreciate. The standout track, however, is "4th of July," penned by Dave Alvin. A wide-screen tale of terminal alienation that holds out little hope of redemption, "4th of July" matches the epic sweep of "Born to Run."

The two-record **Live at the Whisky A Go Go** makes a good case for the band onstage, showcasing pithy axework by Alvin's successor, Tony Gilkyson (ex-Lone Justice). A studio album of new material would have been more welcome, though. (Note that this is not the soundtrack of X's rarely seen feature film, *The Unheard Music*.) With that, X went on indefinite hiatus.

Cervenka's poetry gets an airing on one side of **Twin**

Sisters, a record she shares with Wanda Coleman (who has released several spoken-word album on her own). An excess of pretense and a shortage of wit make the rocker's efforts pretty heavy sledding, with the most notable moments being "Peas and Beans" (which belittles synth bands) and three pieces penned by her late sister Mary.

After X retired, Exene made a record with Tony Gilkyson, who produced, co-wrote and played guitar and mandolin on **Old Wives' Tales**. Dominated by her strong vocals (harmonizing in familiar ways with Gilkyson and others), the tasteful and varied mixture of folk, country, recitation and sturdy rock isn't that great a stylistic leap from the essence of X ("He's Got a She" is, in fact, a carbon copy), although the lyrics aren't exactly what the group generally required ("He carved his initials in her uterus"?).

Running Sacred, again imaginatively produced by Gilkyson with much the same support staff, spans a wider range, with more artistic ambition. There's a gentle acoustic guitar lullaby ("Clinic"), straight country-rock ("Will Jesus Wash the Bloodstains from Your Hands") and full-throttle electric rap-rock ("Real Estate," written by bassist Duke McVinnie). Not everything works, but the discovery of new ways to sing and new things to sing about vaults Cervenka into her artistic own, allowing her some distance from the dormant band. Passing the album's acid test, John Doe sings backup on "Missing Nature" without stirring up the faintest memory of their longtime partnership.

Before making his solo debut, Doe threw himself into a successful acting career, ably appearing in such films as *Slamdance*, *Salvador*, *Roadhouse*, *Border Radio* and *Great Balls of Fire*. It was a wise move, considering the abject failure of **Meet John Doe**. Attempting to make a looselimbed countryish rock record without the off-key camouflage of Exene's voice or roaring punk noise, Doe (with producer Davitt Sigerson—who seems clueless here—and a host of supporters, including guitarist Richard Lloyd) winds up spinning his wheels on a bunch of hangdog songs (mostly originals, but also one by John Hiatt and some old Cervenka lyrics Doe finished off) that don't suit his homely singing and undefined personality enough to be convincing.

At the end of 1990, to prove they hadn't actually broken up, X (with Tony Gilkyson on guitar) played four shows in Los Angeles. [jy/i]

See also *Blasters, Divine Horsemen*.

X

X-Aspirations (Aus. X) 1979 (Aus. Ultimate) 1990
At Home with You (Aus. Major) 1981
And More (Aus. White Label) 1989

Not LA's X nor the current Japanese X (heavy metal girls caught in an explosion at the makeup factory), this X operate(d) in Australia, inventing late-'80s NYC-style post-punk in the waning years of the '70s. **X-Aspirations** couples deep riff repetitive rhythms with scattershot guitar and anguished vocals for a "punk" LP unlike any other, appropriate for a band as distant and isolated from the media focus as one could conceivably get without leaving the planet. In later years, Feedtime

made a point of acknowledging their debt to early X; the band's influence is still readily apparent in Australia's Red Eye and Aberrant stables. (The reissue is remixed and adds a song.)

At Home with You is a more approachable album, transforming the debut's belligerent punk into a sort of fringe rock, but still featuring the high-phlegm Killdozery vocals of Steve Lucus. **And More**, recorded following the '88 death of first-LP drummer Steve Caferio and related fund-raising reunion shows with second-LP drummer Cathy Green, delivers a crowd-pleasing punch of punk aggro and attitude, including an updated but not-so-dissimilar skin-shredding blare culled from the first album. A milestone band, overlooked but hardly forgotten. [ab]

X CLAN

To the East, Blackwards (4th & B'way) 1990 ●

Threatening but never delivering a heavyweight political message, this deeply Afrocentric Brooklyn group—a conceptual attempt to cross Marcus Garvey with George Clinton—parks entertainment on the back burner to make vague statements about history and culture with impressively crisp professorial diction. Evidently better able to express their esoteric views in interview format, X Clan couches its debut album in meaningless argot (calling their efforts "vanglorious" instead of rap, and referring to any dissenter as "sissee"), repeatedly making reference to Africa without any clear point. Typical of the quartet's semi-hollow posturing, Professor X announces "Vanglorious: this is protected by the red, the black and the green" in a ponderous theatrical voice at least a dozen times throughout the record. That's a message? [i]

XMAL DEUTSCHLAND

Incubus Succubus EP (Ger. Zick Zack) 1982
Fetisch (nr/4AD) 1983 ●
Tocsin (nr/4AD) 1984 ●
The Peel Sessions EP (nr/Strange Fruit) 1986
Viva (nr/Phonogram) 1987 ●

The dense, throbbing rock of this Hamburg quintet may be too strong for some; on "Incubus Succubus," the title track of a three-song 12-inch, semi-tonic vocalist Anja Huwe bellows and shrieks with dark drama while the band drones and pounds out an unbelievably heavy track behind her, a horror movie cross between Siouxsie and the Banshees and Hawkwind.

The lineup for **Fetisch**, recorded in England, includes Huwe and three other women (guitar, keyboards, drums) plus a male bassist. With a slightly toned-down attack, Xmal Deutschland's drone loses some of its allure, and a full album's worth of onrushing chaos and numbing noise is more tedious than gripping. The CD adds three songs from a subsequent 12-inch.

Also recorded in London, but this time with mainstream producer Mick Glossop, **Tocsin** tempers the band's ugly side with economy, variety and restraint. They're still loud as hell and do sound in spots like Hawkwind but, at this point, they're also at a nexus with Joy Division, using bleak noise to convey a variety of moods. With the subtlety and dynamics that were previously lacking, **Tocsin** reveals Xmal Deutschland to be cogent and invigorating.

The Peel EP was recorded in April 1985 and contains four selections. [i]

See also *This Mortal Coil*.

X-RAY SPEX
Germ Free Adolescents (nr/EMI Int'l) 1978
POLY STYRENE
Translucence (nr/UA) 1980 (nr/Receiver) 1990 ●
God's & Godesses EP (nr/Awesome) 1986

One of the most exciting groups of its time, X-Ray Spex was at once an ideal and atypical punk band. While boasting as much raw aggression as any of its peers, X-Ray Spex used a distinctively different means of delivery—augmenting Jak Airport's obligatory buzzsaw guitar with Rudi Thompson's (Lora Logic's replacement) even-more-abrasive sax and giving center stage to Poly Styrene (Marion Elliot), a talented teenager who yowled witty lyrics with all the delicacy of a cat in heat.

X-Ray Spex's one LP collects some of the ace singles that made them such an early punk standout, although it doesn't contain their classic first outing, the wild "Oh Bondage, Up Yours!" Styrene's songs focus on the artificiality of modern life; hence such titles as "The Day the World Turned Day-Glo" and "Warrior in Woolworths." Whether the tune is a ballad or a crazed rocker, the band surges as if there were no tomorrow. And for them, there wasn't. A masterpiece!

Styrene always seemed one of punk's most dispossessed souls, so perhaps the solo album that followed the band's dissolution (which sent two members off to form Classix Nouveau) should be viewed as a last stab at finding some sense of place in musical terms. A feeling of alienation still prevails: **Translucence** is so smooth and coolly delivered that one could easily miss the dark side in the lyrics. Jazzy cocktail-hour backing combines with Styrene's childlike visions to make the music's effect most elusive.

Styrene subsequently left music completely to join a British Hare Krishna sect, but resurfaced commercially in early 1986 with a delightful, well-adjusted 12-inch EP. Jak Airport arranged two of the four originals comprising **God's & Godesses**; the record's main musicians are Mick Sweeney and Paul Inder. The anti-cult "Trick of the Witch" has hauntingly echoed vocals and a driving rock beat; synthesized log drum and sitar give the jazzy mantra of "Paramatma" fascinating color. "Big Boy Big Toy" attacks the nuclear arms race with humor and urgency. Welcome back, Poly—please make more records!   [jy/wk/i]

See also *Essential Logic*.

XTC
3D EP (nr/Virgin) 1977 + 1978
White Music (Virgin Int'l) 1978 (Virgin-Epic) 1982
    (Virgin-Geffen) 1984 ●
Go 2 (Virgin Int'l) 1978 (Virgin-Epic) 1982
    (Virgin-Geffen) 1984 ●
Drums and Wires (Virgin) 1979 (Virgin-Epic) 1982
    (Virgin-Geffen) 1984 ●
Generals and Majors EP (nr/Virgin) 1980

Black Sea (Virgin-RSO) 1980 (Virgin-Epic) 1982
    (Virgin-Geffen) 1984 ●
Towers of London EP (nr/Virgin) 1980
5 Senses EP (Can. Virgin) 1981
Senses Working Overtime EP (nr/Virgin) 1982 ●
Ball and Chain EP (nr/Virgin) 1982
English Settlement (nr/Virgin) 1982 (Virgin-Epic) 1982
    (Virgin-Geffen) 1984 ●
Waxworks/Beeswax (nr/Virgin) 1982 (Virgin-Geffen)
    1984
Mummer (nr/Virgin) 1983 (Virgin-Geffen) 1984 ●
The Big Express (Virgin-Geffen) 1984 ●
The Compact XTC—The Singles 1978–85 [CD] (nr/Virgin)
    1985 ●
Skylarking (Virgin-Geffen) 1986 ●
Dear God EP (Virgin-Geffen) 1987 [CD] (nr/Virgin)
    1988 ●
King for a Day EP [tape] (nr/Virgin) 1988
Oranges & Lemons (Virgin-Geffen) 1989 ●
The Mayor of Simpleton EP [CD] (nr/Virgin) 1989 ●
Explode Together: The Dub Experiments 78-80 [CD]
    (nr/Virgin) 1990 ●
Rag & Bone Buffet [CD] (nr/Virgin) 1990 (Virgin-Geffen)
    1991 ●

MR. PARTRIDGE
'Take Away'/'The Lure of Salvage' (nr/Virgin) 1980

DUKES OF STRATOSPHEAR
25 O'Clock EP (nr/Virgin) 1985 ●
Psonic Psunspot (Virgin-Geffen) 1987 ●
You're a Good Man Albert Brown EP (nr/Virgin) 1987
Chips from the Chocolate Fireball [CD] (nr/Virgin) 1987
    (Geffen) 1988 ●

XTC has never been easy to categorize. At first they seemed like one more high-spirited new wave band, gleefully trampling on rock conventions set the day before. On **White Music**, XTC delights in dissonance, unresolved melodic lines and playful lyrics; guitarist Andy Partridge's hiccupping vocals are matched by equally nervous music. Amid hyperactive material like "Radios in Motion," "This Is Pop" and "Spinning Top," only a version of Bob Dylan's "All Along the Watchtower" shows respect for the past. (Packaged in an appropriately stereographic sleeve, the **3D EP** is a 12-inch of "Science Friction" and two other songs; the **White Music** CD appends all three tracks, as well as four early B-sides.)

The follow-up, **Go 2**, is even further out. The songs, mostly by Partridge, excoriate conformism and other hang-ups in kaleidoscopic imagery; the music is alternately herky-jerky and menacing. (If that sounds too coherent, a bonus 12-inch EP called **Go+** pulverizes five of the album's tracks with retitled dub remixes.) Probably XTC's least-known record, **Go 2** yielded no singles whatsoever, although the insidiously wonderful "Are You Receiving Me?," released the same month as the LP, was later added to its CD.

The band settled down on **Drums and Wires**, proving they could make commercial-sounding music without sacrificing their considerable intelligence. The departure of organist Barry Andrews—replaced by guitarist Dave Gregory—seemed to take some helium out of the arrangements. XTC's funhouse world on **Drums and Wires** is more accessible, but still booby-trapped:

"Making Plans for Nigel" (deleted from the Virgin-Epic US edition), "Real by Reel," "Life Begins at the Hop" (a spectacular single added to US editions of the album, both of which have different track sequences from the original LP), "Scissor Man," "Complicated Game." Released in 1991, the US CD puts back "Nigel" and "Day in Day Out" (the UK LP track initially deleted in favor of "Life Begins at the Hop") and appends two obscurities—"Chain of Command" and "Limelight"—from a 1979 single given away with early copies of the album.) As Mr. Partridge, a separately released "solo" album, **'Take Away'/'The Lure of Salvage,'** finds Andy playing more games with tracks from **Drums and Wires**. "This used to be some XTC records," the sleeve notes. "It is now a collection of tracks that have been electronically processed/shattered and layered with other sounds or lyrical pieces." (**Explode Together** combines this record with **Go +** for a complete retrospective of XTC in dub.)

Black Sea refines **Drums and Wires'** approach. Heedless of fashion, XTC builds up the music with multiple strains, undanceable rhythms, intricate interplay and gloriously literate lyrics. The dazzling result is the band's finest achievement up to that point: an album that, like its songs ("Respectable Street," "Generals and Majors," "Towers of London"), unsentimentally employs the past to make new statements. (The CD appends three B-sides, all of them included on **Beeswax**.)

English Settlement continues in the same vein but succumbs to rococo excess. (Five songs were pruned from the original British two-record set to fit it onto one US disc, but the 1984 Geffen reissue returned it to two.) Partridge evidently feels compelled to match musical sophistication with like words; he unfortunately outdoes himself. His prolix lyrics on offbeat but straightforward topics (war, paranoia, even love) read better than they sing and, as recorded, must be read to be understood. **English Settlement** tilts like an over-frosted wedding cake. That it doesn't quite topple is a tribute to the band.

XTC's most winning material, much of it written by bassist Colin Moulding, invariably turns up on their EPs and 45s. **5 Senses** gathers a few non-LP sides (including "Smokeless Zone" and "Wait Till Your Boat Goes Down") from 1980 and '81. But that EP was soon superseded by **Waxworks—Some Singles 1977–1982**, which cleverly assembles the band's 45s, almost all originally drawn from albums, on one superb LP. The accompanying second disc, **Beeswax—Some B-Sides 1977–1982**, collects their non-LP B-sides—not deathless music, but inventive as always and decidedly unpretentious. The advent of new technology a few years later yielded **The Compact XTC**, an eighteen-song CD-only singles compilation which picks up all of **Waxworks** and then continues, starting with "Great Fire" and running up through "Wake Up." (A B-sides and rarities collection—**Rag & Bone Buffet**—followed five years later.)

With drummer Terry Chambers' departure, XTC next found themselves in a precarious position with their British record label, which was reportedly hesitant to release another brilliant but uncommercial album. That hitch delayed the appearance of **Mummer** for quite some time. As far removed as it may be from the quirky pop that originally characterized XTC's music, it's a lovely record, resplendent in a quiet, rural sound and ethos. Co-existing with the invigorating whomp of "Great Fire" and the loud rock and disgusted lyrics of "Funk Pop a Roll," there's Partridge's rustic "Love on a Farmboy's Wages" and Moulding's lazy "Wonderland," offering a perfect summery escape from the pressures and excitement of rock. **Mummer**: Music for Picnics. (The CD has six bonus cuts—all Partridge songs—including two from the UK **Dear God** EP.)

Continuing on as a trio, **The Big Express** returned XTC to the world of urban reality: disgruntled songs about life in the big city, celebrating the alternative ("The Everyday Story of Smalltown") but, more surprisingly, again playing full-blast rock rather than bucolic lyricism. "All You Pretty Girls," incorporating a British folk idiom, is as catchy a number as they've ever done; and the record's overall sense of recharged enthusiasm is quite infectious.

Partridge's regrettable post-release sniping notwithstanding, XTC's collaboration with Todd Rundgren on **Skylarking** yielded an album as good as any in their catalogue. The songs are thoughtful, winsome, introspective and melodic; Rundgren's likeminded production (and sequencing) brings them out in a cavalcade that is resonant and memorable. Moulding's best numbers—"Grass," "The Meeting Place" and "Big Day"—address (respectively) sex al fresco, illicit romance and the dangers of marriage. Partridge, meanwhile, worries about making ends meet in "Earn Enough for Us" and space junk in "Another Satellite." Adult, provocative and plainly brilliant. (A pre-LP UK 12-inch of "Grass" b/w "Extrovert" and "Dear God" focused unexpected attention on Partridge's controversial song about religious skepticism. Those three numbers were then released as an American EP, adding "Earn Enough for Us." Finally, the album was withdrawn and reissued with "Dear God" replacing "Mermaid Smiled," as it does on the CD. The British **Dear God** EP, available only on CD, is entirely different from the American.)

With demerits for an unpleasant electro-drum sound and an overzealous arrangement or three, Sides 1 and 2 of **Oranges & Lemons** are very nearly **Skylarking**'s equal. Unfortunately, it's a double album, and there isn't much in the second half (beyond "Pink Thing," a magical ode to a baby) to rave about. Producer Paul Fox helps the trio tip its sonic hat to the Beatles while giving full attention to the band's usual soaring melodies and inimitable lyrics. (Moulding wrote just three of the fifteen songs; while none is on a musical par with his best, the frank admission of immobilizing insecurity on "One of the Millions" carries an unnerving ring of sincerity.) Making another wonderful and lasting contribution to the XTC classics library, Partridge—in an obviously joyous mood—welcomes a child into the "Garden of Earthly Delights," reaffirms the old hippie faith in "The Loving" and dismisses intelligence as a romantic necessity in "The Mayor of Simpleton."

Some EPs: The **Generals and Majors** and **Towers of London** 12-inches each contain three non-LP tracks. Two of the three songs added to the **Senses Working Overtime** 12-inch (and subsequent 3-inch CD) appear on **Beeswax**; the leftover is Moulding's electronic instrumental, "Egyptian Solution (Homo Safari Series No. 3)." The **Ball and Chain** 12-inch has two B-sides that turn up on **Beeswax**, plus a Partridge remix of the full-length **English Settlement**'s "Down in the Cockpit." **King for a Day** is a cassette single joining that **Oranges & Lemons** track with three oldies, including "Generals and Majors" and "Towers of London." **The Mayor of Simpleton** is a 3-inch CD of a second track from the 1989 LP joined by a pair of home demos and another tune.

Partnered with producer John Leckie, XTC undertook a pseudonymous side project in 1985 as the Dukes of Stratosphear. The day-glo watches and peace symbols on the cover of the carefully appointed satirical **25 O'Clock** mini-album match the six Rutlesque rewrites of '60s classics like "I Had Too Much to Dream Last Night." Unfortunately, the gaily psychedelic put-on is so clever and careful that it winds up less funny than notable for its accomplishment. The full-length **Psonic Psunspot** downplays the pose with a far lighter parodic touch—the most prominent touchstone is **White Album**-era Beatles—and basically amounts to a very casual XTC LP with an intuitive '60s feel rather than a conscious art context. By not striving for specific imitation and merely enjoying the romp, the Dukes have a better time, and so do listeners.

Although **Psonic Psunspot** was issued on its own CD, it was also paired with **25 O'Clock** and released as the CD-only **Chips from the Chocolate Fireball**. Completists can also rest easy about the **You're a Good Man** EP, as it merely contains a pair of selections from each of the group's two records.   [si/i]

See also *Robert Fripp, Shriekback.*

XYMOX

See *Clan of Xymox.*

Y Y Y Y Y Y Y

YACHTS

Yachts (Radar-Polydor) 1979
Yachts Without Radar (Radar-Polydor) 1980

Liverpool's Yachts were capable of alternating a scaled-down version of pomp-rock (faster, more cheaply tricked out, no instrumental exhibitionism) and '60s-influenced rock with leader Henry Priestman's cheesy organ sound. And that in the service of humorously melodramatic caricatures of the usual boy/girl lyric fodder: love by letter ("Box 202"), unfair romantic competition ("Yachting Type," "Semaphore Love," etc.). Despite sympathetic production by Richard Gottehrer, **Yachts** sounds a bit tinny, and the group was unable to equal their mini-classic Stiff debut single ("Suffice to Say"), though the potential to do so is evident.

Not being taken seriously because of funny lyrics may have taken its toll; on **Without Radar**, the jokes and even the previously solid songwriting sound as thin as Martin Rushent's uncharacteristically poor production. [jg]

See also *Christians, It's Immaterial*.

YAZOO (YAZ)

Upstairs at Eric's (Mute-Sire) 1982 ●
You and Me Both (Mute-Sire) 1983 ●

Yazoo (known as Yaz in the US) was one of England's most interesting synth-pop duets, mostly because of the sharp contrast provided by vocalist Alison Moyet's incredibly rich and soulful voice, a more powerful and emotive sound than one generally expected to hear paired with high-tech instrumentation in those days. Along with ex-Depeche Mode synthesist/songwriter Vince Clarke, Yazoo represented a stylistic breakthrough that proved influential in the development of electronic-based dance music.

Unfortunately, while **Upstairs at Eric's** is admirable for its experimentalism, it contains just one really striking song (the beautiful ballad, "Only You"), some moderately interesting quirky pop ("Too Pieces," "Bad Connection"), two solid dance numbers ("Don't Go" and "Situation") made tolerable by the band's talent and strengths and one truly awful piece of tape-looping ("I Before E Except After C").

You and Me Both, on the other hand, offers a better selection, from Moyet's defiant and atmospheric "Nobody's Diary" and funky "Sweet Thing" to Clarke's bouncy "Walk Away from Love." There are some serious low-points to be sure, but in general it's a more even and exciting album, further exploring the blend's possibilities.

Given the dynamic tension of the partnership, it was hardly surprising when Moyet and Clarke decided, after two albums, to go their separate ways: he to form the Assembly (later, Erasure) and she to a successful solo career. [ks/i]

See also *Erasure, Alison Moyet*.

YEAH YEAH NOH

Cottage Industry EP (nr/In Tape) 1984
Weakling Lines EP (nr/In Tape) 1984
Prick Up Your Ears EP (nr/In Tape) 1984
When I Am a Big Girl (nr/In Tape) 1985
Cutting the Heavenly Lawn of Greatness ... Last Rites for the God of Love (nr/In Tape) 1985
Temple of Convenience EP (nr/In Tape) 1985
Fun on the Lawn Lawn Lawn (nr/Vuggum) 1986
The Peel Sessions EP (nr/Strange Fruit) 1987

Like In Tape labelmates the Creepers, this Leicester quartet (later quintet) displays some Fall influence (albeit less harsh) and makes things easy for record buyers by combining several releases onto a single disc. **When I Am a Big Girl** reprises the first three EPs in their entirety and has such highlights as "Cottage Industry," "Prick Up Your Ears" and "Starling Pillowcase and Why" which, like the rest of the record's songs, are unpolished, raw pop gems with smartass lyrics. Cymbal-less drums and chunky bass lines form a foundation for modest guitar work and Derek Hammond's deadpan baritone. Great fun.

Cutting the Heavenly Lawn of Greatness adds some well-placed psychedelic embellishments and a little (but just a wee bit) more production to the homespun sound. Lyrics are sharp as ever: "Home-Ownersexual" is the clever tale of a bored, dissatisfied housewife; "Stealing in the Name of the Lord" decries religious hypocrisy. Some earlier tracks pop up again in new versions, and the LP also contains the title track from the **Temple of Convenience** EP. Sadly, Yeah Yeah Noh disbanded upon that release but left behind a catalogue of great records, permeated with real DIY spirit, warmth and humor.

Fun on the Lawn Lawn Lawn is a posthumous collection of various sessions for John Peel's radio program. (Yeah Yeah Noh were one of his faves. One session, from January 1986, was also released by Strange Fruit.) It includes versions of most of their best tracks ("Home-Ownersexual" is listed as "Another Side of Mrs. Quill") and a few songs that are otherwise unavailable. [dgs]

YELLO

Solid Pleasure (Ralph) 1980 (Mercury) 1988 ●
Claro Que Si (Ralph) 1981 (Mercury) 1988 ●
Bostich EP (Stiff) 1982

748

You Gotta Say Yes to Another Excess (Elektra) 1983
    (Mercury) 1988 ●
Yello EP (Elektra) 1983
Stella (Elektra) 1985 (Mercury) 1988 ●
The New Mix in One Go: 80–'85 (nr/Mercury) 1986 ●
One Second (Mercury) 1987 ●
Flag (Mercury) 1988 ●

Switzerland's Yello (Boris Blank, singer/lyricist Dieter Meier and Carlos Peron—all non-musicians in the finest Brian Eno tradition) harnessed the synthesizer to become one of the most important and creative bands working in the medium.

Solid Pleasure is a record of their exploration of the studio and instruments, surging with discovery and innovation. On this LP, Yello are dark experimenters of the highest order, treading fearlessly through a perilous forest of electronics. The music is a confident cross-pollination of lighthearted pop and avant-garde. Inspired.

Claro Que Si continues Yello's adventurous innovation, but applies it to dance music with stunning results. Meier's vocals, though limited in range, slide blissfully against Blank's synthesizer and backing vocals and Peron's tape effects to create a pop/disco album full of evocative, warm tunes, evincing a dynamism rare in this sort of music. And they stay far away from pretensions, too.

Bostich presents new versions of songs from the albums, with an otherwise unavailable track, "She's Got a Gun," added to the US edition. Remakes aren't normally essential listening, but Yello proves they're one of the few bands capable of transfiguring old material rather than rehashing it, and with exquisite intelligence at that.

Signing to Elektra, Yello made **You Gotta Say Yes to Another Excess**, which contains some of their most accessible dance music, although it would be far from accurate to call Yello commercial or mainstream at this point. "I Love You" pushes a pulsing electro-beat and whispered vocals vaguely about driving, throwing in screeching tires to underscore the point. "No More Words" recites the title over herky-jerky rhythms and little else; "Great Mission" is a suave dramatic travelogue. The 23-minute EP that followed contains remixed, extended versions of three LP tracks plus "Bostich."

Revealing a slimmed-down Yello of just Meier and Blank, **Stella** adopts more of a Euro-disco sound, dropping the reliance on electronics and most of the weirdness to play it relatively straight. Meier's vocals have gone from wondrously strange to cloying; several guest musicians provide vocals, piano, drums and guitar, making this a most routine and non-intriguing release.

Meier and Blank split the chores on **One Second** simply: Boris composed and arranged the music, Dieter wrote and sings the lyrics. Guests include Shirley Bassey and ex-Associate Billy Mackenzie, who provided lyrics for two cuts and vocals for one. Continuing down the conservative path indicated on **Stella**, Yello pushes a reserved, suavely textured sound that is dance-oriented, but not overpowered by rhythm. Polite Latin accents on a few songs provide character; continental excursions and adult pop fill out the program. A pleasant, debonair waste of time. Structurally and stylistically, **Stella** is virtually a re-run of **One Second** (sans

Bassey), and—with the notable exception of the bracing dramatics of "3rd of June"—equally enervating.

The New Mix in One Go is a two-record compilation that includes remixes, remakes of old songs and even some entirely new material.   [sg/i]

YELLOW MAGIC ORCHESTRA
Yellow Magic Orchestra (Jap. Alfa) 1978 (Horizon-A&M) 1979 ●
Solid State Survivor (Jap. Alfa) 1979 (nr/Alfa) 1981 ●
Public Pressure (Jap. Alfa) 1980 ●
X∞ Multiplies (Jap. Alfa) 1980 (nr/Alfa-A&M) 1980
X∞ Multiplies (A&M) 1980
BGM (A&M) 1981 ●
Technodelic (Alfa) 1981 ●
Service (Jap. Alfa) 1983
After Service (Jap. Alfa) 1983
Naughty Boys (Jap. Alfa) 1983 ●
Naughty Boys Instrumental (Hol. Pickup) 1985
Sealed (Jap. Alfa) 1985

For the technology-minded Japanese (who, after all, do have their own musical logic and traditions), the rock medium most suited to adaptation rather than bland mimicry has been electronic-oriented pop. By their third LP, YMO represented to Japanese kids a heterodoxy almost equivalent to the Sex Pistols and, in Japan at least, many times their commercial success.

None of the three members were musical neophytes at YMO's outset. While recording his first solo LP, session keyboardist Ryuichi Sakamoto met drummer Yukihiro Takahashi, who'd not only cut his own album but had been a member of the Sadistic Mika Band (Japan's well-known art-rock export of the early '70s who made three LPs for UK Harvest) and its offshoot, Sadistics. The pair met bassist/producer Haruomi Hosono, a veteran of two historically important Japanese bands, while he was cutting his *fourth* solo LP. (He's done more since but, unlike his two bandmates, Hosono's solo records have never been released in England or America. The 1986 **Video Game Music** employs the electronic sounds of arcade games.)

Despite the pedigree, YMO's first LP is merely inane electro-disco, distinguished only by efforts at diddling video-game blips and squonks into songs. **Solid State Survivor** (their second Japanese LP, issued intact but out of chronological sequence in the UK) is a qualitative leap forward: clever instrumentals and excellent electro-rock tunes with terse, sharp English lyrics by Chris Mosdell. Takahashi's flat, inflexible vocals are a mixed blessing—no silly histrionics, but an air of cool detachment that's, at least initially, off-putting.

X∞ Multiplies has two more fine tracks in the same vein, but the rest of the original Japanese half-hour 10-inch is given over to mostly unfunny comedy skits (and two humorous tries at Archie Bell and the Drells' "Tighten Up"). In the UK, the LP of the same name adds the aural vid-bits from the first LP, but the US release retains only the title and the two good cuts, the rest being the best part of **Solid State Survivor**. **Public Pressure** is a live album.

BGM and **Technodelic** are both mixed bags. On the plus side, they explore new (for YMO) stylistic areas—"Strawberry Fields" gone synth, Germanic bleep strutting, bleak Anglo synth-rap—but little on either is as distinctive or just plain entertaining as Takahashi's or Sakamoto's solo work. Hosono's production (the first six YMO LPs, as well as discs by Sandii and the Sunsetz, Sheena and the Rokkets and others) has clarity but lacks the snap and depth that would make these two records come alive.

Service is a frustrating record; it alternates YMO tracks with cuts just as long as the songs by the comedic (?) theater group S.E.T. As impenetrable as it is to those who don't speak Japanese, even those who do might be annoyed at the non-musical interruptions. It's doubly irksome because the songs are excellent. Wisely, **Naughty Boys** has equally good songs without the comedy. The melodies on both discs are much more accessible and consistently pleasing than any of the previous YMO LPs, with no noticeable shift in songwriting balance. (Beginning with **Service**, Peter Barakan, who's written lyrics for Takahashi's LPs, supplies them to YMO in place of Mosdell. Also, YMO produced these two albums as a group.)

After Service is a double live set, but the name has more to do with the order of its release than its content, drawing on previous records. **Sealed** is a four-disc boxed set.   [jg]

See also *Ryuichi Sakamoto, Yukihiro Takahashi*.

YELLOWMAN
Mister Yellowman (Greensleeves) 1982 ●
Live at Sunsplash (nr/Sunsplash) 1982
Zungguzungguguzungguzeng (Greensleeves) 1983 ●
King Yellowman (CBS) 1984 ●
Nobody Move Nobody Get Hurt (Greensleeves) 1984 ●
Galong Galong Galong (Greensleeves) 1985 ●
Going to the Chapel (Shanachie) 1986 ●
Rambo (Moving Target) 1986 ●
Yellow Like Cheese (RAS) 1987 ●
Don't Burn It Down (Shanachie) 1987 ●
Blueberry Hill (Rohit) 1987 ●
Yellowman Sings the Blues (Rohit) 1988 ●
Yellowman Rides Again (RAS) 1988 ●
One in a Million (Shanachie) 1989 ●
Party (RAS) 1991 ●

YELLOWMAN AND FATHEAD
Bad Boy Skanking (Greensleeves) 1982

YELLOWMAN/CHARLIE CHAPLIN
The Negril Chill [tape] (ROIR) 1988 [CD] (Fr. Danceteria) 1990 ϕ

YELLOWMAN AND GENERAL TREES
A Reggae Calypso Encounter (Rohit) 1987 ●

Albino reggae toaster Yellowman (Winston Foster) parlayed his unusual looks and talent into overnight success. His music is versatile and engagingly comic in a dancehall style. Like his counterparts in American rap, he's often swaggering, boasting about his toasting and his luck with the ladies. Because his strut is goodnatured and backed up by fierce turntable work (his improv and rhythm are extraordinary), he's extremely convincing, and has become quite a sex symbol.

More than two dozen Yellowman albums flooded the market in the early '80s. Many are so-so live sets, collections of singles and outtakes, Jamaican-only releases, or team-ups with other DJs. The listing above contains only some of his most widely available LPs.

Mister Yellowman, the album that helped launch his international fame, remains among his best. Nearly every cut is strong, including "Mister Chin," "Two to Six Supermix" and the *My Fair Lady*-inspired "Yellowman Getting Married" (in the morning). While they often come close, none of his other records equal this consistency and easy versatility.

Zungguzungguguzungguzeng, for instance, isn't even in the same league. For one thing, it's misleading (if not mistitled): seven of ten cuts are actually duets with another DJ (Fathead). They make an okay team, but their rapport is mostly in a rub-a-dub style, and the record bogs down as a result. Best is the title tune, a solo toast to the music of Michigan and Smiley's "Diseases"; worst is "Who Can Make the Dance Ram," a reworking of Sammy Davis Jr.'s "Candy Man."

Admirably, CBS tried to encourage Yellowman's versatility when he signed with the label, but the resulting **King Yellowman** is another mixed success. Most of Side One is fine ("What Dat," for instance), but the flip is a mess. Yellowman meets Material for "Disco Reggae," tries to "Reggae Calypso" and finally covers Frankie Ford's pop hit "Sea Cruise." All of these fusion attempts go wildly astray.

Less contrived versatility is evident on his later Shanachie albums. **Nobody Move** is a bit spotty, but the strong cuts are really great. The title track, as well as "Strictly Mi Belly" and "Why You Bad So" are all cookers, guaranteed to make you rock and groove. **Galong** is also worth investigating, for it features an anti-Michael Jackson number called "Beat It"; "Reggae Win a Grammy," Yellowman's report on his trip to the awards ceremony; and "Skank Quadrille," a toast to Bunny Wailer's "Walk the Proud Land."

Going to the Chapel, on the other hand, lags a bit and is less consistent, although a variety of rhythms are featured and the title cut is a wacko cover of the Dixie Cups' "Chapel of Love." Track for track, **Don't Burn It Down** is stronger, full of energy and fire from first cut (the title song, a ganja anthem) to last (the consummately rude "Dry Head Adassa").

As the '80s progressed, so did Yellowman's label-hopping. **Rambo**, on a Celluloid subsidiary, is a noble experiment featuring Robert Lyn on piano, Sly Dunbar on drums and Robbie Shakespeare going heavy on the bass synthesizer. The backup is unusually high-tech for a Yellowman record, but he raps up a storm, pushing the music aggressively forward like the character commemorated in the title track. (There's another appropriate cut called "Computerize.") **Yellow Like Cheese** returns him to rootsy form: less dance-oriented and with sparser musical backup.

Despite rumors of ill-health, Yellowman has continued to churn out records. While **Don't Burn It Down** contains some of his typically lewd slack lyrics, there's some real fun and noteworthy selections that aren't dirty. The title track, for example, is an anthemic protest against the burning of ganja fields. He condemns violence against women on "Stop Beat Woman" and offers a political opinion about the South African situation in "Free Africa." He delivers his lyrics in a step-lively rock/rap mode geared to rile up his listeners, which he invariably does.

In typically nasty fashion, **Rides Again** contains "Want a Virign," "AIDS" and "Girl You're Too Hot." Yet after such repellent doggerel, Yellowman can draw a card showing his politically conscious side with "Ease Up President Botha," or reveal his sensitivity with an ode to late reggae singers ("In Memory").

Recorded live in concert (1987) at the Negril Tree House in Jamaica, the **Negril Chill** is an actual dancehall session between Mr. Yellow and conscious, roots-culture DJ Charlie Chaplin. It's an authentic slice of life, as the listener becomes part of and a witness to the casual banter between these two contrasting, yet equally talented DJs.

One in a Million (the material on which dates from 1982) contains two of his earliest hits, "Operation Eradication" and "Them a Mad Over Me." [bk/aw]

YOBS

See *Boys*.

YO LA TENGO

Ride the Tiger (Coyote-Twin/Tone) 1986
New Wave Hot Dogs (Coyote-Twin/Tone) 1987 ●
President Yo La Tengo (Coyote) 1989 ●
Fakebook (Bar/None) 1990 ●

SCHRAMMS

Walk to Delphi (OKra) 1990 ●

Led by Hoboken's Ira Kaplan (vocals/guitar) and Georgia Hubley (drums/vocals) plus whomever else they team up with, Yo La Tengo (named for the cry of the Spanish-speaking outfielder) nicely weds the underground noise-rock impulse and the fannish cover-band vibe. Rather than doing the eclectic dilettante bit, Kaplan, Hubley and company work their influences into a surprisingly cohesive and satisfying whole.

Ride the Tiger, produced by ex-Mission of Burma bassist Clint Conley, benefits from Dave Schramm's sterling guitarings which, like Kaplan's reedy (as in Lou) vocals, underline Yo La Tengo's vintage-Velvets connection. The band also covers Ray Davies' "Big Sky," but it's originals like "The Cone of Silence" and "The Forest Green" that make **Ride the Tiger** such a pleasure.

New Wave Hot Dogs suffers a bit from Schramm's absence, but it's more consistent than its predecessor, with distinctive originals ("House Fall Down," "Blocks from Groove St.") and a dead-ringer cover of Lou Reed's "It's Alright (The Way That You Live)."

Gene Holder produced and plays bass on the excellent **President Yo La Tengo** (contained on one CD with **New Wave Hot Dogs**), a strange and noisily electric hodgepodge (two songs were recorded live at CBGB; the material comprises YLT originals as well as an Antietam song and Bob Dylan's "I Threw It All Away") that somehow holds together. Kaplan's "The Evil That Men Do" appears twice: as a concise and twangy '60s guitar'n'organ instrumental and as ten mind-blowing minutes of onstage feedback fury.

Schramm and a standup bassist joined Hubley and Kaplan for **Fakebook**, a delightful low-key collection of (almost all) covers. While reaching across time and space to dredge up an eclectic stack of tuneful arcanities from the Kinks, Flying Burrito Brothers, John Cale, NRBQ, Cat Stevens and the Flamin Groovies, the group also lends an interpretative ear to such lower-profile contemporaries as The Scene Is Now and Daniel Johnston. In a minor conceptual coup, Yo La even covers itself, re-recording a song each from the prior two albums. The simple but imaginative arrangements are ideal for Kaplan's gentle, amateurish singing; Hubley's harmonies likewise contribute to the friendly folks-at-home ambience.

The charming album by Dave Schramm's band—a quartet with **Fakebook** bassist Al Greller, ex-Human Switchboard drummer Ron Metz and a keyboard player—mixes literature and countryish folk-rock to illuminating effect. Besides being a deft and tasteful guitarist, the group's namesake is a winningly plain Dylanesque singer who makes the most of his modest vocal skills. That the Schramms can set Emily Dickinson and Charles Baudelaire poetry to jaunty original music (only on three songs—other than a Tom Paxton cover, the rest of the record is self-penned) and get away without seeming pretentious is only one reason to seek out **Walk to Delphi**. [hd/i]

NEIL YOUNG (AND CRAZY HORSE)

Neil Young (Reprise) 1968 ●
Everybody Knows This Is Nowhere (Reprise) 1969 ●
After the Gold Rush (Reprise) 1970 ●
Harvest (Reprise) 1972 ●
Time Fades Away (Reprise) 1973
On the Beach (Reprise) 1974
Tonight's the Night (Reprise) 1975 ●
Zuma (Reprise) 1975 ●
American Stars 'n Bars (Reprise) 1977
Decade (Reprise) 1977 ●
Comes a Time (Reprise) 1978 ●
Rust Never Sleeps (Reprise) 1979 ●
Live Rust (Reprise) 1979 ●
Hawks & Doves (Reprise) 1980
Re-ac-tor (Reprise) 1981
Trans (Geffen) 1982
Neil and the Shocking Pinks: Everybody's Rockin' (Geffen) 1983
Old Ways (Geffen) 1985
Landing on Water (Geffen) 1986 ●
Life (Geffen) 1987 ●
This Note's for You (Reprise) 1988 ●
Freedom (Reprise) 1989 ●
Ragged Glory (Reprise) 1990 ●

Dirty rock'n'roller and hippie narcissist. Rockabilly hepcat and techno-troubadour. Folkie romantic and bluesy bad boy. Neil Young has been all of these things—and more—in the course of a solo career that's approaching the quarter-century mark. While his output during the '80s was particularly erratic, he's always placed art above commercial success or the need to accommodate fan expectations. Unpredictable and often infuriating, Young is never (well, hardly ever) boring, a state of grace few veteran musicians can claim. Holding to his lyrical axiom that it's better to burn out than fade away, Young is one of the only oldtimers to make real peace with punk-rockers half his age, finding rejuvenation in their fountain of wild youth. Indeed, Young's reckless path demonstrates far less selfconscious orthodoxy than many so-called alternative bands. And virtually alone among his aging peers, Young's intensity, his ability and inclination to throw off cascades of violent guitar fury, hasn't softened one iota.

The self-titled solo debut, released in the wake of Buffalo Springfield's demise, explores a style he hasn't tried since. Apart from "The Last Trip to Tulsa," an awkward, overlong acoustic epic, the album features dense, heavily produced pop tunes, swathed in layers of overdubs. Though "The Loner," "I've Been Waiting for You," etc. now seem a bit overdone, their emotional urgency comes through loud and clear.

Everybody Knows This Is Nowhere marked the first of many radical shifts, turning to the raw, driving rock many feel still suits him best. Backed by Crazy Horse, who display the ratty fervor of punk years before the fact, he yowls and whines with exhilarating abandon, cranking out jagged, overwrought guitar solos like his life depends on it. The catchy "Cinnamon Girl" makes a good single, but the extended melodramas—"Cowgirl in the Sand" and "Down by the River"—offer the biggest thrills.

Enjoying increased exposure after signing on with Crosby, Stills and Nash, Young achieved prominence as a solo artist on **After the Gold Rush**, a mixed-bag of noisy raveups (the infamous "Southern Man," which inspired Lynyrd Skynyrd's "Sweet Home Alabama"), brooding folk-pop ("Tell Me Why") and sappy ballads ("Birds"). **Harvest** temporarily sealed his fate as a mainstream favorite, thanks to the lightweight countryfied chart-topper, "Heart of Gold." The rest of the album ranges from a dreadful orchestral reverie ("A Man Needs a Maid") to a tortured electric lament ("Words"). Both LPs were later issued as a double-play cassette.

Obviously spooked by the tender trap of success, Young abandoned his perch at the top of the heap with **Time Fades Away**. A live album of all-new material, this sloppy, sometimes excruciatingly rough noisefest has the primal directness of John Lennon's Plastic Ono Band. From the title track (his own "Subterranean Homesick Blues") to the aching ballad "Don't Be Denied," Young serves notice he will not grow old gracefully.

The restlessness continued with **On the Beach**. After the snappy leadoff track "Walk On," Young offers edgy, dispirited tales of social decay ("Revolution Blues"), music-biz cynicism ("For the Turnstiles") and other fun stuff. Often riveting, but a downer. Yet it's a barrel of laughs compared to **Tonight's the Night**, Young's most hellish album ever. Featuring guitarist Nils Lofgren and the Crazy Horse rhythm section of Ralph Molina and Billy Talbot, it's a chilling meditation on excess and death, recorded two years prior to its release. The ghostly title cut concerns the 1973 heroin death of a roadie; "Come on Baby Let's Go Downtown" (to score drugs), an older track, is sung from the grave by onetime Crazy Horse guitarist Danny Whitten, who overdosed in 1972. Young and crew sound drunk and exhausted throughout. Essential.

The gloom lifted with **Zuma**, a solid, floor-shaking return to gritty rock. Backed by Crazy Horse (now with Frank Sampedro on rhythm guitar), Young howls the down-home blues ("Don't Cry No Tears") and uncorks some of his most expressive guitar work since "Cowgirl in the Sand" ("Cortez the Killer"). Following a 1976 album with Stephen Stills, his concentration began to drift. There's a precious honkytonk feel to many of the tracks on **American Stars 'n Bars** (a collection of tracks recorded between '74 and '77 with various lineups), although "Like a Hurricane" is a classic guitar showcase and the fascinating, barely-in-tune ballad "Will to Love" finds Neil likening himself to a fish swimming upstream.

The three-disc, two-CD **Decade** makes a persuasive case for Young as one of the most consistently adventurous artists in rock. Besides all the "hits," it includes a generous helping of strong previously unreleased stuff and presages the boxed-set explosion ten years later.

After pausing to tend his gentler side on **Comes a Time**, a largely forgettable outing with prominent harmony vocals from Nicolette Larson, Young got back in the groove with **Rust Never Sleeps**. Joined by Crazy Horse, he turns in some unusually strong ballads ("Thrasher," "Powderfinger") and rocks like the devil, especially on "Hey Hey, My My (Into the Black)," his enthusiastic response to punk. **Live Rust** is a career-spanning double live set that includes lethal versions of "Cortez the Killer," "Like a Hurricane" and "Tonight's the Night," pushed over the edge by Crazy Horse's blazing assault.

Hawks & Doves finds Young back on folk and country turf, offering a few incisive tunes amidst the throwaways. The jaunty title track looks askance at militarism and jingoism, a concern echoed in the acoustic "Captain Kennedy." On **Re-ac-tor**, Young and Crazy Horse reach down deep to get that big nasty electric noise. The material isn't consistent—nine minutes of the disposable "T-Bone" strains one's patience—but "Shots," "Southern Pacific" and others crackle with passion and hot licks.

Young then flipped out, and embarked on a series of genre exercises that seem more arbitrary than heartfelt. **Trans** presents Neil as electro-man, complete with synths, vocoders and songs about computers and future shock; the new version of his Buffalo Springfield classic "Mr. Soul" is particularly odd. **Everybody's Rockin'** salutes rockabilly with a lightweight, good-natured set of originals and oldies, including "Mystery Train" and "Bright Lights, Big City." Then he went back up the country for **Old Ways**, down-home silliness highlighted by a campy cover of "The Wayward Wind" and guest shots by Waylon Jennings and Willie Nelson. **Landing on Water** suggests he'd been listening to the Cars, adding synths and artificial rhythms to standard rock-band sounds. Ill-considered garish production spoils some decent tunes.

Just when it seemed he'd completely lost his marbles, Young reunited with Crazy Horse and made **Life**. While the LP doesn't have the slash-and-burn abandon of **Zuma**—overblown arrangements and production get in the way—"Mideast Vacation," "Cryin' Eyes" and others have a tough edge not glimpsed in years.

After one more stylistic detour—for a pointless set of big-band blues (co-billed with Bluenotes) on **This Note's for You**—Young settled back into his best-known grooves. **Freedom** has a spooky acoustic saga of social strife ("Crime in the City"), a harsh reinterpretation of "On Broadway," strung-out ballads and thundering electric commentary ("Rockin' in the Free World"), among other hearty tracks. Has the "real" Neil Young returned?

Moving from the topical to the personal, **Ragged Glory** offers additional encouragement. Crazy Horse thrash away like there's no tomorrow as Young pulls all sorts of exciting noises from his guitar on "Country Home," "Love to Burn" and others. Although widely regarded as his best in a blue moon, it isn't perfect. A few tracks don't work and the offhand sloppiness occasionally seems forced. But **Ragged Glory** does offer a bracing reminder that Neil Young can still shake the rafters better than most anyone else. Long may he rave.

The essentials: **Everybody Knows This Is Nowhere**, **Time Fades Away**, **Tonight's the Night**, **Zuma**, **Decade**, **Rust Never Sleeps**, **Ragged Glory**.

[jy]

PAUL YOUNG
No Parlez (Columbia) 1983 ●
The Secret of Association (Columbia) 1985 ●
Between Two Fires (Columbia) 1986 ●
The 12″ Tape EP [tape] (nr/CBS) 1986
Other Voices (Columbia) 1990 φ

Q-TIPS
Q-Tips (nr/Chrysalis) 1980 (nr/MFP) 1986
From the ashes of London neo-soulsters the Q-Tips emerged Paul Young, whose smoky voice, singing a mixture of classics and originals, quickly put him in the British, and later, American charts. The choice of songs on **No Parlez** ranges from the prudent ("Love of the Common People," "Wherever I Lay My Hat (That's My Home)," both of which are magnificent) to the surreal (Joy Division's "Love Will Tear Us Apart," which Young slowly mangles beyond recognition). A few of the new compositions are swell as well. The Royal Family (his band) and the Fabulous Wealthy Tarts (singers) supply sympathetic backing; Laurie Latham's wide-screen production is appropriately lush but never abandons the rock basis that anchored classic Motown records of the '60s. Young's first solo outing is promising: a solid pop album by an especially good singer.

The Secret of Association, Young's follow-up as a big star, shows a far more judicious selection process at work, resulting in an exquisite collection that mixes appropriate covers with originals he co-wrote. Items like "Bite the Hand That Feeds," "I'm Gonna Tear Your Playhouse Down" and especially Daryl Hall's "Everytime You Go Away" showcase Young's carefully controlled vocals and Latham's exceptionally subtle production. Each clearly articulated sound functions perfectly in the arrangements, resulting in seamless, emotionally resonant pop-soul creations.

Parting company with Latham, an increasingly self-confident Young co-wrote most of the songs and co-produced **Between Two Fires** with Hugh Padgham and keyboardist Ian Kewley. Although lacking the finely honed impact of **The Secret of Association**, a few tracks (e.g., "Wonderland," "A Certain Passion," "Some People") and the generally high level of appealing quality prove that—in this case, at least—it's possible to tamper with success and not upset the apple cart.

Between Two Fires wasn't a big commercial success in the US, so he reversed the formula for **Other Voices**. Instead of one production team, there are four different producers. Instead of Young co-writing all but two of the songs, he co-wrote three and used covers for the rest. The result is Young's most polished, least cohesive and, oddly, most experimental album, since the producers seem willing to try almost anything to get him a hit. While that mostly means smothering him in an adult-pop sheen or a wash of programmed rhythms, it also leaves the door open for a jazzy duet with Chaka Khan, a fast-rockin' stab at Free's "A Little Bit of Love" (he murders it) and a beautiful reading of the Chi-Lites' "Oh Girl"—the album's most basic and least-produced track—which became a hit. If any lesson was learned from all this, it should bode well for Young's next album. Forget the layers of extraneous production and let the guy sing.

The cassette-only EP contains 12-inch mixes of five singles, including "Wherever I Lay My Hat," "Love of the Common People" and "Everytime You Go Away."

[i/ds]

ROB YOUNGER AND THE RIFLES
See *New Christs*.

YOUNG FRESH FELLOWS
The Fabulous Sounds of the Pacific Northwest (PopLlama Products) 1984 ●
Topsy Turvy (PopLlama Products) 1985 ●
The Men Who Loved Music (PopLlama Products-Frontier) 1987 ●
Refreshments (PopLlama Products-Frontier) 1987 ●
Totally Lost (Frontier) 1988 ●
Beans and Tolerance (PopLlama Products-Frontier) 1989
This One's for the Ladies (Frontier) 1989 ●
Includes a Helmet (nr/Utility) 1990 ●
Electric Bird Digest (Frontier) 1991 ●

MIGHTY SQUIRRELS/NEW AGE URBAN SQUIRRELS
Ernest Anyway and the Mighty Squirrels Sing the Hits of Johnny Kidd and the Pirates/Five Virgins (PopLlama Products) 1986

SQUIRRELS GROUP
What Gives? (PopLlama Products) 1990 ●

JIMMY SILVA
Remnants of the Empty Set (PopLlama Products) 1986

JIMMY SILVA AND THE EMPTY SET
Fly Like a Dog (PopLlama Products) 1987

SCOTT MCCAUGHEY
My Chartreuse Opinion (PopLlama Products) 1989 [CD] (East Side Digital) 1989 ●

From the back cover of **Fabulous Sounds**: "A collector's disc of the sounds that we in the Pacific Northwest live and play by—a high-hearted, medium-fi recording of such nostrums as the whistle of a ferryboat, the hoofbeats of the rodeo, the roar of racing hydroplanes and the musical beat of our symphonies and jazz." Nostrums? From the narrated grooves: mild frivolity like "Power Mowers Theme," "Teenage Dogs in Trouble" and "Rock and Roll Pest Control," played by an adaptable, skillful pop trio with folly in their minds and a tune in their hearts. Perfect.

Topsy Turvy only contains songs, but that's no hazard in light of such bright, well-played numbers as the traveloguish "Searchin' U.S.A." and "You've Got Your Head on Backwards," a "Tobacco Road"-styled beat raveup borrowed from the estimable Sonics. Armed with a winsome sense of nerdiness (check out the teen angst of "Hang Out Right") and a finely tuned grasp of Culture 101 ("The New John Agar"), the Seattle's four Fellows (bassist Jim Sangster's arrival allowed singer/bassist Scott McCaughey to switch to guitar) put a humorous spin on everything they touch here, but not in such a jokey way that they can't be taken seriously. Another delightful outing. (One ESD-label CD manages to contain the first two albums in their entirety.)

The characters assassinated by **The Men Who Loved Music** (entitled **Chicago 19** on the spine: ask for it by name in your local record store) include an assortment of old tube stars (on "TV Dream"), a rueful tune about "Hank, Karen and Elvis" and the white-funking "Amy Grant." But there's nothing cruel about these iconic invocations—it's just the Fellows' way of saying "hey!" The self-deprecating quartet's best LP so far boasts winners in a number of mocking styles, e.g., the stomping "Get Outta My Cave" (a perfect song for the Troggs to cover), "I Got My Mojo Working (And I Thought You'd Like to Know)" and the blues-rocking "I Don't Let the Little Things Get Me Down." Despite their growing underground-band-makes-good coolness, they can still admit to selfconscious geekiness on the power-popping "When the Girls Get Here." (The 21-song **Men Who Loved** CD, with Henry Winkler's face on the disc, appends the previously unreleased "Happy Death Theme" and everything but the remixed version of the first LP's "Young Fresh Fellows Theme" from the subsequent **Refreshments** mini-album.)

Refreshments gathers up seven outtakes and rarities, including "Back Room of the Bar" (recorded for, but omitted from, **Topsy Turvy**), "Beer Money" (included on the **Men Who Loved Music** cassette), "Young Fresh Fellows Update Theme" (an obscure 1985 single) and the previously unissued "Broken Basket."

McCaughey's songs on **Totally Lost** give the Fellows the straightest, least inventively kooky things they've ever done. The LP is by no means bad, merely underwhelming. Despite flashes of familiar lyrical absurdity ("The Universal Trendsetter," "Take My Brain Away," "I'd Say That You Were Upset"), simplification, with a damaging air of haste, eliminates a lot of the band's ebullient personality in favor of guitar-rocking forthrightness. Some of the music preserves the ambitious cross-pollination ("Picky Piggy," "No Help at All," "Little Softy"), but **Totally Lost** as a whole is disappointingly serious and unimaginative. The CD substitutes a longer version of "Totally Lost Theme" and adds "You're Not Supposed to Laugh" and "World Tour '88."

Lead guitarist Chuck Carroll de-Fellowized himself after **Totally Lost**, leaving the "3 Young French Fellows 3" to cut a limited-edition official bootleg variously known as **Beans and Tolerance** or **Simply Wonderful, Wonderfully Simple** (thanks to the lack of a cover or label: the only identifying marks are cryptically scratched in the vinyl around the center hole). Recorded quickly with more enthusiasm than care, the twelve cavalier tunes—most in a gritty and/or psychedelic '60sish vein—add up to a joyous, rock'n'rolling studio party with massed backing vocals, one-take chaos, meandering guitar solos, bum notes and everything else that such great undertakings require.

Guitarist Kurt Bloch (also of the Fastbacks), the newest Fellow, rocks out like crazy and contributes three cool tunes to the loudly melodic **This One's for the Ladies**. Although the LP is a bit slow coming out of the gate, it picks up steam with kicky pop hooks, electric power chords and deft arrangements. A bare-bones version of Ray Davies' "Picture Book" stands out, as do such sturdy originals as "Middle Man of Time," "Miss Lonelyhearts," "The Family Gun," "Lost Track of Time" and the forlorn country corn of "Deep Down and Inbetween," on which Replacements guitarist Slim Dunlap guests.

Includes a Helmet, released on Billy Bragg's Utility label, is an eight-song retrospective—a sketchy but effective introduction that contains few of the songs mentioned above but is still worth hearing if you don't own all the records. (Collectors' alert: **Helmet** includes the otherwise unreleased "A Thing Like That.")

With Dennis Diken of the Smithereens pounding the skins (and members of the extended Fellows family pitching in), Scott McCaughey's lightweight solo record contains more evidence of his flip wit and bizarre imaginings than the band's recent LPs. (Not to mention a delightful version of the Dixie Cups' "People Say.") With unpredictable musical variety ("A Sobering Thought," for one especially weird example, shifts between film noir and **Imagine**-era Lennon, adding garden shears, a hammer and a wacky guitar solo to further confuse things), **My Chartreuse Opinion** offers moderate fun without guilt. (The CD adds four tracks by Jimmy Silva and two songs on which McCaughey is blandly backed by the Ben Vaughn Combo.)

Related (inbred?) projects: As the Mighty Squirrels, the Fellows back singer Rob ("Ernest Anyway") Morgan on a brilliant 1986 dual-concept album. One side covers pre-Beatles classics (intentionally overlooking the best-known "Shakin' All Over" and "Please Don't Touch") by Johnny Kidd and the Pirates. The flip, performed by a mixture of musicians dubbed the New Age Urban Squirrels, attacks representatives of the later '60s (e.g., "Hair" and "Spirit in the Sky"), which they devolve into cocktail lounge laxative sleaze.

The second Squirrels LP, a mad assortment of Fellows-speckled lineups, covers and recording circumstances, is total genius. For such an irreverent assault on pop music, **What Gives?** (some of it retrieved from obscure 45s and compilations) has great playing and production, excellent vocals by Morgan and enough revisionist imagination to cover a dozen such undertakings. After a rollicking rendition of a gospel standard, a spunky revamp of Gilbert O'Sullivan's doggy-do "Get Down," a chaotic monster-heavy assault on Bill Withers' "Lean on Me" (dissolving into Alice Cooper's "Eighteen"), a relatively straight version of Paul Revere and the Raiders' obnoxiously pushy "Let Me!" and the positively inspired (Wizard of) "Oz '90" medley, the handful of Squirrel originals merely ice this monumentally entertaining cake. The perfect antidote to all fifteen volumes of **Have a Nice Day**!

Bay Area singer/guitarist Jimmy Silva, a longtime associate who has written and recorded with the Fellows, gets the favor returned on his second album, **Fly Like a Dog**. McCaughey contributed to the songwriting; the entire band, alongside Dennis Diken, ex-Beau Brummels Sal Valentino and Declan Mulligan and others provide the instrumental backing for Silva's charging rock tunes. (Although the Fellows don't, Diken and Valentino also appear on Silva's first LP which is, nonetheless, memorable and unpretentious power pop.) Two tracks from each are graciously included on McCaughey's **My Chartreuse Opinion** CD.   [i]

See also *Fastbacks*.

YOUNG GODS
The Young Gods (nr/Product Inc.) 1987 (Play It Again Sam) 1989 •
L'Eau Rouge—Red Water (Play It Again Sam) 1989 •
The Young Gods Play Kurt Weill (Play It Again Sam-Caroline) 1991 •

Few bands that can rock as hard as Switzerland's Young Gods are so crafty at sampling technology. Where most mediocre industrialists mix drum machines with real guitars, this trio (who took their name from a Swans song) utilizes an inhuman live drummer and a sampler that produces an incredible array of crunching guitar riffs and cybernetic keyboard tones. That Franz Treichler (the only constant God) sings almost exclusively in husky French is their next biggest asset, adding a palpably sensual and exotic edge to the electronic forays, while Roli Mosimann's stimulating production is so essential he's practically a fourth member.

After the excitement provoked by the thunderous 1986 single "Envoye!" (included on the CD of **The Young Gods**), the eponymous debut—an arid collection of martial beats—is a minor letdown. One tune, "Jimmy," has the same rush of exultant energy as "Envoye!" but an incongruous cover of Gary Glitter's "Did You Miss Me" doesn't aid the cause.

Everything comes into sharp focus on **L'Eau Rouge**, which offers a dense, enthralling mix of neo-metallic riff-driven chargers and subtly symphonic creations. From the opening carnival cabaret strains of "La Fille de la Mort" to the rampaging "Longue Route" and "L'Amourir" singles (the latter on the CD only), Treichler's gravely leer and existential dissertations fit this guitar-heavy material like a leather codpiece. And who could fail to appreciate the audacity of men titling an album and writing a song in honor of menstruation?   [gef]

YOUNG MARBLE GIANTS
Colossal Youth (Rough Trade) 1980 •
Testcard EP (nr/Rough Trade) 1981
The Peel Sessions EP (nr/Strange Fruit) 1988
WEEKEND
La Varieté (nr/Rough Trade) 1982 (Rough Trade) 1990 •
Live at Ronnie Scott's (nr/Rough Trade) 1983
GIST
Embrace the Herd (nr/Rough Trade) 1983

Cardiff's Young Marble Giants—singer Alison Statton and the Moxham brothers, Philip (bass) and Stuart (guitar, organ)—managed to stay together long enough to produce one oddball album before apathy got the upper hand. Using few overdubs, **Colossal Youth** recreates the mythical ambience of a beatnik coffeehouse. Statton's gentleness and the soft accompaniment contribute to a hushed mood that's either soporific or enchanting, depending on your point of view (or blood pressure). Minimalism never had such polite advocates before.

Following YMG, Statton joined Weekend, a trio with guitarists Simon Booth and Spike in which she sang and played bass; the session players on **La Varieté** are uncredited. Well ahead of the mid-'80s pack, the group tried to concoct a jazz-pop genre that a larger range of musical modes than such a concept might suggest. **La Varieté** offers a good outline of Weekend's intentions, as a song that starts out in YMG mode gets transformed into a full-blown samba, complete with horn section. While not all of Weekend's experiments here are similarly successful, the LP is unique and, for the most part, delightful. After Weekend, Booth went on to form and lead the longer-term and more mainstreamed Working Week. Statton returned to Wales and didn't really resurface until the late '80s, in partnership with Ian Devine.

The gist of the Gist is Stuart Moxham, although **Embrace the Herd** involves assistance by Phil on three tracks and contributions from other friends, including Statton. **Embrace the Herd** is a lovely little record that makes good, careful use of unfancy electronics as well as guitar in fragile pop songs and atmospheric (but not all that vague) instrumentals that benefit from Moxham's rare mix of roaming imagination and modest simplicity.   [jy/gk/i]

See also *Devine & Statton*.

YOUNG MC
Stone Cold Rhymin' (Delicious Vinyl) 1989 •

Having made himself invaluable to Delicious Vinyl by cleaning up Tone-Lōc's too-funky lyrics on the chart-topping "Wild Thing" and co-writing "Funky Cold Medina," London-born University of Southern California economics grad Marvin Young helped himself to a hit with "Bust a Move," a goodnatured romantic tale with funny lyrics and a rhythm track built mainly on a bass line for effortless pop accessibility. Putting a more adult spin (except for the high-schooled "Principal's Office," another smash single) on the same kind of friendly middle-class raps that made stars of Jazzy Jeff and the Fresh Prince, Young MC smooths the hardness out of hip-hop and the colorful colloquialisms out of B-boy rhetoric. If **Stone Cold Rhymin'** too frequently succumbs to PG-rated blandness, Young instills this unchallenging platter with enough winning personality to make a good time.   [i]

YOUTH & BEN WATKINS
The Empty Quarter (nr/Illuminated) 1984
BRILLIANT
Kiss the Lips of Life (Atlantic) 1986

BLUE PEARL

Blue Pearl (Big Life-PolyGram) 1990 φ

Three years after opting out of Killing Joke, dread-locked bassist Youth teamed up with former Hitmen vocalist Ben Watkins (now also versed in keyboards, drums and guitar) to record **The Empty Quarter**, the soundtrack to a play. Forceful and musically intelligent, with layers of disembodied sound lunging and pulsing in and out, it's a striking collection of dramatic, largely electronic instrumentals that bear some of Killing Joke's fury, mixed with subtlety and artsiness. Surprising.

Equally unexpected is the sound of the trio Youth subsequently formed with vocalist June Montana (ex-Dream Academy backing singer) and guitarist/keyboardist Jim Cauty (who played with Zodiac Mindwarp and was a leading album/poster designer in the '70s). The Stock-Aitken-Waterman team produced the dismal **Kiss the Lips of Life**, revealing the cynical Brilliant to be into high-tech dance-rock and neo-soul that could just as easily be by the Thompson Twins, Swing Out Sister or Bananarama. And what this bunch does to James Brown's "It's a Man's Man's Man's World" is sad.

After Cauty had gone on to fame and fortune as Bill Drummond's partner in KLF, Youth teamed up with unpleasantly deep-voiced American singer Durga Mc-Broom, and produced, played on and programmed **Blue Pearl**, a muscular but mediocre dance record.   [i]

See also *Justified Ancients of Mu Mu, Killing Joke, Zodiac Mindwarp.*

YOUTH OF TODAY

Can't Close My Eyes EP (Schism) 1985 (Caroline) 1988
Break Down the Walls (Wishing Well) 1986 (Revelation) 1988
We're Not in This Alone (Caroline) 1988
Youth of Today EP (Revelation) 1990

Before he began devoting his energies to the Hare Krishna parade, singer/lyricist Ray Cappo (aka Ray 2 Day) was a cult hero in New York's positive core and straight-edge punk communities. Playing with aggression and conviction, Youth of Today preached self-discipline, scene unity and standing up for one's beliefs, taking a hardline stance against the consumption of drugs, alcohol and meat.

The Youth crew's first release, **Can't Close My Eyes**, was a locally distributed 7-inch of rousing energy if little ingenuity. Each song consists of hyper-speed assaults broken by slow and heavy mosh sections that kick back into another bout of rage. Despite the monotonous ebb and flow, there's a certain inspirational value to lyrics like "Voice your opinion/Just don't sit still/Speak your mind/At your free will." The Caroline edition is a remixed 12-inch.

Break Down the Walls typifies New York straight-edge style, with chants, jetting momentum and self-awareness messages. But Cappo's indecipherable closed-throat rasp makes the LP hard to endure and its intentions hard to understand. The remixed 1988 reissue contains one added track.

Without sacrificing intensity, Cappo's voice is tame enough on **We're Not in This Alone** to blend with the music and have the lyrics come through loud and clear. The band's improved playing introduces dynamic realms that were unknown on previous efforts. Songs address animal rights, friendship and social justice.

Youth of Today splintered after that second album. Cappo joined the Krishnas (not exactly a band) and later fronted Shelter, a Krishna hardcore group; guitarist John Porcell formed Judge. The 1990 release is a posthumous three-song single of their last recordings, ironically some of their best material.   [mg]

YOU'VE GOT FOETUS ON YOUR BREATH

See *Foetus Inc.*

YUNG WU

See *Feelies.*

ZANTEES
Out for Kicks (Bomp!) 1980
Rhythm Bound (Midnight) 1983
The Zantees EP (Midnight) 1984

A-BONES
Tempo Tantrum EP (Ger. Exile) 1986
Free Beer for Life! EP (Norton) 1988
Life of Riley (Norton) 1991

The Zantees, a New York-based rockabilly combo named after an episode of *Outer Limits*, aren't overly serious about their music, which makes **Out for Kicks** delightfully irreverent. Singing and playing with a spirit money can't buy and synthesizers can't replicate, they easily make the oldies ("I Thought It Over," "Cruisin'," three others) their own; the originals ("Gas Up," "Blonde Bombshell," six others) sound like oldies. A futile gesture, perhaps, but a grand one. Poor recording quality adds atmosphere. (Bassist Rob Norris graduated to the Bongos.)

With one-take loose sound on **Rhythm Bound**, method singer Billy Miller barks out such ethnic 'billy originals as "Tic Tac Toe" and "Money to Burn." Drummer Miriam Linna (previously a charter member of the Cramps) also vocalizes on a couple: "I Need a Man" and "I'm Ready." The guitar-picking Statile brothers' proficient chromatic single-string playing provides a dual carburetor rhythm thrust.

The subsequent 12-inch combines two tracks from the second album with a pair of blazing live oldies (one sung each by Miller and Linna).

Besides publishing the luridly wonderful *Kicks* fanzine and running the Norton Records label (home of Hasil Adkins and countless Link Wray reissues), Miller and Linna currently lead the rocking A-Bones. **Tempo Tantrum** is a four-song 10-inch; **Free Beer** is a six-song 12-inch. [si/i]

FRANK ZAPPA AND THE MOTHERS
See *Captain Beefheart and the Magic Band.*

PETER ZAREMBA'S LOVE DELEGATION
See *Fleshtones.*

ZARKONS
See *Alley Cats.*

ZEITGEIST
Translate Slowly (DB) 1985

REIVERS
Saturday (DB-Capitol) 1987 ●
End of the Day (DB-Capitol) 1989 ●
Translate Slowly [CD] (DB) 1989 ●
Pop Beloved (DB) 1991 ●

Out of Austin, Texas came Zeitgeist, two guys and two girls making moody, melodic and occasionally stunning folk-rock with a deep debt to the '60s—although there's plenty of modern angst and a rootsy feel more western than country. On **Translate Slowly**, John Croslin and Kim Longacre work up a Byrdsy guitar drone and evocative vocal interplay that either lulls with a tepid sonic wash ("Cowboys") or explodes with brooding fury ("Things Don't Change") and hot-breath passion ("Araby"). Croslin's dry-as-dust vocals mix equal measures of desire and distance, but Longacre's classically trained harmonies soar on a remake of Willie Nelson's "Blue Eyes Crying in the Rain."

Forced to abandon the Zeitgeist name by a Minneapolis percussion ensemble that had it first, the quartet chose an equally inappropriate new handle. (Capitol stickered the second LP with the band's former name. DB returned the favor by stickering copies of **Translate Slowly** with a wry mention of the new name but later switched the artwork and reissued it as a Reivers record, putting three bonus tracks on the CD.)

Both sides of the Don Dixon-produced **Saturday** begin with hard-edged Pylonesque syncopation, but otherwise the LP consists of unpretentious guitar pop suggesting 10,000 Maniacs with less idiosyncrasy. The band's personality hinges on appealing vocals; ironically, a nutty instrumental ("Karate Party") is one of the record's standouts. The ability to change gears from delicate melodicism ("Electra") to driving rock ("Wait for Time," "Secretariat") is a definite asset. (The CD adds a bonus track.)

End of the Day finds the Reivers moving into adulthood with grace and ease, dropping much of the early discs' otherworldly wispiness in favor of a more measured, down-to-earth feel. The approach is well-suited to Croslin's bittersweet songs, which reflect grown-up dilemmas ("It's About Time," "Cut Above") and irretrievable losses ("Star Telegram," "Discontent of Winter") with insight and empathy. The vocal interplay between Croslin and Longacre truly blossoms here, and Longacre shines on her solo showcases (including "Lazy Afternoon," a Broadway show tune originally performed by Barbra Streisand). There's also yet another nifty guitar instrumental, "Dude Man Hey." [kh/i/hd]

ZERO BOYS
Vicious Circle (Nimrod) 1982 (Toxic Shock) 1988

DATURA SEEDS
Who Do You Want It to Be? (Toxic Shock) 1990

Vicious Circle is yet another example of how US hardcore seemed to peak coast-to-coast in '82. With attention focused on the well-established scenes, however, who would have expected an album this loaded with intensity, zeal, smarts, hooks and chops to come from Indianapolis? The young quartet is surprisingly tight, and recording quality is impeccable, zooming past like an amplified dragster. "Civilization's Dying" (with commentary on the then-recent shootings of John Lennon, Ronald Reagan and the Pope), "Dirty Alleys/Dirty Minds" and "Hightime" all zip by fast and hard (yet crystal clear), while others like "New Generation" and "Livin' in the 80's" are real "My Generation" calls to arms.

The Zero Boys petered out, reuniting from time to time to tour but not doing any further recording. Two members joined Toxic Reasons; singer/guitarist Paul Mahern emerged recently with another sharp hand, the power-poppy Datura Seeds. Recorded as a quartet, **Who Do You Want It to Be?** is a diverse and substantial LP with impressively tuneful songs and spunky delivery.

The reissue of **Vicious Circle** has six bonus cuts tacked on (and this is vinyl!), including three from **The Master Tape, Vol 1** compilation.   [jr]

ZONES

Under Influence (nr/Arista) 1979

This offshoot of Midge Ure's pre-Rich Kids Scottish pop outfit, Slik, had strong players, two of whom—guitarist Willy Gardner and keyboardist Billy McIsaac—wrote good songs and one of whom (Gardner) had an attractive if limited vocal style, like a young hybrid of Mick Ronson and Dave Edmunds. But what to do with it all? Pop? Hard stuff? Commercial new wave? Reggae-pop? The Zones try a little of everything on **Under Influence** without any forceful, unifying personality, despite passing nods to Mott and the Skids (which two Zones later joined). No bad cuts, but only one rises from enjoyable to exciting.   [jg]

ZOVIET FRANCE

Hessian (nr/Red Rhino) 1982 ●
Garista [tape] (nr/Red Rhino) 1982 ф
Norsch (nr/Red Rhino) 1983 ●
Mohnomishe (nr/Red Rhino) 1983 ●
Eostre (nr/Red Rhino) 1984 ●
Popular Soviet Songs and Youth Music [tape] (nr/Red Rhino) 1985
Gris (Ger. No Man's Land) 1985
Misfits, Loony Tunes and Squalid Criminals (nr/Red Rhino) 1986
Lohland [tape] (Hol. Staalplat) 1987
A Flock of Rotations (nr/Red Rhino) 1987
Shouting at the Ground (nr/Red Rhino) 1988 ●
Look into Me (nr/Charrm) 1990 ●
Just an Illusion [CD] (Hol. Staalplat) 1990 ●

One of the most idiosyncratic, original and reclusive groups in new music, Newcastle's Zoviet France issued most of its early records with bizarre handmade covers, using nontraditional materials in lieu of cardboard. (Even as the records have appeared on CD, the group maintains its fondness for odd packages: **Just an Illusion** comes in a balsa box.) As far as the music inside of the sleeves, Zoviet France uses textures and repetitive structures (delay boxes come in useful here) to hypnotize the listener, playing minimal percussion and lots of low-tech electronics.

Hessian, a 12-inch 45 in a screen-printed cloth bag, is enthusiastically primitive and abrasive, with percussion and feedback as well as silly chanting, hyperactive bongo playing and the shrill piping of flutes. Originally issued only on cassette, **Garista** lacks percussion, occasionally gets very silly indeed and is also very murky and industrial sounding. Besides being self-indulgent in parts, the recording quality is poor.

Norsch, a 12-inch 45 wrapped in embossed tinfoil, is the most powerful of Zoviet France's early recordings. Side One begins as screechy nightmare marching music punctuated by tape fragments of some militaristic speech, fading into a rumbly, ominous bad trip. Side Two starts with dreamy Arabian drones then goes pound-happy, with moaning and rudimentary synthesizer howls.

Mohnomishe and **Eostre**, both double-album sets (each available as a single CD), virtually abandon percussion in favor of dense atmospheres of echoey ambient electronics, conjuring up images of thick fog. Packed in masonite, the former (which evinces a growing Can influence) sets you on a coastal highway, propelled along by subtle sequencer action. As dogs bark and cars drone by, repeating blocks of sound—perhaps mangled guitar—come at you in hypnotic waves. Inside the plastic and tissue packaging, **Eostre** traps you on the docks as mammoth ships sail slowly by, clanking and rumbling through dense sheets of mist; whoever's singing on the deck sounds awfully weirded out. Great stuff.

In 1985, to catch up with an increasing backlog of material, the group issued a diverse and haphazard three-hour double-cassette, **Popular Soviet Songs and Youth Music**. The set contains some of the band's best material and some of its worst, sometimes right next to each other. The Zoviets followed that with the 10-inch **Gris**, their most carefully thought-out and best produced work yet. The side-long title track blends entrancing layers of repeating voices, synthesizers and guitar, while the other side is great electronic music, making effective use of a sequencer.

Misfits, Loony Tunes and Squalid Criminals is better recorded, finally achieving commercial quality standards. "They're Eating the Passengers" is probably the closest the group has come to a song, with tapes of hijackers played over attractive pulses, chimings (modified piano?) and restrained percussion. **A Flock of Rotations** is uneven, with some annoying tracks of feedback pinging through electronic delays.

Although the recording quality is poor, the second side of the **Lohland** cassette is spectacular, about 40 minutes of voices singing and howling through flangers, delays and chorus boxes.

Zoviet France reached new heights—in music, instrumental diversity and production polish—with **Shouting at the Ground**, a double album which includes "Shamany Enfluence," a very long piece that might be their finest effort. Nearly as impressive, **Look into Me** contains an even longer magnum opus (the 26-minute "Cair Camouflet"), a combination of industrial grinding, modified guitar and electronics. Other tracks apply electronics and tape loops with far more sophistication and impact than the earlier albums. **Just an Illusion** continues in the same vein, with longer mood pieces and shorter adaptations of Middle Eastern and Oriental music. [sl]

TAPPER ZUKIE

Man Ah Warrior (nr/Klik) 1974 (Mer) 1977
MPLA (Jam. Klik) 1976 (nr/Front Line) 1978
Tapper Roots (nr/Front Line) 1979
Peace in the Ghetto (nr/Front Line) 1979
In Dub (nr/Front Line) 1979
Black Man (nr/Mobiliser) 1979
Raggy Joey Boy (nr/Mobiliser) 1982
Earth Running (nr/Mobiliser) 1983
Ragamuffin (nr/World Enterprise) 1986

Though Tapper (Tappa) Zukie isn't active as a performer in the reggae mainstream, his toasting, which combines staunchly Rasta lyrics and heavy roots accompaniment, has always enjoyed an audience. His rock notoriety was boosted in the late '70s via an association with the Patti Smith Group; **Man Ah Warrior** was reissued by Lenny Kaye on the Mer label. Cuts like "Simpleton Badness," "Viego" (the Jamaican sound system where he got his start) and "A Message to the Pork Eaters" fill the LP with dread, seasoned with irony and humor. Not to be missed.

MPLA is likewise classic and **Tapper Roots** is almost as good. **Peace in the Ghetto**, on the other hand, is lackluster and uninspired; despite the inclusion of the single "Phensic" (retitled "Dangerous Woman"), the rhythms are flabby, the toasting less interesting. Parting company with Virgin/Front Line, Zukie returned to Jamaica.

Black Man is sturdy, as is the first side of **Earth Running**, which features "The General," a tribute to the late General Echo. (Side Two, however, has two unconvincing disco cuts.) **Raggy Joey Boy** has more singing than toasting.

Since the mid-'80s, Zukie has been working mainly as a producer, helming Dennis Brown's "Death Before Dishonour" and Gregory Isaacs' "Hard Drugs," as well as U-Roy's **Line Up and Come** LP, one track of which ("It's About Time") actually features him. [bk/aw]

ZULUS

Down on the Floor (Slash) 1989 ●

Reuniting three members of Boston dance-novelty Human Sexual Response, this quartet dispenses with the jokes on its Bob Mould-produced debut. Unfortunately, it didn't also dispense with Larry Bangor, an insufferable singer with an unpleasant voice and a predilection for theatrical posturing. (Imagine Danny Elfman singing in Perry Farrell's stead, or the other way 'round.) Rich Gilbert's clever guitar moves range from loudly melodic rock to disjointed intricacy, but he only contributes to the album's pointless profusion of personalities. [i]

ZVUKI MU

Zvuki Mu (Opal-Warner Bros.) 1989 ●

This Russian band, produced in Moscow by Brian Eno, sparked Western comparisons to Talking Heads and Captain Beefheart. Maybe. But perhaps they were overwhelmed by Eno's enthusiasm for ambient music; **Zvuki Mu** is awfully enervating. Translations of the lyrics on the inner don't improve things, either: "300 minutes of pleasure with oneself" is admittedly an odd way of referring to masturbation (besides, this album is only 40 minutes, ho ho ho), but there's nothing compelling, nothing that cuts here. [jg]

SOURCES

For more information on non-mainstream music, the following publications—all available by subscription—are recommended, as are the two retail establishments at the end:

Option: This excellent and substantial bi-monthly covers a wide range of alternative musics, from underground to exotic. The articles are generally good, there's always plenty of reviews and the ads are well worth perusing. Sonic Options Network, 2345 Westwood Blvd. #2, Los Angeles CA 90064.

The Big Takeover: Jack Rabid's writing is the backbone of this stimulating and readable fanzine, which has extensive interviews with bands and a lot of provocative record and concert reviews. 249 Eldridge Street, New York NY 10002.

Flipside: Los Angeles' leading punkzine has been going for over a decade, and remains as unspoiled and enthusiastic now as it ever was. Lots of interviews and a great letter section covers the international scene in addition to California. Box 363, Whittier CA 90608.

Rockpool Newsletter: This bi-weekly trade publication has plenty in it for non-industry types. It's not a fun read, but contains dope on new releases and the state of the independent label scene. 83 Leonard Street, New York NY 10013; 212-219-0077.

CMJ New Music Report: This expensive weekly trade magazine oriented towards college radio reviews lots of new records in departments devoted to imports, hip-hop, reggae, worldbeat and metal. The business stuff is boring, but the coverage of new records is timely and knowledgeable. 245 Great Neck Road, Great Neck NY 11021.

Bucketfull of Brains: This amazing British fanzine approaches culty bands from the Saints to Thin White Rope to the Bevis Frond from a record fanatic's perspective. A great source of information with a strong stylistic axe to grind, this is the kind of magazine that will inspire you to buy lots of vinyl. 19 Adela Avenue, New Malden, Surrey KT3 6LF, England.

The Source: America really needs a serious hip-hop magazine, but this will have to do until one comes along. Not quite a trade magazine and not exactly a fanzine, this slick monthly has scene reports, news, features that are occasionally solid and stimulating and record reviews that never quite get around to saying anything. Not yet there, but worth watching. 594 Broadway, New York NY 10012.

Q: This English monthly is everything a rock magazine should be. Largely insulated from the hyper-trendy bullshit that makes the weeklies (*Melody Maker, New Musical Express*) so maddening, this thick glossy takes a more responsible attitude, waits to see what's worth covering and doesn't forget the past. Great features and endless reviews that could sometimes be better written. PO Box 500, Leicester LE99 0AA, England.

See Hear is a unique store that carries nothing but music books and magazines—from hip imports to tiny fanzines. They publish a catalogue and do sales by mail. 59 East 7th Street, New York NY 10003.

Midnight Records has an extremely cool store in New York but also publishes a big mail order catalogue for those in other environs. PO Box 390, Old Chelsea Station, New York NY 10011.

ABOUT THE EDITOR

Ira Robbins co-founded *Trouser Press* magazine in 1974 while completing an electrical engineering degree; he was Publisher and Editorial Director of the music monthly until it ceased to exist ten years and 96 issues later. He has edited and/or contributed to a number of books on rock music, and has written about music and video for countless publications large and small. Born in New York City where he resides with his wife, Regina, three cats—Erasmus, Katie and Bobo—and far too many records, Robbins has been a rock'n'roll fanatic ever since hearing Del Shannon's "Hats off to Larry" on the radio in 1961.